JUL 2008
R
CH/cont

CHILTON®

FORD
SERVICE MANUAL
2008 EDITION
VOLUME I

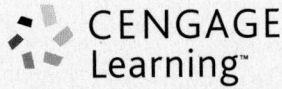

CENGAGE
Learning™

Australia • Brazil • Japan • Korea • Mexico • Singapore • Spain • United Kingdom • United States

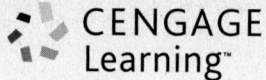

CHILTON®
Ford Service Manual
2008 Edition
Volume I

Vice President,
Technology Professional Business Unit:
 Gregory L. Clayton

Publisher,
Technology Professional Business Unit:
 David Koontz

Director of Marketing:
 Beth A. Lutz

Production Director:
 Patty Stephan

Editorial Assistant:
 Jason Yager

Production Manager:
 Andrew Crouth

Marketing Specialist:
 Jennifer Stall

Marketing Assistant:
 Rachael Conover

Publishing Coordinator:
 Paula Baillie

Sr. Content Project Manager:
 Elizabeth C. Hough

Managing Editor:
 Terry L. Blomquist

Editors:
 Dennis Bailley
 Tim Crain
 Scott Critchfield
 Eugene F. Hannon Jr.
 Tom Mellon
 Kyla Nyjordet
 Christine Sheeky

Graphical Designer:
 Melinda Possinger

For more information contact:
Cengage Learning
Executive Woods
5 Maxwell Drive, PO Box 8007,
Clifton Park, NY 12065-8007
Visit us at **www.chiltononline.com**
For more learning solutions, visit **www.cengage.com**
For permission to use material from
the text or product, contact us by
Tel. (800) 730-2214
Fax (800) 730-2215
www.cengage.com/permissions

Cengage Learning products are represented in Canada by Nelson Education, Ltd.

ISBN-13 : 978-1-4283-2209-7
ISBN-10 : 1-4283-2209-4
ISSN: 1939-621X

NOTICE TO THE READER

Publisher does not warrant or guarantee any of the products described herein or perform any independent analysis in connection with any of the product information contained herein. Publisher does not assume, and expressly disclaims, any obligation to obtain and include information other than that provided to it by the manufacturer.

The reader is expressly warned to consider and adopt all safety precautions that might be indicated by the activities herein and to avoid all potential hazards. By following the instructions contained herein, the reader willingly assumes all risks in connection with such instructions.

The publisher makes no representation or warranties of any kind, including but not limited to, the warranties of fitness for particular purpose or merchantability, nor are any such representations implied with respect to the material set forth herein, and the publisher takes no responsibility with respect to such material. The publisher shall not be liable for any special, consequential, or exemplary damages resulting, in whole or part, from the readers' use of, or reliance upon, this material.

Printed in the United States of America
1 2 3 4 5 xx12 11 10 09 08 07

Table of Contents

Sections

Model Index

USING THIS INFORMATION

Organization

To find where a particular model section or procedure is located, look in the Table of Contents. Main topics are listed with the page number on which they may be found. Following the main topics is an alphabetical listing of all of the procedures within the section and their page numbers.

Manufacturer and Model Coverage

This product covers 2005–2008 Ford Motor Company models that are produced in sufficient quantities to warrant coverage, and which have technical content available from the vehicle manufacturers before our publication date. Although this information is as complete as possible at the time of publication, some manufacturers may make changes which cannot be included here. While striving for total accuracy, the publisher cannot assume responsibility for any errors, changes, or omissions that may occur in the compilation of this data.

Part Numbers & Special Tools

Part numbers and special tools are recommended by the publisher and vehicle manufacturer to perform specific jobs. Before substituting any part or tool for the one recommended, you must be completely satisfied that neither your personal safety, nor the performance of the vehicle will be endangered.

ACKNOWLEDGEMENT

This product contains material that is reproduced and distributed under license from Ford Motor Company. No further reproduction or distribution of the Ford Motor Company material is allowed without express written permission from Ford Motor Company

PRECAUTIONS

Before servicing any vehicle, please be sure to read all of the following precautions, which deal with personal safety, prevention of component damage, and important points to take into consideration when servicing a motor vehicle:

- Always wear safety glasses or goggles when drilling, cutting, grinding or prying.
- Steel-toed work shoes should be worn when working with heavy parts. Pockets should not be used for carrying tools. A slip or fall can drive a screwdriver into your body.
- Work surfaces, including tools and the floor should be kept clean of grease, oil or other slippery material.
- When working around moving parts, don't wear loose clothing. Long hair should be tied back under a hat or cap, or in a hair net.
- Always use tools only for the purpose for which they were designed. Never pry with a screwdriver.
- Keep a fire extinguisher and first aid kit handy.
- Always properly support the vehicle with approved stands or lift.
- Always have adequate ventilation when working with chemicals or hazardous material.
- Carbon monoxide is colorless, odorless and dangerous. If it is necessary to operate the engine with vehicle in a closed area such as a garage, always use an exhaust collector to vent the exhaust gases outside the closed area.
- When draining coolant, keep in mind that small children and some pets are attracted by ethylene glycol antifreeze, and

are quite likely to drink any left in an open container, or in puddles on the ground. This will prove fatal in sufficient quantity. Always drain the coolant into a sealable container.

- To avoid personal injury, do not remove the coolant pressure relief cap while the engine is operating or hot. The cooling system is under pressure; steam and hot liquid can come out forcefully when the cap is loosened slightly. Failure to follow these instructions may result in personal injury. The coolant must be recovered in a suitable, clean container for reuse. If the coolant is contaminated it must be recycled or disposed of correctly.
- When carrying out maintenance on the starting system be aware that heavy gauge leads are connected directly to the battery. Make sure the protective caps are in place when maintenance is completed. Failure to follow these instructions may result in personal injury.
- Do not remove any part of the engine emission control system. Operating the engine without the engine emission control system will reduce fuel economy and engine ventilation. This will weaken engine performance and shorten engine life. It is also a violation of Federal law.
- Due to environmental concerns, when the air conditioning system is drained, the refrigerant must be collected using refrigerant recovery/recycling equipment. Federal law requires that refrigerant be recovered into appropriate recovery equipment and the process be conducted by qualified technicians who have been certified by an approved organization, such as MACS, ASI,

etc. Use of a recovery machine dedicated to the appropriate refrigerant is necessary to reduce the possibility of oil and refrigerant incompatibility concerns. Refer to the instructions provided by the equipment manufacturer when removing refrigerant from or charging the air conditioning system.

- Always disconnect the battery ground when working on or around the electrical system.
- Batteries contain sulfuric acid. Avoid contact with skin, eyes, or clothing. Also, shield your eyes when working near batteries to protect against possible splashing of the acid solution. In case of acid contact with skin or eyes, flush immediately with water for a minimum of 15 minutes and get prompt medical attention. If acid is swallowed, call a physician immediately. Failure to follow these instructions may result in personal injury.
- Batteries normally produce explosive gases. Therefore, do not allow flames, sparks or lighted substances to come near the battery. When charging or working near a battery, always shield your face and protect your eyes. Always provide ventilation. Failure to follow these instructions may result in personal injury.
- When lifting a battery, excessive pressure on the end walls could cause acid to spew through the vent caps, resulting in personal injury, damage to the vehicle or battery. Lift with a battery carrier or with your hands on opposite corners. Failure to follow these instructions may result in personal injury.
- Observe all applicable safety precautions when working around fuel. Whenever

servicing the fuel system, always work in a well-ventilated area. Do not allow fuel spray or vapors to come in contact with a spark, open flame, or excessive heat (a hot drop light, for example). Keep a dry chemical fire extinguisher near the work area. Always keep fuel in a container specifically designed for fuel storage; also, always properly seal fuel containers to avoid the possibility of fire or explosion. Do not smoke or carry lighted tobacco or open flame of any type when working on or near any fuel-related components.

• Fuel injection systems often remain pressurized, even after the engine has been turned OFF. The fuel system pressure must be relieved before disconnecting any fuel lines. Failure to do so may result in fire and/or personal injury.

• The evaporative emissions system contains fuel vapor and condensed fuel vapor. Although not present in large quantities, it still presents the danger of explosion or fire. Disconnect the battery ground cable from the battery to minimize the possibility of an electrical spark occurring, possibly causing a fire or explosion if fuel vapor or liquid fuel is present in the area. Failure to follow these instructions can result in personal injury.

• The EPA warns that prolonged contact with used engine oil may cause a number of skin disorders, including cancer! You should make every effort to minimize your exposure to used engine oil. Protective gloves should be worn when changing oil. Wash your hands and any other exposed skin areas as soon as possible after exposure to used engine oil. Soap and water, or waterless hand cleaner should be used.

• Some vehicles are equipped with an air bag system, often referred to as a Supple-mental Restraint System (SRS) or Supple-mental Inflatable Restraint (SIR) system. The system must be disabled before performing service on or around system components, steering column, instrument panel components, wiring and sensors. Failure to follow safety and disabling procedures could result in accidental air bag deployment, possible personal injury and unnecessary system repairs.

• Always wear safety goggles when working with, or around, the air bag system. When carrying a non-deployed air bag, be sure the bag and trim cover are pointed away from your body. When placing a non-deployed air bag on a work surface, always face the bag and trim cover upward, away from the surface. This will reduce the motion of the module if it is accidentally deployed.

• Electronic modules are sensitive to electrical charges. The ABS module can be damaged if exposed to these charges.

• Brake pads and shoes may contain asbestos, which has been determined to be a cancer-causing agent. Never clean brake surfaces with compressed air. Avoid inhaling brake dust. Clean all brake surfaces with a commercially available brake cleaning fluid.

• When replacing brake pads, shoes, discs or drums, replace them as complete axle sets.

• When servicing drum brakes, disassemble and assemble one side at a time, leaving the remaining side intact for reference.

• Brake fluid often contains polyglycol ethers and polyglycols. Avoid contact with the eyes and wash your hands thoroughly after handling brake fluid. If you do get brake fluid in your eyes, flush your eyes with clean, running water for 15 minutes. If eye irritation persists, or if you have taken brake fluid internally, immediately seek medical assistance.

• Clean, high quality brake fluid from a sealed container is essential to the safe and proper operation of the brake system. You should always buy the correct type of brake fluid for your vehicle. If the brake fluid becomes contaminated, completely flush the system with new fluid. Never reuse any brake fluid. Any brake fluid that is removed from the system should be discarded. Also, do not allow any brake fluid to come in contact with a painted or plastic surface; it will damage the paint.

• Never operate the engine without the proper amount and type of engine oil; doing so will result in severe engine damage.

• Timing belt maintenance is extremely important! Many models utilize an interference-type, non-freewheeling engine. If the timing belt breaks, the valves in the cylinder head may strike the pistons, causing potentially serious (also time-consuming and expensive) engine damage.

• Disconnecting the negative battery cable on some vehicles may interfere with the functions of the on-board computer system (s) and may require the computer to undergo a relearning process once the negative battery cable is reconnected.

• Steering and suspension fasteners are critical parts because they affect performance of vital components and systems and their failure can result in major service expense. They must be replaced with the same grade or part number or an equivalent part if replacement is necessary. Do not use a replacement part of lesser quality or substitute design. Torque values must be used as specified during reassembly to ensure proper retention of these parts.

FORD, LINCOLN AND MERCURY

Aviator • Explorer • Explorer Sport-Trac • Mountaineer

1

SPECIFICATIONS AND MAINTENANCE CHARTS

ENGINE AND VEHICLE IDENTIFICATION

			Engine						Model Year	
Code ①	Liters	Cu. In.	Cyl.	Fuel Sys.	Type	Eng. Mfg.		Code ②		Year
E	4.0	244	6	MFI	SOHC	Ford		5		2005
K	4.0	244	6	MFI	SOHV	Ford		6		2006
8	4.6	281	8	MFI	SOHC	Ford		7		2007
H	4.6	281	8	MFI	DOHC	Ford		8		2008

MFI: (Sequential) Multi-port Fuel Injection

DOHC: Dual Overhead Camshaft

SOHC: Single Overhead Camshaft

① 8th digit of the Vehicle Identification Number (VIN)

② 10th digit of the Vehicle Identification Number (VIN)

22086_EXPL_C0001

GENERAL ENGINE SPECIFICATIONS

Year	Model	Engine Displ. Liters	Engine VIN	Net Horsepower @ rpm	Net Torque @ rpm (ft. lbs.)	Bore x Stroke (in.)	Compression Ratio	Oil Pressure @ rpm
2005	Explorer	4.0	E,K	210@5100	240@3000	3.95x3.32	9.7:1	15@2000
	Explorer	4.6	W	292@5750	282@4000	3.55x3.54	9.8:1	75@2000
	Explorer Sport-Trac	4.0	E,K	210@5100	225@2500	3.81x3.39	9.0:1	15@2000
	Mountaineer	4.0	E,K	210@5250	240@3000	3.81x3.39	9.7:1	15@2000
	Mountaineer	4.6	W	210@5100	282@4000	3.55x3.54	9.8:1	75@2000
	Aviator	4.6	H	292@5750	300@3250	3.55x3.54	10.1:1	20-45@1500
2006	Explorer	4.0	E,K	210@5100	254@3700	3.95x3.32	9.7:1	15@2000
	Explorer	4.6	8	292@5750	300@3950	3.55x3.54	9.8:1	75@2000
	Mountaineer	4.0	E,K	210@5100	254@3700	3.81x3.39	9.7:1	15@2000
	Mountaineer	4.6	8	292@5750	300@3950	3.55x3.54	9.8:1	75@2000
2007	Explorer	4.0	E,K	210@5100	254@3700	3.95x3.32	9.7:1	15@2000
	Explorer	4.6	8	292@5750	300@3950	3.55x3.54	9.8:1	75@2000
	Explorer Sport-Trac	4.0	E,K	210@5100	254@3700	3.81x3.39	9.7:1	15@2000
	Explorer Sport-Trac	4.6	8	292@5750	300@3950	3.55x3.54	9.8:1	75@2000
	Mountaineer	4.0	E,K	210@5100	254@3700	3.81x3.39	9.7:1	15@2000
	Mountaineer	4.6	8	292@5750	300@3950	3.55x3.54	9.8:1	75@2000

22086_EXPL_C0002

GASOLINE ENGINE TUNE-UP SPECIFICATIONS

Year	Engine Displacement Liters	Engine ID/VIN	Spark Plug Gap (in.)	Ignition Timing (deg.) ① MT	AT	Fuel Pressure (psi) ②	Idle Speed (rpm) MT	AT	Valve Clearance In.	Ex.
2005	4.0	E,K	0.061-0.068	—	10B	30-40 ③	①	①	HYD	HYD
	4.6	W	0.052-0.056	—	10B	30-40 ③	①	①	HYD	HYD
	4.6	H	0.052-0.056	—	10B	25-65	①	①	HYD	HYD
2006	4.0	E,K	0.052-0.056	—	10B	30-40	①	①	HYD	HYD
	4.6	8	0.040-0.050	—	10B	30-40	①	①	HYD	HYD
2007	4.0	E,K	0.052-0.056	—	10B	30-40	①	①	HYD	HYD
	4.6	8	0.040-0.050	—	10B	30-40	①	①	HYD	HYD

NOTE: The Vehicle Emission Control Information label often reflects specification changes changes made during production. The label figures must
be used if they differ from those in this chart.

B: Before top dead center

HYD: Hydraulic

① Idle speed and ignition timing are electronically controlled and cannot be adjusted

② Key on; engine off

③ Sport Trac: 60-65 psi

22086_EXPL_C0003

CAPACITIES

Year	Model	Engine Displ. Liters	Engine ID/VIN	Engine Oil with Filter (qts.)	Transmission (pts.) 5-Spd	Auto. ①	Transfer Case (pts.)	Drive Axle Front (pts.)	Rear (pts.)	Fuel Tank (gal.)	Cooling System (qts.)
2005	Explorer	4.0	E,K	5.0	—	25.4	3.0	2.70	3.50	22.5	②
	Explorer	4.6	W	6.5	—	25.4	3.0	2.70	3.50	22.5	③
	Explorer Sport-Trac	4.0	K	4.0	—	④	2.5	3.25	⑤	23.0	14.0
	Mountaineer	4.0	E,K	5.0	—	25.4	3.0	2.70	3.50	22.5	②
	Mountaineer	4.6	W	6.5	—	25.4	3.0	2.70	3.50	22.5	③
	Aviator	4.6	H	6.0	—	25.4	3.0	2.70	3.50	22.5	19.6
2006	Explorer	4.0	E,K	5.0	—	⑥	3.0	2.70	3.50	22.5	⑦
	Explorer	4.6	8	6.5	—	⑥	3.0	2.70	3.50	22.5	⑧
	Mountaineer	4.0	E,K	5.0	—	⑥	3.0	2.70	3.50	22.5	⑦
	Mountaineer	4.6	8	6.5	—	⑥	3.0	2.70	3.50	22.5	⑧
2007	Explorer	4.0	E,K	5.0	—	⑥	3.0	2.70	3.50	22.5	⑦
	Explorer	4.6	8	6.5	—	⑥	3.0	2.70	3.50	22.5	⑧
	Explorer Sport-Trac	4.0	E,K	5.0	—	⑨	3.0	2.70	3.50	22.5	⑦
	Explorer Sport-Trac	4.6	8	6.5	—	⑨	3.0	2.70	3.50	22.5	⑧
	Mountaineer	4.0	E,K	5.0	—	⑥	3.0	2.70	3.50	22.5	⑦
	Mountaineer	4.6	8	6.5	—	⑥	3.0	2.70	3.50	22.5	⑧

NOTE: All capacities are approximate. Add fluid gradually and check to be sure a proper fluid level is obtained.

① Dry fill

② w/o auxiliary heater: 16.3 qts.
w/auxiliary heater: 18.3 qts.

③ w/o auxiliary heater: 18.6 qts.
w/auxiliary heater: 20.1 qts.

④ 4x2: 20.0 pts.
4x4: 20.6 pts.

⑤ With Traction-Lok: 5.25 pts.
Without Traction-Lok: 5.5 pts.

⑥ 5R55S A/T: 25.4 pts.
6R60 A/T: 21.0 pts.

⑦ w/o auxiliary heater: 12.2 qts.
w/auxiliary heater: 14.0 qts.

⑧ w/o auxiliary heater: 14.0 qts.
w/auxiliary heater: 15.7 qts.

⑨ 5R55S A/T: 24.8 pts.
6R60 A/T: 22.0 pts.

22086_EXPL_C0004

FLUID SPECIFICATIONS

Year	Model	Engine Displacement Liters	Engine ID/VIN	Engine Oil	Auto. Trans. ①	Drive Axle	Power Steering Fluid	Brake Master Cylinder
2005	Aviator	4.6L	H	5W-20	①	75W-140	Mercon® ATF	DOT 3
	Explorer	4.0L	E, K	5W-20	①	75W-140	Mercon® ATF	DOT 3
		4.6L	W	5W-20	①	75W-140	Mercon® ATF	DOT 3
	Explorer Sport-Trac	4.0L	E, K	5W-20	①	75W-140	Mercon® ATF	DOT 3
	Mountaineer	4.0L	E, K	5W-20	①	75W-140	Mercon® ATF	DOT 3
		4.6L	W	5W-20	①	75W-140	Mercon® ATF	DOT 3
2006	Explorer	4.0L	E, K	5W-20	① ②	75W-140	Mercon® ATF	DOT 3
		4.6L	8	5W-20	① ②	75W-140	Mercon® ATF	DOT 3
	Mountaineer	4.0L	E, K	5W-20	① ②	75W-140	Mercon® ATF	DOT 3
		4.6L	8	5W-20	① ②	75W-140	Mercon® ATF	DOT 3
2007	Explorer	4.0L	E, K	5W-20	① ②	75W-140	Mercon® ATF	DOT 3
		4.6L	8	5W-20	① ②	75W-140	Mercon® ATF	DOT 3
	Explorer Sport-Trac	4.0L	E, K	5W-20	① ②	75W-140	Mercon® ATF	DOT 3
		4.6L	8	5W-20	① ②	75W-140	Mercon® ATF	DOT 3
	Mountaineer	4.0L	E, K	5W-20	① ②	75W-140	Mercon® ATF	DOT 3
		4.6L	8	5W-20	① ②	75W-140	Mercon® ATF	DOT 3

DOT: Department Of Transpotation
① 5R55E or 5R55S: Mercon V
② 6R60: Mercon SP

22086_EXPL_C0005

VALVE SPECIFICATIONS

Year	Engine Displ. Liters	Engine ID/VIN	Seat Angle (deg.)	Face Angle (deg.)	Spring Test Pressure (lbs. @ in.)	Spring Installed Height (in.)	Stem-to-Guide Clearance (in.) Intake	Stem-to-Guide Clearance (in.) Exhaust	Stem Diameter (in.) Intake	Stem Diameter (in.) Exhaust
2005	4.0	E,K	45	45	202-225@ 1.413-1.445	1.569-1.609	0.0010-0.0020	0.0010-0.0030	0.2740-0.2748	0.2738-0.2742
	4.6	H	45	45.5	160@1.03	1.4228	0.0008-0.0027	0.0018-0.0037	0.2734-0.2754	0.2736-0.2744
	4.6	W	44.5-45	45.5	162-180@ 1.22	1.660	0.0008-0.0027	0.0018-0.0037	0.2352-0.2360	0.2343-0.2351
2006	4.0	E,K	45	45	203-225@ 1.413-1.445	1.569-1.609	0.0010-0.0020	0.0010-0.0030	0.2740-0.2750	0.2730-0.2740
	4.6	8	44.5-45.1	45.25-45.75	162-180@ 1.22	1.660	0.0008-0.0027	0.0018-0.0037	0.2352-0.2360	0.2343-0.2351
2007	4.0	E,K	45	45	203-225@ 1.413-1.445	1.569-1.609	0.0010-0.0020	0.0010-0.0030	0.2740-0.2750	0.2730-0.2740
	4.6	8	44.5-45.1	45.25-45.75	162-180@ 1.22	1.660	0.0008-0.0027	0.0018-0.0037	0.2352-0.2360	0.2343-0.2351

22086_EXPL_C0006

CAMSHAFT AND BEARING SPECIFICATIONS CHART

All measurements are given in inches.

Year	Engine Displ. Liters	Engine VIN	Journal Dia.	Brg. Oil Clearance	Shaft End-play	Runout	Journal Bore	Lobe Height Intake	Lobe Height Exhaust
2005	4.0	E, K	1.099-1.101	0.002-0.004	0.003-0.007	0.002	1.102-1.104	0.259	0.259
	4.6	H	1.0615-1.0605 1.0605	0.00098-0.0030	0.00098-0.0030	0.001	1.0635-1.0625	0.218	0.218
	4.6	W	1.061-1.060	0.00098-0.0030	0.0035-0.0075	0.002	1.063-1.0625	0.2799	0.2951
2006	4.0	E, K	1.099-1.101	0.002-0.004	0.003-0.007	0.002	1.102-1.104	0.259	0.259
	4.6	8	1.126-1.127	0.001-0.003	0.0002-0.009	0.001	1.128-1.129	0.217	0.217
2007	4.0	E, K	1.099-1.101	0.002-0.004	0.003-0.007	0.002	1.102-1.104	0.259	0.259
	4.6	8	1.126-1.127	0.001-0.003	0.0002-0.0009	0.001	1.128-1.129	0.217	0.217

22086_EXPL_C0007

CRANKSHAFT AND CONNECTING ROD SPECIFICATIONS

All measurements are given in inches.

Year	Engine Displ. Liters	Engine ID/VIN	Crankshaft Main Brg. Journal Dia.	Crankshaft Main Brg. Oil Clearance	Crankshaft Shaft End-play	Crankshaft Thrust on No.	Connecting Rod Journal Diameter	Connecting Rod Oil Clearance	Connecting Rod Side Clearance
2005	4.0	E,K	2.2430-2.2440	0.0003-0.0024	0.0020-0.0126	3	2.1250-2.1260	0.0008-0.0012	0.0036-0.0106
	4.6	H	2.6567-2.6576	0.0010-0.0019	0.0051-0.0118	3	2.0859-2.0867	0.0011-0.0027	0.0059-0.0177
	4.6	W	2.6567-2.6576	0.0009-0.0019	0.0030-0.0148	3	2.0867-2.0870	0.0010-0.0027	0.0060-0.0200
2006	4.0	E,K	2.2430-2.2440	0.0003-0.0024	0.0020-0.0126	3	2.1250-2.1260	0.0008-0.0012	0.0036-0.0106
	4.6	8	2.6567-2.6576	0.0009-0.0019	0.0030-0.0148	3	2.0867-2.0870	0.0010-0.0027	0.0060-0.0200
2007	4.0	E,K	2.2430-2.2440	0.0003-0.0024	0.0020-0.0126	3	2.1250-2.1260	0.0008-0.0012	0.0036-0.0106
	4.6	8	2.6567-2.6576	0.0009-0.0019	0.0030-0.0148	3	2.0867-2.0870	0.0010-0.0027	0.0060-0.0200

22086_EXPL_C0009

PISTON AND RING SPECIFICATIONS

All measurements are given in inches.

Year	Engine Displ. Liters	Engine ID/VIN	Piston Clearance	Ring Gap			Ring Side Clearance		
				Top Compression	Bottom Compression	Oil Control	Top Compression	Bottom Compression	Oil Control
2005	4.0	E,K	0.0012-0.0019	0.008-0.018	①	—	0.0016-0.0030	②	SNUG
	4.6	H	0.0004	0.006-0.012	0.012-0.0220	0.006-0.0260	0.0004-0.0009	0.0012-0.0032	SNUG
	4.6	W	0.0007-0.0019	0.006-0.012	0.0098-0.0197	0.006-0.0256	0.0008-0.0020	0.0008-0.0020	SNUG
2006	4.0	E,K	0.0012-0.0019	0.008-0.018	0.016-0.0240	—	0.0016-0.0030	0.0012-0.0026	SNUG
	4.6	8	0.0007-0.0019	0.006-0.012	0.0098-0.0197	0.006-0.0260	0.0008-0.0020	0.0008-0.0020	SNUG
2007	4.0	E,K	0.0012-0.0019	0.008-0.018	0.016-0.0240	—	0.0016-0.0030	0.0012-0.0026	SNUG
	4.6	8	0.0007-0.0019	0.006-0.012	0.0098-0.0197	0.006-0.0260	0.0008-0.0020	0.0008-0.0020	SNUG

① Explorer 4.0L: 0.016-0.024 in.
  Explorer Sport-Trac 4.0L: 0.018-0.028 in.
② Explorer 4.0L: 0.0012-0.0026 in.
  Explorer Sport-Trac 4.0L: 0.0020-0.0030 in.

22086_EXPL_C0008

TORQUE SPECIFICATIONS
All readings in ft. lbs.

	Engine Displ. Liters	Engine ID/VIN	Cylinder Head Bolts	Main Bearing Bolts	Rod Bearing Bolts	Crankshaft Damper Bolts	Flywheel Bolts	Manifold Intake *	Exhaust	Spark Plugs	Oil Pan Drain Plug
2005	4.0	E,K	①	72	②	③	④	8	16	15	19
	4.6	H	⑤	⑥	⑦	⑧	59	7	15	15	10
	4.6	W	⑤	⑥	⑦	⑧	59	18	15	25	19
2006	4.0	E,K	①	72	②	③	④	8	16	15	19
	4.6	8	⑤	⑥	⑦	⑧	59	18	15	25	19
2007	4.0	E,K	①	72	②	③	④	8	16	15	19
	4.6	8	⑤	⑥	⑦	⑧	59	18	15	25	19

NA: Information not available

* NOTE: Applies to Lower Manifold only.

① Step 1: 12mm bolts: 9 ft. lbs.
Step 2: 12mm bolts: 18 ft. lbs.
Step 3: 8mm bolts: 24 ft. lbs.
Step 4: 12mm bolts: plus 90 degrees
Step 5: 12mm bolts: plus an additional 90 degrees

② Step 1: 15 ft. lbs.
Step 2: +90 degrees

③ Step 1: 33 ft. lbs.
Step 2: plus 85 degrees

④ Step 1: 10 ft. lbs.
Step 2: 52 ft. lbs.

⑤ Step 1: 30 ft. lbs.
Step 2: plus 90 degrees
Step 3: back off 1 full turn
Step 4: 30 ft. lbs.
Step 5: plus 90 degrees
Step 6: plus 90 additional degrees

⑥ Bolts 1-20:
Step 1: 89 inch lbs.
Step 2: 18 ft. lbs.
Step 3: 30 ft. lbs.
Step 4: plus 90 degrees
Cross bolts:
Step 1: 30 ft. lbs.
Step 2: plus 90 degrees
Step 3: Plus 90 degrees

⑦ Step 1: 17 ft. lbs.
Step 2: 32 ft. lbs.
Step 3: plus 90-120 degrees

⑧ Step 1: 66 ft. lbs.
Step 2: back off 1 full turn
Step 3: 37 ft. lbs.
Step 4: plus 90 degrees
Do not exceed 148 ft. lbs.

22086_EXPL_C0010

WHEEL ALIGNMENT

Year	Model		Caster Range (+/-Deg.)	Caster Preferred Setting (Deg.)	Camber Range (+/-Deg.)	Camber Preferred Setting (Deg.)	Toe-in (in.)
2005	Aviator	F	1.00	+5.3	0.08	-0.50	0.24+/-0.25
		R	—	—	0.08	-0.95	0.16+/-0.25
	Explorer	F	1.00	L +5.1; R +5.3	0.80	-0.50	0.10+/-0.25
		R	—	—	0.80	-0.90	0.10+/-0.25
	Explorer Sport-Trac	F	1.00	L +3.15; R +4.05	0.70	-0.50	0.12+/-0.25
		R	—	—	—	—	—
	Mountaineer	F	1.00	L +5.1; R +5.3	0.80	-0.50	0.10+/-0.25
		R	—	—	0.80	-0.90	0.10+/-0.25
2006	Explorer	F	0.75	+4.6	0.75	-0.50	0.20+/-0.20
		R	—	—	0.75	-0.50	0.10+/-0.20
	Mountaineer	F	0.75	+4.6	0.75	-0.50	0.20+/-0.20
		R	—	—	0.75	-0.50	0.10+/-0.20
2007	Explorer	F	0.75	+4.6	0.75	-0.50	0.20+/-0.20
		R	—	—	0.75	-0.50	0.05+/-0.20
	Explorer Sport-Trac	F	0.75	+4.6	0.75	-0.50	0.20+/-0.20
		R	—	—	0.75	-0.50	0.05+/-0.20
	Mountaineer	F	0.75	+4.6	0.75	-0.50	0.20+/-0.20
		R	—	—	0.75	-0.50	0.05+/-0.20

22086_EXPL_C0012

TIRE, WHEEL AND BALL JOINT SPECIFICATIONS

Year	Model	OEM Tires Standard	OEM Tires Optional	Tire Pressures (psi) Front	Tire Pressures (psi) Rear	Wheel Size	Ball Joint Inspection	Lug Nut Torque (ft. lbs.)
2005	Aviator	P245/65HR17	none	①	①	7.5	②	100
	Explorer						②	100
	Eddie Bauer	P245/65R17	none	①	①	NA		
	Limited	P245/65R17	none	①	①	NA		
	XLS	P235/70R16	none	①	①	7		
	XLS Sport	P235/70R16	none	①	①	7		
	XLT	P235/70R16	none	①	①	7		
	XLT Sport	P245/65R17	none	①	①	NA		
	XLT Premium	P255/70R16	none	①	①	7		
	Explorer Sport-Trac						②	100
	Adrenalin	P255/70R16	none	①	①	7		
	XLS	P235/70R16	none	①	①	7		
	XLT	P235/70R16	none	①	①	7		
	Mountaineer						②	100
	Convenience	P235/70R16	none	①	①	NA		
	Luxury	P245/65R17	none	①	①	NA		
	Premier	P245/65R17	none	①	①	NA		
2006	Explorer						②	100
	Eddie Bauer	P245/65R17	P235/65R18	①	①	NA		
	Limited	P245/65R17	none	①	①	NA		
	XLS	P235/70R16	none	①	①	7		
	XLT	P235/70R16	P245/65R17	①	①	7		
	Mountaineer						②	100
	Convenience	P245/65R17	none	①	①	NA		
	Luxury	P245/65R17	P235/65R18	①	①	NA		
	Premier	P245/65R17	P235/65R18	①	①	NA		
2007	Explorer						②	100
	Eddie Bauer	P245/65R17	P235/65R18	①	①	NA		
	Limited	P235/65R18	none	①	①	NA		
	Iron Man	P235/65R18	none	①	①	7		
	XLT	P235/70R16	P235/65R17	①	①	7		
	Explorer Sport-Trac						②	100
	XLT	P235/70R16	none	①	①	7		
	Limited	P245/70R17	P235/65R18	①	①	7		
	Mountaineer						②	100
	V6	P245/65R17	none	①	①	NA		
	Premier	P245/65R17	P235/65R18	①	①	NA		

NA: Information not available

OEM: Original Equipment Manufacturer

PSI: Pounds Per Square Inch

STD: Standard

OPT: Optional

① See placard on vehicle

② Upper: 0.008"; Lower: 0.32"

BRAKE SPECIFICATIONS
All measurements in inches unless noted

Year	Model		Brake Disc Original Thickness	Brake Disc Min. Thickness	Brake Disc Max. Runout	Brake Drum Diameter Original Inside Dia.	Brake Drum Diameter Max. Wear Limit	Brake Drum Diameter Max. Machine Dia.	Minimum Lining Thickness	Brake Caliper Bracket Bolts (ft. lbs.)	Brake Caliper Mounting Bolts (ft. lbs.)
2005	Explorer	F	NA	0.960	NA	—	—	—	0.118	100	24
		R	NA	0.430	NA	—	—	—	0.118	—	24
	Explorer	F	NA	0.980	NA	—	—	—	0.118	83	24
	Sport-Trac	R	NA	0.430	NA	—	—	—	0.118	—	20
	Mountaineer	F	NA	0.960	NA	—	—	—	0.118	100	24
		R	NA	0.430	NA	—	—	—	0.118	—	24
	Aviator	F	NA	1.040	NA	—	—	—	0.118	155	32
		R	NA	0.430	NA	—	—	—	0.118	—	24
2006	Explorer	F	NA	1.120	NA	—	—	—	0.118	122	53
		R	NA	0.430	NA	—	—	—	0.118	—	24
	Mountaineer	F	NA	1.120	NA	—	—	—	0.118	122	53
		R	NA	0.430	NA	—	—	—	0.118	—	24
2007	Explorer	F	NA	1.120	NA	—	—	—	0.118	122	53
		R	NA	0.430	NA	—	—	—	0.118	—	24
	Explorer	F	NA	1.120	NA	—	—	—	0.118	122	53
	Sport-Trac	R	NA	0.430	NA	—	—	—	0.118	—	24
	Mountaineer	F	NA	1.120	NA	—	—	—	0.118	122	53
		R	NA	0.430	NA	—	—	—	0.118	—	24

NOTE: Due to changes made during production, refer to manufacturer's specifications if they differ from those in this chart

NA: Information not available

22086_EXPL_C0011

SCHEDULED MAINTENANCE INTERVALS
2005-07 Lincoln Aviator, Ford Explorer, Explorer Sport-Trac, Mercury Mountaineer

TO BE SERVICED	SERVICE	5	10	15	20	25	30	35	40	45	50	55	60	65
		VEHICLE MILEAGE INTERVAL (x1000)												
Engine oil & filter	R	✓	✓	✓	✓	✓	✓	✓	✓	✓	✓	✓	✓	✓
Tires	Rotate	✓	✓	✓	✓	✓	✓	✓	✓	✓	✓	✓	✓	✓
Auto trans. fluid	I			✓			✓			✓			✓	
Brake pads/shoes	I			✓			✓			✓			✓	
Coolant hoses	S/I			✓			✓			✓			✓	
Steering linkage	I			✓			✓			✓			✓	
Suspension, driveshaft	I			✓			✓			✓			✓	
Cabin air filter	R			✓			✓			✓			✓	
Ball joints (2WD)	L			✓			✓			✓			✓	
Wheels ①	I						✓						✓	
Exhaust system	I						✓						✓	
Engine air filter	R						✓						✓	
Fuel filter	R						✓						✓	
Climate controlled seat filter	R						✓						✓	
Accessory drive belts	I	every 100,000 miles												
Premium Gold coolant	R	5 years or 100,000 miles, then every 3 years or 30,000 miles												
Spark plugs	R	every 100,000 miles												
PCV valve	R	every 100,000 miles												
Coolant, exc. Premium Gold	R	every 105,000 miles												
Front wheel bearings and	R	every 150,000 miles if not already done so												
Manual trans. fluid	R	every 120,000 miles												
Auto trans fluid	R	every 150,000 miles												
Differential fluid	R	every 150,000 miles												
Accessory drive belts	R	every 150,000 miles if not already done so												

R: Replace　　　S: Service　　　I: Inspect　　　L: Lubricate

① Inspect wheel ends for end play and noise

Special Operating Condition Requirements

When towing a trailer or using a camper or car-top carrier:

Change engine oil and install a new oil filter every 4,800 km (3,000 miles) or 3 months.

Change transfer case fluid every 96,000 km (60,000 miles).

Change manual transmission fluid as required.

Inspect and lubricate U-joints as required.

During extensive idling and/or low speed driving for long distances, as in heavy commercial use such as delivery, taxi, patrol car or livery:

Change engine oil and install a new oil filter, lube front lower control arm and steering linkage ball joints with

zerk fittings (if equipped) every 4,800 km (3,000 miles) or 3 months.

Inspect brake system and check battery electrolyte level (Patrol cars) every 8,000 km (5,000 miles).

Install a new fuel filter every 24,000 km (15,000 miles).

Change automatic transmission fluid, lubricate 4x2 wheel bearings,

install new grease seals and adjust bearings every 48,000 km (30,000 miles).

Install new spark plugs and change transfer case fluid every 96,000 km (60,000 miles).

Install a new cabin air filter as required.

When operating in dusty conditions such as unpaved or dusty roads:

Change engine oil and install a new oil filter every 4,800 km (3,000 miles) or 3 months.

Install a new fuel filter every 24,000 km (15,000 miles).

Change automatic transmission fluid every 48,000 km (30,000 miles).

22086_EXPL_C0014

SCHEDULED MAINTENANCE INTERVALS
2005-07 Lincoln Aviator, Ford Explorer, Explorer Sport-Trac, Mercury Mountaineer
Footnotes Continued

Change transfer case fluid every 96,000 km (60,000 miles).

Install a new engine air filter as required.

Install a new cabin air filter as required.

When operating in off-road conditions:

Change automatic transmission fluid every 48,000 km (30,000 miles).

Change transfer case fluid every 96,000 km (60,000 miles).

Install a new cabin air filter as required.

Inspect and lubricate U-joints.

Inspect and lubricate steering linkage ball joints with zerk fittings.

22086_EXPL_C0015

PRECAUTIONS

Before servicing any vehicle, please be sure to read all of the following precautions, which deal with personal safety, prevention of component damage, and important points to take into consideration when servicing a motor vehicle:

• Never open, service or drain the radiator or cooling system when the engine is hot; serious burns can occur from the steam and hot coolant.

• Observe all applicable safety precautions when working around fuel. Whenever servicing the fuel system, always work in a well-ventilated area. Do not allow fuel spray or vapors to come in contact with a spark, open flame, or excessive heat (a hot drop light, for example). Keep a dry chemical fire extinguisher near the work area. Always keep fuel in a container specifically designed for fuel storage; also, always properly seal fuel containers to avoid the possibility of fire or explosion. Refer to the additional fuel system precautions later in this section.

• Fuel injection systems often remain pressurized, even after the engine has been turned **OFF**. The fuel system pressure must be relieved before disconnecting any fuel lines. Failure to do so may result in fire and/or personal injury.

• Brake fluid often contains polyglycol ethers and polyglycols. Avoid contact with the eyes and wash your hands thoroughly after handling brake fluid. If you do get brake fluid in your eyes, flush your eyes with clean, running water for 15 minutes. If eye irritation persists, or if you have taken brake fluid internally, IMMEDIATELY seek medical assistance.

• The EPA warns that prolonged contact with used engine oil may cause a number of skin disorders, including cancer. You should make every effort to minimize your exposure to used engine oil. Protective gloves should be worn when changing oil. Wash your hands and any other exposed skin areas as soon as possible after exposure to used engine oil. Soap and water, or waterless hand cleaner should be used.

• All new vehicles are now equipped with an air bag system, often referred to as a Supplemental Restraint System (SRS) or Supplemental Inflatable Restraint (SIR) system. The system must be disabled before performing service on or around system components, steering column, instrument panel components, wiring and sensors. Failure to follow safety and disabling procedures could result in accidental air bag deployment, possible personal injury and unnecessary system repairs.

• Always wear safety goggles when working with, or around, the air bag system. When carrying a non-deployed air bag, be sure the bag and trim cover are pointed away from your body. When placing a non-deployed air bag on a work surface, always face the bag and trim cover upward, away from the surface. This will reduce the motion of the module if it is accidentally deployed. Refer to the additional air bag system precautions later in this section.

• Clean, high quality brake fluid from a sealed container is essential to the safe and proper operation of the brake system. You should always buy the correct type of brake fluid for your vehicle. If the brake fluid becomes contaminated, completely flush the system with new fluid. Never reuse any brake fluid. Any brake fluid that is removed from the system should be discarded. Also, do not allow any brake fluid to come in contact with a painted surface; it will damage the paint.

• Never operate the engine without the proper amount and type of engine oil; doing so WILL result in severe engine damage.

• Timing belt maintenance is extremely important. Many models utilize an interference-type, non-freewheeling engine. If the timing belt breaks, the valves in the cylinder head may strike the pistons, causing potentially serious (also time-consuming and expensive) engine damage. Refer to the maintenance interval charts for the recommended replacement interval for the timing belt, and to the timing belt section for belt replacement and inspection.

• Disconnecting the negative battery cable on some vehicles may interfere with the functions of the on-board computer system(s) and may require the computer to undergo a relearning process once the negative battery cable is reconnected.

• When servicing drum brakes, only disassemble and assemble one side at a time, leaving the remaining side intact for reference.

• Only an MVAC-trained, EPA-certified automotive technician should service the air conditioning system or its components.

BRAKES   ANTI-LOCK BRAKE SYSTEM (ABS)

GENERAL INFORMATION

ANTI-LOCK BRAKE SYSTEM (ABS)

2005 Models

The Anti-lock Brake System (ABS) consists of the following components:
• Hydraulic Control Unit (HCU)
• ABS module
• Rear anti-lock brake sensor
• Rear anti-lock brake sensor ring (integral to the ring gear)
• Front wheel anti-lock brake sensors
• Front wheel anti-lock brake sensor ring (integral to the hub and bearing assembly)
• Yellow ABS warning indicator
• Brake pressure sensor (also called speed control deactivator switch) (ABS only)

➡3-channel systems are used in vehicles with solid rear axles. One wheel speed sensor is installed at each front hub and a third sensor is installed on the rear differential by the ring gear. 4-channel systems have one wheel speed sensor at each of the four wheels.

ANTI-LOCK BRAKE SYSTEM (ABS) WITH STABILITY ASSIST

2005 Models

The Anti-lock Brake System (ABS) with traction control and stability assist consists of these additional components:
• Rear wheel anti-lock brake sensors
• Rear wheel anti-lock brake sensor ring (integral to the half shaft or ring gear)
• Sensor cluster (contains the accelerometer[s] and yaw rate sensor)
• Steering position sensor (integral to the clockspring)
• Primary brake pressure transducer
• Brake pedal travel sensor
• Brake pedal force switch (integral to the brake booster)
• Brake booster solenoid (integral to the brake booster)

2006–07 Models

The Anti-lock Brake System (ABS) with traction control and stability assist consists of these additional components:
• Hydraulic control unit (HCU)
• ABS module
• Stability traction control switch
• Steering wheel rotation sensor
• Stability control sensor cluster (contains the accelerometer[s], roll rate sensor and yaw rate sensor)
• Front wheel speed sensors
• Front wheel speed sensor rings (integral to the wheel bearing and hub assemblies)
• Rear wheel speed sensors
• Rear wheel speed sensor rings (integral to the halfshafts)
• Brake pressure transducer (integral to the ABS module)
• Brake fluid level sensor
• Brake pedal force switch (integral to the brake booster)
• Brake booster solenoid (integral to the brake booster)
• Yellow ABS warning indicator
• Traction control/roll stability control indicator ("sliding car" indicator)

The front wheel speed sensor rings are integral to the front bearing and hub assemblies. The rear wheel speed sensor rings are integral to the rear halfshafts.

FRONT SPEED SENSORS

REMOVAL & INSTALLATION

2005 Aviator, Explorer and Mountaineer

See Figure 1.

1. With the vehicle in NEUTRAL, position it on a hoist.
2. Remove the front brake disc.
3. Disconnect the wheel speed sensor electrical connector.
4. Remove the 3 wheel speed sensor harness retainers.
5. Remove the 2 wheel speed sensor harness pin-type retainers.
6. Remove the wheel speed sensor bolt.

7. Remove the wheel speed sensor and the harness.

To install:
8. Installation is the reverse of the removal procedure.
9. Observe the following tightening specifications:
• Speed sensor bolt 115 inch lbs. (17 Nm)

2005 Explorer Sport-Trac

2WD Models

See Figures 2 and 3.

1. Raise and support the vehicle.
2. Disconnect the electrical connector.
3. Unclip the front anti-lock brake sensor wire from the vehicle frame.
4. Remove the bolt (1).
5. Remove the front anti-lock brake sensor (2).

➡Plug the sensor mount opening and thoroughly clean the mounting surface. Apply grease.

To install:
6. Installation is the reverse of the removal procedure.
7. Observe the following tightening specifications:
• Speed sensor bolt 100 inch lbs. (12 Nm)

4WD Models

See Figures 4 through 6.
See Figure 7.

1. Remove the brake disc shield.
2. Disconnect the front anti-lock brake sensor electrical connector.
3. Unclip the front anti-lock brake sensor wire from the vehicle frame.
4. Remove the bolt.
5. Remove the bolt (1).
   a. Tightening torque 71 inch lbs (8 Nm)
6. Remove the front anti-lock brake sensor (2).

➡Plug the sensor mount opening and thoroughly clean the mounting surface. Apply grease.

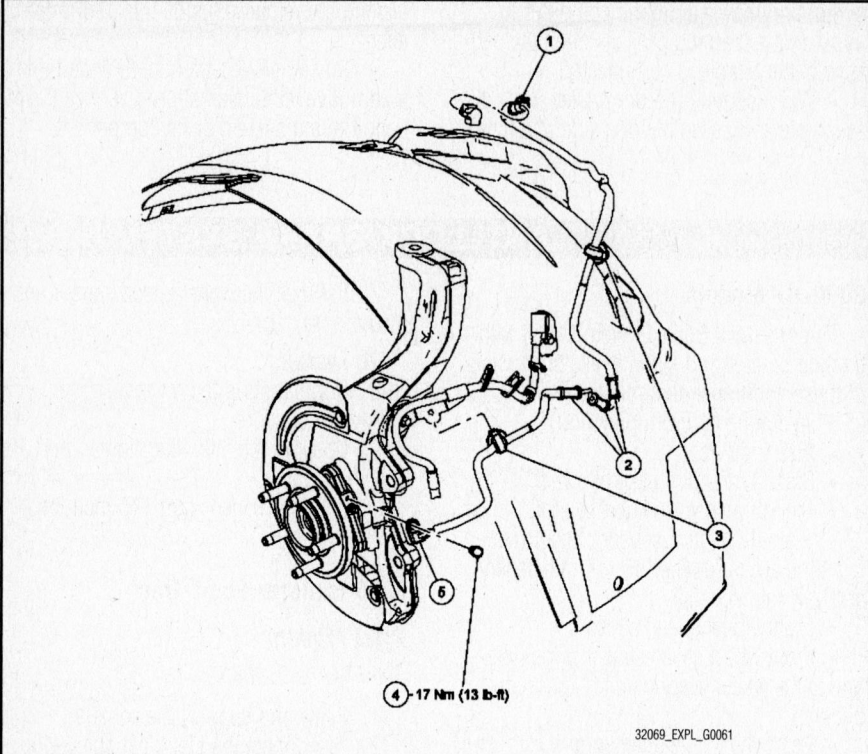

Fig. 1 Wheel speed sensor electrical connector (1), wheel speed sensor harness retainer (2), wheel speed sensor harness pin-type retainer (3), wheel speed sensor bolt (4) and wheel speed sensor (5)

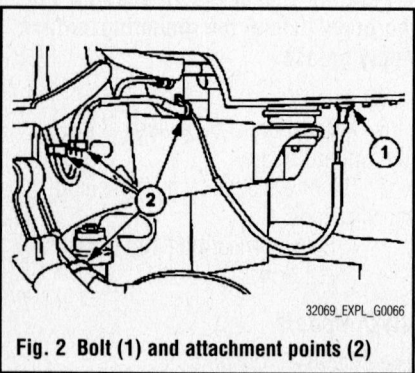

Fig. 2 Bolt (1) and attachment points (2)

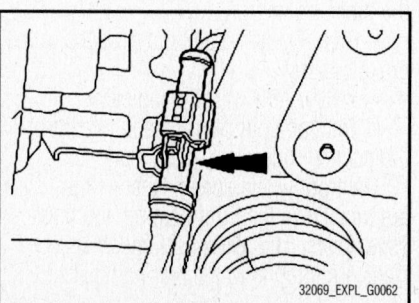

Fig. 4 Front anti-lock brake sensor electrical connector

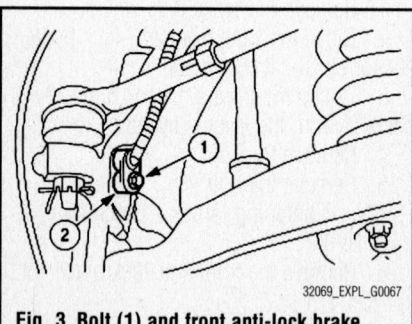

Fig. 3 Bolt (1) and front anti-lock brake sensor (2)

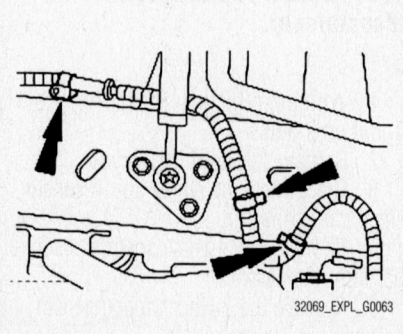

Fig. 5 Anti-lock brake sensor wire attachment points (arrows)

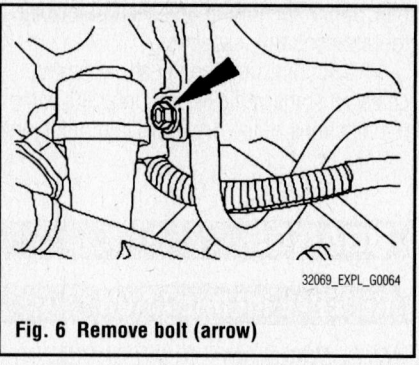

Fig. 6 Remove bolt (arrow)

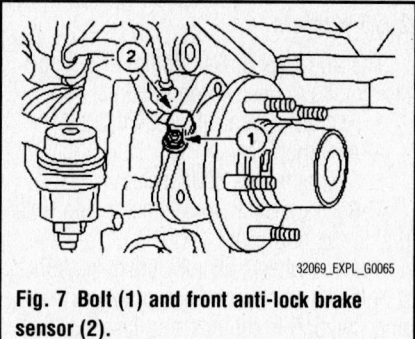

Fig. 7 Bolt (1) and front anti-lock brake sensor (2).

To install:

7. Installation is the reverse of the removal procedure.

8. Observe the following tightening specifications:

- Speed sensor bolt 71 inch lbs. (8 Nm)

2006–07 Explorer and Mountaineer; 2007 Explorer Sport-Trac

1. Remove the front brake disc. See "Brake Disc" under "Front Disc Brakes" section.

2. Disconnect the wheel speed sensor electrical connector.

3. Remove the wheel speed sensor harness bolt.

4. Remove the wheel speed sensor harness pin-type retainers.

5. Remove the wheel speed sensor bolt.

6. Remove the wheel speed sensor and the harness.

7. Installation is the reverse of the removal procedure, tighten the wheel speed sensor bolt to 13 ft. lbs. (17 Nm).

REAR SPEED SENSORS

REMOVAL & INSTALLATION

2005 Aviator, Explorer and Mountaineer

➡The Aviator uses a 4-channel sensor. Refer to the "Rear 4-Channel" procedure below.

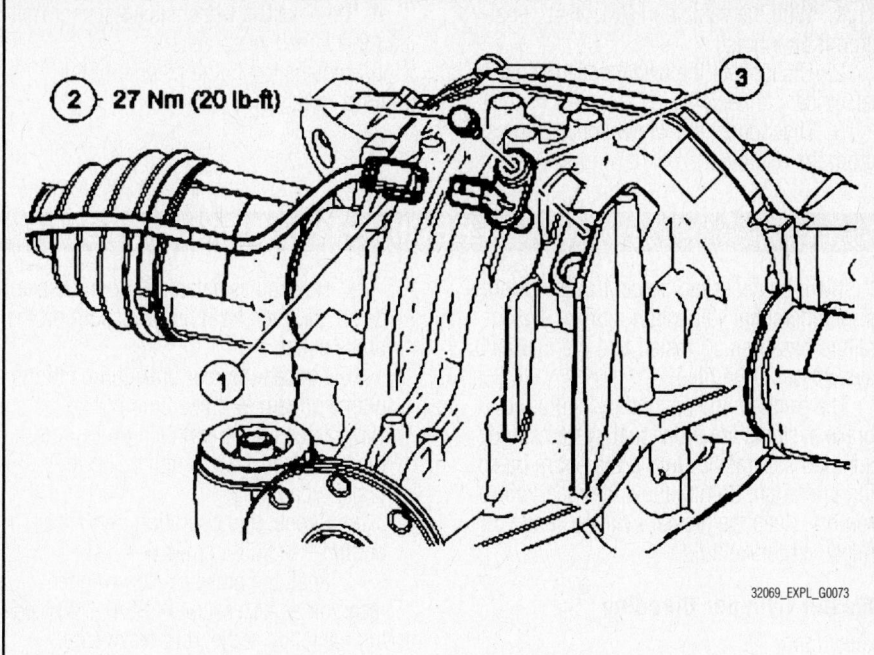

Fig. 8 Wheel speed sensor electrical connector (1), wheel speed sensor bolt (2) and wheel speed sensor (3)

Rear 3-Channel

See Figure 8.

1. With the vehicle in NEUTRAL, position it on a hoist.

➡️**Apply electrical grease to the connector terminals.**

2. Disconnect the wheel speed sensor electrical connector.

3. Remove the wheel speed sensor bolt.

➡️**Install a new O-ring.**

4. Remove the wheel speed sensor.

5. Installation is the reverse of the removal procedure. Tighten the speed sensor bolt to 20 ft. lbs. (27 Nm).

Rear 4-Channel

See Figure 9.

1. With the vehicle in NEUTRAL, position it on a hoist.

2. Disconnect the wheel speed sensor electrical connector.

3. Disconnect the 3 wheel speed sensor harness pin-type retainers.

4. Remove the wheel speed sensor bolt.

5. Remove the wheel speed sensor and harness assembly.

6. Installation is the reverse of the removal procedure. Tighten the speed sensor bolt to 20 ft. lbs. (27 Nm).

2005 Explorer Sport-Trac

See Figure 10.

1. Raise and support vehicle.

➡️**Clean off dirt and foreign material that may have collected around the rear anti-lock brake sensor before removal.**

2. Disconnect the electrical connector.

3. Remove the bolt.

4. Remove the sensor.

5. Thoroughly clean the mounting surface.

➡️**Inspect the anti-lock brake sensor O-ring for damage; lightly lubricate the O-ring with axle lubricant.**

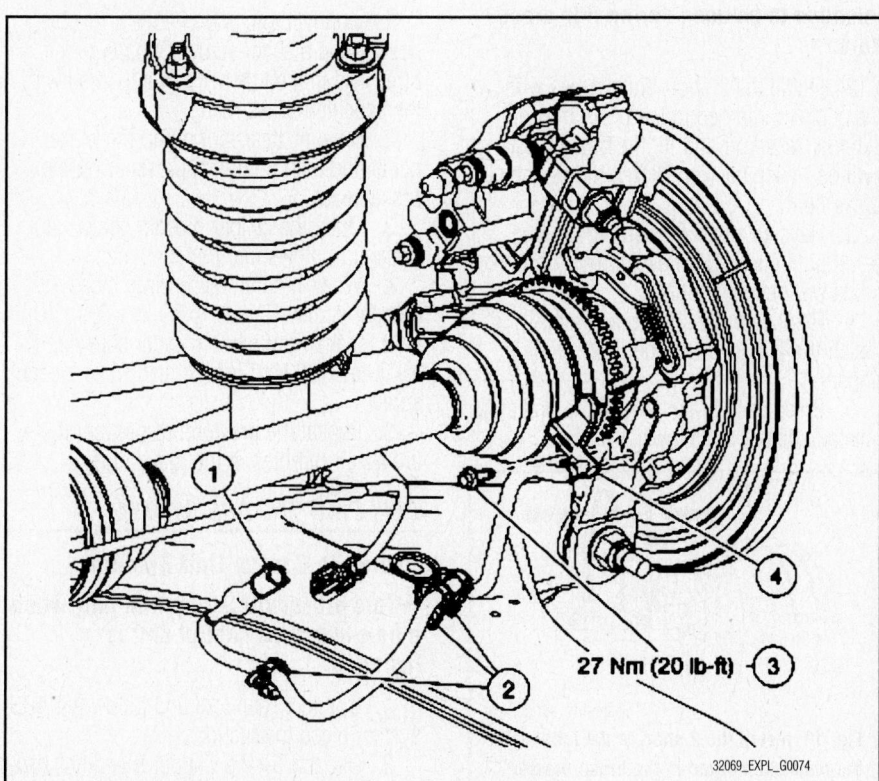

Fig. 9 Wheel speed sensor electrical connector (1), wheel speed sensor harness pin-type retainer (2), wheel speed sensor bolt (3) and wheel speed sensor (4)

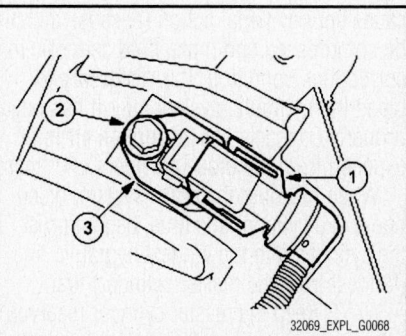

Fig. 10 Rear wheel speed sensor electrical connector (1), bolt (2) and rear wheel speed sensor (3)

6. Installation is the reverse of the removal procedure. Tighten the speed sensor bolt to 20 ft. lbs. (27 Nm).

2006–07 Explorer and Mountaineer; 2007 Explorer Sport-Trac

1. With the vehicle in NEUTRAL, position it on a hoist.
2. Disconnect the wheel speed sensor electrical connector.
3. Disconnect the wheel speed harness from the retainers.

4. Remove the wheel speed sensor bolt and the wheel speed sensor
5. Installation is the reverse of the removal procedure.

BRAKES **BLEEDING THE BRAKE SYSTEM**

BLEEDING PROCEDURE

BRAKE LINE BLEEDING

✳✳ WARNING

Carefully read cautionary information on product label. For EMERGENCY MEDICAL INFORMATION seek medical advice. In the USA or Canada on Ford/Motorcraft products call: 1-800-959-3673. For additional information, consult the product Material Safety Data Sheet (MSDS) if available. Failure to follow these instructions may result in personal injury.

✳ CAUTION

Do not allow the brake master cylinder reservoir to run dry during the bleeding operation. Keep the brake master cylinder reservoir filled with the specified brake fluid. Never reuse brake fluid that has been drained from the hydraulic system.

✳✳ CAUTION

Brake fluid is harmful to painted and plastic surfaces. If brake fluid is spilled onto a painted or plastic surface, immediately wash it with water.

When any part of the hydraulic system has been disconnected for repair or replacement, air may get into the lines and cause spongy pedal action (because air can be compressed and brake fluid cannot). To correct this condition, it is necessary to bleed the hydraulic system after it has been properly connected to be sure all air is expelled from the brake cylinders and lines.

When bleeding the brake system, bleed one brake cylinder at a time, beginning at the cylinder with the longest hydraulic line (farthest from the master cylinder) first. ALWAYS Keep the master cylinder reservoir filled with brake fluid during the bleeding operation. Never use brake fluid that has been drained from the hydraulic system, no matter how clean it is.

It will be necessary to centralize the pressure differential value after a brake system failure has been corrected and the hydraulic system has been bled.

The primary and secondary hydraulic brake systems are individual systems and are bled separately. During the entire bleeding operation, do not allow the reservoir to run dry. Keep the master cylinder reservoir filled with brake fluid.

Master Cylinder Bleeding

See Figure 11.

➡**When a new brake master cylinder has been installed or the system has been emptied or partially emptied, it should be primed to prevent air from getting into the system.**

1. Disconnect the brake master cylinder tubes from the side of the master cylinder.

➡**Original equipment lines are not intended to be used during this procedure.**

2. Install the 2 short brake tubes with the ends submerged in the brake master cylinder reservoir and fill the brake master cylinder reservoir with DOT 3 motor vehicle brake fluid.
3. Have an assistant pump the brake pedal until clear fluid flows from both brake tubes without air bubbles.
4. Remove the 2 short brake tubes and install the 2 master cylinder brake tube fittings.
5. Bleed each brake tube at the brake master cylinder as follows:

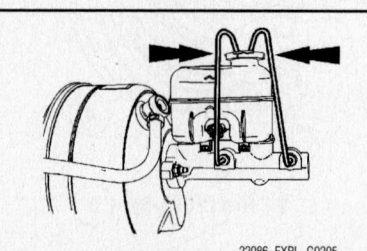

Fig. 11 Install the 2 short brake tubes with the ends submerged in the brake master cylinder reservoir and fill the brake master cylinder reservoir with DOT 3 motor vehicle brake fluid

22086_EXPL_G0205

a. Have an assistant pump the brake pedal and then hold firm pressure on the brake pedal.
b. Loosen the rear brake tube fittings until a stream of brake fluid comes out. Have an assistant maintain pressure on the brake pedal while tightening the brake tube fitting.
c. Repeat this operation until clear, bubble-free fluid comes out.
d. Refill the brake master cylinder reservoir as necessary. REPEAT the bleeding operation at the front brake tube.
6. While the assistant maintains pressure on the brake pedal, tighten the master cylinder brake tubes to 13 ft. lbs. (18 Nm).

Brake Caliper Bleeding

➡**It is not necessary to bleed the entire brake system. It is possible to bleed only the opened part of the system.**

1. Connect one end of a clear flexible hose to the bleeder screw. Submerge the other end in a container partially filled with the specified brake fluid.
2. Have an assistant pump the brake pedal and then hold firm pressure on the brake pedal.
3. Open the caliper bleeder screw until brake fluid flows into the container.
4. When fluid stops flowing, close the bleeder screw. Tighten to 89 inch lbs. (10 Nm) for the front brake bleeder screw and 16 ft. lbs. (22 Nm) for the rear brake bleeder screw.
5. Repeat the previous steps until there are no air bubbles in the brake fluid.

BLEEDING THE ABS SYSTEM

Hydraulic Control Unit Bleeding

➡**This procedure is required only when a new hydraulic control unit is installed.**

1. Connect scan tool and follow the ABS system bleed instructions.
2. Use the "Brake Caliper Bleeding" procedure in this section to bleed the system. Begin at the right rear caliper.

BRAKES

FRONT DISC BRAKES

✳✳ CAUTION

Dust and dirt accumulating on brake parts during normal use may contain asbestos fibers from production or aftermarket brake linings. Breathing excessive concentrations of asbestos fibers can cause serious bodily harm. Exercise care when servicing brake parts. Do not sand or grind brake lining unless equipment used is designed to contain the dust residue. Do not clean brake parts with compressed air or by dry brushing. Cleaning should be done by dampening the brake components with a fine mist of water, then wiping the brake components clean with a dampened cloth. Dispose of cloth and all residue containing asbestos fibers in an impermeable container with the appropriate label. Follow practices prescribed by the Occupational Safety and Health Administration (OSHA) and the Environmental Protection Agency (EPA) for the handling, processing, and disposing of dust or debris that may contain asbestos fibers.

BRAKE CALIPER

REMOVAL & INSTALLATION

Aviator

See Figure 12.

1. Before servicing the vehicle, refer to the "Precautions" section and the "Brake Service Precautions" section.
2. Loosen the wheel lug nuts.
3. Raise and safely support the front of the vehicle. Remove the wheel.
4. Place an 8 in. (203mm) C-clamp on the caliper and tighten the clamp to

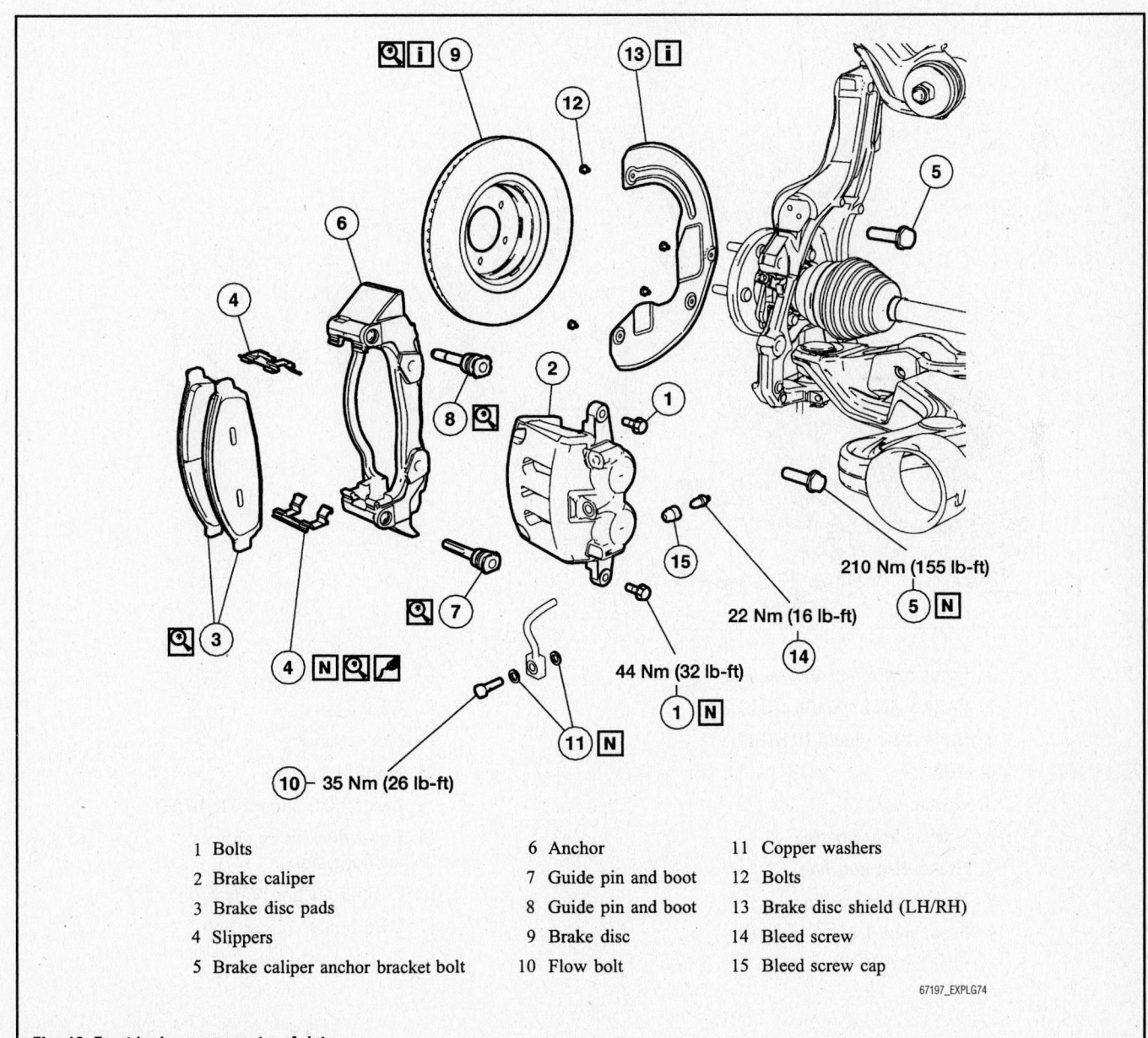

210 Nm (155 lb-ft)
22 Nm (16 lb-ft)
44 Nm (32 lb-ft)
35 Nm (26 lb-ft)

1 Bolts	6 Anchor	11 Copper washers
2 Brake caliper	7 Guide pin and boot	12 Bolts
3 Brake disc pads	8 Guide pin and boot	13 Brake disc shield (LH/RH)
4 Slippers	9 Brake disc	14 Bleed screw
5 Brake caliper anchor bracket bolt	10 Flow bolt	15 Bleed screw cap

67197_EXPLG74

Fig. 12 Front brake components—Aviator

bottom the caliper pistons in their bores. Remove the clamp.

5. Remove the two caliper slide pin bolts and lift the caliper from the anchor plate.

➡**Use care to retain as much of the original caliper slide pin grease as possible.**

6. Position the caliper on a frame member or suspend it with some wire. Do not allow the caliper to hang by the brake hose.

7. Disconnect and plug the brake hose at the caliper. Remove the caliper from the rotor.

To install:

8. Position the caliper over the brake pads and align the slide pin mounting holes.

9. Install the slide pin bolts and tighten them to 32 ft. lbs. (44 Nm).

➡**Tighten the bottom locator pin caliper bolt before tightening the top guide pin caliper bolt.**

10. Install the caliper brake hose using new washers. Tighten the bolt to 26 ft. lbs. (35 Nm).

11. Install the wheel and snug the lug nuts.

12. Lower the vehicle and tighten the lug nuts to 100 ft. lbs. (135 Nm).

➡**The first couple of times you apply the brakes, the pedal may go to the floor. Continue to pump the brake pedal until it feels firm.**

13. Start the engine and apply the brakes several times to readjust the caliper pistons. Ensure that the pedal feels firm before operating the vehicle.

2005 Explorer, Mountaineer and Explorer Sport-Trac

See Figures 13 through 15.

1. Before servicing the vehicle, refer to the "Precautions" section and the "Brake Service Precautions" section.

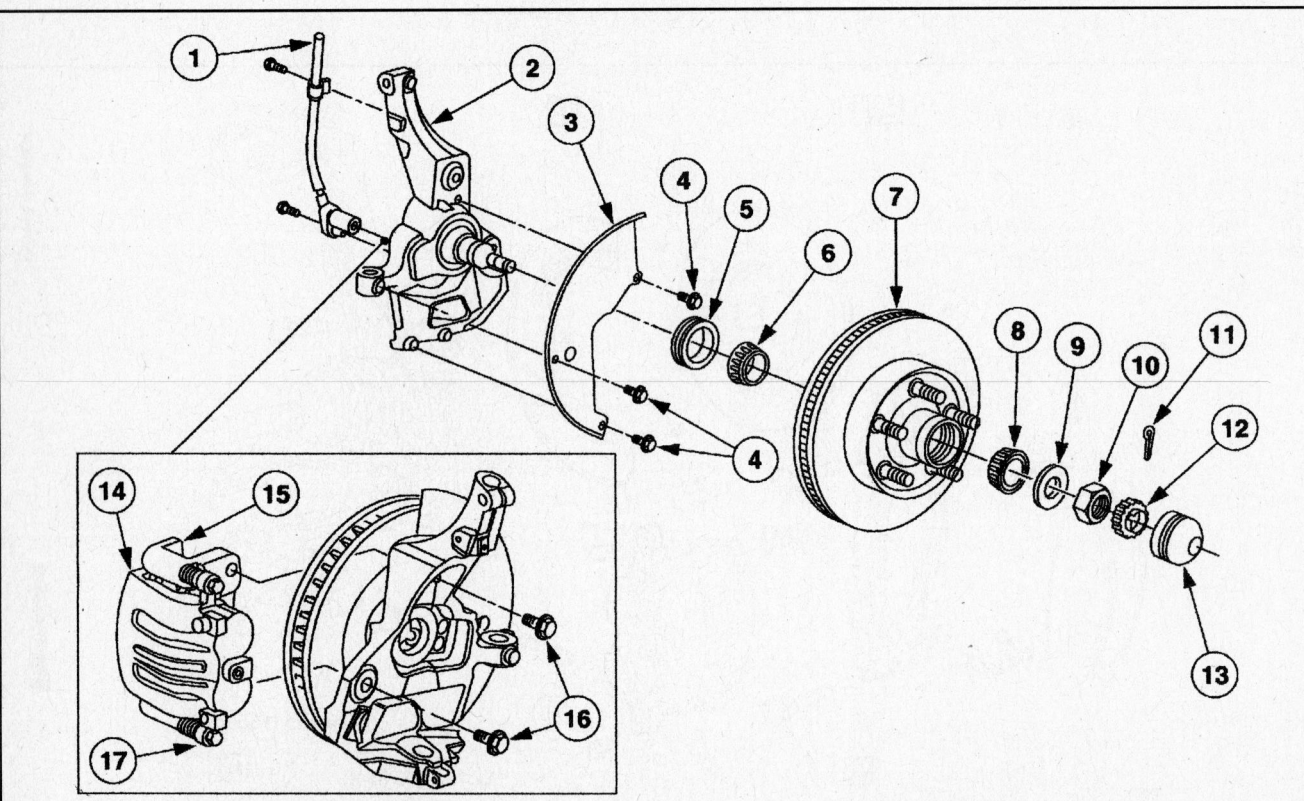

1 Front brake anti-lock sensor
2 Front wheel spindle (RH/LH)
3 Brake disc shield (RH/LH)
4 Bolt
5 Grease seal
6 Front wheel bearing
7 Brake disc and hub
8 Front wheel bearing
9 Front wheel outer bearing retainer washer
10 Hub spindle nut
11 Cotter pin
12 Nut retainer
13 Hub grease cap
14 Disc brake caliper (RH/LH)
15 Front disc brake caliper anchor plate
16 Caliper anchor plate bolts
17 Disc brake caliper bolt

06017-EXPL-G157

Fig. 13 Front brake components—2005 2WD Explorer Sport-Trac

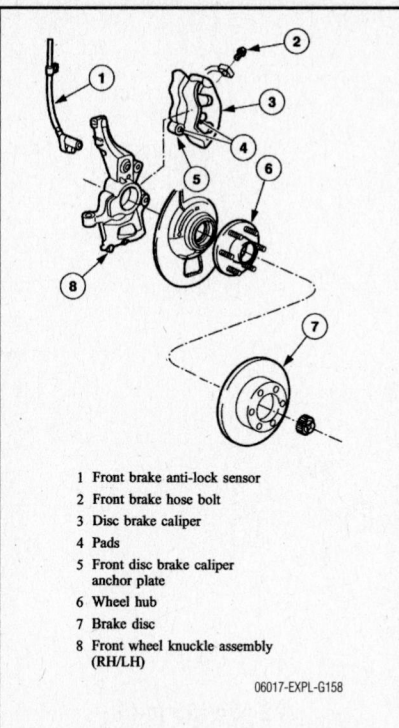

1 Front brake anti-lock sensor
2 Front brake hose bolt
3 Disc brake caliper
4 Pads
5 Front disc brake caliper anchor plate
6 Wheel hub
7 Brake disc
8 Front wheel knuckle assembly (RH/LH)

06017-EXPL-G158

Fig. 14 Front brake components—2005 4WD Explorer Sport-Trac

2. Loosen the wheel lug nuts.

3. Raise and safely support the front of the vehicle. Remove the wheel.

4. Place an 8 in. (203mm) C-clamp on the caliper and tighten the clamp to bottom the caliper pistons in their bores. Remove the clamp.

5. Remove the two caliper slide pin bolts and lift the caliper from the anchor plate.

➡️**Use care to retain as much of the original caliper slide pin grease as possible.**

6. Position the caliper on a frame member or suspend it with some wire. Do not allow the caliper to hang by the brake hose.

7. Disconnect and plug the brake hose at the caliper. Remove the caliper from the rotor.

To install:

8. Position the caliper over the brake pads and align the slide pin mounting holes.

9. Install the slide pin bolts and tighten them to 24 ft. lbs. (32 Nm).

10. Install the caliper brake hose using new washers. Tighten the bolt to 26 ft. lbs. (35 Nm).

11. Install the wheel and snug the lug nuts.

12. Lower the vehicle and tighten the lug nuts to 100 ft. lbs. (135 Nm).

➡️**The first couple of times you apply the brakes, the pedal may go to the floor. Continue to pump the brake pedal until it feels firm.**

13. Start the engine and apply the brakes several times to readjust the caliper pistons. Ensure that the pedal feels firm before operating the vehicle.

2006–07 Explorer and Mountaineer; 2007 Explorer Sport-Trac

See Figure 16.

1. Before servicing the vehicle, refer to the "Precautions" section and the "Brake Service Precautions" section.

2. With the vehicle in NEUTRAL, position it on a hoist.

3. Remove the front wheels.

4. Remove the brake hose flow bolt and position the brake hose aside. Discard the 2 copper washers. Cap the fluid ports.

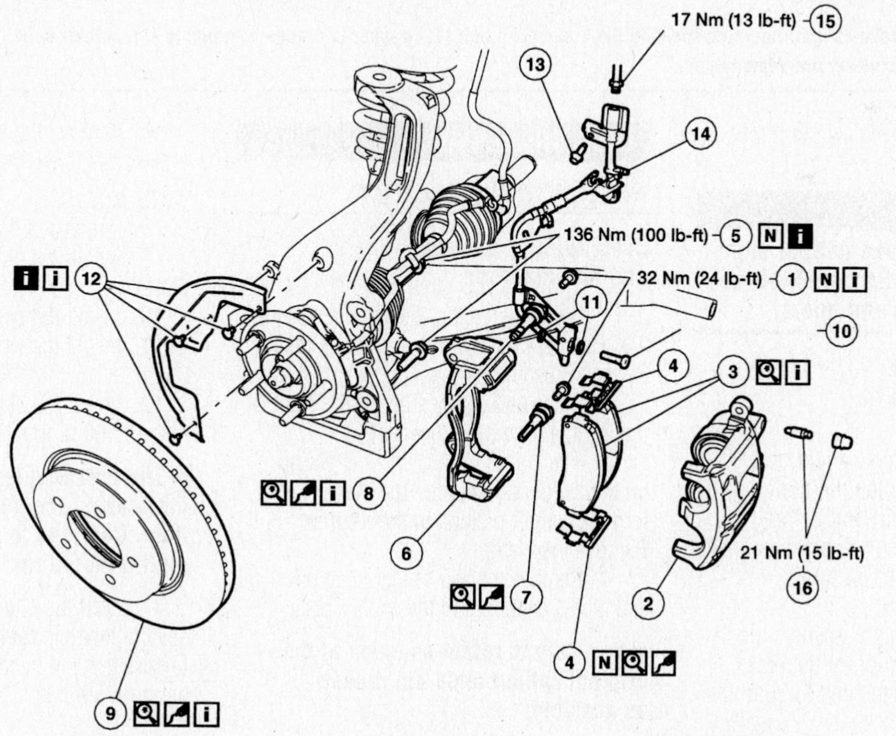

17 Nm (13 lb-ft)
136 Nm (100 lb-ft)
32 Nm (24 lb-ft)
21 Nm (15 lb-ft)

1 Caliper bolts
2 Brake caliper (RH/LH)
3 Brake disc pads
4 Slippers
5 Anchor bracket bolt kit
6 Anchor bracket
7 Guide pin and boot
8 Locating pin and boot
9 Brake disc
10 Flow bolt
11 Copper washers
12 Brake disc shield
13 Brake hose bracket bolt
14 Brake hose (RH/LH)
15 Brake tube

67197EXPLG73

Fig. 15 Front brake components—2005 Explorer and Mountaineer

1. Brake hose flow bolt
2. Copper washers (2 required)
3. Brake hose
4. Brake caliper bolt (2 required)
5. Brake pads
6. Brake caliper

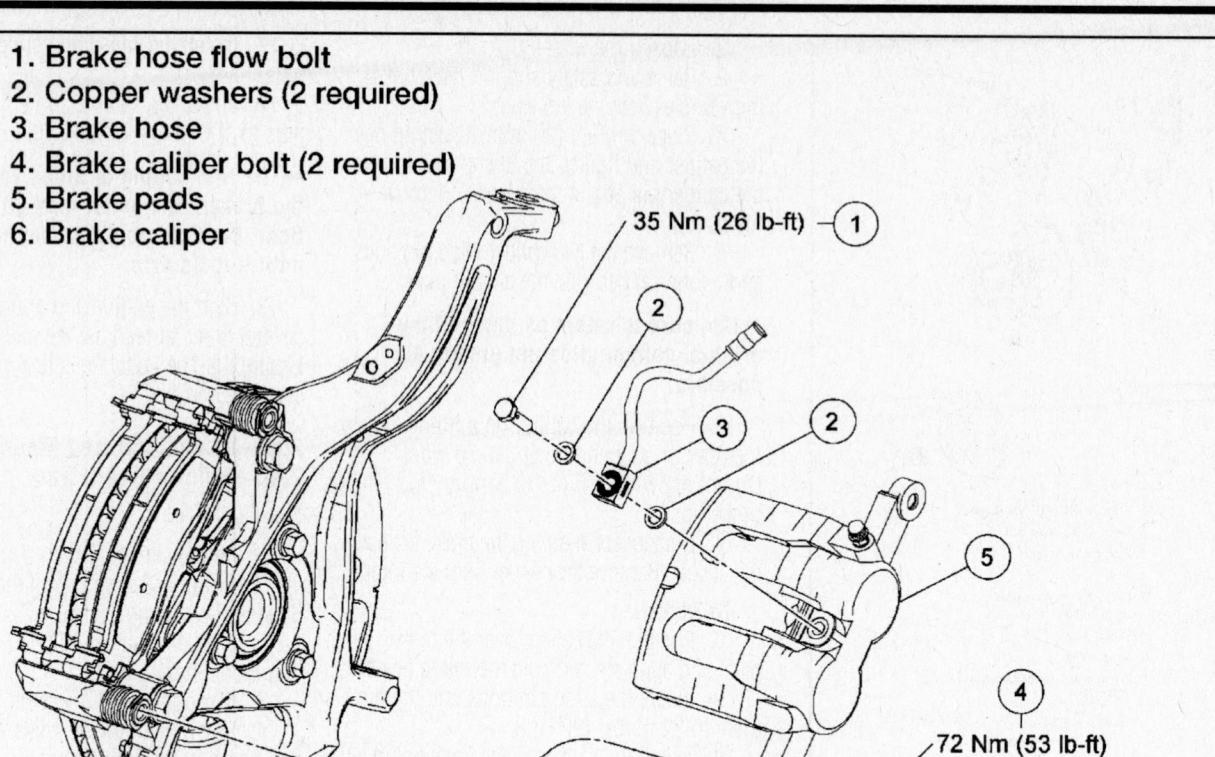

35 Nm (26 lb-ft) — 1

72 Nm (53 lb-ft)

22086_EXPL_G0206

Fig. 16 Showing the brake caliper mounting showing the brake hose bolt (1), washer (2), hose connection (3), caliper bolts (4) and the brake caliper (5)—2006–07 Explorer and Mountaineer

5. Remove the 2 brake caliper bolts and the brake caliper.

❊❊ CAUTION

Do not pry in the brake caliper sight hole to retract the pistons as this can damage the pistons and boots.

6. If leaks or damaged boots are found, install a new brake caliper.

To install:

7. Position the brake caliper and install the 2 bolts. Tighten the bottom locator pin brake caliper bolt before tightening the top guide pin brake caliper bolt. Torque the bolts to 53 ft. lbs. (72 Nm).

8. Using 2 new copper washers, position the brake hose and install the brake hose flow bolt. Tighten the bolt to 26 ft. lbs. (35 Nm).

9. Bleed the brake caliper. See "Brake Caliper Bleeding" above.

10. Install the wheels and lower the vehicle.

11. Test the brake system for normal operation.

DISC BRAKE PAD

REMOVAL & INSTALLATION

2005 Aviator, Explorer and Mountaineer

1. Before servicing the vehicle, refer to the "Precautions" section and the "Brake Service Precautions" section.

2. Raise and safely support the front of the vehicle. Remove the wheel.

3. Place an 8 in. (203mm) C-clamp on the caliper and tighten the clamp to bottom the caliper pistons in their bores. Remove the clamp.

4. Remove the two caliper slide pin bolts and lift the caliper from the anchor plate.

➡ **Use care to retain as much of the original caliper slide pin grease as possible.**

5. Position the caliper on a frame member or suspend it with some wire. Do not allow the caliper to hang by the brake hose.

6. Remove the brake pads and, if necessary, the anti-rattle clips from the anchor plate.

7. Remove the shims, if any, from the brake pads for re-use.

To install:

8. If removed, install the anti-rattle clips.

9. Install the brake pads to the anchor plate.

10. Install the caliper.

11. Install the wheel and snug the lug nuts.

12. Lower the vehicle and tighten the lug nuts to 100 ft. lbs. (135 Nm).

➡ **The first couple of times you apply the brakes, the pedal may go to the floor. Continue to pump the brake pedal until it feels firm.**

13. Start the engine and apply the brakes several times to readjust the caliper pistons. Ensure that the pedal feels firm before operating the vehicle.

2005 Explorer Sport-Trac

1. Before servicing the vehicle, refer to the "Precautions" section and the "Brake Service Precautions" section.

2. Remove brake fluid in the master cylinder reservoir until the reservoir is half full.

3. Raise and support the vehicle.

4. Remove the wheel and tire assembly.

※※ WARNING

Install a new pad if worn to or past the specified thickness above the metal backing plate. Install new pads in complete axle sets.

5. Inspect the pads for wear or contamination.

6. Remove the lower caliper bolt on the right caliper and the upper caliper bolt on the left caliper first. Rotate the disc brake caliper away from the brake disc rotor.

7. Remove the pads.

8. Remove the stainless slippers.

9. Inspect the brake disc:

- If the brake disc is cracked, install a new brake disc.
- If diagnosis has revealed vibration in the steering wheel, seat, or brake pedal while braking, machine the brake disc. Heavily scored brake discs, similar to that caused by linings worn to the backing plate, must also be machined.
- Measure the brake disc for minimum thickness.
- If the brake disc is not within specification, install a new brake disc.

10. Inspect the disc brake caliper for leaks. If leaks are found, disassembly is required.

To install:

11. Use a suitable suction device to remove brake fluid from the master cylinder.

12. Clean the support bracket and slipper surfaces.

13. Install the slippers and the pads.

14. Install the slippers.

15. Install the pads.

➡**If installing new pads, the caliper pistons must be compressed using a C-clamp and a wooden block.**

16. Lower the brake fluid level in the master cylinder if required.

17. Rotate the disc brake caliper into the anchor bracket.

18. Install the caliper bolt.

19. Install the wheel and tire assembly.

20. Check the brake system for correct operation.

2006–07 Explorer and Mountaineer; 2007 Explorer Sport-Trac

※※ CAUTION

Install new brake pads if they are worn past the specified thickness above the metal backing plate or rivets. Install new brake pads in complete axle sets.

1. Before servicing the vehicle, refer to the "Precautions" section and the "Brake Service Precautions" section.

2. Remove brake fluid in the master cylinder reservoir until the reservoir is half full.

3. Raise and support the vehicle.

4. Remove the wheel and tire assembly.

5. Remove the 2 brake caliper bolts and position the brake caliper aside. Support the caliper using mechanic's wire.

6. Inspect the brake pads for wear and contamination.

7. Inspect the brake disc, machine or install a new front brake disc as necessary.

8. Remove the brake pads and clips. Discard the clips.

To install:

9. Install the new brake pad clips and the brake pads.

※※ CAUTION

Protect the piston and boots when pushing the caliper piston into the caliper piston bores.

10. Using a suitable tool (C-clamp) and a worn brake pad, compress the disc brake caliper pistons into the caliper.

11. Position the brake caliper and install the 2 bolts. Tighten the lower bolt and then the upper bolt to 53 ft. lbs. (72 Nm).

12. Install the wheel and tire assembly and lower the vehicle.

13. Fill the brake master cylinder reservoir with clean brake fluid.

14. Test the brakes for normal operation.

BRAKES

※※ CAUTION

Dust and dirt accumulating on brake parts during normal use may contain asbestos fibers from production or aftermarket brake linings. Breathing excessive concentrations of asbestos fibers can cause serious bodily harm. Exercise care when servicing brake parts. Do not sand or grind brake lining unless equipment used is designed to contain the dust residue. Do not clean brake parts with compressed air or by dry brushing. Cleaning should be done by dampening the brake components with a fine mist of water, then wiping the brake components clean with a dampened cloth. Dispose of cloth and all residue containing asbestos fibers in an impermeable container with the
appropriate label. Follow practices prescribed by the Occupational Safety and Health Administration (OSHA) and the Environmental Protection Agency (EPA) for the handling, processing, and disposing of dust or debris that may contain asbestos fibers.

BRAKE CALIPER

REMOVAL & INSTALLATION

Aviator

See Figure 17.

1. Before servicing the vehicle, refer to the "Precautions" section and the "Brake Service Precautions" section.

2. Siphon part of the brake fluid out of the master cylinder to avoid overflow when

REAR DISC BRAKES

the caliper piston is pressed into the caliper bore.

3. Raise the vehicle and support it safely. Remove the wheel and tire assembly.

4. Position an 8 in. (20cm) C-clamp on the caliper and tighten the clamp to move the caliper piston into the bore approximately ⅛ in. (3mm). Remove the clamp.

➡**Do not pry the piston away from the rotor.**

5. Clean excess dirt from the retainer bolt area.

6. Using a Torx® socket, remove the 2 retainer bolts securing the caliper to the bracket and adapter plate.

7. Disconnect and plug the brake hose at the caliper. Remove the caliper from the rotor.

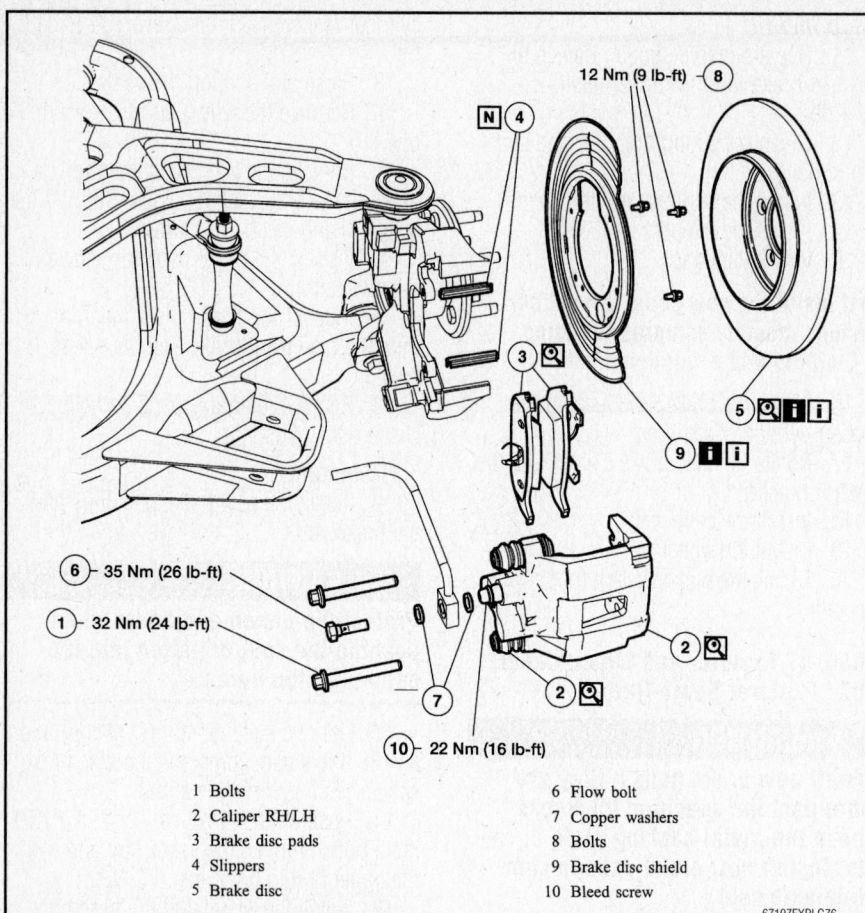

12 Nm (9 lb-ft)

6 - 35 Nm (26 lb-ft)

1 - 32 Nm (24 lb-ft)

10 - 22 Nm (16 lb-ft)

1	Bolts	6	Flow bolt
2	Caliper RH/LH	7	Copper washers
3	Brake disc pads	8	Bolts
4	Slippers	9	Brake disc shield
5	Brake disc	10	Bleed screw

67197EXPLG76

Fig. 17 Rear disc brake components—Aviator

3. Raise the vehicle and support it safely. Remove the wheel and tire assembly.

4. Position an 8 in. (20cm) C-clamp on the caliper and tighten the clamp to move the caliper piston into the bore approximately ⅛ in. (3mm). Remove the clamp.

➡ **Do not pry the piston away from the rotor.**

5. Clean excess dirt from the retainer bolt area.

6. Using a Torx® socket, remove the 2 retainer bolts securing the caliper to the bracket and adapter plate.

7. Disconnect and plug the brake hose at the caliper. Remove the caliper from the rotor.

To install:

8. Make sure the caliper mounting surfaces are free of dirt. Lubricate the caliper grooves with disc brake caliper grease and install the caliper.

9. Position the caliper to the bracket and secure in place with the retainer bolts. Tighten the bolts to 24 ft. lbs. (32 Nm).

10. Install the caliper brake hose using new washers. Tighten the bolt to 26 ft. lbs. (35 Nm).

11. Fill and bleed the brake system.

To install:

8. Make sure the caliper mounting surfaces are free of dirt. Lubricate the caliper grooves with disc brake caliper grease and install the caliper.

9. Position the caliper to the bracket and secure in place with the retainer bolts. Tighten the bolts to 24 ft. lbs. (32 Nm)

10. Install the caliper brake hose using new washers. Tighten the bolt to 26 ft. lbs. (35 Nm).

11. Fill and bleed the brake system.

12. Install the wheel and tire assembly and lower the vehicle. Check the brake fluid level and check the brakes for proper operation.

2005 Explorer, Mountaineer and Explorer Sport-Trac

See Figures 18 and 19.

1. Before servicing the vehicle, refer to the "Precautions" section and the "Brake Service Precautions" section.

2. Siphon part of the brake fluid out of the master cylinder to avoid overflow when the caliper piston is pressed into the caliper bore.

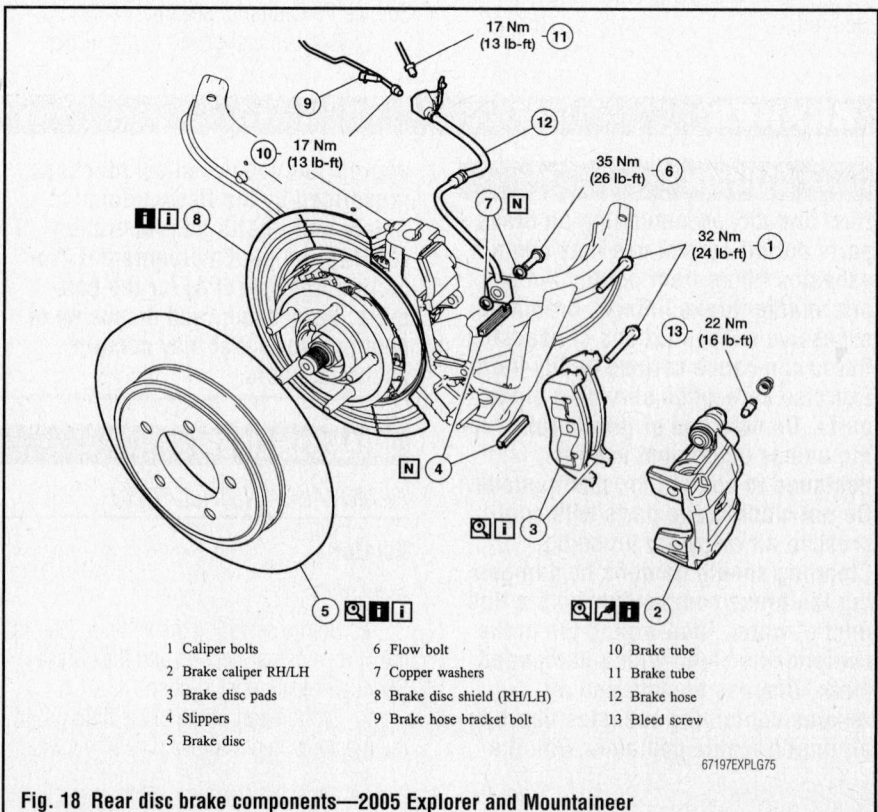

17 Nm (13 lb-ft)

17 Nm (13 lb-ft)

35 Nm (26 lb-ft)

32 Nm (24 lb-ft)

22 Nm (16 lb-ft)

1	Caliper bolts	6	Flow bolt	10	Brake tube
2	Brake caliper RH/LH	7	Copper washers	11	Brake tube
3	Brake disc pads	8	Brake disc shield (RH/LH)	12	Brake hose
4	Slippers	9	Brake hose bracket bolt	13	Bleed screw
5	Brake disc				

67197EXPLG75

Fig. 18 Rear disc brake components—2005 Explorer and Mountaineer

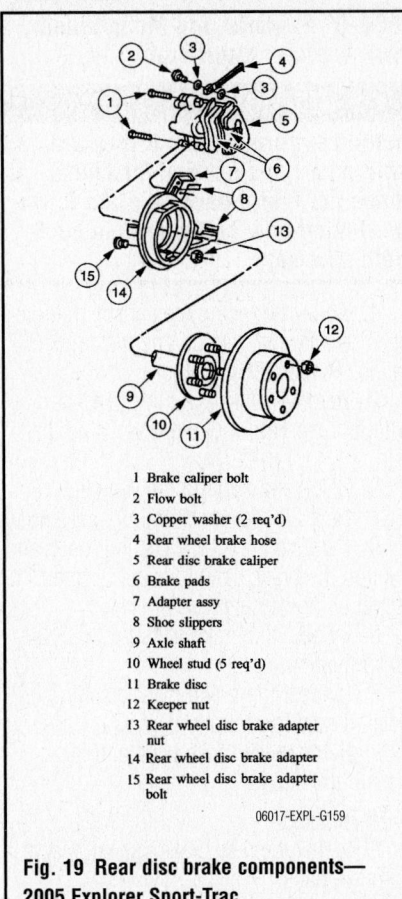

1 Brake caliper bolt
2 Flow bolt
3 Copper washer (2 req'd)
4 Rear wheel brake hose
5 Rear disc brake caliper
6 Brake pads
7 Adapter assy
8 Shoe slippers
9 Axle shaft
10 Wheel stud (5 req'd)
11 Brake disc
12 Keeper nut
13 Rear wheel disc brake adapter nut
14 Rear wheel disc brake adapter
15 Rear wheel disc brake adapter bolt

06017-EXPL-G159

Fig. 19 Rear disc brake components—2005 Explorer Sport-Trac

12. Install the wheel and tire assembly and lower the vehicle. Check the brake fluid level and check the brakes for proper operation.

2006–07 Explorer and Mountaineer; 2007 Explorer Sport-Trac

See Figure 20.

1. Before servicing the vehicle, refer to the "Precautions" section and the "Brake Service Precautions" section.

2. With the vehicle in NEUTRAL, position it on a hoist.

3. Remove the rear wheels.

4. Remove the brake hose flow bolt and position the brake hose aside. Discard the 2 copper washers. Cap the fluid ports.

5. Remove the 2 brake caliper bolts and the brake caliper.

✳✳ CAUTION

Do not pry in the brake caliper sight hole to retract the pistons as this can damage the pistons and boots.

6. If leaks or damaged boots are found, install a new brake caliper.

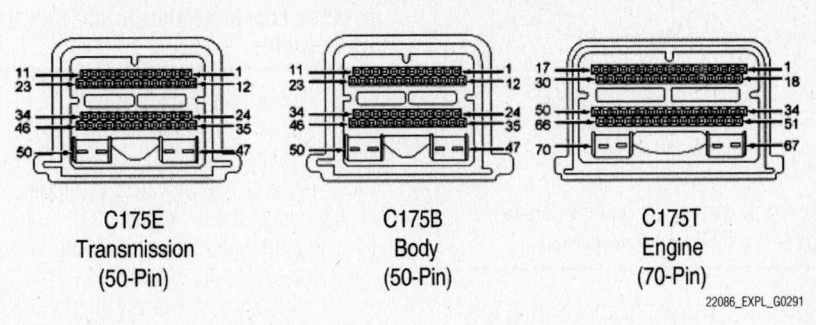

Powertrain Control Module (PCM) Connectors
170-Pin PCM Harness Connectors

C175E
Transmission
(50-Pin)

C175B
Body
(50-Pin)

C175T
Engine
(70-Pin)

22086_EXPL_G0291

Fig. 20 Showing the rear brake caliper mounting—2006–07 Explorer and Mountaineer

To install:

7. Position the brake caliper and install the 2 bolts. Torque the bolts to 24 ft. lbs. (32 Nm).

8. Using 2 new copper washers, position the brake hose and install the brake hose flow bolt. Tighten the bolt to 26 ft. lbs. (35 Nm).

9. Bleed the brake caliper. See "Brake Caliper Bleeding" above.

10. Install the wheels and lower the vehicle.

11. Test the brake system for normal operation.

DISC BRAKE PAD

REMOVAL & INSTALLATION

2005 Aviator, Explorer and Mountaineer

See Figures 21 and 22.

1. Before servicing the vehicle, refer to the "Precautions" section.

2. Siphon part of the brake fluid out of the master cylinder to avoid overflow when the caliper piston is pressed into the caliper bore.

3. Raise the vehicle and support it safely. Remove the wheel and tire assembly.

4. Remove the brake caliper, but do not disconnect the brake hose. Secure the caliper aside with mechanic's wire.

5. Remove the inner and outer brake pad from the caliper.

To install:

6. Bottom out the caliper piston in the caliper bore using an 8 in. (20cm) C-clamp or equivalent and a worn out inner brake pad or block of wood to push against the piston. Do not attempt to bottom out the piston with the outer brake pad installed.

7. Position the inboard brake pad in the

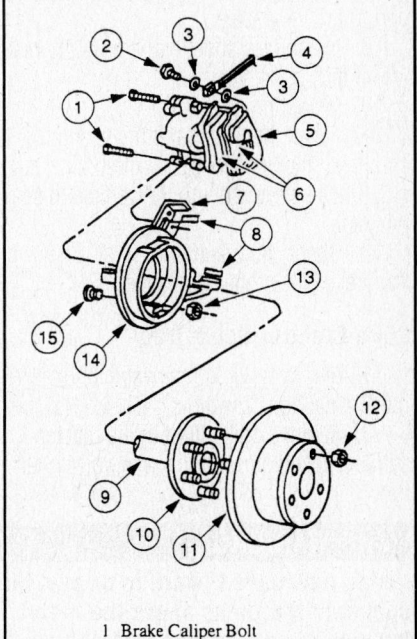

1 Brake Caliper Bolt
2 Flow Bolt
3 Copper Washer (2 Req'd)
4 Rear Wheel Brake Hose
5 Rear Disc Brake Caliper
6 Brake Pads
7 Rear Disc Brake Caliper Anchor Plate
8 Shoe Slippers
9 Axle Shaft
10 Lug Bolt (5 Req'd)
11 Rear Disc Brake Rotor
12 Keeper Nut
13 Rear Wheel Disc Brake Adapter Nut
14 Rear Wheel Disc Brake Adapter
15 Rear Wheel Disc Brake Adapter Bolt

93026G26

Fig. 21 Exploded view of the rear disc brake assembly—Explorer and Mountaineer

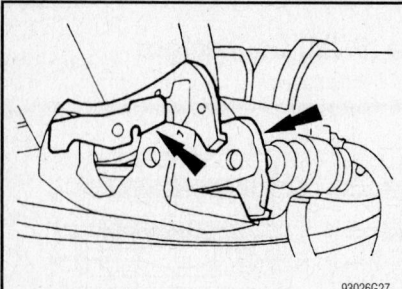

93026G27

Fig. 22 Installing the rear disc brake pads—Explorer and Mountaineer

caliper and press the retainer spring fully into the caliper piston.

8. Start one end of the outboard brake shoe and lining on the caliper and rotate it down until the locating lugs and the retainer spring are fully seated.

9. Install new shoe slippers on the rear wheel disc brake adapter.

10. Install the caliper.

11. Install the wheel and tire assembly and lower the vehicle. Apply the brakes several times before moving the vehicle to seat the pads.

12. Check the brake fluid level. Check the brakes for proper operation.

2005 Explorer Sport-Trac

1. Before servicing the vehicle, refer to the "Precautions" section.

2. Remove brake fluid in the master cylinder reservoir until the reservoir is half full.

❊❊ WARNING
Install new pads if worn to or past the specified thickness above the metal backing plate or rivets. Install new pads in complete axle sets.

3. Inspect the brake pads for wear or contamination. Install new pads if worn to or past specification.

➡It is not necessary to remove the rear wheel brake hose when carrying out this procedure.

4. Remove the rear disc brake caliper.

❊❊ WARNING
Do not allow grease, oil, brake fluid or other contaminants to contact the brake pads.

5. Remove the brake pads.

6. Retract the caliper piston into the rear disc brake caliper.

7. Remove and discard the slippers.

8. Inspect the brake disc:
- If the brake disc is cracked, install a new brake disc.
- If diagnosis has revealed vibration in the steering wheel, seat, or brake pedal while braking, machine the brake disc. Heavily scored brake discs, similar to that caused by linings worn to the backing plate, must also be machined.
- Measure the brake disc for minimum thickness.
- If the brake disc is not within specification, install a new brake disc.

To install:

❊❊ WARNING
New stainless steel slippers must be installed when new brake pads are installed, even if the slippers appear undamaged. Make sure the slippers are correctly positioned with the slipper ends snug against the outboard end of the anchor plate rail.

9. Clean the slipper mating surface, and install the new slippers.

❊❊ WARNING
Install new brake pads in full axle sets. Do not install new brake pads on only one side of the vehicle.

10. Install the brake pads.

11. Install the rear disc brake caliper.

12. Verify correct brake operation.

2006–07 Explorer and Mountaineer; 2007 Explorer Sport-Trac

❊❊ CAUTION
Install new brake pads if they are worn past the specified thickness above the metal backing plate or rivets. Install new brake pads in complete axle sets.

1. Before servicing the vehicle, refer to the "Precautions" section and the "Brake Service Precautions" section.

2. Remove brake fluid in the master cylinder reservoir until the reservoir is half full.

3. Raise and support the vehicle.

4. Remove the wheel and tire assembly.

5. Remove the 2 brake caliper bolts and position the brake caliper aside. Support the caliper using mechanic's wire.

6. Inspect the brake pads for wear and contamination.

7. Inspect the brake disc, machine or install a new front brake disc as necessary.

8. Remove the brake pads and clips. Discard the clips.

To install:

9. Install the new brake pad clips and the brake pads.

❊❊ CAUTION
Protect the piston and boots when pushing the caliper piston into the caliper piston bores.

10. Using a suitable tool (C-clamp) and a worn brake pad, compress the disc brake caliper pistons into the caliper.

11. Position the brake caliper and install the 2 bolts. Tighten the lower bolt and then the upper bolt to 24 ft. lbs. (32 Nm).

12. Install the wheel and tire assembly and lower the vehicle.

13. Fill the brake master cylinder reservoir with clean brake fluid.

14. Test the brakes for normal operation.

BRAKES

PARKING BRAKE

PARKING BRAKE CABLES

ADJUSTMENT

If the parking brake requires adjustment first check for any damaged cables and replace as necessary.

On vehicles with rear disc brakes check for proper operation of the parking brake shoes. Refer to the "Parking Brake Shoes" section.

Parking Brake Cable Tension Release
See Figures 23 and 24.

1. Remove the LH cowl side trim panel.

2. With the help of an assistant, release the parking brake cable tension by pulling down on the intermediate cable at the cable-to-cable connector clip until the parking brake control sector rotates to its stop and a 0.15 inch(4 mm) × 5.9 inch (150 mm) retainer pin can be inserted.

❊❊ CAUTION
Make sure the cable-to-cable connector clip is connected to the front and

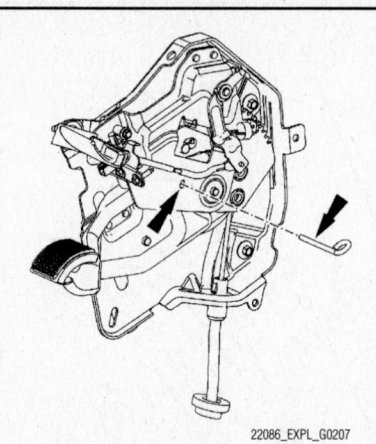

22086_EXPL_G0207

Fig. 23 With the help of an assistant, release the parking brake cable tension by pulling down on the intermediate cable at the cable-to-cable connector clip until the parking brake control sector rotates to its stop and a 0.15 inch (4 mm) × 5.9 inch (150 mm) retainer pin can be inserted

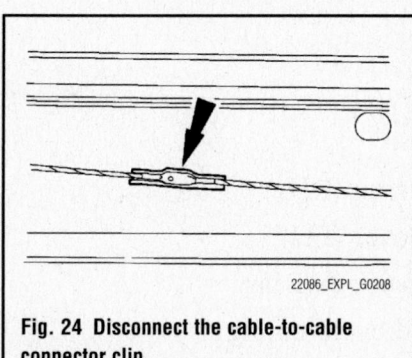

22086_EXPL_G0208

Fig. 24 Disconnect the cable-to-cable connector clip

rear cable before removing the brake control retaining pin, and the cable tension is reloaded slowly.

3. Disconnect the cable-to-cable connector clip.

4. To reload the tension on the parking brake cable, follow the release procedure in reverse.

PARKING BRAKE SHOES

REMOVAL & INSTALLATION

Except 2005 Sport-Trac

See Figures 25 through 27.

1. Before servicing the vehicle, refer to the "Precautions" section and the "Brake Service Precautions" section.

2. Remove the rear brake disc.

3. Remove the parking brake shoe adjusting screw.

06017-EXPL-G160

Fig. 25 Parking brake control—Except 2005 Explorer Sport-Trac

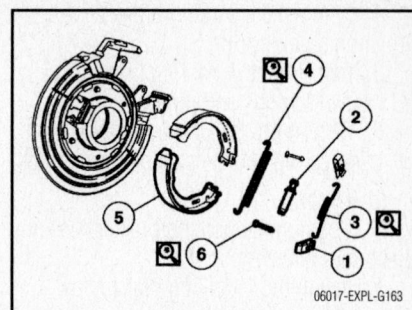

06017-EXPL-G163

Fig. 26 Parking brake shoes—Aviator

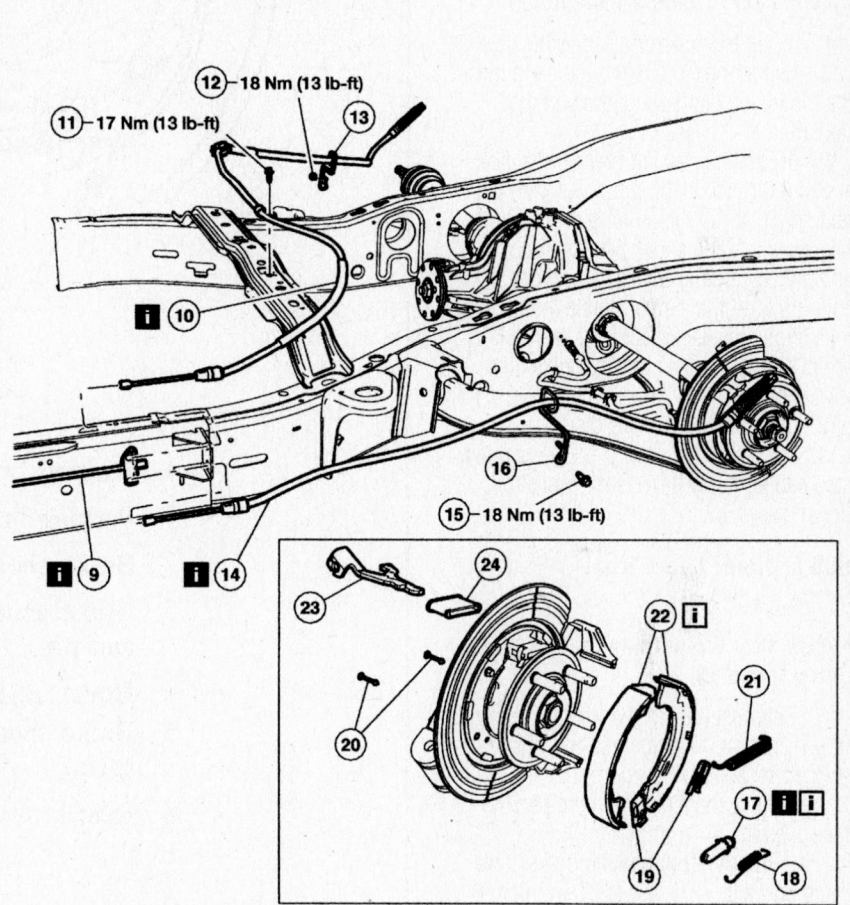

9 Intermediate parking brake cable	17 Brake shoe adjusting screw
10 Rear parking brake cable (RH)	18 Brake shoe adjusting screw spring
11 Rear parking brake cable bracket bolt	19 Brake shoe hold-down spring
12 Wire form retainer bolt	20 Brake shoe hold-down pins
13 Wire form retainer	21 Brake shoe retracting spring
14 Rear parking brake cable (LH)	22 Parking brake shoe kit (one kit required)
15 Wire form retainer bolt	23 Parking brake lever (RH/LH)
16 Wire form retainer	24 Parking brake lever boot

06017-EXPL-G164

Fig. 27 Parking brake shoes and related parts—2005–07 Explorer and Mountaineer; 2007 Explorer Sport-Trac

4. Remove the parking brake shoe adjusting screw spring.

5. Remove the 2 parking brake shoe hold-down springs and pins.

6. Remove the parking brake shoe retracting spring and the parking brake shoes.

To install:

7. Position the parking brake shoes and attach the retracting spring.

8. Install the 2 parking brake shoe hold-down pins and springs.

9. Install the parking brake shoe adjusting screw spring.

➡**Completely retract the parking brake adjusting screw before installation.**

10. Install the brake shoe adjusting screw.

11. Use a brake adjusting gauge to measure the inside diameter of the parking brake drum.

12. Adjust the parking brake shoe clearance of 0.04 inch (1.07 mm) less than the inside diameter of the parking brake drum. Make sure that the parking brake shoes are correctly centered and measure across the center point of the shoes. Rotate the parking brake shoe adjuster wheel to achieve the correct parking brake shoe-to-brake disc clearance.

13. Install the rear brake disc.

14. To reload the tension on the parking brake cable, follow the release procedure in reverse.

2005 Explorer Sport-Trac

See Figures 28 and 29.

➡**Make sure the parking brake control is fully released.**

1. Before servicing the vehicle, refer to the "Precautions" section and the "Brake Service Precautions" section.

2. Relieve the tension on the parking brake system.

  a. Pull the front parking brake cable and conduit.

  b. Insert a 4mm (⁵⁄₃₂ inch) drill bit or equivalent retainer.

3. Raise and support the vehicle.

4. Remove the tire and wheel assembly.

5. Remove the rear brake disc.

6. Remove the brake shoe retracting spring.

7. Remove the brake shoe adjusting screw spring.

8. Remove the brake adjuster screw.

9. Remove the rear brake shoe hold-down springs.

10. Remove the rear brake shoes and linings along with the inboard brake shoe retracting spring.

11. Inspect the components for excessive wear or damage and install new as required.

To install:

➡**Lubricate the brake shoe contact point before installation of rear shoes using grease.**

12. Install the rear brake shoes and linings along with the inboard brake shoe retracting spring.

13. Install the brake shoe hold-down springs.

14. Install the brake adjuster screw.

15. Install the brake shoe adjusting screw spring.

16. Install the outboard brake shoe retracting spring.

17. Using a brake gauge, measure the

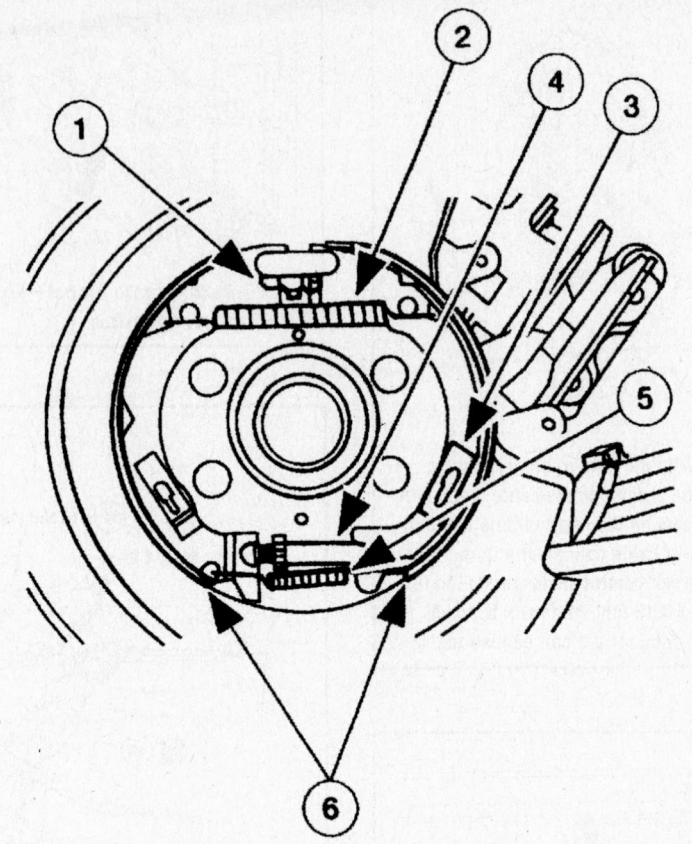

1	Parking brake lever (RH)
1	Parking brake lever (LH)
2	Brake shoe retracting spring
3	Brake shoe hold-down spring and pin
4	Brake adjuster screw
5	Brake shoe adjusting screw spring
6	Rear brake shoe and lining

06017-EXPL-G161

Fig. 28 Parking brake shoes and related parts—2005 Explorer Sport-Trac

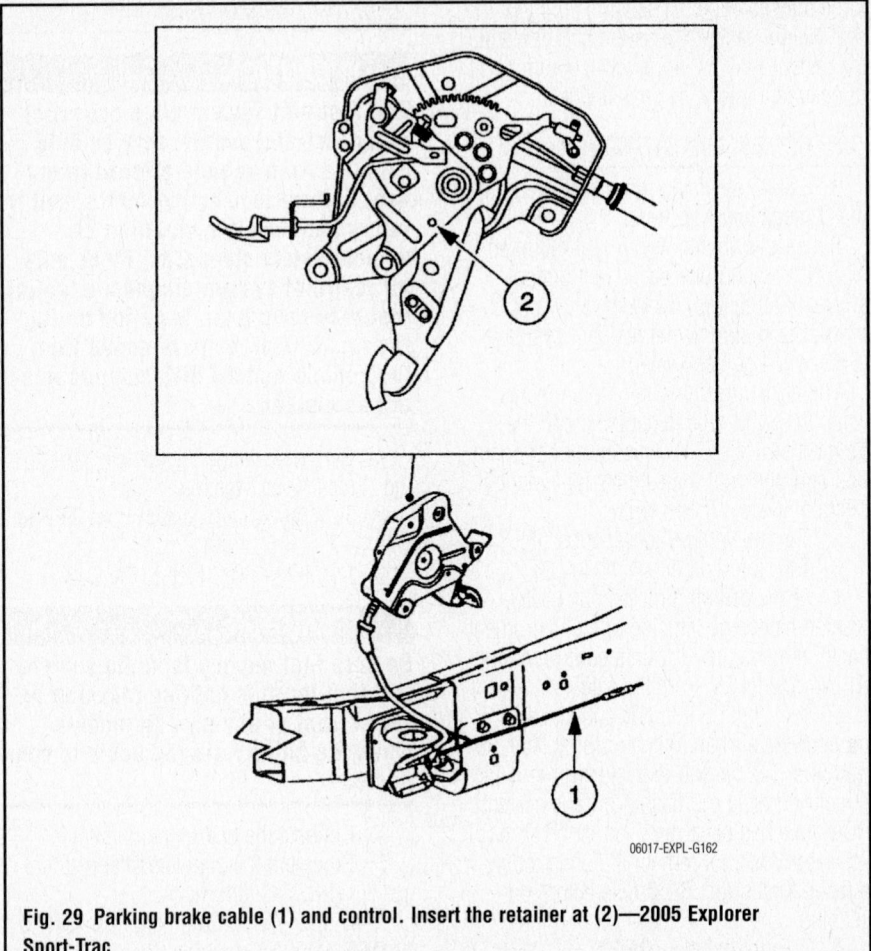

Fig. 29 Parking brake cable (1) and control. Insert the retainer at (2)—2005 Explorer Sport-Trac

inside diameter of the drum portion of the rear brake disc.

18. Using the gauge, set the rear brake shoe and lining diameter to 0.020 inch (0.5mm) less than the inside diameter of the drum portion of the rear brake disc.

19. Install the rear brake disc.

✳✳ CAUTION

Always remove any corrosion, dirt or foreign material present on the mounting surfaces of the wheel or the surface of the wheel hub, brake drum or brake disc that contacts the wheel. Installing wheels without correct metal-to-metal contact at the wheel mounting surfaces can cause the wheel nuts to loosen and come off while the vehicle is in motion, causing loss of control. Failure to follow these instructions may result in personal injury.

20. Clean the wheel hub mounting surface.

21. Install the wheel and tire assembly.

22. Apply tension to the parking brake cable system.

    a. Hold the front parking brake cable and conduit taut.

    b. Remove the retainer from the parking brake control.

23. Check operation of the parking brake.

CHASSIS ELECTRICAL   AIR BAG (SUPPLEMENTAL RESTRAINT SYSTEM)

GENERAL INFORMATION

✳✳ CAUTION

These vehicles are equipped with an air bag system. The system must be disarmed before performing service on, or around, system components, the steering column, instrument panel components, wiring and sensors. Failure to follow the safety precautions and the disarming procedure could result in accidental air bag deployment, possible injury and unnecessary system repairs.

SERVICE PRECAUTIONS

Disconnect and isolate the battery negative cable before beginning any airbag system component diagnosis, testing, removal, or installation procedures. Allow system

capacitor to discharge for two minutes before beginning any component service. This will disable the airbag system. Failure to disable the airbag system may result in accidental airbag deployment, personal injury, or death.

Do not place an intact undeployed airbag face down on a solid surface. The airbag will propel into the air if accidentally deployed and may result in personal injury or death.

When carrying or handling an undeployed airbag, the trim side (face) of the airbag should be pointing towards the body to minimize possibility of injury if accidental deployment occurs. Failure to do this may result in personal injury or death.

Replace airbag system components with OEM replacement parts. Substitute parts may appear interchangeable, but internal differences may result in inferior occupant protection. Failure to do so may result in

occupant personal injury or death.

Wear safety glasses, rubber gloves, and long sleeved clothing when cleaning powder residue from vehicle after an airbag deployment. Powder residue emitted from a deployed airbag can cause skin irritation. Flush affected area with cool water if irritation is experienced. If nasal or throat irritation is experienced, exit the vehicle for fresh air until the irritation ceases. If irritation continues, see a physician.

Do not use a replacement airbag that is not in the original packaging. This may result in improper deployment, personal injury, or death.

The factory installed fasteners, screws and bolts used to fasten airbag components have a special coating and are specifically designed for the airbag system. Do not use substitute fasteners. Use only original equipment fasteners listed in the parts catalog when fastener replacement is required.

During, and following, any child restraint anchor service, due to impact event or vehicle repair, carefully inspect all mounting hardware, tether straps, and anchors for proper installation, operation, or damage. If a child restraint anchor is found damaged in any way, the anchor must be replaced. Failure to do this may result in personal injury or death.

Deployed and non-deployed airbags may or may not have live pyrotechnic material within the airbag inflator.

Do not dispose of driver/passenger/curtain airbags or seat belt tensioners unless you are sure of complete deployment. Refer to the Hazardous Substance Control System for proper disposal.

Dispose of deployed airbags and tensioners consistent with state, provincial, local, and federal regulations.

After any airbag component testing or service, do not connect the battery negative cable. Personal injury or death may result if the system test is not performed first.

If the vehicle is equipped with the Occupant Classification System (OCS), do not connect the battery negative cable before performing the OCS Verification Test using the scan tool and the appropriate diagnostic information. Personal injury or death may result if the system test is not performed properly.

Never replace both the Occupant Restraint Controller (ORC) and the Occupant Classification Module (OCM) at the same time. If both require replacement, replace one, then perform the Airbag System test before replacing the other.

Both the ORC and the OCM store Occupant Classification System (OCS) calibration data, which they transfer to one another when one of them is replaced. If both are replaced at the same time, an irreversible fault will be set in both modules and the OCS may malfunction and cause personal injury or death.

If equipped with OCS, the Seat Weight Sensor is a sensitive, calibrated unit and must be handled carefully. Do not drop or handle roughly. If dropped or damaged, replace with another sensor. Failure to do so may result in occupant injury or death.

If equipped with OCS, the front passenger seat must be handled carefully as well. When removing the seat, be careful when setting on floor not to drop. If dropped, the sensor may be inoperative, could result in occupant injury, or possibly death.

If equipped with OCS, when the passenger front seat is on the floor, no one should sit in the front passenger seat. This uneven force may damage the sensing ability of the seat weight sensors. If sat on and damaged, the sensor may be inoperative, could result in occupant injury, or possibly death.

DISARMING THE SYSTEM

1. Before servicing the vehicle, refer to the "Precautions" section.

If a seat equipped with a seat mounted side air bag and/or a safety belt pretensioner (if equipped) system is being serviced, the supplemental restraint system (SRS) must be depowered.

The air bag warning lamp illuminates when the RCM fuse is removed and the ignition switch is ON. This is normal operation and does not indicate a supplemental restraint system (SRS) fault.

2. Turn all vehicle accessories OFF.
3. Turn the ignition switch to OFF.
4. At the central junction box (CJB), located below the left side of the instrument panel, remove the restraints control module (RCM) fuse (10A) from the CJB.
5. Turn the ignition **ON** and visually monitor the air bag indicator for at least 30 seconds. The air bag indicator will remain lit continuously (no flashing) if the correct RCM fuse has been removed. If the air bag indicator does not remain lit continuously, remove the correct RCM fuse before proceeding.
6. Turn the ignition **OFF**.

✳✳ WARNING

To avoid accidental deployment and possible personal injury, the backup power supply must be depleted before repairing or replacing any front or side air bag supplemental restraint system (SRS) components and before servicing, replacing, adjusting or striking components near the front or side air bag sensors or RCM, such as doors, instrument panel, console, door latches, strikers, seats and hood latches. The side impact sensors (if equipped) are located at or near the base of the B-pillars and C-pillars.

✳✳ CAUTION

To deplete the backup power supply energy, disconnect the battery ground cable and wait at least one minute. Be sure to disconnect auxiliary batteries and power supplies (if equipped). Disconnect the battery ground cable and wait at least one minute.

ARMING THE SYSTEM

✳✳ CAUTION

The restraint system diagnostic tool is for restraint system service only. Remove from vehicle prior to road use. Failure to remove could result in injury and possible violation of vehicle safety standards. Make sure all restraint system diagnostic tool(s) that may have been installed during the repair have been removed from the vehicle and all SRS components are connected.

1. Before servicing the vehicle, refer to the "Precautions" section.
2. Turn the ignition switch from **OFF** to **ON**.
3. Install the RCM fuse to the CJB.

✳✳ CAUTION

Be sure that nobody is in the vehicle and that there is nothing blocking or set in front of any air bag module when the battery ground cable is connected.

4. Connect the battery ground cable.
5. Prove out the supplemental restraint system (SRS) as follows:

a. Turn the ignition key from **ON** to **OFF**. Wait 10 seconds, then turn the key back to ON and visually monitor the air bag indicator with the air bag modules installed. The air bag indicator will light continuously for approximately 6 seconds and then turn off. If an air bag supplemental restraint system (SRS) fault is present, the air bag indicator will:

- Fail to light.
- Remain lit continuously.
- Flash.

b. The flashing might not occur until approximately 30 seconds after the ignition switch has been turned from the **OFF** to the **ON** position. This is the time required for the restraints control module (RCM) to complete the testing of the SRS. If the air bag indicator is inoperative and a SRS fault exists, a chime will sound in a pattern of 5 sets of 5 beeps. If this occurs, the air bag indicator and any SRS fault discovered must be diagnosed and repaired.

6. Clear all continuous DTCs from the restraints control module using a scan tool.

DRIVE TRAIN

AUTOMATIC TRANSMISSION ASSEMBLY

REMOVAL & INSTALLATION

2005 Aviator

2WD Models

1. Before servicing the vehicle, refer to the "Precautions" section.

➡**When the battery has been disconnected and reconnected, some abnormal drive symptoms can occur while the vehicle relearns its adaptive strategy.**

2. Disconnect the negative battery cable.

3. Remove the fan shroud bolts. Do not remove the fan shroud.

4. Raise and support the vehicle.

5. If transmission disassembly or installation of a new transmission is necessary, drain the transmission fluid. Install the drain plug when finished.

6. Remove the 2 right side heat shield bolts and position the shield aside.

7. Disconnect the 2 heated oxygen sensor electrical connectors.

8. Disconnect the 2 catalyst monitor sensor electrical connectors.

9. Remove the right side heat shield bolts.

10. Remove the right side heat shield bolt and remove the heat shield.

11. Remove the left side heat shield bolt.

12. Remove the 2 nuts and the plastic shield on the right side of the crossmember near the fuel tank.

13. Remove the 4 upper crossmember bolts (2 on each side).

14. Remove the bolts, springs, flag nuts and separate the muffler from the converter. Discard the gasket. Discard the flag nuts.

15. Remove the 4 converter-to-manifold nuts.

16. Remove the jack stand and lower the converter assembly with the heat shield.

✳✳ CAUTION

Secure the transmission to the transmission jack with a safety chain. Failure to follow these instructions can result in personal injury.

17. Install a suitable jack under the transmission.

18. Remove the right side crossmember bolts.

19. Remove the left side crossmember bolts.

20. Remove the 2 bolts on the bracket and position aside.

21. Remove the transmission support insulator nuts and remove the crossmember.

➡**This step may require an assistant.**

22. Remove the transmission mounted exhaust hanger and the 3-way converter assembly.

23. Remove the shift cable and bracket and position out of PARK.

24. Index-mark the location of the rear flange and pinion flange. Remove the 4 bolts. Remove the rear driveshaft pinion flange bolts.

➡**Do not use a hammer.**

25. Remove the driveshaft flange from the pinion flange, using a pry bar.

26. Index-mark the driveshaft and the extension housing. Remove the driveshaft from the vehicle.

27. Remove the electrical connector cover.

28. Remove the starter wire and positive battery cable.

29. Remove the starter motor bolts and starter.

30. Remove the flexplate cover.

31. Remove the access cover.

➡**Make an identifying mark on the nut, stud and flexplate to allow for correct installation.**

32. Remove the 4 torque converter nuts.

33. Lower the transmission to gain access to the sensor connectors and the transmission bolts.

34. Disconnect the right side catalyst monitor connector and the fuel lines from the bracket.

35. Disconnect the right side heated oxygen sensor from the transmission.

36. Disconnect the left side heated oxygen sensor and the harness clip from the transmission.

37. Disconnect the left side catalyst monitor connector from the transmission.

38. Move the rubber boot back to gain access to the connector. Disconnect the -digital Transmission Range (TR) sensor connector.

39. Disconnect the Turbine Shaft Speed (TSS) sensor, Output Shaft Speed (OSS) sensor and Intermediate Shaft Speed (ISS) sensor electrical connectors.

➡**Clean the area around connector to prevent contamination of the solenoid body connector.**

40. Remove the screw from the solenoid body connector and disconnect the connector.

41. Disconnect the harness retainers.

✳✳ WARNING

Do not damage the cooler tubes.

42. Disconnect the transmission cooler tubes.

43. Remove the front crossmember.

44. Remove the 7 engine-to-transmission retaining bolts.

45. Lower the transmission assembly from the vehicle.

46. Install special tool 307-346 to hold the torque converter.

47. Carry out the transmission fluid cooler back flushing and cleaning if the transmission is being overhauled or installing a new or remanufactured transmission.

To install

✳✳ CAUTION

Secure the transmission to the transmission jack with a safety chain. Failure to follow these instructions can result in personal injury.

48. Secure the transmission to the transmission jack with a safety chain.

➡**Rotate the torque converter so the orange or green paint daub is in the 12 o'clock position.**

49. Raise and position the transmission to the back of the engine.

50. Install the 7 engine-to-transmission retaining bolts. Tighten to 35 ft. lbs. (48 Nm).

51. Install the 4 torque converter nuts. Tighten to 28 ft. lbs. (38 Nm).

52. Install the access cover.

53. Install the flexplate cover. Tighten to 25 ft. lbs. (34 Nm).

54. Install the starter. Tighten to 18 ft. lbs. (24 Nm).

55. Install the starter motor electrical connectors. Tighten to 115 inch lbs. (13 Nm).

56. Install the starter motor electrical connector cover.

57. Install the front crossmember. Tighten to 62 ft. lbs. (70 Nm).

✳✳ WARNING

Use care not to bend or force the cooler tubes otherwise damage to the cooler tubes and the transmission can result.

58. Install the transmission fluid cooler tubes. Tighten to 22 ft. lbs. (30 Nm).

59. Connect the digital Transmission Range (TR) sensor connector. Move the rubber boot back over the connector.

60. Connect the left side Heated Oxygen Sensor (HO2S) to the transmission and install the wire harness retainer. Position the wire harness and install the retainers.

❊❊ WARNING

Damage will occur to the solenoid body assembly if the screw is tightened above the specification.

➡**Always install new O-ring seals on the vehicle harness connector.**

➡**Clean the area around connector to prevent contamination of the solenoid body connector.**

➡**Use petroleum jelly to lubricate the O-ring seals to aid in the installation process.**

61. Install and lubricate new O-ring seals on the transmission connector and connect the connector. Tighten to 44 inch lbs. (5 Nm).

62. Connect the left side catalyst monitor connector to the transmission.

63. Connect the right side Heated Oxygen Sensor (HO2S) to the transmission.

64. Connect the fuel lines and the right side catalyst monitor connector to the bracket.

65. Connect the Turbine Shaft Speed (TSS) sensor, Output Shaft Speed (OSS) sensor and Intermediate Shaft Speed (ISS) sensor electrical connectors.

➡**This step may require an assistant.**

66. Position the catalytic converter assembly with heat shield and loosely install the 4 converter-to-manifold nuts.

67. Install the rear transmission mount bolts. Tighten to 66 ft. lbs. (90 Nm).

68. Connect the 2 heated oxygen sensor electrical connectors.

69. Connect the 2 catalyst monitor sensor electrical connectors.

70. Position the crossmember in place and loosely install the 2 nuts to hold up the crossmember.

➡**Using a transmission jack, raise the crossmember into place.**

71. Install the right side crossmember bolts. Tighten to 52 ft. lbs. (70 Nm).

72. Install the left side crossmember bolts. Tighten to 52 ft. lbs. (70 Nm).

73. Remove the transmission jack.

74. Install the 4 upper crossmember bolts (2 on each side). Tighten to 52 ft. lbs. (70 Nm).

75. Tighten the rear transmission mount nuts. Tighten to 66 ft. lbs. (90 Nm).

76. Install the cable bracket and 2 bolts. Tighten to 30 ft. lbs. (40 Nm).

77. Install the heat shield bolts. Tighten to 15 ft. lbs. (20 Nm).

78. Install the right side heat shield and 2 bolts. Tighten to 15 ft. lbs. (20 Nm).

79. Install the left side heat shield bolts. Tighten to 15 ft. lbs. (20 Nm).

80. Install the plastic shield on the right side of the crossmember near the fuel tank. Tighten to 80 inch lbs. (9 Nm).

81. Tighten the 4 converter-to-manifold nuts. Tighten to 30 ft. lbs. (40 Nm).

82. Using a new gasket install the converter-to-muffler pipe. Install the bolts, springs and flag nuts. Tighten to 30 ft. lbs. (40 Nm).

83. Align the marks made during removal. Install the front portion of the driveshaft into the transmission.

❊❊ WARNING

If new bolts to retain the driveshaft to the axle are not available, coat the threads of the original bolts with Threadlock and Sealer TA-25 or equivalent meeting Ford specification WSK-M2G351-A5.

❊❊ WARNING

The driveshaft flange fits tightly on the rear axle pinion flange pilot. To make sure that the driveshaft flange seats squarely on the pinion flange, tighten the bolts evenly in a cross pattern as shown.

84. Align the marks made during removal. Install the rear driveshaft and bolts. Tighten to 83 ft. lbs. (112 Nm).

85. Install the shift cable and bracket. Tighten to 30 ft. lbs. (40 Nm).

86. Use the following guidelines for installing the in-line transmission fluid filter:

 a. If the transmission was overhauled and the vehicle was equipped with an in-line fluid filter, install a new in-line fluid filter.

 b. If the transmission was overhauled and the vehicle was not equipped with an in-line fluid filter, install a new in-line fluid filter kit.

 c. If the transmission is being installed for a non-internal repair, do not install an in-line filter or filter kit.

 d. If installing a new or a Ford-authorized remanufactured transmission, install the in-line transmission fluid filter that is supplied.

 e. Prior to lowering the vehicle, install a new in-line transmission filter or a filter kit.

➡**When the battery has been disconnected and reconnected, some abnormal drive symptoms can occur while the vehicle relearns its adaptive strategy. The customer needs to be notified that they can experience slightly different up shifts (either soft or firm) and that this is a temporary condition and will eventually return to normal operating condition.**

87. Connect the battery ground cable.

88. Position the fan shroud and install the bolts.

89. Carry out the fluid level check.

90. Verify that the shift cable is correctly adjusted.

91. Check the operation of the transmission and inspect for leaks.

4WD Models

See Figures 30 through 32.

1. Before servicing the vehicle, refer to the "Precautions" section.

➡**When the battery has been disconnected and reconnected, some abnormal drive symptoms can occur while the vehicle relearns its adaptive strategy.**

2. Disconnect the negative battery cable.

3. Remove the fan shroud bolts. Do not remove the fan shroud.

4. Raise and support the vehicle.

5. If transmission disassembly or installation of new transmission is necessary, drain the transmission fluid. Install the drain plug when finished.

6. Remove the 2 right heat shield bolts and position the right heat shield aside.

7. Disconnect the 2 heated oxygen sensor electrical connectors.

8. Disconnect the 2 catalyst monitor sensor electrical connectors.

9. Remove the right heat shield bolts.

10. Remove the right heat shield bolt and remove the heat shield.

11. Remove the left heat shield bolt.

12. Remove the plastic shield on the right side of the crossmember near the fuel tank.

13. Remove the 4 upper crossmember bolts (2 on each side).

14. Remove the bolts, springs, flag nuts and separate the muffler from the converter. Discard the gasket. Discard the flag nuts.

15. Remove the 4 converter-to-manifold nuts.

16. Install a suitable jack stand under the transfer case.

17. Remove the right side crossmember bolts.

18. Remove the left side crossmember bolts.

19. Remove the transmission support insulator nuts and remove the crossmember.

➡**This step may require an assistant.**

20. Remove the transmission mounted exhaust hanger and the 3-way converter system. Remove the bolt and converter assembly. If required, remove the 2nd bolt and mount.

21. Remove the shift cable and bracket. Position the manual lever out of park.

22. Index-mark the front axle pinion flange and the front driveshaft.

23. Index-mark the front output shaft assembly and the front driveshaft constant velocity (CV) joint.

24. Remove and discard the bolts and washers.

25. Remove and discard the bolts and universal joint retainers.

❋❋ WARNING

Always disconnect the front driveshaft from the transfer case first. Otherwise, the weight of the driveshaft can pinch the boot between the shaft and the boot can and cause the boot to tear.

❋❋ WARNING ·

Tape the bearing cups to the driveshaft to prevent them from falling off of the spider.

➡**The front driveshaft CV-joint is not repairable.**

26. Mark the location of the flanges. Remove the 4 bolts.

27. Remove the rear driveshaft bolts.

➡**Do not use a hammer.**

28. Remove the driveshaft from the flange using a pry bar.

29. Remove the electrical connector cover.

30. Remove the starter wire and the positive battery cable.

31. Remove the starter motor bolts and starter.

32. Remove the flexplate cover.

33. Remove the access cover.

34. Make an identifying mark on the nut, stud and flexplate to allow for correct installation. Remove the 4 torque converter nuts.

35. Lower the transmission to gain access to the sensor connectors and the transmission bolts.

36. Disconnect the right catalyst monitor connector and the fuel lines from the bracket.

37. Disconnect the right heated oxygen sensor from the transmission.

38. If equipped, disconnect the shift motor electrical connector.

39. Disconnect the left heated oxygen sensor and the harness clip from the transmission.

40. Disconnect the left catalyst monitor connector from the transmission.

41. Move the rubber boot back to gain access to the connector. Disconnect the digital Transmission Range (TR) sensor connector.

42. Disconnect the Turbine Shaft Speed (TSS) sensor, Output Shaft Speed (OSS) sensor and Intermediate Shaft Speed (ISS) sensor electrical connectors.

➡**Clean the area around connector to prevent contamination of the solenoid body connector.**

43. Remove the screw from the solenoid body connector and disconnect the connector.

44. Disconnect the harness retainers.

❋❋ WARNING

Do not damage the cooler tubes. Hold the transmission case fittings with a wrench.

45. Disconnect the transmission cooler tubes.

❋❋ CAUTION

Secure the transmission to the transmission jack with a safety chain. Failure to follow these instructions can result in personal injury.

46. Support the transmission with a transmission jack.

47. Remove the jack stand from under the transfer case.

48. Remove the 4 front crossmember bolts and the crossmember.

49. Remove the 7 engine-to-transmission retaining bolts.

50. Lower the transmission and transfer case as an assembly from the vehicle.

51. Install special tool 307-346 to hold the converter.

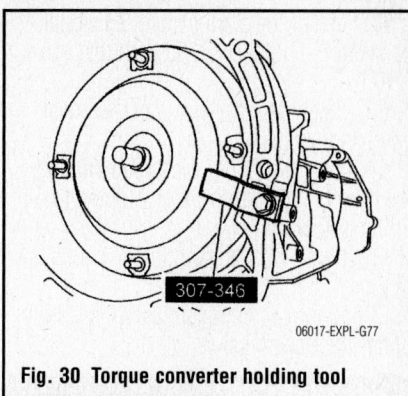

06017-EXPL-G77

Fig. 30 Torque converter holding tool

➡**If the transmission is being serviced, the transfer case will need to be removed.**

52. Remove the transfer case from the back of the transmission.

53. Carry out the transmission fluid cooler back flushing and cleaning if the transmission is being overhauled or installing a new or remanufactured transmission.

To install:

❋❋ CAUTION

Secure the transmission to the transmission jack with a safety chain. Failure to follow these instructions can result in personal injury.

54. If removed, install the transfer case to the back of the transmission, install the bracket and connect the vent hose. Tighten to 30 ft. lbs. (41 Nm)

55. Remove the special tool.

❋❋ CAUTION

Make sure that the transmission and transfer case assembly are secured to the transmission jack with a safety chain. Failure to follow these instructions can result in personal injury.

➡**Rotate the torque converter so the orange or green paint daub is in the 12 o'clock position.**

56. Raise and position the transmission and transfer case to the back of the engine.

57. Install the 7 engine-to-transmission retaining bolts. Tighten to 35 ft. lbs. (48 Nm).

58. Install the 4 torque converter nuts. Tighten to 28 ft. lbs. (38 Nm).

59. Install the access cover.

60. Install the flexplate cover. Tighten to 25 ft. lbs. (34 Nm).

61. Install the starter. Tighten to 18 ft. lbs. (24 Nm).

62. Install the starter motor electrical connectors. Tighten to 115 inch lbs. (13 Nm).

63. Install the starter motor electrical connector cover.

64. Install the front crossmember and the 4 bolts (2 on each side). Tighten to 52 ft. lbs. (70 Nm).

65. Install a jack stand under the transfer case.

66. Remove the transmission jack from under the transmission.

✳✳ WARNING

Use care not to bend or force the cooler tubes otherwise damage to the cooler tubes and the transmission can result.

67. Install the transmission fluid cooler tubes. Tighten to 22 ft. lbs. (30 Nm).

68. Connect the digital Transmission Range (TR) sensor connector. Move the rubber boot back over the connector.

69. Connect the left Heated Oxygen Sensor (HO2S) to the transmission and install the wire harness retainer. Position the wire harness and install the retainers.

✳✳ WARNING

Damage will occur to the solenoid body assembly if the screw is tightened above the specification.

➡Always install new O-ring seals on the vehicle harness connector.

➡Clean the area around connector to prevent contamination of the solenoid body connector.

➡Use petroleum jelly to lubricate the O-ring seals to aid in the installation process.

70. Install and lubricate new O-ring seals on the transmission connector and connect the connector. Tighten to 44 inch lbs. (5 Nm).

71. Connect the left catalyst monitor connector to the transmission.

72. Connect the right Heated Oxygen Sensor (HO2S) to the transmission.

73. Connect the fuel lines and the right catalyst monitor connector to the bracket.

74. Connect the Turbine Shaft Speed (TSS) sensor, Output Shaft Speed (OSS) sensor and Intermediate Shaft Speed (ISS) sensor electrical connectors.

➡This step may require an assistant.

75. Position the catalytic converter assembly with heat shield and loosely install the 4 converter-to-manifold nuts.

76. Install the rear transmission mount bolts. Tighten to 66 ft. lbs. (90 Nm).

77. Connect the 2 heated oxygen sensor electrical connectors.

78. Connect the 2 catalyst monitor sensor electrical connectors.

79. Position the crossmember in place and loosely install the 2 nuts to hold up the crossmember.

80. Install the right side crossmember bolts. Tighten to 52 ft. lbs. (70 Nm).

81. Install the left side crossmember bolts. Tighten to 52 ft. lbs. (70 Nm).

82. Remove the jack stand.

83. Install the 4 upper crossmember bolts (2 on each side). Tighten to 52 ft. lbs. (70 Nm).

84. Tighten the rear transmission mount nuts to 66 ft. lbs. (90 Nm).

85. Install the right heat shield and bolts. Tighten to 15 ft. lbs. (20 Nm).

86. Install the left heat shield bolts. Tighten to 15 ft. lbs. (20 Nm).

87. Install the plastic shield on the right side of the crossmember near the fuel tank. Tighten to 80 inch lbs. (9 Nm).

88. Tighten the 4 converter-to-manifold nuts. Tighten to 30 ft. lbs. (40 Nm).

89. Using a new gasket, install the converter-to-muffler pipe and the heat shield. Install the bolts, springs and flag nuts. Tighten to 30 ft. lbs. (40 Nm).

90. If equipped, connect the shift motor electrical connector.

✳✳ WARNING

The can (domed CV-joint housing cover) is pressed into the CV-joint housing at the factory. When housed correctly, the can will appear as shown in the illustration, top box. Do not reseat the can in the CV-joint housing if the can's flange is above the CV-joint housings shown in the illustration, bottom box.

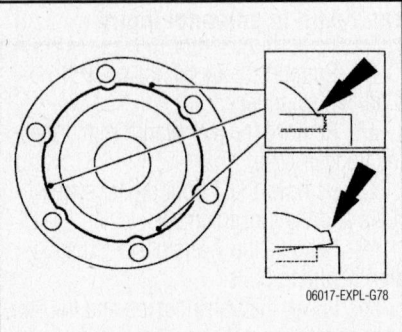

Fig. 31 Proper can installation—2005 Aviator 4WD models

91. Install a new driveshaft.

92. Verify that the can flange is housed correctly in the CV-joint housing as shown in the illustration, top box. Install a new driveshaft if the can flange is not housed correctly.

✳✳ WARNING

Always connect the front driveshaft to the axle first. Otherwise, the weight of the driveshaft can pinch the boot between the shaft and the boot can and cause the boot to tear.

93. Align the index marks. Install the driveshaft.

✳✳ WARNING

Tighten the bolts evenly in a cross pattern or damage will occur to the CV-joint.

➡Install new washers and bolts. If new bolts are not available, coat the threads of the original bolts with threadlock and sealer.

94. Install the new washers and bolts. Tighten the bolts evenly in a cross pattern as shown. Tighten to 22 ft. lbs. (30 Nm).

95. Verify that the CV-joint has seated squarely in the transfer case flange.

   a. Check that the space between the end of the CV-joint cap and the end of the transfer case flange is equal from the top to the bottom of the 2 components.

   b. Rotate the driveshaft ¼ turn.

   c. Check that the space between the end of the CV-joint cap and the end of the transfer case flange is equal from the top to the bottom of the 2 components.

   d. Repeat this procedure several times.

   e. If the space if not equal at any point in the attachment, remove and reinstall the driveshaft as described in this procedure.

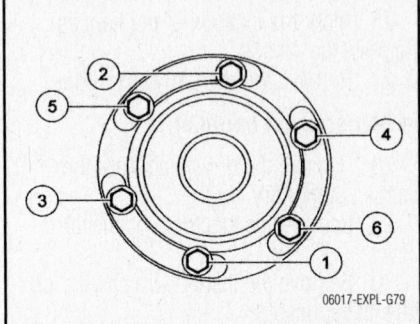

Fig. 32 Driveshaft joint torque sequence—2005 Aviator 4WD Aviator models

➡️**Install new universal joint retainers and bolts. If new bolts are not available, coat the threads of the original bolts with threadlock and sealer.**

96. Align the index marks and install the new universal joint retainer and bolts. Tighten to 13 ft lbs. (18 Nm).

✳✳ WARNING

If new bolts to retain the driveshaft to the axle are not available, coat the threads of the original bolts with Threadlock and Sealer TA-25 or equivalent meeting Ford specification WSK-M2G351-A5.

✳✳ WARNING

The driveshaft flange fits tightly on the rear axle pinion flange pilot. To make sure that the driveshaft flange seats squarely on the pinion flange, tighten the bolts evenly in a cross pattern as shown.

97. Install the rear driveshaft and the 8 bolts. Tighten to 83 ft. lbs. (112 Nm).
98. Install the shift cable and bracket. Tighten to 30 ft. lbs. (40 Nm).
99. Use the following guidelines for installing the in-line transmission fluid filter:

  a. If the transmission was overhauled and the vehicle was equipped with an in-line fluid filter, install a new in-line fluid filter.

  b. If the transmission was overhauled and the vehicle was not equipped with an in-line fluid filter, install a new in-line fluid filter kit.

  c. If the transmission is being installed for a non-internal repair, do not install an in-line filter or filter kit.

  d. If installing a new or a Ford-authorized remanufactured transmission, install the in-line transmission fluid filter that is supplied.

  e. Prior to lowering the vehicle, install a new in-line transmission filter or a filter kit.

➡️**When the battery has been disconnected and reconnected, some abnormal drive symptoms can occur while the vehicle relearns its adaptive strategy. The customer needs to be notified that they can experience slightly different up shifts (either soft or firm) and that this is a temporary condition and will eventually return to normal operating condition.**

100. Connect the battery ground cable.
101. Position the fan shroud and install the bolts.
102. Carry out the fluid level check.
103. Verify that the shift cable is correctly adjusted.
104. Check the operation of the transmission and inspect for leaks.

2005 Explorer And Mountaineer

2WD Models

See Figure 33.

1. Before servicing the vehicle, refer to the "Precautions" section.

➡️**When the battery has been disconnected and reconnected, some abnormal drive symptoms can occur while the vehicle relearns its adaptive strategy.**

2. Disconnect the negative battery cable.
3. Remove the fan shroud bolts. Do not remove the fan shroud.
4. Raise and support the vehicle.
5. If transmission disassembly or installation of new transmission is necessary, drain the transmission fluid. Install the drain plug when finished.
6. Remove the 2 right heat shield bolts and position the right heat shield aside.
7. Disconnect the 2 heated oxygen sensor electrical connectors.
8. Disconnect the 2 catalyst monitor sensor electrical connectors.
9. Remove the right heat shield bolts.
10. Remove the right heat shield bolt and remove the heat shield.
11. Remove the left heat shield bolt.
12. Remove the plastic shield on the right side of the crossmember near the fuel tank.
13. Remove the 2 upper crossmember bolts (2 on each side).
14. Remove the bolts, springs, flag nuts and separate the muffler from the converter. Discard the gasket.
15. Discard the flag nuts.
16. Remove the 4 converter-to-manifold nuts.
17. Install a suitable jack stand under the transfer case.
18. Remove the right side crossmember bolts.
19. Remove the left side crossmember bolts.
20. Remove the transmission support insulator nuts and remove the crossmember.

➡️**This step may require an assistant.**

21. Remove the transmission mounted exhaust hanger and the 3-way converter system.

22. Remove the shift cable and bracket.
23. Position the manual lever out of park.
24. Index-mark the front axle pinion flange and the front driveshaft.
25. Index-mark the front output shaft assembly and the front driveshaft constant velocity (CV) joint.
26. Remove and discard the bolts and washers.
27. Remove and discard the bolts and universal joint retainers.

✳✳ WARNING

Always disconnect the front driveshaft from the transfer case 1st. Otherwise, the weight of the driveshaft can pinch the boot between the shaft and the boot can and cause the boot to tear.

✳✳ WARNING

Tape the bearing cups to the driveshaft to prevent them from falling off of the spider.

➡️**The front driveshaft CV-joint is not repairable.**

28. Remove the driveshaft.
29. Mark the location of the flanges. Remove the rear driveshaft bolts.

➡️**Do not use a hammer.**

30. Remove the driveshaft from the flange using a pry bar.
31. 4.6L engine
  a. Remove the electrical connector cover.
  b. Remove the starter wire and the positive battery cable.
  c. Remove the starter motor bolts and starter.
  d. Remove the flexplate cover.
  e. Remove the access cover.

➡️**Make an identifying mark on the nut, stud and flexplate to allow for correct installation.**

  f. Remove the 4 torque converter nuts.
32. 4.0L engine
  a. Remove the starter and position off to the side.

➡️**Make an identifying mark on the nut, stud and flexplate to allow for correct installation.**

  b. Remove the 4 torque converter nuts.
  c. Remove the lower transmission retaining bolts.

33. All vehicles

a. Lower the transmission to gain access to the sensor connectors and the transmission bolts.

b. Disconnect the right catalyst monitor connector and the fuel lines from the bracket.

c. Disconnect the right heated oxygen sensor from the transmission.

d. If equipped, disconnect the shift motor electrical connector.

e. Disconnect the left heated oxygen sensor and the harness clip from the transmission.

f. Disconnect the left catalyst monitor connector from the transmission.

g. Move the rubber boot back to gain access to the connector.

h. Disconnect the digital Transmission Range (TR) sensor connector.

i. Disconnect the Turbine Shaft Speed (TSS) sensor, Output Shaft Speed (OSS) sensor and Intermediate Shaft Speed (ISS) sensor electrical connectors.

➡Clean the area around connector to prevent contamination of the solenoid body connector.

j. Remove the screw from the solenoid body connector and disconnect the connector.

k. Disconnect the harness retainers.

✳✳ WARNING

Do not damage the cooler tubes. Hold the transmission case fittings with a wrench.

l. Disconnect the transmission cooler tubes.

✳✳ CAUTION

Secure the transmission to the transmission jack with a safety chain. Failure to follow these instructions can result in personal injury.

m. Support the transmission with a transmission jack.

n. Remove the jack stand from under the transfer case.

o. Remove the engine-to-transmission retaining bolts.

p. Lower the transmission and transfer case as an assembly from the vehicle.

q. Install a converter holding tool.

➡If the transmission is being serviced, the transfer case will need to be removed.

r. Remove the transfer case from the back of the transmission.

s. Carry out the transmission fluid cooler back flushing and cleaning if the transmission is being overhauled or installing a new or remanufactured transmission.

To install:

✳✳ CAUTION

Secure the transmission to the transmission jack with a safety chain. Failure to follow these instructions can result in personal injury.

34. Secure the transmission to the transmission jack with a safety chain.

➡Rotate the torque converter so that the torque converter paint mark is in the 12 o'clock position.

35. Raise and position the transmission to the back of the engine.

36. On 2005 4.6L engine, perform the following:

a. Torque the 7 engine-to-transmission retaining bolts: 35 ft. lbs. (48 Nm).

b. Torque the 4 torque converter nuts: 28 ft. lbs. (38 Nm).

c. Install the access cover.

d. Install the flexplate cover to 25 ft. lbs. (34 Nm).

e. Install the starter to 18 ft. lbs. (24 Nm).

f. Install the starter motor electrical connectors. Tighten the cable to 115 inch lbs. (13 Nm). Tighten the wire to 53 inch lbs. (6 Nm).

g. Install the starter motor electrical connector cover.

h. Install the front crossmember bolts to 52 ft. lbs. (70 Nm).

37. On 2005 4.0L engine, perform the following:

a. Position the fuel line bracket in place and install the 6 retaining bolts. Tighten to 35 ft. lbs. (48 Nm).

b. Install the 4 torque converter nuts. Tighten to 28 ft. lbs. (38 Nm).

c. Install the starter motor. Tighten to 18 ft. lbs. (25 Nm).

d. Install the lower transmission retaining bolts. Tighten to 35 ft. lbs. (48 Nm).

38. All vehicles:

✳✳ WARNING

Use care not to bend or force the cooler tubes otherwise damage to the cooler tubes and the transmission can result.

e. Install the transmission fluid cooler tubes. Tighten to 22 ft. lbs. (30 Nm).

f. Connect the digital Transmission Range (TR) sensor connector. Move the rubber boot back over the connector.

g. Connect the left Heated Oxygen Sensor (HO2S) to the transmission and install the wire harness retainer. Position the wire harness and install the retainers.

✳✳ WARNING

Damage will occur to the solenoid body assembly if the screw is tightened above the specification.

➡Always install new O-ring seals on the vehicle harness connector.

➡Clean the area around connector to prevent contamination of the solenoid body connector.

➡Use petroleum jelly to lubricate the O-ring seals to aid in the installation process.

h. Install and lubricate new O-ring seals on the transmission connector and connect the connector. Tighten to 44 inch lbs. (5 Nm).

i. Connect the left catalyst monitor connector to the transmission.

j. Connect the right Heated Oxygen Sensor (HO2S) to the transmission.

k. Connect the fuel lines and the right catalyst monitor connector to the bracket.

l. Connect the Turbine Shaft Speed (TSS) sensor, Output Shaft Speed (OSS) sensor, and Intermediate Shaft Speed (ISS) sensor electrical connectors.

➡This step may require an assistant.

m. Position the catalytic converter assembly with heat shield and loosely install the 4 converter-to-manifold nuts.

n. Install the rear transmission mount bolts. Tighten to 66 ft. lbs. (90 Nm).

o. Connect the 2 heated oxygen sensor electrical connectors.

p. Connect the 2 catalyst monitor sensor electrical connectors.

q. Position the crossmember in place and loosely install the 2 nuts to hold up the crossmember.

➡Using a transmission jack, raise the crossmember into place.

r. Install the right side crossmember bolts. Tighten to 52 ft. lbs. (70 Nm).

s. Install the left side crossmember bolts. Tighten to 52 ft. lbs. (70 Nm).

t. Remove the transmission jack.

u. Install the 2 upper crossmember bolts (2 on each side). Tighten to 52 ft. lbs. (70 Nm).

v. Tighten the rear transmission mount nuts. Tighten to 66 ft. lbs. (90 Nm).

w. Install the cable bracket and 2 bolts. Tighten to 30 ft. lbs. (40 Nm).

x. Install the heat shield bolts. Tighten to 15 ft. lbs. (20 Nm).

y. Install the right heat shield and 3 bolts. Tighten to 15 ft. lbs. (20 Nm).

z. Install the left heat shield bolts. Tighten to 15 ft. lbs. (20 Nm).

aa. Install the plastic shield on the right side of the crossmember near the fuel tank. Tighten to 80 inch lbs. (9 Nm).

bb. Tighten the 4 converter-to-manifold nuts. Tighten to 30 ft. lbs. (40 Nm).

cc. Using a new gasket install the converter-to-muffler pipe. Install the bolts, springs and flag nuts. Tighten to 30 ft. lbs. (40 Nm).

dd. Align the marks made during removal. Install the front portion of the driveshaft into the transmission.

※※ WARNING

If new bolts to retain the driveshaft to the axle are not available, coat the threads of the original bolts with Threadlock and Sealer TA-25 or equivalent meeting Ford specification WSK-M2G351-A5.

※※ WARNING

The driveshaft flange fits tightly on the rear axle pinion flange pilot. To make sure that the driveshaft flange seats squarely on the pinion flange, tighten the bolts evenly in a cross pattern as shown.

ee. Align the marks made during removal. Install the rear driveshaft and bolts. Tighten to 83 ft. lbs. (112 Nm).

ff. Install the shift cable and bracket. Tighten to 30 ft. lbs. (40 Nm).

39. Use the following guidelines for installing the in-line transmission fluid filter:

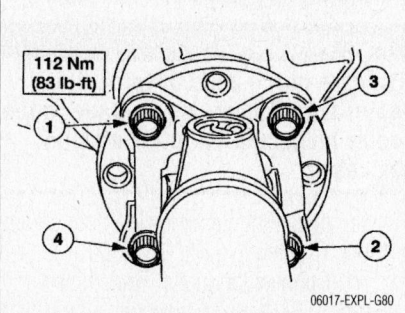

Fig. 33 Rear driveshaft flange torque sequence—2005 Explorer and Mountaineer

a. If the transmission was overhauled and the vehicle was equipped with an in-line fluid filter, install a new in-line fluid filter.

b. If the transmission was overhauled and the vehicle was not equipped with an in-line fluid filter, install a new in-line fluid filter kit.

c. If the transmission is being installed for a non-internal repair, do not install an in-line filter or filter kit.

d. If installing a new or a Ford-authorized remanufactured transmission, install the in-line transmission fluid filter that is supplied.

e. Prior to lowering the vehicle, install a new in-line transmission filter or a filter kit.

➡**When the battery has been disconnected and reconnected, some abnormal drive symptoms can occur while the vehicle relearns its adaptive strategy. The customer needs to be notified that they can experience slightly different up shifts (either soft or firm) and that this is a temporary condition and will eventually return to normal operating condition.**

f. Connect the battery ground cable.

g. Position the fan shroud and install the bolts.

h. Carry out the fluid level check.

i. Verify that the shift cable is correctly adjusted. Check the operation of the transmission and inspect for leaks.

4WD Models

1. Before servicing the vehicle, refer to the "Precautions" section.

➡**When the battery has been disconnected and reconnected, some abnormal drive symptoms can occur while the vehicle relearns its adaptive strategy.**

2. Disconnect the negative battery cable.

3. Remove the fan shroud bolts. Do not remove the fan shroud.

4. Raise and support the vehicle.

5. If transmission disassembly or installation of new transmission is necessary, drain the transmission fluid. Install the drain plug when finished.

6. Remove the 2 right heat shield bolts and position the right heat shield aside.

7. Disconnect the 2 heated oxygen sensor electrical connectors.

8. Disconnect the 2 catalyst monitor sensor electrical connectors.

9. Remove the right heat shield bolts.

10. Remove the right heat shield bolt and remove the heat shield.

11. Remove the left heat shield bolt.

12. Remove the plastic shield on the right side of the crossmember near the fuel tank.

13. Remove the 2 upper crossmember bolts (2 on each side).

14. Remove the bolts, springs, flag nuts and separate the muffler from the converter. Discard the gasket. Discard the flag nuts.

15. Remove the 4 converter-to-manifold nuts.

16. Install a suitable jack stand under the transfer case.

17. Remove the right side crossmember bolts.

18. Remove the left side crossmember bolts.

19. Remove the transmission support insulator nuts and remove the crossmember.

➡**This step may require an assistant.**

20. Remove the transmission mounted exhaust hanger and the 3-way converter system.

21. Remove the shift cable and bracket. Position the manual lever out of park.

22. Index-mark the front axle pinion flange and the front driveshaft.

23. Index-mark the front output shaft assembly and the front driveshaft constant velocity (CV) joint.

24. Remove and discard the bolts and washers.

25. Remove and discard the bolts and universal joint retainers.

※※ WARNING

Always disconnect the front driveshaft from the transfer case 1st. Otherwise, the weight of the driveshaft can pinch the boot between the shaft and the boot can and cause the boot to tear.

※※ WARNING

Tape the bearing cups to the driveshaft to prevent them from falling off of the spider.

➡**The front driveshaft CV-joint is not repairable.**

26. Remove the driveshaft.

➡**The pinion flange is shown, transfer case flange is similar.**

27. Mark the location of the flanges. Remove the rear driveshaft bolts.

➡**Do not use a hammer.**

28. Remove the driveshaft from the flange using a pry bar.

29. For 4.6L engine, perform the following:

a. Remove the electrical connector cover.

b. Remove the starter wire and the positive battery cable.

c. Remove the starter motor bolts and starter.

d. Remove the flexplate cover.

e. Remove the access cover.

➡**Make an identifying mark on the nut, stud and flexplate to allow for correct installation.**

f. Remove the 4 torque converter nuts.

30. For 4.0L engine, perform the following:

a. Remove the starter and position off to the side.

➡**Make an identifying mark on the nut, stud and flexplate to allow for correct installation.**

b. Remove the 4 torque converter nuts.

c. Remove the lower transmission retaining bolts.

31. For all vehicles:

a. Lower the transmission to gain access to the sensor connectors and the transmission bolts.

b. Disconnect the right catalyst monitor connector and the fuel lines from the bracket.

c. Disconnect the right heated oxygen sensor from the transmission.

d. If equipped, disconnect the shift motor electrical connector.

e. Disconnect the left heated oxygen sensor and the harness clip from the transmission.

f. Disconnect the left catalyst monitor connector from the transmission. Move the rubber boot back to gain access to the connector.

g. Disconnect the digital Transmission Range (TR) sensor connector.

h. Disconnect the Turbine Shaft Speed (TSS) sensor, Output Shaft Speed (OSS) sensor and Intermediate Shaft Speed (ISS) sensor electrical connectors.

➡**Clean the area around connector to prevent contamination of the solenoid body connector.**

i. Remove the screw from the solenoid body connector and disconnect the connector.

j. Disconnect the harness retainers.

✳✳ WARNING

Do not damage the cooler tubes. Hold the transmission case fittings with a wrench.

k. Disconnect the transmission cooler tubes.

✳✳ CAUTION

Secure the transmission to the transmission jack with a safety chain. Failure to follow these instructions can result in personal injury.

l. Support the transmission with a transmission jack.

m. Remove the jackstand from under the transfer case.

32. 4.6L engine:

a. Remove the 4 front crossmember bolts and the crossmember.

b. Remove the 7 engine-to-transmission retaining bolts.

33. 4.0L engine:

a. Remove the 6 engine-to-transmission retaining bolts and position the fuel line bracket aside.

34. All vehicles:

a. Lower the transmission and transfer case as an assembly from the vehicle. Install a converter holding tool.

➡**If the transmission is being serviced, the transfer case will need to be removed.**

b. Remove the transfer case from the back of the transmission.

c. Carry out the transmission fluid cooler backflushing and cleaning if the transmission is being overhauled or installing a new or remanufactured transmission

To install:

✳✳ CAUTION

Secure the transmission to the transmission jack with a safety chain. Failure to follow these instructions can result in personal injury.

35. If removed, install the transfer case to the back of the transmission, install the bracket and connect the vent hose. Tighten to 30 ft. lbs. (41 Nm)

36. Remove the special tool.

✳✳ CAUTION

Make sure that the transmission and transfer case assembly are secured to the transmission jack with a safety

chain. Failure to follow these instructions can result in personal injury.

➡**Rotate the torque converter so that the torque converter paint mark is in the 12 o'clock position.**

37. Raise and position the transmission and transfer case to the back of the engine.

38. 4.6L engine:

a. Install the 7 engine-to-transmission retaining bolts. Tighten to 35 ft. lbs. (48 Nm).

b. Install the 4 torque converter nuts. Tighten to 26 ft. lbs. (35 Nm).

c. Install the access cover.

d. Install the flexplate cover. Tighten to 25 ft. lbs. (34 Nm).

e. Install the starter. Tighten to 18 ft. lbs. (24 Nm).

f. Install the starter motor electrical connectors. Tighten the cable to 115 inch lbs. (13 Nm). Tighten the wire to 53 inch lbs. (6 Nm).

g. Install the starter motor electrical connector cover.

➡**right side shown, left side similar.**

h. Install the front crossmember and the 4 bolts (2 on each side). Tighten to 52 ft. lbs. (70 Nm).

39. 4.0L engine:

a. Position the fuel line bracket in place and install the 6 engine-to-transmission retaining bolts. Tighten to 35 ft. lbs. (48 Nm).

b. Install the 4 torque converter nuts. Tighten to 26 ft. lbs. (35 Nm).

c. Install the starter motor. Tighten to 18 ft. lbs. (25 Nm).

d. Install the lower transmission retaining bolts. Tighten to 35 ft. lbs. (48 Nm).

40. All vehicles:

a. Install a jackstand under the transfer case.

b. Remove the transmission jack from under the transmission.

✳✳ WARNING

Use care not to bend or force the cooler tubes otherwise damage to the cooler tubes and the transmission can result.

c. Install the transmission fluid cooler tubes. Tighten to 22 ft. lbs. (30 Nm).

d. Connect the digital Transmission Range (TR) sensor connector. Move the rubber boot back over the connector.

e. Connect the left Heated Oxygen Sensor (HO2S) to the transmission and install the wire harness retainer. Position the wire harness and install the retainers.

> **✳✳ WARNING**
>
> **Damage will occur to the solenoid body assembly if the screw is tightened above the specification.**

➡**Always install new O-ring seals on the vehicle harness connector.**

➡**Clean the area around connector to prevent contamination of the solenoid body connector.**

➡**Use petroleum jelly to lubricate the O-ring seals to aid in the installation process.**

  f. Install and lubricate new O-ring seals on the transmission connector and connect the connector. Tighten to 44 inch lbs. (5 Nm).

  g. Connect the left catalyst monitor connector to the transmission.

  h. Connect the right Heated Oxygen Sensor (HO2S) to the transmission.

  i. Connect the fuel lines and the right catalyst monitor connector to the bracket.

  j. Connect the Turbine Shaft Speed (TSS) sensor, Output Shaft Speed (OSS) sensor, and Intermediate Shaft Speed (ISS) sensor electrical connectors.

➡**This step may require an assistant.**

  k. Position the catalytic converter assembly with heat shield and loosely install the 4 converter-to-manifold nuts.

  l. Position the rear transmission mount and exhaust hanger. Install the rear mount bolts. Tighten to 66 ft. lbs. (90 Nm).

  m. Connect the 2 heated oxygen sensor electrical connectors.

  n. Connect the 2 catalyst monitor sensor electrical connectors.

  o. Position the crossmember in place and loosely install the 2 nuts to hold up the crossmember.

  p. Install the right side crossmember bolts. Tighten to 52 ft. lbs. (70 Nm).

  q. Install the left side crossmember bolts. Tighten to 52 ft. lbs. (70 Nm).

  r. Remove the jackstand.

  s. Install the 2 upper crossmember bolts (2 on each side). Tighten to 52 ft. lbs. (70 Nm).

  t. Tighten the rear transmission mount nuts. Tighten to 66 ft. lbs. (90 Nm).

  u. Install the right heat shield and bolts. Tighten to 15 ft. lbs. (20 Nm).

  v. Install the left heat shield bolts. Tighten to 15 ft. lbs. (20 Nm).

  w. Install the plastic shield on the right side of the crossmember near the fuel tank. Tighten to 80 inch lbs. (9 Nm).

  x. Tighten the 4 converter-to-manifold nuts. Tighten to 30 ft. lbs. (40 Nm).

  y. Using a new gasket, install the converter-to-muffler pipe and the heat shield. Install the bolts, springs and flag nuts. Tighten to 30 ft. lbs. (40 Nm).

  z. If equipped, connect the shift motor electrical connector.

> **✳✳ WARNING**
>
> **The can (domed CV-joint housing cover) is pressed into the CV-joint housing at the factory. When housed correctly, the can will appear as shown in the cut-away illustration, top box. Do not reseat the can in the CV-joint housing if the can's flange is above the CV-joint housings shown in the cut-away illustration, bottom box. Install a new driveshaft.**

  aa. Verify that the can flange is housed correctly in the CV-joint housing as shown in the cut-away illustration, top box. Install a new driveshaft if the can flange is not housed correctly.

> **✳✳ WARNING**
>
> **Always connect the front driveshaft to the axle 1st. Otherwise, the weight of the driveshaft can pinch the boot between the shaft and the boot can and cause the boot to tear.**

➡**Align the index marks.**

  bb. Install the driveshaft.

> **✳✳ WARNING**
>
> **Tighten the bolts evenly in a cross pattern or damage will occur to the CV-joint.**

➡**Install new washers and bolts. If new bolts are not available, coat the threads of the original bolts with threadlock and sealer.**

  cc. Install the new washers and bolts. Tighten the bolts evenly in a cross pattern. Tighten to 22 ft. lbs. (30 Nm).

  dd. Verify that the CV-joint has seated squarely in the transfer case flange.

  ee. Check that the space between the end of the CV-joint cap and the end of the transfer case flange is equal from the top to the bottom of the 2 components.

  ff. Rotate the driveshaft ¼ turn.

  gg. Check that the space between the end of the CV-joint cap and the end of the transfer case flange is equal from the top to the bottom of the 2 components.

  hh. Repeat this procedure several times.

  ii. If the space if not equal at any point in the attachment, remove and reinstall the driveshaft as described in this procedure.

➡**Install new universal joint retainers and bolts. If new bolts are not available, coat the threads of the original bolts with threadlock and sealer.**

  jj. Install the new universal joint retainer and bolts. Tighten to 13 ft lbs. (18 Nm).

> **✳✳ WARNING**
>
> **If new bolts to retain the driveshaft to the axle are not available, coat the threads of the original bolts with Threadlock and Sealer TA-25 or equivalent meeting Ford specification WSK-M2G351-A5.**

> **✳✳ WARNING**
>
> **The driveshaft flange fits tightly on the rear axle pinion flange pilot. To make sure that the driveshaft flange seats squarely on the pinion flange, tighten the bolts evenly in a cross pattern as shown.**

  kk. Install the rear driveshaft and the 8 bolts. Tighten to 83 ft. lbs. (112 Nm).

  ll. Install the shift cable and bracket. Tighten to 30 ft. lbs. (40 Nm).

  41. Use the following guidelines for installing the in-line transmission fluid filter:

  a. If the transmission was overhauled and the vehicle was equipped with an in-line fluid filter, install a new in-line fluid filter.

  b. If the transmission was overhauled and the vehicle was not equipped with an in-line fluid filter, install a new in-line fluid filter kit.

  c. If the transmission is being installed for a non-internal repair, do not install an in-line filter or filter kit.

  d. If installing a new or a Ford-authorized remanufactured transmission, install the in-line transmission fluid filter that is supplied.

  e. Prior to lowering the vehicle, install a new in-line transmission filter or a filter kit.

➡**When the battery has been disconnected and reconnected, some abnormal drive symptoms can occur while the vehicle relearns its adaptive strategy. The customer needs to be notified that they can experience slightly different upshifts (either soft or firm) and that this is a temporary condition and will eventually return to normal operating condition.**

   f. Connect the battery ground cable.
   g. Position the fan shroud and install the bolts.
   h. Carry out the fluid level check.
   i. Verify that the shift cable is correctly adjusted.
   j. Check the operation of the transmission and inspect for leaks.

2006 Explorer And Mountaineer

With 5R55S Transmission

See Figure 34.

   1. Before servicing the vehicle, refer to the "Precautions" section.

➡**When the battery has been disconnected and reconnected, some abnormal drive symptoms can occur while the vehicle relearns its adaptive strategy. The customer needs to be notified that they can experience slightly different upshifts either (soft or firm) and that this is a temporary condition and will eventually return to normal operating condition.**

   2. Disconnect the negative battery cable.
   3. Remove the coolant expansion tank bolts and position it aside.
   4. Remove the fan shroud bolts. Do not remove the fan shroud.
   5. Raise and support the vehicle.
   6. If transmission disassembly or installation of new transmission is necessary, drain the transmission fluid. Install the drain plug when finished.
   7. Remove or disconnect the following:
- 2 RH heat shield bolts and position the right heat shield aside
- 2 heated oxygen sensor electrical connectors
- 2 catalyst monitor sensor electrical connectors
- 2 RH heat shield bolts
- RH heat shield bolt and remove the heat shield
- LH heat shield bolt
- Bolts, springs, flag nuts and separate the muffler from the converter
- 4 converter-to-manifold nuts; repeat for both sides

   8. On 2WD models, install a suitable jack stand under the transmission (2WD) or transfer case (4WD), securing with a safety chain.
   9. Remove the RH and LH side crossmember bolts and nuts.
   10. Remove or disconnect the following:
- 2 bolts and position the bracket aside (mounted on the side of the transmission)
- Transmission support insulator nuts; remove the crossmember

   11. Using an assistant, remove the 3-way converter system.
   12. Remove the shift cable and bracket.
   13. On 2WD models, perform the following:

   a. Index-mark the rear driveshaft flange and the rear pinion flange for proper realignment.
   b. Remove and discard the 4 rear driveshaft bolts.
   c. Remove and discard the bolts and universal joint retainers.
   d. Remove the rear driveshaft from the flange, using a pry bar; do not hammer on the flange or driveshaft.
   14. On 4WD models, perform the following:

   a. If necessary, remove the transmission insulator.
   b. Remove the cable shield by prying on the side of the shield closest to the boot, then sliding the shield away from the boot.
   c. Remove the shift cable and bracket.
   d. Index-mark the front differential pinion flange and the front driveshaft.
   e. Remove and discard the front driveshaft bolts and universal joint retainers.
   f. Index-mark the front output shaft assembly and the front driveshaft constant velocity (CV) joint.
   g. Remove and discard the front driveshaft CV joint bolts and washers.

❊❊ CAUTION

Always disconnect the front driveshaft from the transfer case first. Otherwise, the weight of the driveshaft can pinch the boot between the shaft and the boot can and cause the boot to tear. Also, tape the bearing cups to the driveshaft to prevent them from falling off of the spider.

   h. Remove the driveshaft.
   i. Mark the rear driveshaft pinion flange and the rear transfer case flange for correct alignment during assembly.
   j. Remove the 8 rear driveshaft bolts.

   k. Remove the rear driveshaft from the flange using a pry bar.
   15. Remove ground cable from the starter.
   16. Remove the starter and position aside.

➡**Make an identifying mark on the nut, stud and flexplate to allow for correct installation.**

   17. Remove or disconnect the following:
- 4 torque converter nuts
- Lower transmission retaining bolts
- RH catalyst monitor connector and the fuel lines from the bracket
- RH heated oxygen sensor from the transmission
- If equipped, shift motor electrical connector
- LH heated oxygen sensor and the harness clip from the transmission
- LH catalyst monitor connector from the transmission
- Turbine shaft speed (TSS) sensor, Output Shaft Speed (OSS) sensor and Intermediate Shaft Speed (ISS) sensor electrical connectors.

➡**Clean the area around connector to prevent contamination of the solenoid body connector.**

- Solenoid body connector
- Transmission range (TR) sensor electrical connector
- Wiring harness retainers from the side of the transmission

❊❊ WARNING

Do not damage the cooler tubes. Hold the transmission case fittings with a wrench.

- Transmission cooler tubes
- 6 engine-to-transmission retaining bolts
- Position the fuel line bracket aside
   18. Move the transmission back enough to install the converter holding tool.
   19. Install a converter holding tool, 303-346, to lock the converter in place.
   20. Lower the transmission from the vehicle.
   21. On 4WD models, remove the transfer case from the back of the transmission.

To install:

❊❊ CAUTION

Secure the transmission and transfer case (4WD) to the transmission jacks with a safety chain. Failure to follow these instructions can result in personal injury.

→Rotate the torque converter so that the torque converter paint mark is in the 12 o'clock position.

22. On 4WD, if removed, install the transfer case to the back of the transmission, install the bracket and connect the vent hose.

23. If removed, install the torque converter holding tool.

24. Raise and position the transmission to the back of the engine.

25. Remove the converter holding tool.

26. Position the fuel line bracket.

27. Install and torque the following fasteners:

- 6 engine-to-transmission retaining bolts: 35 ft. lbs. (48 Nm)
- 4 torque converter nuts: 30 ft. lbs. (40 Nm)
- Install the starter: 18 ft. lbs. (24 Nm)
- Starter motor ground cable nut: 10 ft. lbs. (13 Nm)
- 2 lower transmission retaining bolts: 35 ft. lbs. (48 Nm)

✲✲ CAUTION

Ensure transmission and (on 4WD) transfer case are properly supported on jacks and attached to the stand with safety chains.

- Transmission fluid cooler tubes: 30 ft. lbs. (40 Nm)

28. Install or connect the following:
- Wiring harness and retainers to side of transmission
- TR sensor electrical connector (restore rubber cover)
- LH heated oxygen sensor to the transmission; install retainer
- New O-ring seals on transmission connector; tighten connector
- LH catalyst monitor connector
- RH heated oxygen sensor to the transmission
- Fuel line and RH catalyst monitor connector to the bracket
- TSS sensor, OSS sensor and intermediate shaft speed sensor electrical connectors
- Shift cable and bracket; tighten to 30 ft. lbs. (40 Nm)
- Cable shield; if loose on the cable, replace the shield
- Transmission support insulator bolts to 66 ft. lbs. (90 Nm)
- 3-way catalytic converter; loosely install 4 converter-to-manifold nuts
- Both heated oxygen sensor connectors

- Both catalyst monitor sensor connectors

29. Position the crossmember and loosely install 2 nuts in the center of the crossmember.

30. Install the 4 RH crossmember bolts and 1 nut. Torque to 52 ft. lbs. (70 Nm).

31. Repeat for the LH crossmember side.

32. Tighten the rear transmission mount nuts to 66 ft. lbs. (90 Nm).

33. Remove the jack from under the transmission and (on 4WD) transfer case.

34. On 2WD models, install or connect the following:
- Cable bracket and 2 bolts to transmission; tighten to 30 ft. lbs. (40 Nm)
- RH and LH heat shield and bolts; tighten to 15 ft. lbs. (20 Nm)
- 4 converter-to-manifold nuts (on both sides); tighten to 30 ft. lbs. (40 Nm)
- Converter-to-pipe (with new gasket); tighten bolts to 30 ft. lbs. (40 Nm)

✲✲ CAUTION

If new bolts to retain the driveshaft to the axle are not available, coat the threads of the original bolts with threadlock and sealer.

✲✲ CAUTION

The driveshaft flange fits tightly on the rear axle pinion flange pilot. To make sure that the driveshaft flange seats squarely on the pinion flange, tighten the bolts evenly in a cross pattern.

- Rear driveshaft to flange, with marks aligned; tighten the bolts to 83 ft. lbs. (112 Nm)

35. On 4WD models, install or connect the following:
- Rear transmission mount nuts; torque to 66 ft. lbs. (90 Nm)
- RH and LH heat shield and bolts; tighten to 15 ft. lbs. (20 Nm)
- 4 converter-to-manifold nuts (on both sides); tighten to 30 ft. lbs. (40 Nm)
- Converter-to-pipe (with new gasket); tighten bolts to 30 ft. lbs. (40 Nm)
- If equipped, shift motor electrical connector

36. On 4WD models, perform the following:

✲✲ CAUTION

The can (domed CV joint housing cover) is pressed into the CV joint housing at the factory. When housed correctly, the can will appear as shown in the cut-away illustration, top box. Do not reseat the can in the CV joint housing if the can's flange is above the CV joint housings shown in the cut-away illustration, bottom box. Install a new driveshaft.

l. Verify that the can flange is housed correctly in the CV joint housing as shown in the cut-away illustration, top box. Install a new driveshaft if the can flange is not housed correctly.

✲✲ CAUTION

Always connect the front driveshaft to the axle first. Otherwise, the weight of the driveshaft can pinch the boot between the shaft and the boot can and cause the boot to tear.

m. Align the index marks made during removal and install the driveshaft.

n. Install new washers and bolts. If new bolts are not available, coat the threads of the original bolts with threadlock and sealer.

o. Install the new washers and bolts. Tighten the bolts evenly in a cross pattern to 22 ft. lbs. (30 Nm).

p. Verify that the CV joint has seated squarely in the transfer case flange as follows:
- Check that the space between the end of the CV joint cap and the end of the transfer case flange is equal from the top to the bottom of the 2 components.
- Rotate the driveshaft 1/4 turn.

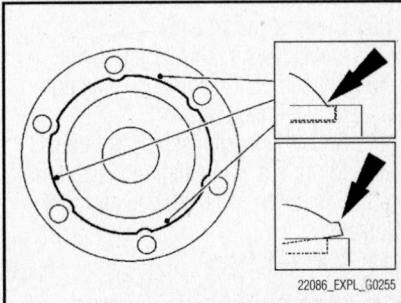

22086_EXPL_G0255

Fig. 34 Verify that the can flange is housed correctly in the CV joint housing as shown in the cut-away illustration, top box; install a new driveshaft if the can flange is not housed correctly

- Check that the space between the end of the CV joint cap and the end of the transfer case flange is equal from the top to the bottom of the 2 components.
- Repeat this procedure several times.
- If the space if not equal at any point in the attachment, remove and reinstall the driveshaft as described in this procedure.

➡**Install new universal joint retainers and bolts. If new bolts are not available, coat the threads of the original bolts with threadlock and sealer.**

q. Install the new universal joint retainer and bolts and tighten to 13 ft. lbs. (18 Nm).

✲✲ CAUTION

The driveshaft flange fits tightly on the rear axle pinion flange pilot. To make sure that the driveshaft flange seats squarely on the pinion flange, tighten the bolts evenly in a cross pattern.

r. With the marks aligned, install the rear driveshaft and bolts to 83 ft. lbs. (112 Nm).

37. Use the following guidelines for installing the in-line transmission fluid filter:

a. If the transmission was overhauled and the vehicle was equipped with an in-line fluid filter, install a new in-line fluid filter.

b. If the transmission was overhauled and the vehicle was not equipped with an in-line fluid filter, install a new in-line fluid filter kit.

c. If the transmission is being installed for a non-internal repair, do not install an in-line filter or filter kit.

d. If installing a new or a Ford-authorized remanufactured transmission, install the in-line transmission fluid filter that is supplied.

38. Connect the negative battery cable.
39. Install the fan shroud and bolts.
40. Reposition the coolant expansion tank and install the bolts.
41. Refill the transmission with fluid.
42. Perform a complete fluid level check.
43. Ensure the shift cable is correctly adjusted.
44. Check for leaks.

With 6R60 Transmission—2WD Models

See Figures 35 through 41.

1. Before servicing the vehicle, refer to the precautions in the beginning of this section.

2. With the vehicle in NEUTRAL, position it on a hoist.
3. Disconnect the negative battery cable.
4. Remove the fluid fill plug fluid level indicator assembly located on the passenger side front portion of the transmission case. Removal of the plug will relieve any vacuum that might have built up in the transmission. This will aid in allowing the fluid pan to be easily removed when the bolts are removed.
5. If transmission disassembly or installation of a new transmission is necessary, remove the transmission fluid pan and allow the fluid to drain.
6. Install the fluid pan and tighten the bolts in a crisscross pattern to 10 ft. lbs. (14 Nm).
7. Mark the driveshaft flange with the output shaft flange for correct alignment during installation.
8. Remove the 4 bolts and position the driveshaft aside.
9. Mark the driveshaft flange with the differential flange for correct alignment during installation.
10. Remove the 4 bolts and the driveshaft.
11. Remove the fuel line bracket bolt from the bracket and position the bracket and lines aside.
12. Disconnect the shift cable end and remove the shift cable bracket bolts and position the cable and bracket aside.
13. Remove or disconnect the following:

- Flexplate inspection cover
- Rubber torque converter nut access plug
- 4 flexplate-to-torque converter nuts (discard nuts)
- Starter motor electrical connectors
- Ground wire from the stud near the starter
- Starter motor

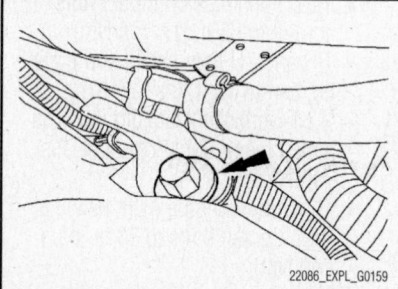

Fig. 35 Remove the fuel line bracket bolt from the bracket and position the bracket and lines aside—2006 6R60 transmission with 2WD

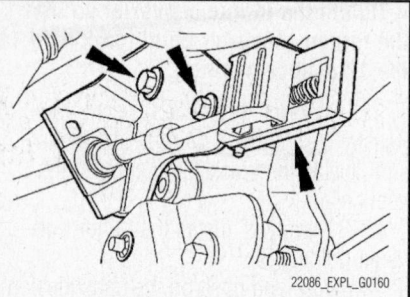
22086_EXPL_G0160

Fig. 36 Disconnect the shift cable end and remove the shift cable bracket bolts and position the cable and bracket aside— 2006 6R60 transmission with 2WD

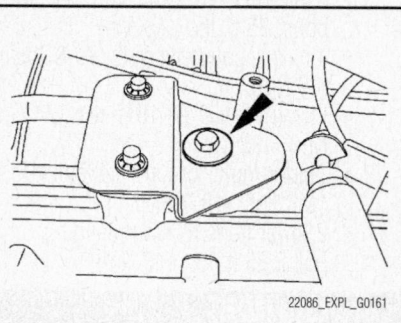
22086_EXPL_G0161

Fig. 37 Remove the transmission fluid cooler tube bracket nut and position the bracket and tubes aside

- Transmission cooler tube bracket bolt
- Engine oil level sensor electrical connector
- Transmission fluid cooler tube bracket nut and position the bracket and tubes aside
- 3 bolts and the RH exhaust heat shield
- LH exhaust heat shield bolt

✲✲ CAUTION

Make sure that the transmission jack makes contact on the outer ribs of the fluid pan, and make sure that the transmission is securely fastened to the transmission jack.

14. Position a suitable high-lift transmission jack under the transmission.
15. Remove or disconnect the following:

- 8 rear crossmember bolts (4 at each end)
- 2 center rear crossmember nuts and the crossmember
- 2 bolts and the transmission insulator
- RH and LH heated oxygen sensors (HO2S) and the catalyst monitor sensor (CMS) electrical connectors

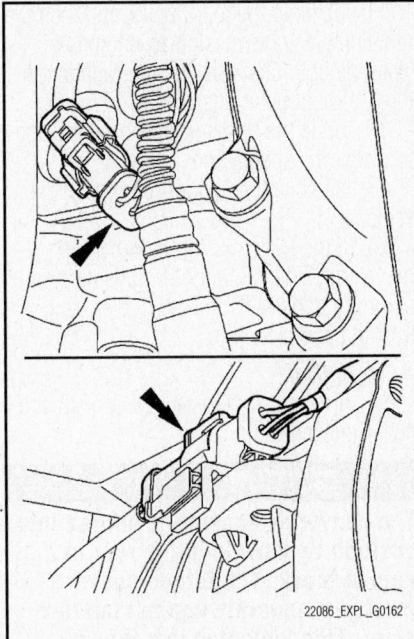

Fig. 38 Remove the RH and LH heated oxygen sensors (HO2S) and the catalyst monitor sensor (CMS) electrical connectors

- RH and LH exhaust flange nuts
- 2 bolts and the dual converter Y-pipe
- CMS electrical connector from the LH side of the transmission
- Wire harness from the top of the transmission
- Main transmission electrical harness by twisting the outer shell and pulling back on the connector

16. Remove the 7 transmission-to-engine bolts.

17. Slide the transmission back far enough to install the converter locking tool.

18. Install the converter locking tool.

19. Remove the transmission from the vehicle.

20. Remove the 4 bolts and the transmission mount bracket.

21. If the transmission is to be overhauled or if installing a new transmission, carry out transmission fluid cooler backflushing and cleaning.

To install:

22. Install the converter locking tool, if it has been removed.

23. Install the transmission insulator bracket to 35 ft. lbs. (48 Nm).

➡ **The converter housing is piloted into position by dowels in the rear of the engine block. The torque converter must rest squarely against the flexplate. This indicates that the converter pilot is not binding in the engine crankshaft.**

24. Position and secure the transmission on the high-lift transmission jack. Raise and position the transmission into the vehicle.

25. Remove the converter locking tool.

✴✴ CAUTION

Make sure the torque converter is fully seated in the transmission before aligning the transmission to the engine.

26. With the transmission in a horizontal position, move it toward the engine. Align the orange balancing marks between the torque converter studs and the flexplate bolt holes.

27. Install the transmission bolts in their correct locations noted during removal.

28. Install the 7 transmission-to-engine bolts around the top of the housing, noting that the top 2 bolts need to be installed prior to installing the rest of the bolts. Torque the bolts to 35 ft. lbs. (48 Nm).

29. Install or connect the following:
- Main transmission electrical harness by pushing it in and twisting the outer shell to lock it in place

- Wire harness to the top of the transmission
- Catalyst monitor sensor (CMS) electrical connector to the LH side of the transmission
- Dual converter Y-pipe; torque the bolts to 30 ft. lbs. (40 Nm)
- LH and RH exhaust flange nuts; torque the nuts to 30 ft. lbs. (40 Nm)
- RH and LH heated oxygen sensors (HO2S) and the CMS electrical connectors
- Transmission insulator; torque the 2 bolts to 59 ft. lbs. (80 Nm)
- Rear crossmember in place and loosely install the transmission insulator nuts in the center
- 8 crossmember bolts; tighten bolts "1" to 59 ft. lbs. (80 Nm) and bolts "2" to 66 ft. lbs. (90 Nm), as shown
- Center crossmember transmission insulator nuts to 66 ft. lbs. (90 Nm)
- LH exhaust heat shield bolt and 2 RH exhaust heat shield bolts; torque to 11 ft. lbs. (15 Nm)
- Transmission cooler tubes in place and install the bracket nut; torque to 20 ft. lbs. (27 Nm)
- Oil level sensor electrical connector
- Transmission cooler tube bracket bolt; torque to 17 ft. lbs. (23 Nm)
- Starter motor; torque to 19 ft. lbs. (26 Nm)
- Ground wire on the stud near the starter; torque to 17 ft. lbs. (23 Nm)
- Starter motor electrical connectors
- Plastic starter motor electrical connector cap
- 4 new flexplate-to-torque converter nuts; torque to 26 ft. lbs. (35 Nm)
- Rubber access plug
- Flexplate inspection cover; torque to 26 ft. lbs. (35 Nm)

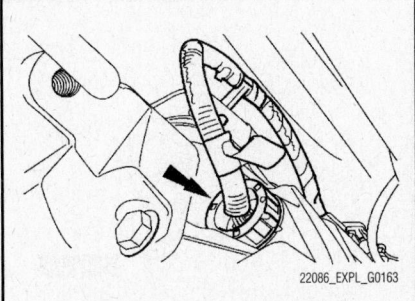

Fig. 39 Remove the main transmission electrical harness by twisting the outer shell and pulling back on the connector

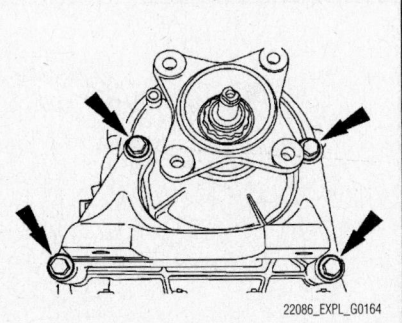

Fig. 40 Install the transmission insulator bracket to 35 ft. lbs. (48 Nm)

Fig. 41 Install the 8 crossmember bolts; tighten bolts "1" to 59 ft. lbs. (80 Nm) and bolts "2" to 66 ft. lbs. (90 Nm)

- Selector lever cable in place, install the bolts and connect the selector lever cable end; torque to 35 ft. lbs. (48 Nm)
- Fuel line in place and install the bolt; torque to 18 ft. lbs. (25 Nm)

➡**To maintain initial driveshaft balance, align the index marks made during removal.**

30. Install the rear driveshaft. Torque the bolts to 60 ft. lbs. (81 Nm).
31. Connect the battery ground cable.
32. Verify that the shift cable is correctly adjusted.
33. Re-flash the transmission control module (TCM) to the latest level of software.
34. Using the refill procedure, fill the transmission with clean automatic transmission fluid.

With 6R60 Transmission—4WD Models

See Figures 42 through 44.

1. Before servicing the vehicle, refer to the precautions in the beginning of this section.
2. With the vehicle in NEUTRAL, position it on a hoist.
3. Disconnect the negative battery cable.
4. Remove the fluid fill plug fluid level indicator assembly located on the passenger side front portion of the transmission case. Removal of the plug will relieve any vacuum that might have built up in the transmission. This will aid in allowing the fluid pan to be easily removed when the bolts are removed.
5. If transmission disassembly or installation of a new transmission is necessary, remove the transmission fluid pan and allow the fluid to drain.
6. Install the fluid pan and tighten the bolts in a crisscross pattern to 10 ft. lbs. (14 Nm).
7. remove the transfer case. See "Transfer Case" section.
8. Position a suitable transmission jack to the transmission. Securely strap the transmission to the jack.
9. Remove or disconnect the following:

- LH and RH exhaust heat shield bolts
- 4 RH and 4 LH side crossmember bolts and the nut
- RH and LH heated oxygen sensors (HO2S) and the catalyst monitor sensor (CMS) electrical connectors
- RH and LH exhaust flange nuts
- Dual converter Y-pipe

- Fuel line bracket bolt; position the bracket and lines aside
- Shift cable end and remove the shift cable bracket bolts; position the cable and bracket aside
- Flexplate inspection cover
- Plastic starter motor electrical connector cap
- Starter motor electrical connectors
- Ground wire from stud near starter
- Starter motor
- Transmission cooler tube bracket bolt
- Oil level sensor electrical connector
- Transmission fluid cooler tube bracket nut and position the bracket and lines aside
- CMS electrical connector from the LH side of the transmission
- Wiring harness from the top of the transmission

10. Disconnect the main transmission electrical harness by twisting the outer shell and pulling back on the connector.

> ✳✳ **CAUTION**
>
> **Do not pull on the wire harness to disconnect the connector or damage to the connector will occur.**

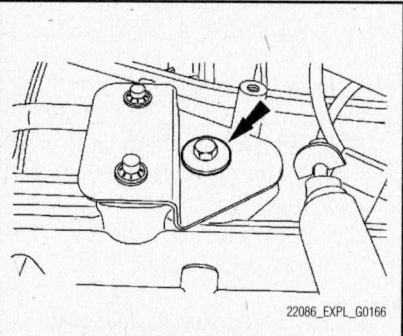

22086_EXPL_G0166

Fig. 42 Showing the location of the transmission cooler tube bracket bolt

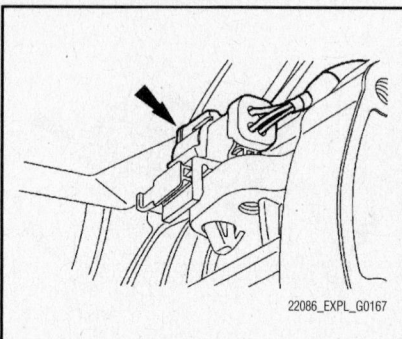

22086_EXPL_G0167

Fig. 43 Showing the location of the CMS electrical connector

11. Remove the top 2 bolts, and then the remaining 5 transmission-to-engine bolts. Note the bolt locations for reinstallation in their original positions.
12. Slide the transmission back enough to install the special tool.
13. Remove the transmission from the vehicle.
14. If the transmission is to be overhauled or if installing a new transmission, carry out transmission fluid cooler backflushing and cleaning.

To install:

15. If removed, reinstall the special converter locking tool.

> ✳✳ **CAUTION**
>
> **The converter housing is piloted into position by dowels in the rear of the engine block. The torque converter must rest squarely against the flexplate. This indicates that the converter pilot is not binding in the engine crankshaft.**

16. Position and secure the transmission on the high-lift transmission jack. Raise and position the transmission into the vehicle.
17. Remove the converter locking tool.

> ✳✳ **CAUTION**
>
> **Make sure the torque converter is fully seated in the transmission before aligning the transmission to the engine.**

18. With the transmission in a horizontal position move it toward the engine. Align the orange balancing marks between the torque converter studs and the flexplate bolt holes.
19. Install the transmission bolts in their correct locations noted during removal. The top 2 bolts need to be

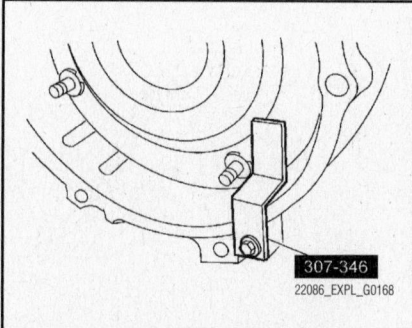

307-346
22086_EXPL_G0168

Fig. 44 Slide the transmission back enough to install the special converter locking tool

installed prior to installing the rest of the bolts.

20. Torque the 7 transmission-to-engine bolts to 35 ft. lbs. (48 Nm).

21. Install or connect the following:

- Main transmission electrical harness by pushing it in and twisting the outer shell to lock it in place
- Catalyst monitor sensor (CMS) electrical connector to the LH side of the transmission
- Transmission cooler tubes in place and install the cooler tube bracket nut to 20 ft. lbs. (27 Nm)
- Engine oil level sensor electrical connector
- Transmission cooler tube bracket bolt to 17 ft. lbs. (23 Nm)
- Starter motor and the 3 bolts to 18 ft. lbs. (23 Nm)
- Ground wire on the stud; tighten the nut to 15 ft. lbs. (20 Nm)
- Starter motor electrical connectors; replace plastic cap
- 4 new torque converter nuts to 26 ft. lbs. (35 Nm)
- Flexplate inspection cover and bolts to 26 ft. lbs. (35 Nm)
- Selector lever bracket and connect the selector lever cable end; tighten retaining bolt to 18 ft. lbs. (25 Nm)
- Fuel line bracket bolt to 18 ft. lbs. (25 Nm)
- Dual converter Y-pipe in place and install the bolts to 30 ft. lbs. (40 Nm)
- LH and RH exhaust flange new nuts to 30 ft. lbs. (40 Nm)
- RH and LH heated oxygen sensors (HO2S) and the CMS electrical connectors
- 4 RH and LH side crossmember bolts and the nut; torque the vertical bolts to 59 ft. lbs. and the horizontal bolts to 66 ft. lbs. (90 Nm)
- RH and LH exhaust heat shields

22. Install the transfer case. See "Transfer Case" section.

23. Connect the battery ground cable.

24. Verify that the shift cable is correctly adjusted.

25. Re-flash the transmission control module (TCM) to the latest level of software.

26. Using the refill procedure, fill the transmission with clean automatic transmission fluid.

TRANSFER CASE ASSEMBLY

REMOVAL & INSTALLATION

See Figures 45 and 46.

1. Before servicing the vehicle, refer to the "Precautions" section.

2. Place the transmission in **Neutral**.

3. Remove or disconnect the following:

- Negative battery cable
- Skid plate, if equipped

➡ **Drain the transfer case if disassembly is necessary.**

➡ **Match-mark the front and rear driveshaft yokes and pinion flange and the rear driveshaft yoke and rear output flange.**

- Rear driveshaft
- Front driveshaft
- Vent tube
- Shift motor electrical connector

4. Using a suitable high lift jack, support the transfer case.

5. Remove or disconnect the following:

- Right crossmember cover, then the four bolts
- The four left crossmember bolts
- Heat shields from the crossmember
- Transmission mount nuts
- The seven bolts and separate the transfer case from the extension housing

6. Lower the transfer case from the vehicle.

7. Remove and discard the transfer case-to-extension housing gasket. Clean the gasket surfaces.

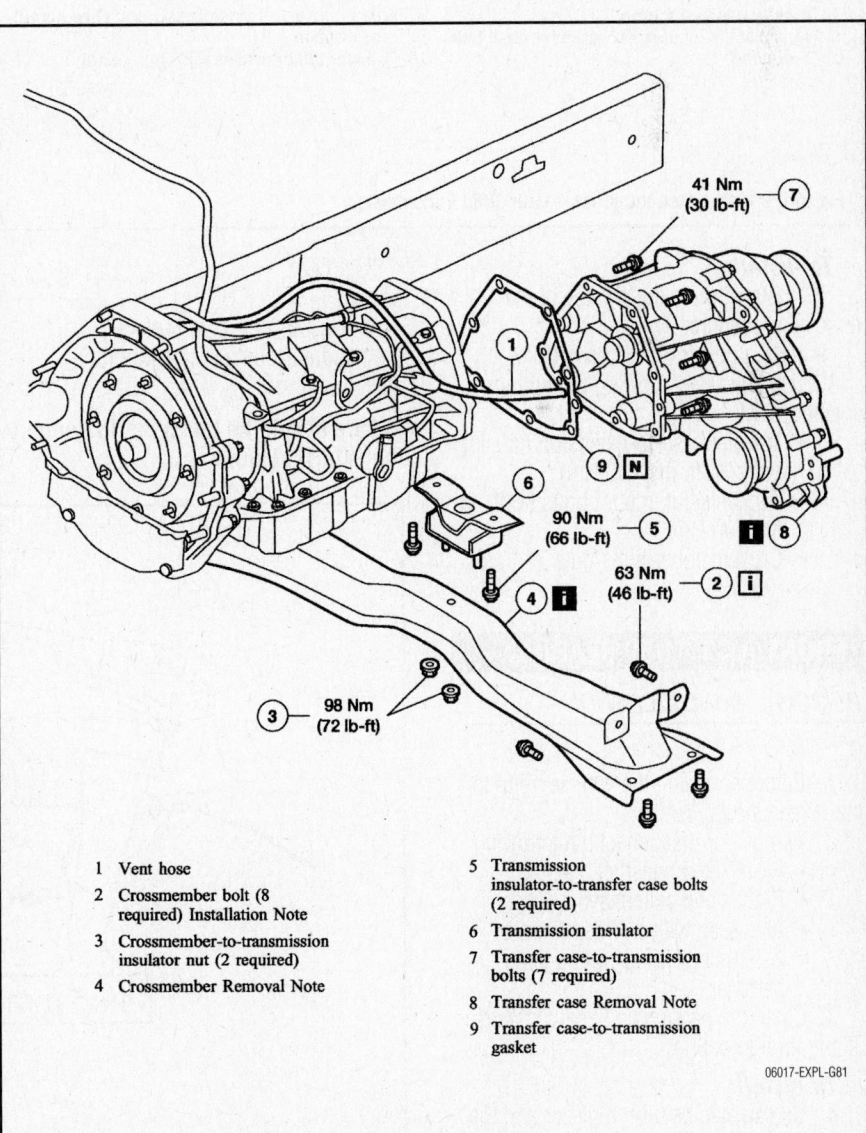

1 Vent hose
2 Crossmember bolt (8 required) Installation Note
3 Crossmember-to-transmission insulator nut (2 required)
4 Crossmember Removal Note
5 Transmission insulator-to-transfer case bolts (2 required)
6 Transmission insulator
7 Transfer case-to-transmission bolts (7 required)
8 Transfer case Removal Note
9 Transfer case-to-transmission gasket

06017-EXPL-G81

Fig. 45 Transfer case mounting—with 5R55 transmission

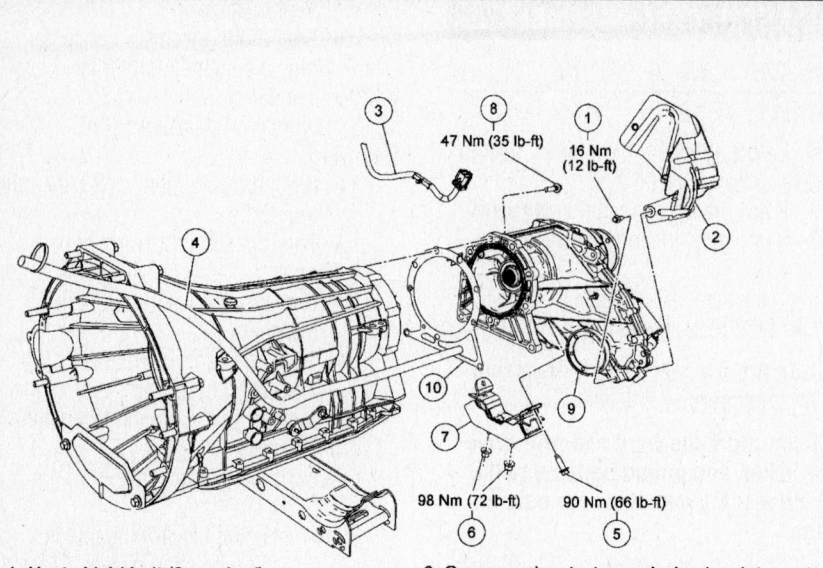

47 Nm (35 lb-ft)
16 Nm (12 lb-ft)
98 Nm (72 lb-ft)
90 Nm (66 lb-ft)

1. Heat shield bolt (3 required)
2. Heat shield
3. Transfer case wire harness
4. Transfer case vent tube
5. Transmission insulator-to-transfer case bolts (2 required)
6. Crossmember-to-transmission insulator nuts (2 required)
7. Transmission insulator
8. Transfer case-to-transmission bolt (7 required)
9. Transfer case
10. Transfer case-to-transmission gasket

22086_EXPL_G0169

Fig. 46 Transfer case mounting—with 6R60 transmission

To install:

8. Installation is the reverse of the removal procedure.

9. Use a new transfer case gasket.

10. Observe the following tightening specifications:

- Transfer case-to-extension housing bolts 30 ft. lbs. (40 Nm).
- Transmission mount bolts 66 ft. lbs. (90 Nm)
- Crossmember bolts/nuts 72 ft. lbs. (98 Nm).

FRONT AXLE TUBE BEARING

REMOVAL & INSTALLATION

See Figure 47.

1. Before servicing the vehicle, refer to the "Precautions" section.

2. Remove or disconnect the following:

- Right-hand halfshaft
- Right-hand axle shaft
- Axle seal, with a slide hammer
- Axle tube bearing, with a slide hammer

3. Clean the bearing and seal surfaces of any foreign debris.

To install:

4. Use an axle bearing replacer and the handle to replace the right axle tube bearing.

5. Check the bearing depth as shown.

6. Use an axle seal replacer and the handle to replace the axle tube seal.

➡Care should be taken not to damage the axle seal surface.

7. Install the axle shaft.

8. Refill the front drive axle to proper level.

9. Install the right halfshaft.

FRONT DRIVESHAFT

REMOVAL & INSTALLATION

See Figures 48 and 50.

1. Before servicing the vehicle, refer to the "Precautions" section.

✳✳ WARNING

Always disconnect the front drive-shaft from the transfer case first. Otherwise, the weight of the driveshaft can pinch the boot between the drive-shaft and the constant velocity (CV) joint flange which can cause the boot to tear.

2. With the vehicle in NEUTRAL, position it on a hoist.

3. Index-mark the front driveshaft to maintain balance.

4. Remove and discard the 6 CV joint bolts and CV joint washers.

5. Remove the 4 universal joint strap bolts and remove the universal joint straps.

6. Remove the front driveshaft.

To install:

7. Install the front driveshaft as follows:

   a. Align the index marks and position the front driveshaft.

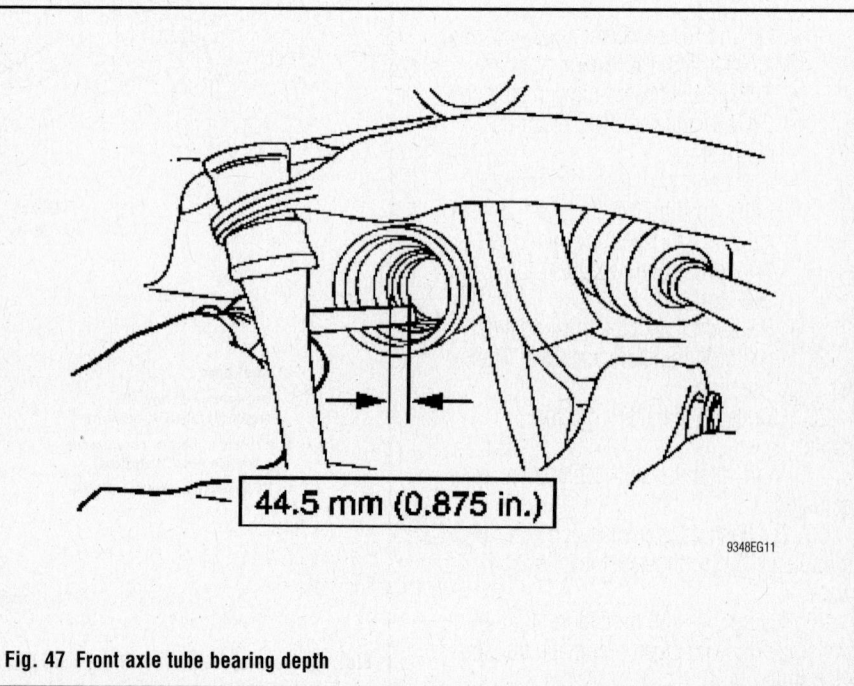

44.5 mm (0.875 in.)

9348EG11

Fig. 47 Front axle tube bearing depth

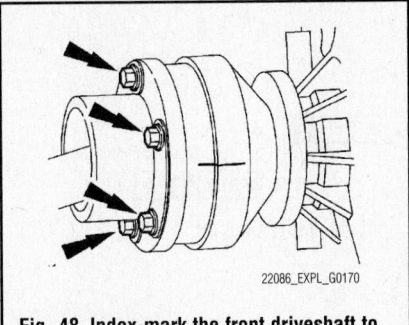

Fig. 48 Index-mark the front driveshaft to maintain balance

22086_EXPL_G0170

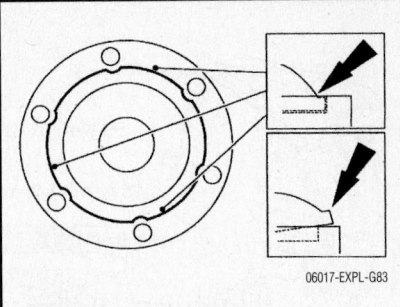

Fig. 50 CV-joint installation—front driveshaft

06017-EXPL-G83

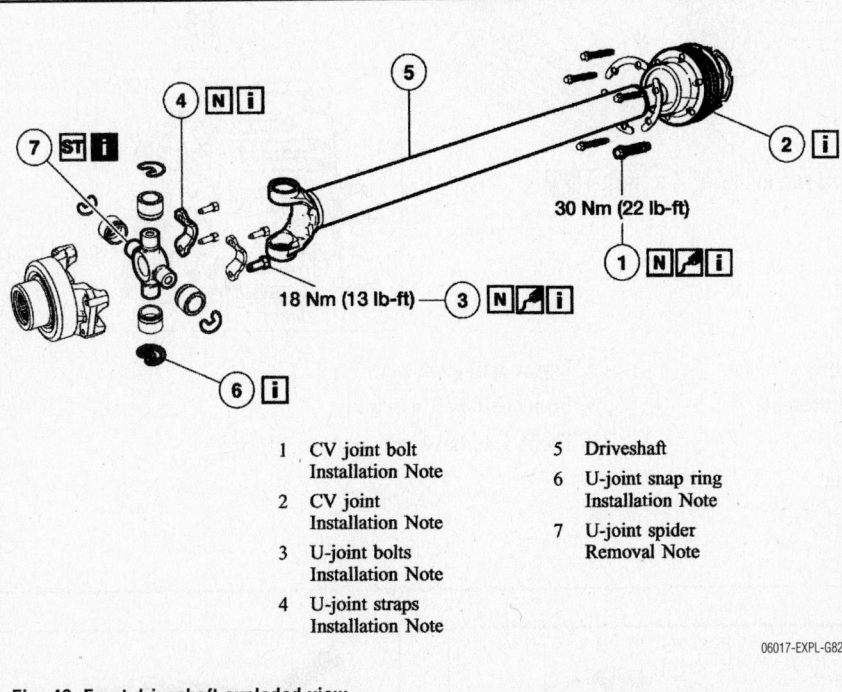

30 Nm (22 lb-ft)

18 Nm (13 lb-ft)

1	CV joint bolt Installation Note	5	Driveshaft
2	CV joint Installation Note	6	U-joint snap ring Installation Note
3	U-joint bolts Installation Note	7	U-joint spider Removal Note
4	U-joint straps Installation Note		

06017-EXPL-G82

Fig. 49 Front driveshaft exploded view

⁂ CAUTION

Always connect the front driveshaft to the axle first. Otherwise, the weight of the driveshaft can pinch the boot between the shaft and the flange and cause the boot to tear.

⁂ CAUTION

Install the driveshaft with new bolts and washers and new bolts and universal joint retainers. If new bolts are not available, coat the threads of the original bolts with threadlock and sealer.

    b. Install 4 new U-joint strap bolts and torque to 14 ft. lbs. (19 Nm).
    c. Install 6 new CV joint bolts and washers. Torque the bolts to 22 ft. lbs. (30 Nm).

FRONT HALFSHAFT

REMOVAL & INSTALLATION

See Figure 51.

    1. Before servicing the vehicle, refer to the "Precautions" section.
    2. Remove or disconnect the following:
    3. Loosen the front axle wheel hub retainer.

- Wheel and tire assembly
- Hub retainer and the washer. Discard the front axle wheel hub retainer.
- The two bolts and position the disc brake caliper aside
- Tie rod end from the knuckle. Discard the nut.
- Stabilizer bar link. Discard the nut.

⁂ WARNING

Do not allow the knuckle to hang freely. It is possible to overextend

and internally separate each inner CV-joint from its housing.

- Upper ball joint from the knuckle

⁂ WARNING

Do not use a hammer to separate the outboard CV-joint from the hub. Damage to the threads and internal CV-joint components may result.

    4. Press the outboard CV-joint until it is loose in the hub.
    5. Remove the outboard CV-joint from the hub.

⁂ WARNING

Do not damage the axle shaft oil seal or the machined sealing surface on the inboard CV-joint housing.

➡A circlip retains the inboard CV-joint housing to the differential side gear in the axle.

    6. On the left side, pry the left inboard CV-joint housing from the differential side gear.
    7. On the right side, disengage the right inboard CV-joint housing from the axle tube.
    8. Pull the halfshaft and the axle shaft away from the axle tube, and separate the inboard CV-joint housing from the axle shaft.
    9. Remove the halfshaft assembly from the vehicle.

⁂ WARNING

Do not damage the axle shaft oil seal, the machined sealing surface on the inboard CV-joint housing, or the axle shaft splines.

To install:
    10. Installation is the reverse of the removal procedure.
    11. Always install the halfshaft with a new retainer circlip and a new front axle wheel hub retainer.
    12. On the right side, check the retainer circlip engagement after reseating the axle shaft and after installing the halfshaft in the axle. On the left side, check the retainer circlip engagement after installing the halfshaft in the axle. When seated, the retainer circlip will lock the axle shaft and the inboard CV-joint housing to the axle.

⁂ WARNING

Never use power tools to tighten the front axle wheel hub retainer. Torque the retainer to 184 ft. lbs. (250 Nm).

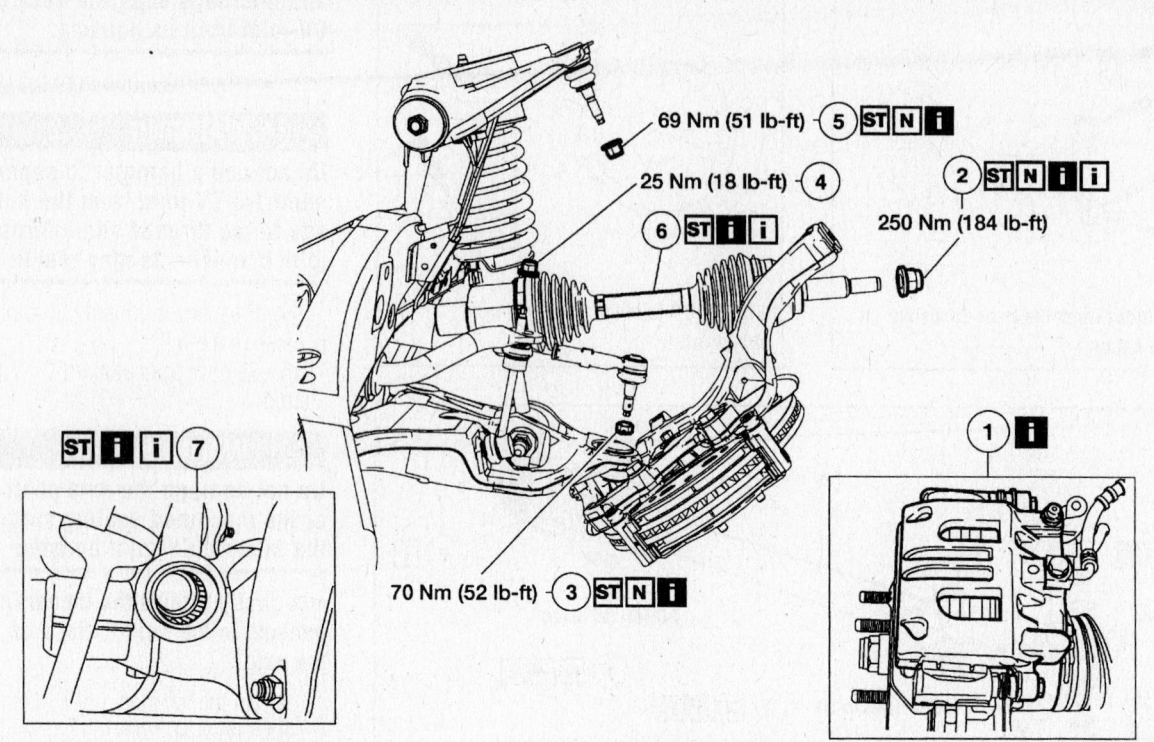

69 Nm (51 lb-ft) 5 ST N i

25 Nm (18 lb-ft) 4

6 ST i i

2 ST N i i

250 Nm (184 lb-ft)

ST i i 7

70 Nm (52 lb-ft) 3 ST N i

1 i

1 Front disc brake caliper
2 Front axle wheel hub retainer
3 Tie-rod end nut
4 Stabilizer bar link nut
5 Upper ball joint nut
6 Front halfshaft assembly
7 Front axle halfshaft seal and bearing

67197EXPLG59

Fig. 51 Front axle halfshaft

➡️It may be necessary to support the front suspension lower arm to be able to connect the upper ball joint to the knuckle.

CV-JOINTS OVERHAUL

See Figures 52 through 58.

1. Before servicing the vehicle, refer to the "Precautions" section.
2. Remove the halfshaft assembly.
3. Remove and discard the boot clamps.
4. Remove the inboard CV-joint housing.
5. Remove and discard the retainer circlip. Slide the boot away from the inboard CV-joint.
6. Using a suitable 3-jaw puller, remove the CV-joint.
7. Remove and discard the inner CV boot.

➡️The outboard CV-joint is not removable from the halfshaft. The boot must be removed or installed from the inboard CV-joint side of the shaft.

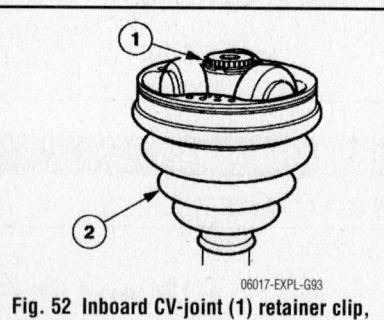

06017-EXPL-G93

Fig. 52 Inboard CV-joint (1) retainer clip, (2) boot

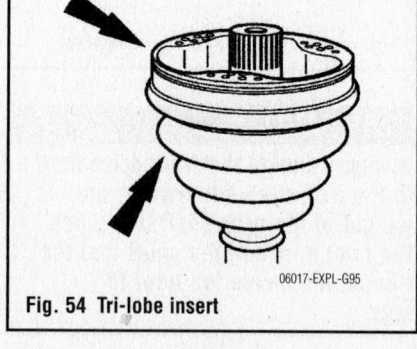

06017-EXPL-G95

Fig. 54 Tri-lobe insert

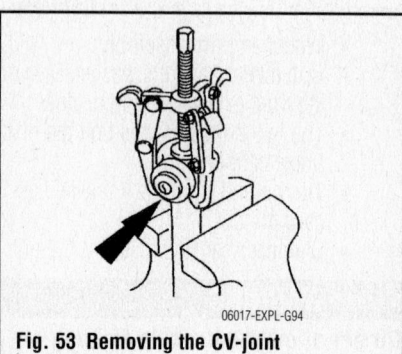

06017-EXPL-G94

Fig. 53 Removing the CV-joint

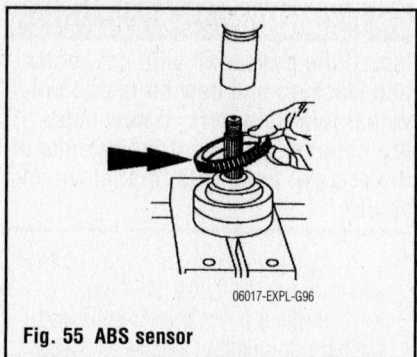

06017-EXPL-G96

Fig. 55 ABS sensor

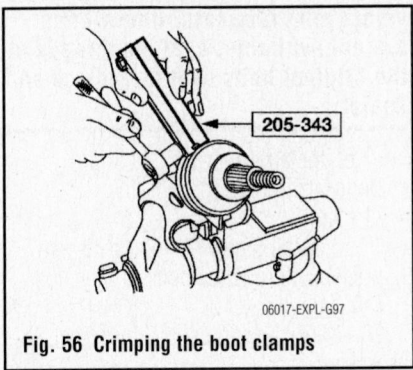

Fig. 56 Crimping the boot clamps

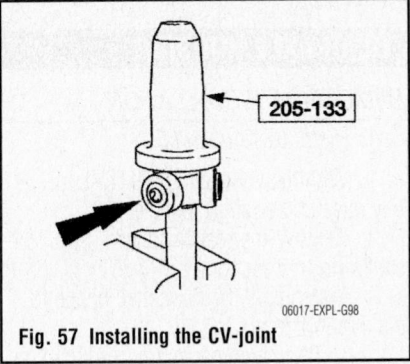

Fig. 57 Installing the CV-joint

8. Remove and discard the outboard CV-joint boot clamps.

9. Remove and discard the boot.

10. If necessary, press the anti-lock brake sensor indicator ring from the outer CV-joint.

To assemble:

11. If removed, install a new anti-lock brake sensor indicator ring on the outer CV-joint.

12. Lubricate the outboard CV-joint. Pack the outboard CV-joint with 185 grams (6.53 oz) of grease. One-third of the grease must be installed in the joint with the remainder placed in the boot. Spread the remaining grease evenly inside the boot.

13. Position the outboard halfshaft boot. Position the boot clamps.

14. Install the outboard CV boot clamps.

15. Position the inboard clamp and boot.

16. Install the CV-joint and snap ring on the halfshaft.

17. Install the stop ring.

18. Fill the inboard CV-joint housing with 210 grams (7.41 oz) of grease. One-

half of the grease must be installed in the joint and the remainder placed in the boot.

19. Position the inboard halfshaft boot in the housing groove. Position the boot clamp.

20. Set the halfshaft assembled length to:
- Aviator, Explorer, Mountaineer: 24.22 inches (615.3mm) for the right side; 26.98 inches (685.3mm) for the left.
- Explorer Sport-Trac: 24.72 inches (618mm) for the left side; 21.92 inches (548mm) for the right side

21. Measure the entire assembly length. Push in or pull out on the inner joint as necessary to adjust the halfshaft assembled length. Hold the inner joint to prevent the assembled length from changing, and insert a small flat-blade screwdriver between the boot and the joint to equalize the pressure.

22. Install the boot clamps.

FRONT PINION SEAL

REMOVAL & INSTALLATION

See Figures 59 through 61.

➡ **This operation disturbs the differential pinion bearing preload. Carefully reset the preload during assembly.**

1. Before servicing the vehicle, refer to the "Precautions" section.

2. With the vehicle in NEUTRAL, position it on a hoist.

➡ **The front wheels and tires and brake calipers must be removed to prevent drag during the pinion bearing preload recording and adjustment.**

3. Remove the front tires and wheels.

4. Remove the front driveshaft as follows:

   a. Index-mark the front driveshaft to maintain balance.

   b. Remove and discard the 6 CV joint bolts and CV joint washers.

   c. Remove the 4 universal joint strap bolts and remove the universal joint straps.

   d. Remove the front driveshaft.

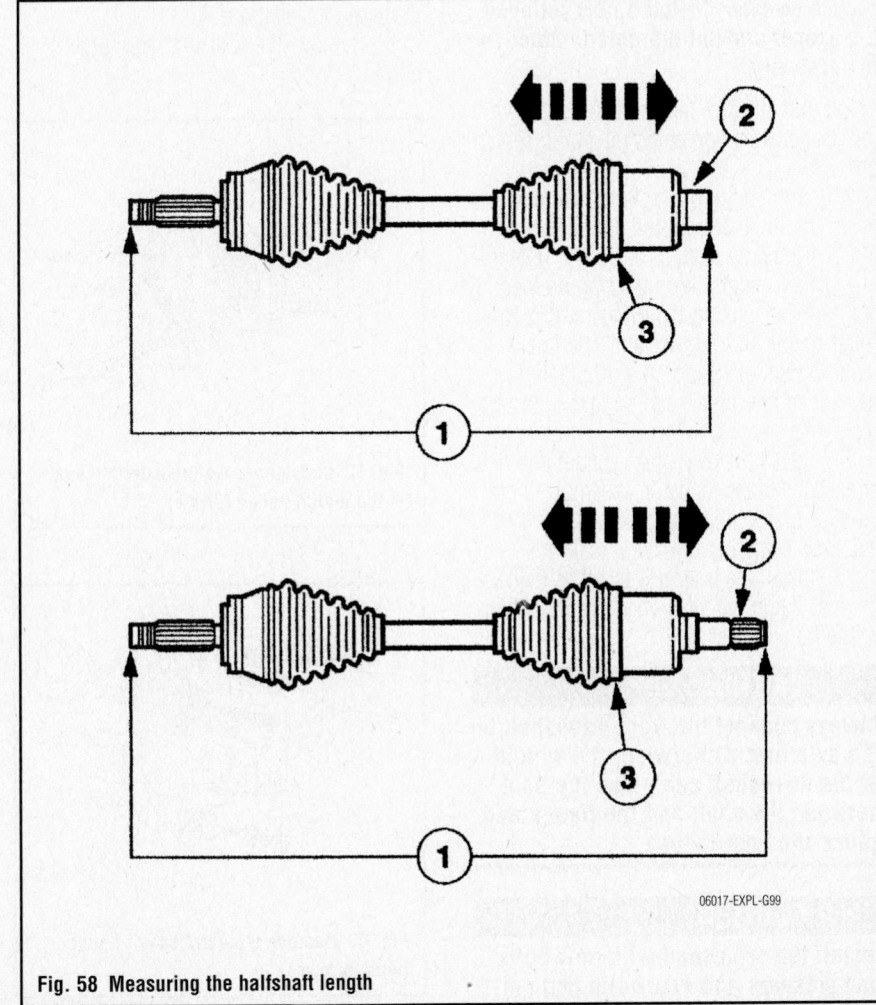

Fig. 58 Measuring the halfshaft length

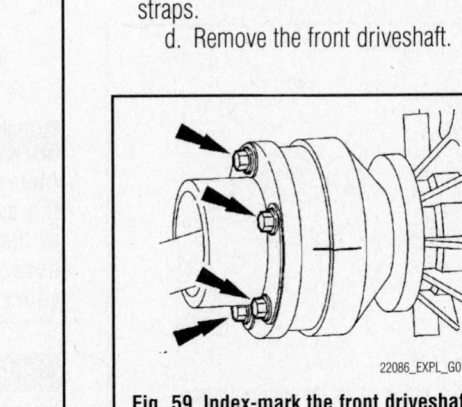

Fig. 59 Index-mark the front driveshaft to maintain balance

5. Remove the disc brake caliper anchor bolts, then remove the disc brake caliper and disc brake caliper anchor as an assembly. Suspend on mechanic's wire.

6. Measure and record the pinion bearing preload. Using a torque wrench, rotate the pinion gear. Measure the torque required to maintain pinion gear rotation.

7. Index-mark the pinion flange and the pinion stem.

8. Hold the pinion flange while removing the nut.

9. Place a drain pan under the differential housing.

10. Using a puller, remove the pinion flange.

11. Inspect the pinion flange for burrs and damage. Inspect the end of the pinion flange that contacts the bearing cone, the nut counterbore, and the seal surface for nicks. Discard the pinion flange as necessary.

12. Using a seal remover and impact slide hammer, remove the pinion seal.

13. Remove the front axle drive pinion shaft oil slinger and the outer pinion bearing.

14. Remove and discard the collapsible spacer.

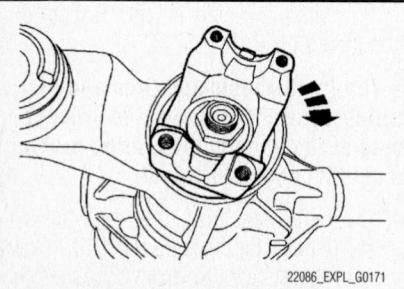

Fig. 60 Measure and record the pinion bearing preload: using a torque wrench, rotate the pinion gear. Measure the torque required to maintain pinion gear rotation

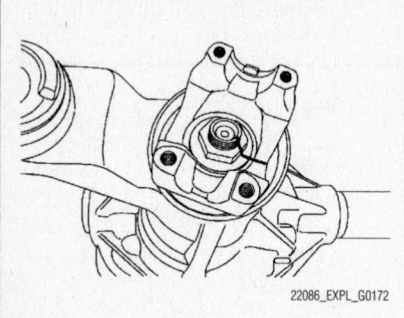

Fig. 61 Index-mark the pinion flange and the pinion stem

To install:

15. Verify that the splines on the pinion stem are free of burrs. If burrs are evident, remove them with a fine crocus cloth. Work in a rotating motion to wipe the pinion clean.

16. Clean the pinion seal bore.

17. Install a new collapsible spacer.

18. Install the pinion bearing and the front axle drive pinion shaft oil slinger.

19. Lubricate the pinion seal with axle lubricant.

20. Install the pinion seal, using a proper seal installer to ensure the seal is fully and evenly seated.

21. Lubricate the pinion flange splines with axle lubricant.

➡**Never use a metal hammer on the pinion flange or install the flange with power tools. If necessary, use a plastic hammer to tap on a tight fitting flange.**

- Align the index marks and install the pinion flange.
- Install the new nut hand-tight.

➡**Do not loosen the pinion nut to reduce preload. Install a new collapsible spacer and nut if preload reduction is necessary.**

22. Use the special tool to hold the pinion flange while tightening the nut to set the preload.

23. Tighten the nut, rotating the pinion occasionally to ensure the differential pinion bearings are seating correctly. Take frequent differential pinion bearing preload readings by rotating the pinion with a Nm (inch-pound) torque wrench. The final reading must be 5 inch lbs. (0.56 Nm) more than the initial reading taken during removal.

24. Install the disc brake caliper and disc brake caliper anchor as an assembly, then the disc brake caliper anchor bolts to 80 ft. lbs. (108 Nm).

25. Install the front driveshaft as follows:
   a. Align the index marks and position the front driveshaft.

✳✳ CAUTION

Always connect the front driveshaft to the axle first. Otherwise, the weight of the driveshaft can pinch the boot between the shaft and the flange and cause the boot to tear.

✳✳ CAUTION

Install the driveshaft with new bolts and washers and new bolts and universal joint retainers. If new bolts are not available, coat the threads of the original bolts with threadlock and sealer.

   b. Install 4 new U-joint strap bolts and torque to 14 ft. lbs. (19 Nm).
   c. Install 6 new CV joint bolts and washers. Torque the bolts to 22 ft. lbs. (30 Nm).

26. Check and adjust the fluid level, if necessary.

27. Lower the vehicle.

REAR AXLE HOUSING

REMOVAL & INSTALLATION

See Figures 62 through 65

1. With the vehicle in NEUTRAL, properly raise and support vehicle.

2. Remove the rear halfshafts. See "Halfshafts" in this section.

3. Matchmark the driveshaft flange to the pinion flange.
   a. The matchmarks are used to align the driveshaft flange to the pinion flange during installation

4. Remove the 4 driveshaft flange bolts.

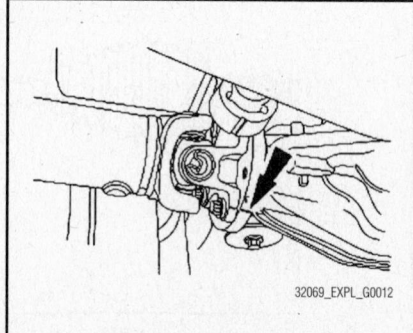

Fig. 62 Matchmark the driveshaft flange to the pinion flange (arrow)

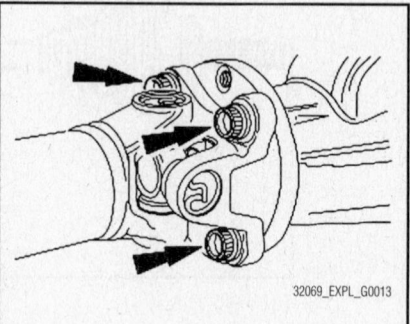

Fig. 63 Remove the 4 driveshaft flange bolts (arrows)

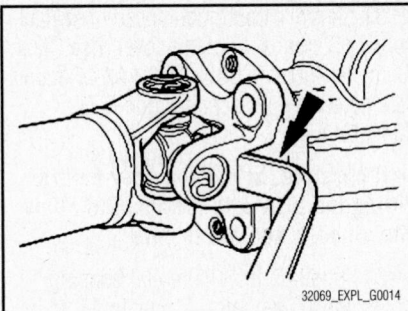

Fig. 64 Pry driveshaft from flange and support shaft with a piece of wire

☆☆ WARNING

The driveshaft flange fits tightly on the pinion flange pilot. Never hammer on the driveshaft or any of its components to disconnect the driveshaft flange from the pinion flange. Pry only in the area shown, with a suitable tool, to disconnect the driveshaft flange from the pinion flange.

5. Using a suitable tool as shown, disconnect the driveshaft flange from the pinion flange, then using mechanic's wire, position aside the driveshaft.

6. Position a suitable transmission jack to the axle housing.

   a. Securely strap the jack to the axle.

7. Remove the axle assembly front lower insulator bolt.

8. Remove the axle assembly rear insulator bolts.

9. Lower the axle assembly from the vehicle.

To install

Install in reverse order of the removal procedure.

☆☆ WARNING

The driveshaft centering socket yoke fits tightly on the pinion flange pilot. To make sure that the yoke seats squarely on the pinion flange, tighten the driveshaft flange bolts evenly in a cross-pattern.

➡If new driveshaft flange bolts are not available, coat the threads of the original driveshaft flange bolts with threadlock and sealer.

➡Align the index marks when installing the driveshaft.

Tightening torques:
  • Axle assembly rear insulator bolts 111 ft. lbs. (150 Nm).
  • Ale assembly front lower insulator bolt 76 ft lbs. (103 Nm).
  • 4 driveshaft flange bolts 83 ft. lbs. (112 Nm).

REAR AXLE SHAFT, BEARING & SEAL

REMOVAL & INSTALLATION

Ford 8.8 inch Ring Gear Solid Axle

See Figures 66 through 68.

1. Before servicing the vehicle, refer to the "Precautions" section.

2. Raise and support the vehicle.

3. Remove the wheel and tire assembly.

4. Loosen the bolts and drain the lubricant from the rear axle housing.

5. Remove the cover bolts.

6. Remove the differential housing cover.

7. Remove the rear brake disc or brake drum and shoes.

☆☆ WARNING

Turning the differential case or an axle shaft with the differential pinion shaft removed will cause the differential pinion gears to fall out of the assembly and damage the components.

8. Remove the differential pinion shaft lock bolt.

9. Remove the differential pinion shaft.

☆☆ WARNING

Do not damage the rubber O-ring in the U-washer groove.

10. Push the axle shaft inboard.

11. Remove the U-washer.

12. Install the differential pinion shaft.

13. Install the differential pinion shaft lock bolt finger-tight.

☆☆ WARNING

Do not damage the wheel bearing oil seal.

14. Remove the axle shaft.

➡If the wheel bearing oil seal is leaking, the axle housing vent may be plugged with foreign material.

➡If only a new seal needs to be installed, use care to avoid damaging the seal bore.

15. Using a suitable seal remover, remove the axle shaft oil seal. Discard the oil seal.

16. Inspect the rear wheel bearing and axle shaft for wear or damage.

17. If necessary, using the special tools, remove the rear wheel bearing.

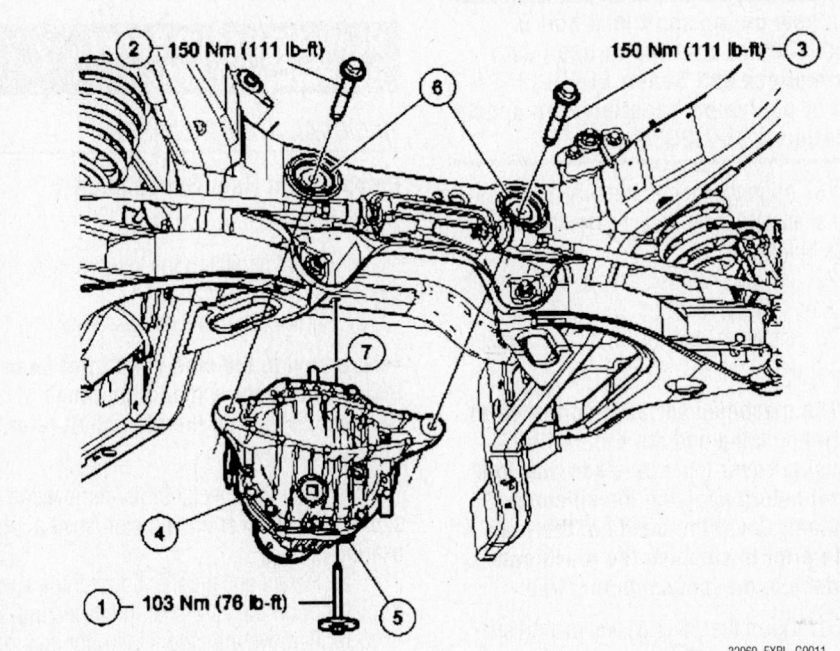

32069_EXPL_G0011

Fig. 65 Differential front lower insulator bolt (1), differential rear insulator bolt (2), differential rear insulator bolt (3), axle assembly (4), differential front lower insulator (5), differential rear insulator (6) and axle vent tube (7)

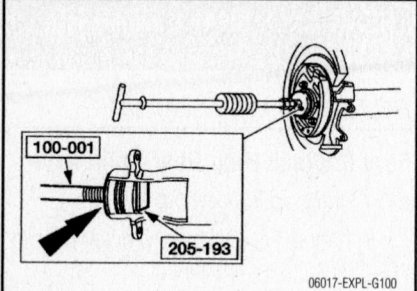

Fig. 66 Rear wheel bearing and seal removal—8.8 inch solid axle

To install:

18. Lubricate the new rear wheel bearing.

   a. For limited slip rear axles, use SAE 75W-140 High Performance Rear Axle Lubricant F1TZ-19580-B or equivalent meeting Ford specification WSL-M2C192-A.

   b. For conventional rear axles, use SAE 80W-90 Premium Rear Axle Lubricant XY-80W90-QL or equivalent meeting Ford specification WSP-M2C197-A.

19. Using a bearing driver, install the rear wheel bearing.

20. Lubricate the lip of the new wheel bearing oil seal. Use Premium Long-Life Grease XG-1-C or equivalent meeting Ford specification ESA-M1C75-B.

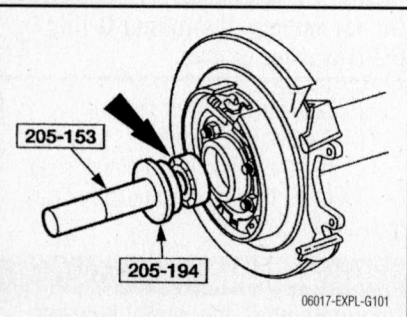

Fig. 67 Rear wheel bearing installation— 8.8 inch solid axle

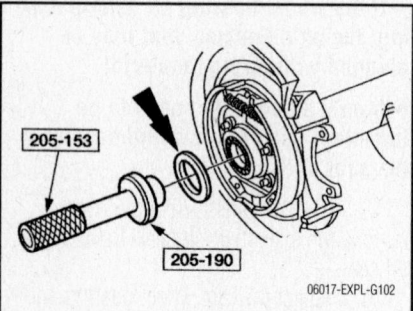

Fig. 68 Rear axle seal installation—8.8 inch solid axle

21. Using a seal driver, install the wheel bearing oil seal.

22. Lubricate the lip of the wheel bearing oil seal. Use Premium Long-Life Grease XG-1-C or equivalent meeting Ford specification ESA-M1C75-B.

✳✳ WARNING

Turning the differential case or an axle shaft with the differential pinion shaft removed will cause the differential pinion gears to fall out of the assembly and damage the components.

23. Remove the differential pinion shaft lock bolt.

24. Remove the differential pinion shaft.

✳✳ WARNING

Do not damage the wheel bearing oil seal.

25. Install the axle shaft.

✳✳ WARNING

Do not damage the rubber O-ring in the U-washer groove.

26. Position the U-washer on the button end of the axle shaft.

27. Pull the axle shaft outward.

✳✳ WARNING

If a new pinion shaft lock bolt is unavailable, coat the threads with Threadlock and Sealer EOAZ-19554-AA or equivalent meeting Ford specification WSK-M2G351-A5.

28. Align the hole in the differential pinion shaft with the differential pinion shaft lock bolt hole.

29. Install a new differential pinion shaft lock bolt. Torque to 22 ft. lbs. (30 Nm).

30. Install the rear brake disc or shoes and drum.

➡The machined surfaces on the differential housing and the differential housing cover must be clean and free of oil before applying the silicone sealant. Cover the inside of the rear axle prior to cleaning the machined surface to prevent contamination.

31. Clean the cover gasket mating surfaces.

➡Install the differential housing cover within 15 minutes of applying the silicone, or it will be necessary to apply new sealant.

32. Apply a continuous bead of sealant to the differential housing cover. Use Clear Silicone Rubber D6AZ-19562-AA or equivalent meeting Ford specification ESB-M4G92-A.

➡If possible, allow one hour before filling the axle with lubricant to allow the silicone sealant to cure.

33. Position the differential housing cover. Install the bolts. Torque to 33 ft. lbs. (45 Nm).

34. Fill the rear axle housing with the specified lubricant type and quantity.

➡For Traction-Lok® axles, first fill the rear axle with 118 ml (4 oz) of Additive Friction Modifier C8AZ-19B546-A or equivalent meeting Ford specification EST-M2C118-A.

➡Service refill capacities are determined by filling the rear axle to the level shown.

35. Fill the rear axle with lubricant and install the fill plug.

   a. For conventional axles, use SAE 80W-90 Premium Rear Axle Lubricant XY-80W90-QL or equivalent meeting Ford specification WSP-M2C197-A.

   b. For Traction-Lok® axles, use SAE 75W-140 Synthetic Rear Axle Lubricant F1TZ-19580-B or equivalent meeting Ford specification WSL-M2C192-A.

36. Install the wheel and tire assembly.

REAR AXLE STUB SHAFT BEARING AND SEAL

REMOVAL & INSTALLATION

Independent Rear Suspension

See Figures 69 through 71.

1. Before servicing the vehicle, refer to the "Precautions" section.

2. Remove the halfshaft assembly.

➡If removing the stub shaft pilot bearing oil seal only, engage the tangs of the special tool on the stub shaft pilot bearing oil seal.

3. Using the special tools, remove the stub shaft pilot bearing and stub shaft pilot bearing oil seal.

   a. Firmly engage the tangs of the special tool on the stub shaft pilot bearing.

   b. Remove the stub shaft pilot bearing and stub shaft pilot bearing oil seal.

4. Inspect the stub shaft pilot bearing oil seal journal for rust, nicks and scratches. Polish the seal journal surface with fine crocus cloth, if necessary.

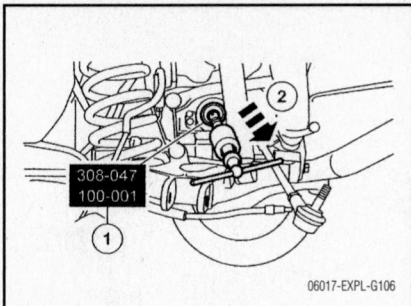

Fig. 69 Stub shaft bearing and seal removal

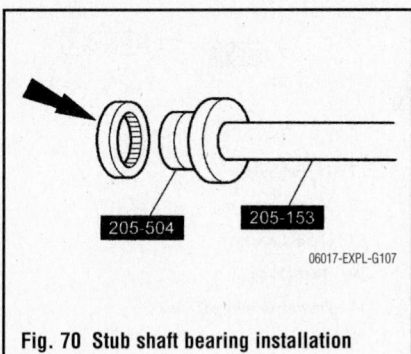

Fig. 70 Stub shaft bearing installation tool

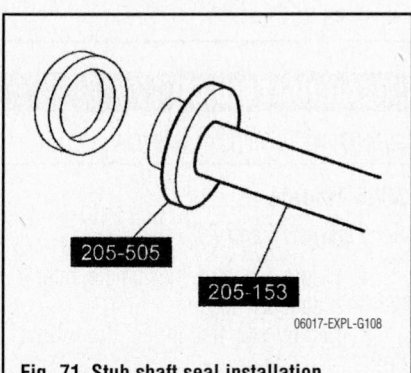

Fig. 71 Stub shaft seal installation

To install:

5. Lubricate the new stub shaft pilot bearing. Use high performance rear axle lubricant.

※※ WARNING

Installation of the stub shaft pilot bearing or stub shaft pilot bearing oil seal without the correct tools can result in early stub shaft pilot bearing or stub shaft pilot bearing oil seal failure. If the stub shaft pilot bearing becomes cocked in the bore during installation, remove it and install a new stub shaft pilot bearing.

6. Place the stub shaft pilot bearing onto the special tools.

7. Install the stub shaft pilot bearing into the rear axle housing bore.

8. Lubricate the lip of the stub shaft pilot bearing oil seal with grease and install the stub shaft pilot bearing oil seal onto the special tools. Use long-life grease.

9. Carefully align the stub shaft pilot bearing oil seal with the housing bore and install the stub shaft pilot bearing oil seal.

※※ WARNING

Install the special tool, to avoid damaging the seal with the halfshaft.

10. Install the halfshaft assembly.

REAR DRIVESHAFT

REMOVAL & INSTALLATION

2WD Models

See Figures 72 through 74.

1. Before servicing the vehicle, refer to the "Precautions" section.

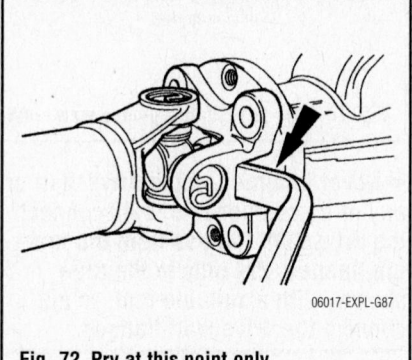

Fig. 72 Pry at this point only

2. With the vehicle in NEUTRAL, position it on a hoist.

➡**Make sure the index marks on the extension housing and driveshaft are aligned before separation.**

➡**After removing the driveshaft, place an index mark on the transmission output shaft that matches the transmission extension housing mark.**

3. Index-mark the driveshaft and the extension housing to maintain driveshaft balance.

4. Index-mark the driveshaft flange to the pinion flange to maintain driveshaft balance.

5. Remove and discard the 4 driveshaft flange bolts.

➡**The driveshaft flange yoke fits tightly on the pinion flange pilot. Never hammer on the driveshaft or any of its components to disconnect the driveshaft flange from the pinion flange.**

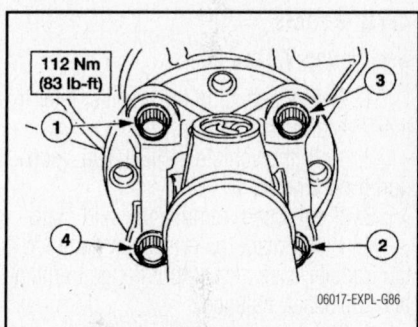

Fig. 74 Rear driveshaft flange torque sequence—2WD models

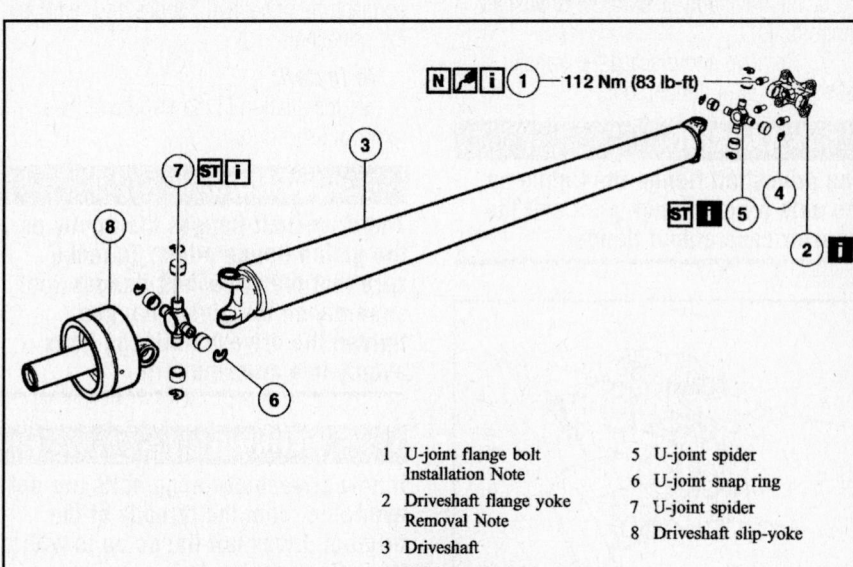

1 U-joint flange bolt Installation Note	5 U-joint spider
2 Driveshaft flange yoke Removal Note	6 U-joint snap ring
3 Driveshaft	7 U-joint spider
4 U-joint snap ring	8 Driveshaft slip-yoke

Fig. 73 Rear driveshaft exploded view—2WD models

6. Use a suitable tool and pry only in the area shown to separate the driveshaft flange yoke from the pinion flange.

To install:

7. Installation is the reverse of the removal procedure

✳✳ WARNING

The driveshaft flange fits tightly on the pinion flange pilot. To make sure that the driveshaft flange seats squarely on the pinion flange, tighten the driveshaft flange bolts evenly in a cross pattern.

✳✳ WARNING

If new driveshaft flange bolts are not available, coat the threads of the original driveshaft flange bolts with a threadlock sealer.

8. Tighten the flange bolts to 83 ft. lbs. (112 Nm).

4WD Models

See Figures 75 and 76.

1. Before servicing the vehicle, refer to the "Precautions" section.
2. With the vehicle in NEUTRAL, position it on a hoist.
3. If equipped, remove the skid plate.
4. Index-mark the driveshaft flange to the transfer case rear output flange to maintain driveshaft balance.
5. Index-mark the driveshaft flange to the pinion flange to maintain driveshaft balance.
6. Remove and discard the driveshaft flange bolts.
7. Remove and discard the transfer case rear output flange bolts.

✳✳ WARNING

The driveshaft flange fits tightly on the axle pinion flange pilot and the transfer case output flange.

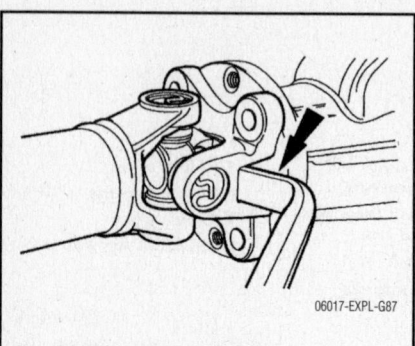

Fig. 75 Pry at this point only

06017-EXPL-G87

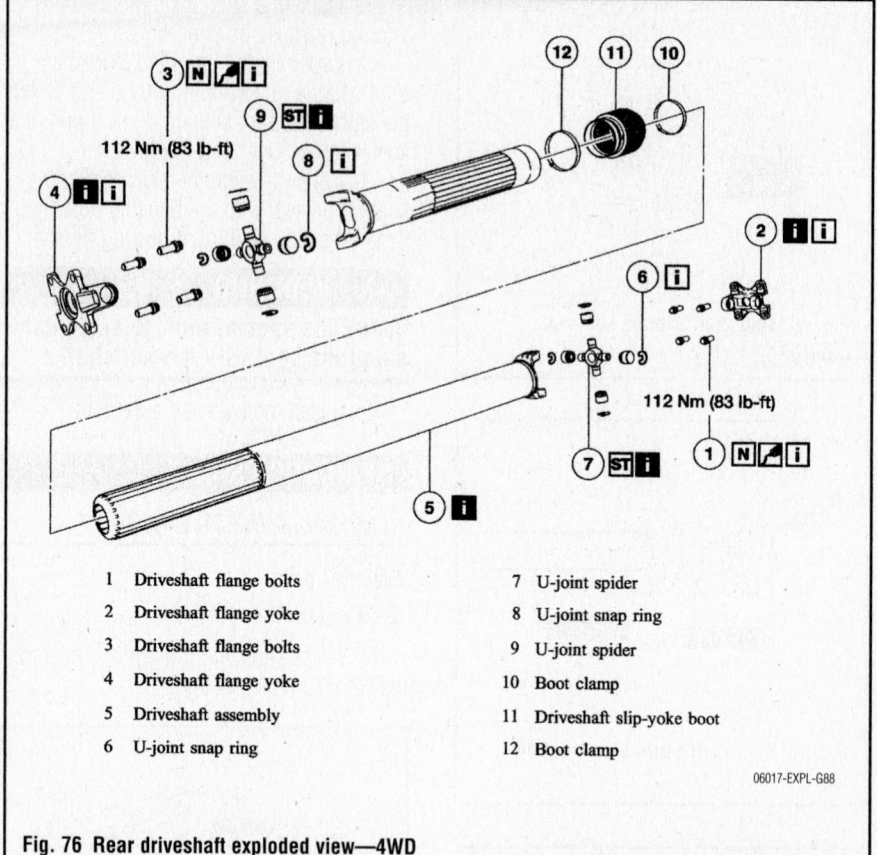

1 Driveshaft flange bolts
2 Driveshaft flange yoke
3 Driveshaft flange bolts
4 Driveshaft flange yoke
5 Driveshaft assembly
6 U-joint snap ring
7 U-joint spider
8 U-joint snap ring
9 U-joint spider
10 Boot clamp
11 Driveshaft slip-yoke boot
12 Boot clamp

06017-EXPL-G88

Fig. 76 Rear driveshaft exploded view—4WD

➡**Never hammer on the driveshaft or any of its components to disconnect the driveshaft flanges from the mating flanges. Pry only in the area shown, with a suitable tool, to disconnect the driveshaft flanges.**

8. Using a suitable tool as shown, disconnect the driveshaft flanges and remove the driveshaft.

To install:

9. Installation is the reverse of the removal procedure

✳✳ WARNING

The driveshaft flanges fits tightly on the pinion flange pilots. To make sure that the driveshaft flanges seat squarely on the pinion flanges, tighten the driveshaft flange bolts evenly in a cross pattern.

✳✳ WARNING

If new driveshaft flange bolts are not available, coat the threads of the original driveshaft flange bolts with a threadlock sealer.

10. Install new fasteners. Torque the flange bolts to 83 ft. lbs. (112 Nm).

REAR HALFSHAFT

REMOVAL & INSTALLATION

2005 Models

See Figures 77 and 78.

1. Before servicing the vehicle, refer to the "Precautions" section.
2. Remove or disconnect the following:

✳✳ WARNING

Do not loosen the rear axle wheel hub retainer until after the wheel and tire assembly are removed from the vehicle. Wheel bearing damage will occur if the wheel bearing is unloaded with the weight of the vehicle applied.

• Wheel and tire assembly

➡**Have an assistant press the brake pedal to keep the axle from rotating.**

• Hub retainer and the washer
• Caliper. Position the disc brake caliper out of the way.
• Brake disc
• Bolt retaining the parking brake cable bracket to the frame

✳✳ WARNING

Using a rubber hose approximately 37.5 mm (1.5 in) long, cover the stabilizer link bolt threads and nut to prevent boot damage when removing the halfshaft assembly from the vehicle.

✳✳ WARNING

The bolt that retains the upper ball joint to the knuckle is longer and it has fewer threads than the bolt that retains the toe link to the knuckle. Switching these bolts during installation will prevent the pinch arms on the knuckle from correctly retaining the toe link to the knuckle. This may cause the toe link to separate from the knuckle during vehicle operation. Failure to follow these instructions may result in personal injury.

- Pinch bolts and disconnect the toe link and upper ball joint from the knuckle

✳✳ WARNING

Using a wood stick, approximately 450 mm (18 in) long and 25 mm (1 in) wide, support the rear suspension upper arm to prevent boot damage when removing the halfshaft assembly from the vehicle

➡Do not use a hammer to separate the outboard CV-joint from the hub. Damage to the threads and internal CV-joint components may result. Once the outboard CV-joint separates from the hub the knuckle will continue to pivot until the brake backing plate presses against the suspension lower arm.

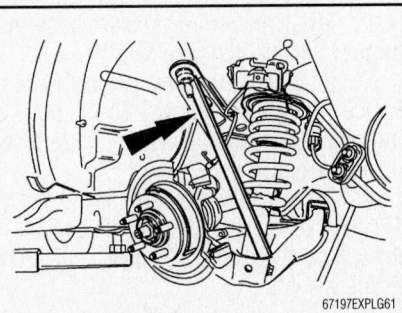

Fig. 77 Using a wood stick, approximately 450 mm (18 in) long and 25 mm (1 in) wide, support the rear suspension upper arm to prevent boot damage when removing the halfshaft assembly from the vehicle

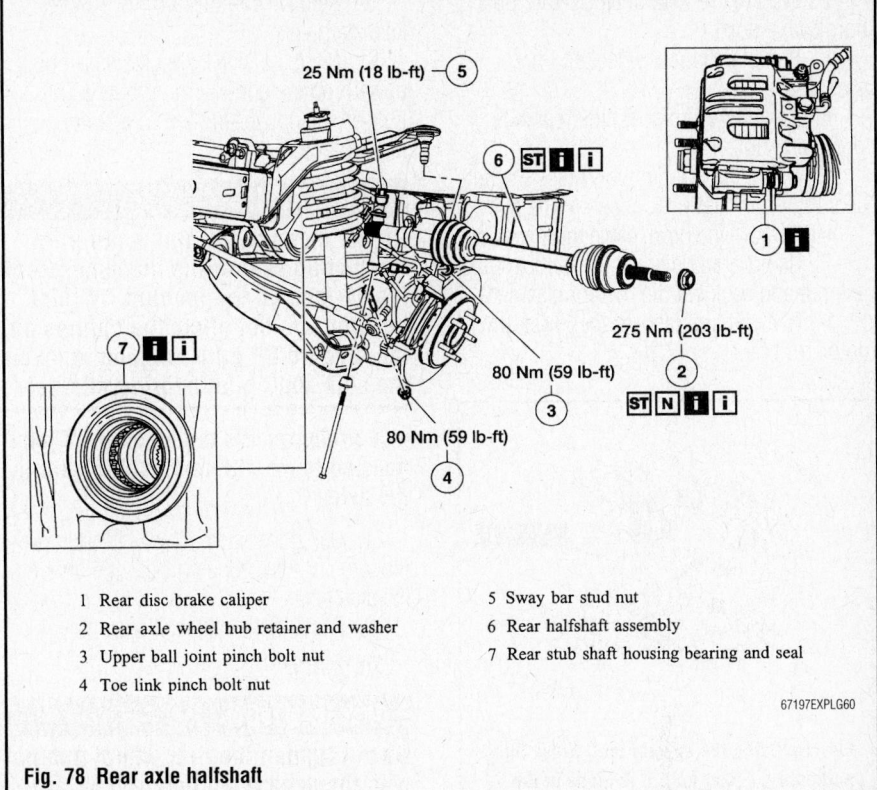

1 Rear disc brake caliper
2 Rear axle wheel hub retainer and washer
3 Upper ball joint pinch bolt nut
4 Toe link pinch bolt nut
5 Sway bar stud nut
6 Rear halfshaft assembly
7 Rear stub shaft housing bearing and seal

67197EXPLG60

Fig. 78 Rear axle halfshaft

To prevent damage to the brake backing plate, immediately after separating the outboard CV-joint from the hub, rest the knuckle on a cushioned support that is tall enough to keep the backing plate from pressing against the suspension lower arm.

3. Press the outboard CV-joint until it is loose in the hub.

4. Separate the outboard CV-joint from the hub.

5. Rest the knuckle on a cushioned support.

✳✳ WARNING

Do not damage the axle shaft oil seal or the machined sealing surface on the inboard CV-joint housing.

➡A circlip retains the inboard CV-joint housing to the differential side gear in the axle.

6. Using the special tool, disengage the inboard CV-joint housing from the differential side gear.

✳✳ WARNING

To prevent damage to the axle shaft oil seal, install the special tool 205-461 (seal protector) before removing the inboard CV-joint housing from the axle.

7. Remove the halfshaft assembly from the vehicle.

To install:

8. Installation is the reverse of the removal procedure.

9. To prevent damage to the axle shaft oil seal, install the seal protector before positioning the inboard CV-joint housing in the axle.

10. Always install the halfshaft with a new retainer circlip and a new rear axle wheel hub retainer.

✳✳ WARNING

Never use power tools to tighten the rear axle wheel hub retainer. Torque the retainer to 203 ft. lbs. (275 Nm).

2006–07 Models

See Figures 79 through 83.

✳✳ CAUTION

Do not loosen the rear axle wheel end nut until after the wheel and tire assembly are removed from the vehicle. Wheel bearing damage will occur if the wheel bearing is unloaded with the weight of the vehicle applied.

1. Before servicing the vehicle, refer to the "Precautions" section.

2. With the vehicle in NEUTRAL, position it on a hoist.

3. Remove the rear wheel and tire assembly.

4. Remove and discard the rear axle wheel end nut.

5. Using the special tool, press the outboard CV joint until it is loose in the hub.

6. Remove the brake cable retainer screw.

7. Remove and discard the outboard toe link nut and back out the bolt for clearance.

8. Remove and discard the lower arm outboard bolt.

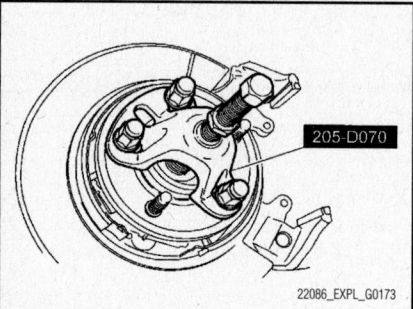

Fig. 79 Using the special tool, press the outboard CV joint until it is loose in the hub

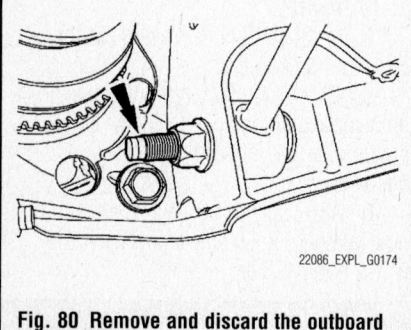

Fig. 80 Remove and discard the outboard toe link nut and back out the bolt for clearance

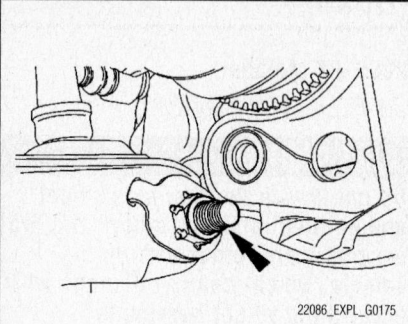

Fig. 81 Remove and discard the lower arm outboard bolt

9. Remove and discard the 3 wheel knuckle bolts.

10. Pivot the wheel knuckle assembly upward on the upper arm outboard bolt. Loosen the upper arm bolt to prevent bushing damage.

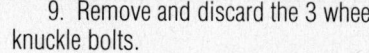
✳✳ WARNING

Do not damage the stub shaft pilot bearing oil seal or the machined sealing surface on the inboard CV joint housing. Do not allow the splines on the inboard CV joint housing to touch the stub shaft pilot bearing oil seal.

➡**A circlip retains the inboard CV joint housing to the differential side gear in the axle.**

11. Using the special tool, disengage the inboard CV joint housing from the differential side gear.

12. Remove the halfshaft assembly.

To install:

✳✳ CAUTION

Do not tighten the rear wheel hub nut with the vehicle on the ground. The nut must be tightened to specification

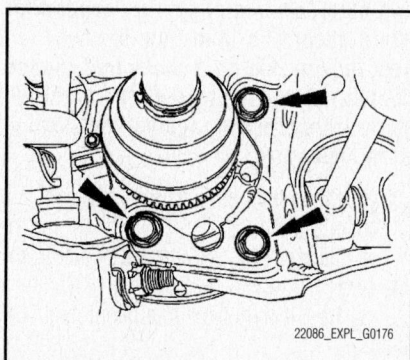

Fig. 82 Remove and discard the 3 wheel knuckle bolts

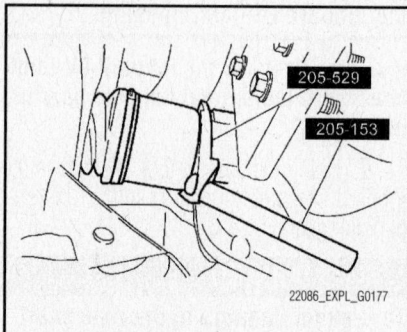

Fig. 83 Using the special tool, disengage the inboard CV joint housing from the differential side gear

before the vehicle is lowered onto the wheels. Wheel bearing damage will occur if the wheel bearing is loaded with the weight of the vehicle applied.

✳✳ CAUTION

Install and tighten the new axle wheel end nut to specification in a continuous rotation. Stopping the rotation during installation will cause the nylon lock to seat incorrectly. This will cause incorrect torque readings while tightening the axle wheel end nut and lead to bearing failure. Always install a new axle wheel end nut, after loosening or when not tightened to specifications, in a continuous rotation.

✳✳ CAUTION

Always install a new differential stub shaft seal whenever the halfshaft is removed.

13. Position the halfshaft in the vehicle.

14. Start one end of the circlip in the groove and work the circlip over the halfshaft and into the groove to prevent the circlip from over-expanding.

✳✳ CAUTION

Make sure the halfshaft is completely seated in the differential side gear by pushing the halfshaft into the rear axle assembly until an audible click is heard or a leak can occur from the axle assembly.

15. Reposition the steering knuckle. Install the upper arm bolt finger-tight (final tightening will be done with vehicle resting on its full weight).

16. Install the 3 wheel knuckle bolts and torque to 203 ft. lbs. (275 Nm).

17. Install the lower arm outboard bolt; torque only snug at this time (final tightening will be done with the vehicle resting on its full weight).

18. Install a new outboard toe link nut. Tighten the bolt only snugly (final tightening will be done with the vehicle resting on its full weight).

19. Install the brake cable retainer screw. Torque to 15 ft. lbs. (20 Nm).

20. Check that the outboard CV joint is properly fit into the hub.

21. Install a new rear axle wheel end nut. Tighten the nut to 203 ft. lbs. (275 Nm).

22. Install the wheel and tire assembly.

23. Lower the vehicle to its full resting weight.

24. Tighten the fasteners as follows:

   a. Wheel lug nuts: 100 ft. lbs. (135 Nm)

   b. Outboard toe link bolt: 259 ft. lbs. (350 Nm)

   c. Lower arm outboard bolt: 203 ft. lbs. (275 Nm)

   d. Upper arm bolt: 203 ft. lbs. (275 Nm)

CV-JOINT OVERHAUL

1. Before servicing the vehicle, refer to the "Precautions" section.

2. Remove or disconnect the following:

3. Remove the halfshaft.

4. For the inboard CV-joint:

   a. Remove and discard the boot clamps.

   b. Remove the inboard CV-joint housing.

   c. Remove and discard the retainer circlip.

   d. Slide the boot away from the CV-joint.

   e. Using a suitable 3-jaw puller, remove the CV-joint.

   f. Remove and discard the tri-lobe insert and the boot.

5. For the outboard CV-joint:

   a. Remove and discard the boot clamps.

   b. Remove and discard the boot.

➡**Do not disassemble the side shaft assembly. Install a new halfshaft assembly, if the components are worn/damaged.**

6. Inspect the grease packed in the inboard CV-joint and the outboard CV-joint for contamination. Rub some of the grease from each joint between two fingers. Any gritty feeling indicates contamination. Wash all of the grease from the inboard CV-joint, the inboard CV-joint housing, the outboard CV-joint, and the interconnecting shaft. Thoroughly dry all of the components, and inspect them for wear and damage. Discard the assembly, if necessary. Proceed as follows only if not discarding the assembly.

7. If necessary, remove and discard the outboard dust seal. Tap uniformly around the seal to separate it from the joint.

8. On the inboard end:

   a. Remove and discard the retainer circlip.

   b. If necessary, remove and discard the inboard dust seal. Tap uniformly around the seal to separate it from the housing.

To assemble:

9. For the outboard CV-joint:

   a. Slide the boot on the interconnecting shaft.

   b. Pack the outboard CV-joint with 5.29 ounces (225 grams) of grease.

   c. Spread any remaining grease evenly inside the boot.

   d. Clean any excess grease from the boot mounting surfaces before installing the boot.

   e. Install the boot by seating it in the groove in the CV-joint housing.

   f. Tighten the through-bolt until the special tool is in the closed position.

   g. Using the special tool, install both boot clamps.

   h. If removed, use the special tools to install the dust seal.

✳✳ WARNING

Do not over-expand or twist the circlip during installation.

   i. Install the retainer circlip.

10. Install the halfshaft in a soft jaw vise.

11. For the inboard CV-joint:

   a. Position the clamp on the interconnecting shaft.

   b. Position the boot on the interconnecting shaft.

➡**The lip on the end of the tri-lobe insert must seat against the end of the boot.**

   c. Install the tri-lobe insert.

➡**One side of the inboard CV-joint has a chamfer cut in the edge of joint at the inner diameter near the splines. Install the inboard CV-joint so that the chamfer faces the outboard end of the halfshaft.**

   d. Install the CV-joint.

   e. Install the retainer circlip.

   f. Pack the inboard CV-joint housing with 7.93 ounces (225 grams) of grease.

   g. Spread any remaining grease evenly inside the boot and on the CV-joint.

   h. Clean any excess grease from the boot mounting surfaces before installing the boot.

   i. Install the inboard CV-joint housing, seating the boot in the groove in the housing.

12. Set the halfshaft assembled length to:

   • Aviator and 2005 Explorer and Mountaineer: right side 33.94 inches (862.1 mm); left side 32.82 inches (833.7mm)

   • 2006–07 Models: right side 34.3 inches (872.7mm); left side 33.2 inches (843.7mm)

13. Hold the inner joint to prevent the assembled length from changing, and insert a wood wand between the boot and the joint to equalize the pressure.

14. Tighten the through-bolt until the special tool is in the closed position.

15. Install both boot clamps.

16. If removed, install the dust seal.

17. Install the halfshaft.

REAR PINION SEAL

REMOVAL & INSTALLATION

1. Before servicing the vehicle, refer to the "Precautions" section.

2. Drain the axle housing fluid.

3. Remove or disconnect the following:

   • Rear wheel and tire assemblies
   • Brake caliper and support bracket from the knuckle as an assembly. Wire the caliper and support bracket assembly out of the way.

➡**Matchmark the driveshaft flange and rear axle pinion flange to maintain initial balance during installation.**

4. Disconnect and position the driveshaft out of the way.

5. Install an inch/pound torque wrench on the nut and record the torque necessary to maintain rotation of the drive pinion gear through several revolutions.

6. Remove and discard the pinion flange nut.

➡**Matchmark the rear axle pinion flange and drive pinion gear stem to maintain initial balance during installation.**

7. Remove the rear axle pinion flange.

8. Force up on the metal flange of the rear axle drive pinion seal. Install gripping pliers and strike with a hammer until the rear axle drive pinion seal is removed.

To install:

9. Lubricate the new rear drive pinion seal with grease.

➡**If the rear axle drive pinion seal becomes misaligned during installation, remove the rear axle drive pinion seal and install a new seal.**

10. Drive in the rear axle drive pinion seal.

11. Inspect the rear axle pinion flange seal journal for rust, nicks and scratches prior to installing the flange. Polish the

seal journal with fine crocus cloth, if necessary.

12. Lubricate the rear axle pinion flange splines.

13. Install the rear axle pinion flange, aligning the matchmarks made during disassembly.

➡Disregard the index marks if installing a new pinion flange.

✳ WARNING

Do not under any circumstance loosen the nut to reduce preload. If it is necessary to reduce preload,

install a new differential drive pinion collapsible spacer and nut.

14. Rotate the pinion occasionally to make sure the pinion bearings seat correctly. Take frequent pinion bearing torque preload readings by rotating the drive pinion gear with an inch/pound torque wrench.

➡Rotational torque must be at least the recorded original torque plus a maximum of 5 inch-pounds.

15. If the preload recorded prior to disassembly is lower than the specification

for used bearings, then tighten the nut to specification. If the preload recorded prior to disassembly is higher than the specification for used bearings, then tighten the nut to the original reading as recorded:

a. Pinion bearing preload: 16–29 inch lbs. (1.8–3.2 Nm)

16. Connect the driveshaft. Torque the bolts to 83 ft. lbs. (112 Nm).

17. Install the rear brake calipers. Torque the bolts to 24 ft. lbs. (32 Nm).

18. Install the rear wheel and tire assemblies.

ENGINE COOLING

ENGINE FAN

REMOVAL & INSTALLATION

2005 Models

Explorer and Mountaineer
See Figures 84 and 85.

1. Remove the upper radiator appearance cover.

2. Vehicles with 4.6L SOHC engine detach the A/C tube from the retainers and position the tube aside.

3. If equipped, remove and discard the fan shroud screws.

4. Remove the bolts and the upper fan shroud.

✳ WARNING

Cardboard must be placed against the radiator when removing the cooling fan. Failure to follow these instructions can result in damage to the vehicle.

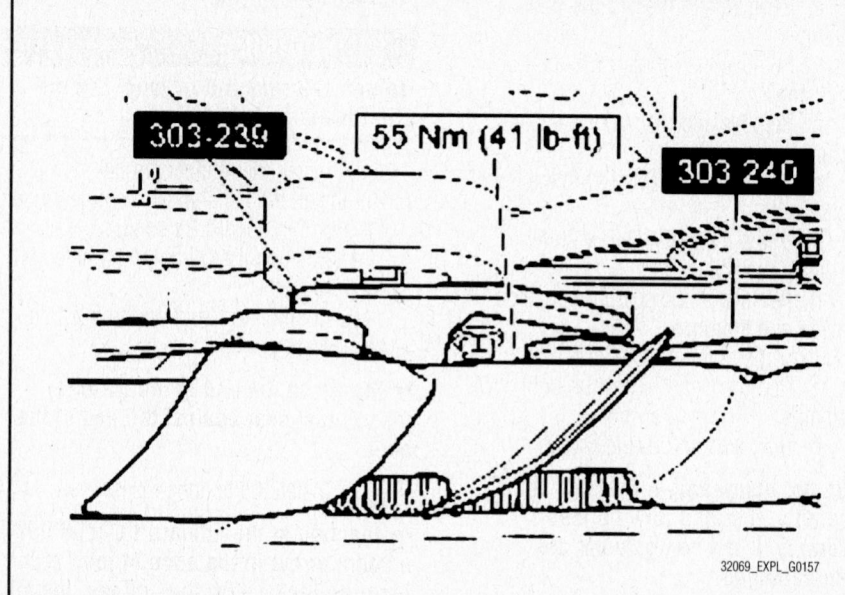

Fig. 85 Removing cooling fan using special tools 303–239 and 303–240

5. Place a piece of cardboard against the radiator to prevent damage while removing the cooling fan.

6. Using the special tools, remove the cooling fan.

To install:

7. Installation is the reverse of the removal procedure.

8. Observe the following tightening specifications:

- Upper fan shroud bolts 62 inch lbs. (7 Nm).
- Cooling fan bolts 41 ft. lbs. (55 Nm).

Explorer Sport-Trac

1. Remove the air cleaner outlet tube (4.6L).

Fig. 84 Detach A/C tube from retainers (arrows)—4.6L SOHC engine

2. Remove the fan blade and clutch assembly.

3. Remove the fan shroud, if necessary.

4. Installation is the reverse of the removal procedure.

5. Tighten the fan blade and clutch assembly mounting bolts to 41 ft. lbs. (55 Nm)

Aviator

1. Raise the vehicle on a hoist.

2. Using a special tool set, remove the large clutch assembly nut right-handed thread while rotating counterclockwise.

3. Remove the lower fan shroud.

4. Remove the cooling fan and clutch assembly.

5. Installation is the reverse of the removal procedure.

6. Tighten the fan mounting bolts to 40 ft. lbs. (55 Nm).

7. Tighten the fan shroud bolts to 89 inch lbs. (10 Nm).

2006–07 Models

1. Remove the air cleaner outlet tube, on models with the 4.6L engine.

2. Remove the coolant expansion tank.

3. Remove the bolt and position the power steering fluid reservoir aside.

4. Remove the bolts, then unclip the upper fan shroud from the lower fan shroud and remove the upper fan shroud.

5. Disconnect the fan clutch electrical connector.

6. Remove the fan clutch wiring harness bracket bolt.

7. Remove the cooling fan.

8. Installation is the reverse of the removal procedure.

9. Torque the cooling fan bolts to 41 ft. lbs. (55 Nm).

10. Torque the power steering reservoir bolt to 89 inch lbs. (10 Nm).

RADIATOR

REMOVAL & INSTALLATION

2005 Models

Aviator, Explorer and Mountaineer

See Figures 86 through 88.

See Figure 89.

1. With the vehicle in NEUTRAL, position it on a hoist.

2. Drain the cooling system.

3. Remove or disconnect the following:

• Upper degas bottle hose
• Upper radiator hose
• Lower radiator hose
• Lower degas bottle hose
• A/C tube from the retainers on top of the radiator (4.6L VIN 8)

4. Remove the safety retainers from the transmission cooler tubes. Using the special tool, disconnect the transmission cooler tubes.

5. If equipped, remove and discard the radiator fan shroud screws.

6. Remove the bolts and the upper radiator fan shroud.

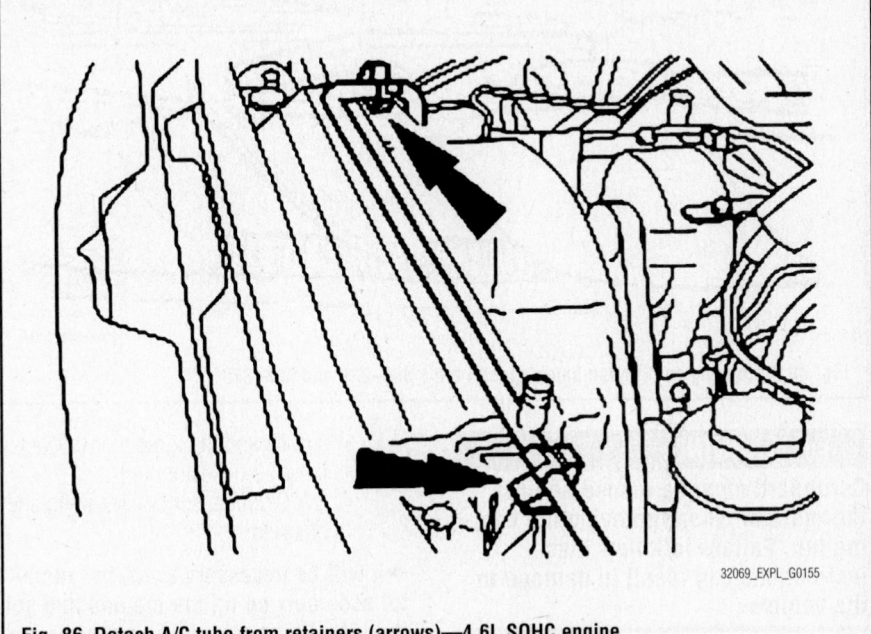

Fig. 86 Detach A/C tube from retainers (arrows)—4.6L SOHC engine

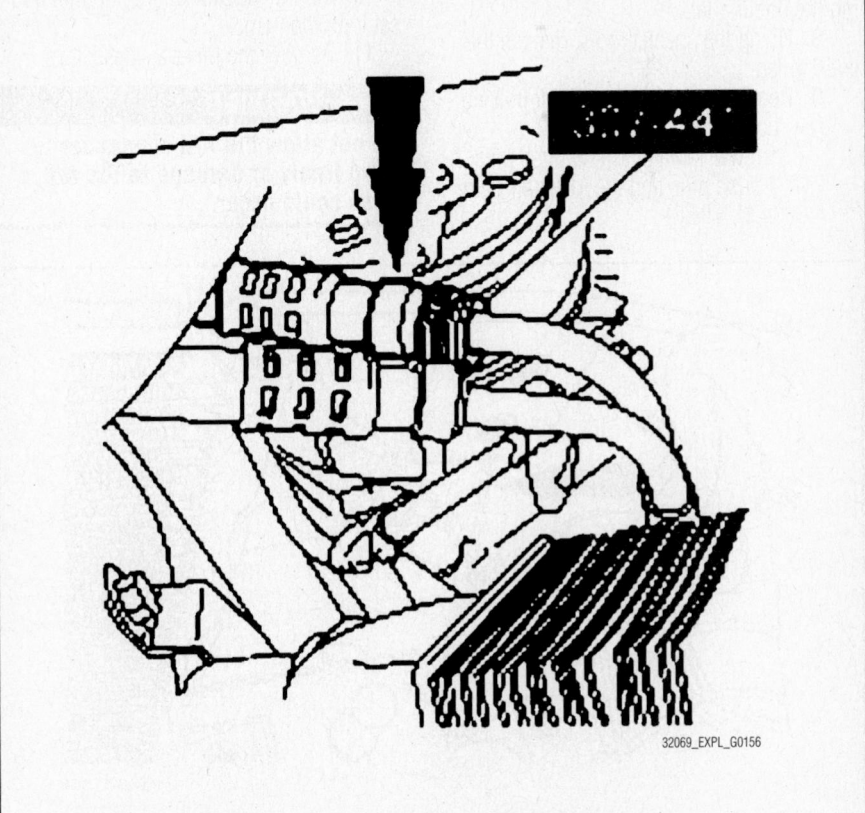

Fig. 87 Disconnecting transmission cooler lines using special tool 307–441

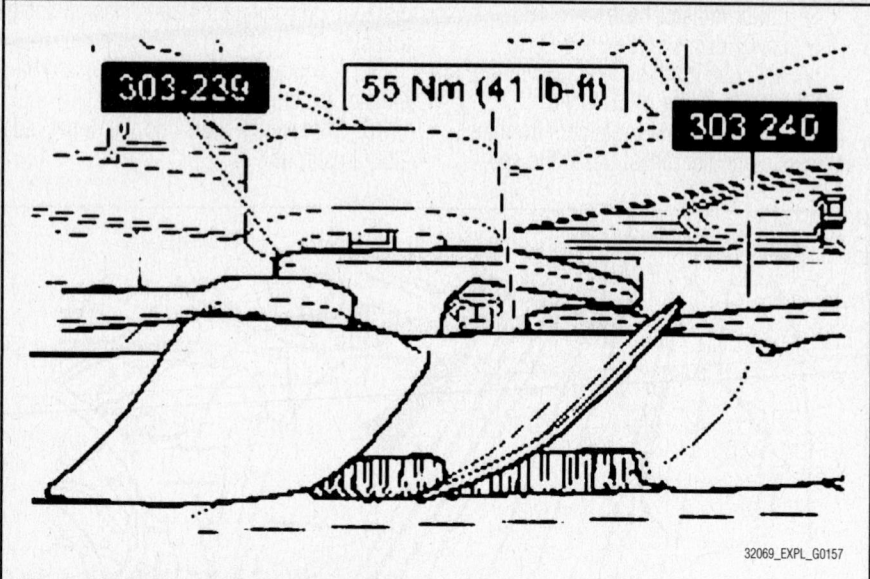

303-239   55 Nm (41 lb-ft)   303 240

32069_EXPL_G0157

Fig. 88 Removing cooling fan using special tools 303–239 and 303–240

✳✳ WARNING

Cardboard must be placed against the radiator when removing the cooling fan. Failure to follow these instructions can result in damage to the vehicle.

7. Place a piece of cardboard against the radiator to prevent damage while removing the cooling fan.
8. Using the special tools, remove the cooling fan.
9. Remove or disconnect the following:
   • Lower fan shroud
   • 3 lower radiator shield push pins
   • 4 push pins and the lower air dam (4.6L VIN 8)

   • 4 bolts and the 2 radiator brackets
   • Inner air deflector
   • 2 A/C condenser bracket bolts and brackets

➡ **It will be necessary to lift the radiator assembly up off the mounts and set it on the frame in order to separate the A/C condenser from the radiator.**

10. Lift the radiator off the mounts and set it on the frame.
11. Remove the inner air deflectors.

✳✳ WARNING

Do not allow the A/C condenser to hang freely or damage to the A/C lines could occur.

12. Using mechanic's wire, support BOTH sides of the A/C condenser.

➡ **It is not necessary to evacuate the A/C system. The A/C condenser can remain in the vehicle, with A/C tubes attached.**

13. Lift the A/C condenser up off the lower support, and move it toward the front of the vehicle.
14. Remove the radiator and transmission cooler as an assembly and place it on a bench.
15. Remove the transmission cooler.
16. Remove the 2 push pins and the splash shield.
17. Loosen the clamp and disconnect the hose.
18. Remove the bolts and the right hand radiator bracket, the left hand radiator bracket and the hose as an assembly.

To install:

19. Install or connect the following:
    • Radiator hose and bracket; tighten to 9 ft. lbs. (12 Nm)
    • Hose with clamp
    • Splash shield with 2 push pins
    • Transmission cooler; tighten the bolts to 89 inch. lbs. (10 Nm)
20. Position the radiator assembly into the vehicle.
21. Reposition the condenser into place.
22. Install or connect the following:
    • Inner air deflector
    • 4 bolts and the 2 radiator brackets
    • 4 push pins and the lower air dam (4.6L VIN 8)
    • 3 lower radiator shield push pins
    • Lower fan and shroud; tighten the fan bolts to 41 ft. lbs. (55 Nm)
23. Remove the cardboard.
24. Install the upper fan shroud. Tighten to 62 inch lbs. (7 Nm).
25. Connect the transmission cooler tubes, using the special tool.
26. Reconnect the remaining degas bottle and radiator hoses.
27. Refill and bleed the cooling system.

Explorer Sport-Trac

1. Drain the cooling system.
2. Remove or disconnect the following:
   • Air cleaner outlet tube
   • Radiator overflow hose
   • Cooling fan shroud
   • Upper and lower radiator hoses from the radiator

32069_EXPL_G0158

Fig. 89 Use wire to support BOTH sides of A/C condenser

- Transmission cooler lines at fittings
- 2 bolts and the radiator

To install:

3. Install or connect the following:
   - Radiator into position; tighten bolts to 62 inch lbs. (8 Nm)
   - Transmission cooler lines; tighten fittings to 18 ft. lbs. (25 Nm)
   - Upper and lower radiator hoses
   - Cooling fan shroud
   - Radiator overflow hose
   - Air cleaner outlet tube
4. Refill and bleed the cooling system.

2006–07 Models

Explorer, Explorer Sport-Trac and Mountaineer

1. Drain the cooling system.
2. Remove or disconnect the following:
   - Air cleaner outlet pipe (4.6L)
   - Coolant expansion tank
   - Power steering fluid reservoir; remove bolts and position aside
   - Upper and lower radiator hoses
   - Transmission cooling hose retainer from radiator support bracket
   - 4 lower radiator air deflector push pins
   - Latch assemblies from the transmission cooler tubes
   - Transmission cooler tubes, using special tool 307-569
   - Upper fan shroud
   - Fan clutch electrical connector
   - Fan clutch wiring harness bracket bolt
   - Cooling fan
   - Lower fan shroud
   - A/C tube from the upper retainer
   - Radiator support bracket-to-body bolts
   - Radiator top seal
3. Deflect the A/C condenser seals and remove the A/C condenser-to-radiator support bracket bolts.
4. Remove the radiator and the radiator support brackets as an assembly.
5. Remove the bolts and separate the radiator support brackets and the radiator.

To install:

6. Install or connect the following:
   - Support brackets to the radiator
   - Radiator into position; tighten the bolts to 9 ft. lbs. (12 Nm)
   - Reposition A/C condenser seals
   - Radiator top seal
   - Radiator support bracket-to-body

bolts; tighten the bolts to 9 ft. lbs. (12 Nm)
   - A/C tube from the upper retainer
   - Lower fan shroud
   - Cooling fan; tighten the bolts to 41 ft. lbs. (55 Nm)
   - Fan clutch wiring harness bracket bolt
   - Fan clutch electrical connector
   - Upper fan shroud
   - Transmission cooler tubes
   - Upper and lower radiator hoses
   - Power steering fluid reservoir; tighten bolts to 89 inch lbs. (10 Nm)
   - Coolant expansion tank
   - Air cleaner outlet pipe (4.6L)
7. Refill and bleed the cooling system.

THERMOSTAT

REMOVAL & INSTALLATION

4.0L Engine

2005–07 Explorer and Mountaineer; 2007 Explorer Sport-Trac

1. Drain the cooling system.
2. Disconnect the upper radiator hose from the thermostat housing.
3. Remove the thermostat housing and the thermostat.
4. Installation is the reverse of the removal procedure.
5. Install a new O-ring seal in the thermostat housing.
6. Torque the thermostat housing bolts to 89 inch lbs. (10 Nm).
7. Fill and bleed the cooling system.

2005 Explorer Sport-Trac

1. Drain the cooling system.
2. Remove the air cleaner outlet tube.
3. Remove the wiring from the alternator and position the harness aside.
4. Disconnect the upper radiator hose from the thermostat housing.
5. Remove the thermostat housing and the thermostat.
6. Installation is the reverse of the removal procedure.
7. Install a new O-ring seal in the thermostat housing.
8. Fill and bleed the cooling system.

4.6L Engine

Aviator

1. Position the vehicle on a hoist.
2. Drain the cooling system.

3. Remove the oil filter drip shield.
4. Remove the coolant inlet connector.
5. Remove the thermostat.
6. Installation is the reverse of the removal procedure.
7. Tighten the coolant inlet connector bolts to 89 inch lbs. (10 Nm).
8. Fill and bleed the cooling system.

2005 Explorer and Mountaineer

1. Drain the cooling system.
2. Remove the bolts and position the thermostat housing out of the way.
3. Remove the thermostat and gasket.
4. Installation is the reverse of the removal procedure.
5. Install a new O-ring seal in the thermostat housing.
6. Torque the thermostat housing bolts to 18 ft. lbs. (25 Nm).
7. Fill and bleed the cooling system.

2006–07 Explorer and Mountaineer; 2007 Explorer Sport-Trac

1. Drain the cooling system.
2. Remove the throttle body. See the "Fuel Systems" section.
3. Disconnect the fuel vapor tube near the thermostat housing.
4. Remove the bolts and position the thermostat housing cover aside.
5. Remove the O-ring seal and the thermostat.
6. Installation is the reverse of the removal procedure.
7. Install the thermostat with the spring facing downward.
8. Install a new O-ring seal and tighten the thermostat housing bolts to 89 inch lbs. (10 Nm).
9. Fill and bleed the cooling system.

WATER PUMP

REMOVAL & INSTALLATION

4.0L (VIN E, K) Engine

Explorer and Mountaineer

See Figure 90.

1. Before servicing the vehicle, refer to the "Precautions" section.
2. Drain the cooling system.
3. Remove or disconnect the following:
   - Fan shroud and cooling fan
   - Accessory drive belt
   - Water pump pulley

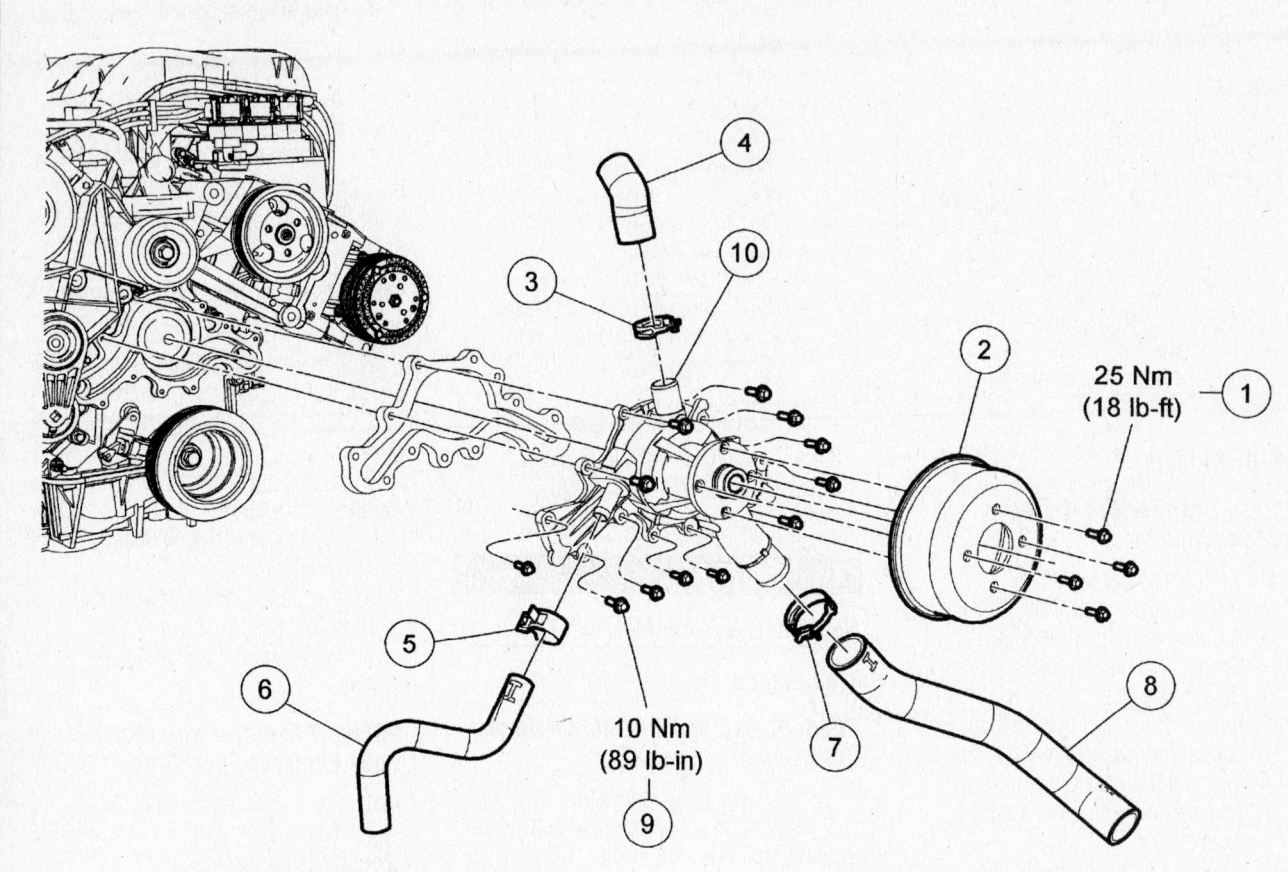

1	Coolant pump pulley bolts (4 required)		6	Heater hose
2	Coolant pump pulley		7	Lower radiator hose clamp
3	Coolant pump bypass hose clamp		8	Lower radiator hose
4	Coolant pump bypass hose		9	Coolant pump bolts (12 required)
5	Heater hose clamp		10	Coolant pump

06017-EXPL-G09

Fig. 90 Typical water pump installation—4.0L engine

- Coolant by-pass hose
- Lower radiator hose
- Water pump

❋❋ WARNING

Use care when scraping the water pump-to-engine block mating surfaces. Gouges in the aluminum could form leak paths.

4. Clean all the sealing surfaces.

To install:

5. Installation is the reverse of the removal procedure.

6. Observe the following tightening specifications:

- Water pump bolts: 89 inch lbs. (10 Nm)
- Pulley bolts: 18 ft. lbs. (25 Nm)

Explorer Sport-Trac

1. Drain the cooling system.

2. Remove or disconnect the following:

- Accessory drive belt
- Cooling fan and shroud
- Accessory drive belt idler pulley
- Water by-pass hose (slide clamp back from water pump connection)
- Lower radiator hose

- Water pump pulley
- Water pump

To install:

3. Installation is the reverse of the removal procedure.

4. Observe the following tightening specifications:

- Water pump mounting bolts: 89 inch lbs. (10 Nm)
- Water pump pulley bolts: 18 ft. lbs. (25 Nm)
- Idler pulley bolt: 33 ft. lbs. (45 Nm)

4.6L (VIN W, H, 8) Engine

See Figure 91.

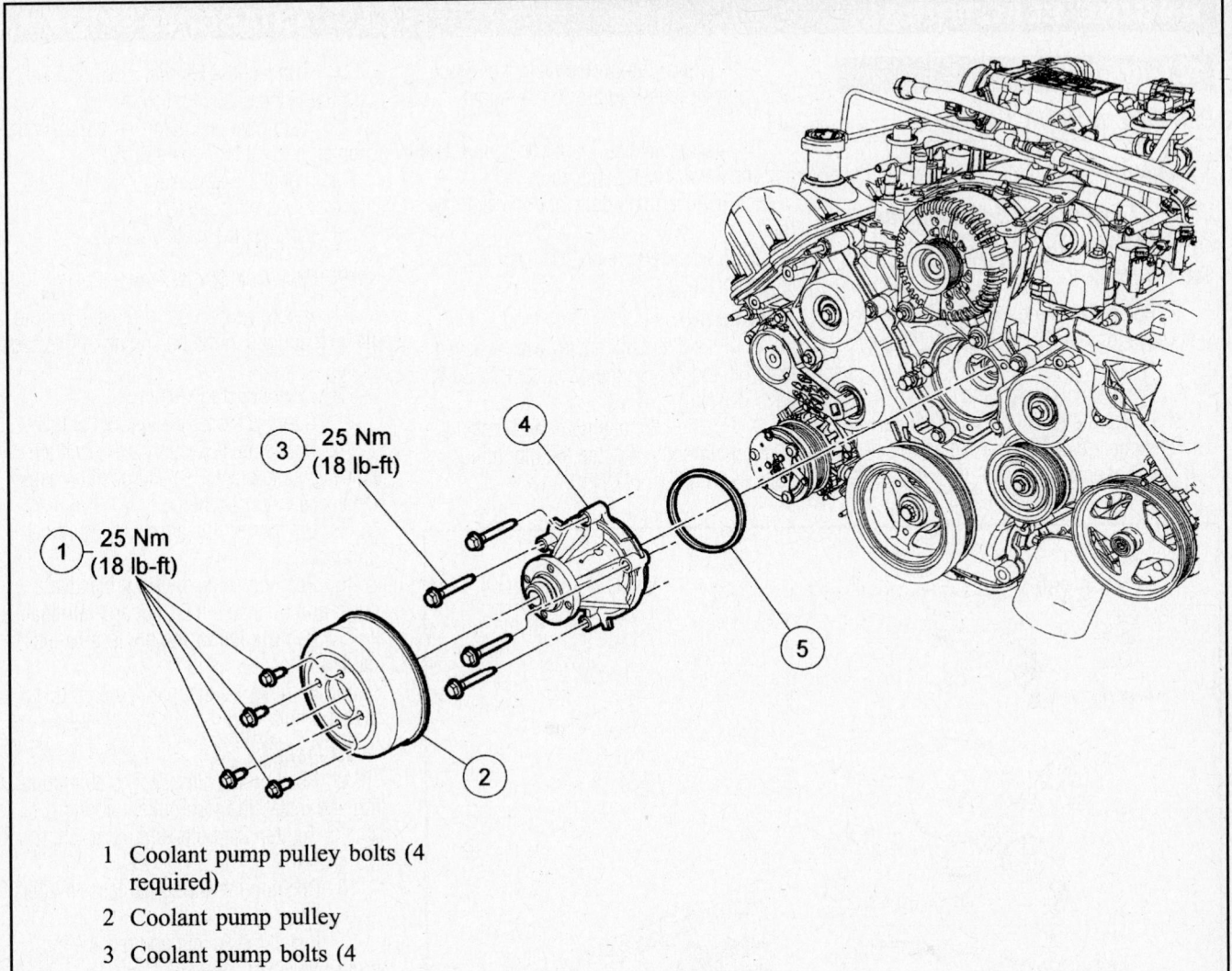

① 25 Nm
(18 lb-ft)

③ 25 Nm
(18 lb-ft)

④

⑤

②

06017-EXPL-G10

1 Coolant pump pulley bolts (4
   required)

2 Coolant pump pulley

3 Coolant pump bolts (4
   required)

4 Coolant pump

5 Coolant pump O-ring

Fig. 91 Water pump installation—4.6L (VIN 8, H) engine

1. Before servicing the vehicle, refer to the "Precautions" section.
2. Drain the cooling system.
3. Remove or disconnect the following:
   - Engine cooling fan
   - Upper fan shroud
   - Water pump pulley bolts (loosen only)
   - Accessory drive belt
   - Water pump pulley
   - Water pump
4. Discard the O-ring seal.

To install:

5. Installation is the reverse of the removal procedure.

6. Install a new O-ring seal and lubricate with engine coolant.
7. Observe the following tightening specifications:
   - Water pump mounting bolts: 18 ft. lbs. (25 Nm).
   - Water pump pulley bolts: 18 ft. lbs. (25 Nm).

ENGINE ELECTRICAL   CHARGING SYSTEM

ALTERNATOR

REMOVAL & INSTALLATION

4.0L Engine

2005–07 Explorer and Mountaineer; 2007 Explorer Sport-Trac

See Figure 92.

1. Before servicing the vehicle, refer to the precautions in the beginning of this section.
2. Disconnect the battery.
3. Rotate the front end accessory drive belt tensioner counterclockwise and position the front end accessory drive belt aside.

4. Position the protective cover aside and remove the alternator B+ terminal nut.
5. Disconnect the alternator B+ terminal and the 2 electrical connectors.
6. Remove the 3 bolts and the alternator.
7. If necessary, remove the nut and the alternator pulley.

To install:

8. If the alternator pulley was removed, install it and tighten the pulley bolt to 80 ft. lbs. (109 Nm).
9. Position the alternator and install the 3 mounting bolts. Tighten the mounting bolts to 35 ft. lbs. (47 Nm).

10. Connect the alternator B+ terminal and both electrical connectors.
11. Install the alternator B+ terminal nut. Tighten it to 80 inch lbs. (9 Nm).
12. Install the accessory drive belt and slowly release the tensioner.
13. Connect the battery cables.

2005 Explorer Sport-Trac

1. Before servicing the vehicle, refer to the precautions in the beginning of this section.
2. Disconnect the battery.
3. Remove the air cleaner outlet tube.
4. Rotate the accessory drive belt tensioner counterclockwise and position aside the accessory drive belt.
5. Disconnect the alternator electrical connectors.
6. Position aside the B+ protective cover and remove the B+ nut and terminal.
7. Remove the wiring harness-to-alternator locator.
8. Remove the alternator, by removing the stud bolts and nut and the shield.

To install:

9. Position the alternator to its mounting and install the stud bolts, nut and shield. Tighten the bolts and nut to 35 ft. lbs. (47 Nm).
10. Position the wiring harness-to-alternator locator.
11. Install the B+ nut and replace the protective cover.
12. Connect the alternator electrical connectors.
13. Install the accessory drive belt and release the tensioner.
14. Install the air cleaner outlet tube.
15. Reconnect the battery.

4.6L Engine

2005 Aviator

See Figures 93 and 94.

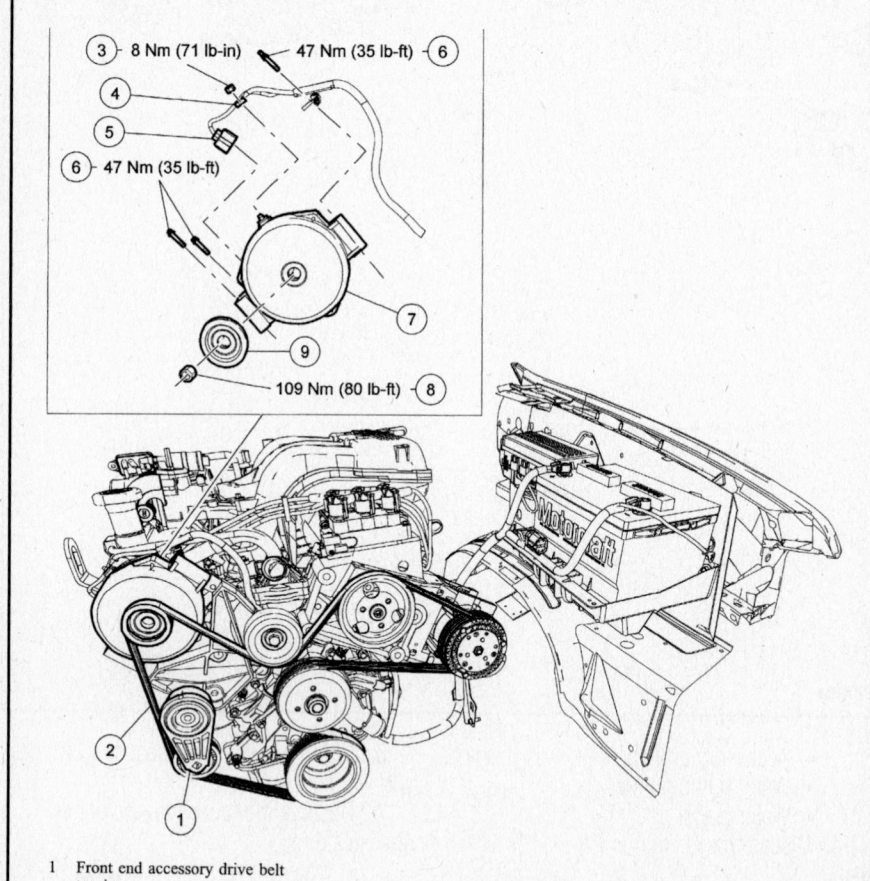

3 — 8 Nm (71 lb-in)   47 Nm (35 lb-ft) — 6
4
5
6 — 47 Nm (35 lb-ft)
7
9
109 Nm (80 lb-ft) — 8
2
1

1 Front end accessory drive belt tensioner
2 Front end accessory drive belt
3 Generator B+ terminal nut
4 Generator B+ terminal
5 Generator electrical connectors
6 Generator bolts
7 Generator
8 Generator pulley nut
9 Generator pulley

06017-EXPL-G02

Fig. 92 Alternator mounting—4.0L engine

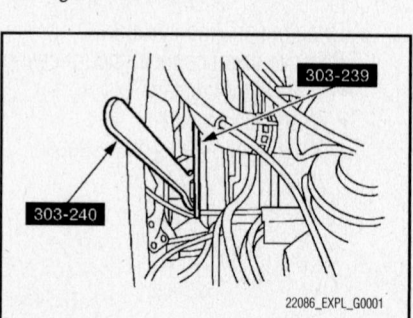

303-239
303-240

22086_EXPL_G0001

Fig. 93 Using the special tools to remove and install the cooling fan clutch nut— 2005 Aviator

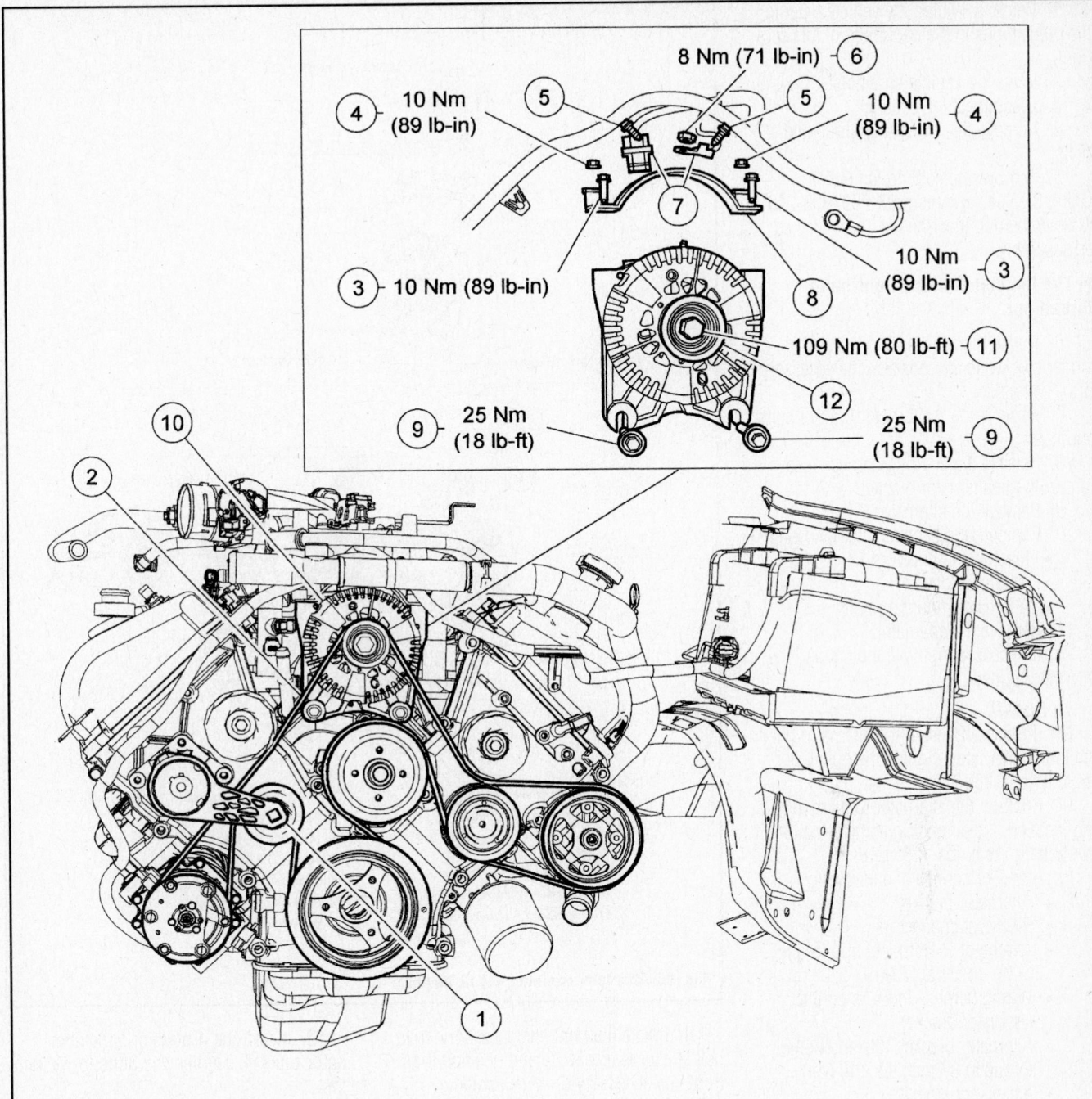

1. Accessory drive belt tensioner
2. Accessory drive belt
3. Generator bracket bolts (2 required)
4. Generator bracket nuts (2 required)
5. Wiring harness locators (2 required)
6. Generator B+ nut
7. Electrical connectors
8. Generator bracket
9. Generator bolts (2 required)
10. Generator
11. Generator pulley nut
12. Generator pulley

06017-EXPL-G04

Fig. 94 A front engine view of the alternator mounting components and the accessory drive belt routing—2005 Aviator

1. Before servicing the vehicle, refer to the precautions in the beginning of this section.

2. Raise the vehicle on a hoist.

3. Disconnect the battery.

4. Remove the lower fan shroud and bolts.

5. Remove the cooling fan clutch. Using the special tools (303-239, 303-240), remove the nut, then the fan and clutch as an assembly.

➡ **The fan clutch has a right-hand thread nut.**

6. Rotate the accessory drive belt tensioner clockwise and position the accessory drive belt aside.

7. Remove the 2 alternator bracket bolts and nuts.

8. Release the 2 wiring harness locators from the alternator bracket.

9. Remove the alternator B+ nut.

10. Remove or disconnect the following:
- Electrical connectors
- Alternator bracket
- Alternator mounting bolts

11. Remove the alternator.

12. If necessary, remove the nut and the alternator pulley.

To install:

13. If removed, install the alternator pulley to the alternator. Tighten the pulley nut to 80 ft. lbs. (109 Nm).

14. Position the alternator to its mounting location. Install and tighten the mounting bolts to 18 ft. lbs. (25 Nm).

15. Install or connect the following:
- Alternator bracket
- Electrical connectors
- Alternator B+ terminal nut; torque to 81 inch lbs. (7 Nm)
- Wiring harness locators on the alternator bracket
- Alternator bracket nuts and bolts; torque to 89 inch lbs. (10 Nm)
- Accessory drive belt

16. Install the cooling fan clutch. Using the special tools (303-239, 303-240), install the nut to 40 ft. lbs. (55 Nm).

17. Install the lower fan shroud and bolts. Tighten the bolts to 89 inch lbs. (10 Nm).

18. Reconnect the battery.

2005 Explorer and Mountaineer

See Figure 95.

1. Before servicing the vehicle, refer to the precautions in the beginning of this section.

2. Disconnect the battery.

3. Remove the nuts and the engine cover assembly.

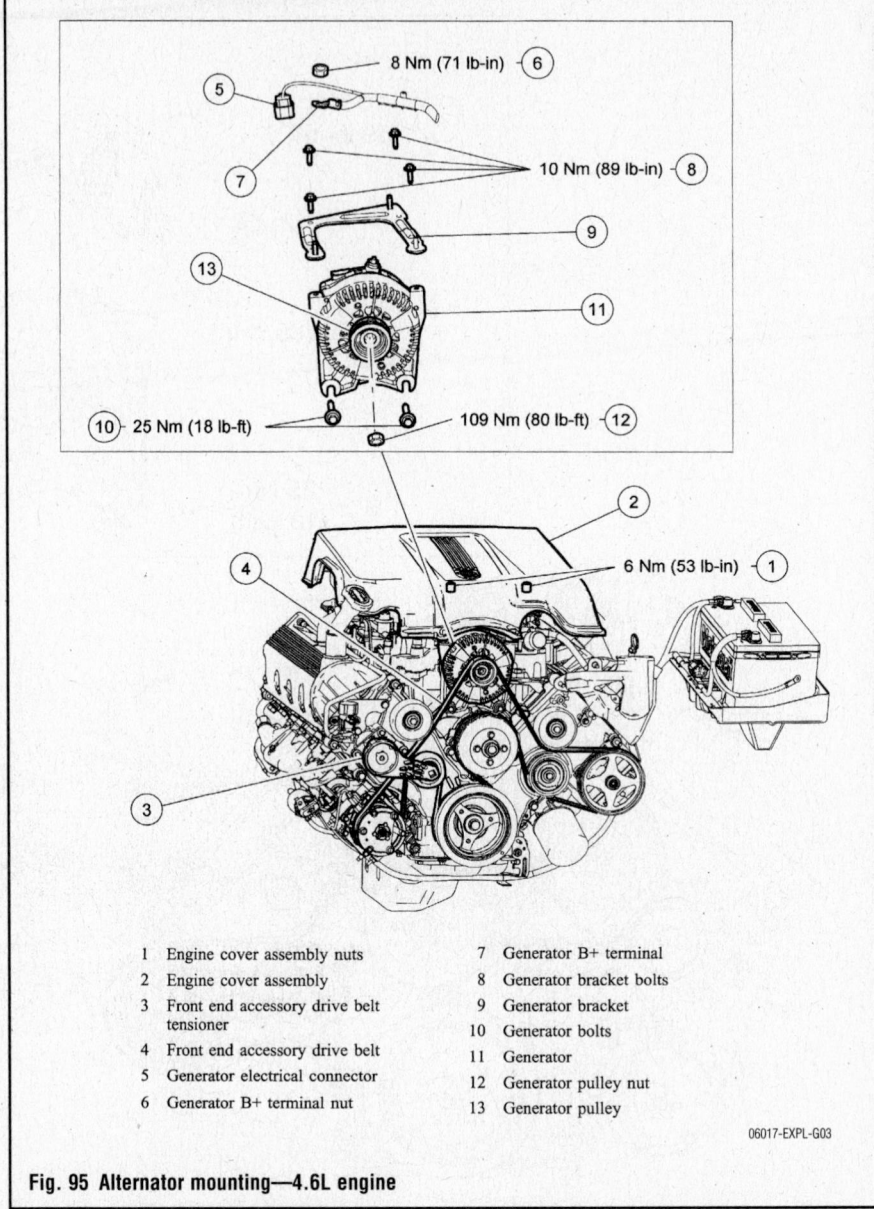

1	Engine cover assembly nuts	7	Generator B+ terminal
2	Engine cover assembly	8	Generator bracket bolts
3	Front end accessory drive belt tensioner	9	Generator bracket
4	Front end accessory drive belt	10	Generator bolts
5	Generator electrical connector	11	Generator
6	Generator B+ terminal nut	12	Generator pulley nut
		13	Generator pulley

06017-EXPL-G03

Fig. 95 Alternator mounting—4.6L engine

4. Rotate the front end accessory drive belt tensioner clockwise and position the front end accessory drive belt aside.

5. Position the protective cover aside and remove the alternator B+ terminal nut.

6. Disconnect the alternator B+ terminal and the electrical connector.

7. Remove the 4 bolts and the alternator bracket.

8. Loosen the 2 bolts and remove the alternator.

9. If necessary, remove the nut and the alternator pulley.

To install:

10. If removed, install the alternator pulley and torque the nut to 80 ft. lbs. (109 Nm).

11. Position the alternator in place and tighten the mounting bolts to 18 ft. lbs. (25 Nm).

12. Install the 4 bolts and the alternator bracket. Tighten the bolts to 89 inch lbs.

13. Connect the B+ terminal connector and the electrical connector. Install the terminal nut to 89 inch lbs. and reposition the protective cover.

14. Install the accessory drive belt and release the tensioner.

15. Install the engine cover. Tighten the nuts to 53 inch lbs. (7 Nm).

16. Connect the battery.

2006–07 Explorer and Mountaineer; 2007 Explorer Sport-Trac

See Figures 96 and 97.

1. Before servicing the vehicle, refer to the precautions in the beginning of this section.

2. Disconnect the battery.

3. Remove the throttle body as follows:

a. Remove the air cleaner outlet pipe.

b. Disconnect the electronic throttle control and throttle position (TP) sensor electrical connectors.

c. Remove the bolts, the throttle body, and the gasket. Discard the gasket.

4. Rotate the front end accessory drive belt tensioner clockwise and position the front end accessory drive belt aside.

5. Remove or disconnect the following:

• 4 bolts and the alternator bracket

• 2 bolts and position the alternator aside

• Protective cover and nut; position the alternator B+ terminal aside

• Remove the alternator.

• If necessary, remove the pulley from the alternator.

To install:

6. If removed, install the pulley onto the alternator. Tighten the pulley nut to 80 ft. lbs. (109 Nm).

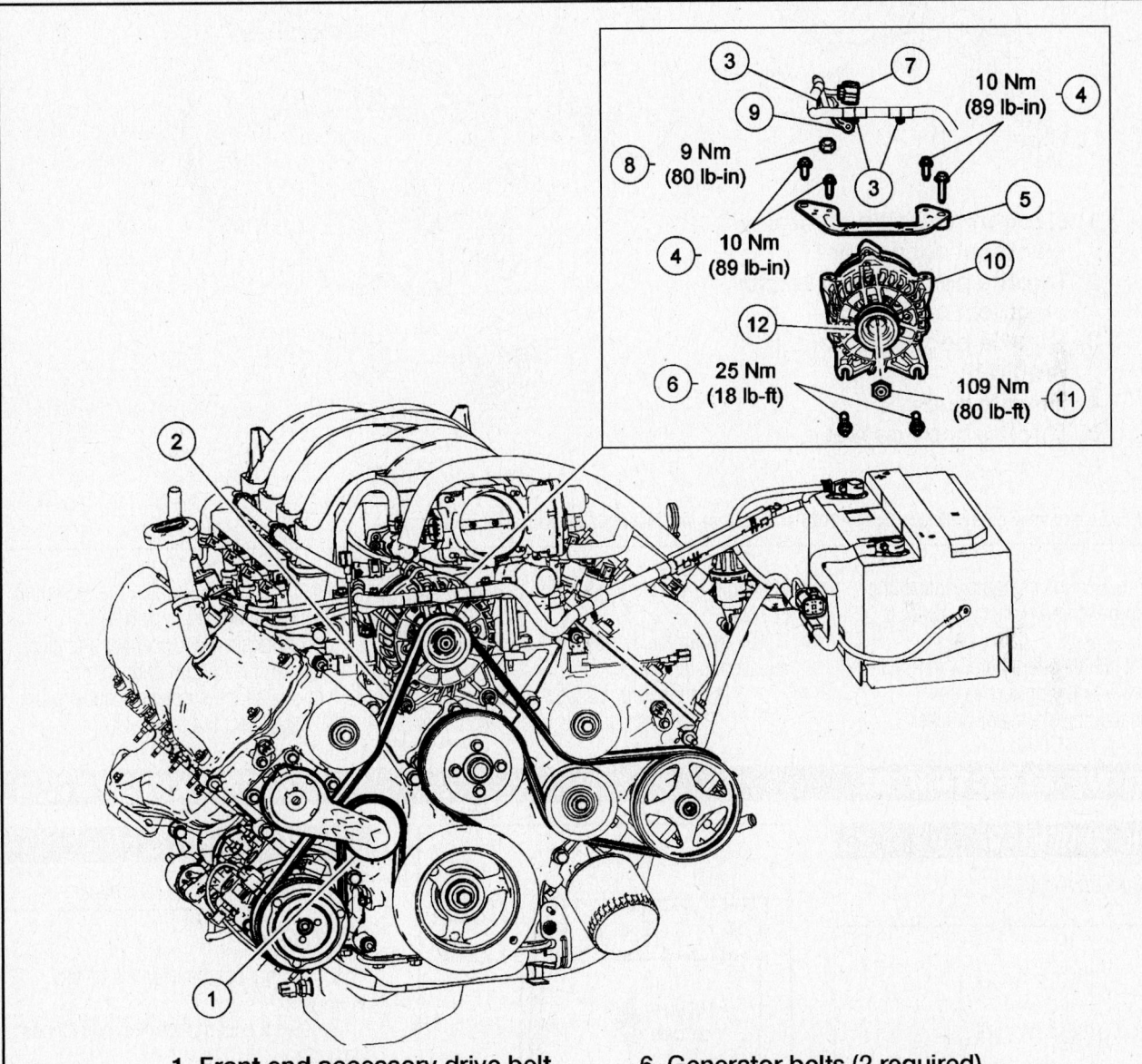

1. Front end accessory drive belt
2. Front end accessory drive belt
3. Generator harness locators (3 required)
4. Generator bracket bolts (4 required)
5. Generator bracket tensioner
6. Generator bolts (2 required)
7. Generator electrical connector
8. Generator B+ terminal nut
9. Generator B+ terminal
10. Generator
11. Generator pulley nut
12. Generator pulley

22086_EXPL_G0003

Fig. 96 A front engine view of the alternator mounting components and the accessory drive belt routing—2006–07 4.6L engine

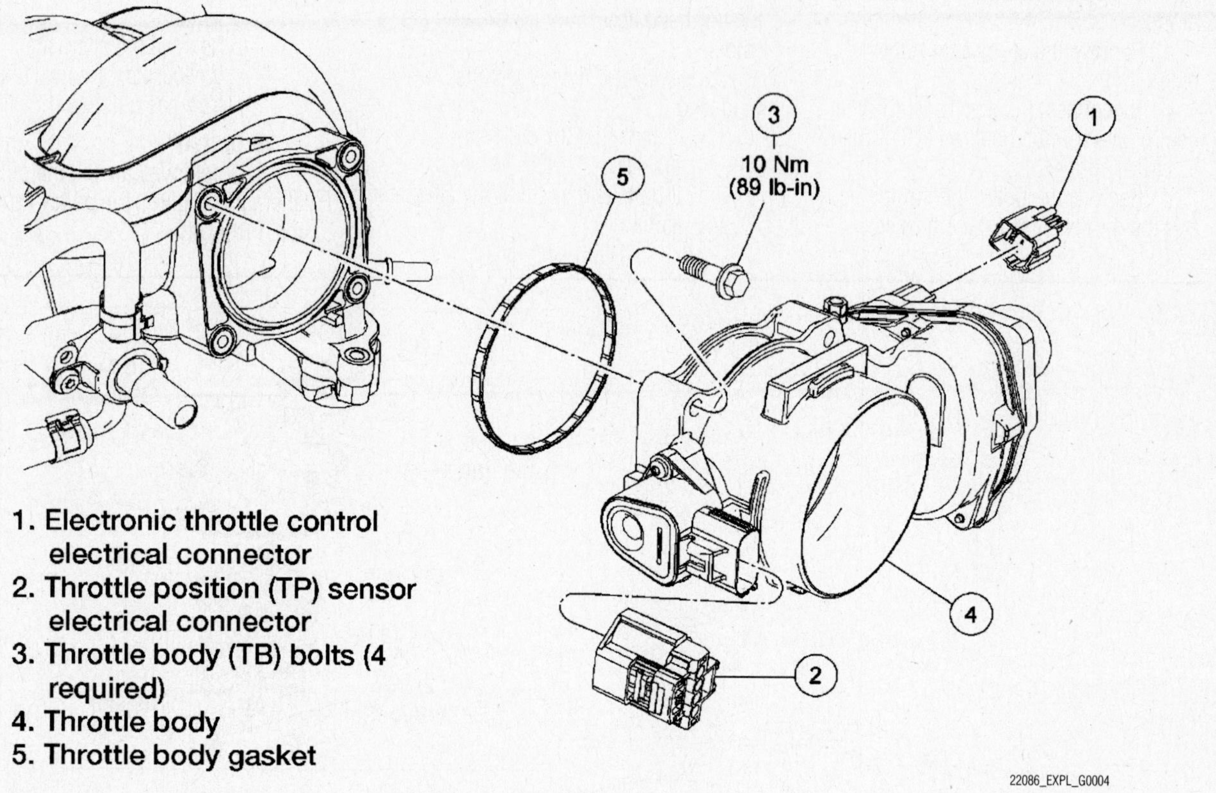

1. Electronic throttle control electrical connector
2. Throttle position (TP) sensor electrical connector
3. Throttle body (TB) bolts (4 required)
4. Throttle body
5. Throttle body gasket

3 10 Nm (89 lb-in)

Fig. 97 Exploded view of the throttle body—2006–07 Explorer and Mountaineer with 4.6L engine

7. Position the alternator. Install the mounting bolts and tighten to 18 lb. ft. (25 Nm).

8. Install the alternator B+ terminal and nut; reposition the protective cover.

9. Install the alternator bracket.

Tighten the 4 bolts to 89 inch lbs. (10 Nm).

10. Install the accessory drive belt and release the tensioner.

11. Install the throttle body as follows:
   a. Position the throttle body, with a new gasket. Install and tighten the mounting bolts to 89 inch lbs. (10 Nm).
   b. Connect the TP sensor and electronic throttle control connectors.
   c. Install the air cleaner outlet pipe.

12. Reconnect the battery.

ENGINE ELECTRICAL

FIRING ORDER

See Figures 98 and 99.

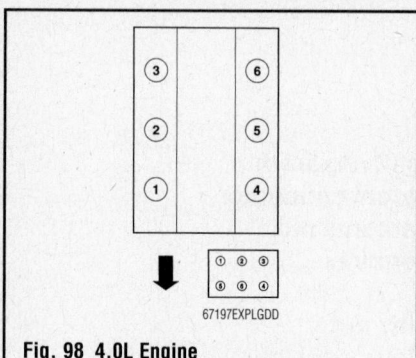

Fig. 98 4.0L Engine
Firing order: 1–4–2–5–3–6
Distributorless ignition system

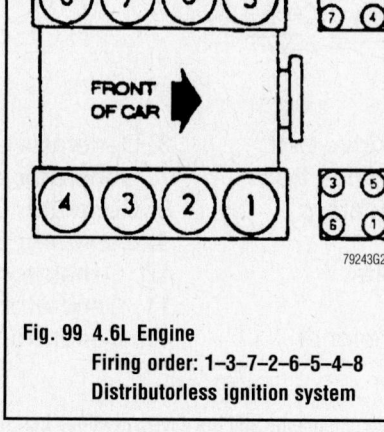

Fig. 99 4.6L Engine
Firing order: 1–3–7–2–6–5–4–8
Distributorless ignition system

oIGNITION SYSTEM

IGNITION COIL

REMOVAL & INSTALLATION

4.0L Engine

1. Disconnect the negative battery cable.

2. Disconnect the ignition coil electrical connector.

3. Disconnect the radio noise suppressor electrical connector, if equipped.

❋❋ WARNING

It is important to twist the spark plug wire boots while pulling upward to avoid possible damage to the spark plug wire.

➥Spark plug wires must be connected to the correct ignition coil terminal. Mark the spark plug wires for installation reference.

4. Squeeze the tabs and twist while pulling upward to disconnect the 6 spark plug wires.

5. Remove the 4 bolts and the ignition coil.

To install:

6. Apply silicone dielectric compound to the inside of the ignition coil boots.

7. Install the ignition coil; tighten the 4 bolts to 53 inch lbs. (6 Nm).

8. Install the spark plug wires to the correct spark plugs, as referenced during removal.

9. Connect the radio noise suppressor electrical connector, if equipped.

10. Connect the ignition coil connector.

11. Connect the battery ground cable.

4.6L Engine

Aviator

1. Disconnect the negative battery cable.

2. Remove the ignition coil cover bolts and remove the covers.

3. Remove the 8 ignition coil connectors and remove the 8 coils from the spark plugs.

To install:

4. Apply silicone dielectric compound to the inside of the ignition coil boots.

5. Connect the ignition coils to the spark plugs.

6. Connect the 8 ignition coil connectors.

7. Install the coil covers and tighten the bolts to 89 inch lbs. (10 Nm).

8. Connect the battery ground cable.

Explorer and Mountaineer

1. Disconnect the negative battery cable.

2. Remove the bolts and the ignition coil-on-plugs.

To install:

3. Apply dielectric compound to the inside of the coil boots before installation.

4. Install the ignition coil-on-plugs and tighten the bolts to 53 inch lbs. (6 Nm).

5. Connect the battery ground cable.

IGNITION TIMING

ADJUSTMENT

The ignition timing is preset to 10 degrees Before Top Dead Center (BTDC) and is not adjustable.

SPARK PLUGS

REMOVAL & INSTALLATION

See Figure 100.

➥Ford recommends replacing standard spark plugs every 100,000 miles.

When you're removing spark plugs, work on one at a time. Don't start by removing the plug wires all at once, because, unless you number them, they may become mixed up. Take a minute before you begin and number the wires with tape. Also, an anti-seize compound should be used before installing the plugs into the cylinder head.

1. Disconnect the negative battery cable, and if the vehicle has been run recently, allow the engine to thoroughly cool.

2. Carefully twist the spark plug wire boot to loosen it, then pull upward and remove the boot from the plug. Be sure to pull on the boot and not on the wire, otherwise the connector located inside the boot may become separated.

3. Using compressed air, blow any water or debris from the spark plug well to assure that no harmful contaminants are allowed to enter the combustion chamber when the spark plug is removed.

➥Remove the spark plugs when the engine is cold, if possible, to prevent damage to the threads. If removal of the plugs is difficult, apply penetrating oil or spray to the area around the base

Fig. 100 Always twist and pull on the spark plug boot, never on the wire

of the plug, and allow it a few minutes to work.

4. Using a spark plug socket that is equipped with a rubber insert to properly hold the plug, turn the spark plug counterclockwise to loosen and remove the spark plug from the bore.

✲✲ WARNING

Be sure not to use a flexible extension on the socket. Use of a flexible extension may allow a shear force to be applied to the plug. A shear force could break the plug off in the cylinder head, leading to costly and frustrating repairs.

To install:

5. Inspect the spark plug boot for tears or damage. If a damaged boot is found, the spark plug wire must be replaced.

➥Coat the spark plug threads with an anti-seize compound before installing it into the cylinder head.

6. Carefully thread the plug into the bore by hand. If resistance is felt before the plug is almost completely threaded, back the plug out and begin threading again. In small, hard to reach areas, an old spark plug wire and boot could be used as a threading tool. The boot will hold the plug while you twist the end of the wire and the wire is supple enough to twist before it would allow the plug to cross-thread.

✲✲ WARNING

Do not use the spark plug socket to thread the plugs. Always carefully thread the plug by hand or using an old plug wire to prevent the possibility of cross-threading and damaging the cylinder head bore.

7. Carefully tighten the spark plug to 15 ft. lbs. (20 Nm).

8. Apply a small amount of silicone dielectric compound to the end of the spark plug lead or inside the spark plug boot to prevent sticking, then install the boot to the spark plug and push until it clicks into place. The click may be felt or heard, then gently pull back on the boot to assure proper contact.

ENGINE ELECTRICAL

STARTING SYSTEM

STARTER

REMOVAL & INSTALLATION

See Figures 101 through 103.

1. With the vehicle in NEUTRAL, raise vehicle on hoist.
2. Disconnect the negative battery cable.
3. On 2005 Sport-Trac, remove the frame damper.
4. Remove the starter solenoid terminal cover.

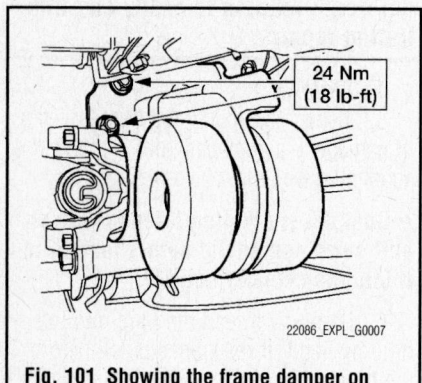

24 Nm (18 lb-ft)

22086_EXPL_G0007

Fig. 101 Showing the frame damper on 2005 Explorer Sport-Trac models

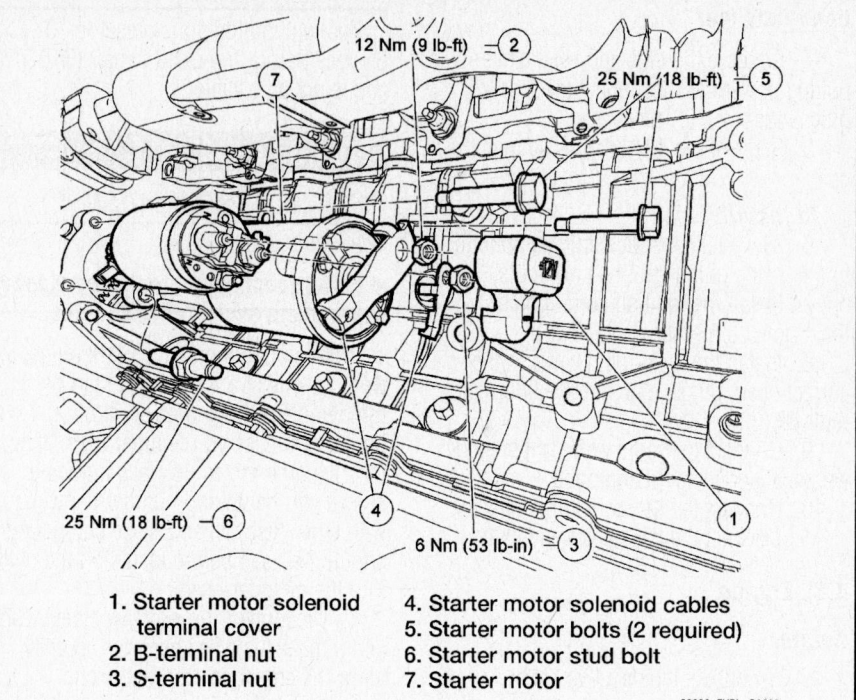

12 Nm (9 lb-ft) — 2
25 Nm (18 lb-ft) — 5
7
25 Nm (18 lb-ft) — 6
4
6 Nm (53 lb-in) — 3
1

1. Starter motor solenoid terminal cover
2. B-terminal nut
3. S-terminal nut
4. Starter motor solenoid cables
5. Starter motor bolts (2 required)
6. Starter motor stud bolt
7. Starter motor

22086_EXPL_G0009

Fig. 103 Starter assembly shown in mounting position—4.6L engine

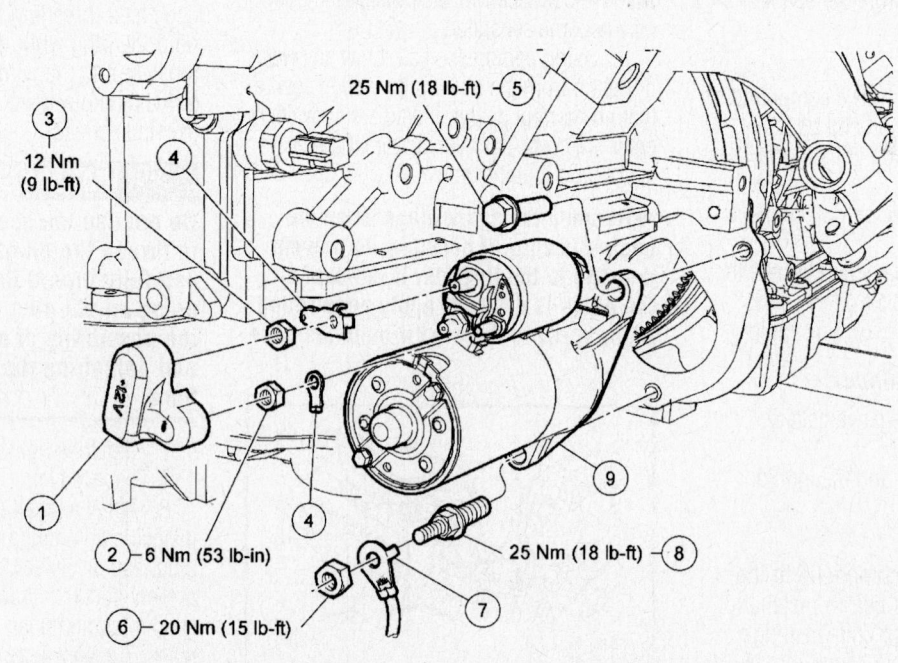

3
12 Nm (9 lb-ft)
4
25 Nm (18 lb-ft) — 5
1
4
9
2 — 6 Nm (53 lb-in)
7
6 — 20 Nm (15 lb-ft)
25 Nm (18 lb-ft) — 8

1. Starter motor solenoid terminal cover
2. Starter motor S-terminal nut
3. Starter motor B-terminal nut
4. Starter motor solenoid cables
5. Starter motor bolt
6. Ground cable nut
7. Ground cable
8. Starter motor stud bolt
9. Starter motor

22086_EXPL_G0008

Fig. 102 Starter assembly shown in mounting position—4.0L engine

5. Remove the nut and disconnect the starter solenoid battery cable.

6. Remove the nut and disconnect the starter solenoid wire.

7. Remove the 3 starter motor bolts and the starter motor.

To install:

8. Position the starter and install and tighten the starter motor bolts to 18 ft. lbs. (25 Nm).

9. Install the solenoid wire and tighten the nut to 44 inch lbs. (6 Nm).

10. Install the solenoid wire and nut. Tighten the nut to 10 ft. lbs. (13 Nm).

11. Install the solenoid terminal cover.

12. If removed, install the frame damper. Tighten the bolts to 18 ft. lbs. (24 Nm).

13. Connect the battery ground cable.

ENGINE MECHANICAL

➡Disconnecting the negative battery cable may interfere with the functions of the on board computer systems and may require the computer to undergo a relearning process, once the negative battery cable is reconnected.

ACCESSORY DRIVE BELTS

ACCESSORY BELT ROUTING

See Figures 104 through 106.

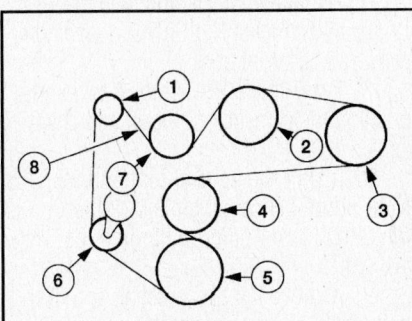

1 Generator pulley
2 Power steering pump pulley
3 A/C compressor pulley
4 Coolant pump pulley
5 Crankshaft damper
6 Drive belt tensioner pulley
7 Belt idler pulley
8 Drive belt

67197EXPLGCC

Fig. 104 Accessory drive belt routing— 4.0L VIN E or VIN K engine

INSPECTION

Inspect the drive belt for signs of glazing or cracking. A glazed belt will be perfectly smooth from slippage, while a good belt will have a slight texture of fabric visible. Cracks will usually start at the inner edge of the belt and run outward. All worn or damaged drive belts should be replaced immediately.

ADJUSTMENT

The belt tensioner automatically set the correct tension on the accessory drive belt. No further adjustment is necessary.

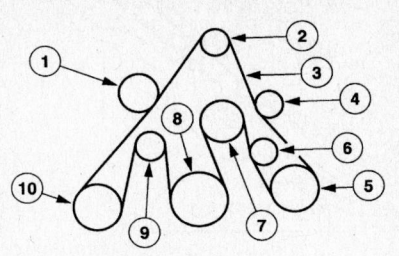

1 Belt idler pulley
2 Generator pulley
3 Drive belt
4 Belt idler pulley
5 Power steering pump pulley
6 Belt idler pulley
7 Coolant pump pulley
8 Crankshaft pulley
9 Drive belt tensioner pulley
10 A/C compressor pulley

67197EXPLGBB

Fig. 105 Accessory drive belt routing— 4.6L VIN W or VIN 8 engine

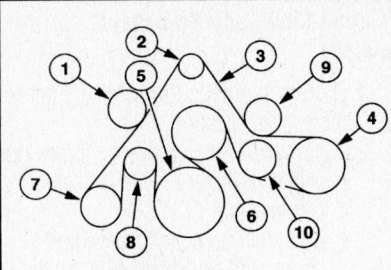

1 Belt idler pulley
2 Generator
3 Drive belt
4 Power steering pump pulley
5 Crankshaft pulley
6 Water pump pulley
7 A/C compressor
8 Drive belt tensioner pulley
9 Belt idler pulley
10 Belt idler pulley

67197EXPLGAA

Fig. 106 Accessory drive belt routing— 4.6L VIN H engine

REMOVAL & INSTALLATION

See Figure 107.

1. Rotate the drive belt tensioner clockwise and remove the drive belt.

⚜ WARNING

Never suddenly let go of the tensioned idler pulley. The force of the spring pressure suddenly released may damage the idler pulley mechanism. Always release the spring pressure gradually.

To install:

2. Route the belt over the pulleys making sure all the grooves in the pulleys and the belt line up correctly. Refer to the accessory belt routing diagrams above.

3. Rotate belt tensioner clockwise and slip drive belt over idler pulley on tensioner.

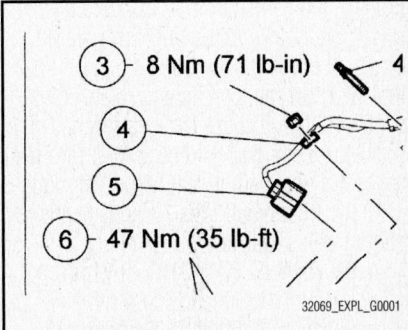

3 - 8 Nm (71 lb-in)
6 - 47 Nm (35 lb-ft)

32069_EXPL_G0001

Fig. 107 Rotate the belt tensioner to relieve tension on the belt—4.6L engine shown, others similar

CAMSHAFT AND VALVE LIFTERS

INSPECTION

Camshaft Lobe Lift

4.0L and 4.6L OHC Engine

See Figure 108.

Check the lift of each lobe in consecutive order and make a note of the readings.

1. Remove the valve covers and spark plugs.

2. Install the Dial Indicator Gauge with Holding Fixture so the rounded tip of indicator is on top of the camshaft lobe and on the same plane as the valve tappet.

3. Rotate the crankshaft using a breaker bar and socket attached to the crankshaft

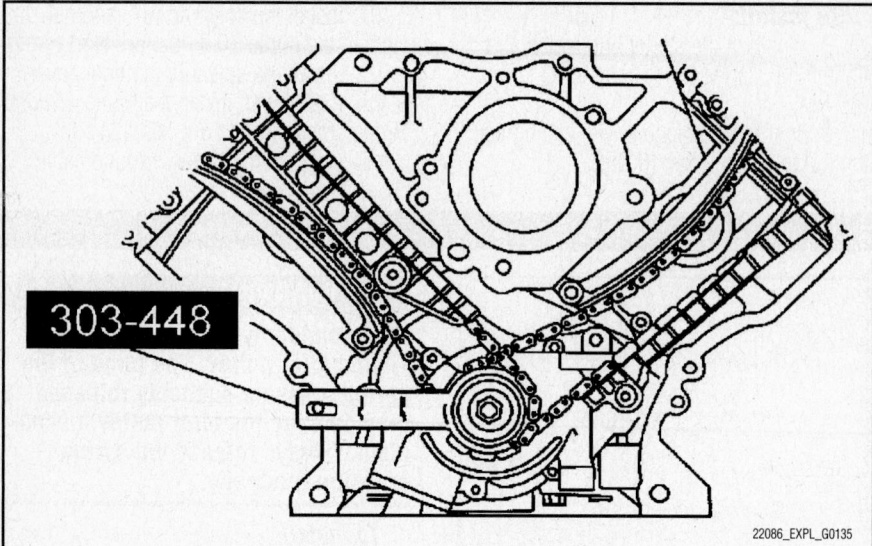

303-448

22086_EXPL_G0135

Fig. 108 Using a dial indicator to measure the amount of camshaft lobe lift—all OHC engines

303-573

22086_EXPL_G0131

Fig. 109 Install the special tool on the crankshaft pulley—4.0L (VIN E, K) SOHC engine

pulley retainer bolt. Rotate the crankshaft until the base circle of the camshaft lobe is reached.

4. Zero the dial indicator. Continue to rotate the crankshaft until the (1) high-lift point of the camshaft lobe is in the fully-raised position (highest indicator reading).

5. To check the accuracy of the original indicator reading, continue to rotate crankshaft until the (2) base circle is reached. The indicator reading should be zero. If zero reading is not obtained, repeat Steps 1 through 6.

6. The camshaft lobe lift specifications should be as follows:

4.0L (VIN E, K) SOHC engine
- Intake: 0.259 inch (6.584 mm)
- Exhaust: 0.259 inch (6.584 mm)
- Maximum allowable lobe lift loss: 0.005 inch (0.127 mm)

4.6L (VIN H) DOHC engine
- Intake: 0.218 inch (5.54 mm)
- Exhaust: 0.218 inch (5.54 mm)
- Maximum allowable lobe lift loss: 0.0051 inch (0.130 mm)

4.6L (VIN 8) SOHC engine
- Intake (2005): 0.2799 inch (7.1104 mm)
- Exhaust (2005): 0.2951 inch (7.4974 mm)
- Maximum allowable lobe lift loss (2005): 0.0000 inch (0.0000 mm)
- Intake (2006–07): 0.2173 inch (5.520 mm)
- Exhaust (2006–07): 0.2168 inch (5.506 mm)
- Maximum allowable lobe lift loss (2006–07): 0.0005 inch (0.0013 mm)

➡If the lift on any lobe is below specified service limits, install a new camshaft, and new camshaft roller followers.

7. Remove the Dial Indicator Gauge with Holding Fixture.

8. Install the spark plugs and valve covers.

REMOVAL & INSTALLATION

4.0L (VIN E, K) SOHC Engine

See Figures 109 through 113.

➡You must carry out the RH and LH camshaft timing procedure when either camshaft is serviced. See "Timing Chain and Sprockets" section.

1. Before servicing the vehicle, refer to the "Precautions" section.

2. Remove or disconnect the following:
- Negative battery cable for safety
- Cooling fan
- Camshaft roller followers; see "Rocker Arms/Shafts (Camshaft Roller Followers)"
- A/C tube bracket (position tube aside)

3. Rotate the crankshaft clockwise to position the number one cylinder at TDC.

✷✷ CAUTION

Do not rotate the engine counterclockwise. Rotating the engine counterclockwise will result in incorrect timing of the engine.

4. Install the special clamping tool, 303-573, onto the crankshaft damper.

5. Install the special tools on the rear of the RH cylinder head and tighten the top 2 clamp bolts to 89 inch lbs. (10 Nm).

✷✷ CAUTION

The RH camshaft sprocket is a LH threaded bolt.

6. Using the special tool and the Camshaft Sprocket Nut Socket, loosen the camshaft sprocket bolt.

7. Remove the RH sprocket bolt and position the camshaft sprocket and chain aside.

8. Install the special tools on the front of the LH camshaft and tighten the 2 top clamp bolts to 89 inch lbs. (10 Nm)

9. Remove the LH camshaft sprocket bolt and position the sprocket and chain aside.

10. On both sides, remove the bolts in the sequence shown and remove the camshaft bearing caps and the oil supply tube.

11. Remove the camshaft.

To install:

12. Lubricate all of the moving parts with clean engine oil.

13. Install camshaft onto the cylinder head.

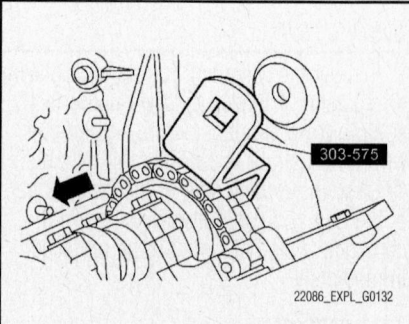

303-575

22086_EXPL_G0132

Fig. 110 Using the special tool with the Camshaft Sprocket Nut Socket 303-565, loosen the RH camshaft sprocket bolt—4.0L (VIN E, K) SOHC engine

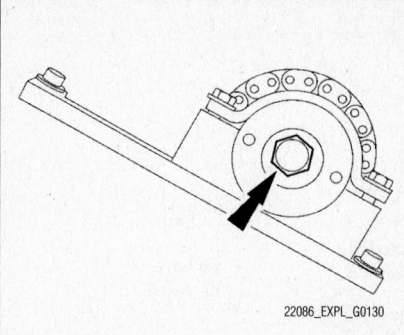

Fig. 111 Install the LH camshaft sprocket special holding tools—4.0L (VIN E, K) SOHC engine

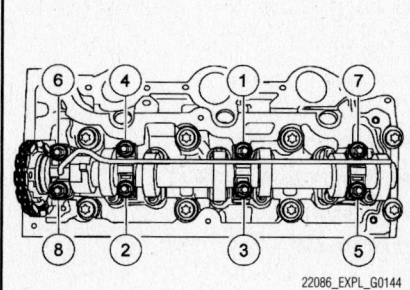

Fig. 112 Remove the bolts in the sequence shown and remove the camshaft bearing caps and the oil supply tube—4.0L (VIN E, K) SOHC engine

14. Install the camshaft bearing caps, in their original locations, and torque the bolts in 2 steps:

   a. Step 1—53.5 inch lbs. (6 Nm).

   b. Step 2—12 ft. lbs. (16 Nm).

15. Install the camshaft oil supply tube.

16. Reposition the camshaft sprocket and chain, for each side, and loosely install the sprocket bolt.

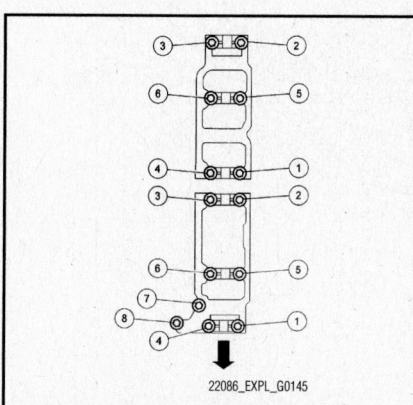

Fig. 113 Camshaft bearing cap torque sequence—4.0L SOHC engine

✳✳ CAUTION

The camshaft gear must turn freely on the camshaft. DO NOT tighten the bolt at this time.

17. Retime the camshafts. See the procedure in "Timing Chain and Sprocket" section.

18. Install or connect the following:
   - Camshaft roller followers
   - A/C tube and bracket
   - Valve covers
   - Cooling fan
   - Negative battery cable

19. Start the engine check for proper operation and leaks. Repair if necessary.

4.6L (VIN W, 8) SOHC Engine

See Figure 114.

1. Before servicing the vehicle, refer to the "Precautions" section.

2. Remove or disconnect the following:

✳✳ WARNING

At no time, when the timing chains are removed and the cylinder heads are installed may the crankshaft or camshaft be rotated. Severe piston and valve damage will occur.

   - Timing chains
   - Camshaft roller followers
   - Camshaft sprocket
   - Camshaft bearing cap bolts (keeping them marked for reinstallation to original locations)
   - Camshaft from the cylinder head

To install:

3. Lubricate the camshaft journals with clean engine oil.

4. Install the camshaft onto the cylinder head.

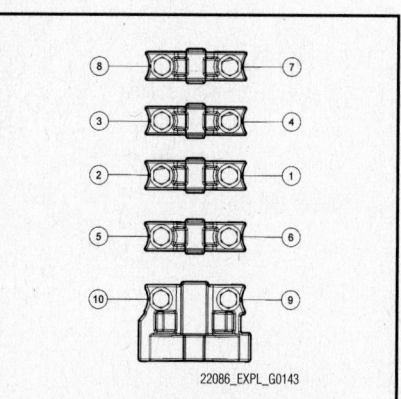

Fig. 114 Camshaft bearing bolt torque sequence—4.6L (VIN 8) SOHC Engine

5. Lubricate the camshaft bearing caps with clean engine oil.

6. Install the camshaft bearing caps and loosely install the bolts.

7. Tighten the bolts in the sequence shown.

8. Install the camshaft sprocket. Tighten the sprocket bolt in two stages.
   - Step 1: Tighten to 30 ft. lbs. (40 Nm)
   - Step 2: Tighten an additional 90 degrees.

9. Install the roller followers

10. Install the timing chains

4.6L (VIN H) DOHC Engine

See Figures 115 through 118.

1. Before servicing the vehicle, refer to the "Precautions" section.

2. Remove the engine front cover, timing gears, chain and tensioners.

3. Remove the valve covers.

4. Remove the roller followers.

5. Remove the spark plugs.

➠Position the piston of the cylinder to be serviced at the bottom of the stroke.

6. Use compressed air in the cylinder to be serviced to hold both valves in position.

7. Install the special tool between the valve spring coils to protect the exhaust valve stem seal from damage.

8. Compress the valve spring. Remove the valve spring retainer keys.

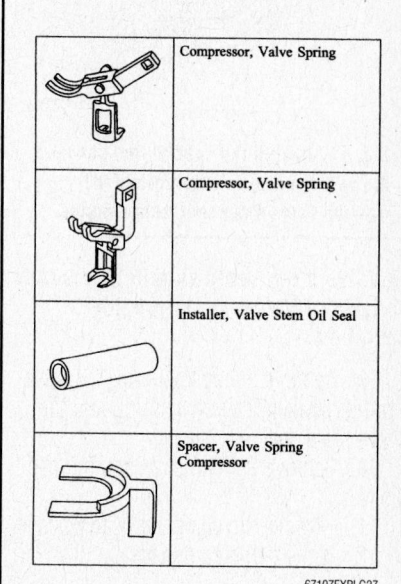

Fig. 115 These tools, or their equivalents, are necessary for camshaft and lifter removal—4.6L DOHC engine

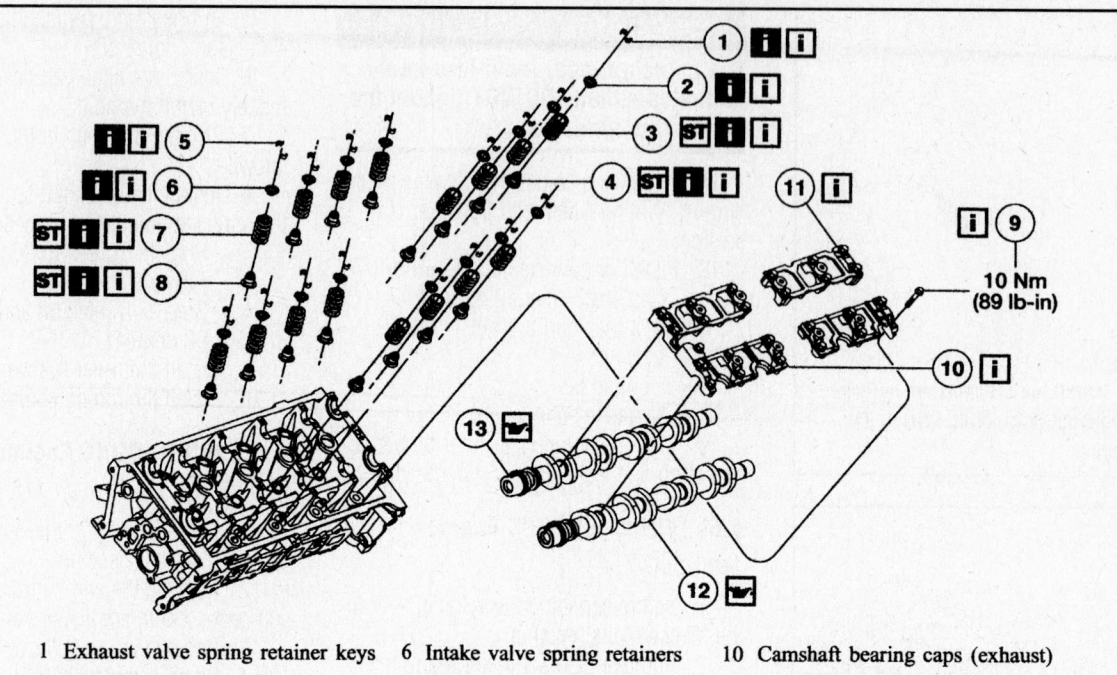

1 Exhaust valve spring retainer keys
2 Exhaust valve spring retainers
3 Exhaust valve springs
4 Exhaust valve stem seals
5 Intake valve spring retainer keys

6 Intake valve spring retainers
7 Intake valve springs
8 Intake valve stem seals
9 Camshaft bearing cap bolts (outboard row)

10 Camshaft bearing caps (exhaust)
11 Camshaft bearing caps (intake)
12 Camshaft (exhaust)
13 Camshaft (intake)

67197EXPLG28

Fig. 116 Valve train exploded view—4.6L DOHC engine

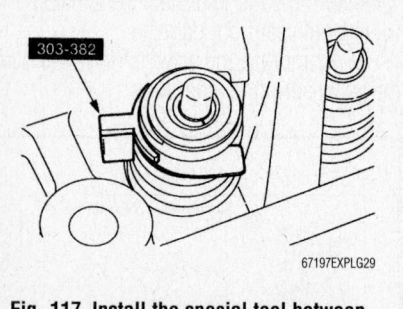

67197EXPLG29

Fig. 117 Install the special tool between the valve spring coils to protect the exhaust valve stem seal from damage

→**Valve stem seals should be visually inspected if new seals are not installed.**

9. Remove the special tool, the valve spring retainer, the valve spring and the valve stem seal.

10. Remove the camshaft bearing cap bolts.

11. Remove the camshaft bearing caps.

12. Remove the camshafts.

To install:

13. Installation is the reverse of the removal procedure.

14. Install the camshaft bearing caps and tighten the fasteners in the sequence shown.

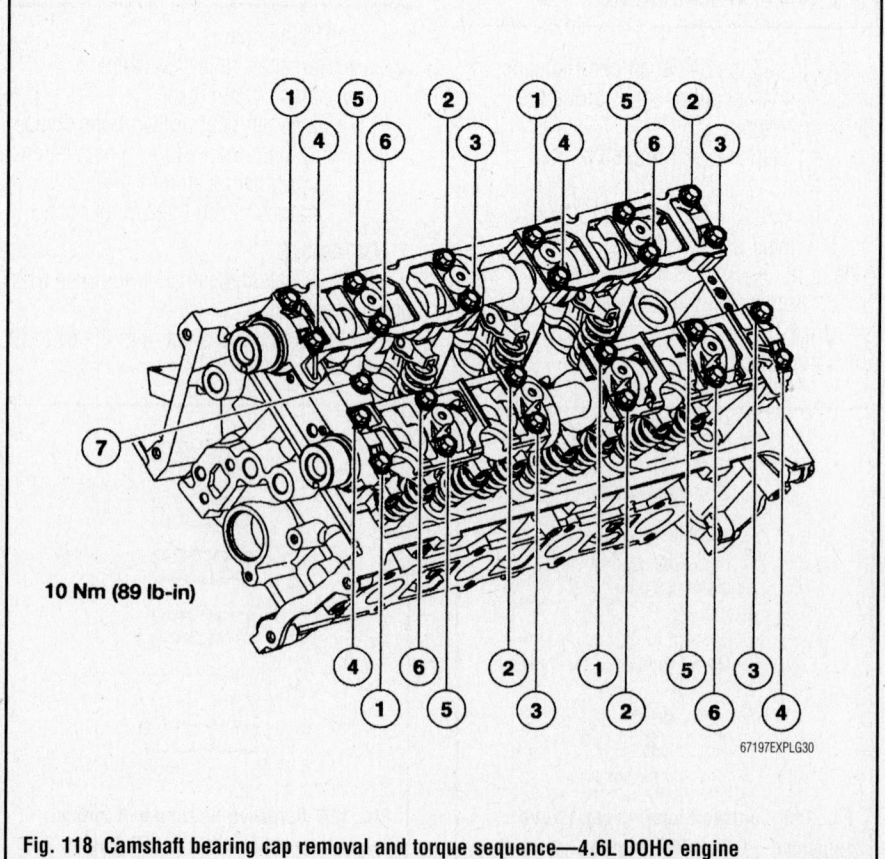

10 Nm (89 lb-in)

67197EXPLG30

Fig. 118 Camshaft bearing cap removal and torque sequence—4.6L DOHC engine

CRANKSHAFT DAMPER

REMOVAL & INSTALLATION

4.0L (VIN E, K) SOHC Engine

1. Remove the engine fan/clutch assembly and shroud.
2. Remove the accessory drive belt.
3. Unbolt and position the power steering cooler aside for clearance, if equipped.
4. Holding the pulley from turning, remove the crankshaft pulley bolt.
5. Use a puller and remove the crankshaft pulley.

To install:

6. Use a crankshaft pulley installation tool, press the pulley onto the crankshaft.

➡**Always use a new damper-to-crankshaft bolt. Do not attempt to re-use the old bolt.**

7. Install the damper-to-crankshaft snout and tighten to:
   a. Step 1: 33 ft. lbs. (45 Nm)
   b. Step 2: additional 85 degrees
8. Reposition the power steering oil cooler, if equipped.
9. Install the accessory drive belt.
10. Install the fan shroud.
11. Run the engine and check for oil leaks.

4.6L (VIN W, 8) SOHC & 4.6L (VIN H) DOHC Engine

1. Remove the engine fan/clutch assembly and shroud.
2. Remove the accessory drive belt.
3. Holding the pulley from turning, remove the crankshaft pulley bolt.
4. Use a puller and remove the crankshaft pulley.

To install:

➡**If the crankshaft pulley is not installed within 4 minutes, the sealant must be removed and the sealing area cleaned.**

5. Apply silicone gasket and sealant to the Woodruff key slot.
6. Use a crankshaft pulley installation tool, press the pulley onto the crankshaft.

➡**Always use a new damper-to-crankshaft bolt. Do not attempt to re-use the old bolt.**

7. Install the crankshaft pulley and tighten the bolt as follows:
   a. Step 1: 66 ft. lbs. (90 Nm)
   b. Step 2: LOOSEN the bolt one full turn

   c. Step 3: 37 ft. lbs. (50 Nm)
   d. Step 4: additional 90 degrees (do not exceed 148 ft. lbs. or 200 Nm of torque)
8. Install the accessory drive belt.
9. Install the fan shroud.
10. Run the engine and check for oil leaks.

CRANKSHAFT FRONT SEAL

REMOVAL & INSTALLATION

4.0L (VIN E, K) SOHC Engine

2005 Explorer and Mountaineer

See Figures 119 through 123.

1. Before servicing the vehicle, refer to the "Precautions" section.
2. Disconnect the battery ground cable
3. Drain the cooling system.
4. Remove the crankshaft front seal.
5. Remove the 2 nuts and detach the power steering pressure hose from the front cover.
6. Remove the 5 oil pan-to-front cover bolts.
7. Release the clamp and disconnect the lower radiator hose.
8. Remove the bolt and the drive belt tensioner.
9. Release the clamp and disconnect the heater hose from the coolant pump.
10. Disconnect the crankshaft position (CKP) sensor electrical connector.
11. Disconnect the alternator electrical connectors and the wiring harness retainer.
12. Remove the 3 alternator bracket bolts and the alternator bracket.
13. Remove the 2 coil bracket-to-left accessory drive bracket bolts.
14. Remove the 4 bolts and the left accessory drive bracket.
15. Remove and discard the CKP sensor wiring harness retainers.
16. Disconnect the engine coolant temperature (ECT) sensor electrical connector.

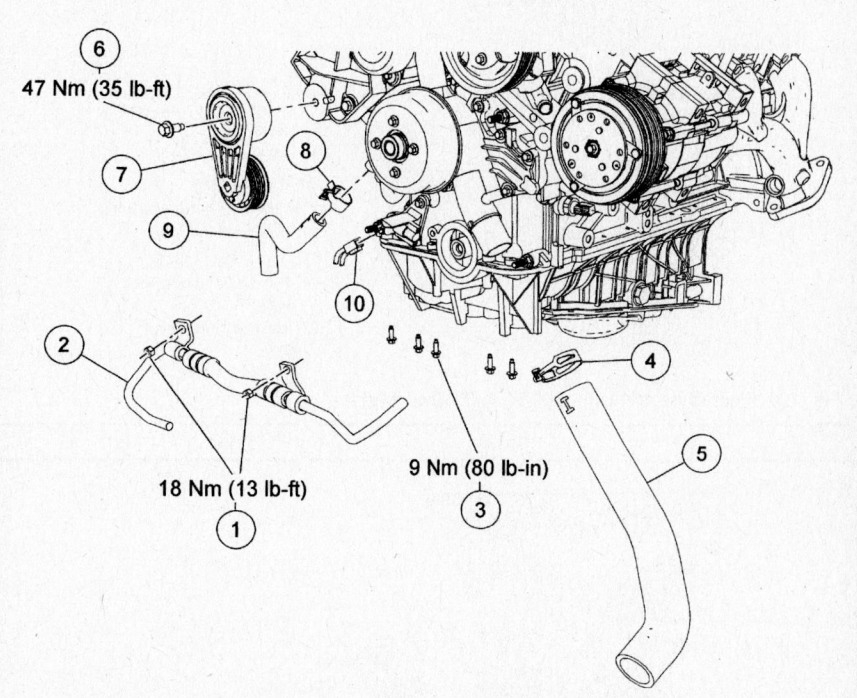

1	A/C hose bracket nuts (2 required)	6	Accessory drive belt tensioner bolt
2	A/C hose	7	Accessory drive belt tensioner
3	Oil pan-to-front cover bolts (5 required)	8	Clamp
4	Lower radiator hose clamp	9	Heater hose
5	Lower radiator hose	10	Crankshaft position sensor electrical connector

06017-EXPL-G45

Fig. 119 Front cover removal, part 1—4.0L SOHC engine

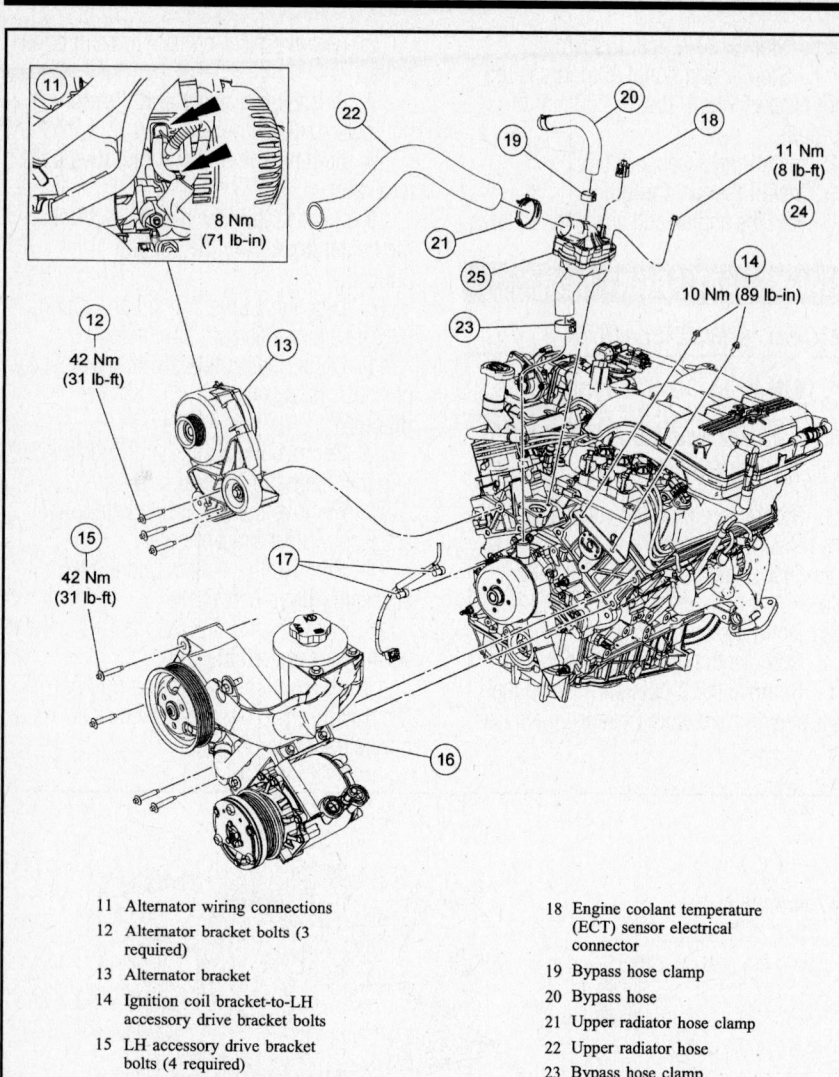

11 Alternator wiring connections
12 Alternator bracket bolts (3 required)
13 Alternator bracket
14 Ignition coil bracket-to-LH accessory drive bracket bolts
15 LH accessory drive bracket bolts (4 required)
16 LH accessory drive bracket
17 Wiring harness routing clips

18 Engine coolant temperature (ECT) sensor electrical connector
19 Bypass hose clamp
20 Bypass hose
21 Upper radiator hose clamp
22 Upper radiator hose
23 Bypass hose clamp
24 Thermostat housing bolts (3 required)
25 Thermostat housing

06017-EXPL-G44

Fig. 120 Front cover removal, part 2—4.0L SOHC engine

25 Engine front cover bolts (10 required)
26 Engine front cover
27 Gasket

06017-EXPL-G46

Fig. 121 Front cover removal—4.0L SOHC engine

17. Release the clamp and disconnect the upper radiator hose from the thermostat housing.

18. Release the clamp and disconnect the heater hose from the thermostat housing.

➡ **The bypass hose will be removed with the thermostat housing.**

19. Release the bypass hose clamp from the coolant pump end.

20. Remove the 3 bolts and the thermostat housing.

➡ **Note the positions of the stud bolts for installation reference**

21. Remove the 10 bolts, the engine front cover and the gasket. Discard the gasket.

To install:

❋❋ **WARNING**

Do not use metal scrapers, wire brushes, power abrasive discs or other abrasive means to clean sealing surfaces. These tools cause scratches and gouges which make leak paths.

22. Clean and inspect the gasket mating surfaces. Use silicone gasket remover and metal surface prep and a plastic or wooden scraping tool. Follow the directions on the packaging.

23. Position the front cover gasket.

❋❋ **WARNING**

If not secured within 4 minutes, the sealant must be removed and the sealing area cleaned. To clean the sealing area, use silicone gasket remover and metal surface prep. Follow the directions on the packaging. Failure to follow this procedure can cause future oil leakage.

24. Apply silicone gasket and sealant to the oil pan and engine block mating surfaces.

06017-EXPL-G47

Fig. 122 Apply silicone gasket and sealant to the oil pan and engine block mating surfaces—4.0L SOHC engine

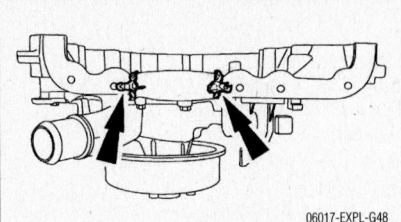

Fig. 123 Apply silicone gasket and sealant to the front cover in 2 places—4.0L SOHC engine

25. Apply silicone gasket and sealant to the front cover in 2 places.

➡**Make sure the stud bolts are installed in their original positions.**

26. Position the front cover and install the 10 bolts. Tighten to 14 ft. lbs. (19 Nm).

➡**Make sure the coolant bypass hose is attached to the coolant pump.**

27. Position the thermostat housing and install the 3 bolts. Tighten to 71 inch lbs. (11 Nm).
28. Position the bypass hose clamp.
29. Connect the upper radiator hose to the thermostat housing and position the clamp.
30. Connect the heater hose to the thermostat housing and position the clamp.
31. Connect the ECT sensor electrical connector.
32. Install new wiring harness retainers and position the CKP sensor wiring.
33. Connect the CKP sensor electrical connector.
34. Position the left accessory drive bracket and install the 4 bolts. Tighten to 31 ft. lbs. (42 Nm).
35. Install the 2 coil bracket-to-left accessory drive bracket bolts. Tighten to 89 inch lbs. (10 Nm).
36. Position the alternator bracket and install the 3 bolts. Tighten to 31 ft. lbs. (42 Nm).
37. Connect the alternator electrical connectors and the wiring harness retainer. Tighten to 71 inch lbs. (8 Nm).
38. Connect the heater hose to the coolant pump and position the clamp.
39. Position the drive belt tensioner and install the bolt. Tighten to 35 ft. lbs. (47 Nm).
40. Connect the lower radiator hose and position the clamp.
41. Install the 5 oil pan-to-front cover bolts. Tighten to 80 inch lbs. (9 Nm).
42. Position the power steering pressure tube and install the 2 nuts. Tighten to 13 ft lbs. (18 Nm).

43. Install the crankshaft front seal.
44. Connect the battery ground cable.
45. Fill the engine cooling system.

2006–07 Explorer and Mountaineer

1. Before servicing the vehicle, refer to the "Precautions" section.
2. Remove the crankshaft pulley. See "Crankshaft Damper" section.
3. Using a proper seal remover, remove the front crankshaft seal.
4. Installation is the reverse of the removal procedure.
5. Lubricate the new seal lip before installation.

2005 Explorer Sport-Trac

1. Before servicing the vehicle, refer to the "Precautions" section.
2. Remove the crankshaft pulley. See "Crankshaft Damper" section.
3. Using a proper seal remover, remove the front crankshaft seal.
4. Installation is the reverse of the removal procedure.
5. Lubricate the new seal lip before installation.

4.6L (VIN W, 8) SOHC & 4.6L (VIN H) DOHC Engine

1. Before servicing the vehicle, refer to the "Precautions" section.
2. Remove the crankshaft pulley. See "Crankshaft Damper" section.
3. Using a proper seal remover, remove the front crankshaft seal.
4. Installation is the reverse of the removal procedure.
5. Lubricate the new seal lip before installation.

CYLINDER HEAD

REMOVAL & INSTALLATION

4.0L (VIN E, K) SOHC Engine

2005 Explorer and Mountaineer

See Figures 124 through 133.

1. Before servicing the vehicle, refer to the "Precautions" section.
2. Disconnect the negative battery cable.
3. With the vehicle in NEUTRAL, position it on a hoist.
4. Drain the engine cooling system.
5. Remove the camshaft roller followers.
6. Remove the accessory drive belt tensioner.
7. On the right side:
   a. Disconnect the alternator electrical connections and disconnect the pushpin.

b. Remove the alternator mounting bracket assembly.
   c. Remove the heater hose from the thermostat housing.
   d. Disconnect the engine coolant temperature (ECT) sensor electrical connector.
   e. Disconnect the upper radiator hose.
   f. Position the coolant bypass hose clamp aside.
   g. Remove the bolts and the thermostat housing.
   h. Remove the engine wiring harness bolts and position the engine wiring harness aside.
   i. Remove the engine ground strap.
8. On the left side:
   a. Disconnect the radio ignition interference capacitor electrical connector.
   b. Remove the bolts.
   c. Remove the bolts and position the accessory bracket aside.
   d. Remove the bolts and the coil bracket.
   e. Remove the oil level indicator tube.

> ❊❊ **WARNING**
>
> **It is important to twist the spark plug wire boots while pulling upward to avoid possible damage to the spark plug wires.**

9. Disconnect all of the spark plug wires from the spark plugs.
10. Remove the engine noise shield.
11. Remove the 4 catalytic converter-to-manifold nuts.
12. Remove both of the exhaust manifolds and gaskets.
13. Discard the gaskets and the retaining nuts.
14. On the right side:
   a. Remove the right side hydraulic chain tensioner.
   b. Install the special tools. Tighten to 89 inch lbs. (10 Nm).
   c. Using the special tool with the Camshaft Sprocket Nut Socket 303-565, remove the right camshaft bolt.
   d. Remove the right side cassette bolt.

> ❊❊ **WARNING**
>
> **Remove the camshaft sprocket from the timing chain to gain clearance to remove the cylinder head.**

➡**Hold the timing chain and cassette with a rubber band to aid in removal and to prevent the timing chain from falling into the cylinder block.**

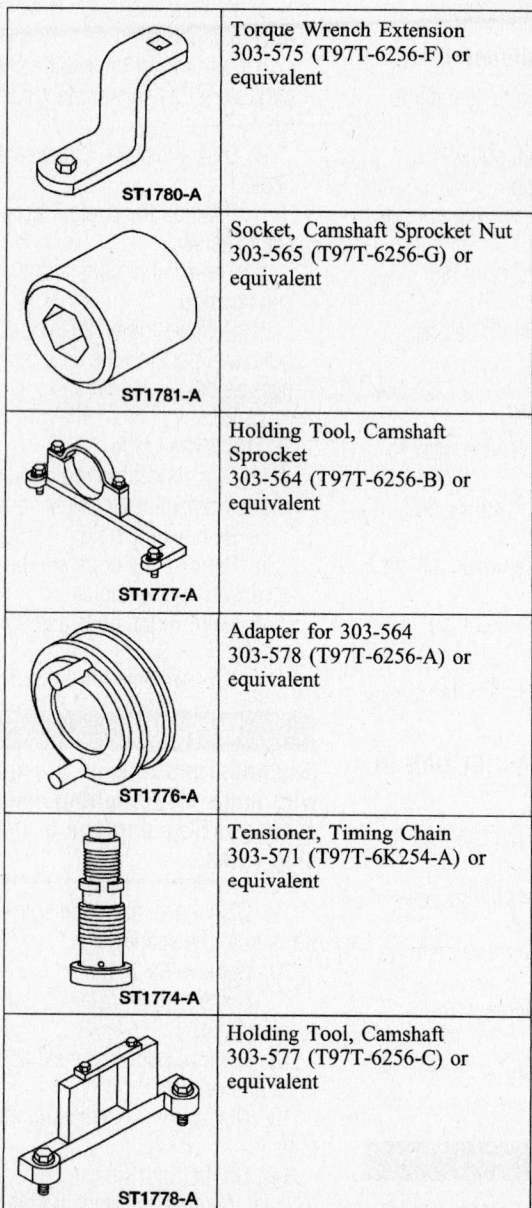

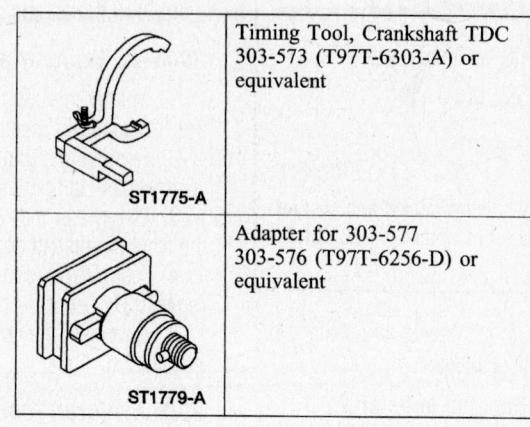

	Torque Wrench Extension 303-575 (T97T-6256-F) or equivalent ST1780-A
	Socket, Camshaft Sprocket Nut 303-565 (T97T-6256-G) or equivalent ST1781-A
	Holding Tool, Camshaft Sprocket 303-564 (T97T-6256-B) or equivalent ST1777-A
	Adapter for 303-564 303-578 (T97T-6256-A) or equivalent ST1776-A
	Tensioner, Timing Chain 303-571 (T97T-6K254-A) or equivalent ST1774-A
	Holding Tool, Camshaft 303-577 (T97T-6256-C) or equivalent ST1778-A
	Timing Tool, Crankshaft TDC 303-573 (T97T-6303-A) or equivalent ST1775-A
	Adapter for 303-577 303-576 (T97T-6256-D) or equivalent ST1779-A

06017-EXPL-G13

Fig. 124 These special tools are necessary for cylinder head removal and installation—2005 4.0L engine

e. Remove the right camshaft sprocket from the timing chain. Install a rubber band around the cassette and the timing chain.

15. On the left side:

a. Remove the left side hydraulic chain tensioner.

b. Install the special tools. Tighten the top clamp bolts to 89 inch lbs. (10 Nm).

c. Remove the left side camshaft sprocket bolt.

d. Remove the left side cassette bolt.

✻✻ WARNING

Remove the camshaft sprocket from the timing chain to gain clearance to remove the cylinder head.

➡Hold the timing chain and cassette with a rubber band to aid in removal and to prevent the timing chain from falling into the cylinder block.

e. Remove the left camshaft sprocket from the timing chain. Install a rubber band around the cassette and the timing chain.

✻✻ WARNING

To avoid damage to the timing chain cassette an assistant will be required to help lift the cylinder head from the vehicle.

✻✻ WARNING

On the left side, when lifting the cylinder head be careful to avoid contacting the A/C tube.

➡**New cylinder head bolts must be installed. They are a torque-to-yield design and cannot be reused.**

16. Remove the cylinder heads.

17. Remove the cylinder head bolts in the sequence shown. Discard all bolts.

18. Remove and discard the head gasket.

✳✳ WARNING

Do not use metal scrapers, wire brushes, power abrasive discs or other abrasive means to clean the sealing surfaces. These tools cause scratches and gouges that make leak paths. Use a plastic scraping tool to remove all traces of the head gasket.

19. Clean and inspect the mating surfaces.

20. Inspect the cylinder head and the cylinder block for flatness

To install:

21. Position the cylinder head gasket on the block.

22. On the right side:

✳✳ WARNING

To avoid damage to the timing chain cassette an assistant will be required to help position the cylinder head in the vehicle.

Fig. 125 Cylinder head bolt loosening sequence—2005 4.0L (VIN E, K) engine

Fig. 126 Right side cylinder head bolt torque sequence—2005 4.0L (VIN E, K) engine

✳✳ WARNING

On the right side, when lifting the cylinder head be careful to avoid contacting the A/C tube.

➡**New cylinder head bolts must be installed. They are a torque-to-yield design and cannot be reused.**

f. Install the cylinder head. Install 8 new 12-mm bolts and tighten in the sequence shown in 2 stages.
- Stage 1: Tighten to 106 inch lbs. (12 Nm).
- Stage 2: Tighten to 18 ft. lbs. (25 Nm).

g. Install 2 new 8-mm bolts. Tighten to 24 ft. lbs. (32 Nm).

h. Tighten the 8 12-mm bolts in the sequence shown in 2 stages.
- Stage 1: Tighten the bolts 90 degrees.
- Stage 2: Tighten the bolts an additional 90 degrees.

✳✳ WARNING

The camshaft gear must turn freely on the camshaft. DO NOT tighten the bolt at this time

i. Remove the rubber band. Install the camshaft sprocket and bolt.

j. Install the right side cassette bolt. Tighten to 106 inch lbs. (12 Nm).

23. On the left side:

✳✳ WARNING

To avoid damage to the timing chain cassette, an assistant will be required to help position the cylinder head in the vehicle.

➡**New cylinder head bolts must be installed. They are a torque-to-yield design and cannot be reused.**

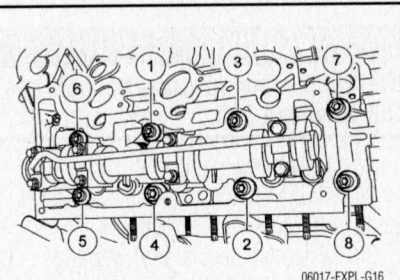

Fig. 127 Left side cylinder head bolt torque sequence—2005 4.0L (VIN E, K) engine

k. Install the cylinder head. Install 8 new 12-mm bolts and tighten in the sequence shown in 2 stages.
- Stage 1: Tighten to 106 inch lbs. (12 Nm).
- Stage 2: Tighten to 18 ft. lbs. (25 Nm).

l. Install 2 new 8-mm bolts. Tighten to 24 ft. lbs. (32 Nm).

m. Tighten the 8 12-mm bolts in the sequence shown in 2 stages.
- Stage 1: Tighten the bolts 90 degrees.
- Stage 2: Tighten the bolts an additional 90 degrees.

✳✳ WARNING

The camshaft gear must turn freely on the camshaft. DO NOT tighten the bolt at this time.

n. Remove the rubber band. Install the camshaft sprocket and bolt.

o. Install the left side cassette bolt. Tighten to 14 ft. lbs. (19 Nm).

24. Install both of the exhaust manifolds gaskets, the exhaust manifolds and the nuts. Tighten to 16 ft. lbs. (22 Nm).

➡**Apply dielectric compound to the inside of the spark plug wire boots.**

25. Connect all of the spark plug wires to the spark plugs.

26. Install the 4 catalytic converter-to-exhaust manifold nuts. Tighten to 30 ft. lbs. (40 Nm).

27. Install the engine noise shield.

28. On the right side:

a. Install the engine ground strap and the bolt. Tighten to 89 inch lbs. (10 Nm).

b. Position the engine wiring harness and install the bolts. Tighten to 35 ft. lbs. (47 Nm).

➡**Inspect the O-ring seal. Install a new O-ring seal if necessary.**

c. Install the thermostat housing and the bolts. Tighten to 71 inch lbs. (11 Nm).

d. Position the coolant bypass hose clamp.

e. Install the upper radiator hose.

f. Connect the engine coolant temperature (ECT) sensor electrical connector.

g. Install the heater hose to the thermostat housing.

h. Install the alternator mounting bracket assembly and the bolts. Tighten to 31 ft. lbs. (42 Nm).

i. Connect the alternator electrical connections and install the pushpin. Tighten to 71 inch lbs. (8 Nm).

29. On the left side:

a. Install the oil level indicator tube and bolt. Tighten to 89 inch lbs. (10 Nm).

b. Install the coil bracket and the bolts. Tighten to 89 inch lbs (10 Nm).

c. Install the accessory bracket and the bolts. Tighten to 31 ft. lbs. (42 Nm).

d. Install the vertical bolts. Tighten to 89 inch lbs. (10 Nm).

e. Connect the radio ignition interference capacitor electrical connector.

30. Install the accessory drive belt tensioner.

➡**You must retime the left and right camshafts when either camshaft is disturbed.**

31. Turn the crankshaft clockwise to position the number one cylinder at top dead center (TDC).

32. Remove the retainer and position the A/C manifold tube bracket aside.

❊❊ **WARNING**

Do not rotate the engine counterclockwise. Rotating the engine counterclockwise will result in incorrect timing of the engine.

➡**The special tool must be installed on the damper and should contact the engine block, this positions the engine at TDC.**

33. Install special tool 303 573 as shown.

➡**Leave the top 2 special tool clamp bolts loose.**

34. Install special tools 303 578 and 303 564 on the rear of the right cylinder head.

➡**The camshaft timing slots are off-center.**

35. Position the camshaft timing slots below the centerline of the camshaft to

Fig. 128 Tool 303-573 installed—2005 4.0L (VIN E, K) engine

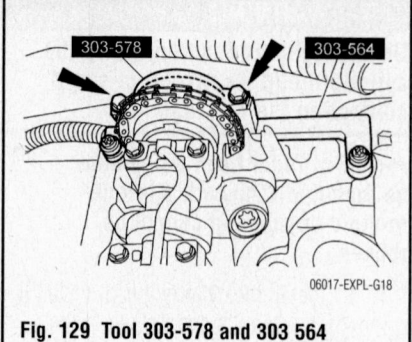

Fig. 129 Tool 303-578 and 303 564 installed—2005 4.0L (VIN E, K) engine

Fig. 130 Tools 303 576 and 303 577 installed—2005 4.0L (VIN E, K) engine

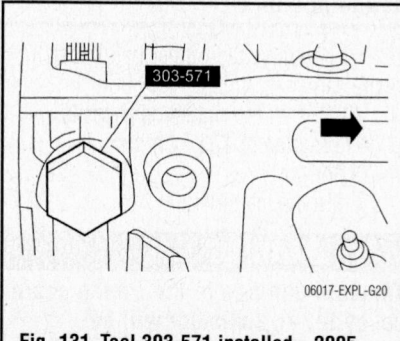

Fig. 131 Tool 303-571 installed—2005 4.0L (VIN E, K) engine

correctly fit the special tools 303 576 and 303 577, and install the special tools on the front of the right cylinder head. Install special tool 303 571.

❊❊ **WARNING**

The right camshaft sprocket bolt is a left threaded bolt.

36. Tighten the bolts.

37. Tighten the special tool top clamp bolts to 89 inch lbs. (10 Nm).

38. Using the special tool with the Camshaft Sprocket Nut Socket 303-565, tighten the camshaft bolt. Tighten to 45 ft. lbs. (61 Nm).

39. Install the right camshaft tensioner. Tighten to 32 ft. lbs. (44 Nm).

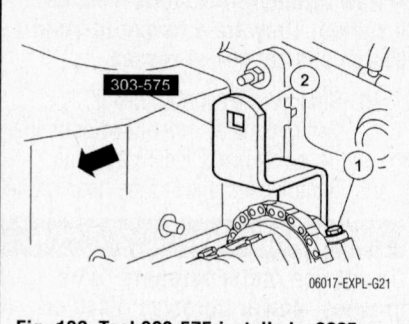

Fig. 132 Tool 303-575 installed—2005 4.0L (VIN E, K) engine

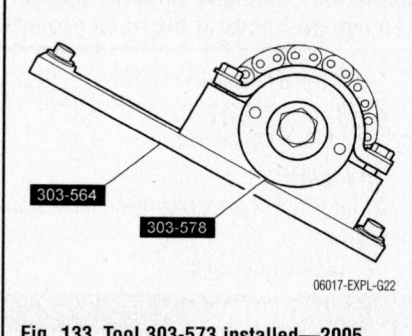

Fig. 133 Tool 303-573 installed—2005 4.0L (VIN E, K) engine

➡**Leave the top 2 special tool clamp bolts loose.**

40. Install special tools 303 564 and 303 578 on the front of the left cylinder head.

➡**The camshaft timing slots are off-center.**

41. Position the camshaft timing slots below the centerline of the camshaft to correctly fit the special tools, and install special tools on the rear of the left cylinder head.

42. Install special tools 303 576 and 303 577. Tighten the bolts.

43. Tighten the special tool top 2 clamp bolts to 89 inch lbs. (10 Nm).

44. Tighten the camshaft bolt. Tighten to 63 ft. lbs. (85 Nm).

45. Install the left camshaft tensioner. Tighten to 32 ft. lbs. (44 Nm).

46. Install the A/C manifold tube assembly bracket and the nut. Tighten to 15 ft. lbs. (20 Nm).

47. Install the roller followers.

48. Fill and bleed the engine cooling system.

2006–07 Explorer and Mountaineer; 2007 Explorer Sport-Trac

See Figures 134 through 138.

1. Before servicing the vehicle, refer to the "Precautions" section.

2. Drain the cooling system.

3. Remove the camshaft roller followers. See "Rocker Arms/Shafts" section.

4. Remove the accessory drive belt.

5. On RH side cylinder head, remove or disconnect the following:
- Heater hose tube bracket (position aside)
- Battery ground cable
- Alternator electrical connections and disconnect the pushpin
- Accessory drive belt tensioner
- Alternator mounting bracket assembly
- Heater hose from the thermostat housing
- ECT sensor electrical connector
- Upper radiator hose
- Coolant bypass hose
- Thermostat housing
- Position the engine wiring harness aside
- Engine ground strap
- Spark plug wires
- Catalytic converter-to-RH exhaust manifold nuts
- RH exhaust manifold and the gasket
- 6 RH exhaust manifold studs
- RH side hydraulic chain tensioner bolt on side of cylinder head
- Holding tool onto RH camshaft
- RH camshaft sprocket nut
- RH camshaft cassette bolt
- RH camshaft sprocket

➡**Use a rubber band around the chain and cassette to hold the chain from falling.**

6. On the LH side cylinder head, remove or disconnect the following:
- Heater hose tube bracket (position aside)
- LH radio interference capacitor connector
- 2 bolts as shown
- Power steering pump bracket (position aside without disconnecting the pump lines)
- Ignition coil bracket
- Oil level indicator tube
- Exhaust pipe from LH exhaust manifold (discard nuts and gasket)
- LH exhaust manifold (discard nuts and gasket)
- 6 LH exhaust manifold studs
- LH camshaft chain tensioner bolt from side of head

7. Install a camshaft sprocket holding tool and remove the sprocket bolt.

8. Remove the LH camshaft cassette bolt in the front of the head.

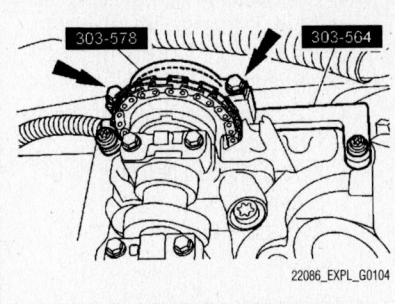

Fig. 134 Install a holding tool onto RH camshaft—2006-07 4.0L Explorer, Sport-Trac & Mountaineer

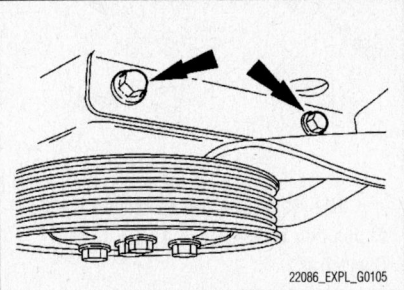

Fig. 135 Remove the 2 bolts as shown—2006-07 4.0L Explorer, Sport-Trac & Mountaineer

9. Wrap a rubber band around the camshaft chain to the cassette to prevent it from falling during removal.

10. Remove the LH camshaft sprocket

⚹⚹ **CAUTION**

To avoid damage to the camshaft cassette, an assistant will be required to lift the cylinder head from the vehicle. Watch the A/C tube on the RH side when lifting the head.

11. For either cylinder head, using the sequence shown, remove and discard the cylinder head bolts.

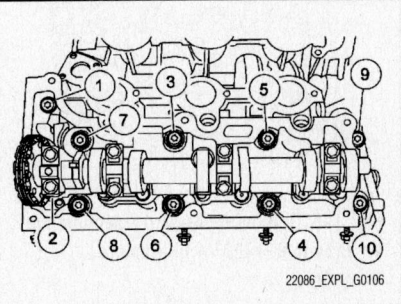

Fig. 136 Remove the cylinder head bolts in the sequence shown—2006-07 4.0L Explorer, Sport-Trac & Mountaineer

12. Lift the cylinder head(s) from the vehicle. Discard the gaskets.

To install:

➡**The installation procedure that follows is for either cylinder head, unless otherwise specified.**

13. Clean all mating surfaces. Clean the bolt holes.

14. Position the new cylinder head gasket on the block mating surface.

15. Carefully set the cylinder head into position, watching for any possible interference with engine components.

16. Install the new 12mm bolts and tighten in 2 stages, in the sequence shown:
   a. Stage 1: 9 ft. lbs. (12 Nm)
   b. Stage 2: 18 ft. lbs. (25 Nm)

17. Install the 2 8mm bolts near the front of the cylinder head. Tighten the bolts to 24 ft. lbs. (32 Nm).

18. Now, retighten the 8 12mm cylinder head bolts, in the same sequence as above, to the following:
   a. Stage 1: 90 degrees additional
   b. Stage 2: 90 degrees additional

19. Install or connect the following:
- Camshaft chain and sprocket
- Camshaft cassette bolt (RH side); tighten to 89 inch lbs. (10 ft. lbs.)

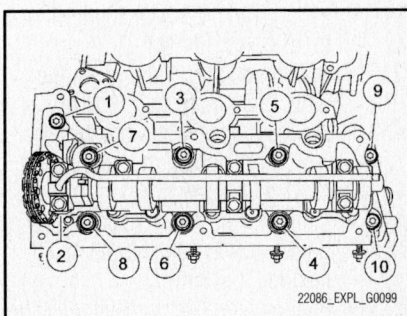

Fig. 137 Cylinder head 12mm bolt tightening sequence—2005 4.0L (VIN E, K) SOHC engine

Fig. 138 Installing the 2 8mm cylinder head bolts—2005 4.0L (VIN E, K) SOHC engine

- New exhaust manifold studs; tighten to 9 ft. lbs. (12 Nm)
- Exhaust manifold; tighten the new nuts to 16 ft. lbs. (22 Nm)
- Exhaust pipe to the manifold; tighten the new nuts to 30 ft. lbs. (40 Nm)
- Spark plug wires to spark plugs (apply dielectric grease inside boots before installation)
- Engine ground strap (RH side)
- Engine wiring harness retaining bolt to side of engine; tighten bolt to 35 ft. lbs. (47 Nm) (RH side)
- Thermostat housing; torque the bolts to 8 ft. lbs. (11 Nm)
- Coolant hose to thermostat housing
- Upper radiator hose
- ECT sensor connector
- Heater hose to thermostat housing
- Oil level indicator tube (LH side)

20. Time the camshafts. See "Camshaft and Valve Lifters" section.

21. Install or connect the following:
- Alternator bracket; tighten the bolts to 31 ft. lbs. (42 Nm)
- Accessory drive belt tensioner; tighten the bolt to 35 ft. lbs. (47 Nm)
- Alternator electrical connections
- Heater hose tube bracket; rear bolt to 17 ft. lbs. (25 Nm) and front bolt to 25 ft. lbs. (34 Nm)
- Ignition coil bracket; tighten the bolts to 89 inch lbs. (10 Nm)
- A/C compressor and power steering pump; tighten mounting bolts to 31 ft. lbs. (42 Nm)
- Ignition coil bracket to accessory drive bracket; tighten bolts to 89 inch lbs. (10 Nm)
- Radio interference capacitor electrical connector
- Accessory drive belt

22. Fill and bleed the cooling system.

2005 Explorer Sport-Trac

See Figures 139 through 144.

See Figures 145 through 152.

1. Before servicing the vehicle, refer to the "Precautions" section.
2. Drain the cooling system.
3. Remove or disconnect the following:
- Negative battery cable
- Intake manifold; see "Intake Manifold" in this section
- Cooling fan shroud
- Accessory drive belt
- Both valve covers
- Alternator electrical connections
- Alternator and bracket

- CKP sensor electrical connector
- Wiring harness from retainers across front of engine (discard retainers)
- ECT sensor electrical connector
- Thermostat housing
- Wiring harness clip on side of engine
- Accessory bracket (position aside)

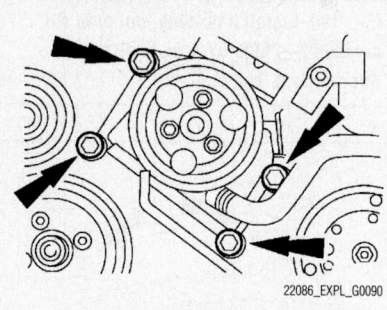

Fig. 139 Removing the accessory bracket to position aside—2005 4.0L Explorer Sport-Trac

- Wiring harness casing from LH cylinder head
- Oil level indicator tube
- LH bank spark plug wires
- Fuel rail and temperature sensor electrical and vacuum connectors

4. Remove the fuel injection supply manifold as follows:

a. Remove the fuel supply tube from the fuel manifold. Position the fuel supply tube aside.

b. Remove the fuel rail bolts. Remove the fuel rail and the fuel injectors as an assembly.

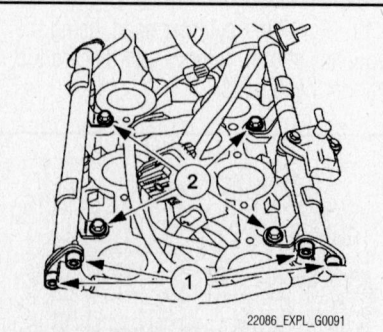

Fig. 140 Removing the fuel injection supply manifold—2005 4.0L Explorer Sport-Trac

5. Remove the camshaft roller followers.
6. Using the special tool 303-573, set the No. 1 piston to TDC.

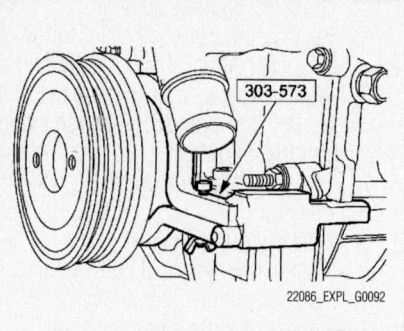

Fig. 141 Using the special tool 303-573, set the No. 1 piston to TDC—2005 4.0L Explorer Sport-Trac

7. On the RH cylinder head, remove or disconnect the following:
- RH fenderwell splash shield
- RH camshaft chain tensioner
- RH exhaust manifold
- Bolt and bracket as shown
- RH camshaft sprocket bolt

➡ **The using of a special holding tool, 303-575, may be necessary.**

- Chain guide bolt
- RH camshaft sprocket (use a heavy

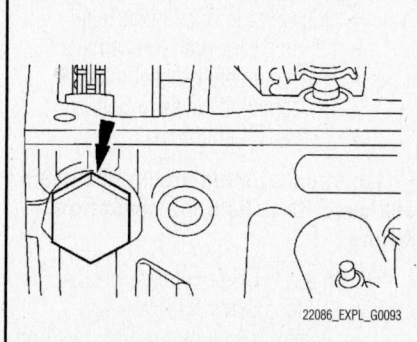

Fig. 142 Remove the RH camshaft chain tensioner—2005 4.0L Explorer Sport-Trac

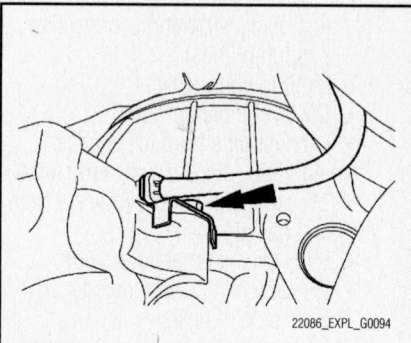

Fig. 143 Remove the bolt and bracket as shown—2005 4.0L Explorer Sport-Trac

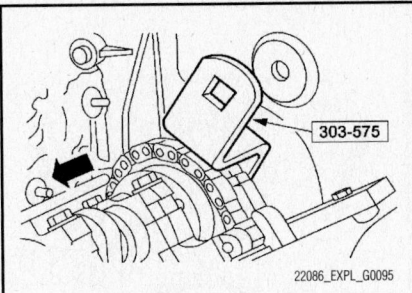

Fig. 144 Using the holding tool while removing the RH camshaft sprocket bolt—2005 4.0L Explorer Sport-Trac

rubber band to hold timing chain on cassette)

8. Remove the 8 12mm bolts and the 2 8mm bolts, in the sequence shown, and remove the RH cylinder head.

9. On the LH cylinder head, remove or disconnect the following:
- LH exhaust manifold
- Ground strap from rear of engine block
- LH hydraulic chain tensioner
- LH camshaft sprocket
- LH camshaft chain guide bolt in front of the block

10. Hold the camshaft chain and

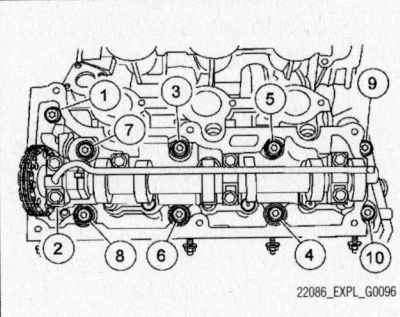

Fig. 145 Cylinder head bolt removal sequence—2005 4.0L Explorer Sport-Trac

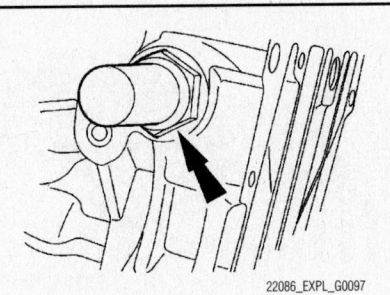

Fig. 146 Showing the location of the LH hydraulic chain tensioner—2005 4.0L Explorer Sport-Trac

cassette with a rubber band, as shown, to aid removal and to prevent chain from falling into the cylinder block.

11. Remove the LH camshaft sprocket from the cassette.

Fig. 147 Holding the chain and cassette with a rubber band during removal—2005 4.0L Explorer Sport-Trac

12. Remove the 8 12mm bolts and the 2 8mm bolts, in the sequence shown, and remove the LH cylinder head.

To install:

➡️**These installation procedures are the same for both cylinder heads, unless specified.**

13. Clean the cylinder head and block mating surfaces. Clean the bolt holes.

14. Position the cylinder head and new gasket onto the block.

15. Install the 12mm bolts and tighten in 2 stages, in the sequence shown:
   a. Stage 1: 9 ft. lbs. (12 Nm)
   b. Stage 2: 18 ft. lbs. (25 Nm)

16. Install the 2 8mm bolts near the front of the cylinder head. Tighten the bolts to 24 ft. lbs. (32 Nm).

17. Now, retighten the 8 12mm cylinder head bolts, in the same sequence as above, to the following:
   a. Stage 1: 90 degrees additional
   b. Stage 2: 90 degrees additional

18. Install or connect the following:

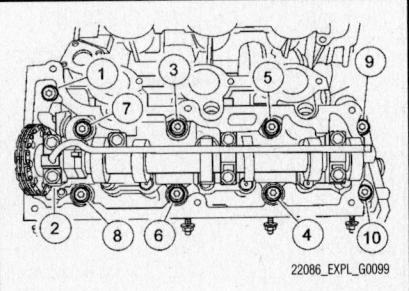

Fig. 148 Cylinder head 12mm bolt tightening sequence—2005 4.0L Explorer Sport-Trac

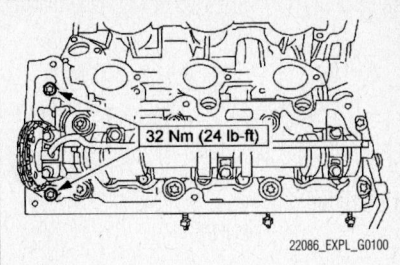

Fig. 149 Installing the 2 8mm cylinder head bolts—2005 4.0L Explorer Sport-Trac

- Camshaft sprocket into the cassette
- Camshaft sprocket bolt into place, but DO NOT tighten at this time
- Chain guide bolt to the side of the sprocket; torque to 89 inch lbs. (10 Nm)
- Bracket and bolt as shown
- Exhaust manifold; see "Exhaust Manifold" in this section

19. If needed, use the camshaft gear torque adapter tool, 303-565, to loosen the sprocket bolt.

20. Position the camshaft timing slots below the centerline of the camshaft and install the camshaft holding tools onto the camshaft, as shown.

21. Install the special holding tool onto the rear of the cylinder head, leaving the top 2 clamp bolts loose.

22. Install the camshaft chain tensioner bolt to the side of the cylinder head.

23. Tighten the top 2 special tool clamp bolts to 89 inch lbs. (10 Nm).

24. Tighten the camshaft bolt, using the special tool, as follows:
   a. LH cylinder head: 45 ft. lbs. (61 Nm)
   b. RH cylinder head: 63 ft. lbs. (85 Nm)

25. Tighten the camshaft tensioner bolt to 32 ft. lbs. (44 Nm).

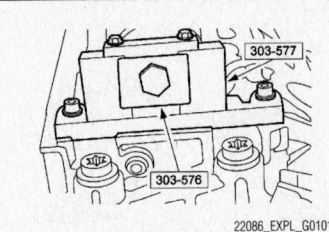

Fig. 150 Position the camshaft timing slots below the centerline of the camshaft and install the camshaft holding tools onto the camshaft, as shown—2005 4.0L Explorer Sport-Trac

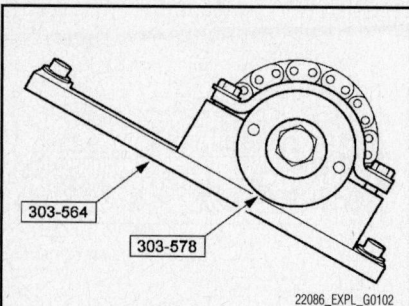

Fig. 151 Install the special holding tool onto the rear of the cylinder head, leaving the top 2 clamp bolts loose—2005 4.0L Explorer Sport-Trac

26. Repeat the above procedure for the other cylinder head, if necessary.

27. Install the camshaft roller followers.

28. Install the fuel injection supply manifold, as follows:

a. Install the fuel injection supply manifold and the fuel injectors as an assembly.

b. Install the fuel supply tube to the fuel manifold.

c. Tighten the bolts, as shown.

29. Install or connect the following:

- Fuel rail pressure and temperature sensor electrical and vacuum connections
- Spark plug wires
- Oil level indicator tube
- Wiring harness retainers
- Accessory bracket
- Thermostat housing and bypass hose
- ECT and CKP sensor connectors
- Alternator and mounting bracket; see "Alternator" section
- Alternator electrical connections
- Valve cover(s); see "Valve (Camshaft) Covers" section
- Accessory drive belt

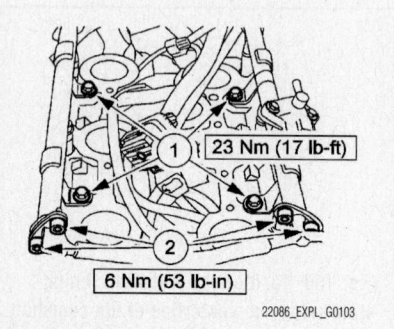

Fig. 152 Tighten the fuel supply manifold bolts, as shown—2005 4.0L Explorer Sport-Trac

- Cooling fan shroud
- Intake manifold; see "Intake Manifold" section
- Refill and bleed the cooling system.

4.6L (VIN W) SOHC Engine

2005 Explorer and Mountaineer

See Figures 153 through 159.

See Figures 160 and 161.

1. Before servicing the vehicle, refer to the "Precautions" section.

➡**Clean all mating surfaces as components are removed during this procedure.**

2. Remove the engine. See "Engine Assembly" section.

3. Transfer the engine to a proper workstand.

4. Remove or disconnect the following for access to the cylinder heads:

- Flexplate and spacer plate
- Accessory drive belt
- Wiring harness bracket behind the crankshaft pulley
- Power steering hose support bracket
- Hoses from the power steering pump
- Power steering pump
- Radio interference capacitor and ground wire from cylinder head
- Power steering reservoir and bracket
- A/C compressor and CKP sensor electrical connectors
- Wiring harness retainers
- A/C tube retainers
- Crankcase air inlet tube
- Upper radiator hose bracket
- Radio interference capacitor (set aside)
- 3 idler pulleys
- Alternator

Fig. 153 Remove the radio interference capacitor and ground wire and position out of the way—2005 4.6L (VIN W) SOHC engine

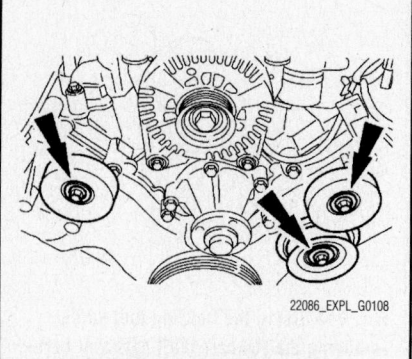

Fig. 154 Remove the 3 idler pulleys—2005 4.6L (VIN W) SOHC engine

- CMP sensor
- Water pump pulley
- EGR tube from across the engine
- RH and LH exhaust manifolds; see "Exhaust Manifold" in this section
- Oil dipstick tube
- Brake booster vacuum hose
- Throttle position sensor and throttle body connectors
- PCV tube and crankcase tube from throttle body adapter
- EGR module and fuel pressure sensor vacuum connections
- EGR module and fuel pressure sensor electrical connections
- Cylinder head temperature (CHT) sensor connector
- Knock sensor connector and wiring harness retainer
- All coolant hoses from the engine
- Electronic throttle body and gasket
- Fuel injectors, ignition coil and ground connections, and wiring harness from both heads
- Ground wire from the manifold
- All remaining wiring harness connections

Fig. 155 Remove the throttle position sensor and throttle body connectors—2005 4.6L (VIN W) SOHC engine

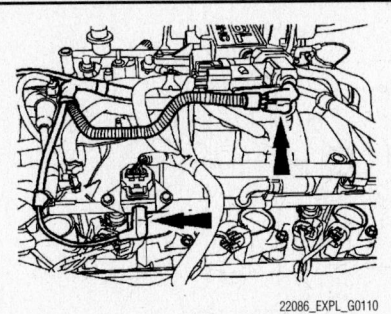

Fig. 156 Remove the EGR module and fuel pressure sensor vacuum connections— 2005 4.6L (VIN W) SOHC engine

- 8 ignition coils
- Thermostat housing
- Intake manifold and gaskets
- Engine mounts
- Cylinder block drain plugs; reinstall after coolant is drained
- Valve covers
- Spark plugs
- Crankshaft pulley
- Crankshaft front oil seal
- Oil pan
- Engine front cover and gaskets
- Crankshaft sensor ring
- Camshaft roller followers; see "Rocker Arms/Shafts (Camshaft Roller Followers)" section
- Both timing chains and guides; see "Timing Chain and Sprockets" section

5. Install lifting handles on each end of the cylinder head.

6. Remove the hydraulic lash adjusters.

7. Remove the coolant tube from between the heads.

8. Remove the cylinder head bolts, cylinder heads and gaskets.

9. Carefully clean all cylinder head mating surfaces and bolt holes.

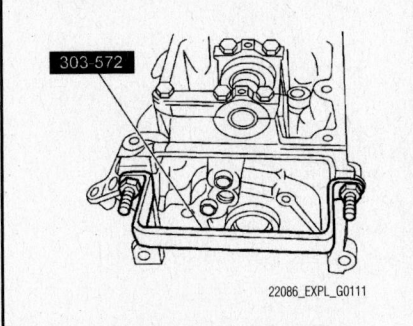

Fig. 157 Install lifting handles on each end of the cylinder head—2005 4.6L (VIN W) SOHC engine

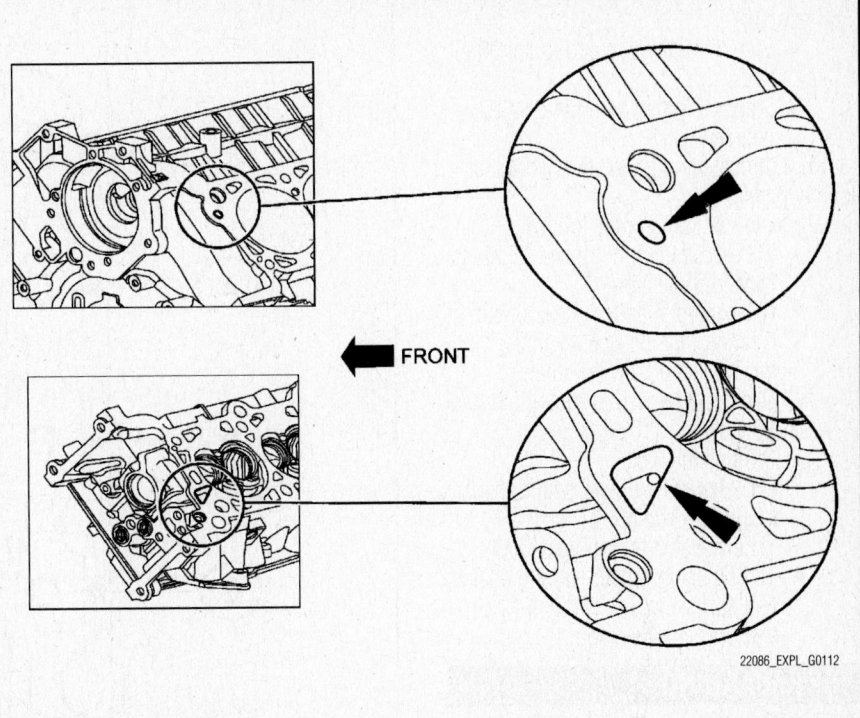

Fig. 158 Inspect the areas shown for any signs of wear, corrosion or deep scratches—2005 4.6L (VIN W) SOHC engine

To install:

10. Carefully clean all cylinder head mating surfaces and bolt holes.

11. Use a straightedge to check the cylinder head surface flatness. Any distortion must be within 0.0004 in. (0.010 mm) from end to end.

12. Inspect the areas shown for any signs of wear, corrosion or deep scratches.

13. Install new cylinder head gaskets over the mounting dowels on the block.

14. Install the cylinder and new bolts. Tighten the bolts, in sequence, in six stages.

- Step 1: Tighten to 30 ft. lbs. (40 Nm).
- Step 2: Tighten an additional 90 degrees.
- Step 3: Back out all bolts one full turn (360 degrees).

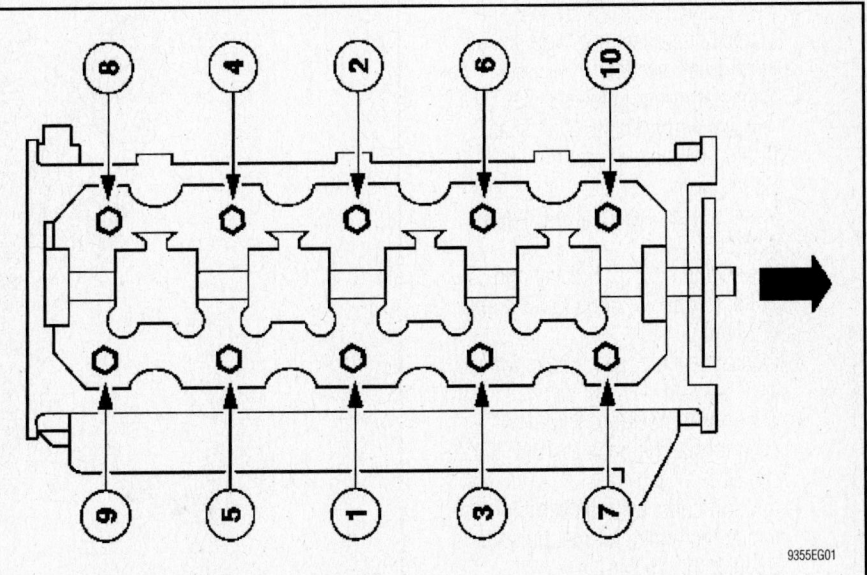

Fig. 159 Left cylinder head bolt torque sequence—2005 4.6L (VIN W) SOHC engine

- Step 4: Tighten to 30 ft. lbs. (40 Nm).
- Step 5: Tighten an additional 90 degrees.
- Step 6: Tighten an additional 90 degrees.

15. Lubricate and install the hydraulic lash adjusters.

16. Install or connect the following:
- RH exhaust manifold; see "Exhaust Manifold" section
- RH exhaust manifold heat shield
- Coolant tube between cylinder heads; install new, lubricated O-rings if needed; torque the nut to 89 inch lbs. (10 Nm)
- Oil dipstick tube
- LH exhaust manifold; see "Exhaust Manifold" section
- LH exhaust manifold heat shield
- Timing chain guides, timing chains and sprockets; see "Timing Chain and Sprocket" section

※※ WARNING

During these procedures, rotate the crankshaft counterclockwise ONLY, and only to the proper position or piston damage will occur. (See "Timing Chain and Sprocket" section.)

- Crankshaft sensor ring onto the crankshaft

17. Apply a 0.32 in. (8 mm) bead of sealant at the points where the cylinder heads meet the block at the vertical front end of the engine.

18. Install new gaskets and the front cover. See "Timing Chain Cover and Seal" section.

19. Install or connect the following:
- New crankshaft front oil seal and crankshaft pulley; see "Crankshaft Front Seal" section
- Camshaft roller followers; see "Rocker Arms/Shafts (Camshaft Roller Followers)" section
- Spark plugs
- Valve covers; see "Valve Covers" section
- RH engine support bracket and bolts; torque the bolts to 53 ft. lbs. (72 Nm)
- Intake manifold; see "Intake Manifold" section
- Thermostat housing, with new O-ring; torque the bolts to 18 ft. lbs. (25 Nm)
- Ignition coils, with dielectric grease inside the boots; torque the bolts to 53 inch lbs. (6 Nm)
- Engine wiring harnesses
- Engine ground wire

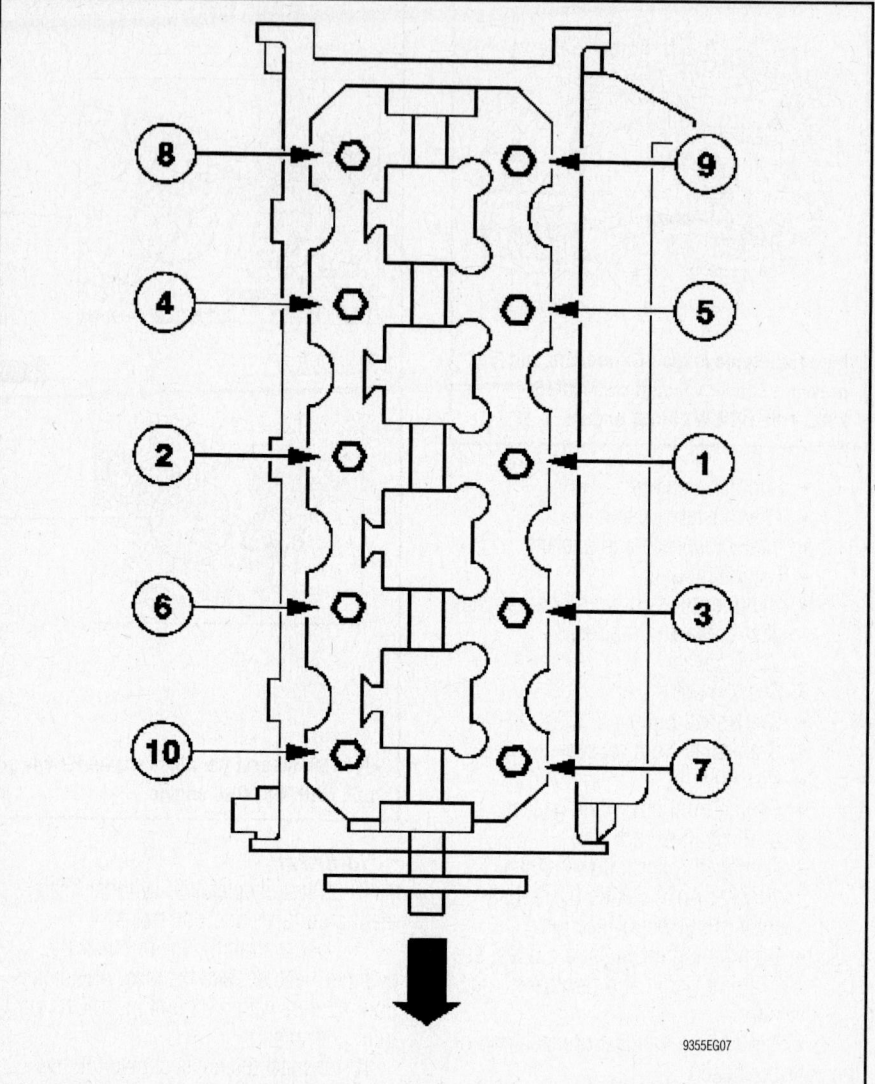

9355EG07

Fig. 160 Right cylinder head bolt torque sequence—2005 4.6L (VIN W) SOHC engine

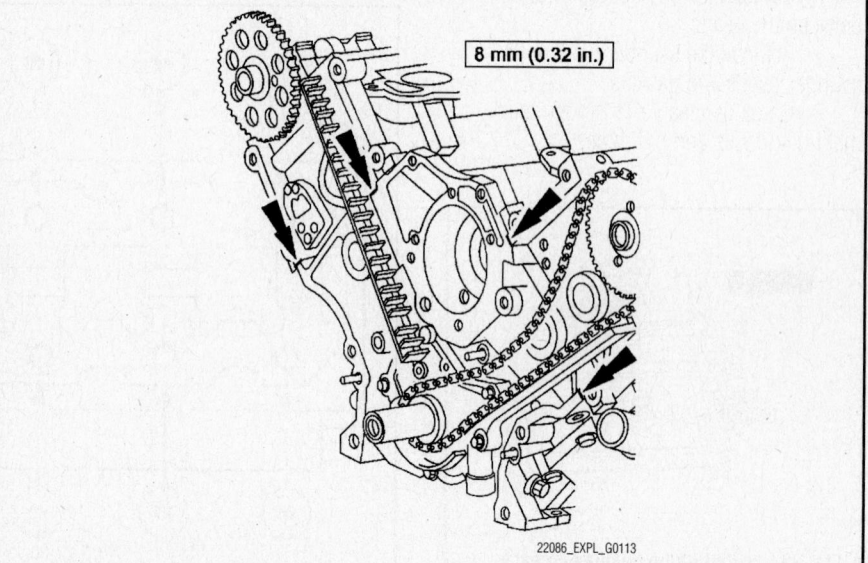

8 mm (0.32 in.)

22086_EXPL_G0113

Fig. 161 Apply a 0.32 in. (8 mm) bead of sealant at the points where the cylinder heads meet the block at the vertical front end of the engine—2005 4.6L (VIN W) SOHC engine

- Wiring harnesses to retainers
- LH and RH fuel injectors and coil-on-plug electrical connectors; attach to wiring retainers
- Throttle body adapter plate
- All coolant hoses
- KS and CHT electrical connectors
- EGR system module and fuel pressure sensor electrical connectors and vacuum connectors
- Brake booster vacuum hose and bolt
- EGR tube; tighten the fitting to 30 ft. lbs. (40 Nm)
- Water pump pulley
- CMP sensor connector
- Alternator; see "Alternator" section
- 3 idler pulleys; torque the bolts to 18 ft. lbs. (25 Nm)
- Bracket on top of the alternator
- Upper radiator hose support bracket and radio interference capacitor
- Crankcase air inlet tube
- A/C compressor and CKP sensor electrical connectors
- Power steering reservoir bracket, radio interference capacitor, and ground cable
- Power steering pump; torque the bolts to 15 ft. lbs. (20 Nm)
- Hoses to power steering pump; new seal in pressure hose fitting; tighten hose fittings to 48 ft. lbs. (65 Nm)
- Power steering hose support bracket
- Oil pressure sensor connector
- Wiring harness bracket behind crankshaft pulley
- Accessory drive belt

20. Install the engine. See "Engine Assembly" section.

21. Refill all fluids. Check for any leaks.

2006–07 Explorer and Mountaineer; 2007 Explorer Sport-Trac

See Figures 162 through 170.

1. Before servicing the vehicle, refer to the "Precautions" section.

➡**Clean all mating surfaces as components are removed during this procedure.**

2. Remove the engine. See "Engine Assembly" section.

3. Transfer the engine to a proper workstand.

4. Remove or disconnect the following for access to the cylinder heads:
- Wiring harness retainers from the RH oil pan bolts
- Crankshaft position sensor electrical connector and detach the wiring harness retainer
- RH and LH camshaft position (CMP) sensor electrical connectors
- RH and LH variable camshaft timing (VCT) solenoid electrical connectors
- Wiring harness retainers from the front end of the engine
- RH radio ignition interference capacitor
- Oil pressure sensor electrical connector
- LH CMP sensor electrical connector and detach the wiring harness retainers
- Cooling fan wiring harness bracket
- LH radio interference capacitor
- Wiring harness retainers from the LH valve cover studs
- 4 RH and 4 LH ignition coil electrical connectors
- Wiring harness retainers from the RH valve cover studs
- Cylinder head temperature (CHT) sensor electrical connector
- Electrical connector retainers and remove the engine wiring harness
- Breather tube from the RH valve cover
- Positive crankcase ventilation (PCV) tube from the LH valve cover
- Oil filter
- 8 ignition coils
- Position the oil level indicator aside
- Valve covers
- Coolant pump pulley and the RH side accessory drive belt idler pulley

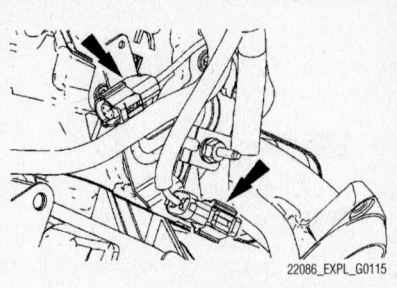

Fig. 163 Remove the electrical connector retainers and remove the engine wiring harness—2006–07 4.6L (VIN 8) SOHC engine

- Crankshaft pulley (discard pulley bolt)
- Front crankshaft seal
- 4 oil pan-to-engine front cover bolts
- Engine front cover
- Crankshaft sensor ring from the crankshaft

5. Position the crankshaft keyway at the 12 o'clock position.

✳✳ CAUTION

If the camshaft lobes are not exactly positioned as shown, the crankshaft will require one full additional rotation to the 12 o'clock position.

6. The No. 1 cylinder camshaft exhaust lobe must be coming up on the exhaust stroke. Verify by noting the position of the 2 intake lobes and the exhaust lobe on the No. 1 cylinder.

7. Remove only the 3 roller followers shown from the RH and LH cylinder heads.

8. Rotate the crankshaft clockwise and position the crankshaft keyway at the 6 o'clock position.

9. Remove the timing chains, guides and sprockets. See "Timing Chain and Sprockets" section.

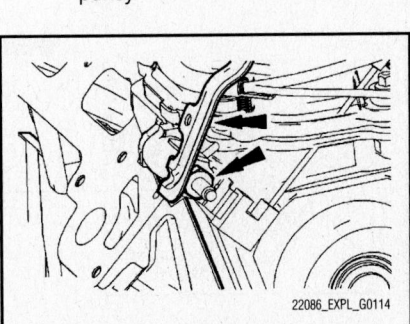

Fig. 162 Remove the cooling fan wiring harness bracket and the LH radio interference capacitor—2006–07 4.6L (VIN 8) SOHC engine

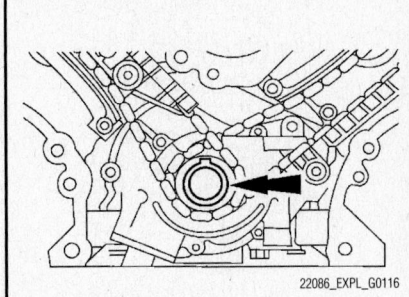

Fig. 164 Position the crankshaft keyway at the 12 o'clock position—2006–07 4.6L (VIN 8) SOHC engine

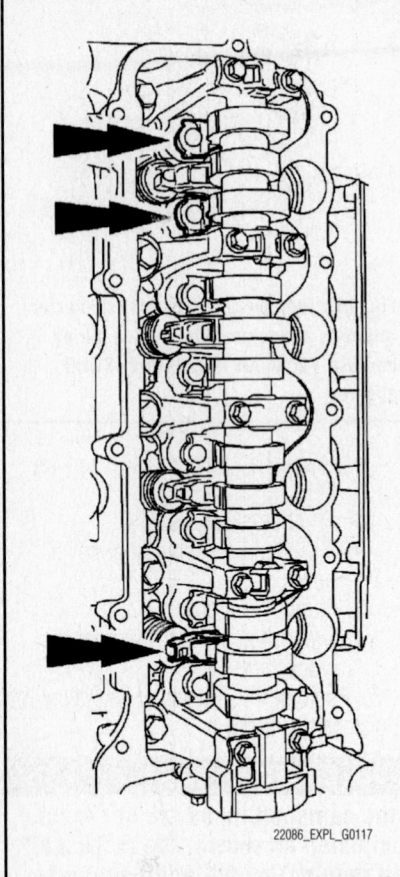

Fig. 165 Remove only the 3 roller followers, as indicated, from the RH cylinder head—2006–07 4.6L (VIN 8) SOHC engine

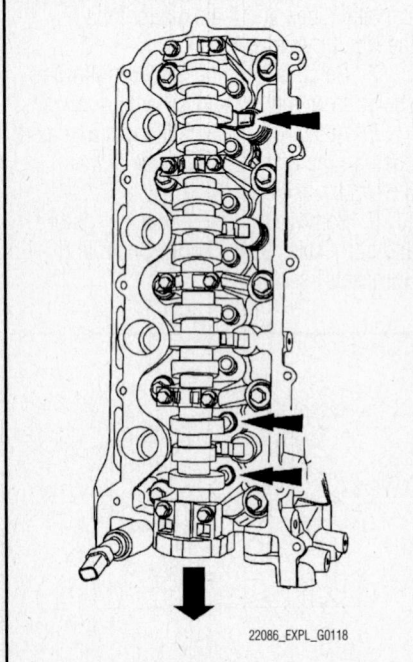

Fig. 166 Remove only the 3 roller followers, as indicated, from the LH cylinder head—2006–07 4.6L (VIN 8) SOHC engine

10. Remove the camshafts. See "Camshaft and Valve Lifter" section.

11. Remove all of the camshaft roller followers and lash adjusters.

12. Install lifting handles on each end of the cylinder heads.

13. Remove the exhaust manifolds.

14. Remove the nut and ground strap from the RH cylinder head.

15. Remove the stud bolt and the heater supply tube and hoses as an assembly from between the cylinder heads.

16. Remove the bolts and lift off the cylinder heads. Remove and discard the gaskets.

To install:

17. Carefully clean all cylinder head mating surfaces and bolt holes.

18. Use a straightedge to check the cylinder head surface flatness. Any distortion must be within 0.0004 in. (0.010 mm) from end to end.

19. Inspect the areas shown for any signs of wear, corrosion or deep scratches.

20. With new gaskets in place, carefully position the LH cylinder head into position. Use locator dowels, if necessary.

21. Install and tighten the cylinder head bolts, in the sequence shown.

22. Tighten the LH cylinder head bolts in 3 steps:

   a. Step 1: 30 ft. lbs. (40 Nm)

   b. Step 2: additional 90 degrees

   c. Step 3: additional 90 degrees

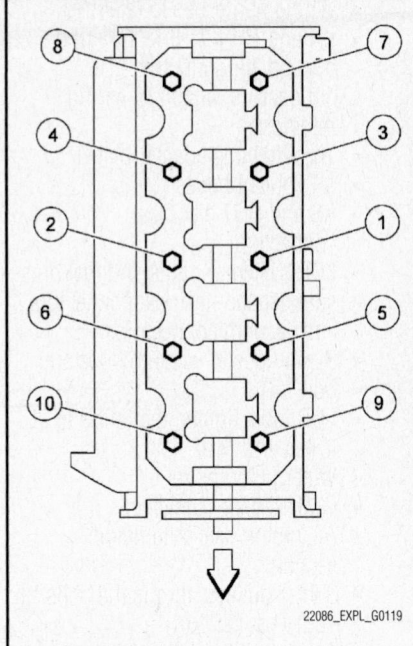

Fig. 168 Tighten the LH cylinder head bolts in the sequence shown—2006–07 4.6L (VIN 8) SOHC engine

23. Remove the cylinder head lifting handles from the end of the cylinder head.

24. Lubricate and install the LH cylinder head lash adjusters in their original positions.

25. With a new O-ring seal, loosely install the oil level indicator tube.

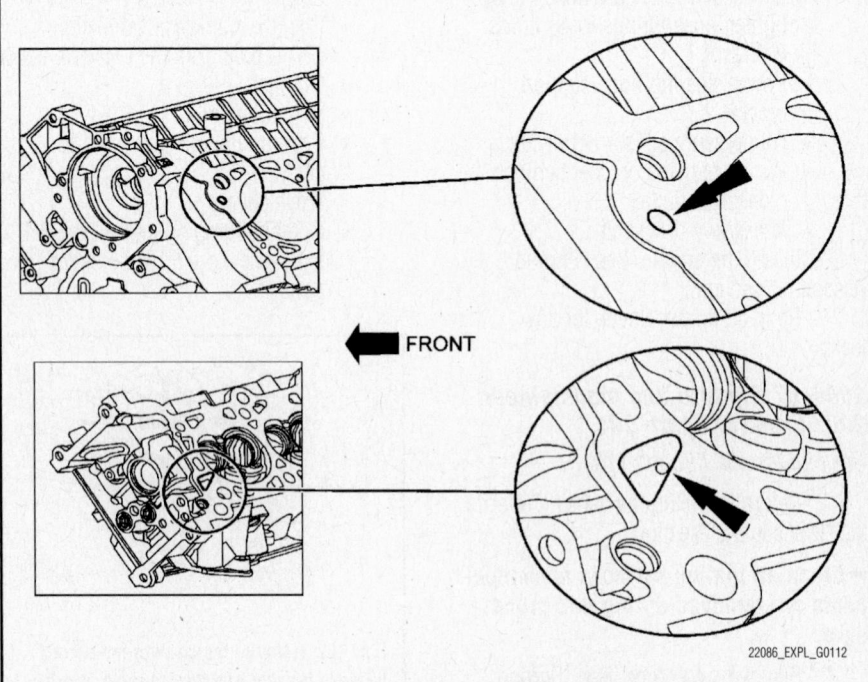

Fig. 167 Inspect the areas shown for any signs of wear, corrosion or deep scratches—2006–07 4.6L (VIN 8) SOHC engine

26. With a new gasket, install the LH exhaust manifold. See "Exhaust Manifold" section for tightening sequence and specifications.

27. With new gaskets in place, carefully position the RH cylinder head into position. Use locator dowels, if necessary.

28. Install and tighten the cylinder head bolts, in the sequence shown.

29. Tighten the RH cylinder head bolts in 3 steps:
   a. Step 1: 30 ft. lbs. (40 Nm)
   b. Step 2: additional 90 degrees
   c. Step 3: additional 90 degrees

30. Remove the cylinder head lifting handles from the end of the cylinder head.

31. Lubricate and install the RH cylinder head lash adjusters in their original positions.

32. With a new gasket, install the RH exhaust manifold. See "Exhaust Manifold" section for tightening sequence and specifications.

33. Install or connect the following:
   - Heater supply tube and the hoses as an assembly
   - Ground strap
   - LH and RH camshafts; see "Camshafts and Valve Lifters" section

34. Install the camshaft phaser sprockets and new camshaft phaser bolts finger-tight.

35. Using the special tool, as shown, tighten the LH and RH camshaft phaser sprocket bolts in 2 stages:

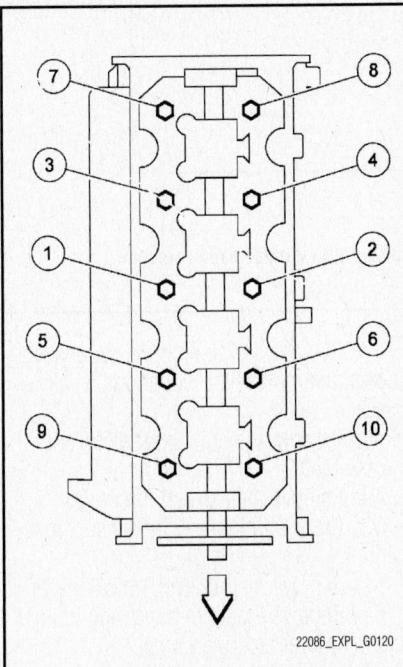

Fig. 169 Tighten the RH cylinder head bolts in the sequence shown—2006–07 4.6L (VIN 8) SOHC engine

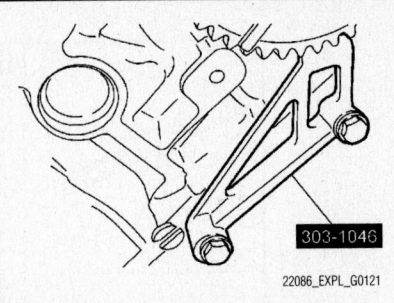

Fig. 170 Using the special tool, as shown, tighten the LH and RH camshaft phaser sprocket bolts—2006–07 4.6L (VIN 8) SOHC engine

   a. Stage 1: 30 ft. lbs. (40 Nm)
   b. Stage 2: additional 90 degrees

36. Install the crankshaft sprocket, making sure the flange faces forward.

37. Rotate the crankshaft to position the crankshaft sprocket timing mark in the 6 o'clock position.

38. Install the camshaft sprockets and timing chains. See "Timing Chain and Sprockets" section.

39. Install the crankshaft sensor ring on the crankshaft.

40. Lubricate and install all of the camshaft roller followers.

41. Install the front cover. See "Timing Chain Cover and Seal" section.

42. Install the 4 bolts to the front of the oil pan. Tighten the bolts to 15 ft. lbs. (20 Nm), then an additional 60 degrees.

43. Install a new front crankshaft oil seal. See "Crankshaft Front Seal" section.

44. Install the crankshaft pulley. Apply silicone to the keyway prior to installation.

45. Tighten the new crankshaft pulley bolt in 4 steps:
   a. Step 1: 66 ft. lbs. (90 Nm)
   b. Step 2: LOOSEN 1 full turn (360 degrees)
   c. Step 3: 37 ft. lbs. (50 Nm)
   d. Step 4: additional 90 degrees

46. Install or connect the following:
   - RH side accessory drive belt idler pulley, the coolant pump pulley and the 5 bolts; tighten the bolts to 18 ft. lbs. (25 Nm)
   - Valve covers; see "Valve Covers" section
   - Tighten the oil level indicator tube bolt to 89 inch lbs. (10 Nm)
   - 8 ignition coils
   - New oil filter
   - Positive crankcase ventilation (PCV) hose to the LH valve cover
   - Breather tube to the RH valve cover
   - Engine wiring harness and attach the electrical connectors to the heater supply tube bracket
   - Cylinder head temperature (CHT) sensor electrical connector
   - Wiring harness retainers to the RH valve cover studs
   - RH and LH ignition coil electrical connectors
   - Wiring harness retainers to the LH valve cover studs
   - LH radio interference capacitor; tighten the nut to 18 ft. lbs. (25 Nm)
   - Cooling fan wiring harness; tighten the nut to 18 ft. lbs. (25 Nm)
   - LH camshaft position sensor and attach the wiring harness retainers
   - Oil pressure sensor electrical connector
   - RH radio interference capacitor; tighten the nut to 18 ft. lbs. (25 Nm)
   - Wiring harness retainers
   - RH and LH variable camshaft timing (VCT) solenoid electrical connectors
   - RH and LH camshaft position (CMP) sensor electrical connectors
   - Crankshaft position sensor electrical connector and attach the wiring harness retainer
   - Wiring harness retainers to the RH oil pan bolts

47. Install the engine. See "Engine Assembly" section.

48. Refill all fluids. Check for leaks.

4.6L (VIN H) DOHC Engine

Aviator

See Figures 171 through 188.

1. Before servicing the vehicle, refer to the "Precautions" section.

2. Remove the engine.

3. Remove the flexplate and the spacer plate.

4. Mount the engine on a suitable engine stand.

5. Remove the two bolts and the pin-type retainer from the power steering reservoir bracket.

6. Remove the power steering reservoir and bracket.

7. Disconnect the battery cable harness ground.

8. Disconnect the electrical connector and the battery cable from the alternator.

9. Disconnect the two retainers from the engine front cover studs.

10. Disconnect the two retainers from the A/C compressor.

11. Remove the bolt and the battery cable harness from the right engine mount.

12. Disconnect the electrical connector and the vacuum hose from the fuel pressure sensor.

13. Disconnect the vacuum harness from the intake manifold and remove the harness.

14. Remove the left and right coil covers.

15. Disconnect the right and left ignition coil electrical connectors.

16. Disconnect the radio interference capacitor electrical connector.

17. Disconnect the eight fuel injector electrical connectors.

18. Separate the fuel charging wiring harness retainers from the fuel injection supply manifold.

19. Disconnect the camshaft position (CMP) sensor electrical connector and the two retainers from the valve cover.

20. Disconnect the oil pressure sensor electrical connector.

21. Disconnect the pin-type retainers from the back of the engine in the locations shown.

22. Disconnect the knock sensor (KS) electrical connector and the pin-type retainer.

23. Disconnect the wiring harness retainer from the stud on the cylinder head.

24. Disconnect the intake manifold runner control (IMRC) electrical connector.

25. Disconnect the exhaust gas recirculation (EGR) system module tube nut from the exhaust manifold.

26. Disconnect the Cylinder Head Temperature (CHT) sensor electrical connector and the two pin-type retainers.

27. Disconnect the positive crankcase ventilation (PCV) electrical connector.

28. Remove the PCV tube.

29. Disconnect the right radio interference capacitor electrical connector and the pin-type retainer.

30. Disconnect the throttle position (TP) sensor and the idle air control (IAC) sensor electrical connectors.

31. Disconnect the two retainers from the right valve cover studs.

32. Disconnect the engine coolant temperature (ECT) sensor electrical connector.

33. Disconnect the A/C compressor and the crankshaft position (CKP) sensor electrical connectors.

34. Remove the upper radiator hose.

35. Remove the coolant bypass-to-thermostat housing hose.

36. Remove the accessory drive belt.

37. Remove the bolts and the alternator support bracket.

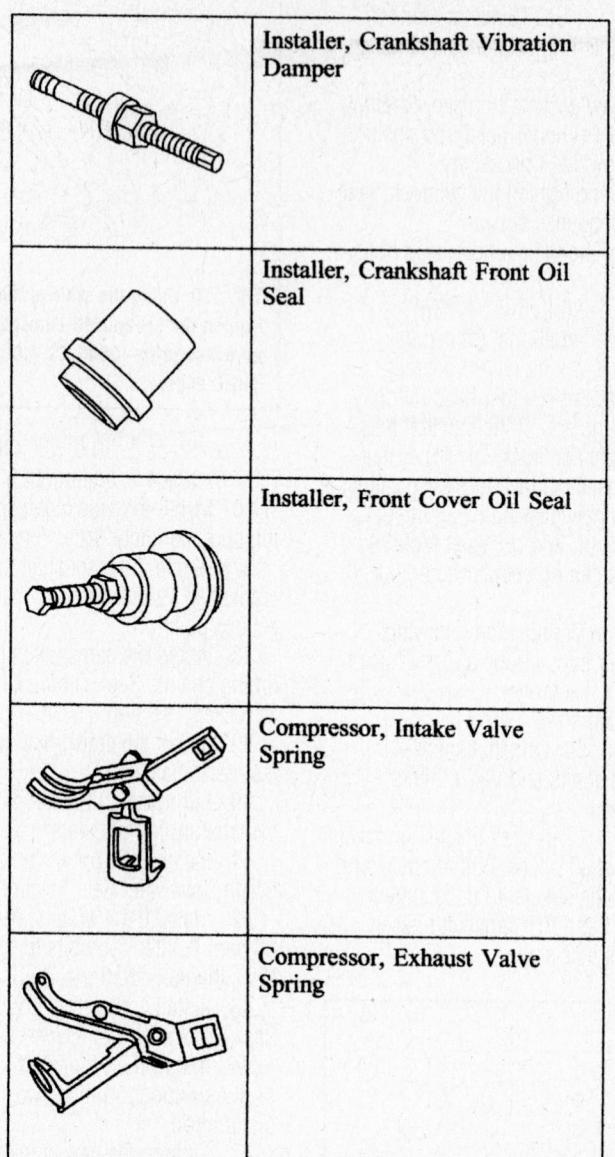

	Installer, Crankshaft Vibration Damper
	Installer, Crankshaft Front Oil Seal
	Installer, Front Cover Oil Seal
	Compressor, Intake Valve Spring
	Compressor, Exhaust Valve Spring

67197EXPLG01

Fig. 171 These tools, or their equivalents, are necessary for cylinder head removal and installation on the 4.6L DOHC engine (1 of 2)

38. Remove the bolts and the alternator.

39. Remove the crossover tube.

40. Remove the eight ignition coils.

41. Remove the nut and the bolt from the oil level indicator tube and position the tube aside.

42. Remove the engine lifting eyes.

43. Remove the bolts and the left valve cover.

44. Remove the coolant hose retainers from the right valve cover.

45. Remove the bolts and the right valve cover.

46. Remove the retainers and the upper-to-lower intake bracket.

47. Remove the bolts in the sequence shown and remove the upper and lower intake.

48. Remove the bolt and the coolant bypass tube.

49. Remove the exhaust manifolds.

50. Clean and inspect the exhaust manifolds.

51. Remove the oil level indicator tube.

52. Remove the three remaining bolts and the power steering pump.

53. Install the special tool.

54. Remove the coolant pump pulley.

55. To remove the crankshaft pulley bolt, remove the upper fan shroud and electric fan.

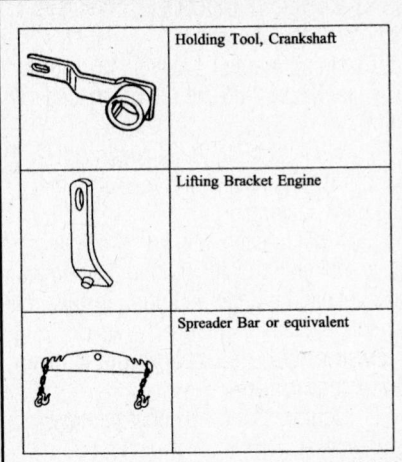

	Holding Tool, Crankshaft
	Lifting Bracket Engine
	Spreader Bar or equivalent

67197EXPLG02

Fig. 172 These tools, or their equivalents, are necessary for cylinder head removal and installation on the 4.6L DOHC engine (2 of 2)

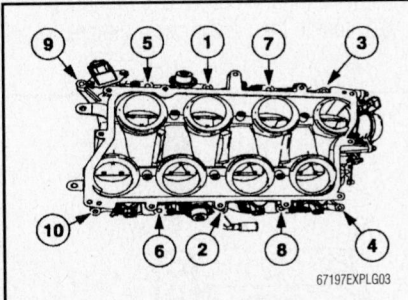

67197EXPLG03

Fig. 173 Intake manifold bolt removal sequence—4.6L DOHC engine

56. Remove the pulley bolt.
57. Remove the crankshaft vibration damper.
58. Remove the crankshaft front seal.
59. Remove the bolt and the belt idler pulley.
60. Remove the four front oil pan-to-timing cover bolts.
61. Remove the engine front cover fasteners in the sequence shown.
62. Remove the crankshaft position sensor pulse wheel.

➡**Mark the roller follower locations. Reused roller followers must be installed in their original locations.**

63. Position the piston of the cylinder in which the roller followers are being removed at the bottom of the stroke and camshaft lobe at the base circle.
64. Compress the intake valve spring and remove the roller follower.
65. Compress the exhaust valve spring and remove the roller follower.

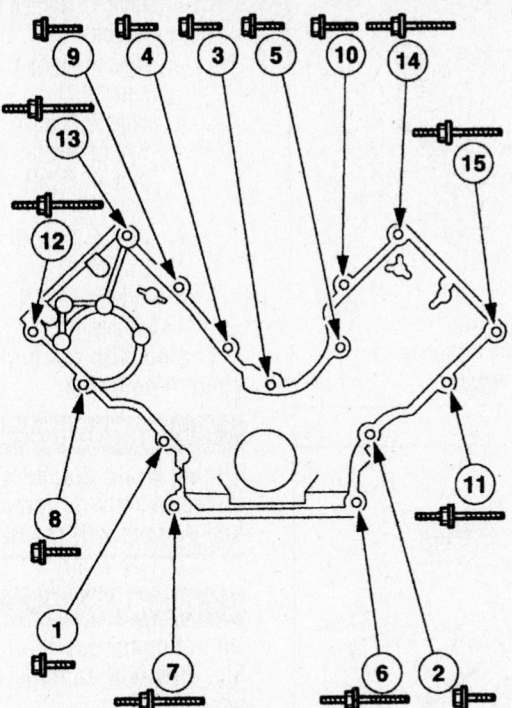

1 Bolt, Hex Flange Head Pilot, M8 x 1.25 x 53
2 Bolt, Hex Flange Head Pilot, M8 x 1.25 x 53
3 Bolt, Hex Flange Head Pilot, M8 x 1.25 x 53
4 Bolt, Hex Flange Head Pilot, M8 x 1.25 x 53
5 Bolt, Hex Flange Head Pilot, M8 x 1.25 x 53
6 Stud, Hex Shldr Pilot, M8 x 1.25 x 50 — M6 x 1 x 10
7 Stud and Washer, Hex Head Pilot, M8 x 1.25 x 60 — M6 x 1 x 26
8 Bolt, Hex Flange Head Pilot, M8 x 1.25 x 53
9 Bolt, Hex Flange Head Pilot, M8 x 1.25 x 53
10 Bolt, Hex Flange Head Pilot, M8 x 1.25 x 53
11 Stud, Hex Shldr Pilot, M8 x 1.25 x 65 — M8 x 1.25 x 26
12 Stud, Hex Head Pilot, M8 x 1.25 x 65 — M8 x 1.25 x 16
13 Stud, Hex Shldr Pilot, M8 x 1.25 x 65 — M8 x 1.25 x 26
14 Stud, Hex Shldr Pilot, M8 x 1.25 x 65 — M8 x 1.25 x 26
15 Stud, Hex Shldr Pilot, M8 x 1.25 x 65 — M8 x 1.25 x 26

67197EXPLG04

Fig. 174 Front cover bolt removal sequence—4.6L DOHC engine

66. Repeat the above steps to remove all the roller followers.
67. Remove the bolts and the right and left timing chain tensioners.
68. Remove the right and left timing chain tensioner arms.
69. Remove the right and the left timing chains and the crankshaft sprocket.
70. Remove the right and left timing chain guides.
71. Remove the right and left cylinder heads. Discard the cylinder head bolts. Discard the cylinder head gaskets.
72. Clean and inspect the cylinder heads.

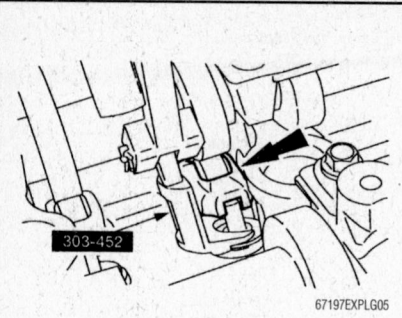

Fig. 175 Compressing the intake valve spring—4.6L DOHC engine

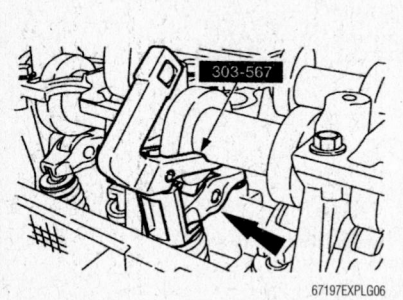

Fig. 176 Compressing the exhaust valve spring—4.6L DOHC engine

To install:

➡Before cylinder head installation, use metal surface cleaner and a suitable plastic or wooden scraper to clean the sealing surfaces. All sealing surfaces must be clean. Make sure coolant and oil passages are clear.

All vehicles
73. Install new cylinder head gaskets.

➡Lubricate the new bolt heads and threads. Use clean engine oil.

74. Install the left and right cylinder heads and tighten the bolts in six stages in the sequence shown.

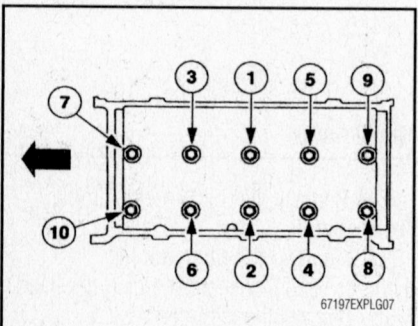

Fig. 177 Cylinder head bolt torque sequence—4.6L DOHC engine

- Stage 1: Tighten to 30 ft. lbs. (40 Nm).
- Stage 2: Tighten an additional 90 degrees.
- Stage 3: Loosen the bolts a minimum of one full turn.
- Stage 4: Tighten to 30 ft. lbs. (40 Nm).
- Stage 5: Tighten an additional 90 degrees.
- Stage 6: Tighten an additional 90 degrees.

Engine with ratcheting timing chain tensioners

> ❋❋ **WARNING**
>
> **Timing chain procedures must be followed exactly or damage to valves and pistons will result.**

> ❋❋ **WARNING**
>
> **Do not compress the ratchet assembly. This will damage the ratchet assembly.**

75. Compress each tensioner plunger, using an edge of a vise.

76. Using a small screwdriver or pick, push back and hold the ratchet mechanism.

77. While holding the ratchet mechanism, push the ratchet arm back into the tensioner housing.

78. Install a paper clip into the hole of each tensioner housing to hold the ratchet assembly and plunger in during installation. Remove the tensioner from the vise.

Engine with non-ratcheting timing chain tensioners

79. Compress the tensioner plunger, using a vise.

80. Install a retaining clip on the tensioner to hold the plunger in during installation.

81. Remove the tensioner from the vise.

All engine

82. If the copper links are not visible, mark one link on one end and one link on the other end, and use as timing marks.

83. Install the timing chain guides.

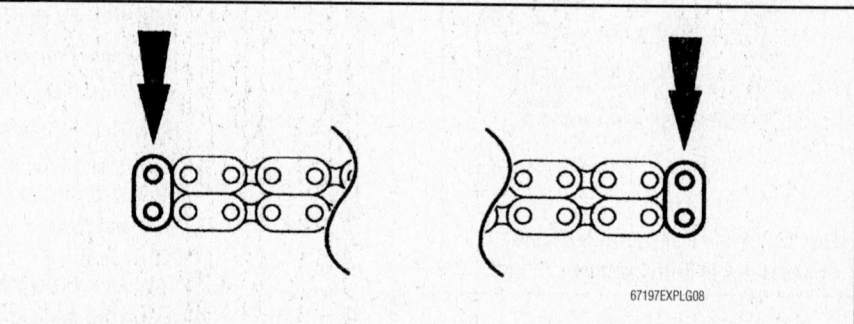

Fig. 178 If the copper links are not visible, mark one link on one end and one link on the other end, and use as timing marks—4.6L DOHC engine

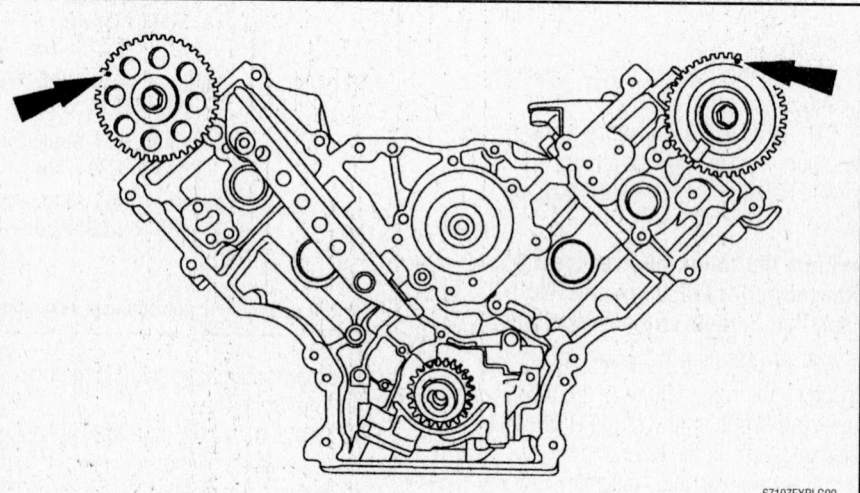

Fig. 179 If the copper links are not visible, mark one link on one end and one link on the other end, and use as timing marks—4.6L DOHC engine

84. Rotate the left camshaft timing sprocket until the timing mark is approximately at the 12 o'clock position. Rotate the right camshaft timing sprocket until the timing mark is at approximately the 11 o'clock position.

✻✻ WARNING

Unless otherwise instructed, at no time when the timing chains are removed and the cylinder heads are installed is the crankshaft or camshaft to be rotated. Severe piston and valve damage will occur.

85. Using the special tool, position the crankshaft.

86. Install the crankshaft sprocket with the flange facing forward.

87. Install the left and right timing chains onto the crankshaft sprocket, aligning the one copper link on the timing chain with the slot on the crankshaft sprocket.

➡ **If necessary, adjust the camshaft sprocket slightly to obtain timing mark alignment.**

88. Position the left and right timing chains on the camshaft sprockets. Make sure the copper-colored links align with the camshaft sprocket timing marks.

89. Position the left and right timing chain tensioner arms on the dowel pins. Position the timing chain tensioner assemblies, and install the bolts.

Engine with ratcheting timing chain tensioners

90. Remove the retaining clip from the timing chain tensioners.

Engine with non-ratcheting timing chain tensioners

91. Remove the retaining clips from the timing chain tensioners.

All engine

92. As a post-check, verify correct alignment of all timing marks.

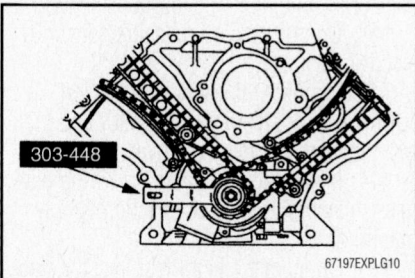

Fig. 180 Using the special tool, position the crankshaft—4.6L DOHC engine

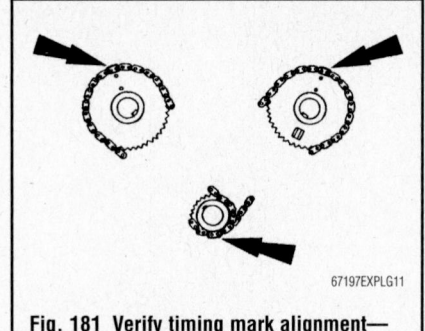

Fig. 181 Verify timing mark alignment— 4.6L DOHC engine

93. Position the crankshaft sensor ring on the crankshaft.

➡ **If the engine front cover is not secured within four minutes, the sealant must be removed and the sealing area cleaned with metal surface cleaner. Allow to dry until there is no sign of wetness, or four minutes, whichever is longer. Failure to follow this procedure can result in future oil leakage.**

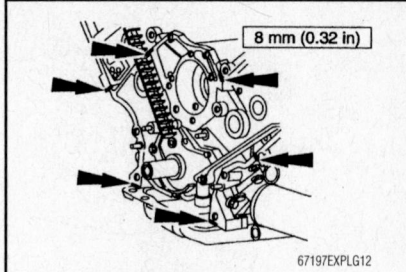

Fig. 182 Apply silicone gasket and sealant in the locations shown—4.6L DOHC engine

94. Apply silicone gasket and sealant in the locations shown.

95. Install the engine front cover and tighten the bolts in the sequence shown.

96. Install the four oil pan bolts and tighten in the sequence shown.
- Stage 1: Tighten to 18 inch lbs. (2 Nm).
- Stage 2: Tighten to 15 ft. lbs. (20 Nm).
- Stage 3: Tighten an additional 60 degrees.

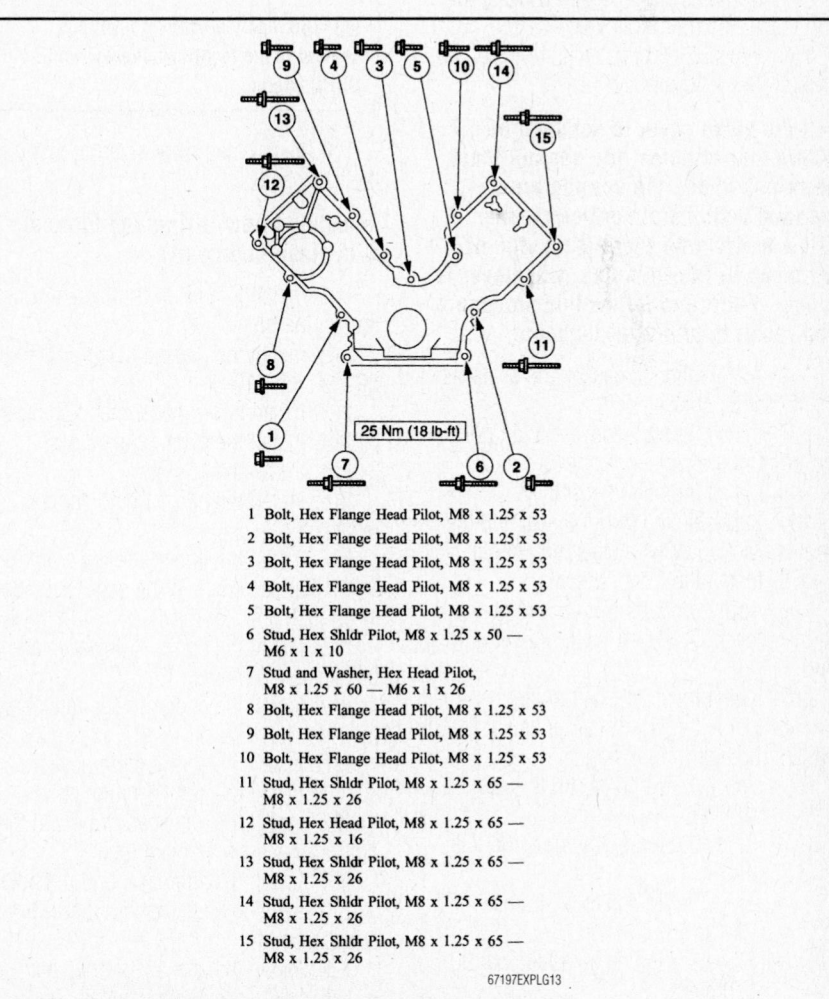

1 Bolt, Hex Flange Head Pilot, M8 x 1.25 x 53
2 Bolt, Hex Flange Head Pilot, M8 x 1.25 x 53
3 Bolt, Hex Flange Head Pilot, M8 x 1.25 x 53
4 Bolt, Hex Flange Head Pilot, M8 x 1.25 x 53
5 Bolt, Hex Flange Head Pilot, M8 x 1.25 x 53
6 Stud, Hex Shldr Pilot, M8 x 1.25 x 50 — M6 x 1 x 10
7 Stud and Washer, Hex Head Pilot, M8 x 1.25 x 60 — M6 x 1 x 26
8 Bolt, Hex Flange Head Pilot, M8 x 1.25 x 53
9 Bolt, Hex Flange Head Pilot, M8 x 1.25 x 53
10 Bolt, Hex Flange Head Pilot, M8 x 1.25 x 53
11 Stud, Hex Shldr Pilot, M8 x 1.25 x 65 — M8 x 1.25 x 26
12 Stud, Hex Head Pilot, M8 x 1.25 x 65 — M8 x 1.25 x 16
13 Stud, Hex Shldr Pilot, M8 x 1.25 x 65 — M8 x 1.25 x 26
14 Stud, Hex Shldr Pilot, M8 x 1.25 x 65 — M8 x 1.25 x 26
15 Stud, Hex Shldr Pilot, M8 x 1.25 x 65 — M8 x 1.25 x 26

Fig. 183 Front cover bolt torque sequence—4.6L DOHC engine

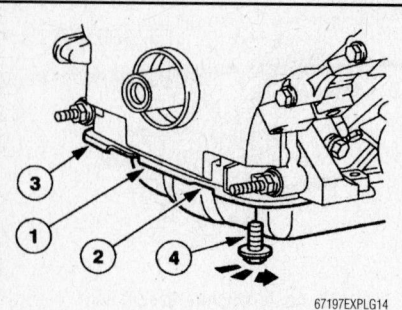

Fig. 184 Install the four oil pan bolts and tighten in the sequence shown—4.6L DOHC engine

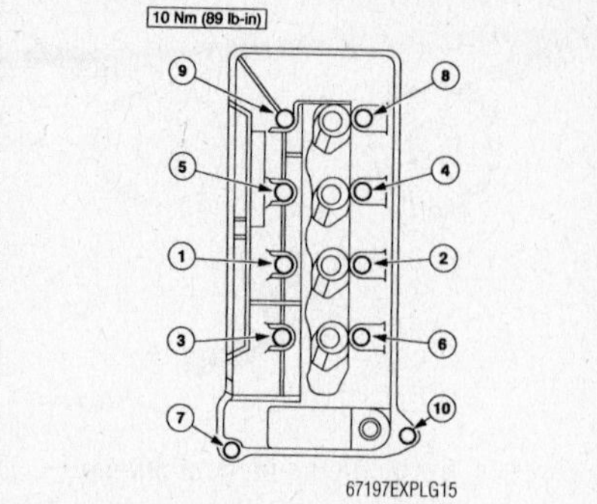

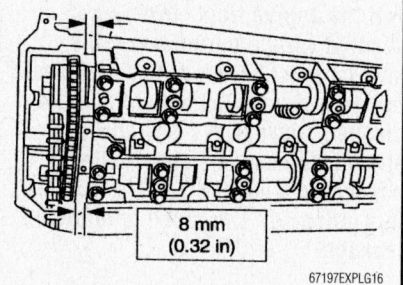

Fig. 185 Valve cover bolt torque sequence—4.6L DOHC engine

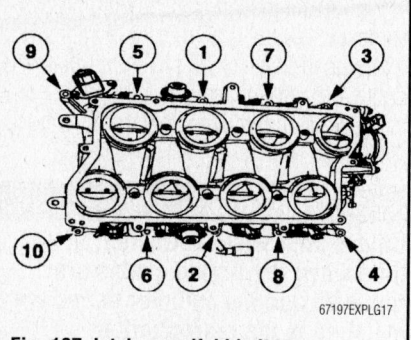

Fig. 187 Intake manifold bolt torque sequence—4.6L DOHC engine

❊❊ WARNING

If reusing the roller followers, install them in their original locations.

97. Position the piston of the cylinder in which the roller followers are being installed at the bottom of the stroke and the camshaft lobe at the base circle.

98. Compress the intake valve spring and install the roller follower.

99. Compress the exhaust valve spring and install the roller follower.

100. Repeat the above steps to install all of the roller followers.

➡**If the valve cover is not secured within four minutes, the sealant must be removed and the sealing area cleaned with metal surface cleaner. Allow to dry until there is no sign of wetness, or four minutes, whichever is longer. Failure to follow this procedure can result in future oil leakage.**

101. Apply silicone gasket and sealant in the locations shown.

102. Install the valve covers and tighten the bolts in the sequence shown.

103. Install the belt idler pulley.

104. Lubricate the front oil seal and the engine front cover with clean engine oil.

105. Install the front oil seal.

106. Apply silicone gasket and sealant to the Woodruff key on the crankshaft pulley.

107. Install the crankshaft pulley.

108. Install the crankshaft pulley bolt and tighten the bolt in four stages.
- Stage 1: Tighten to 66 ft. lbs. (90 Nm).
- Stage 2: Loosen the bolt one full turn.
- Stage 3: Tighten to 37 ft. lbs. (50 Nm).
- Stage 4: Tighten an additional 90 degrees.

109. Install the coolant pump pulley.

Fig. 186 Apply silicone gasket and sealant in the locations shown—4.6L DOHC engine

110. Install the power steering pump and the three bolts.

➡**Install a new O-ring and lubricate with clean engine oil.**

111. Install the oil level indicator tube in the engine block.

112. Install the fasteners and tighten to 89 inch lbs. (10 Nm).

113. Install new exhaust manifold gaskets.

114. Install the exhaust manifolds.

115. Install the 16 nuts.

116. Install the bolt and the coolant bypass tube.

117. Install the upper and lower intake. Tighten all fasteners in the sequence shown to 89 inch lbs. (10 Nm).

118. Install the upper-to-lower intake bracket and the nuts.

119. Install the coolant hose retainers on the right valve cover.

120. Install the engine lifting eyes.

121. Install the eight ignition coils.

122. Install the crossover tube and the nuts. Connect the coolant hose.

123. Install the alternator and the bolts.

124. Install the alternator support bracket and the bolts.

125. Install the accessory drive belt.

126. Install the coolant bypass-to-thermostat housing hose.

127. Install the upper radiator hose.

128. Position the engine wiring harness on the engine.

129. Connect the A/C compressor and the crankshaft position (CKP) sensor electrical connectors.

130. Connect the engine coolant temperature (ECT) sensor electrical connector.

131. Connect the two harness retainers to the right valve cover studs.

132. Connect the throttle position (TP) sensor and the idle air control (IAC) sensor electrical connectors.

133. Connect the right radio interference capacitor electrical connector and the pin-type retainer.

134. Install the positive crankcase ventilation (PCV) tube.

135. Connect the PCV electrical connector.

136. Connect the Cylinder Head Temperature (CHT) sensor electrical connector and the two pin-type retainers.

137. Connect the exhaust gas recirculation (EGR) system module tube to the exhaust manifold.

138. Connect the intake manifold runner control (IMRC) electrical connector.

139. Connect the wiring harness retainer to the stud on the cylinder head.

140. Connect the KS electrical connector and the pin-type retainer.

141. Connect the pin-type retainers to the back of the engine in the locations shown.

142. Connect the oil pressure sensor electrical connector.

143. Connect the camshaft position (CMP) sensor electrical connector and the two retainers to the valve cover.

144. Install the fuel charging wiring harness retainers to the fuel injection supply manifold.

145. Connect the eight fuel injector electrical connectors.

146. Connect the radio interference capacitor electrical connector.

147. Connect the eight ignition electrical connectors.

148. Install the right and left coil covers.

149. Position the vacuum harness and connect it to the intake manifold.

150. Connect the electrical connector and the vacuum hose to the fuel pressure sensor.

151. Install the battery cable harness and the bolt to the right engine mount.

152. Connect the two retainers to the A/C compressor.

153. Connect the two retainers to the engine front cover studs.

154. Connect the electrical connector and the battery cable to the alternator.

155. Connect the battery cable harness ground.

156. Position the power steering reservoir and install the two bolts and the pin-type retainer.

157. Install the remaining bolt and the hose to the power steering reservoir.

158. Remove the engine from the stand.

159. Install the spacer plate and the flexplate.

160. Install the engine.

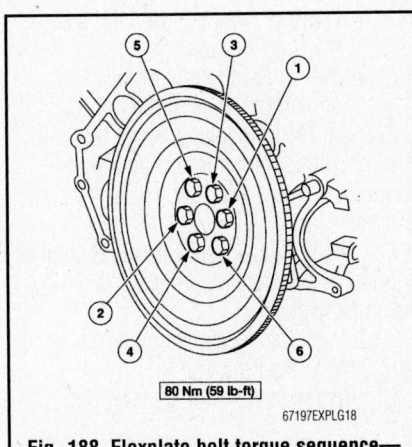

Fig. 188 Flexplate bolt torque sequence—4.6L DOHC engine

80 Nm (59 lb-ft)

67197EXPLG18

ENGINE ASSEMBLY

REMOVAL & INSTALLATION

4.0L (VIN E, VIN K) SOHC Engine

2005 Explorer, Explorer Sport-Trac and Mountaineer

See Figures 189 through 199.

1. Before servicing the vehicle, refer to the precautions in the beginning of this section.

2. Release the fuel system pressure as follows:

   a. Remove the fuel pump relay (located in the battery junction box).

   b. Start the engine and allow it to idle until it stalls.

   c. After the engine stalls, crank the engine for approximately 5 seconds to make sure the fuel rail pressure has been released.

   d. Turn the ignition switch to the OFF position.

3. Remove the fuel line spring-lock coupling.

4. Remove or disconnect the following:
   • Battery cables
   • Engine ground wire from body
   • Wiring harness connector and retainers along the fender

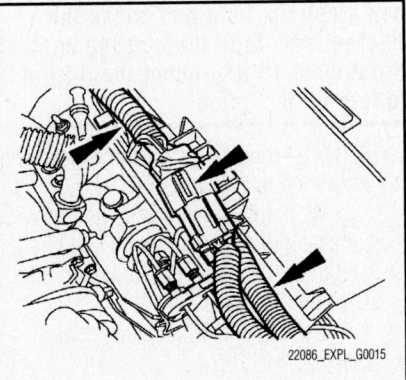

Fig. 189 Identifying the wiring harness connector and retainers to remove

22086_EXPL_G0015

5. Lift the engine compartment relay box cover and disconnect the battery cable from the stud.

6. Drain the cooling system.

7. Recover the A/C system refrigerant.

8. Disconnect the windshield washer hoses from the hood. Mark the hood hinge locations and remove the hinge bolts and the hood.

9. Remove the cooling fan and shroud.

10. Remove or disconnect the following:
    • Accessory drive belt
    • Power steering pump pulley
    • Air cleaner assembly and the outlet pipe
    • Mass air flow (MAF) sensor electrical connector
    • Powertrain Control Module (PCM) electrical connectors
    • Wiring harness clips from the bulkhead
    • Transmission control wiring harness pin-type retainers from the engine wiring harness

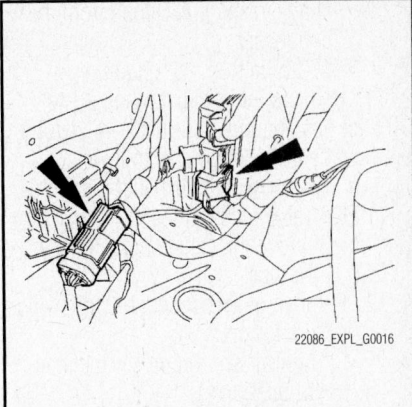

Fig. 190 Disconnect the PCM electrical connectors—4.0L engine (2005 models)

22086_EXPL_G0016

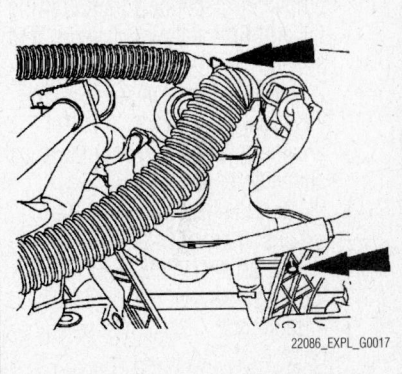

Fig. 191 Disconnect the transmission control wiring harness pin-type retainers from the engine wiring harness —4.0L engine

22086_EXPL_G0017

    • Evaporative emissions (EVAP) tube from the engine connection and position it aside
    • Vacuum hoses at the bulkhead connections (mark for reinstallation)
    • Engine ground wire at the bulkhead
    • Heater control valve vacuum hose and heater hoses from the bulkhead
    • Upper radiator hose and heater hose from the block connections
    • Lower radiator hose at the coolant pump
    • Coolant hoses from the coolant reservoir bottle
    • A/C tube from the accumulator; discard the O-ring seal

➡Cover the accumulator opening to prevent contamination.

    • Low-pressure A/C tube from the condenser; discard the O-ring seal
    • Brake booster vacuum hoses and tubes from the cylinder head cover
    • A/C high-pressure cut-off switch electrical connector

- High-pressure A/C tube from the condenser
- A/C tube from the retainer

11. Remove the exhaust manifold-to-exhaust gas recirculation (EGR) valve tube on the side of the engine as follows:

   a. Disconnect the exhaust manifold-to-EGR valve tube fittings.

   b. Remove the exhaust manifold-to-EGR valve tube.

12. Remove or disconnect the following:
- Starter motor
- Lower air shroud panel (retained with pushpins)
- Battery cable retainer bracket

13. Position a jack stand under the transfer case (4WD) or a transmission jack under the transmission (2WD).

14. Remove or disconnect the following:
- LH and RH catalytic converter heat shields
- 2 heated oxygen sensor (HO2S) electrical connectors
- 2 catalyst monitor sensor electrical connectors
- RH and LH heat shields at the exhaust manifold
- Plastic shield on the right side of the crossmember
- 4 upper and 4 lower crossmember bolts
- Cable bracket from the transmission (2WD only)
- Transmission support insulator nuts and remove the crossmember
- Bolts, springs, flag nuts and separate the muffler from the converter
- 4 converter-to-manifold nuts

15. Remove the transmission-mounted exhaust hanger, the 3-way converter system and the RH heat shield as follows:

   a. Remove the bolt and the converter assembly.

   b. If required, remove the second bolt and mount.

16. Disconnect the shift cable and remove the bracket.

17. On 4WD models, perform the following to remove the front driveshaft:

   a. Index-mark the front axle pinion flange and the front driveshaft.

   b. Index-mark the front output shaft assembly and the front driveshaft constant velocity (CV) joint.

   c. Remove and discard all of the bolts, washers and U-joint nuts from both flanges.

   d. Remove the front driveshaft.

❈❈ CAUTION

Always disconnect the front drive-shaft from the transfer case first. Otherwise, the weight of the driveshaft can pinch the boot and cause the boot to tear. Tape the bearing cups to the driveshaft to prevent them from falling off the spider.

18. On all models, perform the following to remove the rear driveshaft:

   a. Mark the driveshaft flange to the rear axle pinion flange, and if equipped, the transfer case rear output flange for assembly reference.

   b. Remove the 4 rear axle flange bolts.

   c. Index-mark the driveshaft at the 6 o'clock position (2WD).

   d. Remove the 4 transfer case flange bolts (4WD).

   e. Using a suitable tool as shown, disconnect the driveshaft flange and remove the driveshaft.

❈❈ CAUTION

Do not rotate the driveshaft. The driveshaft flange fits tightly on the rear axle pinion flange pilot. Never hammer on the driveshaft or any of its components to disconnect the drive-shaft flange from the pinion flange.

19. For 2WD models, Pull the seal away from the transmission output shaft, and mark the transmission output shaft at the 6 o'clock position.

20. For all models, remove or disconnect the following:
- RH catalyst monitor connector and the fuel tubes from the bracket
- RH HO2S electrical connector from the transmission
- Shift motor electrical connector, if equipped
- LH HO2S electrical connector retainer and the harness clip from the transmission
- LH catalyst monitor connector from the transmission
- 4 torque converter nuts (Rotate the crankshaft to access all the nuts)

➡ **Make an identifying mark on the nut, stud and flexplate to allow for correct installation.**

- Digital transmission range sensor
- Electrical connectors from the side of the transmission housing
- Solenoid body electrical connector (clean the area before disconnecting)
- Harness retainers from the side of the transmission
- Transmission cooler tubes and clips (both ends of the tubes)

21. On 4WD models, support the transmission with a transmission jack and remove the jack stand from under the transfer case.

22. On all models, remove the 8 engine-to-transmission retaining bolts and remove the transmission.

23. Install the special holding tool (307-346) to the flexplate.

24. Remove the power steering return hose.

25. Remove the drain plug and drain the engine oil. Remove the oil filter.

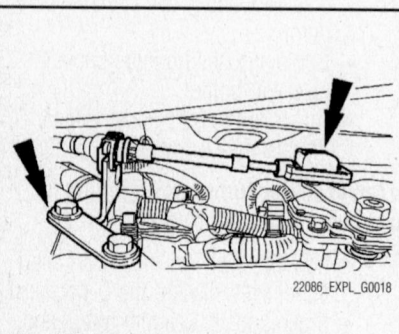

Fig. 192 Disconnect the shift cable and remove the bracket—4.0L engine (2005 models)

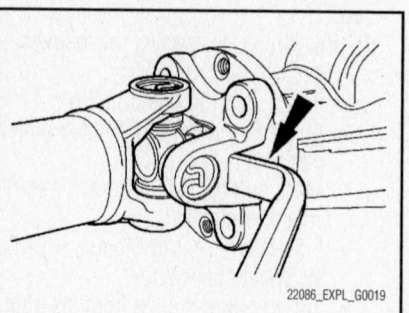

Fig. 193 Using a suitable tool as shown, disconnect the driveshaft flange and remove the driveshaft—4.0L engine

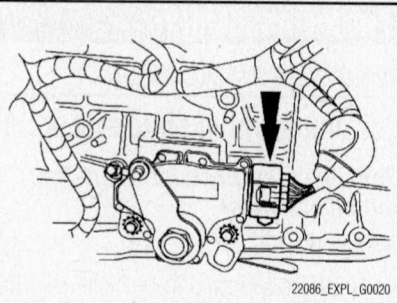

Fig. 194 Pull the boot back and disconnect the digital transmission range sensor—4.0L engine

26. Remove or disconnect the following:
- LH engine support insulator bolt
- Power steering fluid reservoir-to-fluid cooler hose and detach the clip
- Power steering tube support bracket
- Power steering pressure (PSP) tube (discard the O-ring seal)
- RH engine support insulator nuts
- LH and RH radiator support brackets
- RH radiator support bracket
- Radiator and A/C condenser as an assembly

27. Install the lifting hangars on the LH and RH sides of the engine, using bolts on the exhaust manifolds to retain the hangars.

28. Attach the lifting sling, and with a floor crane, remove the engine.

To install:

29. Using the floor crane, carefully lower the engine into the vehicle.

30. Install the RH engine support insulator nuts, and tighten the nuts to 59 ft. lbs. (80 Nm).

31. Install the radiator and A/C condenser as an assembly.

32. Position the RH and LH radiator support brackets and the bolts and tighten to 9 ft. lbs. (12 Nm).

33. Remove the lifting hangars from both sides of the engine.

34. Using the special tool (211-D027) , install a new seal on the power steering pressure (PSP) hose fitting.

35. Connect the PSP hose to the power steering pump. Tighten the fitting to 48 ft. lbs. (65 Nm).

36. Install the PSP hose support bracket and the bolt. Tighten the bolt to 8 ft. lbs. (11 Nm).

37. Install the LH support insulator through bolt. Tighten the bolt to 81 ft. lbs. (110 Nm).

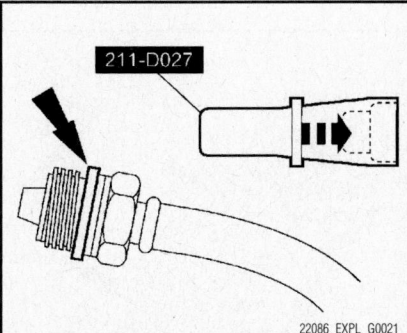

Fig. 195 Using the special tool (211-D027) , install a new seal on the power steering pressure (PSP) hose fitting— 4.0L engine

38. Connect the power steering return hose to the power steering cooler.

39. Remove the holding tool from the flexplate. Make sure the stud and flexplate marks made during removal line up.

40. Position the transmission in the vehicle. Install the 8 engine-to-transmission bolts and tighten to 35 ft. lbs. (48 Nm).

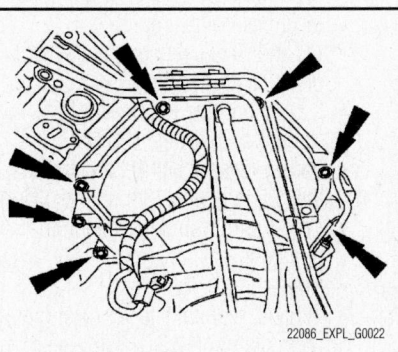

Fig. 196 Position the transmission in the vehicle. Install the 8 engine-to-transmission bolts and tighten to 35 ft. lbs. (48 Nm)—4.0L engine

41. Position the transmission cooler tubes, and the bracket and install the nut. Tighten the nut to 14 ft. lbs. (19 Nm).

42. Connect the transmission cooler tubes to the cooler, and install the tube clips.

43. Connect the cooler tubes to the transmission. Tighten the fittings to 26 ft. lbs. (35 Nm).

44. Install the wiring harness retaining clips onto the side of the transmission housing.

45. Lubricate new O-rings with petroleum jelly. Install new O-ring seals on the transmission body electrical connector, connect the electrical connector and tighten the screw. Tighten the screw to not more than 44 inch lbs. (5 Nm).

✳✳ CAUTION

Damage will occur to the solenoid body assembly if the screw is tightened above the specification.

46. Connect the electrical connectors to the side of the transmission housing.

47. Connect the digital Transmission Range (TR) sensor and move the cover boot back into place.

48. Match the identifying mark on the nut, stud and flexplate to allow for correct installation.

49. Install the 4 torque converter nuts and tighten them to 28 ft. lbs. (38 Nm).

50. Install or connect the following:

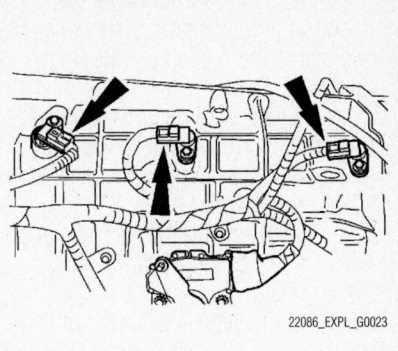

Fig. 197 Connect the electrical connectors to the side of the transmission housing— 4.0L engine

- LH catalyst monitor connector to the transmission
- LH heated oxygen sensor (HO2S) electrical connector retainer and the harness clip to the transmission
- shift motor electrical connector (if equipped)
- RH HO2S electrical connector to the transmission
- RH catalyst monitor connector and the fuel tubes to the bracket

51. Align the marks on the transmission output shaft. Position the driveshaft and install the driveshaft-to-pinion flange bolts in the sequence shown. Torque to 83 ft. lbs. (112 Nm).

➡Use new bolts and washers.

52. On 4WD models, perform the following to install the rear driveshaft:

a. Align the marks made on the flange and driveshaft during removal.

b. Install the rear driveshaft-to-transfer case, with new flange bolts and washers, in the sequence shown. Tighten the bolts to 83 ft. lbs. (112 Nm).

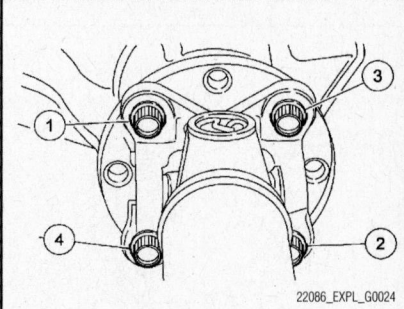

Fig. 198 Align the marks on the transmission output shaft, then position the driveshaft and install the driveshaft-to-pinion flange bolts in the sequence shown (2WD and 4WD models)—4.0L engine

c. Position the front driveshaft flange with the location marks aligned and install the retaining bolts finger-tight.

d. Connect the front driveshaft to the front differential and install new bolts (and new straps). Tighten the bolts to 13 ft. lbs. (18 Nm).

e. Tighten the front driveshaft flange bolts, in the sequence shown, to 22 ft. lbs. (30 Nm).

53. On all models, position the shift cable bracket and install the bolts, Connect the shift cable. Tighten the bolts to 30 ft. lbs. (40 Nm).

54. Install a jack stand under the transfer case, and remove the transmission jack (4WD).

55. Position the transmission-mounted exhaust hanger, the 3-way converter system and RH heat shield, as follows:

a. If removed, position the mount and install the bolt. Tighten the bolt to 66 ft. lbs. (90 Nm).

b. Position the exhaust hanger and the converter assembly and install the bolt. Tighten the bolt to 66 ft. lbs. (90 Nm).

56. Install the 4 converter-to-manifold nuts. Tighten the nuts to 30 ft. lbs. (40 Nm).

57. Connect the LH and RH mufflers to the converters and install the 2 new bolts, 2 springs and 2 new flag nuts. Tighten the bolts and nuts to 30 ft. lbs. (40 Nm).

58. Install the crossmember and the 4 lower and 4 upper bolts. Torque the bolts to 52 ft. lbs. (70 Nm).

59. Remove the jack from under the transfer case (4WD) or from under the transmission (2WD).

60. Install the cable bracket and the bolts to the transmission (2WD). Tighten the bolts to 30 ft. lbs. (40 Nm).

61. Install or connect the following:

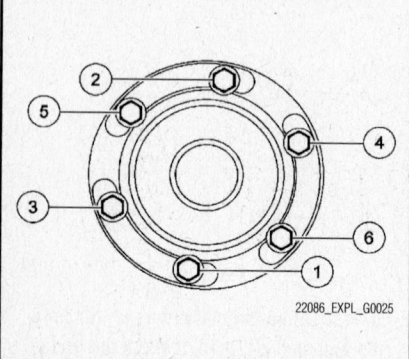

Fig. 199 Tighten the front driveshaft flange bolts, in the sequence shown, to 22 ft. lbs. (30 Nm)—4.0L engine with 4WD

- Plastic shield and the 2 nuts on the right side of the crossmember; torque to 80 inch lbs. (9 Nm)
- Crossmember-to-transmission support insulator nuts; torque to 66 ft. lbs. (90 Nm)
- LH and RH heat shield bolts; torque to 15 ft. lbs. (20 Nm)
- LH and RH catalyst monitor sensor electrical connectors
- LH and RH heated oxygen sensor electrical connectors
- 2 bolts and the RH heat shield; torque to 15 ft. lbs. (20 Nm)
- Battery retainer bracket and install the nut; torque to 15 ft. lbs. (20 Nm)
- Lower air shroud and install the pushpins
- Starter
- Exhaust manifold-to-exhaust gas recirculation (EGR) valve tube and tighten the fittings; torque the fitting to 30 ft. lbs. (40 Nm)
- A/C tube to the condenser and install the nut; torque to 71 inch lbs. (8 Nm)
- A/C tube to the retainer on the side of the condenser
- A/C high pressure cut-off switch electrical connector
- Vacuum hoses to the cylinder head cover
- New O-ring seal, connect the A/C tube to the condenser and install the nut; torque to 71 inch lbs. (8 Nm)
- New O-ring seal, connect the A/C tube to the accumulator and install the nut; torque to 71 inch lbs. (8 Nm)
- Coolant hoses to the coolant reservoir bottle
- Lower radiator hose at the coolant pump
- Upper radiator hose and heater hose to the block connections
- Heater hose bracket and install the bolts; torque to 17 ft. lbs. (23 Nm)
- Vacuum and heater hoses at the bulkhead
- Ground wire and the bolt to the engine; torque to 89 inch lbs. (10 Nm)
- Vacuum hose near the wiring harnesses on the bulkhead
- Evaporative emissions (EVAP) tube
- Fuel line spring lock coupling
- Transmission control wiring harness pin-type retainers to the engine wiring harness
- Engine wiring harness in the clips on the bulkhead
- Powertrain Control Module (PCM) electrical connectors

- Air cleaner
- Mass air flow (MAF) sensor electrical connector
- Hood, the 4 bolts and the hood supports; torque to 9 ft. lbs. (11 Nm)
- Windshield washer hose to the underside of the hood
- Battery cable to the power distribution box and install the nut
- Electrical connector and attach the wiring harness retainer on the fender rail
- Ground wire and the nut on the bulkhead; torque to 80 inch lbs. (9 Nm)
- Cooling fan and shroud
- Air cleaner outlet pipe

62. Fill the engine with clean engine oil.
63. Connect both battery cables.
64. Fill and bleed the cooling system.
65. Fill and purge the power steering system.
66. Evacuate and recharge the A/C system.
67. Start the engine and check for leaks
68. Stop the engine and check all fluid levels.

2006 Explorer and Mountaineer

1. Before servicing the vehicle, refer to the precautions in the beginning of this section.
2. Release the fuel system pressure.
3. Remove the fuel line spring-lock coupling.
4. Remove or disconnect the following:
   - Battery cables
   - Engine ground wire from body
   - Wiring harness connector and retainers along the fender
5. Lift the engine compartment relay box cover and disconnect the battery cable from the stud.
6. Recover the A/C system refrigerant.
7. Drain the cooling system.

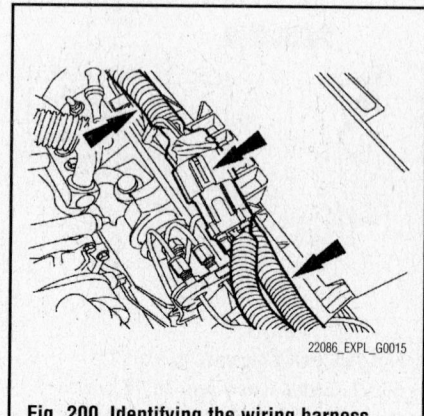

Fig. 200 Identifying the wiring harness connector and retainers to remove

8. Remove the cooling fan and shroud.

9. Remove or disconnect the following:
- Air cleaner and outlet pipe
- Windshield washer hoses from the hood
- Hood.
- Wiring harness electrical connector and the engine wiring harness-to-Powertrain Control Module (PCM) electrical connectors
- Heater hoses and vacuum hose to heater valve at bulkhead
- Engine ground wire at the bulkhead
- Evaporative emissions (EVAP) tube from the engine connection and position it aside
- Upper radiator hose
- Power steering pump pulley bolts
- Accessory drive belt
- Power steering pump pulley
- Lower radiator hose at the coolant pump
- PSP switch electrical connector
- PSP hose and PS pump bracket bolts (position pump aside)
- Brake booster vacuum hoses and tubes from the cylinder head cover
- EVAP canister purge valve connector and EVAP hose
- A/C tubes from compressor
- A/C high-pressure cut-off switch electrical connector
- High-pressure A/C tube from the condenser
- A/C tube from the retainer
- Transmission; see "Transmission" section
- Starter
- Oil filter
- Transmission cooler tube bracket (support with wire)
- Battery cable retainer bracket from frame rail
- LH engine support insulator through-bolt
- RH engine support insulator nuts
- If equipped, block heater electrical connector and retainer
- Heater tube bracket bolt

10. Install the lifting hangars on the LH and RH sides of the engine, using bolts on the exhaust manifolds to retain the hangars.

11. Attach the lifting sling, and with a floor crane, remove the engine.

To install:

12. Using the floor crane, carefully lower the engine into the vehicle.

13. Install the RH engine support insulator nuts, and tighten the nuts to 66 ft. lbs. (90 Nm).

14. Remove the lifting hangar from the RH side of the engine.

15. Install the heater tube bracket bolt. Tighten the bolt to 25 ft. lbs. (34 Nm).

16. Install the block heater electrical connector and wiring harness retainer, if equipped.

17. Remove the lifting hangar from the LH side of the engine.

18. Install or connect the following:
- LH support insulator through bolt; tighten to 76 ft. lbs. (103 Nm)
- Transmission cooler tubes; tighten the nut to 17 ft. lbs. (23 Nm)
- Oil filter
- Transmission; see "Transmission" section
- Starter and terminal connections
- A/C tube and pressure cutout switch; tighten switch to 11 ft. lbs. (15 Nm)
- A/C tubes to the compressor, with new seals
- EVAP hose and purge valve electrical connector
- Brake booster vacuum hose
- Power steering pump; tighten bolts to 18 ft. lbs. (25 Nm)
- PSP hose and PS pump hoses
- PSP switch electrical connector
- Lower radiator hose to the coolant pump
- PS pump pulley; install bolts finger-tight
- Accessory drive belt
- PS pump pulley bolts to 18 ft. lbs. (25 Nm)
- Upper radiator hose
- EVAP hose
- Ground wire; tighten body bolt to 89 inch lbs. (10 Nm)
- Heater hoses to bulkhead connection
- Heater control valve vacuum hose connection
- Wiring harness to PCM electrical connectors
- Hood; align to marks made during removal
- Windshield washer hose to hood
- Air cleaner and outlet pipe
- Battery cables to power distribution center terminals
- Wiring harness in-line connector
- Remaining ground wire to body
- Battery cables to battery
- Fuel supply tube spring-lock coupling

19. Refill the engine with new oil.

20. Fill the cooling system with proper coolant mixture.

21. Evacuate and recharge the A/C system.

22. Start the engine and check for leaks.

23. Stop the engine and check all fluid levels.

2007 Explorer, Explorer Sport-Trac and Mountaineer

See Figures 201 through 205.

1. Before servicing the vehicle, refer to the precautions in the beginning of this section.

2. Release the fuel system pressure as follows:

a. Remove the fuel pump relay (located in the battery junction box).

b. Start the engine and allow it to idle until it stalls.

c. After the engine stalls, crank the engine for approximately 5 seconds to make sure the fuel rail pressure has been released.

d. Turn the ignition switch to the OFF position.

3. Remove the fuel line spring-lock coupling.

4. Remove or disconnect the following:
- Battery cables
- Engine ground wire from body
- Wiring harness connector and retainers along the fender

5. Lift the engine compartment relay box cover and disconnect the battery cable from the stud.

6. Recover the A/C system refrigerant.

7. Drain the cooling system.

8. Remove the cooling fan and shroud as follows:

a. Remove the upper radiator cover.

b. Remove the fan shroud screws.

c. Place a piece of cardboard against the radiator to prevent damage while removing the cooling fan.

d. Remove the cooling fan.

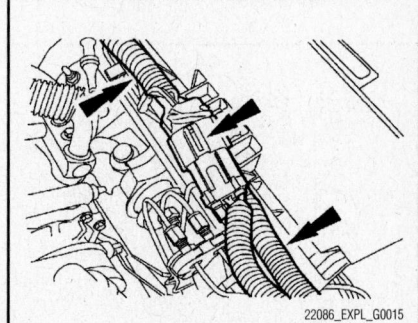

22086_EXPL_G0015

Fig. 201 Identifying the wiring harness connector and retainers to remove from fender—2006-07 4.0L

9. Disconnect the windshield washer hoses from the hood. Mark the hood hinge locations and remove the hinge bolts and the hood.

10. Remove or disconnect the following:
- Air cleaner assembly and the outlet pipe
- Windshield washer hose from the hood clips
- Hood hinge bolts (mark hinge locations for reinstallation)
- Hood
- Wiring harness connector, PCM connectors, harness retainer

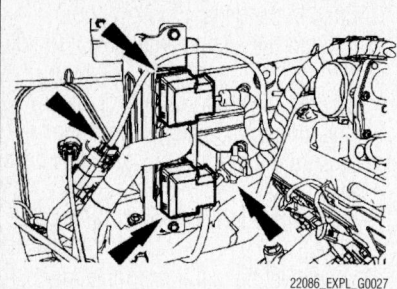

Fig. 202 Disconnect the harness connector, PCM connectors, harness retainer—4.0L engine (2006–07 models)

- Heater control valve vacuum hose and heater hoses from the bulkhead
- Engine ground wire at the bulkhead
- Evaporative emissions (EVAP) tube from the engine connection and position it aside
- Upper radiator hose
- Power steering pump pulley bolts (loosen only)
- Accessory drive belt
- Power steering pump pulley
- Lower radiator hose
- PSP switch electrical connector
- PSP hose and pump supply hose bracket bolts

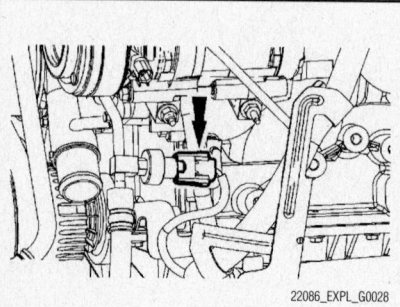

Fig. 203 Disconnect the PSP switch electrical connector—4.0L engine (2007 models)

- Power steering pump; position out of the way
- Brake booster vacuum hose from the cylinder head cover
- EVAP canister purge valve electrical connector
- EVAP hose

Fig. 204 Disconnect the EVAP purge valve electrical connector and EVAP hose—4.0L engine (2007 models)

- A/C tubes from the compressor
- A/C high-pressure switch electrical connector
- High-pressure A/C tube from the condenser

11. Remove the transmission.

12. Remove or disconnect the following:
- Starter motor
- Oil filter
- Transmission cooler tube connector/bracket (suspend with wire)
- Battery cable harness bracket from the frame rail
- LH engine support through-bolt
- RH engine support nuts
- Block heater electrical connector and harness retainer (if equipped)
- Heater tube bracket bolt

13. Install the lifting hangars on the LH and RH sides of the engine, using bolts on the exhaust manifolds to retain the hangars.

14. Attach the lifting sling, and with a floor crane, remove the engine.

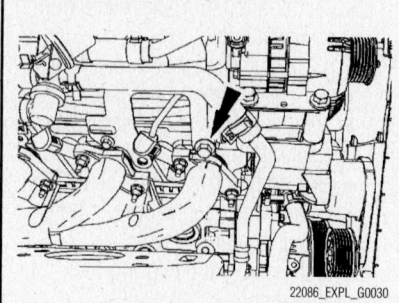

Fig. 205 Remove the heater tube bracket bolt—4.0L engine (2007 models)

To install:

15. Using the floor crane, carefully lower the engine into the vehicle.

16. Install the RH engine support insulator nuts, and tighten the nuts to 66 ft. lbs. (90 Nm).

17. Remove the lifting hangar from the RH side of the engine.

18. Install the heater tube bracket bolt and torque it to 25 ft. lbs. (34 Nm).

19. If equipped, connect the block heater connector and the wiring harness retainer.

20. Remove the LH engine lifting hangar.

21. Install the LH engine support through-bolt and tighten it to 76 ft. lbs. (103 Nm).

22. Install or connect the following:
- Battery cable harness bracket and nut; torque to 11 ft. lbs. (15 Nm)
- Transmission cooler tube bracket; torque nut to 17 ft. lbs. (23 Nm)
- Oil filter
- Transmission
- Starter and wiring
- A/C high-pressure tube to the condenser (with a new gasket and O-ring seal); tighten the fitting to 11 ft. lbs. (15 Nm)
- High-pressure cutoff switch electrical connector
- A/C tubes to the compressor (with new gaskets and new O-ring seals); tighten the tube fitting nuts to 11 ft. lbs. (15 Nm) and the bracket nut to 89 inch lbs. (10 Nm)
- EVAP hose to canister purge valve
- Purge valve electrical connector
- Brake booster vacuum hose to the cylinder head cover
- Power steering pump; torque the bolts to 18 ft. lbs. (25 Nm)
- Power steering pump-to-reservoir hoses
- PSP hose and PSP switch electrical connector
- Lower radiator hose
- Power steering pump pulley; install bolts only finger-tight
- Accessory drive belt
- Power steering pump pulley bolts to 18 ft. lbs. (25 Nm)
- Upper radiator hose
- EVAP hose to connector
- Engine ground wire at body attachment; torque the bolt to 89 inch lbs. (10 Nm)
- Heater hoses and heater valve vacuum hose at bulkhead
- Engine wiring harness-to-Powertrain Control Module (PCM) electrical connectors and the wiring harness electrical connector; wiring harness retainer

- Hood; torque bolts to 9 ft. lbs. (12 Nm)
- Windshield washer hose to hood clips
- Air cleaner and outlet pipe
- Engine cooling fan
- Battery cable connectors and nuts; torque to 9 ft. lbs. (12 Nm)
- Wiring harness connector and retainer at bulkhead
- Engine ground wire at bulkhead; torque nut to 80 inch lbs. (9 Nm)
- Battery cables
- Fuel supply tube spring-lock coupling

23. Refill the engine with clean engine oil.

24. Refill the cooling system.

25. Evacuate and recharge the A/C system.

26. Start the engine and check for leaks. Stop the engine and check all fluid levels.

27. Perform an A/C system leak test.

28. Check the transmission fluid level.

4.6L (VIN H) Engine

2005 Aviator

See Figures 206 through 211.

See Figures 212 through 214.

See Figures 215 through 218.

1. Before servicing the vehicle, refer to the precautions in the beginning of this section.

2. Remove the transmission.

3. Remove the hood (mark the hinge locations for reinstallation).

4. Properly discharge and recover the A/C system.

5. Remove the air cleaner assembly.

6. Remove the engine cooling fan and cooling module.

7. Properly relieve the fuel system pressure as follows:

   a. Remove the fuel line service valve cap.

   b. Install a special tool (pressure gauge with an in-line petcock) and slowly open the petcock to relieve the fuel system pressure into a suitable container.

   c. Remove the special tool.

   d. Immediately cap all fuel system openings to prevent contamination.

8. Drain the engine oil.

9. Disconnect the accelerator cable, the speed control cable and the throttle return spring.

10. Release the speed control cable from the pin-type retainer.

11. Remove the 2 bolts and position the bracket and cables aside.

Fig. 206 Showing the fuel line service valve (1, 2) location—4.6L (VIN H) engine

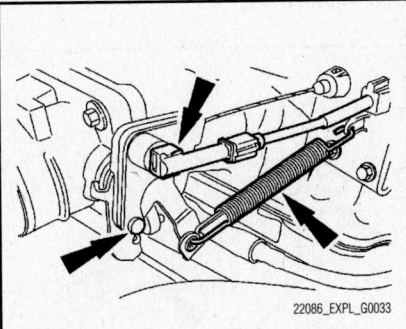

Fig. 207 Disconnect the accelerator cable, the speed control cable and the throttle return spring—4.6L (VIN H) engine

Fig. 208 Release the speed control cable from the pin-type retainer—4.6L (VIN H) engine

12. Remove or disconnect the following:

- Heater hoses from the coolant pump and block
- 2 vacuum hose connections as shown.
- Coolant hose from the retaining clips on the RH valve cover and position aside
- Coolant hose from the intake manifold
- Engine wiring harness and the electrical connector from the Powertrain Control Module (PCM)
- Engine wiring harness from the 3 retaining clips and position aside
- Wiring harness and remove the wiring harness retaining clip

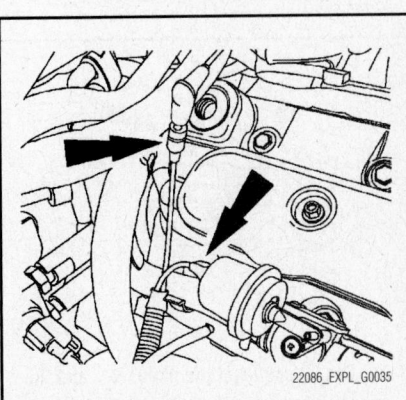

Fig. 209 Disconnect the 2 vacuum hose connections shown—4.6L (VIN H) engine

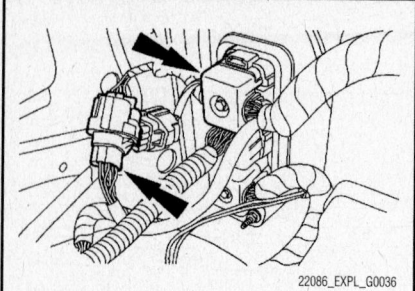

Fig. 210 Disconnect the wiring harness and the electrical connector from the Powertrain Control Module (PCM)—4.6L (VIN H) engine

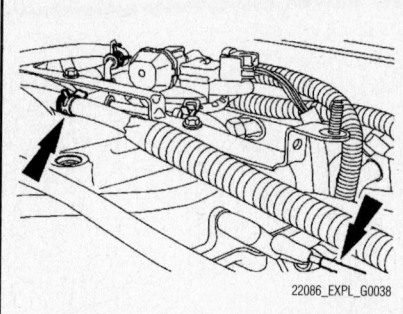

Fig. 212 Disconnect the 2 vacuum hoses from the vapor management (VMV) valve-to-intake manifold—4.6L (VIN H) engine

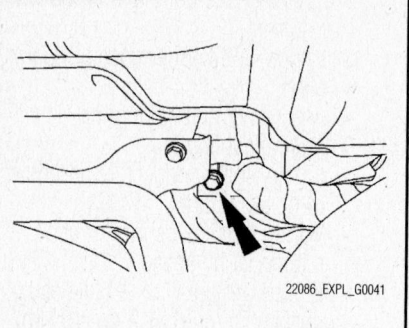

Fig. 215 Remove the bolt and position the A/C compressor manifold assembly aside—4.6L (VIN H) engine

- Ground strap bolt
- Electrical connector and the vacuum hose from the exhaust gas recirculation (EGR) system module
- EGR system module
- Vacuum harness from the retainer clip
- Brake booster hose from the intake manifold
- Fuel tube
- 2 vacuum hoses from the vapor management (VMV) valve-to-intake manifold
- Power distribution supply electrical connector (from inside the box cover)
- Positive and negative battery cables
- Battery cable harness pin-type retainers and position the harness aside
- Power steering reservoir hose from the power steering cooler
- Power steering pressure (PSP) switch electrical connector
- Power steering pressure tube from the power steering pump
- Power steering pressure hose bracket from the front cover

- Power steering pressure hose support bracket and position aside
- Position the A/C compressor manifold assembly aside
- LH engine mount through-bolt
- 2 nuts from the RH engine mount (through the wheel well)

13. Install engine lifting eyes on each side of the block.

14. Using a lifting crane, carefully lift the engine from the vehicle.

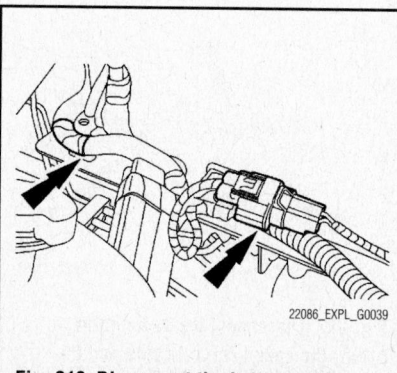

Fig. 213 Disconnect the battery cable harness pin-type retainers and position the harness—4.6L (VIN H) engine

To install:

15. Using the lifting crane, carefully position the engine into the vehicle.

16. Install the 2 nuts to the RH engine mount (through the wheel well). Tighten the nuts to 66 ft. lbs. (90 Nm).

17. Install the LH engine mount through-bolt. Tighten the bolt to 59 ft. lbs. (80 Nm).

18. Remove the crane and the lifting eyes from the engine.

19. Install or connect the following:
- A/C compressor manifold assembly; tighten the bolt to 15 ft. lbs. (20 Nm)
- New O-ring seal on the power steering pressure (PSP) tube fitting
- PSP tube to the power steering pump; tighten the fitting to 48 ft. lbs. (65 Nm)
- PS hose support bracket; tighten the bolt to 89 inch lbs. (10 Nm)
- PSP hose bracket to the front cover
- PSP switch electrical connector
- Power steering reservoir hose to the power steering cooler

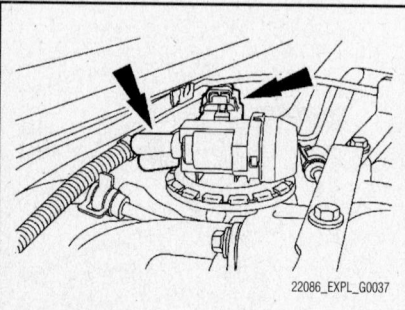

Fig. 211 Disconnect the connector and the vacuum hose from the exhaust gas recirculation (EGR) system module—4.6L (VIN H) engine

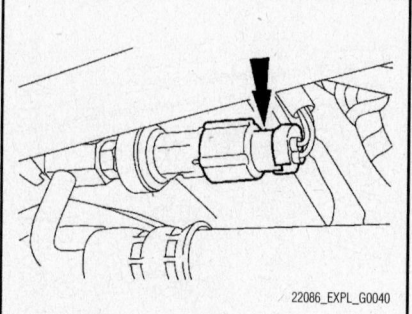

Fig. 214 Disconnect the Power steering pressure (PSP) switch electrical connector—4.6L (VIN H) engine

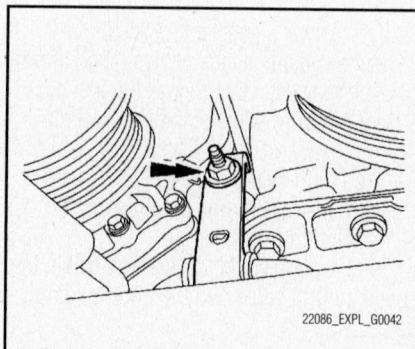

Fig. 216 Install the PS hose support bracket as shown—4.6L (VIN H) engine

- Battery cable harness and install the pin-type retainers

✳✳ CAUTION

Do not connect the negative battery cable at this time.

- Positive battery cable to the battery
- Power distribution power supply electrical connector; tighten the fastener to 89 inch lbs. (10 Nm)
- Power distribution box cover
- 2 vacuum hoses
- Fuel tube
- Brake booster hose to the intake manifold
- Vacuum harness and install it in the retainer
- 2 bolts and the exhaust gas recirculation (EGR) system module; tighten the bolts to 15 ft. lbs. (20 Nm)
- EGR system module tube nut to the EGR system module
- Electrical connector and the vacuum hose to the EGR system module
- Ground strap to the body; tighten the nut to 89 inch lbs. (10 Nm)
- Wiring harness retaining clip and the wiring harness
- Engine wiring harness into the 3 retaining clips
- Engine wiring harness and the electrical connector to the Powertrain Control Module (PCM)
- Coolant hose to the intake manifold
- Coolant hose into the retaining clips on the RH valve cover
- Vacuum harness and install the 2 vacuum hoses
- Coolant hoses to the coolant pump and engine
- Accelerator bracket and cables and install the 2 bolts; tighten the bolts to 89 inch lbs. (10 Nm)

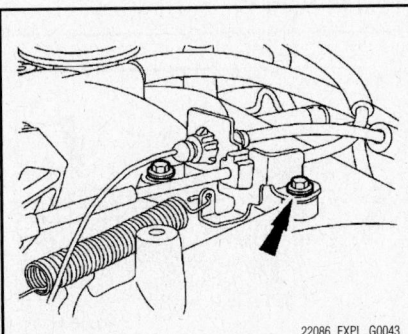

Fig. 217 Connect the accelerator bracket and cables and install the 2 bolts—4.6L (VIN H) engine

Fig. 218 Connect the speed control cable into the pin-type retainer—4.6L (VIN H) engine

- Speed control cable into the pin-type retainer
20. Install the transmission.
21. Install the cooling fan and shroud module.
22. Install the air cleaner assembly.
23. Install a new oil filter and refill the engine with clean engine oil
24. Connect the negative battery cable.
25. Fill and bleed the engine cooling system.
26. Evacuate and recharge the A/C system.
27. Start the engine and check for leaks. Stop the engine and recheck all fluid levels.
28. Perform an A/C system leak check.
29. Perform a transmission fluid level check.
30. Install the hood.

4.6L (VIN W) ENGINE

2005 Explorer, Explorer Sport-Trac and Mountaineer

See Figures 219 through 240.

1. Before servicing the vehicle, refer to the precautions in the beginning of this section.
2. Release the fuel system pressure as follows:
   a. Remove the fuel pump relay (located in the battery junction box).
   b. Start the engine and allow it to idle until it stalls.
   c. After the engine stalls, crank the engine for approximately 5 seconds to make sure the fuel rail pressure has been released.
   d. Turn the ignition switch to the OFF position.
3. Disconnect the fuel tube spring coupling.
4. Disconnect the electrical connector and detach the wiring harness pin-type retainers.

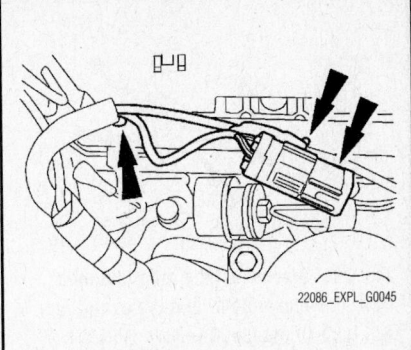

Fig. 219 Disconnect the electrical connector and detach the wiring harness pin-type retainers—4.6L (VIN W) engine

5. Lift the power distribution box cover, remove the nut and disconnect the wiring harness terminals.
6. Drain the cooling system.
7. Properly discharge and recover the A/C system.
8. Remove or disconnect the following:

- Hood
- Air cleaner outlet tube
- Mass Air Flow (MAF) sensor electrical connector
- Air cleaner assembly
- Upper radiator appearance cover
- Upper radiator hose and heater hose from engine connections
- Upper radiator hose and degas bottle vent hose
- Heater hoses from the bulkhead connections
- A/C pressure switch electrical connector
- A/C manifold and tube assembly from the condenser
- A/C tube from the retainers on top of the condenser and position the tube aside

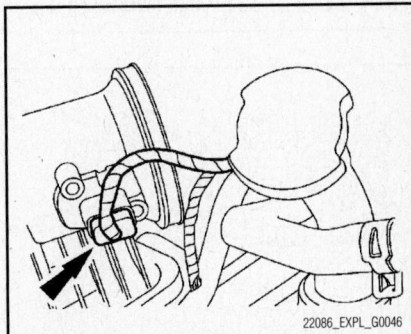

Fig. 220 Disconnect the electrical connector from the MAF sensor—4.6L (VIN W) engine

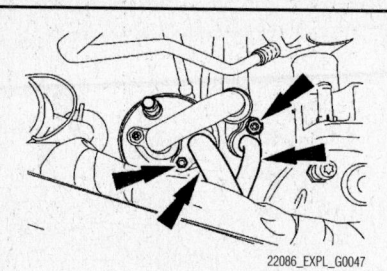

Fig. 221 Disconnect the manifold tube from the accumulator and the auxiliary A/C tube (if equipped)—4.6L (VIN W) engine

✳✳ CAUTION

Immediately cap all A/C system openings to prevent contamination.

- Manifold tube from the accumulator
- Auxiliary A/C tube (if equipped)
- Evaporator tube from the condenser
- 2 bolts and the screw(s) retaining the fan shroud (from both sides)

➡**Some vehicles are equipped with only one retaining screw.**

- Upper fan shroud
- Engine cooling fan
- Heater control valve bracket bolt

- Heater control vacuum supply hose
- Brake booster vacuum hose from the vacuum booster
- Hoses from the evaporative emissions (EVAP) canister purge valve
- Position aside the throttle cable bracket

9. Install the lifting eye tool to the engine as shown.

10. Drain the engine oil. Reinstall the drain plug when finished. Torque the plug to 10 ft. lbs. (14 Nm).

11. Remove or disconnect the following:

- Upper radiator hose from the radiator; remove the hose from the retainer
- Lower radiator hose from the coolant pump
- Lower fan shroud
- Lower air deflector (pin-type retainers)
- Tubes from the transmission cooler (drain the coolant into a suitable container)
- LH and RH radiator support brackets
- Radiator and condenser, as an assembly

12. On 4WD models, position a jack under the transfer case.

13. On 2WD models, support the transmission with a transmission jack. Secure

the transmission to the jack with a safety chain.

14. On all models, remove or disconnect the following:

- RH catalytic converter heat shield
- Both HO2S sensor electrical connectors
- Both catalyst monitor sensor electrical connectors
- RH exhaust heat shield
- LH exhaust heat shield bolt
- 2 nuts and the plastic shield on the RH side of the crossmember
- Crossmember 4 upper bolts and 4 lower bolts

15. On 2WD models, remove the bolts and bracket, as shown.

16. On all models, remove the 2 nuts in the center of the crossmember. Remove the crossmember.

17. Support the dual-converter Y-pipe with a jack stand, then disconnect the muffler from the Y-pipe.

18. Remove the transmission rear mount.

19. Remove the Y-pipe from the exhaust manifold. Remove the jack stand.

20. Disconnect the shift cable and remove the bolts and the bracket.

21. Position the manual shift lever out of the park position by moving it forward.

22. On 4WD models, mark the flanges

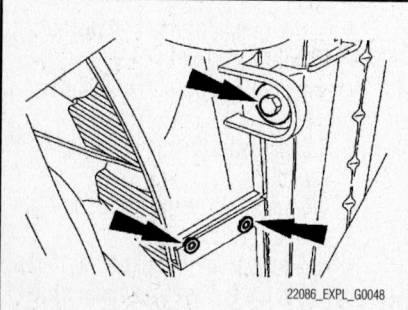

Fig. 222 Remove the 2 bolts and screw(s) from the fan shroud—4.6L (VIN W) engine

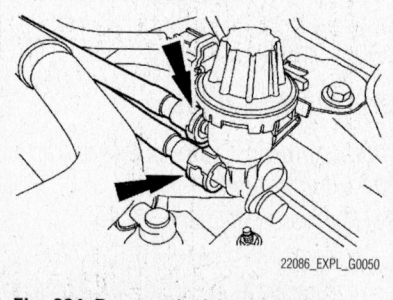

Fig. 224 Remove the hoses from the evaporative emissions (EVAP) canister purge valve—4.6L (VIN W) engine

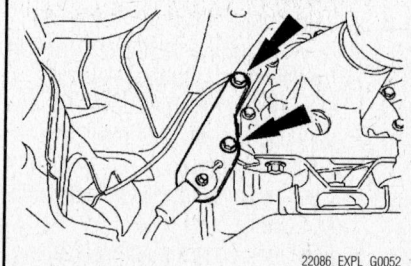

Fig. 226 On 2WD models, remove the bolts and bracket, as shown—4.6L (VIN W) engine

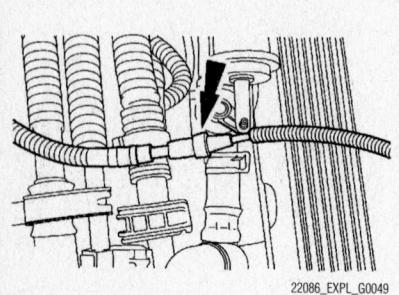

Fig. 223 Remove the heater control vacuum supply hose—4.6L (VIN W) engine

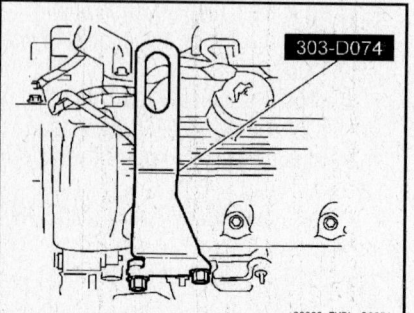

Fig. 225 Install the lifting eye tool to the engine as shown—4.6L (VIN W) engine

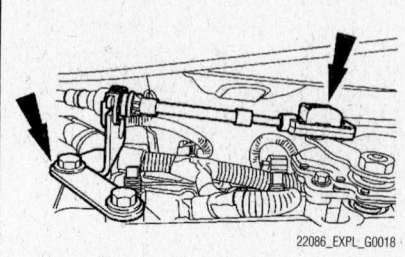

Fig. 227 Disconnect the shift cable and remove the bolts and the bracket—4.6L (VIN W) engine

for installation reference, then remove the front driveshaft.

23. On all models, mark the flanges for installation reference, then remove the rear driveshaft.

24. Disconnect the Turbine Shaft Speed (TSS) sensor, the Output Shaft Speed (OSS) sensor and the Intermediate Shaft Speed (ISS) sensor electrical connectors.

25. Remove or disconnect the following:
- Solenoid body electrical connector
- Transmission range sensor electrical connector (move rubber boot back for access)
- Wiring harness retainers from the side of the transmission
- Both heated oxygen sensor (HO2S) electrical connector retainers from the transmission
- LH catalyst monitor sensor electrical retainer from the transmission
- RH catalyst monitor sensor electrical connector retainer and the fuel tubes from the bracket

Fig. 228 Disconnect the Turbine Shaft Speed (TSS) sensor, the Output Shaft Speed (OSS) sensor and the Intermediate Shaft Speed (ISS) sensor electrical connectors—4.6L (VIN W) engine

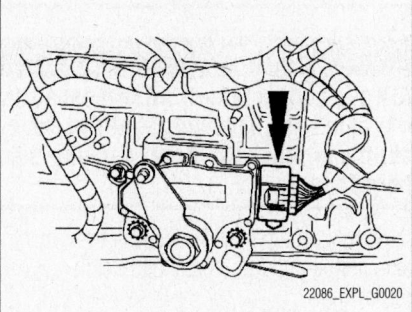

Fig. 229 Disconnect the transmission range sensor electrical connector (move rubber boot back for access)—4.6L (VIN W) engine

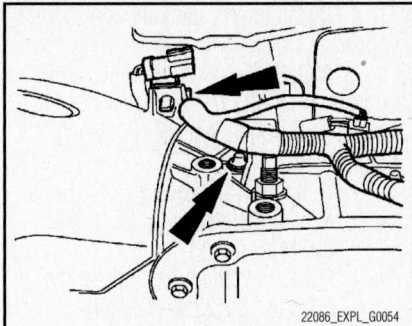

Fig. 230 Disconnect both heated oxygen sensor (HO2S) electrical connector retainers from the transmission—4.6L (VIN W) engine (RH shown; LH similar)

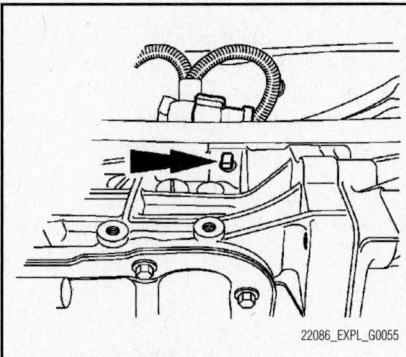

Fig. 231 Disconnect the LH catalyst monitor sensor electrical retainer from the transmission—4.6L (VIN W) engine

26. On 4WD models, perform the following:

a. If equipped, disconnect the shift motor electrical connector and detach the harness pin-type retainer(s).

b. Support the transmission with a transmission jack, and secure the transmission to the jack with a safety chain.

c. Remove the jack stand from the transfer case.

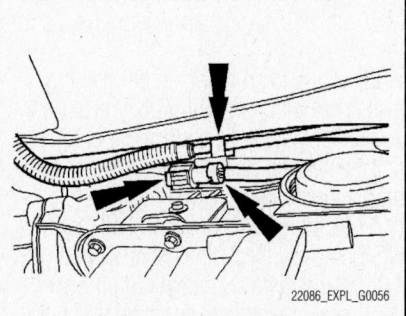

Fig. 232 Disconnect the RH catalyst monitor sensor electrical connector retainer and the fuel tubes from the bracket—4.6L (VIN W) engine

27. On all models, remove or disconnect the following:
- 4 bolts and the front crossmember
- Starter
- 2 rear bolts and the flexplate cover
- Torque converter access cover
- 4 torque converter nuts (mark one stud and the flexplate for assembly reference)
- Transmission cooler tube fittings
- 7 transmission-to-engine bolts

28. Support the engine with a wood block for stability.

29. Lower the transmission and, if equipped, the transfer case.

30. Remove or disconnect the following:
- LH HO2S wiring harness from the retainer
- Nut and the cooler tube bracket (near the flexplate)
- Power steering return hose from the PS cooler (drain the fluid)
- Power steering pressure (PSP) hose
- Nut and washer from the RH engine mount
- Bolt from the LH engine mount
- Fuel charging wiring harness electrical connectors
- Fuel charging wiring harness pin-type retainer
- Harness retaining clip from the ground stud bolt
- Stud bolt and disconnect the ground strap

31. Install the lifting eye to the RH side of the engine as shown.

32. Support the fuel hose with mechanic's wire.

33. Attach a lifting crane and carefully remove the engine.

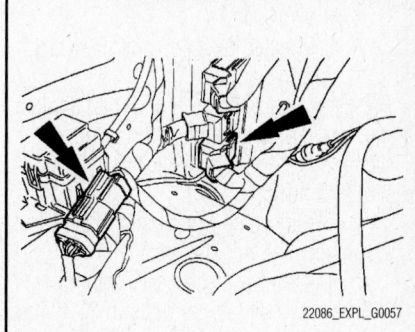

Fig. 233 Disconnect the fuel charging wiring harness electrical connectors—4.6L (VIN W) engine

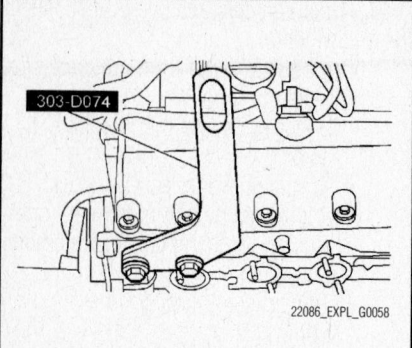

Fig. 234 Install the lifting eye to the engine as shown—4.6L (VIN W) engine

To install:

34. With the lifting crane, carefully position the engine into the vehicle.

35. Remove the lifting crane and sling.

36. Remove the mechanic's wire from the fuel hose.

37. Remove the lifting eye from the RH side of the engine.

38. Install or connect the following:
- Ground strap and install the stud bolt
- Fuel charging wiring harness electrical connectors
- Harness retaining clip to the ground stud bolt
- Fuel charging wiring harness push pins
- LH engine support insulator through-bolt; torque to 76 ft. lbs. (103 Nm)
- Washer and nut on the RH engine support insulator; torque to 66 ft. lbs. (90 Nm)
- New seal on the power steering pressure hose fitting
- Power steering pressure hose; tighten the fitting to 48 ft. lbs. (66 Nm)
- Power steering return hose and clamp
- Power steering cooler tubes and install the nut; torque to 89 inch lbs. (10 Nm)
- LH heated oxygen sensor (HO2S) wiring harness

39. Make sure the stud and the flexplate marks made during removal line up.

40. Install the transmission and transfer case as follows:

a. Position the transmission and, if equipped, the transfer case.

b. Install the 7 engine-to-transmission bolts. Tighten the bolts to 35 ft. lbs. (48 Nm).

c. Remove the wooden support from the front of the engine.

d. Install the 4 torque converter nuts. Tighten the nuts to 28 ft. lbs. (38 Nm).

e. Install the torque converter access cover.

f. Install the flexplate cover and tighten the bolts to 19 ft. lbs. (26 Nm).

41. Install or connect the following:
- Starter
- Transmission fluid cooler tubes; tighten the fittings to 26 ft. lbs. (35 Nm)
- Front crossmember; tighten the bolts to 52 ft. lbs. (70 Nm)

42. Support the transfer case with a suitable jack stand (4WD).

43. Disconnect the safety chain and remove the transmission jack (4WD).

44. If equipped, connect the shift motor electrical connector and wiring harness pin-type retainer(s).

45. Attach the RH catalyst monitor sensor electrical connector and the fuel tubes to the bracket.

46. Attach the LH catalyst monitor sensor electrical connector to the transmission.

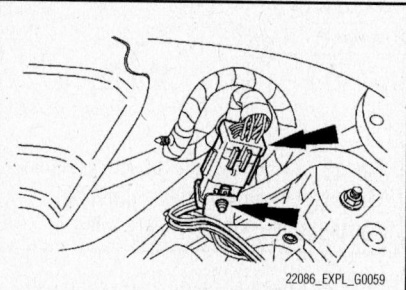

Fig. 235 If equipped, connect the shift motor electrical connector and wiring harness pin-type retainer(s)—4.6L (VIN W) engine

47. Attach the RH and LH HO2S wiring harness retainers to the transmission.

48. Connect the wiring harness retainers to the side of the transmission.

49. Connect the Transmission Range (TR) sensor electrical connector. Reposition the rubber boot.

50. Install and lubricate new O-ring seals on the transmission body electrical connector, connect the electrical connector and tighten the screw. Tighten to not more than 44 inch lbs. (5 Nm).

51. Connect the Turbine Shaft Speed (TSS) sensor, the Output Shaft Speed (OSS) sensor and the Intermediate Shaft Speed (ISS) sensor electrical connectors, on the side of the transmission.

> ✳✳ **CAUTION**
>
> The driveshaft flange fits tightly on the rear axle pinion flange pilot. To

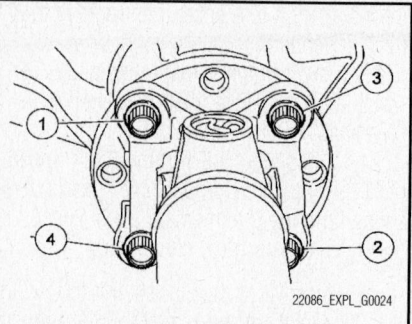

Fig. 236 Showing the driveshaft-to-pinion flange bolt tightening sequence—4.6L (VIN W) engine

make sure that the driveshaft flange seats squarely on the pinion flange, tighten the bolts evenly in the sequence shown.

52. Align the marks made on the flange and driveshaft during removal.

53. Remove the plug placed in the transmission (2WD).

54. Position the driveshaft and install the driveshaft-to-pinion flange bolts. Tighten, in sequence, to 83 ft. lbs. (112 Nm).

55. Verify the can flange is housed correctly in the CV joint housing as shown in the cut-away illustration, top box. Install a new driveshaft if the can flange is not housed correctly.

> ✳✳ **CAUTION**
>
> The can (domed CV joint housing cover) is pressed into the CV joint housing at the factory. When housed correctly, the can will appear as shown in the cut-away illustration, top box. Do not reseat the can in the CV joint housing if the can's flange is above the CV joint housing shown in the cut-away illustration, bottom box. Install a new driveshaft.

> ✳✳ **CAUTION**
>
> Always connect the front driveshaft to the axle first. The weight of the driveshaft can pinch the boot, causing the boot to tear.

56. Align the marks made on the front axle flange and the driveshaft during removal.

57. Install new bolts and washers, in sequence, to 22 ft. lbs. (30 Nm).

58. Install new universal joint retainers and bolts. Tighten the bolts to 13 ft. lbs. (18 Nm).

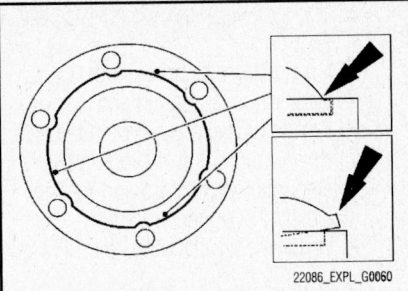

Fig. 237 Verify the can flange is housed correctly in the CV joint housing as shown in the cut-away illustration, top box—4.6L (VIN W) engine

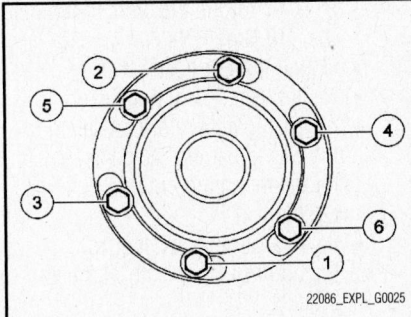

Fig. 238 Install the front axle flange new bolts and washers, in sequence—4.6L (VIN W) engine

59. Place the manual shift lever in the park position by moving it to the rear.

60. Position the shift cable and bracket, install the bolts and connect the cable to the manual shift lever. Tighten the bolts to 30 ft. lbs. (40 Nm).

61. Position the dual converter Y-pipe with the heat shields on a jack stand and loosely install the 4 nuts.

62. Install the transmission rear mount and loosely install the bolts.

63. Using a new gasket, connect the dual converter Y-pipe to the muffler and install the bolts, springs and flag nuts. Tighten the nuts to 30 ft. lbs. (40 Nm).

64. Tighten the 4 dual converter Y-pipe-to-exhaust manifold nuts to 30 ft. lbs. (40 Nm).

65. Tighten the transmission rear mount bolts to 66 ft. lbs. (90 Nm).

66. Remove the jack stand from the dual converter Y-pipe.

67. Connect the LH and RH HO2S electrical connectors.

68. Position the crossmember and loosely install the 2 nuts.

69. Install the 4 crossmember lower bolts and the 4 upper bolts. Tighten to 52 ft. lbs. (70 Nm).

70. On 2WD, position the cable bracket and install the bolts. Tighten the bolts to 18 ft. lbs. (25 Nm).

71. Disconnect the safety chain and remove the transmission jack (2WD).

72. Remove the jack stand from the transfer case (4WD).

73. Tighten the 2 crossmember nuts, near the center, to 66 ft. lbs. (90 Nm).

74. Position the plastic shield on the right side of the crossmember and install the nuts.

75. Position the RH and LH heat shields and install the bolts to 15 ft. lbs. (20 Nm).

76. Install or connect the following:
- Radiator and A/C condenser assembly
- Radiator support brackets and bolts to 9 ft. lbs. (12 Nm).
- Power steering cooler hoses
- Lower air deflector (pin retainers)
- lower fan shroud and install the bolts to 62 inch lbs. (7 Nm)
- Lower radiator hose to coolant pump and into hose retainer

77. Remove the engine lifting brackets.

78. Position the bracket and install the bolts to 15 ft. lbs. (20 Nm).

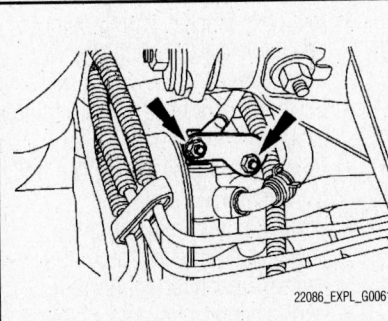

Fig. 239 Position the bracket and install the bolts—2005 Explorer And Mountaineer 4.6L

79. Install or connect the following:
- Evaporative emissions (EVAP) canister purge valve hoses
- Brake booster vacuum hose
- Heater control vacuum supply hose
- Heater control valve bracket and install the bolt to 89 inch lbs. (10 Nm)
- Cooling fan; tighten the bolts to 41 ft. lbs. (55 Nm)
- Upper fan shroud

➡**Do not install the assembly screw holding the upper and lower shrouds together.**

- 2 bolts on each side of the fan shroud

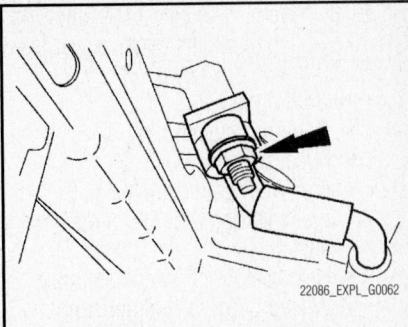

Fig. 240 Install the tube and nut to the radiator—2005 Explorer And Mountaineer 4.6L

- Tube and install the nut
- A/C tubes to the condenser and install the nuts; if equipped, position the auxiliary A/C tube and install the nuts to 71 inch lbs. (8 Nm)
- A/C pressure switch electrical connector
- Heater hose
- Upper radiator and degas vent hoses
- Upper radiator and heater hoses to engine
- Radiator appearance cover
- Air cleaner assembly
- MAF sensor connector
- Air cleaner outlet tube
- Spring-lock coupling on fuel hose
- Wiring terminals at power distribution center
- Wiring harness connectors and retaining clips
- Battery cables
- Hood
- Windshield washer hose to hood

80. Refill engine with clean oil and new oil filter.

81. Fill and bleed the cooling system.

82. Fill the power steering system.

83. Evacuate and recharge the A/C system.

84. Start the engine and check for leaks. Stop the engine and recheck all fluid levels.

85. Perform an A/C system leak check.

2006–07 Explorer and Mountaineer; 2007 Explorer Sport-Trac

See Figure 241.

1. Before servicing the vehicle, refer to the precautions in the beginning of this section.

2. Disconnect the windshield washer hose from the hood.

3. Mark the hood hinges and remove the hood.

4. Remove the intake manifold; see "Intake Manifold".

5. Remove or disconnect the following:
- Wiring terminals under power distribution box cover
- Cooling fan
- Cooling system fluid
- Accessory drive belt
- Electrical connector beneath the A/C tube and A/C pressure switch
- Heated PCV fitting coolant hose
- Wiring harness retainer from the cooling fan wiring harness bracket
- Alternator
- Heater hose from heater control valve
- Upper radiator hose
- Coolant crossover manifold, the gaskets, the heated PCV fitting and the heated PCV fitting coolant hose as an assembly
- Evaporative emission (EVAP) canister purge valve electrical connector
- Heater hose retainer from the RH valve cover
- In-line electrical connector and the 2 Powertrain Control Module (PCM) electrical connectors, and detach the wiring harness pin-type retainer
- Heater hoses
- Engine ground wire from the body terminal
- Transmission; see "Transmission" section
- Inner fender splash shield
- Power steering pressure hose bracket
- Wiring harness brackets near the oil filter and pulley
- Wiring harness retainer from the power steering pump stud bolt
- Stud bolts and position the power steering pump aside
- Lower radiator hose from the oil filter adapter
- A/C clutch electrical connector and detach the wiring harness retainer; remove the nut and detach the A/C hose bracket
- A/C compressor aside
- Engine oil and filter; install the drain plug when finished
- Oil temperature sensor
- Wiring harness bracket from the RH engine support insulator bracket
- RH splash shield
- RH engine support insulator nuts
- Block heater electrical connector (if equipped) and wiring harness retainers

- LH engine support insulator through bolt

6. Install the engine lifting tools and use a suitable floor crane to carefully lift the engine from the vehicle.

To install:

7. Position the engine in the vehicle and remove the floor crane.

8. Remove the lifting tools from the engine.

9. Install or connect the following:
- LH engine support insulator through bolt to 76 ft. lbs. (103 Nm)
- Block heater wiring harness retainers (if equipped) and connect the block heater electrical connector
- RH engine support insulator nuts to 66 ft. lbs. (90 Nm)
- RH splash shield and install the pushpins
- Battery cable bracket on the RH engine support insulator bracket and install the bolt to 11 ft. lbs. (15 Nm)
- Oil temperature sensor to 11 ft. lbs. (15 Nm)
- A/C compressor; torque fasteners to 18 ft. lbs. (25 Nm)
- A/C hose bracket, wiring harness retainer and A/C clutch electrical connector
- Lower radiator hose to the oil filter adapter
- Power steering pump; tighten bolts to 18 ft. lbs. (25 Nm)
- Wiring harness retainer to the power steering pump stud bolt below heater hose connection
- Wiring harness brackets on block
- Power steering pressure hose bracket
- Inner fender splash shield

- Transmission; see "Transmission" section
- Ground wire to body stud
- Heater hoses at bulkhead
- Wiring harness pin-type retainer, 2 Powertrain Control Module (PCM) electrical connectors and in-line electrical connector
- Heater hose retainer to the RH valve cover
- EVAP canister purge valve electrical connector
- Coolant crossover, the heated positive crankcase ventilation (PCV) fitting and the heated PCV fitting hose as an assembly, with new gaskets; torque the bolts to 89 inch lbs. (10 Nm)
- Upper radiator hose
- Heater hose to control valve
- Alternator, alternator bracket and the wiring harness as an assembly; torque mounting nuts to 18 ft. lbs. (25 Nm)
- Wiring harness retainer to the cooling fan wiring harness bracket
- Heated PCV fitting coolant hose
- Electrical connector located beneath the A/C tube and A/C pressure switch
- Accessory drive belt
- Engine cooling fan
- Wiring harness terminals to power distribution center
- Intake manifold; see "Intake Manifold"
- Hood; torque bolts to 9 ft. lbs. (12 Nm)
- Windshield washer hose to hood

10. Refill the engine with clean oil, using a new oil filter.

11. Fill and bleed the cooling system.

22086_EXPL_G0063

Fig. 241 Connect the wiring harness pin-type retainer, 2 Powertrain Control Module (PCM) electrical connectors and in-line electrical connector—2006–07 Explorer And Mountaineer 4.6L

12. Evacuate and recharge the A/C system.

13. Start the engine and check for leaks; stop the engine and recheck all fluid levels.

14. Perform an A/C system leak check.

EXHAUST MANIFOLD

REMOVAL & INSTALLATION

4.0L (VIN E, K) Engine

2005–07 Explorer, Explorer Sport-Trac and Mountaineer

See Figures 242 and 243.

1. Before servicing the vehicle, refer to the "Precautions" section.

2. Remove or disconnect the following:
   - Negative battery cable
   - EGR tube (RH manifold)
   - Exhaust pipe attaching bolts
   - Exhaust manifold and discard the gasket

To install:

3. Clean the gasket mating surfaces.

4. Install or connect the following:
   - New gasket and the exhaust manifold. Torque the bolts to 16 ft. lbs. (22 Nm).

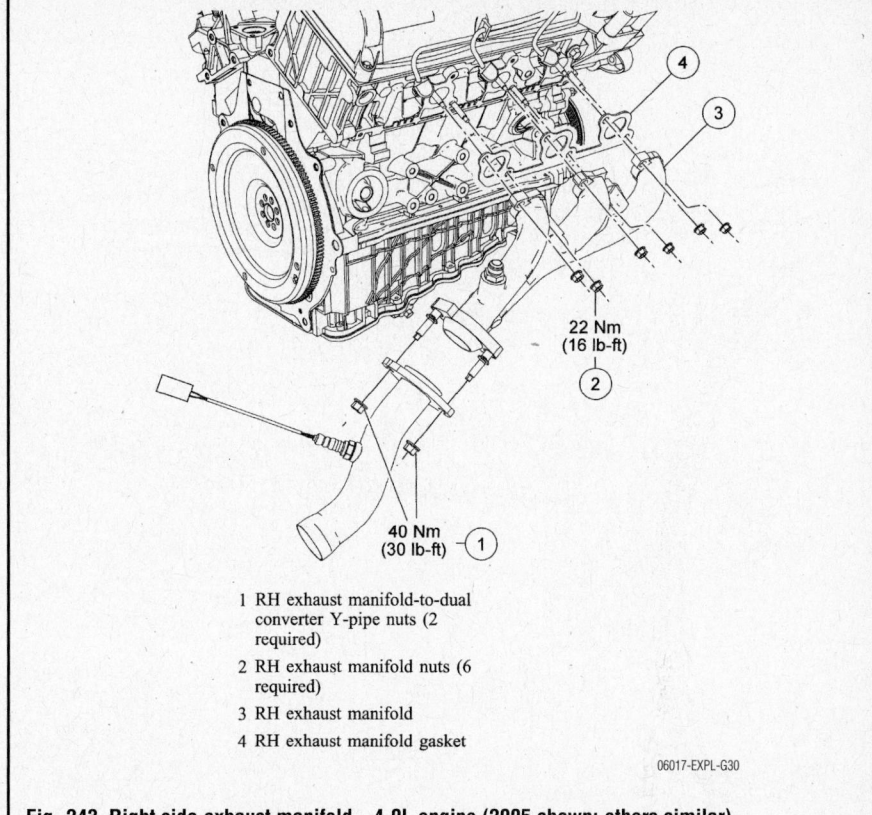

1 RH exhaust manifold-to-dual converter Y-pipe nuts (2 required)

2 RH exhaust manifold nuts (6 required)

3 RH exhaust manifold

4 RH exhaust manifold gasket

06017-EXPL-G30

Fig. 243 Right side exhaust manifold—4.0L engine (2005 shown; others similar)

- Exhaust pipe-to-manifold attaching bolts. Torque the bolts to 30 ft. lbs. (40 Nm).
- EGR tube to the manifold. Torque the fastener to 30 ft. lbs. (40 Nm) (RH manifold)
- Negative battery cable

5. Start the vehicle and check for leaks, repair if necessary.

4.6L (VIN H) Engine

Right Side

See Figure 244.

1. Before servicing the vehicle, refer to the "Precautions" section.

2. Remove or disconnect the following:
   - Tire and wheel
   - Front inner fender well
   - Y-pipe from manifold
   - EGR tube from manifold
   - Heat shield
   - Manifold and gasket

To install:

3. Position the exhaust manifold, with new gaskets, and tighten the new nuts to 15 ft. lbs. (20 Nm).

4. Install or connect the following:
   - Heat shield; tighten the bolts to 8 ft. lbs. (11 Nm)
   - EGR tube to the manifold

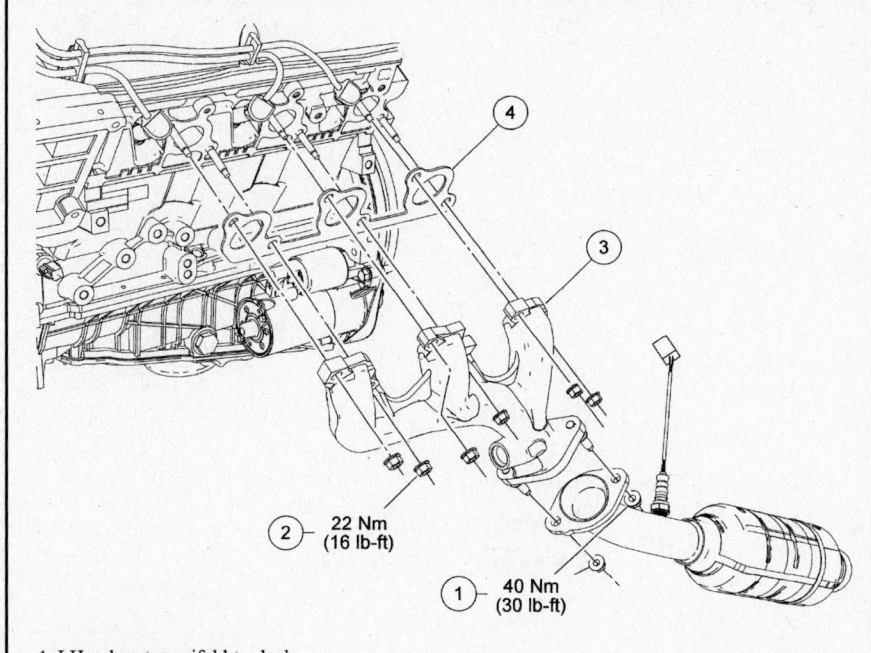

1 LH exhaust manifold-to-dual converter Y-pipe nuts (2 required)

2 LH exhaust manifold nut (6 required)

3 LH exhaust manifold

4 LH exhaust manifold gasket

06017-EXPL-G29

Fig. 242 Left side exhaust manifold—4.0L engine (2005 shown; others similar)

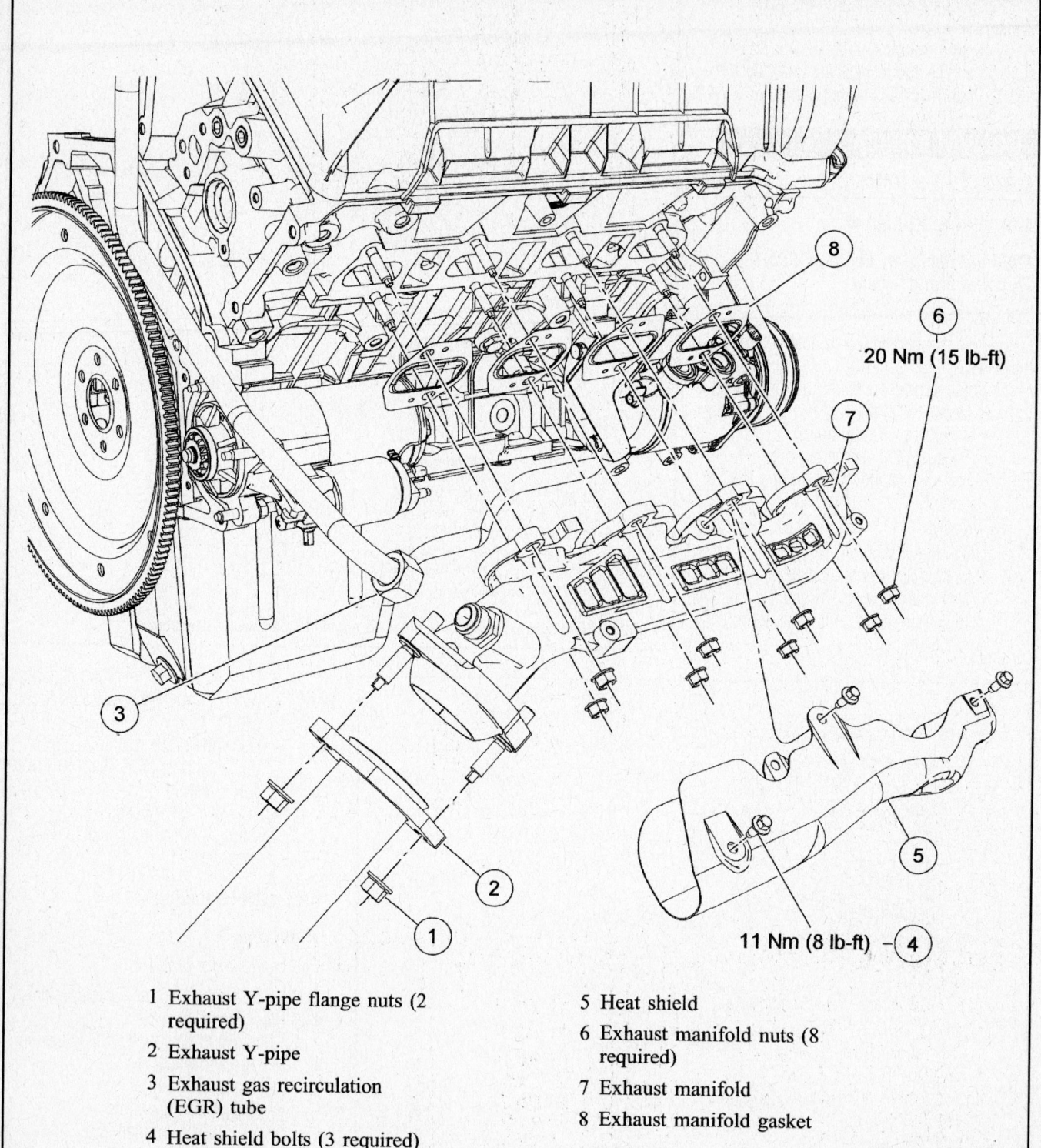

20 Nm (15 lb-ft)

11 Nm (8 lb-ft)

1. Exhaust Y-pipe flange nuts (2 required)
2. Exhaust Y-pipe
3. Exhaust gas recirculation (EGR) tube
4. Heat shield bolts (3 required)
5. Heat shield
6. Exhaust manifold nuts (8 required)
7. Exhaust manifold
8. Exhaust manifold gasket

06017-EXPL-G35

Fig. 244 Right side exhaust manifold and related parts—2005 Aviator 4.6L (VIN H) engine

- Y-pipe to the manifold; tighten the new nuts to 15 ft. lbs. (20 Nm)
- Inner fender well
- Tire and wheel

Left Side
See Figure 245.

1. Before servicing the vehicle, refer to the "Precautions" section.

2. Remove or disconnect the following:
   - Intermediate steering shaft
   - LH front wheel and tire
   - LH front fender well
   - Y-pipe from manifold

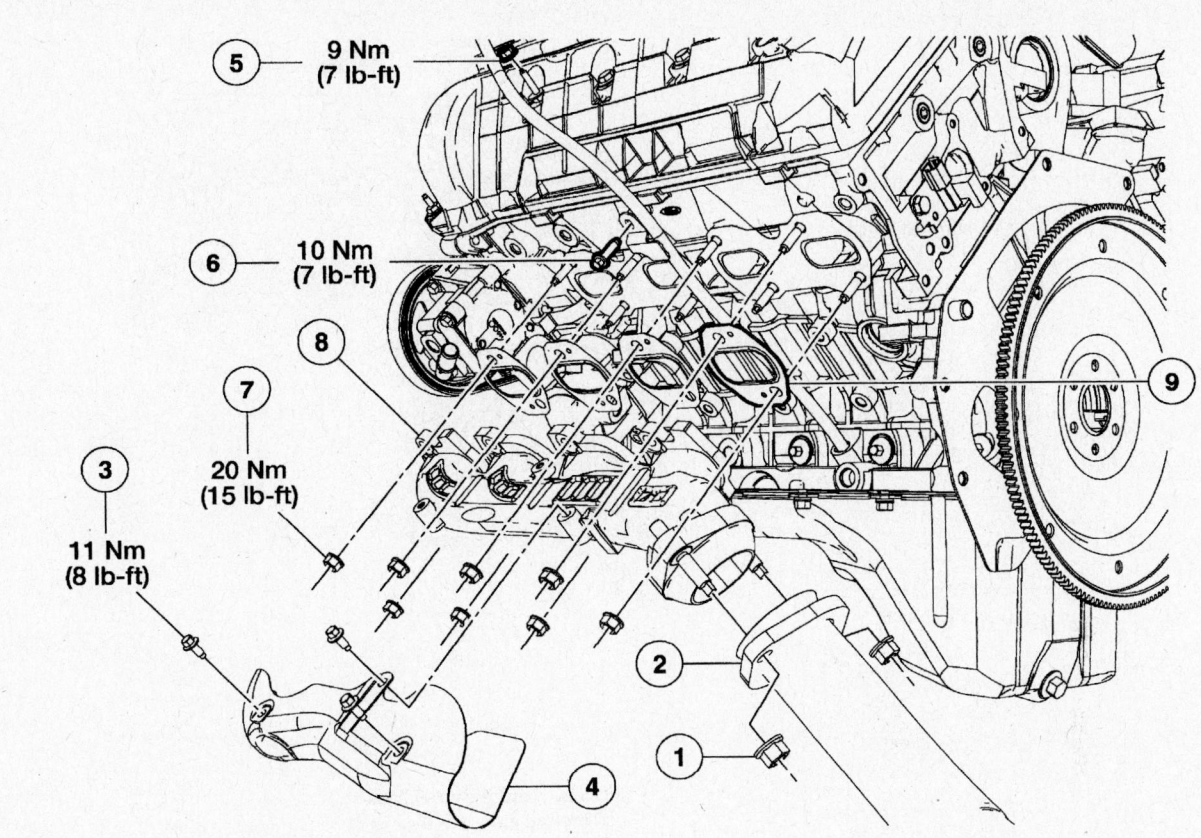

1. Exhaust Y-pipe flange nuts (2 required)
2. Exhaust Y-pipe
3. Heat shield bolts (3 required)
4. Heat shield
5. Oil indicator tube bracket nut
6. Oil indicator bracket bolt
7. Exhaust manifold nuts (8 required)
8. Exhaust manifold
9. Exhaust manifold gasket

06017-EXPL-G34

Fig. 245 Left side exhaust manifold and related parts—2005 Aviator 4.6L (VIN H) engine

- Heat shield
- LH exhaust manifold and gasket

To install:

3. Install the exhaust manifold, with a new gasket and nuts. Tighten the nuts to 15 ft. lbs. (20 Nm).

4. Install or connect the following:
- Heat shield
- Y-pipe to manifold, with new nuts; tighten the nuts to 15 ft. lbs. (20 Nm)
- LH inner fender well
- LH tire and wheel
- Intermediate steering shaft

4.6L (VIN W or VIN 8) Engine

Right Side

See Figures 246 through 248.

1. Before servicing the vehicle, refer to the "Precautions" section.

2. Remove or disconnect the following:
- Front fender splash shield
- EGR tube from the manifold (2005 only)
- RH transmission mount bolt (2005 only)
- Y-pipe from the exhaust manifold
- Heat shield
- Eight nuts and the exhaust manifold

3. Installation is the reverse of the removal procedure.

4. Tighten the exhaust manifold nuts in the sequence shown to the following:
- 2005: 15 ft. lbs. (20 Nm)
- 2006–07: studs—9 ft. lbs. (12 Nm); nuts—18 ft. lbs. (25 Nm)

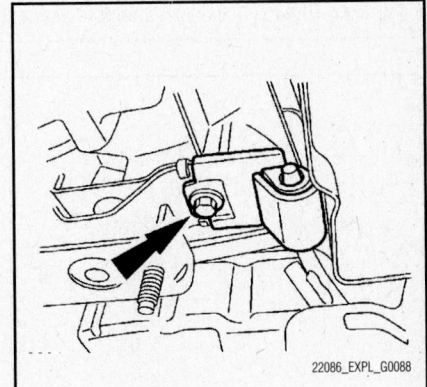

22086_EXPL_G0088

Fig. 246 Remove the RH transmission mount bolt to remove the Y-pipe—2005 4.6L (VIN 8) engine

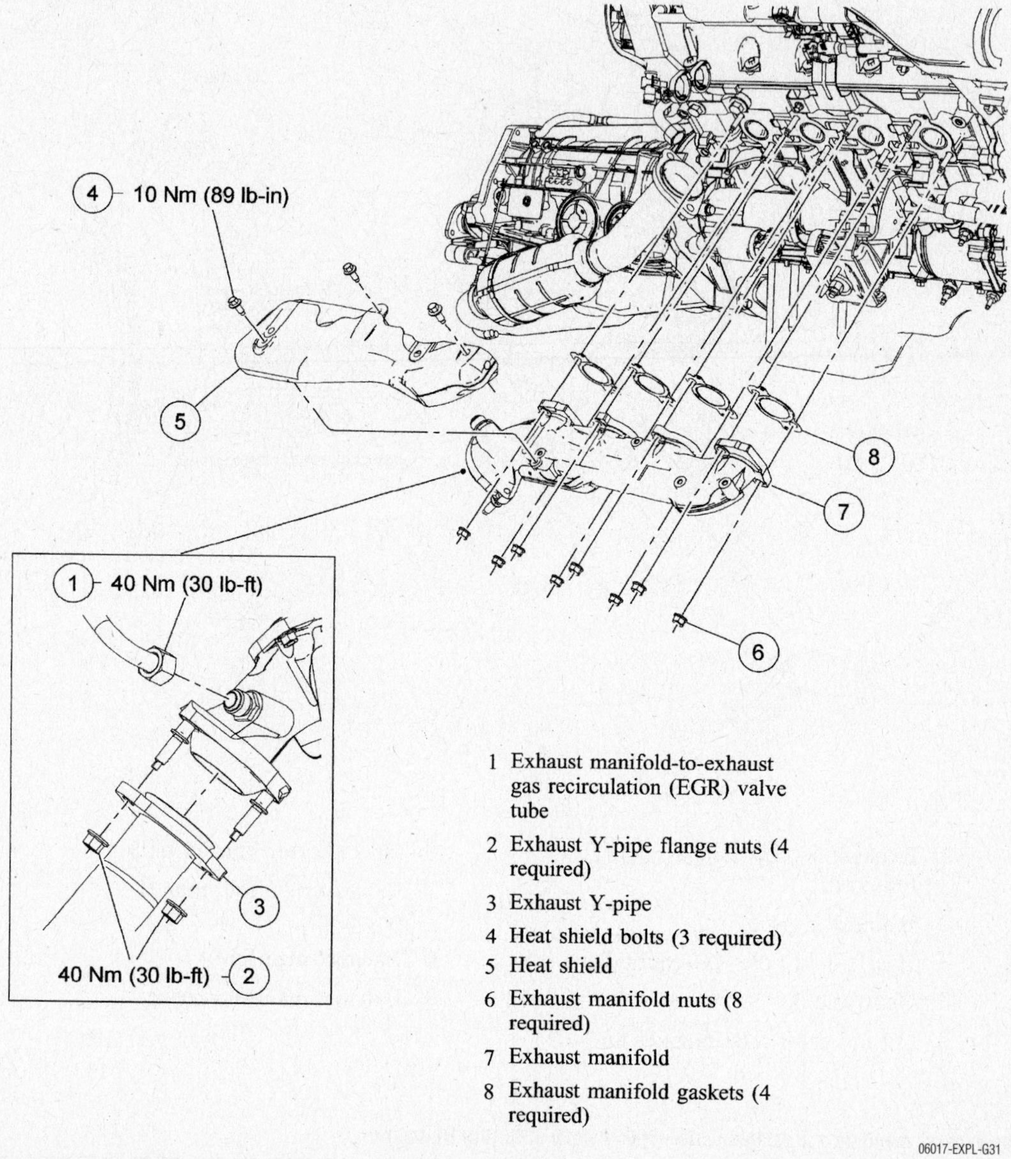

4 — 10 Nm (89 lb-in)

5

8

7

6

1 — 40 Nm (30 lb-ft)

3

40 Nm (30 lb-ft) — 2

1 Exhaust manifold-to-exhaust gas recirculation (EGR) valve tube
2 Exhaust Y-pipe flange nuts (4 required)
3 Exhaust Y-pipe
4 Heat shield bolts (3 required)
5 Heat shield
6 Exhaust manifold nuts (8 required)
7 Exhaust manifold
8 Exhaust manifold gaskets (4 required)

06017-EXPL-G31

Fig. 247 Right side exhaust manifold and related parts—2005 4.6L (VIN W) engine

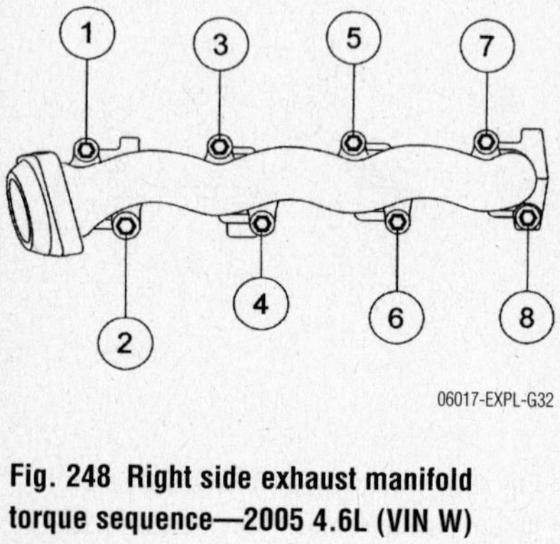

1   3   5   7

2   4   6   8

06017-EXPL-G32

Fig. 248 Right side exhaust manifold torque sequence—2005 4.6L (VIN W) engine

5. Tighten the transmission mount bolt to 66 ft. lbs. (90 Nm) (2005 only)

6. Tighten the Y-pipe new nuts as follows:
- 2005: 15 ft. lbs. (20 Nm)
- 2006–07: 30 ft. lbs. (40 Nm)

Left Side

See Figures 249 through 251.

1. Before servicing the vehicle, refer to the "Precautions" section.

2. Remove or disconnect the following:
- EVAP purge valve from the bracket and position aside (2006–07 models)
- Front fender splash shield

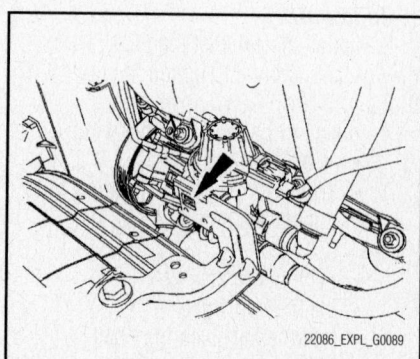

22086_EXPL_G0089

Fig. 249 Remove the EVAP purge valve from the bracket and position aside— 2006–07 4.6L (VIN 8) engine

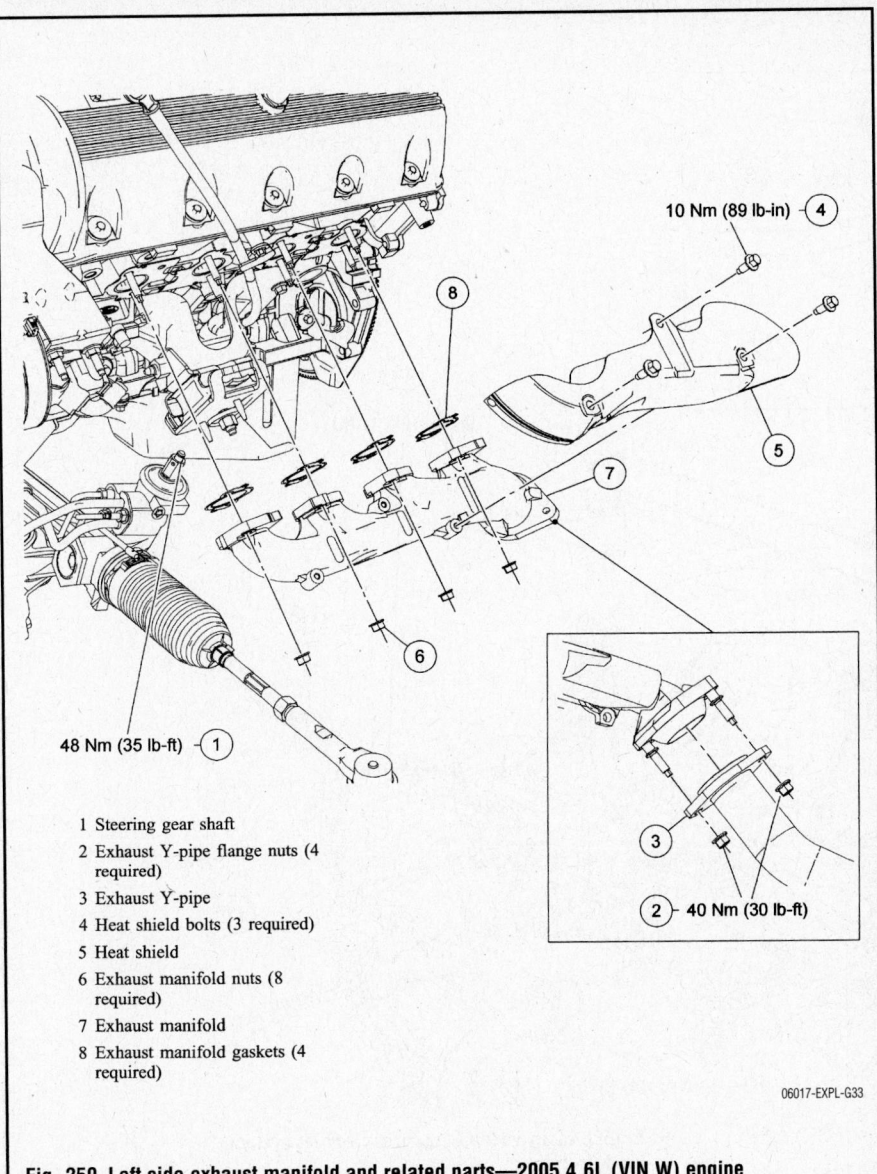

10 Nm (89 lb-in) — 4

48 Nm (35 lb-ft) — 1

40 Nm (30 lb-ft)

1 Steering gear shaft
2 Exhaust Y-pipe flange nuts (4 required)
3 Exhaust Y-pipe
4 Heat shield bolts (3 required)
5 Heat shield
6 Exhaust manifold nuts (8 required)
7 Exhaust manifold
8 Exhaust manifold gaskets (4 required)

06017-EXPL-G33

Fig. 250 Left side exhaust manifold and related parts—2005 4.6L (VIN W) engine

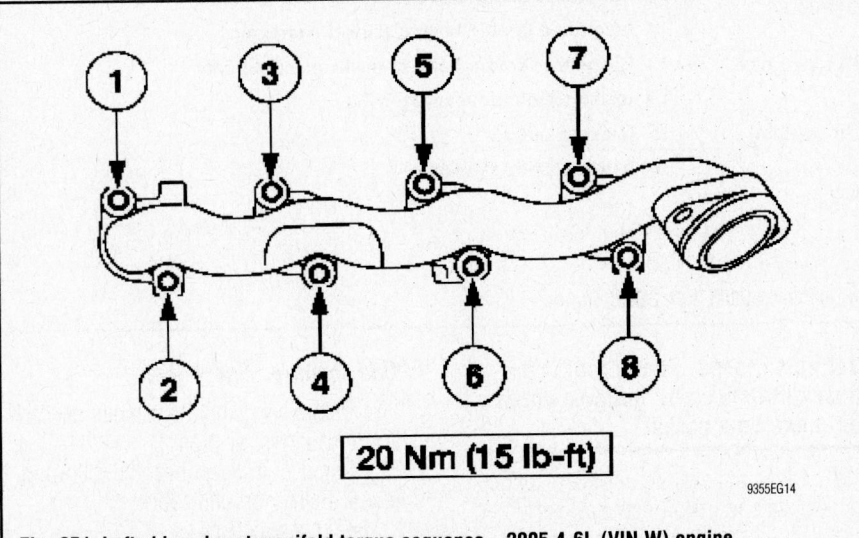

20 Nm (15 lb-ft)

9355EG14

Fig. 251 Left side exhaust manifold torque sequence—2005 4.6L (VIN W) engine

- Lower steering column shaft pinch bolt. Position the lower steering column shaft aside.
- Exhaust manifold heat shield
- 8 nuts and the exhaust manifold

To install:

3. Installation is the reverse of the removal procedure, noting the following:

a. Tighten the nuts in the sequence shown as follows:

- 2005: 15 ft. lbs. (20 Nm)
- 2006–07: studs—9 ft. lbs. (12 Nm); nuts—18 ft. lbs. (25 Nm)

4. Tighten the Y-pipe new nuts as follows:

- 2005: 15 ft. lbs. (20 Nm)
- 2006–07: 30 ft. lbs. (40 Nm)

5. Tighten the intermediate shaft pinch bolt to 35 ft. lbs. (48 Nm).

INTAKE MANIFOLD

REMOVAL & INSTALLATION

4.0L (VIN E, K) Engine

2005 Explorer and Mountaineer

See Figures 252 and 253.

1. Before servicing the vehicle, refer to the "Precautions" section.
2. Disconnect the negative battery cable.
3. Remove the air cleaner outlet pipe.
4. Remove the positive crankcase ventilation (PCV) tube
5. Remove the brake booster vacuum supply hose
6. Remove the engine main vacuum harness-to-intake manifold fitting
7. Remove the evaporative emissions (EVAP) return tube
8. Remove the EVAP tube pin-type retainer
9. Remove the exhaust gas recirculation (EGR) system module electrical connector
10. Remove the wiring harness pin-type retainer
11. Remove the engine main vacuum harness-to-EGR system module fitting
12. Remove the EGR tube fitting
13. Remove the throttle position (TP) sensor electrical connector
14. Remove the electronic throttle body electrical connector
15. Remove the electronic throttle body-to-intake manifold bolt
16. Remove the intake manifold mounting bolts
17. Remove the intake manifold
18. Remove the intake manifold gaskets

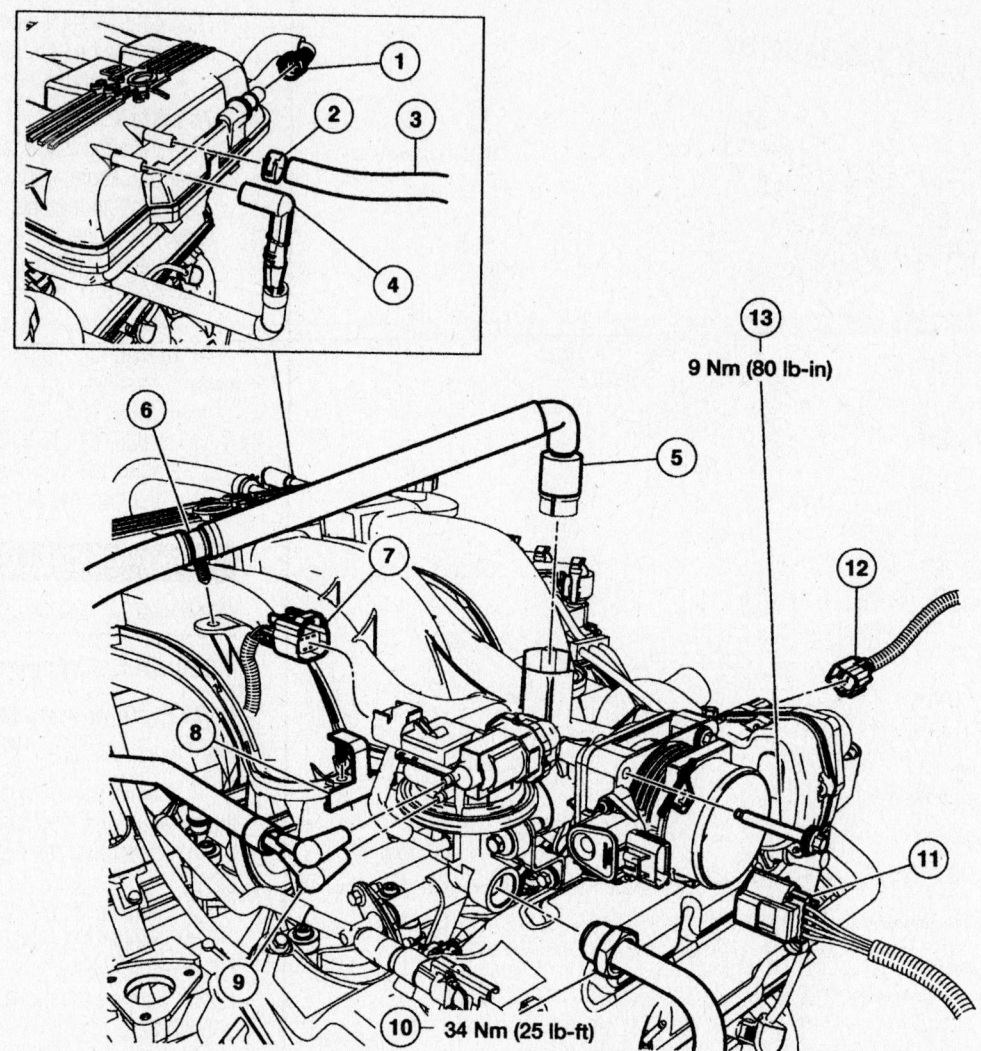

13   9 Nm (80 lb-in)

10   34 Nm (25 lb-ft)

1   Positive crankcase ventilation (PCV) tube
2   Brake booster vacuum supply hose clamp
3   Brake booster vacuum supply hose
4   Engine main vacuum harness-to-intake manifold fitting
5   Evaporative emissions (EVAP) return tube
6   EVAP tube pin-type retainer
7   Exhaust gas recirculation (EGR) system module electrical connector
8   Wiring harness pin-type retainer
9   Engine main vacuum harness-to-EGR system module fitting
10   EGR tube fitting
11   Throttle position (TP) sensor electrical connector
12   Electronic throttle body electrical connector
13   Electronic throttle body-to-intake manifold bolt
14   Intake manifold mounting bolts
15   Intake manifold
16   Intake manifold gaskets

67197EXPLG21

Fig. 252 Parts to be removed prior to intake manifold removal—2005 4.0L SOHC engine

To install:

19. Installation is the reverse of the removal procedure.

⁘ CAUTION

Do not use metal scrapers, wire brushes, power abrasive discs or other abrasive means to clean the

sealing surfaces. These tools can cause scratches and gouges which can make leak paths.

20. Clean the sealing surfaces, inspect the gaskets and install new gaskets if necessary. There is no special torque sequence.

2005 Explorer Sport-Trac

1. Before servicing the vehicle, refer to the "Precautions" section.
2. Remove or disconnect the following:
   • Battery ground cable
   • Engine cover
   • Air cleaner outlet pipe

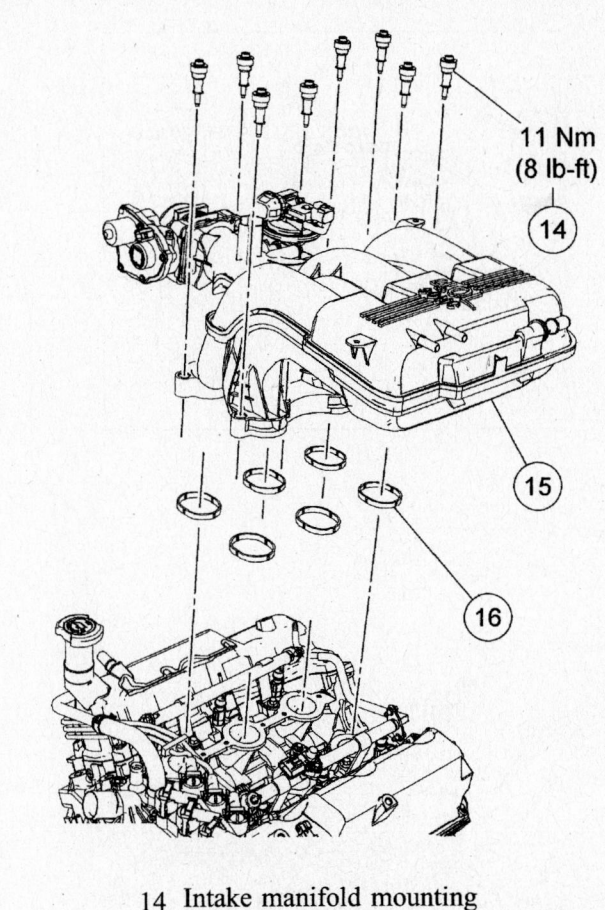

11 Nm
(8 lb-ft)

⑭

⑮

⑯

14 Intake manifold mounting
bolts (8 required)

15 Intake manifold

16 Intake manifold gaskets

06017-EXPL-G27

Fig. 253 Intake manifold removal—2005 4.0L SOHC engine

- Accelerator and speed control cables
- Idle air control valve and TP sensor electrical connectors
- TP sensor wiring routing clip
- EGR vacuum hose and EGR tube from EGR valve
- EGR vacuum regulator solenoid connections
- Fuel vapor hose
- Brake booster vacuum hose
- Spark plug wires (mark locations prior to removal)
- Accelerator cable routing clip and wiring harness
- Ignition coil bracket lower, then upper, bolts; position coil aside
- Remaining vacuum hoses from intake manifold (mark for installation locations)
- Wiring harness retaining nut at bulkhead

- PCM connector
- Ground wires from body connections
- Knock sensor connector
- Intake manifold bolts, and lift up manifold
- Heated PCV hose retainers and PCV fitting

3. Remove intake manifold

To install:

4. Clean the mating surfaces.

5. Position the intake manifold, while installing the PCV fitting and hose retainers.

6. With intake manifold fully in place, tighten the bolts to 89 inch lbs. (10 Nm).

7. Install or connect the following:
- Knock sensor connector
- Ground wires to body connections
- PCM connector

- Wiring harness retaining nut at bulkhead
- Vacuum hoses to intake manifold
- Ignition coil bracket lower, then upper, bolts
- Accelerator cable routing clip and wiring harness
- Spark plug wires
- Brake booster vacuum hose
- Fuel vapor hose
- EGR vacuum regulator solenoid connections
- EGR vacuum hose and EGR tube to EGR valve
- TP sensor wiring routing clip
- Idle air control valve and TP sensor electrical connectors
- Accelerator and speed control cables
- Air cleaner outlet pipe
- Engine cover

8. Connect the battery ground cable.

2006–07 Explorer and Mountaineer

See Figures 254 and 255.

1. Before servicing the vehicle, refer to the "Precautions" section.

2. Remove or disconnect the following:
- Air cleaner outlet pipe
- Knock sensor (KS) electrical connector from the intake manifold
- PCV tube from the intake manifold
- Brake booster vacuum hose from the intake manifold
- Main vacuum harness fitting from the intake manifold
- EVAP tube from the intake manifold
- EGR system module electrical connector
- Wiring harness retainer
- EGR system module vacuum fitting
- Exhaust manifold-to-EGR system module tube from the EGR system module
- TP sensor electrical connector
- Electronic Throttle Body (TB) electrical connector
- Wiring harness bracket from the electronic TB
- Intake manifold and the gaskets

To install:

3. Clean the sealing surfaces and inspect the gaskets. Install new gaskets if necessary.

4. Position the intake manifold and tighten the bolts to 8 ft. lbs. (11 Nm).

5. Install or connect the following:
- Wiring harness bracket to the electronic TB

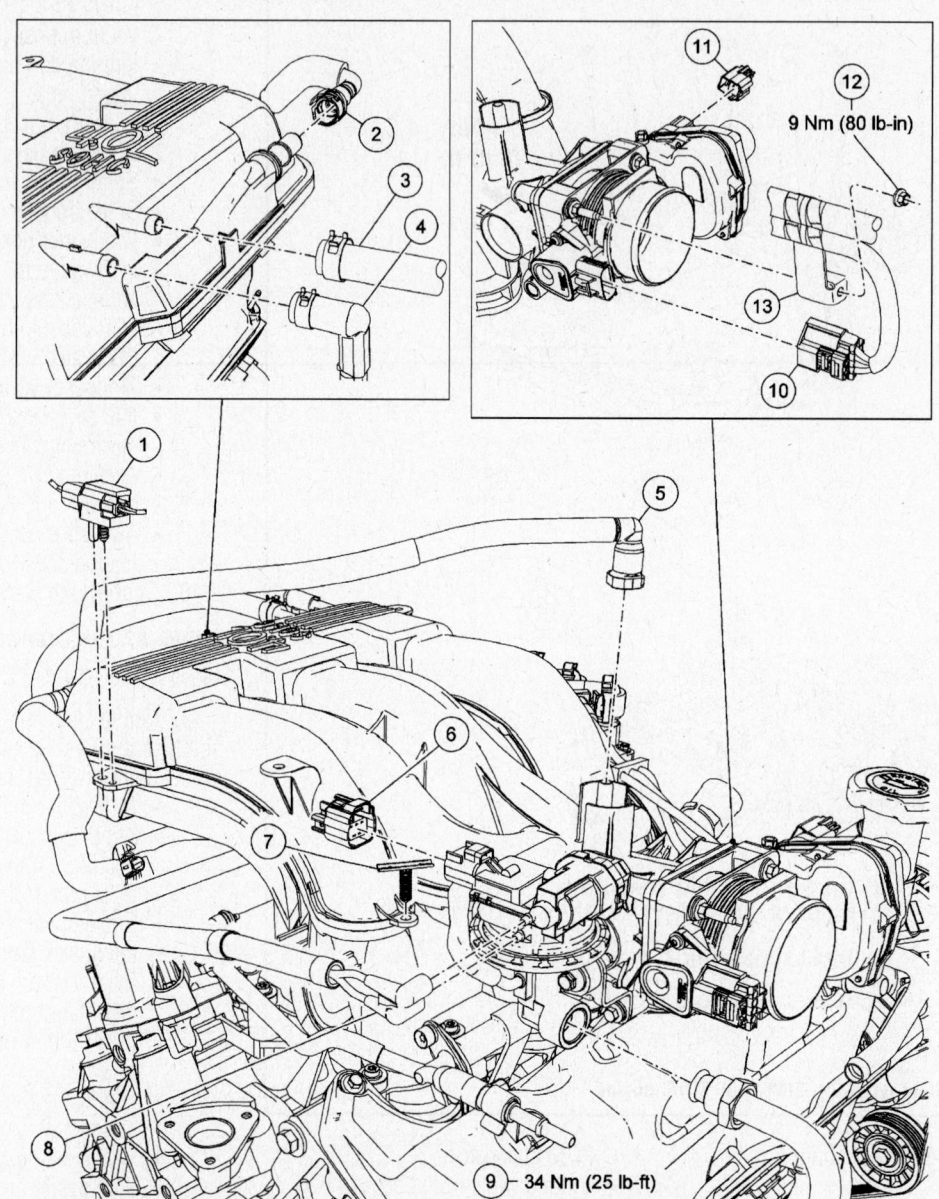

9 Nm (80 lb-in)

9 — 34 Nm (25 lb-ft)

1. Knock sensor (KS) electrical connector
2. Positive crankcase ventilation (PCV) tube
3. Brake booster vacuum supply hose
4. Engine main vacuum harness-to-intake manifold fitting
5. Evaporative emissions (EVAP) tube
6. Exhaust gas recirculation (EGR) system module electrical connector
7. Wiring harness pin-type retainer
8. EGR system module vacuum fitting
9. EGR tube fitting
10. Throttle position (TP) sensor electrical connector
11. Electronic throttle body (TB) electrical connector
12. Wiring harness nut
13. Wiring harness bracket

22086_EXPL_G0081

Fig. 254 Exploded view of the external engine component to remove for intake manifold removal—2006–07 4.0L (VIN E, K) engine

- Electronic TB electrical connector
- TP sensor electrical connector
- Exhaust manifold-to-EGR system module tube to the EGR system module
- EGR system module vacuum fitting
- Wiring harness retainer
- EGR system module electrical connector
- EVAP tube to the intake manifold
- Main vacuum harness fitting to the intake manifold
- Brake booster vacuum hose to the intake manifold
- PCV tube to the intake manifold
- Knock sensor (KS) electrical connector to the intake manifold
- Air cleaner outlet pipe

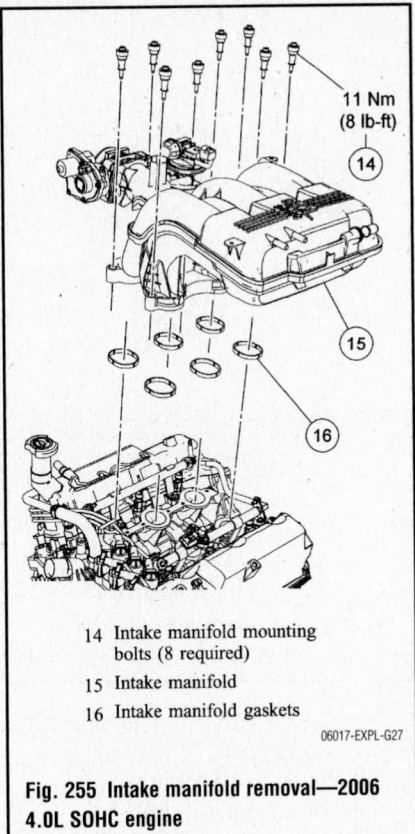

14 Intake manifold mounting
bolts (8 required)

15 Intake manifold

16 Intake manifold gaskets

06017-EXPL-G27

Fig. 255 Intake manifold removal—2006 4.0L SOHC engine

4.6L (VIN W) Engine

2005 Explorer and Mountaineer

See Figures 256 through 259.

1. Before servicing the vehicle, refer to the "Precautions" section.
2. Relieve the fuel system pressure.
3. Drain the cooling system.
4. Remove or disconnect the following:

- Negative battery cable
- Air cleaner outlet pipe
- EGR tube
- Alternator
- Fuel tube spring lock coupling
- Upper radiator hose from the thermostat housing
- Brake booster vacuum tube bracket bolt and disconnect the tube from the throttle body adapter; position the tube aside
- Heater hose from the intake manifold
- Crankcase breather tube
- Heater control vacuum hose fitting
- Vacuum tube from the throttle body adapter
- EGR system module and fuel pressure sensor vacuum fittings
- PCV valve tube
- Thermostat housing cover, the O-ring seal and the thermostat
- Electronic throttle body and throttle

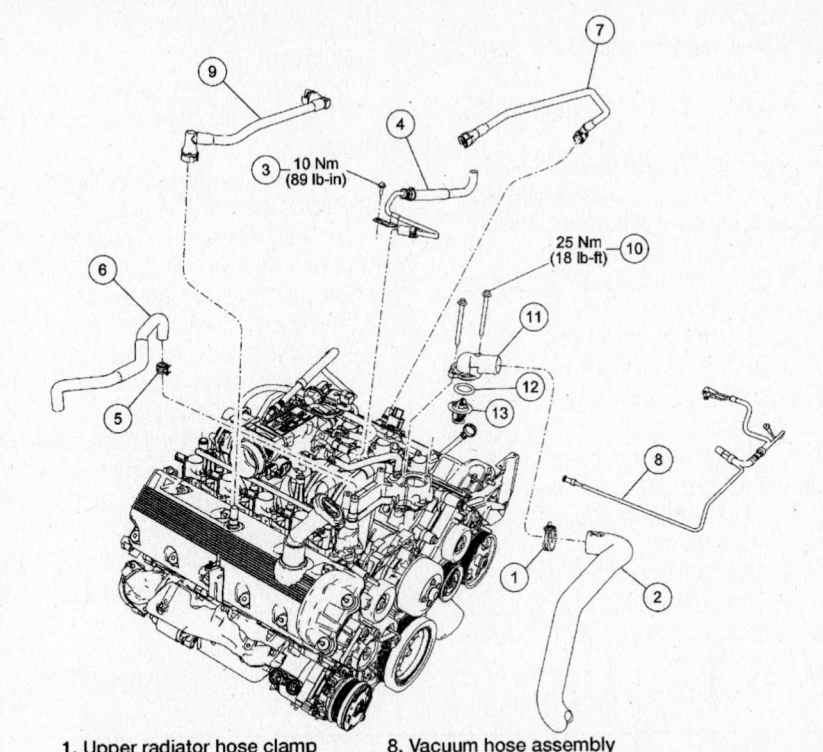

1. Upper radiator hose clamp
2. Upper radiator hose
3. Brake booster vacuum tube bolt
4. Brake booster vacuum tube
5. Heater hose clamp
6. Heater hose
7. Crankcase ventilation tube
8. Vacuum hose assembly
9. Positive crankcase ventilation (PCV) tube
10. Thermostat housing bolts (2 required)
11. Thermostat housing
12. Thermostat housing O-ring seal
13. Thermostat

22086_EXPL_G0082

Fig. 256 External hoses and related parts for intake manifold removal—2005 4.6L (VIN W) engine (1 of 3)

14. Electronic throttle body electrical connector
15. Throttle position (TP) sensor electrical connector
16. Fuel pressure sensor electrical connector
17. Evaporative (EVAP) emissions return tube
18. Coolant inlet hose clamp
19. Coolant inlet hose
20. Coolant outlet hose clamp
21. Coolant outlet hose
22. Exhaust gas recirculation (EGR) system module electrical connector

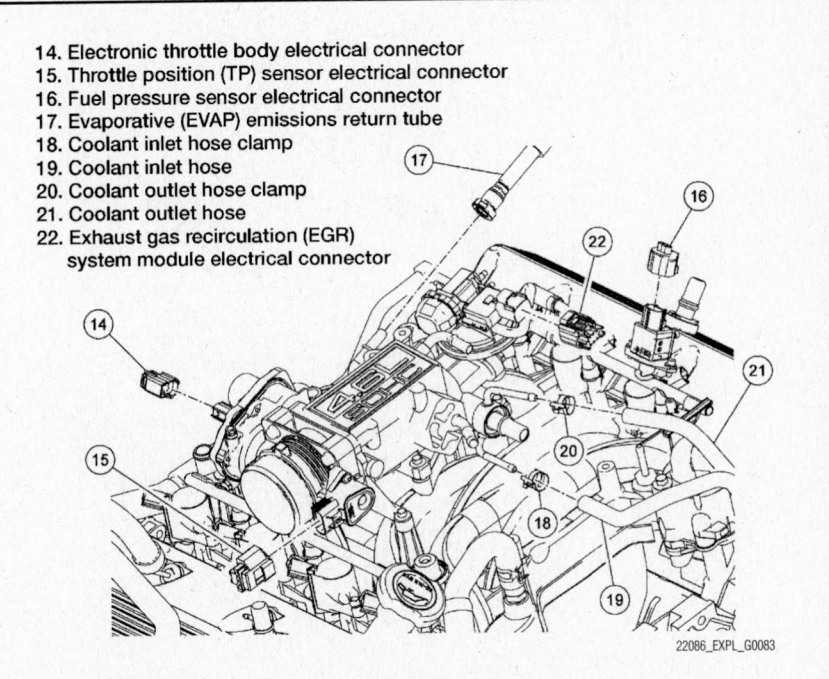

22086_EXPL_G0083

Fig. 257 External related parts for intake manifold removal—2005 4.6L engine (VIN W) (2 of 3)

position (TP) sensor electrical connectors
- Fuel pressure sensor electrical connector
- EVAP tube from the throttle body adapter
- Heated PCV coolant inlet hose
- Heated PCV coolant outlet hose
- Coolant outlet hose anchor from the fuel rail stud
- EGR system module electrical connector
- Ground wire connection
- RH fuel injector, coil pack electrical connectors and the wiring harness retainers
- LH fuel injector and coil pack electrical connectors and the fuel charging wiring harness retainers
- Wire harness locators and the knock sensor (KS) electrical connector from the back of the intake manifold
- All 8 ignition coils

- Intake manifold bolts and intake manifold

To install:

5. Clean all mating surfaces.

6. Position the intake manifold and new gasket.

7. Tighten the intake manifold bolts, in sequence shown, to 18 ft. lbs. (25 Nm).

8. Apply dielectric compound to the inside of the coil boots, then install all 8 ignition coils and the bolts.

9. Install or connect the following:
- Wire harness locators and the KS electrical connector to the back of the intake manifold
- LH fuel injector and coil pack electrical connectors and the fuel charging wiring harness retainers
- RH fuel injector, coil pack electrical connectors and the wiring harness retainers
- Ground wire
- EGR system module electrical connector

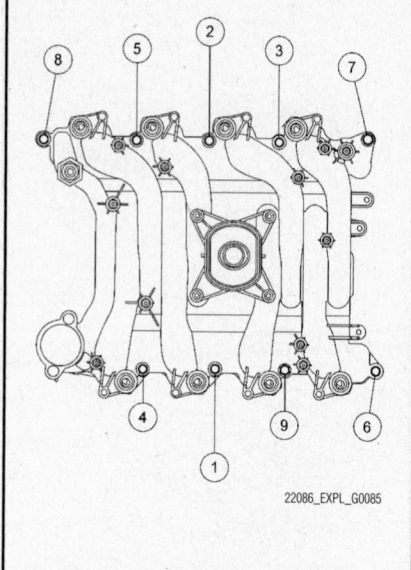

22086_EXPL_G0085

Fig. 259 Intake manifold bolt tightening sequence—4.6L (VIN W) SOHC engine

- Coolant outlet hose anchor to the fuel rail stud
- Heated PCV coolant outlet hose and position the clamp
- Heated PCV coolant inlet hose and position the clamp
- EVAP hose to the throttle body adapter
- Fuel pressure sensor electrical connector
- TP sensor and the electronic throttle body electrical connectors
- Thermostat, with a new O-ring; tighten housing bolts to 18 ft. lbs. (25 Nm)
- PCV valve tube
- Vacuum harness and connect the fuel pressure sensor and EGR system module vacuum fittings
- Vacuum tube to the throttle body adapter
- Heater control vacuum hose fitting
- Crankcase breather tube and connect it to the valve cover
- Heater hose and position the clamp
- Brake booster vacuum tube and connect it to the throttle body adapter, install the vacuum tube bracket bolt
- Upper radiator hose to the thermostat housing
- Fuel tube spring lock coupling
- Alternator
- EGR tube
- Air cleaner outlet pipe
- Battery ground cable

10. Refill and bleed the engine cooling system.

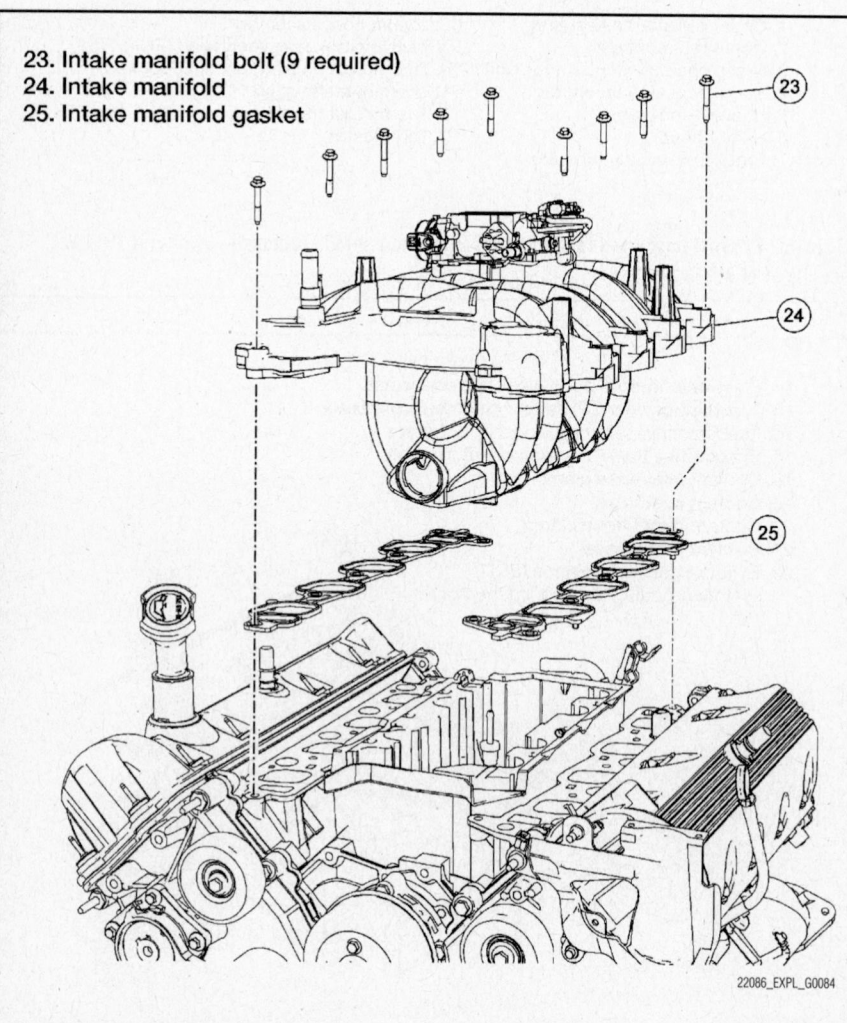

23. Intake manifold bolt (9 required)
24. Intake manifold
25. Intake manifold gasket

22086_EXPL_G0084

Fig. 258 Intake manifold removal—2005 4.6L engine (VIN W) (3 of 3)

4.6L (VIN 8) Engine

2006–07 Models

See Figures 260 and 261.

1. Before servicing the vehicle, refer to the "Precautions" section.
2. Relieve the fuel system pressure.
3. Remove or disconnect the following:
   - Negative battery cable
   - Air cleaner outlet pipe
   - Fuel rail and injectors
   - Electronic Throttle Body (TB) electrical connector
   - EVAP tube from the intake manifold
   - TP sensor electrical connector
   - PCV hose from the heated PCV fitting on the intake manifold
   - Position the heated PCV fitting aside
   - Wiring harness retainers from the intake manifold
   - Charge motion control valve (CMCV) electrical connector
   - Intake manifold bolts and position the intake manifold forward
   - Brake booster vacuum hose from the rear of the intake manifold
   - Vacuum hose from the rear of the intake manifold
4. Remove the intake manifold and gaskets.

To install:

5. Clean and inspect the sealing surfaces.

> ※※ **CAUTION**
>
> **Electrical and vacuum harnesses must not restrict movement of the CMCV control rods at the rear of the intake manifold. Use extreme care during the installation of the intake manifold to prevent any pinching of electrical and vacuum harnesses.**

6. Using new intake manifold gaskets, position the intake manifold.
7. Connect the vacuum hose to the rear of the intake manifold.
8. Connect the brake booster hose to the rear of the intake manifold.
9. Install the intake manifold bolts and tighten the bolts in the sequence shown in 2 stages:
   a. Stage 1: 18 inch lbs. (2 Nm)
   b. State 2: 89 inch lbs. (10 Nm)
10. Install or connect the following:
    - CMCV electrical connector
    - Wiring harness retainers to the intake manifold
    - New O-ring seal, position the heated PCV fitting and install the bolts

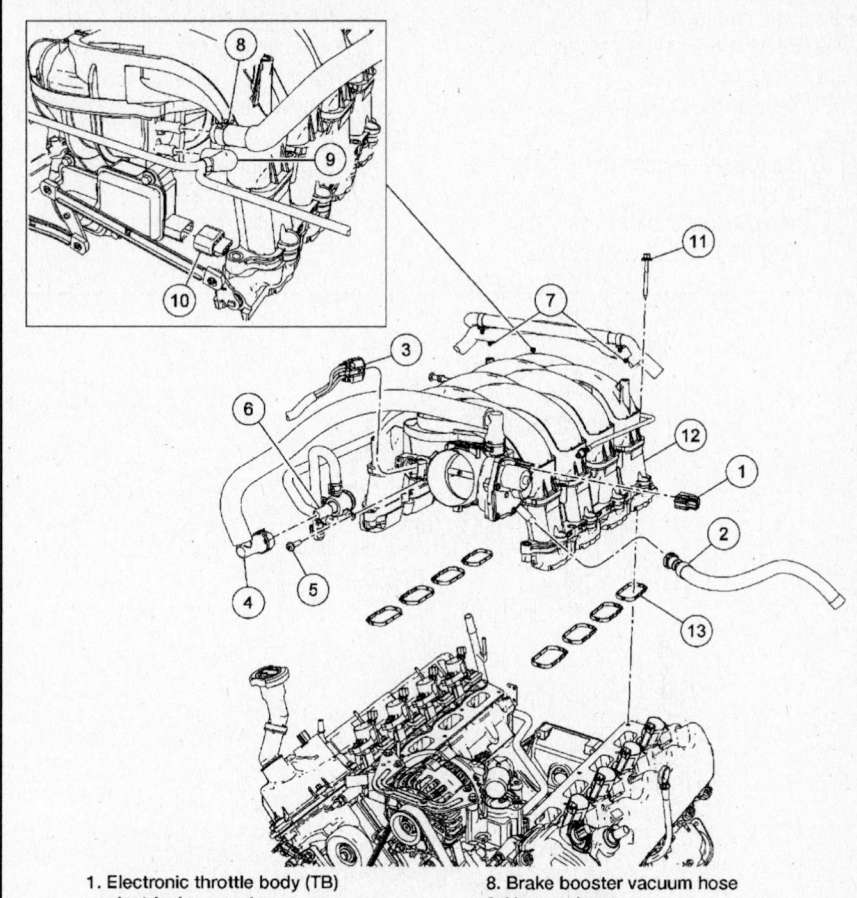

1. Electronic throttle body (TB) electrical connector
2. Evaporative emissions (EVAP) hose
3. Throttle position (TP) sensor electrical connector
4. Positive crankcase ventilation (PCV) hose
5. Heated PCV fitting bolt (2 required)
6. Heated PCV fitting
7. Wiring harness retainers
8. Brake booster vacuum hose
9. Vacuum hose
10. Charge motion control valve (CMCV) electrical connector
11. Intake manifold bolt (10 required)
12. Intake manifold
13. Intake manifold gasket

22086_EXPL_G0086

Fig. 260 Intake manifold and related components—2006–07 4.6L (VIN 8) SOHC engine

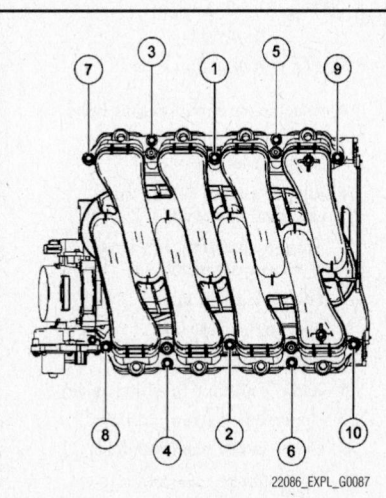

22086_EXPL_G0087

Fig. 261 Intake manifold bolt tightening sequence—2006–07 4.6L (VIN 8) engine

- PCV hose to the heated PCV fitting on the intake manifold
- TP sensor electrical connector
- EVAP hose to the intake manifold
- Electronic TB electrical connector
- Fuel rail and injectors
- Air cleaner outlet pipe
- Negative battery cable

4.6L (VIN H) DOHC Engine

Upper Manifold

See Figures 262 and 263.

1. Before servicing the vehicle, refer to the "Precautions" section.
2. Disconnect the negative battery cable.
3. Drain the cooling system.
4. Remove the air cleaner outlet pipe.

5. Remove the exhaust gas recirculation (EGR) system module.

6. Remove the positive crankcase ventilation (PCV) valve hose.

7. Remove the brake booster vacuum hose.

8. Remove the evaporative emissions (EVAP) hose.

9. Remove the coolant hose clamp.

10. Remove the PCV coolant hose.

11. Remove the coolant hose clamp.

12. Remove the PCV coolant hose.

13. Remove the accelerator cable.

14. Remove the speed control cable.

15. Remove the accelerator cable return spring.

16. Remove the accelerator cable pin-type retainer.

17. Remove the accelerator cable bracket.

18. Remove the idle air control (IAC) valve electrical connector.

19. Remove the throttle position (TP) sensor electrical connector.

20. Remove the fuel rail shield.

21. Remove the radio capacitor.

22. Remove the upper intake manifold bolts.

23. Remove the upper intake manifold studs.

24. Remove the upper intake manifold.

25. Installation is the reverse of the removal procedure. Tighten the bolts and studs in the sequence shown to 89 inch lbs. (10 Nm).

➡**Locations 5 and 9 use studs.**

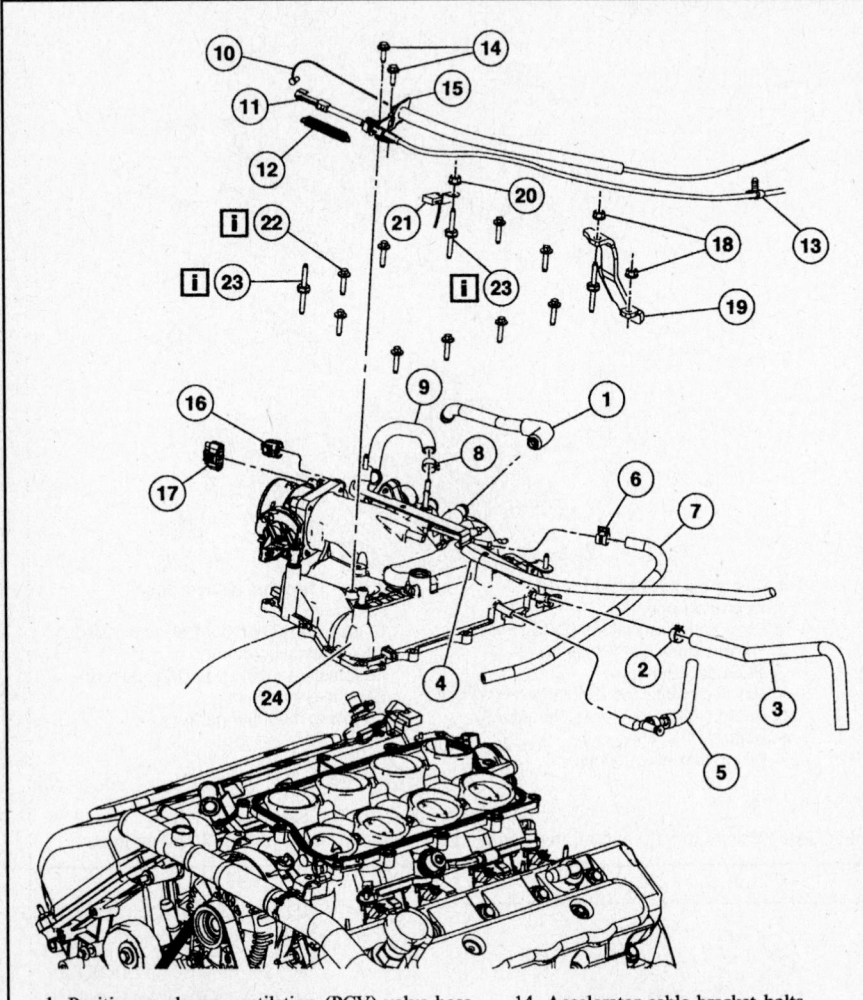

1 Positive crankcase ventilation (PCV) valve hose	14 Accelerator cable bracket bolts
2 Brake booster hose clamp	15 Accelerator cable bracket (position aside)
3 Brake booster vacuum hose	16 Idle air control (IAC) valve electrical connector
4 Evaporative emissions (EVAP) hose	17 Throttle position (TP) sensor electrical connector
5 Vacuum harness connector	18 Fuel rail shield nuts
6 Coolant hose clamp	19 Fuel rail shield
7 PCV coolant hose	20 Radio capacitor nut
8 Coolant hose clamp	21 Radio capacitor (position aside)
9 PCV coolant hose	22 Upper intake manifold bolts
10 Accelerator cable	23 Upper intake manifold studs
11 Speed control cable	24 Upper intake manifold
12 Accelerator cable return spring	
13 Accelerator cable pin-type retainer	

67197EXPLG23

Fig. 262 Upper intake manifold and related parts—4.6L DOHC engine

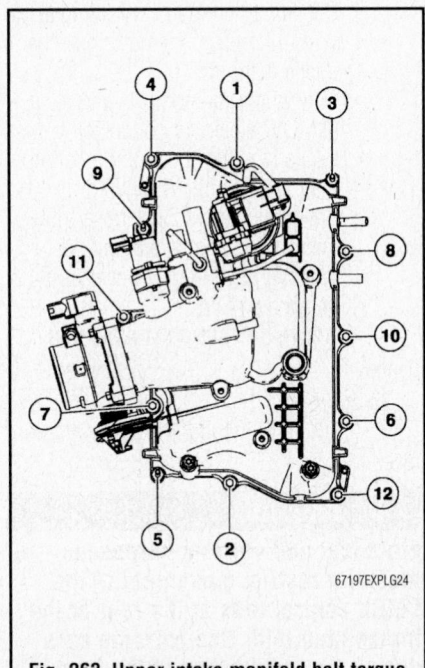

67197EXPLG24

Fig. 263 Upper intake manifold bolt torque sequence—4.6L DOHC engine

Lower Manifold

See Figures 264 and 265.

1. Before servicing the vehicle, refer to the "Precautions" section.

2. Remove the upper intake manifold.

3. Disconnect the spring lock couplings.

4. Remove the cooling fan.

5. Remove the accessory drive belt tensioner.

6. Remove the accessory drive belt.

7. Remove the wire harness retainer.

8. Remove the alternator.

9. Remove the alternator bracket studs.

10. Remove the upper coolant hose.

11. Remove the coolant bypass hose.

12. Remove the thermostat housing coolant hose.

13. Remove the engine coolant temperature (ECT) sensor electrical connector.

14. Remove the coolant crossover tube.

15. Remove the vacuum hose.

16. Remove the engine harness retainers.

17. Remove the fuel rail pressure (FRP) sensor electrical connector.

18. Remove the intake manifold runner control (IMRC) motor electrical connector.

19. Remove the fuel injector connectors.

20. Remove the lower intake manifold bolts.

21. Remove the lower intake manifold assembly.

22. Remove the intake manifold gaskets.

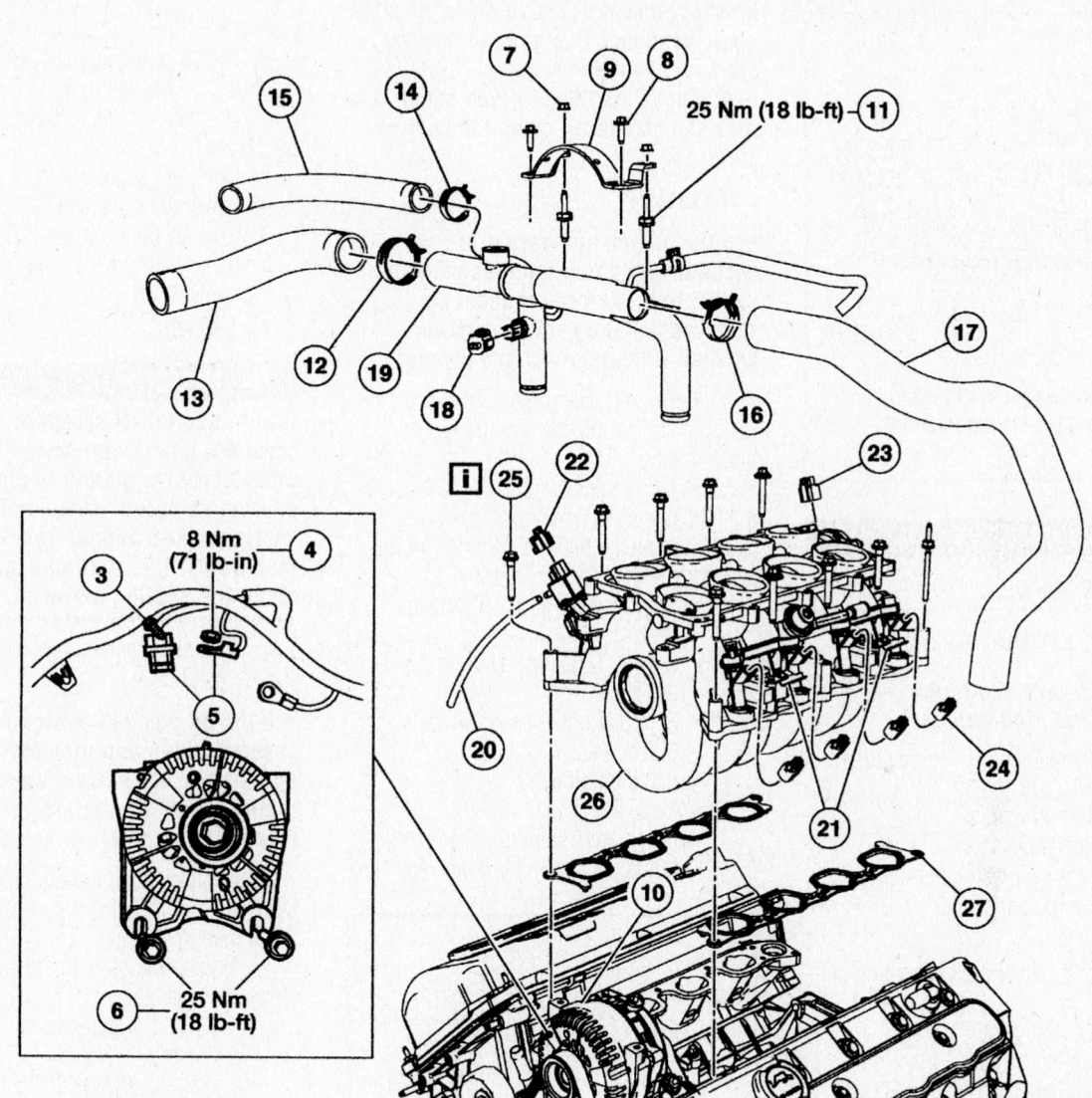

3 Wire harness retainer
4 Generator bracket nuts
5 Electrical connectors (two)
6 Generator bracket bolts
7 Generator bracket nuts
8 Generator bracket bolts
9 Generator bracket
10 Generator
11 Studs
12 Hose clamp

13 Upper coolant hose
14 Hose clamp
15 Coolant hose
16 Hose clamp
17 Thermostat housing coolant hose
18 Engine coolant temperature (ECT) sensor electrical connector
19 Coolant crossover tube
20 Vacuum hose

21 Engine harness retainers
22 Fuel rail pressure (FRP) sensor electrical connector
23 Intake manifold runner control (IMRC) motor electrical connector
24 Fuel injector connectors
25 Lower intake manifold bolts
26 Lower intake manifold assembly
27 Intake manifold gaskets

67197EXPLG25

Fig. 264 Lower intake manifold and related parts—4.6L DOHC engine

23. Installation is the reverse of the removal procedure, noting the following:

➡ **Hand-start all fasteners.**

c. Tighten all fasteners in the sequence shown in the illustration to 89 inch lbs. (10 Nm).

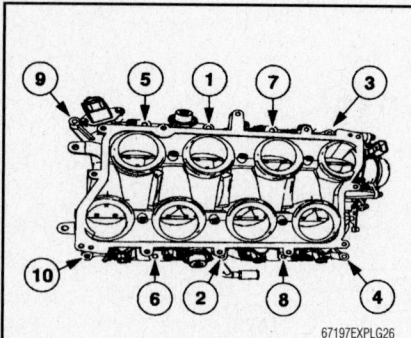

Fig. 265 Lower intake manifold torque sequence—2005 4.6L (VIN H) DOHC engine

OIL PAN

REMOVAL & INSTALLATION

4.0L (VIN E, K) SOHC Engine

2005–06 Explorer, Explorer Sport-Trac and Mountaineer

1. Before servicing the vehicle, refer to the "Precautions" section.
2. Raise the vehicle on a hoist.
3. Drain the engine oil.
4. Remove the oil pan bolts, oil pan and discard the gasket

To install:

5. Clean the pan and block mating surfaces.
6. Install a new gasket.
7. Position the oil pan. Torque the bolts, in an alternating pattern, to 80 inch lbs. (9 Nm).
8. Torque the pan drain bolt to 19 ft. lbs. (26 Nm).
9. Fill the engine with clean oil.
10. Start the vehicle and check for leaks, repair if necessary.

4.6L (VIN H) DOHC Engine

Aviator

See Figure 266.

1. Before servicing the vehicle, refer to the "Precautions" section.
2. Drain the engine oil.
3. Remove or disconnect the following:
   • Front stabilizer bar

• Front axle (on 4WD, support the axle with a jack and lower the axle slightly to access the pan)
• Front crossmember
• Inspection cover (2 bolts)
• Oil pan (16 bolts)

➡ **Do not use metal scrapers, wire brushes, power abrasive discs, or other abrasive means to clean the sealing surfaces. These may cause scratches and gouges resulting in leak paths. Use a plastic scraper to clean the sealing surfaces.**

To install:

➡ **If the oil pan and gasket are not secured within four minutes of sealer application, the sealant must be removed and the sealing surfaces cleaned with metal surface cleaner.**

4. Apply silicone gasket and sealant in the front and rear corners of the pan-to-block mating surface.
5. Position the new oil pan gasket and the oil pan and loosely install the bolts.
6. Tighten the bolts in 3 stages, in the sequence shown, once for each step.
   • Step 1: Tighten to 18 inch lbs. (2 Nm)
   • Step 2: Tighten to 15 ft. lbs. (20 Nm)
   • Step 3: Tighten an additional 60 degrees.
7. Install the following:
   • Inspection cover
   • Front crossmember; torque the through-bolts to 59 ft. lbs. (80 Nm)

Fig. 266 Oil pan bolt tightening sequence—4.6L engine

• Front axle; torque the axle insulator bolts to 74 ft. lbs. (100 Nm)
• Front stabilizer bar; torque the end nuts to 66 ft. lbs. (90 Nm)

4.6L (VIN W) SOHC Engine

2005 Explorer and Mountaineer

See Figure 266.

1. Before servicing the vehicle, refer to the "Precautions" section.
2. With the vehicle in NEUTRAL position on a hoist.
3. Drain the engine oil.
4. Lower the front axle (4WD).
5. Remove the front stabilizer bar.
6. Remove the oil pan bolts, oil pan and gasket.

To install:

✳✳ WARNING

Do not use metal scrapers, wire brushes, power abrasive discs, or other abrasive means to clean the sealing surfaces. These can cause scratches and gouges resulting in leak paths. Use a plastic scraper to clean the sealing surfaces.

7. Clean the sealing surfaces with metal surface cleaner.

➡ **If the oil pan and gasket are not secured within four minutes of sealer application, the sealant must be removed and the sealing surfaces cleaned with metal surface cleaner.**

8. Apply silicone gasket and sealant in two places at the front corner of the pan-to-block mating surface.
9. Tighten the bolts in the sequence shown in three stages:
   • Stage 1: Tighten to 18 inch lbs. (2 Nm).
   • Stage 2: Tighten to 15 ft. lbs. (20 Nm).
   • Stage 3: Tighten an additional 60 degrees.

4.6L (VIN 8) SOHC Engine

2006–07 Explorer and Mountaineer; 2007 Explorer Sport-Trac

See Figure 267.

1. Before servicing the vehicle, refer to the "Precautions" section.
2. With the vehicle in NEUTRAL position on a hoist.
3. Lower the front axle (4WD).
4. Remove the front stabilizer bar.
5. Drain the engine oil.

6. Remove the nut and position the power steering pressure (PSP) hose bracket aside.

7. Remove the nut and position the battery cable bracket aside.

8. Disconnect the oil temperature sensor electrical connector.

9. Remove the bolts and the oil drain splash shield.

10. If equipped with a block heater, detach the block heater wiring harness retainer from the LH side oil pan bolt.

11. Remove the bolts, the oil pan and the gasket.

To install:

✳✳ WARNING

Do not use metal scrapers, wire brushes, power abrasive discs, or other abrasive means to clean the sealing surfaces. These can cause scratches and gouges resulting in leak paths. Use a plastic scraper to clean the sealing surfaces.

12. Clean the sealing surfaces with metal surface cleaner.

➡**If the oil pan and gasket are not secured within four minutes of sealer application, the sealant must be removed and the sealing surfaces cleaned with metal surface cleaner.**

13. Apply silicone gasket and sealant at the front corners and rear corners of the pan-to-block mating surface.

14. Install a new oil pan gasket, position the oil pan and tighten the pan bolts, in the sequence shown, in 3 steps:
    a. Step 1: 18 inch lbs. (2 Nm)
    b. Step 2: 15 ft. lbs. (20 Nm)
    c. Step 3: additional 60 degrees of turn

15. If equipped with a block heater, attach the block heater wiring harness retainer to the LH oil pan bolt.

16. Position the oil drain splash shield and install the bolts.

17. Attach the wiring harness retainers to the RH oil pan bolts.

18. Connect the oil temperature sensor electrical connector.

19. Attach the battery cable bracket and install the nut to 89 inch lbs. (10 Nm).

20. Attach the PSP hose bracket and install the nut to 89 inch lbs. (10 Nm).

21. Install the stabilizer bar. Tighten the stabilizer bar end nut to 26 ft. lbs. (35 Nm) and the clamp bolts to 41 ft. lbs. (55 Nm).

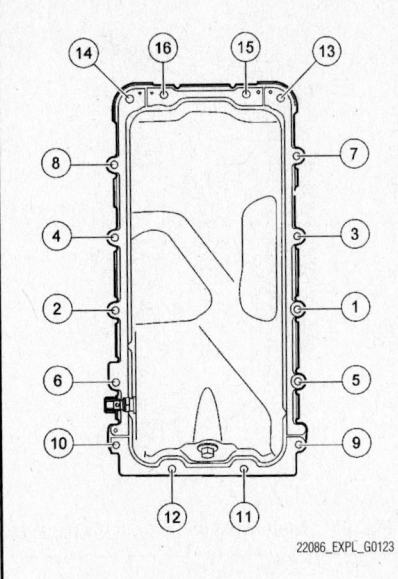

Fig. 267 Oil pan bolt tightening sequence—2006–07 4.6L SOHC engine

22. Install the front axle. Tighten the axle mounting insulator bolts to 74 ft. lbs. (100 Nm).

23. Refill the engine with new oil.

OIL PUMP

REMOVAL & INSTALLATION

4.0L (VIN E, K) SOHC Engine

See Figures 268 through 272.

➡**For the 2005 Explorer Sport-Trac, the oil pump removal requires engine disassembly.**

1. Before servicing the vehicle, refer to the "Precautions" section.

2. With the vehicle in NEUTRAL, position it on a hoist.

3. Remove or disconnect the following:
- Negative battery cable
- Air cleaner outlet tube
- Starter
- Oil pan
- Weatherstrip across front of engine compartment

4. On 2006–07 models, perform the following:
    a. Remove the bolt and position the power steering fluid reservoir aside.
    b. Disconnect the coolant overflow hose. Remove the bolts and the coolant expansion tank.

5. On all models, remove the fan shroud.

6. Remove the heater hose bracket bolt as shown, then install a RH lifting eye, using the previously removed bolt.

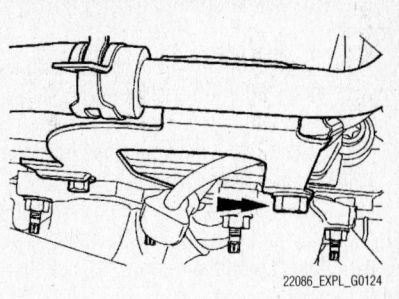

Fig. 268 Remove the heater hose bracket bolt as shown, then install a RH lifting eye, using the previously removed bolt— 4.0L (VIN E, K) Explorer And Mountaineer

➡**This is not a typical setup. Only the right side of the engine will be raised.**

7. Install the engine lifting tools.

8. On AWD models, remove the front stabilizer bar brackets (if equipped) and the crossmember.

9. Remove the RH motor mount insulator nut.

10. Remove the LH motor mount insulator through-bolt.

11. Raise the engine.

12. Remove the 2 bell housing-to-cylinder block cradle bolts.

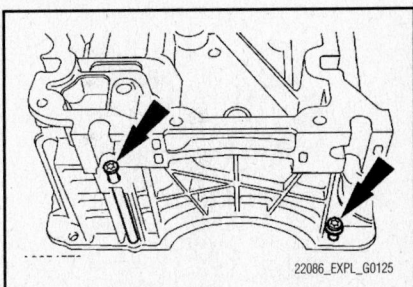

Fig. 269 Remove the 2 Torx® bolts at the rear of the block cradle—4.0L (VIN E, K) Explorer And Mountaineer (shown with block cradle removed for clarity of location)

13. Remove the 2 Torx® bolts at the rear of the block cradle.

14. Remove the 20 bolts and 2 nuts along the outside of the cylinder block cradle. Mark the location of the 2 silver-colored bolts, with washer seals; these must be installed the same position, with new washer seals.

15. Remove the 8 cylinder block cradle inner bolts and 2 washer seals.

16. With the lifting device, raise the engine.

17. On AWD models, perform the following:

   a. Support the front axle with a suitable jack stand and secure with a safety strap or chain.

   b. Disconnect the vent hose from the differential housing vent tube.

   c. Remove and discard the axle housing bolts and nuts. Lower the axle.

18. For all models, remove the cylinder block cradle.

19. Remove the oil pump bolts.

20. Remove the oil pump.

To install:

21. Install the oil pump and tighten the bolts to 15 ft. lbs. (19 Nm).

22. Thoroughly clean all mating surfaces.

✳✳ CAUTION

Do not use metal scrapers, wire brushes, power abrasive discs or other abrasive means to clean the sealing surfaces. These tools cause scratches and gouges which make leak paths. Use a plastic scraping tool to remove all traces of old sealant.

23. Back the set screws off until they are below the cylinder block cradle boss.

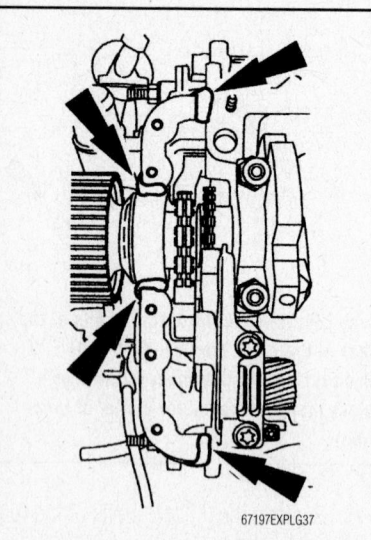

Fig. 270 Back the set screws off until they are below the cylinder block cradle boss—4.0L (VIN E, K) SOHC engine

➡ **If not secured within 4 minutes, the sealant must be removed and the sealing area cleaned.**

24. Apply silicone in the 6 places shown.

25. Position a new gasket and the cylinder block cradle.

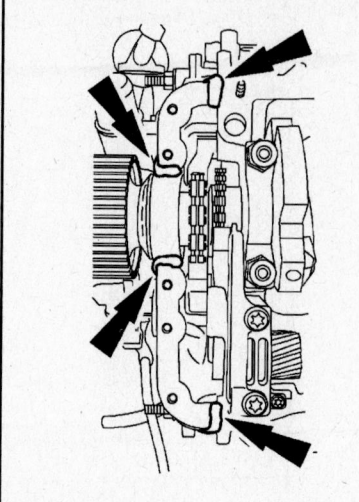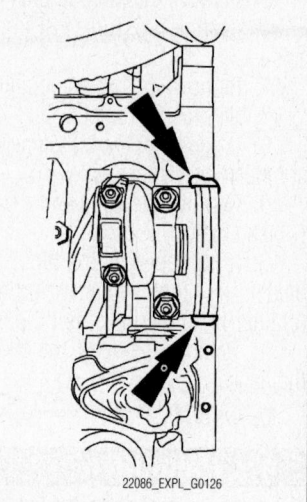

Fig. 271 Apply silicone in the 6 places shown—4.0L SOHC engine

26. Install and hand-tighten the 2 rear Torx® bolts.

27. Install the 2 bell housing-to-cylinder block cradle bolts. Tighten the bolts to 35 ft. lbs. (47 Nm).

28. Tighten the outer 20 bolts and 2 nuts to 89 inch lbs. (10 Nm).

29. Tighten the eight cradle inserts to 27 inch lbs. (3 Nm).

30. Install the two silver-covered bolts and new washer seals. Hand-tighten them at this time.

31. Install and hand-tighten the six remaining inner bolts.

32. Tighten the lower block cradle bolts in two stages:

- Stage 1: Tighten to 11 ft. lbs. (15 Nm).
- Stage 2: Tighten to 25 ft. lbs. (34 Nm).

33. On AWD models, perform the following:

   a. Raise the axle into position. Install new bolts and nuts and tighten to 49 ft. lbs. (66 Nm).

   b. Connect the vent hose to the differential housing.

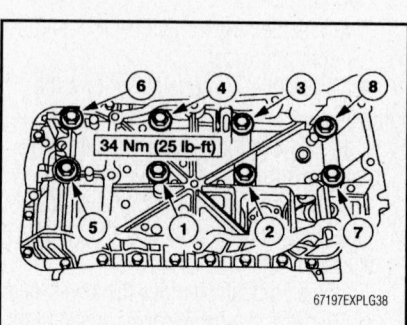

Fig. 272 Cylinder block cradle bolt torque sequence—4.0L SOHC engine

   c. Install the front stabilizer bar brackets and torque the nuts to 41 ft. lbs. (55 Nm).

34. On all models, lower the engine and remove the lifting tools.

35. Install the LH engine support through-bolt and nut. Tighten to 76 ft. lbs. (103 Nm).

36. Install the RH engine support nut and tighten to 66 ft. lbs. (90 Nm).

37. Install the crossmember (AWD models). Tighten the retaining bolts to 52 ft. lbs. (70 Nm).

38. Install the oil pump screen and pickup tube.

39. On 2005 models, perform the following:

   a. Install the starter.

   b. Remove the lifting eye and replace the bolt. Tighten to 17 ft. lbs. (23 Nm).

   c. Install the fan shroud and bolts.

40. On 2006–07 models, perform the following:

   a. Install the fan shroud and bolts.

   b. Install the expansion tank.

   c. Install the power steering reservoir.

41. Install the weatherstrip.

42. Install the air cleaner outlet pipe.

43. Connect the battery ground cable.

44. Fill the engine with clean engine oil.

4.6L (VIN W, 8) SOHC Engine

See Figure 273.

1. Before servicing the vehicle, refer to the "Precautions" section.

2. Drain the engine oil.

3. Remove or disconnect the following:

- Negative battery cable
- Oil pan

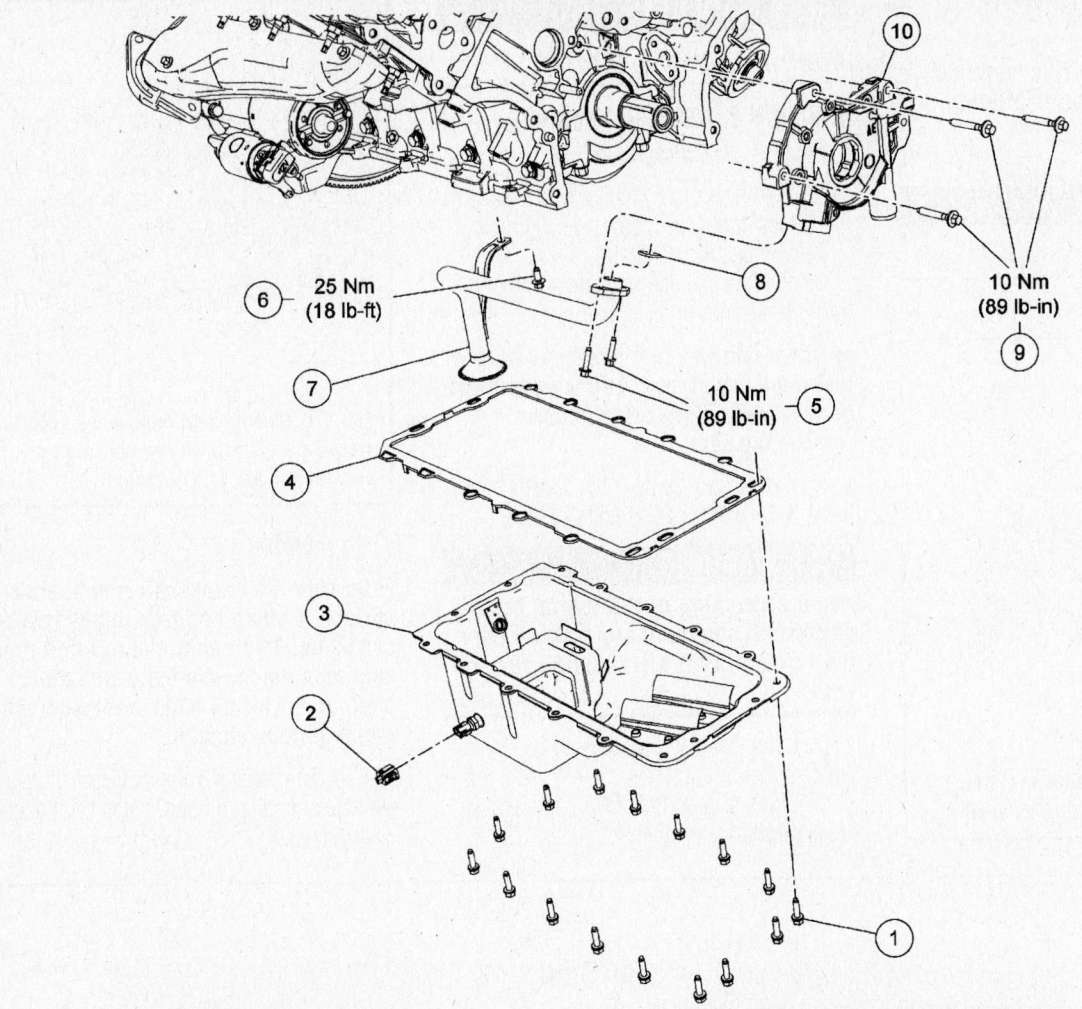

6. 25 Nm (18 lb-ft)

10 Nm (89 lb-in)

10 Nm (89 lb-in)

1. Oil pan bolt (16 required)
2. Oil temperature sensor electrical connector
3. Oil pan
4. Oil pan gasket
5. Oil pump screen and pickup tube-to-oil pump bolts (2 required)
6. Oil pump screen and pickup tube support bracket bolt
7. Oil pump screen and pickup tube
8. Oil pump screen and pickup tube O-ring seal
9. Oil pump bolts (3 required)
10. Oil pump

22086_EXPL_G0127

Fig. 273 Exploded view of the oil pan, oil pickup screen and tube, and the oil pump—4.6L (VIN W, 8) SOHC engine

- Three bolts and the oil pump screen cover and tube
- Timing chains and sprockets; see "Timing Chain and Sprocket" section
- Oil pump

To install:

➡**Lubricate the new O-ring seal with clean engine oil.**

4. Clean and inspect the mating surfaces. Install a new O-ring seal.
5. Position the oil pump.
6. Loosely install the bolts.
7. Tighten the bolts to 89 inch lbs. (10 Nm).

8. Install the timing chains and sprockets; see "Timing Chain and Sprocket" section.
9. Install the three oil pump screen and cover bolts. Torque the bolts to 18 ft. lbs. (25 Nm).
10. Install the oil pan.

4.6L (VIN H) DOHC Engine

1. Before servicing the vehicle, refer to the "Precautions" section.
2. With the vehicle in NEUTRAL position on a hoist.
3. Drain the engine oil.
4. Remove the front stabilizer bar.
5. Remove the timing chain; see "Timing Chain and Sprocket" section

6. Remove the oil pan.
7. Remove the oil pump screen and pickup tube.
8. Remove the oil pump bolts.
9. Remove the oil pump.

To install:

10. Installation is the reverse of the removal procedure.

➡**Oil pump must be held against block until bolts are tightened.**

11. Align the inner rotor of the oil pump assembly to align with the flats on the crankshaft, and slide the oil pump toward the block until it is seated against the block.

12. Rotate the oil pump assembly to align with the bolt holes.

➡Lubricate the new O-ring seal with clean engine oil before installation.

13. Install O-ring seal.

PISTON AND RING

POSITIONING

See Figures 274 and 275.

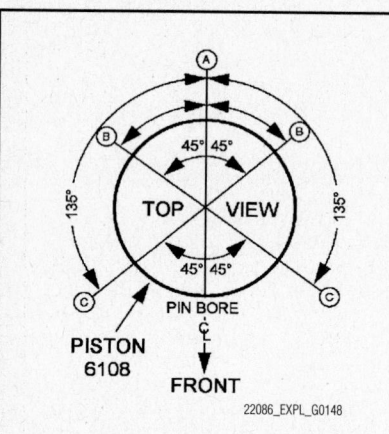

Fig. 274 Piston ring positioning—4.0L (VIN E, K) & 4.6L (VIN W, 8 & H) engine

REAR MAIN SEAL

REMOVAL & INSTALLATION

4.0L (VIN E, K) SOHC Engine

See Figures 276 through 280.

1. Before servicing the vehicle, refer to the "Precautions" section.
2. Remove the flexplate.
3. Remove the spacer plate and the flexplate-to-crankshaft spacer.

➡The crankshaft rear seal may have a metal speedy sleeve. This sleeve must be removed before attempting to remove the seal.

4. If necessary, remove the speedy sleeve using 2 screwdrivers or small pry bars.

※ WARNING

Avoid scratching or damaging the oil crankshaft seal running surface during removal of the crankshaft rear oil seal.

5. Using special tool, 303-514, remove the oil slinger.
6. Using special tool, 303-519, remove the crankshaft rear oil seal.

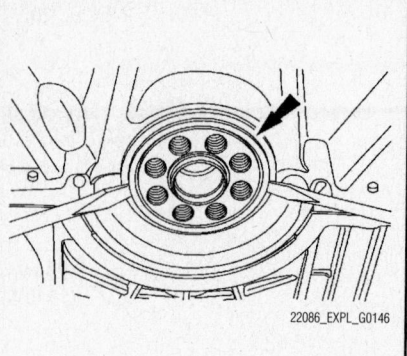

Fig. 276 If necessary, remove the speedy sleeve using 2 screwdrivers or small pry bars—4.0L (VIN E, K) engine

To install:

➡Be sure the crankshaft rear sealing surface is clean and free of any rust or corrosion. To clean the crankshaft rear sealing surface, use extra-fine emery cloth or extra-fine 0000 steel wool with metal surface cleaner.

7. Lubricate the crankshaft rear oil seal with clean engine oil and install on the special tool.

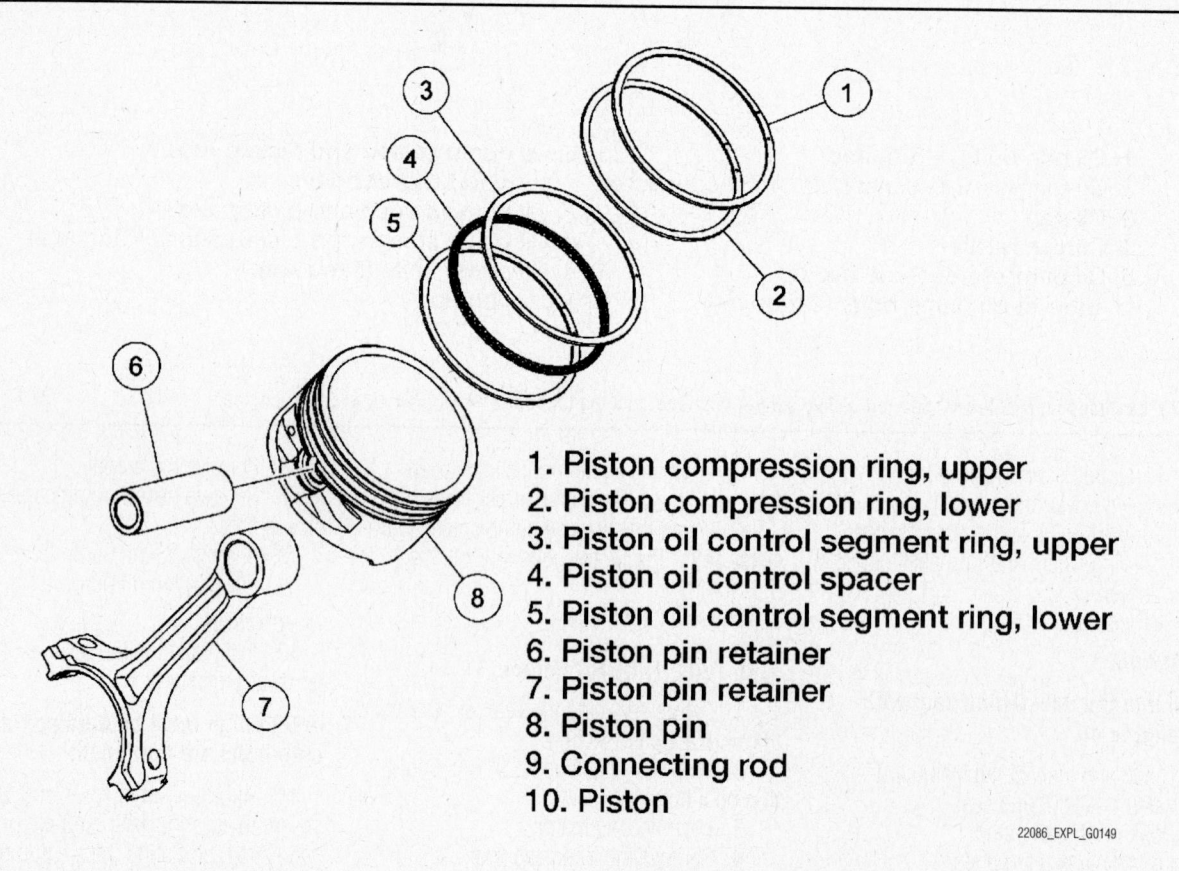

1. Piston compression ring, upper
2. Piston compression ring, lower
3. Piston oil control segment ring, upper
4. Piston oil control spacer
5. Piston oil control segment ring, lower
6. Piston pin retainer
7. Piston pin retainer
8. Piston pin
9. Connecting rod
10. Piston

Fig. 275 Exploded view of the piston, rings and connecting rod—4.0L (VIN E, K) & 4.6L (VIN W, 8, H) engine

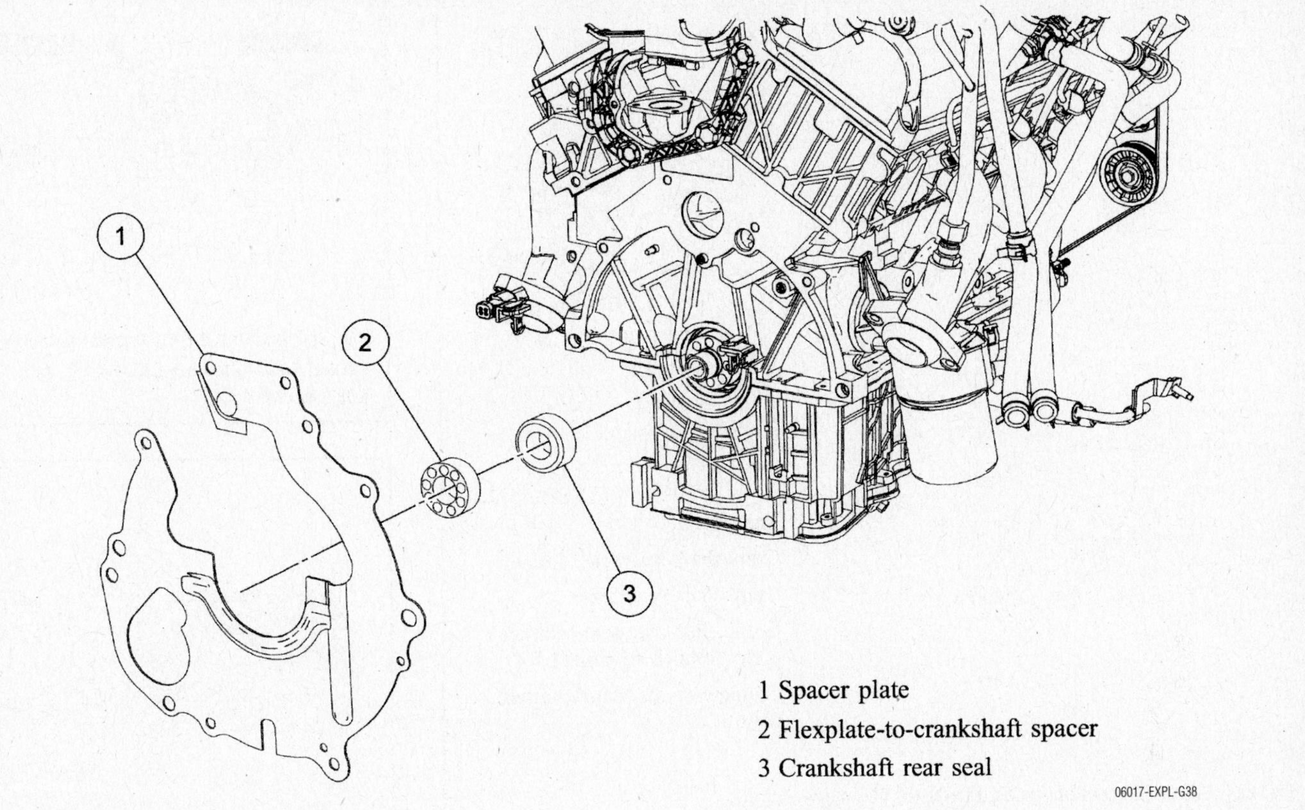

1 Spacer plate
2 Flexplate-to-crankshaft spacer
3 Crankshaft rear seal

06017-EXPL-G38

Fig. 277 Rear main seal and related parts—4.0L engine

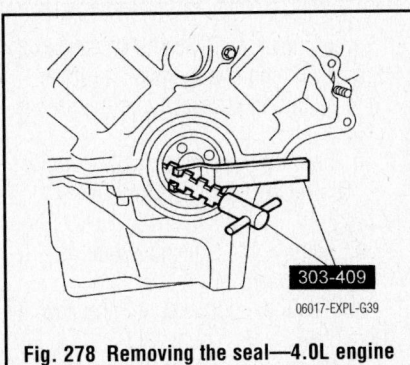

303-409
06017-EXPL-G39

Fig. 278 Removing the seal—4.0L engine

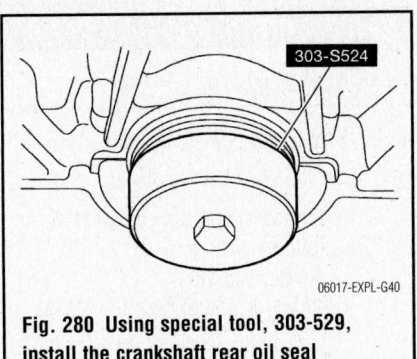

303-S524

06017-EXPL-G40

Fig. 280 Using special tool, 303-529, install the crankshaft rear oil seal

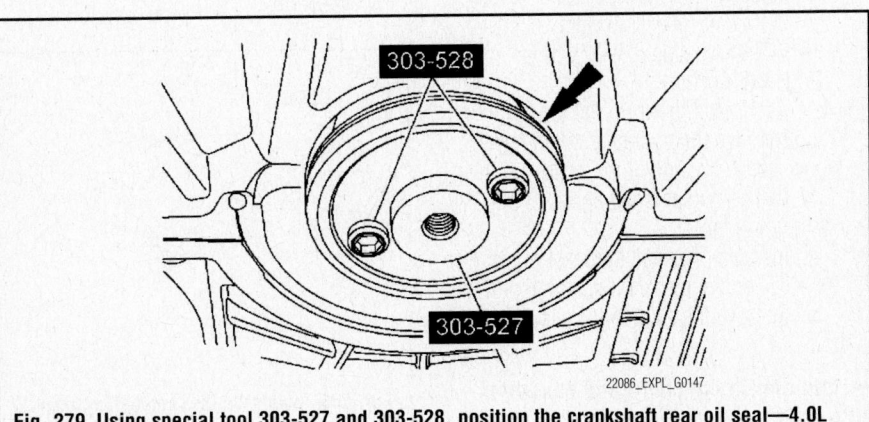

303-528

303-527

22086_EXPL_G0147

Fig. 279 Using special tool 303-527 and 303-528, position the crankshaft rear oil seal—4.0L (VIN E, K) engine

8. Using special tool 303-527 and 303-528, position the crankshaft rear oil seal.

9. Install the flexplate or flexplate.

4.6L SOHC and DOHC Engines

See Figures 281 through 283.

1. Before servicing the vehicle, refer to the "Precautions" section.

2. Remove or disconnect the following:
   - Flexplate
   - Crankshaft rear oil seal slinger with a slide hammer and proper removed tool
   - Rear oil seal with a slide hammer and proper remover tool

To install:

3. Installation is the reverse of the removal procedure. Note the following:
   - Lubricate the inner lip of the rear crankshaft seal with clean engine oil.
   - Use the two Crankshaft Rear Oil Seal Installers to install the rear oil seal.
   - Using the two Crankshaft Rear Oil Seal Installers and the Crankshaft Rear Oil Slinger Installer, install the crankshaft rear oil slinger.

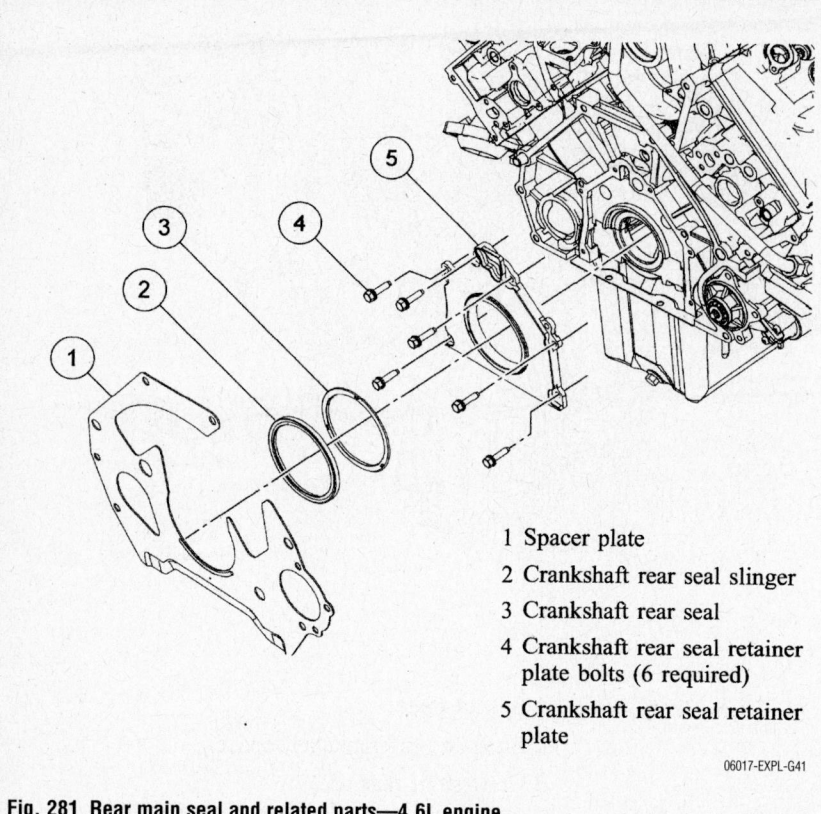

1 Spacer plate
2 Crankshaft rear seal slinger
3 Crankshaft rear seal
4 Crankshaft rear seal retainer plate bolts (6 required)
5 Crankshaft rear seal retainer plate

06017-EXPL-G41

Fig. 281 Rear main seal and related parts—4.6L engine

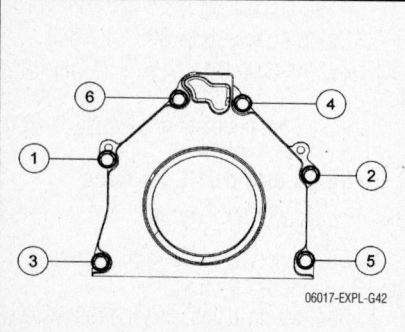

06017-EXPL-G42

Fig. 282 Retainer plate removal and torque sequence—4.6L engine

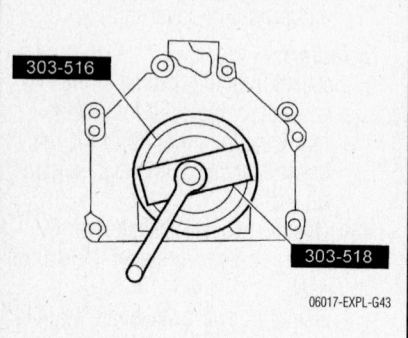

06017-EXPL-G43

Fig. 283 Rear main seal installation—4.6L engine

TIMING CHAIN AND SPROCKETS

REMOVAL & INSTALLATION

4.0L (VIN E, K) SOHC Engine

See Figures 284 through 286.

1. Before servicing the vehicle, refer to the "Precautions" section.
2. Drain the engine oil.
3. Remove or disconnect the following:

- Negative battery cable
- Valve covers
- Camshaft roller followers
- Cylinder heads; see "Cylinder Head" section

4. On RH head, perform the following:

a. Remove the hydraulic chain tensioner bolt from side of the head.

b. Install the camshaft sprocket special holding tools.

c. Install a camshaft sprocket nut tool, 303-575, on the camshaft sprocket nut.

d. Remove the right side cassette bolt.

➡Hold the timing chain and cassette with a rubber band to aid in removal and to prevent the timing chain from falling into the cylinder block.

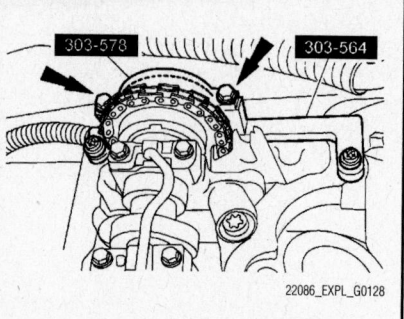

22086_EXPL_G0128

Fig. 284 Install the RH camshaft sprocket special holding tools—4.0L (VIN E, K) SOHC engine

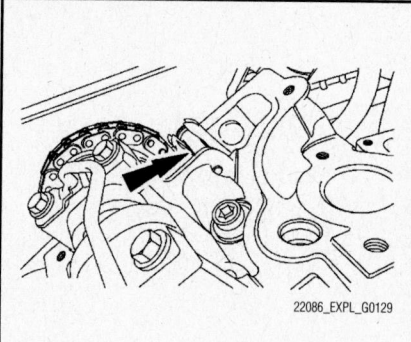

22086_EXPL_G0129

Fig. 285 Remove the right side cassette bolt—4.0L (VIN E, K) SOHC engine

e. Remove the RH camshaft sprocket from the timing chain. Install a rubber band around the cassette and the timing chain.

f. Remove the timing chain.

5. On the LH head, perform the following:

a. Remove the LH side hydraulic chain tensioner bolt.

b. Install the sprocket holding special tools.

c. Remove the LH side camshaft sprocket bolt.

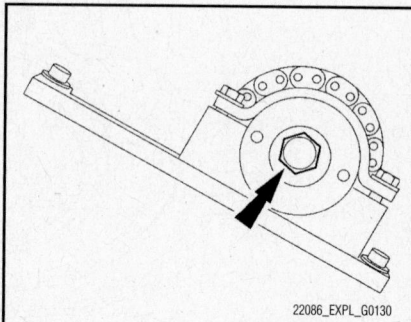

22086_EXPL_G0130

Fig. 286 Install the LH camshaft sprocket special holding tools—4.0L (VIN E, K) SOHC engine

d. Remove the LH side cassette bolt from the front of the engine.

➡**Hold the timing chain and cassette with a rubber band to aid in removal and to prevent the timing chain from falling into the cylinder block.**

e. Remove the LH camshaft sprocket from the timing chain. Install a rubber band around the cassette and the timing chain.

f. Remove the timing chain.

To install:

6. On the RH head, perform the following:

a. Install the timing chain.

b. Install the camshaft sprocket and bolt.

c. Install the RH side cassette bolt and tighten to 9 ft. lbs. (12 Nm).

7. On the LH head, perform the following:

a. Install the timing chain.

b. Install the camshaft sprocket and bolt.

c. Install the LH side cassette bolt to 14 ft. lbs. (19 Nm).

8. Install the following:
• Cylinder heads; see "Cylinder Head" section

9. Perform the "Camshaft Timing Procedure" below.
• Valve covers
• Negative battery cable

10. Fill the engine with clean oil.

11. Start the vehicle, check for leaks and repair if necessary.

CAMSHAFT TIMING PROCEDURE

4.0L (VIN E, K) SOHC Engine

See Figures 287 through 290.

➡**You must retime both camshafts when either camshaft is disturbed.**

1. If installed, remove the camshaft roller followers.

2. On the RH side, perform the following:

a. Turn the crankshaft clockwise to position the number one cylinder at top dead center (TDC).

b. Remove the retainer and position the A/C manifold tube aside.

✳✳ CAUTION

Do not rotate the engine counterclockwise. Rotating the engine counterclockwise will result in incorrect timing of the engine.

➡**The special tool must be installed on the damper and should contact the**

engine block, this positions the engine at TDC.

c. Install the special tool on the crankshaft pulley.

d. Install the special tools to the RH cylinder head and tighten the 2 top clamp bolts to 89 inch lbs. (10 Nm).

e. Using the special tool with the Camshaft Sprocket Nut Socket 303-565, loosen the RH camshaft sprocket bolt.

Fig. 287 Install the special tool on the crankshaft pulley—4.0L (VIN E, K) SOHC engine

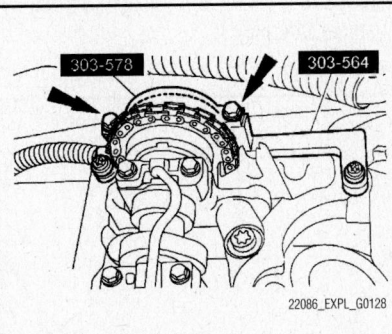

Fig. 288 Install the RH camshaft sprocket special holding tools—4.0L (VIN E, K) SOHC engine

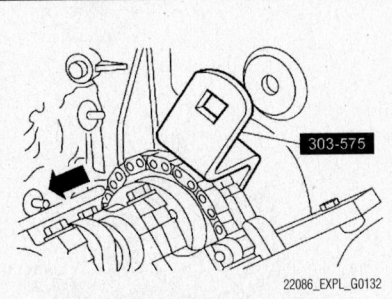

Fig. 289 Using the special tool with the Camshaft Sprocket Nut Socket 303-565, loosen the RH camshaft sprocket bolt—4.0L (VIN E, K) SOHC engine

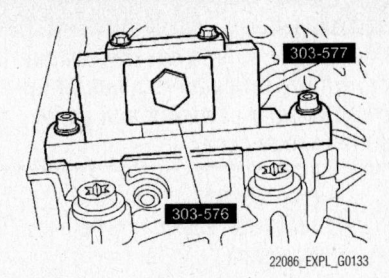

Fig. 290 Position the camshaft timing slots below the centerline of the camshaft to correctly fit the special tools and install the special tools on the front of the RH cylinder head—4.0L (VIN E, K) SOHC engine

f. Loosen the top 2 special tool sprocket clamp bolts.

➡**The camshaft timing slots are off-center.**

g. Position the camshaft timing slots below the centerline of the camshaft to correctly fit the special tools and install the special tools on the front of the RH cylinder head.

h. Remove the RH camshaft tensioner.

i. Install the special tool, 303-571, in place of the RH camshaft tensioner.

✳✳ CAUTION

The RH camshaft sprocket bolt is a LH-threaded bolt.

j. Tighten the sprocket special tool top 2 clamp bolts to 89 inch lbs.(10 Nm).

k. Using the special tool with the Camshaft Sprocket Nut Socket 303-565, tighten the camshaft bolt to 45 ft. lbs. (61 Nm).

l. Remove the special tool from the RH camshaft tensioner hole.

m. Install the RH camshaft tensioner, with a new, lubricated O-ring. Tighten the tensioner to 32 ft. lbs. (44 Nm).

n. Remove the special tools from the RH cylinder head.

3. Repeat the above procedure for the LH cylinder head, using the appropriate special tools where needed.

4. Install the camshaft roller followers.

4.6L (VIN W) SOHC Engine

See Figures 291 through 293.

1. Before servicing the vehicle, refer to the precautions in the beginning of this manual.

2. Remove or disconnect the following:

❄ WARNING

Since the engine is not free-wheeling, timing procedures must be followed exactly or piston and valve damage may occur.

- Front cover
- Crankshaft sensor ring from the crankshaft

3. Rotate the crankshaft until both camshaft key ways are 90 degrees from the valve cover surface. Make sure the copper links line up with the dots on the camshaft sprocket.

4. Install the special tools 303-380 and 303-413 on the camshaft.

5. Remove or disconnect the following:
- Left timing chain tensioner
- Right timing chain tensioner
- Left and right timing chain tensioner arm from the dowel pins
- Timing chains and crankshaft sprocket
- Timing chain guides

To install:

❄ WARNING

Do not compress the ratchet assembly. This will damage the ratchet assembly.

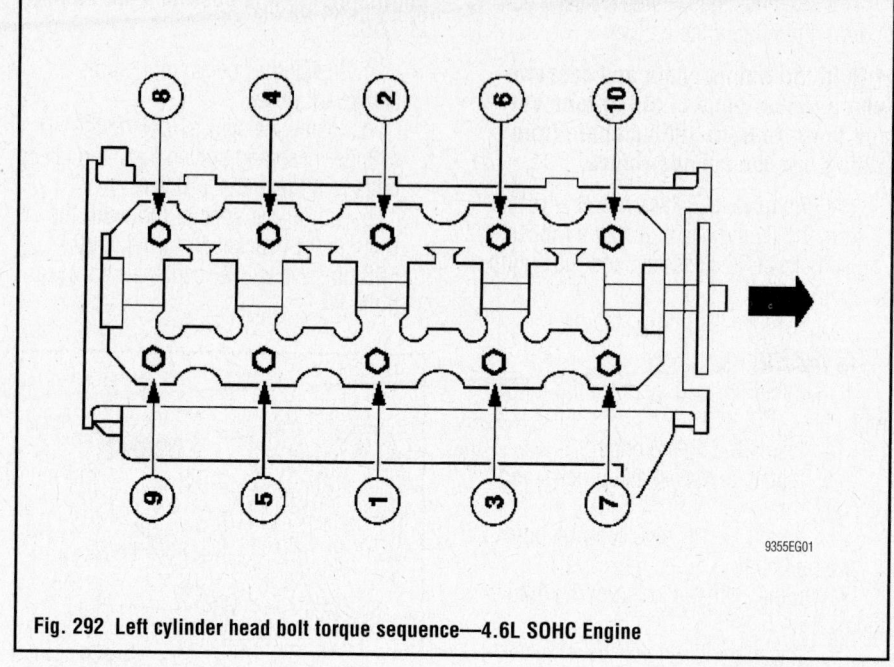

Fig. 292 Left cylinder head bolt torque sequence—4.6L SOHC Engine

6. Compress the tensioner plunger, using an edge of a vise.

7. Using a small screwdriver or pick, push back and hold the ratchet mechanism.

8. While holding the ratchet mechanism, push the ratchet arm back into the tensioner housing.

9. Install a paper clip into the hole in the tensioner housing to hold the ratchet assembly and plunger in during installation.

➡ **If the copper links are not visible, mark one link on one end and one link on the other end, and use as timing marks.**

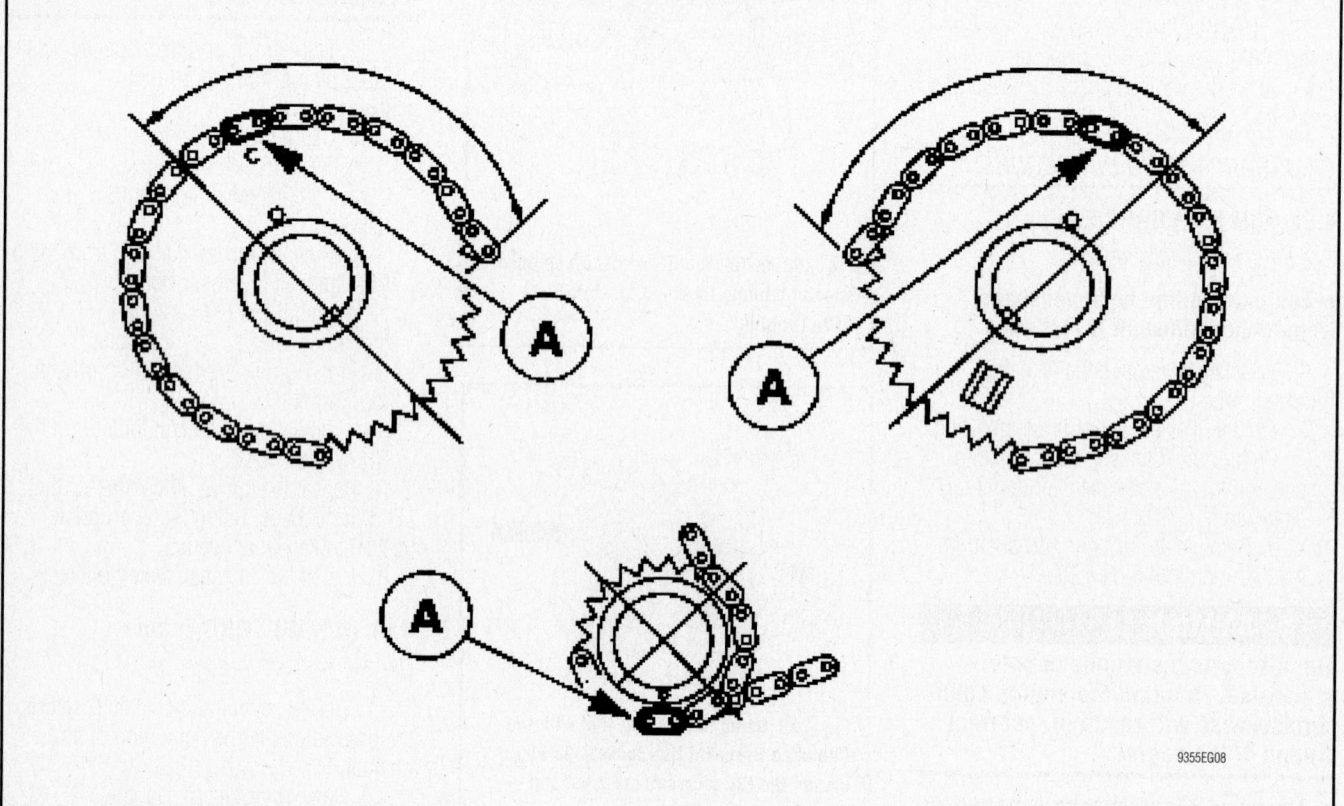

Fig. 291 Copper link alignment—4.6L SOHC Engine

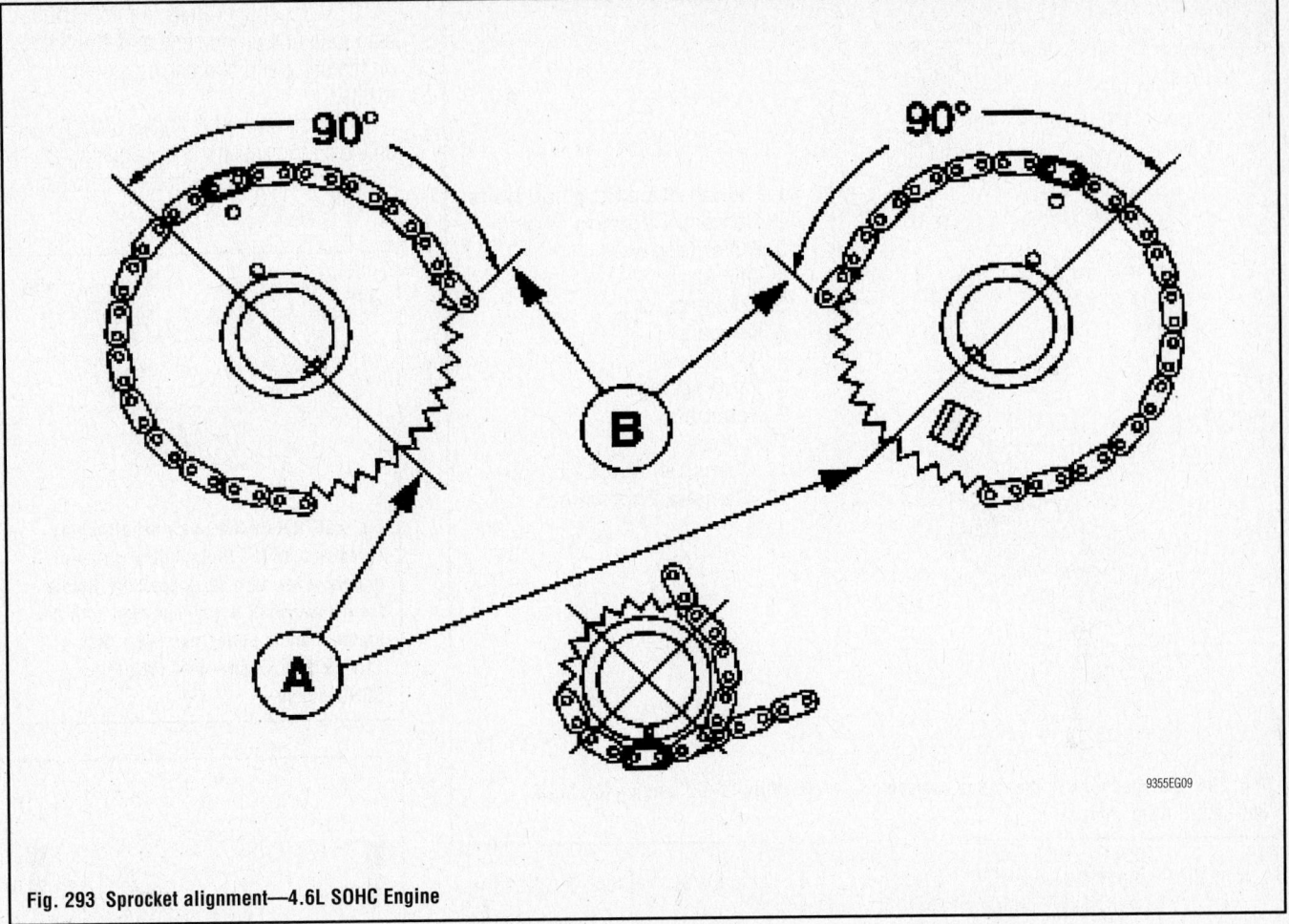

Fig. 293 Sprocket alignment—4.6L SOHC Engine

10. Install or connect the following:
- Crankshaft sprocket, making sure the timing mark faces forward
- Timing chain guides
- Left (inner) timing chain on the crankshaft sprocket, aligning the copper link with the dot on the crankshaft sprocket
- Left (inner) timing chain on the camshaft sprocket, aligning the copper link with the dot on the camshaft sprocket
- Right (outer) timing chain on the crankshaft sprocket, aligning the copper link with the dot on the crankshaft sprocket
- Right (outer) timing chain on the camshaft sprocket, aligning the copper link with the dot on the camshaft sprocket

11. Make sure that the copper marks on the timing chain are lined up with the corresponding dots on the crankshaft sprockets and the camshaft sprockets.

12. Make sure that the camshaft sprocket keyway is 90 degrees from the valve cover mounting surface.

➡The left timing chain tensioner arm has a bump near the dowel hole, for identification.

13. Position the left and right timing chain tensioner arm on the dowel pins.

14. Position the right timing chain tensioner and install the bolts.

15. Position the left timing chain tensioner and install the bolts.

16. Remove both the right and left retaining pins from the timing chain tensioner.

17. Remove the special tools from the camshaft.

18. Install the crankshaft sensor ring on the crankshaft.

19. Install the engine front cover.

4.6L (VIN 8) SOHC Engine

See Figures 294 through 302.

1. Before servicing the vehicle, refer to the "Precautions" section.

2. Remove or disconnect the following:

✵✵ WARNING

Since the engine is not free-wheeling, timing procedures must be fol-lowed exactly or piston and valve damage may occur.

- Front cover; see "Timing Chain Cover and Seal"
- Camshaft roller followers
- Crankshaft sensor ring from the crankshaft

✵✵ WARNING

If one or both of the tensioner mounting bolts are loosened or removed, the tensioner-sealing bead must be inspected for seal integrity. If cracks, tears, separation from the tensioner body or permanent compression of the seal bead is observed, install a new tensioner.

3. Remove the following:
- 2 bolts and the RH timing chain tensioner
- RH timing chain tensioner arm
- 2 bolts and the LH timing chain tensioner
- LH timing chain tensioner arm
- 2 bolts and the RH timing chain guide

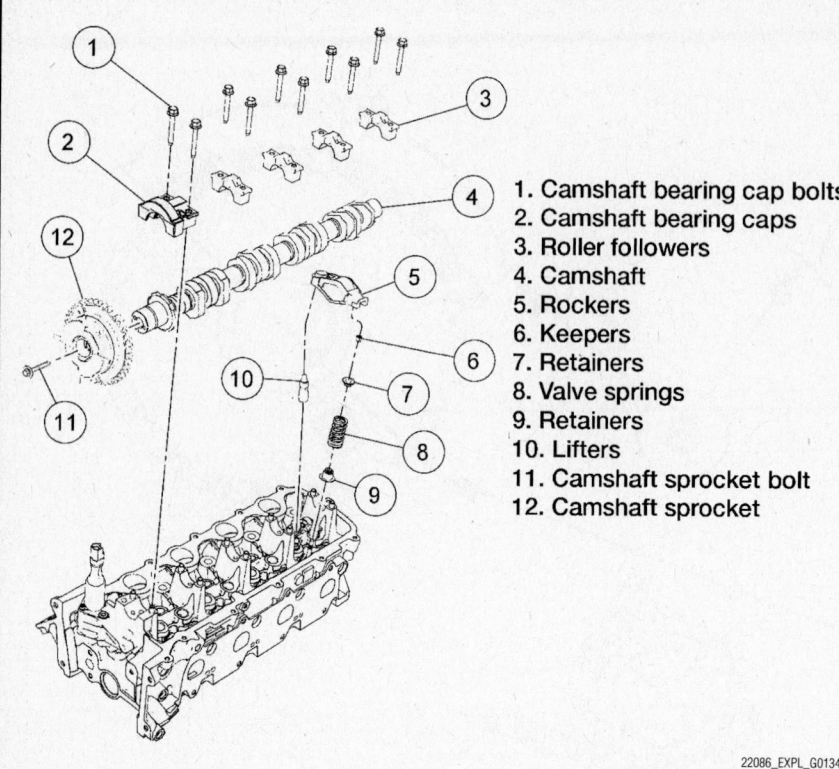

1. Camshaft bearing cap bolts
2. Camshaft bearing caps
3. Roller followers
4. Camshaft
5. Rockers
6. Keepers
7. Retainers
8. Valve springs
9. Retainers
10. Lifters
11. Camshaft sprocket bolt
12. Camshaft sprocket

22086_EXPL_G0134

Fig. 294 Exploded view of the timing components—4.6L (VIN 8) SOHC engine (LH head shown; RH head similar)

- RH timing chain
- 2 bolts and the LH timing chain guide
- LH timing chain
- Crankshaft sprocket

To install:

> ❋❋ **WARNING**
>
> **Rotate the crankshaft counterclockwise only. Do not rotate past the position shown or severe piston and/or valve damage will occur.**

4. Using the special tool, position the crankshaft.

5. Install the crankshaft sprocket with the flange facing forward.

6. Rotate the LH camshaft timing sprocket until the timing mark is approximately at the 12 o'clock position. Rotate the RH camshaft timing sprocket until the timing mark is at approximately the 11 o'clock position.

7. Install the timing chain guides. Tighten the bolts to 89 inch lbs. (10 Nm).

8. If the copper links are not visible, mark one link on one end and one link on the other end and use as timing marks.

9. Position the LH (inner) timing chain on the crankshaft sprocket, aligning the copper (marked) link with the timing mark on the sprocket.

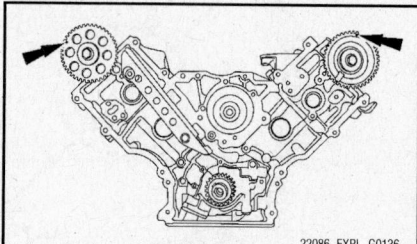

22086_EXPL_G0136

Fig. 296 Rotate the LH camshaft timing sprocket until the timing mark is approximately at the 12 o'clock position. Rotate the RH camshaft timing sprocket until the timing mark is at approximately the 11 o'clock position—4.6L (VIN 8) SOHC engine

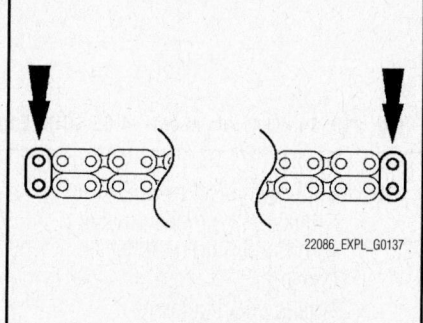

22086_EXPL_G0137

Fig. 297 If the copper links are not visible, mark one link on one end and one link on the other end and use as timing marks—4.6L (VIN 8) SOHC engine

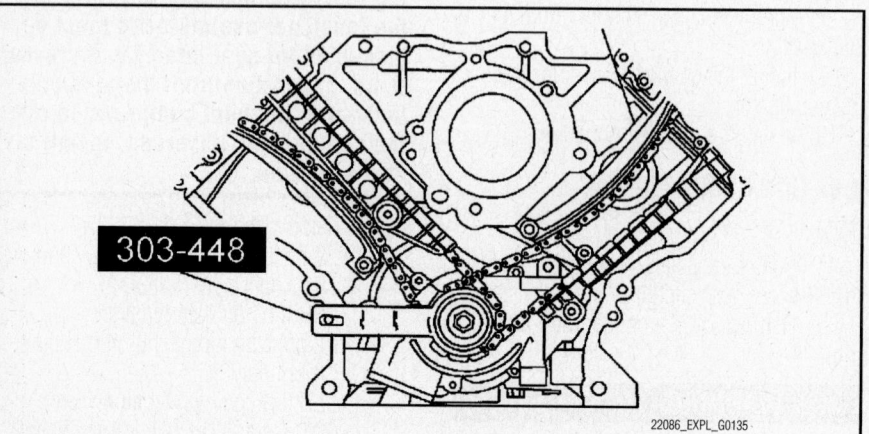

303-448

22086_EXPL_G0135

Fig. 295 Using the special tool, position the crankshaft—4.6L (VIN 8) SOHC engine

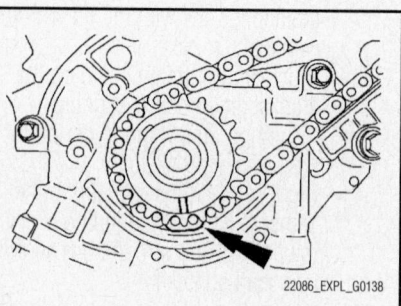

22086_EXPL_G0138

Fig. 298 Position the LH (inner) timing chain on the crankshaft sprocket, aligning the copper (marked) link with the timing mark on the sprocket—4.6L (VIN 8) SOHC engine

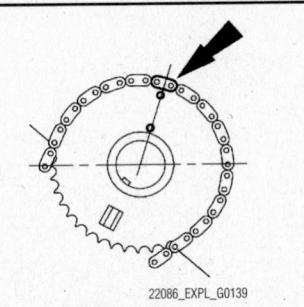

Fig. 299 Position the LH timing chain on the camshaft sprocket. Make sure the copper-colored link aligns with the camshaft sprocket timing mark—4.6L (VIN 8) SOHC engine

➡️If necessary, adjust the camshaft sprocket slightly to obtain timing mark alignment.

10. Position the LH timing chain on the camshaft sprocket. Make sure the copper-colored link aligns with the camshaft sprocket timing mark.

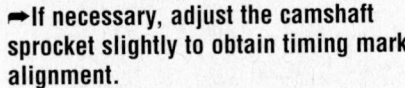

CAUTION

Prior to installation, inspect the tensioner-sealing bead for seal integrity If cracks, tears, separation from the tensioner body or permanent compression of the seal bead is observed, install a new tensioner.

11. Compress the LH tensioner plunger, using a vise.
12. Install a retaining clip on the LH tensioner to hold the plunger in during installation.

➡️The LH timing chain tensioner arm has a bump near the dowel hole for identification.

13. Position the LH timing chain tensioner arm on the dowel pin and install the LH timing chain tensioner and the bolts to 18 ft. lbs. (25 Nm).
14. Remove the retaining clip from the LH timing chain tensioner.
15. Position the RH (outer) timing chain on the crankshaft sprocket, aligning the copper (marked) link with the timing mark on the sprocket.

➡️If necessary, adjust the camshaft sprocket slightly to obtain timing mark alignment.

16. Position the RH timing chain on the camshaft sprocket. Make sure the copper-colored link aligns with the camshaft sprocket timing mark.

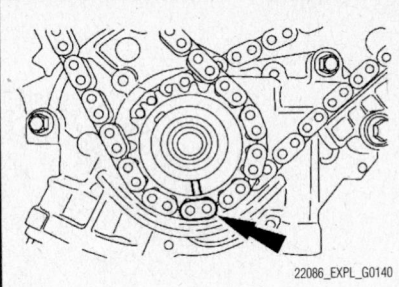

Fig. 300 Position the RH (outer) timing chain on the crankshaft sprocket, aligning the copper (marked) link with the timing mark on the sprocket—4.6L (VIN 8) SOHC engine

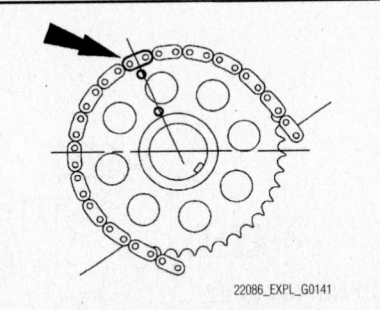

Fig. 301 Position the RH timing chain on the camshaft sprocket. Make sure the copper-colored link aligns with the camshaft sprocket timing mark—4.6L (VIN 8) SOHC engine

CAUTION

Prior to installation, inspect the tensioner-sealing bead for seal integrity. If cracks, tears, separation from the tensioner body or permanent compression of the seal bead is observed, install a new tensioner.

17. Compress the RH tensioner plunger, using a vise.
18. Install a retaining clip on the RH tensioner to hold the plunger in during installation.
19. Position the RH timing chain tensioner arm on the dowel pin and install the RH timing chain tensioner and the bolts to 18 ft. lbs. (25 Nm).
20. Remove the retaining clip from the RH timing chain tensioner.
21. As a post-check, verify correct alignment of all timing marks.
22. Install the sensor ring on the crankshaft.
23. Install the camshaft roller followers.
24. Install the engine front cover.

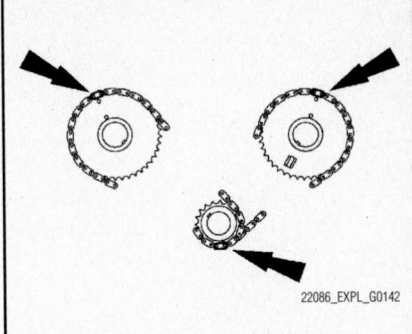

Fig. 302 As a post-check, verify correct alignment of all timing marks—4.6L (VIN 8) SOHC engine

4.6L (VIN H) DOHC Engine

See Figures 303 through 314.

1. Before servicing the vehicle, refer to the "Precautions" section.
2. Remove the crankshaft sensor ignition pulse ring.

WARNING

Since the engine is not free-wheeling, timing procedures must be followed exactly or piston and valve damage can occur.

WARNING

Unless otherwise instructed, at no time when the timing chains are removed and the cylinder heads are installed is the crankshaft or the camshaft to be rotated. Severe piston and valve damage will occur.

3. Using special tool 303-448, position the crankshaft with the keyway at the 12 o'clock position.
4. Install special tool 303-446.
5. Remove the timing chain tensioning system from both timing chains.
   a. Remove the bolts.
   b. Remove the timing chain tensioners.
   c. Remove the timing chain tensioner arms.
6. Remove the right timing chain tensioner arm.
7. Remove the left timing chain tensioner arm.
8. Remove the right camshaft sprocket mounting bolt.
9. Remove the right camshaft sprocket washer.
10. Remove the right camshaft sprocket.

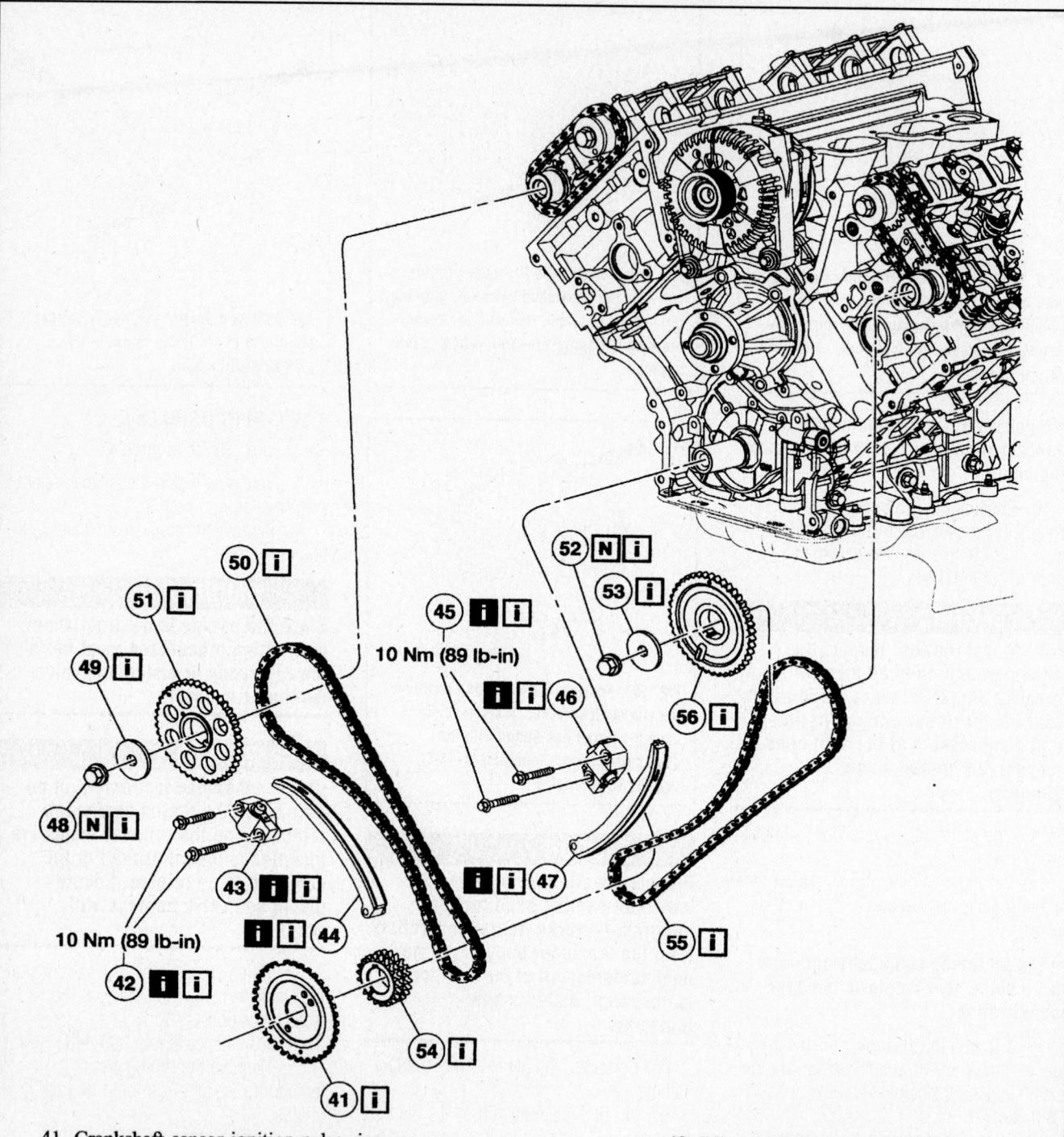

10 Nm (89 lb-in)

10 Nm (89 lb-in)

41 Crankshaft sensor ignition pulse ring

42 RH timing chain tensioner mounting bolts

43 RH timing chain tensioner

44 RH timing chain tensioner arm

45 LH timing chain tensioner mounting bolts

46 LH timing chain tensioner

47 LH timing chain tensioner arm

48 RH camshaft sprocket mounting bolt

49 RH camshaft sprocket washer

50 RH timing chain

51 RH camshaft sprocket

52 LH camshaft sprocket mounting bolt

53 LH camshaft sprocket washer

54 Crankshaft gear

55 LH timing chain

56 LH camshaft sprocket

67197EXPLG45

Fig. 303 Timing chains and related parts—4.6L DOHC engine

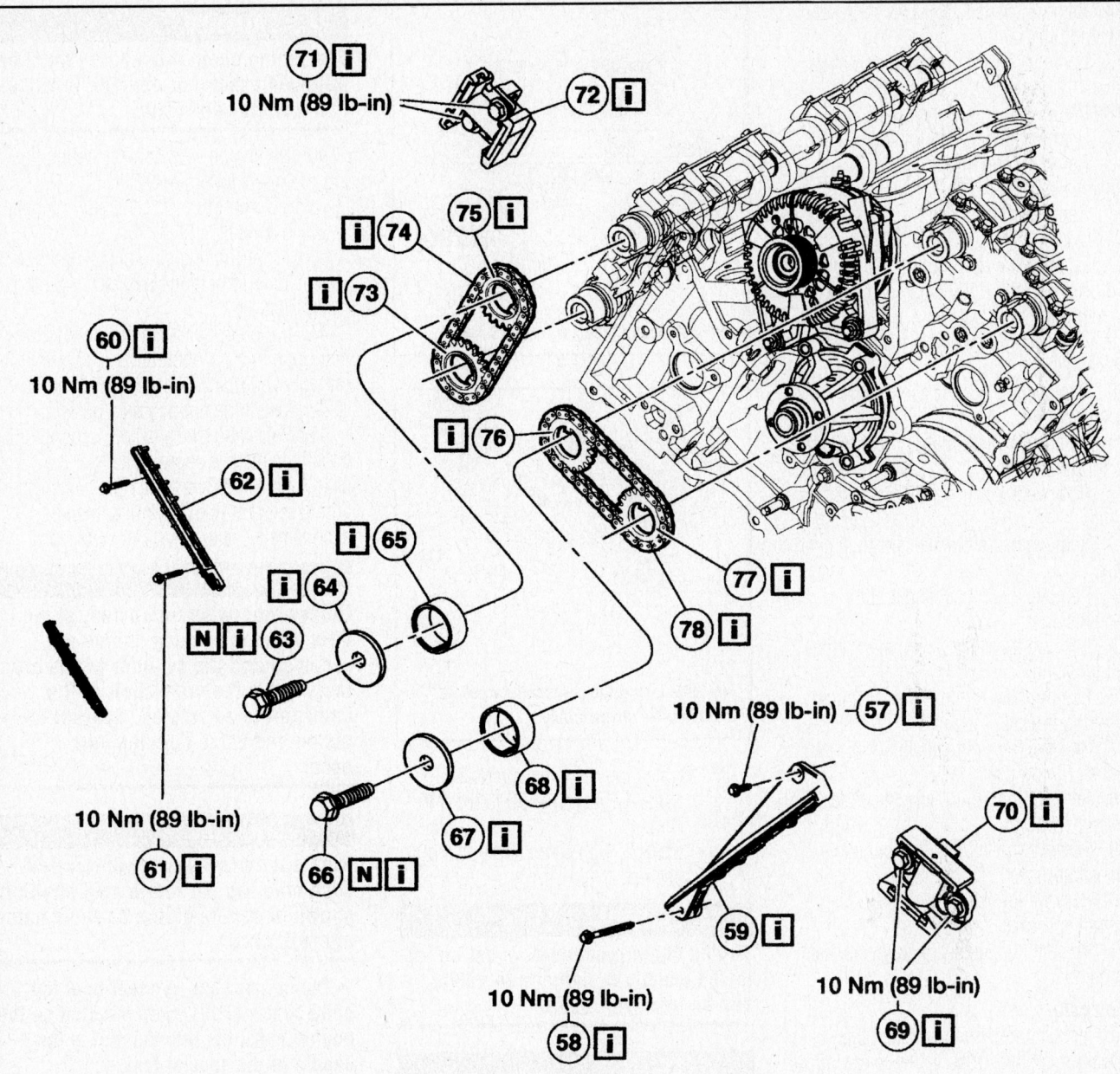

57 LH timing chain guide upper mounting bolt

58 LH timing chain guide lower mounting bolt

59 LH timing chain guide

60 RH timing chain guide upper mounting bolt

61 RH timing chain guide lower mounting bolt

62 RH timing chain guide

63 RH intake camshaft gear mounting bolt

64 RH intake camshaft gear washer

65 RH intake camshaft gear spacer

66 LH intake camshaft gear mounting bolt

67 LH intake camshaft gear washer

68 LH intake camshaft gear spacer

69 LH secondary timing chain tensioner mounting bolts

70 LH secondary timing chain tensioner

71 RH secondary timing chain tensioner mounting bolts

72 RH secondary timing chain tensioner

73 RH exhaust secondary camshaft sprocket

74 RH secondary camshaft timing chain

75 RH intake secondary camshaft sprocket

76 LH intake secondary camshaft sprocket

77 LH exhaust secondary camshaft sprocket

78 LH secondary camshaft timing chain

67197EXPLG46

Fig. 304 Secondary timing chains and related parts—4.6L DOHC engine

11. Remove the left camshaft sprocket mounting bolt.

12. Remove the left camshaft sprocket washer.

13. Remove the crankshaft gear.

14. Remove the left timing chain.

15. Remove the left camshaft sprocket.

16. Remove the left timing chain guide.

17. Remove the right timing chain guide.

18. Remove the right intake camshaft gear mounting bolt.

19. Remove the right intake camshaft gear washer.

20. Remove the right intake camshaft gear spacer.

21. Remove the left intake camshaft gear mounting bolt.

22. Remove the left intake camshaft gear washer.

23. Remove the left intake camshaft gear spacer.

24. Remove the left secondary timing chain tensioner.

25. Remove the right secondary timing chain tensioner.

26. Remove the right exhaust secondary camshaft sprocket.

27. Remove the right secondary camshaft timing chain.

28. Remove the right intake secondary camshaft sprocket.

29. Remove the left intake secondary camshaft sprocket.

30. Remove the left exhaust secondary camshaft sprocket.

31. Remove the left secondary camshaft timing chain.

To install:

32. Installation is the reverse of the removal procedure. Observe the following notes:

Timing Drive Components Installation

33. Compress the tensioner and install the retaining pin. Install the tensioners.

✳✳ CAUTION

Timing marks must be at the 12 o'clock position and indexed at the 6 o'clock position.

34. Install the camshaft sprockets and chain as an assembly.

35. Install special tool 303-446.

36. Install the camshaft spacer, washer and bolt, and hand-tighten the bolt.

37. Install the camshaft gear, washer and bolt, and hand-tighten the bolt.

Fig. 305 Install special tool 303-446

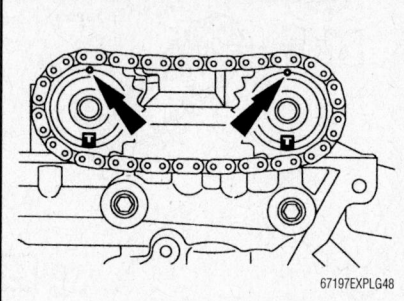

Fig. 306 Install the camshaft sprockets and chain as an assembly

38. Tighten the bolts in two stages:
- Stage 1: Tighten to 30 ft. lbs. (40 Nm).
- Stage 2: Tighten an additional 90 degrees.

✳✳ CAUTION

Timing chain procedures must be followed exactly or damage to valves and pistons will result.

✳✳ CAUTION

Do not compress the ratchet assembly. This will damage the ratchet assembly.

39. On engine with ratcheting timing chain tensioners only.

a. Compress each tensioner plunger, using an edge of a vise.

b. Using a small screwdriver or pick, push back and hold the ratchet mechanism.

c. While holding the ratchet mechanism, push the ratchet arm back into the tensioner housing.

d. Install a paper clip into the hole of each tensioner housing to hold the ratchet assembly and plunger in during installation. Remove the tensioner from the vise.

✳✳ CAUTION

The timing chain procedures must be followed exactly or damage to valves and pistons will result.

40. On engine with non-ratcheting timing chain tensioners only.

a. Compress each tensioner plunger, using a vise.

b. Install a retaining clip on each tensioner to hold the plunger in during installation.

41. If the copper links are not visible, mark one link on one end and one link on the other end, and use as timing marks.

42. Install the timing chain guides.

43. Rotate the left camshaft sprocket until the timing mark is approximately at the 12 o'clock position. Rotate the right camshaft timing sprocket until the timing mark is approximately at the 11 o'clock position.

✳✳ CAUTION

Unless otherwise instructed, at no time when the timing chains are removed and the cylinder heads are installed is the crankshaft or the camshaft to be rotated. Severe piston and valve damage will occur.

✳✳ CAUTION

Rotate the crankshaft counterclockwise only. Do not rotate past position shown or severe piston or valve damage will occur.

➡ The number one cylinder is at top dead center (TDC) when the stud on the engine block fits into the slot in the handle of the special tool.

44. Using special tool 303-448, position the crankshaft so the number one cylinder is at TDC.

45. Remove the special tool.

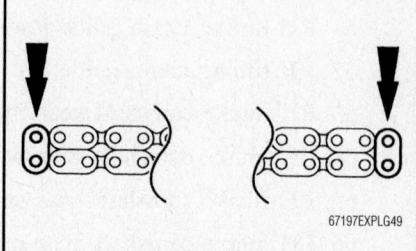

Fig. 307 If the copper links are not visible, mark one link on one end and one link on the other end, and use as timing marks—4.6L DOHC engine

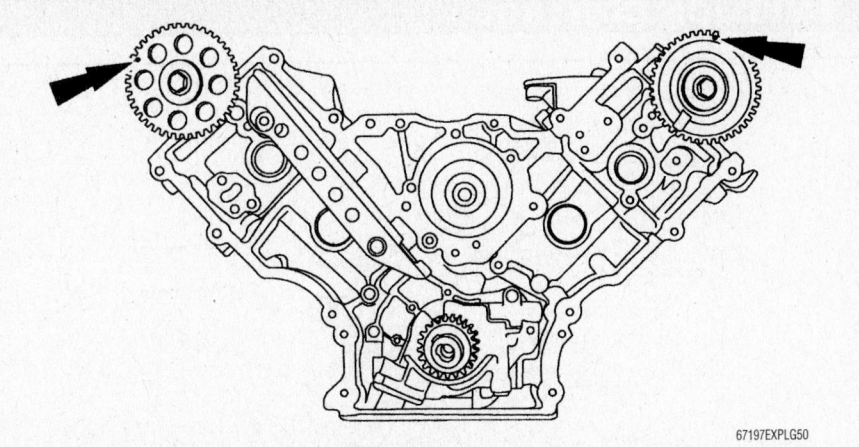

Fig. 308 Rotate the left camshaft sprocket until the timing mark is approximately at the 12 o'clock position. Rotate the right camshaft timing sprocket until the timing mark is approximately at the 11 o'clock position—4.6L DOHC engine

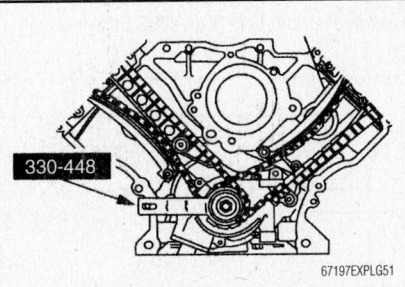

Fig. 309 Using special tool 303-448, position the crankshaft so the number one cylinder is at TDC—4.6L DOHC engine

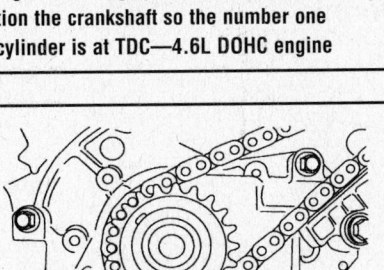

Fig. 310 Position the left (inner) timing chain on the crankshaft sprocket, aligning the copper (marked) link with the timing mark on the sprocket—4.6L DOHC engine

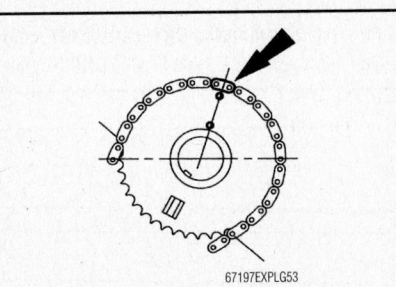

Fig. 311 Install the left timing chain onto the camshaft sprocket, aligning the copper (marked) link with the timing marks on the sprocket—4.6L DOHC engine

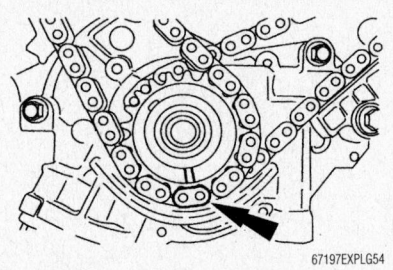

Fig. 312 Position the right (outer) timing chain on the crankshaft sprocket, aligning the copper (marked) link with the timing mark on the sprocket—4.6L DOHC engine

46. Position the left (inner) timing chain on the crankshaft sprocket, aligning the copper (marked) link with the timing mark on the sprocket.

47. Install the left timing chain onto the camshaft sprocket, aligning the copper (marked) link with the timing marks on the sprocket.

➡The left timing chain tensioner arm has a bump near the dowel hole for identification.

48. Position the left timing chain tensioner arms on the dowel pin and install the left timing chain tensioner.

49. On engine with ratcheting timing chain tensioners only, remove the retaining clip from the left timing chain tensioner.

50. On engine with non-ratcheting timing chain tensioners only, remove the retaining clip from the left timing chain tensioner.

51. Position the right (outer) timing chain on the crankshaft sprocket, aligning

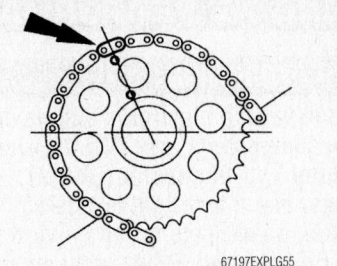

Fig. 313 Install the right timing chain onto the camshaft sprocket, aligning the copper (marked) link with the timing marks on the sprocket—4.6L DOHC engine

the copper (marked) link with the timing mark on the sprocket.

52. Install the right timing chain onto the camshaft sprocket, aligning the copper (marked) link with the timing marks on the sprocket.

53. Position the right timing chain tensioner arms on the dowel pin and install the right timing chain tensioner.

54. On engine with ratcheting timing chain tensioners only, remove the retaining clip from the right timing chain tensioner.

55. On engine with non-ratcheting timing chain tensioners only, remove the retaining clips from the right timing chain tensioner.

➡Applies to all engine.

56. Make sure that the copper (marked) chain links are lined up with the dots on the crankshaft sprockets and the camshaft sprocket.

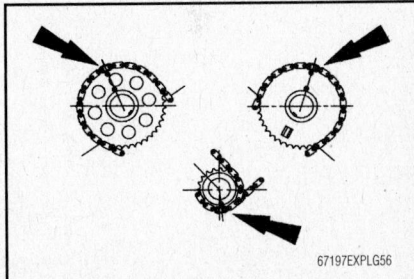

Fig. 314 Make sure that the copper (marked) chain links are lined up with the dots on the crankshaft sprockets and the camshaft sprocket—4.6L engine

VALVE LASH

ADJUSTMENT

The 4.0L and 4.6L engine are equipped with hydraulic lash adjusters. Valve lash is maintained by the hydraulic lifter or hydraulic lash adjuster eliminating the need for any additional manual adjustment. No further adjustment is possible.

ENGINE PERFORMANCE & EMISSION CONTROL

✵✵ WARNING

When testing electronic engine control components, use ONLY a proper Digital Volt Ohmmeter (DVOM). Never use a test light or analog tester, as damage to the Powertrain Control Module (PCM), sensors and other components will occur.

CAMSHAFT POSITION (CMP) SENSOR

LOCATION

4.0L (VIN E, K) SOHC Engine

See Figures 315 and 316.

The Camshaft Position (CMP) sensor is located on the side of the engine, on the cylinder head as shown.

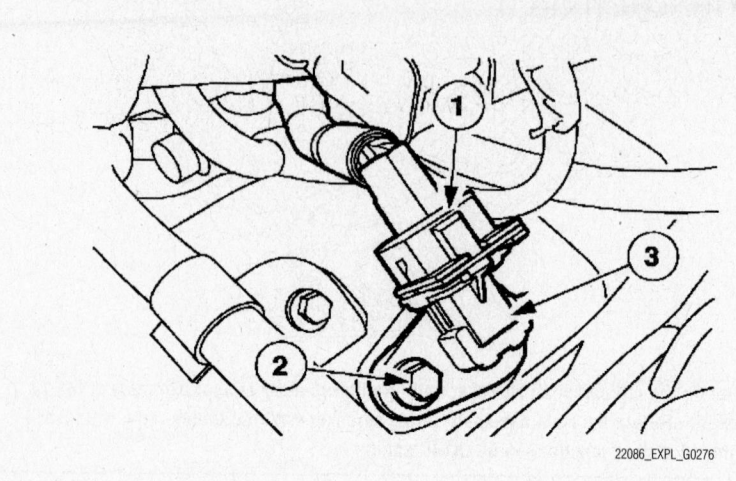

22086_EXPL_G0276

Fig. 316 Showing the CMP sensor (3), connector (1) and retaining bolt (2)—2005 Explorer Sport-Trac–07 4.0L (VIN E, K) SOHC engine

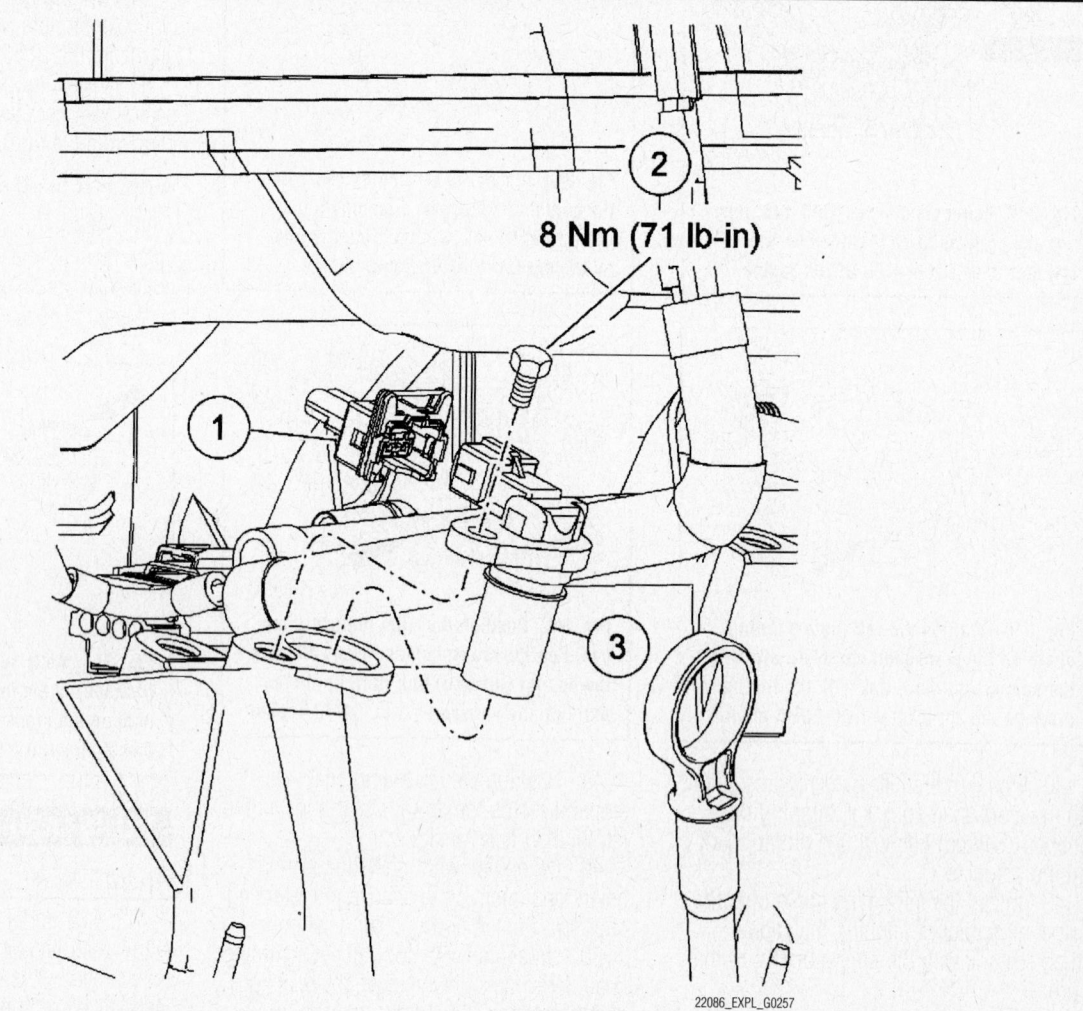

8 Nm (71 lb-in)

22086_EXPL_G0257

Fig. 315 Showing the CMP sensor (3), connector (1) and retaining bolt (2)—2005 Explorer and Mountaineer; 2007 Explorer Sport-Trac–07 4.0L (VIN E, K) SOHC engine

4.6L (VIN 8) SOHC Engine

2005 Models

See Figure 317.

This engine uses a Camshaft Position (CMP) sensor on each cylinder head. The CMP is located on the front of each cylinder head as shown.

2006–07 Models

See Figure 318.

This engine uses a Camshaft Position (CMP) sensor on each cylinder head. The

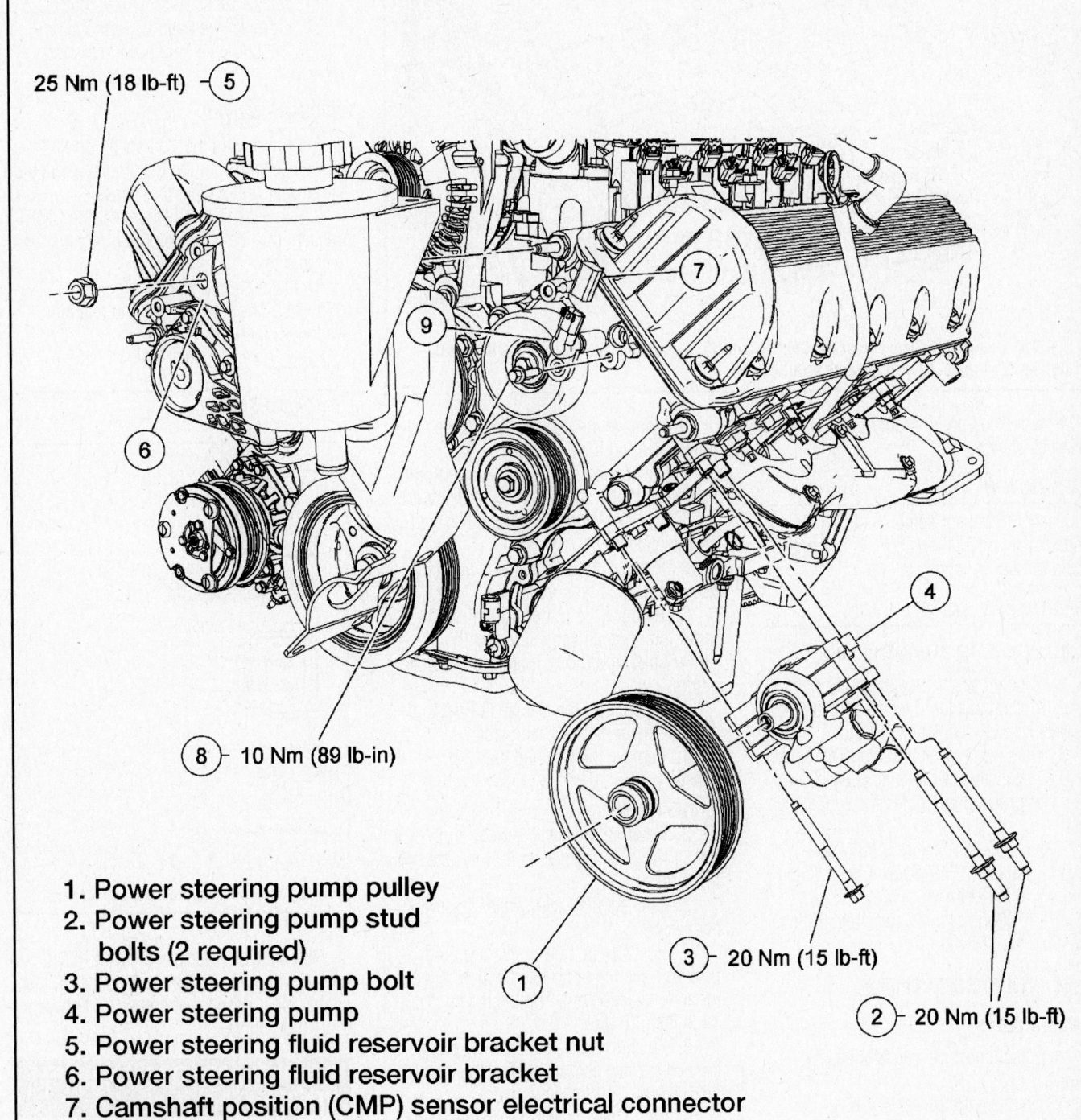

25 Nm (18 lb-ft) — ⑤

⑥

⑨

⑦

④

⑧ — 10 Nm (89 lb-in)

③ — 20 Nm (15 lb-ft)

① ②

② — 20 Nm (15 lb-ft)

1. Power steering pump pulley
2. Power steering pump stud bolts (2 required)
3. Power steering pump bolt
4. Power steering pump
5. Power steering fluid reservoir bracket nut
6. Power steering fluid reservoir bracket
7. Camshaft position (CMP) sensor electrical connector
8. CMP sensor bolt
9. CMP sensor

22086_EXPL_G0258

Fig. 317 Showing the location of the CMP sensor—2005 4.6L (VIN 8) SOHC engine

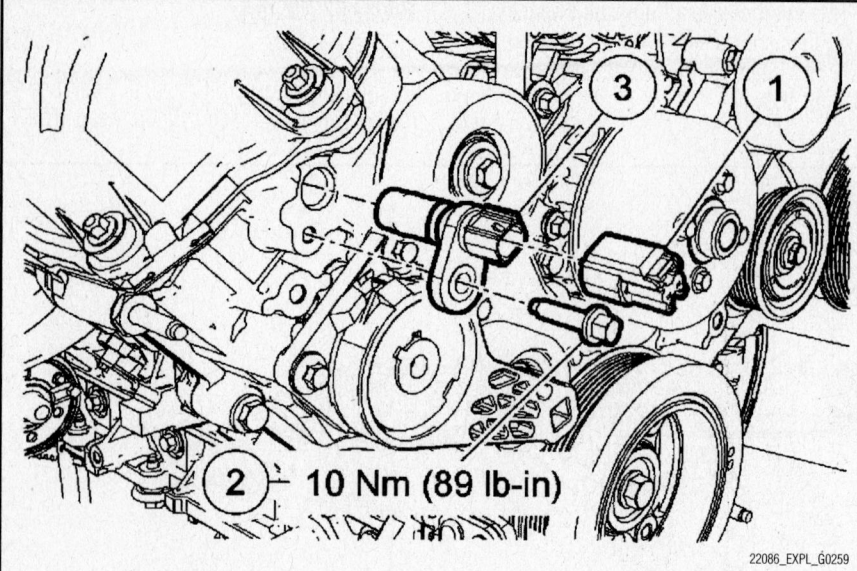

Fig. 318 Showing the location of the CMP sensor (3), electrical connector (1) and the retaining bolt (2)—2006–07 4.6L (VIN 8) SOHC engine

CMP is located on the front of each cylinder head as shown.

OPERATION

The CMP sensor sends the PCM a signal indicating camshaft position. This signal is used for fuel synchronization.

REMOVAL & INSTALLATION

4.0L (VIN E, K) SOHC Engine

1. Disconnect the negative battery cable.
2. Disconnect the Camshaft Position (CMP) sensor electrical connector.
3. Remove the bolt and the CMP sensor.
4. Installation is the reverse of the removal procedure. Tighten the sensor bolt to:
   - 2005–07 Explorer and Mountaineer; 2007 Sport-Trac: 71 inch lbs. (8 Nm)
   - 2005 Explorer Sport-Trac: 53 inch lbs. (6 Nm)

4.6L (VIN 8) SOHC Engine

2005 Models

1. Disconnect the negative battery cable.
2. Remove the accessory drive belt.
3. Using the special tool, remove the power steering pump pulley.
4. Remove the nuts and position the wiring harness bracket and ground cable aside.
5. Remove the power steering pump stud bolts.

6. Remove the nut and detach the power steering hose bracket.
7. Disconnect the power steering pressure hose fitting and remove and discard the O-ring seal. Drain the fluid into a suitable container.
8. Remove the bolt and position the power steering pump aside.
9. Remove the nut and position the radio interference capacitor and the power steering fluid reservoir and bracket aside.
10. Disconnect the Camshaft Position (CMP) sensor electrical connector.
11. Remove the bolt and the CMP sensor.

To install:

12. Position the CMP sensor and install the bolt. Tighten to 89 inch lbs. (10 Nm).
13. Connect the CMP sensor electrical connector.
14. Position the power steering fluid reservoir and the radio interference capacitor and install the nut. Tighten the nut to 18 ft. lbs. (25 Nm).
15. Position the power steering pump, the bolt and the stud bolts. Tighten the bolt to 15 ft. lbs. (20 Nm).
16. Using the special tool, install a new O-ring seal on the power steering pressure hose fitting.
17. Connect the power steering pressure hose fitting. Tighten the fitting to 48 ft. lbs. (65 Nm).
18. Attach the power steering hose bracket and install the nut. Tighten the nut to 8 ft. lbs. (11 Nm).

19. Position the ground wire and the wiring harness bracket and install the nuts. Tighten the nuts to 15 ft. lbs. (20 Nm).
20. Using the special tool, install the power steering pump pulley.
21. Install the accessory drive belt.
22. Connect the battery ground cable.
23. Fill and bleed the power steering system.

2006–07 Models

1. If removing the Camshaft Position (CMP) sensor from the RH side, remove the air cleaner outlet pipe, for access.
2. On either CMP, disconnect the CMP sensor electrical connector and remove the bolt and the CMP sensor.
3. Installation is the, reverse of the removal procedure. Tighten the retaining bolt to 89 inch lbs. (10 Nm)

TESTING

See Figure 319.

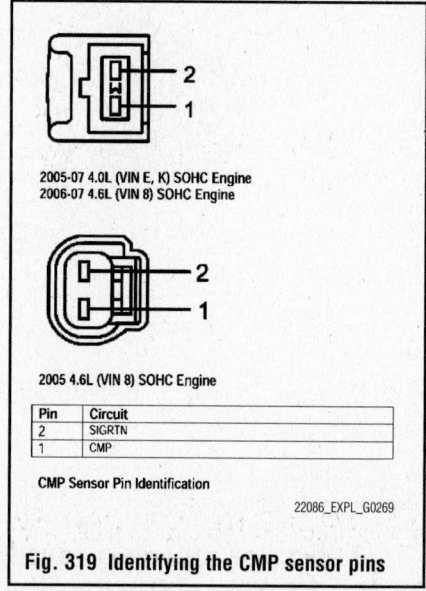

2005-07 4.0L (VIN E, K) SOHC Engine
2006-07 4.6L (VIN 8) SOHC Engine

2005 4.6L (VIN 8) SOHC Engine

Pin	Circuit
2	SIGRTN
1	CMP

CMP Sensor Pin Identification

Fig. 319 Identifying the CMP sensor pins

With the CMP sensor connector disconnected, measure the resistance between the sensor pins. Resistance should be between 250–1000 ohms.

CRANKSHAFT POSITION (CKP) SENSOR

LOCATION

4.0L (VIN E, K) SOHC Engine

See Figures 320 and 321.

The Crankshaft Position (CKP) sensor is located on the front of the engine, near the crankshaft pulley.

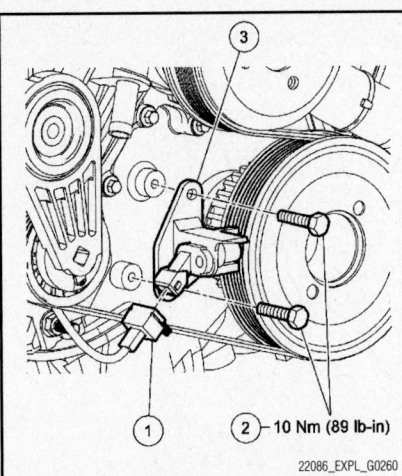

Fig. 320 CKP sensor (3), connector (1) and retaining bolt (2)—2005–07 Explorer and Mountaineer; 2007 Explorer Sport-Trac 4.0L (VIN E, K) SOHC engine

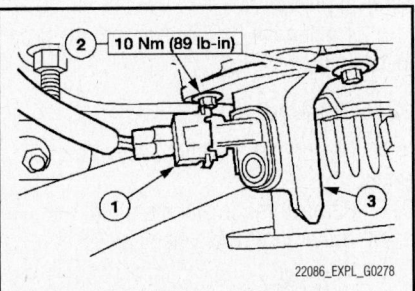

Fig. 321 CKP sensor (3), connector (1) and retaining bolts (2)—2005 Explorer Sport-Trac 4.0L (VIN E, K) SOHC engine

4.6L (VIN 8) SOHC Engine

2005 Models

See Figure 322.

This engine uses a Crankshaft Position (CKP) sensor on each cylinder head. The CKP sensor is located on the front of each cylinder head.

2006–07 Models

See Figure 323.

This engine uses a Crankshaft Position (CKP) sensor located on the front of the block, near the crankshaft pulley.

OPERATION

The CKP sensor sends the PCM a signal indicating crankshaft position. This signal is essential for calculating spark timing.

REMOVAL & INSTALLATION

4.0L (VIN E, K) SOHC Engine

1. With the vehicle in NEUTRAL, position it on a hoist.
2. Disconnect the negative battery cable.
3. Disconnect the Crankshaft Position (CKP) sensor electrical connector.
4. Remove the bolt(s) and the CKP sensor.

To install:

5. Installation is the reverse of the removal procedure, noting the following:

➡**Be sure the sensor wiring is routed away from the battery cable.**

   c. Tighten the sensor bolt(s) to 89 inch lbs. (10 Nm).
6. For Explorer Sport-Trac, note the following:
   a. The new CKP sensor needs to be touching the damper. The new sensor has wear tabs that will wear off after several engine revolutions.
   b. Ensure the sensor wiring is routed away from the battery cable.

4.6L (VIN 8) SOHC Engine

2005 Models

1. With the vehicle in NEUTRAL, position it on a hoist.
2. Disconnect the negative battery cable.
3. Detach the accessory drive belt from the A/C compressor.
4. Disconnect the Crankshaft Position (CKP) sensor electrical connector.
5. Disconnect the A/C compressor electrical connector.
6. Loosen the bolts and slide the A/C compressor down approximately 1 inch (25 mm).
7. To install, tighten to 18 ft. lbs. (25 Nm).
8. Remove the bolt and the CKP sensor.

To install:

9. Install the sensor and tighten the bolt to 89 inch lbs. (10 Nm).
10. Reposition the A/C compressor and tighten the mounting bolts to 18 ft. lbs. (25 Nm).
11. Connect the A/C compressor electrical connector.
12. Connect the Crankshaft Position (CKP) sensor electrical connector.
13. Install the accessory drive belt from the A/C compressor.
14. Connect the battery ground cable.
15. Lower the vehicle.

2006–07 Models

1. With vehicle in NEUTRAL, position it on a hoist.
2. Remove the accessory drive belt.
3. Disconnect the A/C compressor coil electrical connector.
4. Detach the battery cable retainer from the A/C compressor stud bolts.
5. Remove the nut and detach the A/C tube bracket.

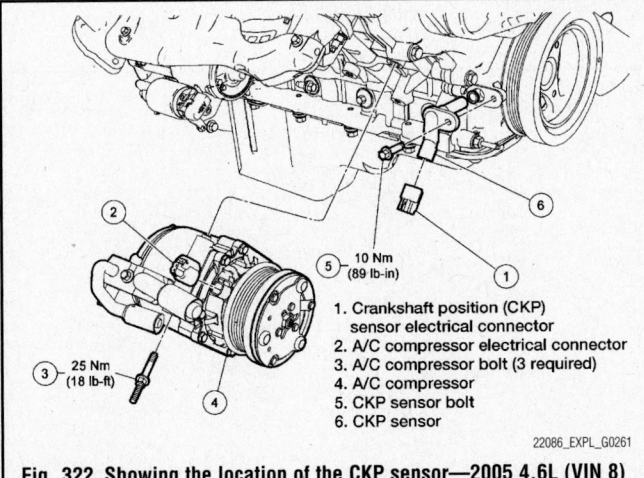

1. Crankshaft position (CKP) sensor electrical connector
2. A/C compressor electrical connector
3. A/C compressor bolt (3 required)
4. A/C compressor
5. CKP sensor bolt
6. CKP sensor

Fig. 322 Showing the location of the CKP sensor—2005 4.6L (VIN 8) SOHC engine

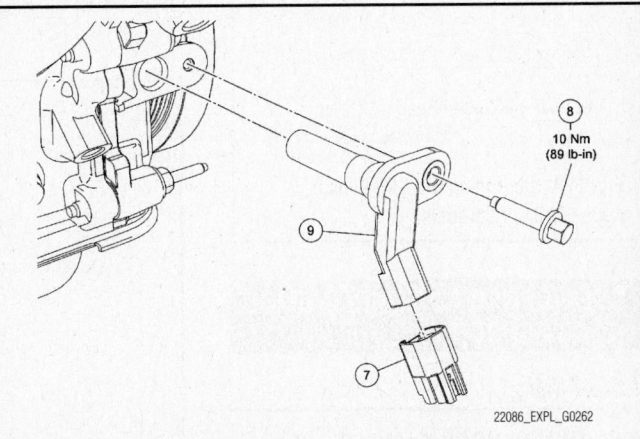

Fig. 323 Showing the location of the CKP sensor (3), electrical connector (1) and the retaining bolt (2)—2006–07 4.6L (VIN 8) SOHC engine

6. Remove the stud bolts and position the A/C compressor aside.

7. Disconnect the Crankshaft Position (CKP) sensor electrical connector.

8. Remove the bolt and the CKP sensor.

To install:

9. Install the CKP sensor. Tighten the bolt to 89 inch lbs. (10 Nm).

10. Connect the CKP sensor electrical connector.

11. Position the A/C compressor and tighten the bolts to 18 ft. lbs. (25 Nm).

12. Install the A/C tube bracket. Tighten the nut to 89 inch lbs. (10 Nm).

13. Attach the battery cable retainer to the A/C compressor stud bolts.

14. Connect the A/C compressor coil electrical connector.

15. Install the accessory drive belt.

TESTING

See Figure 324.

1. With the CKP sensor connector disconnected, the Key ON and the engine OFF, measure the voltage between the sensor pins on the harness side of the connector. Voltage should be between 1–3 volts.

2. With Key in OFF position, disconnect the CKP sensor connector and measure the resistance between the sensor pins. The CKP sensor resistance values change significantly with temperature rise. The resistance should be between 250–1000 ohms.

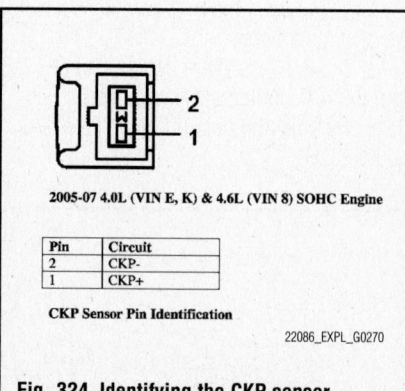

2005-07 4.0L (VIN E, K) & 4.6L (VIN 8) SOHC Engine

Pin	Circuit
2	CKP-
1	CKP+

CKP Sensor Pin Identification

22086_EXPL_G0270

Fig. 324 Identifying the CKP sensor pins—2005–07 models

CYLINDER HEAD TEMPERATURE (CHT) SENSOR

LOCATION

4.6L (VIN 8) SOHC Engine

2005 Models

See Figure 325.

26 Nm (19 lb-ft)

22086_EXPL_G0263

Fig. 325 Showing the location of the CHT sensor (2) and the electrical connector (1)—2005 4.6L (VIN 8) SOHC engine

The Cylinder Head Temperature (CHT) sensor is mounted to the wall of the cylinder head and is not connected to any coolant passages.

2006–07 Models

See Figure 326.

OPERATION

The Cylinder Head Temperature (CHT) sensor sends a signal reading of the current temperature of the cylinder head.

REMOVAL & INSTALLATION

4.6L (VIN 8) SOHC Engine

2005 Models

1. Remove the alternator, as outlined in the Engine Electrical Section.

2. Disconnect the Cylinder Head Temperature (CHT) sensor electrical connector.

3. Remove the CHT sensor.

4. Installation is the reverse of the removal procedure.

5. Tighten the CHT sensor into the head to 19 ft. lbs. (26 Nm).

2006–07 Models

1. Disconnect the negative battery cable.

2. Remove the intake manifold, as outlined in the Engine Mechanical Section.

3. Disconnect the Cylinder Head Temperature (CHT) sensor electrical connector.

4. Remove and discard the CHT sensor.

5. Installation is the reverse of the removal procedure.

➡**Do not reuse the CHT sensor. Install a new sensor.**

6. Tighten the CHT sensor to 19 ft. lbs. (26 Nm).

TESTING

See Figure 327.

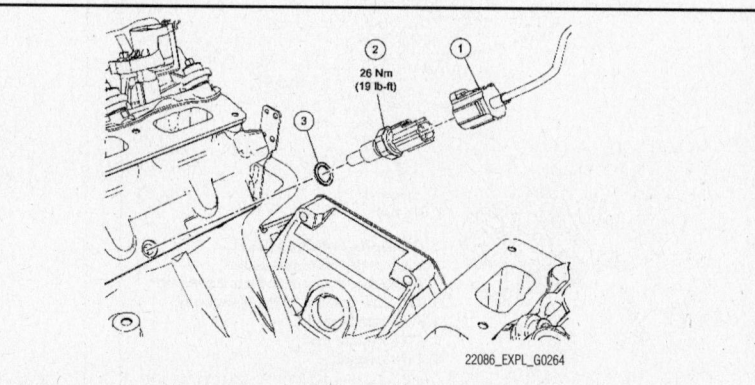

26 Nm (19 lb-ft)

22086_EXPL_G0264

Fig. 326 Showing the location of the CHT sensor (2), the electrical connector (1) and the O-ring seal (3)—2006–07 4.6L (VIN 8) SOHC engine

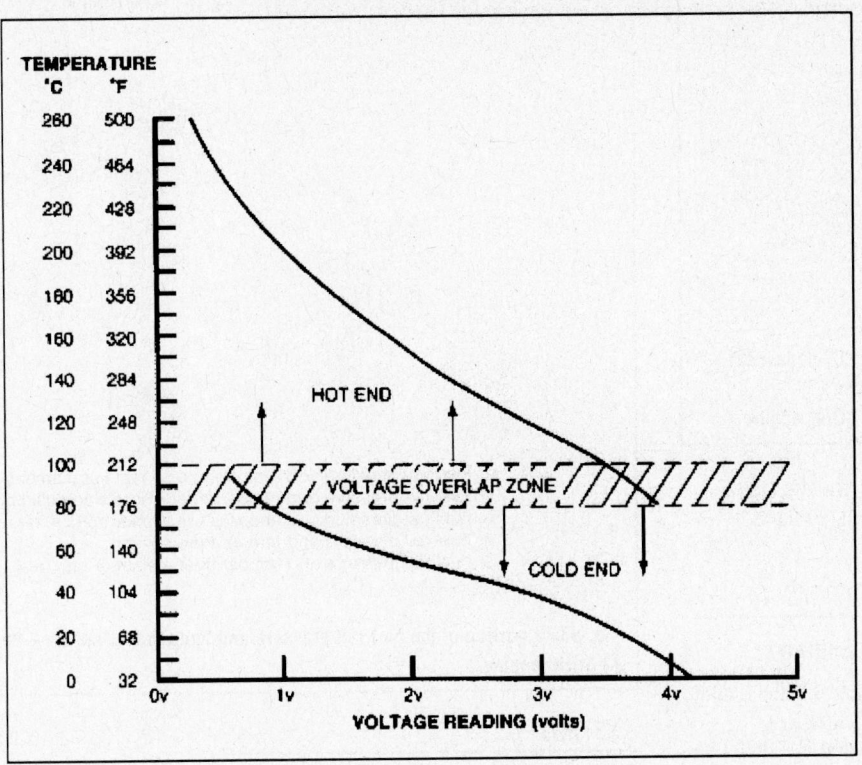

CHT Voltage-Temperature Chart

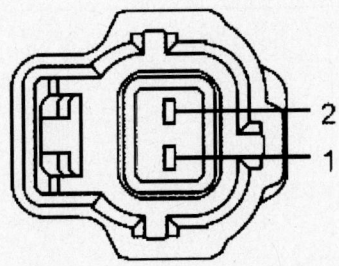

2006-07 CHT Sensor Pins

Pin	Circuit
1	SIGRTN (Signal Return)
2	CHT (Cyl. Head Temperature)

22086_EXPL_G0271

Fig. 327 Identifying the CHT sensor pins—2005–07 4.6L (VIN 8) SOHC engine

1. With the key in OFF position and the CHT sensor connector disconnected, measure the resistance between the sensor pins.

2. Normal resistance at normal operating temperature is approximately 2.75 k-ohms.

ENGINE COOLANT TEMPERATURE (ECT) SENSOR

LOCATION

4.0L (VIN E, K) SOHC Engine

See Figure 328.

The Engine Coolant Temperature (ECT) sensor is located on top of the engine, in the thermostat housing, as shown.

OPERATION

The Engine Coolant Temperature (ECT) sensor sends the PCM a signal indicating

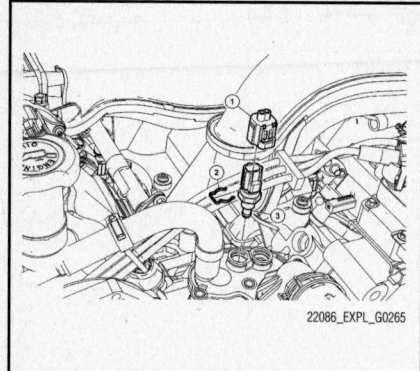

Fig. 328 Location of the ECT sensor (2) and the electrical connector (1)— 2005–07 4.0L (VIN E, K) SOHC engine

engine temperature. The voltage signal from the ECT decreases as coolant temperature increases.

REMOVAL & INSTALLATION

4.0L (VIN E, K) SOHC Engine

1. Disconnect the negative battery cable.
2. Drain the cooling system.
3. Disconnect the Engine Coolant Temperature (ECT) sensor electrical connector.
4. Remove the clip and the ECT sensor.
5. Installation is the reverse of the removal procedure.

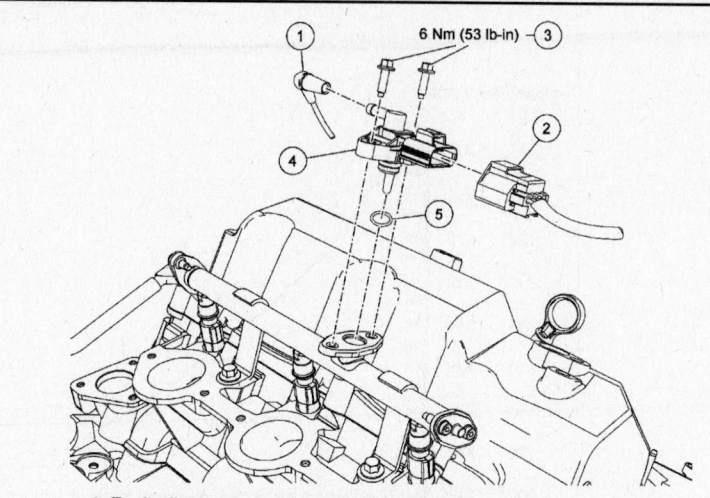

1. Fuel rail pressure and temperature sensor vacuum hose connector
2. Fuel rail pressure and temperature sensor electrical connector
3. Fuel rail pressure and temperature sensor bolts (2 required)
4. Fuel rail pressure and temperature sensor
5. Fuel rail pressure and temperature sensor O-ring seal

Fig. 330 Location of the fuel rail pressure and temperature sensor—2005–07 4.0L (VIN E, K) SOHC engine

TESTING

See Figure 329.

1. With the key in OFF position and the ECT sensor connector disconnected, measure the resistance between the sensor pins.

2. Normal resistance at normal operating temperature is approximately 2.80 k-ohms.

3. With the vehicle at normal operating temperature, the key in the OFF position and the ECT sensor connector disconnected,

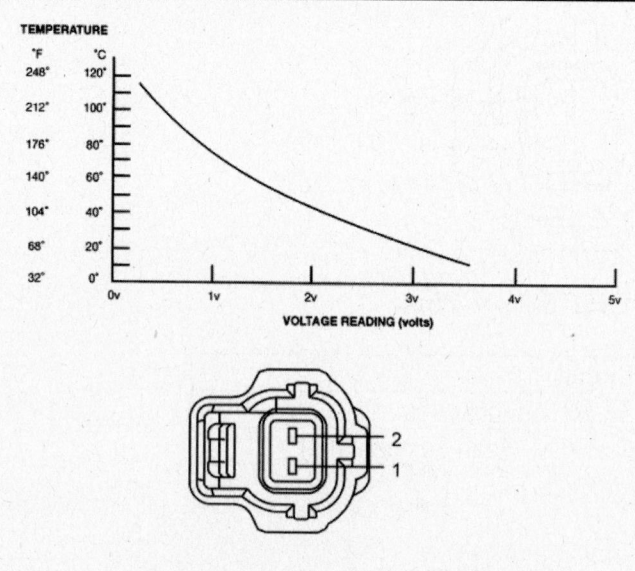

Pin	Circuit
1	ECT (Engine coolant temperature)
2	SIGRTN (Signal return)

ECT Sensor Voltage Chart & Pin Identification

Fig. 329 Identifying the ECT sensor pins and operating parameters—2005–07 4.0L (VIN E, K) SOHC engine

measure the resistance between the pins of the ECT sensor.

4. The resistance values should agree with the charts given.

5. With the ECT sensor connector still disconnected, the key in ON position, measure the voltage between the harness connector pins.

6. The voltage values should agree with the chart given above.

FUEL RAIL PRESSURE AND TEMPERATURE SENSOR

LOCATION

4.0L (VIN E, K) SOHC Engine

The fuel rail pressure and temperature sensor is located on top of the fuel rail, as shown.

4.6L (VIN 8) SOHC Engine

2005 Models

See Figure 331.

The fuel rail pressure and temperature sensor is located on top of the fuel rail, as shown.

➡This components is not used on Explorer Sport-Trac engines.

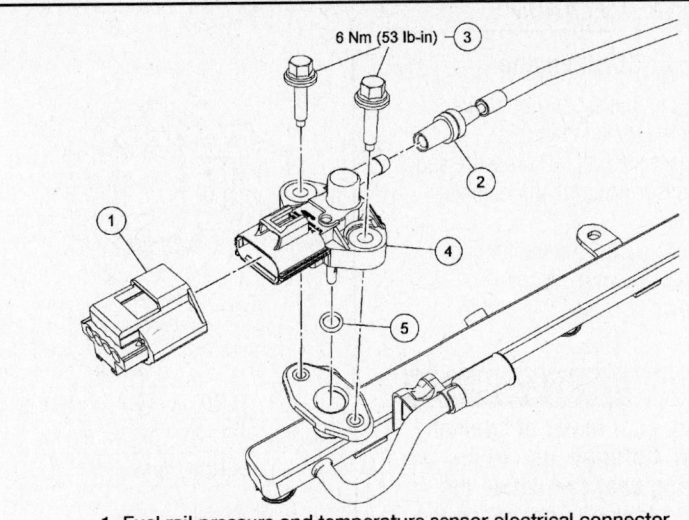

1. Fuel rail pressure and temperature sensor electrical connector
2. Vacuum hose connector
3. Fuel rail pressure and temperature sensor bolts (2 required)
4. Fuel rail pressure and temperature sensor
5. O-ring seal

22086_EXPL_G0268

Fig. 332 Showing the location of the fuel rail pressure and temperature sensor—2006-07 4.6L (VIN 8) SOHC engine

2006–07 Models

See Figure 332.

The fuel rail pressure and temperature sensor is located on top of the fuel rail, as shown.

OPERATION

The fuel rail pressure and temperature sensor monitors these elements of the fuel supply through the fuel rail. It sends a corresponding signal to the PCM.

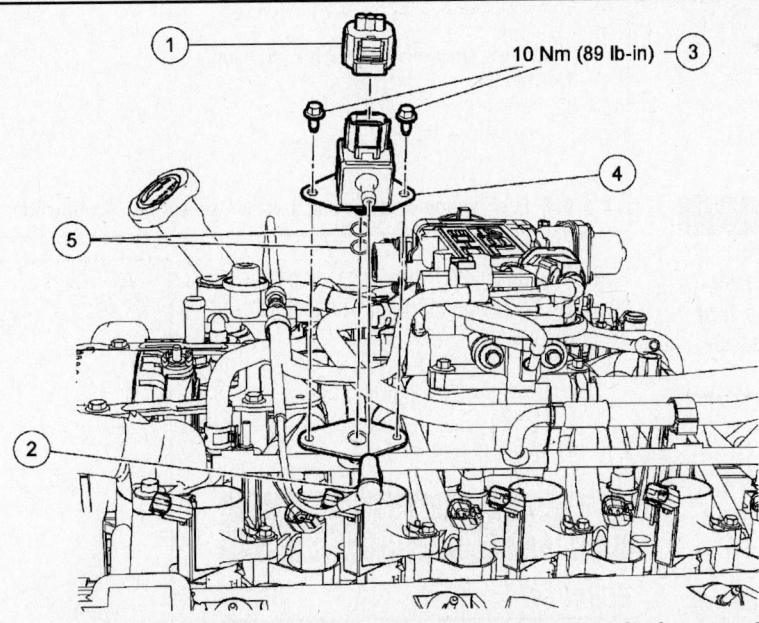

1. Fuel rail pressure and temperature sensor electrical connector
2. Fuel rail pressure and temperature sensor vacuum connector
3. Fuel rail pressure and temperature sensor bolts (2 required)
4. Fuel rail pressure and temperature sensor
5. Fuel rail pressure and temperature sensor O-ring seals (2 required)

22086_EXPL_G0267

Fig. 331 Showing the location of the fuel rail pressure and temperature sensor—2005 4.6L (VIN 8) SOHC engine

REMOVAL & INSTALLATION

4.0L (VIN E, K) SOHC Engine

1. Release the fuel system pressure.
2. Remove the intake manifold.
3. Disconnect the fuel rail pressure and temperature sensor vacuum and electrical connectors.
4. Remove the bolts and the fuel rail pressure and temperature sensor.
5. Remove and discard the O-ring seal.

> ❊❊ **CAUTION**
>
> **Use an O-ring seal made of special fuel resistant material. Use of an ordinary O-ring seal can cause the fuel system to leak. Do not reuse the O-ring seal.**

6. Installation is the reverse of the removal procedure, noting the following:
   - Lubricate the new O-ring seal with clean engine oil
   - Tighten the sensor bolts to 53 inch lbs. (6 Nm)

4.6L (VIN 8) SOHC Engine

2005–07 Models

1. Release the fuel system pressure.
2. Disconnect the negative battery cable.
3. Disconnect the fuel rail pressure and temperature sensor electrical and vacuum connectors.
4. Remove the bolts and the fuel rail pressure and temperature sensor.
5. Remove and discard the O-ring seals.

> ❊❊ **CAUTION**
>
> **Use O-ring seals made of special fuel-resistant material. Use of ordinary O-ring seals can cause the fuel system to leak. Do not reuse the O-ring seals.**

6. Installation is the reverse of the removal procedure, noting the following:
   - Use new O-ring seals.
   - Lubricate the O-ring seals with clean engine oil.
   - Tighten the sensor bolts to 89 inch lbs. (10 Nm).

TESTING

See Figure 333.

1. With the key in OFF position and the FRT sensor connector disconnected, measure the resistance between the sensor pins.

2. Resistance will vary, according to engine (fuel) temperature for this test. Normal readings are:
   - 212°F: 2.073 k-ohms
   - 194°F: 2.80 k-ohms
   - 100°F: 16.12 k-ohms
   - 68°F: 37.332 k-ohms

HEATED OXYGEN SENSOR & CATALYST MONITOR SENSOR

LOCATION

See Figures 334 and 335.

The Heated Oxygen Sensors (HO2S) are located upstream of the catalytic converter. The catalyst monitor sensors are mounted in or downstream of the catalytic converters.

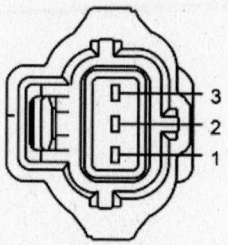

Pin	Circuit
3	FRP (Fuel Rail Pressure)
2	SIGRTN (Signal Return)
1	VREF (Reference Voltage)

Fuel Rail Pressure (FRP) Sensor Connector

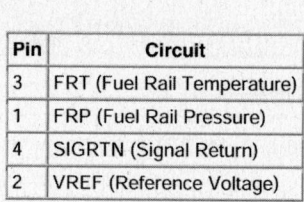

Pin	Circuit
3	FRT (Fuel Rail Temperature)
1	FRP (Fuel Rail Pressure)
4	SIGRTN (Signal Return)
2	VREF (Reference Voltage)

Fuel Rail Pressure/Temperature (FRPT) Sensor Connector

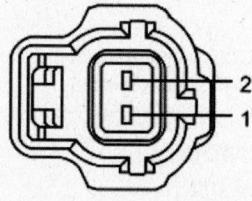

Pin	Circuit
2	SIGRTN (Signal Return)
1	FRT (Fuel Rail Temperature)

Fuel Rail Temperature (FRT) Sensor Connector

22086_EXPL_G0273

Fig. 333 Fuel rail temperature and pressure sensor pin identification

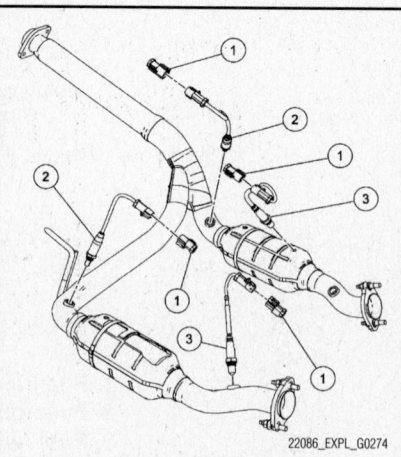

22086_EXPL_G0274

Fig. 334 Locations of the heated oxygen sensors and catalyst monitor sensors: connectors (1), HOS2 (2), catalyst monitor (3)—2005 models

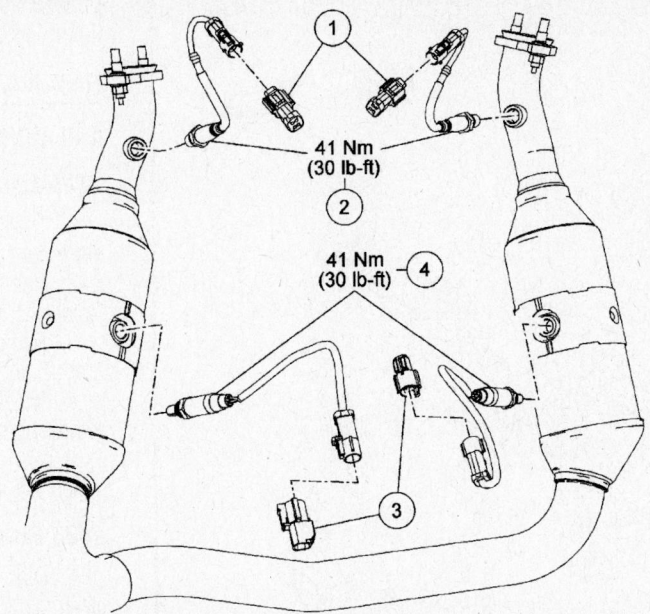

1. Heated oxygen sensor (HO2S) electrical connectors (2 required)
2. HO2S (2 required)
3. Catalyst monitor sensor electrical connectors (2 required)
4. Catalyst monitor sensors (2 required)

22086_EXPL_G0275

Fig. 335 Locations of the heated oxygen sensors and catalyst monitor sensors—2006–07 models

OPERATION

The HO2S perform the following:
• Creates a voltage signal dependent on exhaust oxygen content.
• Provides feedback information to the PCM used to calculate fuel delivery.
The catalyst monitor sensor:
• Monitors oxygen content after it flows through the catalytic converter.
• Provides a voltage to the PCM used to calculate catalytic converter integrity.

REMOVAL & INSTALLATION

HO2S or Catalyst Monitor Sensor

Left side sensor
1. Raise and support the vehicle.
Right side sensor
2. Remove the right front wheel and tire assembly and/or the heat shield.
3. Position aside the right front fender splash shield.
Both sensors

➡**If necessary, lubricate the sensor with lock lubricant to assist in removal.**

4. Detach the electrical connector.
5. Using the special tool, remove the sensor from the exhaust pipe or converter.
6. Installation is the reverse of the removal procedure.

➡**Apply a light coat of anti-seize lubricant to the threads of the sensor.**

c. Tighten the sensor to 30 ft. lbs. (41 Nm).
d. If removed, install the heat shield and tighten the bolts to 15 ft. lbs. (20 Nm).

KNOCK SENSOR (KS)

LOCATION

4.0L (VIN E, K) SOHC Engine

See Figures 336 through 338.

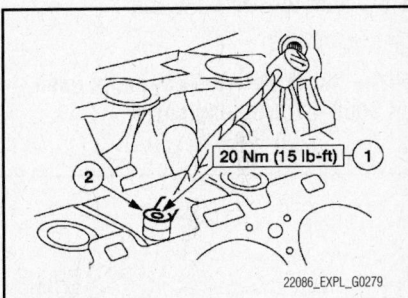

22086_EXPL_G0279

Fig. 337 Location of the Knock Sensor (KS) (2)—2005 Explorer Sport-Trac 4.0L (VIN E, K) SOHC engine

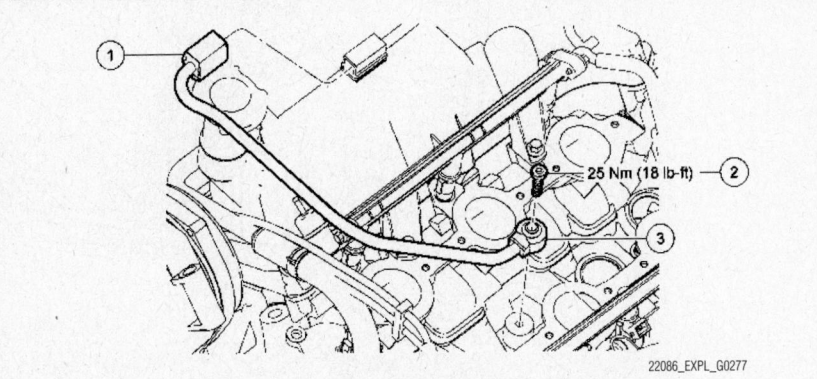

22086_EXPL_G0277

Fig. 336 Location of the Knock Sensor (KS) (3), showing the retaining bolt (2) and the connector (1)—2005 4.0L (VIN E, K) SOHC engine

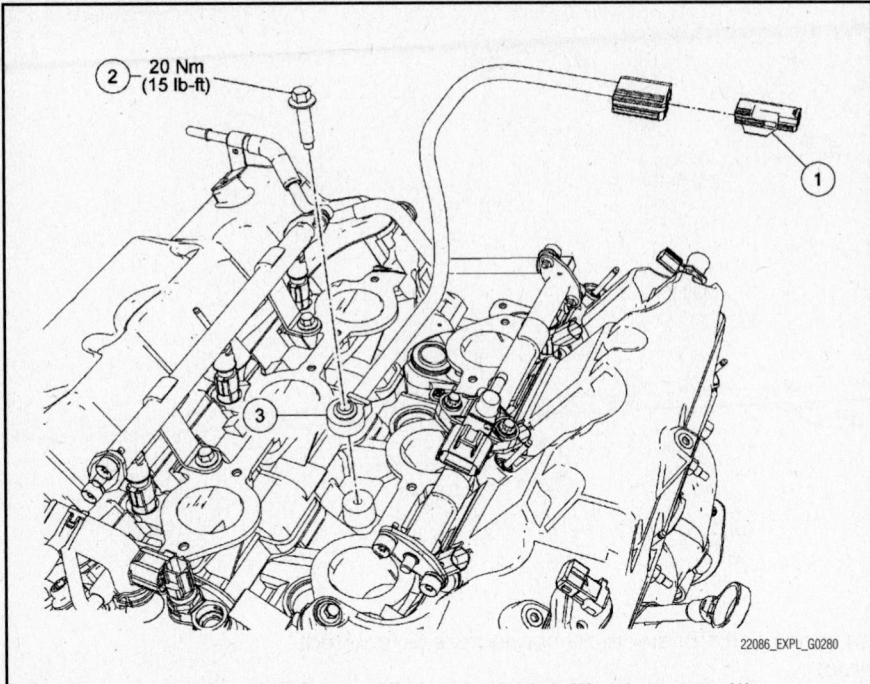

Fig. 338 Location of the Knock Sensor (KS) (3), retaining bolt (2) and connector (1)—2006–07 4.0L (VIN E, K) SOHC engine

Refer to the accompanying illustrations for Knock Sensor (KS) locations.

4.6L (VIN 8) SOHC Engine

See Figure 339.

➥The Knock Sensor (KS) is not used on 2006–07 4.6L engines.

Refer to the accompanying illustrations for Knock Sensor (KS) locations.

OPERATION

The Knock Sensor (KS) is used to detect engine detonation. It sends a voltage signal to the PCM. The knock sensor is able to provide a signal, which retards the ignition timing, as necessary.

REMOVAL & INSTALLATION

4.0L (VIN E, K) SOHC Engine

2005 Explorer and Mountaineer

1. Disconnect the Knock Sensor (KS) electrical connector (1).
2. Remove the intake manifold. See "Intake Manifold" section.
3. Remove the knock sensor retaining bolt (2) and remove the sensor (3).
4. Installation is the reverse of the removal procedure.
   a. Tighten the sensor bolt (2) to 18 ft. lbs. (25 Nm).

2005 Explorer Sport-Trac

1. Disconnect the Knock Sensor (KS) electrical connector.
2. Remove the intake manifold. See "Intake Manifold" section.
3. Remove the KS retaining bolt (1) and remove the sensor (2).
4. Installation is the reverse of the removal procedure.
   a. Tighten the sensor bolt (1) to 15 ft. lbs. (20 Nm).

2006–07 Explorer and Mountaineer; 2007 Explorer Sport-Trac

1. Remove the intake manifold. See "Intake Manifold" section.

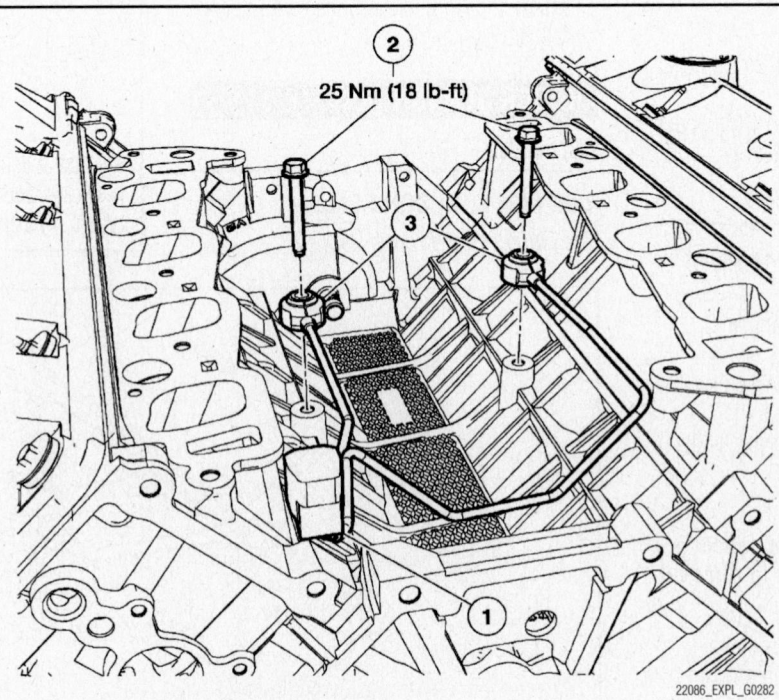

Fig. 339 Location of the Knock Sensors (KS) (3) and the retaining bolts (2)—2005 4.6L (VIN 8) SOHC engine

2. Disconnect the Knock Sensor (KS) electrical connector.

3. Remove the bolt and the KS.

4. Installation is the reverse of the removal procedure

    a. Tighten the retaining bolt to 15 ft. lbs. (20 Nm).

4.6L (VIN 8) SOHC Engine

2005 Explorer and Mountaineer

1. Remove the intake manifold.

2. Disconnect the Knock Sensor (KS) electrical connector.

3. Remove the bolts and the KS.

4. Installation is the reverse of the removal procedure.

    a. Tighten the sensor bolt to 18 ft. lbs. (25 Nm).

TESTING

See Figure 340.

1. Verify the KS is connected and properly installed.

2. With the KS connector disconnected, measure the resistance between the KS pins 1 and 2.

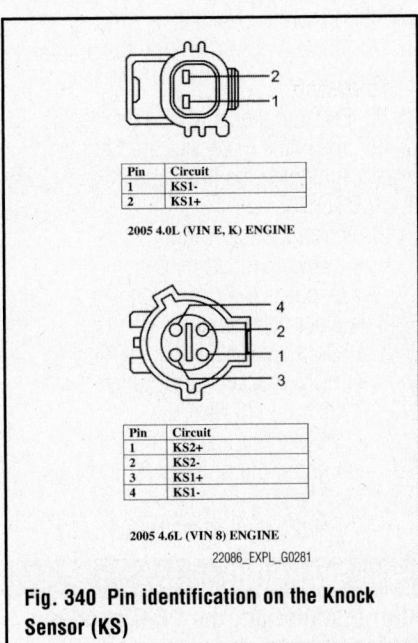

Pin	Circuit
1	KS1-
2	KS1+

2005 4.0L (VIN E, K) ENGINE

Pin	Circuit
1	KS2+
2	KS2-
3	KS1+
4	KS1-

2005 4.6L (VIN 8) ENGINE

22086_EXPL_G0281

Fig. 340 Pin identification on the Knock Sensor (KS)

3. Resistance should be 4.39megaohms–5.35megaohms.

MASS AIR FLOW (MAF) SENSOR

LOCATION

See Figure 341.

Refer to the accompanying illustration for the Mass Air Flow (MAF) sensor location.

22086_EXPL_G0283

Fig. 341 Showing the location of the Mass Air Flow (MAF) sensor (1), the electrical connector (2) and the retaining bolt (3)—4.0L engine shown; 4.6L engine similar

OPERATION

The Mass Air Flow (MAF) sensor uses a hot wire sensing element to measure the amount of air entering the engine. Air passing over the hot wire causes it to cool.

REMOVAL & INSTALLATION

1. Disconnect the negative battery cable.

2. Disconnect the Mass Air Flow (MAF) sensor electrical connector.

3. Remove the bolts and the MAF.

4. Installation is the reverse of the removal procedure.

    a. Tighten the MAF bolts to 18 inch lbs. (2 Nm).

TESTING

See Figure 342.

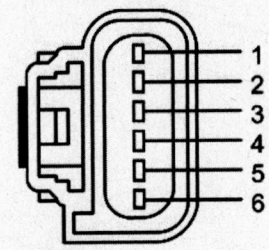

Pin	Circuit
1	IAT
2	SIGRTN
3	MAF
4	MAF RTN
5	PWRGND
6	VPWR

MAF Sensor Pin Connections

22086_EXPL_G0284

Fig. 342 Showing the MAF sensor pin and circuit identification

POWERTRAIN CONTROL MODULE (PCM)

LOCATION

See Figures 343 and 344.

Refer to the accompanying illustrations for PCM location.

OPERATION

The PCM carries out the following functions:

• Accepts input from various engine sensors to compute the fuel flow rate necessary to maintain a prescribed air/fuel ratio throughout the entire engine operational range.

• Outputs a command to the fuel injectors to meter the appropriate quantity of fuel.

REMOVAL & INSTALLATION

2005 Models

> ✳✳ **WARNING**
>
> **Before starting removal procedure, all programmable module information must be downloaded from the PCM using a proper scan tool and software. If you do not have the proper equipment, refer the vehicle to a qualified repair facility for this procedure.**

1. Disconnect the negative battery cable.
2. Loosen the bolts and disconnect the Powertrain Control Module (PCM) electrical connectors.
3. Remove the PCM bracket nuts.
4. Remove the passenger door scuff plate, position the front door weatherstrip aside, and remove the A-pillar lower trim panel.
5. Remove the screws and the glove compartment.
6. Remove the PCM bracket bolt and the PCM and bracket as an assembly.
7. Remove the PCM from the bracket.

To install:

8. Position the PCM into its bracket.
9. Install the PCM and bracket into place and tighten the bracket bolt to 89 inch lbs. (10 Nm).
10. Install the following:
   • Glove compartment
   • A-pillar lower trim panel
   • Door weatherstrip
   • Door scuff plate
   • PCM bracket nuts; tighten to 71 inch lbs. (8 Nm)
   • PCM electrical connectors; tighten the bolts to 62 inch lbs. (7 Nm)
   • Battery ground cable.

> ✳✳ **WARNING**
>
> **After installation, the PCM must be reprogrammed, using proper scan tool and software. If you do not have the proper equipment, refer the vehicle to a qualified repair facility for this procedure.**

2006–07 Models

See Figure 345.

> ✳✳ **WARNING**
>
> **Before starting removal procedure, all programmable module informa-**

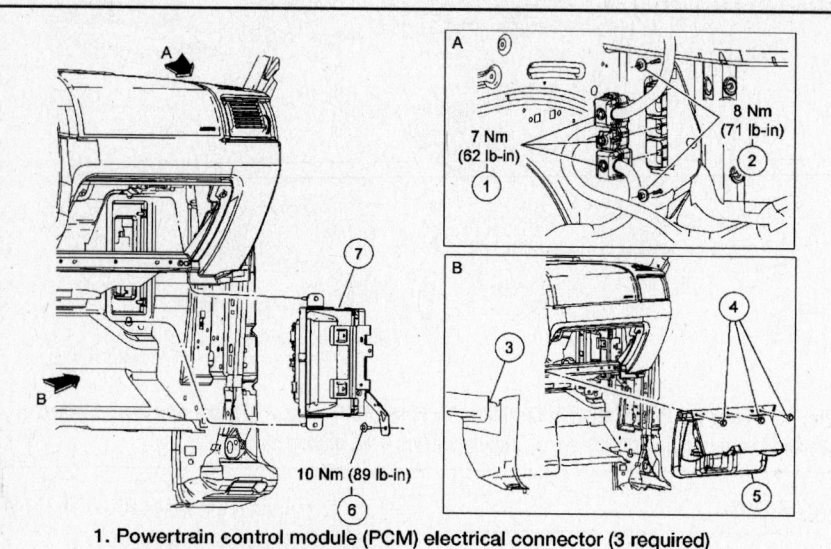

1. Powertrain control module (PCM) electrical connector (3 required)
2. PCM bracket nut (2 required)
3. A-pillar lower trim panel
4. Glove compartment screws (3 required)
5. Glove compartment
6. PCM bracket bolt
7. PCM and mounting bracket

22086_EXPL_G0285

Fig. 343 PCM mounting location—2005 Models

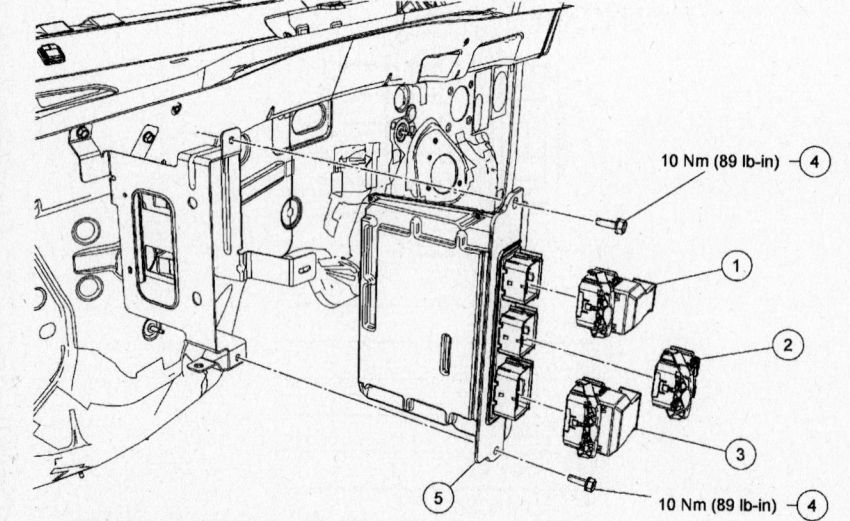

1. Powertrain control module (PCM) electrical connector
2. PCM electrical connector
3. PCM electrical connector
4. PCM bolts (2 required)
5. PCM

22086_EXPL_G0286

Fig. 344 PCM mounting location—2006–07 Models

tion must be downloaded from the PCM using a proper scan tool and software. If you do not have the proper equipment, refer the vehicle to a qualified repair facility for this procedure.

1. Remove the air cleaner (4.6L engine only).
2. Disconnect the RH front wheel speed sensor electrical connector. Remove the nuts and position the A/C tube brackets and wiring harness aside.
3. Disconnect the Powertrain Control Module (PCM) connectors.
4. Remove the bolts and the PCM.

To install:

➡**PCM installation DOES NOT require new keys.**

5. Install the PCM and bolts. Tighten to 89 inch lbs. (10 Nm).
6. Connect the PCM electrical connectors.
7. Position the wiring harness and the A/C tube brackets and install the nuts. Connect the RH front wheel speed sensor electrical connector. Tighten the nuts to 62 inch lbs. (7 Nm).
8. If removed, install the air cleaner.

✳✳ CAUTION

The following steps require special equipment and instructions. Refer the vehicle to a qualified repair facility.

9. Restore the module configuration. Carry out the module configuration restore steps of the Programmable Module Installation procedure.
10. Reprogram the passive anti-theft system (PATS). Carry out the Parameter Reset procedure.

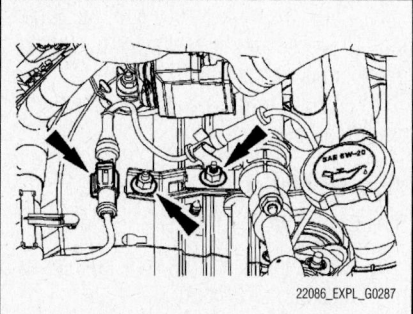

Fig. 345 Disconnect the RH front wheel speed sensor electrical connector. Remove the nuts and position the A/C tube brackets and wiring harness aside

TESTING

See Figure 346.

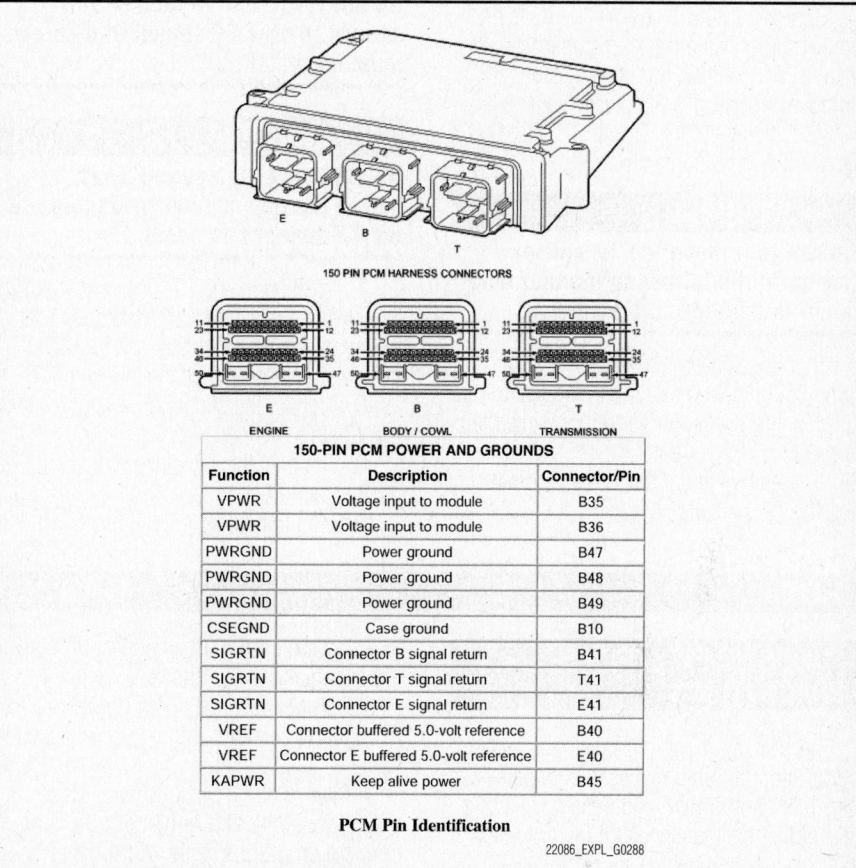

150 PIN PCM HARNESS CONNECTORS

| ENGINE | BODY / COWL | TRANSMISSION |

PCM Pin Identification

150-PIN PCM POWER AND GROUNDS		
Function	Description	Connector/Pin
VPWR	Voltage input to module	B35
VPWR	Voltage input to module	B36
PWRGND	Power ground	B47
PWRGND	Power ground	B48
PWRGND	Power ground	B49
CSEGND	Case ground	B10
SIGRTN	Connector B signal return	B41
SIGRTN	Connector T signal return	T41
SIGRTN	Connector E signal return	E41
VREF	Connector buffered 5.0-volt reference	B40
VREF	Connector E buffered 5.0-volt reference	E40
KAPWR	Keep alive power	B45

22086_EXPL_G0288

Fig. 346 PCM connector pin identification

THROTTLE POSITION (TP) SENSOR

LOCATION

See Figure 347.

OPERATION

The Throttle Position (TP) sensor sends the PCM a signal indicating the throttle plate angle and is the main input to the PCM from the driver.

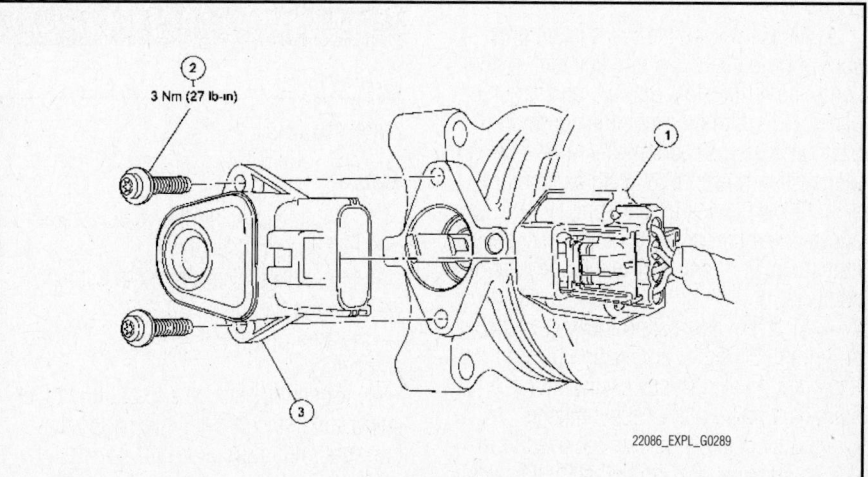

3 Nm (27 lb-in)

22086_EXPL_G0289

Fig. 347 Throttle Position (TP) sensor (3) location, with the bolt (2) and connector (1)—2005 4.0L (VIN E, K) engine

REMOVAL & INSTALLATION

1. Disconnect the negative battery cable.
2. Remove the air cleaner outlet pipe.
3. For 2006–07, remove the bolts and position the heated positive crankcase ventilation (PCV) fitting and hoses aside. Remove and discard the O-ring seal.
4. Disconnect the Throttle Position (TP) sensor electrical connector.

✳✳ WARNING

Failure to remove the TP sensor screws in the following manner will result in damage to the screws.

5. First, loosen the screws 1–2 full turns using a hand tool, and then use a suitable high speed driver to complete the removal.
6. Remove and discard the 2 screws and the TP sensor.

To install:

✳✳ CAUTION

Do not reuse the TP sensor and screws. A new TP sensor and screws must be installed.

✳✳ WARNING

Do not use a high speed driver to install the new screws or damage to the TP sensor can occur.

7. Position the new TP sensor and install the 2 new screws. Make sure that the radial locator tab on the TP sensor is aligned with the radial locator hole on the throttle body.
8. Tighten the sensor screws to 27 inch lbs. (3 Nm).
9. Connect the TP sensor electrical connector.
10. If equipped, install the heated PCV fitting and hoses to original locations, using new O-ring seal.
11. Install the air cleaner outlet pipe.
12. Connect the battery ground cable.

TESTING

See Figure 348.

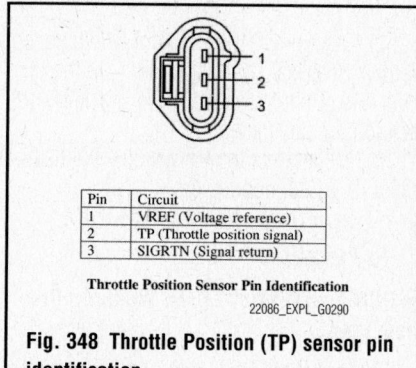

Pin	Circuit
1	VREF (Voltage reference)
2	TP (Throttle position signal)
3	SIGRTN (Signal return)

Throttle Position Sensor Pin Identification

22086_EXPL_G0290

Fig. 348 Throttle Position (TP) sensor pin identification

FUEL   GASOLINE FUEL INJECTION SYSTEM

FUEL SYSTEM SERVICE PRECAUTIONS

Safety is the most important factor when performing not only fuel system maintenance but any type of maintenance. Failure to conduct maintenance and repairs in a safe manner may result in serious personal injury or death. Maintenance and testing of the vehicle's fuel system components can be accomplished safely and effectively by adhering to the following rules and guidelines.

• To avoid the possibility of fire and personal injury, always disconnect the negative battery cable unless the repair or test procedure requires that battery voltage be applied.

• Always relieve the fuel system pressure prior to disconnecting any fuel system component (injector, fuel rail, pressure regulator, etc.), fitting or fuel line connection. Exercise extreme caution whenever relieving fuel system pressure to avoid exposing skin, face and eyes to fuel spray. Please be advised that fuel under pressure may penetrate the skin or any part of the body that it contacts.

• Always place a shop towel or cloth around the fitting or connection prior to loosening to absorb any excess fuel due to spillage. Ensure that all fuel spillage (should it occur) is quickly removed from engine surfaces. Ensure that all fuel soaked cloths or towels are deposited into a suitable waste container.

• Always keep a dry chemical (Class B) fire extinguisher near the work area.

• Do not allow fuel spray or fuel vapors to come into contact with a spark or open flame.

• Always use a back-up wrench when loosening and tightening fuel line connection fittings. This will prevent unnecessary stress and torsion to fuel line piping.

• Always replace worn fuel fitting O-rings with new Do not substitute fuel hose or equivalent where fuel pipe is installed.

Before servicing the vehicle, make sure to also refer to the precautions in the beginning of this section as well.

FUEL SYSTEM PRESSURE

RELIEVING

2005 Models

Aviator

1. Before servicing the vehicle, refer to the "Precautions" section.
2. Remove the cap from the Schrader valve on the fuel line.
3. Install a gauge tool, with a T-fitting and petcock.
4. Open the petcock and drain the fuel into a suitable container, noting the fuel pressure until it drops to zero.
5. When fuel system service and/or repair is complete, remove the special tool and replace the Schrader valve cap.

Explorer, Explorer Sport-Trac and Mountaineer

1. Before servicing the vehicle, refer to the "Precautions" section.

➡**The fuel pump relay is located in the battery junction box (BJB) location C-1051.**

2. Remove the fuel pump relay.
3. Start the engine and allow it to idle until it stalls.
4. After the engine stalls, crank the engine for approximately 5 seconds to make sure the fuel rail pressure has been released.
5. Turn the ignition switch to the OFF position.
6. When the fuel system service is complete, install the fuel pump relay.

➡**It may take more than one key cycle to pressurize the fuel system.**

7. Cycle the ignition key and wait 3 seconds to pressurize the fuel system. Check for leaks before starting the engine.
8. Start the vehicle and check the fuel system for leaks.

2006–07 Models

See Figure 349.

1. Before servicing the vehicle, refer to the "Precautions" section.
2. Remove the front passenger door frame scuff plate (retained by internal metal clips).
3. Remove the front passenger side interior kick panel.

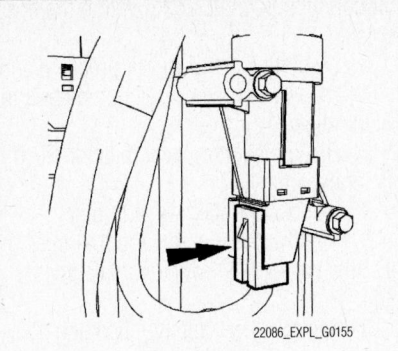

Fig. 349 Disconnect the Inertia Fuel Shut-off (IFS) switch electrical connector—2006 4.0L SOHC engine

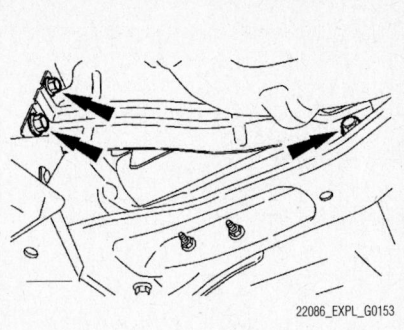

Fig. 350 Removing the fuel filter heat shield—4.0L & 4.6L engines (except 2005 Sport-Trac)

➡️**It may be necessary to reposition the lower end of the door jam weather stripping to remove the front passenger door side interior kick panel.**

4. Disconnect the Inertia Fuel Shutoff (IFS) switch electrical connector.

5. Start the engine and let it idle until it stalls.

6. After the engine stalls, crank it for 5 seconds to ensure all system pressure is relieved.

7. Turn the ignition switch to the OFF position.

8. When the fuel system maintenance and/or repair is complete, reconnect the IFS electrical connector.

FUEL FILTER

REMOVAL & INSTALLATION

Except Explorer Sport-Trac

See Figure 350.

1. Before servicing the vehicle, refer to the "Precautions" section.

2. Disconnect the negative battery cable.

3. Properly relieve the fuel system pressure.

4. Raise the vehicle on a hoist.

5. Remove the bolts and the fuel filter heat shield.

6. Remove the nuts and the fuel filter shield.

7. Disconnect the quick release and spring lock couplings and remove the fuel filter.

To install:

8. Remove any fuel line caps.

9. Install the new fuel filter, connecting the quick-release and spring-lock couplings.

10. Install the fuel filter shield.

11. Install the fuel filter heat shield.

Torque the bolts to 15 ft. lbs. (20 Nm).

12. Reconnect the battery ground cable.

13. Lower the vehicle.

14. Start the vehicle, check for leaks and repair if necessary.

Explorer Sport-Trac

See Figure 351.

1. Before servicing the vehicle, refer to the "Precautions" section.

2. Disconnect the negative battery cable.

3. Properly relieve the fuel system pressure.

4. Disconnect the fuel tube from the front and rear of the fuel filter.

Fig. 351 Removing the fuel filter—2005 Sport-Trac 4.0L SOHC engine

5. Remove the fuel filter.

6. Installation is the reverse of the removal procedure.

FUEL INJECTORS

REMOVAL & INSTALLATION

4.0L (VIN E, K) SOHC Engine

See Figure 352.

✳️ CAUTION

Fuel in the fuel system remains under high pressure even when the engine is not running. Before working on or disconnecting any of the fuel lines or fuel system components, the fuel system pressure must be relieved. Failure to follow these instructions may result in personal injury.

✳️ WARNING

If used as a leverage device, the fuel rail may be damaged. Care must be taken when working around the fuel rail.

1. Before servicing the vehicle, refer to the "Precautions" section.

2. Remove the intake manifold.

3. Disconnect the spring lock coupling.

4. Remove the fuel supply tube bracket bolt.

5. Disconnect the fuel injector electrical connectors.

6. Disconnect the fuel pressure and temperature sensor electrical and vacuum connectors.

7. Remove the bolts and the fuel rail and injectors as an assembly.

✳️ WARNING

O-ring seals are made of special fuel-resistant material. Use of ordinary O-ring seals can cause the fuel system to leak. Do not reuse O-ring seals.

➡️**Install new fuel injector-to-intake manifold O-ring seals and lubricate them with clean engine oil.**

8. Remove the fuel injectors and the fuel injector O-ring seals.

✳️ WARNING

O-ring seals are made of special fuel-resistant material. Use of ordinary O-ring seals can cause the fuel system to leak. Do not reuse O-ring seals.

➡️**Install new fuel injector-to-fuel rail O-ring seals and lubricate them with clean engine oil.**

To install:

9. Installation is the reverse of the removal procedure. Observe the following tightening specifications:

- Fuel rail bolts to 17 ft. lbs. (23 Nm).
- Fuel supply bracket bolt to 71 inch lbs. (8 Nm).

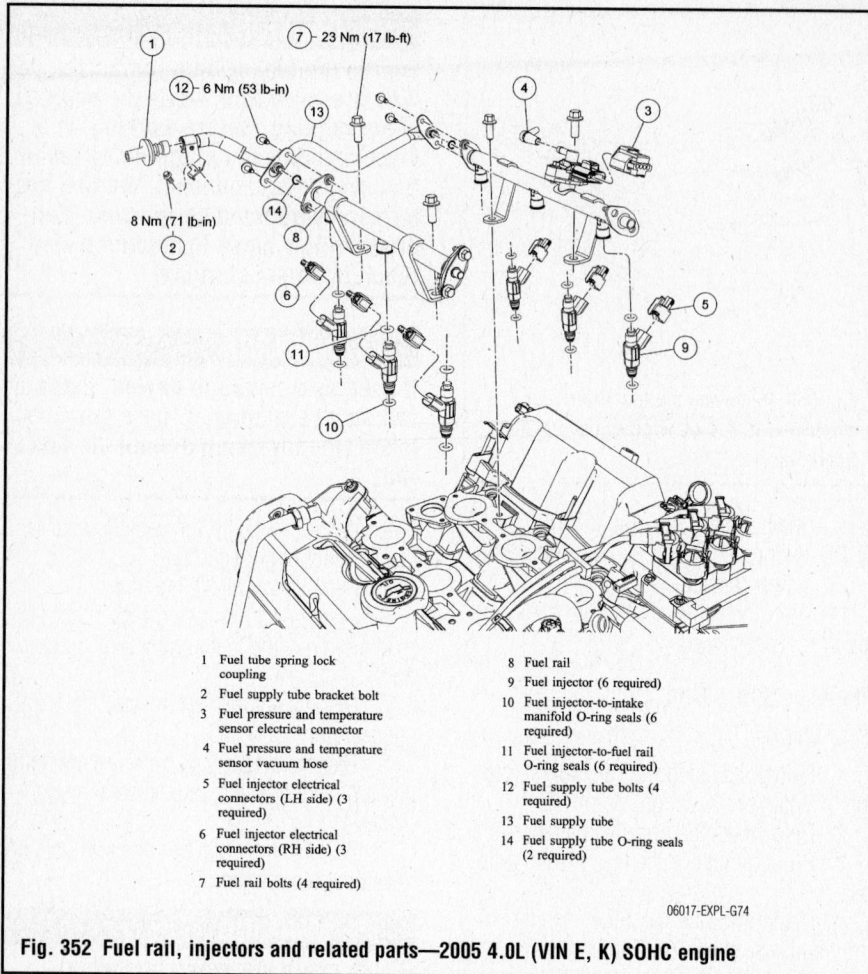

1 Fuel tube spring lock coupling
2 Fuel supply tube bracket bolt
3 Fuel pressure and temperature sensor electrical connector
4 Fuel pressure and temperature sensor vacuum hose
5 Fuel injector electrical connectors (LH side) (3 required)
6 Fuel injector electrical connectors (RH side) (3 required)
7 Fuel rail bolts (4 required)
8 Fuel rail
9 Fuel injector (6 required)
10 Fuel injector-to-intake manifold O-ring seals (6 required)
11 Fuel injector-to-fuel rail O-ring seals (6 required)
12 Fuel supply tube bolts (4 required)
13 Fuel supply tube
14 Fuel supply tube O-ring seals (2 required)

06017-EXPL-G74

Fig. 352 Fuel rail, injectors and related parts—2005 4.0L (VIN E, K) SOHC engine

4.6L (VIN W, 8) SOHC Engine

See Figure 353.

1. Before servicing the vehicle, refer to the "Precautions" section.

2. Release the fuel system pressure.

3. Disconnect the fuel supply tube spring lock coupling.

4. Detach the 2 positive crankcase ventilation (PCV) coolant hose retainers from the fuel rail stud bolts and position the hose aside.

5. Disconnect the fuel rail pressure and temperature sensor electrical connector and vacuum hose.

6. Disconnect the 8 fuel injector electrical connectors.

7. Remove the fuel rail stud bolts.

8. Remove the fuel rail and fuel injectors as an assembly from the intake manifold.

9. Remove the retaining clips and fuel injectors from the fuel rail.

➡The fuel injector clip can be reused if it is not damaged during removal. If the clip is reused, the 2 sides of the clip should be squeezed back into shape by placing it between index finger and thumb.

10. Remove and discard the fuel injector O-ring seals.

To install:

11. Installation is the reverse of the removal procedure, noting the following:
   a. Use new O-ring seals.
   b. Use new fuel injector retaining clips, if needed.
   c. Tighten the fuel rail stud bolts to 89 inch lbs. (10 Nm).

4.6L (VIN H) DOHC Engine

See Figure 354.

> ✳✳ **CAUTION**
>
> Fuel in the system remains under high pressure even when the engine is not running. Before working on or disconnecting any of the fuel lines or fuel system components, the fuel system must be relieved. Failure to follow these instructions can result in personal injury.

1. Before servicing the vehicle, refer to the "Precautions" section.

2. Disconnect the negative battery cable.

3. Remove the air cleaner assembly.

4. Release the fuel system pressure.

5. Disconnect the throttle position (TP) sensor electrical connector.

6. Disconnect the idle air control (IAC) sensor electrical connector.

7. Disconnect the fuel pulse damper electrical connector and vacuum hose.

8. Disconnect the 8 fuel injector electrical connectors.

9. Disconnect the exhaust gas recirculation (EGR) system module electrical connector.

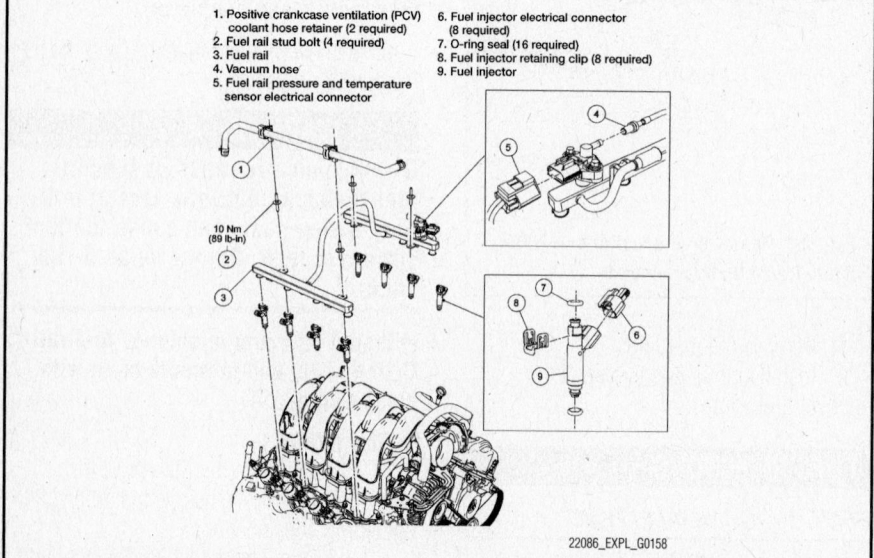

1. Positive crankcase ventilation (PCV) coolant hose retainer (2 required)
2. Fuel rail stud bolt (4 required)
3. Fuel rail
4. Vacuum hose
5. Fuel rail pressure and temperature sensor electrical connector
6. Fuel injector electrical connector (8 required)
7. O-ring seal (16 required)
8. Fuel injector retaining clip (8 required)
9. Fuel injector

22086_EXPL_G0158

Fig. 353 Exploded view of the fuel rail and injector components—4.6L (VIN 8) engine

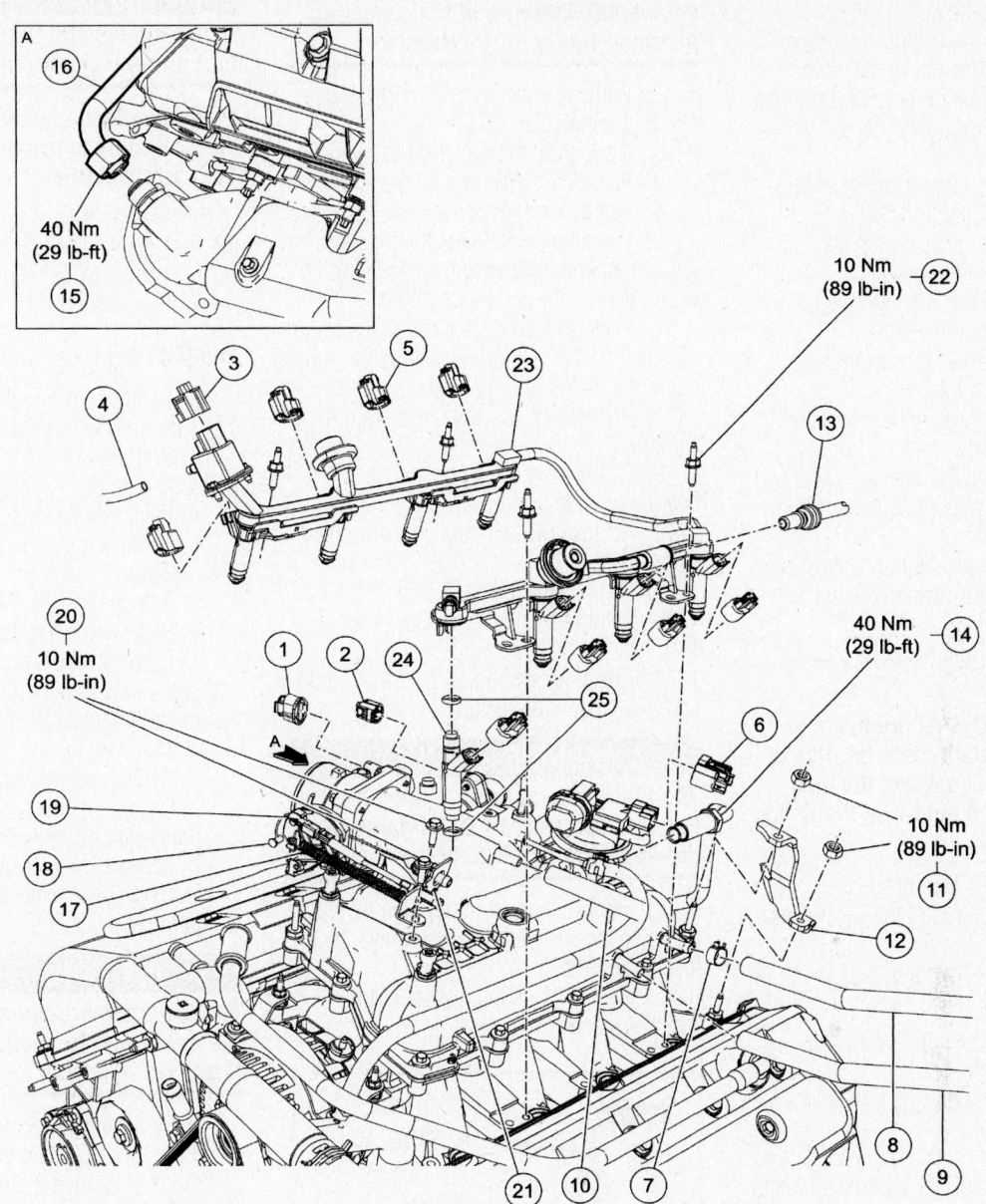

1 Throttle position (TP) sensor electrical connector
2 Idle air control (IAC) sensor electrical connector
3 Fuel pulse damper electrical connector
4 Fuel pulse damper vacuum hose
5 Fuel injector electrical connectors (8 required)
6 Exhaust gas recirculation (EGR) system module electrical connector
7 Brake booster hose clamp
8 Brake booster hose
9 Engine emissions vacuum hose

10 Evaporative emission (EVAP) canister purge valve vacuum hose
11 Upper intake manifold-to-lower intake manifold bracket nuts
12 Upper intake manifold-to-lower intake manifold bracket
13 Fuel tube spring lock coupling
14 EGR system module tube nut-to-EGR system module
15 EGR system module tube nut-to-exhaust manifold
16 EGR system module tube
17 Throttle return spring

18 Accelerator cable
19 Speed control cable
20 Accelerator control assembly bracket bolts
21 Accelerator control assembly bracket (position aside)
22 Fuel injection supply manifold bolts
23 Fuel injection supply manifold and fuel injectors
24 Fuel injectors (8 required)
25 Fuel injector O-rings

06017-EXPL-G72

Fig. 354 Fuel rail, injectors and related parts—4.6L DOHC engine

10. Disconnect the brake booster hose from the intake manifold.

11. Disconnect the engine emissions vacuum hose from the intake manifold.

12. Disconnect the evaporative emission (EVAP) canister purge valve vacuum hose from the intake manifold.

13. Remove the upper intake manifold-to-lower intake manifold bracket nuts.

14. Remove the upper intake manifold-to-lower intake manifold bracket.

15. Remove the fuel tube safety clip.

16. Disconnect the fuel tube.

17. Disconnect the EGR system tube nuts and remove the tube.

18. Disconnect the throttle return spring from the throttle body.

19. Disconnect the accelerator cable and the speed control cable (if equipped) from the throttle body.

20. Remove the accelerator cable assembly bracket bolts and position the bracket and cables aside.

21. Remove the fuel rail bolts and the fuel rail.

➡**Use O-ring seals that are made of special fuel-resistant material. Use of ordinary O-rings can cause the fuel system to leak. Do not reuse the O-ring seals.**

22. Remove the 8 fuel injectors.

23. Remove and discard the O-ring seals.

To install:

24. Installation is the reverse the removal procedure.

25. Install new O-rings and lubricate with clean engine oil.

26. Observe the following tightening specifications:
- Fuel rail bolts: 89 inch lbs. (10 Nm)
- Cable bracket: 89 inch lbs. (10 Nm)
- EGR tube nuts: 30 ft. lbs. (40 Nm)
- Manifold bracket nuts: 89 inch lbs. (10 Nm)

FUEL PUMP

REMOVAL & INSTALLATION

2005 Aviator

See Figure 355.

1. Before servicing the vehicle, refer to the "Precautions" section.

❊❊ **CAUTION**

The fuel in the system remains under high pressure even when the engine is not running. Before repairing or disconnecting any of the fuel lines or fuel system components, the fuel

pressure must be relieved to prevent accidental spraying of fuel, causing personal injury or fire hazard.

2. With the vehicle in NEUTRAL, position it on a hoist.

3. Disconnect the negative battery cable.

4. Release the fuel system pressure.

5. Remove the rear driveshaft.

6. Disconnect the lower fill hose from the fuel intermediate steel by loosening worm gear clamp and pulling it off.

7. Insert a drain hose through the lower fill hose, past the fill tube check valve, and pump fuel out of the fuel tank.

8. Remove the fuel tank skid plate (if equipped).

9. Remove the three bolts at the outboard frame rail.

10. Remove the two nuts on the inboard side.

11. Remove the fuel tank skid plate.

12. Remove the fuel tank. See "Fuel Tank" section.

13. Clean the area around the fuel pump assembly mounting flange.

❊❊ **WARNING**

The fuel pump assembly must be handled carefully to avoid damage to the float arm and the filter.

14. Remove the fuel pump module lock ring with the special tool and remove the fuel pump module.

15. Installation is the reverse of the removal procedure.

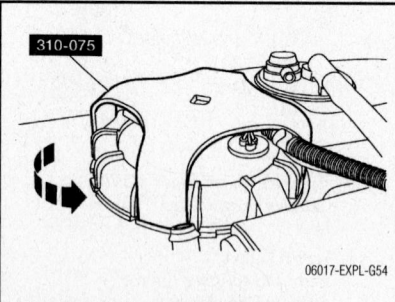

310-075

06017-EXPL-G54

Fig. 355 Fuel pump locking ring— 2005 Aviator

2005 Explorer, Explorer Sport-Trac and Mountaineer

1. Before servicing the vehicle, refer to the "Precautions" section.

2. With the vehicle in NEUTRAL, position it on a hoist.

3. Release the fuel system pressure.

4. Remove the fuel tank. See "Fuel Tank" section.

5. Disconnect the vapor tube fitting.

❊❊ **CAUTION**

Using the special tool, remove the fuel pump locking ring.

➡**The fuel pump module must be handled carefully to avoid damage to the float arm and filter.**

6. Remove the fuel pump module and the O-ring seal. Discard the O-ring seal.

7. Installation is the reverse of the removal procedure.

2006–07 Explorer And Mountaineer

1. Before servicing the vehicle, refer to the "Precautions" section.

2. With the vehicle in NEUTRAL, position it on a hoist.

3. Release the fuel system pressure.

4. Remove the fuel tank. See "Fuel Tank" section.

5. Remove the EVAP canister.

6. Remove the fuel tank shield.

7. Disconnect the fuel pressure sensor and vapor tube assembly-to-fuel pump and the fuel tank vapor valves quick connect couplings.

8. Disconnect the vapor tube fitting.

9. Disconnect the fuel supply tube-to-fuel pump quick connect coupling.

10. Remove the fuel supply tube.

11. Using the special tool, remove the fuel pump locking ring.

❊❊ **CAUTION**

The fuel pump module must be handled carefully to avoid damage to the float arm and filter.

12. Remove the fuel pump module and the O-ring seal. Discard the O-ring seal.

13. Installation is the reverse of the removal procedure.

IDLE SPEED

ADJUSTMENT

Idle speed is maintained by the Powertrain Control Module (PCM). No adjustment is necessary or possible.

THROTTLE BODY

REMOVAL & INSTALLATION

4.0L (VIN E, K) SOHC Engine

2005–07 Explorer and Mountaineer

See Figure 356.

1. Before servicing the vehicle, refer to the "Precautions" section.

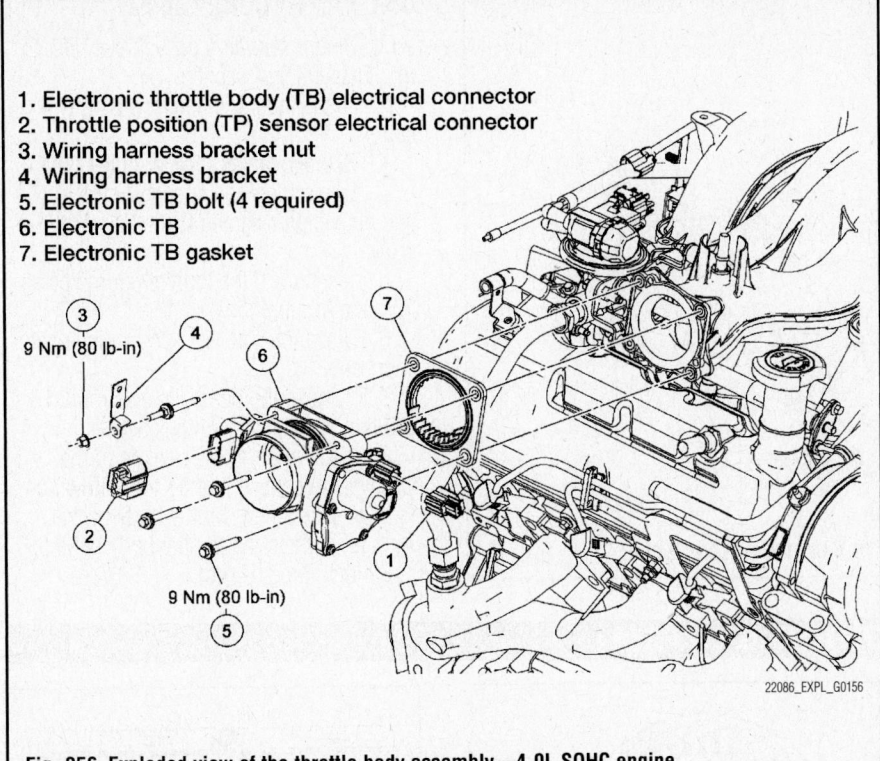

1. Electronic throttle body (TB) electrical connector
2. Throttle position (TP) sensor electrical connector
3. Wiring harness bracket nut
4. Wiring harness bracket
5. Electronic TB bolt (4 required)
6. Electronic TB
7. Electronic TB gasket

9 Nm (80 lb-in)

9 Nm (80 lb-in)

22086_EXPL_G0156

Fig. 356 Exploded view of the throttle body assembly—4.0L SOHC engine

2. Disconnect the negative battery cable.

3. Remove the air cleaner outlet tube.

4. Disconnect the electronic throttle body (TB) electrical connector.

5. Disconnect the throttle position (TP) sensor electrical connector.

6. Remove the nut and position the wiring harness bracket aside (if needed for clearance).

7. Remove the bolts, the electronic TB and the gasket. Discard the gasket.

8. Installation is the reverse of the removal procedure.

9. Note the following:
   a. Use a new throttle body gasket
   b. Tighten the throttle body screws to 80 inch lbs. (9 Nm).

2005 Explorer Sport-Trac

1. Before servicing the vehicle, refer to the "Precautions" section.

2. Disconnect the negative battery cable.

3. Remove the air cleaner outlet tube.

4. Disconnect the throttle position (TP) sensor electrical connector.

5. Disconnect the accelerator cable and the speed control cable (if equipped).

6. Remove the bolts, the electronic TB and the gasket. Discard the gasket.

7. Installation is the reverse of the removal procedure, using a new throttle body gasket

4.6L (VIN W) SOHC Engine

2005 Models

See Figure 357.

1. Before servicing the vehicle, refer to the "Precautions" section.

2. Disconnect the negative battery cable.

3. Remove the air cleaner outlet tube.

4. Disconnect the electronic throttle body (TB) electrical connectors.

5. Remove the bolts, the electronic TB and the gasket. Discard the gasket.

6. Installation is the reverse of the removal procedure, noting the following:
   a. Use a new throttle body gasket.
   b. Tighten the throttle body bolts in 2 steps:
   • Step 1: 80 inch lbs. (9 Nm)
   • Step 2: additional 90 degrees

4.6L (VIN 8) SOHC Engine

2006–07 Models

See Figure 358.

1. Before servicing the vehicle, refer to the "Precautions" section.

2. Disconnect the negative battery cable.

3. Remove the air cleaner outlet tube.

4. Disconnect the electronic throttle body (TB) electrical connectors.

5. Disconnect the throttle position (TP) sensor electrical connector.

6. Remove the bolts, the electronic TB and the gasket. Discard the gasket.

7. Installation is the reverse of the removal procedure, noting the following:
   a. Use a new throttle body gasket.
   b. Tighten the throttle body bolts to 89 inch lbs. (10 Nm).

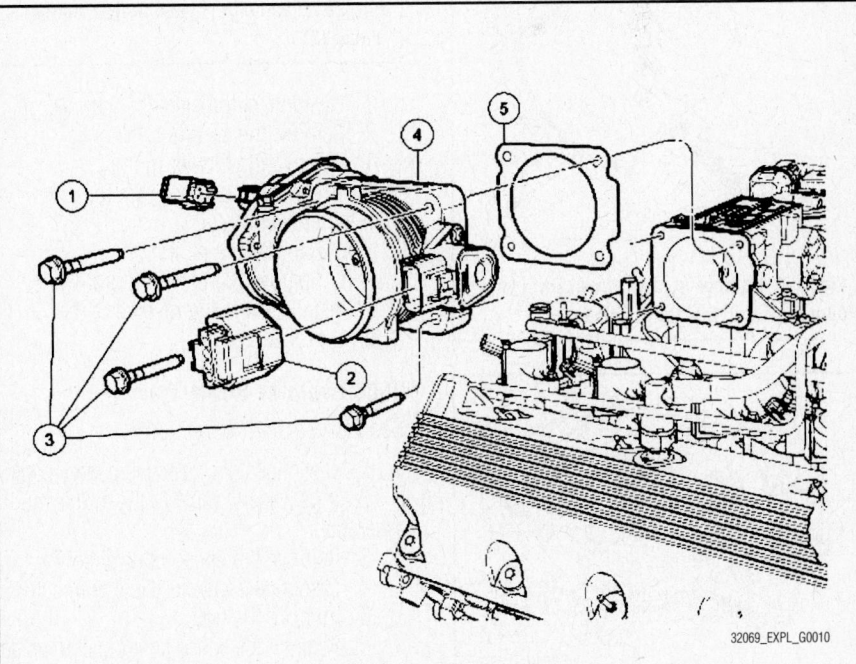

32069_EXPL_G0010

Fig. 357 Exploded view of the throttle body assembly and related components—2005 4.6L (VIN W) SOHC engine

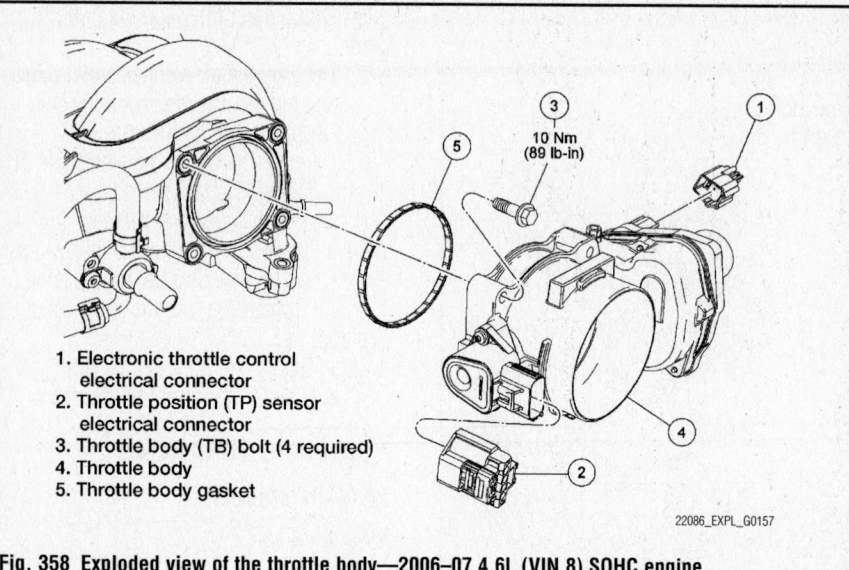

1. Electronic throttle control electrical connector
2. Throttle position (TP) sensor electrical connector
3. Throttle body (TB) bolt (4 required)
4. Throttle body
5. Throttle body gasket

Fig. 358 Exploded view of the throttle body—2006–07 4.6L (VIN 8) SOHC engine

4.6L (VIN H) DOHC Engine

1. Before servicing the vehicle, refer to the "Precautions" section.
2. Disconnect the negative battery cable.
3. Remove the air cleaner outlet tube.
4. Disconnect the speed control and accelerator cables from the throttle body.
5. Disconnect the throttle return spring from the throttle body.
6. Disconnect the TP sensor electrical connector.
7. Remove the bolts, the electronic TB and the gasket. Discard the gasket.
8. Installation is the reverse of the removal procedure, noting the following:
   a. Use a new throttle body gasket.
   b. Tighten the throttle body bolts to 89 inch lbs. (10 Nm).

HEATING & AIR CONDITIONING SYSTEM

BLOWER MOTOR

REMOVAL & INSTALLATION

Except 2005 Explorer Sport-Trac

See Figures 359 through 361.

1. Remove the screw and position aside the vacuum tank.

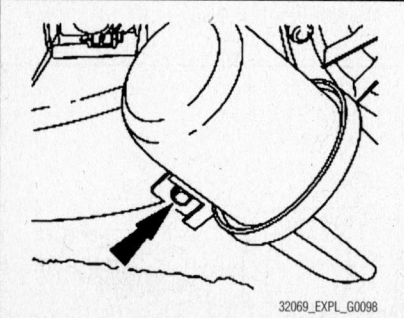

Fig. 359 Remove screw (arrow) from vacuum tank and position it aside

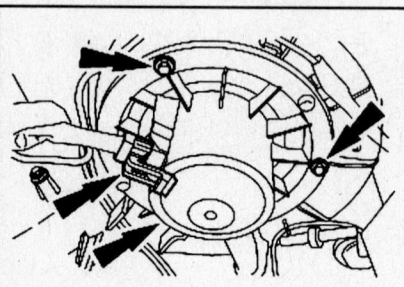

Fig. 360 Blower motor screws and electrical connector

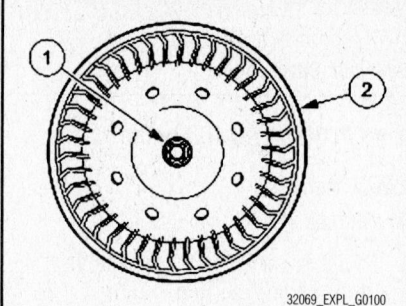

Fig. 361 Push clip (1) and blower motor wheel (2)

2. Disconnect the electrical connector.
3. Remove the screws.
4. Remove the blower motor.
5. To remove the blower motor wheel from the blower motor:
   a. Remove the push clip.
   b. Remove the blower motor wheel.
6. Installation is the reverse of the removal procedure.

2005 Explorer Sport-Trac

See Figures 362 through 364.

1. Disconnect the negative battery cable.
2. If necessary, remove the air cleaner assembly.
3. Remove the speed control servo.
4. Disconnect the electrical connector.
5. Remove the bolt.
6. Position the speed control servo aside.
7. Remove the screws and nuts for the coolant/washer reservoir.
8. Move the coolant/washer reservoir aside.

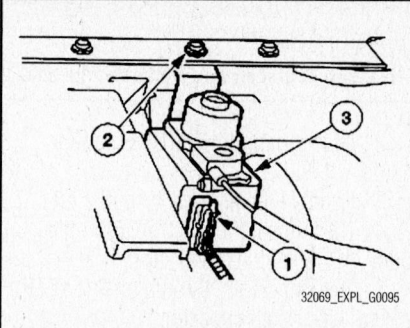

Fig. 362 Electrical connector (1), bolt (2) and speed control servo (3)

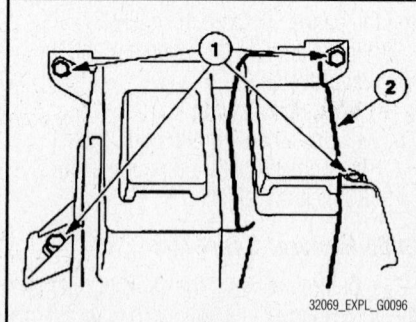

Fig. 363 Screws and nuts (1) and coolant/washer reservoir (2)

9. Disconnect the vent hose.
10. Disconnect the electrical connector.
11. Remove the four screws.
12. Remove the blower motor.

To install:

13. Installation is the reverse of the removal procedure. Observe the following tightening specifications:

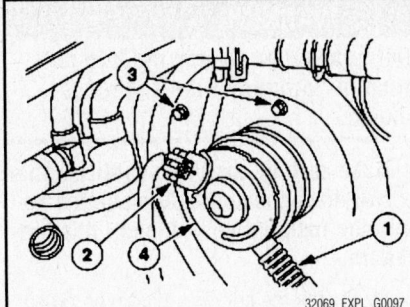

Fig. 364 Vent hose (1), electrical connector (2), screws (3) and blower motor (4)

- Speed control servo bolt 62–80 inch lbs. (7–9 Nm)
- Coolant/washer reservoir screws and nuts 52–71 inch lbs (6–8 Nm)

HEATER CORE

REMOVAL & INSTALLATION

2005 Aviator, Explorer and Mountaineer

Front

See Figure 365.

1. Recover the refrigerant.

➡The air bag warning lamp illuminates when the RCM fuse is removed and the ignition switch is ON. This is normal operation and does not indicate a supplemental restraint system (SRS) fault.

➡After diagnosing or repairing an SRS, the restraint system diagnostic tools must be removed before operating the vehicle over the road.

➡The SRS must be fully operational and free of faults before releasing the vehicle to the customer.

➡Repair is made by installing a new part only. If the new part does not correct the condition, install the original part and perform the diagnostic procedure again.

2. De-power the system.
3. Remove the steering wheel back cover plugs.
4. Remove the driver air bag module bolts.
5. Remove the driver air bag module connectors.
6. Remove the horn switch connector.
7. Remove the driver air bag module.
8. Open the glove compartment.
9. Through the glove compartment opening, release the tab and disconnect the passenger air bag module electrical connector.
10. Remove the parts in the order indicated in the following illustration and table.
11. Remove the passenger air bag module nuts.
12. Reaching one hand into the glove box opening, push out on the passenger air bag module, releasing the clips at the top and remove the passenger air bag module from the instrument panel. Remove the passenger air bag module.

✳✳ WARNING

Do not handle the passenger air bag module by grabbing the edges of the deployment door.

13. Remove the A-pillar trim panels and right cowl side trim panel.

➡After removing the floor console, reconnect the battery to position the front seats back, then disconnect the battery.

14. Remove the floor console.
15. Remove the instrument panel side finish panel (left).
16. Remove the steering column opening cover screws.
17. Remove the steering column opening cover
18. Remove the lower steering column cover.
19. Remove the steering column electrical connector.
20. Remove the bulkhead electrical connector.
21. Remove the body harness electrical connector.
22. Remove the parking brake release handle screws.
23. Remove the instrument panel electrical connector.
24. Remove the instrument panel electrical connector.
25. Remove the pinch bolt.

✳✳ WARNING

To avoid damage to the clockspring, do not allow the steering column shaft to rotate while the intermediate shaft is disconnected.

26. Remove the adjustable pedal electrical connector
27. Remove the instrument panel center brace bolts.
28. Remove the instrument panel center brace nuts.
29. Remove the instrument panel center brace.

30. Remove the transmission range selector lever cable.
31. Remove the bulkhead electrical connector.
32. Remove the body harness electrical connector.
33. Remove the ground strap bolts.
34. Remove the ground straps.
35. Remove the inertia switch electrical connector.
36. Remove the instrument panel electrical connectors.
37. Remove the instrument panel center brace bolts (right).
38. Remove the instrument panel center brace nuts (right).
39. Remove the instrument panel center brace (right).
40. Remove the instrument panel bolt.
41. Remove the instrument panel defroster grille.
42. Remove the sun load sensor electrical connector.

✳✳ WARNING

To avoid damaging the sun load sensor electrical connector, remove the grille just enough to remove the connector.

43. Remove the instrument panel bolts.
44. Remove the antenna lead-in cable.
45. Remove the RCM electrical connector.
46. Remove the ground strap bolt.
47. Remove the instrument panel bolts.

✳✳ WARNING

To avoid damage to the instrument panel, an assistant is required to support the panel before carrying out this step.

✳✳ WARNING

Before removing the instrument panel make sure all electrical connector wiring is free and not hindered.

48. Remove the instrument panel.
49. Drain the engine coolant.
50. Remove the engine appearance cover.
51. Remove the EGR vacuum regulator solenoid electrical connector.
52. Remove the vacuum hoses.
53. Remove the EGR vacuum regulator solenoid mounting nuts.
54. Remove the EGR vacuum regulator solenoid.
55. Remove the wire harness.

56. Remove the heater tube bracket nut.

57. Compress the clamps and disconnect the heater hoses.

58. Remove the A/C line bracket nut at the inner fender well.

59. Remove the A/C line bracket nut at the dash panel.

60. Remove the disconnect the evaporator outlet line fitting.

61. Remove the vacuum connector.

62. Remove the heater core and evaporator core housing nut.

63. Remove the heater core and evaporator core housing.

64. Remove the floor ducts.

65. Remove the housing brace.

66. Remove the heater tube cover.

67. Remove the heater tube seal.

68. Remove the heater core cover.

69. Remove the heater core.

To install:

❊❊ WARNING

The clockspring electrical connectors are unique and cannot be reversed when connected to the driver air bag module. Match the electrical connector key to the keyway in the driver air bag module. Do not force the electrical connectors into the driver air bag module.

70. Match the electrical connector key to the keyway in the driver air bag module and connect the electrical connectors.

❊❊ WARNING

The passenger air bag module nuts must be torqued in the sequence shown.

➡Make sure the battery negative cable is still disconnected before continuing with the installation portion of this procedure.

71. Install the components in the order indicated in the following illustration and table.

72. Install the passenger air bag module.

73. Connect the passenger air bag module electrical connector.

74. Close the glove compartment.

75. Re-power the system.

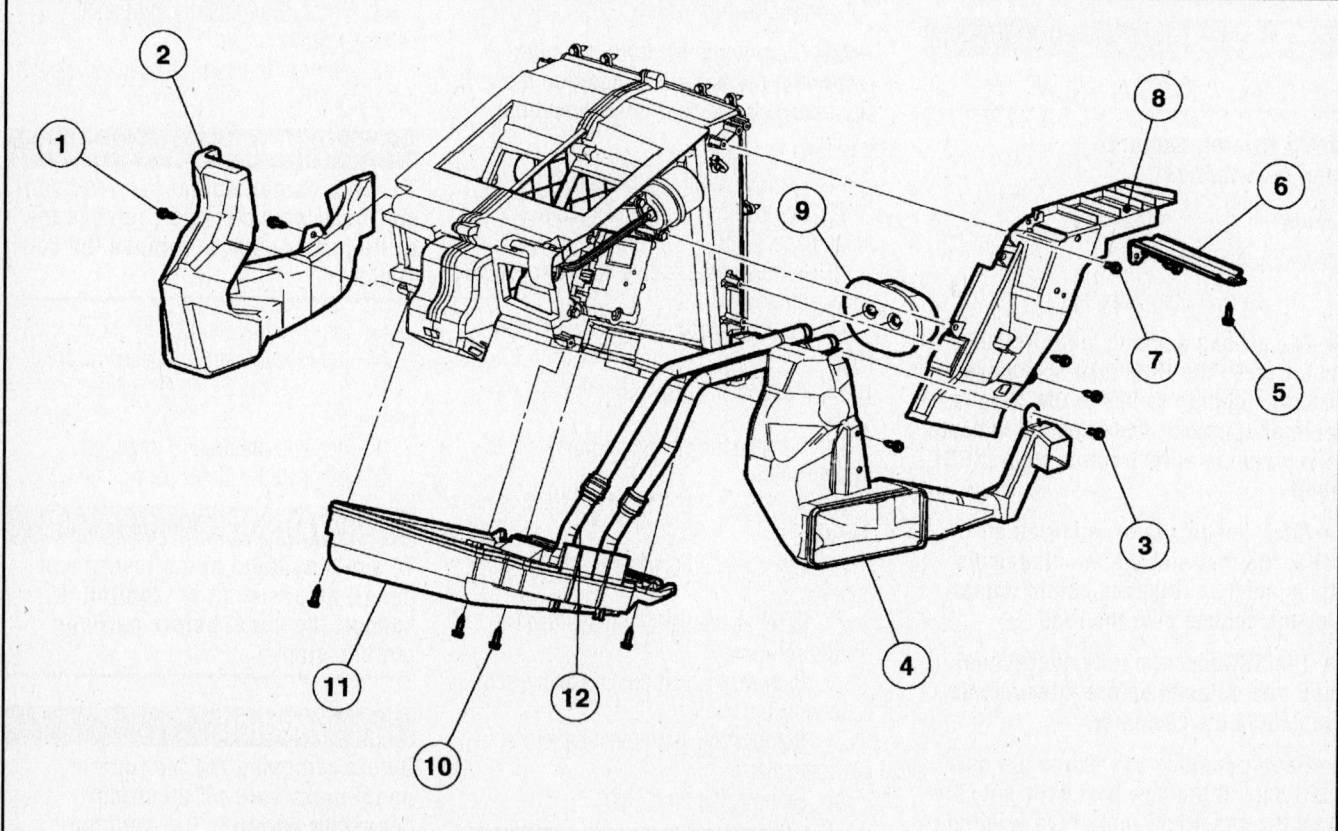

1	LH floor duct screws (2 required)	7	Heater tube cover screw (3 required)
2	LH floor duct	8	Heater tube cover
3	RH floor duct screws (2 required)	9	Heater tube seal
4	RH floor duct	10	Heater core cover screw (4 required)
5	Housing brace screw (3 required)	11	Heater core cover
6	Housing brace	12	Heater core

06017-EXPL-G11

Fig. 365 Front heater core

76. Make sure the retaining clips are in place before positioning the passenger air bag module to the instrument panel.

77. Lubricate the refrigerant system with the correct amount of clean PAG oil.

78. Fill and bleed the engine cooling system.

79. Evacuate, leak test and charge the refrigerant system.

Rear

See Figure 366.

1. Before servicing the vehicle, refer to the "Precautions" section.

➡**Lubricate the coolant hoses with plain water only if needed.**

2. Position the vehicle on a hoist with the gear selector in NEUTRAL.

3. Using suitable tools, clamp-off the underbody heater hoses at the floor pan bracket.

4. Remove the clamps

5. Remove the auxiliary line floor pan bracket nuts.

6. Remove the line bracket screws.

7. Remove the line bracket.

➡**The screw and line bracket are located inside the vehicle above the floor pan line bracket.**

8. Remove the auxiliary harness electrical connector.

9. Remove the auxiliary housing bolts.

10. Remove the auxiliary housing nut.

11. Remove the blend door actuator electrical connector.

12. Remove the blend door actuator screws.

13. Remove the auxiliary blend door actuator.

14. Remove the temperature blend door actuator screws.

15. Remove the auxiliary temperature blend door actuator.

16. Remove the heater core cover.

17. Remove the clamps.

18. Remove the auxiliary heater core.

19. Installation is the reverse of the removal procedure.

20. Fill the engine cooling system.

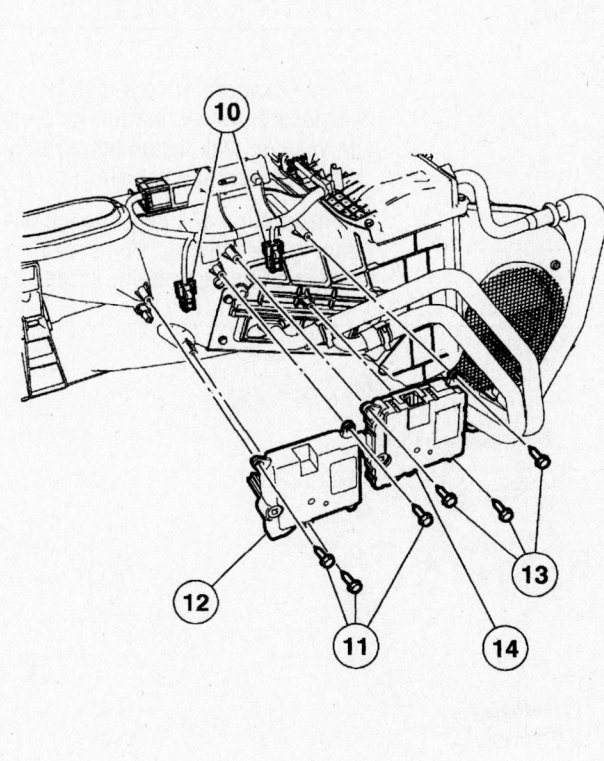
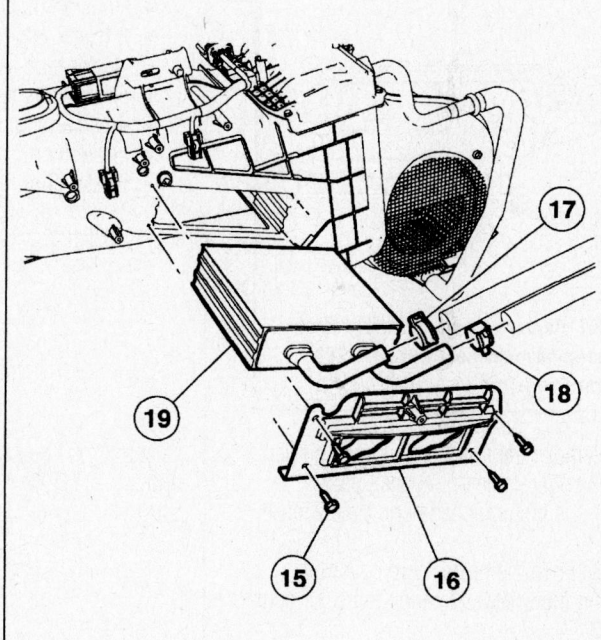

10 Blend door actuator electrical connectors (2 required)

11 Auxiliary blend door actuator screw (3 required)

12 Auxiliary blend door actuator

13 Auxiliary temperature blend door actuator screw (3 required)

14 Auxiliary temperature blend door actuator

15 Heater core cover screw (4 required)

16 Heater core cover

17 Heater core hose clamp

18 Heater core hose clamp

19 Auxiliary heater core

06017-EXPL-G12

Fig. 366 Rear heater core

2005 Explorer Sport-Trac

See Figures 367 and 368.

➡**If a heater core leak is suspected, the heater core must be leak tested before it is removed from the vehicle.**

1. Before beginning service, read the "Precautions" at the beginning of this section.
2. Prepare the vehicle for heater core removal:

    a. Remove the instrument panel. See "Instrument Panel" under the "Body" section.

    b. Remove the A/C evaporator housing. See "HVAC Evaporator Housing" section.

    c. Remove the Powertrain Control Module (PCM).

3. Remove the PCM heat sink:

    a. Remove the ground strap screw.

    b. Remove the heat sink.

Fig. 367 Remove the ground strap screw (1) and remove the heat sink (2)—2005 Explorer Sport-Trac

4. Remove the four heater housing nuts from the engine side of the dash panel. Position the plenum chamber on the vehicle floor.
5. Remove the heater core cover by removing the screws (1) and the heater core cover (2).
6. Remove the heater core.

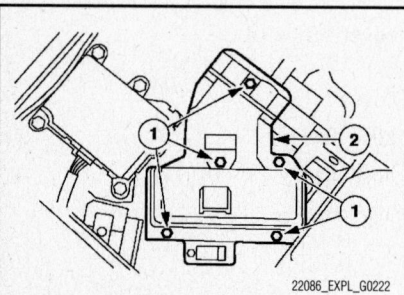

Fig. 368 Remove the heater core cover by removing the screws (1) and the heater core cover (2)—2005 Explorer Sport-Trac

7. Installation is the reverse of the removal procedure.
8. During installation, be sure to install a new oval foam seal around the heater core inlet and outlet tubes.

2006–07 Explorer and Mountaineer; 2007 Explorer Sport-Trac

See Figure 369.

➡**If a heater core leak is suspected, the heater core must be pressure leak tested before it is removed from the vehicle.**

1. Remove the heater core and evaporator core housing (HVAC housing). See "HVAC Housing" section.
2. Remove the following:
   - 2 LH floor duct screws
   - LH floor duct
   - 2 RH floor duct screws
   - RH floor duct
   - 3 housing brace screws
   - Housing brace
   - 3 heater tube cover screws
   - Heater tube cover
   - Heater tube seal
   - 4 heater core cover screws
   - Heater core cover
   - Heater core

To install:

3. Install the following:
   - Heater core
   - Heater core cover
   - 4 heater core cover screws
   - Heater tube seal
   - Heater tube cover
   - 3 heater tube cover screws
   - Housing brace
   - 3 housing brace screws
   - RH floor duct
   - 2 RH floor duct screws
   - LH floor duct
   - 2 LH floor duct screws

4. Install the heater core and evaporator core housing (HVAC housing). See "HVAC Housing" section.

HVAC HOUSING

REMOVAL & INSTALLATION

See Figures 370 through 372.

➡**If an evaporator core leak is suspected, the evaporator core must be vacuum leak tested before it is removed from the vehicle.**

➡**Installation of a new suction accumulator is not required when repairing the air conditioning system, except when**

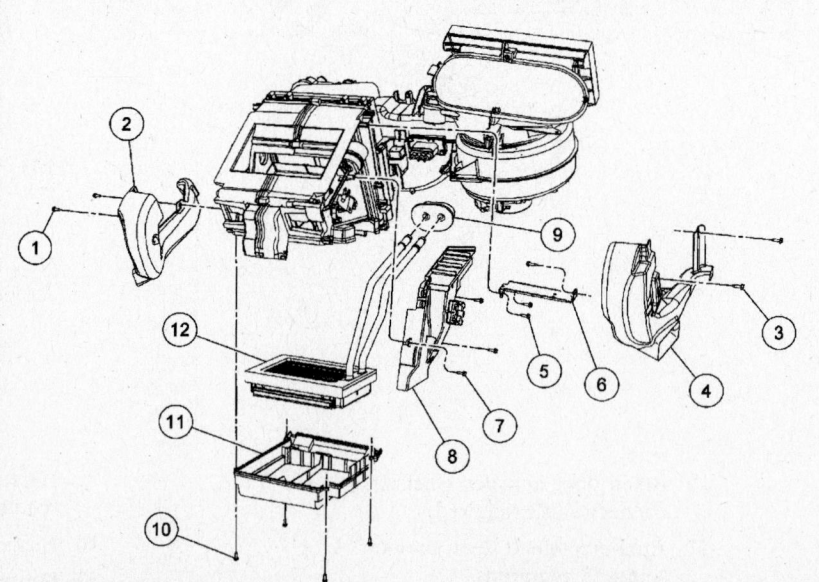

1. LH floor duct screw (2 required)
2. LH floor duct
3. RH floor duct screw (2 required)
4. RH floor duct
5. Housing brace screw (3 required)
6. Housing brace
7. Heater tube cover screw (3 required)
8. Heater tube cover
9. Heater tube seal
10. Heater core cover screw (4 required)
11. Heater core cover
12. Heater core

Fig. 369 Exploded view of the HVAC housing showing the heater core—2006–07 Explorer and Mountaineer; 2007 Explorer Sport-Trac

there is physical evidence of contamination from a failed A/C compressor or damage to the accumulator.

➡**Lubricate the coolant hoses with plain water only if needed.**

1. Recover the refrigerant.
2. Drain the engine coolant.
3. Remove the instrument panel. See "Instrument Panel" under the "Body" section.
4. Detach the wiring harness bracket (above the heater tube bracket) and position the harness aside.
5. Remove the heater tube bracket nut.

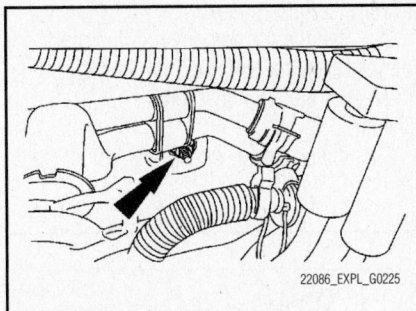

Fig. 370 Remove the heater tube bracket nut

6. Remove the A/C line bracket nut at the dash panel.
7. Disconnect the 2 heater hose clamps at the heater core.

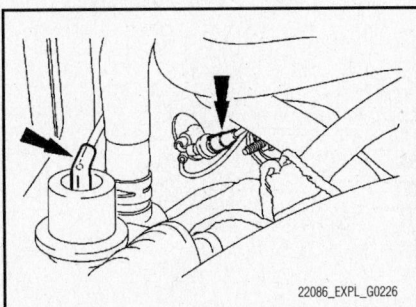

Fig. 371 Disconnect the 2 vacuum connectors

8. Disconnect the evaporator inlet fitting. Discard the O-ring seals.
9. Disconnect the evaporator outlet fitting. Discard the O-ring seals.
10. Disconnect the 2 vacuum connectors.
11. Detach the grommet and push the vacuum lines into the passenger compartment.
12. Remove the 4 HVAC housing nuts.
13. Disconnect the ground terminal bolt.
14. Remove the HVAC housing.

To install:

15. Position the HVAC housing into the vehicle.
16. Disconnect the ground terminal bolt.
17. Install the HVAC housing nuts. Tighten the nuts to 80 inch lbs. (9 Nm).

18. Position the grommet and vacuum lines back into the dash panel.
19. Connect the 2 vacuum connectors.
20. Install new O-ring seals and connect the evaporator inlet and outlet fittings.
21. Connect the heater hoses.
22. Install the A/C line bracket nut at the dash panel.
23. Install the heater tube bracket nut.
24. Attach the wiring harness bracket (above the heater tube bracket)
25. Install the instrument panel. See "Instrument Panel" under the "Body" section.
26. Evacuate and recharge the A/C system.
27. Refill the cooling system.
28. Perform an A/C system leak test.

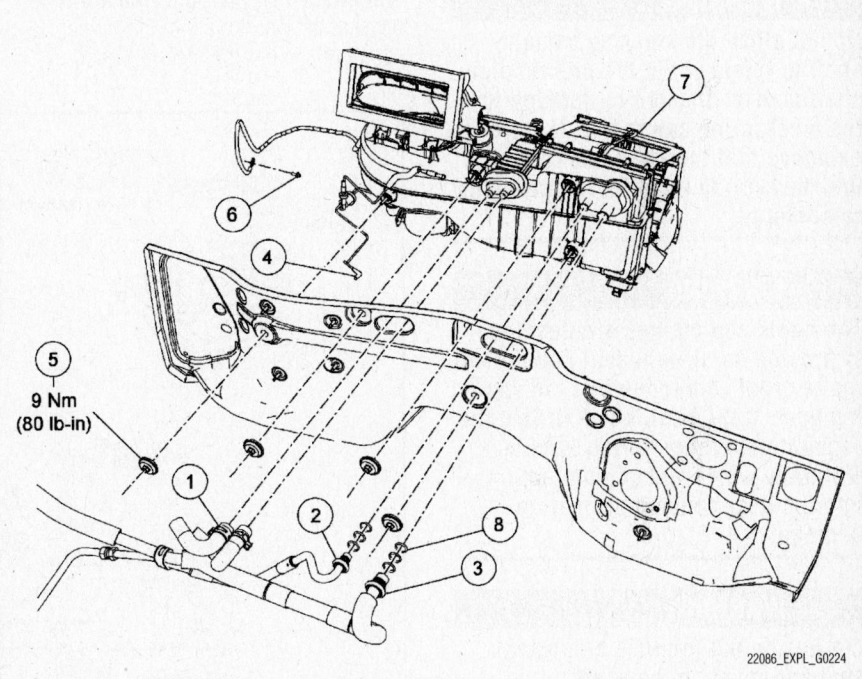

Fig. 372 Exploded view of the HVAC housing assembly: heater hoses (1), pressure hose (2), suction hose (3), vacuum connector (4), retaining nuts (5), screw (6), HVAC housing assembly (7), and O-ring seals (8)

STEERING

POWER STEERING GEAR

REMOVAL & INSTALLATION

2005 Aviator

See Figure 373.

1. Before servicing the vehicle, refer to the "Precautions" section.

➡**New O-ring seals must be installed any time the lines are disconnected from the steering gear.**

2. With the transmission in NEUTRAL, position the vehicle on a hoist.

3. Remove the wheel and tire assembly.

> ⚠ **WARNING**
>
> **Do not allow the steering column shaft to rotate while the intermediate shaft is disconnected or damage to the clockspring can result. If there is evidence that the shaft has rotated, the clockspring must be removed and re-centered.**

> ❄ **WARNING**
>
> **The boots and clamps are designed to provide an airtight seal and protect the internal components of the steering gear. If the seal is not airtight the vacuum generated during turning will draw water and contamination into the gear causing premature damage.**

> ⚠ **WARNING**
>
> **Zip ties do not produce an airtight seal and must not be used.**

> ❄ **WARNING**
>
> **The inner ball joint grease is not compatible with water and contamination trapped in the grease will degrade the life of the joint.**

> ❄ **WARNING**
>
> **If present, the orientation of the vent tube must be noted so the boots and vent tubes can be installed in the correct location.**

4. Remove the lower arm-to-frame nuts.

5. Remove the steering gear mounting bolt

6. Remove the steering gear mounting nut.

7. Remove the steering gear mounting bracket bolt.

8. Remove the steering gear mounting bracket.

9. Remove the steering column pinch bolt.

10. Remove the variable assist power steering (VAPS) switch electrical connector.

11. Remove the power steering hose mounting plate nuts.

12. Disconnect the power steering hoses.

13. Discard the O-rings.

14. Remove the tie rod end-to-knuckle nut. If repairing the right side it will be necessary to pull back the left inner tie rod boot to hold the steering gear.

15. Note the number of times the tie rod ends turn for assembly reference.

16. Remove the brake disc. Rotate the front of the brake rotor outward.

17. Remove the steering gear.

To install:

18. Installation is the reverse of the removal procedure.

19. Final tightening of the front suspension components should be carried out at or near the ride height (curb height) setting.

20. Install new O-ring seals onto the power steering hoses.

21. See the accompanying illustration for relevant fastener torques.

22. Fill and leak test the system.

23. Check and, if necessary, adjust the front toe.

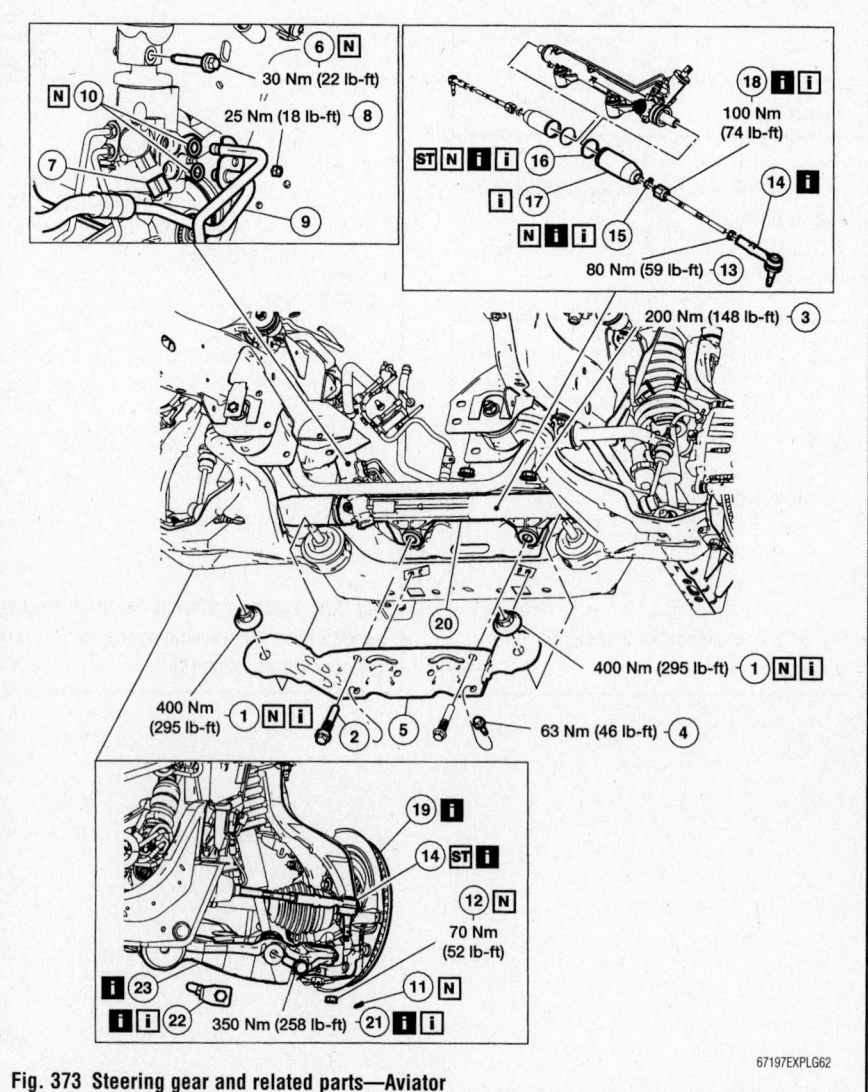

Fig. 373 Steering gear and related parts—Aviator

67197EXPLG62

2005 Explorer Sport-Trac

See Figures 374 through 376.

✻ WARNING

When repairing the power steering system, care should be taken to prevent the entry of contaminants or premature failure of the power steering components can result.

1. Before servicing the vehicle, refer to the "Precautions" section.
2. Turn the wheel to the straight-ahead position and turn the ignition switch to the OFF position.
3. Remove the wheel and tire assemblies.
4. Remove the cooler hose clamp nuts. Loosen the clamp and disconnect the hose. Drain the fluid into a suitable container.
5. Loosen the clamp, disconnect and remove the cooler.
6. Loosen the tie rod end jam nuts.
7. Remove and discard the cotter pins and nuts.

✻ WARNING

Do not damage the tie rod boot when installing the special tool.

➡ **Remove the adapter from the ball end of the special tool. Apply a small amount of grease to the tie rod end stud and the ball of the special tool.**

8. Separate the tie rod ends from the knuckles.
9. Remove the tie rod ends. Count and record the number of turns required to remove the tie rod end.
10. Remove the front stabilizer bar link nuts from the front suspension lower arms.
11. Remove the four stabilizer bar bolts and two brackets.
12. Remove the front stabilizer bar.
13. Remove the stabilizer bar insulators.

✻ WARNING

Do not allow the intermediate shaft to rotate while it is disconnected from the steering gear or damage to the clockspring can result. If there is evidence that the intermediate shaft has rotated, the clockspring must be removed and re-centered.

14. Remove the pinch bolt and detach the intermediate shaft from the gear.
15. Remove the fluid line bracket nut and disconnect the lines.

✻ WARNING

Hold the tops of the steering gear to crossmember stud bolts to avoid damaging the steering gear fluid transfer tubes.

16. Remove the steering gear mounting nuts.
17. Remove the stud bolts and washers.
18. Rotate the steering gear control valve housing toward the front of the vehicle.
19. Turn the steering gear input shaft to the right until the stop is reached.
20. Move the steering gear as far to the right side of the vehicle as possible.
21. Move the left front wheel spindle tie rod forward to clear the frame crossmember.
22. Remove the steering gear from the vehicle.

To install:

➡ **Make sure the steering gear input shaft is turned to the left until the stop is reached.**

➡ Handle the steering gear with caution to avoid damage to fluid transfer tubes and to avoid dimples in the tie rod boots.

23. Turn the steering gear input shaft to the right until the stop is reached. Note the number of turns required.

➡ **Make sure the steering gear control valve housing is turned toward the front of the vehicle.**

24. Install the steering gear into the right opening of the crossmember.

✻ WARNING

Take care not to scuff or tear the inner tie rod boots.

25. Move the steering gear as far to the right side of the vehicle as possible.
26. Move the left front wheel spindle tie rod into the opening in the crossmember and move the steering gear into position.

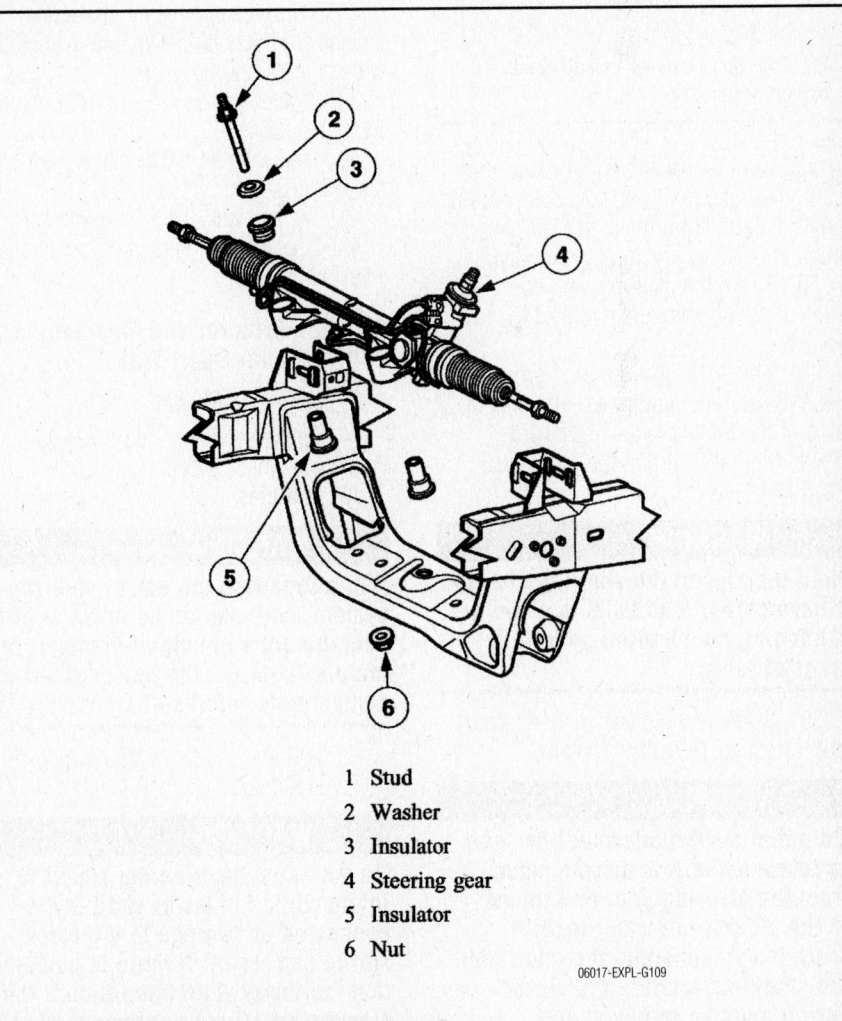

1	Stud
2	Washer
3	Insulator
4	Steering gear
5	Insulator
6	Nut

06017-EXPL-G109

Fig. 374 Steering gear mounting—Explorer Sport-Trac

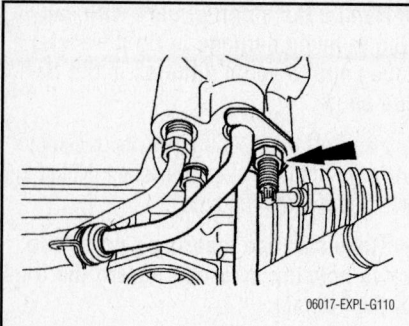

Fig. 375 Steering fluid line bracket nut—Explorer Sport-Trac

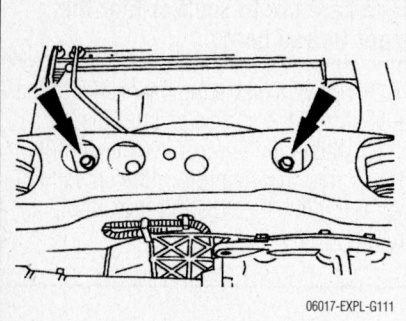

Fig. 376 Steering gear mounting nuts—Explorer Sport-Trac

27. To place the steering gear in the straight-ahead position, turn the steering gear input shaft to the left by half the number of turns previously recorded.

28. Rotate the steering gear control valve housing toward the rear of the vehicle.

29. Install the steering gear crossmember washers and stud bolts. The dished side of the washer faces downward. Install the nuts. Torque to 111 ft. lbs. (150 Nm).

❈❈ WARNING

Hold the tops of the steering gear to crossmember stud bolts to avoid damaging the steering gear fluid transfer tubes.

30. Install the fluid lines and tighten the nut. Torque to 18 ft. lbs. (25 Nm).

❈❈ WARNING

Do not allow the intermediate shaft to rotate while it is disconnected from the steering gear or damage to the clockspring can result. If there is evidence that the intermediate shaft has rotated, the clockspring must be removed and re-centered.

31. Connect the intermediate shaft to the steering gear input shaft. Install a new lower steering column pinch bolt. Torque to 35 ft. lbs. (48 Nm).

32. Install the cooler, hose and clamp. Connect and install the clamp. Install the nuts. Torque to 30 ft. lbs. (40 Nm).

➡ **In the event that the self-tapping bolts cannot be installed in the frame, there is a kit available with flag nuts.**

33. Install the stabilizer bar insulators.

34. Install the front stabilizer bar brackets. Install the bolts. Torque to 25–34 ft. lbs. (34–46 Nm).

35. Install the front stabilizer bar links and the front stabilizer bar bolts.

36. Install the front stabilizer bar link nuts. Torque to 15–20 ft. lbs. (22–29 Nm).

37. Install the tie rod ends on the front wheel spindle tie rods. Rotate the tie rod ends the number of turns recorded during removal.

38. Position the tie rod ends on the steering knuckles. Install the castellated nuts and new cotter pins. Torque to 52 ft. lbs. (72 Nm). Check that the brake dust shields are not bent and are not in contact with the outer tie rod boots.

39. Tighten the tie rod end jam nuts to 59 ft. lbs. (80 Nm).

40. Install the front wheel and tire assemblies

41. Fill and leak check the system.

42. Check and, if necessary, adjust the wheel alignment.

2005–07 Explorer and Mountaineer; 2007 Explorer Sport-Trac

See Figures 377 through 379.

1. Before servicing the vehicle, refer to the "Precautions" section.

All vehicles

❈❈ WARNING

While repairing the power steering system, care should be taken to prevent the entry of contaminants or premature failure of the power steering components can result.

2. With the vehicle in NEUTRAL, position it on a hoist.

❈❈ WARNING

Do not allow the steering wheel to rotate while the lower shaft is disconnected or damage to the clockspring can result. If there is evidence that the lower shaft has rotated, the clockspring must be removed and re-centered.

3. Hold the steering wheel in the straight-ahead position using a suitable device.

4. Using a suitable suction device, drain the power steering fluid reservoir.

5. Remove the 2 bolts and the oil drip shield.

➡ **Install a new lower shaft-to-steering gear bolt.**

6. Remove and discard the lower shaft-to-steering gear bolt.

7. Disconnect the lower shaft from the steering gear.

8. Remove the steering line clamp plate nut.

9. Rotate the steering line clamp plate and disconnect the power steering lines.

➡ **New O-rings must be installed whenever the power steering lines are disconnected.**

10. Remove and discard the 2 O-rings.

➡ **New cotter pins must be installed.**

11. Remove and discard the 2 cotter pins.

➡ **New tie rod end nuts must be installed.**

12. Remove and discard the 2 tie rod end nuts.

❈❈ WARNING

Do not damage the tie rod end boot when installing the special tool.

13. Using the special tool, separate the 2 tie rod ends from the wheel knuckle.

14. Remove the 2 steering gear-to-crossmember nuts and bolts.

15. Remove the 2 bolts and remove the steering gear bracket.

4WD vehicles

➡ **On 4WD vehicles, the following steps (left lower arm only) must be carried out to provide clearance to remove the steering gear.**

❈❈ WARNING

Do not tighten the left lower arm inboard mounting nuts until the installation procedure is complete and the weight of the vehicle is resting on the wheel and tire assemblies. Make sure to tighten the lower arm forward nut before tightening the lower arm-to-frame nuts.

➡ **It is not necessary to disconnect the left lower ball joint.**

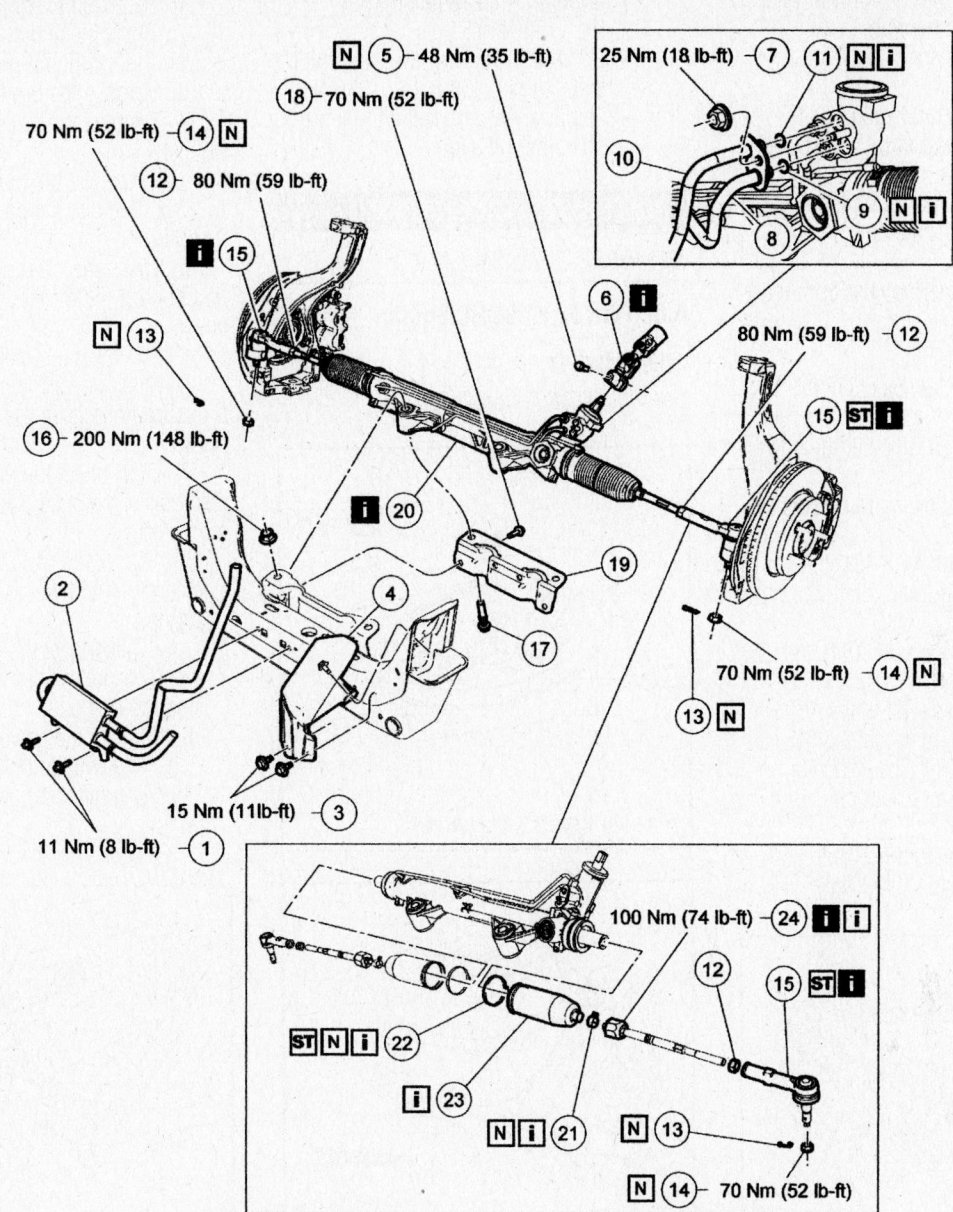

Fig. 377 Steering gear and related parts—Explorer and Mountaineer

1	Fluid cooler-to-crossmember bolts	12	Tie-rod jam nuts (loosen only)
2	Fluid cooler	13	Cotter pins
3	Oil shield-to-crossmember bolts	14	Tie-rod nuts
4	Oil shield	15	Outer tie-rods
5	Intermediate shaft-to-steering gear bolt	16	Steering gear-to-crossmember nuts (2 required)
6	Intermediate shaft (detach only)	17	Steering gear-to-crossmember bolts (2 required)
7	Clamp plate-to-steering gear nut	18	Bracket-to-crossmember bolts (2 required)
8	Power steering high-pressure line	19	Bracket
9	O-ring	20	Steering gear
10	Power steering return line	21	Outer bellows clamp
11	O-ring Installation Note	22	Inner bellows clamp
		23	Steering gear bellows
		24	Spindle tie-rod

06017-EXPL-G112

16. Remove the lower arm forward nut and flag bolt. Discard the nut.

17. Remove and discard the 2 lower arm-to-frame nuts.

18. Remove the shock absorber-to-lower arm bolt and flag nut. Discard the flag nut.

19. Remove the stabilizer bar connecting link nut and disconnect the link.

All vehicles

20. Remove the steering gear from the left side of the vehicle.

To install:

21. Installation is the reverse of the removal procedure.

22. Install 2 new O-rings. Fill the power steering system

23. Observe the following torque specifications:

- Oil drip shield: 11 ft. lbs. (15 Nm).
- Steering pinch bolt: 35 ft. lbs. (48 Nm)
- Fluid line clamp bolt: 18 ft. lbs. (25 Nm)
- Tie rod end nuts: 52 ft. lbs. (70 Nm)
- Steering gear-to-crossmember nuts and bolts: 148 ft. lbs. (200 Nm).
- Steering gear bracket bolts: 52 ft. lbs. (70 Nm).
- Lower arm forward nut and flag bolt: 4295 ft. lbs. (400 Nm).

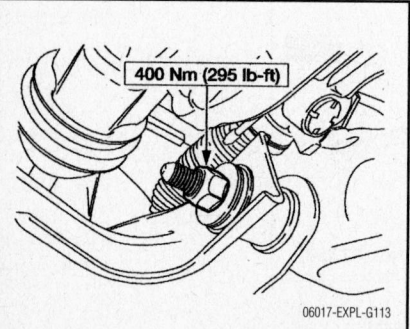

Fig. 378 Lower arm forward nut and flag bolt

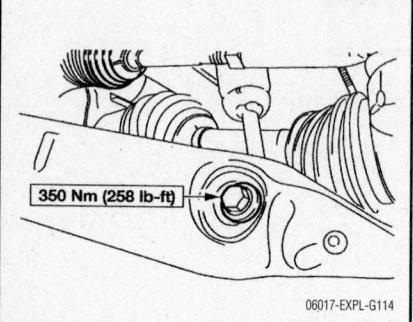

Fig. 379 Shock absorber-to-lower arm bolt and flag nut

- Lower arm-to-frame nuts: 111 ft. lbs. (150 Nm).
- Shock absorber-to-lower arm bolt and flag nut: 258 ft. lbs. (350 Nm).
- Stabilizer bar connecting link nut: 18 ft. lbs. (25 Nm).

POWER STEERING PUMP

REMOVAL & INSTALLATION

4.0L (VIN E, K) SOHC Engine

2005 Models

See Figures 380 through 385.

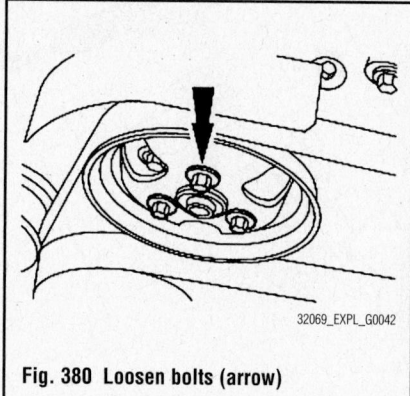

Fig. 380 Loosen bolts (arrow)

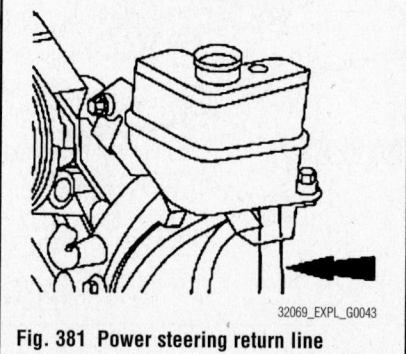

Fig. 381 Power steering return line (arrow)

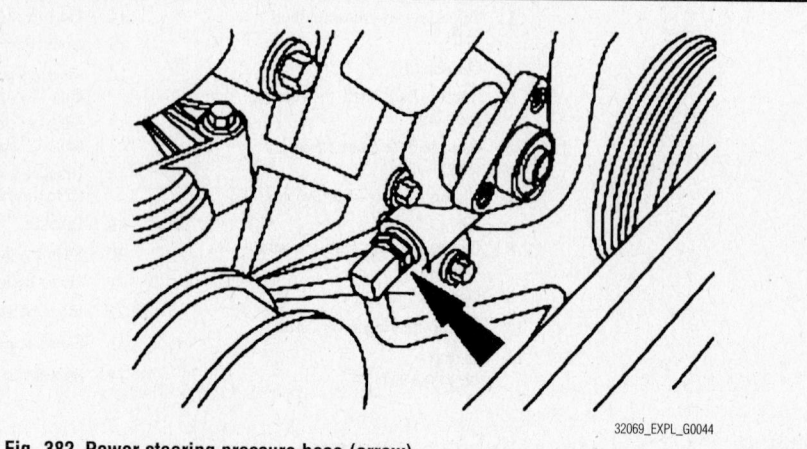

Fig. 382 Power steering pressure hose (arrow)

1. Remove the engine cooling fan.

2. Break loose but do not remove the power steering pump pulley bolts.

3. Remove the drive belt.

4. Remove the power steering pump pulley.

  a. Remove the loosened bolts.

  b. Remove the power steering pump pulley.

5. Disconnect the power steering return line hose at the power steering fluid reservoir.

  c. Allow the system to drain.

6. Disconnect the power steering pressure hose from the power steering pump.

7. Disconnect the power steering fluid reservoir outlet hose from the power steering pump.

  a. Compress and move the power steering fluid reservoir outlet hose clamp.

  b. Disconnect the power steering fluid reservoir outlet hose from the power steering pump.

8. Remove the power steering pump.

  a. Remove the bolts.

  b. Remove the power steering pump.

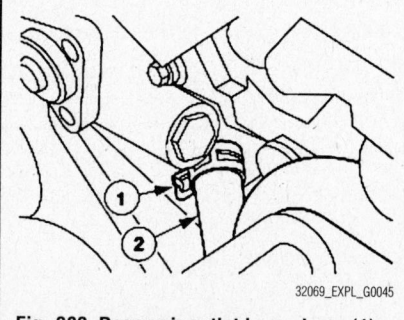

Fig. 383 Reservoir outlet hose clamp (1) and reservoir outlet hose (2)

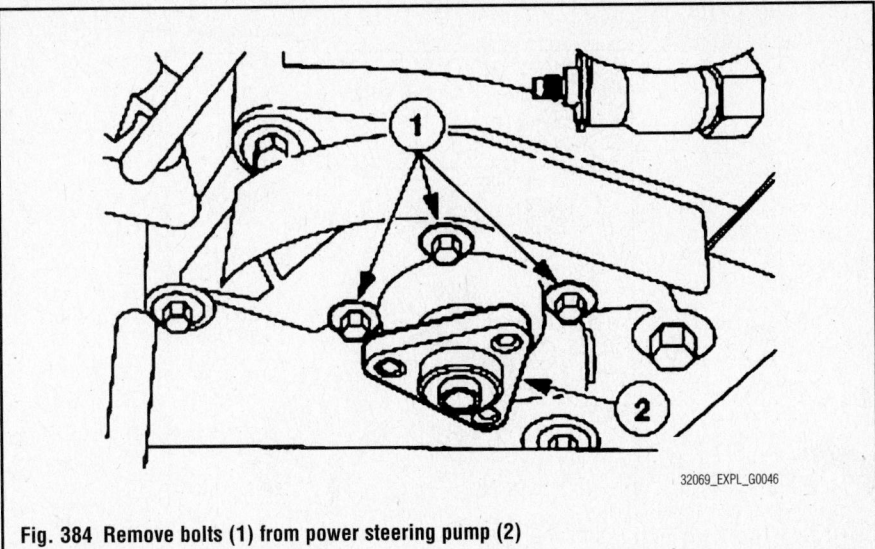

Fig. 384 Remove bolts (1) from power steering pump (2)

32069_EXPL_G0046

To install:

9. Install the power steering pump.
   a. Position the power steering pump.
   b. Install the bolts and tighten to 18 ft. lbs (25 Nm)
10. Connect the power steering fluid reservoir outlet hose to the power steering pump.
   a. Connect the power steering fluid reservoir outlet hose to the power steering pump.
   b. Compress and move the power steering fluid reservoir outlet hose clamp into place.
11. Using the special tool, install a new seal on the power steering pressure hose.
12. Connect the power steering pressure hose to the power steering pump and tighten to 48 ft. lbs. (65 Nm)
13. Connect the power steering return line hose to the power steering fluid reservoir.
14. Install the power steering pump pulley.
   a. Position the power steering pump pulley.
   b. Install the bolts hand-tight.
15. Install the drive belt.
16. Fully tighten the power steering pump pulley bolts to 18 ft. lbs (25 Nm).
17. Install the engine cooling fan.
18. Fill, purge and leak check the system.

2006–07 Models

See Figures 386 and 387.

> ✱✱ **WARNING**
>
> **While repairing the power steering system, care should be taken to prevent the entry of contaminants or premature failure of the power steering components can result.**

1. Using a suitable suction device, drain the power steering fluid reservoir.
2. With the vehicle in NEUTRAL, position it on a hoist.
3. Remove the power steering pump pulley as follows:
   a. Disconnect the fan clutch electrical connector.
   b. Remove the fan clutch wiring harness bracket bolt and position harness aside.
   c. Loosen the 3 power steering pump pulley bolts.
   d. Rotate the tensioner and remove the engine accessory drive belt from the power steering pump pulley.
   e. Remove the 3 bolts and the power steering pump pulley.
4. Remove the pressure line bracket-to-engine bolt.
5. Remove the power steering fluid reservoir-to-pump hose bracket bolt.
6. Release the reservoir-to-pump hose clamp and disconnect the hose.
7. Disconnect the pressure line-to-pump fitting. Remove and discard the Teflon® O-ring seal.
8. Remove the 3 bolts and the power steering pump.

To install:

9. Using the special tool, install a new Teflon® O-ring seal to the pressure line fitting.
10. Position the power steering pump and install the 3 bolts. Torque the bolts to 18 ft. lbs. (25 Nm).
11. Connect the pressure line-to-pump fitting. Tighten the fitting to 48 ft. lbs. (65 Nm).
12. Connect the reservoir-to-pump hose.
13. Install the power steering fluid reservoir-to-pump hose bracket bolt to 8 ft. lbs. (11 Nm).
14. Install the pressure line bracket-to-engine bolt to 8 ft. lbs. (11 Nm).
15. Install the power steering pump pulley as follows:
   a. Install the power steering pump pulley and loosely install the bolts.
   b. Install the engine accessory drive belt to the power steering pump pulley.
   c. Torque the 3 bolts for the power steering pump pulley to 18 ft. lbs. (25 Nm).
   d. Install and tighten the fan clutch wiring harness bracket bolt.
   e. Connect the fan clutch electrical connector.
16. Fill and bleed the power steering system. See "Filling and Bleeding" section.

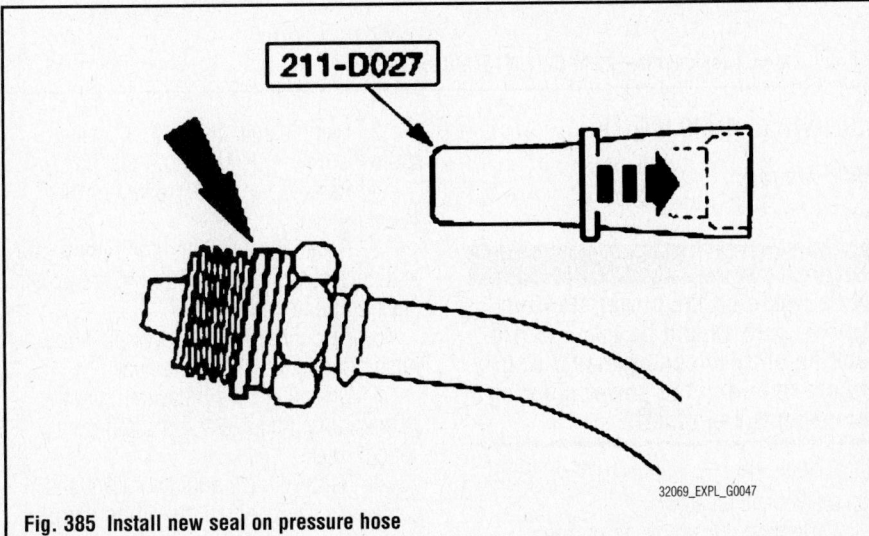

211-D027

Fig. 385 Install new seal on pressure hose

32069_EXPL_G0047

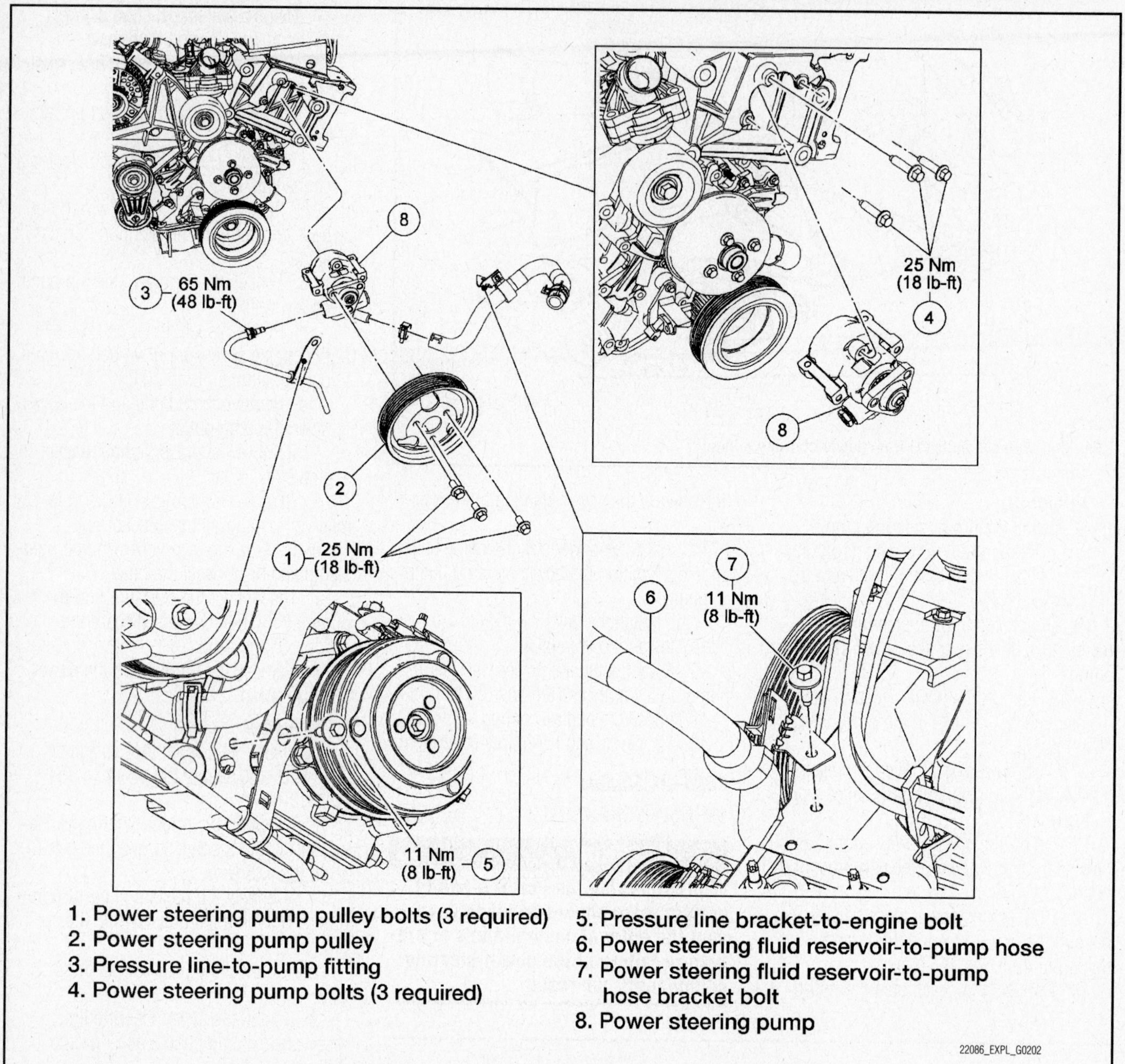

3 — 65 Nm (48 lb-ft)

8

25 Nm (18 lb-ft) — **4**

8

1 — 25 Nm (18 lb-ft)

2

11 Nm (8 lb-ft) — **5**

6

7 — 11 Nm (8 lb-ft)

1. Power steering pump pulley bolts (3 required)
2. Power steering pump pulley
3. Pressure line-to-pump fitting
4. Power steering pump bolts (3 required)
5. Pressure line bracket-to-engine bolt
6. Power steering fluid reservoir-to-pump hose
7. Power steering fluid reservoir-to-pump hose bracket bolt
8. Power steering pump

22086_EXPL_G0202

Fig. 386 Showing the power steering pump, reservoir and related components—2006-07 4.0L SOHC models

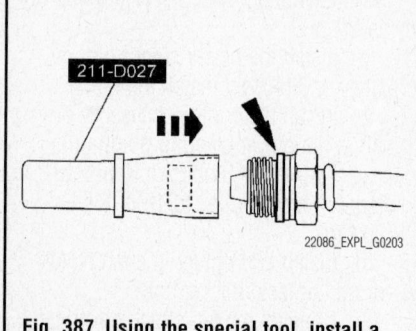

211-D027

22086_EXPL_G0203

Fig. 387 Using the special tool, install a new Teflon® O-ring seal to the pressure line fitting

4.6L (VIN 8) SOHC Engine

2005 Models

See Figure 388.

> ### ❋❋ WARNING
>
> **While repairing the power steering system, care should be taken to prevent the entry of contaminants or premature failure of the power steering components can result.**

1. With the vehicle in NEUTRAL, position the vehicle on a hoist.
2. Remove the engine air cleaner.
3. Using a suitable suction device, drain the power steering fluid reservoir.
4. Remove the pressure line bracket-to-engine nut.
5. Rotate the tensioner and remove the engine accessory drive belt from the power steering pump pulley.
6. Disconnect the reservoir-to-pump hose clamp and remove the hose.
7. Disconnect the pressure line-to-pump fitting. Remove and discard the Teflon® seal.
8. Remove the 2 engine bracket and cable nuts and position the wiring harness aside.

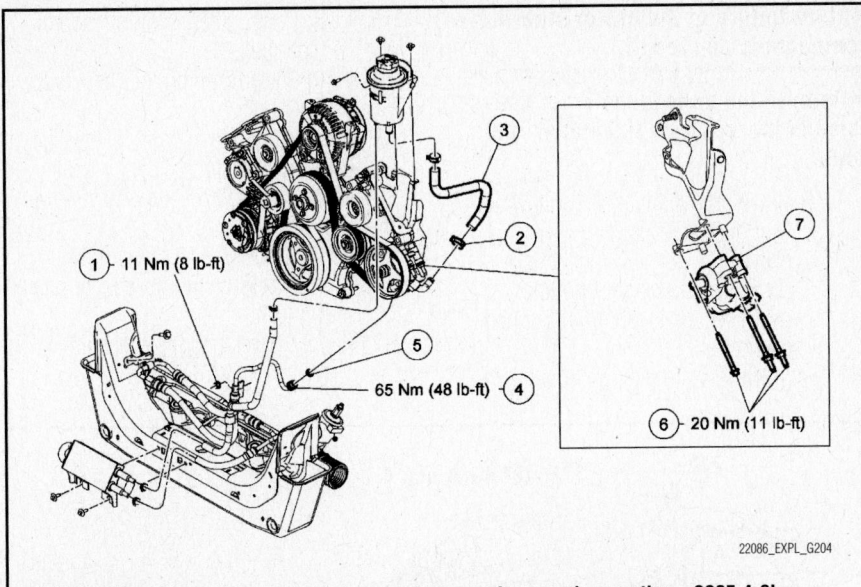

Fig. 388 Showing the power steering pump, hoses and reservoir mounting—2005 4.6L (VIN 8) SOHC Engine

9. Remove the 3 bolts and the power steering pump.

To install:

10. Using the special tool, install a new Teflon® seal on the pressure line-to-pump fitting.

11. Install the power steering pump and the 3 bolts. Torque to 11 ft. lbs. (20 Nm).

12. Install the bracket and cable and the 2 nuts. Torque to 11 ft. lbs. (20 Nm).

13. Connect the pressure line-to-pump fitting. Tighten the fitting to 48 ft. lbs. (65 Nm).

14. Install the reservoir-to-pump hose and connect the clamp.

15. Rotate the tensioner and install the accessory drive belt on the power steering pump pulley.

16. Install the pressure line bracket-to-engine nut. Torque to 8 ft. lbs. (11 Nm).

17. Install the engine air cleaner.

18. Fill and bleed the system. See "Filling and Bleeding" section below.

2006–07 Models

See Figure 389.

1. Using a suitable suction device, drain the power steering fluid reservoir.

2. With the vehicle in NEUTRAL, position it on a hoist.

3. Remove the power steering pump pulley.

4. Remove the pressure line bracket-to-engine nut.

5. Compress the clamp and disconnect the reservoir-to-pump hose.

6. Disconnect the pressure line-to-pump fitting.

7. Remove and discard the Teflon® O-ring seal.

8. Remove the 2 engine wiring bracket nuts and position the wiring harness and ground cable aside.

9. Remove the 3 bolts and the power steering pump.

To install:

10. Using the special tool, install a new Teflon® O-ring seal on the pressure line-to-pump fitting.

11. Position the power steering pump and install the 3 bolts. Tighten to 15 ft. lbs. (20 Nm).

12. Position the ground cable and engine wiring bracket. Install the 2 nuts. Tighten to 15 ft. lbs. (20 Nm).

13. Connect the pressure line-to-pump fitting. Tighten to 48 ft. lbs. (65 Nm).

14. Connect the reservoir-to-pump hose.

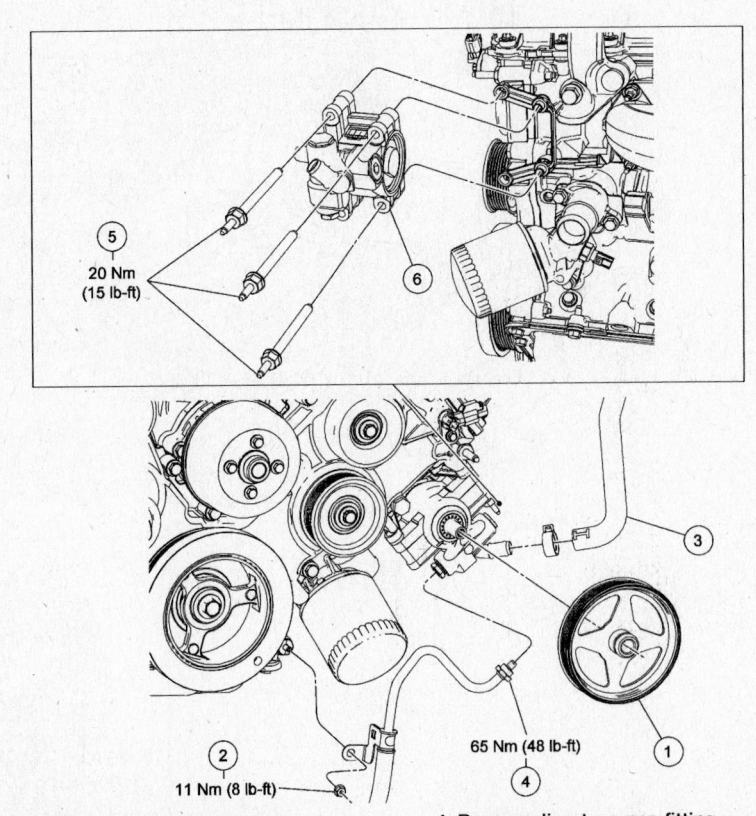

1. Power steering pump pulley
2. Pressure line bracket-to-engine nut
3. Power steering fluid reservoir-to-pump hose
4. Pressure line-to-pump fitting
5. Upper/ lower power steering pump bolts (3 required)
6. Power steering pump

Fig. 389 Showing the power steering pump, hoses and reservoir mounting—2006–07 4.6L (VIN 8) SOHC Engine

15. Install the pressure line bracket-to-engine nut. Tighten to 8 ft. lbs. (11 Nm).

16. Install the power steering pump pulley.

17. Fill the power steering system.

4.6L (VIN H) DOHC Engine

See Figure 390.

✳✳ WARNING

While repairing the power steering system, care should be taken to prevent the entry of contaminants or pre-mature failure of the power steering components can result.

➡**Remove the parts in the order indicated in the following illustration and table.**

1. Remove or disconnect the following:
- (1) Power steering return line clamp
- (2) Power steering return line
- (3) Reservoir-to-pump hose upper clamp
- (4) Reservoir-to-pump hose
- (5) Power steering fluid reservoir upper bolts
- (6) Power steering fluid reservoir lower bolt
- (7) Power steering fluid reservoir
- (8) Belt tensioner
- (9) Reservoir-to-pump hose lower clamp
- (10) Reservoir-to-pump hose
- (11) Pressure line-to-engine retaining nut
- (12) Power steering pressure line

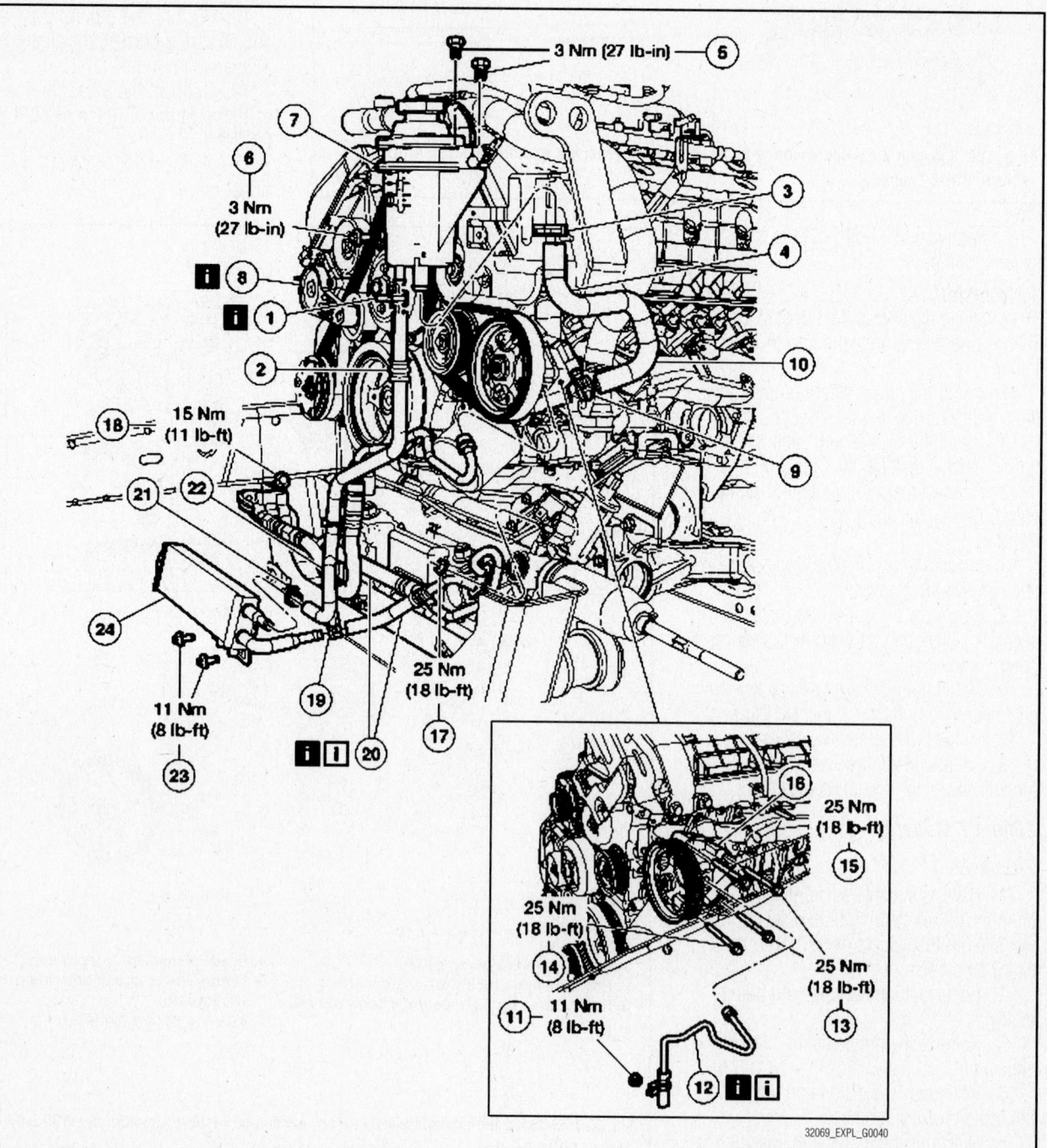

Fig. 390 Removing power steering pump—4.6L (VIN H) DOHC Engine

32069_EXPL_G0040

- (13) Power steering pump bolts (2 required)
- (14) Power steering pump bolt
- (15) Power steering pump bolt
- (16) Power steering pump and pulley
- (17) Pressure line-to-steering gear retaining nut
- (18) Pressure line-to-frame retaining bolt
- (19) Clamp
- (20) Power steering pressure line
- (21) Clamp
- (22) Power steering reservoir-to-cooler return line
- (23) Power steering cooler bolts
- (24) Power steering cooler

2. Installation is the reverse of removal
3. Fill and leak check the system.

FILLING AND BLEEDING

Special tools:
- Vacuum Pump Kit 416-D002 (D95L-7559-A) or equivalent
- Evacuation Cap, Power Steering 211-265 or equivalent

❊❊ WARNING

If the air is not purged from the power steering system correctly, premature power steering pump failure can result. The condition can occur on pre-delivery vehicles with evidence of aerated fluid or on vehicles that have had steering component repairs.

➥A whine heard from the power steering pump can be caused by air in the system. The power steering purge procedure must be carried out prior to any component repair for which power steering noise complaints are accompanied by evidence of aerated fluid.

1. Remove the power steering pump reservoir cap. Check the fluid.
2. Raise the front wheels off the ground.
3. Tightly insert the stopper of the vacuum pump into the reservoir.
4. Start the engine.
5. Install the vacuum pump, apply vacuum, and maintain the maximum vacuum of 20–25 in-Hg (68–85 kPa).
6. If equipped with Hydro-Boost®, apply the brake pedal twice.

❊❊ WARNING

Do not hold the steering wheel against the stops for more than 3 to 5 seconds at a time. Damage to the power steering pump can occur.

7. Cycle the steering wheel fully from stop-to-stop 10 times.
8. Stop the engine.
9. Release the vacuum and remove the vacuum pump.

❊❊ WARNING

Do not overfill the reservoir.

10. Fill the reservoir.
   a. Use approved transmission fluid.
11. Start the engine.
12. Install the vacuum pump. Apply and maintain the maximum vacuum of 20–25 in-Hg (68–85 kPa).

❊❊ WARNING

Do not hold the steering wheel against the stops for more than 3 to 5 seconds at a time. Damage to the power steering pump can occur.

13. Cycle the steering wheel fully from stop-to-stop 10 times.
14. Stop the engine, release the vacuum and remove the vacuum pump.

❊❊ WARNING

Do not overfill the reservoir.

15. Fill the reservoir as needed and install the reservoir cap.
16. Visually inspect the power steering system for leaks.

❊❊ WARNING

Do not overfill the reservoir.

17. Fill the reservoir as needed and visually inspect the power steering system for leaks.
18. Install the reservoir cap.

SUSPENSION   FRONT SUSPENSION

❊❊ WARNING

Suspension fasteners are critical components because they affect performance of vital components and systems and their failure can result in major service expense. New fasteners must be installed with the same component number or an equivalent component if installation is necessary. Do not use a replacement component of lesser quality or substitute design. Torque values must be used as specified during reassembly to make sure of correct retention of these components. Orientation of the fasteners is also important. Make sure the fasteners are installed in the same direction as they were in when removed.

COIL SPRING

REMOVAL & INSTALLATION

Aviator, Explorer and Mountaineer

See Figures 391 through 393.

1. Before servicing the vehicle, refer to the "Precautions" section.
2. Remove the shock absorber and spring assembly.
3. Using a suitable spring compressor, compress the spring until the tension is released from the shock absorber.
4. While holding the flats of the washer, remove and discard the center nut.
5. Remove the shock absorber.
6. Remove the washer.
7. Remove the upper shock absorber mount.

➥Some configurations may have an insulator and support disks under the upper mount.

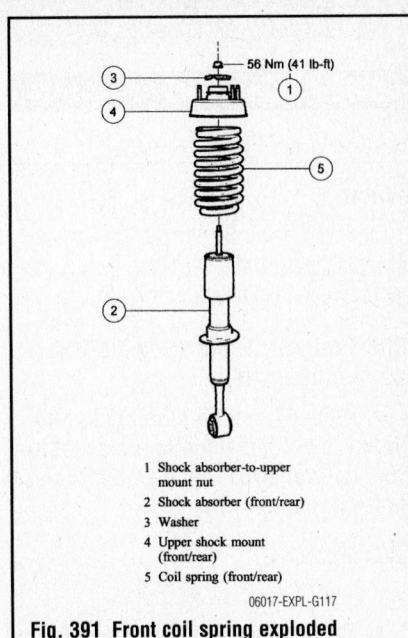

56 Nm (41 lb-ft)

1 Shock absorber-to-upper mount nut
2 Shock absorber (front/rear)
3 Washer
4 Upper shock mount (front/rear)
5 Coil spring (front/rear)

06017-EXPL-G117

Fig. 391 Front coil spring exploded view—Aviator, Explorer and Mountaineer

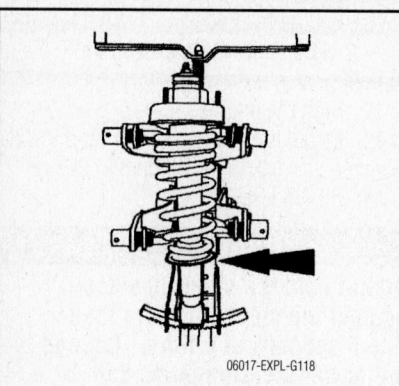

Fig. 392 Spring mounted in compressor—Aviator, Explorer and Mountaineer

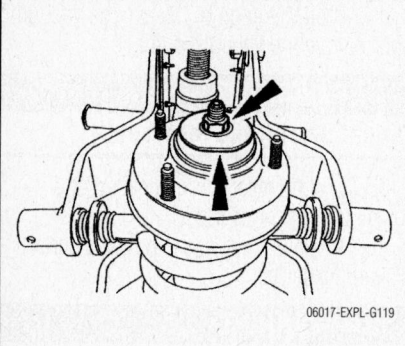

Fig. 393 Center nut removal—Aviator, Explorer and Mountaineer

8. Remove the coil spring.

9. To assemble, reverse the disassembly procedure. Always install a new shock absorber-to-upper mount nut as follows:

   a. 2005: 41 ft. lbs. (56 Nm)
   b. 2006–07: 48 ft. lbs. (65 Nm)

LOWER BALL JOINT

REMOVAL & INSTALLATION

Aviator

The lower ball joints on the Aviator are not replaceable. If the ball requires replacement replace the lower control arm.

2005 Explorer, Explorer Sport-Trac and Mountaineer

➡On 2006–07 models, the lower ball joints are not individually replaceable. If the ball requires replacement replace the lower control arm.

2WD Models

See Figure 394.

1. Before servicing the vehicle, refer to the "Precautions" section.

2. With the vehicle in NEUTRAL, position it on a hoist.

3. Remove the wheel and tire assembly.

> **⁑ WARNING**
>
> **Do not allow the disc brake caliper to hang suspended from the brake hose. Provide a suitable support.**

4. Remove the caliper support bracket bolts, then position the caliper and support bracket aside.

5. Disconnect the ABS electrical connector.

6. Unclip the front ABS wire from the vehicle frame.

7. Using a suitable jack, support the front suspension lower arm.

8. Remove the tie rod end castellated nut. Remove and discard the cotter pin and the castellated nut.

> **⁑ WARNING**
>
> **Do not use a hammer to separate the tie rod from the wheel knuckle or damage to the wheel knuckle will result.**

> **⁑ WARNING**
>
> **Do not damage the tie rod boot when installing the special tool.**

9. Separate the tie rod end from the front wheel knuckle.

10. Remove the lower ball joint castellated nut.

11. Separate the front wheel knuckle from the front suspension lower arm. Then, loosely install the lower ball joint castellated nut.

12. Remove the pinch bolt and nut.

13. Remove the hand-tightened lower ball joint castellated nut, then remove the front wheel knuckle.

14. Remove the snap ring from the ball joint. Discard the snap ring.

15. Using a suitable ball joint remover tool, remove the ball joint.

> **⁑ WARNING**
>
> **Do not damage the ball joint boot when installing the special tool.**

To install:

16. Installation is the reverse of the removal procedure.

➡**Clean and inspect the control arm ball joint bore for damage before installing a new ball joint.**

➡**Make sure the new ball joint snap ring is fully seated.**

17. Always install new castellated nuts and cotter pins.

18. Observe the following ball joint nut torques:

- Explorer Sport-Trac: 98 ft. lbs. (133 Nm)
- Explorer and Mountaineer: 129 ft. lbs. (175 Nm)

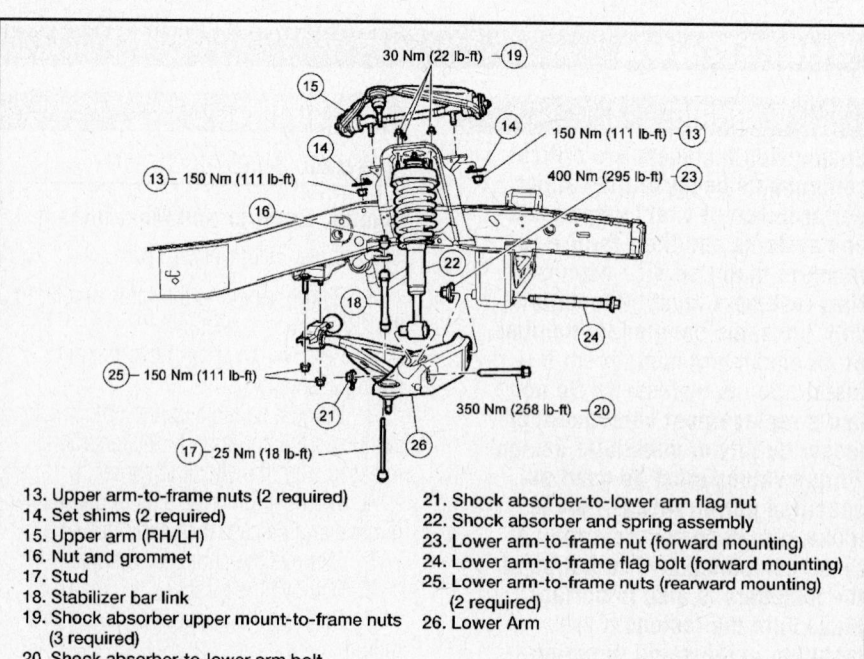

13. Upper arm-to-frame nuts (2 required)
14. Set shims (2 required)
15. Upper arm (RH/LH)
16. Nut and grommet
17. Stud
18. Stabilizer bar link
19. Shock absorber upper mount-to-frame nuts (3 required)
20. Shock absorber-to-lower arm bolt
21. Shock absorber-to-lower arm flag nut
22. Shock absorber and spring assembly
23. Lower arm-to-frame nut (forward mounting)
24. Lower arm-to-frame flag bolt (forward mounting)
25. Lower arm-to-frame nuts (rearward mounting) (2 required)
26. Lower Arm

Fig. 394 Exploded view of the front suspension components—2005 2WD models

19. During installation, torque the remaining fasteners as follows:
- Tie rod end ball stud nut: 52 ft. lbs. (70 Nm)
- Pinch bolt: 41 ft. lbs. (55 Nm)

4WD Models

1. Before servicing the vehicle, refer to the "Precautions" section.
2. With the vehicle in NEUTRAL, position it on a hoist.
3. Remove the wheel and tire assembly.

❊❊ WARNING
Do not reuse the torque prevailing design hub nut and washer assembly.

4. Remove and discard the hub nut and washer assembly.

❊❊ WARNING
Do not allow the disc brake caliper to hang suspended from the brake hose. Provide a suitable support.

5. Remove the caliper support bracket bolts, then position the caliper and support bracket aside.
6. Remove the brake disc.

❊❊ WARNING
Do not use a hammer to separate the outboard front wheel halfshaft joint from the wheel hub. Damage to the outboard CV-joint stub shaft threads and internal CV-joint components may result.

7. Separate the outboard front wheel halfshaft joint from the wheel hub.
8. Disconnect the ABS electrical connector.
9. Unclip the front ABS wire from the vehicle frame.
10. Using a suitable jack, support the front suspension lower arm.

❊❊ WARNING
Secure the front axle shaft to prevent it from overextending. Failure to do so can cause damage to the front axle shaft.

11. Support the front axle shaft with wire.
12. Remove the tie rod end castellated nut. Discard the cotter pin. Discard the castellated nut.

❊❊ WARNING
Do not use a hammer to separate the tie rod from the wheel knuckle or

damage to the wheel knuckle will result.

❊❊ WARNING
Do not damage the tie rod boot when installing the special tool.

13. Separate the tie rod end from the front wheel knuckle.
14. Remove the lower ball joint castellated nut. Discard the cotter pin. Discard the castellated nut.
15. Separate the front wheel knuckle from the front suspension lower arm then, loosely install the lower ball joint castellated nut.
16. Remove the pinch bolt and nut.
17. Remove the hand-tightened lower ball joint castellated nut, then remove the front wheel knuckle.
18. Remove the snap ring from the ball joint. Discard the snap ring.
19. Using a suitable ball joint remover tool, remove the ball joint.

❊❊ WARNING
Do not damage the ball joint boot when installing the special tool.

To install:
20. Installation is the reverse of the removal procedure.

➡ **Clean and inspect the control arm ball joint bore for damage before installing a new ball joint.**

➡ **Make sure the new ball joint snap ring is fully seated.**

21. Always install new castellated nuts and cotter pins. Observe the following torques:
- Hub nut to 162 ft. lbs. (220 Nm) for Explorer Sport-Trac models; 184 ft. lbs. (250 Nm) for Explorer and Mountaineer models.
- Tie rod end nut to 52 ft. lbs. (70 Nm)
- Ball joint nut to 98 ft. lbs. (133 Nm) for Explorer Sport-Trac models; 129 ft. lbs. (175 Nm) for Explorer and Mountaineer models
- Pinch bolt to 41 ft. lbs. (55 Nm).

LOWER CONTROL ARM

REMOVAL AND & INSTALLATION

2005 Aviator, Explorer and Mountaineer

1. Before servicing the vehicle, refer to the "Precautions" section.
2. Remove or disconnect the following:

➡ **For reference during the installation procedure, measure the distance from the lip of the fender to the center of the wheel hub with the vehicle in a level static ground position.**

- Wheel
- Upper shock absorber mounting nuts. Discard the nuts.
- Stabilizer bar connecting link. Discard the nut.
- Bolt, flag nut and the spring and shock assembly. Discard the flag nut.
- Separate the ball joint from the wheel knuckle. Discard the nut.
- Arm-to-frame nuts. Discard the nuts.
- Arm-to-knuckle bolt. Discard the nut.

➡ **On 4×4 vehicles, make sure that the crimped area of the outer CV boot clamp is not positioned downward or it will interfere with the removal of the arm.**

- Lower arm

To install:
3. Installation is the reverse of the removal procedure.

➡ **Using a suitable jack stand, raise the suspension until the distance between the lip of the fender and the center of the wheel hub is equal to the measurement taken in the removal procedure before tightening the inboard lower arm mountings. Make sure that the forward mounting is tightened first.**

4. Observe the following torque specifications:
- Control arm-to-frame flag bolt: 295 ft. lbs. (400 Nm)
- Control arm-to-frame nuts: 111 ft. lbs. (150 Nm)
- Ball joint nut: 129 ft. lbs. (175 Nm) for 4wd Explorer/Mountaineer; 111 ft. lbs. (150 Nm) for Aviator and 2wd Explorer/Mountaineer
- Shock lower flag bolt: 258 ft. lbs. (350 Nm)
- Sway bar link nut: 18 ft. lbs. (25 Nm)
- Upper shock mounting nuts: 22 ft. lbs. (30 Nm)

5. Check and, if necessary, align the front end.

2005 Explorer Sport-Trac

1. Before servicing the vehicle, refer to the "Precautions" section.
2. Remove the wheel and tire assembly.

3. Remove the stabilizer link nut, washer and bushing.

4. Remove the front shock absorber-to-front suspension lower arm nuts.

5. Remove the torsion bar.

6. Remove the cotter pin and the nut.

✳✳ WARNING

Do not use a hammer to separate the ball joint from the wheel knuckle or damage to the wheel knuckle will result. Do not damage the ball joint boot while installing the special tool.

7. Using a puller, separate the front suspension lower arm from the front wheel knuckle/spindle.

8. Remove the front suspension lower arm bolts and nuts.

9. Remove the front suspension lower arm.

To install:

10. Installation is the reverse of the removal procedure.

11. Observe the following torque specifications:

- Stabilizer bar link: 18 ft. lbs. (25 Nm)
- Shock absorber-to-lower arm: 18 ft. lbs. (25 Nm)
- Ball joint stud nut: 98 ft. lbs. (133 Nm)
- Lower arm nuts: 148 ft. lbs. (200 Nm)

12. Check and, if necessary, adjust the ride height.

13. Check and, if necessary, align the front end.

2006–07 Explorer and Mountaineer; 2007 Sport-Trac

See Figure 395.

1. Before servicing the vehicle, refer to the "Precautions" section.

2. With the vehicle in NEUTRAL, position it on a hoist.

3. Remove and discard the lower ball joint nut.

4. Using a proper tool, separate the lower ball joint from the wheel knuckle.

5. Remove the following:
- Stabilizer bar link nut (discard the nut)
- Stabilizer bar link assembly
- Shock absorber lower bolt and flag nut (discard the fasteners)
- Lower arm forward nut and bolt (discard the fasteners)
- Lower arm rearward nut and bolt and the lower control arm

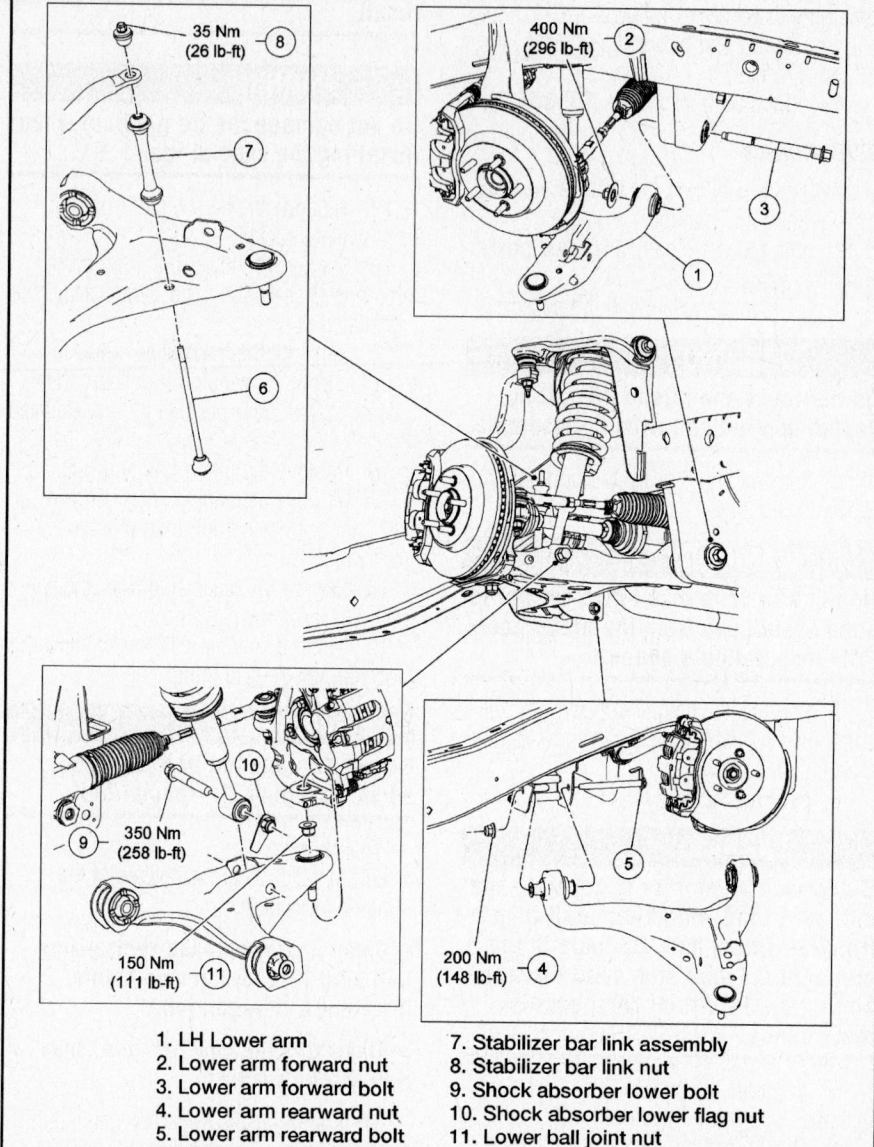

1. LH Lower arm
2. Lower arm forward nut
3. Lower arm forward bolt
4. Lower arm rearward nut
5. Lower arm rearward bolt
6. Stabilizer bar link stud
7. Stabilizer bar link assembly
8. Stabilizer bar link nut
9. Shock absorber lower bolt
10. Shock absorber lower flag nut
11. Lower ball joint nut

22086_EXPL_G0183

Fig. 395 Exploded view of the front suspension, showing the lower control arm and components—2006–07 models

To install:

✳✳ CAUTION

Before tightening any suspension bushing fasteners, use a suitable jack to raise the suspension until the distance between the center of the hub and the lip of the fender is equal to the measurement taken in Step 1 (curb height).

6. Installation is the reverse of the removal procedure, using new fasteners.

7. Note the following tightening specifications:

- Lower control arm rearward nut and bolt: 148 ft. lbs. (200 Nm)
- Lower arm forward nut and bolt: 296 ft. lbs. (400 Nm)
- Shock absorber lower bolt and flag nut: 258 ft. lbs. (350 Nm)
- Stabilizer bar link nut: 26 ft. lbs. (35 Nm)
- Lower ball joint nut: 111 ft. lbs. (150 Nm)

LOWER CONTROL ARM BUSHING REPLACEMENT

The control arm bushings are not serviceable. If they require service, the upper or lower arm must be replaced.

SHOCK ABSORBERS

REMOVAL & INSTALLATION

Aviator, Explorer and Mountaineer

2005 Models

See Figure 396.

1. Before servicing the vehicle, refer to the "Precautions" section.
2. Remove or disconnect the following:
   - Wheel
   - Upper shock mounting nuts. Discard the nuts.
   - Nut and the stabilizer bar link. Discard the nut.
   - Bolt, flag nut and the spring and shock absorber as an assembly. Discard the flag nut.
3. Using a suitable spring compressor, compress the spring until the tension is released from the shock absorber.
4. While holding the flats of the washer, remove the nut.

5. Remove the shock absorber. Discard the nut, remove the washer, bushing and the upper mount.
6. Remove the insulator.
7. Remove the dust shield.

To install:

8. Installation is the reverse of the removal procedure.
9. Observe the following torque specifications:
   - Center nut: 37 ft. lbs. (50 Nm)
   - Lower shock bolt: 258 ft. lbs. (350 Nm).
   - Sway bar link nut: 18 ft. lbs. (25 Nm)
   - Upper shock nuts: 20 ft. lbs. (30 Nm)

2006–07 Models

See Figures 397 and 398.

✳✳ WARNING

All vehicles are equipped with gas-pressurized shock absorbers which will extend unassisted. Do not apply heat or flame to the shock absorbers during removal or component servicing. Failure to follow these instructions may result in personal injury.

1. Before servicing the vehicle, refer to the "Precautions" section.
2. Measure the distance from the center of the hub to the lip of the fender with the vehicle in a level, static ground position (curb height).
3. Remove and discard the 3 shock absorber upper mount nuts.
4. With the vehicle in NEUTRAL, position it on a hoist.
5. Using a suitable jack, support the lower control arm near the lower ball joint.
6. Remove and discard the stabilizer bar link nut and grommet and then remove the stabilizer bar link assembly.
7. Remove the shock absorber lower bolt and flag nut.
8. Remove and discard the upper ball joint nut.

✳✳ CAUTION

Do not use a hammer to separate the ball joint from the wheel knuckle or damage to the wheel knuckle can result.

9. Using the proper separator tool, separate the upper ball joint from the wheel knuckle.
10. While lowering the suspension, remove the shock and spring assembly.

To install:

➡Before tightening any suspension bushing fasteners, use a suitable jack to raise the suspension until the distance between the center of the hub and the lip of the fender is equal to the measurement taken in Step 1 (curb height).

11. Position the shock absorber and spring assembly and raise the suspension into normal position.
12. Install a new upper ball joint nut. Torque to 41 ft. lbs. (55 Nm).
13. Install the lower shock absorber bolt and flag nut. Torque to 258 ft. lbs. (350 Nm).
14. Install a new stabilizer bar link nut and grommet. Torque to 26 ft. lbs. (35 Nm).
15. Install 3 new upper shock mounting nuts. Torque to 22 ft. lbs. (30 Nm).
16. Lower the vehicle.

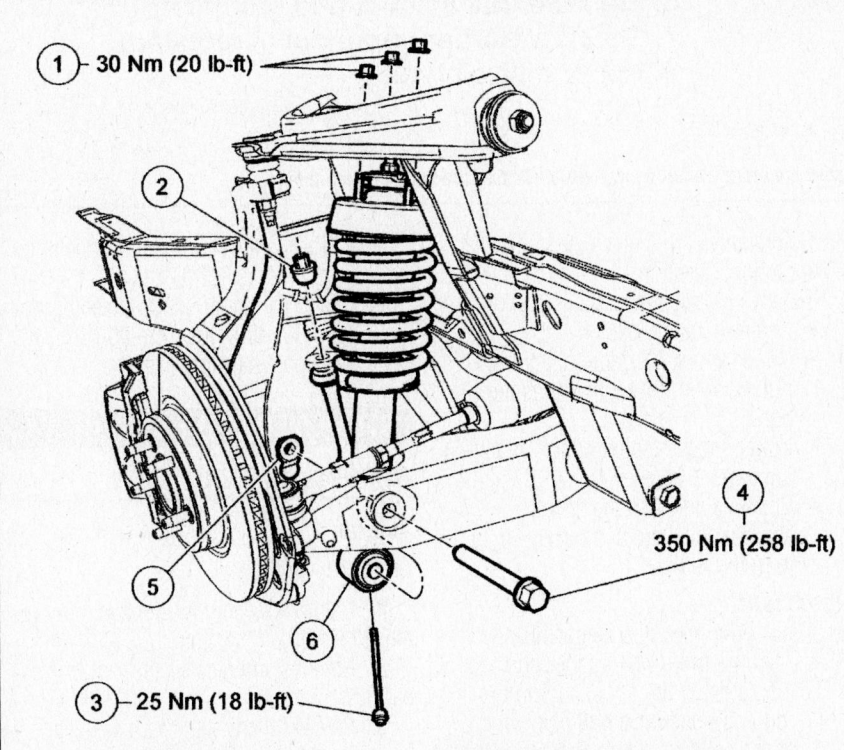

① 30 Nm (20 lb-ft)

350 Nm (258 lb-ft)

③ 25 Nm (18 lb-ft)

1	Shock absorber upper mount-to-frame nuts (3 required)	4	Shock absorber-to-lower arm bolt
2	Nut and grommet	5	Shock absorber-to-lower arm flag nut
3	Stud	6	Shock absorber and spring assembly

06017-EXPL-G115

Fig. 396 Front shock absorber and spring—Aviator, Explorer and Mountaineer

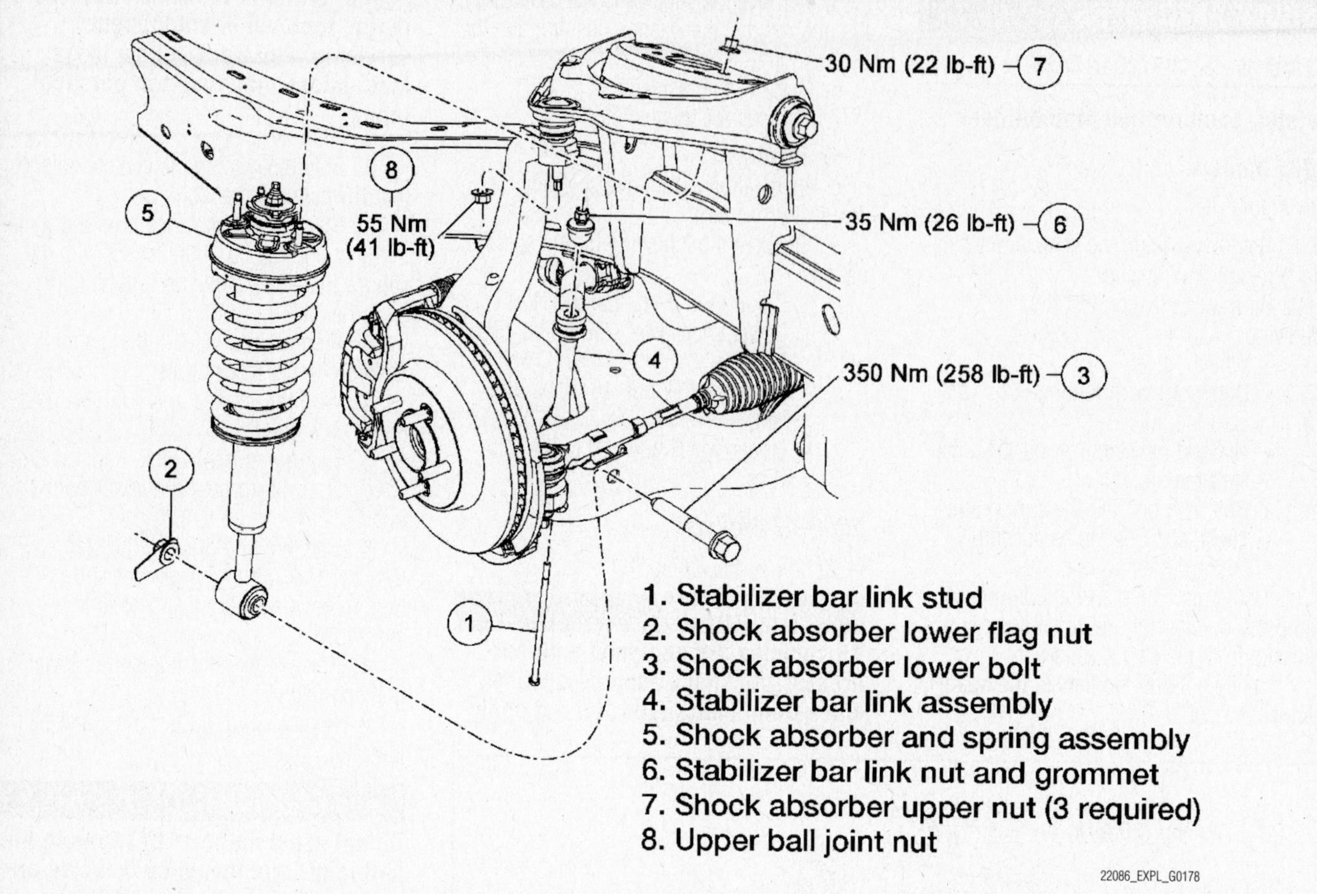

30 Nm (22 lb-ft) — 7

55 Nm (41 lb-ft)

35 Nm (26 lb-ft) — 6

350 Nm (258 lb-ft) — 3

1. Stabilizer bar link stud
2. Shock absorber lower flag nut
3. Shock absorber lower bolt
4. Stabilizer bar link assembly
5. Shock absorber and spring assembly
6. Stabilizer bar link nut and grommet
7. Shock absorber upper nut (3 required)
8. Upper ball joint nut

22086_EXPL_G0178

Fig. 397 Shock absorber and spring assembly and related mounting components—2006–07 Explorer and Mountaineer

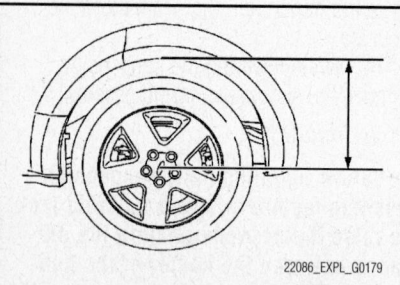

22086_EXPL_G0179

Fig. 398 Measure the distance from the center of the hub to the lip of the fender with the vehicle in a level, static ground position (curb height)—2006–07 Explorer and Mountaineer

Explorer Sport-Trac

2005 Models

➡Low pressure gas shocks are charged with nitrogen gas. Do not attempt to open, puncture or apply heat to them. Prior to installing a new shock absorber, hold it upright and extend it fully. Invert it and fully compress and extend it at least 3 times. This will bleed trapped air.

1. Before servicing the vehicle, refer to the "Precautions" section.
2. Remove or disconnect the following:
   • Negative battery cable
   • Upper shock-to-frame attaching nut, washer and insulator assembly
   • Lower shock-to-control arm attaching nuts
   • Slightly compress the shock absorber by hand and remove it from the vehicle

To install:

3. Install or connect the following:
   • Position the lower washer and insulator on the shock absorber rod and position the shock absorber to the upper frame bracket mount
   • Position the upper insulator and washer on the shock absorber rod and install the attaching nut loosely.
   • Position the lower shock absorber mounting studs into the control arm and install the attaching nuts loosely.

• Torque the lower shock attaching nuts to 15–21 ft. lbs. (21–29 Nm), and the upper shock attaching bolts to 30–40 ft. lbs. (40–55 Nm).
• Negative battery cable

STABILIZER BAR

REMOVAL & INSTALLATION

Aviator

See Figure 399.

1. Before servicing the vehicle, refer to the "Precautions" section.
2. Remove and discard the 2 stabilizer bar nuts.
3. Remove the 2 stabilizer bar links.

➡Inspect and clean the mating surfaces and the internal threads. Make sure all mating surfaces are free of foreign material and remove any thread locking compound from the internal threads.

4. Remove and discard the 4 stabilizer bar-to-frame bolts.
5. Remove the stabilizer bar.

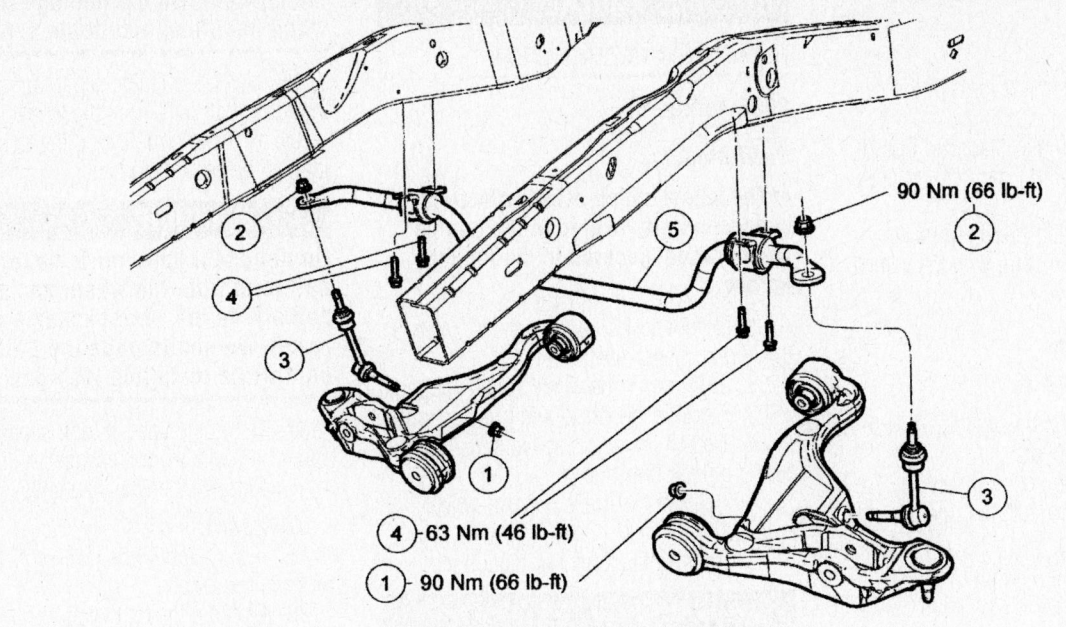

90 Nm (66 lb-ft)

4 - 63 Nm (46 lb-ft)

1 - 90 Nm (66 lb-ft)

1 Stabilizer bar link-to-lower arm nut
2 Stabilizer bar link-to-stabilizer bar nut
3 Stabilizer bar link
4 Stabilizer bar-to-frame bolts
5 Stabilizer bar, bushing and bracket assembly

06017-EXPL-G120

Fig. 399 Front stabilizer bar—Aviator

To install:

6. Installation is the reverse the removal procedure.

7. Always install new stabilizer bar-to-frame bolts.

8. See the accompanying illustration for relevant torque values.

Explorer and Mountaineer

See Figure 400.

1. Before servicing the vehicle, refer to the "Precautions" section.

2. Remove and discard the 2 stabilizer bar nut and grommets.

3. Remove the 2 stabilizer bar studs.

4. Remove the 2 stabilizer bar links.

➡ Inspect and clean the mating surfaces and the internal threads. Make sure all mating surfaces are free of foreign material and remove any thread locking compound from the internal threads.

5. Remove and discard the 4 stabilizer bar-to-frame bolts.

6. Remove the 2 stabilizer bar brackets.

7. Remove the stabilizer bar.

➡ Inspect the bushings for wear or damage. Install new bushings as necessary.

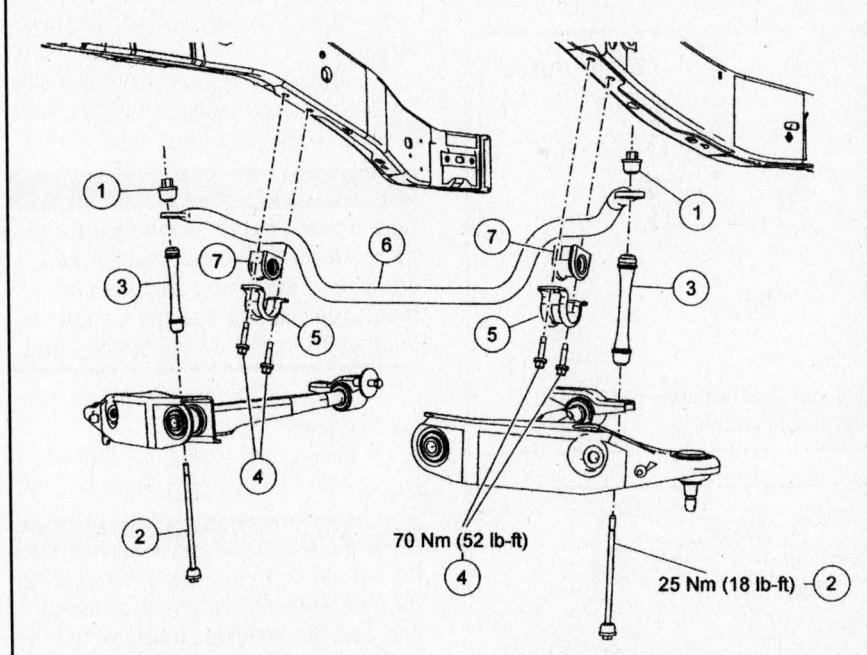

70 Nm (52 lb-ft)

25 Nm (18 lb-ft)

1 Nut and grommet (2 required)
2 Stud (2 required)
3 Stabilizer bar link (2 required)
4 Stabilizer bar-to-frame bolts (4 required)
5 Bracket (2 required)
6 Stabilizer bar
7 Bushing (2 required)

06017-EXPL-G121

Fig. 400 Front stabilizer bar—Explorer and Mountaineer

8. Remove the 2 stabilizer bar bushings.

To install:

9. Installation is the reverse of the removal procedure

10. Always install new stabilizer bar-to-frame bolts and stabilizer bar nut and grommets.

11. Tighten the stabilizer bar bracket bolts to 41 ft. lbs. (55 Nm), with the vehicle at curb weight.

Explorer Sport-Trac

See Figures 401 and 402.

1. Before servicing the vehicle, refer to the "Precautions" section.

2. Raise and support the vehicle.

3. Remove the two nuts and the two stabilizer bar links.

4. Remove the four bolts on the front stabilizer bar brackets and bushings.

To install:

5. Installation is the reverse of the removal procedure

6. Observe the following tightening specifications:

- Link nuts 18 ft. lbs. (25 Nm)
- Bracket bolts 30 ft. lbs. (40 Nm).

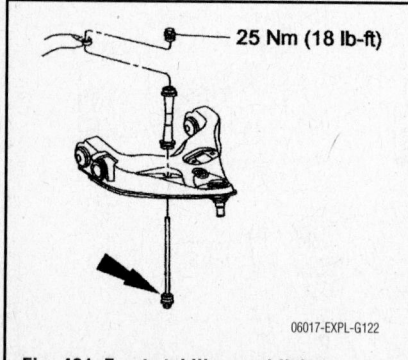

25 Nm (18 lb-ft)

06017-EXPL-G122

Fig. 401 Front stabilizer end links—Explorer Sport-Trac

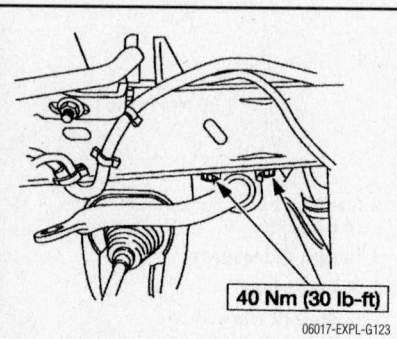

40 Nm (30 lb-ft)

06017-EXPL-G123

Fig. 402 Front stabilizer bar brackets—Explorer Sport-Trac

STEERING KNUCKLE

REMOVAL & INSTALLATION

2005 Aviator

2WD Models

➡The wheel speed sensor electrical connectors are located in the engine compartment secured to the fender aprons.

1. Before servicing the vehicle, refer to the "Precautions" section.
2. Disconnect the wheel speed sensor.
3. Remove the wheel and tire assembly.
4. Detach the wheel speed sensor harness from the brake hose.
5. Remove the brake hose-to-wheel knuckle bolt.
6. Remove the 2 anchor plate bolts.

> ※※ **WARNING**
>
> Do not allow the brake caliper to hang from the hose or damage to the hose can occur.

7. Position the caliper, pads and anchor plate aside.
8. Remove the brake disc.
9. Remove and discard the 3 wheel hub-to-wheel knuckle bolts.
10. Remove the wheel bearing and hub assembly.
11. Remove the discard the 2 cotter pins.
12. Remove and discard the tie rod end-to-wheel knuckle castellated nut.

> ※※ **WARNING**
>
> Do not use a hammer to separate the tie rod from the wheel knuckle or damage to the wheel knuckle can result. Do not damage the tie rod boot while installing the special tool.

13. Using a puller, separate the tie rod from the wheel knuckle.
14. Remove and discard the lower ball joint-to-wheel knuckle castellated nut.

> ※※ **WARNING**
>
> Do not use a prying device or separator fork between the upper or lower arm and the knuckle. Damage to the ball joint or ball joint dust boot can result. Do not strike the wheel knuckle with a hammer to separate the ball joint from the wheel knuckle. Damage to the wheel knuckle can result. Make sure to apply direct force to the end of the ball joint stud when separating the ball joint from

the knuckle. Do not damage the boot when installing a suitable separator.

15. Using a suitable separator, separate the lower ball joint from the wheel knuckle.
16. Remove and discard the upper ball joint-to-wheel knuckle nut.

> ※※ **WARNING**
>
> Do not use a hammer to separate the ball joint from the wheel knuckle or damage to the wheel knuckle can result. Do not damage the ball joint boot while installing the special tool.

17. Using the special tool, separate the upper ball joint from the wheel knuckle.
18. Remove the wheel knuckle.

To install:

19. Installation is the reverse of the removal procedure.

20. Observe the following torque specifications:

- Upper ball joint stud nut: 38 ft. lbs. (52 Nm)
- Lower ball joint stud nut: 111 ft. lbs. (150 Nm)
- Tie rod end stud nut: 52 ft. lbs. (70 Nm)
- Wheel hub-to-wheel knuckle bolts: 83 ft. lbs. (112 Nm)
- Anchor plate bolts: 155 ft. lbs. (210 Nm)

21. Check and, if necessary, align the front end.

22. Always install new:

- Wheel hub-to-wheel knuckle bolts.
- Cotter pins.
- Castellated nuts.
- Upper ball joint-to-wheel knuckle nut.

4WD Models

1. Before servicing the vehicle, refer to the "Precautions" section.
2. Loosen the axle retainer nut.

➡The wheel speed sensor electrical connectors are located in the engine compartment secured to the fender aprons.

3. Disconnect the wheel speed sensor.
4. Remove the wheel and tire assembly.
5. Remove and discard the axle retainer nut.
6. Separate the outboard CV-joint from the wheel hub.
7. Detach the wheel speed sensor harness from the brake hose.
8. Remove the brake hose-to-wheel knuckle bolt.
9. Remove the 2 anchor plate bolts.

> ※※ **WARNING**
>
> **Do not allow the brake caliper to hang from the hose or damage to the hose can occur.**

10. Position the caliper, pads and anchor plate aside.

11. Remove the brake disc.

12. Remove and discard the 3 wheel hub-to-wheel knuckle bolts.

13. Remove the wheel bearing and hub assembly.

14. Remove the discard the 2 cotter pins.

15. Remove and discard the tie rod end-to-wheel knuckle castellated nut.

> ※※ **WARNING**
>
> **Do not use a hammer to separate the tie rod from the wheel knuckle or damage to the wheel knuckle can result. Do not damage the tie rod boot while installing the special tool.**

16. Separate the tie rod from the wheel knuckle.

17. Remove and discard the lower ball joint-to-wheel knuckle castellated nut.

> ※※ **WARNING**
>
> **Do not use a hammer to separate the ball joint from the wheel knuckle or damage to the wheel knuckle can result. Do not damage the ball joint boot while installing the special tool.**

18. Separate the lower ball joint from the wheel knuckle.

19. Remove and discard the upper ball joint-to-wheel knuckle nut.

> ※※ **WARNING**
>
> **Do not use a hammer to separate the ball joint from the wheel knuckle or damage to the wheel knuckle can result. Do not damage the ball joint boot while installing the special tool.**

20. Separate the upper ball joint from the wheel knuckle.

21. Remove the wheel knuckle.

To install:

22. Installation is the reverse of the removal procedure.

23. Observe the following torque specifications:

- Upper ball joint-to-knuckle nut: 41 ft. lbs. (55 Nm)
- Lower ball joint-to-knuckle nut: 111 ft. lbs. (150 Nm)
- Tie rod end-to-knuckle nut: 52 ft. lbs. (70 Nm)

- Wheel hub-to- knuckle bolts: 83 ft. lbs. (112 Nm)
- Anchor plate bolts: 155 ft. lbs. (210 Nm)
- Axle retainer nut: 184 ft. lbs. (250 Nm)

24. Check and, if necessary, align the front end.

25. Always install new:

- Wheel hub-to-wheel knuckle bolts.
- Cotter pins.
- Castellated nuts.
- Upper ball joint-to-wheel knuckle nut.
- Axle retainer nut.

2005 Explorer and Mountaineer

2WD Models

➡ **The wheel speed sensor electrical connectors are located in the engine compartment secured to the fender aprons.**

1. Before servicing the vehicle, refer to the "Precautions" section.

2. Disconnect the wheel speed sensor.

3. Remove the wheel and tire assembly.

4. Detach the wheel speed sensor harness from the brake hose.

5. Remove the brake hose-to-wheel knuckle bolt.

6. Remove the 2 anchor plate bolts.

> ※※ **WARNING**
>
> **Do not allow the brake caliper to hang from the hose or damage to the hose can occur.**

7. Position the caliper, pads and anchor plate aside.

8. Remove the brake disc.

9. Remove and discard the 3 wheel hub-to-wheel knuckle bolts.

10. Remove the wheel bearing and hub assembly.

11. Remove the discard the 2 cotter pins.

12. Remove and discard the tie rod end-to-wheel knuckle castellated nut.

> ※※ **WARNING**
>
> **Do not use a hammer to separate the tie rod from the wheel knuckle or damage to the wheel knuckle can result. Do not damage the tie rod boot while installing the special tool.**

13. Separate the tie rod from the wheel knuckle.

14. Remove and discard the lower ball joint-to-wheel knuckle castellated nut.

> ※※ **WARNING**
>
> **Do not use a hammer to separate the ball joint from the wheel knuckle or damage to the wheel knuckle can result. Do not damage the ball joint boot while installing the special tool.**

15. Separate the lower ball joint from the wheel knuckle.

16. Remove and discard the upper ball joint-to-wheel knuckle nut.

> ※※ **WARNING**
>
> **Do not use a hammer to separate the ball joint from the wheel knuckle or damage to the wheel knuckle can result. Do not damage the ball joint boot while installing the special tool.**

17. Separate the upper ball joint from the wheel knuckle.

18. Remove the wheel knuckle.

To install:

19. Installation is the reverse of the removal procedure.

20. Observe the following torque specifications:

- Upper ball joint-to-knuckle nut: 38 ft. lbs. (52 Nm)
- Lower ball joint-to-knuckle nut: 111 ft. lbs. (150 Nm)
- Tie rod end-to-knuckle nut: 52 ft. lbs. (70 Nm)
- Hub-to-wheel knuckle bolts: 83 ft. lbs. (112 Nm)
- Anchor plate bolts: 83 ft. lbs. (112 Nm)

21. Check and, if necessary, align the front end.

22. Always install new:

- Wheel hub-to-wheel knuckle bolts.
- Cotter pins.
- Castellated nuts.
- Upper ball joint-to-wheel knuckle nut.

4WD Models

1. Before servicing the vehicle, refer to the "Precautions" section.

2. Loosen the axle retainer nut.

➡ **The wheel speed sensor electrical connectors are located in the engine compartment secured to the fender aprons.**

3. Disconnect the wheel speed sensor.

4. Remove the wheel and tire assembly.

5. Remove and discard the axle retainer nut.

6. Using the special tool, separate the outboard CV-joint from the wheel hub.

7. Detach the wheel speed sensor harness from the brake hose.

8. Remove the brake hose-to-wheel knuckle bolt.

9. Remove the 2 anchor plate bolts.

> ✳✳ **WARNING**
>
> **Do not allow the brake caliper to hang from the hose or damage to the hose can occur.**

10. Position the caliper, pads and anchor plate aside.

11. Remove the brake disc.

12. Remove and discard the 3 wheel hub-to-wheel knuckle bolts.

13. Remove the wheel bearing and hub assembly.

14. Remove the discard the 2 cotter pins.

15. Remove and discard the tie rod end-to-wheel knuckle castellated nut.

> ✳✳ **WARNING**
>
> **Do not use a hammer to separate the tie rod from the wheel knuckle or damage to the wheel knuckle can result. Do not damage the tie rod boot while installing the special tool.**

16. Separate the tie rod from the wheel knuckle.

17. Remove and discard the lower ball joint-to-wheel knuckle castellated nut.

> ✳✳ **WARNING**
>
> **Do not use a hammer to separate the ball joint from the wheel knuckle or damage to the wheel knuckle can result. Do not damage the ball joint boot while installing the special tool.**

18. Separate the lower ball joint from the wheel knuckle.

19. Remove and discard the upper ball joint-to-wheel knuckle nut.

> ✳✳ **WARNING**
>
> **Do not use a hammer to separate the ball joint from the wheel knuckle or damage to the wheel knuckle can result. Do not damage the ball joint boot while installing the special tool.**

20. Using the special tool, separate the upper ball joint from the wheel knuckle.

21. Remove the wheel knuckle.

To install:

22. Installation is the reverse of the removal procedure.

23. Observe the following torque specifications:

- Upper ball joint-to-wheel knuckle nut: 38 ft. lbs. (52 Nm)
- Lower ball joint-to-knuckle nut: 129 ft. lbs. (175 Nm)
- Tie rod end-to-knuckle nut: 52 ft. lbs. (70 Nm)
- Hub-to-wheel knuckle bolts: 83 ft. lbs. (112 Nm)
- Anchor plate bolts: 83 ft. lbs. (112 Nm)
- Axle retainer nut: 184 ft. lbs. (250 Nm)

24. Check and, if necessary, align the front end.

25. Always install new:

- Wheel hub-to-wheel knuckle bolts.
- Cotter pins.
- Castellated nuts.
- Upper ball joint-to-wheel knuckle nut.
- Axle retainer nut.

2005 Explorer Sport-Trac

2WD Models

See Figure 403.

1. Before servicing the vehicle, refer to the "Precautions" section.

2. Remove the brake disc and hub .

3. Remove the anti-lock sensor electrical wire from the clamp. Remove the bolt and position the sensor aside.

4. Remove the cotter pin and nut.

5. Using a puller, separate the tie rod end from the spindle.

6. Use a suitable jack stand to support the lower arm.

> ✳✳ **WARNING**
>
> **To avoid possible damage to the front wheel spindle, secure the spindle to keep it from tilting before removing the pinch bolt and nut.**

7. Remove the nut and pinch bolt.

8. Remove the cotter pin and nut.

9. Using a puller, separate the ball joint and remove the spindle.

To install:

10. Installation is the reverse of the removal procedure.

> ✳✳ **WARNING**
>
> **Install the cotter pin into the lower ball joint from outboard to inboard with the fingers bent together at a right angle. Failure to do so can cause damage to the wheel and tire assembly.**

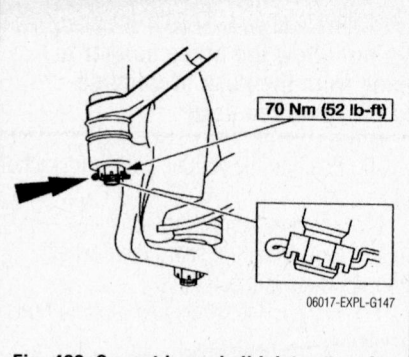

Fig. 403 Correct lower ball joint cotter pin orientation—2005 2WD Explorer Sport-Trac

11. Observe the following torque specifications:

- Lower ball joint stud nut: 98 ft. lbs. (133 Nm)
- Pinch bolt: 41 ft. lbs. (55 Nm)
- Tie rod ball stud nut: 52 ft. lbs. (70 Nm)

4WD Models

1. Before servicing the vehicle, refer to the "Precautions" section.

2. Remove the wheel hub.

3. Remove all tension from the torsion bar. See Torsion Bar Removal & Installation in this Chapter.

> ✳✳ **WARNING**
>
> **Secure the front axle shaft to prevent it from overextending. Failure to do so can cause damage to the front axle shaft.**

4. Suspend the front axle shaft with wire.

5. Remove the tie rod end cotter pin. Remove the tie rod end castellated nut.

6. Separate the tie rod end from the front wheel knuckle.

7. Remove the lower ball joint cotter pin.

8. Remove the lower ball joint castellated nut.

9. Separate the front wheel knuckle from the front suspension lower arm.

10. Remove the pinch bolt and the wheel knuckle.

To install:

11. Installation is the reverse of the removal procedure.

12. Observe the following torque specifications:

- Pinch bolt: 41 ft. lbs. (55 Nm)
- Lower ball joint stud nut: 98 ft. lbs. (133 Nm)

• Tie rod end stud nut: 52 ft. lbs. (70 Nm)

13. Adjust the ride height.

14. Check and if necessary align the front end.

2006–07 Explorer and Mountaineer; 2007 Sport-Trac

✳✳ CAUTION

Suspension fasteners are critical parts because they affect performance of vital components and systems and their failure can result in major service expense. A new part with the same part number or an equivalent part must be installed, if installation is necessary. Do not use a part of lesser quality or substitute design. Torque values must be used as specified during reassembly to make sure of correct retention of these parts.

1. Before servicing the vehicle, refer to the precautions in the beginning of this section.

2. Remove the wheel bearing and hub assembly.

3. Remove the wheel speed sensor harness bracket bolt from the wheel knuckle.

4. Remove and discard the tie rod end nut.

5. Using a proper tool, separate the tie rod end from the wheel knuckle.

6. Remove and discard the lower ball joint nut.

7. Using a proper tool, separate the lower arm ball joint from the wheel knuckle.

8. Remove and discard the upper ball joint nut.

9. Using a proper tool, separate the upper arm ball joint from the wheel knuckle.

10. Remove the wheel knuckle.

To install:

11. Installation is the reverse of the removal procedure.

12. Use new fasteners where indicated.

13. Note the following tightening specifications:

- Upper ball joint nut: 41 ft. lbs. (55 Nm)
- Lower ball joint nut: 111 ft. lbs. (150 Nm)
- Tie rod end nut: 76 ft. lbs. (103 Nm)

14. Check and, if necessary, align the front end.

TORSION BAR

REMOVAL & INSTALLATION

2005 Explorer Sport-Trac

See Figures 404 through 412.

1. Before servicing the vehicle, refer to the "Precautions" section.

2. Raise and support the vehicle.

3. Remove the bolts and the torsion bar cover plate.

➡**Before relieving the torsion bar tension, measure and record the measurement of the torsion bar adjustment bolt. This measurement will be used as the preset depth for the new torsion bar adjustment bolt during installation.**

4. Make preliminary adjustment references. Measure and record the length where indicated.

5. Relieve the torsion bar tension:

a. Position the special tool and adapters.

b. Tighten the special tool until the torsion bar adjuster lifts off the adjustment bolt.

✳✳ WARNING

The torsion bar adjustment bolt is coated with dry adhesive. A new bolt must be installed if it is backed off or removed. Failure to do so can cause the adjustment bolt to loosen during operation and cause a loss of vehicle alignment.

6. Remove the torsion bar adjustment bolt and nut.

7. Loosen the special tool until the tension is removed from the torsion bar.

8. Remove the torsion bar:

a. Mark the torsion bar and the adjuster for reference during installation.

b. Remove the torsion bar insulator.

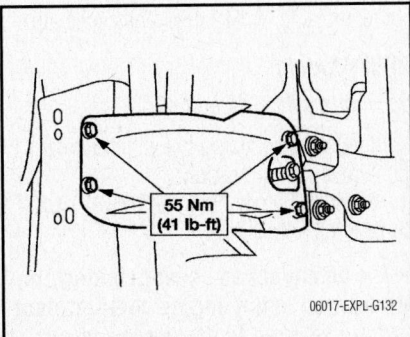

Fig. 404 Torsion bar cover plate—Explorer Sport-Trac

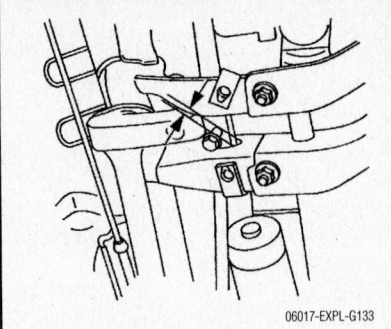

Fig. 405 Measure and record the length where indicated—Explorer Sport-Trac

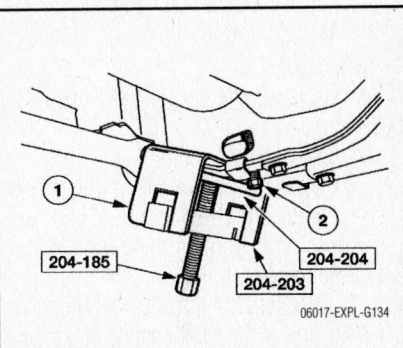

Fig. 406 Relieving torsion bar tension—Explorer Sport-Trac

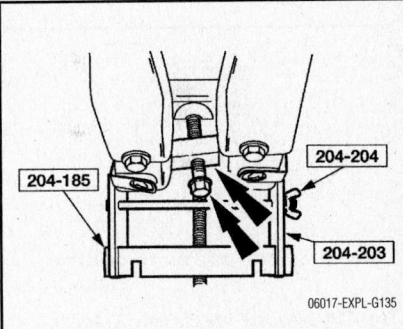

Fig. 407 Removing torsion bar tension bolt and nut—Explorer Sport-Trac

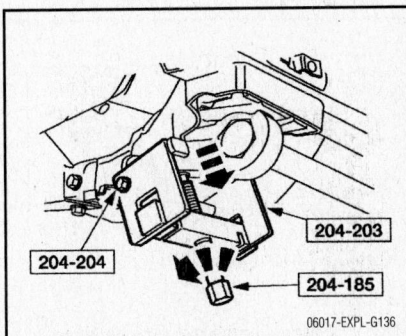

Fig. 408 Removing all tension from the torsion bar—Explorer Sport-Trac

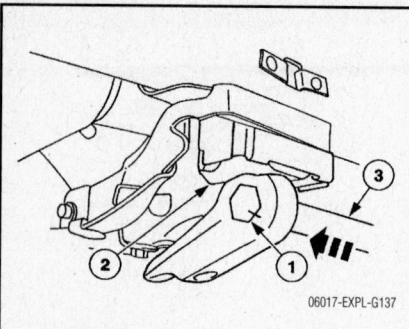

Fig. 409 Removing the torsion bar—Explorer Sport-Trac

c. Grasp the torsion bar, and pull it free from the lower arm.

To install:

9. Installation is the reverse of the removal procedure.

10. Adjust the ride height:

d. Drive the vehicle onto a drive-on lift.

e. Jounce the vehicle's front and rear suspension to normalize the vehicle static ride height.

f. Measure the distance between the center line of the front suspension lower arm bushing bolt and the lift. Record the measurement.

g. Measure the distance between the front wheel spindle (lowest point) and the

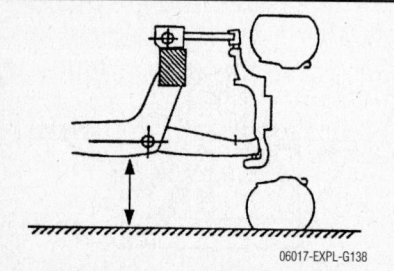

Fig. 410 Measure the distance between the center line of the front suspension lower arm bushing bolt and the lift—Explorer Sport-Trac

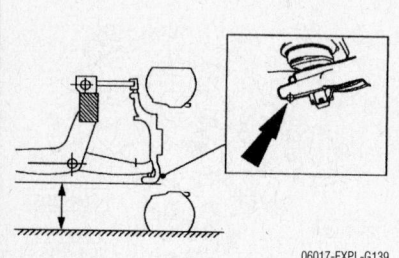

Fig. 411 Measure the distance between the front wheel spindle (lowest point) and the lift—Explorer Sport-Trac

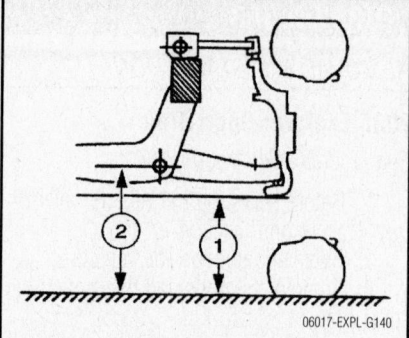

Fig. 412 Subtract measurement 1 from measurement 2—Explorer Sport-Trac

lift. Record the measurement. Take the measurement from the midpoint of the surface shown.

h. Determine ride height. Subtract measurement 1 from measurement 2. This is the ride height.

➡The torsion bar adjusting bolt is coated with adhesive that wears off after disassembly. If the torsion bar system is ever disassembled or the torsion bar adjusting bolt is ever removed, use a new torsion bar adjusting bolt when re-assembling.

i. Adjust the torsion bars (height) as necessary by tightening or loosening the torsion bar adjusting bolt. Tighten the torsion bar adjusting bolt to increase the torque or raise the height. Loosen the torsion bar adjusting bolt to decrease the torque or lower the height.

UPPER BALL JOINT

REMOVAL & INSTALLATION

Aviator and Explorer Sport-Trac

On these models, the upper ball joint is not replaceable. If defective, replace the arm.

2005 Explorer and Mountaineer

On 2006–07 models, the upper ball joint is not replaceable. If defective, replace the arm.

2WD Models

See Figures 413 through 415.

1. Before servicing the vehicle, refer to the "Precautions" section.

2. With the vehicle in NEUTRAL, position it on a hoist.

➡The wheel speed sensor connectors are located in the engine compartment and are secured to the fender aprons.

3. Disconnect the wheel speed sensor connector.

4. Remove the wheel and tire assembly.

5. Detach the harness from the retainers.

❋❋ WARNING

Do not allow the disc brake caliper to hang suspended from the brake hose. Provide suitable support.

6. Remove the bolts and position the brake caliper and support bracket aside.

7. Remove the brake disc.

8. Remove and discard the cotter pin and the outer tie rod end castellated nut.

❋❋ WARNING

Do not use a hammer to separate the tie rod from the wheel knuckle or damage to the wheel knuckle will result.

❋❋ WARNING

Do not damage the tie rod boot when installing the tool.

9. Separate the tie rod from the wheel knuckle.

10. Remove and discard the upper ball joint nut.

❋❋ WARNING

Do not use a hammer to separate the ball joint from the wheel knuckle or damage to the wheel knuckle will result.

❋❋ WARNING

Do not damage the ball joint boot when installing the special tool.

11. Separate the upper ball joint from the wheel knuckle.

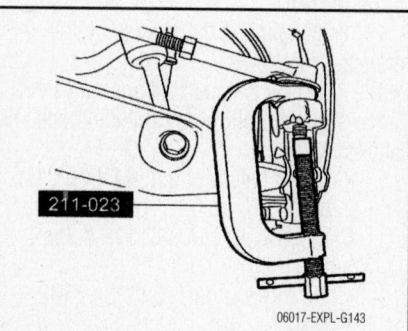

Fig. 413 Separating the tie rod end from the knuckle

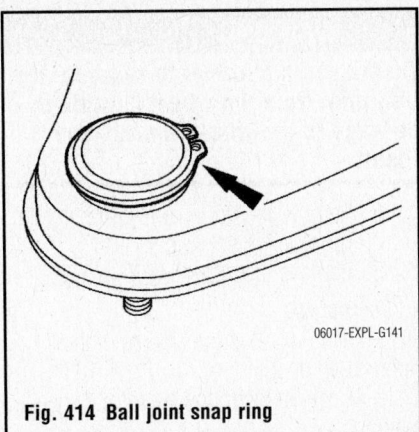

Fig. 414 Ball joint snap ring

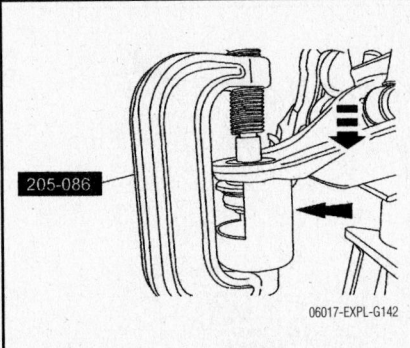

Fig. 415 Removing the ball joint from the control arm

12. Remove and discard the snap ring from the ball joint.

13. Using a suitable ball joint remover tool, remove the ball joint.

✱✱ WARNING

Do not damage the ball joint boot when installing the special tool.

To install:

14. Installation is the reverse of the removal procedure.

➡ **Clean and inspect the control arm ball joint bore for damage before installing a new ball joint.**

➡ **Make sure the new ball joint snap ring is fully seated.**

15. Always install new:
- Snap rings.
- Castellated nuts.
- Cotter pins.
- Upper ball joint nuts.

16. Observe the following torque specifications:
- Outer tie rod end castellated nut: 52 ft. lbs. (70 Nm).
- Upper ball joint nut: 41 ft lbs. (55 Nm).

4WD Models

See Figure 416.

1. Before servicing the vehicle, refer to the "Precautions" section.

2. With the vehicle in NEUTRAL, position it on a hoist.

3. Remove and discard the axle retainer nut.

➡ **The wheel speed sensor connectors are located in the engine compartment and are secured to the fender aprons.**

4. Disconnect the wheel speed sensor connector.

5. Remove the wheel and tire assembly.

6. Detach the harness from the retainers.

✱✱ WARNING

Do not allow the disc brake caliper to hang suspended from the brake hose. Provide a suitable support.

7. Remove the bolts and position the brake caliper and support bracket aside.

8. Remove the brake disc.

✱✱ WARNING

Do not use a hammer to separate the outboard CV-joint from the hub. Damage to the threads and internal CV-joint components can result.

9. Press the outboard CV-joint until it is loose in the hub.

10. Remove and discard the cotter pin and the castellated nut.

✱✱ WARNING

Do not use a hammer to separate the tie rod from the wheel knuckle or damage to the wheel knuckle will result.

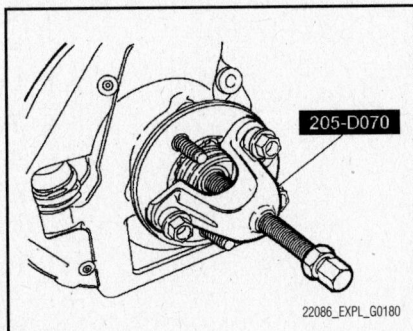

Fig. 416 Press the outboard CV-joint until it is loose in the hub

✱✱ WARNING

Do not damage the tie rod boot when installing the special tool.

11. Separate the tie rod from the wheel knuckle.

12. Remove and discard the upper ball joint nut.

✱✱ WARNING

Secure the front axle shaft to prevent the CV-joint and boots from overextending. Failure to do so can cause damage to the CV-joint and boots.

✱✱ WARNING

Do not use a hammer to separate the ball joint from the wheel knuckle or damage to the wheel knuckle will result.

✱✱ WARNING

Do not damage the ball joint when installing the special tool.

13. Separate the upper ball joint from the wheel knuckle.

14. Remove the hand-tightened lower ball joint castellated nut and remove the wheel knuckle.

15. Remove and discard the snap ring from the ball joint.

16. Using a suitable ball joint remover tool, remove the ball joint.

✱✱ WARNING

Do not damage the ball joint boot when installing the special tool.

To install:

17. Installation is the reverse of the removal procedure.

➡ **Apply a thin coat of silicone sealant to the wheel hub mounting surfaces before installation.**

➡ **Clean and inspect the control arm ball joint bore for damage before installing a new ball joint.**

➡ **Make sure the new ball joint snap ring is fully seated.**

18. Always install new:
- Castellated nuts.
- Cotter pins.
- Snap rings.
- Upper ball joint nuts.
- Axle retainer nut.

19. Observe the following torque specifications:

- Axle retainer nut: 184 ft. lbs. (250 Nm).
- Tie rod end stud nut: 52 ft. lbs. (70 Nm).
- Upper ball joint nut: 41 ft lbs. (55 Nm).

UPPER CONTROL ARM

REMOVAL & INSTALLATION

Aviator, Explorer and Mountaineer

2005 Models

See Figures 417 through 419.

1. Before servicing the vehicle, refer to the "Precautions" section.
2. On 4WD vehicles, loosen the axle retainer nut.

➡ **The wheel speed sensor electrical connectors are located in the engine compartment secured to the fender aprons.**

3. Disconnect the wheel speed sensor.
4. Remove the wheel and tire assembly.
5. Remove the upper ball joint-to-wheel knuckle nut. Separate the ball joint from the knuckle with a ball joint driver.

❋❋ WARNING

Do not use a hammer to separate the ball joint from the wheel knuckle or damage to the wheel knuckle can result.

6. Remove the upper arm-to-frame nuts.
7. Remove the set shims.
8. Remove the upper arm.

To install:

9. Installation is the reverse of the removal procedure.
10. Observe the following torque specifications:

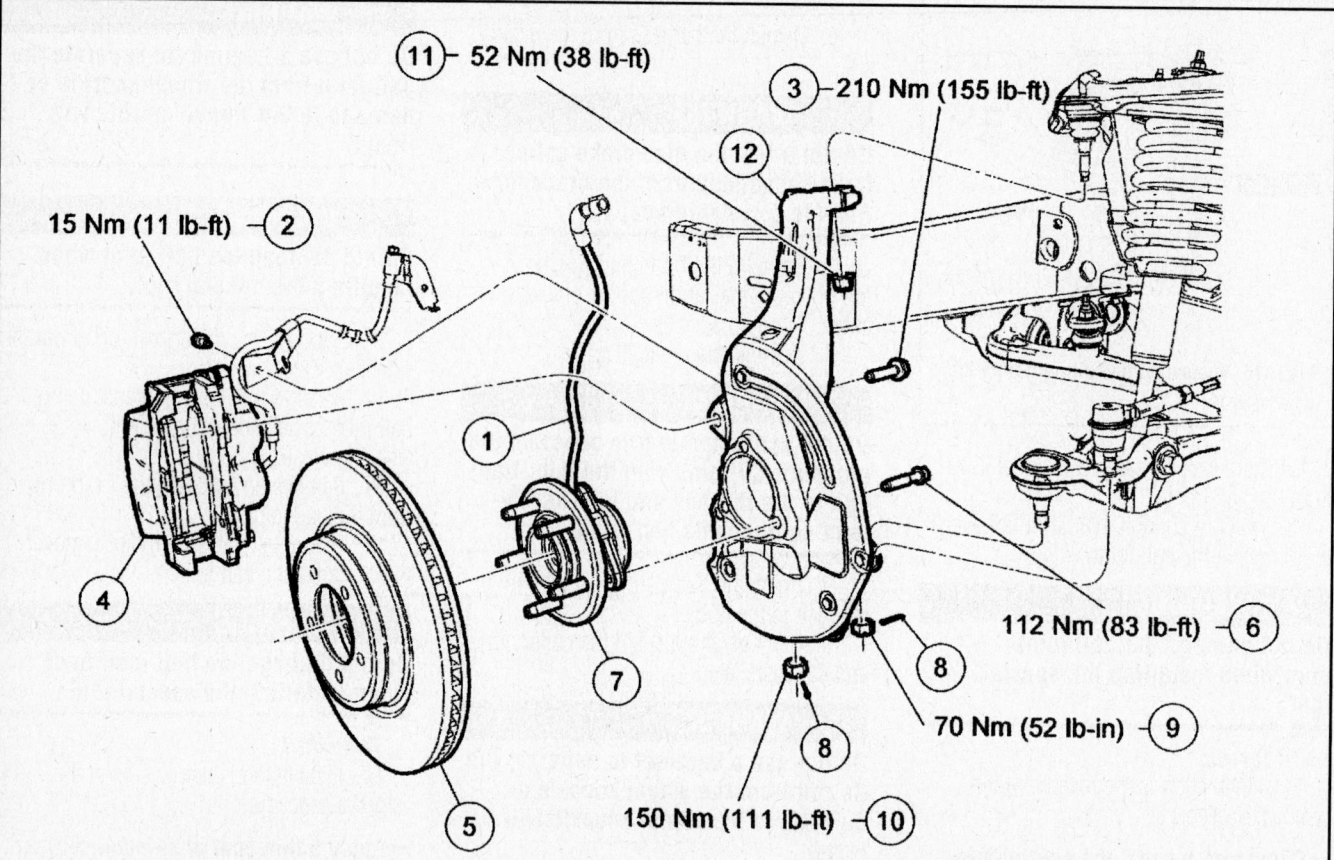

1 Speed sensor harness
2 Brake hose-to-wheel knuckle bolt
3 Anchor plate bolt (2 required)
4 Brake caliper, pads and anchor plate
5 Brake disc
6 Wheel hub-to-wheel knuckle bolt (3 required)

7 Wheel bearing and hub assembly
8 Cotter pins (2 required)
9 Tie-rod end-to-wheel knuckle nut
10 Lower ball joint-to-wheel knuckle nut
11 Upper ball joint-to-wheel knuckle nut
12 Wheel knuckle

06017-EXPL-G145

Fig. 417 Front knuckle and related parts—2WD Aviator

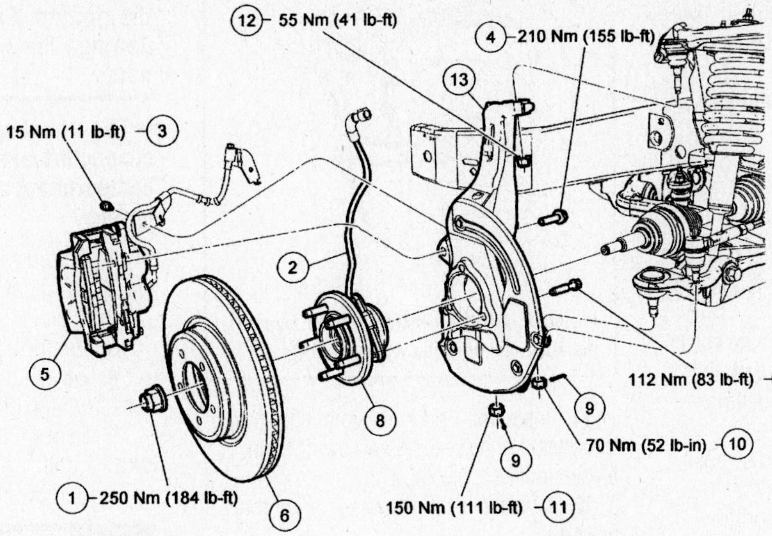

1 Axle-to-wheel hub nut
2 Speed sensor harness
3 Brake hose-to-wheel knuckle bolt
4 Anchor plate bolt (2 required)
5 Brake caliper, pads and anchor plate
6 Brake disc
7 Wheel hub-to-wheel knuckle bolt (3 required)

8 Wheel bearing and hub assembly
9 Cotter pins (2 required)
10 Tie-rod end-to-wheel knuckle nut
11 Lower ball joint-to-wheel knuckle nut
12 Upper ball joint-to-wheel knuckle nut
13 Wheel knuckle

06017-EXPL-G146

Fig. 418 Front knuckle and related parts—4WD Aviator

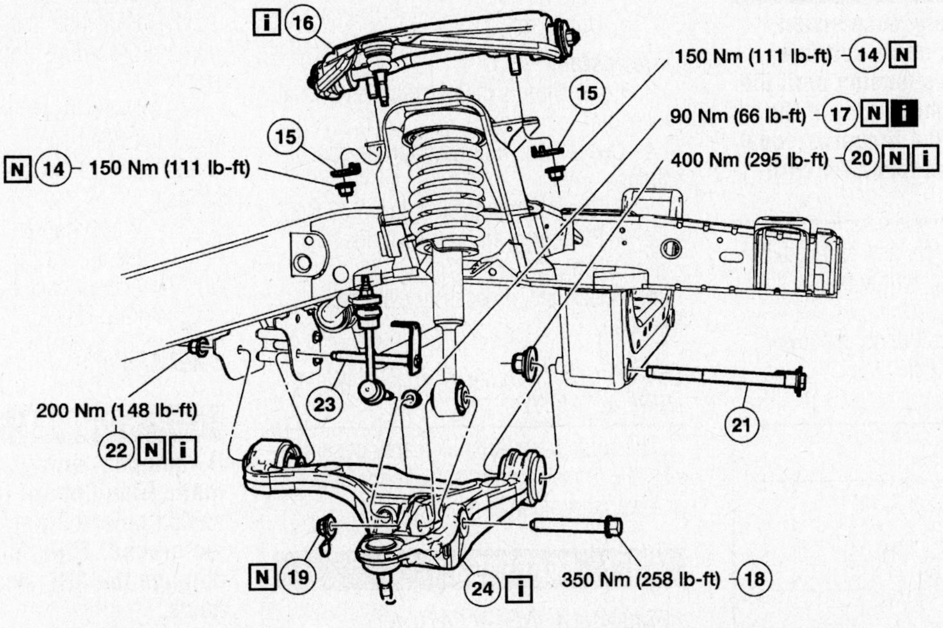

14 Upper arm-to-frame nuts
15 Set shims
16 Upper arm
17 Stabilizer bar link-to-lower arm nut
18 Shock absorber-to-lower arm bolt
19 Shock absorber-to-lower arm flag nut

20 Lower arm-to-frame nut (forward mounting)
21 Lower arm-to-frame flag bolt (forward mounting)
22 Lower arm-to-frame nut (rearward mounting)
23 Lower arm-to-frame flag bolt (rearward mounting)
24 Lower arm

67197EXPLG69

Fig. 419 Front suspension components—Aviator

- Ball joint nut 41 ft. lbs. (55 Nm) for 2wd and 38 ft. lbs. (52 Nm) for 4wd
- Upper arm nuts 111 ft. lbs. (150 Nm).

11. Check and, if necessary, align the front end.

2006–07 Models

See Figures 420 and 421.

1. Before servicing the vehicle, refer to the precautions in the beginning of this section.

2. Measure the distance from the center of the hub to the lip of the fender with the vehicle in a level, static ground position (curb height).

3. With the vehicle in NEUTRAL, position it on a hoist.

4. Using a suitable jack support the lower control arm near the lower ball joint.

5. Remove and discard the upper ball joint nut.

6. Using the proper separator tool, separate the upper ball joint from the wheel knuckle.

7. Using a plastic tie strap, support the suspension at the wheel knuckle.

8. Remove the 2 upper arm bolts and flag nuts and the upper arm.

To install:

> ### ✳✳ CAUTION
>
> **Before tightening any suspension bushing fasteners, use a suitable jack to raise the suspension until the distance between the center of the hub and the lip of the fender is equal to the measurement taken for curb height.**

9. Position the upper arm and install the bolts and flag nuts. Torque to 111 ft. lbs. (150 Nm).

10. With the jack still under the lower arm, remove the plastic tie strap.

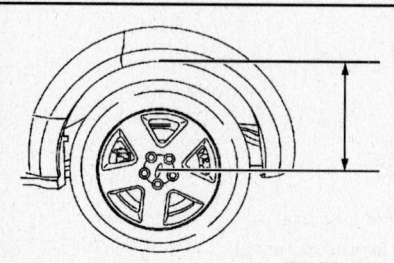

Fig. 420 Measure the distance from the center of the hub to the lip of the fender with the vehicle in a level, static ground position (curb height—2006–07 Explorer and Mountaineer

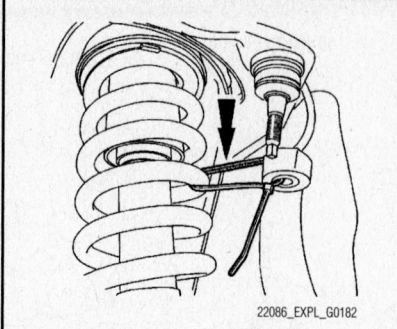

Fig. 421 Using a plastic tie strap, support the suspension at the wheel knuckle

11. Insert the upper ball joint stud into the wheel knuckle. Install a new nut and torque to 41 ft. lbs. (55 Nm).

12. Check and, if necessary, align the front end.

Explorer Sport-Trac

2005 Models

1. Before servicing the vehicle, refer to the "Precautions" section.

2. Remove or disconnect the following:
   - Wheel
   - Pinch bolt and nut from the wheel knuckle. Remove and discard the nut.
   - Arm-to-frame nuts and shims. Discard the nuts.
   - Upper arm

To install:

3. Installation is the reverse the removal procedure.

4. Observe the following torque specifications:
   - Upper arm nuts 98 ft. lbs. (133 Nm).
   - Pinch bolt and nut 41 ft. lbs. (55 Nm).

5. Check and, if necessary, align the front end.

UPPER CONTROL ARM BUSHING REPLACEMENT

The control arm bushings are not serviceable. If they require service, the upper or lower arm must be replaced.

WHEEL BEARINGS

REMOVAL & INSTALLATION

Aviator

2WD Models

> ### ✳✳ WARNING
>
> **If equipped, always turn off the Automatic Ride Control (ARC) service**

switch before lifting the vehicle off of the ground. Failure to do so could damage the ARC system components.

➡ The wheel speed sensor electrical connectors are located in the engine compartment secured to the fender aprons.

1. Before servicing the vehicle, refer to the "Precautions" section.

2. Disconnect the wheel speed sensor.

3. Remove the wheel and tire assembly.

4. Detach the wheel speed sensor harness from the brake hose.

5. Remove the brake hose-to-wheel knuckle bolt.

6. Remove the 2 anchor plate bolts.

> ### ✳✳ WARNING
>
> **Do not allow the brake caliper to hang from the hose or damage to the hose can occur.**

7. Position the caliper, pads and anchor plate aside.

8. Remove the brake disc.

9. Remove and discard the 3 wheel hub-to-wheel knuckle bolts.

10. Remove the wheel bearing and hub assembly.

To install:

11. Installation is the reverse of the removal procedure, noting the following steps:

12. Always install new wheel hub-to-wheel knuckle bolts.

13. Observe the following torque specifications:
   - Wheel hub-to-knuckle bolts: 83 ft. lbs. (112 Nm)
   - Anchor plate bolts: 155 ft. lbs. (210 Nm)

4WD Models

> ### ✳✳ WARNING
>
> **If equipped, always turn off the Automatic Ride Control (ARC) service switch before lifting the vehicle off of the ground. Failure to do so could damage the ARC system components.**

1. Before servicing the vehicle, refer to the "Precautions" section.

2. Loosen the axle retainer nut.

➡ The wheel speed sensor electrical connectors are located in the engine compartment secured to the fender aprons.

3. Disconnect the wheel speed sensor.

4. Remove the wheel and tire assembly.

5. Remove and discard the axle retainer nut.

6. Separate the outboard CV-joint from the wheel hub.

7. Detach the wheel speed sensor harness from the brake hose.

8. Remove the brake hose-to-wheel knuckle bolt.

9. Remove the 2 anchor plate bolts.

❊❊ WARNING

Do not allow the brake caliper to hang from the hose or damage to the hose can occur.

10. Position the caliper, pads and anchor plate aside.

11. Remove the brake disc.

12. Remove and discard the 3 wheel hub-to-wheel knuckle bolts.

13. Remove the wheel bearing and hub assembly.

To install:

14. Installation is the reverse of the removal procedure.

15. Always install new wheel hub-to-wheel knuckle bolts and a new axle retainer nut.

16. Observe the following torque specifications:

- Wheel hub-to-knuckle bolts: 83 ft. lbs. (112 Nm)
- Anchor plate bolts: 155 ft. lbs. (210 Nm)
- Axle retainer nut: 184 ft. lbs. (250 Nm)

2005 Explorer and Mountaineer

2WD Models

❊❊ WARNING

If equipped, always turn off the Automatic Ride Control (ARC) service switch before lifting the vehicle off of the ground. Failure to do so could damage the ARC system components.

1. Before servicing the vehicle, refer to the "Precautions" section.

2. Remove or disconnect the following:

➡**The wheel speed sensor connectors are located in the engine compartment and are secured to the fender aprons.**

- Wheel speed sensor connector
- Brake disc
- Wiring harness from the retainers

- Bolts, wheel hub and sensor as an assembly. Discard the bolts.

To install:

3. Installation is the reverse of the removal procedure.

➡**Apply a thin coat of silicone sealant to the wheel hub mounting surfaces before installation.**

4. Torque the hub-to-knuckle bolts to 83 ft. lbs. (112 Nm)

4WD Models

❊❊ WARNING

If equipped, always turn off the Automatic Ride Control (ARC) service switch before lifting the vehicle off of the ground. Failure to do so could damage the ARC system components.

1. Before servicing the vehicle, refer to the "Precautions" section.

2. Remove or disconnect the following:

- Hub nut. Discard the nut.

➡**The wheel speed sensor connectors are located in the engine compartment and are secured to the fender aprons.**

- Wheel speed sensor connector
- Brake disc

❊❊ WARNING

Do not use a hammer to separate the outboard CV-joint from the hub. Damage to the threads and internal CV-joint components may result.

3. Press the outboard CV-joint until it is loose in the hub.

4. Detach the harness from the retainers.

❊❊ WARNING

Do not overextend the CV-joint and boots when removing the wheel hub.

5. Remove the bolts, wheel hub and sensor as an assembly. Discard the bolts.

To install:

6. Installation is the reverse of the removal procedure.

➡**Apply a thin coat of silicone sealant to the wheel hub mounting surfaces before installation.**

7. Observe the following torque specifications:

- Hub-to-knuckle: 83 ft. lbs. (112 Nm.
- Hub nut: 184 ft. lbs. (250 Nm).

2005 Explorer Sport-Trac

2WD Models

See Figure 422.

1. Before servicing the vehicle, refer to the "Precautions" section.

2. Remove the front disc brake caliper anchor plate.

➡**Match-mark the brake disc and hub.**

3. Remove the hub grease cap.

4. Remove the cotter pin.

5. Remove the nut retainer.

6. Remove the spindle nut.

7. Remove the front wheel outer bearing retainer washer.

8. Remove the outer front wheel bearing.

9. Remove the brake disc and hub.

10. Remove the wheel hub grease seal and inner wheel bearing.

11. Place the hub on a solid wood work surface.

12. Using a suitable drift, drive out the inner bearing race; then, in a similar fashion, drive out the outer bearing race.

To install:

13. Clean and inspect the front wheel bearings and the brake disc and hub. Use Metal Brake Parts Cleaner F6AZ-2C410-AB, or equivalent.

14. Pack the front wheel bearings. Use Premium Long-Life Grease XG-1-C or -K or equivalent meeting Ford specification ESA-M1C75-B.

15. Lubricate the bearing race bore. Using a suitable driver, drive in a new outer bearing race until it fully seats; then, in a similar fashion, drive a new inner race into position.

16. Pack the hub bore with the same grease used to pack the bearings.

17. Install the inner front wheel bearing.

18. Install a new wheel hub grease seal.

19. Position the hub on the spindle.

20. Install the outer front wheel bearing.

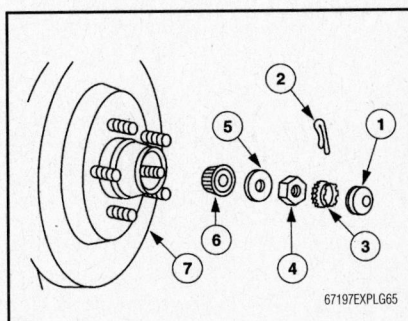

Fig. 422 Front wheel bearings—2WD Explorer Sport-Trac

67197EXPLG65

21. Install the front wheel outer bearing retainer washer.

22. Install the spindle nut.

23. Tighten the spindle nut to 21 ft. lbs. (29 Nm) while rotating the brake disc and hub.

24. Loosen the spindle nut one-half turn.

25. Tighten the spindle nut to 17 inch lbs. (2 Nm) while rotating the brake disc and hub.

26. Install the nut retainer.

27. Install the cotter pin.

28. Install the hub grease cap.

29. Install the front disc brake caliper anchor plate.

4WD Models

1. Before servicing the vehicle, refer to the "Precautions" section.

2. Remove the brake disc.

3. Remove the three bolts and the dust shield.

✳✳ WARNING

Discard the wheel hub retainer nut and washer assembly. It is a torque prevailing design and cannot be reused.

4. Remove the wheel hub retainer nut and washer assembly.

5. Remove the bolts and position the anti-lock sensor aside.

✳✳ WARNING

Do not overextend CV-joint and boots when removing the hub and bearing assembly.

➡ **The CV-joint is a slip fit into the wheel hub and bearing. A puller will not normally be required.**

6. Remove the three bolts and the wheel hub.

To install:

7. Installation is the reverse of the removal procedure.

8. Observe the following torque specifications:

- Wheel hub-to-knuckle: 85 ft. lbs. (115 Nm)
- Axle shaft nut: 162 ft. lbs. (220 Nm)
- Dust shield: 108 inch lbs. (12 Nm)

2006–07 Explorer and Mountaineer; 2007 Sport-Trac

✳✳ CAUTION

Suspension fasteners are critical parts because they affect performance of vital components and systems and their failure can result in major service expense. A new part with the same part number or an equivalent part must be installed, if installation is necessary. Do not use a part of lesser quality or substitute design. Torque values must be used as specified during reassembly to make sure of correct retention of these parts.

2WD Models

1. With the vehicle in NEUTRAL, position it on a hoist.

2. Remove the bolts and position the caliper, pads and anchor plate assembly aside. Discard the bolts. Support the caliper and anchor plate assembly using mechanic's wire.

3. Remove the brake disc.

4. Remove the wheel speed sensor bolt and disconnect the wheel speed sensor from the wheel bearing and hub assembly.

5. Remove the 3 bolts and the wheel bearing and hub assembly.

To install:

6. Install the wheel bearing and hub assembly. Tighten the 3 bolts to 90 ft. lbs. (122 Nm).

7. Install the wheel speed sensor to the wheel bearing and hub assembly. Connect the electrical connector and install the bolt.

8. Install the brake disc.

9. Install the caliper and anchor plate assembly. Tighten the bolts to 122 ft. lbs. (165 Nm).

4WD Models

1. With the vehicle in NEUTRAL, position it on a hoist.

2. Remove and discard the halfshaft nut and washer.

3. separate the outboard CV joint from the wheel hub.

4. Remove the bolts and position the caliper, pads and anchor plate assembly aside. Discard the bolts. Support the caliper and anchor plate assembly using mechanic's wire.

5. Remove the brake disc.

6. Remove the wheel speed sensor bolt and disconnect the wheel speed sensor from the wheel bearing and hub assembly.

7. Remove the 3 bolts and the wheel bearing and hub assembly.

To install:

8. Install the wheel bearing and hub assembly. Tighten the 3 bolts to 90 ft. lbs. (122 Nm).

9. Install the wheel speed sensor to the wheel bearing and hub assembly. Connect the electrical connector and install the bolt.

10. Install the brake disc.

11. Install the caliper and anchor plate assembly. Tighten the bolts to 122 ft. lbs. (165 Nm).

12. Install the outboard CV joint to the wheel hub.

13. Install a new nut and washer to the halfshaft. Tight the nut to 184 ft. lbs. (250 Nm).

14. Lower the vehicle.

ADJUSTMENT

Only the Explorer Sport-Trac 2WD bearings are adjustable. Refer to Removal and Installation procedure in this section for adjusting procedure.

SUSPENSION **REAR SUSPENSION**

COIL SPRING

REMOVAL & INSTALLATION

See Figure 423.

1. Before servicing the vehicle, refer to the "Precautions" section.
2. Remove the shock absorber and spring assembly.
3. Using a suitable spring compressor, compress the spring until the tension is released from the shock absorber.
4. While holding the flats of the washer, remove and discard the center nut.
5. Remove the shock absorber.
6. Remove the upper washer.
7. Remove the upper shock absorber mount and bushing.
8. Carefully release the compressor and remove the coil spring.

To install:

9. Assembly is the reverse of the disassembly procedure.
10. Always install a new shock absorber-to-upper mount nut. Torque as follows:
   - 2005 models: 41 ft. lbs. (56 Nm)
   - 2006-07 models: 48 ft. lbs. (65 Nm)

LEAF SPRING

REMOVAL & INSTALLATION

2005 Explorer Sport-Trac

See Figures 424 through 426.

1. Before servicing the vehicle, refer to the "Precautions" section.
2. Turn the air suspension switch off, if equipped.
3. Remove or disconnect the following:
   - Negative battery cable
   - Rear wheels and support the rear axle
   - Separate the rear spring from the axle and position the spring plate aside
   - Rear spring

To install:

4. Installation is the reverse of the removal procedure, observing the following:

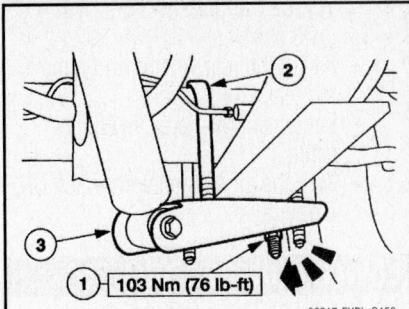

Fig. 425 Rear leaf spring U-bolts

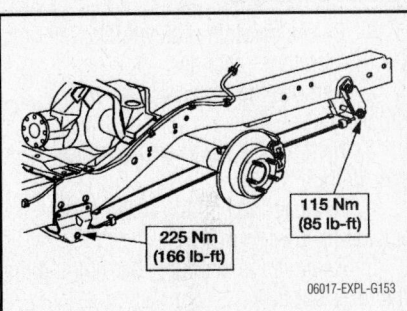

Fig. 426 Leaf spring installation—2005 models

- Torque the forward leaf spring bolt to 166 ft. lbs. (225 Nm) and the rear bolt to 85 ft. lbs. (115 Nm).

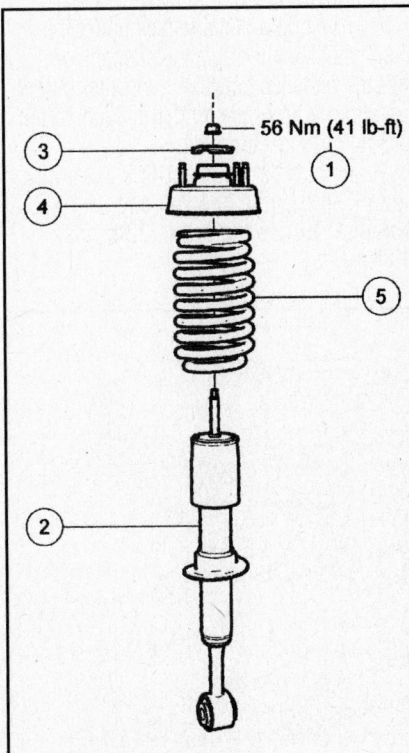

1 Shock absorber-to-upper mount nut
2 Shock absorber (front/rear)
3 Washer
4 Upper shock mount (front/rear)
5 Coil spring (front/rear)

06017-EXPL-G151

Fig. 423 Rear spring removal—Aviator, Explorer and Mountaineer

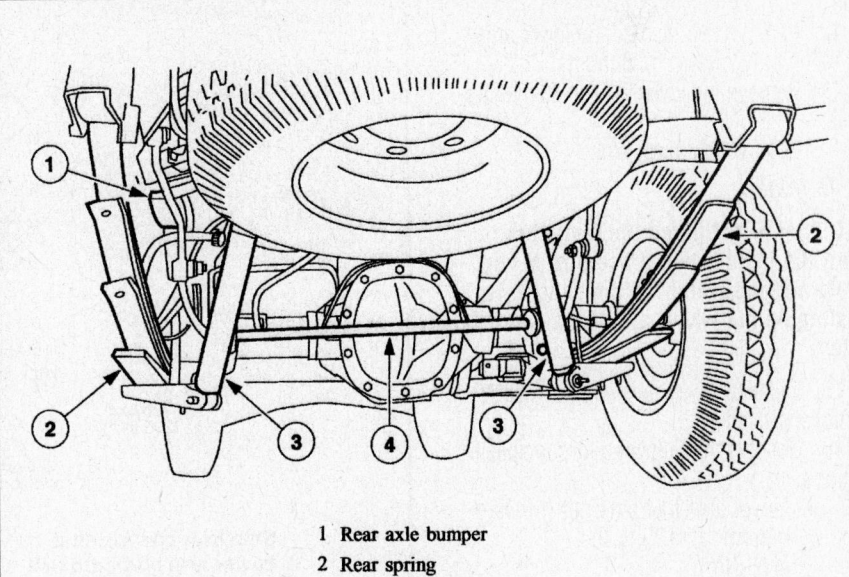

1 Rear axle bumper
2 Rear spring
3 Shock absorber
4 Rear stabilizer bar

06017-EXPL-G116

Fig. 424 Rear suspension—Explorer Sport-Trac

- Properly position the spring plate and install the U-bolts. Torque the bolts to 76 ft. lbs. (103 Nm).
- Install the rear wheels and remove the rear axle support.
- Reconnect the negative battery cable.
- Turn the air suspension switch ON, if equipped.

LOWER CONTROL ARM

REMOVAL & INSTALLATION

2005 Aviator, Explorer and Mountaineer

1. Before servicing the vehicle, refer to the "Precautions" section.
2. Remove the lower arm-to-wheel knuckle nut.
3. Remove the lower arm-to-wheel knuckle bolt.
4. Remove the parking brake cable bracket-to-lower arm bolt.
5. Remove the stabilizer bar nut and the stabilizer bar link.
6. Remove the stabilizer bar stud.
7. Remove the shock absorber-to-lower arm bolt. .
8. Remove and discard the flag nut.
9. Remove and discard the lower arm-to-frame nut (rearward mounting).
10. Remove the set shim.
11. Remove the lower arm-to-frame flag bolt.
12. Remove and discard the lower arm-to-frame nut (forward mounting).
13. Remove the lower arm-to-frame flag bolt.
14. Remove the lower arm.

To install:

➡️**Do not fully tighten the fasteners until the installation procedure is complete and the weight of the vehicle is resting on the wheel and tire assemblies.**

15. Installation is the reverse of the removal procedure.
16. Observe the following torque specifications:
- Lower arm-to-frame nut (forward mounting): 129 ft. lbs. (175 Nm)
- Lower arm-to-frame nut (rearward mounting): 129 ft. lbs. (175 Nm)
- Shock absorber-to-lower arm bolt: 184 ft. lbs. (250 Nm)
- Stabilizer bar stud: 18 ft. lbs. (25 Nm)

- Parking brake cable bracket-to-lower arm bolt: 108 inch lbs. (12 Nm)
- Lower arm-to-wheel knuckle nut: 111 ft. lbs. (150 Nm)
17. Always install a new:
- Flag nut.
- Lower arm-to-frame nut (rearward mounting).
- Lower arm-to-frame nut (forward mounting).

2006–07 Explorer and Mountaineer; 2007 Explorer Sport-Trac

See Figure 427.

1. Before servicing the vehicle, refer to the "Precautions" section.

※※ CAUTION

Orientation of the suspension fasteners is important. Make sure the fasteners are installed in the same direction as they were in when removed.

2. Measure the distance from the center of the hub to the lip of the fender with the vehicle in a level, static ground position (curb height).
3. With the vehicle in NEUTRAL, position it on a hoist.
4. Position a suitable jack under the wheel knuckle and raise the suspension until the distance between the center of the hub and the lip of the fender is equal to the curb height measurement.
5. Remove and discard the lower arm outboard bolt and flag nut.
6. Remove the stabilizer bar link nut and grommet, stud and link assembly. Discard the nut and grommet.
7. Lower the suspension and remove the jack.
8. Remove and discard the shock absorber lower nut and bolt.
9. Remove and discard the lower arm inboard nut and bolt and remove the lower arm.

To install:
10. Position the lower arm and install a new lower arm inboard bolt and nut. Hand-tighten only at this time.
11. Position the lower arm and install a new shock absorber lower bolt and nut. Hand-tighten only at this time.
12. Position a suitable jack under the wheel knuckle and raise the suspension until the distance between the center of the hub and the lip of the fender is equal to the curb height measurement.
13. Install the stabilizer link assembly, the link stud and a new nut and grommet. Torque the nut to 22 ft. lbs. (30 Nm).

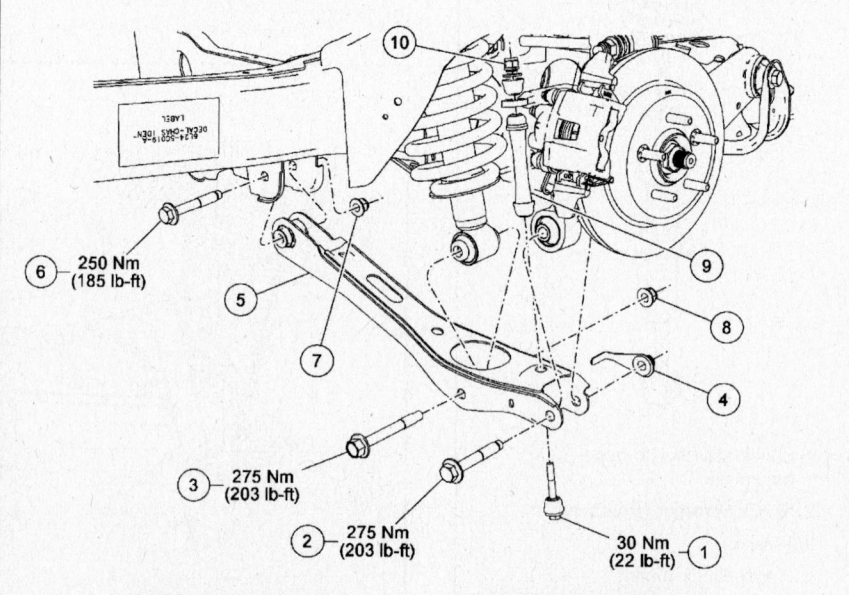

250 Nm (185 lb-ft) — 6
275 Nm (203 lb-ft) — 3
275 Nm (203 lb-ft) — 2
30 Nm (22 lb-ft) — 1

1. Stabilizer bar link stud
2. Lower arm outboard bolt
3. Shock absorber lower bolt
4. Lower arm outboard flag nut
5. Lower arm
6. Lower arm inboard bolt
7. Lower arm inboard nut
8. Shock absorber lower nut
9. Stabilizer bar link assembly
10. Stabilizer bar link nut and grommet

22086_EXPL_G0185

Fig. 427 Lower arm and mounting components

14. Install a new lower arm outboard bolt and flag nut. Torque the nut to 203 ft. lbs. (275 Nm).

15. Tighten the lower arm inboard bolt to 185 ft. lbs. (250 Nm).

16. Tighten the shock absorber lower bolt to 203 ft. lbs. (275 Nm).

17. Lower the suspension and remove the jack.

MCPHERSON STRUT

REMOVAL & INSTALLATION

Aviator, Explorer and Mountaineer

2005 Models

See Figures 428 through 430.

1. Before servicing the vehicle, refer to the "Precautions" section.

2. Remove or disconnect the following:
- Wheels
- Upper shock mounting nuts. Discard the nuts.
- Nut and the stabilizer bar link. Discard the nut.
- Ball joint pinch bolt. Discard the nut.
- Bolt, flag nut and the shock absorber and spring as an assembly. Discard the flag nut.

3. Using a suitable spring compressor, compress the spring until the tension is released from the shock absorber.

4. While holding the flats of the washer, remove the nut.

5. Remove the shock absorber. Discard the nut.

6. Remove the washer, bushing and the upper mount.

7. Remove the insulator.

8. Remove the dust shield.

To install:

9. Installation is the reverse of the removal procedure.

10. Observe the following torque specifications:
- Center nut: 37 ft. lbs. (50 Nm)
- Lower mounting bolt: 184 ft. lbs. (250 Nm)
- Pinch bolt: 111 ft. lbs. (150 Nm)
- Sway bar nut: 18 ft. lbs. (25 Nm)
- Upper shock mounting nuts: 22 ft. lbs. (30 Nm)

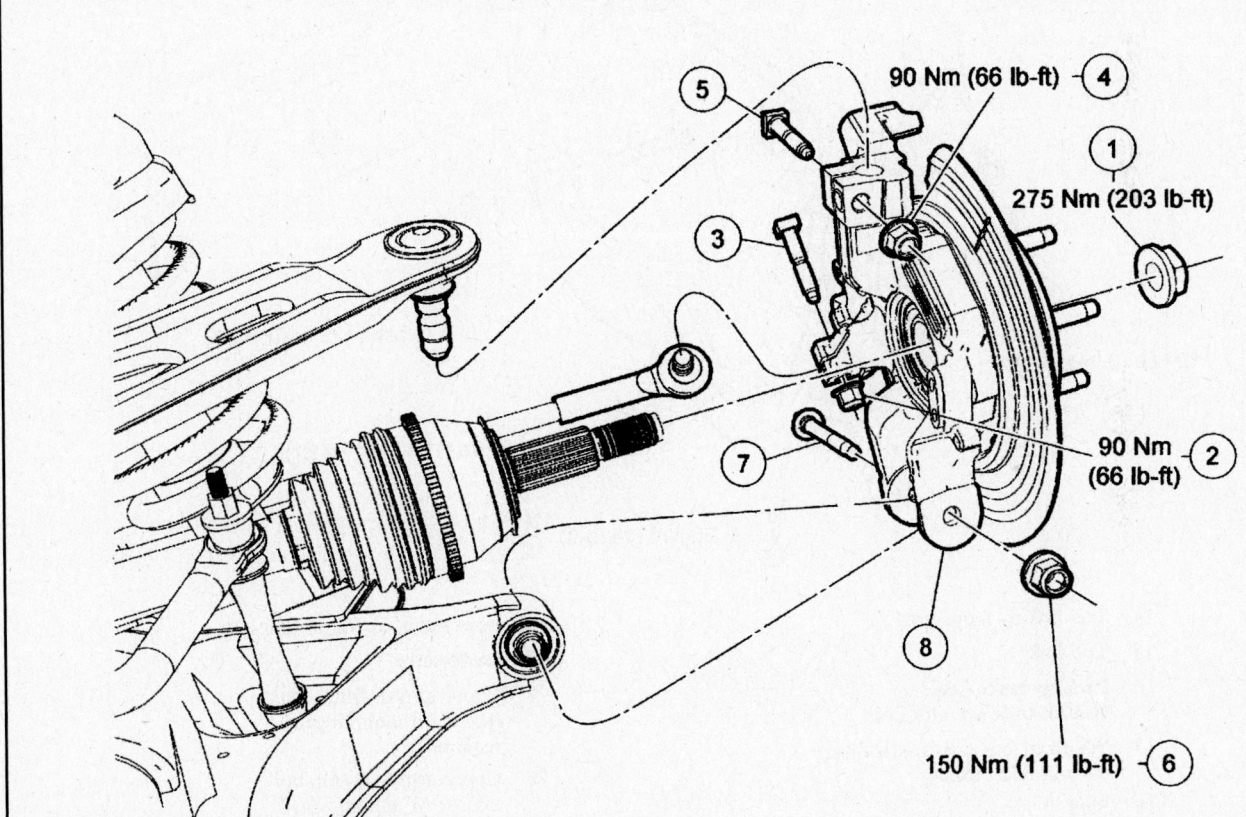

1 Axle nut
2 Toe link-to-wheel knuckle nut
3 Toe link-to-wheel knuckle bolt
4 Upper arm-to-wheel knuckle nut
5 Upper arm-to-wheel knuckle bolt
6 Lower arm-to-wheel knuckle nut
7 Lower arm-to-wheel knuckle bolt
8 Wheel knuckle

06017-EXPL-G148

Fig. 428 Rear hub/knuckle and related parts—Aviator, Explorer and Mountaineer

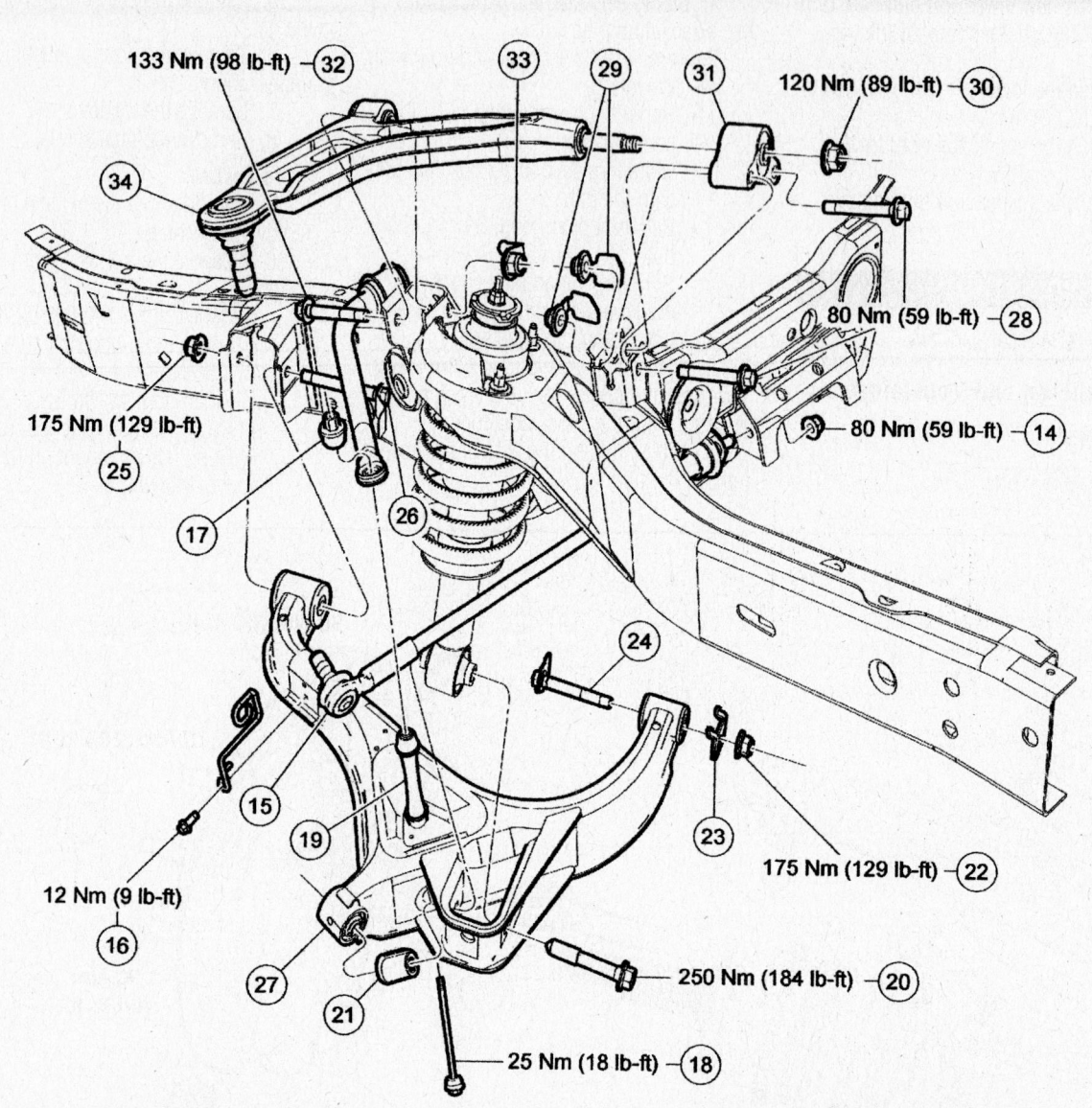

133 Nm (98 lb-ft) — 32
120 Nm (89 lb-ft) — 30
80 Nm (59 lb-ft) — 28
80 Nm (59 lb-ft) — 14
175 Nm (129 lb-ft) — 25
175 Nm (129 lb-ft) — 22
12 Nm (9 lb-ft) — 16
250 Nm (184 lb-ft) — 20
25 Nm (18 lb-ft) — 18

14	Toe link-to-frame nut
15	Toe link
16	Parking brake cable bracket-to-lower arm bolt
17	Stabilizer bar link-to-stabilizer bar nut and bushing
18	Stud
19	Stabilizer bar link
20	Shock absorber-to-lower arm bolt
21	Flag nut
22	Lower arm-to-frame nut (rearward mounting)
23	Set shim
24	Lower arm-to-frame flag bolt
25	Lower arm-to-frame nut (forward mounting)
26	Lower arm-to-frame flag bolt
27	Lower arm
28	Upper arm-to-frame bolt (rearward mounting) (2 required)
28	Upper arm-to-frame bolt (rearward mounting) (2 required)
29	Flag nut (2 required)
30	Upper arm bushing-to-upper arm nut
31	Upper arm bushing (rearward mounting)
32	Upper arm-to-frame bolt (forward mounting)
33	Flag nut
34	Upper arm

06017-EXPL-G149

Fig. 429 Rear suspension—Aviator, Explorer and Mountaineer

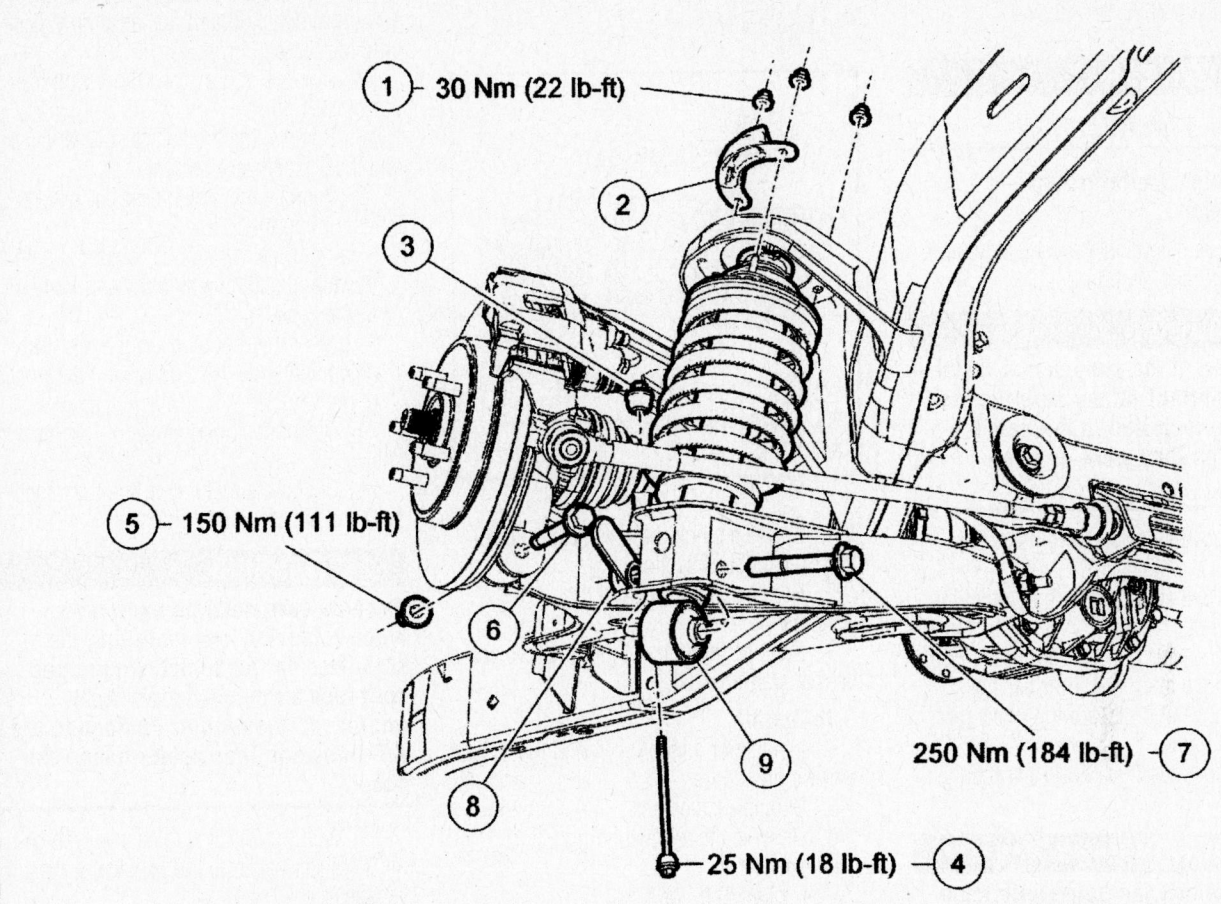

1 — 30 Nm (22 lb-ft)

2

3

5 — 150 Nm (111 lb-ft)

6

8

9

250 Nm (184 lb-ft) — 7

25 Nm (18 lb-ft) — 4

1 Nuts (3 required)
2 Jounce bumper
3 Stabilizer link nut and grommet
4 Stud
5 Lower arm-to-wheel knuckle nut

6 Lower arm-to-wheel knuckle bolt
7 Shock absorber-to-lower arm bolt
8 Shock absorber-to-lower arm flag nut
9 Shock absorber and spring assembly

06017-EXPL-G150

Fig. 430 Rear shock and spring assembly—Aviator, Explorer and Mountaineer

Explorer, Explorer Sport-Trac and Mountaineer

2006–07 Models

1. Before servicing the vehicle, refer to the "Precautions" section.
2. Remove the lower arm. See "Control Arms/Links" section.
3. Remove and discard the 3 shock absorber upper mount nuts and remove the shock absorber and spring assembly.

To install:

4. Install the shock absorber and torque the upper mount nuts to 22 ft. lbs. (30 Nm).

5. Install the lower arm. See "Control Arms/Links" section.

Explorer Sport-Trac

2005 Models

➡Low pressure gas shocks are charged with nitrogen gas. Do not attempt to open, puncture or apply heat to them. Prior to installing a new shock absorber, hold it upright and extend it fully. Invert it and fully compress and extend it at least 3 times. This will bleed trapped air.

1. Before servicing the vehicle, refer to the "Precautions" section.
2. Remove or disconnect the following:
   • Upper shock-to-frame attaching nut
   • Lower shock nut
   • Slightly compress the shock absorber by hand and remove it from the vehicle

To install:

3. Install or connect the following:
   • Shock absorber upper end and nut
   • Shock absorber lower end and nut
   • Torque the upper fasteners to 17 ft. lbs. (23 Nm)

- Torque the lower shock attaching nuts to 46 ft. lbs. (63Nm).

STABILIZER BAR

REMOVAL & INSTALLATION

2005 Aviator, Explorer And Mountaineer

1. Before servicing the vehicle, refer to the "Precautions" section.

⬦ CAUTION

Orientation of the suspension fasteners is important. Make sure the fasteners are installed in the same direction as they were in when removed.

2. Remove the wheel and tire assemblies.
3. Remove and discard the 2 stabilizer bar-to-link nuts.
4. Remove the 2 stabilizer bar studs.
5. Remove the 2 stabilizer bar links.
6. Remove and discard the 4 stabilizer bar-to-frame nuts.
7. Remove the 2 stabilizer bar insulators.

⬦ CAUTION

Do not damage the boot while separating the ball joint from the knuckle.

8. Remove the nut and detach the RH upper ball joint.
9. Remove the bolts and suspend the brake caliper aside with mechanic's wire.
10. Unclip the vapor line from the fuel tank.
11. From the RH side of the vehicle, remove the stabilizer bar.

To install:
12. Position the stabilizer bar into the vehicle.
13. Clip the vapor line to the fuel tank.
14. Position the brake caliper and install and tighten the bolts to 24 ft. lbs. (32 Nm).
15. Reposition the RH upper ball joint and install the nut. Do not fully tighten.
16. Install the 2 stabilizer bar insulators.
17. Install 4 new stabilizer bar-to-frame nuts. Torque the nuts to 41 ft. lbs. (55 Nm).
18. Install the 2 stabilizer bar links and studs. Install new nuts and torque to 18 ft. lbs. (25 Nm).
19. Install the rear wheel and tire assemblies.
20. Lower the vehicle to curb weight and torque the RH upper ball joint nut to 66 ft. lbs. (90 Nm).

2005 Explorer Sport-Trac
See Figure 431.

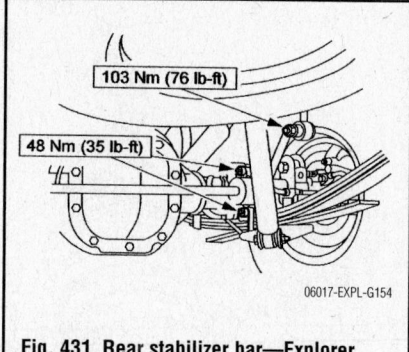

103 Nm (76 lb-ft)

48 Nm (35 lb-ft)

06017-EXPL-G154

Fig. 431 Rear stabilizer bar—Explorer Sport-Trac

1. Before servicing the vehicle, refer to the "Precautions" section.
2. Remove the wheel and tire assembly.
3. Remove the nuts, bolts, brackets and the rear stabilizer bar.

To install:
4. Installation is the reverse of the removal procedure.
5. Use new fasteners.
6. Observe the following tightening specifications:
   - Link 76 ft. lbs. (103 Nm)
   - Clamp 35 ft. lbs. (48 Nm)

2006–07 Explorer And Mountaineer
See Figures 432 through 434.

1. Before servicing the vehicle, refer to the "Precautions" section.

✳ CAUTION

Orientation of the suspension fasteners is important. Make sure the fasteners are installed in the same direction as they were in when removed.

2. Measure the distance from the center of the hub to the lip of the fender with the vehicle in a level, static ground position (curb height).
3. With the vehicle in NEUTRAL, position it on a hoist.
4. Position a suitable jack under the wheel knuckle and raise the suspension until the distance between the | center of the hub and the lip of the fender is equal to the curb height measurement.
5. Remove and discard the outboard nut and bolt from both upper arms.

6. Remove the stabilizer bar link nut and grommet, stud and link assembly. Discard the nut and grommet.
7. Remove and discard the 4 stabilizer bar bracket nuts.
8. Remove the 2 stabilizer bar brackets and the 2 stabilizer bar bushings.
9. Remove the 4 stabilizer bar bracket studs, noting the following:
   a. For the front studs, push the stud down and slide the stud toward the rear of the vehicle.
   b. For the rear studs, push the stud down and slide the stud toward the front of the vehicle.
10. Disconnect the fuel vapor line as shown.
11. Unclip the fuel vapor line from the fuel tank and position aside.

✳ WARNING

Extreme care must be exercised when removing and installing the stabilizer bar on vehicles equipped with rear air conditioning (A/C) and/or rear heating or damage to the A/C lines and rear heater hoses can occur.

12. With the aid of an assistant, remove the stabilizer bar from the LH side of the vehicle.

To install:

✳ WARNING

Extreme care must be exercised when removing and installing the stabilizer bar on vehicles equipped with rear air conditioning (A/C) and/or rear heating or damage to the A/C lines and rear heater hoses can occur.

13. With the aid of an assistant, install the stabilizer bar in through the LH side of the vehicle.

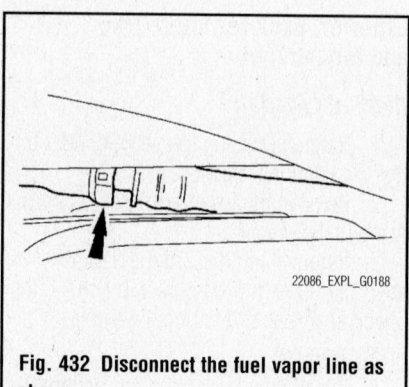

22086_EXPL_G0188

Fig. 432 Disconnect the fuel vapor line as shown

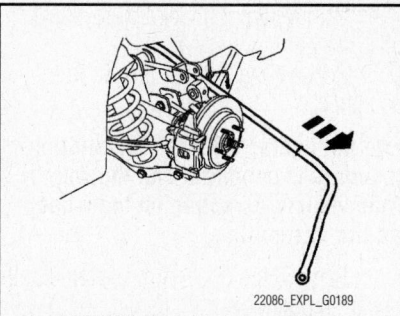

Fig. 433 With the aid of an assistant, remove the stabilizer bar from the LH side of the vehicle

14. Clip the fuel vapor line to the fuel tank.

15. Connect the fuel vapor line.

16. Ensure the jack is under the wheel knuckle and raised until the distance between the center of the hub and the lip of the fender is equal to the curb height measurement.

17. Install the 4 stabilizer bar bracket studs reversing the directions noted in removal.

18. Install the 2 stabilizer bar brackets and the 2 stabilizer bar bushings.

19. Install 4 new stabilizer bar bracket nuts. Torque the nuts to 35 ft. lbs. (48 Nm).

20. Install the stabilizer bar link nut and grommet, stud and link assembly. Torque the nut to 22 ft. lbs. (30 Nm).

21. Install the new outboard nuts and bolts to both upper arms. Torque to 203 ft. lbs. (275 Nm).

2007 Explorer Sport-Trac

See Figures 432, 433, 435 and 436.

1. Before servicing the vehicle, refer to the "Precautions" section.

> **※※ CAUTION**
>
> **Orientation of the suspension fasteners is important. Make sure the fasteners are installed in the same direction as they were in when removed.**

2. Measure the distance from the center of the hub to the lip of the fender with the vehicle in a level, static ground position (curb height).

3. Remove both upper arms. See "Upper Control Arm" section.

4. Remove the LH shock absorber lower bolt to allow more movement of the wheel knuckle when installing the stabilizer bar.

5. Disconnect the purge solenoid electrical connector.

6. Unclip the wiring harness from the frame.

7. Remove the fuel tank filler pipe bracket bolt.

8. Loosen the fuel tank filler pipe hose clamps and disconnect the hose.

9. Remove the stabilizer bar link nut and grommet, stud and link assembly.

10. Remove the wiring harness retainer caps from the stabilizer bar bracket studs.

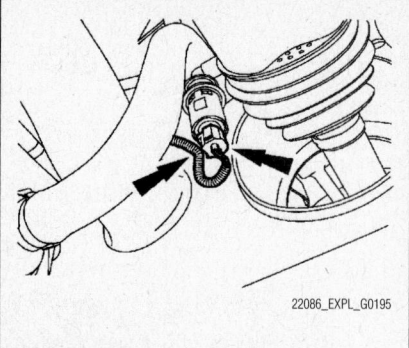

Fig. 435 Disconnect the purge solenoid electrical connector—2007 Explorer Sport-Trac

11. Remove and discard the 4 stabilizer bar bracket nuts.

12. Remove the 2 stabilizer bar brackets and the 2 stabilizer bar bushings.

13. Remove the 4 stabilizer bar bracket studs, noting the following:

   a. For the front studs, push the stud down and slide the stud toward the rear of the vehicle.

   b. For the rear studs, push the stud down and slide the stud toward the front of the vehicle.

14. Disconnect the fuel vapor line as shown.

15. Unclip the fuel vapor line from the fuel tank and position aside.

> **※※ WARNING**
>
> **Extreme care must be exercised when removing and installing the stabilizer bar on vehicles equipped with rear air conditioning (A/C) and/or rear heating or damage to the A/C lines and rear heater hoses can occur.**

16. With the aid of an assistant, remove the stabilizer bar from the LH side of the vehicle.

To install:

➡ Before tightening the stabilizer bar link nuts, use a suitable jack to raise the suspension until the distance between the center of the hub and the lip of the fender is equal to the curb height measurement.

> **※※ WARNING**
>
> **Extreme care must be exercised when removing and installing the stabilizer bar on vehicles equipped with rear air conditioning (A/C) and/or rear heating or damage to the A/C lines and rear heater hoses can occur.**

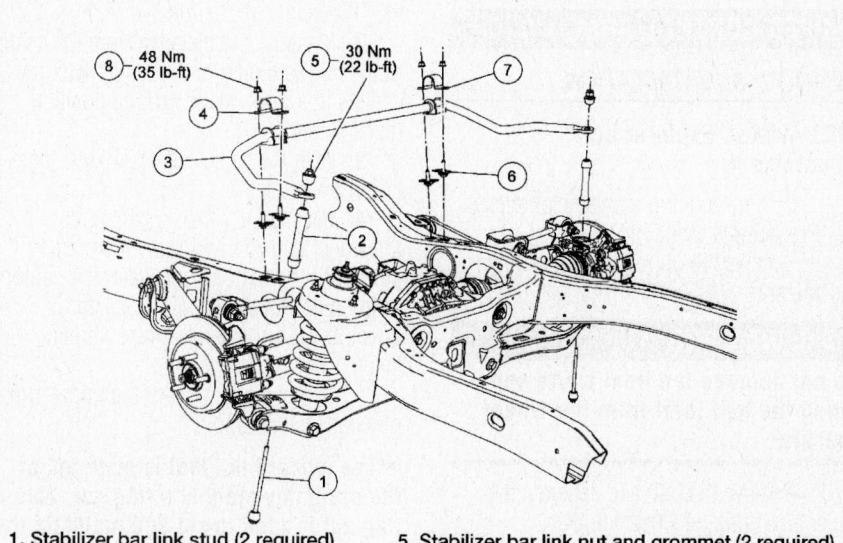

1. Stabilizer bar link stud (2 required)
2. Stabilizer bar link assembly (2 required)
3. Stabilizer bar
4. Stabilizer bar bracket (2 required)
5. Stabilizer bar link nut and grommet (2 required)
6. Stabilizer bar bracket stud (4 required)
7. Stabilizer bar bushing (2 required)
8. Stabilizer bar bracket nut (4 required)

Fig. 434 Showing the stabilizer bar and link and mounting components

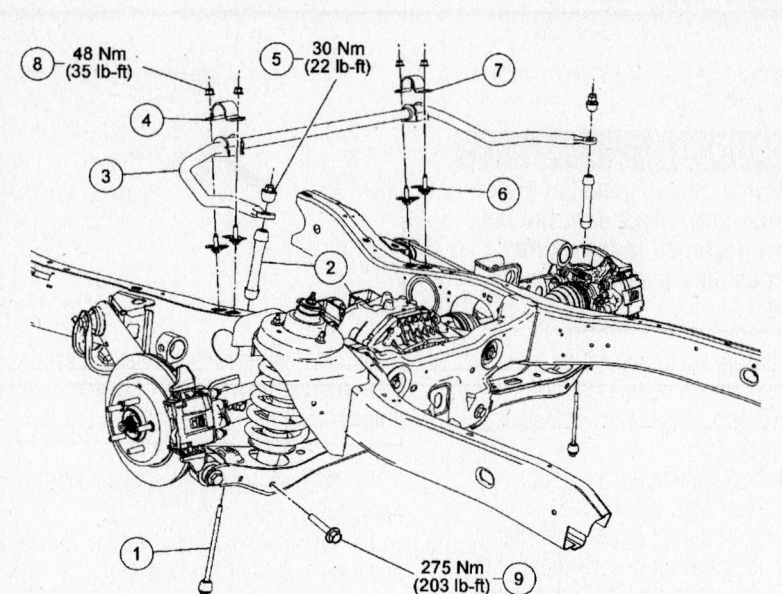

1. Stabilizer bar link stud (2 required)
2. Stabilizer bar link assembly (2 required)
3. Stabilizer bar
4. Stabilizer bar bracket (2 required)
5. Stabilizer bar link nut and grommet (2 required)
6. Stabilizer bar bracket stud (4 required)
7. Stabilizer bar bushing (2 required)
8. Stabilizer bar bracket nut (4 required)
9. Shock absorber lower bolt

22086_EXPL_G0194

Fig. 436 Showing the stabilizer bar and link and mounting components—2007 Explorer Sport-Trac

17. With the aid of an assistant, carefully install the stabilizer bar in through the LH side of the vehicle, watching for interference from wiring and other components.

18. Clip the fuel vapor line to the fuel tank.

19. Connect the fuel vapor line.

20. Ensure the jack is under the wheel knuckle and raised until the distance between the center of the hub and the lip of the fender is equal to the curb height measurement.

21. Install the 4 stabilizer bar bracket studs reversing the directions noted in removal.

22. Install the wiring harness retainer caps to the stabilizer bar bracket studs.

23. Install the stabilizer bar link nut and grommet, stud and link assembly. Torque the nut to 22 ft. lbs. (30 Nm).

24. Reinstall the fuel tank filler pipe hose and connect the hose clamps.

25. Install the fuel tank filler pipe bracket bolt. Torque to 11 ft. lbs. (15 Nm).

26. Clip the wiring harness to the frame.

27. Connect the purge solenoid electrical connector.

28. Install the LH shock absorber lower bolt.

29. Install both upper arms. See "Upper Control Arm" section.

UPPER CONTROL ARM

REMOVAL & INSTALLATION

2005 Aviator, Explorer and Mountaineer

1. Before servicing the vehicle, refer to the "Precautions" section.

2. Remove the upper arm-to-wheel knuckle nut.

✲✲ WARNING

Do not damage the boot while separating the ball joint from the wheel knuckle.

3. Remove the bolt and separate the upper arm from the wheel knuckle.

✲✲ WARNING

Make sure that the upper arm-to-frame mounting bolts are routed through the frame and the bushing before tightening.

4. Remove the 2 upper arm-to-frame bolts (rearward mounting).

5. Remove the 2 upper arm-to-frame flag nuts.

➡**Do not tighten until the installation procedure is complete and the weight of the vehicle is resting on the wheel and tire assemblies.**

6. Remove the upper arm-to-frame bolt (forward mounting).

7. Remove the upper arm-to-frame flag nut.

8. Remove the upper arm.

To install:

➡**Do not tighten the fasteners until the installation procedure is complete and the weight of the vehicle is resting on the wheel and tire assemblies.**

9. Installation is the reverse of the removal procedure.

10. Observe the following tightening specifications:

- Upper arm-to-frame bolt (forward mounting): 98 ft. lbs. (133 Nm)
- Upper arm-to-frame bolts (rearward mounting): 59 ft. lbs. (80 Nm)
- Upper arm-to-wheel knuckle nut: 66 ft. lbs (90 Nm).

2006–07 Explorer and Mountaineer; 2007 Explorer Sport-Trac

See Figure 437.

1. Before servicing the vehicle, refer to the "Precautions" section.

2. Measure the distance from the center of the hub to the lip of the fender with the vehicle in a level, static ground position (curb height).

3. With the vehicle in NEUTRAL, position it on a hoist.

4. Position a suitable jack under the wheel knuckle and raise the suspension until the distance between the center of the hub and the lip of the fender is equal to the curb height measurement taken.

5. Remove and discard the upper arm outboard nut and bolt.

➡**The inboard nut that is installed at the assembly plant is a flag nut. This flag nut is used to set and maintain the rear camber settings. Discard the flag nut and install a non-flag nut to allow the rear camber to be adjusted.**

6. Remove and discard the upper arm inboard bolt and flag nut and remove the upper arm.

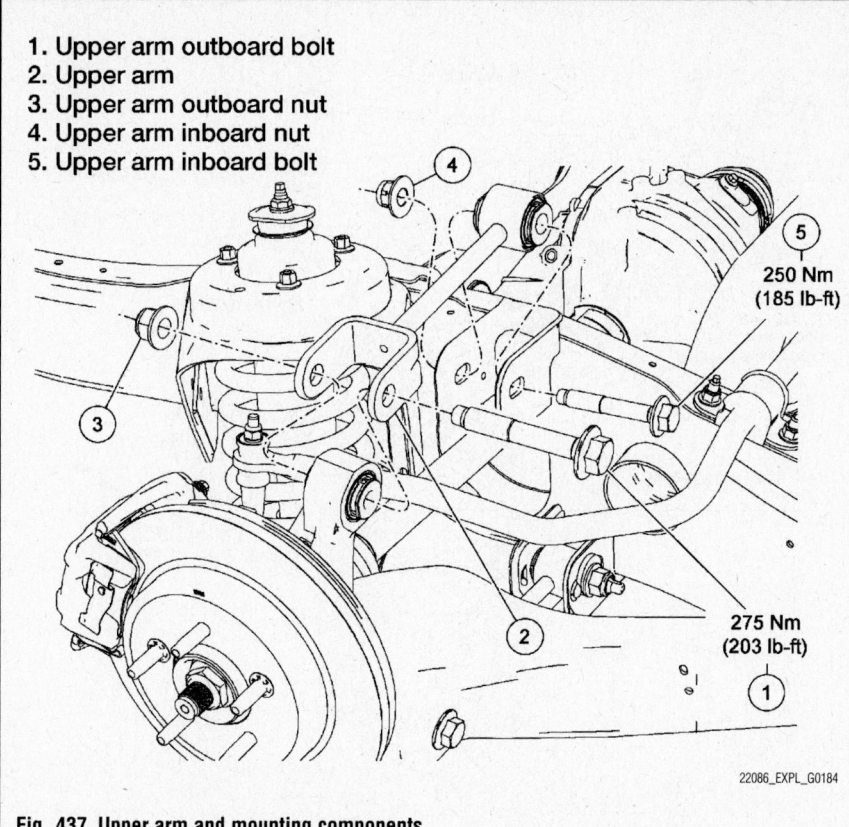

1. Upper arm outboard bolt
2. Upper arm
3. Upper arm outboard nut
4. Upper arm inboard nut
5. Upper arm inboard bolt

250 Nm
(185 lb-ft)

275 Nm
(203 lb-ft)

22086_EXPL_G0184

Fig. 437 Upper arm and mounting components

To install:

7. Ensure the jack is still properly positioned under the wheel knuckle.

8. Position the upper arm and install a new inboard bolt and non-flag nut. Torque the fasteners to 185 ft. lbs. (250 Nm).

❊❊ CAUTION

The upper arm outboard bolt must be installed with the bolt head toward the front of the vehicle or wheel damage can occur.

9. Install a new outboard bolt and nut with the bolt head toward the front of the vehicle. Torque to 203 ft. lbs. (275 Nm).

10. Lower the suspension and remove the jack.

11. Check and, if necessary, align the rear end.

KNUCKLE/SPINDLE

REMOVAL & INSTALLATION

2005 Aviator, Explorer, Mountaineer

❊❊ WARNING

Do not loosen the axle wheel hub retainer until the wheel and tire are removed from the vehicle. Wheel bearing damage will occur if the wheel bearing is unloaded with the weight of the vehicle applied.

➡ **Have an assistant press the brake pedal to keep the axle from turning.**

1. Before servicing the vehicle, refer to the "Precautions" section.

2. Remove the axle-to-wheel hub retainer nut and washer. Discard the nut.

3. Remove the parking brake shoes.

❊❊ WARNING

Do not use a hammer to separate the outboard CV-joint from the hub. Damage to the threads and internal CV-joint components can result.

4. Press the outboard CV-joint until it is loose from the hub.

5. Remove and discard the toe link-to-wheel knuckle nut.

❊❊ WARNING

Do not damage the boot while separating the toe link from the wheel knuckle.

6. Remove the bolt and separate the toe link from the wheel knuckle.

7. Remove and discard the upper arm-to-wheel knuckle nut.

❊❊ WARNING

Do not damage the boot while separating the ball joint from the wheel knuckle.

8. Remove the bolt and separate the upper arm from the wheel knuckle.

9. Remove and discard the lower arm-to-wheel knuckle nut.

10. Remove the lower arm-to-wheel knuckle bolt.

11. Remove the wheel knuckle.

12. Remove the 3 brake shield-to-wheel knuckle bolts.

13. Using a suitable press, remove and discard the wheel hub.

14. Remove the brake shield from the wheel knuckle.

15. Remove and discard the wheel bearing retainer ring.

16. Using a suitable press, remove and discard the wheel bearing.

To install:

17. Installation is the reverse of the removal procedure.

18. Observe the following torque specifications:
- Brake shield-to-wheel knuckle bolts: 115 inch lbs. (13 Nm).
- Lower arm-to-knuckle nut: 111 ft. lbs. (150 Nm).
- Upper arm-to-wheel knuckle nut: 66 ft. lbs. (90 Nm).
- Toe link-to-knuckle nut: 66 ft. lbs. (90 Nm).
- Axle-to-wheel hub retainer nut: 203 ft. lbs. (275 Nm)

19. Always install a new:
- Axle-to-wheel hub retainer nut.
- Toe link-to-wheel knuckle nut.
- Upper arm-to-wheel knuckle nut.
- Lower arm-to-wheel knuckle nut.
- Wheel hub.
- Wheel bearing retainer ring.
- Wheel bearing.

2006–07 Explorer And Mountaineer; 2007 Explorer Sport-Trac

See Figures 438 through 441.

1. Before servicing the vehicle, refer to the "Precautions" section.

2. Measure the distance from the center of the hub to the lip of the fender with the vehicle in a level, static ground position (curb height).

3. If equipped, remove the wheel speed sensor bolt and position the sensor aside.

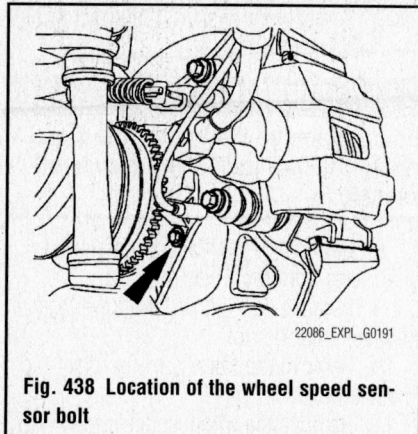

Fig. 438 Location of the wheel speed sensor bolt

❊❊ CAUTION

Do not loosen the halfshaft nut and washer until the wheel and tire are removed from the vehicle. Wheel bearing damage will occur if the wheel bearing is unloaded with the weight of the vehicle applied.

4. Remove the rear wheels.

5. Apply the brake to keep the halfshaft from rotating. Remove and discard the front wheel hub nut.

6. Remove the parking brake shoes.

7. Using a proper tool, press the halfshaft from the hub.

8. Position a suitable jack under the wheel knuckle and raise the suspension until the distance between the center of the hub and the lip of the fender is equal to the curb height measurement.

9. Remove and discard the following:
- toe link outboard nut and bolt
- upper arm outboard nut and bolt
- lower arm outboard nut and bolt
- 3 wheel knuckle bolts

10. Remove the wheel knuckle.

11. If a new wheel knuckle is being installed, remove the wheel bearing and wheel hub.

To install:

12. Position a suitable jack under the wheel knuckle and raise the suspension until the distance between the center of the hub and the lip of the fender is equal to the curb height measurement.

13. Position the wheel knuckle and install 3 new wheel knuckle bolts. Torque the bolts to 203 ft. lbs. (275 Nm).

14. Install a new lower arm outboard bolt and flag nut. Torque the nut to 203 ft. lbs. (275 Nm).

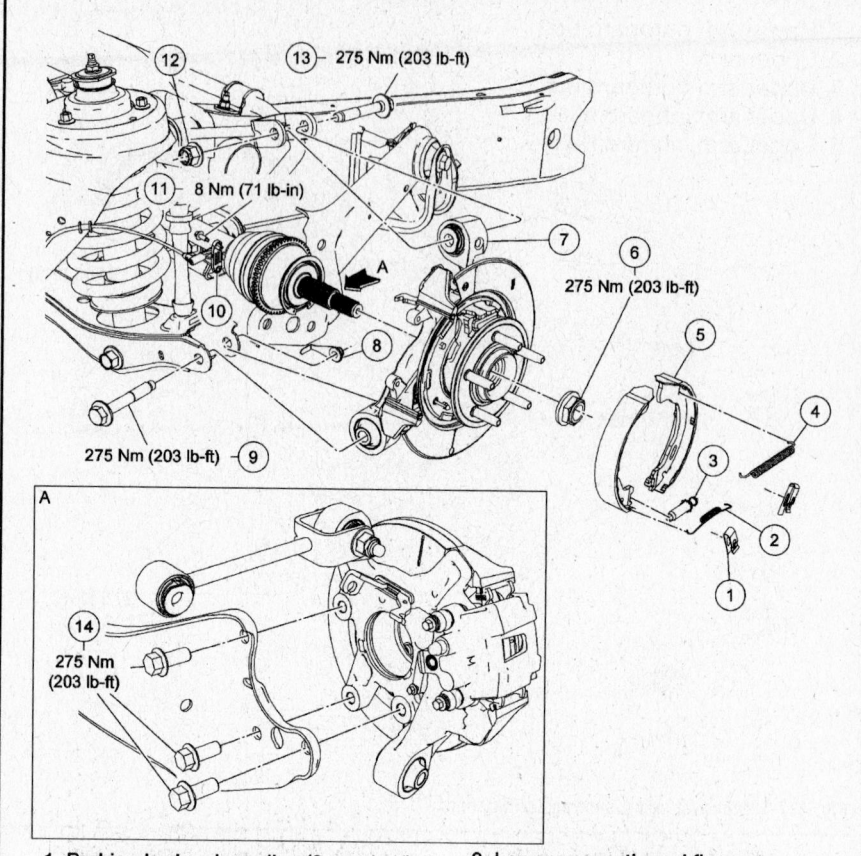

1. Parking brake shoe clips (2 required)
2. Parking brake shoe adjuster spring
3. Parking brake shoe adjuster
4. Parking brake shoe retracting spring
5. Parking brake shoe (2 required)
6. Halfshaft nut and washer
7. LH/RH Wheel knuckle
8. Lower arm outboard flag nut
9. Lower arm outboard bolt
10. Wheel speed sensor
11. Wheel speed sensor bolt
12. Upper arm outboard nut
13. Upper arm outboard bolt
14. Wheel knuckle bolts (3 required)

Fig. 439 Exploded view of the wheel knuckle, spindle, and related mounting components

❊❊ CAUTION

The upper arm outboard bolt must be installed with the bolt head toward the front of the vehicle or wheel damage can occur.

15. Install a new upper arm outboard bolt and nut with the bolt head toward the front of the vehicle. Torque the bolt to 203 ft. lbs. (275 Nm).

16. Position the toe link and install a new toe link outboard bolt and nut.

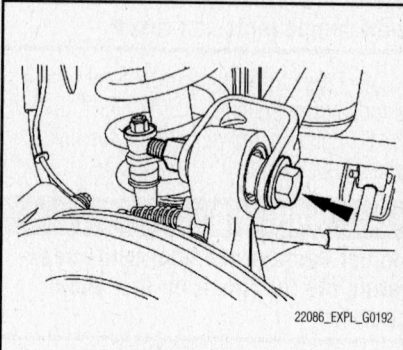

Fig. 440 Showing the proper direction for the upper arm outboard bolt

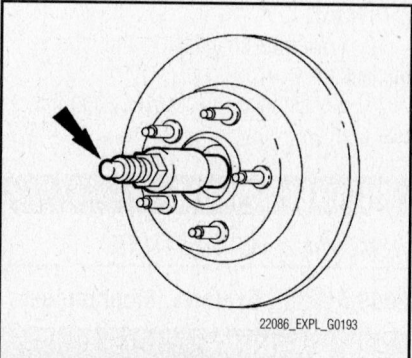

Fig. 441 Using a suitable halfshaft installer tool, install the halfshaft

17. Lower the suspension and remove the jack.

18. Install the parking brake shoes. See "Parking Brake" section.

19. Position the wheel speed sensor and install the bolt.

20. Using a suitable halfshaft installer tool, install the halfshaft.

21. Have an assistant press the brake pedal to keep the axle from turning, then install a new halfshaft nut and washer. Torque the nut to 203 ft. lbs. (275 Nm).

WHEEL HUB AND BEARING

REMOVAL & INSTALLATION

2005 Aviator, Explorer and Mountaineer

See Figures 442 and 443.

❋ WARNING

Do not loosen the axle wheel hub retainer until the wheel and tire are removed from the vehicle.

Wheel bearing damage will occur if the wheel bearing is unloaded with the weight of the vehicle applied.

➡**Have an assistant press the brake pedal to keep the axle from turning.**

1. Before servicing the vehicle, refer to the "Precautions" section.

2. Remove the axle-to-wheel hub retainer nut and washer.

3. Remove the parking brake shoes.

❋ WARNING

Do not use a hammer to separate the outboard CV-joint from the hub. Damage to the threads and internal CV-joint components can result.

4. Press the outboard CV-joint until it is loose from the hub.

5. Remove and discard the toe link-to-wheel knuckle nut.

❋ WARNING

Do not damage the boot while separating the toe link from the wheel knuckle.

6. Remove the bolt and separate the toe link from the wheel knuckle.

7. Remove and discard the upper arm-to-wheel knuckle nut.

❋ WARNING

Do not damage the boot while separating the ball joint from the wheel knuckle.

8. Remove the bolt and separate the upper arm from the wheel knuckle.

9. Remove and discard the lower arm-to-wheel knuckle nut.

10. Remove the lower arm-to-wheel knuckle bolt.

11. Remove the wheel knuckle.

12. Using a suitable press, remove and discard the wheel hub.

13. Remove and discard the wheel bearing retainer ring.

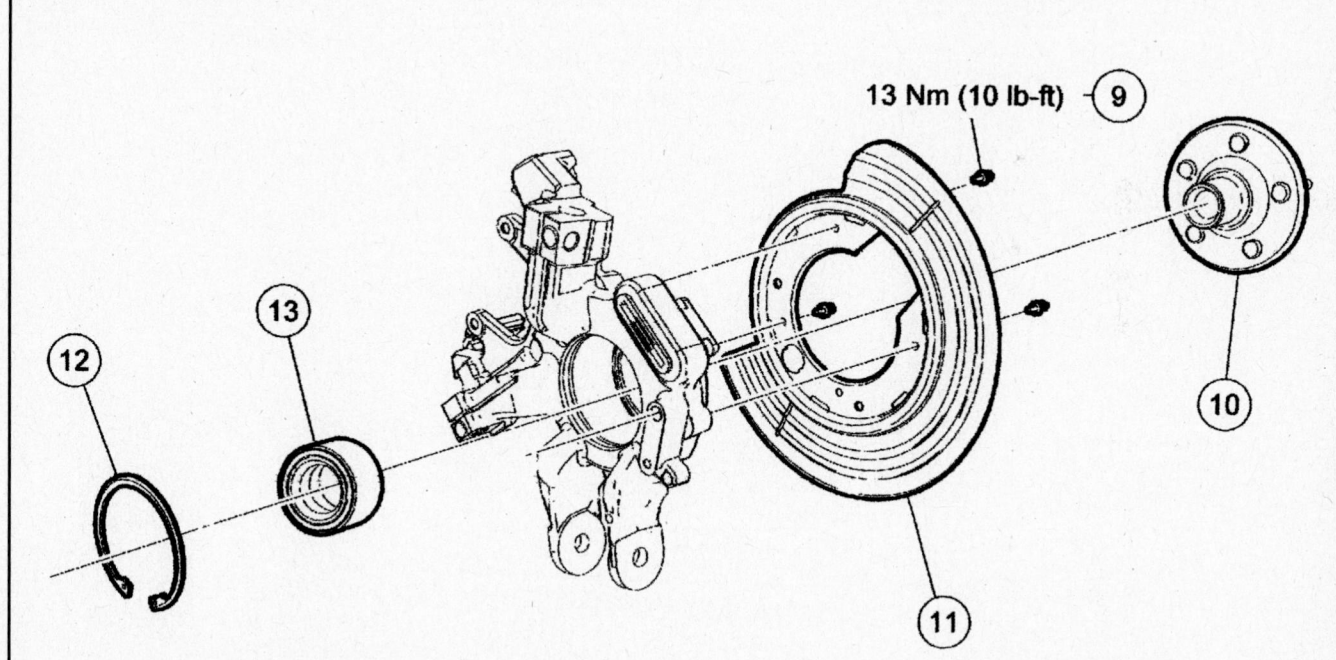

13 Nm (10 lb-ft)

9 **Brake shield-to-wheel knuckle bolts**

10 **Wheel hub**

11 **Brake shield**

12 **Retainer ring**

13 **Wheel bearing**

06017-EXPL-G155

Fig. 442 Rear hub/bearing assembly—Aviator, Explorer and Mountaineer

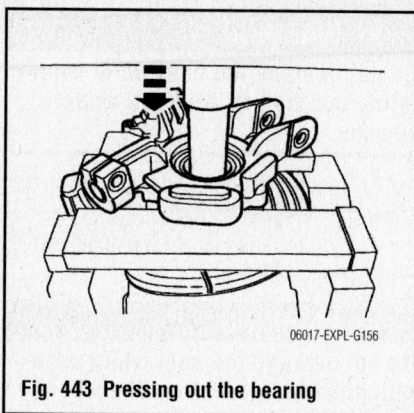

06017-EXPL-G156

Fig. 443 Pressing out the bearing

14. Using a suitable press, remove the wheel bearing.

To install:

15. Installation is the reverse of the removal procedure.

16. Observe the following torque specifications:

- Lower arm-to-wheel knuckle nut: 111 ft. lbs. (150 Nm).
- Upper arm-to-wheel knuckle nut: 66 ft. lbs. (90 Nm).
- Toe link-to-wheel knuckle nut: 66 ft. lbs. (90 Nm).
- Axle-to-hub retainer nut: 203 ft. lbs. (275 Nm).

17. Always install a new:
- Axle-to-wheel hub retainer nut.
- Toe link-to-wheel knuckle nut.
- Upper arm-to-wheel knuckle nut.
- Lower arm-to-wheel knuckle nut.
- Wheel hub.
- Wheel bearing retainer ring.

2006–07 Explorer and Mountaineer; 2007 Explorer Sport-Trac

See Figure 444.

1. Remove the wheel knuckle.
2. Remove the 3 brake disc shield bolts.

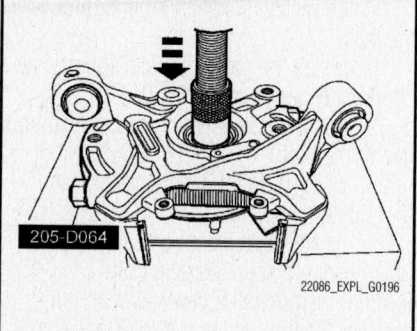

205-D064

22086_EXPL_G0196

Fig. 444 Using the special tool and a suitable press, remove the wheel hub

3. Using the special tool and a suitable press, remove the wheel hub.
4. Remove the snap ring.
5. Using a suitable press and adapters, remove the wheel bearing.
6. Installation is the reverse of the removal procedure.

FORD, LINCOLN AND MERCURY

Crown Victoria • Grand Marquis • Town Car

2

SPECIFICATIONS AND MAINTENANCE CHARTS

ENGINE AND VEHICLE IDENTIFICATION

Code ①	Liters (cc)	Cu. In.	Cyl.	Fuel Sys.	Type	Eng. Mfg.
W	4.6 (4593)	281	8	SFI	SOHC	Ford
V	4.6 (4593)	281	8	SFI	SOHC	Ford

Code ②	Year
5	2005
6	2006
7	2007

SOHC: Single Overhead Camshaft

V: Flex Fuel/E-85 Compliant

① 8th digit of the Vehicle Identification Number (VIN)

② 10th digit of the Vehicle Identification Number (VIN)

22086_CVIC_C0001

GENERAL ENGINE SPECIFICATIONS

Year	Model	Engine Displacement Liters	Engine ID/VIN	Net Horsepower @ rpm	Net Torque @ rpm (ft. lbs.)	Bore x Stroke (in.)	Compression Ratio	Oil Pressure @ rpm
2005	Crown Victoria	4.6	W	①	②	3.60x3.60	③	20-45@1500
	Grand Marquis	4.6	W	①	②	3.60x3.60	9.4:1	20-45@1500
	Town Car	4.6	W	①	②	3.60x3.60	9.4:1	20-45@1500
2006	Crown Victoria	4.6	W,V ④	①	②	3.60x3.60	③	20-45@1500
	Grand Marquis	4.6	W,V ④	①	②	3.60x3.60	9.4:1	20-45@1500
	Town Car	4.6	W,V ④	①	②	3.60x3.60	9.4:1	20-45@1500
2007	Crown Victoria	4.6	W,V ④	①	②	3.60x3.60	③	20-45@1500
	Grand Marquis	4.6	W,V ④	①	②	3.60x3.60	9.4:1	20-45@1500
	Town Car	4.6	W,V ④	①	②	3.60x3.60	9.4:1	20-45@1500

① Single exhaust: 220@4750
Dual exhaust: 235@4000
Crown Victoria with natural gas: 178@4500

② Single exhaust: 265@4000
Dual exhaust: 275@4000
Crown Victoria with natural gas: 237@3500

③ Gasoline engine: 9.4:1
Natural gas engine: 10.0:1

④ VIN V not available on taxi and police models

22086_CVIC_C0002

ENGINE TUNE-UP SPECIFICATIONS

Year	Engine Displacement Liters	Engine ID/VIN	Spark Plug Gap (in.)	Ignition Timing (deg.)	Fuel Pump (psi) ①	Idle Speed (rpm)	Valve Clearance Intake	Valve Clearance Exhaust
2005	4.6	W	0.054	10BTDC	25-40	②	HYD	HYD
2006	4.6	W	0.054	10BTDC	25-40	②	HYD	HYD
	4.6	V	0.054	10BTDC	25-40	②	HYD	HYD
2007	4.6	W	0.054	10BTDC	25-40	②	HYD	HYD
	4.6	V	0.054	10BTDC	25-40	②	HYD	HYD

NOTE: The Vehicle Emission Control Information label may reflect specification changes made during production. The label specifications must be used if they differ from those in this chart.

BTDC: Before Top Dead Center

HYD: Hydraulic

① Fuel pressure with engine running, pressure regulator vacuum hose connected

② Refer to Vehicle Emission Control Information label

22086_CVIC_C0003

CAPACITIES

Year	Model	Engine Displacement Liters	Engine ID/VIN	Engine Oil with Filter (qts.)	Automatic Transmission (pts.) ①	Rear Drive Axle (pts.)	Fuel Tank (gal.)	Cooling System (qts.)
2005	Crown Victoria	4.6	W	5.0	27.2	3.75	19.0	19.2
	Grand Marquis	4.6	W	5.0	28.2	3.75	19.0	19.2
	Town Car	4.6	W	5.0	28.2	3.75	19.0	19.2
2006	Crown Victoria	4.6	W,V	5.0	27.2	3.75	19.0	19.2
	Grand Marquis	4.6	W	5.0	28.2	3.75	19.0	19.2
	Town Car	4.6	W	5.0	28.2	3.75	19.0	19.2
2007	Crown Victoria	4.6	W,V	5.0	27.2	3.75	19.0	19.2
	Grand Marquis	4.6	W	5.0	28.2	3.75	19.0	19.2
	Town Car	4.6	W	5.0	28.2	3.75	19.0	19.2

NOTE: All capacities are approximate. Add fluid gradually and ensure a proper fluid level is obtained.

① Includes torque converter

22086_CVIC_C0004

FLUID SPECIFICATIONS

Year	Model	Engine Displacement Liters	Engine ID/VIN	Engine Oil	Auto. Trans. ①	Drive Axle	Power Steering Fluid	Brake Master Cylinder
2005	Crown Victoria	4.6	W,V ②	5W-20	Mercon V	80W-90	Mercon MP ATF	DOT 3
	Grand Marqis	4.6	W	5W-20	Mercon V	80W-90	Mercon MP ATF	DOT 3
	Town Car	4.6	W	5W-20	Mercon V	80W-90	Mercon MP ATF	DOT 3
2006	Crown Victoria	4.6	W,V ②	5W-20	Mercon V	80W-90	Mercon MP ATF	DOT 3
	Grand Marqis	4.6	W	5W-20	Mercon V	80W-90	Mercon MP ATF	DOT 3
	Town Car	4.6	W	5W-20	Mercon V	80W-90	Mercon MP ATF	DOT 3
2007	Crown Victoria	4.6	W,V ②	5W-20	Mercon V	80W-90	Mercon MP ATF	DOT 3
	Grand Marqis	4.6	W	5W-20	Mercon V	80W-90	Mercon MP ATF	DOT 3
	Town Car	4.6	W	5W-20	Mercon V	80W-90	Mercon MP ATF	DOT 3

① MERCON V = XT-5-QM or XT-5-QMC (US); CXT-5-LM12 (Canada)

② VIN V Not available on taxi and police models

22086_CVIC_C0005

VALVE SPECIFICATIONS

All measurements are given in inches.

Year	Engine Displacement Liters	Engine ID/VIN	Seat Angle (deg.)	Face Angle (deg.)	Spring Test Pressure (lbs. @ in.)	Spring Installed Height (in.)	Stem-to-Guide Clearance (in.) Intake	Stem-to-Guide Clearance (in.) Exhaust	Stem Diameter (in.) Intake	Stem Diameter (in.) Exhaust
2005	4.6	W	45	45.5	132@1.10	1.570	0.0008-0.0027	0.0018-0.0037	0.2746-0.2754	0.2736-0.2744
2006	4.6	W	45	45.5	132@1.10	1.570	0.0008-0.0027	0.0018-0.0037	0.2746-0.2754	0.2736-0.2744
	4.6	V	45	45.5	160@1.03	1.570	0.0008-0.0027	0.0018-0.0037	0.2746-0.275	0.2736-0.2744
2007	4.6	W	45	45.5	132@1.10	1.570	0.0008-0.0027	0.0018-0.0037	0.2746-0.2754	0.2736-0.2744
	4.6	V	45	45.5	160@1.03	1.570	0.0008-0.0027	0.0018-0.0037	0.2746-0.275	0.2736-0.2744

22086_CVIC_C0006

CAMSHAFT AND BEARING SPECIFICATIONS CHART

All measurements are given in inches.

Year	Engine Displ. Liters	Engine ID/VIN	Journal Dia.	Brg. Oil Clearance	Shaft End-play	Runout	Journal Bore	Lobe Height Intake	Lobe Height Exhaust
2005	4.6	W,V	1.0605-1.0615	0.0010-0.0030	0.0011-0.0075	0.0035	1.0625 1.0635	0.2799	0.2952
2006	4.6	W,V	1.0605-1.0615	0.0010-0.0030	0.0011-0.0075	0.0035	1.0625 1.0635	0.2799	0.2952
2007	4.6	W,V	1.0605-1.0615	0.0010-0.0030	0.0011-0.0075	0.0035	1.0625 1.0635	0.2799	0.2952

22086_CVIC_C0007

PISTON AND RING SPECIFICATIONS

All measurements are given in inches.

Year	Engine Displacement Liters	Engine ID/VIN	Piston Clearance ①	Ring Gap Top Compression	Ring Gap Bottom Compression	Ring Gap Oil Control	Ring Side Clearance Top Compression	Ring Side Clearance Bottom Compression	Ring Side Clearance Oil Control
2005	4.6	W	0.0002-0.0010	0.005-0.012	0.012-0.022	0.006-0.026	②	0.008-0.0024	0.0010-0.0077
2006	4.6	W	0.0002-0.0010	0.005-0.012	0.012-0.022	0.006-0.026	②	0.008-0.0024	0.0010-0.0077
	4.6	V	0.0002-0.0010	0.005-0.012	0.012-0.022	0.006-0.026	②	0.008-0.0024	0.0010-0.0077
2007	4.6	W	0.0002-0.0010	0.005-0.012	0.012-0.022	0.006-0.026	②	0.008-0.0024	0.0010-0.0077
	4.6	V	0.0002-0.0010	0.005-0.012	0.012-0.022	0.006-0.026	②	0.008-0.0024	0.0010-0.0077

① Measured 1.96 in. (43mm) from the top
② On 10:1 engines: 0.0012-0.0028 in.
   On 9:1 engines: 0.0008-0.0024 in.

22086_CVIC_C0009

CRANKSHAFT AND CONNECTING ROD SPECIFICATIONS

All measurements are given in inches.

Year	Engine Displacement Liters	Engine ID/VIN	Crankshaft Main Brg. Journal Dia.	Crankshaft Main Brg. Oil Clearance	Crankshaft Shaft End-play	Thrust on No.	Connecting Rod Journal Diameter	Connecting Rod Oil Clearance	Connecting Rod Side Clearance
2005	4.6	W	2.6500-2.6570	0.0009-0.0026	0.0051-0.0119	5	2.0870-2.8670	0.0009-0.0026	0.0006-0.0177
2006	4.6	W	2.6500-2.6570	0.0009-0.0026	0.0051-0.0119	5	2.0870-2.8670	0.0009-0.0026	0.0006-0.0177
	4.6	V	2.6567-2.6577	0.0001-0.0018	0.0051-0.0119	5	2.0859-2.0867	0.0011-0.0027	0.0006-0.0177
2007	4.6	W	2.6500-2.6570	0.0009-0.0026	0.0051-0.0119	5	2.0870-2.8670	0.0009-0.0026	0.0006-0.0177
	4.6	V	2.6567-2.6577	0.0001-0.0018	0.0051-0.0119	5	2.0859-2.0867	0.0011-0.0027	0.0006-0.0177

22086_CVIC_C0008

TORQUE SPECIFICATIONS
All readings in ft. lbs.

Year	Engine Displacement Liters	Engine ID/VIN	Cylinder Head Bolts	Main Bearing Bolts	Rod Bearing Bolts	Crankshaft Damper Bolts	Flywheel Bolts	Manifold Intake	Manifold Exhaust	Spark Plugs	Oil Pan Drain Plug
2005	4.6	W	①	②	③	118	59	18	18	11	10
2006	4.6	W	①	②	③	118	59	18	18	11	10
	4.6	V	①	②	③	118	59	18	18	11	10
2007	4.6	W	①	②	③	118	59	18	18	11	10
	4.6	V	①	②	③	118	59	18	18	11	10

NOTE: Stretch bolts are used in all procedures that require rotating the fastener a certain number of degrees. The bolts stretch and cannot be reused.

For reassembly, replace with new fasteners.

① Step 1: 30 ft. lbs.

Step 2: Rotate 90 degrees

Step 3: Loosen 360 degrees

Step 4: 30 ft. lbs.

Step 5: Rotate 90 degrees

Step 5: Rotate an additional 90 degrees

② Step 1: Main bearing cap bolts: 30 ft. lbs.

Step 2: Rotate each bolt 90 degrees

Step 3: Main bearing cap adjusting screws: 44 in. lbs. then 89 in. lbs.

Step 4: Main bearing cap side bolts: 89 in. lbs. then 15 ft. lbs.

③ Step 1: 32 ft. lbs.

Step 2: 12 ft. lbs.

Step 2: Rotate 90-120 degrees

22086_CVIC_C0010

WHEEL ALIGNMENT

Year	Model		Caster Range (+/-Deg.)	Caster Preferred Setting (Deg.)	Camber Range (+/-Deg.)	Camber Preferred Setting (Deg.)	Toe-in (in.)
2005	Crown Victoria	F	0.75	+0.50	0.75	0	-0.25 +/- 0.25
		R	—	—	—	—	—
	Town Car	F	0.75	0	0.75	0	-0.12 +/- 0.25
		R	—	—	—	—	—
	Grand Marquis	F	0.75	+0.50	0.75	0	-0.13 +/- 0.25
		R	—	—	—	—	—
2006	Crown Victoria	F	0.75	+0.50	0.75	0	-0.25 +/- 0.25
		R	—	—	—	—	—
	Town Car	F	0.75	0	0.75	0	-0.12 +/- 0.25
		R	—	—	—	—	—
	Grand Marquis	F	0.75	+0.50	0.75	0	-0.13 +/- 0.25
		R	—	—	—	—	—
2007	Crown Victoria	F	0.75	+0.50	0.75	0	-0.25 +/- 0.25
		R	—	—	—	—	—
	Town Car	F	0.75	0	0.75	0	-0.12 +/- 0.25
		R	—	—	—	—	—
	Grand Marquis	F	0.75	+0.50	0.75	0	-0.13 +/- 0.25
		R	—	—	—	—	—

Note: Specifications apply to all models, including taxi, police, and vehicles equipped with air suspension

22086_CVIC_C0011

TIRE, WHEEL AND BALL JOINT SPECIFICATIONS

| Year | Model | OEM Tires | | Tire Pressure | | Wheel Size | Ball Joint Inspection | Lug Nut (ft. lbs.) |
		Standard	Optional	Front	Rear			
2005	Crown Victoria	P225/60SR16	P225/60TR16	32	32	7J	U ①	100
			P235/55HR17	35	35		L ①②	
	Crown Victoria Police Special	P225/60SR16	P225/60VR16	35	35	7J	U ①	100
							L ①②	
	Grand Marquis	P225/60SR16	NA	32	32	6-JJ	U ①	100
							L ①②	
	Grand Marquis w/Handling package	P225/60TR16	P225/60VR16	35	35	6-JJ	U ①	100
							L ①②	
	Town Car	P225/60R17	NA	32	32	Std: 7-JJ	U ①	100
							L ①②	
2006	Crown Victoria	P225/60SR16	P225/60TR16	32	32	7J	U ①	100
			P235/55HR17	35	35		L ①②	
	Crown Victoria Police Special	P225/60SR16	P225/60VR16	35	35	7J	U ①	100
							L ①②	
	Grand Marquis	P225/60SR16	NA	32	32	6-JJ	U ①	100
							L ①②	
	Grand Marquis w/Handling package	P225/60TR16	P225/60VR16	35	35	6-JJ	U ①	100
							L ①②	
	Town Car	P225/60R17	NA	32	32	Std: 7-JJ	U ①	100
							L ①②	
2007	Crown Victoria	P225/60SR16	P225/60TR16	32	32	7J	U ①	100
			P235/55HR17	35	35		L ①②	
	Crown Victoria Police Special	P225/60SR16	P225/60VR16	35	35	7J	U ①	100
							L ①②	
	Grand Marquis	P225/60SR16	NA	32	32	6-JJ	U ①	100
							L ①②	
	Grand Marquis w/Handling package	P225/60TR16	P225/60VR16	35	35	6-JJ	U ①	100
							L ①②	
	Town Car	P225/60R17	NA	32	32	Std: 7-JJ	U ①	100
							L ①②	

NA: Not Available

OEM: Original Equipment Manufacturer

PSI: Pounds Per Square Inch

U: Upper

L: Lower

① Replace if any measurable movement is found.

② Do not lift car. Inspect the boss into which the grease fitting is threaded. Replace if the boss is flush or receded below the surface of the ball joint.

22086_CVIC_C0012

BRAKE SPECIFICATIONS
All measurements in inches unless noted

Year	Model	Front Brake Disc Original Thickness	Front Brake Disc Minimum Thickness	Front Brake Disc Maximum Run-out	Rear Brake Disc Original Thickness	Rear Brake Disc Minimum Thickness	Rear Brake Disc Maximum Run-out	Minimum Lining Thickness	Brake Caliper Bracket Bolts (ft. lbs.)	Mounting Bolts (ft. lbs.)
2005	Crown Victoria	1.063	1.037	0.002	NA	0.790	0.003	0.039	118	27
	Grand Marquis	1.063	1.037	0.002	NA	0.790	0.003	0.039	118	27
	Town Car	1.063	1.037	0.002	NA	0.790	0.003	0.039	118	27
2006	Crown Victoria	1.063	1.037	0.002	NA	0.790	0.003	0.039	118	27
	Grand Marquis	1.063	1.037	0.002	NA	0.790	0.003	0.039	118	27
	Town Car	1.063	1.037	0.002	NA	0.790	0.003	0.039	118	27
2007	Crown Victoria	1.063	1.037	0.002	NA	0.790	0.003	0.039	118	27
	Grand Marquis	1.063	1.037	0.002	NA	0.790	0.003	0.039	118	27
	Town Car	1.063	1.037	0.002	NA	0.790	0.003	0.039	118	27

NOTE: Follow specifications stamped on rotor or drum if figures differ from those in this chart.

NA: Not Available

22086_CVIC_C0013

SCHEDULED MAINTENANCE INTERVALS
Ford—Crown Victoria, Mercury—Grand Marquis & Lincoln—Town Car

TO BE SERVICED	TYPE OF SERVICE	5	10	15	20	25	30	35	40	45	50	55	60	65
Engine oil & filter	R	✓	✓	✓	✓	✓	✓	✓	✓	✓	✓	✓	✓	✓
Rotate tires	S/I	✓		✓		✓		✓		✓		✓		✓
Cooling system, hoses, clamps & coolant strength	S/I			✓			✓			✓			✓	
Lubricate steering linkage	S/I			✓			✓						✓	
Air cleaner element	R						✓						✓	
Automatic transaxle fluid & filter	R						✓						✓	
Spark plugs ①	R													
Exhaust heat shields	S/I						✓						✓	
Fuel filter (NGV Crown Victoria) ②	R					✓					✓			
Front & rear brakes	S/I						✓						✓	
Lubricate suspension (Town Car)	S/I						✓						✓	
Engine coolant ③	R										✓			
PCV valve	R												✓	
Accessory drive belt	S/I												✓	

R: Replace   S/I: Service or Inspect

① Replace every 100,000 miles.

② Also drain coalescer assembly. Perform every 24,000 miles for severe service.

③ Change initially at 5 years/100,000 miles, and every 50,000 miles thereafter.

FREQUENT OPERATION MAINTENANCE (SEVERE SERVICE)

If a vehicle is operated under any of the following conditions it is considered severe service:

- Extremely dusty areas.

- 50% or more of the vehicle operation is in 32°C (90°F) or higher temperatures, or constant operation in temperatures below 0°C (32°F).

- Prolonged idling (vehicle operation in stop and go traffic).

- Frequent short running periods (engine does not warm to normal operating temperatures).

- Police, taxi, delivery usage or trailer towing usage.

Oil & filter change: change every 3000 miles.

Rotate tires at 6000 miles & every 9000 miles thereafter.

Automatic transmission fluid & filter: change every 21,000 miles.

22086_CVIC_C0014

PRECAUTIONS

Before servicing any vehicle, please be sure to read all of the following precautions, which deal with personal safety, prevention of component damage, and important points to take into consideration when servicing a motor vehicle:

• Never open, service or drain the radiator or cooling system when the engine is hot; serious burns can occur from the steam and hot coolant.

• Observe all applicable safety precautions when working around fuel. Whenever servicing the fuel system, always work in a well-ventilated area. Do not allow fuel spray or vapors to come in contact with a spark, open flame, or excessive heat (a hot drop light, for example). Keep a dry chemical fire extinguisher near the work area. Always keep fuel in a container specifically designed for fuel storage; also, always properly seal fuel containers to avoid the possibility of fire or explosion. Refer to the additional fuel system precautions later in this section.

• Fuel injection systems often remain pressurized, even after the engine has been turned **OFF**. The fuel system pressure must be relieved before disconnecting any fuel lines. Failure to do so may result in fire and/or personal injury.

• Brake fluid often contains polyglycol ethers and polyglycols. Avoid contact with the eyes and wash your hands thoroughly after handling brake fluid. If you do get brake fluid in your eyes, flush your eyes with clean, running water for 15 minutes. If eye irritation persists, or if you have taken brake fluid internally, IMMEDIATELY seek medical assistance.

• The EPA warns that prolonged contact with used engine oil may cause a number of skin disorders, including cancer. You should make every effort to minimize your exposure to used engine oil. Protective gloves should be worn when changing oil. Wash your hands and any other exposed skin areas as soon as possible after exposure to used engine oil. Soap and water, or waterless hand cleaner should be used.

• All new vehicles are now equipped with an air bag system, often referred to as a Supplemental Restraint System (SRS) or Supplemental Inflatable Restraint (SIR) system. The system must be disabled before performing service on or around system components, steering column, instrument panel components, wiring and sensors. Failure to follow safety and disabling procedures could result in accidental air bag deployment, possible personal injury and unnecessary system repairs.

• Always wear safety goggles when working with, or around, the air bag system. When carrying a non-deployed air bag, be sure the bag and trim cover are pointed away from your body. When placing a non-deployed air bag on a work surface, always face the bag and trim cover upward, away from the surface. This will reduce the motion of the module if it is accidentally deployed. Refer to the additional air bag system precautions later in this section.

• Clean, high quality brake fluid from a sealed container is essential to the safe and proper operation of the brake system. You should always buy the correct type of brake fluid for your vehicle. If the brake fluid becomes contaminated, completely flush the system with new fluid. Never reuse any brake fluid. Any brake fluid that is removed from the system should be discarded. Also, do not allow any brake fluid to come in contact with a painted surface; it will damage the paint.

• Never operate the engine without the proper amount and type of engine oil; doing so WILL result in severe engine damage.

• Timing belt maintenance is extremely important. Many models utilize an interference-type, non-freewheeling engine. If the timing belt breaks, the valves in the cylinder head may strike the pistons, causing potentially serious (also time-consuming and expensive) engine damage. Refer to the maintenance interval charts for the recommended replacement interval for the timing belt, and to the timing belt section for belt replacement and inspection.

• Disconnecting the negative battery cable on some vehicles may interfere with the functions of the on-board computer system(s) and may require the computer to undergo a relearning process once the negative battery cable is reconnected.

• When servicing drum brakes, only disassemble and assemble one side at a time, leaving the remaining side intact for reference.

• Only an MVAC-trained, EPA-certified automotive technician should service the air conditioning system or its components.

BRAKES
ANTI-LOCK BRAKE SYSTEM (ABS)

GENERAL INFORMATION

Vehicles are equipped with a 4-wheel Anti-Lock Brake System (ABS) with optional traction control (TC). The anti-lock brake system prevents wheel lock-up by automatically modulating brake pressure during an emergency stop and allows the driver to maintain steering control and stop the vehicle in the shortest possible distance under most conditions.

The traction control system, if equipped, controls wheelspin by modulating engine torque and applying then releasing the appropriate rear brake to restore traction when driving on slippery or loose surfaces.

SPEED SENSORS

REMOVAL & INSTALLATION

Front Wheel Speed Sensor

See Figure 1.

✳✳ CAUTION

The electrical power to the air suspension system must be turned off prior to hoisting, jacking or towing an air suspension vehicle. Failure to do so can result in unexpected inflation or deflation of the air springs, which can result in shifting of the vehicle during these operations.

✳✳ WARNING

The front wheel speed sensor acts as a wheel bearing seal. Do not operate the vehicle without the front wheel speed sensor installed.

1. Before servicing the vehicle, refer to the precautions in the beginning of this section.
2. Raise and support the vehicle.
3. Disconnect the front anti-lock brake sensor electrical connector.
4. Disconnect the routing clips.
5. Clean the area around the front wheel speed sensor of all dirt and foreign material before removal.

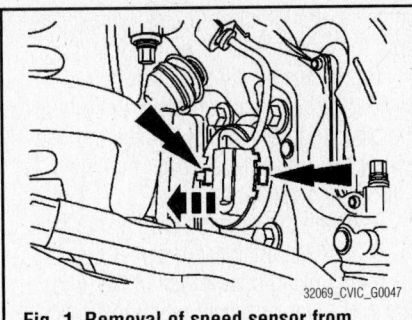

Fig. 1 Removal of speed sensor from housing

6. Remove the front anti-lock brake sensor as follows:
   • Push the tabs inward using a flat-blade screwdriver.
   • Pry the sensor out of its housing.

➡If the front wheel speed sensor wire clips are damaged, repair kit 2C577 is available.

To install:

✳✳ WARNING

Be sure to remove all dirt and foreign material from the area before installation.

7. Press the sensor into its housing until it clicks in place.
8. Reattach the harness routing clips and ABS sensor electrical connector

Rear Wheel Speed Sensor

See Figures 2 and 3.

✳✳ CAUTION

The electrical power to the air suspension system must be turned off prior to hoisting, jacking or towing an air suspension vehicle. Failure to do so can result in unexpected inflation or deflation of the air springs, which can result in shifting of the vehicle during these operations.

1. Before servicing the vehicle, refer to the precautions in the beginning of this section.
2. Remove rear seat bottom.
3. Disconnect the rear anti-lock brake sensor electrical connector.

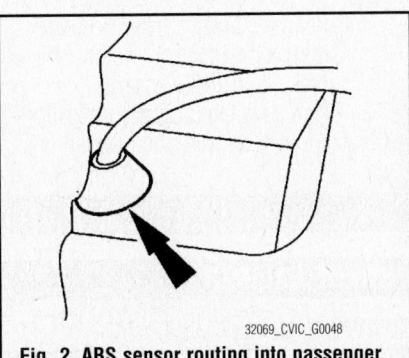
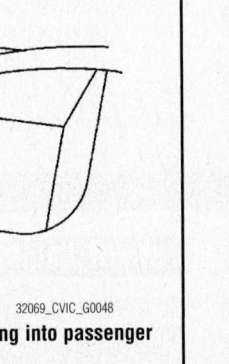

Fig. 2 ABS sensor routing into passenger compartment

4. Push the sensor harness grommet through the passenger compartment floor.
5. Disconnect the routing clips.
6. Remove the rear anti-lock brake sensor as follows:
   • Remove the bolt.
   • Remove the sensor.

To install:

7. Insert the sensor into its housing and torque the bolt to 64 inch lbs. (7 Nm)
8. Route the sensor harness into the passenger compartment and snap the grommet in place.
9. Reattach the routing clips.
10. Attach the sensor electrical connector.
11. Install the rear seat cushion.

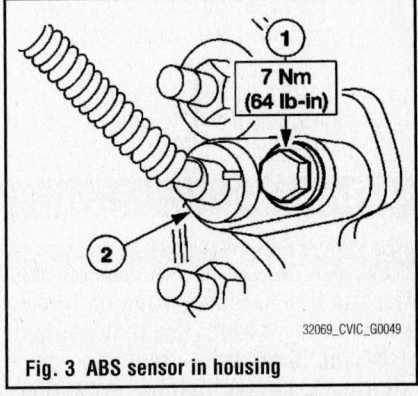

Fig. 3 ABS sensor in housing

BRAKES   BLEEDING THE BRAKE SYSTEM

BLEEDING PROCEDURE

BRAKE LINE BLEEDING

Manual Bleeding

✳✳ WARNING

Use of any brake fluid other than approved DOT 3 will cause permanent damage to brake components and will render the brakes inoperative. Failure to follow these instructions may result in personal injury.

✳✳ CAUTION

Brake fluid contains polyglycol ethers and polyglycols. Avoid contact with eyes. Wash hands thoroughly after handling. If brake fluid contacts eyes, flush eyes with running water for 15 minutes. Get medical attention if irritation persists. If taken internally, drink water and induce vomit-

ing. Get medical attention immediately. Failure to follow these instructions may result in personal injury.

✳✳ WARNING

Do not allow the brake master cylinder reservoir to run dry during the bleeding operation. Keep the brake master cylinder reservoir filled with the specified brake fluid. Never reuse the brake fluid that has been drained from the hydraulic system.

✳✳ WARNING

Brake fluid is harmful to painted and plastic surfaces. If spilled, wipe up immediately before damage to the painted or plastic surfaces occurs.

➡When any part of the hydraulic system has been disconnected for repair or installation of new components, air

can get into the system and cause spongy brake pedal action. This requires bleeding of the hydraulic system after it has been correctly connected.

➡If the hydraulic control unit (HCU) or any component upstream of the HCU are installed new, carry out the brake system bleed procedure first without the diagnostic tool, followed by the brake system bleed procedure using the diagnostic tool. This reduces the risk of trapping air in the HCU.

1. Before servicing the vehicle, refer to the precautions in the beginning of this section.
2. Connect the diagnostic tool DCL cable adapter into the vehicle data link connector (DLC) under the dash and follow the diagnostic tool instructions.
3. Clean all dirt from and remove the brake master cylinder filler cap and fill the

brake master cylinder reservoir with clean motor vehicle brake fluid.

4. For ABS vehicles only, open the master cylinder bleed screw until clear, bubble-free fluid flows from the tube into the cup.

5. Bleed the brake system in the order displayed on the diagnostic tool or bleed from the longest to the shortest brake line. Place a box end wrench on the bleeder screw. Attach a rubber drain tube to the bleeder screw and submerge the free end of the tube in a container partially filled with clean brake fluid.

6. Have an assistant hold firm pressure on the brake pedal.

7. Loosen the bleeder screw until a stream of brake fluid comes out. While the assistant maintains pressure on the brake pedal, tighten the bleeder screw.

- Repeat 3 times until clear, bubble-free fluid comes out.
- Refill the brake master cylinder reservoir with clean motor vehicle brake fluid as necessary.

8. Tighten the bleeder screw.

9. Repeat the for the remaining bleeder screws in the system.

Pressure Bleeding

1. Before servicing the vehicle, refer to the precautions in the beginning of this section.

2. Clean all dirt from and remove the brake master cylinder filler cap and fill the brake master cylinder reservoir with clean motor vehicle brake fluid.

3. Master cylinder pressure bleeder adapter tools are available from various manufacturers of pressure bleeding equipment. Follow the instructions of the manufacturer when installing the adapter.

4. Install the bleeder adapter to the brake master cylinder reservoir, and attach the bleeder tank hose to the fitting on the adapter.

- Refill the brake master cylinder reservoir with clean motor vehicle brake fluid as necessary.

5. Bleed from the longest to the shortest brake line. Make sure the bleeder tank

contains enough clean motor vehicle brake fluid to complete the bleeding operation.

6. Place a box end wrench on the bleeder screw. Attach a rubber drain tube to the bleeder screw, and submerge the free end of the tube in a container partially filled with clean brake fluid.

7. Open the valve on the bleeder tank.

8. Loosen the bleeder screw. Leave open until clear, bubble-free brake fluid flows. Have an assistant pump the brake pedal once every 2 seconds after the diagnostic tool runs the HCU pump. Wait 15 seconds after clear, bubble-free fluid flows through the rubber hose. Then, tighten the bleeder screw and remove the rubber hose.

9. Continue bleeding the rear of the system repeating Step 4 and 5.

10. Close the bleeder tank valve. Remove the tank hose from the adapter, and remove the adapter.

11. Fill the master cylinder reservoir with clean motor vehicle brake fluid

12. Install a new reservoir cap.

BRAKES   FRONT DISC BRAKES

✳ CAUTION

Dust and dirt accumulating on brake parts during normal use may contain asbestos fibers from production or aftermarket brake linings. Breathing excessive concentrations of asbestos fibers can cause serious bodily harm. Exercise care when servicing brake parts. Do not sand or grind brake lining unless equipment used is designed to contain the dust residue. Do not clean brake parts with compressed air or by dry brushing. Cleaning should be done by dampening the brake components with a fine mist of water, then wiping the brake components clean with a dampened cloth. Dispose of cloth and all residue containing asbestos fibers in an impermeable container with the appropriate label. Follow practices prescribed by the Occupational Safety and Health Administration (OSHA) and the Environmental Protection Agency (EPA) for the handling, processing, and disposing of dust or debris that may contain asbestos fibers.

BRAKE CALIPER

REMOVAL & INSTALLATION
See Figure 4.

✳ CAUTION

If the vehicle is equipped with air suspension, the electrical power to the air suspension system must be shut off prior to hoisting, jacking or towing an air suspension vehicle. This can be accomplished by turning off the air suspension switch located in the luggage compartment. Failure to do so can result in unexpected inflation or deflation of the air springs, which can result in shifting of the vehicle during these operations. Failure to follow these instructions may result in personal injury.

→Before continuing with this procedure, make sure to have available, 2 new disc brake caliper guide pin bolts and 2 banjo bolt sealing washers, per caliper. Once removed, these parts loose their torque holding ability or retention capability and must not be reused.

1. If equipped with air suspension, the air suspension switch, located on the right-hand side of the luggage compartment, must be turned to the **OFF** position before raising the vehicle.

2. Remove or disconnect the following:
- Front wheel and tire assembly
- Banjo bolt securing the brake hose from the disc brake caliper. Plug the brake hose. Discard the sealing washers.
- 2 disc brake caliper guide pin bolts and discard. If removing both calipers, mark the right and left sides so they may be reinstalled correctly.
- Disc brake caliper off of the anchor plate

To install:

3. Retract the disc brake caliper piston fully in the piston bore, using an old brake pad or block of wood and a C-clamp.

4. Install or connect the following:
- Disc brake pads to the caliper. Make sure that the brake pad insulators are correctly attached to the brake pad plate.
- Disc brake caliper onto the anchor plate. Make sure the inner and

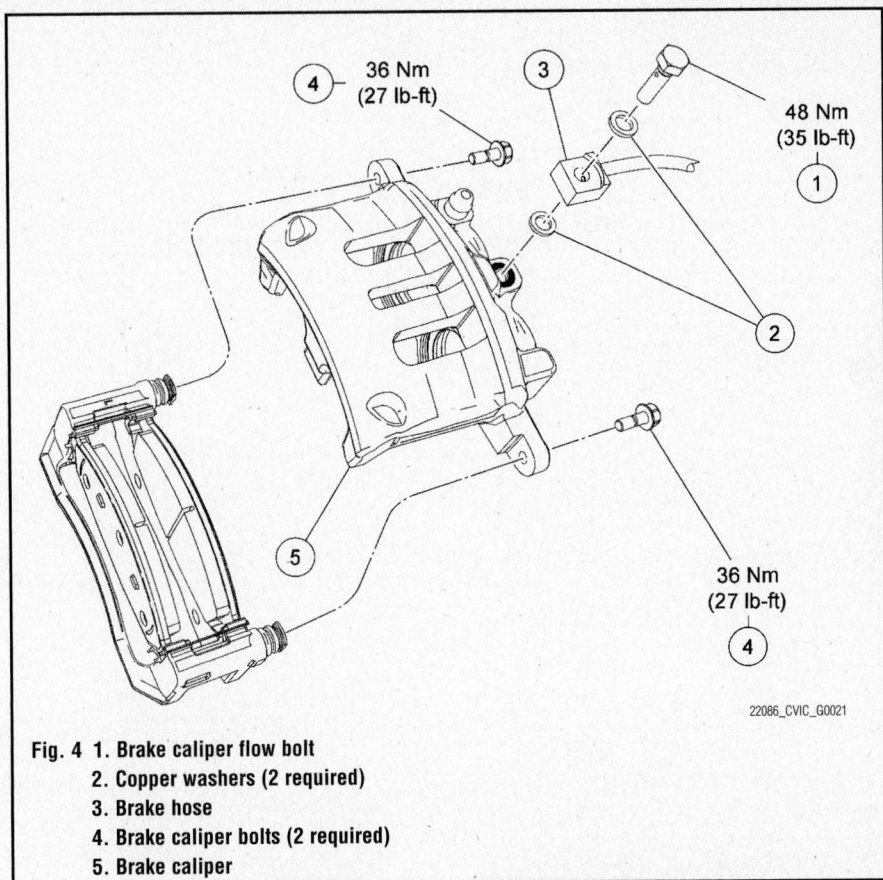

Fig. 4 1. Brake caliper flow bolt
  2. Copper washers (2 required)
  3. Brake hose
  4. Brake caliper bolts (2 required)
  5. Brake caliper

outer pads are properly positioned and the anti-rattle spring is properly positioned. The caliper bleed screw should be positioned on top of the caliper when assembled on the vehicle.

- 2 new caliper guide pin bolts and torque to 27 ft. lbs. (36 Nm)
- Brake hose, after unplugging it, to the disc brake caliper using 2 new copper sealing washers on the banjo bolt. Torque the bolt to 35 ft. lbs. (48 Nm).

5. Bleed the brake system, filling the master cylinder as required. Only use clean DOT 3 brake fluid from a sealed container.

6. Install the wheel and tire assembly. Torque the lug nuts in a star pattern to 100 ft. lbs. (136 Nm).

7. If equipped with air suspension, turn the air suspension switch to the ON position.

8. Pump the brake pedal several times to position the brake pads prior to moving the vehicle.

9. Road test the vehicle and check for proper brake system operation.

DISC BRAKE PADS

REMOVAL AND INSTALLATION

See Figure 5.

✳✳ CAUTION

If the vehicle is equipped with air suspension, the electrical power to the air suspension system must be shut off prior to hoisting, jacking or towing an air suspension vehicle. This can be accomplished by turning off the air suspension switch located in the luggage compartment. Failure to do so can result in unexpected inflation or deflation of the air springs, which can result in shifting of the vehicle during these operations. Failure to follow these instructions may result in personal injury.

➡ Before continuing with this procedure, make sure to have available, 2 new disc brake caliper anchor bracket mounting bolts, per caliper. Once removed, these parts lose their torque

holding ability or retention capability and must not be reused.

1. If equipped with air suspension, the air suspension switch, located on the right-hand side of the luggage compartment, must be turned to the OFF position before raising the vehicle.

2. Remove or disconnect the following:
- ½ of the brake fluid from the brake master cylinder reservoir. Properly dispose of the used brake fluid.
- Front wheel and tire assembly
- 2 disc brake caliper anchor bracket mounting bolts and discard. Lift the caliper assembly from the disc brake rotor using a rotating motion. Suspend the caliper inside the fender housing with wire. Do not allow the caliper to hang from the brake hose.
- Inner and outer disc brake pads. Inspect the rotor braking surfaces for scoring and machine as necessary. Refer to the minimum rotor thickness specification when machining. If machining is not necessary, hand-sand the glaze from the braking surfaces with medium grit sandpaper. Make sure to wear an approved respirator.

To install:

3. Use a C-clamp and an old brake pad, wood block to seat the caliper piston in its bore. Do not allow metal or sharp objects to come into direct contact with the plastic caliper piston surface or damage will result.

4. Remove all rust buildup from the inside of the caliper legs.

5. Make sure the anti-rattle spring is seated in the caliper lining inspection opening and that it is installed from the lining side.

6. Install or connect the following:
- Inner disc brake pad to the caliper piston. Do not bend the pad clips during installation in the piston or distortion and rattles can occur. Install the outer disc brake pad. Make sure the clips are properly seated.
- Caliper over the rotor and install 2 new anchor bracket mounting bolts. Torque the bolts to 118 ft. lbs. (160 Nm).
- Wheel and tire assembly. Torque the lug nuts in a star pattern to 100 ft. lbs. (136 Nm).

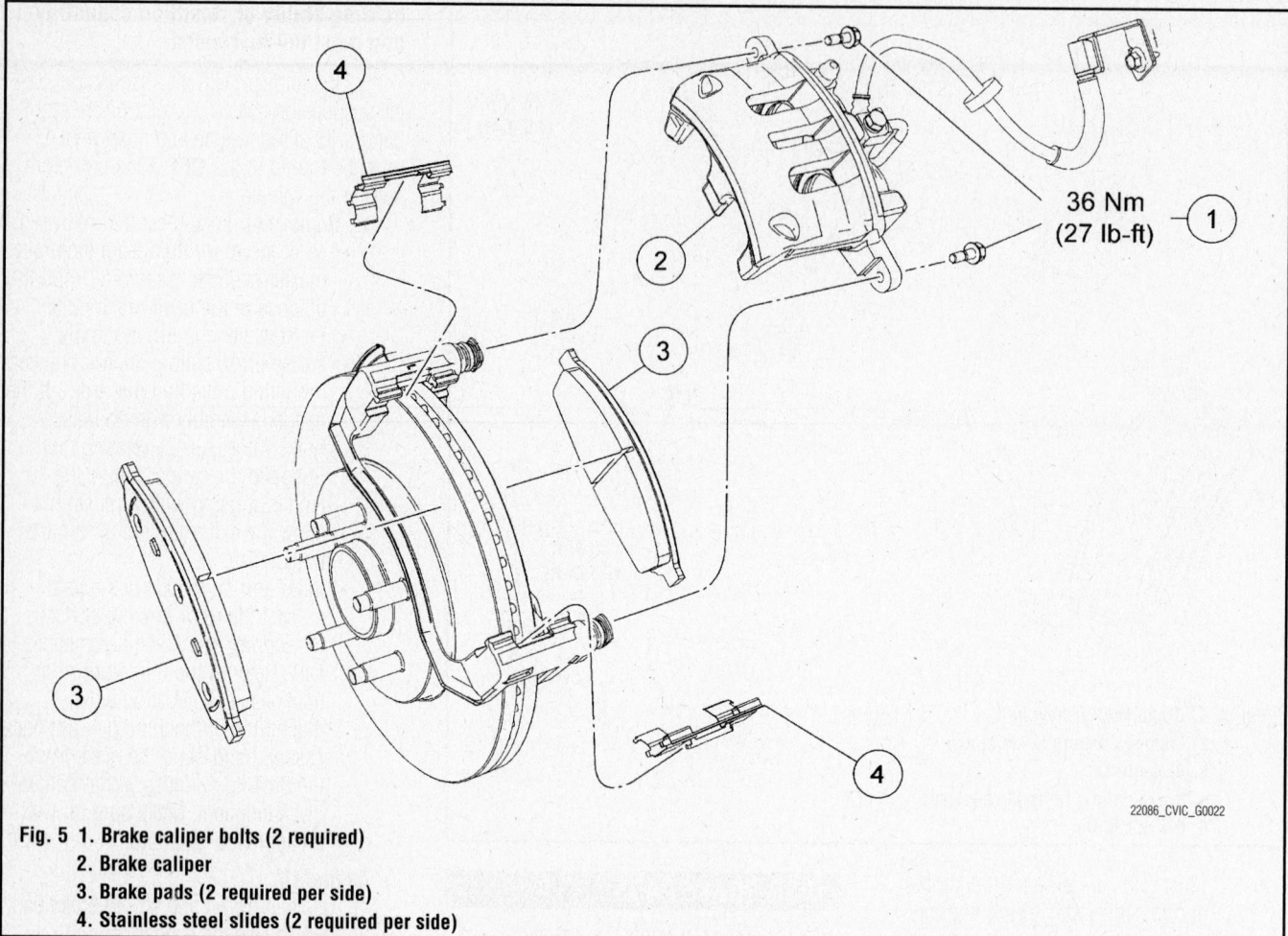

36 Nm
(27 lb-ft)

22086_CVIC_G0022

Fig. 5 1. Brake caliper bolts (2 required)
　　　 2. Brake caliper
　　　 3. Brake pads (2 required per side)
　　　 4. Stainless steel slides (2 required per side)

7. If equipped with air suspension, turn the air suspension switch to the **ON** position.

8. Pump the brake pedal prior to moving the vehicle to seat the brake pads.

9. Fill the master cylinder reservoir with clean DOT 3 brake fluid from a closed container.

10. If the disc brake calipers were replaced or repaired be sure to bleed the system.

11. Road test the vehicle and check for proper brake system operation.

BRAKES

✳✳ CAUTION

Dust and dirt accumulating on brake parts during normal use may contain asbestos fibers from production or aftermarket brake linings. Breathing excessive concentrations of asbestos fibers can cause serious bodily harm. Exercise care when servicing brake parts. Do not sand or grind brake lining unless equipment used is designed to contain the dust residue. Do not clean brake parts with compressed air or by dry brushing. Cleaning should be done by dampening the brake components with a fine mist of water, then wiping the brake components clean with a dampened cloth. Dispose of cloth and all residue containing asbestos fibers in an impermeable container with the appropriate label. Follow practices prescribed by the Occupational Safety and Health Administration (OSHA) and the Environmental Protection Agency (EPA) for the handling, processing, and disposing of dust or debris that may contain asbestos fibers.

BRAKE CALIPER

REMOVAL & INSTALLATION

✳✳ CAUTION

If the vehicle is equipped with air suspension, the electrical power to the air suspension system must be shut off prior to hoisting, jacking or

REAR DISC BRAKES

towing an air suspension vehicle. This can be accomplished by turning off the air suspension switch located in the luggage compartment. Failure to do so can result in unexpected inflation or deflation of the air springs, which can result in shifting of the vehicle during these operations. Failure to follow these instructions may result in personal injury.

➡Before continuing with this procedure, make sure to have available, 2 banjo bolt sealing washers, per caliper. Once removed, these parts loose their torque holding ability or retention capability and must not be reused.

1. If equipped with air suspension, the air suspension switch, located on the right-

hand side of the luggage compartment, must be turned to the **OFF** position before raising the vehicle.

2. Remove or disconnect the following:
- Rear wheel and tire assembly
- Banjo bolt securing the brake hose to the disc brake caliper. Plug the brake hose and discard both sealing washers.
- 2 disc brake caliper locating bolts. Lift the disc brake caliper off the rotor and anchor plate using a rotating motion.

To install:

3. Retract the disc brake caliper piston fully in the piston bore, using an old brake pad or block of wood and a C-clamp.

4. Install or connect the following:
- Disc brake pads on the caliper. Make sure that the pads are on the correct side.
- Caliper assembly above the rotor with the anti-rattle spring located on the lower adapter support arm. Install the caliper over the rotor with a rotating motion.

5. Clean the inner surface of the caliper bushings and locating bolts. Lubricate the caliper locating bolts with a suitable silicone dielectric compound. Install and start the locating bolts by hand only. Torque both bolts to 27 ft. lbs. (36 Nm).
- Brake hose, after unplugging it, to the disc brake caliper using 2 new copper sealing washers on the banjo bolt. Torque the bolt to 35 ft. lbs. (48 Nm).

6. Bleed the brake system, filling the master cylinder as required. Only use clean DOT 3 brake fluid from a sealed container.

7. Replace the rubber rear disc brake bleeder screw cap.

8. Install the wheel and tire assembly. Torque the lug nuts in a star pattern to 100 ft. lbs. (136 Nm).

9. If equipped with air suspension, turn the air suspension switch to the **ON** position.

10. Pump the brake pedal several times to position the brake pads prior to moving the vehicle.

11. Road test the vehicle and check for proper brake system operation.

DISC BRAKE PADS

REMOVAL AND INSTALLATION

See Figures 6 and 7.

✷✷ CAUTION

If the vehicle is equipped with air suspension, the electrical power to

the air suspension system must be shut off prior to hoisting, jacking or towing an air suspension vehicle. This can be accomplished by turning off the air suspension switch located in the luggage compartment. Failure to do so can result in unexpected inflation or deflation of the air springs, which can result in shifting of the vehicle during these operations. Failure to follow these instructions may result in personal injury.

➡Before continuing with this procedure, make sure to have available, 2 new disc brake caliper anchor bracket mounting bolts, per caliper. Once removed, these parts lose their torque holding ability or retention capability and must not be reused.

1. If equipped with air suspension, the air suspension switch, located on the right-hand side of the luggage compartment, must be turned to the **OFF** position before raising the vehicle.

2. Remove or disconnect the following:
- ½ of the brake fluid from the brake master cylinder reservoir. Properly dispose of the used brake fluid.
- Front wheel and tire assembly
- 2 disc brake caliper anchor bracket mounting bolts and discard. Lift the caliper assembly from the disc brake rotor using a rotating motion. Suspend the caliper inside the fender housing with wire. Do not allow the caliper to hang from the brake hose.
- Inner and outer disc brake pads. Inspect the rotor braking surfaces for scoring and machine as necessary. Refer to the minimum rotor thickness specification when machining. If machining is not necessary, hand-sand the glaze from

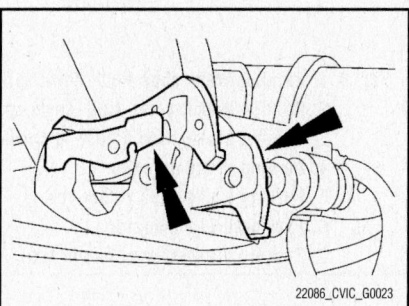

Fig. 6 Removal of rear disc brake pads from caliper

the braking surfaces with medium grit sandpaper. Make sure to wear an approved respirator.

To install:

3. If installing new brake pads, use a C-clamp, and an old brake pad or a wood block to seat the caliper piston in its bore. Do not allow metal or sharp objects to come into direct contact with the plastic caliper piston surface or damage will result.

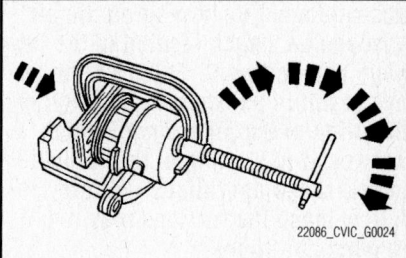

Fig. 7 Compress brake caliper piston as shown

4. Remove all rust buildup from the inside of the caliper legs.

5. Make sure the anti-rattle spring is seated in the caliper lining inspection opening and that it is installed from the lining side.

6. Install or connect the following:
- Inner disc brake pad to the caliper piston. Do not bend the pad clips during installation in the piston or distortion and rattles can occur. Install the outer disc brake pad. Make sure the clips are properly seated.
- Caliper over the rotor and install 2 new anchor bracket mounting bolts. Torque the bolts to 118 ft. lbs. (160 Nm).
- Wheel and tire assembly. Torque the lug nuts in a star pattern to 100 ft. lbs. (136 Nm).

7. If equipped with air suspension, turn the air suspension switch to the **ON** position.

8. Pump the brake pedal prior to moving the vehicle to seat the brake pads.

9. Fill the master cylinder reservoir with clean DOT 3 brake fluid from a closed container.

10. If the disc brake calipers were replaced or repaired be sure to bleed the system.

11. Road test the vehicle and check for proper brake system operation.

BRAKES   PARKING BRAKE

PARKING BRAKE CABLES

ADJUSTMENT

See Figure 8.

> ✳✳ **CAUTION**
>
> **The electrical power to the air suspension system must be shut off prior to hoisting, jacking or towing an air suspension vehicle. This can be accomplished by turning off the air suspension switch located in the luggage compartment. Failure to do so can result in unexpected inflation or deflation of the air springs, which can result in shifting of the vehicle during these operations. Failure to follow these instructions may result in personal injury.**

1. Before servicing the vehicle, refer to the precautions in the beginning of this section.
2. Release the parking brake control using the parking brake release handle.
3. Raise and support the vehicle.
4. Pull the parking brake cable adjuster clip downward. The tensioner spring will take up the cable slack and preload the cables.

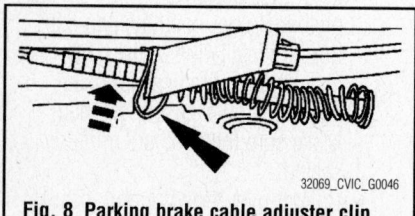

Fig. 8 Parking brake cable adjuster clip

32069_CVIC_G0046

5. Push up on the bottom of the clip to lock the adjustment. If the clip does not slide up, move the assembly slightly to align the closest groove on the parking brake cable adjuster rod with the clip.

➡ **If new cables are installed, allow 20 minutes prior to releasing the parking brake control.**

6. Apply the parking brake control fully and release using the parking brake release handle.
7. Repeat Step 3 and Step 4 to complete the adjustment procedure.

PARKING BRAKE SHOES

REMOVAL & INSTALLATION

See Figure 9.

> ✳✳ **CAUTION**
>
> **The electrical power to the air suspension system must be shut off prior to hoisting, jacking or towing an air suspension vehicle. This can be accomplished by turning off the air suspension switch located in the luggage compartment. Failure to do so can result in unexpected inflation or deflation of the air springs which can result in shifting of the vehicle during these operations. Failure to follow these instructions may result in personal injury.**

1. Before servicing the vehicle, refer to the precautions in the beginning of this section.
2. Disconnect battery negative cable from battery and properly isolate to prevent accidental reconnection.

3. Remove the rear brake disc.
4. Remove the adjuster by removing the brake shoe return spring and the adjusting spring.

➡ **A sharp-pointed tool such as a scratch awl is useful in removing and installing the springs.**

5. Remove the parking brake actuator.
6. Push the parking brake shoes toward each other, then pull the parking brake actuator out. Unhook the parking brake cable end.
7. Remove the brake shoe hold-down springs.
8. Remove the parking brake shoe and linings.

To install:

9. Inspect the components for excessive wear or damage, and install new components as required.
10. Using anti-seize lubricant, lubricate the brake shoe contact point before installation of the rear brake shoes.
11. Lubricate the adjusting screw threads with anti-seize lubricant.

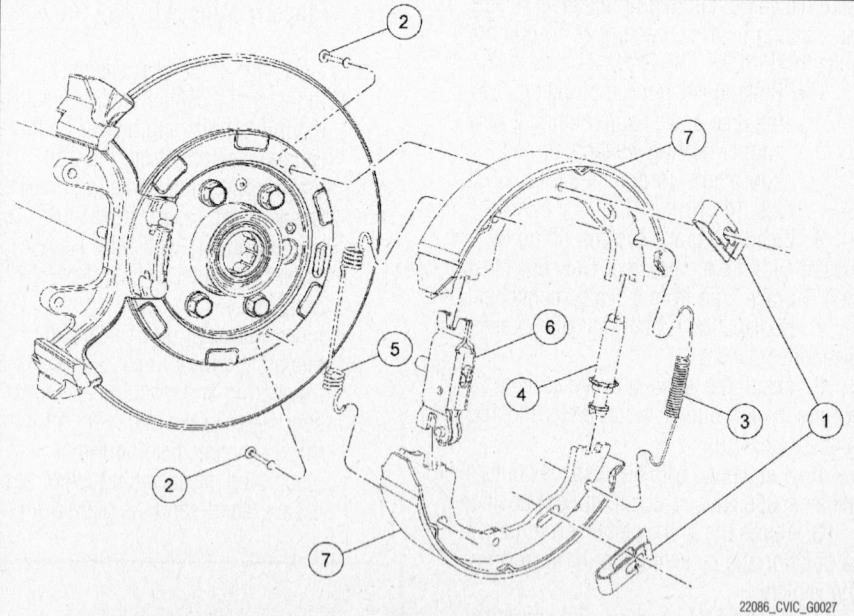

22086_CVIC_G0027

Fig. 9 1. Parking brake shoe hold–down spring (2 required)
    2. Parking brake shoes hold–down spring anchor (2 required)
    3. Parking brake shoe adjusting spring
    4. Parking brake adjuster
    5. Parking brake shoe return spring
    6. Parking brake actuator
    7. Parking brake shoes (2 required)

12. Install the parking brake shoe and linings.

13. Install the parking brake shoe hold-down springs.

14. Connect the parking brake cable and actuator.

15. Using a suitable brake adjusting gauge, set the rear brake shoe and lining diameter to 0.020 inch (0.5 mm) less than the inside diameter of the drum portion of the brake disc.

16. Reinstall the brake rotor.

17. Check the parking brake for normal operation and adjust parking brake cable tension if necessary.

18. Install wheel and tire assemble and lower vehicle.

19. Reconnect negative battery cable.

ADJUSTMENT

See Figure 10.

✳✳ CAUTION

The electrical power to the air suspension system must be shut off prior to hoisting, jacking or towing an air suspension vehicle. This can be accomplished by turning off the air suspension switch located in the luggage compartment. Failure to do so can result in unexpected inflation or deflation of the air springs, which can result in shifting of the vehicle during these operations. Failure to follow these instructions may result in personal injury.

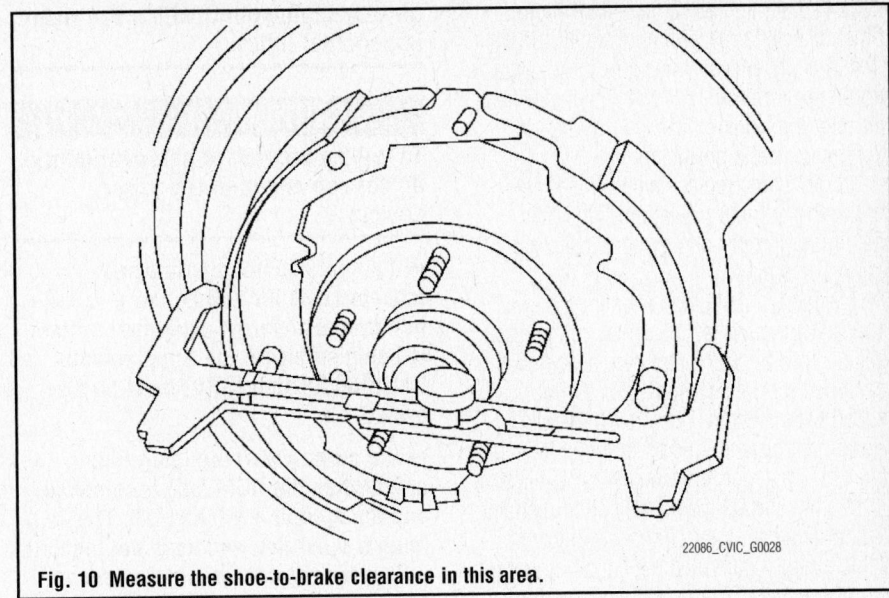

Fig. 10 Measure the shoe-to-brake clearance in this area.

22086_CVIC_G0028

1. Before servicing the vehicle, refer to the precautions in the beginning of this section.

2. Disconnect battery negative cable from battery and properly isolate to prevent accidental reconnection.

3. Using the release handle, release the parking brake control.

➡**Make sure the parking brake is fully released.**

4. Remove the rear brake disc.

5. Inspect the parking brake shoes and drum for wear, damage or oil contamination. Install new components as necessary.

6. If the linings are oil contaminated, install a new rear axle oil seal.

7. Using a suitable brake adjusting gauge, measure the inside diameter of the drum portion of the rear brake disc. Record the measurement.

8. Using a suitable brake adjusting gauge, set the rear brake shoe and lining diameter to 0.020 inch (0.5 mm) less than the inside diameter of the drum portion of the rear brake disc.

9. Install the rear brake disc.

10. Test the parking brake for normal operation.

CHASSIS ELECTRICAL

AIR BAG (SUPPLEMENTAL RESTRAINT SYSTEM)

GENERAL INFORMATION

✳✳ CAUTION

These vehicles are equipped with an air bag system. The system must be disarmed before performing service on, or around, system components, the steering column, instrument panel components, wiring and sensors. Failure to follow the safety precautions and the disarming procedure could result in accidental air bag deployment, possible injury and unnecessary system repairs.

SERVICE PRECAUTIONS

Disconnect and isolate the battery negative cable before beginning any airbag system component diagnosis, testing, removal, or installation procedures. Allow system capacitor to discharge for two minutes before beginning any component service. This will disable the airbag system. Failure to disable the airbag system may result in accidental airbag deployment, personal injury, or death.

Do not place an intact undeployed airbag face down on a solid surface. The airbag will propel into the air if accidentally deployed and may result in personal injury or death.

When carrying or handling an undeployed airbag, the trim side (face) of the airbag should be pointing towards the body to minimize possibility of injury if accidental deployment occurs. Failure to do this may result in personal injury or death.

Replace airbag system components with OEM replacement parts. Substitute parts may appear interchangeable, but internal differences may result in inferior occupant protection. Failure to do so may result in occupant personal injury or death.

Wear safety glasses, rubber gloves, and long sleeved clothing when cleaning powder residue from vehicle after an airbag deployment. Powder residue emitted from a deployed airbag can cause skin irritation. Flush affected area with cool water if irritation is experienced. If nasal or throat irritation is experienced, exit the vehicle for fresh air until the irritation ceases. If irritation continues, see a physician.

Do not use a replacement airbag that is not in the original packaging. This may result in improper deployment, personal injury, or death.

The factory installed fasteners, screws and bolts used to fasten airbag components have a special coating and are specifically designed for the airbag system. Do not use substitute fasteners. Use only original equipment fasteners listed in the parts catalog when fastener replacement is required.

During, and following, any child restraint anchor service, due to impact event or vehicle repair, carefully inspect all mounting hardware, tether straps, and anchors for proper installation, operation, or damage. If a child restraint anchor is found damaged in any way, the anchor must be replaced. Failure to do this may result in personal injury or death.

Deployed and non-deployed airbags may or may not have live pyrotechnic material within the airbag inflator.

Do not dispose of driver/passenger/curtain airbags or seat belt tensioners unless you are sure of complete deployment. Refer to the Hazardous Substance Control System for proper disposal.

Dispose of deployed airbags and tensioners consistent with state, provincial, local, and federal regulations.

After any airbag component testing or service, do not connect the battery negative cable. Personal injury or death may result if the system test is not performed first.

DISARMING THE SYSTEM

❊❊ CAUTION
Always wear safety glasses when repairing an air bag Supplemental Restraint System (SRS) vehicle and when handling an air bag module. This will reduce the risk of injury in the event of an accidental deployment.

❊❊ CAUTION
Never probe the connectors on the air bag module. Doing so can result in

air bag deployment, which can result in personal injury.

❊❊ CAUTION
To reduce the risk of personal injury, do not use any memory saver devices.

➡ If a seat equipped with a seat mounted side air bag and/or a safety belt pretensioner (if equipped) system is being serviced, the Supplemental Restraint System (SRS) must be disarmed.

➡ The air bag warning lamp illuminates when the RCM fuse is removed and the ignition switch is ON. This is normal operation and does not indicate a Supplemental Restraint System (SRS) fault.

1. Turn all vehicle accessories OFF.
2. Turn the ignition switch to **OFF**.
3. At the central junction box (CJB), located on the LH end of the instrument panel, open the kick panel cover and remove the restraints control module (RCM) fuse F2.4 (10A).
4. Turn the ignition ON and visually monitor the air bag indicator for at least 30 seconds. The air bag indicator will remain lit continuously (no flashing) if the correct RCM fuse has been removed. If the air bag indicator does not remain lit continuously, remove the correct RCM fuse before proceeding.
5. Turn the ignition **OFF**.
6. To avoid accidental deployment and possible personal injury, the backup power supply must be depleted before repairing or replacing any front or side air bag Supplemental Restraint System (SRS) components and before servicing, replacing, adjusting or striking components near the front or side air bag sensors or RCM, such as doors, instrument panel, console, door latches, strikers, seats and hood latches. The side impact sensors (if equipped) are located at or near the base of the B-pillars and C-pillars.
7. To deplete the backup power supply energy, disconnect the battery ground cable and wait at least one minute. Be sure to disconnect auxiliary batteries and power supplies (if equipped).
8. Disconnect the battery ground cable (14301) and wait at least one minute.

ARMING THE SYSTEM

❊❊ CAUTION
The restraint system diagnostic tool is for restraint system service only. Remove from vehicle prior to road use. Failure to remove could result in injury and possible violation of vehicle safety standards. Make sure all restraint system diagnostic tool(s) that may have been installed during the repair have been removed from the vehicle and all SRS components are connected.

1. Turn the ignition switch from **OFF** to **ON**.
2. Install the RCM fuse F2.4 (10A) to the CJB and close the cover.

❊❊ CAUTION
Be sure that nobody is in the vehicle and that there is nothing blocking or set in front of any air bag module when the battery ground cable is connected.

3. Connect the battery ground cable.
4. Prove out the Supplemental Restraint System (SRS) as follows:
- Turn the ignition key from **ON** to **OFF**.
- Wait 10 seconds, then turn the key back to **ON**.
- Visually monitor the air bag indicator with the air bag modules installed.
- The air bag indicator will light continuously for approximately six seconds and then turn off.
- If an air bag Supplemental Restraint System (SRS) fault is present, the air bag indicator will either fail to light, remain lit continuously or flash.
- The flashing might not occur until approximately 30 seconds after the ignition switch has been turned from the **OFF** to the **ON** position. This is the time required for the restraints control module (RCM) to complete the testing of the SRS. If the air bag indicator is inoperative and a SRS fault exists, a chime will sound in a pattern of five sets of five.

DRIVE TRAIN

AUTOMATIC TRANSMISSION ASSEMBLY

REMOVAL & INSTALLATION

See Figures 11 through 14.

✳✳ CAUTION

If the vehicle is equipped with air suspension, the electrical power to the air suspension system must be shut off prior to hoisting, jacking or towing an air suspension vehicle. This can be accomplished by turning off the air suspension switch located in the luggage compartment. Failure to do so can result in unexpected inflation or deflation of the air springs, which can result in shifting of the vehicle during these operations. Failure to follow these instructions may result in personal injury.

1. Drain the transmission.
2. If equipped with air suspension, the air suspension switch, located on the right-hand side of the luggage compartment, must be turned to the **OFF** position before raising the vehicle.
3. Remove or disconnect the following:
   - Negative battery cable
   - Exhaust system as necessary for transmission removal
   - Converter bottom access cover and adapter plate bolts
   - Torque converter drain plug, to allow the converter to drain into a container, if equipped. After the converter has drained, reinstall the drain plug and tighten.
   - 4 torque converter-to-flywheel retaining nuts
   - Driveshaft (mark for installation),

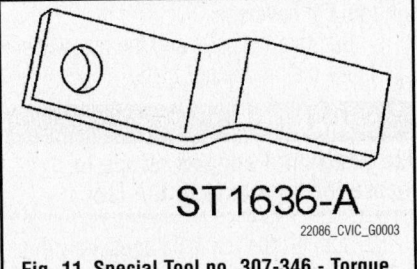

ST1636-A

22086_CVIC_G0003

Fig. 11 Special Tool no. 307-346 - Torque Converter Retainer

plug the transmission extension housing to prevent fluid leakage
   - Vehicle Speed Sensor (VSS) or if equipped, the speedometer cable from the transmission extension housing
   - Shift cable from the transmission manual control lever the throttle valve cable from the transmission throttle valve lever, if equipped
   - Transmission wiring harness connectors.
   - Starter motor retaining bolts and place the starter motor aside
4. Position a transmission jack under the transmission and raise it enough to allow crossmember removal.
5. Remove or disconnect the following:
   - Engine rear support-to-crossmember bolts and the crossmember-to-frame side support retaining bolts
   - Crossmember and transmission support insulator
6. Lower the transmission jack and allow the transmission to hang.
7. Place a jack to the front of the engine and raise the engine enough to gain access to the 2 upper transmission-to-cylinder block retaining bolts. Do not remove the bolts at this time.
8. Remove or disconnect the following:
   - Transmission cooler lines at the transmission. Plug all openings to keep dirt out.
   - Lower transmission-to-cylinder block retaining bolts
   - Transmission fluid fill tube and plug the opening in the transmission

9. Secure the transmission to the transmission jack with a safety strap or chain.
10. Remove the 2 upper transmission-to-cylinder block bolts.
11. Carefully move the transmission rearward to disengage the bell housing from the dowel pins and the torque converter studs from the flywheel.
12. Remove or disconnect the following:
    - Transmission
    - Torque converter to prevent the converter from dropping out of the transmission causing possible damage or personal injury

To install:

13. Remove the safety stand and block of wood supporting the rear of the engine, if installed.
14. Install or connect the following:
    - Torque converter drain plug to 22 ft. lbs. (30 Nm), if equipped
    - Torque converter on the transmission and rotate into position to be sure the drive flats are fully engaged in the pump gear. When fully seated, the center of the torque converter should be about $7/16$–$9/16$ inch (10.2–14.4mm) below the transmission mounting surface
15. Mount the transmission on a transmission jack and secure with a safely strap or chain. Raise the transmission and align with the cylinder block dowel pins.
16. Rotate the converter until the studs and drain plug are in alignment with the holes in the flywheel. Align the orange balancing marks on the converter stud and flywheel bolt hole, if balancing marks are present.

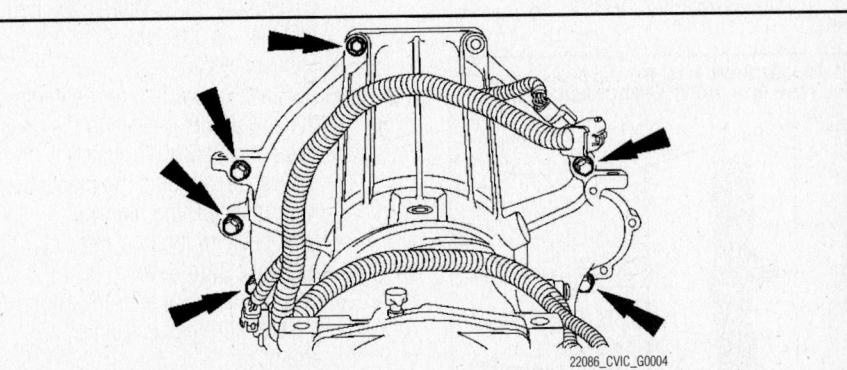

22086_CVIC_G0004

Fig. 12 Make sure that all bell housing bolts have been removed before removing the transmission.

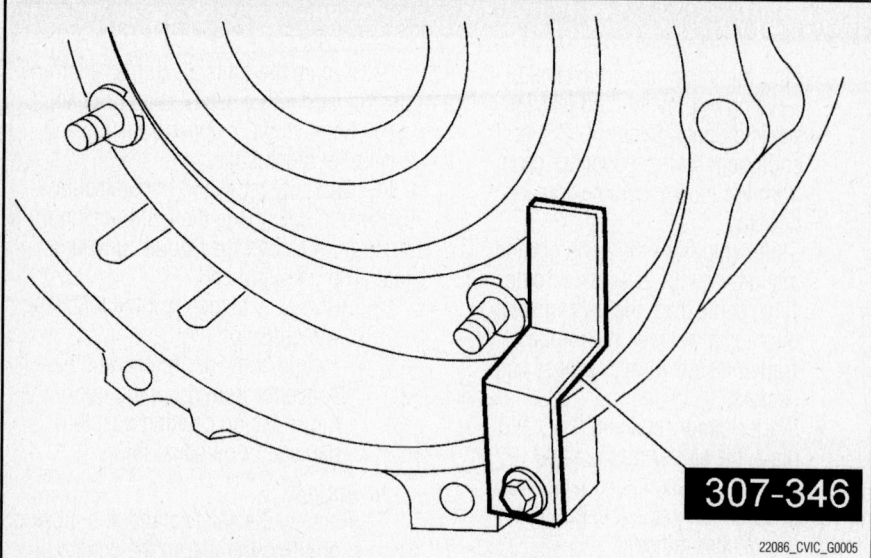

307-346

22086_CVIC_G0005

Fig. 13 Install special tool and be sure that transmission is securely fastened to the transmission jack before tilting transmission.

17. Slide the transmission assembly forward into position, being careful not to damage the flywheel and converter pilot.
18. Install or connect the following:
- 2 transmission housing-to-cylinder block (bell housing) bolts at the engine dowel pin locations. Tighten the bolts to 35 ft. lbs. (48 Nm).
- Transmission housing-to-cylinder block (bell housing) bolts. Tighten the bolts to 35 ft. lbs. (48 Nm).
19. Remove the safety strap or chain from around the transmission.
20. Install or connect the following:
- Transmission fluid fill tube. Tighten the bolt to 35 ft. lbs. (48 Nm).
- Oil cooler lines to the transmission case. Tighten the cooler line fittings to 80 inch lbs. (9 Nm).

DIMENSION A TO BE 10.23-14.43 mm (7/16-9/16 INCH) APPROXIMATELY

A

7922RG24

Fig. 14 To prevent transmission damage, be sure that the torque converter is fully seated in the front pump of the transmission

21. Remove the jack supporting the front of the engine.
22. Install or connect the following:
- Crossmember using the proper jack
- Crossmember and transmission support insulators in position
- Engine rear support-to-crossmember retaining bolts and the crossmember-to-frame side support retaining bolts
23. Remove the transmission jack.
24. Install or connect the following:
- Transmission wiring harness connectors
- Starter motor and wiring
- 4 torque converter-to-flywheel retaining nuts. Tighten to 27 ft. lbs. (36 Nm).
- Torque converter access cover and cover plate bolts. Tighten the bolts to 14 ft. lbs. (19 Nm).
- Exhaust system
- VSS and the wiring, or if equipped, the speedometer cable to the transmission extension housing
- Driveshaft, aligning the marks that were made during removal
- Shift cable to the transmission manual control lever
- Throttle valve cable to the transmission throttle valve lever, if equipped
25. If equipped with air suspension, turn the air suspension switch to the **ON** position.
26. Fill the transmission.
27. Start the engine and check the transmission for leakage.
28. Road test the vehicle and check for proper transmission operation.

AXLE HOUSING

REMOVAL & INSTALLATION
See Figures 15 and 16.

❊❊ WARNING

The electrical power to the air suspension system must be shut off prior to hoisting, jacking or towing an air suspension vehicle. This can be accomplished by turning off the air suspension switch located in the LH side of the luggage compartment. Failure to do so can result in unexpected inflation or deflation of the air springs, which can result in shifting of the vehicle during these operations.

1. Before servicing the vehicle, refer to the precautions in the beginning of this section.
2. Disconnect battery negative cable from battery and properly isolate to prevent accidental reconnection.
3. Remove or disconnect the following:
- Drive pinion
- Parking brake adjuster clip

➡**Pull down on the parking brake cable at the control end. Push up on the parking brake adjuster clip to lock the adjuster.**

- Parking brake rear cables and conduit retainer bolts
- ABS sensor wire harness clips
- Rear stabilizer bar
- Rear height sensor, if equipped with rear air springs

❊❊ WARNING

Take care not to damage the threads on the bellcrank stud.

4. Separate the Watts linkage from the rear axle housing and remove the retainer nut from the bellcrank.
5. Remove the bolts and the rear wheel disc brake caliper anchor plate.

❊❊ CAUTION

Use additional support straps to secure the rear axle to the jack.

6. Support the rear axle housing with a suitable jack.
7. Remove the shock absorber lower nuts, and then remove the shock absorbers from the retainer brackets.
8. Remove the nuts and bolts retaining the LH and RH lower control arms.

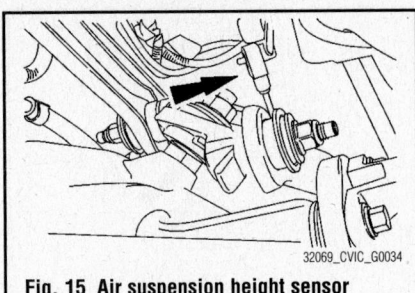

Fig. 15 Air suspension height sensor

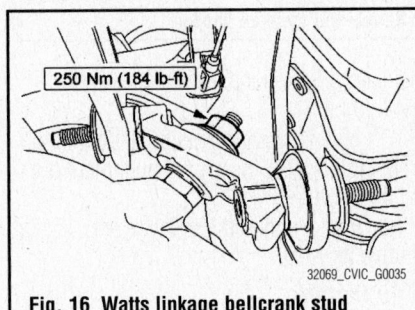

250 Nm (184 lb-ft)

Fig. 16 Watts linkage bellcrank stud

9. Remove the nuts and bolts retaining the LH and RH upper control arms.

10. Unseat the air springs and lower the rear axle from the vehicle.

To install:

11. Raise the rear axle into position using a suitable jack.

12. Seat the air springs.

13. Install or connect the following:
- LH and RH upper control arms and torque the bolts to 69 ft. lbs. (93 Nm)
- Shock absorbers and torque the bolts to 66 ft. lbs. (90 Nm)

14. Remove the axle jack.

15. Install the Watts linkage on the rear axle housing.

16. Install the retainer nut on the bell-crank stud and tighten to 185 ft. lbs. (250 Nm)

17. Install the rear wheel disc brake caliper anchor plate and torque the bolts to 50 ft. lbs. (68 Nm)

18. If equipped with rear air springs, install the height sensor.

19. Install the rear stabilizer bar retainer bolts and tighten to 18 ft. lbs. (25 Nm)

20. Connect the ABS sensor harness routing clips.

21. Install the parking brake rear cables and conduit retainer bolts.

22. Connect the parking brake rear cables and conduit to the parking brake cable connector.

23. Pull down on parking brake cable at the control end, then pull the parking brake adjuster clip downward and release the cable.

24. Push up on the parking brake adjuster clip to lock the adjuster.

25. Install the drive pinion.

26. If equipped with rear air springs, turn on the air suspension switch.

AXLE SHAFT, BEARING & SEAL

REMOVAL & INSTALLATION

See Figures 17, 18 and 19.

❄❄ CAUTION

If the vehicle is equipped with air suspension, the electrical power to the air suspension system must be shut off prior to hoisting, jacking or towing an air suspension vehicle. This can be accomplished by turning off the air suspension switch located in the luggage compartment. Failure to do so can result in unexpected inflation or deflation of the air springs, which can result in shifting of the vehicle during these operations. Failure to follow these instructions may result in personal injury.

1. If equipped, turn the air suspension service switch to the **OFF** position before raising the vehicle.

2. Remove or disconnect the following
- Wheel
- Brake caliper and rotor
- Anti-lock brake speed sensor, if equipped

3. Clean all dirt from the area of the axle housing cover.

4. Place a drain pan under the axle housing.

5. Remove or disconnect the following:
- Axle housing cover retaining bolts and the cover, draining the axle lubricant from the housing
- Differential pinion shaft lock bolt and the differential pinion shaft

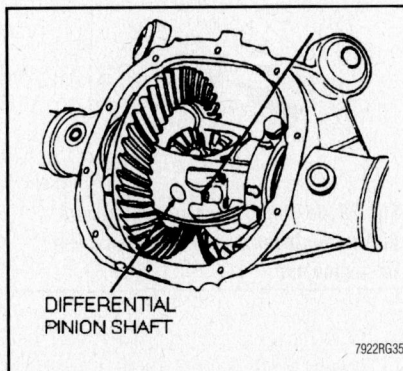

DIFFERENTIAL PINION SHAFT

Fig. 17 Removal of differential pinion shaft

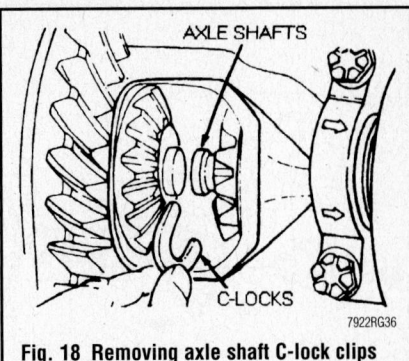

AXLE SHAFTS

C-LOCKS

Fig. 18 Removing axle shaft C-lock clips

6. Push the flanged end of the axle shaft being removed toward the center of the vehicle

7. Remove or disconnect the following:
- C-lock from the button end of the axle shaft
- Axle shaft from the housing, being careful not to damage the oil seal and anti-lock brake sensor ring, if equipped.

8. Insert an axle bearing remover in the axle housing bore and position it behind the wheel bearing so the tangs on the tool engage the bearing outer race.

9. Remove the wheel bearing and seal as an assembly using an impact slide hammer attached to the bearing remover tool

To install:

10. Lubricate the new wheel bearing with rear axle lubricant.

11. Install the wheel bearing into the axle housing bore using a bearing installer.

12. Lubricate the lips of a new wheel bearing oil seal with wheel bearing grease.

13. Install or connect the following:
- New wheel bearing seal using a seal installer
- Axle shaft into the axle housing without damaging the bearing/seal assembly or anti-lock brake sensor ring, if equipped. Start the splines into the side gear and push firmly until the button end of the axle shaft can be seen in the differential case.
- C-lock on the button end of the axle shaft splines, then push the shaft outboard until the shaft splines engage and the C-lock seats in the counterbore of the differential side gear.
- Differential pinion shaft through the case and pinion gears, aligning the hole in the shaft with the lock bolt hole
- Apply a thread locking compound to the lock bolt threads and place in the case and pinion shaft. Tighten to 22 ft. lbs. (30 Nm).

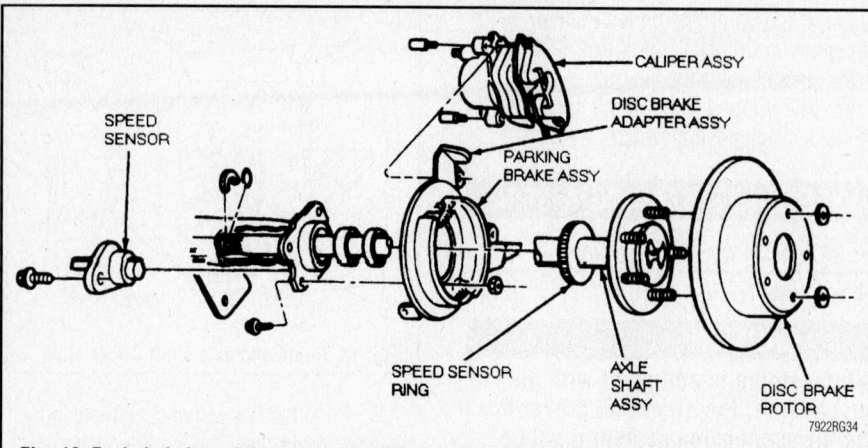

SPEED SENSOR

CALIPER ASSY

DISC BRAKE ADAPTER ASSY

PARKING BRAKE ASSY

SPEED SENSOR RING

AXLE SHAFT ASSY

DISC BRAKE ROTOR

7922RG34

Fig. 19 Exploded view of the rear axle shaft assembly

14. Cover the inside of the differential case with a shop rag and clean the sealing surface of the axle housing and the axle housing cover. Remove the shop rag.

15. Apply a 1/8–3/16 inch (3.18–4.76mm) wide bead of silicone sealer to the cover.

16. Install the axle housing and bolts and tighten in a star pattern. Final torque the cover retaining bolts to 33 ft. lbs. (45 Nm).

17. Add the appropriate rear axle lubricant to the axle housing to a level 1/4–9/16 inch (6–14mm) below the bottom of the fill hole. If equipped with a limited slip differential, add 4 oz. (118.3 ml) of the appropriate friction modifier.

18. Install or connect the following:
- Axle housing fill plug and tighten to 12 ft. lbs. (16 Nm)
- Anti-lock brake speed sensor, if equipped. Tighten the retaining bolt to 53 inch lbs. (6 Nm).
- Brake calipers and rotors
- Wheel

19. If equipped with air suspension, turn the air suspension switch to the **ON** position.

20. Road test the vehicle and check for proper operation.

PINION SEAL

REMOVAL & INSTALLATION

See Figures 20 and 21.

✳✳ CAUTION

If the vehicle is equipped with air suspension, the electrical power to the air suspension system must be shut off prior to hoisting, jacking or towing an air suspension vehicle. This can be accomplished by turning off the air suspension switch located in the luggage compartment. Failure to do so can result in unexpected inflation or deflation of the air springs, which can result in shifting of the vehicle during theseoperations. Failure to follow these instructions may result in personal injury.

1. Remove or disconnect the following:
- Driveshaft
- Rear wheels
- Rear brake calipers

➡ The rear brake calipers must be removed so that there is no additional drag when measuring pinion bearing preload.

2. Use an inch lb. torque wrench and measure the amount of torque required to

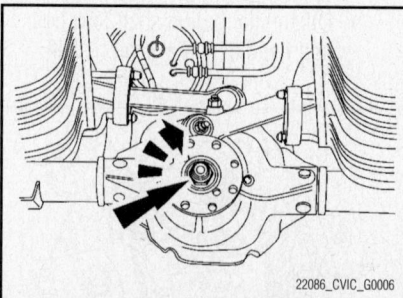

22086_CVIC_G0006

Fig. 20 Be sure to measure and record pinion bearing preload before removing the pinion nut

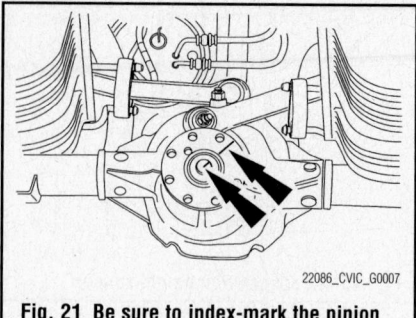

22086_CVIC_G0007

Fig. 21 Be sure to index-mark the pinion flange and stem as shown

maintain pinion rotation through several revolutions.

3. Index mark the pinion flange and the drive pinion stem for correct alignment during installation

4. Remove the pinion flange and remove the seal.

To install:

5. Install or connect the following:
- Pinion seal and flange
- New pinion flange nut

6. Rotate the pinion flange occasionally while tightening the flange nut to make sure the pinion bearings seat correctly.

7. Take frequent bearing preload torque readings.

8. If the preload recorded prior to disassembly is **lower** than the specification for used bearings, then tighten the pinion flange nut to specification. If the preload recorder prior to disassembly is **higher** than the specification for used bearings, then tighten the pinion flange nut to the original reading as recorded.

9. The pinion bearing preload specifications are as follows:
   a. Used bearings: 8–14 inch lbs. (0.9–1.6 Nm).
   b. New bearings: 16–29 inch lbs. (1.8–3.2 Nm).

✳✳ CAUTION

Never loosen the pinion nut to reduce bearing preload. If it is necessary to reduce bearing preload, install a new collapsible spacer and pinion nut.

10. Install or connect the following:
- Driveshaft
- Brake calipers
- Rear wheels

11. Fill the differential with gear lubricant and check for leaks.

ENGINE COOLING

ENGINE FAN

REMOVAL & INSTALLATION

See Figure 22.

1. Before servicing the vehicle, refer to the precautions in the beginning of this section.

2. Disconnect battery negative cable from battery and properly isolate to prevent accidental reconnection.

3. Remove or disconnect the following:
   - Degas bottle

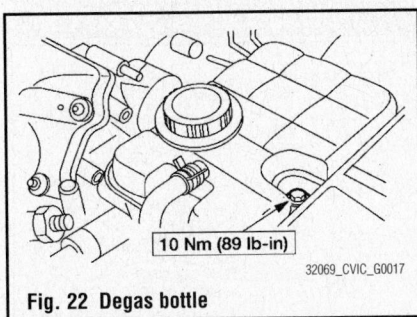

```
10 Nm (89 lb-in)
32069_CVIC_G0017
```

Fig. 22 Degas bottle

   - Power steering reservoir and set aside
   - Fan motor electrical connector
   - Fan blade, motor and shroud assembly

To install:

4. Install or connect the following:
   - Fan blade, motor and shroud assembly and tighten the bolts to 89 inch lbs. (10 Nm)
   - Fan motor electrical connector
   - Power steering reservoir and tighten the bolt to 9 ft. lbs. (12 Nm)
   - Degas bottle and tighten the screws to 89 inch lbs. (10 Nm)

RADIATOR

REMOVAL & INSTALLATION

See Figure 23.

1. Before servicing the vehicle, refer to the precautions in the beginning of this section.

2. Disconnect battery negative cable from battery and properly isolate to prevent accidental reconnection.

3. Drain the engine cooling system.

4. Remove or disconnect the following:
   - Fan blade, fan motor and fan shroud assembly
   - Pin-type retainers and radiator sight shield

   - Upper radiator hose
   - Lower radiator hose
   - Bolts and both radiator support brackets

5. Remove the A/C condenser and transmission cooler bolts and position them away from the radiator.

6. Remove the radiator.

```
32069_CVIC_G0016
```

Fig. 23 Radiator sight shield screw locations

To install:

➡**Do not reuse hose clamps. Instead, use appropriately sized worm-style clamps in place of the constant tension clamps.**

7. Install or connect the following:
   - Radiator
   - A/C condenser and transmission cooler
   - Upper and lower radiator hoses
   - Radiator sight shield
   - Fan blade, fan motor and fan shroud assembly

8. Refill the cooling system.

9. Reconnect the negative battery cable, check for leaks and repair if necessary.

THERMOSTAT

REMOVAL & INSTALLATION

See Figures 24 and 25.

1. Before servicing the vehicle, refer to the precautions in the beginning of this section.

2. Disconnect battery negative cable from battery and properly isolate to prevent accidental reconnection.

3. Drain the coolant below the water thermostat.

4. Remove or disconnect the following:
   - Engine cover

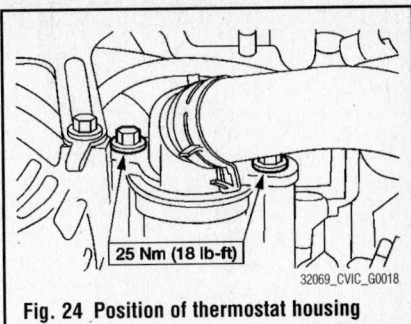

```
25 Nm (18 lb-ft)
32069_CVIC_G0018
```

Fig. 24 Position of thermostat housing

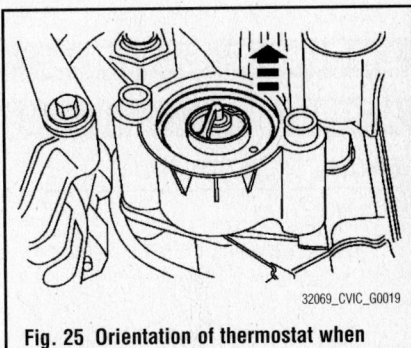

```
32069_CVIC_G0019
```

Fig. 25 Orientation of thermostat when installing

   - Water outlet adapter and position aside
   - Water thermostat and the O-ring seal from the intake manifold

To install:

5. Inspect the O-ring seal install a new seal if necessary.

6. Install or connect the following:
   - Thermostat into the intake manifold
   - Water outlet adapter and torque the bolts to 18 ft. lbs. (25 Nm)
   - Engine cover
   - Refill the cooling system, check for leaks and repair if necessary

WATER PUMP

REMOVAL & INSTALLATION

See Figure 26.

1. Drain the cooling system.

2. Remove or disconnect the following:

   - Negative battery cable
   - Cooling fan and shroud
   - Accessory drive belt
   - 4 water pump pulley-to-water pump bolts
   - Pulley
   - 4 water pump-to-engine bolts
   - Water pump

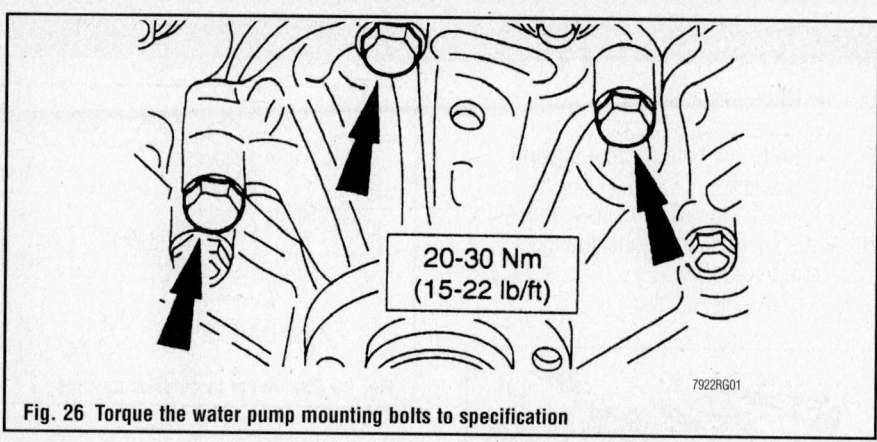

Fig. 26 Torque the water pump mounting bolts to specification

20-30 Nm
(15-22 lb/ft)

7922RG01

To install:

3. Clean the sealing surfaces of the water pump and block.

4. Install or connect the following:
- New O-ring, lubricate it with clean antifreeze prior to installation
- Water pump. Tighten the bolts to 18 ft. lbs. (25 Nm).
- Water pump pulley. Tighten the bolts to 18 ft. lbs. (25 Nm).
- Accessory drive belt

5. Fill the cooling system.

6. Operate the engine to normal operating temperatures and check for leaks.

ENGINE ELECTRICAL

ALTERNATOR

REMOVAL & INSTALLATION

See Figure 27.

1. Before servicing the vehicle, refer to the precautions in the beginning of this section.

2. Remove or disconnect the following:
- Negative battery cable and properly isolate to prevent accidental reconnection.
- Engine cover
- Intake induction silencer
- Accessory drive belt
- Nut and electrical connector
- Mounting bolts

- Alternator bracket
- Alternator

To install:

➡ **Two alternators are available; 130-amp and 200-amp. Their electrical connector torque value is different.**

Install or connect the following:
- Alternator and tighten the mounting bolts to 18 ft. lbs. (25 Nm)
- Alternator bracket and tighten the bolts to 89 inch lbs. (10 Nm)
- Accessory drive belt
- Wire harness and torque the nut to 71 inch lbs. (8 Nm) for vehicles equipped with 130-amp alternator

CHARGING SYSTEM

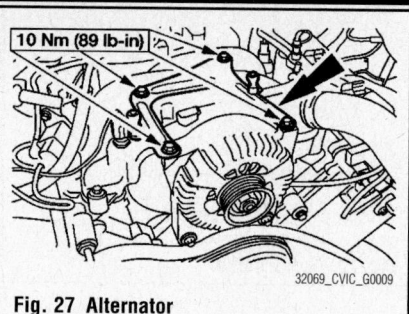

10 Nm (89 lb-in)

Fig. 27 Alternator

32069_CVIC_G0009

- Wire harness and torque the nut to 89 inch lbs. (10 Nm) for vehicles equipped with 200-amp alternator
- Engine cover
- Negative battery cable

ENGINE ELECTRICAL

FIRING ORDER

See Figure 28.

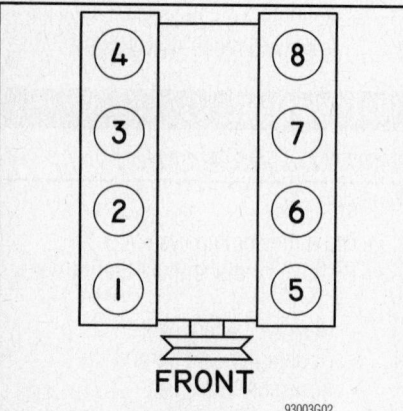

FRONT

93003G02

Fig. 28 4.6L (VIN V and W) Engines
Firing order: 1-3-7-2-6-5-4-8
Distributorless ignition system—One coil per cylinder

IGNITION COIL

REMOVAL & INSTALLATION

See Figure 29.

1. Before servicing the vehicle, refer to the precautions in the beginning of this section.

2. Disconnect battery negative cable from battery and properly isolate to prevent accidental reconnection.

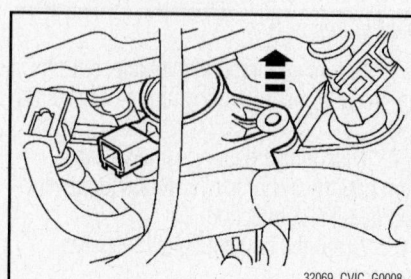

32069_CVIC_G0008

Fig. 29 Ignition coil, plug and bolt location

IGNITION SYSTEM

3. Remove or disconnect the following:
- Air cleaner outlet pipe
- Connector from the ignition coils
- Bolt from the ignition coil
- Ignition coil from spark plug

To install:

4. Install or connect the following:
- Ignition coil to spark plug
- Bolt and torque to 89 inch lbs. (10 Nm)
- Electrical connector
- Air cleaner outlet pipe

IGNITION TIMING

ADJUSTMENT

Ignition timing is controlled by the PCM and is not adjustable. Checking the timing will result in false readings.

SPARK PLUGS

REMOVAL & INSTALLATION

See Figures 30 and 31.

1. Before servicing the vehicle, refer to the precautions in the beginning of this section.
2. Disconnect battery negative cable from battery and properly isolate to prevent accidental reconnection.
3. Remove the ignition coil on plug.

➡**Use compressed air to remove any debris from the spark plug well before removing the spark plugs.**

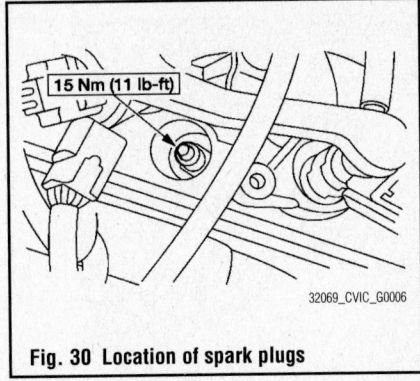

Fig. 30 Location of spark plugs

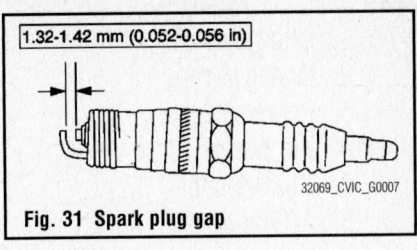

Fig. 31 Spark plug gap

4. Inspect the spark plugs.

To install:
5. Adjust the spark plug gap to 0.052–0.056 inch (1.32–1.42 mm) as required and torque to 11 ft. lbs. (15 Nm)

ENGINE ELECTRICAL

STARTING SYSTEM

STARTER

REMOVAL & INSTALLATION

See Figure 32.

1. Remove or disconnect the following:

- Negative battery cable and properly isolate to prevent accidental reconnection
- Red solenoid safety cap
- Wires from solenoid
- 2 upper bolts
- 1 lower bolt and starter

To install:
2. Install or connect the following:

- Starter (5) and lower mounting bolt (4)
- 2 upper mounting bolts. Tighten all 3 bolts to 18 ft. lbs. (25 Nm)
- Power cable to solenoid. Tighten nut (3) to 9 ft. lbs. (12 Nm)
- Exciter wire to solenoid. Tighten nut (2) to 53 inch lbs. (6 Nm)
- Red solenoid safety cap (1)
- Negative battery cable

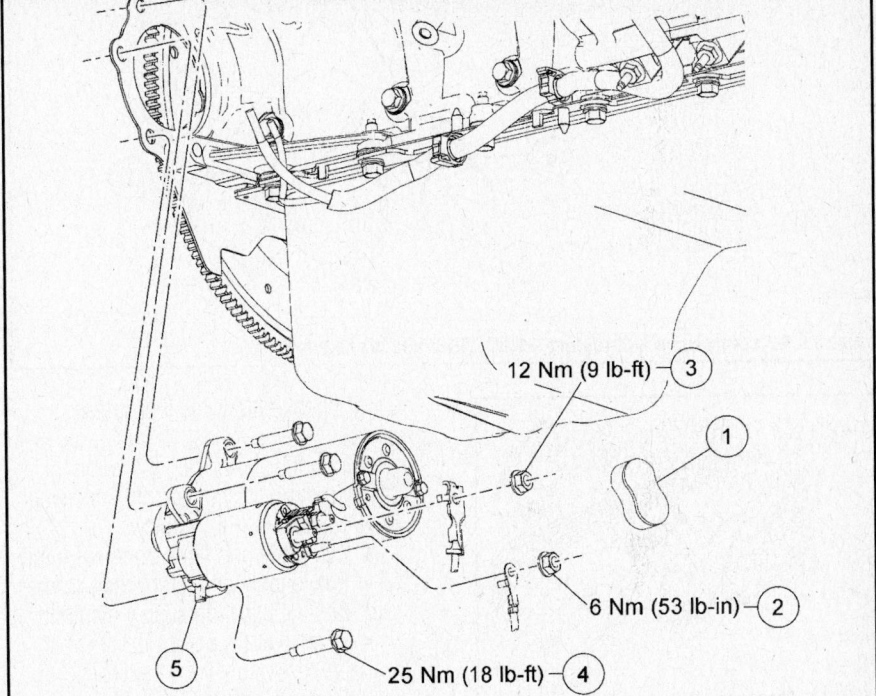

Fig. 32 Starter motor (5), solenoid cap (1), nuts (2, 3) and bolt (4)

ENGINE MECHANICAL

➡**Disconnecting the negative battery cable may interfere with the functions of the on board computer systems and may require the computer to undergo a relearning process, once the negative battery cable is reconnected.**

ACCESSORY DRIVE BELTS

ACCESSORY BELT ROUTING

See Figure 33.

INSPECTION

Inspect the drive belt for signs of glazing or cracking. A glazed belt will be perfectly smooth from slippage, while a good belt will have a slight texture of fabric visible. Cracks will usually start at the inner edge of the belt and run outward. All worn or damaged drive belts should be replaced immediately.

ADJUSTMENT

The accessory drive belt tension is automatically adjusted with a spring-loaded tensioner.

REMOVAL & INSTALLATION

See Figures 33 and 34.

1. Before servicing the vehicle, refer to the precautions in the beginning of this section.
2. Disconnect battery negative cable

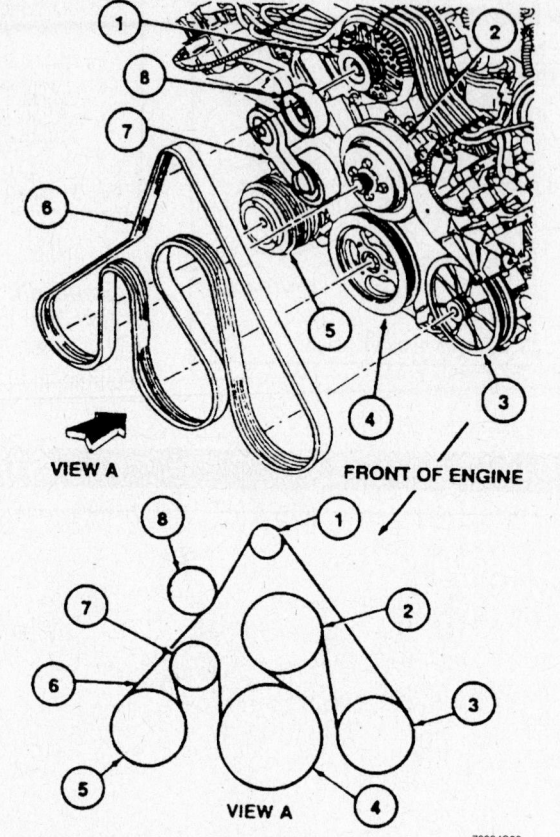

1. Alternator
2. Water pump
3. Power steering pump
4. Crankshaft
5. A/C compressor
6. Drive belt
7. Tensioner
8. Idler pulley

VIEW A   FRONT OF ENGINE

VIEW A

79224G30

Fig. 33 Accessory drive belt routing—4.6L (VIN V and W) engines

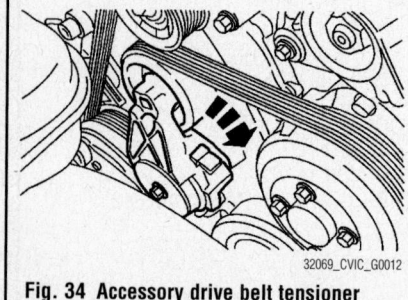

Fig. 34 Accessory drive belt tensioner

from battery and properly isolate to prevent accidental reconnection.

3. Rotate the tensioner clockwise and remove the drive belt.

To install:

4. Rotate the tensioner clockwise.
5. Route the belt around the pulleys.
6. Slowly release the tensioner.

CAMSHAFT AND VALVE LIFTERS

REMOVAL & INSTALLATION

See Figure 35.

1. If equipped with air suspension, the air suspension switch, must be turned to the **OFF** position before raising the vehicle.

2. Properly relieve the fuel system pressure.

3. Drain the engine oil

4. Remove or disconnect the following:
   - Negative battery cable
   - Fan blade and fan shroud assembly
   - Fuel supply and return lines from the fuel injection supply manifold
   - Windshield wiper governor (module) assembly from the vehicle
   - Engine air cleaner outlet tube
   - Accessory drive belt
   - Ignition wires from the spark plugs
   - Ignition wire brackets from the cylinder head cover studs
   - 2 bolts retaining the ignition wire separator to the ignition coil brackets and the bolt retaining the air conditioning pressure line to the right-hand ignition coil bracket
   - Connectors from both ignition coils and the Crankshaft Position (CMP) sensor
   - Ignition coils with brackets attached
   - Electrical connector from the alternator and at the power distribution box
   - Water pump pulley
   - Positive battery cable at the power distribution box

- Bolt from the positive battery cable bracket located on the right-hand cylinder head
- Fuel vapor hose from the EVAP canister purge valve and position the positive battery cable aside
- Positive Crankcase Ventilation (PCV) valve from the cylinder head cover and position aside
- Engine/transmission harness connector from the bracket on the power brake booster
- Crankshaft Position (CKP) sensor and air conditioning clutch harness connectors
- Bolts retaining the power steering pump to the cylinder block and wire the pump aside

➡The front lower bolt on the power steering pump will not come all the way out.

- Oil pan
- Crankshaft pulley bolt and washer and crankshaft pulley
- Engine oil filter
- Power steering control valve actuator and oil pressure sensor
- Oil filter adapter
- Cylinder head covers
- Engine front cover
- Timing chains

5. Rotate the crankshaft counterclockwise no more than 45 degrees from Top Dead Center (TDC) to ensure that all pistons are below the top of the engine block deck face.

6. Install a valve spring compressor under the camshaft and on top of one of the valve spring retainers.

7. Install Valve Spring Spacer T91P-6565-AH between the valve spring coils. Be sure that the valve being compressed is on its base circle. Compress the valve spring and remove the rocker arm. Repeat the procedure until all rocker arms are removed.

8. If required, pull the lash adjusters out of their bores in the cylinder head. Note their locations; they must be installed in the same bore they were removed from.

➡Do not mix the camshaft bearing caps. Note the camshaft bearing cap locations for installation.

9. To remove each camshaft, unfasten the 14 bolts retaining the camshaft bearing caps (cluster assemblies) to the cylinder head. Tap upward on the camshaft bearing caps at points near the upper bearing halves and gradually lift the camshaft bearing cap clusters from the cylinder head.

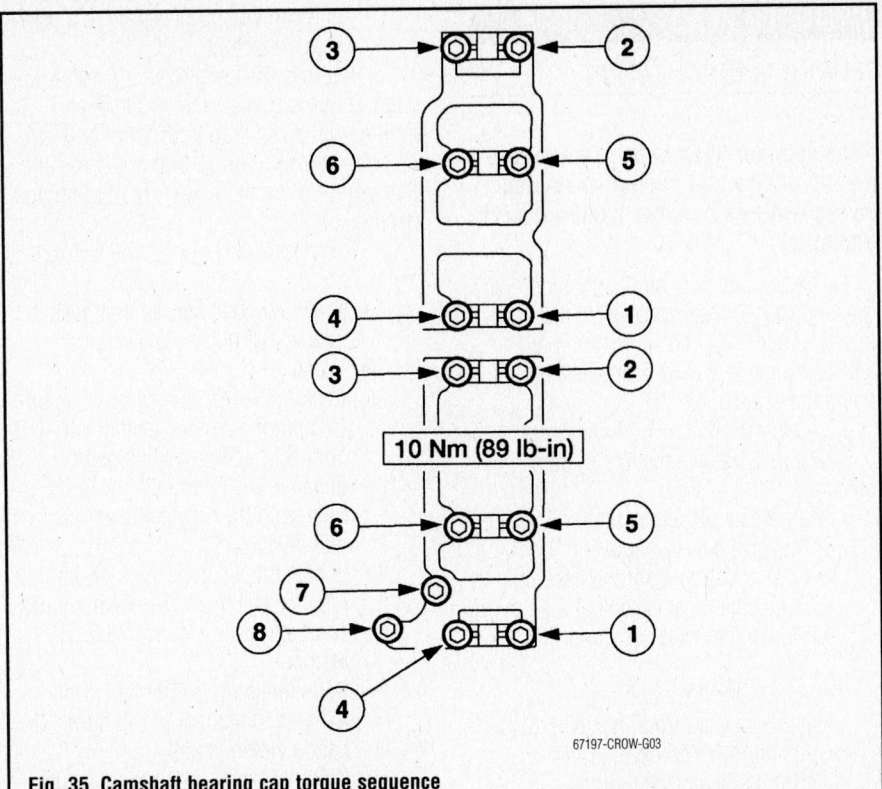

Fig. 35 Camshaft bearing cap torque sequence

10. Repeat the removal procedure for the opposite cylinder head.

11. Remove the camshaft straight upward to avoid bearing damage.

12. Clean and inspect the camshafts and related components for unusual wear or damage.

To install:

13. Clean and inspect the cylinder head covers, engine front cover and cylinder head sealing surfaces.

14. Apply clean engine oil to the camshaft journals and lobes. Position the camshafts on the cylinder heads.

15. Install and seat the camshaft bearing cap cluster assemblies. Install and hand start the retaining bolts. Tighten the camshaft cluster retaining bolts in sequence to 89 inch lbs. (10 Nm). Be sure to tighten each camshaft bearing cap cluster individually.

➡ **Each camshaft bearing cap cluster assembly is tightened individually.**

16. Loosen the camshaft bearing cap cluster retaining bolts approximately 2 turns or until the heads of the bolts are free. Tighten all bolts, again in sequence, to 89 inch lbs. (10 Nm).

17. Repeat the camshaft bearing cap installation for the opposite cylinder head.

➡ **The camshafts should turn freely but with a slight drag.**

18. Check camshaft end-play as follows:

a. Step 1: Install a dial indicator on the front of the engine. Position it so the indicator foot is resting on the camshaft sprocket bolt or the front of the camshaft.

b. Step 2: Push the camshaft toward the rear of the engine and zero the dial indicator.

c. Step 3: Pull the camshaft forward and release it. Specified end-play is 0.0901–0.006 inch (0.025–0.190mm).

d. Step 4: If end-play is too tight, check for binding or foreign material in the camshaft thrust bearing. If end-play is excessive, check for worn camshaft thrust plate and replace the cylinder head, as required.

e. Step 5: Remove the dial indicator.

19. If removed, install the lash adjusters in their original positions.

20. If necessary, install Camshaft Positioning Tools T92P-6256-A on the flats of the camshafts and install the spacers and camshaft sprockets. Install the bolts and washers and tighten to 30 ft. lbs. (40 Nm), then tighten an additional 90 degrees.

21. Install a valve spring compressor under the camshaft and on top of the valve spring retainer.

22. Install Valve Spring Spacer T91P-6565-AH between the valve spring coils. Be sure that the valve being compressed is on its base circle. Compress the valve

spring and install the rocker arm. Repeat the procedure until all rocker arms are installed.

23. Rotate the crankshaft clockwise 45 degrees to position the crankshaft at Top Dead Center (TDC).

➡ **The crankshaft must only be rotated in the clockwise direction and only as far as TDC.**

24. Install or connect the following:
- Timing chains
- Engine front cover
- Cylinder head covers. Tighten the cylinder head cover bolts to 89 inch lbs. (10 Nm).
- Power steering control valve actuator connector
- Oil pressure sensor harness connector

25. Apply silicone sealer to the crankshaft keyway

26. Install the crankshaft pulley and tighten the bolt as follows:

a. Step 1: Tighten to 66 ft. lbs. (90 Nm).

b. Step 2: Loosen one complete turn.

c. Step 3: Tighten to 37 ft. lbs. (50 Nm).

d. Step 4: Tighten an additional 90 degrees.

27. Install or connect the following:
- Engine oil pan
- Power steering pump on the engine and the 4 retaining bolts. Tighten the bolts to 18 ft. lbs. (25 Nm).
- Air conditioning clutch and CKP sensor
- Evaporative emission canister purge valve harness connector
- Engine/transmission harness connectors on the power brake booster retaining bracket
- PCV valve to the right-hand cylinder head cover
- Positive battery cable harness on the right-hand cylinder head
- Bolt retaining the battery cable bracket to the cylinder head
- Evaporative emission hose to the canister purge valve
- Positive battery cable at the power distribution box
- Water pump pulley and tighten the bolts to 18 ft. lbs. (25 Nm)
- Ignition coil brackets and ignition wires to the engine front cover. Tighten the retaining nuts to 18 ft. lbs. (25 Nm).
- Harness connectors to the ignition coils and the CMP sensor

- Air conditioning pressure line on the right-hand ignition coil bracket and the retaining bolt
- Ignition wires to the spark plugs and the brackets onto the cylinder head cover studs
- Accessory drive belt
- Windshield wiper governor
- Fuel supply and return lines
- Fan and shroud assembly
- Negative battery cable

28. Fill the engine cooling system.

29. Fill the crankcase.

30. If equipped with air suspension, turn the air suspension switch to the **ON** position.

31. Start the engine and check for leaks.

32. Road test the vehicle and check for proper engine operation.

CRANKSHAFT FRONT SEAL

REMOVAL & INSTALLATION

See Figure 37.

1. Before servicing the vehicle, refer to the precautions in the beginning of this section.

2. Disconnect battery negative cable from battery and properly isolate to prevent accidental reconnection.

3. Remove the crankshaft pulley.

4. Use special tool 303-107 (T74P-6700-A) or a suitable seal remover to remove the front cover seal.

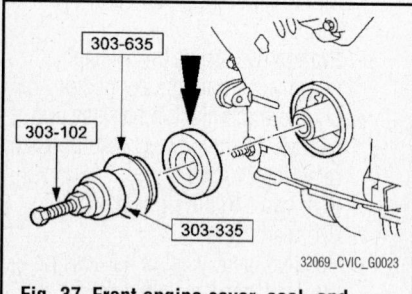

Fig. 37 Front engine cover, seal, and installation tool

To install:

5. Lubricate the engine front cover and the front oil seal inner lip with clean engine oil.

6. Use special tool 303-635 or a suitable seal installer to install the crankshaft front seal into the engine front cover.

7. Install the crankshaft pulley.

8. Reconnect negative battery cable, check for leaks and repair if necessary.

CYLINDER HEAD

REMOVAL & INSTALLATION

See Figures 38 and 39.

➡ **The cylinder head bolts are a torque-to-yield design and cannot be reused. Always use new cylinder head bolts for assembly.**

1. If equipped with air suspension, the air suspension switch, located on the right-hand side of the luggage compartment, must be turned to the **OFF** position before raising the vehicle.

2. Drain the engine cooling system.

3. Properly relieve the fuel system pressure.

4. Remove or disconnect the following:
- Negative battery cable
- Cooling fan and shroud assembly
- Engine air cleaner outlet tube
- Windshield wiper governor (module)
- Accessory drive belt
- Ignition wires from the spark plugs
- Ignition wire brackets from the cylinder head cover studs
- 2 ignition wire tray-to-ignition coil brackets bolts
- Bolt retaining the air conditioning pressure line to the right-hand ignition coil bracket
- Wiring to both ignition coils and the Camshaft Position (CMP) sensor
- Ignition coil brackets-to-engine front cover nuts. Slide the ignition coil brackets and ignition wire assemblies off the mounting studs and from the vehicle
- Water pump pulley
- Alternator wiring harness from the junction block, fender apron and alternator
- Alternator
- Positive battery cable at the power distribution box
- Retaining bolt from the positive battery cable bracket located on the side of the right-hand cylinder head
- Vent hose from the canister purge solenoid and position the positive battery cable aside
- Positive Crankcase Ventilation (PCV) valve from the cylinder head cover
- Engine/transmission harness connector from the retaining bracket on the power brake booster
- Crankshaft Position (CKP) sensor, air conditioning compressor clutch

and canister purge solenoid electrical connectors

5. Remove the bolts retaining the power steering pump to the cylinder block and engine front cover. The front lower bolt on the power steering pump will not come all the way out. Wire the power steering pump aside.

6. Remove or disconnect the following:
- Engine oil pan and oil pan gasket
- Crankshaft pulley retaining bolt
- Pulley
- Power steering control valve actuator and oil pressure sensor wiring connectors and position aside
- Exhaust Gas Recirculation (EGR) tube from the right-hand exhaust manifold
- Exhaust pipes from the exhaust manifolds. Lower the exhaust pipes and hang with wire from the crossmember.
- Bolts retaining the starter wiring harness to the rear of the right-hand cylinder head
- Cylinder head covers to the cylinder heads
- Accelerator and cruise control cables
- Accelerator cable bracket from the intake manifold and position aside
- Vacuum hose from the throttle body elbow vacuum port
- Heated Oxygen Sensor (HO_2S) and the heater water hose
- 2 bolts retaining the thermostat housing to the intake manifold and position the upper hose and thermostat housing aside

➡ **The 2 thermostat housing bolts also retain the intake manifold.**

- 9 intake manifold-to-cylinder heads bolts
- Intake manifold and gaskets
- 7 stud bolts and the 4 bolts attaching the engine front cover to the engine
- Front cover
- Both timing chains
- 10 left-hand cylinder head-to-cylinder block bolts

7. Remove the cylinder head. The lower rear cylinder head bolt must stay in the cylinder head until the cylinder head is removed due to lack of clearance for removal in the vehicle. Use a rubber band to secure the cylinder head bolt in the cylinder head during removal and installation of the cylinder head and to prevent the

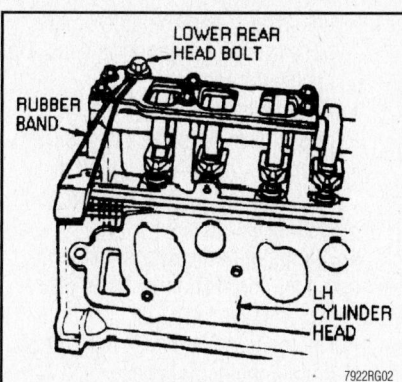

Fig. 38 Use a rubber band to support the rear cylinder head bolt to ease removal of the head

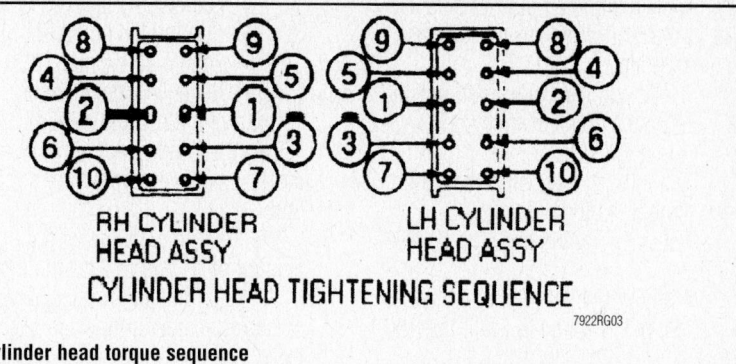

Fig. 39 Cylinder head torque sequence

bolt from damaging the cylinder block or head gasket.

➡The lower rear cylinder head bolt cannot be removed due to interference with the power brake booster. Use a rubber band to hold the bolt away from the cylinder block.

8. Remove or disconnect the following:
- Ground strap, 1 stud and 1 bolt retaining the heater return line to the right-hand cylinder head
- 10 right-hand cylinder head-to-cylinder block bolts

9. Remove the cylinder head. The lower rear cylinder head bolt must stay in the cylinder head until the cylinder head is removed due to lack of clearance for removal in the vehicle. Use a rubber band to secure the cylinder head bolt in the cylinder head during removal and installation of the cylinder head and to prevent the bolt from damaging the cylinder block or head gasket.

➡The lower rear cylinder head bolt cannot be removed due to interference with the evaporator housing. Use a rubber band to hold the bolt away from the cylinder block.

10. Clean all gaskets mating surfaces. Check the cylinder heads and cylinder block for flatness. Check the cylinder heads for scratches near the coolant passages and combustion chambers that could provide leak paths.

To install:

11. Rotate the crankshaft counterclockwise 45 degrees. The crankshaft keyway should be at the 9 o'clock position viewed from the front of the engine. This ensures that all pistons are below the top of the engine block deck face.

12. Rotate the camshaft to a stable posi-

tion where the valves do not extend below the head face.

13. Install or connect the following:
- New head gaskets on the cylinder block
- New bolts in the lower rear bolt holes on both cylinder heads and retain with rubber bands as explained during the removal procedure

14. Position the cylinder heads on the cylinder block dowels, being careful not to score the surface of the head face. Apply clean oil to the new cylinder head bolts, remove the rubber bands from the lower rear bolts and install all bolts hand-tight.

15. Tighten the new cylinder head bolts, in sequence, as follows:
   a. Step 1: 30 ft. lbs. (40 Nm).
   b. Step 2: plus 90 degrees.
   c. Step 3: loosen all bolts at least 1 full turn.
   d. Step 4: 30 ft. lbs. (40 Nm).
   e. Step 5: plus 90 degrees.
   f. Step 6: again, plus 90 degrees.

16. Position the heater return hose and install the 2 retaining bolts.

17. Rotate the camshafts using the flats matched at the center of the camshaft until both are in time. Install Camshaft Positioning Tools T91P-6256-A, on the flats of the camshafts to keep them from rotating.

18. Rotate the crankshaft clockwise 45 degrees to position the crankshaft at Top Dead Center (TDC) for the No. 1 cylinder.

➡The crankshaft must only be rotated in the clockwise direction and only as far as TDC.

19. Install or connect the following:
- Both timing chains
- New engine front cover seal and gasket. Apply silicone sealer to the lower corners of the cover where it meets the junction of the engine oil pan and cylinder block and to the points where the cover contacts the

junction of the cylinder block and the cylinder heads.
- Engine front cover and the bolts. Tighten to 18 ft. lbs. (25 Nm).
- New intake manifold gaskets on the cylinder heads. Be sure the alignment tabs on the gaskets are aligned with the holes in the cylinder heads.
- Intake manifold on the cylinder heads and the retaining bolts. Tighten the bolts in sequence, to 18 ft. lbs. (25 Nm).
- Thermostat, O-ring, thermostat housing and upper hose. Tighten the 2 retaining bolts to 18 ft. lbs. (25 Nm).
- Heater water hose and both HO_2S sensors
- Vacuum hose to the throttle body adapter vacuum port
- Accelerator cable bracket on the intake manifold
- Accelerator and cruise control cables to the throttle body

20. Apply silicone sealer to both places where the engine front cover meets the cylinder heads.
- Cylinder head covers with new gasket on the cylinder heads. Tighten the bolts and stud bolts to 89 inch lbs. (10 Nm).
- Starter motor wiring harness to the right-hand cylinder head and tighten the retaining bolt
- Exhaust pipes to the exhaust manifolds. Tighten the 4 nuts to 25 ft. lbs. (34Nm).

➡Be sure the exhaust system clears the No. 3 crossmember. Adjust as necessary.

- EGR tube to the right-hand exhaust manifold and tighten the line nut to 30 ft. lbs. (40 Nm).
- Power steering control valve actuator and oil pressure sensor electrical connectors

21. Apply a small amount of silicone sealer in the rear of the keyway on the crankshaft pulley.

- Pulley on the crankshaft, making sure the crankshaft key and keyway are aligned.

22. Install the crankshaft pulley and tighten the bolt as follows:

a. Step 1: Tighten to 66 ft. lbs. (90 Nm).

b. Step 2: Loosen one complete turn.

c. Step 3: Tighten to 37 ft. lbs. (50 Nm).

d. Step 4: Tighten an additional 90 degrees.

23. Install or connect the following:

- Engine oil pan and a new gasket
- Power steering pump in position on the cylinder block
- 4 retaining bolts. Tighten the bolts to 18 ft. lbs. (25 Nm).
- Air conditioning compressor, CKP sensor and canister purge solenoid electrical connectors
- Engine/transmission harness connector on the power brake booster
- PCV valve in the right-hand cylinder head cover and connect the canister purge solenoid vent hose
- Positive battery cable harness on the right-hand cylinder head
- Bolt retaining the cable bracket to the cylinder head
- Positive battery cable at the power distribution box and battery
- Alternator and the 2 retaining bolts. Tighten the bolts to 18 ft. lbs. (25 Nm).
- 2 bolts retaining the alternator brace to the intake manifold. Tighten to 89 inch lbs. (10 Nm).
- Water pump pulley. Tighten the bolts to 18 ft. lbs. (25 Nm).
- Ignition coil brackets and ignition wire assemblies onto the mounting studs
- 7 nuts retaining the ignition coil brackets to the engine front cover and tighten to 18 ft. lbs. (25 Nm)
- 2 bolts retaining the ignition wire tray to the ignition coil bracket and tighten to 89 inch lbs. (10 Nm)
- Ignition coil and CMP sensor harness connectors
- Air conditioning pressure line on the right-hand ignition coil bracket and tighten the retaining bolt
- Ignition wires to the spark plugs and the bracket onto the cylinder head cover studs
- Accessory drive belt and the windshield wiper governor

- Fuel supply and return lines
- Cooling fan and shroud
- Engine air cleaner outlet tube
- Negative battery cable

24. Fill the cooling system.

25. If equipped with air suspension, turn the air suspension switch to the **ON** position.

26. Refill the engine with the correct amount of oil and replace the filter.

27. Start the engine and bring to normal operating temperature while checking for leaks.

28. Road test the vehicle and check for proper engine operation.

ENGINE ASSEMBLY

REMOVAL & INSTALLATION

See Figures 40 and 41.

✷✷ CAUTION

If the vehicle is equipped with air suspension, the electrical power to the air suspension system must be shut off prior to hoisting, jacking or towing an air suspension vehicle. This can be accomplished by turning off the air suspension switch located in the luggage compartment. Failure to do so can result in unexpected inflation or deflation of the air springs, which can result in shifting of the vehicle during these operations. Failure to follow these instructions may result in personal injury.

1. Before servicing the vehicle, refer to the precautions in the beginning of this section.

2. Disconnect battery negative cable from battery and properly isolate to prevent accidental reconnection.

3. Drain the engine cooling system.

4. Recover the refrigerant from the air conditioning system.

5. Relieve the fuel system pressure.

6. Drain the engine oil.

7. Remove or disconnect the following:

- Battery
- Hood
- Engine cooling fan, shroud and radiator
- Windshield wiper governor and support bracket
- Engine air cleaner outlet tube
- Engine/transmission harness connector from the retaining bracket
- Accelerator and cruise control cables at the throttle body

- Electrical connector and vacuum hose from the evaporative emission canister purge valve
- Positive battery cable from the power distribution box and harness
- Vacuum supply hose from the throttle body adapter vacuum port
- Both heater hoses
- Alternator harness from the front fender apron and the power distribution box
- Air conditioning hoses from the air conditioning compressor
- Power steering control valve harness connector
- Body ground strap from the dash panel
- Exhaust system from the exhaust manifolds and support with wire hung from the crossmember
- Retaining nut from the transmission line bracket
- 3 bolts and 1 stud retaining the engine to the transmission knee braces
- Starter motor
- 4 bolts retaining the power steering pump to the cylinder block and position aside

8. Transmission housing cover from the cylinder block to access the torque converter nuts. Rotate the crankshaft until each of the 4 nuts is accessible and remove the nuts

9. Remove or disconnect the following:

- 6 transmission-to-engine retaining bolts
- Engine support insulator (mount) through-bolts

10. Support the transmission with a floor jack and a block of wood.

- Bolt retaining the right-hand front engine support insulator to the front engine mount insulator support bracket

11. Install engine lifting bracket to the front of the left-hand cylinder head and to the rear of the right-hand cylinder head. Connect engine lifting equipment to the lifting brackets

12. Raise the engine slightly using a floor crane and carefully separate the engine from the transmission. Do not let the torque converter fall out of the transmission.

13. Carefully lift the engine out of the engine compartment and position on a workstand. Remove the engine lifting equipment.

To install:

14. Engine lifting brackets. Support the engine using a floor crane installed to the

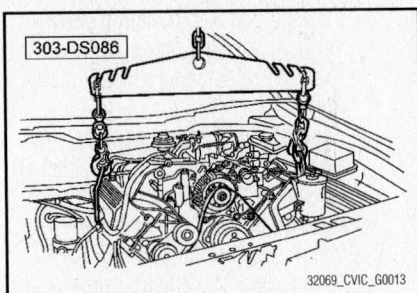

Fig. 40 Slightly lift the engine to access to two top bolts joining the transmission to the engine

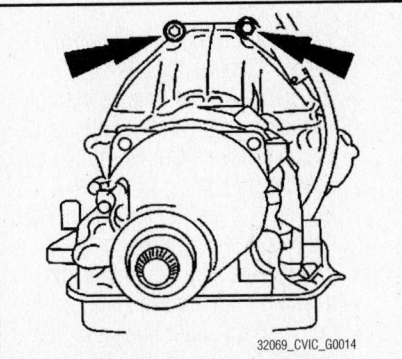

Fig. 41 Top two bolts joining engine to transmission

lifting equipment and remove the engine from the workstand

15. Lower the engine into the engine compartment. Start the converter pilot into the flywheel and align the paint marks on the flywheel and torque converter. Be sure the studs on the torque converter align with the holes in the flywheel.

16. Fully engage the engine to the transmission and lower onto front engine support insulators.

17. Install or connect the following:
- Engine lifting equipment and brackets
- Bolt retaining the right-hand front engine support insulator to the front engine mount insulator support bracket
- 6 engine-to-transmission (bell housing) bolts and tighten to 35 ft. lbs. (48 Nm)
- Front engine support insulator through-bolts and tighten to 18 ft. lbs. (24 Nm)
- 4 torque converter retaining nuts and tighten to 25 ft. lbs. (34 Nm)
- Transmission housing cover to the cylinder block
- Power steering pump on the cylinder block and the 4 retaining nuts. Tighten to 18 ft. lbs. (24 Nm).

- Starter motor
- Engine-to-transmission brace and the 3 bolts and 1 stud. Tighten the bolts and stud to 22 ft. lbs. (30 Nm).
- Transmission line bracket to the brace stud and 1 retaining nut. Tighten to 18 ft. lbs. (24Nm).
- Exhaust system to the exhaust manifolds. Tighten the 4 nuts to 18 ft. lbs. (25 Nm). Be sure the exhaust system clears the No. 3 crossmember. Adjust as necessary.
- Power steering valve harness connector
- Ground strap to the dash panel
- Air conditioning lines to the air conditioning compressor
- Alternator harness at the front fender apron and the power distribution box
- Both heater hoses
- Vacuum supply hose to the throttle body adapter vacuum port
- Positive battery cable to the power distribution box and harness
- Electrical connector and vacuum hose to the evaporative emission canister purge valve
- Accelerator and cruise control cables at the throttle body
- Engine/transmission harness connector to the retaining bracket on the power brake booster
- Windshield wiper governor and support bracket
- Fuel supply and return lines
- Radiator, cooling fan and shroud
- Engine air cleaner outlet tube
- Hood
- Battery

18. Fill the crankcase to the correct level.
19. Fill the cooling system.
20. Start the engine and allow it to reach normal operating temperature.
21. Check for leaks and proper fluid levels.
22. Evacuate and recharge the air conditioning system.
23. Road test the vehicle and check the engine and transmission for proper operation.

EXHAUST MANIFOLD

REMOVAL & INSTALLATION

See Figures 42 and 43.

1. Drain the engine cooling system.
2. Relieve the fuel system pressure.
3. Discharge the air conditioning system

4. Remove or disconnect the following:
- Battery cables
- Engine air inlet tube
- Cooling fan and shroud assembly
- Fuel supply and return lines
- Upper radiator hose
- Windshield wiper governor and support bracket
- Compressor outlet hose at the compressor and the hose assembly-to-right-hand ignition coil bracket bolt. Plug both openings.
- Engine/transmission harness connector from the retaining bracket on the power brake booster
- Heater hose
- Ground strap-to-right-hand cylinder head nut
- Upper stud and lower bolt retaining the heater hose to the right cylinder head and position aside
- Heater blower motor switch resistor
- Bolt retaining the right-hand front engine support insulator to the sub-frame
- Both Heated Oxygen Sensors (HO$_2$S)
- Engine support insulator through-bolts
- Exhaust Gas Recirculation (EGR) valve-to-exhaust manifold tube nut from the right-hand exhaust manifold.
- Catalytic converter pipes from both exhaust manifolds. Lower the exhaust system and hang it from the crossmember with wire.
- Left-hand exhaust manifold
- Front engine support insulator from the cylinder block and the 8 nuts retaining the exhaust manifold
- Left-hand exhaust manifold and the 2 manifold gaskets

5. Position an adjustable jack stand and a block of wood under the engine oil pan, rearward of the oil drain hole. Raise the engine approximately 4 inches (100mm).

6. Install or connect the following:
- 8 exhaust manifold retaining nuts and right-hand exhaust manifold
- Manifold and gasket

To install:

7. If the exhaust manifolds are being replaced, transfer the heated O$_2$ sensors and tighten to 30 ft. lbs. (41 Nm). On the right-hand exhaust manifold, transfer the EGR tube connector and tighten to 35 ft. lbs. (48 Nm).

8. Clean the mating surfaces of the exhaust manifolds and cylinder heads.

9. Install or connect the following:

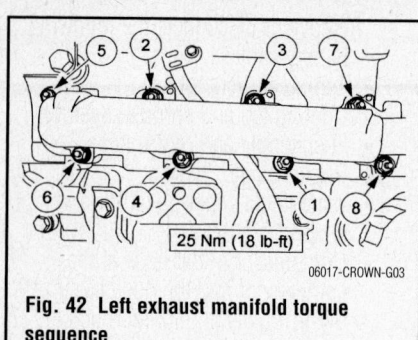

Fig. 42 Left exhaust manifold torque sequence

25 Nm (18 lb-ft)

06017-CROWN-G03

Fig. 43 Right exhaust manifold torque sequence

7922RG09

- Exhaust manifolds, using new gaskets. Tighten the bolts in sequence to 18 ft. lbs. (25 Nm).
- EGR valve and tube assembly to the exhaust manifold. Tighten the line nut to 30 ft. lbs. (40 Nm).
- Left-hand front engine support insulator to the cylinder block and tighten the bolts to 18 ft. lbs. (25 Nm)

10. Lower the engine onto the front engine support insulator and remove the jack.

11. Install or connect the following:
- Left-hand and right-hand engine support insulator through-bolts and tighten to 18 ft. lbs. (25 Nm).
- Catalytic converter pipes to both exhaust manifolds. Tighten the nuts to 25 ft. lbs. (34 Nm).

➡**Be sure the exhaust system clears the No. 3 crossmember. Adjust as necessary.**

- Both HO2S sensors
- Bolt retaining the right-hand front engine support insulator to the subframe. Tighten to 18 ft. lbs. (25 Nm)
- Heater blower motor switch resistor using the 2 retaining screws
- Heater hose in position
- Upper stud and lower bolt and tighten to 18 ft. lbs. (25 Nm)
- Ground strap onto the stud and tighten the nut to 18 ft. lbs. (25 Nm)
- Heater hose
- Engine/transmission harness connector

- Retaining bracket on the power brake booster
- Air conditioning compressor outlet hose to the compressor
- Bolt retaining the hose assembly to the right-hand ignition coil bracket
- Upper radiator hose
- Fuel supply and return lines
- Windshield wiper governor and retaining bracket
- Engine cooling fan blade and fan shroud
- Engine air inlet tube
- Battery cables

12. Fill the cooling system.

13. Start the engine and check for leaks.

14. Properly charge the air conditioning system.

15. Road test the vehicle and check for proper operation.

INTAKE MANIFOLD

REMOVAL & INSTALLATION

See Figure 44.

1. If equipped with air suspension, the air suspension switch, located on the right-hand side of the luggage compartment, must be turned to the **OFF** position before raising the vehicle.

2. Disconnect negative battery cable.

3. Drain the engine cooling system.

4. Properly relieve the fuel system pressure.

5. Remove or disconnect the following:
- Fuel supply and return lines
- Windshield wiper governor (module)
- Engine air cleaner outlet tube
- Accessory drive belt
- Ignition wires from the spark plugs
- Ignition wire brackets from the cylinder head cover studs
- Ignition coils and the Camshaft Position (CMP) sensor
- Ignition wires from both ignition coils
- 2 bolts retaining the ignition wire bracket to the ignition coil brackets
- Ignition wire assembly
- Alternator wiring harness from the junction block at the fender apron and alternator
- Bolts retaining the alternator brace to the intake manifold and the alternator to the cylinder block
- Alternator
- Oil pressure sensor and power steering control valve actuator wiring and position the wiring harness aside

- Exhaust Gas Recirculation (EGR) valve-to-exhaust manifold tube from the right-hand exhaust manifold
- Engine/transmission harness connector from the retaining bracket on the power brake booster
- Air conditioning compressor clutch, Crankshaft position (CKP) sensor and the canister purge solenoid wiring connectors
- Positive Crankcase Ventilation (PCV) valve from the cylinder head cover
- Canister purge vent hose from the PCV valve
- Accelerator and cruise control cables from the throttle body
- Accelerator cable bracket from the intake manifold and position aside
- Vacuum hose from the throttle body adapter port
- Heated Oxygen Sensor (HO2S) and the heater water hose
- 2 bolts retaining the thermostat housing to the intake manifold and position the upper hose and thermostat housing aside

➡**The 2 thermostat housing bolts are also used to retain the intake manifold.**

- 9 bolts retaining the intake manifold to the cylinder heads
- Intake manifold and gaskets

6. If replacing the intake manifold, swap over the necessary parts.

To install:

7. Clean all gaskets mating surfaces.

8. Position new intake manifold gaskets

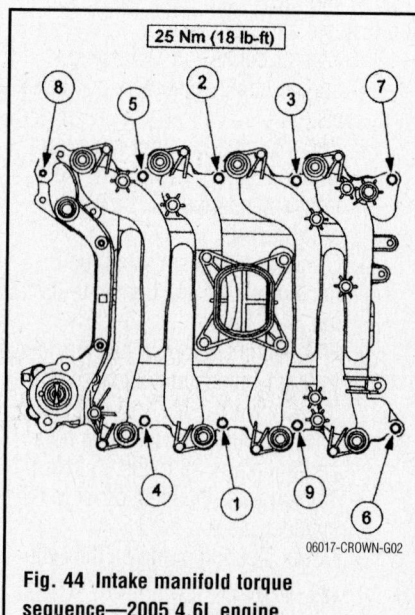

25 Nm (18 lb-ft)

06017-CROWN-G02

Fig. 44 Intake manifold torque sequence—2005 4.6L engine

on the cylinder heads. Be sure the alignment tabs on the gaskets are aligned with the holes in the cylinder heads.

9. Install the intake manifold and the 9 retaining bolts. Hand-tighten the right-rear bolt (viewed from the front of the engine) before final tightening, then tighten the bolts, in sequence, to 18 ft. lbs. (25 Nm).

10. Inspect and if necessary, replace the O-ring seal on the thermostat housing. Position the housing and upper hose and install the 2 retaining bolts. Tighten to 18 ft. lbs. (25 Nm).

11. Install or connect the following:
- Heater water hose
- HO2S sensor
- Vacuum hose to the throttle body adapter vacuum port
- Accelerator cable bracket on the intake manifold
- Accelerator and cruise control cables to the throttle body
- PCV valve in the cylinder head cover
- Canister purge solenoid vent hose
- Air conditioning compressor clutch, CKP sensor and canister purge solenoid wiring connectors
- Engine/transmission harness connector the retaining bracket on the power brake booster
- EGR valve-to-exhaust manifold tube to the right-hand exhaust manifold. Tighten the tube nut to 30 ft. lbs. (40 Nm).
- Power steering control valve actuator
- Oil pressure sensor wiring connectors
- Alternator. Tighten the bolts to 18 ft. lbs. (25 Nm).
- 2 bolts retaining the alternator brace to the intake manifold and tighten to 89 inch lbs. (10 Nm)
- Alternator wiring harness to the alternator, right-hand fender apron and junction block
- Ignition wire assembly on the engine
- 2 bolts retaining the ignition wire bracket to the ignition coil brackets. Tighten the bolts to 89 inch lbs. (10 Nm).
- Ignition wires to the ignition coils
- Ignition wires to the spark plugs
- Ignition wire brackets on the cylinder head cover studs
- Wiring connectors to both ignition coils and the CMP sensor
- Accessory drive belt
- Air cleaner outlet tube
- Windshield wiper governor

- Fuel supply and return lines
- Negative battery cable

12. Fill the engine cooling system.

13. If equipped with air suspension, turn the air suspension switch to the **ON** position.

14. Start the engine and check for leaks.

15. Road test the vehicle and check for proper operation.

OIL PAN

REMOVAL & INSTALLATION
See Figure 45.

✲✲ CAUTION

If the vehicle is equipped with air suspension, the electrical power to the air suspension system must be shut off prior to hoisting, jacking or towing an air suspension vehicle. This can be accomplished by turning off the air suspension switch located in the luggage compartment. Failure to do so can result in unexpected inflation or deflation of the air springs, which can result in shifting of the vehicle during these operations. Failure to follow these instructions may result in personal injury.

1. Drain the engine cooling system

2. Properly discharge the air conditioning system.

3. Relieve the fuel system pressure.

4. Remove or disconnect the following:
- Negative battery cable
- Engine air cleaner outlet tube
- Fuel supply and return lines at the fuel injection supply manifold
- Cooling fan and fan shroud
- Upper radiator hose
- Wiper governor and support bracket
- A/C compressor outlet hose
- Engine/transmission electrical harness connector from the retaining bracket on the power brake booster
- Heater water hose
- Nut retaining the ground strap to the right-hand cylinder head
- Upper stud and loosen the lower bolt retaining the heater outlet hose to the right-hand cylinder head and position aside
- Heater blower motor switch resistor

5. Drain the engine oil and reinstall the oil pan drain plug with a new gasket. Tighten the plug to 10 ft. lbs. (13 Nm).

6. Remove or disconnect the following:
- Bolt retaining the right-hand engine

support insulator to the lower front sub-frame
- Bolts retaining the left-hand and right-hand front engine support insulators to the engine mount supports
- Catalytic converter pipes from both exhaust manifolds. Lower the exhaust system and support it with wire from the transmission cross-member.

7. Position a jack and a block of wood under the oil pan, rearward of the oil drain hole. Raise the engine approximately 4 inches (100mm) and insert 2 wood blocks approximately 2½–2¾ inch (60–70mm) thick under each front engine support insulator. Lower the engine onto the wood blocks and remove the jack.

8. Remove the oil pan.

9. If necessary, remove the 2 bolts retaining the oil pick-up tube to the oil pump and remove the bolt retaining the pick-up tube to the main bearing stud spacer. Remove the pick-up tube.

To install:

10. Clean the engine oil pan and inspect for damage. Clean the sealing surfaces of the front cover and cylinder block. Clean and inspect the oil pick-up tube and replace the O-ring.

11. If removed, position the oil pick-up tube on the oil pump and hand start the 2 retaining bolts. Install the bolt retaining the pick-up tube on the main bearing stud spacer, hand tight.

12. Tighten the pick-up tube-to-oil pump

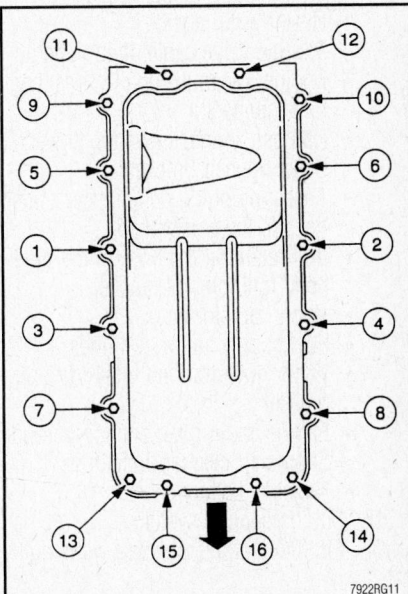

Fig. 45 To prevent oil leaks, tighten the oil pan bolts in the sequence shown

7922RG11

bolts to 89 inch lbs. (10 Nm), then tighten the pick-up tube-to-main bearing stud spacer bolt to 18 ft. lbs. (25 Nm).

13. Position a new gasket on the oil pan. Apply silicone sealer to where the front cover meets the cylinder block and the crankshaft rear oil seal and retainer meets the cylinder block. Position the oil pan to the engine and install the retaining bolts. Tighten the bolts in sequence, to 14 ft. lbs. (20 Nm), then rotate the oil pan retaining bolts, in sequence an additional 60 degrees within 4 minutes of applying the silicone sealer.

14. Position the jack and wood block under the engine oil pan, rearward of the oil drain hole, and raise the engine enough to remove the wood blocks. Lower the engine and remove the jack.

15. Install or connect the following:
- Left-hand and right-hand engine support insulator through-bolts and tighten to 18 ft. lbs. (25 Nm)
- Bolt retaining the right-hand engine support insulator to the lower front sub-frame. Tighten the bolt to 18 ft. lbs. (25 Nm).
- Exhaust system to the exhaust manifolds and tighten the 4 retaining nuts to 25 ft. lbs. (34Nm). Be sure the exhaust system clears the crossmember. Adjust as necessary.
- New engine oil filter
- Heater blower motor switch resistor using the 2 retaining screws
- Heater water hose
- Upper stud and tighten the upper and lower bolts to 18 ft. lbs. (25 Nm)
- Ground strap on the stud and tighten to 18 ft. lbs. (25 Nm)
- Heater water hose
- Throttle valve cable, if equipped
- Engine/transmission electrical harness connector
- Harness connector on the power brake booster bracket
- Air conditioning compressor outlet hose to the compressor
- Bolt retaining the hose to the right-hand ignition coil bracket
- Upper radiator hose
- Fuel supply and return lines
- Wiper governor and retaining bracket
- Engine cooling fan and fan shroud
- Engine air cleaner outlet tube
- Negative battery cable

16. Fill the cooling system.

17. Fill the engine crankcase with engine oil.

18. Start the engine and check for leaks.

19. Properly evacuate and recharge the air conditioning system.

20. Road test the vehicle and check for proper engine operation.

OIL PUMP

REMOVAL & INSTALLATION
See Figure 46.

1. Remove or disconnect the following:
- Negative battery cable
- Cylinder head covers
- Engine front cover
- Engine oil pan
- Timing chains
- 2 bolts retaining the oil pick-up tube to the oil pump and the bolt attaching the oil pick-up tube to the main bearing stud spacer
- Pick-up tube
- 4 bolts retaining the oil pump to the cylinder block
- Oil pump

To install:

2. Rotate the inner rotor of the oil pump to align with the flats on the crankshaft and install the oil pump flush with the cylinder block. Install the 4 retaining bolts and tighten to 89 inch lbs. (10 Nm).

3. Clean the oil pick-up tube and replace the O-ring.

4. Place the pick-up tube on the oil pump and hand start the 2 retaining bolts. Install the bolt retaining the pick-up tube to the main bearing stud spacer hand tight. Tighten the pick-up tube-to-oil pump bolts to 89 inch lbs. (10 Nm). Tighten the pick-up tube to main bearing stud spacer bolt to 18 ft. lbs. (25 Nm).

5. Install or connect the following:

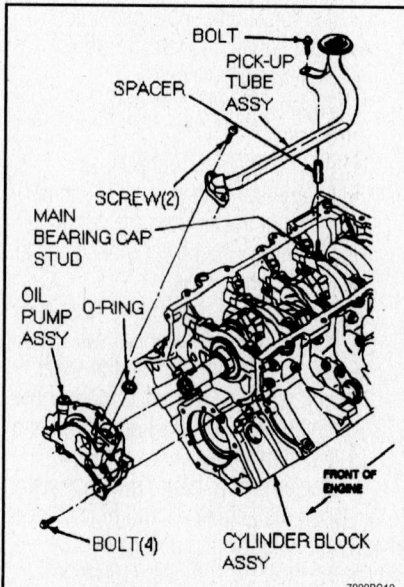

Fig. 46 The oil pump is mounted on the crankshaft at the front of the engine

- New engine oil filter
- Timing chains
- Engine oil pan
- Engine front cover
- Cylinder head covers
- Negative battery cable

6. Fill the crankcase.

7. Start the engine and check for leaks and proper engine oil pressure.

8. Road test the vehicle and check for proper engine operation.

PISTON AND RING

POSITIONING
See Figures 47 and 48.

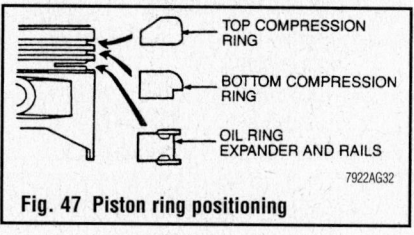

Fig. 47 Piston ring positioning

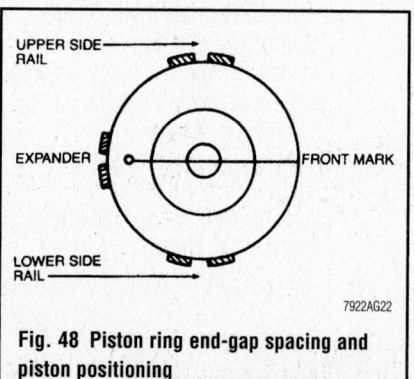

Fig. 48 Piston ring end-gap spacing and piston positioning

REAR MAIN SEAL

REMOVAL & INSTALLATION
See Figures 49 and 50.

✳✳ CAUTION

If the vehicle is equipped with air suspension, the electrical power to the air suspension system must be shut off prior to hoisting, jacking or towing an air suspension vehicle. This can be accomplished by turning off the air suspension switch located in the luggage compartment. Failure to do so can result in unexpected inflation or deflation of the air springs, which can result in shifting of the vehicle during these operations. Failure to follow these instructions may result in personal injury.

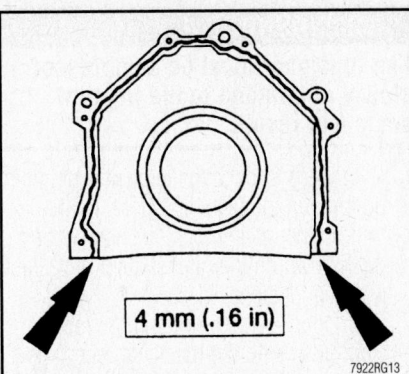

Fig. 49 Apply a continuous bead of silicone sealant to the back of the seal retainer before installing it on the engine

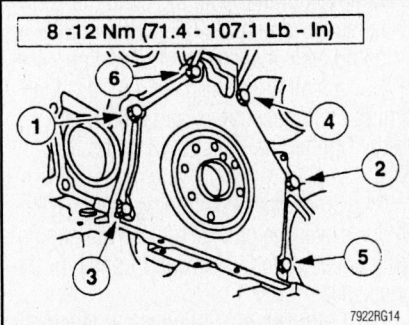

Fig. 50 To avoid leakage, be sure to tighten the crankshaft rear oil seal retainer bolts in the correct sequence

1. Remove or disconnect the following:
   - Transmission
   - Flexplate or flywheel
2. With a sharp awl, carefully punch a small hole in the metal portion of the seal.
3. Remove the seal using a slide hammer with a sheet metal screw attached.

➡**If the oil leak is coming from around the seal retainer, the retainer must also be removed and resealed.**

To install:

4. If the seal retainer was removed, carefully clean the sealant from the retainer and engine block using a plastic scraper. Remove any oil or grease residue from the sealing surfaces with a solvent.
5. Apply silicone sealant to the back of the retainer and immediately install it on the engine block. Tighten the bolts in sequence to 89 inch lbs. (10 Nm).
6. Lubricate the seal and the crankshaft with clean engine oil.
7. Install the seal with the spring side toward the engine.
8. Remove the installation tool.
9. Install or connect the following:
   - Flexplate or flywheel. Tighten the

bolts, in a star pattern, to 59 ft. lbs. (80 Nm).
   - Transmission
   - Negative battery cable
10. Check the engine oil level.
11. Start the engine and check for leaks.

TIMING CHAIN COVER AND SEAL

REMOVAL & INSTALLATION

See Figures 51 thru 57.

1. Drain the engine oil.
2. Remove or disconnect the following:
   - Negative battery cable
   - Cooling fan and shroud
   - Accessory drive belt
   - Water pump pulley
   - Power steering pump
   - Oil pan
   - Crankshaft pulley retaining bolt and washer
   - Crankshaft pulley
   - Bolt retaining the air conditioning pressure line to the right-hand ignition coil bracket
   - Cylinder head covers
   - Wiring at both ignition coils and the Crankshaft Position (CMP) sensor
   - 3 bolts retaining the right-hand ignition coil bracket to the engine front cover. Position the power steering hose aside.
   - 3 nuts retaining the left-hand ignition coil bracket to the engine front cover. Slide both ignition coil brackets and ignition wires off the mounting studs and lay the assembly on top of the engine.
   - Bolts retaining the drive belt idler pulley and the pulley
   - Wiring to the Crankshaft Position (CKP) sensor and the sensor

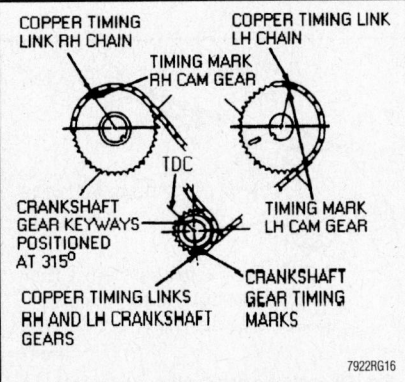

Fig. 51 Be sure that the timing marks are aligned when the No. 1 piston is at TDC on compression cycle

3. If equipped, remove the retainers for the oil cooler from the engine front cover retaining stud bolts and position the oil cooler aside.
   - 9 stud bolts and the 6 standard engine front cover bolts and the cover
   - Crankshaft oil seal from the cover using a seal driver
   - CKP sensor pulse wheel
4. Rotate the engine to set the piston for No. 1 to Top Dead Center (TDC) on its compression stroke.
5. Install Camshaft Positioning Adapters T92P-6256-A on the flats of both camshafts. This will prevent accidental rotation of the camshafts.
6. Remove or disconnect the following:
   - 2 bolts retaining the tensioner to the right-hand cylinder head and the tensioner
   - Right-hand timing chain tensioner arm
   - 2 bolts retaining the right-hand timing chain guide to the cylinder head and remove the timing chain guide.

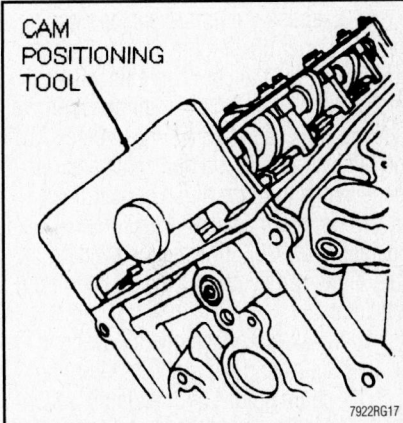

Fig. 52 Use the special tool to maintain camshaft position while installing the timing chains

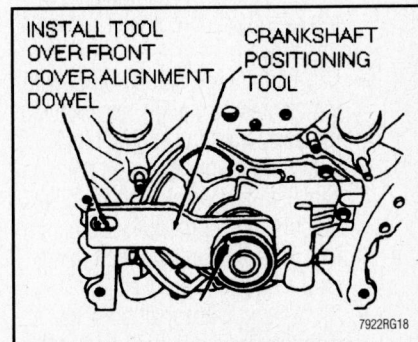

Fig. 53 Install the crankshaft positioning tool to be sure the crankshaft does not turn while installing the timing chains

- Right-hand timing chain from the camshaft and crankshaft sprockets
- Right-hand camshaft sprocket retaining bolt, washer, sprocket and spacer, if necessary
- 2 bolts retaining the timing chain tensioner to the left-hand cylinder head
- Timing chain tensioner
- Left-hand timing chain tensioner arm
- 2 bolts retaining the timing chain guide to the left-hand cylinder head
- Timing chain guide
- Left-hand timing chain from the camshaft and crankshaft sprockets
- Left-hand camshaft sprocket retaining bolt, washer, sprocket and spacer, if necessary

7. If necessary, note the position of the crankshaft sprockets and remove the crankshaft sprockets by sliding them off the front of the crankshaft.

8. Inspect the plastic running face on the tensioner arms and chain guides. If worn or damaged, inspect the engine oil pan for contamination and thoroughly clean the oil pan. Replace the oil pick-up tube.

To install:

9. Examine the timing chains, looking for the copper links. If the copper links are not visible, lay the chain on a flat surface and pull the chain taught until the opposite sides of the chain contact one another. Mark the links at each end of the chain and use these marks in place of the copper links.

10. Be sure Camshaft Positioning Adapters T92P-6256-A are installed on the flats of the camshafts to prevent them from rotating.

11. Install or connect the following:
- Left-hand and right-hand timing chain guides and retaining bolts. Tighten the retaining bolts to 89 inch lbs. (10 Nm).
- Left-hand and right-hand camshaft spacers and sprockets, (if removed) on the camshafts, the washers and retaining bolts but do not tighten at this time.
- Left-hand crankshaft sprocket with the tapered part of the sprocket facing away from the engine block
- Left-hand timing chain on the camshaft and crankshaft sprockets. Be sure the copper links of the timing chain line up with the timing marks on both sprockets.
- Right-hand crankshaft sprocket with the tapered part of the sprocket facing the left-hand crankshaft sprocket, if removed

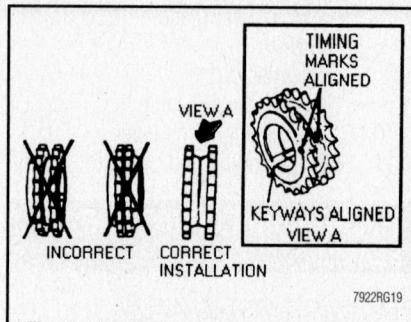

Fig. 54 Install the crankshaft sprockets with the tapered sides facing each other

- Right-hand timing chain on the camshaft and crankshaft sprockets. Be sure the copper links of the timing chain line up with the timing marks on both sprockets.

12. It is necessary to bleed the timing chain tensioners before installation. Proceed as follows:

a. Step 1: position the timing chain tensioner in a soft-jawed vise.

b. Step 2: using a small pick or similar tool, hold the ratchet lock mechanism away from the ratchet stem and slowly compress the tensioner plunger by rotating the vise handle.

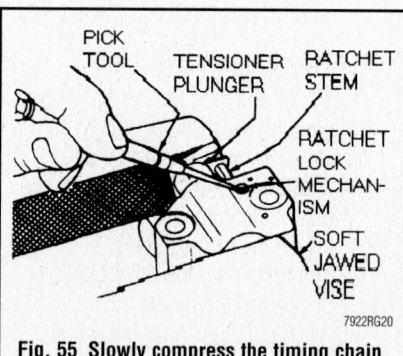

Fig. 55 Slowly compress the timing chain tensioner while holding the ratchet lock away from the stem with a suitable tool

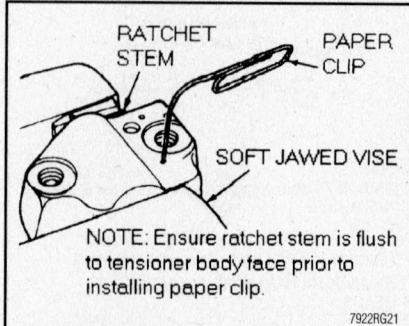

NOTE: Ensure ratchet stem is flush to tensioner body face prior to installing paper clip.

Fig. 56 Install a paper clip or wire into the tensioner to hold the plunger in during assembly

✴✴ WARNING

The tensioner must be compressed slowly or damage to the internal seals will result.

c. Step 3: once the tensioner plunger bottoms in the tensioner bore, continue to hold the ratchet lock mechanism and push down on the ratchet stem until flush with the tensioner face.

d. Step 4: while holding the ratchet stem flush with the tensioner face, release the ratchet lock mechanism and install a paper clip or similar tool in the tensioner body to lock the tensioner in the collapsed position.

e. Step 5: the paper clip must not be removed until the timing chain, tensioner, tensioner arm and timing chain guide are completely installed on the engine.

13. Install the right-hand and left-hand timing chain tensioners and 2 bolts on each. Tighten the bolts to 18 ft. lbs. (25 Nm).

14. Crankshaft Positioning Tool T93P-6265-A over the crankshaft and the engine front cover alignment dowel to position the crankshaft.

15. Lubricate the timing chain tensioner arm contact surfaces with clean engine oil and install the right-hand and left-hand tensioner arms on their dowel pins.

16. Position a C-clamp around the timing chain tensioner arm and timing chain guide to remove all slack from the timing chain. Use care not to bend the timing chain guide.

17. Remove the locking pins or paper clips from the timing chain tensioners and be sure that all timing marks are aligned.

18. Using Camshaft Positioning Adapters T92P-6265-A to align and hold the camshafts, tighten the camshaft sprocket retaining bolts to 30 ft. lbs. (40 Nm), then tighten an additional 90 degrees.

19. Position a dial indicator in the No. 1 cylinder spark plug hole to measure intake valve lift. The intake valve should be at maximum lift when the crankshaft is at 114 degrees after TDC. If the intake valve lift is not at maximum lift, loosen the camshaft sprocket bolt and repeat the steps detailing the installation of the timing chain tensioners to the tightening of the camshaft sprockets.

20. Remove the camshaft and crankshaft positioning tools.

21. Install a new crankshaft seal in the front cover. Apply engine oil to the lip of the seal.

22. Thoroughly clean the sealing sur-

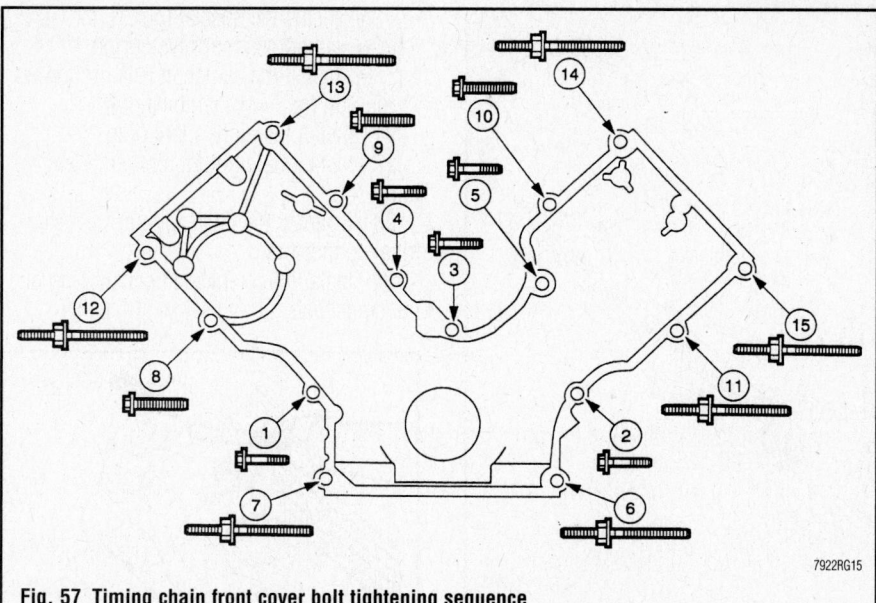

Fig. 57 Timing chain front cover bolt tightening sequence

faces of the front cover, cylinder block and oil pan. Apply silicone sealer to the points where the cylinder head meets the cylinder block.

23. Install or connect the following:
- Front cover in position using new gaskets
- Retaining bolts and studs in their proper locations. Tighten bolts 1 through 5 in sequence to 18 ft. lbs. (25 Nm) and bolt 6 through 15 to 35 ft. lbs. (48 Nm) within 4 minutes of applying the silicone sealer.
- Oil cooler to the front cover retaining stud bolts, if equipped
- CKP sensor and attach the harness connector
- Drive belt idler pulley
- Ignition coil brackets and ignition wires as an assembly onto the mounting studs
- Power steering hose and the nuts retaining the coil brackets to the front cover. Tighten the nuts to 18 ft. lbs. (25 Nm).
- Wiring to both ignition coils and the CMP sensor
- Cylinder head covers
- Air conditioning pressure line on the right-hand ignition coil bracket and tighten the retaining bolt

24. Apply a small amount of silicone sealer in the rear of the keyway in the crankshaft pulley.

25. Install or connect the following:
- Pulley on the crankshaft
- Crankshaft pulley bolt and washer and tighten to 66 ft. lbs. (90 Nm)
- Oil pan
- Power steering pump on the

engine. Tighten the bolts to 18 ft. lbs. (25 Nm).
- Water pump pulley. Tighten the bolts to 18 ft. lbs. (25 Nm).
- Accessory drive belt
- Engine cooling fan and shroud
- Negative battery cable

26. Fill the engine.
27. Start the engine and check for leaks.
28. Road test the vehicle and check for proper engine operation.

TIMING CHAIN AND SPROCKETS

REMOVAL & INSTALLATION
See Figures 58 through 64.

✳✳ CAUTION

Since the engine is not free-wheeling, timing procedures must be followed exactly or piston and valve damage can occur.

1. Before servicing the vehicle, refer to the precautions in the beginning of this section.
2. Disconnect battery negative cable from battery and properly isolate to prevent accidental reconnection.
3. Remove or disconnect the following:
- Engine front cover
- Crankshaft sensor ring from the crankshaft
- Ignition coil electrical connectors
- Ignition coils

➡**Use compressed air to remove any foreign material from the spark plug wells before removing the spark plugs.**

- Spark plugs
4. Position the lobe of the camshaft up.
5. Install the special tool between the valve spring coils to prevent valve stem seal damage.

➡**The roller followers are positional. Mark the followers for installation in their original locations.**

6. Use special tool 303-581 or a suitable on-head valve spring compressor to compress the valve spring and remove the camshaft roller followers.
7. Position the crankshaft with the keyway at the 12 o'clock position.
8. Remove the timing chain tensioning system from both timing chains.
   a. Remove the bolts.
   b. Remove the timing chain tensioners.
   c. Remove the timing chain tensioner arms.
9. Remove the LH and RH timing chains and the crankshaft sprocket as follows:
- Remove the RH timing chain from the camshaft sprocket.
- Remove the RH timing chain from the crankshaft sprocket.
- Repeat for the LH timing chain and crankshaft sprocket.
10. Remove the timing chain guides as follows:
- Remove the bolts.
- Remove the LH timing chain guide.
- Remove the bolts.
- Remove the RH timing chain guide.

To install:
ENGINES WITH RATCHETING TIMING CHAIN TENSIONERS

✳✳ WARNING

Timing chain procedure must be followed exactly or damage to valves and pistons will result.

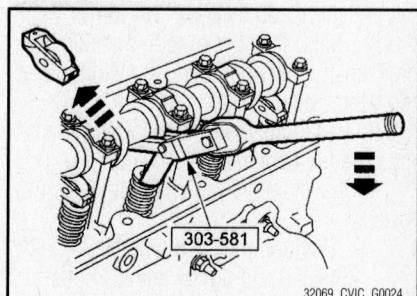

Fig. 58 Compressing valve spring to remove roller follower

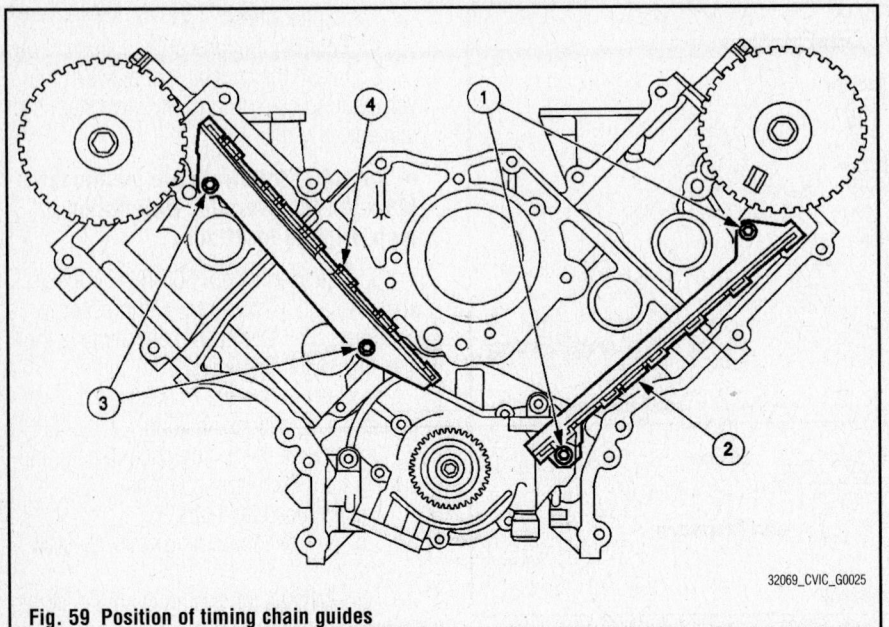

Fig. 59 Position of timing chain guides

⁂ WARNING

Do not compress the ratchet assembly. This will damage the ratchet assembly.

1. Compress each tensioner plunger using an edge of a vise.
2. Using a small screwdriver or pick, push back and hold the ratchet mechanism.
3. While holding the ratchet mechanism, push the ratchet arm back into the tensioner housing.
4. Install a paper clip into the hole of each tensioner housing to hold the ratchet assembly and plunger in during installation.
5. Remove the tensioner from the vise.
6. If the copper links on the timing chain are not visible, mark one link on one end and one link on the other end and use as timing marks.
7. Install the camshaft sprockets and new bolts and tighten in two stages:
   - Stage 1: Tighten the bolt to 30 ft. lbs. (40 Nm).
   - Stage 2: Tighten the bolt an additional 90 degrees (1/4 turn).
8. Using the special tool, position the crankshaft so the number one cylinder is at top dead center (TDC).
9. Install the crankshaft sprocket, making sure the flange faces forward.
10. Install the timing chain guide as follows:
    - Position the LH timing chain guide.
    - Install and tighten the LH bolts.
    - Position the RH timing chain guide.
    - Install and tighten the RH bolts.
11. Rotate the RH camshaft sprocket

until the timing mark is approximately at the 11 o'clock position.
12. Rotate the LH camshaft sprocket until the timing mark is approximately at the 12 o'clock position.
13. Position the LH (inner) timing chain on the crankshaft sprocket, aligning the copper (marked) link with the timing mark on the sprocket.
14. Install the LH timing chain on the sprocket, aligning the copper (marked) link with the timing marks on the sprocket.

➡ **The LH timing chain tensioner arm has a bump near the dowel hole for identification. Position the LH timing chain tensioner arm on the dowel pin and install the LH timing chain tensioner.**

15. Remove the retaining clip from the LH timing chain tensioner.
16. Position the RH (outer) timing chain on the crankshaft sprocket, aligning copper (marked) link with the timing mark on the sprocket.
17. Install the RH timing chain on the camshaft sprocket, aligning the copper (marked) link with the timing marks on the sprocket.
18. Position the RH timing chain tensioner arm on the dowel pin and install the RH timing chain tensioner.
19. Remove the retaining clip from the RH timing chain tensioner.

➡ **Lubricate the camshaft roller followers using clean engine oil.**

20. Install the camshaft roller followers as using this procedure:

- Install the special tool.
- Compress the valve spring.
- Install the camshaft roller followers in their original locations.

21. Install the eight spark plugs.
22. Install the eight ignition coils and bolts.
23. Connect the eight ignition coil electrical connectors.
24. Install the crankshaft sensor ring on the crankshaft.

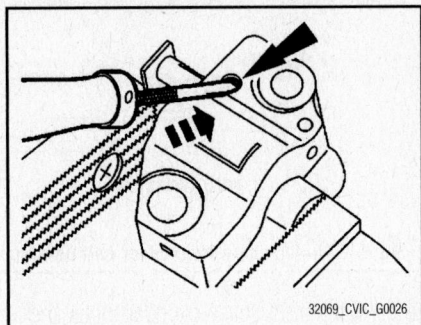

Fig. 60 Releasing the ratcheting timing chain mechanism

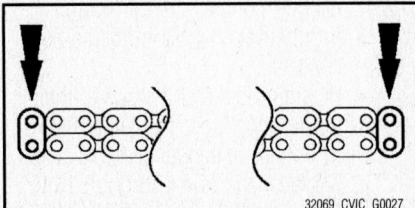

Fig. 61 If the timing chain does not have two copper index links, mark two links as shown

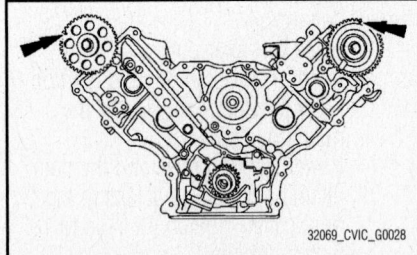

Fig. 62 Position the camshaft sprockets as shown when reinstalling timing chain

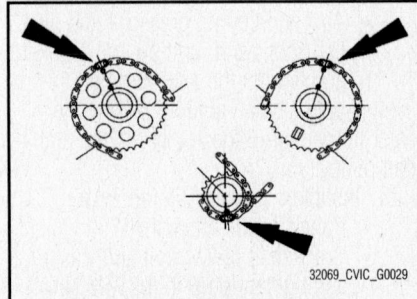

Fig. 63 Position of copper chain links to crank and cam sprockets

25. Install the engine front cover.

26. Reconnect negative battery cable, run engine to check for leaks and repair as necessary.

ENGINES WITH NON-RATCHETING TIMING CHAIN TENSIONERS

❋❋ WARNING

If one or both tensioner mounting bolts are loosened or removed, the tensioner-sealing bead must be inspected for seal integrity. Any cracks, tears, cuts or separation from the tensioner body or permanent compression of the seal bead, will require replacement of the tensioner.

❋❋ WARNING

The timing chain procedure must be followed exactly or damage to valves and pistons will result.

1. Inspect the RH and LH timing chain tensioners and replace as necessary.

2. Compress each tensioner plunger, using a vise.

3. Install a retaining clip on each tensioner to hold the plunger in during installation.

4. If the copper links on the timing chain are not visible, mark one link on one end and one link on the other end and use as timing marks.

5. Install the camshaft sprockets and new bolts and tighten in two stages:
   - Stage 1: Tighten the bolt to 30 ft. lbs. (40 Nm).
   - Stage 2: Tighten the bolt an additional 90 degrees (1/4 turn).

6. Using the special tool, position the crankshaft so the number one cylinder is at top dead center (TDC).

7. Install the crankshaft sprocket, making sure the flange faces forward.

8. Install the timing chain guide as follows:
   - Position the LH timing chain guide.
   - Install and tighten the LH bolts.
   - Position the RH timing chain guide.
   - Install and tighten the RH bolts.

9. Rotate the RH camshaft sprocket until the timing mark is approximately at the 11 o'clock position.

10. Rotate the LH camshaft sprocket until the timing mark is approximately at the 12 o'clock position.

11. Position the LH (inner) timing chain on the crankshaft sprocket, aligning the copper (marked) link with the timing mark on the sprocket.

12. Install the LH timing chain on the sprocket, aligning the copper (marked) link with the timing marks on the sprocket.

➡ **The LH timing chain tensioner arm has a bump near the dowel hole for identification. Position the LH timing chain tensioner arm on the dowel pin and install the LH timing chain tensioner.**

13. Remove the retaining clip from the LH timing chain tensioner.

14. Position the RH (outer) timing chain on the crankshaft sprocket, aligning the copper (marked) link with the timing mark on the sprocket.

15. Install the RH timing chain on the camshaft sprocket, aligning the copper (marked) link with the timing marks on the sprocket.

16. Position the RH timing chain tensioner arm on the dowel pin and install the RH timing chain tensioner.

17. Remove the retaining clip from the RH timing chain tensioner.

18. Make sure that the copper (marked) chain links are lined up with the dots on the crankshaft sprocket and the camshaft sprockets.

19. Rotate the camshaft until the lobe is in the up position.

20. Install the special tool between the valve spring coils to prevent valve stem seal damage.

➡ **Lubricate the camshaft roller followers using clean engine oil.**

21. Install the camshaft roller followers as using this procedure:
   - Install the special tool.
   - Compress the valve spring.
   - Install the camshaft roller followers in their original locations.

22. Install the eight spark plugs.

23. Install the eight ignition coils and bolts.

24. Connect the eight ignition coil electrical connectors.

25. Install the crankshaft sensor ring on the crankshaft.

26. Install the engine front cover.

27. Reconnect negative battery cable, run engine to check for leaks and repair as necessary.

VALVE LASH

ADJUSTMENT

The 4.6L (VIN W and V) engines are equipped with hydraulic lash adjusters. Valve clearance is not adjustable.

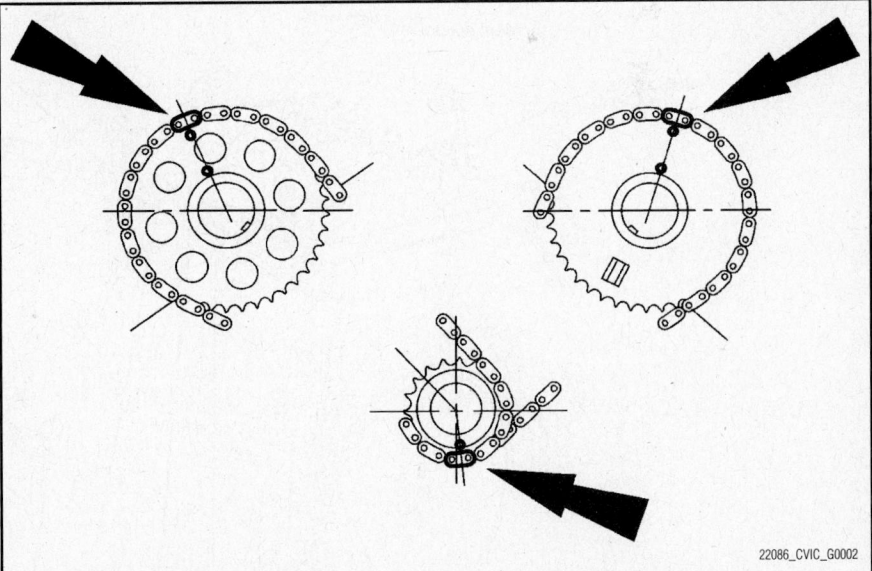

22086_CVIC_G0002

Fig. 64 Make sure that the copper (marked) chain links are lined up with the dots on the crankshaft and camshaft sprockets.

ENGINE PERFORMANCE & EMISSION CONTROL

➡A high-impedance digital multi-meter is required for the following test procedures. Never use a low-imped-ance analog multi-meter or low-imped-ance test light, as damage to electronic components may occur

COMPONENT LOCATIONS

See Figures 65, 66 and 67

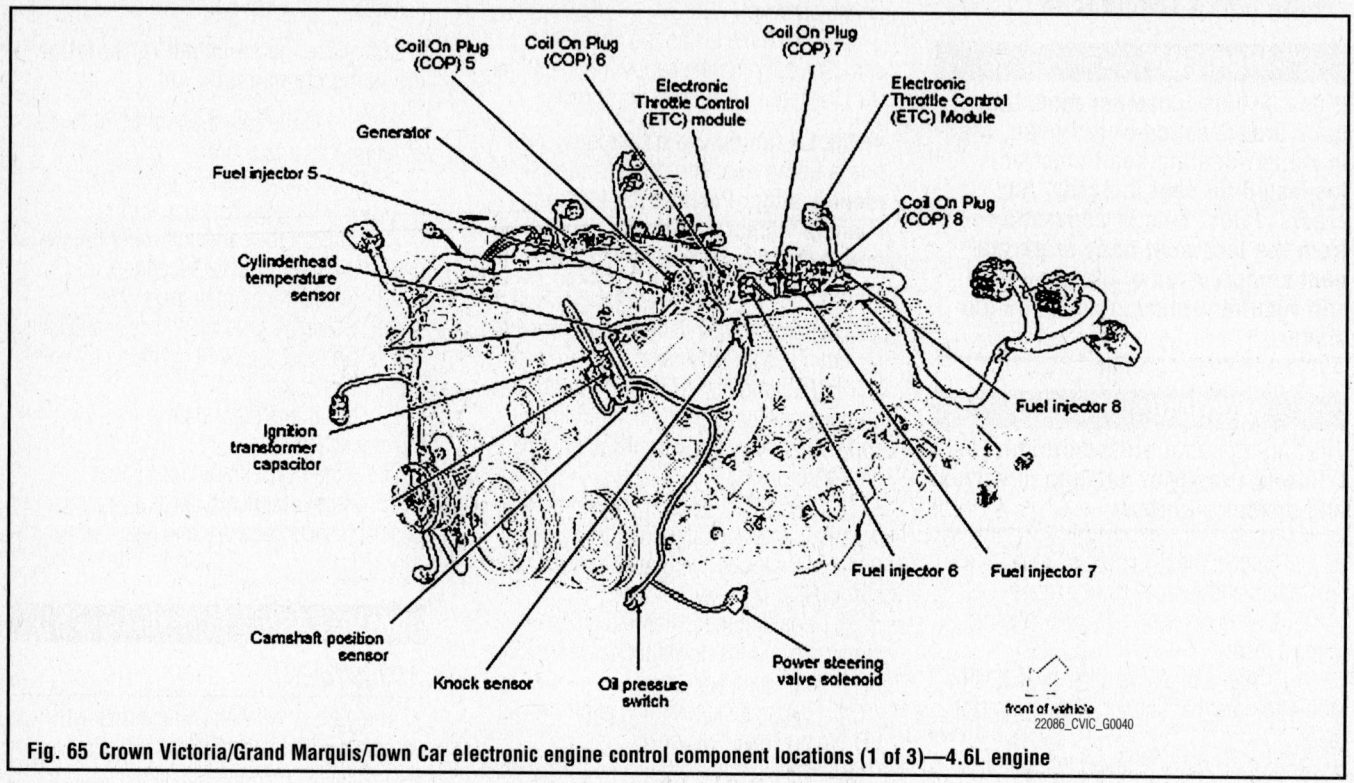

Fig. 65 Crown Victoria/Grand Marquis/Town Car electronic engine control component locations (1 of 3)—4.6L engine

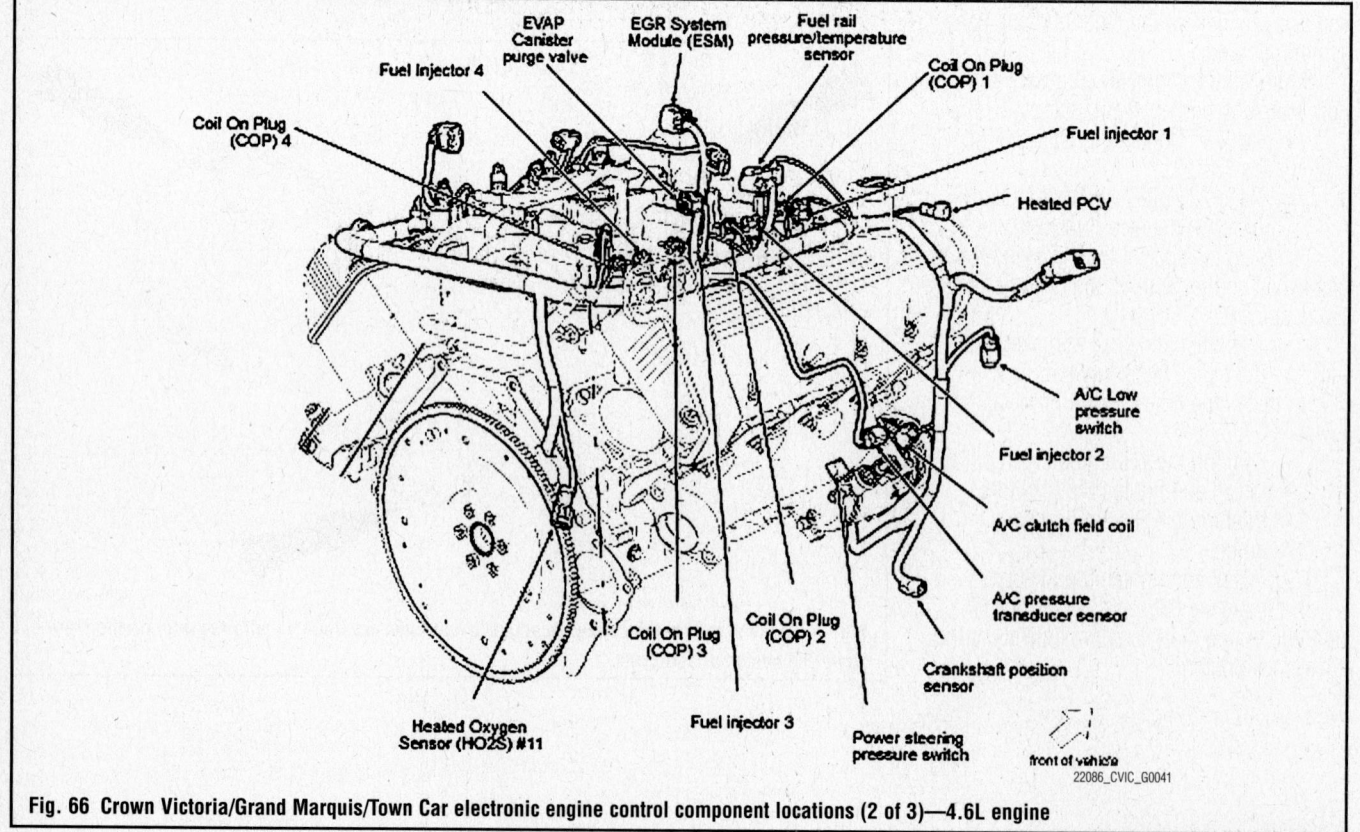

Fig. 66 Crown Victoria/Grand Marquis/Town Car electronic engine control component locations (2 of 3)—4.6L engine

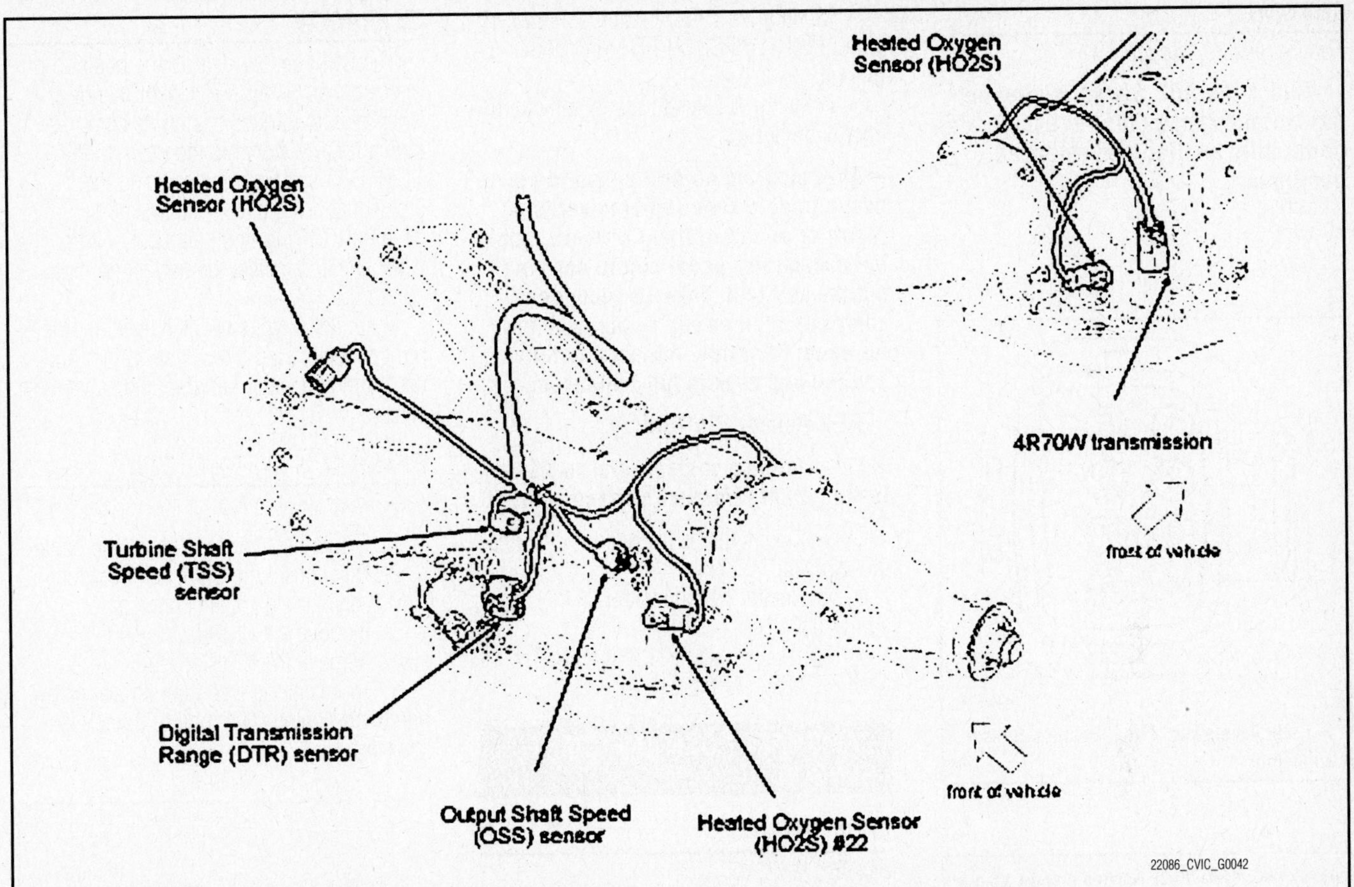

Heated Oxygen
Sensor (HO2S)

Heated Oxygen
Sensor (HO2S)

4R70W transmission

front of vehicle

Turbine Shaft
Speed (TSS)
sensor

Digital Transmission
Range (DTR) sensor

Output Shaft Speed
(OSS) sensor

Heated Oxygen Sensor
(HO2S) #22

front of vehicle

22086_CVIC_G0042

Fig. 67 Crown Victoria/Grand Marquis/Town Car electronic engine control component locations (3 of 3)—4.6L engine

ENGINE PERFORMANCE & EMISSION CONTROL   COMPONENT TESTING

ACCELERATOR PEDAL POSITION (APP) SENSOR

LOCATION
See Figure 68.

22086_CVIC_G0036

Fig. 68 Accelerator Pedal Position Sensor

The Accelerator Pedal Position Sensor is located on top of the accelerator pedal assembly.

OPERATION

The APP sensor is an input to the Powertrain Control Module (PCM) and is used to determine the torque demand. There are 3 pedal position signals in the sensor. Signal 1, APPS1, has a negative slope (increasing angle, decreasing voltage) and signals 2 and 3, APPS2 and APPS3, both have a positive slope (increasing angle, increasing voltage). During normal operation APPS1 is used as the indication of pedal position by the strategy. The 3 pedal position signals make sure the PCM receives a correct input even if 1 signal has a concern. There are 2 reference voltage circuits and 2 signal return circuits for the sensor.

REMOVAL & INSTALLATION
See Figure 69.

1. Disconnect the battery ground cable.
2. Disconnect the accelerator pedal motor electrical connector.

3. Remove the two bolts and the accelerator pedal assembly.
4. To install, reverse the removal procedure.

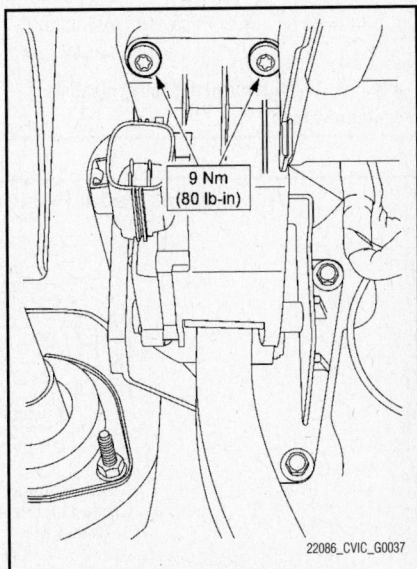

9 Nm
(80 lb-in)

22086_CVIC_G0037

Fig. 69 Remove the two bolts and the accelerator pedal assembly

TESTING

See Figures 70 through 73.

Check the APP Sensor signal output voltage ranges for the accelerator pedal fully applied and released positions.

APPS1 (Pin #2)
APPS2 (Pin #5)
APPS3 (Pin #8)

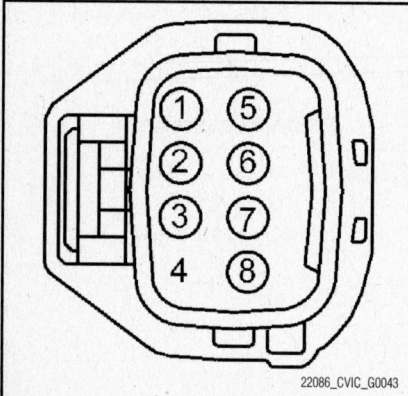

Fig. 70 Accelerator Pedal Position Sensor connector

Accelerator Pedal Fully Applied Voltage Values		
APPS1	**APPS2**	**APPS3**
0.48 - 1.76	2.95 - 4.62	2.43 - 4.02

22086_CVIC_G0038

Fig. 71 Accelerator pedal fully applied voltage values

Accelerator Pedal Fully Released Voltage Values		
APPS1	**APPS2**	**APPS3**
3.43 - 4.69	1.13 - 1.88	0.64 - 1.28

22086_CVIC_G0039

Fig. 72 Accelerator pedal fully released voltage values

• Monitor the voltage readings between pins APPS1, APPS2, APPS3, and body ground.
• Press the accelerator pedal fully to the floor and release.

➡ **After clearing an APP sensor diagnostic trouble code (DTC) to verify a repair or an intermittent concern, apply the accelerator pedal before carrying out the self-test. Take 10 seconds to carry out a full sweep of the accelerator pedal from fully released to fully applied and back to fully released.**

APP Sensor Pin Testing

➡ **For reference values, refer to PCM testing—PCM reference voltage chart**

This pinpoint test is intended to diagnose the following:

• Accelerator pedal position (APP) sensor (9F836)
• Harness circuits: ETCRTN, SIGRTN, ETCREF, APP1, APP2, and APP3

CAMSHAFT POSITION (CMP) SENSOR

LOCATION

See Figure 74.

The Camshaft Position Sensors are located on the timing cover, just below each valve cover.

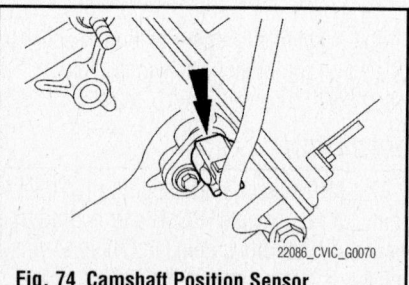

Fig. 74 Camshaft Position Sensor

OPERATION

The CMP sensor detects the position of the camshaft. The CMP sensor identifies when piston number 1 is on its compression stroke. A signal is then sent to the PCM and used for synchronizing the sequential firing of the fuel injectors. Coil-on-plug (COP) ignition applications use the CMP signal to select the correct ignition coil to fire.

There are 2 types of CMP sensors: the 3-pin connector Hall-effect type sensor and the 2-pin connector variable reluctance type sensor.

REMOVAL & INSTALLATION

See Figure 75.

1. Disconnect the battery ground cable.
2. Disconnect the Camshaft Position (CMP) sensor electrical connector.
3. Remove the CMP bolt.
4. Remove the CMP sensor.
5. To install, reverse the removal procedure, and tighten CMP bolt to 89inch lbs. (10 Nm).

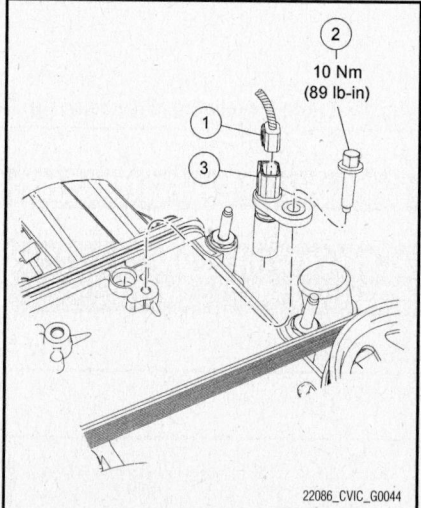

Fig. 75 Camshaft Position (CMP) sensor connector (1), bolt (2) and sensor (3)

TESTING

See Figures 76 and 77.

Before testing, it is necessary to determine if the CMP Sensor is a 2-pin VR type, or a 3-pin Hall-effect Type.

CMP Sensor Pin Testing

This pinpoint test is intended to diagnose the following:

• Camshaft position (CMP) sensor (6B288)
• Harness circuits: CMP, CMP2, SIGRTN, VBPWR, VRSRTN, and VRSRTN2

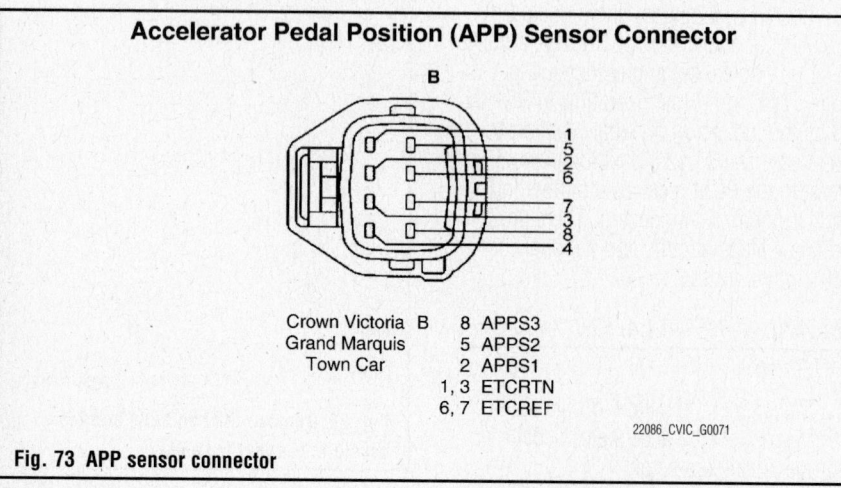

Accelerator Pedal Position (APP) Sensor Connector

B

Crown Victoria B	8	APPS3
Grand Marquis	5	APPS2
Town Car	2	APPS1
	1, 3	ETCRTN
	6, 7	ETCREF

22086_CVIC_G0071

Fig. 73 APP sensor connector

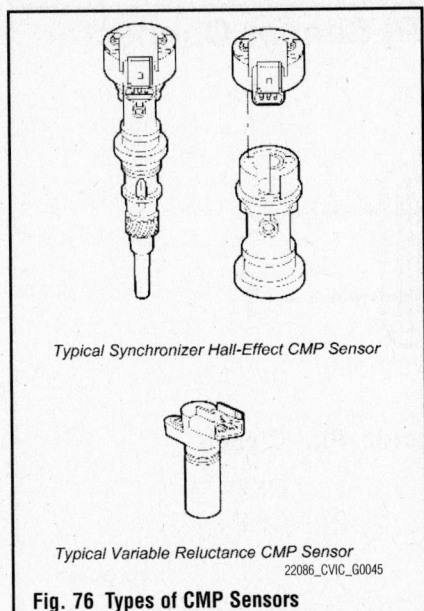

Typical Synchronizer Hall-Effect CMP Sensor

Typical Variable Reluctance CMP Sensor

22086_CVIC_G0045

Fig. 76 Types of CMP Sensors

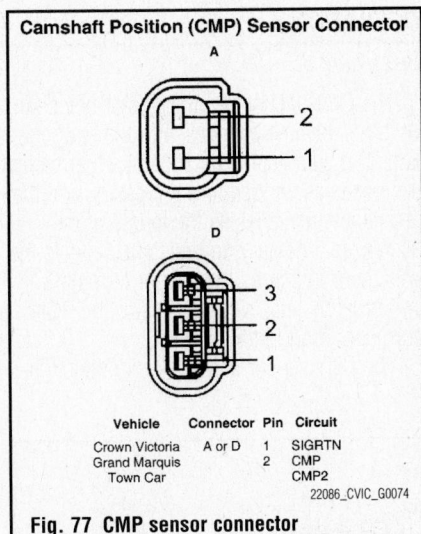

Camshaft Position (CMP) Sensor Connector

A

D

Vehicle	Connector	Pin	Circuit
Crown Victoria	A or D	1	SIGRTN
Grand Marquis		2	CMP
Town Car			CMP2

22086_CVIC_G0074

Fig. 77 CMP sensor connector

➡ **For reference values, refer to PCM testing–PCM reference voltage chart**

CRANKSHAFT POSITION (CKP) SENSOR

LOCATION

See Figure 78.

OPERATION

The CKP sensor is a magnetic transducer mounted on the engine block adjacent to a pulse wheel located on the crankshaft. By monitoring the crankshaft mounted pulse wheel, the CKP is the primary sensor for ignition information to the PCM. The pulse wheel has a total of 35 teeth spaced 10 degrees apart with one

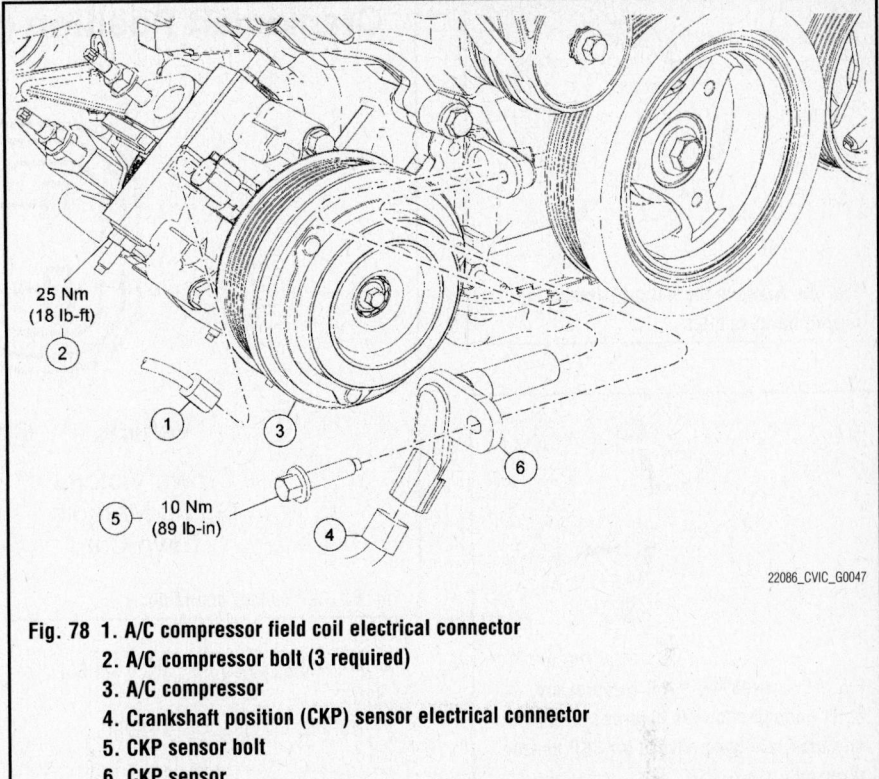

25 Nm
(18 lb-ft)

10 Nm
(89 lb-in)

22086_CVIC_G0047

Fig. 78 1. A/C compressor field coil electrical connector
2. A/C compressor bolt (3 required)
3. A/C compressor
4. Crankshaft position (CKP) sensor electrical connector
5. CKP sensor bolt
6. CKP sensor

empty space for a missing tooth. The 6.8L 10-cylinder pulse wheel has 39 teeth spaced 9 degrees apart and one 9 degree empty space for a missing tooth. By monitoring the pulse wheel, the CKP sensor signal indicates crankshaft position and speed information to the PCM. By monitoring the missing tooth, the CKP sensor is also able to identify piston travel in order to synchronize the ignition system and provide a way of tracking the angular position of the crankshaft relative to a fixed reference for the CKP sensor configuration. The PCM also uses the CKP signal to determine if a misfire has occurred by measuring rapid decelerations between teeth.

REMOVAL & INSTALLATION

See Figures 79, 80 and 81.

⁂ WARNING

If equipped with fire suppression system, disable the system before performing repairs.

1. Disconnect the battery ground cable.
2. Rotate the drive belt tensioner clockwise, and remove the drive belt from the A/C compressor pulley.
3. Disconnect the A/C compressor field coil electrical connector.

4. Disconnect the crankshaft position sensor (CKP) sensor electrical connector.
5. Remove the nut and detach the wiring harness clips. To install, tighten to 80 inch lbs. (9 Nm)
6. Loosen the 3 A/C compressor bolts enough slide the compressor down one inch, allowing access for CKP sensor removal. It is not necessary to completely remove the A/C compressor bolts. To install, tighten to 18 ft. lbs. (25 Nm).
7. Remove the CKP sensor bolt. To install, tighten to 89 inch lbs. (10 Nm).
8. Remove the CKP sensor.

To install, reverse the removal procedure.

⁂ WARNING

If equipped with fire suppression system, enable the system following assembly.

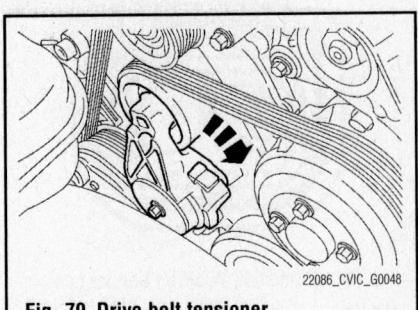

22086_CVIC_G0048

Fig. 79 Drive belt tensioner

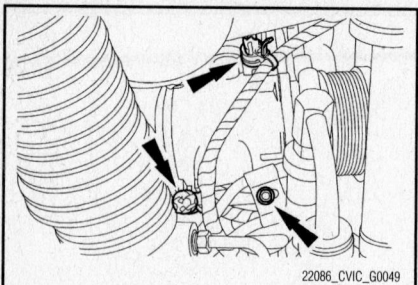

Fig. 80 Remove the nut and detach the wiring harness clips

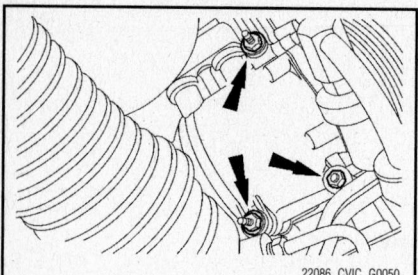

Fig. 81 Loosen the 3 A/C compressor bolts enough slide the compressor down one inch, allowing access for CKP sensor removal

TESTING

See Figures 82 and 83.

Check the CKP Sensor resistance
- Key in OFF position
- Measure the resistance between: CKP+—CKP-

Is resistance between 250—1,000 ohms?

Yes: CKP Sensor resistance is within acceptable limits. Proceed to pin test.

No: Replace the CKP Sensor and verify repair.

CMP Sensor Pin Testing

➡For reference values, refer to PCM testing–PCM reference voltage chart

This pinpoint test is intended to diagnose the following:

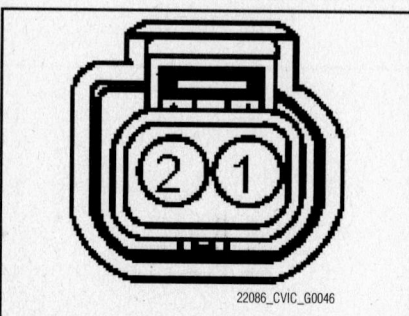

Fig. 82 Crankshaft Position Sensor connector

Crankshaft Position (CKP) Sensor Connector

C

2
1

Vehicle	Connector	Pin	Circuit
Crown Victoria	C	1	CKP-
Grand Marquis		2	CKP+
Town Car			

22086_CVIC_G0075

Fig. 83 CKP sensor connector

- Crankshaft position (CKP) sensor (6C315)
- Harness circuits: CKP(+) and CKP(-)

CYLINDER HEAD TEMPERATURE (CHT) SENSOR

LOCATION

See Figure 84.

The CHT Sensor is located at the front of the engine as shown in illustration.

OPERATION

See Figure 85.

The CHT sensor is a thermistor device in which resistance changes with the temperature. The electrical resistance of a thermistor decreases as temperature increases, and the resistance increases as the temperature decreases. The varying resistance affects the voltage drop across the sensor terminals and provides electrical signals to the PCM corresponding to temperature.

The CHT sensor is installed in the cylin-

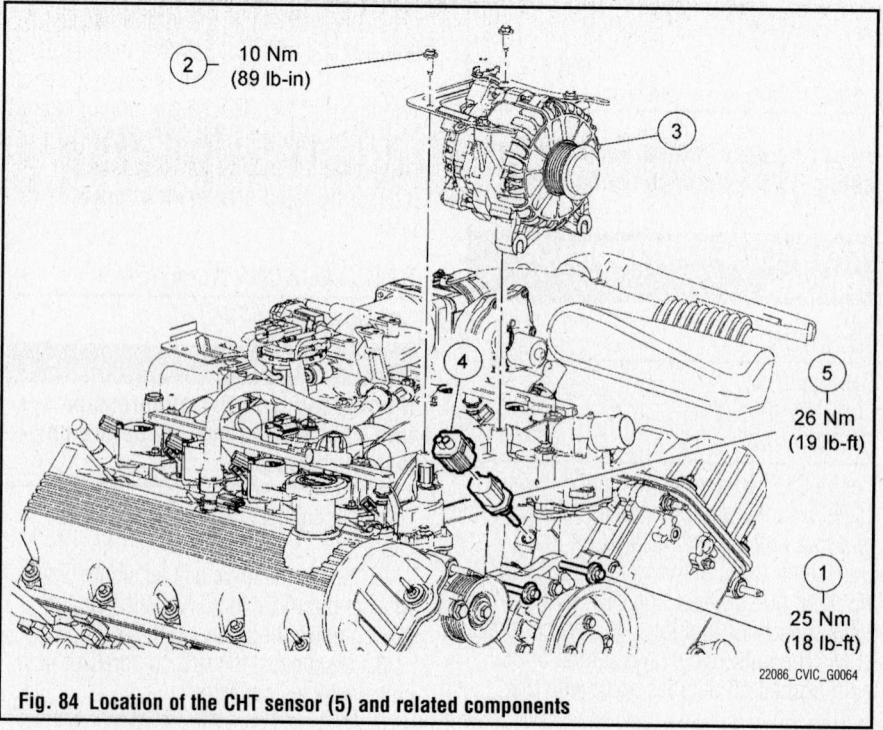

2   10 Nm
(89 lb-in)

3

4

5
26 Nm
(19 lb-ft)

1
25 Nm
(18 lb-ft)

22086_CVIC_G0064

Fig. 84 Location of the CHT sensor (5) and related components

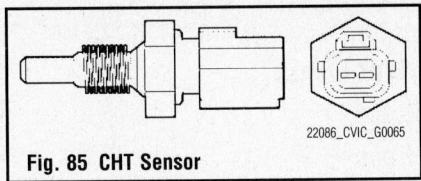

Fig. 85 CHT Sensor

der head and measures the metal temperature. The CHT sensor can provide complete engine temperature information and can be used to infer coolant temperature. If the CHT sensor conveys an overheating condition to the PCM, the PCM initiates a fail-safe cooling strategy based on information from the CHT sensor. A cooling system concern such as low coolant or coolant loss could cause an overheating condition. As a result, damage to major engine components could occur. Using both the CHT sensor and fail-safe cooling strategy, the PCM prevents damage by allowing air-cooling of the engine and limp home capability.

The CHT sensor is mounted into the wall of the cylinder head and is not connected to any coolant passages, and it sends a signal to the PCM indicating the cylinder head temperature.

If the temperature exceeds approximately 121°C (250°F), the PCM disables 4 fuel injectors at a time. The PCM will alternate which fuel injectors are disabled every 32 engine cycles. The 4 cylinders that are not being fuel injected act as air pumps to aid in cooling the engine.

If the temperature exceeds approximately 166°C (330°F), the PCM disables all of the fuel injectors until the engine temperature drops below approximately 154°C (310°F).

If the engine reaches critical temperature, the coolant temperature gauge pointer will read fully hot at approximately 121°C (250°F).

REMOVAL & INSTALLATION

See Figures 86 and 87.

1. Disconnect the battery ground cable.
2. Rotate the tensioner clockwise and position the accessory belt aside.

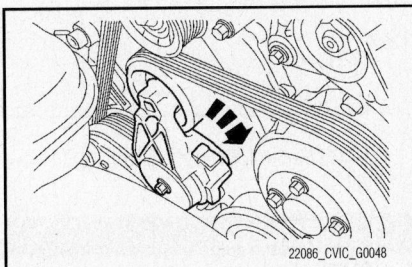

Fig. 86 Rotate the tensioner clockwise and position the accessory belt aside

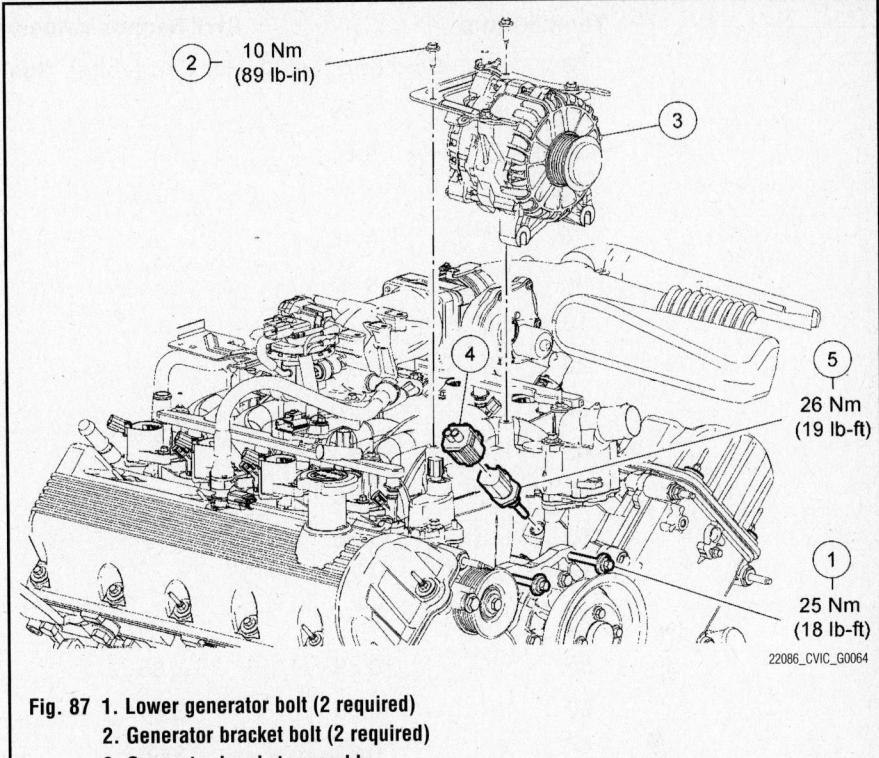

Fig. 87 1. Lower generator bolt (2 required)
2. Generator bracket bolt (2 required)
3. Generator bracket assembly
4. Cylinder head temperature (CHT) sensor electrical conector
5. CHT sensor

3. Loosen the 2 lower generator bolts. To install, tighten to 18 ft. lbs. (25 Nm).
4. Remove the 2 generator bracket bolts and position the generator and bracket aside. To install, tighten to 89 inch lbs. (10 Nm).
5. Disconnect the cylinder head temperature (CHT) sensor electrical connector.
6. Using a 19 mm (0.74 in) 12 point crows foot, remove and discard the CHT sensor. To install, tighten to 19 ft. lbs. (26 Nm).

➡**The CHT sensor is not to be reused. Always install a new sensor.**

To install a new sensor, reverse the removal procedure.

TESTING

See Figures 88 and 89.

On applications that do not use an engine coolant temperature (ECT) sensor, the CHT sensor is used to determine the engine coolant temperature. To cover the entire temperature range of both the CHT and ECT sensors, the PCM has a dual switching resistor circuit on the CHT input. A graph showing the temperature switching from the COLD END line to the HOT END line, with increasing temperature and

back with decreasing temperature is included. Note the temperature to voltage overlap zone. Within this zone it is possible to have either a COLD END or HOT

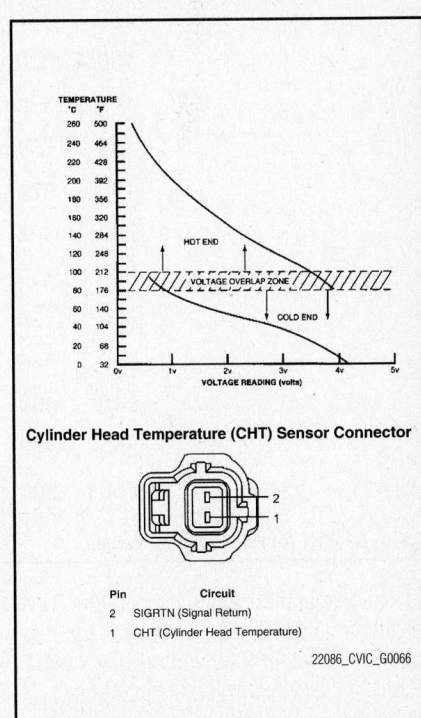

Fig. 88 CHT sensor connector and voltage readings

| Temperature | | CHT Sensor Values | | |
°C	°F	Cold End (volts)	Hot End (volts)	Resistance (K ohms)
-40	-40	4.89	-	965.808
-30	-22	4.81	-	513.019
-20	-4	4.67	-	283.664
-10	14	4.45	-	162.584
0	32	4.14	-	96.255
10	50	3.73	-	59.175
20	68	3.26	-	37.387
30	86	2.74	-	24.215
40	104	2.23	-	16.043
50	122	1.76	-	10.85
60	140	1.36	-	7.487
70	158	1.04	-	5.268
80	176	0.79	3.99	3.775
85	185	0.69	3.86	3.215
90	194	0.60	3.71	2.75
95	203	0.53	3.56	2.361
100	212	0.46	3.41	2.034
110	230	-	3.07	1.523
120	248	-	2.74	1.155
130	266	-	2.41	0.8866
140	284	-	2.10	0.6891
150	302	-	1.81	0.5417
160	320	-	1.55	0.4301
170	338	-	1.33	0.3449
180	356	-	1.13	0.2791
190	374	-	0.96	0.2278
200	392	-	0.82	0.1875
210	410	-	0.70	0.155
220	428	-	0.60	0.130
230	446	-	0.51	0.109
240	464	-	0.44	0.092
250	482		0.35	0.078
260	500		0.33	0.067

22086_CVIC_G0067

Fig. 89 CHT Sensor Expected Values

END voltage at the same temperature. For example, at 90°C (194°F) the voltage could read either 0.60 volt or 3.71 volts. Refer to the table for the temperature to voltage expected values.

Voltage values calculated for VREF = 5 volts. These values can vary by 15% due to sensor and VREF variations.

CHT Sensor Pin Testing

➡For reference values, refer to PCM testing–PCM reference voltage chart

This pinpoint test is intended to diagnose the following:
• Cylinder head temperature (CHT) sensor (6G004)

• Harness circuits: CHT, VREF, and SIGRTN

✳✳ WARNING
The CHT sensor is not to be reused. Always install a new sensor.

EXHAUST GAS RECIRCULATION (EGR) SYSTEM MODULE (ESM)

LOCATION

See Figure 90.

EGR System Components (refer to accompanying illustration)

1. Intake manifold shield retaining bolt (2 required)
2. Intake manifold shield
3. Exhaust gas recirculation system module electrical connector
4. EGR system module
5. EGR system module gasket
6. EGR vacuum connector
7. EGR system module retaining bolt (2 required)
8. EGR tube fitting
9. EGR tube

OPERATION

See Figure 91.

The ESM is an integrated differential pressure feedback EGR system that functions in the same manner as a conventional differential pressure feedback EGR system. The various system components have been integrated into a single component called the ESM. The flange of the valve portion of the ESM bolts directly to the intake manifold with a metal gasket that forms the metering orifice. This arrangement increases system reliability, response time, and system precision. By relocating the EGR orifice from the exhaust to the intake side of the EGR valve, the downstream pressure signal measures manifold absolute pressure (MAP). This MAP signal is used for EGR correction and inferred barometric pressure (BARO) at key on. The system provides the powertrain control module (PCM) with a differential pressure feedback EGR signal, identical to a traditional differential pressure feedback EGR system.

REMOVAL & INSTALLATION

See Figures 92 and 93.

1. Disconnect the exhaust gas recirculation (EGR) system module electrical connector and vacuum connector.
2. Remove the 2 bolts and the intake manifold shield. To install, tighten to 9 ft. lbs. (12 Nm).
3. Disconnect the EGR tube fitting from the EGR system module. To install, tighten to 30 ft. lbs. (40 Nm).
4. Remove the 2 bolts and the EGR system module.
5. To install, tighten to 18 ft. lbs. (25 Nm).

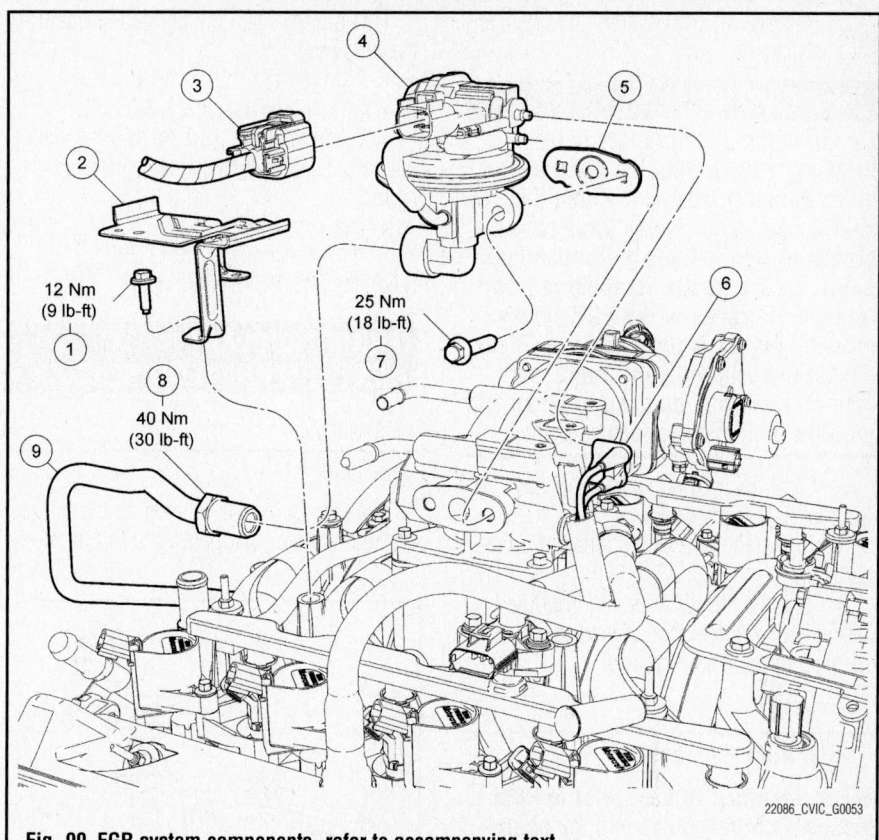

Fig. 90 EGR system components, refer to accompanying text

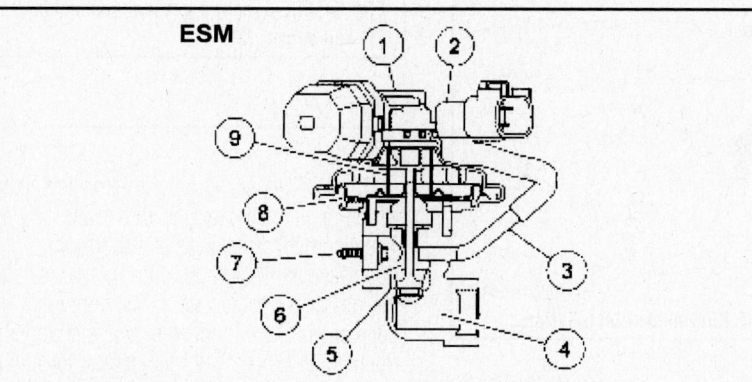

Item	Number	Description
1	—	EGR Vacuum Regulator Integrated into Upper Body
2	—	Differential Pressure Feedback EGR and MAP Sensor
3	—	Upstream Differential Pressure Feedback EGR Port
4	—	Exhaust Flow
5	—	Valve Seat
6	—	Pin/Pintle
7	—	To Intake Manifold Plenum
8	—	Diaphragm
9	—	EGR Spring

Fig. 91 Exhaust Gas Recirculation (EGR) System Module (ESM)

6. Remove the EGR system module gasket and discard.

✳✳ CAUTION

Do not use metal scrapers, wire brushes, power abrasive discs or other abrasive means to clean the sealing surfaces. These tools cause scratches and gouges that make leak paths. Use a plastic scraping tool to remove all traces of the EGR system module gasket. If there is no residual gasket material present, metal surface cleaner may be used to clean and prepare the surfaces for assembly.

7. Clean the mating surfaces of any residual gasket material.

8. To install, reverse the removal procedure.

9. Install a new EGR system module gasket with the side that has the raised circle facing the intake manifold.

TESTING

EGR ESM Pin Testing

➡**For reference values, refer to PCM testing–PCM reference voltage chart**

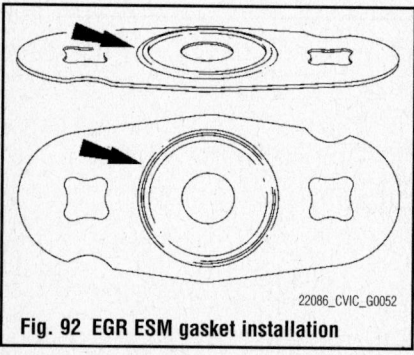

Fig. 92 EGR ESM gasket installation

EGR System Module (ESM) Connector

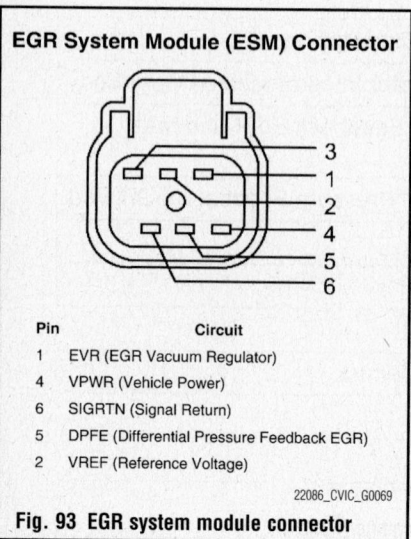

Pin	Circuit
1	EVR (EGR Vacuum Regulator)
4	VPWR (Vehicle Power)
6	SIGRTN (Signal Return)
5	DPFE (Differential Pressure Feedback EGR)
2	VREF (Reference Voltage)

22086_CVIC_G0069

Fig. 93 EGR system module connector

This pinpoint test is intended to diagnose the following:
- ESM (9Y456)
- Orifice tube assembly (9D477)
- Differential pressure feedback exhaust gas recirculation (EGR) sensor pressure hoses
- Vacuum lines
- Harness circuits: VREF, DPFE, SIGRTN, EVR, VPWR and VREF

ENGINE COOLANT TEMPERATURE (ECT) SENSOR

LOCATION

See Figure 94.

The ECT Sensor is located on top of the intake manifold, just below the throttle body.

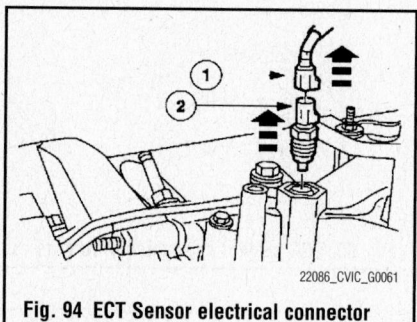

22086_CVIC_G0061

Fig. 94 ECT Sensor electrical connector (1) and sensor (2)

OPERATION

See Figure 95.

The ECT sensor is a thermistor device in which resistance changes with temperature. The electrical resistance of a thermistor decreases as the temperature increases, and the resistance increases as the temperature decreases. The varying resistance changes the voltage drop across the sensor terminals and provides electrical signals to the PCM corresponding to temperature.

Thermistor-type sensors are considered passive sensors. A passive sensor is connected to a voltage divider network so that varying the resistance of the passive sensor causes a variation in total current flow. Voltage that is dropped across a fixed resistor in a series with the sensor resistor determines the voltage signal at the PCM. This voltage signal is equal to the reference voltage minus the voltage drop across the fixed resistor.

The ECT measures the temperature of the engine coolant. The PCM uses the ECT input for fuel control and for cooling fan control. There are 3 types of ECT sensors, threaded, push-in, and twist-lock. The ECT sensor is located in an engine coolant passage.

REMOVAL & INSTALLATION

See Figure 94.

Remove the ECT Sensor as shown in illustration.

TESTING

See Figure 97.

1. Locate and disconnect the ECT sensor.

2. Connect a digital multi-meter between the ECT sensor terminals.

3. With the engine cold and the ignition switch in the ON position, measure and note the ECT sensor resistance.

4. Start the engine and allow the engine to reach normal operating temperature.

5. Monitor and note the ECT sensor resistance through the temperature range, and with the engine hot.

6. Compare the cold and hot ECT sensor resistance measurements with the accompanying chart.

7. If readings do not approximate those in the chart, proceed to the ECM voltage pin test.

ECT Sensor Pin Testing

Engine coolant temperature must be greater than 10°C (50°F) to pass the KOEO self-test and greater than 82°C (180°F) to pass the KOER self-test. to accomplish this, the engine must be at normal operating temperature.

ECT Sensor Pin Testing

This pinpoint test is intended to diagnose the following:
- Engine coolant temperature (ECT) sensor (12A648)
- Harness circuits: ECT and SIGRTN
- Powertrain control module (PCM) (12A650)

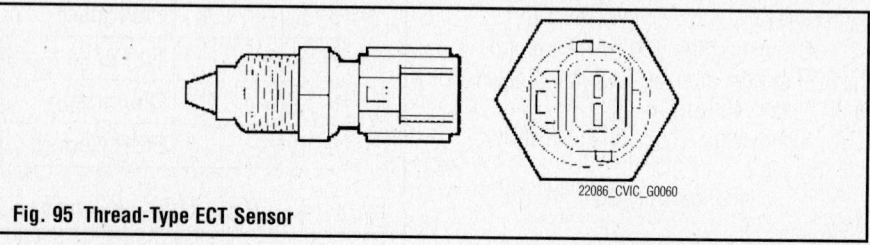

22086_CVIC_G0060

Fig. 95 Thread-Type ECT Sensor

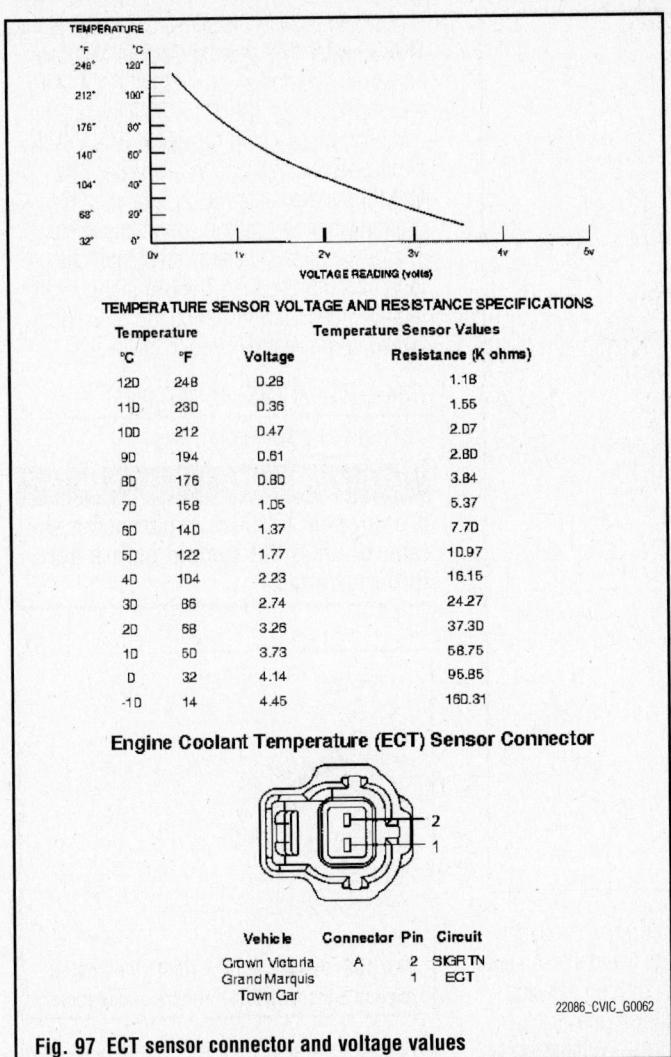

TEMPERATURE SENSOR VOLTAGE AND RESISTANCE SPECIFICATIONS

Temperature		Temperature Sensor Values	
°C	°F	Voltage	Resistance (K ohms)
120	248	0.28	1.18
110	230	0.36	1.55
100	212	0.47	2.07
90	194	0.61	2.80
80	176	0.80	3.84
70	158	1.05	5.37
60	140	1.37	7.70
50	122	1.77	10.97
40	104	2.23	16.15
30	86	2.74	24.27
20	68	3.26	37.30
10	50	3.73	58.75
0	32	4.14	95.85
-10	14	4.45	160.31

Engine Coolant Temperature (ECT) Sensor Connector

Vehicle	Connector	Pin	Circuit
Crown Victoria	A	2	SIGRTN
Grand Marquis		1	ECT
Town Car			

22086_CVIC_G0062

Fig. 97 ECT sensor connector and voltage values

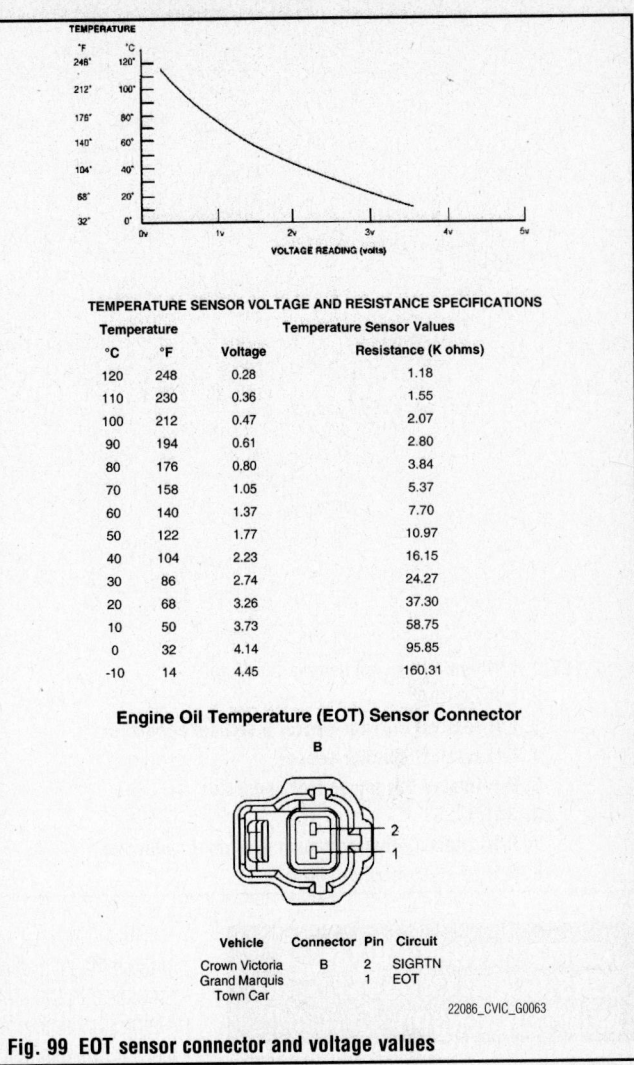

TEMPERATURE SENSOR VOLTAGE AND RESISTANCE SPECIFICATIONS

Temperature		Temperature Sensor Values	
°C	°F	Voltage	Resistance (K ohms)
120	248	0.28	1.18
110	230	0.36	1.55
100	212	0.47	2.07
90	194	0.61	2.80
80	176	0.80	3.84
70	158	1.05	5.37
60	140	1.37	7.70
50	122	1.77	10.97
40	104	2.23	16.15
30	86	2.74	24.27
20	68	3.26	37.30
10	50	3.73	58.75
0	32	4.14	95.85
-10	14	4.45	160.31

Engine Oil Temperature (EOT) Sensor Connector

Vehicle	Connector	Pin	Circuit
Crown Victoria	B	2	SIGRTN
Grand Marquis		1	EOT
Town Car			

22086_CVIC_G0063

Fig. 99 EOT sensor connector and voltage values

Voltage values calculated for VREF = 5 volts. These values can vary by 15% due to sensor and VREF variations.

ENGINE OIL TEMPERATURE (EOT) SENSOR

OPERATION

See Figure 98.

The EOT sensor is a thermistor device in which resistance changes with temperature. The electrical resistance of a thermistor decreases as the temperature increases and the resistance increases as the temperature decreases. The varying resistance changes the voltage drop across the sensor terminals and provides electrical signals to the PCM corresponding to temperature.

Thermistor-type sensors are considered passive sensors. A passive sensor is connected to a voltage divider network so that varying the resistance of the passive sensor causes a variation in total current flow. Volt-age that is dropped across a fixed resistor in a series with the sensor resistor determines the voltage signal at the PCM. This voltage signal is equal to the reference voltage minus the voltage drop across the fixed resistor.

The EOT sensor measures the temperature of the engine oil. The sensor is typically threaded into the engine oil lubrication system. The PCM can use the EOT sensor input to determine the following:

• The PCM can use EOT sensor input in conjunction with other PCM inputs to determine oil degradation.

• The PCM can use EOT sensor input to initiate a soft engine shutdown. To prevent engine damage from occurring as a result of high oil temperatures, the PCM has the ability to initiate a soft engine shutdown. Whenever engine RPM exceeds a calibrated level for a certain period of time, the PCM begins reducing power by disabling engine cylinders.

TESTING

See Figure 99.

EOT Sensor Pin Testing

This pinpoint test is intended to diagnose the following:

• Engine oil temperature (EOT) sensor (12A648)

• Harness circuits: EOT and SIGRTN Powertrain control module (PCM) (12A650)

Engine oil temperature must be greater than 10°C (50°F) to pass the KOEO self-test and greater than 66°C (150°F) to pass the KOER self-test.

Voltage values calculated for VREF = 5 volts. These values can vary by 15% due to sensor and VREF variations.

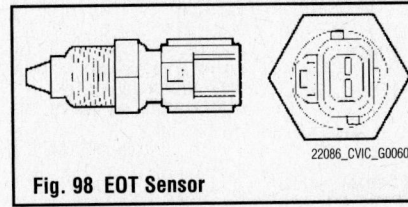

22086_CVIC_G0060

Fig. 98 EOT Sensor

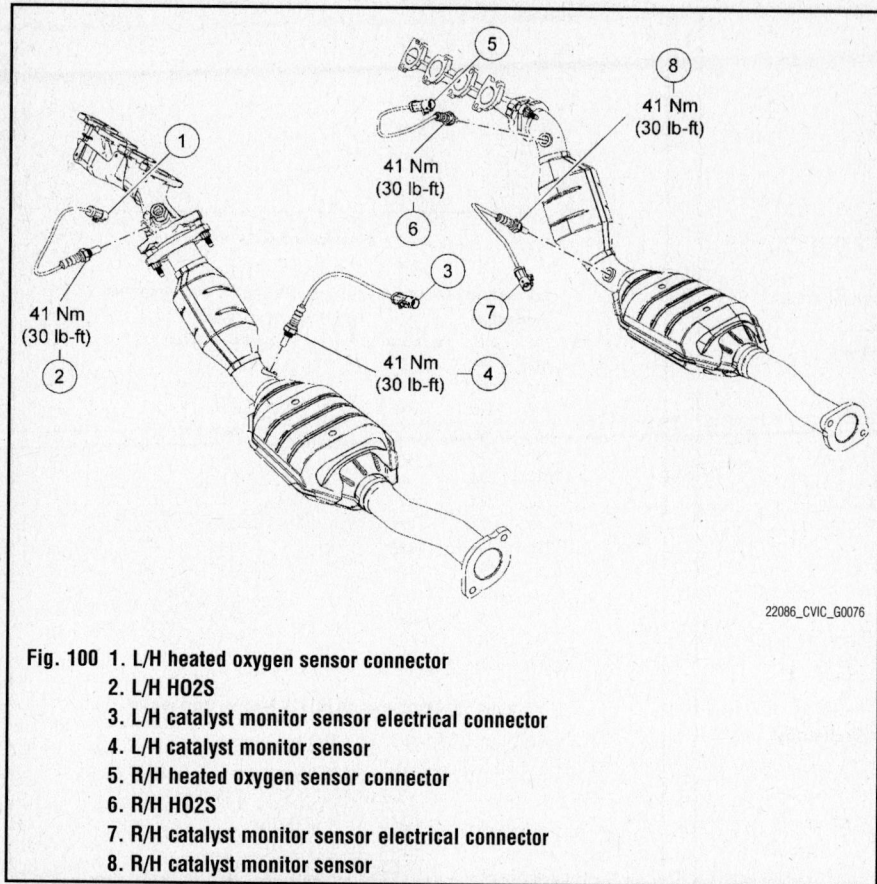

Fig. 100 1. L/H heated oxygen sensor connector
2. L/H HO2S
3. L/H catalyst monitor sensor electrical connector
4. L/H catalyst monitor sensor
5. R/H heated oxygen sensor connector
6. R/H HO2S
7. R/H catalyst monitor sensor electrical connector
8. R/H catalyst monitor sensor

HEATED OXYGEN (HO2S) SENSOR AND CATALYST MONITOR SENSOR

LOCATION

See Figure 100.

OPERATION

See Figure 101.

Heated Oxygen Sensor (HO2S) and Catalyst Monitor Sensor:

The HO2S detects the presence of oxygen in the exhaust and produces a variable voltage according to the amount of oxygen detected. A high concentration of oxygen (lean air/fuel ratio) in the exhaust produces a voltage signal less than 0.4 volt. A low concentration of oxygen (rich air/fuel ratio) produces a voltage signal greater than 0.6 volt. The HO2S provides feedback to the PCM indicating air/fuel ratio in order to achieve a near stoichiometric air/fuel ratio of 14.7:1 during closed loop engine operation. The HO2S generates a voltage between 0.0 and 1.1 volts.

Embedded with the sensing element is the HO2S heater. The heating element heats the sensor to a temperature of 800°C (1,472°F). At approximately 300°C (572°F) the engine can enter closed loop operation. The VPWR circuit supplies voltage to the heater. The PCM turns the heater on by providing the ground when the correct conditions occur. The heater allows the engine to enter closed loop operation sooner. The use of this heater requires the HO2S heater control to be duty cycled, to prevent damage to the heater.

REMOVAL & INSTALLATION

See Figures 102 through 106.

✳✳ WARNING

If equipped with fire suppression system, disable the system before performing repairs.

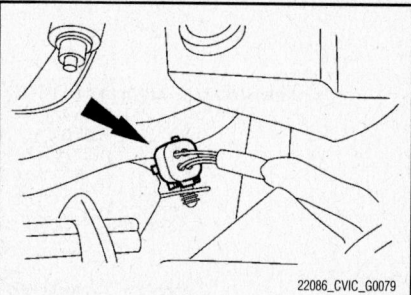

Fig. 102 Disconnect the right side heated oxygen sensor (HO2S) electrical connector

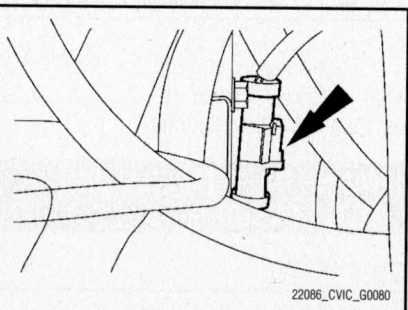

Fig. 103 Disconnect the left side HO2S electrical connector

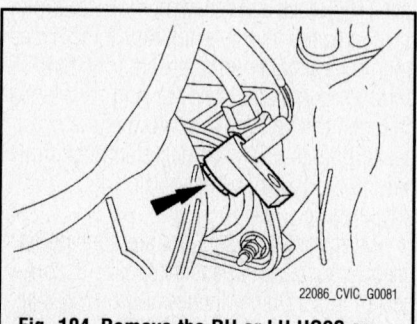

Fig. 104 Remove the RH or LH HO2S as necessary

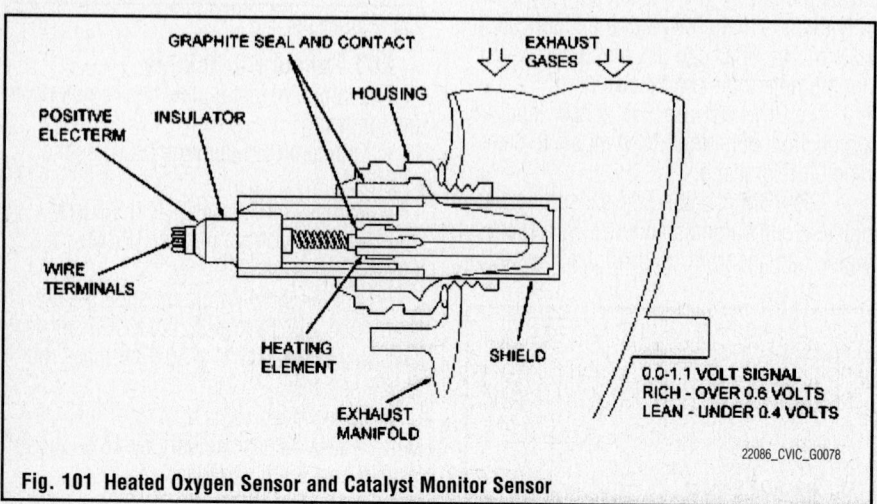

Fig. 101 Heated Oxygen Sensor and Catalyst Monitor Sensor

Heated Oxygen Sensor

1. Disconnect the battery ground cable.

2. Disconnect the right side heated oxygen sensor (HO2S) electrical connector.

3. Disconnect the left side HO2S electrical connector.

4. Remove the RH or LH HO2S as necessary. To install, tighten to 30 ft. lbs. (41 Nm).

To install, reverse the removal procedure. Apply a light coat of ant-seize lubricant to the threads of the HO2S.

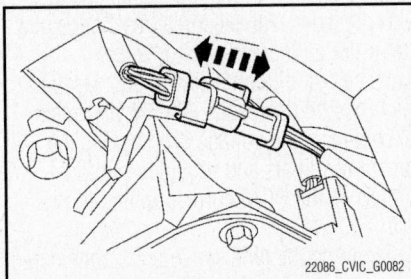

Fig. 105 Disconnect the catalyst monitor electrical connector

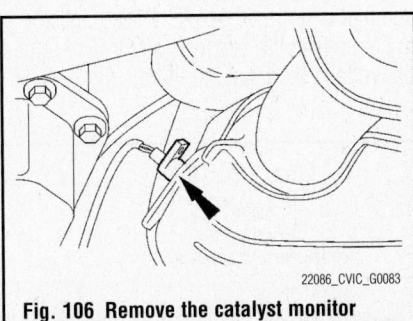

Fig. 106 Remove the catalyst monitor

❊❊ WARNING

If equipped with fire suppression system, enable the system following assembly.

Heated Oxygen Sensor

5. Disconnect the battery ground cable.

6. Disconnect the catalyst monitor electrical connector.

7. Remove the catalyst monitor. To install, tighten to 30 ft. lbs. (41 Nm).

To install, reverse the removal procedure. Apply a light coat of ant-seize lubricant to the threads of the HO2S.

❊❊ WARNING

If equipped with fire suppression system, enable the system following assembly.

Heated Oxygen Sensor (HO2S) Connector

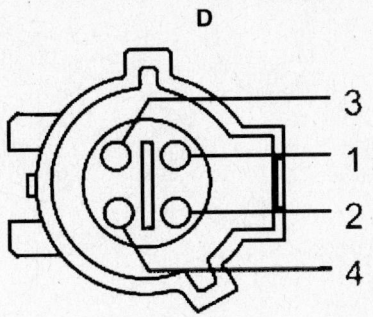

Vehicle	Connector	Pin	Circuit
Crown Victoria	D	1	HO2S Heater
Grand Marquis		4	SIGRTN
Town Car		2	VPWR
		3	HO2S Signal

22086_CVIC_G0077

Fig. 107 HO2S connector

TESTING

See Figure 107.

➡**For reference values, refer to PCM testing–PCM reference voltage chart**

This pinpoint test is intended to diagnose the following:
- HO2S/O2S (9F472)
- HO2S/O2S (9G444)
- Harness circuits: HO2S, HO2S Heater, VPWR, and SIGRTN

IDLE AIR CONTROL (IAC) VALVE

LOCATION

See Figure 108.

The IAC valve is located on the left-hand side of the throttle body.

OPERATION

➡**The IAC valve assembly is not adjustable and cannot be cleaned, also some IAC valves are normally open and others are normally closed. Some IAC**

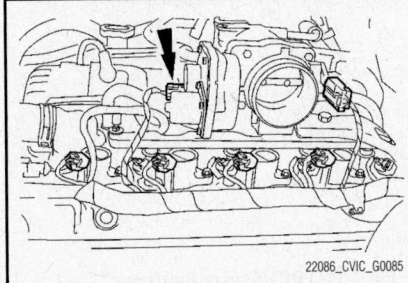

Fig. 108 The IAC Valve is located on the left-hand side of the throttle body

valves require engine vacuum to operate.

The IAC valve assembly controls the engine idle speed and provides a dashpot function. The IAC valve assembly meters intake air around the throttle plate through a bypass within the IAC valve assembly and throttle body. The PCM determines the desired idle speed or bypass air and signals the IAC valve assembly through a specified duty cycle. The IAC valve responds by positioning the IAC valve to control the amount of bypassed air. The PCM monitors engine RPM, and increases or decreases the IAC duty cycle in order to achieve the desired RPM.

The PCM uses the IAC valve assembly to control:
- No touch start
- Cold engine fast idle for rapid warm-up
- Idle (corrects for engine load)
- Stumble or stalling on deceleration (provides a dashpot function)
- Over-temperature idle boost

REMOVAL & INSTALLATION

See Figure 109.

The IAC Valve is part of the Throttle Body, and the entire assembly must be removed for access.

TESTING

See Figure 110.

➡**For reference values, refer to PCM testing–PCM reference voltage chart**

This pinpoint test is intended to diagnose the following:

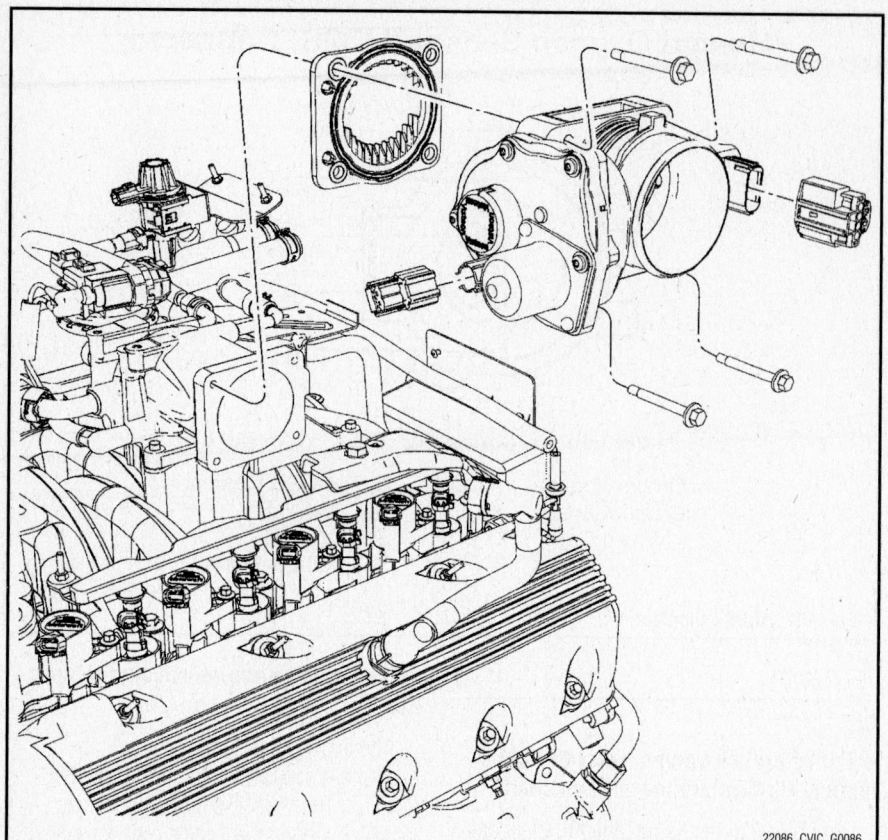

Fig. 109 The IAC Valve is part of the Throttle Body, and the entire assembly must be removed for access

22086_CVIC_G0086

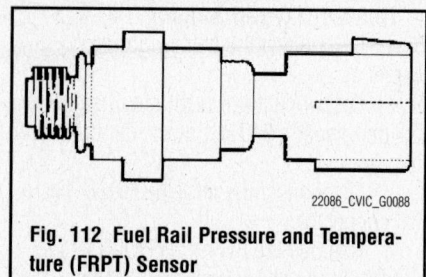

Fig. 112 Fuel Rail Pressure and Temperature (FRPT) Sensor

22086_CVIC_G0088

OPERATION

See Figure 112.

The FRPT sensor is a diaphragm strain gauge device in which resistance changes with pressure. The electrical resistance of a strain gauge increases as pressure increases, and the resistance decreases as the pressure decreases. The varying resistance affects the voltage drop across the sensor terminals and provides electrical signals to the PCM corresponding to pressure.

Strain gauge type sensors are considered passive sensors. A passive sensor is connected to a voltage divider network so that varying the resistance of the passive sensor causes a variation in total current flow. Voltage that is dropped across a fixed resistor in series with the sensor resistor determines the voltage signal at the PCM. This voltage

Idle Air Control (IAC) Connector

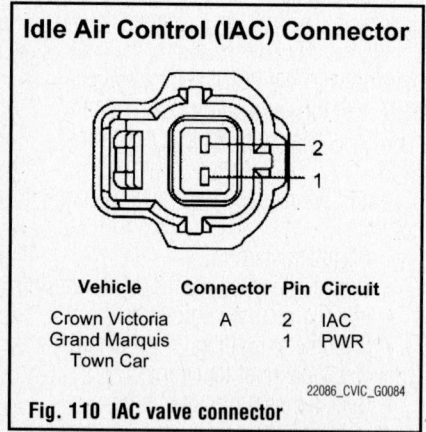

Vehicle	Connector	Pin	Circuit
Crown Victoria	A	2	IAC
Grand Marquis		1	PWR
Town Car			

22086_CVIC_G0084

Fig. 110 IAC valve connector

- Idle air control (IAC) valve (9F715)
- Harness circuits: IAC, PWR and B+ (IAC-RC)

FUEL RAIL PRESSURE AND TEMPERATURE (FRPT) SENSOR

LOCATION

See Figure 111.

The FRPT Sensor is located on the fuel rail, on the passenger's side of the engine.

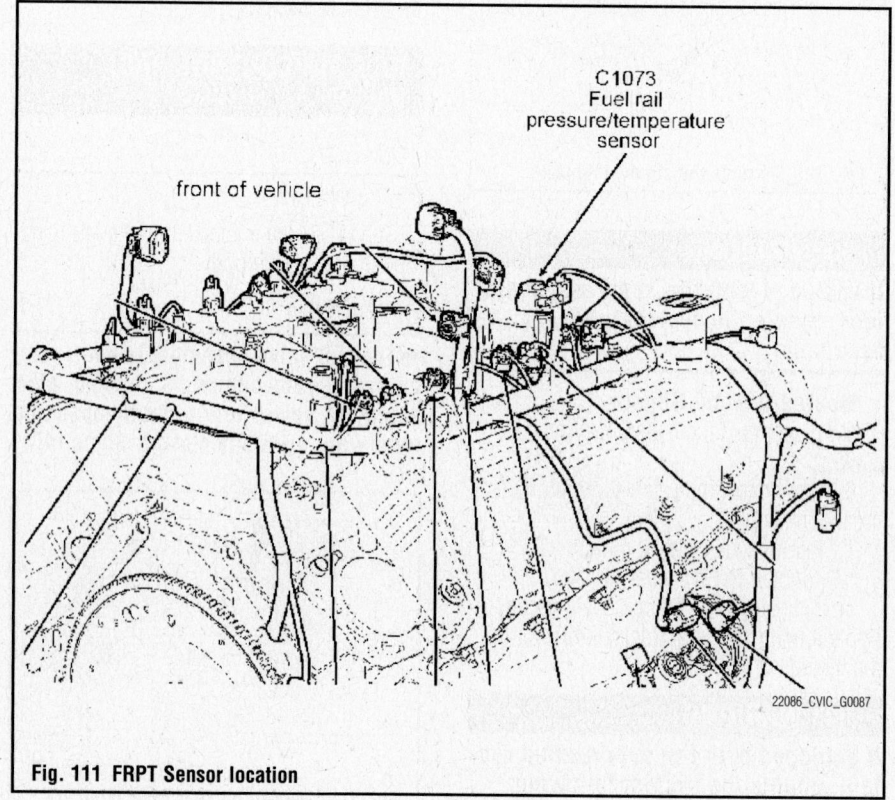

Fig. 111 FRPT Sensor location

22086_CVIC_G0087

signal is equal to the reference voltage minus the voltage drop across the fixed resistor.

The FRPT sensor measures the pressure of the fuel near the fuel injectors. This signal is used by the PCM to adjust the fuel injector pulse width and meter fuel to each engine combustion cylinder.

REMOVAL & INSTALLATION

See Figure 113.

> ### ✳✳ WARNING
>
> **Do not smoke or carry lighted tobacco or open flame of any type when working on or near any fuel-related components. Highly flammable mixtures are always present and can be ignited. Failure to follow these instructions may result in personal injury.**

> ### ✳✳ WARNING
>
> **Do not carry personal electronic devices such as cell phones, pagers, or audio equipment of any type when working on or near any fuel-related components. Highly flammable mixtures are always present and can be ignited. Failure to follow these instructions may result in personal injury.**

1. Disconnect the battery ground cable.
2. Disconnect the fuel rail pressure and temperature sensor electrical connector.
3. Disconnect the fuel rail pressure and temperature sensor vacuum connector.
4. Remove the 2 bolts and the fuel rail

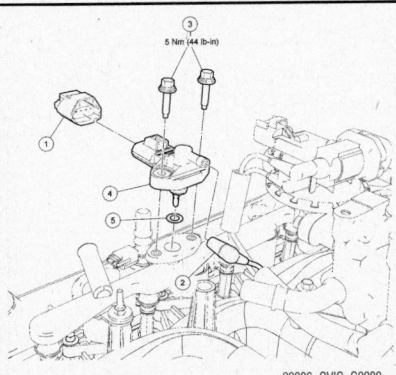

22086_CVIC_G0089

Fig. 113 1. FRPT sensor electrical connector
2. FRPT sensor vacuum connector
3. FRPT sensor bolts (2 required)
4. FRPT sensor
5. O-ring

pressure and temperature sensor. To install, tighten to 44 inch lbs. (5 Nm).

5. Remove and discard the O-ring seal. Install a new O-ring seal and lubricate it with clean engine oil.

6. To install, reverse the removal procedure.

TESTING

See Figure 114.

> ### ✳✳ WARNING
>
> **Vehicle fuel systems are pressurized even when the engine is not running. To avoid fire or personal injury, disable the fuel delivery system and relieve fuel system pressure before removing any fuel system component. Refer to the fuel**

system information at the beginning of pinpoint HC. Failure to follow these instructions may result in personal injury.

➡ With the engine running, the FRPT PID value may be 48-70 kPa (7-10 psi) higher than a fuel pressure reading taken with a mechanical gauge.

FRPT Sensor Pin testing

➡ For reference values, refer to PCM testing–PCM reference voltage chart

This pinpoint test is intended to diagnose the following:
- Fuel rail pressure temperature (FRPT) sensor (9G756)
- Harness circuits: FRPT

Tables and Graphs

FRP AND FRPT SENSOR VOLTAGE AND PRESSURE SPECIFICATIONS

Voltage	Pressure (kPa)	Pressure (psi)
4.5	482	70
3.9	413	60
3.4	344	50
2.8	275	40
2.2	207	30
1.6	138	20
1.1	69	10
0.5	0	0

FRPT SENSOR TEMPERATURE, VOLTAGE, AND RESISTANCE SPECIFICATIONS

Temperature		Sensor	
°C	°F	Volts	K Ohms
100	212	0.47	2.073
95	203	0.54	2.405
90	194	0.61	2.800
85	185	0.70	3.273
80	176	0.80	3.840
75	167	0.92	4.524
70	158	1.06	5.351
65	149	1.21	6.356
60	140	1.38	7.584
55	131	1.56	9.091
50	122	1.77	10.949
45	113	1.99	13.252
40	104	2.23	16.123
35	95	2.48	19.720
30	86	2.74	24.253
25	77	3.00	30.000
20	68	3.26	37.332
15	59	3.50	46.745
10	50	3.73	58.911
5	41	3.95	74.745
0	32	4.13	95.501

Fuel Rail Pressure Temperature (FRPT) Sensor Connector

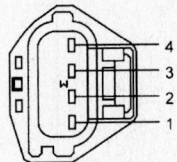

Pin	Circuit
3	FRT (Fuel Rail Temperature)
1	FRP (Fuel Rail Pressure)
4	SIGRTN (Signal Return)
2	VREF (Reference Voltage)

22086_CVIC_G0090

Fig. 114 FRPT sensor connector and graphs

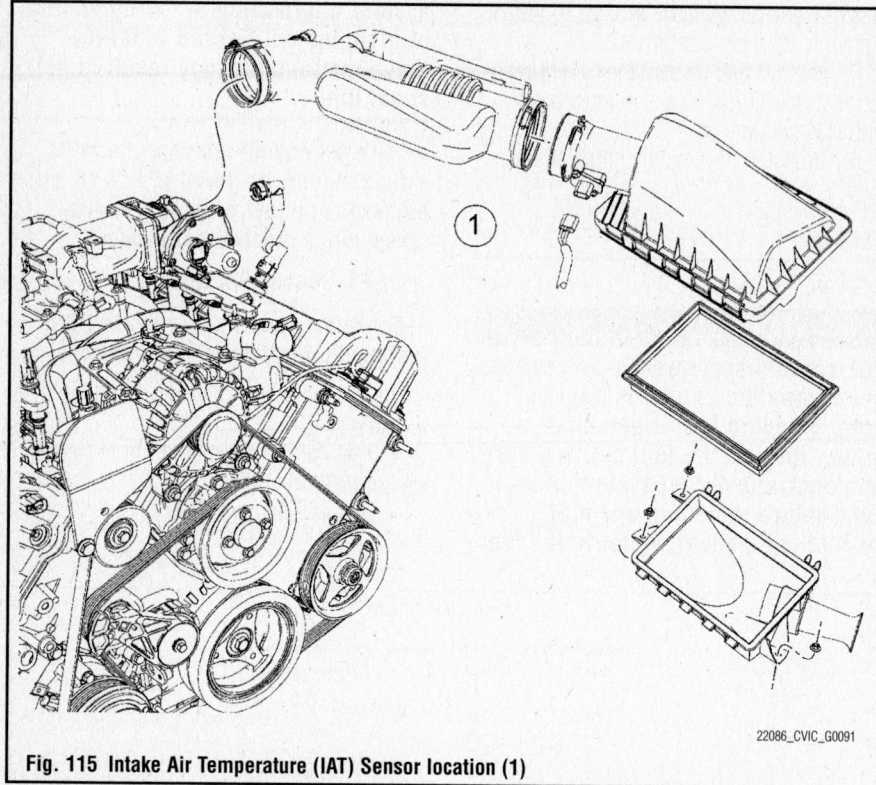

Fig. 115 Intake Air Temperature (IAT) Sensor location (1)

INTAKE AIR TEMPERATURE (IAT) SENSOR

LOCATION

See Figure 115.

The Intake Air Temperature (IAT) Sensor is integrated with the Mass Air Flow (MAF) Sensor, and is located on the inboard side of the air cleaner housing.

OPERATION

See Figure 116.

The Intake Air Temperature (IAT) sensor determines the air temperature inside the intake manifold. Resistance changes in response to the ambient air temperature. The sensor has a negative temperature coefficient. As the temperature of the sensor rises the resistance across the sensor decreases. This provides a signal to the PCM indicating the temperature of the incoming air charge. This sensor helps the PCM to determine spark timing and air/fuel ratio. Information from this sensor is added to the pressure sensor information to calculate the air mass being sent to the cylinders. The IAT is a two wire sensor, a 5-volt reference signal is sent to the sensor and the signal return is based upon the change in the measured resistance due to temperature.

REMOVAL & INSTALLATION

See Figure 117.

1. Disconnect the battery ground cable.
2. Disconnect the intake air temperature/mass air flow (IAT/MAF) sensor electrical connector.

3. Remove the IAT/MAF sensor retaining screws. To install, tighten to 53 inch lbs. (6 Nm).
4. Remove the IAT/MAF sensor.
5. To install, reverse the removal procedure.

TESTING

See Figure 118.

IAT Sensor Pin Testing

➡**For reference values, refer to PCM testing–PCM reference voltage chart**

This pinpoint test is intended to diagnose the following:
- Integrated mass air flow/intake air temperature (MAF/IAT) sensor (12B579)
- Harness circuits: IAT and SIGRTN

Voltage values calculated for VREF equal 5 volts. These values can vary by 15% due to sensor and VREF variations.

KNOCK SENSOR (KS)

LOCATION

See Figure 121.

The Knock Sensors are located in the top of the engine block, under the intake manifold.

OPERATION

See Figure 120.

The operation of the Knock Sensor (KS) is to monitor pre-ignition or "engine

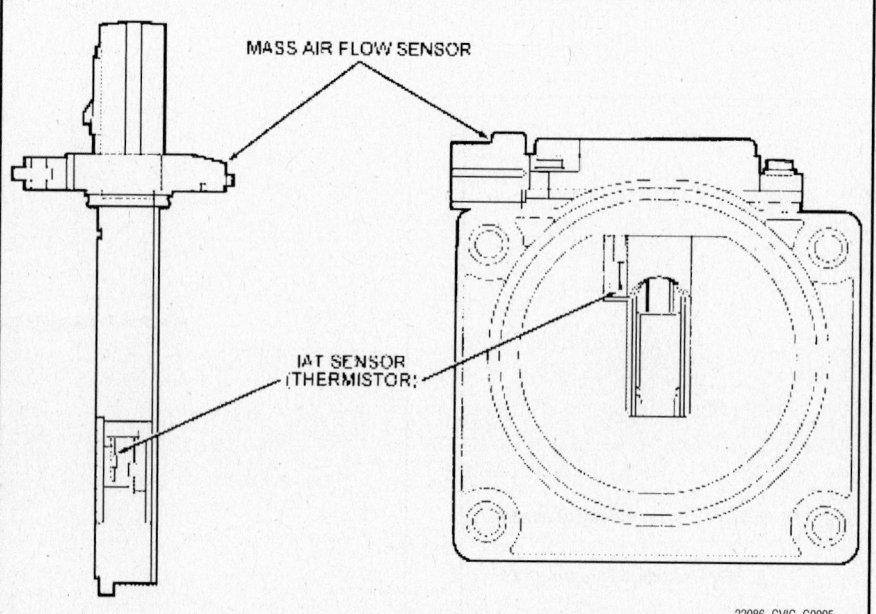

Fig. 116 Integrated Intake Air Temperature (IAT) Sensor Incorporated Into a Drop-in or Flange-type MAF sensor

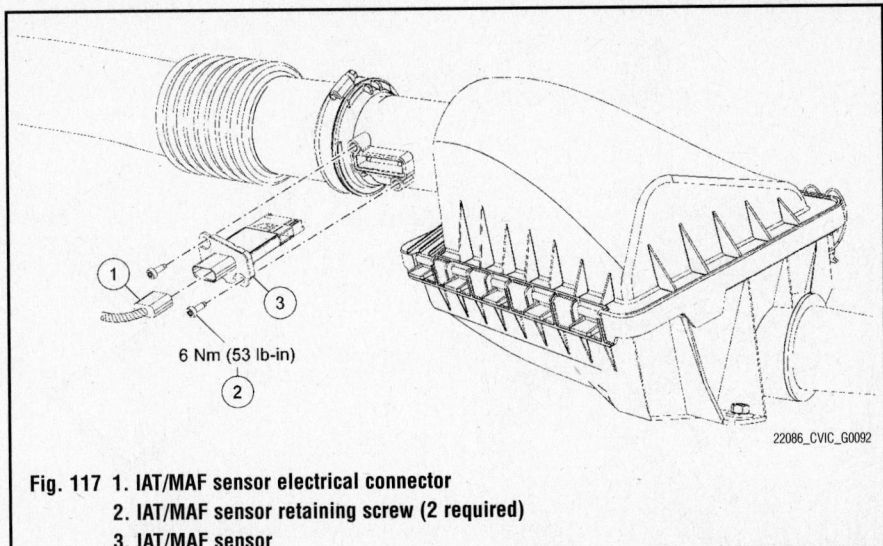

Fig. 117 1. IAT/MAF sensor electrical connector
2. IAT/MAF sensor retaining screw (2 required)
3. IAT/MAF sensor

6 Nm (53 lb-in)

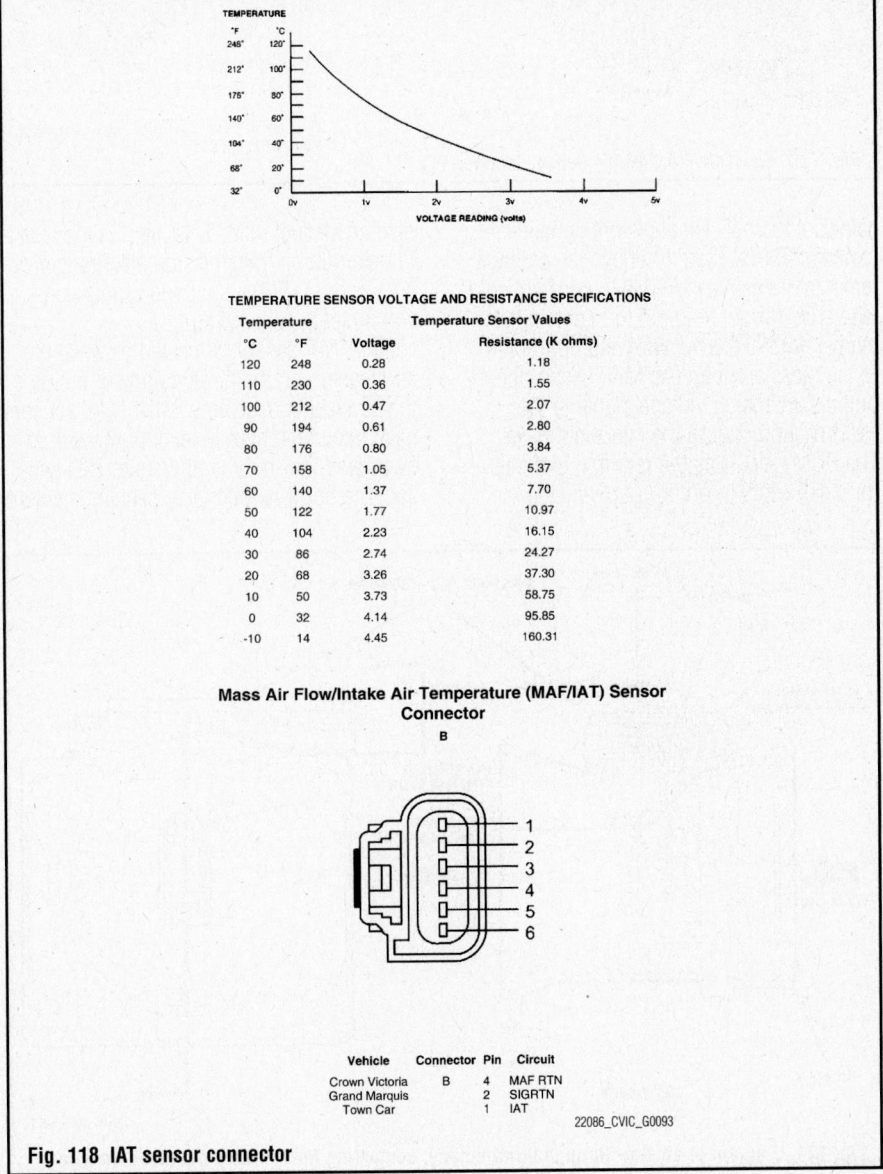

TEMPERATURE SENSOR VOLTAGE AND RESISTANCE SPECIFICATIONS

Temperature		Temperature Sensor Values	
°C	°F	Voltage	Resistance (K ohms)
120	248	0.28	1.18
110	230	0.36	1.55
100	212	0.47	2.07
90	194	0.61	2.80
80	176	0.80	3.84
70	158	1.05	5.37
60	140	1.37	7.70
50	122	1.77	10.97
40	104	2.23	16.15
30	86	2.74	24.27
20	68	3.26	37.30
10	50	3.73	58.75
0	32	4.14	95.85
-10	14	4.45	160.31

Mass Air Flow/Intake Air Temperature (MAF/IAT) Sensor
Connector
B

Vehicle	Connector	Pin	Circuit
Crown Victoria	B	4	MAF RTN
Grand Marquis		2	SIGRTN
Town Car		1	IAT

Fig. 118 IAT sensor connector

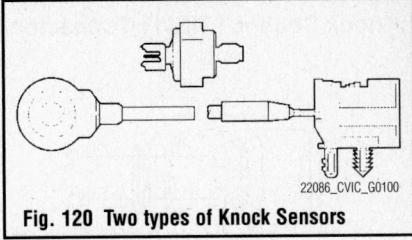

Fig. 120 Two types of Knock Sensors

knocks" and send the signal to the PCM. The PCM responds by adjusting ignition timing until the "knocks" stop. The sensor works by generating a signal produced by the frequency of the knock as recorded by the piezoelectric ceramic disc inside the KS. The disc absorbs the shock waves from the knocks and exerts a pressure on the metal diaphragm inside the KS. This compresses the crystals inside the disc and the disc generates a voltage signal proportional to the frequency of the knocks ranging from zero to 1 volt.

REMOVAL & INSTALLATION

See Figure 121.

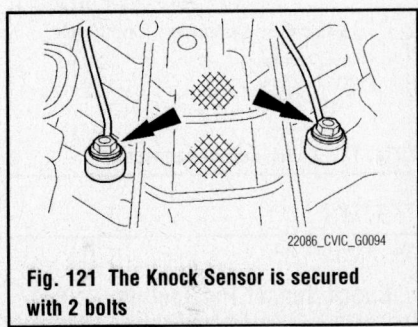

Fig. 121 The Knock Sensor is secured with 2 bolts

✳✳ WARNING

Vehicle fuel systems are pressurized even when the engine is not running. To avoid fire or personal injury, disable the fuel delivery system and relieve fuel system pressure before removing any fuel system component. Refer to the fuel system information at the beginning of pinpoint HC. Failure to follow these instructions may result in personal injury.

For access to the Knock Sensors, refer to Engine Mechanical Components—Intake Manifold—Removal and Installation.

1. Remove the 2 Knock Sensor bolts, and remove the Knock Sensors.
2. To install, tighten the Knock Sensor bolts to 18 ft. lbs. (25 Nm).

Knock Sensor 1 (KS1) Connector

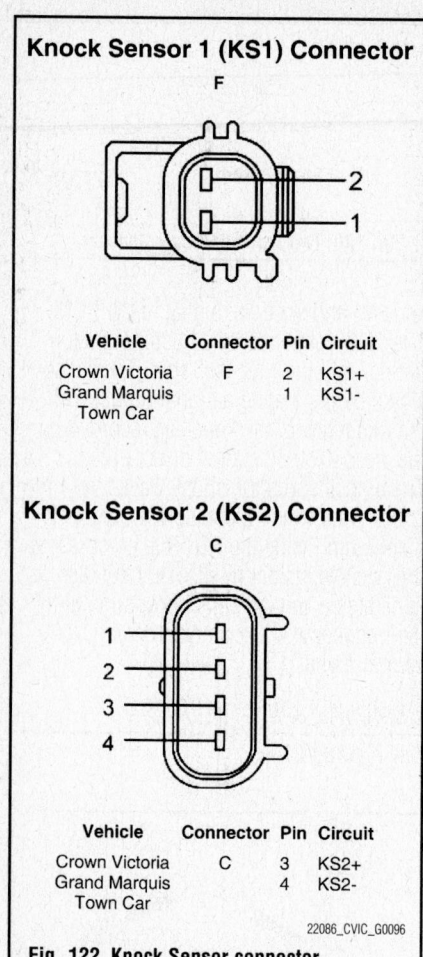

Vehicle	Connector	Pin	Circuit
Crown Victoria	F	2	KS1+
Grand Marquis		1	KS1-
Town Car			

Knock Sensor 2 (KS2) Connector

Vehicle	Connector	Pin	Circuit
Crown Victoria	C	3	KS2+
Grand Marquis		4	KS2-
Town Car			

22086_CVIC_G0096

Fig. 122 Knock Sensor connector

TESTING

See Figure 122.

Knock Sensor Pin Testing

➡**For reference values, refer to PCM testing–PCM reference voltage chart**

This pinpoint test is intended to diagnose the following:
- Knock sensors KS1, KS2 (12A699)
- Harness circuits: KS1+, KS1-, KS2+, and KS2-

MASS AIR FLOW (MAF) SENSOR

LOCATION

See Figure 123.

The Mass Air Flow (MAF) Sensor, and is located on the inboard side of the air cleaner housing.

OPERATION

See Figure 124.

The MAF sensor uses a hot wire sensing element to measure the amount of air entering the engine. Air passing over the hot wire

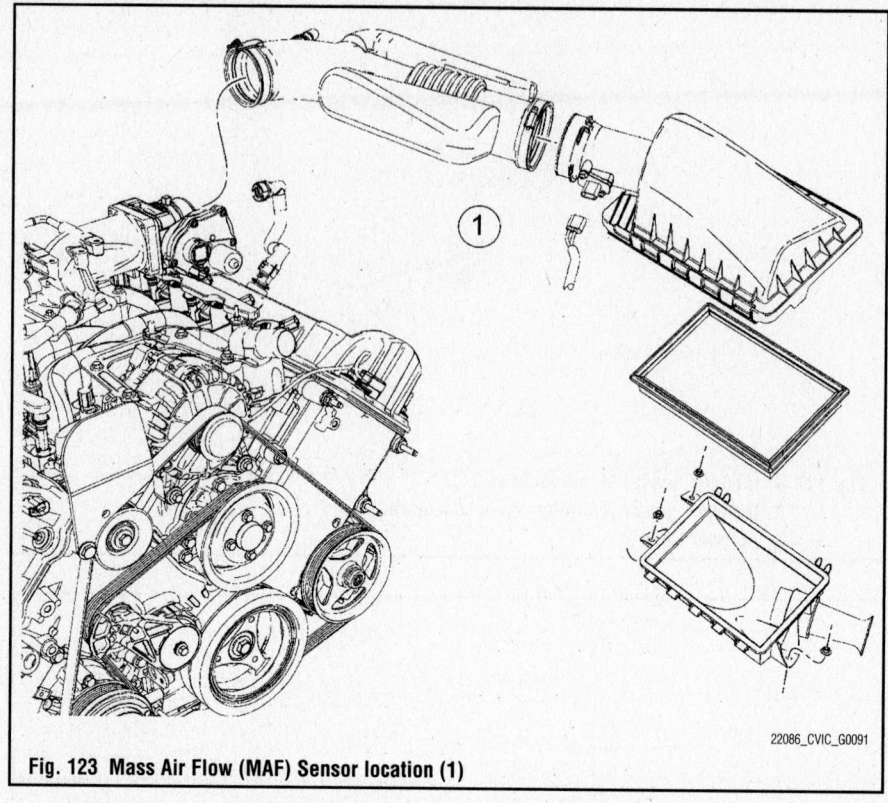

Fig. 123 Mass Air Flow (MAF) Sensor location (1)

22086_CVIC_G0091

causes it to cool. This hot wire is maintained at 200°C (392°F) above the ambient temperature as measured by a constant cold wire. The current required to maintain the temperature of the hot wire is proportional to the mass air flow. The MAF sensor then outputs an analog voltage signal to the PCM proportional to the intake air mass. The PCM calculates the required fuel injector pulse width in order to provide the desired air/fuel ratio. This input is also used in determining transmission electronic pressure control (EPC), shift and torque converter clutch scheduling.

The MAF sensor is located between the air cleaner and the throttle body or inside the air cleaner assembly. Most MAF sensors have integrated bypass technology with an integrated intake air temperature (IAT) sensor. The hot wire electronic sensing element

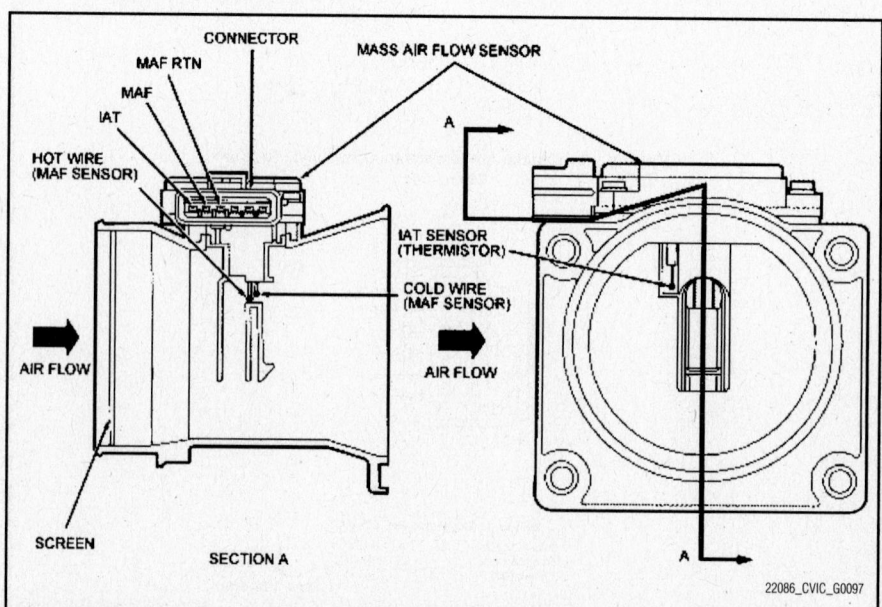

Fig. 124 Diagram of air flow through throttle body, contacting MAF Sensor hot and cold wire (and IAT Sensor wire, where applicable) terminals.

22086_CVIC_G0097

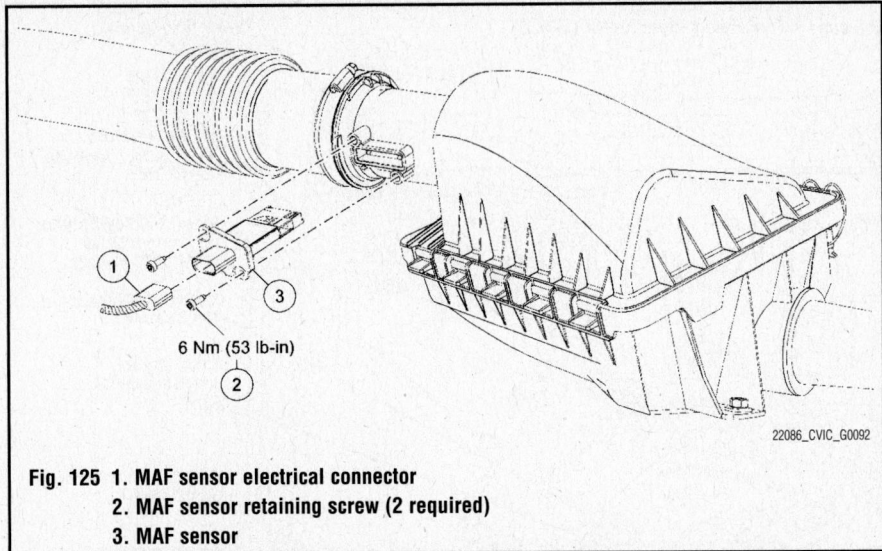

Fig. 125 1. MAF sensor electrical connector
2. MAF sensor retaining screw (2 required)
3. MAF sensor

must be replaced as an assembly. Replacing only the element may change the air flow calibration.

REMOVAL & INSTALLATION

See Figure 125.

1. Disconnect the battery ground cable.
2. Disconnect the mass air flow (MAF) sensor electrical connector.
3. Remove the MAF sensor retaining screws. To install, tighten to 53 inch lbs. (6 Nm).
4. Remove the MAF sensor.
5. To install, reverse the removal procedure.

TESTING

See Figure 126.

MAF Sensor Pin Testing

➡**For reference values, refer to PCM testing–PCM reference voltage chart**

This pinpoint test is intended to diagnose the following:
- Mass air flow sensor (12B579)
- Harness circuits: MAF SIG, MAF RTN, vehicle power (VPWR), power ground (PWRGND), IAT and SIGRTN

MANIFOLD ABSOLUTE PRESSURE (MAP) SENSOR

OPERATION

See Figure 127.

The Manifold Absolute Pressure (MAP) Sensor provides air pressure information to the Powertrain Control Module (PCM). This data is necessary to calculate air density and determine the engine's air mass flow

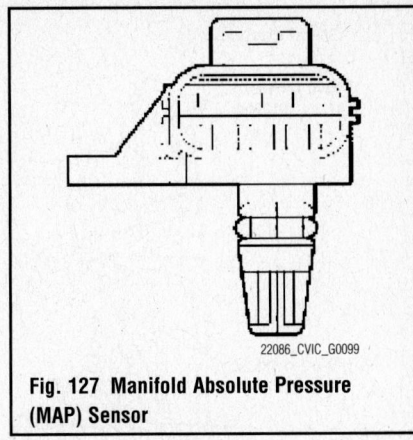

Fig. 127 Manifold Absolute Pressure (MAP) Sensor

rate, which in turn is used to calculate the appropriate air-fuel mixture.

As atmospheric pressure decreases with increasing altitude, vacuum must also decrease to maintain the same MAP in order to maintain the same torque output. This is accomplished by opening the engine's throttle more as altitude increases.

TESTING

See Figure 128.

MAP Sensor Pin Testing

➡**For reference values, refer to PCM testing–PCM reference voltage chart**

This pinpoint test is intended to diagnose the following:
- Manifold absolute pressure (MAP) sensor (9F479)
- Harness circuits: MAP, SIGRTN, VREF

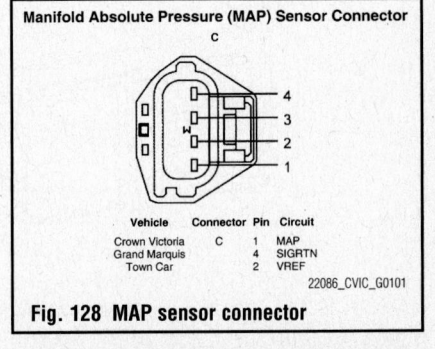

Manifold Absolute Pressure (MAP) Sensor Connector

Vehicle	Connector	Pin	Circuit
Crown Victoria	C	1	MAP
Grand Marquis		4	SIGRTN
Town Car		2	VREF

22086_CVIC_G0101

Fig. 128 MAP sensor connector

POWERTRAIN CONTROL MODULE (PCM)

LOCATION

See Figures 129 and 130.

The Powertrain Control Module (PCM) is located in the engine compartment, driver side, and is fender- mounted.

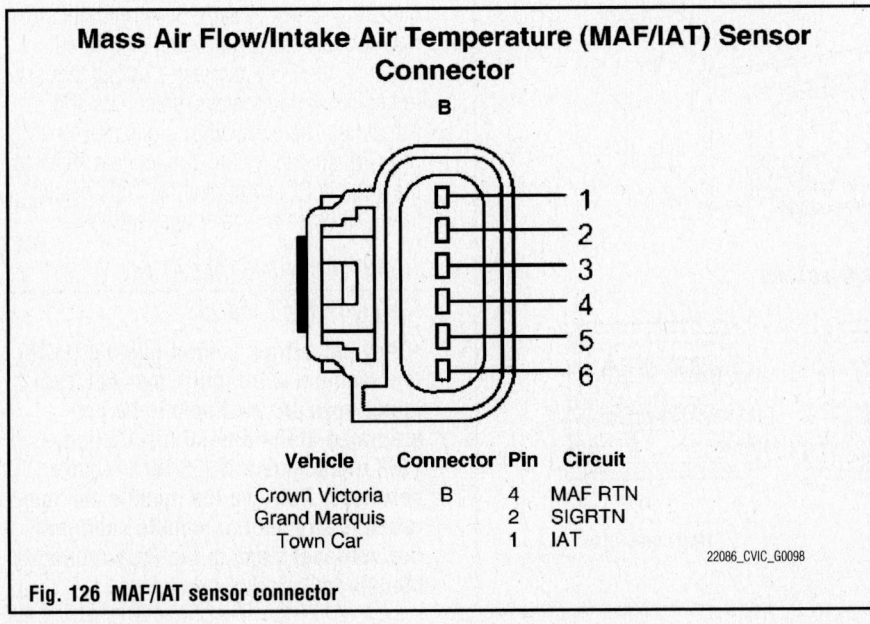

Mass Air Flow/Intake Air Temperature (MAF/IAT) Sensor Connector

B

Vehicle	Connector	Pin	Circuit
Crown Victoria	B	4	MAF RTN
Grand Marquis		2	SIGRTN
Town Car		1	IAT

22086_CVIC_G0098

Fig. 126 MAF/IAT sensor connector

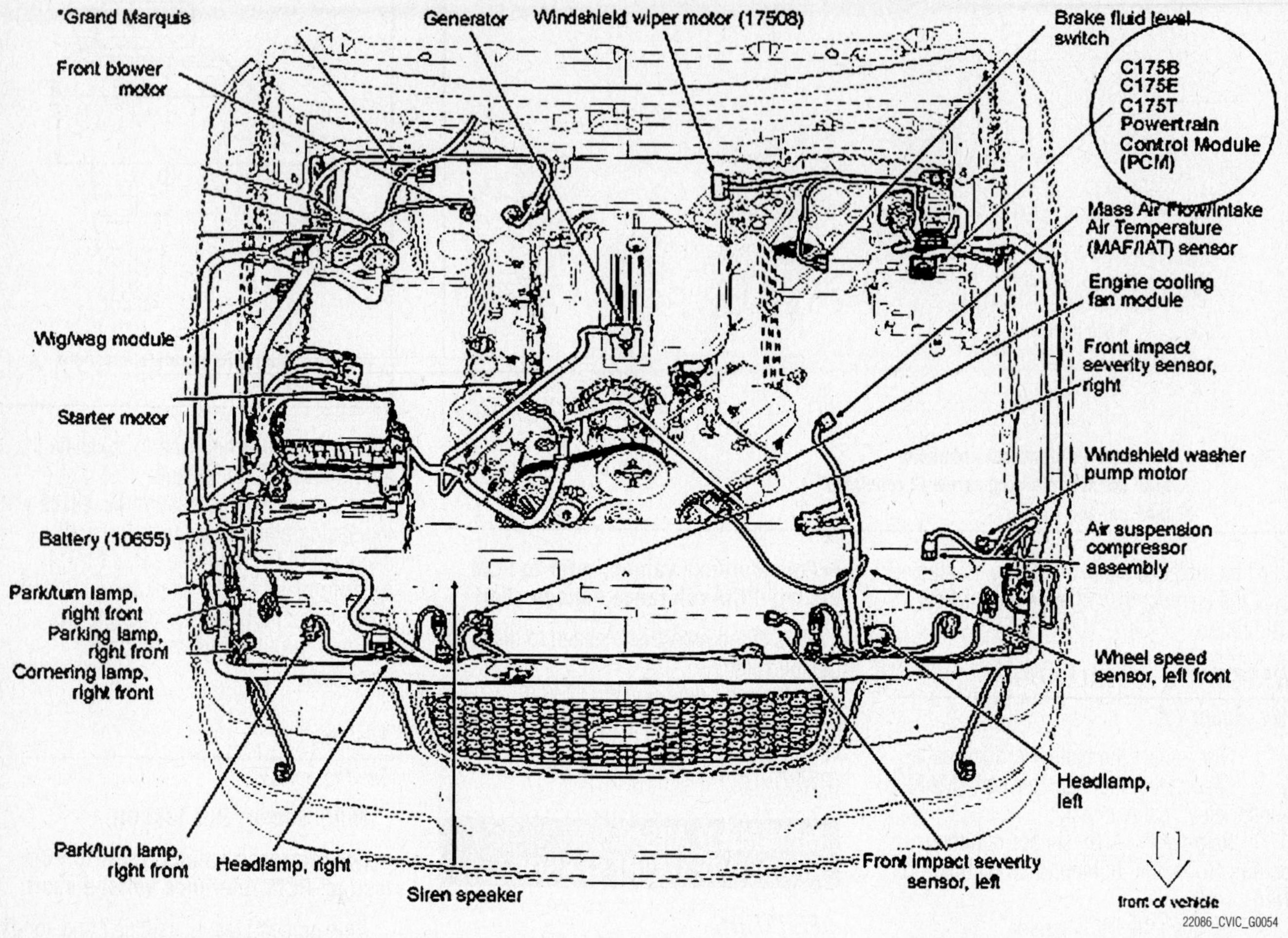

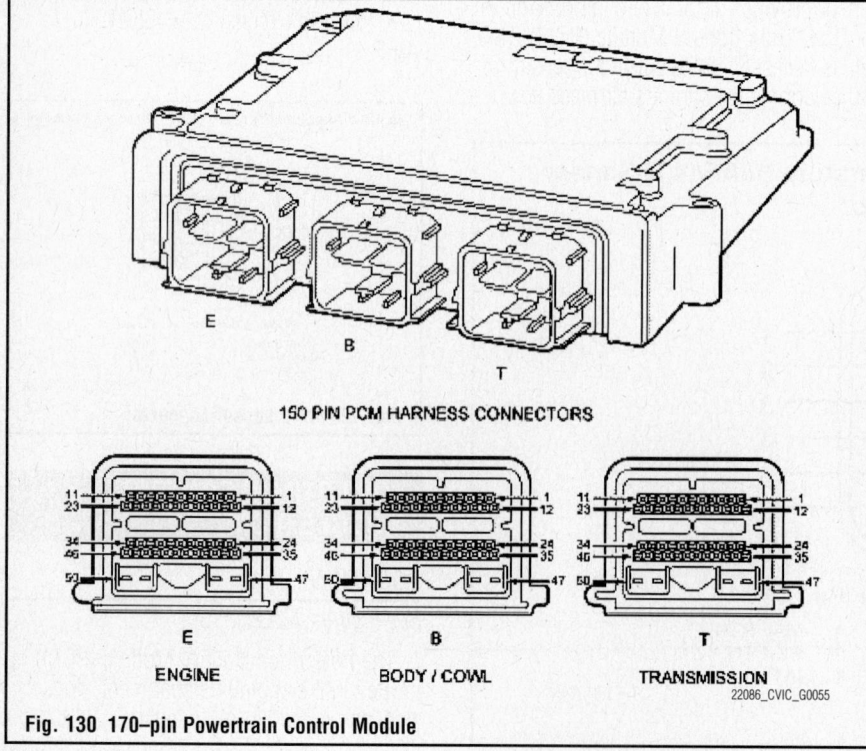

*Grand Marquis
Front blower motor
Wig/wag module
Starter motor
Battery (10655)
Park/turn lamp, right front
Parking lamp, right front
Cornering lamp, right front
Park/turn lamp, right front
Headlamp, right
Siren speaker
Generator
Windshield wiper motor (17508)
Brake fluid level switch
C175B
C175E
C175T
Powertrain Control Module (PCM)
Mass Air Flow/Intake Air Temperature (MAF/IAT) sensor
Engine cooling fan module
Front impact severity sensor, right
Windshield washer pump motor
Air suspension compressor assembly
Wheel speed sensor, left front
Headlamp, left
Front impact severity sensor, left
front of vehicle
22086_CVIC_G0054

Fig. 129 Powertrain Control Module location

E
B
T
150 PIN PCM HARNESS CONNECTORS

11
23
1
12
34
46
24
35
59
47
E
ENGINE

11
23
1
12
34
46
24
35
59
47
B
BODY / COWL

11
23
1
12
34
46
24
35
59
47
T
TRANSMISSION

22086_CVIC_G0055

Fig. 130 170-pin Powertrain Control Module

OPERATION

The center of the electronic engine control (EEC) system is a microprocessor called the PCM. The PCM receives input from sensors and other electronic components (switches, relays). Based on the information received and programmed into its memory, the PCM generates output signals to control various relays, solenoids and actuators. There are several different types of PCMs in use for this model year. Refer to the Vehicle PCM Application Table below for PCM types and their applications.

REMOVAL & INSTALLATION

See Figures 131 and 132.

➡Any powertrain control module (PCM) replacement will require that ALL customer keys are available to be programmed at the time of installation. PCM replacement DOES NOT require new keys. Retrieve the module configuration. Carry out the module configuration retrieval steps of the Programmable Module Installation procedure.

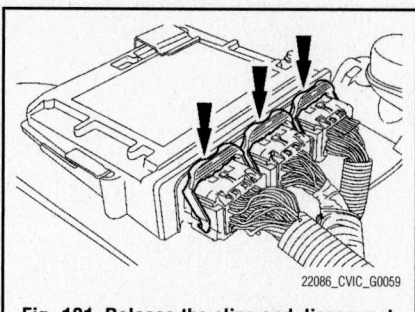

Fig. 131 Release the clips and disconnect the 3 PCM electrical connectors

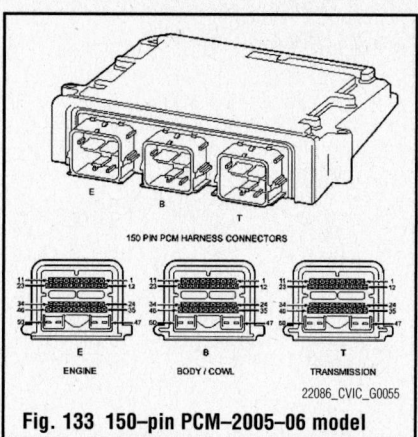

Fig. 133 150–pin PCM–2005–06 model

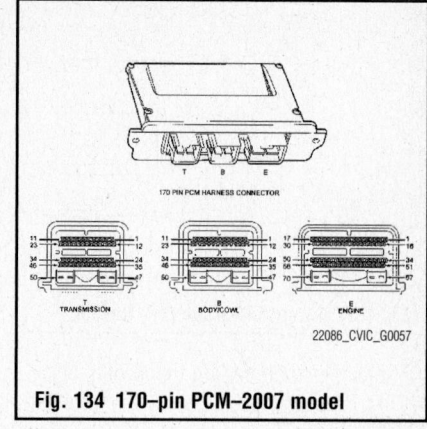

Fig. 134 170–pin PCM–2007 model

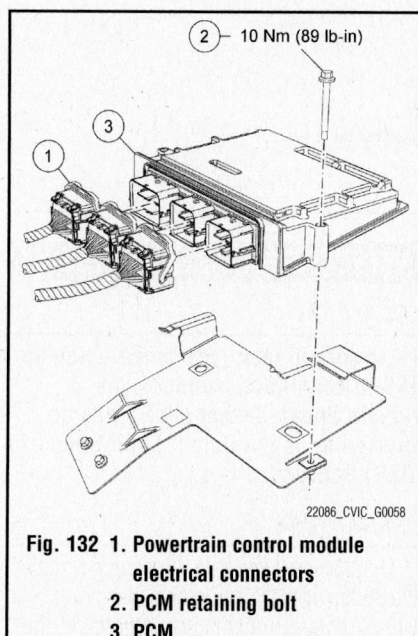

Fig. 132 1. Powertrain control module electrical connectors
2. PCM retaining bolt
3. PCM

1. Release the clips and disconnect the 3 PCM electrical connectors.

To install:
2. Install the PCM and the bolts.
3. Tighten to 89 ft. lbs. (10 Nm).
4. Connect the 3 PCM electrical connectors and install the clips.
5. Restore the module configuration. Carry out the module configuration restore steps of the Programmable Module Installation procedure.
6. Reprogram the Passive Anti-Theft System (PATS). Carry out the Key Programming Using Two Programmed Keys procedure.

TESTING

See Figures 133, 134 and 135.

Using a high-impedance digital multimeter, test the PCM for correct power and ground inputs and outputs, according to the pin location chart.

Function	Description	Connector/Pin
VPWR	Voltage input to module	B35
VPWR	Voltage input to module	B36
PWRGND	Power ground	B47
PWRGND	Power ground	B48
PWRGND	Power ground	B49
PWRGND	Power ground	B50
CSEGND	Case ground	B10
SIGRTN	Connector B signal return	B41
SIGRTN	Connector B signal return	B43
SIGRTN	Connector E signal return	E33
SIGRTN	Connector E signal return	E58
SIGRTN	Connector T signal return	T41
VREF	Connector B buffered 5.0-volt reference	B40
VREF	Connector E buffered 5.0-volt reference	E57
KAPWR	Keep alive power	B45

Fig. 135 Table 1—170–pin PCM Power and ground pin locations

THROTTLE POSITION SENSOR (TPS)

LOCATION

See Figure 136.

The Throttle Position (TP) Sensor is located on the throttle body, towards the rear of the engine.

OPERATION

See Figure 137.

The TP sensor is a rotary potentiometer sensor that provides a signal to the PCM that is linearly proportional to the throttle plate/shaft position. The sensor housing

has a 3-blade electrical connector that may be gold plated. The gold plating increases the corrosion resistance on the terminals and increases the connector durability. The

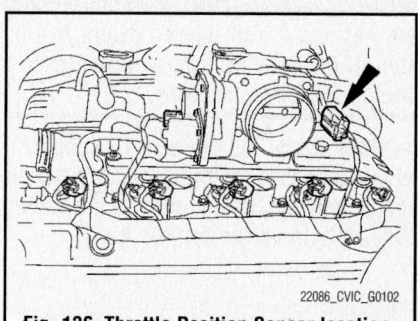

Fig. 136 Throttle Position Sensor location

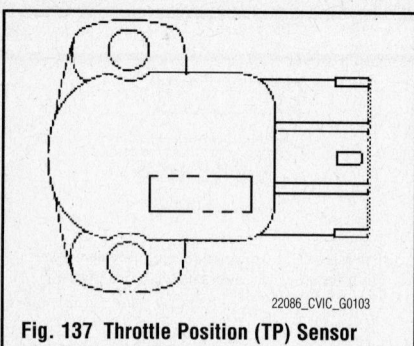

Fig. 137 Throttle Position (TP) Sensor

TP sensor is mounted on the throttle body. As the TP sensor is rotated by the throttle shaft, 4 operating conditions are determined by the PCM from the TP.

The operating conditions are:

- Closed throttle (includes idle or deceleration)
- Part throttle (includes cruise or moderate acceleration)
- Wide open throttle (includes maximum acceleration or de-choke on crank) throttle angle rate

REMOVAL & INSTALLATION

See Figure 138.

1. Disconnect the battery ground cable.
2. Disconnect the throttle position (TP) sensor the throttle body electrical connector.

✦ CAUTION

Failure to remove the TP sensor screws in the following manner will result in damage to the screws.

3. First loosen the screws 1-2 full turns using a hand tool, and then use a suitable high-speed driver to complete the removal.
4. Remove and discard the 2 screws and the TP sensor.

❋❋ CAUTION

Do not reuse the TP sensor and screws. A new TP sensor and screws must be installed.

To install:

✦ CAUTION

Do not use a high-speed driver to install the new screws or damage to the TP sensor can occur.

➡ When installing the new TP sensor, make sure that the radial locator tab on the TP sensor is aligned with the radial locator hole on the throttle body.

5. Position the new TP sensor and install the 2 new screws. Tighten to 27 inch lbs. (3 Nm).

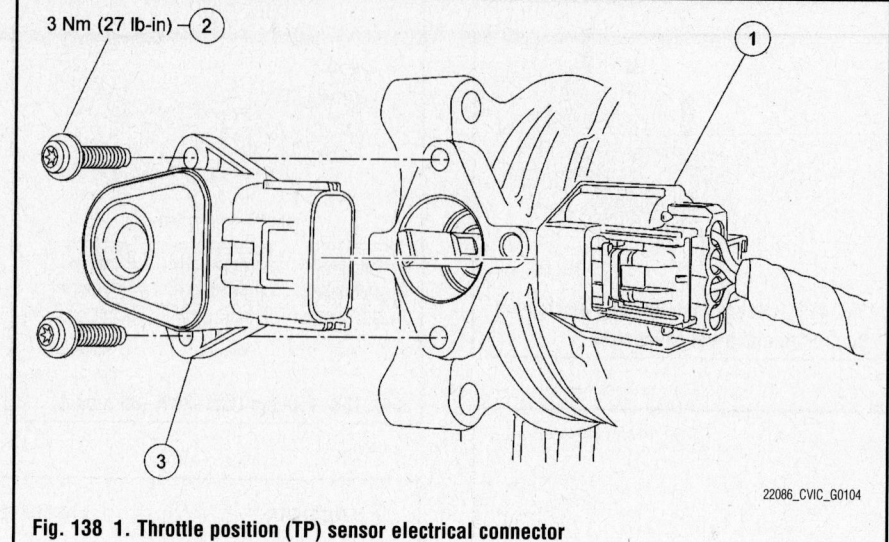

Fig. 138 1. Throttle position (TP) sensor electrical connector
2. TP screws (2 required)
3. TP sensor

6. Connect the TP sensor electrical connector.

TESTING

See Figure 139.

TP Sensor Pin Testing

➡ **For reference values, refer to PCM testing–PCM reference voltage chart**

This pinpoint test is intended to diagnose the following:

- TP sensor (9B989)
- Binding or sticking throttle linkage
- Harness circuits: TP, SIGRTN, VREF, VPWR, and PWRGND

VEHICLE SPEED SENSOR (VSS)

LOCATION

➡ For certain tests, and while using an OBD–II compliant scan tool, the Vehicle Speed Sensor (VSS) may be referred to as the Output Shaft Speed (OSS) Sensor

OPERATION

The VSS is a variable reluctance or hall-effect sensor that generates a waveform with a frequency that is proportional to the speed of the vehicle. If the vehicle is moving at a relatively low velocity, the sensor

Throttle Position (TP) Sensor Connector

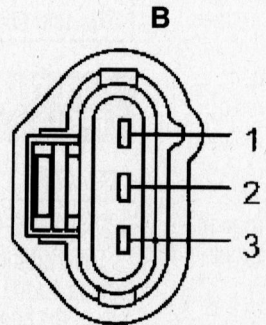

Vehicle	Connector	Pin	Circuit
Crown Victoria	B	2	TP
Grand Marquis		3	SIGRTN
Town Car		1	VREF

Fig. 139 TP sensor connector

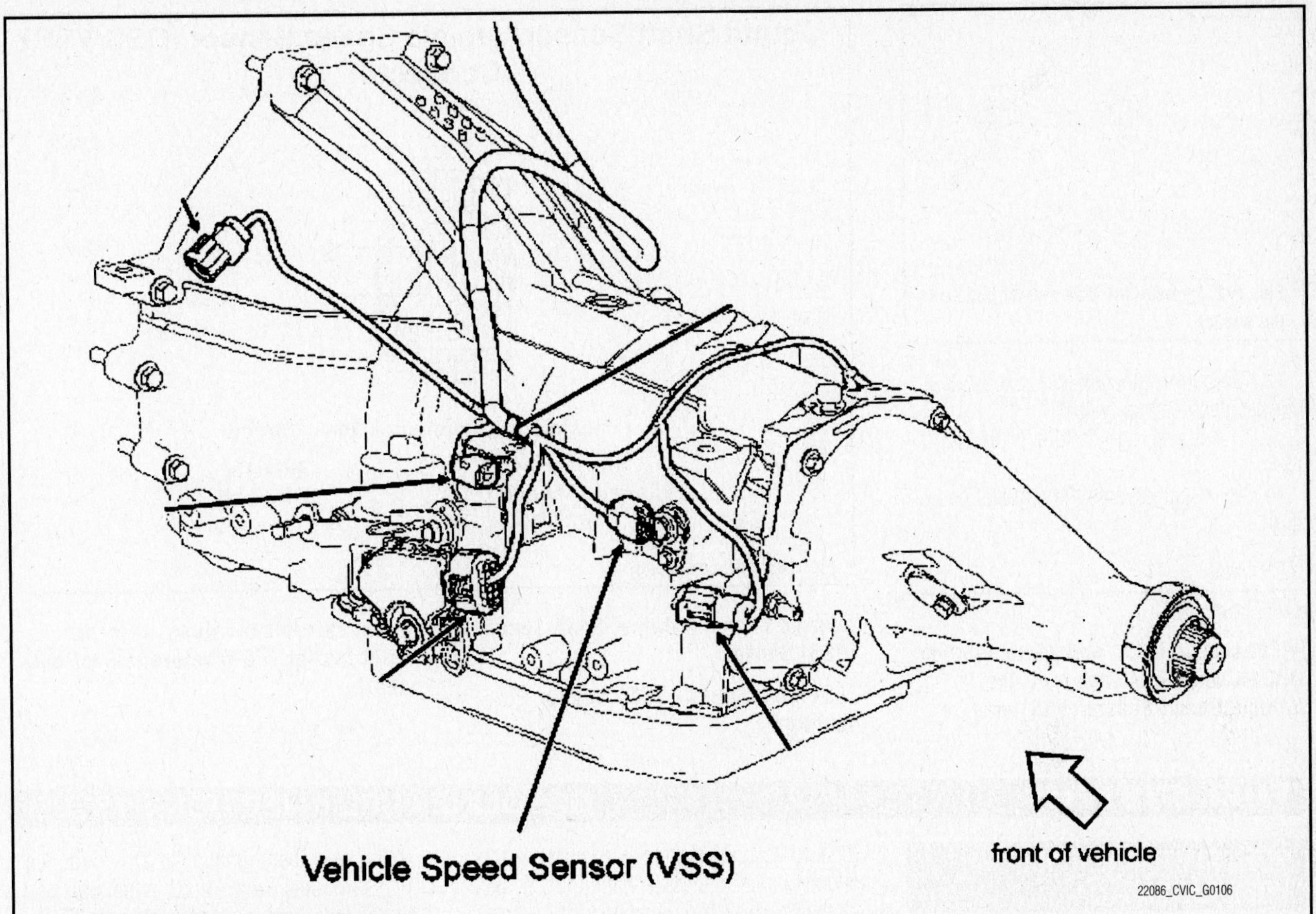

Vehicle Speed Sensor (VSS)

front of vehicle

22086_CVIC_G0106

Fig. 140 Vehicle Speed (VSS) Sensor Location

produces a signal with a low frequency. As the vehicle velocity increases, the sensor generates a signal with a higher frequency. The PCM uses the frequency signal generated by the VSS (and other inputs) to control such parameters as fuel injection, ignition control, transmission/transaxle shift scheduling, and torque converter clutch scheduling.

The VSS provides the PCM with information about the rotational speed of an output shaft. The PCM uses the information to control and diagnose powertrain behavior. In some applications, the sensor is also used as the source of vehicle speed. The sensor may be physically located in different places on the vehicle, depending upon the specific application. The design of each speed sensor is unique and depends on which powertrain control feature uses the information that is generated.

REMOVAL & INSTALLATION

See Figures 141 and 142.

1. Position the vehicle on a hoist, and place the automatic transmission selector into the NEUTRAL position.

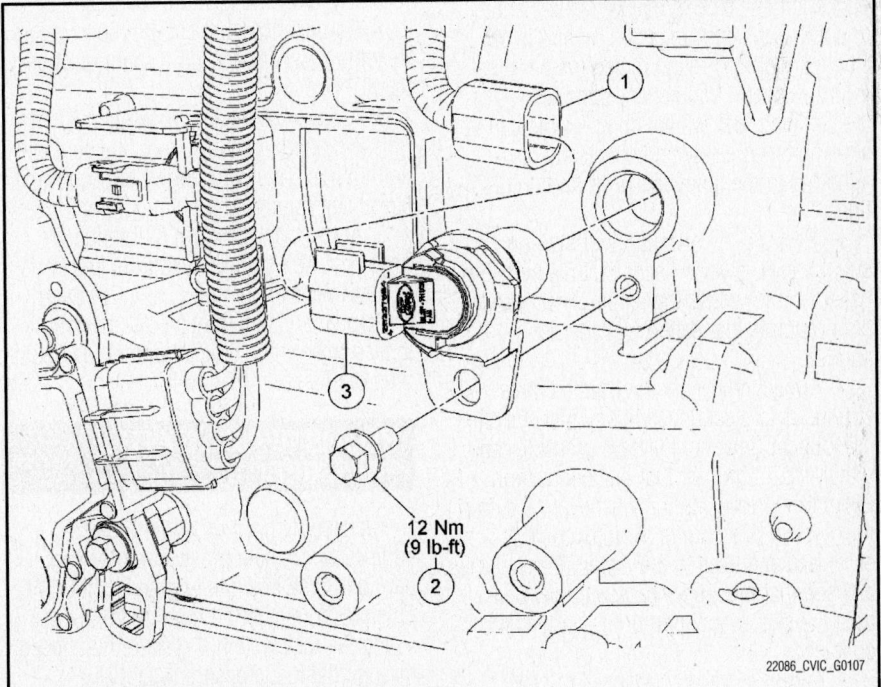

12 Nm
(9 lb-ft)

22086_CVIC_G0107

Fig. 141 1. Vehicle speed sensor electrical connector
2. VSS sensor bolt
3. VSS sensor

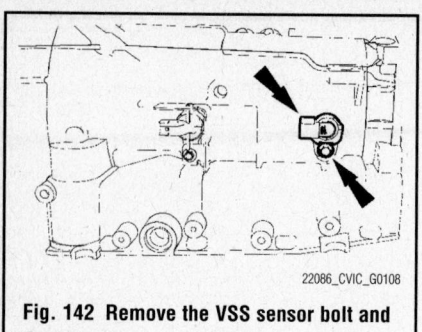

Fig. 142 Remove the VSS sensor bolt and the sensor

2. Disconnect the vehicle speed (VSS) sensor electrical connector.

3. . To install, tighten to 9 ft. lbs (12 Nm).

4. To install, reverse the removal procedure.

TESTING

See Figure 143.

➡For certain tests, and while using an OBD–II compliant scan tool, the Vehicle Speed Sensor (VSS) may be

Output Shaft Sensor/Vehicle Speed Sensor (OSS/VSS) Connector

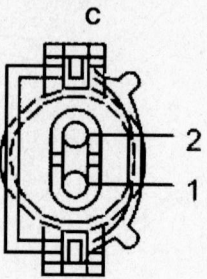

Vehicle	Connector	Pin	Circuit
Crown Victoria	C	1	SIGRTN
Grand Marquis		2	OSS/VSS
Town Car			

22086_CVIC_G0109

Fig. 143 VSS connector

referred to as the Output Shaft Speed (OSS) Sensor

Vehicle Speed (VSS) Sensor Pin Testing

➡For reference values, refer to PCM testing–PCM reference voltage chart

FUEL SYSTEMS

GASOLINE FUEL INJECTION SYSTEM

FUEL SYSTEM SERVICE PRECAUTIONS

Safety is the most important factor when performing not only fuel system maintenance but any type of maintenance. Failure to conduct maintenance and repairs in a safe manner may result in serious personal injury or death. Maintenance and testing of the vehicle's fuel system components can be accomplished safely and effectively by adhering to the following rules and guidelines.

• To avoid the possibility of fire and personal injury, always disconnect the negative battery cable unless the repair or test procedure requires that battery voltage be applied.

• Always relieve the fuel system pressure prior to disconnecting any fuel system component (injector, fuel rail, pressure regulator, etc.), fitting or fuel line connection. Exercise extreme caution whenever relieving fuel system pressure to avoid exposing skin, face and eyes to fuel spray. Please be advised that fuel under pressure may penetrate the skin or any part of the body that it contacts.

• Always place a shop towel or cloth around the fitting or connection prior to loosening to absorb any excess fuel due to spillage. Ensure that all fuel spillage

(should it occur) is quickly removed from engine surfaces. Ensure that all fuel soaked cloths or towels are deposited into a suitable waste container.

• Always keep a dry chemical (Class B) fire extinguisher near the work area.

• Do not allow fuel spray or fuel vapors to come into contact with a spark or open flame.

• Always use a back-up wrench when loosening and tightening fuel line connection fittings. This will prevent unnecessary stress and torsion to fuel line piping.

• Always replace worn fuel fitting O-rings with new Do not substitute fuel hose or equivalent where fuel pipe is installed.

Before servicing the vehicle, make sure to also refer to the precautions in the beginning of this section as well.

RELIEVING FUEL SYSTEM PRESSURE

Fuel supply lines on all fuel injected engines will remain pressurized for some period of time after the engine is shut **OFF**. This pressure must be relieved before servicing the fuel system. Pressure is relieved through the fuel pressure relief valve, located on the fuel rail.

To relieve the fuel system pressure, first remove the fuel tank cap to relieve pressure

in the tank, then remove the cap on the fuel pressure relief valve. Attach a fuel pressure gauge and drain the system through the drain tube into a container. Remove the fuel pressure gauge and replace the cap on the relief valve.

FUEL FILTER

REMOVAL & INSTALLATION

See Figure 144.

1. Disconnect the negative battery cable.

2. Relieve the fuel system pressure.

3. If equipped with air suspension, turn the air suspension switch to the **OFF** position.

4. Remove the hairpin clip push connect fittings from both ends of the fuel filter as follows:

a. Step 1: Inspect the visible internal portion of the fitting for dirt accumulation. If more than a light coating of dust is present, clean the fitting before disassembly.

b. Step 2: Some adhesion between the seals in the fitting and the filter will occur with time. To separate, twist the fitting on the filter, then push and pull the fitting until it moves freely on the filter.

c. Step 3: Remove the hairpin clip from the fitting by first bending and

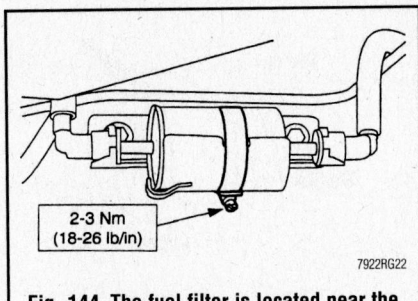

2-3 Nm
(18-26 lb/in)

7922RG22

Fig. 144 The fuel filter is located near the center of the vehicle on the frame rail

breaking the shipping tab. Next, spread the 2 clip legs by hand about ⅛ inch each, to disengage the body and push the legs into the fitting. Lightly pull the triangular end of the clip and work it clear of the filter and fitting.

d. Step 4: Grasp the fitting and pull in an axial direction to remove the fitting from the filter. Be careful on 90 degree elbow connectors, as excessive side loading could break the connector body.

e. Step 5: After disassembly, inspect the inside of the fitting for any internal parts such as O-rings and spacers that may have been dislodged from the fitting. Replace any damaged connector.

5. Remove the filter retaining clamp and remove the fuel filter. Note the direction of the flow arrow on the filter, so the replacement filter can be reinstalled in the same position.

To install:

6. Install or connect the following:
- Fuel filter with the flow arrow facing the proper direction and tighten the filter retaining clamp
- Rubber insulator rings on the new filter. Replace the insulator rings if the filter moves freely after the retainer is installed.
- Filter into the retainer with the flow arrow pointing out the open end of the retainer
- Retainer on the bracket and tighten the mounting bolts to 44 inch lbs. (5 Nm)

7. Install the hairpin clip push connect fittings at both ends of the fuel filter as follows:

a. Step 1: Install a new connector if damage was found. Insert a new clip into any 2 adjacent openings with the triangular portion pointing away from the fitting opening. Install the clip until the legs of the clip are locked on the outside of the body. Piloting with an index finger is necessary.

b. Step 2: Before installing the fitting on the filter, wipe the filter end with a clean cloth. Inspect the inside of the fitting to be sure it is free of dirt and/or obstructions.

c. Step 3: Apply a light coating of engine oil to the filter end. Align the fitting and filter axially and push the fitting onto the filter end. When the fitting is engaged, a definite click will be heard. Pull on the fitting to be sure it is fully engaged.

8. If equipped with air suspension, turn the air suspension switch to the **ON** position.

9. Reconnect the negative battery cable.

10. Start the engine and check for fuel leaks and proper operation.

FUEL INJECTORS

REMOVAL & INSTALLATION

1. Relieve the fuel system pressure.
2. Remove or disconnect the following:
- Injector supply manifold
- Wiring
- Injector by pulling it up and gently rocking it side to side
- O-rings and discard

To install:

3. Lubricate new O-rings with clean engine oil.
4. Install or connect the following:
- O-rings
- Fuel injector using a light, twisting and pushing motion
- Injector supply manifold
- Wiring

FUEL PUMP

REMOVAL & INSTALLATION

See Figure 145.

1. Disconnect the negative battery cable.
2. Relieve the fuel system pressure.
3. Install a hose into the fuel filler pipe and drain or siphon the fuel into a storage tank designed for fuel storage.
4. Remove any dirt that has accumulated around the fuel pump and fuel lines to prevent the entry of contaminants into the tank during fuel pump removal and installation.
5. Remove or disconnect the following:
- Fuel supply and return line fittings at the fuel pump using fuel line disconnect tools

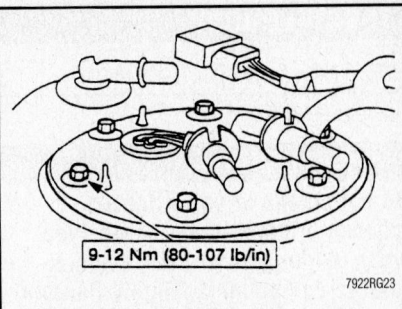

9-12 Nm (80-107 lb/in)

7922RG23

Fig. 145 Tighten the fuel pump mounting bolts to 89 inch lbs. (10 Nm)

- Fuel pump module electrical connector
- 6 retaining bolts around the perimeter of the fuel pump module
- Fuel pump module and seal from the fuel tank

To install:

6. Clean the fuel pump module mounting flange and fuel tank mounting surface.
7. Install or connect the following:
- New seal and the fuel pump module using care not to damage the inlet filter and fuel sending unit float arm
- 6 retaining bolts and tighten to 89 inch lbs. (10 Nm)
- Fuel pump module electrical connector
- Fuel supply and return lines to the fuel pump module. Pull on the fuel line fittings to verify engagement.

8. Add a minimum of 10 gallons (38L) of clean fuel to the fuel tank and check for leaks.

9. Install a Fuel pressure gauge to the Schrader valve on the fuel injection supply manifold.

10. Connect the negative battery cable.

11. Cycle the ignition switch from the **OFF** to **ON** position 5–10 times for 3 second intervals or until the fuel pressure gauge shows at least 35 psi (241 kPa).

12. Check for fuel leaks.

13. Remove the fuel pressure gauge.

14. Start the engine and recheck for fuel leaks.

15. Road test the vehicle and check for proper operation.

IDLE SPEED

ADJUSTMENT

Idle speed is maintained by the Powertrain Control Module (PCM). No adjustment is necessary or possible.

THROTTLE BODY

REMOVAL & INSTALLATION

See Figure 146.

> #### ❄❄ CAUTION
> Do not smoke or carry lighted tobacco or open flame of any type when working on or near any fuel-related components. Highly flammable mixtures are always present and may be ignited. Failure to follow these instructions can result in personal injury.

> #### ❄❄ WARNING
> The throttle body bore and plate area have a special coating and cannot be cleaned.

1. Before servicing the vehicle, refer to the precautions in the beginning of this section.
2. Disconnect battery negative cable from battery and properly isolate to prevent accidental reconnection.
3. Remove or disconnect the following:
   - Air cleaner outlet tube
   - Throttle position (TP) sensor electrical connector
   - Throttle return spring, accelerator and speed control cables

➡ Discard the throttle body (TB) gasket.

   - Four bolts and the throttle body

To install:

4. Install a new throttle body (TB) gasket and the throttle body.

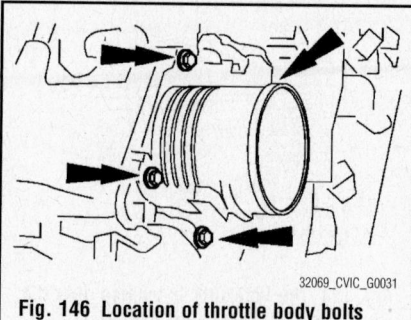
32069_CVIC_G0031
Fig. 146 Location of throttle body bolts

5. Tighten the bolts in two stages:
   - Tighten to 80 inch lbs. (9 Nm)
   - Rotate an additional 90 degrees.
6. Connect the throttle return spring, accelerator and speed control cables.
7. Connect the throttle position (TP) sensor electrical connectors.
8. Install the air cleaner outlet tube.

HEATING & AIR CONDITIONING SYSTEM

BLOWER MOTOR

REMOVAL & INSTALLATION

See Figures 147 and 148.

1. Before servicing the vehicle, refer to the precautions in the beginning of this section.
2. Disconnect battery negative cable from battery and properly isolate to prevent accidental reconnection.
3. Disengage the wire harness connectors from the retainer.
4. Disconnect the blower motor electrical connector.
5. Remove the motor cooling hose.
6. Remove the screws and remove the blower motor.

➡ Prior to removing a wheel that is to be reused, clean any corrosion from the blower motor shaft to prevent damage to the wheel mounting shaft.

7. Remove the wheel from the blower motor as follows:

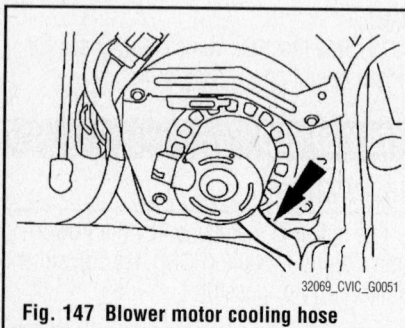
32069_CVIC_G0051
Fig. 147 Blower motor cooling hose

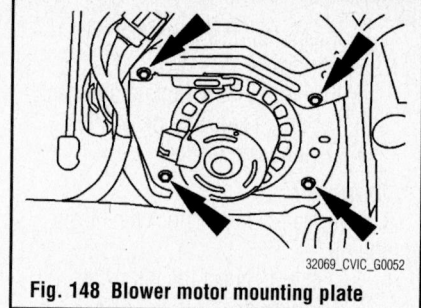
32069_CVIC_G0052
Fig. 148 Blower motor mounting plate

   - Remove the push clip.
   - Remove the wheel from the blower motor.

To install:

8. Install or connect the following:
   - Wheel to the blower motor, if removed.
   - Blower motor and securely tighten the screws.
   - Motor cooling hose
   - Blower motor electrical connector
   - Wire harness retainers

HEATER CORE

REMOVAL & INSTALLATION

See Figures 149 through 153.

1. If equipped, turn the air suspension service switch to the **OFF** position before raising the vehicle.
2. Drain the cooling system.
3. Remove or disconnect the following:
   - Negative battery cable
   - Front seats

   - Carpeting
   - Rear airflow duct
   - Heater hoses
4. Remove the driver's side air bag module by removing or disconnect the following:
   - SRS module-to-steering wheel bolts, from both sides of the steering wheel.
   - SRS module and disconnect the electrical connector
   - Horn switch electrical connector
5. Remove the passenger's side SRS module by removing or disconnecting the following:
   - Open the glove box and disconnect the glove compartment isolator
   - Push inward on the 2 glove box door tabs and lower it
   - SRS module's electrical connector
   - SRS module-to-instrument panel bolts and the module
6. Remove the instrument panel by removing or disconnecting the following:
   - Speed control servo nuts and move the servo aside
   - Bolt and disconnect the left side bulkhead connector
   - Left side bulkhead connector from the dash panel
   - Windshield washer fluid reservoir screw, and position the reservoir aside
   - Blower motor electrical connector
   - Air conditioning pressure cut-off switch electrical connector
   - In-line electrical harness connector

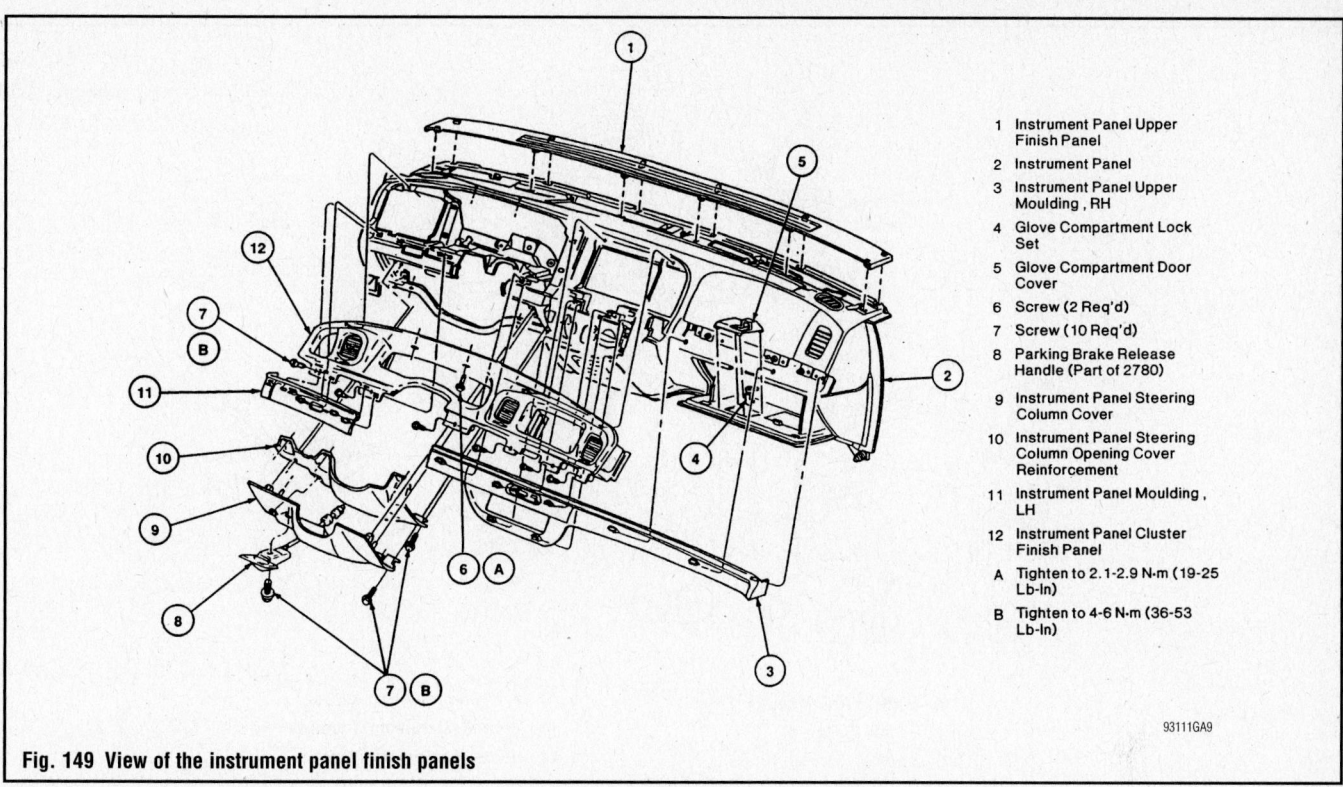

1 Instrument Panel Upper Finish Panel
2 Instrument Panel
3 Instrument Panel Upper Moulding , RH
4 Glove Compartment Lock Set
5 Glove Compartment Door Cover
6 Screw (2 Req'd)
7 Screw (10 Req'd)
8 Parking Brake Release Handle (Part of 2780)
9 Instrument Panel Steering Column Cover
10 Instrument Panel Steering Column Opening Cover Reinforcement
11 Instrument Panel Moulding , LH
12 Instrument Panel Cluster Finish Panel
A Tighten to 2.1-2.9 N·m (19-25 Lb-In)
B Tighten to 4-6 N·m (36-53 Lb-In)

93111GA9

Fig. 149 View of the instrument panel finish panels

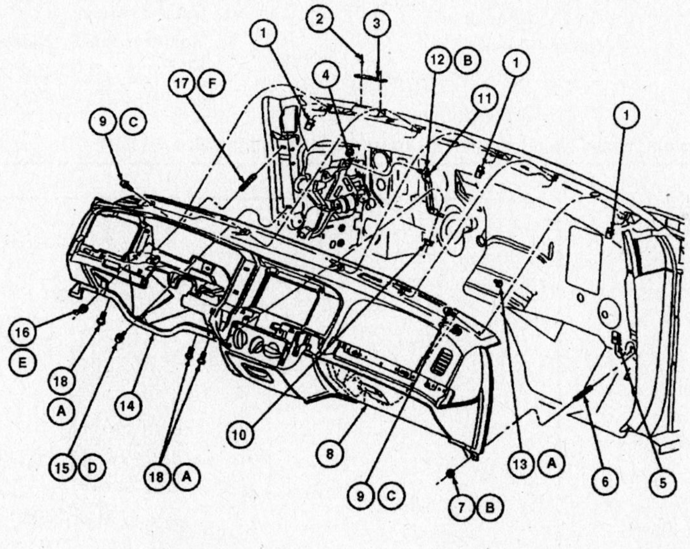

1 Nut (3 Req'd)
2 Rivet (2 Req'd)
3 Vehicle Identification Plate
4 Brake Pedal Support
5 J Nut
6 Stud
7 Nut
8 Instrument Panel
9 Screw (3 Req'd)
10 Steering Column Retaining Nut
11 Bolt (Part of 3F659)
12 Brake Pedal Support Steering Column Brace
13 Bolt (2 Req'd)
14 Instrument Panel Steering Column Opening Cover Reinforcement
15 Bolt (2 Req'd)
16 Nut
17 Stud
18 Bolt (3 Req'd)
A Tighten to 9-14 N·m (80-123 Lb-In)
B Tighten to 10-14 N·m (89-123 Lb-In)
C Tighten to 2-3 N·m (18-26 Lb-In)
D Tighten to 47-63 N·m (35-46 Lb-Ft)
E Tighten to 45-70 N·m (34-51 Lb-Ft)
F Tighten to 22-34 N·m (17-25 Lb-Ft)

93111GA0

Fig. 150 Exploded view of the instrument panel—Crown Victoria and Grand Marquis

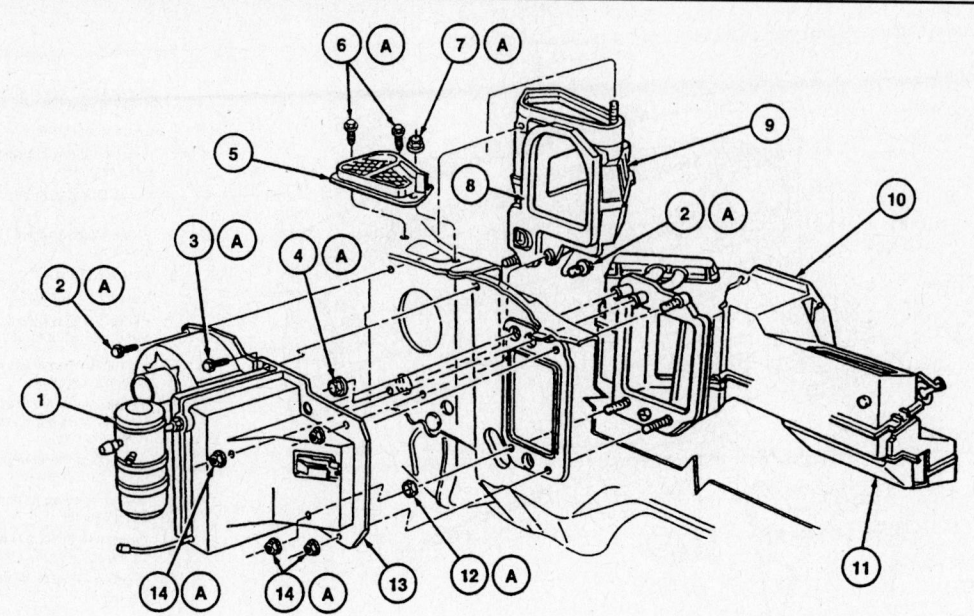

1	Suction Accumulator / Drier	9	A / C Recirculating Air Duct
2	Screw (2 Req'd)	10	Heater Air Plenum Chamber
3	Screw	11	Heater Outlet Floor Duct
4	Nut and Washer Assy	12	Nut
5	A / C Recirculating Air Duct Screen	13	A / C Evaporator Core Housing
6	Screw (2 Req'd)	14	Nut and Washer
7	Nut and Washer	A	Tighten to 2.5-3.2 N·m (23-28 Lb-In)
8	A / C Air Inlet Door Inner Seal		

93111GB1

Fig. 151 Exploded view of the heater air plenum chamber, the evaporator housing and the air inlet duct

- Electronic Automatic Temperature Control (EATC) variable blower motor controller electrical connector
- Right front wheel
- Right front fender splash shield bolts and move the shield away from the cowl
- Wiring harness from the evaporator case
- Wiring harness from the cowl
- Right side instrument panel lower insulator pushpins, disconnect the power point electrical connector, remove the courtesy lamp from the socket and remove the insulator
- Unseat the wiring grommet and feed the wiring harness through the cowl
- Cowl side trim panels and the windshield side garnish moldings from both sides
- Locking clip and the Electronic Crash Sensor (ECS) module electrical connector
- Antenna connector

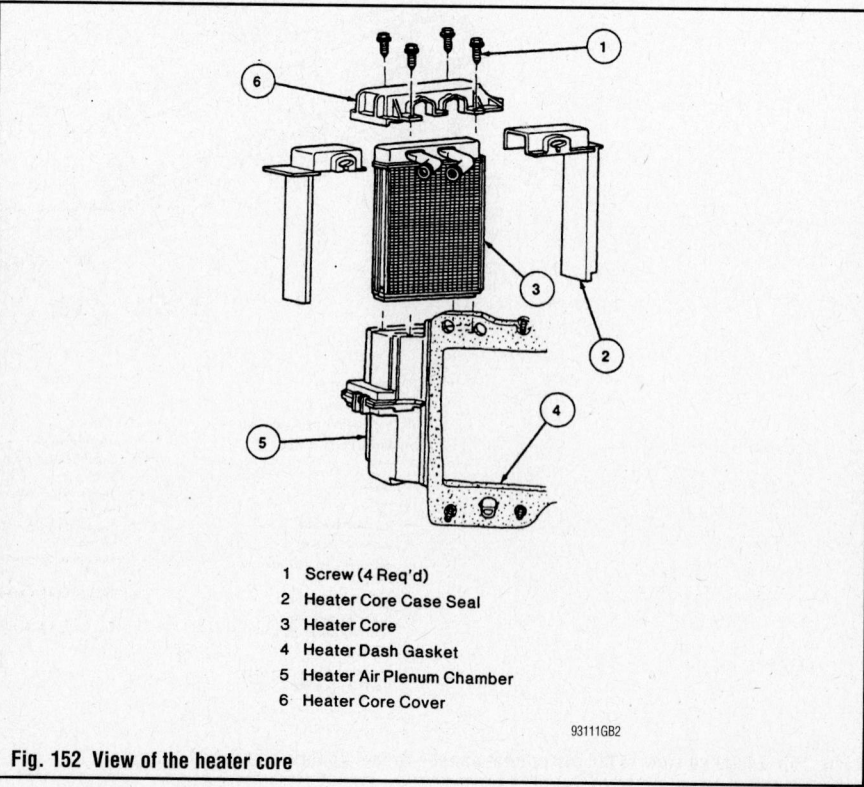

1	Screw (4 Req'd)
2	Heater Core Case Seal
3	Heater Core
4	Heater Dash Gasket
5	Heater Air Plenum Chamber
6	Heater Core Cover

93111GB2

Fig. 152 View of the heater core

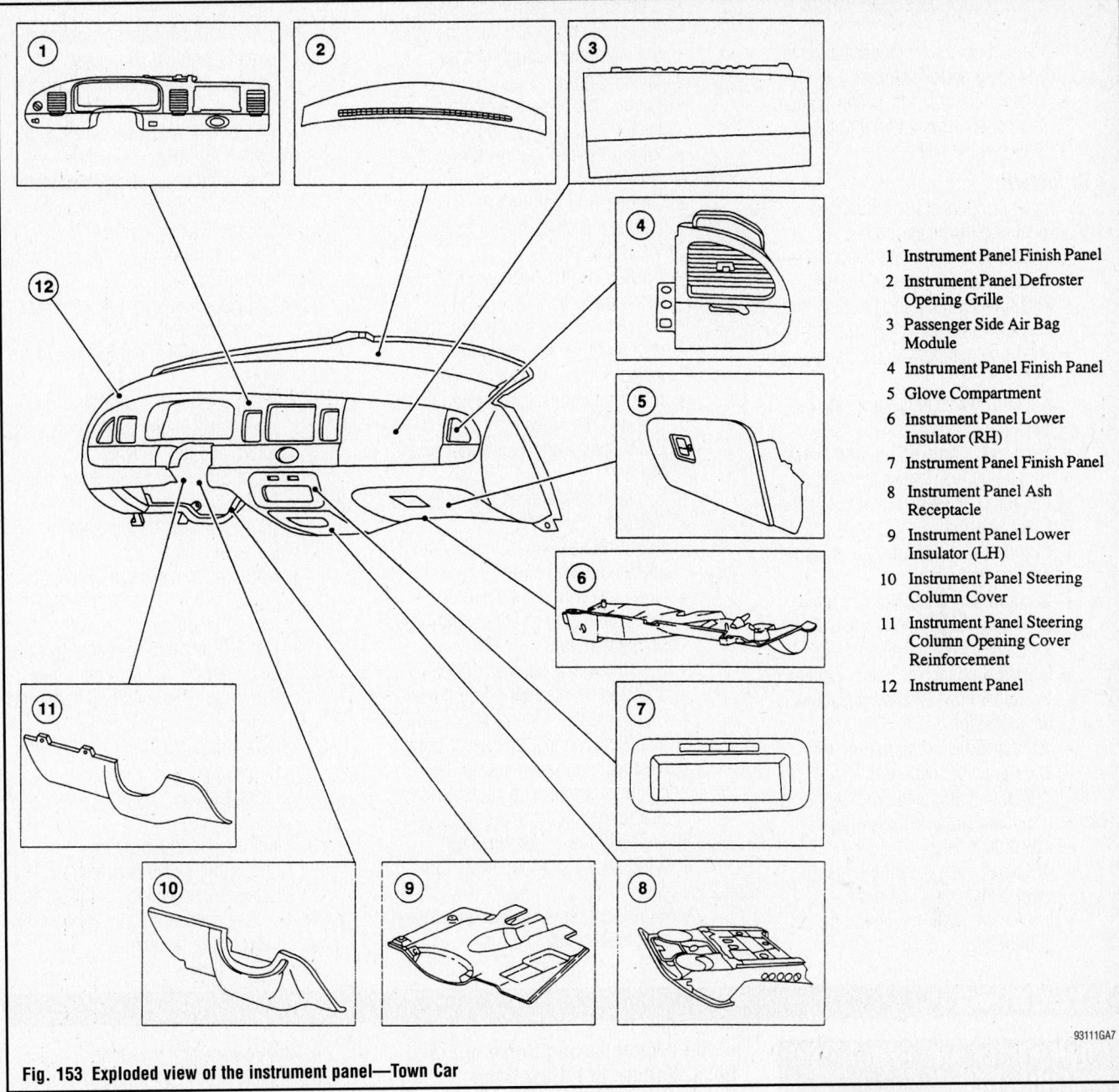

1 Instrument Panel Finish Panel

2 Instrument Panel Defroster
   Opening Grille

3 Passenger Side Air Bag
   Module

4 Instrument Panel Finish Panel

5 Glove Compartment

6 Instrument Panel Lower
   Insulator (RH)

7 Instrument Panel Finish Panel

8 Instrument Panel Ash
   Receptacle

9 Instrument Panel Lower
   Insulator (LH)

10 Instrument Panel Steering
    Column Cover

11 Instrument Panel Steering
    Column Opening Cover
    Reinforcement

12 Instrument Panel

93111GA7

Fig. 153 Exploded view of the instrument panel—Town Car

- Ground wire bolts from the right side
- EATC hose at the evaporator housing
- Bolt and disconnect the bulkhead connector from the right side
- Pull the door weatherstrip seals away from the instrument panel on both sides
- Tunnel brace trim cover
- Climate control head vacuum harness connector
- Instrument panel tunnel brace nuts and the brace
- Ground wire bolts from the left side

- Wiring harness connectors from the left side
- Parking brake switch electrical connector

 d. Pry out the instrument panel defroster opening grille, disconnect the electrical connectors and the remove the grille.

 7. Remove or disconnect the following:

- 3 upper instrument panel screws
- Instrument panel cowl side nut from both sides
- Instrument panel cowl side bolt from the left side
- Instrument panel

- Windshield wiper mounting arm and the pivot shaft
- Electrical connector and remove the upper cowl extension screw and the extension
- Vacuum hoses and the wire harness connector from the evaporative emissions canister purge valve
- Evaporative emissions purge valve nuts and the valve
- Cowl side nut
- Right side rear fender apron screws and reposition the apron
- Evaporator housing nut and screw
- Vacuum hoses and the wiring harness connectors

- Plenum chamber's lower flange nuts
- Plenum chamber's upper flange nut and the plenum chamber
- Heater core cover-to-heater plenum chamber screws and the cover
- Seal and the heater core

To install:

8. Install or connect the following:
- Seal and the heater core
- Heater core cover and the cover-to-heater plenum chamber screws
- Plenum chamber and the plenum chamber's upper flange nut
- Plenum chamber's lower flange nuts
- Vacuum hoses and the wiring harness connectors
- Evaporator housing nut and screw
- Right side rear fender apron and the apron screws
- Cowl side nut
- Evaporative emissions purge valve and the valve nuts
- Vacuum hoses and the wire harness connector to the evaporative emissions canister purge valve
- Electrical connector; then, install the upper cowl extension screw and the extension
- Windshield wiper mounting arm and the pivot shaft

9. Install the instrument panel by installing or connecting the following:
- Instrument panel
- At the left side, install the instrument panel cowl side bolt
- Instrument panel cowl side nut on both sides

- 3 upper instrument panel screws
- Electrical connectors and the install the instrument panel defroster opening grille
- Parking brake switch electrical connector
- Wiring harness connectors on the left side
- Ground wire bolts on the left side
- Instrument panel tunnel brace and the brace nuts
- Climate control head vacuum harness connector
- Install the tunnel brace trim cover.
- Door weatherstrip seals to the instrument panel on both sides
- Bulkhead connector and tighten the bolt on both sides
- EATC hose at the evaporator housing
- Ground wire bolts on the right side
- Antenna connector
- ECS module electrical connector and the locking clip
- Cowl side trim panels and the windshield side garnish moldings on both sides
- Feed the wiring harness through the cowl and seat the wiring grommet
- Right side instrument panel lower insulator, connect the power point electrical connector, install the courtesy lamp to the socket and secure the insulator with pushpins
- Wiring harness from the cowl
- Wiring harness to the evaporator case
- Right front fender splash shield and the shield bolts

- Right front wheel
- EATC variable blower motor controller electrical connector
- In-line electrical harness connector
- Air conditioning pressure cut-off switch electrical connector
- Blower motor electrical connector
- Windshield washer fluid reservoir and the reservoir screw
- Left side bulkhead connector to the dash panel
- Left side bulkhead connector and tighten the bolt
- Speed control servo and the servo nuts
- Right SRS module and torque the module-to-instrument panel bolts to 80 inch lbs. (9 Nm)
- Right SRS module electrical connector
- Glove compartment isolator
- Glove box door
- Horn switch electrical connector
- Electrical connector and install the left SRS module
- Left SRS module-to-steering wheel bolts on both sides of the wheel, and torque the bolts to 9 ft. lbs. (12 Nm)
- Rear airflow duct
- Carpeting
- Front seats
- Heater hoses

10. Refill the cooling system.
11. Connect the negative battery cable.
12. Operate the engine to normal operating temperature. Check the climate control operation and check for leaks.

STEERING

POWER RACK AND PINION STEERING GEAR

REMOVAL & INSTALLATION

See Figures 154, 155 and 156.

✳✳ CAUTION

If the vehicle is equipped with air suspension, the electrical power to the air suspension system must be shut off prior to hoisting, jacking or towing an air suspension vehicle. This can be accomplished by turning off the air suspension switch located in the luggage compartment. Failure to do so can result in unexpected inflation or deflation of the air springs, which can result in shifting

of the vehicle during these operations. Failure to follow these instructions may result in personal injury.

➡ **New O-ring seals must be installed anytime the lines are disconnected from the steering gear.**

✳✳ WARNING

The electrical power to the air suspension system must be turned off prior to hoisting, jacking or towing an air suspension vehicle. Failure to do so can result in unexpected inflation or deflation of the air springs, which can result in shifting of the vehicle during these operations.

1. Before servicing the vehicle, refer to the precautions in the beginning of this section.

2. Disconnect battery negative cable from battery and properly isolate to prevent accidental reconnection.

3. Hold the steering wheel in the straight-ahead position, using a suitable holding device.

✳✳ WARNING

Do not allow the intermediate shaft to rotate while it is disconnected from the steering gear or damage to the clockspring can result. If there is evidence that the intermediate shaft has rotated, the clockspring must be removed and recentered.

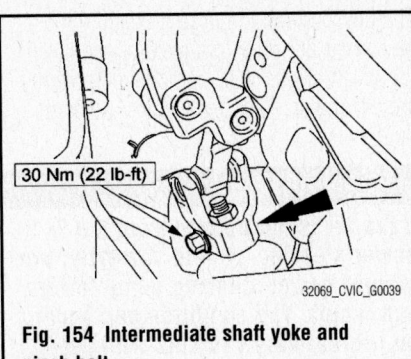

Fig. 154 Intermediate shaft yoke and pinch bolt

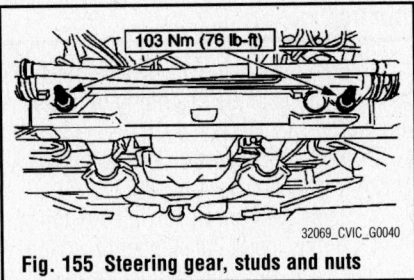

Fig. 155 Steering gear, studs and nuts

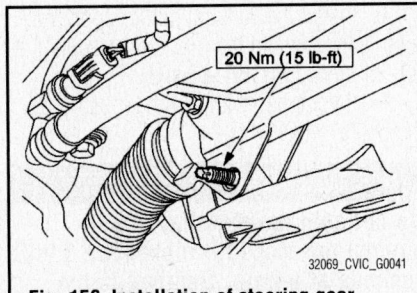

Fig. 156 Installation of steering gear studs

4. From the engine compartment, remove the pinch bolt and detach the intermediate shaft from the gear.

5. Remove the wheel and tire assemblies.

➡The hex holding feature can be used to prevent turning of the stud while removing the nut.

6. Remove the nuts and detach the tie-rods from the wheel knuckles.

7. Remove the clamp plate bolt and disconnect the steering gear lines.

8. Drain the fluid into a suitable container and discard the O-ring seals.

9. Disconnect the electrical connector.

10. Remove the steering gear-to-cross-member nuts.

11. Remove the studs and the steering gear.

To install:

12. Install or connect the following:

- Steering gear studs and torque to 15 ft. lbs. (20 Nm)
- Steering gear and torque the nuts to 76 ft. lbs. (103 Nm)
- Electrical connector
- Power steering hydraulic lines with new O-rings on both the high pressure hose and return hose
- Clamp plate and torque the nuts to 13 ft. lbs. (18 Nm)
- Tie rods and torque the nuts to 59 ft. lbs. (80 Nm)
- Tire and wheel assemblies

13. Lower the vehicle.

14. Install the steering wheel intermediate shaft and torque the pinch bolt to 22 ft. lbs. (30 Nm)

15. Ensure that the wheels and steering wheel are lined up.

16. Refill the power steering system, bleed, check for leaks and repair if necessary.

RECIRCULATING BALL POWER STEERING GEAR

REMOVAL & INSTALLATION

See Figures 157 and 158.

1. If equipped with air suspension, the air suspension switch must be turned to the **OFF** position before raising the vehicle.

2. Center the steering wheel and turn the key to the locked position.

3. Remove or disconnect the following:
- Negative battery cable
- Bolt and the intermediate shaft from the steering gear

4. On Town Car, separate the 2 halves and remove the steering gear cover.

5. Tag the power steering pressure and return lines so they may be reassembled in their original positions.

6. Place a drain pan under the steering gear

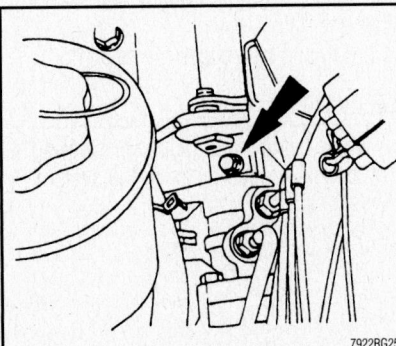

Fig. 157 Remove the bolt and separate the intermediate shaft from the steering gear input shaft

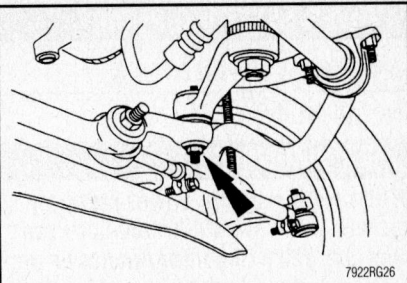

Fig. 158 Remove the locknut and separate the Pitman arm from the center link using the appropriate puller

7. Remove or disconnect the following:
- Pressure and return lines. Plug the lines and ports in the gear to prevent the entry of dirt.
- Pitman arm from the center link using a puller. It is not necessary to remove the Pitman arm from the steering gear.

8. Support the steering gear

9. Remove or disconnect the following:
- Steering gear-to-frame rail retaining bolts
- Steering gear

To install:

10. Install or connect the following:
- Steering gear on the frame rail. Tighten the steering gear-to-frame retaining bolts to 59 ft. lbs. (80 Nm).
- Pitman arm to the center link. Tighten the retaining nut to 59 ft. lbs. (80 Nm).
- Power steering pressure and return lines to the steering gear and tighten the lines to 13 ft. lbs. (18 Nm)
- Intermediate shaft to the steering gear. Tighten the bolt to 35 ft. lbs. (47 Nm).
- Negative battery cable

11. If equipped with air suspension, turn the air suspension switch to the **ON** position.

12. Fill the reservoir with the correct power steering fluid and turn the steering wheel from stop-to-stop to distribute the fluid. Check the fluid level and add fluid, if necessary.

13. Start the engine and turn the steering wheel from left to right. Check for leaks.

14. On Town Car, install the steering gear cover.

POWER STEERING PUMP

REMOVAL & INSTALLATION

See Figures 159 and 160.

> ✳ **WARNING**
>
> **While repairing the power steering system, care should be taken to prevent the entry of contaminants or premature failure of the power steering components can result.**

> ✳ **WARNING**
>
> **The electrical power to the air suspension system must be turned off prior to hoisting, jacking or towing an air suspension vehicle. Failure to do so can result in unexpected inflation or deflation of the air springs, which can result in shifting of the vehicle during these operations.**

1. Before servicing the vehicle, refer to the precautions in the beginning of this section.
2. Remove the power steering pump pulley.

> ✳ **WARNING**
>
> **Installation of a new power steering pump pulley is necessary after being removed and installed two times.**

    e. Remove the drive belt.
    f. Raise the vehicle.

> ✳ **WARNING**
>
> **Do not apply pressure on the power steering pump rotor shaft. Pressure**

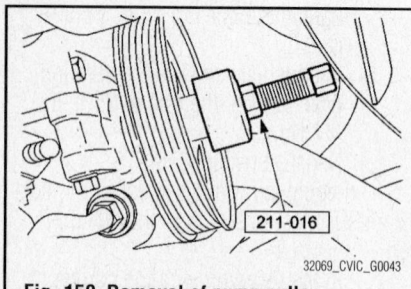

Fig. 159 Removal of pump pulley

211-016

32069_CVIC_G0043

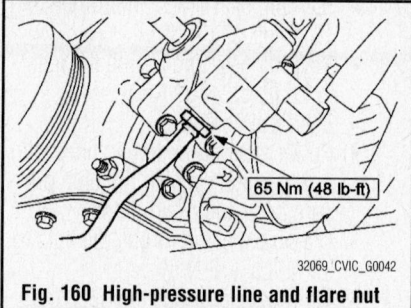

65 Nm (48 lb-ft)

32069_CVIC_G0042

Fig. 160 High-pressure line and flare nut

will damage internal thrust areas of the power steering pump.

    g. Remove the pulley with a suitable puller.
    • Inspect the pulley for paint marks in the web area near the hub. If there are two paint marks, discard the pulley. If there is no paint or one paint mark, use a paint pencil to mark the web area of the pulley near the hub.
3. Loosen the clamp and disconnect the hose and drain the fluid into a suitable container.
4. Remove the nut.
5. Disconnect the high-pressure line.
6. Remove the bolts and the power steering pump.

To install:

7. Install the power steering pump and torque the bolts to 18 ft. lbs. (25 Nm)
8. Install a new Teflon seal on the high-pressure line fitting.
9. Attach the high-pressure line and tighten the flare nut to 48 ft. lbs. (65 Nm)
10. Install the nut and torque to 62 inch lbs. (7 Nm)
11. Attach the low pressure fluid return line.
12. Attach the pump pulley and securely tighten the nut.
13. Fill and leak check the system..

BLEEDING

A whine heard from the power steering pump can be caused by air in the system.

The power steering purge procedure must be carried out prior to any component repair for which power steering noise complaints are accompanied by evidence of aerated fluid.

> ✳ **WARNING**
>
> **If the air is not purged from the power steering system correctly, premature power steering pump failure can result. The condition can occur on pre-delivery vehicles with evidence of aerated fluid or on vehicles that have had steering component repairs.**

1. Before servicing the vehicle, refer to the precautions in the beginning of this section.
2. Remove the power steering pump reservoir cap and check the fluid.
3. Raise the front wheels off the floor.
4. Tightly insert the stopper of a hand-operated vacuum pump into the reservoir.
5. Start the engine.
6. Install the vacuum pump, apply vacuum, and maintain the maximum vacuum of 20–25 inches Hg (68–85 kPa).
7. If equipped with Hydro-Boost, apply the brake pedal twice.

> ✳ **WARNING**
>
> **Do not hold the steering wheel against the stops for more than 3 to 5 seconds at a time. Damage to the power steering pump can occur.**

8. Cycle the steering wheel fully from stop-to-stop 10 times.
9. Stop the engine.
10. Release the vacuum and remove the vacuum pump and refill the reservoir as necessary.
11. Start the engine and repeat the procedure.
12. Visually inspect the power steering system for leaks.
13. Fill the reservoir as needed and visually inspect the power steering system for leaks.
14. Install the reservoir cap.

SUSPENSION **FRONT SUSPENSION**

COIL SPRING

REMOVAL & INSTALLATION

See Figures 161, 162 and 163.

❈❈ CAUTION

If the vehicle is equipped with air suspension, the electrical power to the air suspension system must be shut off prior to hoisting, jacking or towing an air suspension vehicle. This can be accomplished by turning off the air suspension switch located in the luggage compartment. Failure to do so can result in unexpected inflation or deflation of the air springs, which can result in shifting of the vehicle during these operations. Failure to follow these instructions may result in personal injury.

1. If equipped with air suspension, turn the air suspension service switch to the **OFF** position before raising the vehicle.
2. Remove or disconnect the following:
   - Wheel
   - Shock absorber
   - Center link from the Pitman arm
3. Using a spring compressor perform the following steps:
   a. Step 1: install 1 plate with the pivot ball seat facing downward into the coils of the spring. Rotate the plate so it is flush with the upper surface of the lower arm.
   b. Step 2: Install the other plate with the pivot ball seat facing upward into the coils of the spring. Insert the upper ball nut through the coils of the spring, so the nut rests in the upper plate.
   c. Step 3: Insert the compression rod into the opening in the lower arm, through the upper and lower plate and upper ball nut. Insert the securing pin through the upper ball nut and compression rod.
   d. Step 4: With the upper ball nut secured, turn the upper plate so it walks up the coil until it contacts the upper spring seat. Then, back off ½ turn.
   e. Step 5: Install the lower ball nut and thrust washer on the compression rod and screw on the forcing nut. Tighten the forcing nut until the spring is compressed enough so it is free in its seat.
4. Remove or disconnect the following:
   - 2 lower control arm pivot bolts
   - Lower arm from the frame crossmember

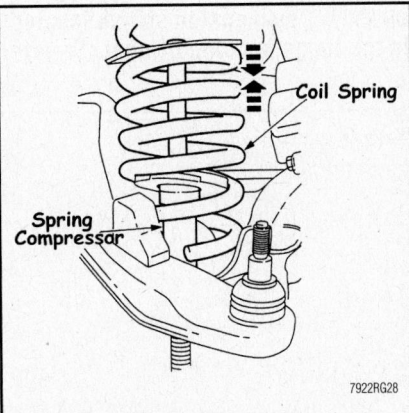

Fig. 162 Compress the coil spring until it moves away from its seat

7922RG28

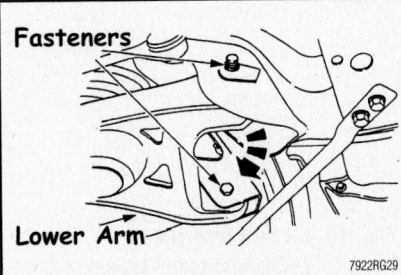

Fig. 163 Remove the fasteners attaching the lower arm to the frame, then lower the arm and remove the spring with the compressor

7922RG29

   - Coil spring
5. If a new coil spring is to be installed, mark the position of the upper and lower plates on the spring with chalk. With an assistant, compress a new spring for installation and measure the compressed length and the amount of curvature of the old spring.
6. Loosen the forcing nut to relieve the spring tension and remove the tools from the spring.

To install:

7. Assemble the spring compressor and locate in the same position as marked during disassembly.
8. Before compressing the coil spring, be sure the upper ball nut securing the pin is inserted properly.
9. Compress the coil spring until the spring height reaches the dimension measured during disassembly.
10. Position the coil spring assembly into the lower arm and position the lower arm into the frame crossmember.
11. Install both the front and rear lower control arm pivot bolts through the frame and lower arm bushings. Tighten the bolts and nuts to 111 ft. lbs. (150 Nm).
12. Remove the spring compressor from the coil spring.
13. Install or connect the following:
   - Drag link to the Pitman arm. Tighten the retaining nut to 60 ft. lbs. (80 Nm).
   - Shock absorber inside the coil spring
   - Retaining bolts
   - Wheel. Tighten the lug nuts in a star pattern to 100 ft. lbs. (136 Nm).
14. Place a washer and retaining nut on the shock absorber top stud. Tighten the nut to 30 ft. lbs. (40 Nm).
15. If equipped with air suspension, turn the air suspension switch to the **ON** position.
16. Check the front end alignment.

LOWER BALL JOINT

REMOVAL & INSTALLATION

See Figures 164 and 165.

❈❈ CAUTION

If the vehicle is equipped with air suspension, the electrical power to the air suspension system must be shut off prior to hoisting, jacking or towing an air suspension vehicle. This can be accomplished by turning

1	Upper Ball	5	Lower Ball Nut
2	Compression Rod	6	Plate
3	Forcing Nut	7	Pin
4	Thrust Washer		

7922RG27

Fig. 161 Exploded view of Spring Compressor D78P-5310-A

off the air suspension switch located in the luggage compartment. Failure to do so can result in unexpected inflation or deflation of the air springs, which can result in shifting of the vehicle during these operations. Failure to follow these instructions may result in personal injury.

→On 2005 models, the ball joint is not serviced separately. If the ball joint is faulty the lower control arm and ball joint are replaced as an assembly.

1. If equipped with air suspension, the air suspension service switch to the **OFF** position before raising the vehicle.
2. Place supports under both sides of the frame behind the lower control arms.
3. Remove or disconnect the following:
   • Wheel
   • Wheel spindle
   • Ball joint boot seal and discard
   • Ball joint

To install:

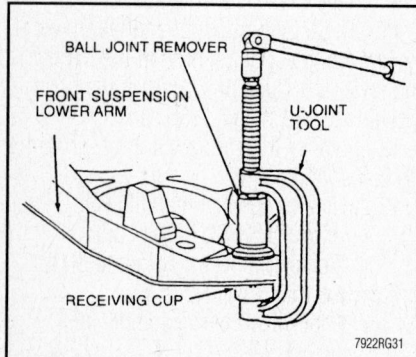

Fig. 164 Use a ball joint press to remove the ball joint from the lower control arm

→When installing a new ball joint, the protective cover should be left on to protect the ball joint seal during installation. It may be necessary to trim the cover so it can pass through the installation tool.

4. Install the ball joint.
5. Discard the protective cover and be sure the new ball joint is fully seated in the lower control arm. Ensure that the ball joint seal is not damaged.
6. Install or connect the following:
   • Wheel spindle
   • Wheel. Tighten the lug nuts in a star pattern to 100 ft. lbs. (136 Nm).
7. If equipped with air suspension, turn the air suspension service switch to the **ON** position.
8. Check the front end alignment.

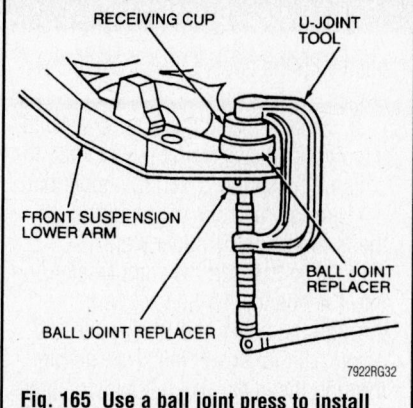

Fig. 165 Use a ball joint press to install the new ball joint into the lower control arm

LOWER CONTROL ARM

REMOVAL AND & INSTALLATION

See Figure 166.

✳✳ CAUTION

If the vehicle is equipped with air suspension, the electrical power to the air suspension system must be shut off prior to hoisting, jacking or towing an air suspension vehicle. This can be accomplished by turning off the air suspension switch located in the luggage compartment. Failure

to do so can result in unexpected inflation or deflation of the air springs, which can result in shifting of the vehicle during these operations. Failure to follow these instructions may result in personal injury.

1. If equipped with air suspension, the air suspension switch, located on the right-hand side of the luggage compartment, must be turned to the **OFF** position before raising the vehicle.
2. Remove or disconnect the following:
   • Front wheel
   • Wheel speed sensor
   • Brake caliper and rotor
   • Sway bar link
   • Shock absorber
   • Drag link
   • Lower ball joint
   • Coil spring
   • Lower control arm pivot bolts
   • Lower control arm

To install:
3. Install or connect the following:
   • Lower control arm. Tighten the pivot bolts to 111 ft. lbs. (150 Nm).
   • Coil spring
   • Lower ball joint. Tighten the nut to 111 ft. lbs. (150 Nm).
   • Shock absorber lower nut and flag

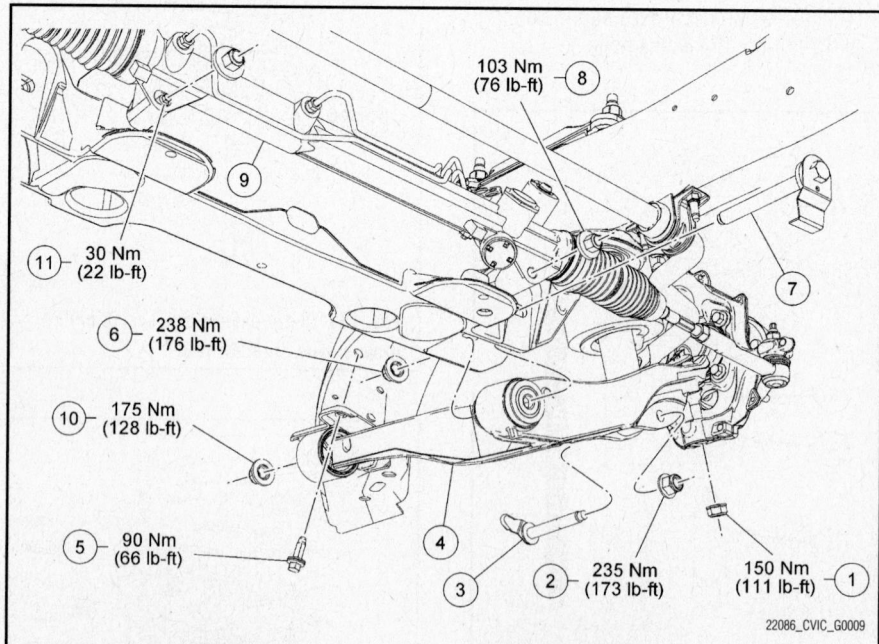

Fig. 166
1. Lower ball joint nut
2. Shock absorber lower nut
3. Shock absorber lower flag bolt
4. Lower arm
5. Lower bushing bracket bolt (3 required)
6. Lower arm cam nut
7. Lower arm cam bolt
8. Steering gear nut (2 required)
9. Steering gear
10. Lower arm bushing nut
11. Steering gear studs (2 required)

bolt. Tighten to 176 ft. lbs. (238 Nm).
- 3 lower arm bracket bolts. Tighten to 66 ft. lbs. (90 Nm).
- 2 steering gear nuts. Tighten to 76 ft. lbs. (103 Nm).
- Power steering rack studs. Tighten to 22 ft. lbs. (30 Nm).
- Brake caliper and rotor
- Wheel speed sensor
- Front wheel

4. If equipped with air suspension, turn the air suspension service switch to the **ON** position.

5. Align the vehicle.

CONTROL ARM BUSHING REPLACEMENT

The control arm bushings are serviced with the control arm as an assembly.

SHOCK ABSORBERS

REMOVAL & INSTALLATION

※ CAUTION

If the vehicle is equipped with air suspension, the electrical power to the air suspension system must be shut off prior to hoisting, jacking or towing an air suspension vehicle. This can be accomplished by turning off the air suspension switch located in the luggage compartment. Failure to do so can result in unexpected inflation or deflation of the air springs, which can result in shifting of the vehicle during these operations. Failure to follow these instructions may result in personal injury.

1. If equipped with air suspension, the air suspension switch, located on the right-hand side of the luggage compartment, must be turned to the **OFF** position before raising the vehicle.

2. Remove or disconnect the following:
- Nut, washer and bushing from the upper end of the shock absorber
- 2 bolts retaining the shock absorber to the lower control arm
- Shock absorber

To install:

3. Prior to installation, prime the new shock absorber. Fully extend the shock absorber while in the right side up (installed) position. Turn the shock absorber upside down and fully compress it. Repeat the procedure at least 3 times to purge any air trapped in the shock absorber.

4. Install or connect the following:

- New bushing and washer on the stud on the top of the new shock absorber and position the unit inside the front coil spring
- 2 lower retaining bolts and tighten them to 10–12 ft lbs. (13–17 Nm).
- New bushing and washer on the shock absorber top stud
- New retaining nut. Tighten the retaining nut to 28 ft. lbs. (40 Nm).

5. If equipped with air suspension, turn the air suspension switch to the **ON** position.

STABILIZER BAR

REMOVAL & INSTALLATION
See Figure 167.

※ WARNING

The electrical power to the air suspension system must be turned off prior to hoisting, jacking or towing an air suspension vehicle. Failure to do so can result in unexpected inflation or deflation of the air springs, which can result in shifting of the vehicle during these operations.

※ WARNING

Suspension fasteners are critical parts because they affect performance of vital components and systems and their failure can result in major service expense. A new part with the same part number must be installed if installation becomes necessary. If substitution is necessary, the part must be of the same finish and property class. Torque values must be used as specified during reassembly to make sure of correct retention of these parts.

1. Before servicing the vehicle, refer to the precautions in the beginning of this section.

2. Disconnect battery negative cable from battery and properly isolate to prevent accidental reconnection.

3. Turn the air suspension service switch off.

4. Raise the vehicle on a hoist.

➡**Use the hex holding feature to prevent the stud from turning while removing the nut.**

5. Remove or disconnect the following:
- Two nuts holding the stabilizer bar end links and discard.
- Stabilizer bar end links

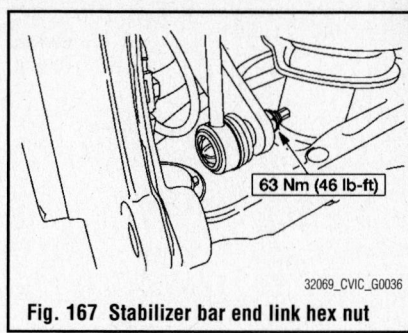
63 Nm (46 lb-ft)

32069_CVIC_G0036

Fig. 167 Stabilizer bar end link hex nut

- Four nuts holding the stabilizer bar brackets and discard.
- Stabilizer bar brackets
- Stabilizer bar

To install:

6. Install or connect the following:
- Stabilizer bar
- Stabilizer bar brackets with new nuts and torque to 46 ft. lbs. (63 Nm)
- Stabilizer bar end links with new nuts and torque to 46 ft. lbs. (63 Nm)

7. Turn air suspension switch on.

STEERING KNUCKLE

REMOVAL & INSTALLATION
See Figure 168.

※ CAUTION

If the vehicle is equipped with air suspension, the electrical power to the air suspension system must be shut off prior to hoisting, jacking or towing an air suspension vehicle. This can be accomplished by turning off the air suspension switch located in the luggage compartment. Failure to do so can result in unexpected inflation or deflation of the air springs, which can result in shifting of the vehicle during these operations. Failure to follow these instructions may result in personal injury.

1. If equipped with air suspension, the air suspension switch, located on the right-hand side of the luggage compartment, must be turned to the **OFF** position before raising the vehicle.

2. Remove or disconnect the following:
- Wheel bearing and hub
- Tie rod from knuckle

3. Raise the suspension arms and place a jack under them to release pressure from the stabilizer bar links.

4. Remove the upper control arm center nut.

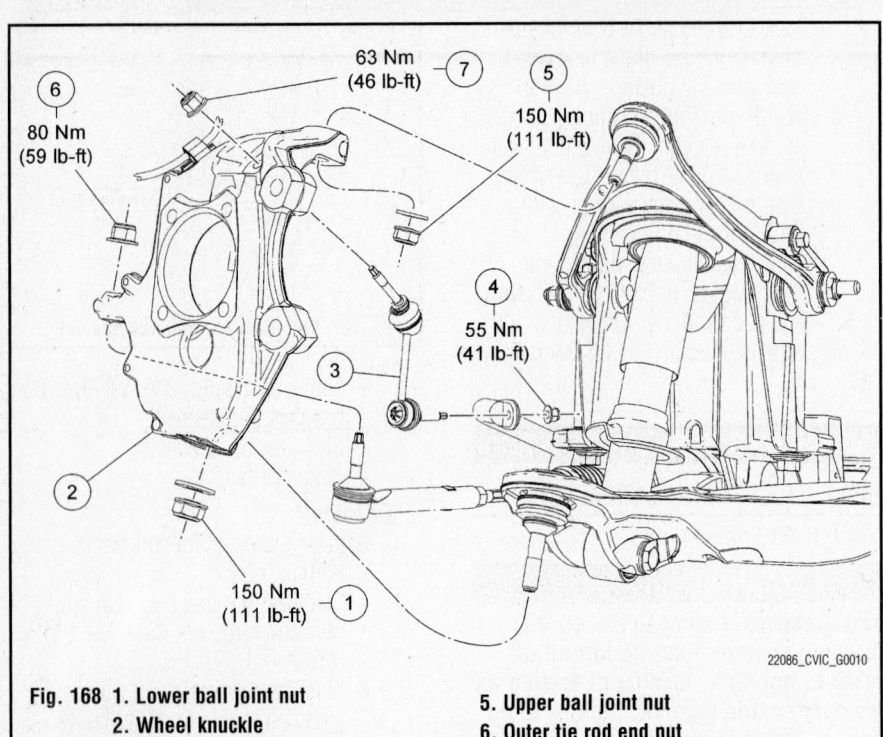

Fig. 168   1. Lower ball joint nut
2. Wheel knuckle
3. Stabilizer bar link
4. Lower stabilizer bar link nut

5. Upper ball joint nut
6. Outer tie rod end nut
7. Upper stabilizer bar link nut

63 Nm (46 lb-ft)
80 Nm (59 lb-ft)
150 Nm (111 lb-ft)
55 Nm (41 lb-ft)
150 Nm (111 lb-ft)

22086_CVIC_G0010

5. Remove the stabilizer bar link nut and discard.

6. Disconnect the brake line retainer.

7. Remove the steering knuckle nuts and remove the steering knuckle.

To install:

8. Install or connect the following:
- Steering knuckle and tighten the nuts to 111 ft. lbs. (150 Nm).
- Brake line retainer.
- Outer stabilizer bar link using a new nut and tighten to 46 ft. lbs. (63 Nm).
- Inner stabilizer bar link using a new nut and tighten to 41 ft. lbs. (55 Nm).
- Upper control arm center nut and tighten to 46 ft. lbs. (63 Nm).
- Tie rod to knuckle and tighten to 59 ft. lbs. (80 Nm).
- Wheel bearing and hub

9. If equipped with air suspension, turn the air suspension switch to the **ON** position.

UPPER BALL JOINT

REMOVAL & INSTALLATION

✳✳ CAUTION

If the vehicle is equipped with air suspension, the electrical power to the air suspension system must be shut off prior to hoisting, jacking or towing an air suspension vehicle. This can be accomplished by turning off the air suspension switch located in the luggage compartment. Failure to do so can result in unexpected inflation or deflation of the air springs, which can result in shifting of the vehicle during these operations. Failure to follow these instructions may result in personal injury.

➡On 2005 models, the ball joint is not serviced separately. If the ball joint is faulty the upper control arm and ball joint are replaced as an assembly.

1. If equipped with air suspension, the air suspension switch to the **OFF** position before raising the vehicle.

2. Place supports under both sides of the frame just behind the lower control arms.

3. Remove the wheel.

4. Place a floor jack under the lower control arm at the lower ball joint area. The floor jack will support the spring load on the lower control arm.

5. Remove the retaining nut and pinch bolt from the upper ball joint stud.

6. Mark the position of the alignment cams. When replacing the upper ball joint this will approximate the current alignment.

7. Remove or disconnect the following:
- 2 nuts retaining the upper ball joint to the upper control arm

- Upper ball joint from the upper control arm and spread the slot in the wheel spindle with a pry bar to remove the ball joint stud from the wheel spindle.

To install:

8. Install or connect the following:
- Upper ball joint to the upper control arm
- Ball stud into the wheel spindle
- Upper ball joint pinch bolt and retaining nut. Tighten to 59 ft. lbs. (80 Nm).
- Alignment cams to the approximate position at removal. If not marked, install in the neutral positions.
- 2 nuts retaining the upper ball joint to the upper control arm. Hold the cams and tighten the nuts to 111 ft. lbs. (150 Nm).
- Wheel and tire assembly. Tighten the lug nuts in a star pattern to 100 ft. lbs. (136 Nm).

9. Remove the floor jack from under the lower control arm.

10. If equipped with air suspension, turn the air suspension switch to the **ON** position.

11. Check and adjust the front wheel alignment.

UPPER CONTROL ARM

REMOVAL & INSTALLATION

See Figure 169.

✳✳ CAUTION

If the vehicle is equipped with air suspension, the electrical power to the air suspension system must be shut off prior to hoisting, jacking or towing an air suspension vehicle. This can be accomplished by turning off the air suspension switch located in the luggage compartment. Failure to do so can result in unexpected inflation or deflation of the air springs, which can result in shifting of the vehicle during these operations. Failure to follow these instructions may result in personal injury.

1. If equipped with air suspension, the air suspension switch, located on the right-hand side of the luggage compartment, must be turned to the **OFF** position before raising the vehicle.

2. Remove or disconnect the following:
- Front wheel
- Upper ball joint. Support the lower control arm.
- Upper control arm pivot bolts

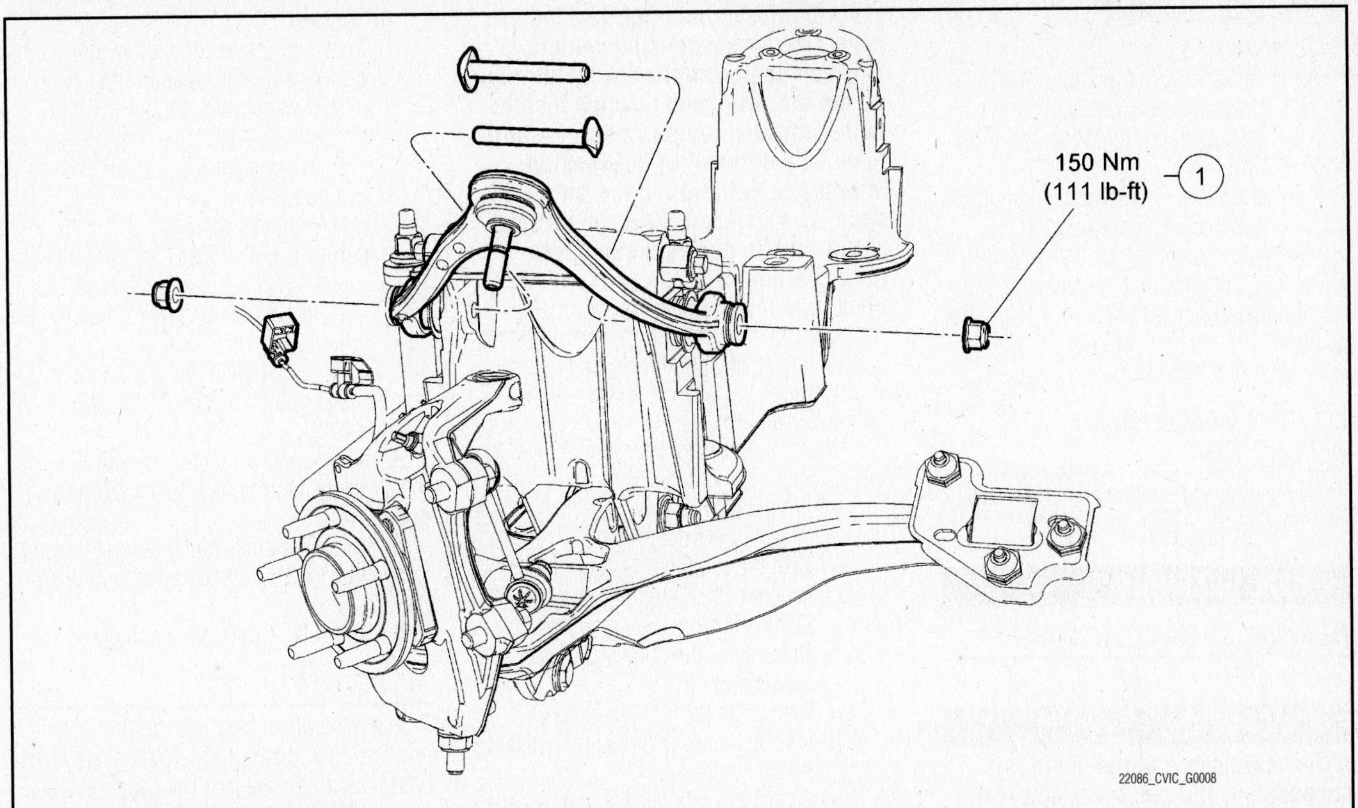

150 Nm
(111 lb-ft) — 1

22086_CVIC_G0008

Fig. 169 Upper control arm assembly

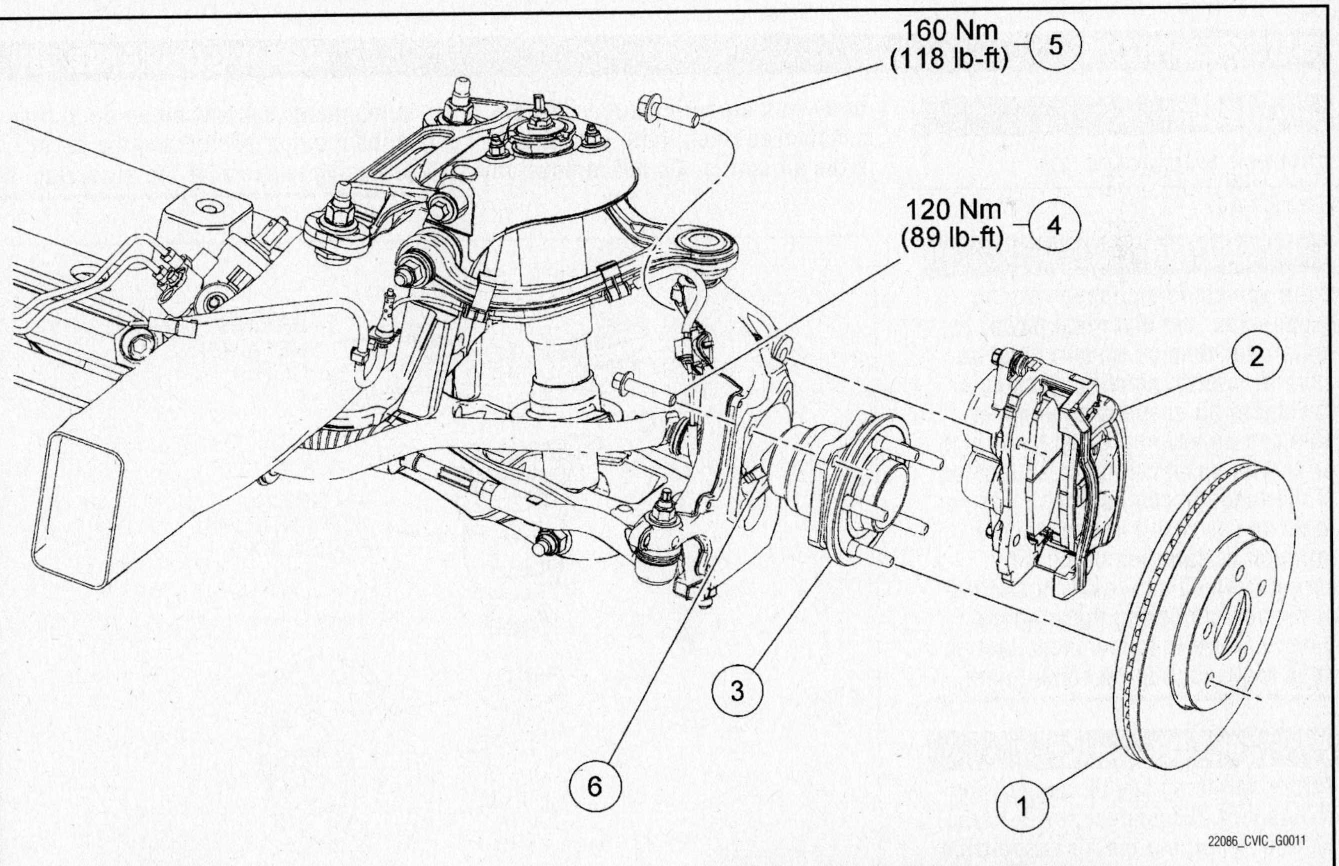

160 Nm
(118 lb-ft) — 5

120 Nm
(89 lb-ft) — 4

22086_CVIC_G0011

Fig. 170 1. Brake disc
2. Brake caliper
3. Wheel bearing and wheel hub assembly
4. Wheel bearing and wheel hub assembly bolt
5. Brake caliper and anchor plate bolt (2 required)
6. Wheel speed sensor electrical connector

- Upper control arm

To install:

3. Install or connect the following:
- Upper control arm. Tighten the pivot bolts (1) to 111 ft. lbs. (150 Nm).
- Upper ball joint. Tighten the pinch bolt to 59 ft. lbs. (80 Nm).
- Front wheel

4. If equipped with air suspension, turn the air suspension service switch to the **ON** position.

5. Align the vehicle.

CONTROL ARM BUSHING REPLACEMENT

The control arm bushings are serviced with the control arm as an assembly.

WHEEL BEARINGS

REMOVAL & INSTALLATION

See Figure 170.

> **✳✳ CAUTION**
>
> If the vehicle is equipped with air suspension, the electrical power to the air suspension system must be

shut off prior to hoisting, jacking or towing an air suspension vehicle. This can be accomplished by turning off the air suspension switch located in the luggage compartment. Failure to do so can result in unexpected inflation or deflation of the air springs, which can result in shifting of the vehicle during these operations. Failure to follow these instructions may result in personal injury.

1. If equipped, turn the air suspension service switch to the **OFF** position before raising the vehicle.

2. Remove or disconnect the following
- Front wheel
- Grease cap from the hub
- Disc brake caliper. Suspend the caliper with a length of wire. Do not let it hang from the brake hose. Discard the disc brake caliper mounting bolts.
- Disc brake rotor. If the factory installed push on nuts are installed, remove them first.
- Wheel hub retainer nut and discard
- Hub and bearing assembly

To install:

3. Install or connect the following:
- Hub and bearing assembly
- New wheel hub retainer nut and tighten to 118 ft. lbs. (160 Nm)
- Disc brake rotor and push on nuts, if equipped
- New grease cap seal
- Disc brake caliper using the 2 new disc brake caliper mounting bolts. Tighten the bolts to 89 ft. lbs. (120 Nm).
- Wheel. Tighten the lug nuts in a star pattern to 100 ft. lbs. (136 Nm).

4. If equipped with air suspension, turn the air suspension switch to the **ON** position.

5. Pump the brake pedal several times to position the brake pads prior to moving the vehicle.

6. Check the front end alignment.

ADJUSTMENT

The front wheel bearings are of a hub unit design and are pre-greased, sealed and require no maintenance. The bearings are preset and cannot be adjusted.

SUSPENSION

AIR SPRING

REMOVAL & INSTALLATION

See Figure 171.

> **✳ CAUTION**
>
> If the vehicle is equipped with air suspension, the electrical power to the air suspension system must be shut off prior to hoisting, jacking or towing an air suspension vehicle. This can be accomplished by turning off the air suspension switch located in the luggage compartment. Failure to do so can result in unexpected inflation or deflation of the air springs, which can result in shifting of the vehicle during these operations. Failure to follow these instructions may result in personal injury.

> **✳ CAUTION**
>
> Before servicing any air suspension component, disconnect power to the system by turning the air suspension service switch OFF or by disconnecting the negative battery cable. Do not

remove an air spring under any circumstances when there is pressure in the air spring. Do not remove any

REAR SUSPENSION

components supporting an air spring without either exhausting the air or providing support for the air spring.

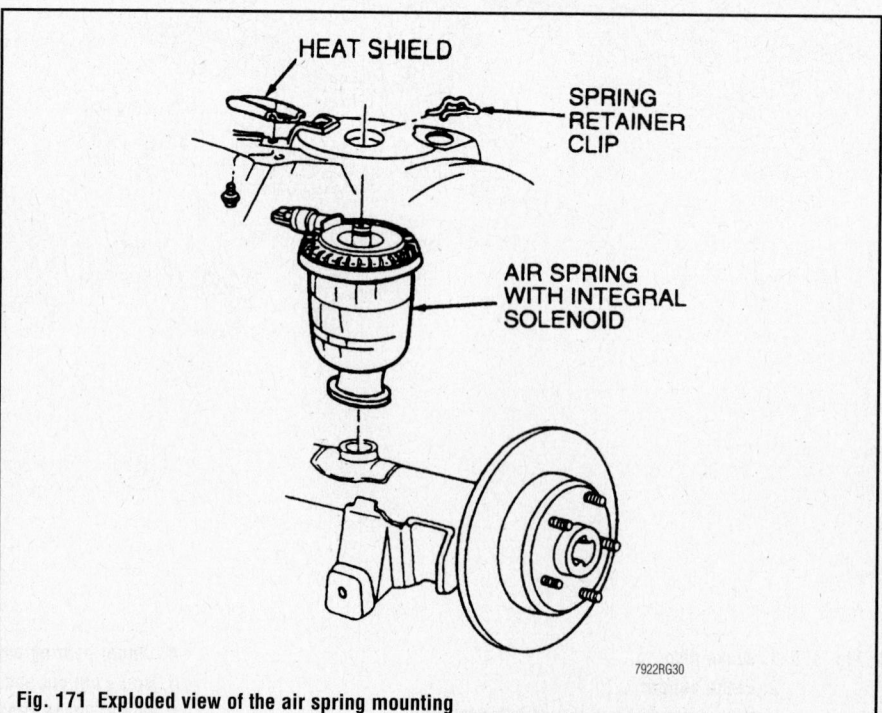

Fig. 171 Exploded view of the air spring mounting

HEAT SHIELD

SPRING RETAINER CLIP

AIR SPRING WITH INTEGRAL SOLENOID

7922RG30

1. Turn the air suspension switch to the **OFF** position.

2. Raise and safely support the vehicle so the suspension is fully down with no load.

3. Remove or disconnect the following:
   - Heat shield, as required
   - Spring retainer clip
   - Air spring solenoid valve electrical connector
   - Air line
   - Air spring solenoid retainer

4. Rotate the solenoid valve counterclockwise to the first stop.

5. Pull the solenoid valve straight out slowly to the second stop to bleed air from the system.

✳✳ CAUTION

Do not fully release the solenoid until the air is completely bled from the air spring or personal injury may result.

6. After the air is fully bled from the system, rotate the solenoid valve counterclockwise to the third stop and remove the solenoid valve from the solenoid housing. Remove the large O-ring from the solenoid housing.

7. Remove the air spring.

To install:

8. Check the solenoid valve O-rings for cuts or abrasions. Replace the O-rings as required. Lightly grease the O-ring area of the solenoid valve and the larger solenoid housing O-ring with silicone dielectric compound.

9. Insert the solenoid into the air spring end cap and rotate clockwise to the third stop, push in to the second stop, then rotate clockwise to the first stop.

10. Install or connect the following:
   - Air spring solenoid retainer. Inspect the wiring harness connector and ensure the rubber gasket is in place at the bottom of the connector cavity
   - Air spring into the frame (upper) spring seat, taking care to keep the solenoid air and electrical connections clean and free of damage
   - Push-on ring spring retainer clip to the knob of the spring cap from the top side of the frame spring seat
   - Air line and electrical connector to the solenoid
   - Heat shield to the frame spring seat, if removed

- Align the air spring piston-to-axle (lower) seat. Squeeze to increase pressure and push downward on the piston, snapping the piston to the axle seat at rebound and supported by the shock absorber.
- Negative battery cable.

✳✳ WARNING

The air springs may be damaged if the suspension is allowed to compress before the spring is inflated.

11. Refill the air spring as follows:
   a. Step 1: Turn the air suspension switch to the **ON** position. The ignition switch must be **ON** and the engine running or a battery charger must be connected to the battery to reduce battery drain.

   b. Step 2: Fold back or remove the right-hand luggage compartment trim panel and connect Super Star II Tester 007-0041-A to the air suspension DLC, which is located near the air suspension switch.

   c. Step 3: Set the tester to EEC-IV/MCU mode. Also set the tester to FAST mode. Release the tester button to the HOLD (up) position and turn the tester **ON**.

   d. Step 4: Depress the tester button to TEST (down) position. A Code 10 will be displayed. Within 2 minutes a Code 13 will be displayed. After Code 13 is displayed, release the tester button to the HOLD (up) position, wait 5 seconds and depress the tester button to TEST (down) position. Ignore any codes displayed.

   e. Step 5: Release the tester button to the HOLD (up) position. Wait at least 20 seconds, and then depress the tester button to TEST (down) position. Within 10 seconds, the codes will be displayed in the order shown.

   f. Step 6: Within 4 seconds after Code 26 is displayed, release the tester button to the HOLD (up) position. Waiting longer than 4 seconds may result in Functional Test 31 being entered. The compressor will fill the air springs with air as long as the tester button is in the HOLD (up) position. To stop filling the air springs, depress the tester button to the TEST (down) position.

   g. Step 7: To exit Functional Test 26, disconnect the tester and turn the ignition switch to the **OFF** position.

12. Install the luggage trim panel, if removed.

COIL SPRING

REMOVAL & INSTALLATION
See Figure 172.

✳✳ CAUTION

If the vehicle is equipped with air suspension, the electrical power to the air suspension system must be shut off prior to hoisting, jacking or towing an air suspension vehicle. This can be accomplished by turning off the air suspension switch located in the luggage compartment. Failure to do so can result in unexpected inflation or deflation of the air springs, which can result in shifting of the vehicle during these operations. Failure to follow these instructions may result in personal injury.

1. Place a hoist under the rear axle housing and raise and safely support the vehicle.

2. Support the frame side rails with 2 jack stands.

3. Remove or disconnect the following:
   - Rear stabilizer bar
   - Lower studs of both rear shock absorbers from the mounting brackets on the axle tube
   - Parking brake cable from the upper arm retainer before lowering the axle housing

4. Lower the axle housing until the coil springs are released. If the axle housing is supported by the hoist, lower the hoist allowing the rear of the vehicle to rest on the jack stands. If the vehicle's axle housing is supported by the jack stands, leave the hoist stationary and lower the jack stands or raise the hoist to release the tension on the coil springs.

5. Remove the coil springs and insulators.

To install:

6. Install or connect the following:
   - Coil spring in the upper and lower seats with an insulator between the upper end of the spring and frame seat
   - Axle housing and connect the lower studs of the shock absorbers to the mounting brackets
   - Parking cable into the upper arm retainer
   - Sway bar

7. Road test the vehicle and check for proper operation.

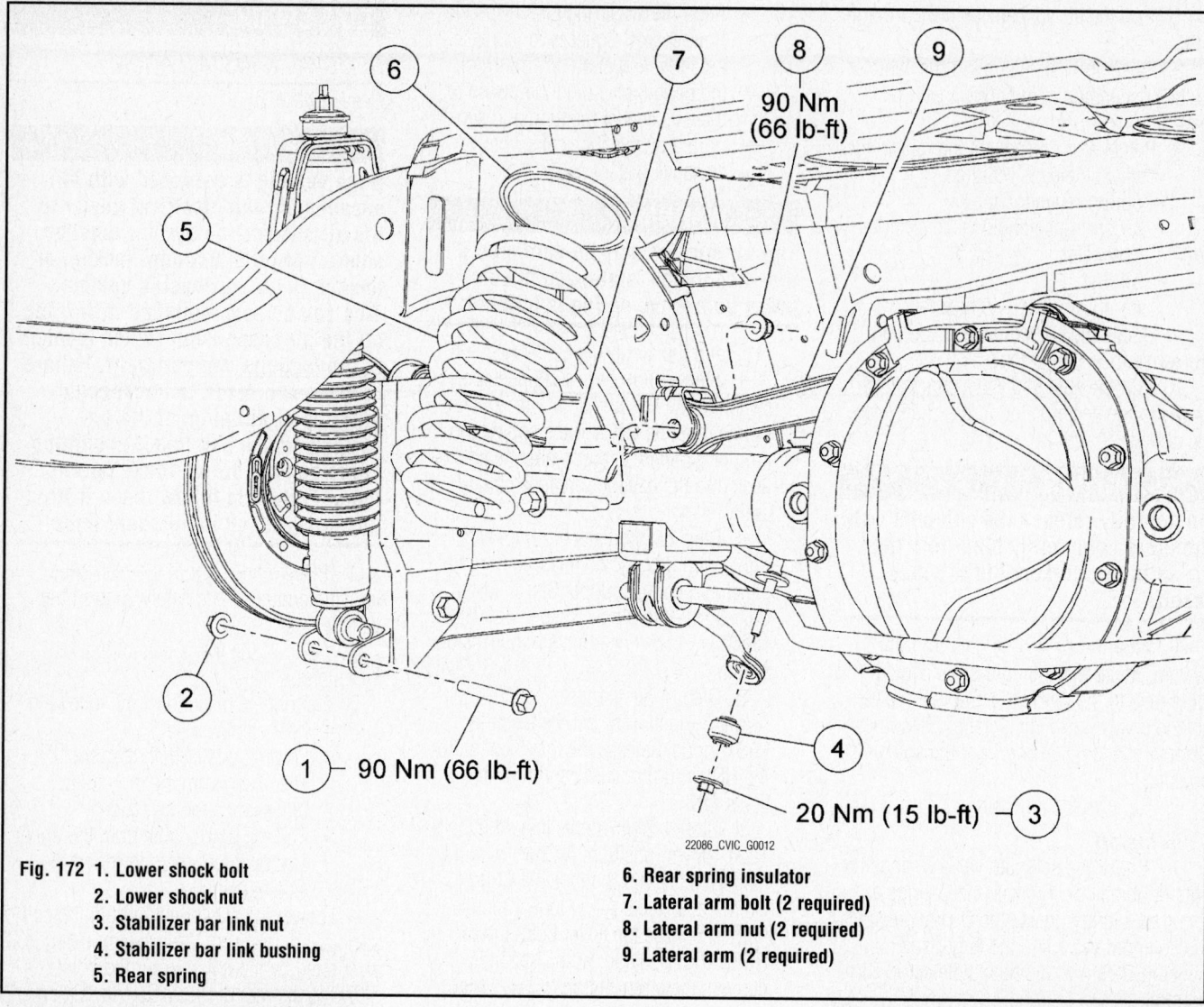

Fig. 172 1. Lower shock bolt
2. Lower shock nut
3. Stabilizer bar link nut
4. Stabilizer bar link bushing
5. Rear spring
6. Rear spring insulator
7. Lateral arm bolt (2 required)
8. Lateral arm nut (2 required)
9. Lateral arm (2 required)

SHOCK ABSORBER

REMOVAL & INSTALLATION
See Figure 173.

✱✱ CAUTION

If the vehicle is equipped with air suspension, the electrical power to the air suspension system must be shut off prior to hoisting, jacking or towing an air suspension vehicle. This can be accomplished by turning off the air suspension switch located in the luggage compartment. Failure to do so can result in unexpected inflation or deflation of the air springs, which can result in shifting of the vehicle during these operations. Failure to follow these instructions may result in personal injury.

1. If equipped with air suspension, turn the air suspension service switch **OFF**.

2. Be sure the ignition switch is in the **OFF** position.
3. Support the rear axle assembly with a jack.
4. Remove or disconnect the following:
   • Top retaining nut, washer and bushing
   • Bottom retaining nut and washer
   • Shock absorber

To install:
5. Install or connect the following:
   • Shock absorber so the upper stud enters the hole in the frame
   • Top bushing, washer and retaining nut. Tighten to 30 ft. lbs. (40 Nm).
6. Extend the shock absorber and place the lower stud through the hole in the bracket
7. Bottom retaining washer and nut. Tighten to 66 ft. lbs. (90 Nm).
8. Remove the jack from the axle assembly.
9. Turn the air suspension service switch to the **ON** position.

WHEEL BEARINGS

REMOVAL & INSTALLATION
See Figures 174, 175 and 176.

✱✱ CAUTION

If the vehicle is equipped with air suspension, the electrical power to the air suspension system must be shut off prior to hoisting, jacking or towing an air suspension vehicle. This can be accomplished by turning off the air suspension switch located in the luggage compartment. Failure to do so can result in unexpected inflation or deflation of the air springs, which can result in shifting of the vehicle during these operations. Failure to follow these instructions may result in personal injury.

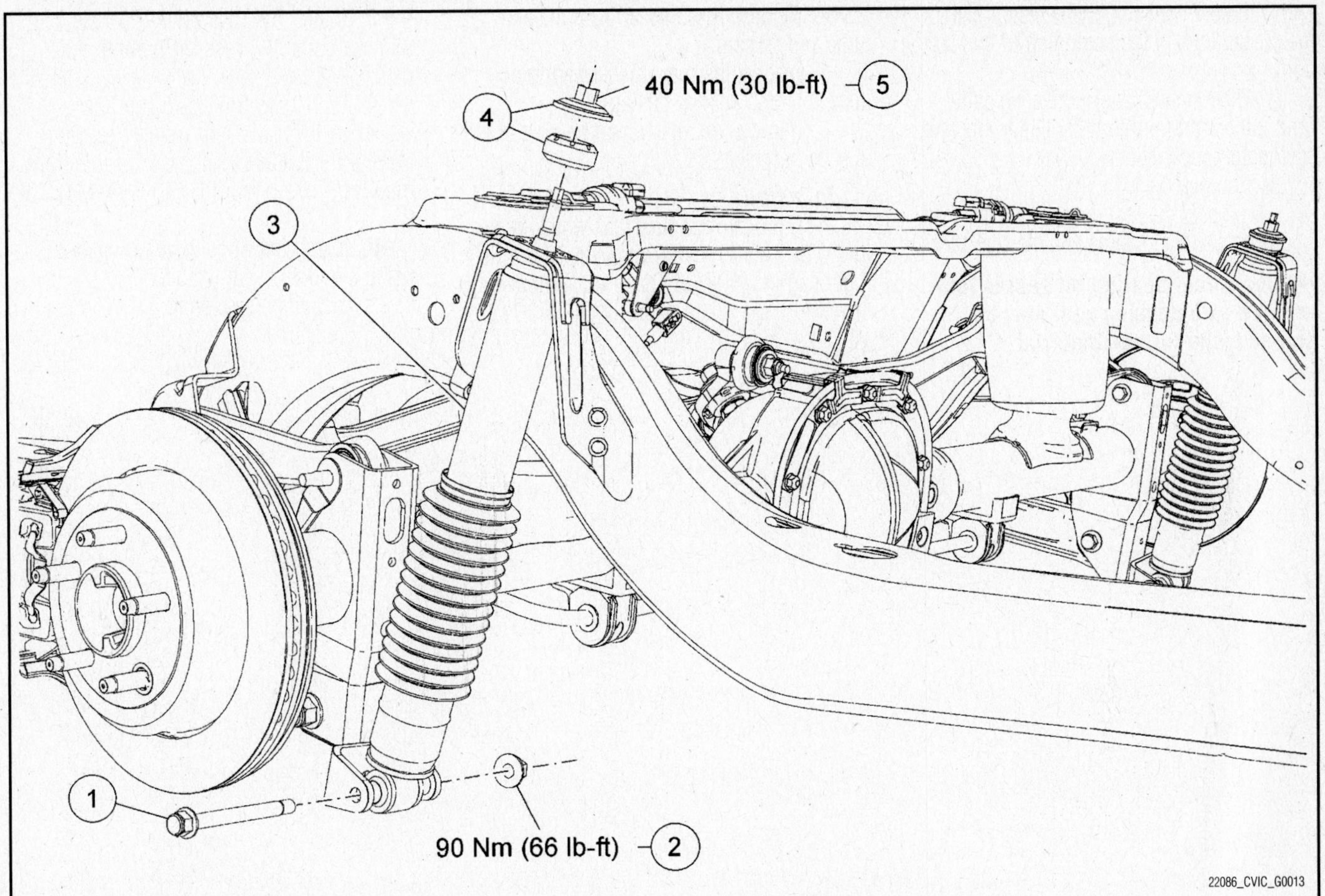

40 Nm (30 lb-ft) — ⑤

④

③

① 90 Nm (66 lb-ft) — ②

22086_CVIC_G0013

Fig. 173 1. Lower shock bolt
2. Lower shock nut
3. Shock absorber assembly

4. Shock washer and insulator
5. Upper shock nut

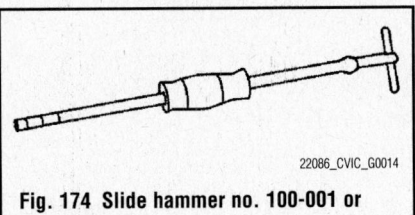

22086_CVIC_G0014

Fig. 174 Slide hammer no. 100-001 or equivalent

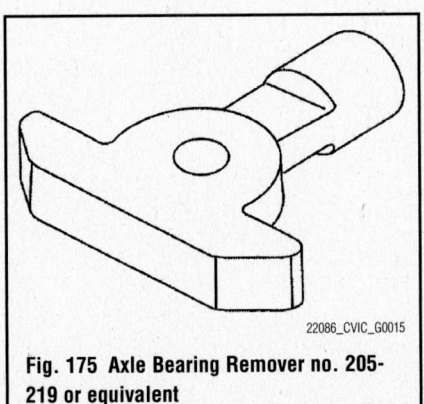

22086_CVIC_G0015

Fig. 175 Axle Bearing Remover no. 205-219 or equivalent

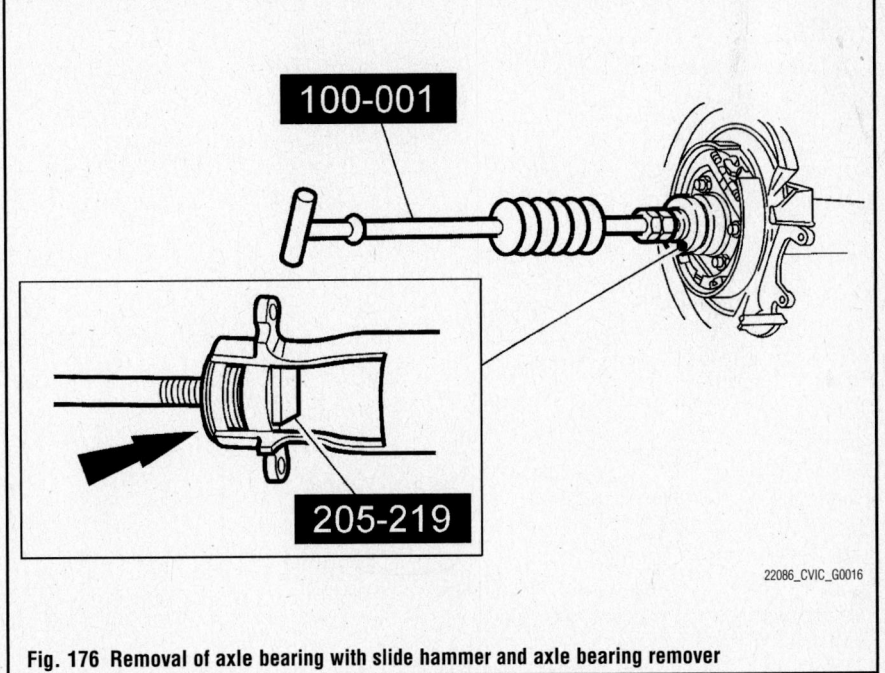

100-001

205-219

22086_CVIC_G0016

Fig. 176 Removal of axle bearing with slide hammer and axle bearing remover

1. Before servicing the vehicle, refer to the precautions in the beginning of this section.

2. Disconnect battery negative cable from battery and properly isolate to prevent accidental reconnection.

3. Remove the axle shaft.

  a. If only the seal needs to be replaced, use care to avoid damaging the seal bore.

➡ **If the wheel bearing oil seal is leaking, the axle housing vent may be plugged with foreign material.**

4. Remove the oil seal from the axle tube and discard.

5. Inspect the rear wheel bearing and axle shaft for wear or damage.

6. Remove the rear wheel bearing using a slide hammer.

To install:

7. Lubricate the new rear wheel bearing with SAE 80W-90 Premium Rear Axle Lubricant XY-80W90-QL or equivalent meeting Ford specification WSP-M2C197-A.

8. Install the rear wheel bearing using a suitable press or hammer and drift.

9. Lubricate the lip of the new wheel bearing oil seal using Premium Long-Life Grease XG-1-C or equivalent meeting Ford specification ESA-M1C75-B.

10. Install the wheel bearing oil seal using a suitable seal installer.

11. Install the axle shaft.

FORD AND LINCOLN

Edge • MKX

3

SPECIFICATIONS AND MAINTENANCE CHARTS

ENGINE AND VEHICLE IDENTIFICATION CHART

		Engine Code					Model Year	
Code	Liters (cc)	Cu. In.	Cyl.	Fuel Sys.	Engine Type	Eng. Mfg.	Code ①	Year
C	3.5 (3500)	214	6	SMFI	DOHC	Ford Motor Co.	7	2007

DOHC: Double Overhead Cam

SMFI: Sequential Multi-port Fuel Injection

① 10th position of VIN

GENERAL ENGINE SPECIFICATIONS

Year	Model	Engine Displacement Liters (VIN)	Net Horsepower @ rpm	Net Torque @ rpm (ft. lbs.)	Bore x Stroke (in.)	Com-pression Ratio	Oil Pressure @ rpm
2007	Edge	3.5 (C)	265@6250	250@4500	3.64x3.41	10.3:1	NA
	MKX	3.5 (C)	265@6250	250@4500	3.64x3.41	10.3:1	NA

NA - Not Available

ENGINE TUNE-UP SPECIFICATIONS

Year	Engine Displacement Liters (VIN)	Spark Plug Gap (in.)	Ignition Timing (deg.) MT	Ignition Timing (deg.) AT	Fuel Pump (psi)	Idle Speed (rpm) MT	Idle Speed (rpm) AT	Valve Clearance (in.) Intake	Valve Clearance (in.) Exhaust
2007	3.5 (C)	0.051-0.057	—	NA	65	—	NA	0.006-0.010	0.012-0.016

NOTE: The Vehicle Emission Control Information label often reflects changes made during production and must be used if they differ from this chart.

NOTE: The fuel pressure readings are with the engine running

NA - Not Available

CAPACITIES

Year	Model	Engine Displacement Liters (VIN)	Engine Oil with Filter (qts.)	Transmission (pts.) 5-Spd	Transmission (pts.) Auto.	Transfer Case (pts.)	Drive Axle Front (pts.)	Drive Axle Rear (pts.)	Fuel Tank (gal.)	Cooling System (qts.)
2007	Edge	3.5 (C)	5.5	—	20.0	①	—	2.43	②	9.7
	MKX	3.5 (C)	5.5	—	20.0	①	—	2.43	②	9.7

NOTE: All capacities are approximate. Add fluid gradually and check to be sure a proper fluid level is obtained.

① 18 ounces
② Front Wheel Drive (FWD): 19 gallons
   All Wheel Drive (AWD): 20 gallons

22086_EDGE_C0004

FLUID SPECIFICATIONS

Year	Model	Engine Displacement Liters (VIN)	Engine Oil	Auto. Trans.	Drive Axle	Power Steering Fluid	Brake Master Cylinder
2007	Edge	3.5 (C)	①	Mercon® ATF Fluid	80W-90	Mercon® ATF Fluid	DOT 3
	MKX	3.5 (C)	①	Mercon® ATF Fluid	80W-90	Mercon® ATF Fluid	DOT 3

DOT: Department Of Transpotation

① 5W-20 Premium Synthetic Blend Motor Oil (US) or 5W-20 Super Premium Motor Oil (Canada)

22086_EDGE_C0005

VALVE SPECIFICATIONS

Year	Engine Displacement Liters (VIN)	Seat Angle (deg.)	Face Angle (deg.)	Spring Test Pressure (lbs. @ in.)	Spring Installed Height (in.)	Stem-to-Guide Clearance (in.) Intake	Stem-to-Guide Clearance (in.) Exhaust	Stem Diameter (in.) Intake	Stem Diameter (in.) Exhaust
2007	3.5 (C)	89.0-91.0	90.50-91.50	115 @ 1.08	1.4500	0.0008-0.0027	0.0013-0.0320	0.2157-0.2164	0.2151-0.2159

NA: Not Available

22086_EDGE_C0006

CAMSHAFT SPECIFICATIONS

All measurements are given in inches

Year	Engine Displacement Liters (VIN)	Journal Diameter	Bearing Oil Clearance	Shaft End-play	Runout	Lobe Height Intake	Lobe Height Exhaust
2007	3.5 (C)	①	②	0.0012-0.0066	0.0015	0.3800	0.3800

① 1st journal: 1.2202-1.2209 in.
   Intermediate journals: 1.021-1.022 in.

② 1st journal: 0.0027 MAX
   Intermediate journals: 0.0029 MAX

22086_EDGE_C0007

CRANKSHAFT AND CONNECTING ROD SPECIFICATIONS

All measurements are given in inches

Year	Engine Displacement Liters (VIN)	Crankshaft Main Brg. Journal Dia.	Crankshaft Main Brg. Oil Clearance	Crankshaft Shaft End-play	Crankshaft Thrust on No.	Connecting Rod Journal Diameter	Connecting Rod Oil Clearance	Connecting Rod Side Clearance
2007	3.5 (C)	2.657	NA	0.0039-0.0114	NA	2.204-2.205	NA	0.0068-0.0167

NA - Not Available

22086_EDGE_C0008

PISTON AND RING SPECIFICATIONS

All measurements are given in inches

Year	Engine Displacement Liters (VIN)	Piston Clearance	Ring Gap Top Compression	Ring Gap Bottom Compression	Ring Gap Oil Control	Ring Side Clearance Top Compression	Ring Side Clearance Bottom Compression	Ring Side Clearance Oil Control
2007	3.5 (C)	0.0003-0.0017	0.0059-0.0098	0.0118-0.0216	0.0059-0.0177	NA	NA	NA

NA: Not Available

22086_EDGE_C0009

TORQUE SPECIFICATIONS
All readings in ft. lbs.

Year	Engine Displacement Liters (VIN)	Cylinder Head Bolts	Main Bearing Bolts	Rod Bearing Bolts	Crankshaft Damper Bolts	Flywheel Bolts	Manifold		Spark Plugs	Oil Pan Drain Plug
							Intake	Exhaust		
2007	3.5 (C)	①	NA	NA	②	59	③	④	11	20

① Step 1: 15 ft. lbs.
Step 2: 26 ft. lbs.
Step 3: +90 degrees
Step 4: +90 degrees
Step 4: +90 degrees

② Step 1: 89 ft. lbs.
Step 2: Loosen one full turn
Step 3: 37 ft. lbs.
Step 4: +90 degrees

③ Upper intake manifold: 89 inch lbs.
Lower intake manfold: 89 inch lbs.

④ Studs: 9 ft. lbs.
Nuts: 15 ft. lbs.

22086_EDGE_C0010

TIRE, WHEEL AND BALL JOINT SPECIFICATIONS

Year	Model	OEM Tires		Tire Pressures (psi)		Wheel Size	Ball Joint Inspection	Lug Nut (ft. lbs.)
		Standard	Optional	Front	Rear			
2007	Edge	P235/65R17	P245/60R18	①	①	NS	NS	100
	MKX	P235/65R17	P245/60R18	①	①	NS	NS	100

OEM: Original Equipment Manufacturer

PSI: Pounds Per Square Inch

NS: Not specified by manufacturer

① See the safety certification label on the driver side door jamb for tire pressures.

22086_EDGE_C0011

BRAKE SPECIFICATIONS
All measurements in inches unless noted

Year	Model		Brake Disc			Brake Drum Diameter			Minimum Lining Thickness		Brake Caliper	
			Original Thickness	Minimum Thickness	Maximum Runout	Original Inside Diameter	Max. Wear Limit	Maximum Machine Diameter	Front	Rear	Bracket Bolts (ft. lbs.)	Mounting Bolts (ft. lbs.)
2007	Edge	F	1.102	1.023	NA	—	—	—	0.118	—	98	65
		R	0.708	0.629	NA	—	—	—	—	0.118	66	19
	MKX	F	1.102	1.023	NA	—	—	—	0.118	—	98	65
		R	0.708	0.629	NA	—	—	—	—	0.118	66	19

F: Front

R: Rear

22086_EDGE_C0012

SCHEDULED MAINTENANCE INTERVALS

FORD EDGE, LINCOLN MKX

TO BE SERVICED	TYPE OF SERVICE	VEHICLE MILEAGE INTERVAL (x1000)											
		10	20	30	40	50	60	70	80	90	100	110	120
Accessory drive belts	I & A			✓			✓			✓			✓
Air cleaner element	R			✓			✓			✓			✓
Air conditioning filter	R			✓			✓			✓			✓
Brake fluid	R											✓	
Brake hoses & lines (including ABS)	I		✓		✓		✓		✓		✓		
Cooling system hoses & connections	I		✓		✓		✓		✓		✓		
Engine coolant	R												✓
Engine oil	R	✓	✓	✓	✓	✓	✓	✓	✓	✓	✓	✓	✓
Engine oil and coolant levels	I	Inspect at each fuel stop											
Engine oil filter	R		✓		✓		✓		✓		✓		
Exhaust system	I		✓		✓		✓		✓		✓		
Fluid levels and condition	I		✓		✓		✓		✓		✓		
Front and rear brakes	I		✓		✓		✓		✓		✓		
Fuel lines & connection	I		✓		✓		✓		✓		✓		
Halfshaft boots	I		✓		✓		✓		✓		✓		
Idle speed	I & A											✓	
Parking brake system	I & A		✓		✓		✓		✓		✓		
Rear differential fluid	R									✓			
Rotate and inspect tires	I	✓	✓	✓	✓	✓	✓	✓	✓	✓	✓	✓	✓
Spark plugs	R											✓	
Suspension components	I		✓		✓		✓		✓		✓		
Tie rod ends, steering gear box & boots	I		✓		✓		✓		✓		✓		
Transmission fluid	R												✓
Valve clearance	I											✓	

R: Replace   I: Inspect   A: Adjust

FREQUENT OPERATION MAINTENANCE (SEVERE SERVICE)

If a vehicle is operated under any of the following conditions it is considered severe service:

- Towing a trailer or using a camper or car-top carrier.
- Repeated short trips of less than 5 miles in temperatures below freezing, or trips of less than 10 miles in any temperature.
- Extensive idling or low-speed driving for long distances as in heavy commercial use, such as delivery, taxi or police cars.
- Operating on rough, muddy or salt-covered roads.
- Operating on unpaved or dusty roads.
- Driving in extremely hot (over 90°) conditions.

Air cleaner element: replace every 15,000 miles

Engine oil and filter: replace every 3750 miles or 6 months, whichever occurs first.

Timing belt: replace every 60,000 miles if the vehicle is regularly driven in temperatures above 110°F or below -20°F.

Transmission fluid: replace every 30,000 miles.

Rear differential fluid: replace every 60,000 miles.

Front and rear brakes: inspect every 7500 miles or 6 months, whichever occurs first.

Locks and hinges: lubricate every 15,000 miles.

Tie rods, steering gear box, boots: inspect every 7500 miles or 6 months, whichever occurs first.

Suspension components: inspect every 7500 miles or 6 months, whichever occurs first.

Halfshaft boots: inspect every 7500 miles or 6 months, whichever occurs first.

PRECAUTIONS

Before servicing any vehicle, please be sure to read all of the following precautions, which deal with personal safety, prevention of component damage, and important points to take into consideration when servicing a motor vehicle:

• Never open, service or drain the radiator or cooling system when the engine is hot; serious burns can occur from the steam and hot coolant.

• Observe all applicable safety precautions when working around fuel. Whenever servicing the fuel system, always work in a well-ventilated area. Do not allow fuel spray or vapors to come in contact with a spark, open flame, or excessive heat (a hot drop light, for example). Keep a dry chemical fire extinguisher near the work area. Always keep fuel in a container specifically designed for fuel storage; also, always properly seal fuel containers to avoid the possibility of fire or explosion. Refer to the additional fuel system precautions later in this section.

• Fuel injection systems often remain pressurized, even after the engine has been turned **OFF**. The fuel system pressure must be relieved before disconnecting any fuel lines. Failure to do so may result in fire and/or personal injury.

• Brake fluid often contains polyglycol ethers and polyglycols. Avoid contact with the eyes and wash your hands thoroughly after handling brake fluid. If you do get brake fluid in your eyes, flush your eyes with clean, running water for 15 minutes. If eye irritation persists, or if you have taken brake fluid internally, IMMEDIATELY seek medical assistance.

• The EPA warns that prolonged contact with used engine oil may cause a number of skin disorders, including cancer. You should make every effort to minimize your exposure to used engine oil. Protective gloves should be worn when changing oil. Wash your hands and any other exposed skin areas as soon as possible after exposure to used engine oil. Soap and water, or waterless hand cleaner should be used.

• All new vehicles are now equipped with an air bag system, often referred to as a Supplemental Restraint System (SRS) or Supplemental Inflatable Restraint (SIR) system. The system must be disabled before performing service on or around system components, steering column, instrument panel components, wiring and sensors. Failure to follow safety and disabling procedures could result in accidental air bag deployment, possible personal injury and unnecessary system repairs.

• Always wear safety goggles when working with, or around, the air bag system. When carrying a non-deployed air bag, be sure the bag and trim cover are pointed away from your body. When placing a non-deployed air bag on a work surface, always face the bag and trim cover upward, away from the surface. This will reduce the motion of the module if it is accidentally deployed. Refer to the additional air bag system precautions later in this section.

• Clean, high quality brake fluid from a sealed container is essential to the safe and proper operation of the brake system. You should always buy the correct type of brake fluid for your vehicle. If the brake fluid becomes contaminated, completely flush the system with new fluid. Never reuse any brake fluid. Any brake fluid that is removed from the system should be discarded. Also, do not allow any brake fluid to come in contact with a painted surface; it will damage the paint.

• Never operate the engine without the proper amount and type of engine oil; doing so WILL result in severe engine damage.

• Timing belt maintenance is extremely important. Many models utilize an interference-type, non-freewheeling engine. If the timing belt breaks, the valves in the cylinder head may strike the pistons, causing potentially serious (also time-consuming and expensive) engine damage. Refer to the maintenance interval charts for the recommended replacement interval for the timing belt, and to the timing belt section for belt replacement and inspection.

• Disconnecting the negative battery cable on some vehicles may interfere with the functions of the on-board computer system(s) and may require the computer to undergo a relearning process once the negative battery cable is reconnected.

• When servicing drum brakes, only disassemble and assemble one side at a time, leaving the remaining side intact for reference.

• Only an MVAC-trained, EPA-certified automotive technician should service the air conditioning system or its components.

BRAKES

GENERAL INFORMATION

The Anti-lock Brake System (ABS) with Roll Stability Control (RSC) and traction assist consists of the following components:
• Hydraulic Control Unit (HCU)
• ABS module (also controls the RSC system and traction assist system)
• Stability/traction control switch
• Steering wheel rotation sensor
• Stability control sensor cluster (contains the accelerometer[s], roll rate sensor and yaw rate sensor)
• Front wheel speed sensors
• Front wheel speed sensor tone rings (integral to the halfshafts)
• Rear wheel speed sensors

• Rear wheel speed sensor tone rings (integral to the halfshafts)
• Brake pressure transducer (integral to the HCU)
• Brake fluid level switch
• Red brake warning indicator
• Yellow ABS warning indicator
• Traction assist/roll stability control indicator ("sliding car" indicator)

SPEED SENSORS

REMOVAL & INSTALLATION

Front

See Figures 1 and 2.

ANTI-LOCK BRAKE SYSTEM (ABS)

1. Disconnect the negative battery cable.
2. Raise and safely support the vehicle.
3. Remove the wheel and tire assembly.
4. Remove the retainers and position the fender splash shield aside.
5. Disconnect the wheel speed sensor electrical connector.
6. Disconnect the 6 pushpin fasteners.
7. Remove the front wheel speed sensor bolt and the wheel speed sensor.

✷✷ WARNING

The wheel speed sensor harness must be routed as shown in the

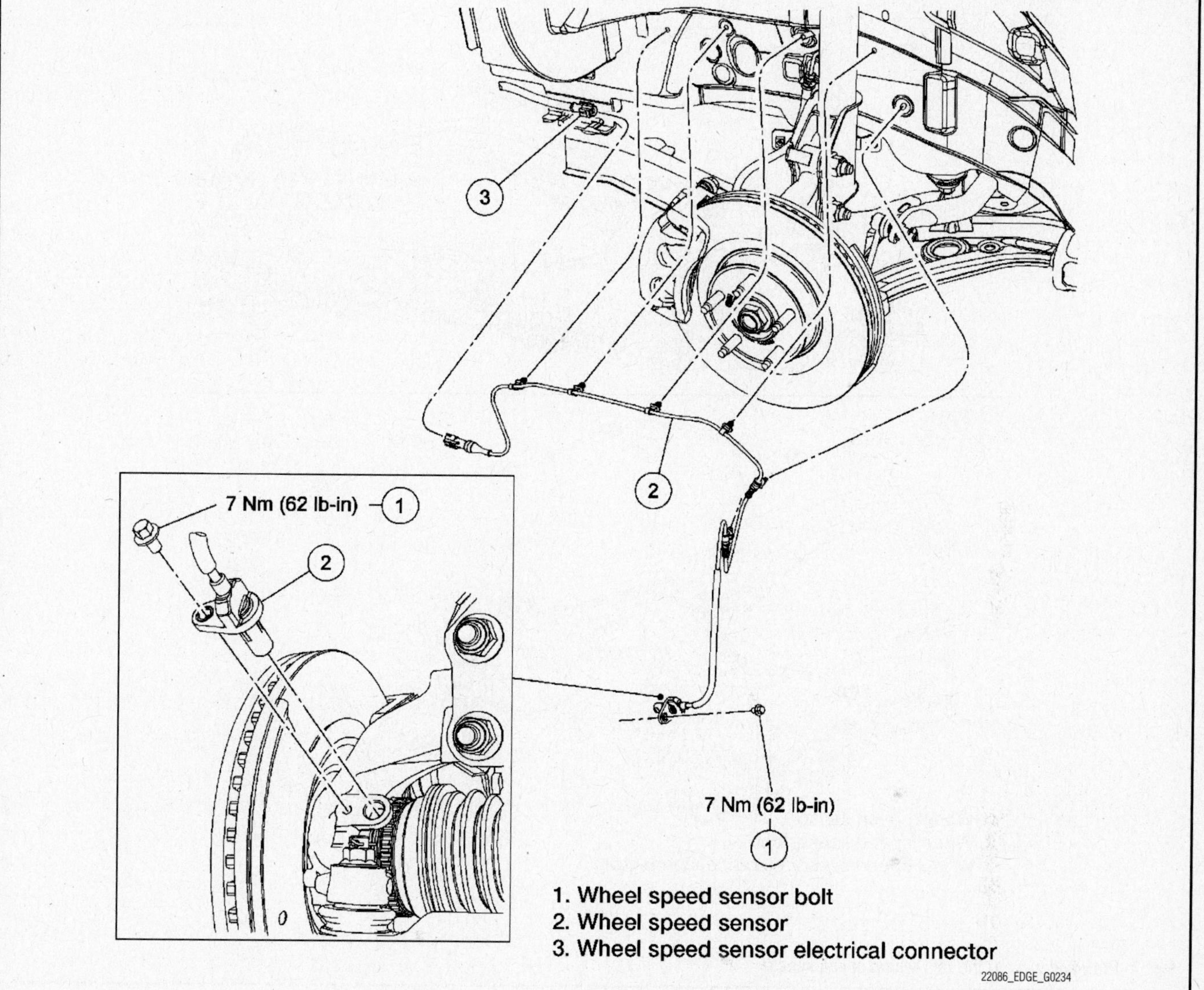

7 Nm (62 lb-in) — ①

② ② ①

7 Nm (62 lb-in)
①

1. Wheel speed sensor bolt
2. Wheel speed sensor
3. Wheel speed sensor electrical connector

22086_EDGE_G0234

Fig. 1 Exploded view of the front wheel speed sensor

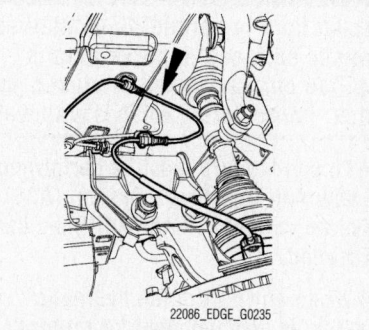

22086_EDGE_G0235

Fig. 2 The wheel speed sensor harness must be properly routed, as shown, or damage to the harness during vehicle jounce and rebound can occur

accompanying illustration, or damage to the harness during vehicle jounce and rebound can occur.

8. Installation is the reverse of the removal procedure. Tighten the speed sensor bolt to 7 Nm (62 inch lbs.).

Rear

See Figure 3.

1. Disconnect the negative battery cable.
2. Raise and safely support the vehicle.
3. Remove the wheel and tire assembly.
4. Disconnect the wheel speed sensor electrical connector.

➡**It is not necessary to remove the harness routing brackets.**

5. Disconnect the wheel speed sensor harness from the brackets
6. Disconnect the pushpin fasteners.
7. Remove the wheel speed sensor bolt and the wheel speed sensor.
8. Installation is the reverse of the removal procedure Tighten the speed sensor bolt to 7 Nm (62 inch lbs.).

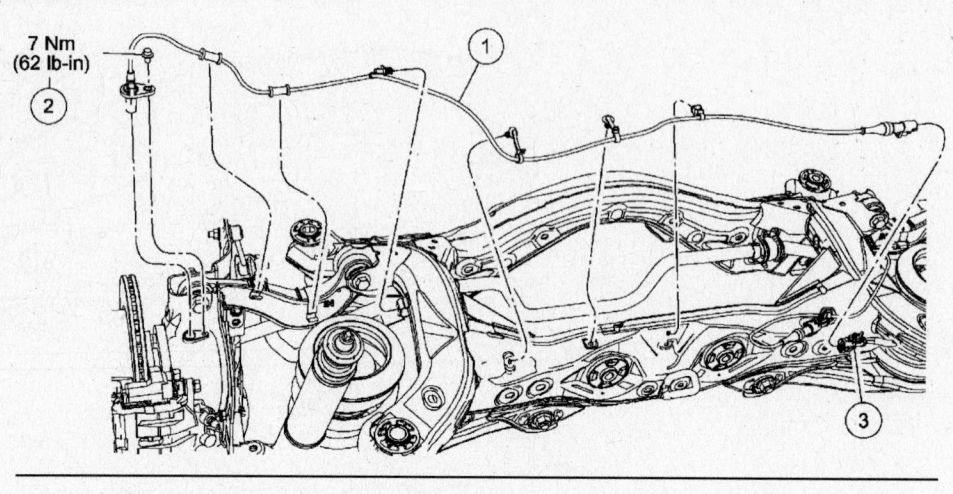

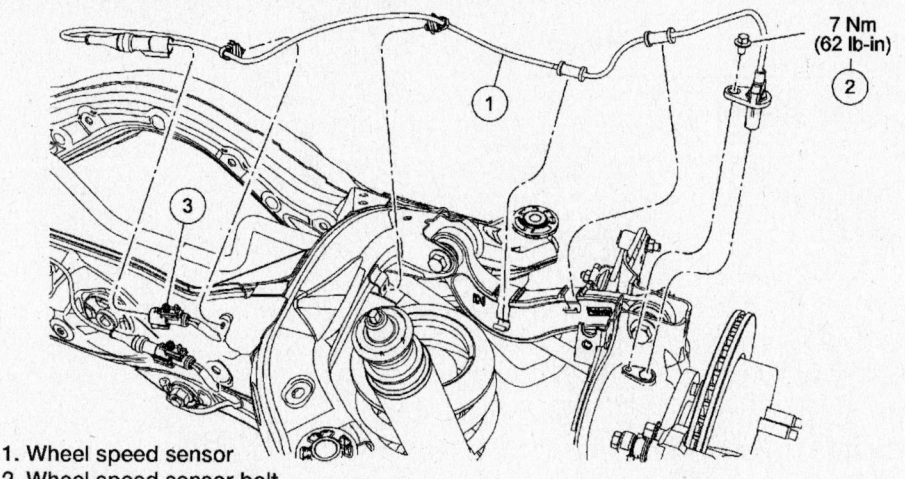

1. Wheel speed sensor
2. Wheel speed sensor bolt
3. Wheel speed sensor electrical connector

22086_EDGE_G0236

Fig. 3 Exploded view of the rear wheel speed sensor

BRAKES   BLEEDING THE BRAKE SYSTEM

BLEEDING PROCEDURE

BLEEDING PROCEDURE

❊❊ CAUTION

Use of any other than approved DOT 3 motor vehicle brake fluid will cause permanent damage to brake components and will render the brakes inoperative. Failure to follow these instructions may result in personal injury.

❊❊ CAUTION

Carefully read all precaution information on product label. For EMERGENCY MEDICAL INFORMATION seek medical advice. In the USA or Canada on Ford/Motorcraft products call: 1-800-959-3673. For additional information, consult the product Material Safety Data Sheet (MSDS) if available. Failure to follow these instructions may result in personal injury.

❊❊ WARNING

Never let the brake master cylinder reservoir run dry during the bleeding operation. Keep the brake master cylinder reservoir filled with clean, specified brake fluid. Never reuse the brake fluid that has been drained from the hydraulic system.

❊❊ WARNING

Brake fluid is harmful to painted and plastic surfaces. If brake fluid is spilled onto a painted or plastic surface, immediately wash it with water.

➡This procedure must be performed if a new Anti-lock Brake System (ABS) Hydraulic Control Unit (HCU) has been installed.

➡When any part of the hydraulic system is disconnected for repair or installation of a new component, air may enter the system and cause spongy a brake pedal. This requires bleeding of the hydraulic system after it has been correctly connected. The hydraulic system can be bled manually or with pressure bleeding equipment.

➡Carrying out the chassis brake bleeding procedure drives trapped air from the otherwise inaccessible lower section of the HCU valves into the upper sections (accessible by bleeding the brakes). Subsequent bleeding removes the air from the system.

➡Bleed the longest brake tube or hose first. Be sure the bleeder tank contains enough specified brake fluid to complete the bleeding operation.

➡Add clean, specified brake fluid as necessary throughout the procedure.

Pressure Bleeding

See Figure 4.

1. If the vehicle is equipped with an ABS, connect the Vehicle Communication Module (VCM) and scan tool into the vehicle Data Link Connector (DLC) under the dash and carry out the chassis brake bleeding procedure.
2. Clean all dirt from the master cylinder filler cap, then remove the cap and fill the brake master cylinder reservoir with clean, specified brake fluid.

➡Master cylinder pressure bleeder adapter tools are available from various manufacturers of pressure bleeding equipment. Follow the manufacturer's instructions when installing the adapter.

3. Install the bleeder adapter to the brake master cylinder reservoir and attach the bleeder tank hose to the fitting on the adapter.
4. Place a box-end wrench on the RH rear disc brake caliper bleeder screw. Attach a rubber hose to the RH rear disc brake caliper bleeder screw and submerge the free end of the hose in a container partially filled with clean, specified brake fluid.
5. Open the valve on the bleeder tank.
6. Loosen the rear disc brake caliper bleeder screw. Leave the bleeder screw open until clear, bubble-free brake fluid flows into the container, then tighten the rear disc brake caliper bleeder screw and remove the rubber hose. Tighten to 8 Nm (71 inch lbs.).
7. Continue bleeding the rest of the system, going in order from the LH rear disc brake caliper to the RH front disc brake caliper, ending with the LH front disc brake caliper.
8. Close the bleeder tank valve and remove the tank hose from the adapter and remove the adapter.

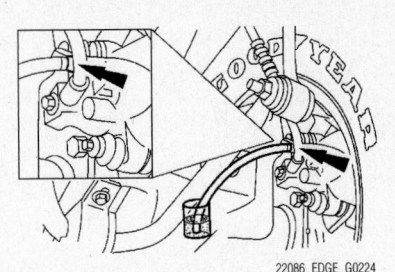

Fig. 4 Place a box-end wrench on the RH rear disc brake caliper bleeder screw. Attach a rubber hose to the RH rear disc brake caliper bleeder screw and submerge the free end of the hose in a container partially filled with clean, specified brake fluid

9. Fill the brake master cylinder reservoir with clean, specified brake fluid and install the cap.

Manual Bleeding

See Figure 4.

1. Clean all dirt from the master cylinder filler cap, then remove the cap and fill the brake master cylinder reservoir with clean, specified brake fluid. Install the master cylinder filler cap.
2. If the vehicle is equipped with an ABS, connect the Vehicle Communication Module (VCM) and scan tool into the vehicle Data Link Connector (DLC) under the dash and carry out the chassis brake bleeding procedure.
3. Place a box-end wrench on the RH rear disc brake caliper bleeder screw. Attach a rubber hose to the RH rear disc brake caliper bleeder screw and submerge the free end of the hose in a container partially filled with clean, specified brake fluid.
4. Have an assistant pump the brake pedal and then hold firm pressure on the brake pedal.
5. Loosen the RH rear disc brake caliper bleeder screw until a stream of brake fluid comes out. Have an assistant maintain pressure on the brake pedal while tightening the RH rear disc brake caliper bleeder screw:
   a. Repeat until clear, bubble-free fluid comes out.
   b. Refill the brake master cylinder reservoir as necessary.
6. Tighten the RH rear disc brake caliper bleeder screw. Tighten to 8 Nm (71 inch lbs.).
7. Repeat Steps 2 through 5 for the LH rear disc brake caliper.

8. Place a box-end wrench on the RH front disc brake caliper bleeder screw. Attach a rubber hose to the RH front disc brake caliper bleeder screw and submerge the free end of the hose in a container partially filled with clean, specified brake fluid.
9. Have an assistant pump the brake pedal and then hold firm pressure on the brake pedal.
10. Loosen the RH front disc brake caliper bleeder screw until a stream of brake fluid comes out. Have an assistant maintain pressure on the brake pedal while tightening the RH front disc brake caliper bleeder screw.
   a. Repeat until clear, bubble-free fluid comes out.
   b. Refill the brake master cylinder reservoir as necessary.
11. Tighten the RH front disc brake caliper bleeder screw to 8 Nm (71 inch lbs.).
12. Repeat Steps 7 through 10 for the LH front disc brake caliper.

Gravity Bleeding

See Figure 4.

1. Clean all dirt from the master cylinder filler cap, then remove the cap and fill the brake master cylinder reservoir with clean, specified brake fluid.
2. If the vehicle is equipped with an ABS, connect the Vehicle Communication Module (VCM) and scan tool into the vehicle Data Link Connector (DLC) under the dash and carry out the chassis brake bleeding procedure.
3. Bleed the rear disc brake calipers:
   a. Place a box-end wrench on the RH rear disc brake caliper bleeder screw.

   Attach a rubber hose to the RH rear disc brake caliper bleeder screw and submerge the free end of the hose in a container partially filled with clean, specified brake fluid.
   b. Open the bleeder screw and leave open until clear bubble-free brake fluid flows into the container.
   c. Repeat for the LH rear disc brake caliper.
4. Tighten the rear disc brake caliper bleeder screws to 8 Nm (71 inch lbs.).
5. Bleed the front disc brake calipers:
   a. Place a box-end wrench on the RH front disc brake caliper bleeder screw.
   b. Attach a rubber hose to the RH front disc brake caliper bleeder screw and submerge the free end of the hose in a container partially filled with clean, specified brake fluid.

c. Open the bleeder screw and leave open until clear bubble-free brake fluid flows.

d. Repeat for the LH front disc brake caliper.

6. Tighten the front disc brake caliper bleeder screws to 8 Nm (71 inch lbs.).

Bleeding the Master Cylinder

See Figure 5.

➡When a new brake master cylinder has been installed or the system has been emptied, or partially emptied, it should be primed to prevent air from getting into the system.

1. Disconnect the brake master cylinder outlet tubes.

2. Install short brake tubes with ends submerged in the brake master cylinder

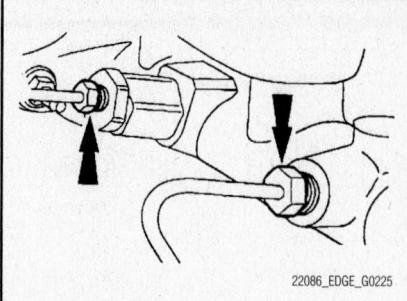

Fig. 5 Disconnect the brake master cylinder outlet tubes

reservoir and fill the brake master cylinder reservoir with clean, specified brake fluid.

3. Have an assistant pump the brake pedal until clear fluid flows from both brake tubes without air bubbles.

4. Remove the short brake tubes and install the brake outlet tubes.

5. Bleed each brake tube at the brake master cylinder as follows:

a. Have an assistant pump the brake pedal and then hold firm pressure on the brake pedal.

b. Loosen the rearmost brake tube fittings until a stream of brake fluid comes out. Have an assistant maintain pressure on the brake pedal while tightening the brake tube fitting.

c. Repeat this operation until clear, bubble-free fluid comes out.

d. Refill the brake master cylinder reservoir as necessary. Repeat the bleeding operation at the front brake tube.

e. While the assistant maintains pressure on the brake pedal, tighten the brake tubes to 28 Nm (21 ft. lbs.).

BRAKES   **FRONT DISC BRAKES**

✳ CAUTION

Dust and dirt accumulating on brake parts during normal use may contain asbestos fibers from production or aftermarket brake linings. Breathing excessive concentrations of asbestos fibers can cause serious bodily harm. Exercise care when servicing brake parts. Do not sand or grind brake lining unless equipment used is designed to contain the dust residue. Do not clean brake parts with compressed air or by dry brushing. Cleaning should be done by dampening the brake components with a fine mist of water, then wiping the brake components clean with a dampened cloth. Dispose of cloth and all residue containing asbestos fibers in an impermeable container with the appropriate label. Follow practices prescribed by the Occupational Safety and Health Administration (OSHA) and the Environmental Protection Agency (EPA) for the handling, processing, and disposing of dust or debris that may contain asbestos fibers.

BRAKE CALIPER

REMOVAL & INSTALLATION
See Figure 6.

✳ CAUTION

Use of any other than approved DOT 3 motor vehicle brake fluid will

cause permanent damage to brake components and will render the brakes inoperative. Failure to follow these instructions may result in personal injury.

✳ CAUTION

Carefully read all precaution information on product label. For EMERGENCY MEDICAL INFORMATION seek medical advice. In the USA or Canada on Ford/Motorcraft products

call: 1-800-959-3673. For additional information, consult the product Material Safety Data Sheet (MSDS) if available. Failure to follow these instructions may result in personal injury.

✳ WARNING

Brake fluid is harmful to painted and plastic surfaces. If brake fluid is spilled onto a painted or plastic surface, immediately wash it with water.

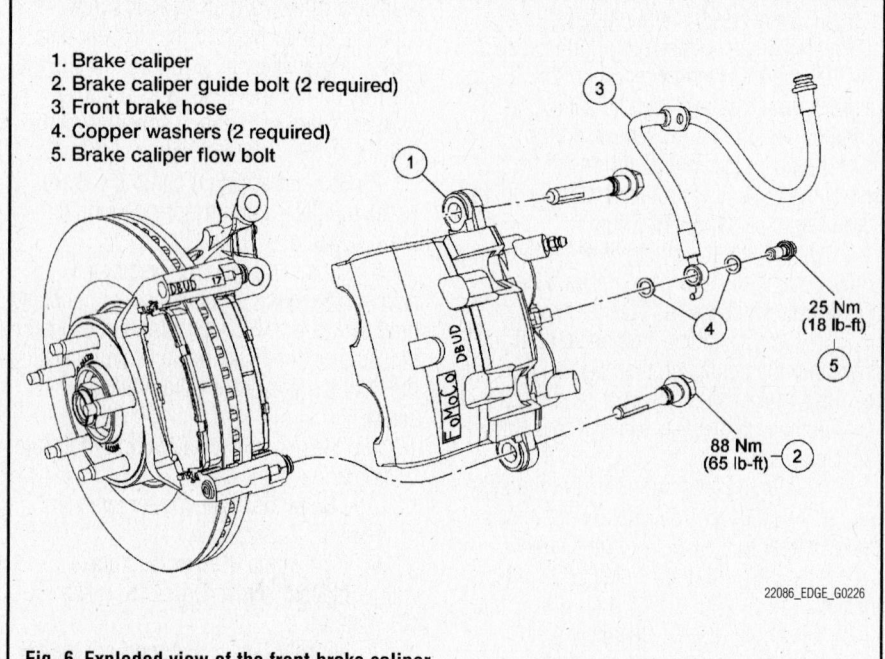

1. Brake caliper
2. Brake caliper guide bolt (2 required)
3. Front brake hose
4. Copper washers (2 required)
5. Brake caliper flow bolt

25 Nm (18 lb-ft)

88 Nm (65 lb-ft)

Fig. 6 Exploded view of the front brake caliper

1. Raise and safely support the vehicle.
2. Remove the wheel and tire assembly.
3. Remove the brake caliper flow bolt and position the hose aside. Discard the 2 copper washers.

➡️**The guide pin bolts are different sizes. The longer/bigger bolt is the upper guide pin bolt.**

4. Remove the 2 brake caliper guide pin bolts.
5. Remove the brake caliper.

To install:

6. Installation is the reverse of the removal procedure, noting the following:
   a. During installation, make sure that the brake caliper hose is not twisted.
   b. Tighten the caliper guide pin bolts to 88 Nm (65 ft. lbs.). Make sure to install the longer/bigger bolt in the upper position.
   c. Use new copper washers, then tighten the brake caliper flow bolts to 25 Nm (18 ft. lbs.).
   d. Bleed the brake system, as outlined in the beginning of the Brake Section.

DISC BRAKE PADS

REMOVAL & INSTALLATION

See Figure 7.

1. Check the brake fluid level in the brake master cylinder reservoir.
2. If necessary, remove the fluid until the brake master cylinder reservoir is 1/2 full.
3. Raise and safely support the vehicle.
4. Remove the wheel and tire assembly.

✴✴ WARNING

Do not pry in the caliper sight hole to retract the pistons as this can damage the pistons and boots.

✴ WARNING

NEVER let the brake caliper hang from the brake hose or damage to the hose can occur.

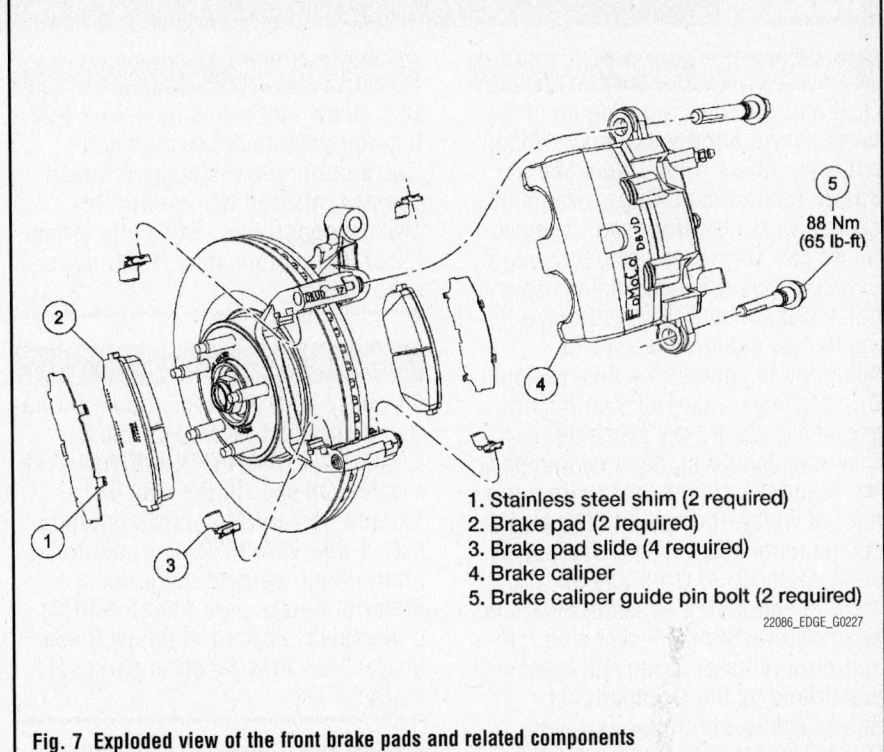

1. Stainless steel shim (2 required)
2. Brake pad (2 required)
3. Brake pad slide (4 required)
4. Brake caliper
5. Brake caliper guide pin bolt (2 required)

88 Nm (65 lb-ft)

22086_EDGE_G0227

Fig. 7 Exploded view of the front brake pads and related components

5. Remove the 2 brake caliper guide pin bolts and position the caliper aside. Support the caliper using a piece of wire.
6. Remove the brake pads, brake pad shims and stainless steel shims.
7. Inspect the brake pads and shims for wear or contamination.
8. Remove the brake pad slides.

To install:

✴✴ WARNING

Protect the caliper piston and boots when pushing the caliper piston into the bores.

✴✴ WARNING

Make sure that the caliper guide pin boots are fully seated or damage to the caliper guide pin boots can occur.

9. If installing new brake pads, using a C-clamp or equivalent suitable tool and a worn brake, compress the disc brake caliper pistons into the caliper.
10. Install the brake pad slides.
11. Apply a thin coating of the supplied grease to the shims and the shim contact area of the brake pads.
12. Install the stainless steel shims to the brake pads.

➡️**The guide pin bolts are different sizes. The longer/bigger bolt is the upper guide pin bolt.**

13. Position the brake caliper and install the 2 guide pin bolts. Tighten to 88 Nm (65 ft. lbs.).
14. Install the wheel and tire assembly.
15. Fill the brake master cylinder reservoir with clean, specified brake fluid.
16. Test the brakes for normal operation.

BRAKES

REAR DISC BRAKES

✳✳ CAUTION

Dust and dirt accumulating on brake parts during normal use may contain asbestos fibers from production or aftermarket brake linings. Breathing excessive concentrations of asbestos fibers can cause serious bodily harm. Exercise care when servicing brake parts. Do not sand or grind brake lining unless equipment used is designed to contain the dust residue. Do not clean brake parts with compressed air or by dry brushing. Cleaning should be done by dampening the brake components with a fine mist of water, then wiping the brake components clean with a dampened cloth. Dispose of cloth and all residue containing asbestos fibers in an impermeable container with the appropriate label. Follow practices prescribed by the Occupational Safety and Health Administration (OSHA) and the Environmental Protection Agency (EPA) for the handling, processing, and disposing of dust or debris that may contain asbestos fibers.

BRAKE CALIPER

REMOVAL & INSTALLATION
See Figure 8.

✳✳ CAUTION

Use of any other than approved DOT 3 motor vehicle brake fluid will cause permanent damage to brake components and will render the brakes inoperative. Failure to follow these instructions may result in personal injury.

✳✳ CAUTION

Carefully read all precaution information on product label. For EMERGENCY MEDICAL INFORMATION seek medical advice. In the USA or Canada on Ford/Motorcraft products call: 1-800-959-3673. For additional information, consult the product Material Safety Data Sheet (MSDS) if available. Failure to follow these instructions may result in personal injury.

✳✳ WARNING

Brake fluid is harmful to painted and plastic surfaces. If brake fluid is spilled onto a painted or plastic surface, immediately wash it with water.

1. Raise and safely support the vehicle.
2. Remove the wheel and tire assembly.

3. Remove the brake caliper flow bolt and position the brake hose aside. Discard the 2 copper washers.
4. Remove the 2 brake caliper guide bolts and the brake caliper.
5. If a leaking or damaged caliper piston boot is found, install a new disc brake caliper.

To install:

✳✳ WARNING

Make sure that the caliper guide pin boots are fully seated or damage to the caliper guide pin boots can occur.

➡Make sure that the brake caliper hose is not twisted during caliper installation.

6. Position the brake caliper onto the anchor plate and brake pads.
7. Install the 2 brake caliper guide pin bolts and tighten to 26 Nm (19 ft. lbs.).
8. Using 2 new copper washers, position the brake hose and install the brake caliper flow bolt. Tighten to 25 Nm (18 ft. lbs.).
9. Install the wheel and tire assembly.
10. Bleed the brake system, as outlined at the beginning of the Brake Section.
11. Test the brakes for normal operation

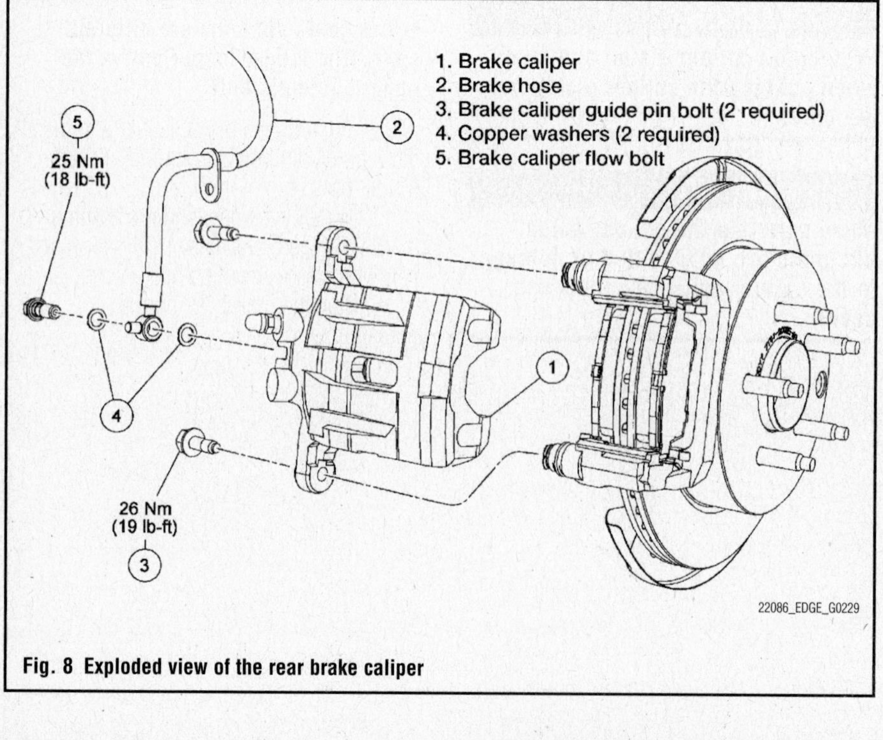

DISC BRAKE PADS

REMOVAL & INSTALLATION
See Figure 9.

✳✳ CAUTION

Use of any other than approved DOT 3 motor vehicle brake fluid will cause permanent damage to brake components and will render the brakes inoperative. Failure to follow these instructions may result in personal injury.

✳✳ CAUTION

Carefully read all precaution information on product label. For EMERGENCY MEDICAL INFORMATION seek medical advice. In the USA or Canada on Ford/Motorcraft products call: 1-800-959-3673. For additional information, consult the product Material Safety Data Sheet (MSDS) if available. Failure to follow these instructions may result in personal injury.

1. Brake caliper
2. Brake hose
3. Brake caliper guide pin bolt (2 required)
4. Copper washers (2 required)
5. Brake caliper flow bolt

25 Nm (18 lb-ft)

26 Nm (19 lb-ft)

22086_EDGE_G0229

Fig. 8 Exploded view of the rear brake caliper

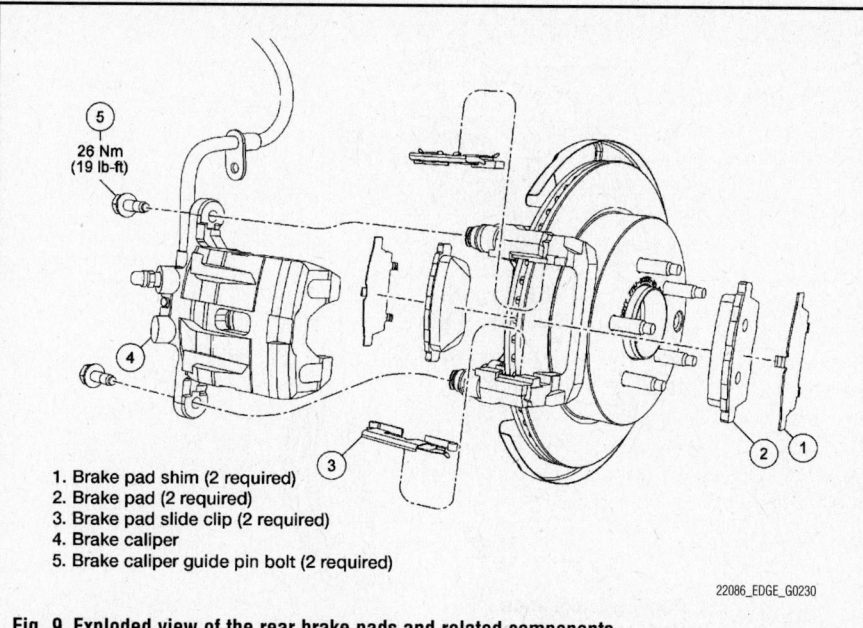

1. Brake pad shim (2 required)
2. Brake pad (2 required)
3. Brake pad slide clip (2 required)
4. Brake caliper
5. Brake caliper guide pin bolt (2 required)

22086_EDGE_G0230

Fig. 9 Exploded view of the rear brake pads and related components

※ **WARNING**

Brake fluid is harmful to painted and plastic surfaces. If brake fluid is spilled onto a painted or plastic surface, immediately wash it with water.

1. Check the brake fluid level in the brake master cylinder reservoir.
2. If necessary, remove the fluid until the brake master cylinder reservoir is 1/2 full.
3. Remove the wheel and tire assembly.

※ **WARNING**

Do not pry in the caliper sight hole to retract the pistons, as this can damage the pistons and boots.

※ **WARNING**

Do not allow the brake caliper to hang from the brake hose or damage to the hose can occur.

4. Remove the 2 brake caliper guide pin bolts and position the caliper aside. Support the caliper using mechanic's wire.

※ **WARNING**

Install new brake pads if they are worn past the specified thickness above the metal backing plates. Install new brake pads in complete axle sets.

5. Remove the 2 brake pads, shims and slide clips. Inspect the brake pads and shims for wear, damage or contamination. Discard the slide clips.

To install:

※ **WARNING**

Protect the caliper piston and boots when pushing the caliper piston into the bores.

➡ **Make sure the caliper piston boot is clean and free of foreign material.**

6. If installing new brake pads, using a suitable tool and a worn brake pad, compress the disc brake caliper pistons into the caliper using a C-clamp..
7. Install the 2 brake pads, shims and new slide clips to the brake caliper anchor plate.

※ **WARNING**

Make sure that the caliper guide pin boots are fully seated or damage to the caliper guide pin boots can occur.

➡ **Make sure that the brake caliper hose is not twisted during caliper installation.**

8. Position the brake caliper on the anchor plate and install the 2 guide pin bolts. Tighten to 26 Nm (19 ft. lbs.).
9. Install the wheel and tire assembly.
10. Fill the brake master cylinder reservoir with clean, specified brake fluid.
11. Test the brakes for normal operation

BRAKES

PARKING BRAKE CABLES

ADJUSTMENT

See Figures 10 and 11.

➡ **Cable tension is adjusted in 2 locations, the first location is at the parking brake control, the second location is at the parking brake cable equalizer. The tension must be adjusted equally at both locations.**

1. Raise and safely support the vehicle.

➡ **The dimension will vary depending on the amount of cable stretch. New cables require cycling the parking brake control 5-10 times to remove the cable slack.**

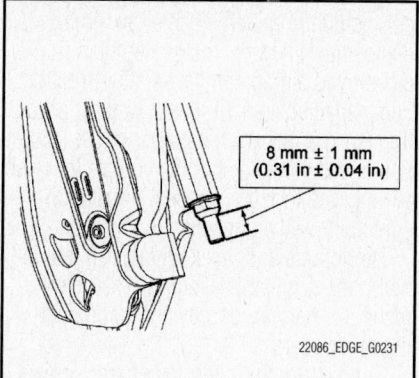

8 mm ± 1 mm
(0.31 in ± 0.04 in)

22086_EDGE_G0231

Fig. 10 Adjust the parking brake control adjustment nut as shown.

PARKING BRAKE

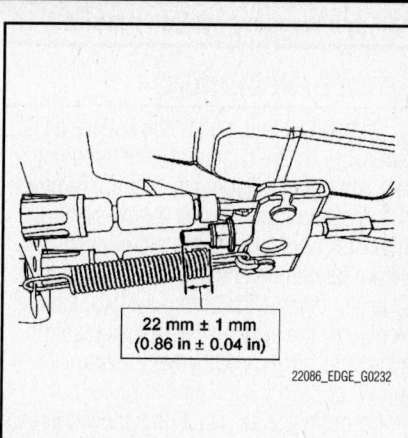

22 mm ± 1 mm
(0.86 in ± 0.04 in)

22086_EDGE_G0232

Fig. 11 Adjust the parking brake cable equalizer adjustment nut as shown

2. Adjust the parking brake control adjustment nut as shown in the accompanying illustration.

3. Adjust the parking brake cable equalizer adjustment nut as shown in the accompanying illustration.

4. Fully apply the parking brake pedal 3 times to verify correct operation of the parking brake system.

5. With the parking brake cable in the fully released position, brake drag should not be present

PARKING BRAKE SHOES

REMOVAL & INSTALLATION

See Figure 12.

1. Remove the rear brake rotor, as outlined in this section.

2. Remove the parking brake shoe return spring.

3. Remove the parking brake shoe.

4. Installation is the reverse of the removal procedure. Check the parking brake for normal operation.

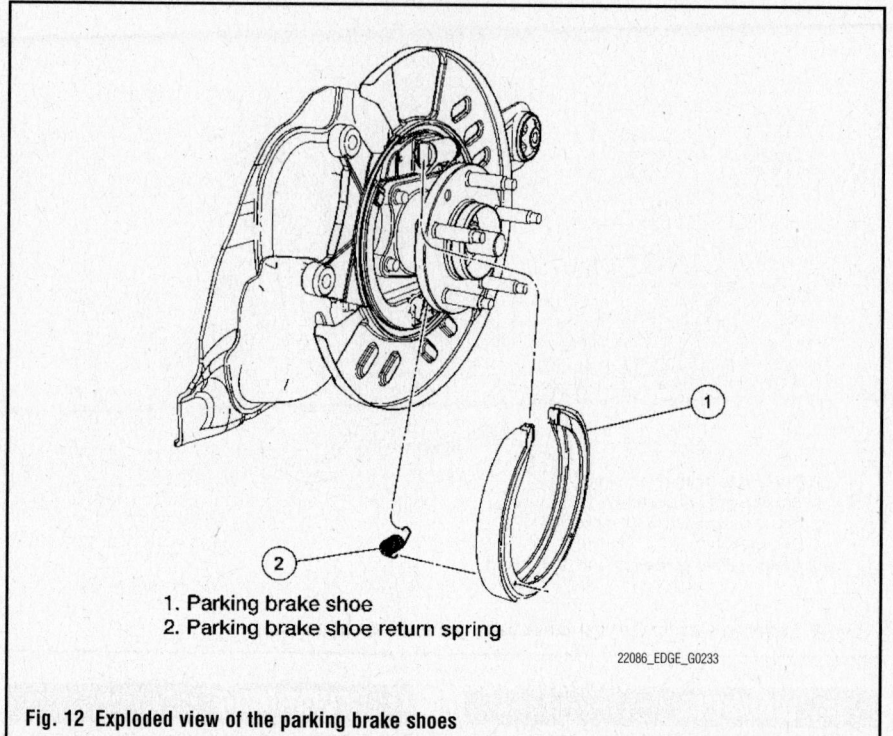

1. Parking brake shoe
2. Parking brake shoe return spring

22086_EDGE_G0233

Fig. 12 Exploded view of the parking brake shoes

CHASSIS ELECTRICAL

AIR BAG (SUPPLEMENTAL RESTRAINT SYSTEM)

GENERAL INFORMATION

❋ CAUTION

These vehicles are equipped with an air bag system. The system must be disarmed before performing service on, or around, system components, the steering column, instrument panel components, wiring and sensors. Failure to follow the safety precautions and the disarming procedure could result in accidental air bag deployment, possible injury and unnecessary system repairs.

SERVICE PRECAUTIONS

Disconnect and isolate the battery negative cable before beginning any airbag system component diagnosis, testing, removal, or installation procedures. Allow system capacitor to discharge for two minutes before beginning any component service. This will disable the airbag system. Failure to disable the airbag system may result in accidental airbag deployment, personal injury, or death.

Do not place an intact undeployed airbag face down on a solid surface. The airbag will propel into the air if accidentally deployed and may result in personal injury or death.

When carrying or handling an undeployed airbag, the trim side (face) of the airbag should be pointing towards the body to minimize possibility of injury if accidental deployment occurs. Failure to do this may result in personal injury or death.

Replace airbag system components with OEM replacement parts. Substitute parts may appear interchangeable, but internal differences may result in inferior occupant protection. Failure to do so may result in occupant personal injury or death.

Wear safety glasses, rubber gloves, and long sleeved clothing when cleaning powder residue from vehicle after an airbag deployment. Powder residue emitted from a deployed airbag can cause skin irritation. Flush affected area with cool water if irritation is experienced. If nasal or throat irritation is experienced, exit the vehicle for fresh air until the irritation ceases. If irritation continues, see a physician.

Do not use a replacement airbag that is not in the original packaging. This may result in improper deployment, personal injury, or death.

The factory installed fasteners, screws and bolts used to fasten airbag components have a special coating and are specifically designed for the airbag system. Do not use substitute fasteners. Use only original equipment fasteners listed in the parts catalog when fastener replacement is required.

During, and following, any child restraint anchor service, due to impact event or vehicle repair, carefully inspect all mounting hardware, tether straps, and anchors for proper installation, operation, or damage. If a child restraint anchor is found damaged in any way, the anchor must be replaced. Failure to do this may result in personal injury or death.

Deployed and non-deployed airbags may or may not have live pyrotechnic material within the airbag inflator.

Do not dispose of driver/passenger/curtain airbags or seat belt tensioners unless you are sure of complete deployment. Refer to the Hazardous Substance Control System for proper disposal.

Dispose of deployed airbags and tensioners consistent with state, provincial, local, and federal regulations.

After any airbag component testing or service, do not connect the battery negative cable. Personal injury or death may result if the system test is not performed first.

If the vehicle is equipped with the Occupant Classification System (OCS), do not connect the battery negative cable before performing the OCS Verification Test using the scan tool and the appropriate diagnostic information. Personal injury or death may result if the system test is not performed properly.

Never replace both the Occupant Restraint Controller (ORC) and the Occupant Classification Module (OCM) at the same time. If both require replacement, replace one, then perform the Airbag System test before replacing the other.

Both the ORC and the OCM store Occupant Classification System (OCS) calibration data, which they transfer to one another when one of them is replaced. If both are replaced at the same time, an irreversible fault will be set in both modules and the OCS may malfunction and cause personal injury or death.

If equipped with OCS, the Seat Weight Sensor is a sensitive, calibrated unit and must be handled carefully. Do not drop or handle roughly. If dropped or damaged, replace with another sensor. Failure to do so may result in occupant injury or death.

If equipped with OCS, the front passenger seat must be handled carefully as well. When removing the seat, be careful when setting on floor not to drop. If dropped, the sensor may be inoperative, could result in occupant injury, or possibly death.

If equipped with OCS, when the passenger front seat is on the floor, no one should sit in the front passenger seat. This uneven force may damage the sensing ability of the seat weight sensors. If sat on and damaged, the sensor may be inoperative, could result in occupant injury, or possibly death.

DISARMING THE SYSTEM

✳✳ CAUTION

Never probe the electrical connectors on air bag, safety canopy or side air curtain modules. Failure to follow this instruction may result in the accidental deployment of these modules, which increases the risk of serious personal injury or death.

✳✳ CAUTION

To reduce the risk of accidental deployment, do not use any memory saver devices. Failure to follow this instruction may result in serious personal injury or death.

➡**The air bag warning indicator illuminates when the Restraints Control Module (RCM) fuse is removed and the ignition switch is ON. This is normal operation and does not indicate a Supplemental Restraints System (SRS) fault.**

1. Turn all vehicle accessories OFF.
2. Turn the ignition switch to the **OFF** position.
3. At the smart power distribution junction box (SPDJB), located in the LH lower kick panel, remove the lower kick panel fuse cover and the restraints control module (RCM) fuse 46 (7.5A) from the (SPDJB).
4. Turn the ignition **ON** and make sure that the air bag warning indicator lights up for at least 30 seconds. The air bag warning indicator will remain lit continuously (no flashing) if the correct RCM fuse has been removed. If the air bag warning indicator does not remain lit continuously, remove the correct RCM fuse before proceeding.
5. Turn the ignition switch to the **OFF** position.

✳✳ WARNING

To avoid accidental deployment and possible personal injury, the backup power supply MUST be depleted before repairing or installing any new front or side air bag SRS components and before servicing, installing, adjusting or striking components near the front or side air bag sensors, such as doors, instrument panel, console, door latches, strikers, seats and hood latches. Failure to follow this instruction may result in serious personal injury. The front impact severity sensors are located on the radiator support under the front bumper cover. The first row side impact sensors are located at or near the base of the B-pillars. The second row side impact sensors are located on the C-pillars.

6. To deplete the backup power supply energy, disconnect the negative battery cable and wait at least one minute. Be sure to disconnect auxiliary batteries and power supplies (if equipped).
7. Disconnect the negative battery cable and wait at least one minute.

ARMING THE SYSTEM

1. Turn the ignition switch from the **OFF** position to the **ON** position.
2. Install RCM fuse 46 (7.5A) to the SPDJB and install the lower kick panel fuse cover.

✳✳ CAUTION

Make sure that nobody is in the vehicle and that there is nothing blocking or set in front of any air bag module when the negative battery

cable is connected. Failure to follow this instruction may result in serious personal injury.

3. Connect the negative battery cable.
4. Prove out the SRS as follows:
   a. Turn the ignition switch from ON to OFF. Wait 10 seconds, then turn the ignition switch back to ON and visually monitor the air bag warning indicator with the air bag modules installed. The air bag warning indicator will light continuously for approximately 6 seconds and then turn OFF. If an air bag SRS fault is present, the air bag warning indicator will:
   • Fail to light.
   • Remain lit continuously.
   • Flash at a 5 Hz rate (RCM not configured).
5. The air bag warning indicator might not light until approximately 30 seconds after the ignition switch has been turned from the OFF to the ON position. This is the time required for the RCM to complete the testing of the SRS. If the air bag warning indicator is inoperative and a SRS fault exists, a chime will sound in a pattern of 5 sets of 5 beeps. If this occurs, the air bag warning indicator and any SRS fault discovered must be diagnosed and repaired.
6. Clear all continuous Diagnostic Trouble Codes (DTCs) from the RCM and Occupant Classification Sensor (OCS) module using a scan tool.

CLOCKSPRING CENTERING

See Figures 13 through 15.

➡**This procedure covers removal and installation, and centering of the clockspring.**

✳✳ CAUTION

To reduce the risk of accidental deployment, do not use any memory saver devices. Failure to follow this instruction may result in serious personal injury or death.

➡**The air bag warning indicator illuminates when the Restraints Control Module (RCM) fuse is removed and the ignition switch is ON. This is normal operation and does not indicate a Supplemental Restraint System (SRS) fault.**

➡**Repair is made by installing a new part only. If the new part does not correct the condition, install the original part and carry out the diagnostic procedure again.**

1. Disarm the SRS, as outlined in this section.

2. Tilt the steering wheel in the downward position and lock the tilt handle.

3. Remove the driver air bag module, as follows:

a. Using a 3-mm Allen wrench or a suitable tool through the access hole on the backside of the steering wheel, position the tool against the spring clip and push in, disengaging the clip from the locking pin. With the spring clip disengaged from the locking pin, gently pull back on that side of the driver air bag module to release it from the steering wheel. Repeat for the other locking pin.

✳✳ WARNING

NEVER pull the driver air bag module electrical connectors out by the locking buttons. Damage to the locking buttons can occur.

b. Using a small screwdriver as shown, lift up and release the locking buttons on the driver air bag module electrical connectors. With the locking buttons released, remove the electrical connectors and the driver air bag module.

✳✳ WARNING

Vehicles with absolute steering angle sensor and/or adaptive headlamps, do not allow the clockspring

rotor to turn from the straight-ahead position after the steering wheel is removed. Failure to follow this instruction may result in component damage and/or system failure.

➡ **Make sure the vehicle's wheels are in the straight-ahead position.**

4. Remove the steering wheel, as outlined in the Steering Section.

5. Tape the clockspring rotor to the steering column shaft to prevent the clockspring rotor from moving out of center.

6. Release the 2 tabs and position the upper steering column shroud upward.

7. Remove the 3 screws and the lower steering column shroud.

8. Disconnect the clockspring electrical connector.

9. Remove the tape from the clockspring rotor to the steering column shaft. Do not allow the clockspring rotor to move from center after tape is removed.

✳✳ WARNING

Vehicles with absolute steering angle sensor and/or adaptive headlamps, do not allow the clockspring rotor to turn from the straight-ahead position after the steering wheel is removed. Failure to follow this instruction may result in component damage and/or system failure.

➡ **Vehicles with absolute steering angle sensor and/or adaptive headlamps, after the clockspring has been removed make sure the arrow on the absolute steering angle sensor ring is lined up with the arrow on the absolute steering angle sensor housing as shown.**

10. Remove the 2 clockspring screws and remove the clockspring.

To install:
Vehicle repairs re-using the same clockspring:

✳✳ CAUTION

If the clockspring is not correctly centralized, it may fail prematurely. If in doubt, repeat the centralizing procedure. Failure to follow these instructions may increase the risk of serious personal injury or death in a crash.

✳✳ WARNING

Make sure the vehicle's wheels are still in the straight-ahead position. Failure to follow this instruction may result in component damage and/or system failure.

11. If the vehicle's clockspring has rotated out of center, follow these steps to center the clockspring.

a. Hold the clockspring outer housing stationary.

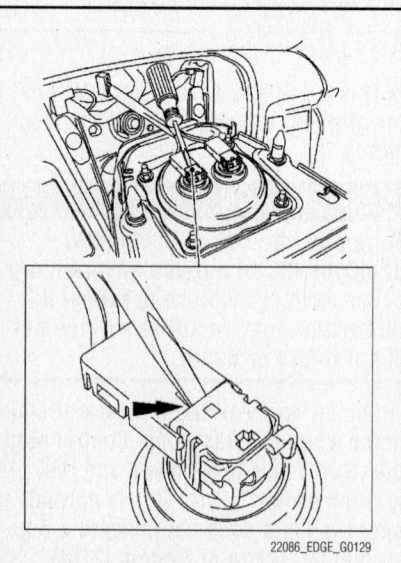

22086_EDGE_G0129

Fig. 13 Using a small screwdriver as shown, lift up and release the locking buttons on the driver air bag module electrical connectors. With the locking buttons released, remove the electrical connectors and the driver air bag module

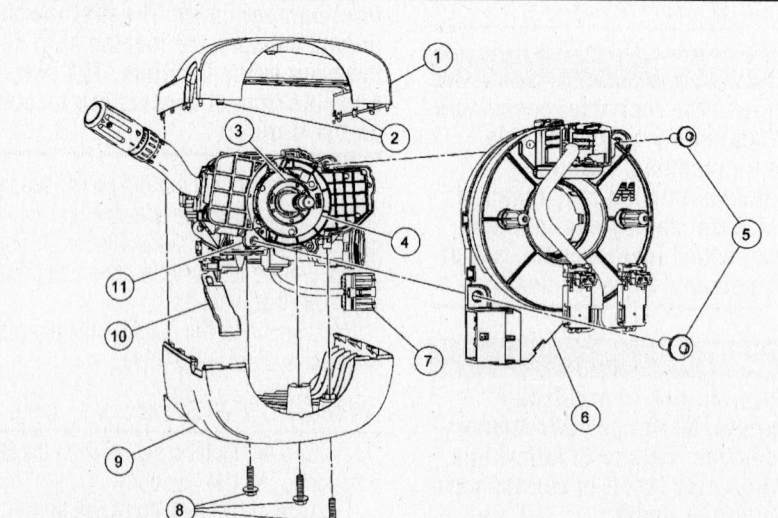

1. Upper steering column shroud
2. Upper steering column shroud tabs (2)
3. Absolute steering angle sensor
4. Absolute steering angle sensor ring
5. Clockspring screws (2)
6. Clockspring
7. Clockspring electrical connector
8. Lower steering column shroud screws (3)
9. Lower steering column shroud
10. Steering column tilt lock/unlock handle
11. Multi-function switch housing

22086_EDGE_G0128

Fig. 14 Exploded view of the SRS clockspring and related components

⁂ WARNING

Overturning will destroy the clock-spring. The internal ribbon wire acts as the stop and can be broken from its internal connection.

b. While turning the rotor counter-clockwise, carefully feel for the ribbon wire to run out of length and for a slight resistance. Stop turning at this point.

c. Turn the clockspring clockwise (approximately 2.25 turns) until the clockspring rotor wiring and connector are in the 12 o'clock position. Clockspring is now centered.

d. Do not allow the rotor to turn from this position.

→Slight rotation of the absolute steering angle sensor ring is allowed to align the 2 arrows.

12. Make sure the sensor ring arrow is lined up with the absolute steering angle sensor housing arrow as shown.

⁂ WARNING

If the clockspring is left unattended between centralizing the clockspring and installing it to the multi-function switch housing, the centralizing procedure must be repeated. Failure to follow this instruction may result in component damage and/or system failure.

→On vehicles with absolute steering angle sensor and/or adaptive head-lamps, slight rotation of the clock-spring rotor might be needed to seat the clockspring 3 locator pins into the absolute steering angle sensor and or adaptive headlamps sensor ring. Very slight rotation is possible on a new clockspring with the sealing key installed.

→Make sure the clockspring is fully seated into the multi-function switch

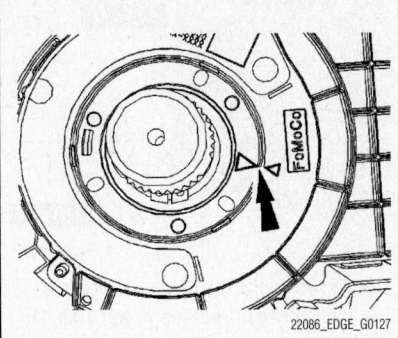

Fig. 15 Make sure the sensor ring arrow is lined up with the absolute steering angle sensor housing arrow as shown

housing before installing the clock-spring screws.

13. Install the clockspring and the 2 screws.
14. Connect the clockspring electrical connector.
15. Install the lower steering column shroud and the 3 screws.
16. Attach the upper steering column shroud to the lower steering column shroud.

⁂ WARNING

If not installing a new clockspring, and the vehicle is left unattended between the installation of the clock-spring to the multi-function switch housing and installing the steering wheel, the centralizing procedure can be repeated at this time with the clockspring being installed in the multi-function switch housing. Failure to follow this instruction may result in component damage and/or system failure.

17. Install the steering wheel.
18. If a new clockspring is being installed, and after the steering wheel installation, remove the clockspring seal-ing key.

19. Install the driver air bag module, as follows:

⁂ WARNING

Do not install the driver air bag module electrical connectors by the lock-ing buttons. Damage to the locking buttons can occur.

⁂ WARNING

The driver air bag module electrical connector locking buttons must be in the released position when the connector is being installed or connector damage may occur.

⁂ WARNING

The driver air bag module electrical connectors are unique and cannot be reversed when connected to the driver air bag module. Match the electrical connector key to the keyway in the driver air bag module. Do not force the electrical connectors into the driver air bag module. Damage to the connector or component may occur.

e. With the locking buttons released, install the driver air bag module electrical connectors fully into the driver air bag module and seat the locking buttons.

→Audible clicks will be heard when both wire clips are seated in the driver air bag module.

Align the driver air bag module locking pins to the steering wheel and, while pushing inward, seat the 2 driver air bag module locking pins to the steering wheel wire clips.

f. When the 2 locking pins are seated in place, there should be an even gap between the driver air bag module trim cover and the steering wheel
20. Rearm the SRS, as outlined in this section.

DRIVE TRAIN

AUTOMATIC TRANSAXLE ASSEMBLY

REMOVAL & INSTALLATION

See Figures 16 through 32.

1. Raise and safely support the vehicle.
2. Disconnect the Mass Air Flow (MAF) sensor electrical connector and the wiring harness fastener from the air cleaner assembly.

3. Disconnect the brake booster vacuum hose from the air cleaner outlet pipe.
4. Disconnect the engine breather from the air cleaner assembly.
5. Remove the air cleaner assembly bracket bolt.
6. Loosen the air cleaner outlet pipe clamp at the throttle body and remove the air cleaner and air cleaner outlet pipe assembly.

7. Disconnect the negative, then the positive battery cable.
8. Remove the battery. Remove the battery tray.
9. Disconnect the wiring harness fasteners.
10. Remove the 3 bolts and the battery tray.
11. Remove the upper intake manifold, as outlined in the Engine Mechanical section.

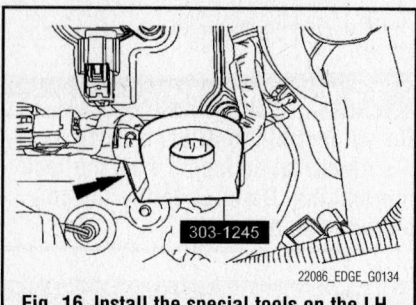

Fig. 16 Install the special tools on the LH cylinder head

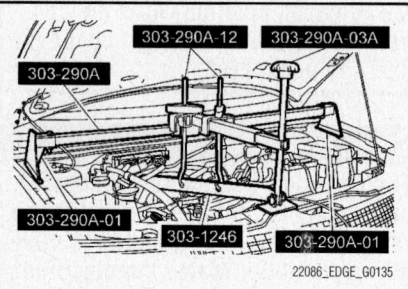

Fig. 17 Install the special tools and support the engine

12. Disconnect the selector lever cable end from the manual lever.

13. Remove the 3 selector lever cable bracket bolts and position aside the selector lever cable.

14. Remove the starter motor electrical terminal cover.

15. Position the starter cable boot back and remove the starter terminals from the starter.

16. Disconnect the wiring harness fastener from the starter motor studbolt.

17. Remove the 2 bolts and the starter.

18. Disconnect the fuel hose routing clip from the transaxle stud and position the fuel hose aside.

19. Disconnect the transaxle electrical connector.

20. Remove the top 4 torque converter housing bolts.

➡**The coolant hoses do not need to be removed from the engine.**

21. Remove the coolant hoses from the transmission fluid filler tube and position aside.

22. Remove the transmission fluid level indicator.

23. Remove the nut, rotate the transmission fluid filler tube counterclockwise 90 degrees and remove the transmission fluid filler tube.

24. Install the special tool on the LH cylinder head.

25. Install the special tools and support the engine.

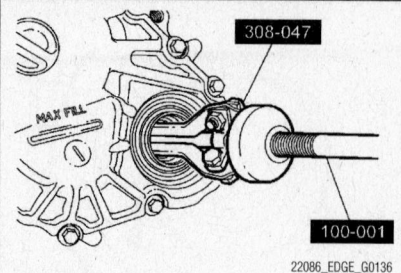

Fig. 18 Using the special tools, remove the halfshaft seal from the Power Transfer Unit (PTU)

26. Remove the transaxle support insulator through bolt.

27. Remove the 3 nuts, the bolt and the transaxle support insulator bracket.

28. Remove the 4 pushpin fasteners and the RH splash shield.

29. Remove the 3 pushpin fasteners, the 7 screws and the front splash shield.

30. Remove the transmission fluid drain plug and allow the transmission fluid to drain.

31. Install the transmission fluid drain plug. Once the fluid has drained, tighten to 9 Nm (80 inch lbs.).

32. Remove the 3 RH subframe-to-lower bumper nuts.

33. Remove the 3 LH subframe-to-lower bumper nuts and separate the front support from the subframe.

34. Remove the 3 power steering tube bracket bolts from the RH side of the subframe and position the power steering tube aside.

35. Remove the 2 sway bar link-to-control arm nuts and separate the sway bar links from the lower control arms.

36. Remove the 2 front halfshaft nuts.

37. Remove the lower control arm-to-knuckle pinch bolts and separate the lower control arms from the knuckles.

38. Using a suitable halfshaft removal tool, separate the halfshafts from the wheel hubs.

39. For All wheel drive (AWD) vehicles, perform the following:

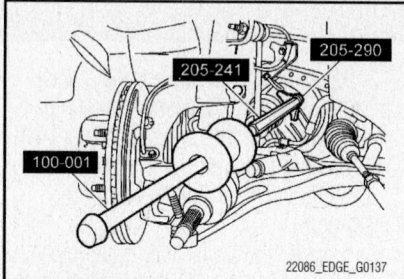

Fig. 19 Using the special tools, remove the LH halfshaft

a. Remove the 2 RH halfshaft bearing support bracket bolts and the RH halfshaft.

b. Inspect the halfshaft hub for wear or damage and replace the halfshaft, if necessary.

c. Inspect the differential seal surface.

d. Inspect the halfshaft bushing surface. If this surface is damaged, inspect the halfshaft bushing for damage.

e. Inspect the differential side gear splines.

➡**A new halfshaft seal must be installed anytime the RH halfshaft is removed.**

➡**The seal deflector will be damaged during removal. Be careful not to damage the cover seal directly behind the seal deflector.**

f. Remove the seal deflector.

g. Using the special tools, remove the halfshaft seal from the Power Transfer Unit (PTU).

40. For Front wheel drive (FWD) vehicles, perform the following:

a. Remove the 2 catalytic converter support bracket bolts.

b. Remove the bolt, the nut and the catalytic converter support bracket.

c. Remove the 2 bolts and the RH halfshaft.

d. Inspect the halfshaft hub for wear or damage and replace the halfshaft, if necessary.

e. Inspect the differential seal surface.

f. Inspect the halfshaft bushing surface. If this surface is damaged, inspect the halfshaft bushing for damage.

g. Inspect the differential side gear splines.

41. Using the special tools, remove the LH halfshaft.

42. Inspect the halfshaft hub for wear or damage and replace the halfshaft, if necessary.

Fig. 20 Remove the 2 nuts, 4 bolts and the subframe support brackets

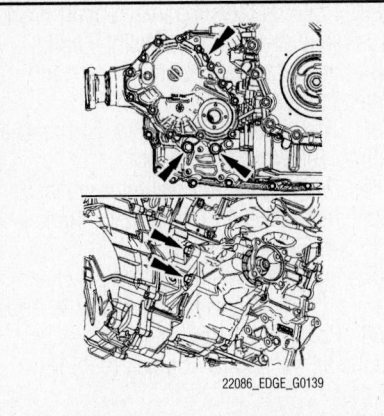

Fig. 21 Remove the 5 bolts and the PTU

43. Inspect the differential seal surface.

44. Inspect the halfshaft bushing surface. If this surface is damaged, inspect the halfshaft bushing for damage.

45. Inspect the differential side gear splines.

46. Loosen the Y-pipe clamp and disconnect the 2 exhaust hangers.

47. Remove the 4 nuts and the Y-pipe assembly.

48. Remove the 4 bolts and position the steering rack aside, using a piece of wire.

49. Remove the 4 bolts and position the sway bar aside, using a piece of wire.

50. Remove the 2 nuts and the roll restrictor heat shield.

51. Remove the 3 bolts from the roll restrictor bracket.

52. Support the subframe using a suitable drivetrain lift.

53. Remove the 2 nuts, 4 bolts and the subframe support brackets.

54. Remove the 2 front subframe nuts.

55. Remove the 2 middle subframe nuts and remove the subframe.

56. Remove the 3 bolts and the roll restrictor bracket.

57. For AWD vehicles, perform the following:

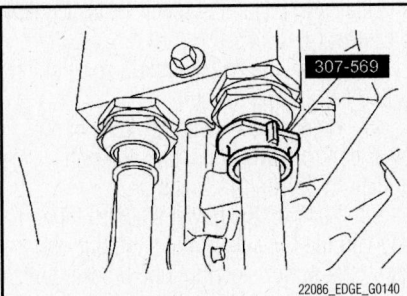

Fig. 22 Using the special tool, disconnect the transmission fluid cooler tubes from the transmission fluid cooler thermal bypass valve

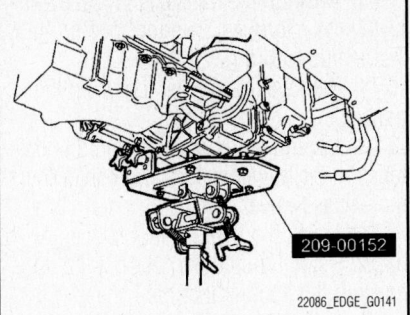

Fig. 23 Using the special tool and a suitable transmission jack, support the transaxle

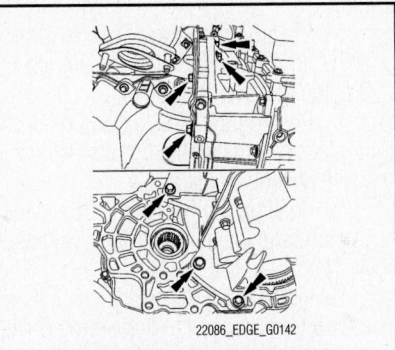

Fig. 24 Remove the 7 torque converter housing bolts and remove the transaxle from the vehicle

a. Index-mark the driveshaft, remove the 4 bolts and position the driveshaft aside.

b. Disconnect the RH catalyst monitor electrical connector.

c. Remove the 2 catalytic converter support bracket bolts.

d. Remove the 4 RH catalytic converter nuts and the RH catalytic converter.

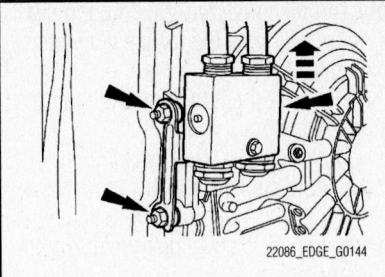

Fig. 26 Remove the 2 nuts, pull the transmission fluid cooler thermal bypass valve and the transmission fluid cooler tubes straight up and remove the assembly from the transaxle

e. Remove the 5 bolts and the PTU support bracket.

f. Remove the 5 bolts and the PTU.

58. Remove the 2 fasteners and the inspection cover.

59. Remove and discard the 3 torque converter bolts.

60. Remove the 2 secondary latches from the transmission fluid cooler tubes at the transmission fluid cooler thermal bypass valve.

61. Using the special tool, disconnect the transmission fluid cooler tubes from the transmission fluid cooler thermal bypass valve.

62. Using the special tool and a suitable transmission jack, support the transaxle.

63. Remove the 7 torque converter housing bolts and remove the transaxle from the vehicle.

64. Check the torque converter housing mating surface to make sure that the dowel pins did not come out of the engine block when the transaxle was removed. If the dowel pin is stuck

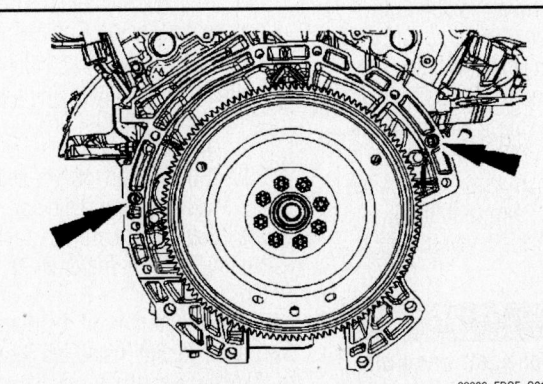

Fig. 25 Check the torque converter housing mating surface to make sure that the dowel pins did not come out of the engine block when the transaxle was removed. If the dowel pin is stuck in the torque converter housing, remove the dowel pin from the torque converter housing

in the torque converter housing, remove the dowel pin from the torque converter housing.

65. Remove the 2 transmission fluid cooler tube bolts.

66. Remove the 2 nuts, pull the transmission fluid cooler thermal bypass valve and the transmission fluid cooler tubes straight up and remove the assembly from the transaxle.

67. Inspect the transaxle case to make sure that the transmission fluid cooler tube seals and backing rings were removed with the transmission fluid cooler tubes and are not stuck in the transaxle case. If the transmission fluid cooler tube seals or backing rings are stuck in the transaxle case, remove the seals and backing rings.

➡If a replacement transaxle assembly is being installed or a new solenoid body is installed, the Powertrain Control Module (PCM) will have to be reflashed with a new solenoid body strategy and ID data file.

To install:

❊❊ **WARNING**

Before installation of a new or overhauled transaxle, the transmission fluid cooler tubes must be cleaned. otherwise transaxle failure can occur.

➡**Before installing a new or overhauled transaxle, flush out the cooler and cooler lines.**

68. Inspect the transmission fluid cooler tube backing rings and seals for damage and install a new backing rings or seals if necessary. Lubricate the transmission fluid cooler tube seals with clean automatic transmission fluid and install the backing rings and seals on the transmission fluid cooler tube.

69. Position the transmission fluid cooler thermal bypass valve and transmission fluid cooler tube assembly in place and install the 2 nuts. Tighten to 9 Nm (80 inch lbs.).

70. Install the 2 transmission fluid cooler tube bolts. Tighten to 11 Nm (8 ft. lbs.).

71. Lubricate the torque converter pilot hub with grease.

❊❊ **WARNING**

If the transaxle is not positioned on the dowel pins, damage to the transaxle can occur.

72. If the dowel pins were pulled out of the engine block during removal, install new dowel pins in the engine block.

73. Position the transaxle in place and install the 7 torque converter housing bolts. Tighten to 48 Nm (35 ft. lbs.).

74. Remove the special tool from the transaxle.

75. Install the transmission fluid cooler tubes in the transmission fluid cooler thermal bypass valve.

76. Install the 2 secondary latches on the transmission fluid cooler tubes at the transmission fluid cooler thermal bypass valve.

77. Install 3 new torque converter bolts and tighten to 55 Nm (41 ft. lbs.).

78. Install the inspection cover and the 2 fasteners.

79. For AWD vehicles , perform the following:

a. Position the Power Transfer Unit (PTU) in place and install the 5 bolts. Tighten to 90 Nm (66 ft. lbs.).

b. Position the PTU support bracket in place and install the 5 bolts. Tighten to 70 Nm (52 ft. lbs.).

c. Position the RH catalytic converter in place and install the 4 nuts. Tighten to 40 Nm (30 ft. lbs.).

d. Install the 2 RH catalytic converter support bracket bolts. Tighten to 20 Nm (15 ft. lbs.).

e. Connect the RH catalyst monitor electrical connector.

f. Line up the index marks on the rear driveshaft to the index marks on the PTU flange made during removal and install the 4 bolts. Tighten to 70 Nm (52 ft. lbs.).

g. Using a suitable driver, install a new intermediate shaft seal. Make sure that the seal is fully seated against the drive gear.

➡**Do not overheat (melt) the seal deflector. If the deflector is damaged, a new one must be used.**

h. Using a suitable heat gun, heat the new seal deflector. Concentrate the heat across the back of the deflector near the white colored tabs. Install the seal deflector immediately after heating.

i. If necessary, use special tools 308-430 and 308-431 to seat the deflector. Make sure the deflector is fully seated and there are no cracks on the face or inner diameter white colored tabs.

80. Position the roll restrictor bracket on the transaxle and install the 3 bolts. Tighten to 90 Nm (66 ft. lbs.).

81. Position the subframe in place and install the 2 middle nuts. Tighten to 150 Nm (111 ft. lbs.).

82. Install the 2 front subframe nuts. Tighten to 150 Nm (111 ft. lbs.).

83. Position the subframe support brackets in place and loosely install the bolts.

84. Install the rear subframe nuts and tighten to 150 Nm (111 ft. lbs.).

85. Tighten the subframe support bracket bolts to 103 Nm (76 ft. lbs.).

86. Position the roll restrictor in place, install the bracket and the 3 bolts. Tighten to 90 Nm (66 ft. lbs.).

87. Install the roll restrictor heat shield and the 2 nuts. Tighten to 11 Nm (8 ft. lbs.).

88. Position the stabilizer bar in place and install the 4 bolts. Tighten to 48 Nm (35 ft. lbs.).

89. Position the power steering rack in place and install the 4 bolts. Tighten to 107 Nm (79 ft. lbs.).

90. Position the exhaust Y-pipe assembly in place and install the 4 nuts. Tighten to 40 Nm (30 ft. lbs.).

91. Install the 2 exhaust hangers and tighten the exhaust clamp. Tighten to 40 Nm (30 ft. lbs.).

92. Position the LH halfshaft in the transaxle and in the steering knuckle.

93. For FWD vehicles, perform the following:

a. Position the RH halfshaft and intermediate shaft support bracket in the transaxle and in the steering knuckle. Install 1 stud bolt and 1 bolt. Tighten to 55 Nm (41 ft. lbs.).

b. Position the catalytic converter support bracket in place and install the bolt and the nut. Tighten the nut to 40 Nm (30 ft. lbs.). Tighten the bolt to 55 Nm (41 ft. lbs.).

c. Install the 2 RH catalytic converter support bracket bolts. Tighten to 20 Nm (15 ft. lbs.).

94. For AWD vehicles, perform the following:

a. Install the RH halfshaft and install the RH halfshaft bearing support bracket bolts. Tighten to 23 Nm (17 ft. lbs.).

95. Install the ball joints in the steering knuckles and install the pinch bolts. Tighten to 55 Nm (41 ft. lbs.).

96. Install the halfshaft nuts and tighten to 350 Nm (258 ft. lbs.).

97. Position the sway bar links in the lower control arms and install the nuts. Tighten to 55 Nm (41 ft. lbs.).

98. Position the power steering tube in place on the RH side of the subframe and install the power steering tube bracket bolts. Tighten to 5 Nm (44 inch lbs.).

99. Position the lower bumper on the subframe and install the 3 LH nuts. Tighten to 10 Nm (89 inch lbs.).

100. Install the 3 RH lower bumper-to-subframe nuts. Tighten to 10 Nm (89 inch lbs.).

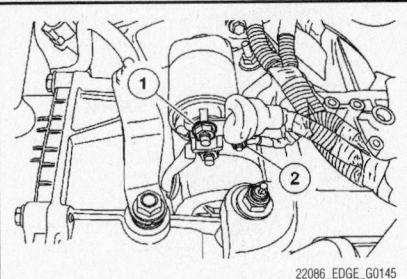

Fig. 27 Connect the starter motor terminals and position the starter terminal boot over the battery cable terminal. Tighten (1) to 12 Nm (9 ft. lbs.) and (2) to 6 Nm (53 inch lbs.), as shown

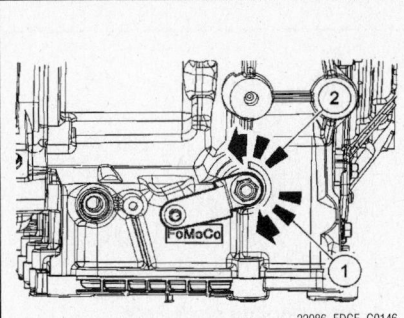

Fig. 28 Rotate the manual lever clockwise until it stops (1), then rotate the manual lever counterclockwise one detent until it stops (2)

101. Install the front splash shield and install the 7 screws and the 3 pushpin fasteners.

102. Install the RH splash shield and the 4 pushpin fasteners.

103. Install the transaxle support insulator bracket, install the bolt and the 3 nuts. Tighten to 63 Nm (46 ft. lbs.).

104. Install the transaxle support insulator through bolt. Tighten to 175 Nm (129 ft. lbs.).

105. Remove the special tools.

106. Remove the special tools from the LH cylinder head.

107. If a new solenoid body was installed, wipe the surface of the existing solenoid body strategy tag on top of the transaxle case clean and install the new solenoid body strategy tag (supplied with the solenoid body service kit) over it.

108. Install the fluid filler tube and the nut. Tighten to 11 Nm (8 ft. lbs.).

109. Install the transmission fluid level indicator.

110. Route the coolant hoses in the transmission fluid filler tube.

111. Install the top 4 torque converter housing bolts. Tighten to 48 Nm (35 ft. lbs.).

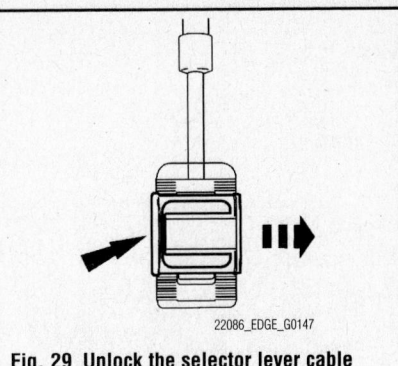

Fig. 29 Unlock the selector lever cable adjuster by sliding the locking tab over

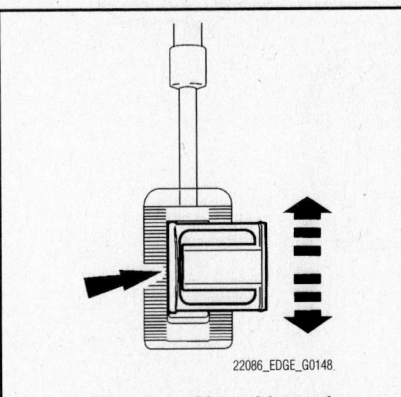

Fig. 30 Slide the cable end forward or backward to align it with the manual lever

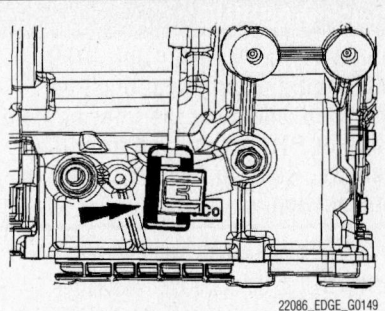

Fig. 31 With the adjuster locking tab released, connect the selector lever cable end to the manual lever

112. Connect the transaxle electrical connector.

113. Position the fuel hose routing clip on the transaxle stud.

114. Install the starter and the 2 bolts. Tighten to 26 Nm (19 ft. lbs.).

115. Install the wiring harness fastener on the starter motor studbolt.

116. Connect the starter motor terminals and position the starter terminal boot over the battery cable terminal. Tighten (1) to 12 Nm (9 ft. lbs.) and (2) to 6 Nm (53 inch lbs.), as shown in the illustration.

117. Install the starter motor electrical terminal cover.

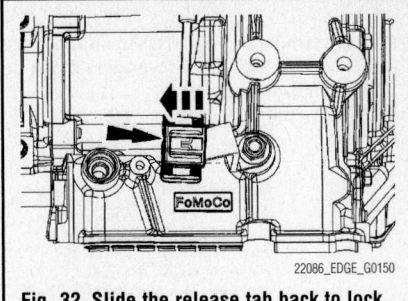

Fig. 32 Slide the release tab back to lock the adjuster

118. Position the selector lever cable and bracket in place and install the 3 bolts. Tighten to 12 Nm (9 ft. lbs.).

119. Place the selector lever in DRIVE.

120. Place the manual lever in DRIVE, as follows:

   a. Rotate the manual lever clockwise until it stops.

   b. Rotate the manual lever counterclockwise one detent until it stops.

121. Unlock the selector lever cable adjuster by sliding the locking tab over.

122. Slide the cable end forward or backward to align it with the manual lever.

123. With the adjuster locking tab released, connect the selector lever cable end to the manual lever.

124. Slide the release tab back to lock the adjuster.

125. Install the upper intake manifold.

126. Install the battery tray. Install the 3 bolts and tighten to 10 Nm (89 inch lbs.).

127. Connect the wiring harness fasteners to the battery tray.

128. Install the battery, then connect the positive, then the negative battery cables.

129. Position the air cleaner assembly in place and install the bolt. Tighten to 11 Nm (8 ft. lbs.).

130. Tighten the air cleaner outlet pipe clamp at the throttle body. Tighten to 5 Nm (44 inch lbs.).

131. Connect the engine breather to the air cleaner assembly.

132. Connect the brake booster vacuum hose to the air cleaner assembly.

133. Connect the MAF sensor electrical connector and connect the electrical harness fastener.

134. Fill with clean automatic transmission fluid to the correct level.

135. If a new solenoid body is installed, the solenoid body strategy and solenoid body ID will need to be updated.

136. If a replacement transaxle assembly is being installed or a new solenoid body is installed, the Powertrain Control Module (PCM) will have to be reflashed with a new solenoid body strategy and ID data file

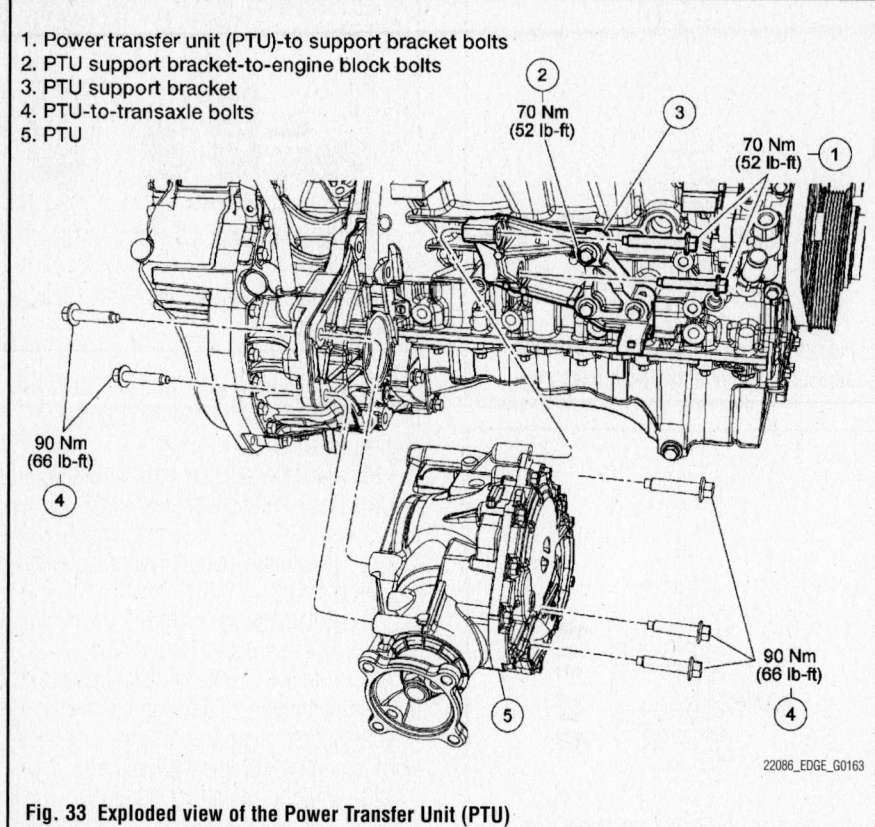

1. Power transfer unit (PTU)-to support bracket bolts
2. PTU support bracket-to-engine block bolts
3. PTU support bracket
4. PTU-to-transaxle bolts
5. PTU

70 Nm (52 lb-ft)
70 Nm (52 lb-ft)
90 Nm (66 lb-ft)
90 Nm (66 lb-ft)

22086_EDGE_G0163

Fig. 33 Exploded view of the Power Transfer Unit (PTU)

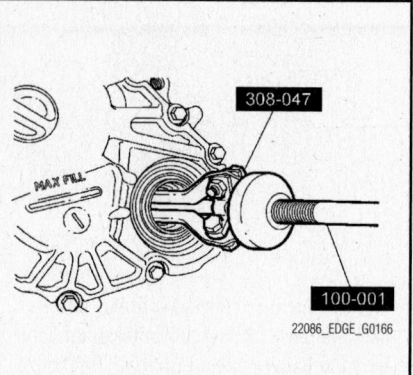

308-047
100-001

22086_EDGE_G0166

Fig. 35 Using the special tools, remove the intermediate shaft seal. Clean the area around the seal deflector and seal

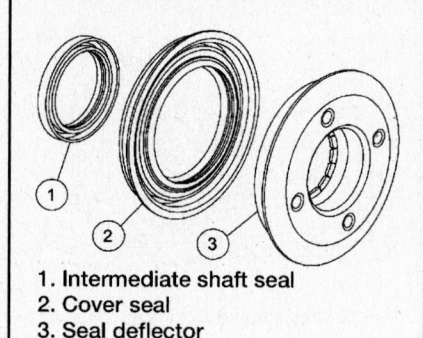

1. Intermediate shaft seal
2. Cover seal
3. Seal deflector

22086_EDGE_G0165

Fig. 36 Exploded view of the seal

TRANSFER CASE ASSEMBLY

REMOVAL & INSTALLATION

See Figure 33.

➡ This procedure covers Removal and Installation of the Power Transfer Unit (PTU).

1. Raise and safely support the vehicle.

✳✳ WARNING

A new Power Transfer Unit (PTU) intermediate shaft seal must be installed whenever the intermediate shaft or PTU is removed from the vehicle. Refer to the procedure in this section.

2. Remove the intermediate shaft.
3. Remove the driveshaft.
4. Remove the exhaust flexible pipe and the RH catalytic converter.
5. Remove the 2 PTU-to-support bracket bolts.
6. Remove the 3 PTU support bracket bolts and the PTU support bracket.
7. Remove the 5 PTU-to-transaxle bolts.
8. Separate the PTU from the transaxle. Remove the PTU.

To install:

✳✳ WARNING

A new Power Transfer Unit (PTU) intermediate shaft seal must be installed whenever the intermediate shaft or PTU is removed from the vehicle. Refer to that procedure in this section.

9. Position the Power Transfer Unit (PTU) to the transaxle. Install the 5 PTU-to-transaxle bolts. Tighten to 90 Nm (66 ft. lbs.).
10. Position the PTU support bracket into place and hand tighten the 5 PTU support bracket bolts:
    a. Tighten the bolts to the transaxle.
    b. Tighten the bolts to the engine.
    c. Tighten to 70 Nm (52 ft. lbs.).
11. Install the intermediate shaft.
12. Install the driveshaft.
13. Install the exhaust flexpipe and RH catalytic converter.
14. Fill the PTU, if necessary.

POWER TRANSFER UNIT SEAL

REMOVAL & INSTALLATION

See Figures 34 through 38.

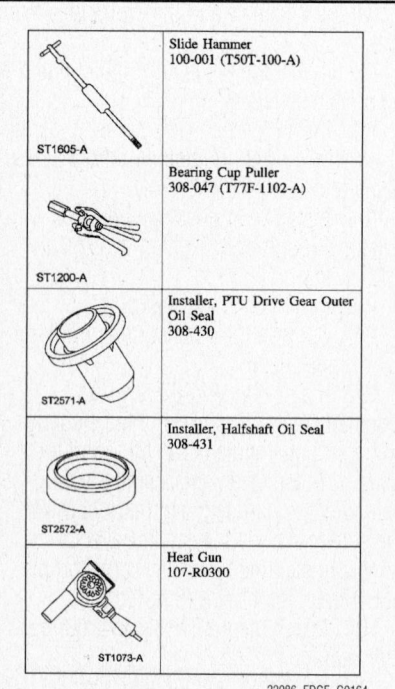

ST1605-A	Slide Hammer 100-001 (T50T-100-A)
ST1200-A	Bearing Cup Puller 308-047 (T77F-1102-A)
ST2571-A	Installer, PTU Drive Gear Outer Oil Seal 308-430
ST2572-A	Installer, Halfshaft Oil Seal 308-431
ST1073-A	Heat Gun 107-R0300

22086_EDGE_G0164

Fig. 34 Special tools are required to remove the PTU seal

➡This procedure will not affect the fluid level of the power transfer unit (PTU). Automatic transmission fluid (ATF) will leak when the intermediate shaft seal is removed. Add ATF to the transmission if necessary.

1. Raise and safely support the vehicle.
2. Remove the intermediate shaft.

➡The seal deflector will be damaged during removal. Be careful not to damage the cover seal directly behind the seal deflector.

3. Using the heat gun, warm the seal deflector. Using a crow's foot bar, remove the seal deflector.

➡The removal of the intermediate shaft can unseat the seal. Check the seal before installing the special tools.

4. Using the special tools, remove the intermediate shaft seal. Clean the area around the seal deflector and seal.

➡There is a bearing inside the PTU, directly behind the cover seal. The bearing is not serviced.

5. If necessary, carefully remove the cover seal.

To install:
6. If necessary, install a new cover seal. Using the special tools, seat the cover seal.
7. Use a suitable socket to install the intermediate shaft seal. The socket should be 39.5 mm (1.5 in) to 40.5 mm (1.6 in) in diameter. Index-mark the socket at 18 mm (0.71 in).
8. Make sure the seal is centered in the bore. Install a new intermediate shaft seal.

❋❋ WARNING

Do not overheat (melt) the seal deflector. If the deflector is damaged, a new one must be used.

9. Using a suitable heat gun, heat the new seal deflector. Concentrate the heat across the back of the deflector near the white colored tabs. Install the seal deflector immediately after heating. An audible snap should be heard.
10. If necessary, use special tools 308-430 and 308-431 to seat the seal deflector. Make sure the deflector is fully seated and there are no cracks on the face or inner diameter white colored tab.
11. An alternate method to heat the seal deflector, place the deflector in boiling water for 3 to 5 minutes. Dry off deflector and install.

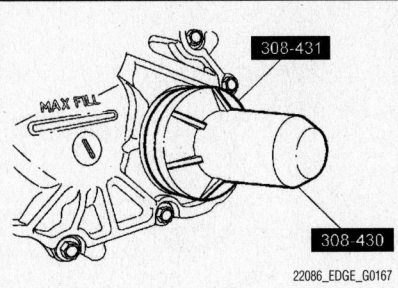

Fig. 37 Using the special tools, seat the cover seal

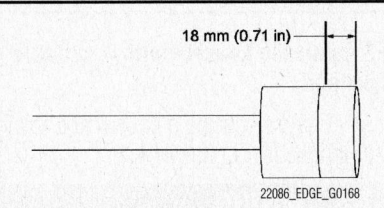

Fig. 38 Use a suitable socket to install the intermediate shaft seal. The socket should be 39.5 mm (1.5 in) to 40.5 mm (1.6 in) in diameter. Index-mark the socket at 18 mm (0.71 in)

12. Make sure the deflector is completely seated all the way around. It is correctly installed when the face of the deflector is recessed into the pocket.
13. Install the intermediate shaft.

FRONT DRIVESHAFT

REMOVAL & INSTALLATION
See Figure 39.

❋❋ CAUTION

The normal operating temperature of the exhaust system is extremely high. NEVER remove any part of the system until it has cooled. Be especially cautious when working around the catalytic converters. The temperature of the converter is very high after only a few minutes of engine operation. Failure to follow these precautions may result in personal injury.

➡Matchmark both the driveshaft flanges.

1. Raise and safely support the vehicle.

❋❋ WARNING

Never reuse the CV joint bolts. Install new bolts or damage to the vehicle may occur.

2. Remove and discard the 4 front driveshaft-to-transfer case bolts.
3. Remove and discard the 4 universal joint flange bolts and remove the front driveshaft.

❋❋ WARNING

Never reuse the bolts for the rear U-joint flange. Install new bolts.

4. Remove and discard the 4 universal joint flange bolts.
5. With the help of an assistant, remove the 4 center bearing support nuts and the driveshaft.

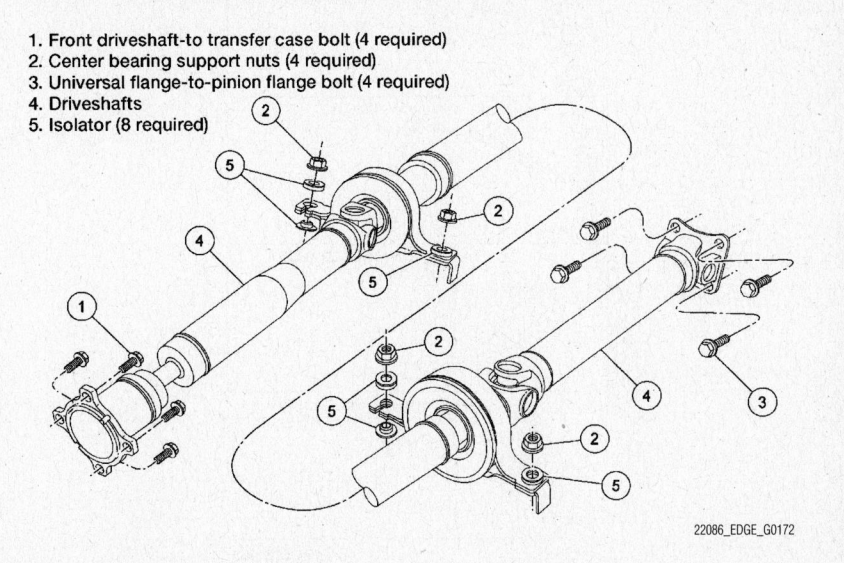

1. Front driveshaft-to transfer case bolt (4 required)
2. Center bearing support nuts (4 required)
3. Universal flange-to-pinion flange bolt (4 required)
4. Driveshafts
5. Isolator (8 required)

Fig. 39 Exploded view of the driveshaft

To install:

➡️ **If a driveshaft is installed and drive-shaft vibration is encountered after installation, index the driveshaft.**

6. Installation is the reverse of the removal procedure, noting the following tightening specifications:

   a. Center bearing support nuts: 40 Nm (30 ft. lbs.)

   b. Universal joint flange bolts: 70 Nm (52 ft. lbs.)

   c. Front driveshaft-to-transfer case bolts: 70 Nm (52 ft. lbs.)

FRONT HALFSHAFT

REMOVAL & INSTALLATION

Left Side

See Figures 40 through 43.

1. Raise and safely support the vehicle.
2. Remove the front tire and wheel.

➡️ **Depress the brake pedal to keep the halfshaft from rotating.**

3. Remove and discard the front wheel hub nut.

4. Remove the ball joint pinch bolt from the knuckle and separate the lower control arm.

5. Remove the stabilizer bar link nuts and position the link aside.

6. Using the special tool, as shown in the accompanying illustration, separate the halfshaft from the wheel hub.

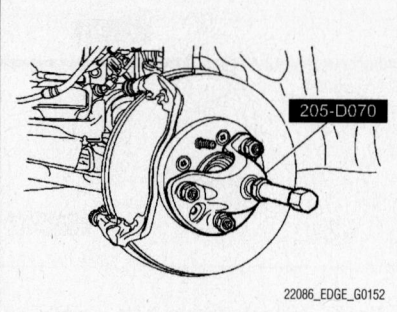

Fig. 41 Using the special tool, separate the halfshaft from the wheel hub

➡️ **Support the knuckle with a suitable jackstand.**

7. Pull the knuckle outboard and rotate it toward the rear of the vehicle.

✳️ CAUTION

The sharp edges on the stub shaft splines can slice or puncture the oil seal. Use care when inserting the stub shaft into the transmission.

8. Using the special tools, as shown in the accompanying illustration, remove the halfshaft from the transmission.

9. Remove and discard the circlip from the stub shaft.

To install:

10. Install a new stub shaft circlip.

11. Insert the halfshaft into the wheel hub.

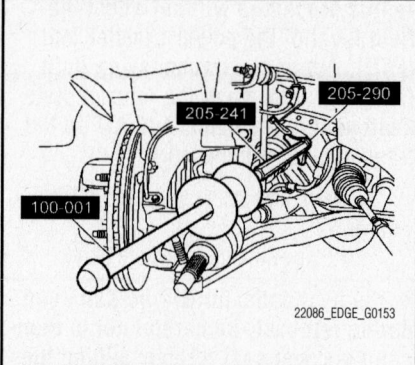

Fig. 42 Using the special tools, remove the halfshaft from the transmission

➡️ **After insertion, pull the halfshaft inner end to make sure the circlip is locked.**

12. Push the stub shaft into the transmission so the circlip locks into the differential side gear.

13. Rotate the knuckle into position.

14. Install the ball joint in the knuckle and install the pinch bolt. Tighten to 55 Nm (41 ft. lbs.).

15. Position the stabilizer bar links and install the link nuts. Tighten to 55 Nm (41 ft. lbs.).

16. Using a suitable tool, install the halfshaft in the wheel hub.

✳️ WARNING

Do not tighten the front wheel hub nut with the vehicle on the ground. The nut must be tightened to specification before the vehicle is lowered onto the wheels. Wheel bearing damage will occur if the wheel bearing is loaded with the weight of the vehicle applied.

➡️ **Depress the brake pedal to keep the halfshaft from rotating.**

17. Install a new front wheel hub nut. Tighten to 350 Nm (258 ft. lbs.).

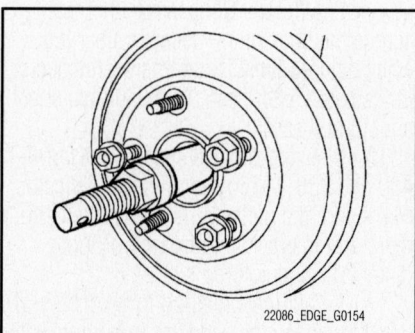

Fig. 43 Using a suitable tool, install the halfshaft in the wheel hub

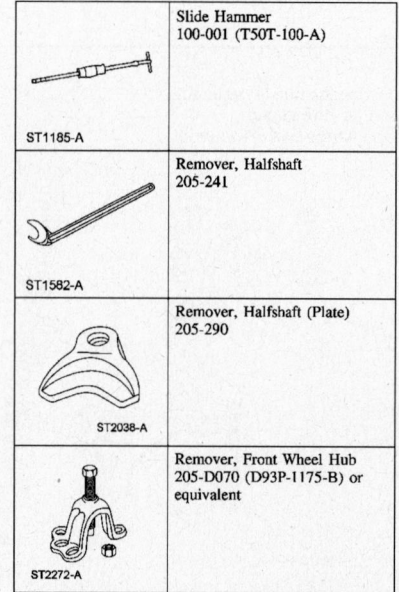

	Slide Hammer 100-001 (T50T-100-A)
ST1185-A	
	Remover, Halfshaft 205-241
ST1582-A	
	Remover, Halfshaft (Plate) 205-290
ST2038-A	
	Remover, Front Wheel Hub 205-D070 (D93P-1175-B) or equivalent
ST2272-A	

Fig. 40 A variety of special tools are required for left halfshaft removal and installation

18. Install the front tire and wheel.
19. Carefully lower the vehicle.

Right Side

See Figures 41 and 43 through 46.

1. Raise and safely support the vehicle.
2. Remove the front tire and wheel.

➡**Depress the brake pedal to keep the halfshaft from rotating.**

3. Remove and discard the front wheel hub nut.
4. Remove the ball joint pinch bolt from the knuckle and separate the lower control arm.
5. Remove the stabilizer bar link nut and position the link aside.
6. Using the special tool, separate the halfshaft from the wheel hub.

➡**Support the knuckle with a suitable jackstand.**

7. Pull the knuckle outboard and rotate it toward the rear of the vehicle.
8. On Front wheel drive (FWD) vehicles, use a brass drift to strike the right side halfshaft, where shown in the accompanying illustration, and separate the RH halfshaft from the intermediate shaft.
9. For all wheel drive (AWD) vehicles, perform the following:
    a. Remove the 2 bearing support bolts.

✳✳ **WARNING**

A new intermediate shaft seal in the Power Transfer Unit (PTU) must be installed whenever the intermediate shaft is removed or leaks from the seal may occur.

    b. Remove the right halfshaft and intermediate shaft as an assembly.
    c. Place the intermediate shaft in a vise and disconnect the halfshaft from

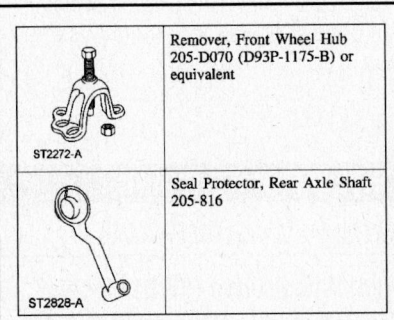

	Remover, Front Wheel Hub 205-D070 (D93P-1175-B) or equivalent
ST2272-A	
	Seal Protector, Rear Axle Shaft 205-816
ST2828-A	

22086_EDGE_G0155

Fig. 44 A variety of special tools are required for right halfshaft removal and installation

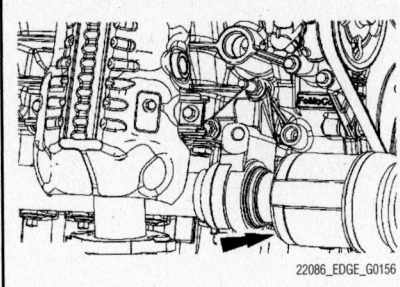

22086_EDGE_G0156

Fig. 45 On FWD vehicles, use a brass drift to strike the right side halfshaft where shown (arrow), and separate the RH halfshaft from the intermediate shaft

the intermediate shaft by striking the joint housing.
10. Remove and discard the circlip from the intermediate shaft.

To install:

11. On FWD vehicles, position the special tool over the halfshaft oil seal.
12. Install a new 30 mm (1.181 in) intermediate shaft circlip.
13. On AWD vehicles, perform the following:
    a. Install a new intermediate shaft seal.

➡**Pull the right side inboard joint outward to make sure the circlip is locked.**

    b. Align the splines on the right side shaft with the intermediate shaft and push the stub shaft in until the circlip locks the shafts together.
    c. Position the assembly in the vehicle aligning the splines on the intermediate shaft with the transmission splines.
    d. Install the 2 intermediate shaft support bearing bolts and tighten to 40 Nm (30 ft. lbs.).

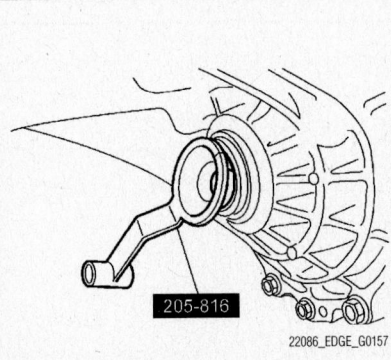

205-816

22086_EDGE_G0157

Fig. 46 On FWD vehicles, position the special tool over the halfshaft oil seal

14. On FWD vehicles, align the splines on the right side shaft with the intermediate shaft and push the stub shaft in until the circlip locks the shafts together.

➡**Pull the right side inboard joint outward to make sure the circlip is locked.**

15. Insert the halfshaft into the wheel hub.
16. Rotate the knuckle into position.
17. Install the ball joint in the knuckle and install the pinch bolt. Tighten to 55 Nm (41 ft. lbs.).
18. Position the stabilizer bar link and install the link nut. Tighten to 55 Nm (41 ft. lbs.).
19. Using a suitable tool, install the halfshaft in the wheel hub.

✳✳ **WARNING**

Do not tighten the front wheel hub nut with the vehicle on the ground. The nut must be tightened to specification before the vehicle is lowered onto the wheels. Wheel bearing damage will occur if the wheel bearing is loaded with the weight of the vehicle applied.

➡**Depress the brake pedal to keep the halfshaft from rotating.**

20. Install a new front wheel hub nut. Tighten to 350 Nm (258 ft. lbs.).
21. Install the front tire and wheel.

CV-JOINTS OVERHAUL

See Figures 47 through 51.

1. Remove the halfshaft assembly, as outlined in this section.
2. For the inboard CV joint, remove and discard the boot clamps.
3. Remove the inboard CV joint retaining ring.

✳✳ **WARNING**

Do not let the roller bearings fall.

4. For the inboard CV joint, carry out the following:
    a. Remove and discard the retainer circlip.
    b. Slide the boot away from the CV joint.
5. Using a suitable 3-jaw puller, remove the CV joint.
6. Remove and discard the inner CV boot.

➡**The outboard CV joint is not removable from the halfshaft. The boot must be removed or installed from the inboard CV joint side of the shaft.**

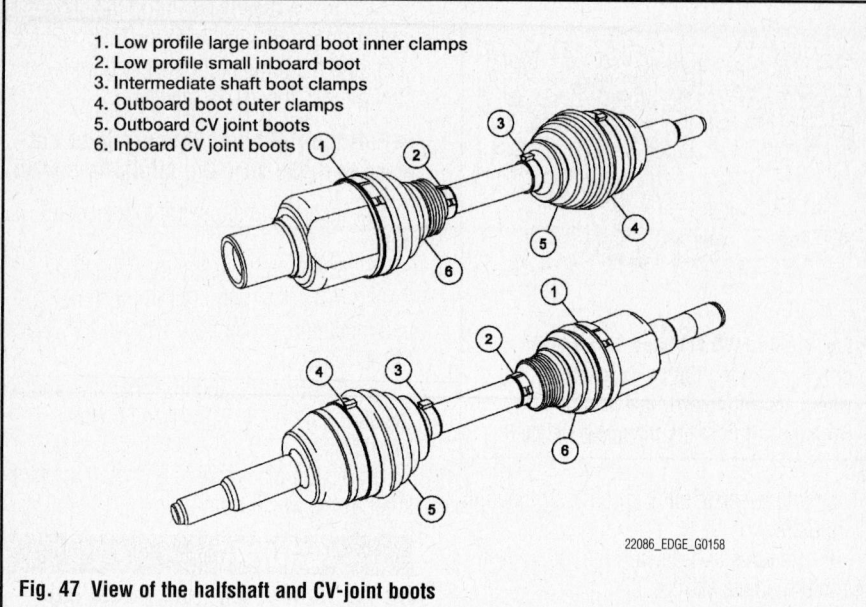

1. Low profile large inboard boot inner clamps
2. Low profile small inboard boot
3. Intermediate shaft boot clamps
4. Outboard boot outer clamps
5. Outboard CV joint boots
6. Inboard CV joint boots

Fig. 47 View of the halfshaft and CV-joint boots

7. For the outboard CV joint, carry out the following:

a. Remove and discard the boot clamps.

b. Remove and discard the boot.

c. If necessary, press the anti-lock brake sensor indicator ring from the outer CV joint.

To assemble:

➡**Do not mix the boot clamps.**

8. If removed, install a new anti-lock brake sensor indicator ring on the outer CV joint.

9. Lubricate the outboard CV joint:

a. Pack the outboard CV joint with grease from the kit. One-third of the grease must be installed in the joint with the remainder placed in the boot.

b. Spread the remaining grease evenly inside the boot.

10. Position the boot so the rib on the boot is located in the groove of the shaft.

11. Position the outboard halfshaft boot and the outboard boot clamps.

12. Install the outboard CV boot clamps, using the special tool as shown.

13. Position the inboard clamp and boot.

14. Install the CV joint and snap ring on the halfshaft.

15. Fill the inboard CV joint housing with grease from the kit. One-half of the grease must be installed in the joint and the remainder placed in the boot.

❋❋ WARNING

Do not let the roller bearings fall.

16. Position the CV housing on the CV joint.

17. Install the retaining ring.

18. Position the inboard halfshaft boot and clamps:

a. Position the boot in the housing groove.

b. Position the boot clamps.

19. Set the halfshaft assembled length

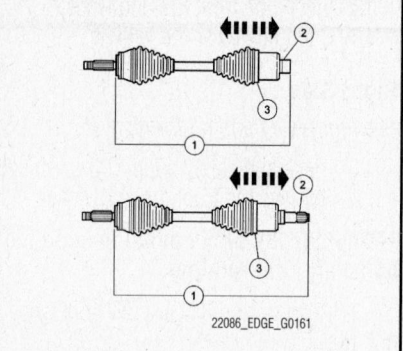

Fig. 50 Setting the halfshaft assembled length to the proper specifications

Item	Specification
Right front halfshaft assembled length (front wheel drive [FWD])	605.4 mm (23.83 in)
Right front halfshaft assembled length (all wheel drive [AWD])	632.4 mm (24.89 in)
Left front halfshaft assembled length	671.8 mm (26.44 in)

Fig. 51 Halfshaft assembled length specifications

to specifications. Refer to the accompanying illustrations, and the following steps:

a. Measure the entire assembly length (item 1 in illustration).

b. Push in or pull out on the inner joint as necessary to adjust the halfshaft assembled length (item 2 in illustration).

c. Hold the inner joint to prevent the assembled length from changing, and insert a small flat-blade screwdriver between the boot and the joint to equalize the pressure (item 3 in illustration).

20. Install the boot clamps.

21. Lever arm to the closed position and use a soft-faced hammer to close the tabs.

22. Install the halfshaft, as outlined in this section.

INTERMEDIATE SHAFT

REMOVAL & INSTALLATION

Front Wheel Drive (FWD) Models

See Figures 52 and 53.

1. Remove the right halfshaft, as outlined in this section.

2. Remove the 2 RH catalytic converter support bracket bolts.

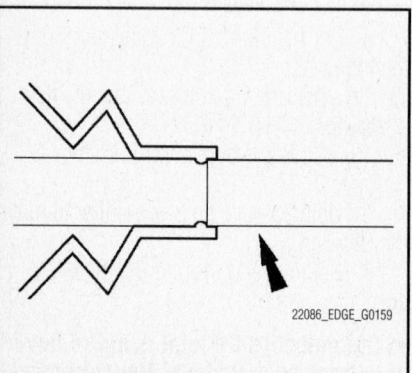

Fig. 48 Position the boot so the rib on the boot is located in the groove of the shaft

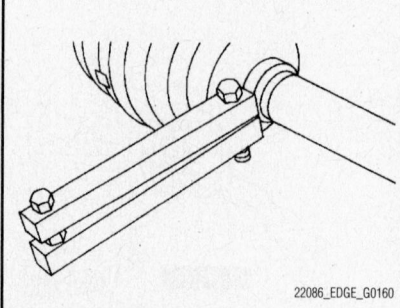

Fig. 49 Install the outboard CV boot clamps, using a suitable CV-Joint Boot Installation tool

3. Remove the bolt, nut and the RH catalytic converter support bracket.

4. Remove the 2 bolts from the intermediate shaft bearing support bracket.

❈❈ WARNING

Do not damage the transaxle seals when removing the intermediate shaft.

5. Carefully remove the intermediate shaft while supporting both ends of the intermediate shaft.

6. Remove and discard the circlip from the outboard end of the intermediate shaft.

To install:

7. Install a new 30 mm (1.181 in) circlip on the outboard end of the intermediate shaft.

8. Position the special tool over the halfshaft oil seal.

9. Position the intermediate shaft in the transaxle and engage the intermediate shaft splines with the transaxle side gears. Make sure the circlip is locked in the gear.

10. Install the 2 intermediate shaft support bracket stud bolts. Tighten to 40 Nm (30 ft. lbs.).

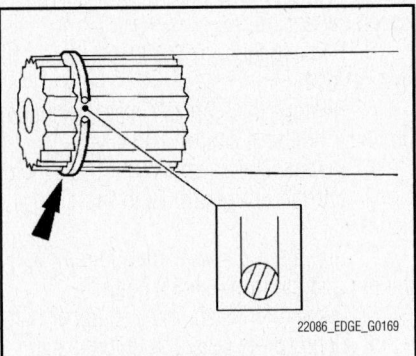

22086_EDGE_G0169

Fig. 52 Install a new 30 mm (1.181 in) circlip on the outboard end of the intermediate shaft as shown

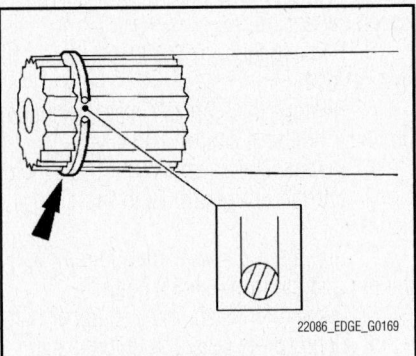

205-816

22086_EDGE_G0170

Fig. 53 Position the special tool over the halfshaft oil seal

11. Install the RH catalytic converter support bracket, nut and bolt. Tighten to 40 Nm (30 ft. lbs.).

12. Install the 2 RH catalytic converter support bracket bolts. Tighten to 20 Nm (15 ft. lbs.).

13. Install the right halfshaft.

All Wheel Drive (AWD) Models
See Figures 52 and 54.

❈❈ WARNING

The intermediate shaft seal in the Power Transfer Unit (PTU) must be replaced whenever the intermediate shaft is removed. Refer to the Power Transfer Unit Seal Replacement procedure under the Transfer Case Section.

1. Remove the right halfshaft assembly.

2. Separate the halfshaft from the intermediate shaft by securing the intermediate shaft in a vise and striking the halfshaft CV housing as shown in the accompanying illustration.

3. Remove and discard the circlip from the outboard end of the intermediate shaft.

To install:

4. Install a new 30 mm (1.181 in) circlip on the outboard end of the intermediate shaft.

5. Install a new intermediate seal in the PTU, as outlined in the Power Transfer Unit Seal procedure.

6. Position the intermediate shaft in the transaxle and engage the intermediate shaft splines with the transaxle side gears. Make sure the circlip is locked in the gear.

7. Install the 2 intermediate shaft support bracket bolts. Tighten to 40 Nm (30 ft. lbs.).

8. Install the right halfshaft.

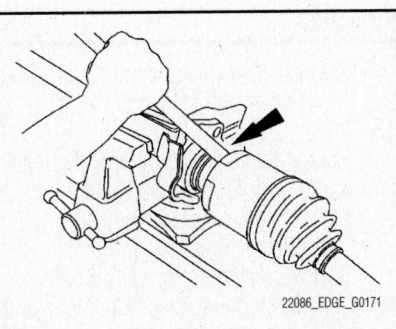

22086_EDGE_G0171

Fig. 54 Mount the intermediate shaft in a vise, then strike the halfshaft CV housing to separate the halfshaft from the intermediate shaft

REAR AXLE HOUSING

REMOVAL & INSTALLATION

1. Remove the rear driveshaft universal joint flange bolts. Support the driveshaft.

2. Remove the rear halfshafts, as outlined in this section.

3. Position a suitable transmission hydraulic jack to the axle housing. Securely strap the jack to the housing.

4. Disconnect the active torque coupling electrical connector at the front of the crossmember.

5. Remove the 4 differential housing-to-front insulator bracket bolts.

6. Loosen the LH front insulator bracket-to-subframe bolt, and rotate the bracket aside.

7. Loosen the RH front insulator bracket-to-subframe bolt and the bracket, and rotate the bracket aside.

8. Remove the 2 RH side insulator bracket-to-rear axle differential bolts and the axle assembly.

9. Remove the 3 LH side insulator or bracket-to-rear axle differential bolts.

10. Lower the rear axle assembly.

To install:

11. Installation is the reverse of the removal procedure, noting the following tightening specifications:

   a. LH side insulator or bracket-to-rear axle differential bolts: 90 Nm (66 ft. lbs.)

   b. RH side insulator bracket-to-rear axle differential bolts: 90 Nm (66 ft. lbs.)

   c. RH front insulator bracket-to-subframe bolt: 90 Nm (66 ft. lbs.)

   d. Differential housing-to-front insulator bracket bolts: 90 Nm (66 ft. lbs.)

   e. Rear driveshaft universal joint flange bolts: 70 Nm (52 ft. lbs.)

REAR AXLE SHAFT, BEARING & SEAL

REMOVAL & INSTALLATION
See Figures 55 through 57.

➡**This procedure covers replacement of the Stub Shaft, Bearing and Seal.**

1. Remove the halfshaft assembly.

2. To remove the seal, use the special tool to remove the stub shaft seal. The stub shaft pilot bearing is not serviced.

To install:

➡**Lubricate the new stub shaft pilot bearing housing seal with grease.**

3. Using the special tools, install the stub shaft pilot bearing housing seal.

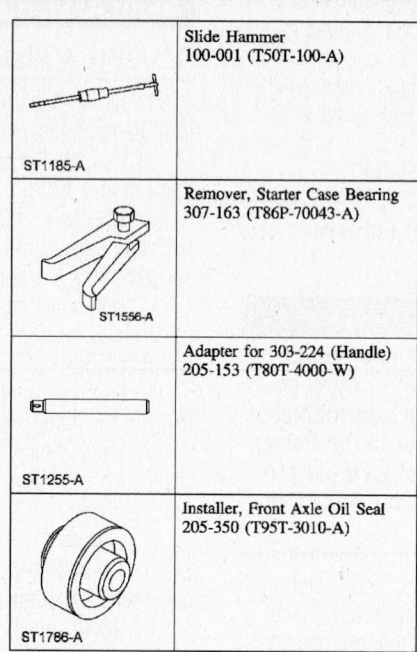 ST1185-A	Slide Hammer 100-001 (T50T-100-A)
ST1556-A	Remover, Starter Case Bearing 307-163 (T86P-70043-A)
ST1255-A	Adapter for 303-224 (Handle) 205-153 (T80T-4000-W)
ST1786-A	Installer, Front Axle Oil Seal 205-350 (T95T-3010-A)

22086_EDGE_G0175

Fig. 55 Special tools needed for seal replacement

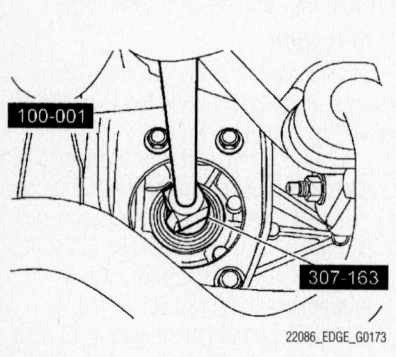

22086_EDGE_G0173

Fig. 56 To remove the seal, use the special tool to remove the stub shaft seal. The stub shaft pilot bearing is not serviced

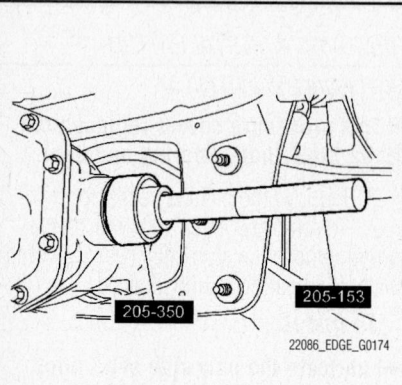

22086_EDGE_G0174

Fig. 57 Using the special tools, install the stub shaft pilot bearing housing seal

✳✳ WARNING

Inspect the inboard CV joint seal journal for rust or nicks/scratches prior to installing the halfshaft. If necessary, polish the seal journal with fine crocus cloth.

4. Install the halfshaft assembly.

REAR HALFSHAFT

REMOVAL & INSTALLATION

See Figures 58 and 59.

✳✳ WARNING

When performing this procedure, please note the following to avoid damaging the halfshaft and/or CV-Joints:

- Never pick up or hold the halfshaft by only the inner or outer Constant Velocity (CV) joint.
- Handle the halfshaft by only the interconnecting shaft to avoid pull-apart and potential damage to the CV joints.
- Do not over-angle the CV joints.
- Damage will occur to an assembled inner CV joint if it is over-plunged outward from the joint housing.
- Never use a hammer to remove or install the halfshafts.
- Never use the halfshaft assembly as a lever to position other components. Always support the free-ends of the halfshaft.

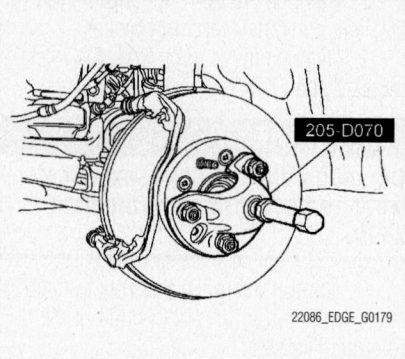

22086_EDGE_G0179

Fig. 58 Using the front hub removal tool, separate the halfshaft from the rear axle hub

- Do not allow the boots to contact sharp edges or hot exhaust components.
- Do not drop assembled halfshafts. The impact may cut the boots from the inside without evidence of external damage.

1. Raise and safely support the vehicle.
2. Remove the tire and wheel.
3. Remove and discard the rear wheel hub nut.
4. Remove the bolt, unclip the 2 retainers and position aside the wheel speed sensor.
5. Remove the brake caliper hose bracket bolt.
6. Remove the 2 anchor plate bolts and position the brake caliper aside.
7. Remove the upper arm outboard bolt.
8. Lift the upper arm from the knuckle.
9. Support the lower arm and remove the nut and the lower shock bolt.
10. Remove the stabilizer link upper nut.
11. Remove the outer toe link nut and bolt.
12. Support the wheel knuckle and remove the lower arm bolt and nut.
13. Using the special tool, separate the halfshaft from the rear axle hub assembly.

✳✳ WARNING

Do not damage the oil seal when removing the axle halfshaft from the differential.

14. Using a suitable pry bar, remove the halfshaft.
15. Position the halfshaft up through the wheel knuckle opening and remove the halfshaft.
16. Remove and discard the circlip from the stub shaft.

To install:

17. Install a new 28 mm (1.102 in) circlip on the stub shaft.

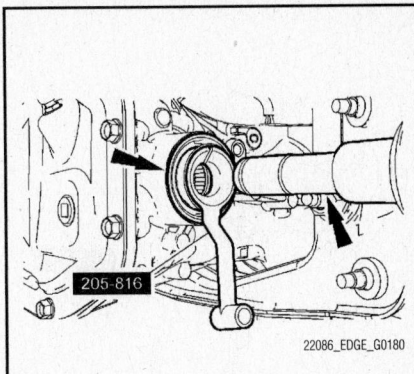

Fig. 59 Using the special tool, install the halfshaft in the differential

❋❋ **WARNING**

Make sure the oil seal protector is correctly aligned with the differential oil seal during installation.

18. Using the special tool, install the halfshaft in the differential.

19. Install the stub shaft in the rear drive unit. Make sure the circlip locks in the side gear.

20. Slide the outboard CV joint down through the knuckle.

21. Position the halfshaft outer CV joint through the hub bearing. Using a suitable tool, install the outer halfshaft end into the hub assembly.

22. Position the upper arm outboard end and install the bolt. Tighten to 110 Nm (81 ft. lbs.).

23. Position the lower arm and install the lower arm bolt and nut. To install, tighten to 101 Nm (74 ft. lbs.).

❋❋ **WARNING**

Do not tighten the rear wheel hub nut with the vehicle on the ground. The nut must be tightened to specification before the vehicle is lowered to the ground. Wheel bearing damage will occur if the wheel bearing is loaded with the weight of the vehicle applied.

24. Install the new rear wheel hub nut. To install, tighten to 275 Nm (203 ft. lbs.).

25. Install the rear toe link bolt. Tighten to 200 Nm (148 ft. lbs.).

26. Install the lower shock absorber bolt. Tighten to 115 Nm (85 ft. lbs.).

27. Install the wheel speed sensor, bolt and clip the retainers. Tighten to 23 Nm (17 ft. lbs.).

28. Install the brake caliper and the 2 anchor plate bolts. Tighten to 70 Nm (52 ft. lbs.).

29. Install the brake caliper hose bracket bolt. Tighten to 15 Nm (11 ft. lbs.).

30. Fill the axle with the specified quantity of the specified lubricant.

31. Install the tire and wheel

CV-JOINTS OVERHAUL

See Figures 60 through 64.

1. Remove the halfshaft assembly.

2. Remove and discard the inboard constant velocity (CV) joint boot clamps.

3. With the inboard CV joint boot removed from the housing, remove the retaining ring.

4. Remove the 8 balls and outer race.

5. Remove the CV joint housing snap ring.

6. Remove and discard the boot.

➡**The outboard CV joint is not removable from the halfshaft. The boot must be removed or installed from the inboard CV joint side of the shaft.**

7. For the outboard CV joint boot, perform the following:

   a. Remove and discard the boot clamps.

   b. Remove and discard the boot.

To install:

8. For the outboard CV joint, perform the following:

   a. Slide the boot on the interconnecting shaft.

   b. Pack the outboard CV joint with 80 g (2.82 oz) of grease.

   c. Spread any remaining grease evenly inside the boot.

   d. Install the boot by seating it in the groove in the CV joint housing.

9. Using the special tool, install the 79.6 mm (3.13 in) boot clamps on the large end of the boot.

10. Install the small clamp on the small end of the boot.

❋❋ **WARNING**

Install a new circlip every time the halfshaft is removed from the axle.

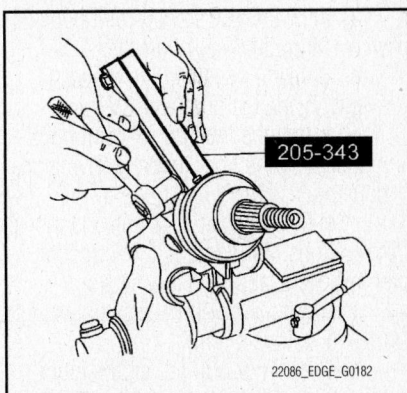

Fig. 61 Using the special tool, install the 79.6 mm (3.13 in) boot clamps on the large end of the boot

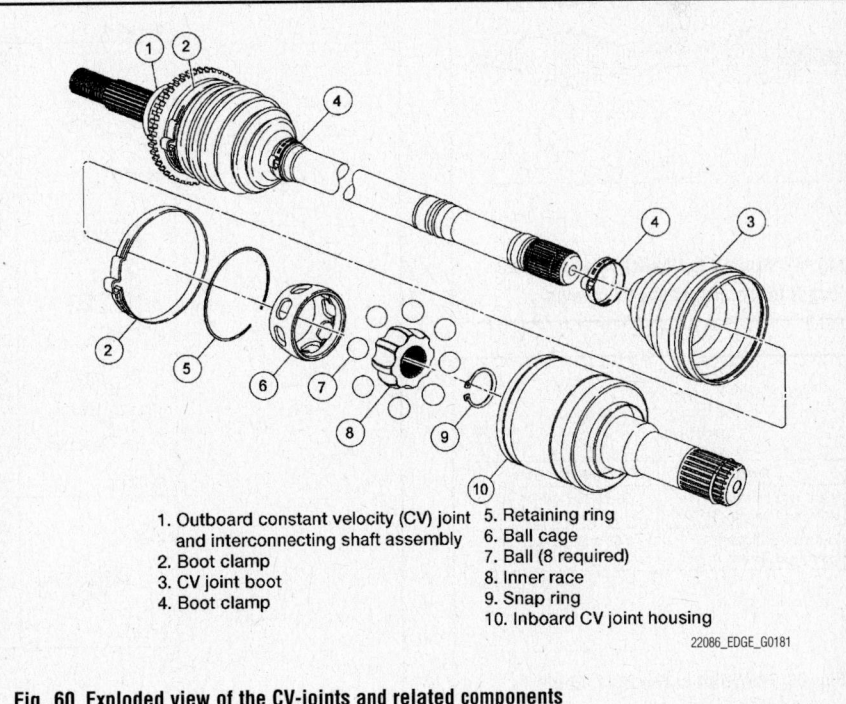

1. Outboard constant velocity (CV) joint and interconnecting shaft assembly
2. Boot clamp
3. CV joint boot
4. Boot clamp
5. Retaining ring
6. Ball cage
7. Ball (8 required)
8. Inner race
9. Snap ring
10. Inboard CV joint housing

Fig. 60 Exploded view of the CV-joints and related components

✳✳ WARNING

Start one end of the circlip in the groove and work the circlip over the halfshaft and into the groove to prevent the circlip from overexpanding.

11. Install a new retainer circlip.

12. Position the small clamp on the interconnecting shaft before installing the boot.

13. Position the boot on the interconnecting shaft.

14. Install the inner race and the retainer snap ring.

15. Install the outer race with 8 balls.

16. Insert the assembly in the housing.

17. Install the retaining ring.

18. For the inboard CV joint, perform the following:

   a. Pack the inboard CV joint housing with 108 g (3.80 oz) of grease.

   b. Spread any remaining grease evenly inside the boot and CV joint.

   c. Install the inboard CV joint housing, seating the boot in the groove in the housing.

19. Set the halfshaft assembled length to specifications. For additional information, refer to Specifications in this section.

   a. Measure the entire assembly length (item 1 in illustration).

   b. Push in or pull out on the inner joint as necessary to adjust the halfshaft assembled length (item 2 in illustration).

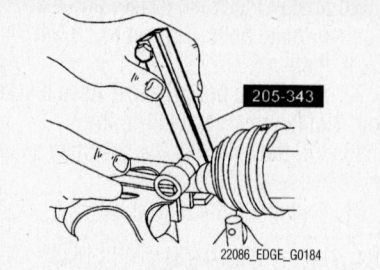

Fig. 64 Using the special tool, install the 77.5 mm (3.05 in) boot clamps on the large end of the boot

   c. Hold the inner joint to prevent the assembled length from changing and insert a soft, flat tool between the boot and the joint to equalize the pressure (item 3 in illustration).

20. Using the special tool, install the 77.5 mm (3.05 in) boot clamps on the large end of the boot.

21. Install the smaller boot clamp.

22. Install the halfshaft as outlined in this section.

REAR PINION SEAL

REMOVAL & INSTALLATION

See Figures 65 through 67.

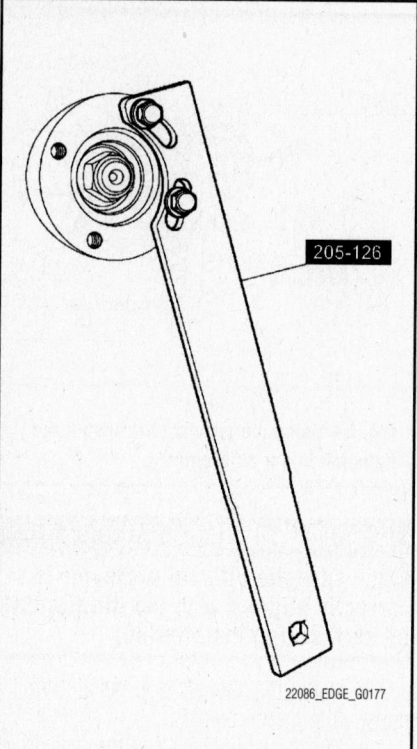

Fig. 66 Using the special tool, hold the pinion flange while removing the nut. Remove the nut, then discard it

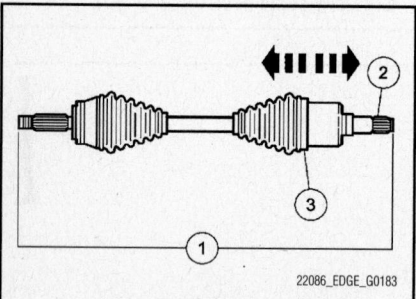

Fig. 62 Setting the halfshaft assembled length to the proper specifications

Item	Specification
Right rear halfshaft assembled length	915.6 mm (36.05 in)
Left rear halfshaft assembled length	863.9 mm (34.01 in)

22086_EDGE_G0185

Fig. 63 Halfshaft assembled length specifications

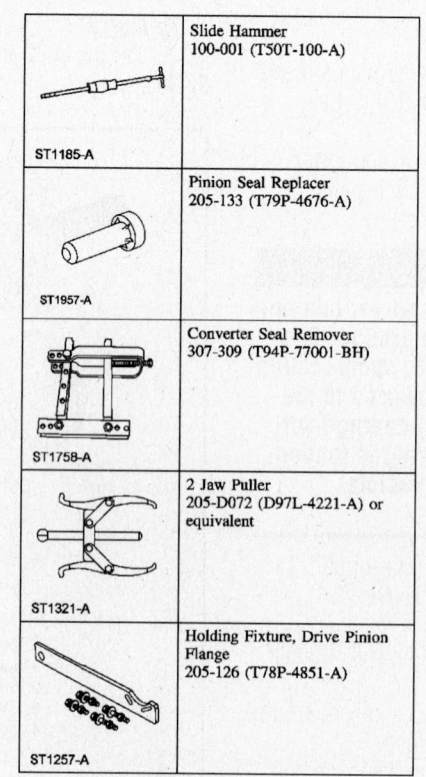

ST1185-A	Slide Hammer 100-001 (T50T-100-A)
ST1957-A	Pinion Seal Replacer 205-133 (T79P-4676-A)
ST1758-A	Converter Seal Remover 307-309 (T94P-77001-BH)
ST1321-A	2 Jaw Puller 205-D072 (D97L-4221-A) or equivalent
ST1257-A	Holding Fixture, Drive Pinion Flange 205-126 (T78P-4851-A)

22086_EDGE_G0176

Fig. 65 View of the special tools needed to remove the pinion seal

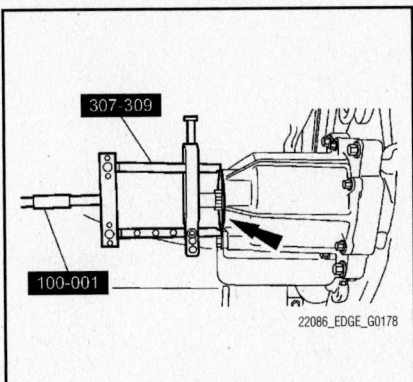

Fig. 67 Using the special tools, remove the seal

1. Raise and safely support the vehicle.
2. Remove and discard the 4 rear driveshaft universal joint flange bolts. Support the driveshaft.

➡ **Discard the nut after removing it. Install a new nut during installation.**

3. Using the special tool, hold the pinion flange while removing the nut. Remove the nut, then discard it.
4. Matchmark the location of the pinion to the yoke.
5. Using a suitable 2-jawed puller, remove the pinion flange.
6. Using the special tools, remove the seal.

To install:

➡ **Make sure that the mating surface is clean before installing the new seal.**

7. Using the special Pinion Seal Installation tool, install the seal.

➡ **Lubricate the pinion flange with premium long-life grease.**

8. Align the matchmarks and position the pinion flange.
9. Using the special tool, install the pinion nut and tighten to 244 Nm (180 ft. lbs.).
10. Align the matchmarks and install the rear driveshaft universal joint flange. Tighten the bolts to 70 Nm (52 ft. lbs.).

ENGINE COOLING

ENGINE FAN

REMOVAL & INSTALLATION

See Figure 68.

1. Disconnect the negative battery cable.
2. Remove the air cleaner assembly.

3. If equipped, detach the 2 block heater wiring clips from the radiator support.
4. Detach the 5 wiring harness retainers and position the harness aside.
5. Position aside the upper radiator hose from the cooling fan motor and shroud.

6. Disconnect the cooling fan motor and shroud electrical connector.
7. If equipped, remove the bolt and position aside the oil cooler bracket.
8. Remove the 2 bolts and the cooling fan motor and shroud.

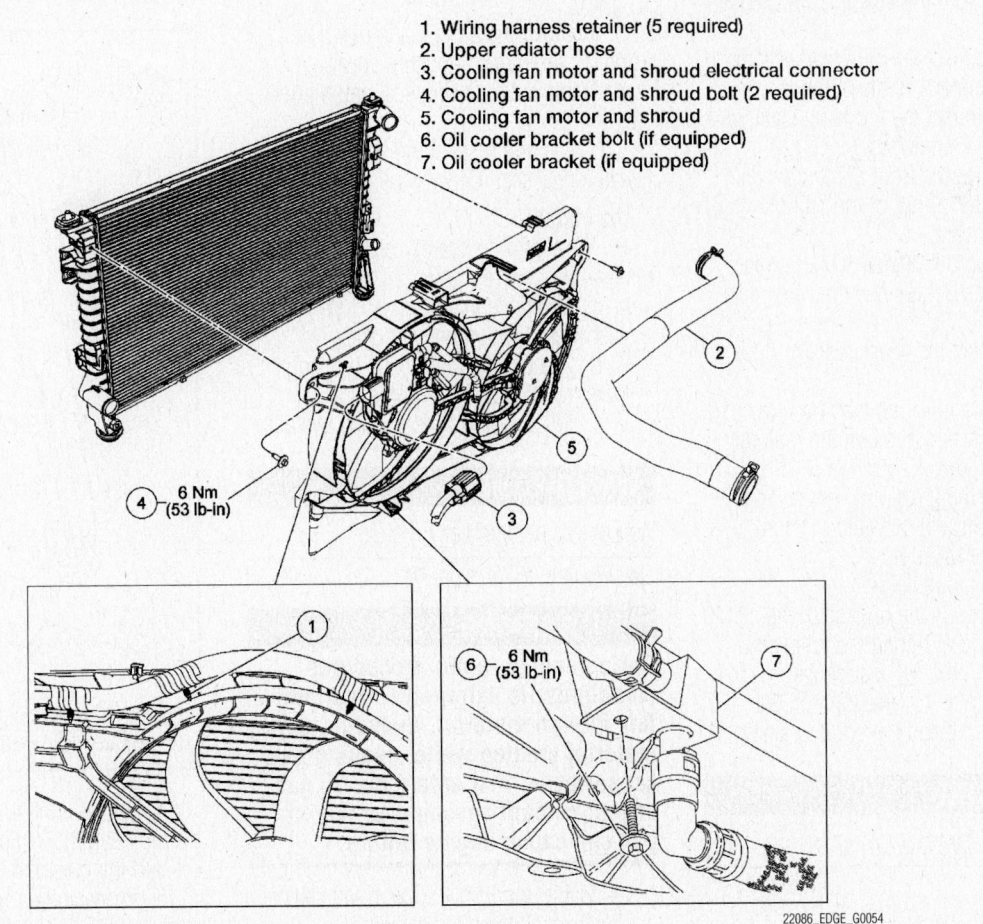

1. Wiring harness retainer (5 required)
2. Upper radiator hose
3. Cooling fan motor and shroud electrical connector
4. Cooling fan motor and shroud bolt (2 required)
5. Cooling fan motor and shroud
6. Oil cooler bracket bolt (if equipped)
7. Oil cooler bracket (if equipped)

Fig. 68 Exploded view of the engine cooling fan and shroud and related components

To install:

9. Installation is the reverse of the removal procedure, noting the following tightening specifications:

    a. Cooling fan motor and shroud bolts: 6 Nm (53 inch lbs.)

    b. Oil cooler bracket bolt: 6 Nm (53 inch lbs.)

RADIATOR

REMOVAL & INSTALLATION

1. Drain the cooling system.
2. Remove the cooling fan motor and shroud, as outlined in this section.
3. Remove the front bumper cover, as follows:

    a. Raise and safely support the vehicle.

    b. Remove the 2 bolts from the top of the radiator grille.

    c. Remove the 4 scrivets from the top of the radiator grille.

    d. Remove the 3 lower pin-type retainers.

    e. Remove the 6 fender splash shield screws (3 each side).

    f. Remove the 4 lower screws (2 each side).

    g. Disconnect the side marker lamp electrical connectors, if equipped.

    h. Disconnect the fog lamp electrical connectors, if equipped.

    i. Remove the front bumper cover.

    j. Pull the corner of the bumper cover from the bracket.

4. Disconnect the upper radiator hose and lower degas bottle hose from the radiator.
5. Disconnect the lower radiator hose from the radiator.
6. Lift and remove the tabs from the radiator support and position the radiator towards the engine.
7. Remove the 2 A/C condenser bolts from the radiator and separate the condenser from the radiator.
8. Remove the radiator.
9. Installation is the reverse of the removal procedure, noting the following:

    a. Tighten the A/C condenser-to-radiator bolts to 10 Nm (89 inch lbs.)

    b. Fill and bleed the cooling system.

THERMOSTAT

REMOVAL & INSTALLATION

See Figure 69.

1. Drain the cooling system.
2. Remove the air cleaner assembly and outlet pipe.

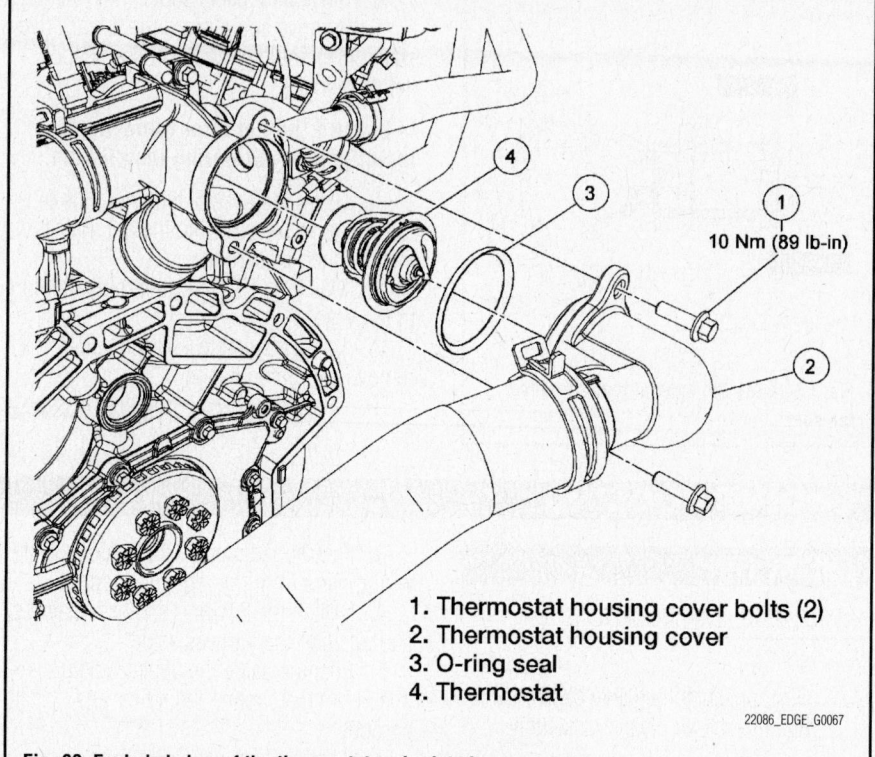

1. Thermostat housing cover bolts (2)
2. Thermostat housing cover
3. O-ring seal
4. Thermostat

22086_EDGE_G0067

Fig. 69 Exploded view of the thermostat and related components

3. Remove the 2 bolts and position aside the thermostat housing cover.
4. Remove the O-ring seal and thermostat.
5. Clean and inspect the O-ring seal. Install a new seal if necessary.

To install:

6. Installation is the reverse of the removal procedure, noting the following:

    a. Lubricate the thermostat O-ring seal with clean engine coolant.

    b. Tighten the thermostat housing cover to 10 Nm (89 inch lbs.).

    c. Fill and bleed the cooling system.

WATER PUMP

REMOVAL & INSTALLATION

See Figures 70 through 72.

✳✳ WARNING

During engine repair procedures, cleanliness is extremely important. Any foreign material, including any material created while cleaning gasket surfaces, that enters the oil passages, coolant passages or the oil pan can cause engine failure.

1. Raise and safely support the vehicle.
2. Drain the cooling system.
3. Loosen the exhaust flexible pipe clamp and disconnect the 2 exhaust hangers.

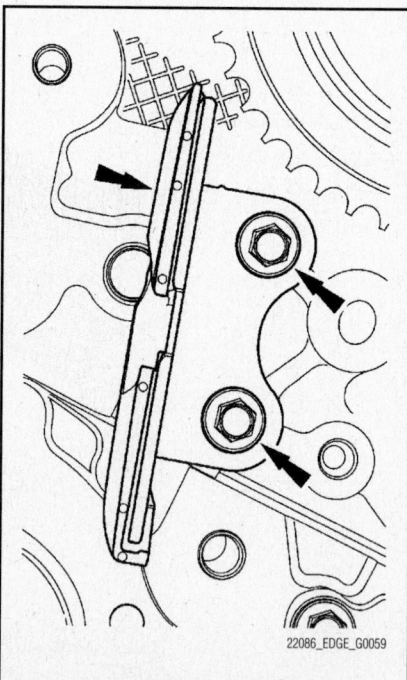

22086_EDGE_G0059

Fig. 70 Remove the 2 bolts and the upper LH primary timing chain guide

4. Remove the 4 nuts, the exhaust flexible pipe and the Y-pipe as an assembly. Discard the nuts and the gasket.
5. Remove the LH and RH catalytic converters. Refer to the Exhaust Manifold procedure for more information on catalytic converter removal.

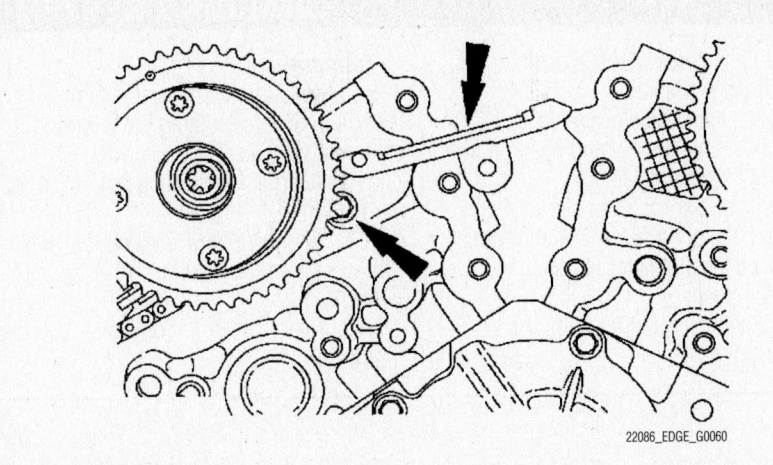

Fig. 71 Loosen the RH primary timing chain guide upper bolt. Rotate the guide and tighten the bolt

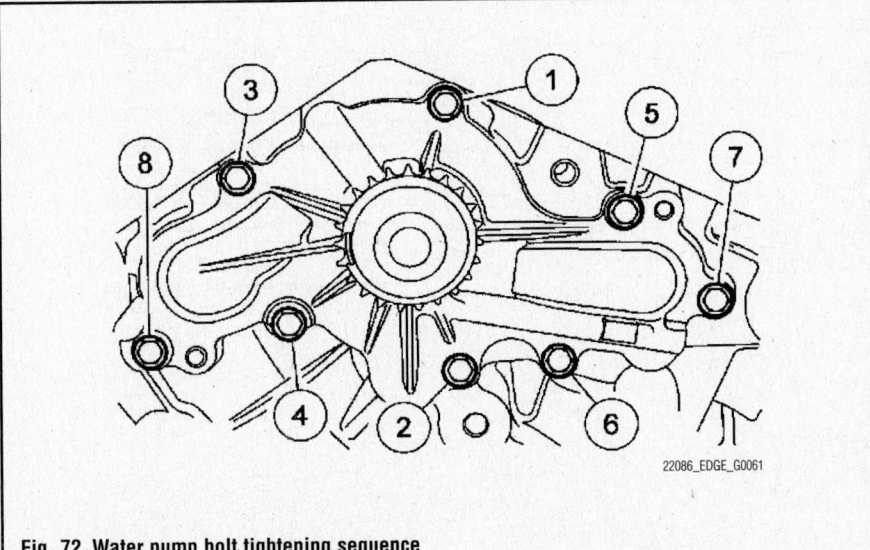

Fig. 72 Water pump bolt tightening sequence

6. If equipped, remove the heat shield and disconnect the block heater electrical connector.

7. Remove the RH cylinder block drain plug or, if equipped, the block heater. Allow the coolant to drain from the cylinder block into a suitable container.

8. Remove the LH cylinder block drain plug. Allow the coolant to drain from the cylinder block into a suitable container.

9. Remove the timing chain (engine front) cover, as outlined in the Engine Mechanical Section.

10. Remove the timing chain, as outlined in the Engine Mechanical Section.

11. Remove the 2 bolts and the upper LH primary timing chain guide.

12. Remove the RH primary timing chain guide lower bolt.

➡ **The RH primary timing chain guide must be repositioned to allow the water pump to be removed.**

13. Loosen the RH primary timing chain guide upper bolt. Rotate the guide and tighten the bolt.

14. Remove the 8 bolts and the water pump.

15. Thoroughly clean and inspect all mating surfaces.

To install:

16. Install the water pump and the 8 bolts. Tighten in the sequence shown to 10 Nm (89 inch lbs.).

17. Loosen the RH primary timing chain guide upper bolt.

18. Position the RH primary timing chain guide and install the lower bolt. Tighten the 2 bolts to 10 Nm (89 inch lbs.).

19. Install the timing chain and front cover, as outlined in the Engine Mechanical Section

20. Install the RH cylinder block drain plug or, if equipped, the block heater. Tighten the cylinder block drain plug to 20 Nm (15 ft. lbs.). Tighten the block heater to 41 Nm (30 ft. lbs.).

➡ **Make sure that the block heater wiring is routed and secured away from rotating or hot components, or damage to the wiring can occur.**

21. If equipped, connect the block heater electrical connector and install the heat shield.

22. Install the LH cylinder block drain plug. Tighten to 20 Nm (15 ft. lbs.) plus an additional 180 degrees.

23. Install the LH and RH catalytic converters.

24. Position the Y-pipe assembly in place and install the 4 nuts. Tighten to 40 Nm (30 ft. lbs.).

25. Install the 2 exhaust hangers and tighten the exhaust clamp. Tighten to 40 Nm (30 ft. lbs.).

26. Fill the engine with clean engine oil.

27. Fill and bleed the cooling system.

ALTERNATOR

REMOVAL & INSTALLATION

See Figure 73.

1. Disconnect the positive and negative battery cables.

2. Remove the engine cooling fan, as outlined in the Engine Mechanical Section..

3. Rotate the accessory drive belt tensioner counterclockwise and position the accessory drive belt aside.

4. Position the alternator protective cover aside, remove the nut and position the alternator B+ terminal aside.

5. Disconnect the alternator electrical connector. Detach the pin-type retainer and wiring

6. Remove the alternator stud nut and the alternator stud.

7. Unfasten the mounting bolts and remove the alternator.

To install:

8. Installation is the reverse of the removal procedure, noting the following tightening specifications:

   a. Alternator mounting bolt: 35 ft. lbs. (47 Nm)

   b. Alternator stud: 71 inch lbs. (8 Nm)

   c. Alternator stud nut: 35 ft. lbs. (47 Nm)

   d. Alternator B+ terminal nut: 9 ft. lbs. (12 Nm)

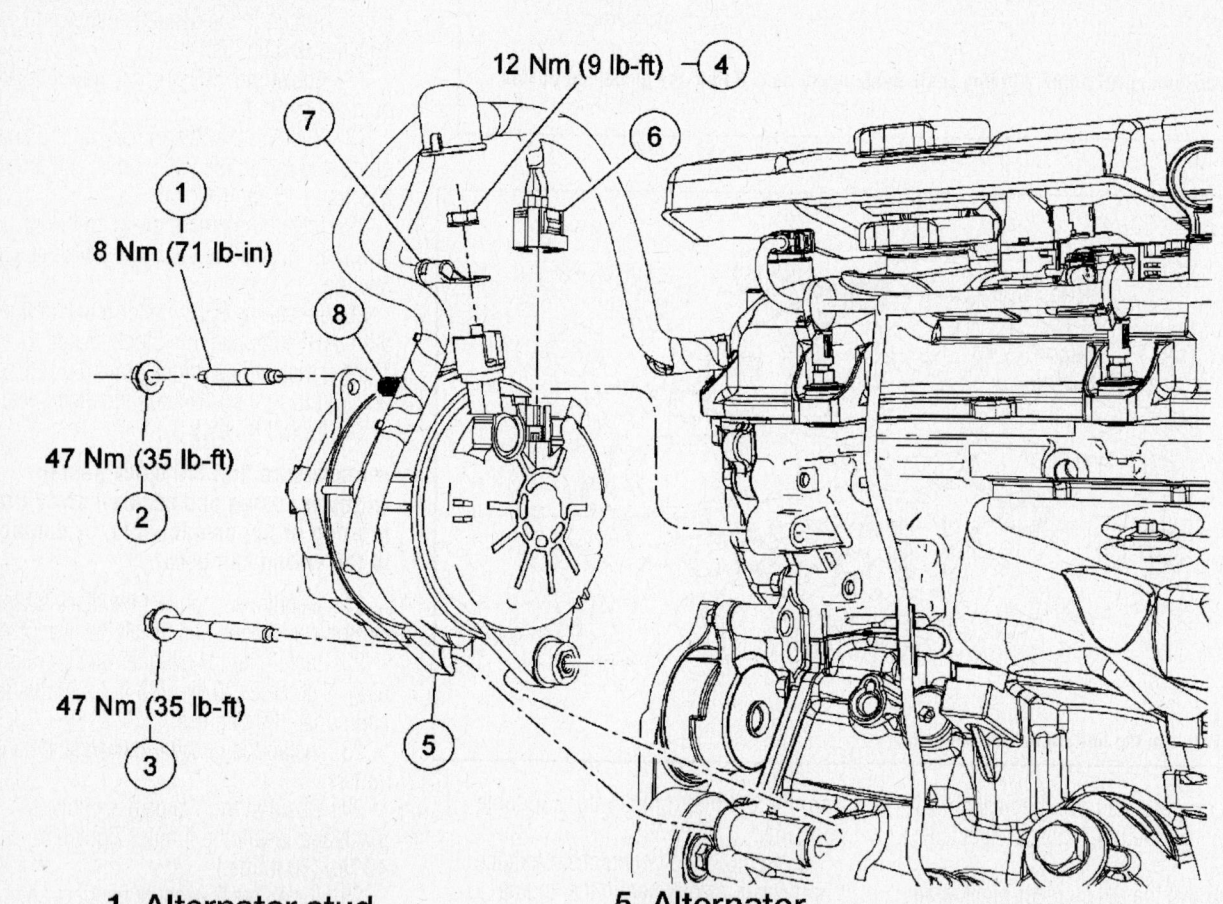

1. Alternator stud
2. Alternator nut
3. Alternator bolt
4. Alternator B+ terminal nut
5. Alternator
6. Alternator electrical connector
7. Alternator B+ terminal
8. Pin-type retainer, wiring harness

22086_EDGE_G0008

Fig. 73 Exploded view of the alternator mounting

ENGINE ELECTRICAL   **IGNITION SYSTEM**

IGNITION COIL

REMOVAL & INSTALLATION

See Figure 74.

1. Disconnect the negative battery cable.
2. If removing the left side ignition coils, disconnect the crankcase vent tube quick connect coupling from the valve cover fitting and position it aside.
3. If removing the right side ignition coils, remove the upper intake manifold, as outlined in the Engine Mechanical Section.

➡ **The upper intake manifold must be removed to access the right side ignition coils only.**

4. Detach the 6 ignition coil-on-plug electrical connectors and unfasten the mounting bolts, then remove the ignition coils from the vehicle.

➡ **When removing the ignition coil-on-plugs, use a slight twisting motion to help break the seal and make removal easier.**

To install:

5. Install the 6 ignition coil-on-plugs and the 6 bolts, then tighten to 62 inch lbs. (7 Nm).
6. Attach the 6 ignition coil-on-plug electrical connectors.

7. If removed, install the upper intake manifold, as outlined in the Engine Mechanical Section.
8. If disconnected, position and connect the crankcase vent tube quick connect coupling to the valve cover
9. Connect the negative battery cable.

IGNITION TIMING

ADJUSTMENT

The ignition timing is controlled by the Powertrain Control Module (PCM). No adjustment is necessary or possible.

SPARK PLUGS

REMOVAL & INSTALLATION

See Figures 74 and 75.

1. Disconnect the negative battery cable.
2. If removing the left side spark plugs, disconnect the crankcase vent tube quick connect coupling from the valve cover fitting and position it aside.
3. If removing the right side spark plugs, remove the upper intake manifold, as outlined in the Engine Mechanical Section.

➡ **The upper intake manifold must be removed to access the right side spark plugs only.**

4. Detach the 6 ignition coil-on-plug electrical connectors and unfasten the mounting bolts, then remove the ignition coils from the vehicle.

➡ **When removing the ignition coil-on-plugs, a slight twisting motion will help break the seal and make removal easier.**

✵ CAUTION

Only use hand tools when removing or installing the spark plugs, or you can damage the spark plug and/or cylinder head. Never use power tools.

➡ **Use compressed air to remove any foreign material in the spark plug well before removing the spark plugs.**

5. Remove the 6 spark plugs.

To install:

6. Adjust the spark plug gap as necessary. The proper spark plug gap is 0.0051–0.0057 in. (1.29–1.45mm).
7. Install the spark plugs and tighten to 11 ft. lbs. (15 Nm).
8. Apply a little dielectric grease to the inside of the ignition coil-on-plug boots before attaching to the spark plugs.
9. Install the 6 ignition coil-on-plugs and the 6 bolts, then tighten to 62 inch lbs. (7 Nm).
10. Attach the 6 ignition coil-on-plug electrical connectors.
11. If removed, install the upper intake manifold, as outlined in the Engine Mechanical Section.
12. If disconnected, position and connect the crankcase vent tube quick connect coupling to the valve cover
13. Connect the negative battery cable.

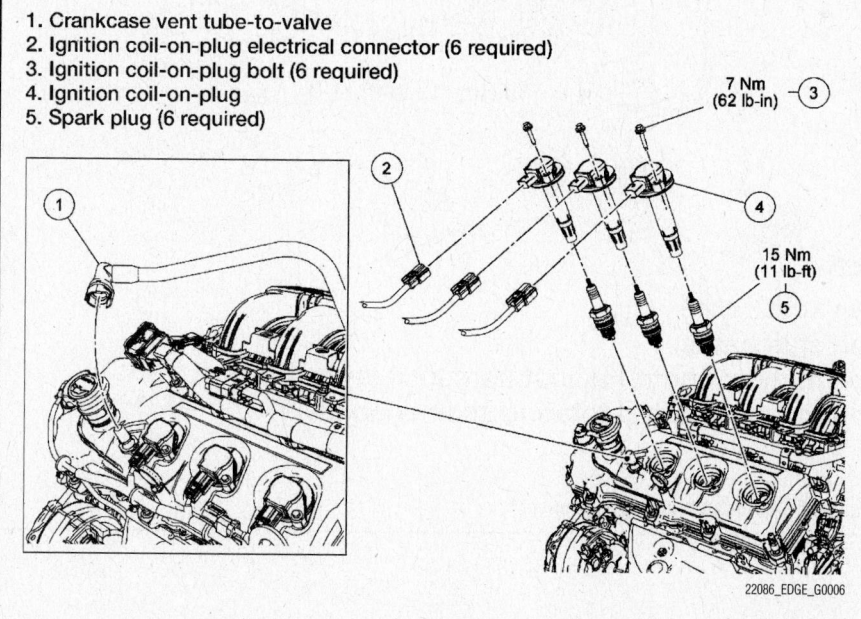

1. Crankcase vent tube-to-valve
2. Ignition coil-on-plug electrical connector (6 required)
3. Ignition coil-on-plug bolt (6 required)
4. Ignition coil-on-plug
5. Spark plug (6 required)

7 Nm (62 lb-in)
15 Nm (11 lb-ft)

22086_EDGE_G0006

Fig. 74 Exploded view of the ignition system components—left side shown, right side similar

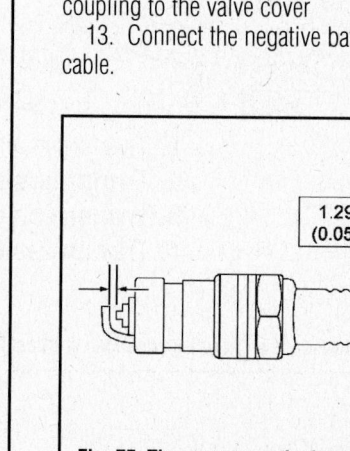

1.29-1.45 mm
(0.051-0.057 in)

22086_EDGE_G0005

Fig. 75 The proper spark plug gap is 0.0051–0.0057 in. (1.29–1.45mm)

ENGINE ELECTRICAL   **STARTING SYSTEM**

STARTER

REMOVAL & INSTALLATION

See Figure 76.

✳✳ CAUTION

When carrying out maintenance on the starting system, be aware that heavy gauge leads are connected directly to the battery. Make sure protective caps are in place when maintenance is completed.

1. Disconnect the negative battery cable.
2. Remove the air cleaner.
3. Disconnect the transmission shift cable and adjustment lock from the transmission manual control lever.
4. Disconnect the transmission shift cable rotating slide snap and position aside the transmission cable.
5. Remove the nut and the transmission manual control lever.
6. Remove the starter motor terminal cover.
7. Remove the starter motor solenoid battery cable nut.
8. Remove the starter motor solenoid wire nut.
9. Disconnect the wiring harness retainer from the starter motor stud bolt and position the wiring harness aside.
10. Unfasten the starter motor stud bolt, then remove the bolt and the starter

To install:

11. Installation is the reverse of the removal procedure, noting the following tightening specifications:

   a. Starter mounting bolt(s) and stud bolt: 20 ft. lbs. (27 Nm)
   b. Starter motor solenoid wire nut: 44 inch lbs. (5 Nm)
   c. Starter motor solenoid battery cable nut: 9 ft. lbs. (12 Nm)
   d. Transmission manual control lever nut: 13 ft. lbs. (18 Nm)

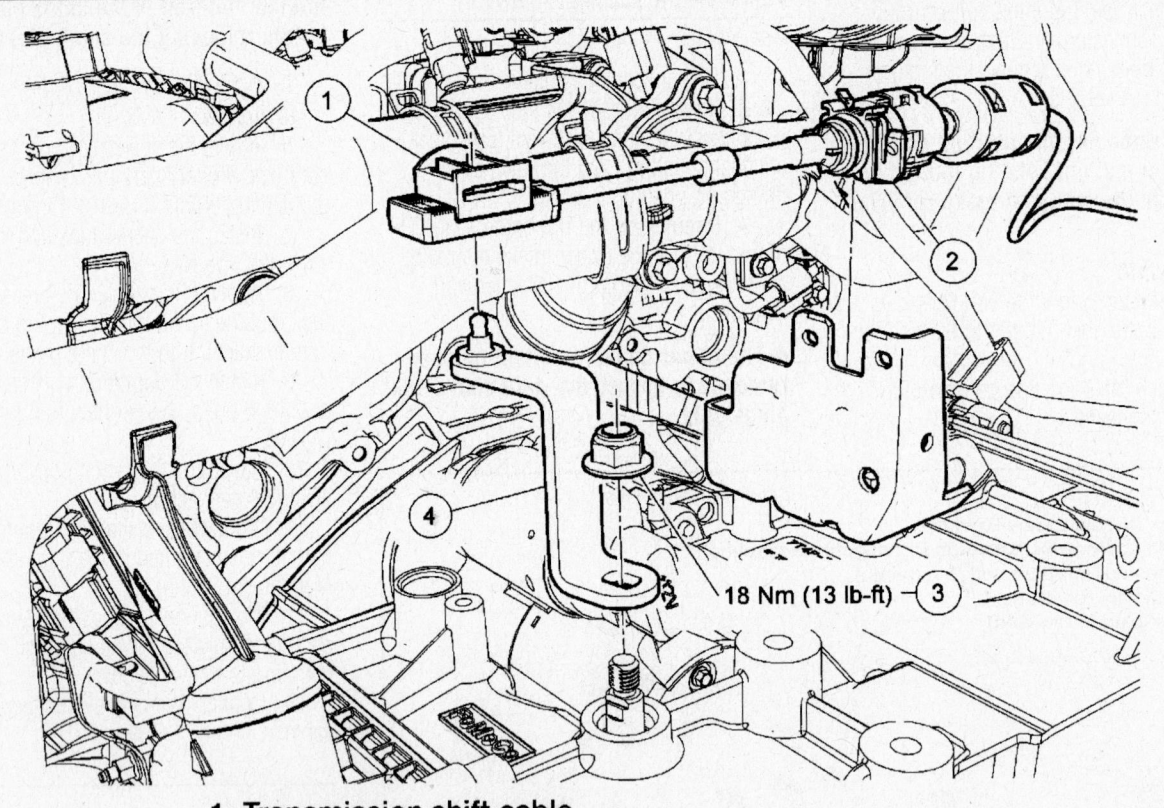

18 Nm (13 lb-ft)

1. Transmission shift cable
2. Transmission shift cable
3. Transmission manual control adjustment lock lever nut
4. Transmission manual control rotating slide snap lever

22086_EDGE_G0011

Fig. 76 Exploded view of the transmission shift cable, control lever and related components

ENGINE MECHANICAL

➡Disconnecting the negative battery cable may interfere with the functions of the on board computer systems and may require the computer to undergo a relearning process, once the negative battery cable is reconnected.

ACCESSORY DRIVE BELTS

ACCESSORY BELT ROUTING

See Figures 77 and 78.

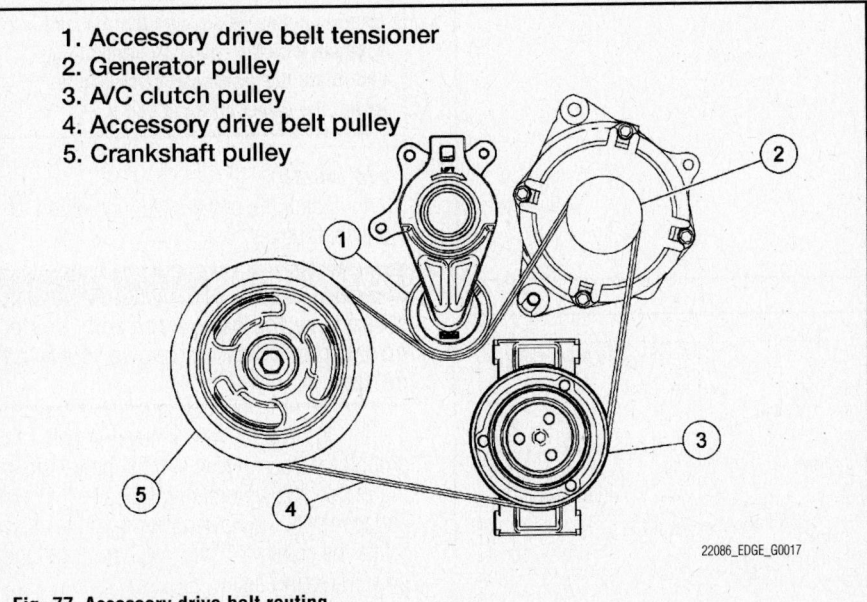

1. Accessory drive belt tensioner
2. Generator pulley
3. A/C clutch pulley
4. Accessory drive belt pulley
5. Crankshaft pulley

22086_EDGE_G0017

Fig. 77 Accessory drive belt routing

INSPECTION

Inspect the drive belt for signs of glazing or cracking. A glazed belt will be perfectly smooth from slippage, while a good belt will have a slight texture of fabric visible. Cracks will usually start at the inner edge of the belt and run outward. All worn or damaged drive belts should be replaced immediately.

ADJUSTMENT

Belt tension is maintained by an automatic belt tensioner. No adjustments are necessary.

REMOVAL & INSTALLATION

Accessory Drive Belt

See Figure 79.

✳✳ WARNING

NEVER lubricate the accessory drive belt, tensioner or pulleys as this will cause potential damage to the belt material and tensioner damping mechanism. Do not apply any fluids or any type of belt dressing to the accessory drive belt or pulleys.

1. Raise and safely support the vehicle.
2. Working from the top of the vehicle, use a suitable belt tensioner release tool to rotate the accessory drive belt tensioner clockwise and remove the accessory drive belt from the alternator pulley.
3. Remove the RH inner fender splash shield.
4. Working from underneath the vehicle, remove the accessory drive belt.

To install:

5. Working from underneath the vehicle, install the accessory drive belt on all pulleys, except the alternator pulley.

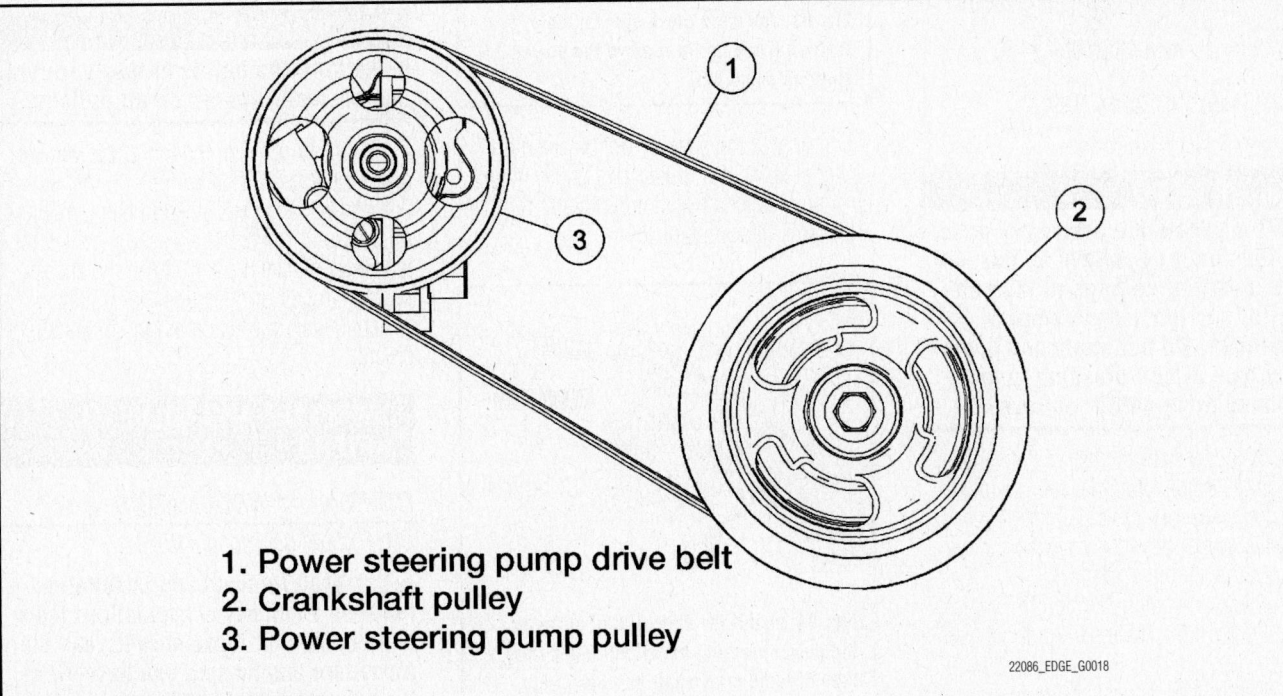

1. Power steering pump drive belt
2. Crankshaft pulley
3. Power steering pump pulley

22086_EDGE_G0018

Fig. 78 Power steering belt routing

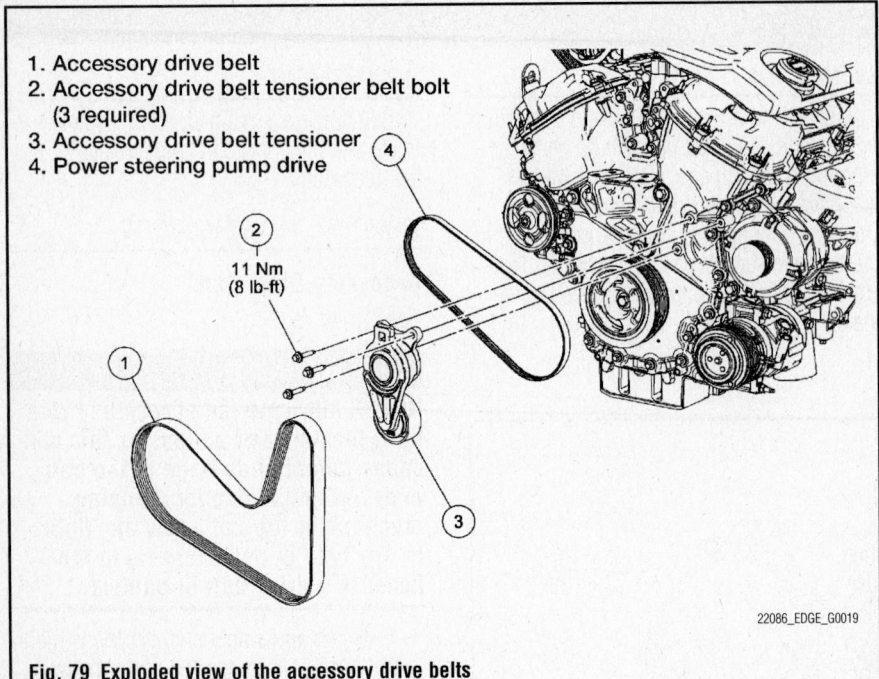

1. Accessory drive belt
2. Accessory drive belt tensioner belt bolt (3 required)
3. Accessory drive belt tensioner
4. Power steering pump drive

11 Nm (8 lb-ft)

22086_EDGE_G0019

Fig. 79 Exploded view of the accessory drive belts

> ✳✳ **WARNING**
>
> **Make sure the belt is properly routed and correctly seated on all pulleys.**

6. Working from the top of the vehicle, position the accessory drive belt on the alternator pulley, then use a suitable belt tensioner release tool to rotate the accessory drive belt tensioner clockwise and install the accessory drive belt on the alternator pulley.

7. Install the RH inner fender splash shield.

8. Carefully lower the vehicle.

Power Steering Pump Belt

See Figures 79 through 82.

> ✳✳ **WARNING**
>
> **NEVER lubricate the accessory drive belt, tensioner or pulleys as this will cause potential damage to the belt material and tensioner damping mechanism. Do not apply any fluids or any type of belt dressing to the accessory drive belt or pulleys.**

1. Working from the top of the vehicle, use a suitable belt tensioner release tool to rotate the accessory drive belt tensioner clockwise and remove the accessory drive belt from the alternator pulley.

2. Raise and safely support the vehicle.

3. Remove the RH inner fender splash shield.

4. Remove the accessory drive belt from the crankshaft pulley.

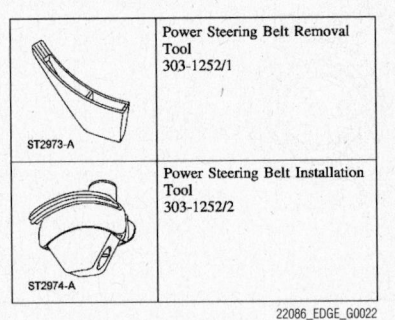

	Power Steering Belt Removal Tool 303-1252/1
ST2973-A	
	Power Steering Belt Installation Tool 303-1252/2
ST2974-A	

22086_EDGE_G0022

Fig. 80 You need these special tools, or their equivalents, to remove the power steering pump belt

5. Install the special tool between the power steering pump belt and pulley, then turn the crankshaft bolt clockwise to remove the power steering belt.

303-1252/1

22086_EDGE_G0020

Fig. 81 Install the special tool between the power steering pump belt and pulley, then turn the crankshaft bolt clockwise to remove the power steering belt

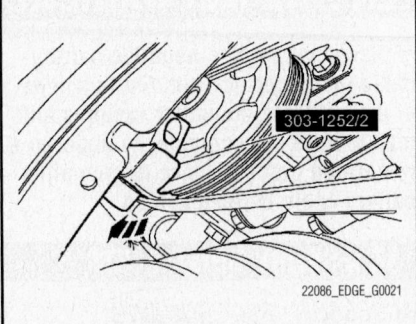

303-1252/2

22086_EDGE_G0021

Fig. 82 Position the power steering belt around the special tool and the power steering pulley. Make sure that the belt is engaged with the power steering pulley and rotate the crankshaft clockwise to install the power steering belt

To install:

6. Install the power steering belt on the crankshaft pulley.

> ✳✳ **WARNING**
>
> **Make sure the belt is correctly seated on the crankshaft and power steering pulleys.**

7. Position the power steering belt around the special tool and the power steering pulley. Make sure that the belt is engaged with the power steering pulley and rotate the crankshaft clockwise to install the power steering belt.

8. Install the accessory drive belt on the crankshaft pulley.

> ✳✳ **WARNING**
>
> **Make sure the belt is properly routed and correctly seated on all pulleys.**

9. Working from the top of the vehicle, place the accessory drive belt on the alternator pulley. Using a suitable belt tensioner release tool, rotate the accessory drive belt tensioner clockwise and install the accessory drive belt on the generator pulley.

10. Install the RH inner fender splash shield.

CAMSHAFT AND VALVE LIFTERS

REMOVAL & INSTALLATION
See Figures 83 through 104.

➡️**Camshaft removal and installation requires a number of specialized tools and equipment. Make sure to read the procedure and be sure you have all of the necessary tools and equipment before beginning the procedure.**

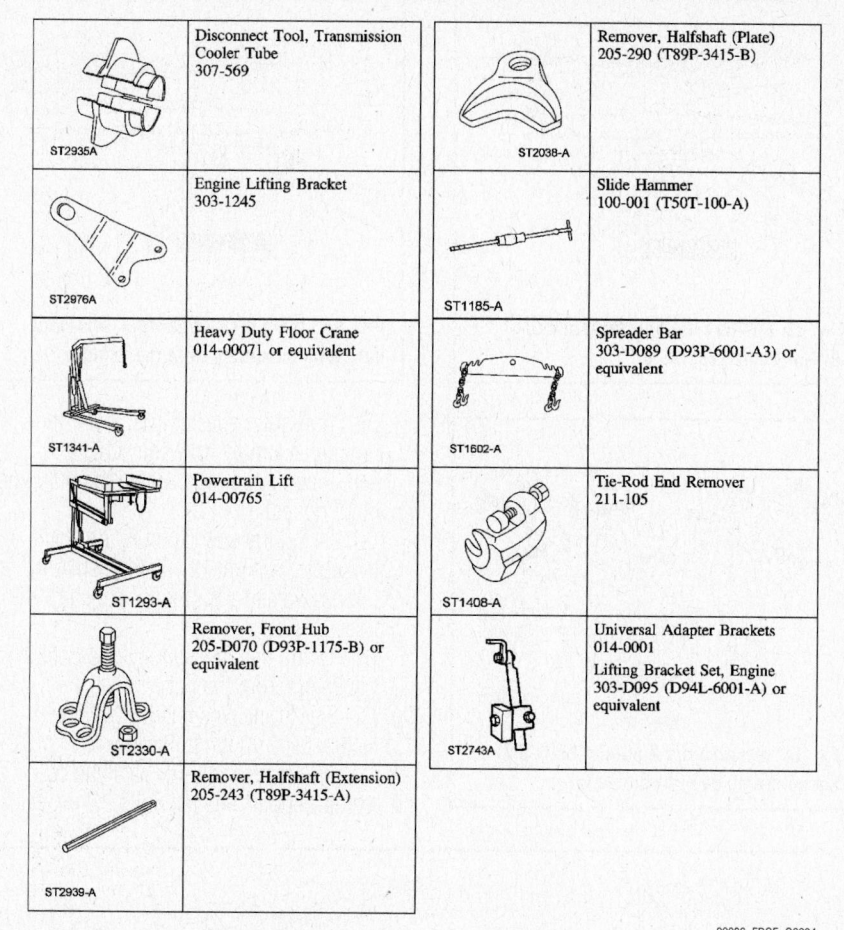

ST2935A	Disconnect Tool, Transmission Cooler Tube 307-569		ST2038-A	Remover, Halfshaft (Plate) 205-290 (T89P-3415-B)
ST2976A	Engine Lifting Bracket 303-1245		ST1185-A	Slide Hammer 100-001 (T50T-100-A)
ST1341-A	Heavy Duty Floor Crane 014-00071 or equivalent		ST1602-A	Spreader Bar 303-D089 (D93P-6001-A3) or equivalent
ST1293-A	Powertrain Lift 014-00765		ST1408-A	Tie-Rod End Remover 211-105
ST2330-A	Remover, Front Hub 205-D070 (D93P-1175-B) or equivalent		ST2743A	Universal Adapter Brackets 014-0001 Lifting Bracket Set, Engine 303-D095 (D94L-6001-A) or equivalent
ST2939-A	Remover, Halfshaft (Extension) 205-243 (T89P-3415-A)			

22086_EDGE_G0034

Fig. 83 Special tools needed for camshaft removal and installation

> ⁂ **WARNING**
>
> **NEVER smoke or carry lighted tobacco or open flame of any type when working on or near any fuel-related components. Highly flammable mixtures are always present and may be ignited. Failure to follow these precautions may result in personal injury or death.**

> ⁂ **WARNING**
>
> **During engine repair procedures, cleanliness is extremely important. Any foreign material, including any material created while cleaning gasket surfaces that enters the oil passages, coolant passages or the oil pan, can cause engine failure.**

1. Raise and safely support the vehicle.
2. Recover the air conditioning system using the proper equipment
3. Release the fuel system pressure, as outlined in the Fuel System Section.
4. Drain the engine cooling system.
5. Remove the accessory drive belt and the power steering belt, as outlined in this section.
6. Disconnect the power steering cooler hose and drain the power steering fluid into a suitable drain pan.
7. Remove the degas bottle.
8. Remove the engine air cleaner and air cleaner outlet pipe.
9. Remove the battery tray.
10. Disconnect the battery harness electrical connector.
11. Remove the nut and disconnect the power feed from the battery terminal.
12. Remove the bolt and the ground wire.
13. Detach the 2 wiring harness retainers from the cowl.
14. Disconnect the vacuum hose from the upper intake manifold.
15. Disconnect the upper Evaporative Emissions (EVAP) tube quick connect coupling from the purge valve.
16. Disconnect the upper radiator hose, lower radiator hose and 2 heater hoses from the thermostat housing.

17. Detach the wiring harness retainer from the transaxle control cable bracket.
18. Disconnect the transaxle control cable from the control lever. Detach the control cable from the bracket.
19. Disconnect the transaxle control electrical connector.
20. If equipped, detach the engine block heater harness retainers from the radiator support and the A/C suction tube.
21. Remove the nut and disconnect the A/C pressure tube fitting. Discard the O-ring seal.
22. Remove the safety clip from the A/C fitting. Disconnect the A/C suction tube fitting.
23. Disconnect the hose from the power steering reservoir.
24. Disconnect the fuel supply tube.
25. Disconnect the fuel hose routing clip from the transaxle stud and position the fuel hose aside.
26. Disconnect the 2 engine wiring harness electrical connectors.
27. Detach the electrical connector from the LH valve cover.
28. Remove the oil level indicator.
29. Detach the wiring harness retainer from the RH valve cover stud bolt.
30. Remove the bolt and the ground wire from the engine front cover.
31. Remove the nut, the ground wire and the radio interference capacitor wire from the engine front cover stud.
32. Loosen the exhaust flexible pipe clamp and disconnect the 2 exhaust hangers.
33. Remove the 4 nuts and the exhaust flexible pipe and Y-pipe as an assembly. Discard the nuts and the gasket.
34. Remove the 3 pin-type retainers, the 7 screws and the radiator splash shield.
35. Remove the LH inner splash shield.
36. Remove the 2 secondary latches from the transmission fluid cooler tubes.
37. Using the special tool shown in the accompanying illustration, disconnect the transaxle cooling tubes.

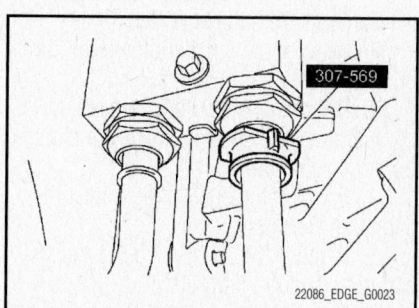

307-569

22086_EDGE_G0023

Fig. 84 Using the special tool shown, disconnect the transaxle cooling tubes

38. Remove the drain plug and drain the engine oil into a suitable container. Install the drain plug and tighten to 27 Nm (20 ft. lbs.).

39. Remove and discard the engine oil filter.

40. Remove the power steering cooler bracket bolt from the RH side of the subframe.

➡**Matchmark the driveshaft for proper alignment during installation.**

41. For All Wheel Drive (AWD) vehicles, remove the 4 bolts and support the driveshaft with a length of mechanic's wire.

42. Remove and discard the RH front halfshaft nut.

43. Remove the 2 nuts and the roll restrictor heat shield.

44. Remove the engine roll restrictor-to-subframe through bolt.

45. Remove and discard the Power Steering Pressure (PSP) tube-to-pump banjo bolt and the 2 seals.

❄ WARNING

Do not allow the intermediate shaft to rotate while it is disconnected from the gear or damage to the clockspring can occur. If there is evidence that the intermediate shaft has rotated, the clockspring must be removed and recentered as outlined in the Chassis Electrical Section.

46. Remove and discard the steering intermediate shaft bolt.

47. Separate the steering intermediate shaft from the steering gear.

48. Remove and discard the cotter pins and tie-rod end nuts.

49. Using a suitable tie rod end removal tool, separate the tie-rod ends from the wheel knuckles.

50. Remove the 2 stabilizer link-to-lower control arm nuts and separate the stabilizer bar links from the lower control arms.

51. Remove the lower control arm-to-knuckle pinch bolts and separate the lower control arms from the knuckles.

52. Remove the 3 RH subframe-to-lower bumper nuts.

53. Remove the 3 LH subframe-to-lower bumper nuts and separate the lower bumper from the subframe.

54. Position the special tool under the subframe assembly.

55. Remove the 2 nuts, 4 bolts and the subframe support brackets.

56. Remove the 2 front subframe nuts.

57. Remove the 2 middle subframe nuts.

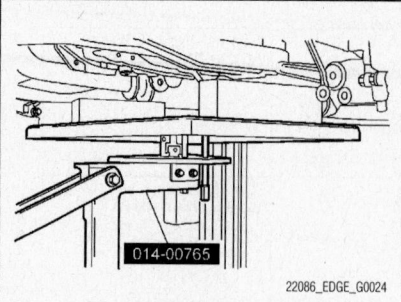

Fig. 85 Position the special tool under the subframe assembly

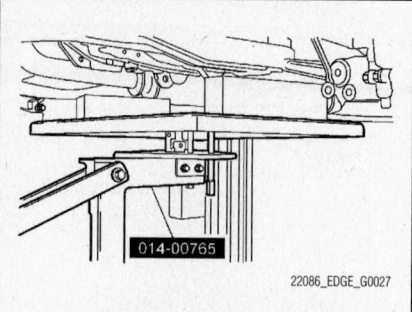

Fig. 88 Using the special tool, lower the subframe assembly from the vehicle

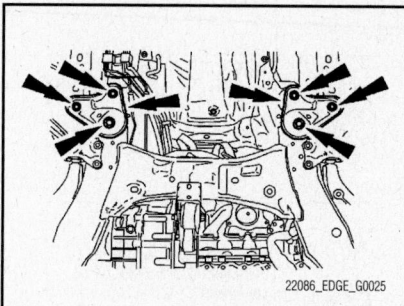

Fig. 86 Remove the 2 nuts, 4 bolts and the subframe support brackets

58. Using the special tool, lower the subframe assembly from the vehicle.

59. If equipped, disconnect the oil cooler coolant hoses.

60. Using the special tools, or their equivalents, separate the LH halfshaft from the transaxle and support the halfshaft with a piece of wire.

61. Using the special tool, separate the RH halfshaft from the hub.

62. For Front Wheel Drive (FWD) vehicles, perform the following:

a. Remove the 2 RH catalytic converter support bracket bolts.

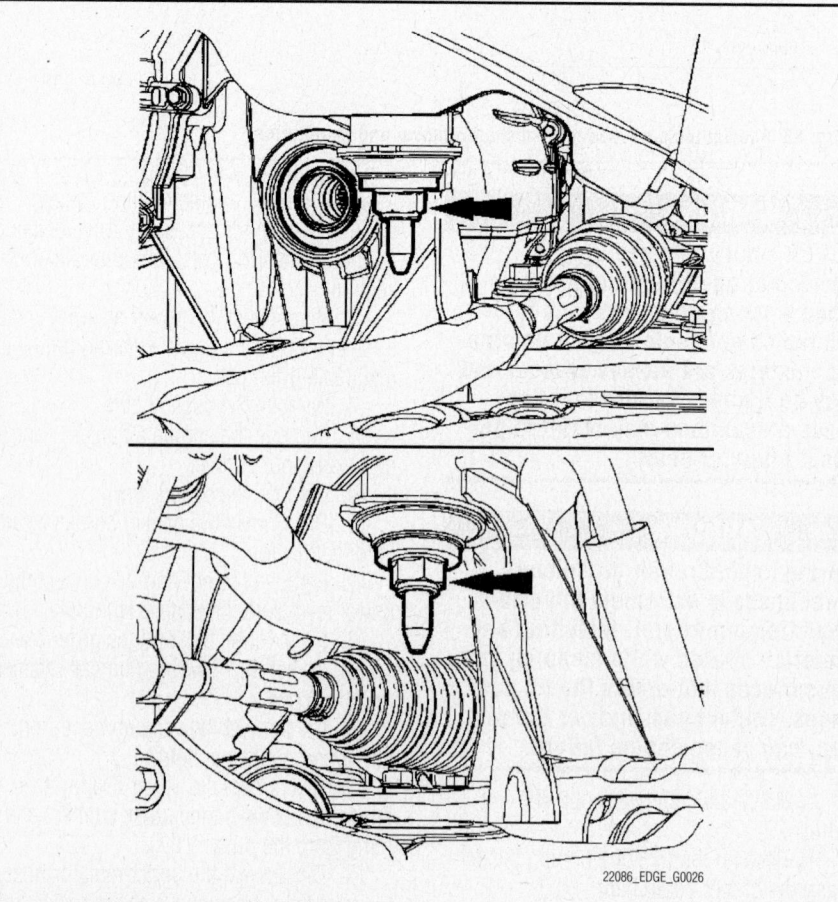

Fig. 87 Remove the 2 middle subframe nuts

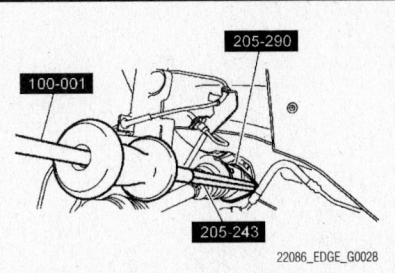

Fig. 89 Using the special tools, separate the LH halfshaft from the transaxle and support the halfshaft with a piece of wire

b. Remove the bolt, the nut and the RH catalytic converter support bracket.

c. Remove the 2 stud bolts and the RH halfshaft/intermediate shaft assembly.

63. For AWD vehicles, remove the 2 RH halfshaft bearing support bracket bolts and the RH halfshaft/intermediate shaft assembly.

64. Position a block of wood under the transaxle. Install the special tools, or their equivalents, as shown in the accompanying illustration.

65. Remove the transaxle support insulator through bolt and nut.

66. Remove the 3 nuts, the bolt and the transaxle support insulator bracket.

67. Remove the nut, bolt and engine mount brace.

68. Remove the 4 engine mount nuts.

69. Remove the 3 bolts and the engine mount.

70. Lower the engine and transaxle assembly from the vehicle.

71. If equipped, detach the engine block heater wiring harness retainers and position the harness aside.

72. Disconnect the Positive Crankcase Ventilation (PCV) fitting electrical connector.

73. Disconnect the PCV hose from the PCV valve.

74. Disconnect the throttle body electrical connector.

75. Detach the wiring harness retainers from the upper intake manifold.

76. Remove the upper intake manifold support bracket bolt.

77. Remove the upper intake manifold support bracket bolt.

78. Remove the 6 bolts and the upper intake manifold. Discard the gaskets.

79. Disconnect the RH catalyst monitor electrical connector.

80. Disconnect the PSP switch electrical connector.

81. Disconnect the RH Variable Camshaft Timing (VCT) solenoid electrical connector.

82. Disconnect the 3 RH coil-on-plug electrical connectors.

83. Disconnect the heated PCV valve electrical connector.

84. Detach all of the wiring harness retainers from the RH valve cover and stud bolts.

85. Disconnect the LH VCT solenoid electrical connector.

86. Disconnect the 3 LH coil-on-plug electrical connectors.

87. Detach all of the wiring harness retainers from the LH valve cover and stud bolts.

88. Remove the 6 bolts and the 6 coil-on-plugs.

89. Remove the 11 stud bolts and the LH valve cover. Discard the gasket.

90. Remove the bolt, the 10 stud bolts and the RH valve cover. Discard the gasket.

91. Inspect the VCT solenoid seals and the spark plug tube seals. Install new seals if damaged. Using the special tools, remove the seal(s).

92. Remove the 3 bolts and the power steering pump.

93. Remove the 3 bolts and the accessory drive belt tensioner.

94. Remove the crankshaft pulley, as outlined in this section.

95. Remove the crankshaft front seal, as outlined in this section.

96. Remove the 2 bolts and the engine mount bracket.

97. Remove the 2 engine mount studs.

98. Remove the 3 bolts and the engine mount bracket.

99. Remove the 22 engine front cover bolts.

100. Install 6 of the engine front cover bolts (finger tight) into the 6 threaded holes in the engine front cover. Tighten the bolts one turn at a time in a criss-cross pattern until the engine front cover-to-cylinder block seal is released. Remove the engine front cover.

❊❊ WARNING

Only use a 3M Roloc® Bristle Disk, (2 inch, white, part number 07528) to clean the engine front cover. Do not use metal scrapers, wire brushes or any other power abrasive disk to clean the engine front cover. These tools cause scratches and gouges that make leak paths.

101. Clean the engine front cover using a 3M Roloc® Bristle Disk, (2 inch, white, part number 07528) in a suitable tool turning at the recommended speed of 15,000 rpm.

102. Thoroughly wash the engine front cover to remove any foreign material, including any abrasive particles created during the cleaning process.

❊❊ WARNING

Place clean, lint free shop towels over exposed engine cavities. Carefully remove the towels so foreign material is not dropped into the engine. Any foreign material (including any material created while cleaning gasket surfaces) that enters the oil passages or the oil pan, can cause engine failure.

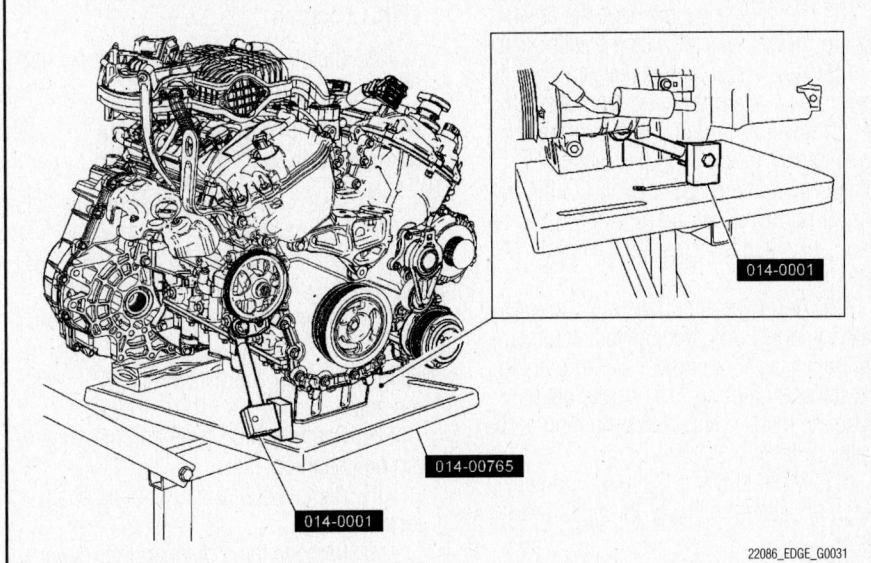

Fig. 90 Position a block of wood under the transaxle. Install the special tools, or their equivalents, as shown

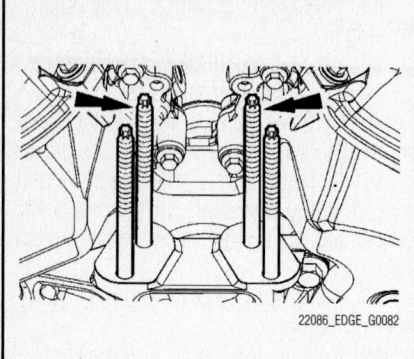

Fig. 91 Remove the 2 engine mount studs (arrows)

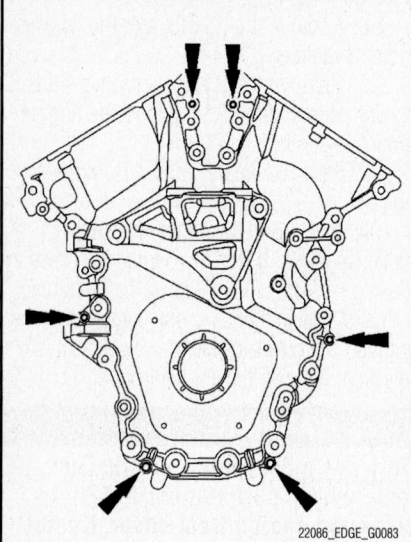

Fig. 92 Install 6 of the engine front cover bolts (finger tight) into the 6 threaded holes in the engine front cover. Tighten the bolts one turn at a time in a criss-cross pattern until the engine front cover-to-cylinder block seal is released

❋❋ WARNING

NEVER use metal scrapers, wire brushes, power abrasive discs or other abrasive means to clean the sealing surfaces. These tools cause scratches and gouges that make leak paths. Use a plastic scraping tool to remove all traces of sealant.

❋❋ WARNING

Observe all warnings or cautions and follow all application directions contained on the packaging of the silicone gasket remover and the metal surface prep.

Fig. 93 Rotate the crankshaft clockwise and align the timing marks on the Variable Camshaft Timing (VCT) assemblies as shown

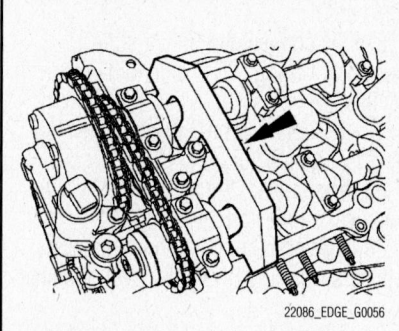

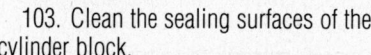

Fig. 94 Install the special tool onto the flats of the camshafts—left side shown, right side similar

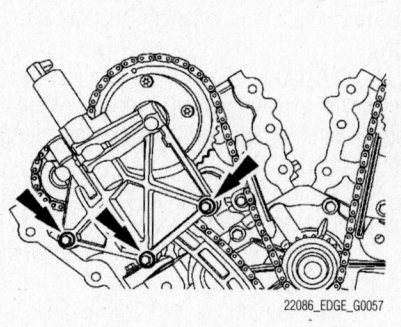

Fig. 95 Remove the 3 bolts and the VCT housing—right side shown, left side similar

103. Clean the sealing surfaces of the cylinder block.

104. Remove any large deposits of silicone or gasket material with a plastic scraper.

105. Apply silicone gasket remover, following package directions, and allow to set for several minutes. Remove the silicone gasket remover with a plastic scraper. A second application of silicone gasket remover may be required if residual traces of silicone or gasket material remain.

106. Apply metal surface prep, following package directions, to remove any remaining traces of oil or coolant and to prepare the surfaces to bond. Do not attempt to make the metal shiny. Some staining of the metal surfaces is normal.

107. Make sure the 2 locating dowel pins are seated correctly in the cylinder block.

108. Rotate the crankshaft clockwise and align the timing marks on the variable camshaft timing (VCT) assemblies as shown.

➡ The special tool will hold the camshafts in the Top Dead Center (TDC) position.

109. Install the special tool onto the flats of the LH camshafts.

➡ The special tool will hold the camshafts in the TDC position.

110. Install the special tool onto the flats of the RH camshafts.

111. Remove the 3 bolts and the RH VCT housing.

112. Remove the 3 bolts and the LH VCT housing.

113. Remove and discard the VCT housing seals.

114. Remove the 2 bolts and the primary timing chain tensioner.

115. Remove the primary timing chain tensioner arm.

116. Remove the 2 bolts and the lower LH primary timing chain guide.

117. Remove the primary timing chain. Refer to the Timing Chain procedure in this section for more details.

118. To remove the LH camshafts, perform the following:

   a. Compress the LH secondary timing chain tensioner and install a suitable lockpin to retain the tensioner in the collapsed position.

➡ **The VCT bolt and the exhaust camshaft bolt must be discarded and new ones installed. However, the exhaust camshaft washer is reusable.**

   b. Remove and discard the LH VCT assembly bolt and the LH exhaust camshaft sprocket bolt.

   c. Remove the LH VCT assembly, secondary timing chain and the LH exhaust camshaft sprocket as an assembly.

➡ **When the special tool is removed, valve spring pressure will rotate the LH camshafts approximately 3 degrees to a neutral position.**

   d. Remove the special tool from the LH camshafts.

❊❊ WARNING

The camshafts must remain in the neutral position during removal.

   e. Verify the LH camshafts are in the neutral position.

❊❊ WARNING

Cylinder head camshaft bearing caps are numbered to verify that they are assembled in their original positions.

   f. Remove the bolts and the LH camshaft bearing caps.

   g. Remove the LH camshafts.

119. To remove the RH camshafts, perform the following:

   a. Compress the RH secondary timing chain tensioner and install a suitable

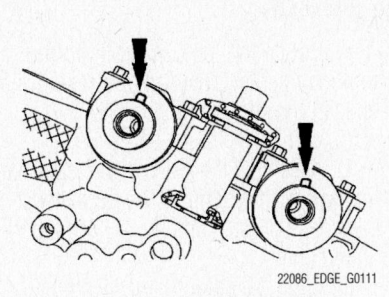

Fig. 97 Verify the camshafts are in the neutral position—left side shown, right side similar

lockpin to retain the tensioner in the collapsed position.

➡ **The VCT bolt and the exhaust camshaft bolt must be discarded and new ones installed. However, the exhaust camshaft washer is reusable.**

   b. Remove and discard the RH VCT assembly bolt and the RH exhaust camshaft sprocket bolt.

   c. Remove the RH VCT assembly, secondary timing chain and the RH exhaust camshaft sprocket as an assembly.

   d. Remove the special tool from the RH camshafts.

➡ **The camshafts must remain in the neutral position during removal.**

   e. Rotate the RH camshafts counterclockwise to the neutral position.

➡ **The cylinder head camshaft bearing caps are numbered to verify that they are assembled in their original positions.**

   f. Remove the bolts and the RH camshaft bearing caps.

   g. Remove the RH camshafts.

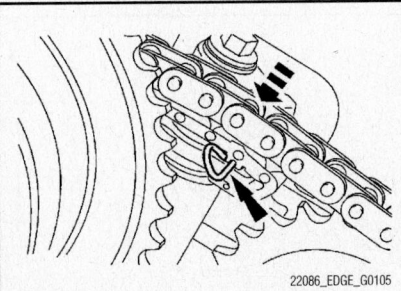

Fig. 96 Compress the secondary timing chain tensioner and install a suitable lockpin to retain the tensioner in the collapsed position—left side shown, right side similar

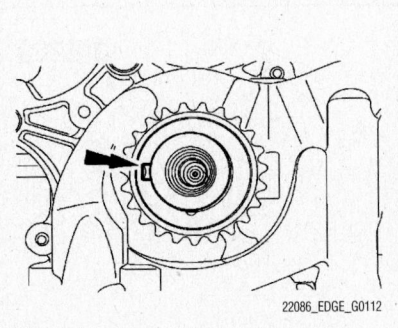

Fig. 98 Rotate the crankshaft counterclockwise until the crankshaft dowel pin is in the 9 o'clock position

To install:

❊❊ WARNING

The crankshaft MUST stay in the free-wheeling position (crankshaft dowel pin at 9 o'clock) until after the camshafts are installed and the valve clearance is checked/adjusted. Do NOT turn the crankshaft until instructed to do so. Failure to follow this process will result in severe engine damage.

120. Rotate the crankshaft counterclockwise until the crankshaft dowel pin is in the 9 o'clock position.

121. To install the LH camshafts, perform the following:

❊❊ WARNING

The camshafts must remain in the neutral position during installation.

➡ **Coat the camshafts with clean engine oil prior to installation.**

   h. Position the camshafts onto the LH cylinder head in the neutral position.

❊❊ WARNING

The cylinder head camshaft bearing caps are numbered to verify that they are assembled in their original positions.

   i. Install the 8 camshaft caps and the 16 bolts. Tighten in the sequence shown to 10 Nm (89 inch lbs.).

122. To install the RH camshafts, perform the following:

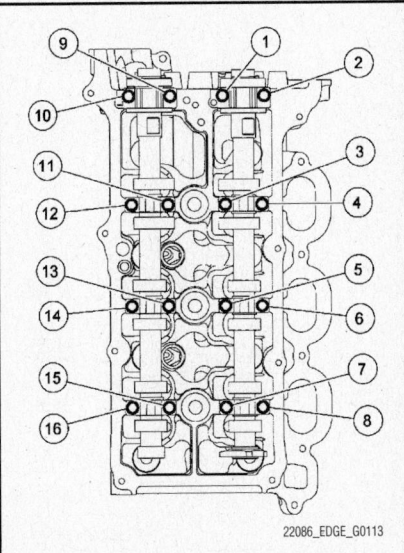

Fig. 99 Camshaft bearing cap tightening sequence—left side

⚙ WARNING

The camshafts must remain in the neutral position during installation.

➡**Coat the camshafts with clean engine oil prior to installation.**

j. Position the camshafts onto the RH cylinder head in the neutral position.

❋❋ WARNING

The cylinder head camshaft bearing caps are numbered to verify that they are assembled in their original positions.

123. Install the 8 camshaft caps and the 16 bolts. Tighten in the sequence shown to 10 Nm (89 inch lbs.).

⚙ WARNING

If any components are installed new, the engine valve clearance must be checked/adjusted or engine damage can occur.

➡**Use a camshaft sprocket bolt to turn the camshafts.**

124. Using a feeler gauge, confirm that the valve tappet clearances are within specification. If valve tappet clearances are not within specification, the clearance must be adjusted by installing new valve tappet(s) of the correct size. Refer to the Valve Lash Adjustment procedure in this section.

125. For LH camshafts, perform the following:

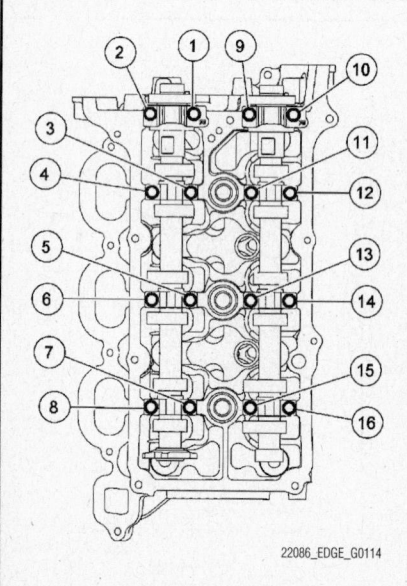

Fig. 100 Camshaft bearing cap tightening sequence—right side

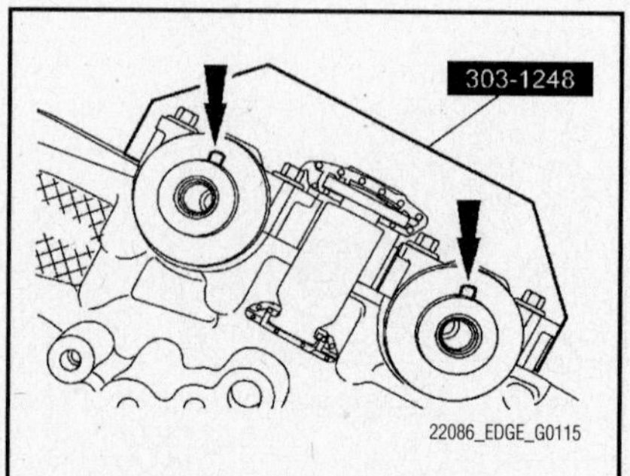

➡**Use a camshaft sprocket bolt to turn the camshafts.**

k. Rotate the LH camshafts to the top dead center position and install the special tool on the flats of the camshafts.

l. Assemble the LH Variable camshaft timing (VCT) assembly, the LH exhaust camshaft sprocket and the LH secondary timing chain.

m. Align the colored links with the timing marks.

n. Position the LH secondary timing assembly onto the camshafts.

o. Install 2 new bolts and the original washer. Tighten in 4 steps, as follows:
- Step 1: Tighten to 40 Nm (30 ft. lbs.).
- Step 2: Loosen one full turn.
- Step 3: Tighten to 10 Nm (89 inch lbs.).
- Step 4: Tighten 90 degrees.

p. Remove the lockpin from the LH secondary timing chain tensioner.

126. For RH camshafts, perform the following:

➡**Use a camshaft sprocket bolt to turn the camshafts.**

q. Rotate the RH camshafts to the top dead center position and install the special tool on the flats of the camshafts.

r. Assemble the RH VCT assembly, the RH exhaust camshaft sprocket and the RH secondary timing chain.

s. Align the colored links with the timing marks.

t. Position the RH secondary timing assembly onto the camshafts.

u. Install 2 new bolts and the original washer. Tighten in 4 Steps.
- Step 1: Tighten to 40 Nm (30 ft. lbs.).
- Step 2: Loosen one full turn.

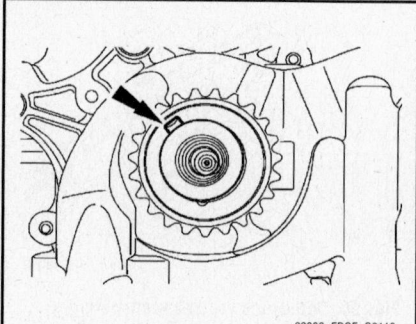

Fig. 101 Rotate the camshafts to the top dead center position and install the special tool on the flats of the camshafts—left side shown, right side similar

- Step 3: Tighten to 10 Nm (89 inch lbs.).
- Step 4: Tighten 90 degrees.

v. Remove the lockpin from the RH secondary timing chain tensioner.

127. Rotate the crankshaft clockwise 60 degrees to the top dead center position (crankshaft dowel pin at 11 o'clock).

128. Install the primary timing chain with the colored links aligned with the timing marks on the VCT assemblies and the crankshaft sprocket.

129. Install the lower LH primary timing chain guide and the 2 bolts. Tighten to 10 Nm (89 inch lbs.).

130. Install the primary timing chain tensioner arm.

131. Reset the primary timing chain tensioner, as follows:

a. Rotate the lever counter clockwise.

b. Using a soft-jawed vise, compress the plunger.

c. Align the hole in the lever with the hole in the tensioner housing.

d. Install a suitable lockpin.

➡**It may be necessary to rotate the crankshaft slightly to remove slack from the timing chain and install the tensioner.**

132. Install the primary tensioner and the 2 bolts. Tighten to 10 Nm (89 inch lbs.).

133. Remove the lockpin.

134. As a post-check, verify correct alignment of all timing marks.

135. Install new VCT housing seals.

❋❋ WARNING

Make sure the dowels on the VCT housing are fully engaged in the cylinder head prior to tightening the bolts.

Fig. 102 Rotate the crankshaft clockwise 60 degrees to the top dead center position (crankshaft dowel pin at 11 o'clock)

136. Install the LH VCT housing and the 3 bolts. Tighten in the sequence shown to 10 Nm (89 inch lbs.).

✳✴ WARNING

Make sure the dowels on the VCT housing are fully engaged in the cylinder head prior to tightening the bolts.

137. Install the RH VCT housing and the 3 bolts. Tighten in the sequence shown to 10 Nm (89 inch lbs.).

138. Install the alignment dowels, or equivalent special tools.

✳✴ WARNING

Failure to use the correct RTV Silicone Sealant (TA-357) may cause the engine oil to foam excessively and result in serious engine damage.

139. Install the timing chain (engine front) cover, as outlined in this section.

140. Install the engine mount bracket and the 2 bolts. Tighten to 24 Nm (18 ft. lbs.).

141. Install the 2 engine mount studs. Tighten to 18 Nm (13 ft. lbs.).

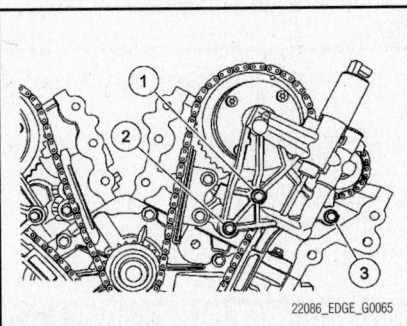

Fig. 103 Install the left side VCT housing and tighten the bolts in the sequence shown

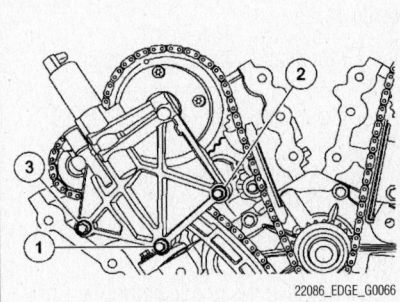

Fig. 104 Install the right side VCT housing and tighten the bolts in the sequence shown

➡**Apply clean engine oil to the crankshaft front seal bore in the engine front cover.**

142. Install a new crankshaft front seal, as outlined in this section.

➡**Lubricate the outside diameter sealing surfaces with clean engine oil.**

143. Install the crankshaft pulley, as outlined in this section.

144. Install the accessory drive belt tensioner and the 3 bolts. Tighten to 11 Nm (8 ft. lbs.).

145. Install the power steering pump and the 3 bolts. Tighten to 24 Nm (18 ft. lbs.).

146. Install the right and left valve covers, as outlined in this section.

147. Install the 6 coil-on-plug assemblies and the 6 bolts. Tighten to 7 Nm (62 inch lbs.).

148. Attach all of the wiring harness retainers to the LH valve cover and stud bolts.

149. Connect the 3 LH coil-on-plug electrical connectors.

150. Connect the LH camshaft VCT solenoid electrical connector.

151. Attach all of the wiring harness retainers to the RH valve cover and stud bolts.

152. Connect the heated PCV valve electrical connector.

153. Connect the 3 RH coil-on-plug electrical connectors.

154. Connect the RH VCT solenoid electrical connector.

155. Connect the Power Steering Pressure (PSP) switch electrical connector.

156. Connect the RH catalyst monitor sensor electrical connector.

157. Using new gaskets, install the upper intake manifold and the 6 bolts. Tighten in the sequence given in the intake manifold procedure, to 10 Nm (89 inch lbs.).

158. Install the upper intake manifold support bracket bolt. Tighten to 10 Nm (89 inch lbs.).

159. Install the upper intake manifold support bracket bolt. Tighten to 10 Nm (89 inch lbs.).

160. Attach the wiring harness retainers to the upper intake manifold.

161. Connect the throttle body electrical connector.

162. Connect the PCV hose to the PCV valve.

163. Connect the PCV fitting electrical connector.

164. If equipped, attach the engine block heater wiring harness retainers.

165. Raise the engine and transaxle assembly into the vehicle.

166. Install the engine mount and the 3 bolts. Tighten to 90 Nm (66 ft. lbs.).

167. Install the 4 engine mount nuts. Tighten to 63 Nm (46 ft. lbs.).

168. Install the engine mount brace, the nut and the bolt. Tighten to 20 Nm (15 ft. lbs.).

169. Install the transaxle support insulator bracket, the 3 nuts and the bolt. Tighten to 63 Nm (46 ft. lbs.).

170. Install the transaxle support insulator through bolt and nut. Tighten to 175 Nm (129 ft. lbs.).

171. For AWD vehicles, perform the following:

✳✴ WARNING

A new Powertrain Transfer Unit (PTU) seal must be installed whenever the intermediate shaft is removed.

e. Install a new PTU seal.

➡**Before installing the halfshaft, inspect the halfshaft sealing surface for wear or damage and install new, if necessary.**

f. Position the RH halfshaft/intermediate shaft assembly in the PTU and in the steering knuckle and install the 2 bolts. Tighten to 40 Nm (30 ft. lbs.).

172. For FWD vehicles, perform the following:

➡**Before installing the halfshaft, inspect the halfshaft sealing surface for wear or damage and install new if necessary.**

g. Position the RH halfshaft/intermediate shaft assembly in the transaxle and in the steering knuckle and install the 2 stud bolts. Tighten to 55 Nm (41 ft. lbs.).

➡**Do not tighten the 2 catalytic converter support bracket bolts at this time.**

h. Install the converter support bracket and the 2 bolts.

i. Install the catalytic converter bracket bolt and the nut. Tighten the nut to 40 Nm (30 ft. lbs.). Tighten the bolt to 55 Nm (41 ft. lbs.).

j. Tighten the 2 RH catalytic converter support bracket bolts to 20 Nm (15 ft. lbs.).

➡**Before installing the halfshaft, inspect the halfshaft sealing surface for wear or damage and install new, if necessary.**

173. Install the LH halfshaft into the transaxle.

174. If equipped, connect the oil cooler coolant hoses.

175. Using the special tool, raise the subframe into the installed position. For more information, refer to the Engine Removal & Installation procedure in this section.

176. Install the 2 middle subframe nuts. Tighten to 133 Nm (98 ft. lbs.).

177. Install the 2 front subframe nuts. Tighten to 133 Nm (98 ft. lbs.).

178. Position the subframe support brackets in place and loosely install the 4 bolts.

179. Install the 2 rear subframe bracket nuts. Tighten to 133 Nm (98 ft. lbs.).

180. Tighten the 4 subframe support bracket bolts. Tighten to 90 Nm (66 ft. lbs.).

181. Position the lower bumper on the subframe and install the 3 LH nuts. Tighten to 9 Nm (80 inch lbs.).

182. Install the 3 RH lower bumper-to-subframe nuts. Tighten to 9 Nm (80 inch lbs.).

183. Install the ball joints in the steering knuckles and install the pinch bolts. Tighten to 55 Nm (41 ft. lbs.).

184. Position the stabilizer bar links in the lower control arms and install the nuts. Tighten to 90 Nm (66 ft. lbs.).

185. Install the tie-rod ends and nuts. Tighten to 48 Nm (35 ft. lbs.). Install new cotter pins.

✳✳ WARNING

Do not let the intermediate shaft rotate while it is disconnected from the gear or damage to the clockspring can occur. If there is evidence that the intermediate shaft has rotated, the clockspring must be removed and recentered, as outlined in the Chassis Electrical Section.

186. Install the intermediate shaft onto the steering gear and install a new bolt. Tighten to 23 Nm (17 ft. lbs.).

187. Using a new banjo bolt and 2 new seals, install the PSP tube. Tighten to 48 Nm (35 ft. lbs.).

188. Install the engine roll restrictor-to-subframe through bolt. Tighten to 103 Nm (76 ft. lbs.).

189. Install the roll restrictor heat shield and the 2 nuts. Tighten to 11 Nm (8 ft. lbs.).

190. Apply the brake to keep the halfshaft from rotating. Install a new RH front half-shaft nut and tighten to 350 Nm (258 ft. lbs.).

191. For AWD vehicles, line up the index marks on the rear driveshaft to the index marks on the PTU flange made during

removal and install the 4 bolts. Tighten to 70 Nm (52 ft. lbs.).

192. Install the power steering cooler bracket bolt to the RH side of the subframe. Tighten to 9 Nm (80 inch lbs.).

193. Connect the power steering cooler hose.

➡**Lubricate the engine oil filter gasket with clean engine oil prior to installing the oil filter.**

194. Install a new engine oil filter. Tighten to 5 Nm (44 inch lbs.) and then rotate an additional 180 degrees.

195. Connect the 2 transmission fluid cooler tubes.

196. Install the 2 secondary latches onto the transmission fluid cooler tubes.

197. Install the LH inner splash shield.

198. Install the radiator splash shield, the 3 pin-type retainers and the 7 screws.

199. Using a new gasket, install the Y-pipe and exhaust flexible pipe assembly and 4 new nuts. Tighten to 40 Nm (30 ft. lbs.).

200. Install the 2 exhaust hangers and tighten the exhaust clamp. Tighten to 40 Nm (30 ft. lbs.).

201. Install the ground wire, the radio interference capacitor wire and the nut to the engine front cover stud. Tighten to 10 Nm (89 inch lbs.).

202. Install the ground wire and bolt to the engine front cover. Tighten to 10 Nm (89 inch lbs.).

203. Attach the wiring harness retainer to the RH valve cover stud bolt.

204. Install the oil level indicator.

205. Connect the 2 engine wiring harness electrical connectors.

206. Attach the electrical connector to the LH valve cover.

207. Connect the fuel hose routing clip to the transaxle stud.

208. Connect the fuel supply tube.

209. Connect the hose to the power steering reservoir.

210. Connect the A/C suction tube fitting. Install the safety clip onto the A/C fitting.

211. Using a new O-ring seal, connect the A/C pressure tube fitting and install the nut. Tighten to 8 Nm (71 inch lbs.).

212. If equipped, attach the engine block heater harness retainers from to the radiator support and the A/C suction tube.

213. Connect the transaxle control electrical connector.

214. Attach the control cable to the bracket. Connect the transaxle control cable to the control lever.

215. Attach the wiring harness retainer to the transaxle control cable bracket.

216. Connect the upper radiator hose, lower radiator hose and 2 heater hoses to the thermostat housing.

217. Connect the upper EVAP tube quick connect coupling. to the purge valve.

218. Connect the vacuum hose to the upper intake manifold.

219. Install the ground wire and the bolt. Tighten to 10 Nm (89 inch lbs.).

220. Attach the 2 wiring harness retainers to the cowl.

221. Connect the power feed to the battery terminal and install the nut. Tighten to 8 Nm (71 inch lbs.).

222. Connect the battery harness electrical connector.

223. Install the battery tray.

224. Install the engine air cleaner and the air cleaner outlet pipe.

225. Install the degas bottle.

226. Install the accessory drive belt and the power steering belt, as outlined in this section.

✳✳ WARNING

Do not expose the RTV Silicone Sealant (TA-357) to engine oil for at least 90 minutes after installing the engine front cover. Failure to follow this instruction may cause oil leakage.

227. Fill the engine with clean engine oil.

228. Fill and bleed the cooling system.

229. Fill the power steering system, as outlined in the Steering Section.

230. Recharge the air conditioning system.

CRANKSHAFT FRONT SEAL

REMOVAL & INSTALLATION

See Figures 105 and 106.

➡**This procedure requires the use of the following special tools or their equivalents:**

- Crankshaft Front Seal Installer 303-1251
- Oil Seal Remover 303-409 (T92C-6700CH)
- Crankshaft Damper Replacer 303-102 (T74P-6316-B)

1. Raise and safely support the vehicle.

2. Remove the crankshaft pulley, as outlined in this section.

3. Using the special tool shown, remove and discard the crankshaft front seal.

4. Thoroughly clean all sealing surfaces with a suitable metal surface cleaner.

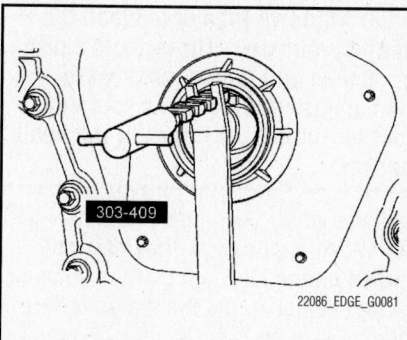

Fig. 105 Using the special tool, remove and discard the crankshaft front seal

To install:

➡ **Apply clean engine oil to the crankshaft front seal bore in the engine front cover.**

5. Using the special tools, install a new crankshaft front seal.

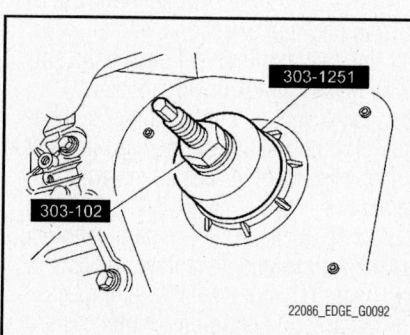

Fig. 106 Using the special tools, install a new crankshaft front seal

6. Install the crankshaft pulley, as outlined in this section.

CRANKSHAFT PULLEY

REMOVAL & INSTALLATION

See Figures 107 through 110.

➡ **This procedure requires the use of the following special tools or their equivalents:**

- 3-Jaw Puller 303-D121
- Front Cover Oil Seal Installer 303-335
- Crankshaft Damper Replacer 303-102 (T74P-6316-B)
- Strap Wrench 303-D055 (D85L-6000-A)

1. Raise and safely support the vehicle.
2. Remove the accessory drive belt and the power steering belt, as outlined in this section.
3. Using the special tool, or equivalent strap wrench to hold the crankshaft, remove

the crankshaft bolt and washer. Discard the bolt.

4. Using the special tool, remove the crankshaft pulley.

To install:

5. Lubricate the crankshaft front seal inner lip with clean engine oil. Lubricate the outside diameter sealing surfaces with clean engine oil.
6. Using the special tools, install the crankshaft pulley.
7. Using the special tool, install the crankshaft pulley washer and new bolt and tighten in 4 steps.
   a. Step 1: Tighten to 120 Nm (89 ft. lbs.).
   b. Step 2: Loosen one full turn.

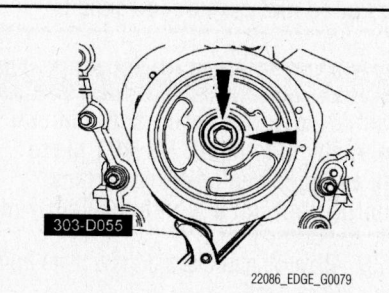

Fig. 107 Using the special tool, remove the crankshaft bolt and washer. Discard the bolt

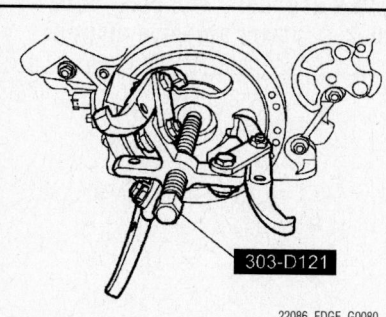

Fig. 108 Using the special tool, remove the crankshaft pulley

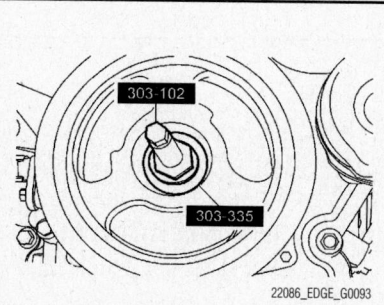

Fig. 109 Using the special tools, install the crankshaft pulley

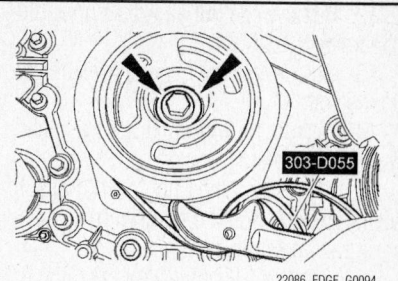

Fig. 110 Using the special tool, install the crankshaft pulley washer and new bolt and tighten in 4 steps

   c. Step 3: Tighten to 50 Nm (37 ft. lbs.).
   d. Step 4: Tighten an additional 90 degrees.
8. Install the accessory drive belt and the power steering belt, as outlined in this section.

CYLINDER HEAD

REMOVAL & INSTALLATION

Left Side

See Figures 111 through 113.

✳✳ WARNING

During engine repair procedures, cleanliness is extremely important. Any foreign material, including any material created while cleaning gasket surfaces that enters the oil passages, coolant passages or the oil pan, can cause engine failure.

1. Remove the LH camshafts, as outlined in this section.
2. If equipped, remove the heat shield and disconnect the block heater electrical connector.
3. Remove the block heater wiring harness from the engine.
4. Tag and detach the 6 fuel injector electrical connectors.
5. Disconnect the Cylinder Head Temperature (CHT) sensor electrical connector.
6. Remove the bolt and position aside the LH radio interference capacitor.
7. Disconnect the LH CMP sensor electrical connector.
8. Disconnect the LH Heated Oxygen Sensor (HO2S) electrical connector.
9. Disconnect the LH catalyst monitor sensor electrical connector.
10. Remove the wiring harness retainer bolt from the rear of the LH cylinder head.
11. Disconnect the A/C compressor electrical connector.

12. Remove the nut and disconnect the generator B+ cable.

13. Disconnect the generator electrical connector.

14. Detach the wiring harness retainer from the generator.

15. Disconnect the Engine Oil Pressure (EOP) switch electrical connector and the wiring harness pin-type retainer.

16. Remove the nut, 2 bolts and the A/C compressor. Position the compressor aside, but DO NOT disconnect the refrigerant lines.

17. Remove the nut, bolt and the generator.

18. Remove the 2 LH catalytic converter bracket bolts.

19. Remove the 4 nuts (3 shown) and the LH catalytic converter. Discard the nuts and the gasket.

20. Remove the 3 bolts and the LH exhaust manifold heat shield.

21. Remove the 6 nuts and the LH exhaust manifold.

22. Discard the nuts and the exhaust manifold gasket.

23. Clean and inspect the LH exhaust manifold, as outlined under the Exhaust Manifold procedure in this section. Remove and discard the 6 LH exhaust manifold studs.

24. Remove the LH cylinder block drain plug. Allow the coolant to drain from the cylinder block into a suitable container.

25. Remove the 2 RH catalytic converter bracket bolts.

26. Remove the 4 nuts and the RH catalytic converter. Discard the nuts and the gasket.

27. Remove the RH cylinder block drain plug or, if equipped, the block heater. Allow the coolant to drain from the cylinder block into a suitable container.

28. Remove the 4 bolts and the fuel rail and injectors as an assembly.

29. Remove the 3 thermostat housing-to-lower intake manifold bolts.

30. Remove the thermostat housing and discard the gasket and O-ring seal.

31. Remove the 10 bolts and the lower intake manifold. Discard the gaskets.

32. Remove the bolt and the LH CMP sensor.

33. Remove the 2 bolts and the upper LH primary timing chain guide.

34. Remove the 2 bolts and the LH secondary timing chain tensioner.

> ❋❋ **WARNING**
>
> **If the components are being reinstalled, they must be installed in the same positions. Mark the**

components for installation into their original positions.

35. Remove the valve tappets from the cylinder head.

36. Remove and discard the M6 bolt.

> ❋❋ **WARNING**
>
> **Place clean rags over any exposed engine cavities. Also, carefully remove the towels so foreign materials do not drop into the engine.**

> ❋❋ **WARNING**
>
> **The cylinder head bolts must be discarded and new bolts must be installed. They are tighten-to-yield designed and cannot be reused.**

> ❋❋ **WARNING**
>
> **Aluminum surfaces are soft and can be easily scratched. Do NOT place the cylinder head gasket surface, unprotected, on a workbench surface.**

37. Remove and discard the 8 bolts from the cylinder head.

38. Remove the cylinder head. Discard the cylinder head gasket.

> ❋❋ **WARNING**
>
> **NEVER use metal scrapers, wire brushes, power abrasive discs or**

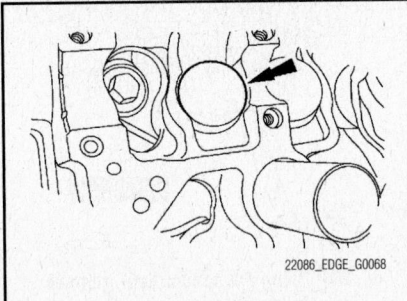

22086_EDGE_G0068

Fig. 111 Remove the valve tappets from the cylinder head

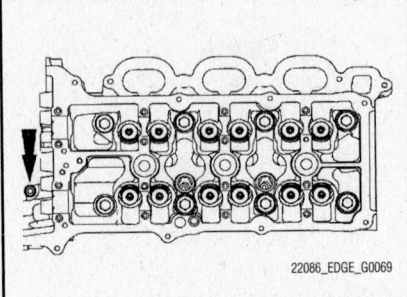

22086_EDGE_G0069

Fig. 112 Remove and discard the M6 bolt

other abrasive means to clean the sealing surfaces. These tools cause scratches and gouges that make leak paths. Use a plastic scraping tool to remove all traces of the head gasket.

➡ Observe all warnings or cautions and follow all application directions contained on the packaging of the silicone gasket remover and the metal surface prep.

➡ If there is no residual gasket material present, metal surface prep can be used to clean and prepare the surfaces.

39. Clean the cylinder head-to-cylinder block mating surfaces of both the cylinder heads and the cylinder block.

40. Remove any large deposits of silicone or gasket material with a plastic scraper.

41. Apply silicone gasket remover, following package directions, and allow to set for several minutes. Remove the silicone gasket remover with a plastic scraper. A second application of silicone gasket remover may be required if residual traces of silicone or gasket material remain.

42. Apply metal surface prep, following package directions, to remove any remaining traces of oil or coolant and to prepare the surfaces to bond with the new gasket. Do not attempt to make the metal shiny. Some staining of the metal surfaces is normal.

43. Support the cylinder head on a bench with the head gasket side up.

➡ The straightedge used must be flat within 0.0051 mm (0.0002 in) per foot of tool length. Inspect all areas of the deck face with a straightedge and feeler gauge. The cylinder head must not have depressions deeper than 0.0254 mm (0.001 in) across a 38.1 mm (1.5 in) square area, or scratches more than 0.0254 mm (0.001 in).

To install:

44. Install a new gasket, the LH cylinder head and 8 new bolts. Tighten in the sequence shown in 5 steps:

    a. Step 1: Tighten to 15 ft. lbs. (20 Nm).

    b. Step 2: Tighten to 26 ft. lbs. (35 Nm).

    c. Step 3: Tighten 90 degrees.

    d. Step 4: Tighten 90 degrees.

    e. Step 5: Tighten 90 degrees.

45. Install the M6 bolt and tighten to 10 Nm (89 inch lbs.).

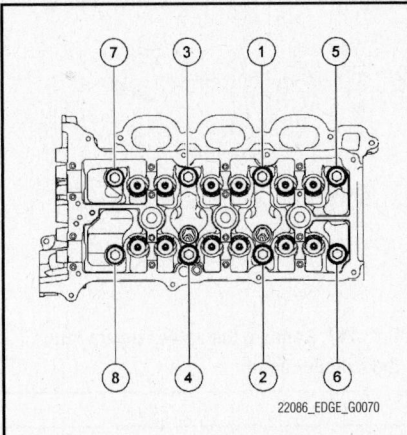

Fig. 113 Cylinder head bolt tightening sequence—left side

⁂ **WARNING**

The valve tappets must be installed in their original positions.

➡ **Coat the valve tappets with clean engine oil prior to installation.**

46. Install the valve tappets in their original positions.

47. Install the LH secondary timing chain tensioner and the 2 bolts. Tighten to 10 Nm (89 inch lbs.).

48. Install the upper LH primary timing chain guide and the 2 bolts. Tighten to 10 Nm (89 inch lbs.).

49. Install LH camshaft position (CMP) sensor and the bolt. Tighten to 10 Nm (89 inch lbs.).

50. Using new gaskets, install the lower intake manifold and the 10 bolts. Tighten in the proper sequence shown to 10 Nm (89 inch lbs.). Refer to the Intake Manifold procedure in this section.

51. Using a new gasket and O-ring seal, install the thermostat housing and the 3 bolts. Tighten to 10 Nm (89 inch lbs.).

⁂ **WARNING**

Make sure to use O-ring seals that are made of special fuel-resistant material. Using regular O-rings can cause the fuel system to leak. Never reuse the O-ring seals.

⁂ **WARNING**

The upper and lower O-ring seals are not interchangeable.

52. Install new fuel injector O-ring seals, as follows:

   a. Remove the retaining clips and separate the fuel injectors from the fuel rail.

   b. Remove and discard the O-ring seals.

   c. Install new O-ring seals and lubricate with clean engine oil.

   d. Install the fuel injectors and the retaining clips onto the fuel rail.

53. Install the fuel rail and injectors as an assembly and install the 4 bolts. Tighten to 10 Nm (89 inch lbs.).

54. Install the RH cylinder block drain plug or, if equipped, the block heater. Tighten to 40 Nm (30 ft. lbs.).

55. Install the 2 RH catalytic converter bracket bolts. Tighten the 4 catalytic converter nuts to 40 Nm (30 ft. lbs.). Tighten the 2 catalytic converter brackets to 20 Nm (15 ft. lbs.).

56. Using a new gasket, install the RH catalytic converter and 4 new nuts. Tighten to 40 Nm (30 ft. lbs.).

57. Install the LH cylinder block drain plug. Tighten to 20 Nm (15 ft. lbs.) plus an additional 180 degrees.

58. Install 6 new LH exhaust manifold studs. Tighten to 12 Nm (9 ft. lbs.).

59. Using a new gasket, install the LH exhaust manifold and 6 new nuts. Tighten in the proper sequence to 20 Nm (15 ft. lbs.). Refer to the Exhaust Manifold procedure in this section.

60. Install the LH exhaust manifold heat shield and the 3 bolts. Tighten to 14 Nm (10 ft. lbs.).

61. Using a new gasket, install the LH catalytic converter and 4 new nuts. Tighten to 40 Nm (30 ft. lbs.).

62. Install the 2 LH catalytic converter bracket bolts. Tighten to 20 Nm (15 ft. lbs.).

63. Install the generator, the bolt and the nut. Tighten to 47 Nm (35 ft. lbs.).

64. Install the A/C compressor, the nut and the 2 bolts. Tighten to 25 Nm (18 ft. lbs.).

65. Connect the EOP switch electrical connector and the wiring harness pin-type retainer.

66. Attach the wiring harness retainer to the generator.

67. Connect the generator electrical connector.

68. Connect the generator B+ cable and install the nut. Tighten to 6 Nm (53 inch lbs.).

69. Connect the A/C compressor electrical connector.

70. Install the wiring harness retainer bolt on the rear of the LH cylinder head. Tighten to 10 Nm (89 inch lbs.).

71. Connect the LH catalyst monitor sensor electrical connector.

72. Connect the LH HO2S electrical connector.

73. Connect the LH CMP sensor electrical connector.

74. Install the LH radio interference capacitor and the bolt. Tighten to 10 Nm (89 inch lbs.).

75. Connect the CHT sensor electrical connector.

76. Connect the 6 fuel injector electrical connectors.

77. If equipped, install the block heater wiring harness onto the engine. Connect the block heater electrical connector and install the heat shield.

78. Install the LH camshafts, as outlined in this section.

Right Side

See Figures 114 through 119.

⁂ **WARNING**

During engine repair procedures, cleanliness is extremely important. Any foreign material, including any material created while cleaning gasket surfaces that enters the oil passages, coolant passages or the oil pan, can cause engine failure.

1. Remove the RH camshafts, as outlined in this section.

2. If equipped, remove the heat shield and disconnect the block heater electrical connector.

3. Remove the block heater wiring harness from the engine.

4. Disconnect the RH Heated Oxygen Sensor (HO2S) electrical connector.

5. Remove the bolt and position aside the RH radio interference capacitor.

6. Disconnect the RH Camshaft Position (CMP) sensor electrical connector.

7. Remove the bolt and the ground cable from the RH cylinder.

8. Tag and detach the 6 fuel injector electrical connectors.

9. Disconnect the Cylinder Head Temperature (CHT) sensor electrical connector.

10. Disconnect the LH catalyst monitor sensor electrical connector.

11. Remove the 2 LH catalytic converter bracket bolts.

12. Remove the 4 nuts (3 shown) and the LH catalytic converter. Discard the nuts and the gasket.

13. Remove the LH cylinder block drain plug. Allow the coolant to drain from the cylinder block into a suitable container.

14. Remove the 2 RH catalytic converter bracket bolts.

15. Remove the 4 nuts and the RH catalytic converter. Discard the nuts and the gasket.

16. Remove the RH cylinder block drain plug or, if equipped, the block heater. Allow the coolant to drain from the cylinder block into a suitable container.

17. Remove the 3 bolts and the RH exhaust manifold heat shield.

18. Remove the 6 nuts and the RH exhaust manifold. Discard the nuts and exhaust manifold gaskets.

19. Clean and inspect the RH exhaust manifold. Refer to the Exhaust Manifold procedure in this section.

20. Remove and discard the 6 RH exhaust manifold studs.

21. Remove the 2 bolts and the RH primary timing chain guide.

22. Remove the 2 bolts and the RH secondary timing chain tensioner.

23. Remove the 2 bolts and the engine lifting eye.

➡Matchmark the installed position of the bracket on the cylinder head for installation.

24. Remove the bolt and the upper intake manifold bracket.

➡Matchmark the installed position of the bracket on the cylinder head for installation.

25. Remove the bolt and the upper intake manifold bracket.

26. Remove the bolt and the RH CMP sensor.

27. Remove the 4 bolts and the fuel rail and injectors as an assembly.

28. Remove the 3 thermostat housing-to-lower intake manifold bolts. Remove the thermostat housing and discard the gasket and O-ring seal.

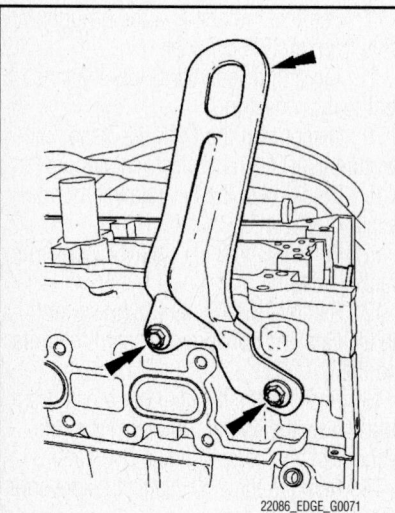

Fig. 114 Remove the 2 bolts and the engine lifting eye

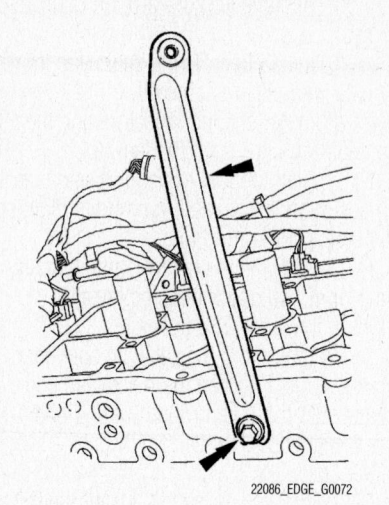

Fig. 115 Matchmark the installed position of the bracket on the cylinder head for installation, then remove the bolt and the upper intake manifold bracket

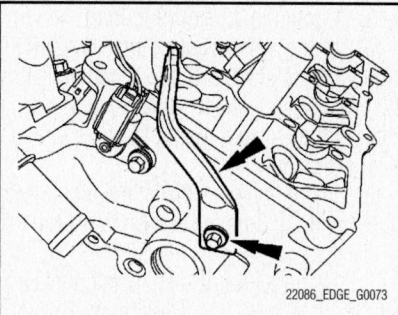

Fig. 116 Matchmark the installed position of the bracket on the cylinder head for installation, then remove the bolt and the upper intake manifold bracket

29. Remove the 10 bolts and the lower intake manifold. Discard the gaskets.

30. Disconnect and remove the CHT sensor jumper harness.

※※ WARNING

If the components are being reinstalled, they must be installed in the same positions. Mark the components for installation into their original positions.

31. Remove the valve tappets from the cylinder head.

32. Remove and discard the M6 bolt.

※※ WARNING

Place clean rags over any exposed engine cavities. Also, carefully remove the towels so foreign materials do not drop into the engine.

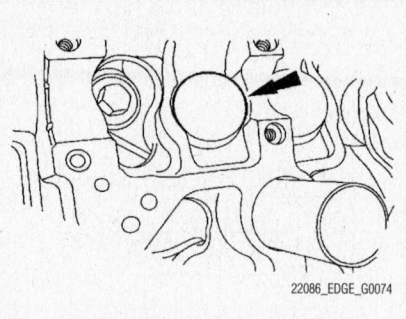

Fig. 117 Remove the valve tappets from the cylinder head

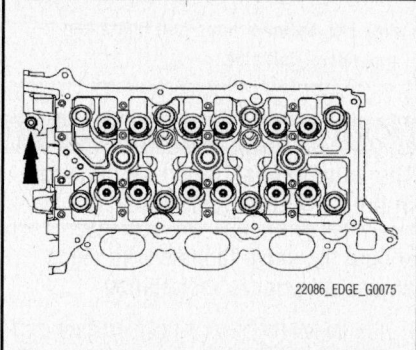

Fig. 118 Remove and discard the M6 bolt

※※ WARNING

The cylinder head bolts must be discarded and new bolts must be installed. They are tighten-to-yield designed and cannot be reused.

※※ WARNING

Aluminum surfaces are soft and can be easily scratched. Do NOT place the cylinder head gasket surface, unprotected, on a workbench surface.

33. Remove and discard the 8 bolts from the cylinder head. Remove the cylinder head. Discard the cylinder head gasket.

※※ WARNING

NEVER use metal scrapers, wire brushes, power abrasive discs or other abrasive means to clean the sealing surfaces. These tools cause scratches and gouges that make leak paths. Use a plastic scraping tool to remove all traces of the head gasket.

➡Observe all warnings or cautions and follow all application directions contained on the packaging of the silicone gasket remover and the metal surface prep.

➡️If there is no residual gasket material present, metal surface prep can be used to clean and prepare the surfaces.

34. Clean the cylinder head-to-cylinder block mating surfaces of both the cylinder heads and the cylinder block.

35. Remove any large deposits of silicone or gasket material with a plastic scraper.

36. Apply silicone gasket remover, following package directions, and allow to set for several minutes.

Remove the silicone gasket remover with a plastic scraper. A second application of silicone gasket remover may be required if residual traces of silicone or gasket material remain.

37. Apply metal surface prep, following package directions, to remove any remaining traces of oil or coolant and to prepare the surfaces to bond with the new gasket. Do not attempt to make the metal shiny. Some staining of the metal surfaces is normal.

38. Support the cylinder head on a bench with the head gasket side up.

➡️The straightedge used must be flat within 0.0051 mm (0.0002 in) per foot of tool length. Inspect all areas of the deck face with a straightedge and feeler gauge. The cylinder head must not have depressions deeper than 0.0254 mm (0.001 in) across a 38.1 mm (1.5 in) square area, or scratches more than 0.0254 mm (0.001 in).

To install:

39. Install a new gasket, the RH cylinder head and 8 new bolts. Tighten in the sequence shown in 5 steps:
   a. Step 1: Tighten to 20 Nm (15 ft. lbs.).
   b. Step 2: Tighten to 35 Nm (26 ft. lbs.).
   c. Step 3: Tighten 90 degrees.
   d. Step 4: Tighten 90 degrees.
   e. Step 5: Tighten 90 degrees.
40. Install the M6 bolt and tighten to 10 Nm (89 inch lbs.).

✳✳ WARNING

The valve tappets must be installed in their original positions.

➡️Coat the valve tappets with clean engine oil prior to installation.

41. Install the valve tappets in their original, installed positions.
42. Install and connect the CHT sensor jumper harness.
43. Using new gaskets, install the lower intake manifold and the 10 bolts. Tighten in

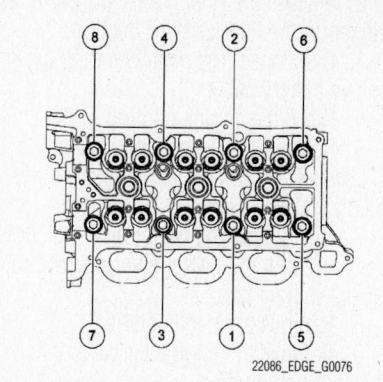

Fig. 119 Cylinder head bolt tightening sequence—right side

the proper sequence to 10 Nm (89 inch lbs.). Refer to the Intake Manifold procedure in this section.

44. Using a new gasket and O-ring seal, install the thermostat housing and the 3 bolts. Tighten to 10 Nm (89 inch lbs.).

✳✳ WARNING

Only use O-ring seals that are made of special fuel-resistant material. Using regular O-rings can cause the fuel system to leak. Never reuse the O-ring seals.

✳✳ WARNING

The upper and lower O-ring seals are not interchangeable.

45. Install new fuel injector O-ring seals, as follows:
   a. Remove the retaining clips and separate the fuel injectors from the fuel rail.
   b. Remove and discard the O-ring seals.
   c. Install new O-ring seals and lubricate with clean engine oil.
   d. Install the fuel injectors and the retaining clips onto the fuel rail.
46. Install the fuel rail and injectors as an assembly and install the 4 bolts. Tighten to 10 Nm (89 inch lbs.).
47. Install the RH CMP sensor and the bolt. Tighten to 10 Nm (89 inch lbs.).

➡️Align the bracket with the index mark made during removal.

48. Install the upper intake manifold bracket and the bolt. Tighten to 10 Nm (89 inch lbs.).

➡️Align the bracket with the index mark made during removal.

49. Install the upper intake manifold

bracket and the bolt. Tighten to 10 Nm (89 inch lbs.).

50. Install the engine lifting eye and the 2 bolts. Tighten to 24 Nm (18 ft. lbs.).

51. Install the RH secondary timing chain tensioner and the 2 bolts. Tighten to 10 Nm (89 inch lbs.).

52. Install the RH primary timing chain guide and the 2 bolts. Tighten to 10 Nm (89 inch lbs.).

53. Install 6 new RH exhaust manifold studs. Tighten to 12 Nm (9 ft. lbs.).

54. Using a new gasket, install the RH exhaust manifold and 6 new nuts. Tighten in the proper sequence to 20 Nm (15 ft. lbs.). Refer to the Exhaust Manifold procedure in this section.

55. Install the RH exhaust manifold heat shield and the 3 bolts. Tighten to 14 Nm (10 ft. lbs.).

56. Install the RH cylinder block drain plug or, if equipped, the block heater. Tighten to 40 Nm (30 ft. lbs.).

➡️Do not tighten the 4 catalytic converter nuts at this time.

57. Using a new gasket, install the RH catalytic converter and 4 new nuts.

58. Install the 2 RH catalytic converter bracket bolts. Tighten the 4 catalytic converter nuts to 40 Nm (30 ft. lbs.). Tighten the 2 catalytic converter brackets to 20 Nm (15 ft. lbs.).

59. Install the LH cylinder block drain plug. Tighten to 20 Nm (15 ft. lbs.) plus an additional 180 degrees.

60. Using a new gasket, install the LH catalytic converter and 4 new nuts (3 shown). Tighten to 40 Nm (30 ft. lbs.).

61. Install the 2 LH catalytic converter bracket bolts. Tighten to 20 Nm (15 ft. lbs.).

62. Connect the LH catalyst monitor sensor electrical connector.

63. Connect the CHT sensor electrical connector.

64. Connect the 6 fuel injector electrical connectors.

65. Install the ground cable and the bolt. Tighten to 10 Nm (89 inch lbs.).

66. Connect the RH CMP sensor electrical connector.

67. Install the RH radio interference capacitor and the bolt. Tighten to 10 Nm (89 inch lbs.).

68. Connect the RH HO2S electrical connector.

69. If equipped, install the block heater wiring harness onto the engine. Connect the block heater electrical connector and install the heat shield.

70. Install the RH camshafts, as outlined in this section.

ENGINE ASSEMBLY

REMOVAL & INSTALLATION

See Figures 120 through 131.

➡**Engine removal and installation requires a number of specialized tools and equipment. Make sure to read the procedure and be sure you have all of the necessary tools and equipment before beginning the procedure.**

❊❊ CAUTION

NEVER smoke or carry lighted tobacco or open flame of any type when working on or near any fuel-related components. Highly flammable mixtures are always present and may be ignited. Failure to follow these instructions may result in personal injury or death.

1. Raise and safely support the vehicle.
2. Recover the air conditioning system.
3. Release the fuel system pressure, as outlined in the Fuel System Section.
4. Disconnect the negative, then the positive battery cables.
5. Drain the engine cooling system.
6. Remove the accessory drive belt and the power steering belt, as outlined in this section.
7. Disconnect the power steering cooler hose and drain the power steering fluid into a suitable drain pan.
8. Remove the degas bottle.
9. Remove the engine air cleaner and air cleaner outlet pipe.
10. Remove the battery and the battery tray.
11. Disconnect the battery harness electrical connector.
12. Remove the nut and disconnect the power feed from the battery terminal.
13. Remove the bolt and the ground wire.
14. Detach the 2 wiring harness retainers from the cowl.
15. Disconnect the vacuum hose from the upper intake manifold.
16. Disconnect the upper Evaporative Emissions (EVAP) tube quick connect coupling from the purge valve.
17. Disconnect the upper radiator hose, lower radiator hose and 2 heater hoses from the thermostat housing.
18. Detach the wiring harness retainer from the transaxle control cable bracket.
19. Disconnect the transaxle control cable from the control lever.
20. Detach the control cable from the bracket.
21. Disconnect the transaxle control electrical connector.
22. If equipped, detach the engine block heater harness retainers from the radiator support and the A/C suction tube.
23. Remove the nut and disconnect the A/C pressure tube fitting.
24. Discard the O-ring seal.
25. Remove the safety clip from the A/C fitting.
26. Disconnect the A/C suction tube fitting.
27. Disconnect the hose from the power steering reservoir.
28. Disconnect the fuel supply tube.
29. Disconnect the fuel hose routing clip from the transaxle stud and position the fuel hose aside.
30. Disconnect the 2 engine wiring harness electrical connectors.
31. Detach the electrical connector from the LH valve cover.
32. Remove the oil level indicator dipstick.
33. Detach the wiring harness retainer from the RH valve cover stud bolt.
34. Remove the bolt and the ground wire from the engine front cover.
35. Remove the nut, the ground wire and the radio interference capacitor wire from the engine front cover stud.
36. Loosen the exhaust flexible pipe clamp and disconnect the 2 exhaust hangers.
37. Remove the 4 nuts and the exhaust flexible pipe and Y-pipe as an assembly.
38. Discard the nuts and the gasket.
39. Remove the 3 pin-type retainers, the 7 screws and the radiator splash shield.
40. Remove the LH inner splash shield.
41. Remove the 2 secondary latches from the transmission fluid cooler tubes.
42. Using the special tool shown in the accompanying illustration, disconnect the transaxle cooling tubes.
43. Remove the 4 oil pan-to-transaxle bolts.
44. Remove the 2 fasteners and the inspection cover.

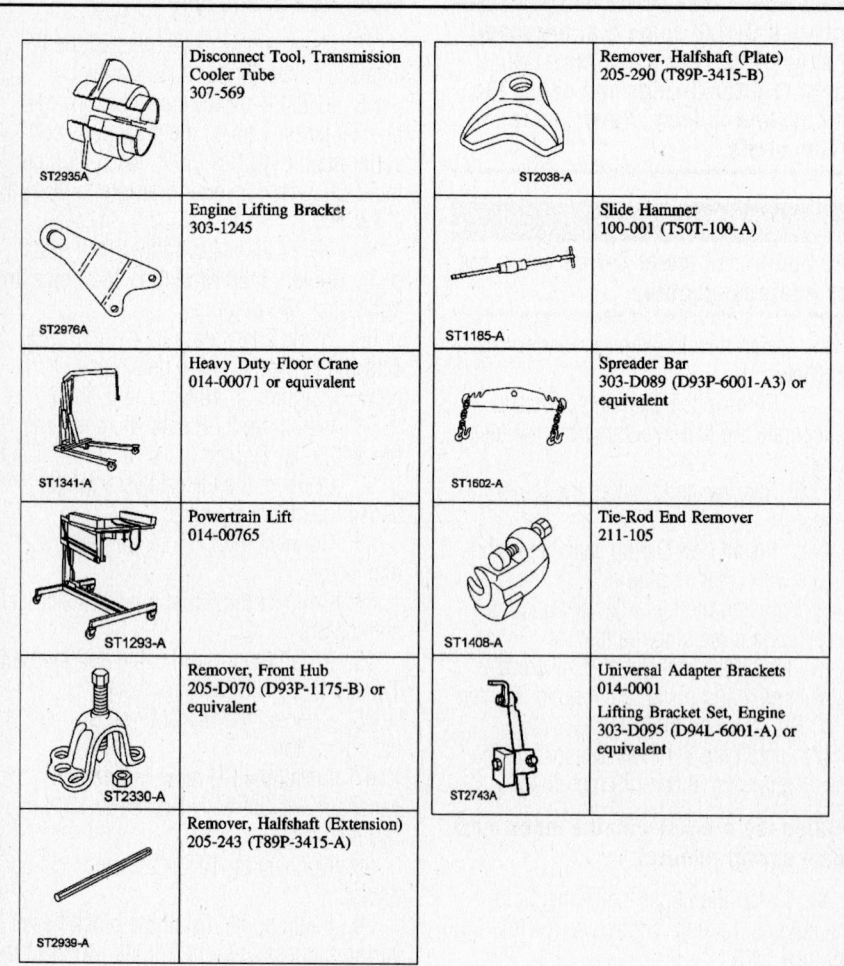

Disconnect Tool, Transmission Cooler Tube 307-569 ST2935A	Remover, Halfshaft (Plate) 205-290 (T89P-3415-B) ST2038-A
Engine Lifting Bracket 303-1245 ST2976A	Slide Hammer 100-001 (T50T-100-A) ST1185-A
Heavy Duty Floor Crane 014-00071 or equivalent ST1341-A	Spreader Bar 303-D089 (D93P-6001-A3) or equivalent ST1602-A
Powertrain Lift 014-00765 ST1293-A	Tie-Rod End Remover 211-105 ST1408-A
Remover, Front Hub 205-D070 (D93P-1175-B) or equivalent ST2330-A	Universal Adapter Brackets 014-0001 Lifting Bracket Set, Engine 303-D095 (D94L-6001-A) or equivalent ST2743A
Remover, Halfshaft (Extension) 205-243 (T89P-3415-A) ST2939-A	

22086_EDGE_G0034

Fig. 120 Special tools needed for engine removal and installation

Fig. 121 Using the special tool shown, disconnect the transaxle cooling tubes

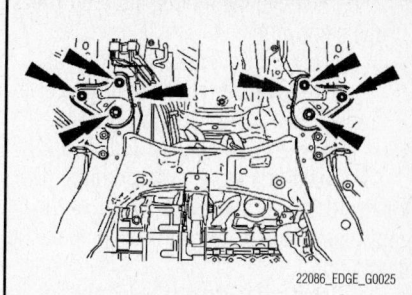

Fig. 123 Remove the 2 nuts, 4 bolts and the subframe support brackets

45. Remove and discard the 3 torque converter bolts.

46. Remove the drain plug and drain the engine oil. Install the drain plug and tighten to 27 Nm (20 ft. lbs.).

47. Remove and discard the engine oil filter.

48. Remove the power steering cooler bracket bolt from the RH side of the subframe.

49. For All Wheel Drive (AWD) vehicles, match mark the driveshaft for installation, then remove the 4 bolts and support the driveshaft with a piece of wire.

50. Remove and discard the RH front halfshaft nut.

51. Remove the 2 nuts and the roll restrictor heat shield.

52. Remove the engine roll restrictor-to-subframe through bolt.

53. Remove and discard the power steering pressure (PSP) tube-to-pump banjo bolt and the 2 seals.

✳✳ WARNING

Do not let the intermediate shaft rotate while it is disconnected from the gear or damage to the clock-spring can occur. If there is evidence that the intermediate shaft has rotated, the clockspring must be removed and recentered, as outlined in the Chassis Electrical Section.

54. Remove and discard the steering intermediate shaft bolt.

55. Separate the steering intermediate shaft from the steering gear.

56. Remove and discard the cotter pins and tie-rod end nuts.

57. Using a suitable puller, separate the tie-rod ends from the wheel knuckles.

58. Remove the 2 stabilizer link-to-lower control arm nuts and separate the stabilizer bar links from the lower control arms.

59. Remove the lower control arm-to-knuckle pinch bolts and separate the lower control arms from the knuckles.

60. Remove the 3 RH subframe-to-lower bumper nuts.

61. Remove the 3 LH subframe-to-lower bumper nuts and separate the lower bumper from the subframe.

62. Position the special tool under the subframe assembly.

63. Remove the 2 nuts, 4 bolts and the subframe support brackets.

64. Remove the 2 front subframe nuts.

65. Remove the 2 middle subframe nuts.

66. Using the special tool, lower the subframe assembly from the vehicle.

67. If equipped, disconnect the oil cooler coolant hoses.

68. Using the special tools, or their equivalents, separate the LH halfshaft from the transaxle and support the halfshaft with a piece of wire.

69. Remove the 2 RH catalytic converter support bracket bolts.

70. Using a suitable puller, separate the RH halfshaft from the hub.

71. For Front wheel drive (FWD) vehicles, perform the following:

a. Remove the bolt, the nut and the RH catalytic converter support bracket.

b. Remove the 2 stud bolts and the RH halfshaft/intermediate shaft assembly.

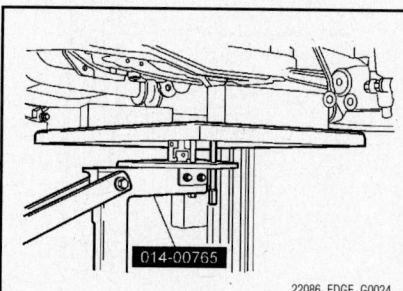

Fig. 122 Position the special tool under the subframe assembly

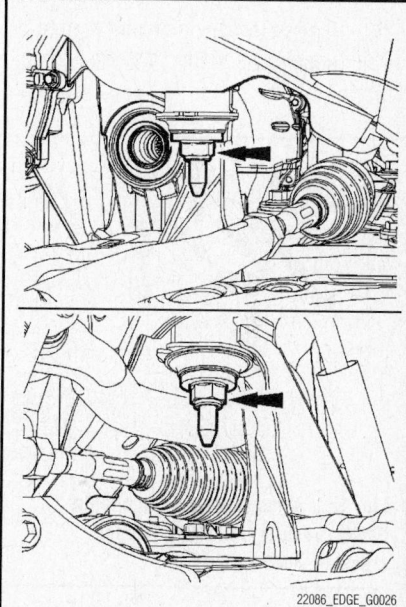

Fig. 124 Remove the 2 middle subframe nuts

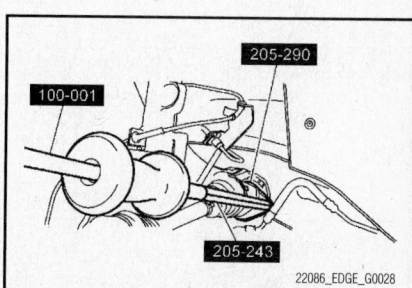

Fig. 126 Using the special tools, separate the LH halfshaft from the transaxle and support the halfshaft with a piece of wire

72. For AWD vehicles, perform the following:

a. Remove the 2 RH halfshaft bearing support bracket bolts and the RH halfshaft/intermediate shaft assembly.

b. Disconnect the RH catalyst monitor electrical connector.

c. Remove the 4 nuts and the RH catalytic converter.

d. Discard the gasket and the nuts.

e. Remove the 5 bolts and the Power Transfer Unit (PTU) support bracket.

f. Remove the 5 bolts and the PTU.

73. Position a block of wood under the transaxle. Install the special tools, or their equivalents, as shown in the accompanying illustration.

74. Remove the transaxle support insulator through bolt and nut.

75. Remove the 3 nuts, the bolt and the transaxle support insulator bracket.

76. Remove the nut, bolt and engine mount brace.

77. Remove the 4 engine mount nuts.

78. Remove the 3 bolts and the engine mount.

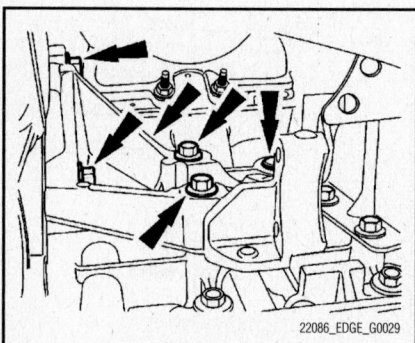

Fig. 127 Remove the 5 bolts and the Power Transfer Unit (PTU) support bracket—AWD models

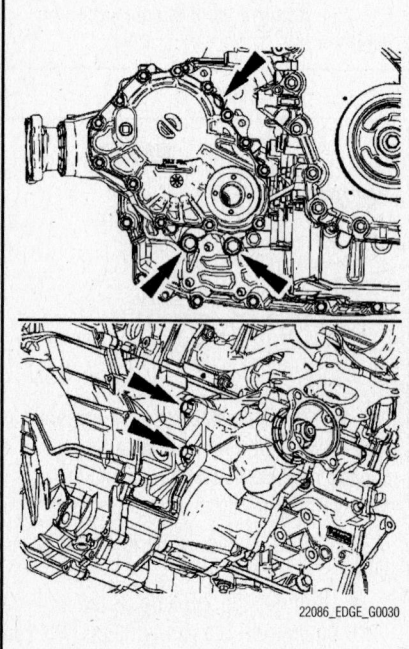

Fig. 128 Remove the 5 bolts and the PTU—AWD models

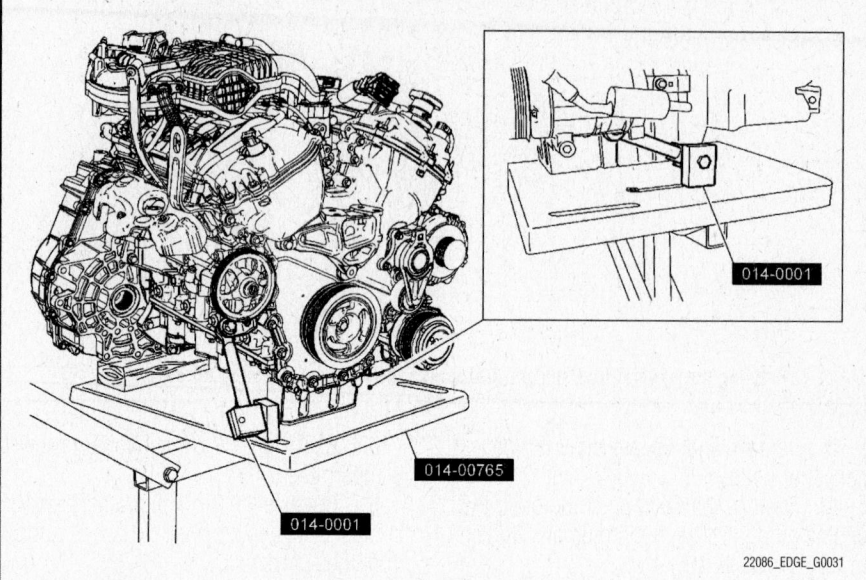

Fig. 129 Position a block of wood under the transaxle. Install the special tools, or their equivalents, as shown

79. Lower the engine and transaxle assembly from the vehicle.

80. Position the starter cable boot back and remove the 2 nuts.

81. Detach the 2 wire terminals from the starter.

82. Disconnect the wiring harness retainer from the starter motor stud bolt.

83. Remove the bolt, stud bolt and the starter.

84. Install the special tool on the LH cylinder head.

85. Using the special tools and a suitable engine crane, remove the engine and transaxle from the lift table.

86. Remove the 2 engine-to-transaxle bolts.

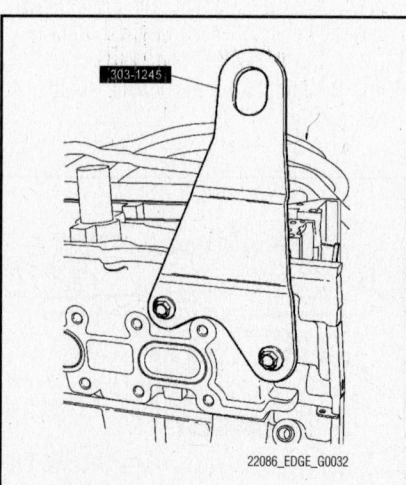

Fig. 130 Install the special tool on the LH cylinder head

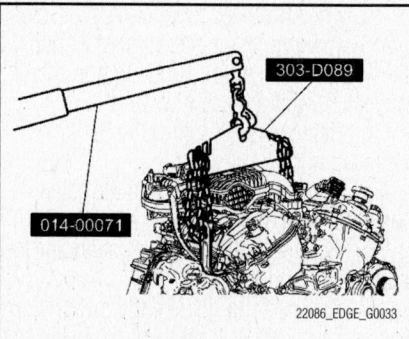

Fig. 131 Using the special tools and a suitable engine crane, remove the engine and transaxle from the lift table

87. Remove the 5 transaxle-to-engine bolts.

88. Separate the transaxle from the engine.

To install:

89. Align the transaxle to the engine.

90. Install the 5 transaxle-to-engine bolts and tighten to 48 Nm (35 ft. lbs.).

91. Install the 2 engine-to-transaxle bolts and tighten to 48 Nm (35 ft. lbs.).

92. Using the special tools, position the engine and transaxle onto the lift table.

93. Position a block of wood under the transaxle. Install the special tools, as shown.

94. Install the starter, the bolt and the stud bolt. Tighten to 27 Nm (20 ft. lbs.).

95. Connect the wiring harness retainer to the starter stud bolt.

96. Attach the starter motor wire terminals and install the 2 nuts. Tighten as follows:

a. Tighten to 12 Nm (9 ft. lbs.).

b. Tighten to 5 Nm (44 inch lbs.).

97. Position the starter terminal boot over the starter terminal.

98. Raise the engine and transaxle assembly into the vehicle.

99. Install the engine mount and the 3 bolts. Tighten to 90 Nm (66 ft. lbs.).

100. Install the 4 engine mount nuts and tighten to 63 Nm (46 ft. lbs.).

101. Install the engine mount brace, the nut and the bolt and tighten to 20 Nm (15 ft. lbs.).

102. Install the transaxle support insulator bracket, the 3 nuts and the bolt. Tighten to 63 Nm (46 ft. lbs.).

103. Install the transaxle support insulator through bolt and nut and tighten to 175 Nm (129 ft. lbs.).

104. For AWD vehicles, perform the following:

a. Position the Power Transfer Unit (PTU) in place and install the 5 bolts. Tighten to 90 Nm (66 ft. lbs.).

b. Position the PTU support bracket in place and install the 5 bolts. Tighten to 70 Nm (52 ft. lbs.).

➡**Do not tighten the 4 catalytic converter nuts at this time.**

c. Using a new gasket, install the RH catalytic converter and 4 new nuts.

d. Install the 2 catalytic converter-to-bracket bolts.

e. Tighten the 4 catalytic converter nuts to 40 Nm (30 ft. lbs.).

f. Tighten the 2 catalytic converter-to-bracket bolts to 20 Nm (15 ft. lbs.).

g. Connect the RH catalyst monitor electrical connector.

✳✳ WARNING

A new PTU seal must be installed whenever the intermediate shaft is removed.

h. Install a new PTU seal.

➡**Before installing the halfshaft, inspect the halfshaft sealing surface for wear or damage and install new, if necessary.**

i. Position the RH halfshaft/intermediate shaft assembly in the PTU and in the steering knuckle and install the 2 bolts. Tighten to 40 Nm (30 ft. lbs.).

105. For FWD vehicles, perform the following:

➡**Before installing the halfshaft, inspect the halfshaft sealing surface for wear or damage and install new if necessary.**

j. Position the RH halfshaft/intermediate shaft assembly in the transaxle and in the steering knuckle and install the 2 stud bolts. Tighten to 55 Nm (41 ft. lbs.).

➡**Do not tighten the 2 catalytic converter support bracket bolts at this time.**

k. Install the converter support bracket and the 2 bolts.

l. Install the catalytic converter bracket bolt and the nut. Tighten the nut to 40 Nm (30 ft. lbs.) and the bolt to 55 Nm (41 ft. lbs.).

m. Tighten the 2 RH catalytic converter support bracket bolts to 20 Nm (15 ft. lbs.).

➡**Prior to installation of the halfshaft, inspect the halfshaft sealing surface for wear or damage and install new, if necessary.**

106. Install the LH halfshaft into the transaxle.

107. If equipped, connect the oil cooler coolant hoses.

108. Using the special tool, raise the subframe into the installed position.

109. Install the 2 middle subframe nuts and tighten to 133 Nm (98 ft. lbs.).

110. Install the 2 front subframe nuts and tighten to 133 Nm (98 ft. lbs.).

111. Position the subframe support brackets in place and loosely install the 4 bolts.

112. Install the 2 rear subframe bracket nuts and tighten to 133 Nm (98 ft. lbs.).

113. Tighten the 4 subframe support bracket bolts to 90 Nm (66 ft. lbs.).

114. Position the lower bumper on the subframe and install the 3 LH nuts. Tighten to 9 Nm (80 inch lbs.).

115. Install the 3 RH lower bumper-to-subframe nuts. Tighten to 9 Nm (80 inch lbs.).

116. Install the ball joints in the steering knuckles and install the pinch bolts. Tighten to 55 Nm (41 ft. lbs.).

117. Position the stabilizer bar links in the lower control arms and install the nuts. Tighten to 90 Nm (66 ft. lbs.).

118. Install the tie-rod ends and nuts and tighten to 48 Nm (35 ft. lbs.). Install new cotter pins.

✳✳ WARNING

Do not let the intermediate shaft to rotate while it is disconnected from the gear or damage to the clockspring can occur. If there is evidence that the intermediate shaft has rotated, the clockspring must be removed and recentered, as outlined in the Chassis Electrical Section.

119. Install the intermediate shaft onto the steering gear and install a new bolt. Tighten to 23 Nm (17 ft. lbs.).

120. Using a new banjo bolt and 2 new seals, install the PSP tube. Tighten to 48 Nm (35 ft. lbs.).

121. Install the engine roll restrictor-to-subframe through bolt and tighten to 103 Nm (76 ft. lbs.).

122. Install the roll restrictor heat shield and the 2 nuts and tighten to 11 Nm (8 ft. lbs.).

➡**Apply the brake to keep the halfshaft from rotating.**

123. Install a new RH front halfshaft nut and tighten to 350 Nm (258 ft. lbs.).

124. For AWD vehicles, align the match-marks on the rear driveshaft to the index marks on the PTU flange made during removal and install the 4 bolts. Tighten the bolts to 70 Nm (52 ft. lbs.).

125. Install the power steering cooler bracket bolt to the RH side of the subframe. Tighten to 9 Nm (80 inch lbs.).

126. Connect the power steering cooler hose.

➡**Lubricate the engine oil filter gasket with clean engine oil before installing the oil filter.**

127. Install a new engine oil filter. Tighten to 5 Nm (44 inch lbs.) and then rotate an additional 180 degrees.

128. Install the 3 new torque converter bolts and tighten to 55 Nm (41 ft. lbs.).

129. Install the inspection cover and the 2 fasteners.

130. Install the 4 oil pan-to-transaxle bolts and tighten to 48 Nm (35 ft. lbs.).

131. Connect the 2 transmission fluid cooler tubes.

132. Install the 2 secondary latches onto the transmission fluid cooler tubes.

133. Install the LH inner splash shield.

134. Install the radiator splash shield, the 3 pin-type retainers and the 7 screws.

135. Using a new gasket, install the Y-pipe and exhaust flexible pipe assembly and 4 new nuts. Tighten to 40 Nm (30 ft. lbs.).

136. Install the 2 exhaust hangers and tighten the exhaust clamp. Tighten to 40 Nm (30 ft. lbs.).

137. Install the ground wire, the radio interference capacitor wire and the nut to the engine front cover stud. Tighten to 10 Nm (89 inch lbs.).

138. Install the ground wire and bolt to the engine front cover. Tighten to 10 Nm (89 inch lbs.).

139. Attach the wiring harness retainer to the RH valve cover stud bolt.

140. Install the oil level indicator.

141. Connect the 2 engine wiring harness electrical connectors.

142. Attach the electrical connector to the LH valve cover.

143. Connect the fuel hose routing clip to the transaxle stud.

144. Connect the fuel supply tube.

145. Connect the hose to the power steering reservoir.

146. Connect the A/C suction tube fitting. Install the safety clip onto the A/C fitting.

147. Using a new O-ring seal, connect the A/C tube fitting and install the nut. Tighten to 8 Nm (71 inch lbs.). If equipped, attach the engine block heater harness retainers to the radiator support and the A/C suction tube.

148. Connect the transaxle control electrical connector.

149. Attach the control cable to the bracket.

150. Connect the transaxle control cable to the control lever.

151. Attach the wiring harness retainer to the transaxle control cable bracket.

152. Connect the upper radiator hose, lower radiator hose and 2 heater hoses to the thermostat housing.

153. Connect the upper EVAP tube quick connect coupling to the purge valve.

154. Connect the vacuum hose to the upper intake manifold.

155. Install the ground wire and the bolt and tighten to 10 Nm (89 inch lbs.).

156. Attach the 2 wiring harness retainers to the cowl.

157. Connect the power feed to the battery terminal and install the nut. Tighten to 8 Nm (71 inch lbs.).

158. Connect the battery harness electrical connector.

159. Install the battery tray and the battery.

160. Install the engine air cleaner and the air cleaner outlet pipe.

161. Install the degas bottle.

162. Install the accessory drive belt and the power steering belt, as outlined in this section.

163. Connect the positive, then the negative battery cables.

164. Fill the engine with clean engine oil.

165. Fill and bleed the cooling system.

166. Fill the power steering system.

167. Recharge the air conditioning system.

EXHAUST MANIFOLD

REMOVAL & INSTALLATION

Left Side

See Figures 132 and 133.

1. Remove the LH catalytic converter, as follows:

a. Raise and safely support the vehicle.

b. Disconnect the catalyst monitor sensor electrical connector.

c. Remove the exhaust Y-pipe.

d. Remove the 2 catalytic converter support bracket-to-transmission bolts.

e. Remove the 4 nuts and the LH catalytic converter.

f. Discard the 4 LH catalytic converter nuts and gasket.

2. Remove the LH Heated Oxygen Sensor (HO2S).

3. Remove the 3 bolts and the LH exhaust manifold heat shield.

4. Remove the 6 nuts and the LH exhaust manifold. Discard the nuts and gasket.

5. Clean and inspect the LH exhaust manifold.

6. Remove and discard the 6 LH exhaust manifold studs.

> ⁑ **WARNING**
>
> **Do not use metal scrapers, wire brushes, power abrasive discs or other abrasive means to clean the sealing surfaces. These may cause scratches and gouges resulting in leak paths. Use a plastic scraper to clean the sealing surfaces.**

7. Clean the exhaust manifold mating surface of the cylinder head with metal surface prep. Follow the directions on the packaging.

To install:

8. Install 6 new LH exhaust manifold studs and tighten to 12 Nm (9 ft. lbs.).

9. Using a new gasket, install the LH exhaust manifold and 6 new nuts. Tighten in the sequence shown to 20 Nm (15 ft. lbs.).

10. Install the LH exhaust manifold heat shield and the 3 bolts and tighten to 14 Nm (10 ft. lbs.).

11. Install the LH HO2S.

➡ **When installing the catalytic converter, always install new fasteners and gaskets. Clean the flange faces prior to new gasket installation to ensure proper sealing.**

12. Install the LH catalytic converter, with new gaskets and nuts, in the reverse of the

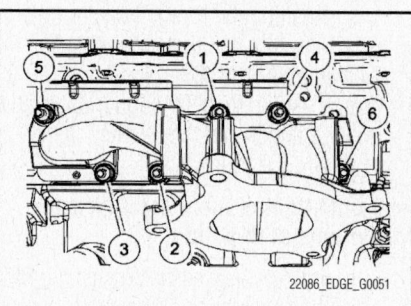

Fig. 133 Exhaust manifold tightening sequence—left side

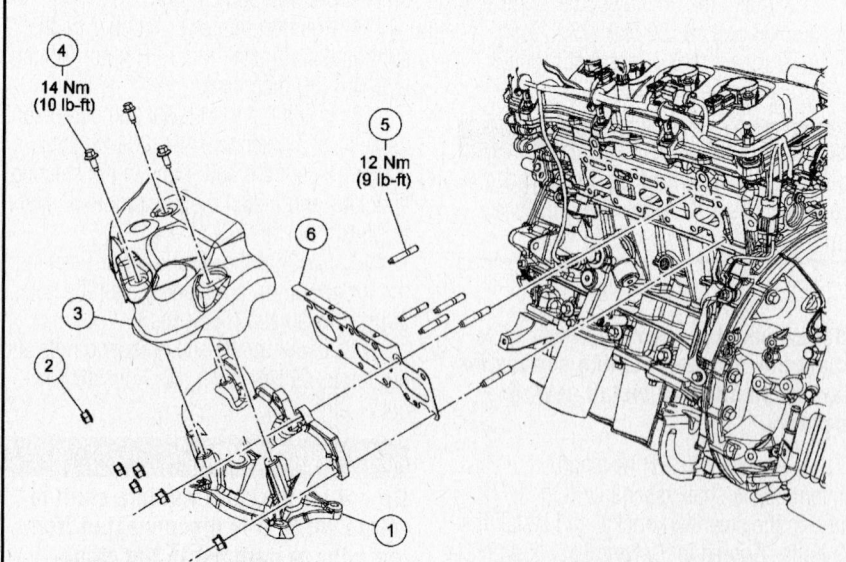

1. LH exhaust manifold
2. LH exhaust manifold nuts (6)
3. LH exhaust manifold heat shield
4. LH exhaust manifold head shield bolts (3)
5. LH exhaust manifold studs (6)
6. LH exhaust manifold gasket

Fig. 132 Exploded view of the left side exhaust manifold and related components

removal procedure. Tighten the retainers as follows:

a. Catalytic converter nuts: 40 Nm (30 ft. lbs.)

b. Catalytic converter support bracket-to-transmission bolts: 48 Nm (35 ft. lbs.)

Right Side

See Figures 134 and 135.

1. Remove the right side catalytic converter, as follows:

a. Raise and safely support the vehicle.

b. Remove the catalyst monitor sensor.

c. Remove the exhaust Y-pipe.

d. For All Wheel Drive (AWD) models, Remove and discard the 4 universal joint (U-joint) flange bolts and separate the front driveshaft and secure it with a piece of wire.

e. For AWD models, remove the RH halfshaft assembly. Remove the 2 catalytic converter support bracket-to-engine block bolts.

f. For Front Wheel Drive (FWD) models, remove the 2 bolts and the power steering rack shield.

g. For FWD models, remove the catalytic converter support bracket-to-engine block bolt and nut.

h. Remove the 2 nuts and the roll restrictor shield.

i. Remove the roll restrictor bolt and rotate the engine forward.

j. Remove the 2 bracket-to-RH catalytic converter bolts.

k. Remove the 4 nuts and the RH catalytic converter.

l. Discard the 4 RH catalytic converter nuts and gasket.

2. Disconnect the RH Heated Oxygen Sensor (HO2S) electrical connector.

3. Remove the 6 nuts and the RH exhaust manifold. Discard the nuts and gasket.

4. Clean and inspect the RH exhaust manifold.

5. Remove and discard the 6 RH exhaust manifold studs.

✳✳ WARNING

NEVER use metal scrapers, wire brushes, power abrasive discs or other abrasive means to clean the sealing surfaces. These may cause scratches and gouges resulting in leak paths. Use a plastic scraper to clean the sealing surfaces.

6. Clean the exhaust manifold mating surface of the cylinder head with metal surface prep. Follow the directions on the packaging.

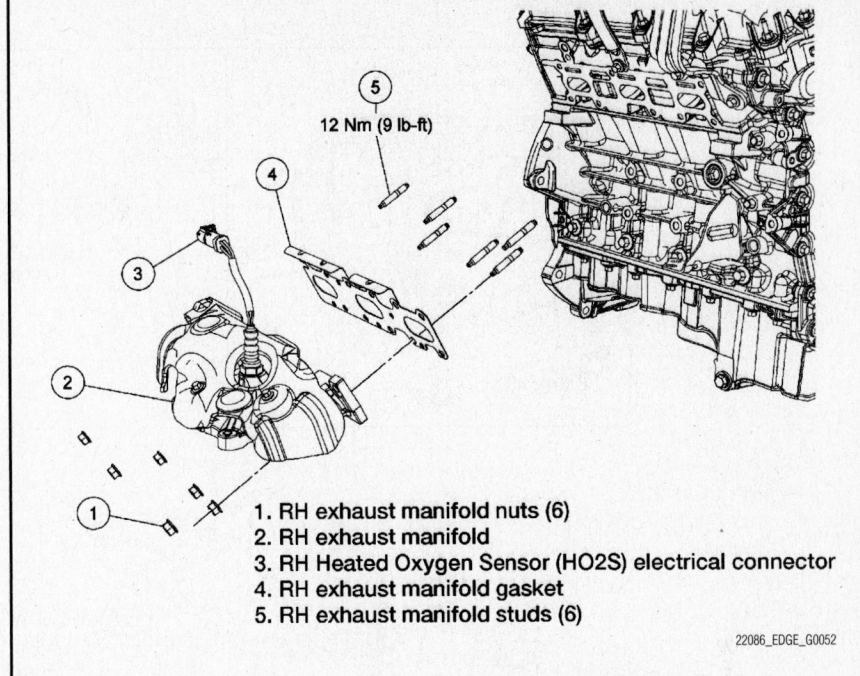

1. RH exhaust manifold nuts (6)
2. RH exhaust manifold
3. RH Heated Oxygen Sensor (HO2S) electrical connector
4. RH exhaust manifold gasket
5. RH exhaust manifold studs (6)

22086_EDGE_G0052

Fig. 134 Exploded view of the right side exhaust manifold and related components

To install:

7. Install 6 new RH exhaust manifold studs and tighten to 12 Nm (9 ft. lbs.).

8. Using a new gasket, install the RH exhaust manifold and 6 new nuts. Tighten in the sequence shown to 20 Nm (15 ft. lbs.).

9. Connect the RH HO2S electrical connector.

➡**When installing the catalytic converter, always install new fasteners and gaskets. Clean the flange faces prior to new gasket installation to ensure proper sealing.**

10. Install the right side catalytic converter, with new gaskets and nuts, in the reverse of the removal procedure. Tighten the retainers as follows:

a. Catalytic converter nuts: 40 Nm (30 ft. lbs.)

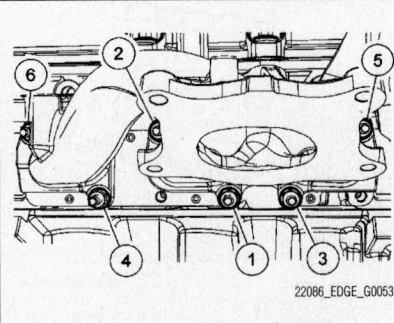

22086_EDGE_G0053

Fig. 135 Exhaust manifold tightening sequence—right side

b. Bracket-to-RH catalytic converter bolts: 20 Nm (15 ft. lbs.)

c. Roll restrictor bolt: 90 Nm (66 ft. lbs.)

d. Roll restrictor shield: 8 ft. lbs. (11 Nm)

e. Catalytic converter support bracket-to-engine block bolt and nut (FWD models): 40 Nm (30 ft. lbs.)

f. Power steering rack shield (FWD models): 15 Nm (11 ft. lbs.)

g. Catalytic converter support bracket-to-engine block bolts (AWD models): 40 Nm (30 ft. lbs.)

h. U-joint flange bolts (AWD models): 70 Nm (52 ft. lbs.)

INTAKE MANIFOLD

REMOVAL & INSTALLATION

Upper Intake Manifold

See Figures 136 through 138.

1. Disconnect the negative battery cable.

2. Remove the air cleaner outlet pipe.

3. Disconnect the throttle body electrical connector.

4. Disconnect the Evaporative Emissions (EVAP) tube from the intake manifold.

5. Disconnect the brake booster vacuum hose from the intake manifold.

6. Disconnect the Positive Crankcase Ventilation (PCV) tube from the PCV valve.

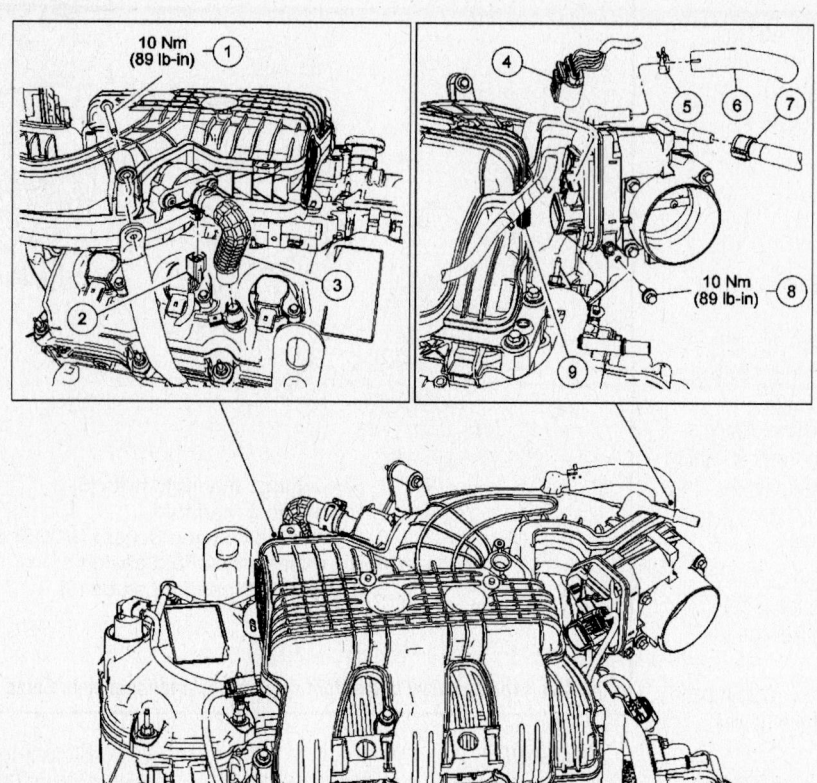

1. Upper intake manifold support bracket bolt
2. PCV fitting electrical connector
3. PCV hose
4. Throttle body electrical connector
5. Brake booster-to-intake manifold vacuum hose clamp
6. Brake booster-to-intake manifold vacuum hose
7. EVAP-to-intake manifold tube
8. Upper intake manifold support bracket bolt
9. Engine control wiring harness retainer

22086_EDGE_G0045

Fig. 136 Installed view of the upper intake manifold and related components

7. Disconnect the PCV fitting electrical connector.

8. Detach the wiring harness retainers from the upper intake manifold.

9. Remove the 2 upper intake manifold support bracket bolts.

10. Remove the 6 bolts and remove the upper intake manifold.

11. Remove and discard the gaskets.

12. Clean and inspect all of the sealing surfaces of the upper and lower intake manifold.

To install:

13. Using new gaskets, install the upper intake manifold and the 6 bolts and tighten to 10 Nm (89 inch lbs.) in the sequence shown in the accompanying illustration.

14. Install the 2 upper intake manifold support bracket bolts. Tighten to 10 Nm (89 inch lbs.).

15. Attach the wiring harness retainers to the upper intake manifold.

16. Connect the PCV fitting electrical connector.

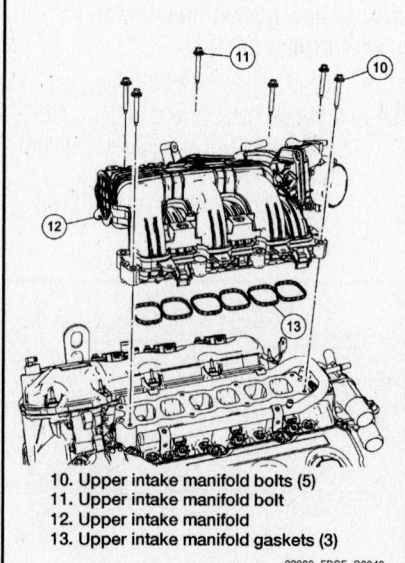

10. Upper intake manifold bolts (5)
11. Upper intake manifold bolt
12. Upper intake manifold
13. Upper intake manifold gaskets (3)

22086_EDGE_G0046

Fig. 137 Exploded view of the upper intake manifold and related components

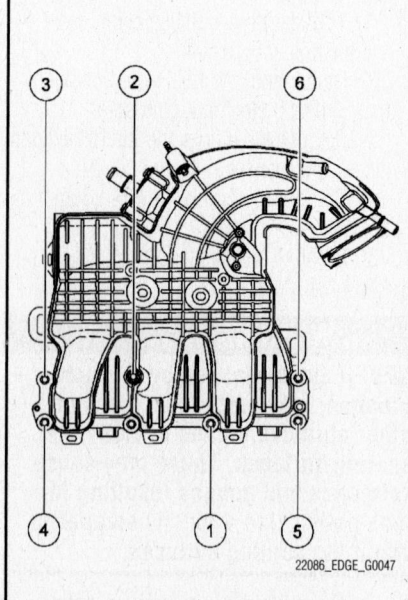

22086_EDGE_G0047

Fig. 138 Upper intake manifold bolt tightening sequence

17. Connect the PCV tube to the PCV valve.

18. Connect the brake booster vacuum hose to the intake manifold.

19. Connect the EVAP tube to the intake manifold.

20. Connect the throttle body electrical connector.

21. Install the air cleaner outlet pipe.

22. Connect the negative battery cable.

Lower Intake Manifold

See Figures 139 and 140.

✳✳ WARNING

During engine repair procedures, cleanliness is extremely important. Any foreign material, including any material created while cleaning gasket surfaces that enters the oil passages, coolant passages or the oil pan, can cause engine failure.

1. Raise and safely support the vehicle.
2. Drain the cooling system.
3. Remove the fuel rail, as outlined in the Fuel System Section.
4. Remove the air cleaner assembly.
5. Remove the 3 thermostat housing-to-lower intake manifold bolts.
6. Unfasten the 10 bolts, then remove the lower intake manifold.

7. Remove and discard the intake manifold and thermostat housing gaskets.

8. Thoroughly clean and inspect all sealing surfaces.

To install:

9. Using new intake manifold and thermostat housing gaskets, install the lower intake manifold and the 10 bolts. Tighten to 10 Nm (89 inch lbs.) in the sequence shown in the accompanying illustration.

10. Install the 3 thermostat housing-to-lower intake manifold bolts. Tighten to 10 Nm (89 inch lbs.).

11. Install the air cleaner assembly.

12. Install the fuel rail.

13. Fill and bleed the cooling system.

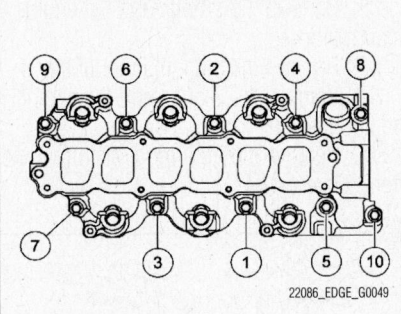

22086_EDGE_G0049

Fig. 140 Lower intake manifold bolt tightening sequence

OIL PAN

REMOVAL & INSTALLATION

See Figures 141 through 154.

➡**This procedure requires engine removal, as well as a variety of specialized tools and equipment.**

1. Remove the engine from the vehicle, as outlined in this section.
2. Remove the 8 bolts and the flex-plate.
3. Remove the crankshaft sensor ring.

✳✳ WARNING

Install the engine stand bolts into the cylinder block only. Do not install the bolts into the oil pan.

4. Mount the engine on a suitable engine stand.
5. If equipped, remove the heat shield and disconnect the block heater electrical connector.
6. Detach all of the engine block heater harness retainers and remove the harness.
7. Disconnect the Positive Crankcase Ventilation (PCV) fitting electrical connector.
8. Disconnect the PCV hose from the PCV valve.
9. Disconnect the throttle body electrical connector.
10. Detach the wiring harness retainers from the upper intake manifold.
11. Remove the upper intake manifold support bracket bolt.
12. Remove the upper intake manifold support bracket bolt.
13. Remove the 6 bolts and the upper intake manifold. Discard the gaskets.
14. Disconnect the Power Steering Pressure (PSP) switch electrical connector.
15. On Front Wheel Drive (FWD) vehicles, disconnect the RH catalyst monitor sensor electrical connector.

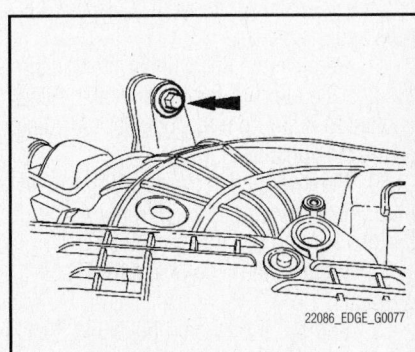

22086_EDGE_G0077

Fig. 141 Remove the upper intake manifold support bracket bolt

1. Thermostat housing-to-lower intake manifold bolts (3)
2. Lower intake manifold gaskets (8)
3. Thermostat housing gasket
4. Lower intake manifold bolts (10)
5. Lower intake manifold

10 Nm (89 lb-in)

22086_EDGE_G0048

Fig. 139 Exploded view of the lower intake manifold and related components

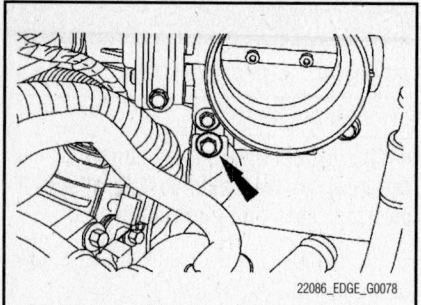

Fig. 142 Remove the upper intake manifold support bracket bolt

22086_EDGE_G0078

16. Disconnect the RH Variable Camshaft Timing (VCT) solenoid electrical connector.

17. Disconnect the 3 RH coil-on-plug electrical connectors.

18. Disconnect the heated PCV valve electrical connector.

19. Detach all of the wiring harness retainers from the RH valve cover and stud bolts.

20. Disconnect the LH catalyst monitor sensor electrical connector.

21. Disconnect the LH VCT solenoid electrical connector.

22. Disconnect the 3 LH coil-on-plug electrical connectors.

23. Detach all of the wiring harness retainers from the LH valve cover and stud bolts.

➡ **The A/C compressor must remain bolted to the engine block before installing the oil pan.**

24. Remove the A/C compressor nut and stud.

25. Remove the 3 bolts and the power steering pump. Do NOT disconnect the fluid lines.

26. Remove the 3 bolts and the accessory drive belt tensioner.

27. Remove the 4 nuts and the LH catalytic converter. Discard the nuts and the gasket.

28. On FWD vehicles, remove the 4 nuts and the RH catalytic converter. Discard the nuts and the gasket.

29. Remove the RH cylinder block drain plug or, if equipped, the block heater. Allow coolant to drain from the cylinder block into a suitable container.

30. Remove the LH cylinder block drain plug. Allow coolant to drain from the cylinder block into a suitable container.

31. Remove the 6 bolts and the 6 coil-on-plugs.

32. Remove the 11 stud bolts and the LH valve cover. Discard the gasket.

33. Remove the bolt, the 10 stud bolts and the RH valve cover. Discard the gasket.

➡ **VCT solenoid seal removal shown, spark plug tube seal removal similar.**

34. Inspect the VCT solenoid seals and the spark plug tube seals. Remove any damaged seals.

   a. Using the special tools, remove the seal(s).

35. Using the special tool, remove the crankshaft bolt and washer. Discard the bolt. Refer to the Crankshaft Pulley procedure in this section.

36. Using the special tool, remove the crankshaft pulley, as outlined in this section.

37. Using the special tool, remove and discard the crankshaft front seal, as outlined in this section.

38. Remove the 2 bolts and the engine mount bracket.

39. Remove the 2 engine mount studs.

40. Remove the 3 bolts and the engine mount bracket.

41. Remove the 22 timing chain (engine front) cover bolts.

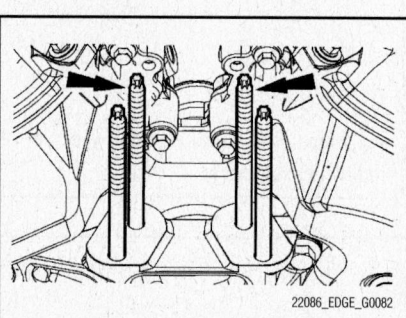

Fig. 143 Remove the 2 engine mount studs (arrows)

22086_EDGE_G0082

42. Install 6 of the engine front cover bolts (finger tight) into the 6 threaded holes in the engine front cover. Tighten the bolts one turn at a time in a criss-cross pattern until the engine front cover-to-cylinder block seal is released.

43. Remove the engine front cover. For more information, refer to the Timing Chain Cover procedure in this section.

44. Remove the 16 oil pan bolts.

45. Install 2 of the oil pan bolts (finger tight) into the 2 threaded holes in the oil pan. Alternately tighten the 2 bolts one turn at a time until the oil pan-to-cylinder block seal is released. Remove the oil pan.

✳✳ WARNING

Only use a 3M Roloc® Bristle Disk, (2 inch, white, part number 07528) to clean the engine front cover and oil pan. Do not use metal scrapers, wire

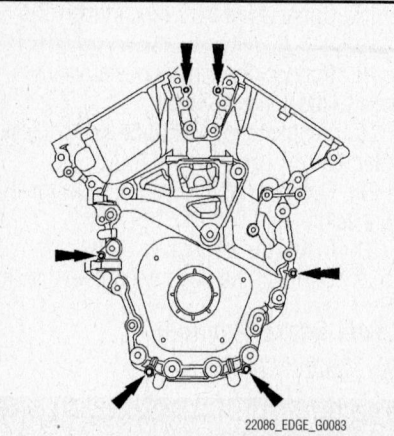

Fig. 144 Install 6 of the engine front cover bolts (finger tight) into the 6 threaded holes in the engine front cover. Tighten the bolts one turn at a time in a criss-cross pattern until the engine front cover-to-cylinder block seal is released

22086_EDGE_G0083

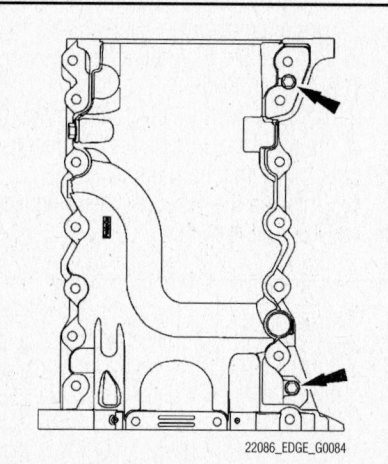

Fig. 145 Install 2 of the oil pan bolts (finger tight) into the 2 threaded holes in the oil pan. Alternately tighten the 2 bolts one turn at a time until the oil pan-to-cylinder block seal is released. Remove the oil pan

22086_EDGE_G0084

brushes or any other power abrasive disk to clean the crankshaft rear seal retainer plate. These tools cause scratches and gouges that make leak paths.

46. Clean the engine front cover and oil pan using a 3M Roloc® Bristle Disk, (2 inch, white, part number 07528) in a suitable tool turning at the recommended speed of 15,000 rpm.

47. Thoroughly wash the engine front cover and oil pan to remove any foreign material, including any abrasive particles created during the cleaning process.

Place clean, lint free shop towels over all exposed engine cavities. Carefully remove the towels so foreign material is not dropped into the engine. Any foreign material (including any material created while cleaning gasket surfaces) that enters the oil passages or the oil pan, can cause engine failure.

Do not use metal scrapers, wire brushes, power abrasive discs or other abrasive means to clean the sealing surfaces. These tools cause scratches and gouges that make leak paths. Use a plastic scraping tool to remove all traces of sealant.

Observe all warnings or cautions and follow all application directions contained on the packaging of the silicone gasket remover and the metal surface prep.

48. Clean the sealing surfaces of the cylinder block.

49. Remove any large deposits of silicone or gasket material with a plastic scraper.

50. Apply silicone gasket remover, following package directions, and allow to set for several minutes. Remove the silicone gasket remover with a plastic scraper. A second application of silicone gasket remover may be required if residual traces of silicone or gasket material remain.

51. Apply metal surface prep, following package directions, to remove any remaining traces of oil or coolant and to prepare the surfaces to bond. Do not attempt to make the metal shiny. Some staining of the metal surfaces is normal.

52. Make sure the 2 locating dowel pins are seated correctly in the cylinder block.

To install:

Failure to use the correct RTV Silicone Sealant (TA-357) may cause the engine oil to foam excessively and result in serious engine damage.

➡The oil pan and the 4 specified bolts must be installed and the oil pan aligned to the cylinder block and A/C

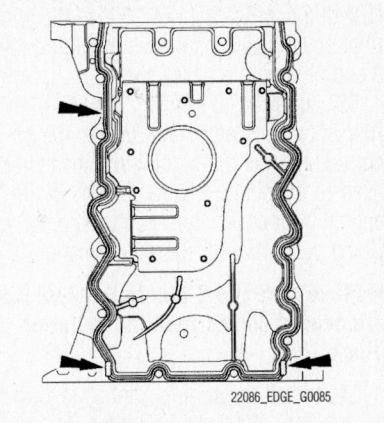

Fig. 146 Silicone sealant locations on the oil pan

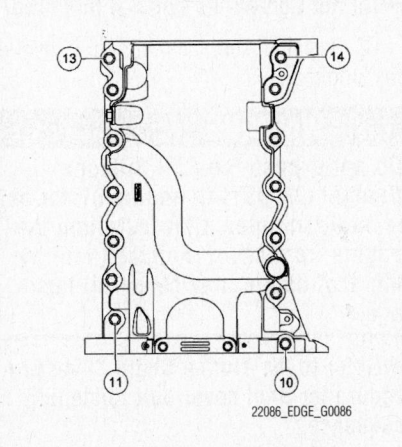

Fig. 147 Location of oil pan bolts 10, 11, 13 and 14

compressor within 4 minutes of sealant application. Final tightening of the oil pan bolts must be carried out within 60 minutes of sealant application.

53. Apply a 3 mm (0.11 in) bead of RTV Silicone Sealant (TA-357) to the sealing surface of the oil pan.

54. Apply a 5.5 mm (0.21 in) bead of RTV Silicone Sealant (TA-357) to the 2 crankshaft seal retainer plate-to-cylinder block joint areas on the sealing surface of the oil pan.

➡The oil pan and the 4 specified bolts must be installed within 4 minutes of the start of sealant application.

55. Install the oil pan and bolts 10, 11, 13 and 14, as shown in the accompanying illustration. Tighten the bolts in the sequence shown to 3 Nm (27 inch lbs.). Loosen the bolts 180 degrees.

56. Align the oil pan to the cylinder block and the A/C compressor.

57. Position the oil pan so the mounting boss is against the A/C compressor and using a straightedge, align the oil pan flush with the rear of the cylinder block at the 2 areas shown in the illustration.

58. Tighten bolts 10, 11, 13 and 14 in the sequence shown, to 3 Nm (27 inch lbs.).

59. Install the remaining oil pan bolts. Tighten all the oil pan bolts in the sequence shown, to the following specifications:

a. Tighten the large bolts (1-14) to 20 Nm (15 ft. lbs.).

b. Tighten the small bolts (15 and 16) to 10 Nm (89 inch lbs.).

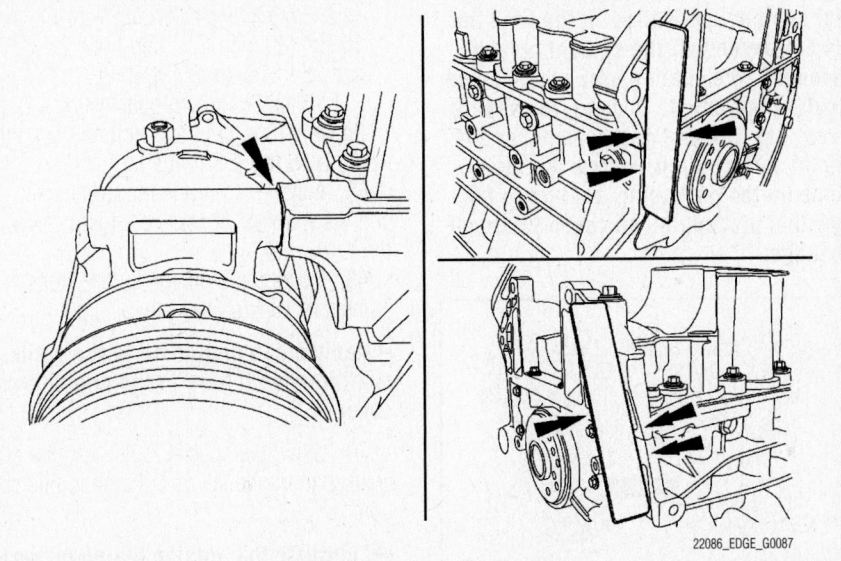

Fig. 148 Position the oil pan so the mounting boss is against the A/C compressor and using a straightedge, align the oil pan flush with the rear of the cylinder block at the 2 areas shown

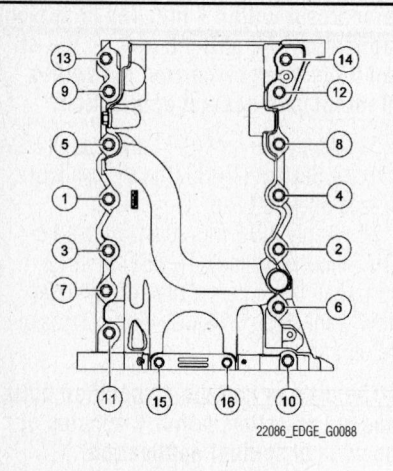

Fig. 149 Oil pan bolt locations and tightening sequence

60. Install the A/C compressor mounting stud and nut. Tighten the stud to 9 Nm (80 inch lbs.) and the nut to 25 Nm (18 ft. lbs.).

61. Install the special alignment pins, or equivalent tools, as shown in the illustration.

❄❄ WARNING

Failure to use the correct RTV Silicone Sealant (TA-357) may cause the engine oil to foam excessively and result in serious engine damage.

➥The engine front cover and bolts 17, 18, 19 and 20 must be installed within 4 minutes of the initial sealant application. The remainder of the engine front cover bolts and the engine mount bracket bolts must be installed and tightened within 35 minutes of the initial sealant application. If the time limits are exceeded, the sealant must be removed, the sealing area cleaned and sealant reapplied. To clean the sealing area, use silicone gasket remover and metal surface prep. Follow the directions on the packaging. Failure to follow this procedure can cause future oil leakage.

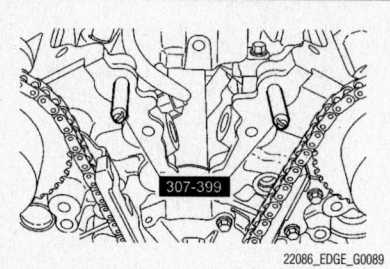

307-399

Fig. 150 Install the alignment pins, or equivalent special tools as shown

62. Apply a 3.0 mm (0.11 in) bead of RTV Silicone Sealant (TA-357) to the engine front cover sealing surfaces including the 3 engine mount bracket bosses.

63. Apply a 5.5 mm (0.21 in) bead of RTV Silicone Sealant (TA-357) to the oil pan-to-cylinder block joint and the cylinder head-to-cylinder block joint areas of the engine front cover. Refer to the Timing Chain procedure for more information.

➥**Make sure the 2 locating dowel pins are seated correctly in the cylinder block.**

64. Install the engine front cover and bolts 17, 18, 19 and 20. Tighten in sequence to 3 Nm (27 inch lbs.).

65. Remove the special tools (alignment pins).

➥**Do not tighten the bolts at this time.**

66. Install the engine mount bracket and the 3 bolts.

❄❄ WARNING

Do not expose the RTV Silicone Sealant (TA-357) to engine oil for at least 90 minutes after installing the engine front cover. Failure to follow this instruction may cause oil leakage.

➥Refer to the Timing Chain Cover procedure for front cover bolt tightening sequence.

67. Install the remaining engine front cover bolts. Tighten all of the engine front cover bolts and engine mount bracket bolts in sequence, in 2 steps:
   a. Step 1: Tighten bolts 1 thru 22 to 10 Nm (89 inch lbs.) and bolts 23, 24 and 25 to 15 Nm (11 ft. lbs.).
   b. Step 2: Tighten bolts 1 thru 22 to 24 Nm (18 ft. lbs.) and bolts 23, 24 and 25 to 75 Nm (55 ft. lbs.).

68. Install the engine mount bracket and the 2 bolts. Tighten to 24 Nm (18 ft. lbs.).

69. Install the 2 engine mount studs. Tighten to 18 Nm (13 ft. lbs.).

➥**Apply clean engine oil to the crankshaft front seal bore in the engine front cover.**

70. Using the special tools, install a new crankshaft front seal, as outlined in this section.

➥**Lubricate the outside diameter sealing surfaces with clean engine oil.**

71. Using the special tools, install the crankshaft pulley. Refer to the Crankshaft

Pulley procedure in this section for more information.

72. Using the special tool, install the crankshaft pulley washer and new bolt and tighten in 4 steps.
   a. Step 1: Tighten to 120 Nm (89 ft. lbs.).
   b. Step 2: Loosen one full turn.
   c. Step 3: Tighten to 50 Nm (37 ft. lbs.).
   d. Step 4: Tighten an additional 90 degrees.

➥**Installation of new seals is only required if damaged seals were removed during disassembly of the engine.**

73. Using the special tools, install new VCT solenoid and/or spark plug tube seals.

❄❄ WARNING

Failure to use the correct RTV Silicone Sealant (TA-357) may cause the engine oil to foam excessively and result in serious engine damage.

➥**If the valve cover is not installed and the fasteners tightened within 4 minutes, the sealant must be removed and the sealing area cleaned. To clean the sealing area, use silicone gasket remover and metal surface prep. Follow the directions on the packaging. Failure to follow this procedure can cause future oil leakage.**

74. Apply a 8 mm (0.31 in) bead of RTV Silicone Sealant (TA-357) to the engine front cover-to-RH cylinder head joints.

75. Using a new gasket, install the RH valve cover, bolt and the 10 stud bolts. Tighten in the sequence shown to 10 Nm (89 inch lbs.).

76. Apply a 8 mm (0.31 in) bead of RTV Silicone Sealant (TA-357) to the engine front cover-to-LH cylinder head joints.

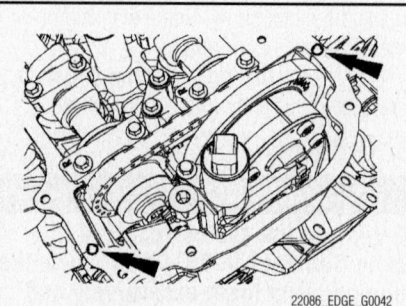

Fig. 151 Apply an 8 mm (0.31 in) bead of RTV Silicone Sealant (TA-357) to the engine front cover-to-RH cylinder head joints

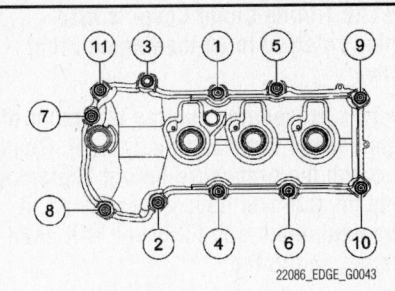

Fig. 152 Right side valve cover bolt tightening sequence

77. Using a new gasket, install the LH valve cover and 11 stud bolts. Tighten in the sequence shown to 10 Nm (89 inch lbs.).

78. Install the 6 coil-on-plug assemblies and the 6 bolts. Tighten to 7 Nm (62 inch lbs.).

79. Install the LH cylinder block drain plug. Tighten to 20 Nm (15 ft. lbs.) plus an additional 180 degrees.

80. Install the RH cylinder block drain plug or, if equipped, the block heater. Tighten to 40 Nm (30 ft. lbs.).

81. On FWD vehicles, using a new gasket, install the RH catalytic converter and 4 new nuts. Tighten to 40 Nm (30 ft. lbs.).

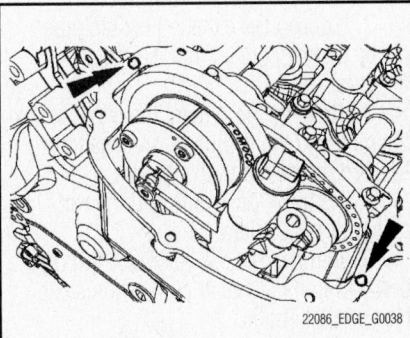

Fig. 153 Apply a 8mm (0.31 in) bead of RTV Silicone Sealant (TA-357, or equivalent) to the engine front cover-to-LH cylinder head joints

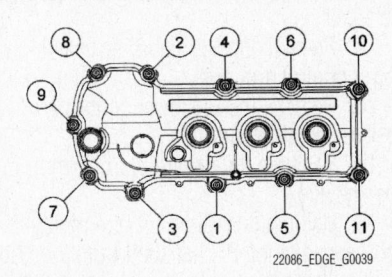

Fig. 154 Left side valve cover bolt tightening sequence

82. Using a new gasket, install the LH catalytic converter and 4 new nuts (3 shown). Tighten to 40 Nm (30 ft. lbs.).

83. Install the accessory drive belt tensioner and the 3 bolts. Tighten to 11 Nm (8 ft. lbs.).

84. Install the power steering pump and the 3 bolts. Tighten to 24 Nm (18 ft. lbs.).

85. Attach all of the wiring harness retainers to the LH valve cover and stud bolts. Connect the 3 LH coil-on-plug electrical connectors.

86. Connect the LH camshaft VCT solenoid electrical connector.

87. Connect the LH catalyst monitor sensor electrical connector.

88. Attach all of the wiring harness retainers to the RH valve cover and stud bolts.

89. Connect the heated PCV valve electrical connector.

90. Connect the 3 RH coil-on-plug electrical connectors.

91. Connect the RH VCT solenoid electrical connector.

92. On FWD vehicles, connect the RH catalyst monitor sensor electrical connector.

93. Connect the PSP switch electrical connector.

94. Using new gaskets, install the upper intake manifold and the 6 bolts. Tighten, in sequence, to 10 Nm (89 inch lbs.). Refer to the Intake Manifold procedure for tightening sequence.

95. Install the upper intake manifold support bracket bolt. Tighten to 10 Nm (89 inch lbs.).

96. Install the upper intake manifold support bracket bolt. Tighten to 10 Nm (89 inch lbs.).

97. Attach the wiring harness retainers to the upper intake manifold.

98. Connect the throttle body electrical connector.

99. Connect the PCV hose to the PCV valve.

100. Connect the PCV fitting electrical connector.

101. If equipped, position the engine block heater harness on the engine and attach all of the harness retainers. Connect the engine block heater electrical connector and install the heat shield.

102. Using the special tools, remove the engine from the stand.

103. Install the crankshaft sensor ring.

104. Install the flexplate and the 8 bolts. Tighten to 80 Nm (59 ft. lbs.).

105. Install the engine in the vehicle, as outlined in this section.

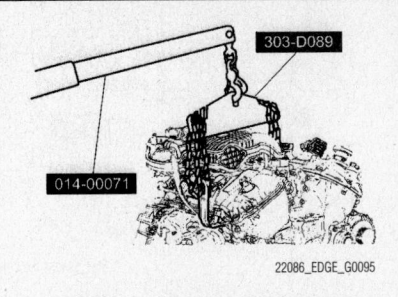

Fig. 155 Using the special tools, remove the engine from the stand

OIL PUMP

REMOVAL & INSTALLATION
See Figures 156 and 157.

> ❈❈ **WARNING**
>
> **During engine repair procedures, cleanliness is extremely important. Any foreign material, including any material created while cleaning gasket surfaces, that enters the oil passages, coolant passages or the oil pan may cause engine failure.**

1. Remove the engine front cover, as outlined in the Timing Chain Cover procedure in this section.

2. Remove the timing chain, as outlined in this section.

3. Remove the crankshaft timing chain sprocket.

4. Remove the 2 oil pump screen and pickup tube bolts.

5. Remove the 3 oil pump bolts. Rotate the oil pump clockwise and separate the oil pump from the oil pump screen and pickup tube. Remove the oil pump. Discard the oil pump screen and pickup tube O-ring seal.

To install:

➡**Install a new oil pump screen and pickup tube O-ring seal before installing the oil pump.**

6. Position the oil pump onto the crankshaft and rotate counterclockwise to position the pump onto the oil pump screen and pickup tube. Install the 3 bolts and tighten to 10 Nm (89 inch lbs.).

7. Install the 2 oil pump screen and pickup tube bolts. Tighten to 10 Nm (89 inch lbs.).

8. Install the crankshaft timing chain sprocket.

9. Install the timing chain, as outlined in this section.

10. Install the engine front cover, as outlined in the Timing Chain Cover procedure in this section.

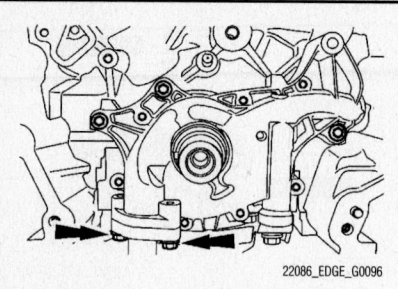

Fig. 156 Remove the 2 oil pump screen and pickup tube bolts

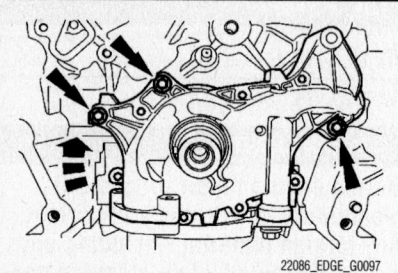

Fig. 157 Remove the 3 oil pump bolts. Rotate the oil pump clockwise and separate the oil pump from the oil pump screen and pickup tube. Remove the oil pump. Discard the oil pump screen and pickup tube O-ring seal

REAR MAIN SEAL

REMOVAL & INSTALLATION

See Figures 158 through 160.

→This procedure requires the use of the following special tools, or their equivalents:

- Handle 205-153 (T80T-4000-W)
- Crankshaft Rear Seal Installer 303-1250
- Crankshaft Rear Seal Remover 303-519 (T95P-6701-EH)
- Slide Hammer 307-005 (T59L-100-B)

1. Raise and safely support the vehicle.
2. Remove the flexplate, as outlined in this section.
3. Remove the crankshaft sensor ring.
4. Using the special tools shown in the illustration, remove and discard the crankshaft rear seal.
5. Clean all sealing surfaces with metal surface cleaner.

To install:

→Lubricate the seal lips and bore with clean engine oil prior to installation.

6. Position the special tool onto the end of the crankshaft and slide a new crankshaft rear seal onto the tool.

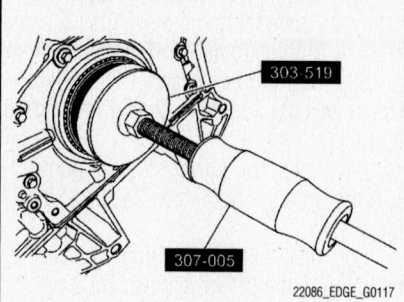

Fig. 158 Using the special tools shown in the illustration, remove and discard the crankshaft rear seal

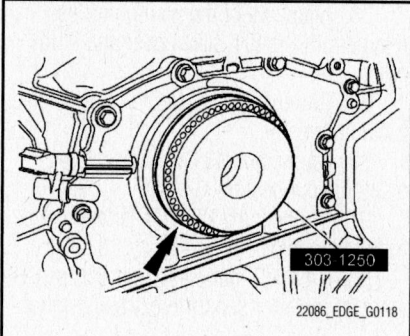

Fig. 159 Position the special tool onto the end of the crankshaft and slide a new crankshaft rear seal onto the tool

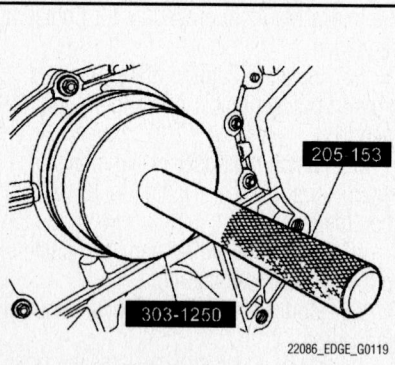

Fig. 160 Using the special tools, install the new crankshaft rear seal

7. Using the special tools, install the new crankshaft rear seal.
8. Install the crankshaft sensor ring.
9. Install the flexplate, as outlined in this section.

TIMING CHAIN COVER AND SEAL

REMOVAL & INSTALLATION

See Figures 161 through 168.

→The Timing Chain Cover is also often referred to as the Engine Front Cover.

→This procedure requires a number of specialized tools and equipment. Read through the procedure before beginning and be sure you have access to all of the equipment and tools you will need before beginning.

✳✳ WARNING

During engine repair procedures, cleanliness is extremely important. Any foreign material, including any material created while cleaning gasket surfaces that enters the oil passages, coolant passages or the oil pan, may cause engine failure.

1. Raise and safely support the vehicle.
2. Recover the air conditioning system, using the proper equipment.
3. Disconnect the negative battery cable.
4. Remove the accessory drive belt, tensioner and the power steering belt, as outlined in this section.
5. Remove the crankshaft pulley, as outlined in this section.
6. Remove and discard the crankshaft front seal, as outlined in this section.
7. Loosen the exhaust flexible pipe clamp and disconnect the 2 exhaust hangers.
8. Remove the 4 nuts, the exhaust flexible pipe and the Y-pipe as an assembly. Discard the nuts and the gasket.
9. Remove the 2 nuts and the roll restrictor heat shield.
10. Remove the roll restrictor through bolt and the 2 roll restrictor-to-transaxle bracket plate bolts.
11. Loosen the roll restrictor-to-subframe through bolt.
12. Position the roll restrictor and transaxle bracket plate aside.
13. Remove the 3 bolts and the transaxle bracket.
14. Remove and discard the RH front halfshaft nut.
15. Remove the RH stabilizer link-to-lower control arm nut.
16. Remove the RH lower control arm-to-knuckle pinch bolt.
17. Separate the lower control arm from the knuckle.
18. Using a suitable front hub removal tool, separate the RH halfshaft from the hub.
19. Using the special tools, separate the RH halfshaft from the intermediate shaft. Remove the RH halfshaft.

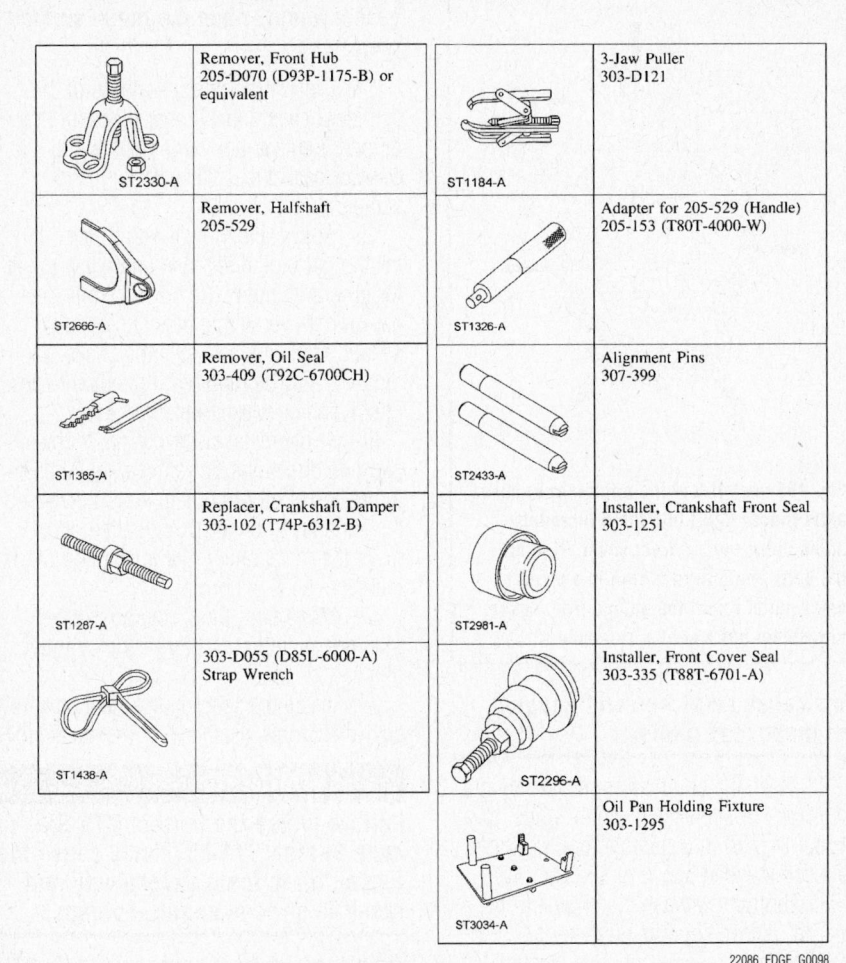

Fig. 161 Timing chain (front cover) replacement requires many special tools

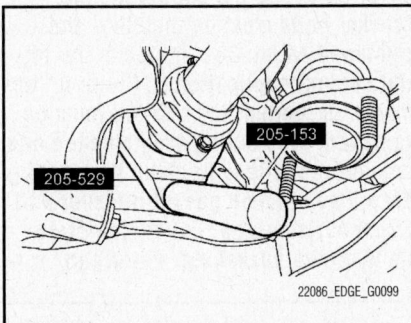

Fig. 162 Using the special tools, separate the RH halfshaft from the intermediate shaft. Remove the RH halfshaft

20. Remove the drain plug and drain the engine oil. Install the drain plug and tighten to 27 Nm (20 ft. lbs.).

21. If equipped, detach the engine block heater harness from the radiator support, the A/C suction tube and the engine wiring harness.

22. Remove the engine air cleaner and air cleaner outlet pipe.

23. Remove the LH and RH valve covers, as outlined in this section.

24. Remove the safety clip from the A/C suction tube fitting.

25. Disconnect the A/C suction tube fitting and position the tube aside.

26. Remove the A/C pressure tube bracket bolt.

27. Remove the nut and disconnect the A/C pressure tube fitting. Discard the O-ring seal. Position the A/C pressure tube aside.

28. Disconnect the 2 engine wiring harness connectors.

29. Remove the bolt and the ground wire from the engine front cover.

30. Remove the nut, the ground wire and the radio interference capacitor wire from the engine front cover stud.

31. Remove the nut, the ground wire and the radio interference capacitor from the cowl stud.

32. Disconnect the purge valve electrical connector.

33. Disconnect the 3 Powertrain Control Module (PCM) electrical connectors and position the wiring harness aside.

34. Remove the 3 bolts and position the degas bottle aside.

➡**The area between the front of the engine and the body of the vehicle must be unobstructed in order to properly remove and install the engine front cover.**

35. Remove the 2 power steering reservoir nuts. Support the power steering reservoir and hose away from the front of the engine with a piece of wire.

36. Remove the 3 power steering pump bolts.

37. Support the power steering pump and hose away from the front of the engine with a piece of wire.

38. Remove the bolts, the LH and the RH VCT solenoids.

✳✳ WARNING

The special tool must be carefully aligned to the mounting bosses on the oil pan. Failure to follow these instructions may result in damage to the oil pan.

➡**The special tool and floor jack are used to raise and lower the engine to access the engine front cover and engine mount bracket fasteners.**

39. Position a floor jack and the special tool under the oil pan.

✳✳ WARNING

The transaxle through bolt must be loosened prior to removing the engine mount and lowering the front of the engine. Failure to follow these instructions may cause internal damage to the hydraulic transaxle mount and possible fluid leakage.

40. Loosen the transaxle mount through bolt.

41. Remove the nut, bolt and engine mount brace.

42. Remove the 4 engine mount nuts.

43. Remove the 3 bolts and the engine mount.

44. Remove the 2 bolts and the engine mount bracket.

45. Remove the 2 engine mount studs.

46. Remove the 2 upper engine mount bracket bolts.

47. Lower the engine to access the lower engine mount bracket bolt.

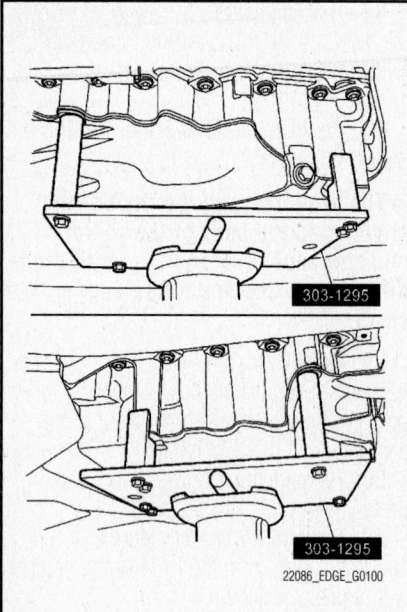

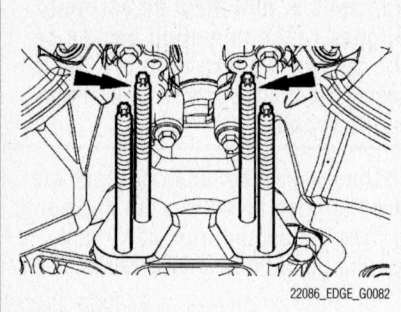

Fig. 163 Position a floor jack and the special tool under the oil pan

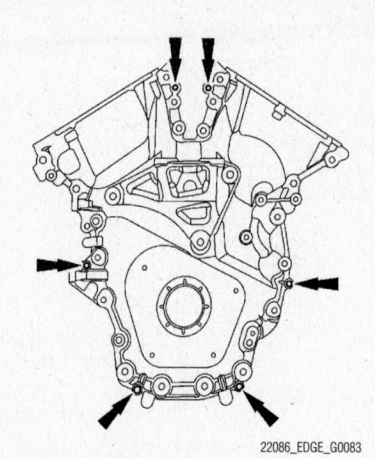

Fig. 165 Install 6 of the engine front cover bolts (finger tight) into the 6 threaded holes in the engine front cover. Tighten the bolts one turn at a time in a criss-cross pattern until the engine front cover-to-cylinder block seal is released

tools cause scratches and gouges that make leak paths.

52. Clean the engine front cover using a 3M Roloc® Bristle Disk, (2 inch, white, part number 07528) in a suitable tool turning at the recommended speed of 15,000 rpm.

53. Thoroughly wash the engine front cover to remove any foreign material, including any abrasive particles created during the cleaning process.

✴✴ WARNING

Place clean, lint-free shop towels over exposed engine cavities. Carefully remove the towels so foreign material is not dropped into the engine. Any foreign material (including any material created while cleaning gasket surfaces) that enters the oil passages or the oil pan, can cause engine failure.

✴✴ WARNING

NEVER use metal scrapers, wire brushes, power abrasive discs or other abrasive means to clean the sealing surfaces. These tools cause scratches and gouges that make leak paths. Use a plastic scraping tool to remove all traces of sealant, including any sealant from the inner surface of the cylinder block and cylinder head.

➡Observe all warnings or cautions and follow all application directions con-

tained on the packaging of the silicone gasket remover and the metal surface prep.

54. Clean the sealing surfaces of the cylinder heads, the cylinder block and the oil pan. Remove any large deposits of silicone or gasket material with a plastic scraper.

55. Apply silicone gasket remover, following package directions and allow to set for several minutes. Remove the silicone gasket remover with a plastic scraper. A second application of silicone gasket remover may be required if residual traces of silicone or gasket material remain.

56. Apply metal surface prep, following package directions, to remove any remaining traces of oil or coolant and to prepare the surfaces to bond. Do not attempt to make the metal shiny. Some staining of the metal surfaces is normal.

57. Make sure the 2 locating dowel pins are seated correctly in the cylinder block.

58. Install the special alignment pins, or equivalent tools, as shown in the illustration.

✴✴ WARNING

Failure to use the correct RTV Silicone Sealant (TA-357) may cause the engine oil to foam excessively and result in serious engine damage.

➡The engine front cover and bolts 17, 18, 19 and 20 must be installed within 4 minutes of the initial sealant application. The remainder of the engine front cover bolts and the engine mount bracket bolts must be installed and tightened within 35 minutes of the initial sealant application. If the time limits are exceeded, the sealant must be removed, the sealing area cleaned and sealant reapplied. To clean the sealing area, use silicone gasket remover and metal surface prep. Follow the directions on the packaging. Failure to

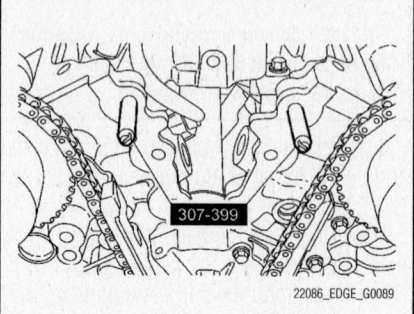

Fig. 166 Install the alignment pins, or equivalent special tools as shown

Fig. 164 Remove the 2 engine mount studs (arrows)

48. Loosen the lower engine mount bracket bolt and remove the engine mount bracket and bolt as an assembly.

49. Remove the 22 engine front cover bolts.

50. Install 6 of the engine front cover bolts (finger tight) into the 6 threaded holes in the engine front cover. Tighten the bolts one turn at a time in a criss-cross pattern until the engine front cover-to-cylinder block seal is released. Remove the engine front cover.

To install:

51. Raise the engine to the installed position.

✴✴ WARNING

Only use a 3M Roloc® Bristle Disk, (2 inch, white, part number 07528) to clean the engine front cover. Do not use metal scrapers, wire brushes or any other power abrasive disk to clean the engine front cover. These

follow this procedure can cause future oil leakage.

59. Apply a 3.0 mm (0.11 in) bead of RTV Silicone Sealant (TA-357) to the engine front cover sealing surfaces including the 3 engine mount bracket bosses.

60. Apply a 5.5 mm (0.21 in) bead of RTV Silicone Sealant (TA-357) to the oil pan-to-cylinder block joint and the cylinder head-to-cylinder block joint areas of the engine front cover in 5 places as indicated.

➡️**Make sure the 2 locating dowel pins are seated correctly in the cylinder block.**

61. Install the engine front cover and bolts 17, 18, 19 and 20. Tighten in sequence to 3 Nm (27 inch lbs.).

62. Remove the special tools (alignment pins).

➡️**Do not tighten the bolt at this time.**

63. Lower the engine to allow installation of the engine mount bracket and lower bolt.

64. Install the engine mount bracket and lower bolt as an assembly.

➡️**Do not tighten the bolts at this time.**

65. Raise the engine to the installed position.

66. Install the 2 upper engine mount bracket bolts.

✳✳ WARNING

Do not expose the RTV Silicone Sealant (TA-357) to engine oil for at least 90 minutes after installing the engine front cover. Failure to follow this instruction may cause oil leakage. Install the remaining engine

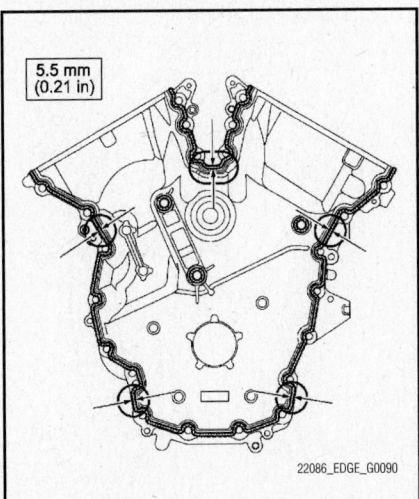

Fig. 167 Front cover sealant application locations

front cover bolts. Tighten all of the engine front cover bolts and engine mount bracket bolts in the sequence shown in 2 steps:

e. Step 1: Tighten bolts 1 thru 22 to 10 Nm (89 inch lbs.) and bolts 23, 24 and 25 to 15 Nm (11 ft. lbs.).

f. Step 2: Tighten bolts 1 thru 22 to 24 Nm (18 ft. lbs.) and bolts 23, 24 and 25 to 75 Nm (55 ft. lbs.).

67. Install the engine mount bracket and the 2 bolts. Tighten to 24 Nm (18 ft. lbs.).

68. Install the 2 engine mount studs. Tighten to 18 Nm (13 ft. lbs.).

69. Install the engine mount and the 3 bolts. Tighten to 90 Nm (66 ft. lbs.).

70. Install the 4 engine mount nuts. Tighten to 63 Nm (46 ft. lbs.).

71. Install the engine mount brace, nut and bolt. Tighten to 20 Nm (15 ft. lbs.).

72. Tighten the transaxle mount through bolt to 175 Nm (129 ft. lbs.).

73. Install the LH and RH VCT solenoids and bolts. Tighten to 10 Nm (89 inch lbs.).

74. Install the power steering pump and the 3 bolts. Tighten to 24 Nm (18 ft. lbs.).

75. Install the power steering reservoir and the 2 nuts. Tighten to 8 Nm (71 inch lbs.).

76. Install the degas bottle and the 3 bolts. Tighten to 9 Nm (80 inch lbs.).

77. Connect the 3 PCM electrical connectors.

78. Connect the purge valve electrical connector.

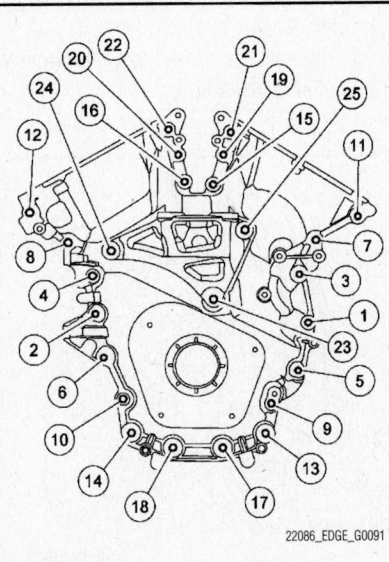

Fig. 168 Front cover bolt locations and tightening sequence

79. Install the radio interference capacitor, the ground wire and the nut to the cowl stud. Tighten to 10 Nm (89 inch lbs.).

80. Install the radio interference capacitor wire, the ground wire and the nut to the engine front cover stud. Tighten to 10 Nm (89 inch lbs.).

81. Install the ground wire and bolt on the engine front cover. Tighten to 10 Nm (89 inch lbs.).

82. Connect the 2 engine wiring harness connectors.

83. Using a new O-ring seal, connect the A/C pressure tube fitting and install the nut. Tighten to 8 Nm (71 inch lbs.).

84. Install the A/C pressure tube bracket and bolt. Tighten to 8 Nm (71 inch lbs.).

85. Connect the A/C suction tube fitting. Install the safety clip onto the fitting.

86. Install the LH and RH valve covers, as outlined in this section.

87. Install the engine air cleaner and air cleaner outlet pipe.

88. If equipped, attach the engine block heater harness to the radiator support, the A/C suction tube and the engine wiring harness.

89. Align the RH halfshaft splines with the intermediate shaft and push the halfshaft on until the circlip locks the shafts together.

90. Pull the inboard halfshaft outward to make sure the circlip is locked.

➡️**Do not tighten the halfshaft nut at this time.**

91. Install the RH halfshaft into the hub and install a new halfshaft nut.

92. Install the RH lower ball joint into the steering knuckle and install the pinch bolt. Tighten to 55 Nm (41 ft. lbs.).

93. Install the RH stabilizer bar link into the lower control arm and install the nut. Tighten to 90 Nm (66 ft. lbs.).

94. Apply the brake to keep the halfshaft from rotating, then tighten the RH halfshaft nut to 350 Nm (258 ft. lbs.).

95. Install and the transaxle bracket and the 3 bolts. Tighten to 90 Nm (66 ft. lbs.).

96. Position the roll restrictor and transaxle bracket plate and install the 3 bolts. Tighten to 90 Nm (66 ft. lbs.).

97. Tighten the engine roll restrictor-to-subframe through bolt to 103 Nm (76 ft. lbs.).

98. Install the roll restrictor heat shield and the 2 nuts. Tighten to 11 Nm (8 ft. lbs.).

99. Position the Y-pipe assembly in place and install the 4 nuts. Tighten to 40 Nm (30 ft. lbs.).

100. Install the 2 exhaust hangers and tighten the exhaust clamp. Tighten to 40 Nm (30 ft. lbs.).

➡️**Apply clean engine oil to the crankshaft front seal bore in the engine front cover.**

101. Install a new crankshaft front seal, as outlined in this section.

➡️**Lubricate the outside diameter sealing surfaces with clean engine oil.**

102. Install the crankshaft pulley, as outlined in this section.

103. Install the accessory drive belt, tensioner and the power steering belt, as outlined in this section.

104. Fill the engine with clean engine oil.

105. Connect the negative battery cable.

106. Evacuate and recharge the air conditioning system.

TIMING CHAIN AND SPROCKETS

REMOVAL & INSTALLATION

See Figures 169 through 187.

✷ WARNING

During engine repair procedures, cleanliness is extremely important. Any foreign material, including any material created while cleaning gasket surfaces that enters the oil passages, coolant passages or the oil pan may cause engine failure.

1. Remove the engine front (timing chain) cover, as outlined in this section.

2. Rotate the crankshaft clockwise and align the timing marks on the Variable Camshaft Timing (VCT) assemblies as shown.

➡️**The special tool will hold the camshafts in the Top Dead Center (TDC) position.**

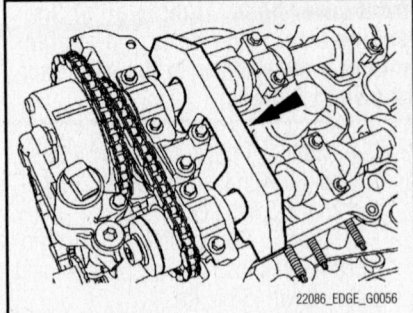

Fig. 170 Install the special tool onto the flats of the camshafts—left side shown, right side similar

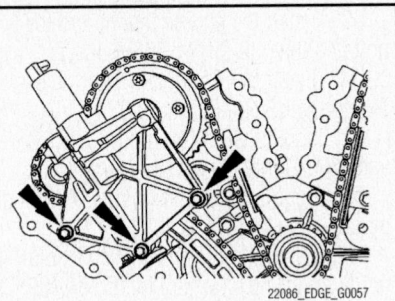

Fig. 171 Remove the 3 bolts and the VCT housing—right side shown, left side similar

3. Install the special tool onto the flats of the LH camshafts.

4. Install the special tool onto the flats of the RH camshafts.

5. Remove the 3 bolts and the RH VCT housing.

6. Remove the 3 bolts and the LH VCT housing.

7. Remove and discard the VCT housing seals.

8. Remove the 2 bolts and the primary timing chain tensioner.

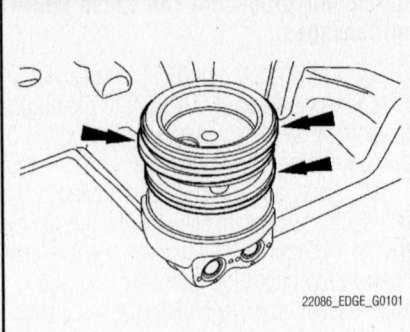

Fig. 172 Remove and discard the VCT housing seals

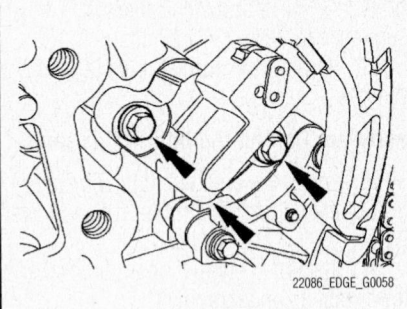

Fig. 173 Remove the 2 bolts and the primary timing chain tensioner

9. Remove the primary timing chain tensioner arm.

10. Remove the 2 bolts and the lower LH primary timing chain guide.

11. Remove the primary timing chain.

12. Remove the crankshaft timing chain sprocket.

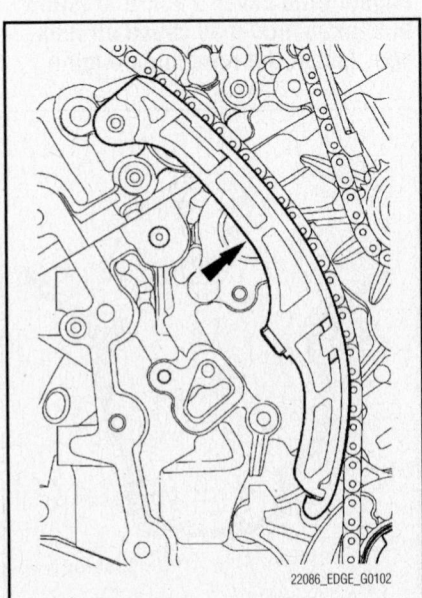

Fig. 174 Remove the primary timing chain tensioner arm

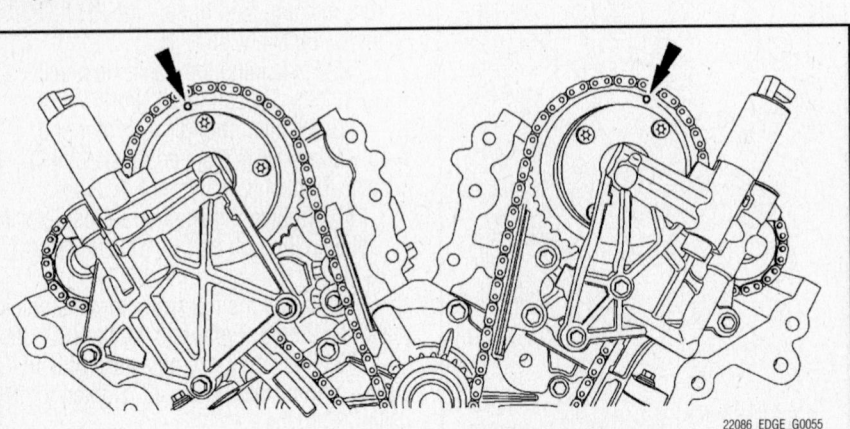

Fig. 169 Rotate the crankshaft clockwise and align the timing marks on the Variable Camshaft Timing (VCT) assemblies as shown

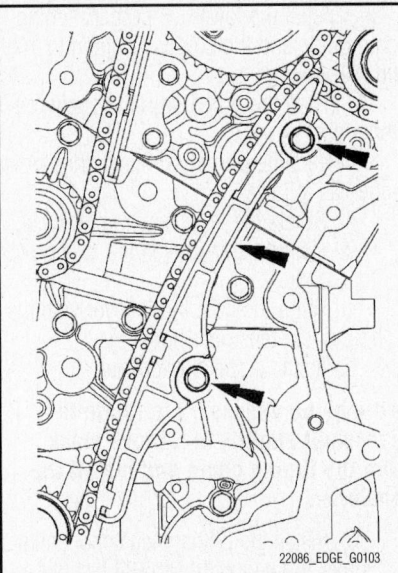

Fig. 175 Remove the 2 bolts and the lower LH primary timing chain guide

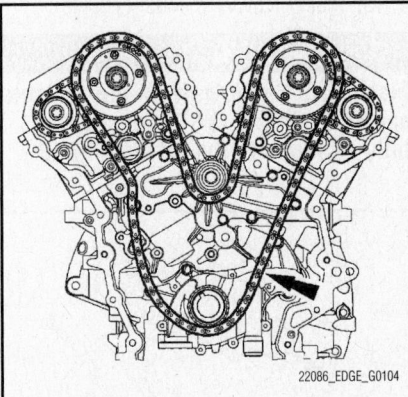

Fig. 176 Remove the primary timing chain

13. Remove the 2 bolts and the upper LH primary timing chain guide.

14. Compress the LH secondary timing chain tensioner and install a suitable lockpin to retain the tensioner in the collapsed position.

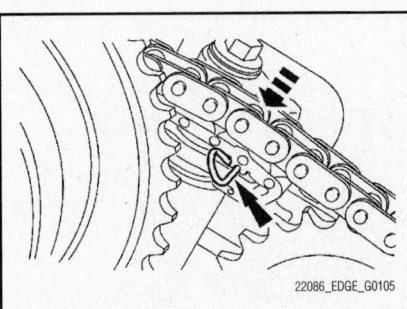

Fig. 177 Compress the LH secondary timing chain tensioner and install a suitable lockpin to retain the tensioner in the collapsed position

➡**The VCT bolt and the exhaust camshaft bolt must be discarded and new ones installed. However, the exhaust camshaft washer is reusable.**

15. Remove and discard the LH VCT assembly bolt and the LH exhaust camshaft sprocket bolt.

16. Remove the LH VCT assembly, secondary timing chain and the LH exhaust camshaft sprocket as an assembly.

➡**It is necessary to tilt the special tool toward the rear of the engine to access the rearmost secondary timing chain tensioner bolt.**

17. Remove the 2 bolts and the LH secondary timing chain tensioner.

18. Compress the RH secondary timing chain tensioner and install a suitable lockpin to retain the tensioner in the collapsed position.

➡**The VCT bolt and the exhaust camshaft bolt must be discarded and new ones installed. However, the exhaust camshaft washer is reusable.**

19. Remove and discard the RH VCT assembly bolt and the RH exhaust camshaft sprocket bolt.

20. Remove the RH VCT assembly, secondary timing chain and the RH exhaust camshaft sprocket as an assembly.

➡**It is necessary to tilt the special tool toward the rear of the engine to access the rearmost secondary timing chain tensioner bolt.**

21. Remove the 2 bolts and the RH secondary timing chain tensioner.

22. Remove the 2 bolts and the RH primary timing chain guide.

To install:

23. Install the RH primary timing chain guide and the 2 bolts. Tighten to 10 Nm (89 inch lbs.).

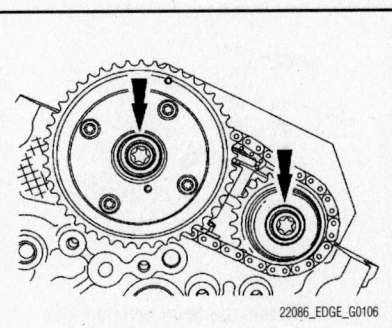

Fig. 178 Remove the LH VCT assembly, secondary timing chain and the LH exhaust camshaft sprocket as an assembly

➡**It is necessary to tilt the special tool toward the rear of the engine to access the rearmost secondary timing chain tensioner bolt.**

24. Install the RH secondary timing chain tensioner and the 2 bolts. Tighten to 10 Nm (89 inch lbs.).

25. Assemble the RH VCT assembly, the RH exhaust camshaft sprocket and the RH secondary timing chain.

26. Align the colored links with the timing marks.

27. Position the RH secondary timing assembly onto the camshafts.

28. Install the new VCT bolt and new exhaust camshaft bolt and the original washers. Tighten in 4 steps, as follows:

   a. Step 1: Tighten to 40 Nm (30 ft. lbs.).

   b. Step 2: Loosen one full turn.

   c. Step 3: Tighten to 10 Nm (89 inch lbs.).

   d. Step 4: Tighten 90 degrees.

29. Remove the lockpin from the RH secondary timing chain tensioner.

➡**It is necessary to tilt the special tool toward the rear of the engine to access the rearmost secondary timing chain tensioner bolt.**

30. Install the LH secondary timing chain tensioner and the 2 bolts. Tighten to 10 Nm (89 inch lbs.).

31. Assemble the LH VCT assembly, the LH exhaust camshaft sprocket and the LH secondary timing chain.

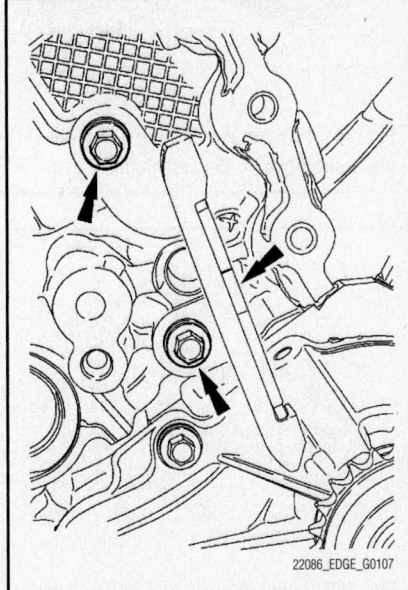

Fig. 179 Remove the 2 bolts and the RH primary timing chain guide

32. Align the colored links with the timing marks.

33. Position the LH secondary timing assembly onto the camshafts.

34. Install the new VCT bolt and new exhaust camshaft bolt and the original washers. Tighten in 4 steps.

    a. Step 1: Tighten to 40 Nm (30 ft. lbs.).

    b. Step 2: Loosen one full turn.

    c. Step 3: Tighten to 10 Nm (89 inch lbs.).

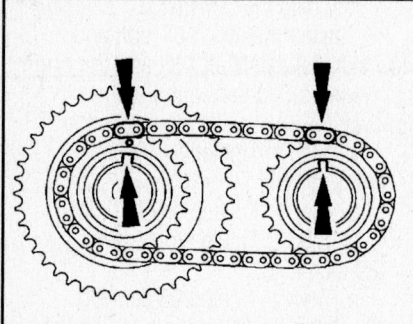

Fig. 180 Align the colored links with the timing marks

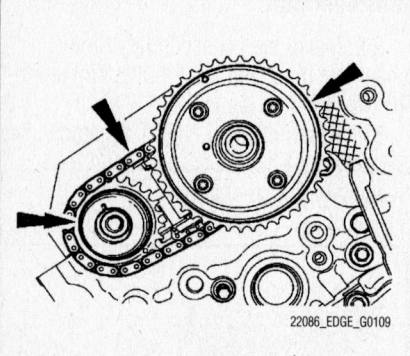

Fig. 181 Position the RH secondary timing assembly onto the camshafts

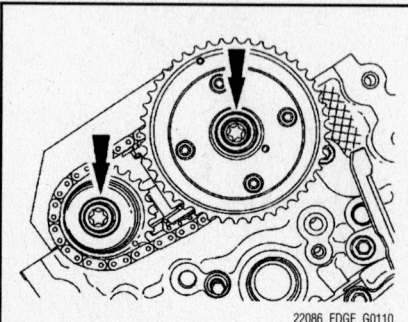

Fig. 182 Install the new VCT bolt and new exhaust camshaft bolt and the original washers

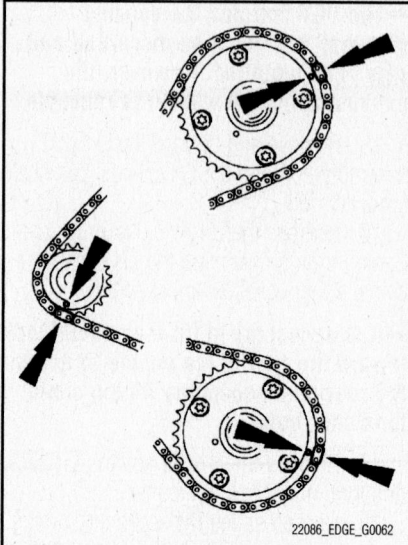

Fig. 183 Install the primary timing chain with the colored links aligned with the timing marks on the VCT assemblies and the crankshaft sprocket

    d. Step 4: Tighten 90 degrees.

35. Remove the lockpin from the LH secondary timing chain tensioner.

36. Install the crankshaft timing chain sprocket.

37. Install the primary timing chain with the colored links aligned with the timing marks on the VCT assemblies and the crankshaft sprocket.

38. Install the upper LH primary timing chain guide and the 2 bolts. Tighten to 10 Nm (89 inch lbs.).

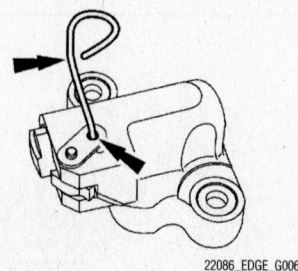

Fig. 184 Rotate the lever counterclockwise. Using a soft-jawed vise, compress the plunger. Align the hole in the lever with the hole in the tensioner housing, then insert a lock pin

39. Install the lower LH primary timing chain guide and the 2 bolts. Tighten to 10 Nm (89 inch lbs.).

40. Install the primary timing chain tensioner arm.

41. Reset the primary timing chain tensioner, as follows:

    a. Rotate the lever counterclockwise.

    b. Using a soft-jawed vise, compress the plunger.

    c. Align the hole in the lever with the hole in the tensioner housing.

    d. Install a suitable lockpin.

➡It may be necessary to rotate the crankshaft slightly to remove slack from the timing chain and install the tensioner.

    e. Install the primary tensioner and the 2 bolts. Tighten to 10 Nm (89 inch lbs.).

    f. Remove the lock pin.

42. As a post-check, verify correct alignment of all timing marks.

43. Install new VCT housing seals.

❊❊ WARNING

Make sure the dowels on the variable camshaft timing (VCT) housing are fully engaged in the cylinder head

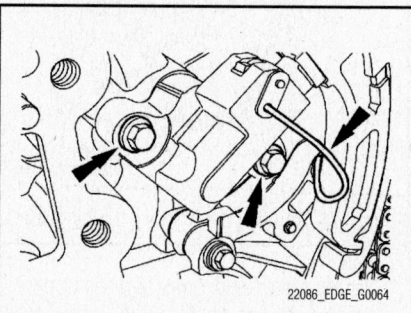

Fig. 185 Install the primary tensioner, secure with the 2 bolts, then remove the lock pin

Fig. 186 Install the left side VCT housing and tighten the bolts in the sequence shown

prior to tightening the bolts. Failure to follow this process will result in severe engine damage.

44. Install the LH VCT housing and the 3 bolts. Tighten in the sequence shown to 10 Nm (89 inch lbs.).

> ✲✲ **WARNING**

Make sure the dowels on the VCT housing are fully engaged in the cylinder head prior to tightening the bolts.

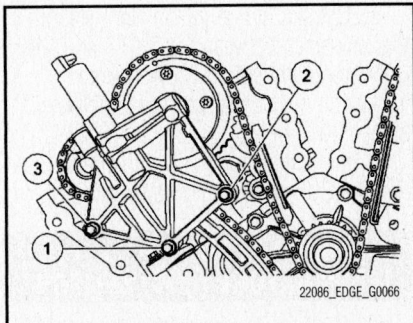

22086_EDGE_G0066

Fig. 187 Install the right side VCT housing and tighten the bolts in the sequence shown

45. Install the RH VCT housing and the 3 bolts. Tighten in the sequence shown to 10 Nm (89 inch lbs.).

46. Install the engine front (timing chain) cover, as outlined in this section.

VALVE LASH

INSPECTION/ADJUSTMENT

See Figure 188.

1. Remove the valve covers.

➡ **The valve clearance must be measured with the camshaft at base circle. The engine will have to be rotated with the crankshaft pulley bolt to bring each valve to base circle.**

2. Use a feeler gauge to measure the clearance of each valve and record its location. A midrange clearance is the most desirable:

    a. Intake: 0.15–0.25 mm (0.006–0.01 in)

    b. Exhaust: 0.300–0.400 mm (0.0118–0.0157 in)

➡ **The number on the valve tappet reflects the thickness of the valve tap-**

pet. For example, a tappet with the number 3.310 has the thickness of 3.31 mm (0.13 in).

3. If any of the valve clearances are out of specification, select new tappets using this formula: tappet thickness = measured clearance + the base tappet thickness − most desirable thickness.

4. Select the tappets and mark the installation location.

5. If required, install the new selected valve tappets in the marked locations.

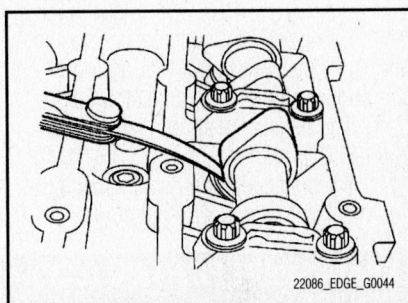

22086_EDGE_G0044

Fig. 188 Use a feeler gauge to measure the clearance of each valve and record its location. A midrange clearance is the most desirable

ENGINE PERFORMANCE & EMISSION CONTROL

CAMSHAFT POSITION (CMP) SENSOR

LOCATION

See Figure 189.

Refer to the accompanying illustration for Camshaft Position (CMP) sensor locations.

OPERATION

The Camshaft Position (CMP) sensor sends the PCM a signal indicating

camshaft position used for fuel synchronization

REMOVAL & INSTALLATION

See Figure 189.

1. To remove the RH Camshaft Position (CMP) sensor, remove the air cleaner outlet pipe.

2. To remove the LH CMP sensor, remove the air cleaner assembly.

3. Disconnect the CMP electrical connector.

4. Remove the bolt and the CMP sensor.

5. Installation is the reverse of the removal procedure, noting the following:

    a. Lubricate the CMP O-ring seal with clean engine oil.

    b. Tighten the CMP sensor bolt to 10 Nm (89 lb-in).

TESTING

See Figure 190.

1. Turn the ignition to the **OFF** position.

2. Disconnect the Camshaft Position Sensor (CMP) electrical connector.

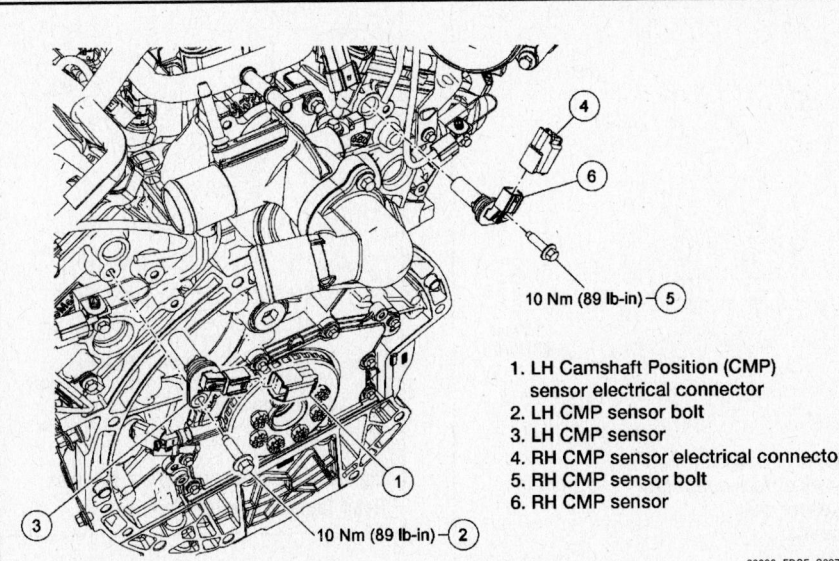

10 Nm (89 lb-in) ─ 5

1. LH Camshaft Position (CMP) sensor electrical connector
2. LH CMP sensor bolt
3. LH CMP sensor
4. RH CMP sensor electrical connector
5. RH CMP sensor bolt
6. RH CMP sensor

10 Nm (89 lb-in) ─ 2

22086_EDGE_G0277

Fig. 189 Exploded view of the Camshaft Position (CMP) sensor

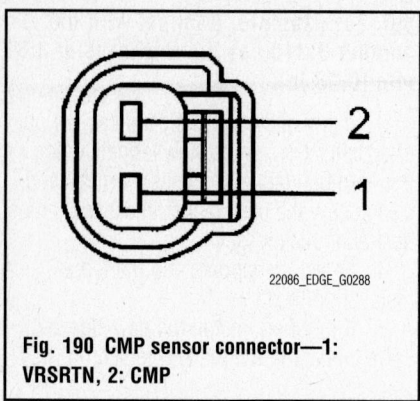

Fig. 190 CMP sensor connector—1: VRSRTN, 2: CMP

3. Using a digital multimeter, measure the resistance between the CMP + and CMP - at component side of the connector.

4. The resistance should fall between 250—1,000 ohms.

5. If resistance is not within specification the CMP sensor may be faulty.

CRANKSHAFT POSITION (CKP) SENSOR

LOCATION

See Figure 191.

The Crankshaft Position (CKP) sensor is located under the heat shield. Refer to the accompanying illustration for sensor location.

OPERATION

The Crankshaft Position (CKP) sensor sends the PCM a signal indicating crankshaft position and is essential for calculating spark timing

REMOVAL & INSTALLATION

See Figure 191.

1. Raise and safely support the vehicle.
2. Remove the LH catalytic converter.
3. Remove the bolt, nut and the heat shield.
4. Remove the rubber grommet cover.
5. Disconnect the Crankshaft Position (CKP) sensor electrical connector.
6. Remove the bolt and the CKP sensor.

To install:

7. Installation is the reverse of the removal procedure, noting the following:
   a. Tighten the CKP sensor bolt to 10 Nm (89 lb-in).
   b. Tighten the heat shield bolt and nut to 10 Nm (89 lb-in).

TESTING

See Figure 192.

1. Turn the ignition to the **OFF** position.
2. Disconnect the Crankshaft Position Sensor (CKP) electrical connector.

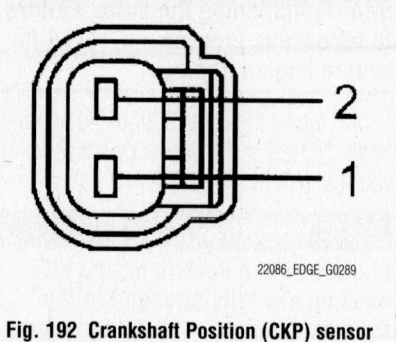

Fig. 192 Crankshaft Position (CKP) sensor connector—1: CKP-, 2: CKP+

3. Using a digital multimeter measure the resistance between the CKP + and CKP - at component side of the connector.

4. The resistance should fall between 250—1,000 ohms.

5. If resistance is not within specification the CKP sensor may be faulty.

CYLINDER HEAD TEMPERATURE (CHT) SENSOR

LOCATION

See Figure 193.

Refer to the accompanying illustration for Cylinder Head Temperature (CHT) sensor location.

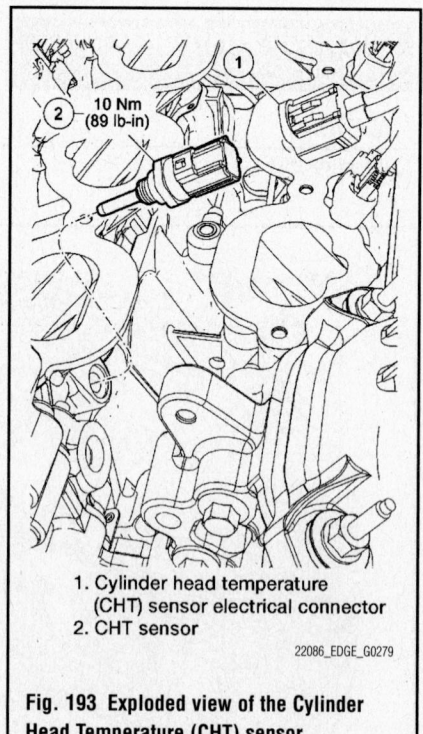

1. Cylinder head temperature (CHT) sensor electrical connector
2. CHT sensor

Fig. 193 Exploded view of the Cylinder Head Temperature (CHT) sensor

OPERATION

The Cylinder Head Temperature (CHT) sensor, sends the PCM a signal indicating

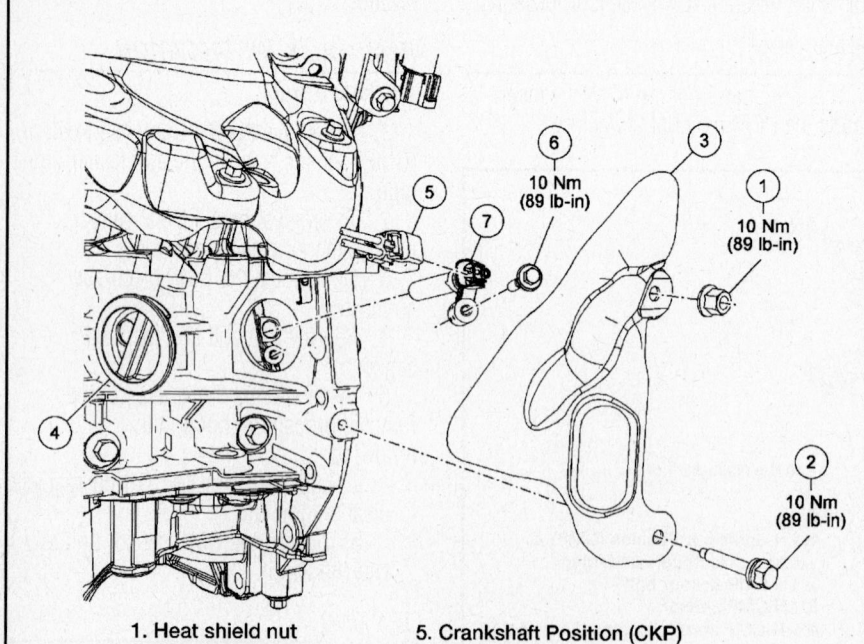

1. Heat shield nut
2. Heat shield bolt
3. Heat shield
4. Rubber grommet cover
5. Crankshaft Position (CKP) sensor electrical connector
6. CKP sensor bolt
7. CKP sensor

Fig. 191 Exploded view of the Crankshaft Position (CKP) sensor

cylinder head temperature. Its resistance decreases as coolant temperature increases

REMOVAL & INSTALLATION

See Figure 193.

1. Disconnect the negative battery cable.
2. Remove the lower intake manifold, as outlined in the Engine Mechanical Section.
3. Disconnect the Cylinder Head Temperature (CHT) sensor electrical connector.
4. Remove and discard the CHT sensor.

To install:

5. Installation is the reverse of the removal procedure, noting the following:
   a. Do not reuse the CHT sensor, install a new sensor
   b. Tighten the CHT sensor to 10 Nm (89 lb-in).

TESTING

See Figures 194 through 196.

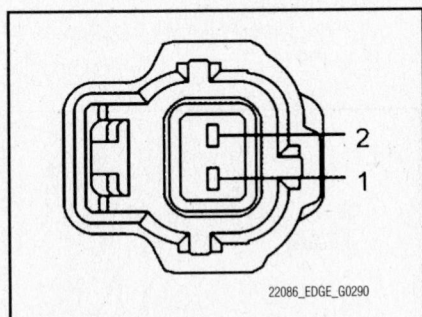

Fig. 194 CHT sensor connector—Pin 1: CHT, Pin 2: SIGRTN (Signal Return)

Cylinder Head Temperature Sensor Expected Values				
Temperature		CHT Sensor Values		
°C	°F	Cold End (volts)	Hot End (volts)	Resistance (K ohms)
-40	-40	4.89	-	965.808
-30	-22	4.81	-	513.019
-20	-4	4.67	-	283.664
-10	14	4.45	-	162.584
0	32	4.14	-	96.255
10	50	3.73	-	59.175
20	68	3.26	-	37.387
30	86	2.74	-	24.215
40	104	2.23	-	16.043
50	122	1.76	-	10.85
60	140	1.36	-	7.487
70	158	1.04	-	5.268
80	176	0.79	3.99	3.775
85	185	0.69	3.86	3.215
90	194	0.60	3.71	2.75
95	203	0.53	3.56	2.361
100	212	0.46	3.41	2.034
110	230	-	3.07	1.523
120	248	-	2.74	1.155
130	266	-	2.41	0.8866
140	284	-	2.10	0.6891
150	302	-	1.81	0.5417
160	320	-	1.55	0.4301
170	338	-	1.33	0.3449
180	356	-	1.13	0.2791
190	374	-	0.96	0.2278
200	392	-	0.82	0.1875
210	410	-	0.70	0.155
220	428	-	0.60	0.130
230	446	-	0.51	0.109
240	464	-	0.44	0.092
250	482		0.35	0.078
260	500		0.33	0.067

Fig. 196 Temperature voltage and resistance specification chart

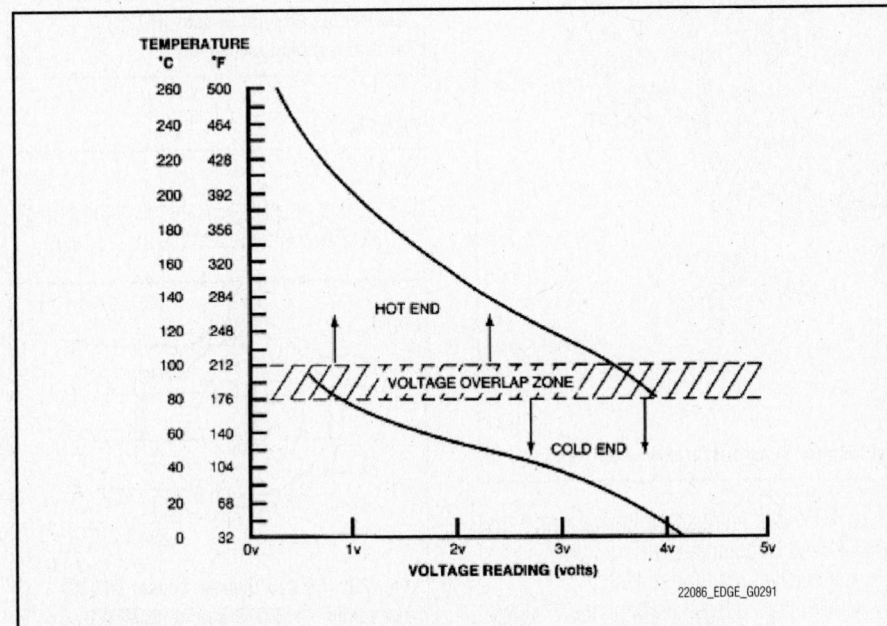

Fig. 195 Cylinder Head Temperature (CHT) sensor temperature-to-voltage table

1. Turn the ignition switch to the **OFF** position.
2. Disconnect the Cylinder Head Temperature (CHT) sensor electrical connector.
3. Measure the resistance between CHT + pin 1 and CHT - pin 2 on sensor side of connector.
4. If resistance is not within specification replace sensor.

HEATED OXYGEN SENSOR (HO2S) & CATALYST MONITOR SENSOR

LOCATION

See Figures 197 and 198.

The Heated Oxygen Sensors (HO2S) are located upstream of the catalytic converter. The catalyst monitor sensors are mounted in or downstream of the catalytic converters.

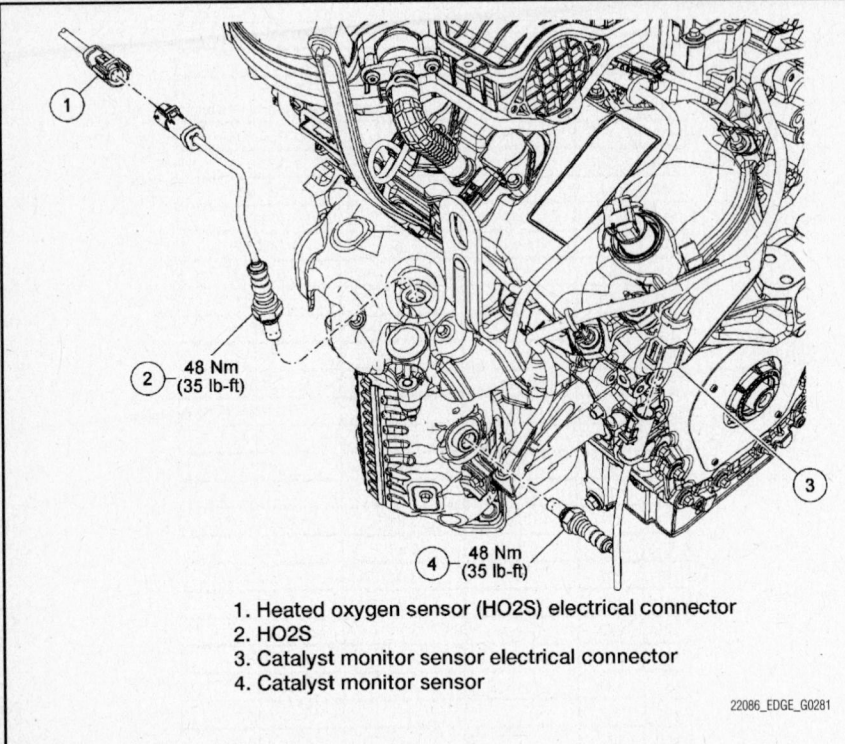

1. Heated oxygen sensor (HO2S) electrical connector
2. HO2S
3. Catalyst monitor sensor electrical connector
4. Catalyst monitor sensor

22086_EDGE_G0281

Fig. 197 Heated Oxygen Sensor (HO2S) and Catalyst Monitor Sensor locations—right side

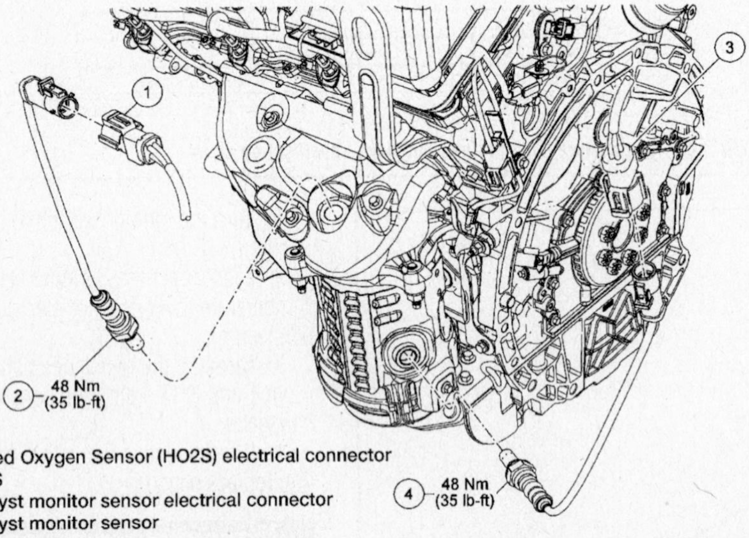

1. Heated Oxygen Sensor (HO2S) electrical connector
2. HO2S
3. Catalyst monitor sensor electrical connector
4. Catalyst monitor sensor

22086_EDGE_G0282

Fig. 198 Heated Oxygen Sensor (HO2S) and Catalyst Monitor Sensor locations—left side

OPERATION

The Heated Oxygen Sensors (HO2S) perform the following:
• Creates a voltage signal dependent on exhaust oxygen content.

• Provides feedback information to the PCM used to calculate fuel delivery.
The catalyst monitor sensors:
• Monitors oxygen content after it flows through the catalytic converter.

• Provides voltage to the PCM used to calculate catalytic converter integrity.

REMOVAL & INSTALLATION

See Figure 199.

1. Disconnect the negative battery cable.
2. If removing the RH sensor, raise and safely support the vehicle.
3. Disconnect the sensor electrical connector(s).

➡**If necessary, lubricate the sensor threads with penetrating and lock lubricant to make removal easier.**

4. Using Special Tool 303-476, or equivalent HO2S sensor socket, remove the sensor.

To install:

5. Installation is the reverse of the removal procedure, noting the following:
   a. Apply a light coat of anti-seize lubricant to the threads of the sensor before installing it.
   b. Tighten the sensor to 48 Nm (35 lb-ft).

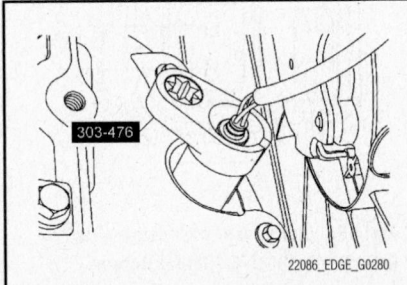

22086_EDGE_G0280

Fig. 199 Use the special socket to remove the Heated Oxygen Sensor (HO2S) or Catalyst Monitor sensor

TESTING

See Figure 200.

1. Disconnect the Heated Oxygen Sensor (HO2S) connector. Measure the resis-

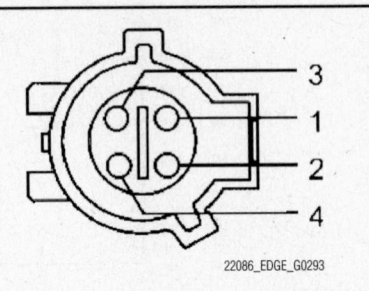

22086_EDGE_G0293

Fig. 200 Heated Oxygen Sensor (HO2S) connector—1: HO2S heater, 2: VPWR, 3: HO2S signal, 4: SIGRTN

tance between the HO2S heater and VPWR on sensor side of harness. The reading should be approximately 3—30 ohms. If resistance is not within specifications, the sensor may be faulty.

2. With the engine running and HO2S sensor in place measure the voltage with digital multimeter between terminals HO2S and SIGRTN at the sensor harness. The voltage should read approximately 0.01—1.0V. If the reading is off or the voltage fluctuation is very slow suspect faulty sensor.

3. Check for unmetered air leaks at intake manifold gasket leaks, hoses connecting to the mass air flow (MAF) sensor assembly, PCV system. Fuel calculations can be affected by unmetered air leaks.

KNOCK SENSOR (KS)

LOCATION

See Figure 201.

Refer to the accompanying illustration for Knock Sensor (KS) location.

OPERATION

The Knock Sensor (KS) is used to detect engine detonation. It sends a voltage signal to the PCM. The knock sensor is able to provide a signal, which retards the ignition timing, as necessary.

REMOVAL & INSTALLATION

See Figure 201.

1. Remove the thermostat housing. Refer to the Thermostat procedure in the Engine Mechanical Section.
2. Remove the lower intake manifold, as outlined in the Engine Mechanical Section
3. Remove the coolant tube. Discard the O-ring.
4. Disconnect the Knock Sensor (KS) electrical connector.
5. Remove the 2 bolts and the KS.

To install:

6. Installation is the reverse of the removal procedure, noting the following:
   a. Lubricate the new O-ring with clean engine coolant before installing it.
   b. Tighten the KS bolts to 20 Nm (15 lb-ft).

TESTING

See Figure 202.

➡ Appropriate repair methods and procedures are essential for the safe, reliable operation of all motor vehicles, as well as the personal safety of the individual doing the work. This procedure provides general directions for repairing vehicles with tested, effective techniques. Following them helps to establish reliability. There are numerous variations in procedures, techniques, tools, and parts for repairing vehicles, as well as in the skill of the individual doing the work. This manual cannot possibly anticipate all such variations and provide advice or cautions as to each. Accordingly, anyone who departs from the instructions provided in this procedure must first establish that they compromise neither their personal safety nor the vehicle integrity by their choice of methods, tools, or parts.

1. Make sure the Knock Sensor (KS) is installed properly.

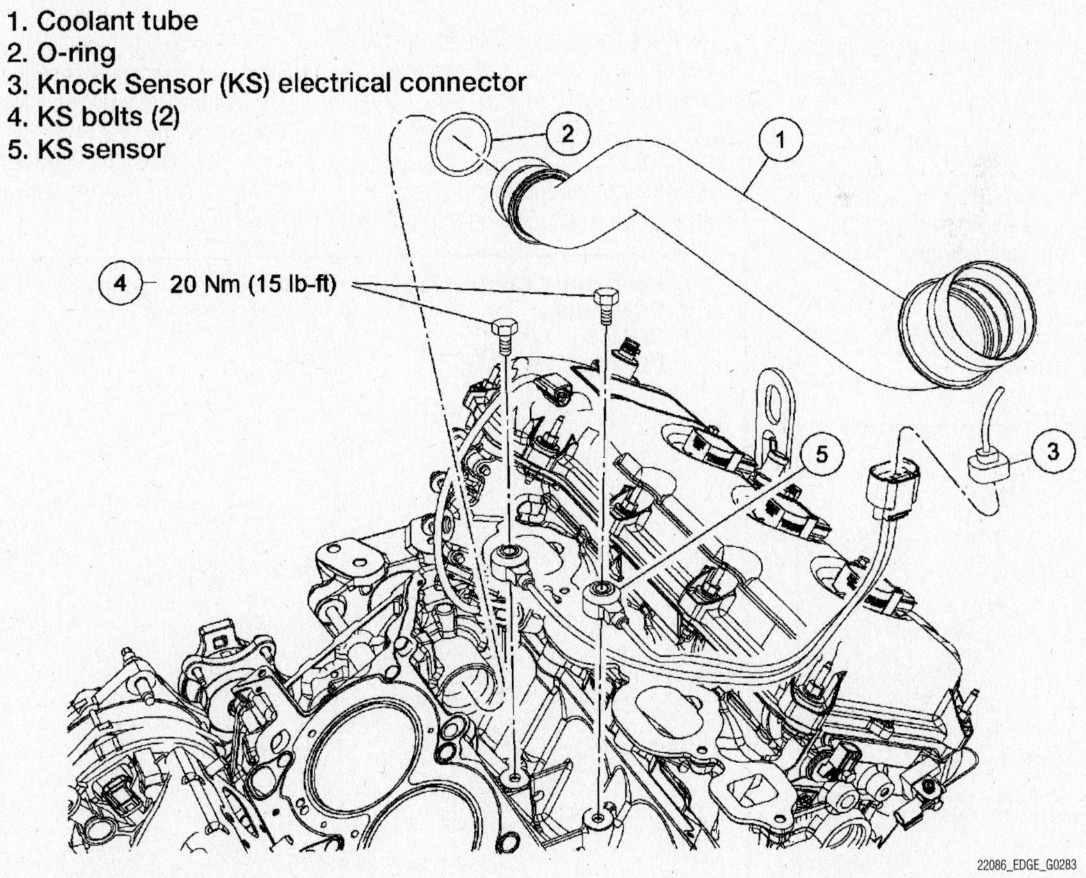

1. Coolant tube
2. O-ring
3. Knock Sensor (KS) electrical connector
4. KS bolts (2)
5. KS sensor

4 — 20 Nm (15 lb-ft)

22086_EDGE_G0283

Fig. 201 Exploded view of the Knock Sensor (KS)

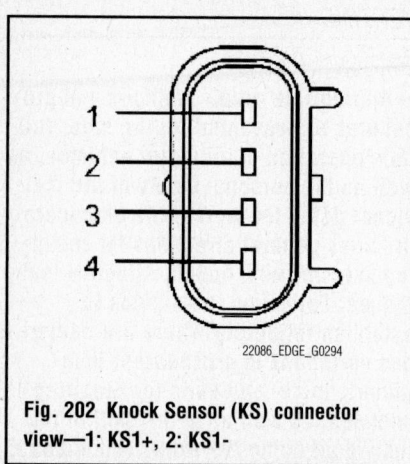

Fig. 202 Knock Sensor (KS) connector view—1: KS1+, 2: KS1-

2. Disconnect the KS harness connector and measure the resistance between KS + and KS - on the component side. The resistance should read between 4.39—5.35 megaohms. If resistance reading is not within specifications suspect a faulty KS.

MASS AIR FLOW (MAF) SENSOR

LOCATION

See Figure 203.

Refer to the accompanying illustration for the Mass Air Flow (MAF) sensor location.

OPERATION

The Mass Air Flow (MAF) sensor uses a hot wire sensing element to measure the amount of air entering the engine. Air passing over the hot wire causes it to cool.

REMOVAL & INSTALLATION

See Figure 203.

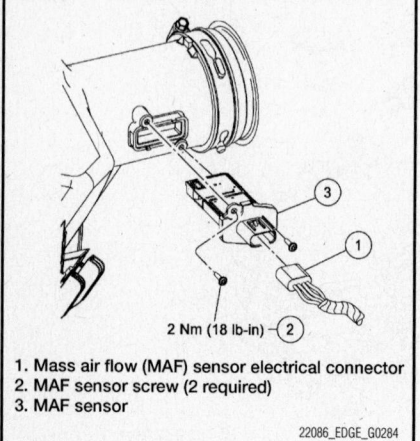

1. Mass air flow (MAF) sensor electrical connector
2. MAF sensor screw (2 required)
3. MAF sensor

Fig. 203 Exploded view of the Mass Air Flow (MAF) sensor

1. Disconnect the negative battery cable.
2. Disconnect the Mass Air Flow (MAF) sensor electrical connector.
3. Remove the 2 screws and the MAF sensor.
4. Installation is the reverse of the removal procedure. Tighten the MAF sensor screws to 18 inch lbs. (2 Nm).

TESTING

See Figure 204.

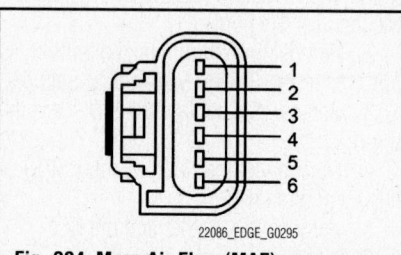

Fig. 204 Mass Air Flow (MAF) sensor connector—1: IAT, 2: SIGRTN, 3: MAF 4: MAF RTN, 5: PWRGND, 6: VPWR

POWERTRAIN CONTROL MODULE (PCM)

LOCATION

See Figure 205.

The Powertrain Control Module (PCM) is located on the passenger side of the vehicle, mounted to the cowl.

OPERATION

The center of the Electronic Engine Control (EEC) system is a microprocessor called the Powertrain Control Module (PCM). The PCM receives input from sensors and other electronic components (switches, relays). Based on the information received and programmed into its memory, the PCM generates output signals to control various relays, solenoids and actuators. The Edge and MKX use a 190-pin PCM.

REMOVAL & INSTALLATION

See Figure 205.

➡ PCM replacement DOES NOT require new keys or programming of keys.

1. Retrieve the module configuration. Carry out the module configuration retrieval steps of the Programmable Module Installation procedure.
2. Disconnect the 3 Powertrain Control Module (PCM) electrical connectors.
3. Remove the 2 nuts and the PCM.
4. Remove the gasket.

To install:

5. Install the gasket and the PCM.
6. Install the 2 PCM nuts and tighten to 5 Nm (44 lb-in).
7. Connect the 3 PCM electrical connectors.
8. Restore the module configuration. Carry out the module configuration restore steps of the Programmable Module Installation procedure.
9. Reprogram the Passive Anti-Theft System (PATS). Carry out the Parameter Reset procedure

1. **Powertrain Control Module (PCM) electrical connector**
2. **PCM nuts**
3. **PCM**
4. **PCM gasket**

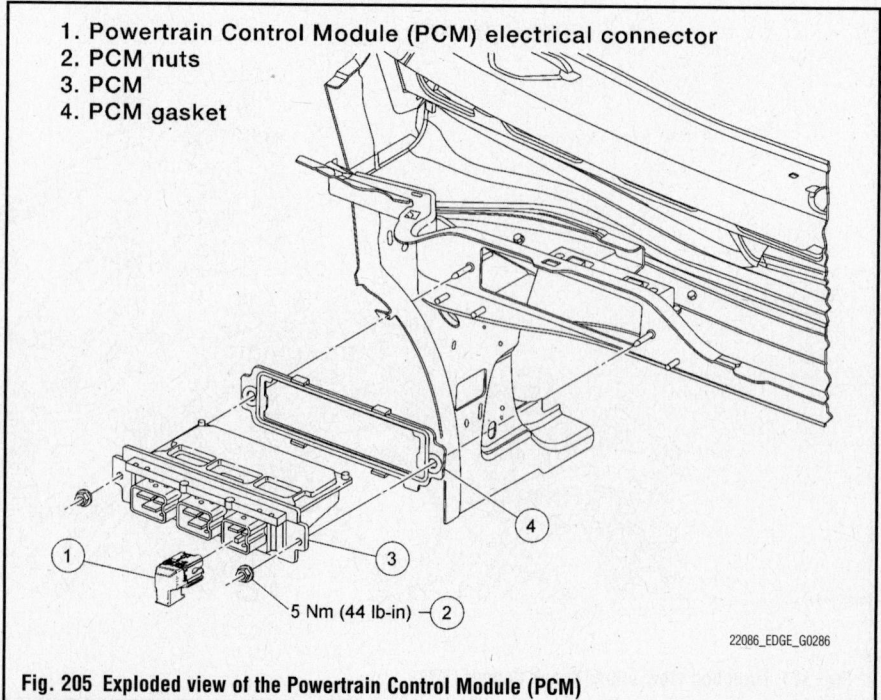

Fig. 205 Exploded view of the Powertrain Control Module (PCM)

TESTING

See Figures 206 and 207.

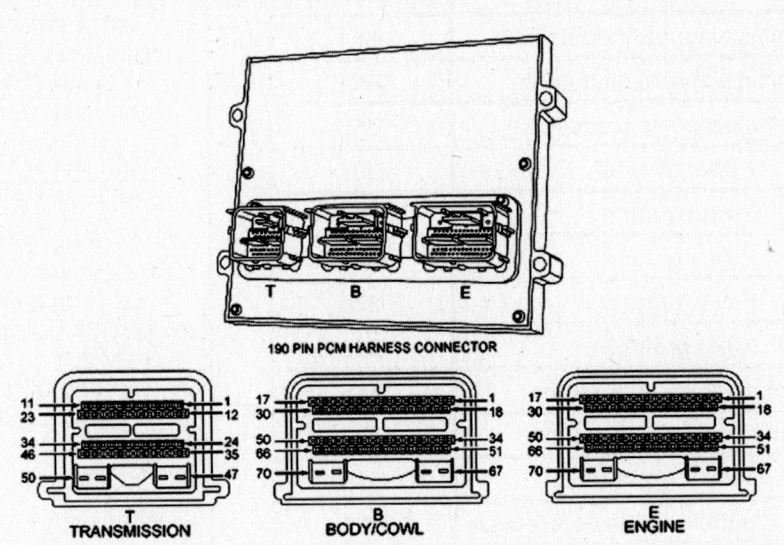

TABLE 1 — 190-PIN PCM POWER AND GROUNDS

Function	Description	Connector/Pin
VPWR	Voltage input to module	B51
VPWR	Voltage input to module	B52
VPWR	Voltage input to module	B53
PWRGND	Power ground	B67
PWRGND	Power ground	B68
PWRGND	Power ground	B69
PWRGND	Power ground	B70
CSEGND	Case ground	B66
SIGRTN	Connector B signal return	B58
SIGRTN	Connector T signal return	T43
SIGRTN	Connector E signal return	E58
VREF	Connector B buffered 5.0-volt reference	B29
VREF	Connector E buffered 5.0-volt reference	E57
KAPWR	Keep alive power	B54

22086_EDGE_G0296

Fig. 206 PCM connector view

TABLE 1 — 190-PIN PCM POWER AND GROUNDS

Function	Description	Connector/Pin
VPWR	Voltage input to module	B51
VPWR	Voltage input to module	B52
VPWR	Voltage input to module	B53
PWRGND	Power ground	B67
PWRGND	Power ground	B68
PWRGND	Power ground	B69
PWRGND	Power ground	B70
CSEGND	Case ground	B66
SIGRTN	Connector B signal return	B58
SIGRTN	Connector T signal return	T43
SIGRTN	Connector E signal return	E58
VREF	Connector B buffered 5.0-volt reference	B29
VREF	Connector E buffered 5.0-volt reference	E57
KAPWR	Keep alive power	B54

22086_EDGE_G0297

Fig. 207 PCM voltage and power pin location chart

1. Check the power and grounds for the Powertrain Control Module (PCM). Check all the connector pins for corrosion or contact problems. Refer to PCM connectors, power and ground chart.

VARIABLE CAMSHAFT TIMING (VCT) OIL CONTROL SOLENOID

LOCATION

See Figure 208.

The Variable Camshaft Timing (VCT) Oil Control Solenoids are located under the left or right valve covers, as applicable.

OPERATION

The Variable Camshaft Timing (VCT) oil control solenoid is an electrically controlled hydraulic valve that directs engine oil to the camshaft phaser. Once the PCM

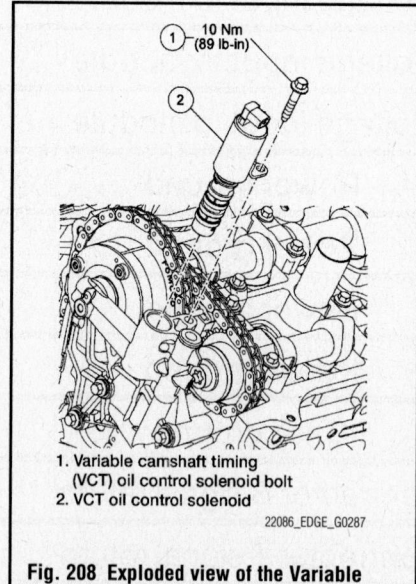

1. Variable camshaft timing (VCT) oil control solenoid bolt
2. VCT oil control solenoid

22086_EDGE_G0287

Fig. 208 Exploded view of the Variable Camshaft Timing (VCT) oil control solenoid

transmits a signal, the solenoid moves a valve spool, directing oil into the camshaft phaser cavity. This action changes valve timing by either inducing an advance or retard condition. The camshaft is, thereby repositioned in relation to crankshaft timing and allows for optimum engine performance and lower emissions.

REMOVAL & INSTALLATION

See Figure 208.

1. Remove the LH or RH valve cover, as applicable
2. Remove the bolt and the Variable Camshaft Timing (VCT) oil control solenoid.
3. Installation is the reverse of the removal procedure. Tighten the VCT oil control solenoid to 10 Nm (89 lb-in).

TESTING

See Figure 209.

1. Turn the ignition switch to the **OFF** position.
2. Disconnect the VCT1 or VCT2 sensor electrical connector, as applicable.
3. Measure the resistance between VCT + and VCT - on the component side.
4. If resistance is not within 5–14 ohms, replace sensor.

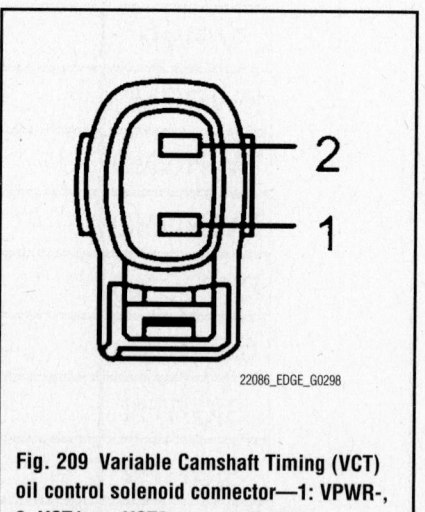

22086_EDGE_G0298

Fig. 209 Variable Camshaft Timing (VCT) oil control solenoid connector—1: VPWR-, 2: VCT1+ or VCT2+, as applicable

FUEL

GASOLINE FUEL INJECTION SYSTEM

FUEL SYSTEM SERVICE PRECAUTIONS

Safety is the most important factor when performing not only fuel system maintenance but any type of maintenance. Failure to conduct maintenance and repairs in a safe manner may result in serious personal injury or death. Maintenance and testing of the vehicle's fuel system components can be accomplished safely and effectively by adhering to the following rules and guidelines.

• To avoid the possibility of fire and personal injury, always disconnect the negative battery cable unless the repair or test procedure requires that battery voltage be applied.

• Always relieve the fuel system pressure prior to disconnecting any fuel system component (injector, fuel rail, pressure regulator, etc.), fitting or fuel line connection. Exercise extreme caution whenever relieving fuel system pressure to avoid exposing skin, face and eyes to fuel spray. Please be advised that fuel under pressure may penetrate the skin or any part of the body that it contacts.

• Always place a shop towel or cloth around the fitting or connection prior to loosening to absorb any excess fuel due to spillage. Ensure that all fuel spillage (should it occur) is quickly removed from engine surfaces. Ensure that all fuel soaked cloths or towels are deposited into a suitable waste container.

• Always keep a dry chemical (Class B) fire extinguisher near the work area.

• Do not allow fuel spray or fuel vapors to come into contact with a spark or open flame.

• Always use a back-up wrench when loosening and tightening fuel line connection fittings. This will prevent unnecessary stress and torsion to fuel line piping.

• Always replace worn fuel fitting O-rings with new Do not substitute fuel hose or equivalent where fuel pipe is installed.

Before servicing the vehicle, make sure to also refer to the precautions in the beginning of this section as well. ·

RELIEVING FUEL SYSTEM PRESSURE

See Figure 210.

❋❋ CAUTION

Observe all applicable safety precautions when working around fuel. Whenever servicing the fuel system, always work in a well ventilated area. Do not allow fuel spray or

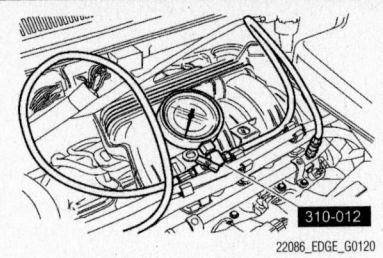

Fig. 210 Install a suitable fuel pressure gauge and slowly open the manual valve to relieve the fuel system pressure

vapors to come in contact with a spark or open flame. Keep a dry chemical fire extinguisher near the work area. Always keep fuel in a container specifically designed for fuel storage; also, always properly seal fuel containers to avoid the possibility of fire or explosion.

❋❋ CAUTION

Do not carry personal electronic devices such as cell phones, pagers or audio equipment of any type when working on or near any fuel-related components. Highly flammable mixtures are always present and may be ignited. Failure to follow these instructions may result in personal injury.

❋❋ CAUTION

Fuel in the fuel system remains under high pressure, even when the engine is not running. Before servicing or disconnecting any of the fuel lines or fuel system components, the fuel system pressure must be relieved to prevent accidental spraying of fuel, which may cause personal injury or a fire hazard.

1. Remove the Schrader valve cap.

➥This step will drain some fuel out of the system. Place the fuel in a suitable container.

2. Install a suitable fuel pressure gauge and slowly open the manual valve to relieve the fuel system pressure.

FUEL INJECTORS

REMOVAL & INSTALLATION

See Figure 211.

❋❋ CAUTION

Observe all applicable safety precautions when working around fuel. Whenever servicing the fuel system, always work in a well ventilated area. Do not allow fuel spray or vapors to come in contact with a spark or open flame. Keep a dry chemical fire extinguisher near the work area. Always keep fuel in a container specifically designed for fuel storage; also, always properly seal fuel containers to avoid the possibility of fire or explosion.

1. Disconnect the negative battery cable.

2. Relieve the fuel system pressure, as outlined in this section.

3. Remove the upper intake manifold. Refer to the Intake Manifold procedure in the Engine Mechanical Section.

4. Disconnect the fuel tube-to-fuel rail quick connect coupling.

5. Disconnect the 6 fuel injector electrical connectors.

6. Remove the 4 fuel rail bolts.

7. Remove the fuel rail and injectors as an assembly.

8. Remove the 6 fuel injector clips and the 6 fuel injectors.

9. Remove and discard the 12 fuel injector O-ring seals.

To install:

❋❋ WARNING

Only use O-ring seals that are made of special fuel-resistant material. Using regular O-rings can cause the fuel system to leak. Do not reuse the O-ring seals.

❋❋ WARNING

The upper and lower O-ring seals are not interchangeable.

➥Install new fuel injector O-ring seals and lubricate them with clean engine oil.

10. Install the 6 fuel injectors and the 6 fuel injector clips into the fuel rail.

11. Install the fuel rail and fuel injectors as an assembly.

12. Install the 4 fuel rail bolts. Tighten to 10 Nm (89 inch lbs.).

13. Connect the 6 fuel injector electrical connectors.

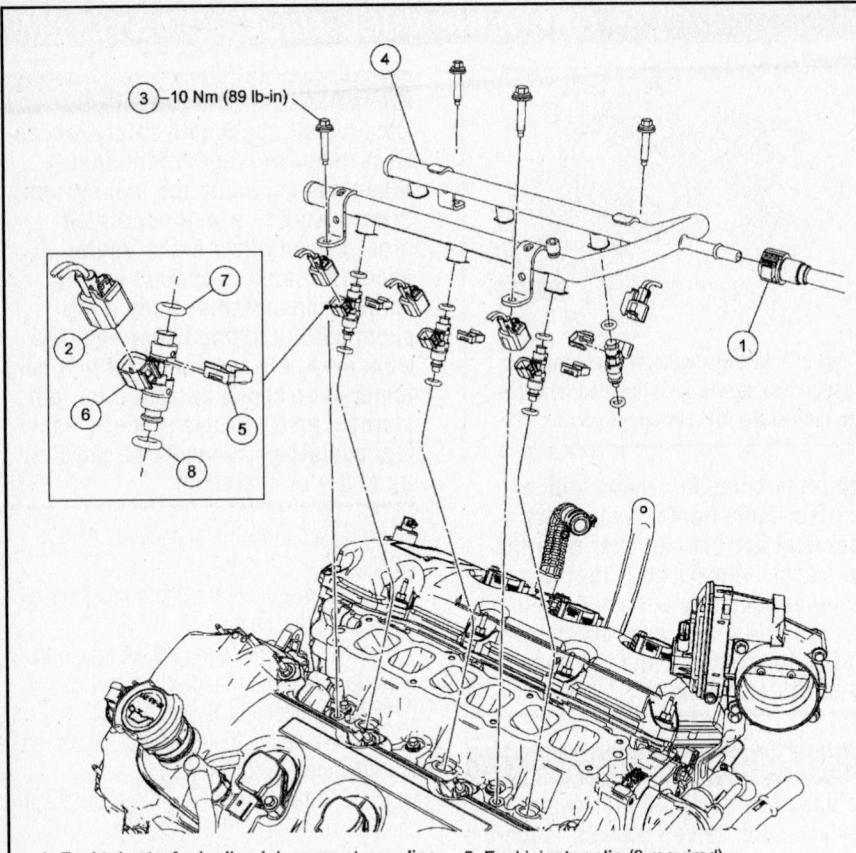

3 —10 Nm (89 lb-in)

1. Fuel tube-to-fuel rail quick connect coupling
2. Fuel injector electrical connector (6 required)
3. Fuel rail bolt (4 required)
4. Fuel rail
5. Fuel injector clip (6 required)
6. Fuel injector (6 required)
7. Upper fuel injector O-ring seal (6 required)
8. Lower fuel injector O-ring seal (6 required)

22086_EDGE_G0124

Fig. 211 Exploded view of the fuel rail, injectors and related components

14. Connect the fuel tube-to-fuel rail quick connect coupling.
15. Install the upper intake manifold.
16. Connect the negative battery cable.

FUEL PUMP

REMOVAL & INSTALLATION

See Figures 212 and 213.

✳✳ CAUTION

Observe all applicable safety precautions when working around fuel. Whenever servicing the fuel system, always work in a well ventilated area. Do not allow fuel spray or vapors to come in contact with a spark or open flame. Keep a dry chemical fire extinguisher near the work area. Always keep fuel in a container specifically designed for fuel storage; also, always properly seal fuel containers to avoid the possibility of fire or explosion.

✳✳ CAUTION

Do not carry personal electronic devices such as cell phones, pagers or audio equipment of any type when working on or near any fuel-related components. Highly flammable mixtures are always present and may be ignited. Failure to follow these instructions may result in personal injury.

✳✳ CAUTION

Fuel in the fuel system remains under high pressure, even when the engine is not running. Before servicing or disconnecting any of the fuel lines or fuel system components, the fuel system pressure must be relieved to prevent accidental spraying of fuel, which may cause personal injury or a fire hazard.

1. Relieve the fuel system pressure, as outlined in this section.

2. Disconnect the negative battery cable.
3. Release the fuel tank filler cap and position aside.
4. Insert a suitable fuel drain tube into the fuel tank filler pipe until it reaches the fuel tank inlet spout.
5. Attach the fuel storage tanker to the fuel drain tube and remove any residual fuel remaining in the fuel tank filler pipe.
6. Remove the rear seat.
7. Position the carpet and/or any insulation covering the fuel pump module access cover aside.
8. Remove the 4 screws and the fuel pump module access cover.
9. Disconnect the fuel pump module electrical connector.
10. Disconnect the fuel tank supply tube-to-fuel pump module quick connect coupling.

✳✳ WARNING

Place absorbent pads on the floor pan in the immediate area in case of fuel spills. Carefully remove the fuel pump module from the vehicle to avoid fuel spillage inside the vehicle.

11. Using the special tool, remove the fuel pump module lock ring retainer.
12. On All Wheel Drive (AWD) vehicles, perform the following:

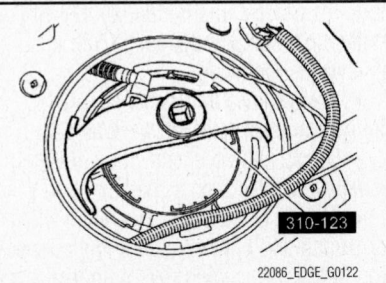

310-123

22086_EDGE_G0122

Fig. 212 Using the special tool, remove the fuel pump module lock ring retainer

✳✳ WARNING

The fuel pump module must be handled carefully to avoid damage to the fuel pump module and/or float arm.

c. Carefully lift the fuel pump module out of the fuel tank enough to access and disconnect the fuel tank crossover tube-to-fuel pump module quick connect coupling.

✳✳ WARNING

The fuel pump module will have residual fuel remaining internally, drain into a suitable container.

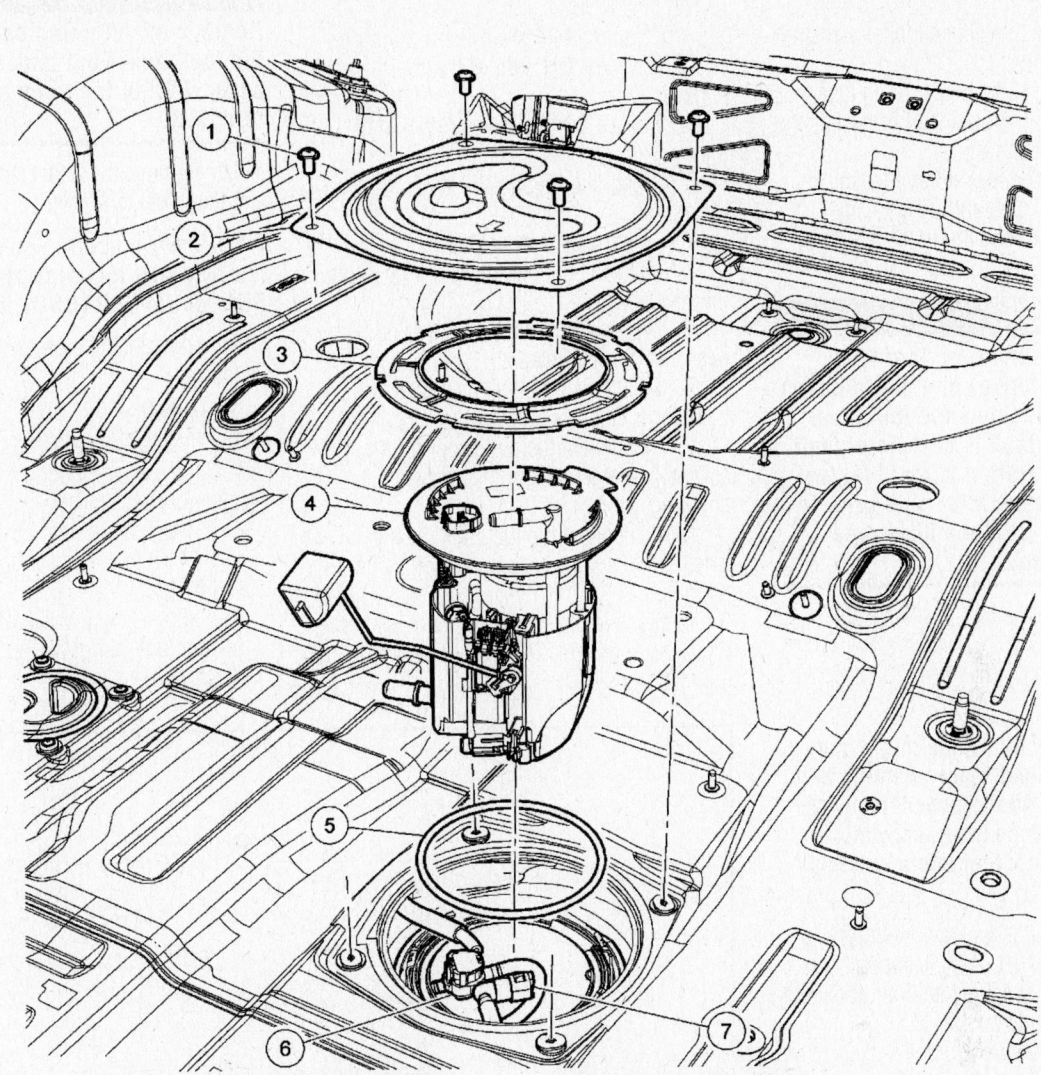

1. Fuel pump (FP) module access cover retainer screw (4 required)
2. FP module access cover
3. FP module lock ring
4. FP module
5. FP module O-ring
6. FP module electrical connector
7. Fuel supply tube quick connect coupling

22086_EDGE_G0121

Fig. 213 Exploded view of the fuel pump module and related components—AWD model shown, FWD similar

13. Completely remove the fuel pump module from the fuel tank.

❋❋ WARNING

Inspect the mating surfaces of the fuel pump module flange and the fuel tank O-ring seal contact surfaces. Do not polish or adjust the O-ring seal contact area of the fuel tank flange or the fuel tank. Install a new fuel pump module or fuel tank if the O-ring seal contact area is bent, scratched or corroded.

❋❋ WARNING

Make sure to install a new fuel pump module O-ring seal. Install a new lock ring if it is bent, damaged or corroded.

➡**Apply clean engine oil to the O-ring seal before installing the O-ring.**

14. Remove the fuel pump module O-ring seal.

➡**Make sure the alignment tab on the fuel pump module and the fuel tank**

meet before tightening the fuel pump module lock ring.

15. Installation is the reverse of the removal procedure.

FUEL TANK

REMOVAL & INSTALLATION

See Figures 214 and 215.

1. Drain the fuel tank, as follows:
   a. Raise and safely support the vehicle.
   b. Relieve the fuel system pressure, as outlined in this section.

c. Disconnect the negative battery cable.

d. Release the fuel tank filler cap and position it aside.

e. Insert a suitable fuel drain tube into the fuel tank filler pipe until it reaches the fuel tank inlet spout.

f. Attach the fuel storage tanker to the fuel drain tube and remove any residual fuel remaining in the fuel tank filler pipe.

❋❋ WARNING

The fuel pump module, fuel level sensor (if equipped) and the fuel tank inlet spout are below the fuel level when the fuel tank is completely full. Make sure to drain any residual fuel from the fuel tank filler pipe prior to removing the fuel tank filler pipe clamp and hose.

g. Release the fuel tank filler pipe hose-to-fuel tank inlet spout clamp.

To install, tighten to 4 Nm (35 inch lbs.).

➡ **The fuel tank filler pipe might contain some residual fuel remaining in it after draining. After disconnecting the fuel tank filler pipe hose, carefully drain the residual fuel into a suitable container.**

h. Remove the fuel tank filler pipe hose from the fuel tank inlet spout.

i. Insert a suitable fuel drain tube into the fuel tank inlet spout.

j. Attach the fuel storage tanker to the fuel drain tube and drain the fuel from the fuel tank.

2. On All Wheel Drive (AWD) vehicles only, perform the following additional fuel draining steps:

a. Remove the rear seats.

b. Position aside the carpet and any insulation covering the fuel level sensor access cover.

c. Remove the 4 screws and the fuel level sensor access cover.

d. Disconnect the fuel level sensor electrical connector.

➡ **Place absorbent pads in the general work area in case of fuel spillage.**

e. Clean the surrounding area of the fuel level sensor mounting flange.

f. Release the lock tab, and using a suitable tool, rotate the fuel level sensor counterclockwise approximately 1/4 turn, lift and position aside.

g. Install a suitable fuel drain tube into the fuel level sensor aperture in the fuel tank.

h. Completely drain the remaining fuel from the RH side of the fuel tank.

3. For All Wheel Drive (AWD) vehicles:

a. Remove the muffler and tailpipe.

b. Remove the driveshaft.

4. Install a suitable lifting device under the fuel tank.

5. Disconnect the fuel tank wiring harness electrical connector.

6. Disconnect the fuel tank pressure transducer electrical connector.

7. Disconnect the fuel vapor tube assembly-to-fuel tank quick connect coupling. z

8. Disconnect the fuel tank supply tube-to-fuel supply tube quick connect coupling.

9. Remove the 2 emergency brake cable bracket-to-fuel tank flange bolts and position cables aside.

❋❋ WARNING

Remove all retaining bolts to lower the fuel tank. Fuel tank damage can occur if all of the bolts are not removed.

10. Remove the 2 fuel tank bracket bolts and the 4 fuel tank bolts.

➡ **For AWD models, you must position the fuel tank forward, past the Rear Differential Unit (RDU), then lowered.**

11. Completely lower and remove the fuel tank.

To install:

12. Installation is the reverse of the removal procedure, noting the following tightening specifications:

a. Fuel tank bolts: 25 Nm (18 ft. lbs.)

b. Fuel tank bracket bolts: 25 Nm (18 ft. lbs.)

c. Emergency brake cable bracket-to-fuel tank flange bolts: 23 Nm (17 ft. lbs.)

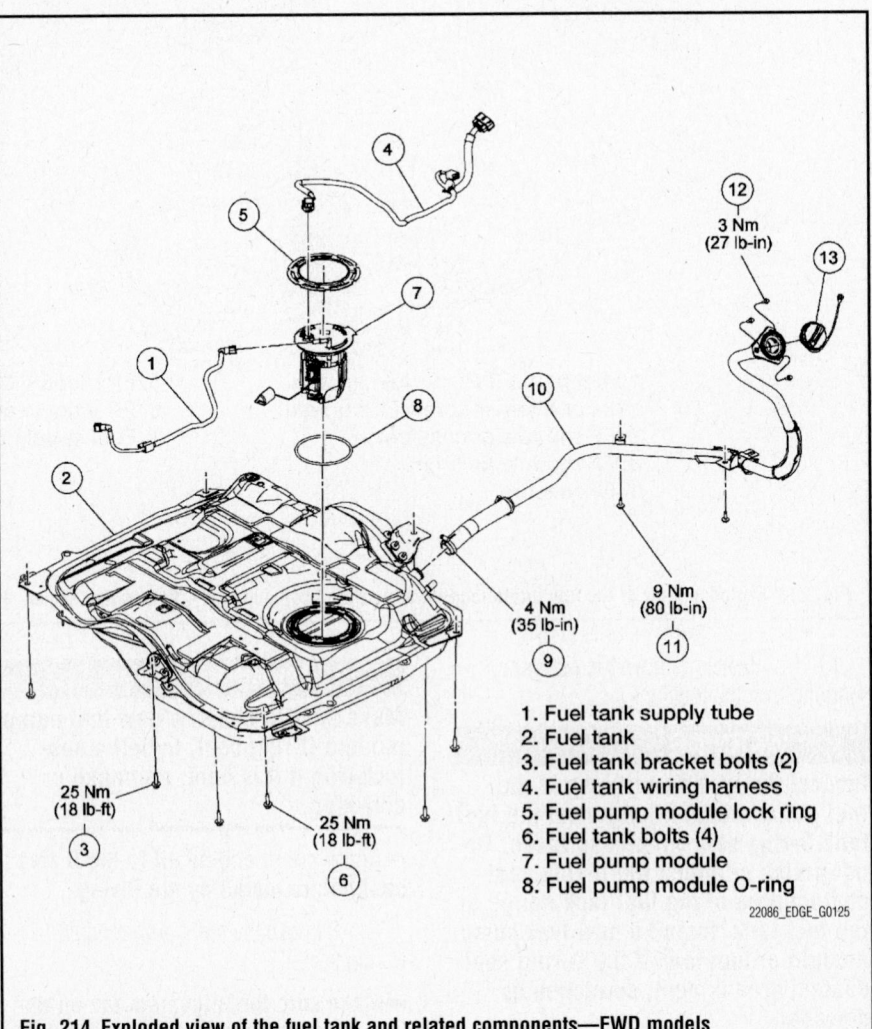

1. Fuel tank supply tube
2. Fuel tank
3. Fuel tank bracket bolts (2)
4. Fuel tank wiring harness
5. Fuel pump module lock ring
6. Fuel tank bolts (4)
7. Fuel pump module
8. Fuel pump module O-ring

22086_EDGE_G0125

Fig. 214 Exploded view of the fuel tank and related components—FWD models

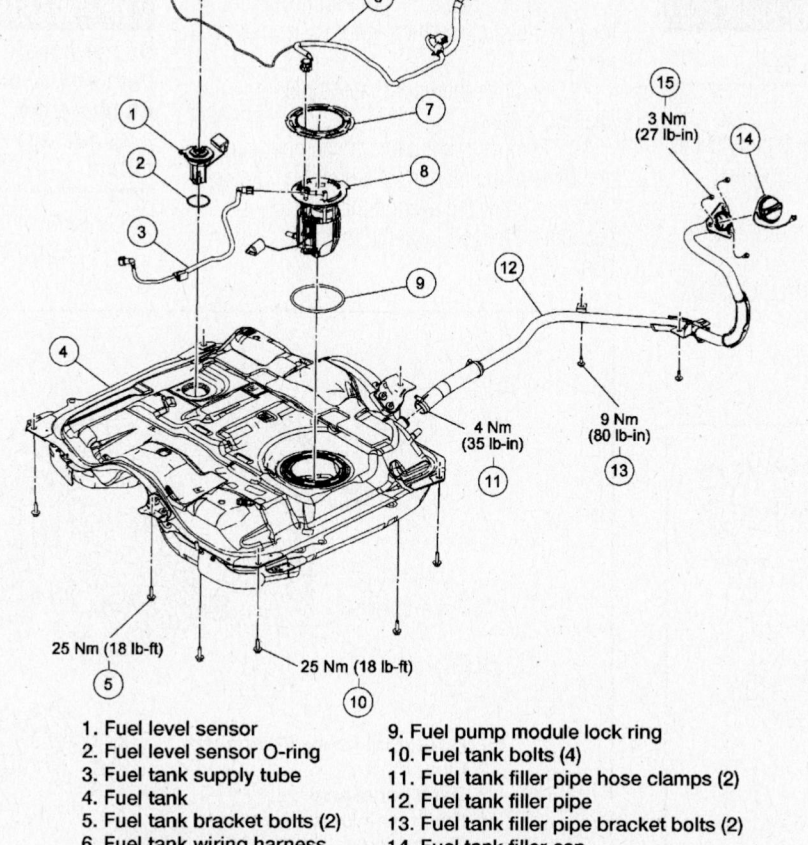

1. Fuel level sensor
2. Fuel level sensor O-ring
3. Fuel tank supply tube
4. Fuel tank
5. Fuel tank bracket bolts (2)
6. Fuel tank wiring harness
7. Fuel pump module lock ring
8. Fuel pump module
9. Fuel pump module lock ring
10. Fuel tank bolts (4)
11. Fuel tank filler pipe hose clamps (2)
12. Fuel tank filler pipe
13. Fuel tank filler pipe bracket bolts (2)
14. Fuel tank filler cap
15. Fuel tank filler pipe flange screws (3)

22086_EDGE_G0126

Fig. 215 Exploded view of the fuel tank and related components—AWD models

IDLE SPEED

ADJUSTMENT

Idle speed is maintained by the Powertrain Control Module (PCM). No adjustment is necessary or possible.

THROTTLE BODY

REMOVAL & INSTALLATION

See Figure 216.

1. Remove the air cleaner outlet pipe.
2. Disconnect the electronic throttle control electrical connector.
3. Remove the 4 bolts and the throttle body. Discard the throttle body gasket.

To install:

4. Install a new throttle gasket.
5. Install the throttle body and tighten to 10 Nm (89 inch lbs.).
6. Attach the electronic throttle control electrical connector.
7. Install the air cleaner outlet pipe.

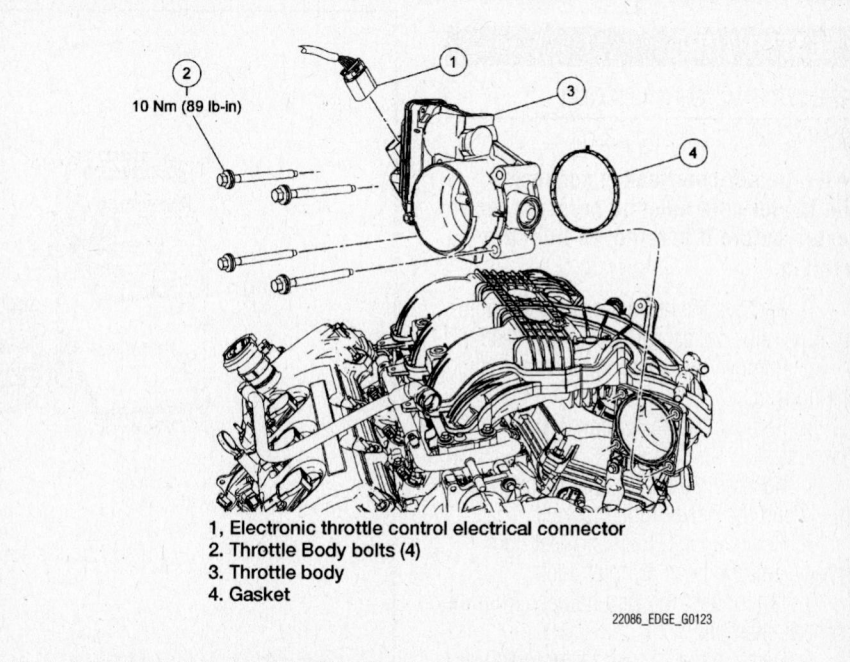

1. Electronic throttle control electrical connector
2. Throttle Body bolts (4)
3. Throttle body
4. Gasket

22086_EDGE_G0123

Fig. 216 Exploded view of the throttle body and related components

HEATING & AIR CONDITIONING SYSTEM

BLOWER MOTOR

REMOVAL & INSTALLATION

See Figure 217.

1. Disconnect the negative battery cable.
2. Remove the RH lower instrument panel insulator.
3. Disconnect the blower motor electrical connector.
4. Remove the 3 blower motor screws.
5. Remove the blower motor.
6. Installation is the reverse of the removal procedure.

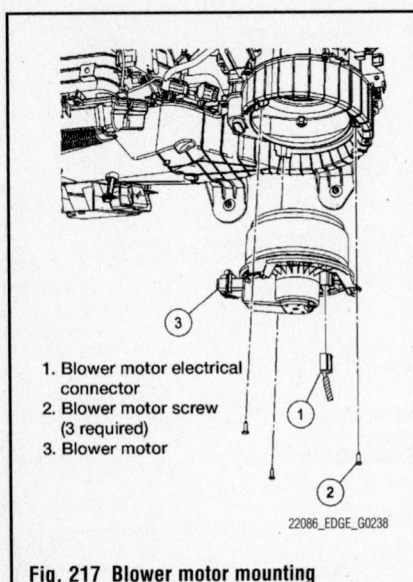

1. Blower motor electrical connector
2. Blower motor screw (3 required)
3. Blower motor

22086_EDGE_G0238

Fig. 217 Blower motor mounting

HEATER CORE

REMOVAL & INSTALLATION

See Figures 218 through 220.

➡If a heater core leak is suspected, the heater core must be pressure leak tested before it is removed from the vehicle.

1. Remove the heater core and evaporator core housing, as outlined in this section.
2. Remove the 6 floor duct screws and the floor duct.
3. Remove the heater core tube dash panel seal.
4. Remove the heater tube bracket screw and the heater tube bracket.
5. Remove the 5 fresh air inlet duct screws and the fresh air inlet duct.
6. Disconnect the wire harness from the plenum chamber.
7. Remove the 7 lower facing plenum chamber screws.

8. Adjust the heater core and evaporator core housing so the plenum chamber is upright.
9. Remove the upper facing plenum chamber screw.
10. Remove the 2 plenum chamber clips and remove the plenum chamber being careful not to allow the evaporator core to become dislodged from the installed position.

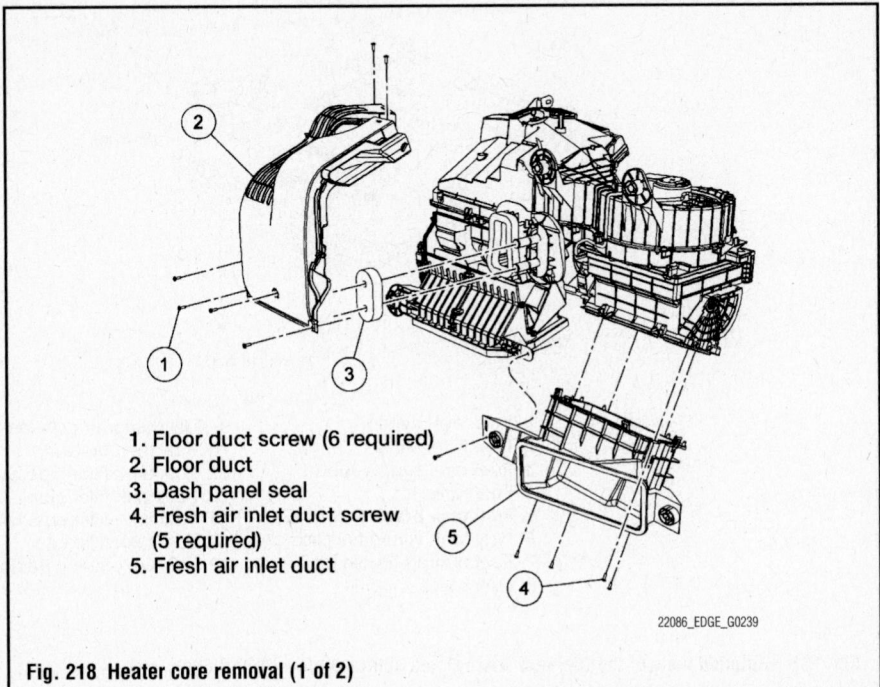

1. Floor duct screw (6 required)
2. Floor duct
3. Dash panel seal
4. Fresh air inlet duct screw (5 required)
5. Fresh air inlet duct

22086_EDGE_G0239

Fig. 218 Heater core removal (1 of 2)

✲✲ WARNING

Do not handle the heater core by the inlet and/or outlet tube to remove. Handling the heater core by the tubes may damage the joints and lead to failure of the heater core.

11. Remove the heater core, as follows:
    a. Grasp the heater core by the core-

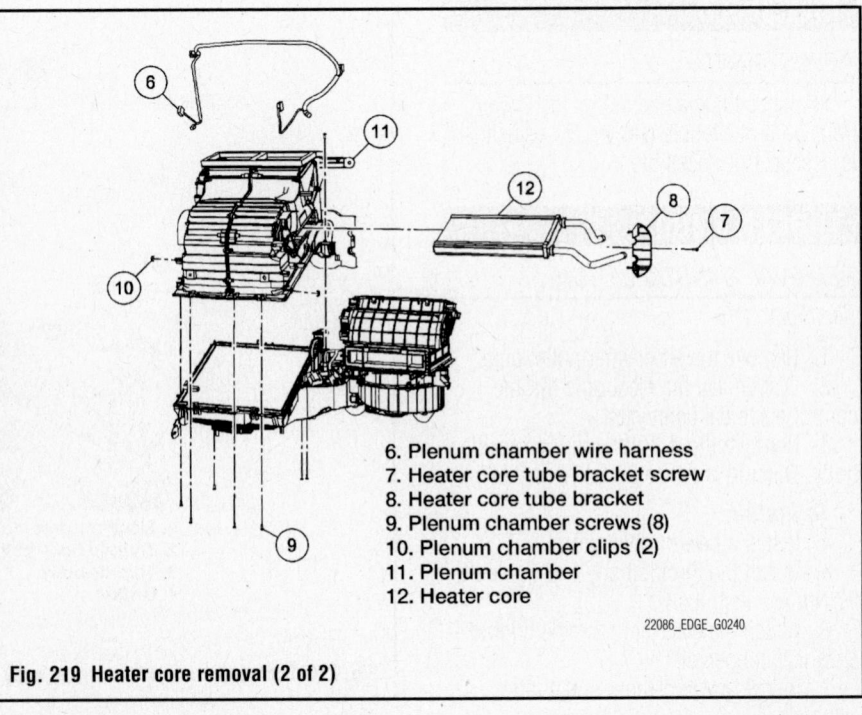

6. Plenum chamber wire harness
7. Heater core tube bracket screw
8. Heater core tube bracket
9. Plenum chamber screws (8)
10. Plenum chamber clips (2)
11. Plenum chamber
12. Heater core

22086_EDGE_G0240

Fig. 219 Heater core removal (2 of 2)

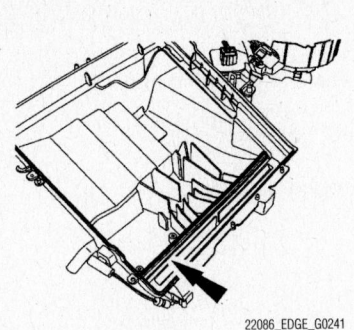

Fig. 220 If the evaporator core has been moved at any point during heater core removal, remove the evaporator core, verify that the drain seal is installed in the correct position and install the evaporator core in the correct position

side of the heater tube connections and partially remove it from the plenum chamber.

b. Grasp the heater core by the top of the core and remove it from the plenum chamber.

➡**It is not necessary to perform this step if the evaporator core has not become dislodged from the installed position during this procedure.**

12. If the evaporator core has been moved at any point during heater core removal, remove the evaporator core, verify that the drain seal is installed in the correct position and install the evaporator core in the correct position.

13. Installation is the reverse of the removal procedure.

HEATER CORE AND EVAPORATOR CORE HOUSING

REMOVAL & INSTALLATION

See Figures 221 and 222.

➡**Installation of a new receiver/drier desiccant bag is not required when repairing the air conditioning system except when there is physical evidence of system contamination from a failed A/C compressor or damage to the receiver/drier desiccant bag.**

➡**The O-ring seals used on this vehicle are not interchangeable with all similarly sized O-ring seals used on other Ford products. Use only the O-ring seals specified for this vehicle in the Ford master parts catalog.**

1. Recover the refrigerant.
2. Drain the engine coolant.
3. Remove the instrument panel, as outlined in this section.
4. Remove the 3 driver side carpet pin-type retainers and position the driver side front carpet aside.
5. Remove the 4 LH rear footwell duct pin-type retainers and the LH rear footwell duct.
6. Remove the 2 passenger front carpet pin-type retainers and position the passenger front carpet aside enough to access the 2 front pin-type retainers on the RH rear footwell duct.
7. Remove the 2 front pin-type retainers on the RH rear footwell duct and detach the RH rear footwell duct from the heater core and evaporator core housing.
8. Release the 2 heater hose clamps at the heater core and disconnect the heater hoses.
9. Remove the Thermostatic eXpansion Valve (TXV) fitting nut and detach the A/C lines from the TXV. Discard the O-ring seals.

❋❋ WARNING

The retaining clips on the plastic evaporator drain tube elbow will break if the elbow is removed from inside the vehicle. If the evaporator drain tube elbow must be removed, the retaining clips must be detached from below the vehicle. If the plastic evaporator drain tube elbow does not need to be removed, only detach the evaporator drain tube from the elbow.

10. Disconnect the evaporator drain tube from the elbow at the floorpan.
11. Remove the 5 heater core and evaporator core housing nuts.
To install, tighten to 9 Nm (80 inch lbs.).
12. Remove the heater core and evaporator core housing.

To install:

13. Installation is the reverse of the removal procedure, noting the following:
a. Install new O-ring seals lubricated in clean PAG oil.
b. Lubricate the refrigerant system with the correct amount of clean PAG oil.
c. Tighten the heater core and evaporator core housing nuts to 9 Nm (80 inch lbs.).
d. Tighten the TXV fitting nut to 8 Nm (71 inch lbs.).
e. Fill the engine coolant level.
f. Evacuate, leak test and charge the refrigerant system

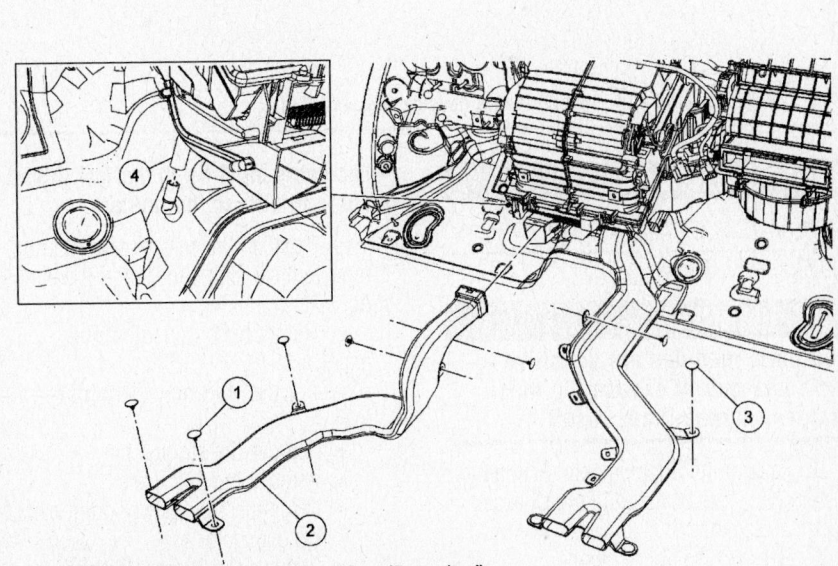

1. LH rear footwell duct pin-type retainer (5 required)
2. LH rear footwell duct
3. RH rear footwell duct front pin-type retainer (2 required)
4. Evaporator drain tube

Fig. 221 Heater core and evaporator core housing removal (1 of 2)

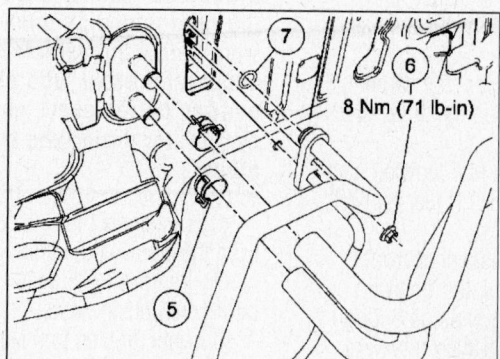

5. Heater hose clamp (2 required)
6. Thermostatic expansion valve (TXV) fitting nut
7. O-ring seal (2 required)
8. Heater core and evaporator core housing nut (5 required)
9. Heater core and evaporator core housing

8 Nm (71 lb-in)

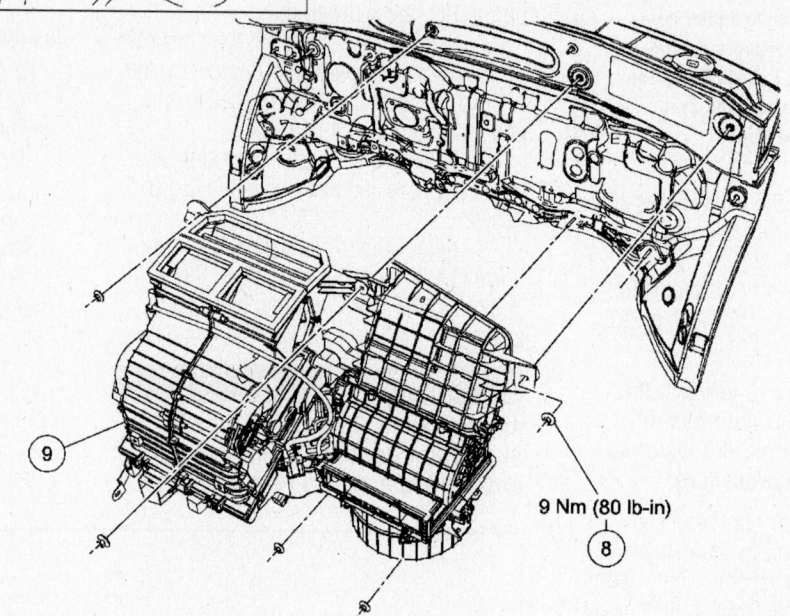

9 Nm (80 lb-in)

22086_EDGE_G0243

Fig. 222 Heater core and evaporator core housing removal (2 of 2)

INSTRUMENT PANEL

REMOVAL & INSTALLATION
See Figures 223 through 226.

✴✴ WARNING

Electronic modules are sensitive to static charges. If exposed to these charges, damage may result.

1. Disarm the Supplemental Restraint System (SRS), as outlined in the Chassis Electrical Section.
2. Remove the floor console:
   a. Position the gear shift lever to NEUTRAL.

➡**The seats must be in the full raised position to access the bolts.**

   b. Position the seats forward and remove the 2 rear bolts.
   c. Remove the 2 console side panels.

➡**The seats must be in the full raised position to access the bolts.**

   d. Position the seats rearward and remove the 2 side panels and 2 center bolts.
   e. Remove the console finish panel.
   f. For the MKX only, perform the following:
   • Remove the storage bin.
   • Remove the 2 scrivets.
   • Disconnect the power point electrical connector.
   • Remove the 2 console front side bolts.
   g. Remove the 2 console-to-instrument panel bolts.
   h. Disconnect the floor console electrical connector from the lower right front wiring harness.
   i. Remove the floor console.
3. Remove the weatherstripping from the front door openings near the instrument panel.
4. Remove the LH and RH instrument panel end trim panels.
5. Remove the LH and RH A-pillar trim panels:

➡**The A-pillar trim panel is held in place by a clip/tether that is snapped to the back of the panel. A new clip must be installed when installing the existing trim panel.**

   j. Remove the A-pillar trim panel and disconnect the tether
6. Remove the LH and RH cowl panels.
7. Remove the steering column cover, as follows:
   a. Remove the 2 column cover screws.
   b. Disengage the steering column cover from the retaining clips.

c. Disconnect the electrical connector and hose, if equipped.

8. Remove the bolt and the hood opening handle. Position the handle aside.

9. Disconnect the LH bulkhead electrical connector from under the steering column.

10. Disconnect the RH bulkhead electrical connector from under the steering column.

11. Disconnect the 2 electrical connectors from the left cowl panel side.

12. Disconnect the electrical connectors and the antenna lead-in cable from the right cowl panel side. Remove the harness from the retainers.

13. Disconnect the 2 A/C electrical connectors from inside the glove compartment.

14. Disconnect the blower motor resistor or blower motor speed control electrical connector from the top of the heater core and evaporator core housing.

15. Disconnect the shift cable from the ball stud on the shifter.

16. Remove the shift cable from the retaining clips.

17. Remove the 4 screws (2 each side) from the inner floor console support.

18. Remove the screws from the front inner floor console support-to-instrument panel.

19. Disconnect the electrical connectors from the front inner floor console.

20. Remove the inner floor console support.

21. Disconnect the Restraints Control Module (RCM) small electrical connector.

22. Remove the LH pushpin retainer and position the carpet aside.

23. Remove the LH pushpin retainer from the instrument panel-to-A/C duct.

24. Remove the 2 LH instrument panel-to-floor bolts.

25. Remove the RH pushpin retainer and position the carpet aside.

26. Remove the screw from the RH instrument panel brace-to-A/C duct.

27. Remove the RH instrument panel brace-to-floor bolt.

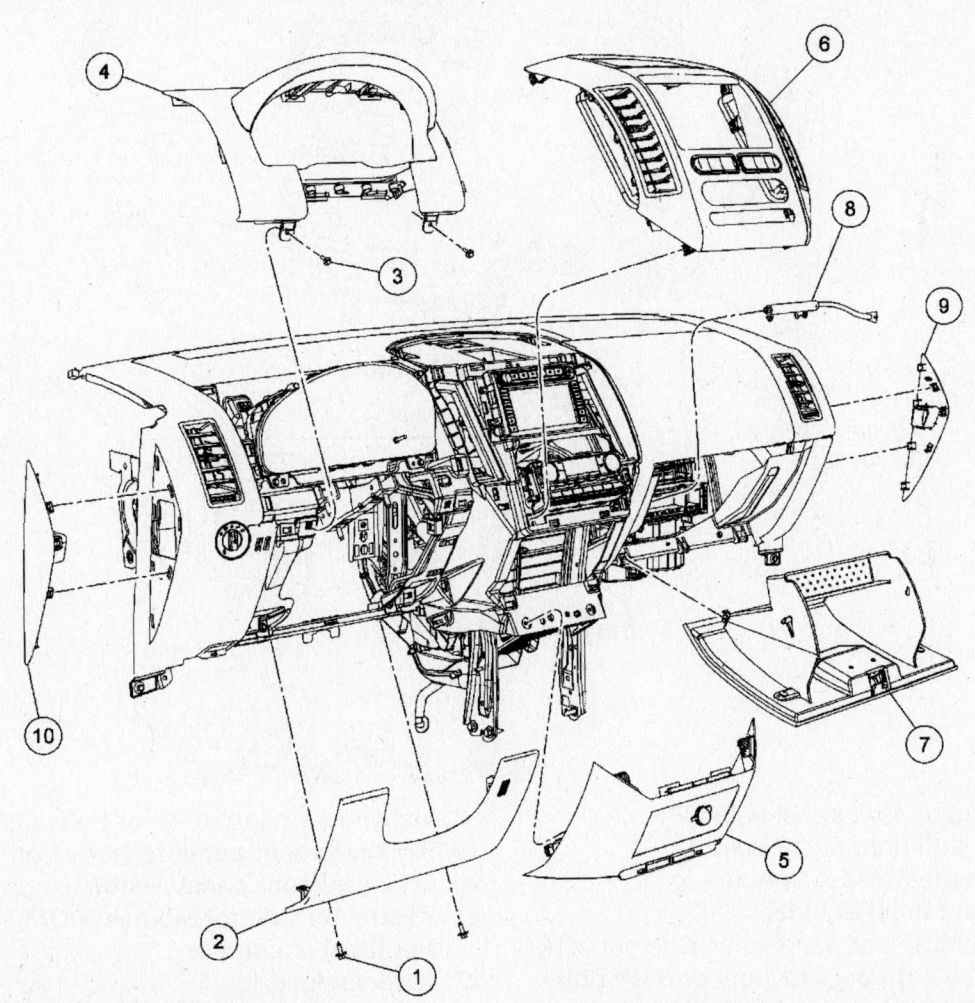

1. Steering column cover screws (2)
2. Steering column cover
3. Instrument panel cluster finish panel screws (2)
4. Instrument panel cluster finish panel
5. Instrument panel lower center finish panel
6. Instrument panel upper center finish panel
7. Glove compartment
8. Glove compartment dampener
9. RH instrument panel end trim panel
10. LH instrument panel end trim panel

22086_EDGE_G0264

Fig. 223 Exploded view of the instrument panel (1 of 2)—Edge

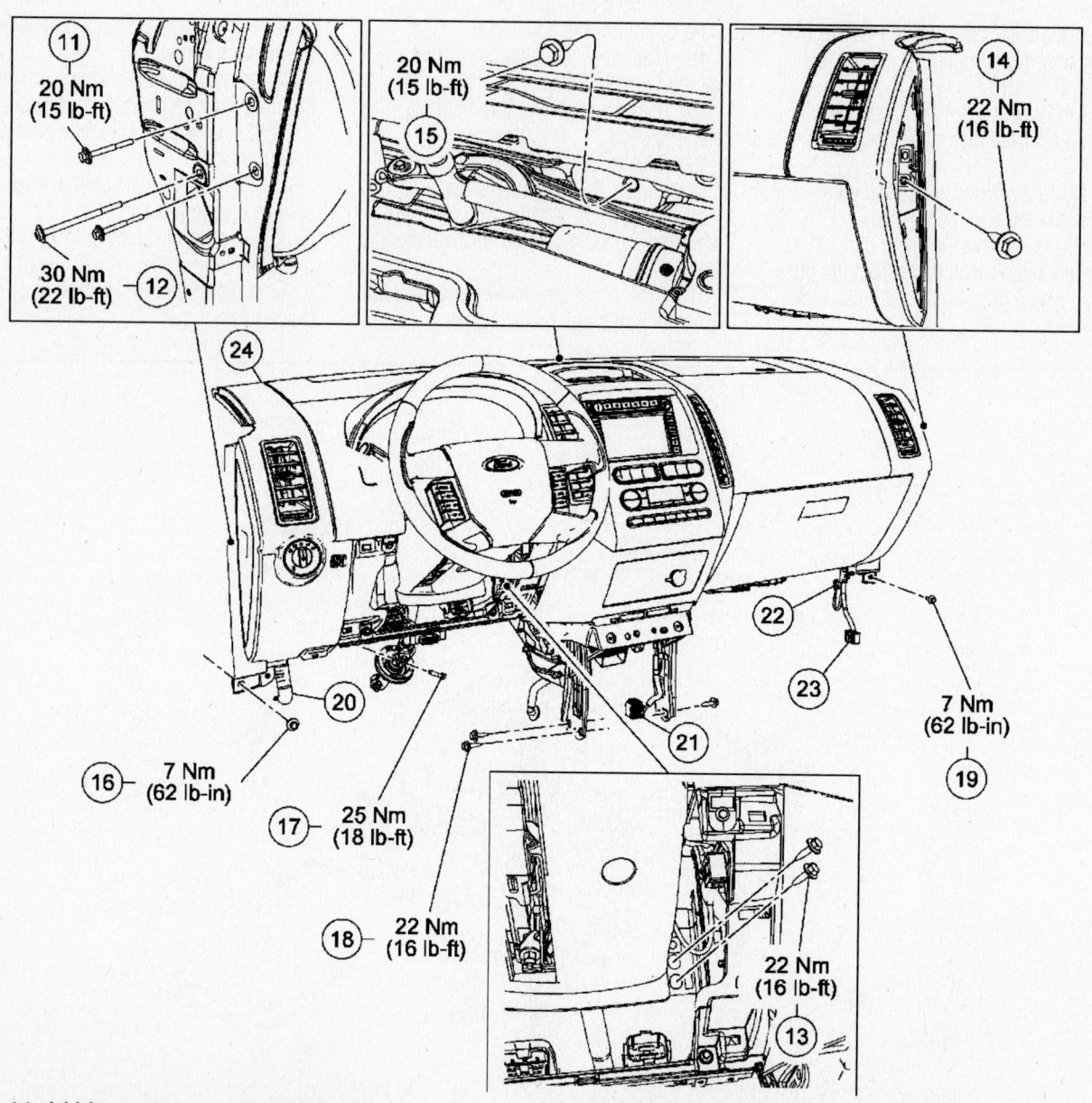

11. LH instrument panel bolts (2)
12. LH instrument panel bolts
13. Instrument panel-to-steering column bracket bolts (2)
14. RH instrument panel cowl side panel bolt
15. Instrument panel-to-front of dash body
16. LH instrument panel-to-body bolt
17. Steering column pinch bolt
18. Instrument panel-to-floor bolts (3)
19. RH instrument panel-to-body bolt
20. LH instrument panel electrical connectors
21. Restraints Control Module (RCM) electrical connector
22. Antenna lead-in
23. RH instrument panel electrical connector
24. Instrument panel

22086_EDGE_G0265

Fig. 224 Exploded view of the instrument panel (2 of 2)—Edge

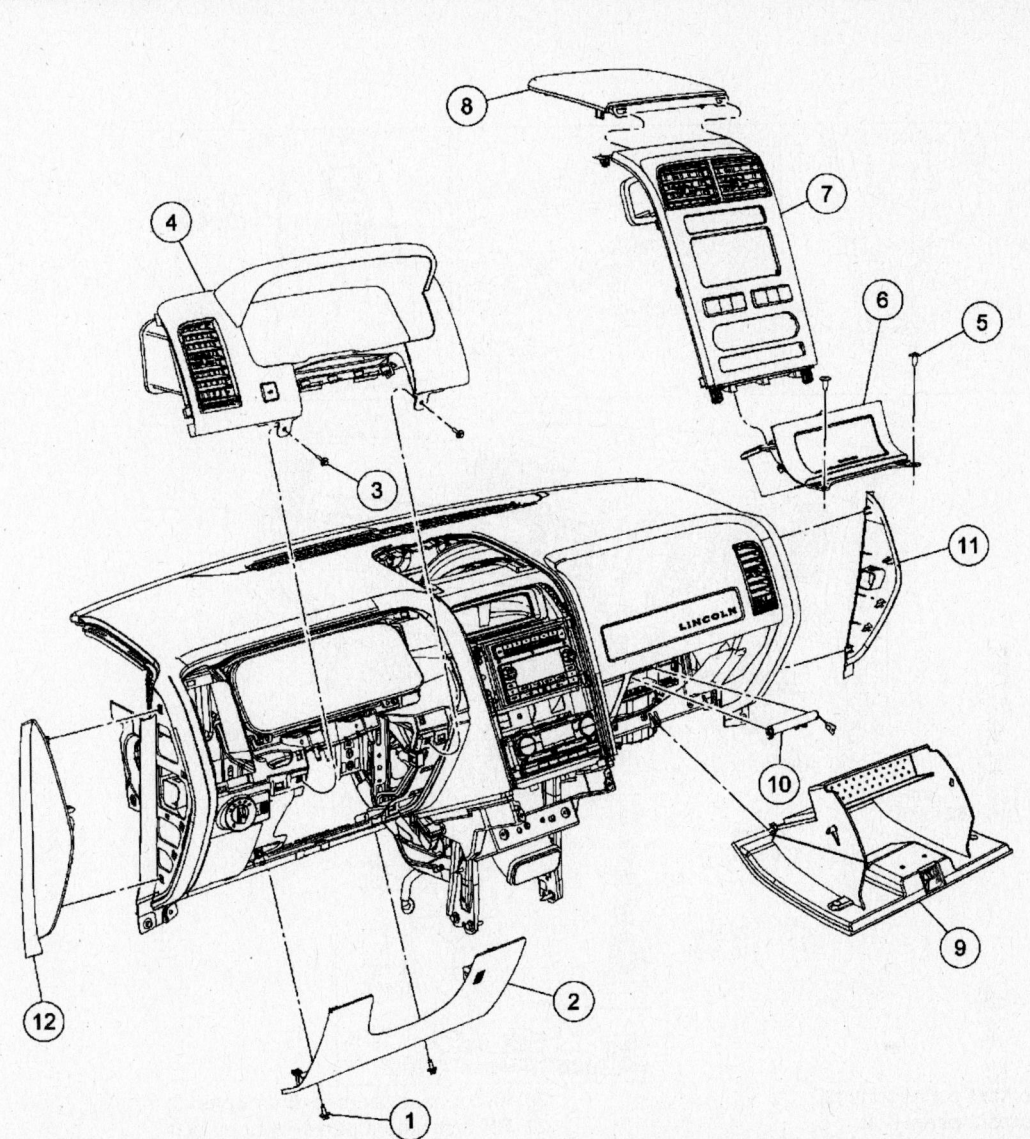

1. Steering column cover screws (2)
2. Steering column cover
3. Instrument panel cluster finish panel screws (2)
4. Instrument panel cluster finish panel
5. Instrument panel storage bin screws (2)
6. Instrument panel storage bin
7. Instrument panel lower center finish panel
8. Instrument panel upper center finish panel
9. Glove compartment
10. Glove compartment dampener
11. RH instrument panel end trim panel
12. LH instrument panel end trim panel

22086_EDGE_G0266

Fig. 225 Exploded view of the instrument panel (1 of 2)—MKX

28. Remove the 2 nuts and the LH instrument panel brace-to-A/C duct.

29. Remove the steering column pinch bolt.

30. Remove the upper cowl panel grille:

a. Remove the RH cowl side outer panel.

b. Remove the LH cowl side outer panel.

c. Remove the 2 scrivets from the RH upper cowl panel grille.

d. Remove the 2 bolts from the RH upper cowl grille panel and remove the RH upper cowl grille panel.

e. Remove the 2 scrivets from the LH upper cowl grille panel.

f. Remove the 2 bolts from the LH upper cowl grille panel and remove the LH upper cowl grille panel.

31. Remove the bolt from the front of dash.

32. Remove the front driver seat.

➡The Torx® head bolt is not completely removed. The bolt is pulled outward far enough to allow for clearance when removing the instrument panel.

33. Remove the Torx® head bolt from inside the LH door.

34. Remove the 2 bolts from inside the LH door.

35. Remove the 2 bolts from the bracket under the steering column.

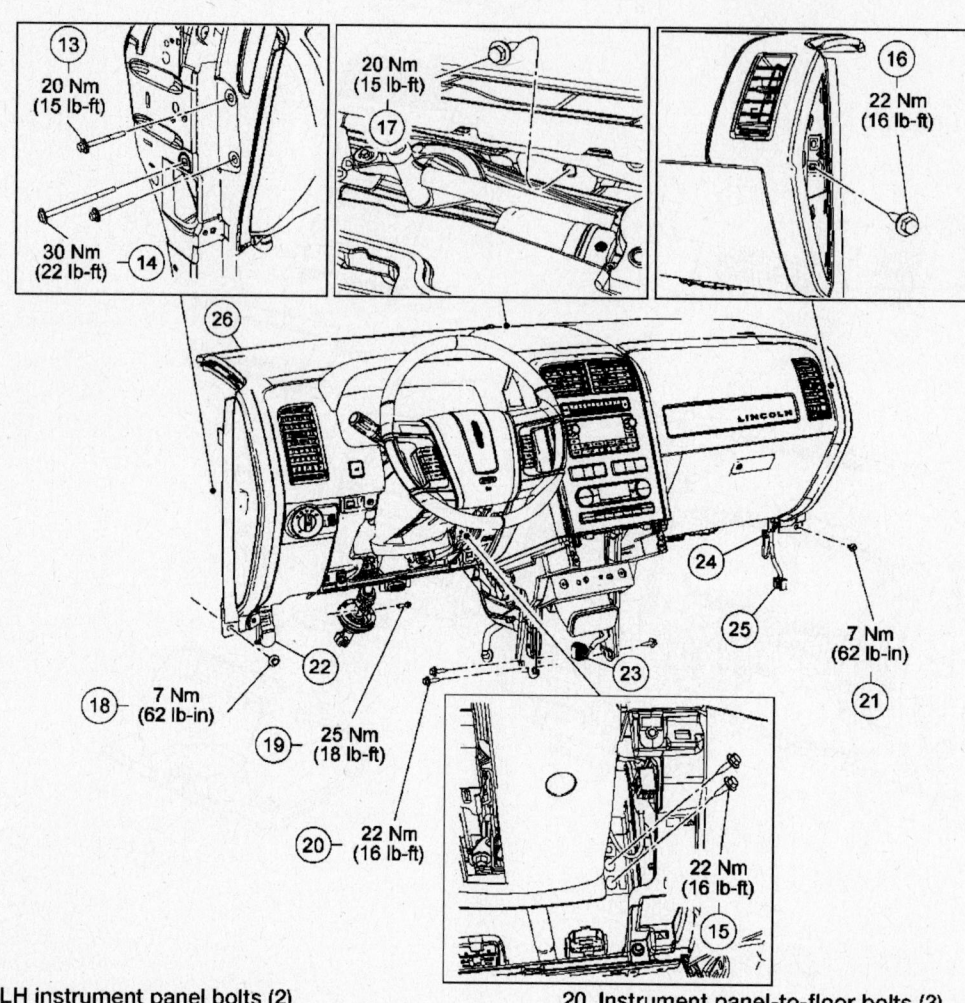

13. LH instrument panel bolts (2)
14. LH instrument panel bolt
15. Instrument panel-to-steering column bracket bolts (2)
16. RH instrument panel cowl side panel bolt
17. Instrument panel-to-front of dash bolt
18. LH instrument panel-to-body bolt
19. Steering column pinch bolt

20. Instrument panel-to-floor bolts (3)
21. RH instrument panel-to-body bolt
22. LH instrument panel electrical connectors
23. Restraints Control Module (RCM) electrical connector.
24. Antenna lead-in
25. RH instrument panel electrical connector
26. Instrument panel

22086_EDGE_G0267

Fig. 226 Exploded view of the instrument panel (2 of 2)—MKX

36. Remove the bolt from the RH instrument panel cowl side panel.

37. Remove the bolt and the hood opening handle. Position the handle aside.

✷✷ WARNING

To avoid damage to the instrument panel, this next step requires the help of an assistant.

38. Remove the instrument panel, with the aid of an assistant.

To install:

39. Installation is the reverse of the removal procedure, noting the following tightening specifications:

a. Instrument panel-to-body bolts (both sides): 7 Nm (62 inch lbs.)

b. RH instrument panel cowl side panel: 22 Nm (16 ft. lbs.)

c. Steering column bracket bolts: 22 Nm (16 ft. lbs.)

d. LH door inside bolts: 20 Nm (15 ft. lbs.)

e. Inside LH door Torx® bolt: 30 Nm (22 ft. lbs.)

f. Front of dash bolt: 20 Nm (15 ft. lbs.)

g. Steering column pinch bolt: 25 Nm (18 ft. lbs.)

h. Instrument panel brace-to-floor bolts (both sides): 22 Nm (16 ft. lbs.)

STEERING

POWER STEERING GEAR

REMOVAL & INSTALLATION

See Figures 227 and 228.

> ❉❉ **WARNING**
>
> **When repairing the power steering system, care should be taken to prevent the entry of contaminants or premature failure of the power steering components may result.**

1. Remove the stabilizer bar.
2. Remove the power steering pressure line-to-steering gear banjo bolt. Discard the 2 seals.
3. Release the clamp and disconnect the return hose from the steering gear.
4. Remove the 2 bolts and the steering gear heat shield.
5. Remove the 3 power steering pressure line-to-steering gear bracket bolts.
6. Remove and discard the 4 steering gear bolts.
7. Remove the steering gear.

To install:

8. Position the steering gear and tighten the 4 steering gear bolts to 103 Nm (76 ft. lbs.) in the sequence shown.

> ❉❉ **WARNING**
>
> **New seals must be installed any time the power steering pressure line is**

disconnected from the power steering pump and/or the steering gear or a fluid leak may occur.

9. Install the power steering pressure line-to-steering gear banjo bolt. Tighten to 48 Nm (35 ft. lbs.).
10. Install the 3 power steering pressure line-to-steering gear bracket bolts. Tighten to 9 Nm (80 inch lbs.).
11. Release the clamp and connect the return hose to the steering gear.
12. When installing a new steering gear, install a new steering gear turn tube heat wrap.
13. Install the steering gear heat shield and the 2 bolts. Tighten to 6 Nm (53 inch lbs.).

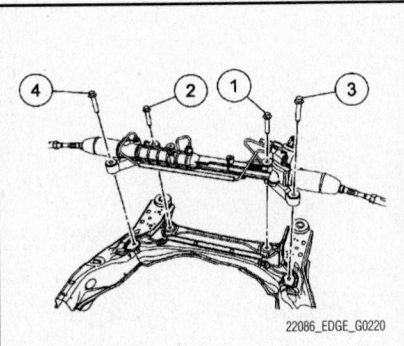

Fig. 228 Steering gear bolt tightening sequence

14. Install the stabilizer bar.
15. Fill the power steering system, as outlined under Power Steering Pump, Bleeding.

POWER STEERING PUMP

REMOVAL & INSTALLATION

See Figures 229 through 231.

> ❉❉ **WARNING**
>
> **When working on the power steering system, do not let any contaminants enter the system or premature failure of the power steering components may occur.**

1. Raise and safely support the vehicle.
2. Using a suitable suction device, siphon the power steering fluid from the power steering fluid reservoir.
3. Remove the RH inner fender splash shield.
4. Using the special tool, disengage the power steering pump belt from the power steering pump pulley and position it aside:
   a. Install the removal tool between the belt and the pulley and turn the crankshaft bolt clockwise to disengage the belt.
5. For All wheel drive (AWD) vehicles, remove the 4 bolts and position the driveshaft aside.
6. Using a suitable jack, support the rear of the subframe.
7. Remove the 2 nuts, 4 bolts and the subframe support brackets.
8. Remove the 2 middle subframe nuts.
9. Lower the rear of the subframe.

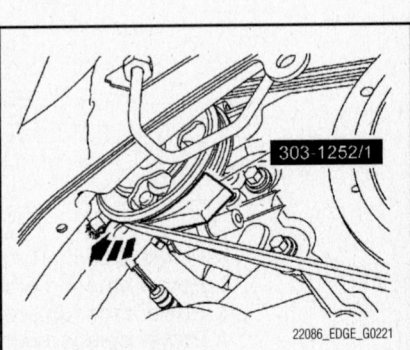

Fig. 229 Install the removal tool between the belt and the pulley and turn the crankshaft bolt clockwise to disengage the belt

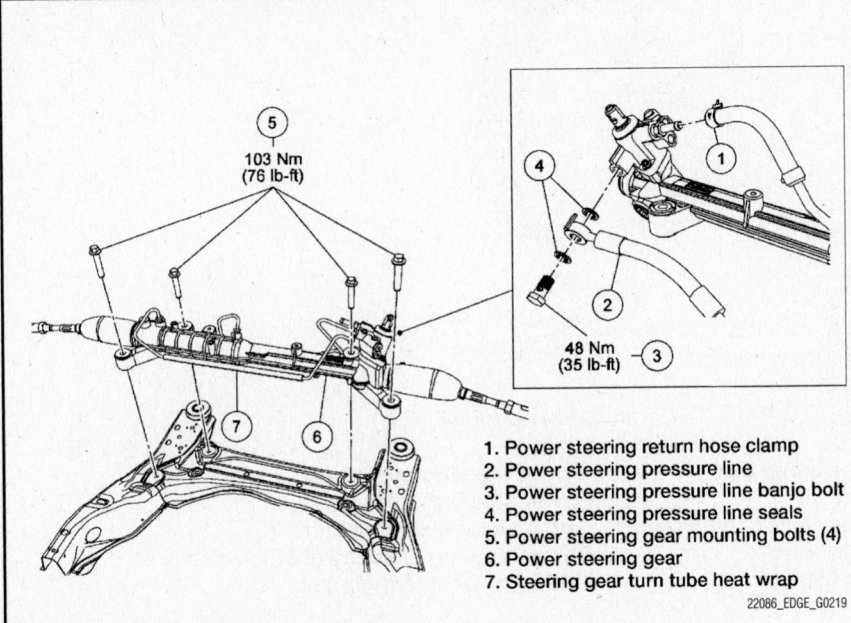

1. Power steering return hose clamp
2. Power steering pressure line
3. Power steering pressure line banjo bolt
4. Power steering pressure line seals
5. Power steering gear mounting bolts (4)
6. Power steering gear
7. Steering gear turn tube heat wrap

22086_EDGE_G0219

Fig. 227 Exploded view of the steering gear mounting

10. Release the clamp and disconnect the power steering pump supply hose from the power steering pump.

11. Disconnect the Power Steering Pressure (PSP) switch electrical connector.

12. Remove the power steering pressure line banjo bolt and disconnect the line from the power steering pump. Discard the 2 seals.

13. Remove the 3 power steering pump bolts and the power steering pump.

To install:

14. Position the power steering pump and install the 3 bolts. Tighten to 24 Nm (18 ft. lbs.).

☀ WARNING
New seals must be installed any time the power steering pressure line is disconnected from the power steering pump or a fluid leak may occur.

15. Position the power steering pressure line and install the banjo bolt and seals. Tighten to 48 Nm (35 ft. lbs.).

16. Connect the PSP switch electrical connector.

17. Connect the power steering pump supply hose and secure the clamp.

18. Using the jack, raise the rear of the subframe.

19. Install the 2 middle subframe nuts. Tighten to 150 Nm (111 ft. lbs.).

20. Install the 2 nuts, 4 bolts and the subframe support brackets. Tighten the nuts to 150 Nm (111 ft. lbs.). Tighten the bolts to 103 Nm (76 ft. lbs.).

21. For AWD vehicles, position the driveshaft and install the 4 bolts. Tighten to 70 Nm (52 ft. lbs.).

☀ WARNING
After installation, make sure the belt is correctly seated on the crankshaft and power steering pulley or damage to the belt may occur.

22. Using the special tool, install the power steering belt onto the power steering pump pulley:

   a. Position the belt around the special tool and the power steering pump pulley. Make sure that the belt is engaged with the pulley and rotate the crankshaft clockwise to install the belt.

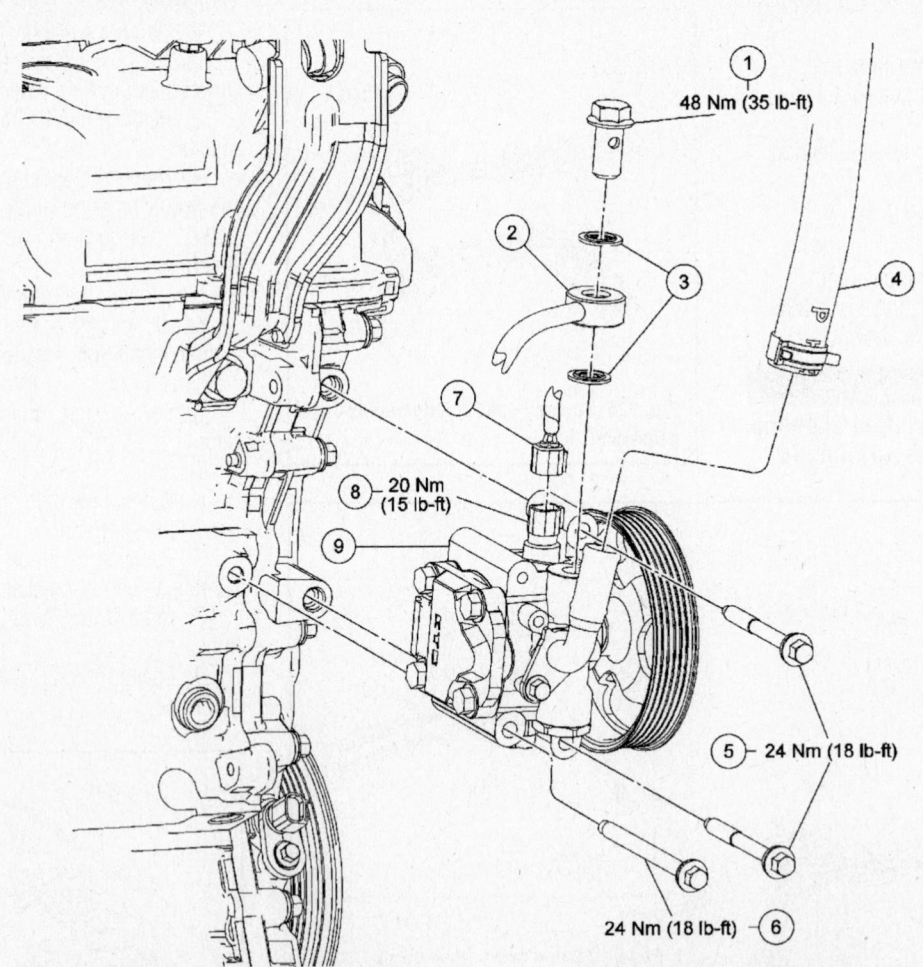

1. Power steering pressure line banjo bolt
2. Power steering pressure line kit
3. Power steering pressure line seals (2 required)
4. Power steering pump supply hose
5. Power steering pump bolts (2 required)
6. Power steering pump bolt
7. Power steering pressure switch electrical connector
8. Power steering pressure (PSP) switch
9 3A696 Power steering pump

22086_EDGE_G0223

Fig. 230 Exploded view of the power steering pump mounting

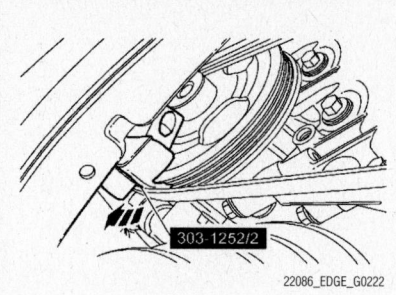

Fig. 231 Position the belt around the special tool and the power steering pump pulley. Make sure that the belt is engaged with the pulley and rotate the crankshaft clockwise to install the belt

23. Install the RH inner fender splash shield.

24. Fill the power steering system, as outlined under Bleeding in this section.

BLEEDING

❊❊ WARNING

If the air is not purged from the power steering system correctly, premature power steering pump failure can result. The condition can occur on pre-delivery vehicles with evidence of aerated fluid or on vehicles that have had steering component repairs.

1. Remove the power steering pump reservoir cap.

2. Tightly install the evacuation cap to the power steering pump reservoir.

3. Install the hose from the fill adapter manifold tee to the evacuation cap on the power steering pump reservoir.

4. Install the vacuum pump to the fill adapter manifold control valve.

5. Install the hose to the opposite fill adapter manifold control valve and submerge the open end of the hose into a container of new power steering fluid.

➡**The fill adapter manifold control valves are in the open position when the point of the handles face the center of the fill adapter manifold.**

6. Close the fill adapter manifold control valve connected to the power steering fluid container.

7. Open the fill adapter manifold control valve connected to the vacuum pump.

8. Using the vacuum pump, apply 68-85 kPa (20-25 in-Hg) of vacuum to the power steering system.

9. Observe the vacuum gauge for 30 seconds.

10. If the vacuum gauge reading drops more than 3 kPa (0.88 in-Hg), correct any leaks in the power steering system or the filling tools before proceeding.

➡**The vacuum pump gauge reading will drop slightly during this step.**

11. Slowly open the fill adapter manifold control valve connected to the power steering fluid container until power steering fluid completely fills the hose.

12. Close the fill adapter manifold control valve connected to the power steering fluid container.

13. Using the vacuum pump, apply 68-85 kPa (20-25 in-Hg) of vacuum to the power steering system.

14. Close the fill adapter manifold - control valve connected to the vacuum pump.

15. Slowly open the fill adapter manifold control valve connected to the power steering fluid container.

16. When the power steering fluid has drained from the hose connected to the power steering fluid container, close the fill adapter manifold control valve connected to the power steering fluid container.

17. Remove the tools from the vehicle.

18. Install the power steering reservoir cap.

❊❊ WARNING

Do not hold the steering wheel against the stops for more than 3 to 5 seconds at a time. Damage to the power steering pump can occur.

➡**There will be a slight drop in the power steering fluid level in the power steering fluid reservoir when the engine is started.**

19. Start the engine and turn the steering wheel from stop-to-stop.

20. If equipped with Hydro-Boost®, apply the brake pedal twice.

21. Turn the ignition switch to the **OFF** position.

❊❊ WARNING

Do not overfill the reservoir.

22. Remove the power steering reservoir cap and fill the reservoir.

23. Install the power steering reservoir cap

SUSPENSION

LOWER CONTROL ARM

REMOVAL & INSTALLATION

See Figure 232.

❊❊ WARNING

Suspension fasteners are critical parts because they affect performance of vital parts and systems and their failure can result in major service expense. A new part with the same part number must be installed if installation becomes necessary. NEVER use a replacement part of lesser quality or substitute design. Torque values must be adhered to during reassembly to ensure correct retention of these parts.

1. Raise and safely support the vehicle.

2. Remove the wheel and tire assembly.

3. Remove and discard the stabilizer bar link lower nut.

4. Remove and discard the lower ball joint nut and bolt.

❊❊ WARNING

Do not tighten any suspension bushing fasteners until the installation procedure is complete and the weight of the vehicle is resting on the wheel and tire assemblies.

5. Remove the lower arm-to-frame forward bolt and spacer. Discard the bolt.

FRONT SUSPENSION

6. Remove the 2 lower arm-to-frame rearward bolts and remove the lower arm. Discard the bolt.

To install:

❊❊ WARNING

Do not tighten any suspension bushing fasteners until the installation procedure is complete and the weight of the vehicle is resting on the wheel and tire assemblies.

7. Installation is the reverse of the removal procedure, noting the following tightening specifications:

　a. Lower arm-to-frame rearward bolts: 80 Nm (59 ft. lbs.)

　b. Lower arm-to-frame forward bolt: 50 Nm (111 ft. lbs.)

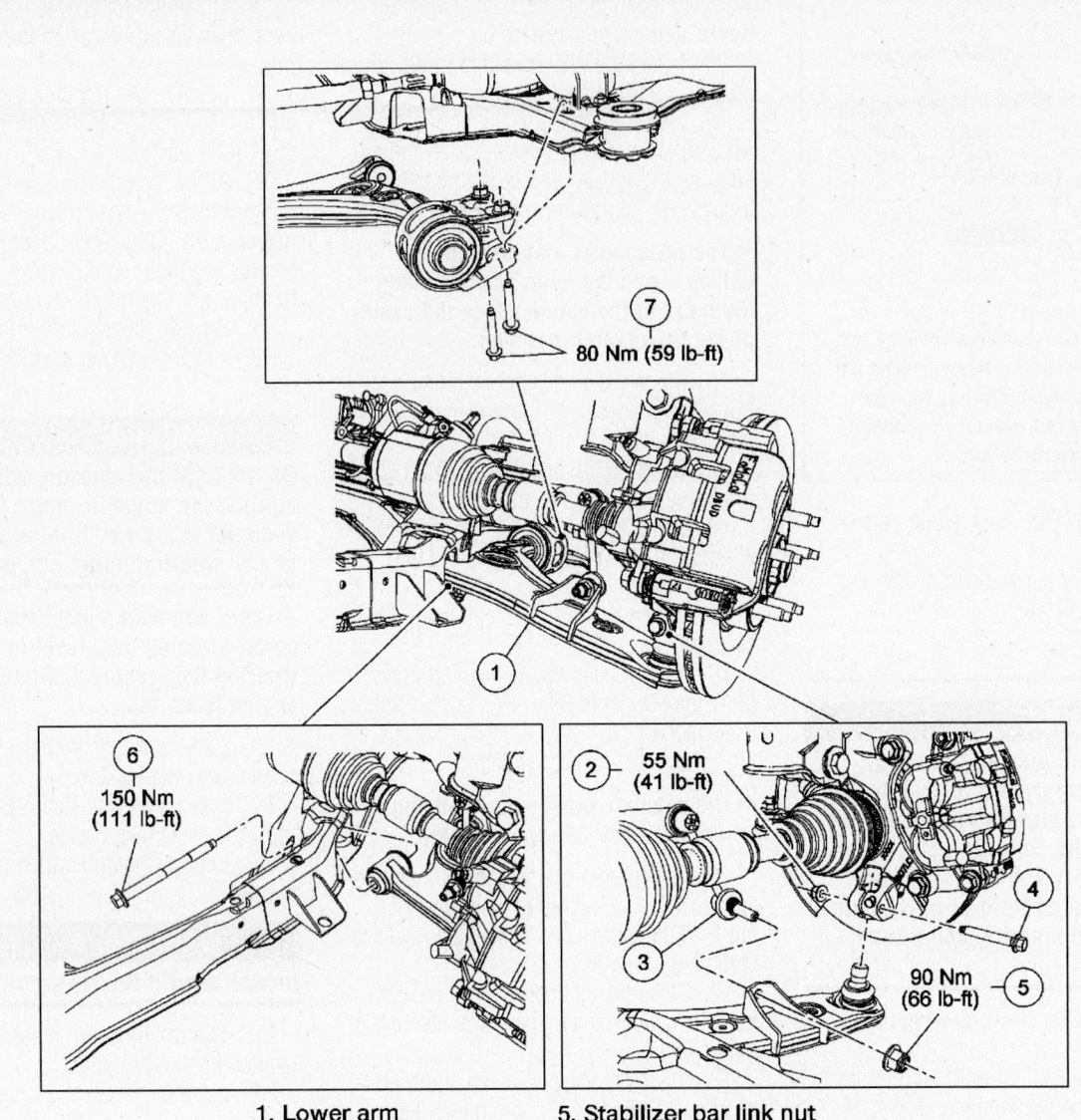

1. Lower arm
2. Lower ball joint nut
3. Stabilizer bar link
4. Lower ball joint bolt
5. Stabilizer bar link nut
6. Lower arm-to-frame forward bolt
7. Lower arm-to-frame
   rearward bolts (2 required)

22086_EDGE_G0191

Fig. 232 Exploded view of the lower control arm and related components

c. Lower ball joint nut and bolt: 55 Nm (41 ft. lbs.)

d. Stabilizer bar link lower nut: 90 Nm (66 ft. lbs.)

8. Check and if necessary, adjust the alignment.

MACPHERSON STRUT

REMOVAL & INSTALLATION

See Figure 233.

❊❊ **WARNING**

Suspension fasteners are critical parts because they affect perfor-mance of vital parts and systems and their failure can result in major service expense. A new part with the same part number must be installed if installation becomes necessary. NEVER use a replacement part of lesser quality or substitute design. Torque values must be adhered to during reassembly to ensure correct retention of these parts.

1. Remove and discard the 4 shock absorber upper mount nuts.

2. Remove the wheel and tire assembly.

3. Remove the shock absorber lower nuts, flag bolts and the shock absorber and spring assembly. Discard the nuts and flag bolts.

To install:

4. Installation is the reverse of the removal procedure, noting the following tightening specifications:

a. Shock absorber lower nuts and flag bolts: 225 Nm (166 ft. lbs.)

b. Shock absorber upper mount nuts: 30 Nm (22 ft. lbs.)

5. Check and if necessary, adjust the alignment

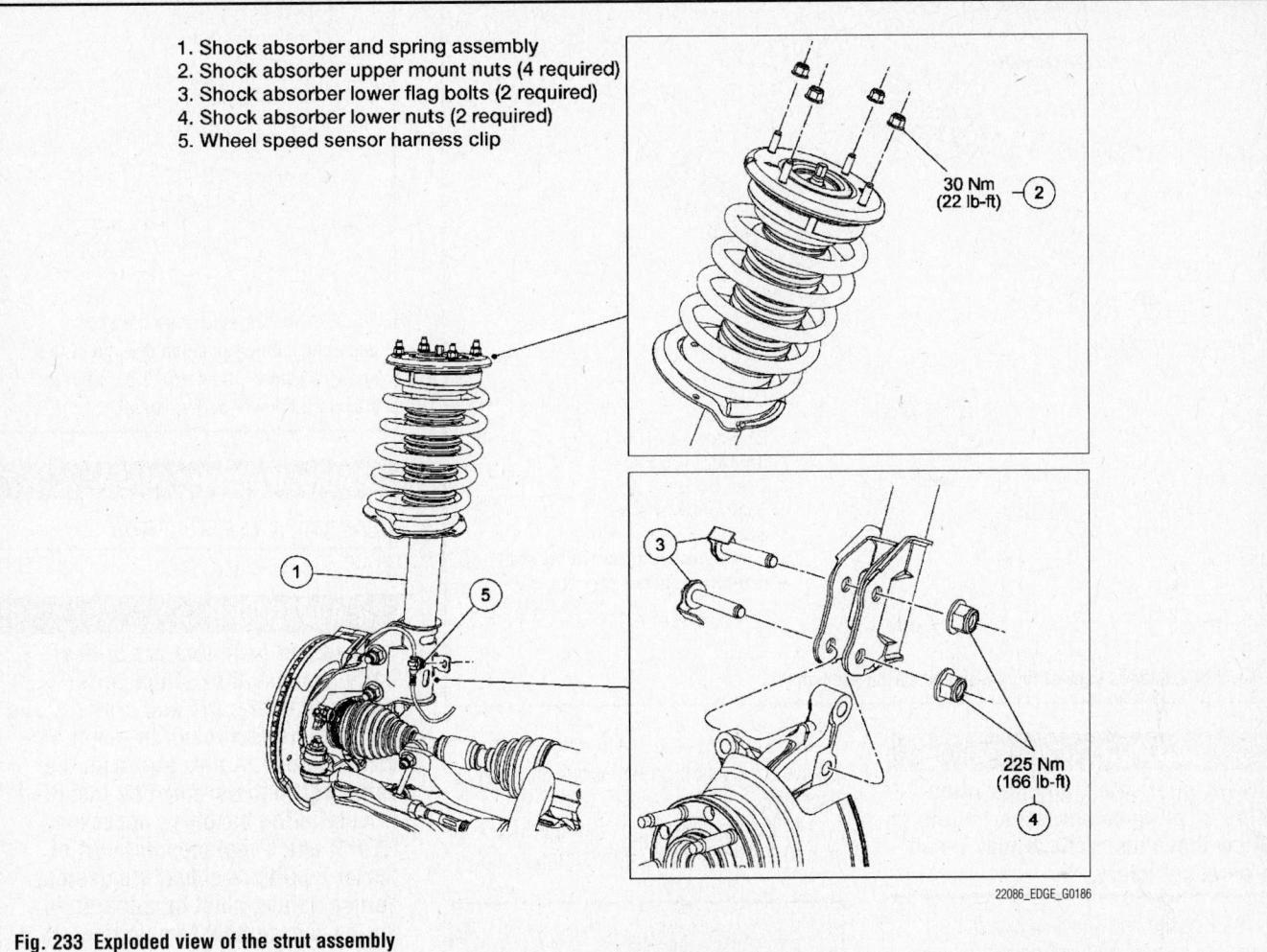

1. Shock absorber and spring assembly
2. Shock absorber upper mount nuts (4 required)
3. Shock absorber lower flag bolts (2 required)
4. Shock absorber lower nuts (2 required)
5. Wheel speed sensor harness clip

30 Nm
(22 lb-ft)

225 Nm
(166 lb-ft)

22086_EDGE_G0186

Fig. 233 Exploded view of the strut assembly

OVERHAUL

See Figures 234 through 237.

✳ CAUTION

These vehicles are equipped with gas-pressurized shock absorbers which will extend unassisted. Do not apply heat or flame to the shock absorbers during removal or component servicing. Failure to follow these instructions may result in personal injury.

✳ CAUTION

The spring is under extreme compression, care must be taken at all times. Failure to follow this instruction may result in personal injury.

✳ CAUTION

The coil spring is coated with long-term corrosion protective paint. Do not damage the paint during component servicing.

✳ CAUTION

Suspension fasteners are critical parts because they affect performance of vital parts and systems and their failure can result in major service expense. A new part with the same part number must be installed if installation becomes necessary. Do not use a replacement part of lesser quality or substitute design. Torque values must be used as specified during reassembly to make sure of correct retention of these parts.

1. Remove the MacPherson Strut (shock absorber and spring assembly), as outlined in this section

✳ CAUTION

Always wear safety goggles when using a spring compressor. Failure to follow these instructions may result in personal injury.

2. Position the shock and spring assembly in a suitable spring compressor.

3. Compress the spring enough to relieve the tension on the shock and spring assembly.

✳ WARNING

Never use an impact wrench on the shock absorber rod nut.

➡ Use the holding feature to prevent the shock absorber rod from turning while removing the nut.

4. While holding the shock absorber rod, remove and discard the rod nut.
5. Remove the shock absorber assembly and spring lower seat.
6. Remove the dust boot and jounce bumper.
7. Remove the shock absorber upper mount and spring upper seat.
8. Carefully release the tension on the spring compressor and remove the spring.

To assemble:

9. Install the lower spring seat, jounce bumper and dust boot onto the shock absorber.

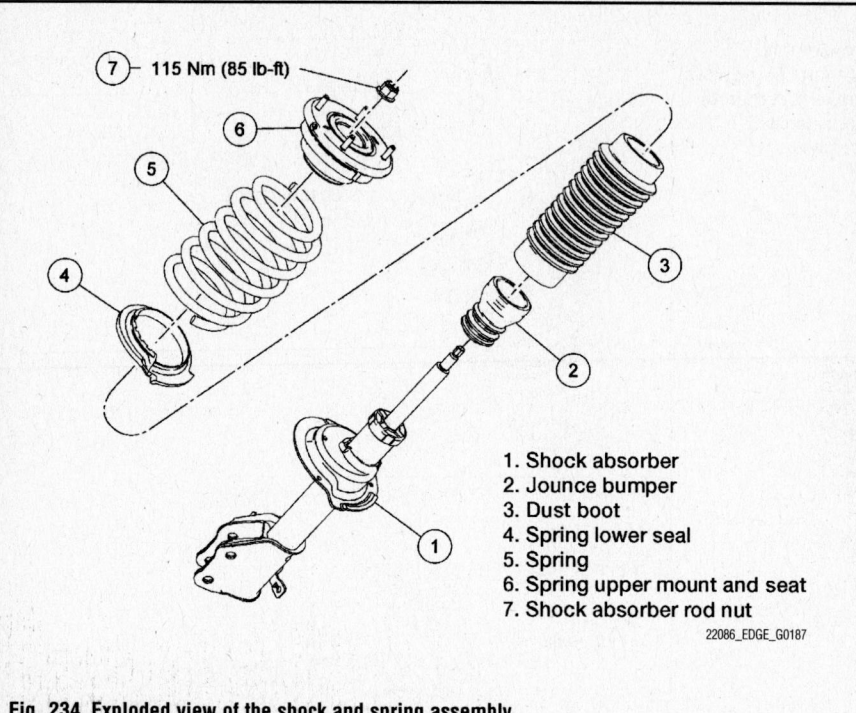

1. Shock absorber
2. Jounce bumper
3. Dust boot
4. Spring lower seal
5. Spring
6. Spring upper mount and seat
7. Shock absorber rod nut

22086_EDGE_G0187

Fig. 234 Exploded view of the shock and spring assembly

✳✳ CAUTION

Always wear safety goggles when using a spring compressor. Failure to follow these instructions may result in personal injury.

10. Position the shock and spring assembly in a suitable spring compressor.

11. Install the spring, shock absorber upper mount and spring upper seat.

12. Align the arrow on the upper mount perpendicular to the center of the shock absorber lower mount.

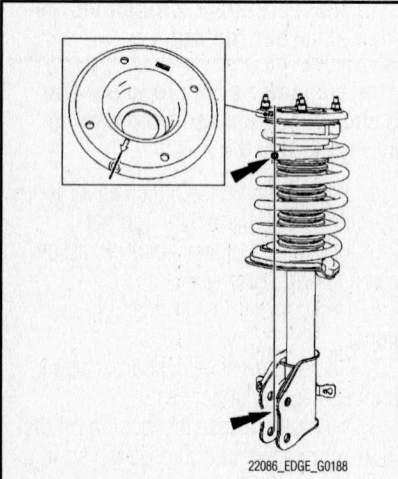

22086_EDGE_G0188

Fig. 235 Align the arrow on the upper mount perpendicular to the center of the shock absorber lower mount

13. Compress the spring enough to relieve the tension on the shock and spring assembly.

14. Position the end of spring within 0–10 mm (0–0.39 in) of the upper spring mount.

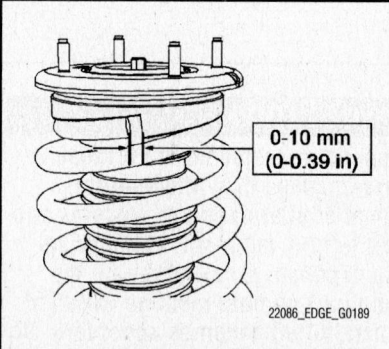

0–10 mm
(0–0.39 in)

22086_EDGE_G0189

Fig. 236 Position the end of spring within 0–10 mm (0–0.39 in) of the upper spring mount

➡ Before tightening the shock absorber rod nut, position the end of the spring within 0–10 mm (0–0.39 in) of the step on the lower spring mount.

➡ Use the holding feature to prevent the shock absorber rod from turning while installing the nut.

15. Install the shock absorber rod nut and tighten to 115 Nm (85 ft. lbs.).

16. Release the tension on the shock and spring assembly.

17. Install the strut assembly

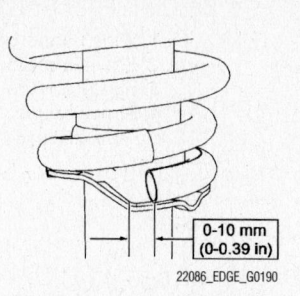

0–10 mm
(0–0.39 in)

22086_EDGE_G0190

Fig. 237 Before tightening the shock absorber rod nut, position the end of the spring within 0–10 mm (0–0.39 in) of the step on the lower spring mount

STABILIZER BAR

REMOVAL & INSTALLATION

See Figures 238 and 239.

✳✳ WARNING

Suspension fasteners are critical parts because they affect performance of vital parts and systems and their failure can result in major service expense. A new part with the same part number must be installed if installation becomes necessary. NEVER use a replacement part of lesser quality or substitute design. Torque values must be adhered to during reassembly to ensure correct retention of these parts.

1. Raise and safely support the vehicle.

2. Remove the wheel and tire assembly.

3. Remove the lower steering shaft coupler bolt and disconnect the coupler from the steering gear.

4. Matchmark the installed position of the front subframe to the underbody at the mounting locations.

5. Remove the RH fender splash shield.

6. Remove the 3 pushpin fasteners, the 7 screws and the front splash shield.

7. Remove the 3 RH front lower bumper-to-subframe nuts.

8. Remove the 3 LH front lower bumper-to-subframe nuts and separate the lower bumper from the subframe.

9. Remove the power steering cooler hose bracket bolt.

10. Loosen the Y-pipe clamp and disconnect the 2 exhaust hangers.

11. Remove the 2 nuts and separate the flex pipe from the Y-pipe assembly.

12. For All Wheel Drive (AWD) vehicles, matchmark the driveshaft, remove the 4 bolts and position the driveshaft aside.

➡Use the holding feature to prevent the ball stud from turning while removing or installing the stabilizer bar link nuts.

13. Remove the stabilizer link upper and lower nuts and the stabilizer links. Discard the nuts.

14. Remove the 2 outer tie-rod end nuts (1 each side).

15. Using the special tool, separate the outer tie-rod ends from the wheel knuckles.

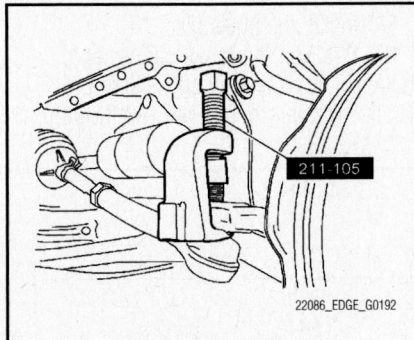

211-105

22086_EDGE_G0192

Fig. 238 Use a suitable tool to separate the outer tie-rod ends from the knuckles—right side shown, left side similar

16. Remove the 2 lower ball joint bolts and nuts and separate the lower ball joints from the wheel knuckles. Discard the bolts and nuts.

17. Remove the nut and the engine roll restrictor heat shield.

18. Remove the engine roll restrictor-to-subframe bolt.

19. Using a suitable jack, support the subframe. Support the subframe in the center rear area of the subframe.

20. Remove the 2 nuts, 4 bolts and the subframe support brackets. Discard the nuts and bolts.

21. Remove and discard the 4 front subframe nuts.

22. Using the jack, lower the subframe about 76.2 mm (3 in).

23. Remove the 4 bolts, 2 stabilizer bar brackets and bushings. Discard the bolts.

24. Remove the stabilizer bar.

To install:

➡During installation, the subframe brackets are loosely installed with the support bracket bolts.

➡Align the matchmarks made during removal, then tighten the rear subframe nuts prior to tightening the support bracket bolts.

25. Installation is the reverse of the

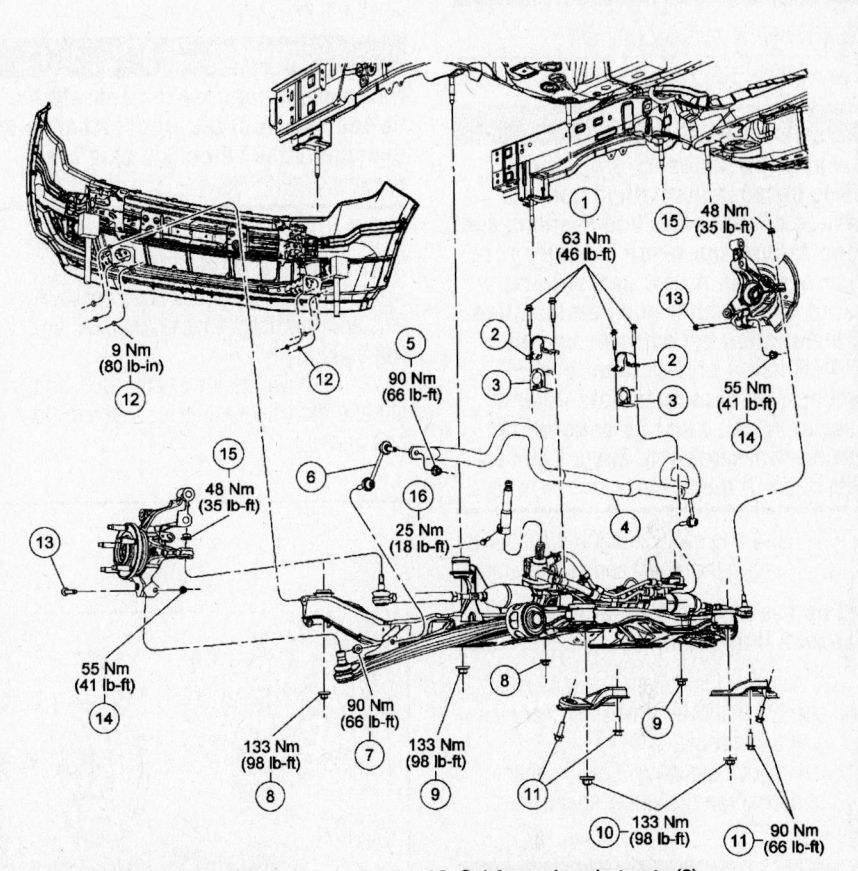

1. Stabilizer bar bracket bolts (4 required)
2. Stabilizer bar brackets
3. Stabilizer bar bushings
4. Stabilizer bar
5. Stabilizer bar link upper nut
6. Stabilizer bar link (2 required)
7. Stabilizer bar link lower nut
8. Front subframe mounting nuts
9. Front subframe mounting nuts
10. Subframe bracket nuts (2)
11. Subframe bracket bolts (4)
12. Front lower bumper-to-subframe nuts (6)
13. Lower ball joint bolt
14. Lower ball joint nuts
15. Tie-rod end nuts
16. Lower steering shaft coupler bolt

22086_EDGE_G0193

Fig. 239 Exploded view of the stabilizer

removal procedure. Make sure to properly align the components matchmarked during removal, replace any specified fasteners, and note the following tightening specifications:

a. Stabilizer bar bracket bolts and nuts: 63 Nm (46 ft. lbs.)

b. Front subframe nuts: 133 Nm (98 ft. lbs.)

c. Subframe support bracket bolts: 90 Nm (66 ft. lbs.)

d. Subframe support bracket nuts: 133 Nm (98 ft. lbs.)

e. Engine roll restrictor-to-subframe bolt: 90 Nm (66 ft. lbs.)

f. Engine roll restrictor heat shield nut: 11 Nm (8 ft. lbs.)

g. Lower ball joint bolts and nuts: 55 Nm (41 ft. lbs.)

h. Outer tie-rod end nuts (1 each side): 48 Nm (35 ft. lbs.)

i. Stabilizer link upper and lower nuts: 90 Nm (66 ft. lbs.)

j. Driveshaft bolts (AWD vehicles): 70 Nm (52 ft. lbs.)

k. Flex pipe-to-Y-pipe bolts: 40 Nm (30 ft. lbs.)

l. Y-pipe clamp: 40 Nm (30 ft. lbs.)

m. Power steering cooler hose bracket bolt: 9 Nm (80 inch lbs.)

n. Front lower bumper-to-subframe nuts: 9 Nm (80 inch lbs.)

o. Lower steering shaft coupler bolt: 25 Nm (18 ft. lbs.)

26. Check, and if necessary, adjust the alignment

STEERING KNUCKLE

REMOVAL & INSTALLATION

See Figures 238, 240 and 241.

> ※※ **WARNING**
>
> **Suspension fasteners are critical parts because they affect performance of vital parts and systems and their failure can result in major service expense. A new part with the same part number must be installed if installation becomes necessary. NEVER use a replacement part of lesser quality or substitute design. Torque values must be adhered to during reassembly to ensure correct retention of these parts.**

1. Raise and safely support the vehicle.
2. Remove the wheel and tire assembly.

→**Depress the brake pedal to keep the halfshaft from rotating.**

3. Remove the halfshaft nut, halfshaft hub seal and halfshaft washer. Discard the nut, seal and washer.
4. Remove the wheel speed sensor bolt and position the wheel speed sensor aside.

> ※※ **WARNING**
>
> **Do not let the caliper and anchor plate assembly hang from the brake hose or damage to the hose can occur.**

5. Remove the 2 bolts and position the caliper and anchor plate assembly aside.
6. Support the caliper and anchor plate assembly using a piece of wire.
7. Remove the brake disc.
8. Using the special tool, separate the halfshaft from the wheel hub.

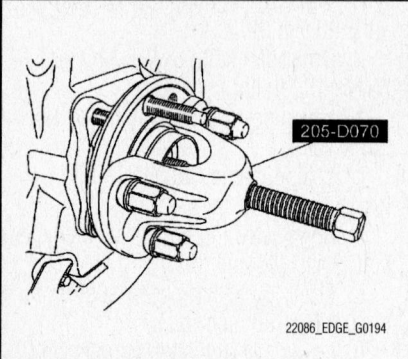

Fig. 240 Use a suitable puller to separate the halfshaft from the hub

22086_EDGE_G0194

9. Remove and discard the tie-rod end cotter pin and nut.

> ※※ **WARNING**
>
> **Never use a hammer to separate the tie-rod end from the wheel knuckle or damage to the wheel knuckle can result.**

10. Using the special tool, separate the tie-rod end from the wheel knuckle.
11. Remove the shock absorber lower nuts and flag bolts. Discard the nuts and flag bolts.
12. Remove the lower ball joint bolt, nut and the wheel knuckle. Discard the bolt and nut.

To install:

13. Position the wheel knuckle and install the lower ball joint bolt and nut. Tighten the nut to 55 Nm (41 ft. lbs.).
14. Install the shock absorber lower nuts and flag bolts. Tighten to 225 Nm (166 ft. lbs.).
15. Position the tie-rod end and install the nut and cotter pin. Tighten to 48 Nm (35 ft. lbs.).
16. Position the wheel speed sensor and install the bolt. Tighten to 7 Nm (62 inch lbs.).
17. Install the brake disc.
18. Position the brake caliper and anchor plate assembly and install the 2 bolts. Tighten to 133 Nm (98 ft. lbs.).

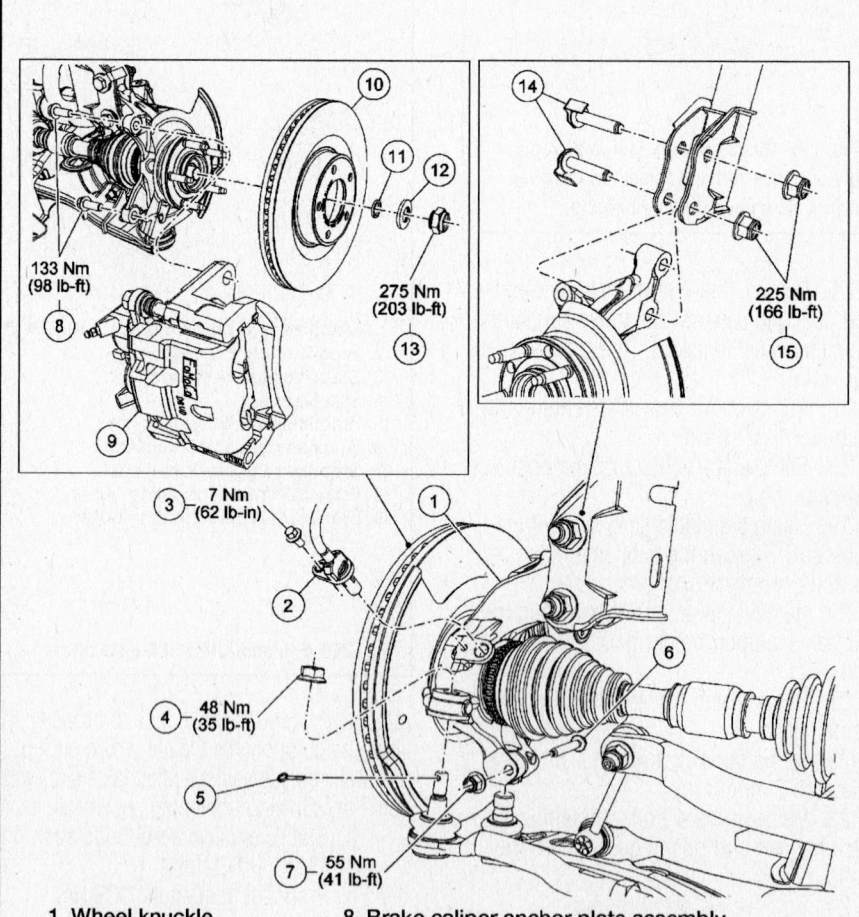

1. Wheel knuckle	8. Brake caliper anchor plate assembly
2. Wheel speed sensor	9. Brake caliper and anchor
3. Wheel speed sensor bolt	10. Brake disc
4. Tie-rod end nut	11. Halfshaft hub seal
5. Tie-rod end cotter pin	12. Halfshaft hub washer
6. Lower ball joint bolt	13. Halfshaft nut
7. Lower ball joint nut	14. Lower shock absorber flag bolts (2 required)

Fig. 241 Exploded view of the steering knuckle and related components

22086_EDGE_G0195

19. Using a suitable installation tool, install the halfshaft into the wheel hub.

✸ WARNING

Never tighten the halfshaft nut with the vehicle on the ground. The nut must be tightened to specification before the vehicle is lowered onto the wheels. Wheel bearing damage will occur if the wheel bearing is loaded with the weight of the vehicle applied.

➡**Apply the brake to keep the halfshaft from rotating.**

20. Install the halfshaft hub seal, washer and nut. Tighten to 225 Nm (185 ft. lbs.).
21. Install the wheel and tire assembly.
22. Check and if necessary, adjust the alignment.

WHEEL HUB AND BEARING

REMOVAL & INSTALLATION
See Figures 242 through 247.

✸ WARNING

Suspension fasteners are critical parts because they affect performance of vital parts and systems and their failure can result in major service expense. A new part with the same part number must be installed if installation becomes necessary. NEVER use a replacement part of lesser quality or substitute design. Torque values must be adhered to during reassembly to ensure correct retention of these parts.

➡**If removing the wheel hub, the wheel bearing must be replaced.**

1. Remove the steering knuckle, as outlined in this section.
2. Using the special tool, press the wheel hub from the wheel bearing.

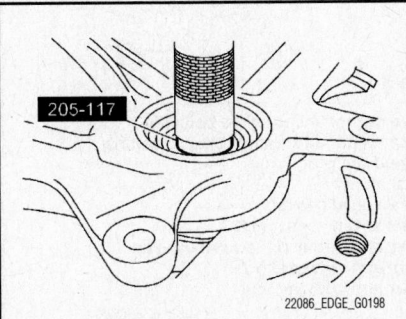

Fig. 242 Using the special tool, press the wheel hub from the wheel bearing

➡**This step may not be necessary if the inner wheel bearing race remains in the wheel knuckle after removing the wheel hub.**

3. Using the special tool, press the inner wheel bearing race from the wheel hub.
4. Remove the snap ring.
5. Using the special tool, press the outer wheel bearing race from the wheel knuckle.

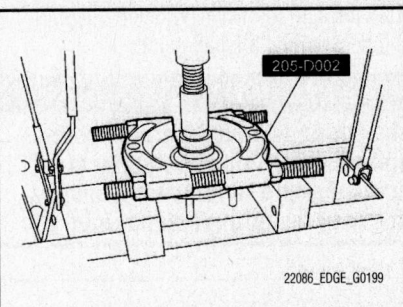

Fig. 243 Using the special tool, press the inner wheel bearing race from the wheel hub

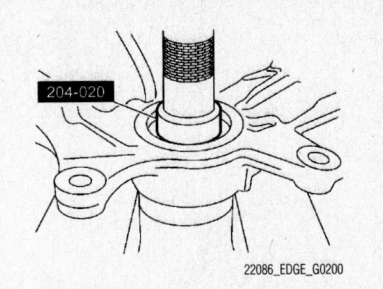

Fig. 244 Using the special tool, press the outer wheel bearing race from the wheel knuckle

To install:

6. Using the special tool, press the wheel bearing into the wheel knuckle.
7. Install the snap ring.
8. Using the special tools, press the wheel hub into the wheel bearing.
9. Install the steering knuckle, as outlined in this section.

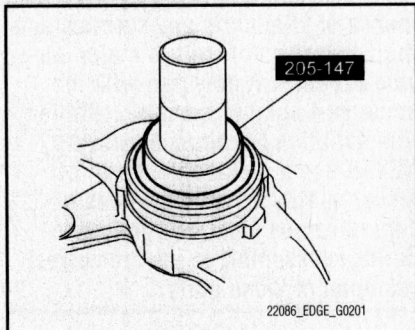

Fig. 246 Using the special tool, press the wheel bearing into the wheel knuckle

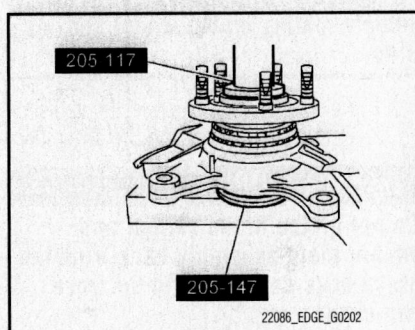

Fig. 247 Using the special tools, press the wheel hub into the wheel bearing

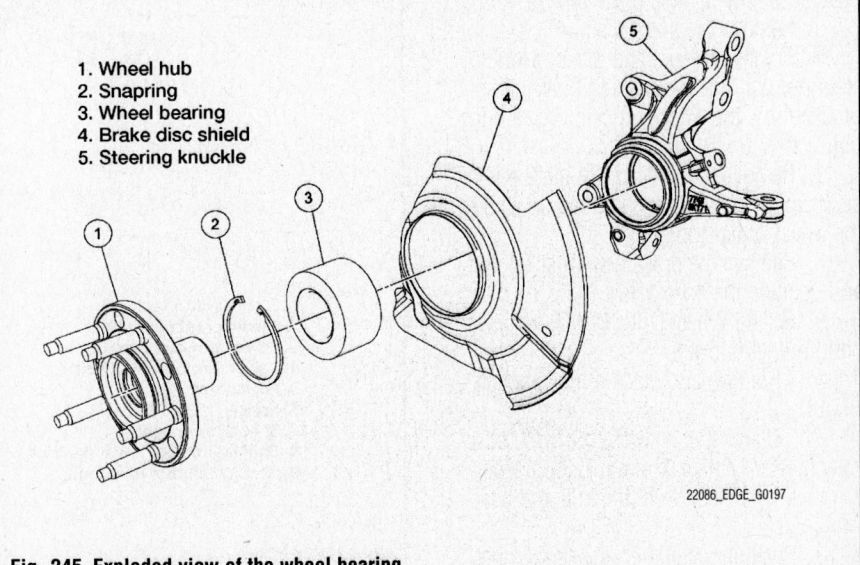

1. Wheel hub
2. Snapring
3. Wheel bearing
4. Brake disc shield
5. Steering knuckle

Fig. 245 Exploded view of the wheel bearing

SUSPENSION

COIL SPRING

REMOVAL & INSTALLATION
See Figures 248 through 250.

❋ WARNING

Suspension fasteners are critical parts because they affect performance of vital parts and systems and their failure can result in major service expense. A new part with the same part number must be installed if installation becomes necessary. NEVER use a replacement part of lesser quality or substitute design. Torque values must be adhered to during reassembly to ensure correct retention of these parts.

❋ WARNING

Suspension bushing fasteners must be tightened with the weight of the vehicle resting on the wheel and tires.

1. Raise and safely support the vehicle.
2. Remove the wheel and tire assembly.

❋ WARNING

Do not let the brake caliper and anchor plate assembly hang from the brake hose or damage to the hose can occur.

3. Remove the 2 anchor plate bolts and position the brake caliper and anchor plate assembly aside.
4. Support the brake caliper and anchor plate assembly using a piece of wire.
5. Remove the brake disc.
6. Remove the nut and disconnect the stabilizer bar link and parking brake cable bracket from the wheel knuckle. Discard the nut.
7. Remove the bolt, unclip the 2 retainers from the upper arm and position aside the wheel speed sensor.
8. Remove the brake hose bracket bolt and position the hose aside.
9. For All Wheel Drive (AWD) vehicles, perform the following:
   a. Remove and discard the halfshaft nut.
   b. Using special tool 205-D070 or equivalent halfshaft removal tool, separate the halfshaft from the hub and bearing.
10. Position a suitable jackstand under the lower arm.

11. Remove and discard the lower shock nut and flag bolt.
12. Remove and discard the upper arm outboard bolt and nut.
13. Remove and discard the toe link outboard bolt and nut.
14. Lower and remove the jackstand.
15. For AWD vehicles, position the halfshaft through the wheel knuckle opening and secure the halfshaft aside.

❋ CAUTION

The spring is under extreme compression, care must be taken at all times. Failure to follow this instruction may result in personal injury.

16. Position the jackstand under the lower arm.
17. Remove and discard the lower arm outboard bolt and nut.

❋ CAUTION

The spring is under extreme compression, care must be taken at all times. Failure to follow this instruction may result in personal injury.

18. Pull outward on the wheel knuckle while lowering the jack stand and remove the spring.
19. Inspect the spring upper and lower seats, install new seats as necessary.

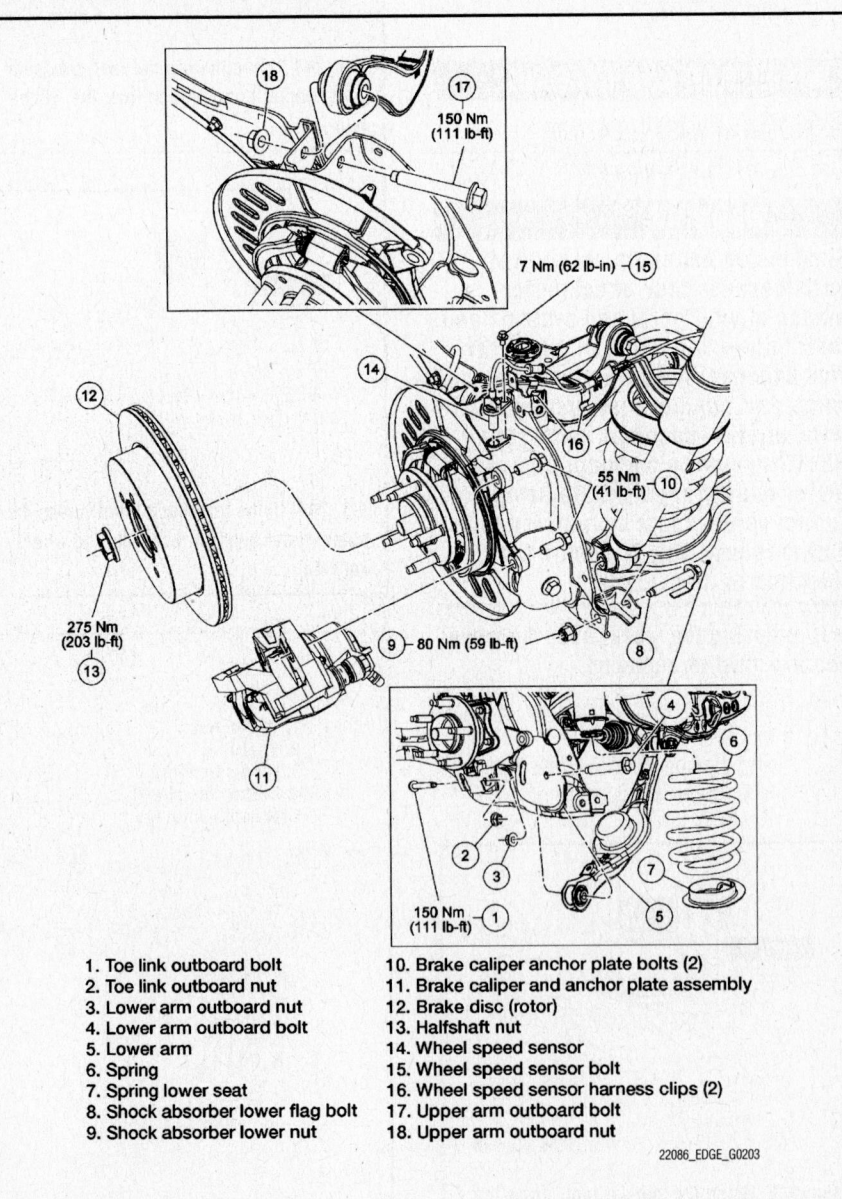

1. Toe link outboard bolt
2. Toe link outboard nut
3. Lower arm outboard nut
4. Lower arm outboard bolt
5. Lower arm
6. Spring
7. Spring lower seat
8. Shock absorber lower flag bolt
9. Shock absorber lower nut
10. Brake caliper anchor plate bolts (2)
11. Brake caliper and anchor plate assembly
12. Brake disc (rotor)
13. Halfshaft nut
14. Wheel speed sensor
15. Wheel speed sensor bolt
16. Wheel speed sensor harness clips (2)
17. Upper arm outboard bolt
18. Upper arm outboard nut

22086_EDGE_G0203

Fig. 248 Exploded view of the rear spring and related components

Suspension bushing fasteners must be tightened with the weight of the vehicle resting on the wheels and tires.

➡️**Use a suitable installation tool when installing the halfshaft into the wheel hub.**

To install:

20. Installation is the reverse of the removal procedure, noting the following:

    a. If removed, position the spring lower seat into the lower arm aligning the recess in the seat with the projection on the lower arm.

    b. During installation, position the spring onto the lower arm with the end of the spring 0–10 mm (0–0.39 in) from the step on the spring seat.

21. Tighten the retainers as follows:

    a. Lower arm outboard bolt and nut: 80 Nm (59 ft. lbs.), plus an additional 90 degrees

    b. Toe link outboard bolt and nut: 150 Nm (111 ft. lbs.)

    c. Upper arm outboard bolt and nut: 150 Nm (111 ft. lbs.)

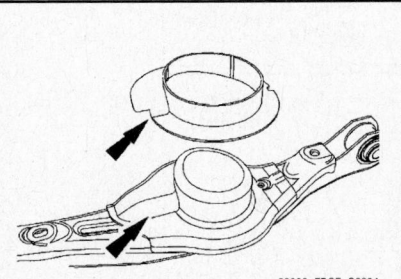

22086_EDGE_G0204

Fig. 249 If removed, position the spring lower seat into the lower arm aligning the recess in the seat with the projection on the lower arm

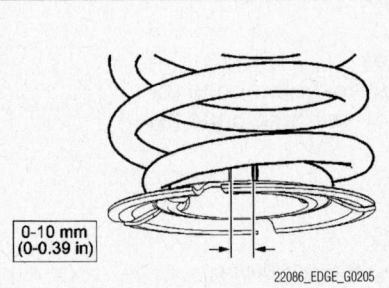

0-10 mm
(0-0.39 in)

22086_EDGE_G0205

Fig. 250 During installation, position the spring onto the lower arm with the end of the spring 0–10 mm (0–0.39 in) from the step on the spring seat

    d. Lower shock nut and flag bolt: 80 Nm (59 ft. lbs.)

    e. Halfshaft nut (AWD models): 275 (203 ft. lbs.)

    f. Brake hose bracket bolt: 7 Nm (62 inch lbs.)

    g. Wheel speed sensor: 7 Nm (62 inch lbs.)

    h. Stabilizer bar link and parking brake cable bracket: 35 Nm (26 ft. lbs.).

    i. Brake caliper and anchor plate assembly bolts: 55 Nm (41 ft. lbs.)

22. Check, and if necessary, align the vehicle.

KNUCKLE

REMOVAL & INSTALLATION

See Figure 251.

Suspension fasteners are critical parts because they affect performance of vital parts and systems and their failure can result in major service expense. A new part with the same part number must be installed if installation becomes necessary. NEVER use a replacement part of lesser quality or substitute design. Torque values must be adhered to during reassembly to ensure correct retention of these parts.

1. Raise and safely support the vehicle.
2. Remove the wheel and tire assembly.

Never let the brake caliper and anchor plate assembly hang from the brake hose or damage to the hose can occur.

3. Remove the 2 anchor plate bolts and position the brake caliper and anchor plate assembly aside.
4. Support the brake caliper and anchor plate assembly using a piece of wire.
5. Remove the brake disc.
6. Disconnect the parking brake shoe retaining spring and remove the spring and brake shoe assembly.
7. Remove the 2 bolts and disconnect the parking brake cable.
8. Remove the nut and disconnect the stabilizer bar link and parking brake cable bracket from the wheel knuckle. Discard the nut.
9. Remove the bolt, unclip the 2 retainers and position aside the wheel speed sensor.

10. Remove the brake hose bracket bolt.
11. For All Wheel Drive (AWD) vehicles, perform the following:

    a. Remove and discard the halfshaft nut.

    b. Using special tool 205-D070, or equivalent front hub removal tool, separate the halfshaft from the wheel bearing and wheel hub.

12. Position a suitable jackstand under the lower arm.
13. Remove and discard the lower shock bolt and nut.
14. Remove and discard the upper arm outboard bolt and nut.
15. Remove and discard the lower arm outboard bolt and nut.
16. Remove and discard the toe link outboard bolt and nut.
17. For AWD vehicles, position the halfshaft through the wheel knuckle opening and secure the halfshaft aside.
18. Remove the 5 wheel knuckle bracket-to-frame bolts and the wheel knuckle. Discard the bolts.

To install:

Suspension bushing fasteners must be tightened with the weight of the vehicle resting on the wheel and tires.

19. Position the wheel knuckle and install the 5 wheel knuckle bracket-to-frame bolts. Tighten the bolts to 47 Nm (35 ft. lbs.).
20. For AWD vehicles, position the halfshaft into the wheel bearing and hub.
21. Position the wheel knuckle onto the toe link and lower arm.

➡️**Do not tighten the lower arm forward bolt at this time.**

22. Loosely install the lower arm forward bolt.

➡️**Do not tighten the toe link forward bolt at this time.**

23. Loosely install the toe link forward bolt.

➡️**Do not tighten the shock absorber lower bolt at this time.**

24. Loosely install the shock absorber lower bolt.
25. Using the jack, raise the suspension and install the upper arm outboard bolt and nut. Tighten to 150 Nm (111 ft. lbs.).

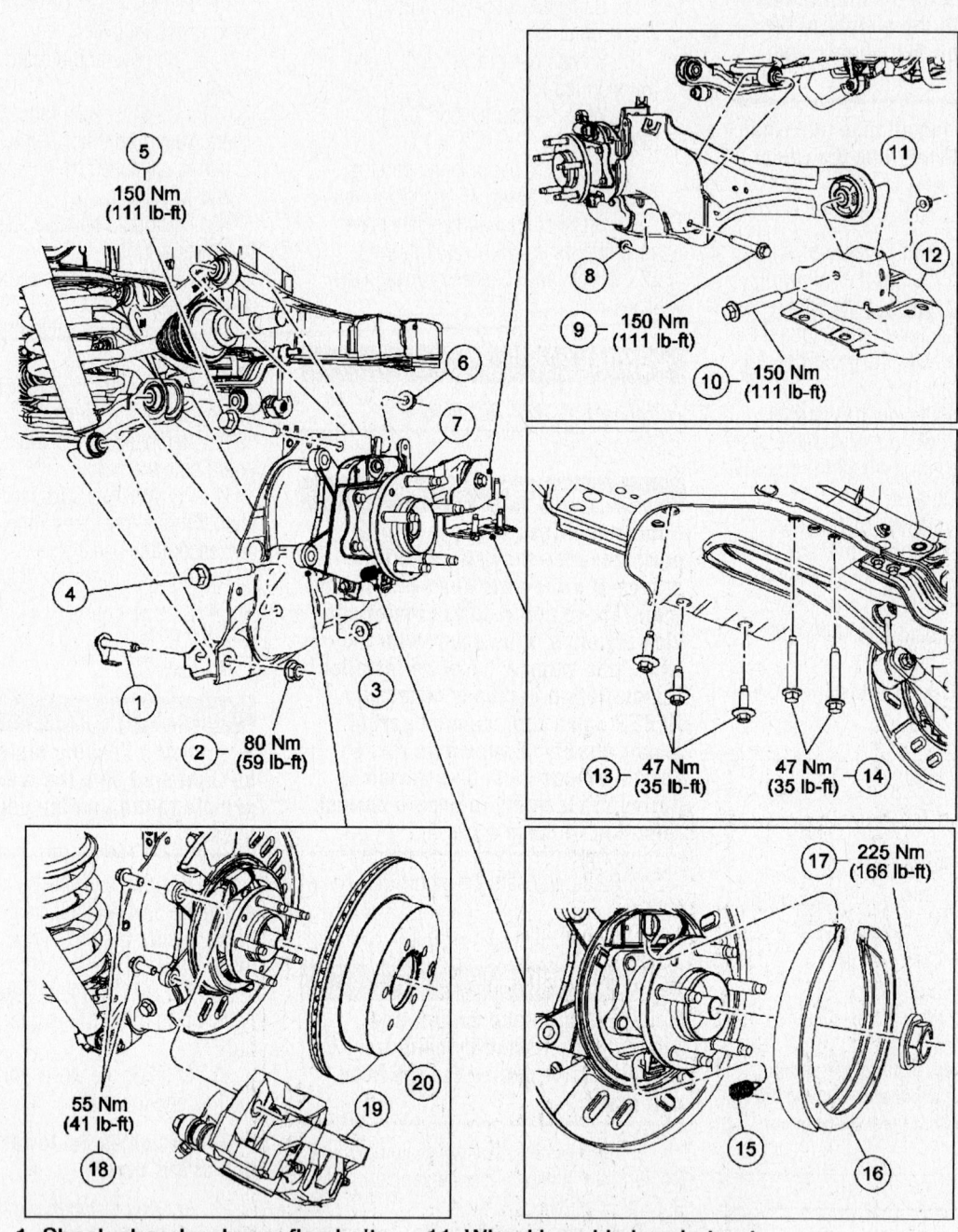

1. Shock absorber lower flag bolt
2. Shock absorber lower nut
3. Lower arm outboard nut
4. Lower arm outboard bolt
5. Upper arm outboard bolt
6. Upper arm outboard nut
7. Wheel knuckle
8. Toe link outboard nut
9. Toe link outboard bolt
10. Wheel knuckle bracket bolt
11. Wheel knuckle bracket nut
12. Wheel knuckle arm bracket
13. Wheel knuckle arm bracket-to-frame bolts (2)
14. Wheel knuckle arm bracket-to-frame bolts (3)
15. Parking brake spring
16. Parking brake shoe
17. Halfshaft nut
18. Brake anchor plate bolts (2)
19. Brake caliper and anchor plate assembly
20. Brake disc (rotor)

22086_EDGE_G0208

Fig. 251 Exploded view of the knuckle and related components—AWD model shown, FWD similar

26. If installing a new wheel knuckle, perform the following:

a. Tighten the lower arm outboard bolt to 150 Nm (111 ft. lbs.). Loosen the bolt 180 degrees.

b. Tighten the bolt to 80 Nm (59 ft. lbs.).

c. Tighten the bolt an additional 90 degrees.

27. If installing the original wheel knuckle, perform the following:

a. Tighten the lower arm outboard bolt to 80 Nm (59 ft. lbs.).

b. Tighten the bolt an additional 90 degrees.

c. Tighten the toe link outboard bolt to 150 Nm (111 ft. lbs.).

d. Tighten the shock absorber lower nut to 80 Nm (59 ft. lbs.).

28. For AWD vehicles, perform the following:

a. Using a suitable installation tool, install the halfshaft into the wheel hub.

b. Install the halfshaft nut and tighten to 225 Nm (166 ft. lbs.).

29. Install the brake hose bracket bolt. Tighten to 7 Nm (62 inch lbs.).

30. Position the wheel speed sensor, clip the 2 retainers to the upper arm and install the bolt. Tighten to 7 Nm (62 inch lbs.).

➡ **The parking brake cable bracket is fastened to the wheel knuckle with the same bolt as the stabilizer bar link.**

31. Install the parking brake cable bracket and the stabilizer bar link to the wheel knuckle. Tighten the bolt to 35 Nm (26 ft. lbs.).

32. Connect the parking brake cable and install the 2 bolts. Tighten to 18 Nm (13 ft. lbs.).

33. Install the parking brake shoe and retaining spring.

34. Install the brake disc.

35. Position the brake caliper and anchor plate assembly and install the anchor plate bolts. Tighten to 55 Nm (41 ft. lbs.).

36. Install the wheel and tire assembly

LOWER CONTROL ARM

REMOVAL & INSTALLATION

1. Remove the Coil Spring, as outlined in this section.

2. Remove the cam adjuster nut, cam adjuster and cam bolt. Discard the cam bolt and nut.

3. Remove the lower arm.

4. Installation is the reverse of the removal procedure. Tighten the cam adjuster bolt and nut to 150 Nm (111 ft. lbs.).

SHOCK ABSORBER

REMOVAL & INSTALLATION
See Figure 252.

✳ WARNING

Suspension fasteners are critical parts because they affect performance of vital parts and systems and their failure can result in major service expense. A new part with the same part number must be installed if installation becomes necessary. NEVER use a replacement part of lesser quality or substitute design. Torque values must be adhered to during reassembly to ensure correct retention of these parts.

➡ **New OEM shock absorbers are shipped with a strap securing it in the compressed position.**

1. Remove the quarter trim panel.

2. Remove and discard the shock absorber upper nuts.

3. Raise and safely support the vehicle.

4. Remove the wheel and tire assembly.

5. Position a suitable jackstand under the lower arm.

6. Remove the shock absorber lower bolt, flagnut and shock absorber. Discard the bolt and flagnut.

✳ WARNING

Suspension bushing fasteners must be tightened with the weight of the vehicle resting on the wheel and tires.

To install:

7. Installation is the reverse of the removal procedure. Tighten the retainers as follows:

a. Shock absorber lower bolt and flagnut: 80 Nm (59 ft. lbs.)

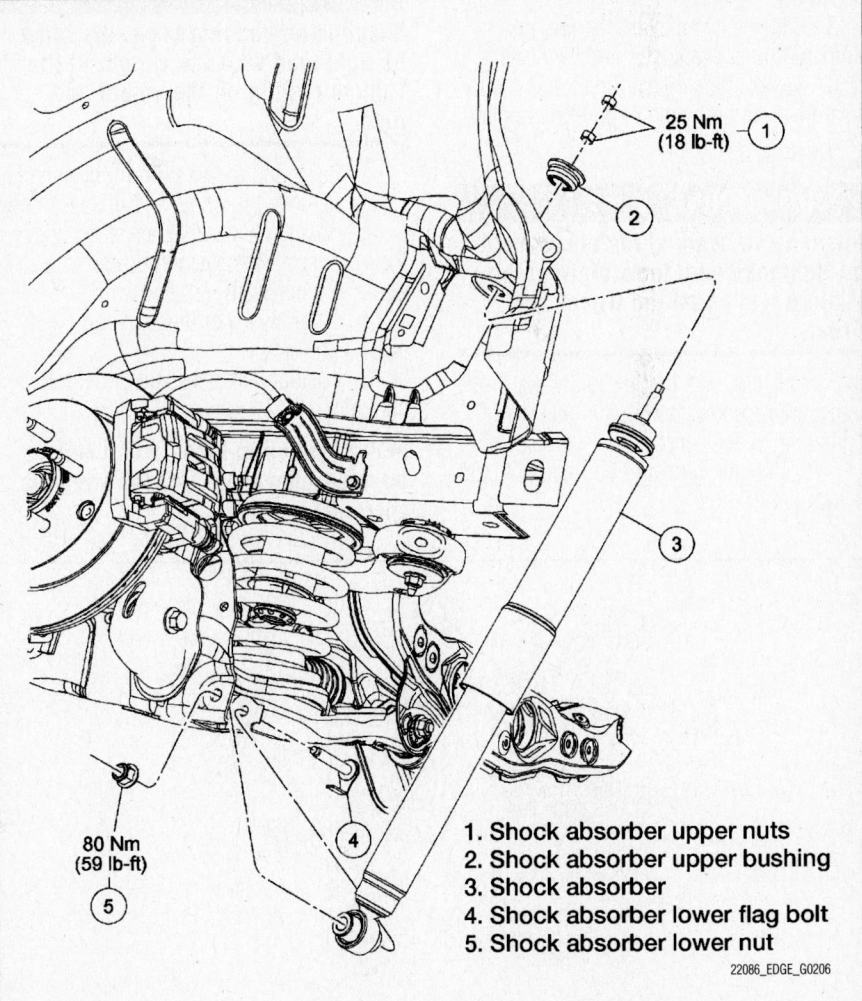

25 Nm (18 lb-ft) — ①
②
③
④
80 Nm (59 lb-ft) ⑤

1. Shock absorber upper nuts
2. Shock absorber upper bushing
3. Shock absorber
4. Shock absorber lower flag bolt
5. Shock absorber lower nut

22086_EDGE_G0206

Fig. 252 Exploded view of the shock absorber and related components

b. Shock absorber upper nuts: 25 Nm (18 ft. lbs.)

TOE LINK

REMOVAL & INSTALLATION
See Figure 253.

✳✳ WARNING

Suspension fasteners are critical parts because they affect performance of vital parts and systems and their failure can result in major service expense. A new part with the same part number must be installed if installation becomes necessary. NEVER use a replacement part of lesser quality or substitute design. Torque values must be adhered to during reassembly to ensure correct retention of these parts.

1. Raise and safely support the vehicle.
2. Remove the wheel and tire assembly.
3. Remove and discard the toe link inboard nut, cam adjuster and cam bolt.
4. Remove and discard the toe link outboard bolt and nut then remove the toe link.

To install:

✳✳ WARNING

Suspension bushing fasteners must be tightened with the weight of the vehicle resting on the wheel and tires.

5. Installation is the reverse of the removal procedure, noting the following tightening specifications:
   a. Toe link outboard bolt and nut: 150 Nm (111 ft. lbs.)

b. Toe link inboard nut, cam adjuster and cam bolt: 200 Nm (148 ft. lbs.)
6. Check and, if necessary, adjust the rear toe

UPPER CONTROL ARM

REMOVAL & INSTALLATION

✳✳ WARNING

Suspension fasteners are critical parts because they affect performance of vital parts and systems and their failure can result in major service expense. A new part with the same part number must be installed if installation becomes necessary. NEVER use a replacement part of lesser quality or substitute design. Torque values must be adhered to during reassembly to ensure correct retention of these parts.

✳✳ WARNING

Suspension bushing fasteners must be tightened with the weight of the vehicle resting on the wheel and tires.

1. Raise and safely support the vehicle.
2. Remove the wheel and tire assembly.
3. Position a suitable jackstand under the lower arm. Remove and discard the upper arm outboard bolt and nut.
4. Carefully lower the lower arm and remove the jack.
5. Position the jackstand under the subframe.

➡ **The upper arm inboard bolt cannot be removed without first lowering the subframe.**

6. Remove and discard the 2 subframe bushing brace-to-body bolts.
7. Remove the subframe forward mounting nut.

➡ **The upper arm inboard bolt cannot be removed without first lowering the subframe.**

✳✳ WARNING

The rear springs are under pressure. The jack must be lowered slowly while relieving the spring pressure.

8. Remove the subframe rearward mounting nut and lower the jack.
9. Remove and discard the upper arm inboard bolt and nut.
10. Remove the upper arm.

To install:

✳✳ WARNING

Suspension bushing fasteners must be tightened with the weight of the vehicle resting on the wheel and tires.

11. Installation is the reverse of the removal procedure. Note the following tightening specifications:
   a. Upper arm inboard bolt and nut: 150 Nm (111 ft. lbs.)
   b. Subframe forward mounting nut and bolts: 90 Nm (66 ft. lbs.)
   c. Subframe bushing brace-to-body bolts: 25 Nm (18 ft. lbs.)
   d. Upper arm outboard bolt and nut: tighten to 150 Nm (111 ft. lbs.)

STABILIZER BAR

REMOVAL & INSTALLATION

✳✳ WARNING

Suspension fasteners are critical parts because they affect performance of vital parts and systems and their failure can result in major service expense. A new part with the same part number must be installed if installation becomes necessary. NEVER use a replacement part of lesser quality or substitute design. Torque values must be adhered to during reassembly to ensure correct retention of these parts.

1. Raise and safely support the vehicle..
2. Remove and discard the stabilizer bar link upper nuts.
3. Remove and discard the stabilizer bar link lower nuts and remove the stabilizer bar links.

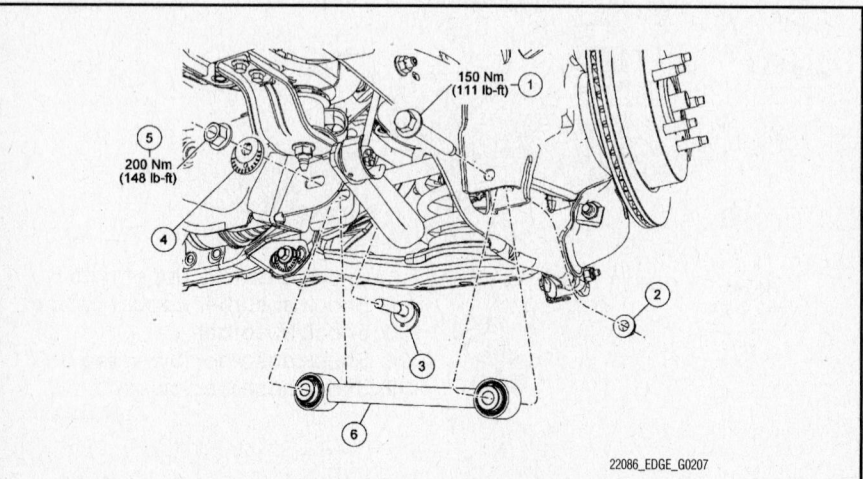

22086_EDGE_G0207

Fig. 253 Exploded view of the toe link and related components

4. Remove and discard the stabilizer bar bracket nuts and remove the stabilizer bar brackets and the stabilizer bar.

5. Inspect the stabilizer bar bushings and install a new bushing(s) if necessary.

To install:

6. Installation is the reverse of the removal procedure, noting the following tightening specifications:

   a. Stabilizer bar bracket nuts: 55 Nm (41 ft. lbs.)

   b. Stabilizer bar link upper and lower nuts: 35 Nm (26 ft. lbs.)

WHEEL HUB AND BEARING

REMOVAL & INSTALLATION

See Figure 254.

✳ WARNING

Suspension fasteners are critical parts because they affect performance of vital parts and systems and their failure can result in major service expense. A new part with the same part number must be installed if installation becomes necessary. NEVER use a replacement part of lesser quality or substitute design. Torque values must be adhered to during reassembly to ensure correct retention of these parts.

1. Raise and safely support the vehicle.

2. Remove the wheel and tire assembly.

✳ WARNING

Do not let the brake caliper and anchor plate assembly hang from the brake hose or damage to the hose can occur.

3. Remove the 2 anchor plate bolts and position the brake caliper and anchor plate assembly aside.

4. Support the brake caliper and anchor plate assembly using a piece of wire.

5. Remove the brake disc.

6. For All Wheel Drive (AWD) vehicles, perform the following:

   a. Remove and discard the halfshaft nut.

   b. Using special tool 205-D070, or equivalent hub removal tool, separate the

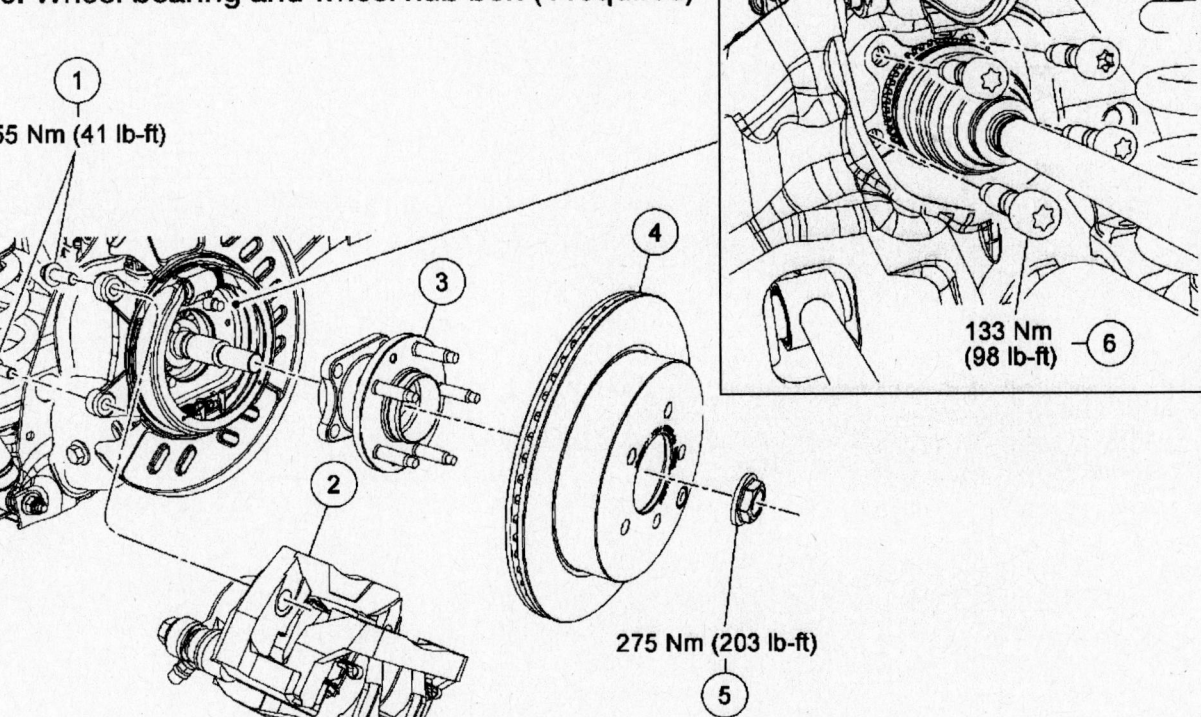

1. Brake caliper anchor plate bolts (2 required)
2. Brake caliper and anchor plate assembly
3. Wheel hub and bearing assembly
4. Brake disc
5. Halfshaft nut
6. Wheel bearing and wheel hub bolt (4 required)

55 Nm (41 lb-ft)

133 Nm (98 lb-ft)

275 Nm (203 lb-ft)

Fig. 254 Exploded view of the rear hub and bearing—AWD model shown

\22086_EDGE_G0209

halfshaft from the hub and bearing assembly.

7. Remove the 4 bolts and the wheel bearing and wheel hub. Discard the bolts.

To install:

8. Install the wheel bearing and new wheel hub bolts. Tighten to 133 Nm (98 ft. lbs.).

9. Position the brake caliper and anchor plate assembly and install the 2 bolts. To install, tighten to 55 Nm (41 ft. lbs.).

10. Install the brake disc.

11. For AWD vehicles, perform the following:

a. Using a suitable installation tool, install the halfshaft into the wheel bearing and wheel hub.

b. Install the halfshaft hub nut. Tighten to 275 Nm (203 ft. lbs.)

FORD AND LINCOLN

F-150 • F-250 • F-350 • Mark LT

SPECIFICATIONS AND MAINTENANCE CHARTS

ENGINE AND VEHICLE IDENTIFICATION

Engine							Model Year	
Code ①	Liters (cc)	Cu. In.	Cyl.	Fuel Sys.	Type	Eng. Mfg.	Code ②	Year
2	4.2 (4195)	256	6	EFI	OHV	Ford	5	2005
5	5.4 (5409)	330	8	EFI	SOHC	Ford	6	2006
L	5.4 (5409)	330	8	EFI	SOHC	Ford	7	2007
P	6.0 (5921)	365	8	TDI	OHV	Navistar		
S	6.8 (6802)	415	10	MFI	SOHC	Ford		
V ③	5.4 (5409)	330	8	④	SOHC	Ford		
V ④	6.8 (6802)	415	10	MFI	SOHC	Ford		
W	4.6 (4588)	280	8	EFI	SOHC	Ford		
Y	6.8 (6802)	415	10	EFI	SOHC	Ford		

MFI: Multi-port Fuel Injection

TDI: Direct Injection Turbo-Diesel

EFI: Electronic Fuel Injection

OHV: Overhead Valve

SOHC: Single Overhead Camshaft

① 8th digit of the Vehicle Identification Number (VIN)

② 10th digit of the Vehicle Identification Number (VIN)

③ 3 valves per cylinder Flex-Fuel engine

④ 3 valves per cylinder

22086_FTRK_C0001

GENERAL ENGINE SPECIFICATIONS

Year	Model	Engine Displ. Liters	Engine VIN	Net Horsepower @ rpm	Net Torque @ rpm (ft. lbs.)	Bore x Stroke (in.)	Compression Ratio	Oil Pressure @ rpm
2005	F-150	4.2	2	202@4800	255@3400	3.81x3.74	9.3:1	40@2500
		4.6	W	210@4400	290@3250	3.55x3.54	9.0:1	40@2500
		5.4	5	300@5000	365@3750	3.55x4.17	9.8:1	75@2000
	F-250, F-350	5.4	L	235@4250	330@3000	3.55x4.17	9.0:1	40-70@1500
		6.0 ①	P	325@3300	560@2000	3.74x4.13	18.0:1	24@1200
		6.8	S	265@4250	410@2750	4.09x4.17	9.0:1	40-70@1500
		6.8	V	362@4750	465@3300	4.09x4.17	9.2:1	40-75@2000
2006	F-150	4.2	2	202@4800	255@3400	3.81x3.74	9.3:1	40@2500
		4.6	W	210@4400	290@3250	3.55x3.54	9.0:1	40@2500
		5.4 ②	V	300@5000	365@3750	3.55x4.17	9.8:1	40@2000
		5.4	5	300@5000	365@3750	3.55x4.17	9.8:1	75@2000
	Mark LT	5.4	5	300@5000	365@3750	3.55x4.17	9.8:1	75@2000
	F-250, F-350	5.4	5	300@5000	365@3750	3.55x4.17	9.8:1	75@2000
		6.0 ①	P	325@3300	560@2000	3.74x4.13	18.0:1	24@1200
		6.8	Y	362@4750	465@3300	4.09x4.17	9.2:1	40-75@2000
2007	F-150	4.2	2	202@4800	255@3400	3.81x3.74	9.3:1	40@2500
		4.6	W	210@4400	290@3250	3.55x3.54	9.0:1	40@2500
		5.4 ②	V	300@5000	365@3750	3.55x4.17	9.8:1	40@2000
		5.4	5	300@5000	365@3750	3.55x4.17	9.8:1	75@2000
	Mark LT	5.4	5	300@5000	365@3750	3.55x4.17	9.8:1	75@2000
	F-250, F-350	5.4	5	300@5000	365@3750	3.55x4.17	9.8:1	75@2000
		6.0 ①	P	325@3300	560@2000	3.74x4.13	18.0:1	24@1200
		6.8	V	362@4750	465@3300	4.09x4.17	9.2:1	40-75@2000

① Turbo diesel

② Flex-Fuel

22086_FTRK_C0002

GASOLINE ENGINE TUNE-UP SPECIFICATIONS

Year	Engine Displacemen Liters	Engine VIN	Spark Plug Gap (in.)	Ignition Timing (deg.) ①		Fuel Pump (psi) ②	Idle Speed (rpm)		Valve Clearance	
				MT	AT		MT	AT	In.	Ex.
2005	4.2	2	0.052-0.056	10B	10B	30-45	③	③	HYD	HYD
	4.6	W	0.040-0.050	10B	10B	30-45	③	③	HYD	HYD
	5.4	5	0.040-0.050	10B	10B	28-45	③	③	HYD	HYD
	5.4	L	0.040-0.050	10B	10B	28-45	③	③	HYD	HYD
	6.8	S	0.052-0.056	10B	10B	28-45	③	③	HYD	HYD
	6.8	V	0.040-0.050	10B	10B	28-45	③	③	HYD	HYD
2006	4.2	2	0.052-0.056	10B	10B	30-45	③	③	HYD	HYD
	4.6	W	0.040-0.050	10B	10B	30-45	③	③	HYD	HYD
	5.4	5	0.040-0.050	10B	10B	28-45	③	③	HYD	HYD
	5.4	V ④	0.040-0.050	10B	10B	28-45	③	③	HYD	HYD
	6.8	Y	0.040-0.050	10B	10B	28-45	③	③	HYD	HYD
2007	4.2	2	0.052-0.056	10B	10B	30-45	③	③	HYD	HYD
	4.6	W	0.040-0.050	10B	10B	30-45	③	③	HYD	HYD
	5.4	5	0.040-0.050	10B	10B	28-45	③	③	HYD	HYD
	5.4	V ④	0.040-0.050	10B	10B	28-45	③	③	HYD	HYD
	6.8	Y	0.040-0.050	10B	10B	28-45	③	③	HYD	HYD

NOTE: The Vehicle Emission Control Information label often reflects specification changes changes made during production. The label figures must be used if they differ from this chart.

B: Before top dead center

HYD: Hydraulic

NA: Information not Available

① Ignition timing is preset and cannot be adjusted

② With engine running

③ Idle speed is electronically controlled and cannot be adjusted

④ Flex-fuel engine

22086_FTRK_C0003

DIESEL ENGINE TUNE-UP SPECIFICATIONS

Year	Engine Displ. Liters	Engine VIN	Valve Clearance		Injection Pump Setting (deg.)	Injection Nozzle Pressure (psi)		Idle Speed (rpm)	Cranking Compression Pressure (psi)
			Intake (in.)	Exhaust (in.)		New	Used		
2005	6.0	P	HYD	HYD	①	②	②	③	④
2006	6.0	P	HYD	HYD	①	②	②	③	④
2007	6.0	P	HYD	HYD	①	②	②	③	④

NOTE: The Vehicle Emission Control Information label often reflects specification changes made during production. The label figures must be used if they differ from those in this chart

HYD: Hydraulic

NA: Not Available

① PCM controlled

② Pump output pressure: 450-4,000 psi

③ See underhood emission label

④ Compression pressure in the lowest cylinder must be at least 75% of the highest cylinder

   Minimum pressure: 195 psi

   Maximum pressure: 440 psi

22086_FTRK_C0004

CAPACITIES

Year	Model	Engine Displ. Liters	Engine VIN	Engine Oil with Filter (qts.)	Transmission (pts.)		Transfer Case (pts.)	Drive Axle		Fuel Tank (gal.)	Cooling System (qts.)
					MT	Auto.*		Front (pts.)	Rear (pts.)		
2005	F-150	4.2	2	6.0	7.6	27.8	4.0	3.7	①	②	20.1
		4.6	W	6.0	③	27.8	4.0	3.7	①	②	19.8
		5.4	5	7.0	③	27.8	4.0	3.7	①	②	20.6
	F-250, F350	5.4	L	7.0	③	19.2 ④	③	6.38	⑤	⑥	26.4
		6.0	P	15.0	③	19.2 ④	③	6.38	⑤	⑥	27.5
		6.8	S	7	③	19.2 ④	③	6.38	⑤	⑥	27.5
		6.8	V	③	6.38	⑤	⑥	27.5	⑤	⑥	27.5
2006	F-150	4.2	2	6.0	7.6	27.8	4.0	3.7	①	②	20.1
		4.6	W	6.0	③	27.8	4.0	3.7	①	②	19.8
		5.4	V ⑦	7	③	19.2 ④	③	6.38	⑤	⑥	27.5
	F-150, Mark LT	5.4	5	7.0	③	27.8	4.0	3.7	①	②	20.6
	F-250, F-350	5.4	5	7.0	③	27.8	4.0	3.7	①	②	20.6
		6.0	P	15.0	③	19.2 ④	③	6.38	⑤	⑥	27.5
		6.8	Y	③	6.38	⑤	⑥	27.5	⑤	⑥	27.5
2007	F-150	4.2	2	6.0	7.6	27.8	4.0	3.7	①	②	20.1
		4.6	W	6.0	③	27.8	4.0	3.7	①	②	19.8
		5.4	V ⑦	7	③	19.2 ④	③	6.38	⑤	⑥	27.5
	F-150, Mark LT	5.4	5	7.0	③	27.8	4.0	3.7	①	②	20.6
	F-250, F-350	5.4	5	7.0	③	27.8	4.0	3.7	①	②	20.6
		6.0	P	15.0	③	19.2 ④	③	6.38	⑤	⑥	27.5
		6.8	Y	③	6.38	⑤	⑥	27.5	⑤	⑥	27.5

NA: Information not available

NOTE: All capacities are approximate. Add fluid gradually and check to be sure a proper fluid level is obtained.

* Overhaul

① 8.8 and 9.75 inch axles: 5.5 pts.

   10.25 inch axle: 6.9 pts.

② Regular cab w/126 in. wheel base and 6.5 ft. bed: 26.0

   Super cab w/132 inch wheel base and 5.5 ft. bed: 26.0

   Crew cab w/138 in. wheel base and 5.5 ft. bed: 30.0

   Regular cab w/144 in. wheel base and 8 ft. bed: 27.0

   SuperCab w/163 in. wheel base and 8 ft. bed: 27.0

   Optional for SuperCab w/144 in. wheel base and 6.5 ft. bed: 35.7

   Optional for Regular Cab w/144 in. wheel base and 8 ft. bed: 35.7

   Optional for SuperCab w/163 in. wheel base and 8 ft. bed: 35.7

③ Fill to bottom of oil fill hole.

④ Dry fill capacity given; always check fluid level during refill.

⑤ 10.5 inch: 6.9 pts.

   Dana 80: 8.5 pts.

   Dana 80 with Trac Loc: 8.0 pts.

   Dana S110 and S130: 16.0 pts.

⑥ Super Cab and Club Cab with 142 in. or 156 in. wheel base: 30.5

   Regular Cab, SuperCab and Club Cab with 137 in., 158 in. or 172 in. wheelbase: 38.0

   Optional narrow frame chassis cab aft-of-axle tank: 40.0

   Optional narrow frame chassis cab midship tank: 19.0

⑦ Flex-fuel engine

FLUID SPECIFICATIONS

Year	Model	Engine Displacement Liters	Engine ID/VIN	Engine Oil	Man. Trans.	Auto. Trans. ①	Drive Axle	Power Steering Fluid	Brake Master Cylinder
2005	F-150	4.2	2	5W-20	②	③	④	MERCON ATF	DOT 3
		4.6	W	5W-20	②	③	④	MERCON ATF	DOT 3
		5.4	5	5W-20	②	③	④	MERCON ATF	DOT 3
	F-250, F-350	5.4	L	5W-20	②	③	④	MERCON ATF	DOT 3
		6.0	P	15W-40	②	③	④	MERCON ATF	DOT 3
		6.8	S	5W-20	②	③	④	MERCON ATF	DOT 3
		6.8	V	5W-20	②	③	④	MERCON ATF	DOT 3
2006	F-150	4.2	2	5W-20	②	③	④	MERCON ATF	DOT 3
		4.6	W	5W-20	②	③	④	MERCON ATF	DOT 3
	F-150, Mark LT	5.4	5, V	5W-20	②	③	④	MERCON ATF	DOT 3
	F-250, F-350	5.4	5	5W-20	②	③	④	MERCON ATF	DOT 3
		6.0	P	15W-40	②	③	④	MERCON ATF	DOT 3
		6.8	Y	5W-20	②	③	④	MERCON ATF	DOT 3
2007	F-150	4.2	2	5W-20	②	③	④	MERCON ATF	DOT 3
		4.6	W	5W-20	②	③	④	MERCON ATF	DOT 3
	F-150, Mark LT	5.4	5, V	5W-20	②	③	④	MERCON ATF	DOT 3
	F-250, F-350	5.4	5	5W-20	②	③	④	MERCON ATF	DOT 3
		6.0	P	15W-40	②	③	④	MERCON ATF	DOT 3
		6.8	Y	5W-20	②	③	④	MERCON ATF	DOT 3

DOT: Department Of Transpotation

① Type 9601 may be substituted

② MERCON Type XD-2-QDX ATF

③ MERCON -SP Type XD-6-QSP ATF

④ Fluid type varies per axle type usage:

With Ford 8.8 in. and Ford 9.75 in.: Motorcraft SAE 75W-140 Synthetic Rear Axle Lubricant XY-75W140-QL (US); CXY-75W140-1L (Canada)

With Ford 10.25 in.: SAE 75W-140 High Performance Rear Axle Lubricant F1TZ-19580-B

With DANA 80: SAE 75W-90 Premium Synthetic Transaxle Lubricant XT-75W90-QGT

With DANA S110 and S130: Motorcraft SAE 75W-140 High Performance Rear Axle Lubricant XY-75W140-QL (Vehicles w/ trailer towing option or 4:10 ratio)

With front driveshafts: Motorcraft 80W-90 Premium Rear Axle Lubricant XY-80W90-QL (US); CXY-80W90-1L (Canada) (

22086_FTRK_C0006

VALVE SPECIFICATIONS

Year	Engine Displ. Liters	Engine VIN	Seat Angle (deg.)	Face Angle (deg.)	Spring Test Pressure (lbs. @ in.)	Spring Installed Height (in.)	Stem-to-Guide Clearance (in.) Intake	Stem-to-Guide Clearance (in.) Exhaust	Stem Diameter (in.) Intake	Stem Diameter (in.) Exhaust
2005	4.2	2	44.75	45.675	225@1.15	1.610	0.0008-0.0027	0.0015-0.0033	0.2738-0.2751	0.2728-0.2741
	4.6	W	45.5	45.25-45.75	132@1.103	1.5630-1.5866	0.0008-0.0027	0.0018-0.0037	0.2754-0.2746	0.2744-0.2736
	5.4	5, L	44.5-45	45.5	79@1.66	1.660	0.0010-0.0020	0.0030-0.0040	0.2350-0.2360	0.2340-0.2350
	6.0	P	①	①	191@1.51	1.820	0.0055 max.	0.0055 max.	0.2720-0.2735	0.2720-0.2735
	6.8	S, V	44.5-45	45.5	171@1.66	1.660	0.0010-0.0030	0.0020-0.0040	0.2350-0.2360	0.2340-0.2350
2006	4.2	2	44.75	45.675	225@1.15	1.610	0.0008-0.0027	0.0015-0.0033	0.2738-0.2751	0.2728-0.2741
	4.6	W	45.5	45.25-45.75	132@1.103	1.5630-1.5866	0.0008-0.0027	0.0018-0.0037	0.2754-0.2746	0.2744-0.2736
	5.4	5, V	44.5-45	45.5	79@1.66	1.660	0.0010-0.0020	0.0030-0.0040	0.2350-0.2360	0.2340-0.2350
	6.0	P	①	①	191@1.51	1.820	0.0055 max.	0.0055 max.	0.2720-0.2735	0.2720-0.2735
	6.8	Y	44.5-45	45.5	171@1.66	1.660	0.0010-0.0030	0.0020-0.0040	0.2350-0.2360	0.2340-0.2350
2007	4.2	2	44.75	45.675	225@1.15	1.610	0.0008-0.0027	0.0015-0.0033	0.2738-0.2751	0.2728-0.2741
	4.6	W	45.5	45.25-45.75	132@1.103	1.5630-1.5866	0.0008-0.0027	0.0018-0.0037	0.2754-0.2746	0.2744-0.2736
	5.4	5, V	44.5-45	45.5	79@1.66	1.660	0.0010-0.0020	0.0030-0.0040	0.2350-0.2360	0.2340-0.2350
	6.0	P	①	①	191@1.51	1.820	0.0055 max.	0.0055 max.	0.2720-0.2735	0.2720-0.2735
	6.8	Y	44.5-45	45.5	171@1.66	1.660	0.0010-0.0030	0.0020-0.0040	0.2350-0.2360	0.2340-0.2350

① Intake: 30
Exhaust: 37.5

22086_FTRK_C0007

CAMSHAFT AND BEARING SPECIFICATIONS
All measurements are given in inches.

Year	Engine Displ. Liters	Engine VIN	Journal Diameter	Brg. Oil Clearance	Shaft End-play	Runout	Journal Bore	Lobe Lift	
								Intake	Exhaust
2005	4.2	2	2.0505-2.0515	0.0010-0.0030	0.0010-0.0060	0.002	①	0.2449	0.2587
	4.6	W	1.0605-1.0615	0.0010-0.0030	0.0035-0.0075	0.002	1.0625-1.0635	0.2560	0.2560
	5.4	5	1.1260-1.1270	0.0010-0.0030	0.0035-0.0075	0.001	1.1280-1.1290	0.2173	0.2168
	5.4	L	1.1260-1.1270	0.0010-0.0030	0.0035-0.0075	0.001	1.1280-1.1290	0.2173	0.2168
	6.0	P	2.4400-2.4410	0.0015-0.0060	0.0020-0.0080	NA	2.4430-2.4460	0.2261	0.2296
	6.8	S, V	1.1260-1.1270	0.0009-0.0029	0.0013-0.0019	0.004	1.1280-1.1290	0.2156	0.2173
2006	4.2	2	2.0505-2.0515	0.0010-0.0030	0.0010-0.0060	0.002	①	0.2449	0.2587
	4.6	W	1.0605-1.0615	0.0010-0.0030	0.0035-0.0075	0.002	1.0625-1.0635	0.2560	0.2560
	5.4	5	1.1260-1.1270	0.0010-0.0030	0.0035-0.0075	0.001	1.1280-1.1290	0.2173	0.2168
	5.4	V ②	1.1260-1.1270	0.0010-0.0030	0.0035-0.0075	0.001	1.1280-1.1290	0.2173	0.2168
	6.0	P	2.4400-2.4410	0.0015-0.0060	0.0020-0.0080	NA	2.4430-2.4460	0.2261	0.2296
	6.8	Y	1.1260-1.1270	0.0009-0.0029	0.0013-0.0019	0.001	1.1280-1.1290	0.2156	0.2173
2007	4.2	2	2.0505-2.0515	0.0010-0.0030	0.0010-0.0060	0.002	①	0.2449	0.2587
	4.6	W	1.0605-1.0615	0.0010-0.0030	0.0035-0.0075	0.002	1.0625-1.0635	0.2560	0.2560
	5.4	5	1.1260-1.1270	0.0010-0.0030	0.0035-0.0075	0.001	1.1280-1.1290	0.2173	0.2168
	5.4	V ②	1.1260-1.1270	0.0010-0.0030	0.0035-0.0075	0.001	1.1280-1.1290	0.2173	0.2168
	6.0	P	2.4400-2.4410	0.0015-0.0060	0.0020-0.0080	NA	2.4430-2.4460	0.2261	0.2296
	6.8	Y	1.1260-1.1270	0.0009-0.0029	0.0013-0.0019	0.001	1.1280-1.1290	0.2156	0.2173

NA: Information not available

① Intake: 1.8532-1.8542 in.
   Exhaust: 1.5635-1.5645 in.

② Flex-fuel engine

22086_FTRK_C0010

CRANKSHAFT AND CONNECTING ROD SPECIFICATIONS
All measurements are given in inches.

Year	Engine Displ. Liters	Engine VIN	Crankshaft				Connecting Rod		
			Main Brg. Journal Dia.	Main Brg. Oil Clearance	Shaft End-play	Thrust on No.	Journal Dia.	Oil Clearance	Side Clearance
2005	4.2	2	2.5190-2.5198	0.0005-0.0023	0.004-0.0080	3	NA	0.0010-0.0014	0.0043-0.0193
	4.6	W	2.6570-2.6576	0.0011-0.0026	0.0051-0.0120	5	2.0859-2.0867	0.0010-0.0027	0.0006-0.0177
	5.4	5, L	2.6568-2.6576	0.0009-0.0019	0.0030-0.0148	5	2.0859-2.0867	0.0010-0.0025	0.0049-0.0187
	6.0	P	3.1500-3.1880	0.0008-0.0034	0.0200	NA	2.7160-2.7170	0.0008-0.0033	0.0120-0.0240
	6.8	S, V	2.6568-2.6576	0.0009-0.0019	0.0015-0.0030	5	2.0859-2.0867	0.0010-0.0025	0.0006-0.0177
2006	4.2	2	2.5190-2.5198	0.0005-0.0023	0.004-0.0080	3	NA	0.0010-0.0014	0.0043-0.0193
	4.6	W	2.6570-2.6576	0.0011-0.0026	0.0051-0.0120	5	2.0859-2.0867	0.0010-0.0027	0.0006-0.0177
	5.4	5	2.6568-2.6576	0.0009-0.0019	0.0030-0.0148	5	2.0859-2.0867	0.0010-0.0025	0.0049-0.0187
	5.4	V ①	2.6568-2.6576	0.0009-0.0019	0.0030-0.0148	5	2.0859-2.0867	0.0010-0.0025	0.0049-0.0187
	6.0	P	3.1500-3.1880	0.0008-0.0034	0.0200	NA	2.7160-2.7170	0.0008-0.0033	0.0120-0.0240
	6.8	Y	2.6568-2.6576	0.0009-0.0019	0.0015-0.0030	5	2.0859-2.0867	0.0010-0.0025	0.0049-0.0187
2007	4.2	2	2.5190-2.5198	0.0005-0.0023	0.004-0.0080	3	NA	0.0010-0.0014	0.0043-0.0193
	4.6	W	2.6570-2.6576	0.0011-0.0026	0.0051-0.0120	5	2.0859-2.0867	0.0010-0.0027	0.0006-0.0177
	5.4	5	2.6568-2.6576	0.0009-0.0019	0.0030-0.0148	5	2.0859-2.0867	0.0010-0.0025	0.0049-0.0187
	5.4	V ①	2.6568-2.6576	0.0009-0.0019	0.0030-0.0148	5	2.0859-2.0867	0.0010-0.0025	0.0049-0.0187
	6.0	P	3.1500-3.1880	0.0008-0.0034	0.0200	NA	2.7160-2.7170	0.0008-0.0033	0.0120-0.0240
	6.8	Y	2.6568-2.6576	0.0009-0.0019	0.0015-0.0030	5	2.0859-2.0867	0.0010-0.0025	0.0049-0.0187

NA: Information not available

① Flex-fuel engine

22086_FTRK_C0009

PISTON AND RING SPECIFICATIONS

All measurements are given in inches.

	Engine Displ. Liters	Engine VIN	Piston Clearance	Ring Gap			Ring Side Clearance		
				Top Compression	Bottom Compression	Oil Control	Top Compression	Bottom Compression	Oil Control
2005	4.2	2	0.0007-0.0017	0.0067-0.0130	0.0118-0.0217	0.006-0.026	0.0012-0.0032	0.0012-0.0031	SNUG
	4.6	W	0.0005-0.0001	0.010-0.020	0.010-0.020	0.006-0.026	0.0012-0.0028	0.0012-0.0028	0.0018-0.0077
	5.4	5, L	0.0010-0.0018	0.006-0.012	0.0098-0.0197	0.006-0.026	0.0008-0.0031	0.0012-0.0028	SNUG
	6.0	P	0.0017-0.0036	0.011-0.0210	0.055-0.0650	0.009-0.0190	NA	NA	NA
	6.8	S, V	0.0002-0.0010	0.0059-0.0118	0.010-0.0200	0.006-0.026	0.0012-0.0020	0.0012-0.0031	SNUG
2006	4.2	2	0.0007-0.0017	0.0067-0.0130	0.0118-0.0217	0.006-0.026	0.0012-0.0032	0.0012-0.0031	SNUG
	4.6	W	0.0005-0.0001	0.010-0.020	0.010-0.020	0.006-0.026	0.0012-0.0028	0.0012-0.0028	0.0018-0.0077
	5.4	5	0.0010-0.0018	0.006-0.012	0.0098-0.0197	0.006-0.026	0.0008-0.0031	0.0012-0.0028	SNUG
	5.4	V ①	0.0010-0.0018	0.006-0.012	0.0098-0.0197	0.006-0.026	0.0008-0.0031	0.0012-0.0028	SNUG
	6.0	P	0.0017-0.0036	0.011-0.0210	0.055-0.0650	0.009-0.0190	NA	NA	NA
	6.8	Y	0.0002-0.0010	0.0059-0.0118	0.010-0.0200	0.006-0.026	0.0012-0.0020	0.0012-0.0031	SNUG
2007	4.2	2	0.0007-0.0017	0.0067-0.0130	0.0118-0.0217	0.006-0.026	0.0012-0.0032	0.0012-0.0031	SNUG
	4.6	W	0.0005-0.0001	0.010-0.020	0.010-0.020	0.006-0.026	0.0012-0.0028	0.0012-0.0028	0.0018-0.0077
	5.4	5	0.0010-0.0018	0.006-0.012	0.0098-0.0197	0.006-0.026	0.0008-0.0031	0.0012-0.0028	SNUG
	5.4	V ①	0.0010-0.0018	0.006-0.012	0.0098-0.0197	0.006-0.026	0.0008-0.0031	0.0012-0.0028	SNUG
	6.0	P	0.0017-0.0036	0.011-0.0210	0.055-0.0650	0.009-0.0190	NA	NA	NA
	6.8	Y	0.0002-0.0010	0.0059-0.0118	0.010-0.0200	0.006-0.026	0.0012-0.0020	0.0012-0.0031	SNUG

① Flex-fuel engine

22086_FTRK_C0008

TORQUE SPECIFICATIONS
All readings in ft. lbs.

	Engine Displ. Liters	Engine VIN	Cylinder Head Bolts	Main Bearing Bolts	Rod Bearing Bolts	Crankshaft Damper Bolts	Flywheel Bolts	Manifold		Spark Plugs	Oil Pan Drain Plug
								Intake *	Exhaust		
2005	4.2	2	①	②	④	118	59	⑤	24	11	19
	4.6	W	⑥	⑦	⑧	⑨	59	⑩	18	11	10
	5.4	5	⑥	⑪	⑫	⑨	59	⑬	18	25	10
	5.4	L	⑥	⑦	⑭	⑨	59	⑬	18	25	10
	6.0	P	⑮	⑯	⑰	⑱	69	8	28 ⑲	—	18
	6.8	S, V	⑥	⑪	⑮	⑨	59	⑬	18	25	17
2006	4.2	2	①	②	④	118	59	⑤	24	11	19
	4.6	W	⑥	⑦	⑧	⑨	59	⑩	18	11	10
	5.4	5	⑥	⑪	⑫	⑨	59	⑬	18	25	10
	5.4	V	⑥	⑪	⑫	⑨	59	⑬	18	25	10
	6.0	P	⑮	⑯	⑰	⑱	69	8	28 ⑲	—	18
	6.8	Y	⑳	⑪	⑭	⑨	59	⑬	18	25	10
2007	4.2	2	①	②	④	118	59	⑤	24	11	19
	4.6	W	⑥	⑦	⑧	⑨	59	⑩	18	11	10
	5.4	5	⑥	⑪	⑫	⑨	59	⑬	18	25	10
	5.4	V	⑥	⑪	⑫	⑨	59	⑬	18	25	10
	6.0	P	⑮	⑯	⑰	⑱	69	8	28 ⑲	—	18
	6.8	Y	⑳	⑪	⑭	⑨	59	⑬	18	25	10

NA: Information not available

* NOTE: Applies to Lower Manifold only. For Upper Manifold, see the text.

① See the procedure in the text

② Step 1: 37 ft. lbs.
  Step 2: Plus 120 degrees

③ Tighten bolts to 71-101 inch lbs.

④ Step 1: 18 ft. lbs.
  Step 2: 33 ft. lbs.
  Step 3: plus 90-120 degrees

⑤ Step 1: 44 inch lbs.
  Step 2: 89 inch lbs.

⑥ Step 1: 30 ft. lbs.
  Step 2: Plus 85-95 degrees
  Step 3: Plus 85-95 degrees

⑦ Vertical bolts:
  Step 1: 30 ft. lbs.
  Step 2: Plus 90 degrees
  Jack screws:
  Step 1: 44 inch lbs.
  Step 2: 89 inch lbs.
  Side bolts: 15 ft. lbs.

⑧ Step 1: 32 ft. lbs.
  Step 2: 105 degrees

⑨ Step 1: 66 ft. lbs.
  Step 2: loosen 1 full turn
  Step 3: 37 ft. lbs.
  Step 4: + 90 deg. Without exceeding 148 ft. lbs.

⑩ 89 inch lbs.

⑪ Vertical bolts:
  Step 1: 30 ft. lbs.
  Step 2: plus 90 degrees
  Side bolts:
  Step 1: 22 ft. lbs.
  Step 2: plus 90 degrees

⑫ Step 1: 18 ft. lbs.
  Step 2: 33 ft. lbs.
  Step 3: plus 90-120 degrees

⑬ Step 1: 18 inch lbs.
  Step 2: 89 inch lbs.

⑭ Step 1: 32 ft. lbs.
  Step 2: 105 degrees

⑮ See procedure in text.

⑯ Step 1: 90 ft. lbs.
  Step 2: 120 ft. lbs.
  Step 3: 170 ft. lbs.
  Lower crankcase bolts: 23 ft. lbs.

⑰ Step 1: 33 ft. lbs.
  Step 2: 50 ft. lbs.

⑱ Step 1: 50 ft. lbs.
  Step 2: plus 90 degrees
  See the text for torque sequence

⑲ Apply anti-seize compound to bolt threads.

⑳ Step 1: 30 ft. lbs.
  Step 2: plus 90 degrees
  Step 3: plus 90 degrees

22086_FTRK_C0011

WHEEL ALIGNMENT

Year	Model	Style	Caster Range (+/-Deg.)	Caster Preferred Setting (Deg.)	Camber Range (+/-Deg.)	Camber Preferred Setting (Deg.)	Toe-in Front ① (Deg.)
2005	F-150 Reg. Cab	4x2	1.00	+4.4	0.75	-0.20	0.15+/-0.25
	F-150 Super Cab	4x2	1.00	+4.6	0.75	-0.20	0.15+/-0.25
	F-150 Crew Cab	4x2	1.00	+4.6	0.75	-0.20	0.15+/-0.25
	F-150 Reg. Cab	4x4	1.00	+4.3	0.75	-0.20	0.15+/-0.25
	F-150 Super Cab	4x4	1.00	+4.6	0.75	-0.20	0.15+/-0.25
	F-150 Crew Cab	4x4	1.00	+4.6	0.75	-0.20	0.15+/-0.25
	F-250/350	4x2	1.20	+3.8	0.75	L+0.62 R+0.67	0.10+/-0.25
	F-250 Std. Susp.	4x4	1.20	+3.3	0.75	+0.15	0.10+/-0.25
	F-250 HD Susp.	4x4	1.30	+2.6	0.75	+0.15	0.10+/-0.25
	F-350 SRW Std. Susp.	4x4	1.20	+2.5	0.75	+0.15	0.10+/-0.25
	F-350 SRW HD Susp.	4x4	1.30	+1.8	0.75	+0.15	0.10+/-0.25
	F-350 DRW Std. Susp.	4x4	1.20	+3.0	0.75	+0.15	0.10+/-0.25
	F-350 DRW HD Susp.	4x4	1.30	+2.4	0.75	+0.15	0.10+/-0.25
	F-350 Chassis/Cab SRW Std. Susp.	4x4	1.20	+2.8	0.75	+0.15	0.10+/-0.25
	F-350 Chassis/Cab SRW HD Susp.	4x4	1.30	+2.3	0.75	+0.15	0.10+/-0.25
	F-350 Chassis/Cab DRW Std. Susp.	4x4	1.20	+2.5	0.75	+0.15	0.10+/-0.25
	F-350 Chassis/Cab DRW HD Susp.	4x4	1.30	+1.9	0.75	+0.15	0.10+/-0.25
2006	F-150 & Mark LT Reg. Cab	4x2	1.00	②	0.75	-0.2	0.15+/-0.25
	F-150 & Mark LT Super Cab	4x2	1.00	③	0.75	0.0	0.15+/-0.20
	F-150 & Mark LT Crew Cab	4x2	1.00	④	0.75	-0.2	0.15+/-0.20
	F-150 & Mark LT Reg. Cab	4x4	1.00	⑤	0.75	-0.2	0.15+/-0.20
	F-150 & Mark LT Super Cab	4x4	1.00	⑥	0.75	-0.2	0.15+/-0.20
	F-150 & Mark LT Crew Cab	4x4	1.00	⑦	0.75	-0.2	0.15+/-0.20
	F-250, F-350	4x2	1.20	3.3	0.75	0.62	0.10+/-0.25
	F-250 Std. Susp.	4x4	1.20	3.3	0.75	0.15	0.10+/-0.25
	F-250 H.D. Susp.	4x4	1.30	2.6	0.75	0.15	0.10+/-0.25
	F-350 Std. Susp., Sgl. Rear Wheel	4x4	1.20	2.5	0.75	0.15	0.10+/-0.25
	F-350 H.D. Susp., Sgl. Rear Wheel	4x4	1.30	1.8	0.75	0.15	0.10+/-0.25
	F-350 Std. Susp., Dual Rear Wheel	4x4	1.20	3.0	0.75	0.15	0.10+/-0.25
	F-350 H.D. Susp., Dual Rear Wheel	4x4	1.30	2.4	0.75	0.15	0.10+/-0.25
	F-350 Chassis Cab, Std. Susp., Sgl. Rear Wheel	4x4	1.20	2.8	0.75	0.15	0.10+/-0.25
	F-350 Chassis Cab, H.D. Susp., Sgl. Rear Wheel	4x4	1.30	2.3	0.75	0.15	0.10+/-0.25
	F-350 Chassis Cab, Std. Susp., Dual Rear Wheel	4x4	1.20	2.5	0.75	0.15	0.10+/-0.25
	F-350 Chassis Cab, H.D. Susp., Dual Rear Wheel	4x4	1.30	1.9	0.75	0.15	0.10+/-0.25

NOTE: See next chart for footnote explanations.

22086_FTRK_C0012

WHEEL ALIGNMENT

Year	Model	Style	Caster Range (+/-Deg.)	Caster Preferred Setting (Deg.)	Camber Range (+/-Deg.)	Camber Preferred Setting (Deg.)	Toe-in Front ① (Deg.)
2007	F-150 & Mark LT Reg. Cab	4x2	1.00	②	0.75	0.0	0.20+/-0.20
	F-150 & Mark LT Super Cab	4x2	1.00	③	0.75	-0.2	0.20+/-0.20
	F-150 & Mark LT Crew Cab	4x2	1.00	④	0.75	-0.2	0.20+/-0.20
	F-150 & Mark LT Reg. Cab	4x4	1.00	⑤	0.75	-0.2	0.20+/-0.20
	F-150 & Mark LT Super Cab	4x4	1.00	⑥	0.75	-0.2	0.20+/-0.20
	F-150 & Mark LT Crew Cab	4x4	1.00	⑦	0.75	-0.2	0.20+/-0.20
	F-250, F-350	4x2	1.20	3.8	0.75	0.62	0.1+/-0.25
	F-250 Std. Susp.	4x4	1.20	3.3	0.75	0.15	0.1+/-0.25
	F-250 H.D. Susp.	4x4	1.30	2.6	0.75	0.15	0.1+/-0.25
	F-350 Std. Susp., Sgl. Rear Wheel	4x4	1.20	2.5	0.75	0.15	0.1+/-0.25
	F-350 H.D. Susp., Sgl. Rear Wheel	4x4	1.30	1.8	0.75	0.15	0.1+/-0.25
	F-350 Std. Susp., Dual Rear Wheel	4x4	1.20	3.0	0.75	0.15	0.1+/-0.25
	F-350 H.D. Susp., Dual Rear Wheel	4x4	1.30	2.4	0.75	0.15	0.1+/-0.25
	F-350 Chassis Cab, Std. Susp., Sgl. Rear Wheel	4x4	1.20	2.8	0.75	0.15	0.1+/-0.25
	F-350 Chassis Cab, H.D. Susp., Sgl. Rear Wheel	4x4	1.30	2.3	0.75	0.15	0.1+/-0.25
	F-350 Chassis Cab, Std. Susp., Dual Rear Wheel	4x4	1.20	2.5	0.75	0.15	0.1+/-0.25
	F-350 Chassis Cab, H.D. Susp., Dual Rear Wheel	4x4	1.30	1.9	0.75	0.15	0.1+/-0.25

NA: Information not available

① 2005-06 4x4 rear wheel toe-in:

   F-150/Mk LT: 0.0+/-0.20

   F-250, F-350: 0.0+/-0.6

   2007 all model rear wheel toe-in: 0.0+./-0.20

② Left: +4.1

   Right: +4.5

③ Left: 4.3

   Right: 4.7

   With 20 in. or 22 in. tires:

   Left: 3.9

   Right: 4.3

④ Left: 4.4

   Right: 4.8

   With 20 in. or 22 in. tires:

   Left: 4.0

   Right: 4.0

⑤ Left: 4.1

   Right: 4.5

⑥ Left: 4.4

   Right: 4.8

⑦ Left: 4.5

   Right: 4.9

⑧ Left: 4.3

   Right: 4.7

   With 20 in. or 22 in. tires:

   Left: 3.9

   Right

22086_FTRK_C0013

TIRE, WHEEL AND BALL JOINT SPECIFICATIONS

Year	Model	OEM Tires Standard	OEM Tires Optional	Tire Pressures (psi.) Front	Tire Pressures (psi.) Rear	Wheel Size	Ball Joint Inspection	Lug Nut Torque (ft. lbs.)
2005	F-150 Reg. Cab							
	XL 2wd	P235/70R17	P255/65R17	①	①	NA	0.060 in. ②	150
	XL 4wd	P235/75R17	P255/70R17	①	①	NA	0.060 in. ②	150
	XLT 2wd	P235/70R17	P255/65R17	①	①	NA	0.060 in. ②	150
	XLT 4wd	P235/75R17	P255/70R17	①	①	NA	0.060 in. ②	150
	STX 2wd	P255/65R17	none	①	①	NA	0.060 in. ②	150
	STX 4wd	P255/70R17	none	①	①	NA	0.060 in. ②	150
	FX4	P255/70R17	LT245/65R18	①	①	NA	0.060 in. ②	150
			P275/65R18	①	①	NA	0.060 in. ②	150
	F-150 SuperCab							
	XL 2wd	P235/70R17	P255/65R17	①	①	NA	0.060 in. ②	150
	XL 4wd	P235/75R17	P255/70R17	①	①	NA	0.060 in. ②	150
	XLT 2wd	P235/70R17	P255/65R17	①	①	NA	0.060 in. ②	150
	XLT 4wd	P235/75R17	P255/70R17	①	①	NA	0.060 in. ②	150
	STX 2wd	P255/65R17	none	①	①	NA	0.060 in. ②	150
	STX 4wd	P255/70R17	none	①	①	NA	0.060 in. ②	150
	Lariat 2wd	P265/60R18	LT245/65R18	①	①	NA	0.060 in. ②	150
	Lariat 4wd	P275/65R18	LT245/65R18	①	①	NA	0.060 in. ②	150
	FX4	P255/70R17	LT245/65R18	①	①	NA	0.060 in. ②	150
			P275/65R18	①	①	NA	0.060 in. ②	150
	F-150 Crew Cab							
	XLT 2wd	P255/65R17	none	①	①	NA	0.060 in. ②	150
	XLT 4wd	P255/70R17	none	①	①	NA	0.060 in. ②	150
	Lariat 2wd	P265/60R18	LT245/65R18	①	①	NA	0.060 in. ②	150
	Lariat 4wd	P275/65R18	LT245/65R18	①	①	NA	0.060 in. ②	150
	FX4	P255/70R17	LT245/65R18	①	①	NA	0.060 in. ②	150
			P275/65R18	①	①	NA	0.060 in. ②	150
	F-250 Lariat	LT265/75R16E	none	①	①	NA	0.030 in. ②	165
	F-250 XL, XLT	LT235/85R16E	LT265/75R16E	①	①	NA	0.030 in. ②	165
	F-350 SRW	LT265/75R16E	none	①	①	NA	0.030 in. ②	165
	F-350 DRW	LT235/85R16E	none	①	①	NA	0.030 in. ②	165
2006	F-150 4x2 ③	P235/70R17	④	①	①	NA	⑤	150
	F-150 4x4 ③	P235/75R17	④	①	①	NA	⑤	150
	Mark LT 4x2 ③	2wd P265/60R18	④	①	①	NA	0.060 in. ②	150
	Mark LT 4x4 ③	4wd P275/65R18	④	①	①	NA	0.060 in. ②	150
	F-250 4x4	P265/70R17	④	①	①	NA	⑥	165
	F-350 4x4	P275/70R18	④	①	①	NA	⑥	165
2007	F-150 4x2 ③	P235/70R17	④	①	①	NA	⑤	150
	F-150 4x4 ③	P235/75R17	④	①	①	NA	⑤	150
	Mark LT 4x2 ③	2wd P265/60R18	④	①	①	NA	0.060 in. ②	150
	Mark LT 4x4 ③	4wd P275/65R18	④	①	①	NA	0.060 in. ②	150
	F-250 4x4	P245/75R17E	④	①	①	NA	⑥	165
	F-350 4x4	P265/70R17E	④	①	①	NA	⑥	165

NA: Information not available

OEM: Original Equipment Manufacturer

PSI: Pounds Per Square Inch

STD: Standard

OPT: Optional

SRW: Single rear wheels

DRW: Dual rear wheels

① See placard on vehicle

② Both upper and lower

③ All cabs with TPMS

④ Multiple optional tires available; consult tire dealer.

⑤ Upper: 0.0.032 in.; Lower: 0.008 in.

⑥ Upper: 0.0.024 in.; Lower: 0.004 in.

22086_FTRK_C0014

BRAKE SPECIFICATIONS

All measurements in inches unless noted

Year	Model		Brake Disc			Brake Drum Diameter			Brake Caliper	
			Original Thickness	Minimum Thickness	Maximum Runout	Original Inside Diameter	Max. Wear Limit	Maximum Machine Diameter	Bracket Bolts (ft. lbs.)	Mounting Bolts (ft. lbs.)
2005	F-150	F	NA	1.12	NA	—	—	—	148	47
		R	NA	0.72	NA	—	—	—	60	22
	F-250	F	NA	1.43	NA	—	—	—	166	56
		R	NA	1.27	NA	—	—	—	①	②
	F-350	F	NA	1.43	NA	—	—	—	166	56
		R	NA	1.27	NA	—	—	—	①	②
2006	F-150, Mark LT	F	NA	1.12	NA	—	—	—	148	55
		R	NA	0.72	NA	—	—	—	60	22
	F-250	F	NA	1.43	NA	—	—	—	166	56
		R	NA	1.27	NA	—	—	—	①	②
	F-350	F	NA	1.43	NA	—	—	—	166	56
		R	NA	1.27	NA	—	—	—	①	②
2007	F-150, Mark LT	F	NA	1.12	NA	—	—	—	148	55
		R	NA	0.72	NA	—	—	—	60	22
	F-250	F	NA	1.43	NA	—	—	—	166	56
		R	NA	1.27	NA	—	—	—	①	②
	F-350	F	NA	1.43	NA	—	—	—	166	56
		R	NA	1.27	NA	—	—	—	①	②

NOTE: Due to changes made during production, refer to manufacturer's specifications if they differ from those in this chart

NA: Information not available

① Caliper support bolts: 101 ft. lbs.
  Anchor plate bolts: 203 ft. lbs.

② F-250 and F-350 Single Rear Wheel: 26 ft. lbs.
  F-350 Dual Rear Wheels: 56 ft. lbs.

22086_FTRK_C0016

SCHEDULED MAINTENANCE INTERVALS
F-150, F-250 and F-350 Series with Gasoline Engines

TO BE SERVICED	TYPE OF SERVICE	VEHICLE MILEAGE INTERVAL (x1000)												
		5	10	15	20	25	30	35	40	45	50	55	60	65
Engine oil & filter	R	✓	✓	✓	✓	✓	✓	✓	✓	✓	✓	✓	✓	✓
Tires	Rotate	✓	✓	✓	✓	✓	✓	✓	✓	✓	✓	✓	✓	✓
Wheels	I ①			✓			✓			✓			✓	
Auto trans. fluid	I			✓			✓			✓			✓	
Brake pads/shoes	I			✓			✓			✓			✓	
Coolant hoses	S/I			✓			✓			✓			✓	
Steering linkage	I			✓			✓			✓			✓	
Suspension	I			✓			✓			✓			✓	
Driveshaft	I			✓			✓			✓			✓	
Cabin air filter	R			✓			✓			✓			✓	
Ball joints (2wd)	L			✓			✓			✓			✓	
Front drive axle U-joints	I/L			✓			✓			✓			✓	
NGV fuel filter	R					✓					✓			
Exhaust system	I						✓						✓	
Engine air filter	R						✓						✓	
Fuel filter	R						✓						✓	
Auto trans fluid (4R100 and	R						✓						✓	
Manual trans. fluid	R												✓	
Front wheel bearings (2wd)	L/Adj												✓	
Front wheel bearings grease	R												✓	
Accessory drive belts	I	every 100,000 miles												
Spark plugs	R	every 100,000 miles												
PCV valve ②	R	every 100,000 miles												
Premium Gold coolant	R	every 3 years or 100,000 miles												
Auto trans fluid (all exc. 4R100 and TorqShift)	R	every 120,000 miles												
PCV valve (5.4L 3v)	I	every 150,000 miles												
Front wheel bearings (2wd)	R	at 150,000 miles, if not previously done so												
Front drive axle needle bearings (F-Super Duty)	L	every 150,000 miles												
Fuel tank	I	every 150,000 miles												
Front drive axle fluid	R	every 150,000 miles												
Rear drive axle fluid	R	every 150,000 miles												
Transfer case fluid	R	every 150,000 miles												
Accessory drive belts	R	every 150,000 miles, if not previously done so												

NOTE: See next chart for footnotes.

SCHEDULED MAINTENANCE INTERVALS
F-150, F-250 and F-350 Series with Gasoline Engines
Footnotes

R: Replace   S: Service   I: Inspect   L: Lubricate

NGV: Natural gas vehicle

① Inspect for end play and noise

② Vehicles under 6,000 lbs. GVW, exc. 5.4L 3v engines

Special Operating Condition Requirements

When towing a trailer or using a camper or car-top carrier:

Change engine oil and install a new oil filter every 4,800 km (3,000 miles), 3 months or 200 hours of engine operation (whichever occurs first).

Change transfer case fluid every 96,000 km (60,000 miles).

Change manual transmission fluid as required.

Inspect and lubricate U-joints as required.

During extensive idling and/or low speed driving for long distances, as in heavy commercial use such as delivery, taxi, patrol car or livery:

Change engine oil and install a new oil filter every 4,800 km (3,000 miles), 3 months or 200 hours of engine operation (whichever occurs first).

Lube front lower control arm and steering linkage ball joints with zerk fittings (if equipped) every 4,800 km (3,000 miles) or 3 months.

Inspect brake system and check battery electrolyte level (Patrol cars) every 8,000 km (5,000 miles).

Install a new fuel filter every 24,000 km (15,000 miles).

Change automatic transmission fluid, lubricate 4x2 wheel bearings, install new grease seals and adjust bearings every 48,000 km (30,000 miles). If equipped, change the in-line service installed transmission fluid filter.

Install new spark plugs and change transfer case fluid every 96,000 km (60,000 miles).

Install a new cabin air filter as required.

When operating in dusty conditions such as unpaved or dusty roads:

Change engine oil and install a new oil filter every 4,800 km (3,000 miles) or 3 months.

Install a new fuel filter every 24,000 km (15,000 miles).

Change automatic transmission fluid every 48,000 km (30,000 miles). If equipped, change the in-line service installed transmission fluid filter.

Change transfer case fluid every 96,000 km (60,000 miles).

Install a new engine air filter as required.

Install a new cabin air filter as required.

When operating in off-road conditions:

Change automatic transmission fluid every 48,000 km (30,000 miles). If equipped, change the in-line service installed transmission fluid filter.

Change transfer case fluid every 96,000 km (60,000 miles).

Install a new cabin air filter as required.

Inspect and lubricate U-joints.

Inspect and lubricate steering linkage ball joints with zerk fittings.

Short trips in cold operating conditions:

Inspect and lubricate 4x2 ball joints and steering idler arms every 8,000 km (5,000 miles).

Change transfer case fluid every 96,000 km (60,000 miles).

22086_FTRK_C0018

SCHEDULED MAINTENANCE INTERVALS
All Vehicles with the 6.0L Diesel Engine

TO BE SERVICED	TYPE OF SERVICE	7.5	15	22.5	30	37.5	45	52.5	60	67.5	75	82.5	90	97.5
		VEHICLE MILEAGE INTERVAL (x1000)												
Engine oil & filter	R	✓	✓	✓	✓	✓	✓	✓	✓	✓	✓	✓	✓	✓
Tires	Rotate	✓	✓	✓	✓	✓	✓	✓	✓	✓	✓	✓	✓	✓
Air filter minder	I ①	✓	✓	✓	✓	✓	✓	✓	✓	✓	✓	✓	✓	✓
Wheels	I ②		✓		✓		✓		✓		✓		✓	
Brake pads, hoses, etc.	I		✓		✓		✓		✓		✓		✓	
Coolant hoses	I		✓		✓		✓		✓		✓		✓	
Steering linkage and suspension	I/L		✓		✓		✓		✓		✓		✓	
Cabin air filter	R						✓						✓	
Ball joints (2wd)	L		✓		✓		✓		✓		✓		✓	
Driveshaft	I/L		✓		✓		✓		✓		✓		✓	
4x4 front axle U-joints	L		✓		✓		✓		✓		✓		✓	
Exhaust system and heat shields	I		✓		✓		✓		✓		✓		✓	
Engine air filter	R		✓		✓		✓		✓		✓		✓	
Fuel filters ③	R		✓		✓		✓		✓		✓			
Auto trans fluid ④	R				✓				✓				✓	
4x2 front wheel bearings	L							✓						
4x2 front wheel bearing grease seals	R							✓						
Accessory drive belts	I													✓
Manual trans. fluid	R							✓						
Rear differential fluid ⑤	R													✓
Coolant (Premium Gold)	R	every 105,000 miles												
Front drve axle fluid	R	every 150,000 miles												
Transfer case fluid	R	every 150,000 miles												
Accessory drive belts	R	every 150,000 miles, if not previously done so												

R: Replace   S: Service   I: Inspect   L: Lubricate   Adj: adjust

① Reset after new filter is installed
② Inspect for end play and noise
③ Frame-mounted and engine
④ Including external and in-line filters
⑤ Dana axles using non-synthetic fluid only

When towing a trailer or using a camper or car-top carrier:

Change engine oil and install a new oil filter every 4,800 km (3,000 miles), 3 months or 200 hours of engine operation (whichever occurs first).

Change transfer case fluid every 96,000 km (60,000 miles).

Change manual transmission fluid as required.

Inspect and lubricate U-joints as required.

During extensive idling and/or low speed driving for long distances, as in heavy commercial use such as delivery, taxi, patrol car or livery:

Change engine oil and install a new oil filter every 4,800 km (3,000 miles), 3 months or 200 hours of engine operation (whichever occurs first).

Lube front lower control arm and steering linkage ball joints with zerk fittings (if equipped) every 4,800 km (3,000 miles) or 3 months.

Inspect brake system and check battery electrolyte level (Patrol cars) every 8,000 km (5,000 miles).

Install a new fuel filter every 24,000 km (15,000 miles).

Change automatic transmission fluid, lubricate 4x2 wheel bearings, install new grease seals and adjust bearings every 48,000 km (30,000 miles). If equipped, change the in-line service installed transmission fluid filter.

Change transfer case fluid every 96,000 km (60,000 miles).

Install a new cabin air filter as required.

SCHEDULED MAINTENANCE INTERVALS
All Vehicles with the 6.0L Diesel Engine
Footnotes continued

When operating in dusty conditions such as unpaved or dusty roads:

Change engine oil and install a new oil filter every 4,800 km (3,000 miles) or 3 months.

Install a new fuel filter every 24,000 km (15,000 miles).

Change automatic transmission fluid every 48,000 km (30,000 miles). If equipped, change the in-line service installed transmission fluid filter.

Change transfer case fluid every 96,000 km (60,000 miles).

Install a new engine air filter or cabine air filter as required.

When operating in off-road conditions:

Change automatic transmission fluid every 48,000 km (30,000 miles). If equipped, change the in-line service installed transmission fluid filter.

Change transfer case fluid every 96,000 km (60,000 miles).

Install a new cabin air filter as required.

Inspect and lubricate U-joints.

Inspect and lubricate steering linkage ball joints with zerk fittings.

22086_FTRK_C0022

SCHEDULED MAINTENANCE INTERVALS
Lincoln Mark LT

TO BE SERVICED	SERVIC	VEHICLE MILEAGE INTERVAL (x1000)												
		5	10	15	20	25	30	35	40	45	50	55	60	65
Engine oil & filter	R	✓	✓	✓	✓	✓	✓	✓	✓	✓	✓	✓	✓	✓
Tires	Rotate	✓	✓	✓	✓	✓	✓	✓	✓	✓	✓	✓	✓	✓
Wheels	I ①			✓			✓			✓			✓	
Brake fluid level	S/I	✓	✓	✓	✓	✓	✓	✓	✓	✓	✓	✓	✓	✓
Tire pressure and wear	S/I	✓	✓	✓	✓	✓	✓	✓	✓	✓	✓	✓	✓	✓
Auto trans. fluid	I			✓			✓			✓			✓	
Power steering fluid level	S/I	✓	✓	✓	✓	✓	✓	✓	✓	✓	✓	✓	✓	✓
Washer fluid level	S/I	✓	✓	✓	✓	✓	✓	✓	✓	✓	✓	✓	✓	✓
Battery performance	I	✓	✓	✓	✓	✓	✓	✓	✓	✓	✓	✓	✓	✓
Exterior lights	I	✓	✓	✓	✓	✓	✓	✓	✓	✓	✓	✓	✓	✓
Brake pads/shoes	I			✓			✓			✓			✓	
Coolant hoses	S/I	✓	✓	✓	✓	✓	✓	✓	✓	✓	✓	✓	✓	✓
A/C hoses	I	✓	✓	✓	✓	✓	✓	✓	✓	✓	✓	✓	✓	✓
Engine air filter	I	✓	✓	✓	✓	✓	✓	✓	✓	✓	✓	✓	✓	✓
Steering linkage	I			✓			✓			✓			✓	
Suspension	I/L			✓			✓			✓			✓	
Halfshafts	I			✓			✓			✓			✓	
Driveshaft	I			✓			✓			✓			✓	
Cabin air filter	R			✓			✓			✓			✓	
Ball joints (2wd)	L			✓			✓			✓			✓	
Front drive axle U-joints	I/L			✓			✓			✓			✓	
Exhaust system	I	✓	✓	✓	✓	✓	✓	✓	✓	✓	✓	✓	✓	✓
Engine air filter	R						✓						✓	
Fuel filter	R						✓						✓	
Climate controlled seat filters	R						✓						✓	
Front wheel bearings (2wd)	L/Adj									✓				
Accessory drive belts	I	every 100,000 miles												
Spark plugs	R	every 100,000 miles												
Premium Gold coolant	R	every 5 years or 100,000 miles												
PCV valve	R	every 100,000 miles												
Auto trans fluid	R	every 150,000 miles												
Front wheel bearings (2wd)	R	at 150,000 miles, if not previously done so												
Fuel tank	I	every 150,000 miles												
Front drive axle fluid	R	every 150,000 miles												
Rear drive axle fluid	R	every 150,000 miles												
Transfer case fluid	R	every 150,000 miles												
Accessory drive belts	R	every 150,000 miles, if not previously done so												

NOTE: See next chart for footnotes.

22086_FTRK_C0020

SCHEDULED MAINTENANCE INTERVALS
Lincoln Mark LT
Footnotes

R: Replace   S: Service   I: Inspect   L: Lubricate

NGV: Natural gas vehicle

① Inspect for end play and noise

Special Operating Condition Requirements

When towing a trailer or using a camper or car-top carrier:

Change engine oil and install a new oil filter every 4,800 km (3,000 miles), 3 months or 200 hours of engine operation (whichever occurs first).

Change transfer case fluid every 96,000 km (60,000 miles).

Change manual transmission fluid as required.

Inspect and lubricate U-joints as required.

During extensive idling and/or low speed driving for long distances, as in heavy commercial use such as delivery, taxi, patrol car or livery:

Change engine oil and install a new oil filter every 4,800 km (3,000 miles), 3 months or 200 hours of engine operation (whichever occurs first).

Lube front lower control arm and steering linkage ball joints with zerk fittings (if equipped) every 4,800 km (3,000 miles) or 3 months.

Inspect brake system and check battery electrolyte level (Patrol cars) every 8,000 km (5,000 miles).

Install a new fuel filter every 24,000 km (15,000 miles).

Change automatic transmission fluid, lubricate 4x2 wheel bearings, install new grease seals and adjust bearings every 48,000 km (30,000 miles). If equipped, change the in-line service installed transmission fluid filter.

Install new spark plugs and change transfer case fluid every 96,000 km (60,000 miles).

Install a new cabin air filter as required.

When operating in dusty conditions such as unpaved or dusty roads:

Change engine oil and install a new oil filter every 4,800 km (3,000 miles) or 3 months.

Install a new fuel filter every 24,000 km (15,000 miles).

Change automatic transmission fluid every 48,000 km (30,000 miles). If equipped, change the in-line service installed transmission fluid filter.

Change transfer case fluid every 96,000 km (60,000 miles).

Install a new engine air filter as required.

Install a new cabin air filter as required.

When operating in off-road conditions:

Change automatic transmission fluid every 48,000 km (30,000 miles). If equipped, change the in-line service installed transmission fluid filter.

Change transfer case fluid every 96,000 km (60,000 miles).

Install a new cabin air filter as required.

Inspect and lubricate U-joints.

Inspect and lubricate steering linkage ball joints with zerk fittings.

Short trips in cold operating conditions:

Inspect and lubricate 4x2 ball joints and steering idler arms every 8,000 km (5,000 miles).

Change transfer case fluid every 96,000 km (60,000 miles).

22086_FTRK_C0021

PRECAUTIONS

Before servicing any vehicle, please be sure to read all of the following precautions, which deal with personal safety, prevention of component damage, and important points to take into consideration when servicing a motor vehicle:

• Never open, service or drain the radiator or cooling system when the engine is hot; serious burns can occur from the steam and hot coolant.

• Observe all applicable safety precautions when working around fuel. Whenever servicing the fuel system, always work in a well-ventilated area. Do not allow fuel spray or vapors to come in contact with a spark, open flame, or excessive heat (a hot drop light, for example). Keep a dry chemical fire extinguisher near the work area. Always keep fuel in a container specifically designed for fuel storage; also, always properly seal fuel containers to avoid the possibility of fire or explosion. Refer to the additional fuel system precautions later in this section.

• Fuel injection systems often remain pressurized, even after the engine has been turned **OFF**. The fuel system pressure must be relieved before disconnecting any fuel lines. Failure to do so may result in fire and/or personal injury.

• Brake fluid often contains polyglycol ethers and polyglycols. Avoid contact with the eyes and wash your hands thoroughly after handling brake fluid. If you do get brake fluid in your eyes, flush your eyes with clean, running water for 15 minutes. If eye irritation persists, or if you have taken brake fluid internally, IMMEDIATELY seek medical assistance.

• The EPA warns that prolonged contact with used engine oil may cause a number of skin disorders, including cancer. You should make every effort to minimize your exposure to used engine oil. Protective gloves should be worn when changing oil. Wash your hands and any other exposed skin areas as soon as possible after exposure to used engine oil. Soap and water, or waterless hand cleaner should be used.

• All new vehicles are now equipped with an air bag system, often referred to as a Supplemental Restraint System (SRS) or Supplemental Inflatable Restraint (SIR) system. The system must be disabled before performing service on or around system components, steering column, instrument panel components, wiring and sensors. Failure to follow safety and disabling procedures could result in accidental air bag deployment, possible personal injury and unnecessary system repairs.

• Always wear safety goggles when working with, or around, the air bag system. When carrying a non-deployed air bag, be sure the bag and trim cover are pointed away from your body. When placing a non-deployed air bag on a work surface, always face the bag and trim cover upward, away from the surface. This will reduce the motion of the module if it is accidentally deployed. Refer to the additional air bag system precautions later in this section.

• Clean, high quality brake fluid from a sealed container is essential to the safe and proper operation of the brake system.

You should always buy the correct type of brake fluid for your vehicle. If the brake fluid becomes contaminated, completely flush the system with new fluid. Never reuse any brake fluid. Any brake fluid that is removed from the system should be discarded. Also, do not allow any brake fluid to come in contact with a painted surface; it will damage the paint.

• Never operate the engine without the proper amount and type of engine oil; doing so WILL result in severe engine damage.

• Timing belt maintenance is extremely important. Many models utilize an interference-type, non-freewheeling engine. If the timing belt breaks, the valves in the cylinder head may strike the pistons, causing potentially serious (also time-consuming and expensive) engine damage. Refer to the maintenance interval charts for the recommended replacement interval for the timing belt, and to the timing belt section for belt replacement and inspection.

• Disconnecting the negative battery cable on some vehicles may interfere with the functions of the on-board computer system(s) and may require the computer to undergo a relearning process once the negative battery cable is reconnected.

• When servicing drum brakes, only disassemble and assemble one side at a time, leaving the remaining side intact for reference.

• Only an MVAC-trained, EPA-certified automotive technician should service the air conditioning system or its components.

BRAKES

GENERAL INFORMATION

PRECAUTIONS

The anti-lock brake system consists of the following components:
• Hydraulic Control Unit (HCU)
• Anti-lock Brake System (ABS) module
• Rear wheel speed sensor
• Rear wheel speed sensor ring
• Front wheel speed sensors
• Front wheel speed sensor rings
• Yellow ABS warning indicator
• Stop lamp switch

The front wheel speed sensor rings are integral to the front hub and bearing assemblies.

The rear wheel speed sensor ring is integral to the rear axle.

SPEED SENSORS

REMOVAL & INSTALLATION

F-150 and Mark LT

Front—2-Wheel Drive

See Figure 1.

ANTI-LOCK BRAKE SYSTEM (ABS)

1. Raise and safely support the vehicle.

➡ **The harness connector is located in the engine compartment secured to the fender apron.**

2. Disconnect the wheel speed sensor electrical connector.
3. Remove the 3 wheel speed sensor harness retainers.
4. Remove the bolt and the wheel speed sensor.
5. To install, reverse the removal procedure. Tighten to 9 Nm (80 inch lbs.).

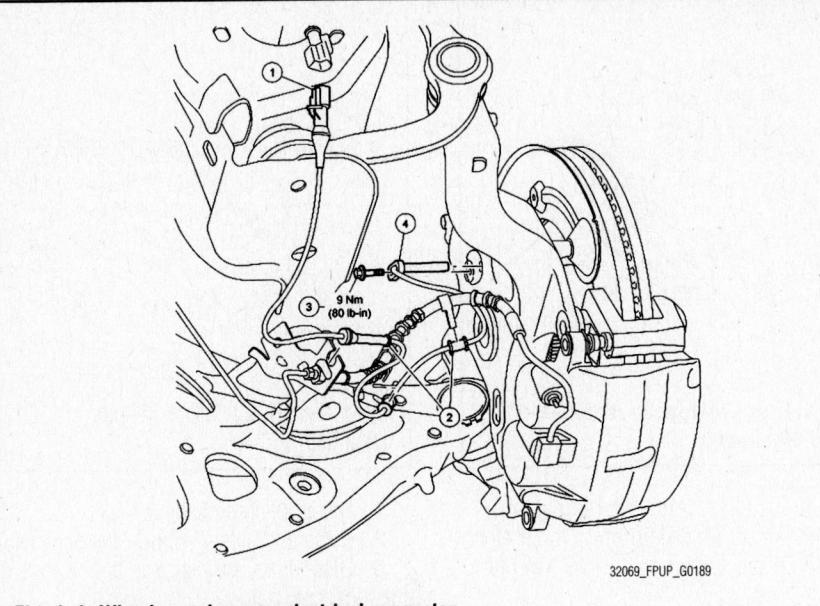

32069_FPUP_G0189

Fig. 1 1. Wheel speed sensor electrical connector
2. Wheel speed sensor harness retainers
3. Wheel speed sensor bolt
4. Wheel speed sensor
Front wheel speed sensor—F-150 and Mark LT w/2WD

Front—4-Wheel Drive

See Figure 2.

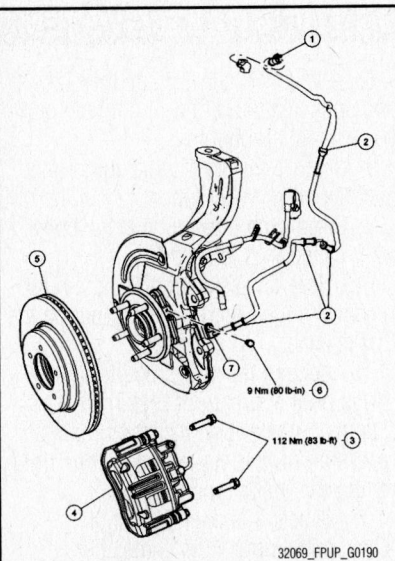

32069_FPUP_G0190

Fig. 2 1. Wheel speed sensor electrical connector
2. Wheel speed sensor harness retainers
3. Front brake caliper anchor plate bolts
4. Front brake caliper assembly
5. Front brake disc
6. Wheel speed sensor bolt
7. Wheel speed sensor
Front wheel speed sensor—F-150 and Mark LT w/4WD

❊❊ WARNING

When removing the front disc brake components, never allow them to hang from the brake hose.

1. Raise and safely support the vehicle.

➡ **The harness connector is located in the engine compartment secured to the fender apron.**

2. Disconnect the wheel speed sensor electrical connector.
3. Remove the 4 wheel speed sensor harness retainers.
4. Remove the 2 bolts and position the front brake caliper assembly aside. See Brake Caliper R&I.

➡ **Match mark the front disc brake rotor and front wheel hub flange before removing the front disc brake rotor.**

5. Remove the brake disc. For additional information, refer to Brake Rotor R&I.
6. Remove the bolt and the front wheel speed sensor.
7. To install, reverse the removal procedure. Tighten to 9 Nm (80 inch lbs.).

Rear

See Figure 3.

1. Raise and safely support the vehicle.
2. Disconnect the rear axle speed sensor electrical connector.
3. Remove the rear axle speed sensor bolt.

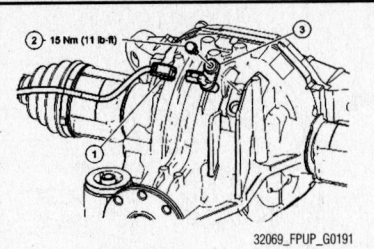

32069_FPUP_G0191

Fig. 3 1. Rear axle speed sensor electrical connector
2. Rear axle speed sensor bolt
3. Rear axle speed sensor
Rear wheel speed sensor—F-150 and Mark LT

➡ **Install a new O-ring before installing the rear axle speed sensor.**

4. Remove the rear axle speed sensor.
5. To install, reverse the removal procedure. Tighten to 15 Nm (11 ft. lbs.).

F-250 and F-350

Front—2-Wheel Drive

See Figure 4.

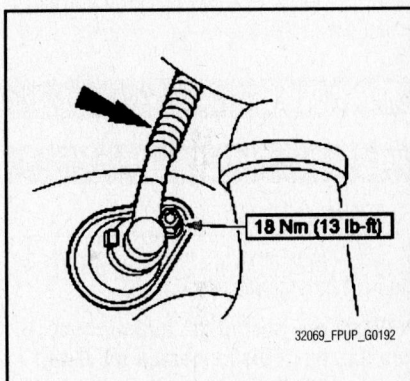

32069_FPUP_G0192

Fig. 4 Front wheel speed sensor—F-250 and F-350 w/2WD

1. Raise and safely support the vehicle.
2. Disconnect the front wheel speed sensor electrical connector.
3. Separate the wheel speed sensor harness from the brake hose clips.
4. Remove the bolt and the front wheel speed sensor.
5. To install, reverse the removal procedure. Torque the bolt to 18 Nm (13 ft. lbs.).

Front—4-Wheel Drive

See Figures 5 and 6.

1. Remove the brake disc. For additional information, refer to Brake Rotor R&I.

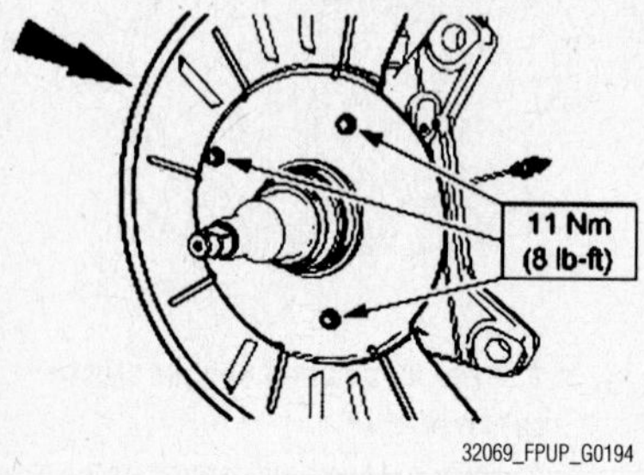

Fig. 5 Brake disc shield—F-250 and F-350 w/4WD

2. Remove the brake disc shield screws and the brake disc shield.
3. Disconnect the front wheel speed sensor electrical connector.

⁂ WARNING

Make sure the ABS harness is properly routed to prevent the disc from cutting the ABS harness.

4. Remove the 2 screws and the front wheel speed sensor.

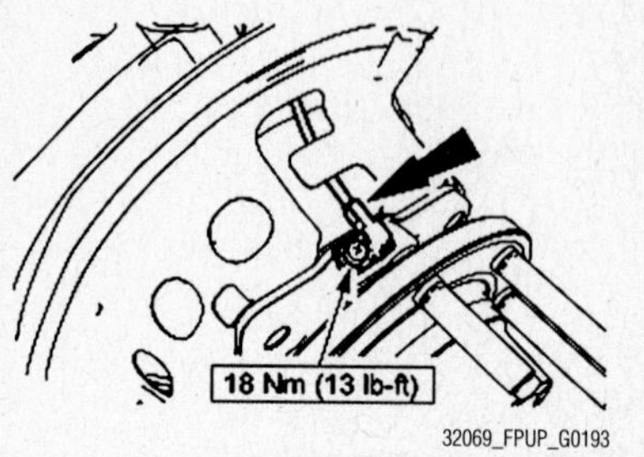

Fig. 6 Front wheel speed sensor—F-250 and F-350 w/4WD

5. To install, reverse the removal procedure. Torque the shield bolts to 11 Nm (8 ft. lbs.); the sensor bolt to 18 Nm (13 ft. lbs.).

Rear

See Figure 7.

➡Clean off dirt and debris that may have collected around the rear axle speed sensor before removal to prevent fluid contamination.

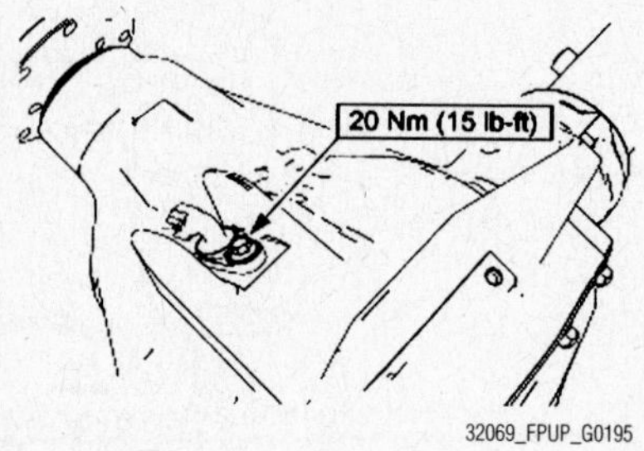

Fig. 7 Rear speed sensor—F-250 and F-350

1. Disconnect the battery.
2. Raise and safely support the vehicle.
3. Disconnect the rear axle speed sensor electrical connector.

➡Do not apply force to the plastic rear axle speed sensor connector.

4. Remove the bolt and the rear axle speed sensor.
5. To install, reverse the removal procedure. Torque to 20 Nm (15 ft. lbs.).

BRAKES — BLEEDING THE BRAKE SYSTEM

BLEEDING PROCEDURE

BLEEDING PROCEDURE

1. Before servicing the vehicle, refer to the Precautions Section.

➡When any part of the hydraulic system has been disconnected for repair or new installation, air may get into the system and cause spongy brake pedal action. This requires bleeding of the hydraulic system after it has been correctly connected. The hydraulic system can be gravity bled, manually bled or with pressure bleeding equipment.

Master Cylinder, Bench

2. Support the brake master cylinder body in a vise and fill the brake master cylinder reservoir with specified brake fluid.

➡Original equipment lines are not intended to be used during this procedure.

3. Install short brake tubes with the ends submerged in the brake master cylinder reservoir.
4. Slowly press the primary piston until clear fluid flows from both brake tubes, without air bubbles.
5. Remove the short brake tubes and plug the brake tube ports.

Master Cylinder—In Vehicle

⁂ WARNING

Do not allow the brake master cylinder reservoir to run dry during the bleeding operation. Keep the brake master cylinder reservoir filled with the specified brake fluid. Never reuse the brake fluid that has been drained from the hydraulic system.

➡When a new brake master cylinder has been installed or the system has been emptied, or partially emptied, it should be primed to prevent air from getting into the system.

6. Disconnect the brake master cylinder outlet tubes.

➡Original equipment lines are not intended to be used during this procedure.

7. Install short brake tubes with ends submerged in the brake master cylinder reservoir and fill the brake master cylinder reservoir with brake fluid.
8. Have an assistant pump the brake pedal until clear fluid flows from both brake tubes without air bubbles.
9. Remove the short brake tubes and install the brake outlet tubes.
10. Bleed each brake tube at the brake master cylinder as follows:
    a. Have an assistant pump the brake pedal and then hold firm pressure on the brake pedal.
    b. Loosen the rear brake tube fittings until a stream of brake fluid comes out. Have an assistant maintain pressure on the brake pedal while tightening the brake tube fitting.
    c. Repeat this operation until clear, bubble-free fluid comes out.
    d. Refill the brake master cylinder reservoir as necessary. Repeat the bleeding operation at the front brake tube.
11. While the assistant maintains pressure on the brake pedal, tighten the brake tubes.

Gravity Bleeding

⁂ WARNING

Do not allow the brake master cylinder reservoir to run dry during the bleeding operation. Keep the brake

master cylinder reservoir filled with the specified brake fluid. Never reuse the brake fluid that has been drained from the hydraulic system.

➡When a new brake master cylinder has been installed or the system has been emptied, or partially emptied, it should be primed to prevent air from getting into the system.

12. Fill the brake master cylinder reservoir with brake fluid.

13. Connect a clear tube to the right rear disc brake caliper bleeder screw and the other end in a container partially filled with recommended brake fluid.

14. Open the bleeder screw and leave open until clear bubble-free brake fluid flows.

15. Refill the brake master cylinder reservoir as necessary.

16. Tighten the disc brake caliper bleeder screw.

17. Repeat Steps 1 through 4 for the three remaining brake calipers, going in order from the left rear disc brake caliper to the right front disc brake caliper ending with the left front disc brake caliper.

18. If the brake pedal feels spongy, repeat the bleed procedure.

Manual Bleeding

✳✳ WARNING

Do not allow the brake master cylinder reservoir to run dry during the bleeding operation. Keep the brake

master cylinder reservoir filled with the specified brake fluid. Never reuse the brake fluid that has been drained from the hydraulic system.

19. Fill the brake master cylinder reservoir with brake fluid.

20. Connect a clear tube to the right rear disc brake caliper bleeder screw and the other end in a container partially filled with recommended brake fluid.

21. Have an assistant pump the brake pedal and then hold firm pressure on the brake pedal.

22. Loosen the disc brake caliper bleeder screw until a stream of brake fluid comes out. Have an assistant maintain pressure on the brake pedal while tightening the disc brake caliper bleeder screw. Repeat until clear, bubble-free fluid comes out. Refill the brake master cylinder reservoir as necessary.

23. Tighten the disc brake caliper bleeder screw.

24. Repeat Steps 1 through 5 for the three remaining brake calipers, going in order from the left rear disc brake caliper to the right front disc brake caliper ending with the left front disc brake caliper.

25. If the brake pedal feels spongy, repeat the bleed procedure.

Anti-Lock Brake System Hydraulic Control Unit Bleeding

➡This procedure is only required when a new hydraulic control unit is installed.

26. Connect diagnostic tool Worldwide Diagnostic System (WDS) 418-F224, New Generation STAR (NGS) Tester 418-F052, or equivalent diagnostic tool and follow the ABS system bleed instructions.

27. Use the gravity bleed or manual bleed procedure(s) to bleed the system. Begin at the right rear caliper.

BLEEDING THE ABS SYSTEM

Anti-Lock Brake System (ABS) Hydraulic Control Unit Bleeding

➡This procedure is required only when a new hydraulic control unit is installed. A diagnostic tool, such as the Worldwide Diagnostic System, or equivalent, in necessary.

➡When any part of the hydraulic system has been disconnected for repair or new installation, air may get into the system and cause spongy brake pedal action. This requires bleeding of the hydraulic system after it has been correctly connected. See Bleeding the Brake System, under Brake Operating Systems.

1. Connect the diagnostic tool and follow the ABS system bleed instructions.

2. Use the manual bleed procedure(s) to bleed the system. Begin at the right rear caliper.

BRAKES

✳✳ CAUTION

Dust and dirt accumulating on brake parts during normal use may contain asbestos fibers from production or aftermarket brake linings. Breathing excessive concentrations of asbestos fibers can cause serious bodily harm. Exercise care when servicing brake parts. Do not sand or grind brake lining unless equipment used is designed to contain the dust residue. Do not clean brake parts with compressed air or by dry brushing. Cleaning should be done by dampening the brake components with a fine mist of water, then wiping the brake components clean with a dampened cloth. Dispose of cloth and all residue containing asbestos fibers in an impermeable container with

the appropriate label. Follow practices prescribed by the Occupational Safety and Health Administration (OSHA) and the Environmental Protection Agency (EPA) for the handling, processing, and disposing of dust or debris that may contain asbestos fibers.

BRAKE CALIPER

REMOVAL & INSTALLATION

F-150 and Mark LT

See Figures 8 and 9.

1. Before servicing the vehicle, refer to the Precautions Section.

2. Remove the wheel and tire assembly.

3. Remove the caliper bolts.

4. Remove the brake caliper.

FRONT DISC BRAKES

✳✳ WARNING

Do not allow the brake caliper to hang by the flexible brake hose.

5. Support the caliper to the vehicle.

6. Remove the flow bolt.

7. Remove the copper washers.

8. Remove the brake line.

To install:

9. To install, reverse the removal procedure. Tighten the bottom caliper bolt and then the top caliper bolt. Always use new copper washers.

10. Observe the following torques:
- Caliper mounting bolts: 47 ft. lbs. (64 Nm).
- Brake line flow bolt: 26 ft. lbs. (35 Nm).

11. Bleed the brake system.

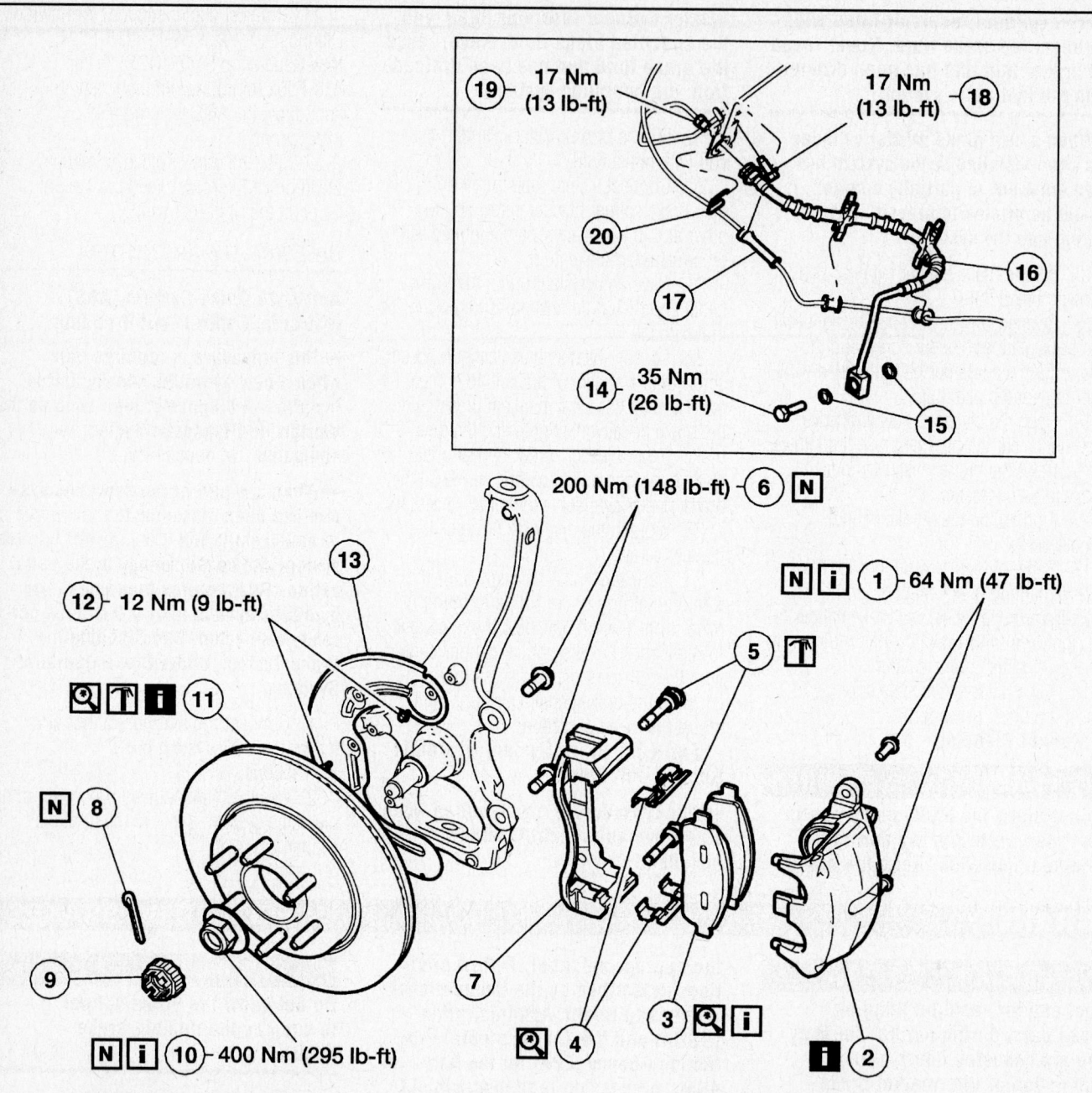

1 Caliper bolt (2 required for each side)
2 Brake caliper (RH/LH)
3 Brake disc pads (1 kit LH and RH)
4 Slippers
5 Guide pin and boot (2 required for each side)
6 Anchor bracket bolts (2 required for each side)
7 Anchor bracket
8 Cotter pin
9 Retainer
10 Spindle nut (1 each side)

11 Brake disc (heavy duty and light duty)
12 Dust shield bolts (3 required each side)
13 Dust shield (RH/LH)
14 Flow bolt
15 Copper washers (2 required each side)
16 Brake line (RH/LH)
17 Anti-lock brake sensor cable
18 Brake line bracket bolt
19 Brake line fitting
20 Retainer clip

67197-EFSE-G201

Fig. 8 Front disc brake components—2WD F-150 and Mark LT

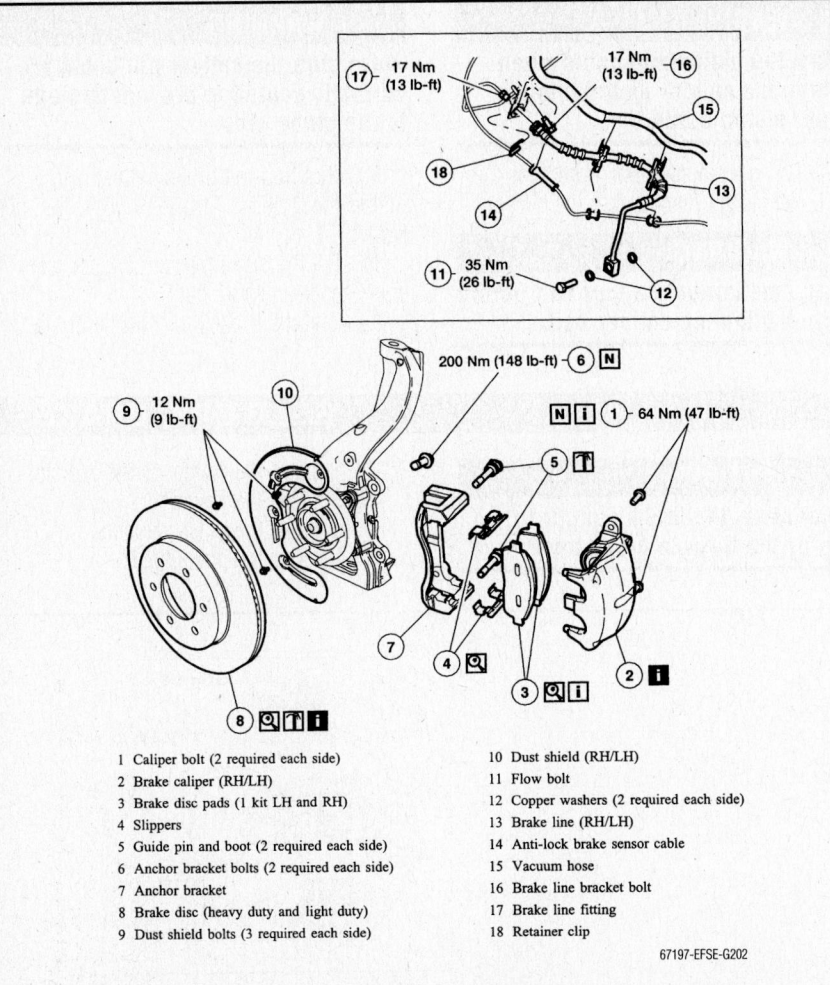

1 Caliper bolt (2 required each side)
2 Brake caliper (RH/LH)
3 Brake disc pads (1 kit LH and RH)
4 Slippers
5 Guide pin and boot (2 required each side)
6 Anchor bracket bolts (2 required each side)
7 Anchor bracket
8 Brake disc (heavy duty and light duty)
9 Dust shield bolts (3 required each side)
10 Dust shield (RH/LH)
11 Flow bolt
12 Copper washers (2 required each side)
13 Brake line (RH/LH)
14 Anti-lock brake sensor cable
15 Vacuum hose
16 Brake line bracket bolt
17 Brake line fitting
18 Retainer clip

67197-EFSE-G202

Fig. 9 Front disc brake components—4WD F-150 and Mark LT

F-250 and F-350

1. Before servicing the vehicle, refer to the Precautions Section.
2. Raise and safely support the vehicle.
3. Remove the brake flexible hose flow bolt and position the brake flexible hose aside. Discard the 2 copper washers.

⁂ WARNING

Do not pry in the caliper sight hole to retract the pistons as this can damage the pistons and boots.

4. Remove the 2 brake caliper bolts and the brake caliper. If leaks or damaged boots are found, install a new disc brake caliper.

To install:

⁂ WARNING

Tighten the bottom caliper bolt before tightening the top caliper bolt.

⁂ WARNING

Make sure the caliper pin boots are correctly seated to prevent damage to the guide pins.

5. Position the brake caliper and install the 2 bolts. Torque to 56 ft. lbs. (76 Nm).
6. Using 2 new copper washers, position the brake flexible hose and install the brake caliper flow bolt. Torque to 35 ft. lbs. (48 Nm).
7. Bleed the brake caliper.
8. Test the brake system for normal operation.

DISC BRAKE PADS

REMOVAL & INSTALLATION

F-150 and Mark LT

See Figures 8 and 9.

1. Before servicing the vehicle, refer to the Precautions Section.
2. Remove the wheel and tire assembly.
3. Remove the caliper bolt.
4. Remove the brake caliper.

⁂ CAUTION

Do not allow the brake caliper to hang by the flexible brake hose.

5. Support the caliper to the vehicle.
6. Remove the brake disc pads.
7. Remove the slippers.
8. To install, reverse the removal procedure. If replacing the brake pads, remove the brake fluid in the master cylinder reservoir until it is half filled.
9. If replacing the brake pads, use a suitable tool to push the brake caliper pistons into the caliper bore.

➡**Tighten the bottom caliper bolt first and then the top caliper bolt. Torque to 47 ft. lbs. (64 Nm).**

10. If the hydraulic system was opened, bleed the brake system.

F-250 and F-350

1. Before servicing the vehicle, refer to the Precautions Section.
2. Check the brake fluid level in the brake master cylinder reservoir. If required, remove the fluid until the brake master cylinder reservoir is half full.
3. Raise and safely support the vehicle.

⁂ WARNING

Do not pry in the caliper sight hole to retract the pistons, as this can damage the pistons and boots.

⁂ WARNING

Do not allow the brake caliper to hang from the brake caliper flexible hose. Use a suitable tool to support the brake caliper.

4. Remove the 2 brake caliper bolts and position the caliper aside.
5. Remove the 2 brake pads and if equipped, remove the 4 retraction clips. Discard the retraction clips.
6. Measure the front brake disc thickness. Install a new front brake disc if it is not within specification.

⁂ WARNING

Install new brake pads if they are worn past the specified thickness above the metal backing plates. Install new brake pads in complete axle sets.

7. Inspect the brake pads for wear and contamination.

To install:

❊❊ WARNING

Do not allow grease, oil, brake fluid or other contaminants to contact the pad lining material. Do not install contaminated pads.

➡ **Install all new hardware as supplied with the brake pad kit.**

8. Install the 4 new retracting clips and the 2 brake pads.

❊❊ WARNING

Protect the piston and boots when pushing the caliper piston into the caliper piston bores.

9. Using a suitable tool, compress the disc brake caliper pistons into the caliper.

❊❊ WARNING

Tighten the bottom caliper bolt before tightening the top caliper bolt.

❊❊ WARNING

Make sure the caliper pin boots are correctly seated to prevent damage to the guide pins.

10. Position the brake caliper and install the 2 bolts. Torque to 56 ft. lbs. (76 Nm).
11. Fill the brake master cylinder reservoir with clean brake fluid.
12. Test the brakes for normal operation.

BRAKES   REAR DISC BRAKES

❊❊ CAUTION

Dust and dirt accumulating on brake parts during normal use may contain asbestos fibers from production or aftermarket brake linings. Breathing excessive concentrations of asbestos fibers can cause serious bodily harm. Exercise care when servicing brake parts. Do not sand or grind brake lining unless equipment used is designed to contain the dust residue. Do not clean brake parts with compressed air or by dry brushing. Cleaning should be done by dampening the brake components with a fine mist of water, then wiping the brake components clean with a dampened cloth. Dispose of cloth and all residue containing asbestos fibers in an impermeable container with the appropriate label. Follow practices prescribed by the Occupational Safety and Health Administration (OSHA) and the Environmental Protection Agency (EPA) for the handling, processing, and disposing of dust or debris that may contain asbestos fibers.

❊❊ CAUTION

Do not allow the brake caliper to hang by the flexible brake hose.

5. Support the caliper to the vehicle.
6. Remove the flow bolt.
7. Remove the brass washers.
8. Remove the brake hose.

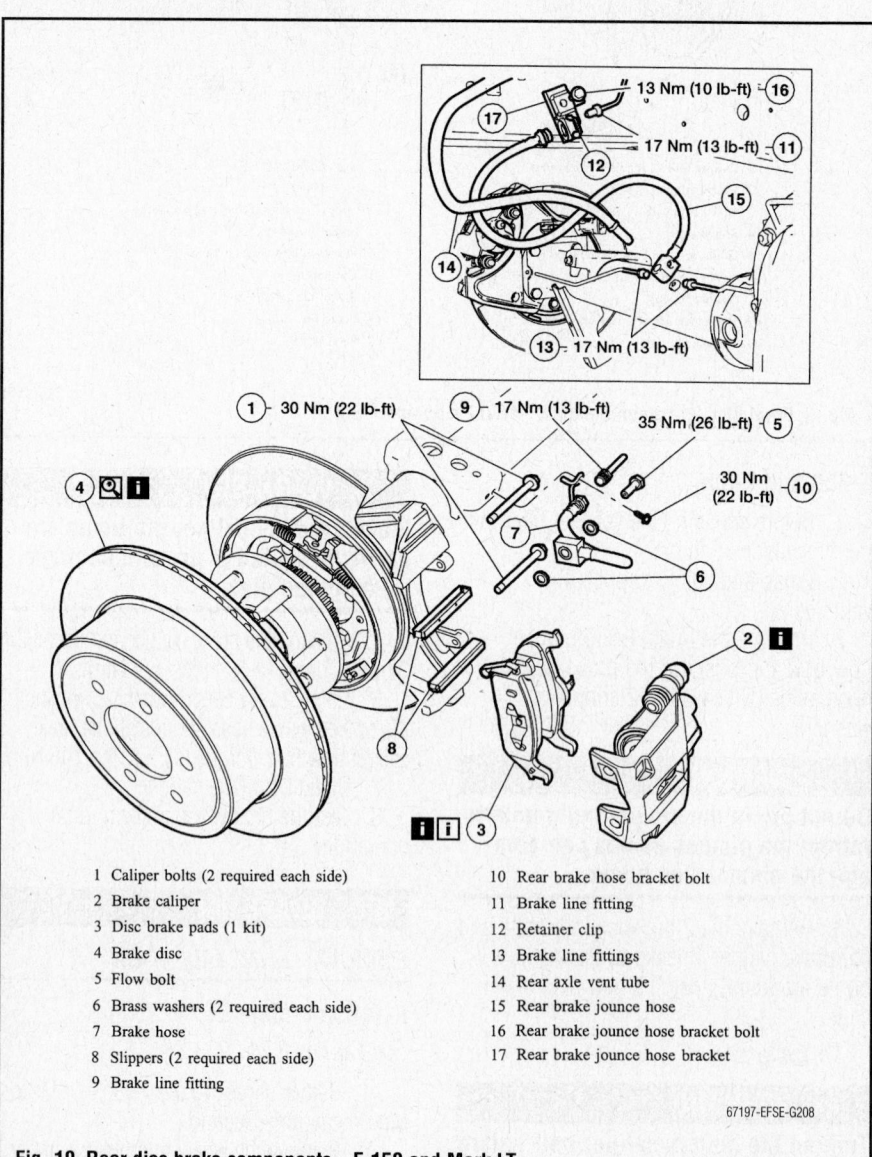

1 Caliper bolts (2 required each side)
2 Brake caliper
3 Disc brake pads (1 kit)
4 Brake disc
5 Flow bolt
6 Brass washers (2 required each side)
7 Brake hose
8 Slippers (2 required each side)
9 Brake line fitting
10 Rear brake hose bracket bolt
11 Brake line fitting
12 Retainer clip
13 Brake line fittings
14 Rear axle vent tube
15 Rear brake jounce hose
16 Rear brake jounce hose bracket bolt
17 Rear brake jounce hose bracket

67197-EFSE-G208

Fig. 10 Rear disc brake components—F-150 and Mark LT

BRAKE CALIPER

REMOVAL & INSTALLATION

F-150 and Mark LT

See Figure 10.

1. Before servicing the vehicle, refer to the Precautions Section.
2. Remove the rear wheel and tire assembly.
3. Remove the caliper bolts.
4. Remove the brake caliper.

To install:

9. To install, reverse the removal procedure. Observe the following torques:
- Caliper pin bolts: 22 ft. lbs. (30 Nm).
- Flow bolt: 26 ft. lbs. (35 Nm).

10. If the hydraulic system has been opened, bleed the brake system.

F-250 and F-350

1. Before servicing the vehicle, refer to the Precautions Section.
2. Raise and support the vehicle.
3. Remove the brake caliper flow bolt and discard the 2 copper washers.

❋❋ WARNING

Do not pry in the caliper sight hole to retract the pistons, as this can damage the pistons and boots.

4. Remove the 2 brake caliper bolts and the caliper.

To install:

5. Position the brake caliper and install the 2 brake caliper bolts.
- For F-250, F-350 single rear wheel caliper, tighten to 35 Nm (26 ft. lbs.).
- For F-350 dual rear wheel caliper, tighten to 76 Nm (56 ft. lbs.).

6. Position the brake flexible hose, install the brake caliper flow bolt and 2 new copper washers. Torque to 26 ft. lbs. (35 Nm).
7. Bleed the brake system.

DISC BRAKE PADS

REMOVAL & INSTALLATION

F-150 and Mark LT

See Figure 10.

1. Before servicing the vehicle, refer to the Precautions Section.
2. Remove the rear wheel and tire assembly.

3. Remove the caliper bolts.
4. Remove the brake caliper.

❋❋ WARNING

Do not allow the brake caliper to hang by the flexible brake hose.

5. Support the caliper to the vehicle.
6. Remove the disc brake pads.

❋❋ WARNING

Do not us any tools to separate the inner brake pad away from the caliper piston. Damage to the caliper piston may occur.

7. Remove the rear brake pads from the caliper.
8. To install, reverse the removal procedure.

❋❋ CAUTION

Install a new lining if worn to or past the specified thickness above the metal backing plate or if the pad is damaged. Install new pads in complete axle sets.

9. If replacing the brake pads, use a suitable suction device, remove the brake fluid in the master cylinder reservoir until it is half filled.
10. If replacing the brake pads, use a suitable tool to push the brake caliper pistons into the caliper bore.
11. If the hydraulic system has been opened, bleed the brake system.

F-250 and F-350

1. Before servicing the vehicle, refer to the Precautions Section.
2. If necessary, remove the brake fluid until the brake master cylinder reservoir is half full.
3. Remove the wheel and tire assembly.

❋❋ WARNING

Do not pry in caliper sight hole to retract pistons as this can damage the pistons and boots.

❋❋ WARNING

When removing the brake caliper, never allow it to hang from the brake flexible hose. Provide a suitable support.

4. Remove the 2 brake caliper bolts and position the caliper aside.

➡**Install a new pads if they are worn past the specified thickness. Install new pads in complete axle sets.**

5. Remove the brake pads and retraction clips.
6. Measure the brake disc thickness. Install a new brake disc if not within specification.
7. Inspect the disc brake caliper for leaks. If leaks are found a new caliper must be installed.
8. Inspect the disc brake anchor plate assembly.
- Check the guide pin boots for damage.
- Check the guide pins for binding and damage.
- Replace worn or damaged pins. Lube pins with Silicone Brake Caliper Compound.

To install:

➡**Make sure to correctly locate the retraction clip.**

9. Install the brake pads and retraction clips.
10. Position the brake caliper and install the 2 brake caliper bolts.
- For F-250, F-350 single rear wheel caliper, tighten to 35 Nm (26 ft. lbs.).
- For F-350 dual rear wheel caliper, tighten to 76 Nm (56 ft. lbs.).

BRAKES   **PARKING BRAKE**

PARKING BRAKE CABLES

ADJUSTMENT

The parking brake system utilizes an automatic adjuster. No adjustment is necessary.

PARKING BRAKE SHOES

REMOVAL & INSTALLATION

F-150 and Mark LT

See Figure 11.

1. Before servicing the vehicle, refer to the Precautions Section.

➡**One parking brake shoe kit contains the linings required for both the left and right side.**

➡**Make sure the parking brake control is fully released.**

2. Relieve the tension on the parking brake cable.

a. With the vehicle in NEUTRAL, position it on the hoist.

b. Remove the left A-pillar lower trim panel.

c. With an assistant, release the parking brake cable tension by pulling down on the intermediate cable at the cable-to-cable union until the parking brake control sector rotates to its stop and a 4 mm (0.15 in.) x 150 mm (5.9 in.) retainer pin can be inserted.

d. Disconnect the cable at the cable-to-cable union.

3. Remove the rear brake disc.

4. Remove the brake shoe adjuster screw.

5. Remove the brake shoe adjuster screw spring.

6. Remove the 2 brake shoe hold down springs and 2 pins.

7. Remove the brake shoe retracting spring and the parking brake shoes.

To install:

➡**Lubricate the parking brake shoes where the shoe contacts the wear pad on the backing plate.**

8. Position the parking brake shoes and attach the retracting spring.

9. Install the 2 brake shoe hold-down pins and springs.

10. Install the brake shoe adjusting screw spring.

➡**Completely retract the parking brake adjusting screw before installation.**

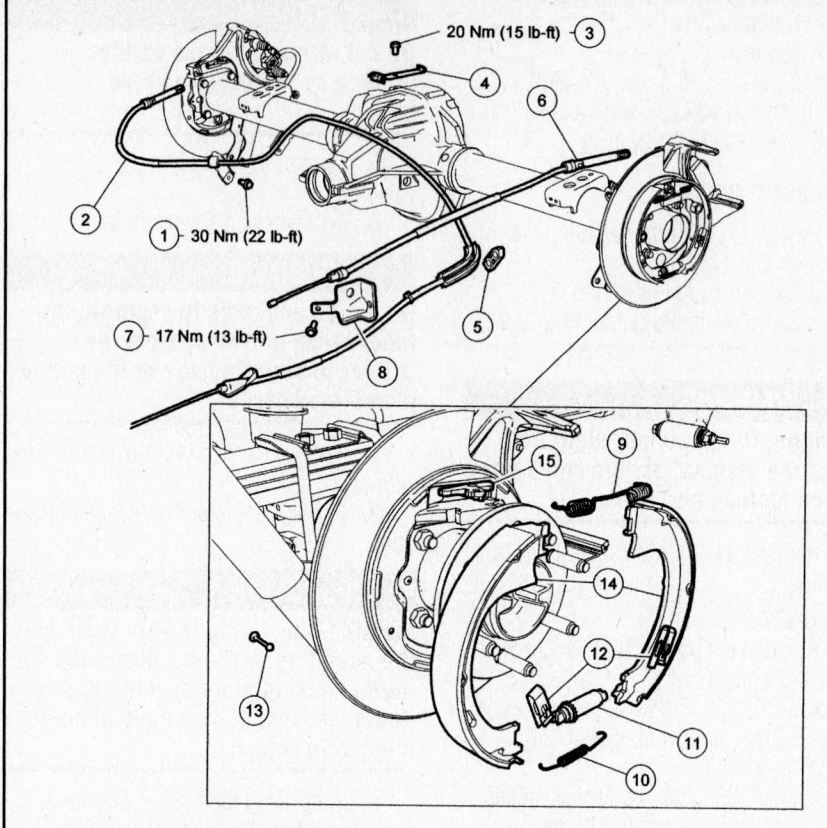

1 Parking brake cable bracket bolt (RH)
2 Rear parking brake cable (RH)
3 Parking brake cable differential bracket bolt (RH)
4 Parking brake cable differential bracket
5 Double cable clamp
6 Parking brake cable (LH)
7 Parking brake cable bracket bolt (LH)
8 Parking brake cable bracket (LH)
9 Parking brake shoe return spring
10 Parking brake shoe adjuster spring
11 Parking brake shoe adjuster
12 Parking brake shoe retainer spring clip (2 required)
13 Parking brake shoe retainer pin (2 required)
14 Parking brake shoe kit (1 kit required)
15 Actuator lever kit (LH/RH)

06017-F150-G282

Fig. 11 Parking brake exploded view—F-150 and Mark LT

11. Install the brake shoe adjusting screw.

12. Measure the inside diameter of the parking brake drum.

13. Adjust the parking brake shoe clearance to 0.6 mm (0.02 in.) less than the inside diameter of the parking brake drum.

14. Make sure that the parking brake shoes are correctly centered by measuring across the center point of the shoes.

15. Rotate the parking brake shoe adjuster wheel to achieve the correct parking brake shoe-to-brake disc clearance.

16. Install the rear brake disc.

17. Reload the tension on the parking brake cable.

F-250 and F-350

1. Before servicing the vehicle, refer to the Precautions Section.

2. Remove the brake disc.

3. Release the tension on the parking brake system.

a. Remove the left lower A-pillar trim panel.

b. With an assistant, release the parking brake cable tension by pulling down on the intermediate cable at the cable-to-cable union until the parking brake control sector rotates to its stop and a 4 mm

(0.15 in.) x 150 mm (5.9 in.) retainer pin can be inserted.

  c. Disconnect the cable at the cable-to-cable union.

➥**Make sure the cable-to-cable union is connected to the front and rear cable before removing the brake control retaining pin, and the cable tension is reloaded slowly.**

  4. Separate the parking brake cables at the parking brake equalizer.

  5. Release the parking brake cable from the left and right parking brake bracket assembly.

  6. Rotate the parking brake cable 90 degrees to release it from the parking brake actuating lever.

  7. Remove the 2 brake shoe hold-down clips and the 2 retaining pins.

  8. Remove the brake shoe adjusting screw and the adjusting spring.

  9. Remove the outboard brake shoes and the retracting spring.

  10. To install, reverse the removal procedure. Inspect the components for excessive wear or damage and install new as required. To reload the tension on the parking brake cable, reverse the release procedure.

ADJUSTMENT

F-150 and Mark LT

Parking brake shoe adjustment is part of the parking brake shoe installation procedure.

F-250 and F-350

See Figure 12.

  1. Raise and support the vehicle.
  2. Remove the wheel and tire assembly.

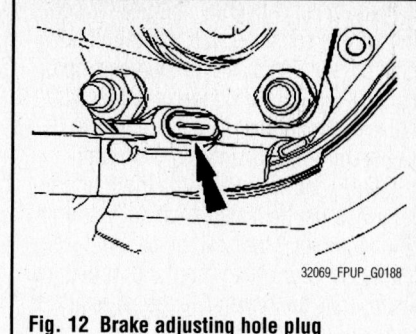

32069_FPUP_G0188

Fig. 12 Brake adjusting hole plug

  3. Remove the brake adjusting hole cover from the backing plate.
  4. Turn the brake adjuster screw to expand the parking brake shoe and linings until they drag against the drum-in-hat rotor.
  5. Back off the brake adjuster screw until no drag is evident.

CHASSIS ELECTRICAL

AIR BAG (SUPPLEMENTAL RESTRAINT SYSTEM)

GENERAL INFORMATION

✳✳ CAUTION

These vehicles are equipped with an air bag system. The system must be disarmed before performing service on, or around, system components, the steering column, instrument panel components, wiring and sensors. Failure to follow the safety precautions and the disarming procedure could result in accidental air bag deployment, possible injury and unnecessary system repairs.

SERVICE PRECAUTIONS

Disconnect and isolate the battery negative cable before beginning any airbag system component diagnosis, testing, removal, or installation procedures. Allow system capacitor to discharge for two minutes before beginning any component service. This will disable the airbag system. Failure to disable the airbag system may result in accidental airbag deployment, personal injury, or death.

Do not place an intact undeployed airbag face down on a solid surface. The airbag will propel into the air if accidentally deployed and may result in personal injury or death.

When carrying or handling an undeployed airbag, the trim side (face) of the airbag should be pointing towards the body to minimize possibility of injury if accidental

deployment occurs. Failure to do this may result in personal injury or death.

Replace airbag system components with OEM replacement parts. Substitute parts may appear interchangeable, but internal differences may result in inferior occupant protection. Failure to do so may result in occupant personal injury or death.

Wear safety glasses, rubber gloves, and long sleeved clothing when cleaning powder residue from vehicle after an airbag deployment. Powder residue emitted from a deployed airbag can cause skin irritation. Flush affected area with cool water if irritation is experienced. If nasal or throat irritation is experienced, exit the vehicle for fresh air until the irritation ceases. If irritation continues, see a physician.

Do not use a replacement airbag that is not in the original packaging. This may result in improper deployment, personal injury, or death.

The factory installed fasteners, screws and bolts used to fasten airbag components have a special coating and are specifically designed for the airbag system. Do not use substitute fasteners. Use only original equipment fasteners listed in the parts catalog when fastener replacement is required.

During, and following, any child restraint anchor service, due to impact event or vehicle repair, carefully inspect all mounting hardware, tether straps, and anchors for proper installation, operation, or damage. If a child restraint anchor is found damaged in any way, the anchor must be replaced. Failure to do this may result in personal injury or death.

Deployed and non-deployed airbags may or may not have live pyrotechnic material within the airbag inflator.

Do not dispose of driver/passenger/curtain airbags or seat belt tensioners unless you are sure of complete deployment. Refer to the Hazardous Substance Control System for proper disposal.

Dispose of deployed airbags and tensioners consistent with state, provincial, local, and federal regulations.

After any airbag component testing or service, do not connect the battery negative cable. Personal injury or death may result if the system test is not performed first.

If the vehicle is equipped with the Occupant Classification System (OCS), do not connect the battery negative cable before performing the OCS Verification Test using the scan tool and the appropriate diagnostic information. Personal injury or death may result if the system test is not performed properly.

Never replace both the Occupant Restraint Controller (ORC) and the Occupant Classification Module (OCM) at the same time. If both require replacement, replace one, then perform the Airbag System test before replacing the other.

Both the ORC and the OCM store Occupant Classification System (OCS) calibration data, which they transfer to one another when one of them is replaced. If both are replaced at the same time, an irreversible fault will be set in both modules and the OCS may malfunction and cause personal injury or death.

If equipped with OCS, the Seat Weight Sensor is a sensitive, calibrated unit and must be handled carefully. Do not drop or handle roughly. If dropped or damaged, replace with another sensor. Failure to do so may result in occupant injury or death.

If equipped with OCS, the front passenger seat must be handled carefully as well. When removing the seat, be careful when setting on floor not to drop. If dropped, the sensor may be inoperative, could result in occupant injury, or possibly death.

If equipped with OCS, when the passenger front seat is on the floor, no one should sit in the front passenger seat. This uneven force may damage the sensing ability of the seat weight sensors. If sat on and damaged, the sensor may be inoperative, could result in occupant injury, or possibly death.

DISARMING THE SYSTEM

1. Before servicing the vehicle, refer to the Precautions Section.
2. Turn all vehicle accessories OFF.
3. Turn the ignition switch to OFF.
4. At the central junction box (CJB), located below the instrument panel, remove the trim panel, the cover, and the restraints control module (RCM) fuse from the CJB. See your Owner's Manual for fuse identification.
5. Turn the ignition ON and visually monitor the air bag indicator for at least 30 seconds. The air bag indicator will remain lit continuously (no flashing) if the correct RCM fuse has been removed. If the air bag indicator does not remain lit continuously, remove the correct RCM fuse before proceeding.
6. Turn the ignition OFF.

✳✳ CAUTION

To avoid accidental deployment and possible personal injury, the backup power supply must be depleted before repairing or replacing any front or side air bag supplemental restraint system (SRS) components and before servicing, replacing, adjusting or striking components near the front or side air bag sensors, such as doors, instrument panel, console, door latches, strikers, seats and hood latches.

7. To deplete the backup power supply energy, disconnect the battery ground cable and wait at least 1 minute. Be sure to disconnect auxiliary batteries and power supplies (if equipped).
8. Disconnect the battery ground cable and wait at least 1 minute.

ARMING THE SYSTEM

1. Before servicing the vehicle, refer to the Precautions Section.
2. Turn the ignition switch from OFF to ON.
3. Install the RCM fuse to the CJB and install the cover and trim panel.

✳✳ CAUTION

Be sure that nobody is in the vehicle and that there is nothing blocking or set in front of any air bag module when the battery ground cable is connected.

4. Connect the battery ground cable.
5. Prove out the supplemental restraint system (SRS) as follows:
6. Turn the ignition key from ON to OFF. Wait 10 seconds, then turn the key back to ON and visually monitor the air bag indicator with the air bag modules installed. The air bag indicator will light continuously for approximately 6 seconds and then turn off. If an air bag supplemental restraint system (SRS) fault is present, the air bag indicator will either:
   - fail to light.
   - remain lit continuously.
   - flash.
7. The flashing might not occur until approximately 30 seconds after the ignition switch has been turned from the OFF to the ON position. This is the time required for the restraints control module (RCM) to complete the testing of the SRS. If the air bag indicator is inoperative and a SRS fault exists, a chime will sound in a pattern of 5 sets of 5 beeps. If this occurs, the air bag indicator and any SRS fault discovered must be diagnosed and repaired.
8. Clear all continuous DTCs from the restraints control module using a diagnostic tool.

REMOVAL, CENTERING AND INSTALLATION

F-150 and Mark LT

See Figure 13.

✳✳ CAUTION

Always wear safety glasses when repairing an air bag supplemental restraint system (SRS) vehicle and when handling an air bag module. This will reduce the risk of injury in the event of an accidental deployment.

✳✳ CAUTION

To reduce the risk of personal injury, do not use any memory saver devices.

➡The air bag warning lamp illuminates when the RCM fuse is removed and the ignition switch is ON. This is normal operation and does not indicate a supplemental restraint system (SRS) fault.

➡Repair is made by installing a new part only. If the new part does not correct the condition, install the original part and perform the diagnostic procedure again.

1. Before servicing the vehicle, refer to the precautions in the beginning of this section.
2. Depower the system. For additional information, refer to the procedures in this section.
3. Make sure the road wheels are in the straight-ahead position.
4. Remove the driver air bag module. For additional information, refer to Steering Wheel R&I in this section.
5. Remove the steering wheel. For additional information, refer to Steering Wheel R&I in this section.
6. Remove the screw and lower steering column shroud.
7. Remove the 2 upper steering column shroud screws and upper steering column shroud.
8. If installing the same clockspring, apply 2 strips of masking tape across the clockspring to prevent accidental rotation when the clockspring is removed.
9. Remove the multi-function switch screw.
10. Remove the screw and the multi-function switch. While releasing the retaining tab at the top of the multi-function switch, slide the multi-function switch up and out of the way.
11. Disconnect the clockspring electrical connectors.
12. Release the 3 clips and remove the clockspring.
13. Check the clockspring mounting bracket for damage and install a new mounting bracket as necessary.

To install:

✳✳ WARNING

Incorrect centralization may result in premature component failure. If in doubt when centralizing the cloc spring, repeat the centralizing

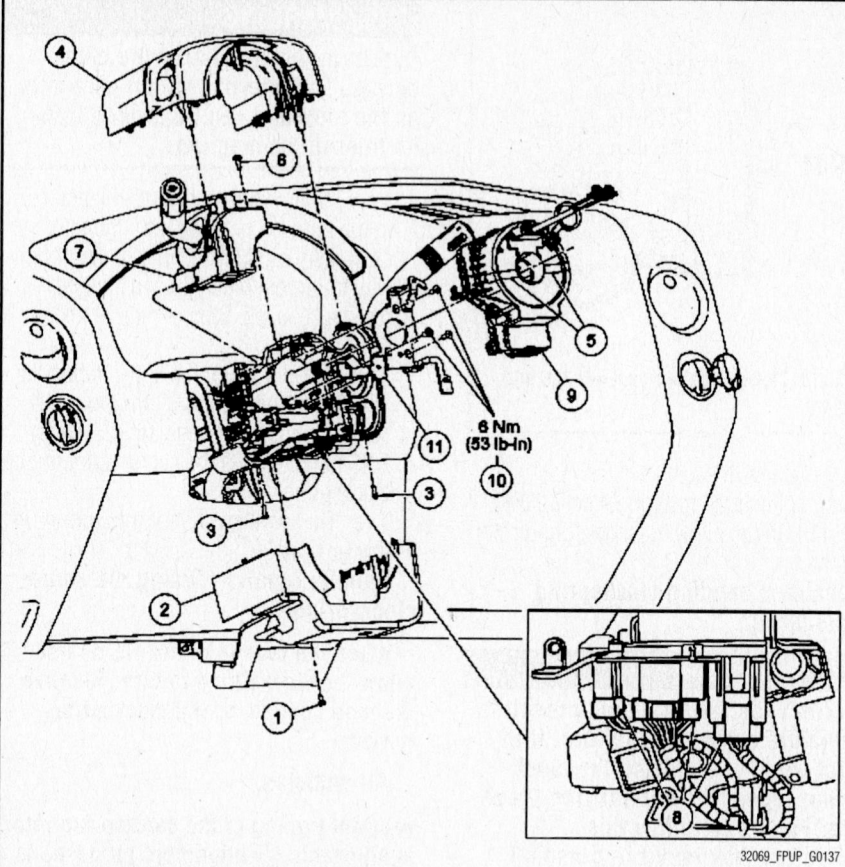

32069_FPUP_G0137

Fig. 13
1. Lower steering column shroud screw
2. Lower steering column shroud
3. Upper steering column shroud screws
4. Upper steering column shroud
5. Tape
6. Multi-function switch screw
7. Multi-function switch
8. Clockspring connectors
9. Clockspring
10. Clockspring mounting bracket screws
11. Clockspring mounting bracket

Clockspring and related components—F-150 and Mark LT

18. With the flats of the clockspring aligned to the flats of the steering column, slide the clockspring onto the steering column.

19. For vehicles receiving a new clockspring, remove the retaining pin.

20. For vehicles reusing the clockspring that was removed, remove the tape.

21. Connect the clockspring electrical connectors. Make sure to align and completely seat the electrical connectors.

22. Install the multi-function switch and screw.

23. Install the upper steering column shroud and shroud screw.

24. Install the lower steering column shroud and screw.

25. Install the steering wheel.

26. Install the driver air bag module.

27. Repower the system.

F-250 and F-350

See Figures 14 through 17.

1. Before servicing the vehicle, refer to the precautions in the beginning of this section.

2. Depower the system. For additional information, refer to procedures in this section.

➡ **Make sure the wheels are in the straight-ahead position.**

3. Remove the two steering wheel back cover plugs.

4. Remove the two driver air bag module bolts.

5. Disconnect the horn electrical connector.

6. Disconnect the clockspring electrical connector.

7. Remove the driver air bag module.

8. Remove the steering wheel. For additional information, refer to Steering Wheel R&I.

procedure. Failure to follow this instruction may result in personal injury.

✳✳ WARNING

Make sure the road wheels are in the straight-ahead position.

14. If the vehicle's clockspring has rotated out of center, follow these steps to center the clockspring.

15. Hold the clockspring outer housing stationary.

✳✳ WARNING

Overturning will destroy the clockspring. The internal ribbon wire acts as the stop and can be broken from its internal connection.

16. While turning the rotor counterclockwise, carefully feel for the ribbon wire to run out of length and for a slight resistance. Stop turning at this point.

17. Turn the clockspring clockwise approximately 3 turns. This is the center point of the clockspring. Do not allow the rotor to turn from this position. To prevent accidental rotation until the clockspring is installed, 2 pieces of tape may be applied to the clockspring.

➡ **Slight turning of the clockspring rotor is allowable for alignment purposes to the steering column.**

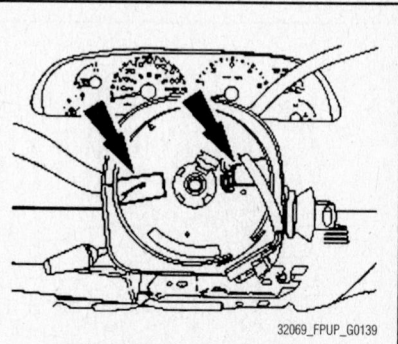

32069_FPUP_G0139

Fig. 14 Apply two strips of masking tape across the clockspring to prevent accidental rotation—F-250 and F-350

9. Apply two strips of masking tape across the clockspring to prevent accidental rotation.

10. Twist the tilt wheel handle and shank and remove.

11. Remove the steering column opening lower finish panel.

   a. Turn the retaining clips a quarter-turn counterclockwise to release.

   b. Remove the steering column opening lower finish panel.

12. Remove the lower steering column shroud.

   a. Remove the three screws.

   b. Remove the steering column shroud.

13. Position the lock cylinder to RUN.

14. Using a suitable tool, push upward on the cylinder release tab while pulling the cylinder outward.

15. Remove the upper steering column shroud.

Vehicles with a passive anti-theft system:

   c. Remove the PATS transmitter retaining screw.

   d. Remove the PATS transmitter.

16. Remove the key-in-ignition warning indicator switch.

17. Remove the clockspring electrical connectors and wire harness from the side of the steering column.

18. Remove the clockspring electrical connectors from the bracket. Disconnect the remaining electrical connector.

19. Remove the wire harness from the retainers.

20. Release the retaining clips. Remove the clockspring.

To install:

Vehicles receiving a new clockspring:

➡A new clockspring is supplied in a centralized position and held there with a key.

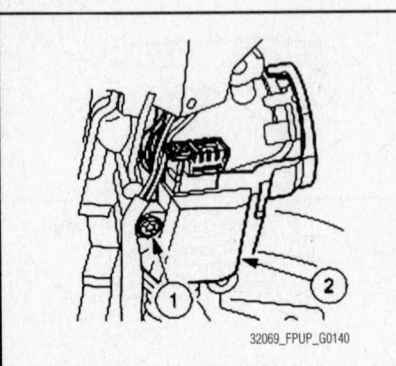

Fig. 15 PATS transmitter—F-250 and F-350

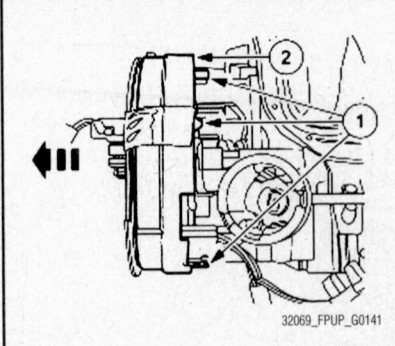

Fig. 16 Clockspring removal—F-250 and F-350

21. Remove the key from the clockspring, holding the rotor in its centralized position. Do not allow the clockspring rotor to turn.

Vehicles needing clockspring re-centering:

⚹⚹ **WARNING**

Incorrect centralization may result in premature component failure. If in doubt when centralizing the clockspring, repeat the centralizing procedure. Failure to follow this instruction may result in personal injury.

⚹⚹ **WARNING**

Make sure the road wheels are in the straight ahead position.

➡If a clockspring has rotated out of center, follow through with this step.

22. Centralize the clockspring.

   a. Hold the clockspring outer housing stationary.

   b. Push and release the anti-rotation tab.

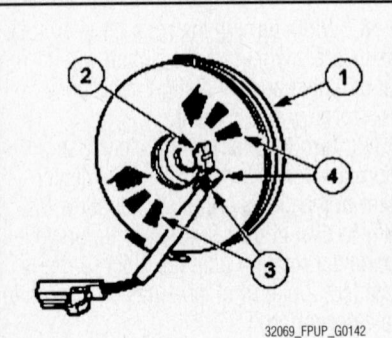

Fig. 17 Centralizing the clockspring—F-250 and F-350

⚹⚹ **WARNING**

Overturning will destroy the clockspring. The internal ribbon wire acts as the stop and can be broken from its internal connection.

   c. While holding the anti-rotation tab in the released position, turn the rotor clockwise, carefully feeling for the ribbon wire to run out of length and a slight resistance is felt. Stop turning at this point.

   d. While holding the anti-rotation tab in the released position, turn the clockspring counterclockwise approximately 2.25 turns. This is the center point of the clockspring.

   e. Do not allow the rotor to turn from this position.

Vehicle repairs reusing the same clockspring:

➡When the tape is removed, do not allow the clockspring to turn. Remove the tape applied during clockspring removal.

All vehicles:

➡Slight turning of the clockspring rotor is allowable for alignment purposes to the steering column.

23. Install the clockspring.

   a. With the flats of the clockspring aligned to the flats of the steering column, slide the clockspring onto the steering column.

   b. Engage the retaining tabs.

24. Install the clockspring wire harness and electrical connectors.

   a. Route the clockspring wire harness down the side of the steering column and into the holders.

   b. Connect the clockspring electrical connectors. Install the electrical connectors into the bracket.

25. Install the key-in-ignition warning indicator switch.

Vehicles with a passive anti-theft system:

   a. Position the PATS transmitter.

   b. Install the PATS transmitter retaining screw.

All vehicles:

26. Install the upper steering column shroud.

27. Position the ignition switch lock cylinder to the RUN position.

28. Insert the ignition switch lock cylinder into the steering column.

29. Make sure the ignition switch lock cylinder is fully seated and aligned in the

interlocking washer before turning the key to the OFF position.

30. Make sure the ignition switch lock cylinder retaining pin is seated in the hole in the steering column.

31. Rotate the ignition switch lock cylinder through all positions to verify operation.

32. Position the lower steering column shroud. Install the screws.

33. Align the steering column opening lower finish panel to the instrument panel. Turn the retaining clips a quarter-turn clockwise to install.

34. Install the tilt wheel handle and shank.

35. Install the steering wheel. Do not install the driver air bag module at this time.

36. Connect the horn electrical connector.

37. Connect the driver air bag module electrical connector.

38. Position the driver air bag module into the steering wheel.

39. Install the two bolts.

40. Install the two steering wheel back cover plugs.

41. Repower the system.

DRIVETRAIN

AUTOMATIC TRANSMISSION ASSEMBLY

REMOVAL & INSTALLATION

F-150 and Mark LT

2-Wheel Drive

See Figures 18 and 19.

1. Before servicing the vehicle, refer to the Precautions Section.

2. Disconnect the battery ground cable.

3. With the vehicle in **Neutral**, position it on a hoist.

4. Remove the rear driveshaft.

5. Drain the transmission fluid.

6. Loosen the transmission fluid pan bolts and allow the fluid to drain. After the fluid has drained, remove the bolts.

7. Remove the transmission fluid pan and transmission fluid pan gasket. Drain the rest of the fluid from the pan.

➡The transmission fluid pan gasket is reusable. Clean and inspect for damage. If not damaged, the gasket should be reused.

8. Install the transmission fluid pan and gasket.

➡If removing the transmission for a transmission related failure, it is not necessary to torque the transmission fluid pan back onto the transmission case. If removing the transmission for a non-related transmission failure it is necessary to re-torque the transmission fluid pan.

9. Install the bolts.

10. Remove the starter motor solenoid terminal cover.

11. Disconnect the starter motor electrical connectors and the ground wire.

12. Remove the starter motor.

13. Remove the rubber plug to access the nuts.

14. Remove the four torque converter nuts. Rotate either the front of the crankshaft

or the flexplate to access all of the torque converter retaining nuts.

15. Remove the transmission inspection cover.

16. Remove the shift cable and bracket.

17. Disconnect the transmission electrical connectors.

18. Disconnect the solenoid body assembly electrical connector.

19. Using a suitable transmission jack, support the transmission and secure the transmission to it with a safety strap.

20. Remove the left bolt retaining the heat shield to the transmission support crossmember.

21. Remove the right bolt retaining the heat shield to the transmission support crossmember.

22. Loosen, but do not remove, the transmission mount-to-crossmember nuts.

23. Remove the two bolts for the exhaust hanger.

24. Remove the four crossmember-to-frame nuts and bolts (two on each side).

25. Remove the transmission mount-to-crossmember nuts, and remove the crossmember.

26. Remove the two bolts and the rear transmission mount.

27. Remove the exhaust hanger.

28. Disconnect the transmission fluid cooler tubes.

29. Remove the seven transmission-to-engine bolts.

30. Position the fuel lines and bracket aside.

✷✷ CAUTION

The torque converter is heavy and can result in injury if it falls out of the transmission. Secure the torque converter in the transmission. If the torque converter is dropped, a new one must be installed.

31. Slide the transmission rearward enough to install the holding tool.

✷✷ CAUTION

The transmission must be secured with a safety chain or strap.

➡The front of the transmission must be lowered for the transmission to clear the exhaust system during removal.

32. Continue moving the transmission rearward, while gradually lowering the front of the transmission. As the transmission jack is being lowered, move the transmission forward and remove it from the vehicle.

33. If the transmission is to be overhauled or if installing a new transmission, carry out transmission backflushing and cleaning.

To install:

✷✷ WARNING

The torque converter cover is piloted into position to the engine crankshaft by dowels in the rear of the engine block. The torque converter must rest squarely and loosely against the flexplate. This indicates that the torque converter pilot is not binding in the engine crankshaft.

✷✷ CAUTION

The transmission must be secured with a safety chain or strap.

✷✷ CAUTION

The torque converter is heavy and can result in injury if it falls out of the transmission. Secure the torque converter in the transmission. If the torque converter is dropped, a new one must be installed.

➡The front of the transmission must be lowered for the transmission to clear the exhaust system during installation.

34. Continue moving the transmission rearward, while gradually raising the front of the transmission. As the transmission jack

is being raised, move the transmission back and install it in the vehicle.

35. Align the orange balancing marks between the torque converter studs and the flexplate bolt holes.

36. Remove the special tool.

➡**While positioning the transmission to the back of the engine, use the transmission filler tube as a guide and install the transmission filler tube into the case.**

37. Install the seven transmission-to-engine bolts. Torque to 35 ft. lbs. (48 Nm).

38. Position the fuel line and bracket.

39. Install the bolts.

40. Connect the transmission fluid cooler tubes.

41. Position the rear transmission insulator and install the bolts. Torque to 59 ft. lbs. (80 Nm).

42. Install the exhaust hanger onto the exhaust crossover pipe.

43. Position the crossmember and loosely install the mount-to-crossmember nuts.

44. Install the four crossmember-to-frame nuts and bolts (two on each side). Torque to 66 ft. lbs. (90 Nm).

45. Tighten the rear transmission mount nuts. Torque to 76 ft. lbs. (103 Nm).

46. Install the bolt retaining the left heat shield to the transmission support crossmember.

47. Install the bolt retaining the right heat shield to the transmission support crossmember.

48. Install the bolts retaining the exhaust hanger to the crossmember. Torque to 30 ft. lbs. (40 Nm).

49. Connect the solenoid body assembly electrical connector.

50. Connect the transmission electrical connectors.

51. Install the shift cable bracket and connect the transmission shift linkage.

52. Install the transmission inspection cover.

53. Install the torque converter nuts. Torque to 27 ft. lbs. (36 Nm).

54. Install the rubber access plug.

55. Install the starter motor.

56. Connect the starter motor electrical connectors and the ground wire.

57. Install the starter motor solenoid terminal cover.

58. Install the rear driveshaft.

59. Use the following guidelines for the in-line transmission fluid filter:

   a. If the transmission was overhauled and the vehicle was equipped with an in-line fluid filter, install a new in-line fluid filter.

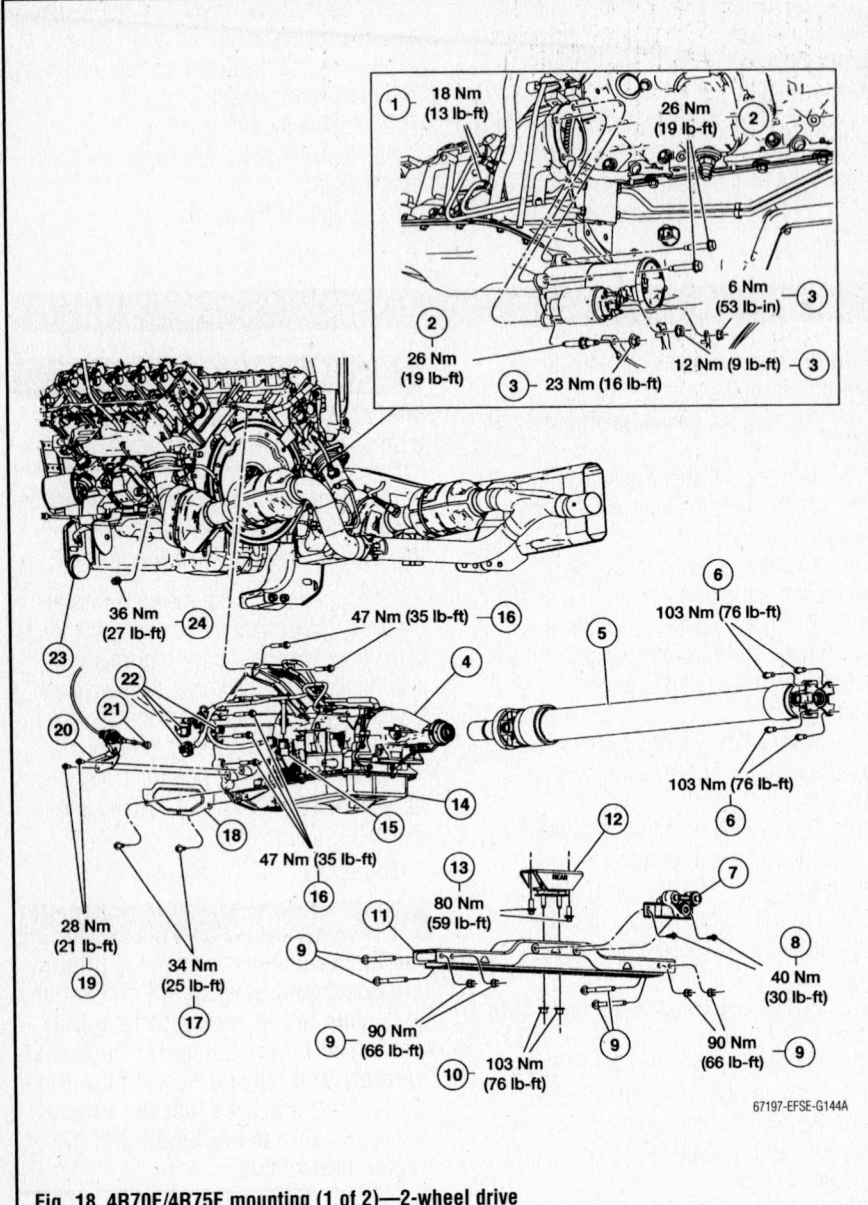

Fig. 18 4R70E/4R75E mounting (1 of 2)—2-wheel drive

67197-EFSE-G144A

1 Transmission fluid cooler tube nuts	13 Transmission rear support bolts
2 Starter motor bolts	14 Transmission fluid pan
3 Electrical connector nuts	15 Transmission solenoid body connector
4 Transmission assembly	16 Transmission retaining bolts
5 Rear driveshaft	17 Inspection cover shield bolts
6 Rear driveshaft retaining bolts	18 Inspection cover
7 Exhaust hanger	19 Transmission range selector lever cable bolts
8 Exhaust hanger bolts	20 Transmission range selector lever cable and bracket
9 Rear crossmember bolts and nuts	21 Transmission range selector lever cable end
10 Rear transmission mount nuts	22 Transmission electrical connectors
11 Rear crossmember	23 Torque converter nut rubber access plug
12 Transmission rear support	24 Torque converter nuts

67197-EFSE-G144B

Fig. 19 Keylist (2 of 2)

b. If the transmission was overhauled and the vehicle was not equipped with an in-line fluid filter, install a new in-line fluid filter kit.

c. If the transmission is being installed for a non-internal repair, do not install an in-line filter or filter kit.

d. If installing a new or a Ford authorized remanufactured transmission, install the in-line transmission fluid filter that is supplied.

60. Prior to lowering the vehicle, install a new in-line transmission filter or a filter kit.

61. Connect the battery ground cable.

62. Fill the transmission with clean automatic transmission fluid and inspect for correct operation.

63. Check the fluid filter for any leaks.

4-Wheel Drive

See Figures 20 and 21.

1. Before servicing the vehicle, refer to the Precautions Section.

2. Disconnect the battery ground cable.

3. With the vehicle in **Neutral**, position it on a hoist.

4. Drain the transmission fluid.

5. Loosen the transmission fluid pan bolts and allow the fluid to drain. After the fluid has drained, remove the bolts.

6. Remove the transmission fluid pan and transmission fluid pan gasket. Drain the rest of the transmission fluid from the fluid pan.

➡**The transmission fluid pan gasket is reusable. Clean and inspect for damage. If not damaged, the gasket should be reused.**

7. Install the transmission fluid pan and gasket.

8. Position the transmission fluid pan gasket.

9. Position the transmission fluid pan.

➡**If removing the transmission for a transmission related failure, it is not necessary to torque the transmission fluid pan back onto the transmission case. If removing the transmission for a non-related transmission failure it is necessary to re-torque the transmission fluid pan.**

10. Install the bolts.

11. Using a suitable transmission jack, support the transmission and secure the transmission to it with a safety strap.

12. Index-mark the front flange of the front driveshaft.

13. Index-mark the rear flange of the front driveshaft at the transfer case.

14. Remove the front driveshaft shield.

15. Remove the transfer case.

16. Remove the front driveshaft.

17. Remove the left bolt retaining the heat shield to the transmission support crossmember.

18. Remove the right bolt retaining the heat shield to the transmission support crossmember.

19. Loosen, but do not remove, the transmission mount-to-crossmember nuts.

20. Remove the two bolts for the exhaust hanger.

21. Remove the four crossmember-to-frame nuts and bolts (two on each side).

22. Remove the transmission mount-to-crossmember nuts, and remove the crossmember.

23. Remove the two bolts and the rear transmission mount.

24. Remove the exhaust hanger.

25. Remove the starter motor solenoid terminal cover.

26. Disconnect the starter motor electrical connectors and the ground wire.

27. Remove the starter motor.

28. Remove the rubber plug to access the nuts.

29. Remove the four nuts. Rotate the crankshaft/flexplate assembly to access all the nuts.

30. Remove the transmission inspection cover.

31. Remove the shift cable and bracket.

32. Disconnect the solenoid body assembly electrical connector.

33. Disconnect the transmission electrical connectors.

34. Disconnect the transmission fluid cooler tubes.

35. Remove the seven transmission-to-engine bolts.

36. Position the fuel lines and bracket aside.

✳✳ CAUTION

The torque converter is heavy and can result in injury if it falls out of the transmission. Secure the torque converter in the transmission. If the torque converter is dropped, a new one must be installed.

37. Slide the transmission rearward enough to install a torque converter holding tool.

✳✳ CAUTION

The transmission must be secured with a safety chain or strap.

➡**The front of the transmission must be lowered for the transmission to clear the exhaust system during removal.**

38. Continue moving the transmission rearward, while gradually lowering the front of the transmission. As the transmission jack is being lowered, move the transmission forward and remove it from the vehicle.

39. If the transmission is to be overhauled or if installing a new transmission, carry out transmission backflushing and cleaning.

To install:

✳✳ CAUTION

The torque converter cover is piloted into position to the engine crankshaft by dowels in the rear of the engine block. The torque converter must rest squarely and loosely against the flexplate. This indicates that the torque converter pilot is not binding in the engine crankshaft.

40. When installing a new transmission, install a torque converter holding tool.

✳✳ CAUTION

The transmission must be secured with a safety chain or strap.

✳✳ CAUTION

The torque converter is heavy and can result in injury if it falls out of the transmission. Secure the torque converter in the transmission. If the torque converter is dropped, a new one must be installed.

➡**The front of the transmission must be lowered for the transmission to clear the exhaust system during installation.**

41. Continue moving the transmission rearward, while gradually raising the front of the transmission. As the transmission jack is being raised, move the transmission back and install it in the vehicle.

42. Align the orange balancing marks between the torque converter studs and the flexplate bolt holes.

43. Remove the special tool.

➡**While positioning the transmission to the back of the engine use the transmission filler tube as a guide and install the transmission filler tube into the case.**

44. Install the seven transmission-to-engine bolts. Torque to 35 ft. lbs. (48 Nm).

45. Position the fuel line and bracket.

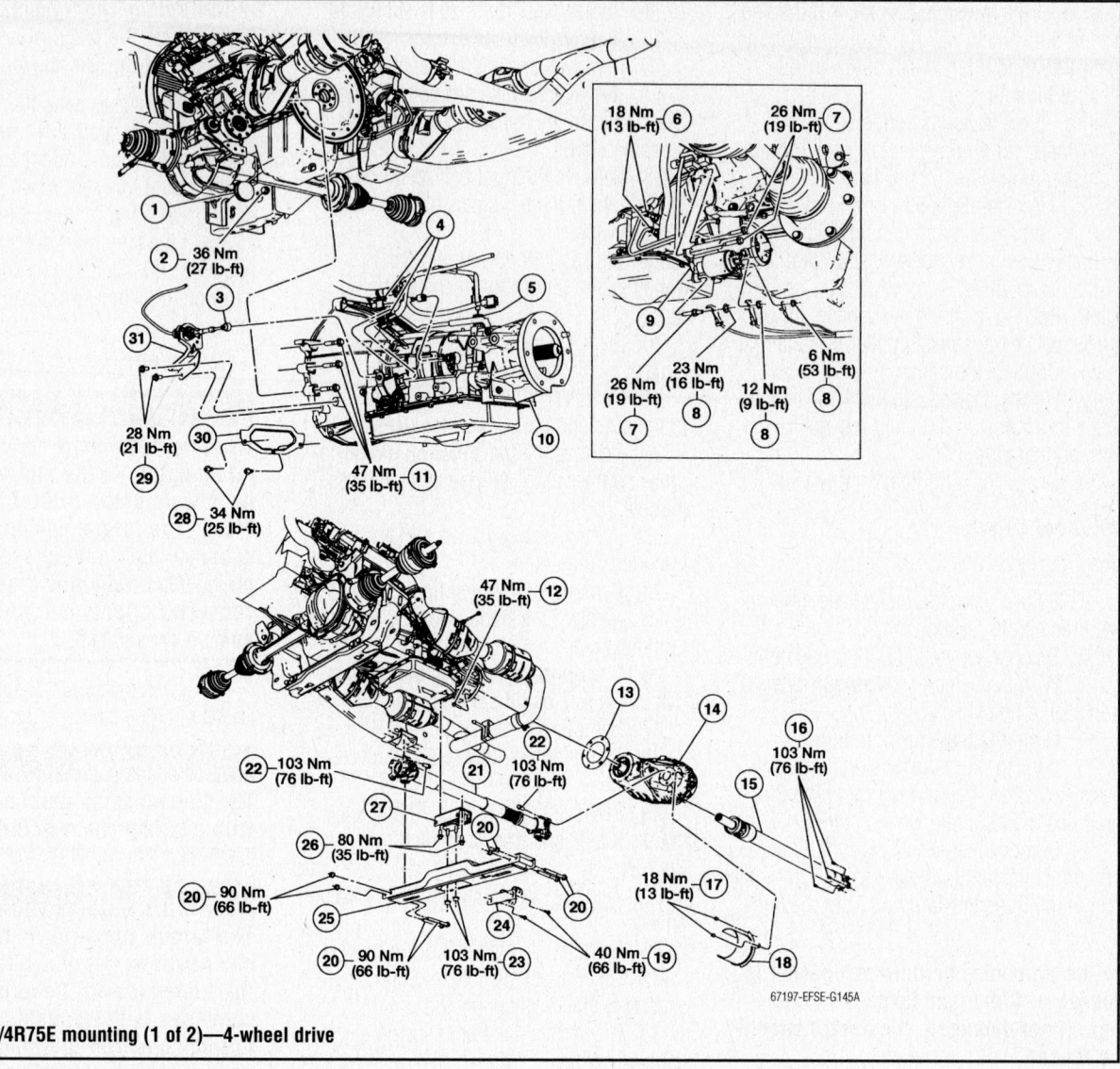

Fig. 20 4R70E/4R75E mounting (1 of 2)—4-wheel drive

67197-EFSE-G145A

1 Torque converter nut rubber access plug	17 Front driveshaft shield nuts
2 Torque converter nuts	18 Front driveshaft shield
3 Transmission range selector lever cable end	19 Exhaust hanger bolts
4 Transmission electrical connectors	20 Rear crossmember bolts and nuts
5 Transmission solenoid body connector	21 Front driveshaft
6 Transmission fluid cooler tube nuts	22 Front driveshaft retaining bolts
7 Starter motor bolts	23 Rear transmission mount nuts
8 Starter motor electrical connector nuts	24 Exhaust hanger
9 Starter motor	25 Rear crossmember
10 Transmission assembly	26 Transmission rear support bolts
11 Transmission retaining bolts	27 Transmission rear support
12 Transfer case retaining bolts	28 Inspection cover shield bolts
13 Transfer case gasket	29 Transmission range selector lever cable bracket bolts
14 Transfer case	30 Inspection cover shield
15 Rear driveshaft	31 Transmission range selector lever cable bracket
16 Rear driveshaft retaining bolts	

67197-EFSE-G145B

Fig. 21 Keylist (2 of 2)

46. Install the bolts.

47. Connect the transmission fluid cooler tubes.

48. Install the exhaust hanger onto the exhaust crossover pipe.

49. Position the rear transmission insulator and install the bolts. Torque to 59 ft. lbs. (80 Nm).

50. Position the crossmember and loosely install the mount-to-crossmember nuts.

51. Install the four crossmember-to-frame nuts and bolts (two on each side). Torque to 66 ft. lbs. (90 Nm).

52. Tighten the rear transmission mount nuts. Torque to 76 ft. lbs. (103 Nm).

53. Install the bolt retaining the left heat shield to the transmission support crossmember.

54. Install the bolt retaining the right heat shield to the transmission support crossmember.

55. Install the bolts retaining the exhaust hanger to the crossmember.

56. Connect the solenoid body assembly electrical connector.

57. Connect the transmission electrical connectors.

58. Install the shift cable bracket and connect the transmission shift linkage.

59. Install the transmission inspection cover.

60. Install the torque converter nuts. Torque to 27 ft. lbs. (36 Nm).

61. Install the rubber access plug.

62. Install the starter motor.

63. Connect the starter motor electrical connectors and the ground wire.

64. Install the starter motor solenoid terminal cover.

65. Position the front driveshaft in place.

66. Install the transfer case.

67. Align the marks made during removal, install the front driveshaft flange and the four bolts.

68. Align the marks made during removal, install the rear driveshaft flange and the four bolts.

69. Install the front driveshaft shield.

70. Install the rear driveshaft.

71. Use the following guidelines for the in-line transmission fluid filter:

a. If the transmission was overhauled and the vehicle was equipped with an in-line fluid filter, install a new in-line fluid filter.

b. If the transmission was overhauled and the vehicle was not equipped with an in-line fluid filter, install a new in-line fluid filter kit.

c. If the transmission is being installed for a non-internal repair, do not install an in-line filter or filter kit.

d. If installing a new or a Ford authorized remanufactured transmission, install the in-line transmission fluid filter that is supplied.

72. Prior to lowering the vehicle, install a new in-line transmission filter or a filter kit.

73. Connect the battery ground cable.

74. Fill the transmission with clean automatic transmission fluid and inspect for correct operation.

75. Check the fluid filter for any leaks.

Torqshift

1. Before servicing the vehicle, refer to the Precautions Section.

2. With the vehicle in **Neutral**, position it on a hoist.

3. Disconnect both battery ground cables.

4x4 vehicles

4. Remove the transfer case assembly.

4x2 vehicles

5. Remove the driveshaft.

All vehicles

6. If transmission disassembly is required, drain the transmission fluid. Remove the drain plug and allow the fluid to drain.

7. Install the drain plug.

8. Install a suitable high-lift transmission jack.

4x4 vehicles

9. Remove the jack stand from under the extension housing after installing the transmission jack.

4x2 vehicles

10. Remove the wire harness from the rear crossmember.

11. Remove the rear transmission mount nuts.

All vehicles

12. Remove the shift cable.

13. Disconnect the shift cable from the manual lever.

14. Remove the bolts and position the shift cable and bracket out of the way.

15. Loosen the bolt and disconnect the solenoid body electrical connector.

16. Disconnect the output shaft speed (OSS) sensor electrical connector.

17. Disconnect the turbine shaft and intermediate shaft combination speed sensor electrical connector.

18. Disconnect the right and left wire harness from the side of the transmission.

4x2 vehicles

19. Remove the left crossmember bolts and nuts.

20. Loosen, but do not remove, the bolt and nut indicated.

21. Remove the right crossmember bracket bolts and nuts.

22. Remove the bracket bolts and nuts.

23. Remove the bracket.

24. Remove the right crossmember bolts and nuts.

25. Remove the left crossmember bolt, nut and the crossmember.

26. Remove the bolt and nut.

27. Remove the crossmember.

28. Remove the rear transmission mount from the extension housing.

29. If equipped with dual alternators, rotate the tensioner and remove the outer accessory drive belt from the crankshaft pulley.

All vehicles

30. Remove the cylinder block opening cover in order to gain access to the torque converter nuts.

➡**Using a suitable strap wrench, rotate the crankshaft pulley to gain access to the torque converter nuts.**

31. Remove and discard the torque converter nuts.

32. While holding the case fitting, disconnect the rear fluid cooler tube nut and tube.

33. While holding the case fitting, disconnect the front fluid cooler tube nut and tube.

34. Remove the nine transmission-to-engine mounting bolts.

35. Slide the transmission back enough to install the special tool.

36. If the transmission is being overhauled or if installing a new or remanufactured transmission, carry out the transmission fluid cooler backflushing and cleaning.

To install:

⁂ **CAUTION**

Prior to the installation of a new or overhauled transmission, the fluid cooler lines must be cleaned. Otherwise transmission failure can occur.

⁂ **CAUTION**

Prior to the installation of a new or overhauled transmission, a new transmission fluid cooler remote filter must be installed. Otherwise transmission failure can occur.

37. If necessary, install a new transmission fluid cooler remote filter.

⁂ **CAUTION**

Prior to the installation of the assembly, the torque converter pilot hub must be correctly lubricated or damage to the torque converter or the engine crankshaft can occur.

38. Lubricate the torque converter pilot hub with multi-purpose grease.

39. If the holding special tool has not been installed during the assembly of the transmission, install the tool to hold the torque converter in place while moving and positioning the transmission in place. Once the transmission is in place, prior to bolting it to the engine, remove the special tool.

40. Position the transmission in place. While raising the transmission up into the engine compartment, align the fluid filler tube with the stub tube on the transmission using the fluid level indicator as a guide.

41. While installing the transmission to the engine, align the torque converter studs with the mounting holes in the flexplate.

42. Install nine transmission-to-engine bolts. Torque to 35 ft. lbs. (47 Nm).

43. Using a suitable strap wrench to rotate the crankshaft and pulley, install the new torque converter-to-flexplate nuts. Torque to 26 ft. lbs. (35 Nm).

44. Install the cylinder block opening cover.

45. If equipped with dual alternators, rotate the tensioner and install the outer accessory drive belt onto the crankshaft pulley.

All applications

46. Install the front transmission fluid cooler tube.

47. Install the rear transmission fluid cooler tube.

4x4 applications

48. Support the extension housing with a jack stand and remove the transmission jack.

4x2 applications

49. Install the transmission mount. Torque to 69 ft. lbs. (94 Nm).

50. Position the crossmember to the transmission mount and loosely install the nut.

51. Install the left crossmember bolts. Torque to 60 ft. lbs. (81 Nm).

52. Install the right crossmember bolts. Torque to 60 ft. lbs. (81 Nm).

53. Install the bracket and loosely install the bolts.

54. Install the bracket.

55. Loosely install the bolts.

56. Tighten the right crossmember bolts. Torque to 60 ft. lbs. (81 Nm).

57. Tighten the rear insulator nuts. Torque to 69 ft. lbs. (94 Nm).

All applications

58. Connect the right and left wiring harness to the side of the transmission.

59. Connect the output shaft speed (OSS) sensor electrical connector.

60. Connect the intermediate shaft and turbine shaft combination speed sensor electrical connector.

61. Connect the solenoid body electrical connector.

➡️**If the vehicle is equipped with a power take-off unit, all or part of the PTO unit will need to be installed.**

62. Connect the shift cable.

63. Install the cable housing bracket.

64. Install the shift cable to the manual lever.

4x2 applications

65. Reconnect the wire harness to the frame.

4x4 applications

66. If equipped, install the transfer case.

4x2 applications

67. Install the rear driveshaft.

All applications

➡️**Use the following guidelines for the in-line transmission filter:**

e. If the transmission was overhauled and the vehicle was equipped with an in-line fluid filter, install a new in-line fluid filter.

f. If the transmission was overhauled and the vehicle was not equipped with the in-line fluid filter, install a new in-line fluid filter.

g. If the transmission is being installed for a non-internal repair, do not install an in-line filter or filter kit.

h. If installing a new or a Ford-authorized remanufactured transmission, install the in-line transmission fluid filter that is supplied.

68. Prior to lowering the vehicle, install a new in-line transmission filter or a filter kit.

69. Connect the battery ground cable.

70. Adjust the shift linkage. Verify that the vehicle starts in **Park** and **Neutral** and the **Reverse** lamps illuminate in **Reverse**.

71. With the engine running and the transmission at normal operating temperature 66–77°C (150–170°F), check and adjust the transmission fluid level, and check for any leaks. If fluid is needed, add fluid in increments of 0.24L (0.5 pint) until the correct level is achieved (fluid should be in the cross-hatched area of the fluid level indicator).

F-250 and F-350

1. Before servicing the vehicle, refer to the Precautions Section.

All vehicles

2. Raise and safely support the vehicle.

3. Remove the exhaust pipe between the exhaust manifolds and the exhaust flange.

4x4 vehicles

4. Remove the transfer case assembly.

4x2 vehicles

5. Remove the driveshaft.

All vehicles

6. If transmission disassembly is required, drain the transmission fluid. Remove the drain plug and allow the fluid to drain.

7. Install the drain plug. Torque to 18 ft. lbs. (25 Nm).

8. Install a suitable high-lift transmission jack.

4x4 vehicles

9. Remove the jack stand from under the extension housing after installing the transmission jack.

4x2 vehicles

10. Remove the wire harness from the rear crossmember.

11. Remove the rear transmission mount nuts.

All vehicles

12. Disconnect the shift cable from the manual lever.

13. Remove the bolts and position the shift cable and bracket out of the way.

14. Loosen the bolt and disconnect the solenoid body electrical connector.

15. Disconnect the output shaft speed (OSS) sensor electrical connector.

16. Disconnect the turbine shaft and intermediate shaft combination speed sensor electrical connector.

17. Disconnect the right and left wire harness from the side of the transmission.

4x2 vehicles

18. Remove the left crossmember bolts and nuts. Loosen, but do not remove, the lower bolt.

19. Remove the right crossmember bracket bolts and nuts.

20. Remove the right crossmember bolts and nuts.

21. Remove the left crossmember bolt, nut and the crossmember.

22. Remove the rear transmission mount from the extension housing.

23. If equipped with dual alternators, rotate the tensioner and remove the outer accessory drive belt from the crankshaft pulley.

All vehicles

24. Remove the cylinder block opening cover in order to gain access to the torque converter nuts.

➡️**Using a suitable strap wrench, rotate the crankshaft pulley to gain access to the torque converter nuts.**

25. Remove and discard the torque converter nuts.

26. While holding the case fitting, disconnect the rear fluid cooler tube nut and tube.

27. While holding the case fitting, disconnect the front fluid cooler tube nut and tube.

28. Remove the nine transmission-to-engine mounting bolts.

29. Slide the transmission back enough to install the torque converter holding tool.

30. Carefully lower the transmission assembly.

31. If the transmission is being overhauled or if installing a new or remanufactured transmission, carry out the transmission fluid cooler backflushing and cleaning.

To install:
All vehicles

> ❋❋ **WARNING**
>
> **Prior to installation of a new or overhauled transmission, the fluid cooler lines must be cleaned. Otherwise transmission failure can occur.**

> ❋❋ **WARNING**
>
> **Prior to installation of a new or overhauled transmission, a new transmission fluid cooler remote filter element must be installed. Otherwise transmission failure can occur.**

32. If necessary, install a new transmission fluid cooler remote filter element.

> ❋❋ **WARNING**
>
> **Prior to installation of the assembly, the torque converter pilot hub must be correctly lubricated or damage to the torque converter or the engine crankshaft can occur.**

33. Lubricate the torque converter pilot hub with multi-purpose grease.

34. Rotate the torque converter so the green or orange paint daub on the converter is in the 12 o'clock position.

35. If the special tool has not been installed during the assembly of the transmission, install the special tool to hold the torque converter in place while moving and positioning the transmission in place. Once the transmission is in place, prior to bolting it to the engine, remove the special tool.

36. Position the transmission in place. While raising the transmission up into the engine compartment, align the fluid filler tube with the stub tube on the transmission using the fluid level indicator as a guide.

37. While installing the transmission to the engine, align the torque converter studs with the mounting holes in the flexplate.

38. Install nine transmission-to-engine bolts. Torque to 35 ft. lbs. (47 Nm).

39. Using a suitable strap wrench to rotate the crankshaft and pulley, install the new torque converter-to-flexplate nuts. Torque to 26 ft. lbs. (35 Nm).

40. Install the cylinder block opening cover.

41. If equipped with dual alternators, rotate the tensioner and install the outer accessory drive belt onto the crankshaft pulley.

42. Install the front transmission fluid cooler tube. Torque to 30 ft. lbs. (40 Nm).

43. Install the rear transmission fluid cooler tube. Torque to 30 ft. lbs. (40 Nm).

4x4 vehicles
44. Support the extension housing with a jack stand and remove the transmission jack.

4x2 vehicles
45. Install the transmission mount. Torque to 69 ft. lbs. (94 Nm).

46. Position the crossmember to the transmission mount and loosely install the nut.

47. Install the left crossmember bolts. Torque to 60 ft. lbs. (81 Nm).

48. Install the right crossmember bolts. Torque to 60 ft. lbs. (81 Nm).

49. Install the bracket and loosely install the bolts.

50. Tighten the right crossmember bolts. Torque to 60 ft. lbs. (81 Nm).

51. Tighten the rear insulator nuts. Torque to 69 ft. lbs. (94 Nm).

All vehicles
52. Connect the right and left wiring harness to the side of the transmission.

53. Connect the output shaft speed (OSS) sensor electrical connector.

54. Connect the intermediate shaft and turbine shaft combination speed sensor electrical connector.

55. Connect the solenoid body electrical connector.

➡ **If the vehicle is equipped with a power take-off (PTO) unit, all or part of the PTO unit will need to be installed.**

56. Install the shift cable housing bracket. Torque to 18 ft. lbs. (25 Nm).

57. Install the shift cable to the manual lever.

4x2 vehicles
58. Reconnect the wire harness to the frame.

59. Install the exhaust pipe between the exhaust manifold and the exhaust flange.

4x4 vehicles
60. If equipped, install the transfer case.
4x2 vehicles
61. Install the rear driveshaft.
All vehicles

➡ **Use the following guidelines for the in-line transmission filter:**

- If the transmission was overhauled and the vehicle was equipped with an in-line fluid filter, install a new in-line fluid filter.
- If the transmission was overhauled and the vehicle was not equipped with the in-line fluid filter, install a new in-line fluid filter.
- If the transmission is being installed for a non-internal repair, do not install an in-line filter or filter kit.
- If installing a new or a Ford-authorized remanufactured transmission, install the in-line transmission fluid filter that is supplied.

62. Prior to lowering the vehicle, install a new in-line transmission filter or a filter kit.

63. Adjust the shift linkage. Verify that the vehicle starts in PARK and NEUTRAL and the REVERSE lamps illuminate in REVERSE.

64. With the engine running and the transmission at normal operating temperature 66–77°C (150–170°F), check and adjust the transmission fluid level, and check for any leaks. If fluid is needed, add fluid in increments of 0.24 liter (0.5 pint) until the correct level is achieved (fluid should be in the cross-hatched area of the fluid level indicator).

MANUAL TRANSMISSION ASSEMBLY

REMOVAL & INSTALLATION

F-150

1. Before servicing the vehicle, refer to the Precautions Section.

2. Disconnect the battery ground cable.

3. Unclip the console cover, then slide the cover and boot assembly up.

4. Remove the gearshift lever nut.

5. Install the gearshift lever nut on the left side of the lever, then, tighten the nut to remove the eccentric stud out of the gearshift lever. Remove the upper gearshift lever.

6. Remove the 4 screws and the lower boot.

7. Remove the 4 bolts and the lower gearshift lever.

8. Raise and safely support the vehicle.

9. If transmission disassembly is required, remove the drain plug and drain the transmission fluid. Install the drain plug after draining all the fluid. Tighten to 48 Nm (35 ft. lbs.).

10. Remove the right catalytic converter.

11. Remove the 2 starter motor bolts and the starter motor. Using mechanic's wire, position the starter motor aside.

12. Disconnect the wire harness from the transmission and disconnect both of the heated oxygen (HEGO) sensor electrical connectors.

13. Disconnect the reverse lamp switch electrical connector.

14. Disconnect the vehicle speed sensor (VSS) electrical connector.

15. Remove the front stabilizer bar.

16. Remove the 2 nuts and disconnect the fuel lines and the wire harness from the rear of the transmission. Position them aside.

17. Using the special tool, disconnect the clutch hydraulic line.

18. Position a suitable jack under the transmission. Secure the transmission to the jack with a safety strap.

19. Remove the 2 exhaust hanger bolts.

20. Remove the 2 exhaust heat shield bolts.

21. Remove the 4 crossmember bolts.

22. Remove the 2 transmission mount nuts and the crossmember.

23. Lower the transmission enough to gain access to the upper transmission-to-engine bolts.

24. Remove 9 transmission-to-engine bolts.

25. Pull the transmission rearward until the input shift is clear of the pressure plate, then lower the transmission from the vehicle.

26. To install, reverse the removal procedure. Note the following:

  a. Before securing the engine to the transmission, connect the hydraulic line to the clutch slave cylinder.

  b. Make sure the exhaust system is correctly aligned.

  c. Align the index marks when installing the rear driveshaft.

  d. Check and, if necessary, fill the transmission with the specified type and quantity of fluid.

27. Observe the following torques:

- Transmission-to-engine bolts: 60 Nm (44 ft. lbs.).
- Transmission mount nuts: 98 Nm (72 ft. lbs.).
- The 4 crossmember bolts: 90 Nm (66 ft. lbs.).
- The 2 exhaust heat shield bolts: 15 Nm (11 ft. lbs.).
- The 2 starter motor bolts: 33 Nm (24 ft. lbs.).

F-250 and F-350

1. Before servicing the vehicle, refer to the Precautions Section.

All vehicles

2. Remove the four screws and the outer shift lever boot.

3. Remove the upper gearshift lever.

4. Remove the lower shift lever boot.

5. Remove the lower gearshift and shift housing.

Vehicles with a manual shift transfer case

6. Shift the transfer case into 4H.

7. Remove the screws that attach the bezel and boot assembly to the floor.

8. Remove the bolt that attaches the shift lever to the transfer case control lever assembly, and remove the shift lever, and the bezel and boot assembly.

All vehicles

9. Raise and support the vehicle.

10. If the transmission is being disassembled, drain the transmission fluid.

11. Remove the catalytic converter.

12. Remove the starter.

➡ Index-mark the driveshaft to the transfer case flange. Remove and discard the driveshaft bolts.

13. Disconnect the rear driveshaft and position it aside.

14. Remove the transfer case, if equipped.

15. Disconnect the fuel lines from the transmission.

16. Remove any power take-off (PTO) equipment, if equipped.

17. Using a transmission jack, support the transmission.

❊❊ CAUTION

Securely strap the jack to the transmission.

18. Remove the right crossmember nuts.

19. Remove the left crossmember bolts.

20. Disconnect the wire harness from the crossmember.

21. Remove the transmission mount nuts and the crossmember.

22. Disconnect the reverse lamp switch electrical connector.

23. Disconnect wiring harness from the transmission.

24. Push the clutch slave cylinder inward, then rotate counterclockwise 45 degrees to remove.

25. Disconnect the transmission cooling tubes.

26. Remove the dust cover bolts. 6.0L equipped vehicles do not have a dust cover.

27. Remove the transmission-to-engine bolts.

28. Move the transmission rearward until the input shaft is clear of the clutch, then lower from the vehicle.

To install:
All vehicles

29. Using the transmission jack, raise and position the transmission to the engine and clutch.

30. Install the transmission-to-engine bolts. Torque to 46 ft. lbs. (63 Nm). Vehicles equipped with diesel engines have six bolts. Those equipped with gasoline engines, have seven bolts.

31. Position the crossmember in the vehicle. Install the transmission mount nuts. Torque to 60 ft. lbs. (81 Nm).

32. Install the left crossmember bolts. Torque to 52 ft. lbs. (70 Nm).

33. Install the right crossmember nuts. Torque to 52 ft. lbs. (70 Nm).

34. Attach the wire harness to the crossmember.

35. Install the dust cover bolts. Torque to 21 ft. lbs. (28 Nm).

➡ 6.0L equipped vehicles do not have a dust cover.

36. Remove the transmission jack.

37. Connect the transmission cooler tubes. Torque to 20 ft. lbs. (27 Nm).

38. Install the clutch slave cylinder. Rotate the clutch slave cylinder clockwise 45 degrees to lock in position.

39. Install the starter.

40. Install the catalytic converter.

41. Install the transfer case, if equipped. If the transfer case control lever assembly was removed from the transmission, it must be correctly aligned.

42. Connect the driveshaft.

43. Install any power take-off (PTO) equipment, if equipped.

44. Connect the fuel lines to the transmission.

45. Connect the reverse lamp switch electrical connector.

46. Connect the wiring harness to the transmission.

47. Refill the transmission to specification.

48. Lower the vehicle.

❊❊ WARNING

Do not use a silicone sealing compound.

➡ Do not wait longer than ten minutes to tighten the six bolts due to the rapid cure time of the sealant.

49. Install the lower gearshift lever and shift housing assembly. Apply gasket maker to the shift housing and the main case. Torque to 17 ft. lbs. (23 Nm).

50. Install the lower shift lever boot.

51. Apply threadlock and sealer to the gearshift lever bolts. Install the upper gearshift lever. Torque to 21 ft. lbs. (28 Nm).

52. Install the screws.

Vehicles with a manual shift transfer case

53. Position the shift lever with the bezel and boot assembly and install the bolt. Torque to 20 ft. lbs. (27 Nm).

54. Position the bezel and boot assembly and install the screws.

55. Verify the shift sequence from 2H to 4L to 2H.

CLUTCH DRIVEN DISC & PRESSURE PLATE

REMOVAL & INSTALLATION

F-150

See Figures 22 and 23.

1. Before servicing the vehicle, refer to the Precautions Section.

2. Remove the transmission.

3. If the original components are to be installed, index-mark the clutch pressure plate and the flywheel.

4. Remove the clutch pressure plate bolts, clutch pressure plate and the clutch disc.

To install:

➡ The self-adjusting clutch pressure plate should always be adjusted before installation.

5. Place the flywheel and the clutch pressure plate in a press. Using a suitable adapter, compress the clutch diaphragm fingers until the adjusting ring moves.

6. Adjust the clutch pressure plate as follows:

    e. Rotate the adjusting ring counter-clockwise until the tension springs are compressed.

    f. Hold the adjusting ring, then, release the pressure on the clutch pressure plate fingers.

7. Using an aligning tool, position the clutch disc on the flywheel.

➡ If installing the original clutch pressure plate, use the index marks made during removal.

8. Position the clutch pressure plate on the dowels, install the clutch pressure plate bolts and remove the aligning tool. Apply Threadlock and Sealer TA-25 meeting Ford specification WSK-M2G351-A5 to the clutch pressure plate bolt threads. Tighten to 55 Nm (41 ft. lbs.).

9. Install the transmission. Before securing the transmission to the engine, install the hydraulic line to the clutch slave cylinder.

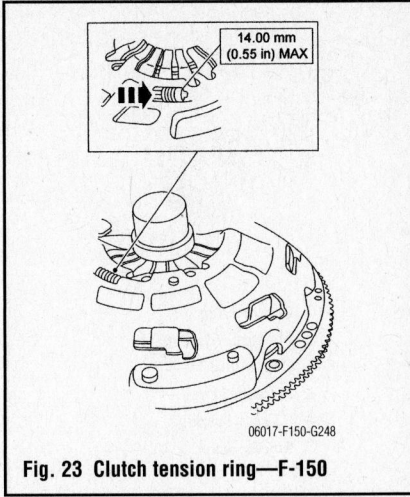

14.00 mm (0.55 in) MAX

06017-F150-G248

Fig. 23 Clutch tension ring—F-150

10. Operate the vehicle to check clutch operation.

F-250 and F-350

See Figures 24 through 26.

1. Before servicing the vehicle, refer to the Precautions Section.

2. Remove the transmission.

3. Index-mark the clutch pressure plate and the flywheel, if reinstalling these parts.

4. Remove the bolts, the clutch pressure plate, and the clutch disc.

5. Inspect the transmission input shaft pilot bearing for:

    a. Misalignment and looseness in the crankshaft (gasoline engine) or flywheel (7.3L diesel engine).

    b. Needle rollers for scoring, discoloration, wear, and broken rollers.

    c. Seal for damage and lubricant leakage.

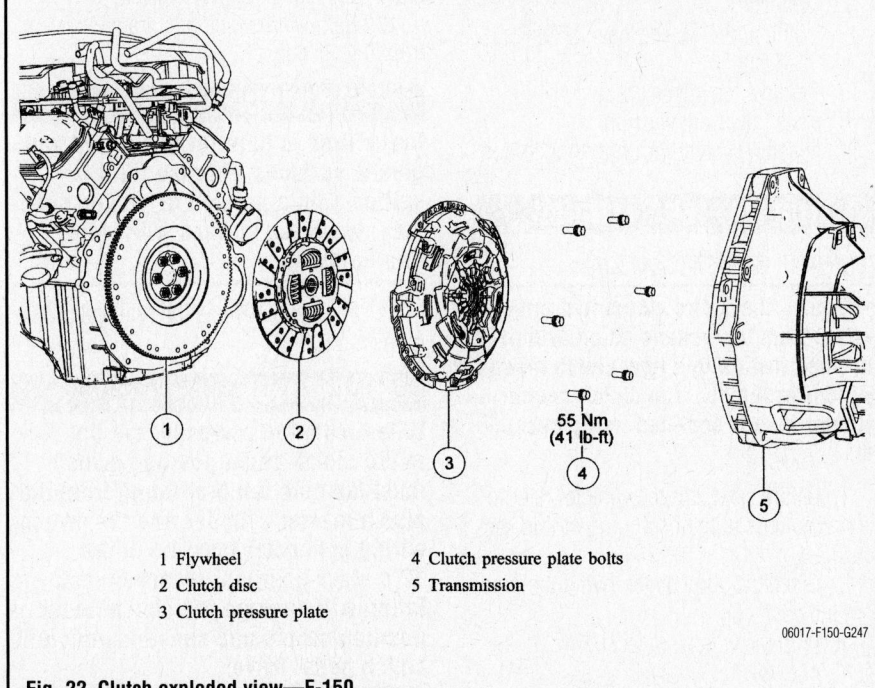

55 Nm
(41 lb-ft)

1 Flywheel
2 Clutch disc
3 Clutch pressure plate
4 Clutch pressure plate bolts
5 Transmission

06017-F150-G247

Fig. 22 Clutch exploded view—F-150

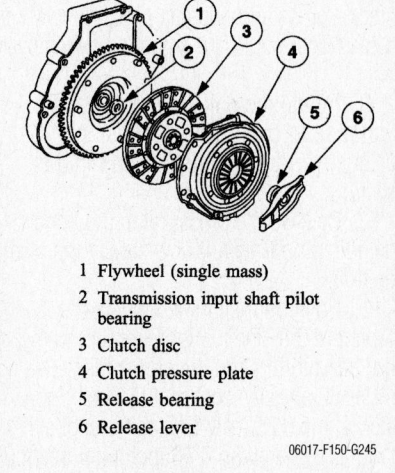

1 Flywheel (single mass)
2 Transmission input shaft pilot bearing
3 Clutch disc
4 Clutch pressure plate
5 Release bearing
6 Release lever

06017-F150-G245

Fig. 24 Clutch exploded view—F-250 and F-350 exc. 6.0L Diesel Engine

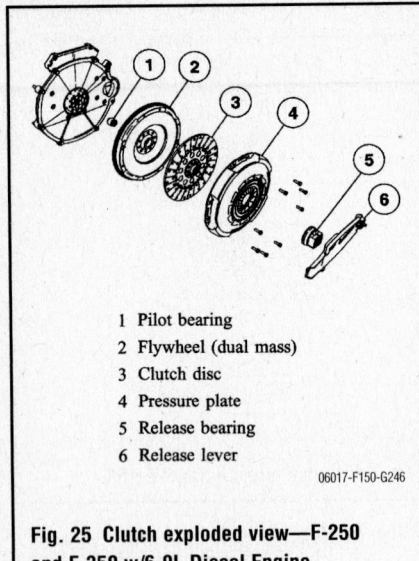

1 Pilot bearing
2 Flywheel (dual mass)
3 Clutch disc
4 Pressure plate
5 Release bearing
6 Release lever

06017-F150-G246

Fig. 25 Clutch exploded view—F-250 and F-350 w/6.0L Diesel Engine

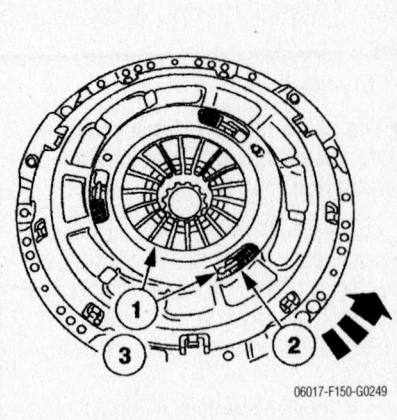

06017-F150-G0249

Fig. 26 Rotate the adjusting ring counterclockwise to compress the tension springs—F-250 and F-350

6. Install a new transmission input shaft pilot bearing if any of these conditions are present.

To install:

➥Sometimes, when removing the transmission, the input shaft will remove a considerable amount of lubricant from the transmission input shaft pilot bearing.

7. Lubricate the transmission input shaft pilot bearing, as necessary. Use Krytox® High-Temperature Grease.

✳✳ WARNING

When installing the original clutch pressure plate on 5.4L, 6.0L and 6.8L applications, reset the wear indicator before installing the clutch pressure plate on the flywheel.

8. Reset the wear indicator. Using a suitable press and adapter, press downward on the fingers until the adjusting ring moves freely.

9. Rotate the adjusting ring counterclockwise to compress the tension springs. Hold the adjusting ring in this position.

10. Release the pressure on the fingers. The adjusting ring will now stay in the reset position.

11. Position the clutch disc on the flywheel and the clutch alignment tool in the pilot bearing to align the clutch disc. The 5.4L/6.8L engines accept a 1¼ inch input shaft. The 6.0L Diesel Engines accept a 1⅜ inch input shaft with 0.98 inch pilot bearing inner diameter. The 7.3L engines accept a 1⅜ inch input shaft with 0.67 inch pilot bearing inner diameter.

➥Align the index marks if installing the original clutch pressure plate and flywheel.

12. Install the clutch pressure plate. Position the clutch pressure plate on the dowels.

➥The 7.3L diesel engine flywheel has two dowels. The gasoline engine flywheel has three dowels.

13. Using a clutch alignment tool, align the clutch disc and the pressure plate.

14. Install the bolts and tighten in a star pattern sequence to:
- 5.4L and 6.8L engines: 33 ft. lbs. (45 Nm)
- 6.0L and 7.3L engines: 21 ft. lbs. (28 Nm)

15. Remove the special tool.
16. Install the transmission.
17. Test the system for normal operation.

CLUTCH MASTER CYLINDER

REMOVAL & INSTALLATION

➥Remove the entire clutch hydraulic system from the vehicle as an assembly when installing a new clutch master cylinder assembly. The clutch master cylinder is only serviced in the assembly.

1. Before servicing the vehicle, refer to the precautions in the beginning of this section.

2. Disconnect the clutch hydraulic tube from the dash clip.

3. With the vehicle in NEUTRAL, position it on a hoist.

4. The 5.4L and 6.8L clutch control

system has a heat shield that covers most of the tube and clutch slave cylinder. To unlock the slave cylinder, slide the heat shield back and off of the slave cylinder. Slide the heat shield over the tube.

5. Compress and twist the clutch slave cylinder counterclockwise to unlock it from the transmission.

6. Disconnect the clutch hydraulic tube from the floor pan clip. Position the clutch slave cylinder and hydraulic tube forward below the left engine bank. This will make it easier to unlock the clutch master cylinder from the clutch pedal and support bracket by reducing tension on the hydraulic tube.

7. Lower the vehicle.

✳✳ WARNING

The clutch pedal is under spring tension.

8. Unlock the push rod retaining clips and separate the clutch master cylinder push rod from the clutch pedal.

9. Remove and discard the clutch master cylinder push rod bushing.

10. Remove the switch cover and the clutch pedal position switch from the clutch master cylinder push rod.

11. Separate the power distribution box from the bracket to gain access to the clutch master cylinder.

12. Compress and twist the clutch master cylinder clockwise 45 degrees to unlock it from the clutch pedal and support bracket. Remove the clutch master cylinder from the clutch pedal and support bracket.

13. Remove the clutch hydraulic system from the vehicle.

✳✳ CAUTION

Brake fluid is harmful to painted and plastic surfaces. If brake fluid is spilled onto a painted or plastic surface, wash the surface with water immediately.

14. To install, reverse the removal procedure.

✳✳ CAUTION

When installed correctly, the flat side of the clutch pedal position switch must face the tab protruding from the clutch master cylinder and the switch wiring connector must be in the 12 o'clock position. Incorrect installation will damage the clutch pedal position switch and cause insufficient clutch pedal travel.

✻ CAUTION

The push rod is not removable after installing it in the clutch master cylinder.

15. Install the new push rod in the clutch master cylinder.

16. Install a new push rod bushing.

17. For 5.4L and 6.8L clutch control systems, make sure to slide the heat shield forward and over the slave cylinder until it contacts the transmission case.

18. Press the clutch pedal to seat the push rod in the clutch master cylinder.

19. Test the system for normal operation.

CLUTCH SLAVE CYLINDER

➡The clutch slave cylinder, the clutch master cylinder and the hydraulic lines make up the clutch hydraulic system. The clutch slave cylinder is only serviced in the assembly.

TRANSFER CASE ASSEMBLY

REMOVAL & INSTALLATION

F-150 and Mark LT

Mechanical Shift

See Figure 27.

1. Before servicing the vehicle, refer to the Precautions Section.

➡**To maintain initial driveshaft balance, index-mark the rear driveshaft.**

2. Remove the rear driveshaft.

3. Remove the skid plate, if equipped.

4. Drain the fluid if the transfer case is to be disassembled.

5. Disconnect the transfer case wire harness.

6. Remove the front driveshaft shield.

7. Remove the front driveshaft.

8. Remove the transfer case shift linkage.

9. Remove the vent tube.

10. Position a suitable transmission jack to the transfer case. Securely strap the transfer case to the jack.

11. Remove the transfer case.

12. Clean the mating surfaces of the transfer case and the transmission.

13. To install, reverse the removal procedure.

14. Tighten the transmission-to-transfer case bolts evenly in a star pattern to 35 ft. lbs. (47 Nm).

15. Fill the transfer case.

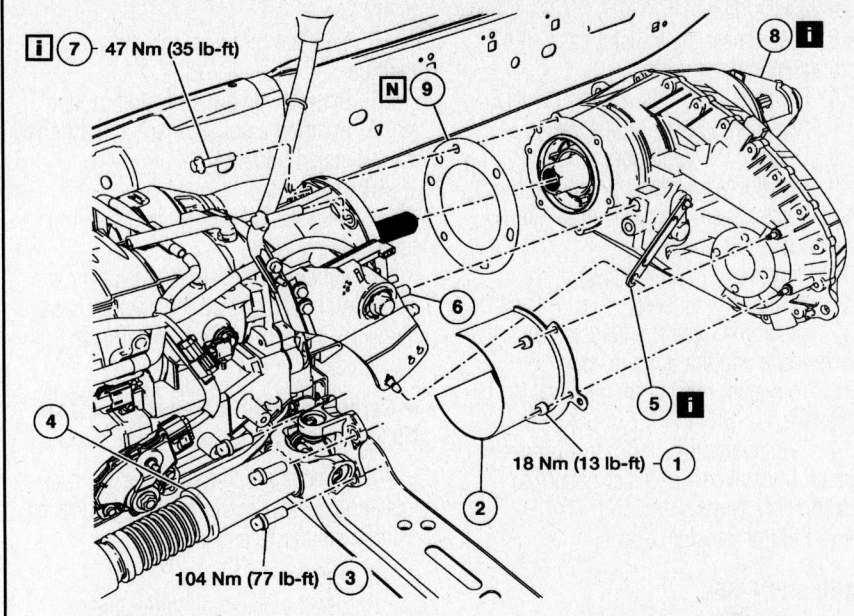

1 Front driveshaft shield nut	4 Front driveshaft	7 Transmission-to-transfer case bolts
2 Front driveshaft shield	5 Transfer case shift linkage	8 Transfer case
3 Front driveshaft bolt	6 Transfer case vent tube	9 Transfer case-to-transmission gasket

67197-EFSE-G146

Fig. 27 Mechanical shift transfer case—F-150

Electronic Shift

See Figure 28.

1. Before servicing the vehicle, refer to the Precautions Section.

➡**To maintain initial driveshaft balance, index-mark the rear driveshaft.**

2. Remove the rear driveshaft.

3. Remove the skid plate, if equipped.

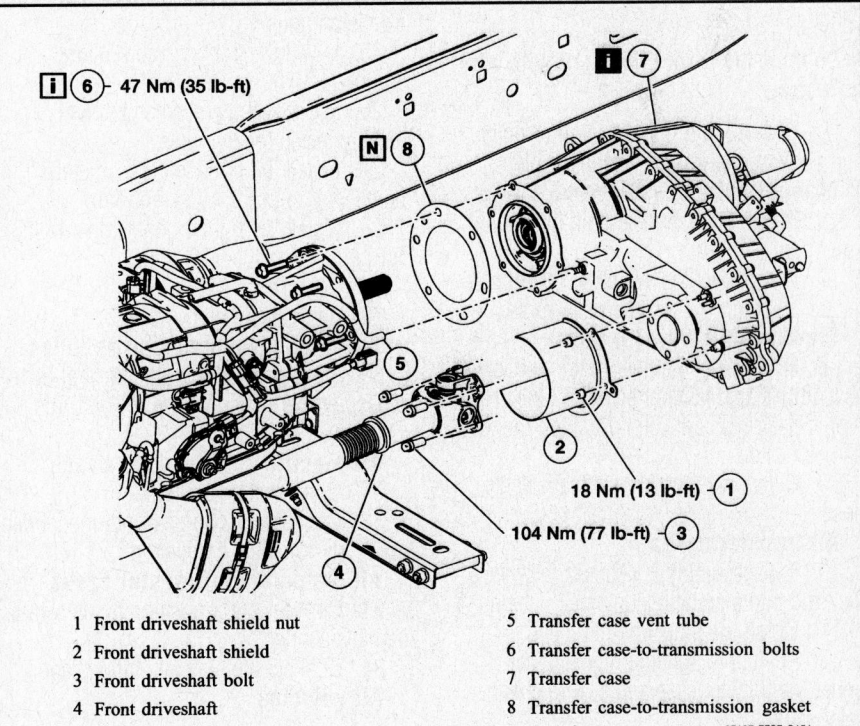

1 Front driveshaft shield nut	5 Transfer case vent tube
2 Front driveshaft shield	6 Transfer case-to-transmission bolts
3 Front driveshaft bolt	7 Transfer case
4 Front driveshaft	8 Transfer case-to-transmission gasket

67197-EFSE-G151

Fig. 28 Electronic shift transfer case—F-150

4. Drain the fluid if the transfer case is to be disassembled.

5. Disconnect the transfer case shift motor electrical connector.

6. Remove the front driveshaft shield.

7. Remove the front driveshaft.

8. Remove the vent tube.

9. Position a suitable transmission jack to the transfer case. Securely strap the transfer case to the jack.

10. Remove the transfer case.

11. Remove the gasket.

12. Clean the mating surfaces of the transfer case and the transmission.

13. To install, reverse the removal procedure.

14. Tighten the transfer case-to-transmission bolts evenly in a star pattern to 35 ft. lbs. (47 Nm).

15. Fill the transfer case.

F-250 and F-350

1. Before servicing the vehicle, refer to the Precautions Section.

➡ **Shift the transfer case to 2W HI.**

2. Raise and support the vehicle.

3. Remove the four bolts and the skid plate, if equipped.

➡ **Index-mark the driveshaft to maintain driveline balance.**

4. Remove the rear driveshaft. Index-mark the front driveshaft to the transfer case flange.

➡ **Support the front driveshaft with wire or a strap.**

5. Remove and discard the four bolts and position the front driveshaft aside.

Manual shift transfer case

6. Remove the manual shift linkage, if equipped.

7. Disconnect the switch electrical connector. Position the wire harness aside.

Electric shift transfer case

8. Disconnect the gear motor encoder assembly electrical connector and the gear motor electrical connector. Position the wire harness aside.

9. Disconnect the transfer case vent hose.

All transfer cases

10. If disassembly is necessary, drain the fluid into a suitable container.

11. Install the plug when finished.

12. Position a suitable high-lift jack under the transfer case and secure it with safety straps.

With automatic transmission

13. Remove the four right crossmember bolts.

14. Remove the three left crossmember bolts.

15. Remove the nuts and the crossmember.

16. Remove the transmission mount.

17. Position a suitable jack stand under the extension housing.

All vehicles

18. Remove the six transfer case-to-transmission bolts.

19. Separate the transfer case from the extension housing. Pull the transfer case rearward, then lower the transfer case from the vehicle.

➡ **Carefully clean the gasket surfaces. Nicks and gouges cause fluid leaks.**

20. Remove the transfer case-to-transmission gasket. Clean the mating surfaces, using metal surface cleaner.

To install:

21. Install a new mounting gasket.

✳✳ CAUTION

Secure the transfer case to the high-lift jack with a safety strap.

22. Raise the transfer case into position.

23. Install the six bolts retaining the transfer case to the extension housing. Torque to 37 ft. lbs. (50 Nm).

Automatic transmission vehicles

24. Remove the jack stand from the extension housing.

25. Install the transmission mount. Torque to 70 ft. lbs. (95 Nm).

26. Position the crossmember and loosely install the two nuts.

27. Install the three left crossmember bolts. Torque to 52 ft. lbs. (70 Nm).

28. Install the right crossmember bolts. Torque to 52 ft. lbs. (70 Nm).

All vehicles

29. Remove the high-lift jack.

Automatic transmission vehicles

30. Tighten the transmission mount-to-crossmember nuts. Torque to 69 ft. lbs. (92 Nm).

All electric shift transfer cases

31. Connect the vent hose.

32. Connect the two gear motor encoder assembly electrical connectors.

All manual shift transfer cases

33. Connect the 3-position mode switch harness connector.

34. Connect the manual shift linkage.

All vehicles

➡ **Align the index-marks when installing the driveshaft.**

35. Connect the front driveshaft to the

transfer case and install the four new bolts. Torque to 82 ft. lbs. (111 Nm).

36. Install the rear driveshaft.

37. If equipped, install the skid plate and the four bolts.

38. If drained, fill the transfer case.

FRONT AUTOMATIC LOCKING HUBS

REMOVAL & INSTALLATION

F-150 and Mark LT

See Figure 29.

1. Before servicing the vehicle, refer to the precautions in the beginning of this section.

2. With the vehicle in NEUTRAL, position it on a hoist.

3. Remove the dust cap.

4. Remove and discard the wheel end nut.

5. Remove the vacuum and vent line at the vacuum and vent port of the integrated wheel end.

6. Remove the 3 integrated wheel end bolts.

7. Remove the tie-rod nut and separate the tie rod from the knuckle.

8. Remove the upper ball joint nut and separate the upper ball joint from the knuckle.

✳✳ CAUTION

Do not damage the hub seal.

➡ **Allow the steering knuckle to swing outward while keeping the halfshaft pushed inward.**

9. Once clearance is available, remove the halfshaft outboard end and integrated wheel end from the hub bearing.

10. Remove the integrated wheel end from the halfshaft outboard end.

11. To install, reverse the removal procedure. Use new a wheel end nut, tie-rod nut, and upper ball joint nut.

✳✳ CAUTION

Do not install the integrated wheel end in the knuckle. It must be installed on the outer constant velocity joint housing.

✳✳ CAUTION

Do not dislodge the integrated wheel end seal spring when installing the integrated wheel end on the outer constant velocity joint housing.

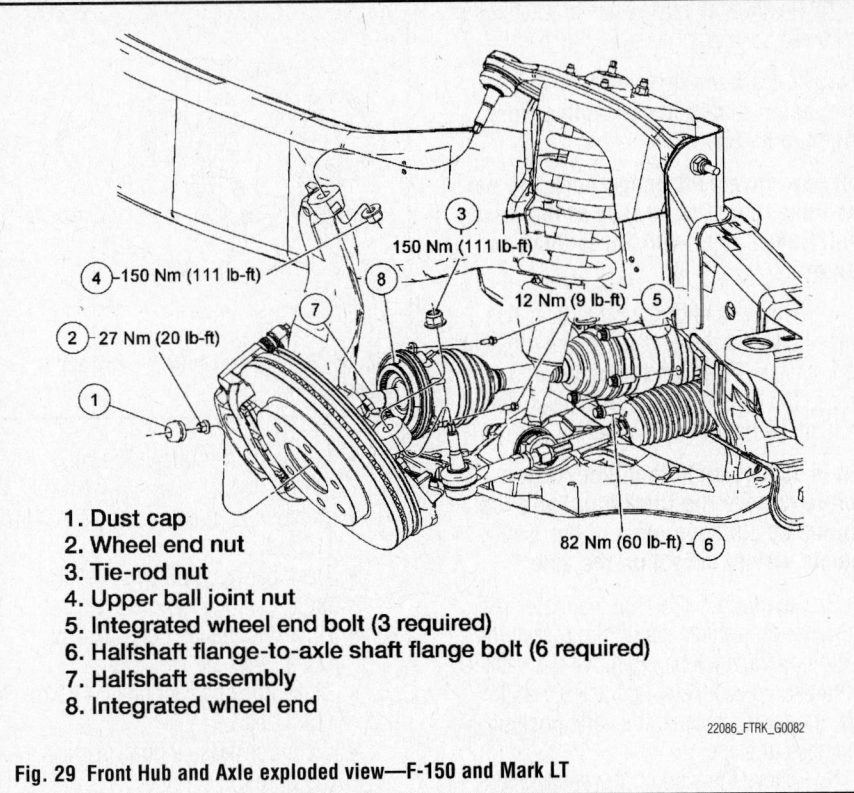

1. Dust cap
2. Wheel end nut
3. Tie-rod nut
4. Upper ball joint nut
5. Integrated wheel end bolt (3 required)
6. Halfshaft flange-to-axle shaft flange bolt (6 required)
7. Halfshaft assembly
8. Integrated wheel end

4 — 150 Nm (111 lb-ft)
2 — 27 Nm (20 lb-ft)
1
7
8
3
150 Nm (111 lb-ft)
12 Nm (9 lb-ft)
5
82 Nm (60 lb-ft) — 6

22086_FTRK_G0082

Fig. 29 Front Hub and Axle exploded view—F-150 and Mark LT

➡ **Compress the integrated wheel end and install a vacuum cap on the vacuum port.**

FRONT MANUAL LOCKING HUBS

REMOVAL & INSTALLATION

F-250 and F-350

1. Before servicing the vehicle, refer to the precautions in the beginning of this section.
2. Remove the front wheel.
3. Remove the hub extender nuts and the hub extender, if equipped.
4. Loosen the hub lock screws one to two turns.
5. Use a small pry bar around the entire hub flange to release the gasket.
6. Remove and discard the hub lock screws.

➡ **Wiggle the axle shaft while sliding the hub lock off of the splines to ease removal.**

7. Use a small pry bar around the entire hub flange and remove the hub lock from the wheel hub.
8. Remove the old gasket material completely and discard the O-ring.
9. Clean the O-ring seal contact area as necessary to provide a good seal.

To install:

10. Install a new gasket and O-ring on the hub lock.
11. Rotate the hub lock dial clockwise to the LOCK position, then apply grease to the inner and outer splines.

➡ **Wiggle the axle shaft while sliding the hub lock on the splines to ease installation.**

12. Slowly rotate the wheel hub while installing the hub lock into the hub.
13. Push the hub lock in firmly by hand to seat the O-ring seal completely.
14. Rotate the hub lock dial counterclockwise to the AUTO position.
15. Be sure that the axle shaft turns freely.
16. Tighten the new hub lock screws to 6 Nm (53 lb-in).
17. Install the front wheel hub extender and nuts, if equipped and tighten to 176 Nm (130 lb-ft).
18. Install the front wheel.

FRONT AXLE HOUSING

REMOVAL & INSTALLATION

F-150 and Mark LT

See Figures 30 through 34.

1. Raise and safely support the vehicle.
2. If equipped, remove the front skid plate nuts and the front skid plate.

3. Remove the front driveshaft. For additional information, refer to the procedure in this section.

⁂ **WARNING**

Do not allow the halfshaft to hang unsupported.

4. Remove the 12 halfshaft flange-to-axle shaft flange bolts, and disconnect the front halfshafts from the axle shafts.
5. Remove the 4 crossmember bolts and the crossmember.
6. Use a high-lift jack to support the axle assembly.

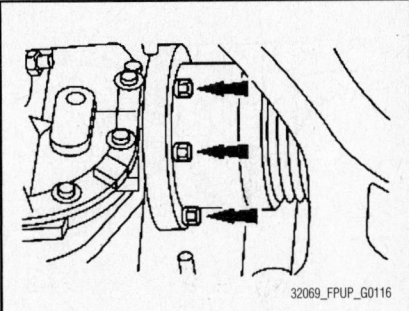

32069_FPUP_G0116

Fig. 30 Remove the 12 halfshaft flange-to-axle shaft flange bolts—F-150 and Mark LT

32069_FPUP_G0117

Fig. 31 Remove the 4 crossmember bolts—F-150 and Mark LT

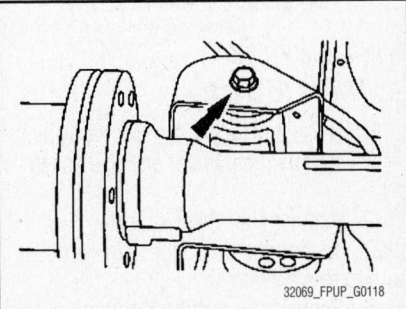

32069_FPUP_G0118

Fig. 32 Remove the axle tube bushing nut and axle tube bushing bolt—F-150 and Mark LT

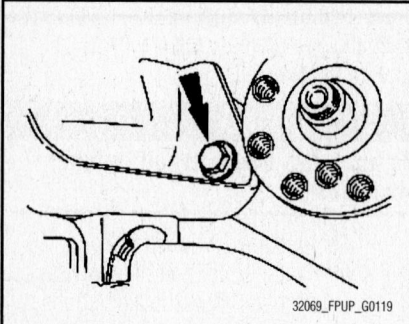

Fig. 33 Remove the lower mounting bushing bolt—F-150 and Mark LT

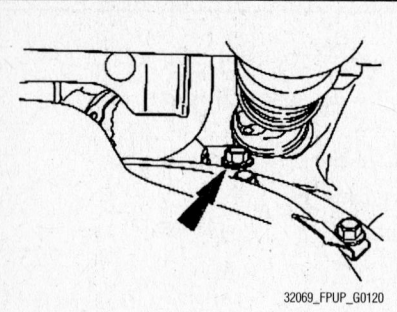

Fig. 34 Remove the upper mounting bushing bolt—F-150 and Mark LT

7. Remove the axle tube bushing nut and axle tube bushing bolt.

8. Remove the lower mounting bushing bolt.

9. Remove the upper mounting bushing bolt.

10. Carefully lower the axle assembly.

11. Disconnect the vent hose from the axle vent.

12. To install, reverse the removal procedure. Observe the following torques:
- All axle mounting bolts/nuts: 115 Nm (85 ft. lbs.)
- Crossmember bolts: 90 Nm (66 ft. lbs.)
- Halfshaft bolts: 82 Nm (60 ft. lbs.)
- Skidplate: 15 Nm (11 ft. lbs.)

F-250 and F-350

See Figures 35 and 36.

1. Raise and safely support the vehicle.

2. Remove the wheel and tire assembly.

3. Remove the wheel knuckles. For additional information, refer to the procedure in this section.

4. Remove the stabilizer bar link nuts and disconnect the stabilizer bar links from the frame.

5. Disconnect the anti-lock brake system (ABS) wire from the radius arms.

6. Remove the brake hose bracket bolts and brake hose brackets from the axle.

➡ **Index-mark the driveshaft to the companion flange to maintain proper driveline balance.**

➡ **If new driveshaft flange bolts are not available, coat the threads of the driveshaft flange bolts with Threadlock and Sealer.**

7. Remove and discard the driveshaft flange bolts and disconnect the driveshaft at the front axle. Wrap electrical tape around the bearing cups and using mechanic's wire, position the front driveshaft aside.

➡ **It is necessary to load the suspension to remove the track bar. Load the springs by allowing most of the front vehicle weight to rest on the axle.**

8. Support the axle with a suitable jack, and lower the vehicle enough to relieve the tension on the track bar. Remove the track bar nut and disconnect the track bar at the axle, then using mechanic's wire, position the track bar aside.

9. Relieve the load on the suspension after disconnecting the track bar.

10. Leave the jack supporting the axle for removal from the vehicle.

11. Disconnect the vent tube and the routing clip.

12. Position aside the Hublock vacuum hoses. On the LH side of the axle, remove the Hublock vacuum hose bolt.

13. Remove the lower shock bolts.

14. Lower the axle.

15. Remove the front coil springs.

16. Remove the trailing arm bolts.

17. Lower the axle from the vehicle.

18. To install, reverse the removal procedure. Check and, if necessary, fill the axle with the specified lubricant. Observe the following torques:
- Trailing arm bolts: 300 Nm (221 ft. lbs.).

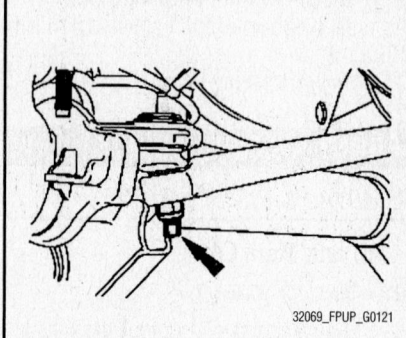

Fig. 35 Track bar nut—F-250 and F-350

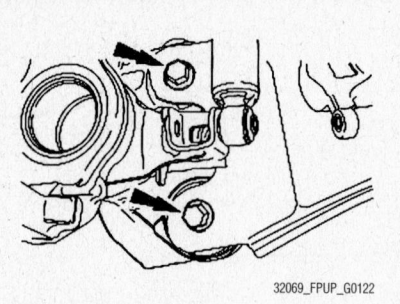

Fig. 36 Trailing arm bolts—F-250 and F-350

- Lower shock bolts: 150 Nm (111 ft. lbs.).
- Hublock vacuum hose bolt: 20 Nm (15 ft. lbs.).
- Track bar nut: 250 Nm (184 ft. lbs.).
- Driveshaft flange bolts: 35 Nm (26 ft. lbs.).
- Brake hose bracket bolts: 18 Nm (13 ft. lbs.).
- Stabilizer bar link nuts: 80 Nm (59 ft. lbs.).

FRONT AXLE SHAFT, BEARING & SEAL

REMOVAL & INSTALLATION

See the Front Hub and Bearing procedure in this section.

FRONT HALFSHAFT

REMOVAL & INSTALLATION

F-150 and Mark LT

See Figure 37.

1. Before servicing the vehicle, refer to the Precautions Section.

2. Position the vehicle on a hoist.

3. Remove the front wheel and tire assembly.

4. Remove the dust cap and axle shaft nut.

5. Disconnect the tie rod end.

6. Disconnect the upper ball joint.

7. Remove the integrated wheel end disconnect retaining bolts.

8. Remove the halfshaft flange retaining bolts.

✱✱ WARNING

Do not damage the hub seal.

➡ **Allow the steering knuckle to swing outboard while keeping the constant velocity shaft pushed inboard.**

9. Once clearance is available, remove the constant velocity shaft joint outboard end and integrated wheel end disconnect from the steering knuckle hub bearing.

10. Separate the halfshaft assembly from the axle assembly and remove the halfshaft assembly from the vehicle.

11. Carefully remove the integrated wheel end disconnect from the outboard constant velocity joint housing to avoid damage to the vacuum chamber.

12. To install, reverse the removal procedure. Take note of the following:

➡ **Maintain a clean work surface.**

13. Compress the integrated wheel end disconnect on the bench to collapse the vacuum chamber.

14. While the integrated wheel end disconnect is collapsed, install a vacuum cap on the vacuum port.

✳✳ WARNING

Do not install the integrated wheel end disconnect in the knuckle. It must be installed on the outer constant velocity joint housing.

✳✳ WARNING

Do not dislodge the integrated wheel end disconnect seal spring when installing the integrated wheel end on the outer constant velocity joint housing.

15. Install the integrated wheel end disconnect on the outer constant velocity joint housing.

16. Install the front axle halfshaft in the vehicle. Install the halfshaft flange retaining bolts.

✳✳ WARNING

Verify the spline engagement by checking for spline lash before tightening the retainers of the integrated wheel end disconnect and the front axle halfshaft retaining nut.

17. Install and tighten the integrated wheel end disconnect retaining bolts.

18. Verify the front axle lubricant level is to specifications.

19. Observe the following torques:
- Tie rod stud nut: 111 ft. lbs. (150 Nm)
- Axle halfshaft (wheel end) nut: 20 ft. lbs. (27 Nm)
- Upper ball joint stud nut: 111 ft. lbs. (150 Nm)
- Integrated wheel end disconnect bolts: 108 inch lbs. (12 Nm)
- Halfshaft flange bolts: 60 ft. lbs. (82 Nm)

CV-JOINTS OVERHAUL

➡ **Before continuing with this procedure, make sure to have available a new CV-joint boot kit, for each CV-joint being serviced. The outer CV-joint**
cannot be disassembled, only the boot can be replaced.

Inner CV-Joint And Boot

1. Before servicing the vehicle, refer to the Precautions Section.

2. Remove the halfshaft assembly from the vehicle.

3. Clamp the halfshaft in a vise equipped with jaw caps to prevent damage to machined surfaces. Do not allow the vise jaws to contact the boot or its clamp.

4. Slide 2 inboard clamp protectors off the boot clamps.

5. Carefully remove 2 boot clamps, and slide the boot off the inner CV-joint and housing.

6. Remove the CV-joint retaining ring and remove the housing.

7. Mark the inner race and the ball cage for assembly.

8. Remove 6 cage balls.

9. Remove the snapring.

10. Remove the inner race and ball cage.

11. Clean all parts in suitable parts cleaning solvent and inspect for wear.

To install:

12. Place the boot and the small boot clamp and protector on the shaft.

13. Place the ball cage on the shaft with the tapered end toward the outer CV-joint.

➡ **Line up the marks made at disassembly.**

14. Position the inner race on the driveshaft in the position marked on disassembly.

15. Install the snapring.

16. Lubricate and position 6 balls with suitable CV-joint grease.

17. Place the boot protector and boot clamp on the CV-joint housing. Fill the housing with 8.29 ounces of suitable CV-joint grease.

18. Place the housing to the cage and bearings and install the retaining ring.

19. Remove any excess grease from the mating surface and position the boot and clamp.

20. Adjust the CV-joint to boot spacing to 16.93 in. (429.92mm).

21. After adjusting the CV-joint to boot spacing, insert a dull bladed screwdriver blade to relieve built up air pressure in the boot.

22. Use CV Boot Clamp Installer T95P-3514-A or equivalent, to install the boot clamps.

23. Place the clamp protectors over the boot clamps.

24. Install the halfshaft into the vehicle.

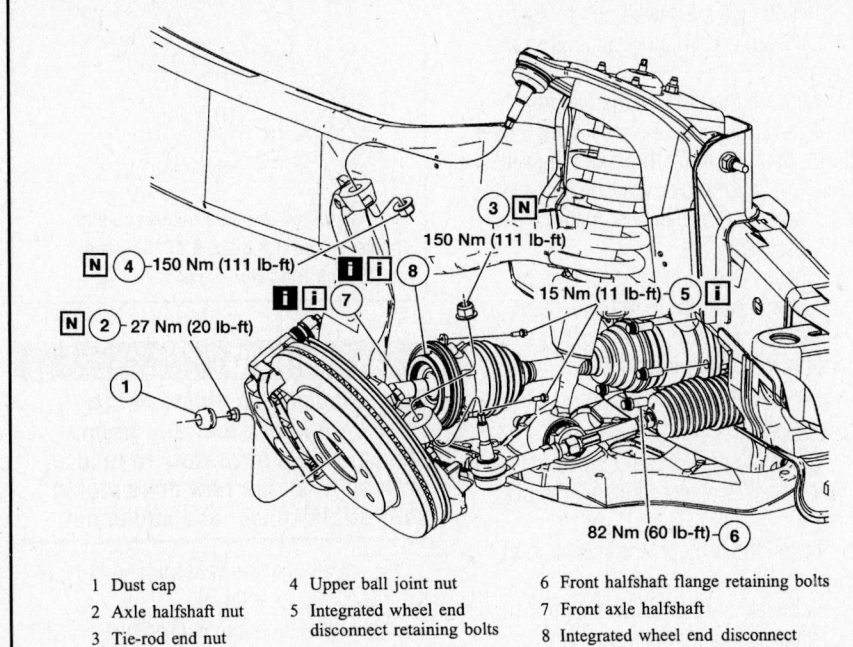

N (4) - 150 Nm (111 lb-ft)
N (2) - 27 Nm (20 lb-ft)
(1)
(3) N
150 Nm (111 lb-ft)
15 Nm (11 lb-ft) (5)
82 Nm (60 lb-ft) (6)
(7) (8)

1 Dust cap
2 Axle halfshaft nut
3 Tie-rod end nut
4 Upper ball joint nut
5 Integrated wheel end disconnect retaining bolts
6 Front halfshaft flange retaining bolts
7 Front axle halfshaft
8 Integrated wheel end disconnect

67197-EFSE-G152

Fig. 37 Front axle halfshaft assembly—F-150 and Mark LT

25. Road test the vehicle and check for proper operation.

Outer Boot

1. Before servicing the vehicle, refer to the Precautions Section.
2. Remove the inner CV-joint and housing from the halfshaft.
3. Remove the inner boot from the halfshaft.
4. Remove the outer boot clamp protectors and carefully remove the boot clamps.
5. Remove the outer boot from the halfshaft and inspect the grease for contamination.
6. If the grease is contaminated, clean and inspect the joint for wear. Replace the joint and shaft if worn or damaged.

To install:

7. Place the new CV-joint boot on the shaft.
8. Using 5.82 ounces (165 grams) of suitable CV-joint grease, pack the outer CV-joint with grease, then spread the remaining grease inside the boot.
9. Clean the boot mounting surface and position the boot in the joint grooves.
10. Place the clamps in position and use CV Boot Clamp Installer T95P-3514-A or equivalent, to install the boot clamps.
11. Place the clamp protectors over the boot clamps.
12. Install the inner boot on the halfshaft.
13. Install the inner CV-joint and housing on the halfshaft.
14. Install the halfshaft in the vehicle.
15. Road test the vehicle and check for proper operation.

FRONT PINION SEAL

REMOVAL & INSTALLATION

F-150

See Figures 38 39 and 40.

1. Before servicing the vehicle, refer to the Precautions Section.

✳✳ WARNING

This operation disturbs the pinion bearing preload. Carefully reset the preload during assembly.

➡ The front drive axle must be in Neutral before beginning this procedure.

2. Raise and support the vehicle.
3. Remove the front differential support.
4. Match-mark the front driveshaft to the axle universal joint flange.

✳✳ WARNING

Do not allow the driveshaft to hang unsupported.

5. Disconnect and support the front driveshaft.
6. Using an Nm (inch-pound) torque wrench, measure the torque necessary to maintain pinion rotation. Record the measurement for reference during installation.
7. Match-mark the axle universal joint flange to the pinion stem.
8. Install a holding tool, and loosen, but do not remove the pinion nut.

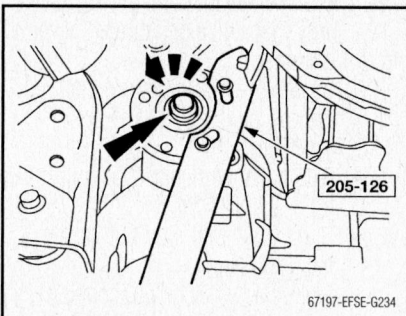

Fig. 38 Flange holding tool—Ford 8.8 inch, 9.75 inch and 10.25 inch Ring Gear Axle

✳✳ WARNING

Before proceeding, place a drain pan under the differential carrier.

9. With the pinion nut still engaged by a few threads, use a 2-jawed pull to separate the axle universal joint flange from the pinion gear.
10. Remove the nut and the flange.
11. Inspect the axle universal joint flange for burrs, the nut counterbore and the seal contact surface for nicks, and the bearing cone contact area for damage. Install a new flange if necessary.
12. Check the pinion stem splines for burrs. If burrs are evident, remove them with a fine crocus cloth. Working in a rotating motion, wipe the pinion clean.
13. Remove the pinion seal.

To install:

14. Clean the pinion seal bore, and use the Pinion Seal Replacer to install the pinion seal.
15. Install the front axle universal joint flange.
16. Lubricate the axle universal joint flange splines and the pinion seal. Use Motorcraft SAE 75W-90 Premium 4x4 Front Axle Lubricant XY-75W90-TQL or equivalent meeting Ford specification WSP-M2C201-A.

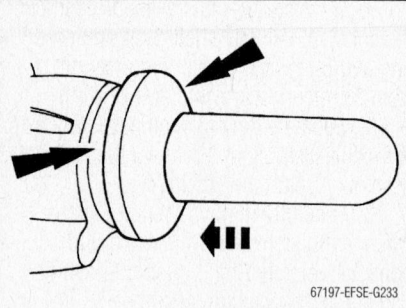

Fig. 39 Installing the pinion seal—Ford 8.8 inch, 9.75 inch and 10.25 inch Ring Gear Axle

✳✳ WARNING

Never install the axle universal joint flange with a hammer or power tools.

➡ Disregard the scribe marks if installing a new flange.

17. Align the index-marks and position the axle universal joint flange on the pinion shaft.

➡ Rotate the pinion gear occasionally to make sure the pinion bearings seat correctly.

18. Using the special tool, install the axle universal joint flange.

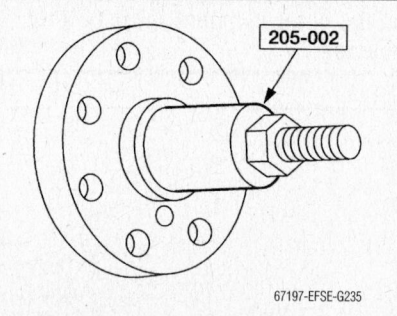

Fig. 40 Install the axle universal joint flange—Ford 8.8 inch, 9.75 inch and 10.25 inch Ring Gear Axle

✳✳ WARNING

Do not loosen the pinion nut to reduce preload under any circumstance. If it is necessary to reduce preload, install a new drive pinion collapsible spacer and pinion nut.

19. Install the special tool, and tighten the pinion nut as follows:

a. Rotate the pinion gear occasionally to make sure the pinion bearings are seating correctly. Take frequent pinion bearing torque preload readings by rotating the pinion gear with a Nm (inch/pound) torque wrench.

b. If the preload recorded prior to disassembly is lower than the specification for used bearings, then tighten the pinion nut to the specification. If the preload recorded prior to disassembly is higher than the specification for used bearings, then tighten the pinion nut to the original reading as recorded.

- Pinion bearing torque preload (used pinion bearing): 0.9–1.5 Nm (8–14 inch lbs.)
- Pinion bearing torque preload (new pinion bearing): 1.8–3.3 Nm (16–29 inch lbs.)

20. Align the index-marks then attach the front driveshaft.

21. Install the front differential support.

22. Check and, if necessary, fill the differential. Use Motorcraft SAE 75W-90 Premium 4x4 Front Axle Lubricant XY-75W90-TQL, or equivalent, meeting Ford specification WSP-M2C201-A.

23. Lower the vehicle.

F-250 and F-350 Dana 50 and 60 Axles

See Figures 41 through 43.

1. Before servicing the vehicle, refer to the Precautions Section.

2. With the vehicle in **Neutral**, raise and support the vehicle.

3. Match-mark the front driveshaft and the front axle flange to maintain driveline balance.

4. Disconnect the front driveshaft from the front axle flange, and position it aside.

5. Rotate the pinion with a Nm (inch lb.) torque wrench. Record the torque necessary to maintain rotation of the pinion through several revolutions.

6. Remove and discard the nut and washer. Use the special tool to prevent the flange from turning while removing the nut.

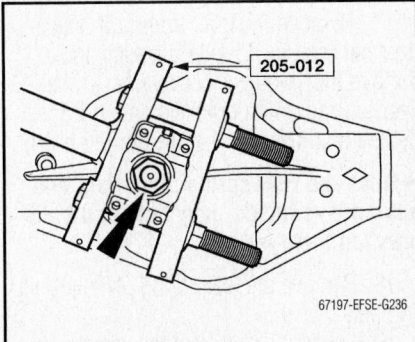

Fig. 41 Flange holding tool—F-250 and F-350 Dana 50 and 60 Axles

➡**Match-mark the flange and the pinion shaft.**

7. Using the special tool, remove the flange.

8. Using the special tools, remove the pinion seal. Discard the seal.

9. Clean and inspect the following:

a. The seal mounting surface.

b. The flange lugs and the flange end that contacts the bearing cone.

c. Verify that the flange nut counterbore and the seal contact surfaces are smooth and free of nicks.

To install:

10. Using a suitable driver, install the pinion seal. Lightly coat the pinion seal lip with lubricant.

✳✳ WARNING

Never use a metal hammer on the pinion flange or install the flange with power tools. If necessary, use a plastic hammer to tap on a tight fitting flange.

➡**Align the index marks.**

11. Lightly coat the flange splines and seal mating area with lubricant, then install the flange with a new washer and nut.

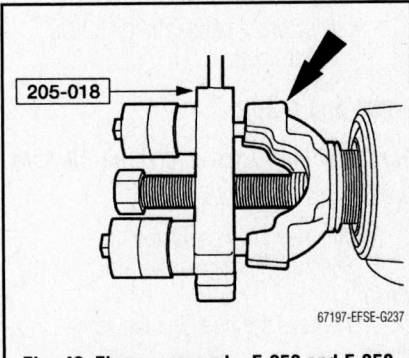

Fig. 42 Flange removal—F-250 and F-350 Dana 50 and 60 Axles

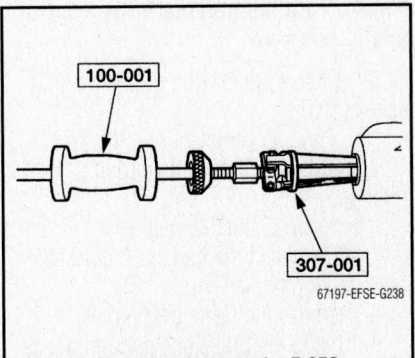

Fig. 43 Pinion seal removal—F-250 and F-350 Dana 50 and 60 Axles

✳✳ WARNING

Never back off the pinion nut to reduce preload. If preload reduction is necessary, install a new collapsible spacer and pinion nut.

12. Tighten the pinion nut as follows:

a. Use the special tool to prevent the flange from turning while tightening the nut. Remove the special tool when taking pinion bearing torque preload readings.

b. Take frequent pinion bearing torque preload readings.

➡**Never back off the pinion nut to reduce preload. If preload reduction is necessary, install a new collapsible spacer and pinion nut.**

c. For new pinion bearing installation, tighten the pinion nut to a rotating torque of 1.7–3.4 Nm (15–30 inch lbs.) Pinion nut torque range is 217–678 Nm (160–500 ft. lbs.).

d. For original pinion bearing installation, the reading must be 0.56 Nm (5 inch lbs.) more than the initial reading taken during the disassembly procedure.

13. Connect the front driveshaft to the front axle flange. Torque to 26 ft. lbs. (35 Nm).

14. Check and, if necessary, fill the axle with the specified lubricant.

15. Lower the vehicle.

REAR AXLE HOUSING

REMOVAL & INSTALLATION

F-150 and Mark LT

Ford 8.8 Inch Axle, 9.75 Inch Axle And 10.25 Inch Axle

See Figures 44 through 46.

1. Raise and safely support the vehicle.

2. Remove the disc brake caliper bolts and the disc brake caliper. Using mechanics wire, position aside the disc brake caliper.

3. Index-mark the driveshaft flange and pinion flange for correct alignment during installation.

4. Remove the 4 driveshaft flange bolts.

✳✳ WARNING

The driveshaft centering socket yoke fits tightly on the pinion flange pilot. Never hammer on the driveshaft or any of its components to disconnect the driveshaft centering socket yoke from the pinion flange. Pry only in the area shown with a suitable tool to disconnect the driveshaft centering socket yoke from the pinion flange.

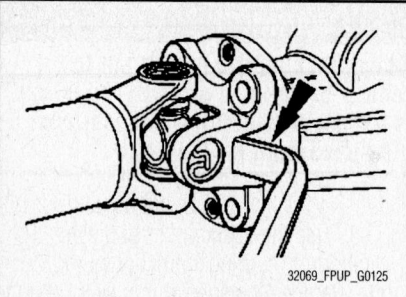

Fig. 44 Using a suitable tool as shown, disconnect the driveshaft centering socket yoke from the pinion flange—F-150 and Mark LT

5. Using a suitable tool as shown, disconnect the driveshaft centering socket yoke from the pinion flange. Using mechanic's wire, position the driveshaft aside.

6. Disconnect the disc brake anti-lock sensor from the axle.

➡**If the vent hose is disconnected from the vehicle body, a new retainer must be installed.**

7. Remove the vent hose.

8. Remove the brake hose junction block bolt.

9. Separate the parking brake cables from the axle housing.

10. Remove the brake line bracket bolt, then remove the brake line from the brake line retaining clips.

11. Support the axle with a suitable transmission jack.

12. Remove the lower shock absorber nuts and bolts.

13. Remove the spring plate nuts.

14. Remove the 2 spring plate U-bolts.

15. Remove the spring plate.

16. Repeat the procedure for the other side.

17. Lower the axle housing from the vehicle.

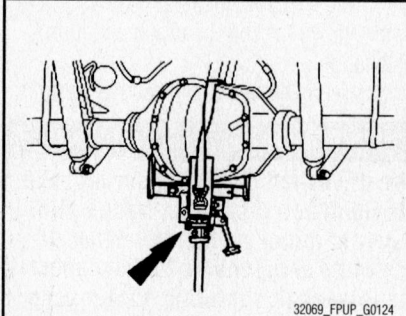

Fig. 45 Use a suitable transmission jack to support the axle—F-150 and Mark LT

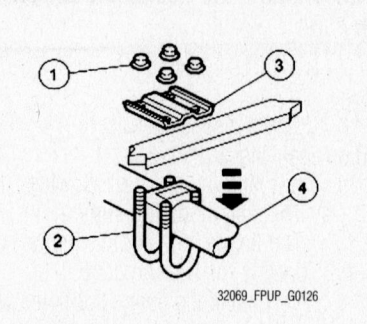

Fig. 46 Axle U-bolts and spring plate—F-150 and Mark LT

18. To install the original assembly, reverse the removal procedure. To install a factory replacement axle assembly, remove the new disc brake calipers and the vent plug. Check the rear axle fluid level after installation. Observe the following torques:

- U-bolts: 115 Nm (85 ft. lbs.)
- Lower shock absorber nuts and bolts: 8.8 inch axle 70 Nm (52 ft. lbs.); 9.75 and 10.25 inch axle 90 Nm (66 ft. lbs.)
- Brake line bracket bolt: 25 Nm (18 ft. lbs.).
- Parking brake cables to the axle housing: 25 Nm (18 ft. lbs.).
- Brake hose junction block bolt: 18 Nm (13 ft. lbs.).
- Disc brake caliper bolts: 32 Nm (24 ft. lbs.).

F-250 and F-350

Ford 105 Inch Axle And Dana 80 Axle

See Figures 47 and 48.

1. Remove the wheels and tires.

2. Disconnect the rear anti-lock brake sensor.

3. Remove the nuts and the stone shield.

4. Remove the caliper pin bolts.

5. Remove the rear disc brake caliper.

➡**Make sure the parking brake control is fully released.**

6. Release the tension on the parking brake system.

e. Have an assistant pull the front parking brake cable and conduit to its full range.

f. Insert a suitable retainer.

7. Disconnect the parking brake cable at the parking brake lever.

8. Remove the cable clamp bolt.

9. Unclip the brake line and remove the retainer from the parking brake cable bracket and position the cable aside.

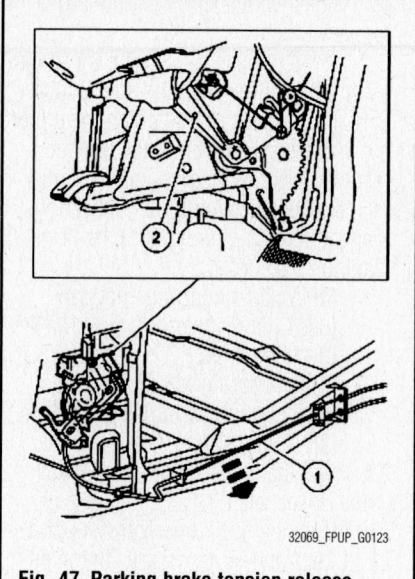

Fig. 47 Parking brake tension release—F-250 and F-350

10. Remove the bolt from the brake hose bracket.

11. Remove the vent hose at the brake hose junction block.

12. Remove the brake junction block from the rear axle housing and let it hang.

13. Remove the brake lines from the rear axle housing tie strap (but not from the disc brake calipers) and let the tubing hang.

❊❊ CAUTION

Strap the axle securely to the jack.

14. Use a suitable transmission jack to support the axle.

15. Remove the lower shock absorber nuts and bolts.

16. Loosen the nuts from both lower ends of the stabilizer bar links.

➡**When lowering or raising the differential housing, position the sway bar forward to clear the front of the differential housing.**

17. Remove the nuts from both stabilizer bar retainer-to-axle brackets and remove the stabilizer bar retainers, stabilizer bar mounting brackets and U-bolts. Let the stabilizer bar hang from the links.

➡**Once the rear spring plate nuts and bolts are removed, new nuts and bolts must be installed.**

18. Remove the rear spring plate U-bolts and nuts.

19. Lower the axle from the vehicle.

20. To install, reverse the removal procedure. Observe the following torques:

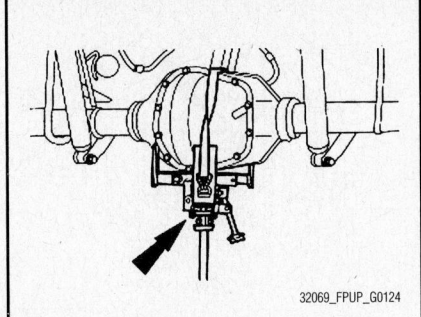

Fig. 48 Use a suitable transmission jack to support the axle—F-250 and F-350

- Spring plate U-bolt nuts: 251 Nm (186 ft. lbs.)
- Caliper pin bolts: 36 Nm (27 ft. lbs.)
- Stone shield nuts: 62 Nm (46 ft. lbs.)
- Shock absorber bolts: 63 Nm (47 ft. lbs.)
- Stabilizer bar bracket U-bolt nuts: 30 ft. lbs. (40 Nm)
- End links top and bottom: 52 ft. lbs. (70 Nm)

REAR AXLE SHAFT, BEARING & SEAL

REMOVAL & INSTALLATION

Ford 8.8 Inch Ring Gear, 9.75 Inch Ring Gear And 10.25 Inch Ring Gear Axles

See Figures 49 through 53.

1. Before servicing the vehicle, refer to the Precautions Section.
   All Vehicles
2. Raise and support the vehicle.
3. Remove the wheel and tire assembly.

➡Empty the lubricant into a clean container for reuse.

4. Remove the 10 differential housing cover bolts and drain the lubricant from the rear axle housing.
5. Remove the differential housing cover.
   Vehicles with drum brakes
6. Remove the rear brake drums.
   Vehicles with disc brakes
7. Remove the rear disc brake caliper. Wire the rear disc brake caliper aside.
8. Remove the rear brake disc.
   All vehicles
9. Remove and discard the differential pinion shaft lock bolt.
10. Remove the differential pinion shaft.

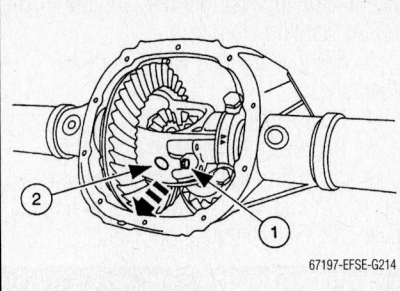

Fig. 49 Lock bolt (1); pinion shaft (2)—Ford 8.8 inch, 9.75 inch ring gear, and 10.25 inch ring gear axles

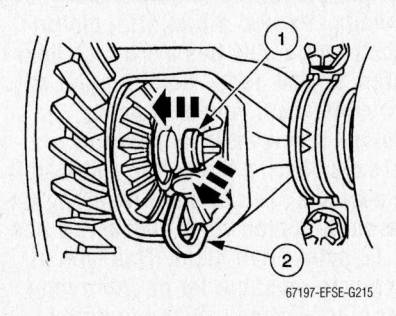

Fig. 50 Axle shaft (1); U-washer (2)—Ford 8.8 inch, 9.75 inch ring gear and 10.25 inch ring gear axles

✳✳ WARNING
Do not damage the rubber O-rings in the axle shaft grooves.

11. Push in the axle shafts.
12. Remove the U-washers.

✳✳ WARNING
Do not damage the wheel bearing oil seal.

13. Remove the axle shaft.

➡If the wheel bearing oil seal is leaking, the axle housing vent may be plugged with foreign material.

➡If only a new seal needs to be installed, use care to avoid damaging the seal bore.

14. Using a suitable seal remover, remove the axle shaft oil seal. Discard the oil seal.
15. Inspect the rear wheel bearing and axle shaft for wear or damage.
16. If necessary, using the special tools, remove the rear wheel bearing.

To install:
17. Lubricate the new rear wheel bearing with rear axle lubricant.
18. Using the special tools, install the rear wheel bearing.

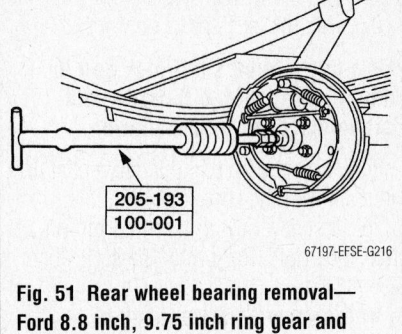

Fig. 51 Rear wheel bearing removal—Ford 8.8 inch, 9.75 inch ring gear and 10.25 inch ring gear axles

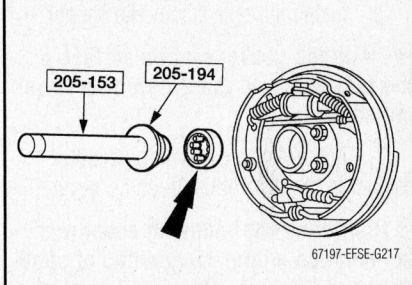

Fig. 52 Rear wheel bearing installation—Ford 8.8 inch, 9.75 inch ring gear and 10.25 inch ring gear axles

19. Lubricate the lip of the new wheel bearing oil seal with grease.
20. Using the special tools, install the wheel bearing oil seal.
    All vehicles

✳✳ WARNING
Do not damage the wheel bearing oil seal.

21. Install the axle shaft.

✳✳ WARNING
Do not damage the rubber O-rings in the U-washer grooves.

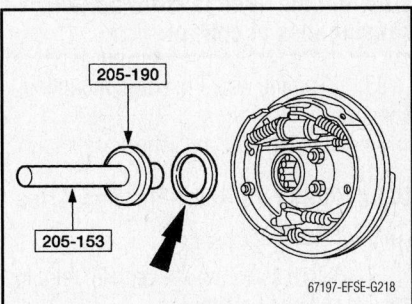

Fig. 53 Oil seal installation—Ford 8.8 inch, 9.75 inch ring gear and 10.25 inch ring gear axles

22. Position the two U-washers on the button end of the axle shafts.

23. Pull the axle shafts outward.

➡**If a new pinion shaft lock bolt is unavailable coat the threads with Threadlock prior to installation.**

24. Align the hole in the differential pinion shaft with the case lock bolt hole.

25. Install a new differential pinion shaft lock bolt. Torque to 15–30 ft. lbs. (20–40 Nm).

Vehicles with drum brakes

26. Install the rear brake drums.

Vehicles with disc brakes

27. Install the rear brake disc.

28. Install the rear disc brake caliper.

➡**Clean the gasket mating surface of the rear axle and the differential housing cover.**

29. Apply a new continuous bead of sealant to the differential housing cover.

➡**The differential housing cover must be installed within 15 minutes of application of the silicone, or new sealant must be applied. If possible, allow one hour before filling with lubricant to make sure the silicone sealant has correctly cured.**

30. Install the differential housing cover.

31. Install the 10 differential housing cover bolts. Torque to 33 ft. lbs. (45 Nm).

32. Fill the rear axle housing with 2.37 liters (5 pints) with the specified lubricant.

❋❋ CAUTION

Always remove any corrosion, dirt or foreign material present on the mounting surfaces of the wheel or the surface of the wheel hub or brake drum or disc that contacts the wheel. Installing wheels without correct metal-to-metal contact at the wheel mounting surfaces can cause the lug nut to loosen and the wheel to come off while the vehicle is in motion, causing loss of control.

33. Clean the wheel hub and mounting surfaces.

34. Install the tire and wheel assembly.

Dana 60 And 70 Semi-Floating Axles

See Figures 54 through 60.

1. Before servicing the vehicle, refer to the Precautions Section.

2. Raise the vehicle on a hoist or raise the rear end of the vehicle with a jack. Install safety stands under the frame rails and lower the jack or hoist enough to allow

the rear axle to drop into the rebound position for working clearance.

3. Remove the rear wheel and tire assembly.

4. Remove the brake disc.

5. Remove the differential housing cover and drain the lubricant. Clean the gasket material from the differential housing cover and the differential housing.

❋❋ WARNING

The differential assembly is equipped with either a Loctite® coated differential pinion shaft lock screw or a differential pinion shaft lock screw with torque prevailing threads. The Loctite® treated differential pinion shaft lock screw has a $\frac{5}{32}$ inch hexagram socket head. Never, under any circumstance, reuse a Loctite® coated screw after removing it. Always discard the screw and install a new one. The torque prevailing differential pinion shaft lock screw has a 12-point drive head. This type of screw is reusable for no more than four installations. When in doubt about the number of installations of a torque prevailing differential pinion shaft lock screw, discard it and install a new screw.

6. Remove the lock screw.

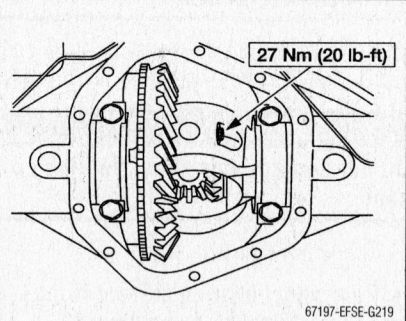

Fig. 54 Lock screw—Dana 60 and 70 semi-floating axle

7. Remove the differential pinion shaft. The pinion shaft is a slip-fit design and is removable by hand.

8. Push the flanged end of the axle shaft toward the center of the axle and remove the U-washer.

❋❋ WARNING

Do not damage the wheel bearing oil seal when removing the axle shaft.

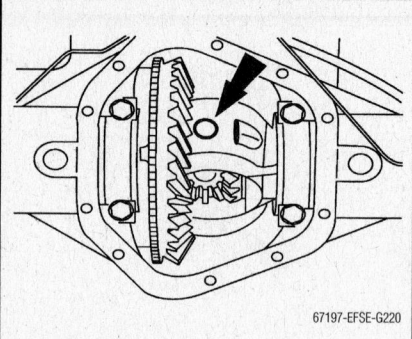

Fig. 55 Pinion shaft—Dana 60 and 70 semi-floating axle

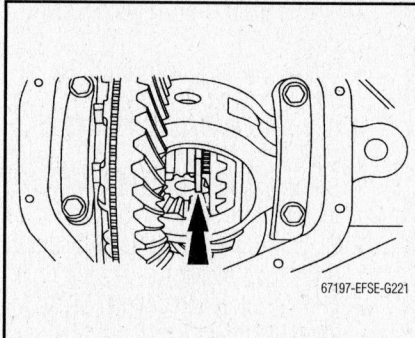

Fig. 56 U-washer—Dana 60 and 70 semi-floating axle

❋❋ WARNING

Do not rotate the differential side gears when removing the axle shaft. Rotating the differential side gears causes the differential pinion gears and differential pinion thrust washers to turn to the differential case opening and fall out of the differential case.

9. Remove the axle shaft.

❋❋ WARNING

Install the differential pinion shaft and the old lock screw (finger-tight) to prevent the differential side gears and differential pinion gears from rotating and falling out of the differential case.

10. Install the differential pinion shaft and the old lock screw in the differential case.

❋❋ WARNING

It is not necessary to remove the rear wheel bearing if only installing a new wheel bearing oil seal. To remove only the wheel bearing oil seal, pry it from the axle tube. Do not damage

the seal seating surface. If removing the rear wheel bearing and the oil seal, proceed to the following step.

11. Remove the wheel bearing oil seal from the axle tube. Discard the seal.

❈❈ CAUTION

Make sure protective eyewear is in place. Failure to follow these instructions may result in personal injury.

12. Using the special tools, remove the rear wheel bearing and the wheel bearing oil seal as a unit. Discard the seal and the bearing.

❈❈ WARNING

The bearing and seal seating surfaces must be free from burrs, nicks, and spalling.

13. Clean and inspect the bore in the axle tube. Wipe the bore in the axle tube with emery cloth to smooth the surface. Clean the bore with a standard metal-cleaning solvent. Wipe the bore with a soft, lint free cloth to remove any foreign material.

To install:

14. If removed, lubricate the new rear wheel bearing with the specified axle lubricant.

❈❈ WARNING

Install the rear wheel bearing with the identification numbers facing outward.

❈❈ WARNING

Do not cock the rear wheel bearing in the axle tube.

15. Using the special tools, install the rear wheel bearing.

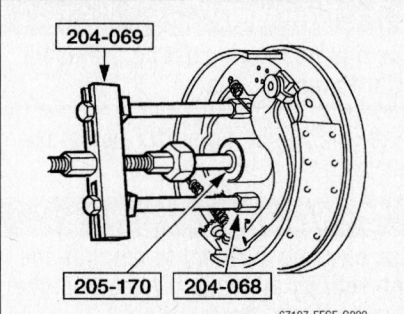

Fig. 57 Rear wheel bearing removal— Dana 60 and 70 semi-floating axle

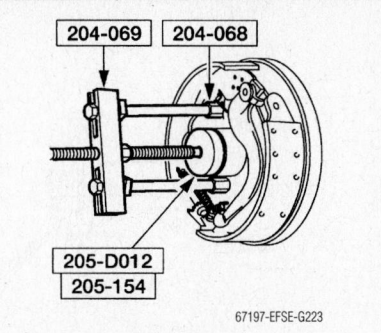

Fig. 58 Rear wheel bearing installation— Dana 60 and 70 semi-floating axle

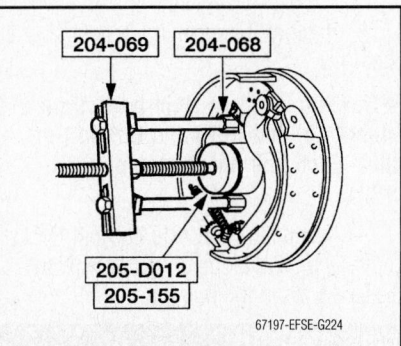

Fig. 59 Oil seal installation—Dana 60 and 70 semi-floating axle

❈❈ WARNING

Do not cock the wheel bearing oil seal in the axle tube.

➡ **The following step shows an alternate method for installing the wheel bearing oil seal.**

16. Using the special tools, install the new wheel bearing oil seal.

❈❈ WARNING

Do not cock the wheel bearing oil seal in the axle tube bore.

➡ **This step is an alternate method for installing the wheel bearing oil seal. Carry out this step if wheel bearing oil seal installation was not done in the previous step.**

17. Using the special tools, install the new wheel bearing oil seal.

18. Lubricate the cavity between the wheel bearing oil seal lips and the rear wheel bearing with grease.

19. Remove the lock screw and the differential pinion shaft.

❈❈ WARNING

Do not damage the wheel bearing oil seal when installing the axle shaft.

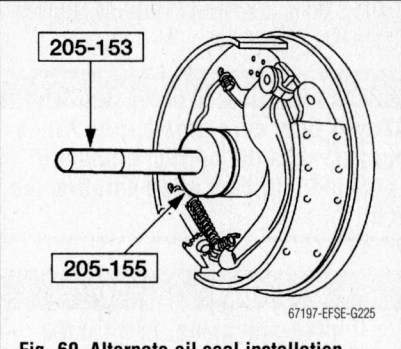

Fig. 60 Alternate oil seal installation— Dana 60 and 70 semi-floating axle

20. Push the axle shaft into the axle tube and engage the differential side gear with the shaft splines.

21. Push the axle shaft toward the center of the axle and install the U-washer. Pull the axle shaft outward until the U-washer locks into the differential side gear.

22. Align the differential pinion shaft lock screw hole with the hole in the differential case. Correctly position the differential pinion thrust washers. Install the differential pinion shaft.

➡ **The threads in the differential case and on the lock screw must be free of dirt and oil.**

23. Install the new lock screw. Torque to 20 ft. lbs. (27 Nm).

❈❈ WARNING

Clean the mounting surface on the differential housing cover and the differential housing with a suitable solvent to remove all traces of oil film.

❈❈ WARNING

The differential housing cover uses silicone rubber sealant material as a gasket. Install the differential housing cover within 15 minutes of applying the silicone or it will be necessary to apply new sealant.

24. Apply a continuous bead of silicone sealant to the differential housing cover mounting surface.

25. Assemble two bolts into the differential housing cover at the eight o'clock and two o'clock positions. Using the two bolts as a guide, position the differential housing cover on the differential housing.

26. Install the remaining bolts. Tighten the bolts alternately and evenly. Tighten

Grade 5 bolts to 47 Nm (35 ft. lbs. Tighten Grade 8 bolts to 61 Nm (45 ft. lbs.

✳✳ WARNING

Allow 1 hour cure time before filling the axle with the correct amount of specified lubricant and operating the vehicle.

✳✳ WARNING

For limited-slip axles, first fill the axle with 7 ounces of friction modifier.

27. Fill the differential housing with 3.0L (6.3 pints) of the specified rear axle lubricant. For additional information, refer to Specifications.

28. Install the brake disc.

29. Install the wheel and tire assembly.

30. Lower the vehicle.

Ford Full-Floating Axle

See Figures 61 through 64.

1. Before servicing the vehicle, refer to the Precautions Section.

2. Set the parking brake.

3. Loosen the retaining bolts.

4. Raise the vehicle to the desired working height, keeping the axle parallel with the floor.

5. Release the parking brake.

6. Remove the wheel(s).

7. Remove the brake caliper and rotor on the single rear wheel axle.

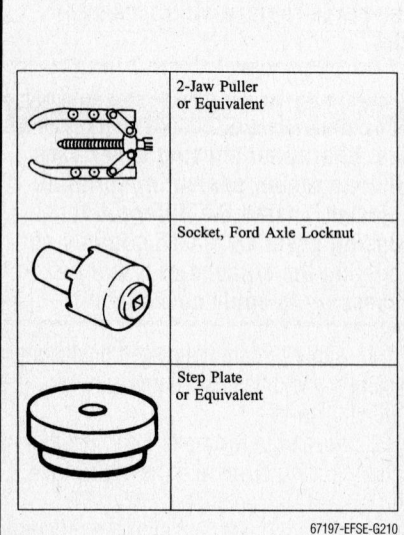

Fig. 61 Tools needed for the following hub removal on the Ford Full-Floating axle

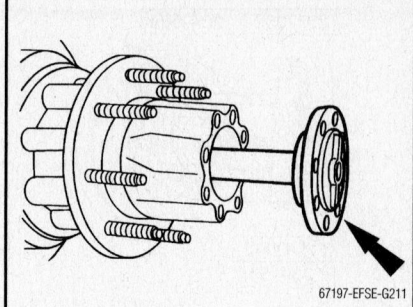

67197-EFSE-G211

Fig. 62 Axle shaft removal—Ford full-floating axle

8. Remove the retaining bolts and axle shaft.

➡️**The hub nuts are right-hand thread (right hub) and left-hand thread (left hub). Each hub nut is stamped RH or LH.**

9. Install the Ford Axle Locknut Socket so that the drive tangs of the tool engage the four slots in the hub nut.

✳✳ WARNING

Discard the hub nut if the hub nut comes apart during removal.

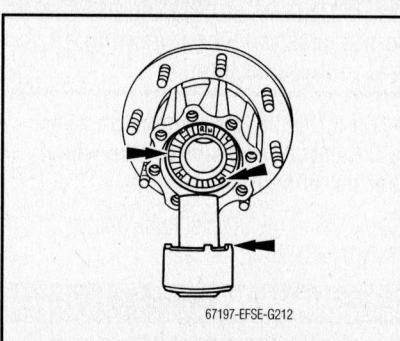

67197-EFSE-G212

Fig. 63 Install the Ford Axle Locknut Socket so that the drive tangs of the tool engage the four slots in the hub nut

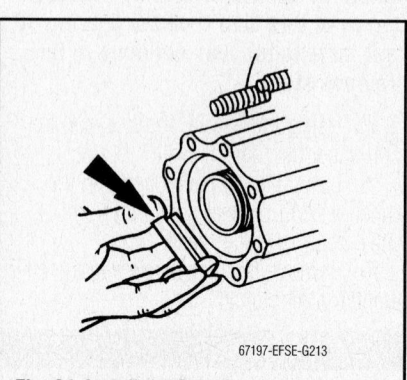

67197-EFSE-G213

Fig. 64 Install the Step Plate—Ford full-floating axle

✳✳ WARNING

Under no circumstances are power tools to be used when performing these operations.

➡️**The hub nut will ratchet during this operation.**

10. Remove the hub nut (counterclockwise for right-hand thread; clockwise for left-hand thread).

11. Install the Step Plate.

12. Install the 2-Jaw Puller and loosen the rear hub to the point of removal.

✳✳ WARNING

Do not drop the outer hub bearing when removing the hub.

13. Remove the rear hub assembly.

✳✳ WARNING

Install a new hub seal each time the hub assembly is removed.

➡️**The inner bearing is located behind the hub seal.**

14. Pack each bearing and replace the hub seals.

✳✳ WARNING

Use extreme care not to scratch or gouge the seal or bearing surfaces.

15. If after hub removal, the hub seal or seal inner sleeve remains on the spindle, remove using the Step Plate and the 2-Jaw Puller.

16. Inspect the seal surface and inner shoulder for scratches and damage. Remove all scratches, gouges or galling damage with No. 600 or finer crocus cloth.

To install:

➡️**Clean the spindle thoroughly after removing the rear hub.**

17. Coat the spindle with axle lubricant.

✳✳ WARNING

The hub bearings must be prelubed prior to installation.

18. Fill the hub cavity with 1 oz. of axle lubricant.

✳✳ WARNING

Use extreme care not to damage the hub seal by allowing it to contact the spindle during installation.

➡️**Coat the spindle and hub seal inside diameter with axle lubricant.**

➡️Installing the rear hub in this manner causes the outer bearing to act as a pilot making the installation easier.

19. Push the rear hub and outer bearing onto the spindle as an assembly. Hold the outer bearing seated and use the bearing as a pilot.

❋❋ **WARNING**

Install a new hub nut if the hub nut comes apart during installation.

➡️Make sure the hub nut tab is located in the keyway prior to thread engagement.

20. Install the hub nut on the spindle. Turn the hub nut clockwise for right-hand thread or counterclockwise for left-hand thread.
21. Position the Ford Axle Locknut Socket on the hub nut.

❋❋ **WARNING**

Under no circumstances are power tools to be used when performing these operations.

➡️The hub nut will ratchet as torque is applied.

22. Tighten the hub nut, rotating the rear hub occasionally while tightening. Torque to 60 ft. lbs. (81 Nm).
23. Adjust hub nuts as follows:
   a. For new bearings, ratchet back five teeth or notches (⅛ turn) on the hub nut. Five notches must be felt during this operation in order to have performed it correctly.
   b. For used bearings, ratchet back seven teeth or notches (⅙ turn) on the hub nut. Seven notches must be felt during this operation to have performed it correctly.
24. Inspect the axle shaft O-ring seal for cracks, nicks or wear and replace it if required.

➡️Lubricate the O-ring seal with lubricant prior to installation of axle shaft.

25. Install the axle shaft.

➡️Coat the threads of the retaining bolts with Stud and Bearing Mount E0AZ-19554-BA or equivalent meeting Ford specification WSK-M2G349-A1.

26. Install and tighten the retaining bolts until they seat.

❋❋ **WARNING**

Remember, the last step of this procedure is to tighten the axle shaft

bolts to specification, after the wheel lug nuts have been tightened.

27. Install the brake rotor and caliper on the single rear wheel axles.
28. Install the wheels and tires but do not tighten the lug nuts to specification at this time.
29. Check the axle lubricant level.
30. Lower the vehicle.
31. Tighten the wheel lug nuts.
32. Tighten the axle shaft retaining bolts. Torque to 80 ft. lbs. (109 Nm).

Dana Axle Full-Floating Axle

See Figures 65 and 66.

1. Before servicing the vehicle, refer to the Precautions Section.
All vehicles
2. Remove the tire and wheel assembly.
3. Remove the anchor plate.
4. Remove the axle shaft.

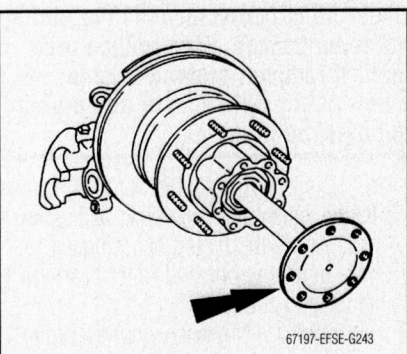

67197-EFSE-G243

Fig. 65 Remove the axle shaft—Dana Axle Full-Floating Axle

Dana 70

➡️Make sure that the drive tangs on the special tool engage the four slots of the hub nut.

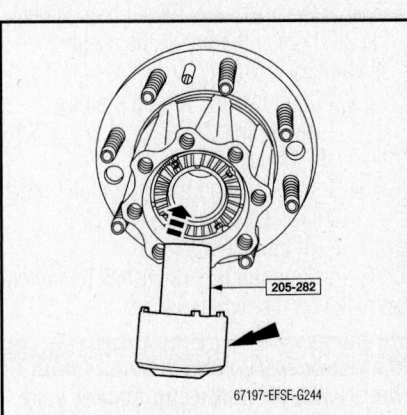

205-282

67197-EFSE-G244

Fig. 66 Using special tool 205-282, or equivalent, remove the hub nut—Dana Axle Full-Floating Axle

5. Using special tool 205-282, or equivalent, remove the hub nut.
All vehicles
6. Remove the outer rear wheel bearing.
7. Remove the rear hub and brake disc assembly.
8. Remove the bolts and separate the rear hub from the rear brake disc.
9. Inspect the rear hub for the following:
   • Cracks and damage around the bolt holes.
   • Oversized holes.

To install:

❋❋ **WARNING**

Install a new rear hub seal after removing the rear hub from the axle. A damaged or worn seal can permit bearing lubricant to reach the brake linings, resulting in ineffective brake operation. Failure to follow these instructions may result in personal injury.

❋❋ **WARNING**

Clean and remove any dirt or foreign material in the rear hub bolt holes.

10. Install a new rear hub seal.
11. Position the rear brake disc on the rear hub and install the bolts. Torque to 66–88 ft. lbs. (89–119 Nm).

❋❋ **WARNING**

Thoroughly clean the spindle. Wrap the spindle threads with electrician's tape to prevent damage while installing the rear hub and brake disc assembly.

❋❋ **WARNING**

Lightly coat the spindle and pack each rear wheel bearing with Premium Long-Life Grease XG-1-C or equivalent meeting Ford specification ESA-M1C75-B.

12. Prepare the spindle for rear hub installation.
13. Slide the rear hub and brake disc assembly over the axle housing spindle. Remove the electrician's tape.
14. Install the outer rear wheel bearing.
15. Start the hub nut making sure that the tab aligns correctly in the keyway prior to thread engagement.

➡️Apply inward pressure to the socket to separate the ratcheting components of the hub nut.

16. To adjust the bearings, tighten the nut to 70 ft. lbs. (95 Nm).

17. Back off the nut 90 degrees.

18. Tighten the nut to 18 ft. lbs. (24 Nm). To verify that there is no side-to-side end play, attach a magnetically mounted dial indicator to the spindle end and place the dial indicator tip on the outboard surface of the hub. Check for side-to-side end play. Final bearing adjustment has zero end play. The maximum torque to rotate the hub is 2.3 Nm (20 inch lbs.) when end play is zero.

19. Install the axle shaft.

20. Install the anchor plate.

21. Install the tire and wheel assembly.

REAR PINION SEAL

REMOVAL & INSTALLATION

Ford 8.8 inch, 9.75 inch and 10.25 inch Ring Gear Axle

1. Before servicing the vehicle, refer to the Precautions Section.

2. Raise and support the vehicle.

3. Remove the rear wheel and tire assemblies.

> ❈❈ **WARNING**
>
> **Remove the brake drums or discs to prevent brake drag during drive pinion bearing preload adjustment.**

4. Remove the brake discs or drums.

5. Mark the driveshaft flange and pinion flange for correct alignment during installation.

6. Remove the four bolts.

> ❈❈ **WARNING**
>
> **The driveshaft centering socket yoke fits tightly on the rear axle pinion flange pilot. Never hammer on the driveshaft or any of its components to disconnect the yoke from the flange.**

7. Disconnect the driveshaft centering socket yoke from the rear axle pinion flange. Position the driveshaft out of the way.

8. Install a Nm (inch-pound) torque wrench on the pinion nut and record the torque required to maintain rotation of the pinion through several revolutions.

> ❈❈ **WARNING**
>
> **After removal of the pinion nut, discard it. A new nut must be used for installation.**

9. Use the special tool to hold the pinion flange while removing the pinion nut.

10. Mark the driveshaft pinion flange in relation to the drive pinion stem to make sure of correct alignment during installation.

11. Using the special tool, remove the pinion flange.

To install:

12. Lubricate the pinion flange splines. Use SAE 75W-140 High Performance Rear Axle Lubricant F1TZ-19580-B or equivalent meeting Ford specification WSL-M2C192-A.

➡**Disregard the scribe marks if a new pinion flange is being installed.**

13. Align the pinion flange with the drive pinion shaft.

14. With the drive pinion in place in the rear axle housing, install the pinion flange using the special tool.

15. Position the new pinion nut.

> ❈❈ **WARNING**
>
> **Under no circumstances is the pinion nut to be backed off to reduce preload. If reduced preload is required, a new collapsible spacer and pinion nut must be installed.**

16. Using the special tool to hold the pinion flange, tighten the pinion nut as follows:

   a. Rotate the pinion occasionally to make sure the cone and roller bearings are seating correctly.

   b. Install a Nm (inch-pound) torque wrench on the pinion nut.

   c. Rotating the pinion through several revolutions, take frequent cone and roller bearing torque preload readings until the original recorded preload reading is obtained.

   d. If the original recorded preload is lower than specifications, tighten to the appropriate specifications for used bearings. If the preload is higher than specification, tighten the nut to the original reading as recorded.

   • Pinion bearing torque preload (used pinion bearing): 0.9–1.5 Nm (8–14 inch lbs.)

   • Pinion bearing torque preload (new pinion bearing): 1.8–3.3 Nm (16–29 inch lbs.)

17. Position the rear driveshaft and align the marks on the pinion flange.

> ❈❈ **WARNING**
>
> **The driveshaft centering socket yoke fits tightly on the rear axle pinion flange pilot. To make sure that the yoke seats squarely on the flange,** tighten the bolts evenly in a cross pattern as shown.

18. Install the bolts and tighten to 83 ft. lbs. (112 Nm).

19. Install the brake disc or drum.

20. Install the rear wheel and tire assemblies.

Ford 10.5 inch Ring Gear Axle

See Figures 67 through 69.

1. Before servicing the vehicle, refer to the Precautions Section.

➡**The rear wheels and brake calipers must be removed to prevent brake drag during drive pinion bearing preload adjustment.**

2. Remove the rear brake calipers.

3. Remove the driveshaft.

4. Install an Nm (inch-pound) torque wrench on the pinion nut, and record the rotational torque required to maintain rotation of the pinion through several revolutions.

➡**After removal of the pinion nut, discard it. A new nut must be used for installation.**

5. Use a flange holder to hold the pinion flange while removing the pinion nut.

6. Mark the pinion flange in relation to the drive pinion stem to ensure proper alignment during installation.

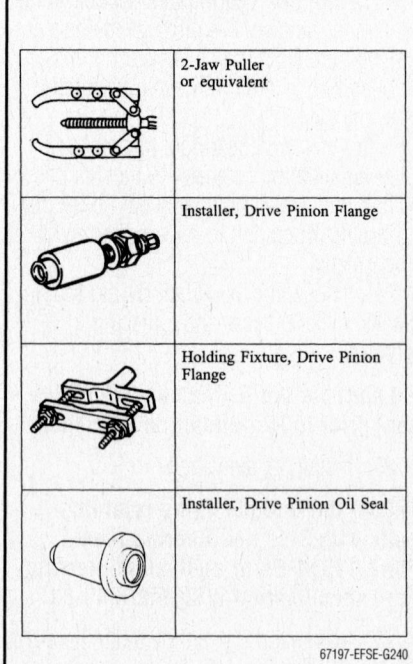

	2-Jaw Puller or equivalent
	Installer, Drive Pinion Flange
	Holding Fixture, Drive Pinion Flange
	Installer, Drive Pinion Oil Seal

67197-EFSE-G240

Fig. 67 Tools necessary for this job—Ford 10.5 inch ring gear axle pinion seal replacement

7. Use a 2-jaw puller to remove the pinion flange.

8. Force up on the metal flange of the rear axle drive pinion seal. Install locking pliers to the seal flange and strike with a hammer until the rear axle drive pinion seal is removed.

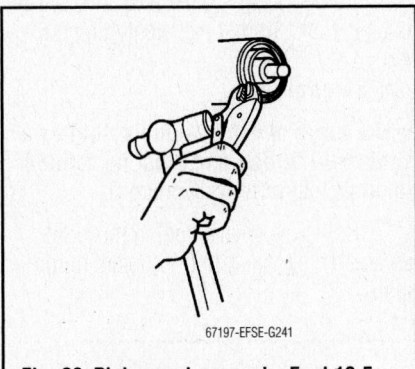

Fig. 68 Pinion seal removal—Ford 10.5 inch ring gear axle

To install:

9. Lubricate the new pinion seal. Use Premium Long-Life Grease XG-1-C or equivalent meeting Ford specification ESA-M1C75-B.

➡If the rear axle drive pinion seal becomes misaligned during installation, remove the rear axle drive pinion seal and replace it with a new seal.

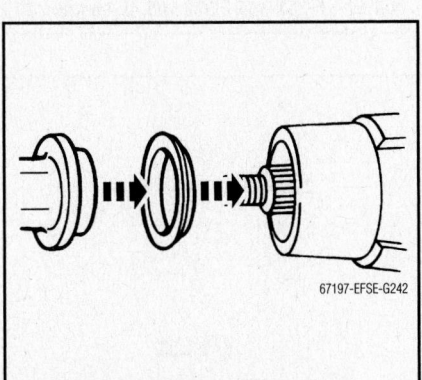

Fig. 69 Pinion seal installation—Ford 10.5 inch ring gear axle

10. Use the Pinion Seal Replacer to install the rear axle drive pinion seal.

11. Lubricate the pinion flange splines. Use SAE 75W-140 Synthetic Rear Axle Lubricant F1TZ-19580-B or equivalent meeting Ford specification WSL-M2C192-A.

➡Disregard the scribe marks if a new pinion flange is being installed.

12. Align the pinion flange with the drive pinion shaft.

13. With the pinion flange in place in the rear axle housing, install the pinion flange using the Companion Flange Replacer.

14. Position the new pinion nut.

➡Under no circumstances is the pinion nut to be backed off to reduce preload. If reduced preload is required, a new collapsible spacer and pinion nut must be installed.

15. Use the Flange Holder to hold the pinion flange while tightening the pinion nut.

a. Tighten the pinion nut, rotating the pinion occasionally to make sure the cone and roller bearings are seating properly. Take frequent cone and roller bearing torque preload readings until the originally recorded preload reading is obtained by rotating the pinion with an Nm (inch-pound) torque wrench.

b. If the original recorded preload is lower than specifications, tighten to the appropriate specification for used bearings. If the preload is higher than specification, tighten the nut to the original reading as recorded.

c. Pinion bearing preload (used pinion bearing): 0.9–1.5Nm (8–14 inch lbs).

d. Pinion bearing preload (new pinion bearing): 1.8–3.3Nm (16–29 inch lbs.).

e. Initial minimum breakaway torque (Traction-Lok®): 27Nm (20 ft. lbs)

16. Install the driveshaft.

17. Install the brake calipers.

Dana 80 Rear Axle
See Figure 70.

1. Before servicing the vehicle, refer to the Precautions Section.

2. Raise the vehicle on a hoist or raise the rear end of the vehicle with a jack. Install safety stands under the frame rails and lower the jack or hoist far enough to allow the rear axle to drop into the rebound position for working clearance.

➡To maintain driveline balance, mark the driveshaft components so they can be reinstalled in their original positions.

3. Disconnect the driveshaft at the rear axle, and position it aside.

➡Index-mark the flange to the pinion shaft.

4. While using a flange holding tool to prevent the flange or yoke from turning, remove the pinion nut.

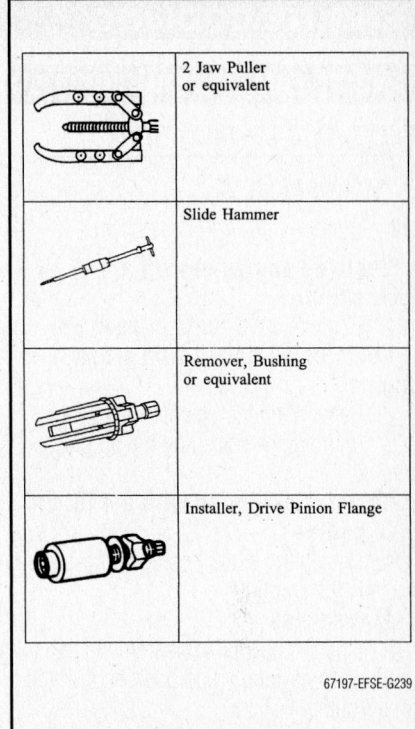

Fig. 70 Tools necessary for this job— Dana 80 axle

5. Using a 2-jaw puller, remove the flange or yoke.

6. Using a bushing remover and slide hammer, remove the pinion seal.

7. Clean the rear axle pinion seal seat.

To install:

➡If the pinion seal becomes cocked during installation, remove the seal and install a new one. Make sure the garter spring remains in place during assembly. If the spring is dislodged, a new pinion seal must be installed.

8. Install the seal using a suitable driver. Coat the pinion seal rubber lips with lubricant.

9. Using the special tool, 205-285, or equivalent, install the pinion flange.

✳✳ WARNING

Always install a new washer and locknut.

10. Install the new washer and locknut. Torque to 470 ft. lbs. (637 Nm).

11. Install the driveshaft at the rear axle. Observe the following torques:
- Split pin yoke: 26 ft. lbs. (35 Nm)
- Circular flange: 82 ft. lbs. (111 Nm)

ENGINE COOLING

ENGINE FAN AND SHROUD

REMOVAL & INSTALLATION

F-150 and Mark LT

See Figures 71 through 73.

Vehicles equipped with a 4.2L or 4.6L engine

1. Remove the air cleaner outlet pipe.

Vehicles equipped with a 5.4L engine

2. Remove the air cleaner intake pipe.
3. Remove the bolts and the air cleaner bracket.

Vehicles equipped with a 4.6L or 5.4L engine

4. Detach the battery cable harness from the radiator shroud.

All vehicles

5. sing the special tools, remove the cooling fan assembly and position it in the fan shroud.

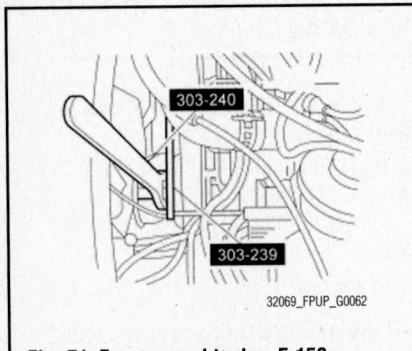

Fig. 71 Fan removal tools—F-150

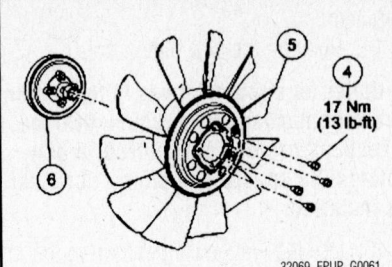

Fig. 73 Cooling fan and clutch—F-150—4. Fan clutch bolts, 5. Cooling fan, 6. Fan clutch

6. Remove the bolts and the fan shroud and fan.
7. If necessary, remove the bolts and separate the fan and the fan clutch.
8. To install, reverse the removal procedure. Tighten the fan-to-clutch bolts to 17 Nm (13 ft. lbs.). Tighten the fan shroud bolts to 6 Nm (53 inch lbs.). Tighten the fan center bolt to 55 Nm (41 ft. lbs.).

F-250 and F-350 w/Gasoline Engines

See Figures 74 through 76.

All engines:

1. Drain the cooling system.
2. Remove the air cleaner outlet tube.
3. Disconnect the upper radiator hose and the degas bottle (coolant reservoir) hose.

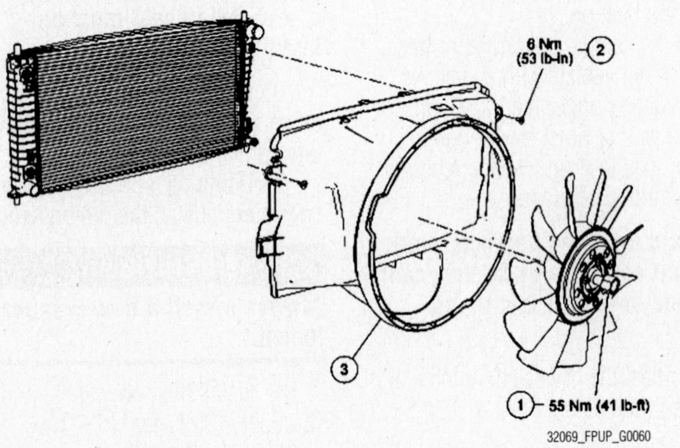

Fig. 72 1. Cooling fan assembly
2. Cooling fan shroud bolts
3. Cooling fan shroud
Fan and shroud assembly—F-150 and Mark LT

5.4L engines:

➡The large clutch assembly nut has a right-hand thread and must be rotated counterclockwise to remove it.

4. Using the special tool, remove the fan and fan clutch from the coolant pump pulley.

6.8L engines:

➡The large clutch assembly nut has a right-hand thread and must be rotated counterclockwise to remove it.

5. Using the special tool, remove the fan and fan clutch from the coolant pump pulley.

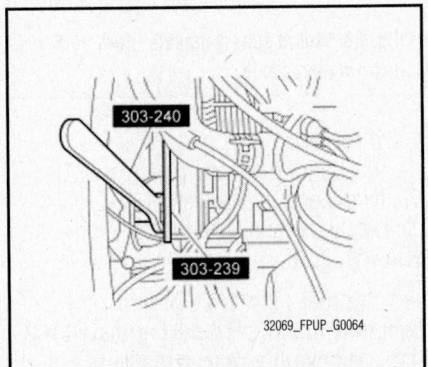

Fig. 74 Using the special tool, remove the fan and fan clutch from the coolant pump pulley—F-250 and F-350 w/5.4L engine

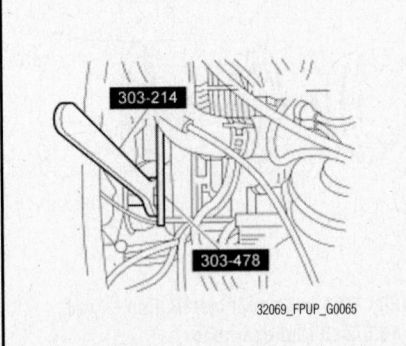

Fig. 75 Using the special tool, remove the fan and fan clutch from the coolant pump pulley—F-250 and F-350 w/6.8L engine

All engines:

6. Carefully position the fan and the fan clutch into the shroud.
7. Remove the 2 cooling fan shroud bolts, the shroud, fan and clutch.
8. To install, reverse the removal procedure. Tighten the fan clutch-to-pump bolt to 133 Nm (98 ft. lbs.).

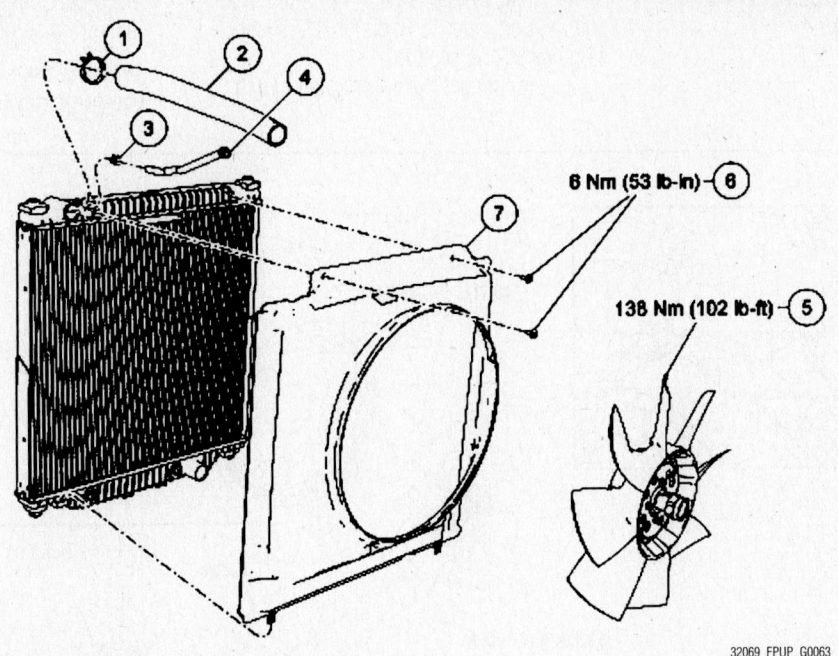

Fig. 76 Radiator fan and shroud—F-250 and F-350 w/Gasoline Engines
1. Upper radiator hose clamp
2. Upper radiator hose
3. Degas bottle (coolant reservoir) hose clamp
4. Degas bottle (coolant reservoir) hose
5. Cooling fan assembly
6. Radiator shroud bolts
7. Radiator shroud

F-250 and F-350 w/Diesel Engines

Fan Shroud

See Figure 77.

1. Raise and safely support the vehicle.
2. Drain the engine cooling system.
3. Remove the 4 bolts and the 2 radiator support brackets.
4. Remove the 4 pin-type retainers and pull back the sight shield.
5. With the sight shield pulled back, remove the 3 pin-type retainers and the 2 wiring retainers and position the harness rearward out of the way.
6. Remove the 2 upper shroud bolts.
7. Disconnect the upper radiator hose and the radiator overflow hose.
8. Move the radiator forward.
9. Pull up on the shroud evenly, and remove the shroud from the radiator.

➡**When installing the shroud, make sure that the aligning tabs are installed correctly in the slots.**

10. To install, reverse the removal procedure. Torque the support bracket bolts to

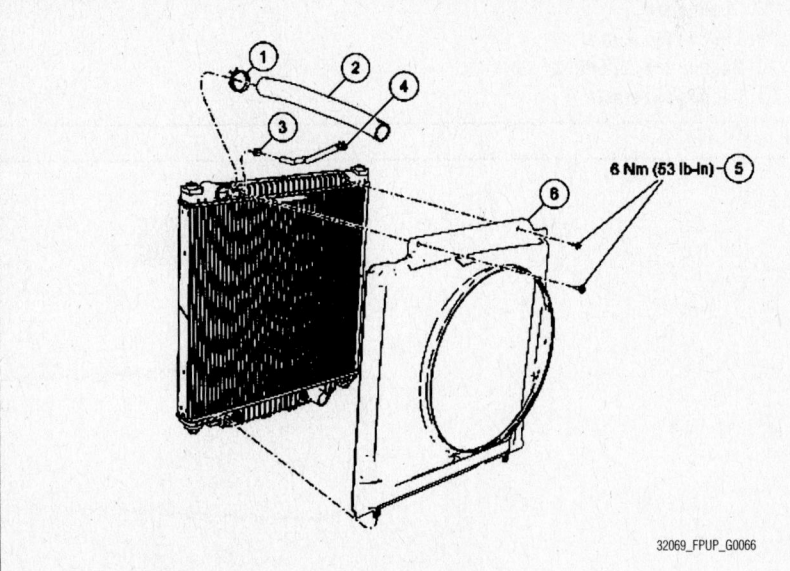

Fig. 77 Fan shroud—F-250 and F-350 w/6.0L diesel
1. Upper radiator hose clamp
2. Upper radiator hose
3. Degas bottle (coolant reservoir) hose clamp
4. Degas bottle (coolant reservoir) hose
5. Radiator shroud bolts
6. Radiator shroud

12 Nm (9 ft. lbs.) and the upper shroud bolts to 6 Nm (53 inch lbs.).

Fan

See Figures 78 and 79.

1. Remove the radiator. For additional information, refer to Radiator R&I Diesel Engines in this section.
2. Disconnect the cooling fan clutch electrical connector. Unclip and position the fan wiring aside.

➡**Use a hole in the fan hub to prevent the fan from turning.**

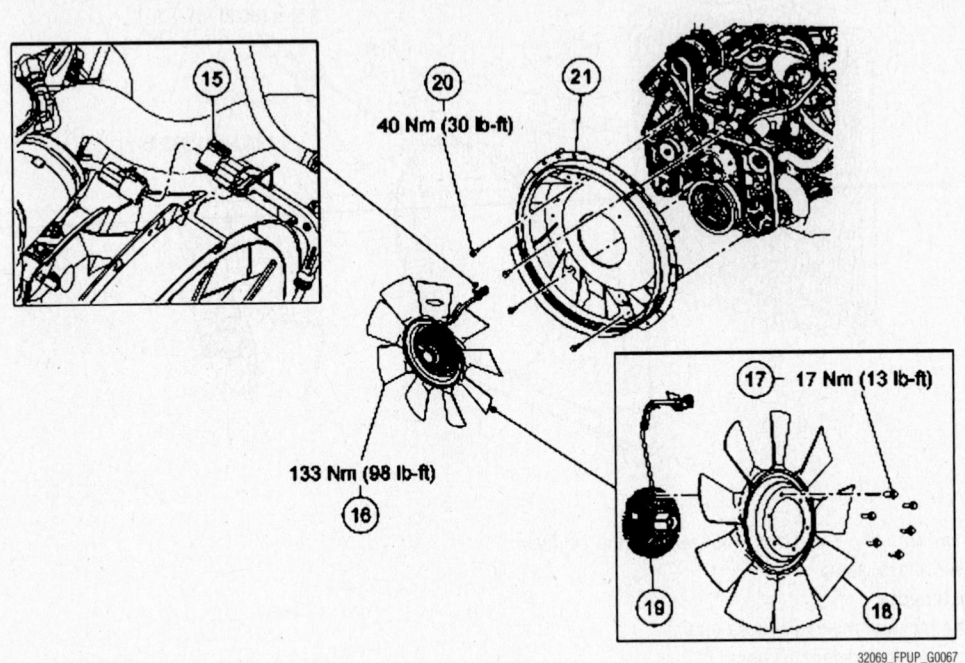

32069_FPUP_G0067

Fig. 78 Engine cooling fan and related parts—F-250 and F-350 w/6.0L diesel

15. Cooling fan electrical connector
16. Cooling fan and clutch assembly
17. Cooling fan-to-clutch bolts
18. Cooling fan
19. Cooling fan clutch
20. Cooling fan stator bolts
21. Cooling fan stator

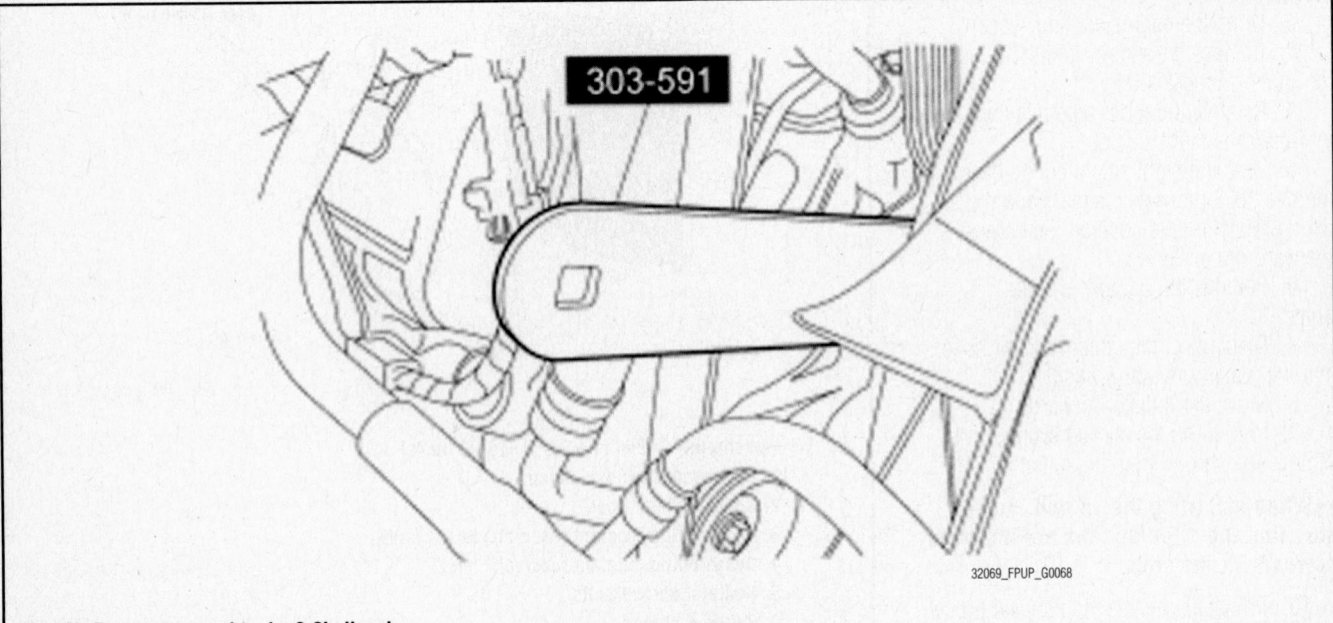

303-591

32069_FPUP_G0068

Fig. 79 Fan nut removal tool—6.0L diesel

3. Using the special tool, remove the cooling fan and clutch.

4. If necessary, remove the bolts and separate the cooling fan and the clutch.

5. To install, reverse the removal procedure. Torque the fan retaining nut to 133 Nm (98 ft. lbs.) and the fan-to-clutch bolts to 17 Nm (13 ft. lbs.).

RADIATOR

REMOVAL & INSTALLATION

F-150 and Mark LT

See Figures 80 and 81.

1. Drain the engine cooling system.

2. Remove the cooling fan and shroud.

3. Release the clamp and disconnect the upper radiator hose.

4. Release the clamp and disconnect the upper degas bottle (coolant reservoir) hose.

5. Release the clamp and disconnect the lower radiator hose.

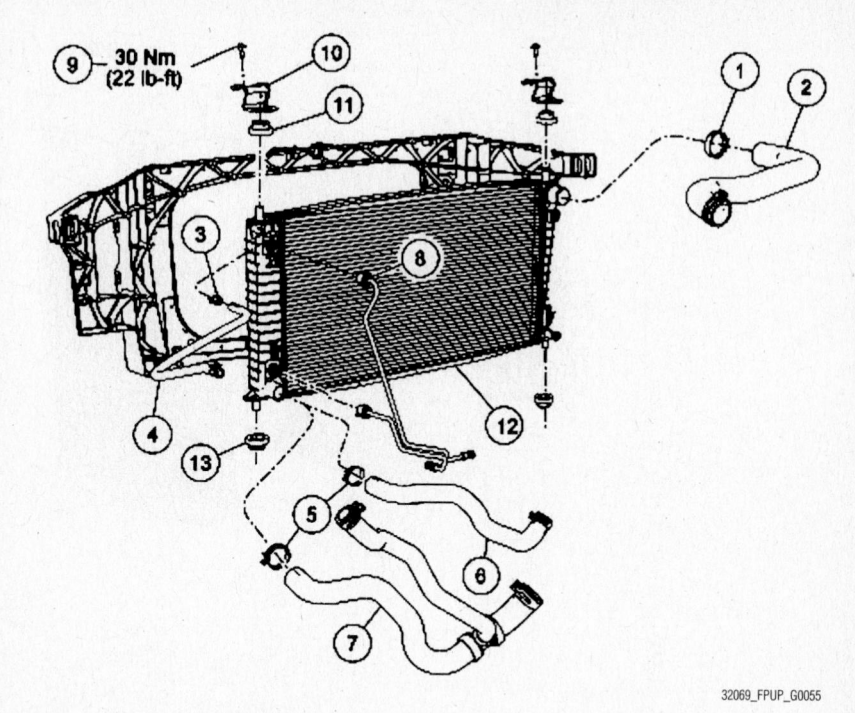

32069_FPUP_G0055

Fig. 81 1. **Upper radiator hose clamp**
    2. **Upper radiator hose**
    3. **Upper degas bottle (coolant reservoir) hose clamp**
    4. **Upper degas bottle (coolant reservoir) hose**
    5. **Lower radiator hose clamp**
    6. **Lower radiator hose 4.6L (2V) and 5.4L (3V)**
    7. **Lower radiator hose 4.2L**
    8. **Transmission cooler tubes**
    9. **Radiator support bracket bolts**
    10. **Radiator support bracket**
    11. **Upper radiator insulators**
    12. **Radiator**
    13. **Lower radiator insulators**
    Radiator and related parts—F-150 and Mark LT

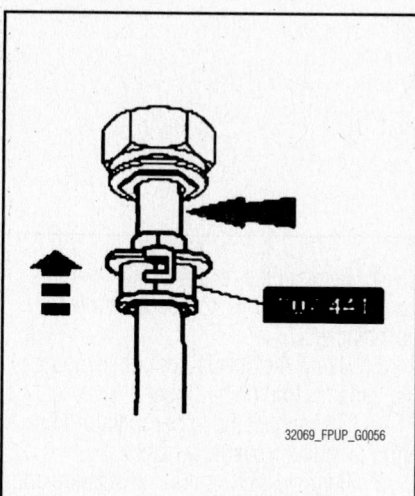

32069_FPUP_G0056

Fig. 80 Using the special tool, disconnect the transmission cooler tubes

6. Using the special tool, disconnect the transmission cooler tubes.

7. Remove the bolts, the radiator support brackets and the upper radiator insulators.

8. Remove the radiator.

9. Remove the lower radiator insulators.

10. To install, reverse the removal procedure. Tighten the radiator support brackets to 30 Nm (22 ft. lbs.).

F-250 and F-350

With Gasoline Engines

See Figures 82 and 83.

1. Remove the cooling fan shroud. For additional information, refer to Engine Fan and Shroud, 5.4L, 6.8L in this section.

2. Disconnect the lower radiator coolant hose.

3. Push the special tool into the fitting to release the tube retaining clip and remove the transmission cooler lines from the radiator.

4. Remove the 4 bolts and the 2 radiator support brackets.

5. Remove the radiator and the radiator insulators.

6. To install, reverse the removal procedure. Tighten the 2 radiator support brackets to 30 Nm (22 ft. lbs.).

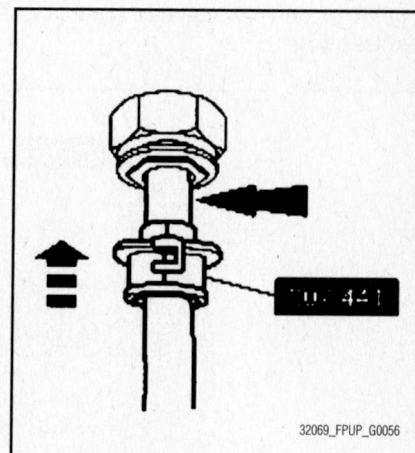

32069_FPUP_G0056

Fig. 82 Using the special tool, disconnect the transmission cooler tubes

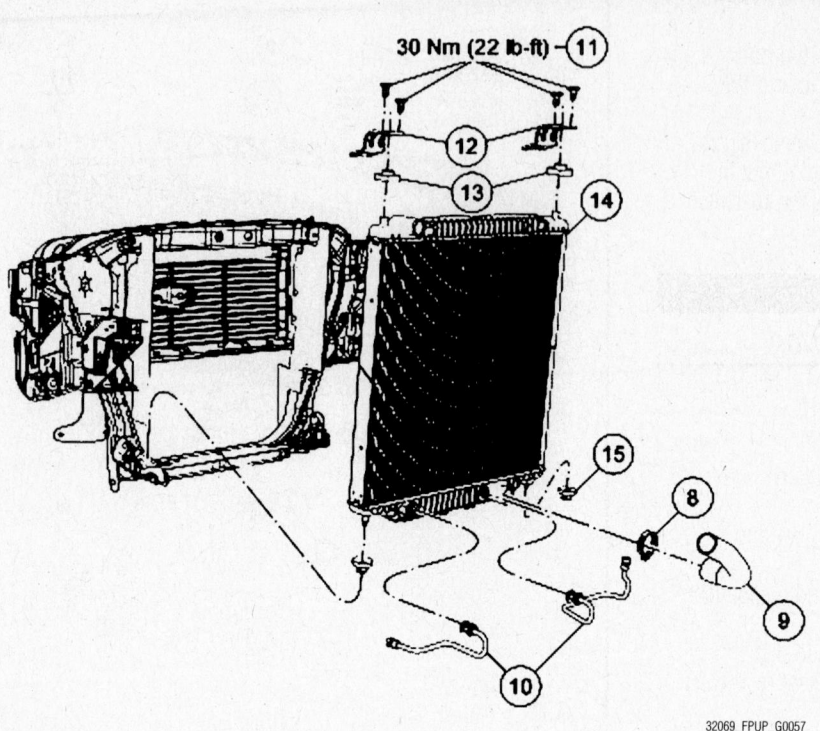

Fig. 83 8. Lower radiator hose clamp
9. Lower radiator hose
10. Transmission cooler lines
11. Radiator support bracket bolts
12. Radiator support bracket
13. Upper radiator insulators
14. Radiator
15. Lower radiator insulators
Radiator mounting—F-250 and F-350 w/gasoline engines

With Diesel Engines

See Figures 84 and 85.

➡ When adding engine coolant, use a 50/50 mixture of engine coolant and distilled water.

1. Raise and safely support the vehicle.
2. Drain the engine cooling system.
3. Disconnect the lower radiator hose.

4. Remove the retaining clips and disconnect the transmission cooler tube support brackets.
5. Using the special tool, disconnect the transmission cooler tubes.
6. Disconnect the upper radiator hose and the radiator overflow hose.
7. Remove the 2 bolts and separate the cooling fan shroud from the radiator.
8. Remove the 4 bolts and the 2 radiator support brackets.
9. Remove the 4 pin-type retainers and pull back the sight shield.
10. Disconnect the 3 pin-type retainers and 2 wiring harness retainers. Position the cable so that the radiator can be moved forward.
11. Remove the radiator assembly.
12. To install, reverse the removal procedure. Check and top off the transmission fluid level. Torque the radiator support bracket bolts to 12 Nm (9 ft. lbs.). Torque the shroud bolts to 6 Nm (53 inch lbs.).

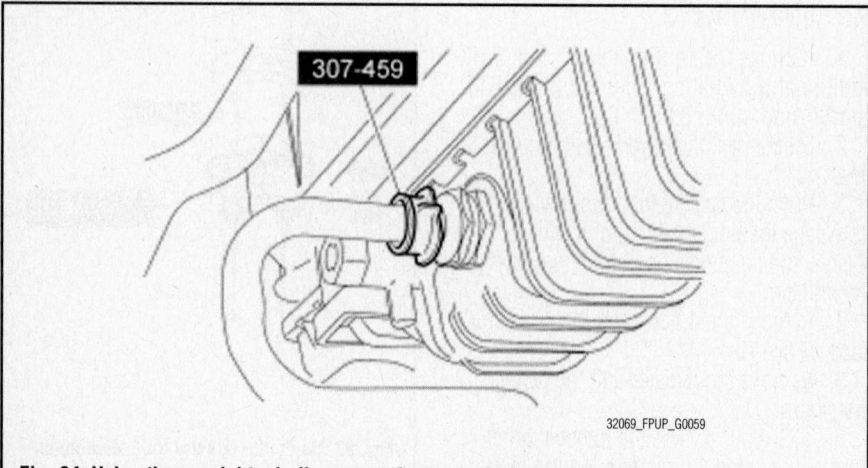

Fig. 84 Using the special tool, disconnect the transmission cooler tubes

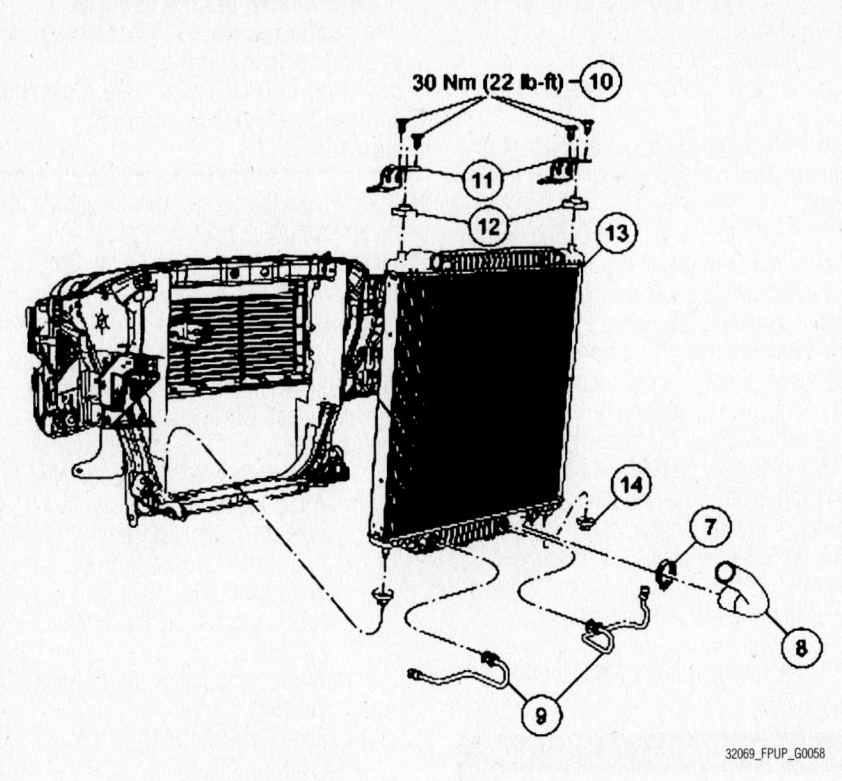

Fig. 85 **7. Lower radiator hose clamp**
8. Lower radiator hose
9. Transmission cooler lines
10. Radiator support bracket bolts
11. Radiator support bracket
12. Upper radiator insulators
13. Radiator
14. Lower radiator insulators
Radiator mounting—F-250 and F-350 w/diesel engines

THERMOSTAT

REMOVAL & INSTALLATION

4.2L Engine

See Figure 86.

1. Drain the cooling system.
2. Release the clamp and disconnect the upper radiator hose from the coolant outlet connection.
3. Remove the bolts and the coolant outlet connection.
4. Remove the gasket and the thermostat.

To install:

✳✳ WARNING

Do not use metal scrapers, wire brushes, power abrasive discs, or other abrasive means to clean the sealing surfaces. These may cause scratches and gouges resulting in

leak paths. Use a plastic scraper to clean the sealing surfaces.

5. Clean the gasket mating surfaces with a plastic scraper and metal surface cleaner. Follow the directions on the packaging.

➡**The thermostat is indexed and must be installed as shown.**

6. Install the thermostat in the water outlet connection and rotate the thermostat either clockwise or counterclockwise to engage the cam on the thermostat securely. The thermostat vent must be located either at the 11 o'clock or 1 o'clock position.
7. Position a new gasket and the coolant outlet connection and install the bolts. Tighten the bolts in 2 stages.
   - Stage 1: Tighten to 8 Nm (71 inch lbs.).
   - Stage 2: Tighten an additional 60 degrees.
8. Connect the upper radiator hose and position the clamp.
9. Fill and bleed the cooling system.

4.6L Engine

1. Drain the engine cooling system.
2. Remove the air cleaner outlet pipe.
3. Release the upper radiator hose clamp and disconnect the radiator hose from the thermostat housing.
4. Remove the power steering upper bracket-to-thermostat housing bolt.
5. Remove the power steering upper bracket-to-intermediate bracket bolts and the power steering upper bracket.
6. Remove the bolts and the thermostat housing.

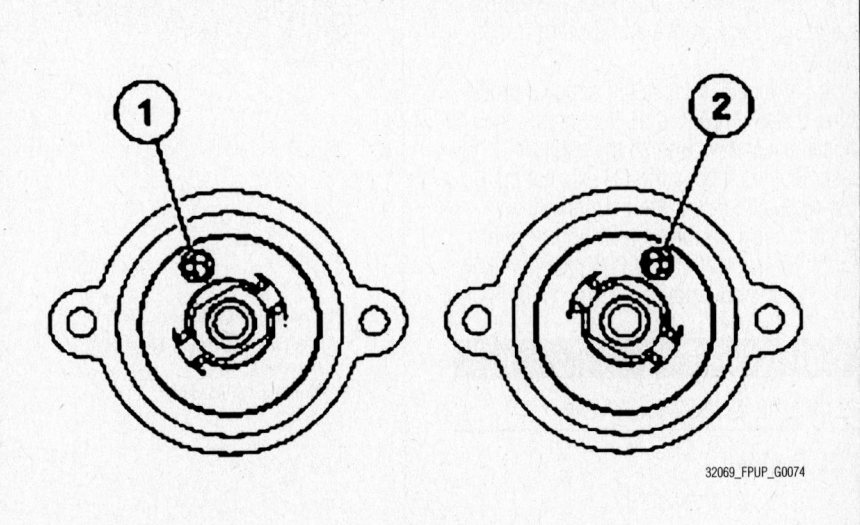

Fig. 86 **Correct thermostat positioning—4.2L engine**

7. Remove the thermostat and the O-ring seal. Discard the O-ring seal.

8. To install, reverse the removal procedure. Install a new O-ring seal and lubricate it with clean coolant. Tighten the power steering upper bracket-to-thermostat housing bolt to 11 Nm (8 ft. lbs.). Tighten the power steering upper bracket-to-intermediate bracket bolts to 17 Nm (13 ft. lbs.). Tighten the thermostat housing bolts to 25 Nm (18 ft. lbs.).

5.4L and 6.8L Engines

1. Drain the engine cooling system.
2. Remove the air cleaner intake pipe.
3. Release the clamp and disconnect the upper radiator hose from the thermostat housing.
4. Remove the bolts and the thermostat housing.
5. Remove the thermostat and the O-ring seal. Discard the O-ring seal.
6. To install, reverse the removal procedure. Install a new O-ring seal and lubricate it with clean coolant. Torque the housing bolts to 10 Nm (89 inch lbs.).
7. Fill and bleed the cooling system.

6.0L Diesel Engine

1. Drain the engine cooling system.
2. Remove the air cleaner assembly.
3. Loosen the clamps and remove the charge air cooler duct.
4. Disconnect and position the upper radiator hose aside.
5. Disconnect the exhaust backpressure sensor electrical connector.
6. Disconnect the exhaust backpressure tube at the LH exhaust manifold.
7. Remove the 2 nuts and exhaust backpressure sensor and bracket as an assembly.
8. Remove the 2 stud bolts and thermostat assembly. Remove and discard the O-ring seal.
9. To install, reverse the removal procedure. Install a new O-ring seal on the thermostat assembly. Tighten the exhaust backpressure tube at the LH exhaust manifold to 30 Nm (22 ft. lbs.). Tighten the 2 exhaust backpressure sensor and bracket nuts to 31 Nm (23 ft. lbs.). Tighten the thermostat housing bolts to 27 Nm (17 ft. lbs.).

WATER PUMP

REMOVAL & INSTALLATION

4.2L Engine

See Figures 87 through 90.

1. Before servicing the vehicle, refer to the Precautions Section.
2. Drain the cooling system.

3. Remove the engine cooling fan and the fan shroud.
4. Remove the drive belt.
5. Remove the bolts and the coolant pump pulley.
6. Remove the bolt and disconnect the heater outlet tube assembly from the coolant pump.
7. Clean and inspect the O-ring seal. Install a new O-ring seal if necessary.
8. Remove the nuts for the A/C compressor mounting bracket support.
9. Remove the A/C compressor mounting bracket support upper bolt. Loosen the A/C compressor mounting bracket support lower bolt. Position the bracket and bolt forward until they contact the power steering pump pulley. Position the A/C compressor mounting bracket aside.
10. Release the clamp and disconnect the lower radiator hose.
11. Remove the fasteners and the coolant pump.
12. Remove and discard the coolant pump gasket.

✳✳ WARNING

Do not use metal scrapers, wire brushes, power abrasive discs, or other abrasive means to clean the sealing surfaces. These may cause scratches and gouges resulting in leak paths. Use a plastic scraper to clean the sealing surfaces.

13. Clean the coolant pump gasket mating surfaces with a plastic scraper and metal surface prep. Follow the directions on the packaging.

To install:

14. To install, reverse the removal procedure. Lubricate the O-ring seal with clean engine coolant. Observe the following torques:

- Water pump: 21 ft. lbs. (28 Nm)
- A/C compressor support bracket nuts: 21 ft. lbs. (28 Nm)
- A/C compressor support bracket bolts: 35 ft. lbs. (48 Nm)
- Heater outlet tube: 89 inch lbs. (10 Nm)
- Water pump pulley: 89 inch lbs. (10 Nm)
- Fan-to-fan clutch: 13 ft. lbs. (17 Nm)
- Fan shroud: 53 inch lbs. (6 Nm)
- Fan hub: 41 ft. lbs. (55 Nm)

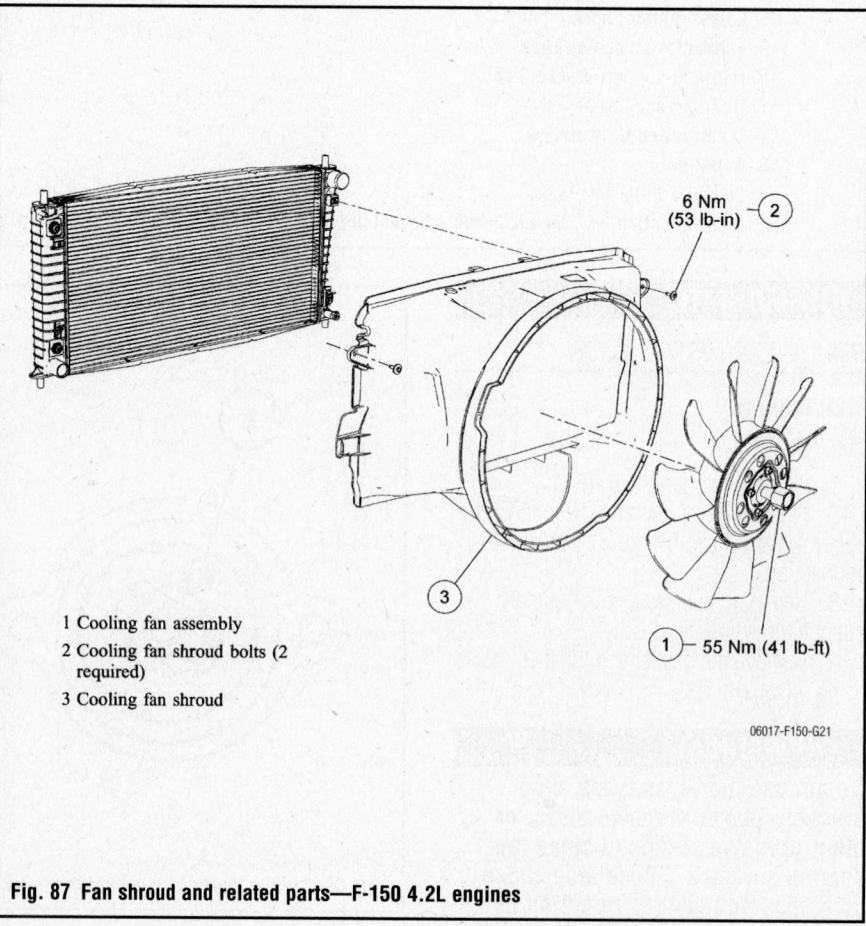

1 Cooling fan assembly
2 Cooling fan shroud bolts (2 required)
3 Cooling fan shroud

06017-F150-G21

Fig. 87 Fan shroud and related parts—F-150 4.2L engines

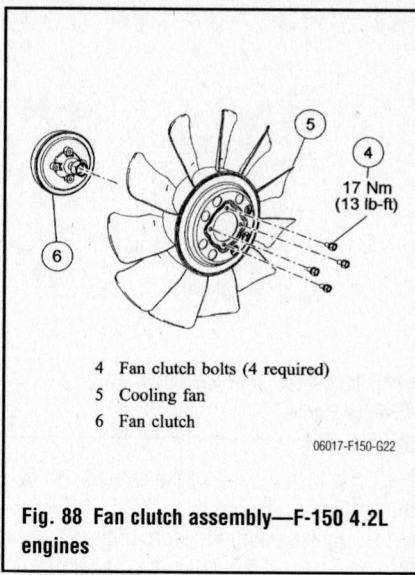

4 Fan clutch bolts (4 required)
5 Cooling fan
6 Fan clutch

06017-F150-G22

Fig. 88 Fan clutch assembly—F-150 4.2L engines

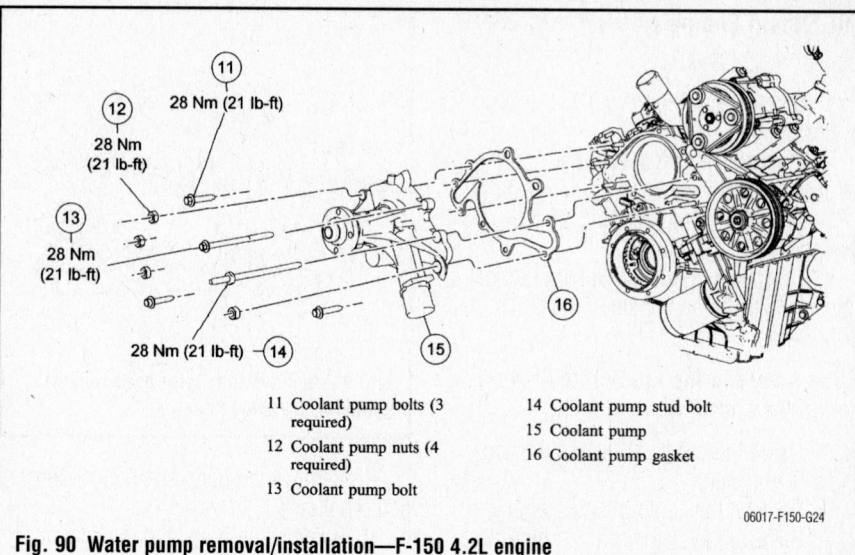

11 Coolant pump bolts (3 required)
12 Coolant pump nuts (4 required)
13 Coolant pump bolt
14 Coolant pump stud bolt
15 Coolant pump
16 Coolant pump gasket

06017-F150-G24

Fig. 90 Water pump removal/installation—F-150 4.2L engine

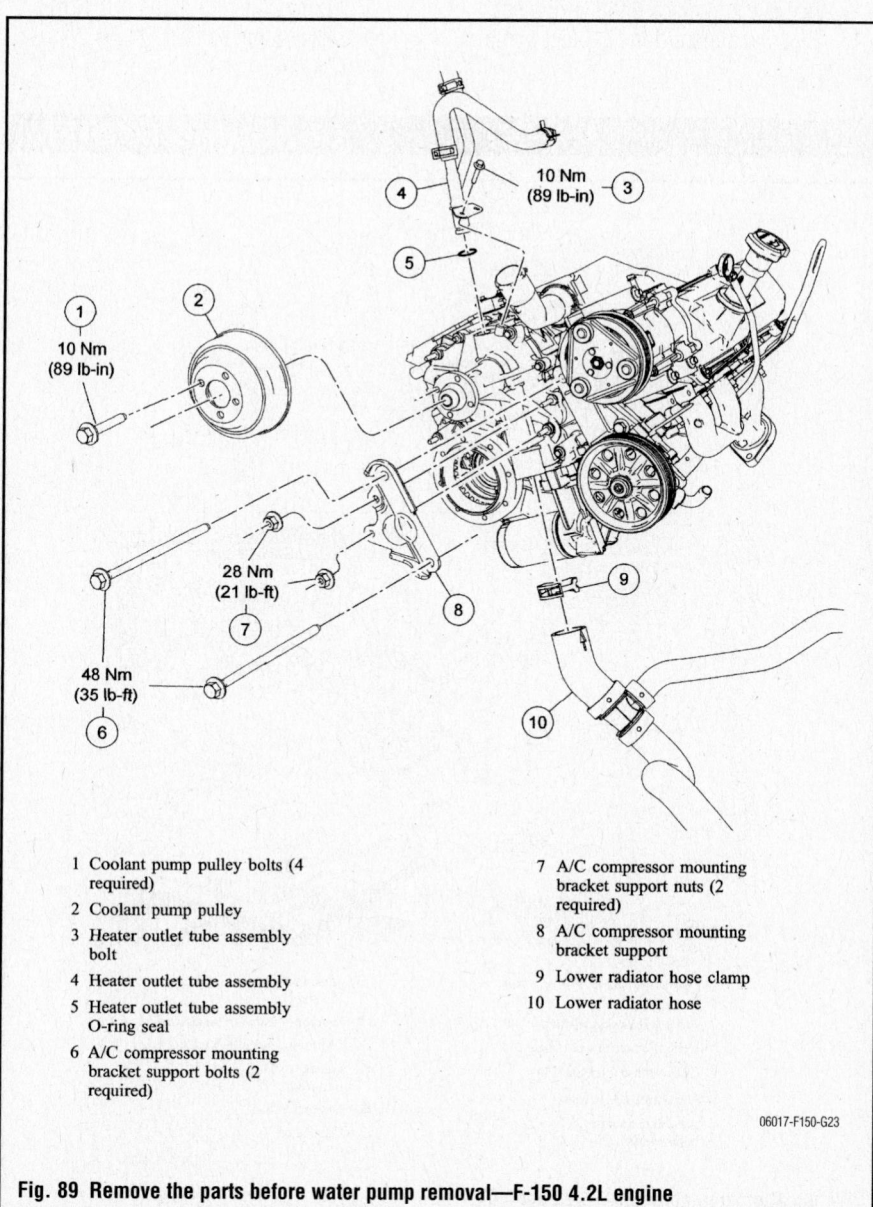

1 Coolant pump pulley bolts (4 required)
2 Coolant pump pulley
3 Heater outlet tube assembly bolt
4 Heater outlet tube assembly
5 Heater outlet tube assembly O-ring seal
6 A/C compressor mounting bracket support bolts (2 required)

7 A/C compressor mounting bracket support nuts (2 required)
8 A/C compressor mounting bracket support
9 Lower radiator hose clamp
10 Lower radiator hose

06017-F150-G23

Fig. 89 Remove the parts before water pump removal—F-150 4.2L engine

F-250 and F-350 5.4L and 6.8L Engines

1. Before servicing the vehicle, refer to the Precautions Section.

2. Drain the cooling system.

3. Remove the air cleaner outlet tube.

4. Disconnect the upper radiator hose and the degas bottle (coolant reservoir) hose.

✳✳ WARNING

The large clutch assembly nut has a right-hand thread and must be rotated counterclockwise to remove it.

5. Using a hub wrench set, remove the fan and fan clutch from the coolant pump pulley.

6. Carefully position the fan and the fan clutch into the shroud.

7. Remove the 2 cooling fan shroud bolts, the shroud, fan and clutch.

8. Remove the accessory drive belt.

9. Remove the 4 bolts and the coolant pump pulley.

10. Remove the 4 bolts and the coolant pump. Discard the O-ring seal.

11. Installation is the reverse of removal. Install a new O-ring seal. Lubricate the O-ring seal with clean engine coolant prior to installation. Clean the sealing surfaces with metal surface prep. Observe the following torques:

- Water pump: 18 ft. lbs. (25 Nm)
- Water pump pulley: 18 ft. lbs. (25 Nm)
- Fan shroud: 53 inch lbs. (6 Nm)
- Fan hub nut: 98 ft. lbs. (133 Nm)

6.0L Diesel Engine

See Figures 91 and 92.

1. Before servicing the vehicle, refer to the Precautions Section.

2. With the vehicle in **Neutral**, position it on a hoist.

3. Remove the radiator and shroud assembly.

4. Disconnect the cooling fan electrical connector. Unclip and position the fan wiring aside.

➡**Use a hole in the fan hub to prevent the fan from turning.**

5. Using the hub tool, loosen the cooling fan and clutch.

6. Remove the cooling fan assembly.

7. Remove the stator bolts and the stator.

8. Rotate the accessory drive belt tensioner clockwise and position the drive belt aside.

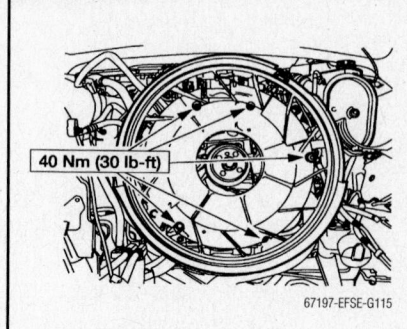

Fig. 91 Remove the stator bolts and the stator—6.0L Diesel Engine

9. Remove the bolts and the coolant pump pulley.

10. Remove the bolts and the coolant pump.

11. Remove and discard the O-ring seal.

12. Clean and inspect the coolant pump mounting.

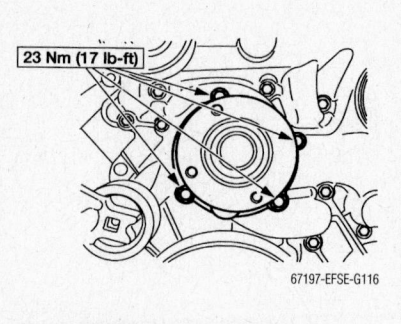

Fig. 92 Water pump mounting—6.0L Diesel Engine

13. To install, reverse the removal procedure.

14. Observe the following torques:
- Stator bolts: 30 ft. lbs. (40 Nm)
- Pulley bolts: 23 ft. lbs. (31 Nm)
- Water pump bolts: 17 ft. lbs. (23 Nm)

ENGINE ELECTRICAL

CHARGING SYSTEM

ALTERNATOR

REMOVAL & INSTALLATION

4.2L Engine

See Figure 93.

1. Before servicing the vehicle, refer to the Precautions Section.

2. Remove or disconnect the following:
- Negative battery cable
- Drive belt
- Alternator electrical connectors
- Alternator B+ nut and the cable
- A/C line bracket (position aside)
- Alternator harness bracket (position bracket aside)
- Alternator bolts and the alternator

To install:

3. Install or connect the following:
- Alternator and tighten the bolts to 35 ft. lbs. (47 Nm)
- Alternator harness bracket; tighten the nut to 18 ft. lbs. (25 Nm)
- A/C line bracket; tighten the nut to 18 ft. lbs. (25 Nm)
- Alternator B+ cable nut
- Alternator stator and voltage regulator connectors
- Alternator electrical connectors
- Drive belt
- Negative battery cable

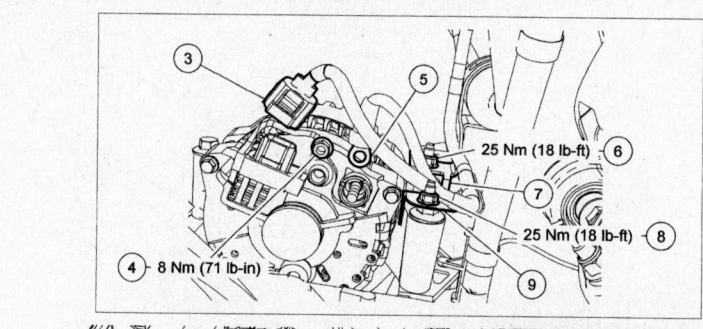

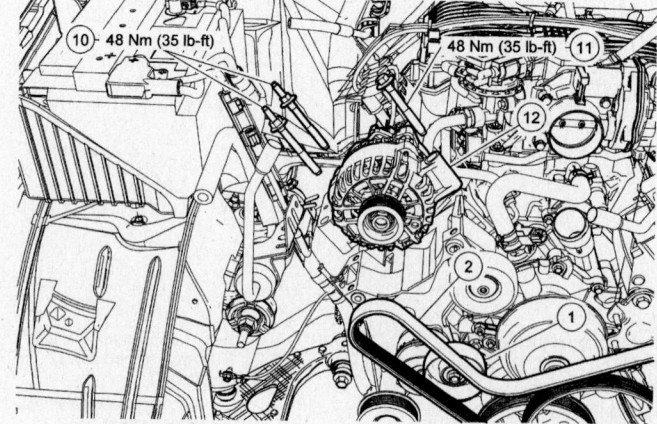

1	Front end accessory drive belt tensioner	7	Air conditioning (A/C) line bracket
2	Front end accessory drive belt	8	Generator harness bracket nut
3	Generator electrical connector	9	Generator harness bracket
4	Generator B+ terminal nut	10	Generator stud bolts (2 required)
5	Generator B+ terminal	11	Generator bolt
6	Air conditioning (A/C) line bracket nut	12	Generator

Fig. 93 Alternator mounting—4.2L engine

4.6L and 5.4L Engines

See Figure 94.

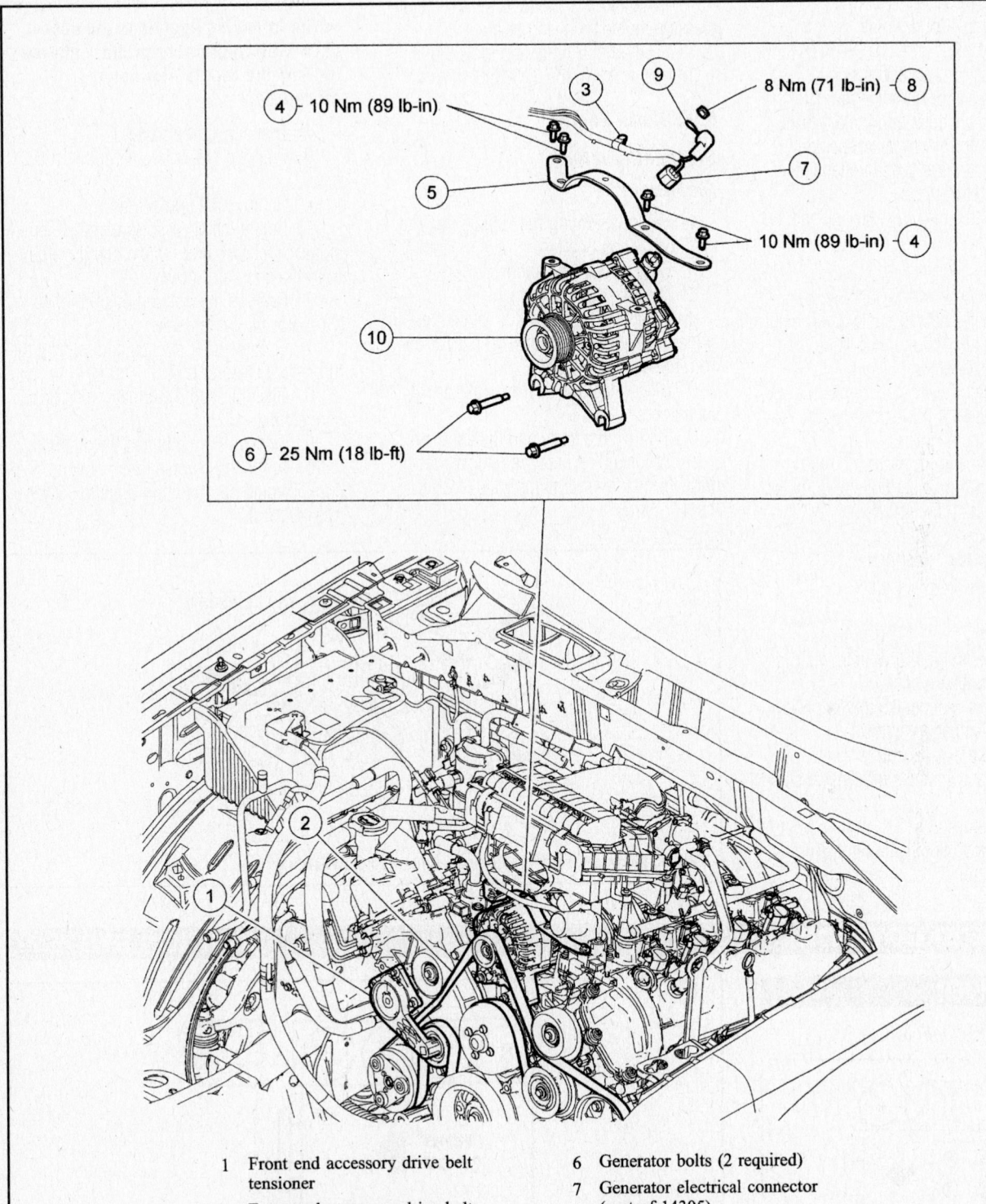

1　Front end accessory drive belt tensioner
2　Front end accessory drive belt
3　Generator harness locator
4　Generator bracket bolts (4 required)
5　Generator bracket
6　Generator bolts (2 required)
7　Generator electrical connector (part of 14305)
8　Generator B+ terminal nut
9　Generator B+ terminal
10　Generator

06017-F150-G014

Fig. 94 Alternator mounting—5.4L engine; 4.6L similar

1. Before servicing the vehicle, refer to the Precautions Section.
2. Remove or disconnect the following:
   - Negative battery cable
   - Air cleaner outlet pipe
   - Drive belt
   - Alternator bracket bolts
   - Ignition wire from the alternator
   - Alternator bolts and the alternator
   - Alternator electrical connectors
   - Alternator stator and voltage regulator connectors
   - Alternator battery cable nut and the cable

To install:

3. Install or connect the following:
   - Alternator battery cable and the nut
   - Alternator stator and voltage regulator connectors
   - Alternator electrical connectors
   - Alternator and the bolts, tighten to 18 ft. lbs. (25 Nm)
   - Ignition wire from the alternator
   - Alternator bracket bolts and tighten to 89 inch lbs. (10 Nm)
   - Drive belt
   - Air cleaner outlet pipe
   - Negative battery cable

6.8L Engines

1. Before servicing the vehicle, refer to the Precautions Section.
2. Remove or disconnect the following:
   - Negative battery cable
   - Accessory drive belt
   - Alternator harness bracket (position aside)
   - Alternator bolts
   - Alternator electrical connectors
   - Alternator

To install:

3. Before servicing the vehicle, refer to the Precautions Section.
4. Installation is the reverse of removal, please note the following torques:
   a. Alternator bolts and the alternator. Tighten to 18 ft. lbs. (25 Nm).

6.0L Diesel Engine

Single Alternator

See Figure 95.

1. Before servicing the vehicle, refer to the Precautions Section.
2. Disconnect the batteries.
3. Remove the cooling fan.
4. Rotate the accessory drive belt tensioner clockwise and remove the drive belt from the alternator pulley.
5. Disconnect the alternator electrical connectors.
6. Remove the bolts and the alternator.
7. To install, reverse the removal procedure. Torque the mounting bolts to 35 ft. lbs. (47 Nm).

Dual Alternators

1. Before servicing the vehicle, refer to the Precautions Section.

➡The following applies to the secondary alternator. For primary alternator, see the Single Alternator procedure.

2. Disconnect the batteries.
3. Remove the charge air cooler (CAC) pipe.
4. Remove the coolant fan.
5. Rotate the accessory drive belt tensioner clockwise and remove the drive belt from the alternator pulley.
6. Remove the nut and position the alternator B+ cable aside.
7. Loosen the 2 clamps and remove the turbo-to-air cooler pipe.
8. Disconnect the alternator electrical connectors.
9. Remove the bolts and the alternator.
10. To install, reverse the removal procedure. Torque the mounting bolts to 35 ft. lbs. (47 Nm).

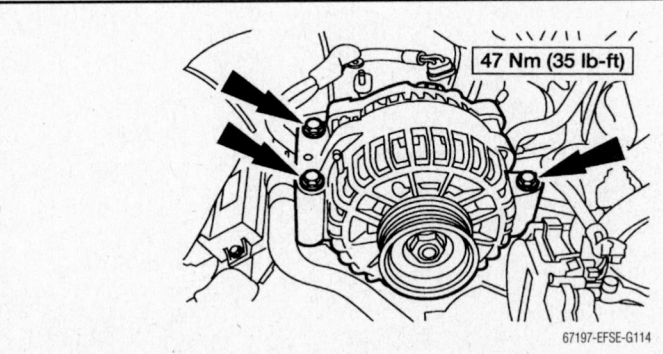

47 Nm (35 lb-ft)

67197-EFSE-G114

Fig. 95 Single alternator mounting—6.0L w/single alternator

ENGINE ELECTRICAL

IGNITION SYSTEM

FIRING ORDER

See Figures 96 through 99.

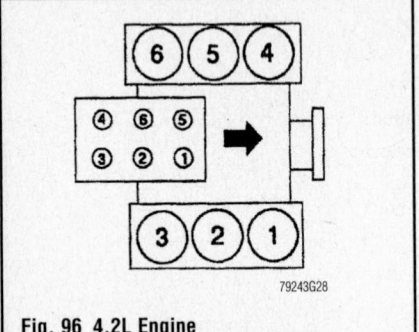

79243G28

Fig. 96 4.2L Engine
Firing Order: 1–4–2–5–3–6
Distributorless ignition system

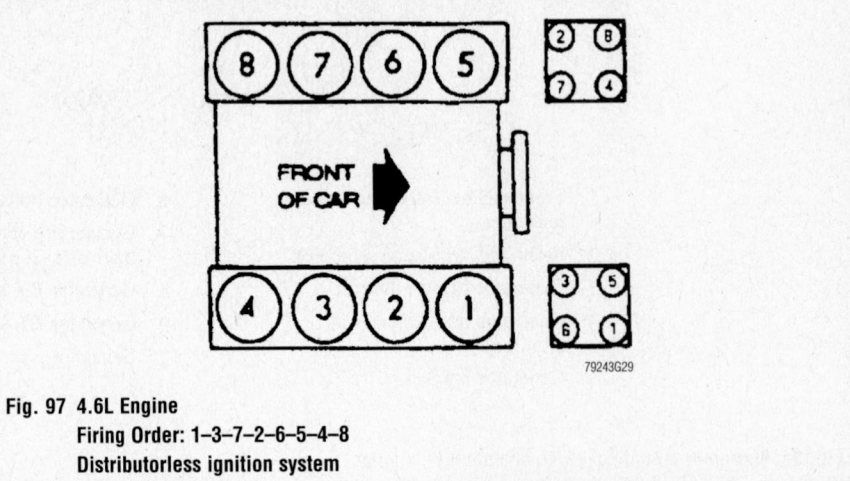

FRONT OF CAR

79243G29

Fig. 97 4.6L Engine
Firing Order: 1–3–7–2–6–5–4–8
Distributorless ignition system

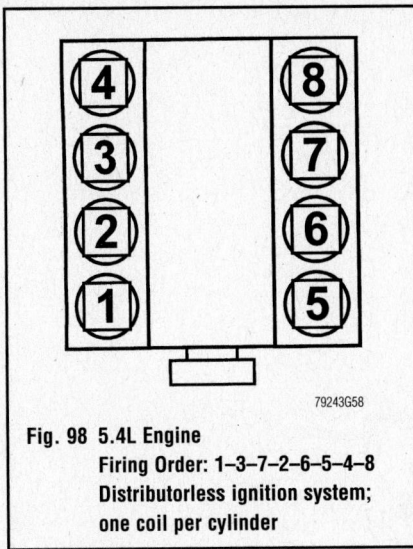

Fig. 98 5.4L Engine
Firing Order: 1–3–7–2–6–5–4–8
Distributorless ignition system;
one coil per cylinder

79243G58

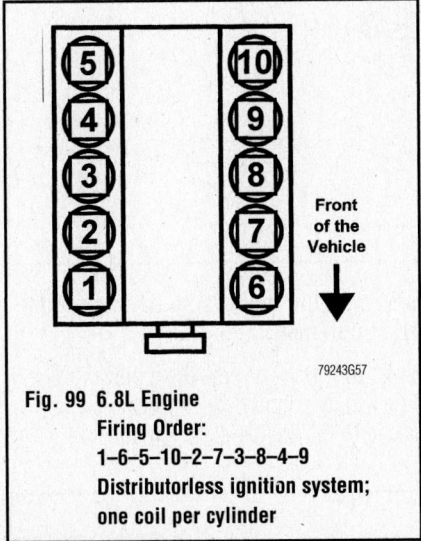

Front
of the
Vehicle

79243G57

Fig. 99 6.8L Engine
Firing Order:
1–6–5–10–2–7–3–8–4–9
Distributorless ignition system;
one coil per cylinder

➥The firing order for 6.0L diesel engine is: 1–2–7–3–4–5–6–8. An illustration is not available for this engine.

IGNITION COIL

REMOVAL & INSTALLATION

4.2L Engine

See Figure 100.

1. Disconnect the ignition coil electrical connector.

✳✳ WARNING

It is important to twist the spark plug wire boots while pulling upward to avoid possible damage to the spark plug wires. The spark plug wires must be connected in the correct firing order.

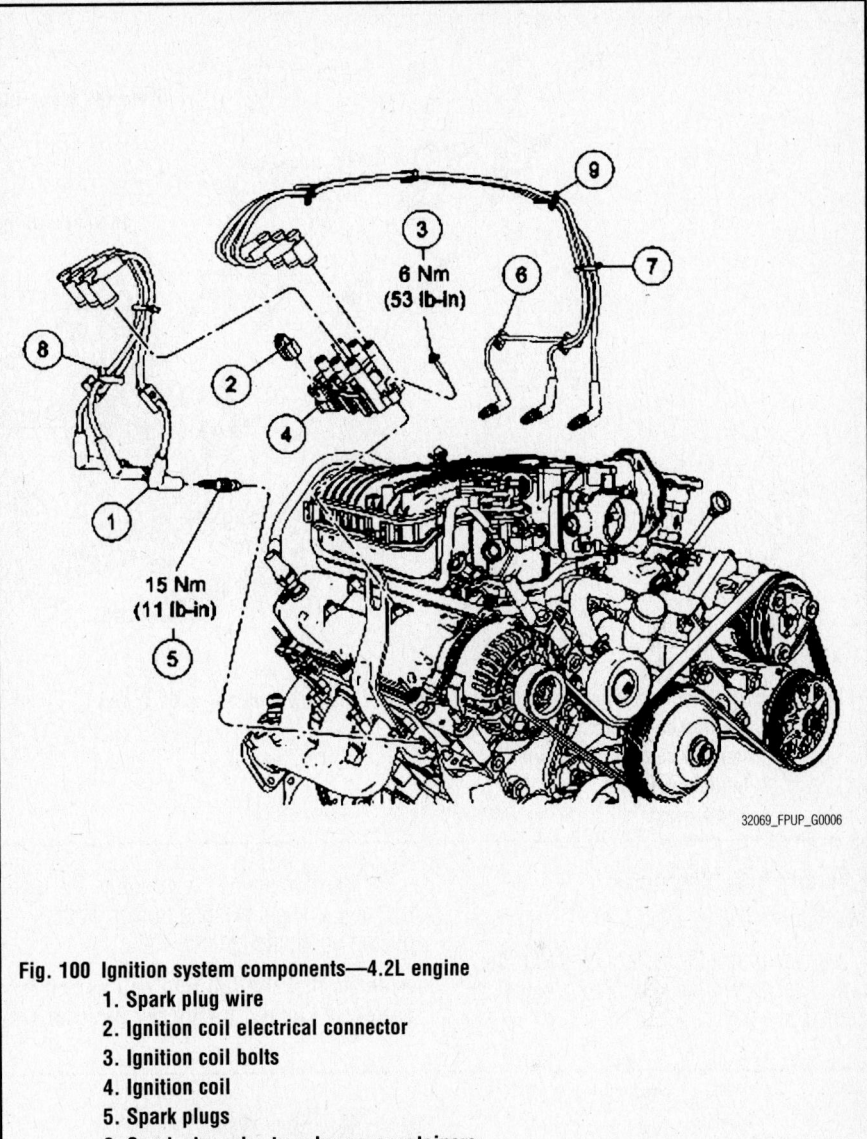

6 Nm
(53 lb-in)

15 Nm
(11 lb-in)

32069_FPUP_G0006

Fig. 100 Ignition system components—4.2L engine
1. Spark plug wire
2. Ignition coil electrical connector
3. Ignition coil bolts
4. Ignition coil
5. Spark plugs
6. Spark plug wire-to-valve cover retainers
7. Spark plug wire separators
8. Spark plug wire separator
9. Spark plug wire-to-intake manifold retainers

2. Disconnect the spark plug wires from the ignition coil by twisting while pulling upward.

3. Remove the bolts and the ignition coil.

4. Inspect the ignition coil for carbon tracks or damage.

5. To install, reverse the removal procedure. Tighten to 6 Nm (53 inch lbs.). Apply silicone brake caliper grease and dielectric compound to the inside of the spark plug wire boots.

4.6L Engine

See Figure 101.

1. Disconnect the battery ground cable.

2. Disconnect the ignition coil electrical connector.

3. Remove the ignition coil retaining bolt.

4. Rotate the ignition coil clockwise 30–40 degrees to clear the fuel injection supply manifold. Use a twisting motion while pulling up on the ignition coil and remove.

➥Verify that the ignition coil spring is correctly located inside the ignition coil boot and that there is no damage to the tip of the boot.

5. To install, reverse the removal procedure. Apply dielectric compound to the inside of the coil boots before installing. Torque the ignition coil retaining bolt to 10 Nm (89 inch lbs.).

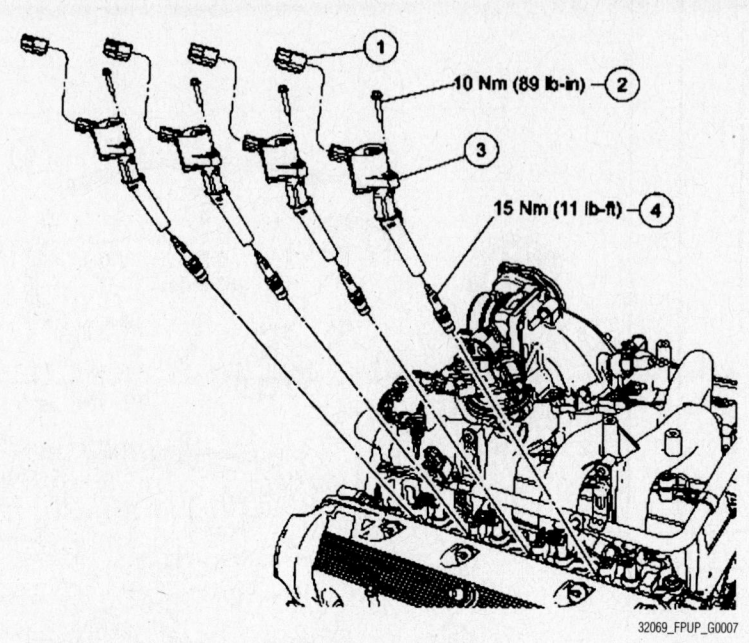

Fig. 101 Ignition system components. Left side shown; right side similar—4.6L engine
1. Ignition coil electrical connector
2. Ignition coil retaining bolt
3. Ignition coil
4. Spark plugs

5.4L and 6.8L Engines

See Figures 102 and 103.

1. Disconnect the battery ground cable.
2. Disconnect the ignition coil electrical connector.

3. Remove the bolt and remove the ignition coil, using a twisting motion while pulling up on the ignition coil.

➡**Verify that the ignition coil spring is correctly located inside the ignition coil** boot and that there is no damage to the tip of the boot.

4. To install, reverse the removal procedure. Apply a light coat of dielectric compound to the inside of the ignition coil

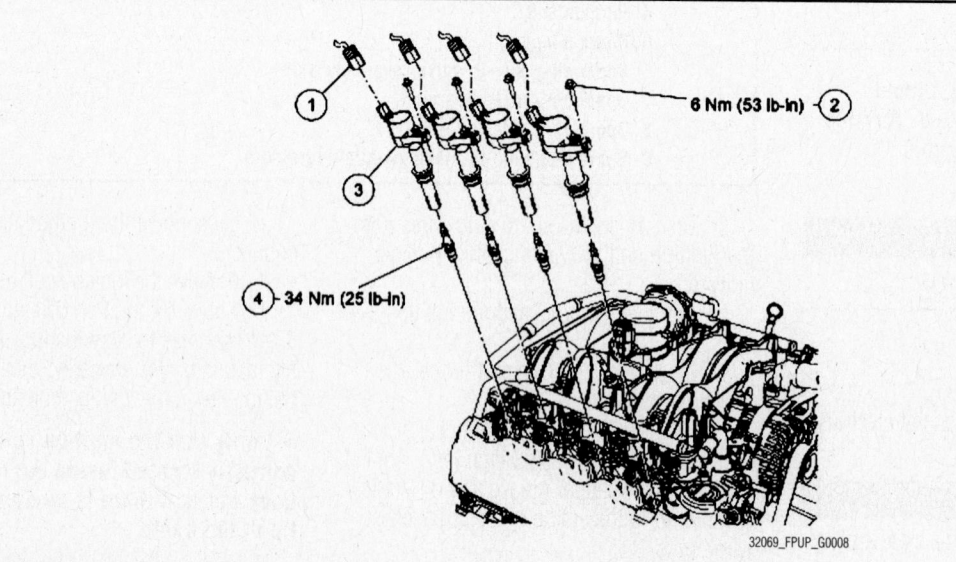

Fig. 102 Ignition system components. Right side shown; left side similar—5.4L engine
1. Ignition coil electrical connectors
2. Ignition coil retaining bolts
3. Ignition coils
4. Spark plugs

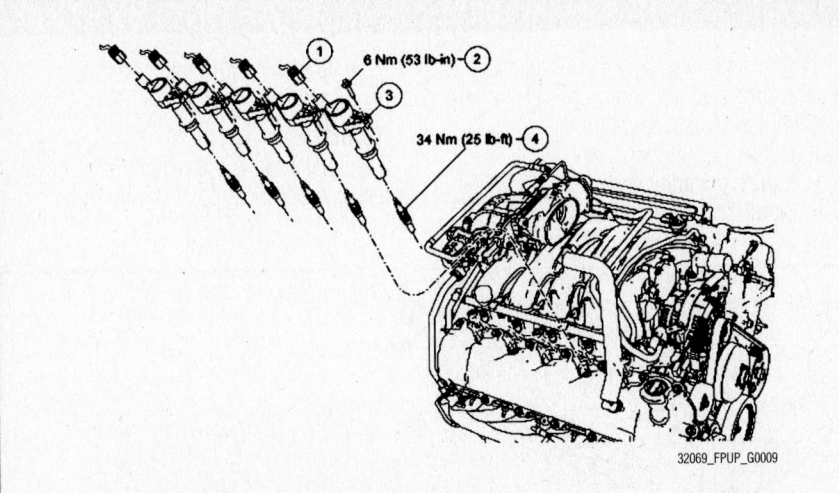

Fig. 103 Ignition system components. Right side shown; left side similar—6.8L engine
1. Ignition coil electrical connectors
2. Ignition coil retaining bolts
3. Ignition coils
4. Spark plugs

boots. Tighten the coil bolt to 6 Nm (53 inch lbs.).

GNITION TIMING

ADJUSTMENT

Base timing for distributorless ignition engines is set at the factory at 10 degrees BTDC and is not adjustable.

SPARK PLUGS

REMOVAL & INSTALLATION

4.2L Engine

See Figure 104.

✳✳ WARNING

Spark plug wires must be connected in the correct firing order.

✳✳ WARNING

It is important to twist the spark plug wire boots while pulling upward to avoid possible damage to the spark plug wire.

1. Using the special tool shown, or equivalent, with a twisting motion pull the spark plug wire off the spark plug.

➡ **Use compressed air to remove any foreign material in the spark plug well before removing the spark plugs.**

➡ **If an original spark plug is reused, make sure it is installed in the same cylinder from which it was taken.**

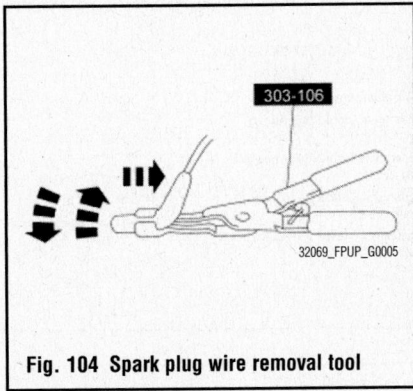

Fig. 104 Spark plug wire removal tool

New spark plugs can be used in any cylinder.

2. Remove the spark plug.
3. Inspect the spark plug firing tip.
4. Adjust the spark plug gap as necessary.

➡ **Apply silicone brake caliper grease and dielectric compound to the inside of the spark plug wire boots.**

5. To install, reverse the removal procedure. See the torque Specifications Chart for spark plug tightening.

4.6L Engines

1. Disconnect the battery ground cable.
2. Disconnect the ignition coil electrical connector.
3. Remove the ignition coil retaining bolt.
4. Rotate the ignition coil clockwise 30–40 degrees to clear the fuel injection supply manifold. Use a twisting motion while pulling up on the ignition coil and remove.

➡ **Verify that the ignition coil spring is correctly located inside the ignition coil boot and that there is no damage to the tip of the boot.**

➡ **Use compressed air to remove any foreign material from the spark plug well before removing the spark plugs.**

➡ **If an original spark plug is used, make sure it is installed in the same cylinder from which it was taken. New spark plugs can be used in any cylinder.**

5. Remove the spark plugs.
6. Inspect the spark plugs. Install new spark plugs as necessary.
7. To install, reverse the removal procedure. Apply dielectric compound to the inside of the coil boots before installing. See the torque Specifications Chart for spark plug tightening. Torque the ignition coil retaining bolt to 10 Nm (89 inch lbs.).

5.4L and 6.8L Engines

1. Disconnect the battery ground cable.
2. Disconnect the ignition coil electrical connector.
3. Remove the bolt and remove the ignition coil, using a twisting motion while pulling up on the ignition coil.

➡ **Verify that the ignition coil spring is correctly located inside the ignition coil boot and that there is no damage to the tip of the boot.**

➡ **Use compressed air to remove any foreign material from the spark plug well before removing the spark plugs.**

➡ **If an original spark plug is used, make sure it is installed in the same cylinder from which it was taken.**

4. New spark plugs can be used in any cylinder.
5. Remove the spark plugs.

✳✳ WARNING

The spark plug gap is NOT adjustable. Damage can occur to the ceramic if the gap is adjusted. Replace the spark plug if the gap is out of specification.

6. Inspect the spark plugs. Install new spark plugs as necessary.
7. To install, reverse the removal procedure. Apply a light coat of dielectric compound to the inside of the ignition coil boots. See the torque Specifications Chart for spark plug tightening. Tighten the coil bolt to 6 Nm (53 inch lbs.).

ENGINE ELECTRICAL   **STARTING SYSTEM**

STARTER

REMOVAL & INSTALLATION

4.2L, 4.6L, 5.4L and 6.8L Engines

See Figures 105 and 106.

1. Before servicing the vehicle, refer to the Precautions Section.
2. Remove or disconnect the following:
   - Negative battery cable
   - Starter motor electrical connections
   - Starter motor bolts and the motor

To install:

3. Installation is the reverse of removal, tighten the starter motor bolts to 18 ft. lbs. (25 Nm).

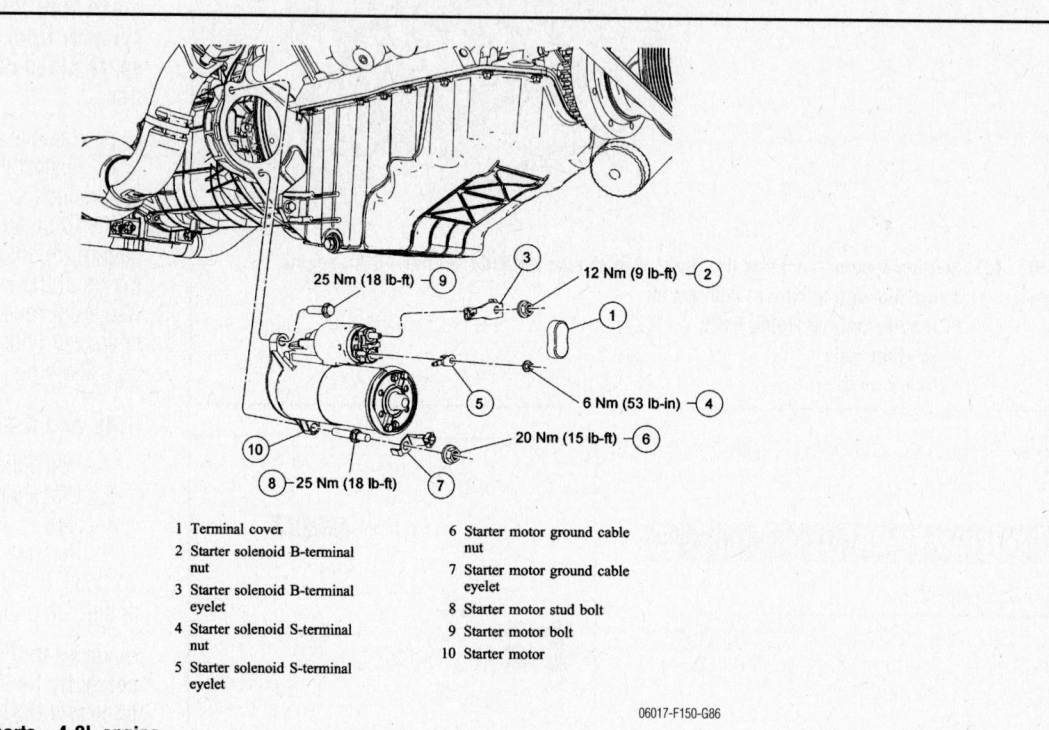

1 Terminal cover
2 Starter solenoid B-terminal nut
3 Starter solenoid B-terminal eyelet
4 Starter solenoid S-terminal nut
5 Starter solenoid S-terminal eyelet
6 Starter motor ground cable nut
7 Starter motor ground cable eyelet
8 Starter motor stud bolt
9 Starter motor bolt
10 Starter motor

06017-F150-G86

Fig. 105 Starter and related parts—4.2L engine

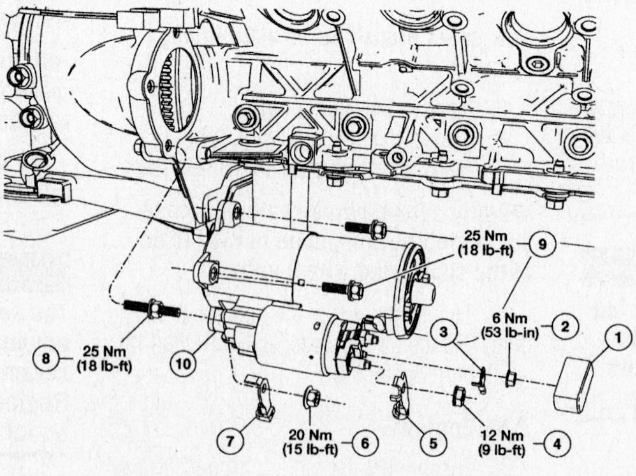

1 Terminal cover
2 Starter solenoid S-terminal nut
3 Starter solenoid S-terminal eyelet
4 Starter solenoid B-terminal nut
5 Starter solenoid B-terminal eyelet
6 Starter motor ground cable nut
7 Starter motor ground cable eyelet
8 Starter motor mounting stud bolt
9 Starter motor mounting bolt (2 required)
10 Starter motor

06017-F150-G87

Fig. 106 Starter and related parts—4.6L, 5.4L and 6.8L engines

6.0L Diesel Engine

1. Before servicing the vehicle, refer to the Precautions Section.

✳✳ WARNING

When performing maintenance on the starting system, be aware heavy

gauge leads are connected to the battery. Make sure protective caps are in place when maintenance is complete.

2. Disconnect the battery ground cable.

3. Raise and support the vehicle.

4. Remove starter solenoid protective cap.

5. Disconnect the starter motor electrical connections.

6. Remove the bolts and the starter.

7. To install, reverse the removal procedure. Torque the bolts to 18 ft. lbs. (25Nm).

ENGINE MECHANICAL

➡**Disconnecting the negative battery cable may interfere with the functions of the on board computer systems and may require the computer to undergo a relearning process, once the negative battery cable is reconnected.**

ACCESSORY DRIVE BELTS

ACCESSORY BELT ROUTING

See Figures 107 through 111.

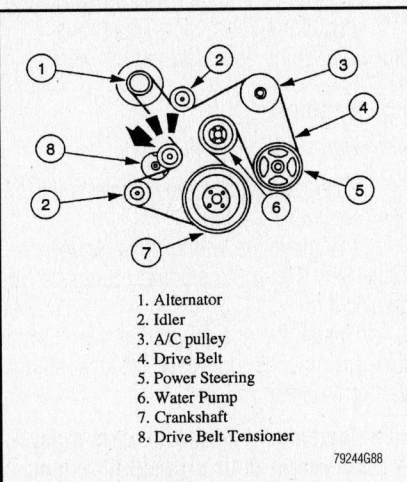

1. Alternator
2. Idler
3. A/C pulley
4. Drive Belt
5. Power Steering
6. Water Pump
7. Crankshaft
8. Drive Belt Tensioner

79244G88

Fig. 107 Accessory drive belt routing— 4.2L engine with A/C

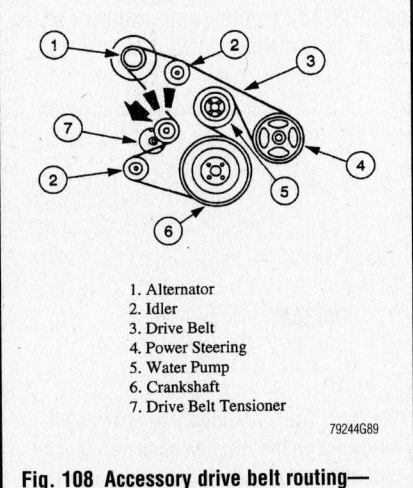

1. Alternator
2. Idler
3. Drive Belt
4. Power Steering
5. Water Pump
6. Crankshaft
7. Drive Belt Tensioner

79244G89

Fig. 108 Accessory drive belt routing— 4.2L engine without A/C

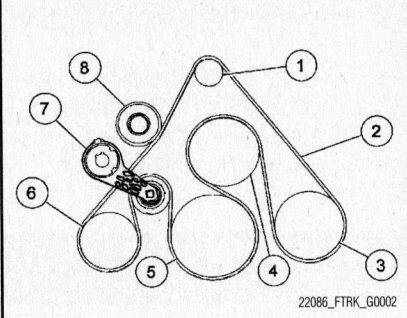

22086_FTRK_G0002

Fig. 109 Accessory drive belt routing— 4.6L, 5.4L and 6.8L engines with A/C

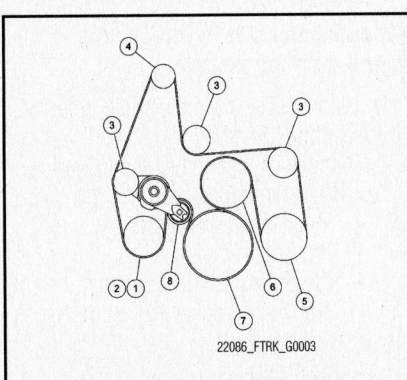

22086_FTRK_G0003

Fig. 110 Accessory drive belt routing— 6.0L diesel engine with single alternator

INSPECTION

Inspect the drive belt for signs of glazing or cracking. A glazed belt will be perfectly smooth from slippage, while a good belt will have a slight texture of fabric visible. Cracks will usually start at the inner edge of the belt and run outward. All worn or damaged drive belts should be replaced immediately.

REMOVAL & INSTALLATION

4.2L Engine

See Figure 112.

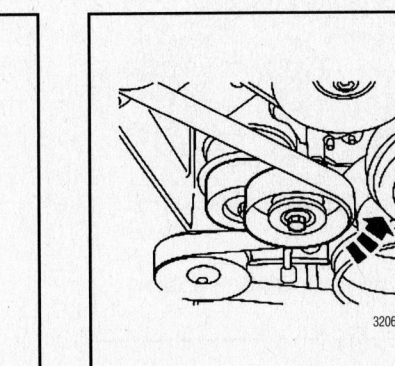

32069_FPUP_G0012

Fig. 112 Accessory drive belt removal— 4.2L engine

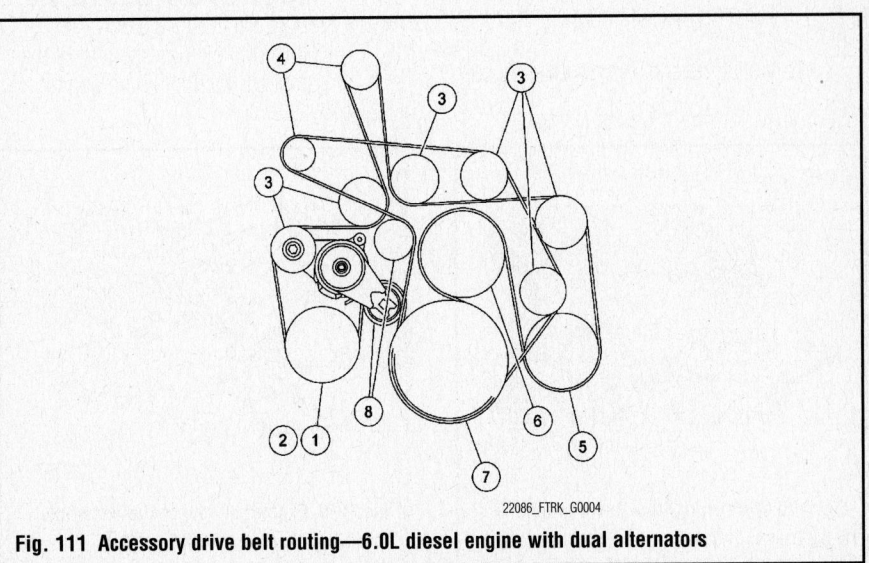

22086_FTRK_G0004

Fig. 111 Accessory drive belt routing—6.0L diesel engine with dual alternators

1. Rotate the tensioner counterclockwise and remove the drive belt.

2. To install, reverse the removal procedure.

4.6L Engine

See Figure 113.

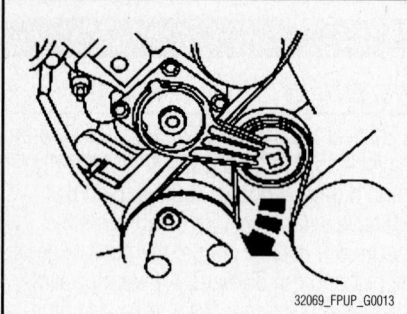

Fig. 113 Accessory drive belt removal—4.6L, 5.4L and 6.8L engines

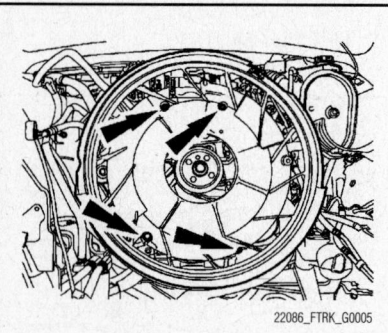

Fig. 114 Cooling fan stator—6.0L Diesel Engine

1. Remove the engine cooling fan and shroud.

2. Rotate the drive belt tensioner clockwise and remove the accessory drive belt.

3. To install, reverse the removal procedure.

Fig. 115 Accessory drive belt removal—6.0L Diesel Engine

5.4L and 6.8L Engines

1. Remove the air cleaner intake pipe.

2. Rotate the drive belt tensioner clockwise and remove the accessory drive belt.

3. To install, reverse the removal procedure.

6.0L Diesel Engine

See Figures 114 and 115.

1. Remove the cooling fan.

2. Remove the 4 bolts and cooling fan stator.

3. Rotate the drive belt tensioner clockwise and remove the accessory drive belt.

4. To install, reverse the removal procedure. Tighten the stator bolts to 40 Nm (30 ft. lbs.).

CAMSHAFT AND VALVE LIFTERS

REMOVAL & INSTALLATION

4.2L Engine

See Figure 116.

➡ **It may be easier to remove the engine from the vehicle.**

1. Before servicing the vehicle, refer to the Precautions Section.

2. Remove or disconnect the following:
- Negative battery cable
- Lower intake manifold
- Rocker arm cover
- Rocker arm hold-down bolt, then remove the rocker arm from the cylinder head.
- Pushrods
- Valve lifters by pulling them up out of their bores
- Timing chain and sprockets; see procedure in this section
- Camshaft key from the end of the camshaft, then slide the engine

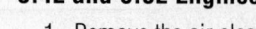

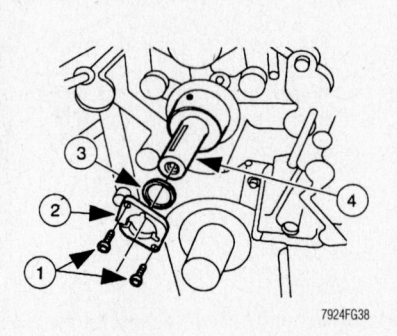

Fig. 116 Exploded view of the camshaft retaining hardware—4.2L engine

dynamic balance shaft drive gear off the camshaft.
- The 2 camshaft thrust plate retaining bolts (1), then remove the thrust plate (2).

3. Remove the camshaft spacer (3), then slide the camshaft (4) out of the front of the engine block. Be cautious not to gouge or scratch the camshaft bearing journals.

To install:

4. Lubricate the camshaft with engine oil prior to installation.

5. Carefully slide the camshaft into the camshaft bore. Do not scratch the bearing surfaces.

6. Install the camshaft thrust plate with the spacer. Tighten the thrust plate mounting bolts to 72–120 inch lbs. (8–14 Nm).

7. Slide the engine dynamic balance shaft drive gear onto the camshaft. Install the camshaft key to the camshaft groove.

8. Install the timing chain and sprockets.

9. Install the valve lifters, pushrods, intake manifolds and rocker arm covers.

4.6L Engines

See Figures 117 through 119.

1. Before servicing the vehicle, refer to the Precautions Section.

2. Remove the timing drive components. See "Timing Chain and Sprockets" in this section.

3. Install the special tool between the valve spring coils to protect the valve stem seal from damage.

➡ **The camshaft roller followers must be installed in their original locations. Record the camshaft roller follower locations.**

➡ **The 3 rearmost camshaft roller followers on the RH side must use special tool 303-567 in the same manner as is shown in the illustration.**

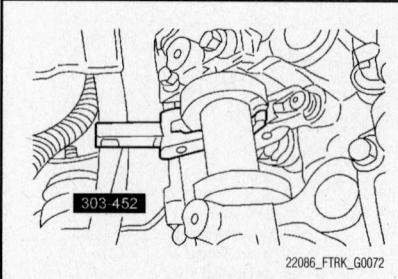

Fig. 117 The 3 rearmost camshaft roller followers on the RH side must use special tool 303-567 in the same manner as is shown

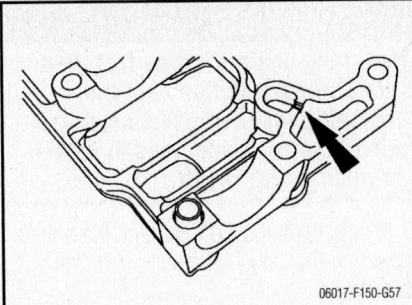

Fig. 118 One of the bearing caps contains an oil flow restriction groove—4.6L engine

4. Using the special tool, compress the valve spring and remove the camshaft roller follower.

5. Remove all of the camshaft roller followers from the camshaft being serviced.

6. Remove the bolt, camshaft sprocket and camshaft sprocket spacer from the camshaft being serviced.

7. Remove the special tools from the camshaft being serviced.

8. Remove the bolts, camshaft bearing caps and the camshaft.

9. Clean and inspect the camshaft bearing caps.

10. One of the bearing caps contains an oil flow restriction groove. Make sure the groove is free of foreign material.

11. Clean and inspect the camshaft bearing caps. One of the bearing caps contains an oil flow restriction groove. Make sure the groove is free of foreign material.

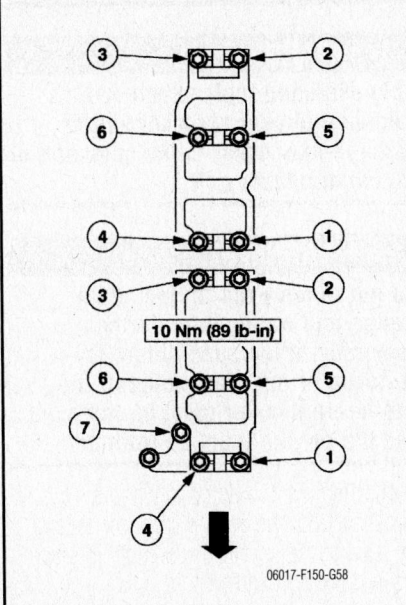

Fig. 119 Camshaft bearing cap torque sequence—4.6L engine

To install:

12. Install the camshaft and the camshaft bearing caps in their original locations, performing the following:

    a. Lubricate the camshaft with clean engine oil.

    b. Position the camshaft.

    c. Lubricate the camshaft bearing caps with clean engine oil.

    d. Position the camshaft bearing caps.

    e. Install the bolts loosely.

13. Tighten the bolts in the sequence shown to 89 inch lbs. (10 Nm).

14. Install the camshaft sprocket. Install and tighten the bolt.

- Tighten in two stages.
- Stage 1: Tighten to 40 Nm (30 ft. lbs.).
- Stage 2: Tighten an additional 90 degrees.

15. Install the timing chains.

16. Install the camshaft roller followers.

5.4L Engines

Left Side

See Figures 120 through 125.

1. Before servicing the vehicle, refer to the Precautions Section.

> ※※ **WARNING**
>
> **The camshaft procedure must be followed exactly or damage to the valves and pistons will result.**

2. Remove the cooling fan shroud.

3. Position the crankshaft damper spoke at the 12 o'clock position and the timing mark indentation at the 1 o'clock position.

4. Remove the left valve cover.

> ※※ **WARNING**
>
> **Damage to the camshaft phaser sprocket assembly will occur if mis-**

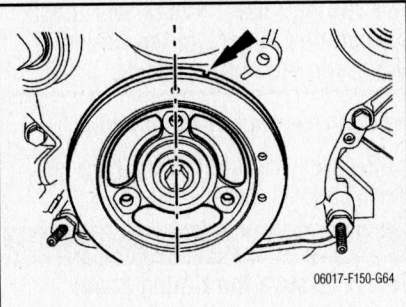

Fig. 120 Position the crankshaft damper spoke at the 12 o'clock position and the timing mark indentation at the 1 o'clock position—5.4L engine

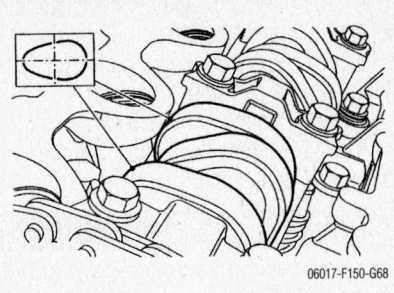

Fig. 121 The number 5 cylinder camshaft exhaust lobe must be coming up on the exhaust stroke. Verify by noting the position of the 2 intake camshaft lobes and the exhaust lobe on the number 5 cylinder—5.4L engine

handled or used as a lifting or leveraging device.

5. Loosen and back off the left camshaft phaser bolt 1 full turn.

6. Disconnect the left camshaft position (CMP) sensor electrical connector.

7. Remove the left CMP sensor and the bolt.

> ※※ **WARNING**
>
> **If servicing both camshafts, do not rotate the crankshaft. Camshaft position has been established earlier.**

→ If the camshaft lobes are not exactly positioned as shown, the crankshaft keyway will require 1 full additional rotation to 12 o'clock.

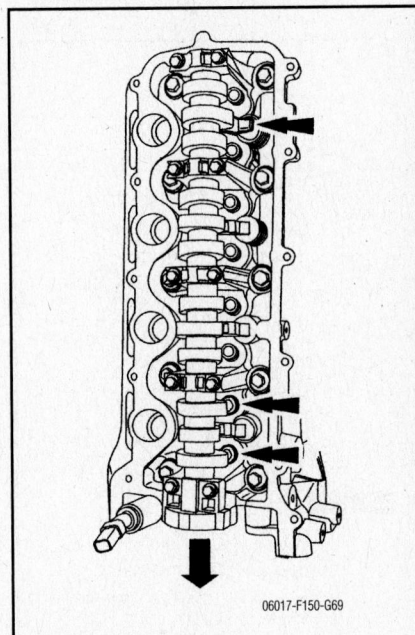

Fig. 122 Remove only these 3 roller followers at this time—5.4L engine

8. The number 5 cylinder camshaft exhaust lobe must be coming up on the exhaust stroke. Verify by noting the position of the 2 intake camshaft lobes and the exhaust lobe on the number 5 cylinder.

9. Remove only the 3 roller followers shown in the illustration.

⚙ WARNING

Do not allow the valve keepers to fall off the valve or the valve may drop into the cylinder.

➡ The camshaft roller followers must be installed in their original locations. Record camshaft roller follower locations.

➡ It may be necessary to push the valve down while compressing the spring.

10. Using special tool 303-1039, remove only the 3 designated roller followers from the previous step.

⚙ WARNING

The crankshaft cannot be moved past the 6 o'clock position once set.

11. Rotate the crankshaft clockwise, as viewed from the front, positioning the crankshaft damper spoke at the 6 o'clock position and the timing mark indentation at the 7 o'clock position.

❊ WARNING

Engine is not freewheeling. Camshaft procedure must be followed exactly

Fig. 123 Using special tool 303-1039—5.4L engine

06017-F150-G71

Fig. 124 Rotate the crankshaft clockwise, as viewed from the front, positioning the crankshaft damper spoke at the 6 o'clock position and the timing mark indentation at the 7 o'clock position—5.4L engine

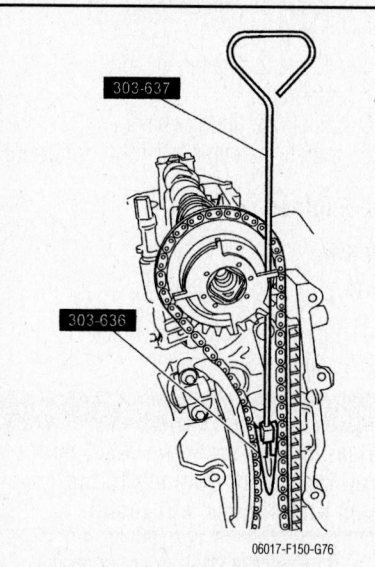

06017-F150-G76

Fig. 125 The Timing Chain Wedge tool must be installed square to the timing chain and the engine block—5.4L engine

or damage to valves and pistons will result.

❊ WARNING

The Timing Chain Wedge tool must be installed square to the timing chain and the engine block.

➡ Front cover removed for clarity.

12. Install the special tools in the left timing chain as shown.

❊ WARNING

Do not remove the timing chain wedge tool at any time during assembly. If the special tool is removed or out of placement, the engine front cover must be removed and the engine must be retimed.

❊ WARNING

The timing chain must be installed in its original position onto the camshaft phaser sprocket using the scribed marks, or damage to valves and pistons will result.

13. Scribe a location mark on the timing chain and the camshaft phaser sprocket assembly.

❊ WARNING

Remove the front thrust camshaft bearing cap straight upward from the bearing towers, or the bearing cap may be damaged from side loading.

➡ The camshaft bearing caps must be installed in their original locations. Record camshaft bearing cap locations.

14. Remove the bolts in the sequence shown and remove the front camshaft bearing cap and then the remaining bearing caps.

15. Clean and inspect the left camshaft bearing caps. The camshaft front thrust bearing cap contains an oil metering groove. Make sure the groove is free of foreign material.

❊ WARNING

Damage to the camshaft phaser sprocket assembly will occur if mishandled or used as a lifting or leveraging device.

❊ WARNING

Only use hand tools to remove the camshaft phaser sprocket bolt or damage may occur to the camshaft or camshaft phaser unit.

❊ WARNING

Do not remove the timing chain wedge tool at any time during assembly. If the special tool is removed or out of placement, the engine front cover must be removed and the engine must be retimed.

16. Remove the bolt and withdraw the camshaft from the phaser sprocket assembly leaving the sprocket assembly in place. Discard the bolt and washer.

To install:

17. Lubricate the camshaft and camshaft journals with clean engine oil.

> **※※ WARNING**
>
> **Do not remove the timing chain wedge tool at any time during assembly. If the special tool is removed or out of placement, the engine front cover must be removed and the engine must be retimed.**

> **※※ WARNING**
>
> **Damage to the camshaft phaser sprocket assembly will occur if mishandled or used as a lifting or leveraging device.**

> **※ WARNING**
>
> **Do not allow the roller followers to move out of position when installing the camshaft.**

18. Install the camshaft into the camshaft phaser sprocket assembly and onto the head.

19. Install a new camshaft phaser bolt finger tight.

> **※ WARNING**
>
> **Do not remove the timing chain wedge tool at any time during assembly. If the special tool is removed or out of placement, the engine front cover must be removed and the engine must be retimed.**

> **※ WARNING**
>
> **The timing chain must be installed in its original position onto the camshaft phaser sprocket using the scribed marks, or damage to valves and pistons will result. Verify the camshaft phaser sprocket and timing chain scribe marks are still in alignment.**

> **※ WARNING**
>
> **Do not allow the roller followers to move out of position when installing the camshaft.**

20. Lubricate the camshaft bearing caps with clean engine oil.

21. Position the front camshaft bearing cap.

22. Position the remaining camshaft bearing caps.

23. Install the bolts loosely.

24. Tighten the bolts in the sequence shown. Tighten to 10 Nm (89 inch lbs.).

25. Remove the special tools.

26. Rotate the crankshaft a half turn counterclockwise and position the crankshaft damper spoke at the 12 o'clock position and the timing mark indentation at the 1 o'clock position.

27. Verify correct cam position by noting the position of the number 5 cylinder intake and exhaust camshaft lobes.

28. Using the special tool, install the 3 originally removed roller followers.

29. Install the CMP sensor and the bolt.

30. Connect the CMP electrical connector.

> **※※ WARNING**
>
> **Only use hand tools to install the camshaft phaser sprocket assembly or damage may occur to the camshaft or camshaft phaser unit.**

> **※※ WARNING**
>
> **Damage to the camshaft phaser sprocket assembly will occur if mishandled or used as a lifting or leveraging device.**

31. Tighten the camshaft phaser bolt in 2 stages:

- Stage 1: Tighten to 40 Nm (30 ft. lbs.).
- Stage 2: Tighten an additional 90 degrees.

32. Install the left valve cover.

33. Install the cooling fan shroud.

Right Side

See Figures 126 through 132.

1. Before servicing the vehicle, refer to the Precautions Section.

> **※※ WARNING**
>
> **The camshaft procedure must be followed exactly or damage to the valves and pistons will result.**

2. Remove the cooling fan shroud.

3. Position the crankshaft damper spoke at the 12 o'clock position and the timing mark indentation at the 1 o'clock position.

4. Remove the right valve cover.

> **※※ WARNING**
>
> **Damage to the camshaft phaser sprocket assembly will occur if mishandled or used as a lifting or leveraging device.**

5. Loosen and back off the right camshaft phaser bolt 1 full turn.

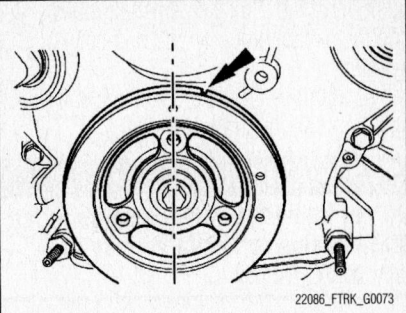

22086_FTRK_G0073

Fig. 126 The number 1 cylinder camshaft exhaust lobe must be coming up on the exhaust stroke. Verify by noting the position of the 2 intake camshaft lobes and the exhaust lobe on the number 1 cylinder—5.4L engine

6. Disconnect the right camshaft position (CMP) sensor electrical connector.

7. Remove the bolt and the right CMP sensor.

➡️**If the camshaft lobes are not exactly positioned as shown, the crankshaft will require 1 full additional rotation to 12 o'clock.**

8. The number 1 cylinder camshaft exhaust lobe must be coming up on the exhaust stroke. Verify by noting the

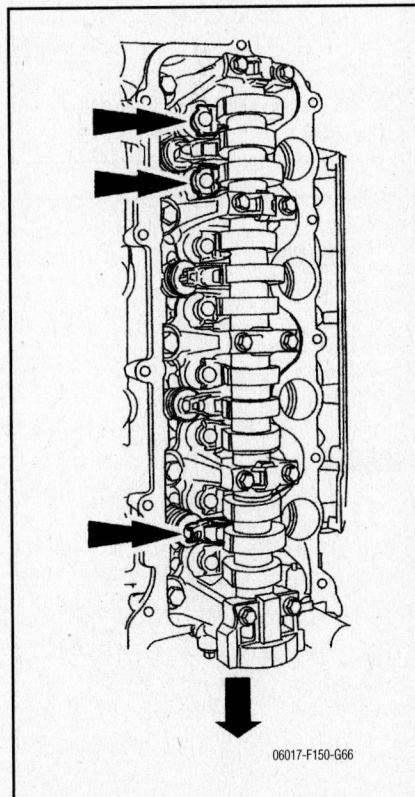

06017-F150-G66

Fig. 127 Remove only these 3 roller followers at this time—5.4L engine

position of the 2 intake camshaft lobes and the exhaust lobe on the number 1 cylinder.

9. Remove only the 3 roller followers shown in the illustration.

❊❊ WARNING

Do not allow the valve keepers to fall off the valve or the valve may drop into the cylinder.

➡The camshaft roller followers must be installed in their original locations. Record camshaft roller follower locations.

➡It may be necessary to push the valve down while compressing the spring.

10. Using special tool 303-1039, remove only the 3 designated roller followers from the previous step.

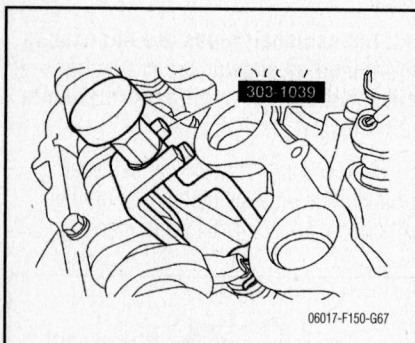

Fig. 128 Using special tool 303-1039— 5.4L engine

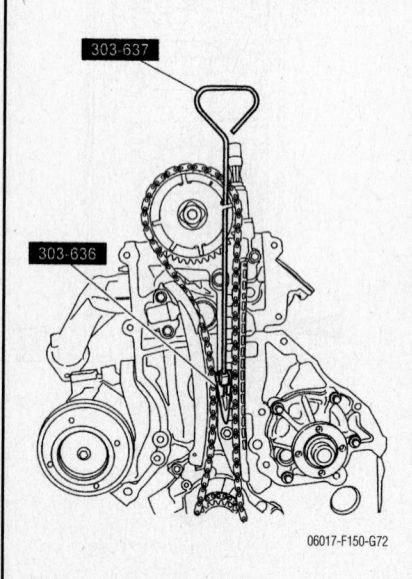

Fig. 129 Timing chain wedge tool installed—5.4L engine

❊❊ WARNING

The crankshaft cannot be moved past the 6 o'clock position once set.

11. Rotate the crankshaft clockwise, as viewed from the front, positioning the crankshaft damper spoke at the 6 o'clock position and the timing mark indentation at the 7 o'clock position.

❊❊ WARNING

Engine is not freewheeling. Camshaft procedure must be followed exactly or damage to valves and pistons will result.

❊❊ WARNING

The Timing Chain Wedge tool must be installed square to the timing chain and the engine block.

➡Front cover removed for clarity.

12. Install the special tools in the right timing chain as shown.

❊❊ WARNING

Do not remove the timing chain wedge tool at any time during assembly. If the special tool is removed or out of placement, the engine front cover must be removed and the engine must be retimed.

❊❊ WARNING

The timing chain must be installed in its original position onto the camshaft phaser sprocket using the scribed marks, or damage to valves and pistons will result.

13. Scribe a location mark on the timing chain and the camshaft phaser sprocket assembly.

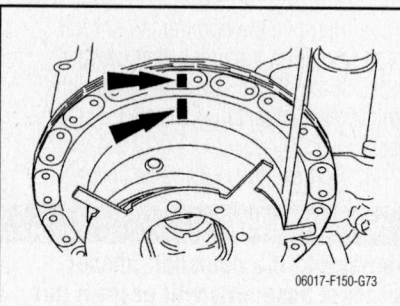

Fig. 130 Scribe a location mark on the timing chain and the camshaft phaser sprocket assembly—5.4L engine

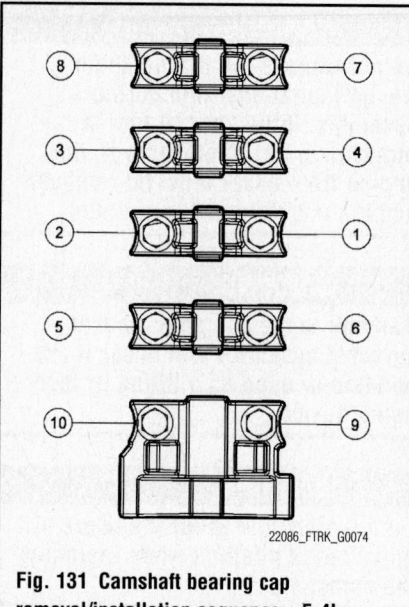

Fig. 131 Camshaft bearing cap removal/installation sequence—5.4L engine

❊❊ WARNING

Remove the front thrust camshaft bearing cap straight upward from the bearing towers, or the bearing cap may be damaged from side loading.

➡The camshaft bearing caps must be installed in their original locations. Record camshaft bearing cap locations.

14. Remove the bolts in the sequence shown and remove the front camshaft bearing cap and then the remaining bearing caps.

15. Clean and inspect the right camshaft bearing caps. The camshaft front thrust bearing cap contains an oil metering groove. Make sure the groove is free of foreign material.

❊❊ WARNING

Damage to the camshaft phaser sprocket assembly will occur if mishandled or used as a lifting or leveraging device.

❊❊ WARNING

Only use hand tools to remove the camshaft phaser sprocket bolt or damage may occur to the camshaft or camshaft phaser unit.

❊❊ WARNING

Do not remove the timing chain wedge tool at any time during assembly. If the special tool is removed or out of placement, the

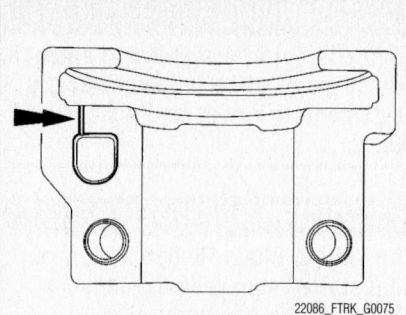

Fig. 132 The camshaft front thrust bearing cap contains an oil metering groove—5.4L engine

engine front cover must be removed and the engine must be retimed.

16. Remove the bolt and withdraw the camshaft from the phaser sprocket assembly leaving the sprocket assembly in place. Discard the bolt and washer.

To install:

17. Lubricate the camshaft and camshaft journals with clean engine oil.

✺✺ WARNING

Do not remove the timing chain wedge tool at any time during assembly. If the special tool is removed or out of placement, the engine front cover must be removed and the engine must be retimed.

✺✺ WARNING

Damage to the camshaft phaser sprocket assembly will occur if mishandled or used as a lifting or leveraging device.

✺✺ WARNING

Do not allow the roller followers to move out of position when installing the camshaft.

18. Install the camshaft into the camshaft phaser sprocket assembly and onto the head.
19. Install a new camshaft phaser bolt finger tight.

✺✺ WARNING

Do not remove the timing chain wedge tool at any time during assembly. If the special tool is removed or out of placement, the engine front cover must be removed and the engine must be retimed.

✺✺ WARNING

The timing chain must be installed in its original position onto the camshaft phaser sprocket using the scribed marks, or damage to valves and pistons will result.

20. Verify the camshaft phaser sprocket and timing chain scribe marks are still in alignment.

✺✺ WARNING

Do not allow the roller followers to move out of position when installing the camshaft.

21. Lubricate the camshaft bearing caps with clean engine oil.
22. Position the front camshaft bearing cap.
23. Position the remaining camshaft bearing caps.
24. Install the bolts loosely.
25. Tighten the bolts in the sequence shown. Tighten to 10 Nm (89 inch lbs.).
26. Remove the special tools.
27. Rotate the crankshaft a half turn counterclockwise and position the crankshaft damper spoke at the 12 o'clock position and the timing mark indentation at the 1 o'clock position.
28. Verify correct cam position by noting the position of the number 1 cylinder intake and exhaust camshaft lobes.
29. Using the special tool, install the 3 originally removed roller followers.
30. Install the CMP sensor and the bolt.
31. Connect the CMP electrical connector.

✺✺ WARNING

Only use hand tools to install the camshaft phaser sprocket assembly or damage may occur to the camshaft or camshaft phaser unit.

✺✺ WARNING

Damage to the camshaft phaser sprocket assembly will occur if mishandled or used as a lifting or leveraging device.

32. Tighten the camshaft phaser bolt in 2 stages:
  • Stage 1: Tighten to 40 Nm (30 ft. lbs.).
  • Stage 2: Tighten an additional 90 degrees.
33. Install the right valve cover.

6.8L Engine

Left Side

See Figures 133 through 140.

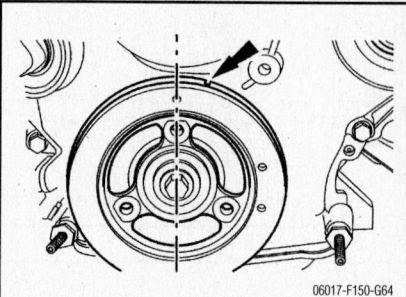

Fig. 133 Position the crankshaft damper spoke at the 12 o'clock position and the timing mark indentation at the 1 o'clock position—6.8L engine

1. Before servicing the vehicle, refer to the Precautions Section.

✺✺ WARNING

The camshaft procedure must be followed exactly or damage to the valves and pistons will result.

2. Remove the cooling fan shroud.
3. Position the crankshaft damper spoke at the 12 o'clock position and the timing mark indentation at the 1 o'clock position.
4. Remove the left valve cover.
5. Remove the 6 bolts in the sequence shown, the 3 bearing caps and the balance shaft.

➡**Keep caps in exact order as removed for reinstallation.**

✺✺ WARNING

Damage to the camshaft sprocket assembly will occur if mishandled or used as a lifting or leveraging device.

6. Loosen and back off the left camshaft bolt 1 full turn.

✺✺ CAUTION

If servicing both camshafts, do not rotate the crankshaft. Camshaft position has been established in the proper step in this procedure.

➡**If the camshaft lobes are not exactly positioned as shown, the crankshaft keyway will require one full additional rotation to 12 o'clock. Do not rotate the crankshaft if servicing both camshafts.**

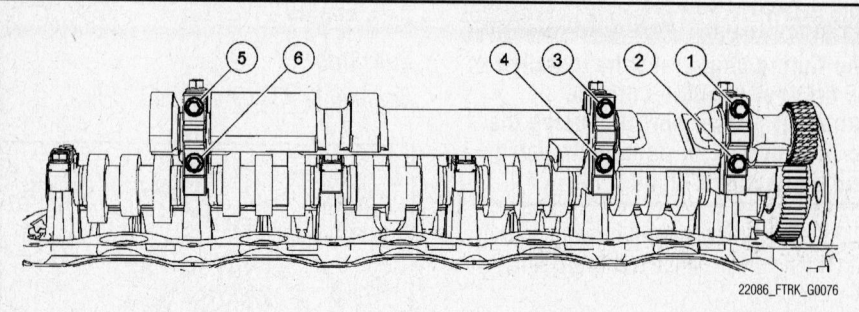

Fig. 134 Remove the 6 bolts in the sequence shown, the 3 bearing caps and the balance shaft

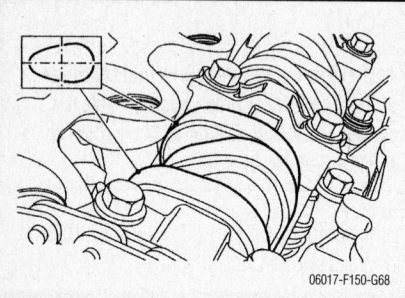

Fig. 135 The number 6 cylinder camshaft exhaust lobe must be coming up on the exhaust stroke. Verify by noting the position of the 2 intake camshaft lobes and the exhaust lobe on the number 6 cylinder—6.8L engine

7. The No. 6 cylinder camshaft exhaust lobe must be coming up on the exhaust stroke. Verify by noting the position of the 2 intake camshaft lobes and the exhaust lobe on the No. 6 cylinder.

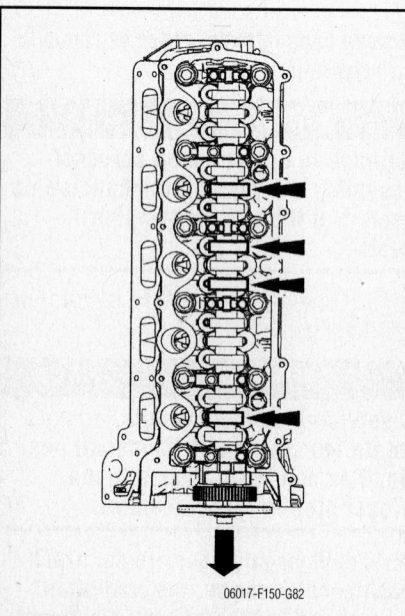

Fig. 136 Remove only these 3 roller followers at this time—6.8L engine

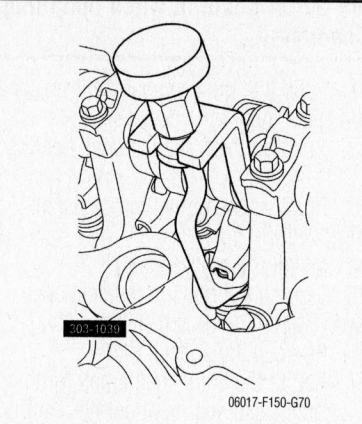

Fig. 137 Using special tool 303-1039—6.8L engine

8. Remove only the 3 roller followers shown in the illustration.

✳✳ WARNING

Do not allow the valve keepers to fall off the valve or the valve may drop into the cylinder.

➡The camshaft roller followers must be installed in their original locations. Record camshaft roller follower locations.

➡It may be necessary to push the valve down while compressing the spring.

9. Using special tool 303-1039, remove only the 3 designated roller followers from the previous step.

✳✳ WARNING

The crankshaft cannot be moved past the 6 o'clock position once set.

10. Rotate the crankshaft clockwise, as viewed from the front, positioning the crankshaft damper spoke at the 6 o'clock position and the timing mark indentation at the 7 o'clock position.

✳✳ WARNING

Engine is not freewheeling. Camshaft procedure must be followed exactly or damage to valves and pistons will result.

✳✳ WARNING

The Timing Chain Wedge tool must be installed square to the timing chain and the engine block.

➡Front cover removed for clarity.

11. Install the special tools in the left timing chain as shown.

✳✳ WARNING

Do not remove the timing chain wedge tool at any time during assembly. If the special tool is

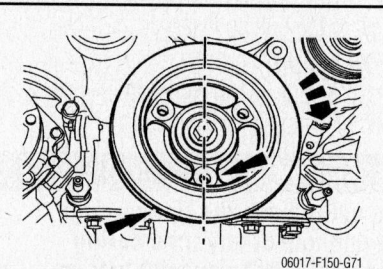

Fig. 138 Rotate the crankshaft clockwise, as viewed from the front, positioning the crankshaft damper spoke at the 6 o'clock position and the timing mark indentation at the 7 o'clock position—6.8L engine

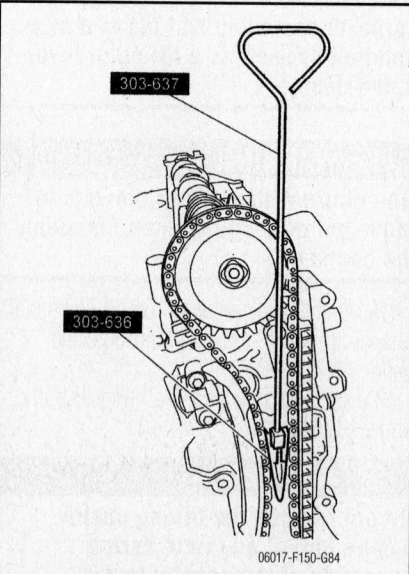

Fig. 139 The Timing Chain Wedge tool must be installed square to the timing chain and the engine block—6.8L engine

removed or out of placement, the engine front cover must be removed and the engine must be retimed.

> ✳✳ **WARNING**
>
> The timing chain must be installed in its original position onto the camshaft phaser sprocket using the scribed marks, or damage to valves and pistons will result.

12. Scribe a location mark on the timing chain and the camshaft phaser sprocket assembly.

> ✳✳ **WARNING**
>
> Remove the front thrust camshaft bearing cap straight upward from the bearing towers, or the bearing cap may be damaged from side loading.

→The camshaft bearing caps must be installed in their original locations. Record camshaft bearing cap locations.

13. Remove the bolts in the sequence shown and remove the front camshaft bearing cap and then the remaining bearing caps.

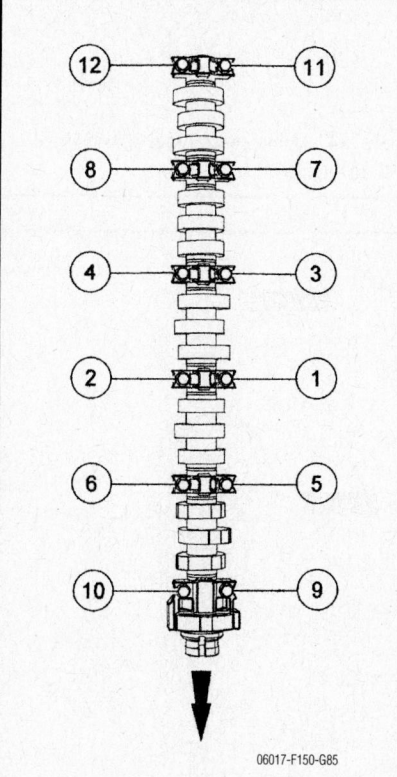

Fig. 140 Camshaft bearing cap removal/installation torque sequence—6.8L engine

06017-F150-G85

14. Clean and inspect the left camshaft bearing caps. The camshaft front thrust bearing cap contains an oil metering groove. Make sure the groove is free of foreign material.

> ✳✳ **WARNING**
>
> Damage to the camshaft phaser sprocket assembly will occur if mishandled or used as a lifting or leveraging device.

> ✳✳ **WARNING**
>
> Only use hand tools to remove the camshaft phaser sprocket bolt or damage may occur to the camshaft or camshaft phaser unit.

> ✳✳ **WARNING**
>
> Do not remove the timing chain wedge tool at any time during assembly. If the special tool is removed or out of placement, the engine front cover must be removed and the engine must be retimed.

15. Remove the bolt and withdraw the camshaft from the phaser sprocket assembly leaving the sprocket assembly in place. Discard the bolt and washer.

To install:

16. Lubricate the camshaft and camshaft journals with clean engine oil.

> ✳✳ **WARNING**
>
> Do not remove the timing chain wedge tool at any time during assembly. If the special tool is removed or out of placement, the engine front cover must be removed and the engine must be retimed.

> ✳✳ **WARNING**
>
> Damage to the camshaft phaser sprocket assembly will occur if mishandled or used as a lifting or leveraging device.

> ✳✳ **WARNING**
>
> Do not allow the roller followers to move out of position when installing the camshaft.

17. Install the camshaft into the camshaft phaser sprocket assembly and onto the head.

18. Install a new camshaft phaser bolt finger tight.

> ✳✳ **WARNING**
>
> Do not remove the timing chain wedge tool at any time during assembly. If the special tool is removed or out of placement, the engine front cover must be removed and the engine must be retimed.

> ✳✳ **WARNING**
>
> The timing chain must be installed in its original position onto the camshaft phaser sprocket using the scribed marks, or damage to valves and pistons will result. Verify the camshaft phaser sprocket and timing chain scribe marks are still in alignment.

> ✳✳ **WARNING**
>
> Do not allow the roller followers to move out of position when installing the camshaft.

19. Lubricate the camshaft bearing caps with clean engine oil.

20. Position the front camshaft bearing cap.

21. Position the remaining camshaft bearing caps.

22. Install the bolts loosely.

23. Tighten the bolts in the sequence shown. Tighten to 10 Nm (89 inch lbs.).

24. Remove the special tools.

25. Rotate the crankshaft a half turn counterclockwise and position the crankshaft damper spoke at the 12 o'clock position and the timing mark indentation at the 1 o'clock position.

26. Verify correct cam position by noting the position of the number 5 cylinder intake and exhaust camshaft lobes.

27. Using the special tool, install the 3 originally removed roller followers.

28. Install the CMP sensor and the bolt.

29. Connect the CMP electrical connector.

> ✳✳ **WARNING**
>
> Only use hand tools to install the camshaft phaser sprocket assembly or damage may occur to the camshaft or camshaft phaser unit.

> ✳✳ **WARNING**
>
> Damage to the camshaft phaser sprocket assembly will occur if mishandled or used as a lifting or leveraging device.

30. Tighten the camshaft phaser bolt in 2 stages:
- Stage 1: Tighten to 40 Nm (30 ft. lbs.).
- Stage 2: Tighten an additional 90 degrees.

31. Install the left valve cover.
32. Install the cooling fan shroud.

Right Side

See Figures 141 through 147.

1. Before servicing the vehicle, refer to the Precautions Section.

> **⁂ WARNING**
>
> **The camshaft procedure must be followed exactly or damage to the valves and pistons will result.**

2. Remove the cooling fan shroud.
3. Position the crankshaft damper spoke at the 12 o'clock position and the timing mark indentation at the 1 o'clock position.
4. Remove the right valve cover.

> **⁂ WARNING**
>
> **Damage to the camshaft phaser sprocket assembly will occur if mishandled or used as a lifting or leveraging device.**

5. Loosen and back off the right camshaft phaser bolt 1 full turn.
6. Disconnect the right camshaft position (CMP) sensor electrical connector.
7. Remove the bolt and the right CMP sensor.

➡ If the camshaft lobes are not exactly positioned as shown, the crankshaft will require 1 full additional rotation to 12 o'clock.

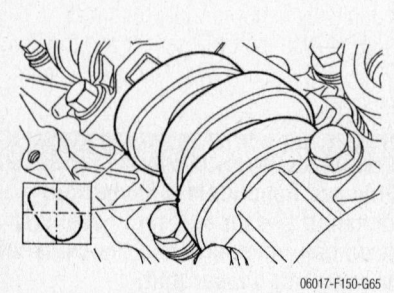

Fig. 141 The number 1 cylinder camshaft exhaust lobe must be coming up on the exhaust stroke. Verify by noting the position of the 2 intake camshaft lobes and the exhaust lobe on the number 1 cylinder—6.8L engine

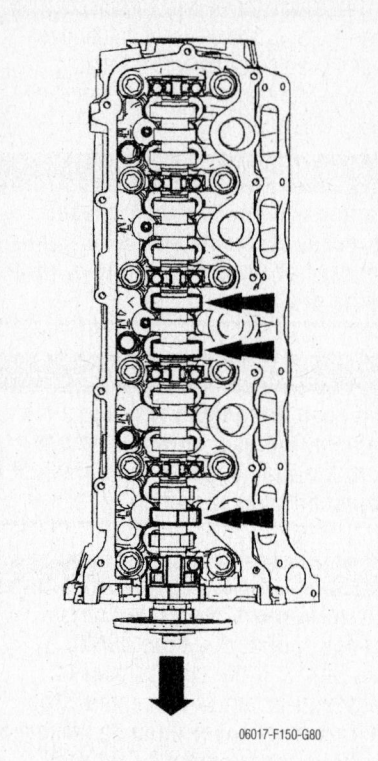

Fig. 142 Remove only these 3 roller followers at this time—6.8L engine

8. The number 1 cylinder camshaft exhaust lobe must be coming up on the exhaust stroke. Verify by noting the position of the 2 intake camshaft lobes and the exhaust lobe on the number 1 cylinder.
9. Remove only the 3 roller followers shown in the illustration.

> **⁂ WARNING**
>
> **Do not allow the valve keepers to fall off the valve or the valve may drop into the cylinder.**

➡ The camshaft roller followers must be installed in their original locations. Record camshaft roller follower locations.

➡ It may be necessary to push the valve down while compressing the spring.

10. Using special tool 303-1039, remove only the 3 designated roller followers from the previous step.

> **⁂ WARNING**
>
> **The crankshaft cannot be moved past the 6 o'clock position once set.**

11. Rotate the crankshaft clockwise, as viewed from the front, positioning the crankshaft damper spoke at the 6 o'clock

position and the timing mark indentation at the 7 o'clock position.

> **⁂ WARNING**
>
> **Engine is not freewheeling. Camshaft procedure must be followed exactly or damage to valves and pistons will result.**

> **⁂ WARNING**
>
> **The Timing Chain Wedge tool must be installed square to the timing chain and the engine block.**

➡ Front cover removed for clarity.

12. Install the special tools in the right timing chain as shown.

> **⁂ WARNING**
>
> **Do not remove the timing chain wedge tool at any time during**

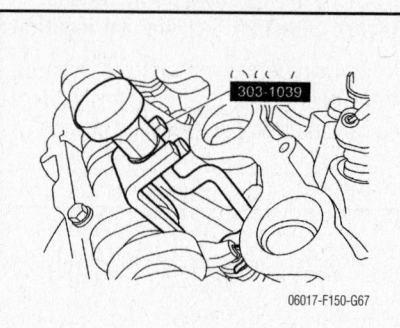

Fig. 143 Using special tool 303-1039—6.8L engine

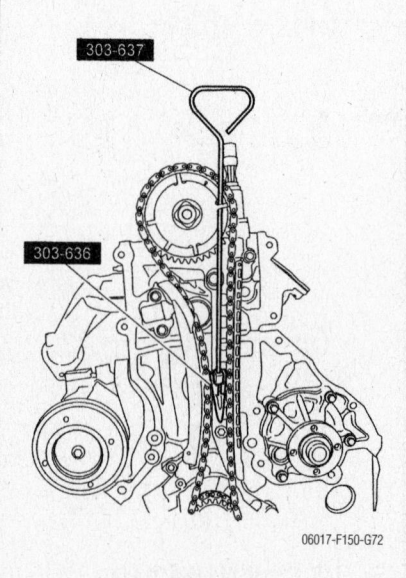

Fig. 144 Timing chain wedge tool installed—6.8L engine

assembly. If the special tool is removed or out of placement, the engine front cover must be removed and the engine must be retimed.

> ❋ **WARNING**
>
> The timing chain must be installed in its original position onto the camshaft phaser sprocket using the scribed marks, or damage to valves and pistons will result.

13. Scribe a location mark on the timing chain and the camshaft phaser sprocket assembly.

> ❋ **WARNING**
>
> Remove the front thrust camshaft bearing cap straight upward from the bearing towers, or the bearing cap may be damaged from side loading.

➡ The camshaft bearing caps must be installed in their original locations. Record camshaft bearing cap locations.

14. Remove the bolts in the sequence shown and remove the front camshaft bearing cap and then the remaining bearing caps.

15. Clean and inspect the right camshaft bearing caps. The camshaft front thrust bearing cap contains an oil metering groove. Make sure the groove is free of foreign material.

> ❋ **WARNING**
>
> Damage to the camshaft phaser sprocket assembly will occur if mishandled or used as a lifting or leveraging device.

> ❋ **WARNING**
>
> Only use hand tools to remove the camshaft phaser sprocket bolt or

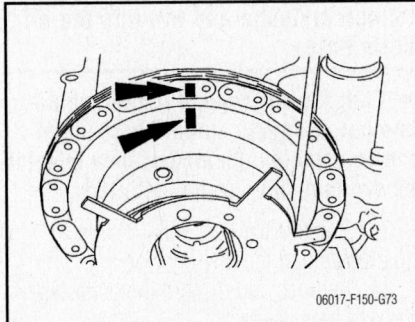

Fig. 145 Scribe a location mark on the timing chain and the camshaft phaser sprocket assembly—6.8L engine

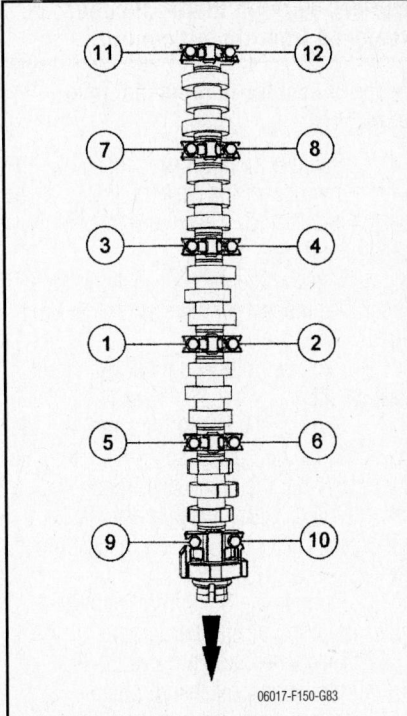

06017-F150-G83

Fig. 146 Camshaft bearing cap removal/installation sequence—6.8L engine

damage may occur to the camshaft or camshaft phaser unit.

> ❋ **WARNING**
>
> Do not remove the timing chain wedge tool at any time during assembly. If the special tool is removed or out of placement, the engine front cover must be removed and the engine must be retimed.

16. Remove the bolt and withdraw the camshaft from the phaser sprocket assembly leaving the sprocket assembly in place. Discard the bolt and washer.

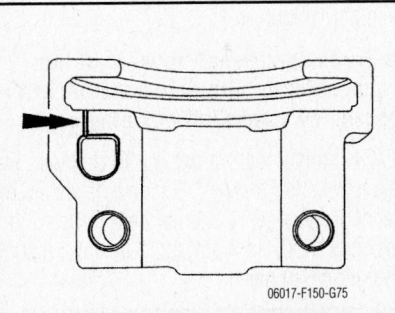

06017-F150-G75

Fig. 147 The camshaft front thrust bearing cap contains an oil metering groove—6.8L engine

To install:

17. Lubricate the camshaft and camshaft journals with clean engine oil.

> ❋ **WARNING**
>
> Do not remove the timing chain wedge tool at any time during assembly. If the special tool is removed or out of placement, the engine front cover must be removed and the engine must be retimed.

> ❋ **WARNING**
>
> Damage to the camshaft phaser sprocket assembly will occur if mishandled or used as a lifting or leveraging device.

> ❋ **WARNING**
>
> Do not allow the roller followers to move out of position when installing the camshaft.

18. Install the camshaft into the camshaft phaser sprocket assembly and onto the head.

19. Install a new camshaft phaser bolt finger tight.

> ❋ **WARNING**
>
> Do not remove the timing chain wedge tool at any time during assembly. If the special tool is removed or out of placement, the engine front cover must be removed and the engine must be retimed.

> ❋ **WARNING**
>
> The timing chain must be installed in its original position onto the camshaft phaser sprocket using the scribed marks, or damage to valves and pistons will result.

20. Verify the camshaft phaser sprocket and timing chain scribe marks are still in alignment.

> ❋ **WARNING**
>
> Do not allow the roller followers to move out of position when installing the camshaft.

21. Lubricate the camshaft bearing caps with clean engine oil.

22. Position the front camshaft bearing cap.

23. Position the remaining camshaft bearing caps.

24. Install the bolts loosely.

25. Tighten the bolts in the sequence shown. Tighten to 10 Nm (89 inch lbs.).

26. Remove the special tools.

27. Rotate the crankshaft a half turn counterclockwise and position the crankshaft damper spoke at the 12 o'clock position and the timing mark indentation at the 1 o'clock position.

28. Verify correct cam position by noting the position of the number 1 cylinder intake and exhaust camshaft lobes.

29. Using the special tool, install the 3 originally removed roller followers.

30. Install the CMP sensor and the bolt.

31. Connect the CMP electrical connector.

☀ WARNING

Only use hand tools to install the camshaft phaser sprocket assembly or damage may occur to the camshaft or camshaft phaser unit.

☀ WARNING

Damage to the camshaft phaser sprocket assembly will occur if mishandled or used as a lifting or leveraging device.

32. Tighten the camshaft phaser bolt in 2 stages:
- Stage 1: Tighten to 40 Nm (30 ft. lbs.).
- Stage 2: Tighten an additional 90 degrees.

33. Install the right valve cover.

6.0L Diesel Engine

See Figure 148.

1. Before servicing the vehicle, refer to the Precautions Section.

2. Mount the engine on an engine stand.

3. Remove the serpentine belt idler.

4. Remove the serpentine belt tensioner.

5. Remove and discard the O-rings from the oil filter base.

6. Remove the exhaust gas recirculation (EGR) cooler coolant supply port cover. Clean and inspect the gaskets. Install new gaskets if necessary. Clean and inspect the sealing surfaces.

☀ WARNING

In the event of a catastrophic engine failure, always install a new oil cooler cover assembly (with oil cooler). Foreign material cannot be removed from the oil cooler.

➡ **The oil cooler is replaced as an assembly.**

7. Remove the oil cooler assembly. Clean and inspect the gaskets. Install a new gasket if necessary. Clean and inspect the sealing surfaces.

8. Remove the oil pump inlet strainer. Clean and inspect for tears and other damage.

9. Remove bolts and the turbocharger heat shield.

10. Remove the high-pressure oil pump cover. Use a thin gasket scraper to separate the cover from the crankcase. Clean and inspect the gaskets. Install a new gasket if necessary. Clean and inspect the sealing surfaces.

11. Remove the bolts from the high-pressure oil pump discharge pipe.

12. Disconnect and remove the high-pressure oil pump discharge pipe.

13. Remove and discard the D-ring seal.

14. Remove and discard the high-pressure pump O-ring seal.

15. Remove the bolts and the high-pressure oil pump.

16. Remove and discard the lower O-ring seal.

17. Remove the glow plug buss bar.

18. Remove the eight glow plugs.

➡ **Mark the location of the stud bolts.**

19. Remove the valve covers. Clean and inspect the gaskets. Install a new gasket if necessary. Clean and inspect the sealing surfaces.

20. Remove the bolts and the coolant pump pulley.

21. Remove the coolant pump.

22. If equipped, remove the bolts and the dual alternator pulley.

23. Prior to removing the crankshaft damper, check the crankshaft vibration damper runout.

➡ **Pry the crankshaft forward at the same point to eliminate possible error caused by crankshaft end play.**

24. Rotate the crankshaft 90 degrees. Pry the crankshaft forward. Record the measurement. Repeat every 90 degrees. If the runout exceeds 0.002 inch, install a new crankshaft vibration damper.

☀ WARNING

To prevent engine damage, you must always replace all four bolts when installing the vibration damper.

☀ CAUTION

To avoid personal injury, support the vibration damper during mounting bolt removal. The damper can slide off the nose of the crankshaft very easily.

25. Remove the bolts and the crankcase vibration damper. Discard the bolts.

26. Punch two holes in the seal. Remove the crankshaft seal with a slidehammer.

➡ **Production engine will not have a wear sleeve. If equipped, remove the crankshaft damper wear sleeve.**

27. Remove the oil pump body. Remove and discard the O-ring seal.

➡ **Mark the front of each drive rotor for correct reassembly orientation.**

28. Remove the inner and outer oil pump drive rotors.

29. Remove the engine front cover. Clean and inspect the gaskets. Install new gaskets if necessary. Clean and inspect the sealing surfaces.

30. Using a quick-disconnect tool, disconnect the high-pressure oil rail supply line at the high-pressure oil rail.

31. Remove the bolts and the high pressure oil rail. Disconnect and remove the high-pressure oil supply line.

☀ WARNING

Do not attempt to put battery voltage to the fuel injector or damage to the fuel injector will occur.

32. Using a 19 mm socket, push the fuel injector electrical connector out of the rocker arm carrier.

☀ WARNING

To prevent engine damage, do not use air tools to remove the fuel injectors. The clip that extracts the injector can dislodge and fall into the oil drain hole.

➡ **If engine oil is found in the engine coolant or engine coolant is found in the combustion chambers, new injector sleeve may need to be installed.**

33. Remove the bolt, the fuel injector hold down and the fuel injector.

34. Remove and discard the crankcase-to-head tube assembly.

35. Remove the inner head bolts from both cylinder heads.

36. Remove the 16 bolts and the rocker arm assemblies.

37. Remove the rocker arm carrier from the cylinder head. Clean and inspect the gaskets. Install new gaskets if necessary. Clean and inspect the sealing surfaces.

➡**Mark the location of the valve bridges before removing.**

38. Remove the 16 valve bridges.

✳✳ WARNING

To prevent engine damage, keep the push rods in the order in which they were removed. Install all push rods back in their original positions.

39. Mark the location and remove the 16 push rods.

40. Remove the 10 outer head bolts.

41. Remove the cylinder heads.

42. Remove and discard the cylinder head gasket.

43. Remove and discard the four cylinder head dowel sleeves.

44. Remove the bolts from the rear engine tube assembly.

45. Remove the bolt and the rear engine tube assembly.

✳ WARNING

To prevent engine damage, keep the cam followers in the order in which they were removed. Install all cam followers back in their original positions.

46. Remove the bolts and the roller follower guides. Remove the hydraulic cam followers.

47. Install the special tool and measure the camshaft gear backlash. Install a new camshaft gear if backlash is not within specification.

48. Install a dial indicator and measure the camshaft end play. Install a new camshaft thrust plate if end play is not within 0.002–0.008 inch.

49. Remove the bolt and the camshaft position (CMP) sensor.

✳ WARNING

Do not knick or scratch the camshaft bearings with the camshaft lobes or engine damage will occur.

50. Remove the thrust plate mounting bolts and remove the camshaft and gear.

To install:

➡**Check alignment of the oil holes after installing the bearings.**

51. If removed, install the camshaft bearings.

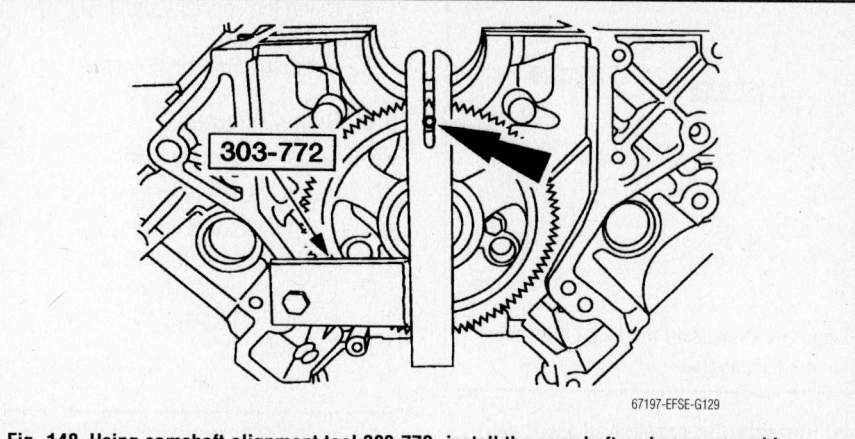

Fig. 148 Using camshaft alignment tool 303-772, install the camshaft and gear assembly

✳✳ WARNING

Do not nick or scratch the camshaft bearings with the camshaft lobes or engine damage can occur.

➡**Apply clean engine oil to the camshaft prior to installing.**

52. Using camshaft alignment tool 303-772, install the camshaft and gear assembly. Aligning it with the crankshaft. Install the thrust plate mounting bolts. Torque to 23 ft. lbs. (31 Nm).

53. The remainder of installation is the reverse of removal.

CRANKSHAFT FRONT SEAL

REMOVAL & INSTALLATION

4.2L Engine

See Figures 149 through 151.

Fig. 150 Crankshaft front seal removal— 4.2L engine

1. Remove the crankshaft pulley.

2. Using the special tool, remove the crankshaft front seal. Discard the crankshaft front seal.

To install:

3. Inspect the crankshaft damper and the engine front cover for damage that may cause the crankshaft front seal to fail.

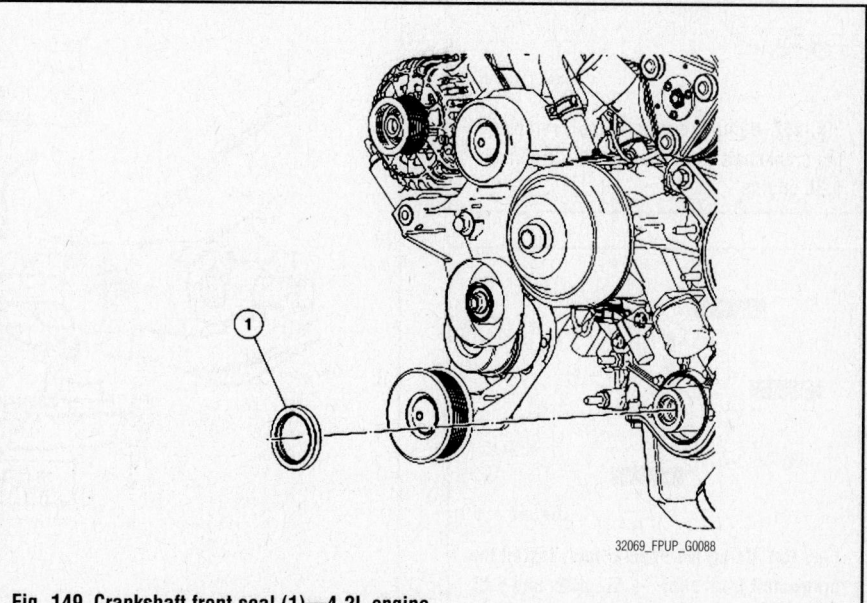

Fig. 149 Crankshaft front seal (1)—4.2L engine

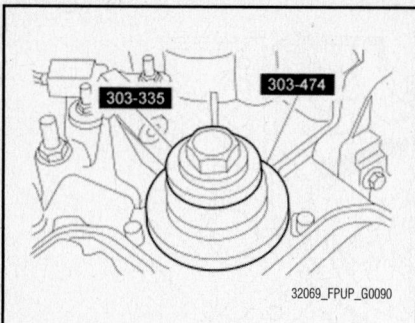

Fig. 151 Crankshaft front seal installation—4.2L engine

➡**Lubricate the crankshaft front seal with clean engine oil.**

4. Using the special tools, install the crankshaft front seal.

5. Install the crankshaft pulley. For additional information, refer to "Crankshaft Damper" in this section.

4.6L, 5.4L and 6.8L Engines

See Figures 152 and 153.

1. Remove the crankshaft pulley.
2. Using the special tool, remove the crankshaft front seal.

To install:

3. Lubricate the engine front cover and the crankshaft front seal inner lip with clean engine oil.

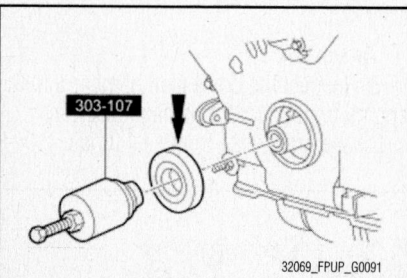

Fig. 152 Using the special tool, remove the crankshaft front seal—4.6L, 5.4L and 6.8L engine

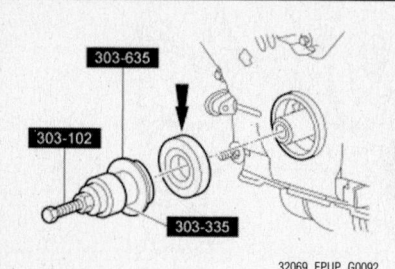

Fig. 153 Using the special tool, install the crankshaft front seal—4.6L, 5.4L and 6.8L engine

4. Using the special tools, install the crankshaft front seal.

5. Install the crankshaft pulley.

6.0L Diesel Engine

See Figures 154 through 156.

1. Remove the crankshaft vibration damper. For additional information, refer to Crankshaft Damper in this section.
2. Punch two holes in the seal.
3. Using the special tool, remove the crankshaft seal.

➡**Production engines will not have a wear sleeve.**

4. If equipped, remove the crankshaft seal wear sleeve.

To install:

5. Thoroughly clean the crankshaft front seal mounting surface.
6. Apply High Strength Threadlocker to the outer circumference of the leading edge of the crankshaft.

➡**New seal and wear sleeve must not be separated.**

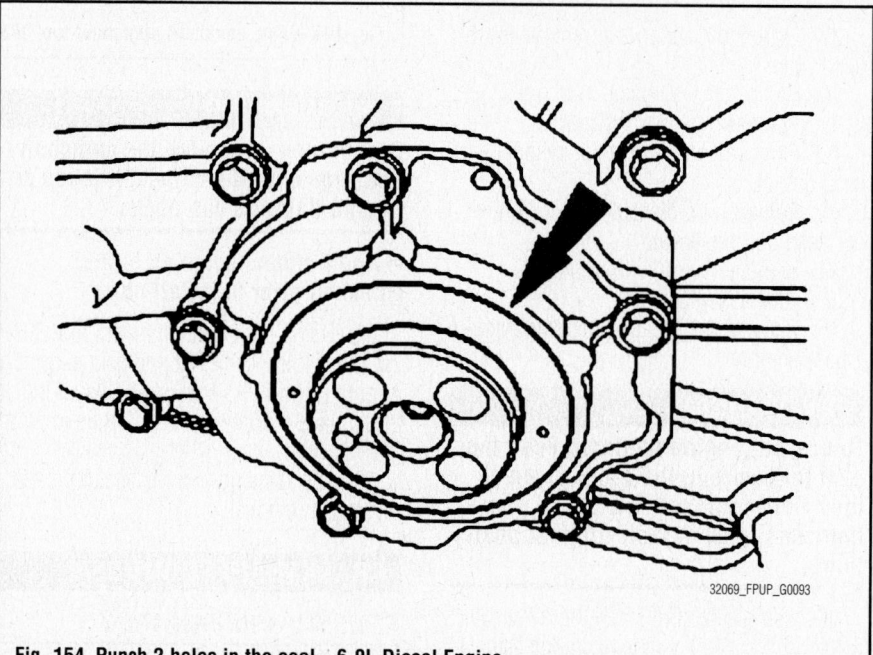

Fig. 154 Punch 2 holes in the seal—6.0L Diesel Engine

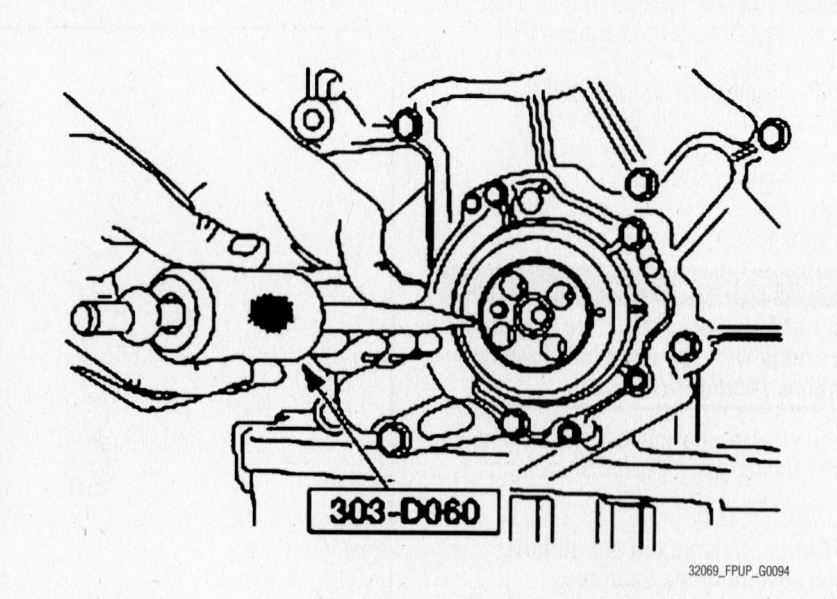

Fig. 155 Using the special tool, remove the crankshaft seal—6.0L Diesel Engine

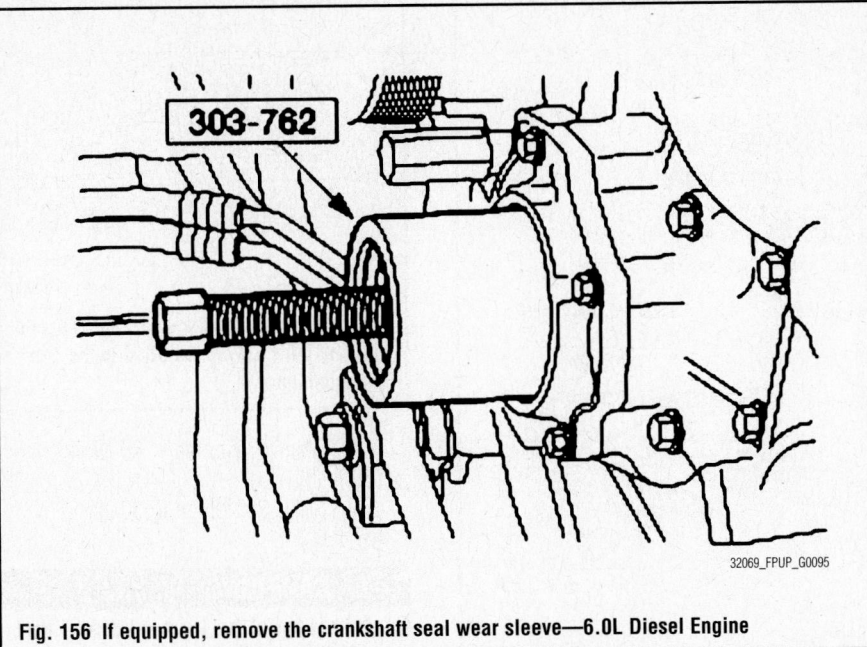

Fig. 156 If equipped, remove the crankshaft seal wear sleeve—6.0L Diesel Engine

7. Using the special tool, install the oil seal and wear sleeve assembly.

8. Install the crankshaft damper. For additional information, refer to Crankshaft Damper in this section.

CYLINDER HEAD

REMOVAL & INSTALLATION

4.2L Engine

See Figures 157 through 160.

> **✳✳ CAUTION**
>
> **Fuel injection systems remain under pressure, even after the engine has been turned OFF. The fuel system pressure must be relieved before disconnecting any fuel lines. Failure to do so may result in fire and/or personal injury.**

1. Before servicing the vehicle, refer to the Precautions Section.

> **✳✳ CAUTION**
>
> **During engine repair procedures, cleanliness is extremely important. Any foreign material, including any material created while cleaning gasket surfaces, that enters the oil passages, coolant passages or the oil pan can cause engine failure.**

Both cylinder heads

2. With the vehicle in NEUTRAL, position it on a hoist.

3. Remove the lower intake manifold.

4. Rotate the accessory drive belt tensioner counterclockwise and remove the accessory drive belt.

RH cylinder head

5. Remove the bolt and the upper idler pulley.

6. Remove the 4 bolts and position the generator bracket, the generator, the accessory drive belt tensioner and the accessory drive belt idler pulley aside as an assembly.

7. Remove the bolt and position the radio interference capacitor aside.

8. Remove the RH exhaust manifold.

9. Detach the heated oxygen sensor (HO2S) electrical connector retainer from the rear of the RH cylinder head. Remove the bolt and detach the ground wire.

10. Remove the push rods from the RH cylinder head.

LH cylinder head

11. If equipped, remove the A/C compressor.

12. Remove the nuts for the A/C compressor and power steering bracket brace.

13. Remove the A/C compressor mounting and power steering bracket brace upper bolt. Loosen the lower bolt and position it forward until it contacts the power steering pulley. Position the A/C compressor and power steering bracket brace aside.

14. Loosen the remaining bolt in the A/C compressor and power steering bracket. Position it forward until it contacts the power steering pulley and position the A/C compressor and power steering bracket aside.

15. Remove the LH exhaust manifold.

16. Disconnect the KS and CHT sensor electrical connectors. Detach the HO2S electrical connector retainer from the rear of the LH cylinder head.

17. Remove the push rods from the LH cylinder head.

Both cylinder heads

18. Remove the 2 cylinder block coolant drain plugs.

19. Remove and discard the 4 short and 4 long cylinder head bolts.

20. Remove the cylinder head and the gasket. Discard the gasket.

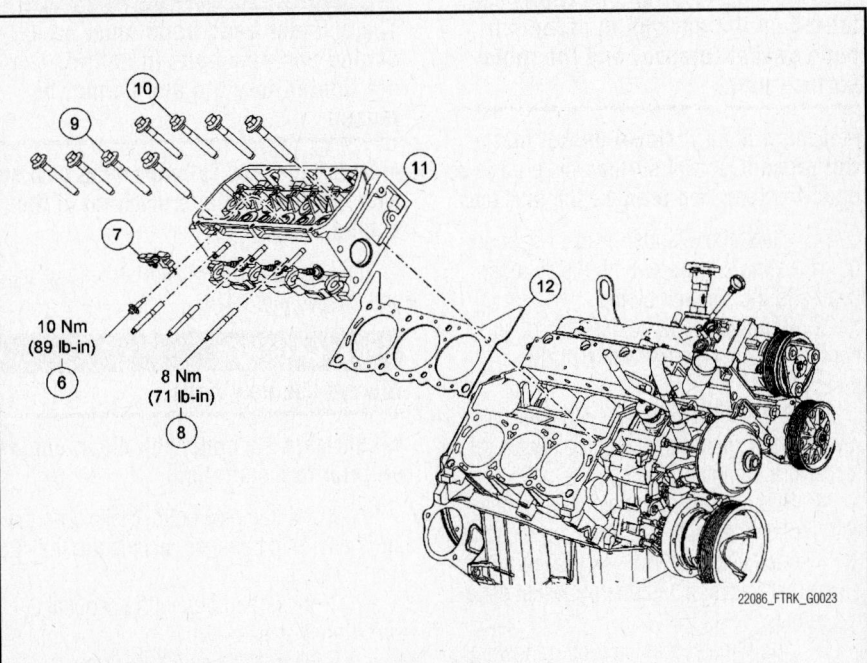

Fig. 157 Removing the RH cylinder head—4.2L engine

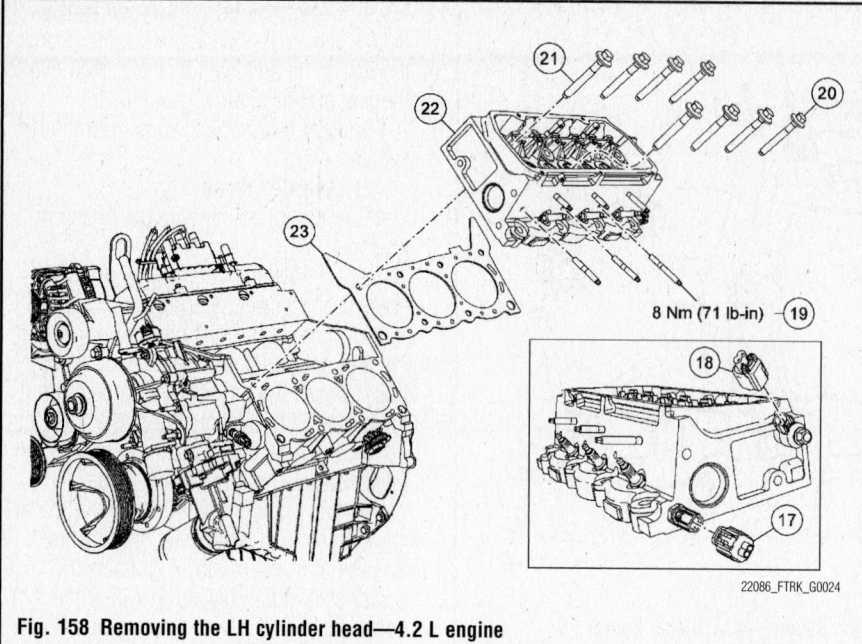

Fig. 158 Removing the LH cylinder head—4.2 L engine

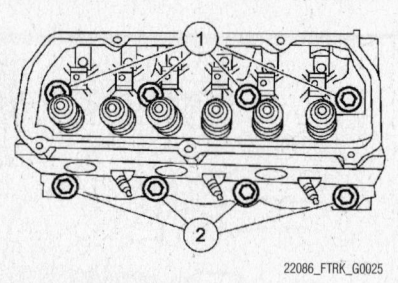

Fig. 159 Make sure the short bolts (1) and the long bolts (2) are installed in the correct locations

To install:

> ❋❋ **CAUTION**
>
> Do not use metal scrapers, wire brushes, power abrasive discs or other abrasive means to clean the sealing surfaces. These tools cause scratches and gouges that make leak paths. Use a plastic scraping tool to remove all traces of the head gasket.

> ❋❋ **CAUTION**
>
> Observe all warnings or cautions and follow all application directions contained on the packaging of the silicone gasket remover and the metal surface prep.

➥If there is no residual gasket material present, metal surface prep can be used to clean and prepare the surfaces.

21. Clean the cylinder head-to-cylinder block mating surface of both the cylinder head and the cylinder block.

22. Remove any large deposits of silicone or gasket material with a plastic scraper.

23. Apply silicone gasket remover, following package directions and allow to set for several minutes.

24. Remove the silicone gasket remover with a plastic scraper. A second application of silicone gasket remover may be required if residual traces of silicone or gasket material remain.

25. Apply metal surface prep, following package directions, to remove any traces of

oil or coolant and to prepare the surfaces to bond with the new gasket. Do not attempt to make the metal shiny. Some staining of the metal surfaces is normal.

26. Inspect the cylinder head for distortion.

> ❋❋ **CAUTION**
>
> The use of sealing aids (aviation cement, copper spray and glue) is not permitted. The gasket must be installed dry.

> ❋❋ **CAUTION**
>
> The cylinder head bolts must be discarded and new bolts installed. They are tighten-to-yield and cannot be reused.

➥Install the new cylinder head gaskets with the small hole to the front of the engine.

27. Position a new cylinder head gasket and the cylinder head.

> ❋❋ **CAUTION**
>
> Always use new bolts.

➥Lubricate the bolts with clean engine oil prior to installation.

28. Install the new bolts. Make sure the short and long bolts are installed in the correct locations.

29. Tighten the bolts in the sequence shown in 3 stages:
   a. Stage 1: Tighten to 20 Nm (15 lb-ft).

   b. Stage 2: Tighten to 40 Nm (30 lb-ft).
   c. Stage 3: Tighten to 50 Nm (37 lb-ft).

> ❋❋ **CAUTION**
>
> Each bolt must be loosened and the final tightening carried out prior to working on the next bolt in the sequence. Do not loosen all of the bolts at one time.

30. Carry out the following final tightening process on each bolt in the sequence shown:

   Long bolts:
   a. Loosen and back out 3 turns.
   b. Tighten to 45 Nm (33 lb-ft).
   c. Tighten an additional 180 degrees.
   d. Continue on to the next bolt in the sequence.

   Short bolts
   a. Loosen and back out 3 turns.
   b. Tighten to 25 Nm (18 lb-ft).

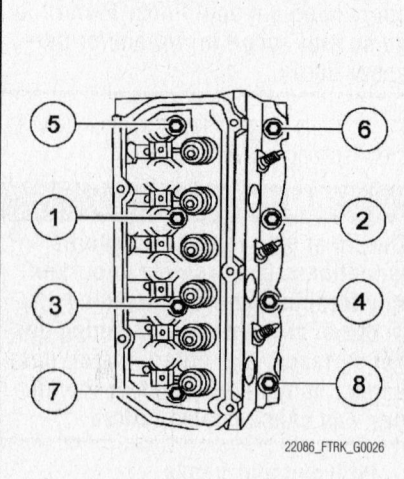

Fig. 160 Cylinder head bolt tightening sequence—4.2L engine

c. Tighten an additional 180 degrees.

d. Continue on to the next bolt in the sequence.

31. Apply thread sealant to the drain plug threads and install the 2 cylinder block coolant drain plugs. Tighten to 32 Nm (24 lb-ft).

LH cylinder head

32. Install the push rods in the LH cylinder head.

33. Connect the KS and CHT electrical connectors. Attach the HO2S electrical connector to the rear of the LH cylinder head.

34. Install the LH exhaust manifold.

35. Position back the A/C compressor and power steering bracket and loosely install the bolt.

36. Position back the A/C compressor and power steering bracket brace and install the 2 bolts. Tighten the 3 bolts. Tighten to 48 Nm (35 lb-ft).

37. Install the nuts for the A/C compressor and power steering bracket brace. Tighten to 25 Nm (18 lb-ft).

38. Install the A/C compressor.

RH cylinder head

39. Install the push rods in the RH cylinder head.

40. Attach the HO2S electrical connector retainer to the rear of the RH cylinder head. Position the ground wire and install the bolt. Tighten to 89 inch lbs. (10 Nm).

41. Install the RH exhaust manifold.

42. Position the radio interference capacitor and install the bolt. Tighten to 89 inch lbs. (10 Nm).

43. Position the generator bracket, the generator, the accessory drive belt tensioner and the accessory drive belt idler pulley as an assembly and install the 3 bolts. Tighten to 48 Nm (35 lb-ft).

44. Position the upper idler pulley and install the bolt. Tighten the bolt to 55 Nm (41 lb-ft).

Both cylinder heads

45. Rotate the accessory drive belt tensioner counterclockwise and install the accessory drive belt.

46. Install the lower intake manifold.

4.6L Engine

See Figures 161 through 182.

1. Before servicing the vehicle, refer to the Precautions Section.

2. Remove the engine. See "Engine Assembly" in this section.

3. Remove the bolts and the flexplate or the flywheel.

4. Install the engine onto a suitable engine stand.

5. Remove the 3 bolts and the RH engine support insulator.

6. Remove the cylinder block drain plugs and drain the coolant into a suitable container. Reinstall the cylinder block drain plugs.

7. Remove or disconnect the following:

- Engine oil pressure (EOP) sensor electrical connector
- Knock sensor (KS) electrical connector and the wiring harness pin-type retainer
- Camshaft position (CMP) sensor electrical connector
- Crankshaft position (CKP) sensor electrical connector
- Upper radiator hose bracket.
- LH radio ignition interference capacitor and cylinder head temperature (CHT) sensor electrical connectors
- RH radio ignition interference capacitor electrical connector
- Engine wiring harness retainers from the valve cover studs and remove the electrical harness from the engine assembly
- 2 radio interference capacitors
- CMP sensor and the CKP sensor
- Valve covers
- Accessory drive belt tensioner

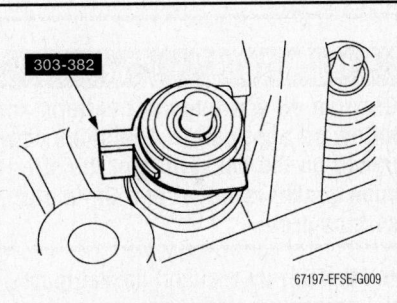

Fig. 161 Install the special tool between the valve spring coils to prevent valve stem seal damage

Fig. 162 Using the special tool, compress the valve springs and remove the camshaft roller followers

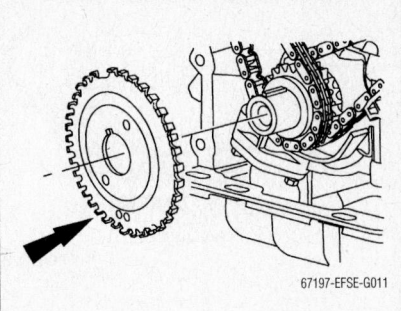

Fig. 163 Remove the crankshaft sensor ring from the crankshaft

- Crankshaft pulley bolt and washer (discard the bolt)
- Crankshaft pulley
- Crankshaft front seal
- 4 front oil pan bolts

8. Remove the engine front cover bolts engine and front cover from the front cover to cylinder.

9. Remove the 8 spark plugs.

10. Install the special tool between the valve spring coils to prevent valve stem seal damage.

11. The camshaft roller followers must be reinstalled in their original locations. Record the camshaft roller follower locations.

➡ Position the cam lobe away from the camshaft roller follower prior to removing each camshaft roller follower.

12. Using the special tool, compress the valve springs and remove the camshaft roller followers.

13. Repeat the previous steps for each of the roller followers.

14. Remove the crankshaft sensor ring from the crankshaft.

15. Rotate the crankshaft until the timing mark on the RH camshaft sprocket is approximately at the 11 o'clock position and the timing mark on the LH camshaft sprocket is approximately at the 12 o'clock position.

✳✳ CAUTION

If one or both of the tensioner mounting bolts are loosened or removed, the tensioner-sealing bead must be inspected for seal integrity. If cracks, tears, separation from the tensioner body or permanent compression of the seal bead is observed, install a new tensioner.

16. Remove the timing chain tensioning system from both timing chains.

17. Remove the bolts and the timing chain tensioners.

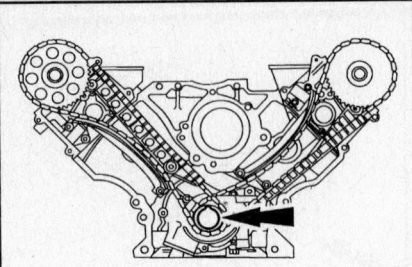

67197-EFSE-G012

Fig. 164 Rotate the crankshaft until the timing mark on the RH camshaft sprocket is approximately at the 11 o'clock position and the timing mark on the LH camshaft sprocket is approximately at the 12 o'clock position

18. Remove the timing chain tensioner arms.

19. Remove the timing chains and crankshaft sprocket.

20. Remove the timing chain guides:

    a. Remove the bolts.

    b. Remove the LH timing chain guide.

    c. Remove the bolts.

    d. Remove the RH timing chain guide.

LH cylinder head

21. Remove the LH exhaust manifold.

22. Remove the bolt and the oil level indicator tube.

RH cylinder head

23. Remove the RH exhaust manifold.

24. Disconnect the coolant hoses from the heater outlet tube and studs.

25. Remove the heater outlet tube and discard the O-ring seal.

All cylinder heads

26. Install the special lifting handles on both ends of the cylinder head being serviced.

✳✳ CAUTION

The cylinder head must be cool before removing it from the engine. Cylinder head warpage can result if a warm or hot cylinder head is removed.

✳✳ CAUTION

Place clean shop towels over exposed engine cavities. Carefully remove the towels so foreign material is not dropped into the engine.

✳✳ CAUTION

The cylinder head bolts must be discarded and new bolts must be installed. They are tighten-to-yield designed and cannot be reused.

✳✳ CAUTION

Do not use metal scrapers, wire brushes, power abrasive discs or other abrasive means to clean the sealing surfaces. These tools cause scratches and gouges that make leak paths. Use a plastic scraping tool to remove all traces of the head gasket.

✳✳ CAUTION

Aluminum surfaces are soft and can be scratched easily. Never place the cylinder head gasket surface, unprotected, on a bench surface.

27. Remove the bolts and the cylinder head. Discard the gasket and bolts.

✳✳ CAUTION

Do not use metal scrapers, wire brushes, power abrasive discs or other abrasive means to clean the sealing surfaces. These tools cause scratches and gouges that make leak paths. Use a plastic scraping tool to remove all traces of the head gasket.

✳✳ CAUTION

Observe all warnings or cautions and follow all application directions contained on the packaging of the silicone gasket remover and the metal surface prep.

➡ If there is no residual gasket material present, metal surface prep can be used to clean and prepare the surfaces.

28. Clean the cylinder head-to-cylinder block mating surfaces of both the cylinder head and the cylinder block.

29. Remove any large deposits of silicone or gasket material with a plastic scraper.

30. Apply silicone gasket remover, following package directions, and allow to set for several minutes.

31. Remove the silicone gasket remover with a plastic scraper. A second application of silicone gasket remover may be required if residual traces of silicone or gasket material remain.

32. Apply metal surface prep, following package directions, to remove any remaining traces of oil or coolant and to prepare the surfaces to bond with the new gasket. Do not attempt to make the metal shiny. Some staining of the metal surfaces is normal.

➡ Make sure all cylinder head surfaces are clear of any gasket material, RTV, oil and coolant. The cylinder head surface must be clean and dry before running a flatness check.

➡ Use a straightedge that is calibrated by the manufacturer to be flat with 0.005 mm (0.0002 in) per running foot length. For example, if the straightedge is 61 cm (24 in) long, the machine edge must be flat with 0.010 mm (0.0004 in) from end to end.

33. Support the cylinder head on a bench with the head gasket side up. Inspect all areas of the deck face with a straightedge, paying particular attention to the oil pressure feed area. The cylinder head must not have depressions deeper than 0.0254 mm (0.001 in) across a 38.1 mm (1.5 in) square area, or scratches more than 0.0254 mm (0.001 in).

To install:
All cylinder heads

✳✳ WARNING

Make sure all coolant residue and foreign material are cleaned from the block surface and cylinder bore.

✳✳ WARNING

The use of sealing aids. The gasket must be installed dry.

✳✳ WARNING

The cylinder head bolts must be discarded and new bolts installed. They are tighten-to-yield designed and cannot be reused.

➡ Do not turn the crankshaft until instructed to do so.

34. Using the lifting tools, position the cylinder head gaskets and cylinder heads over the dowels and install the cylinder head bolts loosely.

35. Tighten the bolts in the sequence shown.

    a. Stage 1: Tighten to 40 Nm (30 ft. lbs.).

    b. Stage 2: Tighten an additional 90 degrees.

    c. Stage 3: Tighten an additional 90 degrees.

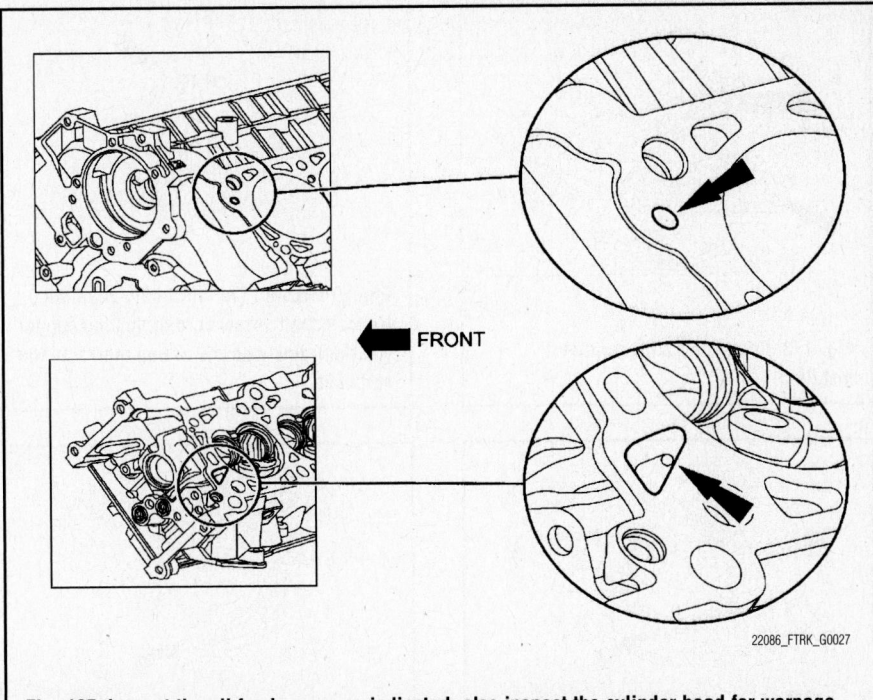

Fig. 165 Inspect the oil feed areas, as indicated; also inspect the cylinder head for warpage

All cylinder heads

❊❊ WARNING

Timing chain procedures must be followed exactly or damage to valves and pistons will result.

36. Compress the tensioner plunger, using a vise.
37. Install a retaining clip on the tensioner to hold the plunger in during installation.

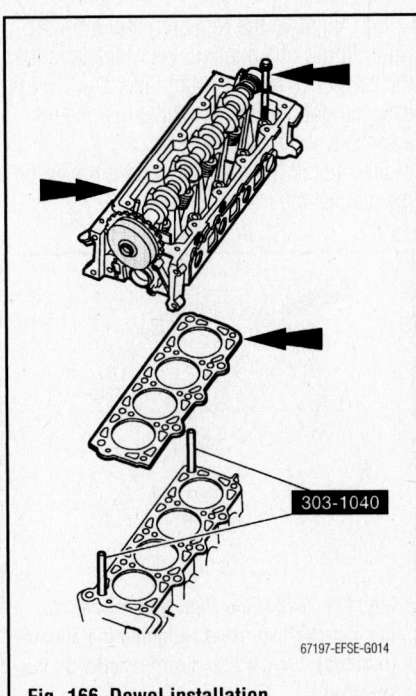

Fig. 166 Dowel installation

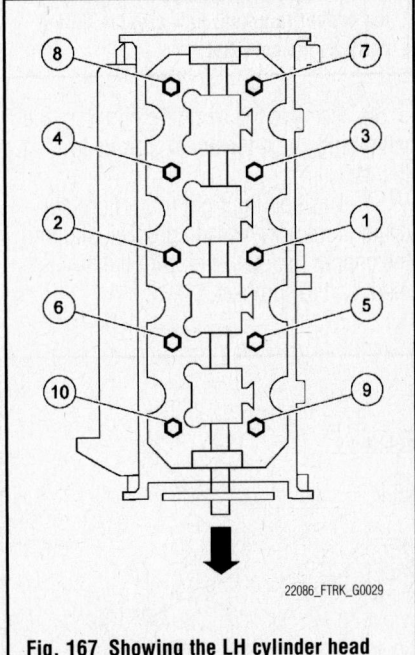

Fig. 167 Showing the LH cylinder head bolt tightening sequence

38. Remove the tensioner from the vise. If the copper links are not visible, mark one link on one end and one link on the other end, and use as timing marks.
39. Install the crankshaft sprocket, making sure the flange faces forward.
40. Position the left timing chain guide.
41. Install and tighten the left bolts.
42. Position the right timing chain guide.

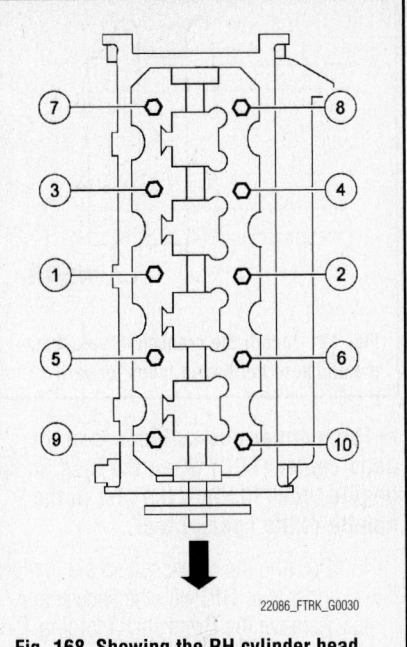

Fig. 168 Showing the RH cylinder head bolt tightening sequence

43. Install and tighten the right bolts.
44. Rotate the right camshaft sprocket until the timing mark is approximately at the 11 o'clock position. Rotate the left camshaft sprocket until the timing mark is approximately at the 12 o'clock position.

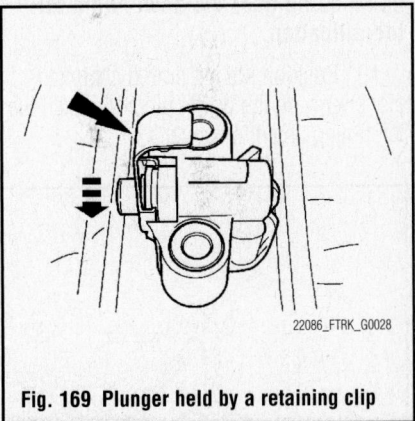

Fig. 169 Plunger held by a retaining clip

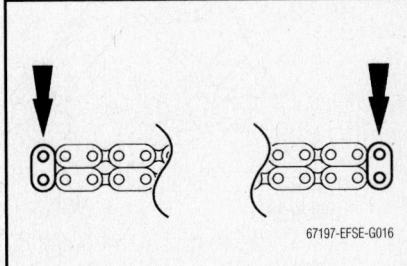

Fig. 170 If the copper links are not visible, mark one link on one end and one link on the other end, and use as timing marks

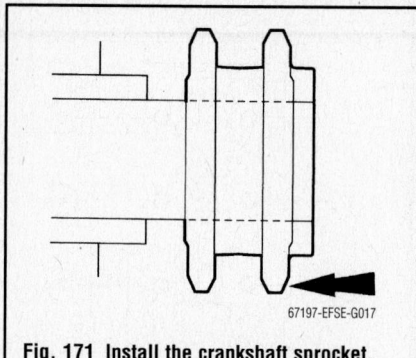

Fig. 171 Install the crankshaft sprocket, making sure the flange faces forward

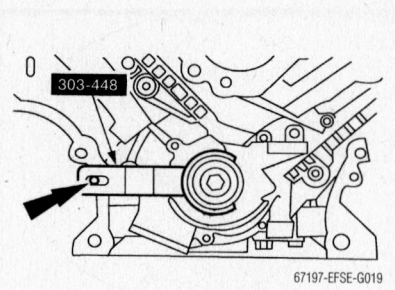

Fig. 173 Crankshaft alignment tool installed

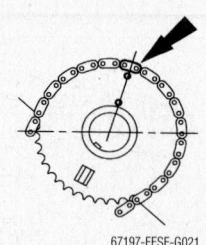

Fig. 175 Install the left timing chain on the camshaft sprocket, aligning the copper (marked) link with the timing marks on the sprocket

➡ **The number one cylinder is at top dead center (TDC) when the stud on the engine block fits into the slot in the handle of the special tool.**

45. Position the crankshaft so the number one cylinder is at TDC with the special tool.

46. Remove the Crankshaft Holding Tool.

47. Position the left (inner) timing chain on the crankshaft sprocket, aligning the copper (marked) link with the timing mark on the sprocket.

48. Install the left timing chain on the camshaft sprocket, aligning the copper (marked) link with the timing marks on the sprocket.

➡ **The left timing chain tensioner arm has a bump near the dowel hole for identification.**

49. Position the left timing chain tensioner arm on the dowel pin and install the left timing chain tensioner.

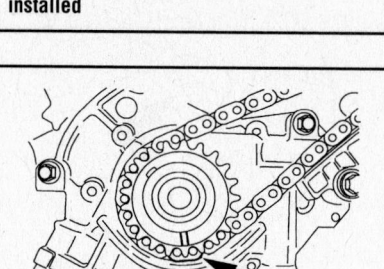

Fig. 174 Position the left (inner) timing chain on the crankshaft sprocket, aligning the copper (marked) link with the timing mark on the sprocket

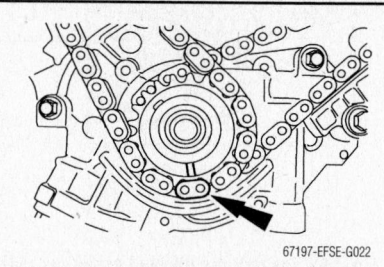

Fig. 176 Position the right (outer) timing chain on the crankshaft sprocket, aligning the copper (marked) link with the timing mark on the sprocket

50. Remove the retaining clip from the left timing chain tensioner. Torque to 18 ft. lbs. (25 Nm).

51. Position the right (outer) timing chain on the crankshaft sprocket, aligning the copper (marked) link with the timing mark on the sprocket.

52. Install the right timing chain on the camshaft sprocket, aligning the copper (marked) link with the timing marks on the sprocket.

53. Position the right timing chain tensioner arm on the dowel pin and install the right timing chain tensioner. Torque to 18 ft. lbs. (25 Nm).

54. Remove the retaining clip from the right timing chain tensioner. Make sure that the copper (marked) chain links are lined up with the dots on the crankshaft sprockets and the camshaft sprocket.

55. Install the crankshaft sensor ring on the crankshaft.

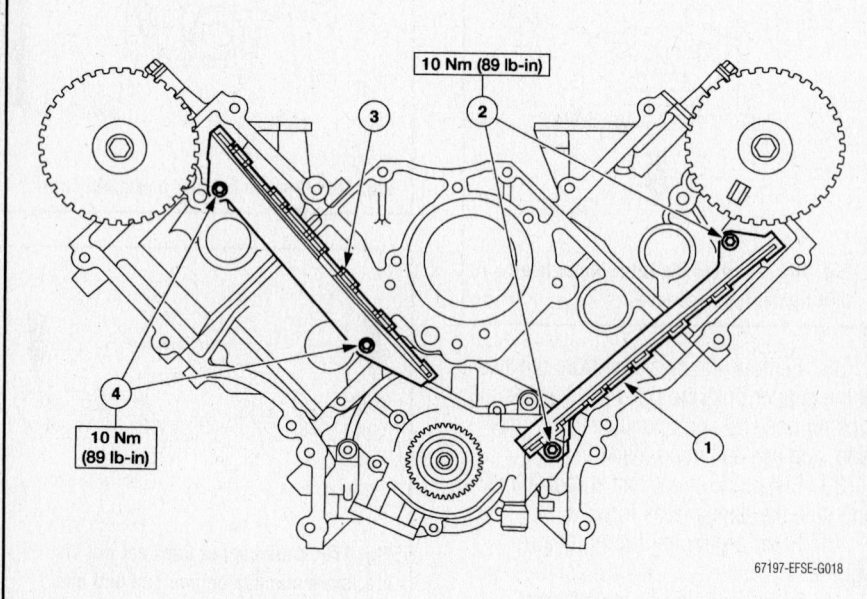

Fig. 172 Timing chain guide installation

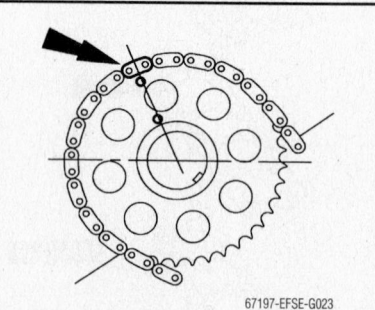

Fig. 177 Install the right timing chain on the camshaft sprocket, aligning the copper (marked) link with the timing marks on the sprocket

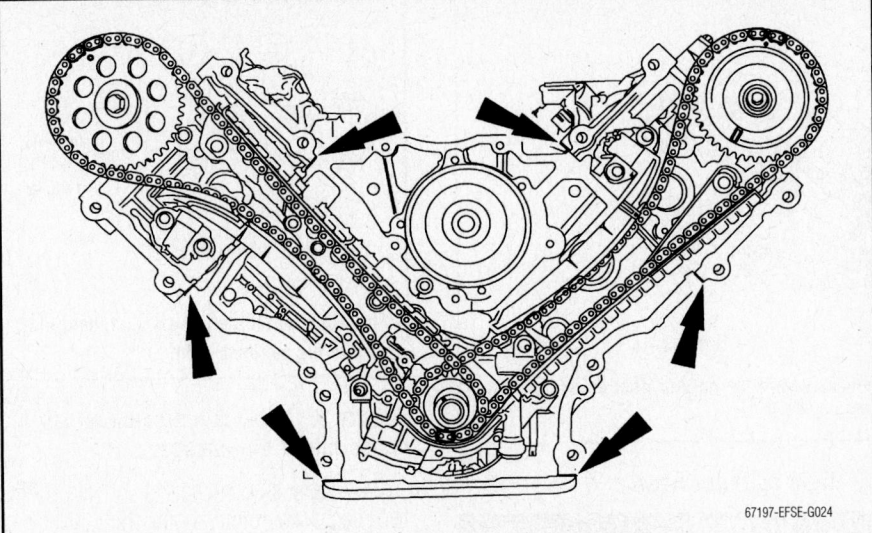

Fig. 178 Apply a bead of silicone gasket and sealant along the cylinder head-to-cylinder block surface and the oil pan-to-cylinder block surface, at the locations shown

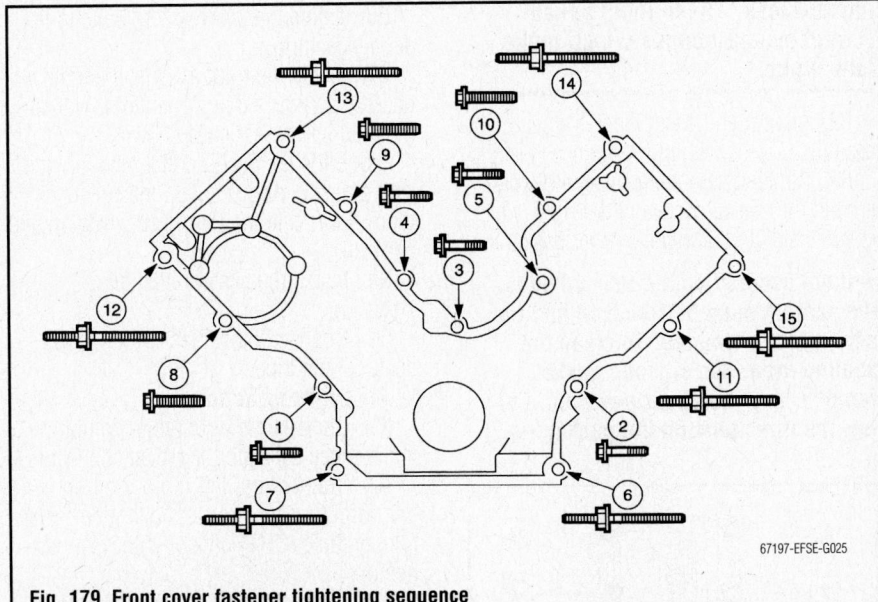

Fig. 179 Front cover fastener tightening sequence

✳✳ WARNING

Do not use metal scrapers, wire brushes, power abrasive discs or other abrasive means to clean the sealing surfaces. These tools cause scratches and gouges which make leak paths. Use a plastic scraping tool to remove all traces of old sealant.

➡If the engine front cover is not secured within four minutes, the sealant must be removed and the sealing area cleaned. To clean the sealing area, use silicone gasket remover and metal surface prep. Follow the directions on the packaging. Failure to follow this procedure can cause future oil leakage.

➡Make sure that the engine front cover gasket is in place on the engine front cover before installation.

56. Apply a bead of silicone gasket and sealant along the cylinder head-to-cylinder block surface and the oil pan-to-cylinder block surface, at the locations shown.

57. Install a new engine front cover gasket on the engine front cover. Position the engine front cover. Install the fasteners finger-tight.

58. Tighten the engine front cover fasteners in sequence in three stages.

a. Stage 1: Tighten fasteners 1 through 5 to 25 Nm (18 ft. lbs.).
b. Stage 2: Tighten fasteners 6 and 7 to 25 Nm (18 ft. lbs.).
c. Stage 3: Tighten fasteners 8 through 15 to 25 Nm (18 ft. lbs.).

59. Install the left camshaft position (CMP) sensor and the bolt.

60. Lubricate the new O-ring seal with clean engine oil prior to installation.

61. Lubricate the engine front cover and the crankshaft seal inner lip with clean engine oil. Use a driver to install the crankshaft seal into the engine front cover.

➡If not secured within four minutes, the sealant must be removed and the sealing area cleaned. To clean the sealing area, use silicone gasket remover and metal surface prep. Follow the directions on the packaging. Failure to follow this procedure can cause future oil leakage.

62. Apply silicone gasket and sealant to the Woodruff key slot on the crankshaft pulley. Use the special tool to install the crankshaft pulley.

63. Tighten the new crankshaft pulley bolt in four stages.

a. Stage 1: Tighten to 90 Nm (66 ft. lbs.).
b. Stage 2: Loosen 360 degrees.
c. Stage 3: Tighten to 50 Nm (37 ft. lbs.).
d. Stage 4: Tighten an additional 90 degrees.

64. Install the three accessory drive belt idler pulleys, the coolant pump pulley and the bolts.

65. Position the accessory drive belt tensioner and install the bolts.

66. Install a suitable tool between the valve spring coils to prevent valve stem seal damage.

➡The camshaft roller followers must be reinstalled in their original locations.

➡Position the cam lobe away from the valve stem prior to installing each camshaft roller follower.

67. Use a suitable tool to compress the valve springs, and install the camshaft roller follower. Remove the special tool.

➡The camshaft roller followers must be reinstalled in their original locations.

68. Repeat the previous four steps for each of the camshaft roller followers.

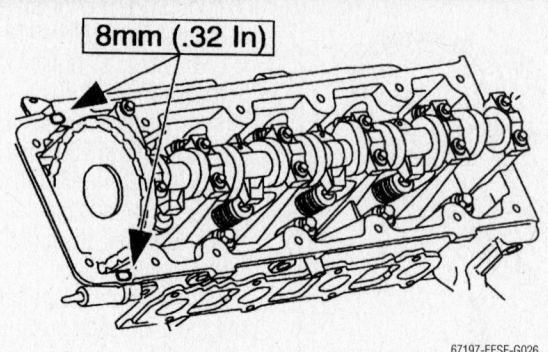

Fig. 180 Apply silicone gasket and sealant in two places where the engine front cover meets the cylinder head

69. Install the radio frequency interference capacitors.

Left cylinder head

⁂ **WARNING**

Do not use metal scrapers, wire brushes, power abrasive discs or other abrasive means to clean sealing surfaces. These tools cause scratches and gouges which make leak paths.

70. Inspect and clean the valve cover sealing surfaces with metal surface cleaner.
71. Apply instant adhesive completely around the gasket groove in the left valve cover.
72. Install the new valve cover gasket.

➡ **If not secured within four minutes, the sealant must be removed and the sealing area cleaned. To clean the sealing area, use silicone gasket remover and metal surface prep.**

73. Follow the directions on the packaging. Failure to follow this procedure can cause future oil leakage.
74. Apply silicone gasket and sealant in two places where the engine front cover meets the cylinder head.
75. Position the left valve cover and gasket on the cylinder head and install the bolts loosely.
76. Tighten the valve cover bolts in the sequence shown.

➡ **Lubricate the O-ring seal with clean engine oil.**

77. Install the oil level indicator tube.
78. Install a new O-ring seal on the oil level indicator tube.
79. Install the oil level indicator tube.
80. Install the bolt.
81. Install the left exhaust manifold and the exhaust manifold gasket. Tighten the nuts in the sequence shown.

Right cylinder head

⁂ **WARNING**

Do not use metal scrapers, wire brushes, power abrasive discs or other abrasive means to clean sealing surfaces. These tools cause scratches and gouges which make leak paths.

82. Inspect and clean the valve cover sealing surfaces with metal surface cleaner.
83. Apply instant adhesive completely around the gasket groove in the right valve cover. Install the new valve cover gasket.

➡ **If not secured within four minutes, the sealant must be removed and the sealing area cleaned. To clean the sealing area, use silicone gasket remover and metal surface prep. Follow the directions on the packaging.**

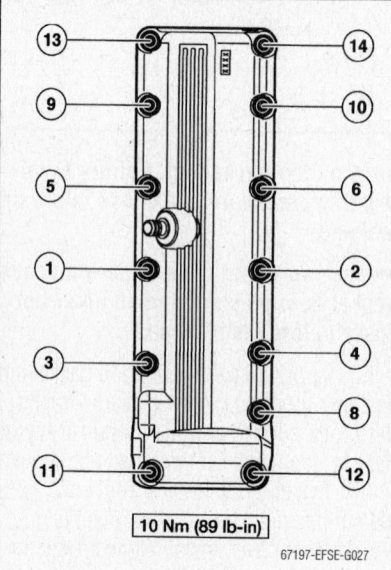

Fig. 181 Tighten the valve cover bolts in the sequence shown

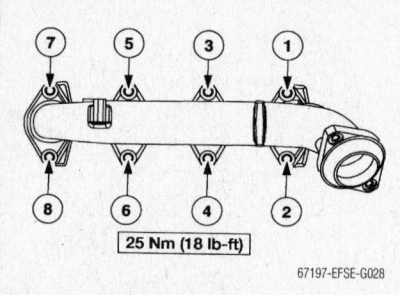

Fig. 182 Install the left exhaust manifold nuts in the sequence shown

Failure to follow this procedure can cause future oil leakage.

84. Apply silicone gasket and sealant in two places where the engine front cover meets the cylinder head.
85. Position the right valve cover and gasket on the cylinder head and install the bolts loosely.
86. Tighten the valve cover bolts in the sequence shown.
87. Install the right exhaust manifold gaskets and the exhaust manifold. Tighten the nuts in the sequence shown.
88. Slide the heater outlet tube forward with a new O-ring seal into the cylinder block. Lubricate the O-ring seal with engine coolant.
89. Install the heater outlet tube studs.
90. Connect the coolant hoses to the heater outlet tube.

All cylinder heads

91. Connect the right radio ignition interference capacitor electrical connector.
92. Connect the left radio ignition interference capacitor and cylinder head temperature (CHT) sensor electrical connectors.
93. Connect the CMP sensor electrical connectors.
94. Connect the CKP sensor electrical connector.
95. Install a suitable tool.
96. Using a suitable floor crane, remove the engine from the engine stand.
97. Install the flexplate or the flywheel and bolts. Tighten the bolts in the sequence shown.
98. Install the engine.

5.4L Engine

See Figures 183 through 204.

1. Before servicing the vehicle, refer to the Precautions Section.
2. Remove the engine.
3. Remove the bolts and the flexplate or the flywheel.

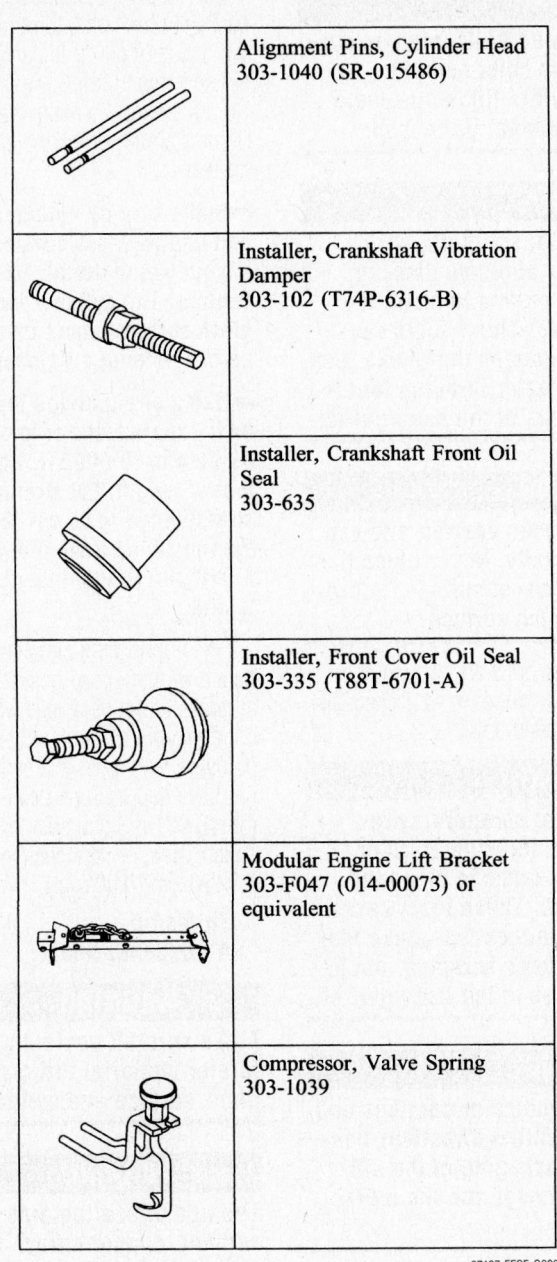

	Alignment Pins, Cylinder Head 303-1040 (SR-015486)
	Installer, Crankshaft Vibration Damper 303-102 (T74P-6316-B)
	Installer, Crankshaft Front Oil Seal 303-635
	Installer, Front Cover Oil Seal 303-335 (T88T-6701-A)
	Modular Engine Lift Bracket 303-F047 (014-00073) or equivalent
	Compressor, Valve Spring 303-1039

67197-EFSE-G033

Fig. 183 Special tools needed for this procedure. These tools are referred to in the following procedure

4. Install the engine onto a suitable engine stand.
5. Remove the special tool.

Left cylinder head

6. Remove the left exhaust manifold.
7. Remove the bolt and the oil level indicator tube.
8. Remove the engine wiring harness retainers from the left valve cover studs.

> ❄❄ **WARNING**
>
> **When removing the valve cover, make sure to avoid damaging the variable camshaft timing (VCT) solenoid.**

9. Remove the bolts and the left valve cover.

Right cylinder head

10. Remove the right exhaust manifold.
11. Remove the nuts.
12. Remove the right exhaust manifold.
13. Remove and discard the right exhaust manifold gasket.
14. Remove the engine wiring harness retainers from the right valve cover studs.

> ❄❄ **WARNING**
>
> **When removing the valve cover, make sure to avoid damaging the variable camshaft timing (VCT) solenoid.**

15. Remove the bolts and the right valve cover.
16. Remove the stud.

All cylinder heads

17. Remove the bolts, the coolant pump pulley and the accessory drive belt idler pulleys.
18. Remove the bolt and washer and using a puller set, remove the crankshaft pulley. Discard the crankshaft bolt.
19. Using a suitable tool, remove the crankshaft seal.
20. Remove the bolts and the accessory drive belt tensioner.
21. Disconnect the left and right radio ignition interference capacitor electrical connectors.
22. Remove the nuts and the two radio interference capacitors.
23. Disconnect the camshaft position (CMP) sensor electrical connectors.
24. Remove the bolt and the right CMP sensor.
25. Remove the bolt and the left CMP sensor.
26. Disconnect the crankshaft position (CKP) sensor electrical connector.
27. Remove the oil pan front bolts.
28. Remove the bolts.

> ❄❄ **WARNING**
>
> **Do not use metal scrapers, wire brushes, power abrasive discs or other abrasive means to clean the sealing surfaces. These tools cause scratches and gouges which make leak paths. Use a plastic scraping tool to remove all traces of old sealant.**

29. Remove the engine front cover from the front cover-to-cylinder block dowels.
30. Remove the engine front cover gaskets.
31. Clean the mating surfaces with silicone gasket remover and metal surface prep. Follow the directions on the packaging.
32. Inspect the mating surfaces.

> ❄❄ **WARNING**
>
> **Do not allow the valve keepers to fall off of the valve or the valve can drop into the cylinder.**

➡It may be necessary to push the valve down while compressing the valve spring.

➡The roller followers must be installed in their original positions.

33. Using a suitable tool, remove all of the roller followers. Record the roller follower positions.
34. Position the crankshaft keyway at the 12 o'clock position.
35. Remove the bolts, the left timing chain tensioner and tensioner arm.
36. Remove the bolts, the right timing chain tensioner and tensioner arm.
37. Remove the ignition pulse wheel from the crankshaft.
38. Remove the right timing chain from the camshaft sprocket.
39. Remove the right timing chain from the crankshaft sprocket.
40. Remove the left timing chain from the camshaft sprocket.
41. Remove the left timing chain and crankshaft sprocket.
42. Remove both timing chain guides.

**** WARNING**

Use only hand tools to remove the camshaft phaser sprocket assembly or damage can occur to the camshaft or camshaft phaser sprocket.

43. If disassembly of the cylinder head is required, using a suitable tool, loosen the camshaft phaser sprocket bolt.
44. Install a suitable tool onto the left cylinder head. Install a suitable tool onto the right cylinder head.

**** WARNING**

The cylinder head must be cool before removing it from the engine. Cylinder head warpage can result if a warm or hot cylinder head is removed.

**** WARNING**

Do not use the variable camshaft timing (VCT) phaser sprocket as a lifting point or leveraging device when removing the cylinder head or damage to the VCT phaser sprocket can occur.

**** WARNING**

Place clean shop towels over exposed engine cavities. Carefully remove the towels so foreign material is not dropped into the engine.

**** WARNING**

The cylinder head bolts must be discarded and new bolts must be installed. They are tighten-to-yield designed and cannot be reused.

**** WARNING**

Do not use metal scrapers, wire brushes, power abrasive discs or other abrasive means to clean the sealing surfaces. These tools cause scratches and gouges that make leak paths. Use a plastic scraping tool to remove all traces of the head gasket.

**** WARNING**

Aluminum surfaces are soft and can be scratched easily. Never place the cylinder head gasket surface, unprotected, on a bench surface.

45. Remove the bolts and the cylinder head. Discard the cylinder head gasket. Discard the cylinder head bolts.

**** WARNING**

Do not use metal scrapers, wire brushes, power abrasive discs or other abrasive means to clean the sealing surfaces. These tools cause scratches and gouges that make leak paths. Use a plastic scraping tool to remove all traces of the head gasket.

**** WARNING**

Observe all warnings or cautions and follow all application directions contained on the packaging of the silicone gasket remover and the metal surface prep.

➡If there is no residual gasket material present, metal surface prep can be used to clean and prepare the surfaces.

46. Clean the cylinder head-to-cylinder block mating surfaces of both the cylinder head and the cylinder block.
47. Remove any large deposits of silicone or gasket material with a plastic scraper.
48. Apply silicone gasket remover, following package directions, and allow to set for several minutes.
49. Remove the silicone gasket remover with a plastic scraper. A second application of silicone gasket remover may be required if residual traces of silicone or gasket material remain.
50. Apply metal surface prep, following package directions, to remove any remaining traces of oil or coolant, and to prepare the surfaces to bond with the new gasket. Do not attempt to make the metal shiny. Some staining of the metal surfaces is normal.

➡Make sure all cylinder head surfaces and engine block surfaces are clear of any gasket material, RTV, oil and coolant. The cylinder head and engine block surfaces must be clean and dry before running a flatness check.

➡Use a straightedge that is calibrated by the manufacturer to be flat within 0.005 mm (0.0002 in.) per running foot of length. For example, if the straightedge is 61 cm (24 in.) long, the machined edge must be flat with 0.010 mm (0.0004 in.) from end to end.

51. Support the cylinder head on a bench with the head gasket side up. Inspect all areas of the deck face with a straightedge, paying particular attention to the oil pressure feed area. The cylinder head must not have depressions deeper than 0.0254 mm (0.001 in.) across a 38.1 mm (1.5 in.) square area, or scratches more than 0.0254 mm (0.001 in.).

To install:

All cylinder heads

**** WARNING**

Make sure all coolant residue and foreign material are cleaned from the block surface and cylinder bore.

**** WARNING**

The use of sealing aids (aviation cement, copper spray, and glue) is not permitted. The gasket must be installed dry.

**** WARNING**

The cylinder head bolts must be discarded and new bolts installed. They are tighten-to-yield designed and cannot be reused.

**** WARNING**

Do not allow the cylinder head alignment pins to contact the cylinder head gasket or cylinder head sealing surfaces or damage can occur to the cylinder head or cylinder head gasket.

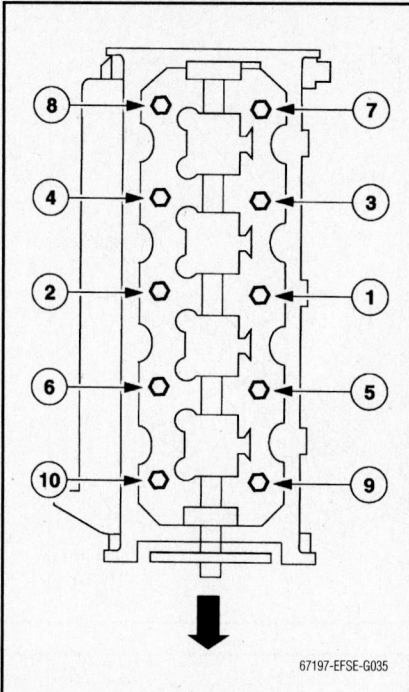

Fig. 184 Left cylinder head torque sequence—5.4L engine (RH cylinder head similar)

➡**Do not turn the crankshaft until instructed to do so.**

52. Using the cylinder head alignment pins, position the cylinder head gasket and cylinder head onto the dowels and install the cylinder head bolts loosely.

53. Tighten the bolts in the sequence shown.

    a. Stage 1: Tighten to 40 Nm (30 ft. lbs.).

    b. Stage 2: Tighten an additional 90 degrees.

    c. Stage 3: Tighten an additional 90 degrees.

54. Remove the cylinder head lifting handle tools.

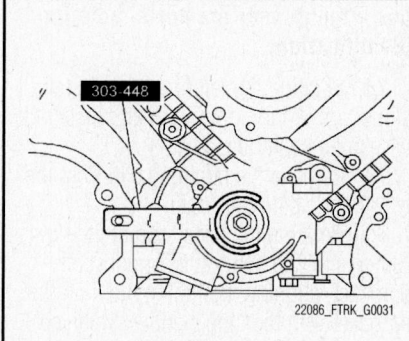

Fig. 185 Position the crankshaft with the special tool, then remove the tool

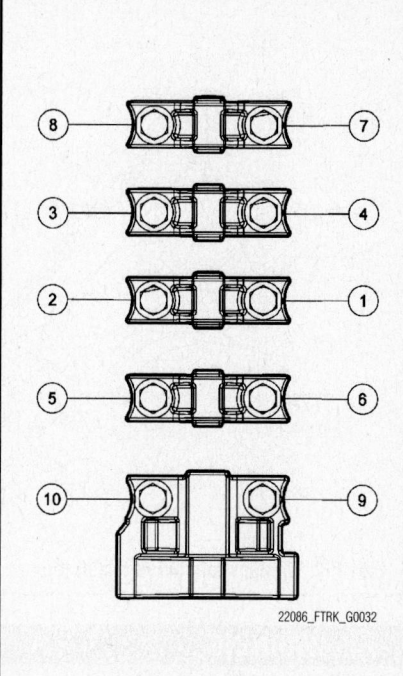

Fig. 186 Install the camshafts and tighten the bearing caps in the sequence shown

55. Remove the special tool from the cylinder head.

56. Install the hydraulic lash adjusters into the cylinder head. Lubricate the hydraulic lash adjusters with clean engine oil prior to installation.

57. Position a new gasket and the exhaust manifold and tighten the 8 nuts in the sequence shown. Tighten to 18 ft. lbs. (25 Nm).

58. Install the exhaust manifold shield and the 2 nuts. Tighten to 89 inch lbs. (10 Nm).

59. Position the crankshaft with the special tool, then remove the tool.

60. Install the LH and RH camshafts. Lubricate the camshaft and camshaft journals with clean engine oil prior to installation.

61. Install the LH and RH camshaft bearing caps in their original locations.

    a. Lubricate the camshaft bearing caps with clean engine oil.

    b. Position the front camshaft bearing cap.

    c. Position the remaining camshaft bearing caps.

    d. Install the bolts loosely.

    e. Tighten to 89 inch lbs. (10 Nm) in the sequence shown.

✳✳ **CAUTION**

Damage to the variable camshaft timing (VCT) phaser sprocket

assembly will occur if mishandled or used as a lifting or leveraging device.

62. Install the VCT phaser sprockets and new VCT phaser sprocket bolts finger tight.

✳✳ **CAUTION**

Only use hand tools to remove the VCT phaser sprocket assembly or damage may occur to the camshaft or VCT phaser sprocket.

63. Using the special tool, tighten the LH and RH VCT phaser sprocket bolts in 2 stages:

    a. Stage 1: Tighten to 30 ft. lbs. (40 Nm).

    b. Stage 2: Tighten an additional 90 degrees.

✳✳ **WARNING**

Timing chain procedures must be followed exactly or damage to valves and pistons will result.

64. Compress the tensioner plunger, using a vice.

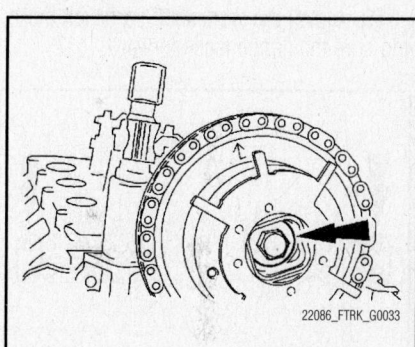

Fig. 187 Install the VCT phaser sprockets and new VCT phaser sprocket bolts finger tight

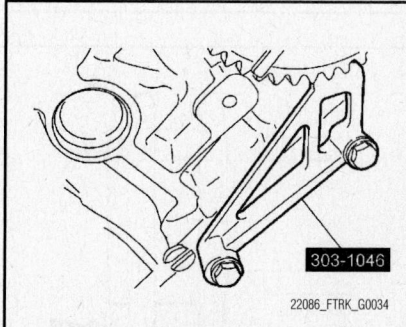

Fig. 188 Using the special tool, tighten the LH and RH VCT phaser sprocket bolts in 2 stages

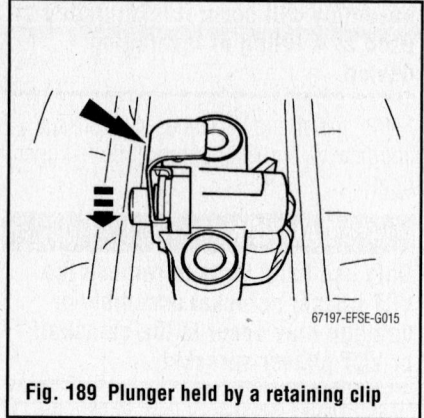

Fig. 189 Plunger held by a retaining clip

65. Install a retaining clip on the tensioner to hold the plunger in during installation.

66. Remove the tensioner from the vise. If the copper links are not visible, mark two links on one end and one link on the other end, and use as timing marks.

✳✳ WARNING

Crankshaft keyway must be in the 12 o'clock position.

67. Install the timing chain guides.
68. Position the left timing chain guide.
69. Install the crankshaft sprocket, making sure the flange faces forward.

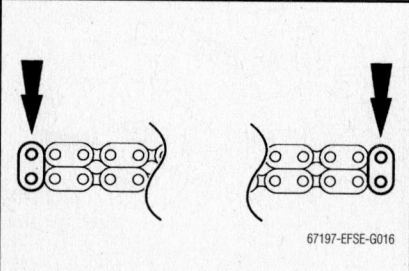

Fig. 190 If the copper links are not visible, mark one link on one end and one link on the other end, and use as timing marks

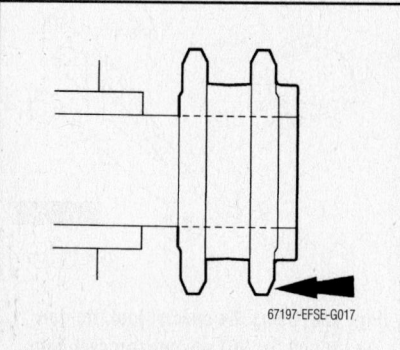

Fig. 191 Install the crankshaft sprocket, making sure the flange faces forward

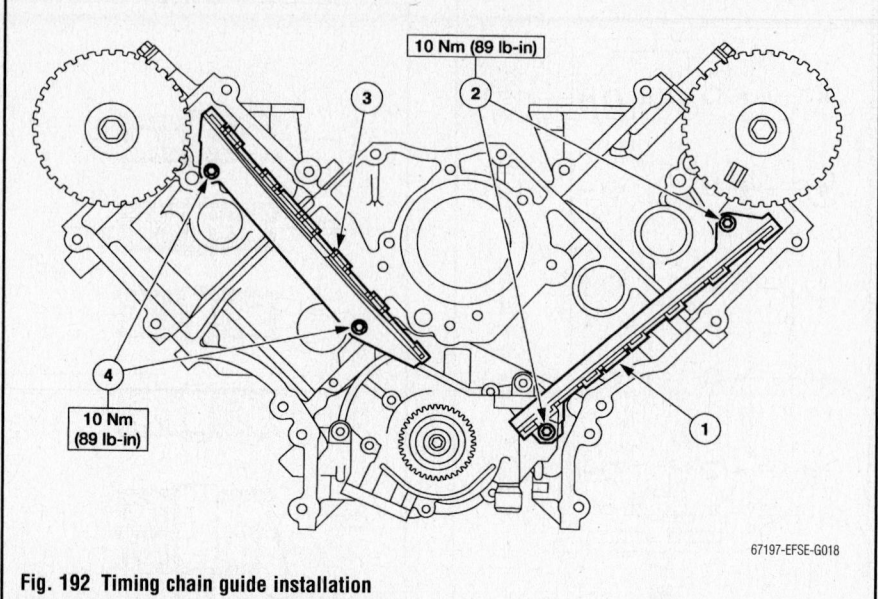

Fig. 192 Timing chain guide installation

✳✳ WARNING

Only use hand tools to install the camshaft phaser sprocket assembly or damage may occur to the camshaft or camshaft phaser unit.

➡ **This step is only required if cylinder head was disassembled.**

70. Using a suitable tool, tighten the bolts in two stages:
    a. Stage 1: Tighten to 40 Nm (30 ft. lbs.).
    b. Stage 2: Tighten an additional 90 degrees.
71. Remove the special tool.
72. Position the lower end of the left (inner) timing chain on the crankshaft sprocket, aligning the timing mark on the outer flange of the crankshaft sprocket with the single copper (marked) link on the chain.

➡ **Make sure the upper half of the timing chain is below the tensioner arm dowel.**

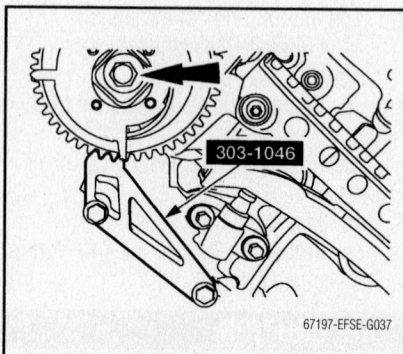

Fig. 193 Camshaft phaser sprocket holding tool—5.4L engine

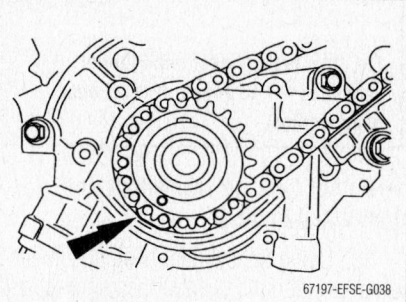

Fig. 194 Position the lower end of the left (inner) timing chain on the crankshaft sprocket, aligning the timing mark on the outer flange of the crankshaft sprocket with the single copper (marked) link on the chain—5.4L engine

73. Position the timing chain on the camshaft sprocket with the camshaft sprocket timing mark positioned between the two copper (marked) chain links.

➡ **The left timing chain tensioner arm has a bump near the dowel hole for identification.**

74. Position the left timing chain tensioner arm on the dowel pin and install the left timing chain tensioner.
75. Remove the retaining clip from the left timing chain tensioner.
76. Position the lower end of the right (outer) timing chain on the crankshaft sprocket, aligning the timing mark on the sprocket with the single copper (marked) chain link.

➡ **The lower half of the timing chain must be positioned above the tensioner arm dowel.**

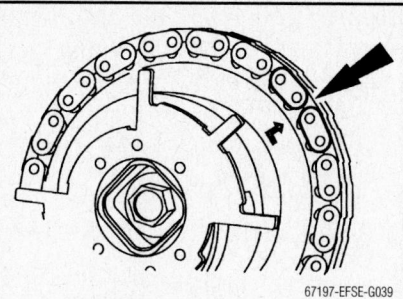

Fig. 195 Position the timing chain on the camshaft sprocket with the camshaft sprocket timing mark positioned between the two copper (marked) chain links— 5.4L engine

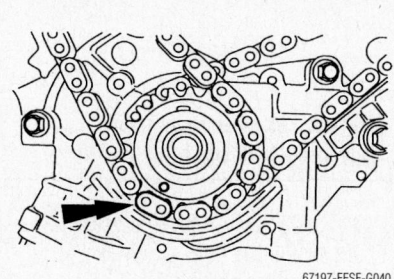

Fig. 196 Position the lower end of the right (outer) timing chain on the crankshaft sprocket, aligning the timing mark on the sprocket with the single copper (marked) chain link

77. Position the right timing chain on the camshaft sprocket. Make sure the camshaft sprocket timing mark is positioned between the two copper (marked) chain links.

78. Position the right timing chain tensioner arm on the dowel pin and install the right timing chain tensioner.

79. Remove the retaining clip from the right timing chain tensioner.

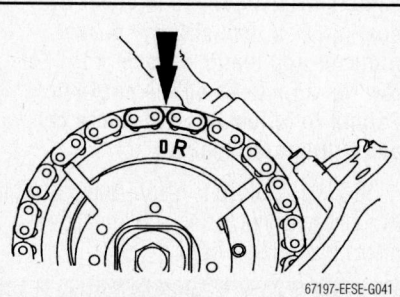

Fig. 197 Position the right timing chain on the camshaft sprocket. Make sure the camshaft sprocket timing mark is positioned between the two copper (marked) chain links

➡Both camshaft phaser sprockets are identical. Refer to the R timing mark to identify the right camshaft phaser sprocket and the L timing mark to identify the left camshaft phaser sprocket.

80. As a post-check, verify correct alignment of all timing marks. Make sure the R and L timing marks on the sprockets correspond to the above note.

81. Install the crankshaft sensor ring on the crankshaft.

➡Lubricate the camshaft roller followers using clean engine oil.

➡Using the mark on each camshaft roller follower, make sure it is returned to its original position.

82. Using a suitable tool, install all of the camshaft roller followers.

✳✳ WARNING

Do not use metal scrapers, wire brushes, power abrasive discs or other abrasive means to clean the sealing surfaces. These tools cause scratches and gouges which make leak paths. Use a plastic scraping tool to remove all traces of old sealant.

➡If the engine front cover is not secured within four minutes, the sealant must be removed and the sealing area cleaned. To clean the sealing area, use silicone gasket remover and metal surface prep. Follow the directions on the packaging. Failure to follow this procedure can cause future oil leakage.

➡Make sure that the engine front cover gasket is in place on the engine front cover before installation.

83. Apply a bead of silicone gasket and sealant along the cylinder head-to-cylinder block surface and the oil pan-to-cylinder block surface, at the locations shown.

84. Install a new engine front cover gasket on the engine front cover. Position the engine front cover. Install the fasteners finger-tight.

85. Tighten the engine front cover fasteners in sequence in two stages.
   a. Stage 1: Tighten fasteners 1 through 15 to 25 Nm (18 ft. lbs.).
   b. Stage 2: Tighten fasteners 6 and 7 to 48 Nm (35 ft. lbs.).
   c. Loosely install the pan-to-case bolts, then tighten the bolts in two stages, in the sequence shown.
   d. Stage 1: Tighten to 20 Nm (15 ft. lbs.).
   e. Stage 2: Tighten an additional 60 degrees.

86. Install the left camshaft position (CMP) sensor and the bolt.

87. Lubricate the new O-ring seal with clean engine oil prior to installation.

88. Install the right CMP sensor and the bolt.

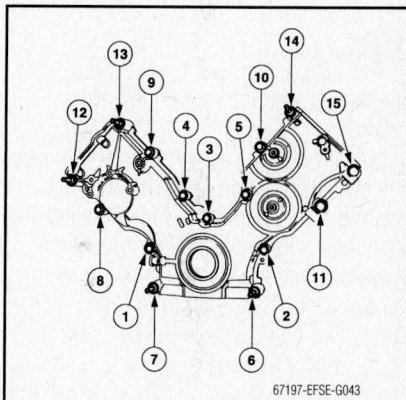

Fig. 199 Front cover fastener tightening sequence

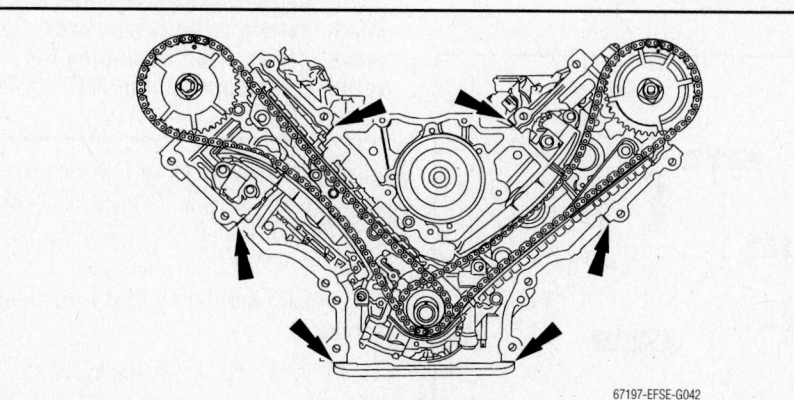

Fig. 198 Apply a bead of silicone gasket and sealant along the cylinder head-to-cylinder block surface and the oil pan-to-cylinder block surface, at the locations shown—5.4L engine

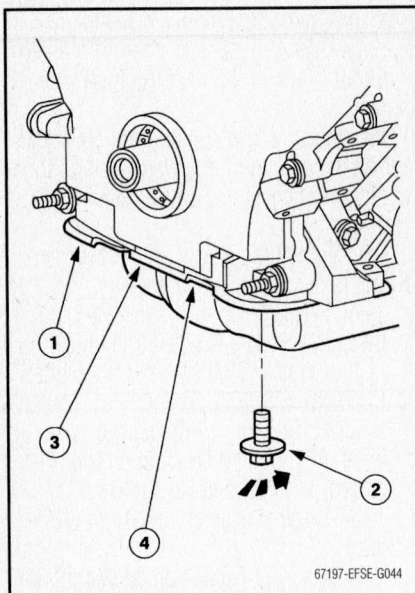

Fig. 200 Loosely install the pan-to-case bolts, then tighten the bolts in two stages, in the sequence shown

89. Lubricate the new O-ring seal with clean engine oil prior to installation.

90. Lubricate the engine front cover and the crankshaft seal inner lip with clean engine oil.

91. Use the special tools to install the crankshaft seal into the engine front cover.

92. If not secured within four minutes, the sealant must be removed and the sealing area cleaned. To clean the sealing area, use silicone gasket remover and metal surface prep. Follow the directions on the packaging. Failure to follow this procedure can cause future oil leakage.

93. Apply silicone gasket and sealant to the Woodruff key slot on the crankshaft pulley. Use a suitable tool to install the crankshaft pulley.

94. Tighten the new crankshaft pulley bolt in four stages.

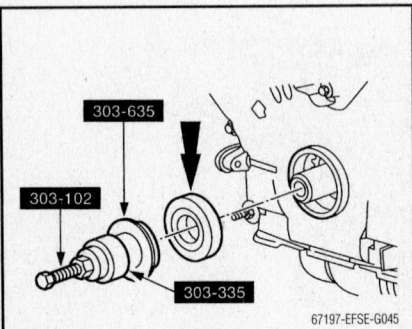

Fig. 201 Crankshaft seal installation tools

a. Stage 1: Tighten to 90 Nm (66 ft. lbs.).
b. Stage 2: Loosen 360 degrees.
c. Stage 3: Tighten to 50 Nm (37 ft. lbs.).
d. Stage 4: Tighten an additional 90 degrees.

95. Install the three accessory drive belt idler pulleys, the coolant pump pulley and the bolts. Torque all bolts to 18 ft. lbs. (25 Nm).

96. Position the accessory drive belt tensioner and install the bolts. Torque all bolts to 18 ft. lbs. (25 Nm).

97. Install the radio frequency interference capacitors.

Left cylinder head

> ✳✳ **WARNING**
>
> Do not use metal scrapers, wire brushes, power abrasive discs or other abrasive means to clean sealing surfaces. These tools cause scratches and gouges which make leak paths. Use a plastic scraping tool to remove all traces of old sealant. Inspect and clean the valve cover sealing surfaces with silicone gasket remover and metal surface prep. Follow the directions on the packaging.

➡ **If not secured within four minutes, the sealant must be removed and the sealing area cleaned. To clean the sealing area, use silicone gasket remover and metal surface prep. Follow the directions on the packaging. Failure to follow this procedure can cause future oil leakage.**

98. Apply silicone gasket and sealant in two places where the engine front cover meets the cylinder head.

> ✳✳ **WARNING**
>
> When installing the valve cover, make sure to avoid damaging the variable camshaft timing (VCT) solenoid.

99. Position the left valve cover and gasket on the cylinder head and install the bolts loosely. Tighten the bolts in the sequence shown.

➡ **Lubricate the O-ring seal with clean engine oil.**

100. Install the oil level indicator tube.

101. Install a new O-ring seal on the oil level indicator tube.

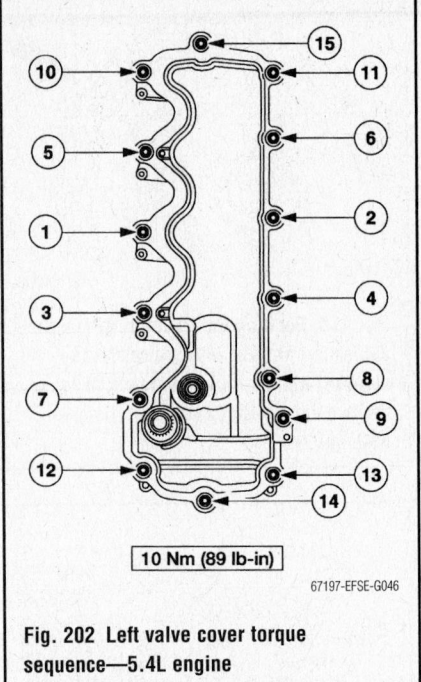

Fig. 202 Left valve cover torque sequence—5.4L engine

`10 Nm (89 lb-in)`

102. Install the oil level indicator tube.
103. Install the bolt.

Right cylinder head

> ✳✳ **WARNING**
>
> Do not use metal scrapers, wire brushes, power abrasive discs or other abrasive means to clean sealing surfaces. These tools cause scratches and gouges which make leak paths. Use a plastic scraping tool to remove all traces of old sealant. Inspect and clean the valve cover sealing surfaces with silicone gasket remover and metal surface prep. Follow the directions on the packaging.

➡ **If not secured within four minutes, the sealant must be removed and the sealing area cleaned. To clean the sealing area, use silicone gasket remover and metal surface prep. Follow the directions on the packaging. Failure to follow this procedure can cause future oil leakage.**

104. Apply silicone gasket and sealant in two places where the engine front cover meets the cylinder head.

> ✳✳ **WARNING**
>
> When installing the valve cover, make sure to avoid damaging the variable camshaft timing (VCT) solenoid.

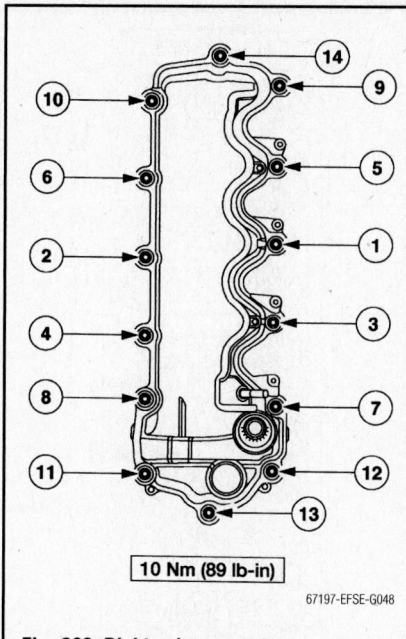

Fig. 203 Right valve cover torque sequence—5.4L engine

105. Position the right valve cover and gasket on the cylinder head and install the bolts loosely. Tighten the bolts in the sequence shown.

106. Install the heater outlet tube stud.

All cylinder heads

107. Position the electrical harness on the valve cover and connect the engine wiring harness retainers to the valve cover studs.

108. Connect the right radio ignition interference capacitor electrical connector.

109. Connect the left radio ignition

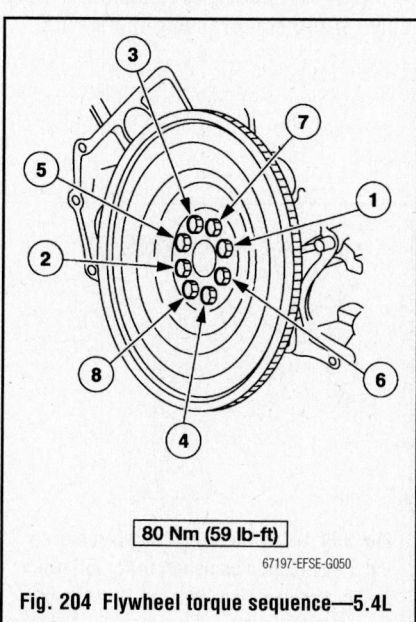

Fig. 204 Flywheel torque sequence—5.4L engine

interference capacitor and cylinder head temperature (CHT) sensor electrical connectors.

110. Connect the CMP sensor electrical connectors.

111. Connect the CKP sensor electrical connector.

112. Install a suitable tool.

113. Using a suitable floor crane remove the engine from the engine stand.

114. Install the flexplate or the flywheel and bolts. Tighten the bolts in the sequence shown.

115. Install the engine.

6.8L Engine

See Figures 205 through 235.

1. Before servicing the vehicle, refer to the Precautions Section.

2. Remove the engine.

3. Remove the bolts and the flexplate or the flywheel.

❋❋ CAUTION

Do not use the oil pan to support the engine.

4. Lower and support the engine assembly on wood blocks.

5. Using the special tools, remove and discard the crankshaft rear oil slinger.

6. Using the special tools, remove and discard the crankshaft rear seal.

7. Remove the bolts and the crankshaft rear seal retainer plate.

8. Mount the engine on a suitable work stand.

9. Remove the right engine mount.

10. Remove the cylinder block drain plugs and drain the coolant into a suitable container.

11. Disconnect the camshaft position (CMP) electrical connector.

12. Disconnect the right radio frequency interference capacitor electrical connector and the capacitor.

13. Disconnect the electrical connector retainer from the coolant tube support bracket.

14. Disconnect the 10 ignition coil electrical connectors.

15. Remove the 10 bolts and the 10 ignition coils.

16. Disconnect the cylinder head temperature (CHT) sensor electrical connector.

17. Disconnect the engine oil pressure (EOP) sensor electrical connector.

18. Remove the nut and the LH radio ignition interference capacitor.

19. Disconnect the crankshaft position (CKP) sensor electrical connector.

20. Remove the nuts and position the wiring harness aside.

21. Remove the rear oil indicator tube and bracket.

22. Disconnect and remove the CMP sensor.

23. Remove the CKP sensor.

➡The bolts are part of the valve cover and should not be removed.

24. Loosen the 16 fasteners in an alternating sequence and remove the valve cover and gasket.

25. Clean the valve cover mating surface of the cylinder head with silicone gasket remover and metal surface prep. Follow the directions on the packaging.

26. Discard the valve cover gasket. Clean the valve cover gasket groove with soap and water or a suitable solvent.

27. Clean the valve cover mating surface of the cylinder head with silicone gasket remover and metal surface prep. Follow the directions on the packaging.

28. Inspect the valve cover gasket. If the gasket is damaged, remove and discard the gasket. Clean the valve cover gasket groove with soap and water or a suitable solvent.

29. Clean the valve cover mating surfaces of the cylinder head with silicone gasket remover and metal surface prep. Follow the directions on the packaging.

30. Inspect the valve cover gasket. If the gasket is damaged, remove and discard the gasket. Clean the valve cover gasket groove with soap and water or a suitable solvent.

31. Remove the bolt and the idler pulley.

32. Remove the coolant pump pulley.

33. Remove the bolts and the accessory drive belt tensioner.

34. Using a suitable tool, remove and discard the crankshaft pulley bolt. Remove the crankshaft pulley.

35. Using a suitable tool, remove the crankshaft front seal.

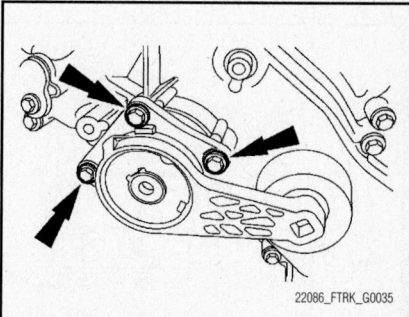

Fig. 205 Remove the bolts and the accessory drive belt tensioner

36. Remove the front four oil pan bolts.

➡ **Correct engine front cover fastener location is essential for assembly procedure. Record fastener location.**

37. Remove the engine front cover fasteners.

38. Remove the engine front cover from the cylinder block.

❋❋ CAUTION

Only use hand tools to loosen the camshaft sprocket bolt or damage may occur to the camshaft or camshaft sprocket.

39. Loosen and back off the RH camshaft sprocket bolt 1 full turn.

40. Loosen the LH camshaft sprocket bolt.

➡ **The balance shaft caps must be marked for installation in their original locations or damage to the engine may occur.**

41. Remove the six bolts, in the sequence shown, and remove the balance shaft bearing caps.

42. Remove the balance shaft.

43. Remove the crankshaft sensor ring from the crankshaft.

44. Position the crankshaft with the keyway at the 12 o'clock position.

➡ **If the camshaft lobes are not exactly positioned as shown, the crankshaft will require one full additional rotation to 12 o'clock.**

➡ **The No. 1 cylinder camshaft exhaust lobe must be coming up on the exhaust stroke. Verify by noting the position of the 2 intake camshaft lobes and the exhaust lobe on the No. 1 cylinder.**

❋❋ CAUTION

If the components are to be reinstalled, they must be installed in the same positions. Mark the compo-

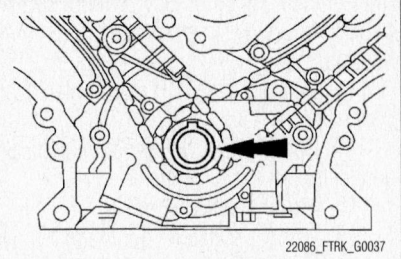

Fig. 207 Position the crankshaft with the keyway at the 12 o'clock position—6.8L engine

nents for installation into the original locations.

45. Remove only the 3 camshaft roller followers shown in the illustration from the RH cylinder head.

❋❋ CAUTION

Do not allow the valve keepers to fall off the valve or the valve may drop into the cylinder.

➡ **It may be necessary to push the valve down while compressing the spring.**

46. Using the special tool, remove the 3 designated camshaft roller followers in the previous step from the RH cylinder head.

❋❋ CAUTION

If the components are to be reinstalled, they must be installed in the same positions. Mark the components for installation into the original locations.

47. Remove only the 4 camshaft roller followers shown in the illustration from the LH cylinder head.

❋❋ CAUTION

Do not allow the valve keepers to fall off the valve or the valve may drop into the cylinder.

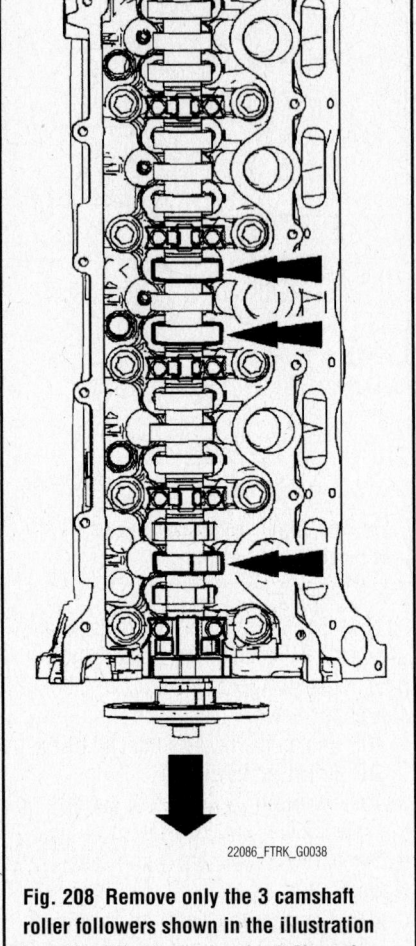

Fig. 208 Remove only the 3 camshaft roller followers shown in the illustration from the RH cylinder head—6.8L engine

➡ **It may be necessary to push the valve down while compressing the spring.**

48. Using the special tool, remove the 4 designated camshaft roller followers in the previous step from the LH cylinder head.

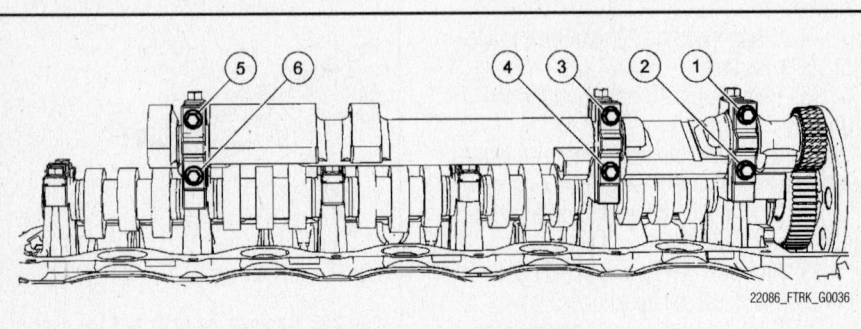

Fig. 206 Balance shaft cap bolt removal sequence—6.8L engine

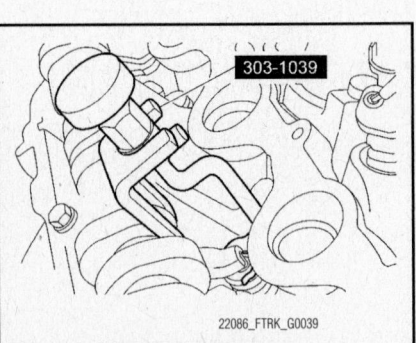

Fig. 209 Using the special tool, remove the 3 designated camshaft roller followers in the previous step from the RH cylinder head—6.8L engine

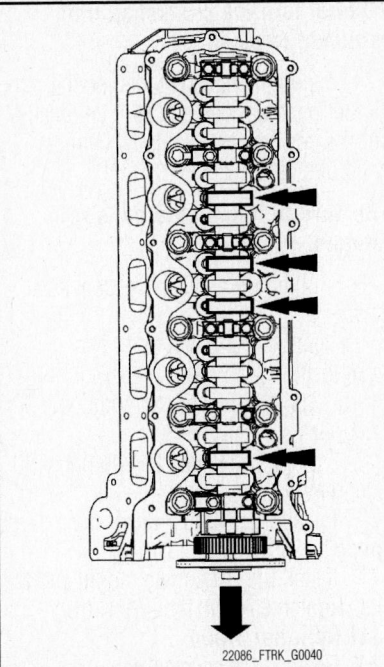

Fig. 210 Remove only the 4 camshaft roller followers shown in the illustration from the LH cylinder head—6.8L engine

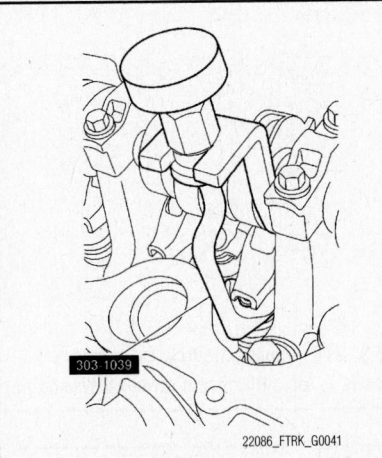

Fig. 211 Using the special tool, remove the 4 designated camshaft roller followers in the previous step from the LH cylinder head—6.8L engine

※※ **CAUTION**

The crankshaft cannot be moved past the 6 o'clock position once set.

49. Rotate the crankshaft clockwise and position the crankshaft keyway at the 6 o'clock position.

※※ **CAUTION**

If one or both of the tensioner mounting bolts are loosened or removed, the tensioner-sealing bead must be

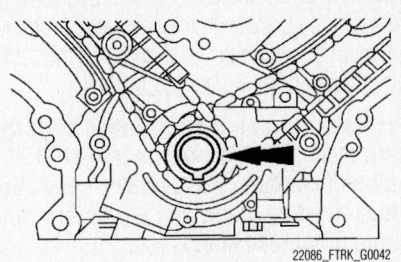

Fig. 212 Rotate the crankshaft clockwise and position the crankshaft keyway at the 6 o'clock position—6.8L engine

inspected for seal integrity. If cracks, tears, separation from the tensioner body or permanent compression of the seal bead is observed, install a new tensioner.

50. Remove the bolts, the LH and RH timing chain tensioner and tensioner arm.

51. Remove the timing chains. Where necessary, remove the crankshaft sprocket with the chain.

52. Remove the 4 bolts and the timing chain guides.

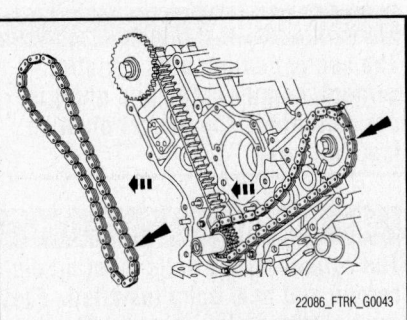

Fig. 213 Remove the timing chains; where necessary, remove the crankshaft sprocket with the chain—6.8L engine

53. Remove the bolts and the RH and LH camshaft sprockets.

54. Remove the balance shaft drive gear from the LH camshaft.

※※ **CAUTION**

Remove the front thrust camshaft bearing cap straight upward from the bearing towers, or the bearing cap may be damaged from sideloading.

➡The camshaft bearing caps must be installed in their original locations. Record camshaft bearing cap locations.

55. Remove the bolts in the sequence shown and remove the RH cylinder head front camshaft bearing cap and then the remaining bearing caps.

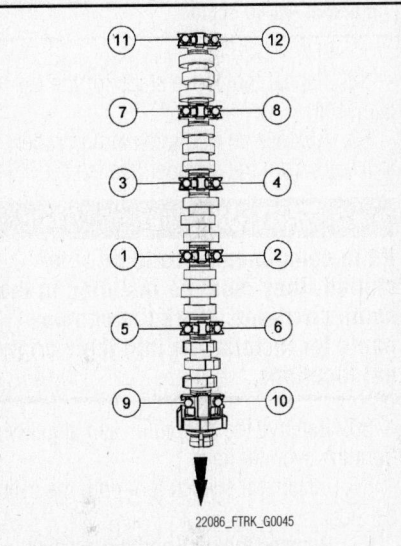

Fig. 215 Remove the bolts in the sequence shown and remove the RH cylinder head front camshaft bearing cap and then the remaining bearing caps—6.8L engine

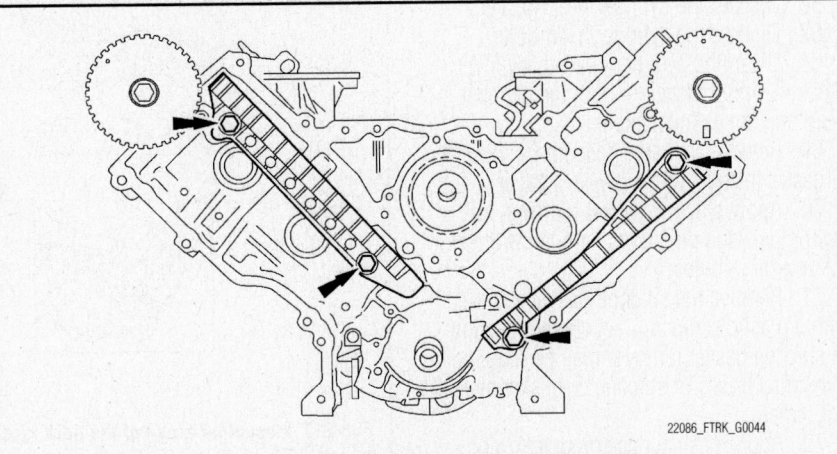

Fig. 214 Remove the 4 bolts and the timing chain guides—6.8L engine

56. Clean and inspect the RH camshaft bearing caps.

57. The camshaft front thrust bearing cap contains an oil metering groove. Make sure the groove is free of foreign material.

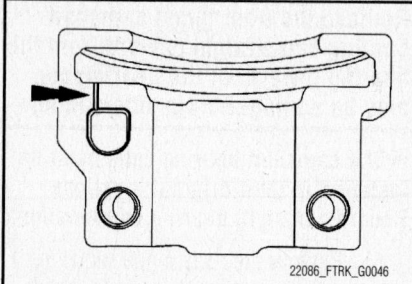

Fig. 216 The camshaft front thrust bearing cap contains an oil metering groove; make sure the groove is free of foreign material—6.8L engine

58. Repeat the above steps for the LH camshaft.

59. Remove all of the remaining roller followers from the cylinder heads.

✳✳ CAUTION

If the components are to be reinstalled, they must be installed in the same positions. Mark the components for installation into their original locations.

60. Remove the hydraulic lash adjusters from the cylinder head.

61. Install the special tool onto the cylinder head.

62. Remove the nuts and the exhaust manifold. Discard the gasket.

63. Remove the stud bolt and the coolant tube.

64. Discard the O-ring seals.

65. Remove the bolts and the cylinder head.

66. Discard the cylinder head gasket.

67. Discard the cylinder head bolts.

68. Clean the cylinder head-to-cylinder block mating surfaces of both the cylinder head and the cylinder block.

69. Remove any large deposits of silicone or gasket material with a plastic scraper.

70. Apply silicone gasket remover, following package directions, and allow to set for several minutes.

71. Remove the silicone gasket remover with a plastic scraper. A second application of silicone gasket remover may be required if residual traces of silicone or gasket material remain.

72. Apply metal surface prep, following package directions, to remove any remaining

traces of oil or coolant, and to prepare the surfaces to bond with the new gasket. Do not attempt to make the metal shiny. Some staining of the metal surfaces is normal.

➡ **Make sure all cylinder head surfaces are clear of any gasket material, RTV, oil and coolant. The cylinder head surface must be clean and dry before running a flatness check.**

➡ **Use a straightedge that is calibrated by the manufacturer to be flat within 0.0002 inch (0.005 mm) per running foot length. For example, if the straightedge is 24 inch (61 cm) long, the machined edge must be flat within 0.0004 inch (0.010 mm) from end to end.**

73. Support the cylinder head on a bench with the head gasket side up. Inspect all areas of the deck face with a straightedge, paying particular attention to the oil pressure feed area. The cylinder head must not have depressions deeper than 0.001 inch (0.0254 mm) across a 1.5 inch (38.1 mm) square area, or scratches longer than 0.001 inch (0.0254 mm).

To install:

✳✳ CAUTION

The use of sealing aids (aviation cement, copper spray and glue) is not permitted. The gasket must be installed dry.

✳✳ CAUTION

The cylinder head bolts must be discarded and new bolts installed. They are tighten-to-yield designed and cannot be reused.

➡ **Do not turn the crankshaft until instructed to do so.**

74. Using the special tools, position the cylinder head gaskets and cylinder heads over the dowels and install the cylinder head bolts loosely.

➡ **Be sure to tighten the bolts in 3 stages.**

75. Tighten the bolts in the sequence shown.

   a. Stage 1: Tighten to 40 Nm (30 lb-ft).

   b. Stage 2: Tighten an additional 90 degrees.

   c. Stage 3: Tighten an additional 90 degrees.

76. Install the cylinder block drain plugs. Tighten to 18 ft. lbs. (24 Nm).

77. Install the RH engine mount and the bolts. Tighten to 46 ft. lbs. (63 Nm).

LH Cylinder Head

78. Remove the special lifting tool from the LH cylinder head.

79. Install the hydraulic lash adjusters into the LH cylinder head. Lubricate the

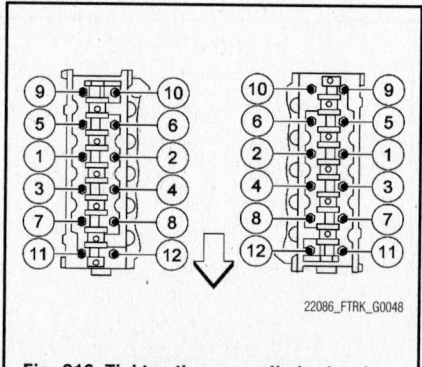

Fig. 218 Tighten the new cylinder head bolts in the sequence shown—6.8L engine

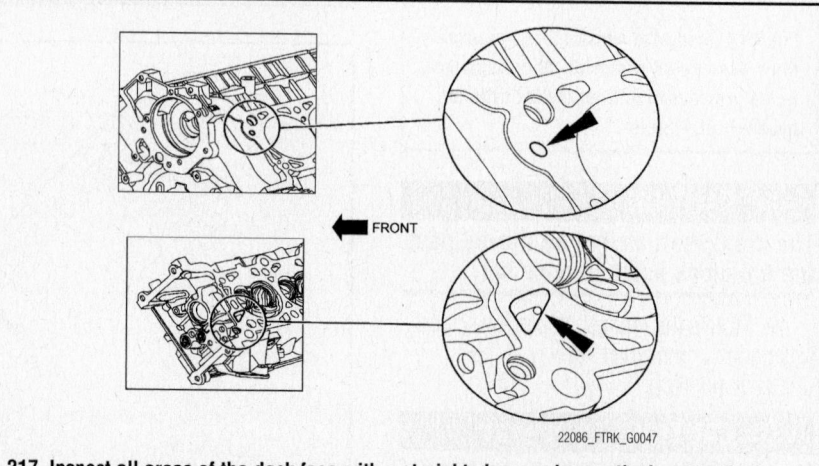

Fig. 217 Inspect all areas of the deck face with a straightedge, paying particular attention to the oil pressure feed area—6.8L engine

hydraulic lash adjusters with clean engine oil prior to installation.

80. Position a new gasket, the LH exhaust manifold and tighten the 10 nuts in the sequence shown. Tighten to 18 ft. lbs. (25 Nm).

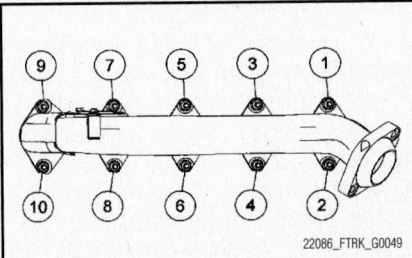

Fig. 219 Tighten the LH exhaust manifold nuts in the sequence shown—6.8L engine

RH Cylinder Head

81. Remove the special lifting tool from the RH cylinder head.

82. Install the hydraulic lash adjusters into the RH cylinder head. Lubricate the hydraulic lash adjusters with clean engine oil prior to installation.

83. Position a new gasket, the RH exhaust manifold and tighten the 10 nuts in the sequence shown. Tighten to 18 ft. lbs. (25 Nm).

84. Install the coolant tube and the stud bolt. Tighten to 89 inch lbs. (10 Nm).

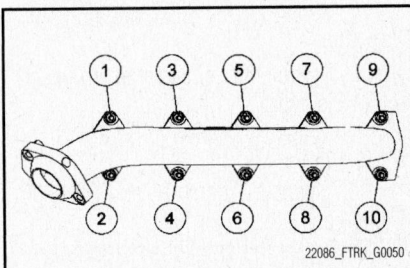

Fig. 220 Tighten the RH exhaust manifold nuts in the sequence shown—6.8L engine

All Cylinder Heads

✻✻ CAUTION

If the components are to be reinstalled, they must be installed into their original locations.

➡**Lubricate the camshaft roller followers with clean engine oil prior to installation.**

85. Install only the identified camshaft roller followers onto the RH cylinder head.

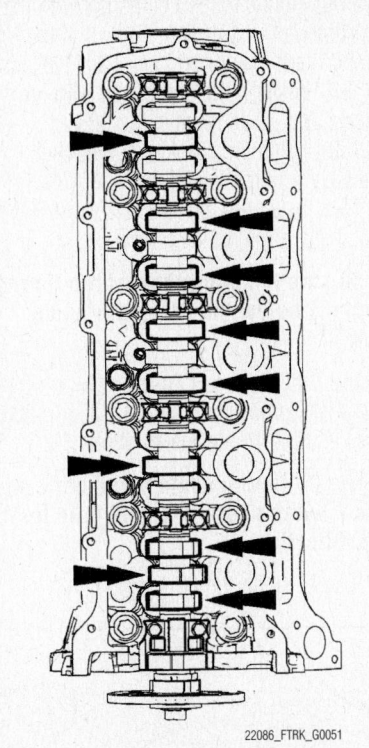

Fig. 221 Install only the identified camshaft roller followers onto the RH cylinder head (camshaft shown installed to clarify camshaft roller follower position)—6.8L engine

✻✻ CAUTION

If the components are to be reinstalled, they must be installed into their original locations.

➡**Lubricate the camshaft roller followers with clean engine oil prior to installation.**

86. Install only the identified camshaft roller followers onto the LH cylinder head.

87. Install the LH and RH camshafts. Lubricate the camshaft and camshaft journals with clean engine oil prior to installation.

88. Install the LH and RH camshaft bearing caps in their original locations. Lubricate the camshaft bearing caps with clean engine oil.

89. Position the front camshaft bearing cap. Position the remaining camshaft bearing caps. Install the bolts loosely.

90. Tighten the LH camshaft bearing cap bolts in 2 stages:

    a. Stage 1: Tighten to 71 inch lbs. (8 Nm) in the sequence shown.

    b. Stage 2: Tighten an additional 45 degrees.

91. Tighten the RH camshaft bearing cap bolts in 2 stages:

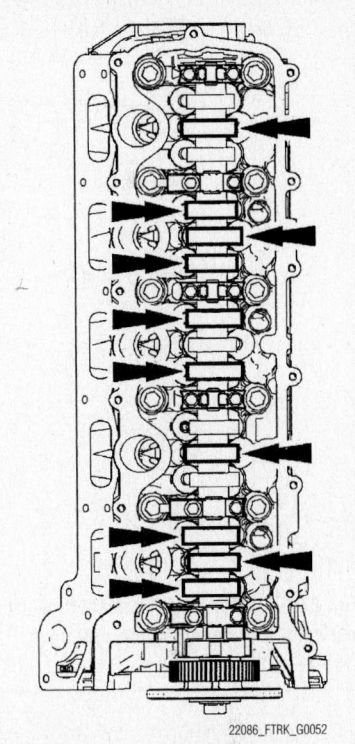

Fig. 222 Install only the identified camshaft roller followers onto the LH cylinder head (camshaft shown installed to clarify camshaft roller follower position)—6.8L engine

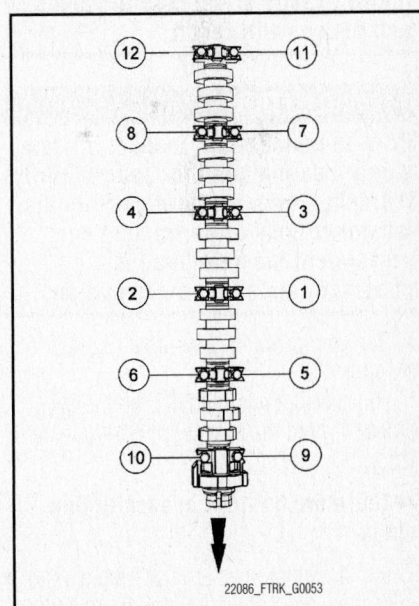

Fig. 223 Tighten the LH camshaft bearing cap bolts in 2 stages, in the sequence shown—6.8L engine

    a. Stage 1: Tighten to 8 Nm (71 lb-in) in the sequence shown.

    b. Stage 2: Tighten an additional 45 degrees.

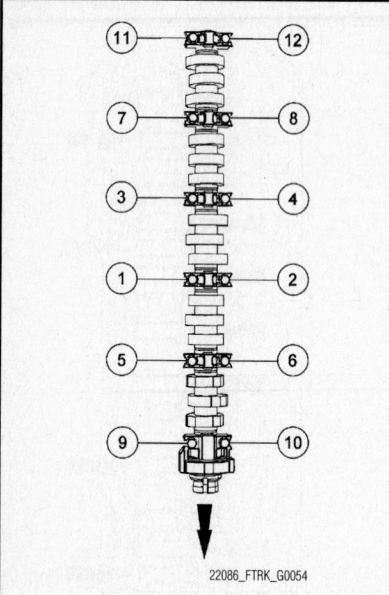

Fig. 224 Tighten the RH camshaft bearing cap bolts in 2 stages, in the sequence shown—6.8L engine

92. Install the balance shaft drive gear onto the LH camshaft.

93. Install both camshaft sprockets and camshaft sprocket bolts finger tight.

> ✳✳ **CAUTION**
>
> **Timing chain procedures must be followed exactly or damage to valves and pistons will result.**

> ✳✳ **CAUTION**
>
> **Prior to installation, inspect the tensioner-sealing bead for seal integrity. If cracks, tears, separation from the tensioner body or permanent compression of the seal bead is observed, install a new tensioner.**

94. Compress the tensioner plunger, using a vise.

95. Install a retaining clip on the tensioner to hold the plunger in during installation.

➡ **There are 61 links in each timing chain.**

96. If copper links are not visible, mark 2 links on one end and 1 link on the other end, and use as timing marks.

97. Install the timing chain guides and the 4 bolts. Tighten to 89 inch lbs. (10 Nm).

98. Preposition the camshafts:
   a. Rotate the LH camshaft with the Camshaft Positioning Tool until the timing mark is approximately at 12 o'clock.

b. Rotate the RH camshaft with the Camshaft Positioning Tool until the timing mark is approximately at 11 o'clock.

99. Position the crankshaft with the special tool, then remove the tool.

100. Install the crankshaft sprocket, marking sure the flange faces forward.

101. Install the lower end of the LH timing chain, aligning the timing marks.

➡ **Be sure the upper half of the timing chain is below the tensioner guide dowel.**

102. Install the LH timing chain on the camshaft sprocket with the 2 chain (marked) links and the timing marks aligned.

➡ **The LH timing chain tensioner arm has a bump near the dowel hole for identification.**

103. Position the LH timing chain ten-

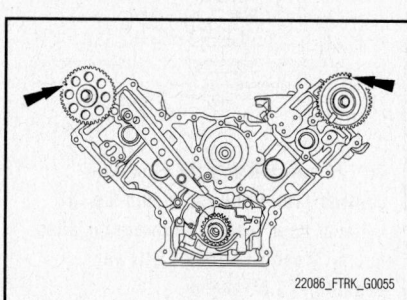

Fig. 225 Preposition the camshafts as shown—6.8L engine

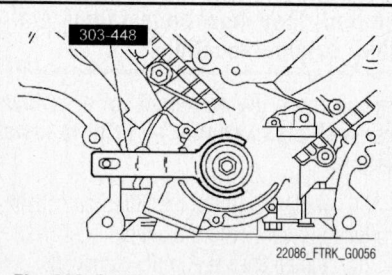

Fig. 226 Position the crankshaft with the special tool, then remove the tool—6.8L engine

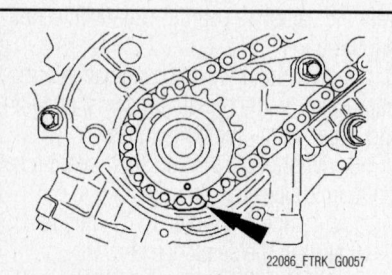

Fig. 227 Install the lower end of the LH timing chain, aligning the timing marks—6.8L engine

sioner arm on the dowel pin and install the LH timing chain tensioner and bolts. Tighten to 18 ft. lbs. (25 Nm).

➡ **Be sure the chain link and crankshaft sprocket timing marks are aligned. The lower half of the timing chain must be positioned above the dowel.**

104. Install the RH (outer) timing chain on the crankshaft sprocket.

105. Position the timing chain on the camshaft sprocket. Make sure the 2 copper-colored (marked) links align with the camshaft sprocket timing mark.

106. Position the RH timing chain tensioner arm on the dowel pin and install the RH timing chain tensioner and bolts. Tighten to 18 ft. lbs. (25 Nm).

107. Remove the retaining clips from the RH and LH timing chain tensioners.

108. Check for correct alignment of all timing marks.

109. Install the crankshaft sensor ring on the crankshaft.

> ✳✳ **CAUTION**
>
> **Only use hand tools to tighten the camshaft sprocket bolt or damage may occur to the camshaft or camshaft sprocket.**

110. Tighten the RH camshaft sprocket bolt in 2 stages:
   a. Stage 1: Tighten to 30 ft. lbs. (40 Nm).
   b. Stage 2: Tighten an additional 90 degrees.

111. Tighten the LH camshaft sprocket bolt in 2 stages:
   a. Stage 1: Tighten to 30 ft. lbs. (40 Nm).
   b. Stage 2: Tighten an additional 90 degrees.

112. Rotate the crankshaft clockwise and position the crankshaft keyway at the 6 o'clock position.

113. Remove the 2 bolts and the camshaft bearing cap.

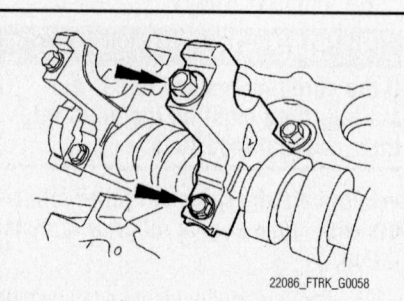

Fig. 228 Remove the 2 bolts and the camshaft bearing cap—6.8L engine

If the components are to be reinstalled, they must be installed into their original locations or damage to the engine may occur.

114. Using the special tool, install the roller follower. Lubricate the camshaft roller follower with clean engine oil prior to installation.

115. Position the camshaft bearing cap and install the bolts in 2 stages:

   a. Stage 1: Tighten to 71 inch lbs. (8 Nm).

   b. Stage 2: Tighten an additional 45 degrees.

116. Repeat for the remaining roller followers with similar bearing cap.

117. Using the special tool, install all of the remaining camshaft roller followers. Lubricate the camshaft roller followers with clean engine oil prior to installation.

118. Rotate the crankshaft counterclockwise and position the crankshaft keyway at the 11 o'clock position.

119. Lubricate the balance shaft journals with clean engine oil.

120. Using the index mark on the balance shaft, mark the corresponding gear tooth with chalk.

121. Position the balance shaft on the journals.

➡ **It may be necessary to use an inspection mirror to see the marks.**

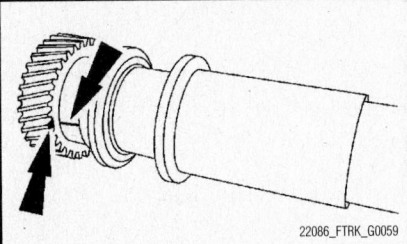

Fig. 229 Using the index mark on the balance shaft, mark the corresponding gear tooth with chalk—6.8L engine

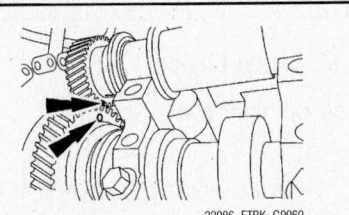

Fig. 230 Position the balance shaft on the journals and align the chalk mark on the balance shaft with the camshaft timing mark as shown—6.8L engine

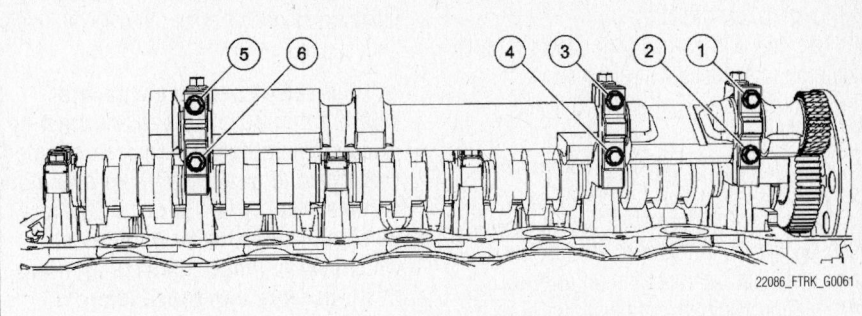

Fig. 231 Install the balance shaft bolts and tighten in the sequence shown—6.8L engine

122. Position the balance shaft on the journals and align the chalk mark on the balance shaft with the camshaft timing mark as shown.

➡ **Install the balance shaft bearing caps in their original locations.**

123. Install the bolts and tighten in the sequence shown. Tighten to 89 inch lbs. (10 Nm).

Do not use metal scrapers, wire brushes, power abrasive discs or other abrasive means to clean the sealing surfaces. These tools cause scratches and gouges which make leak paths. Use a plastic scraping tool to remove all traces of old sealant.

➡ **If the engine front cover is not secured within 4 minutes, the sealant must be removed and the sealing area cleaned. To clean the sealing area, use silicone gasket remover and metal surface prep. Follow the directions on the packaging. Allow to dry until there is no sign of wetness, or 4 minutes, whichever is longer. Failure to follow this procedure can cause future oil leakage.**

➡ **Make sure that the engine front cover gasket is in place on the engine front cover before installation.**

124. Apply a bead of silicone gasket and sealant along the cylinder head-to-cylinder block surface at the locations shown.

125. Install a new engine front cover gasket on the engine front cover. Position the engine front cover onto the dowels. Install the fasteners finger-tight.

126. Tighten the engine front cover fasteners, in sequence, in 2 stages.

   a. Stage 1: Tighten fasteners 1 through 15 to 18 ft. lbs. (25 Nm).

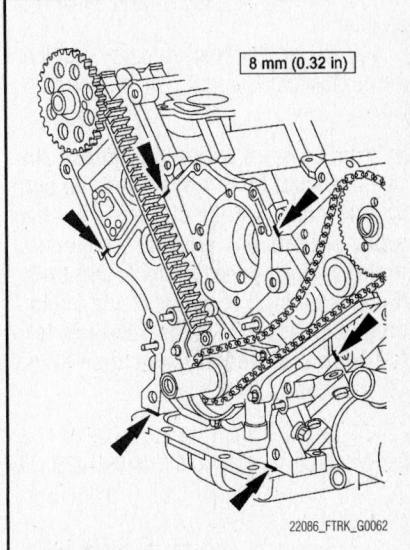

Fig. 232 Apply a bead of silicone gasket and sealant along the cylinder head-to-cylinder block surface at the locations shown—6.8L engine

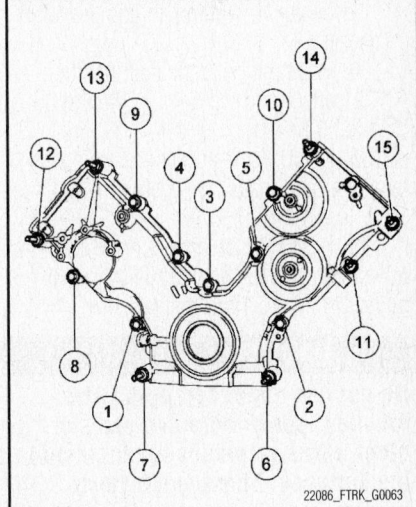

Fig. 233 Tighten the engine front cover fasteners, in sequence, in 2 stages—6.8L engine

b. Stage 2: Tighten fasteners 6 and 7 to 35 ft. lbs. (48 Nm).

127. Install the front 4 oil pan bolts in an alternating sequence, in 2 stages:

   a. Stage 1: Tighten to 15 ft. lbs. (20 Nm).

   b. Stage 2: Tighten an additional 60 degrees.

128. Install the camshaft position (CMP) sensor and the bolt. Lubricate the new O-ring seal with clean engine oil prior to installation. Tighten the sensor to 89 inch lbs. (10 Nm).

129. Lubricate the engine front cover and the crankshaft seal inner lip with clean engine oil.

130. Using the special tools, install a new crankshaft seal into the engine front cover.

➡ If not secured within 4 minutes, the sealant must be removed and the sealing area cleaned. To clean the sealing area, use silicone gasket remover and metal surface prep. Allow to dry until there is no sign of wetness, or 4 minutes, whichever is longer. Failure to follow this procedure can cause future oil leakage.

131. Apply silicone gasket and sealant to the Woodruff key slot on the crankshaft pulley.

132. Use the special tool to install the crankshaft pulley.

133. Tighten the new crankshaft pulley bolt in 4 stages.

   a. Stage 1: Tighten to 66 ft. lbs. (90Nm).

   b. Stage 2: Loosen 360 degrees.

   c. Stage 3: Tighten to 37 ft. lbs. (50 Nm).

   d. Stage 4: Tighten an additional 90 degrees.

134. Position the crankshaft position (CKP) sensor and the bolt. Tighten to 89 inch lbs. (10 Nm).

135. Position the accessory drive belt tensioner and install the 3 bolts. Tighten to 18 ft. lbs. (25 Nm).

136. Install the accessory drive belt idler pulley bolt and the coolant pump pulley bolts. Tighten to 18 ft. lbs. (25 Nm).

✳✳ CAUTION

Do not use metal scrapers, wire brushes, power abrasive discs or other abrasive means to clean sealing surfaces. These tools cause scratches and gouges which make leak paths. Use a plastic scraping tool to remove all traces of old sealant.

137. Clean the valve cover mating surface with silicone gasket remover and metal surface prep.

➡ If the valve cover is not secured within 4 minutes, the sealant must be removed and the sealing area cleaned with silicone gasket remover and metal surface prep. Allow to dry until there is no sign of wetness, or 4 minutes, whichever is longer. Failure to follow this procedure can cause future oil leakage.

138. Apply a bead of silicone gasket and sealant in 2 places where the engine front cover meets the cylinder head.

139. Position the RH valve cover and new gasket on the cylinder head and tighten the 16 fasteners in the sequence shown. Tighten to 89 inch lbs. (10 Nm).

140. Repeat for the LH valve cover.

141. Position the oil level indicator and tube and install the bolt. Install a new O-ring seal and lubricate with clean engine oil prior to installation. Tighten to 89 inch lbs. (10 Nm).

142. Install the oil level indicator and tube front bolt. Tighten to 18 ft. lbs. (25 Nm).

143. Position the electrical harness on the engine assembly and connect the engine wiring harness retainers to the valve cover studs.

144. Connect the CKP sensor electrical connector.

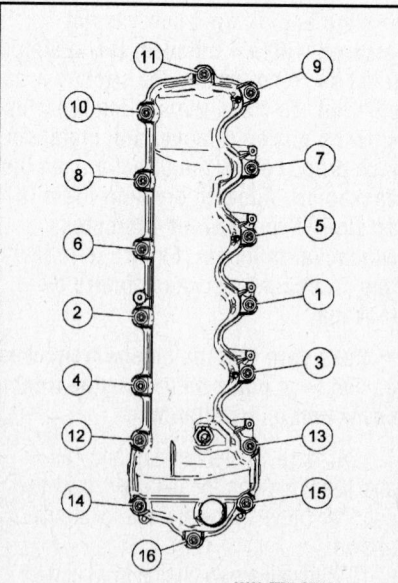

Fig. 234 Position the valve cover and new gasket on the cylinder head and tighten the 16 fasteners in the sequence shown— 6.8L engine (RH cover shown; LH cover sequence similar)

145. Position the electrical harness on the engine assembly and connect the engine wiring harness retainers to the valve cover studs.

146. Install the 10 ignition coils and the 10 bolts.

147. Connect the 10 ignition coil electrical connectors.

148. Install the LH radio ignition interference capacitor and the stud bolt. Tighten to 18 ft. lbs. (25 Nm).

149. Connect the engine oil pressure (EOP) sensor electrical connector.

150. Connect the cylinder head temperature (CHT) sensor electrical connector.

151. Connect the electrical connector retainer to the coolant tube.

152. Install the RH radio ignition interference capacitor and the stud bolt. Tighten to 18 ft. lbs. (25 Nm).

153. Connect the CMP sensor electrical connector.

154. Using a suitable floor crane, remove the engine from the engine stand.

155. Lower and support the engine assembly on wood blocks.

156. Install the special engine lifting tool.

157. Using a suitable floor crane raise the engine.

158. Install the flexplate or flywheel and the 8 bolts in the sequence shown. Tighten to 59 ft. lbs. (80 Nm).

159. Install the engine.

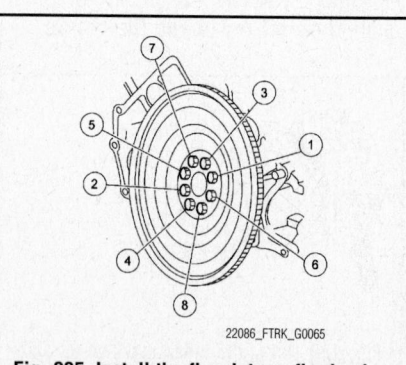

Fig. 235 Install the flexplate or flywheel and the 8 bolts in the sequence shown— 6.8L engine (RH cover shown; LH cover sequence similar)

6.0L Diesel Engine

Left Cylinder Head

See Figures 236 and 237.

1. Before servicing the vehicle, refer to the Precautions Section.

2. With the vehicle in **Neutral**, position it on a hoist.

3. Drain the engine oil.

4. Remove the intake manifold.

5. Remove the left cylinder block drain plug.

6. Remove the fuel injector control module mounting bracket.

7. Disconnect the glow plug connector and position aside.

8. Remove the nut and position the oil level indicator and tube aside.

➡**Mark the position of the valve cover bolts for valve cover bolt installation.**

9. Remove the eleven bolts and the valve cover. Remove the valve cover gasket.

Early build

10. Disconnect the high-pressure oil rail supply line at the high-pressure oil rail.

11. Remove the bolts and the high-pressure oil rail.

12. Disconnect and remove the high-pressure oil supply line.

13. Remove and discard the crankcase-to-head tube assembly.

14. Remove the glow plug buss bar.

Late build

➡**Do not remove the oil rail end plugs or acoustic wave attenuator port fitting. Service parts are not available to support the components.**

15. Remove the bolts and the high-pressure oil rail.

➡**The rings on the crankcase-to-head tube are to be used to pry the tube assembly from the branch tube assembly or the oil rail assembly.**

16. Remove the crankcase-to-head tube assembly.

17. Remove and discard the O-rings.

✳✳ WARNING

Do not pull on the glow plug wire or damage may occur.

18. Remove the glow plug harness.

All vehicles

19. Remove the four glow plugs.

✳✳ WARNING

Do not attempt to apply battery voltage to the fuel injector or damage to the fuel injector will occur.

20. Using a 19 mm socket, push the fuel injector electrical connector out of the rocker arm carrier.

21. Prior to removing the injector assembly, insert clean shop towels in the oil drain holes adjacent to each glow plug.

✳✳ WARNING

Failure to account for all snaprings or pieces prior to placing the vehicle back in service can cause engine damage. A missing snapring can be ingested into the lube oil system causing severe engine damage.

✳✳ WARNING

To prevent engine damage, do not use air tools to remove the fuel injectors. The snapring that extracts the injector can dislodge and fall into the oil drain hole.

➡**There is no need to drain the fuel rail.**

➡**If engine oil is found in the engine coolant or engine coolant is found in the combustion chambers, a new injector sleeve may need to be installed.**

22. Remove the bolt, fuel injector hold-down and fuel injector.

➡**If a snapring or piece of a snapring is missing from the injector hold-down assembly, it must be located prior to removing the shop towels.**

23. Remove the shop towels.

24. Remove the nuts and bolts from the turbocharger adapter pipe.

25. Remove the turbocharger adapter pipe.

➡**Remove and discard the O-ring.**

26. Remove the oil level indicator and tube.

27. Remove the bolts and turbocharger heat shield.

28. Disconnect the exhaust backpressure tube at the exhaust manifold.

29. Remove the retaining nuts. Remove the exhaust backpressure bracket assembly.

30. Remove the retaining bolt from the fuel line bracket and position the fuel lines aside.

31. Remove the bolt and the idler pulley.

32. Disconnect the heater hose from the front cover and position aside.

33. Remove the fan shroud mounting stud.

➡**Remove and discard the sealing washers.**

34. Remove the banjo fitting and the fuel line.

35. Remove and discard the inner cylinder head bolts.

36. Remove the eight bolts and the rocker arm assemblies.

37. Mark the eight valve bridges with a permanent marker and remove.

✳✳ WARNING

To prevent engine damage, keep the push rods in the order in which they were removed. Install all push rods back in their original positions.

38. Mark the location and remove the eight push rods.

39. Remove the outer cylinder head bolts.

40. Install the special tool and the lifting crane. With the help of an assistant, remove the cylinder from the vehicle.

41. Remove and discard the cylinder head gasket and dowels.

42. Clean and inspect the gasket sealing surfaces.

To install:
All vehicles, late build

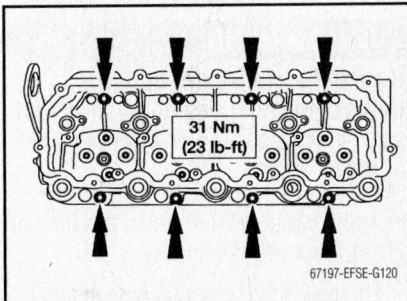

Fig. 236 Rocker arm carrier installation—6.0L Diesel Engine

✳✳ WARNING

Install new D-ring seals on the crankcase-to-head tube. It requires several hours after installation for the D-ring seals to relax back to their original size. If the tube assembly is installed before the D-ring seals have relaxed, damage to the D-ring seals can occur.

43. Install new D-ring seals on each end of the crankcase to head tube assemblies.

➡**Use care to avoid scratching the blue compound on the cylinder head gasket.**

44. Install the gasket with the part number facing upward and verify the five top holes and head gasket push rod holes line up.

45. Install the dowels and the cylinder head gasket.

➡**Position the fuel lines in place before the cylinder head is installed.**

46. Using the special tools and with the help of an assistant, install the cylinder

head on the engine. Remove the special tools.

47. Install the outer cylinder head bolts finger-tight.

⊗ WARNING

To prevent engine damage, keep the push rods in the order in which they were removed. Install all push rods back in their original positions.

➡ **Higher mileage engines require push rods to be cleaned so the copper colored end of the push rod can be identified.**

48. Apply clean engine oil to each end of the push rod. Insert them into their respective positions with the copper-colored end up.

➡ **Coat the end of each valve stem with clean engine oil.**

49. Install the eight valve bridges.

⊗ WARNING

Rotate the crankshaft until the damper locating dowel notch is in the six o'clock position or engine damage can occur.

➡ **Apply clean engine oil to the top center of each valve bridge.**

50. Install the rocker arm assemblies and eight bolts.

✳ WARNING

Using too much engine oil on the threads of the cylinder head bolts can cause damage to the threads and poor sealing. Using anti-seize compounds, grease or any other lubricants other than engine oil on the cylinder head bolt threads can affect the true torque value of the bolts.

➡ **Lightly lubricate the new cylinder head bolt threads and flanges with clean engine oil.**

51. Install the 10 cylinder head retaining bolts finger-tight.
52. Tighten the head bolts in the following sequence.
   a. Tighten bolts 1 through 10 to 88 Nm (65 ft. lbs.).
   b. Tighten bolts 1, 3, 5, 7 and 9 to 115 Nm (85 ft. lbs.).
   c. Tighten bolts in sequence 1 through 10, clockwise 90 degrees.
   d. Tighten bolts in sequence 1 through 10, a second time, clockwise 90 degrees.

   e. Tighten bolts in sequence 1 through 10, a third time, clockwise 90 degrees.
   f. Tighten bolts 11 through 15 an to 24 Nm (18 ft. lbs.).
   g. Tighten bolts 11 through 15 to 31 Nm (23 ft. lbs.).

➡ **Install new sealing washers.**

53. Install the fuel line and the banjo fitting.
54. Install the fan shroud mounting stud.
55. Position back and connect the heater hose.
56. Install the idler pulley and bolt.
57. Position the exhaust backpressure bracket assembly and install the retaining nuts.
58. Tighten the exhaust backpressure tube fitting at the exhaust manifold.
59. Position the fuel lines and install the fuel line bracket retaining bolt.

➡ **Install a new O-ring and apply clean engine oil.**

60. Install the oil level indicator and tube.
61. Install the turbocharger heat shield and bolts.
62. Position the turbocharger adapter pipe.

➡ **Apply anti-seize lubricants to the bolt threads prior to installing the bolts.**

➡ **Do not tighten until after the turbocharger is installed.**

63. Install the nuts and bolts in the adapter pipe.
64. Install the four glow plugs.

✳ WARNING

If the fuel injector oil inlet D-ring is damaged, a new fuel injector must be installed.

➡ **Lubricate the fuel injector and O-rings liberally with clean engine oil.**

65. Install new O-rings and copper washer on the fuel injector.

✳ WARNING

To prevent engine damage, do not use air tools to install the fuel injectors. The snapring that extracts the injector can dislodge and fall into the oil drain hole.

66. Install the fuel injector, fuel injector hold-down and bolt. Torque to 24 ft. lbs. (33 Nm).

✳ WARNING

To prevent engine damage, be sure the injector wiring is clear of all moving parts.

67. Install the fuel injector electrical connector into the rocker carrier.
68. Apply engine oil to the top fuel injector O-rings.
   Early build

➡ **Install a new lower O-ring.**

69. Install a new crankcase to head tube assembly. Torque to 33 ft. lbs. (45 Nm).
70. Install the high-pressure oil rail and bolts.
71. Install the high-pressure oil rail.
72. Install the bolts finger tight.
73. Tighten the bolts in the sequence shown.

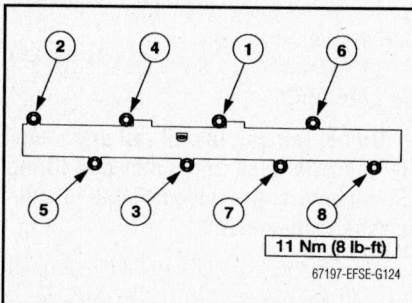

Fig. 237 High pressure oil rail torque installation—6.0L Diesel Engine

74. Install the high-pressure oil line.

➡ **Clean and inspect the O-rings and install new as necessary.**

➡ **Apply clean engine oil to the O-rings before installing.**

75. Install the glow plug buss bar.
   Late build

✳ WARNING

To prevent engine damage, check that the crankcase-to-head tube assemblies bottom out in the branch tube assembly. The oil rail, crankcase-to-head tube and the fuel injectors will not function correctly if the tube is not bottomed out.

➡ **Install new O-rings and .**

76. Apply clean engine oil and install the crankcase-to-head tube assembly.

➡ **Apply clean engine oil to the top fuel injector D-ring before installing the high pressure oil rail.**

77. Position the oil rail on the fuel injectors.

78. Place the oil rail on top of the carrier so that the four single ball tubes are engaging the injector lead angle.

79. Insert three guide bolts, two on the ends of the straight side of the oil rail and one in the middle of the wavy side of the oil rail. Install the guide studs six to seven turns.

80. Press the oil rail into the fuel injectors.

81. Inspect that the oil rail mounting feet are flat against the mounting surface.

82. Loosely install the six bolts.

83. Install the oil rail retaining bolts.

84. Remove the three guide bolts.

85. Loosely install the three remaining bolts.

86. Tighten the bolts in the sequence shown.

➡ Clean and inspect the O-rings and install new as necessary.

➡ Apply clean engine oil to the O-rings prior to installing.

87. Install the glow plug harness.
All vehicles

✳✳ WARNING

To prevent engine damage, do not use air powered tools when installing the valve cover.

➡ Clean and inspect the valve cover gasket. Install a new gasket if necessary.

88. Position the valve cover gasket. Install the valve cover and 11 bolts.

89. Position back the oil level indicator and install the nut.

90. Connect the glow plug connector.

91. Install the fuel injector control module mounting bracket.

➡ Install a new oil filter.

92. Fill the crankcase with clean engine oil.

➡ Lightly lubricate the O-ring with clean engine oil before installing.

93. Install the cylinder block drain plug.

94. Install the intake manifold.

Right Cylinder Head

See Figure 238.

1. Before servicing the vehicle, refer to the Precautions Section.
All vehicles
2. With the vehicle in **Neutral**, position it on a hoist.
3. Drain the engine oil.

4. Remove the intake manifold.

5. Remove the fuel injectors.

6. Remove the starter.

7. Remove the cylinder drain block.

8. Remove the nuts and bolts from the turbocharger adapter pipe.

9. Remove the turbocharger adapter pipe.
Early build
10. Remove and discard the crankcase to head tube assembly.

11. Remove the glow plug buss bar.
Late build

➡ The rings on the crankcase-to-head tube are to be used to pry the tube assembly from the branch tube assembly or the oil rail assembly.

12. Remove the crankcase-to-head tube assembly.

13. Remove and discard the O-rings.

✳✳ WARNING

Do not pull on the wiring to remove the glow plug connector or damage may occur.

14. Remove the glow plug harness.
All vehicles
15. Remove the four glow plugs.

16. Remove and discard the 10 inner cylinder head bolts.

17. Remove the eight bolts and the rocker arm assemblies.

18. Mark the eight valve bridges with a permanent marker and remove.

✳✳ WARNING

To prevent engine damage, keep the push rods in the order in which they were removed. Install all push rods back in their original positions.

19. Mark the location and remove the eight push rods.

20. Remove the outer cylinder head bolts.

21. Install the special tool and the lifting crane. With the help of an assistant, remove the cylinder head from the vehicle.

22. Remove and discard the cylinder head gasket and dowels.

23. Clean and inspect the gasket sealing surfaces.

To install:
All vehicles, late build

✳✳ WARNING

Install new D-ring seals on the crankcase-to-head tube. It requires several hours after installation for the D-ring seals to relax back to their

original size. If the tube assembly is installed before the D-ring seals have relaxed, damage to the D-ring seals can occur.

24. Install new D-ring seals on each end of the crankcase to head tube assemblies.

➡ Use care to avoid scratching the blue compound on the cylinder head gasket.

25. Install a new cylinder head gasket with the part number facing up and verify the top five holes and the head gasket push rod holes line up.

26. Install the dowels and the cylinder head gasket.

27. Using the special tools and with the help of an assistant, install the cylinder head on the engine. Remove the special tools.

28. Install the outer cylinder head bolts finger-tight.

✳✳ WARNING

To prevent engine damage, keep the push rods in the order in which they were removed. Install all push rods back in their original positions.

➡ Higher mileage engines require push rods to be cleaned so the copper colored end of the push rod can be identified.

29. Apply clean engine oil to each end of the push rod. Insert them into their respective positions with the copper colored end up.

➡ Coat the end of each valve stem with clean engine oil.

30. Install the eight valve bridges.

✳✳ WARNING

Rotate the crankshaft until the damper locating dowel notch is in the six o'clock position or engine damage can occur.

➡ Apply clean engine oil to the top center of each valve bridge.

31. Install the rocker arm assemblies and eight bolts.

✳✳ WARNING

Using too much engine oil on the threads of the cylinder head bolts can cause damage to the threads and poor sealing. Using anti-seize compounds, grease or any other lubricants other than engine oil on the cylinder head bolt threads can affect the true torque value of the bolts.

➡Lightly lubricate the new cylinder head bolt threads and flanges with clean engine oil.

32. Install the 10 inner cylinder head retaining bolts finger-tight.

33. Tighten the head bolts in the following sequence.

    a. Tighten bolts 1 through 10 to 88 Nm (65 ft. lbs.).

    b. Tighten bolts 1, 3, 5, 7 and 9 to 115 Nm (85 ft. lbs.).

    c. Tighten bolts in sequence 1 through 10, clockwise 90 degrees.

    d. Tighten bolts in sequence 1 through 10, a second time, clockwise 90 degrees.

    e. Tighten bolts in sequence 1 through 10, a third time, clockwise 90 degrees.

    f. Tighten bolts 11 through 15 to 24 Nm (18 ft. lbs.).

    g. Tighten bolts 11 through 15 to 31 Nm (23 ft. lbs.).

34. Install the four glow plugs.

Late build

➡Clean and inspect the glow plug connector O-rings and install new as necessary.

➡Apply clean engine oil to the O-rings.

35. Install the glow plug harness.

❊❊ WARNING

To prevent engine damage, check that the crankcase-to-head tube assemblies bottom out in the branch tube assembly. The oil rail, crankcase-to-head tube and the fuel injectors will not function correctly if the tube is not bottomed out.

36. Apply clean engine oil and install the crankcase-to-head tube assembly.

Early build

➡Clean and inspect the glow plug buss bar O-rings and install new as necessary.

➡Apply clean engine oil to the O-rings before installing.

37. Install the glow plug buss bar.

➡Install a new lower O-ring.

38. Install a new crankcase to head tube assembly.

All vehicles

39. Position the turbocharger adapter pipe.

➡Apply anti-seize lubricants to the bolt threads prior to installing the bolts.

➡Do not tighten until after the turbocharger is installed.

40. Install the nuts and bolts in the adapter pipe.

➡Apply clean engine oil to the O-ring prior to installing.

41. Install the cylinder block drain plug.

42. Install the starter.

43. Install the fuel injectors.

44. Install the intake manifold.

➡Install a new oil filter.

45. Fill the crankcase with clean engine oil.

ENGINE ASSEMBLY

REMOVAL & INSTALLATION

F-150 and Mark LT 4.2L Engine

1. Before servicing the vehicle, refer to the Precautions Section.

All vehicles

2. Raise and safely support the vehicle.

3. Release the fuel system pressure.

4. Disconnect the battery ground cable.

5. Drain the cooling system.

6. Remove the hood.

7. Remove the cowl panel grille.

8. Remove the powertrain control module (PCM).

9. Detach the electrical connector, the wiring harness retainer and the washer hose from the cowl extension panel.

Vehicles equipped with a manual transmission

10. Remove the push pins and position the clutch master cylinder reservoir aside.

11. Disconnect the fuel vapor tubes from the purge valve.

All vehicles

12. Remove the 7 bolts and the cowl extension panel.

13. Remove the 9 push pins and the radiator sight shield.

14. Remove the upper intake manifold.

15. Remove the radiator, the cooling fan and the shroud.

16. Remove the air cleaner.

17. Release the clamp and disconnect the upper radiator hose from the thermostat housing. Remove the hose from the vehicle.

18. Release the clamps, disconnect the heater hoses and position the heater hoses aside.

19. Release the clamp and disconnect the lower radiator hose from the coolant pump.

20. Disconnect the intake manifold runner control (IMRC) actuator and the fuel charging wiring harness electrical connectors.

21. Disconnect the fuel supply spring lock coupling.

22. Remove the 4 bolts and the fuel rail, the fuel injectors, the fuel charging wiring harness and the vacuum harness as an assembly.

Vehicles equipped with an automatic transmission

23. Disconnect the fuel vapor tubes from the purge valve.

All vehicles

24. Using the special tool, with a twisting motion, pull the left spark plug wires off the spark plugs.

25. Detach the left spark plug wire retainers and remove the left spark plug wires.

26. Remove the bolts and position the power steering fluid reservoir aside.

27. If equipped, remove the compressor manifold and tube assembly.

28. Rotate the accessory drive belt

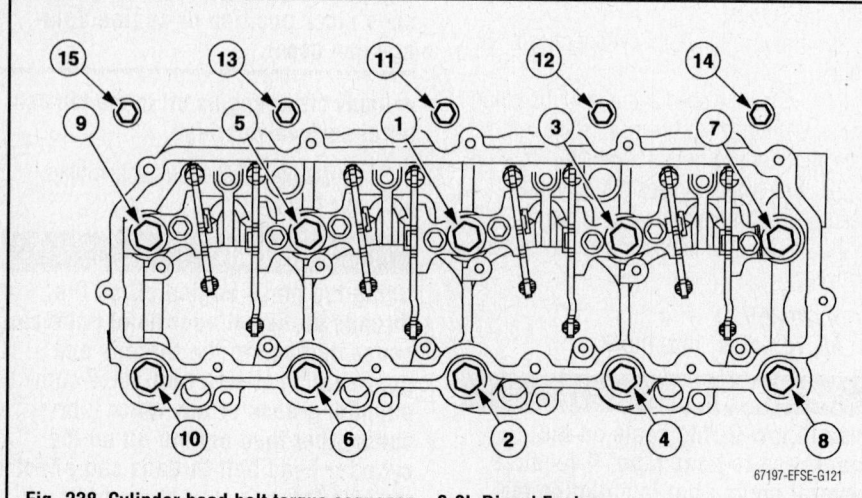

Fig. 238 Cylinder head bolt torque sequence—6.0L Diesel Engine

67197-EFSE-G121

tensioner counterclockwise and remove the accessory drive belt.

29. Remove the 2 power steering pump upper bolts.

30. Disconnect the alternator.

31. Detach the wiring harness retainer.

32. Using the special tool, with a twisting motion, pull the right spark plug wires off the spark plugs.

33. Detach the right spark plug wire retainers.

34. Disconnect the coil electrical connector.

35. Remove the bolts, the coil and the right spark plug wires as an assembly.

36. Disconnect the positive crankcase ventilation (PCV) valve hose from the PCV valve and remove the hose.

37. Disconnect the wiring harness in-line connector.

38. Remove the bolt and detach the ground wire.

39. Detach the wiring harness retainer from the rear of the right cylinder head.

40. Remove the power steering pressure hose bracket nut.

➡**The front bolt cannot be removed from the power steering pump with the pressure hose in place. Remove the rear bolt first, then slide the power steering pump out while removing the second bolt.**

41. Remove the bolts and position the power steering pump aside.

42. Drain the engine oil. Install the drain plug when finished. Tighten to 23 Nm (17 ft. lbs.).

43. Remove the oil filter.

Vehicles equipped with an automatic transmission

44. Detach the transmission cooler tubes from the bracket.

All vehicles

45. Remove the nut and position the starter wiring harness aside.

46. If equipped, disconnect the engine block heater electrical connector.

47. Remove the 4 3-way catalytic converter-to-exhaust manifold nuts.

48. Remove the starter motor.

Vehicles equipped with an automatic transmission

49. Remove the cylinder block opening cover.

➡**Rotate the crankshaft using the crankshaft pulley bolt to access all of the torque converter nuts.**

➡**Mark the flexplate and one torque converter stud for installation reference.**

50. Remove the 4 torque converter nuts.

51. Remove the 3 oil pan-to-transmission bolts.

52. Remove the transmission-to-engine bolts.

53. Remove the left engine support insulator through bolt.

54. Remove the right engine support insulator nuts.

55. Remove the stud bolt, the bolts and the power steering fluid reservoir bracket.

56. Remove the nuts and the right engine lifting eye.

57. Install the lifting eye on the right side of the engine.

58. Remove the nuts and the left engine lifting eye.

59. Install the lifting eye on the left side of the engine.

➡**Use 2 10mm (⅜ inch) spring links to connect the Engine Lifting Bracket 303-F047 to the Lifting Bracket, Engine 303-050.**

60. Install the lifting bracket.

61. Connect an engine crane to the special tool and lift the engine approximately 75 mm (3 in.).

62. Remove the bolts and the left engine support insulator.

63. Remove the bolts and the right engine support insulator.

64. Support the transmission with a floor jack and a wood block.

Vehicles equipped with an automatic transmission

65. Remove the engine from the vehicle.

Vehicles equipped with a manual transmission

66. Lift the engine while pulling the engine forward until the alternator pulley is above the radiator upper support.

67. Rotate the engine 90 degrees to the left and remove the engine from the vehicle.

To install:
Vehicles equipped with an automatic transmission

➡**Make sure the marks made on the torque converter stud and the flexplate are lined up.**

68. Position the engine in the vehicle and mate it to the transmission.

Vehicles equipped with a manual transmission

69. Position the engine with the front of the engine facing the left side of the vehicle.

70. Lower the engine until the alternator pulley is slightly higher than the radiator upper support.

71. Turn the engine 90 degrees to the right, lower the engine and mate it to the transmission.

All vehicles

72. Install the right engine support insulator and the bolts. Tighten to 63 Nm (46 ft. lbs.).

73. Install the left engine support insulator and the bolts. Tighten to 63 Nm (46 ft. lbs.).

74. Remove the floor jack and wood block from the transmission.

75. Lower the engine into position and remove the floor crane and the special tools.

76. Position the power steering fluid reservoir bracket and install the bolts and the stud bolt. Tighten to 20 Nm (15 inch lbs.).

77. Install the right engine support insulator nuts. Tighten to 175 Nm (129 ft. lbs.).

78. Install the left engine support insulator through bolt. Tighten to 175 Nm (129 ft. lbs.).

79. Install the transmission-to-engine bolts. Tighten to 47 Nm (35 ft. lbs.).

80. Install the 3 oil pan-to-transmission bolts. Tighten to 34 Nm (24 ft. lbs.).

Vehicles equipped with an automatic transmission

➡**Rotate the crankshaft using the crankshaft pulley bolt to access all of the torque converter nuts.**

81. Install the 4 torque converter nuts. Tighten to 36 Nm (27 ft. lbs.).

82. Install the cylinder block opening cover.

All vehicles

83. Install the starter motor.

84. Install the 4 3-way catalytic converter nuts. Tighten to 40 Nm (30 ft. lbs.).

85. If equipped, connect the engine block heater electrical connector.

86. Position the starter wiring harness bracket and install the nut. Tighten to 20 Nm (15 ft. lbs.).

Vehicles equipped with an automatic transmission

87. Attach the transmission cooler tubes to the bracket.

All vehicles

88. Install a new oil filter. Tighten to 12 Nm (9 ft. lbs.).

➡**Do not tighten the bolts until the 2 upper bolts are installed.**

➡**Make sure the power steering pressure hose bracket is installed on the stud.**

89. Position the power steering pump and install the bolts finger tight. Install the nut. Tighten to 10 Nm (89 inch lbs.).

90. Attach the wiring harness retainer to the rear of the right cylinder head.

91. Position the ground wire and install the bolt.

92. Connect the wiring harness in-line connector.

93. Connect the positive crankcase ventilation (PCV) valve hose to the PCV valve.

94. Position the coil and the right spark plug wires as an assembly and install the bolts. Tighten to 7 Nm (62 inch lbs.).

95. Connect the coil electrical connector.

96. Attach the right spark plug wire retainers.

97. Apply silicone dielectric compound to the inside of the spark plug wire boots.

98. Connect the spark plug wires to the spark plugs. Attach the wiring harness retainer.

99. Connect the alternator.

➡ **Tighten the lower bolts at this time.**

100. Install the power steering pump upper bolts. Tighten to 25 Nm (18 ft. lbs.).

101. Rotate the accessory drive belt tensioner counterclockwise and install the accessory drive belt.

102. If equipped, install the compressor manifold and tube assembly.

103. Position the power steering fluid reservoir and install the bolts. Tighten to 10 Nm (89 inch lbs.).

104. Position the left spark plug wires and attach the left spark plug wire retainers.

105. Apply silicone dielectric compound to the inside of the spark plug wire boots.

106. Connect the spark plug wires to spark plugs.

Vehicles equipped with an automatic transmission

107. Connect the fuel vapor tubes to the purge valve.

All vehicles

108. Position the fuel rail, the fuel injectors, the fuel charging wiring harness and the vacuum harness as an assembly and install the bolts. Tighten to 10 Nm (89 inch lbs.).

109. Connect the fuel supply spring lock coupling.

110. Connect the intake manifold runner control (IMRC) actuator and the fuel charging wiring harness electrical connectors.

111. Connect the lower radiator hose to the coolant pump.

112. Connect the heater hoses.

113. Connect the upper radiator hose to the thermostat housing.

114. Install the air cleaner.

115. Install the radiator and the cooling fan and shroud.

116. Install the upper intake manifold.

117. Position the radiator sight shield and install the 9 push pins.

118. Position the cowl extension panel and install the 7 bolts.

Vehicles equipped with a manual transmission

119. Connect the fuel vapor tubes to the purge valve. Position the clutch master cylinder reservoir and install the push pins.

All vehicles

120. Attach the windshield washer hose, the wiring harness retainer and the electrical connector to the cowl extension panel.

121. Install the powertrain control module (PCM).

122. Install the cowl panel grille.

123. Position the hood and install the bolts. Tighten to 30 Nm (22 ft. lbs.).

124. Connect the battery ground cable.

125. Fill the engine with clean engine oil.

126. Fill and bleed the cooling system.

127. If equipped, evacuate and charge the A/C system.

F-150 and Mark LT 4.6L Engine

1. Before servicing the vehicle, refer to the Precautions Section.

2. Raise and safely support the vehicle.

3. Remove the hood.

4. Remove the intake manifold. See "Intake Manifold" in this section.

5. Remove the radiator.

6. Remove the powertrain control module (PCM) and the support bracket.

7. Remove the cowl panel grille.

8. Detach the wiring harness and the windshield washer hose from the cowl panel extension.

9. Remove the bolts and the cowl panel extension.

10. Disconnect the electrical connector and remove the bolt and the ground strap.

11. Disconnect the heater hose.

12. Remove the nut and the A/C manifold and tube assembly support bracket.

13. Disconnect the A/C compressor electrical connector.

14. Disconnect the degas bottle (coolant reservoir) coolant hose.

15. Remove the bolts and position the power steering reservoir assembly aside.

16. Using the special tool, remove the power steering pump pulley.

17. Disconnect the power steering pressure tube. Drain the power steering fluid into a suitable container.

18. Remove the nut and position aside the power steering pressure tube.

19. Remove the power steering pump bolts and position the power steering pump assembly aside.

20. Remove the starter.

21. Disconnect the crankcase position (CKP) sensor electrical connector and harness retainer.

22. If equipped, remove the nut and the transmission cooler tube support bracket.

23. Remove the bolts and position the A/C compressor aside.

24. If equipped, disconnect the block heater electrical connector.

25. Detach the starter electrical harness support from the cylinder block.

26. Remove the drain plug and drain the engine oil.

27. Remove the oil filter.

28. Remove the bolts and the flexplate inspection cover.

29. Remove the cylinder block opening cover.

30. Remove the torque converter-to-flexplate nuts. Discard the nuts.

31. Disconnect the left heated exhaust gas oxygen sensor (HO2S) electrical connector and detach the electrical connector retainer.

32. Disconnect the shift cable and remove the shift cable bracket.

➡ **The left upper transmission-to-engine bolt will be removed later.**

33. Remove the 6 transmission-to-engine bolts.

34. Remove the bolt and position the transmission fluid filler tube aside.

35. Remove the 4 exhaust manifold flange nuts.

36. Remove the right motor mount nuts.

37. Remove the left motor mount bolt.

38. Support the transmission.

➡ **On 4x4 vehicles, it may be necessary to reposition the transfer case vent hose to access the bolt.**

39. Remove the left upper transmission-to-engine bolt.

40. Install the lifting bracket.

➡ **Raise the engine and position forward to disconnect the transmission wiring harness retainer at the rear of the right cylinder head and disconnect the right heated exhaust gas oxygen sensor (HO2S) electrical connector and detach the electrical connector retainer.**

41. Using a suitable floor crane, remove the engine assembly from the vehicle.

To install:

❈❈ WARNING

Clean the engine support insulator-to-frame mating surfaces of any dirt

or foreign material prior to engine installation.

→**Position the engine assembly forward to connect the right heated exhaust gas oxygen sensor (HO₂S) electrical connector and the transmission harness retainers at the rear of the cylinder head.**

42. Using a suitable floor crane, position the engine assembly into the vehicle.

43. Apply High Strength Threadlocker to the bolt threads and install the left engine support insulator bolt.

   a. If the engine support insulator nut is missing or damaged, install a new nut using service part number W709375.

   b. If the engine support insulator nut cage is damaged or missing, install a new nut using service part number W520516-S301. Tighten to 175 Nm (129 ft. lbs.).

44. Apply High Strength Threadlocker to the bolt threads and install the right engine support insulator washer and nuts. Tighten to 175 Nm (129 ft. lbs.).

45. Install the 6 transmission-to-engine bolts. Tighten to 60 Nm (44 ft. lbs.).

46. Connect the shift cable and install the shift cable bracket and the bolts. Tighten to 25 Nm (18 ft. lbs.).

47. Connect the left heated exhaust gas oxygen sensor (HO₂S) electrical connector and attach the electrical connector retainer.

→**Lubricate the O-ring seals with clean transmission fluid.**

48. Position the transmission fluid filler tube and install the bolt. Tighten to 12 Nm (9 ft. lbs.).

49. Install the 4 exhaust manifold-to-catalytic converter nuts. Tighten to 40 Nm (30 ft. lbs.).

50. Install the torque converter-to-flexplate nuts. Tighten to 35 Nm (26 ft. lbs.).

51. Install the cylinder block opening cover.

52. Install the flexplate inspection cover. Tighten to 34 Nm (25 ft. lbs.).

53. Install a new oil filter.

54. Install the drain plug. Tighten to 14 Nm (10 ft. lbs.).

55. Attach the starter electrical harness support to the cylinder block. Tighten to 10 Nm (89 inch lbs.).

56. If equipped, connect the block heater electrical connector.

57. Position the A/C compressor and install the bolts. Tighten to 25 Nm (18 ft. lbs.).

58. Install the starter.

59. Position the power steering reservoir and install the 2 lower bolts. Tighten to 23 Nm (17 ft. lbs.).

60. Position the power steering pump and install the bolts. Tighten to 25 Nm (18 ft. lbs.).

61. Using the special tool, install a new O-ring seal on the pressure line fitting.

62. Connect the power steering pressure tube. Tighten to 65 Nm (48 ft. lbs.).

63. Position the power steering pressure tube support bracket and install the nut. Tighten to 10 Nm (89 inch lbs.).

✳✳ WARNING

If the pulley has been removed and installed twice, install a new power steering pump pulley.

64. Install the power steering pump pulley. Inspect the pulley for paint marks in the web area near the hub. If there are 2 paint marks, install a new pulley. If there is one paint mark or none at all, use a pencil to mark the web area of the pulley near the hub.

65. If equipped, install the transmission cooler tube support bracket and nut. Tighten to 10 Nm (89 inch lbs.).

66. Connect the degas bottle (coolant reservoir) coolant hose.

67. Connect the A/C compressor electrical connector.

68. Connect the crankcase position (CKP) sensor electrical connector and the harness retainer.

69. Position the A/C manifold and tube assembly support bracket and install the nut. Tighten to 10 Nm (89 inch lbs.).

70. Remove the lifting bracket.

71. Install the upper transmission-to-engine bolts. Tighten to 60 Nm (44 ft. lbs.).

72. Connect the heater coolant hose.

73. Install the ground strap and the bolt and connect the electrical connector. Tighten to 10 Nm (89 inch lbs.).

74. Install the cowl panel extension.

75. Attach the wiring harness and the windshield washer hose to the cowl panel extension.

76. Install the cowl panel grill.

77. Install the powertrain control module (PCM) and the support bracket.

78. Install the intake manifold.

79. Install the radiator.

80. Install the hood and the 4 bolts. Tighten to 30 Nm (22 ft. lbs.).

81. Fill the engine with clean engine oil.

82. Fill and bleed the engine cooling system.

F-150 and Mark LT 5.4L Engine

1. Before servicing the vehicle, refer to the Precautions Section.

All vehicles

2. Raise and safely support the vehicle.

3. Remove the hood.

4. Remove the intake manifold. See "Intake Manifold" in this section.

5. Remove the accessory drive belt.

6. Recover the A/C system.

7. Remove the radiator.

8. Remove the powertrain control module (PCM) and the support bracket.

9. Remove the cowl panel grille.

10. Detach the wiring harness and the windshield washer hose retainers from the cowl panel extension.

11. Remove the bolts and the cowl extension panel.

12. Disconnect the electrical connector and remove the bolt and the ground strap.

13. Disconnect the heater hose.

14. Remove the nut, disconnect the A/C manifold and tube assembly and position aside.

15. Remove the nut and the A/C manifold and tube assembly and support bracket.

16. Disconnect the coolant hose.

17. Remove the bolt and position the power steering reservoir assembly aside.

18. Disconnect the alternator wiring harness retainer from the right cylinder head.

19. Disconnect the A/C compressor and the A/C high pressure cut-off switch electrical connectors.

20. Disconnect the alternator wiring harness retainer from the right cylinder head and position the harness aside.

21. Disconnect the crankshaft position (CKP) sensor wiring harness retainer from the starter motor wiring harness.

22. Remove the nut and position aside the power steering pressure hose support bracket.

23. Using a puller, remove the power steering pump pulley.

24. Disconnect the power steering pressure tube. Drain the power steering fluid into a suitable container.

25. Remove the 3 bolts and position the power steering pump aside.

Manual transmission vehicles

26. Remove the clutch.

Automatic transmission vehicles

27. Remove the nut and position aside the transmission cooler tube support bracket.

28. Remove the starter.

29. Remove the 2 bolts and the flexplate inspection cover.

30. Remove the cylinder block opening cover.

31. Remove the 4 torque converter-to-flexplate nuts. Discard the nuts.

32. Disconnect the shift cable and remove the shift cable bracket.

➡ **The upper 2 transmission-to-engine bolts will be removed later.**

33. Remove the lower 5 transmission-to-engine bolts.

34. Remove the bolt and position the transmission fluid filler tube aside.

All vehicles

35. Remove the drain plug and drain the engine oil.

36. Disconnect the right heated oxygen sensor (HO$_2$S) electrical connector and detach the wiring harness retainer.

37. Disconnect the left heated exhaust gas oxygen sensor electrical connector and detach the electrical connector retainer.

38. Remove the oil filter.

39. Disconnect the oil temperature sensor electrical connector.

40. Remove the bolts and position the A/C compressor aside.

41. If equipped, disconnect the block heater electrical connector.

42. Detach the starter electrical harness support from the cylinder block.

43. Remove the 4 exhaust manifold flange nuts.

44. Remove the right engine support insulator nuts and washer.

45. Remove the left engine support insulator bolt.

Automatic transmission vehicles

46. Support the transmission.

➡ **On 4WD vehicles, it may be necessary to reposition the transfer case vent hose to access the bolts.**

47. Remove the upper 2 transmission-to-engine bolts.

All vehicles

48. Install the lifting bracket.

49. Using a suitable floor crane, remove the engine assembly from the vehicle.

To install:
All vehicles

50. Using a suitable floor crane, position the engine assembly into the vehicle.

✳✳ WARNING

Only use hand tools when installing the left engine mount bolt or damage to the engine mount can occur.

➡ **Early build vehicles are equipped with an M14 through bolt. Late build vehicles are equipped with an M18 through bolt.**

51. Apply high strength threadlocker to the bolt threads and install the left engine support insulator bolt.

  a. If the M14 through bolt engine support insulator nut is missing or damaged, install a new nut using service part number W709375.

  b. If the M14 through bolt engine support insulator nut cage is damaged or missing, install a new nut using service part number W520516-S301.

  c. Early build vehicles, tighten to 220 Nm (162 ft. lbs.); Late build vehicles, tighten to 350 Nm (258 ft. lbs.).

✳✳ WARNING

Only use hand tools when installing the right engine mount nuts or damage to the engine mount can occur.

52. Apply high strength threadlocker to the stud threads and install the right engine support insulator washer and nuts. Tighten to 250 Nm (184 ft. lbs.).

53. Remove the lifting bracket.

Manual transmission vehicles

54. Install the clutch.

Automatic transmission vehicles

➡ **The upper 2 transmission-to-engine bolts will be installed later.**

55. Install the lower 5 transmission-to-engine bolts. Tighten to 60 Nm (44 ft. lbs.).

56. Position the shift cable bracket and install the bolts and connect the shift cable. Tighten to 25 Nm (18 ft. lbs.).

57. Install 4 new torque converter-to-flexplate nuts. Tighten to 36 Nm (27 ft. lbs.).

58. Install the cylinder block opening cover.

59. Install the flexplate inspection cover and the 2 bolts. Tighten to 34 Nm (25 ft. lbs.).

60. Install the starter.

61. Position the transmission cooler tube support bracket and install the bolt. Tighten to 10 Nm (89 inch lbs.).

All vehicles

62. If equipped, connect the block heater electrical connector.

63. Connect the left and right heated exhaust gas oxygen sensor (HO$_2$S) electrical connector and attach the electrical connector retainer.

64. Attach the starter electrical harness support bracket.

65. Connect the oil temperature sensor electrical connector.

66. Position the A/C compressor and install the 3 bolts. Tighten to 25 Nm (18 ft. lbs.).

67. Install the 4 exhaust manifold flange nuts. Tighten to 40 Nm (30 ft. lbs.).

Automatic transmission vehicles

68. Install the upper 2 transmission-to-engine bolts. Tighten to 60 Nm (44 ft. lbs.).

69. Position the transmission filler tube and install the bolt. Tighten to 20 Nm (15 ft. lbs.).

All vehicles

70. Connect the crankshaft position (CKP) sensor wiring harness retainer to the starter motor wiring harness.

71. Connect the alternator wiring harness retainer to the right cylinder head.

72. Connect the A/C compressor and the A/C high pressure cut-off switch electrical connectors.

73. Connect the alternator wiring harness retainer to the right cylinder head.

74. Position the power steering pump assembly and install the 3 bolts. Tighten to 25 Nm (18 ft. lbs.).

75. Install a new O-ring seal on the pressure line fitting.

76. Connect the power steering pressure tube. Tighten to 65 Nm (48 ft. lbs.).

77. Install the power steering pump pulley.

78. Position the power steering pressure hose support bracket and install the nut. Tighten to 10 Nm (89 inch lbs.).

79. Position the power steering reservoir assembly and install the bolt. Tighten to 23 Nm (17 ft. lbs.).

80. Using a new O-ring seal, connect the A/C manifold and tube assembly and install the nut. Tighten to 25 Nm (18 ft. lbs.).

81. Position the A/C manifold and tube assembly support bracket and install the nut. Tighten to 25 Nm (18 ft. lbs.).

82. Connect the heater hose.

83. Disconnect the coolant hose.

84. Connect the electrical connector and position the ground strap and install the bolt. Tighten to 10 Nm (89 inch lbs.).

85. Position the cowl extension panel and install the bolts.

86. Attach the wiring harness and the windshield washer hose retainers to the cowl panel extension.

87. Install the intake manifold.

88. Install the radiator.

89. Install the powertrain control module (PCM).

90. Install the cowl.

91. Install the hood.

92. Fill the crankcase with clean engine oil.

93. Evacuate and charge the A/C system.

94. Fill and bleed the power steering system.

F-250 and F-350 5.4L Engine

All vehicles

1. Raise and safely support the vehicle.
2. Remove the hood.
3. Remove the cowl vent grille.
4. Remove the radiator.
5. Remove the degas bottle (coolant reservoir).
6. Remove the intake manifold. See "Intake Manifold" in this section.
7. Remove the powertrain control module (PCM).
8. Remove the accessory drive belt.
9. Drain the engine oil.
10. Disconnect the degas bottle (coolant reservoir) coolant hose.
11. Disconnect the 2 electrical connectors on the left fender splash shield.
12. Remove the 3 bolts and position the power steering pump assembly aside.
13. Disconnect the alternator wiring harness retainer from the right cylinder head.
14. Disconnect the A/C compressor and the A/C high pressure cut-off switch electrical connectors.
15. Disconnect the alternator wiring harness retainer from the right cylinder head and position the harness aside.
16. Disconnect the crankshaft position (CKP) sensor wiring harness retainer from the starter motor wiring harness.
17. Disconnect the engine wiring harness retainer from the evaporative emissions (EVAP) canister purge valve bracket.
18. Disconnect the vacuum hose and engine wiring harness retainers.
19. Disconnect the EVAP tube quick connect couplings and the electrical connector from EVAP canister purge valve.
20. Remove the 3 nuts and remove the EVAP canister purge valve and bracket assembly.
21. Disconnect the body wiring harness retainer from the degas bottle (coolant reservoir) support bracket.
22. Remove the 3 nuts and the degas bottle (coolant reservoir) support bracket.
23. Remove the 2 nuts and the air cleaner outlet tube support bracket.
24. Disconnect the heater hose.

Manual transmission vehicles

25. Remove the clutch and pressure plate.

Automatic transmission vehicles

26. Remove the starter.
27. Remove the nut and position the transmission oil cooler lines and bracket aside.
28. Remove the 2 bolts and the flexplate inspection cover.
29. Remove the cylinder block opening cover.

30. Remove the 4 torque converter-to-flexplate nuts. Discard the nuts.

➡**The upper 2 transmission-to-engine bolts will be removed later.**

31. Remove the 5 transmission-to-engine bolts.
32. Remove the nut, the ground cable and position the transmission fluid filler tube aside.

All vehicles

33. If equipped, disconnect the block heater electrical connector.
34. Remove the stud bolt and position the ground strap aside.
35. Disconnect the oil temperature sensor electrical connector.
36. Remove the 3 bolts and position the A/C compressor aside.
37. Disconnect the 2 heated exhaust gas oxygen sensor (HO2S) electrical connectors.
38. Remove the 4 exhaust manifold flange nuts.
39. Remove the 6 right and left motor mount nuts.

Automatic transmission vehicles

40. Remove the upper 2 transmission-to-engine bolts.

All vehicles

41. Install the lifting bracket.
42. Using a suitable floor crane, remove the engine assembly from the vehicle.

To install:

All vehicles

43. Using a suitable floor crane, position the engine assembly into the vehicle.

⁕⁕ WARNING

Only use hand tools when installing the right engine mount nut or damage to the engine mount can occur.

➡**Align the engine-to-transmission dowels before installing the engine mount bolt.**

44. Install the 6 engine mount nuts. Tighten to 175 Nm (129 ft. lbs.).
45. Remove the lifting bracket.

Manual transmission vehicles
46. Install the clutch.

Automatic transmission vehicles

➡**The upper 2 transmission-to-engine bolts will be installed later.**

47. Install the lower 5 transmission-to-engine bolts. Tighten to 35 Nm (26 ft. lbs.).
48. Install 4 new torque converter-to-flexplate nuts. Tighten to 35 Nm (26 ft. lbs.).
49. Install the cylinder block opening cover.

50. Install the flexplate inspection cover and the 2 bolts. Tighten to 34 Nm (25 ft. lbs.).
51. Install the transmission fluid filler tube, the ground strap and the nut. Tighten to 12 Nm (9 ft. lbs.).
52. Install the starter.

All vehicles

53. If equipped, connect the block heater electrical connector.
54. Position the starter electrical harness support bracket and install the bolt. Tighten to 10 Nm (89 inch lbs.).
55. Position the ground strap and install the stud bolt. Tighten to 10 Nm (89 inch lbs.).
56. Connect the oil temperature sensor electrical connector.
57. Position the A/C compressor and install the 3 bolts. Tighten to 25 Nm (18 ft. lbs.).
58. Install the 4 exhaust manifold flange nuts. Tighten to 40 Nm (30 ft. lbs.).
59. Connect the 2 heated exhaust gas oxygen sensor (HO2S) electrical connectors.

Automatic transmission vehicles

60. Install the transmission cooler tube support bracket and the nut. Tighten to 10 Nm (89 inch lbs.).
61. Install the upper 2 transmission-to-engine bolts. Tighten to 48 Nm (35 ft. lbs.).

All vehicles

62. Position the degas bottle (coolant reservoir) support bracket and install the 3 nuts. Tighten to 10 Nm (89 inch lbs.).
63. Connect the body wiring harness retainer to the degas bottle (coolant reservoir) support bracket.
64. Position the evaporative emissions (EVAP) canister purge valve and bracket assembly, and install the 3 nuts. Tighten to 10 Nm (89 inch lbs.).
65. Connect the electrical connector and the EVAP tube quick connect couplings to the EVAP canister purge valve.
66. Connect the engine wiring harness retainer to the EVAP canister purge valve bracket.
67. Connect the crankshaft position (CKP) sensor wiring harness retainer to the starter motor wiring harness.
68. Connect the alternator wiring harness retainer to the right cylinder head.
69. Connect the A/C compressor and the A/C high pressure cut-off switch electrical connectors.
70. Connect the alternator wiring harness retainer to the right cylinder head.
71. Position the power steering pump and install the 3 bolts. Tighten to 25 Nm (18 ft. lbs.).

72. Position the air cleaner outlet tube support bracket and install the 2 nuts. Tighten to 25 Nm (18 ft. lbs.).

73. Connect the 2 electrical connectors on the left fender splash shield.

74. Connect the degas bottle (coolant reservoir) coolant hose.

75. Install the intake manifold.

76. Install the radiator.

77. Install the degas bottle (coolant reservoir).

78. Install the powertrain control module (PCM).

79. Install the cowl vent grille.

80. Install the hood.

81. Fill the crankcase with clean engine oil.

82. Evacuate and charge the A/C system.

83. Fill and bleed the power steering system.

F-250 and F-350 6.8L Engine

1. Before servicing the vehicle, refer to the Precautions Section.

All vehicles

2. Raise and safely support the vehicle.

3. Remove the hood.

4. Remove the radiator grille support.

5. Remove the A/C condenser core.

6. Remove the cowl vent grille.

7. Remove the radiator, fan shroud and engine cooling fan.

8. Remove the intake manifold.

9. Remove the degas bottle (coolant reservoir).

10. Remove the powertrain control module (PCM).

11. Disconnect the degas bottle (coolant reservoir) coolant hose.

12. Disconnect the 2 electrical connectors on the left fender splash shield.

13. If equipped, disconnect the block heater electrical connector.

14. Remove the 3 bolts and position the power steering pump aside.

15. Disconnect the alternator wiring harness retainer from the right cylinder head.

16. Disconnect the A/C compressor and the A/C high pressure cut-off switch electrical connectors.

17. Disconnect the alternator wiring harness retainer from the right cylinder head and position the harness aside.

18. Disconnect the crankshaft position (CKP) sensor wiring harness retainer from the starter motor wiring harness.

19. Disconnect the engine wiring harness retainer from the evaporative emissions (EVAP) canister purge valve bracket.

20. Disconnect EVAP tube quick connect couplings and the electrical connector from EVAP canister purge valve.

21. Remove the 3 nuts and remove EVAP canister purge valve and bracket assembly.

22. Disconnect the heater hose at the rear of the engine.

23. Disconnect the body wiring harness retainer from the degas bottle (coolant reservoir) support bracket.

24. Remove the 3 nuts and the degas bottle (coolant reservoir) support bracket.

25. Drain the engine oil.

26. Remove the 4 exhaust manifold-to-catalytic converter nuts.

27. Disconnect the 2 heated exhaust gas oxygen sensor (HO$_2$S) electrical connectors.

28. Remove the nut and the ground cable.

29. Remove the 3 bolts and position the A/C compressor aside.

Manual transmission vehicles

30. Remove the clutch.

All vehicles

31. Remove and discard the oil filter.

32. Disconnect the coolant hoses from the oil cooler.

33. Loosen the threaded shaft and remove the oil cooler. Discard the oil cooler.

Automatic transmission vehicles

34. Remove the starter motor.

35. Remove the transmission filler tube.

36. Remove the bolts and position the transmission oil cooler lines and bracket aside.

All vehicles

37. Remove the stud bolt and position the ground strap aside.

38. Remove the nut and position the starter electrical harness support bracket aside.

Automatic transmission vehicles

39. Remove the 2 bolts and the flexplate inspection cover.

40. Remove the access plug.

41. Remove the 6 torque converter-to-flexplate nuts. Discard the nuts.

42. Remove the 5 lower transmission-to-engine bolts.

Automatic transmission vehicles

43. Remove the upper 2 transmission-to-engine bolts.

All vehicles

44. Install the lifting bracket and support the engine with a suitable floor crane.

✳✳ WARNING

Only use hand tools when removing the engine mount nut or damage to the engine mount can occur.

45. Remove the 4 engine mount nuts.

Automatic transmission vehicles

46. Support the transmission with a jack.

All vehicles

47. Using a suitable floor crane, remove the engine assembly from the vehicle.

To install:

All vehicles

48. Using a suitable floor crane, position the engine assembly into the vehicle.

✳✳ WARNING

Only use hand tools when installing the right engine mount nut or damage to the engine mount can occur.

➡**Align the engine-to-transmission dowels before installing the engine mount bolt.**

49. Install the 4 engine mount nuts. Tighten to 175 Nm (129 ft. lbs.).

50. Remove the lifting bracket.

Manual transmission vehicles

51. Install the clutch.

Automatic transmission vehicles

➡**The upper 2 transmission-to-engine bolts will be installed later.**

52. Install the lower 5 transmission-to-engine bolts. Tighten to 35 Nm (26 ft. lbs.).

53. Install 6 new torque converter-to-flexplate nuts. Tighten to 35 Nm (26 ft. lbs.).

54. Install the cylinder block opening cover.

55. Install the flexplate inspection cover and the 2 bolts. Tighten to 34 Nm (25 ft. lbs.).

56. Install the starter.

57. Install the transmission filler tube.

All vehicles

58. Install the ground strap and the nut. Tighten to 10 Nm (89 inch lbs.).

59. If equipped, connect the block heater electrical connector.

60. Position the starter electrical harness support bracket and install the bolt. Tighten to 10 Nm (89 inch lbs.).

61. Position the ground strap and install the stud bolt. Tighten to 10 Nm (89 inch lbs.).

62. Position the A/C compressor and install the 3 bolts. Tighten to 25 Nm (18 ft. lbs.).

63. Install the 4 exhaust manifold flange nuts. Tighten to 40 Nm (30 ft. lbs.).

64. Connect the 2 heated exhaust gas oxygen sensor (HO$_2$S) electrical connectors.

Automatic transmission vehicles

65. Install the transmission cooler tube support bracket and the nut. Tighten to 10 Nm (89 inch lbs.).

66. Install the upper 2 transmission-to-engine bolts. Tighten to 48 Nm (35 ft. lbs.).

All vehicles

67. Position the degas bottle (coolant reservoir) support bracket and install the 3 nuts. Tighten to 10 Nm (89 inch lbs.).

68. Connect the heater hose at the rear of the engine.

69. Connect the body wiring harness retainer to the degas bottle (coolant reservoir) support bracket.

70. Position the evaporative emissions (EVAP) canister purge valve and bracket assembly, and install the 3 nuts. Tighten to 10 Nm (89 inch lbs.).

71. Connect the electrical connector and the EVAP tube quick connect couplings to the EVAP canister purge valve.

72. Connect the engine wiring harness retainer to the EVAP canister purge valve bracket.

73. Connect the crankshaft position (CKP) sensor wiring harness retainer to the starter motor wiring harness.

74. Connect the alternator wiring harness retainer to the right cylinder head.

75. Connect the A/C compressor and the A/C high pressure cut-off switch electrical connectors.

76. Connect the alternator wiring harness retainer to the right cylinder head.

77. Position the power steering pump and install the 3 bolts. Tighten to 25 Nm (18 ft. lbs.).

78. Connect the 2 electrical connectors on the left fender splash shield.

79. Connect the degas bottle (coolant reservoir) coolant hose.

80. Install the intake manifold.

81. Install the radiator, fan shroud and engine cooling fan.

82. Install the degas bottle (coolant reservoir).

83. Install the powertrain control module (PCM).

84. Install the cowl vent grille.

85. Install the radiator grille support.

86. Install the A/C condenser core.

87. Install the hood.

88. Fill the crankcase with clean engine oil.

F-250 and F-350 6.0L Diesel Engine

1. Before servicing the vehicle, refer to the Precautions Section.

2. With the vehicle in **Neutral**, position it on a hoist.

3. Disconnect the left and right battery ground cables.

Vehicles with manual transmission

➡**On vehicles equipped with manual transmissions, the transmission must be removed before the engine can be removed.**

4. Remove the transmission.

5. Remove the clutch.

All vehicles

6. Remove the air cleaner assembly.

7. Remove the radiator.

8. Remove the charge air cooler.

Vehicles with A/C

9. Remove the A/C condenser assembly.

All vehicles

10. Remove the parking lamp and the headlamp assemblies.

11. Remove the radiator grille, the radiator grille opening panel, and the upper radiator core supports.

12. Remove the front bumper.

13. Disconnect the transmission cooler hoses.

14. Remove the bolts and the transmission oil cooler.

15. Remove the bolts and position the power steering cooler out of the way.

16. Remove the intake manifold.

17. Remove the accessory drive idler pulley and bolt.

18. Disconnect the heater hose at the coolant pump.

19. Remove the battery cable cover.

20. Remove the nut and position the cable out of the way.

21. Disconnect the left glow plug electrical connector and wire retainer.

22. Disconnect the camshaft position (CMP) sensor electrical connector.

23. Remove the clips and disconnect the fuel lines.

24. Remove the lower radiator hose clamp and the hose.

25. Remove the power steering upper mounting bolts.

➡**Bolts need to be removed evenly.**

26. Remove the bolts and position the power steering pump out of the way.

27. Remove the nut and the battery cable bracket.

28. Remove the ground stud and the ground cable.

29. If equipped, disconnect the injection control pressure (ICP) sensor electrical connector.

30. Disconnect the glow plug electrical connectors.

31. Disconnect the right glow plug electrical connector and wire retainer.

Vehicles with A/C

32. Disconnect the A/C high pressure switch and the A/C clutch electrical connectors.

33. Disconnect the air conditioning manifold lines from the A/C compressor.

34. Remove the A/C compressor.

All vehicles

35. Disconnect the crankshaft position (CKP) sensor electrical connector and position the wiring aside.

Vehicles with automatic transmission

36. Remove the automatic transmission fluid indicator and tube.

All vehicles

37. Remove the ground strap at the back of the right head.

38. Remove the solenoid cap and disconnect the starter wiring.

39. Disconnect the block heater electrical connector.

40. Position the block heater and starter wiring harness out of the way.

Vehicles with automatic transmission

41. Remove the torque converter cover.

42. Remove the torque converter nuts.

All vehicles

43. Remove the bolts for the turbocharger adapter pipe.

44. Remove the motor mount nuts.

45. Loosen the nuts at the turbocharger adapter pipe flange.

Vehicles with automatic transmission

46. Remove the nine bell housing bolts.

All vehicles

47. Remove the turbocharger adapter pipe.

48. Remove the nuts and the fuel injector control module bracket.

49. Remove the left rear valve cover stud.

50. Remove the transmission cooler line bracket.

51. Secure the turbocharger outlet pipe.

52. Remove the manufacturer's lifting eye.

53. Install the engine lifting eye on the right cylinder head.

54. Install the front lifting brackets.

Vehicles with automatic transmission

55. Position a suitable jack under the transmission.

All vehicles

56. Install the Heavy Duty Floor Crane and Diesel Engine Lifting Bracket on the engine.

57. Raise the engine high enough to clear the No. 1 crossmember and pull the engine forward and clear of the vehicle.

To install:
All vehicles

58. With the vehicle in **Neutral**, position it on a hoist.

59. Raise the engine high enough to clear the No. 1 crossmember, then position the engine into the vehicle.

Vehicles with automatic transmission

60. Align the torque converter studs with the holes in the engine flywheel, then lower the engine onto the engine mount towers.

Vehicles with manual transmission

61. Lower the engine onto the engine mount towers.

All vehicles

62. Remove the Heavy Duty Floor Crane and the Diesel Engine Lifting Bracket.

Vehicles with automatic transmission

63. Remove the transmission jack.

64. Install the transmission-to-engine mounting bolts. Torque to 35 ft. lbs. (47 Nm).

65. Install the torque converter-to-flywheel retaining nuts. Torque to 26 ft. lbs. (35 Nm).

66. Install the flywheel housing cover.

All vehicles

67. Install the left and right side engine mount retaining nuts. Torque to 76 ft. lbs. (103 Nm).

68. Remove the engine lifting eye from the right side cylinder head.

69. Install the manufacturer's lifting bracket.

70. Remove the two engine lift adapters.

71. Position the turbocharger outlet pipe.

72. Install the transmission cooler tube bracket and nut.

73. Install the left rear valve cover stud.

74. Install the fuel injector control module bracket and nuts.

75. Position the turbocharger adapter pipe.

➡ **Do not tighten bolts at this time.**

➡ **Apply anti-seize lubricant to the threads prior to installing the bolts.**

76. Install the bolts for the turbocharger adapter pipe.

77. Position back the block heater and starter wiring.

78. Connect the block heater electrical connector.

79. Connect the starter wiring and install the solenoid cap.

80. Connect the ground strap on the right head and install the bolt.

Vehicles with automatic transmission

81. Install the automatic transmission fluid indicator and tube.

All vehicles

82. Position back the wiring and connect the crankshaft position (CKP) sensor electrical connector.

Vehicles with A/C

83. Install the A/C compressor. Torque to 18 ft. lbs. (25 Nm).

84. Position the A/C compressor manifold and install the bolt. Torque to 15 ft. lbs. (21 Nm).

85. Connect the A/C high pressure switch and the clutch electrical connectors.

All vehicles

86. Connect the right glow plug electrical connector and wire retainer.

87. Connect the glow plug module electrical connectors.

88. If equipped, connect the injection control pressure (ICP) sensor electrical connector.

89. Connect the ground cable and the ground stud.

90. Install the battery cable bracket and the nut.

➡**The lower bolts need to be installed evenly.**

91. Position the power steering pump and install the lower bolts. Torque to 18 ft. lbs. (25 Nm).

92. Install the power steering pump upper bolts. Torque to 18 ft. lbs. (25 Nm).

93. Install the lower radiator hose and clamp.

94. Connect the fuel lines and install the clips.

95. Connect the camshaft position (CMP) sensor electrical connector.

96. Connect the left glow plug electrical connector and wire retainer.

97. Connect the battery crossover cable.

98. Install the battery cable cover.

99. Connect the heater hose at the coolant pump.

100. Install the accessory drive idler pulley and bolt. Torque to 35 ft. lbs. (47 Nm).

101. Install the intake manifold.

102. Tighten the turbocharger adapter pipe at the flanges. Torque to 20 ft. lbs. (27 Nm).

103. Tighten the nuts at the turbocharger adapter pipe flange. Torque to 35 ft. lbs. (47 Nm).

104. Position and install the power steering cooler and bolts.

105. Install the transmission oil cooler.

106. Connect the transmission cooler hoses.

107. Install the front bumper.

108. Install the upper radiator core support, radiator grill opening panel and the radiator grill.

109. Install the headlamp and the parking lamp assemblies.

Vehicles with A/C

110. Install the A/C condenser assembly.

All vehicles

111. Install the charge air cooler.

112. Install the radiator.

113. Install the air cleaner assembly.

Vehicles with manual transmission

114. Install the clutch assembly.

115. Install the transmission.

All vehicles

116. Fill the motor with clean engine oil.

117. Connect the left and right battery cables.

118. Fill the cooling system.

Vehicles with automatic transmission

119. Check and fill the automatic transmission.

EXHAUST MANIFOLD

REMOVAL & INSTALLATION

4.2L Engine

See Figures 239 and 240.

1. Before servicing the vehicle, refer to the Precautions Section.

2. Remove or disconnect the following:
   - Negative battery cable.
   - For the right-hand manifold: the EGR valve-to-exhaust manifold tube.
   - For the left-hand manifold: the oil level indicator tube bracket nut, then remove the oil level indicator tube. Remove and discard the oil level indicator tube O-ring.
   - Oxygen Sensor (O_2S) electrical connector.
   - The 2 catalytic converter-to-exhaust manifold nuts, then disconnect the Y-pipe from the left-hand exhaust manifold.
   - Exhaust manifold stud bolts, then remove the manifold mounting bolts.
   - Exhaust manifold. Remove and discard the exhaust manifold gasket.

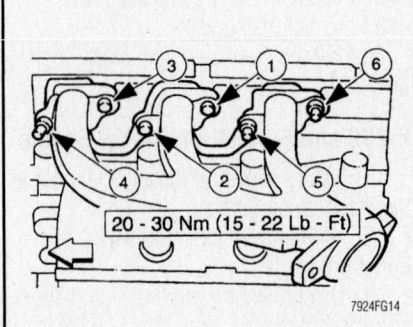

Fig. 239 Tighten the left-hand exhaust manifold bolts in the order shown—4.2L engine

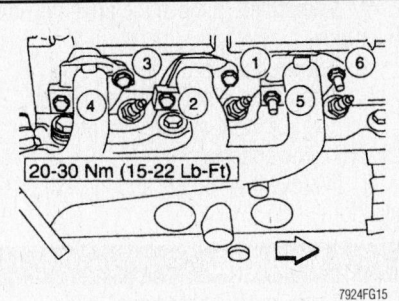

Fig. 240 Tighten the right-hand exhaust manifold bolts in the order shown—4.2L engine

To install:

3. Install or connect the following:
- New exhaust manifold gasket onto the engine, then install the exhaust manifold. Tighten the bolts and stud bolts in the sequence shown to 15–22 ft. lbs. (20–30 Nm).
- Y-pipe to the exhaust manifold, then install and tighten the catalytic converter nuts to 25–34 ft. lbs. (34–46 Nm).
- O_2S connector, then lower the vehicle.
- Left-hand exhaust manifold: a new oil level indicator tube O-ring onto the tube. Insert the tube into the engine block and tighten the bracket retaining nut to 15–22 ft. lbs. (20–30 Nm).
- For the right-hand exhaust manifold: the EGR valve-to-exhaust manifold tube. Tighten the upper and lower fittings to 25–34 ft. lbs. (34–47 Nm).
- Negative battery cable.

4.6L Engine

Right Side

See Figure 241.

1. Before servicing the vehicle, refer to the Precautions Section.
2. With the vehicle in **Neutral**, position it on a hoist.
3. Remove the starter.
4. Remove the right inner fenderwell.
5. Disconnect the Y-pipe at the manifold.
6. Remove the manifold. Discard the gasket.

➡**Do not use metal scrapers, wire brushes, power abrasive discs, or other abrasive means to clean the sealing surfaces. These may cause scratches and gouges resulting in leak paths. Use**

a plastic scraper to clean the sealing surfaces.

7. Clean the sealing surfaces with metal surface prep.

To install:

➡**Install a new exhaust manifold gasket.**

8. Position the right exhaust manifold and tighten the nuts in the sequence shown.
9. To install, reverse the removal procedure.

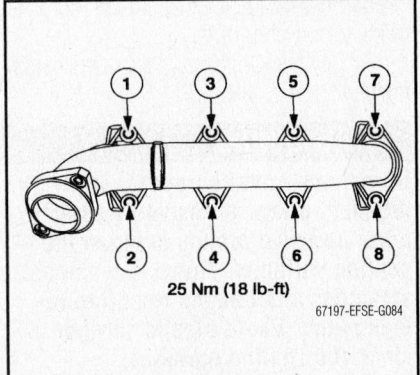

Fig. 241 Right exhaust manifold torque sequence—4.6L engine

Left Side

See Figure 242.

1. Before servicing the vehicle, refer to the Precautions Section.
2. With the vehicle in **Neutral**, position it on a hoist.
3. Remove the left inner fenderwell.
4. Disconnect the Y-pipe at the manifold.
5. Disconnect the EGR tube.
6. Remove the manifold. Discard the gasket.

➡**Do not use metal scrapers, wire brushes, power abrasive discs, or other abrasive means to clean the sealing surfaces. These may cause scratches and gouges resulting in leak paths. Use a plastic scraper to clean the sealing surfaces.**

7. Clean the sealing surfaces with metal surface prep.

To install:

➡**Install a new exhaust manifold gasket.**

8. Position the left exhaust manifold and tighten the exhaust manifold nuts in the sequence shown.
9. To install, reverse the removal procedure.

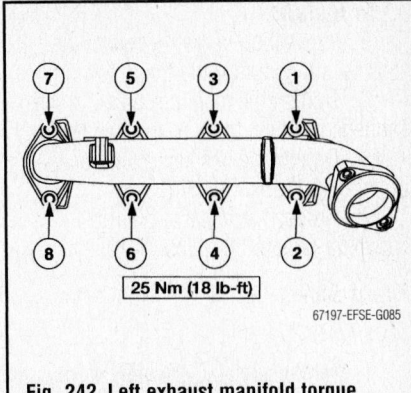

Fig. 242 Left exhaust manifold torque sequence—4.6L engines

5.4L Engine

Left Side

See Figure 243.

1. Before servicing the vehicle, refer to the Precautions Section.
2. With the vehicle in **Neutral**, position it on a hoist.
3. Remove the front and rear oxygen sensors.
4. Disconnect the exhaust pipes from the catalytic converters and the crossmember brackets.
5. Remove the manifold. Discard the gasket.

➡**Do not use metal scrapers, wire brushes, power abrasive discs, or other abrasive means to clean the sealing surfaces. These may cause scratches and gouges resulting in leak paths. Use a plastic scraper to clean the sealing surfaces.**

6. Clean the sealing surfaces with metal surface prep.
7. Install the manifold with a new gasket.
8. Tighten the exhaust manifold nuts in the sequence shown.

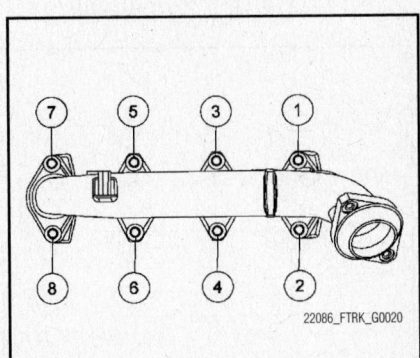

Fig. 243 Right side exhaust manifold nut tightening sequence—2005 4.6L engine

To install:

9. Installation is the reverse of the removal procedure. Note the following:

10. Tighten the manifold bolts, in the sequence shown, to 18 ft. lbs. (25 Nm).

11. Tighten the exhaust pipe bracket bolts to 18 ft. lbs. (25 Nm).

12. Tighten the exhaust pipe-to-converter nuts to 30 ft. lbs. (40 Nm).

Right Side

See Figure 244.

1. Before servicing the vehicle, refer to the Precautions Section.

2. With the vehicle in **Neutral**, position it on a hoist.

3. Remove the starter.

4. Remove the right side inner fender well.

5. Disconnect the exhaust pipes at the manifolds and catalytic converters.

6. If equipped, remove the mounting bolts and position the sway bar aside.

7. Remove the manifold. Discard the gasket.

➡Do not use metal scrapers, wire brushes, power abrasive discs, or other abrasive means to clean the sealing surfaces. These may cause scratches and gouges resulting in leak paths. Use a plastic scraper to clean the sealing surfaces.

8. Clean the sealing surfaces with metal surface prep.

9. Tighten the right exhaust manifold nuts in the sequence shown.

To install:

10. Installation is the reverse of the removal procedure. Note the following:

11. Tighten the manifold bolts, in the sequence shown, to 18 ft. lbs. (25 Nm).

12. If removed, install the sway bar nuts to 22 ft. lbs. (30 Nm).

13. Tighten the exhaust pipe flange and converter nuts to 30 ft. lbs. (40 Nm).

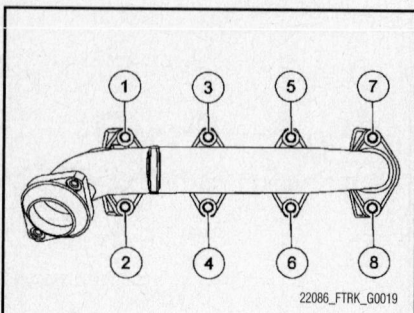

Fig. 244 Right side exhaust manifold nut tightening sequence—2005 4.6L engine

6.8L Engines

Left Side

See Figure 245.

1. Before servicing the vehicle, refer to the Precautions Section.

2. Raise and safely support the vehicle.

3. Remove the air cleaner housing.

4. Remove the 2 bolts and position the degas bottle (coolant reservoir) aside.

5. Disconnect and position the brake tube retainer aside.

6. Remove the 4 exhaust manifold-to-catalytic converter nuts.

7. Remove the 10 nuts and the exhaust manifold.

✳✳ WARNING

Do not use metal scrapers, wire brushes, power abrasive discs or other abrasive means to clean the sealing surfaces. These may cause scratches and gouges resulting in leak paths. Use a plastic scraper to clean the sealing surfaces.

➡Clean the sealing surfaces with metal surface prep. Follow the directions on the packaging.

8. Remove and discard the exhaust manifold gaskets. Clean the sealing surfaces with metal surface prep.

9. To install, reverse the removal procedure.

10. Torque the manifold nuts to 18 ft. lbs. (25 Nm).

11. Torque the exhaust pipe-to-manifold nuts to 30 ft. lbs. (40 Nm).

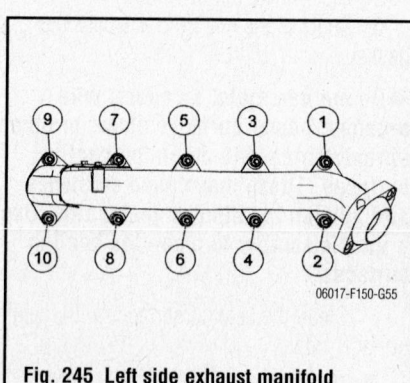

Fig. 245 Left side exhaust manifold torque sequence—6.8L engine

Right Side

See Figure 246.

1. Before servicing the vehicle, refer to the Precautions Section.

2. Raise and safely support the vehicle.

3. If equipped, remove the transmission filler tube.

4. Remove the starter.

5. Remove the right inner fenderwell.

6. Remove the 4 exhaust manifold-to-catalytic converter nuts.

7. Remove the 10 nuts and the exhaust manifold.

✳✳ WARNING

Do not use metal scrapers, wire brushes, power abrasive discs or other abrasive means to clean the sealing surfaces. These may cause scratches and gouges resulting in leak paths. Use a plastic scraper to clean the sealing surfaces.

➡Clean the sealing surfaces with metal surface prep. Follow the directions on the packaging.

8. Remove and discard the exhaust manifold gaskets. Clean the sealing surfaces with metal surface prep.

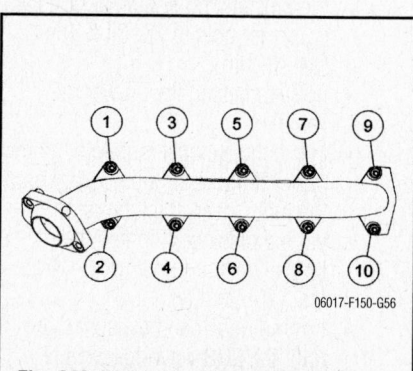

Fig. 246 Right side exhaust manifold torque sequence—6.8L engine

9. To install, reverse the removal procedure. Torque the manifold nuts to 18 ft. lbs. (25 Nm). Torque the exhaust pipe-to-manifold nuts to 30 ft. lbs. (40 Nm).

6.0L Diesel Engine

Left Side

See Figure 247.

1. Before servicing the vehicle, refer to the Precautions Section.

2. With the vehicle in NEUTRAL, position it on a hoist.

3. Prior to removing the exhaust manifold, inspect the exhaust manifold for warpage with a feeler gauge between the manifold and the cylinder head.

4. Record the measurement and compare with the specifications.

5. Remove the 2 LH exhaust manifold-to-turbocharger adapter pipe nuts.

6. Disconnect the exhaust pressure (EP) sensor tube from the LH exhaust manifold.

7. Remove the 8 bolts, 8 spacers and the LH exhaust manifold.

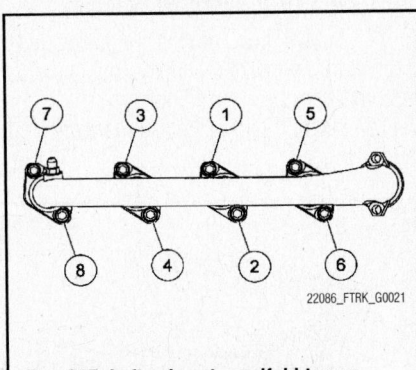

Fig. 247 Left exhaust manifold torque sequence—6.0L Diesel Engine

To install:

➡ **Start installing the bolts with the second bolt from the rear on the top. The hole diameter is smaller, therefore allowing alignment of the remaining bolts. When installing the exhaust manifolds, only use prevailing torque hex flange bolts with an interference fit.**

8. Apply anti-seize lubricant to the bolt threads prior to installing the bolts.

9. Install the LH exhaust manifold and tighten the 8 bolts in the sequence shown. Tighten to 28 ft. lbs. (38 Nm).

10. Install the 2 LH exhaust manifold-to-turbocharger adapter pipe nuts. Tighten to 20 ft. lbs. (27 Nm).

11. Connect the EP sensor tube to the exhaust manifold. Tighten to 22 ft. lbs. (30 Nm).

12. Connect the LH and RH battery ground cables.

Right Side

See Figure 248.

1. Position the vehicle in NEUTRAL, position it on a hoist.

2. Disconnect the LH and RH battery ground cables.

Vehicles with automatic transmission

3. Remove the transmission fluid indicator. Remove the retaining nut and position the transmission fluid tube off the stud.

4. Separate the transmission fluid tube and position aside.

All vehicles

5. Prior to removing the exhaust manifold, inspect the exhaust manifold for warpage with a feeler gauge between the manifold and

the cylinder head. Record the measurement and compare with the specifications.

6. Remove the 2 RH exhaust manifold-to-turbocharger adapter pipe nuts.

7. Remove the 8 bolts and the RH exhaust manifold.

To install:
All vehicles

➡ **Start installing the bolts with the second bolt from the rear on the top. The hole diameter is smaller, therefore allowing alignment of the remaining bolts. When installing the exhaust manifolds, only use prevailing torque hex flange bolts with an interference fit.**

8. Apply anti-seize lubricant to the bolt threads prior to installing the bolts.

9. Install the RH exhaust manifold and tighten the 8 bolts in the sequence shown. Tighten to 28 ft. lbs. (38 Nm).

10. Install the 2 RH exhaust manifold-to-turbocharger adapter pipe nuts. Tighten to 20 ft. lbs. (27 Nm).

Vehicles with automatic transmission

11. Position back and install the transmission fluid tube.

12. Position the transmission fluid tube on the stud and install the retaining nut. Install the transmission fluid indicator.

All vehicles

13. Connect the LH and RH battery ground cables.

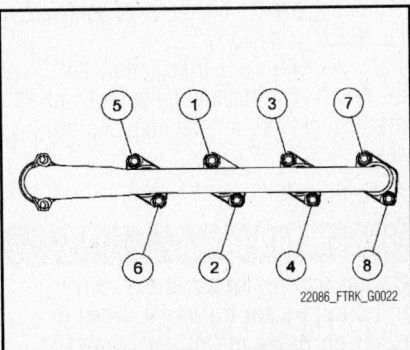

Fig. 248 Right exhaust manifold torque sequence—6.0L Diesel Engine

INTAKE MANIFOLD

REMOVAL & INSTALLATION

➡ **When the battery is disconnected and reconnected, some abnormal drive symptoms may occur while the vehicle relearns its adaptive strategy. The vehicle may need to be driven 10 miles (16 km) or more to relearn the strategy.**

4.2L Engine

Upper

See Figure 249.

1. Before servicing the vehicle, refer to the Precautions Section.

2. Drain the engine cooling system.

3. Disconnect the battery ground cable.

4. Remove the air cleaner outlet pipe.

5. Remove the bolt and position the heater hoses aside.

✱✱ WARNING

It is important to twist the spark plug wire boots while pulling upward to avoid possible damage to the spark plug wire.

➡ **Spark plug wires must be connected to the correct ignition coil terminal. Mark the spark plug wires for installation reference.**

6. Disconnect the 3 left spark plug wires from the ignition coil, disconnect the 2 spark plug wire retainers from the upper intake manifold and position the left spark plug wires aside.

7. Disconnect the exhaust gas recirculation (EGR) system module electrical and vacuum connectors.

8. Disconnect the exhaust manifold-to-EGR system module tube from the EGR system module.

9. Disconnect the electronic throttle body electrical connector.

10. Release the clamp and disconnect the fuel vapor tube from the upper intake manifold.

11. Disconnect the 5 wiring harness retainers from the upper intake manifold.

12. Release the clamp and disconnect the brake booster vacuum hose from the upper intake manifold.

13. Disconnect the vacuum hose connector from the rear of the upper intake manifold.

14. Release the clamps and disconnect the 2 heated positive crankcase ventilation (PCV) coolant hoses from the rear of the upper intake manifold.

15. Disconnect the PCV valve hose from the rear of the upper intake manifold.

16. Detach the fuel charging wiring harness-to-main engine wiring harness electrical connector retainer from the rear of the upper intake manifold.

17. Remove the 8 bolts and the upper intake manifold.

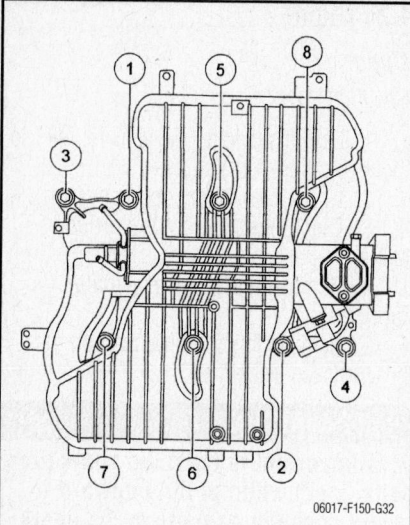

Fig. 249 Upper intake manifold torque sequence—4.2Lengine

To install:

18. Inspect the 6 upper intake manifold gaskets. Install new gaskets, if necessary.

19. Position the upper intake manifold and install the bolts. Tighten the bolts in the sequence shown in 2 stages.
- Stage 1: Tighten to 6 Nm (53 inch lbs.).
- Stage 2: Tighten to 10 Nm (89 inch lbs.).

20. Attach the fuel charging wiring harness-to-main engine wiring harness electrical connector retainer to the rear of the upper intake manifold.

21. Connect the PCV valve hose to the rear of the upper intake manifold.

22. Connect the 2 heated PCV coolant hoses to the rear of the upper intake manifold and position the clamps.

23. Connect the vacuum hose connector to the rear of the upper intake manifold.

24. Connect the brake booster vacuum hose to the upper intake manifold and position the clamp.

25. Connect the 5 wiring harness retainers to the upper intake manifold.

26. Connect the fuel vapor hose to the upper intake manifold and position the clamp.

27. Connect the electronic throttle body electrical connector.

28. Connect the exhaust manifold-to-EGR system module tube to the EGR system module. Tighten to 40 Nm (30 ft. lbs.).

29. Connect the EGR system module electrical and vacuum connectors.

➥ Apply silicone brake caliper grease and dielectric compound to the inside of the spark plug wire boots.

➥ Spark plug wires must be connected to the correct ignition coil terminals.

30. Position the spark plug wires, connect the 2 spark plug wire retainers to the upper intake manifold and connect the 3 spark plug wires to the ignition coil.

31. Position the heater hoses and install the bolt. Tighten to 5 Nm (44 inch lbs.).

32. Install the air cleaner outlet pipe.

33. Connect the battery ground cable.

34. Fill and bleed the engine cooling system.

Lower

See Figures 250 and 251.

1. Before servicing the vehicle, refer to the Precautions Section.

2. Relieve the fuel system pressure.

3. Disconnect the fuel supply spring lock coupling.

4. Remove the upper intake manifold. See the procedure above.

5. Disconnect the fuel charging wiring harness-to-main engine wiring harness and the intake manifold runner control (IMRC) actuator electrical connectors.

6. Remove the bolts and the fuel rail, the fuel charging wiring harness and the engine vacuum hose harness as an assembly.

7. Release the clamp and disconnect the heater outlet hose.

8. Release the clamp and disconnect the upper radiator hose.

9. Release the clamp and disconnect the bypass hose.

10. Release the clamp and disconnect the heater inlet hose.

11. Remove the 6 long and 8 short bolts, the lower intake manifold, the lower intake manifold gaskets and the front and rear seals.

To install:

✷✷ WARNING

Do not use metal scrapers, wire brushes, power abrasive discs or other abrasive means to clean the sealing surfaces. These tools cause scratches and gouges which make leak paths. Use a plastic scraping tool to remove all traces of old sealant.

12. Using a plastic scraping tool, silicone gasket remover and metal surface prep, clean the gasket mating surfaces. Follow the directions on the packaging.

➥ If the lower intake manifold is not secured within 4 minutes, the sealant must be removed and the sealing area

cleaned. To clean the sealing area, use silicone gasket remover and metal surface prep. Follow the directions on the packaging. Failure to follow this procedure can cause future oil leakage.

13. Apply a bead of silicone gasket and sealant to the intake manifold front and rear seal mounting points as indicated.

14. Install the lower intake manifold front and rear seals.

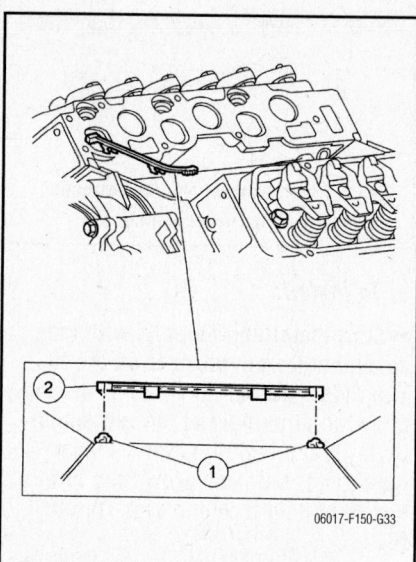

Fig. 250 Intake manifold seal RTV sealer application points—4.2L engine

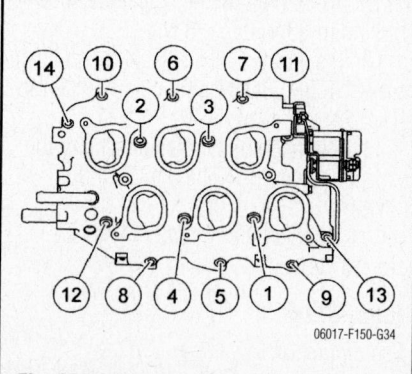

Fig. 251 Intake manifold bolt torque sequence—4.2Lengine

4.6L Engine

2005

See Figures 252 and 253.

1. Before servicing the vehicle, refer to the Precautions Section.

2. Release the fuel system pressure.

3. Disconnect the battery ground cable.

4. Drain the cooling system.

5. Remove the air cleaner outlet tube.

6. Release the upper radiator hose clamp and position the upper radiator hose aside.

7. Release the heater hose clamp and remove and position the heater hose aside.

8. Disconnect the vapor tube quick connect fitting.

9. Disconnect the throttle position (TP) sensor electrical connector.

10. Remove the power steering reservoir support bracket bolt.

11. Remove the 2 power steering reservoir support bracket bolts and the power steering reservoir support bracket.

12. Disconnect the injection pressure (IPR) sensor electrical connector.

13. Disconnect the IPR sensor vacuum connector.

14. Remove the brake booster bracket nut and disconnect the brake booster tube and position aside the brake booster bracket and tube.

15. Remove the exhaust gas recirculation (EGR) system module-to-exhaust manifold tube.

16. Disconnect the EGR system module vacuum and electrical connectors.

17. Disconnect the fuel tube spring lock coupling.

18. Disconnect the positive crankcase ventilation (PCV) tube quick release fitting.

19. Rotate the tensioner clockwise and remove the accessory drive belt.

20. If equipped, disconnect the vacuum hose.

21. Disconnect the throttle body (TB) spacer coolant hose from the intake manifold.

22. Disconnect the alternator electrical connector.

23. Remove the alternator battery cable nut and the alternator battery cable.

24. Release the alternator wiring harness retainer.

25. Remove the 4 alternator support bracket bolts and the alternator support bracket.

26. Remove the 2 lower alternator bolts and the alternator.

27. Disconnect the 8 fuel injector electrical connectors.

28. Disconnect the 8 ignition coil electrical connectors.

29. Remove the 8 ignition coil bolts and the 8 ignition coils.

30. Disconnect the electronic throttle control electrical connector.

31. Release the PCV coolant hose clamp and remove the PCV coolant return hose.

32. Remove the 2 thermostat housing bolts and the thermostat housing and discard the O-ring seal.

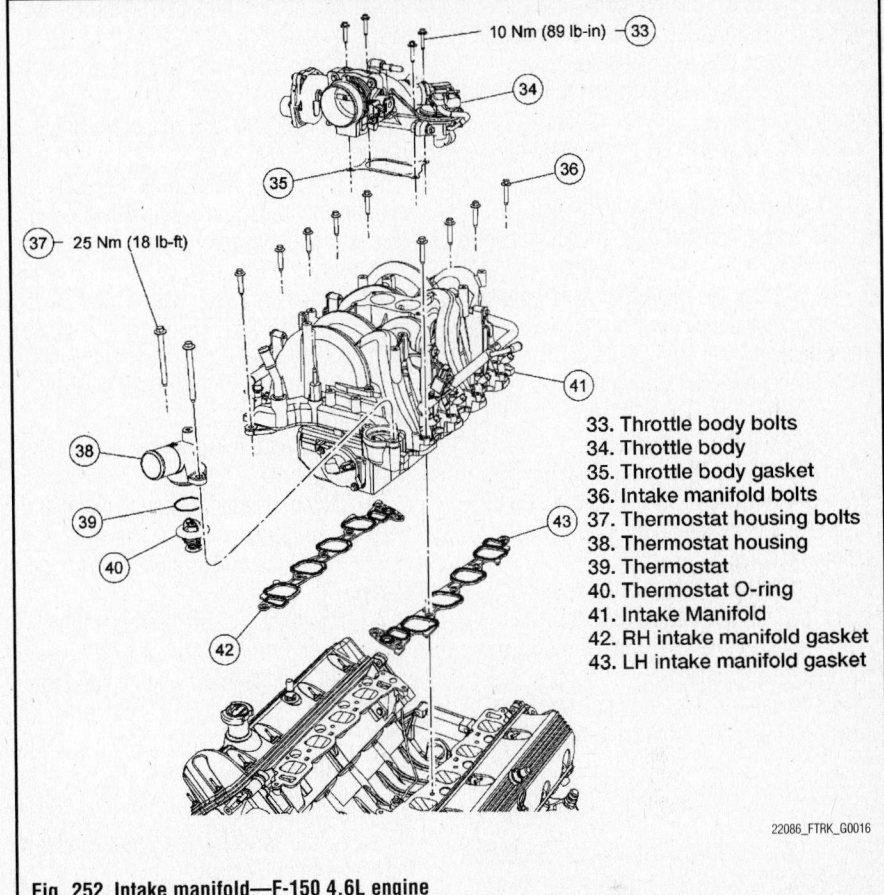

33. Throttle body bolts
34. Throttle body
35. Throttle body gasket
36. Intake manifold bolts
37. Thermostat housing bolts
38. Thermostat housing
39. Thermostat
40. Thermostat O-ring
41. Intake Manifold
42. RH intake manifold gasket
43. LH intake manifold gasket

Fig. 252 Intake manifold—F-150 4.6L engine

33. Remove the thermostat.

34. Detach the wiring harness from the left valve cover and position aside.

35. Remove the 9 intake manifold bolts.

36. Remove the intake manifold and discard the RH and LH intake manifold gaskets.

To install:

37. Before servicing the vehicle, refer to the Precautions Section.

✳✳ WARNING

Do not use metal scrapers, wire brushes, power abrasive discs or other abrasive means to clean the sealing surfaces. These tools cause scratches and gouges which make leak paths. Use a plastic scraping tool to remove all traces of old sealant.

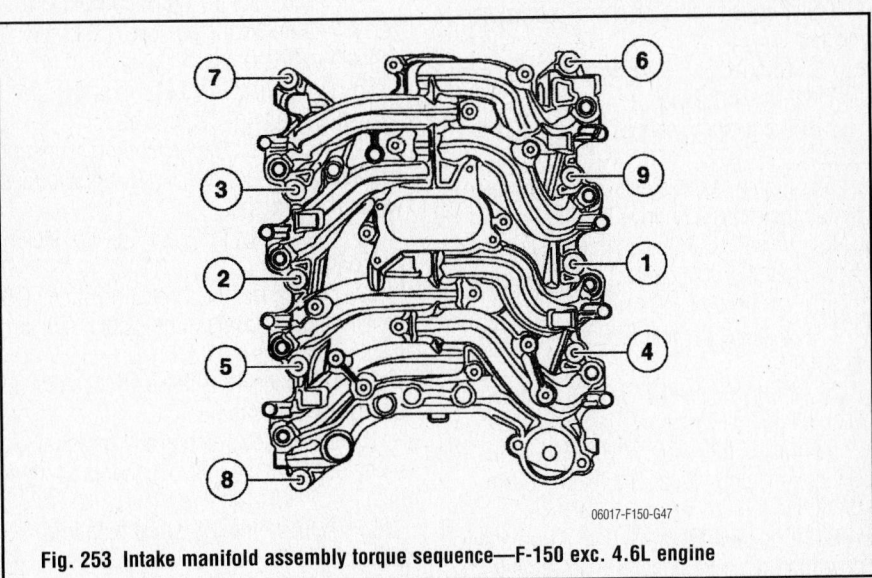

Fig. 253 Intake manifold assembly torque sequence—F-150 exc. 4.6L engine

38. Clean the mating surfaces of the cylinder head and the intake manifold with metal surface prep and silicone gasket remover. Follow the directions on the packaging.

39. Position the new intake manifold gaskets.

40. Position the intake manifold.

41. Loosely install the 9 intake manifold bolts.

42. Tighten the intake manifold bolts in the sequence shown. Tighten to 10 Nm (89 inch lbs.).

43. Attach the wiring harness to the left valve cover.

44. Install the thermostat.

45. Install the thermostat housing and the thermostat housing O-ring seal. Apply clean engine coolant to the O-ring seal before installation.

46. Install the 2 thermostat housing bolts. Tighten to 25 Nm (18 ft. lbs.).

47. Connect the electronic throttle control electrical connector.

48. Install the 8 ignition coil and the 8 ignition coils bolts. Tighten to 6 Nm (53 inch lbs.).

49. Connect the 8 ignition coil electrical connectors.

50. Connect the 8 fuel injector electrical connectors.

51. Install the alternator and the 2 lower alternator bolts. Tighten to 25 Nm (18 ft. lbs.).

52. Install the alternator support bracket and the 4 alternator support bracket bolts. Tighten to 10 Nm (89 inch lbs.).

53. Attach the alternator wiring harness retainer.

54. Install the alternator battery cable and the alternator battery cable nut. Tighten to 10 Nm (89 inch lbs.).

55. Connect the alternator electrical connector.

56. Connect the TB spacer coolant hose to the intake manifold.

57. If equipped, connect the vacuum hose.

58. Rotate the tensioner clockwise and install the accessory drive belt.

59. Install the PCV coolant return hose and install the PCV coolant hose clamp.

60. Connect the PCV tube.

61. Connect the fuel tube spring lock coupling.

62. Connect the EGR system module vacuum and electrical connectors.

63. Install the EGR system module-to-exhaust manifold tube. Tighten to 40 Nm (30 ft. lbs.).

64. Connect the brake booster tube and position the brake booster bracket and

install the nut. Tighten to 10 Nm (89 inch lbs.).

65. Connect the IPR sensor vacuum connector.

66. Connect the IPR sensor electrical connector.

67. Install the power steering reservoir support bracket and the 2 power steering reservoir support bracket bolts. Tighten to 17 Nm (13 ft. lbs.).

68. Install the power steering reservoir support bracket bolt. Tighten to 11 Nm (8 ft. lbs.).

69. Connect the TP sensor electrical connector.

70. Connect the vapor tube quick connect fitting.

71. Install the heater hose and install the heater hose clamp.

72. Install the upper radiator hose and clamp.

73. Install the air cleaner outlet tube.

74. Connect the battery ground cable.

75. Fill and bleed the engine cooling system.

5.4L Engine

See Figure 254.

1. Before servicing the vehicle, refer to the Precautions Section.

2. Drain the cooling system.

3. Release the fuel system pressure.

4. Remove the alternator.

5. Remove the air cleaner.

6. Disconnect the upper radiator hose from the thermostat housing.

7. Disconnect the heater coolant hose from the coolant bypass tube.

8. Disconnect the quick connect coupling and remove the evaporative emissions (EVAP) tube from the intake manifold.

9. Disconnect the quick connect coupling and remove the positive crankcase ventilation (PCV) tube.

10. Disconnect the fuel supply spring lock coupling from the fuel rail.

11. Disconnect the fuel rail pressure and temperature sensor electrical connector and vacuum connector.

12. Disconnect the 8 fuel injector electrical connectors.

13. Disconnect the throttle position (TP) sensor and electronic throttle control electrical connectors.

14. Disconnect the heated PCV element electrical connector.

15. Disconnect the brake booster vacuum hose from the intake manifold vacuum tube.

16. Remove the 10 intake manifold bolts.

✳✳ WARNING

Do not use metal scrapers, wire brushes, power abrasive discs or other abrasive means to clean the sealing surfaces. These tools cause scratches and gouges which make leak paths. Use a plastic scraping tool to remove all traces of old sealant.

17. Remove the 3 bolts, the coolant bypass tube and discard the gaskets.

18. Clean and inspect the sealing surfaces with metal surface prep. Follow the directions on the packaging.

19. Disconnect the charge motion control valve (CMCV) electrical connector.

20. Disconnect the intake manifold vacuum tube from the valve cover stud and the support bracket.

21. Disconnect the cylinder head temperature (CHT) sensor jumper harness electrical connector.

22. Disconnect the LH and RH knock sensor (KS) electrical connectors.

23. Remove the nut and disconnect the engine wiring harness retainer from the CMCV stud.

✳✳ WARNING

Do not use metal scrapers, wire brushes, power abrasive discs or other abrasive means to clean the sealing surfaces. These tools cause scratches and gouges which make leak paths. Use a plastic scraping tool to remove all traces of old sealant.

24. Remove the intake manifold and discard the gaskets.

25. Clean and inspect the sealing surfaces with metal surface prep. Follow the directions on the packaging.

To install:

➡**Electrical and vacuum harnesses must not restrict movement of the CMCV control rods at the rear of the intake manifold. Use extreme care on installation of the intake manifold to prevent any pinching of electrical and vacuum harnesses.**

26. Using new intake manifold gaskets, position the intake manifold.

27. Using new gaskets, position the coolant crossover and install the 3 bolts. Tighten to 10 Nm (89 inch lbs.).

28. Install the intake manifold bolts and tighten in 2 stages in the sequence shown.

- Stage 1: Tighten to 2 Nm (18 inch lbs.).
- Stage 2: Tighten to 10 Nm (89 inch lbs.).

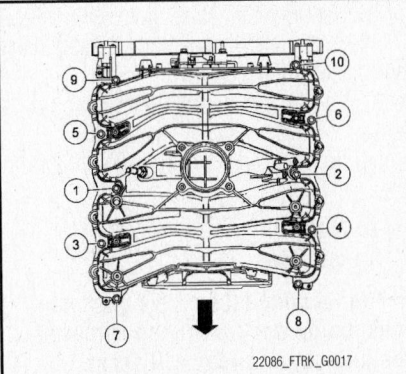

Fig. 254 Intake manifold bolt tightening sequence—5.4L engine

29. Connect the engine wiring harness retainer to the CMCV stud and install the nut. Tighten to 10 Nm (89 inch lbs.).

30. Connect the CMCV electrical connector.

31. Connect the CHT sensor jumper harness electrical connector.

32. Connect the LH and RH KS electrical connectors.

33. Connect the intake manifold vacuum tube to the support bracket and the valve cover stud.

34. Connect the brake booster vacuum hose to the intake manifold vacuum tube.

35. Connect the heated PCV element electrical connector.

36. Connect the TP sensor and electronic throttle control electrical connectors.

37. Connect the 8 fuel injector electrical connectors.

38. Connect the fuel rail pressure and temperature sensor electrical connector and vacuum connector.

39. Connect the fuel supply spring lock coupling to the fuel rail.

40. Position the PCV tube and connect the quick connect coupling.

41. Position the EVAP tube and connect the quick connect coupling to the intake manifold.

42. Connect the heater coolant hose to the coolant bypass.

43. Connect the upper radiator hose to the thermostat housing.

44. Install the alternator.

45. Install the air cleaner.

46. Fill and bleed the engine cooling system.

6.8L Engine

See Figure 255.

⁂ WARNING

Fuel in the fuel system remains under high pressure, even when the engine is not running.

1. Before servicing the vehicle, refer to the Precautions Section.

2. Relieve the fuel system pressure.

3. Disconnect the fuel supply spring lock coupling from the fuel rail.

4. Drain the cooling system.

5. Remove the alternator. See the "Alternator" section.

6. Remove the air cleaner outlet pipe.

7. Disconnect the upper radiator hose from the thermostat housing.

8. Disconnect the heater coolant hose from the coolant crossover assembly.

9. Disconnect the intake manifold runner control (IMRC) actuator electrical connector.

10. Disconnect the fuel rail pressure and temperature sensor electrical connector and vacuum connector.

11. Disconnect the 10 fuel injector electrical connectors.

12. Disconnect the positive crankcase ventilation (PCV) tube quick connect coupling from the intake manifold.

13. Disconnect the quick connect couplings and remove the evaporative emissions (EVAP) tube.

14. Disconnect the brake booster and engine vacuum hose connections from the rear of the intake manifold and position aside.

15. Disconnect the 2 heated PCV coolant hoses from the intake manifold.

16. Disconnect the throttle position (TP) sensor and electronic throttle control electrical connectors.

17. Disconnect the engine wiring harness position retainers from the intake manifold.

18. Remove the 12 intake manifold bolts.

⁂ CAUTION

Do not use metal scrapers, wire brushes, power abrasive discs or other abrasive means to clean the sealing surfaces. These tools cause scratches and gouges which make leak paths. Use a plastic scraping tool to remove all traces of old sealant.

19. Remove the 2 bolts, the coolant crossover tube and discard the gaskets.

20. Clean and inspect the sealing sur-

faces with metal surface prep and silicone gasket remover. Follow the directions on the packaging.

21. Remove the intake manifold and discard the gaskets.

22. Clean and inspect the sealing surfaces with metal surface prep and silicone gasket remover.

To install:

23. Using new intake manifold gaskets, position the intake manifold.

24. Using new gaskets, position the coolant crossover tube and install the 2 bolts. Tighten to 89 inch lbs. (10 Nm).

25. Install the intake manifold bolts and tighten in 2 stages in the sequence shown, to the following:

  a. Stage 1: Tighten to 2 Nm (18 lb-in).

  b. Stage 2: Tighten to 89 inch lbs. (10 Nm).

26. Connect the throttle position (TP) sensor and electronic throttle control electrical connectors.

27. Connect the engine wiring harness position retainers to the intake manifold.

28. Connect the brake booster and engine vacuum hose connections to the rear of the intake manifold.

29. Connect the positive crankcase ventilation (PCV) tube quick connect coupling to the intake manifold.

30. Position the evaporative emissions (EVAP) tube and connect the quick connect couplings.

31. Connect the 2 heated PCV coolant hoses to the intake manifold.

32. Connect the 10 fuel injector electrical connectors.

33. Connect the fuel rail pressure and temperature sensor electrical connector and vacuum connector.

34. Connect the intake manifold runner control (IMRC) actuator electrical connector.

35. Connect the fuel supply spring lock coupling to the fuel rail.

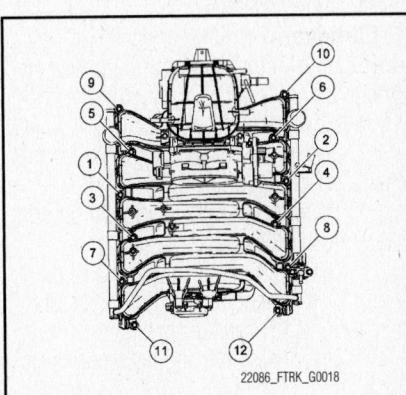

Fig. 255 Intake manifold bolt tightening sequence—6.8L engine

36. Connect the heater coolant hose to the coolant crossover assembly.

37. Connect the heated PCV coolant hose to the coolant crossover assembly.

38. Connect the upper radiator hose to the thermostat housing.

39. Install the alternator. See the "Alternator" section.

40. Install the air cleaner outlet pipe.

41. Fill and bleed the engine cooling system.

6.0L Diesel Engine

See Figures 256 and 257.

1. Before servicing the vehicle, refer to the Precautions Section.

2. Remove the auxiliary battery.

3. Remove the cooling fan stator.

4. Remove the degas bottle (coolant reservoir).

5. Remove the upper radiator hose.

6. Remove the turbocharger-to-charge air cooler duct.

Vehicles with dual alternators

7. Remove the accessory drive belt.

8. Remove the bolt and the accessory drive belt tensioner.

9. Remove the accessory drive belt.

10. Remove the bolts, bracket and accessory drive belt idler pulley.

11. Remove the bolts and the accessory drive belt tensioner.

12. Disconnect the wire retainer, alternator electrical connector and B+ wire.

13. Remove the bolts and the alternator with mounting bracket.

Vehicles with single alternator

14. Remove the accessory drive belt.

All vehicles

15. Position the boot back and disconnect the alternator B+ wire and electrical connector.

16. Remove the three bolts and the alternator.

17. Remove the turbocharger and the turbocharger pedestal.

Early build

18. Loosen the clamps and remove the charge air cooler duct.

Late build

19. Loosen the clamps and remove the charge air cooler duct.

20. Remove the bolts and position the heater hose tube aside.

21. Remove and discard the O-ring.

22. Disconnect the manifold absolute pressure (MAP) sensor hose.

23. Disconnect the engine coolant vent hose.

24. Remove the fuel injector control module.

25. Remove or position aside the heat insulating wrap.

26. Disconnect the wiring retainer, injector pressure regulator valve and injector control pressure (ICP) sensor (if equipped) electrical connectors.

27. Disconnect the exhaust gas recirculation (EGR) valve electrical connector.

28. Disconnect the engine oil pressure (EOP) sensor electrical connector.

29. Disconnect the engine oil temperature sensor electrical connector.

30. Disconnect the exhaust gas recirculation (EGR) throttle position control module electrical connector.

31. Disconnect the EGR throttle position sensor electrical connector.

32. Disconnect the pin-type retainer and engine coolant temperature (ECT) sensor.

33. Disconnect the intake air temperature (IAT2) sensor electrical connector and wiring connector.

34. Disconnect the exhaust backpressure sensor and retaining clip.

35. Disconnect the eight fuel injectors electrical connectors. Remove the nut and the fuel injector wiring harness.

➡**It is necessary to remove the fuel filter and drain the housing.**

36. Disconnect the fuel line fittings.

➡**It is necessary to remove the oil filter and drain the housing.**

37. Remove the four bolts and the oil filter housing.

38. Remove the bolt and the oil filter return tube.

39. Remove the fuel line.

40. Remove the bolt, and the banjo fitting from the fuel line.

41. Discard the sealing washers and remove the fuel line.

➡**Align the flat edge with the index feature located on the coolant supply port.**

42. Pull the EGR cooler clamp forward, twist and then slide the EGR cooler hose rearward to remove.

Early build

43. Remove the nuts and the turbocharger heat shield.

➡**Intake removed for clarity.**

44. Remove the EGR cooler V-clamp and gasket.

45. Remove the bolts and the intake manifold.

Late build

46. Remove the nuts and the turbocharger heat shield.

47. Remove the EGR cooler V-clamp and gasket.

48. Remove the bolts and the intake manifold.

All vehicles

49. Remove the intake manifold gaskets.

50. Clean and inspect the gaskets. Install new gaskets if necessary.

51. Clean and inspect the sealing surfaces.

52. Remove and discard the front module O-ring seal.

To install:
All vehicles

➡**The locating tabs on the gaskets must be up and toward the center of the engine, or a leak will occur.**

53. Install the intake manifold gaskets and front module O-ring seal.

Late build

54. Install the intake manifold and bolts and tighten in the following sequence.
   a. Loosely install bolts 1–8.
   b. Tighten bolts 9–16 to 11 Nm (8 ft. lbs.).
   c. Tighten all bolts to 11 Nm (8 ft. lbs.) in the sequence shown.

55. Install the gasket and the EGR cooler V-clamp.

56. Install the turbocharger heat shield and the nuts.

Early build

57. Install the intake manifold and bolts and tighten in the following sequence.
   a. Loosely install bolts 1–8.
   b. Tighten bolts 9–16 to 11 Nm (8 ft. lbs.).

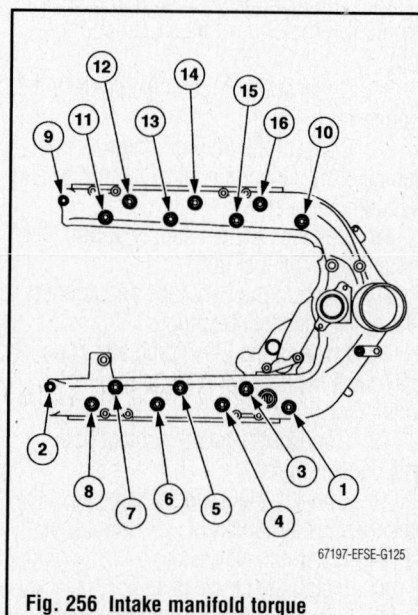

67197-EFSE-G125

Fig. 256 Intake manifold torque sequence—6.0L Diesel Engine

c. Tighten all bolts to 11 Nm (8 ft. lbs.) in the sequence shown.

58. Install the gasket and the EGR cooler V-clamp.

59. Install the turbocharger heat shield and the nuts.

All vehicles

60. Slide the EGR cooler hose forward and rotate flat to lock.

61. Install the fuel line.

62. Install new sealing washers.

63. Install the fuel line.

64. Install the banjo fitting and the bolt.

65. Install the oil filter return tube and bolt.

66. On new oil filter return tubes, tighten to 6 Nm (53 inch lbs.).

67. On used oil filter return tubes, tighten to 3 Nm (27 inch lbs.).

68. Install the oil filter housing and the four bolts.

69. Clean and inspect the housing O-rings. Install new O-rings if necessary.

70. Connect the fuel line fittings.

71. Position the fuel injector harness and install the retaining nut. Connect the eight fuel injectors electrical connectors.

72. Connect the retaining clip and exhaust backpressure sensor electrical connector.

73. Connect the wiring retainer and the IAT2 sensor electrical connector.

74. Connect the engine coolant temperature (ECT) sensor and the pin-type retainer.

75. Connect the EGR throttle position sensor electrical connector.

76. Connect the EGR throttle position control module electrical connector.

77. Connect the engine oil temperature (EOT) sensor electrical connector.

78. Connect the engine oil pressure (EOP) sensor electrical connector.

79. Connect the EGR valve electrical connector.

80. Connect the wiring retainer, injector pressure regulator and ICP sensor (if equipped) electrical connectors.

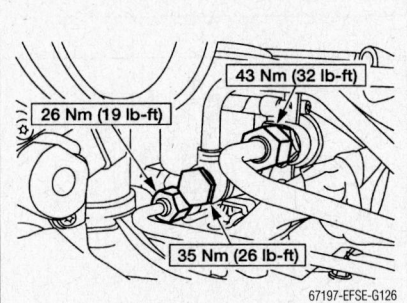

Fig. 257 Reposition and connect the fuel tubes at the fuel filter housing

81. Position back or install the heat insulating wrap.

82. Install the fuel injector control module.

83. Connect the engine coolant vent hose and clamp.

84. Connect the MAP sensor hose.

➡**Install a new O-ring on the heater hose tube.**

85. Install the heater hose tube and bolts.

Early build

86. Install the charge air cooler duct and tighten the clamps.

Late build

87. Install the charge air cooler duct and tighten the clamp.

88. Install the turbocharger pedestal and turbocharger.

89. Install the alternator and the three bolts.

90. Connect the alternator B+ wire land electrical connector and position the boot back.

Vehicles with single alternator

91. Install the accessory drive belt.

Vehicles with dual alternators

92. Install the alternator with mounting bracket and bolts.

93. Connect the B+ wire, alternator electrical connector and wire retainer.

94. Install the accessory drive belt tensioner and bolts.

95. Position the accessory drive belt idler pulley. Install the bracket and bolts.

96. Install the accessory drive belt.

97. Install the accessory drive belt tensioner and bolt.

98. Install the accessory drive belt.

All vehicles

99. Install the turbocharger-to-charge air cooler duct.

100. Install the upper radiator hose.

101. Install the degas bottle (coolant reservoir).

102. Install the auxiliary battery.

103. Install the cooling fan stator.

OIL PAN

REMOVAL & INSTALLATION

F-150 and Mark LT

4.2L Engine

See Figure 258.

1. Before servicing the vehicle, refer to the Precautions Section.

☼☼ WARNING

During engine repair procedures, cleanliness is extremely important.

Any foreign material, including any material created while cleaning gasket surfaces, that enters the oil passages, coolant passages or the oil pan can cause engine failure.

2. Raise and safely support the vehicle.

3. Remove the starter.

4. Drain the engine oil. Install the drain plug when finished.

5. Remove the 4 bolts and the cross-member.

6. Remove the 3 oil pan-to-transmission bolts.

7. Remove the 17 bolts and the oil pan.

8. Remove and discard the oil pan rear seal.

To install:

☼☼ WARNING

Do not use metal scrapers, wire brushes, power abrasive discs or other abrasive means to clean the sealing surfaces. These tools cause scratches and gouges which make leak paths. Use silicone gasket remover and a plastic scraping tool to remove all traces of old sealant. Follow the directions on the packaging.

9. Clean the gasket mating surfaces using silicone gasket remover, a plastic scraping tool and metal surface prep. Follow the directions on the packaging.

➡**If the oil pan is not secured within 4 minutes, the sealant must be removed and the sealing areas cleaned. To clean the sealing area, use silicone gasket remover and metal surface prep. Follow the directions on the packaging. Failure to follow this procedure can cause future oil leakage.**

10. Apply silicone gasket and sealant to the oil pan sealing areas shown and install the oil pan rear seal.

11. Apply silicone gasket and sealant to the rear main bearing cap.

12. Install the oil pan rear seal.

13. Apply a bead of silicone gasket and sealant to the oil pan mating surface.

14. Position the oil pan and install the bolts. Tighten the bolts in the sequence shown. Tighten to 10 Nm (89 inch lbs.).

15. Install the 3 oil pan-to-transmission bolts. Tighten to 34 Nm (25 ft. lbs)

16. Install the starter.

17. Position the crossmember and install the 4 bolts. Tighten to 90 Nm (66 ft. lbs.).

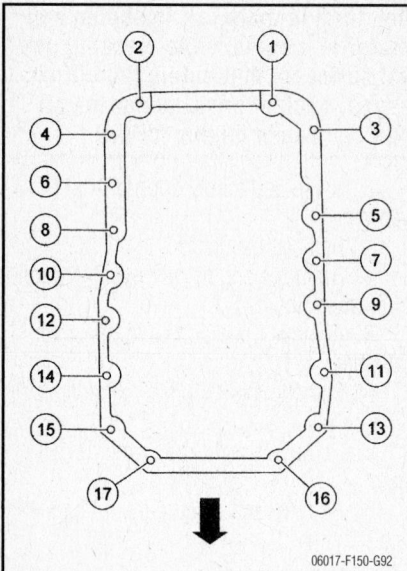

Fig. 258 Oil pan torque sequence—4.2L engine

4.6L or 5.4L Engine With 2-Wheel Drive

See Figure 259.

1. Before servicing the vehicle, refer to the Precautions Section.
2. Raise and safely support the vehicle.
3. Drain the engine oil.
4. If equipped, remove the 4 skid plate bolts and the skid plate.
5. Remove the bolts and the crossmember.

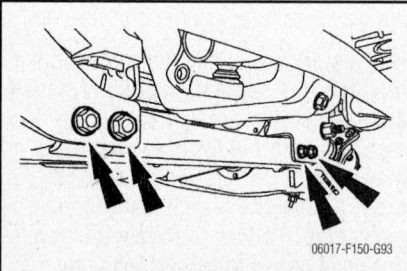

Fig. 259 Remove the bolts and the crossmember—F-150 and Mark LT 5.4L Engine

❊❊ WARNING

Do not use metal scrapers, wire brushes, power abrasive discs, or other abrasive means to clean the sealing surfaces. These may cause scratches and gouges resulting in leak paths. Use a plastic scraper to clean the sealing surfaces.

6. Remove the 16 oil pan bolts and the oil pan, discard the oil pan gasket. Clean the sealing surfaces with silicone gasket remover and metal surface prep. Follow the directions on the packaging. Inspect the mating surfaces.

To install:

➡ If the oil pan is not secured within 4 minutes, the sealant must be removed and the sealing area cleaned. To clean the sealing area, use silicone gasket remover and metal surface prep. Follow the directions on the packaging. Failure to follow this procedure can cause future oil leakage.

7. Apply the silicone gasket and sealant at the engine front cover-to-cylinder block mating surface.

➡ If the oil pan is not secured within 4 minutes, the sealant must be removed and the sealing area cleaned. To clean the sealing area, use silicone gasket remover and metal surface prep. Follow the directions on the packaging. Failure to follow this procedure can cause future oil leakage.

8. Apply silicone gasket and sealant in the locations shown.
9. Position the new oil pan gasket and the oil pan and loosely install the 16 bolts.
10. Tighten the bolts in 3 stages in the sequence shown.
   - Stage 1: Tighten to 2 Nm (18 inch lbs.).
   - Stage 2: Tighten to 20 Nm (15 ft. lbs.).
   - Stage 3: Tighten an additional 60 degrees.
11. Install the crossmember and the 4 bolts. Tighten to 90 Nm (66 ft. lbs.).
12. If equipped, install the skid plate and the 4 bolts. Tighten to 25 Nm (18 ft. lbs.).
13. Install the engine oil pan drain plug and fill the engine with clean engine oil. Tighten to 14 Nm (10 ft. lbs.).

4.6L or 5.4L Engine With 4-Wheel Drive

See Figures 260 through 264.

1. Raise and safely support the vehicle.
2. Drain the engine oil.
3. If equipped, remove the 4 skid plate bolts and the skid plate.
4. Remove the bolts and the crossmember.
5. Position a suitable hydraulic jack under the front axle. Securely strap the jack to the axle.

➡ Rotate the steering column so the pinch bolt for the steering column coupling allows clearance for the isolator bolt.

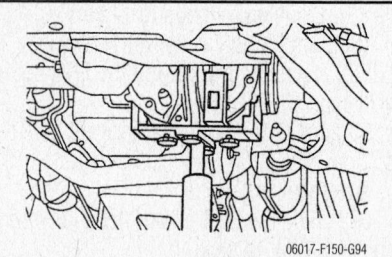

Fig. 260 Position a suitable hydraulic jack under the front axle—F-150 4WD

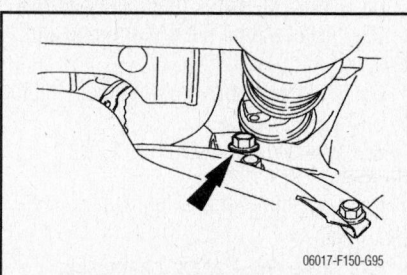

Fig. 261 Remove the upper front axle carrier mounting bushing bolt—F-150 4WD

6. Remove the upper front axle carrier mounting bushing bolt.
7. Remove the axle shaft housing carrier bushing bolt.
8. Remove the lower front axle carrier mounting bushing bolt.
9. Partially lower the front axle assembly.

❊❊ WARNING

Do not use metal scrapers, wire brushes, power abrasive discs, or

Fig. 262 Remove the axle shaft housing carrier bushing bolt—F-150 4WD

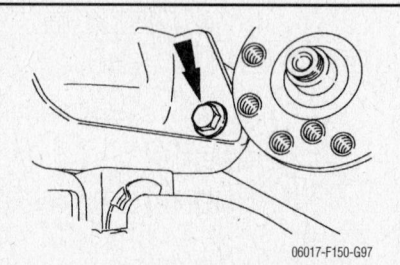

Fig. 263 Remove the lower front axle carrier mounting bushing bolt—F-150 4WD

other abrasive means to clean the sealing surfaces. These may cause scratches and gouges resulting in leak paths. Use a plastic scraper to clean the sealing surfaces.

10. Remove the 16 oil pan bolts and the oil pan, discard the oil pan gasket. Clean the sealing surfaces with silicone gasket remover and metal surface prep. Follow the directions on the packaging. Inspect the mating surfaces.

To install:

➡️**If the oil pan is not secured within 4 minutes, the sealant must be removed and the sealing area cleaned. To clean the sealing area, use silicone gasket remover and metal surface prep. Follow the directions on the packaging. Failure to follow this procedure can cause future oil leakage.**

11. Apply the silicone gasket and sealant at the engine front cover-to-cylinder block mating surface.

➡️**If the oil pan is not secured within 4 minutes, the sealant must be removed and the sealing area cleaned. To clean the sealing area, use silicone gasket remover and metal surface prep. Follow the directions on the packaging. Failure to follow this procedure can cause future oil leakage.**

12. Apply silicone gasket and sealant in the locations shown.
13. Position the new oil pan gasket and the oil pan and loosely install the 16 bolts.
14. Tighten the bolts in 3 stages in the sequence shown.
- Stage 1: Tighten to 2 Nm (18 inch lbs.).
- Stage 2: Tighten to 20 Nm (15 ft. lbs.).

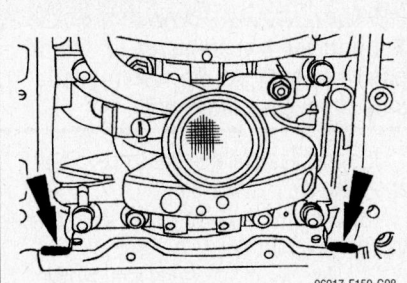

Fig. 264 Apply silicone gasket and sealant in the locations shown— F-150 4.6L or 5.4L engine

06017-F150-G98

- Stage 3: Tighten an additional 60 degrees.
15. Position the front axle.

➡️**Rotate the steering column so the pinch bolt for the steering column coupling allows clearance for the isolator bolt.**

16. Install the upper front axle carrier mounting bushing bolt. Tighten to 90 Nm (66 ft. lbs.).
17. Install the axle shaft housing carrier bushing nut and bolt. Tighten to 90 Nm (66 ft. lbs.).
18. Install the lower front axle carrier mounting bushing bolt. Tighten to 90 Nm (66 ft. lbs.).
19. Install the crossmember and the 4 bolts. Tighten to 90 Nm (66 ft. lbs.).
20. If equipped, install the skid plate and the 4 bolts. Tighten to 25 Nm (18 ft. lbs.).
21. Install the engine oil pan drain plug and fill the engine with clean engine oil. Tighten to 14 Nm (10 ft. lbs.).

F-250 and F-350

5.4L Engine

1. Before servicing the vehicle, refer to the Precautions Section.
2. Remove the transmission.
3. Drain the engine oil.
4. Disconnect the engine oil temperature (EOT) sensor electrical connector.
5. Remove the nut and the starter wiring harness support bracket.
6. Remove the nut and position the transmission oil cooler lines and bracket aside.
7. Remove the 16 bolts and lower the oil pan onto the crossmember.
8. Remove the 3 bolts and position the oil pump screen and pickup tube into the oil pan.

➡️**Be careful when removing the oil pan gasket. It is reusable.**

9. Remove the oil pan and the oil pump screen and pickup tube.
10. Inspect the oil pan gasket for damage. If damaged, discard the oil pan gasket and the oil pan-to-oil pump gaskets. Discard the oil pump screen and pickup tube O-ring seal.

To install:

❄️❄️ **WARNING**

Do not use metal scrapers, wire brushes, power abrasive discs or other abrasive means to clean the sealing surfaces. These tools cause

scratches and gouges, which make leak paths. Use a plastic scraping tool to remove all traces of old sealant.

11. Inspect the oil pan. Clean the mating surface for the oil pan with silicone gasket remover and metal surface prep. Follow the directions on the packaging.
12. Position the oil pump screen and pickup tube in the oil pan and position the oil pan into the vehicle.

❄️❄️ **WARNING**

Make sure to install a new O-ring seal. A missing or damaged O-ring seal can cause foam in the lubrication system, low oil pressure and severe engine damage.

➡️**Clean and inspect the mating surfaces and install a new O-ring seal. Lubricate the O-ring seal with clean engine oil prior to installation.**

13. Position the oil pump screen and pickup tube and install the bolts.
14. Tighten the oil pump screen and pickup tube-to-oil pump bolts to 10 Nm (89 inch lbs.).
15. Tighten the oil pump screen and pickup tube-to-spacer bolt to 25 Nm (18 ft. lbs.).

➡️**If not secured within 4 minutes, the sealant must be removed and the sealing area cleaned. To clean the sealing area, use silicone gasket remover and metal surface prep. Follow the directions on the packaging. Failure to follow this procedure can cause future oil leakage.**

16. Apply silicone gasket and sealant at the crankshaft rear seal retainer plate-to-cylinder block sealing surface.

➡️**If not secured within 4 minutes, the sealant must be removed and the sealing area cleaned. To clean the sealing area, use silicone gasket remover and metal surface prep. Follow the directions on the packaging. Failure to follow this procedure can cause future oil leakage.**

17. Apply silicone gasket and sealant at the engine front cover-to-cylinder block sealing surface.
18. Install the oil pan gasket and the oil pan and loosely install the 16 bolts.
19. Tighten the bolts in 3 stages, in the sequence shown.
- Stage 1: Tighten to 2 Nm (18 inch lbs.).

- Stage 2: Tighten to 20 Nm (15 ft. lbs.).
- Stage 3: Tighten an additional 60 degrees.

20. Install the wire harness bracket and the bolt. Tighten to 10 Nm (89 inch lbs.).

21. Position the starter wiring harness support bracket and install the nut. Tighten to 10 Nm (89 inch lbs.).

22. Connect the engine oil temperature (EOT) sensor electrical connector.

23. Install the transmission.

24. Fill the crankcase with clean engine oil.

F-250 and F-350

6.8L Engine With Manual Transmission

1. Before servicing the vehicle, refer to the Precautions Section.

2. Remove the flywheel.

3. Remove the nut and the starter wiring harness support bracket.

4. Remove the 18 bolts and partially lower the oil pan.

5. Remove the 3 bolts and position the oil pump screen and pickup tube into the oil pan.

➡ **Be careful when removing the oil pan gasket. It is reusable.**

6. Remove the oil pan and the oil pump screen and pickup tube.

7. Inspect the oil pan gasket for damage. If damaged, discard the oil pan gasket and the oil pan-to-oil pump gaskets. Discard the oil pump screen and pickup tube O-ring seal.

To install:

> ✳ **WARNING**
>
> **Do not use metal scrapers, wire brushes, power abrasive discs or other abrasive means to clean the sealing surfaces. These tools cause scratches and gouges, which make leak paths. Use a plastic scraping tool to remove all traces of old sealant.**

8. Inspect the oil pan. Clean the mating surface for the oil pan with silicone gasket remover and metal surface prep. Follow the directions on the packaging.

9. Position the oil pump screen and pickup tube in the oil pan and position the oil pan into the vehicle.

> ✳ **WARNING**
>
> **Make sure to install a new O-ring seal. A missing or damaged O-ring**

seal can cause foam in the lubrication system, low oil pressure and severe engine damage.

➡ **Clean and inspect the mating surfaces and install a new O-ring seal. Lubricate the O-ring seal with clean engine oil prior to installation.**

10. Position the oil pump screen and pickup tube and install the bolts.

11. Tighten the oil pump screen and pickup tube-to-oil pump bolts to 10 Nm (89 inch lbs.).

12. Tighten the oil pump screen and pickup tube-to-spacer bolt to 25 Nm (18 ft. lbs.).

➡ **If not secured within 4 minutes, the sealant must be removed and the sealing area cleaned. To clean the sealing area, use silicone gasket remover and metal surface prep. Follow the directions on the packaging. Failure to follow this procedure can cause future oil leakage.**

13. Apply silicone gasket and sealant at the crankshaft rear seal retainer plate-to-cylinder block sealing surface.

➡ **If not secured within 4 minutes, the sealant must be removed and the sealing area cleaned. To clean the sealing area, use silicone gasket remover and metal surface prep. Follow the directions on the packaging. Failure to follow this procedure can cause future oil leakage.**

14. Apply silicone gasket and sealant at the engine front cover-to-cylinder block sealing surface.

15. Install the oil pan gasket and the oil pan and loosely install the 18 bolts.

16. Tighten the bolts in 3 stages, in the sequence shown.

- Stage 1: Tighten to 2 Nm (18 inch lbs.).
- Stage 2: Tighten to 20 Nm (15 ft. lbs.).
- Stage 3: Tighten an additional 60 degrees.

17. Install the transmission cooler tube support bracket and the nut. Tighten to 10 Nm (89 inch lbs.).

18. Install the flywheel.

6.8L Engine With Automatic Transmission

1. Before servicing the vehicle, refer to the Precautions Section.

2. Raise and safely support the vehicle.

3. Remove the air cleaner outlet tube.

4. Remove the alternator.

5. Remove the cooling fan shroud.

6. Remove the starter.

7. Install the an engine crane and support the engine.

> ✳✳ **WARNING**
>
> **Only use hand tools when removing the transmission mount-to-crossmember nuts or damage to the transmission mount can occur.**

8. Remove the transmission mount-to-crossmember nuts.

> ✳✳ **WARNING**
>
> **Only use hand tools when installing the right engine mount nut or damage to the engine mount can occur.**

9. Remove the 6 engine mount nuts.

10. Remove the 4 exhaust manifold-to-catalytic converter nuts. To install, tighten to 40 Nm (30 ft. lbs.).

11. Remove the nut and the starter wiring harness support bracket.

12. Remove the nut and position the transmission oil cooler lines and bracket aside.

> ✳✳ **WARNING**
>
> **Damage to the TSS/OSS may occur and cause the transmission or torque converter operational concerns if the transmission is raised prior to removing TSS/OSS.**

> ✳✳ **WARNING**
>
> **Sensor bosses must be cleaned prior to removal and then plugged to prevent contamination from damaging internal components.**

13. If the vehicle is equipped with turbine shaft speed (TSS) and output shaft sensors (OSS), remove the sensors and install plugs in the transmission.

14. Using the crane, raise the engine.

> ✳✳ **WARNING**
>
> **Support the transmission on the oil pan rails only or internal transmission damage can occur.**

15. Install a suitable transmission jack and raise the transmission.

16. Remove the 2 bolts and the flywheel inspection plate.

17. Remove the 18 bolts and partially lower the oil pan.

18. Remove the 3 bolts and position the oil pump screen and pickup tube into the oil pan.

➤Be careful when removing the oil pan gasket. It is reusable.

19. Remove the oil pan and the oil pump screen and pickup tube.

20. Inspect the oil pan gasket for damage. If damaged, discard the oil pan gasket and the oil pan-to-oil pump gaskets. Discard the oil pump screen and pickup tube O-ring seal.

To install:

✳ WARNING

Do not use metal scrapers, wire brushes, power abrasive discs or other abrasive means to clean the sealing surfaces. These tools cause scratches and gouges, which make leak paths. Use a plastic scraping tool to remove all traces of old sealant.

21. Inspect the oil pan. Clean the mating surface for the oil pan with silicone gasket remover and metal surface prep. Follow the directions on the packaging.

22. Position the oil pump screen and pickup tube in the oil pan and position the oil pan into the vehicle.

✳ WARNING

Make sure to install a new O-ring seal. A missing or damaged O-ring seal can cause foam in the lubrication system, low oil pressure and severe engine damage.

➤Clean and inspect the mating surfaces and install a new O-ring seal. Lubricate the O-ring seal with clean engine oil prior to installation.

23. Position the oil pump screen and pickup tube and install the bolts.

24. Tighten the oil pump screen and pickup tube-to-oil pump bolts to 10 Nm (89 inch lbs.).

25. Tighten the oil pump screen and pickup tube-to-spacer bolt to 25 Nm (18 ft. lbs.).

➤If not secured within 4 minutes, the sealant must be removed and the sealing area cleaned. To clean the sealing area, use silicone gasket remover and metal surface prep. Follow the directions on the packaging. Failure to follow this procedure can cause future oil leakage.

26. Apply silicone gasket and sealant at the crankshaft rear seal retainer plate-to-cylinder block sealing surface.

➤If not secured within 4 minutes, the sealant must be removed and the sealing area cleaned. To clean the sealing area, use silicone gasket remover and metal surface prep. Follow the directions on the packaging. Failure to follow this procedure can cause future oil leakage.

27. Apply silicone gasket and sealant at the engine front cover-to-cylinder block sealing surface.

28. Install the oil pan gasket and the oil pan and loosely install the 18 bolts.

29. Tighten the bolts in 3 stages, in the sequence shown.
- Stage 1: Tighten to 2 Nm (18 inch lbs.).
- Stage 2: Tighten to 20 Nm (15 ft. lbs.).
- Stage 3: Tighten an additional 60 degrees.

30. Install the flexplate inspection cover and the 2 bolts. Tighten to 34 Nm (25 ft. lbs.).

31. Lower the transmission.

32. Align the engine mount studs and lower the engine. Remove the special tool.

✳ WARNING

Only use hand tools when installing the right engine mount nut or damage to the engine mount can occur.

➤Align the engine-to-transmission dowels before installing the engine mount bolt.

33. Install the 6 engine mount nuts. Tighten to 175 Nm (129 ft. lbs.).

✳ WARNING

Only use hand tools when removing the transmission mount-to-crossmember nuts or damage to the transmission mount can occur.

34. Install the transmission mount-to-crossmember nuts. Tighten to 25 Nm (18 ft. lbs.).

35. Install the transmission cooler tube support bracket and the nut. Tighten to 10 Nm (89 inch lbs.).

36. Install the 4 exhaust manifold flange nuts. Tighten to 40 Nm (30 ft. lbs.).

37. If the vehicle is equipped with TSS and turbine/OSS, remove the plugs and install the sensors in the transmission.

38. Install the starter.

39. Install the alternator.

40. Install the cooling fan shroud.

41. Install the air cleaner outlet tube.

42. Fill the crankcase with clean engine oil.

6.0L Diesel Engine

Lower Oil Pan

See Figure 265.

1. Before servicing the vehicle, refer to the Precautions Section.

2. With the vehicle in **Neutral**, position it on a hoist.

3. Disconnect the negative battery cable.

✳ WARNING

Never remove the pressure relief cap while the engine is operating or when the cooling system is hot. Failure to follow these instructions can result in damage to the cooling system or engine or result in personal injury. To avoid having scalding hot coolant or steam blow out of the degas bottle (coolant reservoir) when removing the pressure relief cap, wait until the engine has cooled then wrap a thick cloth around the pressure relief cap and turn it slowly. Step back while the pressure is released from the cooling system. When certain all the pressure has been released, (still with a cloth) turn and remove the pressure relief cap. Failure to follow these instructions can result in personal injury.

✳ CAUTION

The coolant must be removed in a suitable, clean container for reuse. If the coolant is contaminated, it must be recycled or disposed of correctly and the system filled with new coolant.

➤Less than 80% of coolant capacity can be recovered with the engine in the vehicle. Dirty, rusty, or contaminated coolant requires replacement.

4. Place a suitable container below the radiator draincock. If equipped, disconnect the coolant return hose at the fluid cooler.

5. Remove the fill cap from the degas bottle (coolant reservoir).

6. Remove the oil pan drain plug and drain the engine oil.

7. Loosen the exhaust pipe retaining nuts.

8. Remove the motor mount retaining nuts.

9. Open the radiator draincock.

10. Disconnect the lower radiator hose.

11. Disconnect the transmission cooler tubes.

12. Remove the air cleaner assembly.

13. On vehicles with metal ducts, remove the charge air cooler duct.

14. On vehicles with blow molded ducts, loosen the clamps and remove the charge air cooler duct.

15. Remove the radiator support brackets.

16. Remove the 4 pin-type retainers and pull back the sight shield.

17. With the sight shield pulled back, remove the 3 pin-type retainers and the 2 wiring retainers and position the harness rearward out of the way.

18. Disconnect the upper radiator hose and the radiator overflow hose.

19. Remove the radiator and shroud as an assembly.

20. Disconnect the cooling fan electrical connector. Unclip and position the fan and wiring aside.

➡**Use a hole in the fan hub to prevent the fan from turning.**

21. Using the special tool 303-591, or equivalent, loosen the fan clutch. Remove the cooling fan.

22. Remove the bolts from the stator, remove the stator.

23. On vehicles with dual alternator perform the following:

    a. Remove the secondary accessory drive belt.

    b. Remove the bolt and the secondary accessory drive belt tensioner.

    c. Remove the primary accessory drive belt.

    d. Remove the bolts, bracket and secondary accessory drive belt idler pulley.

    e. Remove the bolts and the primary accessory drive belt tensioner.

    f. Disconnect the wire retainer, secondary alternator electrical connector and B+ wire.

    g. Remove the bolts and the secondary alternator with mounting bracket.

24. On vehicles with single alternator, remove the primary accessory drive belt.

25. Remove the bolts and position the alternator back.

26. Support the hood and disconnect the hood lift assemblies.

27. Install two lifting eyes 303-D030, or equivalent, on the right hand cylinder head.

28. Remove the retaining bolt for the fuel lines.

29. Disconnect the heater hose at the coolant pump.

30. Remove the fan shroud mounting stud.

31. Install one lifting eye 303-D030 on the left hand cylinder head.

⚠ CAUTION

Do not use the special tool to raise the engine. Damage to the special tool or vehicle may occur.

➡**The ball studs may have to be removed.**

➡**This procedure requires a second bolt hook assembly. The tools are available through Rotunda tools with the following numbers: bolt hook 303-F070-6, handle 303-F070-8, bracket 303-F070-7 and washer 303-F070-12004.**

32. Install the special tool.

➡**The engine must be raised evenly.**

33. Using a lifting crane, raise the engine until the turbo charger is about to touch the cowl. Secure the engine with the special tool.

34. Remove the transmission cooler line bracket.

35. Remove the bolts and position back the oil pan until the oil pick-up tube bolts are accessible.

36. Remove the bolts and let the oil pick-up tube go into the oil pan. Remove the oil pan.

37. Remove the press-in-place gasket and discard.

38. Clean and inspect the sealing surfaces.

39. Remove and discard the oil pick-up tube O-ring.

To install:

40. Install a new O-ring on the oil pick-up tube and position the oil pick-up tube in the oil pan.

41. Install a new press-in-place gasket into the upper oil pan.

42. Position the oil pan in the vehicle.

43. Install the oil pick-up tube and bolts. Tighten to 10 ft. lbs. (13 Nm).

44. Position the oil pan and install the bolts. Install the long bolts first. Tighten to 10 ft. lbs. (13 Nm).

45. Install the transmission cooler tube bracket and nut. Tighten to 18 inch lbs. (10 Nm).

46. Using the special tool 303-F070, lower the engine.

47. Remove the lifting eyes 303-D030 and the special tool.

48. Install the fan shroud mounting stud. Tighten to 30 ft. lbs. (40 Nm).

49. Connect the heater hose at the coolant pump.

50. Install the retaining bolt for the fuel lines. Tighten to 10 ft. lbs. (10 Nm).

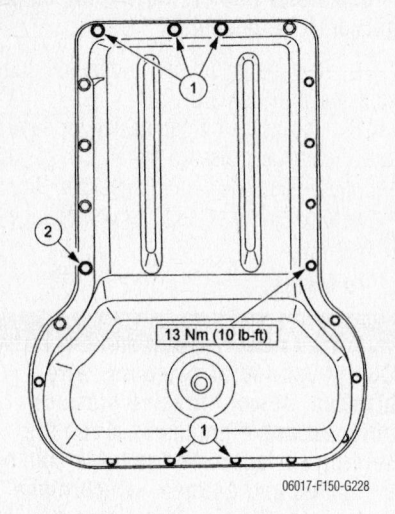

06017-F150-G228

Fig. 265 Lower oil pan installation. (1) indicates the long bolts—6.0L Diesel Engine lower oil pan

51. If removed, install the ball studs.

52. Connect the hood lifts and remove the hood support.

53. Position the primary alternator and install the bolts.

54. On a vehicle with a single alternator, install the primary accessory drive belt.

55. On vehicles with dual alternators, perform the following:

    a. Install the secondary alternator with mounting bracket and bolts. Tighten to 35 ft. lbs. (47 Nm).

    b. Connect the B+ wire, secondary alternator electrical connector and wire retainer.

    c. Install the primary accessory drive belt tensioner and bolts. Tighten to 18 ft. lbs. (25 Nm).

    d. Position the secondary accessory drive belt idler pulley. Install the bracket and bolts. Tighten to 18 ft. lbs. (25 Nm).

    e. Install the primary accessory drive belt.

    f. Install the secondary accessory drive belt tensioner and bolt. Tighten to 18 ft. lbs. (25 Nm).

    g. Install the secondary accessory drive belt.

56. Install the stator and stator bolts. Tighten to 30 ft. lbs. (40 Nm).

57. Install the cooling fan clutch. Use the special tool 303-591 to tighten the cooling fan clutch. Tighten to 98 ft. lbs. (133 Nm).

58. Position and clip the cooling fan wiring. Connect the cooling fan electrical connector.

59. Install the radiator and shroud as an assembly.

60. Connect the upper radiator hose and the radiator overflow hose.

61. Position the harness wiring, install the 2 wiring retainers and 3 pin-type retainers.

62. Position the sight shield and install the 4 pin-type retainers.

63. Install the radiator support brackets. Tighten to 22 ft. lbs. (30 Nm).

64. On vehicles with metal ducts, install the charge air cooler duct and tighten the clamps.

65. On vehicles with blow molded ducts, install the charge air cooler duct and tighten the clamps.

66. Install the air cleaner assembly.

67. Connect the transmission cooler tubes. Tighten to the specifications illustrated.

68. Close the radiator draincock. Connect the lower radiator hose.

69. Install the motor mount retaining nuts. Tighten to 76 ft. lbs. (103 Nm).

70. Tighten the exhaust pipe retaining nuts to 35 ft. lbs. (47 Nm).

71. Clean and inspect the oil pan drain plug and gasket, install new if necessary.

72. Install the oil pan drain plug and tighten to 18 ft. lbs. (25 Nm).

73. Connect the negative battery cables.

74. Fill the engine with clean engine oil.

75. Fill the coolant system.

76. Run the engine and check for leaks.

Upper Oil Pan

See Figure 266.

1. Before servicing the vehicle, refer to the Precautions Section.

2. Remove the oil pan.

3. Remove the bolts and the upper oil pan. Remove and discard the press-in-place gasket.

4. Clean and inspect the sealing surfaces.

To install:

➡ **Install a new press-in-place gasket.**

5. Install the upper oil pan and bolts.

6. Install the lower oil pan.

OIL PUMP

REMOVAL & INSTALLATION

4.2L Engine

See Figure 267.

1. Before servicing the vehicle, refer to the Precautions Section.

2. Raise and safely support the vehicle.

3. Drain the engine oil. Install the drain plug when finished.

4. Remove and discard the oil filter.

5. Remove the 6 bolts and the oil pump.

❄❄ WARNING

Do not reuse the oil pump seal. A new service seal must be installed.

6. Remove and discard the oil pump seal.

7. Remove and inspect the oil pump drive gear, the driven gear and the cover. Install new components if necessary.

8. Inspect the face of the oil pump for flatness.

To install:

9. Install a new service oil pump seal on the oil pump.

➡ **Lubricate the parts with clean engine oil before assembly.**

10. Install the oil pump drive gear, the driven gear and the cover.

11. Position the oil pump and install the bolts. Tighten the bolts as shown.

- Bolts numbered 1: Tighten to 10 Nm (89 inch lbs.).
- Bolts numbered 2: Tighten to 25 Nm (18 ft. lbs.).

12. Install a new oil filter.

13. Fill the engine with clean engine oil.

4.6L, 5.4L and 6.8L Engine

See Figures 268 and 269.

1. Before servicing the vehicle, refer to the Precautions Section.

2. Raise and safely support the vehicle.

3. Remove the timing drive components.

4. Remove the oil pan.

5. Remove the 3 bolts, the oil pump screen and pickup tube and the spacer.

6. Remove the 3 bolts and the oil pump.

To install:

➡ **Lubricate the new O-ring seal with clean engine oil.**

7. Clean and inspect the mating surfaces and install a new O-ring seal.

❄❄ WARNING

The oil pump must be primed prior to starting the engine.

8. Install the oil pump and loosely install the 3 bolts. Tighten the bolts in the sequence shown to 10 Nm (89 inch lbs.).

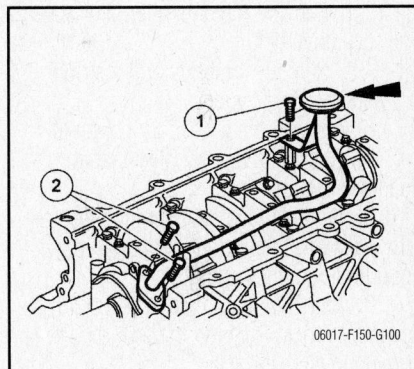

06017-F150-G100

Fig. 268 Pickup tube and spacer—4.6L, 5.4L and 6.8L engines

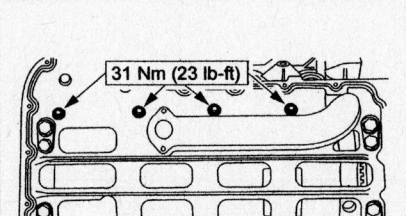

06017-F150-G229

Fig. 266 Upper oil pan fasteners—6.0L Diesel Engine

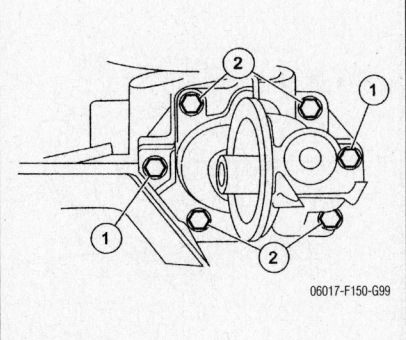

06017-F150-G99

Fig. 267 Oil pump fasteners—4.2L engine

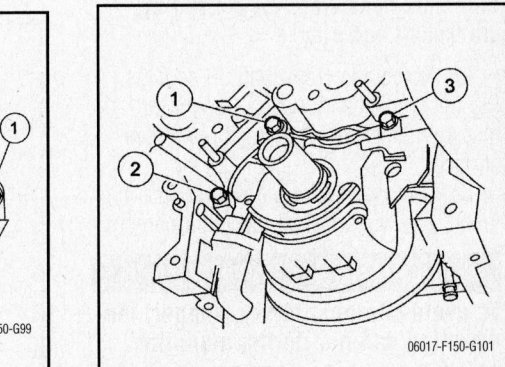

06017-F150-G101

Fig. 269 Oil pump fasteners—4.6L, 5.4L and 6.8L engines

❊❊ WARNING

Make sure the O-ring is in place and not damaged. A missing or damaged O-ring can cause foam in the lubrication system, low oil pressure and severe engine damage.

➡ **Install a new O-ring and lubricate with clean engine oil.**

9. Install the pick up tube spacer, oil pump screen and pickup tube and the 3 bolts. Tighten bolt 1 to 25 Nm (18 ft. lbs.). Tighten bolts 2 to 10 Nm (89 inch lbs.).

10. Install the oil pan.

11. Install the timing drive components.

6.0L Diesel Engine

See Figure 270.

1. Before servicing the vehicle, refer to the Precautions Section.

2. With the vehicle in **Neutral**, position it on a hoist.

3. Disconnect the battery ground cable(s).

4. Remove the cooling fan.

5. On vehicles with dual alternator, perform the following:

   a. Remove the dual alternator accessory drive belt.

   b. Remove the bolts and the dual alternator pulley.

6. Remove the accessory drive belt.

7. Check the crankshaft vibration damper runout.

8. Remove the paint from the face of the crankshaft vibration damper at four points 90 degrees apart.

9. Attach dial indicator 100-002 to the cylinder block. Position the tool on one of the unpainted surfaces.

10. Using a suitable tool, pry the crankshaft forward. Zero the dial indicator.

➡ **Pry the crankshaft forward only to eliminate possible error caused by crankshaft end play.**

11. Rotate the crankshaft 90 degrees. Pry the crankshaft forward. Record the measurement. Repeat at each unpainted surface.

12. If the runout exceeds specification, install a new crankshaft vibration damper.

❊❊ CAUTION

To avoid personal injury, support the vibration damper during mounting bolt removal. The damper can slide off the nose of the crankshaft very easily.

13. Remove the bolts and the crankshaft vibration damper.

14. Discard the bolts.

15. Punch two holes in the seal.

16. Using the special tool 303-D060, remove the crankshaft seal.

➡ **Production engine will not have a wear sleeve.**

17. If equipped, remove the crankshaft damper wear sleeve using tool 303-762.

18. Remove the bolts and the gerotor cover. Remove and discard the O-ring seal.

➡ **Mark the front of the inner and outer gerotor for correct reassembly.**

19. Remove the inner and outer gerotors.

20. Inspect the oil pump components and replace as necessary.

21. Inspect the oil pump for excessive metal particles.

22. Inspect the oil pump for gouging, cracks or deep scratches.

23. Inspect the oil pump inner and outer gear rotors for damage or excessive wear.

To install:

➡ **Install the gears with marks pointing outward.**

24. Lubricate the inner gear with lithium assembly grease and install onto the crankshaft. Lubricate the outer gear with lithium assembly grease and mesh with the inner gear rotor in the oil pump housing. Wipe off the excess assembly grease.

25. Install a new O-ring seal.

26. Install the gerotor cover and bolts. Tighten to 71 inch lbs. (8 Nm).

27. Thoroughly clean the crankshaft front seal mounting surface.

28. Apply Threadlock 262® to the outer circumference of the leading edge of the crankshaft.

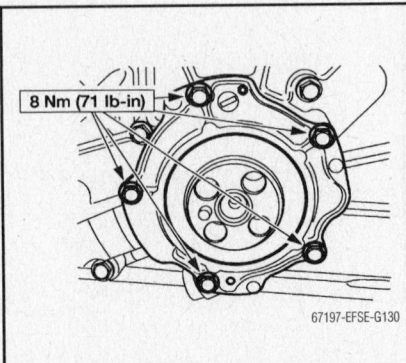

Fig. 270 Oil pump mounting—6.0L Diesel Engine

67197-EFSE-G130

➡ **New seal and wear sleeve must not be separated.**

29. Using the special tool 303-361, install the oil seal and wear sleeve assembly.

❊❊ CAUTION

To prevent engine damage, you must always install four new bolts when installing the vibration damper.

➡ **Do not use anti-seize compounds, grease or any lubricants. Lubricants have an adverse effect on the torque results.**

30. Install the crankshaft vibration damper and bolts.

31. Tighten the bolts in a criss-cross sequence as follows:

   a. Tighten the bolts to 50 ft. lbs. (68 Nm).

   b. Tighten the bolts an additional 90 degrees.

32. Install the accessory drive belt.

33. On vehicles with dual alternator, perform the following:

   a. Install the dual alternator pulley and bolts. Tighten to 35 ft. lbs. (47 Nm).

   b. Install the dual alternator accessory drive belt.

34. Install the cooling fan stator.

35. Connect the battery ground cables.

PISTON AND RING

POSITIONING

See Figures 271 through 273.

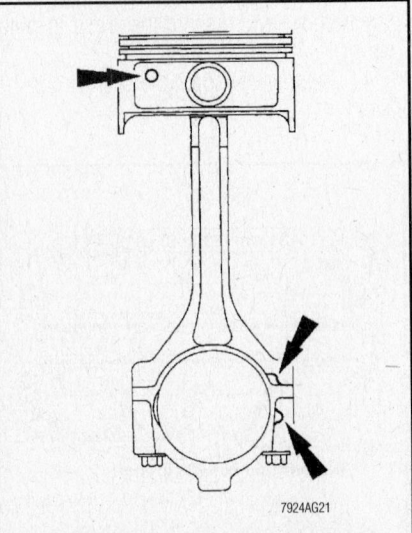

Fig. 271 Piston connecting rod to bearing cap orientation—all gasoline engines

7924AG21

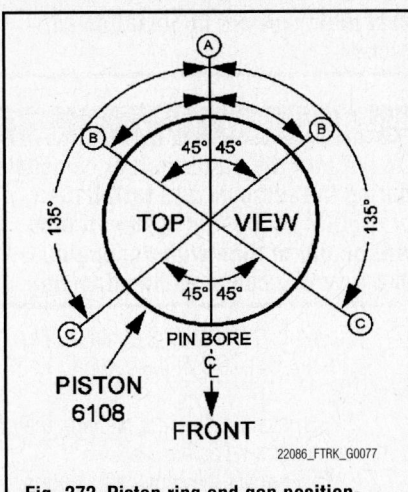

Fig. 272 Piston ring end gap positioning—all gasoline engines

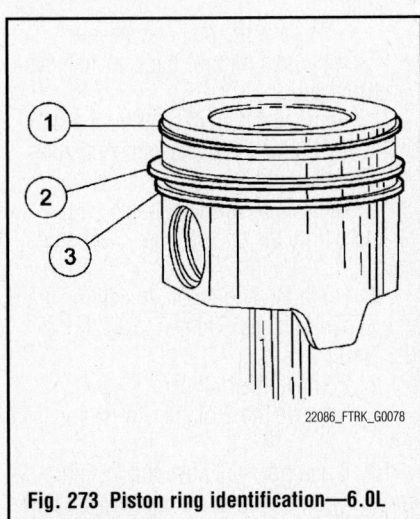

Fig. 273 Piston ring identification—6.0L diesel engine

REAR MAIN SEAL

REMOVAL & INSTALLATION

4.2L Engine

See Figures 274 through 277.

If the crankshaft rear oil seal replacement is the only operation being performed, it can be done in the vehicle as detailed in the following procedure. If the oil seal is being replaced in conjunction with a rear main bearing replacement, the engine must be removed from the vehicle and installed on a work stand.

1. Before servicing the vehicle, refer to the Precautions Section.
2. Disconnect the negative battery cable.
3. Remove the transmission from the vehicle.
4. Remove the flywheel/flexplate.

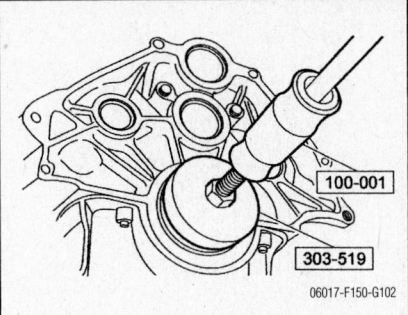

Fig. 274 Rear main seal removal—4.2L engine

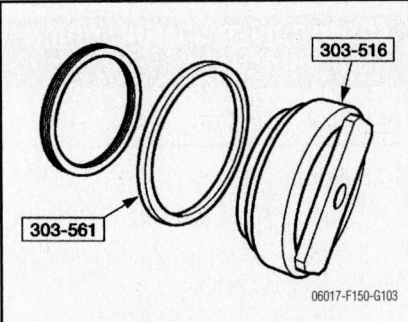

Fig. 275 Assembling the rear main seal and tools—4.2L engine

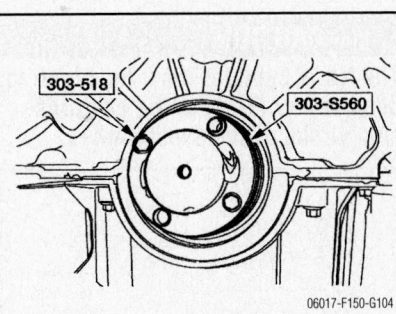

Fig. 276 Install tools 303-518 and 303-S560 on the crankshaft—4.2L engine

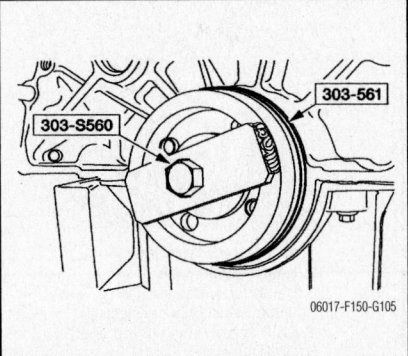

Fig. 277 Installing the seal—4.2L engine

5. Use an appropriate seal removal tool to extract the rear crankshaft seal.
6. Clean the oil seal mating surface.

To install:

7. Coat the new oil seal and the crankshaft with a light film of engine oil.
8. Assemble the oil seal to the installer tool.
9. Install the oil seal until fully seated.
10. Install flywheel.
11. Install the transmission, following the recommended procedure.
12. Install the negative battery cable.

4.6L, 5.4L and 6.8L Engine

1. Remove the transmission.
2. Remove the 6 flexplate bolts and the flexplate.
3. Remove the engine rear cover plate.
4. Using the special tools, remove and discard the crankshaft oil slinger.
5. Using the special tools, remove and discard the crankshaft rear seal.

To install:

6. Lubricate the crankshaft rear seal with clean engine oil prior to installation.
7. Using the special tools, install a new crankshaft rear seal.
8. Lubricate the crankshaft oil slinger with clean engine oil prior to installation.
9. Using the special tools, install a new crankshaft oil slinger.
10. Install the engine rear cover plate.
11. Install the flexplate and the 6 bolts. Tighten the bolts in 2 stages in a criss-cross pattern:
    a. Stage 1: Tighten to 20 Nm (15 lb-ft).
    b. Stage 2: Tighten to 80 Nm (59 lb-ft).
12. Install the transmission.

6.0L Diesel Engine

See Figures 278 through 280.

1. Before servicing the vehicle, refer to the Precautions Section.
2. Remove the transmission.
3. Remove the bolts.
4. Remove the flexplate or flywheel.

➡**Use extreme care when removing the flywheel front adapter to prevent damage to the alignment dowel pin.**

5. Remove the flywheel front adapter.

❉❉ CAUTION

To prevent engine damage, do not remove the rear primary crankshaft flange bolts under any circumstances. If the flange is removed and reinstalled, it will result in engine vibration and premature transmission component wear.

6. Punch two holes in the rear main seal, across from each other.

7. Using the puller tool 100-001, remove the rear main seal.

➡ **Production engines will not have a wear sleeve.**

8. If equipped with a crankshaft wear sleeve, use the tool 303-771 to remove the crankshaft rear wear sleeve.

9. Clean and inspect the crankshaft sealing surface.

To install:

➡ **The crankshaft rear oil seal and wear sleeve are installed as an assembly.**

➡ **Lubricate the outer diameter of the rubber seal with a solution of dish soap and water (approximately 50/50 mix) prior to assembly. Do not use any other type of lubricant.**

10. Apply a bead of Threadlock 262® around the circumference of the outer rear edge of the secondary crankshaft flange.

11. Using tool 303-770, install the crankshaft rear oil seal.

12. Install the flywheel front adapter.

13. Install the flexplate or flywheel.

14. Install the bolts. Snug all bolts to 44 inch lbs. (5 Nm), then tighten all bolts to 69 ft. lbs. (94 Nm) in the sequence illustrated.

15. Install the transmission.

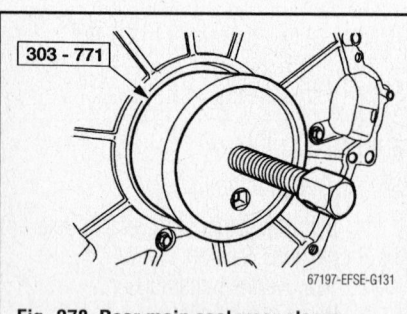

Fig. 278 Rear main seal wear sleeve removal—6.0L Diesel Engine

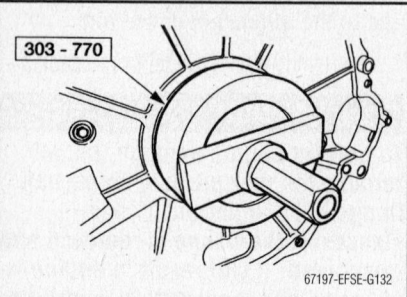

Fig. 279 Rear main seal installation— 6.0L Diesel Engine

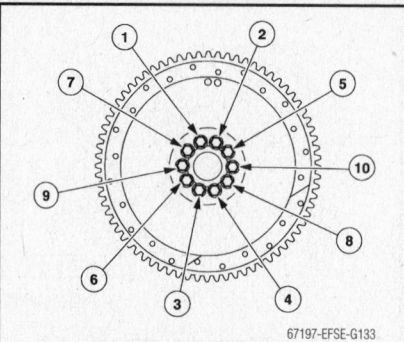

Fig. 280 Flywheel installation torque sequence—6.0L Diesel Engine

FRONT COVER, TIMING CHAIN AND SPROCKETS

REMOVAL & INSTALLATION

4.2L Engine

See Figures 281 through 286.

1. Before servicing the vehicle, refer to the Precautions Section.

2. Remove the coolant pump.

3. Remove the camshaft synchronizer:
   a. Disconnect the battery ground cable.
   b. Drain the engine cooling system.

✳ CAUTION

The No. 1 cylinder must be set on top dead center (TDC) of the compression stroke or the synchronizer

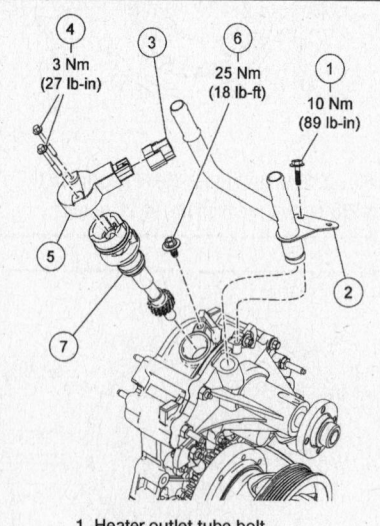

1. Heater outlet tube bolt
2. Heater outlet tube
3. Camshaft position (CMP) sensor electrical connector
4. CMP sensor bolts (2 required)
5. CMP sensor
6. Camshaft synchronizer bolt and washer assembly
7. Camshaft synchronizer

Fig. 281 Exploded view of the camshaft synchronizer and components

assembly will not be installed correctly.

✳ CAUTION

Do not turn the crankshaft or camshaft during the removal and installation procedure or the fuel system timing will be out of time with the engine and possibly cause engine damage.

c. Rotate the crankshaft until the No. 1 cylinder is at TDC of the compression stroke.

d. Remove the bolt and position the heater outlet tube aside.

e. Disconnect the camshaft position (CMP) sensor electrical connector.

f. Remove the bolts and the CMP sensor.

g. Remove the bolt and washer assembly and remove the camshaft synchronizer.

4. Remove the crankshaft front seal.

5. Disconnect the crankshaft position (CKP) sensor electrical connector.

6. Detach the wiring harness retainers from the engine front cover stud bolts.

7. Drain the engine oil. Install the drain plug when finished. Tighten to 17 ft. lbs. (23 Nm).

8. Remove the oil filter.

9. Remove the 2 oil pan-to-engine front cover bolts.

10. If equipped, remove the retaining nut and position the transmission coolant tube support bracket aside.

11. Remove the bolt and the accessory drive belt tensioner.

12. Loosen the 4 power steering pump bolts and slide the power steering pump out approximately 25 mm (1 in).

13. Remove the bolt and the A/C compressor and power steering pump bracket brace.

✳ CAUTION

The cap screw is concealed by the oil pump housing. Failure to remove this

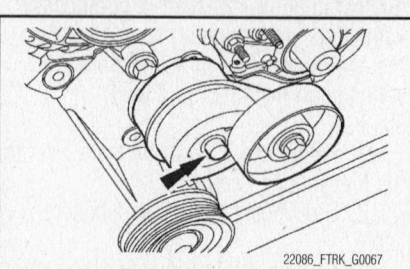

Fig. 282 Remove the bolt and the accessory drive belt tensioner

retainer will result in damage to the engine front cover.

14. Remove the bolt and the stud bolts. Slide the engine front cover from the studs. Remove and discard the gasket.

➥There are 2 different studs. Note the locations of the studs for installation reference.

15. Remove the 4 studs.
16. Remove the camshaft synchronizer drive gear:
    a. Remove the bolt.
    b. Remove the camshaft synchronizer drive gear.
17. Rotate the crankshaft until the timing marks and keyways align.
18. Compress and install a retaining pin to hold the timing chain tensioner.
19. Remove the camshaft sprocket, the crankshaft sprocket and the timing chain as an assembly.
20. Remove the bolts and the timing chain tensioner.

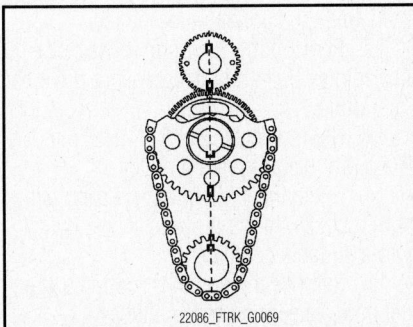

Fig. 283 Remove the bolt and the accessory drive belt tensioner

To install:
21. Install the timing chain tensioner and the bolts. Tighten to 9 ft. lbs. (12 Nm).
22. If necessary, retract the tensioner pad retracting mechanism and insert a retaining pin.
23. Rotate the crankshaft so the No. 1 piston is at top dead center (TDC) and the key is at the 12 o'clock position.
24. Turn the camshaft sprocket so that the timing mark is at the 12 o'clock position and is lined up with the timing mark on the balance shaft at the 6 o'clock position.
25. Install the timing chain, the camshaft sprocket and the crankshaft sprocket.
26. Make sure that the timing marks and the keyways are aligned.
27. Remove the retaining pin.
28. Install the camshaft synchronizer drive gear and the bolt. Tighten to 33 ft. lbs. (45 Nm).

❋❋ CAUTION

In order to prevent foreign material from contaminating the engine block or the engine front cover, it is necessary to seal the coolant and oil passages of both components. Failure to follow these directions will result in engine damage.

❋❋ CAUTION

Do not use metal scrapers, wire brushes, power abrasive discs or other abrasive means to clean the sealing surfaces. These tools cause scratches and gouges which make leak paths. Use a plastic scraping tool to remove all traces of old sealant.

29. Clean and inspect the engine block and engine front cover as follows:
    a. Pack the exposed portion of the oil pan with clean shop towels.
    b. Plug the oil and coolant passages.
    c. Clean the gasket surfaces. Use silicone gasket remover and metal surface prep.
    d. Using compressed air, remove any remaining foreign material from the engine block and front cover.
    e. Remove the shop towels from the oil pan.
    f. Remove the plugs or seals from the oil and coolant passages.
30. Apply thread sealant to the threads on the studs and the cap screw.
31. Install the engine front cover studs. Tighten to 62 inch lbs. (7 Nm).

➥If the engine front cover is not secured within 4 minutes, the sealant must be removed and the sealing areas cleaned. To clean the sealing area, use silicone gasket remover and metal surface prep. Failure to follow this procedure can cause future oil leakage.

32. Apply silicone gasket and sealant as shown.

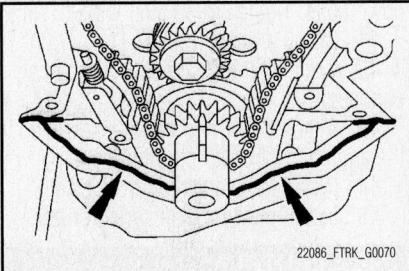

Fig. 285 Apply silicone gasket and sealant to the areas shown

33. Install the engine front cover gasket.

❋❋ CAUTION

The coolant pump and gasket must be installed at this time to correctly tighten all of the engine front cover fasteners in sequence.

34. Install the engine front cover and coolant pump.
35. Position the engine front cover and install the bolt, the stud bolts and the cap screw finger tight.
36. Position a new coolant pump gasket and the coolant pump and install the fasteners finger tight.
37. Tighten the fasteners in the sequence shown

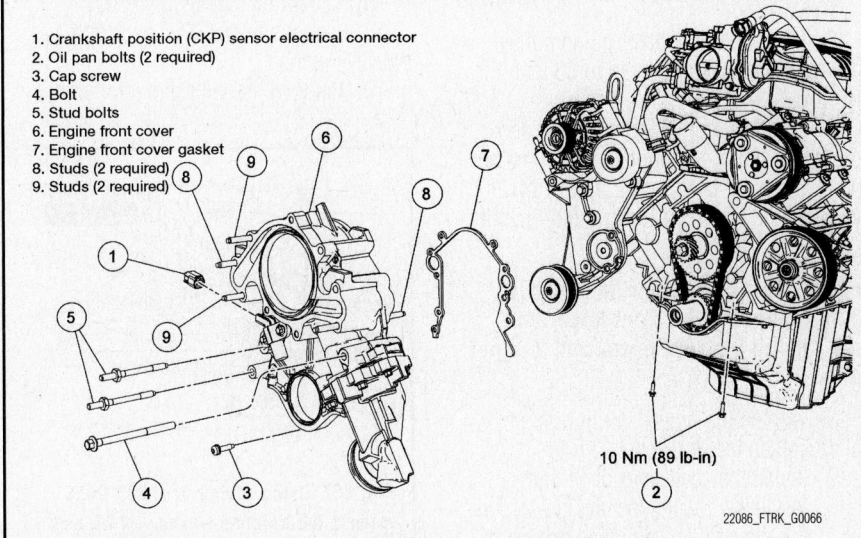

1. Crankshaft position (CKP) sensor electrical connector
2. Oil pan bolts (2 required)
3. Cap screw
4. Bolt
5. Stud bolts
6. Engine front cover
7. Engine front cover gasket
8. Studs (2 required)
9. Studs (2 required)

10 Nm (89 lb-in)

Fig. 284 Exploded view of the engine front cover and components

a. Tighten capscrew No. 12 to 89 inch lbs. (10 Nm).

b. Tighten all other fasteners to 28 Nm (21 lb-ft).

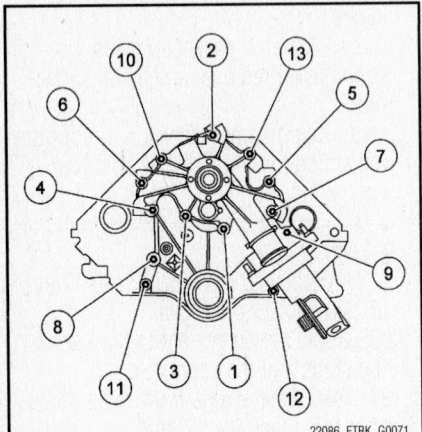

Fig. 286 Tighten the front cover screws in the sequence shown

38. If equipped, position the transmission cooler tube bracket and install the nut. Tighten to 15 ft. lbs. (20 Nm).

39. Install the accessory drive belt tensioner and the bolt. Tighten to 41 ft. lbs. (55 Nm).

40. Install the 2 oil pan-to-engine front cover bolts. Tighten to 89 inch lbs. (10 Nm).

41. Install a new oil filter.

42. Connect the CKP sensor electrical connector.

43. Attach the wiring harness retainers to the engine front cover stud bolts.

44. Install the crankshaft front seal.

45. Install the camshaft synchronizer:

✶ CAUTION

After installation, do not loosen the synchronizer bolt and rotate the synchronizer assembly. The synchronizer assembly is not adjustable. Do not loosen the synchronizer bolt after the alignment tool has been removed in order to align the CMP sensor electrical connector for any reason. If the electrical connector is not in the correct position, the synchronizer assembly must be removed, the alignment tool and the assembly reinstalled if the engine has not been rotated from TDC of the compression stroke on the No. 1 cylinder.

✶ CAUTION

Do not turn the crankshaft or camshaft during the removal and installation procedure or the fuel sys-

tem timing will be out of time with the engine and possibly cause engine damage.

✶✶ CAUTION

A synchronizer alignment gauge must be used during the installation of the synchronizer assembly. Failure to follow these procedures will result in the fuel system being out of time with the engine and possibly cause engine damage.

c. Install the special tool on the camshaft synchronizer by rotating the tool until it engages the notch on the camshaft synchronizer housing.

➡ Coat the synchronizer drive gear with clean engine oil prior to installation.

➡ During installation, the arrow in the synchronizer alignment tool will rotate clockwise as the gears engage.

d. Install the camshaft synchronizer so the arrow on the synchronizer alignment gauge is 54 degrees from the centerline of the engine.

e. Install the camshaft synchronizer bolt and washer assembly. Tighten to 18 ft. lbs. (25 Nm).

f. Install the CMP sensor and the bolts.

g. Connect the CMP sensor electrical connector.

➡ Clean and inspect the heater tube O-ring seal. Install a new O-ring seal if necessary. Lubricate the O-ring seal with clean engine coolant.

h. Position the heater outlet tube and install the bolt. Tighten to 89 inch lbs. (10 Nm).

46. Position the coolant pump pulley and install the bolts. Tighten to 89 inch lbs. (10 Nm).

47. Position the A/C compressor and power steering pump pulley bracket brace and install the 2 bolts and 2 nuts. Tighten the bolts to 35 ft. lbs. (48 Nm) and the nuts to 18 ft. lbs. (25 Nm).

➡ Slide the power steering pump in while tightening the front lower bolt, then tighten the rear lower and 2 upper bolts.

48. Tighten the power steering pump bolts. Tighten to 18 ft. lbs. (25 Nm).

49. Install the accessory drive belt.

50. Install the cooling fan and fan shroud.

51. Fill the engine with clean engine oil.

52. Fill and bleed the cooling system.

4.6L Engine and 5.4L Engine

See Figures 287 through 315.

1. Before servicing the vehicle, refer to the Precautions Section.

2. Raise and safely support the vehicle.

3. Disconnect the battery ground cable.

4. Drain the engine oil.

5. Remove the cooling fan.

6. Remove the right valve cover.

7. Remove the left valve cover.

8. Rotate the tensioner clockwise and remove the drive belt. Using special tool 303-D055, remove the bolt and washer and discard the bolt.

✶✶ WARNING

This bolt is torque-to-yield and cannot be reused.

9. Using special tool 303-099, remove the crankshaft pulley.

10. Using special tool 303-107, remove the crankshaft front seal.

11. Remove the 4 coolant pump pulley bolts and the coolant pump pulley.

12. Remove the accessory drive belt idler pulley bolt and the accessory drive belt idler pulley.

13. Using special tool 211-016, remove the power steering pump pulley.

14. Disconnect the power steering pressure tube. Drain the power steering fluid into a suitable container.

15. Remove the nut and position aside the power steering pressure tube.

16. Remove the power steering pump bolts and position the power steering pump assembly aside.

17. Disconnect the camshaft position (CMP) sensor electrical connector.

18. Remove the CMP sensor bolt and the CMP sensor.

19. Remove the left radio interference

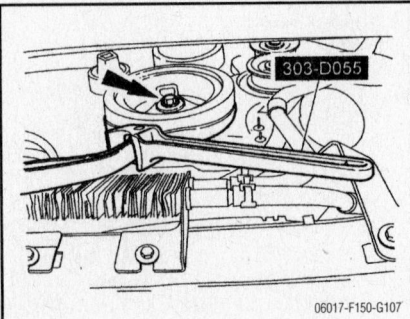

Fig. 287 Using special tool 303-D055, remove the bolt and washer—4.6L and 5.4L engine

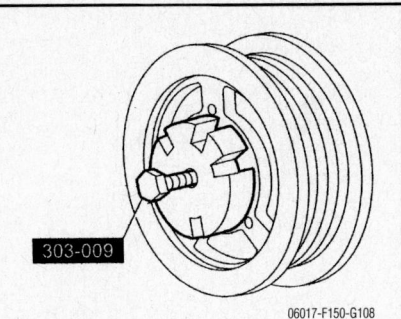

Fig. 288 Using special tool 303-099, remove the crankshaft pulley—4.6L and 5.4L engine

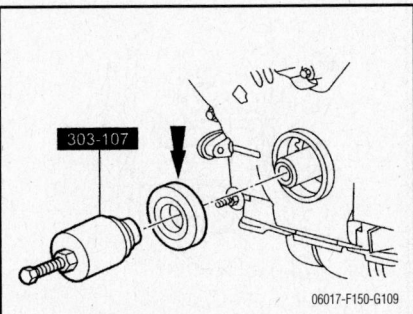

Fig. 289 Using special tool 303-107, remove the crankshaft front seal—4.6L and 5.4L engine

capacitor nut and position the left radio interference capacitor aside.

20. Remove the nut and the upper radiator hose bracket.

21. Remove the right radio interference capacitor nut and position the right radio interference capacitor aside.

22. Disconnect the crankshaft position (CKP) sensor electrical connector.

23. Remove the 4 oil pan bolts.

24. Remove the nut and the A/C manifold and tube assembly support bracket.

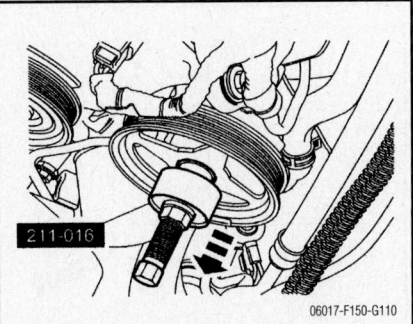

Fig. 290 Using special tool 211-016, remove the power steering pump pulley—4.6L and 5.4L engine

25. If equipped, remove the nut and the transmission cooler tube support bracket.

26. Remove the bolts and the studs.

❋❋ WARNING

Do not use metal scrapers, wire brushes, power abrasive discs or other abrasive means to clean the sealing surfaces. These tools cause scratches and gouges which make leak paths. Use a plastic scraping tool to remove all traces of old sealant.

27. Remove the engine front cover from the front cover-to-cylinder block dowel.

28. Remove the engine front cover gaskets.

29. Clean the mating surfaces with silicone gasket remover and metal surface prep. Follow the directions on the packaging.

30. Inspect the mating surfaces.

31. Remove the CKP sensor bolt and the CKP sensor.

32. Remove the crankshaft sensor ring from the crankshaft.

33. Rotate the crankshaft until the timing

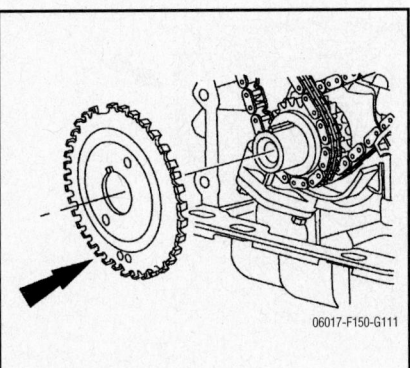

Fig. 291 Crankshaft sensor ring—4.6L and 5.4L engine

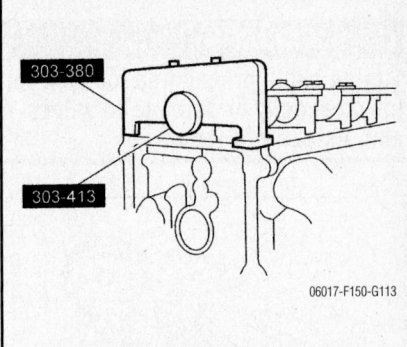

Fig. 293 Install the special tools on the camshaft—4.6L and 5.4L engine

mark on the right camshaft sprocket is approximately at the 11 o'clock position and the timing mark on the left camshaft sprocket is approximately at the 12 o'clock position.

34. Install the special tools on the camshaft as shown.

❋❋ WARNING

If one or both of the tensioner mounting bolts are loosened or removed, the tensioner-sealing bead must be inspected for seat integrity. If cracks, tears or separation from the tensioner body or permanent compression of the seal bead is observed, install a new tensioner.

35. Remove the bolts (1). Remove the timing chain tensioners (2). Remove the timing chain tensioner arms (3).

36. Remove the timing chains and crankshaft sprocket.

37. Remove the bolts (1). Remove the left timing chain guide (2).

38. Remove the bolts (3). Remove the right timing chain guide (4).

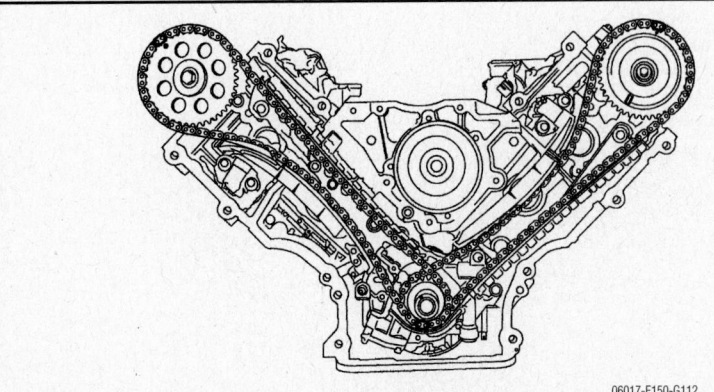

Fig. 292 Rotate the crankshaft until the timing mark on the right camshaft sprocket is approximately at the 11 o'clock position and the timing mark on the left camshaft sprocket is approximately at the 12 o'clock position—4.6L and 5.4L engine

To install:

✻✻ WARNING

Timing chain procedures must be followed exactly or damage to valves and pistons will result.

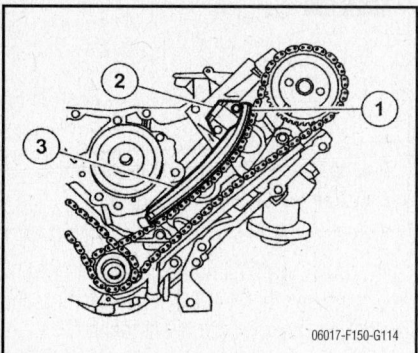

Fig. 294 Removing the tensioners and tensioner arms—4.6L and 5.4L engine

✻✻ WARNING

Prior to installation, inspect the tensioner-sealing bead for seal integrity. If cracks, tears, separation from the tensioner body or permanent compression of the seal bead is observed, install a new tensioner.

39. Compress the tensioner plunger, using a vise.
40. Install a retaining clip on the tensioner to hold the plunger in during installation.
41. If the copper links are not visible, mark one link on one end and one link on the other end, and use as timing marks.
42. Install the crankshaft sprocket, making sure the flange faces forward.
43. Position the left timing chain guide.
44. Install and tighten the left bolts. Tighten to 10 Nm (89 inch lbs.).

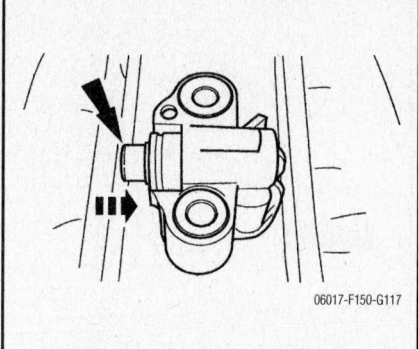

Fig. 297 Compress the tensioner plunger, using a vise—4.6L and 5.4L engine

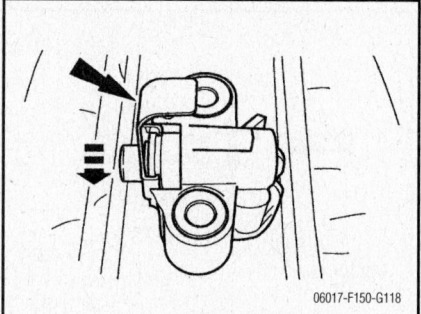

Fig. 298 Install a retaining clip on the tensioner to hold the plunger in during installation—4.6L and 5.4L engine

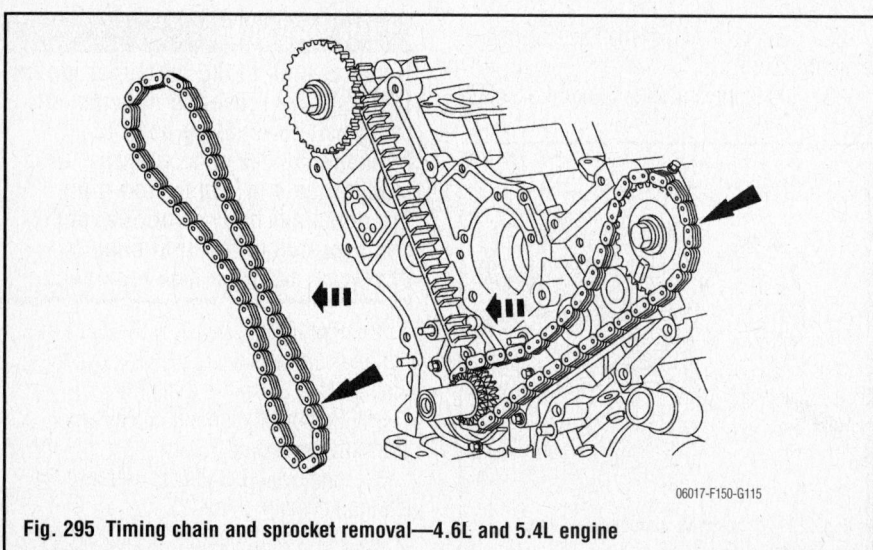

Fig. 295 Timing chain and sprocket removal—4.6L and 5.4L engine

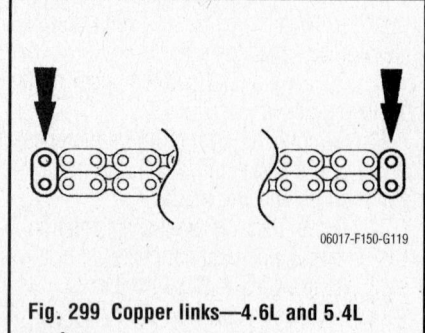

Fig. 299 Copper links—4.6L and 5.4L engine

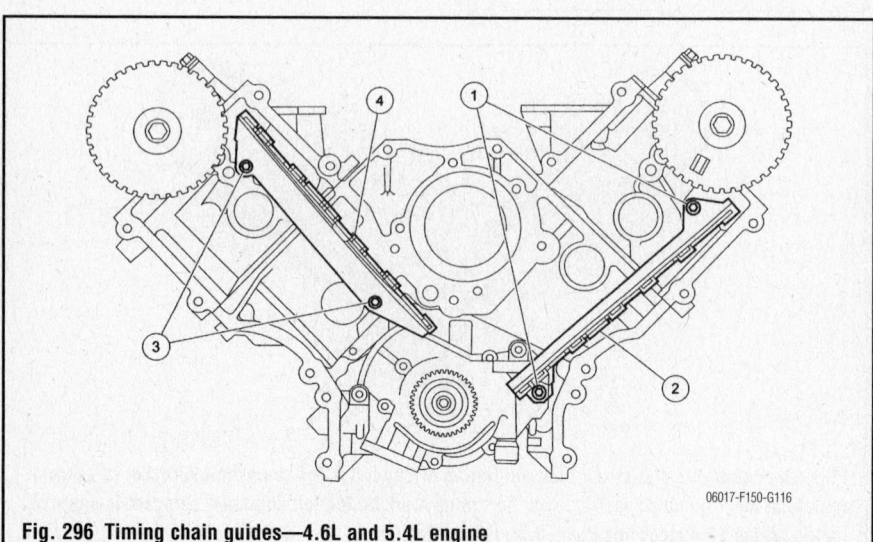

Fig. 296 Timing chain guides—4.6L and 5.4L engine

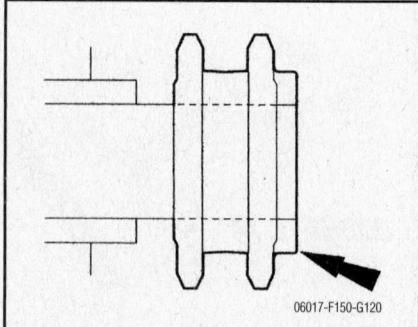

Fig. 300 Install the crankshaft sprocket, making sure the flange faces forward—4.6L and 5.4L engine

45. Position the right timing chain guide.

46. Install and tighten the right bolts. Tighten to 10 Nm (89 inch lbs.).

�֍ WARNING

Unless otherwise instructed, do not rotate either the crankshaft or the camshafts, when the timing chains are removed and the cylinder heads are installed. Severe piston and valve damage will occur.

➡The number one cylinder is at top dead center (TDC) when the stud on the engine block fits into the slot in the handle of the special tool.

47. Remove the Crankshaft Holding Tool.

48. Position the left (inner) timing chain on the crankshaft sprocket, aligning the copper (marked) link with the timing mark on the sprocket.

49. Install the left timing chain on the camshaft sprocket, aligning the copper (marked) link with the timing marks on the sprocket.

➡The left timing chain tensioner arm has a bump near the dowel hole for identification.

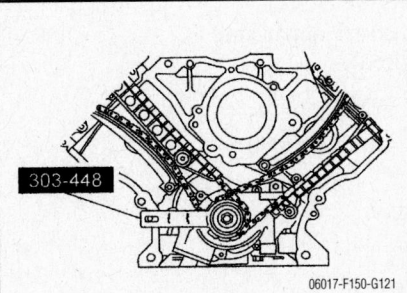

Fig. 301 Using the special tool, position the crankshaft so the number one cylinder is at TDC—4.6L and 5.4L engine

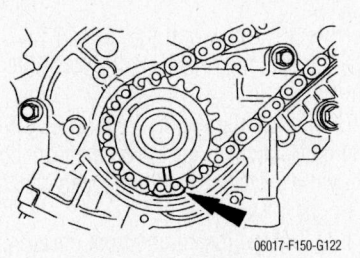

Fig. 302 Position the left (inner) timing chain on the crankshaft sprocket, aligning the copper (marked) link with the timing mark on the sprocket—4.6L and 5.4L engine

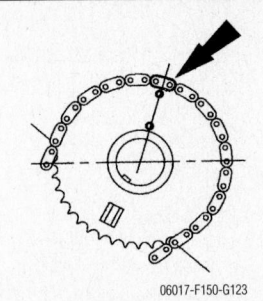

Fig. 303 Install the left timing chain on the camshaft sprocket, aligning the copper (marked) link with the timing marks on the sprocket—4.6L and 5.4L engine

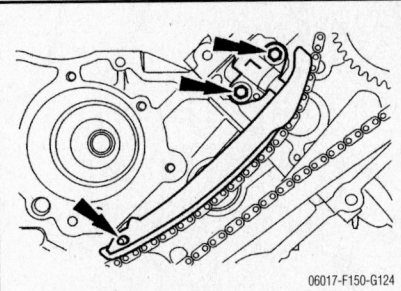

Fig. 304 Position the left timing chain tensioner arm on the dowel pin and install the left timing chain tensioner—4.6L and 5.4L engine

50. Position the left timing chain tensioner arm on the dowel pin and install the left timing chain tensioner. Tighten to 25 Nm (18 ft. lbs.).

51. Remove the retaining clip from the left timing chain tensioner.

52. Position the right (outer) timing chain on the crankshaft sprocket, aligning the copper (marked) link with the timing mark on the sprocket.

54. Install the right timing chain on the camshaft sprocket, aligning the copper (marked) link with the timing marks on the sprocket.

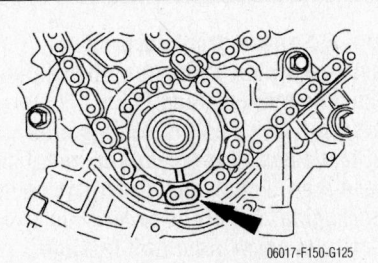

Fig. 305 Position the right (outer) timing chain on the crankshaft sprocket, aligning the copper (marked) link with the timing mark on the sprocket—4.6L and 5.4L engine

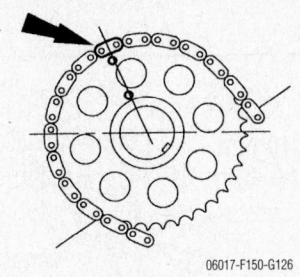

Fig. 306 Install the right timing chain on the camshaft sprocket, aligning the copper (marked) link with the timing marks on the sprocket—4.6L and 5.4L engine

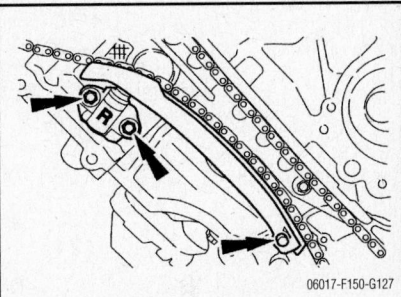

Fig. 307 Position the right timing chain tensioner arm on the dowel pin and install the right timing chain tensioner—4.6L and 5.4L engine

55. Position the right timing chain tensioner arm on the dowel pin and install the right timing chain tensioner. Tighten to 25 Nm (18 ft. lbs.).

56. Remove the retaining clip from the right timing chain tensioner.

57. Make sure that the copper (marked) chain links are lined up with the dots on the crankshaft sprockets and the camshaft sprocket.

58. Remove the special tools from the camshaft.

59. Install the crankshaft sensor ring on the crankshaft.

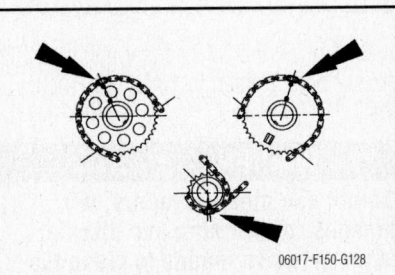

Fig. 308 Make sure that the copper (marked) chain links are lined up with the dots on the crankshaft sprockets and the camshaft sprocket—4.6L and 5.4L engine

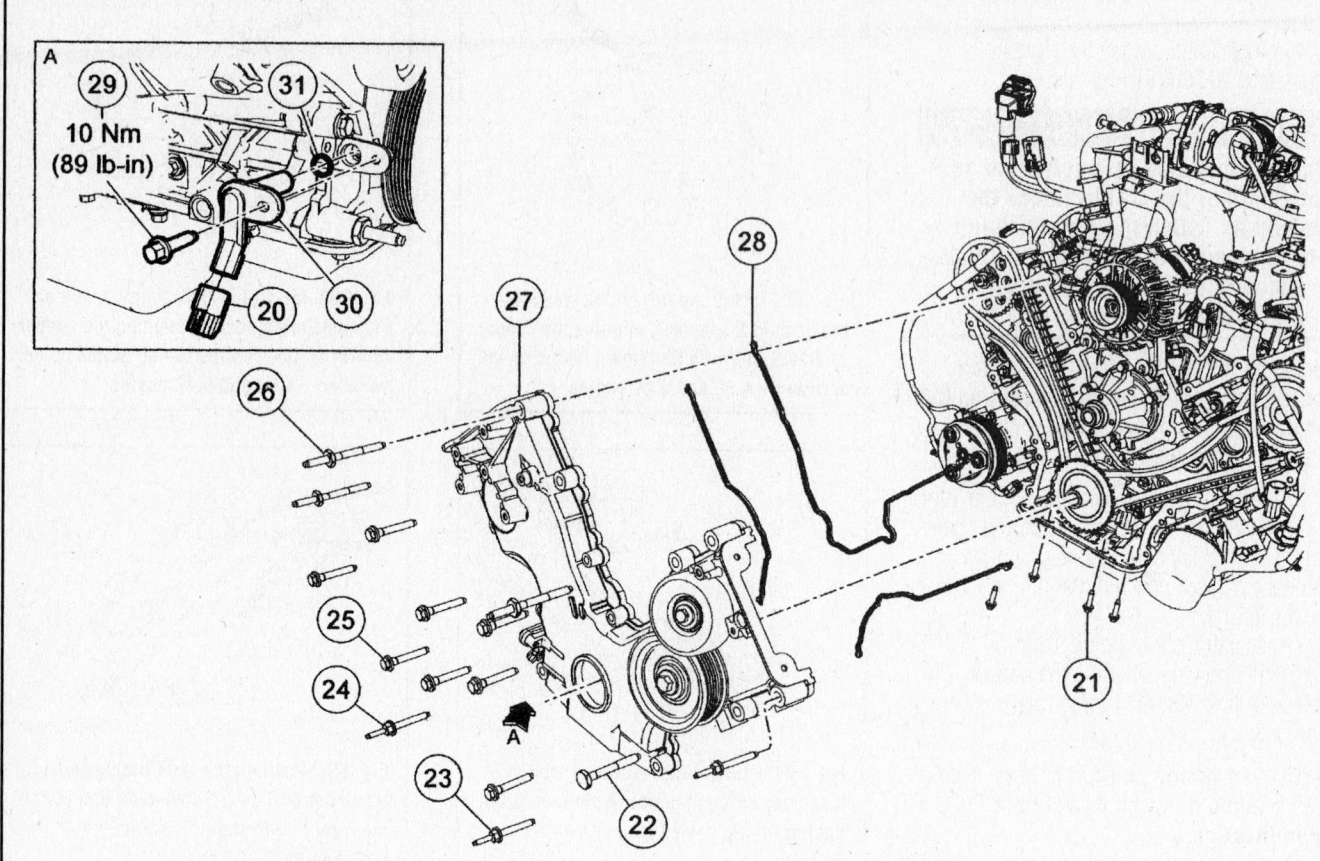

20 Crankshaft position (CKP) sensor electrical connector

21 Oil pan bolts (4 required)

22 Engine front cover bolt

23 Engine front cover lower stud bolt

24 Engine front cover lower stud bolt

25 Engine front cover bolts (8 required)

26 Engine front cover upper stud bolts (4 required)

27 Engine front cover

28 Engine front cover gaskets (3 required)

29 CKP sensor bolt

30 CKP sensor

31 CKP sensor O-ring seal

06017-F150-G129

Fig. 309 Front cover and related parts—4.6L and 5.4L engine

60. Install the CKP sensor and the CKP sensor bolt. Tighten to 10 Nm (89 inch lbs.).

⁂ WARNING

Do not use metal scrapers, wire brushes, power abrasive discs or other abrasive means to clean the sealing surfaces. These tools cause scratches and gouges which make leak paths. Use a plastic scraping tool to remove all traces of old sealant.

➡ If the engine front cover is not secured within 4 minutes, the sealant must be removed and the sealing area cleaned. To clean the sealing area, use silicone gasket remover and metal surface prep. Follow the directions on the packaging. Failure to follow this procedure can cause future oil leakage.

➡ Make sure that the engine front cover gasket is in place on the engine front cover before installation.

61. Apply a bead of silicone gasket and sealant along the cylinder head-to-cylin-

der block surface and the oil pan-to-cylinder block surface, at the locations shown.

62. Install the engine front cover with the engine front cover gasket on the front cover-to-cylinder block dowel and loosely install the bolts.

63. Tighten the engine front cover fasteners in the sequence shown.

64. Loosely install the oil pan-to-front cover bolts, then tighten the bolts in 2 steps, in the sequence shown.

• Step 1: Tighten to 20 Nm (15 ft. lbs.).

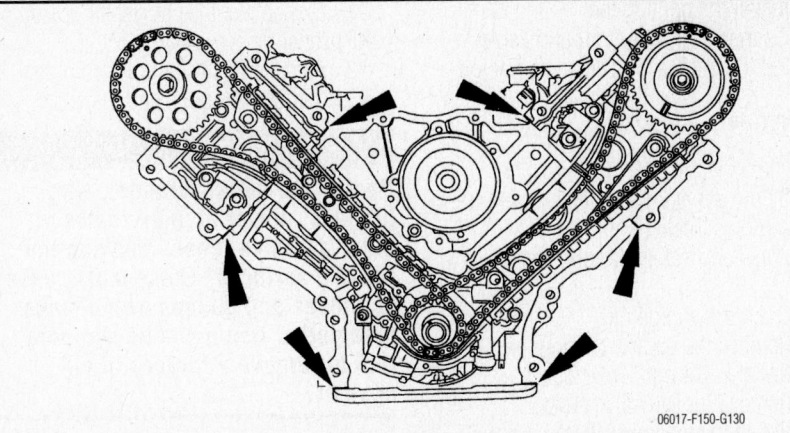

Fig. 310 Apply a bead of silicone gasket and sealant along the cylinder head-to-cylinder block surface and the oil pan-to-cylinder block surface, at the locations indicated—4.6L and 5.4L engine

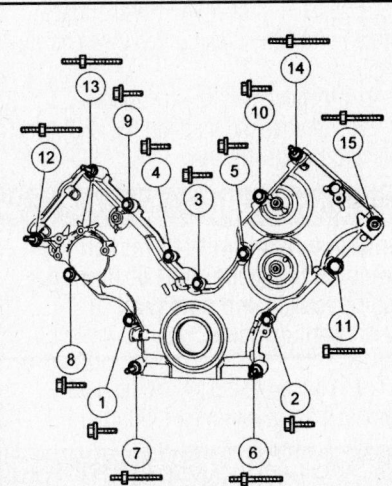

1. Bolt, Hex Flange Head Pilot, M8 x 1.25 x 53
2. Bolt, Hex Flange Head Pilot, M8 x 1.25 x 53
3. Bolt, Hex Flange Head Pilot, M8 x 1.25 x 53
4. Bolt, Hex Flange Head Pilot, M8 x 1.25 x 53
5. Bolts, Hex Flange Head Pilot, M8 x 1.25 x 53
6. Stud Hex Shoulder Pilot, M8 x 1.25 x 50— M6 x 1 x 10
7. Stud and Washer, Hex Head Pilot, M8 x 1.25 — M6 x 1 x 86.35
8. Bolt, Hex Flange Head Pilot, M8 x 1.25 x 53
9. Bolt, Hex Flange Head Pilot, M8 x 1.25 x 53
10. Bolt, Hex Flange Head Pilot, M8 x 1.25 x 53
11. Bolt, Hex Head Pilot, M8 x 1.25 x 53
12. Stud Hex Shoulder Pilot, M8 x 1.25 x 1.25 x 91.1
13. Stud Hex Shoulder Pilot, M8 x 1.25 x 1.25 x 91.1

06017-F150-G131

Fig. 311 Front cover fastener identification—4.6L and 5.4L engine

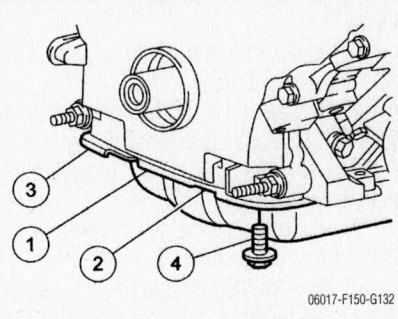

06017-F150-G132

Fig. 312 Oil pan-to-front cover bolt torque sequence—4.6L and 5.4L engine

- Step 2: Tighten an additional 60 degrees.

65. If equipped, install the transmission cooler tube support bracket and nut. Tighten to 10 Nm (89 inch lbs.).

66. Install the A/C manifold and tube assembly support bracket and nut. Tighten to 10 Nm (89 inch lbs.).

67. Connect the CKP sensor electrical connector.

68. Position the right radio interference capacitor and install the nut. Tighten to 10 Nm (89 inch lbs.).

69. Position the upper radiator hose bracket and install the nut. Tighten to 10 Nm (89 inch lbs.).

70. Install the left radio interference capacitor and install the left radio interference capacitor nut. Tighten to 10 Nm (89 inch lbs.).

71. Install the CMP sensor and the bolt. Tighten to 10 Nm (89 inch lbs.).

72. Connect the CMP sensor electrical connector.

73. Position the power steering pump and install the bolts. Tighten to 25 Nm (18 ft. lbs.).

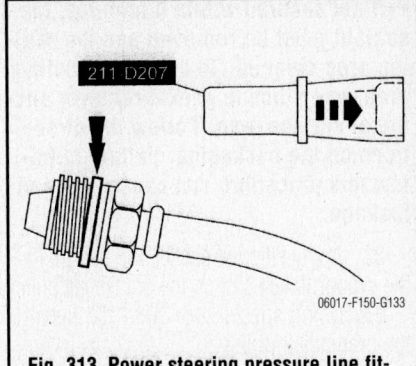

06017-F150-G133

Fig. 313 Power steering pressure line fitting connection—4.6L and 5.4L engine

74. Using special tool 211-D207, install a new O-ring seal on the pressure line fitting.

75. Connect the power steering pressure tube. Tighten to 65 Nm (48 ft. lbs.).

76. Position the power steering pressure tube support bracket and install the nut. Tighten to 10 Nm (89 inch lbs.).

❄❄ WARNING

If the pulley has been removed and installed twice, install a new power steering pump pulley.

77. Using special tool 211-185, install the power steering pump pulley. Inspect the pulley for paint marks in the web area near the hub. If there are 2 paint marks, install a new pulley. If there is 1 paint mark or none at all, use a pencil to mark the web area of the pulley near the hub.

78. Install the accessory drive belt idler pulley and the 3 bolts. Tighten to 25 Nm (18 ft. lbs.).

79. Install the coolant pump pulley and the 4 bolts. Tighten to 25 Nm (18 ft. lbs.).

80. Lubricate the engine front cover and the crankshaft front seal inner lip with clean engine oil.

81. Using the special tools shown, install the crankshaft front seal.

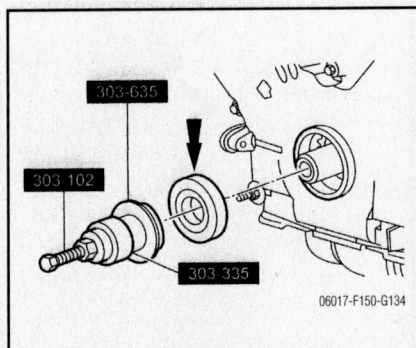

06017-F150-G134

Fig. 314 Crankshaft front seal installation—4.6L and 5.4L engine

➡If not secured within 4 minutes, the sealant must be removed and the sealing area cleaned. To clean the sealing area, use silicone gasket remover and metal surface prep. Follow the directions on the packaging. Failure to follow this procedure can cause future oil leakage.

82. Apply silicone gasket and sealant to the Woodruff key slot on the crankshaft pulley.

83. Using special tool 303-102, install the crankshaft pulley.

84. Using a new crankshaft pulley bolt, install the crankshaft pulley bolt and washer.

85. Using the special tool to hold the crankshaft pulley, tighten the bolt in 4 steps:
- Step 1: Tighten the bolt to 90 Nm (66 ft. lbs.).
- Step 2: Loosen the bolt one full turn.
- Step 3: Tighten the bolt to 50 Nm (37 ft. lbs.).
- Step 4: Tighten the bolt an additional 90 degrees without exceeding 200 Nm (148 ft. lbs.).

86. Rotate the tensioner clockwise and install the drive belt.

87. Install the left valve cover.

88. Install the right valve cover.

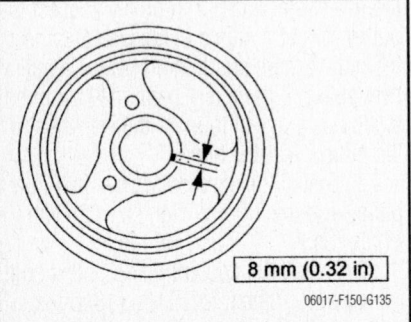

Fig. 315 Apply silicone gasket and sealant to the Woodruff key slot on the crankshaft pulley—4.6L and 5.4L engine

8 mm (0.32 in)

06017-F150-G135

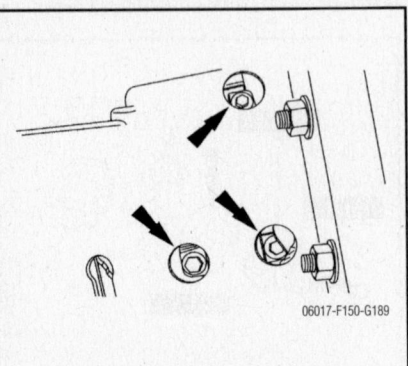

Fig. 316 Remove these 3 bolts from the A/C compressor—6.8L engine

06017-F150-G189

89. Install the cooling fan.

90. Connect the battery ground cable.

91. Fill the engine with clean engine oil.

6.8L Engine

See Figures 316 through 340.

1. Before servicing the vehicle, refer to the Precautions Section.

2. Raise and safely support the vehicle.

3. Drain the engine oil.

4. Remove the engine cooling fan.

5. Remove the right valve cover.

6. Remove the left valve cover.

7. Rotate the tensioner clockwise and remove the accessory drive belt.

8. Remove the 3 bolts and position the power steering pump aside.

9. Remove the nut and position the starter electrical harness support bracket aside.

10. Remove the 3 bolts and position the A/C compressor aside.

11. Remove the crankshaft pulley bolt and washer. Discard the crankshaft pulley bolt.

12. Using the special tool, remove the crankshaft pulley.

13. Using the special tool, remove the crankshaft front seal.

14. Remove the bolt and the accessory drive idler pulley.

15. Remove the 4 bolts and the coolant pump pulley.

16. Remove the 3 bolts and the accessory drive belt tensioner.

17. Disconnect the camshaft position (CMP) sensor electrical connector.

18. Remove the bolt and the CMP sensor. Discard the O-ring seal.

19. Disconnect the right and left radio ignition interference capacitor electrical connectors.

20. Remove the nut and the right and left radio ignition interference capacitors.

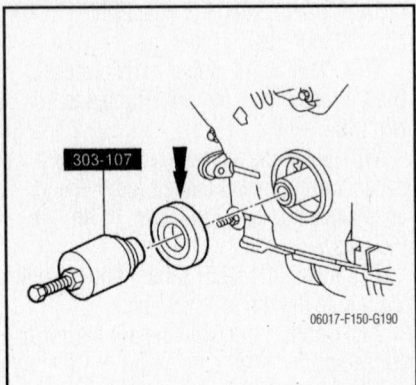

Fig. 317 Front seal removal—6.8L engine

303-107

06017-F150-G190

21. Disconnect the crankshaft position (CKP) sensor electrical connector.

22. Remove the 4 front oil pan bolts.

23. Remove the bolts and the studs.

✳✳ WARNING

Do not use metal scrapers, wire brushes, power abrasive discs or other abrasive means to clean the sealing surfaces. These tools cause scratches and gouges which make leak paths. Use a plastic scraping tool to remove all traces of old sealant.

24. Remove the engine front cover from the front cover to cylinder block dowel.

25. Remove the engine front cover gaskets.

26. Clean the mating surfaces with silicone gasket remover and metal surface prep. Follow the directions on the packaging.

27. Inspect the mating surfaces.

28. Remove the bolt and the CKP sensor. Discard the O-ring seal.

✳✳ WARNING

Only use hand tools to loosen the camshaft sprocket bolt or damage may occur to the camshaft or camshaft sprocket.

29. Loosen and back off the right camshaft sprocket bolt 1 full turn.

✳✳ WARNING

Only use hand tools to loosen the sprocket bolt or damage may occur to the camshaft or camshaft sprocket.

30. Loosen the left camshaft sprocket bolt.

➡The balance shaft bearing caps must be installed in their original locations. Record camshaft bearing cap locations.

31. Remove the 6 bolts in the sequence shown, the 3 bearing caps and the balance shaft.

32. Remove the crankshaft sensor ring from the crankshaft.

33. Position the crankshaft keyway at the 12 o'clock position.

➡If the camshaft lobes are not exactly positioned as shown, the crankshaft will require one full additional rotation to 12 o'clock.

34. The number 1 cylinder camshaft exhaust lobe must be coming up on the exhaust stroke. Verify by noting the position

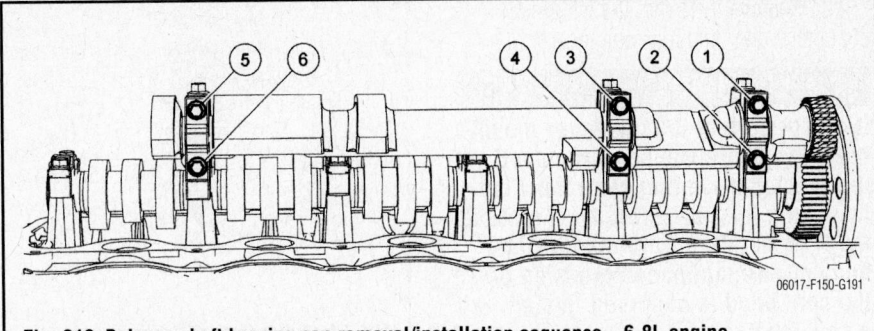

Fig. 318 Balance shaft bearing cap removal/installation sequence—6.8L engine

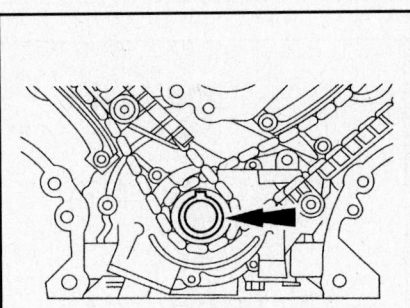

Fig. 319 Position the crankshaft keyway at the 12 o'clock position—6.8L engine

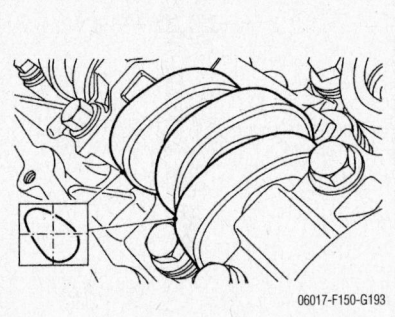

Fig. 320 The number 1 cylinder camshaft exhaust lobe must be coming up on the exhaust stroke. Verify by noting the position of the 2 intake camshaft lobes and the exhaust lobe on the number 1 cylinder—6.8L engine

of the 2 intake camshaft lobes and the exhaust lobe on the number 1 cylinder.

✳✳ WARNING

If the components are to be reinstalled, they must be installed in the same positions.

35. Mark the components for installation into the original locations.

36. Remove only the 3 roller followers shown in the illustration from the right cylinder head.

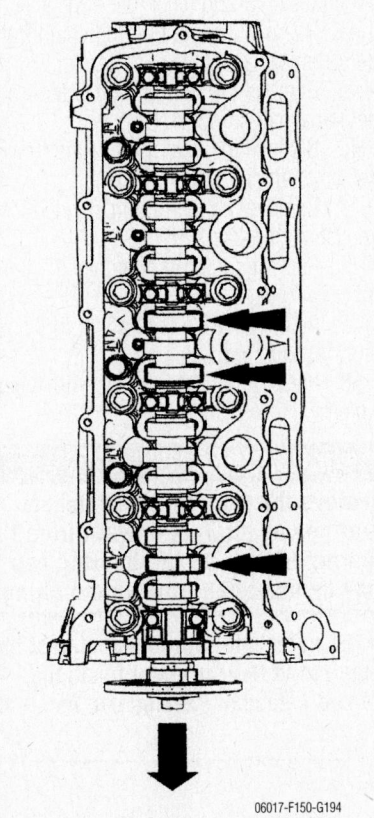

Fig. 321 Remove only these 3 roller followers from the right cylinder head—6.8L engine

Fig. 322 Using special tool 303-1039— 6.8L engine

✳✳ WARNING

Do not allow the valve keepers to fall off the valve or the valve may drop into the cylinder.

➡️ It may be necessary to push the valve down while compressing the spring.

37. Using special tool 303-1039, remove the 3 designated roller followers in the previous step from the right cylinder head.

✳✳ WARNING

If the components are to be reinstalled, they must be installed in the same positions.

38. Mark the components for installation into the original locations.

39. Remove only the 4 roller followers shown in the illustration from the left cylinder head.

✳✳ WARNING

Do not allow the valve keepers to fall off the valve or the valve may drop into the cylinder.

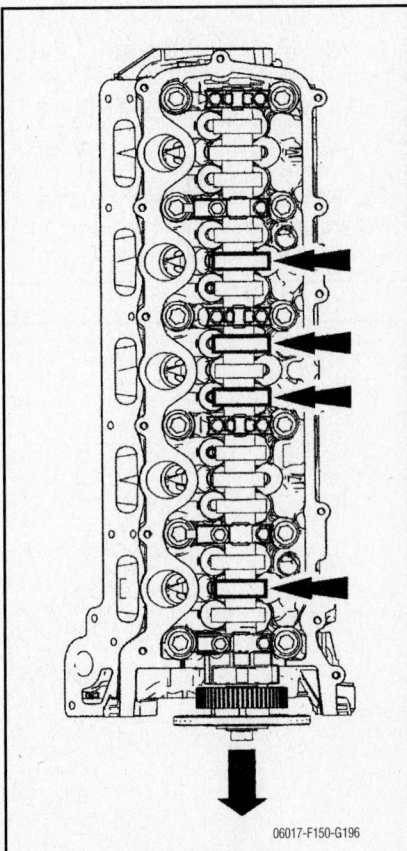

Fig. 323 Remove only these 4 roller followers from the left cylinder head—6.8L engine

➡It may be necessary to push the valve down while compressing the spring.

40. Using the special tool, remove the 4 designated roller followers in the previous step from the left cylinder head.

✳✳ WARNING

The crankshaft cannot be moved past the 6 o'clock position once set.

41. Rotate the crankshaft clockwise and position the crankshaft keyway at the 6 o'clock position.

✳✳ WARNING

If one or both of the tensioner mounting bolts are loosened or removed, the tensioner-sealing bead must be inspected for seal integrity. If cracks, tears, separation from the tensioner body or permanent compression of the seal bead is observed, install a new tensioner.

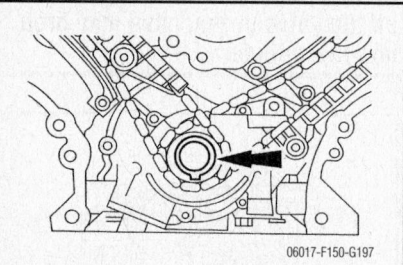

06017-F150-G197

Fig. 324 Rotate the crankshaft clockwise and position the crankshaft keyway at the 6 o'clock position—6.8L engine

42. Remove the bolts, the left timing chain tensioner and tensioner arm.

✳✳ WARNING

If one or both of the tensioner mounting bolts are loosened or removed, the tensioner-sealing bead must be inspected for seal integrity. If cracks, tears, separation from the tensioner body or permanent compression of the seal bead is observed, install a new tensioner.

43. Remove the bolts, the right timing chain tensioner and tensioner arm.
44. Remove the right timing chain from the camshaft sprocket.
45. Remove the right timing chain from the crankshaft sprocket.
46. Remove the left timing chain from the camshaft sprocket.
47. Remove the left timing chain and the crankshaft sprocket.
48. Remove the bolts. Remove the timing chain guides.
49. Remove the bolts and the right and left camshaft sprockets.
50. Remove the balance shaft drive gear from the left camshaft.

✳✳ WARNING

Remove the front thrust camshaft bearing cap straight upward from the bearing towers, or the bearing cap may be damaged from side loading.

➡The camshaft bearing caps must be installed in their original locations. Record camshaft bearing cap locations.

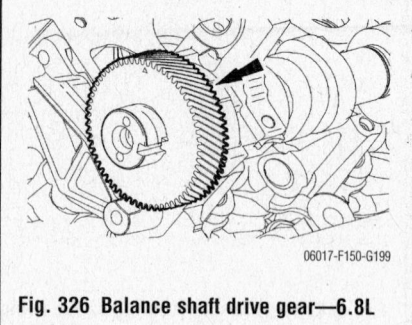

06017-F150-G199

Fig. 326 Balance shaft drive gear—6.8L engine

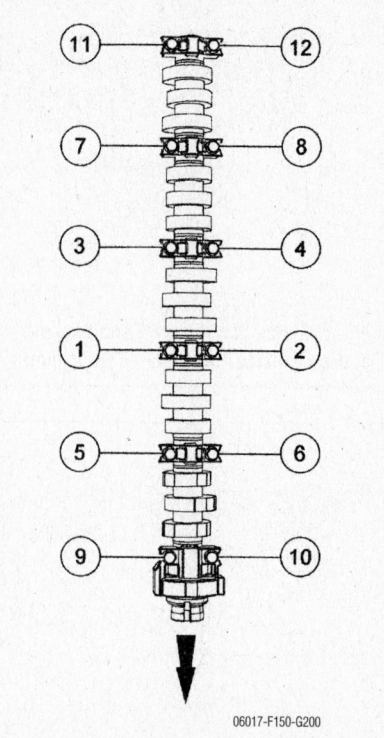

06017-F150-G200

Fig. 327 Right side camshaft bearing cap removal/installation sequence—6.8L engine

51. Remove the bolts in the sequence shown and remove the right cylinder head front camshaft bearing cap and then the remaining bearing caps.
52. Clean and inspect the right camshaft bearing caps. The camshaft front thrust bearing cap contains an oil metering groove. Make sure the groove is free of foreign material.
53. Remove the right camshaft.

✳✳ WARNING

Remove the front thrust camshaft bearing cap straight upward from the bearing towers, or the bearing cap may be damaged from side loading.

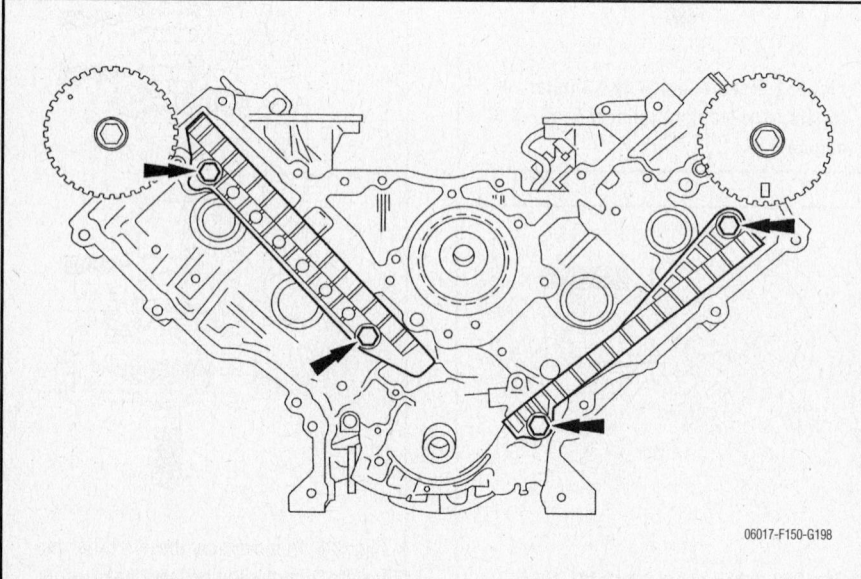

06017-F150-G198

Fig. 325 Timing chain guide bolts—6.8L engine

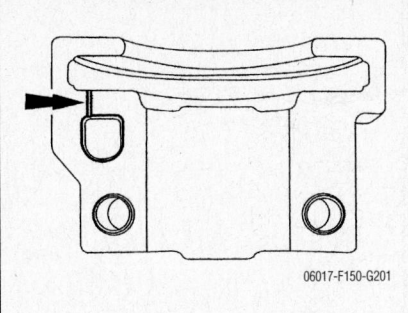

Fig. 328 The camshaft front thrust bearing cap contains an oil metering groove—6.8L engine

➡️The camshaft bearing caps must be installed in their original locations. Record camshaft bearing cap locations.

54. Remove the bolts in the sequence shown and remove the left cylinder head front camshaft bearing cap and then the remaining bearing caps.

55. Clean and inspect the left camshaft bearing caps. The camshaft front thrust bearing cap contains an oil metering groove. Make sure the groove is free of foreign material.

56. Remove the left camshaft.

❉ WARNING

If the components are to be reinstalled, they must be installed in the same positions.

57. Mark the components for installation into their original locations.

58. Remove all of the remaining roller followers from the cylinder heads.

To install:

❉❉ WARNING

Timing chain procedures must be followed exactly or damage to valves and pistons will result.

❉ WARNING

If the components are to be reinstalled, they must be installed into their original locations.

➡️Camshaft shown installed to clarify roller follower position.

59. Install only the identified camshaft roller followers onto the right cylinder head.

❉❉ WARNING

If the components are to be reinstalled, they must be installed into their original locations.

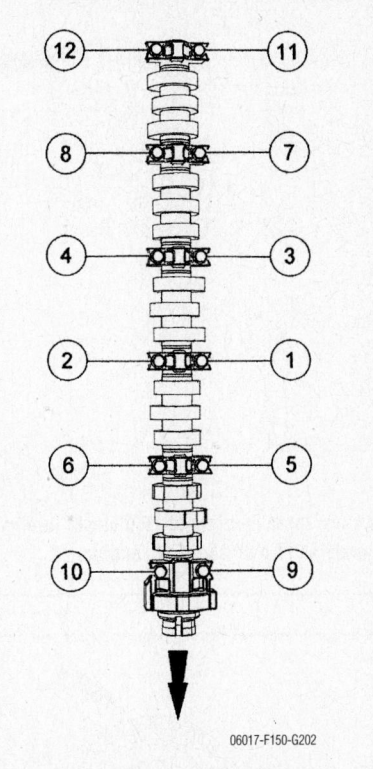

Fig. 329 Left side camshaft bearing cap removal/installation sequence—6.8L engine

➡️Camshaft shown installed to clarify camshaft roller follower position.

60. Install only the identified camshaft roller followers onto the left cylinder head.

61. Install the left and right camshafts.

62. Lubricate the camshaft and camshaft journals with clean engine oil prior to installation.

63. Lubricate the camshaft bearing caps with clean engine oil.

64. Position the front camshaft bearing cap.

65. Position the remaining camshaft bearing caps.

66. Install the bolts loosely.

67. Tighten the left camshaft bearing cap bolts in 2 steps:
- Step 1: Tighten to 8 Nm (71 inch lbs.) in the sequence shown.
- Step 2: Tighten an additional 45 degrees.

68. Tighten the right camshaft bearing cap bolts in 2 steps:
- Step 1: Tighten to 8 Nm (71 inch lbs.) in the sequence shown.
- Step 2: Tighten an additional 45 degrees.

69. Install the balance shaft drive gear onto the left camshaft.

70. Install the camshaft sprockets and camshaft sprocket bolts finger tight.

❉❉ WARNING

Timing chain procedures must be followed exactly or damage to valves and pistons will result.

❉❉ WARNING

Prior to installation, inspect the tensioner-sealing bead for seal integrity. If cracks, tears, separation from the tensioner body or permanent compression of the seal bead is observed, install a new tensioner.

71. Compress the tensioner plunger, using a vise.

72. Install a retaining clip on the tensioner to hold the plunger in during installation.

➡️There are 61 links in each timing chain.

73. If copper links are not visible, mark 2 links on one end and one link on the other end, and use as timing marks.

74. Install the timing chain guides and the 4 bolts. Tighten to 10 Nm (89 inch lbs.).

75. Rotate the left camshaft until the timing mark is approximately at 12 o'clock.

76. Rotate the right camshaft until the timing mark is approximately at 11 o'clock.

❉❉ WARNING

Rotate the crankshaft counterclockwise only. Do not rotate past the position shown or severe piston and/or valve damage can occur.

77. Position the crankshaft with special tool 303-448, then remove the tool.

78. Install the crankshaft sprocket, making sure the flange faces forward.

79. Install the lower end of the left timing chain, aligning the timing marks.

➡️Be sure the upper half of the timing chain is below the tensioner guide dowel.

80. Install the left timing chain on the camshaft sprocket with the 2 chain (marked) links and the timing marks aligned.

➡️The left timing chain tensioner arm has a bump near the dowel hole for identification.

81. Position the left timing chain tensioner arm on the dowel pin and install the

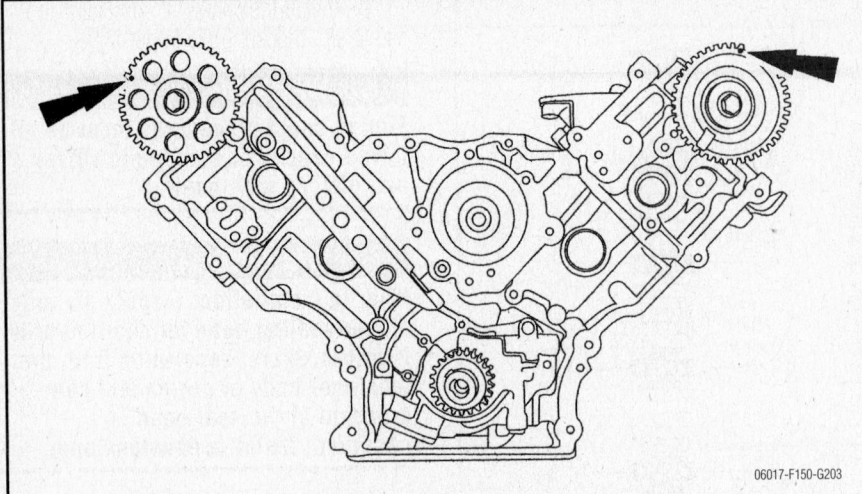

Fig. 330 Rotate the left camshaft until the timing mark is approximately at 12 o'clock. Rotate the right camshaft until the timing mark is approximately at 11 o'clock—6.8L engine

06017-F150-G203

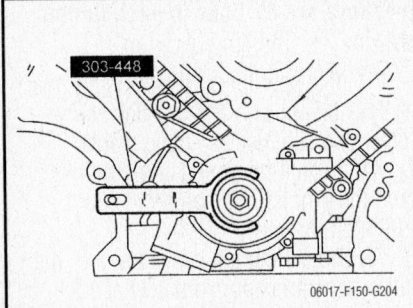

Fig. 331 Position the crankshaft with special tool 303-448—6.8L engine

06017-F150-G204

left timing chain tensioner and bolts. Tighten to 25 Nm (18 ft. lbs.).

➡ Be sure the chain link and crankshaft sprocket timing marks are aligned.

➡ The lower half of the timing chain must be positioned above the dowel.

82. Install the right (outer) timing chain on the crankshaft sprocket.

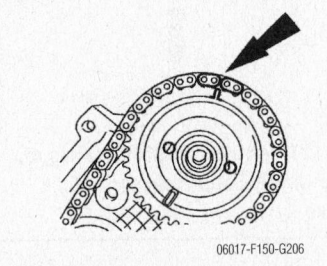

Fig. 333 Install the left timing chain on the camshaft sprocket with the 2 chain (marked) links and the timing marks aligned—6.8L engine

06017-F150-G206

83. Position the timing chain on the camshaft sprocket. Make sure the 2 copper-colored (marked) links align with the camshaft sprocket timing mark.

84. Position the right timing chain tensioner arm on the dowel pin and install the right timing chain tensioner and bolts. Tighten to 25 Nm (18 ft. lbs.).

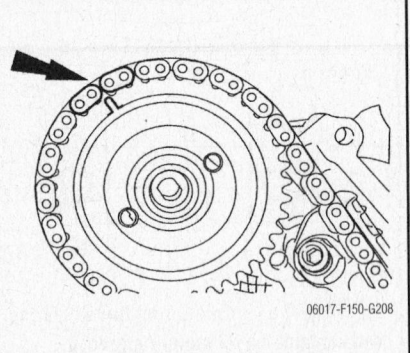

Fig. 335 Position the timing chain on the camshaft sprocket. Make sure the 2 copper-colored (marked) links align with the camshaft sprocket timing mark—6.8L engine

06017-F150-G208

85. Remove the retaining clips from the right and left timing chain tensioners.

86. Check for correct alignment of all timing marks.

87. Install the crankshaft sensor ring on the crankshaft.

88. Lubricate the balance shaft journals with clean engine oil.

89. Using the index mark on the balance shaft, mark the corresponding gear tooth with chalk.

90. Position the balance shaft on the journals.

➡ It may be necessary to use an inspection mirror to see the marks.

91. Position the balance shaft on the journals and align the chalk mark on the balance shaft with the camshaft timing mark as shown.

➡ Install the bearing caps in their original locations.

92. Install the bolts and tighten the bolts in the sequence shown. Tighten to 10 Nm (89 inch lbs.).

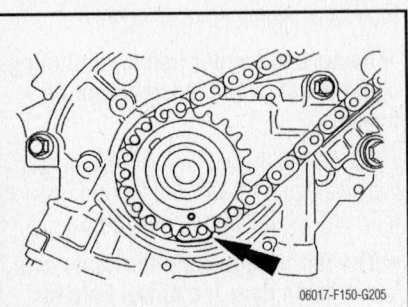

Fig. 332 Install the lower end of the left timing chain, aligning the timing marks—6.8L engine

06017-F150-G205

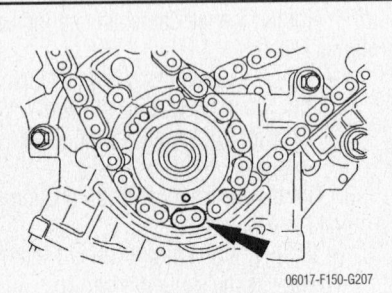

Fig. 334 Install the right (outer) timing chain on the crankshaft sprocket—6.8L engine

06017-F150-G207

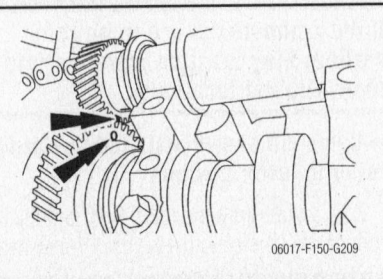

Fig. 336 Position the balance shaft on the journals and align the chalk mark on the balance shaft with the camshaft timing mark—6.8L engine

06017-F150-G209

⁂ WARNING

Only use hand tools to tighten the camshaft sprocket bolt or damage may occur to the camshaft or camshaft sprocket.

93. Tighten the right camshaft sprocket bolt in 2 steps:
- Step 1: Tighten to 40 Nm (30 ft. lbs.) in the sequence shown.
- Step 2: Tighten an additional 90 degrees.

⁂ WARNING

Only use hand tools to tighten the camshaft sprocket bolt or damage may occur to the camshaft or camshaft sprocket.

94. Tighten the left camshaft sprocket bolt in 2 steps:
- Step 1: Tighten to 40 Nm (30 ft. lbs.) in the sequence shown.
- Step 2: Tighten an additional 90 degrees.

⁂ WARNING

If the components are to be reinstalled, they must be installed into their original locations.

95. Using the special tool, install all of the remaining camshaft roller followers.
96. Lubricate the roller followers with clean engine oil prior to installation.

⁂ WARNING

Do not use metal scrapers, wire brushes, power abrasive discs or other abrasive means to clean the sealing surfaces. These tools cause scratches and gouges which make leak paths. Use a plastic scraping tool to remove all traces of old sealant.

➡ **If the engine front cover is not secured within 4 minutes, the sealant must be removed and the sealing area cleaned. To clean the sealing area, use silicone gasket remover and metal surface prep. Follow the directions on the packaging. Failure to follow this procedure can cause future oil leakage.**

➡ **Make sure that the engine front cover gasket is in place on the engine front cover before installation.**

97. Apply a bead of silicone gasket and sealant along the cylinder head-to-cylinder block surface and the oil pan-to-cylinder block surface, at the locations shown.

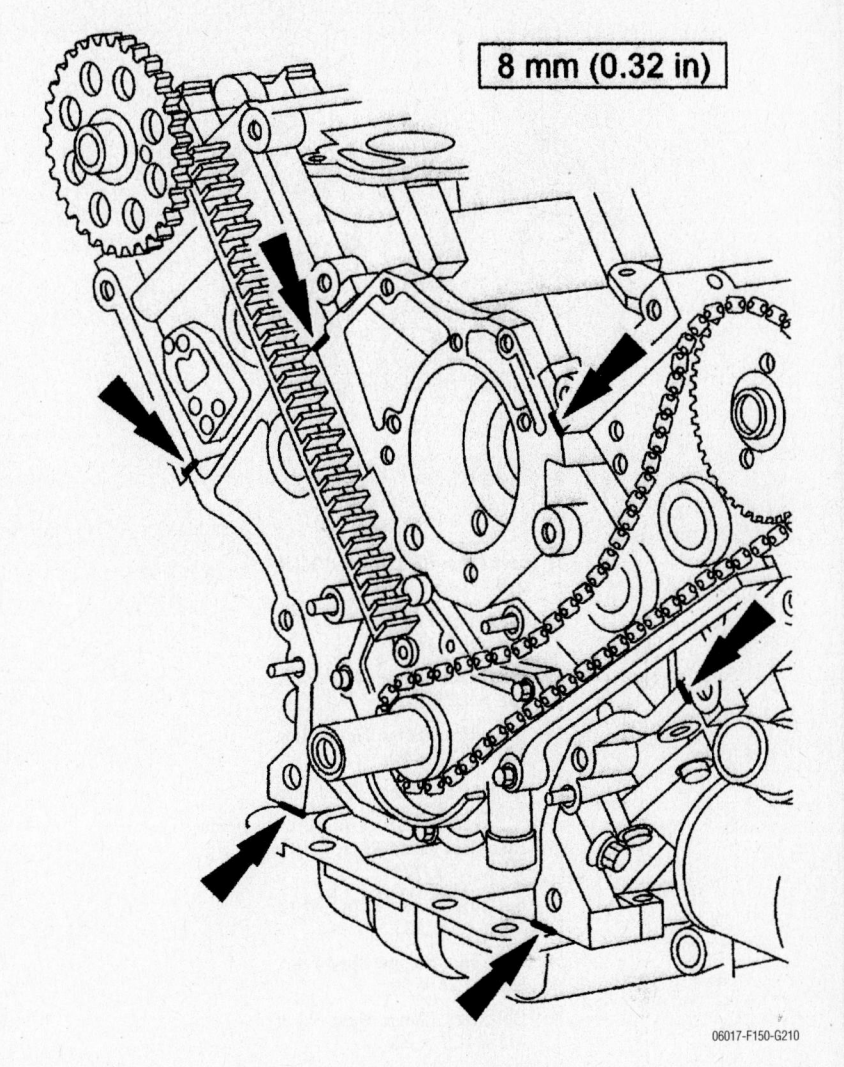

8 mm (0.32 in)

06017-F150-G210

Fig. 337 Apply a bead of silicone gasket and sealant along the cylinder head-to-cylinder block surface and the oil pan-to-cylinder block surface—6.8L engine

98. Install a new engine front cover gasket on the engine front cover. Position the engine front cover onto the dowels. Install the fasteners finger tight.
99. Tighten the engine front cover fasteners in sequence in 2 steps.
- Step 1: Tighten fasteners 1 through 15 to 25 Nm (18 ft. lbs.).
- Step 2: Tighten fasteners 6 and 7 to 48 Nm (35 ft. lbs.).
100. Loosely install the oil pan-to-front cover bolts, then tighten the bolts in 2 steps, in the sequence shown.
- Step 1: Tighten to 20 Nm (15 ft. lbs.).
- Step 2: Tighten an additional 60 degrees.
101. Using a new O-ring seal, install the crankshaft position (CKP) sensor and the bolt.

102. Lubricate the new O-ring seal with clean engine oil prior to installation. Tighten to 10 Nm (89 inch lbs.).
103. Connect the CKP sensor electrical connector.
104. Position the A/C compressor and install the 3 bolts. Tighten to 25 Nm (18 ft. lbs.).
105. Position the power steering pump and install the 3 bolts. Tighten to 25 Nm (18 ft. lbs.).
106. Position the starter electrical harness support bracket and install the bolt. Tighten to 10 Nm (89 inch lbs.).

➡ **Lubricate the O-ring seal with clean engine oil prior to installation.**

107. Using a new O-ring seal, install the camshaft position (CMP) sensor and the bolt.

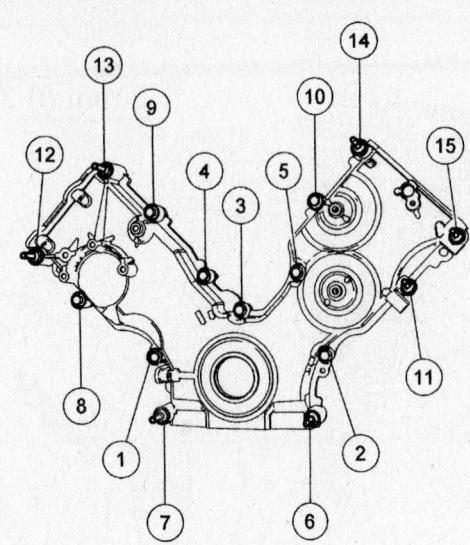

1 Bolt, Hex Flange Head Pilot,
   M8 x 1.25 x 50

2 Bolt, Hex Flange Head Pilot,
   M8 x 1.25 x 50

3 Bolt, Hex Flange Head Pilot,
   M8 x 1.25 x 50

4 Bolt, Hex Flange Head Pilot,
   M8 x 1.25 x 50

5 Bolts, Hex Flange Head Pilot,
   M8 x 1.25 x 50

6 Stud, Hex Head Pilot, M10 x
   1.5 x 1.5 x 103

7 Stud, Hex Head Pilot, M10 x
   1.5 x 1.5 x 103

8 Bolt, Hex Flange Head Pilot,
   M8 x 1.25 x 50

9 Bolt, Hex Flange Head Pilot,
   M8 x 1.25 x 50

10 Bolt, Hex Flange Head Pilot,
   M8 x 1.25 x 50

11 Stud and Washer, Hex Head
   Pilot, M8 x 1.25 x 1.25 x 94

12 Stud and Washer, Hex Head
   Pilot, M8 x 1.25 x 1.25 x 94

13 Stud and Washer, Hex Head
   Pilot, M8 x 1.25 x 1.25 x 94

14 Stud and Washer, Hex Head
   Pilot, M8 x 1.25 x 1.25 x 94

15 Stud and Washer, Hex Head
   Pilot, M8 x 1.25 x 56

06017-F150-G211

Fig. 338 Front cover torque sequence—6.8L engine

108. Tighten to 10 Nm (89 inch lbs.).
109. Connect the CMP sensor electrical connector.
110. Install the left radio ignition interference capacitor and the nut. Tighten to 10 Nm (89 inch lbs.).
111. Install the right radio ignition interference capacitor and the nut. Tighten to 10 Nm (89 inch lbs.).

112. Connect the radio ignition interference capacitor electrical connectors.
113. Install the accessory drive belt tensioner and the 3 bolts. Tighten to 25 Nm (18 ft. lbs.).
114. Install the coolant pump pulley and the 4 bolts. Tighten to 25 Nm (18 ft. lbs.).
115. Install the accessory drive idler pulley and the 3 bolts. Tighten to 25 Nm (18 ft. lbs.).

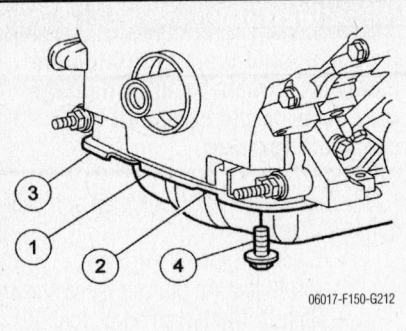

06017-F150-G212

Fig. 339 Oil pan-to-front cover bolt torque sequence—6.8L engine

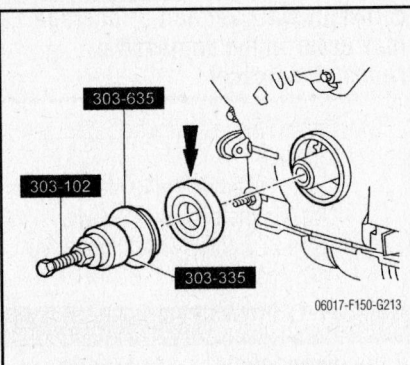

06017-F150-G213

Fig. 340 Front cover seal installation—6.8L engine

116. Lubricate the engine front cover and the crankshaft seal inner lip with clean engine oil.
117. Using the special tools, install the crankshaft seal into the engine front cover.

➡If not secured within 4 minutes, the sealant must be removed and the sealing area cleaned. To clean the sealing area, use silicone gasket remover and metal surface prep. Follow the directions on the packaging. Failure to follow this procedure can cause future oil leakage.

118. Apply silicone gasket and sealant to the Woodruff key slot on the crankshaft pulley.
119. Use the special tool to install the crankshaft pulley.
120. Tighten the new crankshaft pulley bolt in 4 steps.
  • Step 1: Tighten to 90 Nm (66 ft. lbs.).
  • Step 2: Loosen 360 degrees.
  • Step 3: Tighten to 50 Nm (37 ft. lbs.).
  • Step 4: Tighten an additional 90 degrees.
121. Rotate the tensioner clockwise and install the accessory drive belt.

122. Install the right valve cover.

123. Install the left valve cover. Install the engine cooling fan.

124. Fill the crankcase with clean engine oil.

FRONT COVER, SEAL AND TIMING GEARS

REMOVAL & INSTALLATION

6.0L Diesel Engine

1. Before servicing the vehicle, refer to the Precautions Section.

2. Remove the intake manifold.

➡ **Remove the thermostat housing only if a new front cover is being installed.**

3. Remove the stud bolts and the thermostat housing.

4. Remove and discard the O-ring.

5. Disconnect the engine coolant fill hose.

6. Disconnect the lower radiator hose.

7. Remove the stator stand-off bolt.

➡ **Upper bolts shown, lower bolts similar.**

8. Remove the four bolts and position aside the power steering pump.

9. Remove the bolts and the accessory drive belt tensioner.

10. Remove the bolts and the accessory drive idler pulleys.

➡ **Remove the coolant pump pulley only if a new front cover is being installed.**

11. Remove the coolant pump pulley.

➡ **Remove the coolant pump only if a new front cover is being installed.**

12. Remove the bolts and the coolant pump.

13. Remove and discard the O-ring.

14. Remove the nut and the battery cable bracket.

15. Remove the oil pump.

16. Check the crankshaft vibration damper runout.

17. Remove the paint from the face of the crankshaft vibration damper at four points 90 degrees apart.

18. Attach the special tool to the cylinder block. Position the special tool on one of the unpainted surfaces.

19. Using a suitable tool, pry the crankshaft forward. Zero the dial indicator.

➡ **Pry the crankshaft forward at the same point to eliminate possible error caused by crankshaft end play.**

20. Rotate the crankshaft 90 degrees. Pry the crankshaft forward. Record the measurement. Repeat at each unpainted surface. If the runout exceeds specification, install a new crankshaft vibration damper.

❈❈ **WARNING**

To prevent engine damage, you must always install four new bolts when installing the vibration damper.

❈❈ **WARNING**

To avoid personal injury, support the vibration damper during mounting bolt removal. The damper can slide off the nose of the crankshaft very easily.

21. Remove the bolts and the crankcase vibration damper.

22. Discard the bolts.

23. Remove the bolts and the front cover.

❈❈ **WARNING**

Sealant is used where the crankcase and lower crankcase meet. Failure to cut the sealant could result in pulling the lower crankcase seal out while removing the front cover gasket.

24. Use a thin blade scraper to cut the sealant where the crankcase and the lower crankcase meet. Remove and discard the front cover gasket.

25. Clean and inspect the sealing surfaces.

26. Punch two holes in the seal.

27. Using the special tool, remove the crankshaft seal.

➡ **Production engine will not have a wear sleeve.**

28. If equipped, remove the crankshaft damper wear sleeve.

29. Remove the thrust plate mounting bolts and remove the camshaft and gear.

To install:

30. Install the camshaft and gear assembly. Using the special tool, align the camshaft timing mark as shown. Install the thrust plate mounting bolts.

31. Thoroughly clean the crankshaft front seal mounting surface.

32. Apply Threadlock 262® to the outer circumference of the leading edge of the crankshaft.

➡ **New seal and wear sleeve must not be separated.**

33. Using the special tool, install the oil seal and wear sleeve assembly.

34. If removed, install the front cover crankcase dowels into the cylinder block.

➡ **Use guide studs to aid in installation. Studs must be fabricated locally.**

35. Install the guide studs.

36. Apply a bead of sealant at the seam where the crankcase and the lower crankcase meet.

37. Install a new engine front cover gasket.

38. Install the engine front cover and bolts.

❈❈ **WARNING**

To prevent engine damage, you must always install four new bolts when installing the vibration damper.

➡ **Do not use anti-seize compounds, grease or any lubricants. Lubricants have an adverse effect on the torque results.**

39. Install the crankshaft vibration damper and bolts.

40. Tighten the bolts in the sequence shown.

   a. Tighten the bolts to 68 Nm (50 ft. lbs.).

   b. Tighten the bolts an additional 90 degrees.

41. Install the oil pump.

42. Install the battery cable bracket and nut.

➡ **Install a new O-ring on the coolant pump pulley.**

43. If removed, install the coolant pump and bolts.

44. If removed, install the coolant pump pulley and bolts.

45. Install the accessory drive idler pulleys and bolts.

46. Install the accessory drive belt tensioner and bolts.

47. Position back the power steering pump and install the bolts.

48. Install the stator stand-off bolt.

49. Connect the lower radiator coolant hose.

50. Connect the engine coolant hose.

➡ **Install a new O-ring.**

51. If removed, install the thermostat housing and stud bolts.

52. Install the intake manifold.

TURBOCHARGER

REMOVAL & INSTALLATION

6.0L Diesel Engines

1. Before servicing the vehicle, refer to the Precautions Section.
2. Remove the air cleaner assembly.
3. Disconnect the engine vent and radiator vent hoses.
4. Remove the bolts and position the degas bottle (coolant reservoir) aside.
5. Loosen the clamp at the turbocharger.
6. Remove the nuts and the turbocharger intake tube.
7. Disconnect the Charge Air Cooler (CAC) inlet pipe.
8. Remove the push pins from the shield above the turbocharger.
9. Disconnect the two wiring harness push pins and position aside.
10. Disconnect the turbocharger variable vane hydraulic control valve electrical connector.
11. Remove the bolts for the turbocharger oil supply tube.
12. Remove and discard the gasket.
13. Remove the bolt and the wire retainer from the turbocharger.
14. Remove the clamp from the turbocharger outlet.
15. Remove the clamp from the turbocharger inlet.

Early build

16. Remove the rear turbocharger mounting bolt.

Late build

17. Remove the bolt and turbocharger oil supply tube.

18. Remove and discard the O-ring.
19. Remove the rear turbocharger mounting bolt.

All vehicles

20. Remove the front mounting bolts.
21. Position the turbocharger and remove the turbocharger drain tube.
22. Remove and discard the drain tube O-rings.
23. Remove the turbocharger. Remove the bolts and the turbocharger pedestal.

To install:

All vehicles

24. Position the turbocharger on the turbocharger pedestal.

➡**Install new O-rings and apply clean engine oil.**

25. Position the turbocharger and install the turbocharger drain tube.

Late build

26. Install the turbocharger and the rear mounting bolt. Torque to 28 ft. lbs. (38 Nm).

➡**Install a new O-ring and apply clean engine oil.**

27. Install the oil supply tube. Torque to 10 ft. lbs. (13 Nm).
28. Position the locking bracket and install the bolt.

Early build

29. Install the turbocharger and the rear mounting bolt. Torque to 28 ft. lbs. (38 Nm).
30. Install the oil feed tube.

All vehicles

31. Install the turbocharger front mounting bolts. Torque to 28 ft. lbs. (38 Nm).

32. Install the turbocharger inlet clamp.
33. Install the turbocharger exhaust clamp.
34. Position the wire retainer and install the bolt.
35. Pre-lubricate the oil inlet hole of the turbocharger assembly with clean engine oil and spin the compressor wheel several times to coat the bearing with oil.
36. Position the oil feed tube and install the bolts.
37. Install a new gasket.
38. Connect the turbocharger variable vane hydraulic control valve electrical connector.
39. Position the wiring harness and connect the push pins.
40. Install the push pins.
41. Connect the charge air cooler inlet pipe.
42. Install the turbocharger intake tube.

VALVE LASH

ADJUSTMENT

The 4.2L, 4.6L, 5.4L and 6.8L engines do not require valve lash adjusting, because they utilize hydraulic lash components in their valve actuation systems. The 4.2L engine uses hydraulic valve lifters, whereas the 4.6L, 5.4L and 6.8L engines utilize hydraulic lash adjusters, all of which automatically adjust the valve lash. No valve lash adjustment is necessary.

Valve lash on the diesel engine is not adjustable.

ENGINE PERFORMANCE & EMISSION CONTROL

MALFUNCTION INDICATOR LIGHT (MIL) RESET PROCEDURES

To turn off the MIL after a repair, a reset command from the diagnostic tool must be sent, or 3 consecutive drive cycles must be completed without a fault.

DRIVE CYCLE

1. Install scan tool. Turn key on with the engine off. Cycle key off, then on. Select appropriate Vehicle & Engine qualifier. Clear all DTCs/ Perform a PCM Reset.
2. Begin to monitor the following PIDs: ECT, EVAPDC, FLI (if available) and TP MODE. Start vehicle WITHOUT returning to Key Off.

3. Idle vehicle for 15 seconds. Drive at 64 Km/h (40 MPH) until ECT is at least 76.7°C (170° F).
4. Is IAT within 4.4 to 37.8°C (40 to 100° F)? If Not, complete the following steps but, note that step 14 will be required to "bypass " the Evap monitor and clear the P1000.
5. Cruise at 64 Km/h (40 MPH) for up to 4 minutes.
6. Cruise at 72 to 104 Km/h (45 to 65 MPH) for 10 minutes (avoid sharp turns and hills) Note, to initiate the monitor: TP MODE should =PT, EVAPDC must be>75%, and FLI must be between 15 and 85%
7. Drive in stop and go traffic conditions. Include five different constant cruise speeds, ranging from 40 to 72 Km/h (25 to 45 MPH) over a 10 minute period.

8. From a stop, accelerate to 72 Km/h (45 MPH) at 1/2 to 3/4 throttle. Repeat 3 times.
9. Bring the vehicle to a stop. Idle with transmission in drive (neutral for M/T) for 2 minutes.
10. For M/T, accelerate from 0 to 80 Km/h (o to 50 MPH), continue to step 11. For A/T, from a stop and in overdrive, moderately accelerate to 80 Km/h (50 MPH) and cruise for at least 15 seconds. Stop vehicle and repeat without overdrive to 64 Km/h (40 MPH) cruising for at least 30 seconds. While at 64 Km/h (40 MPH) , activate overdrive and accelerate to 80 Km/h (50 MPH) and cruise for at least 15 seconds. Stop for at least 20 seconds and repeat step 10 five times.
11. From a stop, accelerate to 104 Km/h (65 MPH). Decelerate at closed throttle until

64 Km/h (40 MPH) (no brakes). Repeat this 3 times.

12. Access the ON-Board System Readiness (OBDII monitor status) function on the scan tool. Determine whether all non-continuous monitors have completed. If not, go to step 13.

13. With the scan tool, check for pending codes. Conduct normal repair procedures for any pending code concern. Otherwise, rerun any incomplete monitor.

➡If the EVAP monitor is not complete AND IAT was out of the 4.4 to 37.8° C (40 to 100° F) temperature range in step #4, or the altitude is over 2438 m. (8000 ft.), the Evap "bypass" procedure must be followed. Proceed to step 14.

14. Park vehicle for a minimum of 8 hours. Repeat steps 2 through 12. DO NOT REPEAT STEP 1.

COMPONENT LOCATIONS

See Figures 341 through 365.

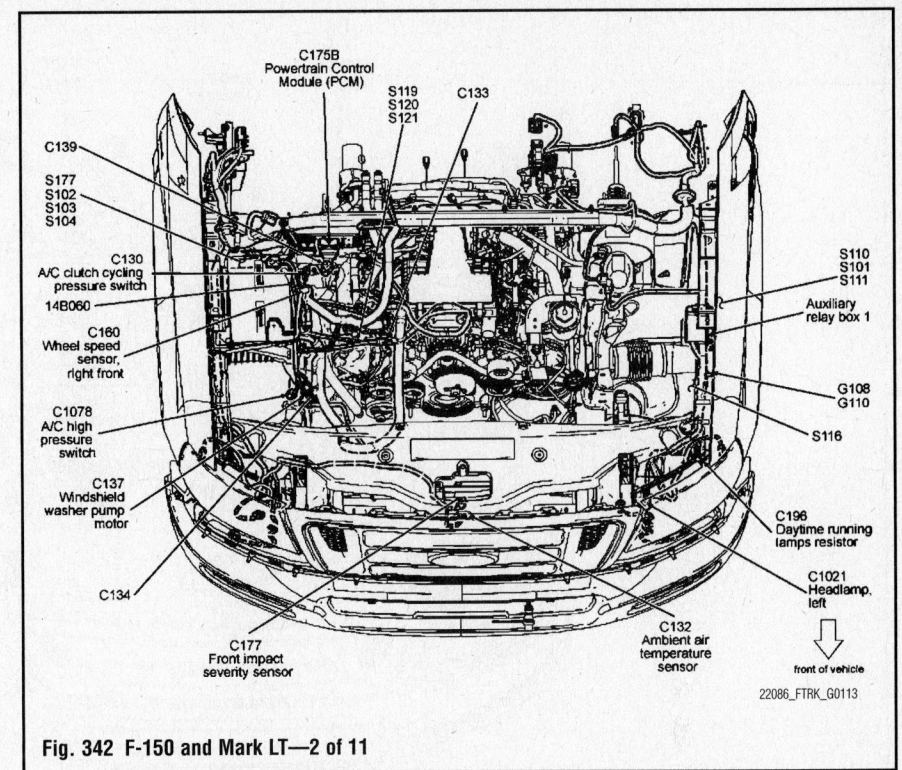

Fig. 342 F-150 and Mark LT—2 of 11

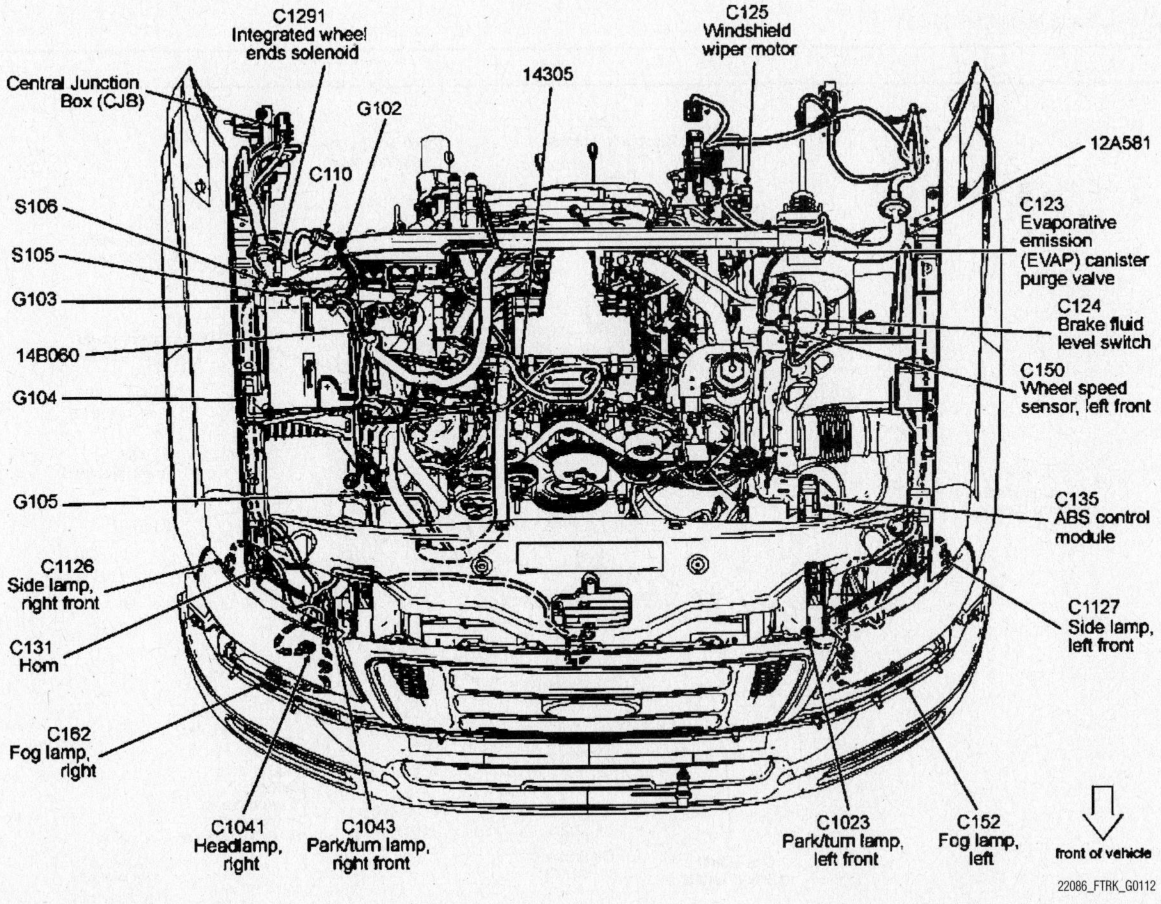

Fig. 341 F-150 and Mark LT—1 of 11

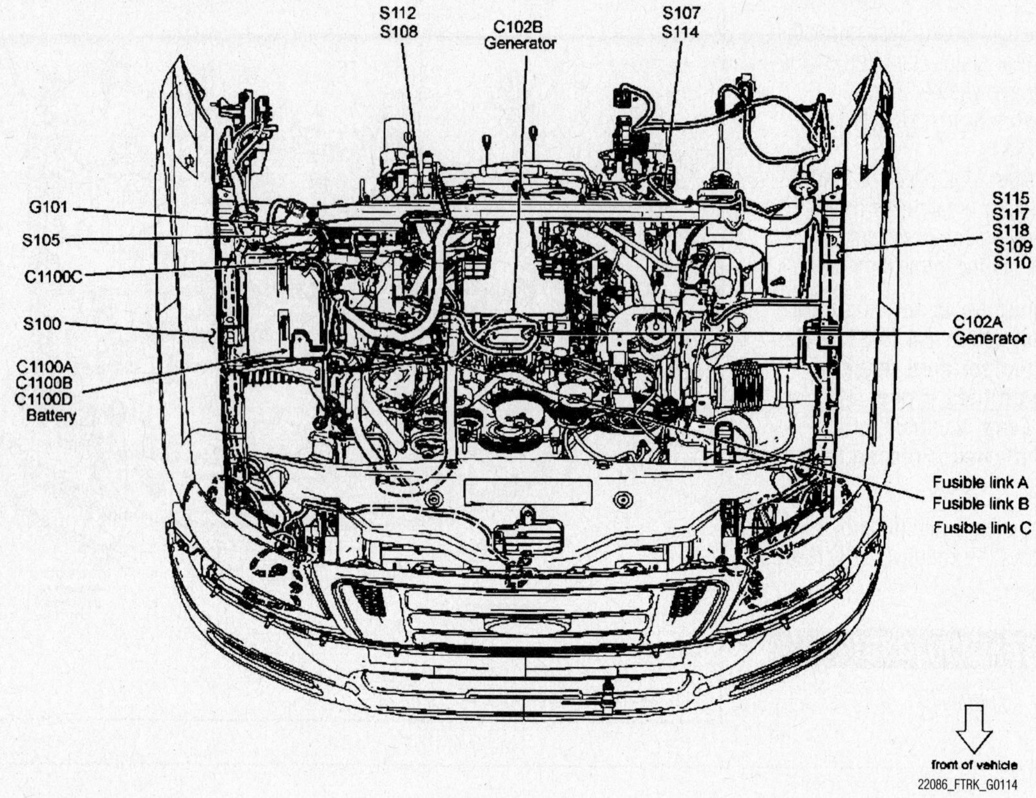

S112
S108

C102B
Generator

S107
S114

G101

S105

C1100C

S100

C1100A
C1100B
C1100D
Battery

S115
S117
S118
S109
S110

C102A
Generator

Fusible link A
Fusible link B
Fusible link C

front of vehicle
22086_FTRK_G0114

Fig. 343 F-150 and Mark LT—3 of 11

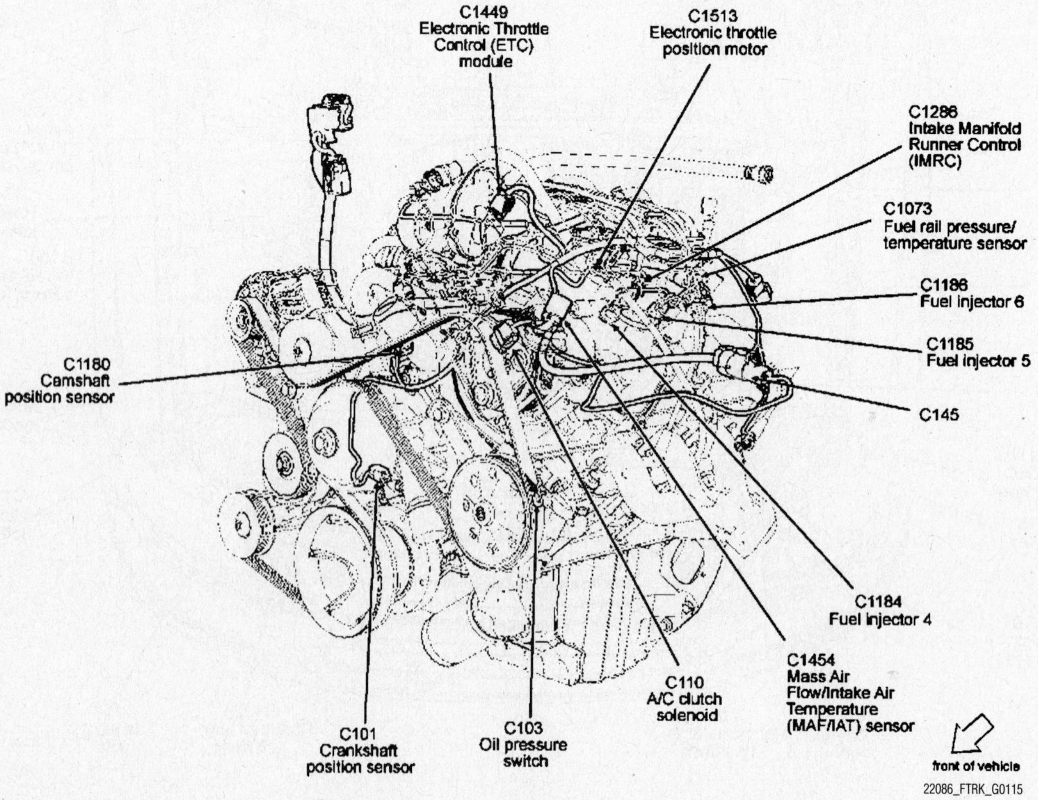

C1449
Electronic Throttle
Control (ETC)
module

C1513
Electronic throttle
position motor

C1286
Intake Manifold
Runner Control
(IMRC)

C1073
Fuel rail pressure/
temperature sensor

C1186
Fuel injector 6

C1185
Fuel injector 5

C145

C1180
Camshaft
position sensor

C1184
Fuel injector 4

C110
A/C clutch
solenoid

C1454
Mass Air
Flow/Intake Air
Temperature
(MAF/IAT) sensor

C101
Crankshaft
position sensor

C103
Oil pressure
switch

front of vehicle
22086_FTRK_G0115

Fig. 344 F-150 and Mark LT—4 of 11

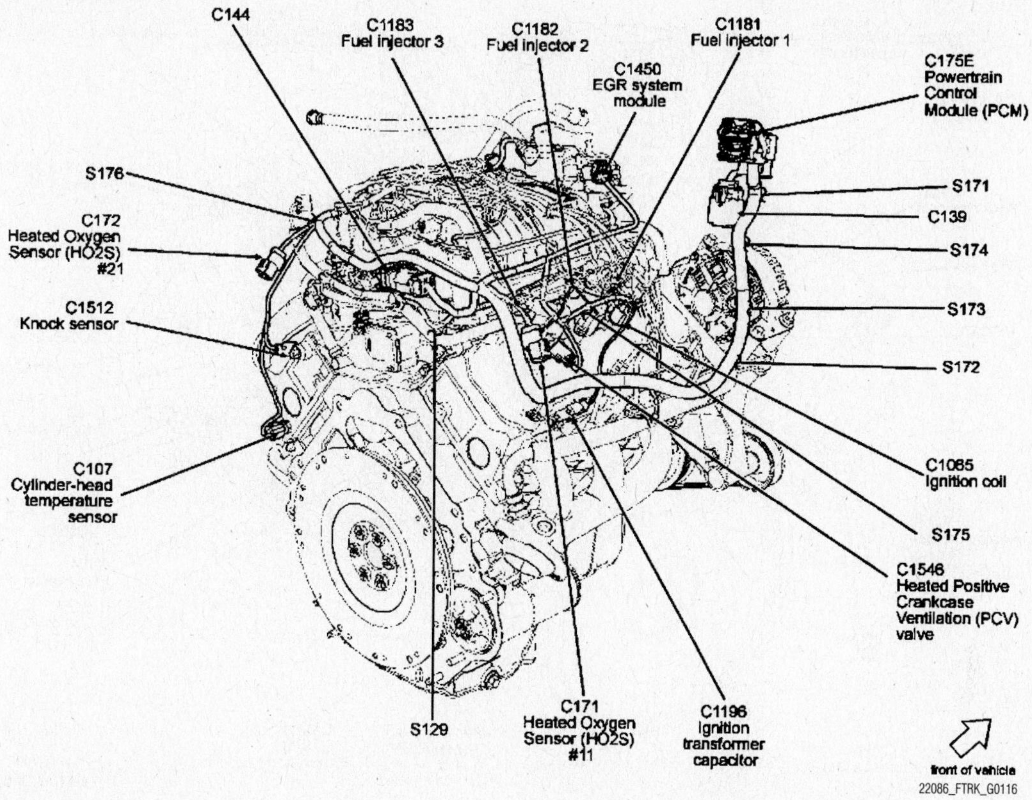

C144

C1183
Fuel injector 3

C1182
Fuel injector 2

C1181
Fuel injector 1

C1450
EGR system
module

C175E
Powertrain
Control
Module (PCM)

S176

C172
Heated Oxygen
Sensor (HO2S)
#21

C1512
Knock sensor

C107
Cylinder-head
temperature
sensor

S171

C139

S174

S173

S172

C1085
Ignition coil

S175

C1546
Heated Positive
Crankcase
Ventilation (PCV)
valve

S129

C171
Heated Oxygen
Sensor (HO2S)
#11

C1196
Ignition
transformer
capacitor

front of vehicle
22086_FTRK_G0116

Fig. 345 F-150 and Mark LT—5 of 11

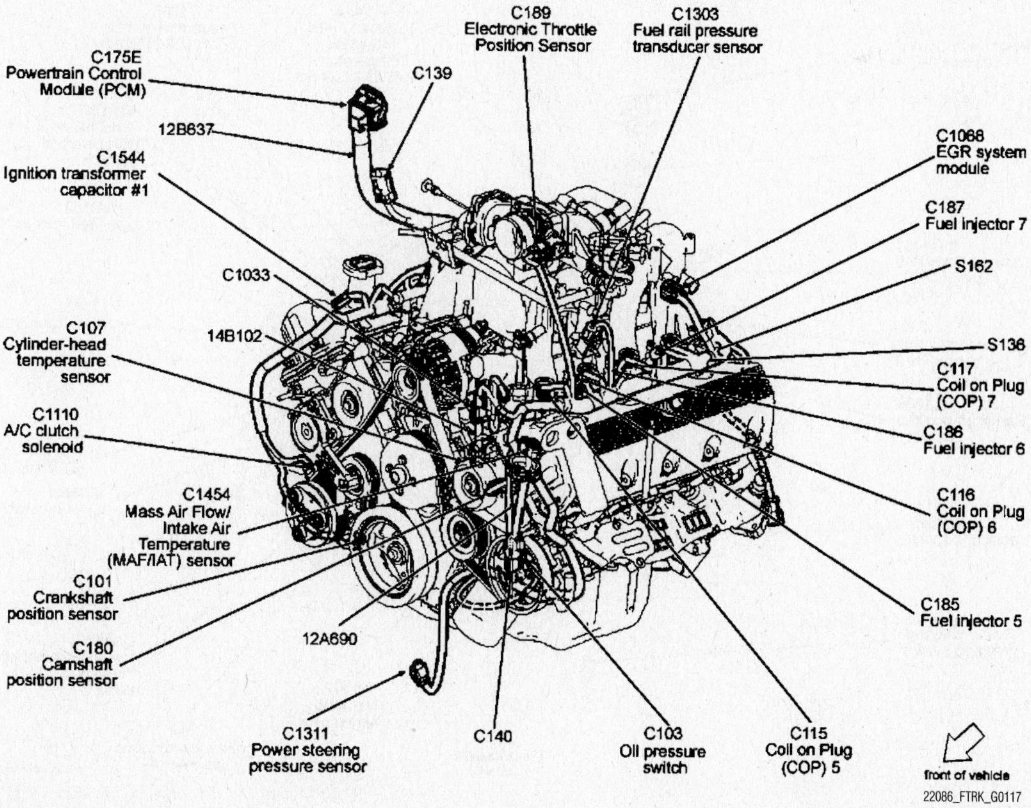

C189
Electronic Throttle
Position Sensor

C1303
Fuel rail pressure
transducer sensor

C175E
Powertrain Control
Module (PCM)

C139

12B637

C1544
Ignition transformer
capacitor #1

C1068
EGR system
module

C187
Fuel injector 7

S162

C1033

C107
Cylinder-head
temperature
sensor

14B102

S136

C117
Coil on Plug
(COP) 7

C1110
A/C clutch
solenoid

C186
Fuel injector 6

C1454
Mass Air Flow/
Intake Air
Temperature
(MAF/IAT) sensor

C116
Coil on Plug
(COP) 6

C101
Crankshaft
position sensor

C180
Camshaft
position sensor

12A690

C185
Fuel injector 5

C1311
Power steering
pressure sensor

C140

C103
Oil pressure
switch

C115
Coil on Plug
(COP) 5

front of vehicle
22086_FTRK_G0117

Fig. 346 F-150 and Mark LT—6 of 11

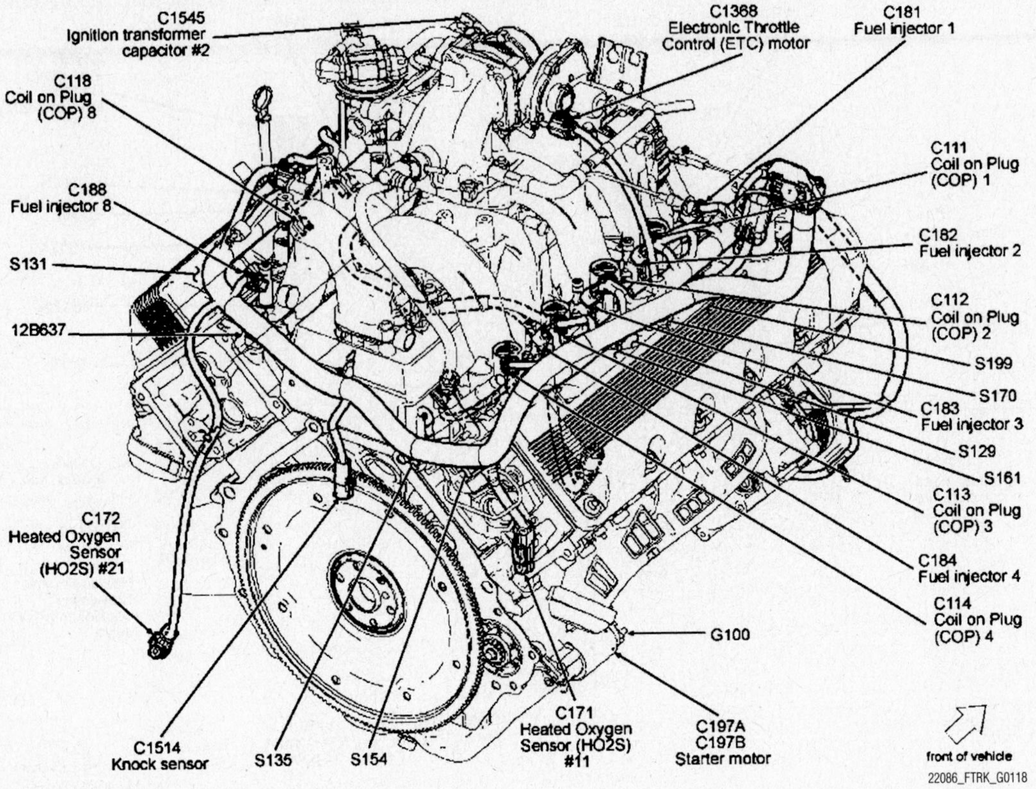

C1545
Ignition transformer
capacitor #2

C118
Coil on Plug
(COP) 8

C188
Fuel injector 8

S131

12B637

C172
Heated Oxygen
Sensor
(HO2S) #21

C1514
Knock sensor

S135

S154

C1368
Electronic Throttle
Control (ETC) motor

C181
Fuel injector 1

C111
Coil on Plug
(COP) 1

C182
Fuel injector 2

C112
Coil on Plug
(COP) 2

S199

S170

C183
Fuel injector 3

S129

S161

C113
Coil on Plug
(COP) 3

C184
Fuel injector 4

C114
Coil on Plug
(COP) 4

G100

C171
Heated Oxygen
Sensor (HO2S)
#11

C197A
C197B
Starter motor

front of vehicle
22086_FTRK_G0118

Fig. 347 F-150 and Mark LT—7 of 11

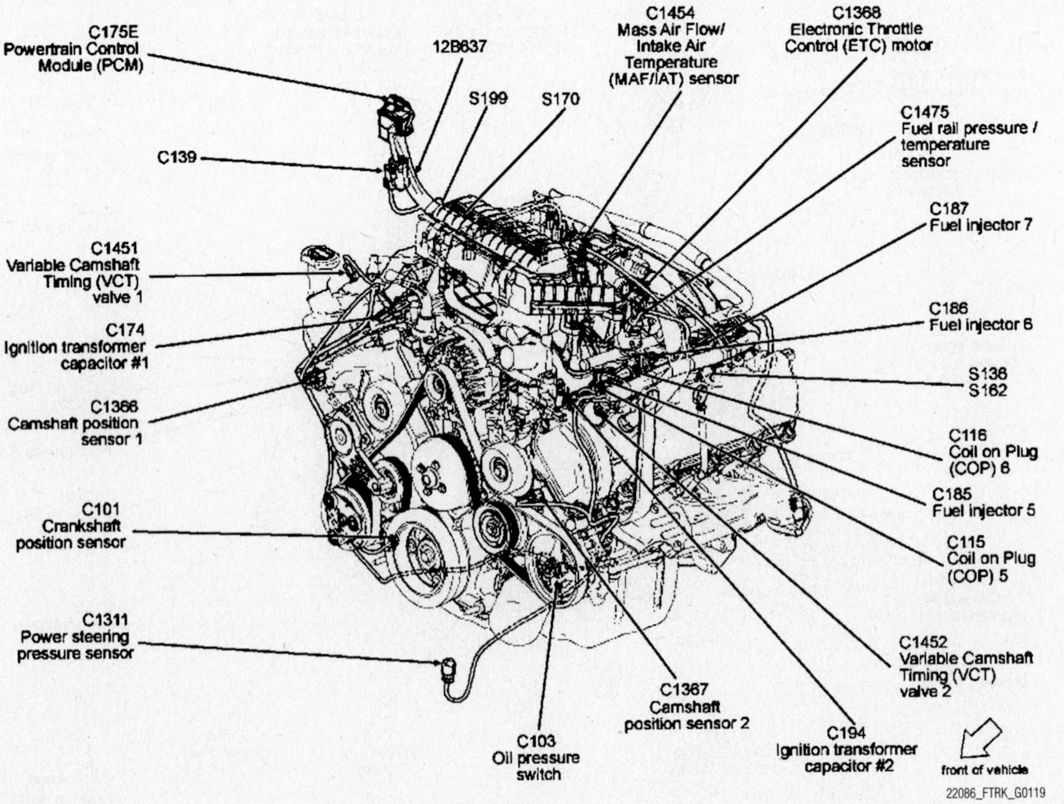

C175E
Powertrain Control
Module (PCM)

C139

C1451
Variable Camshaft
Timing (VCT)
valve 1

C174
Ignition transformer
capacitor #1

C1366
Camshaft position
sensor 1

C101
Crankshaft
position sensor

C1311
Power steering
pressure sensor

12B637

S199

S170

C1454
Mass Air Flow/
Intake Air
Temperature
(MAF/IAT) sensor

C1368
Electronic Throttle
Control (ETC) motor

C1475
Fuel rail pressure /
temperature
sensor

C187
Fuel injector 7

C186
Fuel injector 6

S138
S162

C116
Coil on Plug
(COP) 6

C185
Fuel injector 5

C115
Coil on Plug
(COP) 5

C1452
Variable Camshaft
Timing (VCT)
valve 2

C194
Ignition transformer
capacitor #2

C103
Oil pressure
switch

C1367
Camshaft
position sensor 2

front of vehicle
22086_FTRK_G0119

Fig. 348 F-150 and Mark LT—8 of 11

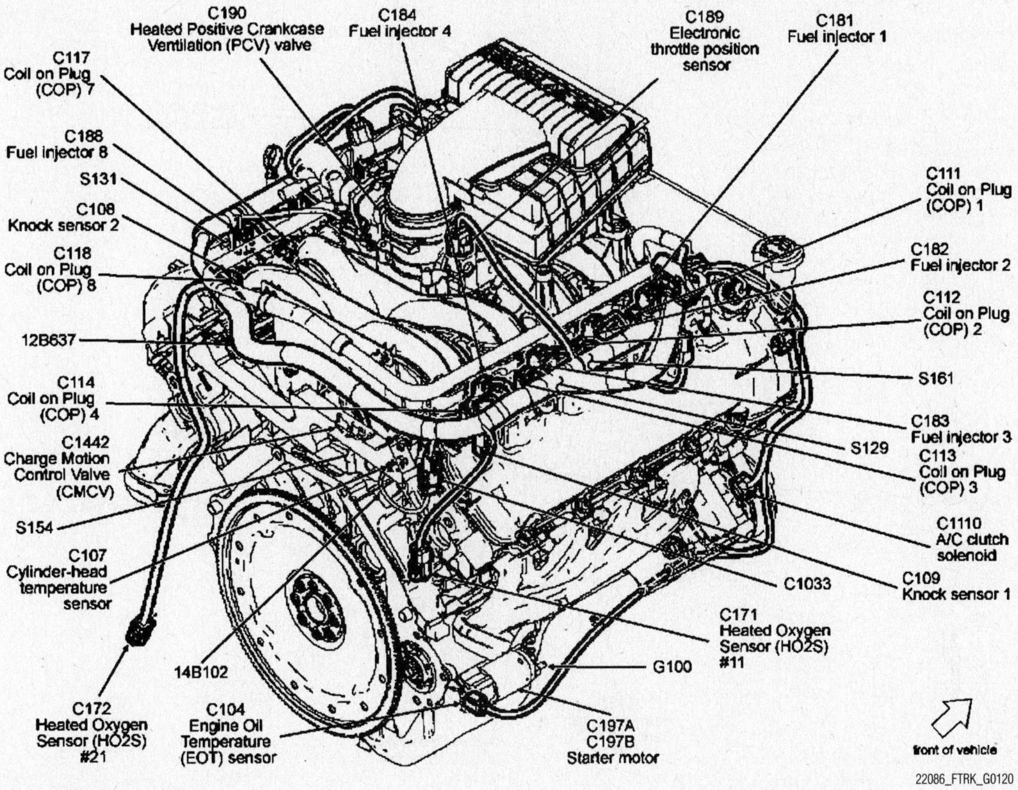

C190
Heated Positive Crankcase
Ventilation (PCV) valve

C184
Fuel injector 4

C189
Electronic
throttle position
sensor

C181
Fuel injector 1

C117
Coil on Plug
(COP) 7

C188
Fuel injector 8

S131

C108
Knock sensor 2

C118
Coil on Plug
(COP) 8

12B637

C114
Coil on Plug
(COP) 4

C1442
Charge Motion
Control Valve
(CMCV)

S154

C107
Cylinder-head
temperature
sensor

C172
Heated Oxygen
Sensor (HO2S)
#21

14B102

C104
Engine Oil
Temperature
(EOT) sensor

C197A
C197B
Starter motor

G100

C171
Heated Oxygen
Sensor (HO2S)
#11

C1033

C109
Knock sensor 1

C1110
A/C clutch
solenoid

C113
Coil on Plug
(COP) 3

S129

C183
Fuel injector 3

S161

C112
Coil on Plug
(COP) 2

C182
Fuel injector 2

C111
Coil on Plug
(COP) 1

front of vehicle

22086_FTRK_G0120

Fig. 349 F-150 and Mark LT—9 of 11

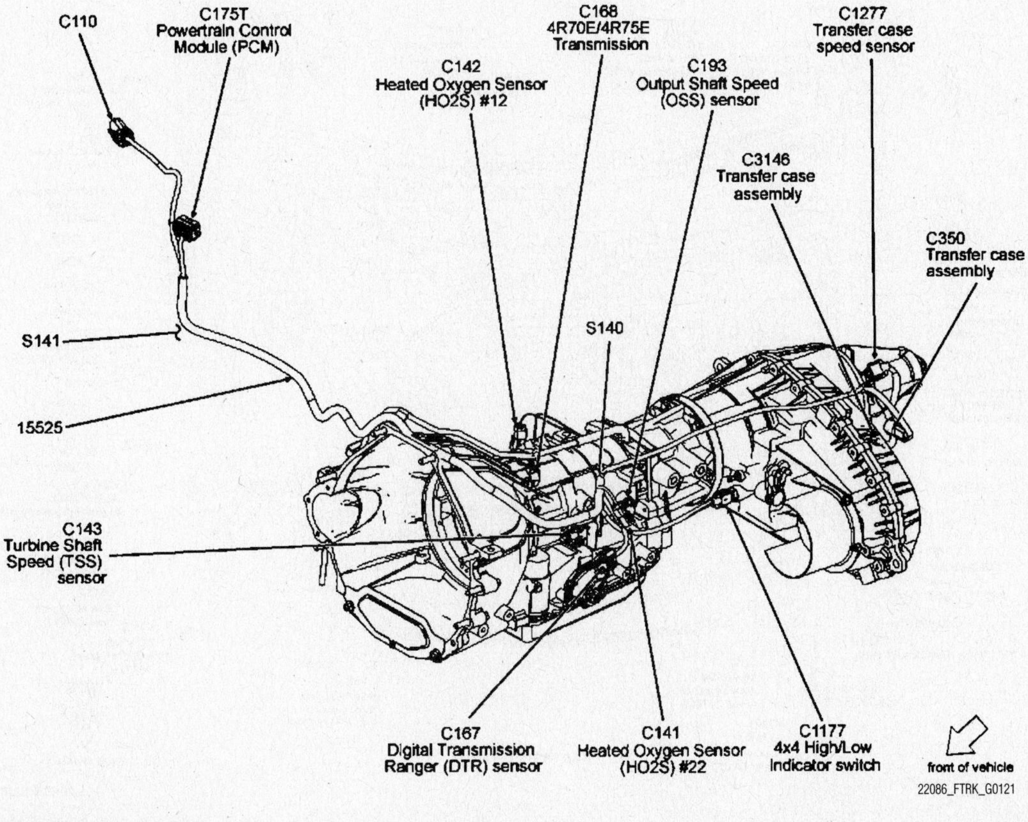

C110

C175T
Powertrain Control
Module (PCM)

C142
Heated Oxygen Sensor
(HO2S) #12

C168
4R70E/4R75E
Transmission

C193
Output Shaft Speed
(OSS) sensor

C1277
Transfer case
speed sensor

C3146
Transfer case
assembly

C350
Transfer case
assembly

S141

15525

S140

C143
Turbine Shaft
Speed (TSS)
sensor

C167
Digital Transmission
Ranger (DTR) sensor

C141
Heated Oxygen Sensor
(HO2S) #22

C1177
4x4 High/Low
Indicator switch

front of vehicle

22086_FTRK_G0121

Fig. 350 F-150 and Mark LT—10 of 11

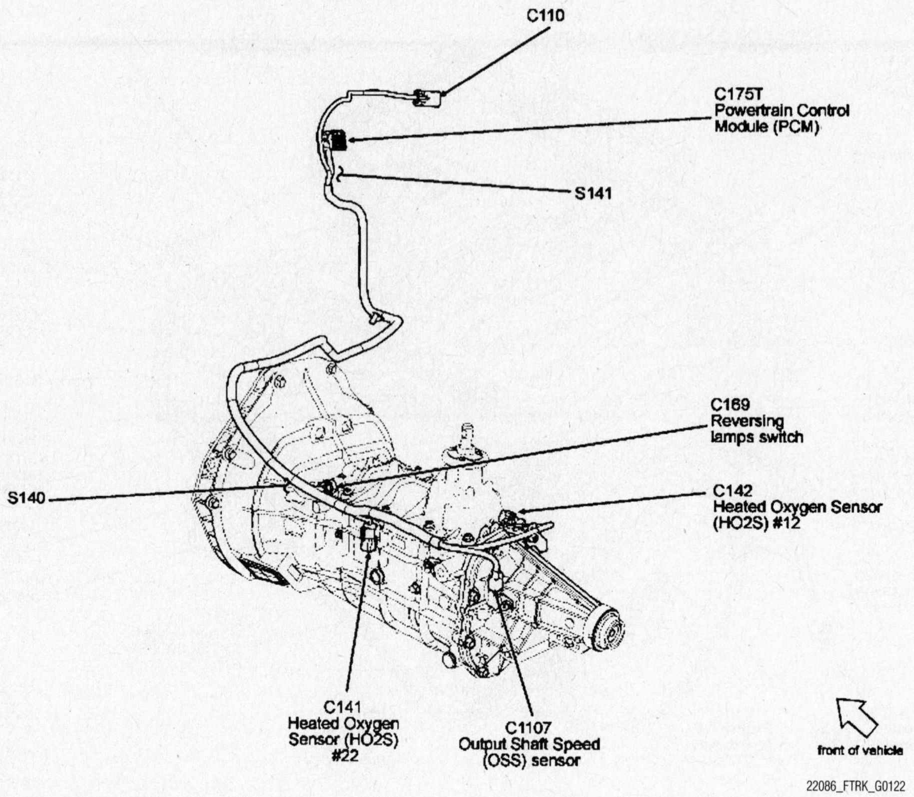

C110

C175T
Powertrain Control
Module (PCM)

S141

C169
Reversing
lamps switch

C142
Heated Oxygen Sensor
(HO2S) #12

S140

C141
Heated Oxygen
Sensor (HO2S)
#22

C1107
Output Shaft Speed
(OSS) sensor

front of vehicle

22086_FTRK_G0122

Fig. 351 F-150 and Mark LT—11 of 11

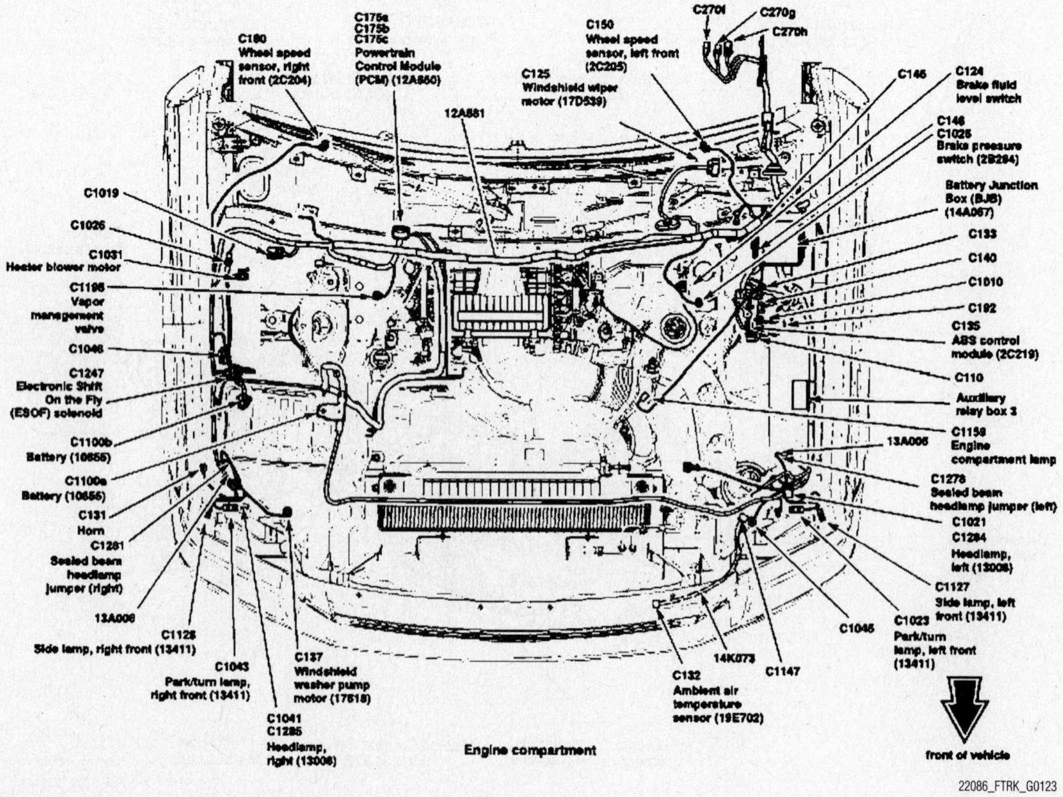

C175a
C175b
C175c
Powertrain
Control Module
(PCM) (12A650)

C180
Wheel speed
sensor, right
front (2C204)

C150
Wheel speed
sensor, left front
(2C205)

C125
Windshield wiper
motor (17D539)

C270i
C270g
C270h

C145

C124
Brake fluid
level switch

12A651

C146
C1025
Brake pressure
switch (2B264)

Battery Junction
Box (BJB)
(14A067)

C1019

C133

C1026

C140

C1031
Heater blower motor

C1010

C1198
Vapor
management
valve

C192

C135
ABS control
module (2C219)

C1046

C110

C1247
Electronic Shift
On the Fly
(ESOF) solenoid

Auxiliary
relay box 3

C1100b
Battery (10655)

13A006

C1159
Engine
compartment lamp

C1100e
Battery (10655)

C1278
Sealed beam
headlamp jumper (left)

C131
Horn

C1021

C1281
Sealed beam
headlamp
jumper (right)

C1284
Headlamp,
left (13008)

C1127
Side lamp, left
front (13411)

13A006

C1023
Park/turn
lamp, left front
(13411)

C1128
Side lamp, right front (13411)

C1045

C1043
Park/turn lamp,
right front (13411)

C137
Windshield
washer pump
motor (17618)

C132
Ambient air
temperature
sensor (19E702)

14K073

C1147

C1041
C1285
Headlamp,
right (13008)

Engine compartment

front of vehicle

22086_FTRK_G0123

Fig. 352 F-250 and F-350—1 of 14

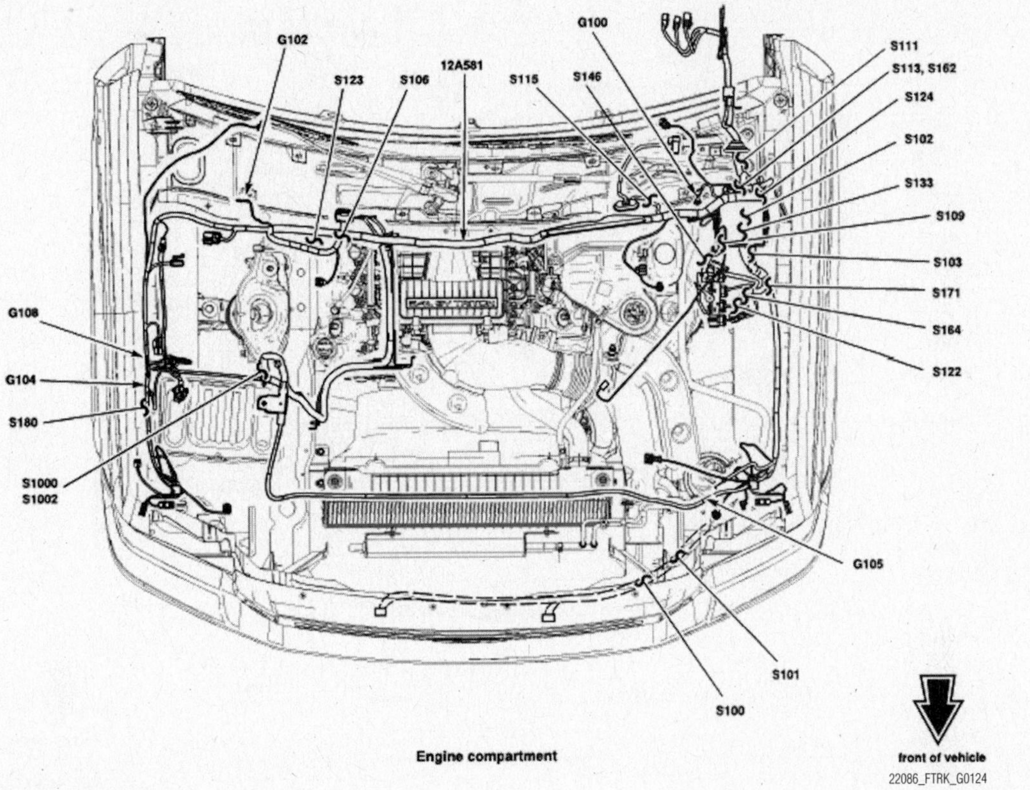

Engine compartment

front of vehicle

22086_FTRK_G0124

Fig. 353 F-250 and F-350—2 of 14

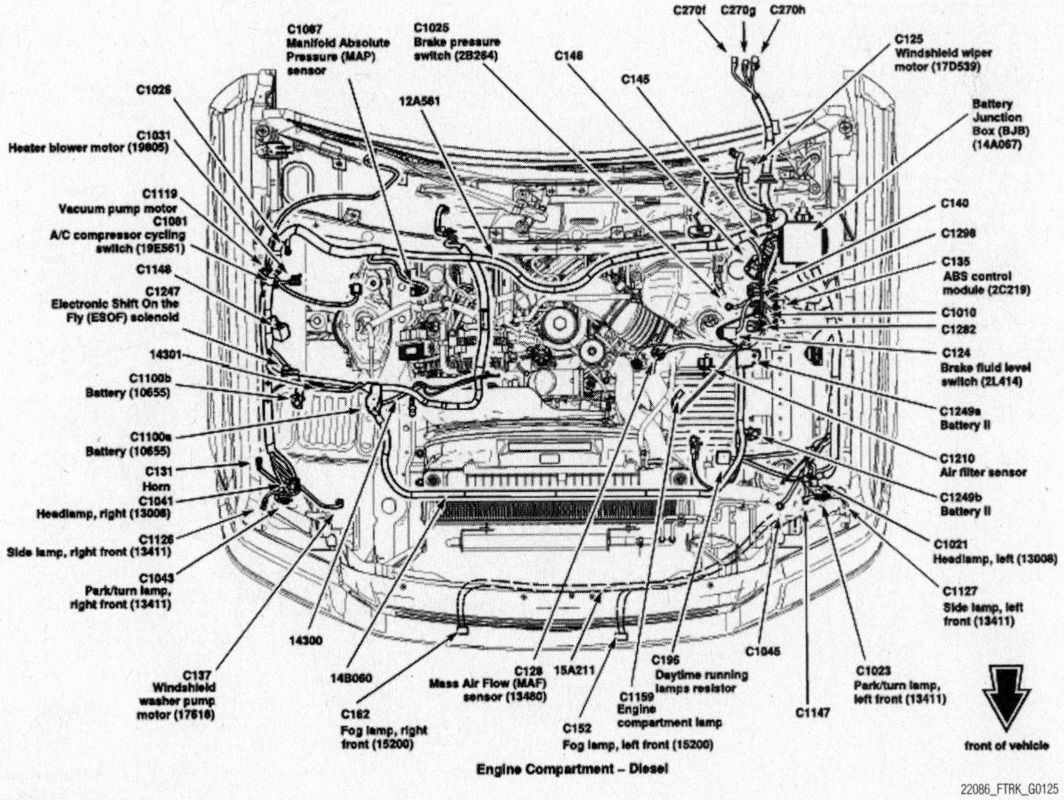

Engine Compartment – Diesel

front of vehicle

22086_FTRK_G0125

Fig. 354 F-250 and F-350—3 of 14

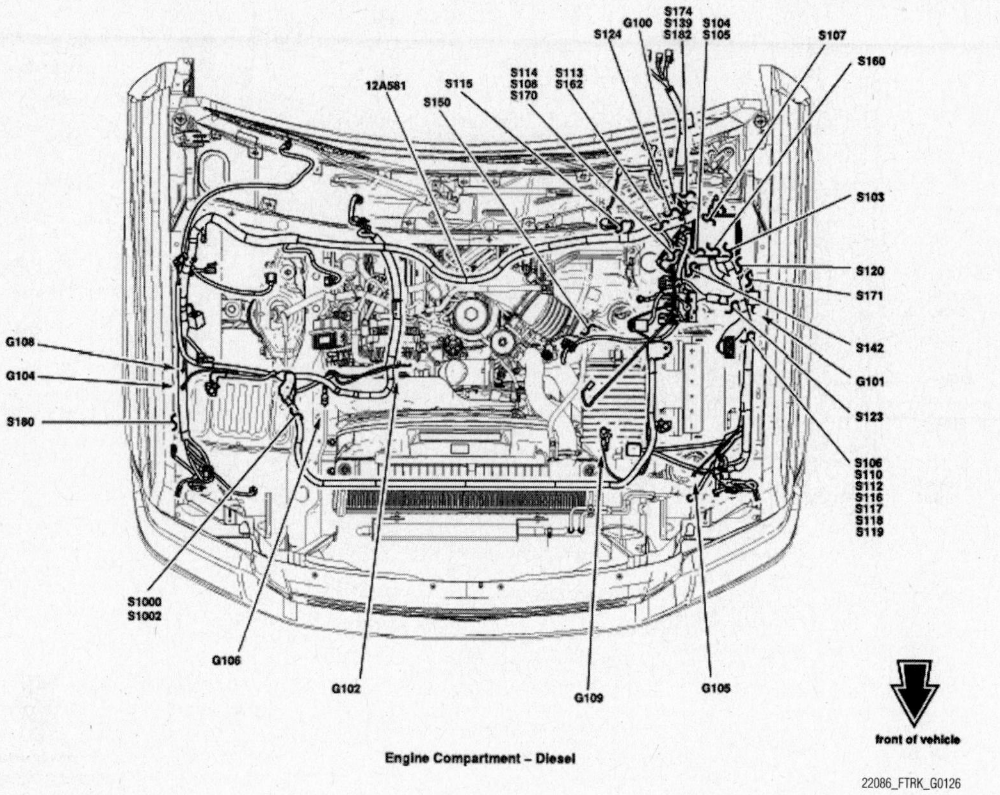

S174
G100 S139 S104
S124 S182 S105 S107
S160
12A581 S114 S113
S115 S108 S162
S150 S170
S103
G108
G104 S120
S180 S171
S142
G101
S123
S1000 S106
S1002 S110
S112
G106 S116
S117
S118
G102 S119
G109 G105

front of vehicle

Engine Compartment – Diesel

22086_FTRK_G0126

Fig. 355 F-250 and F-350—4 of 14

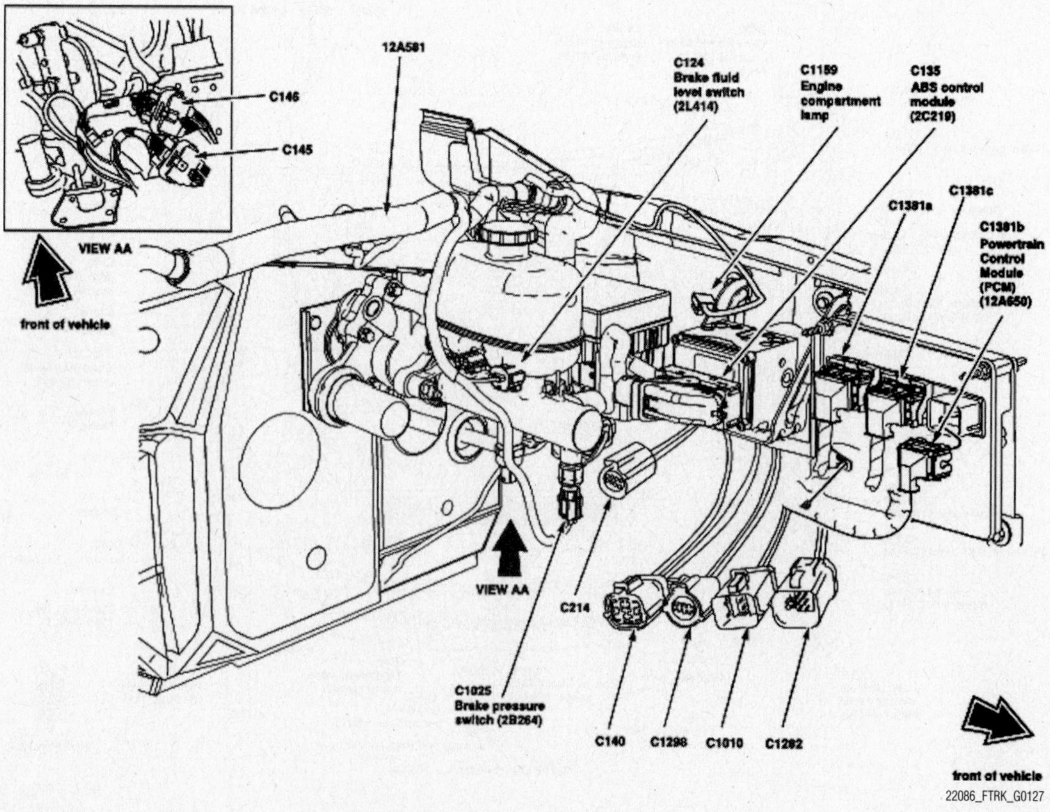

C146
C145

VIEW AA

front of vehicle

12A581
C124 Brake fluid level switch (2L414)
C1159 Engine compartment lamp
C135 ABS control module (2C219)
C1381c
C1381a
C1381b Powertrain Control Module (PCM) (12A650)

VIEW AA

C214
C1025 Brake pressure switch (2B264)
C140 C1298 C1010 C1282

front of vehicle

22086_FTRK_G0127

Fig. 356 F-250 and F-350—5 of 14

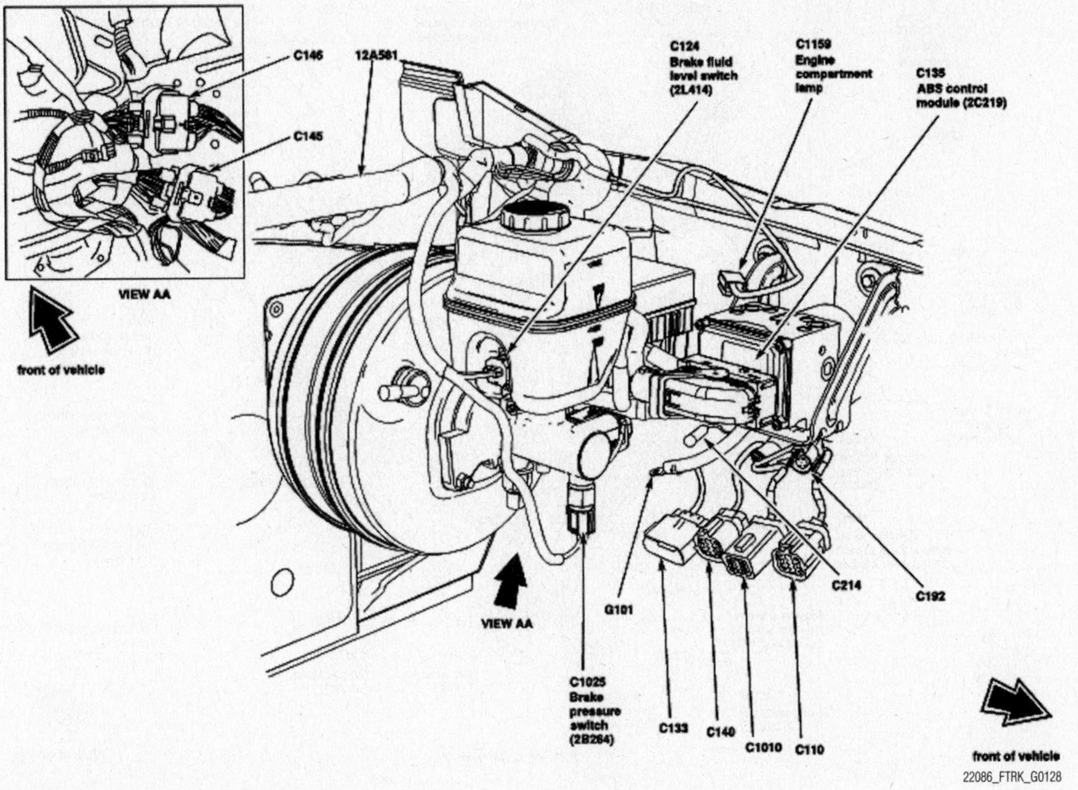

C146

C145

VIEW AA

front of vehicle

12A581

C124
Brake fluid
level switch
(2L.414)

C1159
Engine
compartment
lamp

C135
ABS control
module (2C219)

C214

C192

VIEW AA

G101

C1025
Brake
pressure
switch
(2B264)

C133

C140

C1010

C110

front of vehicle

22086_FTRK_G0128

Fig. 357 F-250 and F-350—6 of 14

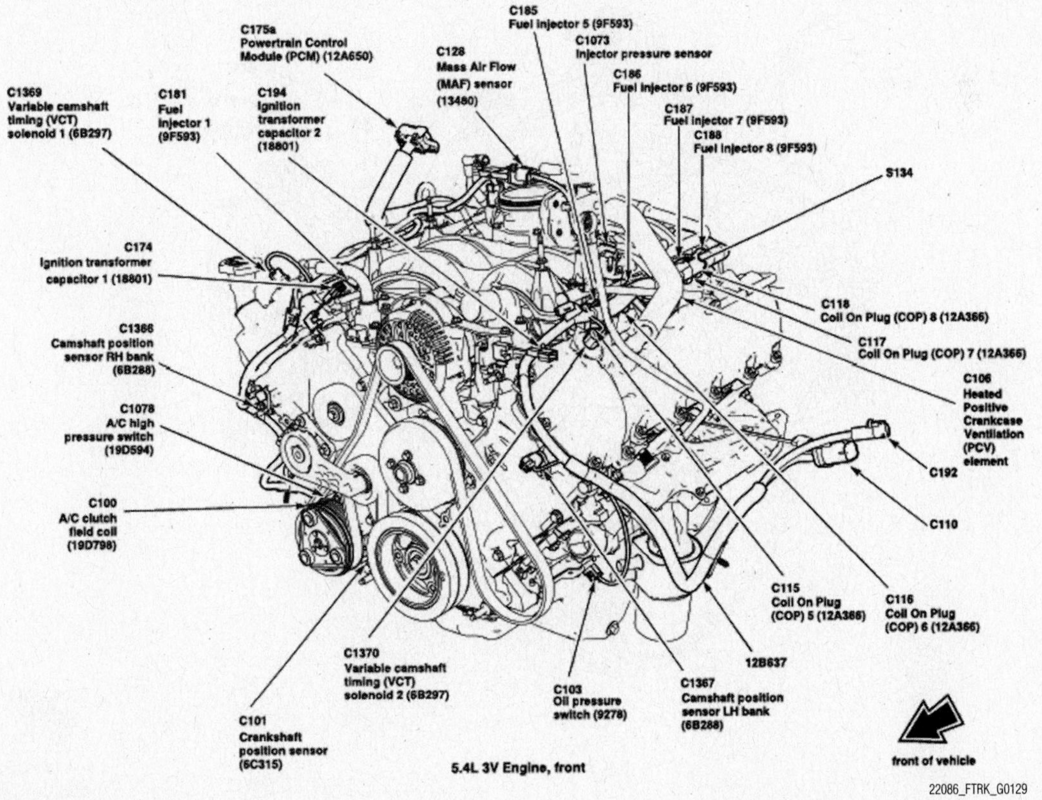

C1369
Variable camshaft
timing (VCT)
solenoid 1 (6B297)

C181
Fuel
injector 1
(9F593)

C194
Ignition
transformer
capacitor 2
(18801)

C175a
Powertrain Control
Module (PCM) (12A650)

C128
Mass Air Flow
(MAF) sensor
(13480)

C185
Fuel injector 5 (9F593)

C1073
Injector pressure sensor

C186
Fuel injector 6 (9F593)

C187
Fuel injector 7 (9F593)

C188
Fuel injector 8 (9F593)

S134

C174
Ignition transformer
capacitor 1 (18801)

C1366
Camshaft position
sensor RH bank
(6B288)

C1078
A/C high
pressure switch
(19D594)

C100
A/C clutch
field coil
(19D798)

C118
Coil On Plug (COP) 8 (12A366)

C117
Coil On Plug (COP) 7 (12A366)

C106
Heated
Positive
Crankcase
Ventilation
(PCV)
element

C192

C110

C115
Coil On Plug
(COP) 5 (12A366)

C116
Coil On Plug
(COP) 6 (12A366)

12B637

C1370
Variable camshaft
timing (VCT)
solenoid 2 (6B297)

C103
Oil pressure
switch (9278)

C1367
Camshaft position
sensor LH bank
(6B288)

C101
Crankshaft
position sensor
(6C315)

5.4L 3V Engine, front

front of vehicle

22086_FTRK_G0129

Fig. 358 F-250 and F-350—7 of 14

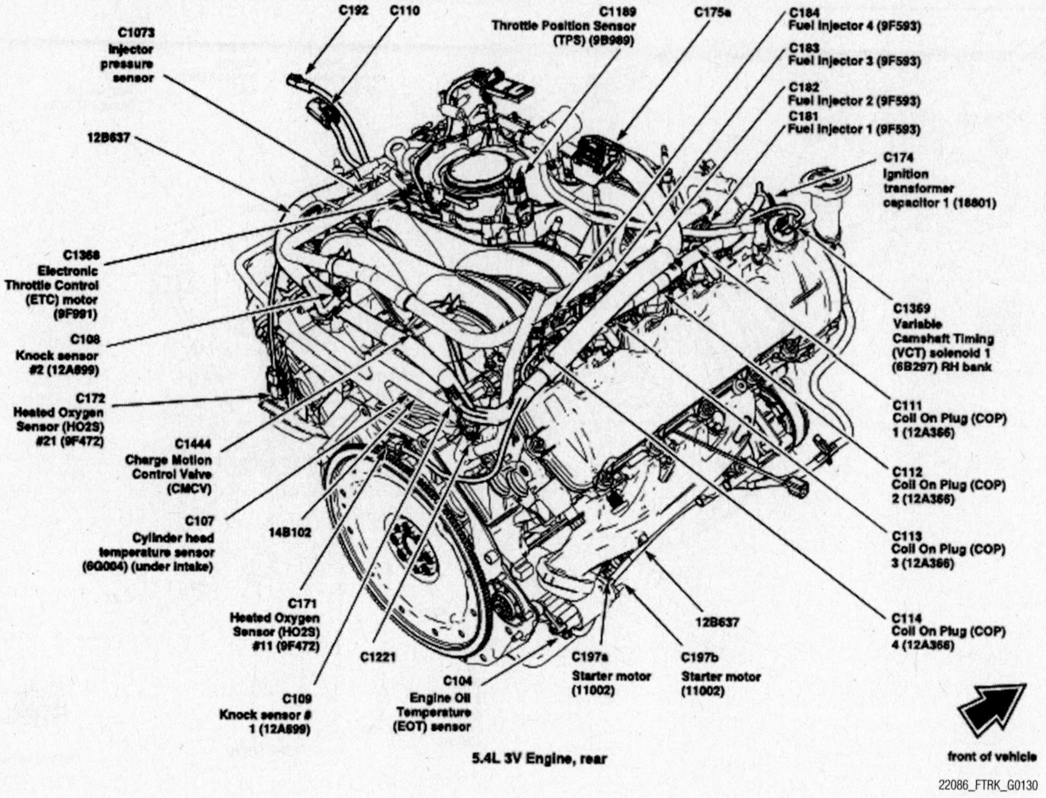

C192 C110

C1073
Injector
pressure
sensor

12B637

C1368
Electronic
Throttle Control
(ETC) motor
(9F991)

C108
Knock sensor
#2 (12A699)

C172
Heated Oxygen
Sensor (HO2S)
#21 (9F472)

C1444
Charge Motion
Control Valve
(CMCV)

C107
Cylinder head
temperature sensor
(6G004) (under intake)

14B102

C171
Heated Oxygen
Sensor (HO2S)
#11 (9F472)

C1221

C104
C109
Knock sensor #
1 (12A699)

C197a
Engine Oil
Temperature
(EOT) sensor

C1189
Throttle Position Sensor
(TPS) (9B989)

C175a

C184
Fuel Injector 4 (9F593)

C183
Fuel Injector 3 (9F593)

C182
Fuel Injector 2 (9F593)

C181
Fuel Injector 1 (9F593)

C174
Ignition
transformer
capacitor 1 (18801)

C1369
Variable
Camshaft Timing
(VCT) solenoid 1
(6B297) RH bank

C111
Coil On Plug (COP)
1 (12A366)

C112
Coil On Plug (COP)
2 (12A366)

C113
Coil On Plug (COP)
3 (12A366)

C114
Coil On Plug (COP)
4 (12A366)

12B637

Starter motor
(11002)

C197b
Starter motor
(11002)

front of vehicle

5.4L 3V Engine, rear

22086_FTRK_G0130

Fig. 359 F-250 and F-350—8 of 14

12B637

S143

S145

S132

S136

S135

5.4L 3V Engine, rear

front of vehicle

22086_FTRK_G0131

Fig. 360 F-250 and F-350—9 of 14

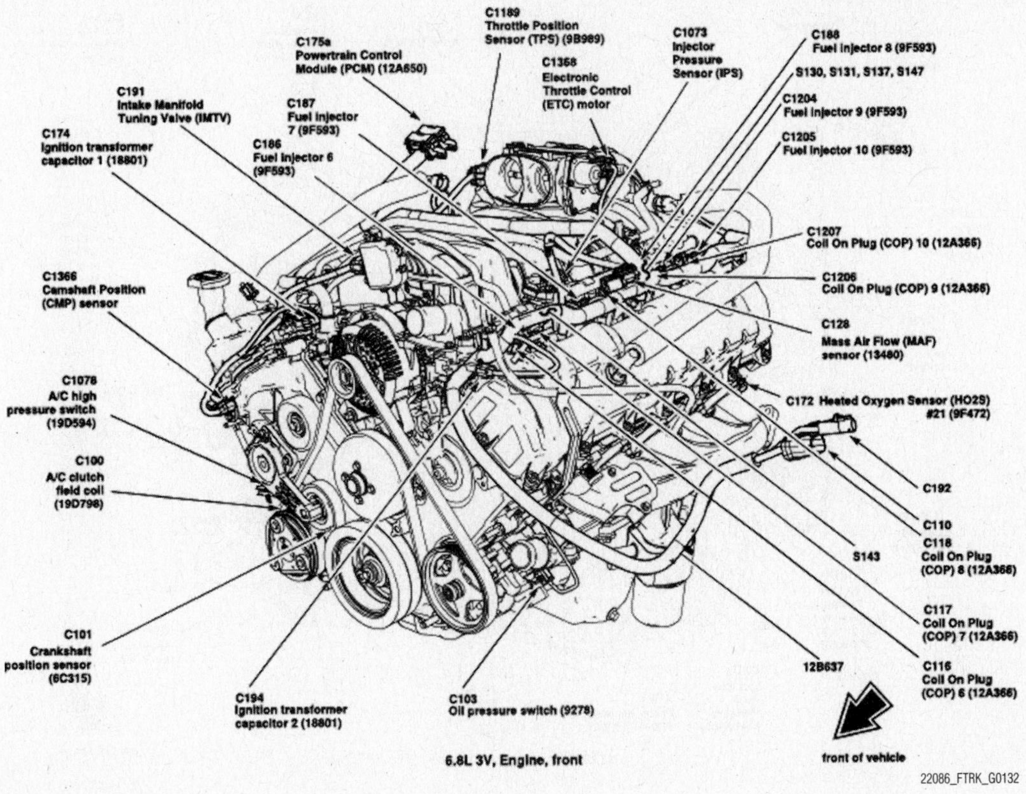

C1189
Throttle Position
Sensor (TPS) (9B989)

C175a
Powertrain Control
Module (PCM) (12A650)

C1073
Injector
Pressure
Sensor (IPS)

C1368
Electronic
Throttle Control
(ETC) motor

C188
Fuel injector 8 (9F593)

S130, S131, S137, S147

C1204
Fuel injector 9 (9F593)

C1205
Fuel injector 10 (9F593)

C191
Intake Manifold
Tuning Valve (IMTV)

C187
Fuel Injector
7 (9F593)

C174
Ignition transformer
capacitor 1 (18801)

C186
Fuel Injector 6
(9F593)

C1366
Camshaft Position
(CMP) sensor

C1078
A/C high
pressure switch
(19D594)

C100
A/C clutch
field coil
(19D798)

C101
Crankshaft
position sensor
(6C315)

C194
Ignition transformer
capacitor 2 (18801)

C103
Oil pressure switch (9278)

C1207
Coil On Plug (COP) 10 (12A366)

C1206
Coil On Plug (COP) 9 (12A366)

C128
Mass Air Flow (MAF)
sensor (13480)

C172 Heated Oxygen Sensor (HO2S)
#21 (9F472)

C192

C110

C118
Coil On Plug
(COP) 8 (12A366)

C117
Coil On Plug
(COP) 7 (12A366)

S143

12B637

C116
Coil On Plug
(COP) 6 (12A366)

6.8L 3V, Engine, front

front of vehicle

22086_FTRK_G0132

Fig. 361 F-250 and F-350—10 of 14

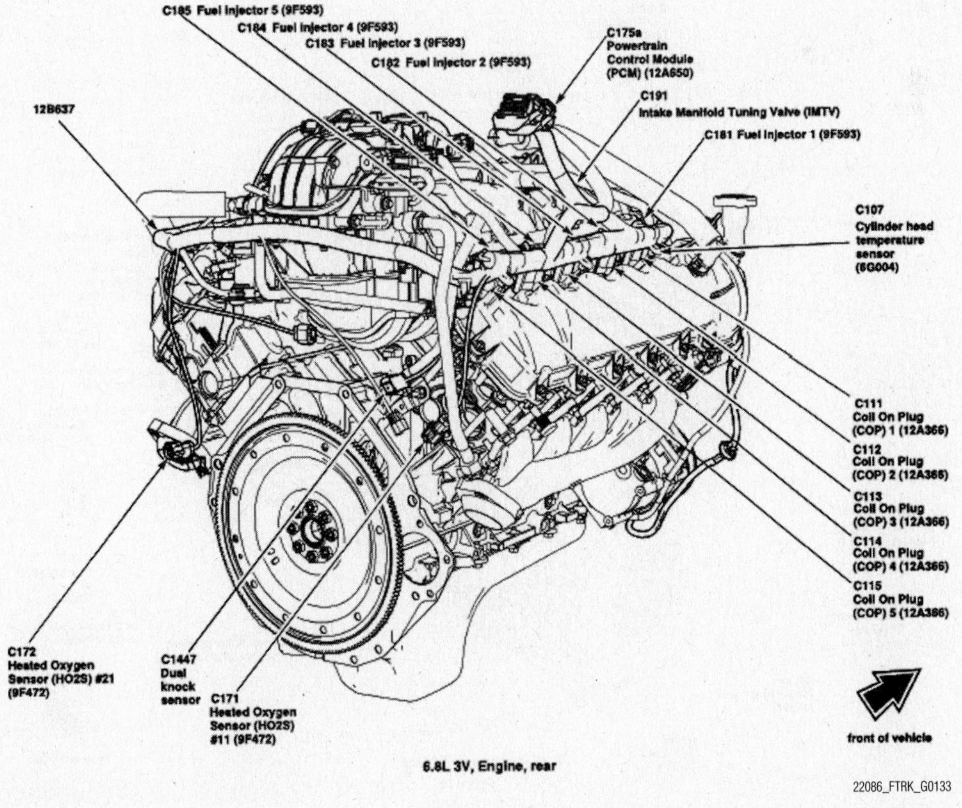

C185 Fuel Injector 5 (9F593)

C184 Fuel Injector 4 (9F593)

C183 Fuel Injector 3 (9F593)

C182 Fuel Injector 2 (9F593)

C175a
Powertrain
Control
Module
(PCM) (12A650)

C191
Intake Manifold Tuning Valve (IMTV)

C181 Fuel Injector 1 (9F593)

12B637

C107
Cylinder head
temperature
sensor
(6G004)

C111
Coil On Plug
(COP) 1 (12A366)

C112
Coil On Plug
(COP) 2 (12A366)

C113
Coil On Plug
(COP) 3 (12A366)

C114
Coil On Plug
(COP) 4 (12A366)

C115
Coil On Plug
(COP) 5 (12A366)

C172
Heated Oxygen
Sensor (HO2S) #21
(9F472)

C1447
Dual
knock
sensor

C171
Heated Oxygen
Sensor (HO2S)
#11 (9F472)

6.8L 3V, Engine, rear

front of vehicle

22086_FTRK_G0133

Fig. 362 F-250 and F-350—11 of 14

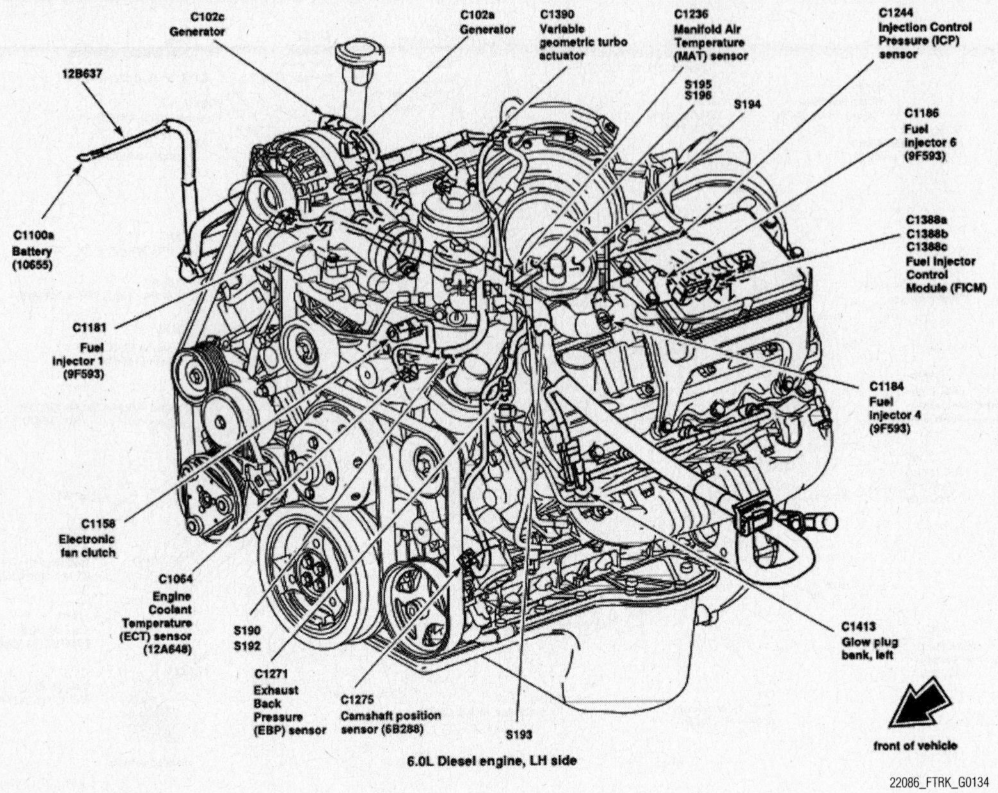

C102c
Generator

C102a
Generator

C1390
Variable
geometric turbo
actuator

C1236
Manifold Air
Temperature
(MAT) sensor

C1244
Injection Control
Pressure (ICP)
sensor

12B637

S195
S196

S194

C1186
Fuel
injector 6
(9F593)

C1100a
Battery
(10655)

C1388a
C1388b
C1388c
Fuel Injector
Control
Module (FICM)

C1181
Fuel
Injector 1
(9F593)

C1184
Fuel
Injector 4
(9F593)

C1158
Electronic
fan clutch

C1064
Engine
Coolant
Temperature
(ECT) sensor
(12A648)

S190
S192

C1271
Exhaust
Back
Pressure
(EBP) sensor

C1275
Camshaft position
sensor (6B288)

S193

C1413
Glow plug
bank, left

6.0L Diesel engine, LH side

front of vehicle

22086_FTRK_G0134

Fig. 363 F-250 and F-350—12 of 14

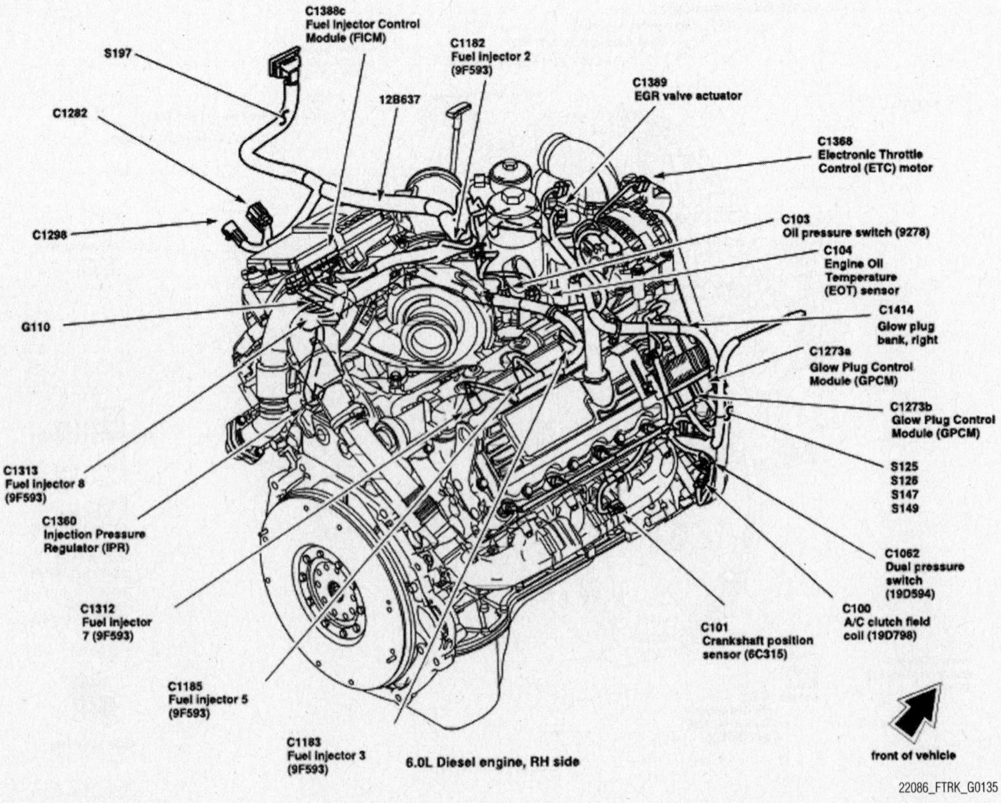

C1388c
Fuel Injector Control
Module (FICM)

C1182
Fuel injector 2
(9F593)

C1389
EGR valve actuator

S197

C1282

12B637

C1368
Electronic Throttle
Control (ETC) motor

C1298

C103
Oil pressure switch (9278)

C104
Engine Oil
Temperature
(EOT) sensor

G110

C1414
Glow plug
bank, right

C1273a
Glow Plug Control
Module (GPCM)

C1273b
Glow Plug Control
Module (GPCM)

C1313
Fuel injector 8
(9F593)

S125
S126
S147
S149

C1360
Injection Pressure
Regulator (IPR)

C1062
Dual pressure
switch
(19D594)

C1312
Fuel injector
7 (9F593)

C100
A/C clutch field
coil (19D798)

C1101
Crankshaft position
sensor (6C315)

C1185
Fuel injector 5
(9F593)

C1183
Fuel injector 3
(9F593)

6.0L Diesel engine, RH side

front of vehicle

22086_FTRK_G0135

Fig. 364 F-250 and F-350—13 of 14

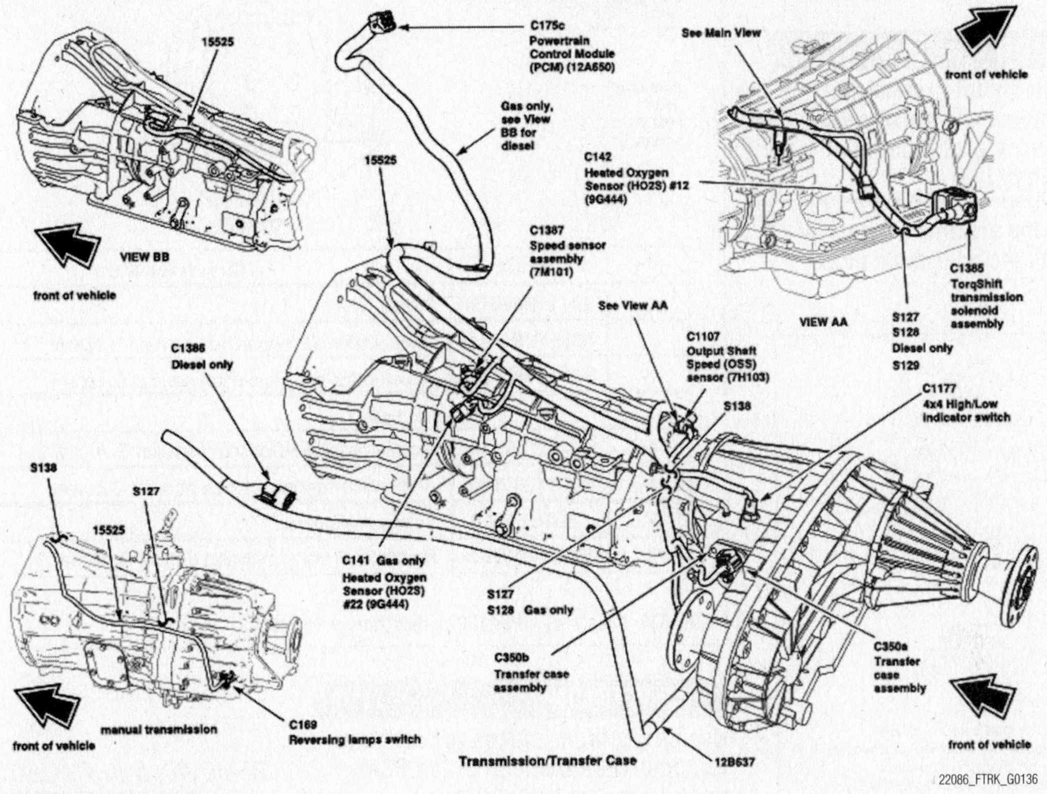

15525

C175c
Powertrain
Control Module
(PCM) (12A650)

See Main View

front of vehicle

15525

Gas only,
see View
BB for
diesel

C142
Heated Oxygen
Sensor (HO2S) #12
(9G444)

C1387
Speed sensor
assembly
(7M101)

See View AA

C1385
TorqShift
transmission
solenoid
assembly

VIEW BB

front of vehicle

C1386
Diesel only

C1107
Output Shaft
Speed (OSS)
sensor (7H103)

VIEW AA   S127
S128
Diesel only
S129

S138

C1177
4x4 High/Low
indicator switch

S138

S127

15525

C141 Gas only
Heated Oxygen
Sensor (HO2S)
#22 (9G444)

S127
S128 Gas only

C350b
Transfer case
assembly

C350a
Transfer
case
assembly

manual transmission

C169
Reversing lamps switch

front of vehicle

Transmission/Transfer Case   12B637

front of vehicle

22086_FTRK_G0136

Fig. 365 F-250 and F-350—14 of 14

ACCELERATOR PEDAL POSITION (APP) SENSOR

LOCATION

Part of the accelerator pedal assembly.

OPERATION

The APP sensor is a 3-track potentiometer that is used to calculate driver demand for power based on the rotation angle of the accelerator pedal. The sensor receives a reference voltage from the powertrain control module (PCM) and provides a variable voltage signal directly proportional to the accelerator pedal position. The PCM uses the 3 APP sensor inputs to calculate the desired fuel quantity, injection timing, and the correct injection control pressure. A concern with the APP sensor illuminates the powertrain malfunction indicator (wrench). Normal engine operation is permitted if the PCM detects a concern on one of the 3 sensor signals. If the PCM detects a concern on two of the 3 sensor signals, the PCM only allows the engine to operate at idle.

REMOVAL & INSTALLATION

With Fixed Pedal

See Figure 366.

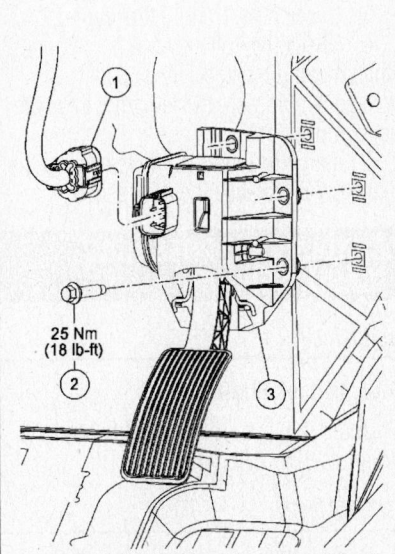

25 Nm
(18 lb-ft)

1. Accelerator pedal and position sensor assembly electrical connector
2. Accelerator pedal and position sensor assembly bolts (3 required)
3. Accelerator pedal and position sensor assembly

22086_FTRK_G0170

Fig. 366 Fixed Accelerator Pedal Assembly

1. Before servicing the vehicle, refer to the precautions in the beginning of this section.
2. Disconnect the battery ground cable.
3. Disconnect the accelerator pedal and position sensor assembly electrical connector.
4. Remove the 3 bolts and the accelerator pedal and position sensor assembly.
5. To install, reverse the removal procedure.

With Adjustable Pedal

See Figure 367.

1. Before servicing the vehicle, refer to the precautions in the beginning of this section.
2. Disconnect the battery ground cable.
3. Disconnect the accelerator pedal and position sensor assembly electrical connector.
4. Disconnect the adjustable pedal motor electrical connector.
5. Disconnect the adjustable pedal motor drive cable from the brake pedal assembly.
6. Remove the 3 nuts and the accelerator pedal and position sensor assembly.
7. Remove the 3 bolts and the adjustable pedal motor and bracket assembly.

8. To install, reverse the removal procedure.

> ❊❊ **CAUTION**
>
> **The adjustable pedal system must be indexed whenever the brake pedal assembly or accelerator pedal assembly is installed.**

→ Make sure the electrical connector is connected to the adjustable pedal motor.

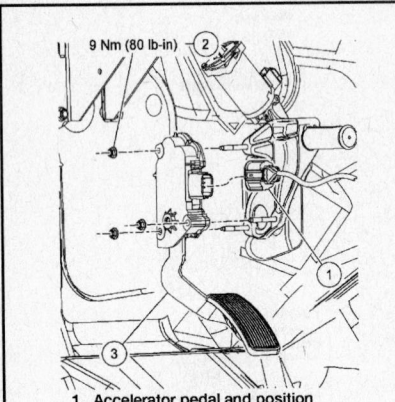

1. Accelerator pedal and position sensor assembly electrical connector
2. Accelerator pedal and position sensor assembly nuts (3 required)
3. Accelerator pedal and position sensor assembly

22086_FTRK_G0171

Fig. 367 Adjustable Accelerator Pedal Assembly

9. Disconnect the adjustable pedal motor drive cable from the brake pedal drive.

10. Operate the accelerator pedal to the full rearward position.

11. Connect the adjustable pedal motor drive cable to the adjustable brake pedal drive.

12. Operate the adjustable pedals to the full forward position.

13. Disconnect the adjustable pedal motor drive cable from the adjustable brake pedal assembly.

14. Operate the adjustable accelerator pedal to the full forward position.

15. Connect the adjustable pedal motor drive cable to the adjustable brake pedal drive.

16. Check that the brake and accelerator pedals can be fully adjusted forward and rearward.

TESTING

See Figure 368.

1. Before servicing the vehicle, refer to the precautions in the beginning of this section.

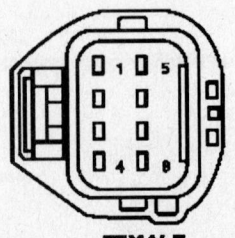

C2040 (GY)

Accelerator pedal position sensor

FEMALE

Pin	Circuit	Circuit function
1	3011 (BK/OG)	Signal return
2	3835 (YE/WH)	Accelerator pedal position sensor 1, signal
3	3014 (BK/WH)	Accelerator pedal position sensor 3, return
4	–	not used
5	3012 (WH)	Accelerator pedal position sensor 2, signal
6	3013 (GY/BK)	Accelerator pedal position sensor, 3 power
7	3010 (TN)	Voltage reference
8	3015 (WH/RD)	Accelerator pedal position sensor 3, signal

22086_FTRK_G0176

Fig. 368 Accelerator Pedal Position Sensor Connector

> ❊❊ **WARNING**
>
> **Use only a high-impedance multimeter, otherwise damage to the PCM and/or sensors can result.**

2. With the key **ON** and the engine **OFF**, check pins 6 and 7 for reference voltage (4.5–5.5 VDC).

3. Check pins 1 and 3 for ground.

4. Check the voltage at pins 2, 5, and 8 while moving the accelerator pedal. The voltage should rise and fall smoothly with pedal movement.

5. If any measurement falls outside the range given, replace the APP sensor.

BAROMETRIC PRESSURE (BARO) SENSOR

LOCATION

6.0L Diesel Engine

Under the instrument panel behind the lower steering column cover.

OPERATION

6.0L Diesel Engine

The BARO pressure sensor is a variable capacitor sensor that processes a signal indicating atmospheric pressure. This allows the PCM to compensate for altitude. The PCM uses this information to calculate injection timing and glow plug control. At higher altitudes, glow plug on time is increased to reduce start-up smoke. The BARO sensor is located behind the lower steering column opening finish panel.

REMOVAL & INSTALLATION

6.0L Diesel Engine

See Figure 369.

> ❊❊ **CAUTION**
>
> **Make sure the ignition switch is in the OFF position prior to working on the electronic engine controls.**

1. Before servicing the vehicle, refer to the precautions in the beginning of this section.

2. Turn the ignition switch to the OFF position.

> ❊❊ **CAUTION**
>
> **Use care when removing the instrument panel steering column cover or damage to the cover locating tab can occur.**

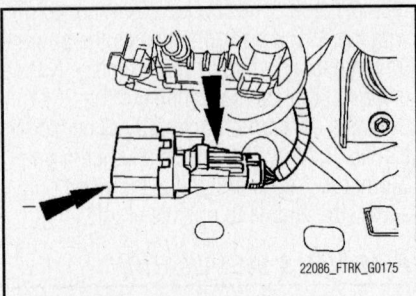

22086_FTRK_G0175

Fig. 369 Barometric Pressure sensor and harness connector

3. Remove the instrument panel steering column cover.

4. Unlock the retainers.

5. Remove the instrument panel steering column cover.

6. Disconnect the BARO sensor electrical connector.

7. Release the clip and remove the BARO sensor.

8. To install, reverse the removal procedure.

TESTING

6.0L Diesel Engine

See Figure 370.

➡ Most weather reports include a local barometric pressure that has been corrected to factor in sea level. However, the BARO PID reports the barometric pressure for the vehicle's actual altitude. Local weather conditions (high or low pressure) change the local barometric pressure by several inches of mercury.

1. Before servicing the vehicle, refer to the precautions in the beginning of this section.

2. Key ON, engine OFF.

3. Access the PCM and monitor the BARO and MAP PIDs.

4. Record the BARO and MAP values.

5. Verify that the BARO PID reading is approximately the same as the barometric pressure reading for the location, day, and altitude where the vehicle is being repaired.

6. If the BARO PID reading does not compare with the daily barometric report for the local area, replace the BARO sensor and retest.

7. Key ON, engine running.

8. Access the PCM and monitor the BARO PID.

9. Compare the BARO and MAP value with the KOEO value.

10. If the BARO PID value is not equal to the recorded value, replace the BARO sensor and retest.

CAMSHAFT POSITION (CMP) SENSOR

LOCATION

4.2L Engine

Front of the engine, near the heater outlet tube.

4.6L Engine

At the front of the left cylinder head.

5.4L and 6.8L Engines

One at the front of each cylinder head.

6.0L Diesel Engine

On the engine, under the power steering pump.

OPERATION

The CMP sensor detects the position of the camshaft. The CMP sensor identifies when piston number 1 is on its compression stroke. A signal is then sent to the PCM and used for synchronizing the sequential firing of the fuel injectors. Coil-on-plug (COP) ignition applications use the CMP signal to select the correct ignition coil to fire.

REMOVAL & INSTALLATION

4.2L Engine

See Figure 371.

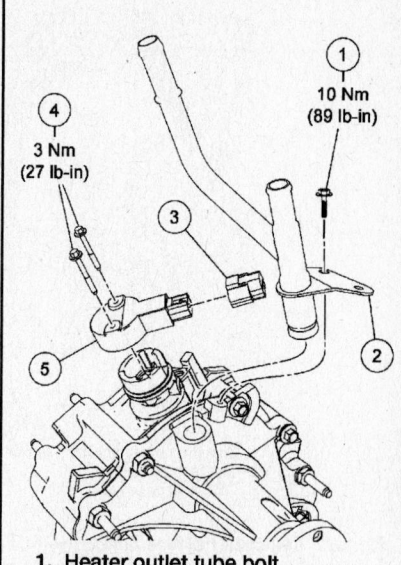

1. Heater outlet tube bolt
2. Heater outlet tube
3. Camshaft position (CMP) sensor electrical connector
4. CMP sensor bolts (2 required)
5. CMP sensor

Fig. 371 Camshaft Position Sensor—4.2L Engine

1. Before servicing the vehicle, refer to the precautions in the beginning of this section.

2. Disconnect the battery ground cable.

3. Drain the engine cooling system.

➡Clean and inspect the heater outlet tube O-ring seal. Install a new O-ring seal if necessary. Lubricate the O-ring seal with clean engine coolant.

4. Remove the bolt and position the heater outlet tube aside.

5. Disconnect the camshaft position sensor (CMP) sensor electrical connector.

6. Remove the bolts and the CMP sensor.

7. To install, reverse the removal procedure.

4.6L Engine

See Figure 372.

1. Before servicing the vehicle, refer to the precautions in the beginning of this section.

2. Disconnect the battery ground cable.

3. Disconnect the camshaft position sensor (CMP) sensor electrical connector.

4. Remove the bolt and the CMP sensor.

5. To install, reverse the removal procedure.

C2256 (BK)

Barometric Absolute Pressure (BAP) switch

FEMALE

Pin	Circuit	Circuit function
1	3011 (BK/OG)	Signal return
2	3010 (TN)	Reference voltage
3	356 (DB/LG)	Sensor signal
4	—	not used

Fig. 370 BARO sensor connector—6.0L Diesel Engine

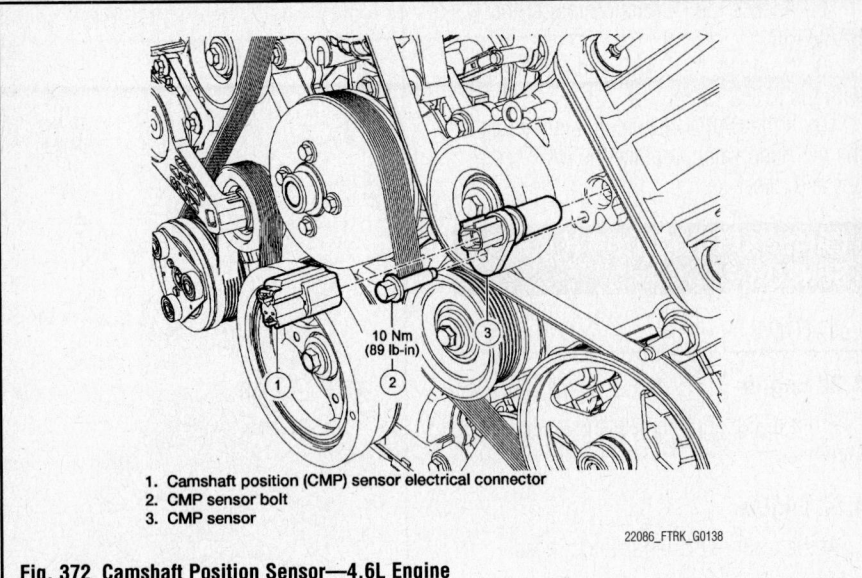

1. Camshaft position (CMP) sensor electrical connector
2. CMP sensor bolt
3. CMP sensor

10 Nm (89 lb-in)

22086_FTRK_G0138

Fig. 372 Camshaft Position Sensor—4.6L Engine

5.4L Engine

See Figures 373 and 374.

1. Before servicing the vehicle, refer to the precautions in the beginning of this section.

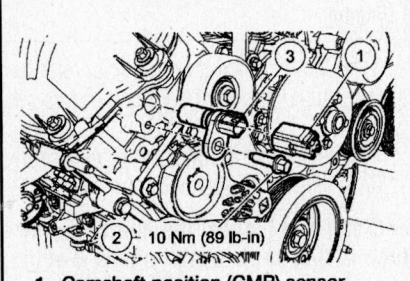

2. 10 Nm (89 lb-in)

1. Camshaft position (CMP) sensor electrical connector
2. CMP sensor bolt
3. CMP sensor

22086_FTRK_G0139

Fig. 373 Right Camshaft Position Sensor—5.4L Engine

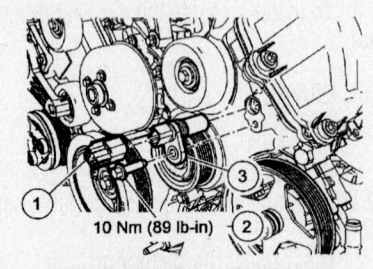

10 Nm (89 lb-in)

1. Camshaft position (CMP) sensor electrical connector
2. CMP sensor bolt
3. CMP sensor

22086_FTRK_G0140

Fig. 374 Left Camshaft Position Sensor—5.4L Engine

2. Disconnect the battery ground cable.
3. For the left camshaft position (CMP) sensor, remove the air cleaner inlet pipe and resonator.
4. Disconnect the CMP sensor electrical connector.
5. Remove the bolt and the CMP sensor.
6. To install, reverse the removal procedure.

6.8L Engine

See Figure 375.

1. Before servicing the vehicle, refer to the precautions in the beginning of this section.
2. Disconnect the battery ground cable.
3. Disconnect the camshaft position (CMP) sensor electrical connector.

4. Remove the bolt and the CMP sensor. Discard the O-ring seal.
5. Lubricate a new O-ring seal with clean engine oil prior to installation.
6. To install, reverse the removal procedure.

6.0L Diesel Engine

See Figure 376.

1. Before servicing the vehicle, refer to the precautions in the beginning of this section.
2. With the vehicle in NEUTRAL, position it on a hoist.

❊❊ CAUTION

Make sure the ignition switch is in the OFF position prior to working on the electronic engine controls.

3. Turn the ignition switch to the OFF position.
4. Rotate the accessory drive belt tensioner clockwise and remove the accessory drive belt from the power steering pump pulley.
5. Remove the 3 bolts and position the power steering pump aside.

➡ **The camshaft position (CMP) sensor is located behind the power steering pump.**

6. Disconnect the CMP sensor electrical connector.
7. Remove the bolt, the CMP sensor and discard the O-ring seal.

➡ **Apply clean engine oil to the new O-ring seal prior to installation.**

8. To install, reverse the removal procedure.

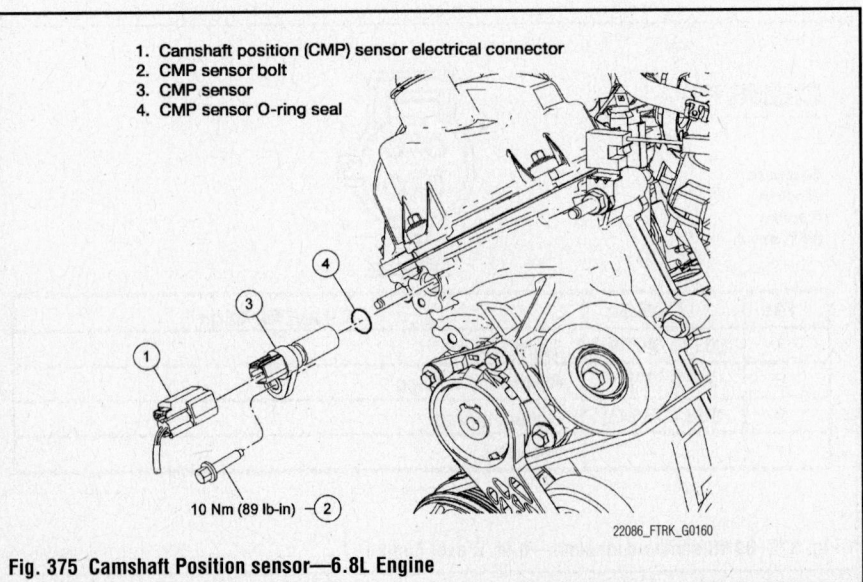

1. Camshaft position (CMP) sensor electrical connector
2. CMP sensor bolt
3. CMP sensor
4. CMP sensor O-ring seal

10 Nm (89 lb-in)

22086_FTRK_G0160

Fig. 375 Camshaft Position sensor—6.8L Engine

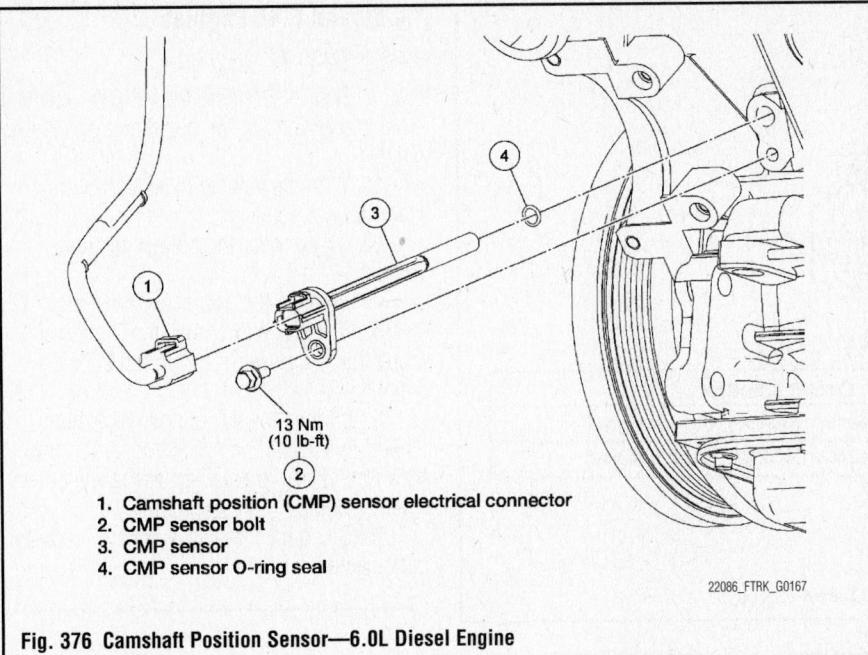

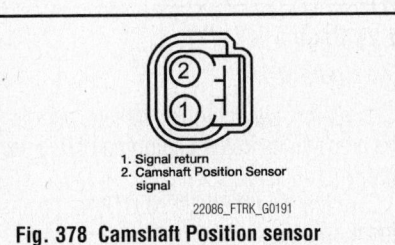

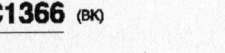

13 Nm
(10 lb-ft)

1. Camshaft position (CMP) sensor electrical connector
2. CMP sensor bolt
3. CMP sensor
4. CMP sensor O-ring seal

22086_FTRK_G0167

Fig. 376 Camshaft Position Sensor—6.0L Diesel Engine

9. Verify that the accessory drive belt is correctly seated on the pulleys.

TESTING

4.2L Engine

See Figure 377.

1. Before servicing the vehicle, refer to the precautions in the beginning of this section.

⁜ **WARNING**

Use only a high-impedance multimeter, otherwise damage to the PCM and/or sensors can result.

2. With the key **OFF**, disconnect the CMP sensor harness connector.
3. Measure the resistance between pins 2 and 3 of the CMP sensor. Specification is 300–425 ohms.

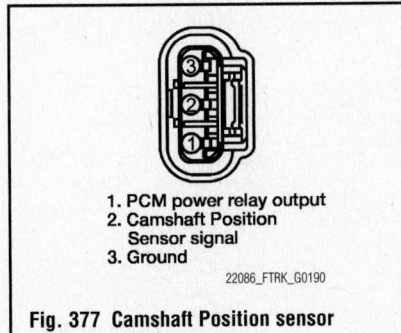

1. PCM power relay output
2. Camshaft Position Sensor signal
3. Ground

22086_FTRK_G0190

Fig. 377 Camshaft Position sensor connector—4.2L Engine

4.6L, 5.4L and 6.8L Engines

See Figures 378 and 379.

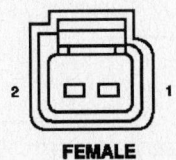

1. Signal return
2. Camshaft Position Sensor signal

22086_FTRK_G0191

Fig. 378 Camshaft Position sensor connector—4.6L Engine

1. Before servicing the vehicle, refer to the precautions in the beginning of this section.

⁜ **WARNING**

Use only a high-impedance multimeter, otherwise damage to the PCM and/or sensors can result.

2. With the key **OFF**, disconnect the CMP sensor harness connector.
3. Measure the resistance of the CMP sensor. Specification is 250–1000 ohms.

6.0L Diesel Engine

See Figure 380.

1. Before servicing the vehicle, refer to the precautions in the beginning of this section.

⁜ **WARNING**

Use only a high-impedance multimeter, otherwise damage to the PCM and/or sensors can result.

2. With the key **OFF**, disconnect the CMP sensor harness connector.
3. Measure the resistance of the CMP sensor. Specification is 800–1000 ohms.

C1366 (BK)

Camshaft
position sensor
RH bank

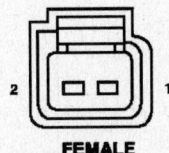

FEMALE

Pin	Circuit	Circuit function
1	359 (GY/RD)	Signal return
2	282 (DB/OG)	Camshaft position sensor 1 (6B288) control

C1367 (BK)

Camshaft
position sensor
LH bank

FEMALE

Pin	Circuit	Circuit function
1	359 (GY/RD)	Signal return
2	365 (OG)	Camshaft position sensor 2 (6B288) control

22086_FTRK_G0192

Fig. 379 Camshaft Position sensor connector—5.4L and 6.8L Engines

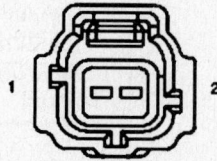

C1275 (BK)

Camshaft position sensor

FEMALE

Pin	Circuit	Circuit function
1	50 (RD)	Camshaft position sensor (6B288), Sensor signal +
2	49 (OG)	Camshaft position sensor (6B288), Sensor signal −

22086_FTRK_G0178

Fig. 380 Camshaft Position sensor connector—6.0L Diesel Engine

CRANKSHAFT POSITION (CKP) SENSOR

LOCATION

F-150 and Mark LT

Front of the engine, above the crankshaft damper.

F-250 and F-350

Front of the engine, passenger side of the crankshaft pulley.

OPERATION

The CKP sensor is a magnetic transducer mounted on the engine block adjacent to a pulse wheel located on the crankshaft. By monitoring the crankshaft mounted pulse wheel, the CKP is the primary sensor for ignition information to the PCM. The pulse wheel has a total of 35 teeth spaced 10 degrees apart with one empty space for a missing tooth. The 6.8L 10-cylinder pulse wheel has 39 teeth spaced 9 degrees apart and one 9 degree empty space for a missing tooth. By monitoring the pulse wheel, the CKP sensor signal indicates crankshaft position and speed information to the PCM. By monitoring the missing tooth, the CKP sensor is also able to identify piston travel in order to synchronize the ignition system and provide a way of tracking the angular position of the crankshaft relative to a fixed reference for the CKP sensor configuration. The PCM also uses the CKP signal to determine if a misfire has occurred by measuring rapid decelerations between teeth.

REMOVAL & INSTALLATION

4.2L Engine

See Figure 381.

1. Before servicing the vehicle, refer to the precautions in the beginning of this section.
2. With the vehicle in NEUTRAL, position it on a hoist.
3. Disconnect the battery ground cable.
4. Disconnect the crankshaft position (CKP) sensor electrical connector.
5. Remove the bolts and the CKP sensor.
6. To install, reverse the removal procedure.

4.6L and 5.4L Engines

See Figure 382.

1. Before servicing the vehicle, refer to the precautions in the beginning of this section.
2. With the vehicle in NEUTRAL, position it on a hoist.
3. Disconnect the battery ground cable.
4. Remove the accessory drive belt.
5. If equipped, remove the 2 bolts and position the power steering fluid cooler aside.
6. Loosen the A/C compressor bolts enough to slide the A/C compressor down 25 mm (1 in), to allow access to the crankshaft position (CKP) sensor.
7. Disconnect the CKP sensor electrical connector.

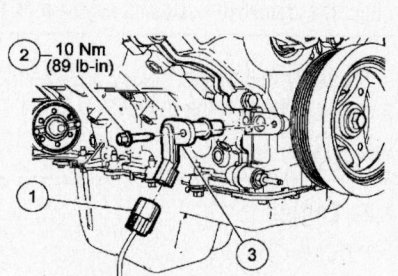

1. Crankshaft position (CKP) sensor electrical connector
2. CKP sensor bolt
3. CKP sensor

22086_FTRK_G0142

Fig. 382 Crankshaft Position Sensor—4.6L and 5.4L Engines

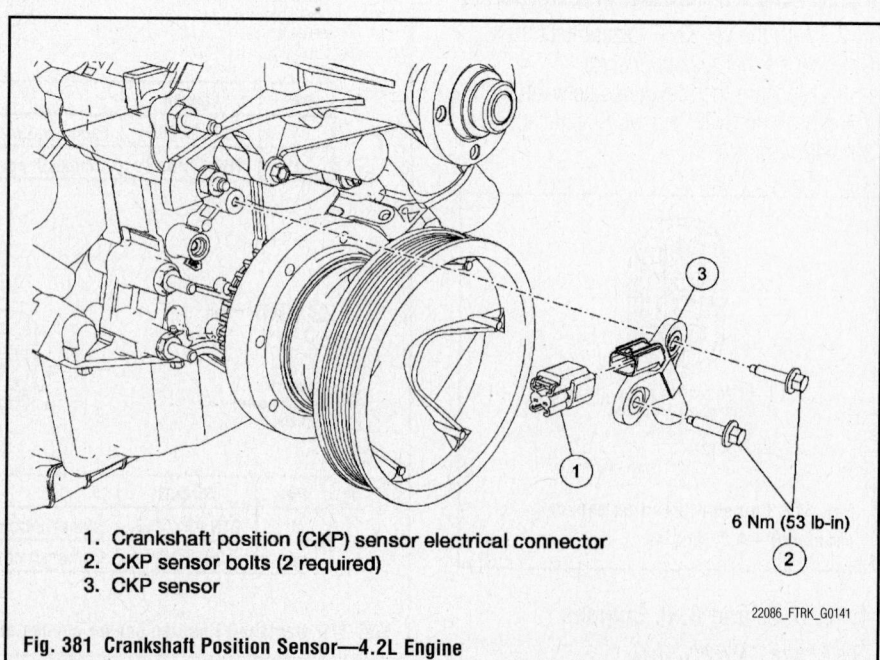

1. Crankshaft position (CKP) sensor electrical connector
2. CKP sensor bolts (2 required)
3. CKP sensor

6 Nm (53 lb-in)

22086_FTRK_G0141

Fig. 381 Crankshaft Position Sensor—4.2L Engine

8. Remove the bolt and the CKP sensor.

9. To install, reverse the removal procedure.

6.8L Engine

See Figure 383.

1. Before servicing the vehicle, refer to the precautions in the beginning of this section.

2. With the vehicle in NEUTRAL, position it on a hoist.

3. Disconnect the battery ground cable.

4. Remove the accessory drive belt.

5. Disconnect the A/C compressor electrical connector.

6. Remove the 3 bolts and position the A/C compressor aside.

7. Disconnect the crankshaft position (CKP) sensor electrical connector.

8. Remove the bolt and the CKP sensor. Discard the O-ring seal.

9. Lubricate the new O-ring seal with clean engine oil prior to installation.

10. To install, reverse the removal procedure.

6.0L Diesel Engine

See Figure 384.

1. Before servicing the vehicle, refer to the precautions in the beginning of this section.

2. With the vehicle in NEUTRAL, position it on a hoist.

✳✳ CAUTION

Make sure the ignition switch is in the OFF position prior to working on the electronic engine controls.

3. Turn the ignition switch to the OFF position.

➡ **The crankshaft position (CKP) sensor is located underneath the air conditioning compressor.**

4. Remove the nut and position the positive battery cable and support bracket aside.

5. Remove the stud bolt and position the battery negative cable aside.

6. Disconnect the CKP sensor electrical connector.

7. Remove the bolt, the CKP sensor and discard the O-ring seal.

➡ **Apply clean engine oil to the O-ring seal prior to installation.**

8. To install, reverse the removal procedure.

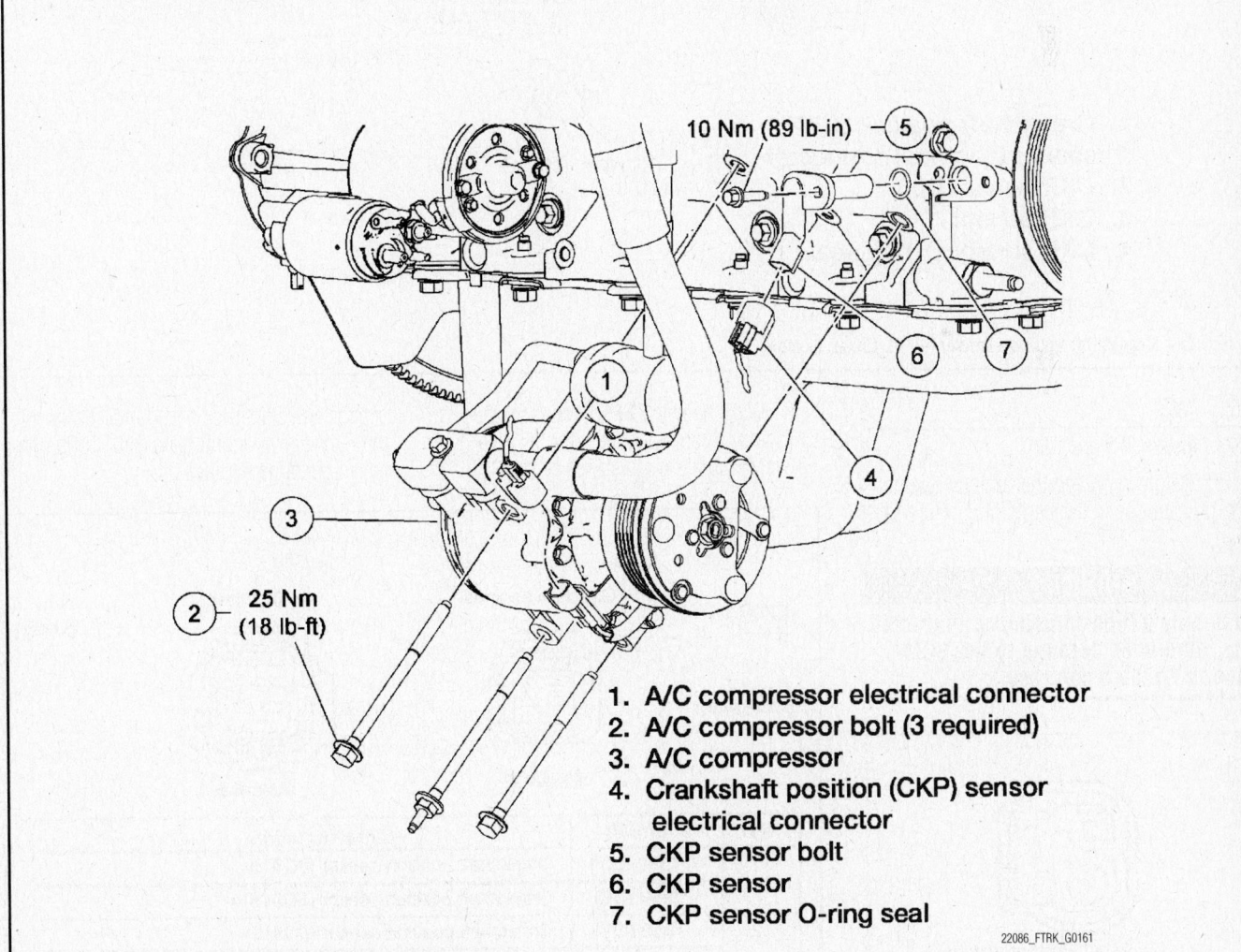

10 Nm (89 lb-in)

25 Nm (18 lb-ft)

1. A/C compressor electrical connector
2. A/C compressor bolt (3 required)
3. A/C compressor
4. Crankshaft position (CKP) sensor electrical connector
5. CKP sensor bolt
6. CKP sensor
7. CKP sensor O-ring seal

22086_FTRK_G0161

Fig. 383 Crankshaft Position sensor—6.8L Engine

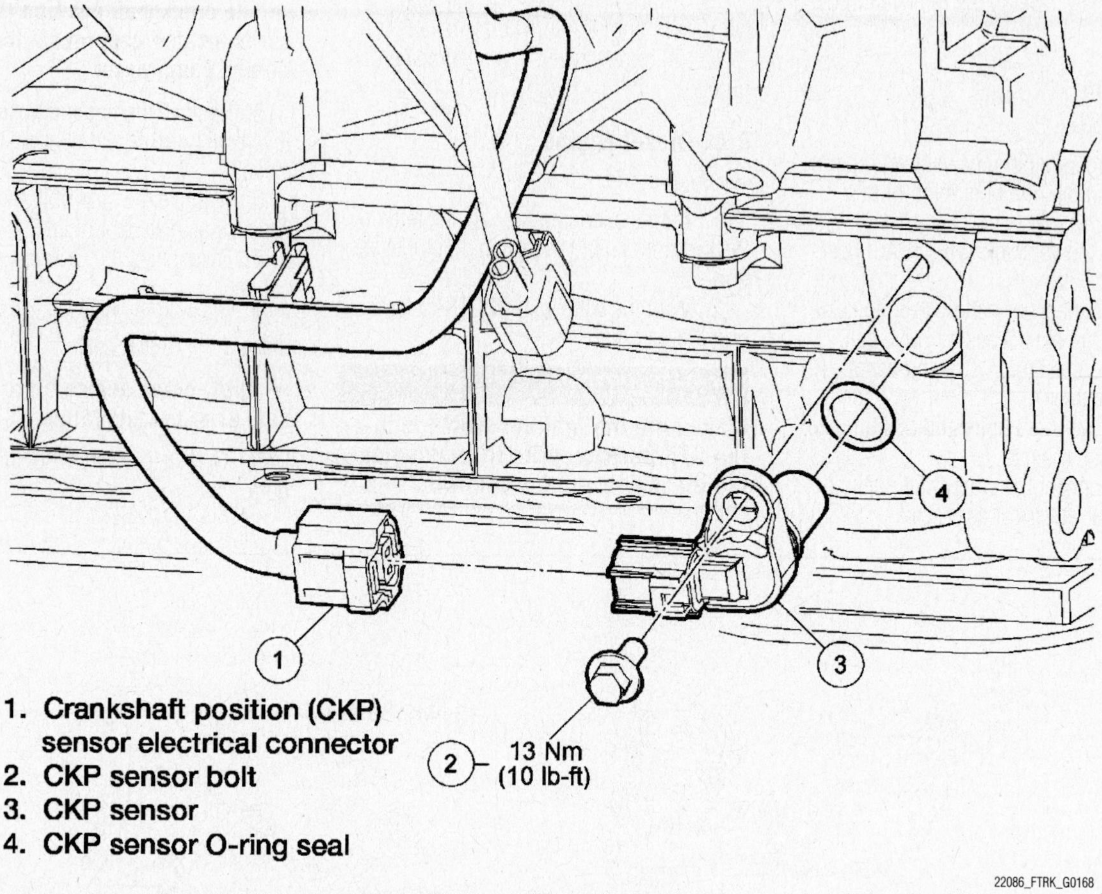

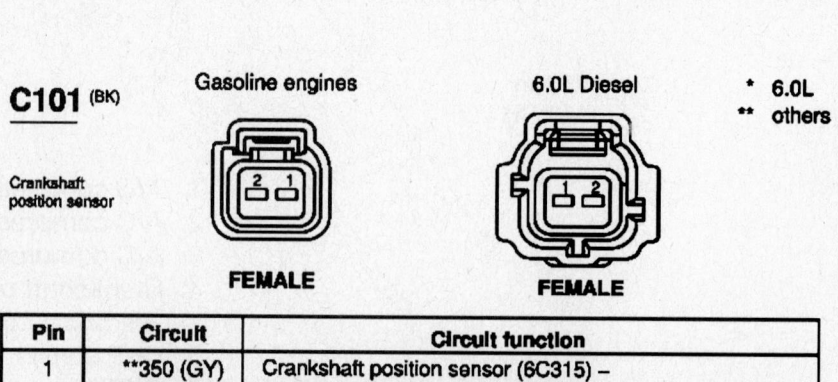

1. **Crankshaft position (CKP) sensor electrical connector**
2. **CKP sensor bolt**
3. **CKP sensor**
4. **CKP sensor O-ring seal**

13 Nm (10 lb-ft)

22086_FTRK_G0168

Fig. 384 Crankshaft Position sensor—6.0L Diesel Engine

TESTING

See Figures 385 and 386.

1. Before servicing the vehicle, refer to the precautions in the beginning of this section.

✳✳ WARNING

Use only a high-impedance multimeter, otherwise damage to the PCM and/or sensors can result.

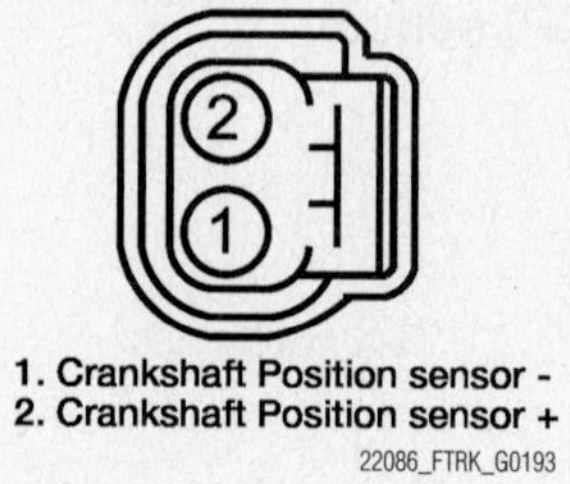

1. Crankshaft Position sensor -
2. Crankshaft Position sensor +

22086_FTRK_G0193

Fig. 385 Crankshaft Position sensor connector—F-150 and Mark LT

2. With the key **OFF**, disconnect the CKP sensor harness connector.

3. Measure the resistance of the CKP sensor. Specification is 300–400 ohms for the 6.0L diesel engine, and 250–1000 ohms for all gasoline engines.

C101 (BK)

Crankshaft position sensor

Gasoline engines — FEMALE

6.0L Diesel — FEMALE

* 6.0L
** others

Pin	Circuit	Circuit function
1	**350 (GY)	Crankshaft position sensor (6C315) −
	*349 (DB)	Crankshaft position sensor (6C315) +
2	*350 (GY)	Crankshaft position sensor (6C315) −
	**349 (DB)	Crankshaft position sensor (6C315) +

22086_FTRK_G0179

Fig. 386 Crankshaft Position sensor connector—F-250 and F-350

CYLINDER HEAD TEMPERATURE SENSOR (CHT)

LOCATION

F-150 and Mark LT

At the rear of the left cylinder head.

F-250 and F-350

Under the intake manifold.

OPERATION

The CHT sensor is a thermistor device in which resistance changes with the temperature. The electrical resistance of a thermistor decreases as temperature increases, and the resistance increases as the temperature decreases. The varying resistance affects the voltage drop across the sensor terminals and provides electrical signals to the PCM corresponding to temperature.

The CHT sensor is installed in the cylinder head and measures the metal temperature. The CHT sensor can provide complete engine temperature information and can be used to infer coolant temperature. If the CHT sensor conveys an overheating condition to the PCM, the PCM initiates a fail-safe cooling strategy based on information from the CHT sensor. A cooling system concern such as low coolant or coolant loss could cause an overheating condition. As a result, damage to major engine components could occur. Using both the CHT sensor and fail-safe cooling strategy, the PCM prevents damage by allowing air cooling of the engine and limp home capability.

REMOVAL & INSTALLATION

4.2L Engine

See Figure 387.

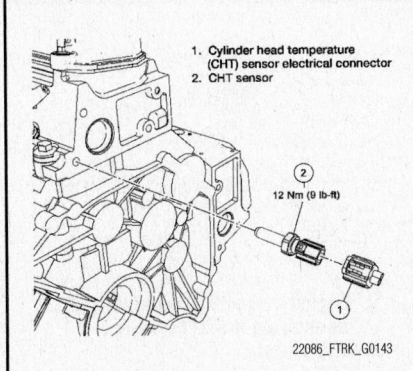

1. Cylinder head temperature (CHT) sensor electrical connector
2. CHT sensor

12 Nm (9 lb-ft)

22086_FTRK_G0143

Fig. 387 Cylinder Head Temperature Sensor—4.2L Engine

1. Before servicing the vehicle, refer to the precautions in the beginning of this section.
2. With the vehicle in NEUTRAL, position it on a hoist.
3. Disconnect the battery ground cable.
4. Disconnect the cylinder head temperature (CHT) sensor electrical connector.
5. Remove the CHT sensor.
6. To install, reverse the removal procedure.

4.6L Engine

See Figure 388.

1. Before servicing the vehicle, refer to the precautions in the beginning of this section.
2. Remove the generator.
3. Disconnect the cylinder head temperature (CHT) sensor electrical connector.
4. Remove the CHT sensor.
5. To install, reverse the removal procedure.

➡Apply anti-seize to the threads of the CHT sensor.

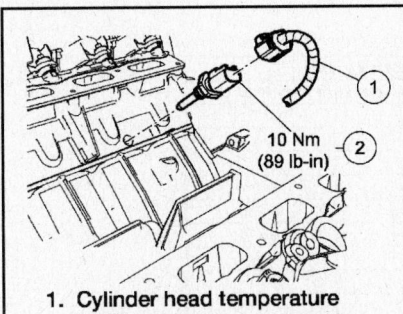

1. Cylinder head temperature (CHT) sensor jumper harness
2. CHT sensor

10 Nm (89 lb-in)

22086_FTRK_G0144

Fig. 388 Cylinder Head Temperature Sensor—4.6L Engine

5.4L and 6.8L Engines

See Figure 389.

1. Before servicing the vehicle, refer to the precautions in the beginning of this section.
2. Remove the intake manifold.
3. Disconnect the cylinder head temperature (CHT) sensor electrical connector.
4. Remove the CHT.
5. To install, reverse the removal procedure.

➡Apply anti-seize to the threads of the CHT sensor.

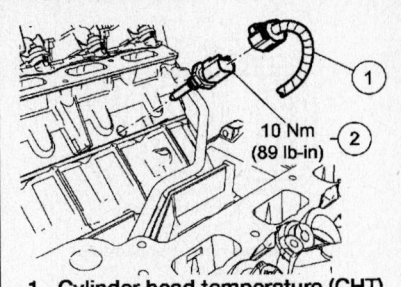

1. Cylinder head temperature (CHT) sensor jumper harness
2. CHT sensor

10 Nm (89 lb-in)

22086_FTRK_G0145

Fig. 389 Cylinder Head Temperature Sensor—5.4L and 6.8L Engines

TESTING

See Figures 390 through 392.

➡The CHT sensor is used to determine the engine coolant temperature. To cover the entire temperature range of both the CHT and ECT sensors, the PCM has a dual switching resistor circuit on the CHT input. A graph showing the temperature switching from the COLD END line to the HOT END line, with increasing temperature and back with decreasing temperature is included. Note the temperature to voltage overlap zone. Within this zone it is possible to have either a COLD END or HOT END voltage at the same temperature. For example, at 90°C (194°F) the voltage could read either 0.60 volt or 3.71 volts. Refer to the table for the temperature to voltage expected values.

1. Before servicing the vehicle, refer to the precautions in the beginning of this section.

✳✳ WARNING

Use only a high-impedance multimeter, otherwise damage to the PCM and/or sensors can result.

2. With the key **OFF**, disconnect the CHT sensor harness connector and measure the resistance of the sensor. Compare the resistance and the temperature with the illustration.
3. Connect the CHT sensor harness and backprobe the connection.
4. With the key **ON**, compare the voltage measurement and the temperature with the illustration.
5. If the measurements are not as listed, replace the CHT sensor.

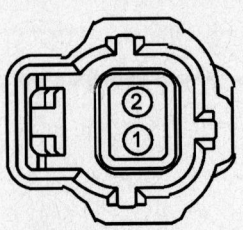

1. Cylinder Head Temperature
   sensor signal
2. Signal return

22086_FTRK_G0195

Fig. 390 Cylinder Head Temperature Sensor Connector—F-150 and Mark LT

C107 (WH)

Cylinder head
temperature
sensor

FEMALE

Pin	Circuit	Circuit function
1	1102 (YE/LG)	Cylinder head temperature sensor signal
2	359 (GY/RD)	Signal return

22086_FTRK_G0196

Fig. 391 Cylinder Head Temperature Sensor Connector—F-250 and F-350

CYLINDER HEAD TEMPERATURE SENSOR EXPECTED VALUES

Temperature		CHT Sensor Values		
°C	°F	COLD END (volts)	HOT END (volts)	Resistance (K ohms)
-40	-40	4.89	-	965.808
-30	-22	4.81	-	513.019
-20	-4	4.67	-	283.664
-10	14	4.45	-	162.584
0	32	4.14	-	96.255
10	50	3.73	-	59.175
20	68	3.26	-	37.387
30	86	2.74	-	24.215
40	104	2.23	-	16.043
50	122	1.76	-	10.85
60	140	1.36	-	7.487
70	158	1.04	-	5.268
80	176	0.79	3.99	3.775
85	185	0.69	3.86	3.215
90	194	0.60	3.71	2.75
95	203	0.53	3.56	2.361
100	212	0.46	3.41	2.034
110	230	-	3.07	1.523
120	248	-	2.74	1.155
130	266	-	2.41	0.8866
140	284	-	2.10	0.6891
150	302	-	1.81	0.5417
160	320	-	1.55	0.4301
170	338	-	1.33	0.3449
180	356	-	1.13	0.2791
190	374	-	0.96	0.2278
200	392	-	0.82	0.1875
210	410	-	0.70	0.155
220	428	-	0.60	0.130
230	446	-	0.51	0.109
240	464	-	0.44	0.092
250	482	-	0.35	0.078
260	500	-	0.33	0.067

22086_FTRK_G0194

Fig. 392 CHT Temperature, Resistance and Voltage Table

ENGINE COOLANT TEMPERATURE (ECT) SENSOR

LOCATION

Front and top of engine, near thermostat housing.

OPERATION

The ECT sensor is a thermistor device in which resistance changes with temperature. The electrical resistance of a thermistor decreases as the temperature increases, and resistance increases as the temperature decreases. The varying resistance affects the voltage drop across the sensor terminals and provides electrical signals to the PCM corresponding to temperature.

If the PCM receives a high engine temperature signal from the ECT, it adjusts fueling rates to protect the engine from damage due to overheating.

REMOVAL & INSTALLATION

6.0L Diesel Engine

See Figure 393.

> ※※ **CAUTION**
>
> **Make sure the ignition switch is in the OFF position prior to working on the electronic engine controls.**

1. Before servicing the vehicle, refer to the precautions in the beginning of this section.
2. Turn the ignition switch to the OFF position.
3. Drain the engine cooling system.
4. Disconnect the cooling fan electrical connector.
5. Disconnect the engine coolant temperature (ECT) electrical connector.
6. Remove the ECT sensor and discard the O-ring seal.

To install:

➡ **Apply clean engine oil to the new O-ring seal prior to installation.**

7. Using a new O-ring seal, install the ECT sensor.
8. Tighten to 18 Nm (13 lb-ft).
9. Connect the ECT sensor electrical connector.
10. Connect the cooling fan electrical connector.
11. Fill and bleed the engine cooling system.

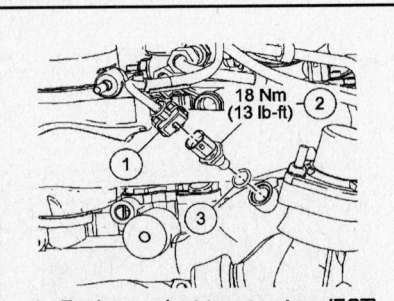

1. Engine coolant temperature (ECT) sensor electrical connector
2. ECT sensor
3. ECT sensor O-ring seal

22086_FTRK_G0169

Fig. 393 Engine Coolant Temperature sensor

TESTING

6.0L Diesel Engine

See Figures 394 and 395.

1. Before servicing the vehicle, refer to the precautions in the beginning of this section.

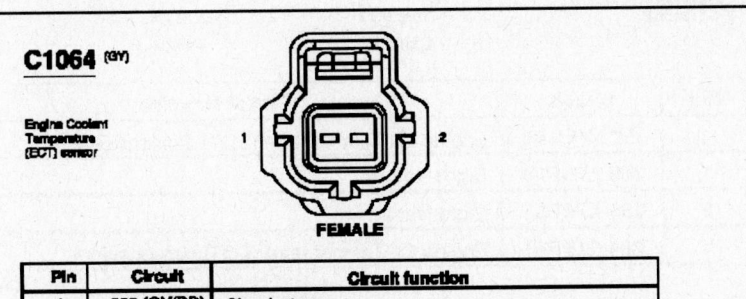

C1064 (GY)

Engine Coolant
Temperature
(ECT) sensor

1   2

FEMALE

Pin	Circuit	Circuit function
1	359 (GY/RD)	Signal return
2	3076 (YE/WH)	Reference voltage

22086_FTRK_G0180

Fig. 394 Engine Coolant Temperature sensor connector—6.0L Diesel Engine

**TEMPERATURE VS.
RESISTANCE VALUES
(APPROXIMATE)**

Degrees C	Degrees F	Ohms
100	212	2,080
90	194	2,803
80	176	3,836
70	158	5,337
60	140	7,556
50	122	10,908
45	113	13,216
40	104	16,092
35	95	19,696
30	86	24,329
25	77	30,000
20	68	37,352
15	59	46,797
10	50	59,016
5	41	79,940
0	32	95,851
-5	23	124,485
-10	14	160,313
-15	5	209,816
-20	-4	276,959
-30	-22	496,051
-40	-40	925,021

22086_FTRK_G0197

Fig. 395 Engine Coolant Temperature Sensor resistance and temperature table—6.0L Diesel Engine

> **⁂ WARNING**
>
> **Use only a high-impedance multimeter, otherwise damage to the PCM and/or sensors can result.**

2. With the key **OFF**, disconnect the ECT sensor harness connector and measure the resistance of the sensor. Compare the resistance and the temperature with the illustration.

3. If the measurements are not as listed, replace the ECT sensor.

ENGINE OIL TEMPERATURE (EOT) SENSOR

LOCATION

Right side of engine, near the starter.

OPERATION

The EOT sensor is a thermistor device in which resistance changes with temperature. The electrical resistance of a thermistor decreases as the temperature increases and the resistance increases as the temperature decreases. The varying resistance changes the voltage drop across the sensor terminals and provides electrical signals to the PCM corresponding to temperature.

Thermistor-type sensors are considered passive sensors. A passive sensor is connected to a voltage divider network so that varying the resistance of the passive sensor causes a variation in total current flow. Voltage that is dropped across a fixed resistor in a series with the sensor resistor determines the voltage signal at the PCM. This voltage signal is equal to the reference voltage minus the voltage drop across the fixed resistor.

REMOVAL & INSTALLATION

6.8L Engine

See Figure 396.

1. Before servicing the vehicle, refer to the precautions in the beginning of this section.

2. With the vehicle in NEUTRAL, position it on a hoist.

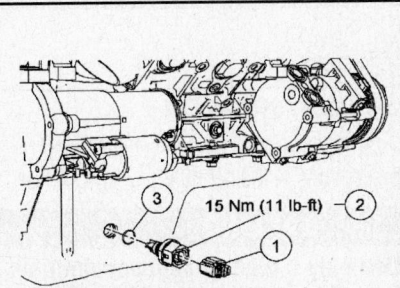

15 Nm (11 lb-ft)

1. Engine oil temperature (EOT) sensor electrical connector
2. EOT sensor
3. EOT sensor O-ring seal

22086_FTRK_G0172

Fig. 396 Engine Oil Temperature sensor—6.8L Engine

3. Disconnect the battery ground cable.

4. Drain the engine oil.

5. Disconnect the engine oil temperature (EOT) sensor electrical connector.

6. Remove the EOT sensor. Discard the O-ring seal.

7. Install a new O-ring seal. Lubricate the new O-ring seal with clean engine oil prior to installation.

8. To install, reverse the removal procedure.

6.0L Diesel Engine

See Figure 397.

✳✳ CAUTION

Make sure the ignition switch is in the OFF position prior to working on the electronic engine controls.

1. Before servicing the vehicle, refer to the precautions in the beginning of this section.

2. Turn the ignition switch to the OFF position.

3. Disconnect the engine oil temperature (EOT) sensor.

4. Remove the EOT sensor.

5. To install, reverse the removal procedure. Tighten the EOT sensor to 18 Nm (13 lb-ft).

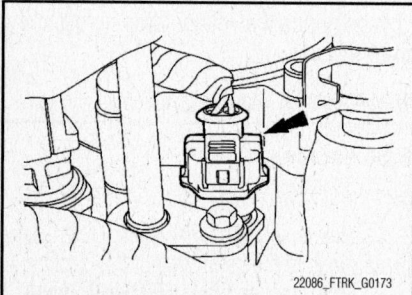

Fig. 397 Engine Oil Temperature sensor— 6.0L Diesel Engine

TESTING

See Figures 398 and 399.

1. Before servicing the vehicle, refer to the precautions in the beginning of this section.

✳✳ WARNING

Use only a high-impedance multimeter, otherwise damage to the PCM and/or sensors can result.

2. With the key **OFF**, disconnect the EOT sensor harness connector and measure the resistance of the sensor. Compare the resistance and the temperature with the illustration.

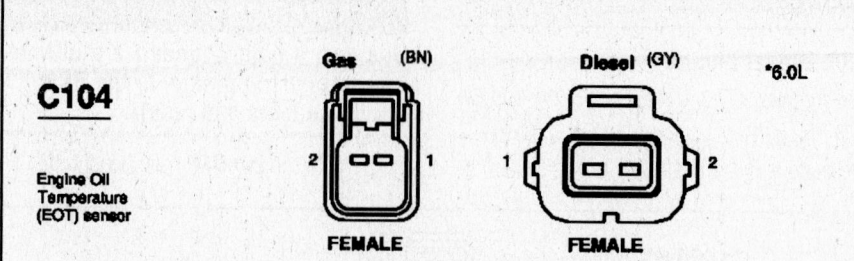

C104

Engine Oil Temperature (EOT) sensor

Gas (BN) — FEMALE

Diesel (GY) *6.0L — FEMALE

Pin	Circuit	Circuit function
1	263 (YE/LB)	Engine Oil Temperature (EOT) sensor, signal
*1	359 (GY/RD)	Signal return
2	359 (GY/RD)	Signal return
*2	354 (LG/RD)	Engine Oil Temperature (EOT) sensor, signal

22086_FTRK_G0181

Fig. 398 Engine Oil Temperature sensor connector—All Engines

TEMPERATURE VS. RESISTANCE VALUES (APPROXIMATE)

°C	°F	Ohms
100	212	2,080
90	194	2,083
90	176	2,836
70	158	5,337
60	140	7,556
50	122	10,908
45	113	13,216
40	104	16,092
35	95	19,696
30	86	24,329
25	77	30,000
20	68	37,352
15	59	46,797
10	50	59,016
5	41	79,940
0	32	95,851
-5	23	124,485
-10	14	160,313
-15	5	209,816
-20	-4	276,959
-30	-22	496,051
-40	-40	925,021

22086_FTRK_G0198

Fig. 399 Engine Oil Temperature Sensor resistance and temperature table—6.0L Diesel Engine

3. If the measurements are not as listed, replace the EOT sensor.

EXHAUST BACKPRESSURE SENSOR

LOCATION

Front of the engine, left side.

OPERATION

Measures analog output indicating exhaust back pressure. PCM uses information to control back pressure under cold conditions.

REMOVAL & INSTALLATION

6.0L Diesel Engine

See Figure 400.

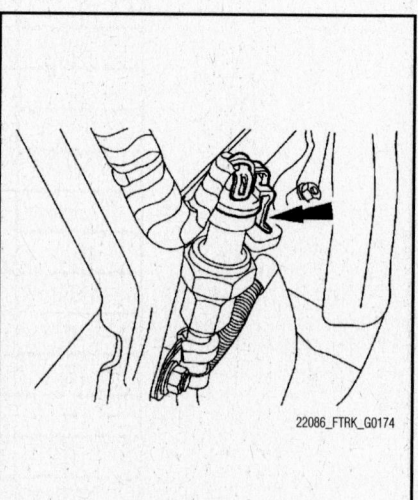

22086_FTRK_G0174

Fig. 400 Exhaust Backpressure sensor— 6.0L Diesel Engine

❋❋ CAUTION

Make sure the ignition switch is in the OFF position prior to working on the electronic engine controls.

1. Before servicing the vehicle, refer to the precautions in the beginning of this section.
2. Turn the ignition switch to the OFF position.
3. Disconnect the exhaust pressure (EP) sensor electrical connector.

➡ **Support the EP sensor tube flange nut when removing the EP sensor.**

4. Remove the EP sensor.
5. To install, reverse the removal procedure. Tighten to 20 Nm (15 lb-ft).

TESTING

6.0L Diesel Engine

See Figures 401 and 402.

1. Before servicing the vehicle, refer to the precautions in the beginning of this section.
2. With the key **OFF**, disconnect the EP sensor.
3. Install the ICP/EBC Adapter Cable D94T-50-A or equivalent between the EP sensor and the vehicle harness.
4. Start the engine and measure the voltage between the EP signal circuit and ground on the ICP/EBC Adapter Cable D94T-50-A.
5. Accelerate the engine to wide open throttle (WOT) several times. The voltage should be above 1.35 VDC during acceleration.

kPa	psi	EP (volts)
43.8	6.4	0.05
70.5	10.2	0.45
101.5	14.7	0.90
325.5	47.2	4.14
365.4	53	4.75

22086_FTRK_G0199

Fig. 402 Exhaust Pressure Sensor pressure and voltage table

HEATED OXYGEN (HO2S) SENSOR

LOCATION

See Figures 403 and 404.

C1271 (BK)

Exhaust Back Pressure (EBP) sensor

FEMALE

Pin	Circuit	Circuit function
1	359 (GY/RD)	Signal return
2	351 (BN/WH)	Reference voltage
3	553 (VT/LB)	Pressure sense

22086_FTRK_G0182

Fig. 401 Exhaust Backpressure sensor connector—6.0L Diesel Engine

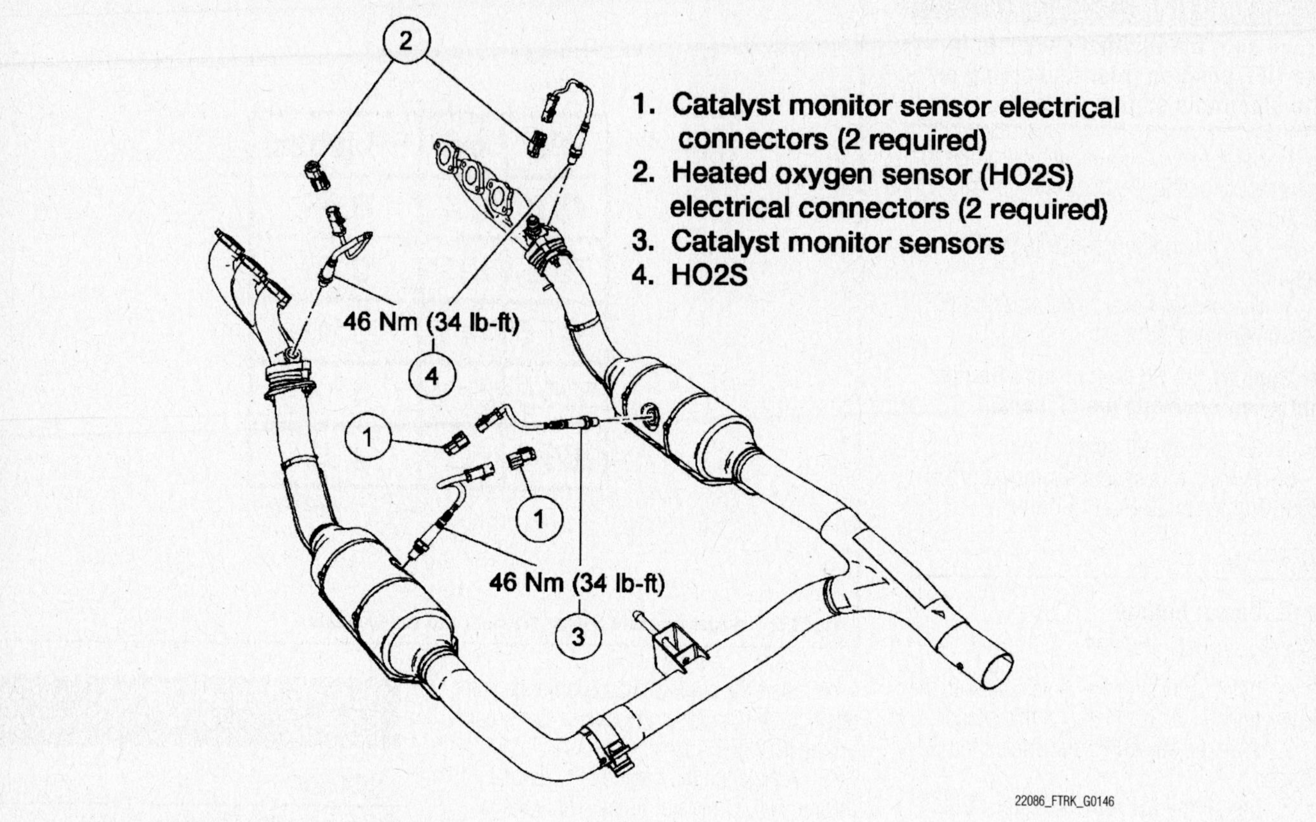

1. **Catalyst monitor sensor electrical connectors (2 required)**
2. **Heated oxygen sensor (HO2S) electrical connectors (2 required)**
3. **Catalyst monitor sensors**
4. **HO2S**

46 Nm (34 lb-ft)

46 Nm (34 lb-ft)

22086_FTRK_G0146

Fig. 403 Heated Oxygen Sensors—4.2L Engine

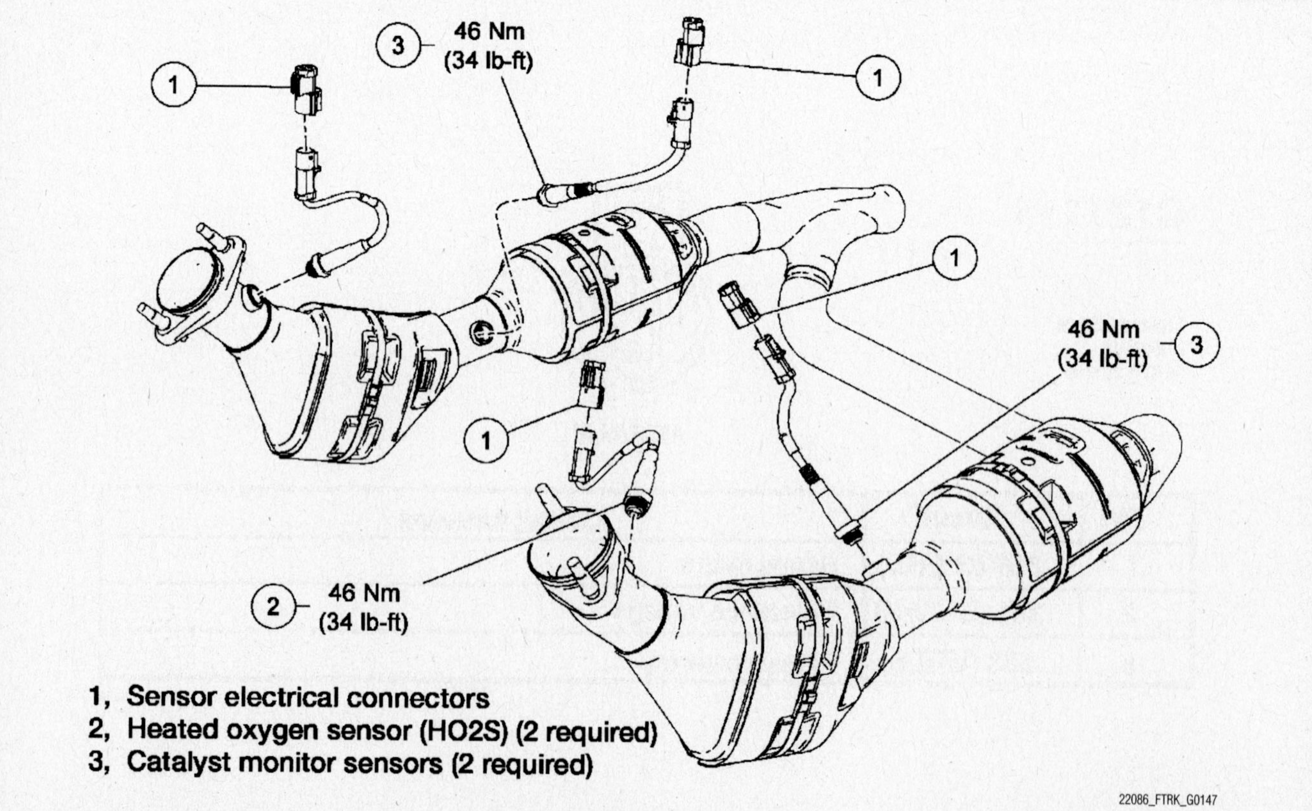

3 — 46 Nm (34 lb-ft)

46 Nm (34 lb-ft)

2 — 46 Nm (34 lb-ft)

1, **Sensor electrical connectors**
2, **Heated oxygen sensor (HO2S) (2 required)**
3, **Catalyst monitor sensors (2 required)**

22086_FTRK_G0147

Fig. 404 Heated Oxygen Sensors—5.4L Engine shown, 4.6L and 6.8L Engines similar

OPERATION

The HO2S detects the presence of oxygen in the exhaust and produces a variable voltage according to the amount of oxygen detected. A high concentration of oxygen (lean air/fuel ratio) in the exhaust produces a voltage signal less than 0.4 volt. A low concentration of oxygen (rich air/fuel ratio) produces a voltage signal greater than 0.6 volt. The HO2S provides feedback to the PCM indicating air/fuel ratio in order to achieve a near stoichiometric air/fuel ratio of 14.7:1 during closed loop engine operation. The HO2S generates a voltage between 0.0 and 1.1 volts.

Embedded with the sensing element is the HO2S heater. The heating element heats the sensor to a temperature of 800°C (1,472°F). At approximately 300°C (572°F) the engine can enter closed loop operation. The VPWR circuit supplies voltage to the heater. The PCM turns the heater on by providing the ground when the correct conditions occur. The heater allows the engine to enter closed loop operation sooner. The use of this heater requires the HO2S heater control to be duty cycled, to prevent damage to the heater.

REMOVAL & INSTALLATION

4.2L Engine

See Figure 405.

1. Before servicing the vehicle, refer to the precautions in the beginning of this section.
2. With the vehicle in NEUTRAL, position it on a hoist.
3. Disconnect the battery ground cable.
4. If necessary, detach the electrical connector from the RH inner fender splash shield.
5. If necessary, remove the 6 screws, the pushpin and the RH inner fender splash shield.
6. Disconnect the heated oxygen sensor (HO2S) electrical connector.

➡ **If necessary, lubricate the HO2S with lock lubricant to assist in removal.**

7. Remove the HO2S.
8. To install, reverse the removal procedure.

➡**Apply anti-seize to the threads of the HO2S.**

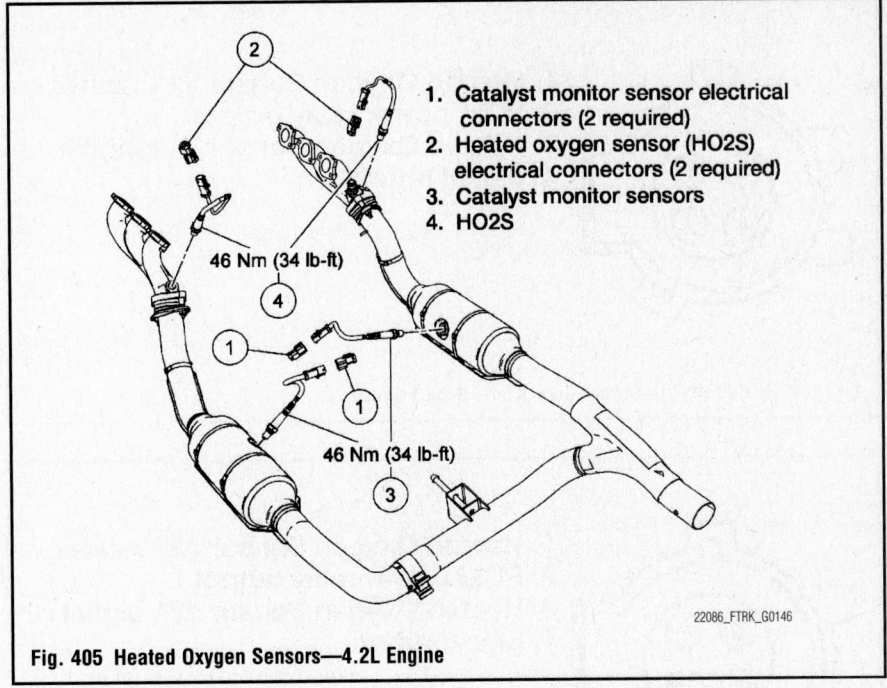

1. Catalyst monitor sensor electrical connectors (2 required)
2. Heated oxygen sensor (HO2S) electrical connectors (2 required)
3. Catalyst monitor sensors
4. HO2S

46 Nm (34 lb-ft)

46 Nm (34 lb-ft)

22086_FTRK_G0146

Fig. 405 Heated Oxygen Sensors—4.2L Engine

4.6L, 5.4L and 6.8L Engines

See Figure 406.

1. Before servicing the vehicle, refer to the precautions in the beginning of this section.
2. With the vehicle in NEUTRAL, position it on a hoist.
3. Disconnect the battery ground cable.

➡ **If necessary, lubricate the HO2S with penetrating and lock lubricant to assist in removal**

4. Remove the HO2S.
5. To install, reverse the removal procedure.

➡**Apply anti-seize to the threads of the HO2S.**

TESTING

F-150 and Mark LT

See Figures 407 through 410.

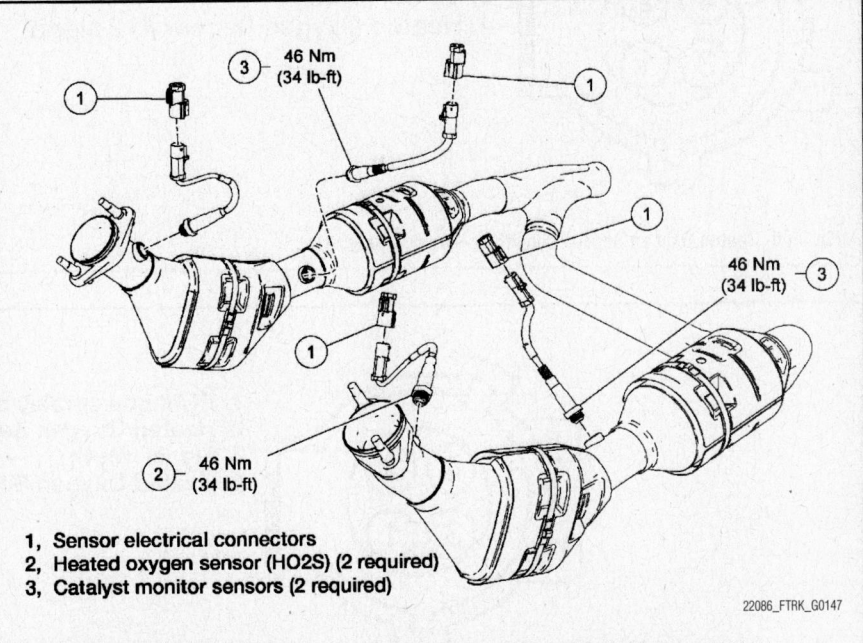

46 Nm (34 lb-ft)

46 Nm (34 lb-ft)

46 Nm (34 lb-ft)

1. Sensor electrical connectors
2. Heated oxygen sensor (HO2S) (2 required)
3. Catalyst monitor sensors (2 required)

22086_FTRK_G0147

Fig. 406 Heated Oxygen Sensors—5.4L Engine shown, 4.6L and 6.8L Engines similar

1. Heated Oxygen Sensor #11 heater -
2. PCM power relay output
3. Heated Oxygen Sensor #11 signal
4. Signal return

22086_FTRK_G0200

Fig. 407 Heated Oxygen Sensor Connector—Bank 1 Sensor 1

1. Heated Oxygen Sensor #21 heater -
2. PCM power relay output
3. Heated Oxygen Sensor #21 signal
4. Signal return

22086_FTRK_G0201

Fig. 408 Heated Oxygen Sensor Connector—Bank 2 Sensor 1

1. PCM power relay output
2. Heated Oxygen Sensor #12 heater
3. Signal return
4. Heated Oxygen Sensor #12 signal

22086_FTRK_G0202

Fig. 409 Heated Oxygen Sensor Connector—Bank 1 Sensor 2

1. PCM power relay output
2. Heated Oxygen Sensor #12 heater
3. Signal return
4. Heated Oxygen Sensor #12 signal

22086_FTRK_G0203

Fig. 410 Heated Oxygen Sensor Connector—Bank 2 Sensor 2

1. Before servicing the vehicle, refer to the precautions in the beginning of this section.

✳✳ WARNING

Use only a high-impedance multimeter, otherwise damage to the PCM and/or sensors can result.

✳✳ WARNING

Do not measure resistance between pins 3 and 4. Damage to the HO2S will result.

2. With the key **OFF**, disconnect the HO2S harness connector.
3. Measure the HO2S sensor resistances as follows:
   - Pins 1 and 2: 3–30 ohms
   - Pins 1 and 4: Greater than 10M ohms
   - Pin 1 and battery negative: Greater than 10M ohms.
4. If any measurement is outside the range given, replace the HO2S.

F-250 and F-350

See Figures 411 through 414.

1. Before servicing the vehicle, refer to the precautions in the beginning of this section.

✳✳ WARNING

Use only a high-impedance multimeter, otherwise damage to the PCM and/or sensors can result.

✳✳ WARNING

Do not measure resistance between pins 3 and 4. Damage to the HO2S will result.

2. With the key **OFF**, disconnect the HO2S harness connector.

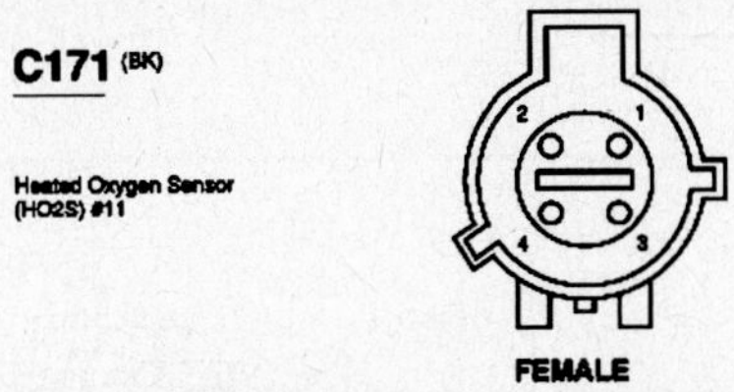

C171 (BK)

Heated Oxygen Sensor
(HO2S) #11

FEMALE

Pin	Circuit	Circuit function
1	391 (RD/YE)	PCM power relay, switched power
2	387 (RD/WH)	Heated Oxygen Sensor (HO2S) #11 (9F472), heater
3	359 (GY/RD)	Signal return
4	74 (GY/LB)	Heated Oxygen Sensor (HO2S) #11 (9F472), input

22086_FTRK_G0204

Fig. 411 Heated Oxygen Sensor Connector—Bank 1 Sensor 1

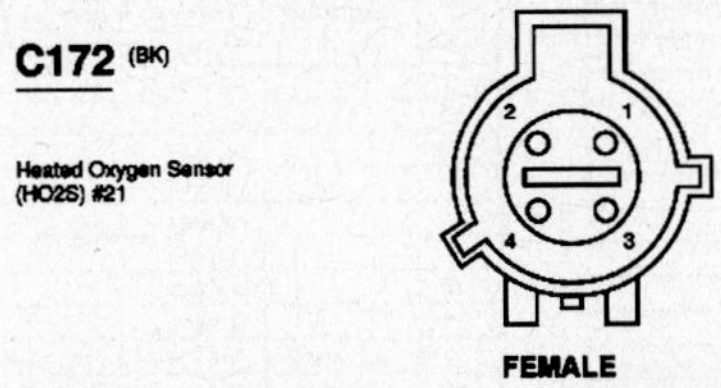

C172 (BK)

Heated Oxygen Sensor
(HO2S) #21

FEMALE

Pin	Circuit	Circuit function
1	391 (RD/YE)	PCM power relay, switched power
2	388 (YE/LB)	Heated Oxygen Sensor (HO2S) #21 (9F472), heater
3	359 (GY/RD)	Signal return
4	94 (RD/BK)	Heated Oxygen Sensor (HO2S) #21 (9F472), input

22086_FTRK_G0205

Fig. 412 Heated Oxygen Sensor Connector—Bank 2 Sensor 1

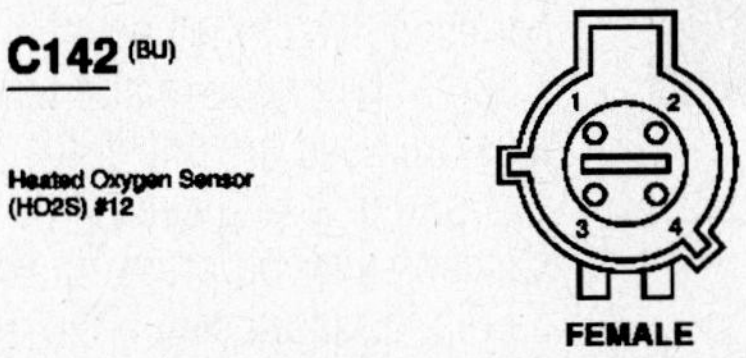

C142 (BU)

Heated Oxygen Sensor
(HO2S) #12

FEMALE

Pin	Circuit	Circuit function
1	389 (WH/BK)	Heated Oxygen Sensor (HO2S) #12 (9G444), heater
2	391 (RD/YE)	PCM power relay, switched power
3	392 (RD/LG)	Heated Oxygen Sensor (HO2S) #12 (9G444), input
4	1704 (VT/LG)	Signal return

122086_FTRK1_G0206

Fig. 413 Heated Oxygen Sensor Connector—Bank 1 Sensor 2

C141 (BU)

Heated Oxygen
Sensor (HO2S)
#22

FEMALE

Pin	Circuit	Circuit function
1	390 (TN/YE)	Heated Oxygen Sensor (HO2S) #22 (9G444), heater
2	391 (RD/YE)	PCM power relay, switched power
3	393 (VT/LG)	Heated Oxygen Sensor (HO2S) #22 (9G444), input
4	1704 (VT/LG)	Signal return

22086_FTRK_G0207

Fig. 414 Heated Oxygen Sensor Connector—Bank 2 Sensor 2

3. Measure the HO2S sensor resistances as follows:
- Pins 1 and 2: 3–30 ohms
- Pins 1 and 4: Greater than 10M ohms
- Pin 1 and battery negative: Greater than 10M ohms.

4. If any measurement is outside the range given, replace the HO2S.

INJECTOR DRIVER MODULE (IDM)

LOCATION

Left side of engine, above valve cover.

OPERATION

Also referred to as the Fuel Injector Control Module (FICM).

The FICM requires a 12-volt power source. The FICM receives power from the vehicle batteries through the FICM relay contacts each time the key is turned to the ON position. As the key is turned to the ON position, the FICM provides an internal ground to the coil side of the FICM relay. This closes the relay contacts and provides the FICM with the necessary power. The PCM communicates with the FICM using the CAN protocol. The CAN protocol is an international standards organization (ISO) standard for serial data communication. The CAN protocol standard includes a physical layer using differential transmission on a twisted pair of wires and a data link layer that defines different message types, arbitration rules for bus access, methods for concern detection and concern confinement. The FICM receives information from the PCM, including the volume of fuel desired, RPM, engine oil temperature, injection control pressure, and others. The FICM uses those signals to calculate fuel injection and duration. After calculating injector fuel delivery time, the FICM sends 48 volts at a 20-amp pulse to the correct injector so that the correct amount of fuel is delivered to the cylinder at the correct time.

REMOVAL & INSTALLATION

✸ CAUTION

Make sure the ignition switch is in the OFF position prior to working on the electronic engine controls.

1. Before servicing the vehicle, refer to the precautions in the beginning of this section.

2. Turn the ignition switch to the OFF position.

❈❈ WARNING

Never remove the pressure relief cap while the engine is operating or when the cooling system is hot. Failure to follow these instructions can result in damage to the cooling system or engine or result in personal injury. To avoid having scalding hot coolant or steam blow out of the degas bottle when removing the pressure relief cap, wait until the engine has cooled, then wrap a thick cloth around the pressure relief cap and turn it slowly. Step back while the pressure is released from the cooling system. When certain all the pressure has been released, (still with a cloth) turn and remove the pressure relief cap. Failure to follow these instructions can result in personal injury.

3. Relieve the cooling system pressure. Disconnect and plug or cap the engine vent hose and radiator vent hose.

4. Remove the 2 bolts and position the degas bottle aside.

5. Release the 2 exhaust pressure (EP) sensor harness pin-type retainers.

6. Disconnect the EP sensor electrical connector and position the harness aside.

7. Remove the fuel injector control module (FICM) nuts and bracket.

8. Remove the FICM bolts.

❈❈ CAUTION

Make sure both latches are released before removing the electrical connectors or connector damage can occur.

9. Position out the FICM and disconnect the electrical connectors. Remove the FICM.

❈❈ CAUTION

With the engine cold, fill vehicles with a yellow fill level decal to within the yellow cold fill range shown on the decal. If the decal is missing, fill the degas bottle only to the molded line. The correct fill level on these vehicles is between the molded line and 15 mm (0.59 inch) below the line. These fill levels will allow for coolant expansion. Overfilling the degas bottle may result in damage to the pressure cap, which can cause the engine to overheat.

10. To install, reverse the removal procedure.

TESTING

See Figure 415.

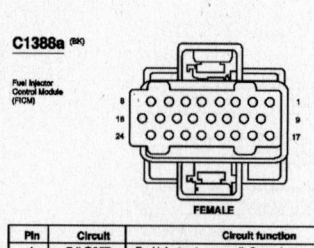
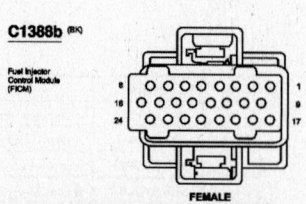

Pin	Circuit	Circuit function
1	7 (LG/YE)	Fuel Injector 4, open coil, Ground
2	3 (LG/WH)	Fuel Injector 1, open coil, Ground
3	11 (TN/YE)	Fuel Injector 7, open coil, Ground
4	15 (RD/YE)	Fuel Injector 6, open coil, Ground
5	2 (WH/LB)	Fuel Injector 1, close coil, Ground
6	6 (YE/LG)	Fuel Injector 4, close coil, Ground
7	14 (BN)	Fuel Injector 6, close coil, Ground
8	10 (LG/RD)	Fuel Injector 7, close coil, Ground
9	–	not used
10	–	not used
11	–	not used
12	–	not used
13	–	not used
14	–	not used
15	–	not used
16	–	not used
17	12 (LG/BK)	Fuel Injector 7, open coil, Power
18	9 (LG/OG)	Fuel Injector 7, close coil, Power
19	4 (WH/BK)	Fuel Injector 1, open coil, Power
20	1 (DB)	Fuel Injector 1, close coil, Power
21	16 (RD/LG)	Fuel Injector 6, open coil, Power
22	13 (RD/BK)	Fuel Injector 6, close coil, Power
23	33 (WH/PK)	Fuel Injector 4, open coil, Power
24	5 (OG/LB)	Fuel Injector 4, close coil, Power

Pin	Circuit	Circuit function
1	23 (TN/LG)	Fuel Injector 5, open coil, Ground
2	19 (LB/RD)	Fuel Injector 2, open coil, Ground
3	31 (WH/RD)	Fuel Injector 8, open coil, Ground
4	27 (OG/LG)	Fuel Injector 3, open coil, Ground
5	22 (LB/BK)	Fuel Injector 5, close coil, Ground
6	18 (OG/YE)	Fuel Injector 2, close coil, Ground
7	30 (BK/LG)	Fuel Injector 8, close coil, Ground
8	26 (WH/VT)	Fuel Injector 3, close coil, Ground
9	–	not used
10	–	not used
11	–	not used
12	–	not used
13	–	not used
14	–	not used
15	–	not used
16	–	not used
17	20 (WH/LB)	Fuel Injector 2, open coil, Power
18	17 (WH)	Fuel Injector 2, close coil, Power
19	28 (BK/PK)	Fuel Injector 3, open coil, Power
20	25 (DG/VT)	Fuel Injector 3, close coil, Power
21	24 (DB/OG)	Fuel Injector 5, open coil, Power
22	21 (DG/LG)	Fuel Injector 5, close coil, Power
23	32 (RD/LB)	Fuel Injector 8, open coil, Power
24	29 (YE/WH)	Fuel Injector 8, close coil, Power

22086_FTRK_G0183

Fig. 415 Injector Driver Module connectors—6.0L Diesel Engine

INJECTION CONTROL PRESSURE (ICP) SENSOR

LOCATION

4.2L and 5.4L Engines

Attached to the left fuel rail.

4.6L and 6.8L Engines

Attached to the right fuel rail.

OPERATION

The FRPT sensor measures the pressure and temperature of the fuel in the fuel rail and sends these signals to the PCM. The sensor uses the intake manifold vacuum as a reference to determine the pressure difference between the fuel rail and the intake manifold. The relationship between fuel pressure and fuel temperature is used to determine the possible presence of fuel vapor in the fuel rail.

The temperature sensing portion of the FRPT sensor is a thermistor device in which resistance changes with temperature. The electrical resistance of the thermistor decreases as the temperature increases, and the resistance increases as the temperature decreases. The varying resistance changes the voltage drop across the sensor terminals and provides electrical signals to the PCM corresponding to temperature.

Both the pressure and temperature signals are used to control the speed of the fuel pump. The speed of the fuel pump sustains fuel rail pressure which preserves fuel in its liquid state. The dynamic range of the fuel injectors increase because of the higher rail pressure, which allows the injector pulse width to decrease.

REMOVAL & INSTALLATION

4.2L Engine

See Figure 416.

❈❈ WARNING

Do not smoke or carry lighted tobacco or open flame of any type when working on or near any fuel-related components. Highly flammable mixtures are always present and can be ignited. Failure to follow these instructions may result in personal injury.

❈❈ WARNING

Fuel in the fuel system remains under high pressure even when the engine is not running. Before working

on or disconnecting any of the fuel lines or fuel system components, the fuel system pressure must be relieved. Failure to follow these instructions may result in personal injury.

1. Before servicing the vehicle, refer to the precautions in the beginning of this section.

2. Release the fuel system pressure.

3. Disconnect the battery ground cable.

4. Disconnect the fuel rail pressure and temperature sensor electrical connector.

5. Disconnect the fuel rail pressure and temperature sensor vacuum connector.

6. Remove the bolts and the fuel rail pressure and temperature sensor.

7. Remove and discard the O-ring seal.

8. To install, reverse the removal procedure.

➡ Install a new O-ring seal and lubricate with clean engine oil prior to installation.

4.6L Engine

See Figure 417.

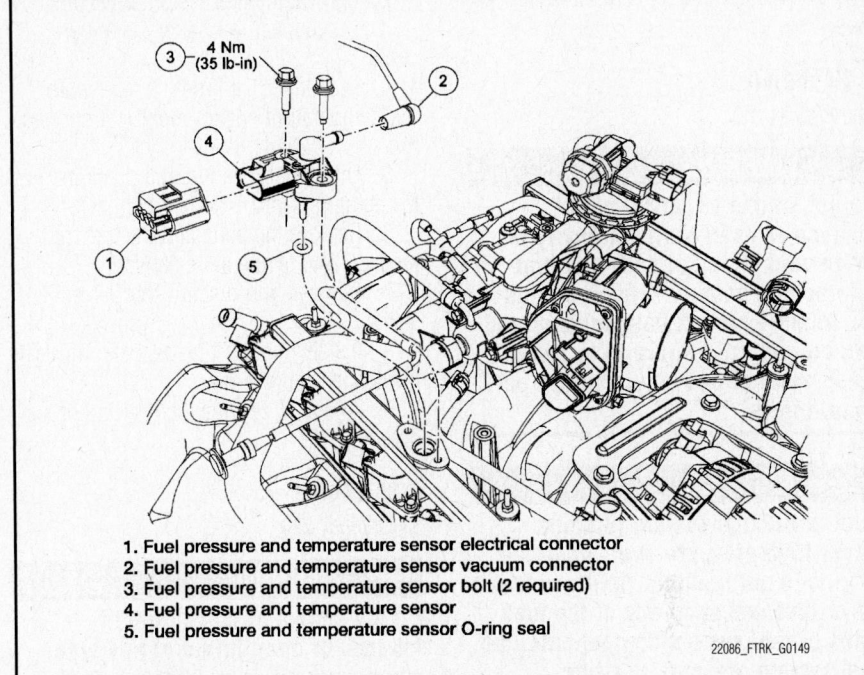

1. Fuel pressure and temperature sensor electrical connector
2. Fuel pressure and temperature sensor vacuum connector
3. Fuel pressure and temperature sensor bolt (2 required)
4. Fuel pressure and temperature sensor
5. Fuel pressure and temperature sensor O-ring seal

22086_FTRK_G0149

Fig. 417 Fuel Rail Pressure and Temperature Sensor—4.6L Engine

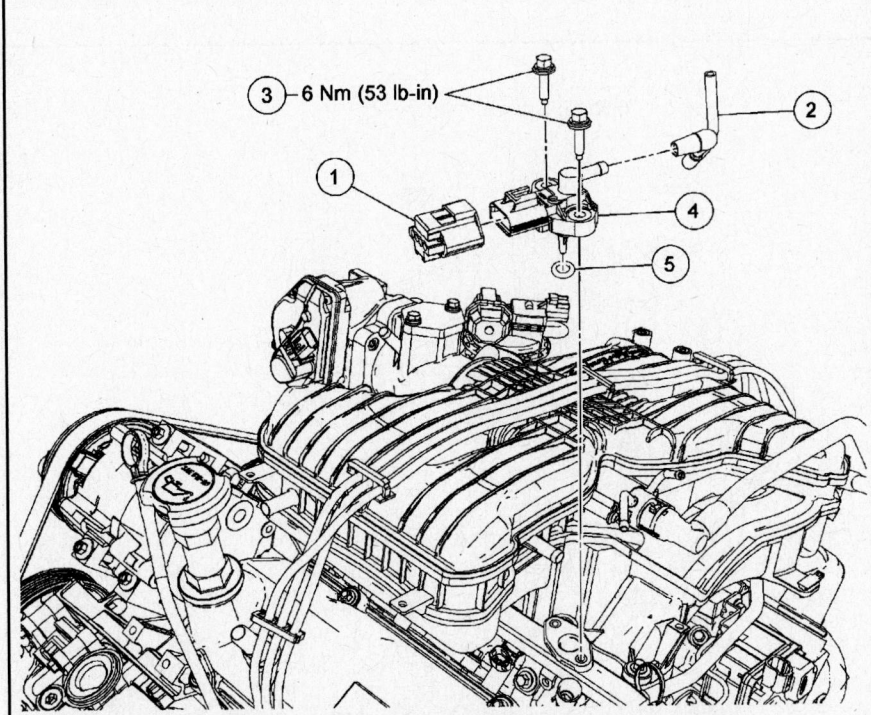

1. Fuel rail pressure and temperature sensor electrical connector
2. Fuel rail pressure and temperature sensor vacuum connector
3. Fuel rail pressure and temperature sensor bolts (2 required)
4. Fuel rail pressure and temperature sensor

22086_FTRK_G0148

Fig. 416 Fuel Rail Pressure and Temperature Sensor—4.2L Engine

❋❋ WARNING

Do not smoke or carry lighted tobacco or open flame of any type when working on or near any fuel-related components. Highly flammable mixtures are always present and can be ignited. Failure to follow these instructions may result in personal injury.

❋❋ WARNING

Fuel in the fuel system remains under high pressure even when the engine is not running. Before working on or disconnecting any of the fuel lines or fuel system components, the fuel system pressure must be relieved. Failure to follow these instructions may result in personal injury.

1. Before servicing the vehicle, refer to the precautions in the beginning of this section.

2. Release the fuel system pressure.

3. Disconnect the fuel pressure and temperature sensor electrical connector.

4. Disconnect the fuel pressure and temperature sensor vacuum connector.

5. Remove the bolts and the fuel pressure and temperature sensor.

6. Remove and discard the O-ring seal.

7. Install a new O-ring seal and lubricate with clean engine oil prior to installation.

8. To install, reverse the removal procedure.

5.4L Engine

See Figure 418.

> ※※ **WARNING**
>
> **Do not smoke or carry lighted tobacco or open flame of any type when working on or near any fuel-related components. Highly flammable mixtures are always present and can be ignited. Failure to follow these instructions may result in personal injury.**

> ※※ **WARNING**
>
> **Fuel in the fuel system remains under high pressure even when the engine is not running. Before working on or disconnecting any of the fuel lines or fuel system components, the fuel system pressure must be relieved. Failure to follow these instructions may result in personal injury.**

1. Before servicing the vehicle, refer to the precautions in the beginning of this section.

2. Release the fuel system pressure.

3. Disconnect the battery ground cable.

4. Disconnect the fuel rail pressure and temperature sensor electrical connector.

5. Disconnect the fuel rail pressure and temperature sensor vacuum connector.

6. Remove the bolts and the fuel rail pressure and temperature sensor.

7. Remove and discard the O-ring seal.

8. Install a new O-ring seal and lubricate it with clean engine oil.

9. To install, reverse the removal procedure.

6.8L Engine

See Figure 419.

> ※※ **WARNING**
>
> **Do not smoke or carry lighted tobacco or open flame of any type when working on or near any fuel-related components. Highly flammable mixtures are always present and can be ignited. Failure to follow**

these instructions may result in personal injury.

> ※※ **WARNING**
>
> **Fuel in the fuel system remains under high pressure even when the engine is not running. Before working on or disconnecting any of the fuel lines or fuel system components, the fuel system pressure must be relieved. Failure to follow these instructions may result in personal injury.**

1. Before servicing the vehicle, refer to the precautions in the beginning of this section.

2. Release the fuel system pressure.

3. Disconnect the battery ground cable.

4. Disconnect the fuel rail pressure and temperature sensor electrical and vacuum connectors.

5. Remove the 2 bolts and the fuel rail pressure and temperature sensor and discard the O-ring seal.

6. Lubricate the new O-ring seal with clean engine oil prior to installation.

7. To install, reverse the removal procedure.

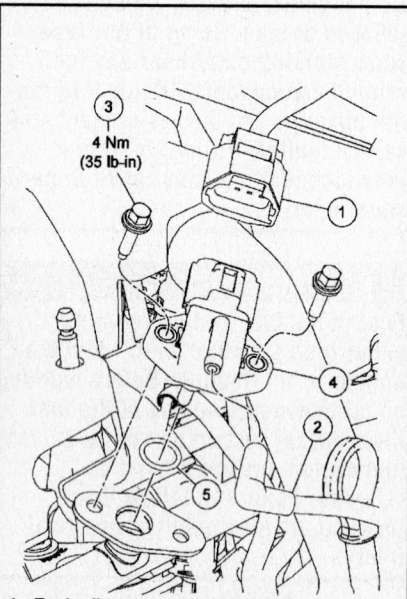

1. Fuel rail pressure and temperature sensor electrical connector
2. Fuel rail pressure and temperature sensor vacuum connector
3. Fuel rail pressure and temperature sensor bolts
4. Fuel rail pressure and temperature sensor

22086_FTRK_G0150

Fig. 418 Fuel Rail Pressure and Temperature Sensor—5.4L Engine

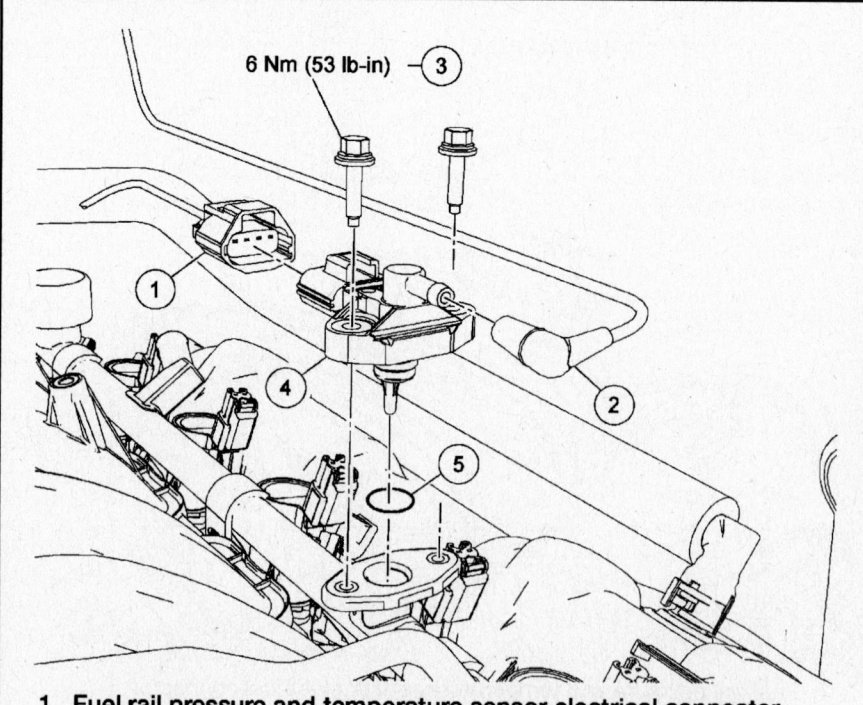

1. Fuel rail pressure and temperature sensor electrical connector
2. Fuel rail pressure and temperature sensor vacuum connector
3. Fuel rail pressure and temperature sensor bolt (2 required)
4. Fuel rail pressure and temperature sensor

22086_FTRK_G0164

Fig. 419 Fuel Rail Pressure and Temperature Sensor—6.8L Engine

TESTING

See Figures 420 through 423.

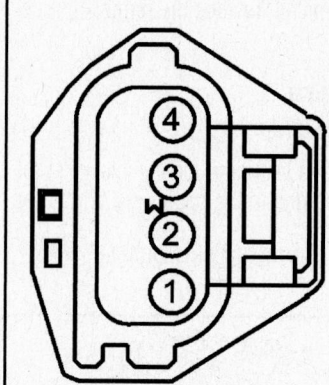

1. Fuel rail pressure transducer sensor signal
2. Reference voltage
3. Temperature sensor signal
4. Signal return

22086_FTRK_G0209

Fig. 420 Fuel Rail Pressure and Temperature sensor connector—F-150 and Mark LT

C1073 (BK)

Injector
Pressure
Sensor (IPS)

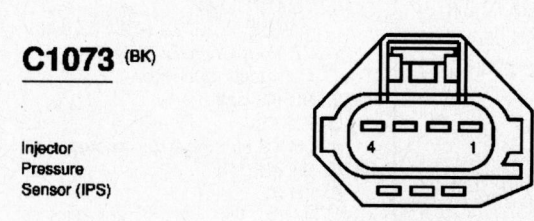

FEMALE

Pin	Circuit	Circuit function
1	1289 (OG/LG)	Fuel rail pressure sensor signal
2	3073 (RD/WH)	Fuel rail pressure sensor reference voltage
3	225 (BK/YE)	Fuel rail temperature sensor signal
4	359 (GY/RD)	Signal return

22086_FTRK_G0210

Fig. 421 Fuel Rail Pressure and Temperature sensor connector—F-250 and F-350

Voltage	Pressure (kPa)	Pressure (psi)
4.5	482	70
3.9	413	60
3.4	344	50
2.8	275	40
2.2	207	30
1.6	138	20
1.1	69	10
0.5	0	0

22086_FTRK_G0211

Fig. 422 FRPT sensor pressure specification table

1. Before servicing the vehicle, refer to the precautions in the beginning of this section.

FRPT SENSOR TEMPERATURE, VOLTAGE, AND RESISTANCE SPECIFICATIONS

Temperature		Sensor	
°C	°F	Volts	K Ohms
100	212	0.47	2.073
95	203	0.54	2.405
90	194	0.61	2.800
85	185	0.70	3.273
80	176	0.80	3.840
75	167	0.92	4.524
70	158	1.06	5.351
65	149	1.21	6.356
60	140	1.38	7.584
55	131	1.56	9.091
50	122	1.77	10.949
45	113	1.99	13.252
40	104	2.23	16.123
35	95	2.48	19.720
30	86	2.74	24.253
25	77	3.00	30.000
20	68	3.26	37.332
15	59	3.50	46.745
10	50	3.73	58.911
5	41	3.95	74.745
0	32	4.13	95.501

22086_FTRK_G0212

Fig. 423 FRPT sensor temperature specification table

2. Connect a mechanical fuel pressure gauge.

3. With the key **ON** and engine running, backprobe the FRPT sensor pins 1 and 4.

4. Compare the voltage and pressure readings with the specifications table.

5. Backprobe FRPT sensor pins 3 and 4.

6. Compare the voltage and temperature with the specification table.

INJECTION PRESSURE REGULATOR (IPR)

LOCATION

Rear center of the engine.

OPERATION

Regulates high pressure oil used for controlling fuel injectors.

TESTING

See Figure 424.

C1360 (BK)

Injection
Pressure
Regulator
(IPR)

FEMALE

Pin	Circuit	Circuit function
A	361 (RD)	PCM power relay, switched power
B	552 (YE/RD)	Switched ground

22086_FTRK_G0185

Fig. 424 Injection Pressure Regulator connector—6.0L Diesel Engine

INTAKE AIR TEMPERATURE (IAT) SENSOR

Part of the Mass Air Flow Sensor.

KNOCK SENSOR (KS)

LOCATION

4.2L Engine

Rear of the left cylinder head.

4.6L, 5.4L and 6.8L Engines

Under the intake manifold.

OPERATION

The KS is a tuned accelerometer on the engine which converts engine vibration to an electrical signal. The PCM uses this signal to determine the presence of engine knock and to retard spark timing.

REMOVAL & INSTALLATION

4.2L Engine

See Figure 425.

1. Before servicing the vehicle, refer to the precautions in the beginning of this section.
2. With the vehicle in NEUTRAL, position it on a hoist.
3. Disconnect the battery ground cable.
4. Remove the bolt and position the fuel tube bracket aside.
5. Disconnect the knock sensor (KS) electrical connector.
6. Remove the bolt and the KS.
7. To install, reverse the removal procedure.

4.6L Engine

See Figure 426.

1. Before servicing the vehicle, refer to the precautions in the beginning of this section.

2. Remove the intake manifold.
3. Disconnect the knock sensor (KS) electrical connector.
4. Remove the bolt and the KS.
5. To install, reverse the removal procedure.

5.4L Engine

See Figure 427.

1. Before servicing the vehicle, refer to the precautions in the beginning of this section.
2. Remove the intake manifold.

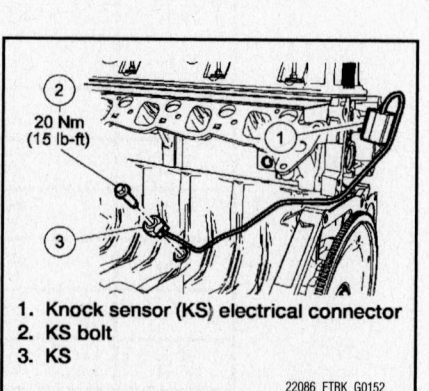

1. RH knock sensor (KS) electrical connector
2. RH KS bolt
3. RH KS
4. LH KS electrical connector
5. LH KS bolt
6. LH KS

22086_FTRK_G0153

Fig. 427 Knock Sensor—5.4L Engine

3. Disconnect the knock sensor (KS) electrical connectors.
4. Remove the bolts and the 2 KS.
5. To install, reverse the removal procedure.

6.8L Engine

See Figure 428.

1. Before servicing the vehicle, refer to the precautions in the beginning of this section.
2. Remove the intake manifold.

1. Knock sensor (KS) electrical connector
2. KS bolt
3. KS

22086_FTRK_G0152

Fig. 426 Knock Sensor—4.6L Engine

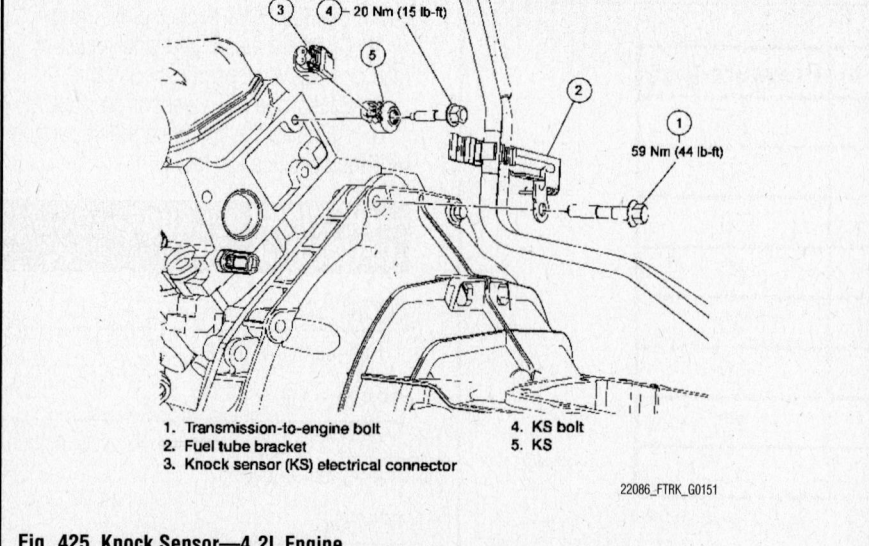

1. Transmission-to-engine bolt
2. Fuel tube bracket
3. Knock sensor (KS) electrical connector
4. KS bolt
5. KS

22086_FTRK_G0151

Fig. 425 Knock Sensor—4.2L Engine

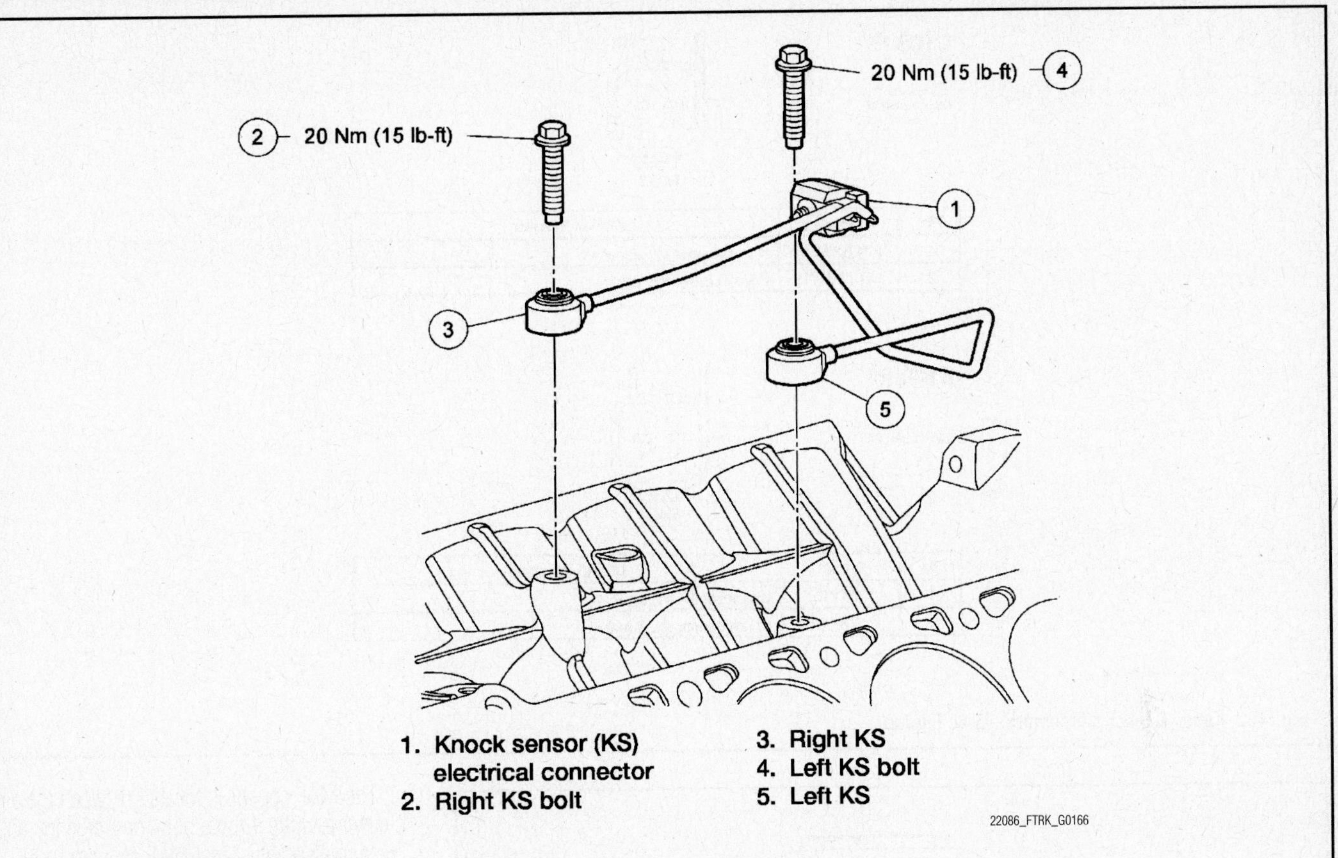

2 — 20 Nm (15 lb-ft)

20 Nm (15 lb-ft) — 4

1

3

5

1. Knock sensor (KS) electrical connector
2. Right KS bolt
3. Right KS
4. Left KS bolt
5. Left KS

22086_FTRK_G0166

Fig. 428 Knock Sensor—6.8L Engine

3. Disconnect the knock sensor (KS) electrical connectors.

4. Remove the bolts and the 2 KS.

5. To install, reverse the removal procedure.

TESTING

F-150 and Mark LT

See Figures 429 through 431.

1. Before servicing the vehicle, refer to the precautions in the beginning of this section.

> ※※ **WARNING**
>
> **Use only a high-impedance multimeter, otherwise damage to the PCM and/or sensors can result.**

2. With the key **ON** and the engine **OFF**, disconnect the knock sensor.

3. Measure resistance of the knock sensor. Standard value is 4.39M ohms—5.35M ohms. If not, replace the knock sensor.

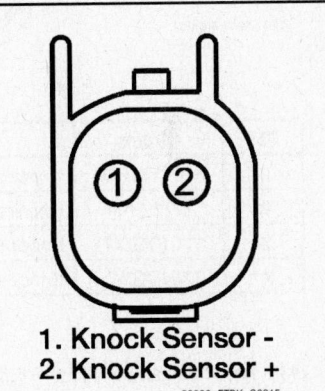

1. Knock Sensor -
2. Knock Sensor +

22086_FTRK_G0215

Fig. 431 Knock Sensor connector—5.4L Engine

F-250 and F-350

See Figures 432 and 433.

1. Before servicing the vehicle, refer to the precautions in the beginning of this section.

> ※※ **WARNING**
>
> **Use only a high-impedance multimeter, otherwise damage to the PCM and/or sensors can result.**

2. With the key **ON** and the engine **OFF**, disconnect the knock sensor.

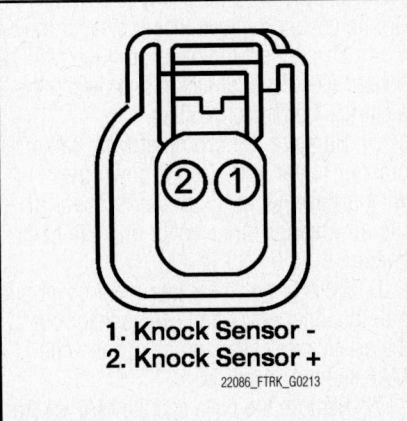

1. Knock Sensor -
2. Knock Sensor +

22086_FTRK_G0213

Fig. 429 Knock Sensor connector—4.2L Engine

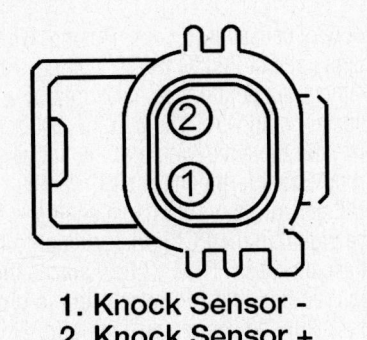

1. Knock Sensor -
2. Knock Sensor +

22086_FTRK_G0214

Fig. 430 Knock Sensor connector—4.6L Engine

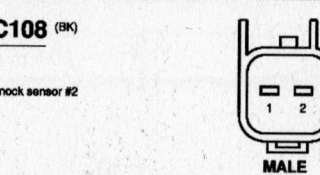

C108 (BK)

Knock sensor #2

MALE

Pin	Circuit	Circuit function
1	1274 (DG/WH)	Knock sensor #2, signal −
2	311 (DG/VT)	Knock sensor #2, signal +

C109 (BK)

Knock sensor #1

MALE

Pin	Circuit	Circuit function
1	1273 (YE)	Knock sensor #1, signal −
2	310 (YE/RD)	Knock sensor #1, signal +

22086_FTRK_G0216

Fig. 432 Knock Sensor connectors—5.4L Engine

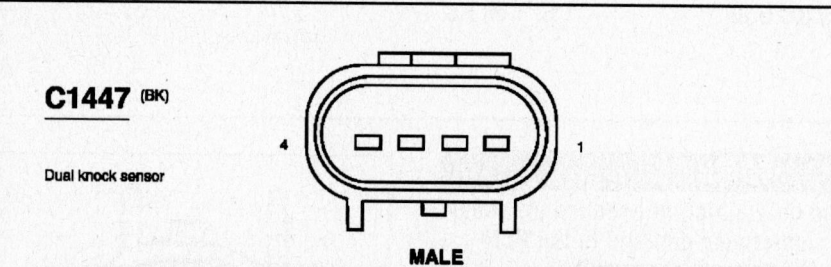

C1447 (BK)

Dual knock sensor

MALE

Pin	Circuit	Circuit function
1	310 (YE/RD)	Knock sensor #1, signal +
2	1273 (YE)	Knock sensor #1, signal −
3	311 (DG/VT)	Knock sensor #2, signal +
4	1274 (DG/WH)	Knock sensor #2, signal −

22086_FTRK_G0217

Fig. 433 Knock Sensor connector—6.8L Engine

3. Measure resistance of the knock sensor. Standard value is 4.39M ohms—5.35M ohms. If not, replace the knock sensor.

MASS AIR FLOW (MAF) SENSOR

LOCATION

Attached to the air filter assembly.

OPERATION

The MAF sensor uses a hot wire sensing element to measure the amount of air entering the engine. Air passing over the hot wire causes it to cool. This hot wire is maintained at 200°C (392°F) above the ambient temperature as measured by a constant cold wire. The current required to maintain the temperature of the hot wire is proportional to the mass air flow. The MAF sensor then outputs an analog voltage signal to the PCM proportional to the intake air mass. The PCM calculates the required fuel injector pulse width in order to provide the desired air/fuel ratio. This input is also used in determining transmission electronic pressure control (EPC), shift and torque converter clutch scheduling.

The MAF sensor is located between the air cleaner and the throttle body or inside the air cleaner assembly. Most MAF sensors have integrated bypass technology with an integrated intake air temperature (IAT) sensor. The hot wire electronic sensing element must be replaced as an assembly. Replacing only the element may change the air flow calibration.

REMOVAL & INSTALLATION

4.2L Engine

See Figure 434.

1. Before servicing the vehicle, refer to the precautions in the beginning of this section.

2. Release the clamp and detach the air cleaner cover from the air cleaner tray.

3. Lift the air cleaner tray from the grommets and remove the air cleaner tray.

4. Disconnect the mass air flow (MAF) sensor electrical connector and detach the electrical connector retainer.

5. Remove the grommet from the air cleaner cover and slide it down the wiring harness to allow the removal of the air cleaner inner cover and the MAF sensor.

6. Detach the air cleaner inner cover and pull the inner cover and MAF sensor out of the air cleaner cover and disconnect the MAF sensor jumper wire.

7. Remove the bolts and the MAF sensor.

8. To install, reverse the removal procedure.

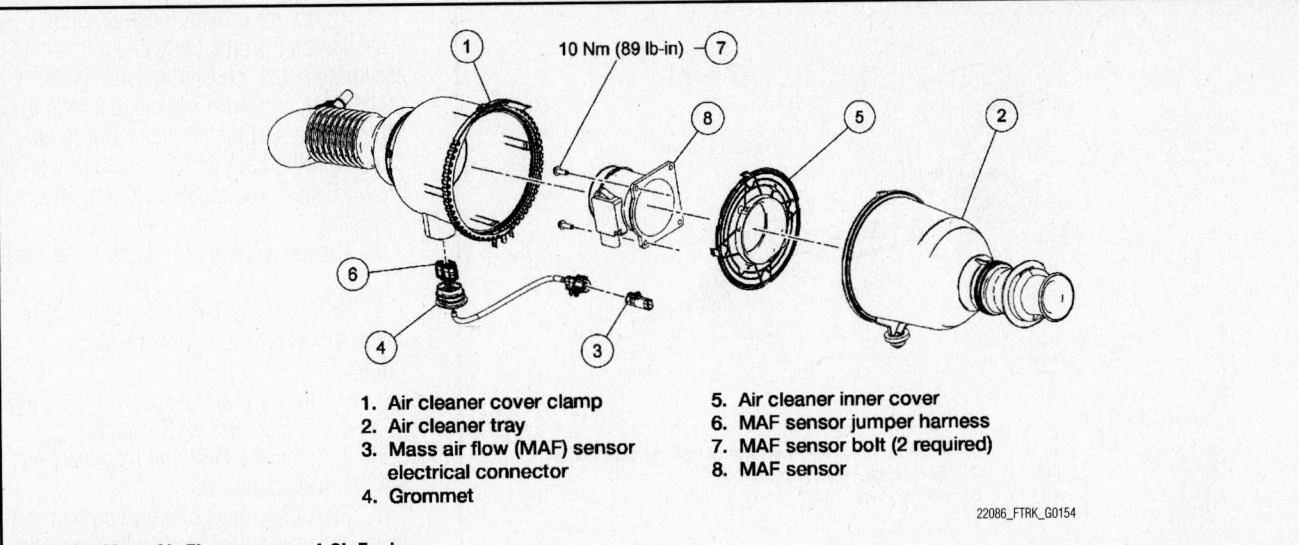

1. Air cleaner cover clamp
2. Air cleaner tray
3. Mass air flow (MAF) sensor electrical connector
4. Grommet
5. Air cleaner inner cover
6. MAF sensor jumper harness
7. MAF sensor bolt (2 required)
8. MAF sensor

22086_FTRK_G0154

Fig. 434 Mass Air Flow sensor—4.2L Engine

4.6L Engine

See Figure 435.

1. Before servicing the vehicle, refer to the precautions in the beginning of this section.

2. Open the clamp on the air cleaner and separate the tray from the cover.

3. Disconnect the mass air flow (MAF) sensor electrical connector and detach the connector retainer.

4. Remove the grommet from the air cleaner cover and slide it down the electrical harness.

5. Pull the air cleaner inner cover and MAF sensor out of the air cleaner cover.

6. Disconnect the MAF sensor electrical connector and remove the inner cover and MAF sensor assembly.

7. Remove the bolts and the MAF sensor.

8. To install, reverse the removal procedure.

5.4L Engine

See Figure 436.

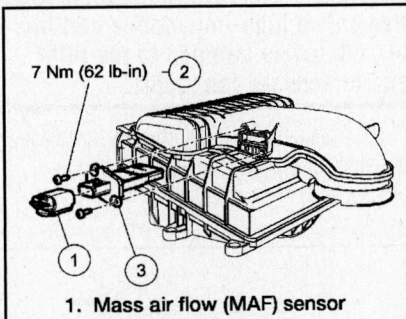

1. Mass air flow (MAF) sensor electrical connector
2. MAF sensor bolt (2 required)
3. MAF sensor

22086_FTRK_G0156

Fig. 436 Mass Air Flow sensor—5.4L Engine

1. Before servicing the vehicle, refer to the precautions in the beginning of this section.

2. Disconnect the mass air flow (MAF) sensor electrical connector.

3. Remove the bolts and the MAF sensor.

4. To install, reverse the removal procedure.

6.8L Engine

See Figure 437.

1. Before servicing the vehicle, refer to the precautions in the beginning of this section.

2. Disconnect the battery ground cable. Disconnect the mass air flow (MAF) sensor electrical connector.

3. Remove the 2 bolts and the MAF sensor.

4. To install, reverse the removal procedure.

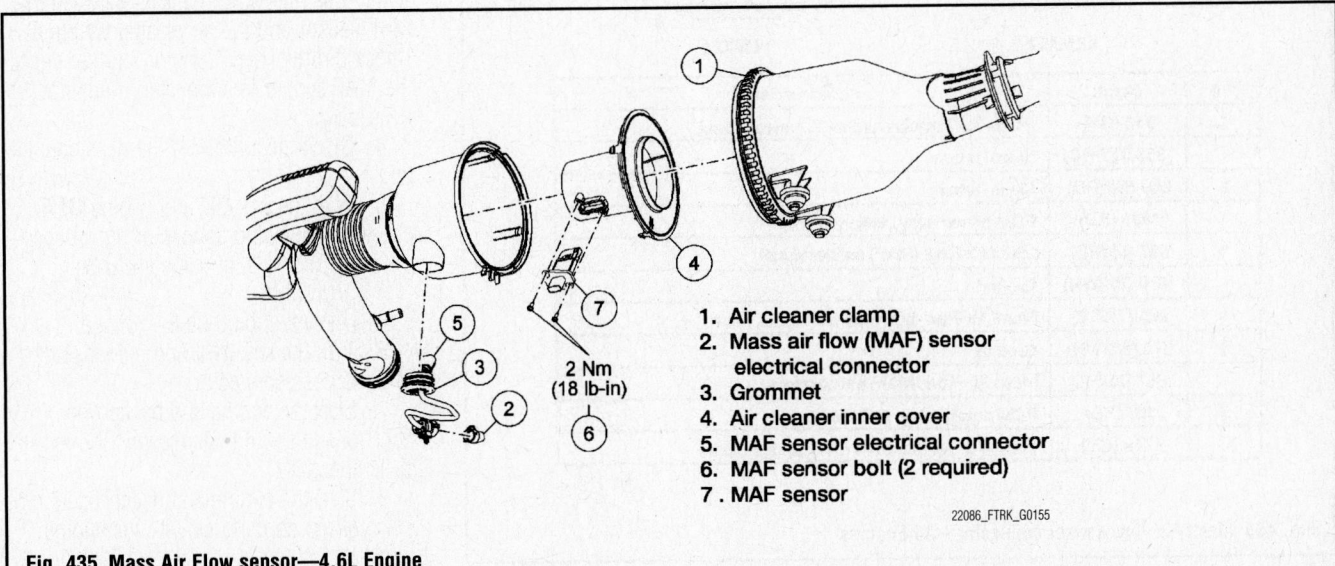

1. Air cleaner clamp
2. Mass air flow (MAF) sensor electrical connector
3. Grommet
4. Air cleaner inner cover
5. MAF sensor electrical connector
6. MAF sensor bolt (2 required)
7. MAF sensor

22086_FTRK_G0155

Fig. 435 Mass Air Flow sensor—4.6L Engine

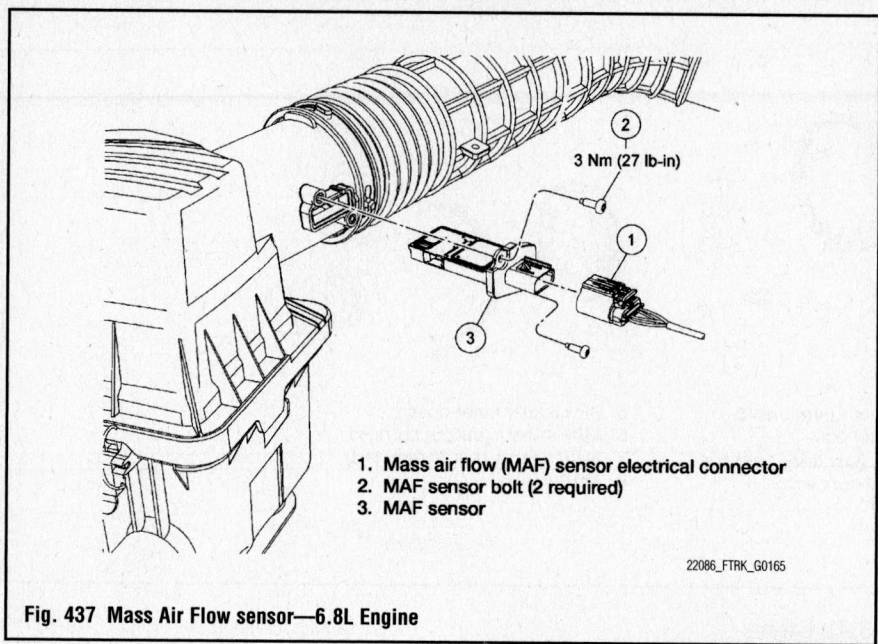

1. Mass air flow (MAF) sensor electrical connector
2. MAF sensor bolt (2 required)
3. MAF sensor

22086_FTRK_G0165

Fig. 437 Mass Air Flow sensor—6.8L Engine

TESTING

4.2L 4.6L, 5.4L and 6.8L Engines

See Figure 438.

1. Before servicing the vehicle, refer to the precautions in the beginning of this section.

> ※ **WARNING**
>
> **Use only a high-impedance multimeter, otherwise damage to the PCM and/or sensors can result.**

2. Check the air inlet system (air cleaner, housing, ductwork) for obstructions or blockage.

C128 (BK)

Mass Air Flow (MAF) sensor (13450)

12B637	12A581
Gasoline	Diesel
FEMALE	FEMALE

* Diesel

Pin	Circuit	Circuit function
1	743 (GY)	Intake Air Temperature (IAT) sensor signal
	*359 (GY/RD)	Signal return
2	359 (GY/RD)	Signal return
	*381 (RD)	PCM power relay, switched power
3	967 (LB/RD)	Mass Air Flow (MAF) sensor signal
	*570 (BK/WH)	Ground
4	968 (TN/LB)	Mass Air Flow (MAF) sensor signal, return
5	570 (BK/WH)	Ground
	*967 (LB/RD)	Mass Air Flow (MAF) sensor signal
6	381 (RD)	PCM power relay, switched power
	*743 (GY)	Intake Air Temperature (IAT) sensor signal

22086_FTRK_G0184

Fig. 438 Mass Air Flow sensor connector—All Engines

3. Check for broken/loose air outlet tube clamps (throttle body and air cleaner assembly ends), cracks/holes in the air outlet tube, and worn gaskets between the MAF sensor and the air cleaner assembly. Check throttle body bore for sludge. Verify the MAF sensor is connected. Repair as necessary.

4. Disconnect the MAF harness connector.

5. With the key **ON** and engine **OFF**, check the following connector pin values:
- Pins 2, 4, and 5 should be ground.
- Pin 6 should be B+ voltage.

6. Turn the key **OFF** and reconnect the MAF harness connector.

7. Start the engine and backprobe pin 1. This voltage should change with the intake air temperature.

8. Start the engine and backprobe pin 3. This voltage should rise with the engine rpm.

6.0L Diesel Engine

See Figure 438.

1. Before servicing the vehicle, refer to the precautions in the beginning of this section.

> ※ **WARNING**
>
> **Use only a high-impedance multimeter, otherwise damage to the PCM and/or sensors can result.**

2. Check the air inlet system (air cleaner, housing, ductwork) for obstructions or blockage.

3. Check for broken/loose air outlet tube clamps (throttle body and air cleaner assembly ends), cracks/holes in the air outlet tube, and worn gaskets between the MAF sensor and the air cleaner assembly. Check throttle body bore for sludge. Verify the MAF sensor is connected. Repair as necessary.

4. Disconnect the MAF harness connector.

5. With the key **ON** and engine **OFF**, check the following connector pin values:
- Pins 1, 3, and 4 should be ground.
- Pin 2 should be B+ voltage.

6. Turn the key **OFF** and reconnect the MAF harness connector.

7. Start the engine and backprobe pin 6. This voltage should change with the intake air temperature.

8. Start the engine and backprobe pin 5. This voltage should rise with the engine rpm.

MANIFOLD ABSOLUTE PRESSURE (MAP) SENSOR

LOCATION

Passenger side of the engine, near the cowl.

OPERATION

The MAP sensor is a variable capacitor sensor that is supplied a 5-volt reference signal by the PCM and returns a voltage signal to the PCM relative to the intake manifold pressure. The sensor voltage increases as the pressure increases. The MAP sensor allows the PCM to determine the engine boost to calculate fuel quantity. In addition, the MAP signal is used to control smoke by limiting fuel quantity during acceleration until a specified boost pressure is obtained, and is used by the PCM for EGR system calculations and control.

A MAP signal concern detected by the PCM causes the PCM to calculate an estimated manifold pressure based on known engine conditions.

REMOVAL & INSTALLATION

6.0L Diesel Engine

✳✳ CAUTION

Make sure the ignition switch is in the OFF position prior to working on the electronic engine controls.

1. Before servicing the vehicle, refer to the precautions in the beginning of this section.
2. Turn the ignition switch to the OFF position.
3. Disconnect the manifold absolute pressure (MAP) sensor.
4. Disconnect the pressure hose.
5. Disconnect the electrical connector.
6. Remove the mounting screws and the MAP sensor.
7. To install, reverse the removal procedure.

TESTING

6.0L Diesel Engine

See Figures 439 and 440.

1. Before servicing the vehicle, refer to the precautions in the beginning of this section.

✳✳ WARNING

Use only a high-impedance multimeter, otherwise damage to the PCM and/or sensors can result.

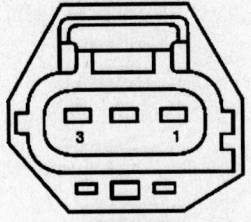

C1087 (BK)

Manifold Absolute Pressure (MAP) sensor

FEMALE

Pin	Circuit	Circuit function
1	351 (BN/WH)	Reference voltage
2	358 (LG/BK)	Manifold Absolute Pressure (MAP) sensor, to, Powertrain Control Module (PCM) (12A650)
3	359 (GY/RD)	Signal return

22086_FTRK_G0186

Fig. 439 Manifold Absolute Pressure sensor connector—6.0L Diesel Engine

MAP Sensor

Volts	kPa	psi
0.02	20	2.9
0.5	50	7.25
0.92	76.6	11.1
3.8	255.9	37.1
4.49	299	43.4
5	300	43.5

22086_FTRK_G0218

Fig. 440 MAP sensor pressure/voltage table

2. Disconnect the pressure hose from the MAP sensor.
3. With the key ON, engine OFF, connect the Pressure Adapter Kit 014-00761, or equivalent (gauge bar), and apply pressure to the MAP sensor.
4. Backprobe MAP sensor connector pin 2 and measure the voltage between pin 2 and ground.
5. Compare the values with the pressure/voltage table.

POWERTRAIN CONTROL MODULE (PCM)

LOCATION

All Except 6.0L Diesel Engine

Passenger side of the engine compartment, mounted to the cowl.

6.0L Diesel Engine

Underhood, on the left inner fender.

OPERATION

The center of the electronic engine control (EEC) system is a microprocessor called the PCM. The PCM receives input from sensors and other electronic components (switches, relays). Based on the information received and programmed into its memory, the PCM generates output signals to control various relays, solenoids and actuators.

REMOVAL & INSTALLATION

F-150 and Mark LT

See Figure 441.

➡ **Any powertrain control module (PCM) replacement will require that ALL customer keys are available to be reprogrammed at the time of installation. PCM replacement DOES NOT require new keys.**

1. Before servicing the vehicle, refer to the precautions in the beginning of this section.
2. Retrieve the module configuration. Carry out the module configuration retrieval steps of the Programmable Module Installation procedure.
3. Disconnect the PCM electrical connectors.
4. Remove the bolts and the PCM.
5. If necessary, remove the bolts and the PCM bracket.

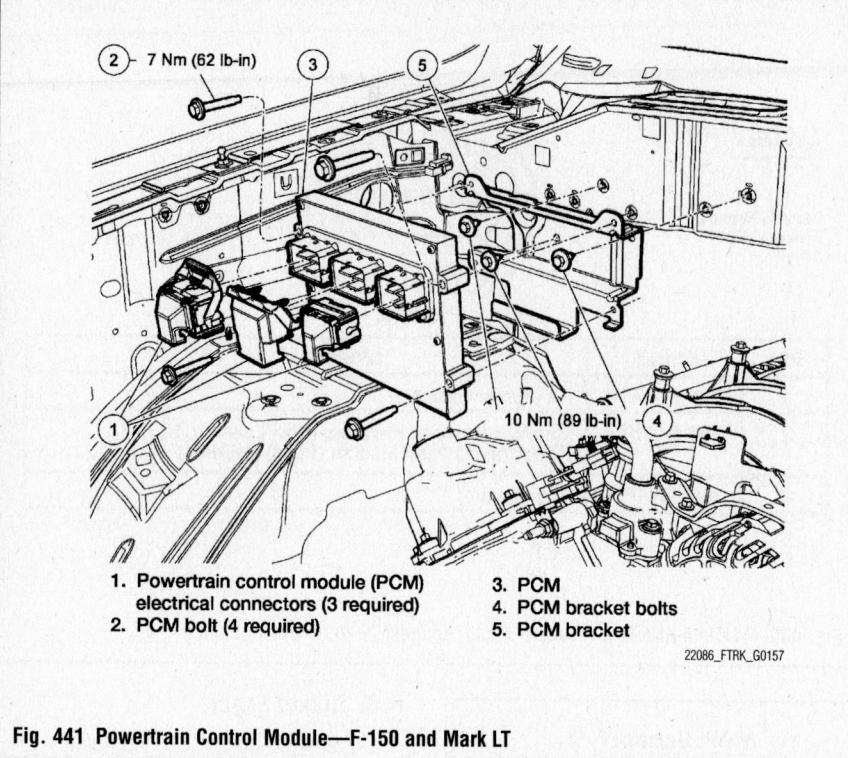

1. Powertrain control module (PCM) electrical connectors (3 required)
2. PCM bolt (4 required)
3. PCM
4. PCM bracket bolts
5. PCM bracket

22086_FTRK_G0157

Fig. 441 Powertrain Control Module—F-150 and Mark LT

To install:

6. If necessary, install the PCM bracket and the bolts.

7. Install the PCM and the bolts.

8. Connect the PCM electrical connectors.

9. Restore the module configuration. Carry out the module configuration restore steps of the Programmable Module Installation procedure.

10. Reprogram the passive anti-theft system (PATS). Carry out the Key Programming Using Two Programmed Keys procedure.

F-250 and F-350

With 5.4L And 6.8L Engines

See Figure 442.

➡**If servicing the powertrain control module (PCM), connect the scan tool to the vehicle. Allow the scan tool to identify the vehicle and obtain configuration data.**

1. Before servicing the vehicle, refer to the precautions in the beginning of this section.

2. Disconnect the battery ground cable.

3. Disconnect the powertrain control module (PCM) electrical connectors.

4. Remove the 2 bolts and the PCM.

5. To install, reverse the removal procedure.

With 6.0L Diesel Engine

❄❄ **CAUTION**

Always disconnect the battery ground cable prior to working on the electronic engine controls.

1. Before servicing the vehicle, refer to the precautions in the beginning of this section.

2. Disconnect the battery ground cable.

3. Disconnect the auxiliary battery positive cable (LH side of the engine compartment).

4. Remove the auxiliary battery cover.

5. Unlatch and disconnect the powertrain control module (PCM) electrical connectors.

6. Remove the 2 bolts and the PCM.

7. To install, reverse the removal procedure.

PROGRAMMABLE MODULE INSTALLATION (PMI) USING THE INTEGRATED DIAGNOSTIC SYSTEM (IDS)

When The Original Module Is Available

➡**If PMI fails on the first attempt, exit the diagnostic tool PMI application and carry out the procedure again.**

1. Connect the IDS and ID the vehicle as normal.

2. From the Toolbox icon, select and highlight Module Programming and press the check mark.

3. Select and highlight Programmable Module Installation.

4. Follow the on-screen instructions, turn the ignition key to the OFF position, and press the check mark.

5. INSTALL the new module and press the check mark.

6. Turn the headlamp switch to the OFF position.

7. Turn the ignition key to the RUN position.

8. Open the driver's door.

9. Unlock the doors using the interior trim switch.

10. Follow the on-screen instructions, turn the ignition key to the ON position, and press the check mark.

11. The module configuration is complete.

12. Test the module for correct operation.

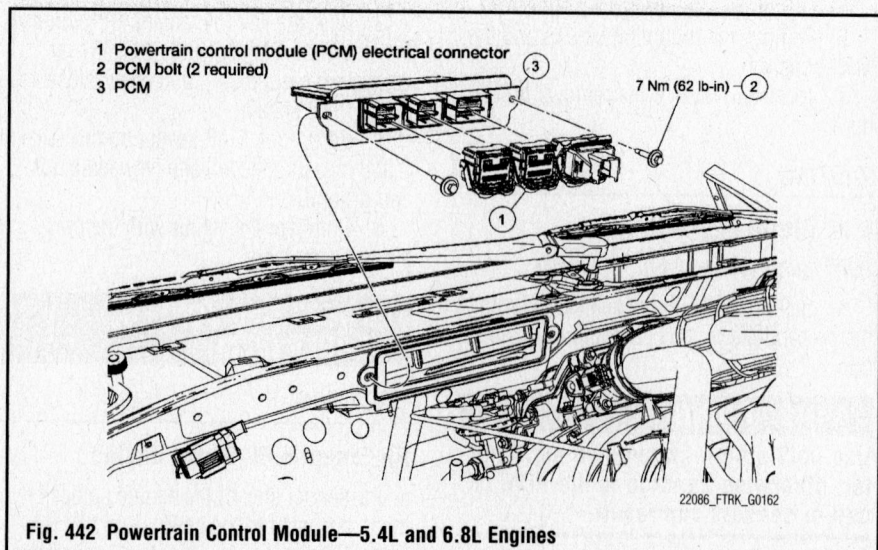

1. Powertrain control module (PCM) electrical connector
2. PCM bolt (2 required)
3. PCM

7 Nm (62 lb-in)

22086_FTRK_G0162

Fig. 442 Powertrain Control Module—5.4L and 6.8L Engines

When The Original Module Is Not Available

➡ **If PMI fails on the first attempt, exit the diagnostic tool PMI application and carry out the procedure again.**

1. Install the new module.
2. Connect the IDS and ID the vehicle as normal.
3. From the Toolbox icon, select and highlight Module Programming. Then highlight the module that was installed and press the check mark.
4. Select and highlight Programmable Module Installation. Then highlight the module that was installed and press the check mark.
5. Turn the headlamp switch to the OFF position.
6. Turn the ignition key to the RUN position.
7. Open the driver's door.
8. Unlock the doors using the interior trim switch.
9. Follow the on-screen instructions, turn the ignition key to the RUN position and press the check mark.
10. The IDS retrieves the module data, automatically downloads the data into the new module, and displays Module Configuration Complete.
11. If the data is not available in the module, the IDS displays a screen stating to contact the As-Built Data Center. Retrieve the data from WWW.FMCDEALER.COM at this time and press the check mark.
12. Enter the module data (the module address and line are displayed to the left of the 3 entry boxes) and press the check mark.
13. The IDS downloads the data into the new module and displays Operation Successful — Programming Complete.
14. Test the module for correct operation.

KEY PROGRAMMING USING TWO PROGRAMMED KEYS

➡ **This procedure works only if 2 or more programmed ignition keys are available.**

➡ **If the programming procedure is successful, the new key(s) will start the vehicle and the anti-theft indicator will prove-out for approximately 3 seconds. If the programming procedure is not successful and the new key(s) does not start the engine, leave the key in the ON position for at least 3 seconds, then turn the key off. Repeat the key programming procedure from Step 1.**

➡ **A minimum of 2 PATS keys must be programmed into the PCM before the vehicle will start.**

➡ **If the vehicle is in unlimited key mode, this spare key programming procedure still functions. Any 2 keys that can start the vehicle can be used to program an additional unlimited key.**

➡ **If additional keys are to be programmed, and the remaining keys are with the customer, or are not available, instruct the customer to refer to the Owner's Literature for instructions on programming the remaining keys.**

➡ **If the steps are not carried out as outlined, the programming procedure will end.**

➡ **Ignition keys must have a correct mechanical key cut for the vehicle and must be PATS encoded keys (contain a transponder).**

1. Insert the first programmed key into the ignition lock cylinder and turn the key from the OFF position to the ON position (maintain the key in the ON position for a minimum of 3 seconds and less than 10 seconds).
2. Turn the key to the OFF position and remove the first key from the ignition lock cylinder.
3. Within 5 seconds of turning the key to the OFF position, insert the second programmed key into the ignition lock cylinder and turn the key from the OFF position to the ON position (maintain the key in the ON position for a minimum of 3 seconds and less than 10 seconds).
4. Turn the key to the OFF position and remove the key from the ignition lock cylinder.
5. Within 10 seconds of turning the key to the OFF position, insert the unprogrammed key (the new key) into the ignition lock cylinder and turn the key from the OFF position to the ON position (maintain the key in the ON position for a minimum of 3 seconds and less than 10 seconds).
6. If it is desired to program additional key(s) (only up to 8 keys total can be programmed into the PCM), repeat Steps 1 - 5 for each additional key that needs to be programmed.
7. Start the vehicle with the new key(s).

THROTTLE POSITION SENSOR (TPS)

LOCATION

Mounted on the throttle body.

OPERATION

As resistance varies according to accelerator pedal angle, PCM applies voltage to sensor and measures voltage drop to calculate fuel delivery.

REMOVAL & INSTALLATION

5.4L Engine

See Figure 443.

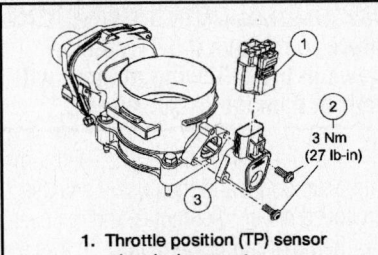

1. Throttle position (TP) sensor electrical connector
2. TP sensor screws (2 required)
3. TP sensor

22086_FTRK_G0158

Fig. 443 Throttle Position Sensor—5.4L Engine

1. Before servicing the vehicle, refer to the precautions in the beginning of this section.
2. Disconnect the throttle position (TP) sensor electrical connector.

✳✳ CAUTION

Failure to remove the TP sensor screws in the following manner will result in damage to the screws.

3. First loosen the screws 1-2 full turns using a hand tool and then use a suitable high speed driver to complete the removal.
4. Remove and discard the 2 screws and the TP sensor.

To install:

✳✳ CAUTION

Do not reuse the TP sensor and screws. A new TP sensor and screws must be installed.

✳✳ CAUTION

Do not use a high speed driver to install the new screws or damage to the TP sensor can occur.

➡**When installing the new TP sensor, make sure that the radial locator tab on the TP sensor is aligned with the radial locator hole on the throttle body (TB).**

5. Position the new TP sensor and install the 2 new screws.

6. Tighten to 3 Nm (27 lb-in).
7. Connect the TP sensor electrical connector.

6.8L Engine
See Figure 444.

1. Before servicing the vehicle, refer to the precautions in the beginning of this section.
2. Disconnect the throttle position (TP) sensor electrical connector.

> **⊗ CAUTION**
>
> **Failure to remove the TP sensor screws in the following manner will result in damage to the screws.**

3. First loosen the screws 1-2 full turns using a hand tool and then use a suitable high speed driver to complete the removal.
4. Remove and discard the 2 screws and the TP sensor.

To install:

> **❋❋ CAUTION**
>
> **Do not reuse the TP sensor and screws. A new TP sensor and screws must be installed.**

> **⊗ CAUTION**
>
> **Do not use a high speed driver to install the new screws or damage to the TP sensor can occur.**

➡ When installing the new TP sensor, make sure that the radial locator tab on the TP sensor is aligned with the radial locator hole on the throttle body (TB).

5. Position the new TP sensor and install the 2 new screws.

6. Tighten to 3 Nm (27 lb-in).
7. Connect the TP sensor electrical connector.

TESTING
See Figure 445.

1. Before servicing the vehicle, refer to the precautions in the beginning of this section.

> **❋❋ WARNING**
>
> **Use only a high-impedance multimeter, otherwise damage to the PCM and/or sensors can result.**

2. With the key **ON** and engine **OFF**, backprobe the TPS connector and check for the following values:
- Pin 2: 5 volt reference voltage
- Pins 1 and 4: Change with throttle position
- Pin 3: Signal return

VARIABLE CAMSHAFT TIMING OIL CONTROL SOLENOID

LOCATION
Front of the cylinder head, under the valve cover.

OPERATION
The VCT solenoid valve is an integral part of the VCT system. The solenoid valve controls the flow of engine oil in the VCT actuator assembly. As the PCM controls the duty cycle of the solenoid valve, oil pressure/flow advances or retards the cam timing. Duty cycles near 0% or 100% represent rapid movement of the camshaft. Retaining a fixed camshaft position is accomplished by dithering (oscillating) the solenoid valve duty cycle.

The PCM calculates and determines the desired camshaft position. It will continually

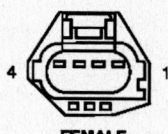

Pin	Circuit	Circuit function
1	357 (YE/WH)	Throttle Position Sensor (TPS) signal 2
2	1945 (VT/WH)	Throttle Position Sensor (TPS) Reference voltage
3	1946 (OG/LB)	Throttle Position Sensor (TPS) Signal return
4	355 (GY/WH)	Throttle Position Sensor (TPS) signal 1

22086_FTRK_G0189

Fig. 445 Throttle Position sensor connector—5.4L and 6.8L Engines

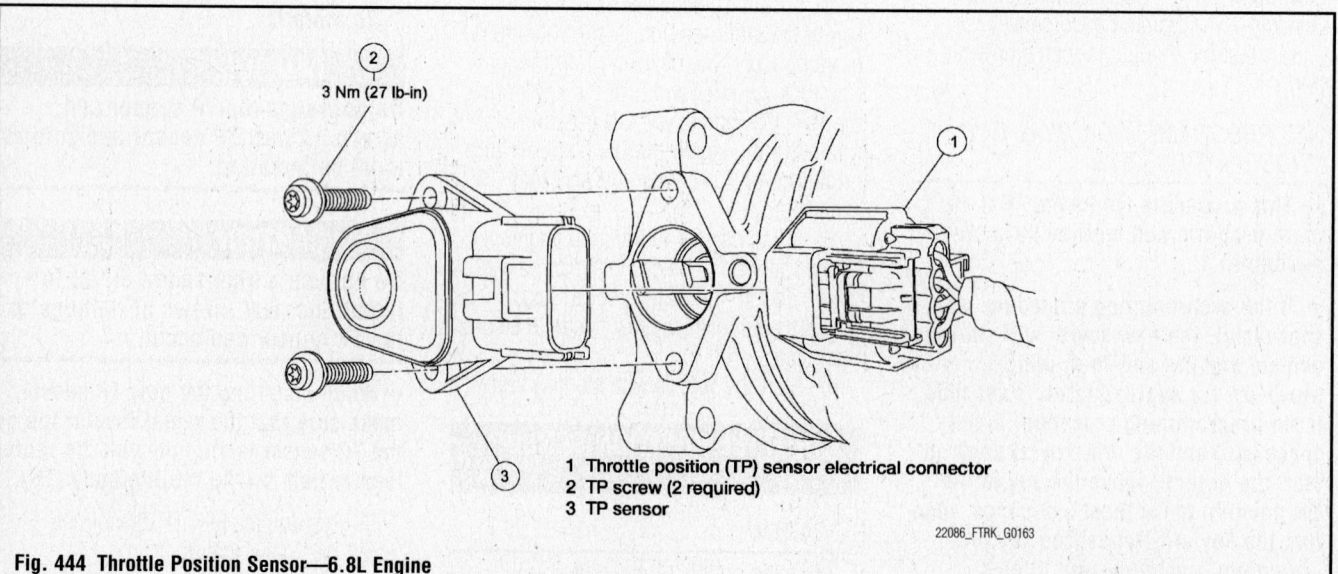

1 Throttle position (TP) sensor electrical connector
2 TP screw (2 required)
3 TP sensor

22086_FTRK_G0163

Fig. 444 Throttle Position Sensor—6.8L Engine

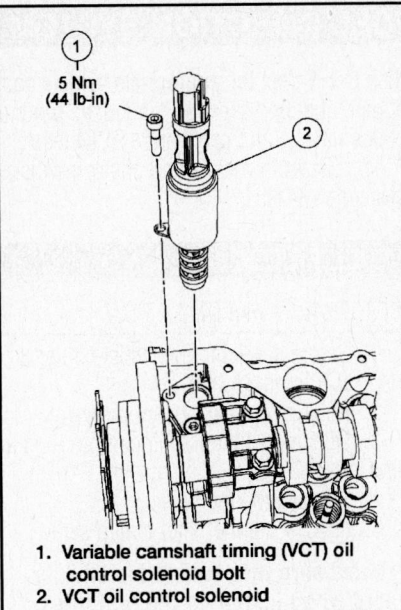

1. Variable camshaft timing (VCT) oil control solenoid bolt
2. VCT oil control solenoid

22086_FTRK_G0159

Fig. 446 Variable Camshaft Timing Oil Control Solenoid—5.4L Engine

update the VCT solenoid duty cycle until the desired position is achieved. A difference between the desired and actual camshaft position represents a position error in the PCM VCT control loop. The PCM will disable the VCT and place the camshaft in a default position if a fault is detected. A related DTC will also be set when the fault is detected.

REMOVAL & INSTALLATION

5.4L Engine

See Figure 446.

1. Before servicing the vehicle, refer to the precautions in the beginning of this section.
2. Remove the valve cover - LH or valve cover - RH.
3. Remove the bolt and the VCT oil control solenoid.
4. To install, reverse the removal procedure.

TESTING

1. Before servicing the vehicle, refer to the precautions in the beginning of this section.
2. With the key **OFF**, disconnect the VCT solenoid connector.
3. Measure the resistance of the VCT solenoid. Specification is 5–14 ohms.
4. Measure the resistance between VTC solenoid pin 1 and ground. Specification is infinite resistance.

5. Replace the VCT solenoid if any tests are out of specifications.

VEHICLE SPEED SENSOR (VSS)

LOCATION

Rear of the transmission, near the output shaft.

OPERATION

Also called the Output Shaft Speed (OSS) Sensor.

The Output Shaft Speed (OSS) sensor is a Hall effect type sensor located on the extension housing. The OSS input to the PCM is used for shift scheduling, timing, and TCC operation. The OSS has bi-directional capability and has a digital output.

REMOVAL & INSTALLATION

See Figure 447.

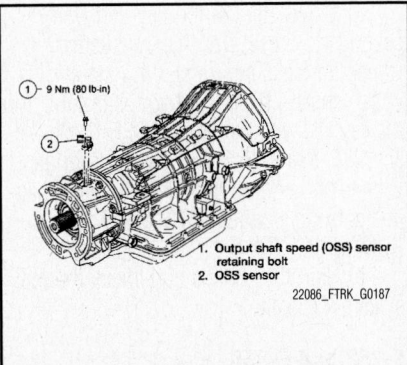

1. Output shaft speed (OSS) sensor retaining bolt
2. OSS sensor

22086_FTRK_G0187

Fig. 447 Output Shaft Speed sensor

1. Before servicing the vehicle, refer to the precautions in the beginning of this section.
2. With the vehicle in NEUTRAL, position it on a hoist.
3. Disconnect the output shaft speed (OSS) sensor electrical connector.

➡ **Prior to removing the speed sensor, make sure that the area around the sensor is free of foreign material to prevent contamination of the transmission.**

4. Remove the OSS sensor.

To install:

5. Lubricate the O-ring with clean automatic transmission fluid and install the OSS sensor.
6. Install the bolt and tighten to 9 Nm (80 lb-in).
7. Connect the OSS sensor electrical connector.

TESTING

See Figure 448.

1. Before servicing the vehicle, refer to the precautions in the beginning of this section.
2. Disconnect the Output Shaft Speed (OSS) sensor harness connector.
3. Measure the resistance between sensor pins 2 and 1, 3 and ground. Specification is no continuity.
4. Measure the resistance between pins 2 and 3. Specification is 400–1250 ohms.
5. If any measurement is outside specifications, replace the OSS sensor.

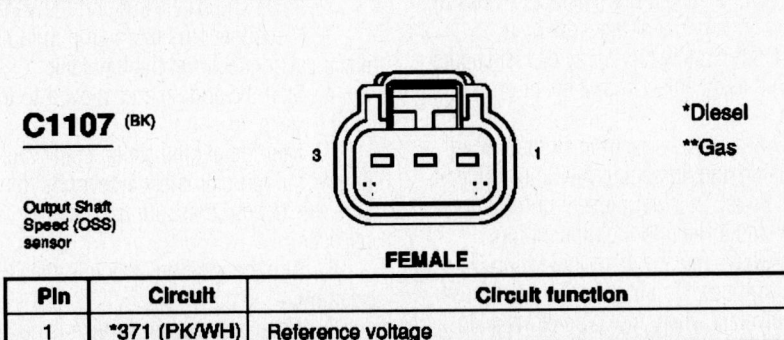

C1107 (BK)

Output Shaft Speed (OSS) sensor

3   1

FEMALE

*Diesel
**Gas

Pin	Circuit		Circuit function
1	*371 (PK/WH)		Reference voltage
	**3087 (DG/VT)		Reference voltage
2	136 (DB/YE)		Output Shaft Speed (OSS) sensor (7H103), signal
3	*570 (BK/WH)		Signal return
	**1704 (VT/LG)		Signal return

22086_FTRK_G0188

Fig. 448 Output Shaft Speed sensor connector

FUEL   **GASOLINE FUEL INJECTION SYSTEM**

FUEL SYSTEM SERVICE PRECAUTIONS

Safety is the most important factor when performing not only fuel system maintenance but any type of maintenance. Failure to conduct maintenance and repairs in a safe manner may result in serious personal injury or death. Maintenance and testing of the vehicle's fuel system components can be accomplished safely and effectively by adhering to the following rules and guidelines.

• To avoid the possibility of fire and personal injury, always disconnect the negative battery cable unless the repair or test procedure requires that battery voltage be applied.

• Always relieve the fuel system pressure prior to disconnecting any fuel system component (injector, fuel rail, pressure regulator, etc.), fitting or fuel line connection. Exercise extreme caution whenever relieving fuel system pressure to avoid exposing skin, face and eyes to fuel spray. Please be advised that fuel under pressure may penetrate the skin or any part of the body that it contacts.

• Always place a shop towel or cloth around the fitting or connection prior to loosening to absorb any excess fuel due to spillage. Ensure that all fuel spillage (should it occur) is quickly removed from engine surfaces. Ensure that all fuel soaked cloths or towels are deposited into a suitable waste container.

• Always keep a dry chemical (Class B) fire extinguisher near the work area.

• Do not allow fuel spray or fuel vapors to come into contact with a spark or open flame.

• Always use a back-up wrench when loosening and tightening fuel line connection fittings. This will prevent unnecessary stress and torsion to fuel line piping.

• Always replace worn fuel fitting O-rings with new Do not substitute fuel hose or equivalent where fuel pipe is installed.

Before servicing the vehicle, make sure to also refer to the precautions in the beginning of this section as well.

FUEL SYSTEM PRESSURE

RELIEVING

F-150 and Mark LT

1. Before servicing the vehicle, refer to the Precautions Section.

➡**The splash shield is located on the LH frame rail under the driver side door.**

2. Disconnect the splash shield and position aside.
3. Disconnect the electrical connector.
4. Start the engine and allow it to idle until it stalls.
5. After the engine stalls, crank the engine for approximately 5 seconds to make sure the fuel rail pressure has been released.
6. Turn the ignition switch to the OFF position.
7. When fuel system service is complete, connect the electrical connector.
8. Reposition the splash shield and install a new push pin.

➡**It may take more than one key cycle to pressurize the fuel system.**

9. Cycle the ignition key and wait 3 seconds to pressurize the fuel system. Check for leaks before starting the engine.
10. Install the WDS diagnostic tool. Turn the key ON with the engine OFF. Cycle the key OFF, then ON. Select the appropriate vehicle and engine qualifier. Clear all diagnostic trouble codes (DTCs) and carry out a PCM reset.
11. Start the vehicle and check the fuel system for leaks.

F-250 and F-350

1. Before servicing the vehicle, refer to the Precautions Section.
2. Raise and safely support the vehicle.
3. Disconnect the fuel pump module electrical connector at the fuel tank.
4. Start the engine and allow it to idle until it stalls.
5. After the engine stalls, crank the engine for approximately 5 seconds to make sure the fuel rail pressure has been released.
6. Turn the ignition switch to the OFF position.
7. When fuel system service is complete, connect the fuel pump module electrical connector.

➡**It may take more than one key cycle to pressurize the fuel system.**

8. Cycle the ignition key and wait three seconds to pressurize the fuel system. Check for leaks before starting the engine.
9. Install the scan tool. Turn the key ON with the engine OFF. Cycle the key OFF,

then ON. Select the appropriate vehicle and engine qualifier. Clear all diagnostic trouble codes (DTCs) and carry out a PCM reset.
10. Start the vehicle and check the fuel system for leaks.

FUEL FILTER

REMOVAL & INSTALLATION

1. Before servicing the vehicle, refer to the Precautions Section.
2. Relieve the fuel system pressure.
3. Disconnect the fuel lines from the fuel filter.
4. Remove the fuel filter.
5. Loosen the fuel filter clamp screw.

➡**Make sure that an audible click is heard when installing the fuel lines. Pull back on the fuel lines to confirm engagement.**

6. To install, reverse the removal procedure.

FUEL INJECTORS

REMOVAL & INSTALLATION

4.2L Engine

1. Before servicing the vehicle, refer to the Precautions Section.
2. Release the fuel system pressure.
3. Disconnect the battery ground cable.
4. Disconnect the spring lock coupling at the fuel rail.
5. Remove the upper intake manifold.
6. Disconnect the fuel rail pressure sensor vacuum and electrical connectors.
7. Disconnect the 6 fuel injector electrical connectors.
8. Remove the wire tie.
9. Detach the wiring harness retainers from the fuel rail.
10. Remove the 4 bolts and the fuel rail and injectors as an assembly.
11. Remove and discard the fuel injector O-ring seals.
12. To install, reverse the removal procedure. Tighten the fuel rail bolts to 89 inch lbs. (10 Nm).

➡**Lubricate the new O-ring seals with clean engine oil.**

4.6L Engine

See Figure 449.

1. Before servicing the vehicle, refer to the Precautions Section.
2. Release the fuel system pressure.

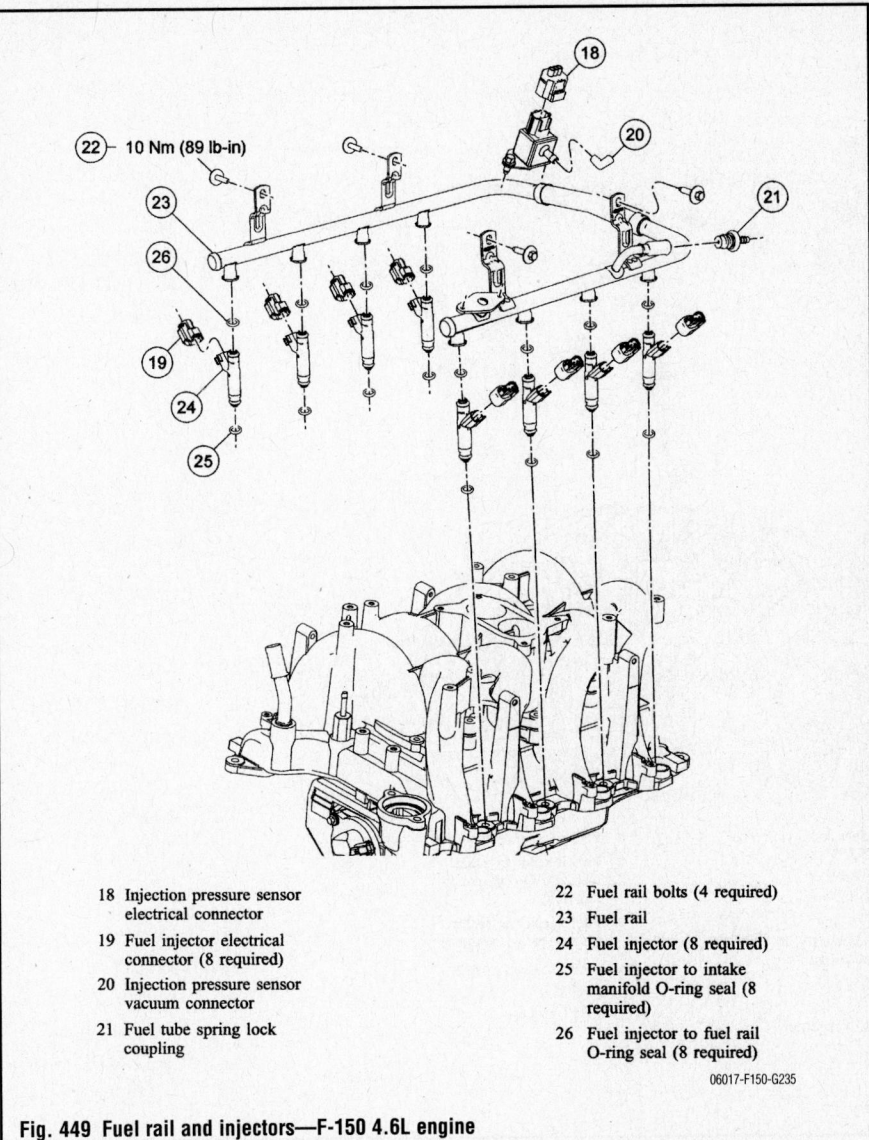

18 Injection pressure sensor
    electrical connector

19 Fuel injector electrical
    connector (8 required)

20 Injection pressure sensor
    vacuum connector

21 Fuel tube spring lock
    coupling

22 Fuel rail bolts (4 required)

23 Fuel rail

24 Fuel injector (8 required)

25 Fuel injector to intake
    manifold O-ring seal (8
    required)

26 Fuel injector to fuel rail
    O-ring seal (8 required)

06017-F150-G235

Fig. 449 Fuel rail and injectors—F-150 4.6L engine

3. Disconnect the battery ground cable.

4. Remove the air cleaner outlet pipe.

5. Disconnect the exhaust gas recirculation (EGR) system module tube upper fitting.

6. Loosen the EGR system module tube lower fitting and rotate to position aside.

7. Disconnect the brake booster vacuum hose.

8. Disconnect the throttle position (TP) sensor electrical connector.

9. Disconnect the upper vapor tube and position aside.

10. Disconnect the EGR system module vacuum and electrical connector.

11. Disconnect the crankcase vent hose quick-release fitting at the rear of the intake manifold.

12. Disconnect the crankcase vent hose quick-release fitting at the RH valve cover.

13. Disconnect the electronic throttle control electrical connector.

14. Disconnect the throttle body spacer vacuum hose.

15. Release the heated TB coolant hose clamp and remove and plug the coolant hose.

16. Release the heated TB coolant hose clamp and remove and plug the coolant hose.

17. Remove the 4 throttle body spacer bolts and the throttle body assembly and discard the gasket.

18. Disconnect the injection pressure sensor electrical connector.

19. Disconnect the 8 fuel injector electrical connectors.

20. Disconnect the injection pressure sensor vacuum connector.

21. Disconnect the fuel tube spring lock coupling.

22. Remove the 4 fuel rail bolts.

23. Remove the fuel rail.

24. Remove the 8 fuel injectors.

25. Remove and discard the 8 upper fuel injector O-ring seals and the 8 lower fuel injector O-ring seals

26. To install, reverse the removal procedure. Torque the 4 fuel rail bolts to 10 Nm (89 inch lbs.). Torque the 4 throttle body spacer bolts to 10 Nm (89 inch lbs.). Torque the EGR system module tube fittings 40 Nm (30 ft. lbs.).

➡**Install new O-ring seals on the fuel injectors. Lubricate the new fuel injector O-ring seals with clean engine oil prior to installing the fuel rail.**

5.4L Engine

See Figure 450.

1. Before servicing the vehicle, refer to the Precautions Section.

2. Release the fuel system pressure.

3. Disconnect the battery ground cable.

4. Remove the air cleaner and air cleaner intake pipe.

5. Disconnect the fuel vapor quick connect fitting from the evaporative emission (EVAP) canister purge valve and position aside.

6. Disconnect the heated positive crankcase ventilation (PCV) valve electrical connector.

7. Disconnect the PCV hose from the intake manifold and position aside.

8. Disconnect the electronic throttle control electrical connector.

9. Disconnect the throttle position (TP) sensor electrical connector.

10. Disconnect the vacuum hose near the rear of the right valve cover.

11. Disconnect the fuel rail pressure and temperature (FRPT) sensor electrical connector.

12. Disconnect the FRPT sensor vacuum hose.

13. Disconnect the 8 fuel injector electrical connectors.

14. Disconnect the spring lock couplings at the fuel rail.

15. Remove the 4 fuel rail bolts.

✳✳ WARNING

When installing the fuel injectors, make sure that the injectors are fully engaged in the fuel injector cups.

16. Remove the fuel rail and injectors as an assembly.

17. Remove the 8 fuel injectors and discard the 8 lower and 8 upper fuel injector O-ring seals.

➡**Lubricate the O-ring seal with clean engine oil.**

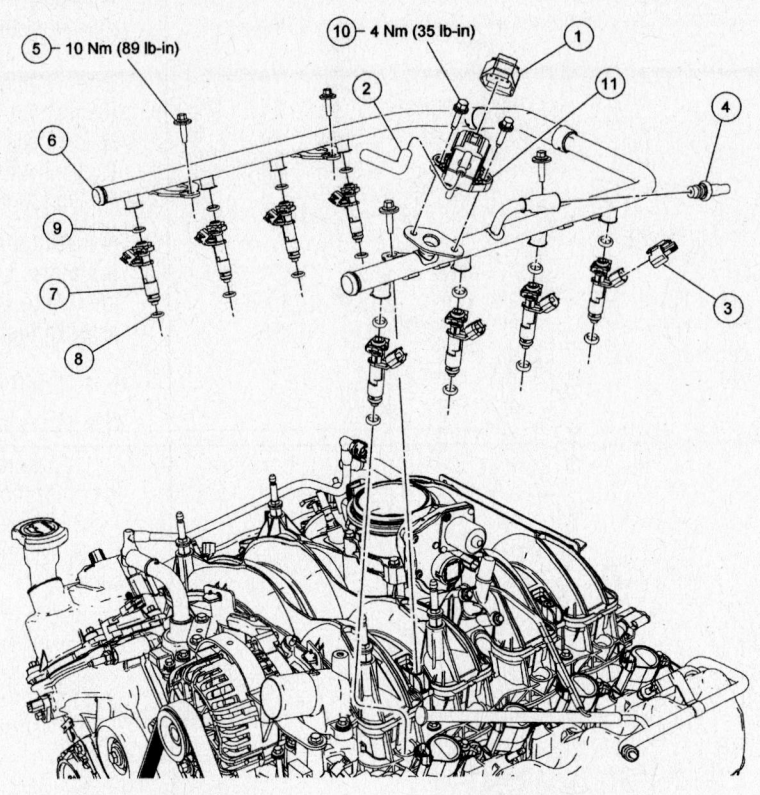

⑤ 10 Nm (89 lb-in)   ⑩ 4 Nm (35 lb-in)

1	Fuel rail pressure and temperature (FRPT) sensor electrical connector	7	Fuel injector (8 required)
2	FRPT sensor vacuum connector	8	Fuel injector to intake manifold O-ring seal (8 required)
3	Fuel injector electrical connector (8 required)	9	Fuel injector to fuel rail O-ring seal (8 required)
4	Fuel tube spring lock couplings	10	FRPT sensor bolts (2 required)
5	Fuel rail bolts (4 required)	11	FRPT sensor
6	Fuel rail		

06017-F150-G236

Fig. 450 F-Series 5.4L engine fuel rail and injectors

18. If installing a new fuel rail, remove the 2 FRPT bolts and remove the FRPT sensor.

19. Inspect the O-ring seal and install a new seal if necessary.

20. To install, reverse the removal procedure.

➡**Install new O-ring seals on the fuel injectors. Lubricate the new fuel injector O-ring seals with clean engine oil prior to installing the fuel injectors.**

21. Torque the 2 FRPT bolts to 4 Nm (35 inch lbs.).

22. Torque the 4 fuel rail bolts to 10 Nm (89 inch lbs.).

6.8L Engine

See Figure 451.

1. Before servicing the vehicle, refer to the Precautions Section.

2. Release the fuel system pressure.

3. Disconnect the battery ground cable.

4. Remove the air cleaner outlet pipe.

5. Disconnect the fuel supply tube spring lock coupling.

6. Disconnect the 2 electrical connectors from the throttle body (TB).

7. Disconnect the positive crankcase ventilation (PCV) tube from the TB spacer.

8. Disconnect the 2 vacuum lines from the TB spacer.

9. Disconnect the fuel rail pressure and temperature sensor electrical and vacuum connectors.

10. Disconnect the 10 fuel injector electrical connectors.

11. Detach the main engine wiring harness retainer from the RH valve cover.

12. Detach the 2 main engine wiring harness retainers from the intake manifold and position the harness for access to remove the fuel rail.

➡**When removing the fuel rail, leave the fuel injectors in the intake manifold. This will make removal of the fuel rail easier.**

13. Remove the 6 fuel rail bolts and the fuel rail.

✳✳ WARNING

Use O-ring seals that are made of special fuel-resistant material. Use of ordinary O-rings can cause the fuel system to leak. Do not reuse the O-ring seals. Lubricate the O-ring seals with clean engine oil prior to installation.

14. Remove the fuel injectors and the fuel injector O-ring seals. Discard the O-ring seals.

15. To install, reverse the removal procedure. Torque the 6 fuel rail bolts to 10 Nm (89 inch lbs.)

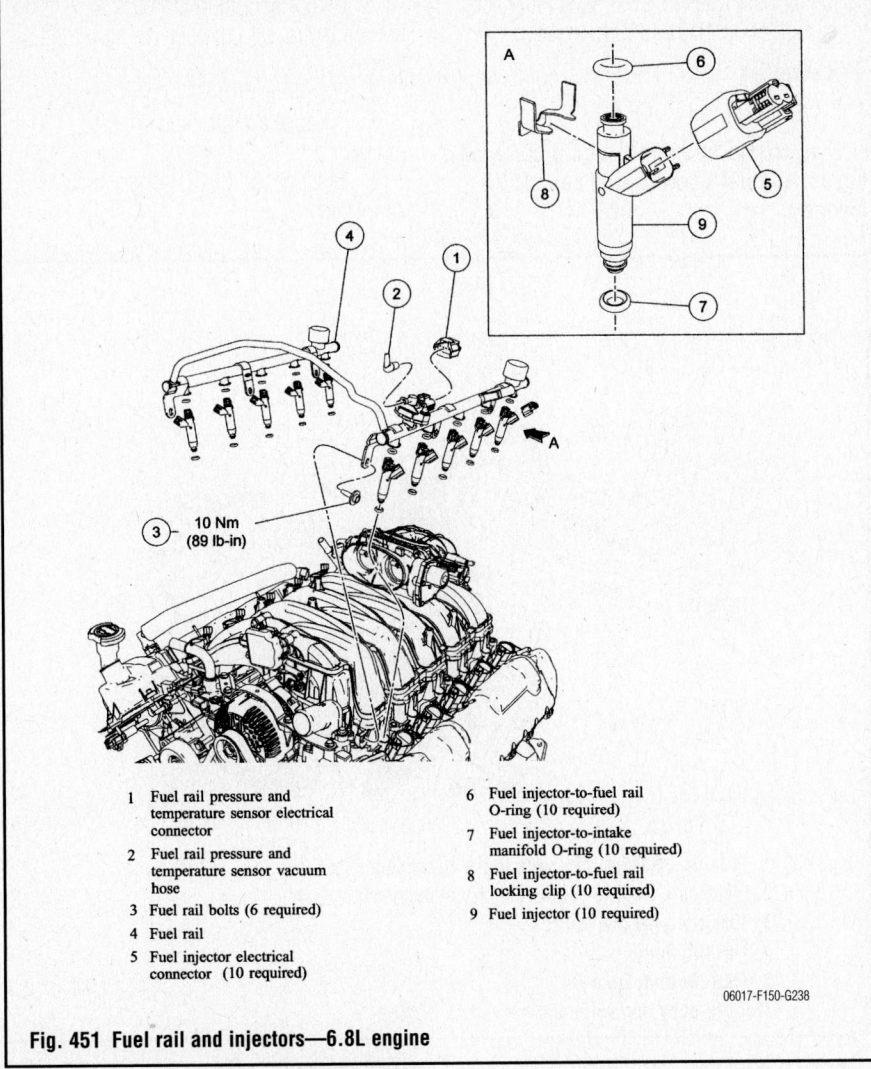

1 Fuel rail pressure and temperature sensor electrical connector
2 Fuel rail pressure and temperature sensor vacuum hose
3 Fuel rail bolts (6 required)
4 Fuel rail
5 Fuel injector electrical connector (10 required)
6 Fuel injector-to-fuel rail O-ring (10 required)
7 Fuel injector-to-intake manifold O-ring (10 required)
8 Fuel injector-to-fuel rail locking clip (10 required)
9 Fuel injector (10 required)

10 Nm (89 lb-in)

06017-F150-G238

Fig. 451 Fuel rail and injectors—6.8L engine

FUEL PUMP

REMOVAL & INSTALLATION

✳✳ CAUTION

Fuel injection systems remain under pressure, even after the engine has been turned OFF. The fuel system pressure must be relieved before disconnecting any fuel lines. Failure to do so may result in fire and/or personal injury.

1. Before servicing the vehicle, refer to the Precautions Section.
2. Remove or disconnect the following:
   - Negative battery cable
   - Fuel pressure
   - Fuel tank skid plate bolts and lower the skid plate.
   - Fuel
   - Fuel tank filler pipe hose from the tank
   - Fuel tank filler pipe vent hose from the tank
   - Fuel lines from the fuel pump
   - Front fuel tank connections
   - Rear Evaporative Emissions (EVAP) hose clamp and the hose
   - Electrical connector from the fuel pump
3. Support the fuel tank with a jack.
   - Fuel tank support strap bolts and the fuel tank straps
   - Fuel tank
   - Fuel pump bolts, if equipped with a metal tank
   - Fuel pump retaining ring, if equipped with a plastic tank
4. Squeeze the locking tabs and remove the fuel pump.

To install:
5. Install the fuel pump, using a new O-ring or gasket. With plastic tanks, make sure the alignment arrows match.
6. Installation is the reverse of removal. Note the following torques:

   a. Tighten the fuel tank strap bolts to:
   - F-150: 35 ft. lbs. (47 Nm)
   - F-250 and F-350 mid-ships tank: 30 ft. lbs. (40 Nm)
   - F-250 and F-350 aft-of-axle tank: 66 ft. lbs. (90 Nm)
   - Mark LT: 35 ft. lbs. (47 Nm)
7. Tighten the skid plate bolts to:
   - F-150: 15 ft. lbs. (20 Nm)
   - F-250 and F-350 mid-ships tank shield: 15 ft. lbs. (20 Nm)
   - F-250 and F-350 aft-of-axle tank cover: 66 ft. lbs. (90 Nm)
   - Mark LT: 15 ft. lbs. (20 Nm)
8. Connect the negative battery cable.

FUEL TANK

REMOVAL & INSTALLATION

✳✳ CAUTION

Fuel injection systems remain under pressure, even after the engine has been turned OFF. The fuel system pressure must be relieved before disconnecting any fuel lines. Failure to do so may result in fire and/or personal injury.

1. Before servicing the vehicle, refer to the Precautions Section.
2. Remove or disconnect the following:
   - Negative battery cable
   - Fuel pressure
   - Fuel tank skid plate bolts and lower the skid plate.
   - Fuel
   - Fuel tank filler pipe hose from the tank
   - Fuel tank filler pipe vent hose from the tank
   - Fuel lines from the fuel pump
   - Front fuel tank connections
   - Rear Evaporative Emissions (EVAP) hose clamp and the hose
   - Electrical connector from the fuel pump
3. Support the fuel tank with a jack.
   - Fuel tank support strap bolts and the fuel tank straps
   - Fuel tank

To install:
4. Installation is the reverse of removal. Note the following torques:

   a. Tighten the fuel tank strap bolts to:
   - F-150: 35 ft. lbs. (47 Nm)
   - F-250 and F-350 mid-ships tank: 30 ft. lbs. (40 Nm)
   - F-250 and F-350 aft-of-axle tank: 66 ft. lbs. (90 Nm)
   - Mark LT: 35 ft. lbs. (47 Nm)

5. Tighten the skid plate bolts to:
- F-150: 15 ft. lbs. (20 Nm)
- F-250 and F-350 mid-ships tank shield: 15 ft. lbs. (20 Nm)
- F-250 and F-350 aft-of-axle tank cover: 66 ft. lbs. (90 Nm)
- Mark LT: 15 ft. lbs. (20 Nm)

6. Connect the negative battery cable.

IDLE SPEED

ADJUSTMENT

Idle speed is maintained by the Powertrain Control Module (PCM). No adjustment is necessary or possible.

THROTTLE BODY

REMOVAL & INSTALLATION

4.2L Engine

See Figure 452.

➡The throttle body bore and plate area have a special coating and cannot be cleaned.

1. Before servicing the vehicle, refer to the precautions in the beginning of this section.
2. Remove the air cleaner outlet tube.
3. Disconnect the electronic throttle body electrical connector.
4. Remove the bolts and the electronic throttle body.
5. Inspect the throttle body gasket. Install a new gasket, if necessary.

6. To install, reverse the removal procedure. Tighten to 10 Nm (89 inch lbs.).

4.6L Engine

See Figure 453.

➡The throttle body bore and plate area have a special coating and cannot be cleaned.

1. Before servicing the vehicle, refer to the precautions in the beginning of this section.
2. Disconnect the battery ground.
3. Remove the air cleaner outlet pipe.
4. Disconnect the TP sensor electrical connector.

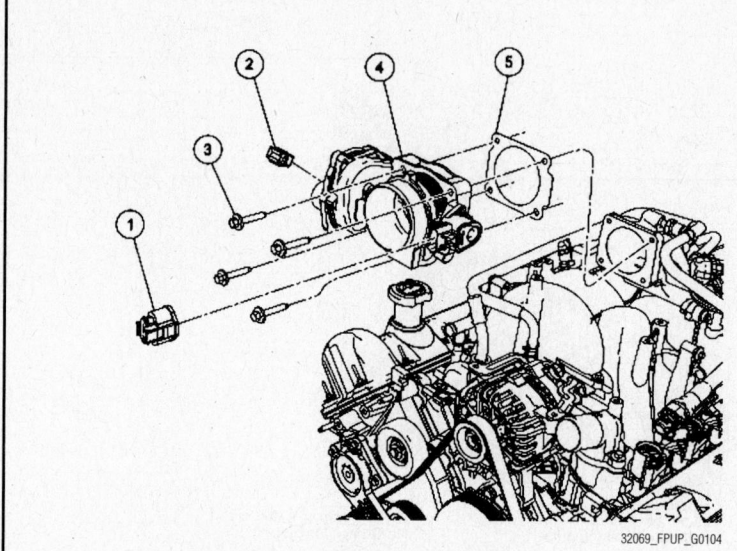

Fig. 453 1. Throttle position (TP) sensor electrical connector
2. Electronic throttle control electrical connector
3. Throttle body (TB) bolts
4. Throttle body
5. Throttle body gasket
Throttle body and related parts—4.6L engine

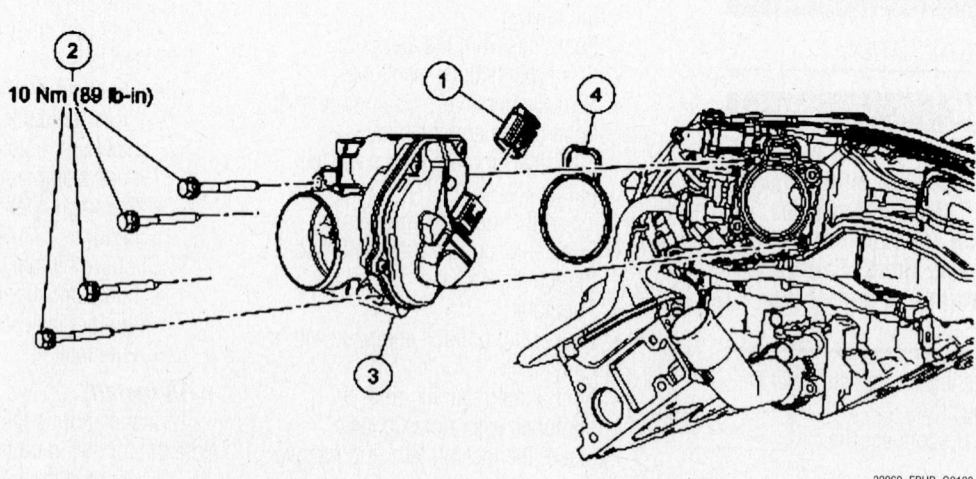

Fig. 452 1. Electronic throttle body electrical connector
2. Electronic throttle body bolts
3. Electronic throttle body
4. Electronic throttle body gasket
Throttle body and related parts—4.2L engine

5. Disconnect the electronic throttle control electrical connector.

6. Remove the TB bolts and the TB and discard the gasket.

7. To install, reverse the removal procedure. Install a new TB gasket. To install, tighten to 9 Nm (80 inch lbs.). Tighten an additional 90 degrees.

5.4L Engine

See Figure 454.

➡**The throttle body bore and plate area have a special coating and cannot be cleaned.**

1. Before servicing the vehicle, refer to the precautions in the beginning of this section.

2. Disconnect the battery ground cable.

3. Remove the air cleaner and air cleaner intake pipe.

4. Disconnect the electronic throttle control electrical connector.

5. Disconnect the throttle position (TP) sensor electrical connector.

6. Remove the 4 throttle body (TB) bolts and the TB and discard the TB O-ring seal.

7. To install, reverse the removal procedure. To install, tighten to 9 Nm (80 inch lbs.). Tighten an additional 90 degrees.

6.8L Engine

See Figure 455.

1. Before servicing the vehicle, refer to the precautions in the beginning of this section.

2. Disconnect the battery ground cable.

3. Remove the air cleaner outlet tube.

4. Disconnect the electronic throttle control electrical connector.

5. Disconnect the TP sensor electrical connector.

6. Remove the 4 throttle body bolts and the throttle body and discard the throttle body gasket.

7. To install, reverse the removal procedure. To install, tighten to 9 Nm (80 inch lbs.). Tighten an additional 90 degrees.

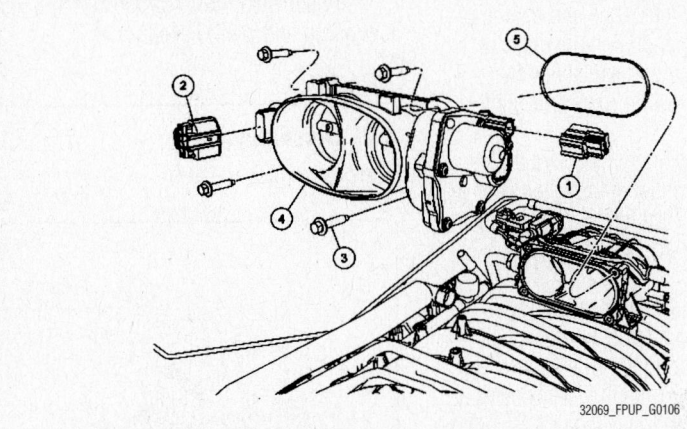

32069_FPUP_G0106

Fig. 455 1. Electronic throttle control electrical connector
2. Throttle position (TP) sensor electrical connector
3. Throttle body bolts
4. Throttle body
5. Throttle body gasket
Throttle body and related parts—6.8L engine

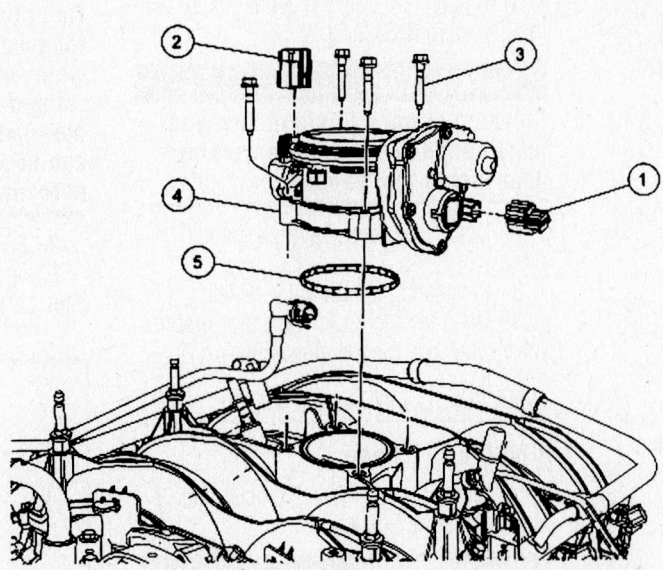

32069_FPUP_G0105

Fig. 454 1. Electronic throttle control electrical connector
2. Throttle position (TP) sensor electrical connector
3. Throttle body (TB) bolts
4. TB
5. TB O-ring seal
Throttle body and related parts—5.4L engine, exc. supercharged engines

FUEL

FUEL SYSTEM SERVICE PRECAUTIONS

Safety is the most important factor when performing not only fuel system maintenance but any type of maintenance. Failure to conduct maintenance and repairs in a safe manner may result in serious personal injury or death. Maintenance and testing of the vehicle's fuel system components can be accomplished safely and effectively by adhering to the following rules and guidelines.

• To avoid the possibility of fire and personal injury, always disconnect the negative battery cable unless the repair or test procedure requires that battery voltage be applied.

• Always relieve the fuel system pressure prior to disconnecting any fuel system component (injector, fuel rail, pressure regulator, etc.), fitting or fuel line connection. Exercise extreme caution whenever relieving fuel system pressure to avoid exposing skin, face and eyes to fuel spray. Please be advised that fuel under pressure may penetrate the skin or any part of the body that it contacts.

• Always place a shop towel or cloth around the fitting or connection prior to loosening to absorb any excess fuel due to spillage. Ensure that all fuel spillage (should it occur) is quickly removed from engine surfaces. Ensure that all fuel soaked cloths or towels are deposited into a suitable waste container.

• Always keep a dry chemical (Class B) fire extinguisher near the work area.

• Do not allow fuel spray or fuel vapors to come into contact with a spark or open flame.

• Always use a back-up wrench when loosening and tightening fuel line connection fittings. This will prevent unnecessary stress and torsion to fuel line piping.

• Always replace worn fuel fitting O-rings with new. Do not substitute fuel hose or equivalent where fuel pipe is installed.

Before servicing the vehicle, make sure to also refer to the precautions in the beginning of this section as well.

FUEL SYSTEM PRESSURE

RELIEVING

6.0L Diesel Engine

1. Before servicing the vehicle, refer to the Precautions Section.

2. Raise and safely support the vehicle.
3. Disconnect both battery ground cables.
4. Open the fuel/water separator drain valve to release the fuel pressure.

FUEL CONDITIONING MODULE

The Fuel Condition Module contains the fuel pump and water separator.

DRAINING

6.0L Diesel Engine

See Figure 456.

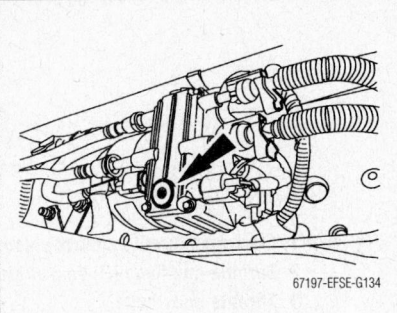

67197-EFSE-G134

Fig. 456 Fuel/water separator drain valve—6.0L Diesel Engine

1. Before servicing the vehicle, refer to the Precautions Section.

✳✳ CAUTION

Smoking or open flame of any type must not be present when working near fuel or fuel vapor.

2. Disconnect both battery ground cables.
3. Raise and support the vehicle.
4. Open the fuel/water separator drain valve to release the fuel pressure.

REMOVAL & INSTALLATION

6.0L Diesel Engine

1. Before servicing the vehicle, refer to the Precautions Section.

✳✳ CAUTION

Smoking or open flame of any type must not be present when working near fuel or fuel vapor.

2. Disconnect both battery ground cables.
3. Raise and support the vehicle.

4. Open the fuel/water separator drain valve to release the fuel pressure.
5. Disconnect the electrical connectors.
6. Disconnect the fuel pump electrical connector.
7. Disconnect the fuel warmer electrical connector.
8. Disconnect the water-in-fuel electrical connector.
9. Disconnect the fuel hoses.
10. Remove the fuel hose retaining clips and discard. Disconnect the fuel hoses from the fuel pump.
11. Press in the retaining clips and release the fuel hoses.
12. Remove the mounting nuts and the fuel conditioning module.
13. To install, reverse the removal procedure. Torque the nuts to 11 ft. lbs. (15 Nm).

FUEL FILTER

REMOVAL & INSTALLATION

6.0L Diesel Engine

See Figure 457.

1. Before servicing the vehicle, refer to the Precautions Section.

✳✳ CAUTION

Do not smoke or carry lighted tobacco or open flame of any type when working on or near any fuel related component. Highly flammable mixtures are always present and can be ignited, resulting in possible personal injury.

2. Relieve the fuel system pressure.
3. Disconnect the fuel lines from the fuel filter.

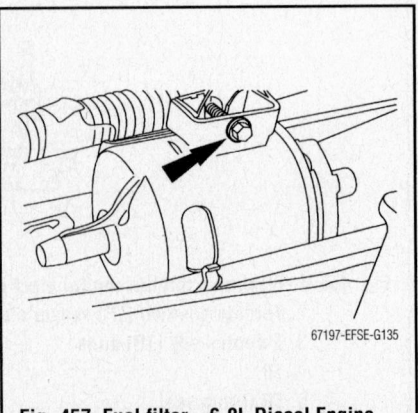

67197-EFSE-G135

Fig. 457 Fuel filter—6.0L Diesel Engine

4. Remove the fuel filter.
5. Loosen the fuel filter clamp screw.

➡**Make sure that an audible click is heard when installing the fuel lines. Pull back on the fuel lines to confirm engagement.**

6. To install, reverse the removal procedure.

DRAINING WATER FROM THE SYSTEM

See Figure 458.

1. Before servicing the vehicle, refer to the precautions in the beginning of this section.
2. With the vehicle in NEUTRAL, position it on a hoist.
3. Disconnect both battery ground cables.
4. Drain the fuel conditioning module by removing the drain plug.
5. Reinstall the drain plug once the fuel conditioning module is drained.

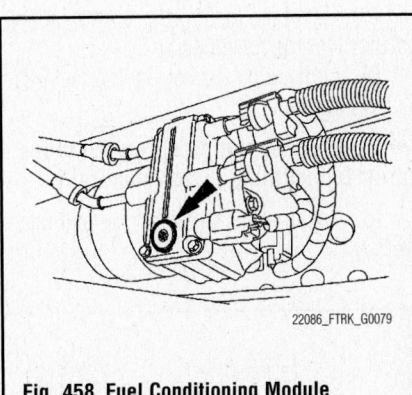

22086_FTRK_G0079

Fig. 458 Fuel Conditioning Module drain plug

FUEL SYSTEM PURGING

6.0L Diesel Engine

Fuel pressure in the cylinder head fuel galleries is controlled by a fuel pressure regulator. The fixed orifice is an air bleed. It is the highest point in the fuel system. It allows the air behind the fuel pressure regulator to be vented to the fuel tank rather than ingested in the fuel galleries. The fuel pressure regulator contains a spring-loaded poppet valve, which opens to allow excess fuel to return to the fuel-conditioning module.

FUEL INJECTORS

REMOVAL & INSTALLATION

✳ CAUTION

Observe all applicable safety precautions when working around fuel.

Whenever servicing the fuel system, always work in a well ventilated area. Do not allow fuel spray or vapors to come in contact with a spark or open flame. Keep a dry chemical fire extinguisher near the work area. Always keep fuel in a container specifically designed for fuel storage; also, always properly seal fuel containers to avoid the possibility of fire or explosion.

6.0L Diesel Engine

Early Build

See Figures 459 through 461.

1. Before servicing the vehicle, refer to the Precautions Section.
2. If removing the right fuel injectors, remove the evaporator case.
3. Remove the valve cover.
4. Disconnect the fuel injector electrical connector.
5. Disconnect the high-pressure oil rail supply line at the high-pressure oil rail.
6. Remove the bolts and the high-pressure oil rail.
7. Disconnect and remove the high-pressure oil supply line.

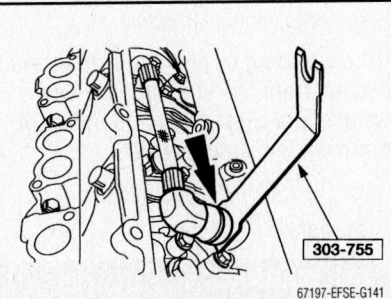

303-755

67197-EFSE-G141

Fig. 459 Disconnect the high-pressure oil rail supply line at the high-pressure oil rail—6.0L Diesel Engine

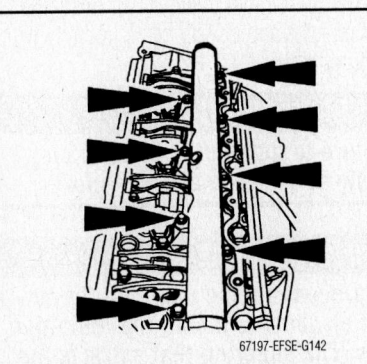

67197-EFSE-G142

Fig. 460 Remove the bolts and the high-pressure oil rail—6.0L Diesel Engine

✳✳ WARNING

Do not attempt to apply battery voltage to the fuel injector or damage to the fuel injector will occur.

8. Using a 19 mm socket, push the fuel injector electrical connector out of the rocker arm carrier.

✳✳ WARNING

To prevent engine damage, do not use air tools to remove the fuel injectors. The clip that extracts the injector can dislodge and fall into the oil drain hole.

➡**There is no need to drain the fuel rail.**

➡**If engine coolant is found in the combustion chambers, It may be necessary to install a new injector sleeve.**

9. Remove the bolt, fuel injector hold-down clamp and fuel injector.

To install:

✳✳ WARNING

If the fuel injector oil inlet D-shaped O-ring is damaged, a new fuel injector must be installed.

10. Install new O-ring seals and copper washer on the fuel injector. Lubricate the fuel injector and O-ring seals liberally with clean engine oil.

✳✳ WARNING

To prevent engine damage, do not use air tools to install the fuel injectors. The clip that extracts the injector can dislodge and fall into the oil drain hole.

11. Install the fuel injector, fuel injector hold-down clamp and bolt. Torque to 24 ft. lbs. (33 Nm).

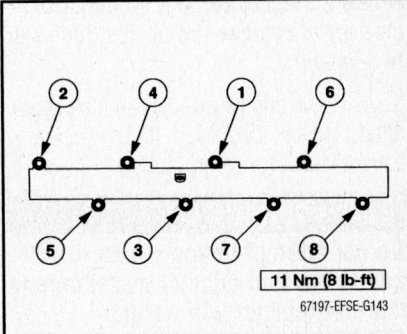

11 Nm (8 lb-ft)

67197-EFSE-G143

Fig. 461 High pressure oil rail torque sequence—early build 6.0L Diesel Engine

12. Install the fuel injector electrical connector into the rocker carrier.

13. Apply engine oil to the top fuel injector O-ring seals.

14. Install the high-pressure oil rail and bolts.

15. Install the high-pressure oil rail.

16. Install the bolts finger tight.

17. Tighten the bolts in the sequence shown.

18. Install the high-pressure oil line.

19. Connect the fuel injector electrical connector.

20. Install the valve covers.

21. If removed, install the evaporator case.

Late Build

See Figures 462, 463, and 464

1. Before servicing the vehicle, refer to the Precautions Section.

2. Remove the valve cover.

3. Disconnect the fuel injector electrical connector.

✳✳ WARNING

To prevent engine damage, it is recommended that a new crankcase-to-head tube to installed each time it is removed. The D-rings are not replaceable. If you reuse the crankcase-to-head tube, you assume the risk for leakage. You must inspect each D-ring carefully for evidence of cutting, abrasion or twisting and never reuse a tube exhibiting any of these conditions.

4. Remove the crankcase-to-head tube assembly.

➡Do not remove the oil rail end plugs or acoustic wave attenuator port fitting. Service parts are not available to support the components.

5. Remove the bolts and the high-pressure oil rail.

➡Use a shop towel and brake parts cleaner to remove the oil residue prior to removal.

6. If the crankcase-to-head tube separated, use the special tool to remove the lower crankcase-to-head tube.

✳✳ WARNING

Do not attempt to apply battery voltage to the fuel injector or damage to the fuel injector will occur.

7. Using the special tool, push the fuel injector electrical connector out of the rocker arm carrier.

8. Prior to removing the injector assembly, insert clean shop towels in the oil drain holes adjacent to each glow plug.

✳✳ WARNING

Failure to account for all snaprings or pieces prior to placing the vehicle back in service can cause engine damage. A missing snapring can be ingested into the lube oil system, causing severe engine damage.

✳✳ WARNING

To prevent engine damage, do not use air tools to remove the fuel injectors. The snapring that extracts the injector can dislodge and fall into the oil drain hole.

➡There is no need to drain the fuel rail.

➡If engine coolant is found in the combustion chambers, it may be necessary to install a new injector sleeve.

➡Use a tool like Snap-On® SDMT440 Torx®to avoid damaging the fuel injector plastic and to avoid interference with the evaporator case.

9. Remove the bolt, fuel injector hold-down clamp and fuel injector.

➡If a snapring or piece of a snapring is missing from the injector hold-down assembly, it must be located prior to removing the shop towels.

10. Remove the shop towels.

To install:

✳✳ WARNING

If the fuel injector oil inlet D-shaped O-ring is damaged, a new fuel injector must be installed.

11. Install new O-ring seals and copper washer on the fuel injector. Lubricate the fuel injector and O-ring seals liberally with clean engine oil.

✳✳ WARNING

Failure to tighten the injector correctly can lead to engine failure.

✳✳ WARNING

To prevent engine damage, do not use air tools to install the fuel injectors. The snapring that extracts the injector can dislodge and fall into the oil drain hole.

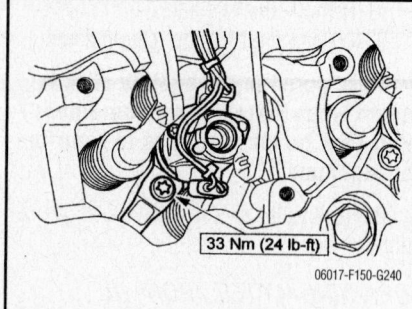

Fig. 462 Injector installation—6.0L Diesel Engine

12. Install the fuel injector, fuel injector hold-down clamp and bolt. Torque to 24 ft. lbs. (33 Nm).

✳✳ WARNING

Make sure the injector wiring is clear of all moving parts or engine damage can occur.

13. Install the fuel injector electrical connector into the rocker carrier.

14. Apply engine oil to the top fuel injector O-ring seals.

➡Apply clean engine oil on the tubes prior to installing the oil manifold.

15. Position the oil rail on the fuel injectors.

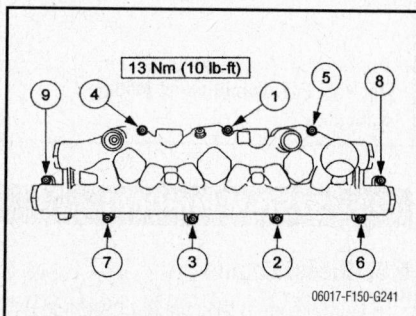

Fig. 463 Oil rail bolt torque sequence—late build 6.0L Diesel Engine

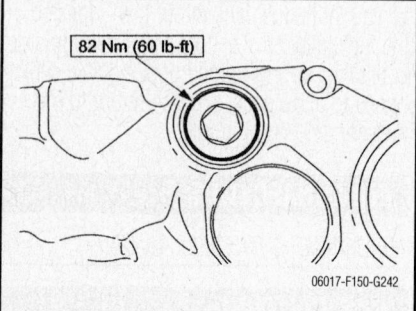

Fig. 464 Crankcase-to-head tube assembly—late build 6.0L Diesel Engine

a. Place the oil rail on top of the carrier so that the four single ball tubes are engaging the injector lead angle.

b. Insert three bolts, two on the ends of the straight side of the oil rail and one in the middle of the wavy side of the rail. Install the guide studs six to seven turns.

c. Press the oil rail into the fuel injectors.

d. Make sure that the oil rail mounting feet are flat against the mounting surface.

e. Loosely install the six bolts.

16. Install the oil rail retaining bolts.

a. Remove the three guide bolts.

b. Loosely install three remaining bolts.

c. Tighten the nine bolts in the sequence shown to 10 ft. lbs. (13 Nm).

※ WARNING

To prevent engine damage, it is recommended that a new crankcase-to-head tube to installed each time it is removed. The D-rings are not replaceable. If you reuse the crankcase-to-head tube, you assume the risk for leakage. You must inspect each D-ring carefully for evidence of cutting, abrasion or twisting and never reuse a tube exhibiting any of these conditions.

➡**Apply clean engine oil to the crankcase-to-head tube prior to installation.**

17. Install the crankcase-to-head tube assembly. Torque to 60 ft. lbs. (82 Nm).

18. Connect the fuel injector electrical connector.

19. Install the valve covers.

FUEL INJECTOR CONTROL MODULE

REMOVAL & INSTALLATION

6.0L Diesel Engine

See Figure 465.

※ WARNING

Make sure the ignition switch is in the OFF position prior to working on the electronic engine controls.

1. Before servicing the vehicle, refer to the precautions in the beginning of this section.

2. Turn the ignition switch to the OFF position.

※ CAUTION

Never remove the pressure relief cap while the engine is operating or when the cooling system is hot. Failure to follow these instructions can result in damage to the cooling system or engine or result in personal injury. To avoid having scalding hot coolant or steam blow out of the degas bottle (coolant reservoir) when removing the pressure relief cap, wait until the engine has cooled, then wrap a thick cloth around the pressure relief cap and turn it slowly. Step back while the pressure is released from the cooling system. When certain all the pressure has been released, (still with a cloth) turn and remove the pressure relief cap. Failure to follow these instructions can result in personal injury.

3. Relieve the cooling system pressure. Disconnect and plug or cap the engine vent hose and radiator vent hose.

4. Remove the bolts and position the degas (coolant reservoir) bottle aside.

5. On late build vehicles: Disconnect the two exhaust pressure (EP) sensor harness pin-type retainers. Disconnect the EP sensor electrical connector and position the harness aside.

6. Remove the two bolts, two nuts and turbocharger intake tube bracket.

7. Remove the fuel injector control module (FICM) bolts.

※ WARNING

Make sure both latches are released before removing the electrical con-

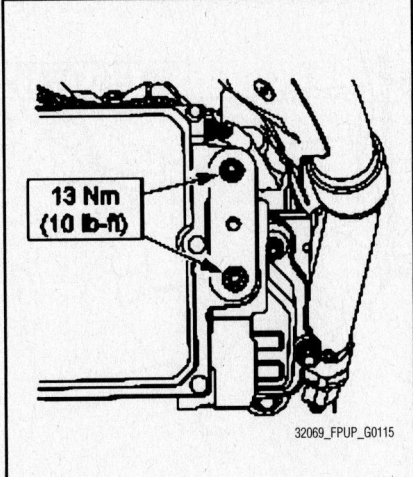

Fig. 465 FICM bolts—6.0L Diesel Engine

nectors or connector damage can occur.

8. Position out the FICM and disconnect the electrical connectors. Remove the FICM.

9. To install, reverse the removal procedure.

FUEL PRESSURE REGULATOR

REMOVAL & INSTALLATION

Pressure Regulator

See Figure 466.

1. Before servicing the vehicle, refer to the precautions in the beginning of this section.

2. Remove the secondary fuel filter and remove all fuel from the fuel filter housing.

3. Disconnect the fuel return tube from the regulator cover.

※ CAUTION

Clean all fuel residue from the engine compartment. Failure to follow these instructions may result in personal injury.

4. Remove the screws and the fuel pressure regulator cover.

5. Remove and discard the fuel pressure regulator cover O-ring seal.

6. Remove the restrictor, spring and poppet valve.

7. Clean the fuel pressure regulator bore in the fuel filter housing.

8. To install, reverse the removal procedure. Tighten the fuel line fitting to 43 Nm (32 ft. lbs.).

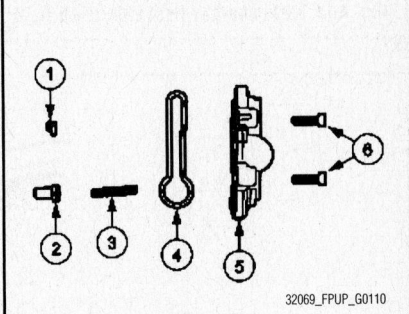

Fig. 466 1. Fixed orifice
2. Poppet valve and O-ring seal
3. Spring
4. O-ring seal
5. Cover
6. Screw, Torx®M5
Fuel pressure regulator—6.0L Diesel Engine

Injection Pressure Regulator

Early Build

See Figures 467 and 468.

1. Before servicing the vehicle, refer to the precautions in the beginning of this section.
2. Raise and safely support the vehicle.
3. Vehicles with automatic transmission: Remove the fluid level indicator. Remove the transmission fluid fill tube nut. Position aside the transmission fluid filler tube.
4. Remove the turbocharger heat shield.

➡**It will be necessary to position aside or remove the heat insulating wrap.**

5. Disconnect the injector pressure regulator (IPR) valve electrical connector.

➡**Use a 1⅜ inch 12-point deep flare nut crowfoot wrench to remove the valve.**

6. Remove the IPR valve.
7. To install, reverse the removal procedure. Apply clean engine oil to the IPR valve prior to installing it. Torque the IPR to 50 Nm (37 ft. lbs.).

Late Build

See Figures 469 and 470.

1. Before servicing the vehicle, refer to the precautions in the beginning of this section.

Fig. 469 Rear FICM bracket—6.0L Diesel Engine

2. Remove the turbocharger intake tube.
3. Remove the fuel injector control module (FICM). For additional information, refer to the procedure in this section.
4. Remove the retaining nuts and the rear FICM bracket.
5. Remove the retaining nuts from the heat shield bracket. Position the ground wire aside.
6. Disconnect the wiring retainer from the back of the heat shield bracket.
7. Remove the bolts and the heat shield bracket.
8. Remove the intake manifold stud.
9. Position back the injection pressure regulator (IPR) valve electrical connector heat insulating wrap.
10. Disconnect the IPR valve electrical connector.
11. Disconnect the snap and remove the heat insulating wrap.
12. Remove the IPR valve.

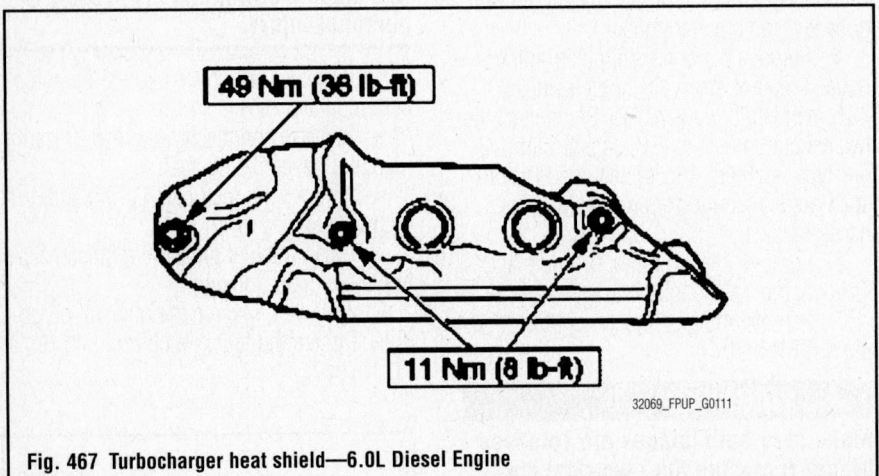

Fig. 467 Turbocharger heat shield—6.0L Diesel Engine

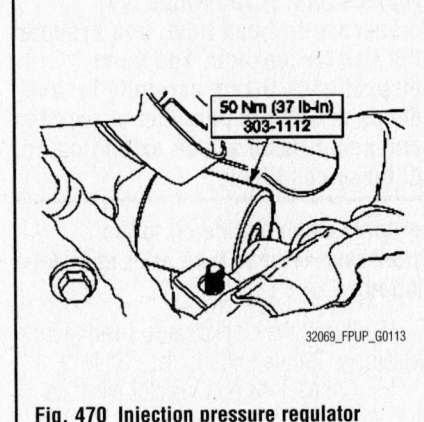

Fig. 470 Injection pressure regulator valve—late build 6.0L Diesel Engines

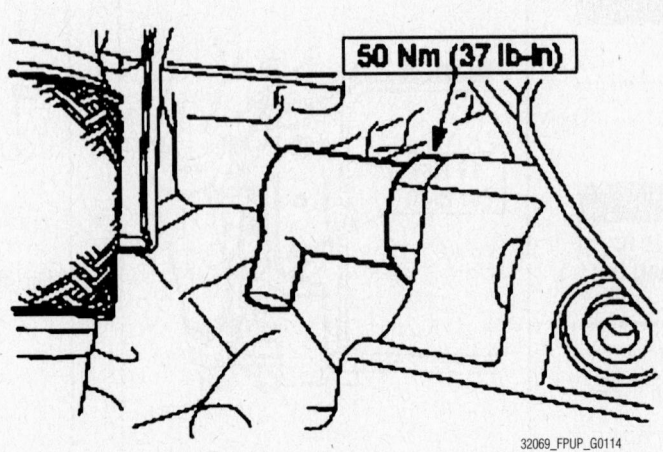

Fig. 468 Injection pressure regulator valve—early build 6.0L Diesel Engines

→It is necessary to re-install the heat insulating wrap on the IPR valve.

13. To install, reverse the removal procedure. Apply clean engine oil to the IPR valve prior to installing. Observe the following torques:

- IPR: 50 Nm (37 ft. lbs.)
- Intake manifold stud: 11 Nm (8 ft. lbs.)
- FICM bracket: 8 Nm (71 inch lbs.)

FUEL SUPPLY PUMP

REMOVAL & INSTALLATION

6.0L Diesel Engine

The fuel pump is located in the fuel conditioning module.

GLOW PLUGS

REMOVAL & INSTALLATION

6.0L Diesel Engine

Early Build

See Figure 471.

1. Before servicing the vehicle, refer to the Precautions Section.
2. If servicing the right glow plugs, remove the evaporator core housing.
3. Disconnect the glow plug electrical connector.
4. Remove the glow plug buss bar.

→If coolant residue is found on the glow plug, a new glow plug sleeve may have to be installed.

5. Remove the glow plug.

To install:
6. Install the glow plug. Torque to 14 ft. lbs. (19 Nm).
7. Clean and inspect the O-rings and install new if necessary.

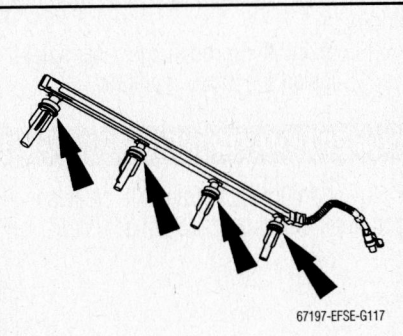

Fig. 471 Apply clean engine oil to the O-rings—early build 6.0L Diesel Engines

8. Apply clean engine oil to the O-rings.
9. Install the glow plug buss bar.
10. Connect the glow plug electrical connector.
11. If removed, install the evaporator core housing.

Late Build

See Figure 472.

1. Before servicing the vehicle, refer to the Precautions Section.
2. Disconnect the glow plug electrical connector.

❊❊ WARNING

Do not pull on the wiring to remove the glow plug connector or damage may occur.

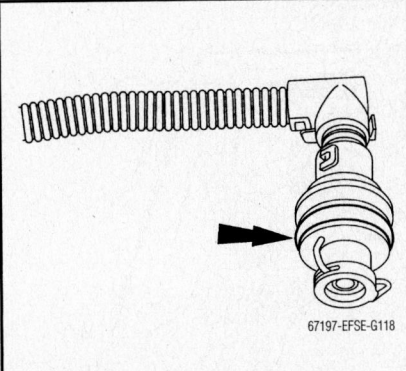

Fig. 472 Apply clean engine oil to the O-rings—late build 6.0L Diesel Engines

3. Remove the glow plug harness.

→If coolant residue is found on the glow plug, a new glow plug sleeve may have to be installed.

4. Remove the glow plug.

To install:
5. Install the glow plug. Torque to 14 ft. lbs. (19 Nm).
6. Clean and inspect the O-rings and install new if necessary.
7. Apply clean engine oil to the O-rings.
8. Install the glow plug harness.
9. Connect the glow plug electrical connector.

HIGH PRESSURE OIL PUMP

REMOVAL & INSTALLATION

6.0L Diesel Engine

Early Build

See Figures 473 through 477.

1. Before servicing the vehicle, refer to the Precautions Section.
2. Remove the intake manifold.
3. Remove the turbocharger heat shield.
4. Remove the bolts and the high-pressure oil pump cover. Use a thin gasket scraper to separate the cover from the crankcase.
5. Remove and discard the press-in-place gasket.
6. Position the dial indicator with bracketry onto the oil pump drive and check the oil pump drive gear backlash.

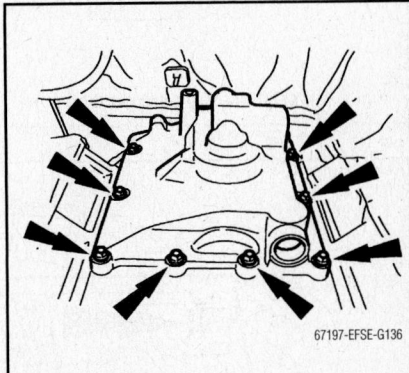

Fig. 473 Remove the high-pressure oil pump cover

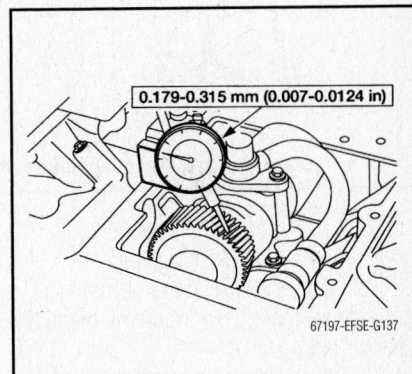

Fig. 474 Check the oil pump drive gear backlash

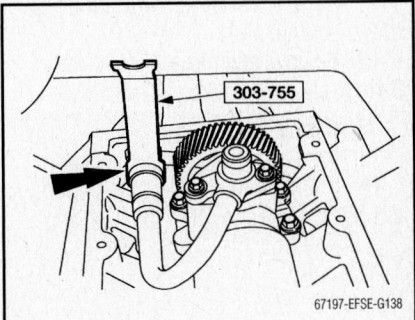

Fig. 475 Using the special tool, disconnect and remove the high-pressure oil pump discharge pipe

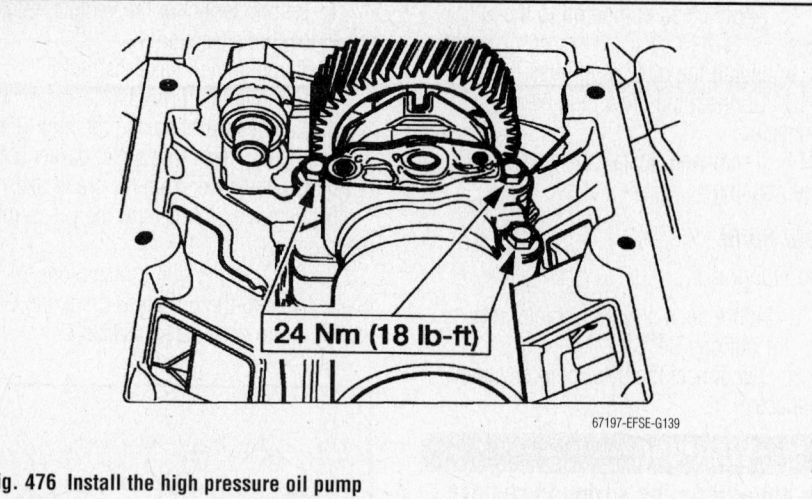

Fig. 476 Install the high pressure oil pump

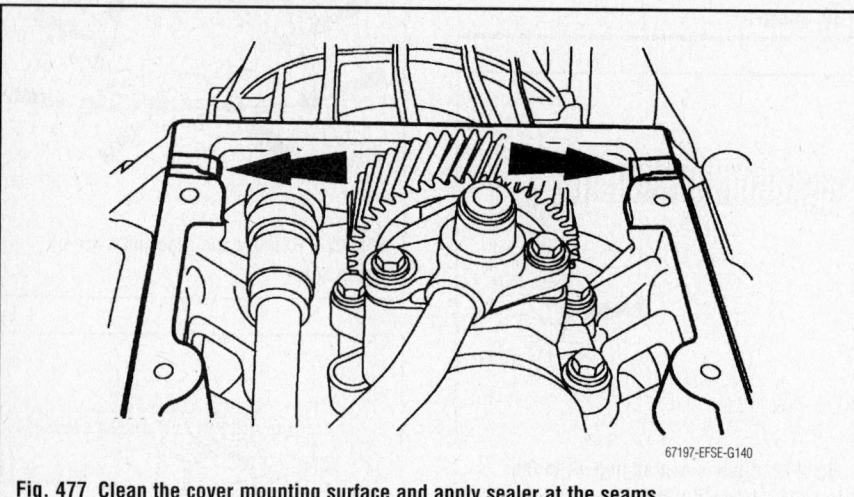

Fig. 477 Clean the cover mounting surface and apply sealer at the seams

7. Remove the bolts from the high-pressure oil pump discharge pipe.

8. Using the special tool, disconnect and remove the high-pressure oil pump discharge pipe.

9. Remove and discard the D-shaped O-ring seal.

10. Remove and discard the high-pressure pump O-ring seal.

11. Remove the bolts and the high-pressure oil pump.

12. Remove and discard the lower O-ring seal.

To install:

13. Install a new lower O-ring seal.

14. Install the high-pressure oil pump and bolts. Torque to 18 ft. lbs. (24 Nm).

15. Install the high-pressure pump O-ring seal.

16. Install the oil pump discharge pipe.

17. Install the bolts for the oil discharge pipe.

18. Position the dial indicator with bracketry onto the oil pump drive and check the oil pump drive gear backlash.

19. Install a new D-ring seal on the high-pressure discharge pipe. Torque to 71 inch lbs. (8 Nm).

20. Install a new press-in-place gasket in the high-pressure pump cover.

21. Clean the cover mounting surface and apply sealer at the seams.

22. Install the high-pressure pump cover and bolts. Torque to 8 ft. lbs. (11 Nm).

23. Install the turbocharger heat shield.

24. Install the intake manifold.

Late Build

1. Before servicing the vehicle, refer to the Precautions Section.

2. Remove the intake manifold.

3. Remove the turbocharger heat shield.

4. Remove the bolts and the high-pressure oil pump cover.

5. Use a thin gasket scraper to separate the cover from the crankcase.

6. Remove and discard the press-in-place gasket.

7. Position the dial indicator with bracketry onto the oil pump drive and check the oil pump drive gear backlash.

8. Remove the bolts from the high-pressure oil pump discharge pipe. Position the high-pressure discharge pipe aside.

9. Remove and discard the high-pressure pump O-ring seal.

10. Remove the bolts and the high-pressure oil pump.

11. Remove and discard the lower O-ring seal.

To install:

12. Install a new lower O-ring seal.

13. Install the high-pressure oil pump and bolts.

14. Install the high-pressure pump O-ring seal.

15. Position back the high-pressure discharge tube and install the bolts.

16. Position the dial indicator with bracketry onto the oil pump drive and check the oil pump drive gear backlash.

17. Install a new D-ring seal on the high-pressure discharge pipe.

18. Install a new press-in-place gasket in the high-pressure pump cover. Clean the cover mounting surface and apply sealer at the seams.

19. Install the high-pressure pump cover and bolts.

20. Install the turbocharger heat shield.

21. Install the intake manifold.

INJECTION TIMING

Injection timing for the 6.0L diesels is computer controlled and not adjustable.

HEATING & AIR CONDITIONING SYSTEM

BLOWER MOTOR

REMOVAL & INSTALLATION

F-150 and Mark LT

See Figure 478.

1. Remove the RH lower A-pillar trim panel.
2. Position aside the carpet below the blower motor.
3. Disconnect the blower motor electrical connector.
4. Remove the 3 blower motor screws.
5. Remove the blower motor.
6. Remove the blower motor wheel clip.
7. Remove the blower motor wheel.
8. To install, reverse the removal procedure.

F-250 and F-350

See Figures 479 through 482.

Fig. 479 Remove the retainers and the insulator—F-250 and F-350 w/6.0L diesel

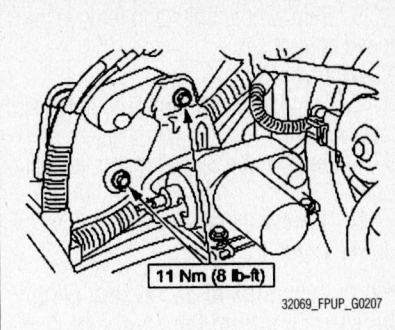

11 Nm (8 lb-ft)

32069_FPUP_G0207

Fig. 480 Vacuum pump—F-250 and F-350 w/6.0L diesel

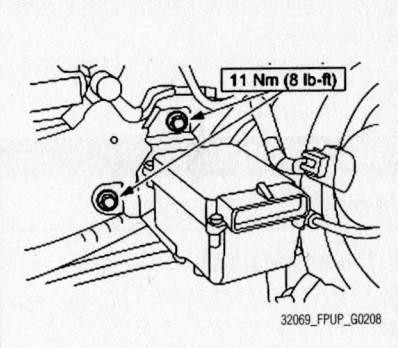

11 Nm (8 lb-ft)

32069_FPUP_G0208

Fig. 481 Speed control servo—F-250 and F-350 w/5.4L and 6.8L engines

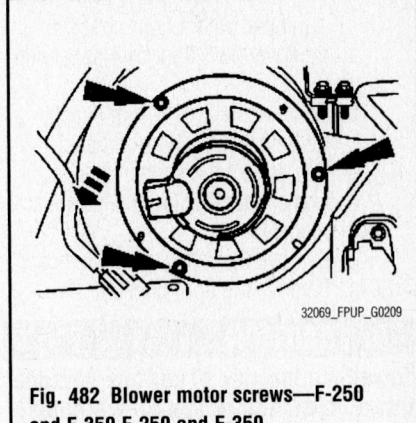

32069_FPUP_G0209

Fig. 482 Blower motor screws—F-250 and F-350 F-250 and F-350

Vehicles with 6.0L Diesel:

1. Remove the retainers and the insulator.
2. Disconnect the electrical connector from the vacuum pump.
3. Remove the bolts.
4. Disconnect the vacuum hose and remove the vacuum pump and mounting bracket.

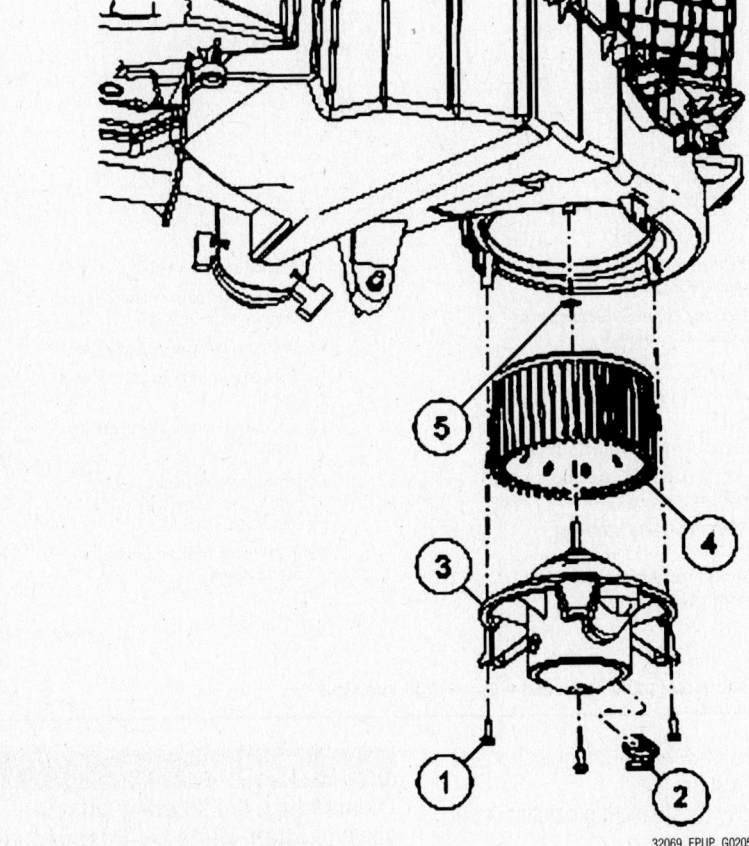

Fig. 478 1. Blower motor screw
2. Blower motor electrical connector
3. Blower motor
4. Blower motor wheel
5. Blower motor wheel clip
Blower motor—F-150 and Mark LT

Vehicles with 5.4L and 6.8L:

5. Disconnect the speed control servo connector.

6. Remove the bolts and remove the speed control servo.

All vehicles:

7. Disconnect the blower motor electrical connector.

8. Remove the blower motor ventilation tube.

9. Remove the screws and remove the blower motor.

➡**If the wheel is to be reused, clean the corrosion from the shaft end prior to removing the wheel.**

10. Remove the wheel from the blower motor.

11. Remove the push clip.

12. Remove the wheel from the blower motor.

13. To install, reverse the removal procedure.

HEATER CORE

REMOVAL & INSTALLATION

F-150 and Mark LT

See Figures 483, 484, 485, 486, 487, 488 and 489.

1. Before servicing the vehicle, refer to the Precautions Section.

2. If equipped with adjustable pedals, move the pedals to the full forward position.

3. If equipped with a floor console:

a. Remove the 3 floor trim panel push pins.

b. Remove the 2 floor trim panels.

c. Remove the shifter trim panel.

d. Disconnect the shifter cable.

e. Disconnect the floor console electrical connector.

f. Remove the 4 floor console bolts.

g. Remove the floor console.

✳✳ CAUTION

To reduce the risk of serious personal injury, read and follow all warnings, cautions, notes and instructions in the supplemental restraint system (SRS) deactivation/reactivation procedure.

4. De-power the supplemental restraint system (SRS). For additional information, refer to Steering.

5. Position the left and right door weatherstrip seals aside.

6. Remove the A-pillar trim panels and right cowl side trim panel.

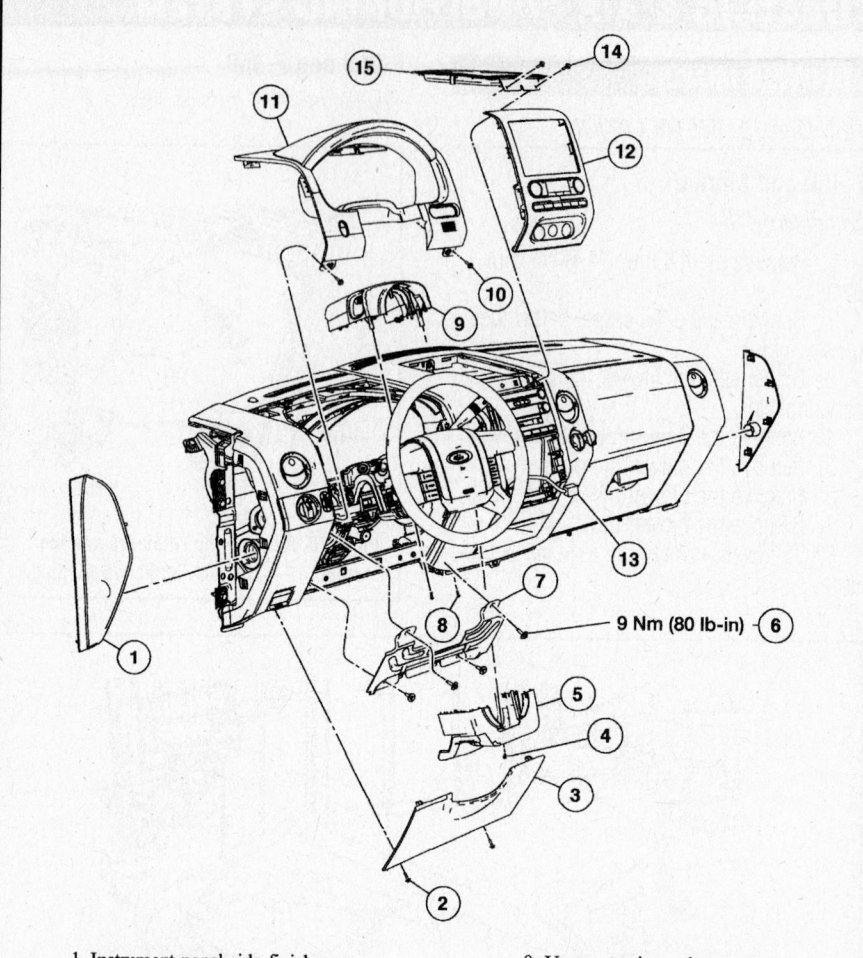

1 Instrument panel side finish panel (RH/LH)

2 Steering column opening trim screws (2 required)

3 Steering column opening trim

4 Lower steering column cover screw

5 Lower steering column cover

6 Steering column opening panel screws (4 required)

7 Steering column opening panel

8 Upper steering column cover screws (2 required)

9 Upper steering column cover

10 Instrument cluster finish panel screws (2 required)

11 Instrument cluster finish panel

12 Instrument panel center finish panel

13 Climate control electrical connector

14 Instrument cluster center finish panel screws (2 required)

15 Instrument cluster center finish panel

06017-F150-G25

Fig. 483 Instrument panel exploded view—F-150 and Mark LT

7. Remove the left and right instrument panel side finish panels.

8. Remove the 2 steering column opening trim screws.

9. Remove the steering column opening trim.

✳✳ WARNING

Removing the steering wheel without using a puller can damage the column bearings.

✳✳ WARNING

Do not allow the steering column shaft to rotate while the intermediate shaft is disconnected or damage to the clockspring can result. If there is evidence that the shaft has rotated, the clockspring must be removed and re-centered.

10. Place the steering wheel in the straight-ahead position and turn the ignition switch to the OFF position.

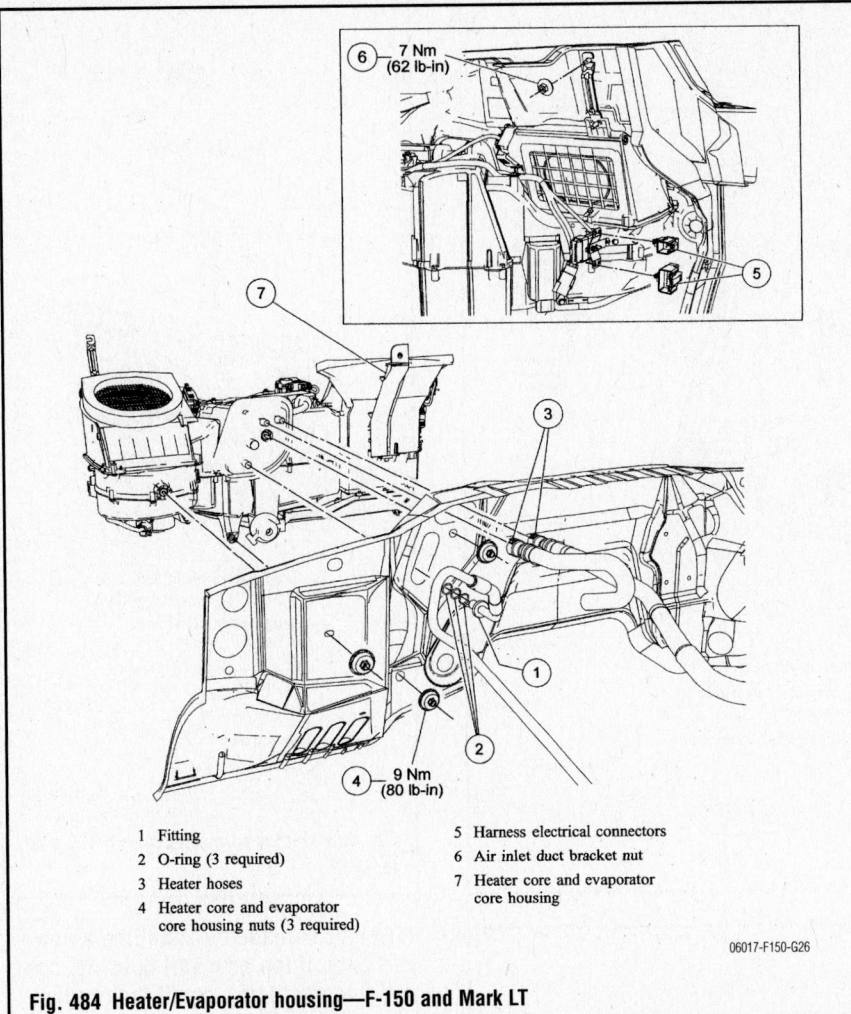

1 Fitting
2 O-ring (3 required)
3 Heater hoses
4 Heater core and evaporator core housing nuts (3 required)
5 Harness electrical connectors
6 Air inlet duct bracket nut
7 Heater core and evaporator core housing

06017-F150-G26

Fig. 484 Heater/Evaporator housing—F-150 and Mark LT

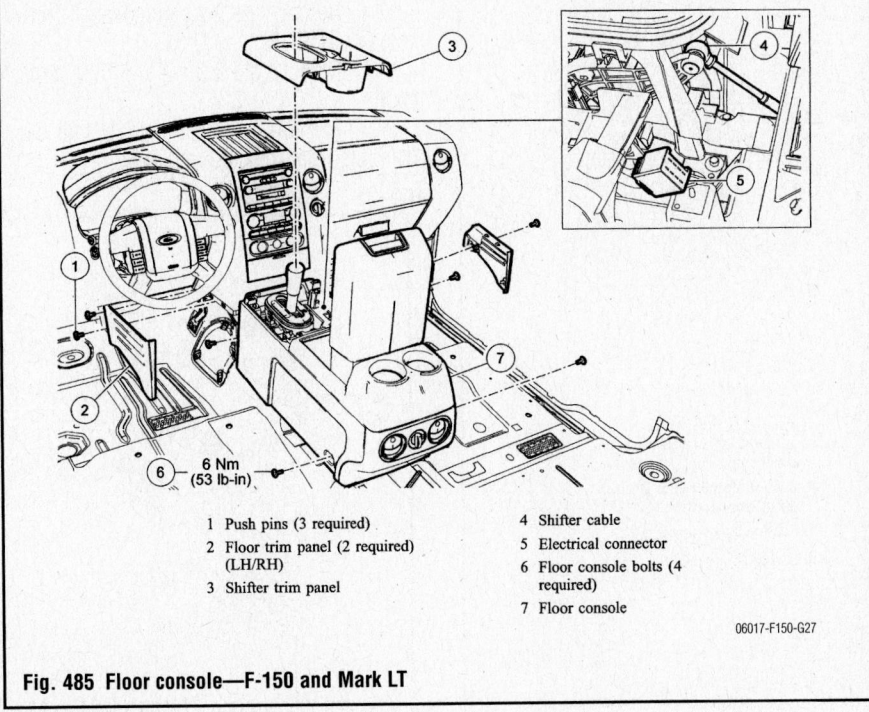

1 Push pins (3 required)
2 Floor trim panel (2 required) (LH/RH)
3 Shifter trim panel
4 Shifter cable
5 Electrical connector
6 Floor console bolts (4 required)
7 Floor console

06017-F150-G27

Fig. 485 Floor console—F-150 and Mark LT

✳✳ CAUTION

Always wear safety glasses when repairing an air bag supplemental restraint system (SRS) vehicle and when handling an air bag module. This will reduce the risk of injury in the event of an accidental deployment.

✳✳ CAUTION

Carry a live air bag module with the air bag and trim cover pointed away from your body. This will reduce the risk of injury in the event of an accidental deployment.

✳✳ CAUTION

Do not set a live air bag module down with the trim cover face down. This will reduce the risk of injury in the event of an accidental deployment.

✳✳ CAUTION

After deployment, the air bag surface can contain deposits of sodium hydroxide, a product of the gas generant combustion that is irritating to the skin. Wash your hands with soap and water afterwards.

✳✳ CAUTION

Never probe the connectors on the air bag module. Doing so can result in air bag deployment, which can result in personal injury.

✳✳ CAUTION

Air bag modules with discolored or damaged trim covers must be replaced, not repainted.

✳✳ CAUTION

To reduce the risk of personal injury, do not use any memory saver devices.

➤The air bag warning lamp illuminates when the RCM fuse is removed and the ignition switch is ON. This is normal operation and does not indicate a supplemental restraint system (SRS) fault.

➤The SRS must be fully operational and free of faults before releasing the vehicle to the customer.

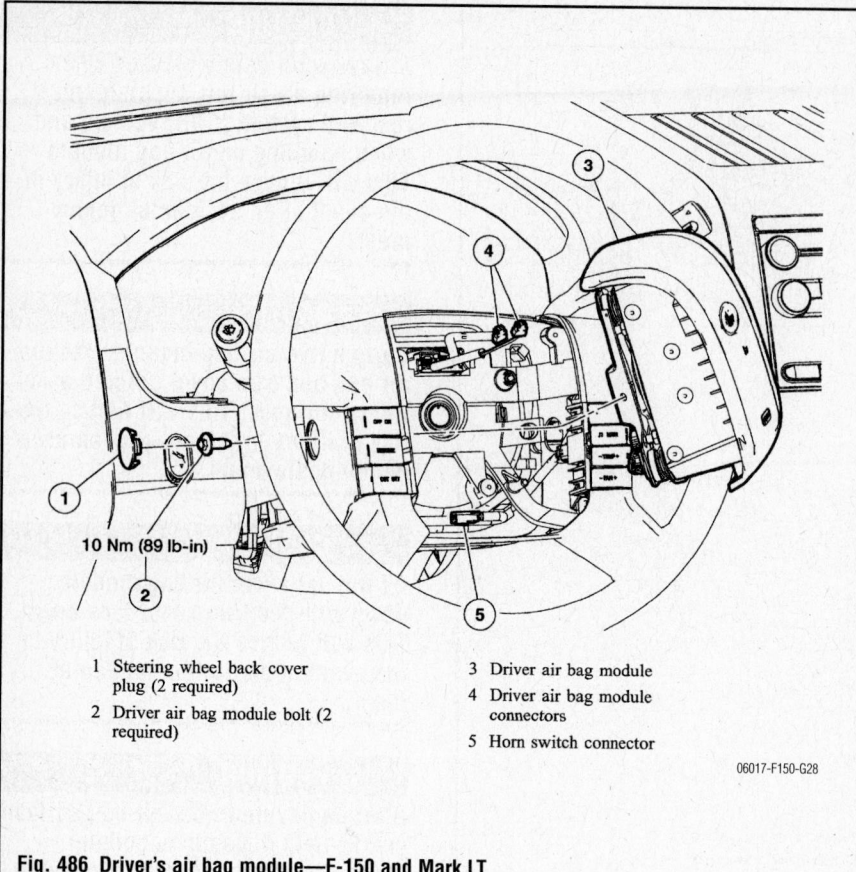

10 Nm (89 lb-in)

1 Steering wheel back cover plug (2 required)
2 Driver air bag module bolt (2 required)
3 Driver air bag module
4 Driver air bag module connectors
5 Horn switch connector

06017-F150-G28

Fig. 486 Driver's air bag module—F-150 and Mark LT

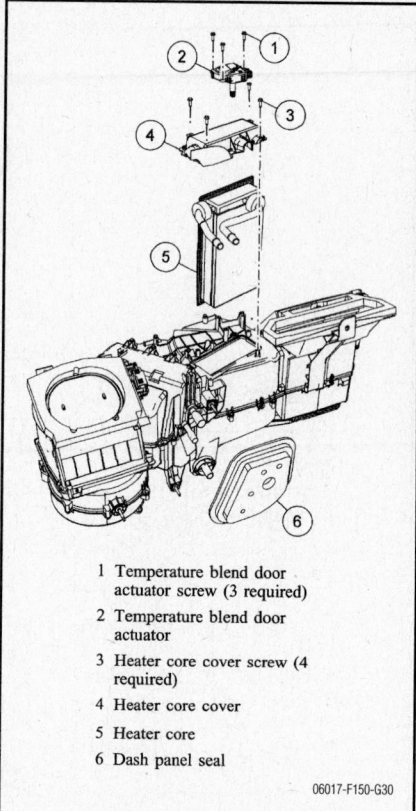

1 Temperature blend door actuator screw (3 required)
2 Temperature blend door actuator
3 Heater core cover screw (4 required)
4 Heater core cover
5 Heater core
6 Dash panel seal

06017-F150-G30

Fig. 488 Heater core removal—F-150 and Mark LT

➡ **Repair is made by installing a new part only. If the new part does not correct the condition, install the original part and perform the diagnostic procedure again.**

11. Remove the 2 steering wheel back cover plugs.

12. Remove the 2 driver's air bag module bolts.

13. Partially remove the driver's air bag module from the steering wheel.

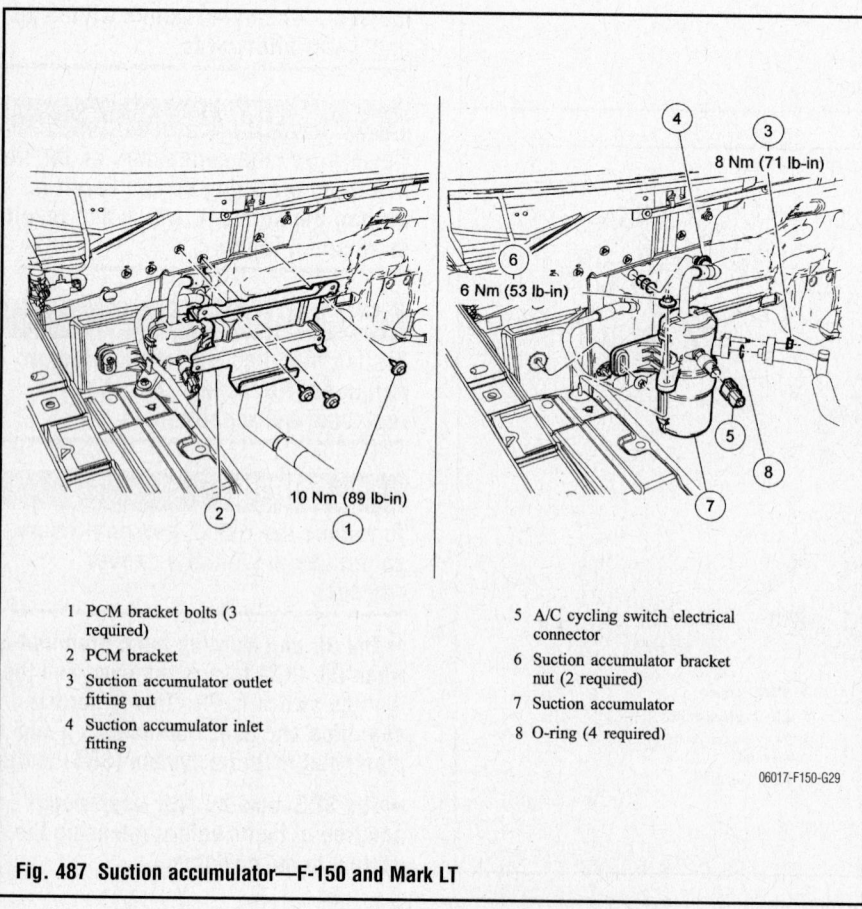

10 Nm (89 lb-in)
8 Nm (71 lb-in)
6 Nm (53 lb-in)

1 PCM bracket bolts (3 required)
2 PCM bracket
3 Suction accumulator outlet fitting nut
4 Suction accumulator inlet fitting
5 A/C cycling switch electrical connector
6 Suction accumulator bracket nut (2 required)
7 Suction accumulator
8 O-ring (4 required)

06017-F150-G29

Fig. 487 Suction accumulator—F-150 and Mark LT

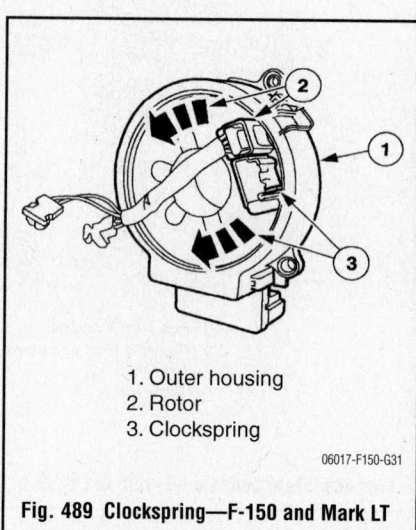

1. Outer housing
2. Rotor
3. Clockspring

06017-F150-G31

Fig. 489 Clockspring—F-150 and Mark LT

✳✳ **WARNING**

The clockspring electrical connectors are unique and cannot be reversed when connected to the driver's air bag module. Match the electrical connector key to the keyway in the driver's air bag module. Do not force the electrical connectors into the driver's air bag module during installation.

14. Disconnect the driver's air bag module electrical connectors.

15. Disconnect the horn switch electrical connector and remove the driver's air bag module.

➡**Do not remove the bolt until the steering wheel has been separated from the column.**

16. Loosen the steering wheel bolt.

17. Using a puller, separate the steering wheel from the steering column assembly.

18. Remove the steering wheel bolt and the steering wheel.

19. Remove the lower steering column cover screw.

20. Remove the lower steering column cover.

21. Remove the 2 upper steering column cover screws.

22. Remove the upper steering column cover.

23. Remove the instrument cluster finish panel.

24. Remove the instrument panel center finish panel.

25. Remove the instrument cluster center finish panel.

26. Remove the parking brake release handle bolt.

27. Position aside the parking brake release handle. Remove the parking brake release handle pin-type retainer.

28. Remove the hood release handle bolt.

29. Position aside the hood release handle.

30. Loosen the electrical connector screw and disconnect the bulkhead electrical connector.

31. Remove the ground bolt.

32. Disconnect the electrical connectors.

33. Position aside the front carpet.

34. Remove the 4 left center brace bolts.

35. Remove the left center brace.

36. If equipped, disconnect the transmission range indicator cable and position aside.

✳✳ **WARNING**

To avoid damage to the clockspring, do not allow the steering column shaft to rotate while the intermediate shaft is disconnected.

37. Remove the steering column pinch bolt and disconnect the steering column intermediate shaft.

38. Disconnect the steering column electrical connector.

39. Remove the ground bolt.

40. Disconnect the radio antenna.

41. Disconnect the 4 PDB (B1, B2, L1 and L2) electrical connectors.

42. Disconnect the ETAC electrical connector.

43. Disconnect the instrument panel electrical connectors.

44. Position aside the front carpet.

45. Remove the 4 right center brace bolts.

46. Remove the right center brace.

➡**If equipped with a floor console, remove the third center brace.**

47. If equipped, remove the 4 third center brace bolts.

48. If equipped, remove the third center brace.

49. Remove the 2 defrost grilles.

50. Disconnect the wiring harness pin-type retainer.

✳✳ **WARNING**

To avoid damage to the instrument panel, an assistant is required to support the panel before carrying out this step.

51. Remove the 9 instrument panel bolts.

✳✳ **WARNING**

Before removing the instrument panel, make sure all electrical connector wiring is free and not hindered.

52. Remove the instrument panel.

➡**Installation of a new suction accumulator is not required when repairing the air conditioning system, except when there is physical evidence of contamination from a failed A/C compressor or damage to the suction accumulator.**

53. Recover the refrigerant.

54. Remove the powertrain control module (PCM).

55. Remove the battery and battery tray.

56. Remove the PCM bracket.

57. Remove the suction accumulator outlet fitting nut and disconnect the fitting.

58. Discard the O-ring seal.

59. Disconnect the suction accumulator inlet fitting. Discard the O-ring seals.

60. Remove the 2 suction accumulator bracket nuts.

61. Remove the suction accumulator.

62. Disconnect the evaporator core spring lock coupling. Discard the O-ring seals.

63. Clamp off and disconnect the 2 heater core quick disconnect fittings.

64. Remove the 3 heater core and evaporator core housing nuts.

65. Disconnect the 2 harness electrical connectors.

66. Remove the air inlet duct bracket nut.

67. Remove the bolt and position the junction box aside.

68. Loosen the nut and remove the heater core and evaporator core housing.

69. Remove the dash panel seal from the heater core tubes.

70. Position the temperature blend door actuator aside.

71. Remove the heater core cover.

72. Remove the heater core.

➡**The heater core seal must be correctly installed to prevent airflow from bypassing the heater core.**

✳✳ **CAUTION**

Incorrect centralization may result in premature component failure. If in doubt when centralizing the clockspring, repeat the centralizing procedure. Failure to follow this instruction may result in personal injury.

✳✳ **WARNING**

Make sure the road wheels are in the straight-ahead position.

73. If the vehicle's clockspring has rotated out of center, follow these steps to center the clockspring.

a. Hold the clockspring outer housing stationary.

✳✳ **WARNING**

Overturning will destroy the clockspring. The internal ribbon wire acts as the stop and can be broken from its internal connection.

b. While turning the rotor counterclockwise, carefully feel for the ribbon wire to run out of length and for a slight resistance. Stop turning at this point.

c. Turn the clockspring clockwise approximately 3 turns. This is the center point of the clockspring. Do not allow the rotor to turn from this position. To prevent accidental rotation until the clockspring is installed, 2 pieces of tape may be applied to the clockspring.

➡**Slight turning of the clockspring rotor is allowable for alignment purposes to the steering column.**

d. With the flats of the clockspring aligned to the flats of the steering column, slide the clockspring onto the steering column. For vehicles receiving a new clockspring, remove the retaining pin. For vehicles reusing the clockspring that was removed, remove the tape.

74. To install, reverse the removal procedure. Evacuate, charge and leak test the system. Install new O-ring seals. Lubricate the refrigerant system with the correct amount of clean PAG oil.

75. Observe the following torques:
  • Heater core nut: 62 inch lbs. (7 Nm)
  • Air inlet duct bracket: 62 inch lbs. (7 Nm)
  • Heater core and evaporator core housing nuts: 80 inch lbs. (9 Nm)
  • Suction accumulator bracket nuts: 53 inch lbs. (6 Nm)
  • Suction accumulator outlet fitting nut: 71 inch lbs. (8 Nm)
  • PCM bracket: 89 inch lbs. (10 Nm)
  • Instrument panel bolts: 15 ft. lbs. (20 Nm)
  • Steering column pinch bolt: 30 ft. lbs. (40 Nm)

  • Steering wheel bolt and the steering wheel: 30 ft. lbs. (40 Nm)
  • Driver's air bag module bolts: 89 inch lbs. (10 Nm)
76. Fill the engine cooling system.

F-250 and F-350
See Figures 490 and 491.

1. Before servicing the vehicle, refer to the Precautions Section.
2. Clamp off and disconnect the heater water hoses from the heater core.
3. Disengage the stops and lower the glove compartment door.

➡**Do not attempt to bend any part of the panel/floor door lever. It is brittle and will break.**

4. Remove the panel/floor door vacuum control motor.
5. Remove the electronic blend door actuator and bracket assembly.
6. Remove the core cover screws.

➡**The heater core cover must be raised vertically before removal to avoid damage to the heater core housing.**

7. Raise the heater core cover.
8. Remove the heater core cover.
9. Remove the heater core.

➡**Position the temperature blend door manually to correctly align the actuator and the door. Do not power the actuator electrically. If it is not engaged with the temperature blend door, damage to the actuator can occur.**

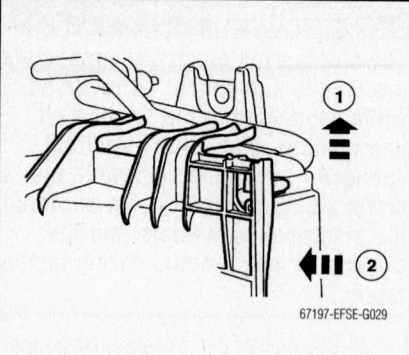

67197-EFSE-G029

Fig. 490 Remove the heater core cover— F-250 and F-350

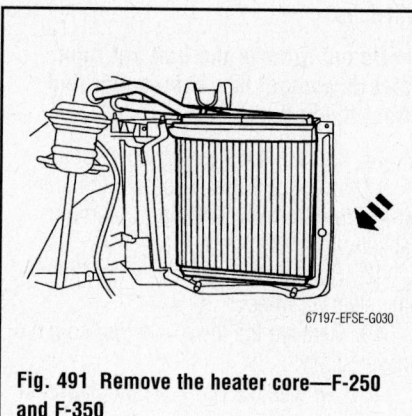

67197-EFSE-G030

Fig. 491 Remove the heater core—F-250 and F-350

➡**Add gasket between housing and cover before installing cover.**

10. To install, reverse the removal procedure.
11. Fill the engine cooling system.

STEERING

POWER STEERING GEAR

REMOVAL & INSTALLATION

F-150 and Mark LT
See Figures 492 and 493.

1. Before servicing the vehicle, refer to the Precautions Section.

➡**New O-ring seals must be installed any time the lines are disconnected from the steering gear.**

2. With the transmission in **Neutral**, raise and support the vehicle.
3. Remove the skid plate.

⁂ **WARNING**

The boots and clamps are designed to produce an airtight seal and protect the internal components of the

steering gear. If the seal is not airtight, the vacuum generated during turning will draw water and contamination into the gear, causing premature damage.

⁂ **WARNING**

Zip ties do not provide an airtight seal and must not be used.

⁂ **WARNING**

The inner ball joint grease is not compatible with water, and contamination trapped in the grease will degrade the life of the joint.

⁂ **WARNING**

If present, the orientation of the vent tube must be noted so the boots and

vent tubes can be installed in the correct location.

4. Remove the tire and wheel assembly.
5. Remove the lower shaft-to-steering gear bolt.
6. Disconnect the lower shaft.

➡**Do not allow the steering column shaft to rotate while the lower shaft is disconnected or damage to the clockspring can result. If there is evidence that the shaft has rotated, the clockspring must be removed and re-centered. Follow these steps to center the clockspring.**

e. Hold the clockspring outer housing stationary.

⁂ **WARNING**

Overturning will destroy the clockspring. The internal ribbon wire acts

as the stop and can be broken from its internal connection.

f. While turning the rotor counter-clockwise, carefully feel for the ribbon wire to run out of length and for a slight resistance. Stop turning at this point.

g. Turn the clockspring clockwise approximately three turns. This is the center point of the clockspring.

h. Do not allow the rotor to turn from this position. Two pieces of tape may be applied to the clockspring to prevent accidental rotation, until the clockspring is installed.

7. Remove the clamp plate-to-steering gear bolt

8. Remove the power steering high pressure hose.

9. Remove the O-ring seal.

10. Remove the power steering return hose

11. Remove the O-ring seal.

12. Remove the tie-rod nuts.

13. Remove the outer tie-rods. When repairing the right side, it is necessary to pull back the left inner tie-rod boot to hold the steering gear. Note the number of times the tie-rod ends turn for assembly reference. After removing the tie-rod end, remove the tie-rod end jam nut from the front wheel spindle tie-rod

14. Remove the bracket-to-crossmember nuts.

15. Remove the bracket-to-crossmember bolts.

16. Remove the steering gear-to-crossmember nuts.

17. Remove the steering gear-to-crossmember bolts.

18. Remove the bracket.

19. Remove the steering gear. Remove the steering gear through the left side wheel opening.

20. To install, reverse the removal procedure.

21. Fill and leak test the system.

22. Check and, if necessary, align the front end.

23. Install new O-ring seals onto the power steering hoses.

24. Observe the following torques:
- The 2 steering gear bracket-to-gear bolts and nuts: 150 Nm (111 ft. lbs.).
- The 2 steering gear bracket-to-crossmember bolts and nuts: 103 Nm (76 ft. lbs.).
- The 2 outer tie-rod end nuts: 150 Nm (111 ft. lbs.).
- The 2 outer tie-rod end lock nuts: 103 Nm (76 ft. lbs.).

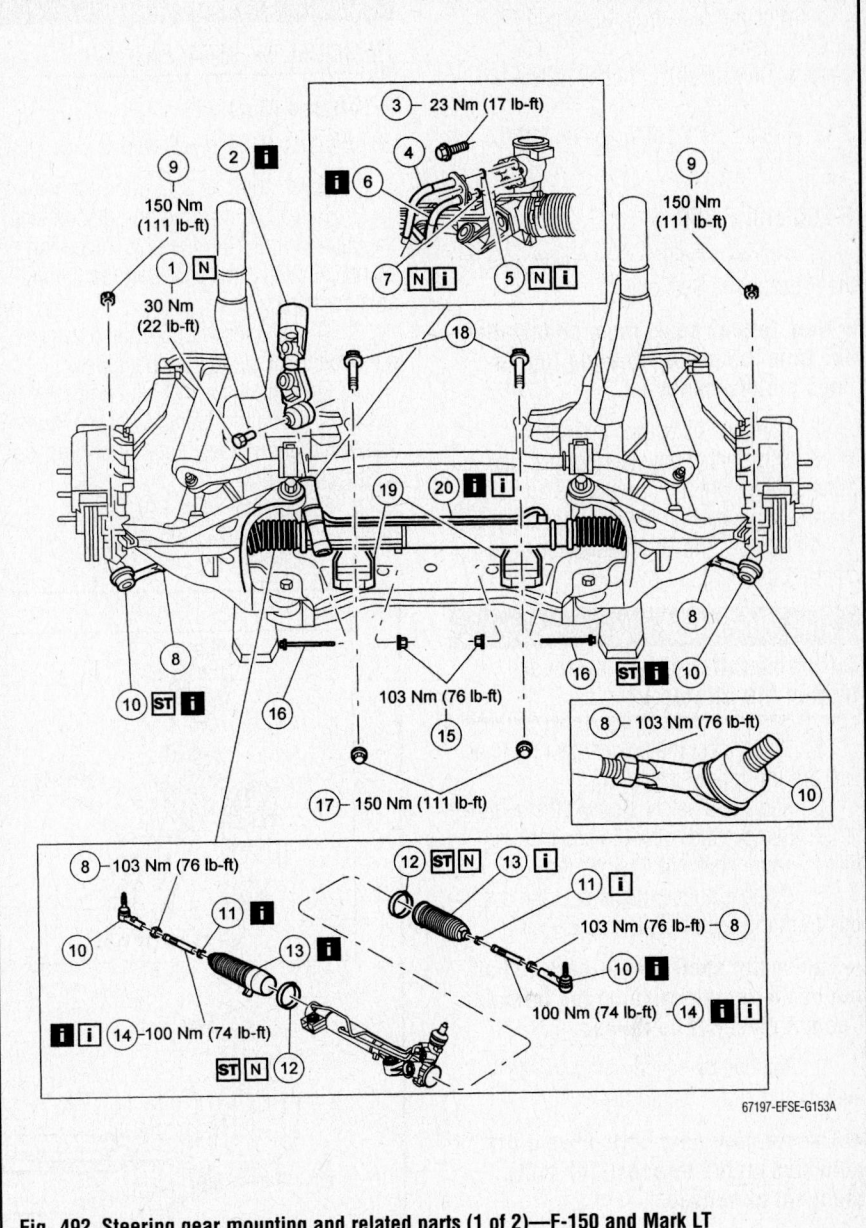

Fig. 492 Steering gear mounting and related parts (1 of 2)—F-150 and Mark LT

1	Lower shaft-to-steering gear bolt	11	Outer bellows clamp
2	Lower shaft (disconnect only)	12	Inner bellows clamp
3	Clamp plate-to-steering gear bolt	13	Steering gear bellows
4	Power steering high pressure hose	14	Inner tie-rod
5	O-ring seal	15	Bracket-to-crossmember nuts
6	Power steering return hose	16	Bracket-to-crossmember bolts
7	O-ring seal	17	Steering gear-to-crossmember nuts
8	Tie-rod lock nuts (loosen only)	18	Steering gear-to-crossmember bolts
9	Tie-rod nuts	19	Bracket
10	Outer tie-rods	20	Steering gear

67197-EFSE-G153B

Fig. 493 Keylist (2 of 2)

- Power steering high pressure line clamp plate bolt: 23 Nm (17 ft. lbs.).
- Oil drip shield bolts: 10 Nm (89 inch lbs.).
- Skid plate bolts: 25 Nm (18 ft. lbs.).

F-250 and F-350

1. Before servicing the vehicle, refer to the Precautions Section.

➡**New Teflon® seals must be installed any time the power steering line fittings are disconnected.**

2. Remove the engine air cleaner.
3. Disconnect the steering gear coupling shield from the line fittings and slide the shield upward on the intermediate shaft.
4. Remove the intermediate shaft-to-steering gear bolt.

✳✳ WARNING

During installation, do not over-tighten the fittings.

5. Disconnect the power steering lines. Discard the Teflon® seals.
6. Raise and safely support the vehicle.
7. Remove the cotter pin and the drag link-to-sector shaft nut. Discard the cotter pin.
8. Using a puller, disconnect the drag link from the sector shaft arm.

➡**The sector shaft arm-to-sector shaft nut has a dry adhesive on the threads. The nut must not be reused.**

9. Remove the sector shaft arm-to-sector shaft nut. Discard the nut.

➡**The steering gear bolts have a dry adhesive on the threads. The bolts must not be reused.**

10. Remove the 3 bolts and the steering gear. Discard the bolts.
11. Using a puller, remove the sector shaft arm.
12. To install, reverse the removal procedure. Note the following:
    - Using special tool 211-D027, install 2 new Teflon® seals on the power steering line fittings.
    - intermediate shaft-to-steering gear bolt 36 ft. lbs. (48 Nm)
    - power steering lines: 26 ft. lbs. (35 Nm)
    - drag link-to-sector shaft nut: 148 ft. lbs. (200 Nm)
    - sector shaft arm-to-sector shaft nut: 350 ft. lbs. (475 Nm)
    - steering gear: 111 ft. lbs. (150 Nm)
    - Fill the power steering system.

POWER STEERING PUMP

REMOVAL & INSTALLATION

F-150 and Mark LT

See Figures 494 through 496.

1. Raise and safely support the vehicle.
2. Release the clamp and disconnect the suction line from the power steering pump. Allow the fluid to drain into a suitable container.
3. On vehicles with 5.4L engine, remove the air cleaner intake pipe.
4. On vehicles with 4.6L engine, remove the cooling fan and shroud. For additional information, refer to Engine Fan & Shroud R&I.
5. On vehicles with 4.2L engine, remove the air cleaner outlet pipe.

6. Rotate the accessory drive belt tensioner clockwise and remove the accessory drive belt from the power steering pump pulley.
7. Using the special tool, remove the power steering pump pulley.
8. Disconnect the pressure line fitting-to-pump and position the high pressure line aside. Discard the Teflon® seal.
9. Remove the power steering pump.
10. On 4.6L, 5.4L engines, remove the 3 power steering pump bolts.
11. On 4.2L engines, remove the 4 power steering pump bolts.

To install:

12. Using the special tool, install a new Teflon® seal on the pressure line fitting.

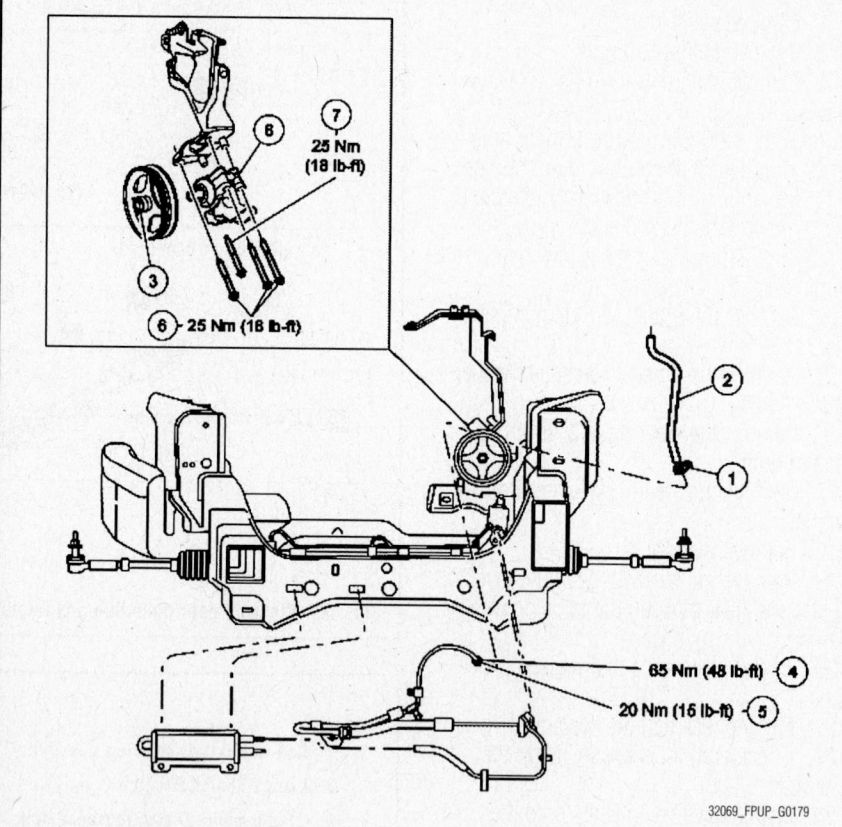

32069_FPUP_G0179

Fig. 494 1. Suction line-to-power steering pump clamp
 2. Suction line
 3. Power steering pump pulley
 4. Pressure line fitting-to-pump (4.6L, 5.4L engines)
 5. Pressure line fitting-to-pump (4.2L engine)
 6. Power steering pump bolts
 7. Power steering pump bolt (4.2L engine)
 8. Power steering pump
 Power steering pump and related parts—F-150 and Mark LT, 4.6L and 5.4L engine shown, 4.2L engine similar

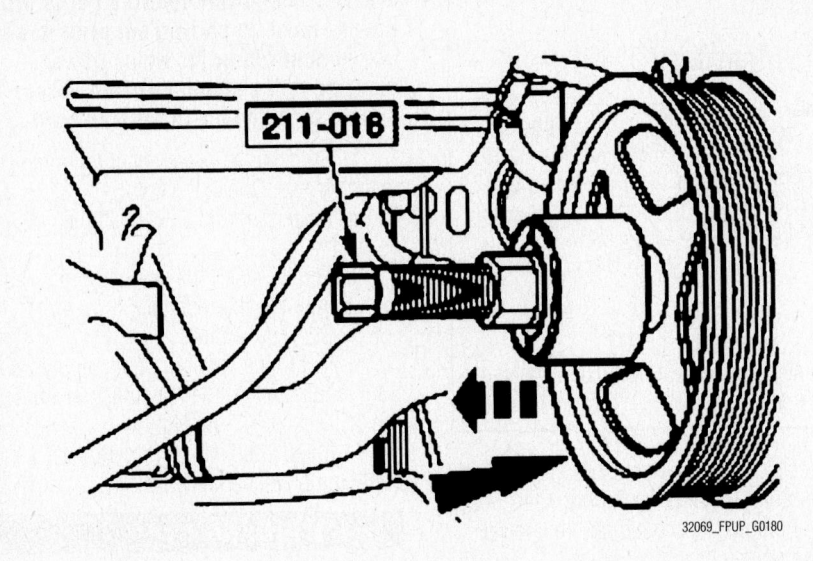

Fig. 495 Using the special tool, remove the power steering pump pulley—F-150 and Mark LT

13. On 4.6L, 5.4L engines, position the power steering pump and install the 3 bolts. Tighten to 25 Nm (18 ft. lbs.).

14. On 4.2L engines, position the power steering pump and install the 4 bolts. Tighten to 25 Nm (18 ft. lbs.).

15. Position the high pressure line and connect the fitting to the power steering pump.

- If equipped with a 4.6L or 5.4L engine, tighten to 65 Nm (48 ft. lbs.).
- If equipped with a 4.2L engine, tighten to 20 Nm (15 ft. lbs.).

16. Connect the suction line and install the clamp.

➡**Make sure the pulley is flush with the end of the power steering pump shaft.**

17. Using the special tool, install the power steering pump pulley.

18. Rotate the accessory drive belt tensioner and install the accessory drive belt on the power steering pump pulley.

19. On vehicles with 4.2L engine, install the air cleaner outlet pipe.

20. On vehicles with 4.6L engine, install the cooling fan and shroud.

21. On vehicles with 5.4L engine, Install the air cleaner intake pipe.

22. Install the power steering pump pulley. Fill the power steering system.

F-250 and F-350

See Figures 497, 498, 499, 500, 501, and 502.

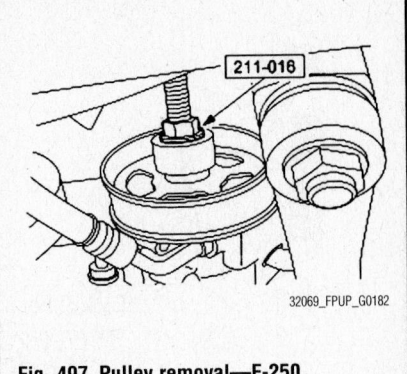

Fig. 497 Pulley removal—F-250 and F-350

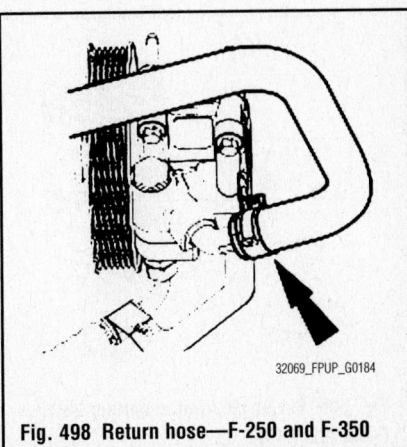

Fig. 498 Return hose—F-250 and F-350

❋❋❋ **WARNING**

While repairing the power steering system, care should be taken to prevent the entry of contaminants or premature failure of the power steering components can result.

➡**New Teflon® seals must be installed any time the power steering line fittings are disconnected.**

1. On vehicles with 6.0L Diesel Engine, remove the engine cooling fan. For additional information, refer to Engine Fan and Shroud in this section.

2. Rotate the tensioner and remove the accessory drive belt from the power steering pump pulley. For vehicles with air conditioning, rotate the tensioner clockwise. For vehicles without air conditioning, rotate the tensioner counterclockwise.

3. On vehicles with 5.4L and 6.8L engine, with the vehicle in NEUTRAL, position it on a hoist.

4. Using the special tool, remove the pulley. Inspect the pulley for paint marks in the web area near the hub. If there are 2 paint marks, discard the pulley. If there is no

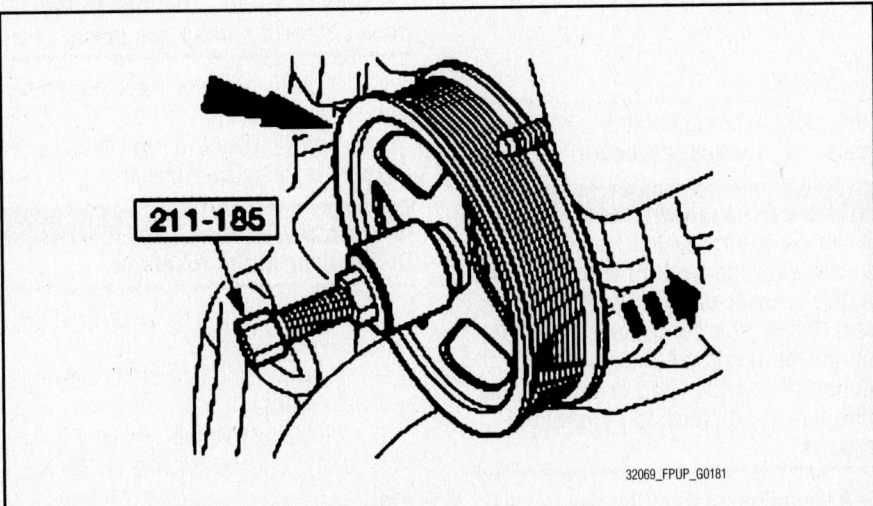

Fig. 496 Pulley installation—F-150 and Mark LT

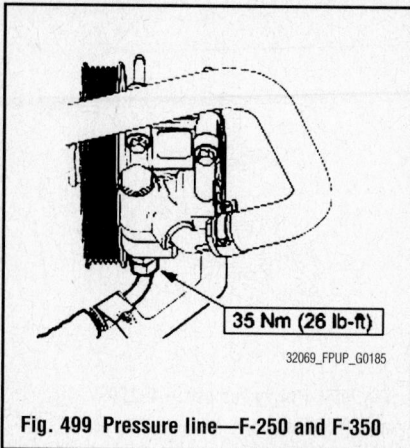

Fig. 499 Pressure line—F-250 and F-350

35 Nm (26 lb-ft)

32069_FPUP_G0185

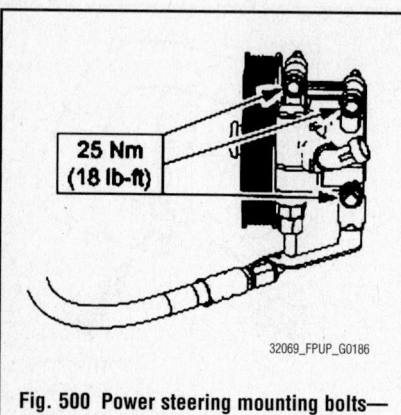

Fig. 500 Power steering mounting bolts—F-250 and F-350

25 Nm (18 lb-ft)

32069_FPUP_G0186

paint or 1 paint mark, use a paint pencil to mark the web area of the pulley near the hub.

5. Disconnect the return hose.

➡ **Thoroughly clean all debris from the pressure line-to-pump threads before installing the fitting.**

➡ **To prevent fluid leakage be sure to insert the pressure line into the quick connect before positioning the pressure line bracket and tightening the lower power steering pump bolt.**

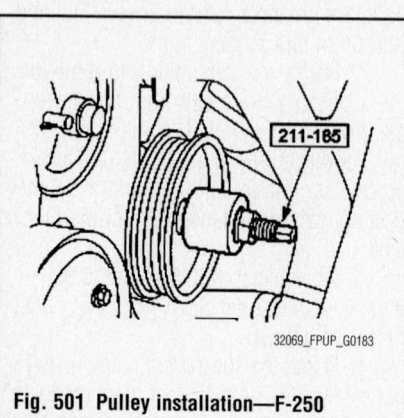

Fig. 501 Pulley installation—F-250 and F-350

211-185

32069_FPUP_G0183

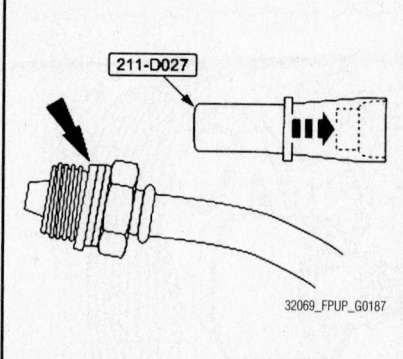

Fig. 502 Teflon® seal installation—F-250 and F-350

211-D027

32069_FPUP_G0187

6. Disconnect the pressure line-to-pump fitting. Discard the Teflon® seal.

7. Remove the 3 bolts and the power steering pump.

To install:

➡ **Replacement of the power steering pump pulley is necessary after being removed and installed 2 times.**

8. Using the special tool, install the power steering pump pulley.

➡ **Vehicle with air conditioning shown; vehicles without air conditioning similar.**

9. Rotate the tensioner and install the accessory drive belt on the power steering pump pulley. For vehicles with air conditioning, rotate the tensioner clockwise. For vehicles without air conditioning, rotate the tensioner counterclockwise.

10. On vehicles with 6.0L Diesel Engine, install the engine cooling fan.

11. The remainder of installation is the reverse of the removal procedure.

12. Using the special tool, install a new Teflon® seal on the pressure line fitting.

13. Fill the power steering system.

BLEEDING

➡ **A vacuum pump kit and adapter are necessary for this procedure.**

⁂ **WARNING**

If the air is not purged from the power steering system correctly, premature power steering pump failure can result. The condition can occur on pre-delivery vehicles with evidence of aerated fluid or on vehicles that have had steering component repairs.

➡ **A whine heard from the power steering pump can be caused by air in the**

system. The power steering purge procedure must be carried out prior to any component repair for which power steering noise complaints are accompanied by evidence of aerated fluid.

1. Remove the power steering pump reservoir cap. Check the fluid.

2. Raise the front wheels off the floor.

3. Tightly insert the stopper of the vacuum pump into the reservoir.

4. Start the engine.

5. Install the vacuum pump, apply vacuum, and maintain the maximum vacuum of 68–85 kPa (20–25 in. Hg).

6. If equipped with Hydro-Boost®, apply the brake pedal twice.

⁂ **WARNING**

Do not hold the steering wheel against the stops for more than 3 to 5 seconds at a time. Damage to the power steering pump can occur.

7. Cycle the steering wheel fully from stop-to-stop 10 times.

8. Stop the engine.

9. Release the vacuum and remove the vacuum pump.

➡ **Do not overfill the reservoir.**

10. Fill the reservoir. Use approved transmission fluid.

11. Start the engine.

12. Install the vacuum pump. Apply and maintain the maximum vacuum of 68–85 kPa (20–25 in. Hg).

⁂ **WARNING**

Do not hold the steering wheel against the stops for more than 3 to 5 seconds at a time. Damage to the power steering pump can occur.

13. Cycle the steering wheel fully from stop-to-stop 10 times.

14. Stop the engine, release the vacuum and remove the vacuum pump.

⁂ **WARNING**

Do not overfill the reservoir.

15. Fill the reservoir as needed and install the reservoir cap.

16. Visually inspect the power steering system for leaks.

17. Fill the reservoir as needed and visually inspect the power steering system for leaks.

18. Install the reservoir cap.

SUSPENSION

FRONT SUSPENSION

✳✳ CAUTION

Suspension fasteners are critical parts because they affect performance of vital components and systems and their failure can result in major service expense. They must be replaced with the same part number or an equivalent part if replacement is necessary. Do not use a replacement part of lesser quality or substitute design. Torque values must be used as specified during reassembly to ensure proper retention of these parts.

BALL JOINTS

REMOVAL & INSTALLATION

F-150 and Mark LT

The upper and lower ball joints are serviced with the upper and lower control arms as assemblies.

2-Wheel Drive F-250 and F-350

Upper And Lower

1. Before servicing the vehicle, refer to the Precautions Section.
2. Raise and support the vehicle.
3. Remove the wheel and tire assembly.
4. Remove the disc brake caliper and the front disc brake hub and rotor.
5. Remove the front disc brake rotor shield.
6. If equipped, remove the ABS sensor retaining bolt, ABS sensor harness retaining bolt and the ABS sensor. Position out of the way.
7. Disconnect the tie rod end.
   a. Remove and discard the cotter pin.
   b. Remove the castellated nut.
   c. Using the Pitman Arm Puller, remove the tie rod end.
8. Remove the pinch bolt.
9. Remove the camber adjuster.

✳✳ WARNING

To prevent damage to the ball joint seal and the ball joint socket, do not use a pickle fork-type remover to loosen the ball joints.

10. Remove the front wheel spindle.
    a. Remove and discard the cotter pin.
    b. Loosen, but do not remove, the castellated nut.

c. Strike the lower end of the front axle to loosen the ball joint.
    d. Remove the castellated nut and the front wheel spindle.
11. Position the front wheel spindle in a vise, and remove the snapring from the lower ball joint.

✳✳ WARNING

To avoid damage to the components, do not use heat to aid ball joint removal.

12. Using the ball joint press tool and suitable receiver cup, remove the lower ball joint from the front wheel spindle.
13. Using the ball joint press tool and suitable receiver cup, remove the upper ball joint.

To install:

✳✳ WARNING

To avoid damage to components, do not use heat to aid installation.

➡ **Clean the wheel knuckle ball joint bores.**

➡ **The lower ball joint must be installed first.**

14. Using the ball joint press with suitable receiver cups, install the lower ball joint.
15. Using the ball joint press with suitable receiver cups, install the upper ball joint.
16. Install the snapring in the groove at the bottom of the ball joint.

➡ **Tighten the ball joint nut further, if necessary, in order to insert a new cotter pin.**

17. Using new fasteners, follow the removal procedure in reverse order.
18. Check the front end alignment. Observe the following torques:
   • Ball joint stud nut: 99 ft. lbs. (133 Nm)
   • Pinch bolt: 60 ft. lbs. (80 Nm)
   • Tie rod end stud nut: 67 ft. lbs. (90 Nm)

4-Wheel Drive F-250 and F-350

Upper

See Figures 503 through 507.

1. Before servicing the vehicle, refer to the Precautions Section.
2. Raise and support the vehicle.
3. Remove the wheel and tire assembly.

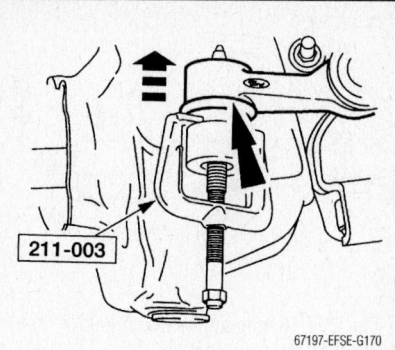

211-003

67197-EFSE-G170

Fig. 503 Disconnect the tie-rod end from the wheel knuckle—4WD F-250 and F-350

4. Remove the front brake disc.
5. Remove the wheel hub and bearing.
6. Using a drift, drive the axle shaft main seal out of the wheel knuckle.
7. Remove the axle shaft and main seal.
8. Remove the tie-rod end castellated nut.
9. Disconnect the tie-rod end from the wheel knuckle.
10. Remove the upper ball joint castellated nut and the insert.
11. Remove the lower ball joint nut.
12. Remove the knuckle.
13. Clean and inspect the wheel knuckle ball joint bores.
14. Place the wheel knuckle into a suitable vise.

➡ **Always remove the lower ball joint first.**

15. Remove the lower ball joint.
16. Using a suitable ball joint press, remove the upper ball joint.

To install:

17. Clean the wheel knuckle ball joint bores.
18. Using a suitable ball joint press, install the upper ball joint.
19. Install the lower ball joint.
20. Install the wheel knuckle.
21. Position the wheel knuckle onto the axle housing.
22. Install the nut onto the lower ball joint. Do not tighten the nut at this time.
23. Install the insert and the castellated nut onto the upper ball joint. Do not tighten the nut at this time.
24. Tighten the lower ball joint retaining nut. Pre-tighten the nut to 47 Nm (35 ft. lbs.).

➡ **Do not loosen the castellated nut to install the cotter pin.**

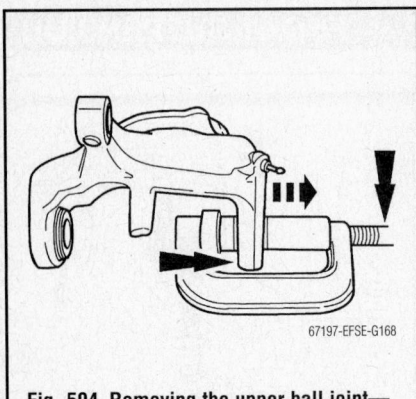

Fig. 504 Removing the upper ball joint—4WD F-250 and F-350

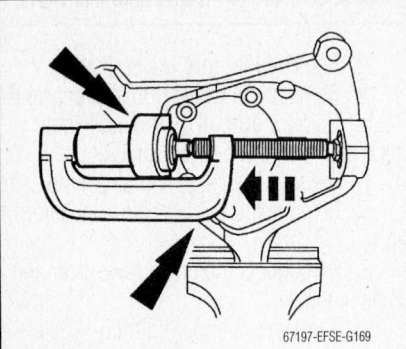

Fig. 505 Installing the upper ball joint—4WDF-250 and F-350

25. Tighten the upper ball joint castellated nut. Torque to 69 ft. lbs. (94 Nm).

26. Install the cotter pin. If necessary, tighten the castellated nut until the cotter pin can be installed.

27. Tighten the lower ball joint nut to 204 Nm (150 ft. lbs.).

28. Position the tie-rod end into the wheel knuckle.

29. Install and tighten the castellated nut. Torque to 52 ft. lbs. (70 Nm).

30. Install the cotter pin.

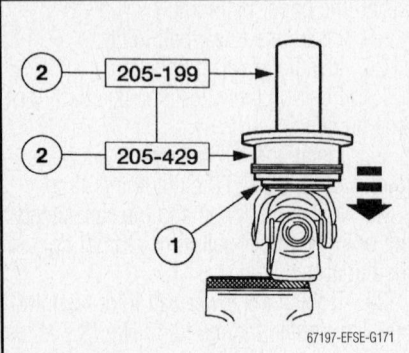

Fig. 506 Seat the main seal onto the axle shaft—4WD F-250 and F-350

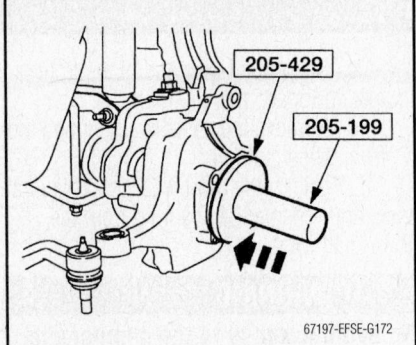

Fig. 507 Install the main seal into the wheel knuckle—4WD F-250 and F-350

31. Position the main seal onto the axle shaft.

32. Using the special tools and a hammer, seat the main seal onto the axle shaft.

33. Position the axle shaft into the axle housing.

34. Using the special tools and a hammer, install the main seal into the wheel knuckle.

35. Install the wheel hub and bearing.

36. Install the front brake disc.

37. Install the wheel and tire assembly.

Lower

See Figures 503, 508 and 509.

1. Raise and support the vehicle.

2. Remove the wheel and tire assembly.

3. Remove the front brake disc.

4. Remove the wheel hub and bearing.

5. Using a drift, drive the axle shaft main seal out of the wheel knuckle.

6. Remove the axle shaft and main seal.

7. Remove the tie-rod end castellated nut.

8. Disconnect the tie-rod end from the wheel knuckle.

9. Remove the upper ball joint castellated nut and the insert.

10. Remove the lower ball joint nut.

11. Remove the knuckle.

12. Clean and inspect the wheel knuckle ball joint bores.

13. Place the wheel knuckle into a suitable vise.

14. Remove the lower ball joint.

To install:

15. Clean the wheel knuckle ball joint bores.

16. Install the lower ball joint.

17. Install the wheel knuckle.

18. Position the wheel knuckle onto the axle housing.

19. Install the nut onto the lower ball joint. Do not tighten the nut at this time.

20. Install the insert and the castellated nut onto the upper ball joint. Do not tighten the nut at this time.

21. Tighten the lower ball joint retaining nut. Pre-tighten the nut to 47 Nm (35 ft. lbs.).

➡ **Do not loosen the castellated nut to install the cotter pin.**

22. Tighten the upper ball joint castellated nut. Torque to 69 ft. lbs. (94 Nm).

23. Install the cotter pin. If necessary, tighten the castellated nut until the cotter pin can be installed.

24. Tighten the lower ball joint nut to 204 Nm (150 ft. lbs.).

25. Position the tie-rod end into the wheel knuckle.

26. Install and tighten the castellated nut. Torque to 52 ft. lbs. (70 Nm).

27. Install the cotter pin.

28. Position the main seal onto the axle shaft.

29. Using the special tools and a hammer, seat the main seal onto the axle shaft.

30. Position the axle shaft into the axle housing.

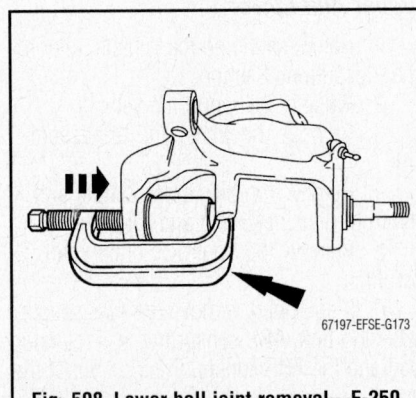

Fig. 508 Lower ball joint removal—F-250 and F-350

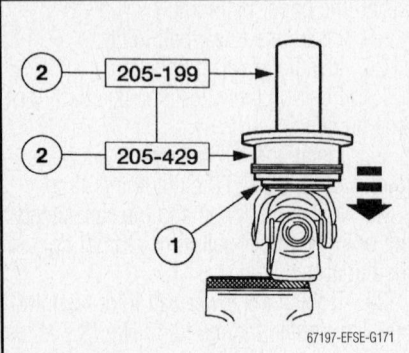

Fig. 509 Lower ball joint installation—F-250 and F-350

31. Using the special tools and a hammer, install the main seal into the wheel knuckle.
32. Install the wheel hub and bearing.
33. Install the front brake disc.
34. Install the wheel and tire assembly.

COIL SPRING

REMOVAL & INSTALLATION

F-250 and F-350

2-Wheel Drive

1. Before servicing the vehicle, refer to the Precautions Section.

※※ CAUTION

Suspension fasteners are critical parts because they affect performance of vital components and systems and their failure can result in major service expense. Install new parts with the same part number or an equivalent part if installation is necessary. Do not install a part of lesser quality or substitute design. Torque values must be used as specified during reassembly to ensure correct retention of these parts.

2. Remove the wheel and tire assembly.
3. Using a suitable jack, support the front axle assembly.
4. Remove the nut and detach the shock from the mounting stud.
5. Remove the upper spring retainer.
6. Lower the front axle until the spring is free of the upper spring seat.
7. Using an extension through the top of the spring, remove the lower spring retainer.
8. Remove the front spring.
9. Using new fasteners, reverse the removal procedure. Tighten the lower spring retainer to 99 ft. lbs. (133 Nm); the upper retainer to 26 ft. lbs. (35 Nm).

4-Wheel Drive

1. Before servicing the vehicle, refer to the Precautions Section.

※※ CAUTION

All vehicles are equipped with gas-pressurized shock absorbers which will extend unassisted. Do not apply heat or flame to the shock absorbers during removal or component servicing.

2. Raise and safely support the vehicle.
3. Remove the wheel and tire assembly.

4. Position jack stands under the axle housing.
5. Remove the front shock absorber lower mounting bolt and nut.
6. Lower the axle and remove the spring.
7. Remove the spring insulator and retain for reinstallation.
8. To install, reverse the removal procedure.

LOWER CONTROL ARM

REMOVAL & INSTALLATION

F-150 and Mark LT

2-Wheel Drive

1. Before servicing the vehicle, refer to the Precautions Section.
2. Disconnect the wheel speed sensor.
3. Remove the wheel and tire assembly.

➡Use the hex holding feature to prevent the ball studs (upper control arm, lower control arm tie-rod end, and stabilizer bar links) from turning while removing and installing the nuts.

※※ WARNING

Do not hammer the ball studs to separate them from the wheel knuckle or stabilizer bar. Doing so can cause damage. Lightly tap the wheel knuckle or stabilizer bar to loosen the joints.

4. Remove the anchor plate bolt.
5. Remove the brake caliper, pads and anchor plate.

※※ WARNING

Do not allow the brake caliper to hang by the flexible brake hose.

6. Support the caliper to the vehicle.
7. Remove the axle-to-wheel hub nut, retainer and cotter pin.
8. Remove the brake disc.
9. Remove the tie-rod end-to-wheel knuckle nut.
10. Remove the lower ball joint-to-wheel knuckle nut.
11. Remove the upper ball joint-to-wheel knuckle nut.
12. Remove the wheel knuckle.
13. Remove the strut-to-lower arm nut.
14. Remove the strut-to-lower arm bolt.
15. Remove the lower arm-to-frame nut.
16. Remove the lower arm-to-frame bolt.
17. Remove the lower arm.
18. To install, reverse the removal procedure. Observe the following torques:

- Control arm-to-frame: 222 ft. lbs. (300 Nm)
- Upper control arm-to-knuckle: 85 ft. lbs. (115 Nm)
- Lower control arm-to-knuckle: 111 ft. lbs. (150 Nm)
- Tie rod end-to-knuckle: 111 ft. lbs. (150 Nm)
- Hub nut: 296 ft. lbs. (400 Nm)
- Anchor plate bolts: 148 ft. lbs. (200 Nm)

※※ CAUTION

Do not apply lubricant to the threaded part of the axle.

19. To ease installation, lubricate the inner race of the bearing assembly using the specified lubricant.

4-Wheel Drive

1. Before servicing the vehicle, refer to the Precautions Section.
2. Loosen the axle retainer nut.

➡The wheel speed sensor electrical connectors are located in the engine compartment secured to the fender aprons.

3. Disconnect the wheel speed sensor.
4. Remove the wheel and tire assembly.

※※ WARNING

Use the hex holding feature to prevent the ball studs (upper control arm, lower control arm tie-rod end, and stabilizer bar links) from turning while removing and installing the nuts.

※※ WARNING

Do not hammer the ball studs to separate them from the wheel knuckle or stabilizer bar. Doing so can cause damage. Lightly tap the wheel knuckle or stabilizer bar to loosen the joints.

5. Remove the axle-to-wheel hub nut. Remove the nut and separate the outboard CV-joint from the wheel hub.
6. Remove the wheel speed sensor harness connector.
7. Remove the anchor plate bolt.
8. Remove the brake caliper, pads and anchor plate .

※※ WARNING

Do not allow the brake caliper to hang from the hose or damage to the hose can occur.

9. Position the caliper, pads and anchor plate aside.

10. Remove the brake disc.

11. Remove the wheel hub-to-wheel knuckle bolts.

12. Remove the wheel bearing and hub assembly.

13. Remove the tie-rod end-to-wheel knuckle nut.

14. Remove the lower ball joint-to-wheel knuckle nut.

15. Remove the upper ball joint-to-wheel knuckle nut.

16. Remove the wheel knuckle.

17. Remove the shock absorber-to-lower arm nut.

18. Remove the shock absorber-to-lower arm bolt.

19. Remove the lower arm-to-frame nut.

20. Remove the lower arm-to-frame bolt.

21. Remove the lower arm.

➡ **Do not tighten the control arm nuts until the installation procedure is complete and the weight of the vehicle is resting on the wheel and tire assemblies.**

22. To install, reverse the removal procedure.

23. Observe the following torques:
- Lower arm-to-frame: 222 ft. lbs. (300 Nm)
- Strut-to-lower arm: 351 ft. lbs. (475 Nm)
- Upper arm-to-knuckle: 85 ft. lbs. (115 Nm)
- Lower arm-to-knuckle: 111 ft. lbs. (150 Nm)
- Tie rod end-to-knuckle: 111 ft. lbs. (150 Nm)
- Anchor plate: 148 ft. lbs. (200 Nm)

24. Check and, if necessary, align the front end.

RADIUS ARM

REMOVAL & INSTALLATION

F-250 and F-350

1. Before servicing the vehicle, refer to the Precautions Section.

2. Raise and support the vehicle.

3. Remove the wheel and tire assembly.

4. Remove the front disc brake caliper, front disc brake hub and rotor and front disc brake rotor shield.

5. If equipped, remove the front disc brake ABS sensor retainer bolt and the ABS sensor harness bracket bolt from the front wheel spindle. Position the ABS sensor out of the way.

6. Remove the cotter pin and the castellated nut from the tie rod end. Discard the cotter pin.

7. Using a Pitman arm puller, remove the tie rod end.

8. Remove the cotter pin and the lower ball joint castellated nut. Discard the cotter pin.

9. Remove the pinch bolt and the camber adjuster from the upper ball joint.

❉❉ WARNING

To prevent damage to the ball joint seal and the ball joint socket, do not use a pickle fork-type remover to loosen the ball joints.

10. Remove the front wheel spindle.
   a. Strike the lower end of the axle to loosen the ball joint.
   b. Remove the front wheel spindle.

11. Using a suitable jack, support the front axle.

12. Remove the front coil spring.

13. Remove the lower spring insulator.

14. Remove the lower spring seat.

15. Remove the radius arm-to-axle bolt and nut.

16. Remove the radius arm-to-frame bracket pivot bolt and nut. Remove the radius arm.

➡ **In order to obtain clearance for the pivot bolt removal when servicing the right front axle, it may be necessary to raise the side of the vehicle to relieve the weight on the suspension.**

17. Remove the pivot nut and bolt.

To install:

18. Inspect the pivot bushing for wear or damage. Replace as necessary.

19. Position the front axle into the pivot bracket and install a new pivot bolt and nut hand-tight.

20. Inspect the radius arm pivot bushing for wear or damage. Replace as necessary.

21. Install a new radius arm-to-axle bolt and nut hand-tight.

22. Install a new radius arm-to-frame bracket pivot bolt and nut. Tighten to 221 ft. lbs. (300 Nm).

23. Tighten the radius arm-to-axle bolt and nut to 295 ft. lbs. (400 Nm).

24. Install the lower spring seat.

25. Install the lower spring insulator.

26. Install the front coil spring.

➡ **Tighten the ball joint nut further, if necessary, in order to insert the new cotter pin.**

27. Using new fasteners, install the front wheel spindle in the front axle.
   a. Position the front wheel spindle in the front axle.
   b. Install the ball joint nut and tighten to 60 ft. lbs (80 Nm).
   c. Install the new cotter pin.

28. Install the camber adjuster and a new pinch bolt. Tighten to 60 ft. lbs (80 Nm).

29. Install the front disc brake rotor shield, front disc brake hub and rotor and the front disc brake caliper.

30. If equipped, install the front disc brake ABS sensor, retainer bolt and the ABS sensor harness bracket bolt.

31. Install the tie rod end in the front wheel spindle using a new nut and a new cotter pin. Torque to 67 ft. lbs. (90 Nm).

32. Install the tire and wheel assembly.

33. Lower the vehicle and with the vehicle weight on the suspension, tighten the axle pivot bolt and nut to 130 ft. lbs. (175 Nm).

34. Perform front end alignment.

SHOCK ABSORBERS

REMOVAL & INSTALLATION

F-250 and F-350

2-Wheel Drive

1. Before servicing the vehicle, refer to the Precautions Section.

❉❉ CAUTION

All vehicles are equipped with gas-pressurized shock absorbers which will extend unassisted. Do not apply heat or flame to the shock absorbers during removal or component servicing.

❉❉ CAUTION

Suspension fasteners are critical parts because they affect performance of vital components and systems and their failure can result in major service expense. They must be replaced with the same part number or an equivalent part if replacement is necessary. Do not use a replacement part of lesser quality or substitute design. Torque values must be used as specified during reassembly to ensure proper retention of these parts.

2. Raise the hood and remove the upper shock absorber retaining nut and upper shock absorber insulator.

3. Raise and support the vehicle.

4. Remove the lower shock absorber retaining nut and remove the shock absorber.

5. Using new fasteners, follow the removal procedure in reverse order. Observe the following torques:

- Upper nut: 30 ft. lbs. (40 Nm)
- Lower nut: 60 ft. lbs. (80 Nm)

4-Wheel Drive

See Figures 510 through 512.

1. Before servicing the vehicle, refer to the Precautions Section.

2. Raise and support the vehicle.

3. Disconnect the shock absorber lower mount.

4. Disconnect the shock absorber upper mount.

5. To install, reverse the removal procedure. Tighten to:

- Upper: 46 ft. lbs. (63 Nm)
- Lower: 111 ft. lbs. (150 Nm)

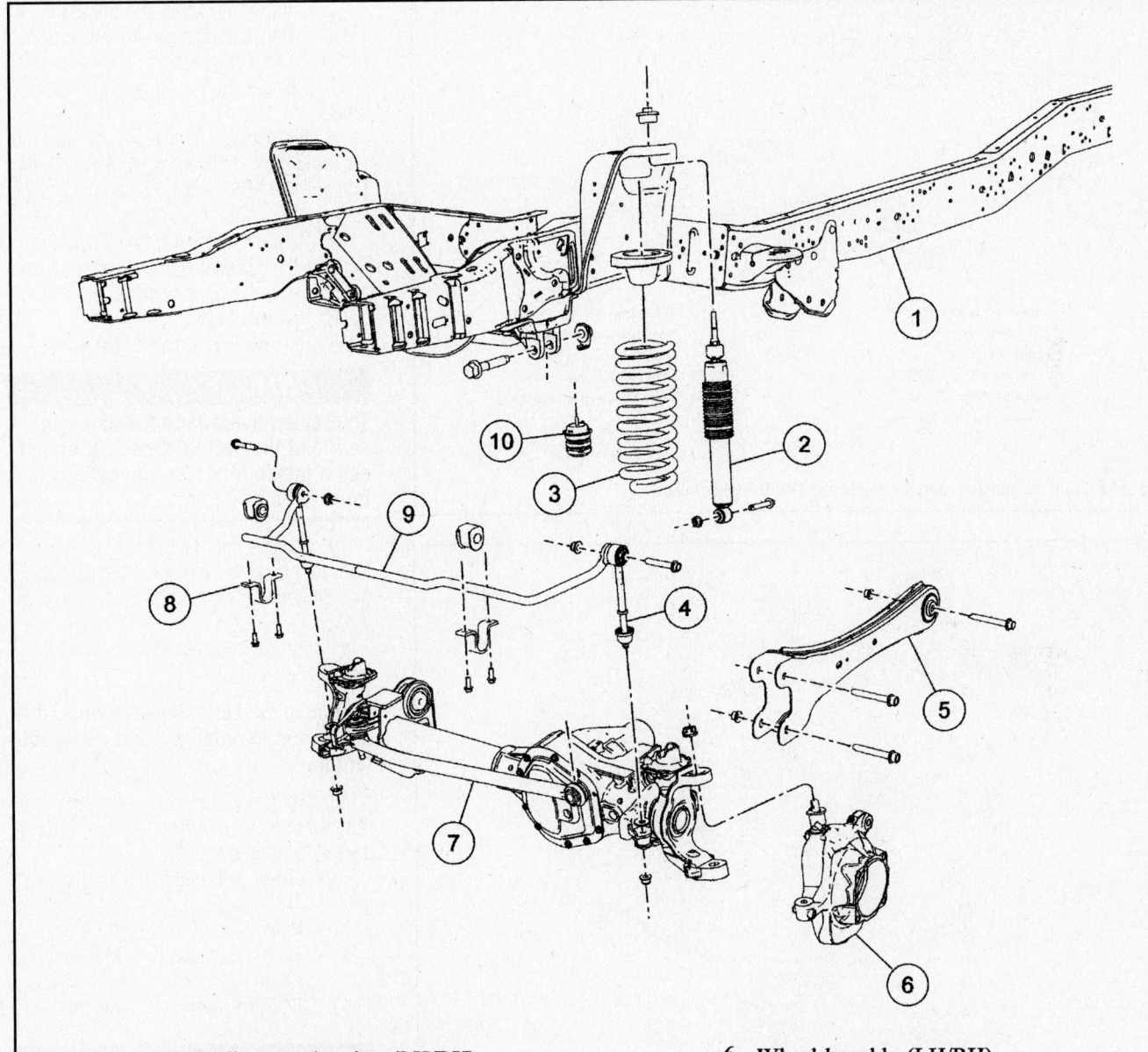

1 Radius arm bracket (LH/RH)	6 Wheel knuckle (LH/RH)
2 Shock absorber	7 Track bar
3 Coil spring	8 Stabilizer bar retainer
4 Stabilizer bar link	9 Stabilizer bar
5 Radius arm (LH/RH)	10 Jounce bumper

06017-F150-G268

Fig. 510 Front suspension—F-250 and F-350 4-wheel drive

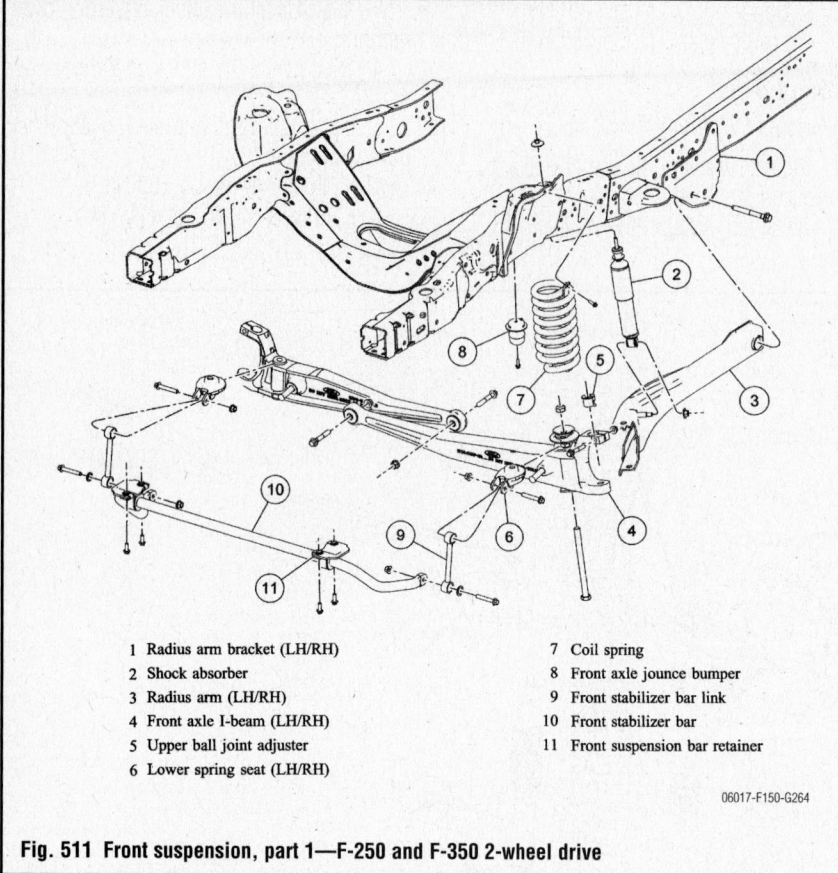

1	Radius arm bracket (LH/RH)	7	Coil spring
2	Shock absorber	8	Front axle jounce bumper
3	Radius arm (LH/RH)	9	Front stabilizer bar link
4	Front axle I-beam (LH/RH)	10	Front stabilizer bar
5	Upper ball joint adjuster	11	Front suspension bar retainer
6	Lower spring seat (LH/RH)		

06017-F150-G264

Fig. 511 Front suspension, part 1—F-250 and F-350 2-wheel drive

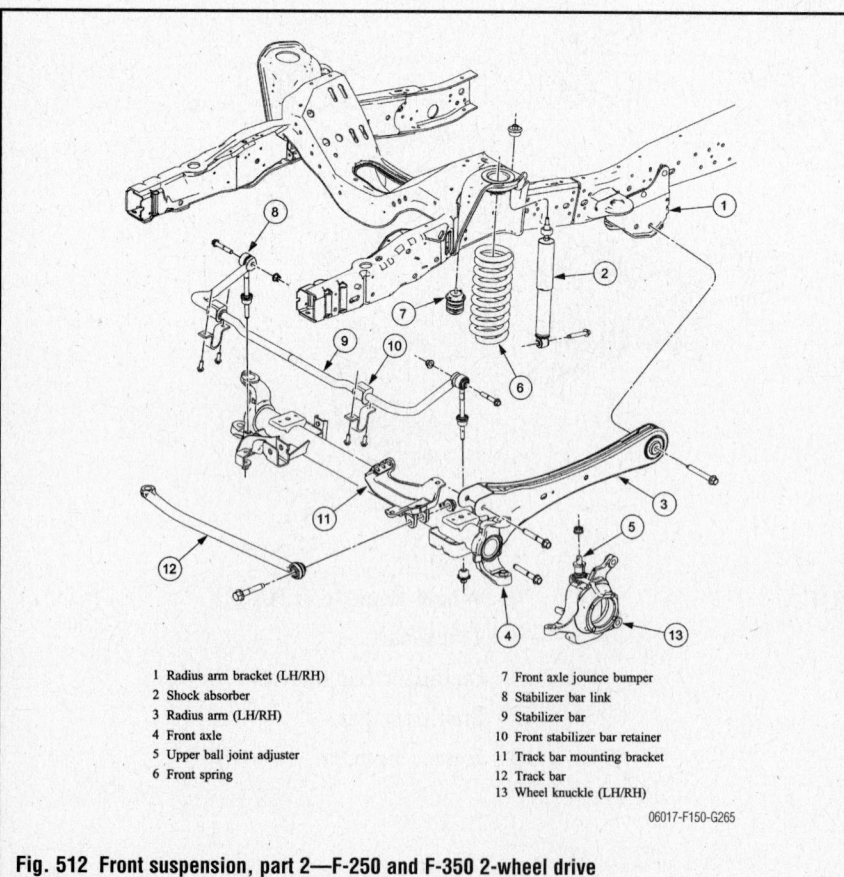

1	Radius arm bracket (LH/RH)	7	Front axle jounce bumper
2	Shock absorber	8	Stabilizer bar link
3	Radius arm (LH/RH)	9	Stabilizer bar
4	Front axle	10	Front stabilizer bar retainer
5	Upper ball joint adjuster	11	Track bar mounting bracket
6	Front spring	12	Track bar
		13	Wheel knuckle (LH/RH)

06017-F150-G265

Fig. 512 Front suspension, part 2—F-250 and F-350 2-wheel drive

SPINDLE

REMOVAL & INSTALLATION

F-250 and F-350

2-Wheel Drive

1. Before servicing the vehicle, refer to the Precautions Section.
2. Raise and support the vehicle.
3. Remove the wheel and tire assembly.
4. Remove the disc brake caliper and the front disc brake hub and rotor.
5. Remove the front disc brake rotor shield.
6. If equipped, remove the ABS sensor retaining bolt, ABS sensor harness retaining bolt and the ABS sensor. Position out of the way.
7. Remove and discard the cotter pin. Remove the castellated nut. Using a pitman arm puller, remove the tie rod end.
8. Remove the pinch bolt.
9. Remove the camber adjuster.

✳✳ WARNING

To prevent damage to the ball joint seal and the ball joint socket, do not use a pickle fork-type remover to loosen the ball joints.

10. Remove and discard the cotter pin. Loosen, but do not remove, the castellated nut. Strike the lower end of the front axle to loosen the ball joint.
11. Remove the castellated nut and the front wheel spindle.

➡**Tighten the ball joint nut further, if necessary, in order to insert a new cotter pin.**

12. Using new fasteners, follow the removal procedure in reverse order. Observe the following torques:
   - Lower ball joint nut: 99 ft. lbs. (133 Nm)
   - Pinch bolt: 60 ft. lbs. (80 Nm)
   - Tie rod ball stud nut: 67 ft. lbs. (90 Nm)
13. Check the front end alignment.

STABILIZER BAR

REMOVAL & INSTALLATION

F-150 and Mark LT
See Figures 513 and 514.

1. Before servicing the vehicle, refer to the Precautions Section.

➡**Use the hex holding feature to prevent the ball studs (upper ball joint,**

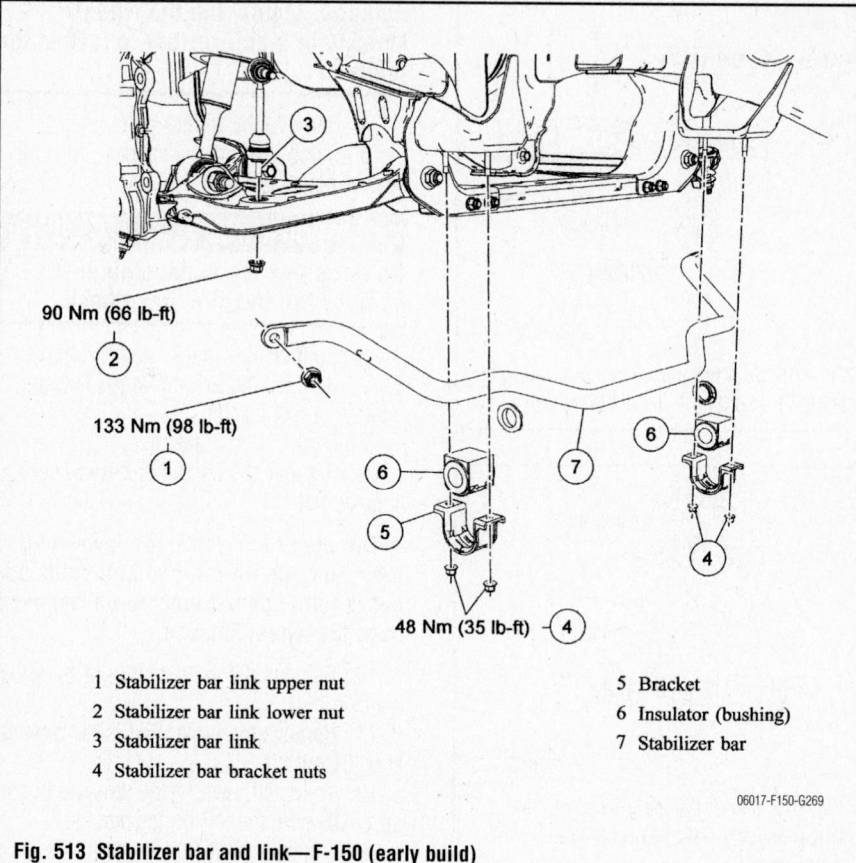

1 Stabilizer bar link upper nut
2 Stabilizer bar link lower nut
3 Stabilizer bar link
4 Stabilizer bar bracket nuts
5 Bracket
6 Insulator (bushing)
7 Stabilizer bar

06017-F150-G269

Fig. 513 Stabilizer bar and link—F-150 (early build)

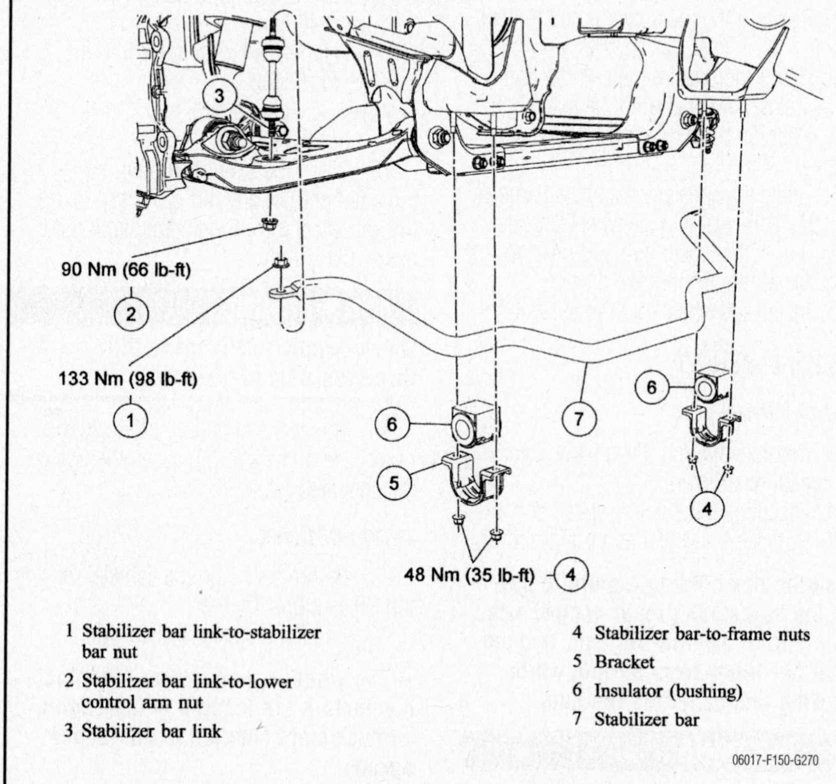

1 Stabilizer bar link-to-stabilizer bar nut
2 Stabilizer bar link-to-lower control arm nut
3 Stabilizer bar link
4 Stabilizer bar-to-frame nuts
5 Bracket
6 Insulator (bushing)
7 Stabilizer bar

06017-F150-G270

Fig. 514 Stabilizer bar and link—F-150 (late build) and Mark LT

lower ball joint, tie-rod end and stabilizer bar links) from turning while removing and installing the nuts.

※ WARNING

Do not hammer the ball studs to separate them from the wheel knuckle or stabilizer bar. Doing so can cause damage. Lightly tap the wheel knuckle or stabilizer bar to loosen the joints.

2. Remove the stabilizer bar link upper nuts.
3. Remove the stabilizer bar link lower nuts.
4. Remove the stabilizer bar links.
5. Remove the stabilizer bar bracket nuts, then, remove the stabilizer bar.
6. To install, reverse the removal procedure. Observe the following torques:
- Stabilizer bar bracket nuts: 48 Nm (35 ft. lbs.)
- Stabilizer bar link lower nuts: 90 Nm (66 ft. lbs.)
- Stabilizer bar link upper nuts: 133 Nm (98 ft. lbs.)

F-250 and F-350

2-Wheel Drive

1. Before servicing the vehicle, refer to the Precautions Section.
2. Raise and safely support the vehicle.
3. Remove the bolts and the retainer brackets.
4. Remove the nuts, bolts, washers and the stabilizer bar and links.
5. To install, reverse the removal procedure. Torque the fasteners as follows:
- Upper and lower link nuts: 85 ft. lbs. (115 Nm)
- Bracket bolts: 35 ft. lbs. (48 Nm)

4-Wheel Drive

1. Before servicing the vehicle, refer to the Precautions Section.
2. Remove the nuts, washers, and bolts, and then disconnect the stabilizer bar links.
3. Remove the nuts and the stabilizer bar.
4. To install, reverse the removal procedure. Observe the following torques:
- Bracket nuts: 41 ft. lbs. (55 Nm)
- End link nuts to 80 ft. lbs. (109 Nm)

F-250 and F-350

4-Wheel Drive

1. Before servicing the vehicle, refer to the Precautions Section.

2. Remove the nuts and bolts and then disconnect the stabilizer bar links.

3. Remove the nuts and the stabilizer bar.

4. To install, reverse the removal procedure. Torque the bracket bolts to 35 ft. lbs. (48 Nm). Torque the link nuts to 111 ft. lbs. (150 Nm).

STEERING KNUCKLE

REMOVAL & INSTALLATION

F-250 and F-350

4-Wheel Drive

See Figures 515 and 516.

1. Before servicing the vehicle, refer to the Precautions Section.

2. Raise and support the vehicle.

3. Remove the wheel and tire assembly.

4. Remove the front brake disc.

5. Remove the wheel hub and bearing.

6. Using a drift, drive the axle shaft main seal out of the wheel knuckle.

7. Remove the axle shaft and main seal.

8. Remove the tie-rod end castellated nut.

9. Using the special tool, disconnect the tie-rod end from the wheel knuckle.

10. Remove the upper ball joint castellated nut and the insert.

11. Remove the lower ball joint nut.

12. Remove the knuckle.

13. Clean and inspect the wheel knuckle ball joint bores.

To install:

14. Position the wheel knuckle onto the axle housing.

15. Install the nut onto the lower ball joint. Do not tighten the nut at this time.

16. Install the insert and the castellated nut onto the upper ball joint. Do not tighten the nut at this time.

17. Tighten the lower ball joint retaining nut. Pre-tighten the nut to 47 Nm (35 ft. lbs.).

➡Do not loosen the castellated nut to install the cotter pin.

18. Tighten the upper ball joint castellated nut. Torque to 69 ft. lbs. (94 Nm).

19. Install the cotter pin. If necessary, tighten the castellated nut until the cotter pin can be installed.

20. Tighten the lower ball joint nut to 204 Nm (150 ft. lbs.).

21. Position the tie-rod end into the wheel knuckle.

22. Install and tighten the castellated nut. Torque to 52 ft. lbs. (70 Nm).

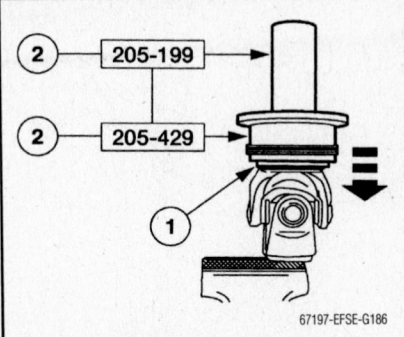

67197-EFSE-G186

Fig. 515 Seat the main seal onto the axle shaft—F-250 and F-350 4-Wheel Drive

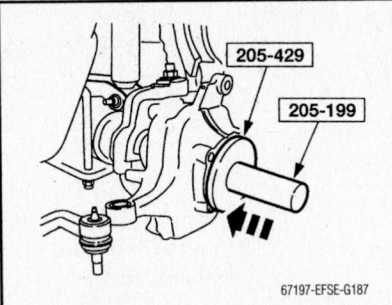

67197-EFSE-G187

Fig. 516 Install the main seal into the wheel knuckle—F-250 and F-350 4-Wheel Drive

23. Install the cotter pin.

24. Position the main seal onto the axle shaft.

25. Using the special tools and a hammer, seat the main seal onto the axle shaft.

26. Position the axle shaft into the axle housing.

27. Using the special tools and a hammer, install the main seal into the wheel knuckle.

28. Install the wheel hub and bearing.

29. Install the front brake disc.

30. Install the wheel and tire assembly.

F-150 and Mark LT

2-Wheel Drive

1. Before servicing the vehicle, refer to the Precautions Section.

2. Disconnect the wheel speed sensor.

3. Remove the wheel and tire assembly.

➡Use the hex holding feature to prevent the ball studs (upper control arm, lower control arm tie-rod end, and stabilizer bar links) from turning while removing and installing the nuts.

✻✻ WARNING

Do not hammer the ball studs to separate them from the wheel knuckle or stabilizer bar. Doing so can cause

damage. Lightly tap the wheel knuckle or stabilizer bar to loosen the joints.

4. Remove the anchor plate bolts.

5. Remove the brake caliper, pads and anchor plate.

✻✻ WARNING

Do not allow the brake caliper to hang by the flexible brake hose.

6. Support the caliper to the vehicle.

7. Remove the axle-to-wheel hub nut, retainer and cotter pin.

8. Remove the brake disc.

9. Remove the tie-rod end-to-wheel knuckle nut.

➡The upper ball joint, the lower ball joint, and the tie-rod end ball studs do not require special tools to be removed from the wheel knuckle.

10. Remove the lower ball joint-to-wheel knuckle nut.

11. Remove the upper ball joint-to-wheel knuckle nut.

12. To install, reverse the removal procedure. Observe the following torques:

- Anchor plate bolts: 148 ft. lbs. (200 Nm)
- Hub nut: 296 ft. lbs. (400 Nm)
- Lower ball joint nut: 111 ft. lbs. (148 Nm)
- Upper ball joint nut: 85 ft. lbs. (115 Nm)
- Tie rod end stud nut: 111 ft. lbs. (148 Nm)

13. Clean the axle (including the threaded end) of any dirt or grease using the specified solvent before installing the brake disc.

✻✻ WARNING

Do not apply lubricant to the threaded part of the axle.

14. To ease installation, lubricate the inner race of the bearing assembly using the specified lubricant.

4-Wheel Drive

1. Before servicing the vehicle, refer to the Precautions Section.

2. Loosen the axle retainer nut.

➡The wheel speed sensor electrical connectors are located in the engine compartment secured to the fender aprons.

3. Disconnect the wheel speed sensor.

4. Remove the wheel and tire assembly.

> ※※ **WARNING**
>
> **Use the hex holding feature to prevent the ball studs (upper control arm, lower control arm tie-rod end, and stabilizer bar links) from turning while removing and installing the nuts.**

> ※ **WARNING**
>
> **Do not hammer the ball studs to separate them from the wheel knuckle or stabilizer bar. Doing so can cause damage. Lightly tap the wheel knuckle or stabilizer bar to loosen the joints.**

5. Remove the axle-to-wheel hub nut. Separate the outboard CV joint from the wheel hub.
6. Remove the wheel speed sensor harness connector.
7. Remove the anchor plate bolt.
8. Remove the brake caliper, pads and anchor plate.

> ※ **WARNING**
>
> **Do not allow the brake caliper to hang from the hose or damage to the hose can occur.**

9. Position the caliper, pads and anchor plate aside.
10. Remove the brake disc.
11. Remove the wheel hub-to-wheel knuckle bolts.
12. Remove the wheel bearing and hub assembly.
13. Remove the tie-rod end-to-wheel knuckle nut.
14. Remove the lower ball joint-to-wheel knuckle nut.
15. Remove the upper ball joint-to-wheel knuckle nut.
16. Remove the knuckle.
17. To install, reverse the removal procedure. Observe the following torques:
   - Axle hub nut: 20 ft. lbs. (27 Nm)
   - Anchor plate bolt: 148 ft. lbs. (200 Nm)
   - Hub-to-knuckle bolts: 148 ft. lbs. (200 Nm)
   - Lower ball joint nut: 111 ft. lbs. (150 Nm)
   - Upper ball joint nut: 85 ft. lbs. (115 Nm)
18. Check and, if necessary, align the front end.

STRUT

REMOVAL & INSTALLATION

F-150 and Mark LT

2-Wheel Drive

See Figure 517.

1. Before servicing the vehicle, refer to the Precautions Section.
2. Remove the wheel and tire assembly.

➡**Use the hex holding feature to prevent the ball studs (upper control arm, lower control arm tie-rod end, and stabilizer bar links) from turning while removing and installing the nuts.**

> ※※ **WARNING**
>
> **Do not hammer the ball studs to separate them from the wheel knuckle or stabilizer bar. Doing so can cause damage. Lightly tap the wheel knuckle or stabilizer bar to loosen the joints.**

3. Remove the strut upper mount nuts.
4. Remove the lower mount nut/bolt.

5. Remove the nut and detach the tie-rod from the wheel knuckle. Discard the nut.
6. Remove the strut.
7. To install, reverse the removal procedure. Tighten the upper strut nuts to 35 ft. lbs. (48 Nm); the lower strut-to-arm bolts to 351 ft. lbs. (475 Nm). Torque the tie rod stud nut to 111 ft. lbs. (150 Nm).
8. Do not tighten the fasteners until the installation procedure is complete and the weight of the vehicle is resting on the wheel and tire assemblies.

4-Wheel Drive

See Figure 517.

1. Before servicing the vehicle, refer to the Precautions Section.
2. Remove the wheel and tire assembly.
3. Remove and discard the 4 strut upper mount-to-frame nuts.

> ※※ **WARNING**
>
> **Do not hammer the ball stud to separate it from the wheel knuckle. Doing so can cause damage. Lightly tap the wheel knuckle to loosen the joint.**

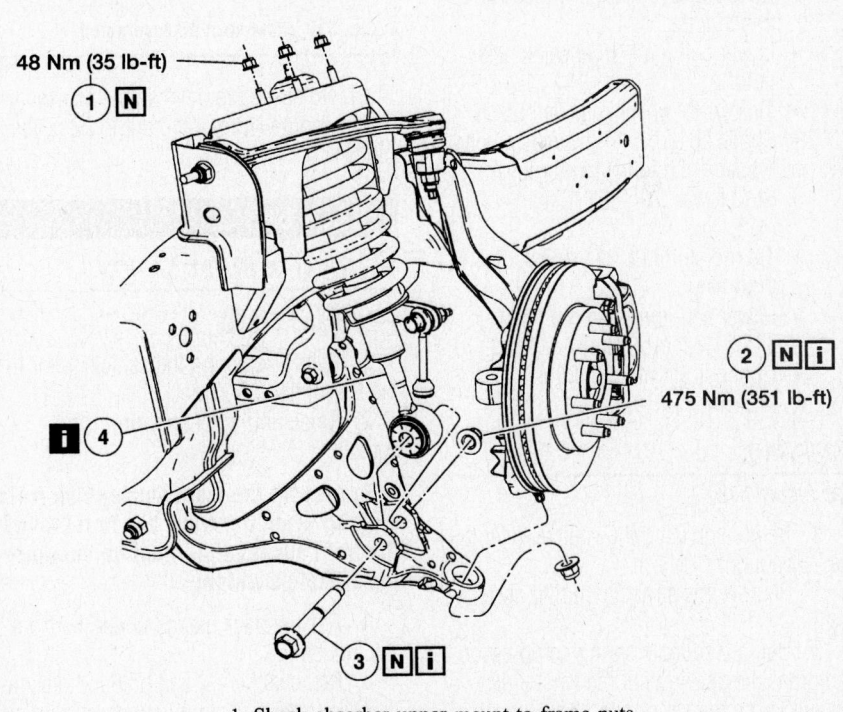

48 Nm (35 lb-ft)

475 Nm (351 lb-ft)

1 Shock absorber upper mount-to-frame nuts
2 Shock absorber-to-lower arm nut
3 Shock absorber-to-lower arm bolt
4 Shock absorber and spring assembly

67197-EFSE-G156

Fig. 517 Front strut mounting—F-150 and Mark LT

4. Remove and discard the lower ball joint-to-wheel knuckle nut.

5. Separate the lower ball joint from the wheel knuckle.

❉❉ WARNING

Use the hex holding feature to prevent the ball studs (upper control arm, lower control arm and tie rod end, and stabilizer bar links) from turning while removing and installing the nuts.

6. Remove and discard the tie rod-to-wheel knuckle nut.

7. Separate the tie-rod from the wheel knuckle.

8. Remove and discard the strut-to-lower arm bolt.

9. Remove the strut and spring assembly from the vehicle.

➡**Do not tighten the nuts until the installation procedure is complete and the weight of the vehicle is resting on the wheel and tire assemblies.**

10. To install, reverse the removal procedure.

  a. Always install new:
- Shock absorber upper mount-to-frame nuts.
- Lower ball joint-to-wheel knuckle nuts.
- Tie-rod-to-wheel knuckle nuts.
- Shock absorber-to-lower arm bolts.

  b. Observe the following torques:
- Strut lower bolt: 351 ft. lbs. (475 Nm)
- Tie rod stud nut: 111 ft. lbs. (150 Nm)
- Lower ball joint stud nut: 111 ft. lbs. (150 Nm)
- Upper strut nuts: 35 ft. lbs. (48 Nm)

OVERHAUL

See Figure 518.

1. Before servicing the vehicle, refer to the Precautions Section.

2. Remove the strut and spring assembly.

3. Using a suitable spring compressor, compress the spring until the tension is released from the shock absorber.

4. Remove the shock absorber-to-upper mount nut

5. Remove the upper shock mount

6. Remove the isolator

7. Remove the dust tube

8. Remove the coil spring

9. Remove the shock absorber

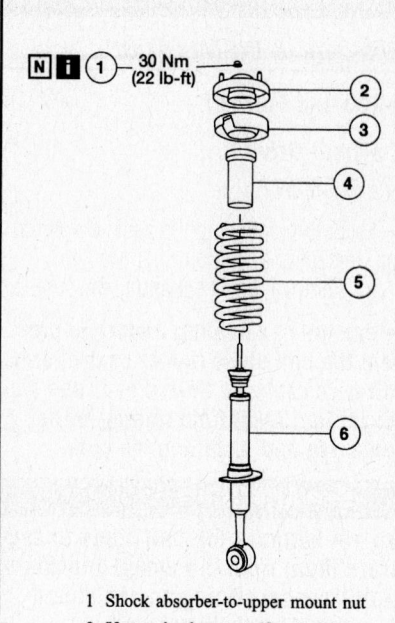

1 Shock absorber-to-upper mount nut
2 Upper shock mount (front/rear)
3 Isolator
4 Dust tube
5 Coil spring (front)
6 Shock absorber (front/rear)

67197-EFSE-G157

Fig. 518 Front strut disassembled

10. To assemble, reverse the disassembly procedure. Torque the nut to 22 ft. lbs. (30 Nm).

TRACK BAR

REMOVAL & INSTALLATION

F-250 and F-350

1. Before servicing the vehicle, refer to the Precautions Section.

2. Raise and safely support the vehicle.

➡**To prevent the front suspension from shifting when the track bar is removed, the front suspension must be supporting vehicle's weight.**

3. Position jack stands under the front axle housing.

4. Remove the nut and bolt and disconnect the track bar from the upper mounting bracket.

5. Remove the nut, then disconnect and remove the track bar.

6. To install, reverse the removal procedure. Torque the upper end nut to 406 ft. lbs. (550 Nm); the lower end nut to 183 ft. lbs. (250 Nm).

UPPER CONTROL ARM

REMOVAL & INSTALLATION

F-150 and Mark LT

2-Wheel Drive

See Figures 519 and 520.

1. Before servicing the vehicle, refer to the Precautions Section.

2. Disconnect the wheel speed sensor.

3. Remove the wheel and tire assembly.

➡**Use the hex holding feature to prevent the ball studs (upper control arm, lower control arm tie-rod end, and stabilizer bar links) from turning while removing and installing the nuts.**

❉❉ WARNING

Do not hammer the ball studs to separate them from the wheel knuckle or stabilizer bar. Doing so can cause damage. Lightly tap the wheel knuckle or stabilizer bar to loosen the joints.

4. Remove the anchor plate bolt.

5. Remove the brake caliper, pads and anchor plate.

❉❉ WARNING

Do not allow the brake caliper to hang by the flexible brake hose.

6. Support the caliper to the vehicle.

7. Remove the axle-to-wheel hub nut, retainer and cotter pin.

8. Remove the brake disc.

9. Remove the tie-rod end-to-wheel knuckle nut.

10. Remove the lower ball joint-to-wheel knuckle nut.

11. Remove the upper ball joint-to-wheel knuckle nut.

12. Remove the wheel knuckle.

13. Remove the strut-to-lower arm nut.

14. Remove the strut-to-lower arm bolt.

15. Remove the upper arm-to-frame nut.

16. Remove the upper arm-to-frame bolt.

17. Remove the upper arm.

18. To install, reverse the removal procedure. Observe the following torques:
- Control arm-to-frame: 114 ft. lbs. (155 Nm)
- Upper control arm-to-knuckle: 85 ft. lbs. (115 Nm)
- Lower control arm-to-knuckle: 111 ft. lbs. (150 Nm)
- Tie rod end-to-knuckle: 111 ft. lbs. (150 Nm)
- Hub nut: 296 ft. lbs. (400 Nm)

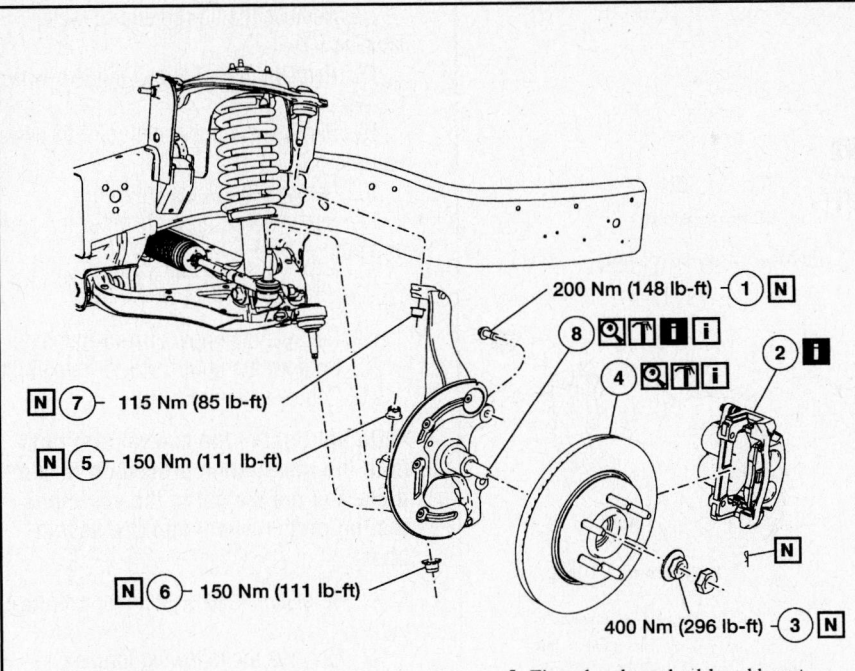

N ⑦ — 115 Nm (85 lb-ft)

N ⑤ — 150 Nm (111 lb-ft)

N ⑥ — 150 Nm (111 lb-ft)

⑧ 🔍 T i i

④ 🔍 T i i

200 Nm (148 lb-ft) ① **N**

② i

N

400 Nm (296 lb-ft) ③ **N**

1 Anchor plate bolt
2 Brake caliper, pads and anchor plate
3 Axle-to-wheel hub nut (retainer/cotter pin)
4 Brake disc

5 Tie-rod end-to-wheel knuckle nut
6 Lower ball joint-to-wheel knuckle nut
7 Upper ball joint-to-wheel knuckle nut
8 Wheel knuckle

67197-EFSE-G177

Fig. 519 Spindle and hub components—F-150 and Mark LT

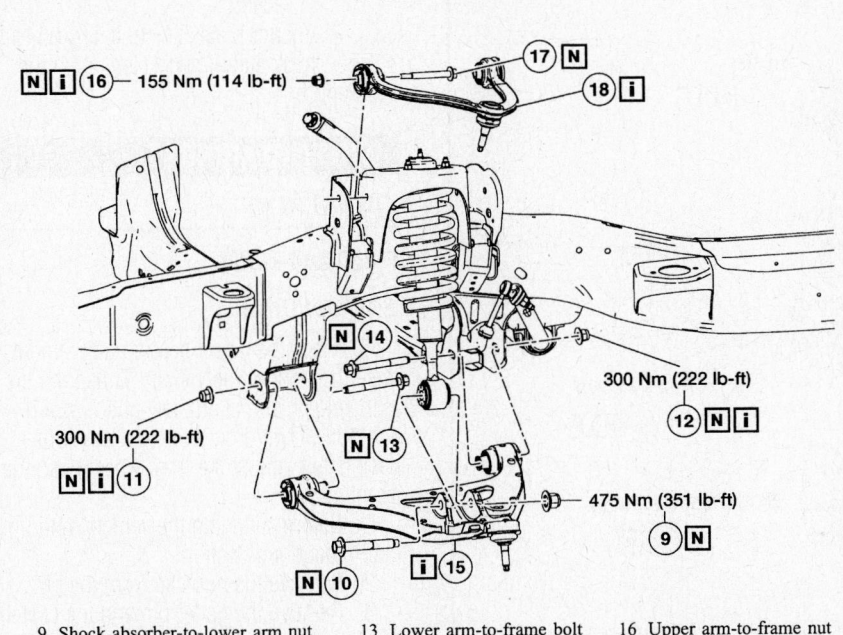

N i ⑯ — 155 Nm (114 lb-ft)

⑰ **N**

⑱ i

N ⑭

300 Nm (222 lb-ft)
⑫ **N** i

300 Nm (222 lb-ft)
N i ⑪

N ⑬

475 Nm (351 lb-ft)
⑨ **N**

N ⑩

i ⑮

9   Shock absorber-to-lower arm nut
10 Shock absorber-to-lower arm bolt
11 Lower arm-to-frame nut
12 Lower arm-to-frame nut

13 Lower arm-to-frame bolt
14 Lower arm-to-frame bolt
15 Lower arm

16 Upper arm-to-frame nut
17 Upper arm-to-frame bolt
18 Upper arm RH/LH

67197-EFSE-G178

Fig. 520 Front suspension components—F-150 and Mark LT

- Anchor plate bolts: 148 ft. lbs. (200 Nm)

❋❋ CAUTION

Do not apply lubricant to the threaded part of the axle.

19. To ease installation, lubricate the inner race of the bearing assembly using the specified lubricant.

4-Wheel Drive

See Figures 521 and 522.

1. Before servicing the vehicle, refer to the Precautions Section.
2. Loosen the axle retainer nut.

➡**The wheel speed sensor electrical connectors are located in the engine compartment secured to the fender aprons.**

3. Disconnect the wheel speed sensor.
4. Remove the wheel and tire assembly.

❋❋ WARNING

Use the hex holding feature to prevent the ball studs (upper control arm, lower control arm tie-rod end, and stabilizer bar links) from turning while removing and installing the nuts.

❋❋ WARNING

Do not hammer the ball studs to separate them from the wheel knuckle or stabilizer bar. Doing so can cause damage. Lightly tap the wheel knuckle or stabilizer bar to loosen the joints.

5. Remove the axle-to-wheel hub nut. Remove the nut and separate the outboard CV-joint from the wheel hub.
6. Remove the wheel speed sensor harness connector.
7. Remove the anchor plate bolt.
8. Remove the brake caliper, pads and anchor plate .

❋❋ WARNING

Do not allow the brake caliper to hang from the hose or damage to the hose can occur.

9. Position the caliper, pads and anchor plate aside.
10. Remove the brake disc.
11. Remove the wheel hub-to-wheel knuckle bolts.
12. Remove the wheel bearing and hub assembly.

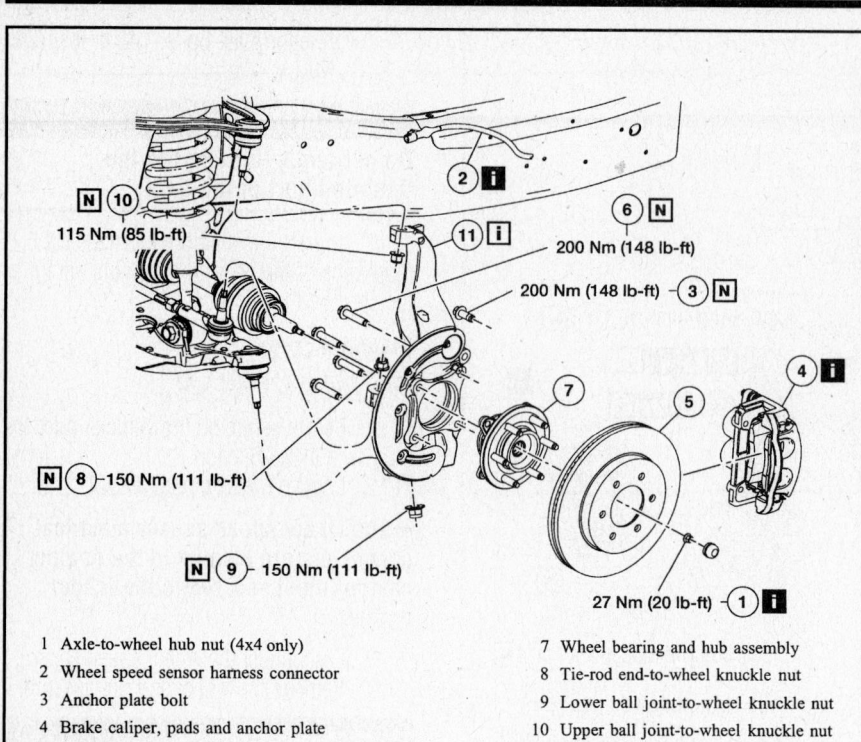

1 Axle-to-wheel hub nut (4x4 only)
2 Wheel speed sensor harness connector
3 Anchor plate bolt
4 Brake caliper, pads and anchor plate
5 Brake disc
6 Wheel hub-to-wheel knuckle bolts
7 Wheel bearing and hub assembly
8 Tie-rod end-to-wheel knuckle nut
9 Lower ball joint-to-wheel knuckle nut
10 Upper ball joint-to-wheel knuckle nut
11 Wheel knuckle

67197-EFSE-G179

Fig. 521 Spindle and hub components—4WD F-150 and Mark LT

12 Shock absorber-to-lower arm nut
13 Shock absorber-to-lower arm bolt
14 Lower arm-to-frame nut
15 Lower arm-to-frame nut
16 Lower arm-to-frame bolt
17 Lower arm-to-frame bolt
18 Lower arm
19 Upper arm-to-frame nut
20 Upper arm-to-frame bolt
21 Upper arm RH/LH

67197-EFSE-G180

Fig. 522 Front suspension components—4WD F-150 and Mark LT

13. Remove the tie-rod end-to-wheel knuckle nut.

14. Remove the lower ball joint-to-wheel knuckle nut.

15. Remove the upper ball joint-to-wheel knuckle nut.

16. Remove the wheel knuckle.

17. Remove the shock absorber-to-lower arm nut.

18. Remove the shock absorber-to-lower arm bolt.

19. Remove the upper arm-to-frame nut.

20. Remove the upper arm-to-frame bolt.

21. Remove the upper arm.

➡Do not tighten the control arm nuts until the installation procedure is complete and the weight of the vehicle is resting on the wheel and tire assemblies.

22. To install, reverse the removal procedure.

23. Observe the following torques:
- Upper arm-to-frame: 114 ft. lbs. (155 Nm)
- Strut-to-lower arm: 351 ft. lbs. (475 Nm)
- Upper arm-to-knuckle: 85 ft. lbs. (115 Nm)
- Lower arm-to-knuckle: 111 ft. lbs. (150 Nm)
- Tie rod end-to-knuckle: 111 ft. lbs. (150 Nm)
- Anchor plate: 148 ft. lbs. (200 Nm)

24. Check and, if necessary, align the front end.

WHEEL BEARINGS

ADJUSTMENT

F-250 and F-350

2-Wheel Drive

To check the wheel bearing adjustment, raise the front of the vehicle. Grasp the tire at the sides, and alternately push inward and pull outward on the tire. If any looseness is felt, adjust the front wheel bearings as follows.

1. Before servicing the vehicle, refer to the Precautions Section.

2. Remove the hub cap from the hub.

3. Remove the cotter pin and the castellated nut.

4. While rotating the wheel, tighten the adjusting nut to 21 ft. lbs. (28 Nm) to seat the bearings.

5. Back off the adjusting nut until loose (120–180 degrees).

6. While rotating the wheel, tighten the adjusting nut to 18 inch lbs. (2Nm). Torque

required to rotate the hub should be 18 inch lbs. (2 Nm).

7. Install the castellated nut and insert a new cotter pin.

8. Install the hub cap.

REMOVAL & INSTALLATION

F-150 and Mark LT

2-Wheel Drive

See Figure 523.

1. Before servicing the vehicle, refer to the Precautions Section.

2. Disconnect the wheel speed sensor.

3. Remove the wheel and tire assembly.

4. Remove the anchor plate bolts.

5. Remove the brake caliper, pads and anchor plate. Support the caliper to the vehicle.

6. Remove the axle-to-wheel hub nut, retainer and cotter pin.

7. Remove the brake disc/hub assembly.

8. To install, reverse the removal procedure.

> ☀☀ **CAUTION**
>
> **Do not apply lubricant to the threaded part of the axle.**

9. To ease installation, lubricate the inner race of the bearing assembly using the specified lubricant.

10. Observe the following torques:
- Hub nut: 296 ft. lbs. (400 Nm)
- Anchor plate bolts: 148 ft. lbs. (200 Nm)

4-Wheel Drive

See Figure 524.

1. Before servicing the vehicle, refer to the Precautions Section.

2. Loosen the axle retainer nut.

➡ **The wheel speed sensor electrical connectors are located in the engine compartment secured to the fender aprons.**

3. Disconnect the wheel speed sensor.

4. Remove the wheel and tire.

5. Remove the axle-to-wheel hub nut and, using a puller, separate the outboard CV joint from the wheel hub. assembly.

6. Remove the wheel speed sensor harness connector.

7. Remove the anchor plate bolts.

8. Remove the brake caliper, pads and anchor plate.

> ☀☀ **CAUTION**
>
> **Do not allow the brake caliper to hang from the hose or damage to the hose can occur.**

9. Position the caliper, pads and anchor plate aside.

10. Remove the brake disc.

11. Remove the wheel hub-to-wheel knuckle bolts.

12. Remove the wheel bearing and hub assembly.

13. To install, reverse the removal procedure.

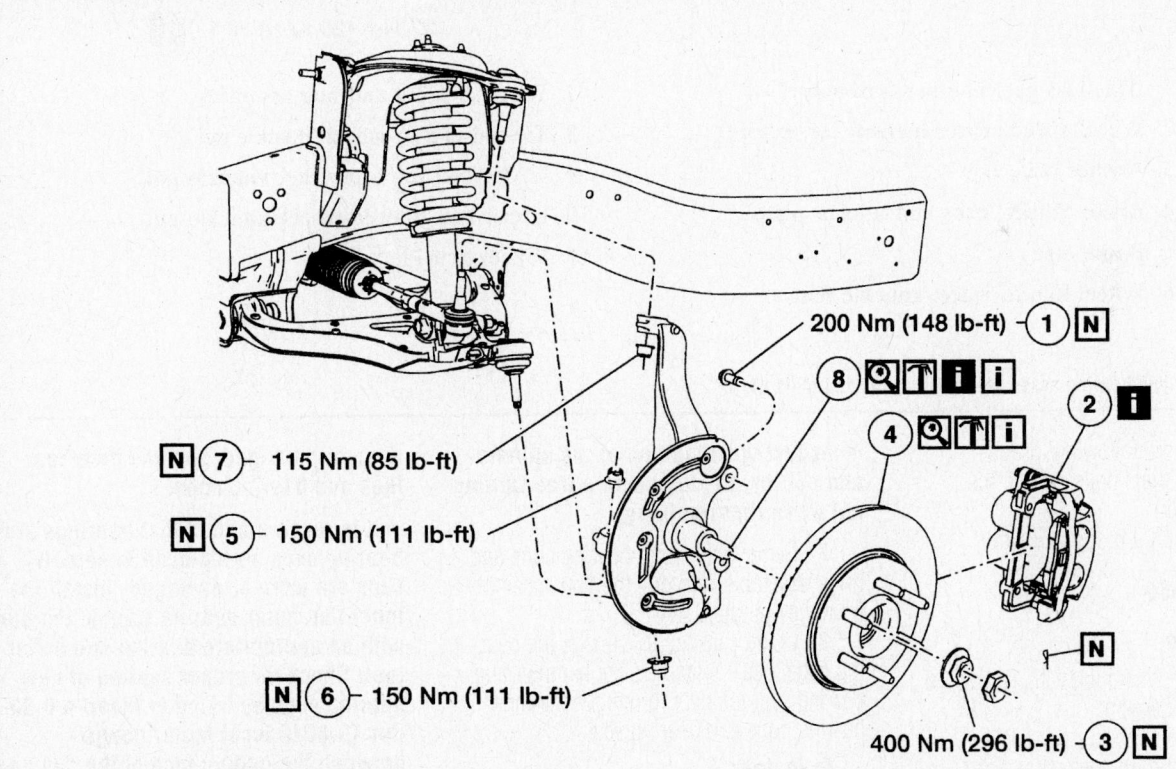

1 Anchor plate bolt
2 Brake caliper, pads and anchor plate
3 Axle-to-wheel hub nut (retainer/cotter pin)
4 Brake disc
5 Tie-rod end-to-wheel knuckle nut
6 Lower ball joint-to-wheel knuckle nut
7 Upper ball joint-to-wheel knuckle nut
8 Wheel knuckle

67197-EFSE-G193

Fig. 523 Front hub/bearing installation—2WD F-150 and Mark LT

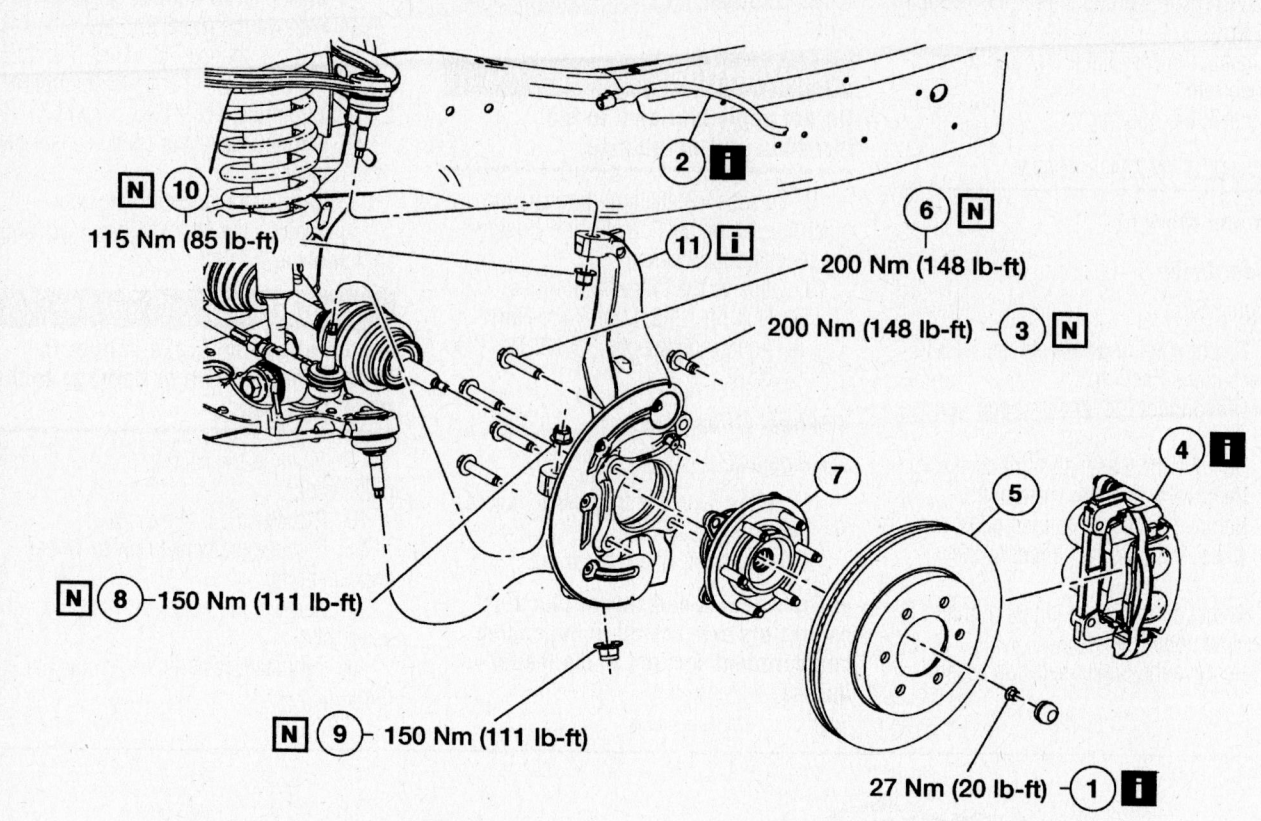

1 Axle-to-wheel hub nut (4x4 only)
2 Wheel speed sensor harness connector
3 Anchor plate bolt
4 Brake caliper, pads and anchor plate
5 Brake disc
6 Wheel hub-to-wheel knuckle bolts

7 Wheel bearing and hub assembly
8 Tie-rod end-to-wheel knuckle nut
9 Lower ball joint-to-wheel knuckle nut
10 Upper ball joint-to-wheel knuckle nut
11 Wheel knuckle

67197-EFSE-G194

Fig. 524 Front hub/bearing assembly—4WD F-150 and Mark LT

14. Observe the following torques:
- Anchor plate bolts: 148 ft. lbs. (200 Nm)
- Hub nut: 20 ft. lbs. (27 Nm)

F-250 and F-350

2-Wheel Drive

1. Before servicing the vehicle, refer to the Precautions Section.

2. Raise and support the vehicle.

3. Remove the front wheel and tire assemblies.

4. Remove the front disc brake caliper and rotor, and position the caliper out of the way.

5. Remove the hub cap from the hub assembly.

6. Remove the cotter pin, adjusting nut and flat washer.

➡Inspect the condition of the spindle and nut threads to ensure a free turning nut when reassembling.

7. Remove the outer bearing cone and roller assembly, and pull the hub assembly from the spindle.

8. Using care not to damage the bearing cage, use a suitable slide hammer and bearing seal remover to remove the inner bearing cone and bearing seal.

To install:

➡Do not spin the bearing dry with compressed air.

➡Remove all traces of lubricant from the bearings, hub and axle spindle. Inspect bearings and bearing cups for pitting, spalling or unusual wear. If either bearings or bearing cups are

worn or damaged, replace both bearings and bearing cups.

➡It is recommended that bearings and bearing cups be replaced in sets. If cups are worn or damaged, install the inner and outer bearing cups in the hub with an appropriate bearing cup driver tool. Check for proper seating of new bearing cups by trying to insert a 0.38-mm (0.0015 inch) feeler gauge between the bottom face of the cup and wheel hub seat. You should not be able to insert the feeler gauge.

9. Remove all burrs, nicks or scratches from the shoulder of the spindle and seal bore in the hub with emery cloth.

10. Pack the inside of the hub with lithium-base wheel bearing grease such as Motorcraft Premium Long-Life Grease

XG-1-C or -K or equivalent meeting Ford specification ESA-M1C75-B. Fill the hub until the grease is flush with the inside diameters of both bearing cups.

11. Pack the bearing cone and roller assemblies with wheel bearing grease. Use a bearing packer for this operation. If a packer is not available, work as much lubricant as possible between the rollers and cages.

⁂ WARNING

Keep the hub centered on the spindle to prevent damage to the grease seal or spindle threads.

12. Place the inner bearing cone and roller assembly in the inner cup and install the wheel bearing hub seal, using a suitable seal replacer. Make sure seal is fully seated and lubricated.
13. Install the hub assembly.
14. Install the outer bearing cone and roller assembly and the flat washer on the spindle and install the adjusting nut. Adjust the bearings. Install a new cotter pin.
15. Install the hub cap.
16. Install the front disc brake caliper and rotor.
17. Install the front wheel and tire assemblies.
18. Lower the vehicle.

4-Wheel Drive

1. Before servicing the vehicle, refer to the Precautions Section.
All vehicles
2. Remove the wheel and tire assembly.
3. Remove the two front disc brake caliper anchor plate bolts.
4. Remove the front disc brake caliper anchor plate and position aside.

➡**If excessive force must be used during brake rotor removal, the brake rotors should be checked for lateral runout prior to installation.**

5. On F-250 and F-350 4x4 SRW vehicles, remove the rotor.

6. On DRW vehicles, remove the eight hub plate nuts. Remove the hub plate. Remove the rotor.
7. Remove the retainer ring. Pull outward and remove the hub lock.
8. Remove the snapring. Remove the three thrust washers.
Vehicles equipped with ABS
➡**Do not remove the ABS sensor from the bearing.**
9. Disconnect the ABS wheel sensor harness.
All vehicles
➡**The wheel hub and bearing is a slip fit design and should not require a puller to remove it.**
10. Remove the four lock nuts. Remove the wheel hub and bearing.
11. If necessary, remove the brake disc shield.
Vehicles with ABS
12. If necessary, remove the bolt and the ABS sensor.
All vehicles
➡**If necessary, position the hub in a soft-jawed vise.**
13. Install two nuts on the studs and use the inner nut to remove the studs.
14. Remove and discard the O-ring.

To install:
All vehicles
➡**Any time the wheel hub is removed for any reason, a new O-ring seal must be installed. Failure to do so can cause a vacuum leak and loss of four wheel drive operations.**
15. Install a new O-ring.
➡**Position the hub in a soft-jawed vise.**
16. Install two nuts on the studs and use the outer nut to install the studs.
Vehicles equipped with ABS
17. Position the ABS sensor and install the bolt. Torque to 13 ft. lbs. (18 Nm).
All vehicles
18. Position the brake disc shield.

➡**Apply a coat of Ford High Temperature 4x4 Front Axle and Wheel Bearing Grease E8TZ-19590-A meeting Ford specification ESA-M1C198-A to the O-ring area of the wheel hub and bearing before installing the hub and bearing.**

19. Position the wheel hub and bearing. Install the four lock nuts. Torque to 133 ft. lbs. (180 Nm).
Vehicle equipped with ABS
20. Connect the ABS sensor harness.
All vehicles

⁂ CAUTION

The non-metallic thrust washer must be installed between the two metal thrust washers. Failure to do so will cause severe wear to the non-metallic thrust washer, allowing the axle shaft to travel further in and out during torque thrust causing damage to the wheel hub and bearing, the axle shaft end seal and the axle shaft.

21. Position the three thrust washers onto the axle shaft. Install the snapring.

➡**Any time the hub lock is removed, a new O-ring seal must be installed. Failure to do so can cause a vacuum leak and loss of four wheel drive functions.**

22. Install a new O-ring.
23. Position the hub lock.
24. Install the retainer ring.
25. Position the front disc brake rotor to the wheel hub. Make sure the wheel hub and the front disc brake rotor braking and mounting surfaces are clean. Use brake parts cleaner to clean the front disc brake rotor.
26. For DRW vehicles, install the front wheel hub extender and nuts. Torque to 130 ft. lbs. (176 Nm).
27. Position back the front disc brake caliper and anchor plate. Install the front disc brake caliper anchor plate bolts. Torque to 166 ft. lbs. (225 Nm).
28. Install the wheel and tire assembly.
29. Test the system for normal operation.

SUSPENSION **REAR SUSPENSION**

LEAF SPRING

REMOVAL & INSTALLATION

F-150 and Mark LT

1. Before servicing the vehicle, refer to the Precautions Section.
2. Remove the wheel and tire assembly.

✳✳ WARNING

Lower the rear axle only enough to gain access to the rear spring.

3. Use the jack to support and lower the rear axle housing assembly.
4. Remove the brake caliper and bolts

✳✳ WARNING

Do not allow the brake caliper to hang from the brake hose.

5. Position the brake caliper aside using mechanic's wire.
6. Disconnect the shock absorber at the lower end.
7. Remove the spring front eye bolt and nut.

➡Lower the fuel tank to gain access to the spring shackle bolt.

8. Remove the spring shackle bolt and nut (rear)
9. Remove the U-bolt nuts
10. Remove the U-bolt plate
11. Remove the U-bolts
12. Remove the rear spring assembly
13. To install, reverse the removal procedure.

➡Tighten the U-bolt nuts in a cross pattern in 3 even steps.

14. Observe the following torques:
   - U-bolt nuts. Light duty, in 3 equal steps: 85 ft. lbs. (115 Nm)

   - U-bolt nuts. Heavy duty, in 3 equal steps: 184 ft. lbs. (250 Nm)
   - Spring front eye bolt: 222 ft. lbs. (300 Nm)
   - Spring rear shackle bolt: 98 ft. lbs. (133 Nm)
   - Shock absorber nut: (66 ft. lbs. (90 Nm)

F-250 and F-350

See Figure 525.

1. Before servicing the vehicle, refer to the Precautions Section.

2. Raise and safely support the vehicle.
3. Remove the wheel and tire assembly.
4. Support the rear axle with a suitable jack.
5. Remove and discard the U-bolt retaining nuts and the U-bolts.
6. Remove the rear spring upper plate.
7. Remove the nut and bolt from the rear spring front hanger bracket.

➡If the rear spring has an auxiliary spring and spacer, it is serviced as part of the rear spring assembly.

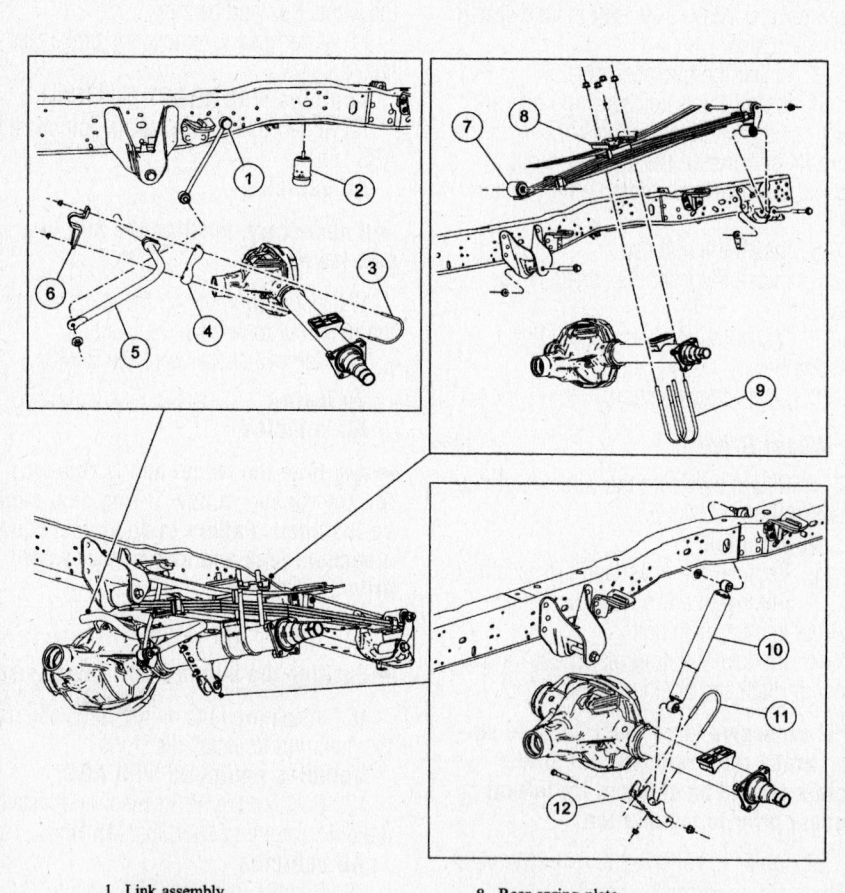

1 Link assembly
2 Rear axle bumper assembly
3 U-bolt, M10-1.75 x 137.5/161.5 (Ford axle only)
4 Rear stabilizer bar bracket (Ford axle only)
5 Stabilizer bar assembly
6 Rear stabilizer bar retainer
7 Rear spring assembly
8 Rear spring plate
9 U-bolt, M16-2.0 x 108/225 (narrow frame 4 required, wide frame 6 required)
10 Rear shock absorber
11 U-bolt, M10-1.50 x 101/136.7 (Ford axle only) (LH/RH)
12 Lower shock bracket (Ford axle only)

06017-F150-G274

Fig. 525 F-250 and F-350 rear suspension

8. Remove the lower nut and bolt from the rear spring shackle bracket. Remove the rear spring assembly.

To install:

9. To install, follow the removal procedure in reverse order, using new fasteners.

10. Use the following procedure to correctly install the U-bolts.

   a. Install the U-bolts and U-bolt retaining nuts. Do not tighten the fasteners at this time.

   b. Align the U-bolts so they are as vertical as possible.

   c. Tighten the nuts evenly in a cross-type pattern to:

- Step 1: 37 ft. lbs. (50 Nm)
- Step 2: 74 ft. lbs. (100 Nm)
- Step 3: 111 ft. lbs. (150 Nm)
- Step 4: 148 ft. lbs. (200 Nm).

11. Observe the following torques:

- Spring-to-front shackle, exc. waxed bracket: 277 ft. lbs. (375 Nm)
- Spring-to-front shackle, waxed bracket: 222 ft. lbs. (300 Nm)
- Spring-to-rear shackle: 185 ft. lbs. (250 Nm)
- Rear shackle-to-frame: 185 ft. lbs. (250 Nm)

SHOCK ABSORBER

REMOVAL & INSTALLATION

F-150 and Mark LT

See Figure 526.

1. Before servicing the vehicle, refer to the Precautions Section.

2. Raise the vehicle and secure on support stands.

3. Remove the self-locking nut, steel washer, and rubber bushings at the upper end of the shock absorber.

4. Remove the bolt and nut at the lower end and remove the shock absorber. If needed, raise the rear axle assembly slightly with a jack.

To install:

5. Installation is the reverse of removal. Tighten the upper and lower mounting nuts to 66 ft. lbs. (90 Nm).

F-250 and F-350

> ❊❊ **WARNING**
>
> **Suspension fasteners are critical parts because they affect performance of vital components and systems and their failure can result in major service expense. Install new parts with the same part number or**

an equivalent part if installation is necessary. Do not use an installation part of lesser quality or substitute design. Torque values must be used as specified during reassembly to make sure of correct retention of these parts.

1. Before servicing the vehicle, refer to the Precautions Section.

> ❊❊ **WARNING**
>
> **The low pressure gas shock absorbers are charged with nitrogen gas. Do not attempt to open, punc-**

ture or apply heat to shock absorbers.

2. Raise and support the vehicle.

3. Using a suitable jack, support the rear axle.

4. Remove the shock absorber lower retaining nut and bolt.

5. Remove the nut from the upper shock absorber mounting bracket and remove the shock.

6. To install, follow the removal procedure in reverse order, using new fasteners. Torque the upper bolt/nut to 46 ft. lbs. (62 Nm); the lower bolt/nut to 66 ft. lbs. (90 Nm).

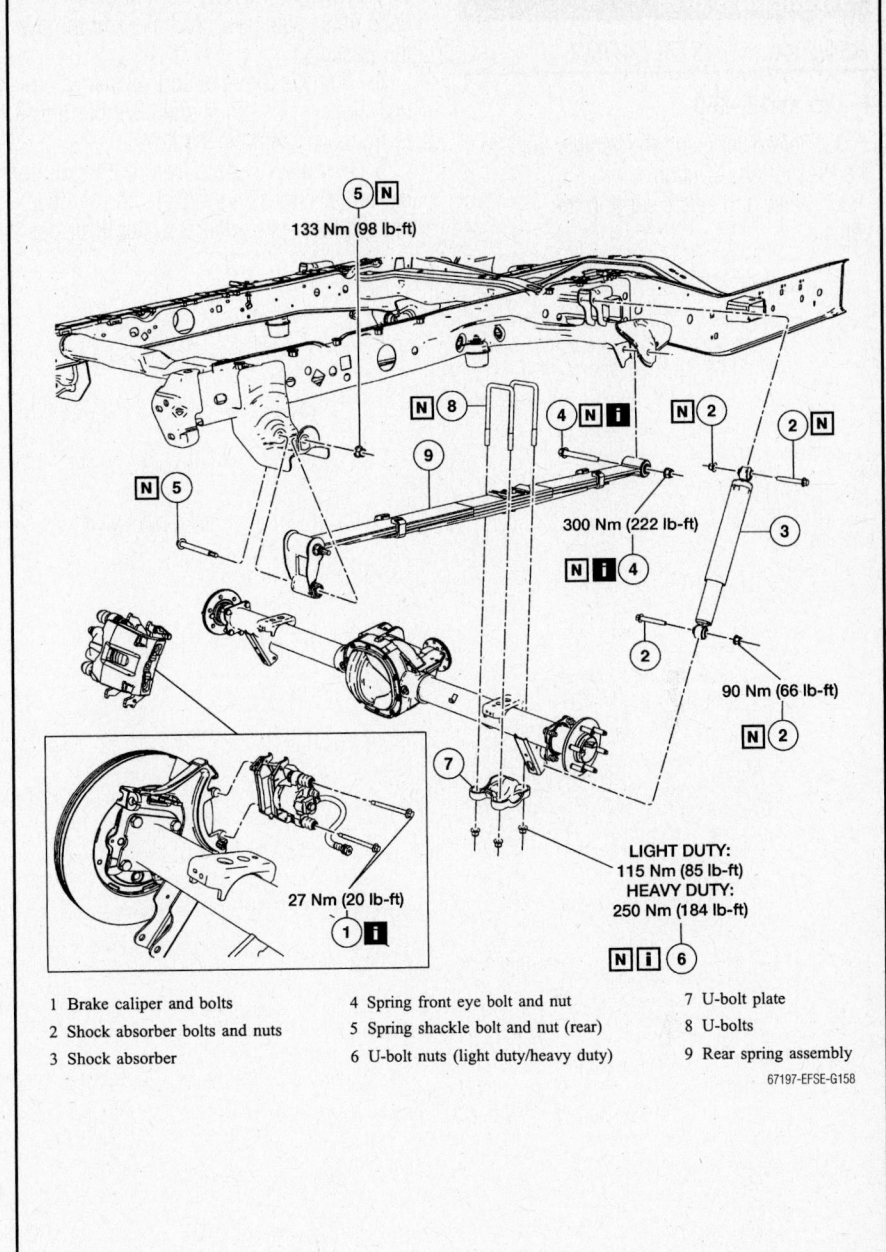

133 Nm (98 lb-ft)

300 Nm (222 lb-ft)

90 Nm (66 lb-ft)

27 Nm (20 lb-ft)

LIGHT DUTY:
115 Nm (85 lb-ft)
HEAVY DUTY:
250 Nm (184 lb-ft)

1 Brake caliper and bolts	4 Spring front eye bolt and nut
2 Shock absorber bolts and nuts	5 Spring shackle bolt and nut (rear)
3 Shock absorber	6 U-bolt nuts (light duty/heavy duty)
	7 U-bolt plate
	8 U-bolts
	9 Rear spring assembly

67197-EFSE-G158

Fig. 526 Rear suspension components—F-150 and Mark LT

STABILIZER BAR

REMOVAL & INSTALLATION

F-250 and F-350

1. Before servicing the vehicle, refer to the Precautions Section.

2. Raise and safely support the vehicle.

3. Remove the nuts from both lower ends of the stabilizer bar links and remove the washers.

4. Remove the nuts and washers from both upper ends of the stabilizer bar links-to-frame and remove the links.

5. Remove the nuts from both stabilizer bar retainer-to-axle brackets and remove the stabilizer bar retainers, stabilizer bar mounting brackets, U-bolts and the stabilizer bar.

6. To install, reverse the removal procedure, using new fasteners. Observe the following torques:

- Bracket U-bolt nuts: 30 ft. lbs. (40 Nm)
- End links top and bottom: 52 ft. lbs. (70 Nm)

FORD

5

E-150 • E-250 • E-350

SPECIFICATIONS AND MAINTENANCE CHARTS

ENGINE AND VEHICLE IDENTIFICATION

Engine							Model Year	
Code ①	Liters (cc)	Cu. In.	Cyl.	Fuel Sys.	Type	Eng. Mfg.	Code ②	Year
L	5.4 (5409)	330	8	EFI	SOHC	Ford	5	2005
P	6.0 (5921)	365	8	TDI	OHV	Navistar	6	2006
S	6.8 (6802)	415	10	MFI	SOHC	Ford	7	2007
W	4.6 (4588)	280	8	MFI	SOHC	Ford		

MFI: Multi-port Fuel Injection

TDI: Direct Injection Turbo-Diesel

EFI: Electronic Fuel Injection

SFI: Sequential Fuel Injection

OHV: Overhead Valve

SOHC: Single Overhead Camshaft

① 8th digit of the Vehicle Identification Number (VIN)

② 10th digit of the Vehicle Identification Number (VIN)

22086_ETRK_C0001

GENERAL ENGINE SPECIFICATIONS

Year	Model	Engine Displ. Liters	Engine VIN	Net Horsepower @ rpm	Net Torque @ rpm (ft. lbs.)	Bore x Stroke (in.)	Compression Ratio	Oil Pressure @ rpm
2005	E-150 Wagon	4.6	W	210@4400	290@3250	3.55x3.54	9.0:1	20-45@1500
		5.4	L	235@4250	330@3000	3.55x4.17	9.0:1	40-70@1500
	E-350 Wagon	5.4	L	235@4250	330@3000	3.55x4.17	9.0:1	40-70@1500
		6.0	P	325@3300	560@2000	3.74x4.13	18.0:1	24@1200
		6.8	S	265@4250	410@2750	4.09x4.17	9.0:1	40-75@2000
	E-150 Cargo	4.6	W	210@4400	290@3250	3.55x3.54	9.0:1	20-45@1500
		5.4	L	235@4250	330@3000	3.55x4.17	9.0:1	40-70@1500
		6.0	P	325@3300	560@2000	3.74x4.13	18.0:1	24@1200
	E-250 Cargo	4.6	W	210@4400	290@3250	3.55x3.54	9.0:1	20-45@1500
		5.4	L	235@4250	330@3000	3.55x4.17	9.0:1	40-70@1500
		6.0	P	325@3300	560@2000	3.74x4.13	18.0:1	24@1200
	E-350 Cargo	5.4	L	235@4250	330@3000	3.55x4.17	9.0:1	40-70@1500
		6.0	P	325@3300	560@2000	3.74x4.13	18.0:1	24@1200
		6.8	S	265@4250	410@2750	4.09x4.17	9.0:1	40-75@2000
2006	E-150 Wagon	4.6	W	210@4400	290@3250	3.55x3.54	9.0:1	20-45@1500
		5.4	L	235@4250	330@3000	3.55x4.17	9.0:1	40-70@1500
	E-350 Wagon	5.4	L	235@4250	330@3000	3.55x4.17	9.0:1	40-70@1500
		6.0	P	325@3300	560@2000	3.74x4.13	18.0:1	24@1200
		6.8	S	265@4250	410@2750	4.09x4.17	9.0:1	40-75@2000
	E-150 Cargo	4.6	W	210@4400	290@3250	3.55x3.54	9.0:1	20-45@1500
		5.4	L	235@4250	330@3000	3.55x4.17	9.0:1	40-70@1500
		6.0	P	325@3300	560@2000	3.74x4.13	18.0:1	24@1200
	E-250 Cargo	4.6	W	210@4400	290@3250	3.55x3.54	9.0:1	20-45@1500
		5.4	L	235@4250	330@3000	3.55x4.17	9.0:1	40-70@1500
		6.0	P	325@3300	560@2000	3.74x4.13	18.0:1	24@1200
	E-350 Cargo	5.4	L	235@4250	330@3000	3.55x4.17	9.0:1	40-70@1500
		6.0	P	325@3300	560@2000	3.74x4.13	18.0:1	24@1200
		6.8	S	265@4250	410@2750	4.09x4.17	9.0:1	40-75@2000
2007	E-150 Wagon	4.6	W	210@4400	290@3250	3.55x3.54	9.0:1	20-45@1500
		5.4	L	235@4250	330@3000	3.55x4.17	9.0:1	40-70@1500
	E-350 Wagon	5.4	L	235@4250	330@3000	3.55x4.17	9.0:1	40-70@1500
		6.0	P	325@3300	560@2000	3.74x4.13	18.0:1	24@1200
		6.8	S	265@4250	410@2750	4.09x4.17	9.0:1	40-75@2000
	E-150 Cargo	4.6	W	210@4400	290@3250	3.55x3.54	9.0:1	20-45@1500
		5.4	L	235@4250	330@3000	3.55x4.17	9.0:1	40-70@1500
		6.0	P	325@3300	560@2000	3.74x4.13	18.0:1	24@1200
	E-250 Cargo	4.6	W	210@4400	290@3250	3.55x3.54	9.0:1	20-45@1500
		5.4	L	235@4250	330@3000	3.55x4.17	9.0:1	40-70@1500
		6.0	P	325@3300	560@2000	3.74x4.13	18.0:1	24@1200
	E-350 Cargo	5.4	L	235@4250	330@3000	3.55x4.17	9.0:1	40-70@1500
		6.0	P	325@3300	560@2000	3.74x4.13	18.0:1	24@1200
		6.8	S	265@4250	410@2750	4.09x4.17	9.0:1	40-75@2000

22086_ETRK_C0002

GASOLINE ENGINE TUNE-UP SPECIFICATIONS

Year	Engine Displacement Liters	Engine VIN	Spark Plug Gap (in.)	Ignition Timing (deg.) ① MT	AT	Fuel Pump (psi) ②	Idle Speed (rpm) MT	AT	Valve Clearance In.	Ex.
2005	4.6	W	0.052-0.056	—	10B	30-45	—	③	HYD	HYD
	5.4	L	0.052-0.056	—	10B	28-45	—	③	HYD	HYD
	6.8	S	0.052-0.056	—	10B	28-45	—	③	HYD	HYD
2006	4.6	W	0.052-0.056	—	10B	30-45	—	③	HYD	HYD
	5.4	L	0.052-0.056	—	10B	28-45	—	③	HYD	HYD
	6.8	S	0.052-0.056	—	10B	28-45	—	③	HYD	HYD
2007	4.6	W	0.052-0.056	—	10B	30-45	—	③	HYD	HYD
	5.4	L	0.052-0.056	—	10B	28-45	—	③	HYD	HYD
	6.8	S	0.052-0.056	—	10B	28-45	—	③	HYD	HYD

NOTE: The Vehicle Emission Control Information label often reflects specification changes changes made during production. The label figures must be used if they differ from this chart.

B: Before top dead center

HYD: Hydraulic

① Ignition timing is preset and cannot be adjusted

② With engine running

③ Idle speed is electronically controlled and cannot be adjusted

22086_ETRK_C0003

DIESEL ENGINE TUNE-UP SPECIFICATIONS

Year	Engine Displ. Liters	Engine VIN	Valve Clearance Intake (in.)	Exhaust (in.)	Injection Pump Setting (deg.)	Injection Nozzle Pressure (psi) New	Used	Idle Speed (rpm)	Cranking Compression Pressure (psi)
2005	6.0	P	HYD	HYD	①	②	②	③	NA
2006	6.0	P	HYD	HYD	①	②	②	③	NA
2007	6.0	P	HYD	HYD	①	②	②	③	NA

NOTE: The Vehicle Emission Control Information label often reflects specification changes made during production. The label figures must be used if they differ from those in this chart

NA: Not Available

① PCM controlled

② Pump output pressure: 450-4,000 psi

③ See underhood emission label

22086_ETRK_C0004

CAPACITIES

Year	Model	Engine Displ. Liters	Engine VIN	Engine Oil with Filter (qts.)	Transmission (pts.)		Transfer Case (pts.)*	Drive Axle		Fuel Tank (gal.)	Cooling System (qts.)
					MT	Auto.		Front (pts.)	Rear (pts.)		
2005	E-150 Wagon	4.6	W	6.0	—	①	—	—	②	35.0	③
		5.4	L	6.0	—	①	—	—	②	35.0	④
	E-350 Wagon	5.4	L	6.0	—	①	—	—	②	35.0	④
		6.0	P	15.0	—	①	—	—	②	35.0	⑤
		6.8	S	6.0	—	①	—	—	②	35.0	⑥
	E-150 Cargo	4.6	W	6.0	—	①	—	—	②	35.0	③
		5.4	L	6.0	—	①	—	—	②	35.0	④
		6.0	P	15.0	—	①	—	—	②	35.0	⑤
	E-250 Cargo	4.6	W	6.0	—	①	—	—	②	35.0	③
		5.4	L	6.0	—	①	—	—	②	35.0	④
		6.0	P	15.0	—	①	—	—	②	35.0	⑥
	E-350 Cargo	5.4	L	6.0	—	①	—	—	②	⑦	③
		6.0	P	15.0	—	①	—	—	②	⑦	④
		6.8	S	6.0	—	①	—	—	②	⑦	⑥
2006	E-150 Wagon	4.6	W	6.0	—	①	—	—	②	35.0	③
		5.4	L	6.0	—	①	—	—	②	35.0	④
	E-350 Wagon	5.4	L	6.0	—	①	—	—	②	35.0	④
		6.0	P	15.0	—	①	—	—	②	35.0	⑤
		6.8	S	6.0	—	①	—	—	②	35.0	⑥
	E-150 Cargo	4.6	W	6.0	—	①	—	—	②	35.0	③
		5.4	L	6.0	—	①	—	—	②	35.0	④
		6.0	P	15.0	—	①	—	—	②	35.0	⑤
	E-250 Cargo	4.6	W	6.0	—	①	—	—	②	35.0	③
		5.4	L	6.0	—	①	—	—	②	35.0	④
		6.0	P	15.0	—	①	—	—	②	35.0	⑥
	E-350 Cargo	5.4	L	6.0	—	①	—	—	②	⑦	③
		6.0	P	15.0	—	①	—	—	②	⑦	④
		6.8	S	6.0	—	①	—	—	②	⑦	⑥

22086_ETRK_C0019

CAPACITIES

Year	Model	Engine Displ. Liters	Engine VIN	Engine Oil with Filter (qts.)	Transmission (pts.)		Transfer Case (pts.)*	Drive Axle		Fuel Tank (gal.)	Cooling System (qts.)
					MT	Auto.		Front (pts.)	Rear (pts.)		
2007	E-150 Wagon	4.6	W	6.0	—	①	—	—	②	35.0	③
		5.4	L	6.0	—	①	—	—	②	35.0	④
	E-350 Wagon	5.4	L	6.0	—	①	—	—	②	35.0	④
		6.0	P	15.0	—	①	—	—	②	35.0	⑤
		6.8	S	6.0	—	①	—	—	②	35.0	⑥
	E-150 Cargo	4.6	W	6.0	—	①	—	—	②	35.0	③
		5.4	L	6.0	—	①	—	—	②	35.0	④
		6.0	P	15.0	—	①	—	—	②	35.0	⑤
	E-250 Cargo	4.6	W	6.0	—	①	—	—	②	35.0	③
		5.4	L	6.0	—	①	—	—	②	35.0	④
		6.0	P	15.0	—	①	—	—	②	35.0	⑥
	E-350 Cargo	5.4	L	6.0	—	①	—	—	②	⑦	③
		6.0	P	15.0	—	①	—	—	②	⑦	④
		6.8	S	6.0	—	①	—	—	②	⑦	⑥

NA: Information not available

NOTE: All capacities are approximate. Add fluid gradually and check to be sure a proper fluid level is obtained.

* Overhaul

① 4R100: 34.2 pts.
4R70W/4R75W: 27.8 pts.
TorqShift: 38.4 pts.

② Ford 8.8 inch: 5.7 pts.
Ford 9.5 inch: 5.7 pts.
Traction-Lok includes 4 oz. of friction modifier
Dana 60-1U: 6.3 pts.
Dana 70-2U: 6.6 pts.
Dana 70-HD: 7.4
Limited slip includes 7 oz. of friction modifier

③ Without rear heat: 23.8 qts.
With rear heat: 26.0 qts.

④ Without rear heat: 27.8 quarts
With rear heat: 29.8 quarts

⑤ Without rear heat: 22.2 qts.
With rear heat: 24.9 qts.

⑥ Without rear heat: 29.4 qts.
With rear heat: 31.6 qts.

⑦ E-350 Cargo: 35.0
Commercial chassis-cab: 37.0 standard; 55.0 optional

22086_ETRK_C0005

FLUID SPECIFICATIONS

Year	Model	Engine Displacement Liters	Engine ID/VIN	Engine Oil	Auto. Trans.	Drive Axle	Power Steering Fluid	Brake Master Cylinder
2005	E-150 Wagon	4.6	W	①	②	③	④	DOT 3
		5.4	L	①	②	③	④	DOT 3
	E-350 Wagon	5.4	L	①	②	③	④	DOT 3
		6.0	P	①	②	③	④	DOT 3
		6.8	S	①	②	③	④	DOT 3
	E-150 Cargo	4.6	W	①	②	③	④	DOT 3
		5.4	L	①	②	③	④	DOT 3
		6.0	P	①	②	③	④	DOT 3
	E-250 Cargo	4.6	W	①	②	③	④	DOT 3
		5.4	L	①	②	③	④	DOT 3
		6.0	P	①	②	③	④	DOT 3
	E-350 Cargo	5.4	L	①	②	③	④	DOT 3
		6.0	P	①	②	③	④	DOT 3
		6.8	S	①	②	③	④	DOT 3
2006	E-150 Wagon	4.6	W	①	②	③	④	DOT 3
		5.4	L	①	②	③	④	DOT 3
	E-350 Wagon	5.4	L	①	②	③	④	DOT 3
		6.0	P	①	②	③	④	DOT 3
		6.8	S	①	②	③	④	DOT 3
	E-150 Cargo	4.6	W	①	②	③	④	DOT 3
		5.4	L	①	②	③	④	DOT 3
		6.0	P	①	②	③	④	DOT 3
	E-250 Cargo	4.6	W	①	②	③	④	DOT 3
		5.4	L	①	②	③	④	DOT 3
		6.0	P	①	②	③	④	DOT 3
	E-350 Cargo	5.4	L	①	②	③	④	DOT 3
		6.0	P	①	②	③	④	DOT 3
		6.8	S	①	②	③	④	DOT 3
2007	E-150 Wagon	4.6	W	①	②	③	④	DOT 3
		5.4	L	①	②	③	④	DOT 3
	E-350 Wagon	5.4	L	①	②	③	④	DOT 3
		6.0	P	①	②	③	④	DOT 3
		6.8	S	①	②	③	④	DOT 3
	E-150 Cargo	4.6	W	①	②	③	④	DOT 3
		5.4	L	①	②	③	④	DOT 3
		6.0	P	①	②	③	④	DOT 3
	E-250 Cargo	4.6	W	①	②	③	④	DOT 3
		5.4	L	①	②	③	④	DOT 3
		6.0	P	①	②	③	④	DOT 3
	E-350 Cargo	5.4	L	①	②	③	④	DOT 3
		6.0	P	①	②	③	④	DOT 3
		6.8	S	①	②	③	④	DOT 3

DOT: Department Of Transpotation

① Motorcraft SAE 5W-20 Premium Synthetic Blend Motor Oil XO-5W20-QSP

② Motorcraft MERCON® V Automatic Transmission Fluid XT-5-QM

③ Dana 60 and 70 Axles: XY-80W90-QL

    Dana 80 and Ford 8.8/9.75: SAE 75W-140 High Performance Rear Axle Lubricant F1TZ-19580-B

    Additive Friction Modifier C8AZ-19B546-A

④ MERCON® Multi-Purpose Transmission Fluid XT-2-QDX

VALVE SPECIFICATIONS

Year	Engine Displ. Liters	Engine VIN	Seat Angle (deg.)	Face Angle (deg.)	Spring Test Pressure (lbs. @ in.)	Spring Installed Height (in.)	Stem-to-Guide Clearance (in.)		Stem Diameter (in.)	
							Intake	Exhaust	Intake	Exhaust
2005	4.6	W	45.5	45.25-45.75	132@1.103	1.563-1.586	0.0008-0.0027	0.0018-0.0037	0.2754-0.2746	0.2744-0.2736
	5.4	L	45.5	45.25-45.75	171@1.34	1.6654-1.689	0.0008-0.0027	0.0018-0.0037	0.2754-0.2746	0.2744-0.2736
	6.0	P	①	①	191@1.51	1.820	0.0055 max.	0.0055 max.	0.2720-0.2735	0.2720-0.2735
	6.8	S	44.5-45	45.25-45.75	150@1.10	1.575	0.0008-0.0027	0.0018-0.0037	0.2754-0.2746	0.2744-0.2736
2006	4.6	W	45.5	45.25-45.75	132@1.103	1.563-1.586	0.0008-0.0027	0.0018-0.0037	0.2754-0.2746	0.2744-0.2736
	5.4	L	45.5	45.25-45.75	171@1.34	1.6654-1.689	0.0008-0.0027	0.0018-0.0037	0.2754-0.2746	0.2744-0.2736
	6.0	P	①	①	191@1.51	1.820	0.0055 max.	0.0055 max.	0.2720-0.2735	0.2720-0.2735
	6.8	S	44.5-45	45.25-45.75	150@1.10	1.575	0.0008-0.0027	0.0018-0.0037	0.2754-0.2746	0.2744-0.2736
2007	4.6	W	45.5	45.25-45.75	132@1.103	1.563-1.586	0.0008-0.0027	0.0018-0.0037	0.2754-0.2746	0.2744-0.2736
	5.4	L	45.5	45.25-45.75	171@1.34	1.6654-1.689	0.0008-0.0027	0.0018-0.0037	0.2754-0.2746	0.2744-0.2736
	6.0	P	①	①	191@1.51	1.820	0.0055 max.	0.0055 max.	0.2720-0.2735	0.2720-0.2735
	6.8	S	44.5-45	45.25-45.75	150@1.10	1.575	0.0008-0.0027	0.0018-0.0037	0.2754-0.2746	0.2744-0.2736

NA: Information not available

① Intake: 30 degrees
  Exhaust: 37.5 degrees

22086_ETRK_C0007

CAMSHAFT AND BEARING SPECIFICATIONS CHART

All measurements are given in inches.

Year	Engine Displ. Liters	Engine VIN	Journal Dia.	Brg. Oil Clearance	Shaft End-play	Runout	Journal Bore	Lobe Lift	
								Intake	Exhaust
2005	4.6	W	1.0605-1.0615	0.0010-0.0030	0.0035-0.0075	0.002	1.0625-1.0635	0.2560	0.2560
	5.4	L	1.1260-1.1270	0.0010-0.0030	0.0035-0.0075	0.001	1.1280-1.1290	0.2173	0.2168
	6.0	P	2.4400-2.4420	0.0015-0.0060	0.0020-0.0080	NA	2.4430-2.4460	0.2261	0.2296
	6.8	S	1.1260-1.1270	0.0009-0.0029	0.0013-0.0019	0.001	1.1280-1.1290	0.2156	0.2173
2006	4.6	W	1.0605-1.0615	0.0010-0.0030	0.0035-0.0075	0.002	1.0625-1.0635	0.2560	0.2560
	5.4	L	1.1260-1.1270	0.0010-0.0030	0.0035-0.0075	0.001	1.1280-1.1290	0.2173	0.2168
	6.0	P	2.4400-2.4420	0.0015-0.0060	0.0020-0.0080	NA	2.4430-2.4460	0.2261	0.2296
	6.8	S	1.1260-1.1270	0.0009-0.0029	0.0013-0.0019	0.001	1.1280-1.1290	0.2156	0.2173
2007	4.6	W	1.0605-1.0615	0.0010-0.0030	0.0035-0.0075	0.002	1.0625-1.0635	0.2560	0.2560
	5.4	L	1.1260-1.1270	0.0010-0.0030	0.0035-0.0075	0.001	1.1280-1.1290	0.2173	0.2168
	6.0	P	2.4400-2.4420	0.0015-0.0060	0.0020-0.0080	NA	2.4430-2.4460	0.2261	0.2296
	6.8	S	1.1260-1.1270	0.0009-0.0029	0.0013-0.0019	0.001	1.1280-1.1290	0.2156	0.2173

NA: Information not available

① Intake: 1.8532-1.8542 in.

　Exhaust: 1.5635-1.5645 in.

22086_ETRK_C0008

CRANKSHAFT AND CONNECTING ROD SPECIFICATIONS

All measurements are given in inches.

Year	Engine Displ. Liters	Engine VIN	Crankshaft				Connecting Rod		
			Main Brg. Journal Dia.	Main Brg. Oil Clearance	Shaft End-play	Thrust on No.	Journal Dia.	Oil Clearance	Side Clearance
2005	4.6	W	2.6500-2.6570	0.0011-0.0026	0.0051-0.0120	5	2.0859-2.0867	0.0010-0.0027	0.0006-0.0177
	5.4	L	2.6568-2.6576	0.0009-0.0019	0.0030-0.0148	5	2.0859-2.0867	0.0010-0.0025	0.0049-0.0187
	6.0	P	3.1500-3.1880	NA	0.0087	NA	2.7160-2.7170	NA	0.0120-0.0240
	6.8	S	2.6568-2.6576	0.0009-0.0019	0.0015-0.0030	5	2.0859-2.0867	0.0010-0.0025	0.0006-0.0177
2006	4.6	W	2.6500-2.6570	0.0011-0.0026	0.0051-0.0120	5	2.0859-2.0867	0.0010-0.0027	0.0006-0.0177
	5.4	L	2.6568-2.6576	0.0009-0.0019	0.0030-0.0148	5	2.0859-2.0867	0.0010-0.0025	0.0049-0.0187
	6.0	P	3.1500-3.1880	NA	0.0087	NA	2.7160-2.7170	NA	0.0120-0.0240
	6.8	S	2.6568-2.6576	0.0009-0.0019	0.0015-0.0030	5	2.0859-2.0867	0.0010-0.0025	0.0006-0.0177
2007	4.6	W	2.6500-2.6570	0.0011-0.0026	0.0051-0.0120	5	2.0859-2.0867	0.0010-0.0027	0.0006-0.0177
	5.4	L	2.6568-2.6576	0.0009-0.0019	0.0030-0.0148	5	2.0859-2.0867	0.0010-0.0025	0.0049-0.0187
	6.0	P	3.1500-3.1880	NA	0.0087	NA	2.7160-2.7170	NA	0.0120-0.0240
	6.8	S	2.6568-2.6576	0.0009-0.0019	0.0015-0.0030	5	2.0859-2.0867	0.0010-0.0025	0.0006-0.0177

NA: Information not available

22086_ETRK_C0010

PISTON AND RING SPECIFICATIONS

All measurements are given in inches.

Year	Engine Displ. Liters	Engine VIN	Piston Clearance	Ring Gap			Ring Side Clearance		
				Top Compression	Bottom Compression	Oil Control	Top Compression	Bottom Compression	Oil Control
2005	4.6	W	0.0005-0.0010	0.010-0.020	0.010-0.020	0.006-0.026	0.0012-0.0028	0.0012-0.0028	0.0018-0.0077
	5.4	L	0.0000-0.0010	0.006-0.0150	0.010-0.020	0.006-0.026	0.0002-0.0013	0.0012-0.0031	SNUG
	6.0	P	0.0017-0.0036	0.011-0.0210	0.055-0.0650	0.009-0.0190	NA	NA	NA
	6.8	S	0.0000-0.0010	0.0059-0.0118	0.010-0.016	0.006-0.026	0.0012-0.0037	0.0012-0.0037	SNUG
2006	4.6	W	0.0005-0.0010	0.010-0.020	0.010-0.020	0.006-0.026	0.0012-0.0028	0.0012-0.0028	0.0018-0.0077
	5.4	L	0.0000-0.0010	0.006-0.0150	0.010-0.020	0.006-0.026	0.0002-0.0013	0.0012-0.0031	SNUG
	6.0	P	0.0017-0.0036	0.011-0.0210	0.055-0.0650	0.009-0.0190	NA	NA	NA
	6.8	S	0.0000-0.0010	0.0059-0.0118	0.010-0.016	0.006-0.026	0.0012-0.0037	0.0012-0.0037	SNUG
2007	4.6	W	0.0005-0.0010	0.010-0.020	0.010-0.020	0.006-0.026	0.0012-0.0028	0.0012-0.0028	0.0018-0.0077
	5.4	L	0.0000-0.0010	0.006-0.0150	0.010-0.020	0.006-0.026	0.0002-0.0013	0.0012-0.0031	SNUG
	6.0	P	0.0017-0.0036	0.011-0.0210	0.055-0.0650	0.009-0.0190	NA	NA	NA
	6.8	S	0.0000-0.0010	0.0059-0.0118	0.010-0.016	0.006-0.026	0.0012-0.0037	0.0012-0.0037	SNUG

NA: Information not available

22086_ETRK_C0009

TORQUE SPECIFICATIONS
All readings in ft. lbs.

	Engine Displ. Liters	Engine VIN	Cylinder Head Bolts	Main Bearing Bolts	Rod Bearing Bolts	Crankshaft Damper Bolts	Flywheel Bolts	Manifold Intake *	Manifold Exhaust	Spark Plugs	Oil Pan Drain Plug
2005	4.6	W	①	②	③	④	59	⑤	18	11	10
	5.4	L	①	⑥	③	④	59	⑦	18	10	10
	6.0	P	⑧	⑨	⑩	⑪	69	8	28 ⑫	—	18
	6.8	S	①	⑥	③	④	59	⑬	18	10	10
2006	4.6	W	①	②	③	④	59	⑤	18	11	10
	5.4	L	①	⑥	③	④	59	⑦	18	10	10
	6.0	P	⑧	⑨	⑩	⑪	69	8	28 ⑫	—	18
	6.8	S	①	⑥	③	④	59	⑬	18	10	10
2007	4.6	W	①	②	③	④	59	⑤	18	11	10
	5.4	L	①	⑥	③	④	59	⑦	18	10	10
	6.0	P	⑧	⑨	⑩	⑪	69	8	28 ⑫	—	18
	6.8	S	①	⑥	③	④	59	⑬	18	10	10

NA: Information not available

* NOTE: Applies to Lower Manifold only. For Fpper Manifold, see the text.

① Step 1: 30 ft. lbs.
Step 2: Plus 85-95 degrees
Step 3: Plus 85-95 degrees

② Vertical bolts:
Step 1: 30 ft. lbs.
Step 2: Plus 90 degrees
Jack screws:
Step 1: 44 inch lbs.
Step 2: 89 inch lbs.
Side bolts: 15 ft. lbs.

③ Step 1: 32 ft. lbs.
Step 2: 105 degrees

④ Step 1: 66 ft. lbs.
Step 2: loosen 1 full turn
Step 3: 37 ft. lbs.
Step 4: plus 90 deg. Without exceeding 148 ft. lbs.

⑤ Step 1: 18 inch lbs.
Step 2: 18 ft. lbs.

⑥ Vertical bolts:
Step 1: 30 ft. lbs.
Step 2: plus 90 degrees
Side bolts:
Step 1: 22 ft. lbs.
Step 2: plus 90 degrees

⑦ Step 1: 18 inch lbs
Step 2: 18 ft. lbs.

⑧ See the procedure in the text

⑨ Step 1: 90 ft. lbs.
Step 2: 120 ft. lbs.
Step 3: 170 ft. lbs.
Lower crankcase bolts: 23 ft. lbs.

⑩ Step 1: 33 ft. lbs.
Step 2: 50 ft. lbs.

⑪ Step 1: 50 ft. lbs.
Step 2: plus 90 degrees
See the text for torque sequence

⑫ Apply high temp nickel anti-seize to the threads

⑬ Step 1: 18 inch lbs.
Step 2 18 ft. lbs.

22086_ETRK_C0011

WHEEL ALIGNMENT

Year	Model		Caster Range (+/-Deg.)	Caster Preferred Setting (Deg.)	Camber Range (+/-Deg.)	Camber Preferred Setting (Deg.)	Toe-in (Deg.)
2005	E-150	Left	2.75	+4.00	0.50	+0.25	0.06+/-0.25
		Right	2.75	+4.50	—	—	—
	E-250	Left	2.75	+4.00	0.50	+0.50	0.06+/-0.25
		Right	2.75	+4.50	—	—	—
	E-350	Left	2.75	+4.00	0.50	+0.50	0.06+/-0.25
		Right	2.75	+4.50	—	—	—
	E-Super Duty	Left	2.75	+4.00	0.50	+0.50	0.06+/-0.25
		Right	2.75	+4.50	—	—	—
2006	E-150	Left	2.75	+4.00	0.50	+0.25	0.06+/-0.25
		Right	2.75	+4.50	—	—	—
	E-250	Left	2.75	+4.00	0.50	+0.50	0.06+/-0.25
		Right	2.75	+4.50	—	—	—
	E-350	Left	2.75	+4.00	0.50	+0.50	0.06+/-0.25
		Right	2.75	+4.50	—	—	—
	E-Super Duty	Left	2.75	+4.00	0.50	+0.50	0.06+/-0.25
		Right	2.75	+4.50	—	—	—
2007	E-150	Left	2.75	+4.00	0.50	+0.25	0.06+/-0.25
		Right	2.75	+4.50	—	—	—
	E-250	Left	2.75	+4.00	0.50	+0.50	0.06+/-0.25
		Right	2.75	+4.50	—	—	—
	E-350	Left	2.75	+4.00	0.50	+0.50	0.06+/-0.25
		Right	2.75	+4.50	—	—	—
	E-Super Duty	Left	2.75	+4.00	0.50	+0.50	0.06+/-0.25
		Right	2.75	+4.50	—	—	—

22086_ETRK_C0012

TIRE, WHEEL AND BALL JOINT SPECIFICATIONS

Year	Model	OEM Tires Standard	OEM Tires Optional	Tire Pressures (psi.) Front	Tire Pressures (psi.) Rear	Wheel Size	Ball Joint Inspection	Lug Nut Torque (ft. lbs.)
2005	E-150 Wagon	P235/70R16	none	①	①	NA	0.030 in. ②	③
	E-350 Wagon	LT225/75R16E	none	①	①	NA	0.030 in. ②	③
	E-350 Ext. Wagon	LT245/75R16E	none	①	①	NA	0.030 in. ②	③
	E-150 Cargo	P235/70R16	none	①	①	NA	0.030 in. ②	③
	E-250 Cargo	LT245/75R16E	none	①	①	NA	0.030 in. ②	③
	E-350 cargo	LT245/75R16E	none	①	①	NA	0.030 in. ②	③
2006	E-150 Wagon	P235/70R16	none	①	①	NA	0.030 in. ②	③
	E-350 Wagon	LT225/75R16E	none	①	①	NA	0.030 in. ②	③
	E-350 Ext. Wagon	LT245/75R16E	none	①	①	NA	0.030 in. ②	③
	E-150 Cargo	P235/70R16	none	①	①	NA	0.030 in. ②	③
	E-250 Cargo	LT245/75R16E	none	①	①	NA	0.030 in. ②	③
	E-350 cargo	LT245/75R16E	none	①	①	NA	0.030 in. ②	③
2007	E-150 Wagon	P235/70R16	none	①	①	NA	0.030 in. ②	③
	E-350 Wagon	LT225/75R16E	none	①	①	NA	0.030 in. ②	③
	E-350 Ext. Wagon	LT245/75R16E	none	①	①	NA	0.030 in. ②	③
	E-150 Cargo	P235/70R16	none	①	①	NA	0.030 in. ②	③
	E-250 Cargo	LT245/75R16E	none	①	①	NA	0.030 in. ②	③
	E-350 cargo	LT245/75R16E	none	①	①	NA	0.030 in. ②	③

NA: Information not available

OEM: Original Equipment Manufacturer

PSI: Pounds Per Square Inch

① See placard on vehicle

② Both upper and lower

③ 5 lug: 74-133 ft. lbs.

   8 lug: 126-170 ft. lbs.

22086_ETRK_C0013

BRAKE SPECIFICATIONS
All measurements are given in inches.

| Year | Model | | Brake Disc | | | Brake Drum Diameter | | | Brake Caliper | |
			Original Thickness	Minimum Thickness	Maximum Runout	Original Inside Diameter	Max. Wear Limit	Maximum Machine Diameter	Bracket Bolts (ft. lbs.)	Mounting Bolts (ft. lbs.)
2005	E-150	F	NA	1.15	NA	—	—	—	129	24
		R	NA	0.80	NA	—	—	—	129	24
	E-250	F	NA	1.10	NA	—	—	—	166	23
		R	NA	1.10	NA	—	—	—	①	27
	E-350	F	NA	1.10	NA	—	—	—	166	23
		R	NA	1.10	NA	—	—	—	①	27
2006	E-150	F	NA	1.15	NA	—	—	—	129	24
		R	NA	0.80	NA	—	—	—	129	24
	E-250	F	NA	1.10	NA	—	—	—	166	23
		R	NA	1.10	NA	—	—	—	①	27
	E-350	F	NA	1.10	NA	—	—	—	166	23
		R	NA	1.10	NA	—	—	—	①	27
2007	E-150	F	NA	1.15	NA	—	—	—	129	24
		R	NA	0.80	NA	—	—	—	129	24
	E-250	F	NA	1.10	NA	—	—	—	166	23
		R	NA	1.10	NA	—	—	—	①	27
	E-350	F	NA	1.10	NA	—	—	—	166	23
		R	NA	1.10	NA	—	—	—	①	27

NOTE: Due to changes made during production, refer to manufacturer's specifications if they differ from those in this chart

NA: Information not available

① Support bracket support bolts: 100 ft. lbs.

22086_ETRK_C0014

SCHEDULED MAINTENANCE INTERVALS
2005–07 E-Series with Gasoline Engines

TO BE SERVICED	TYPE OF SERVICE	VEHICLE MILEAGE INTERVAL (x1000)												
		5	10	15	20	25	30	35	40	45	50	55	60	65
Engine oil & filter	R	✓	✓	✓	✓	✓	✓	✓	✓	✓	✓	✓	✓	✓
Tires	Rotate	✓	✓	✓	✓	✓	✓	✓	✓	✓	✓	✓	✓	✓
Wheels	I ①			✓			✓			✓			✓	
Auto trans. fluid	I			✓			✓			✓			✓	
Brake pads/shoes	I			✓			✓			✓			✓	
Coolant hoses	S/I			✓			✓			✓			✓	
Steering linkage	I			✓			✓			✓			✓	
Suspension	I			✓			✓			✓			✓	
Driveshaft	I			✓			✓			✓			✓	
Cabin air filter	R			✓			✓			✓			✓	
Ball joints	L			✓			✓			✓			✓	
NGV fuel filter	R					✓					✓			
Exhaust system	I						✓						✓	
Engine air filter	R						✓						✓	
Fuel filter	R						✓						✓	
Auto trans fluid (4R100 and Torqshift)	R						✓						✓	
Front wheel bearings	L/Ådj												✓	
Front wheel bearings grease seal	R												✓	
Accessory drive belts	I	every 100,000 miles												
Spark plugs	R	every 100,000 miles												
PCV valve ②	R	every 100,000 miles												
Premium Gold coolant	R	every 3 years or 100,000 miles												
Auto trans fluid (all exc. 4R100 and TorqShift)	R	every 120,000 miles												
PCV valve (5.4L 3v)	I	every 150,000 miles												
Front wheel bearings	R	at 150,000 miles, if not previously done so												
Fuel tank	I	every 150,000 miles												
Rear drive axle fluid	R	every 150,000 miles												
Accessory drive belts	R	every 150,000 miles, if not previously done so												

R: Replace   S: Service   I: Inspect   L: Lubricate

NGV: Natural gas vehicle

① Inspect for end play and noise

② Vehicles under 6,000 lbs. GVW, exc. 5.4L 3v engines

Special Operating Condition Requirements

When towing a trailer or using a camper or car-top carrier:

Change engine oil and install a new oil filter every 4,800 km (3,000 miles), 3 months or 200 hours of engine operation (whichever occurs first).

Inspect and lubricate U-joints as required.

During extensive idling and/or low speed driving for long distances, as in heavy commercial use such as delivery, taxi, patrol car or livery:

Change engine oil and install a new oil filter every 4,800 km (3,000 miles), 3 months or 200 hours of engine operation (whichever occurs first).

Lube front lower control arm and steering linkage ball joints with zerk fittings (if equipped) every 4,800 km (3,000 miles) or 3 months.

Inspect brake system and check battery electrolyte level (Patrol cars) every 8,000 km (5,000 miles).

Install a new fuel filter every 24,000 km (15,000 miles).

SCHEDULED MAINTENANCE INTERVALS
2005–07 E-Series with Gasoline Engines
Footnotes continued

Change automatic transmission fluid, lubricate 4x2 wheel bearings, install new grease seals and adjust bearings every 48,000 km (30,000 miles). If equipped, change the in-line service installed transmission fluid filter.

Install new spark plugs every 96,000 km (60,000 miles).

Install a new cabin air filter as required.

When operating in dusty conditions such as unpaved or dusty roads:

Change engine oil and install a new oil filter every 4,800 km (3,000 miles) or 3 months.

Install a new fuel filter every 24,000 km (15,000 miles).

Change automatic transmission fluid every 48,000 km (30,000 miles). If equipped, change the in-line service installed transmission fluid filter.

Install a new engine air filter as required.

Install a new cabin air filter as required.

When operating in off-road conditions:

Change automatic transmission fluid every 48,000 km (30,000 miles). If equipped, change the in-line service installed transmission fluid filter.

Install a new cabin air filter as required.

Inspect and lubricate U-joints.

Inspect and lubricate steering linkage ball joints with zerk fittings.

Short trips in cold operating conditions:

22086_ETRK_C0016

SCHEDULED MAINTENANCE INTERVALS
2005–07 E-Series with 6.0L Diesel Engines

TO BE SERVICED	TYPE OF SERVICE	VEHICLE MILEAGE INTERVAL (x1000)												
		7.5	15	22.5	30	37.5	45	52.5	60	67.5	75	82.5	90	97.5
Engine oil & filter	R	✓	✓	✓	✓	✓	✓	✓	✓	✓	✓	✓	✓	✓
Tires	Rotate	✓	✓	✓	✓	✓	✓	✓	✓	✓	✓	✓	✓	✓
Air filter minder	I ①	✓	✓	✓	✓	✓	✓	✓	✓	✓	✓	✓	✓	✓
Wheels	I ②		✓		✓		✓		✓		✓		✓	
Brake pads, hoses, etc.	I		✓		✓		✓		✓		✓		✓	
Coolant hoses	I		✓		✓		✓		✓		✓		✓	
Steering linkage and suspension	I/L		✓		✓		✓		✓		✓		✓	
Cabin air filter	R						✓						✓	
Ball joints	L		✓		✓		✓		✓		✓		✓	
Driveshaft	I/L		✓		✓		✓		✓		✓		✓	
Exhaust system and heat shields	I		✓		✓		✓		✓		✓		✓	
Engine air filter	R		✓		✓		✓		✓		✓		✓	
Fuel filters ③	R		✓		✓		✓		✓		✓		✓	
Auto trans fluid ④	R				✓				✓				✓	
Front wheel bearings	L								✓					
Front wheel bearing grease seals	R								✓					
Accessory drive belts	I													✓
Rear differential fluid ⑤	R													✓
Coolant (Premium Gold)	R	every 105,000 miles												
Accessory drive belts	R	every 150,000 miles, if not previously done so												

R: Replace   S: Service   I: Inspect   L: Lubricate   Adj: adjust

① Reset after new filter is installed
② Inspect for end play and noise
③ Frame-mounted and engine
④ Including external and in-line filters
⑤ Dana axles using non-synthetic fluid only

Special Operating Condition Requirements

When towing a trailer or using a camper or car-top carrier:

Change engine oil and install a new oil filter every 4,800 km (3,000 miles), 3 months or 200 hours of engine operation (whichever occurs first).

Inspect and lubricate U-joints as required.

During extensive idling and/or low speed driving for long distances, as in heavy commercial use such as delivery, taxi, patrol car or livery:

Change engine oil and install a new oil filter every 4,800 km (3,000 miles), 3 months or 200 hours of engine operation (whichever occurs first).

Lube front lower control arm and steering linkage ball joints with zerk fittings (if equipped) every 4,800 km (3,000 miles) or 3 months.

Inspect brake system and check battery electrolyte level (Patrol cars) every 8,000 km (5,000 miles).

Install a new fuel filter every 24,000 km (15,000 miles).

Change automatic transmission fluid, lubricate 4x2 wheel bearings, install new grease seals and adjust bearings every 48,000 km (30,000 miles). If equipped, change the in-line service installed transmission fluid filter.

Install a new cabin air filter as required.

22086_ETRK_C0017

SCHEDULED MAINTENANCE INTERVALS
2005–07 E-Series with 6.0L Diesel Engines
Footnotes continued

When operating in dusty conditions such as unpaved or dusty roads:

Change engine oil and install a new oil filter every 4,800 km (3,000 miles) or 3 months.

Install a new fuel filter every 24,000 km (15,000 miles).

Change automatic transmission fluid every 48,000 km (30,000 miles). If equipped, change the in-line service installed transmission fluid filter.

Install a new engine air filter as required.

Install a new cabin air filter as required.

When operating in off-road conditions:

Change automatic transmission fluid every 48,000 km (30,000 miles). If equipped, change the in-line service installed transmission fluid filter.

Install a new cabin air filter as required.

Inspect and lubricate U-joints.

Inspect and lubricate steering linkage ball joints with zerk fittings.

22086_ETRK_C0018

PRECAUTIONS

Before servicing any vehicle, please be sure to read all of the following precautions, which deal with personal safety, prevention of component damage, and important points to take into consideration when servicing a motor vehicle:

• Never open, service or drain the radiator or cooling system when the engine is hot; serious burns can occur from the steam and hot coolant.

• Observe all applicable safety precautions when working around fuel. Whenever servicing the fuel system, always work in a well-ventilated area. Do not allow fuel spray or vapors to come in contact with a spark, open flame, or excessive heat (a hot drop light, for example). Keep a dry chemical fire extinguisher near the work area. Always keep fuel in a container specifically designed for fuel storage; also, always properly seal fuel containers to avoid the possibility of fire or explosion. Refer to the additional fuel system precautions later in this section.

• Fuel injection systems often remain pressurized, even after the engine has been turned **OFF**. The fuel system pressure must be relieved before disconnecting any fuel lines. Failure to do so may result in fire and/or personal injury.

• Brake fluid often contains polyglycol ethers and polyglycols. Avoid contact with the eyes and wash your hands thoroughly after handling brake fluid. If you do get brake fluid in your eyes, flush your eyes with clean, running water for 15 minutes. If eye irritation persists, or if you have taken brake fluid internally, IMMEDIATELY seek medical assistance.

• The EPA warns that prolonged contact with used engine oil may cause a number of skin disorders, including cancer. You should make every effort to minimize your exposure to used engine oil. Protective gloves should be worn when changing oil. Wash your hands and any other exposed skin areas as soon as possible after exposure to used engine oil. Soap and water, or waterless hand cleaner should be used.

• All new vehicles are now equipped with an air bag system, often referred to as a Supplemental Restraint System (SRS) or Supplemental Inflatable Restraint (SIR) system. The system must be disabled before performing service on or around system components, steering column, instrument panel components, wiring and sensors. Failure to follow safety and disabling procedures could result in accidental air bag deployment, possible personal injury and unnecessary system repairs.

• Always wear safety goggles when working with, or around, the air bag system. When carrying a non-deployed air bag, be sure the bag and trim cover are pointed away from your body. When placing a non-deployed air bag on a work surface, always face the bag and trim cover upward, away from the surface. This will reduce the motion of the module if it is accidentally deployed. Refer to the additional air bag system precautions later in this section.

• Clean, high quality brake fluid from a sealed container is essential to the safe and proper operation of the brake system. You should always buy the correct type of brake fluid for your vehicle. If the brake fluid becomes contaminated, completely flush the system with new fluid. Never reuse any brake fluid. Any brake fluid that is removed from the system should be discarded. Also, do not allow any brake fluid to come in contact with a painted surface; it will damage the paint.

• Never operate the engine without the proper amount and type of engine oil; doing so WILL result in severe engine damage.

• Timing belt maintenance is extremely important. Many models utilize an interference-type, non-freewheeling engine. If the timing belt breaks, the valves in the cylinder head may strike the pistons, causing potentially serious (also time-consuming and expensive) engine damage. Refer to the maintenance interval charts for the recommended replacement interval for the timing belt, and to the timing belt section for belt replacement and inspection.

• Disconnecting the negative battery cable on some vehicles may interfere with the functions of the on-board computer system(s) and may require the computer to undergo a relearning process once the negative battery cable is reconnected.

• When servicing drum brakes, only disassemble and assemble one side at a time, leaving the remaining side intact for reference.

• Only an MVAC-trained, EPA-certified automotive technician should service the air conditioning system or its components.

BRAKES

BLEEDING THE BRAKE SYSTEM

BLEEDING PROCEDURE

BLEEDING PROCEDURE

1. Before servicing the vehicle, refer to the Precautions Section.

➡When any part of the hydraulic system has been disconnected for repair or new installation, air may get into the system and cause spongy brake pedal action. This requires bleeding of the hydraulic system after it has been correctly connected. The hydraulic system can be gravity bled, manually bled or with pressure bleeding equipment.

Master Cylinder, Bench

2. Support the brake master cylinder body in a vise and fill the brake master cylinder reservoir with specified brake fluid.

➡Original equipment lines are not intended to be used during this procedure.

3. Install short brake tubes with the ends submerged in the brake master cylinder reservoir.

4. Slowly press the primary piston until clear fluid flows from both brake tubes, without air bubbles.

5. Remove the short brake tubes and plug the brake tube ports.

Master Cylinder—In Vehicle

❋❋ WARNING

Do not allow the brake master cylinder reservoir to run dry during the bleeding operation. Keep the brake master cylinder reservoir filled with the specified brake fluid. Never

reuse the brake fluid that has been drained from the hydraulic system.

➡When a new brake master cylinder has been installed or the system has been emptied, or partially emptied, it should be primed to prevent air from getting into the system.

6. Disconnect the brake master cylinder outlet tubes.

➡Original equipment lines are not intended to be used during this procedure.

7. Install short brake tubes with ends submerged in the brake master cylinder reservoir and fill the brake master cylinder reservoir with brake fluid.

8. Have an assistant pump the brake pedal until clear fluid flows from both brake tubes without air bubbles.

9. Remove the short brake tubes and install the brake outlet tubes.

10. Bleed each brake tube at the brake master cylinder as follows:

   a. Have an assistant pump the brake pedal and then hold firm pressure on the brake pedal.

   b. Loosen the rear brake tube fittings until a stream of brake fluid comes out. Have an assistant maintain pressure on the brake pedal while tightening the brake tube fitting.

   c. Repeat this operation until clear, bubble-free fluid comes out.

   d. Refill the brake master cylinder reservoir as necessary. Repeat the bleeding operation at the front brake tube.

11. While the assistant maintains pressure on the brake pedal, tighten the brake tubes.

Gravity Bleeding

> ❄ **WARNING**
>
> **Do not allow the brake master cylinder reservoir to run dry during the bleeding operation. Keep the brake master cylinder reservoir filled with the specified brake fluid. Never reuse the brake fluid that has been drained from the hydraulic system.**

➡ **When a new brake master cylinder has been installed or the system has been emptied, or partially emptied, it should be** primed to prevent air from getting into the system.

12. Fill the brake master cylinder reservoir with brake fluid.

13. Connect a clear tube to the right rear disc brake caliper bleeder screw and the other end in a container partially filled with recommended brake fluid.

14. Open the bleeder screw and leave open until clear bubble-free brake fluid flows.

15. Refill the brake master cylinder reservoir as necessary.

16. Tighten the disc brake caliper bleeder screw.

17. Repeat Steps 1 through 4 for the three remaining brake calipers, going in order from the left rear disc brake caliper to the right front disc brake caliper ending with the left front disc brake caliper.

18. If the brake pedal feels spongy, repeat the bleed procedure.

Manual Bleeding

> ❄ **WARNING**
>
> **Do not allow the brake master cylinder reservoir to run dry during the bleeding operation. Keep the brake master cylinder reservoir filled with the specified brake fluid. Never reuse the brake fluid that has been drained from the hydraulic system.**

19. Fill the brake master cylinder reservoir with brake fluid.

20. Connect a clear tube to the right rear disc brake caliper bleeder screw and the other end in a container partially filled with recommended brake fluid.

21. Have an assistant pump the brake pedal and then hold firm pressure on the brake pedal.

22. Loosen the disc brake caliper bleeder screw until a stream of brake fluid comes out. Have an assistant maintain pressure on the brake pedal while tightening the disc brake caliper bleeder screw. Repeat until clear, bubble-free fluid comes out. Refill the brake master cylinder reservoir as necessary.

23. Tighten the disc brake caliper bleeder screw.

24. Repeat Steps 1 through 5 for the three remaining brake calipers, going in order from the left rear disc brake caliper to the right front disc brake caliper ending with the left front disc brake caliper.

25. If the brake pedal feels spongy, repeat the bleed procedure.

Anti-Lock Brake System Hydraulic Control Unit Bleeding

➡ **This procedure is only required when a new hydraulic control unit is installed.**

26. Connect diagnostic tool Worldwide Diagnostic System (WDS) 418-F224, New Generation STAR (NGS) Tester 418-F052, or equivalent diagnostic tool and follow the ABS system bleed instructions.

27. Use the gravity bleed or manual bleed procedure(s) to bleed the system. Begin at the right rear caliper.

BRAKES

> ❄ **CAUTION**
>
> **Dust and dirt accumulating on brake parts during normal use may contain asbestos fibers from production or aftermarket brake linings. Breathing excessive concentrations of asbestos fibers can cause serious bodily harm. Exercise care when servicing brake parts. Do not sand or grind brake lining unless equipment used is designed to contain the dust residue. Do not clean brake parts with compressed air or by dry brushing. Cleaning should be done by dampening the brake components with a fine mist of water, then wiping the brake components clean with a dampened cloth. Dispose of cloth and all residue containing asbestos fibers in an impermeable** container with the appropriate label. Follow practices prescribed by the Occupational Safety and Health Administration (OSHA) and the Environmental Protection Agency (EPA) for the handling, processing, and disposing of dust or debris that may contain asbestos fibers.

BRAKE CALIPER

REMOVAL & INSTALLATION

E-150

See Figure 1.

1. Before servicing the vehicle, refer to the Precautions Section.

2. Remove the tire and wheel assembly.

3. Release the speed sensor wiring from the front brake hose.

FRONT DISC BRAKES

> ❄ **CAUTION**
>
> **To prevent contamination and reduce air entry, always plug a disconnected front brake hose.**

4. Disconnect the front brake hose from the disc brake caliper.

   a. Remove the flow bolt.

   b. Disconnect the front brake hose.

   c. Remove and discard the copper washers.

5. Remove the two disc brake caliper bolts.

6. Remove the disc brake caliper from the front disc brake caliper anchor plate.

7. Inspect the disc brake caliper for brake fluid leakage. If the disc brake caliper is leaking, it must be rebuilt or installed new.

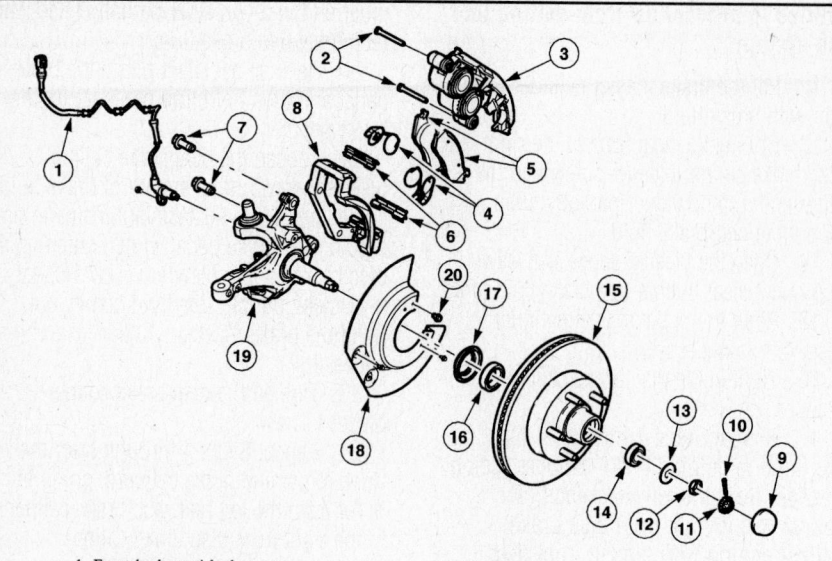

1 Front brake anti-lock sensor
2 Disc brake caliper bolt
3 Disc brake caliper
4 Disc brake pad retaining springs
5 Front disc pads
6 Disc brake pad anti-rattle clip
7 Disc brake caliper anchor bracket bolts
8 Disc brake caliper anchor bracket
9 Hub grease cap
10 Cotter pin

11 Nut retainer
12 Spindle nut
13 Front wheel outer bearing retainer washer
14 Front wheel bearing/cup
15 Brake disc and hub
16 Front wheel bearing/cup
17 Grease seal
18 Backing plate
19 Front wheel spindle
20 Backing plate screw

67197-EFSE-G198

Fig. 1 Front disc brake components—E-150

eyes, flush eyes with running water for 15 minutes. Get medical attention if irritation persists. If taken internally, drink water and induce vomiting. Get medical attention immediately. Failure to follow these instructions may result in personal injury.

1. Before servicing the vehicle, refer to the Precautions Section.
2. Raise and support the vehicle.
3. Remove the tire and wheel assembly.
4. If so equipped, unclip the speed sensor wiring from the front brake hose.

❋❋ CAUTION

To prevent contamination and reduce air entry, always plug a disconnected front brake hose.

5. Disconnect the front brake hose from the disc brake caliper.
   a. Remove the flow bolt.
   b. Disconnect the front brake hose.
   c. Remove and discard the copper washers.
6. Remove the two disc brake caliper bolts.
7. Remove the disc brake caliper from the anchor plate.

To install:

❋❋ CAUTION

To prevent deterioration of the caliper sleeve boots, do not use petroleum-based lubricant.

8. Fill the rubber caliper sleeve boots with caliper grease.
9. Position the disc brake caliper in the front disc brake caliper anchor plate.
10. Install and tighten the disc brake caliper bolts. Torque to 24 ft. lbs. (32 Nm).
11. Using new copper washers, install the front brake hose and the bolt. Torque to 26 ft. lbs. (35 Nm).
12. Attach the speed sensor wiring to the front brake hose.
13. Bleed the brake system.
14. Install the wheel and tire assembly.
15. Inspect the brake system operation.

E-250 and E-350

See Figures 2 and 3.

❋❋ CAUTION

Brake fluid contains polyglycol ethers and polyglycols. Avoid contact with eyes. Wash hands thoroughly after handling. If brake fluid contacts

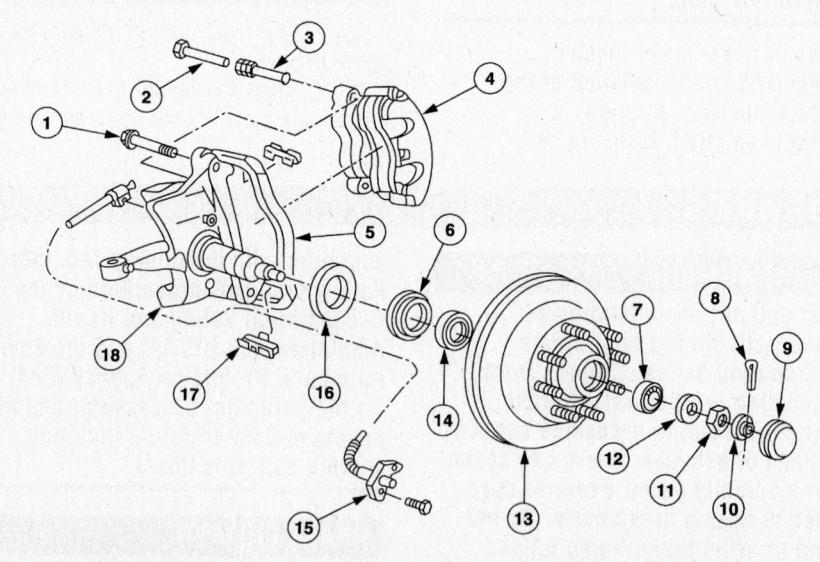

1 Anchor bracket-to-spindle bolt
2 Disc brake caliper bolt
3 Caliper bolt sleeve
4 Disc brake caliper
5 Front disc brake caliper anchor plate
6 Wheel hub grease seal
7 Front wheel bearing
8 Cotter pin
9 Hub grease cap
10 Nut retainer
11 Spindle nut
12 Front wheel outer bearing retainer washer
13 Brake disc and hub
14 Bearing cone and roller
15 Front brake anti-lock sensor
16 Front brake splash shield gasket
17 Disc brake pad anti-rattle clip
18 Front wheel spindle

67197-EFSE-G196

Fig. 2 Front disc brake components—E-250, 350 single rear wheel

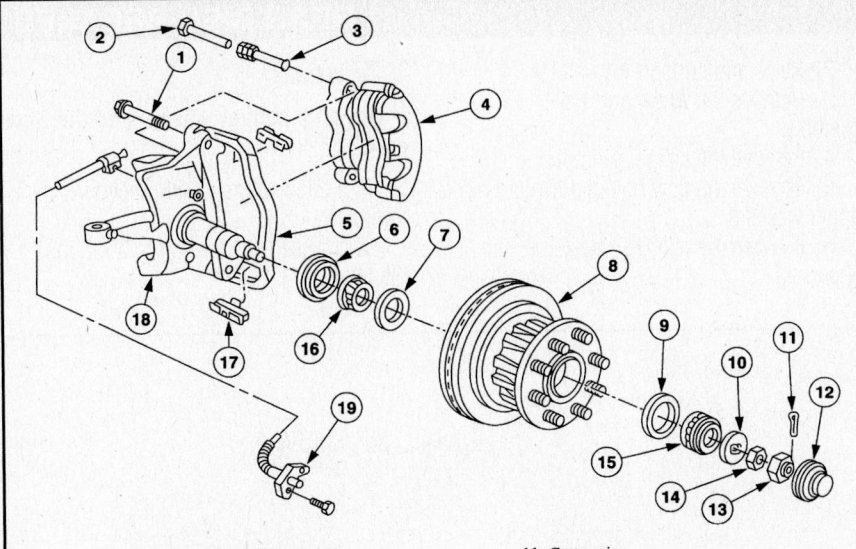

1 Anchor bracket-to-spindle bolt
2 Disc brake caliper bolt
3 Caliper bolt sleeve
4 Disc brake caliper
5 Front disc brake caliper anchor plate
6 Wheel hub grease seal
7 Bearing cup, inner
8 Brake disc and hub (dual rear wheel)
9 Bearing cup, outer
10 Front wheel outer bearing retainer washer

11 Cotter pin
12 Hub grease cap
13 Nut retainer
14 Spindle nut
15 Front wheel bearing (outer)
16 Front wheel bearing (inner)
17 Disc brake pad anti-rattle clip
18 Front wheel spindle
19 Front brake anti-lock sensor

67197-EFSE-G197

Fig. 3 Front disc brake components—E-250, 350 dual rear wheel

8. Inspect the disc brake caliper for brake fluid leakage. If the disc brake caliper is leaking, it must be rebuilt or replaced.

To install:

✳ CAUTION

To prevent deterioration of the caliper sleeve boots, do not use petroleum-based lubricant.

9. Fill the rubber caliper sleeve boots with silicone brake caliper grease.
10. Install the disc brake caliper and the front brake hose.
   a. Position the disc brake caliper on the anchor plate.
   b. Install and tighten the disc brake caliper bolts. Torque to 23 ft. lbs. (31 Nm).

   c. Using new copper washers, install the front brake hose and the bolt. Torque to 28 ft. lbs. (35 Nm).
11. If so equipped, attach the speed sensor wiring to the front brake hose.
12. Bleed the brake system.
13. Install the wheel and tire assembly.
14. Inspect the brake system operation.

DISC BRAKE PADS

REMOVAL & INSTALLATION

See Figures 1 through 3.

1. Before servicing the vehicle, refer to the Precautions Section.
2. Remove and discard enough brake fluid from the brake master cylinder to allow room for the brake fluid displaced when the caliper piston is pressed to the bottom of the caliper bore.
3. Remove the tire and wheel assembly.
4. Release the speed sensor wiring from the front brake hose.
5. Remove the two disc brake caliper bolts.

✳ WARNING

Do not allow the disc brake caliper to hang from the front brake hose. Use wire to support the disc brake caliper from a convenient underbody component.

6. Remove and support the disc brake caliper.
7. On E-150, remove the brake pad retaining springs.
8. Remove the brake pads from the brake caliper anchor bracket.

To install:

➡**Bottoming of the caliper piston is not necessary if reusing the original pads.**

9. If installing new pads, use a suitable tool and a pad to press the caliper piston to the bottom of the caliper bore.

✳ CAUTION

To prevent deterioration of the caliper sleeve boots, do not use petroleum-based lubricant.

10. Fill the rubber caliper sleeve boots with caliper grease.
11. Install the brake pads.
12. On E-150, install the brake pad retaining springs.
13. Install the disc brake caliper. Install and tighten the disc brake caliper bolts.
14. Attach the speed sensor wiring to the front brake hose.
15. Install the tire and wheel assembly.

❊❊ CAUTION

Dust and dirt accumulating on brake parts during normal use may contain asbestos fibers from production or aftermarket brake linings. Breathing excessive concentrations of asbestos fibers can cause serious bodily harm. Exercise care when servicing brake parts. Do not sand or grind brake lining unless equipment used is designed to contain the dust residue. Do not clean brake parts with compressed air or by dry brushing. Cleaning should be done by dampening the brake components with a fine mist of water, then wiping the brake components clean with a dampened cloth. Dispose of cloth and all residue containing asbestos fibers in an impermeable container with the appropriate label. Follow practices prescribed by the Occupational Safety and Health Administration (OSHA) and the Environmental Protection Agency (EPA) for the handling, processing, and disposing of dust or debris that may contain asbestos fibers.

BRAKE CALIPER

REMOVAL & INSTALLATION

E-150

1. Before servicing the vehicle, refer to the Precautions Section.
2. Remove the wheel and tire assembly.
3. Remove the brake hose flow bolt and position the brake hose aside. Discard the copper washers.
4. Remove the caliper pin bolts.
5. Remove the rear disc brake caliper.

➡Use new copper washers on the brake hose flow bolt.

6. Bleed the brake system.
7. To install, reverse the removal procedure.
8. Observe the following torques:
   • Flow bolt: 26 ft. lbs. (35 Nm)
   • Caliper pin bolts: 24 ft. lbs. (32 Nm)

E-250, 350

See Figures 4 through 6.

1. Before servicing the vehicle, refer to the Precautions Section.

2. Raise and support the vehicle.
3. Remove the wheel and tire assembly.
4. Remove the caliper pin bolts.
5. Remove the flow bolt and discard the copper washers.
6. Remove the rear disc brake caliper.

To install:

➡Use new copper washers on the flow bolt.

7. Follow the removal procedure in reverse order.
8. Torque the flow bolt to 26 ft. lbs. (35 Nm).

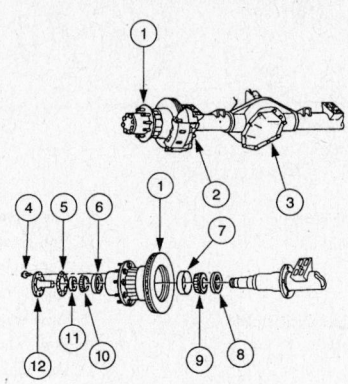

1 Rear brake disc and hub assembly
2 Rear disc brake caliper
3 Dana full-floating axle — Model 80
4 Axle shaft-to-rear hub bolt
5 Rear wheel gasket
6 Outer bearing cup
7 Inner bearing cup
8 Inner hub seal
9 Rear wheel bearing inner cone and roller
10 Rear wheel bearing outer cone and roller
11 Wheel bearing lock nut
12 Axle shaft

67197-EFSE-G204

Fig. 4 Rear disc brake exploded view—E-250, 350

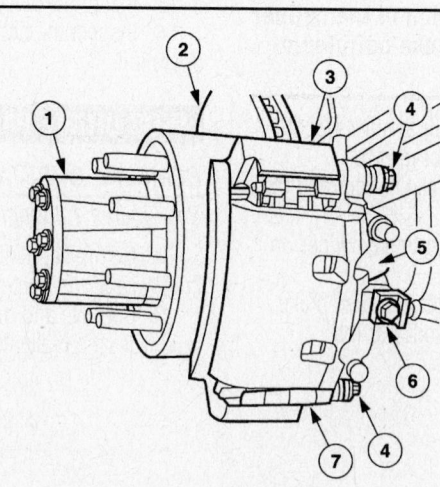

1 Hub		5 Caliper	
2 Brake disc		6 Brake hose	
3 Caliper anchor plate		7 Stainless steel slippers	
4 Caliper pin bolts			

67197-EFSE-G205

Fig. 5 Rear disc brake caliper—E-250, 350

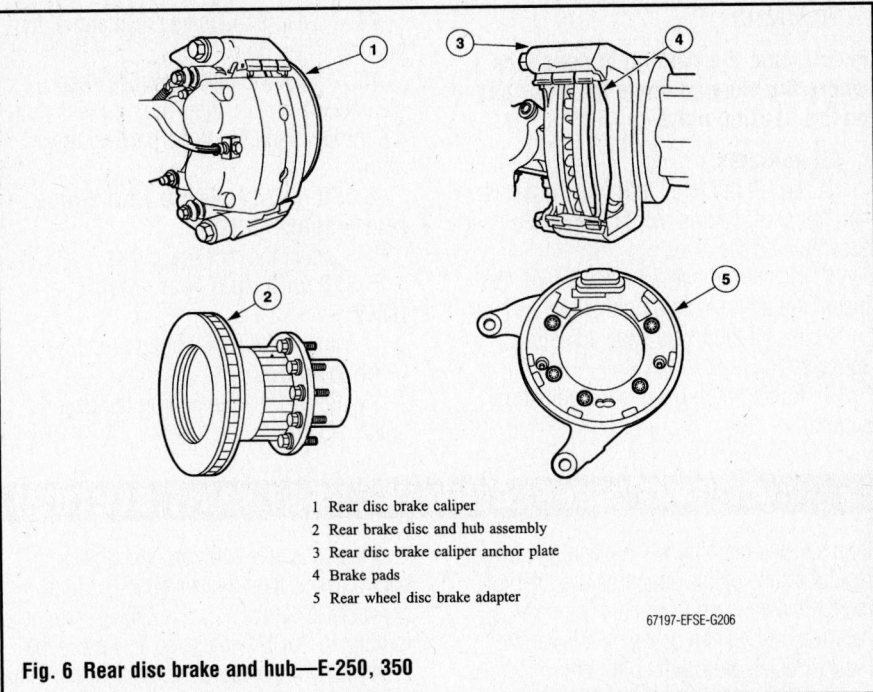

1 Rear disc brake caliper
2 Rear brake disc and hub assembly
3 Rear disc brake caliper anchor plate
4 Brake pads
5 Rear wheel disc brake adapter

67197-EFSE-G206

Fig. 6 Rear disc brake and hub—E-250, 350

9. Torque the caliper pin bolts to 27 ft. lbs. (36 Nm).

10. Bleed the brake system.

DISC BRAKE PADS

REMOVAL & INSTALLATION

E-150

1. Before servicing the vehicle, refer to the Precautions Section.

2. Clean the area and remove the brake cylinder filler cap. Check the brake fluid level in the brake master cylinder reservoir. Remove the fluid until the brake master cylinder reservoir is half full.

3. Remove the wheel and tire assembly.

4. Inspect the brake pads for wear or contamination. If worn, damaged or past specification, install new brake pads.

5. Remove the caliper pin bolts.

✳✳ CAUTION

Never allow the rear disc brake caliper to hang from the brake hose. Provide suitable support.

6. Position aside the rear disc brake caliper aside.

7. Remove the brake pad clips and the brake pads.

8. If installing new brake pads, use

a suitable tool to push the brake caliper pistons into the caliper bore.

9. Inspect the rear disc brake caliper for leaks. If leaks are found, disassembly is required.

10. To install, reverse the removal procedure. Torque the caliper pin bolts to 24 ft. lbs. (32 Nm).

E-250, 350

See Figures 4 through 6.

1. Before servicing the vehicle, refer to the Precautions Section.

2. Remove the brake master cylinder filler cap. Check brake fluid level in brake master cylinder reservoir. Remove fluid until brake master cylinder reservoir is half full.

3. Raise and support the vehicle.

4. Remove the wheel and tire assembly.

5. Inspect the brake pads for wear or contamination. If worn, damaged or past specification, install new components.

6. Remove the caliper pin bolts.

✳✳ CAUTION

Never allow the rear disc brake caliper to hang from the brake hose. Provide suitable support.

7. Remove the rear disc brake caliper.

8. Remove the brake pads and rail clips.

9. Inspect the disc brake caliper for leaks. If leaks are found, disassembly is required.

10. Installation is the reverse of removal. Observe the following torques:

- Caliper bolts: 27 ft. lbs. (36 Nm)

BRAKES

PARKING BRAKE SHOES

REMOVAL, INSTALLATION & ADJUSTMENT

See Figure 7.

1. Before servicing the vehicle, refer to the Precautions Section.

➡**One parking brake she kit contains the linings required for both the LH and RH side.**

All vehicles

➡**Make sure the parking brake control is fully released.**

2. Relieve the tension on the parking brake cable.

a. Raise and safely support the vehicle.

b. Remove the left A-pillar lower trim panel.

c. With an assistant, release the parking brake cable tension by pulling down on the intermediate cable at the cable-to-cable union until the parking brake control sector rotates to its stop and a 4 mm (0.15 in) x 150 mm (5.9 in) retainer pin can be inserted.

d. Disconnect the cable at the cable-to-cable union.

E-350 with dual rear wheels (DRW)

3. Remove the wheel hub assembly.

E-150, E-250, E-350 with single rear wheels (SRW)

4. Remove the brake disc.

PARKING BRAKE

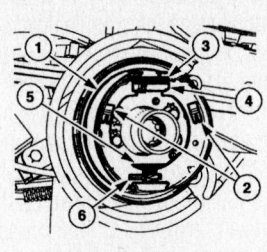

1 Brake shoe and lining
2 Brake shoe hold-down spring
3 Brake shoe adjusting screw spring
4 Brake adjuster screw
5 Brake shoe retracting spring
6 Parking brake lever

06017-F150-G279

Fig. 7 Parking brake assembly—E-Series

All vehicles

5. Remove the brake shoe adjusting screw.

6. Remove the brake shoe adjusting screw spring.

7. Remove the brake shoe hold-down clips and pins.

8. Position the brake shoes apart and remove the brake shoes and the retracting spring assembly from the axle.

9. Remove the inner and outer retraction springs from the brake shoes.

To install:

→**Lubricate the parking brake shoes where the shoe contacts the wear pad on the backing plate.**

All vehicles

10. Install the inner and outer retraction springs and position the parking brake shoe assembly on the axle.

11. Position the 2 hold-down pins and install the 2 brake shoe hold-down springs.

12. Install the brake shoe adjusting screw spring.

13. Position the brake shoe adjusting screw.

14. Measure the inside diameter of the parking brake drum.

15. Adjust the parking brake shoe clearance to 0.375 mm (0.01 in) less than the inside diameter of the parking brake drum.

E-150, E-250, E-350 with single rear wheels (SRW)

16. Install the rear brake disc.

E-350 with dual rear wheels (DRW)

17. Install the wheel hub assembly.

All vehicles

18. Reload the tension on the parking brake cable.

CHASSIS ELECTRICAL

AIR BAG (SUPPLEMENTAL RESTRAINT SYSTEM)

GENERAL INFORMATION

❋❋ CAUTION

These vehicles are equipped with an air bag system. The system must be disarmed before performing service on, or around, system components, the steering column, instrument panel components, wiring and sensors. Failure to follow the safety precautions and the disarming procedure could result in accidental air bag deployment, possible injury and unnecessary system repairs.

SERVICE PRECAUTIONS

Disconnect and isolate the battery negative cable before beginning any airbag system component diagnosis, testing, removal, or installation procedures. Allow system capacitor to discharge for two minutes before beginning any component service. This will disable the airbag system. Failure to disable the airbag system may result in accidental airbag deployment, personal injury, or death.

Do not place an intact undeployed airbag face down on a solid surface. The airbag will propel into the air if accidentally deployed and may result in personal injury or death.

When carrying or handling an undeployed airbag, the trim side (face) of the airbag should be pointing towards the body to minimize possibility of injury if accidental deployment occurs. Failure to do this may result in personal injury or death.

Replace airbag system components with OEM replacement parts. Substitute parts may appear interchangeable, but internal differences may result in inferior occupant protection. Failure to do so may result in occupant personal injury or death.

Wear safety glasses, rubber gloves, and long sleeved clothing when cleaning powder residue from vehicle after an airbag deployment. Powder residue emitted from a deployed airbag can cause skin irritation. Flush affected area with cool water if irritation is experienced. If nasal or throat irritation is experienced, exit the vehicle for fresh air until the irritation ceases. If irritation continues, see a physician.

Do not use a replacement airbag that is not in the original packaging. This may result in improper deployment, personal injury, or death.

The factory installed fasteners, screws and bolts used to fasten airbag components have a special coating and are specifically designed for the airbag system. Do not use substitute fasteners. Use only original equipment fasteners listed in the parts catalog when fastener replacement is required.

During, and following, any child restraint anchor service, due to impact event or vehicle repair, carefully inspect all mounting hardware, tether straps, and anchors for proper installation, operation, or damage. If a child restraint anchor is found damaged in any way, the anchor must be replaced. Failure to do this may result in personal injury or death.

Deployed and non-deployed airbags may or may not have live pyrotechnic material within the airbag inflator.

Do not dispose of driver/passenger/curtain airbags or seat belt tensioners unless you are sure of complete deployment. Refer to the Hazardous Substance Control System for proper disposal.

Dispose of deployed airbags and tensioners consistent with state, provincial, local, and federal regulations.

After any airbag component testing or service, do not connect the battery negative cable. Personal injury or death may result if the system test is not performed first.

If the vehicle is equipped with the Occupant Classification System (OCS), do not connect the battery negative cable before performing the OCS Verification Test using the scan tool and the appropriate diagnostic information. Personal injury or death may result if the system test is not performed properly.

Never replace both the Occupant Restraint Controller (ORC) and the Occupant Classification Module (OCM) at the same time. If both require replacement, replace one, then perform the Airbag System test before replacing the other.

Both the ORC and the OCM store Occupant Classification System (OCS) calibration data, which they transfer to one another when one of them is replaced. If both are replaced at the same time, an irreversible fault will be set in both modules and the OCS may malfunction and cause personal injury or death.

If equipped with OCS, the Seat Weight Sensor is a sensitive, calibrated unit and must be handled carefully. Do not drop or handle roughly. If dropped or damaged, replace with another sensor. Failure to do so may result in occupant injury or death.

If equipped with OCS, the front passenger seat must be handled carefully as well. When removing the seat, be careful when setting on floor not to drop. If dropped, the sensor may be inoperative, could result in occupant injury, or possibly death.

If equipped with OCS, when the passenger front seat is on the floor, no one should sit in the front passenger seat. This uneven force may damage the sensing ability of the seat weight sensors. If sat on and damaged, the sensor may be inoperative, could result in occupant injury, or possibly death.

DEACTIVATION

1. Before servicing the vehicle, refer to the Precautions Section.

2. Turn all vehicle accessories OFF.

3. Turn the ignition switch to OFF.

4. At the central junction box (CJB), located below the instrument panel, remove the trim panel, the cover, and the restraints control module (RCM) fuse from the CJB. See your Owner's Manual for fuse identification.

5. Turn the ignition ON and visually monitor the air bag indicator for at least 30 seconds. The air bag indicator will remain lit continuously (no flashing) if the correct RCM fuse has been removed. If the air bag indicator does not remain lit continuously, remove the correct RCM fuse before proceeding.

6. Turn the ignition OFF.

❋ CAUTION

To avoid accidental deployment and possible personal injury, the backup power supply must be depleted before repairing or replacing any front or side air bag supplemental restraint system (SRS) components and before servicing, replacing, adjusting or striking components near the front or side air bag sensors, such as doors, instrument panel, console, door latches, strikers, seats and hood latches.

7. To deplete the backup power supply energy, disconnect the battery ground cable and wait at least 1 minute. Be sure to disconnect auxiliary batteries and power supplies (if equipped).

8. Disconnect the battery ground cable and wait at least 1 minute.

REACTIVATION

1. Before servicing the vehicle, refer to the Precautions Section.

2. Turn the ignition switch from OFF to ON.

3. Install the RCM fuse to the CJB and install the cover and trim panel.

❋ CAUTION

Be sure that nobody is in the vehicle and that there is nothing blocking or set in front of any air bag module when the battery ground cable is connected.

4. Connect the battery ground cable.

5. Prove out the supplemental restraint system (SRS) as follows:

6. Turn the ignition key from ON to OFF. Wait 10 seconds, then turn the key back to ON and visually monitor the air bag indicator with the air bag modules installed. The air bag indicator will light continuously for approximately 6 seconds and then turn off. If an air bag supplemental restraint system (SRS) fault is present, the air bag indicator will either:

- fail to light.
- remain lit continuously.
- flash.

7. The flashing might not occur until approximately 30 seconds after the ignition switch has been turned from the OFF to the ON position. This is the time required for the restraints control module (RCM) to complete the testing of the SRS. If the air bag indicator is inoperative and a SRS fault exists, a chime will sound in a pattern of 5 sets of 5 beeps. If this occurs, the air bag indicator and any SRS fault discovered must be diagnosed and repaired.

8. Clear all continuous DTCs from the restraints control module using a diagnostic tool.

DRIVETRAIN

AUTOMATIC TRANSMISSION ASSEMBLY

REMOVAL & INSTALLATION

4R100 Transmission

1. Before servicing the vehicle, refer to the Precautions Section.

2. Disconnecting the negative battery cable on some vehicles may interfere with the functions of the on-board computer system(s) and may require the computer to undergo a relearning process once the negative battery cable is reconnected.

3. Remove or disconnect the following:

- Air cleaner air intake duct assembly
- Transmission fluid level indicator
- Engine cover
- Vapor management valve assembly and position it aside, gas engines only
- Fluid filler tube from the short fluid inlet tube, and secure it aside
- Electrical harness connectors

➡**Note the length of each bolt for correct location during installation.**

- Transmission-to-engine retaining bolts
- Driveshaft

- Transmission-mounted parking brake assembly, if equipped
- Vehicle Speed Sensor (VSS)
- Transmission Range (TR) sensor connector
- Heat shield, if equipped
- Solenoid body connector
- Shift cable at the transmission and position it aside
- Starter motor
- Cylinder block opening cover
- Torque converter-to-flexplate retaining nuts and discard

❋ CAUTION

Be sure not to raise the back of the transmission too high. If it makes contact with the underbody, damage to the TSS sensor can occur.

4. Install a high lift transmission jack with the special jack adapter 014-0763 to the transmission.

- Rear transmission mount nuts
- Transmission support crossmember
- Fluid cooler tubes at the Cooler Bypass Valve (CBV), plug all fittings and position the tubes aside
- Right and left hand transmission-to-engine bolts

- Flexplate inspection cover
- Transmission-to-engine bolts
- Transmission from the vehicle

To install:

5. Installation is the reverse of removal, please note the following specs:

6. Transmission-to-engine bolts to 45 ft. lbs. (61 Nm).

7. Torque converter-to-flexplate nuts to 26 ft. lbs. (35 Nm).

8. Flexplate inspection cover nuts to 25 ft. lbs. (34 Nm).

9. Fluid filler tube into the short fluid inlet tube. Tighten the nut to 26 ft. lbs. (35 Nm).

10. Refill all transmissions with the correct amount of Motorcraft MERCON® automatic transmission fluid.

11. Connect the negative battery cable.

4R70W Transmission

1. Before servicing the vehicle, refer to the Precautions Section.

2. Disconnecting the negative battery cable on some vehicles may interfere with the functions of the on-board computer system(s) and may require the computer to undergo a relearning process once the negative battery cable is reconnected.

3. Remove or disconnect the following:
- Air cleaner air intake duct assembly
- Transmission fluid level indicator
- Engine cover
- Fluid filler tube
- Electrical harness connectors
- Torque converter housing-to-engine retaining bolts. Position the fuel and electrical harness bracket aside.
- Fluid cooler tubes and plug all fittings and position the tubes aside

4. Mark the driveshaft flange and the rear companion flange for correct alignment during assembly.
- Driveshaft
- Shift cable and bracket
- Access plugs
- Starter motor
- Fasteners and the front A/C deflector assembly, if equipped
- Four torque converter-to-flexplate retaining nuts and discard the bolts
- Catalyst monitoring sensor harness connectors, if equipped
- Right hand heat shield
- Exhaust Gas Recirculation (EGR) vacuum reservoir from the frame and position aside, if equipped

5. Attach a high lift transmission jack to the transmission.
- Crossmember

6. Support the transmission support crossmember.
- Transmission insulator and retainer-to-crossmember retaining nuts and the transmission support crossmember
- Clamp and hanger assembly, if equipped
- Transmission range sensor electrical connector
- Output Shaft Speed (OSS) sensor connector
- Solenoid body connector
- Flexplate inspection plate
- Transmission bolts

✳✳ CAUTION

Watch for clearance between the transmission and the right side heat shield retaining bracket as well as other obstructions.

7. Separate and back the transmission away from the engine, positioning the extension housing above the exhaust crossover pipe.

8. Hold the torque converter firmly in its installed position.

✳✳ CAUTION

Watch for clearance between the transmission and the engine.

9. Carefully tilt the front of the transmission downward.

✳✳ CAUTION

Watch for clearance between the transmission and the exhaust crossover pipe.

10. Lower the transmission enough to clear the engine. Then, carefully pull the jack with the transmission toward the front of the vehicle, lowering the transmission as required until it is clear of the exhaust crossover pipe.

11. Tilt the front of the transmission upward until level.

12. Remove the transmission with the jack from under the vehicle.

To install:

13. Installation is the reverse of removal, please note the following specs:

14. Transmission-to-engine bolts to 45 ft. lbs. (61 Nm).

15. Torque converter-to-flexplate nuts to 26 ft. lbs. (35 Nm).

16. Flexplate inspection cover nuts to 15 ft. lbs. (20 Nm).

17. Refill all transmissions with the correct amount of Motorcraft MERCON® automatic transmission fluid.

18. Connect the negative battery cable.

E40D Transmission

See Figure 8.

1. Before servicing the vehicle, refer to the Precautions Section.

2. Disconnecting the negative battery cable on some vehicles may interfere with the functions of the on-board computer system(s) and may require the computer to undergo a relearning process once the negative battery cable is reconnected.

➡ **On vehicles equipped with an auxiliary battery, both the negative and positive battery cables must be disconnected.**

3. Disconnect the negative battery cable.

4. Remove or disconnect the following:
- Air cleaner air intake duct assembly
- Transmission fluid level indicator
- Engine cover
- Vapor management valve assembly and position it aside, gas engines only

- Fluid filler tube from the short fluid inlet tube, and secure it aside
- Electrical harness connectors

➡ **Note the length of each bolt for correct location during installation.**

- Transmission-to-engine retaining bolts
- Driveshaft
- Transmission-mounted parking brake assembly, if equipped
- Vehicle Speed Sensor (VSS)
- Transmission Range (TR) sensor connector
- Heat shield, if equipped
- Front air deflector, if equipped
- Solenoid body connector
- Shift cable at the transmission and position it aside
- Starter motor
- Cylinder block opening cover
- Torque converter-to-flexplate retaining nuts and discard

✳✳ CAUTION

Be sure not to raise the back of the transmission too high. If it makes contact with the underbody, damage to the coolant bypass valve can occur.

5. Install a high lift transmission jack with the special jack adapter 014-0763 to the transmission.
- Rear transmission mount nuts
- Transmission support crossmember
- Exhaust crossover pipe and heat shields
- Fluid cooler tubes at the Cooler Bypass Valve (CBV), plug all fittings and position the tubes aside
- Right and left hand transmission-to-engine bolts
- Flexplate inspection cover
- Transmission-to-engine bolts
- Transmission from the vehicle

To install:

6. Installation is the reverse of removal, please note the following specs:

7. Transmission-to-engine bolts to 35 ft. lbs. (47 Nm).

8. Torque converter-to-flexplate nuts to 26 ft. lbs. (35 Nm).

9. Flexplate inspection cover nuts to 25 ft. lbs. (34 Nm).

10. Tighten the crossmember bolts as shown in the illustration.

11. Fluid filler tube into the short fluid inlet tube. Tighten the nut to 26 ft. lbs. (35 Nm).

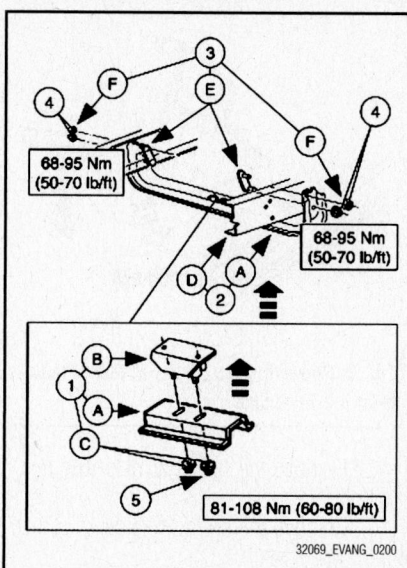

Fig. 8 Transmission crossmember bolt tightening—E40D transmission

12. Refill all transmissions with the correct amount of Motorcraft MERCON® automatic transmission fluid.

13. Connect the negative battery cable.

Torqshift

1. Before servicing the vehicle, refer to the Precautions Section.

2. With the vehicle in **Neutral**, position it on a hoist.

3. Disconnect both battery ground cables.

4. Remove the fluid level indicator.

5. Remove the driveshaft.

6. If transmission disassembly is required, drain the transmission fluid. Remove the drain plug and allow the fluid to drain

7. Install the drain plug.

8. Install a suitable high-lift transmission jack.

9. If equipped, remove the two wire harness retainers from the rear crossmember and position the wire harness out of the way.

10. If equipped, disconnect the transmission-mounted parking brake linkage.

11. Disconnect the return spring from the pin.

12. Remove the hair pin retaining clip from the pin.

13. Remove the pin from the actuating lever and move the actuating cable away from the actuating lever.

14. Compress the spring on the actuating cable and remove the cable from the cable housing.

15. Disconnect the transmission fluid cooler tubes form the filter assembly.

16. Remove the shift cable.

17. Remove the transmission fluid filter bracket nut.

18. Remove the transmission fluid filter bracket bolt, position the bracket aside.

19. Disconnect the shift cable from the manual lever.

20. Disconnect the wire harness from the shift cable bracket.

21. Remove the bolts and position the shift cable and bracket aside.

22. Disconnect the oil cooler tubes from the filter housing.

23. Remove the bolts and remove the filter housing.

24. Loosen the bolt and disconnect the solenoid body electrical connector.

25. Disconnect and position the wire harness out of the way.

26. Disconnect the output shaft speed (OSS) sensor electrical connector.

27. Disconnect the turbine shaft and intermediate shaft combination speed sensor electrical connector.

28. Disconnect the wire harness from the side of the transmission.

29. Remove the cylinder block opening cover in order to gain access to the torque converter nuts.

30. Use a suitable tool to rotate the crankshaft in order to gain access to the flexplate nuts.

31. Remove and discard the six torque nuts.

32. Remove the left crossmember nuts.

33. Remove the left crossmember bracket.

34. Remove the right crossmember nuts.

35. Remove the right crossmember bracket.

36. Remove the rear transmission mount nuts and remove the crossmember.

37. Remove the rear transmission mount from the extension housing.

38. Disconnect the wire harness from the bracket.

39. Remove the nine transmission-to-engine mounting bolts and position the wire harness bracket out of the way.

40. Slide the transmission back enough to install the special tool.

41. If equipped, remove the transmission-mounted parking brake.

42. Remove the transmission-mounted parking retaining bolts.

43. Keeping the vent in an upward position, remove the transmission-mounted parking brake assembly.

44. Remove and discard the transmission-mounted parking brake gasket.

45. Disconnect the transmission fluid cooler tubes and filter housing from the case.

46. If overhauling the transmission or installing a new transmission, carry out the transmission fluid cooler backflushing and cleaning.

To install:

47. Loosely position the fluid cooler tubes in place.

48. Loosely install the fluid filter bracket and bolt.

49. Tighten the transmission fluid cooler tube nuts and remove the bracket bolt. Torque to 30 ft. lbs. (40 Nm).

50. If equipped, install the transmission-mounted parking brake.

51. Install a new transmission-mounted parking brake gasket.

52. Keeping the vent in an upward position, install the transmission-mounted parking brake assembly.

53. Install the transmission-mounted parking retaining bolts. Torque to 41 ft. lbs. (55 Nm).

> **✳✳ WARNING**
>
> **Prior to the installation of the assembly, the torque converter pilot hub must be correctly lubricated or damage to the torque converter or the engine crankshaft can occur.**

54. Lubricate the torque converter pilot hub with multi-purpose grease.

55. If the special tool has not been installed during the assembly of the transmission, install the special tool to hold the torque converter in place while moving and positioning the transmission in place. Once the transmission is in place, prior to bolting it to the engine, remove the special tool.

56. Position the transmission in place. While raising the transmission up into the engine compartment, align the fluid filler tube with the stub tube on the transmission using the fluid level indicator as a guide.

57. While installing the transmission to the engine, align the torque converter studs with the mounting holes in the flexplate.

58. Position the electrical wiring harness bracket in place and install the eight transmission-to-engine bolts. Torque to 35 ft. lbs. (47 Nm).

59. Connect the wire harness to the bracket.

60. Using the special tool, rotate the crankshaft to gain access to the torque converter studs.

61. Install the new torque converter-to-flexplate nuts. Torque to 26 ft. lbs. (35 Nm).

62. Install the cylinder block opening cover.

63. Install the wire harness retaining clip into the transmission on the left side.

64. Connect the wire harness on the right side of the transmission.

65. Install the oil filter housing.

66. Connect the oil cooler lines.

67. Install the transmission mount. Torque to 69 ft. lbs. (94 Nm).

68. Position the crossmember to the transmission mount and loosely install the nut.

69. Install the left crossmember bracket.

70. Install the left crossmember nuts. Torque to 60 ft. lbs. (81 Nm).

71. Install the right crossmember bracket.

72. Install the right crossmember nuts. Torque to 60 ft. lbs. (81 Nm).

73. Tighten the rear insulator nuts. Torque to 69 ft. lbs. (94 Nm).

74. Connect the output shaft speed (OSS) sensor electrical connector.

75. Connect the intermediate shaft and turbine shaft combination speed sensor electrical connector.

76. Connect the solenoid body electrical connector.

77. Connect the shift cable.

78. Install the cable housing bracket with one stud bolt and one bolt.

79. Install the bolt and nut for the filter housing and bracket.

80. Connect the wire harness to the bracket.

81. Install the shift cable to the manual lever.

82. Install the fluid cooler lines to the filter housing.

83. If equipped, install the wire harness and install the two retaining clips to the rear of the crossmember.

84. If equipped, connect the transmission-mounted parking brake.

85. Install the parking cable into the bracket.

86. Position the cable end onto the lever.

87. Install the retaining pin and clip.

88. Install the return spring.

89. Install the rear driveshaft.

✳✳ WARNING

If installing a newly overhauled or a new transmission, a new transmission fluid cooler remote filter must be installed. Otherwise transmission failure can occur.

90. Install a new transmission fluid cooler remote filter.

91. Use the following guidelines for the in-line transmission fluid filter:

a. If the transmission was overhauled and the vehicle was equipped with an in-line fluid filter, install a new in-line fluid filter.

b. If the transmission was overhauled and the vehicle was not equipped with an in-line fluid filter, install a new in-line fluid filter kit.

c. If the transmission is being installed for a non-internal repair, do not install an in-line filter or filter kit.

d. If installing a new or a Ford authorized remanufactured transmission, install the in-line transmission fluid filter that is supplied.

92. Prior to lowering the vehicle, install a new in-line transmission filter or a filter kit.

93. Connect the battery ground cable.

94. Adjust the shift linkage. Verify that the vehicle starts in **Park** and **Neutral** and the **Reverse** lamps illuminate in **Reverse**.

95. Install the fluid level indicator.

96. With the engine running and the transmission at normal operating temperature 66–77°C (150–170°F), check and adjust the transmission fluid level, and check for any leaks. If fluid is needed, add fluid in increments of 0.24 liter (0.5 pint) until the correct level is achieved (fluid should be in the cross-hatched area of the fluid level indicator).

FRONT AXLE

REMOVAL & INSTALLATION

See Figure 9.

1. Raise and support the vehicle.

2. Remove the wheel and tire assembly.

3. Remove the disc brake caliper and brake disc and hub.

4. Remove the brake disc shield.

5. Remove the cotter pin and the castellated nut.

6. Using the Pitman Arm Puller disconnect the tie rod end.

7. Remove the cotter pin and the lower ball joint nut. Discard the cotter pin,

8. Remove the pinch bolt and the camber adjuster.

✳✳ CAUTION

To prevent damage to the ball joint seal and the ball joint socket, do not use a pickle fork-type remover to loosen the ball joints.

9. Strike the lower end of the axle to loosen the ball joint.

10. Remove the front wheel spindle.

11. Remove the front coil spring.

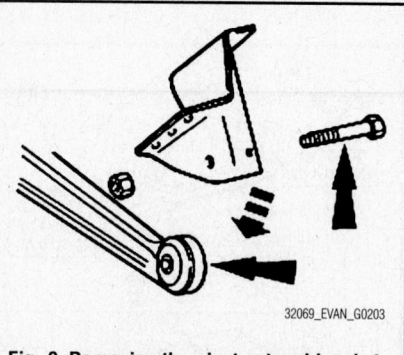

Fig. 9 Removing the pivot nut and bracket from the front axle

32069_EVAN_G0203

12. Remove the radius arm-to-axle nut and bolt.

13. Remove the spring retainer and insulator.

14. Remove the nut.

15. Remove the washer and rear insulator.

16. Remove the radius arm from the bracket, and remove the spacer, insulator and washer.

17. In order to obtain clearance for the pivot bolt removal when servicing the RH front axle, it may be necessary to raise the LH side of the vehicle to relieve the weight on the suspension.

18. Remove the pivot nut and bolt and remove the axle.

To install:

19. Inspect the pivot bushing for wear or damage. Replace as necessary.

20. Position the front axle into the pivot bracket and install the pivot bolt and nut hand-tight.

21. Inspect the radius arm insulators for wear or damage. Replace as necessary.

22. Install the washer, insulator and spacer and pull the radius arm through the bracket.

23. Install the rear insulator, washer and nut and tighten hand-tight.

24. Install the spring retainer and insulator.

25. Install the radius arm-to-axle nut and bolt.

26. Tighten the radius arm-to-axle nut and bolt to 220 ft. lbs. (298 Nm).

27. Tighten the rear radius arm nut to 98 ft. lbs. (133 Nm).

28. Install the front coil spring.

29. Position the front wheel spindle in the front axle.

30. Install the ball joint nut and tighten to 130 ft. lbs. (176 Nm).

31. Install the new cotter pin.

32. Install the camber adjuster and pinch bolt and tighten to 76 ft. lbs. (100 Nm).

33. Install the brake disc shield.

34. Install the brake disc and hub and the disc brake caliper.

35. Using a new cotter pin, install the tie rod end in the front wheel spindle and tighten to 66 ft. lbs. (90 Nm).

36. Install the tire and wheel assembly.

37. Lower the vehicle and, with the vehicle weight on the suspension, tighten the axle pivot bolt and nut to 130 ft. lbs. (176 Nm).

38. Perform front end alignment.

REAR AXLE HOUSING

REMOVAL & INSTALLATION

Ford 8.8 Inch and 9.75 Inch Ring Gear Axle

1. Before servicing the vehicle, refer to the Precautions Section.

2. Raise and support the vehicle.

3. Mark the driveshaft flange and rear axle companion flange for correct alignment during installation.

4. Remove the four driveshaft bolts and disconnect the driveshaft.

➡**Prior to disconnecting the rear parking brake cables, note left and right side cable routing. Also, to maintain proper adjustment, measure and record the distance from the top of the parking brake cable equalizer adjusting nut to the end of the stud.**

5. Disconnect the parking brake cable.

6. Loosen the adjusting nut at the parking brake cable equalizer until the right side (upper) and left side (lower) cable anchors are free from the equalizer retaining slots. Disconnect the cables at the equalizer.

7. Slide the boxed end of a 13 mm wrench over the rear parking brake cable and onto the cable conduit retainer. Depress the retainer locking tabs and pull the cable conduit toward the rear of the vehicle and out from the parking brake cable support bracket. Repeat for the opposite cable.

8. Separate the left side rear parking brake cable from the support spring at the frame rail. Tie-wrap the cable to the axle.

9. Use care so as not to dislodge the cable support spring from the frame rail.

10. Separate the right side rear parking brake cable from the support spring.

11. Disconnect the right side rear parking brake cable from the retainers at the axle. Separate the cable from the frame and pull the cable around the front of the axle. Tie-wrap the cable to the axle.

12. Disconnect the rear brake anti-lock sensor electrical connector.

13. Disconnect the rear axle brake hose and rear axle vent tube at the frame.

14. Remove the two lower shock absorber nuts only (one on each side). Do not remove the bolts yet.

15. Lower the vehicle until the tires are in contact with the floor. Support the front of the rear axle housing.

16. Remove the lower shock absorber bolts.

17. Remove the rear axle U-bolt assembly.

18. Raise the vehicle until clear of the rear axle and remove the rear axle.

To install:

19. Installation is the reverse of the removal procedure noting the following torque specifications:
- Spring plate U-bolts: 85 ft. lbs. (115 Nm)
- Shock absorber bolts: 52 ft. lbs. (70 Nm)
- Driveshaft bolts: 82 ft. lbs. (112 Nm)

Dana Model 60, 70 and 80 Axle

1. Before servicing the vehicle, refer to the Precautions Section.

2. Release the tension on the parking brake cables.

3. Raise and support the vehicle.

4. Remove the rear tire and wheel assemblies.

5. Remove the drive pinion.

6. Remove the brake cable bolt from the lower shock mounting on both sides.

7. Remove the bolts retaining the anchor plate to the axle. Position the rear brake caliper aside. Repeat for the opposite side.

8. Position the brake tube, harness and cable out of the way.

9. Use a suitable transmission jack to support the axle. Strap the axle securely to the jack.

10. Remove the nut and bolt retaining shock absorber to the axle on both sides.

11. Remove the nuts and the axle U-bolts.

12. Lower the axle from the vehicle.

To install:

13. Installation is the reverse of the removal procedure noting the following torque specifications:
- Spring plate U-bolts: 130 ft. lbs. (221 Nm)
- Shock absorber bolts: 58 ft. lbs. (79 Nm)
- Caliper bolts: 128 ft. lbs. (173 Nm)

REAR AXLE SHAFT, BEARING & SEAL

REMOVAL & INSTALLATION

Ford 8.8 and 9.75 Inch Ring Gear Axles

See Figures 10 through 14.

1. Before servicing the vehicle, refer to the Precautions Section.

All Vehicles

2. Raise and support the vehicle.

3. Remove the wheel and tire assembly.

➡**Empty the lubricant into a clean container for reuse.**

4. Remove the 10 differential housing cover bolts and drain the lubricant from the rear axle housing.

5. Remove the differential housing cover.

Vehicles with drum brakes

6. Remove the rear brake drums.

Vehicles with disc brakes

7. Remove the rear disc brake caliper. Wire the rear disc brake caliper aside.

8. Remove the rear brake disc.

All vehicles

9. Remove and discard the differential pinion shaft lock bolt.

10. Remove the differential pinion shaft.

✳✳ WARNING

Do not damage the rubber O-rings in the axle shaft grooves.

11. Push in the axle shafts.

12. Remove the U-washers.

✳✳ WARNING

Do not damage the wheel bearing oil seal.

13. Remove the axle shaft.

➡**If the wheel bearing oil seal is leaking, the axle housing vent may be plugged with foreign material.**

➡**If only a new seal needs to be installed, use care to avoid damaging the seal bore.**

14. Using a suitable seal remover, remove the axle shaft oil seal. Discard the oil seal.

15. Inspect the rear wheel bearing and axle shaft for wear or damage.

16. If necessary, using the special tools, remove the rear wheel bearing.

To install:

17. Lubricate the new rear wheel bearing with rear axle lubricant.

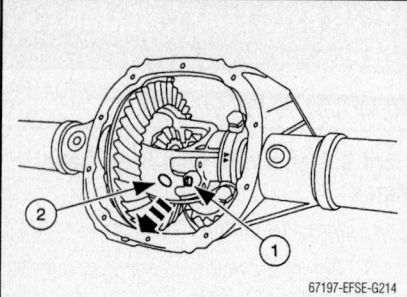

Fig. 10 Lock bolt (1); pinion shaft (2)—Ford 8.8 inch and 9.75 inch ring gear axles

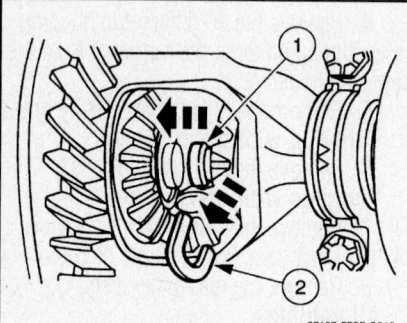

Fig. 11 Axle shaft (1); U-washer (2)—Ford 8.8 inch and 9.75 inch ring gear axles

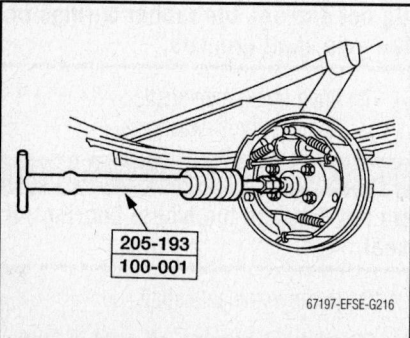

Fig. 12 Rear wheel bearing removal—Ford 8.8 inch and 9.75 inch ring gear axles

18. Using the special tools, install the rear wheel bearing.
19. Lubricate the lip of the new wheel bearing oil seal with grease.
20. Using the special tools, install the wheel bearing oil seal.
All vehicles

Do not damage the wheel bearing oil seal.

21. Install the axle shaft.

Do not damage the rubber O-rings in the U-washer grooves.

22. Position the two U-washers on the button end of the axle shafts.
23. Pull the axle shafts outward.

➡**If a new pinion shaft lock bolt is unavailable coat the threads with Threadlock prior to installation.**

24. Align the hole in the differential pinion shaft with the case lock bolt hole.
25. Install a new differential pinion shaft lock bolt. Torque to 15–30 ft. lbs. (20–40 Nm).
Vehicles with drum brakes
26. Install the rear brake drums.
Vehicles with disc brakes
27. Install the rear brake disc.
28. Install the rear disc brake caliper.

➡**Clean the gasket mating surface of the rear axle and the differential housing cover.**

29. Apply a new continuous bead of sealant to the differential housing cover.

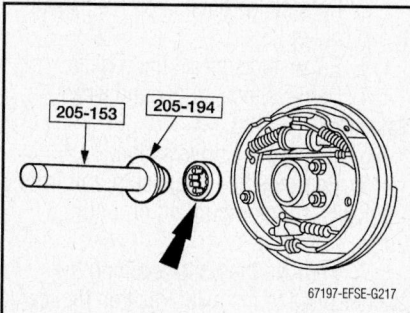

Fig. 13 Rear wheel bearing installation—Ford 8.8 inch and 9.75 inch ring gear axles

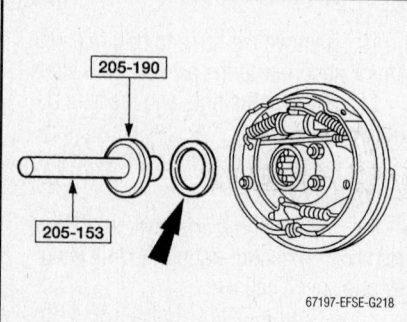

Fig. 14 Oil seal installation—Ford 8.8 inch and 9.75 inch ring gear axles

➡**The differential housing cover must be installed within 15 minutes of application of the silicone, or new sealant must be applied. If possible, allow one hour before filling with lubricant to make sure the silicone sealant has correctly cured.**

30. Install the differential housing cover.
31. Install the 10 differential housing cover bolts. Torque to 33 ft. lbs. (45 Nm).
32. Fill the rear axle housing with 2.37 liters (5 pints) with the specified lubricant.

Always remove any corrosion, dirt or foreign material present on the mounting surfaces of the wheel or the surface of the wheel hub or brake drum or disc that contacts the wheel. Installing wheels without correct metal-to-metal contact at the wheel mounting surfaces can cause the lug nut to loosen and the wheel to come off while the vehicle is in motion, causing loss of control.

33. Clean the wheel hub and mounting surfaces.
34. Install the tire and wheel assembly.

Dana 60 And 70 Semi-Floating Axles
See Figures 15 through 21.

1. Before servicing the vehicle, refer to the Precautions Section.
2. Raise the vehicle on a hoist or raise the rear end of the vehicle with a jack. Install safety stands under the frame rails and lower the jack or hoist enough to allow the rear axle to drop into the rebound position for working clearance.
3. Remove the rear wheel and tire assembly.
4. Remove the brake disc.
5. Remove the differential housing cover and drain the lubricant. Clean the gasket material from the differential housing cover and the differential housing.

The differential assembly is equipped with either a Loctite® coated differential pinion shaft lock screw or a differential pinion shaft lock screw with torque prevailing threads. The Loctite® treated differential pinion shaft lock screw has a 5/32 inch hexagram socket head. Never, under any circumstance, reuse

a Loctite® coated screw after removing it. Always discard the screw and install a new one. The torque prevailing differential pinion shaft lock screw has a 12-point drive head. This type of screw is reusable for no more than four installations. When in doubt about the number of installations of a torque prevailing differential pinion shaft lock screw, discard it and install a new screw.

6. Remove the lock screw.

7. Remove the differential pinion shaft. The pinion shaft is a slip-fit design and is removable by hand.

8. Push the flanged end of the axle shaft toward the center of the axle and remove the U-washer.

❉❉ WARNING

Do not damage the wheel bearing oil seal when removing the axle shaft.

❉❉ WARNING

Do not rotate the differential side gears when removing the axle shaft. Rotating the differential side gears causes the differential pinion gears and differential pinion thrust washers to turn to the differential case opening and fall out of the differential case.

9. Remove the axle shaft.

❉❉ WARNING

Install the differential pinion shaft and the old lock screw (finger-tight) to prevent the differential side gears and differential pinion gears from rotating and falling out of the differential case.

10. Install the differential pinion shaft and the old lock screw in the differential case.

❉❉ WARNING

It is not necessary to remove the rear wheel bearing if only installing a new wheel bearing oil seal. To remove only the wheel bearing oil seal, pry it from the axle tube. Do not damage the seal seating surface. If removing the rear wheel bearing and the oil seal, proceed to the following step.

11. Remove the wheel bearing oil seal from the axle tube. Discard the seal.

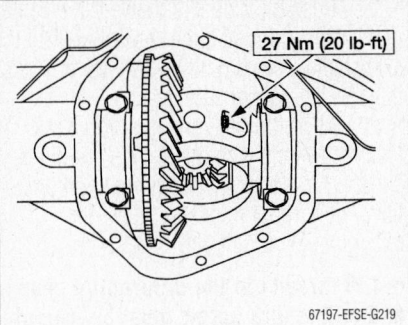

Fig. 15 Lock screw—Dana 60 and 70 semi-floating axle

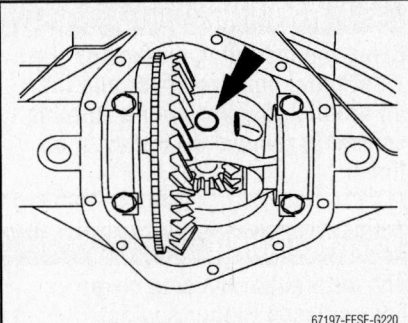

Fig. 16 Pinion shaft—Dana 60 and 70 semi-floating axle

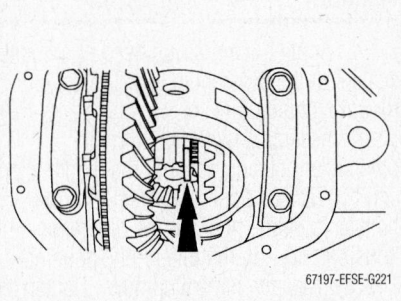

Fig. 17 U-washer—Dana 60 and 70 semi-floating axle

❉❉ CAUTION

Make sure protective eyewear is in place. Failure to follow these instructions may result in personal injury.

12. Using the special tools, remove the rear wheel bearing and the wheel bearing oil seal as a unit. Discard the seal and the bearing.

❉❉ WARNING

The bearing and seal seating surfaces must be free from burrs, nicks, and spalling.

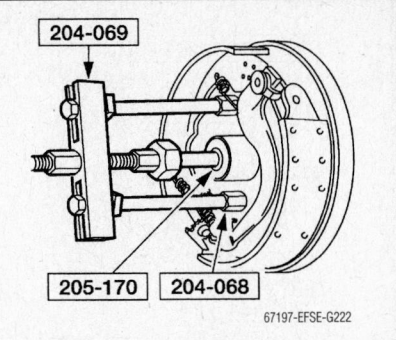

Fig. 18 Rear wheel bearing removal—Dana 60 and 70 semi-floating axle

13. Clean and inspect the bore in the axle tube. Wipe the bore in the axle tube with emery cloth to smooth the surface. Clean the bore with a standard metal-cleaning solvent. Wipe the bore with a soft, lint free cloth to remove any foreign material.

To install:

14. If removed, lubricate the new rear wheel bearing with the specified axle lubricant.

❉❉ WARNING

Install the rear wheel bearing with the identification numbers facing outward.

❉❉ WARNING

Do not cock the rear wheel bearing in the axle tube.

15. Using the special tools, install the rear wheel bearing.

❉❉ WARNING

Do not cock the wheel bearing oil seal in the axle tube.

➡The following step shows an alternate method for installing the wheel bearing oil seal.

16. Using the special tools, install the new wheel bearing oil seal.

❉❉ WARNING

Do not cock the wheel bearing oil seal in the axle tube bore.

➡This step is an alternate method for installing the wheel bearing oil seal. Carry out this step if wheel bearing oil seal installation was not done in the previous step.

17. Using the special tools, install the new wheel bearing oil seal.

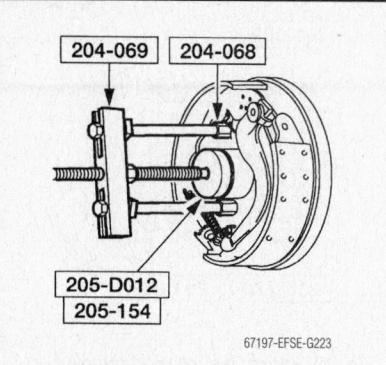

Fig. 19 Rear wheel bearing installation—Dana 60 and 70 semi-floating axle

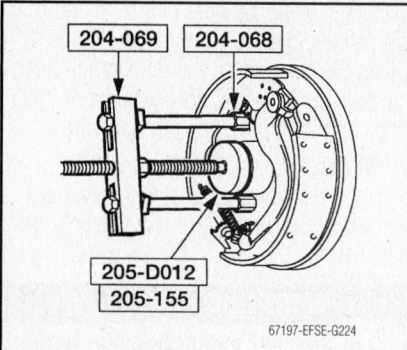

Fig. 20 Oil seal installation—Dana 60 and 70 semi-floating axle

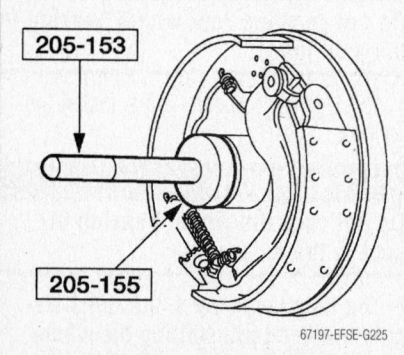

Fig. 21 Alternate oil seal installation—Dana 60 and 70 semi-floating axle

18. Lubricate the cavity between the wheel bearing oil seal lips and the rear wheel bearing with grease.

19. Remove the lock screw and the differential pinion shaft.

※※ WARNING

Do not damage the wheel bearing oil seal when installing the axle shaft.

20. Push the axle shaft into the axle tube and engage the differential side gear with the shaft splines.

21. Push the axle shaft toward the center of the axle and install the U-washer. Pull the axle shaft outward until the U-washer locks into the differential side gear.

22. Align the differential pinion shaft lock screw hole with the hole in the differential case. Correctly position the differential pinion thrust washers. Install the differential pinion shaft.

➡**The threads in the differential case and on the lock screw must be free of dirt and oil.**

23. Install the new lock screw. Torque to 20 ft. lbs. (27 Nm).

※※ WARNING

Clean the mounting surface on the differential housing cover and the diferential housing with a suitable solvent to remove all traces of oil film.

※※ WARNING

The differential housing cover uses silicone rubber sealant material as a gasket. Install the differential housing cover within 15 minutes of applying the silicone or it will be necessary to apply new sealant.

24. Apply a continuous bead of silicone sealant to the differential housing cover mounting surface.

25. Assemble two bolts into the differential housing cover at the eight o'clock and two o'clock positions. Using the two bolts as a guide, position the differential housing cover on the differential housing.

26. Install the remaining bolts. Tighten the bolts alternately and evenly. Tighten Grade 5 bolts to 47 Nm (35 ft. lbs. Tighten Grade 8 bolts to 61 Nm (45 ft. lbs.

※※ WARNING

Allow 1 hour cure time before filling the axle with the correct amount of specified lubricant and operating the vehicle.

※※ WARNING

For limited-slip axles, first fill the axle with 7 ounces of friction modifier.

27. Fill the differential housing with 3.0L (6.3 pints) of the specified rear axle lubricant. For additional information, refer to Specifications.

28. Install the brake disc.
29. Install the wheel and tire assembly.
30. Lower the vehicle.

Dana Axle Full-Floating Axle

See Figures 22 and 23.

1. Before servicing the vehicle, refer to the Precautions Section.

All vehicles

2. Remove the tire and wheel assembly.
3. Remove the anchor plate.
4. Remove the axle shaft.

➡**Make sure that the drive tangs on the special tool engage the four slots of the hub nut.**

5. Using special tool 205-282, or equivalent, remove the hub nut.

All vehicles

6. Remove the outer rear wheel bearing.
7. Remove the rear hub and brake disc assembly.
8. Remove the bolts and separate the rear hub from the rear brake disc.
9. Inspect the rear hub for the following:
   - Cracks and damage around the bolt holes.
   - Oversized holes.

To install:

※※ WARNING

Install a new rear hub seal after removing the rear hub from the axle. A damaged or worn seal can permit bearing lubricant to reach the brake linings, resulting in ineffective brake operation. Failure to follow these instructions may result in personal injury.

※※ WARNING

Clean and remove any dirt or foreign material in the rear hub bolt holes.

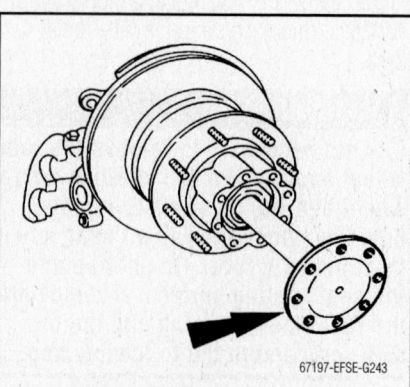

Fig. 22 Remove the axle shaft— Dana Axle Full-Floating Axle

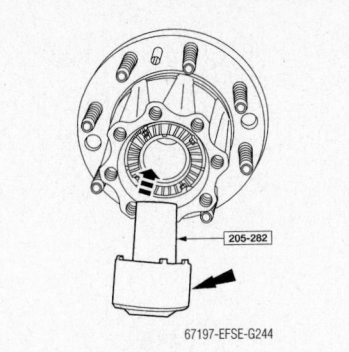

Fig. 23 Using special tool 205-282, or equivalent, remove the hub nut—Dana Axle Full-Floating Axle

67197-EFSE-G244

10. Install a new rear hub seal.

11. Position the rear brake disc on the rear hub and install the bolts. Torque to 66–88 ft. lbs. (89–119 Nm).

✳✳ WARNING

Thoroughly clean the spindle. Wrap the spindle threads with electrician's tape to prevent damage while installing the rear hub and brake disc assembly.

✳✳ WARNING

Lightly coat the spindle and pack each rear wheel bearing with Premium Long-Life Grease XG-1-C or equivalent meeting Ford specification ESA-M1C75-B.

12. Prepare the spindle for rear hub installation.

13. Slide the rear hub and brake disc assembly over the axle housing spindle. Remove the electrician's tape.

14. Install the outer rear wheel bearing.

15. Start the hub nut making sure that the tab aligns correctly in the keyway prior to thread engagement.

➡**Apply inward pressure to the socket to separate the ratcheting components of the hub nut.**

16. To adjust the bearings, tighten the nut to 70 ft. lbs. (95 Nm).

17. Back off the nut 90 degrees.

18. Tighten the nut to 18 ft. lbs. (24 Nm). To verify that there is no side-to-side end play, attach a magnetically mounted dial indicator to the spindle end and place the dial indicator tip on the outboard surface of the hub. Check for side-to-side end play. Final bearing adjustment has zero end play. The maximum torque to rotate the hub is 2.3 Nm (20 inch lbs.) when end play is zero.

19. Install the axle shaft.
20. Install the anchor plate.
21. Install the tire and wheel assembly.

REAR DRIVESHAFT

REMOVAL & INSTALLATION

One-Piece Shaft

See Figures 24 and 25.

1. Before servicing the vehicle, refer to the Precautions Section.

2. Raise and safely support the vehicle.

3. Index-mark the driveshaft flange to the pinion flange to maintain alignment during installation.

4. Index mark the driveshaft to the extension housing to maintain alignment during installation.

5. Remove and discard the 4 driveshaft flange bolts.

✳✳ WARNING

The driveshaft flange fits tightly on the flange pilot. Never hammer on the driveshaft or any of its components to disconnect the driveshaft flange from the flange pilot. Pry only in the area shown with a suitable tool to disconnect the driveshaft flange from the flange pilot.

6. Using a suitable tool as shown, disconnect the driveshaft flange from the flange pilot and remove the driveshaft.

7. Plug the extension housing to prevent fluid loss.

➡**The driveshaft flanges fits tightly on the pinion flange pilots. To make sure**

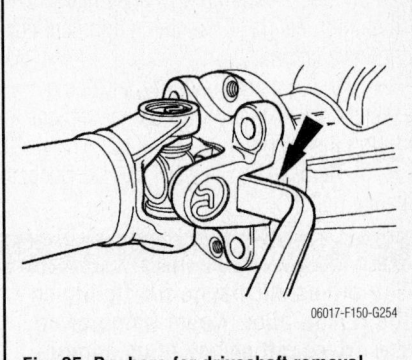

Fig. 25 Pry here for driveshaft removal

06017-F150-G254

that the driveshaft flanges seat squarely on the pinion flange pilots, tighten the driveshaft flange bolts evenly in a cross pattern.

✳✳ WARNING

If new bolts are not available, coat the threads of the original driveshaft flange bolts with Threadlock and Sealer.

➡**Align the index marks made during removal.**

8. To install, reverse the removal procedure. Install new driveshaft flange bolts. Torque the flange bolts to 83 ft. lbs. (112 Nm)

E-150 Two-Piece Shaft

See Figure 26.

1. Before servicing the vehicle, refer to the Precautions Section.

2. Raise and safely support the vehicle.

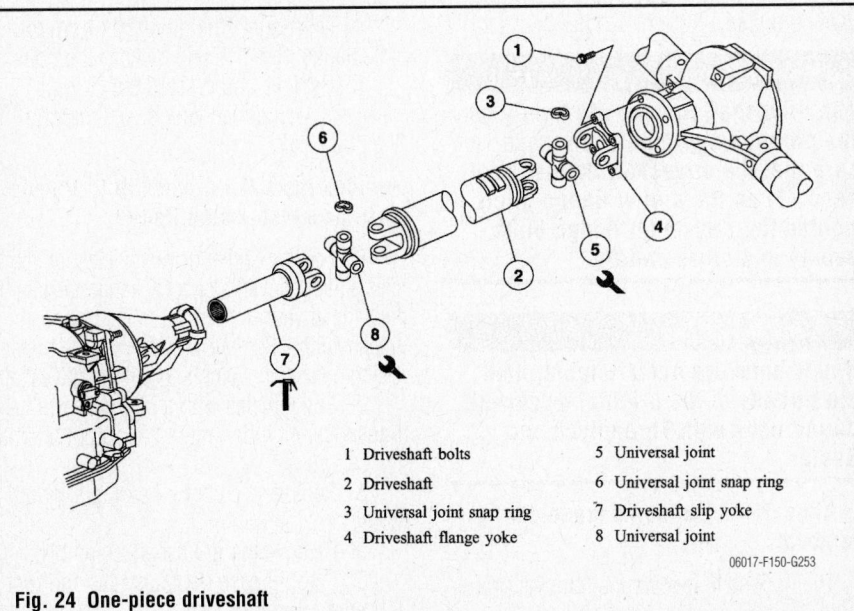

1 Driveshaft bolts	5 Universal joint
2 Driveshaft	6 Universal joint snap ring
3 Universal joint snap ring	7 Driveshaft slip yoke
4 Driveshaft flange yoke	8 Universal joint

06017-F150-G253

Fig. 24 One-piece driveshaft

3. Index-mark the driveshaft flange to the pinion flange to maintain alignment during installation.

4. Index-mark the driveshaft to the extension housing to maintain alignment during installation.

5. Remove and discard the 4 driveshaft flange bolts.

✳✳ WARNING

The driveshaft flange fits tightly on the flange pilot. Never hammer on the driveshaft or any of its components to disconnect the driveshaft flange from the flange pilot. Pry only in the area shown with a suitable tool, to disconnect the driveshaft flange from the flange pilot.

6. Using a suitable tool as shown, disconnect the driveshaft flange from the flange pilot.

7. On models with a transmission mounted parking brake, support the coupling shaft and remove the center bearing bolts.

8. Lock the parking brake.

9. Remove the coupling shaft bolts from the parking brake assembly by removing the four U-joint retainer bolts.

10. Separate the coupling shaft from the parking brake assembly.

11. On models without a transmission mounted parking brake, remove the driveshaft center bearing bolts and remove the driveshaft.

12. Remove the driveshaft center bearing bolts.

13. Lower the driveshaft and slide the driveshaft slip yoke rearward off of the output shaft.

14. Plug the extension housing to prevent fluid loss.

✳✳ WARNING

The driveshaft flanges fits tightly on the pinion flange pilots. To make sure that the driveshaft flanges seat squarely on the pinion flange pilots, tighten the driveshaft flange bolts evenly in a cross pattern.

✳✳ WARNING

If new bolts are not available, coat the threads of the original driveshaft flange bolts with Threadlock and Sealer.

➡**Align the index marks made during removal.**

15. To install, reverse the removal procedure.

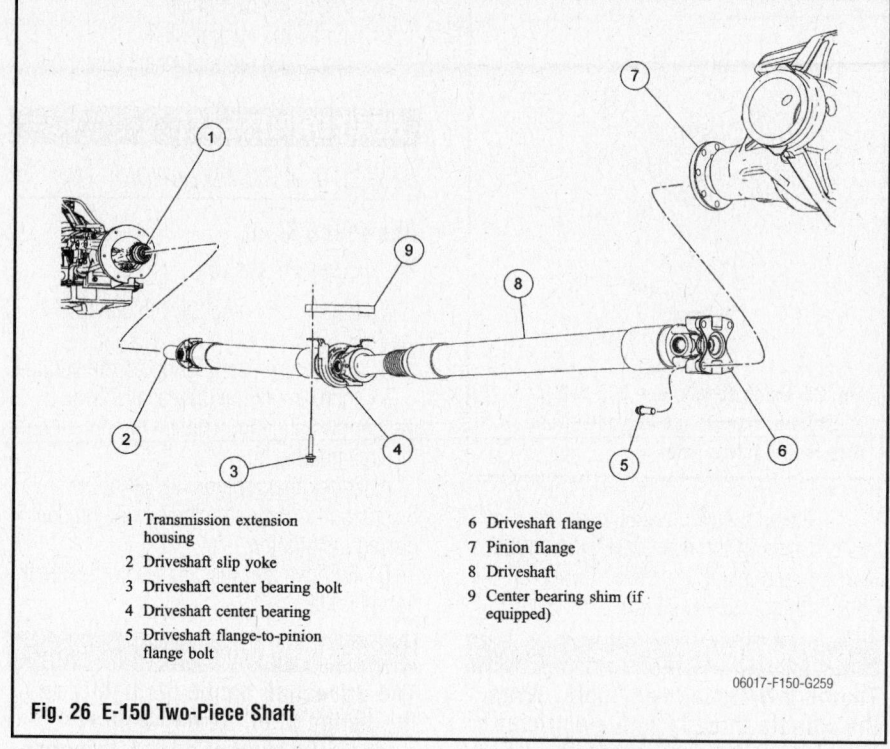

1 Transmission extension housing	6 Driveshaft flange
2 Driveshaft slip yoke	7 Pinion flange
3 Driveshaft center bearing bolt	8 Driveshaft
4 Driveshaft center bearing	9 Center bearing shim (if equipped)
5 Driveshaft flange-to-pinion flange bolt	

06017-F150-G259

Fig. 26 E-150 Two-Piece Shaft

16. Install new driveshaft flange bolts. Torque the bolts to 76 ft. lbs. (103 Nm)

17. Torque the center bearing bolts to 35 ft. lbs. (48 Nm)

18. Torque the U-joint caps and bolts to 32 ft. lbs. (43 Nm).

E-250/350 w/Two-Piece Shaft
See Figure 27.

1. Before servicing the vehicle, refer to the Precautions Section.

2. Raise and support the vehicle.

3. Index-mark the driveshaft at the axle flange.

4. Disconnect the driveshaft from the axle flange. Remove and discard the bolts.

5. Remove and discard the U-joint retainers. Using mechanic's wire, support the driveshaft.

➡**Index-mark the driveshaft to transfer case or transmission flange.**

6. For four-wheel drive vehicles, or vehicles equipped with a circular flange, disconnect the driveshaft from the transfer case or transmission. Remove and discard the bolts. Using mechanic's wire, support the driveshaft.

7. For vehicles with a slip yoke at the transmission, index-mark the output shaft to the slip yoke.

8. Remove the center bearing support bolts.

9. Remove the driveshaft assembly.

10. Clean grease deposits, dirt and rust from the following:

- The driveshaft flange yoke areas.
- All driveshaft slip yoke areas.

11. Inspect the following:

- The driveshaft slip yoke boot for rips or holes. Install a new boot if necessary.
- The driveshaft center bearing support for wear or rough action. If roughness or wear is evident, install a new driveshaft center bearing support.
- The center bearing rubber insulator for evidence of hardening, cracking or deterioration. Install a new insulator if necessary.

12. Note the following:

- Inspect the transmission, transfer case and axle seals for damage. Install new components as necessary.
- Lubricate the slip yoke splines with grease.
- Install the driveshaft so that the index marks made before removal.
- Install new bolts and retainers.
- Bolt direction is vehicle application dependent.

13. To install, reverse the removal procedure. Observe the following torques:

- Flange bolts: 76 ft. lbs. (102 Nm)
- U-joint retainer bolts: 26 ft. lbs. (35 Nm)
- Center bearing bolts: 47 ft. lbs. (63 Nm)

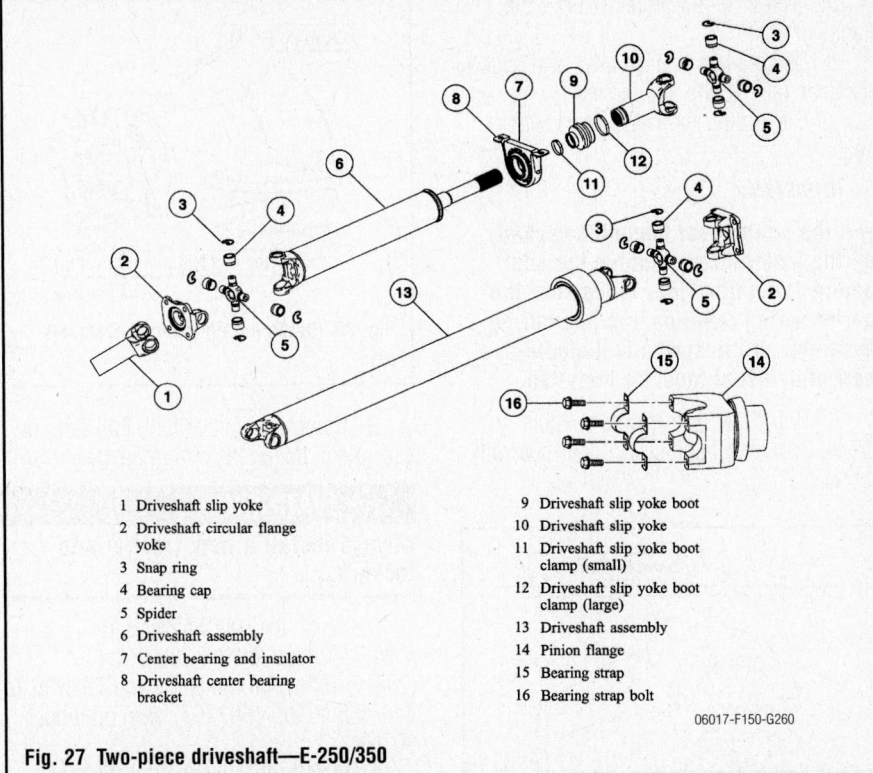

1 Driveshaft slip yoke	9 Driveshaft slip yoke boot
2 Driveshaft circular flange yoke	10 Driveshaft slip yoke
3 Snap ring	11 Driveshaft slip yoke boot clamp (small)
4 Bearing cap	12 Driveshaft slip yoke boot clamp (large)
5 Spider	13 Driveshaft assembly
6 Driveshaft assembly	14 Pinion flange
7 Center bearing and insulator	15 Bearing strap
8 Driveshaft center bearing bracket	16 Bearing strap bolt

06017-F150-G260

Fig. 27 Two-piece driveshaft—E-250/350

REAR PINION SEAL

REMOVAL & INSTALLATION

Ford 8.8 Inch and 9.75 Inch Ring Gear Axle

1. Before servicing the vehicle, refer to the Precautions Section.
2. Raise and support the vehicle.
3. Remove the rear wheel and tire assemblies.

✳✳ WARNING

Remove the brake drums or discs to prevent brake drag during drive pinion bearing preload adjustment.

4. Remove the brake discs or drums.
5. Mark the driveshaft flange and pinion flange for correct alignment during installation.
6. Remove the four bolts.

✳✳ WARNING

The driveshaft centering socket yoke fits tightly on the rear axle pinion flange pilot. Never hammer on the driveshaft or any of its components to disconnect the yoke from the flange.

7. Disconnect the driveshaft centering socket yoke from the rear axle pinion flange. Position the driveshaft out of the way.
8. Install a Nm (inch-pound) torque wrench on the pinion nut and record the torque required to maintain rotation of the pinion through several revolutions.

✳✳ WARNING

After removal of the pinion nut, discard it. A new nut must be used for installation.

9. Use the special tool to hold the pinion flange while removing the pinion nut.
10. Mark the driveshaft pinion flange in relation to the drive pinion stem to make sure of correct alignment during installation.
11. Using the special tool, remove the pinion flange.

To install:
12. Lubricate the pinion flange splines. Use SAE 75W-140 High Performance Rear Axle Lubricant F1TZ-19580-B or equivalent meeting Ford specification WSL-M2C192-A.

➡**Disregard the scribe marks if a new pinion flange is being installed.**

13. Align the pinion flange with the drive pinion shaft.
14. With the drive pinion in place in the rear axle housing, install the pinion flange using the special tool.
15. Position the new pinion nut.

✳✳ WARNING

Under no circumstances is the pinion nut to be backed off to reduce pre-

load. If reduced preload is required, a new collapsible spacer and pinion nut must be installed.

16. Using the special tool to hold the pinion flange, tighten the pinion nut as follows:
   a. Rotate the pinion occasionally to make sure the cone and roller bearings are seating correctly.
   b. Install a Nm (inch-pound) torque wrench on the pinion nut.
   c. Rotating the pinion through several revolutions, take frequent cone and roller bearing torque preload readings until the original recorded preload reading is obtained.
   d. If the original recorded preload is lower than specifications, tighten to the appropriate specifications for used bearings. If the preload is higher than specification, tighten the nut to the original reading as recorded.
   • Pinion bearing torque preload (used pinion bearing): 0.9–1.5 Nm (8–14 inch lbs.)
   • Pinion bearing torque preload (new pinion bearing): 1.8–3.3 Nm (16–29 inch lbs.)

17. Position the rear driveshaft and align the marks on the pinion flange.

✳✳ WARNING

The driveshaft centering socket yoke fits tightly on the rear axle pinion flange pilot. To make sure that the yoke seats squarely on the flange, tighten the bolts evenly in a cross pattern as shown.

18. Install the bolts and tighten to 83 ft. lbs. (112 Nm)
19. Install the brake disc or drum.
20. Install the rear wheel and tire assemblies.

Dana 60, 70 and 80 Rear Axle

See Figures 28 through 30.

1. Before servicing the vehicle, refer to the Precautions Section.
2. Raise the vehicle on a hoist or raise the rear end of the vehicle with a jack. Install safety stands under the frame rails and lower the jack or hoist far enough to allow the rear axle to drop into the rebound position for working clearance.

➡**To maintain driveline balance, mark the driveshaft components so they can be reinstalled in their original positions.**

3. Remove the nuts and two U-bolts (Models 60 and 70) or four bolts (Model 80)

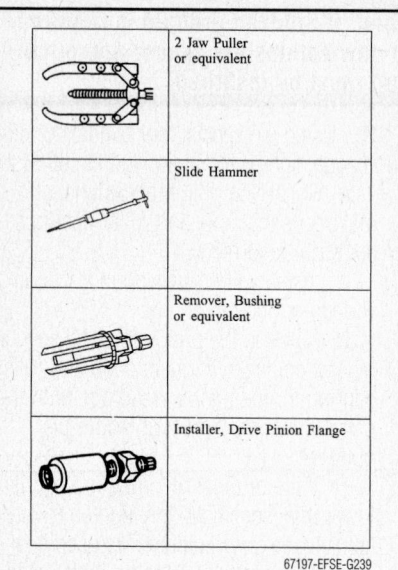

Fig. 28 Tools necessary for this job—Dana 80 axle

from the rear axle universal joint flange and disconnect the driveshaft. Wire the drive-shaft to the frame.

➡**Index-mark the flange to the pinion shaft.**

4. While using a flange holding tool to prevent the flange or yoke from turning, remove the pinion nut.

5. Using a 2-jaw puller, remove the flange or yoke.
6. Using a bushing remover and slide hammer, remove the pinion seal.
7. Clean the rear axle pinion seal seat.

To install:

➡**If the pinion seal becomes cocked during installation, remove the seal and install a new one. Make sure the garter spring remains in place during assembly. If the spring is dislodged, a new pinion seal must be installed.**

8. Install the seal using a suitable driver. Coat the pinion seal rubber lips with lubricant.

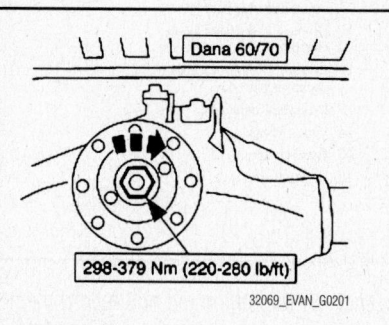

Fig. 29 Pinion nut tightening—Dana 60 and 70 axle

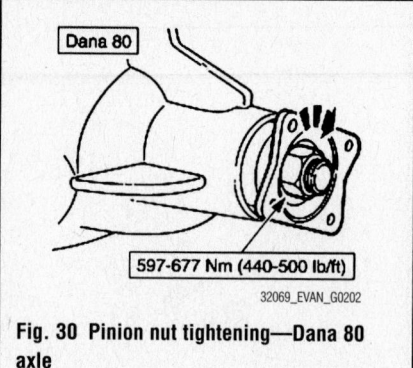

Fig. 30 Pinion nut tightening—Dana 80 axle

9. Using the special tool, 205-285, or equivalent, install the pinion flange.

✳✳ WARNING
Always install a new washer and locknut.

10. Install the new washer and locknut. Torque to 220–280 ft. lbs. (298–379 Nm) on model 60 and 70 axles or 440–500 ft. lbs. (597–677 Nm) on model 80 axle.
11. Install the driveshaft at the rear axle.
12. Tighten the split pin yoke to 26 ft. lbs. (35 Nm) and the circular flange to 82 ft. lbs. (111 Nm).

ENGINE COOLING

ENGINE FAN

REMOVAL & INSTALLATION

Except 6.0L Diesel

See Figures 31 and 32.

➡**The fan, fan clutch and shroud must be removed and installed together due to insufficient clearance to remove them separately.**

1. Before servicing the vehicle, refer to the Precautions Section.
2. Drain the cooling system.
3. Remove the air cleaner assembly.
4. Disconnect the radiator upper hose from the radiator. Position the radiator hose aside.
5. Disconnect the overflow hose from the radiator.
6. Disconnect the coolant degas bottle hose from the shroud.

✳✳ WARNING
The clutch assembly nut has a right-hand thread and must be

rotated counterclockwise to remove it.

7. Using the special tools, loosen the fan clutch.
8. Carefully rotate the fan and fan clutch assembly counterclockwise until the assembly is free from the water pump. Place the fan and fan clutch into the shroud opening.
9. If equipped, disconnect the retaining clips from the fan shroud.

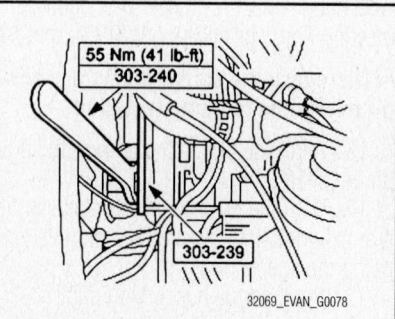

Fig. 31 Fan clutch tool—4.6L and 5.4L engines

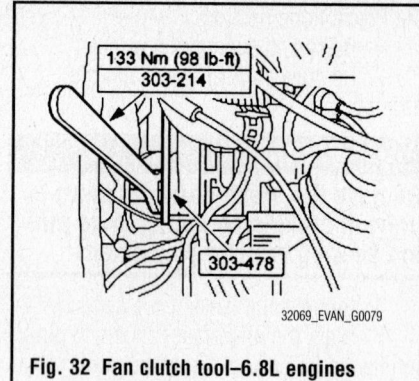

Fig. 32 Fan clutch tool—6.8L engines

10. Raise and support the vehicle.
11. Disconnect the lower radiator hose retaining clamp from the shroud.
12. If equipped, disconnect the underbody splash shield from the shroud.
13. Lower the vehicle.

✳✳ WARNING
Use extreme care when removing or installing the fan, fan clutch and shroud. Failure to do so will cause damage to the radiator.

14. Remove the mounting bolts, and the fan, fan clutch and shroud.

15. To install, reverse the removal procedure. Install an appropriately sized worm drive-type clamp in place of the constant tension clamp. Observe the tightening torques shown in the accompanying illustrations.

ENGINE FAN AND STATOR

REMOVAL & INSTALLATION

6.0L Diesel

See Figures 33 and 34.

1. Before servicing the vehicle, refer to the Precautions Section.
2. Remove the radiator.
3. Disconnect the electrical connector. Release the wiring from the stator.

➡ **Use a hole in the fan hub to prevent the fan from turning.**

4. Using the special tool, loosen the fan clutch by turning the wrench counterclockwise. Remove the cooling fan and clutch.

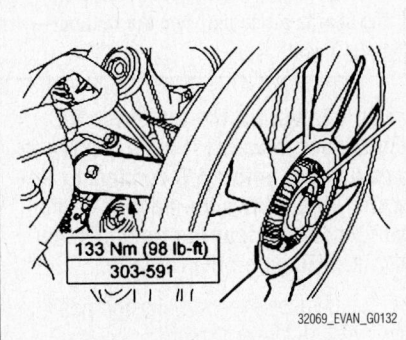

133 Nm (98 lb-ft)
303-591

32069_EVAN_G0132

Fig. 33 Using the special tool, loosen the fan clutch by turning the wrench counterclockwise—6.0L engine

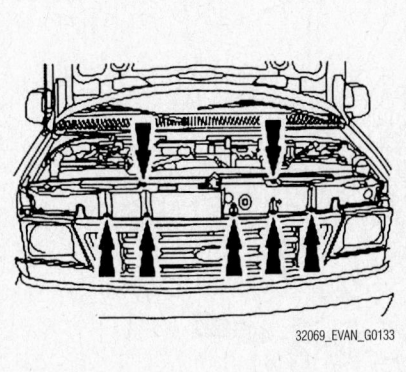

32069_EVAN_G0133

Fig. 34 Remove the bolts and cooling fan stator assembly

5. Remove the bolts and cooling fan stator assembly.

6. To install, reverse the removal procedure. Torque the stator bolts to 40 Nm (30 ft. lbs.) and the fun clutch to 133 Nm (98 ft. lbs.).

RADIATOR AND SHROUD

REMOVAL & INSTALLATION

Except 6.0L Diesel

See Figures 35 through 37.

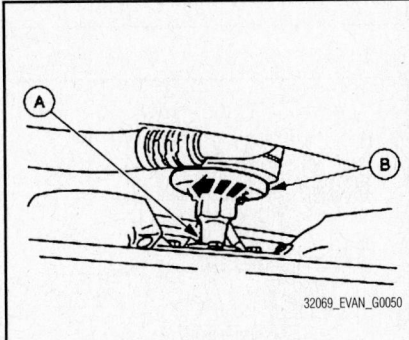

32069_EVAN_G0050

Fig. 35 Remove the (A) fan and fan clutch from the (B) water pump pulley

1. Before servicing the vehicle, refer to the Precautions Section.
2. Drain the cooling system.
3. Remove the air cleaner assembly.
4. Remove the plastic rivet retainers and the air deflector from the vehicle.
5. Disconnect the upper radiator hose from the radiator.
6. Disconnect the overflow hose from the radiator.

➡ **The large clutch assembly nut has a right-hand thread and must be rotated counterclockwise to remove it.**

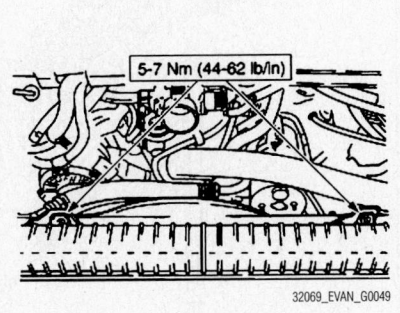

5-7 Nm (44-62 lb/in)

32069_EVAN_G0049

Fig. 36 Remove the bolts and lift the fan shroud, and fan and fan clutch from the vehicle

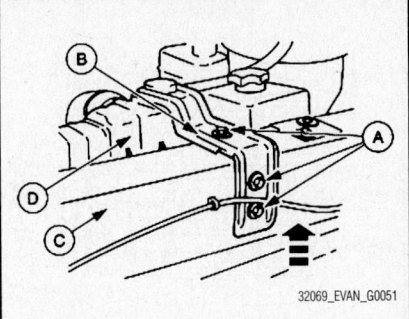

32069_EVAN_G0051

Fig. 37 Remove the (A) bolts retaining the (B) support brackets to the (C) radiator support. Lift the radiator support brackets upwards and away from the (D) radiator

7. Remove the (A) fan and fan clutch from the (B) water pump pulley.
8. Remove the (A) bolts and lift the (B) fan shroud, and fan and fan clutch from the vehicle.
F9. Raise the vehicle.
10. Remove the underbody splash shield, if so equipped.
11. Compress the clamps and slide away from the radiator. Twist the transmission oil cooler hoses and remove from the radiator.
12. Disconnect the lower radiator hose from the radiator.
13. Lower the vehicle.
14. Remove the (A) bolts retaining the (B) support brackets to the (C) radiator support. Lift the radiator support brackets upwards and away from the (D) radiator.
15. Remove the radiator from the vehicle.
16. Follow the removal procedure in reverse order.

6.0L Diesel

See Figures 38 through 46.

1. Before servicing the vehicle, refer to the Precautions Section.
2. With the vehicle in NEUTRAL, position it on a hoist.
3. Drain the cooling system.
4. Remove the pushpin retainers and upper air deflector.
5. Remove the bolts for the power steering reservoir bracket.
6. Remove the bolts and power steering fluid indicator. Remove the power steering reservoir mounting bracket. Install the power steering fluid indicator and position aside.
7. Disconnect the coolant hoses from the air cleaner outlet tube.
8. Loosen the clamps and remove the air cleaner outlet tube.
9. Loosen the clamps and remove the charge air cooler pipe.

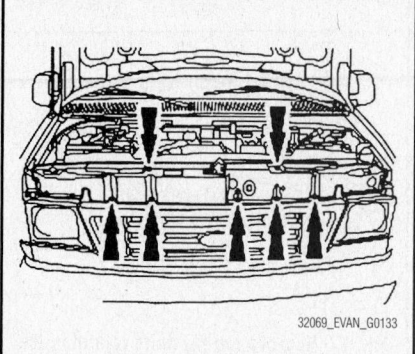

Fig. 38 Remove the pushpin retainers and upper air deflector—6.0L Diesel

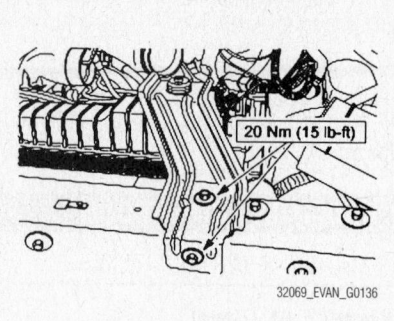

Fig. 41 Remove the bolts and the radiator mounting brackets—6.0L Diesel

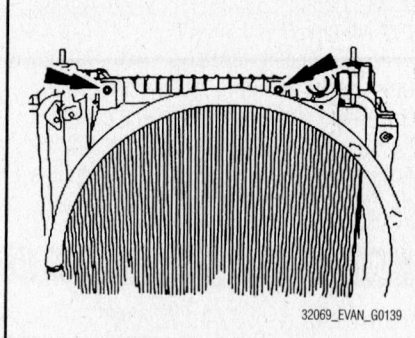

Fig. 44 Remove the bolts and fan shroud—6.0L Diesel

Fig. 39 Remove the bolts for the power steering reservoir bracket—6.0L Diesel

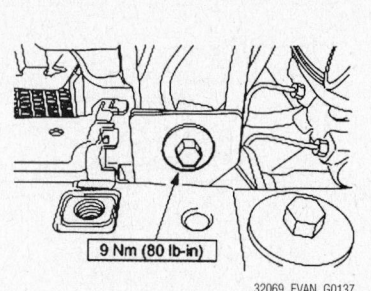

Fig. 42 Remove the two bolts and position the A/C condenser forward—6.0L Diesel

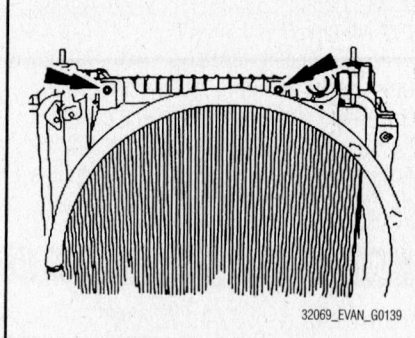

Fig. 45 Remove the bolts and separate the charge air cooler from the radiator—6.0L Diesel

➡️**If there is any oil residue, clean both connecting ports and the inside surface of the charge air cooler hose to prevent the hose from blowing off.**

10. Loosen the clamps and remove the charge air cooler hose.

11. Disconnect the radiator vent hose.

12. Disconnect and remove the upper radiator hose.

13. Remove the pushpin retainers and lower air deflector.

14. Disconnect the transmission cooler hoses. Plug or cap the lines as needed.

15. Disconnect the lower radiator hose.

16. Remove the two bolts and the lower shroud.

17. Disconnect the transmission cooler hoses and remove the lower shroud.

18. Remove the bolts and the radiator mounting brackets.

➡️**Do not just tilt the top of the A/C condenser forward. It is necessary to position the entire A/C condenser forward. This allows the bottom of the condenser to clear the transmission cooler fittings on the radiator.**

19. Remove the two bolts and position the A/C condenser forward.

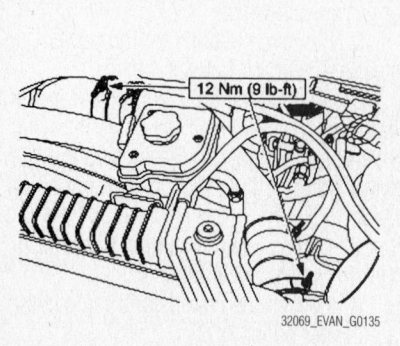

Fig. 40 Loosen the clamps and remove the charge air cooler pipe—6.0L Diesel

Fig. 43 Remove the push pin and radiator air deflector—6.0L Diesel

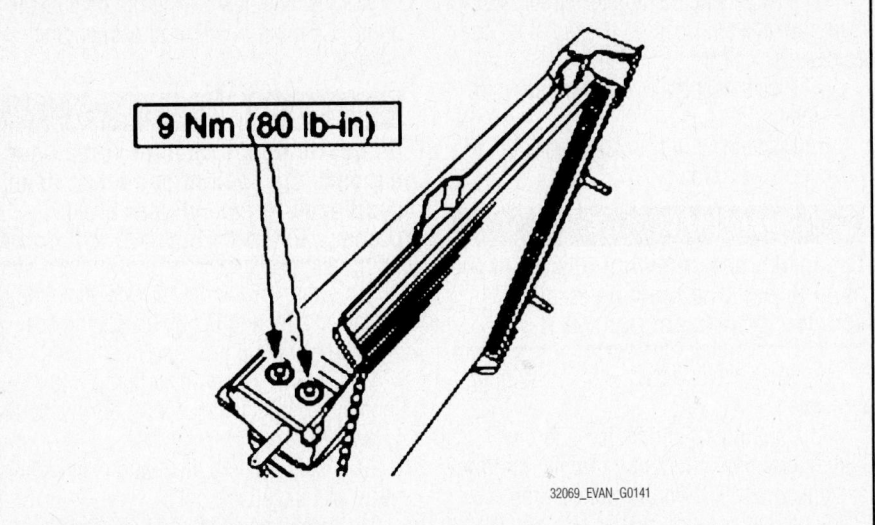

9 Nm (80 lb-in)

32069_EVAN_G0141

Fig. 46 Remove the bolts and brackets from the radiator—6.0L Diesel

20. Disconnect the oil level indicator and tube.

➡️The cooling module (radiator, charge air cooler and fan shroud) is removed as an assembly. If it is necessary to separate the radiator from the cooling module, refer to Disassembly and Assembly in this section.

21. Remove the cooling module from the vehicle.

22. Remove the push pin and radiator air deflector.

23. Remove the bolts and fan shroud.

24. Remove the bolts and separate the charge air cooler from the radiator.

➡️Right side shown, left side similar.

25. Remove the bolts and brackets from the radiator.

26. To install, reverse the removal procedure.

THERMOSTAT

REMOVAL & INSTALLATION

4.6L Engine

1. Drain the engine cooling system.
2. Remove the air cleaner outlet pipe.
3. Release the upper radiator hose clamp and disconnect the radiator hose from the thermostat housing.
4. Remove the power steering upper bracket-to-thermostat housing bolt.
5. Remove the power steering upper bracket-to-intermediate bracket bolts and the power steering upper bracket.
6. Remove the bolts and the thermostat housing.

7. Remove the thermostat and the O-ring seal. Discard the O-ring seal.

8. To install, reverse the removal procedure. Install a new O-ring seal and lubricate it with clean coolant. Tighten the power steering upper bracket-to-thermostat housing bolt to 11 Nm (8 ft. lbs.). Tighten the power steering upper bracket-to-intermediate bracket bolts to 17 Nm (13 ft. lbs.). Tighten the thermostat housing bolts to 25 Nm (18 ft. lbs.).

5.4L and 6.8L Engines

1. Drain the engine cooling system.
2. Remove the air cleaner intake pipe.
3. Release the clamp and disconnect the upper radiator hose from the thermostat housing.
4. Remove the bolts and the thermostat housing.
5. Remove the thermostat and the O-ring seal. Discard the O-ring seal.
6. To install, reverse the removal procedure. Install a new O-ring seal and lubricate it with clean coolant. Torque the housing bolts to 10 Nm (89 inch lbs.).
7. Fill and bleed the cooling system.

6.0L Diesel Engine

1. Drain the engine cooling system.
2. Remove the air cleaner assembly.
3. Loosen the clamps and remove the charge air cooler duct.
4. Disconnect and position the upper radiator hose aside.
5. Disconnect the exhaust backpressure sensor electrical connector.
6. Disconnect the exhaust backpressure tube at the LH exhaust manifold.
7. Remove the 2 nuts and exhaust backpressure sensor and bracket as an assembly.

8. Remove the 2 stud bolts and thermostat assembly. Remove and discard the O-ring seal.

9. To install, reverse the removal procedure. Install a new O-ring seal on the thermostat assembly. Tighten the exhaust backpressure tube at the LH exhaust manifold to 30 Nm (22 ft. lbs.). Tighten the 2 exhaust backpressure sensor and bracket nuts to 31 Nm (23 ft. lbs.). Tighten the thermostat housing bolts to 27 Nm (17 ft. lbs.).

WATER PUMP

REMOVAL & INSTALLATION

4.6L and 5.4L Engines

1. Before servicing the vehicle, refer to the Precautions Section.

➡️The fan, fan clutch and shroud must be removed and installed together due to insufficient clearance to remove them separately.

2. Drain the cooling system.
3. Remove the air cleaner assembly.
4. Disconnect the radiator upper hose from the radiator. Position the radiator hose aside.
5. Disconnect the overflow hose from the radiator.
6. Disconnect the coolant degas bottle hose from the shroud.

✳✳ WARNING

The clutch assembly nut has a right-hand thread and must be rotated counterclockwise to remove it.

7. Using the special tools, loosen the fan clutch.
8. Carefully rotate the fan and fan clutch assembly counterclockwise until the assembly is free from the water pump. Place the fan and fan clutch into the shroud opening.
9. If equipped, disconnect the retaining clips from the fan shroud.
10. Raise and support the vehicle.
11. Disconnect the lower radiator hose retaining clamp from the shroud.
12. If equipped, disconnect the underbody splash shield from the shroud.
13. Lower the vehicle.

✳✳ WARNING

Use extreme care when removing or installing the fan, fan clutch and shroud. Failure to do so will cause damage to the radiator.

14. Remove the mounting bolts, and the fan, fan clutch and shroud.

15. Remove the accessory drive belt.

16. Remove the bolts. Remove the coolant pump pulley.

17. Remove the bolts. Remove the coolant pump from the cylinder block.

To install:

※ WARNING

Always fill the cooling system with the same coolant that is present in the system. Do not mix coolant types.

18. Install a new O-ring on the coolant pump. Coat the new O-ring with engine coolant.

※ WARNING

Do not rotate the coolant pump housing once the coolant pump has been positioned in the cylinder block. Damage to the O-ring seal will occur.

19. Lubricate the new O-ring seal using engine coolant and install the O-ring seal onto the coolant pump.

20. Position the coolant pump into the engine block. Install the bolts. Torque to 18 ft. lbs. (25 Nm).

21. Position the pulley onto the coolant pump and install the bolts.

22. Install the accessory drive belt.

23. Install the fan and fan clutch.

24. To install, reverse the removal procedure. Torque the fan shroud fasteners to 53 inch lbs. (6 Nm). Torque the fan clutch to 41 ft. lbs. (55 Nm). Install an appropriately sized worm drive-type clamp in place of the constant tension clamp.

6.8L Engine

→The fan, fan clutch and shroud must be removed and installed together due to insufficient clearance to remove them separately.

1. Drain the cooling system.

2. Remove the air cleaner assembly.

3. Disconnect the radiator upper hose from the radiator. Position the radiator hose aside.

4. Disconnect the overflow hose from the radiator.

5. Disconnect the coolant degas bottle hose from the shroud.

※ WARNING

The clutch assembly nut has a right-hand thread and must be rotated counterclockwise to remove it.

6. Using the special tools, loosen the fan clutch.

7. Carefully rotate the fan and fan clutch assembly counterclockwise until the assembly is free from the water pump. Place the fan and fan clutch into the shroud opening.

8. If equipped, disconnect the retaining clips from the fan shroud.

9. Raise and support the vehicle.

10. Disconnect the lower radiator hose retaining clamp from the shroud.

11. If equipped, disconnect the underbody splash shield from the shroud.

12. Lower the vehicle.

※ WARNING

Use extreme care when removing or installing the fan, fan clutch and shroud. Failure to do so will cause damage to the radiator.

13. Remove the mounting bolts, and the fan, fan clutch and shroud.

14. Remove the accessory drive belt.

15. Remove the bolts. Remove the coolant pump pulley.

16. Remove the bolts. Remove the coolant pump from the cylinder block.

To install:

※ WARNING

Always fill the cooling system with the same coolant that is present in the system. Do not mix coolant types.

17. Install a new O-ring on the coolant pump. Coat the new O-ring with engine coolant.

※ WARNING

Do not rotate the coolant pump housing once the coolant pump has been positioned in the cylinder block. Damage to the O-ring seal will occur.

18. Lubricate the new O-ring seal using engine coolant and install the O-ring seal onto the coolant pump.

19. Position the coolant pump into the engine block. Install the bolts. Torque to 18 ft. lbs. (25 Nm).

20. Position the pulley onto the coolant pump and install the bolts.

21. Install the accessory drive belt.

22. Install the fan and fan clutch.

23. To install, reverse the removal procedure. Torque the fan shroud fasteners to 53 inch lbs. (6 Nm). Torque the fan clutch to 98 ft. lbs. (133 Nm). Install an appropriately sized worm drive-type clamp in place of the constant tension clamp.

6.0L Diesel Engine

1. Before servicing the vehicle, refer to the Precautions Section.

2. Remove the radiator.

3. Disconnect the electrical connector. Release the wiring from the stator.

→Use a hole in the fan hub to prevent the fan from turning.

4. Using the special tool, loosen the fan clutch by turning the wrench counterclockwise. Remove the cooling fan and clutch.

5. Remove the bolts and cooling fan stator assembly.

6. Remove the accessory drive belt.

7. Remove the bolts and the coolant pump pulley.

8. Remove the bolts and the coolant pump.

9. Remove and discard the O-ring seal.

10. Clean and inspect the coolant pump mounting.

11. To install, reverse the removal procedure.

ENGINE ELECTRICAL

CHARGING SYSTEM

ALTERNATOR

REMOVAL & INSTALLATION

4.6L and 5.4L Engines

See Figure 47.

1. Before servicing the vehicle, refer to the Precautions Section.
2. Remove or disconnect the following:
   - Negative battery cable
   - Drive belt
   - Alternator bracket bolts
   - Ignition wire from the alternator
   - Alternator bolts and the alternator
   - Alternator electrical connectors
   - Alternator stator and voltage regulator connectors
   - Alternator battery cable nut and the cable

To install:

3. Install or connect the following:
   - Alternator battery cable and the nut
   - Alternator stator and voltage regulator connectors
   - Alternator electrical connectors
   - Alternator and the bolts, tighten to 18 ft. lbs. (25 Nm)
   - Ignition wire from the alternator
   - Alternator bracket bolts and tighten to 89 inch lbs. (10 Nm)
   - Drive belt
   - Negative battery cable

6.8L Engines

1. Before servicing the vehicle, refer to the Precautions Section.
2. Remove or disconnect the following:
   - Negative battery cable
   - Air cleaner assembly
   - Mass Air Flow (MAF) sensor electrical connector
   - Accessory drive belt
   - Alternator electrical connectors
   - Bolts retaining the upper intake plenum to the alternator bracket
   - Alternator bolts and the alternator

To install:

3. Before servicing the vehicle, refer to the Precautions Section.
4. Installation is the reverse of removal, please note the following torques:
   a. Bolts retaining the upper intake plenum to the alternator bracket. Tighten to 80–106 inch lbs. (7–9 Nm).
   b. Alternator bolts and the alternator. Tighten to 16–21 ft. lbs. (22–28 Nm).

6.0L Diesel Engine

Single Alternator

1. Before servicing the vehicle, refer to the Precautions Section.

➡**This procedure also applies to the primary alternator of the dual alternator system.**

2. Disconnect the dual batteries.
3. Position the cowl wire harness aside.
4. Remove the bolt and position the manifold absolute pressure (MAP) sensor aside.
5. Remove the bolt and position the ground strap aside.
6. Remove the 2 bolts and position the power steering fluid reservoir aside.
7. Remove the 3 bolts and position the cowl wire harness aside.
8. Remove the 3 bolts, 2 nuts and the intercooler tube bracket.
9. Loosen the 2 clamps and remove the intercooler tube.
10. Rotate the accessory drive belt tensioner clockwise and remove the drive belt from the alternator pulley.
11. Remove the transmission dipstick tube bracket nut from the alternator stud bolt and position the bracket aside.
12. Remove the alternator.

➡**Make sure to install the engine-to-body ground strap under the front alternator stud bolt.**

13. To install, reverse the removal procedure. Torque the mounting bolts to 35 ft. lbs. (47 Nm).

Dual Alternators

1. Before servicing the vehicle, refer to the Precautions Section.

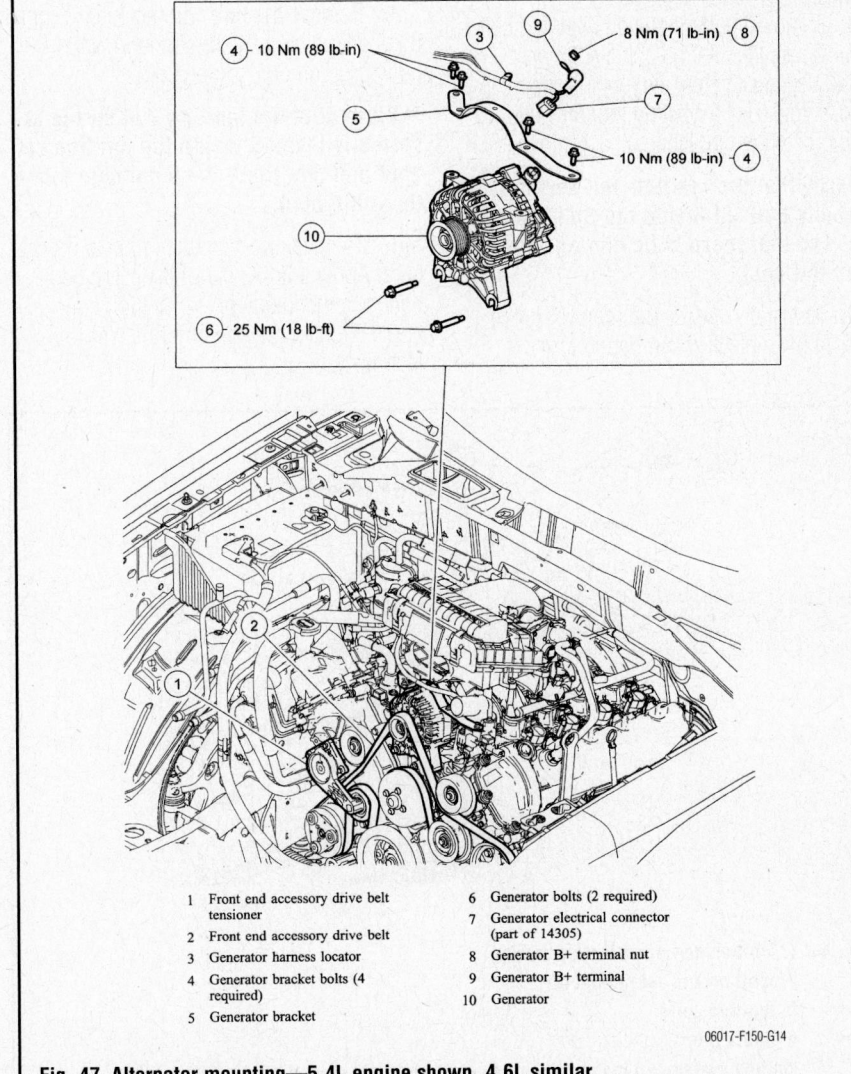

1	Front end accessory drive belt tensioner
2	Front end accessory drive belt
3	Generator harness locator
4	Generator bracket bolts (4 required)
5	Generator bracket
6	Generator bolts (2 required)
7	Generator electrical connector (part of 14305)
8	Generator B+ terminal nut
9	Generator B+ terminal
10	Generator

06017-F150-G14

Fig. 47 Alternator mounting—5.4L engine shown, 4.6L similar

➡This procedure applies to the secondary alternator of the dual alternator system.

2. Disconnect the dual batteries.

3. Position the cowl wire harness aside.

4. Remove the bolt and position the manifold absolute pressure (MAP) sensor aside.

5. Remove the bolt and position the ground strap aside.

6. Remove the 2 bolts and position the power steering fluid reservoir aside.

7. Remove the 3 bolts and position the cowl wire harness aside.

8. Remove the 3 bolts, 2 nuts and the intercooler tube bracket.

9. Loosen the 2 clamps and remove the intercooler tube.

10. Rotate the accessory drive belt tensioner clockwise and remove the drive belt from the alternator pulley.

11. Disconnect the alternator electrical connectors.

12. Remove the bolts and the alternator.

13. To install, reverse the removal procedure. Torque the mounting bolts to 35 ft. lbs. (47 Nm).

ENGINE ELECTRICAL

FIRING ORDER

See Figures 48 through 50.

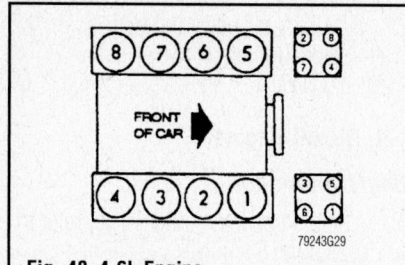

Fig. 48 4.6L Engine
Firing Order: 1–3–7–2–6–5–4–8
Distributorless ignition system

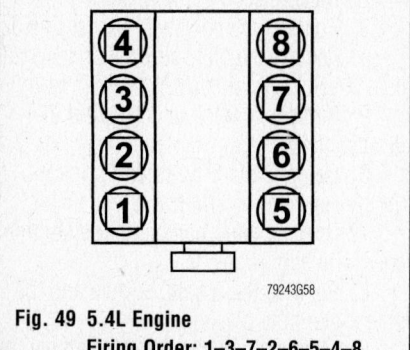

Fig. 49 5.4L Engine
Firing Order: 1–3–7–2–6–5–4–8
Distributorless ignition system;
one coil per cylinder

Fig. 50 6.8L Engine
Firing Order:
1–6–5–10–2–7–3–8–4–9
Distributorless ignition system;
one coil per cylinder

IGNITION COIL

REMOVAL & INSTALLATION

4.6L Engine
See Figure 51.

1. Before servicing the vehicle, refer to the Precautions Section.

2. Disconnect the battery ground cable..

3. Disconnect the ignition coil electrical connector.

4. Remove the ignition coil retaining bolt.

5. Rotate the ignition coil clockwise 30–40 degrees to clear the fuel injection supply manifold. Use a twisting motion while pulling up on the ignition coil and remove.

➡Verify that the ignition coil spring is correctly located inside the ignition coil boot and that there is no damage to the tip of the boot.

6. To install, reverse the removal procedure. Apply dielectric compound to the

IGNITION SYSTEM

inside of the coil boots before installing. Torque the ignition coil retaining bolt to 10 Nm (89 inch lbs.).

5.4L and 6.8L Engines
See Figures 52 and 53.

1. Before servicing the vehicle, refer to the Precautions Section.

2. Disconnect the battery ground cable.

3. Disconnect the ignition coil electrical connector.

4. Remove the bolt and remove the ignition coil, using a twisting motion while pulling up on the ignition coil.

➡Verify that the ignition coil spring is correctly located inside the ignition coil boot and that there is no damage to the tip of the boot.

5. To install, reverse the removal procedure. Apply a light coat of dielectric compound to the inside of the ignition coil boots. Tighten the coil bolt to 6 Nm (53 inch lbs.).

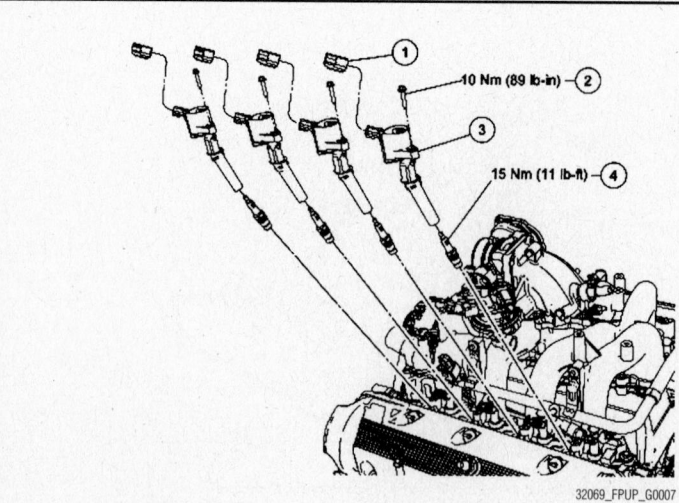

Fig. 51 1. Ignition coil electrical connector
2. Ignition coil retaining bolt
3. Ignition coil
4. Spark plugs
Ignition system components. Left side shown; right side similar—4.6L engine

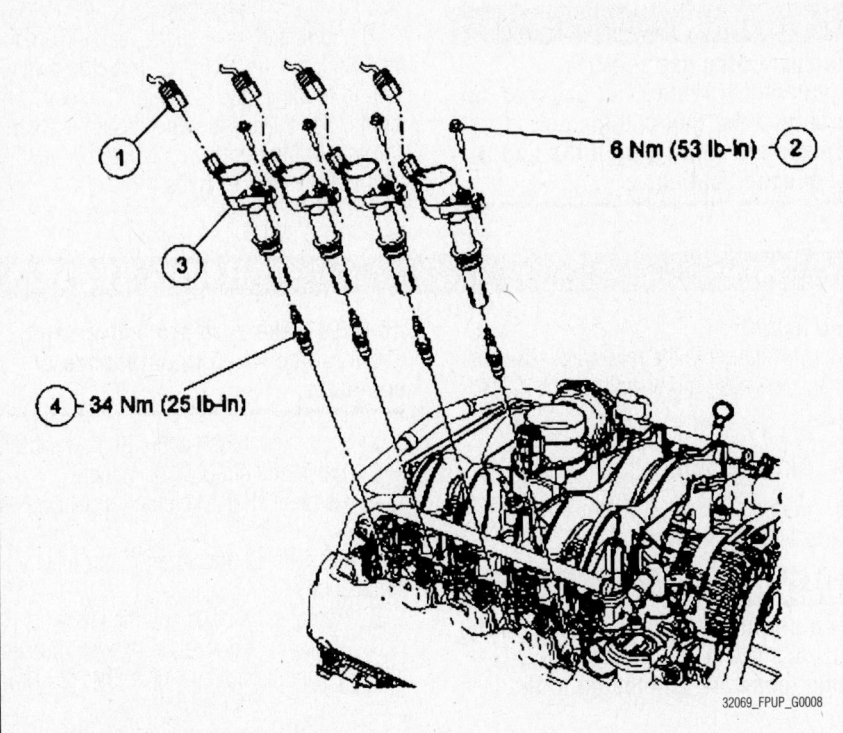

Fig. 52 1. Ignition coil electrical connectors
2. Ignition coil retaining bolts
3. Ignition coils
4. Spark plugs
Ignition system components. Right side shown; left side similar—5.4L engine

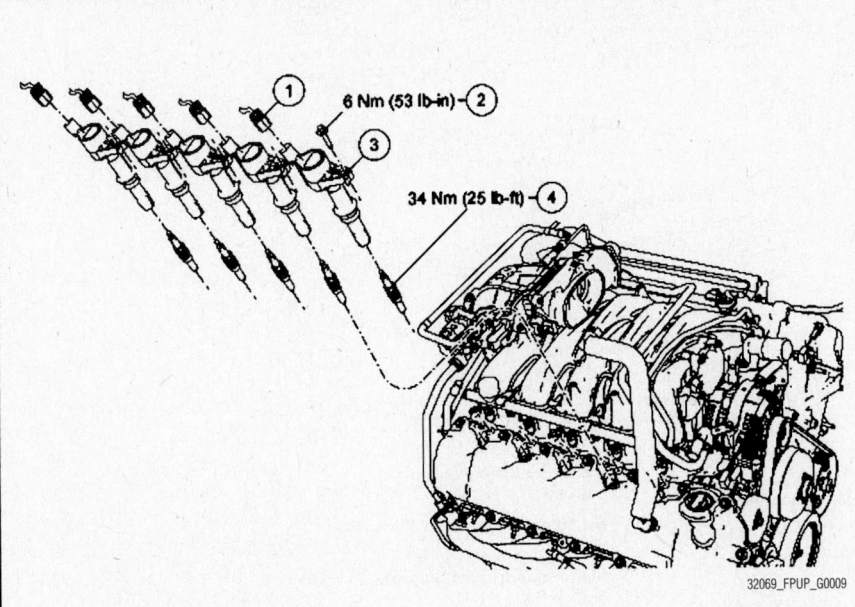

Fig. 53 1. Ignition coil electrical connectors
2. Ignition coil retaining bolts
3. Ignition coils
4. Spark plugs
Ignition system components. Right side shown; left side similar—6.8L engine

IGNITION TIMING

ADJUSTMENT

The ignition timing is controlled by the Powertrain Control Module (PCM). No adjustment is necessary or possible.

SPARK PLUGS

REMOVAL & INSTALLATION

4.6L Engines

1. Before servicing the vehicle, refer to the Precautions Section.
2. Disconnect the battery ground cable..
3. Disconnect the ignition coil electrical connector.
4. Remove the ignition coil retaining bolt.
5. Rotate the ignition coil clockwise 30–40 degrees to clear the fuel injection supply manifold. Use a twisting motion while pulling up on the ignition coil and remove.

➡ **Verify that the ignition coil spring is correctly located inside the ignition coil boot and that there is no damage to the tip of the boot.**

➡ **Use compressed air to remove any foreign material from the spark plug well before removing the spark plugs.**

➡ **If an original spark plug is used, make sure it is installed in the same cylinder from which it was taken. New spark plugs can be used in any cylinder.**

6. Remove the spark plugs.
7. Inspect the spark plugs. Install new spark plugs as necessary.
8. To install, reverse the removal procedure. Apply dielectric compound to the inside of the coil boots before installing. See the Torque Specifications Chart for spark plug tightening. Torque the ignition coil retaining bolt to 10 Nm (89 inch lbs.).

5.4L and 6.8L Engines

1. Before servicing the vehicle, refer to the Precautions Section.
2. Disconnect the battery ground cable.
3. Disconnect the ignition coil electrical connector.
4. Remove the bolt and remove the ignition coil, using a twisting motion while pulling up on the ignition coil.

➡ **Verify that the ignition coil spring is correctly located inside the ignition coil boot and that there is no damage to the tip of the boot.**

→Use compressed air to remove any foreign material from the spark plug well before removing the spark plugs.

→If an original spark plug is used, make sure it is installed in the same cylinder from which it was taken.

5. New spark plugs can be used in any cylinder.

6. Remove the spark plugs.

✳✳ WARNING

The spark plug gap is NOT adjustable. Damage can occur to the ceramic if the gap is adjusted. Replace the spark plug if the gap is out of specification.

7. Inspect the spark plugs. Install new spark plugs as necessary.

8. To install, reverse the removal procedure. Apply a light coat of dielectric compound to the inside of the ignition coil boots. See the Torque Specifications Chart for spark plug tightening. Tighten the coil bolt to 6 Nm (53 inch lbs.).

ENGINE ELECTRICAL

STARTER

REMOVAL & INSTALLATION

4.6L, 5.4L and 6.8L Engines

See Figure 54.

1. Before servicing the vehicle, refer to the Precautions Section.
2. Remove or disconnect the following:
   • Negative battery cable
   • Starter motor electrical connections
   • Starter motor bolts and the motor

To install:

3. Installation is the reverse of removal, tighten the starter motor bolts to 18 ft. lbs. (25 Nm).

6.0L Diesel Engine

1. Before servicing the vehicle, refer to the Precautions Section.

✳✳ WARNING

When performing maintenance on the starting system, be aware heavy gauge leads are connected to the

STARTING SYSTEM

battery. Make sure protective caps are in place when maintenance is complete.

2. Disconnect the battery ground cable.
3. Raise and support the vehicle.
4. Remove starter solenoid protective cap.
5. Disconnect the starter motor electrical connections.
6. Remove the bolts and the starter.
7. To install, reverse the removal procedure. Torque the bolts to 18 ft. lbs. (25 Nm).

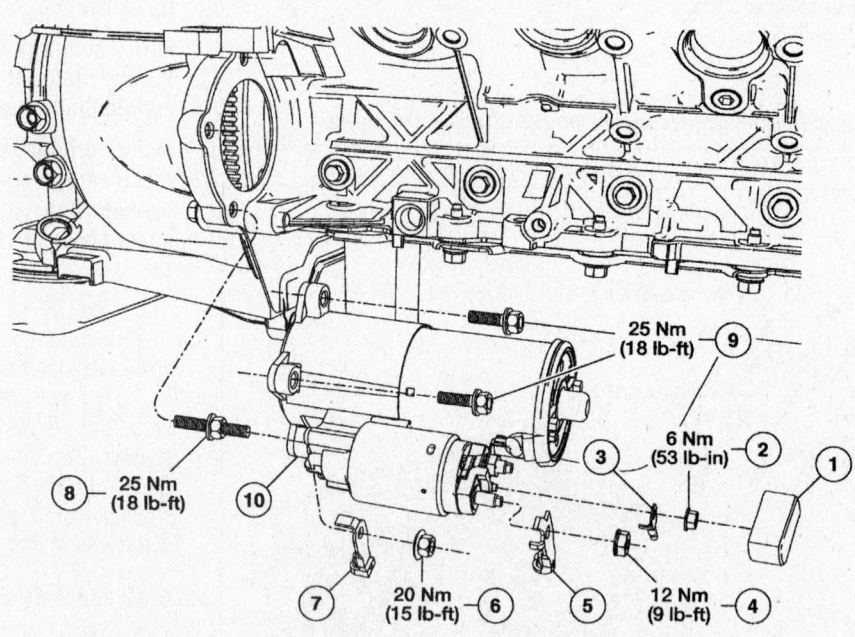

1 Terminal cover	6 Starter motor ground cable nut
2 Starter solenoid S-terminal nut	7 Starter motor ground cable eyelet
3 Starter solenoid S-terminal eyelet	8 Starter motor mounting stud bolt
4 Starter solenoid B-terminal nut	9 Starter motor mounting bolt (2 required)
5 Starter solenoid B-terminal eyelet	10 Starter motor

06017-F150-G87

Fig. 54 Starter and related parts—4.6L, 5.4L and 6.8L engines

ENGINE MECHANICAL

➡Disconnecting the negative battery cable may interfere with the functions of the on board computer systems and may require the computer to undergo a relearning process, once the negative battery cable is reconnected.

ACCESSORY DRIVE BELTS

ACCESSORY BELT ROUTING

See Figures 55 and 56.

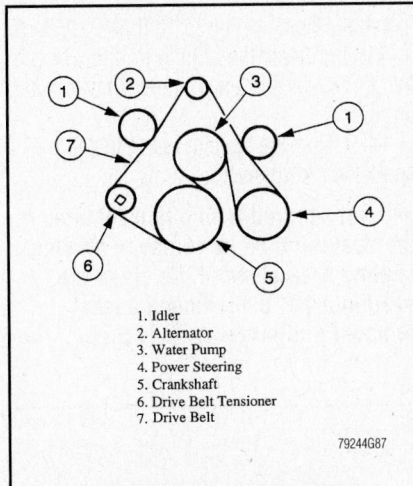

1. Idler
2. Alternator
3. Water Pump
4. Power Steering
5. Crankshaft
6. Drive Belt Tensioner
7. A/C Pulley
8. Drive Belt

79244G86

Fig. 55 Accessory drive belt routing— 4.6L, 5.4L and 6.8L engines with A/C

1. Idler
2. Alternator
3. Water Pump
4. Power Steering
5. Crankshaft
6. Drive Belt Tensioner
7. Drive Belt

79244G87

Fig. 56 Accessory drive belt routing— 4.6L, 5.4L and 6.8L engines without A/C

INSPECTION

Inspect the drive belt for signs of glazing or cracking. A glazed belt will be perfectly smooth from slippage, while a good belt will have a slight texture of fabric visible. Cracks will usually start at the inner edge of the belt and run outward. All worn or damaged drive belts should be replaced immediately.

REMOVAL & INSTALLATION

4.6L Engine

See Figure 57.

1. Before servicing the vehicle, refer to the Precautions Section.
2. Remove the engine cooling fan and shroud.
3. Rotate the drive belt tensioner clockwise and remove the accessory drive belt.
4. To install, reverse the removal procedure.

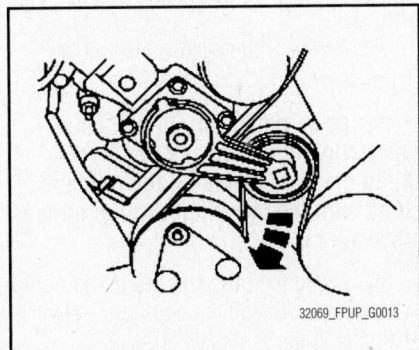

32069_FPUP_G0013

Fig. 57 Accessory drive belt removal— 4.6L, 5.4L and 6.8L engines

5.4L and 6.8L Engines

1. Before servicing the vehicle, refer to the Precautions Section.
2. Remove the air cleaner intake pipe.
3. Rotate the drive belt tensioner clockwise and remove the accessory drive belt.
4. To install, reverse the removal procedure.

6.0L Diesel Engine

See Figures 58 and 59.

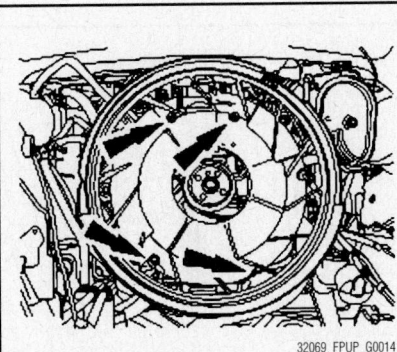

32069_FPUP_G0014

Fig. 58 Cooling fan stator—6.0L engine

32069_FPUP_G0015

Fig. 59 Accessory drive belt removal— 6.0L engine

1. Before servicing the vehicle, refer to the Precautions Section.
2. Remove the cooling fan.
3. Remove the 4 bolts and cooling fan stator.
4. Rotate the drive belt tensioner clockwise and remove the accessory drive belt.
5. To install, reverse the removal procedure. Tighten the stator bolts to 40 Nm (30 ft. lbs.).

BALANCE SHAFT

REMOVAL & INSTALLATION

6.8L Engine

See Figures 60 through 67.

1. Before servicing the vehicle, refer to the Precautions Section.
2. Remove the engine.
3. Remove the bolts and the flexplate or the flywheel.
4. Mount the engine on a suitable work stand.
5. Remove the right engine mount.
6. Remove the cylinder block drain plugs and drain the coolant into a suitable container.
7. Disconnect the left radio frequency interference capacitor and cylinder head temperature (CHT) sensor electrical connectors.
8. Disconnect the camshaft position (CMP) electrical connector.
9. Disconnect the right radio frequency interference capacitor electrical connector.
10. Disconnect the knock sensor electrical connector.
11. Disconnect the crankshaft position (CKP) sensor electrical connector.
12. Disconnect the oil pressure switch electrical connector.

13. Remove the nuts and position the wiring harness aside.

14. Disconnect all of the harness routing clips and connector retainers. Remove the engine control sensor wiring harness.

15. Remove the nuts and the two radio interference capacitors.

16. Remove the crankcase ventilation tube from the left valve cover.

17. Remove the positive crankcase ventilation (PCV) valve and hose from the right valve cover.

➡ **Do not use metal scrapers, wire brushes, power abrasive discs or other abrasive means to clean the sealing surfaces. These tools cause scratches and gouges which make leak paths. Use a plastic scraping tool to remove all traces of old sealant.**

➡ **The bolts are part of the valve cover and should not be removed.**

18. Fully loosen the bolts and remove the left valve cover.

19. Clean the valve cover mating surface of the cylinder head with silicone gasket remover and metal surface prep. Follow the directions on the packaging.

20. Inspect the valve cover gasket. If the gasket is damaged, remove and discard the gasket. Clean the valve cover gasket groove with soap and water or a suitable solvent.

➡ **Do not use metal scrapers, wire brushes, power abrasive discs or other abrasive means to clean the sealing surfaces. These tools cause scratches and gouges which make leak paths. Use a plastic scraping tool to remove all traces of old sealant.**

➡ **The bolts are part of the valve cover and should not be removed.**

21. Fully loosen the bolts and remove the right valve cover.

22. Clean the valve cover mating surfaces of the cylinder head with silicone gasket remover and metal surface prep. Follow the directions on the packaging.

23. Inspect the valve cover gasket. If the gasket is damaged, remove and discard the gasket. Clean the valve cover gasket groove with soap and water or a suitable solvent.

24. Remove the bolt and the idler pulley.

25. Remove the coolant pump pulley.

26. Using a suitable tool remove and discard the crankshaft pulley bolt.

27. Using a suitable tool, remove the crankshaft front seal.

28. Remove the four oil pan bolts.

➡ **Correct fastener location is essential for assembly procedure. Record fastener location.**

29. Remove the fasteners.

30. Remove the engine front cover from the cylinder block.

31. Remove the crankshaft sensor ring from the crankshaft.

➡ **The caps must be marked for installation in their original locations or damage to the engine may occur.**

32. Remove the six bolts and remove the balance shaft bearing caps.

33. Remove the balance shaft.

To install:

34. Using the index mark on the balance shaft, mark the corresponding gear tooth with chalk.

35. Position the balance shaft on the journals.

➡ **It may be necessary to use an inspection mirror to see the marks. Align the chalk mark on the balance shaft with the camshaft timing mark as shown.**

36. Install the bearing caps in their original locations. Install the bolts and tighten the bolts in the sequence shown.

37. Install the crankshaft sensor ring on the crankshaft.

➡ **If the front cover is not secured within four minutes, the sealant must be removed and the sealing area cleaned. To clean the sealing area, use silicone gasket remover and metal surface prep. Follow the directions on the packaging. Failure to follow this procedure can cause future oil leakage.**

38. Apply a bead of silicone gasket and sealant along the cylinder head-to-cylinder block surface and the oil pan-to-cylinder block surface, at the locations shown.

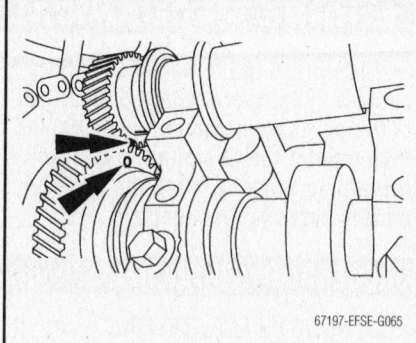

67197-EFSE-G065

Fig. 61 It may be necessary to use an inspection mirror to see the marks. Align the chalk mark on the balance shaft with the camshaft timing mark as shown—6.8L engine

39. Install a new front cover gasket on the engine front cover. Position the engine front cover. Install the fasteners.

40. Tighten the engine front cover fasteners in sequence in two steps.

   a. Step 1: Tighten fasteners 1 through 7 to 25 Nm (18 ft. lbs.).

   b. Step 2: Tighten fasteners 6 through 15 to 48 Nm (35 ft. lbs.).

41. Loosely install the bolts, then tighten in two steps in the sequence shown.

   a. Step 1: Tighten to 20 Nm (15 ft. lbs.).

   b. Step 2: Tighten an additional 60 degrees.

42. Position the belt idler pulley and install the bolt. Torque to 18 ft. lbs. (25 Nm).

43. Lubricate the engine front cover and the crankshaft front seal inner lip with clean engine oil.

44. Using the special tools, install the crankshaft front seal.

➡ **If not secured within four minutes, the sealant must be removed and the sealing area cleaned. To clean the sealing area, use silicone gasket remover and metal surface prep.**

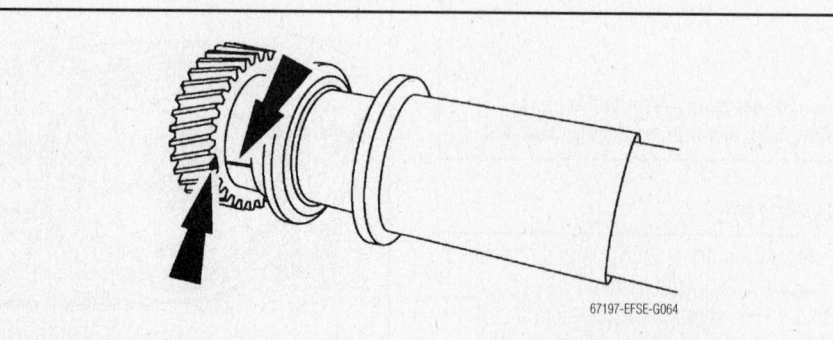

67197-EFSE-G064

Fig. 60 Using the index mark on the balance shaft, mark the corresponding gear tooth with chalk—6.8L engine

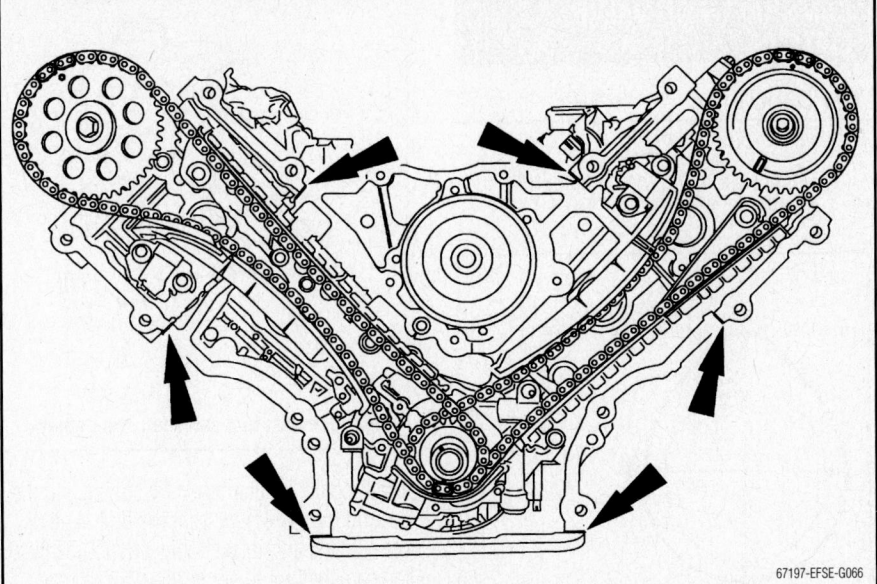

Fig. 62 Apply a bead of silicone gasket and sealant along the cylinder head-to-cylinder block surface and the oil pan-to-cylinder block surface, at the locations shown—6.8L engine

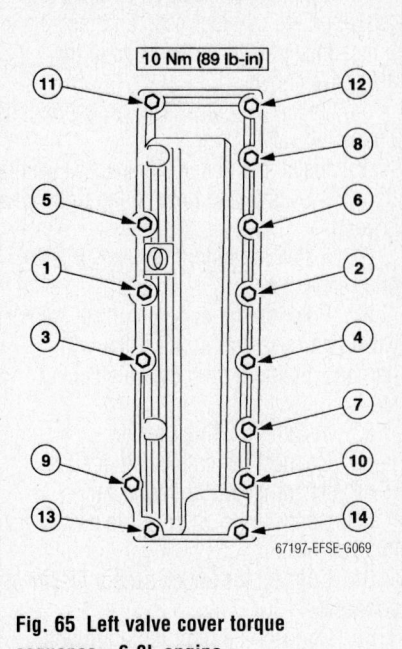

Fig. 65 Left valve cover torque sequence—6.8L engine

Follow the directions on the packaging. Failure to follow this procedure can cause future oil leakage.

45. Apply silicone gasket and sealant to the Woodruff key slot on the crankshaft pulley. Use a suitable tool to install the crankshaft pulley.

➡**Use a suitable strap wrench to hold the pulley while tightening the bolt.**

46. Tighten the new crankshaft bolt in four steps.
   a. Step 1: Tighten to 90 Nm (66 ft. lbs.).
   b. Step 2: Loosen 360 degrees.
   c. Step 3: Tighten to 50 Nm (37 ft. lbs.).
   d. Step 4: Tighten an additional 90 degrees.
47. Position the water pump pulley on the water pump and install the bolts. Torque to 18 ft. lbs. (25 Nm).

48. If a new gasket is being installed, apply instant adhesive completely around the gasket groove in the left valve cover. Install the new valve cover gasket.

➡**If not secured within four minutes, the sealant must be removed and the sealing area cleaned. To clean the sealing area, use silicone gasket remover and metal surface prep.**

49. Follow the directions on the packaging. Failure to follow this procedure can cause future oil leakage.
50. Apply silicone gasket and sealant in two places where the engine front cover meets the cylinder head.
51. Position the left valve cover and gasket on the cylinder head and install the bolts loosely. Tighten the bolts in the sequence shown. If a new gasket is being installed, apply instant adhesive completely around the gasket groove in the

right valve cover. Install the new valve cover gasket.

➡**If not secured within four minutes, the sealant must be removed and the sealing area cleaned. To clean the sealing area, use silicone gasket remover and metal surface prep. Follow the directions on the packaging. Failure to follow this procedure can cause future oil leakage.**

52. Apply silicone gasket and sealant in two places where the engine front cover meets the cylinder head.

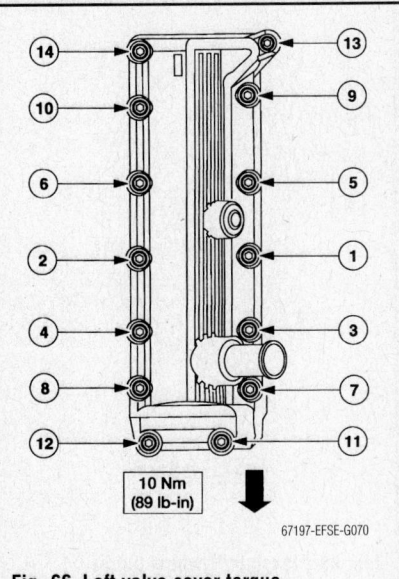

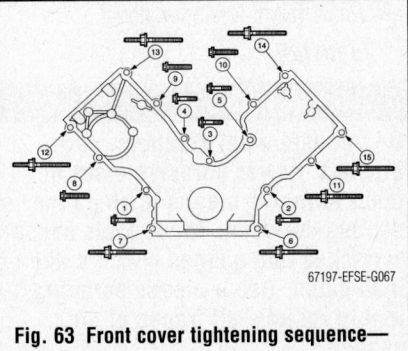

Fig. 63 Front cover tightening sequence—6.8L engine

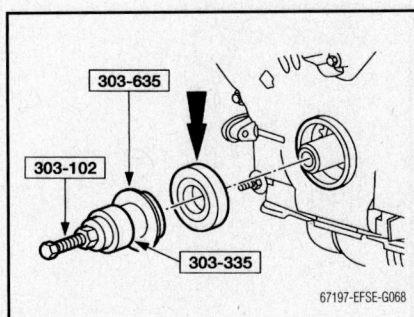

Fig. 64 Crankshaft front seal installation—6.8L engine

Fig. 66 Left valve cover torque sequence—6.8L engine

53. Position the right valve cover and gasket on the cylinder head and install the bolts loosely. Tighten the bolts in the sequence shown.
54. Install the crankcase ventilation tube on the left valve cover.
55. Install the positive crankcase ventilation (PCV) valve and hose in the right valve cover.
56. Install the radio frequency interference capacitors.
57. Position the engine control sensor wiring harness and connect the wiring harness retainers onto the valve cover studs.
58. Install the lifting bracket.
59. Connect the crankshaft position (CKP) sensor electrical connector.
60. Connect the oil pressure switch electrical connector.
61. Connect the knock sensor electrical connector.
62. Connect the right radio ignition interference capacitor electrical connector.
63. Connect the CMP electrical connector.
64. Connect the left radio ignition interference capacitor and cylinder head temperature (CHT) sensor electrical connectors.
65. Install the cylinder block drain plugs.
66. Install the right engine mount. Tighten the bolts to 63 Nm (46 ft. lbs.).
67. Install a suitable tool and remove the engine from the work stand.
68. Install the flexplate or the flywheel and the bolts in the sequence shown.
69. Install the engine.

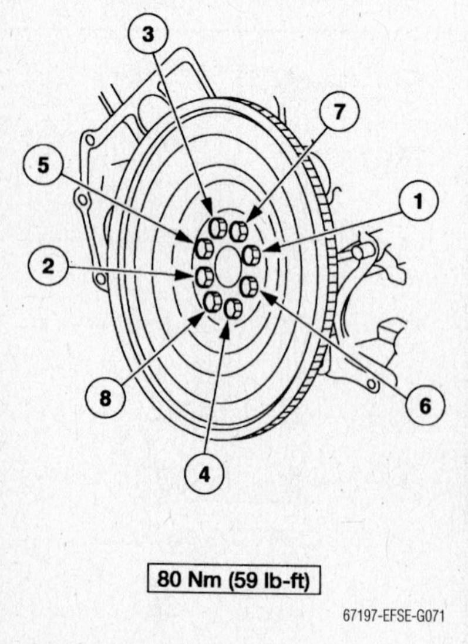
3
7
5
1
2
8
6
4
80 Nm (59 lb-ft)
67197-EFSE-G071
Fig. 67 Flexplate/flywheel torque sequence—6.8L engine

CAMSHAFT AND VALVE LIFTERS

INSPECTION

See Figures 68 through 70.

1. Before servicing the vehicle, refer to the Precautions Section.

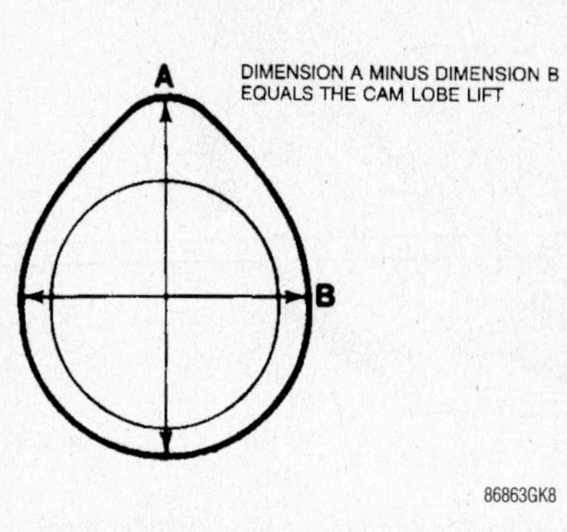
A
DIMENSION A MINUS DIMENSION B EQUALS THE CAM LOBE LIFT
B
86863GK8
Fig. 68 Measuring camshaft lobe lift

Using solvent, degrease the camshaft and clean out all of the oil holes. Visually inspect the cam lobes and bearing journals for excessive wear. If a lobe is questionable, check all of the lobes as indicated. If a journal or lobe is worn, the camshaft MUST BE or replaced.

➡**If a journal is worn, there is a good chance that the bearings or journals are worn and need replacement.**

If the lobes and journals appear intact, place the front and rear journals in V-blocks and rest a dial indicator on the center journal. Rotate the camshaft to check the straightness. If deviation exceeds 0.001 in. (0.0254mm), replace the camshaft.

Check the camshaft lobes with a micrometer, by measuring the lobes from the nose to the base and again at 90° (see illustration).

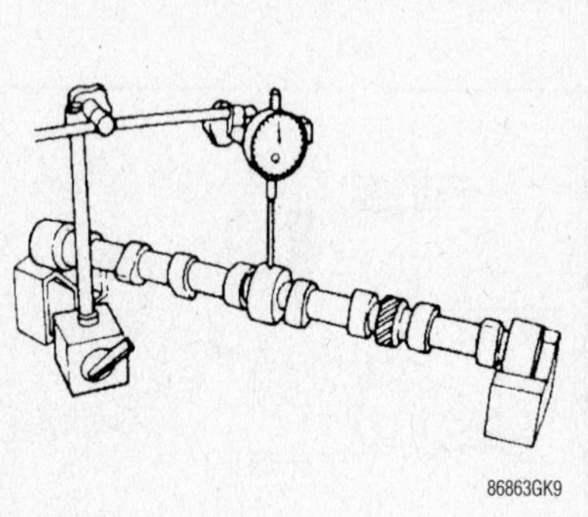
86863GK9
Fig. 69 Measuring camshaft run-out

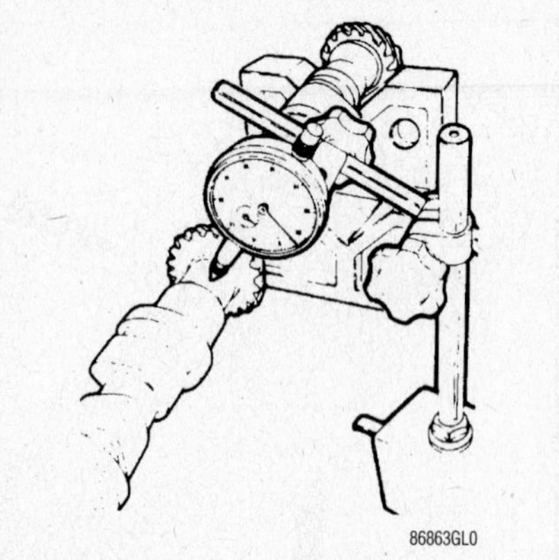
86863GL0
Fig. 70 Measuring camshaft straightness

The lobe lift is determined by subtracting the second measurement from the first. If all of the exhaust and intake lobes are not identical, the camshaft must be reground or replace.

REMOVAL & INSTALLATION

4.6L Engine

See Figures 71 and 72.

1. Before servicing the vehicle, refer to the Precautions Section.
2. Remove the camshaft roller followers.

WARNING

At no time, when the timing chains are removed and the cylinder heads are installed may the crankshaft or camshaft be rotated. Severe piston and valve damage will occur.

3. Remove the timing chains
4. Remove the bolt. Remove the camshaft sprocket.

➡**The camshaft bearing caps must be installed in their original location. Record camshaft bearing cap location.**

5. Remove the bolts, the bearing caps and the camshaft.
6. Clean and inspect the camshaft bearing caps. One of the bearing caps contains an oil flow restriction groove. Make sure the groove is free of foreign material.

To install:

WARNING

Do not use metal scrapers, wire brushes, power abrasive discs or other abrasive means to clean the sealing surfaces. These tools cause scratches and gouges which make leak paths. Use a plastic scraping tool to remove all traces of old sealant.

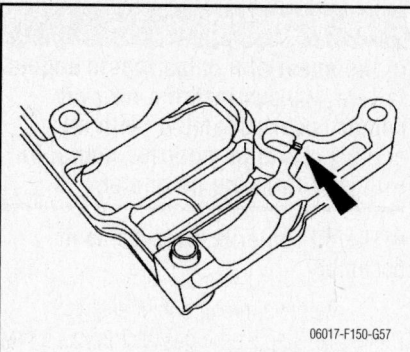

Fig. 71 One of the bearing caps contains an oil flow restriction groove—4.6L engine

7. Clean the valve cover mating surface of the cylinder head with silicone gasket remover and metal surface prep. Follow the directions on the packaging.

8. Lubricate the camshaft bearing caps with clean engine oil.

9. Position the camshaft bearing caps.

10. Install the bolts loosely.

11. Tighten the bolts in the sequence shown to 89 inch lbs. (10 Nm).

12. Install the camshaft sprocket.

13. Install and tighten the bolt.
   - Tighten in two stages.
   - Stage 1: Tighten to 40 Nm (30 ft. lbs.).
   - Stage 2: Tighten an additional 90 degrees.

14. Install the timing chains.

15. Install the camshaft roller followers.

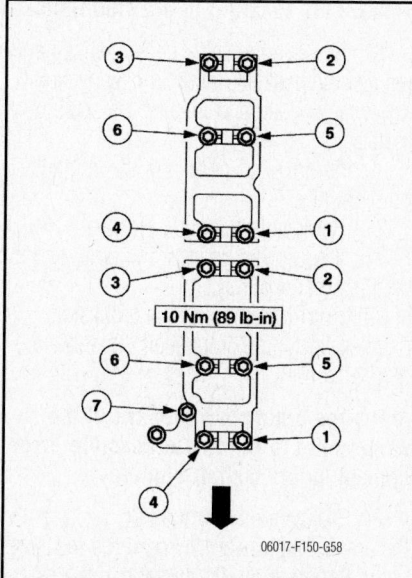

Fig. 72 Camshaft bearing cap torque sequence—4.6L engine

5.4L Engine

See Figures 73 and 74.

1. Before servicing the vehicle, refer to the Precautions Section.

2. Remove the camshaft roller followers.

> ❊❊ **WARNING**
>
> **At no time, when the timing chains are removed and the cylinder heads are installed, may the crankshaft or camshaft be rotated. Severe piston and valve damage will occur.**

3. Remove the timing chains.

➡ **The camshaft bearing caps must be installed in their original location. Record camshaft bearing cap location.**

4. Remove the bolts, the bearing caps and the camshaft.

5. Clean and inspect the camshaft bear-

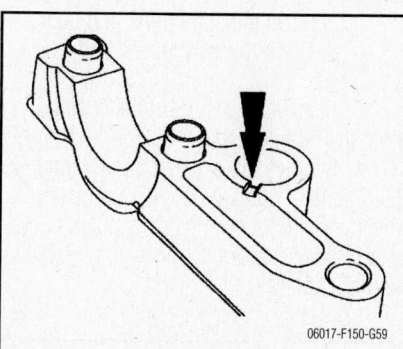

Fig. 73 One of the bearing caps contains an oil flow restriction groove—5.4L Engine

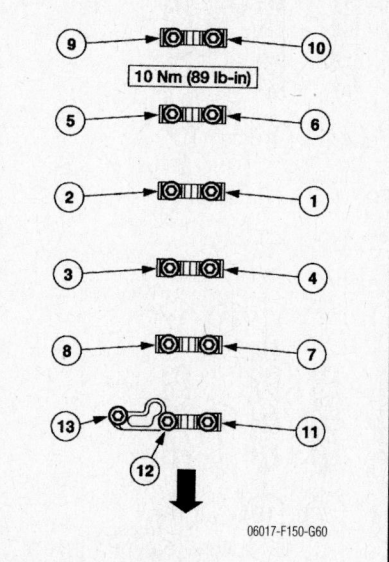

Fig. 74 Camshaft bearing torque sequence—5.4L Engine

ing caps. One of the bearing caps contains an oil flow restriction groove. Make sure the groove is free of foreign material.

To install:

> ❊❊ **WARNING**
>
> **Do not use metal scrapers, wire brushes, power abrasive discs or other abrasive means to clean the sealing surfaces. These tools cause scratches and gouges which make leak paths. Use a plastic scraping tool to clean sealing surfaces.**

6. Clean the valve cover mating surface of the cylinder head with silicone gasket remover and metal surface prep. Follow the directions on the packaging.

7. Lubricate the camshaft journals with clean engine oil.

8. Install the camshaft sprocket.

9. Install and tighten the bolt in two stages.
   - Stage 1: Tighten to 40 Nm (30 ft. lbs.).
   - Stage 2: Tighten an additional 90 degrees.

10. Lubricate the camshaft bearing caps with clean engine oil.

11. Position the camshaft bearing caps.

12. Install the bolts loosely.

13. Tighten the bolts in the sequence shown to 89 inch lbs. (10 Nm).

14. Install the timing chains.

15. Install the camshaft roller followers.

6.8L Engine

See Figures 75 through 77.

1. Before servicing the vehicle, refer to the Precautions Section.

2. Disconnect the battery ground cable.

3. Remove the intake manifold.

4. Remove the timing drive components.

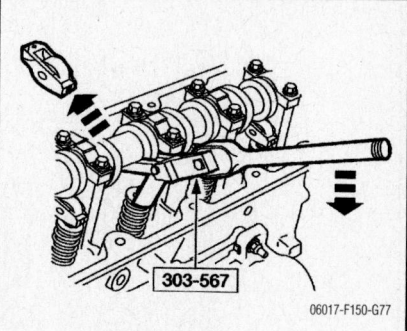

Fig. 75 Use special tool 303-567 to compress the valve springs and remove the camshaft roller followers—6.8L engine

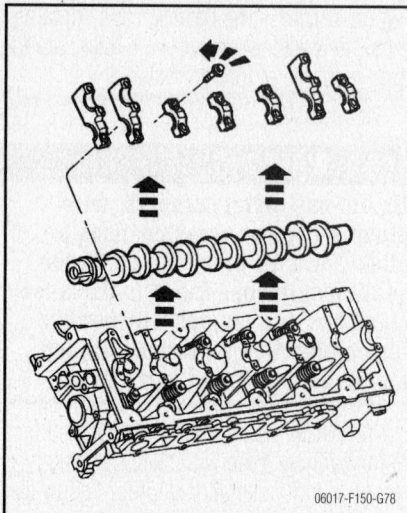

Fig. 76 Camshaft and bearing caps—6.8L engine

5. Use special tool 303-567 to compress the valve springs and remove the camshaft roller followers.

✳✳ WARNING

The bearing caps must be marked for installation in their original location or engine damage can occur.

6. Remove the bolts, the camshaft bearing caps and the camshaft from the cylinder block.

To install:

7. Lubricate the camshaft journals with clean engine oil.

8. Install the camshaft and the camshaft bearing caps in their original locations onto the cylinder head. Loosely install the fifteen bolts.

9. Tighten the bolts in the sequence shown to 89 inch lbs. (10 Nm).

10. Use the special tool to compress the valve springs and install the camshaft roller followers.

11. Install the timing drive components.

12. Install the intake manifold.

13. Connect the battery ground cable.

6.0L Diesel Engine

See Figure 78.

1. Before servicing the vehicle, refer to the Precautions Section.

2. Mount the engine on an engine stand.

3. Remove the serpentine belt idler.

4. Remove the serpentine belt tensioner.

5. Remove and discard the O-rings from the oil filter base.

6. Remove the exhaust gas recirculation (EGR) cooler coolant supply port cover. Clean and inspect the gaskets. Install new gaskets if necessary. Clean and inspect the sealing surfaces.

✳✳ WARNING

In the event of a catastrophic engine failure, always install a new oil cooler cover assembly (with oil cooler). Foreign material cannot be removed from the oil cooler.

➡ **The oil cooler is replaced as an assembly.**

7. Remove the oil cooler assembly. Clean and inspect the gaskets. Install a new gasket if necessary. Clean and inspect the sealing surfaces.

8. Remove the oil pump inlet strainer. Clean and inspect for tears and other damage.

9. Remove bolts and the turbocharger heat shield.

10. Remove the high-pressure oil pump cover. Use a thin gasket scraper to separate the cover from the crankcase. Clean and inspect the gaskets. Install a new gasket if necessary. Clean and inspect the sealing surfaces.

11. Remove the bolts from the high-pressure oil pump discharge pipe.

12. Disconnect and remove the high-pressure oil pump discharge pipe.

13. Remove and discard the D-ring seal.

14. Remove and discard the high-pressure pump O-ring seal.

15. Remove the bolts and the high-pressure oil pump.

16. Remove and discard the lower O-ring seal.

17. Remove the glow plug buss bar.

18. Remove the eight glow plugs.

➡ **Mark the location of the stud bolts.**

19. Remove the valve covers. Clean and inspect the gaskets. Install a new gasket if necessary. Clean and inspect the sealing surfaces.

20. Remove the bolts and the coolant pump pulley.

21. Remove the coolant pump.

22. If equipped, remove the bolts and the dual alternator pulley.

23. Prior to removing the crankshaft damper, check the crankshaft vibration damper runout.

➡ **Pry the crankshaft forward at the same point to eliminate possible error caused by crankshaft end play.**

24. Rotate the crankshaft 90 degrees. Pry the crankshaft forward. Record the measurement. Repeat every 90 degrees. If the runout exceeds 0.002 inch, install a new crankshaft vibration damper.

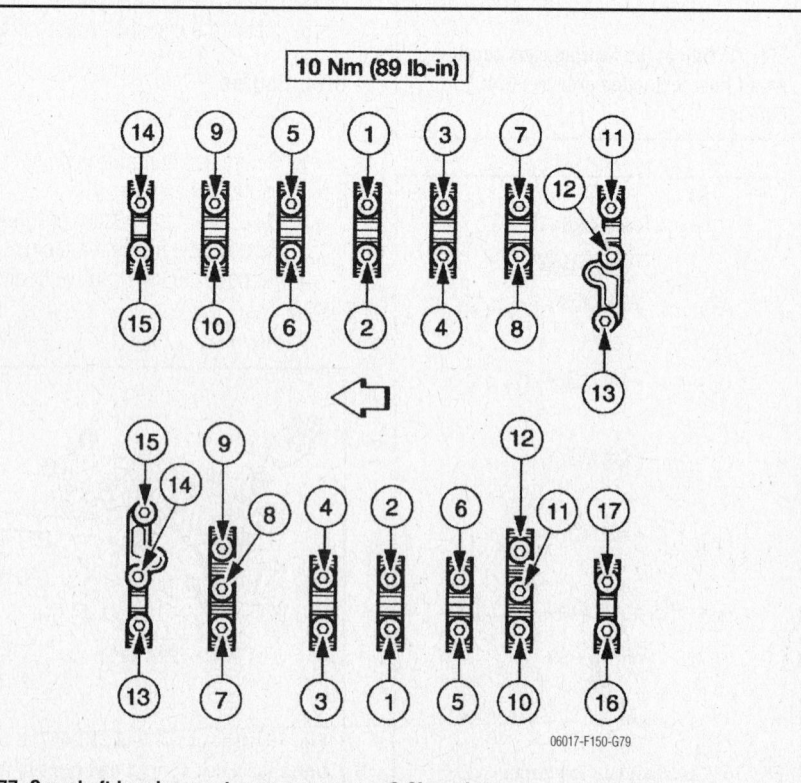

Fig. 77 Camshaft bearing cap torque sequence—6.8L engine

❋❋ **WARNING**

To prevent engine damage, you must always replace all four bolts when installing the vibration damper.

❋❋ **CAUTION**

To avoid personal injury, support the vibration damper during mounting bolt removal. The damper can slide off the nose of the crankshaft very easily.

25. Remove the bolts and the crankcase vibration damper. Discard the bolts.

26. Punch two holes in the seal. Remove the crankshaft seal with a slide-hammer.

➡Production engine will not have a wear sleeve. If equipped, remove the crankshaft damper wear sleeve.

27. Remove the oil pump body. Remove and discard the O-ring seal.

➡Mark the front of each drive rotor for correct reassembly orientation.

28. Remove the inner and outer oil pump drive rotors.

29. Remove the engine front cover. Clean and inspect the gaskets. Install new gaskets if necessary. Clean and inspect the sealing surfaces.

30. Using a quick-disconnect tool, disconnect the high-pressure oil rail supply line at the high-pressure oil rail.

31. Remove the bolts and the high pressure oil rail. Disconnect and remove the high-pressure oil supply line.

❋❋ **WARNING**

Do not attempt to put battery voltage to the fuel injector or damage to the fuel injector will occur.

32. Using a 19 mm socket, push the fuel injector electrical connector out of the rocker arm carrier.

❋❋ **WARNING**

To prevent engine damage, do not use air tools to remove the fuel injectors. The clip that extracts the injector can dislodge and fall into the oil drain hole.

➡If engine oil is found in the engine coolant or engine coolant is found in the combustion chambers, new injector sleeve may need to be installed.

33. Remove the bolt, the fuel injector hold down and the fuel injector.

34. Remove and discard the crankcase-to-head tube assembly.

35. Remove the inner head bolts from both cylinder heads.

36. Remove the 16 bolts and the rocker arm assemblies.

37. Remove the rocker arm carrier from the cylinder head. Clean and inspect the gaskets. Install new gaskets if necessary Clean and inspect the sealing surfaces.

➡Mark the location of the valve bridges before removing.

38. Remove the 16 valve bridges.

❋❋ **WARNING**

To prevent engine damage, keep the push rods in the order in which they were removed. Install all push rods back in their original positions.

39. Mark the location and remove the 16 push rods.

40. Remove the 10 outer head bolts.

41. Remove the cylinder heads.

42. Remove and discard the cylinder head gasket.

43. Remove and discard the four cylinder head dowel sleeves.

44. Remove the bolts from the rear engine tube assembly.

45. Remove the bolt and the rear engine tube assembly.

❋❋ **WARNING**

To prevent engine damage, keep the cam followers in the order in which they were removed. Install all cam followers back in their original positions.

46. Remove the bolts and the roller follower guides. Remove the hydraulic cam followers.

47. Install the special tool and measure the camshaft gear backlash. Install a new camshaft gear if backlash is not within specification.

48. Install a dial indicator and measure the camshaft end play. Install a new camshaft thrust plate if end play is not within 0.002–0.008 inch.

49. Remove the bolt and the camshaft position (CMP) sensor.

❋❋ **WARNING**

Do not knick or scratch the camshaft bearings with the camshaft lobes or engine damage will occur.

50. Remove the thrust plate mounting bolts and remove the camshaft and gear.

To install:

➡Check alignment of the oil holes after installing the bearings.

51. If removed, install the camshaft bearings.

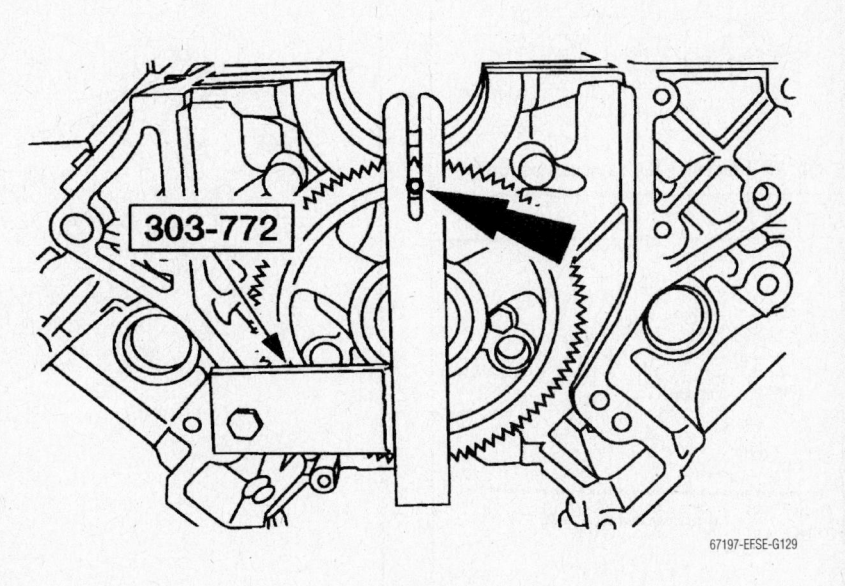

303-772

67197-EFSE-G129

Fig. 78 Using camshaft alignment tool 303-772, install the camshaft and gear assembly

✳✳ WARNING

Do not nick or scratch the camshaft bearings with the camshaft lobes or engine damage can occur.

➡**Apply clean engine oil to the camshaft prior to installing.**

52. Using camshaft alignment tool 303-772, install the camshaft and gear assembly. Aligning it with the crankshaft. Install the thrust plate mounting bolts. Torque to 23 ft. lbs. (31 Nm).

53. The remainder of installation is the reverse of removal.

CAMSHAFT BEARING REPLACEMENT

OHV Engines

See Figures 79 through 83.

If excessive camshaft wear is found, or if the engine is completely rebuilt, the camshaft bearings should be replaced.

➡**The front and rear bearings should be removed last, and installed first.**

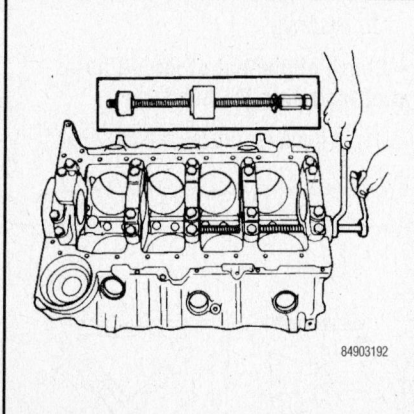

Fig. 79 Removing the camshaft bearings

A. Bearing tool
B. Pilot
C. Nut
D. Puller screw

Fig. 80 Replacing the inner camshaft bearing

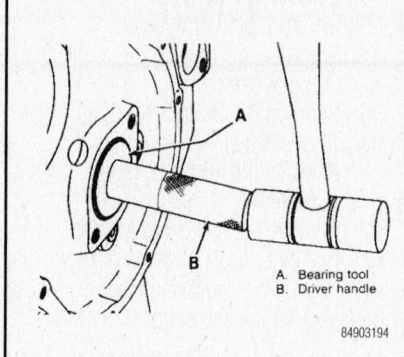

A. Bearing tool
B. Driver handle

Fig. 81 Installing the outer camshaft bearing

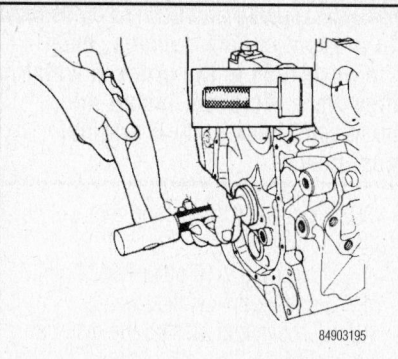

Fig. 82 Installing the front camshaft bearing on the diesel. The bearing tool is shown in the inset

Those bearings act as guides for the other bearings and pilot.

1. Before servicing the vehicle, refer to the Precautions Section.

2. Drive the camshaft rear plug from the block.

3. Assemble the removal puller with its shoulder on the bearing to be removed. Gradually tighten the puller nut until the bearing is removed.

4. Remove the remaining bearings, leaving the front and rear for last. To remove these, reverse the position of the puller, so as to pull the bearings towards the center of the block. Leave the tool in this position, pilot the new front and rear bearings on the installer, and pull them into position.

5. Return the puller to its original position and pull the remaining bearings into position.

➡**You must make sure that the oil holes of the bearings and block align when installing the bearings. If they don't align, the camshaft will not get proper lubrication and may seize or at least be seriously damaged. To check for correct oil hole alignment, use a piece of brass rod with a 90° bend in the end as shown in the illustration. Check all oil hole openings. The wire must enter each hole,**

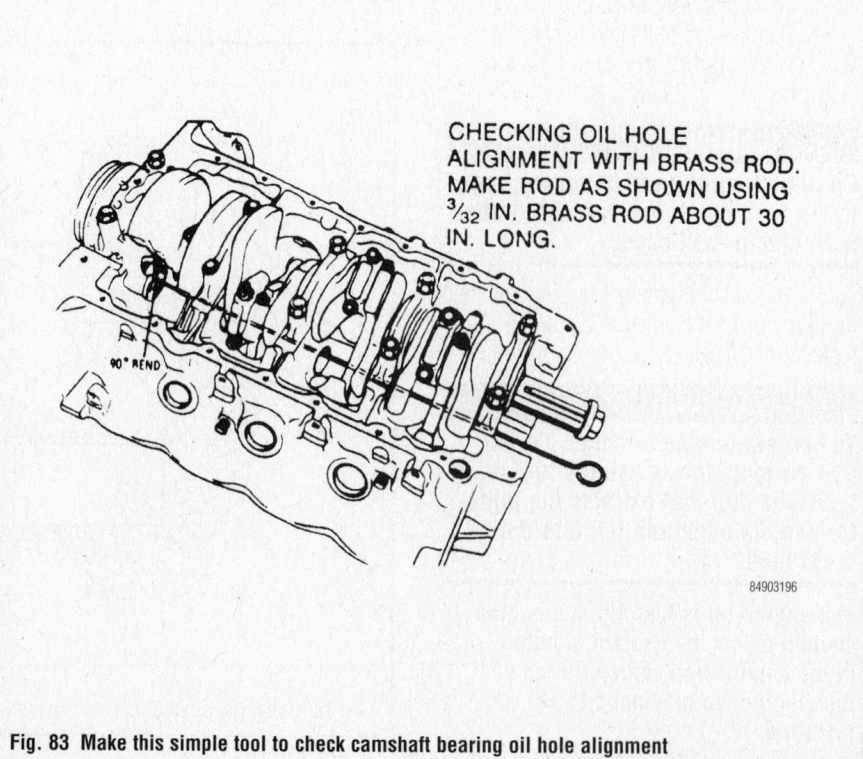

CHECKING OIL HOLE ALIGNMENT WITH BRASS ROD. MAKE ROD AS SHOWN USING 3/32 IN. BRASS ROD ABOUT 30 IN. LONG.

90° BEND

Fig. 83 Make this simple tool to check camshaft bearing oil hole alignment

or the hole is not properly aligned.

6. Replace the camshaft rear plug, and stake it into position. On the diesel, coat the outer diameter of the new plug with GM sealant #1052080 or equivalent, and install it flush to 1/32 in. (0.794mm) deep.

CRANKSHAFT FRONT SEAL

REMOVAL & INSTALLATION

4.6L, 5.4L and 6.8L Engines

See Figures 84 and 85.

1. Before servicing the vehicle, refer to the Precautions Section.
2. Remove the crankshaft pulley. For additional information, refer to Crankshaft Pulley in this section.
3. Using the special tool, remove the crankshaft front seal.

To install:

4. Lubricate the engine front cover and the crankshaft front seal inner lip with clean engine oil.
5. Using the special tools, install the crankshaft front seal.
6. Install the crankshaft pulley.

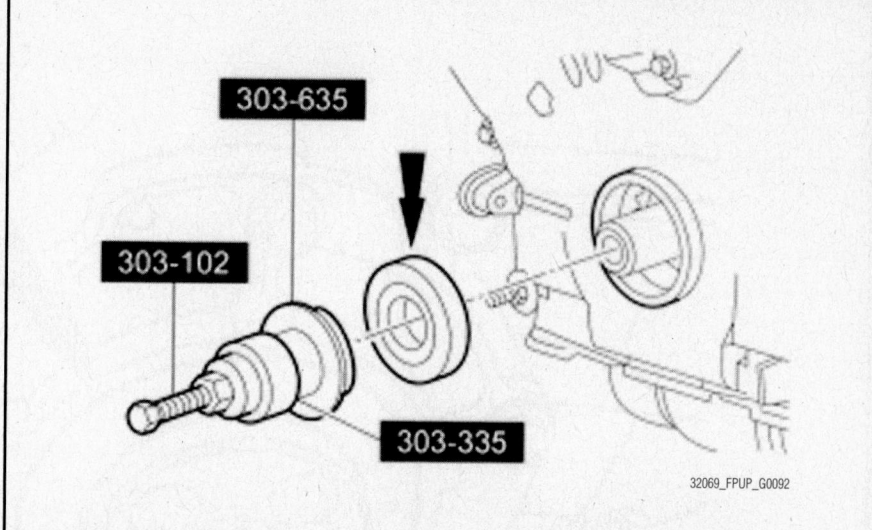

Fig. 85 Using the special tool, install the crankshaft front seal—4.6L, 5.4L SOHC and 6.8L engine

6.0L Diesel Engine

See Figures 86 through 88.

1. Before servicing the vehicle, refer to the Precautions Section.
2. Remove the crankshaft vibration damper. For additional information, refer to Crankshaft Pulley in this section.

3. Punch two holes in the seal.
4. Using the special tool, remove the crankshaft seal.

➡**Production engines will not have a wear sleeve.**

5. If equipped, remove the crankshaft seal wear sleeve.

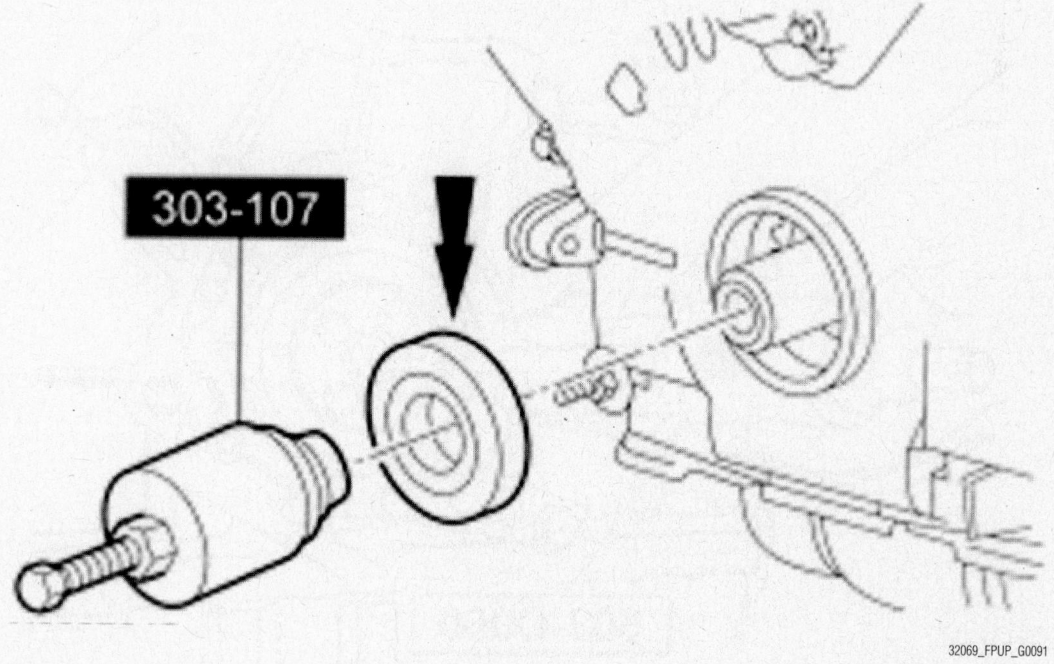

Fig. 84 Using the special tool, remove the crankshaft front seal—4.6L, 5.4L and 6.8L engine

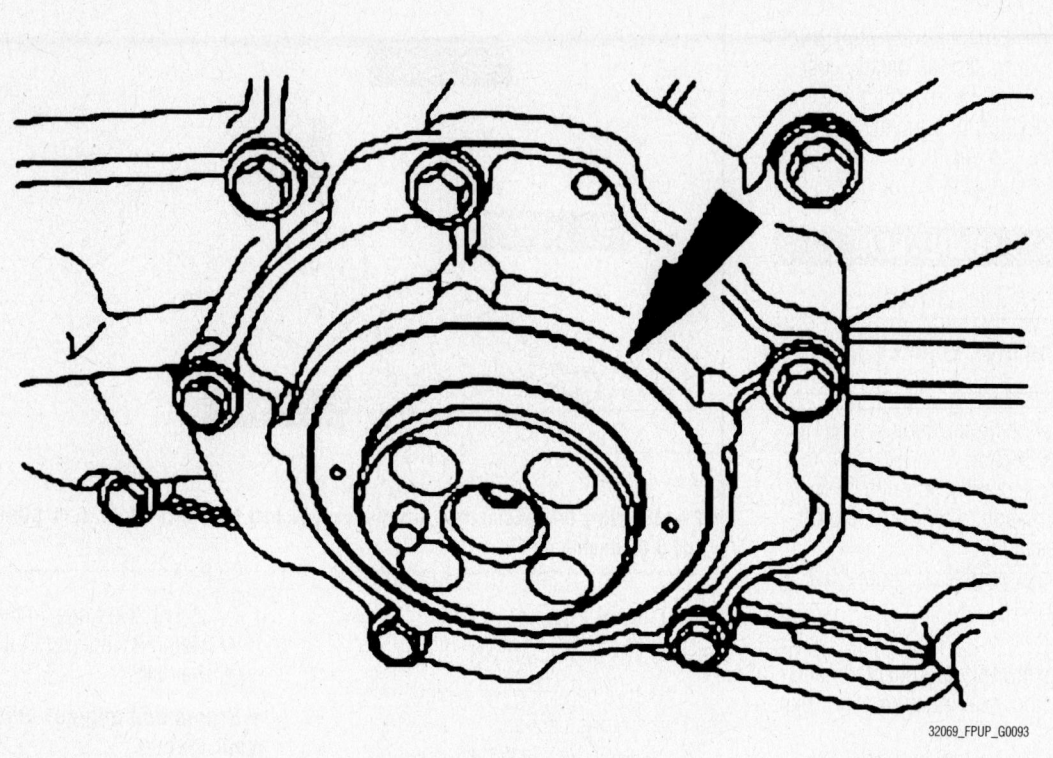

Fig. 86 Punch 2 holes in the seal—6.0L engine

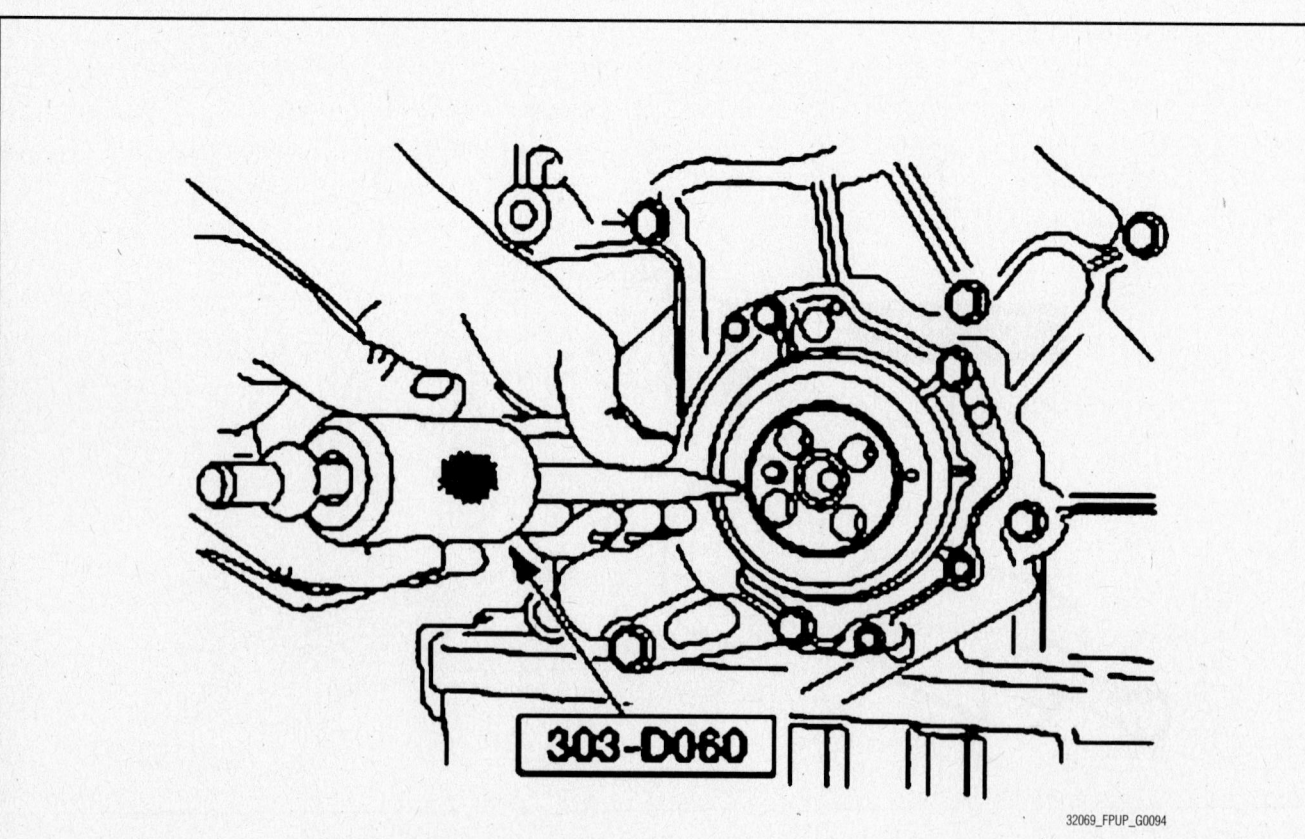

Fig. 87 Using the special tool, remove the crankshaft seal—6.0L engine

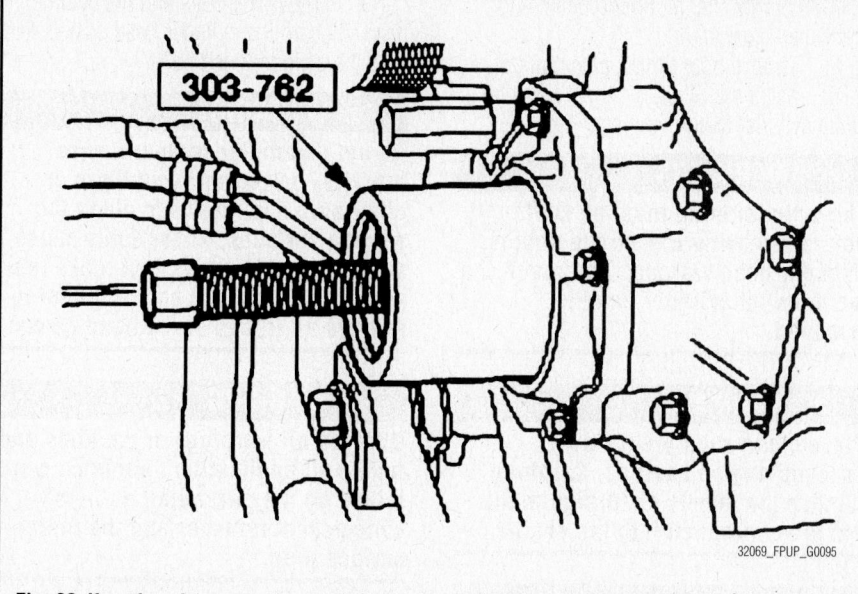

Fig. 88 If equipped, remove the crankshaft seal wear sleeve—6.0L engine

32069_FPUP_G0095

To install:

6. Thoroughly clean the crankshaft front seal mounting surface.

7. Apply High Strength Threadlocker to the outer circumference of the leading edge of the crankshaft.

➡**New seal and wear sleeve must not be separated.**

8. Using the special tool, install the oil seal and wear sleeve assembly.

9. Install the crankshaft damper. For additional information, refer to Crankshaft Pulley in this section.

CYLINDER HEAD

REMOVAL & INSTALLATION

4.6L Engine

See Figures 89 through 108.

1. Before servicing the vehicle, refer to the Precautions Section.

2. Remove the engine.

3. Remove the bolts and the flexplate or the flywheel.

4. Install the engine onto a suitable engine stand.

Left cylinder head

5. Remove the left exhaust manifold.

6. Remove the bolt and the oil level indicator tube.

7. Remove the engine wiring harness retainers from the left valve cover studs.

➡**The bolts are part of the valve cover and should not be removed.**

8. Remove the bolts and the left valve cover.

Right cylinder head

9. Remove the right exhaust manifold.

10. Remove the engine wiring harness retainers from the right valve cover studs.

➡**The bolts are part of the valve cover and should not be removed.**

11. Remove the bolts and the right valve cover.

12. Disconnect the coolant hoses from the heater outlet tube.

13. Remove the heater outlet tube studs.

14. Remove the heater outlet tube and discard the O-ring seal.

All cylinder heads

15. Remove the bolts, the coolant pump pulley and the accessory drive belt idler pulleys.

16. Remove the bolts and the accessory drive belt tensioner.

17. Disconnect the left and right radio ignition interference capacitor electrical connectors.

18. Remove the nuts and the two radio interference capacitors.

19. Remove the bolt and the left CMP sensor.

20. Connect the crankshaft position (CKP) sensor electrical connector.

21. Remove the bolt and washer and using a suitable tool, remove the crankshaft pulley. Discard the crankshaft bolt.

22. Using a suitable tool, remove the crankshaft seal.

23. Remove the four oil pan front bolts.

24. Remove the bolts.

25. Remove the engine front cover from the front cover to cylinder block dowel.

26. Remove the engine front cover gaskets.

27. Clean the mating surfaces with silicone gasket remover and metal surface prep. Follow the directions on the packaging.

28. Inspect the mating surfaces.

➡**Use compressed air to remove any foreign material from the spark plug well before removing the spark plugs.**

29. Remove the eight spark plugs.

30. Install a suitable tool between the valve spring coils to prevent valve stem seal damage.

➡**The camshaft roller followers must be reinstalled in their original locations. Record the camshaft roller follower locations.**

➡**Position the cam lobe away from the camshaft roller follower prior to removing each camshaft roller follower.**

31. Use a suitable tool to compress the valve springs, and remove the camshaft roller followers.

32. Remove the special tool.

➡**The camshaft roller followers must be reinstalled in their original locations.**

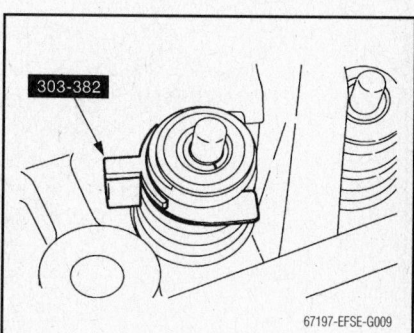

67197-EFSE-G009

Fig. 89 Special tool installation—4.6L Engine

Fig. 90 Special tool installation to compress the valve spring—4.6L Engine

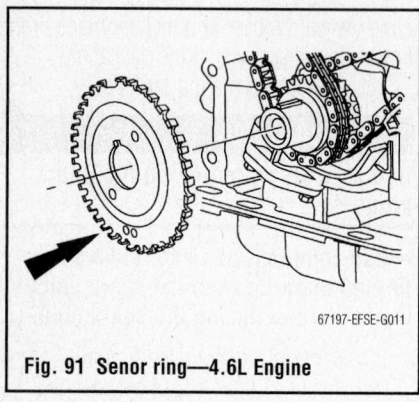

Fig. 91 Senor ring—4.6L Engine

33. Repeat the previous three steps for each of the roller followers.

34. Remove the crankshaft sensor ring from the crankshaft.

35. Position the crankshaft with the keyway at the 12 o'clock position.

36. Remove the timing chain tensioning system from both timing chains.

37. Remove the right timing chain from the camshaft sprocket.

38. Remove the right timing chain from the crankshaft sprocket.

39. Remove the left timing chain from the camshaft sprocket.

40. Remove the left timing chain and crankshaft sprocket(s).

41. Remove both timing chain guides.

42. Install the lifting tools on both ends of the cylinder head being serviced.

❋❋ WARNING

The cylinder head must be cool before removing it from the engine. Cylinder head warpage can result if a warm or hot cylinder head is removed.

❋❋ WARNING

Place clean shop towels over exposed engine cavities. Carefully remove the towels so foreign material is not dropped into the engine.

❋❋ WARNING

The cylinder head bolts must be discarded and new bolts must be installed. They are tighten-to-yield designed and cannot be reused.

❋❋ WARNING

Do not use metal scrapers, wire brushes, power abrasive discs or other abrasive means to clean the sealing surfaces. These tools cause scratches and gouges that make leak paths. Use a plastic scraping tool to remove all traces of the head gasket.

❋❋ WARNING

Aluminum surfaces are soft and can be scratched easily. Never place the cylinder head gasket surface, unprotected, on a bench surface.

43. Remove the bolts and the cylinder head. Discard the cylinder head gasket. Discard the cylinder head bolts.

❋❋ WARNING

Do not use metal scrapers, wire brushes, power abrasive discs or other abrasive means to clean the sealing surfaces. These tools cause scratches and gouges that make leak paths. Use a plastic scraping tool to remove all traces of the head gasket.

❋❋ WARNING

Observe all warnings or cautions and follow all application directions contained on the packaging of the silicone gasket remover and the metal surface prep.

➡If there is no residual gasket material present, metal surface prep can be used to clean and prepare the surfaces.

44. Clean the cylinder head-to-cylinder block mating surfaces of both the cylinder head and the cylinder block.

45. Remove any large deposits of silicone or gasket material with a plastic scraper.

46. Apply silicone gasket remover, following package directions, and allow to set for several minutes.

47. Remove the silicone gasket remover with a plastic scraper. A second application of silicone gasket remover may be required if residual traces of silicone or gasket material remain.

48. Apply metal surface prep, following package directions, to remove any remaining traces of oil or coolant, and to prepare the surfaces to bond with the new gasket. Do not attempt to make the metal shiny. Some staining of the metal surfaces is normal.

➡Make sure all cylinder head surfaces are clear of any gasket material, RTV, oil and coolant. The cylinder head surface must be clean and dry before running a flatness check.

➡Use a straightedge that is calibrated by the manufacturer to be flat with 0.005 mm (0.0002 in.) per running foot length. For example, if the straightedge is 61 cm (24 in.) long, the machine edge must be flat with 0.010 mm (0.0004 in.) from end to end.

49. Support the cylinder head on a bench with the head gasket side up. Inspect all areas of the deck face with a straightedge, paying particular attention to the oil pressure feed area. The cylinder head must not have

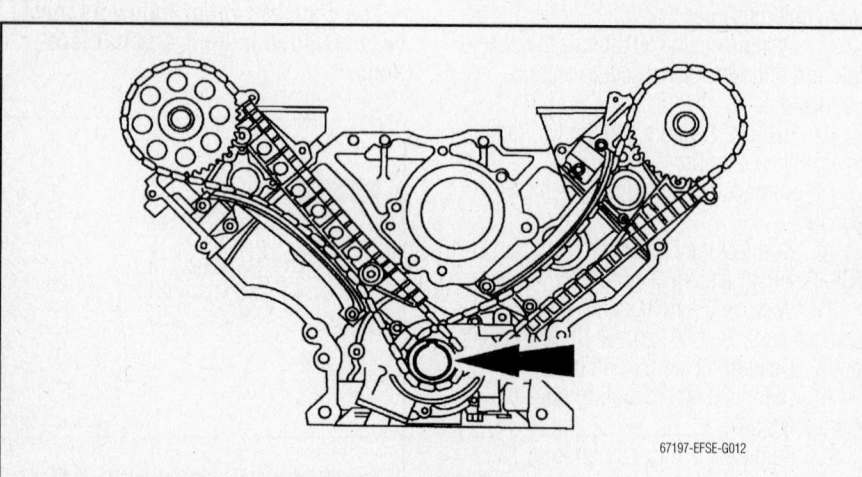

Fig. 92 Keyway at the 12 o'clock position—4.6L Engine

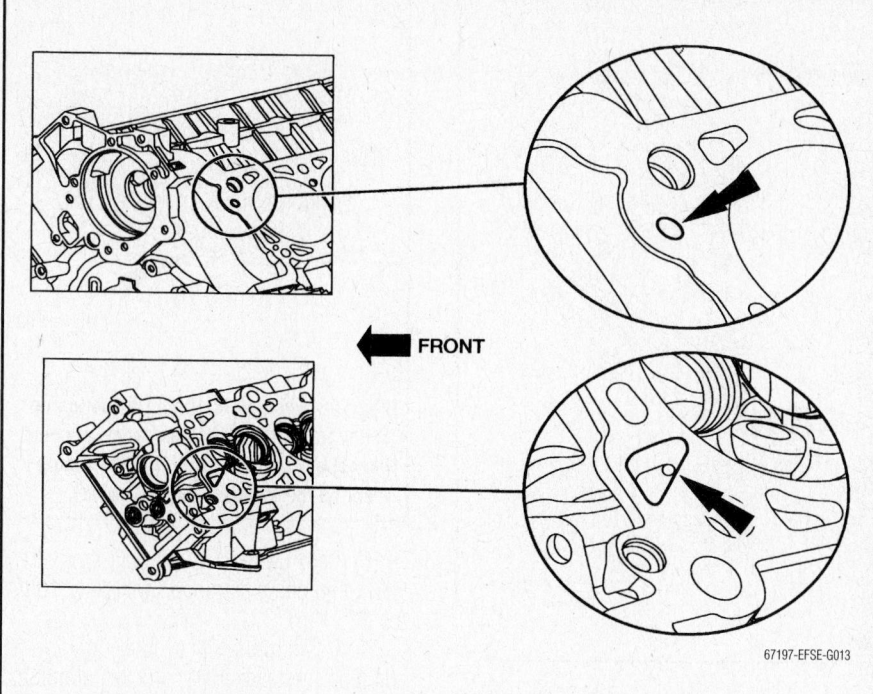

FRONT

Fig. 93 When checking flatness, pay particular attention to these areas—4.6L Engine

67197-EFSE-G013

depressions deeper than 0.0254 mm (0.001 in.) across a 38.1 mm (1.5 in.) square area, or scratches more than 0.0254 mm (0.001 in.).

To install:
All cylinder heads

⁕ **WARNING**

Make sure all coolant residue and foreign material are cleaned from the block surface and cylinder bore.

⁕ **WARNING**

The use of sealing aids. The gasket must be installed dry.

⁕ **WARNING**

The cylinder head bolts must be discarded and new bolts installed. They are tighten-to-yield designed and cannot be reused.

➡ Do not turn the crankshaft until instructed to do so.

50. Using the lifting tools, position the cylinder head gaskets and cylinder heads over the dowels and install the cylinder head bolts loosely.

51. Tighten the bolts in the sequence shown.

    a. Stage 1: Tighten to 40 Nm (30 ft. lbs.).

    b. Stage 2: Tighten an additional 90 degrees.

    c. Stage 3: Tighten an additional 90 degrees.

All cylinder heads

⁕ **WARNING**

Timing chain procedures must be followed exactly or damage to valves and pistons will result.

52. Compress the tensioner plunger, using a vise.

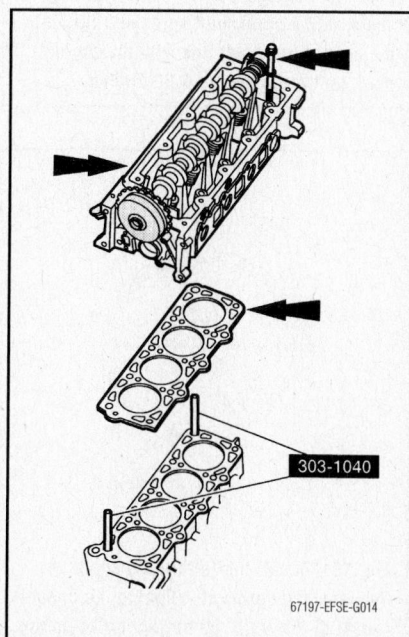

303-1040

67197-EFSE-G014

Fig. 94 Dowel installation—4.6L Engine

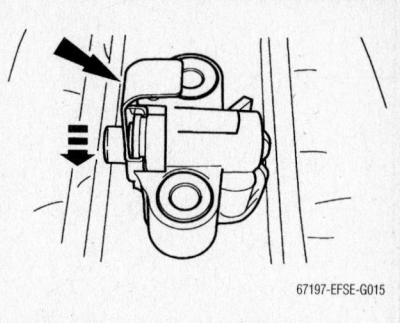

67197-EFSE-G015

Fig. 95 Plunger held by a retaining clip—4.6L Engine

53. Install a retaining clip on the tensioner to hold the plunger in during installation.

54. Remove the tensioner from the vise. If the copper links are not visible, mark one link on one end and one link on the other end, and use as timing marks.

55. Install the crankshaft sprocket, making sure the flange faces forward.

56. Position the left timing chain guide.

57. Install and tighten the left bolts.

58. Position the right timing chain guide.

59. Install and tighten the right bolts.

60. Rotate the right camshaft sprocket until the timing mark is approximately at the 11 o'clock position. Rotate the left

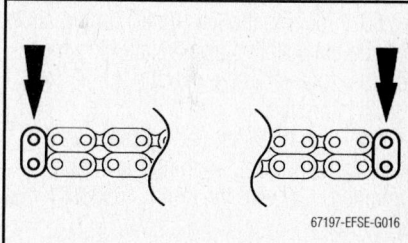

67197-EFSE-G016

Fig. 96 If the copper links are not visible, mark one link on one end and one link on the other end, and use as timing marks—4.6L Engine

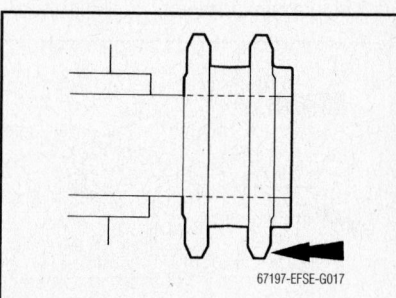

67197-EFSE-G017

Fig. 97 Install the crankshaft sprocket, making sure the flange faces forward—4.6L Engine

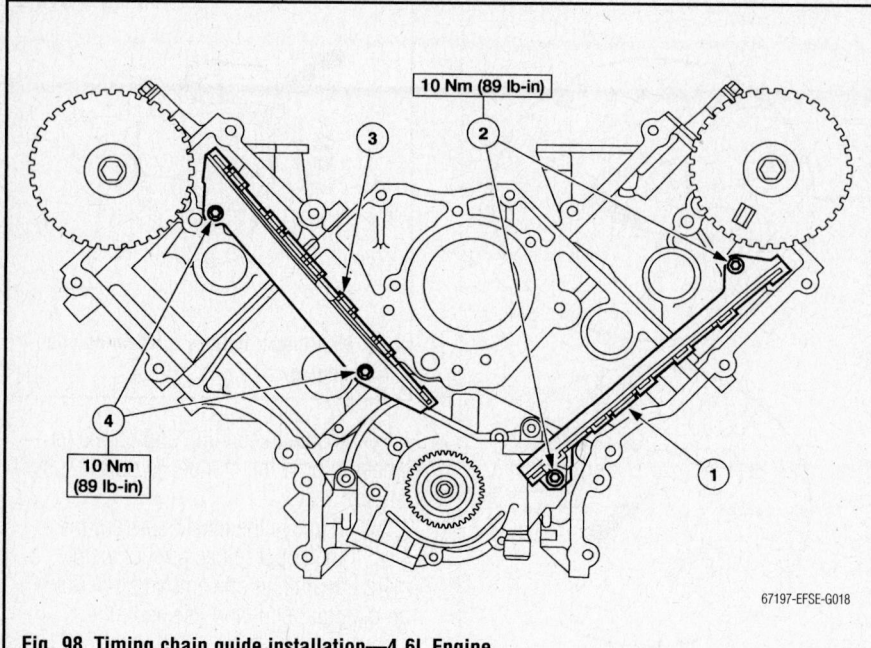

Fig. 98 Timing chain guide installation—4.6L Engine

camshaft sprocket until the timing mark is approximately at the 12 o'clock position.

➡**The number one cylinder is at top dead center (TDC) when the stud on the engine block fits into the slot in the handle of the special tool.**

61. Position the crankshaft so the number one cylinder is at TDC with the special tool.
62. Remove the Crankshaft Holding Tool.
63. Position the left (inner) timing chain on the crankshaft sprocket, aligning the copper (marked) link with the timing mark on the sprocket.
64. Install the left timing chain on the camshaft sprocket, aligning the copper (marked) link with the timing marks on the sprocket.

➡**The left timing chain tensioner arm has a bump near the dowel hole for identification.**

65. Position the left timing chain tensioner arm on the dowel pin and install the left timing chain tensioner.

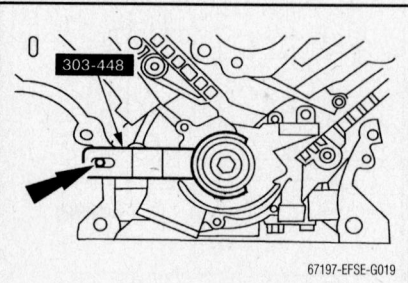

Fig. 99 Crankshaft alignment tool installed—4.6L Engine

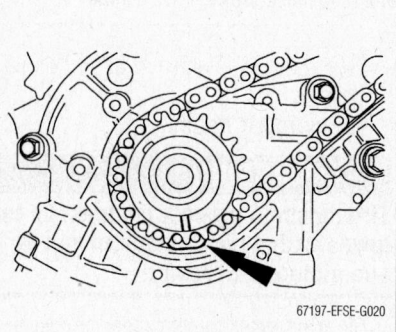

Fig. 100 Position the left (inner) timing chain on the crankshaft sprocket, aligning the copper (marked) link with the timing mark on the sprocket—4.6L Engine

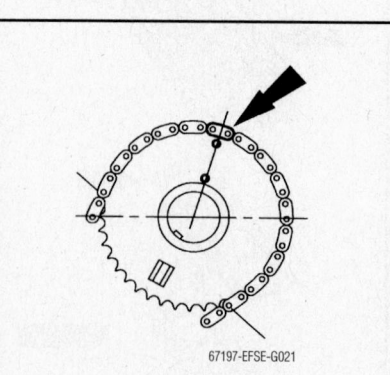

Fig. 101 Install the left timing chain on the camshaft sprocket, aligning the copper (marked) link with the timing marks on the sprocket—4.6L Engine

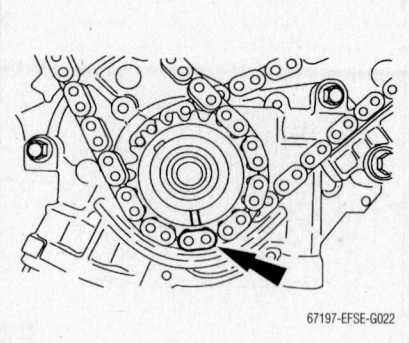

Fig. 102 Position the right (outer) timing chain on the crankshaft sprocket, aligning the copper (marked) link with the timing mark on the sprocket—4.6L Engine

66. Remove the retaining clip from the left timing chain tensioner. Torque to 18 ft. lbs. (25 Nm).
67. Position the right (outer) timing chain on the crankshaft sprocket, aligning the copper (marked) link with the timing mark on the sprocket.
68. Install the right timing chain on the camshaft sprocket, aligning the copper (marked) link with the timing marks on the sprocket.
69. Position the right timing chain tensioner arm on the dowel pin and install the right timing chain tensioner. Torque to 18 ft. lbs. (25 Nm).
70. Remove the retaining clip from the right timing chain tensioner. Make sure that the copper (marked) chain links are lined up with the dots on the crankshaft sprockets and the camshaft sprocket.
71. Install the crankshaft sensor ring on the crankshaft.

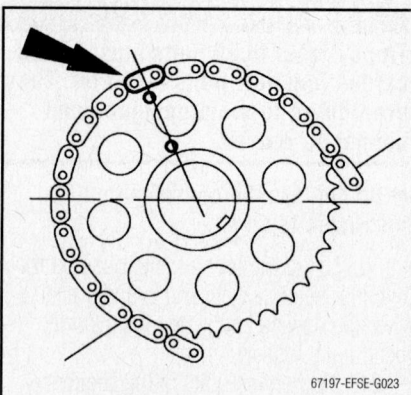

Fig. 103 Install the right timing chain on the camshaft sprocket, aligning the copper (marked) link with the timing marks on the sprocket—4.6L Engine

※※ WARNING

Do not use metal scrapers, wire brushes, power abrasive discs or other abrasive means to clean the sealing surfaces. These tools cause scratches and gouges which make leak paths. Use a plastic scraping tool to remove all traces of old sealant.

➡️If the engine front cover is not secured within four minutes, the sealant must be removed and the sealing area cleaned. To clean the sealing area, use silicone gasket remover and metal surface prep. Follow the directions on the packaging. Failure to follow this procedure can cause future oil leakage.

➡️Make sure that the engine front cover gasket is in place on the engine front cover before installation.

72. Apply a bead of silicone gasket and sealant along the cylinder head-to-cylinder block surface and the oil pan-to-cylinder block surface, at the locations shown.

73. Install a new engine front cover gasket on the engine front cover. Position the engine front cover. Install the fasteners finger-tight.

74. Tighten the engine front cover fasteners in sequence in three stages.

 a. Stage 1: Tighten fasteners 1 through 5 to 25 Nm (18 ft. lbs.).

 b. Stage 2: Tighten fasteners 6 and 7 to 25 Nm (18 ft. lbs.).

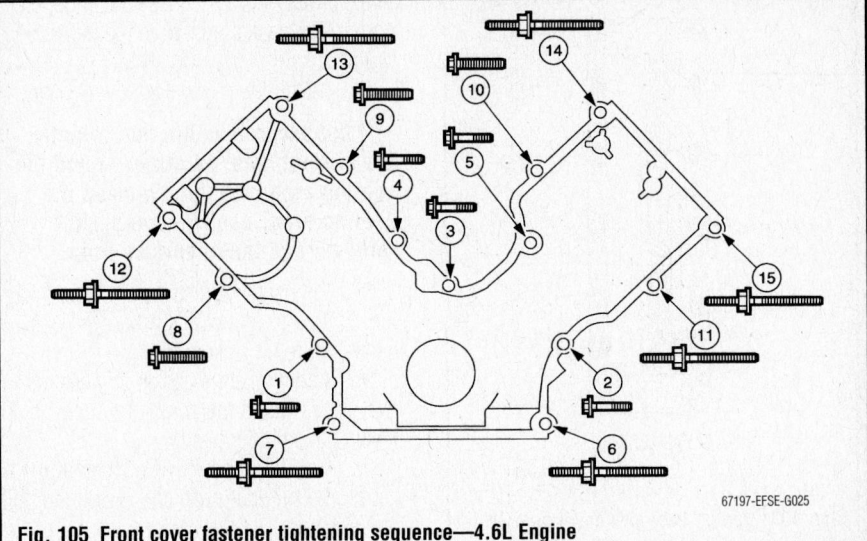

Fig. 105 Front cover fastener tightening sequence—4.6L Engine

 c. Stage 3: Tighten fasteners 8 through 15 to 25 Nm (18 ft. lbs.).

75. Install the left camshaft position (CMP) sensor and the bolt.

76. Lubricate the new O-ring seal with clean engine oil prior to installation.

77. Lubricate the engine front cover and the crankshaft seal inner lip with clean engine oil. Use a driver to install the crankshaft seal into the engine front cover.

➡️If not secured within four minutes, the sealant must be removed and the sealing area cleaned. To clean the sealing area, use silicone gasket remover and metal surface prep. Follow the directions on the packaging. Failure to follow this procedure can cause future oil leakage.

78. Apply silicone gasket and sealant to the Woodruff key slot on the crankshaft pulley. Use the special tool to install the crankshaft pulley.

79. Tighten the new crankshaft pulley bolt in four stages.

 a. Stage 1: Tighten to 90 Nm (66 ft. lbs.).

 b. Stage 2: Loosen 360 degrees.

 c. Stage 3: Tighten to 50 Nm (37 ft. lbs.).

 d. Stage 4: Tighten an additional 90 degrees.

80. Install the three accessory drive belt idler pulleys, the coolant pump pulley and the bolts.

81. Position the accessory drive belt tensioner and install the bolts.

82. Install a suitable tool between the valve spring coils to prevent valve stem seal damage.

➡️The camshaft roller followers must be reinstalled in their original locations.

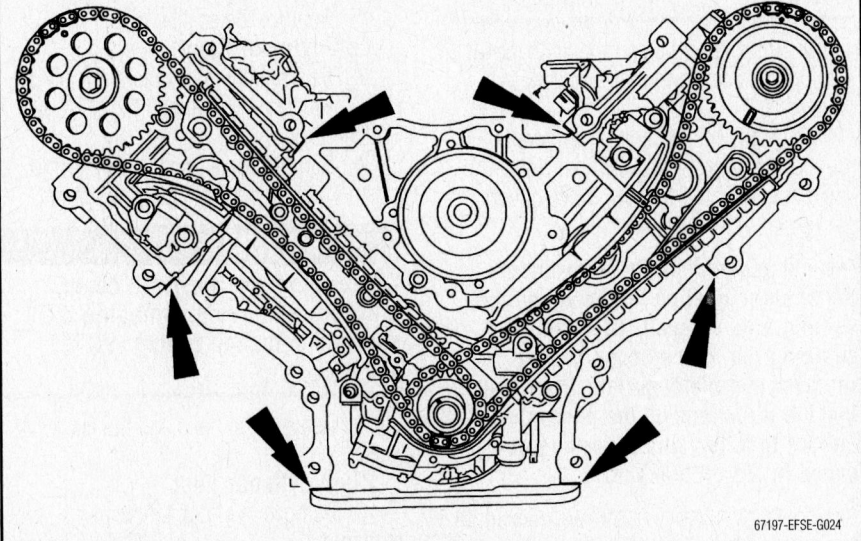

Fig. 104 Apply a bead of silicone gasket and sealant along the cylinder head-to-cylinder block surface and the oil pan-to-cylinder block surface, at the locations shown—4.6L Engine

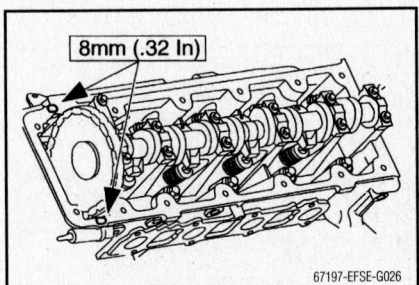

Fig. 106 Apply silicone gasket and sealant in two places where the engine front cover meets the cylinder head—4.6L Engine

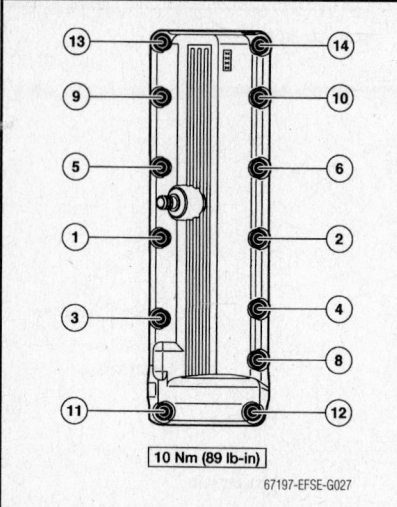

10 Nm (89 lb-in)

67197-EFSE-G027

Fig. 107 Tighten the valve cover bolts in the sequence shown—4.6L Engine

➡**Position the cam lobe away from the valve stem prior to installing each camshaft roller follower.**

83. Use a suitable tool to compress the valve springs, and install the camshaft roller follower. Remove the special tool.

➡**The camshaft roller followers must be reinstalled in their original locations.**

84. Repeat the previous four steps for each of the camshaft roller followers.

85. Install the radio frequency interference capacitors.

Left cylinder head

✳✳ WARNING

Do not use metal scrapers, wire brushes, power abrasive discs or other abrasive means to clean sealing surfaces. These tools cause scratches and gouges which make leak paths.

86. Inspect and clean the valve cover sealing surfaces with metal surface cleaner.

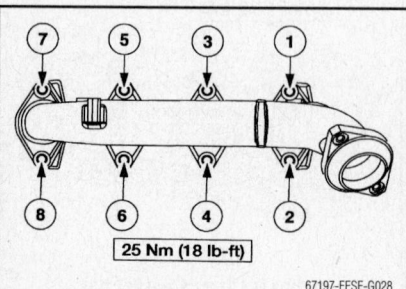

25 Nm (18 lb-ft)

67197-EFSE-G028

Fig. 108 Install the left exhaust manifold nuts in the sequence shown—4.6L Engine

87. Apply instant adhesive completely around the gasket groove in the left valve cover.

88. Install the new valve cover gasket.

➡**If not secured within four minutes, the sealant must be removed and the sealing area cleaned. To clean the sealing area, use silicone gasket remover and metal surface prep.**

89. Follow the directions on the packaging. Failure to follow this procedure can cause future oil leakage.

90. Apply silicone gasket and sealant in two places where the engine front cover meets the cylinder head.

91. Position the left valve cover and gasket on the cylinder head and install the bolts loosely.

92. Tighten the valve cover bolts in the sequence shown.

➡**Lubricate the O-ring seal with clean engine oil.**

93. Install the oil level indicator tube.

94. Install a new O-ring seal on the oil level indicator tube.

95. Install the oil level indicator tube.

96. Install the bolt.

97. Install the left exhaust manifold and the exhaust manifold gasket. Tighten the nuts in the sequence shown.

Right cylinder head

✳✳ WARNING

Do not use metal scrapers, wire brushes, power abrasive discs or other abrasive means to clean sealing surfaces. These tools cause scratches and gouges which make leak paths.

98. Inspect and clean the valve cover sealing surfaces with metal surface cleaner.

99. Apply instant adhesive completely around the gasket groove in the right valve cover. Install the new valve cover gasket.

➡**If not secured within four minutes, the sealant must be removed and the sealing area cleaned. To clean the sealing area, use silicone gasket remover and metal surface prep. Follow the directions on the packaging. Failure to follow this procedure can cause future oil leakage.**

100. Apply silicone gasket and sealant in two places where the engine front cover meets the cylinder head.

101. Position the right valve cover and gasket on the cylinder head and install the bolts loosely.

102. Tighten the valve cover bolts in the sequence shown.

103. Install the right exhaust manifold gaskets and the exhaust manifold. Tighten the nuts in the sequence shown.

104. Slide the heater outlet tube forward with a new O-ring seal into the cylinder block. Lubricate the O-ring seal with engine coolant.

105. Install the heater outlet tube studs.

106. Connect the coolant hoses to the heater outlet tube.

All cylinder heads

107. Connect the right radio ignition interference capacitor electrical connector.

108. Connect the left radio ignition interference capacitor and cylinder head temperature (CHT) sensor electrical connectors.

109. Connect the CMP sensor electrical connectors.

110. Connect the CKP sensor electrical connector.

111. Install a suitable tool.

112. Using a suitable floor crane, remove the engine from the engine stand.

113. Install the flexplate or the flywheel and bolts. Tighten the bolts in the sequence shown.

114. Install the engine.

5.4L Engine

See Figures 109 through 130.

1. Before servicing the vehicle, refer to the Precautions Section.

2. Remove the engine.

3. Remove the bolts and the flexplate or the flywheel.

4. Install the engine onto a suitable engine stand.

5. Remove the special tool.

Left cylinder head

6. Remove the left exhaust manifold.

7. Remove the bolt and the oil level indicator tube.

8. Remove the engine wiring harness retainers from the left valve cover studs.

✳✳ WARNING

When removing the valve cover, make sure to avoid damaging the variable camshaft timing (VCT) solenoid.

9. Remove the bolts and the left valve cover.

Right cylinder head

10. Remove the right exhaust manifold.

11. Remove the nuts.

12. Remove the right exhaust manifold.

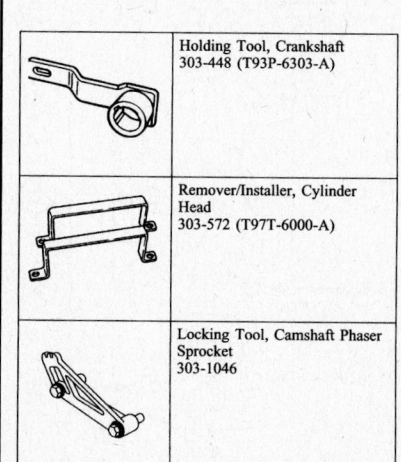

	Alignment Pins, Cylinder Head 303-1040 (SR-015486)
	Installer, Crankshaft Vibration Damper 303-102 (T74P-6316-B)
	Installer, Crankshaft Front Oil Seal 303-635
	Installer, Front Cover Oil Seal 303-335 (T88T-6701-A)
	Modular Engine Lift Bracket 303-F047 (014-00073) or equivalent
	Compressor, Valve Spring 303-1039

67197-EFSE-G033

Fig. 109 Special tools needed for this procedure. These tools are referred to in the following procedure

	Holding Tool, Crankshaft 303-448 (T93P-6303-A)
	Remover/Installer, Cylinder Head 303-572 (T97T-6000-A)
	Locking Tool, Camshaft Phaser Sprocket 303-1046

67197-EFSE-G034

Fig. 110 Special tools needed for this procedure. These tools are referred to in the following procedure

13. Remove and discard the right exhaust manifold gasket.

14. Remove the engine wiring harness retainers from the right valve cover studs.

> ❋❋ **WARNING**
>
> **When removing the valve cover, make sure to avoid damaging the variable camshaft timing (VCT) solenoid.**

15. Remove the bolts and the right valve cover.

16. Remove the stud.

All cylinder heads

17. Remove the bolts, the coolant pump pulley and the accessory drive belt idler pulleys.

18. Remove the bolt and washer and using a puller set, remove the crankshaft pulley. Discard the crankshaft bolt.

19. Using a suitable tool, remove the crankshaft seal.

20. Remove the bolts and the accessory drive belt tensioner.

21. Disconnect the left and right radio ignition interference capacitor electrical connectors.

22. Remove the nuts and the two radio interference capacitors.

23. Disconnect the camshaft position (CMP) sensor electrical connectors.

24. Remove the bolt and the right CMP sensor.

25. Remove the bolt and the left CMP sensor.

26. Disconnect the crankshaft position (CKP) sensor electrical connector.

27. Remove the oil pan front bolts.

28. Remove the bolts.

> ❋❋ **WARNING**
>
> **Do not use metal scrapers, wire brushes, power abrasive discs or other abrasive means to clean the sealing surfaces. These tools cause scratches and gouges which make leak paths. Use a plastic scraping tool to remove all traces of old sealant.**

29. Remove the engine front cover from the front cover-to-cylinder block dowels.

30. Remove the engine front cover gaskets.

31. Clean the mating surfaces with silicone gasket remover and metal surface prep. Follow the directions on the packaging.

32. Inspect the mating surfaces.

> ❋❋ **WARNING**
>
> **Do not allow the valve keepers to fall off of the valve or the valve can drop into the cylinder.**

➡ **It may be necessary to push the valve down while compressing the valve spring.**

➡ **The roller followers must be installed in their original positions.**

33. Using a suitable tool, remove all of the roller followers. Record the roller follower positions.

34. Position the crankshaft keyway at the 12 o'clock position.

35. Remove the bolts, the left timing chain tensioner and tensioner arm.

36. Remove the bolts, the right timing chain tensioner and tensioner arm.

37. Remove the ignition pulse wheel from the crankshaft.

38. Remove the right timing chain from the camshaft sprocket.

39. Remove the right timing chain from the crankshaft sprocket.

40. Remove the left timing chain from the camshaft sprocket.

41. Remove the left timing chain and crankshaft sprocket.

42. Remove both timing chain guides.

> ❋❋ **WARNING**
>
> **Use only hand tools to remove the camshaft phaser sprocket assembly or damage can occur to the camshaft or camshaft phaser sprocket.**

43. If disassembly of the cylinder head is required, using a suitable tool, loosen the camshaft phaser sprocket bolt.

44. Install a suitable tool onto the left cylinder head. Install a suitable tool onto the right cylinder head.

> ❋❋ **WARNING**
>
> **The cylinder head must be cool before removing it from the engine. Cylinder head warpage can result if a warm or hot cylinder head is removed.**

> ❋❋ **WARNING**
>
> **Do not use the variable camshaft timing (VCT) phaser sprocket as a lifting point or leveraging device when removing the cylinder head or damage to the VCT phaser sprocket can occur.**

✥ WARNING

Place clean shop towels over exposed engine cavities. Carefully remove the towels so foreign material is not dropped into the engine.

✥ WARNING

The cylinder head bolts must be discarded and new bolts must be installed. They are tighten-to-yield designed and cannot be reused.

✥ WARNING

Do not use metal scrapers, wire brushes, power abrasive discs or other abrasive means to clean the sealing surfaces. These tools cause scratches and gouges that make leak paths. Use a plastic scraping tool to remove all traces of the head gasket.

✥ WARNING

Aluminum surfaces are soft and can be scratched easily. Never place the cylinder head gasket surface, unprotected, on a bench surface.

45. Remove the bolts and the cylinder head. Discard the cylinder head gasket. Discard the cylinder head bolts.

✥ WARNING

Do not use metal scrapers, wire brushes, power abrasive discs or other abrasive means to clean the sealing surfaces. These tools cause scratches and gouges that make leak paths. Use a plastic scraping tool to remove all traces of the head gasket.

✥ WARNING

Observe all warnings or cautions and follow all application directions contained on the packaging of the silicone gasket remover and the metal surface prep.

➡ If there is no residual gasket material present, metal surface prep can be used to clean and prepare the surfaces.

46. Clean the cylinder head-to-cylinder block mating surfaces of both the cylinder head and the cylinder block.

47. Remove any large deposits of silicone or gasket material with a plastic scraper.

48. Apply silicone gasket remover, following package directions, and allow to set for several minutes.

49. Remove the silicone gasket remover with a plastic scraper. A second application of silicone gasket remover may be required if residual traces of silicone or gasket material remain.

50. Apply metal surface prep, following package directions, to remove any remaining traces of oil or coolant, and to prepare the surfaces to bond with the new gasket. Do not attempt to make the metal shiny. Some staining of the metal surfaces is normal.

➡ Make sure all cylinder head surfaces and engine block surfaces are clear of any gasket material, RTV, oil and coolant. The cylinder head and engine block surfaces must be clean and dry before running a flatness check.

➡ Use a straightedge that is calibrated by the manufacturer to be flat within 0.005 mm (0.0002 in) per running foot of length. For example, if the straightedge is 61 cm (24 in) long, the machined edge must be flat with 0.010 mm (0.0004 in) from end to end.

51. Support the cylinder head on a bench with the head gasket side up. Inspect all areas of the deck face with a straightedge, paying particular attention to the oil pressure feed area. The cylinder head must not have depressions deeper than 0.0254 mm (0.001 in) across a 38.1 mm (1.5 in) square area, or scratches more than 0.0254 mm (0.001 in).

To install:
All cylinder heads

✳✳ WARNING

Make sure all coolant residue and foreign material are cleaned from the block surface and cylinder bore.

✳✳ WARNING

The use of sealing aids (aviation cement, copper spray, and glue) is not permitted. The gasket must be installed dry.

✳✳ WARNING

The cylinder head bolts must be discarded and new bolts installed. They are tighten-to-yield designed and cannot be reused.

✳✳ WARNING

Do not allow the cylinder head alignment pins to contact the cylinder head gasket or cylinder head sealing surfaces or damage can occur to the cylinder head or cylinder head gasket.

➡ Do not turn the crankshaft until instructed to do so.

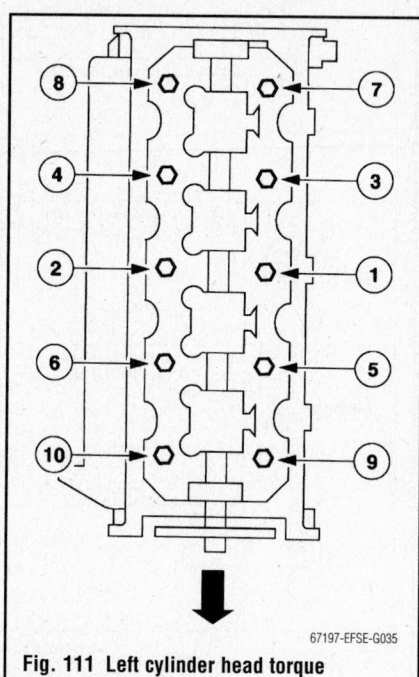

67197-EFSE-G035

Fig. 111 Left cylinder head torque sequence—5.4L engine

67197-EFSE-G036

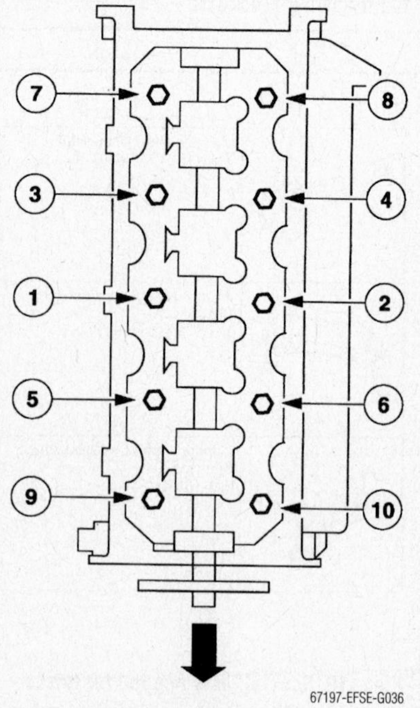

Fig. 112 Right cylinder head torque sequence—5.4L engine

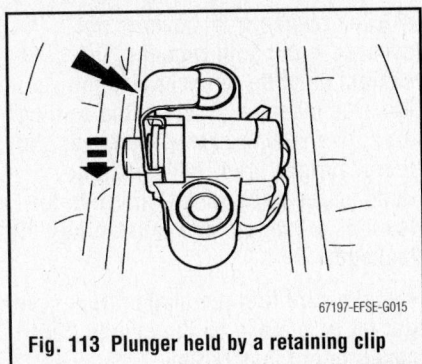

Fig. 113 Plunger held by a retaining clip

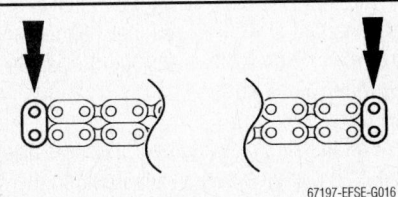

Fig. 114 If the copper links are not visible, mark one link on one end and one link on the other end, and use as timing marks

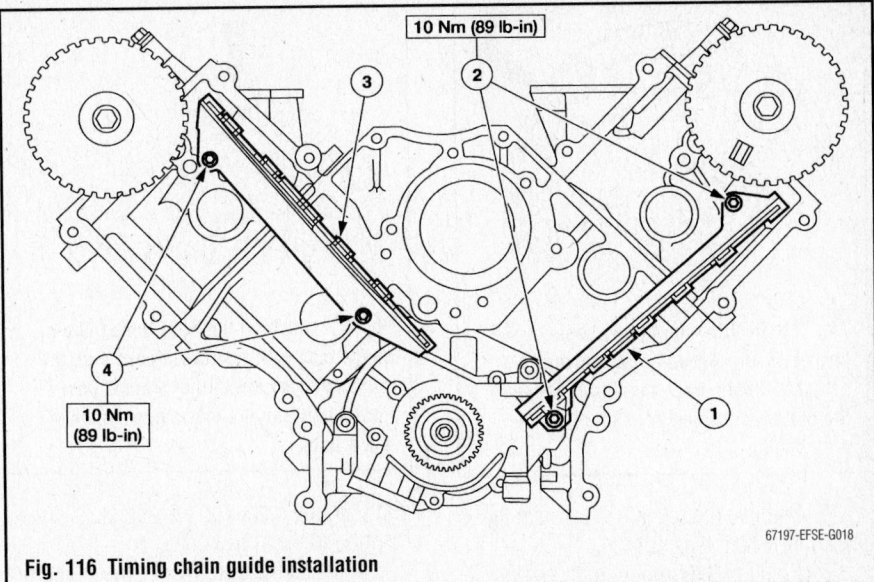

Fig. 116 Timing chain guide installation

52. Using the cylinder head alignment pins, position the cylinder head gasket and cylinder head onto the dowels and install the cylinder head bolts loosely.

53. Tighten the bolts in the sequence shown.

    a. Stage 1: Tighten to 40 Nm (30 ft. lbs.).

    b. Stage 2: Tighten an additional 90 degrees.

    c. Stage 3: Tighten an additional 90 degrees.

54. Remove the special tool.

❋❋ WARNING

Timing chain procedures must be followed exactly or damage to valves and pistons will result.

55. Compress the tensioner plunger, using a vice.

56. Install a retaining clip on the tensioner to hold the plunger in during installation.

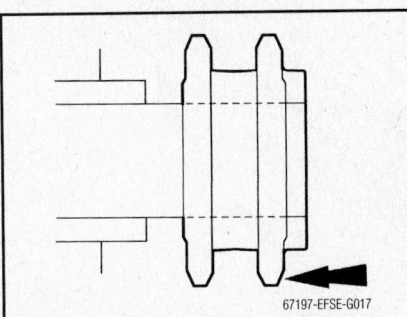

Fig. 115 Install the crankshaft sprocket, making sure the flange faces forward

57. Remove the tensioner from the vise. If the copper links are not visible, mark two links on one end and one link on the other end, and use as timing marks.

❋❋ WARNING

Crankshaft keyway must be in the 12 o'clock position.

58. Install the timing chain guides.

59. Position the left timing chain guide.

60. Install the crankshaft sprocket, making sure the flange faces forward.

❋❋ WARNING

Only use hand tools to install the camshaft phaser sprocket assembly or damage may occur to the camshaft or camshaft phaser unit.

➡ **This step is only required if cylinder head was disassembled.**

61. Using a suitable tool, tighten the bolts in two stages:

    a. Stage 1: Tighten to 40 Nm (30 ft. lbs.).

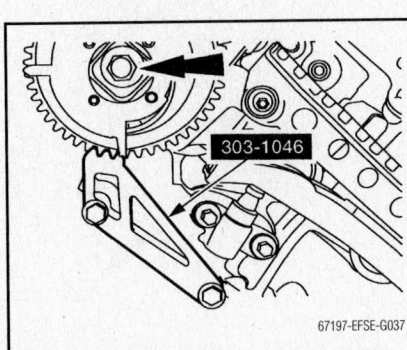

Fig. 117 Camshaft phaser sprocket holding tool—5.4L engine

    b. Stage 2: Tighten an additional 90 degrees.

62. Remove the special tool.

63. Position the lower end of the left (inner) timing chain on the crankshaft sprocket, aligning the timing mark on the outer flange of the crankshaft sprocket with the single copper (marked) link on the chain.

➡ **Make sure the upper half of the timing chain is below the tensioner arm dowel.**

64. Position the timing chain on the camshaft sprocket with the camshaft sprocket timing mark positioned between the two copper (marked) chain links.

➡ **The left timing chain tensioner arm has a bump near the dowel hole for identification.**

65. Position the left timing chain tensioner arm on the dowel pin and install the left timing chain tensioner.

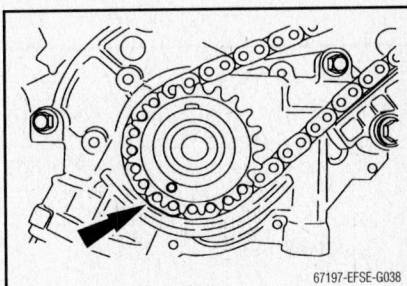

Fig. 118 Position the lower end of the left (inner) timing chain on the crankshaft sprocket, aligning the timing mark on the outer flange of the crankshaft sprocket with the single copper (marked) link on the chain—5.4L engine

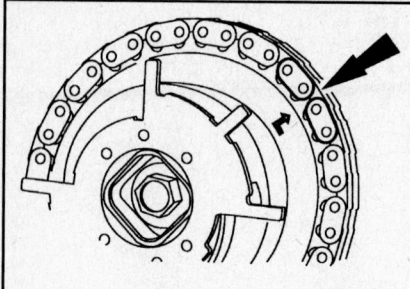

Fig. 119 Position the timing chain on the camshaft sprocket with the camshaft sprocket timing mark positioned between the two copper (marked) chain links— 5.4L engine

66. Remove the retaining clip from the left timing chain tensioner.

67. Position the lower end of the right (outer) timing chain on the crankshaft sprocket, aligning the timing mark on the sprocket with the single copper (marked) chain link.

➡**The lower half of the timing chain must be positioned above the tensioner arm dowel.**

68. Position the right timing chain on the camshaft sprocket. Make sure the camshaft sprocket timing mark is positioned between the two copper (marked) chain links.

69. Position the right timing chain tensioner arm on the dowel pin and install the right timing chain tensioner.

70. Remove the retaining clip from the right timing chain tensioner.

➡**Both camshaft phaser sprockets are identical. Refer to the R timing mark to identify the right camshaft phaser sprocket and the L timing mark to identify the left camshaft phaser sprocket.**

71. As a post-check, verify correct alignment of all timing marks. Make sure the R

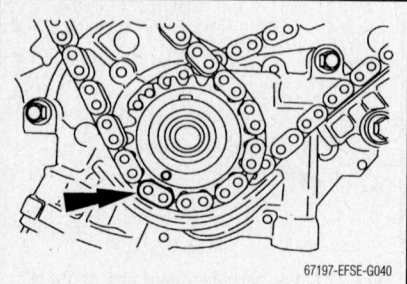

Fig. 120 Position the lower end of the right (outer) timing chain on the crankshaft sprocket, aligning the timing mark on the sprocket with the single copper (marked) chain link

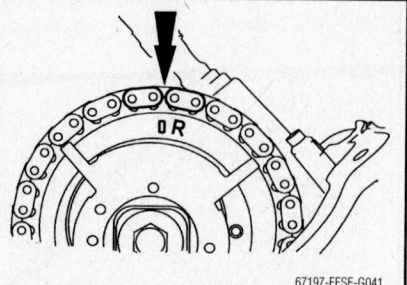

Fig. 121 Position the right timing chain on the camshaft sprocket. Make sure the camshaft sprocket timing mark is positioned between the two copper (marked) chain links

and L timing marks on the sprockets correspond to the above note.

72. Install the crankshaft sensor ring on the crankshaft.

➡**Lubricate the camshaft roller followers using clean engine oil.**

➡**Using the mark on each camshaft roller follower, make sure it is returned to its original position.**

73. Using a suitable tool, install all of the camshaft roller followers.

✳✳ WARNING

Do not use metal scrapers, wire brushes, power abrasive discs or other abrasive means to clean the sealing surfaces. These tools cause scratches and gouges which make leak paths. Use a plastic scraping tool to remove all traces of old sealant.

➡If the engine front cover is not secured within four minutes, the sealant must be removed and the sealing area cleaned. To clean the sealing area, use silicone gasket remover and metal surface prep. Follow the directions on the packaging. Failure to follow this procedure can cause future oil leakage.

➡Make sure that the engine front cover gasket is in place on the engine front cover before installation.

74. Apply a bead of silicone gasket and sealant along the cylinder head-to-cylinder block surface and the oil pan-to-cylinder block surface, at the locations shown.

75. Install a new engine front cover gasket on the engine front cover. Position the engine front cover. Install the fasteners finger-tight.

76. Tighten the engine front cover fasteners in sequence in two stages.
   a. Stage 1: Tighten fasteners 1 through 15 to 25 Nm (18 ft. lbs.).
   b. Stage 2: Tighten fasteners 6 and 7 to 48 Nm (35 ft. lbs.).
   c. Loosely install the pan-to-case bolts, then tighten the bolts in two stages, in the sequence shown.
   d. Stage 1: Tighten to 20 Nm (15 ft. lbs.).
   e. Stage 2: Tighten an additional 60 degrees.

77. Install the left camshaft position (CMP) sensor and the bolt.

78. Lubricate the new O-ring seal with clean engine oil prior to installation.

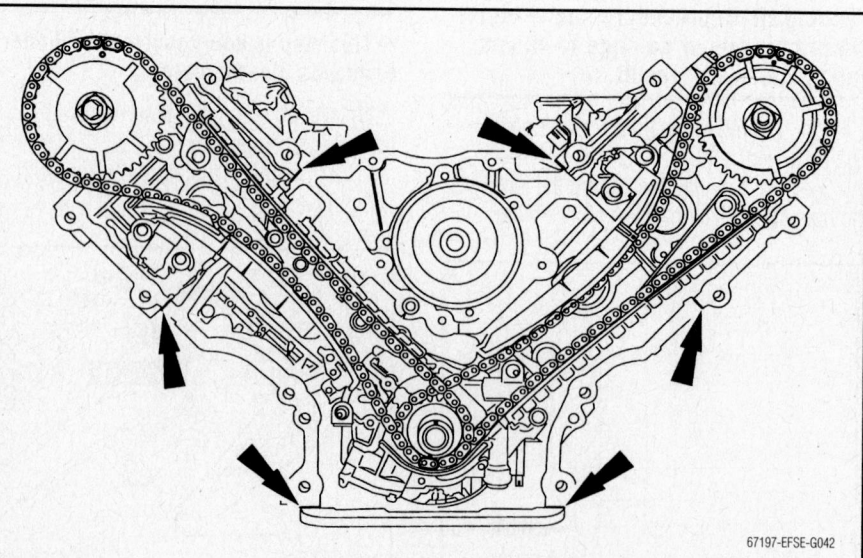

Fig. 122 Apply a bead of silicone gasket and sealant along the cylinder head-to-cylinder block surface and the oil pan-to-cylinder block surface, at the locations shown—5.4L engine

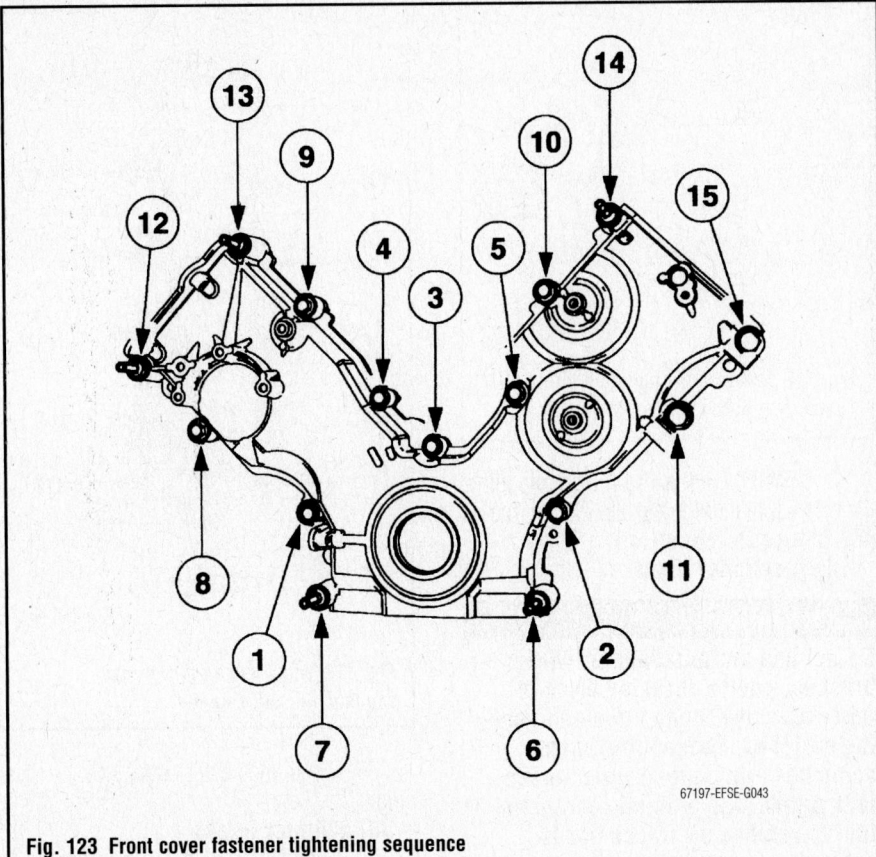

Fig. 123 Front cover fastener tightening sequence

79. Install the right CMP sensor and the bolt.

80. Lubricate the new O-ring seal with clean engine oil prior to installation.

81. Lubricate the engine front cover and the crankshaft seal inner lip with clean engine oil.

82. Use the special tools to install the crankshaft seal into the engine front cover.

83. If not secured within four minutes, the sealant must be removed and the sealing area cleaned. To clean the sealing area, use silicone gasket remover and metal surface prep. Follow the directions on the packaging. Failure to follow this procedure can cause future oil leakage.

84. Apply silicone gasket and sealant to the Woodruff key slot on the crankshaft pulley. Use a suitable tool to install the crankshaft pulley.

85. Tighten the new crankshaft pulley bolt in four stages.

    a. Stage 1: Tighten to 90 Nm (66 ft. lbs.).

    b. Stage 2: Loosen 360 degrees.

    c. Stage 3: Tighten to 50 Nm (37 ft. lbs.).

    d. Stage 4: Tighten an additional 90 degrees.

86. Install the three accessory drive belt idler pulleys, the coolant pump pulley and the bolts. Torque all bolts to 18 ft. lbs. (25 Nm).

87. Position the accessory drive belt tensioner and install the bolts. Torque all bolts to 18 ft. lbs. (25 Nm).

88. Install the radio frequency interference capacitors.

Left cylinder head

✱✱ WARNING

Do not use metal scrapers, wire brushes, power abrasive discs or other abrasive means to clean sealing surfaces. These tools cause scratches and gouges which make leak paths. Use a plastic scraping tool to remove all traces of old sealant. Inspect and clean the valve cover sealing surfaces with silicone gasket remover and metal surface prep. Follow the directions on the packaging.

➡**If not secured within four minutes, the sealant must be removed and the sealing area cleaned. To clean the sealing area, use silicone gasket remover and metal surface prep. Follow the directions on the packaging. Failure to follow this procedure can cause future oil leakage.**

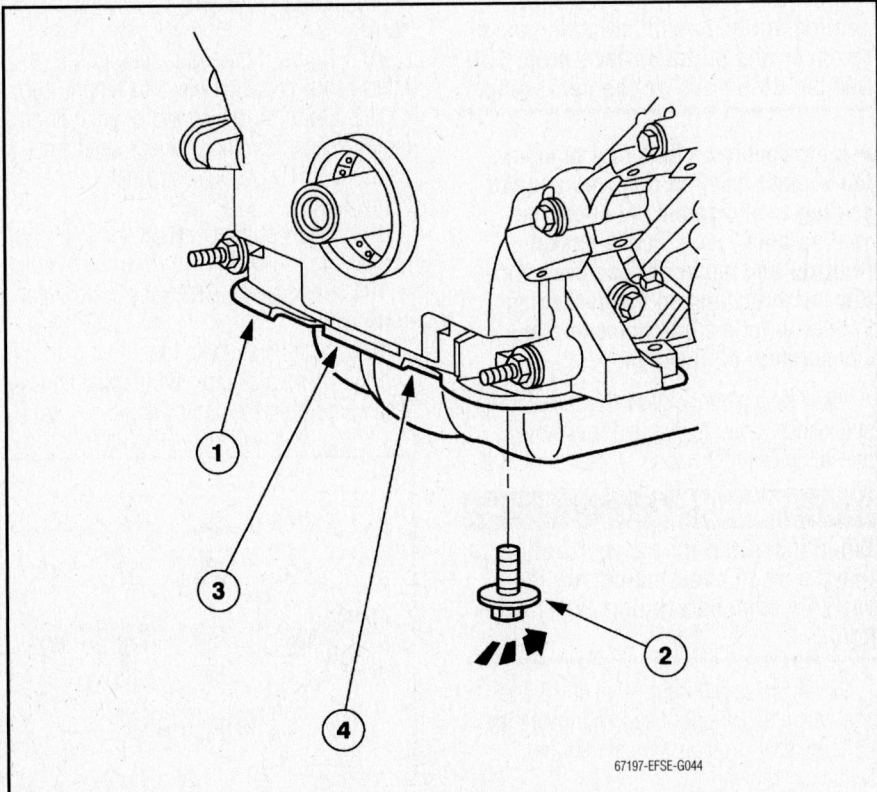

Fig. 124 Loosely install the pan-to-case bolts, then tighten the bolts in two stages, in the sequence shown

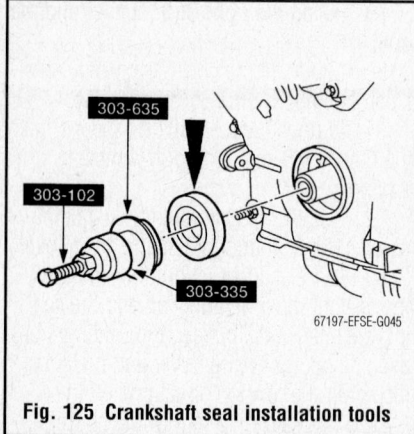

Fig. 125 Crankshaft seal installation tools

89. Apply silicone gasket and sealant in two places where the engine front cover meets the cylinder head.

✳✳ WARNING

When installing the valve cover, make sure to avoid damaging the variable camshaft timing (VCT) solenoid.

90. Position the left valve cover and gasket on the cylinder head and install the bolts loosely. Tighten the bolts in the sequence shown.

➡**Lubricate the O-ring seal with clean engine oil.**

91. Install the oil level indicator tube.
92. Install a new O-ring seal on the oil level indicator tube.
93. Install the oil level indicator tube.
94. Install the bolt.

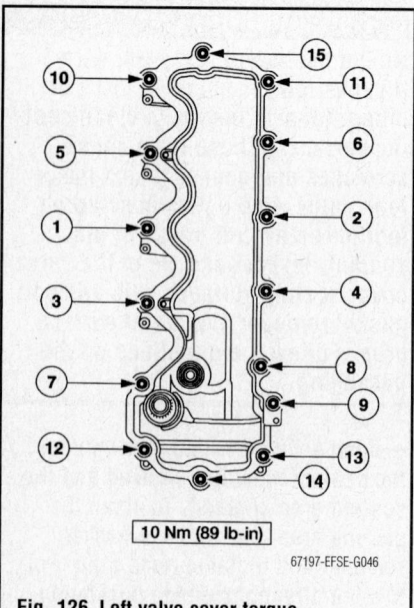

Fig. 126 Left valve cover torque sequence—5.4L engine

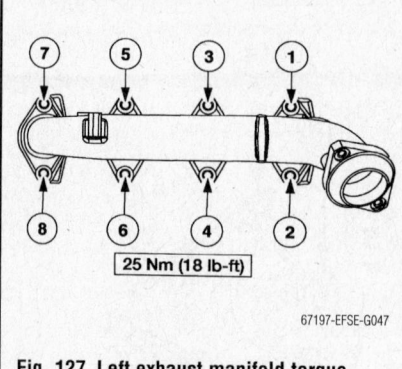

Fig. 127 Left exhaust manifold torque sequence—5.4L engine

95. Install the left exhaust manifold and the exhaust manifold gaskets. Tighten the nuts in the sequence shown.
Right cylinder head

✳✳ WARNING

Do not use metal scrapers, wire brushes, power abrasive discs or other abrasive means to clean sealing surfaces. These tools cause scratches and gouges which make leak paths. Use a plastic scraping tool to remove all traces of old sealant.

Inspect and clean the valve cover sealing surfaces with silicone gasket remover and metal surface prep. Follow the directions on the packaging.

➡**If not secured within four minutes, the sealant must be removed and the sealing area cleaned. To clean the sealing area, use silicone gasket remover and metal surface prep. Follow the directions on the packaging. Failure to follow this procedure can cause future oil leakage.**

96. Apply silicone gasket and sealant in two places where the engine front cover meets the cylinder head.

✳✳ WARNING

When installing the valve cover, make sure to avoid damaging the variable camshaft timing (VCT) solenoid.

97. Position the right valve cover and gasket on the cylinder head and install the bolts loosely. Tighten the bolts in the sequence shown.
98. Install the right exhaust manifold gaskets and the exhaust manifold. Tighten the nuts in the sequence shown.

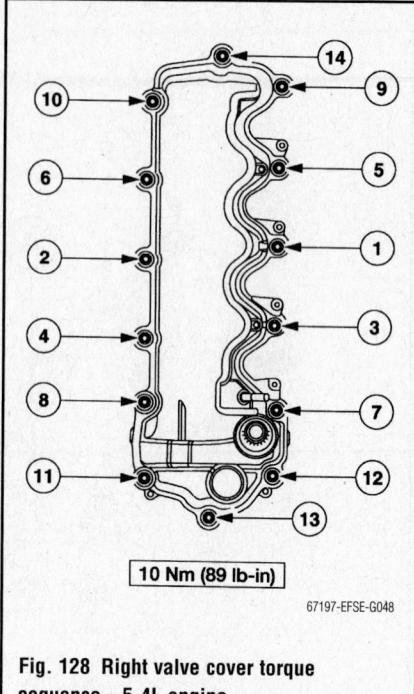

Fig. 128 Right valve cover torque sequence—5.4L engine

99. Install the heater outlet tube stud.
All cylinder heads
100. Position the electrical harness on the valve cover and connect the engine wiring harness retainers to the valve cover studs.
101. Connect the right radio ignition interference capacitor electrical connector.
102. Connect the left radio ignition interference capacitor and cylinder head temperature (CHT) sensor electrical connectors.
103. Connect the CMP sensor electrical connectors.
104. Connect the CKP sensor electrical connector.
105. Install a suitable tool.
106. Using a suitable floor crane remove the engine from the engine stand.

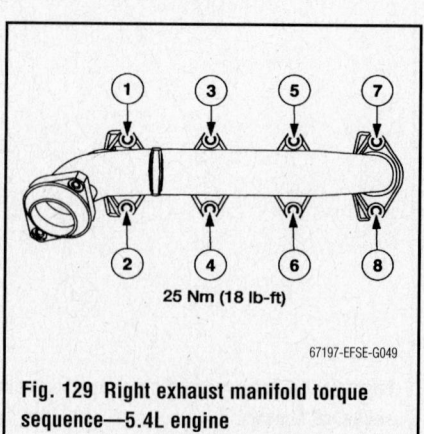

Fig. 129 Right exhaust manifold torque sequence—5.4L engine

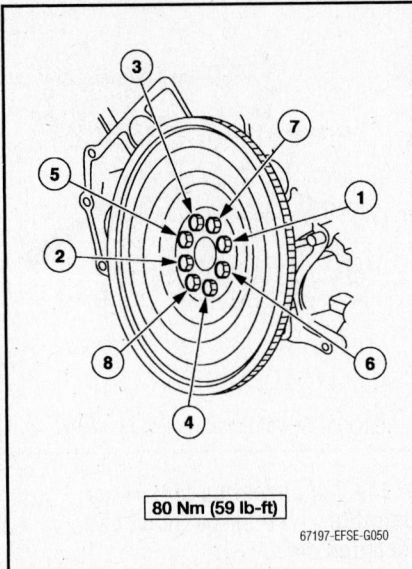

80 Nm (59 lb-ft)

67197-EFSE-G050

Fig. 130 Flywheel torque sequence—5.4L engine

107. Install the flexplate or the flywheel and bolts. Tighten the bolts in the sequence shown.

108. Install the engine.

6.8L Engine

See Figures 131 through 151.

1. Before servicing the vehicle, refer to the Precautions Section.

2. Remove the engine.

3. Remove the bolts and the flexplate or the flywheel.

4. Mount the engine on a suitable work stand.

5. Remove the right engine mount.

6. Remove the cylinder block drain plugs and drain the coolant into a suitable container.

7. Disconnect the left radio frequency interference capacitor and cylinder head temperature (CHT) sensor electrical connectors.

8. Disconnect the camshaft position (CMP) electrical connector.

9. Disconnect the right radio frequency interference capacitor electrical connector.

10. Disconnect the knock sensor electrical connector.

11. Disconnect the crankshaft position (CKP) sensor electrical connector.

12. Disconnect the oil pressure switch electrical connector.

13. Remove the nuts and position the wiring harness aside.

14. Disconnect all of the harness routing clips and connector retainers. Remove the engine control sensor wiring harness.

15. Remove the nuts and the two radio interference capacitors.

16. Remove the crankcase ventilation tube from the left valve cover.

17. Remove the positive crankcase ventilation (PCV) valve and hose from the right valve cover.

➡️**Do not use metal scrapers, wire brushes, power abrasive discs or other abrasive means to clean the sealing surfaces. These tools cause scratches and gouges which make leak paths. Use a plastic scraping tool to remove all traces of old sealant.**

➡️**The bolts are part of the valve cover and should not be removed.**

18. Fully loosen the bolts and remove the left valve cover.

19. Clean the valve cover mating surface of the cylinder head with silicone gasket remover and metal surface prep. Follow the directions on the packaging.

20. Inspect the valve cover gasket. If the gasket is damaged, remove and discard the gasket. Clean the valve cover gasket groove with soap and water or a suitable solvent.

➡️**Do not use metal scrapers, wire brushes, power abrasive discs or other abrasive means to clean the sealing surfaces. These tools cause scratches and gouges which make leak paths. Use a plastic scraping tool to remove all traces of old sealant.**

➡️**The bolts are part of the valve cover and should not be removed.**

21. Fully loosen the bolts and remove the right valve cover.

22. Clean the valve cover mating surfaces of the cylinder head with silicone gasket remover and metal surface prep. Follow the directions on the packaging.

23. Inspect the valve cover gasket. If the gasket is damaged, remove and discard the gasket. Clean the valve cover gasket groove with soap and water or a suitable solvent.

24. Remove the bolt and the idler pulley.

25. Remove the coolant pump pulley.

26. Using a suitable tool remove and discard the crankshaft pulley bolt.

27. Using a suitable tool, remove the crankshaft front seal.

28. Remove the four oil pan bolts.

➡️**Correct fastener location is essential for assembly procedure. Record fastener location.**

29. Remove the fasteners.

30. Remove the engine front cover from the cylinder block.

31. Remove the crankshaft sensor ring from the crankshaft.

➡️**The caps must be marked for installation in their original locations or damage to the engine may occur.**

32. Remove the six bolts and remove the balance shaft bearing caps.

33. Remove the balance shaft.

➡️**Use care when removing the spark plugs.**

➡️**Use compressed air to remove any foreign material from the spark plug well before removing the spark plugs.**

34. Remove the 10 spark plugs.

35. Install a suitable tool between the valve spring coils to prevent valve stem seal damage.

➡️**The camshaft roller followers must be reinstalled in their original locations. Record the camshaft roller follower locations.**

➡️**Position the cam lobe away from the camshaft roller follower prior to removing each camshaft roller follower.**

36. Use a suitable tool to compress the valve springs and remove the camshaft roller followers.

37. Position the crankshaft with the keyway at the 12 o'clock position.

38. Remove the timing chain tensioning system from both timing chains.

39. Remove the right timing chain from the camshaft sprocket.

40. Remove the right timing chain from the crankshaft sprocket.

41. Remove the left timing chain from the camshaft sprocket.

42. Remove the left timing chain from the crankshaft sprocket.

43. Remove both timing chain guides.

Right cylinder head

44. Remove the right exhaust manifold.

Left cylinder head

45. Remove the left exhaust manifold.

46. Remove the bolt and the oil level indicator tube.

Both cylinder heads

47. Clean and inspect the exhaust manifolds.

48. Install lifting on both ends of the cylinder head.

➡️**The hydraulic lash adjusters must be reinstalled in their original locations. Record the hydraulic lash adjuster locations.**

49. Remove the hydraulic lash adjusters.

Right cylinder head

➡️**The cylinder head must be cool before removing it from the engine.**

Cylinder head warpage can result if a warm or hot cylinder head is removed.

➡Place clean shop towels over exposed engine cavities. Carefully remove the towels so foreign material is not dropped into the engine.

➡The cylinder head bolts must be discarded and new bolts installed. They are tighten-to-yield and cannot be reused.

➡Do not use metal scrapers, wire brushes, power abrasive discs or other abrasive means to clean the sealing surfaces. These tools cause scratches and gouges which make leak paths. Use a plastic scraping tool to remove all traces of the head gasket.

➡Aluminum surfaces are soft and can be scratched easily. Never place the cylinder head gasket surface, unprotected, on a bench surface.

50. Remove the bolts and the right cylinder head. Discard the cylinder head gasket. Discard the cylinder head bolts.

Left cylinder head

➡The cylinder head must be cool before removing it from the engine. Cylinder head warpage can result if a warm or hot cylinder head is removed.

➡Place clean shop towels over exposed engine cavities. Carefully remove the towels so foreign material is not dropped into the engine.

➡The cylinder head bolts must be discarded and new bolts installed. They are tighten-to-yield and cannot be reused.

➡Do not use metal scrapers, wire brushes, power abrasive discs or other abrasive means to clean the sealing surfaces. These tools cause scratches and gouges which make leak paths. Use a plastic scraping tool to remove all traces of the head gasket.

➡Aluminum surfaces are soft and can be scratched easily. Never place the cylinder head gasket surface, unprotected, on a bench surface.

51. Remove the bolts and the left cylinder head. Discard the cylinder head gasket. Discard the cylinder head bolts.

Both cylinder heads

➡Do not use metal scrapers, wire brushes, power abrasive discs or other abrasive means to clean the sealing surfaces. These tools cause scratches

and gouges which make leak paths. Use a plastic scraping tool to remove all traces of the head gasket.

➡Observe all warnings or cautions and follow all application directions contained on the packaging of the silicone gasket remover and the metal surface prep.

➡If there is no residual gasket material present, metal surface prep can be used to clean and prepare surfaces.

52. Clean the cylinder head-to-cylinder block mating surfaces of both the cylinder head and the cylinder block.

53. Remove any large deposits of silicone or gasket material with a plastic scraper.

54. Apply silicone gasket remover, following package directions, and allow to set for several minutes.

55. Remove the silicone gasket remover with a plastic scraper. A second application of silicone gasket remover may be required if residual traces of silicone or gasket material remain.

56. Apply metal surface prep, following package directions, to remove any remaining traces of oil or coolant, and to prepare the surfaces to bond with the new gasket. Do not attempt to make the metal shiny. Some staining of the metal surface is normal.

➡Make sure all cylinder head surfaces are clear of any gasket material, RTV, oil and coolant. The cylinder head surface must be clean and dry before running a flatness check.

➡Use a straightedge that is calibrated by the manufacturer to be flat with 0.005 mm (0.0002 in.) per running foot length. For example, if the straightedge is 61 cm (24 in.) long, the machined edge must be flat with 0.010 mm (0.0004 in.) from end to end.

57. Support the cylinder head on a bench with the head gasket side up. Inspect all areas of the deck face with a straightedge, paying particular attention to the oil pressure feed area. The cylinder head must not have depressions deeper than 0.0254 mm (0.001 in.) across a 38.1 mm (1.5 in.) square area, or scratches more than 0.0254 mm (0.001 in.).

To install:
Both cylinder heads

➡Make sure all coolant residue and foreign material is cleaned from the block surface and the cylinder bore.

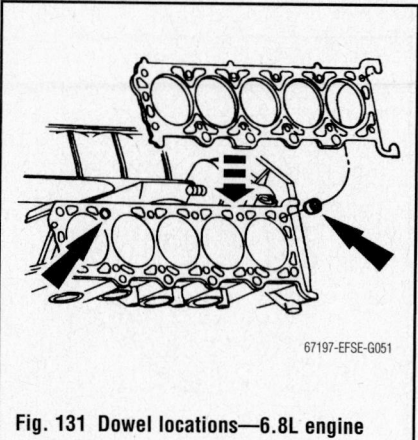

Fig. 131 Dowel locations—6.8L engine

➡The use of sealing aids is not permitted. The gasket must be installed dry.

➡The new gasket has a film coating which is crucial to the gasket's ability to seal properly. Do not scratch the gasket.

58. Install the head gaskets over the dowel pins. Position the heads.

➡The new cylinder head bolts must be lightly oiled with a rag and allowed to

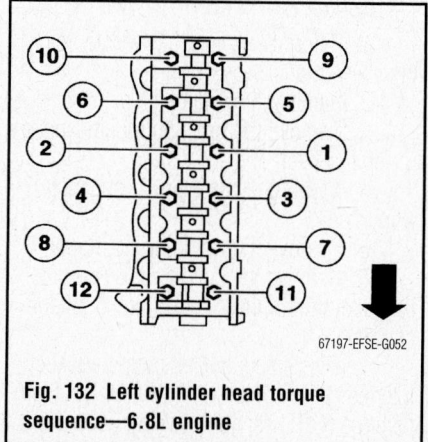

Fig. 132 Left cylinder head torque sequence—6.8L engine

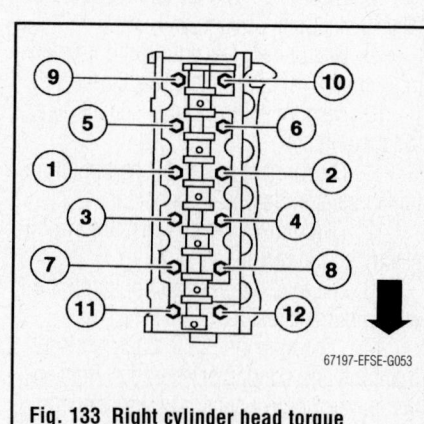

Fig. 133 Right cylinder head torque sequence—6.8L engine

drain for a few minutes prior to installation.

59. Loosely install cylinder head bolts.

60. Tighten the cylinder head bolts in three steps in the sequence shown.

    a. Step 1: Tighten the bolts to 40 Nm (30 ft. lbs.).

    b. Step 2: Tighten the bolts an additional 90 degrees.

    c. Step 3: Tighten the bolts an additional 90 degrees.

61. Remove the Lifting Handles from both ends of the cylinder head.

➡**Lubricate the hydraulic lash adjusters with clean engine oil.**

62. Install the hydraulic lash adjusters in their original locations.

Right cylinder head

63. Using a new gasket, install the right exhaust manifold. Tighten the nuts in the sequence shown.

Left cylinder head

➡**Lubricate the O-ring seal with clean engine oil.**

64. Install the oil level indicator tube.

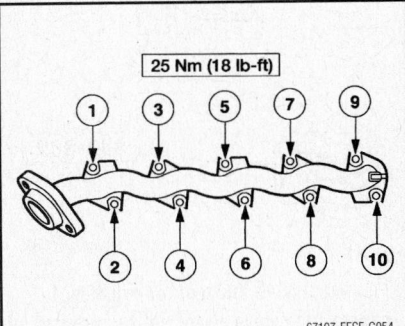

Fig. 134 Right exhaust manifold torque sequence—6.8L engine

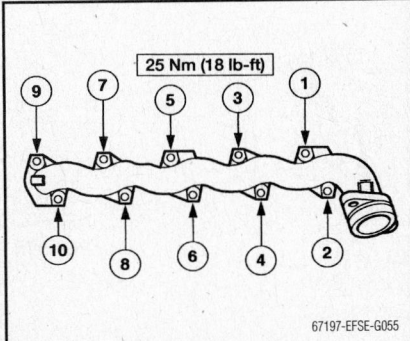

Fig. 135 Left exhaust manifold torque sequence—6.8L engine

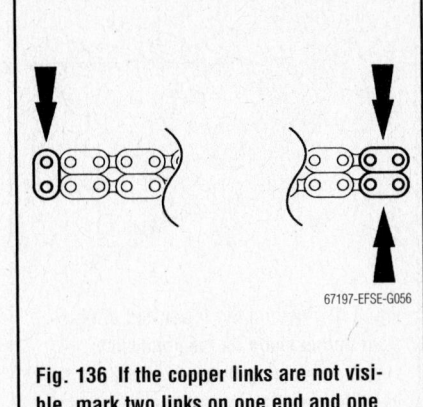

Fig. 136 If the copper links are not visible, mark two links on one end and one link on the other end, and use as timing marks

65. Using a new gasket, install the left exhaust manifold. Tighten the nuts in the sequence shown.

Both cylinder heads

➡**The timing chain procedures must be followed exactly or damage to the valves and pistons will result.**

66. Compress the tensioner plunger, using an edge of a vise.

67. Install a retaining clip on the tensioner to hold the plunger in during installation.

68. Remove the tensioner from the vise.

69. If the copper links are not visible, mark two links on one end and one link on the other end, and use as timing marks.

70. Install the timing chain guides.

71. Pre-position the camshafts. Rotate the left camshaft until the timing mark is approximately at 12 o'clock. Rotate the right camshaft until the timing mark is approximately at 11 o'clock.

➡**Rotate the crankshaft counterclockwise only. Do not rotate past position shown or severe piston and valve damage can occur.**

➡**The number one piston is at top dead center (TDC) when the stud on the engine block fits into the slot in the handle of the crankshaft alignment tool 303-448, or equivalent.**

72. Position the crankshaft so the number one cylinder is at TDC with a suitable tool.

73. Remove the crankshaft holding tool.

74. Install the crankshaft sprocket, making sure the flange faces forward.

75. Position the lower end of the left timing chain on the crankshaft sprocket, aligning the timing mark on the outer flange of the crankshaft sprocket with the single copper (marked) link on the chain.

➡**Make sure the upper half of the timing chain is below the tensioner arm dowel.**

76. Position the timing chain on the camshaft sprocket with the camshaft sprocket timing mark positioned between the two copper (marked) chain links.

➡**The left timing chain tensioner arm has a bump near the dowel hole for identification.**

77. Position the left timing chain tensioner arm on the dowel pin and install the left timing chain tensioner.

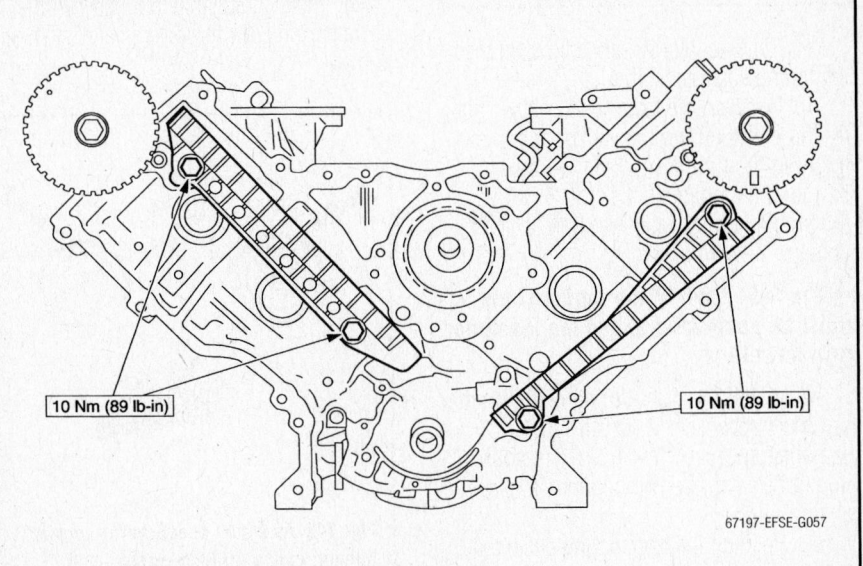

Fig. 137 Timing chain guides installed—6.8L engine

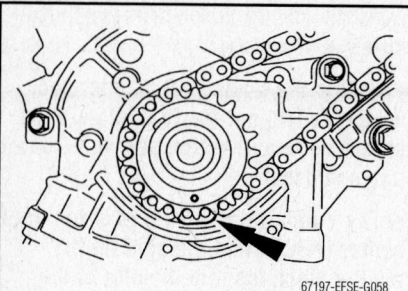

Fig. 138 Position the lower end of the left timing chain on the crankshaft sprocket, aligning the timing mark on the outer flange of the crankshaft sprocket with the single copper (marked) link on the chain—6.8L engine

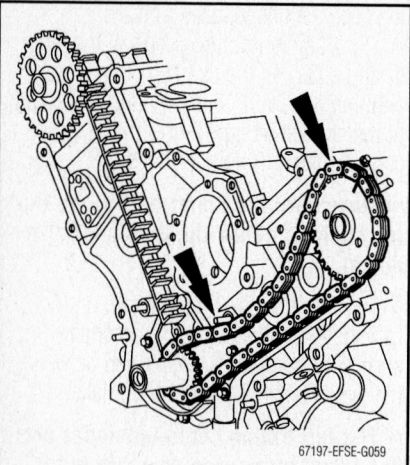

Fig. 139 Position the timing chain on the camshaft sprocket with the camshaft sprocket timing mark positioned between the two copper (marked) chain links—6.8L engine

78. Remove the retaining clip from the left timing chain tensioner.

79. Position the lower end of the right timing chain on the crankshaft sprocket, aligning the timing mark on the outer flange of the crankshaft sprocket with the single copper (marked) link on the chain.

➡ **The lower half of the timing chain must be positioned above the tensioner arm dowel.**

80. Install the right timing chain on the camshaft sprocket. Make sure the camshaft sprocket timing mark is positioned between the two copper (marked) chain links.

81. Position the right timing chain tensioner arm on the dowel pin and install the right timing chain tensioner.

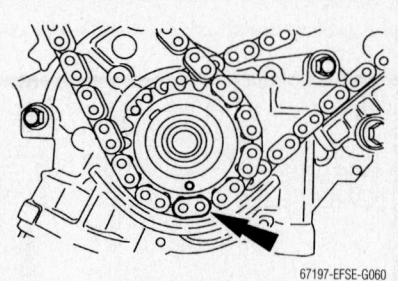

Fig. 140 Position the lower end of the right timing chain on the crankshaft sprocket, aligning the timing mark on the outer flange of the crankshaft sprocket with the single copper (marked) link on the chain—6.8L engine

Fig. 141 Install the right timing chain on the camshaft sprocket. Make sure the camshaft sprocket timing mark is positioned between the two copper (marked) chain links—6.8L engine

82. Remove the retaining clip from the right timing chain tensioner.

83. As a post-check, verify correct alignment of all timing marks.

84. Install a suitable tool between the valve spring coils to prevent valve stem seal damage.

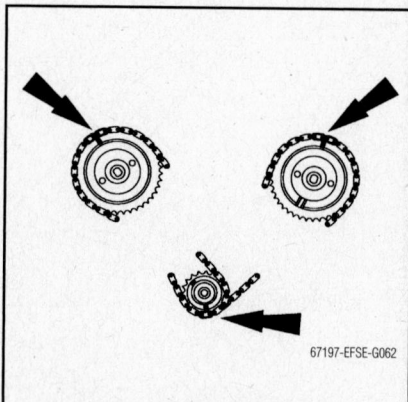

Fig. 142 As a post-check, verify correct alignment of all timing marks—6.8L engine

➡ Lubricate the camshaft roller followers, using clean engine oil.

➡ Position the cam lobe away from the camshaft roller follower location prior to installing each camshaft roller follower.

85. Install a suitable tool. Compress the valve spring. Install the camshaft roller followers in their original locations. Remove the tool.

➡ **When installing the spark plugs, use care not to exceed the recommended torque.**

86. Install the 10 spark plugs. Tighten the spark plugs to 18 Nm (13 ft. lbs.).

87. Using the index mark on the balance shaft, mark the corresponding gear tooth with chalk.

88. Position the balance shaft on the journals.

➡ **It may be necessary to use an inspection mirror to see the marks. Align the chalk mark on the balance**

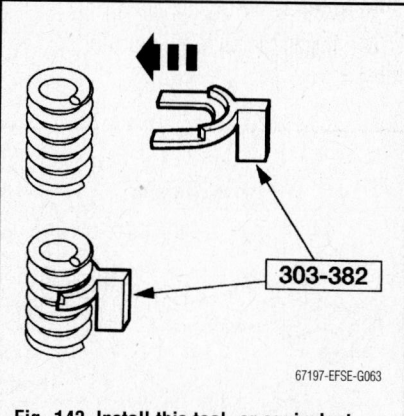

Fig. 143 Install this tool, or equivalent, between the valve spring coils to prevent valve stem seal damage—6.8L engine

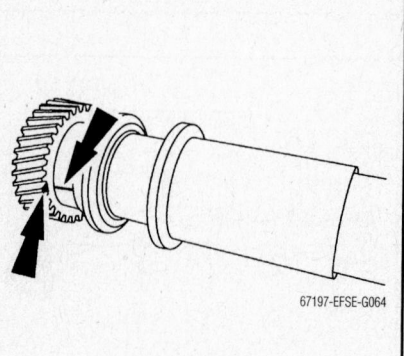

Fig. 144 Using the index mark on the balance shaft, mark the corresponding gear tooth with chalk—6.8L engine

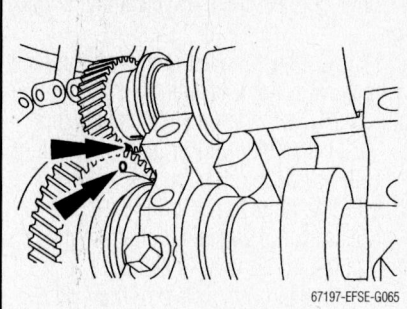

Fig. 145 It may be necessary to use an inspection mirror to see the marks. Align the chalk mark on the balance shaft with the camshaft timing mark as shown—6.8L engine

shaft with the camshaft timing mark as shown.

89. Install the bearing caps in their original locations. Install the bolts and tighten the bolts in the sequence shown.

90. Install the crankshaft sensor ring on the crankshaft.

➡**If the front cover is not secured within four minutes, the sealant must be removed and the sealing area cleaned. To clean the sealing area, use silicone gasket remover and metal surface prep. Follow the directions on the packaging. Failure to follow this procedure can cause future oil leakage.**

91. Apply a bead of silicone gasket and sealant along the cylinder head-to-cylinder block surface and the oil pan-to-

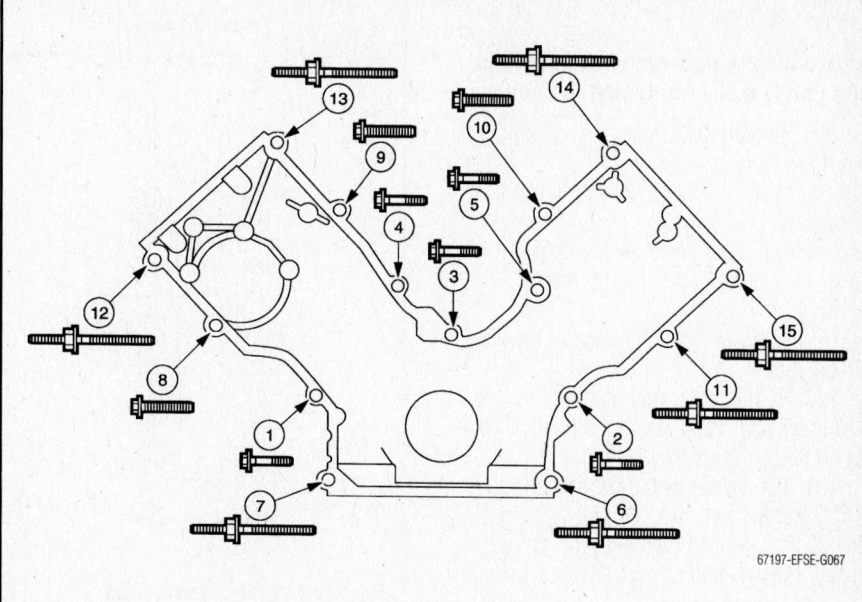

Fig. 147 Front cover tightening sequence—6.8L engine

cylinder block surface, at the locations shown.

92. Install a new front cover gasket on the engine front cover. Position the engine front cover. Install the fasteners.

93. Tighten the engine front cover fasteners in sequence in two steps.

    a. Step 1: Tighten fasteners 1 through 7 to 25 Nm (18 ft. lbs.).

    b. Step 2: Tighten fasteners 6 through 15 to 48 Nm (35 ft. lbs.).

94. Loosely install the bolts, then tighten in two steps in the sequence shown.

    a. Step 1: Tighten to 20 Nm (15 ft. lbs.).

    b. Step 2: Tighten an additional 60 degrees.

95. Position the belt idler pulley and install the bolt. Torque to 18 ft. lbs. (25 Nm).

96. Lubricate the engine front cover and the crankshaft front seal inner lip with clean engine oil.

97. Using the special tools, install the crankshaft front seal.

➡**If not secured within four minutes, the sealant must be removed and the sealing area cleaned. To clean the sealing area, use silicone gasket remover and metal surface prep. Follow the directions on the packaging. Failure to follow this procedure can cause future oil leakage.**

98. Apply silicone gasket and sealant to the Woodruff key slot on the crankshaft

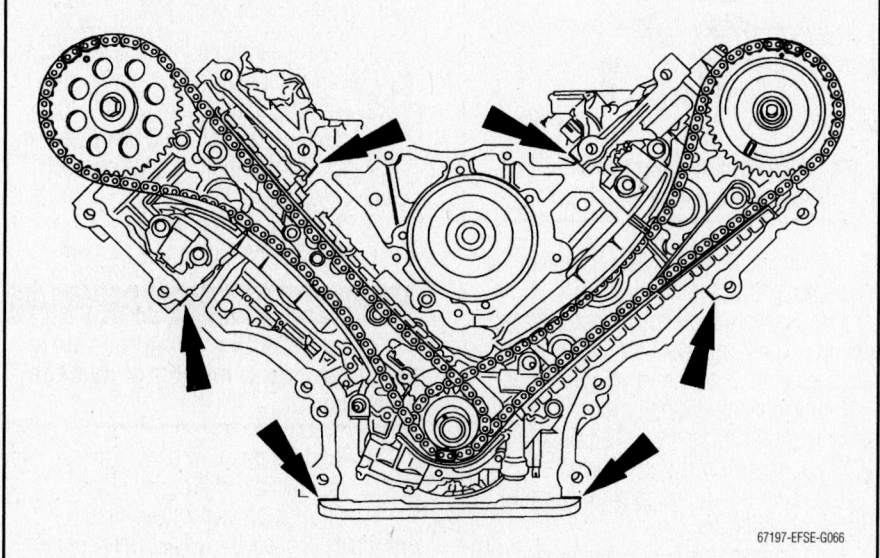

Fig. 146 Apply a bead of silicone gasket and sealant along the cylinder head-to-cylinder block surface and the oil pan-to-cylinder block surface, at the locations shown—6.8L engine

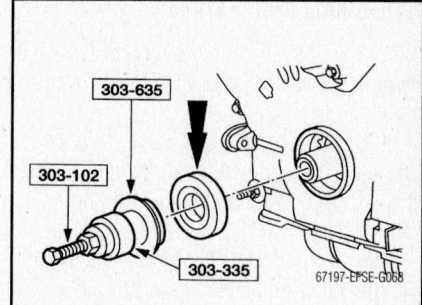

Fig. 148 Crankshaft front seal installation—6.8L engine

pulley. Use a suitable tool to install the crankshaft pulley.

➡**Use a suitable strap wrench to hold the pulley while tightening the bolt.**

99. Tighten the new crankshaft bolt in four steps.

    a. Step 1: Tighten to 90 Nm (66 ft. lbs.).

    b. Step 2: Loosen 360 degrees.

    c. Step 3: Tighten to 50 Nm (37 ft. lbs.).

    d. Step 4: Tighten an additional 90 degrees.

100. Position the water pump pulley on the water pump and install the bolts. Torque to 18 ft. lbs. (25 Nm).

101. If a new gasket is being installed, apply instant adhesive completely around the gasket groove in the left valve cover. Install the new valve cover gasket.

➡**If not secured within four minutes, the sealant must be removed and the sealing area cleaned. To clean the sealing area, use silicone gasket remover and metal surface prep.**

102. Follow the directions on the packaging. Failure to follow this procedure can cause future oil leakage.

103. Apply silicone gasket and sealant in two places where the engine front cover meets the cylinder head.

104. Position the left valve cover and gasket on the cylinder head and install the bolts loosely. Tighten the bolts in the sequence shown. If a new gasket is being installed, apply instant adhesive completely around the gasket groove in the right valve cover. Install the new valve cover gasket.

➡**If not secured within four minutes, the sealant must be removed and the sealing area cleaned. To clean the sealing area, use silicone gasket remover and metal surface prep. Follow the directions on the packaging. Failure to follow this procedure can cause future oil leakage.**

105. Apply silicone gasket and sealant in two places where the engine front cover meets the cylinder head.

106. Position the right valve cover and gasket on the cylinder head and install the bolts loosely. Tighten the bolts in the sequence shown.

107. Install the crankcase ventilation tube on the left valve cover.

108. Install the positive crankcase ventilation (PCV) valve and hose in the right valve cover.

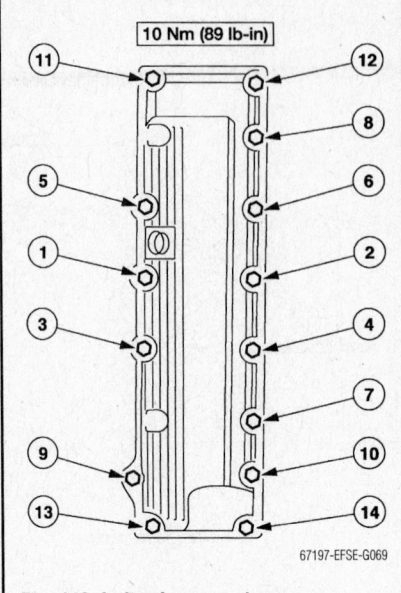

Fig. 149 Left valve cover torque sequence—6.8L engine

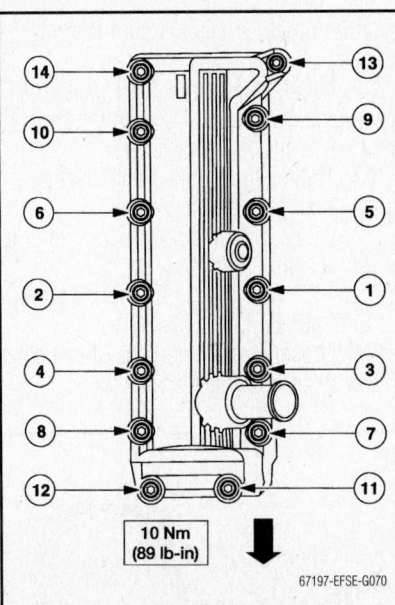

Fig. 150 Left valve cover torque sequence—6.8L engine

109. Install the radio frequency interference capacitors.

110. Position the engine control sensor wiring harness and connect the wiring harness retainers onto the valve cover studs.

111. Install the lifting bracket.

112. Connect the crankshaft position (CKP) sensor electrical connector.

113. Connect the oil pressure switch electrical connector.

114. Connect the knock sensor electrical connector.

115. Connect the right radio ignition interference capacitor electrical connector.

116. Connect the CMP electrical connector.

117. Connect the left radio ignition interference capacitor and cylinder head temperature (CHT) sensor electrical connectors.

118. Install the cylinder block drain plugs.

119. Install the right engine mount. Tighten the bolts to 63 Nm (46 ft. lbs.).

120. Install a suitable tool and remove the engine from the work stand.

121. Install the flexplate or the flywheel and the bolts in the sequence shown.

122. Install the engine.

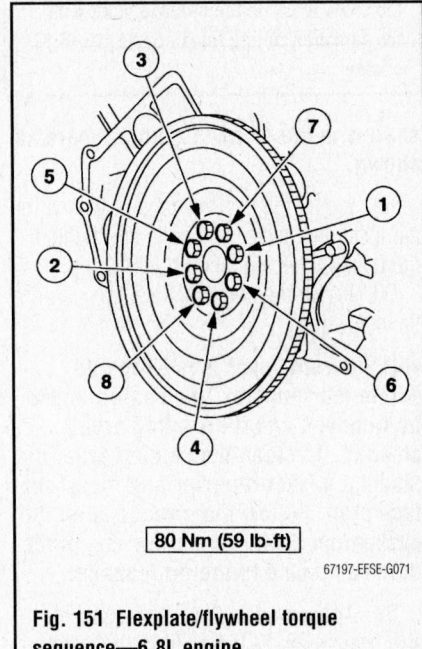

Fig. 151 Flexplate/flywheel torque sequence—6.8L engine

6.0L Diesel Engine

See Figures 152 through 154.

1. Before servicing the vehicle, refer to the Precautions Section.

2. Remove the engine.

3. Remove the bolts and flexplate.

4. Mount the engine on an engine stand.

5. Remove the rear lifting eye.

6. Remove the lifting tools.

❄❄ **WARNING**

Do not pull on the wiring to remove the glow plug connector or damage may occur.

7. Remove the glow plug harness.

8. Remove the eight glow plugs.

9. Prior to removing the exhaust manifolds, inspect the exhaust manifold for warpage with a feeler gauge between the manifold and cylinder head. Record the measurement and compare with the specifications.

10. Remove the bolts and the exhaust manifolds.

Left cylinder head

11. Remove the left cylinder head banjo fitting and fuel line. Discard the sealing washers.

12. Remove the bolts and turbocharger heat shield.

13. Remove the protective covering from the left cylinder head.

Right cylinder head

➡**Mark the location of the stud bolts.**

14. Remove the right valve cover.

15. Remove the stud bolts, bolts and valve cover.

16. Clean and inspect the gaskets.

17. Install a new gasket if necessary.

18. Clean and inspect the sealing surfaces.

19. Remove the right high pressure oil rail-to-valve cover gasket.

Both cylinder heads

20. Remove the bolts and the high pressure oil rail.

> ※※ **WARNING**
>
> **Do not attempt to apply battery voltage to the fuel injector or damage to the fuel injector will occur.**

21. Using a 19 mm (0.74 in.) socket, push the fuel injector electrical connector out of the rocker arm carrier.

➡**If engine oil is found in the engine coolant or engine coolant is found in the combustion chambers, new injector sleeves may need to be installed.**

22. Remove the bolt, the fuel injector hold down and the fuel injector.

23. Remove the crankcase-to-head tube assembly.

24. Remove and discard the O-ring seals.

25. Remove and discard the 20 inner cylinder head bolts.

26. Remove the 16 bolts and the rocker arm assemblies.

27. Remove the bolts and rocker arm carrier.

28. Clean and inspect the gasket.

29. Install new gaskets if necessary.

30. Clean and inspect the sealing surfaces.

31. Mark the 16 valve bridges with a permanent marker and remove.

32. Mark and remove the 16 push rods.

33. Remove the outer cylinder head bolts.

34. Install the lifting tool.

35. Remove the cylinder head.

36. Remove and discard the cylinder head gasket and dowels.

37. Clean and inspect the gasket sealing surfaces.

To install:
Both cylinder heads

➡**Use care to avoid scratching the blue compound on the cylinder head gasket.**

38. Install a new cylinder head gasket with the part number facing upward and verify the top five holes and the head gasket push rod holes line up.

39. Install new dowels and the cylinder head gasket.

40. Using the special tools, install the cylinder head on the engine.

41. Install the lifting bracket.

42. Install the bolts.

43. Install the cylinder head.

44. Install the outer cylinder head bolts finger-tight.

➡**Higher mileage engines require push rods to be cleaned so the copper colored end of the push rod can be identified.**

45. Apply clean engine oil to each end of the push rod. Insert them into their respective positions with the copper colored end up.

➡**Coat the end of each valve stem with clean engine oil.**

46. Install the 16 valve bridges.

47. Install the rocker arm carrier.

48. Install the press-in-place gasket.

49. Install the rocker arm carrier and bolts.

> ※※ **WARNING**
>
> **Rotate the crankshaft until the damper locating dowel notch is in the six o'clock position or engine damage can occur.**

➡**Apply clean engine oil to the top center of each valve bridge.**

50. Install the rocker arm assemblies and 16 bolts. Torque to 23 ft. lbs. (31 Nm).

> ※※ **WARNING**
>
> **Using too much engine oil on the threads of the cylinder head bolts can cause damage to the threads and poor sealing. Using anti-seize compounds, grease or any other lubricants other than engine oil on the cylinder head bolt threads can affect the true torque value of the bolts.**

➡**Lightly lubricate the new cylinder head bolt threads and flanges with clean engine oil.**

51. Install the 20 inner cylinder head retaining bolts finger-tight.

52. Tighten the head bolts in the following sequence.

 a. Tighten bolts 1 through 10 to 88 Nm (65 ft. lbs.).

 b. Tighten bolts 1, 3, 5, 7 and 9 to 115 Nm (85 ft. lbs.).

 c. Tighten bolts in sequence 1 through 10, clockwise 90 degrees.

 d. Tighten bolts in sequence 1 through 10, a second time, clockwise 90 degrees.

31 Nm (23 lb-ft)

67197-EFSE-G120

Fig. 152 Rocker arm carrier installation—6.0L engine

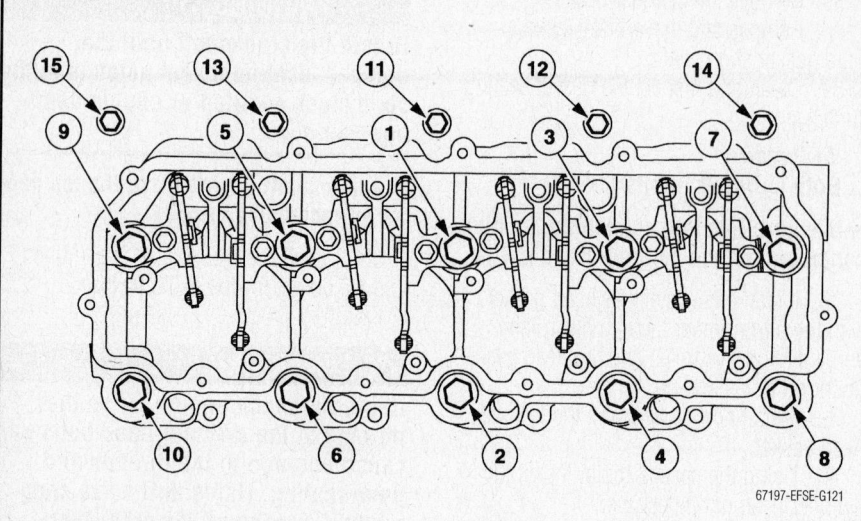

Fig. 153 Cylinder head bolt torque sequence—6.0L engine

e. Tighten bolts in sequence 1 through 10, a third time, clockwise 90 degrees.

f. Tighten bolts 11 through 15 to 24 Nm (18 ft. lbs.).

g. Tighten bolts 11 through 15 to 31 Nm (23 ft. lbs.).

➡**Install new O-ring seals and apply clean engine oil.**

53. Install a crankcase-to-head tube assembly.

✳✳ WARNING
If the fuel injector oil inlet D-ring is damaged, a new fuel injector must be installed.

➡**Lubricate the fuel injector and O-ring seals liberally with clean engine oil.**

54. Install new O-ring seals and a copper washer on the fuel injector.

55. Install the fuel injector, the fuel injector hold-down and bolt.

✳✳ WARNING
Be sure the injector wiring is clear of all moving parts or engine damage can occur.

56. Install the fuel injector electrical connector into the rocker carrier.

➡**Apply clean engine oil to the top fuel injector O-ring seals before installing the high pressure oil rail.**

57. Position the high pressure oil rail on the injectors.

58. Place the high pressure oil rail on top of the carrier so that the four single ball

tubes are engaging the fuel injector lead angle.

59. Insert three guide bolts, two on the ends of the straight side of the high pressure oil rail and one in the middle of the wavy side of the high pressure rail. Install the guide studs six to seven turns.

60. Press the high pressure oil rail into the fuel injectors.

61. Inspect that the high pressure oil rail mounting feet are flat against the mounting surface.

62. Loosely install the six bolts.

63. Install the remaining bolts and tighten.

64. Remove the three guide bolts.

65. Loosely install the three remaining bolts.

66. Tighten the nine bolts in the sequence shown.

Right cylinder head
67. Install the right high pressure oil rail-to-valve cover gasket.

✳✳ WARNING
To prevent engine damage, do not use air powered tools when installing the valve cover.

68. Install the right valve cover. Torque to 71 inch lbs. (8 Nm).

69. Install the right exhaust manifold and the bolts.

➡**Apply anti-seize lubricant to the bolt threads prior to installing. Torque to 28 ft. lbs. (39 Nm).**

➡**Start installing the bolts with the second bolt from the rear on the top. The hole diameter is smaller, therefore allowing alignment of the remaining bolts.**

Left cylinder head
70. Cover the left cylinder head with an appropriate covering.

71. Install the turbocharger heat shield and bolts.

➡**Install new sealing washers.**

72. Install the left cylinder head fuel line. Torque to 28 ft. lbs. (39 Nm).

➡**Start installing the bolts with the second bolt from the rear on the top. The hole diameter is smaller, therefore allowing alignment of the remaining bolts.**

➡**Apply anti-seize lubricant to the bolt threads prior to installing.**

73. Install the left exhaust manifold and the bolts. Torque to 28 ft. lbs. (39 Nm).

Both cylinder heads
74. Install the eight glow plugs.

➡**Clean and inspect the glow plug connector O-ring seals and install new as necessary.**

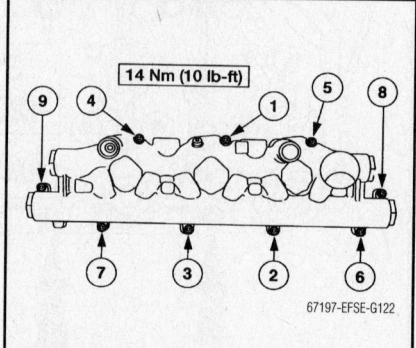

Fig. 154 High pressure oil rail torque sequence—6.0L engine

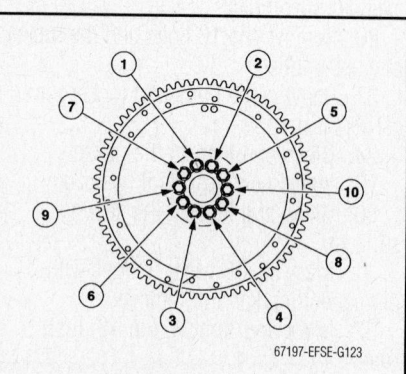

Fig. 155 Flexplate torque sequence—6.0L engine

➡**Apply clean engine oil to the O-ring seals.**

75. Install the glow plug harness.
76. Install the special tools.
77. Install the special tool.
78. Install the lifting crane and remove the engine from the engine stand.
79. Install the flexplate and the bolts.
80. Tighten the bolts in the following sequence.
   a. Tighten all bolts to 5 Nm (44 inch lbs.).
   b. Tighten all bolts to 94 Nm (69 ft. lbs.) in the sequence shown.
81. Install the engine.

ENGINE ASSEMBLY

REMOVAL & INSTALLATION

4.6L and 5.4L Engines

1. Before servicing the vehicle, refer to the Precautions Section.
2. Recover the air conditioning system.
3. With the vehicle in **Neutral**, position it on a hoist.
4. Remove the intake manifold.
5. Remove the front bumper.
6. Disconnect the lower radiator hose from the radiator.
7. Remove the pushpin retainers and the splash shield.
8. Disconnect the transmission cooler hoses and drain the fluid into a suitable container.
9. Disconnect the exhaust system from the left and right exhaust manifolds.
10. Drain the engine oil.
11. Disconnect the oil cooler hoses and set aside.
12. Remove the oil filter.
13. Loosen the threaded insert and remove the oil cooler from the oil filter adapter.
14. Remove the starter motor solenoid terminal cover.
15. Disconnect the starter motor electrical connections.
16. Remove the starter motor.
17. Remove the flexplate inspection cover.
18. Remove the cylinder block opening cover.
19. Remove the four nuts retaining the torque converter to the flexplate. Rotate the crankshaft to access all of the torque converter nuts. Discard the torque converter nuts.

Vehicles equipped with 4R70E transmission

20. Disconnect the shift cables and the mounting bracket.

All vehicles

21. Remove the two transmission-to-engine bolts and position the shifter cable support bracket, mounting bracket and cable aside.
22. Remove the right lower transmission-to-engine bolt.
23. Remove the four engine mount nuts.
24. Disconnect the power steering reservoir hose and the power steering pressure tube at the power steering pump.
25. Remove the nut and position the transmission fluid cooler support bracket aside.
26. Remove the valance panel.
27. Disconnect the upper radiator hose and the degas hose from the radiator.

> ❊❊ **CAUTION**
>
> **The large clutch assembly nut has a right-hand thread and must be rotated counterclockwise to remove it.**

28. Remove the fan blade assembly and fan clutch.
29. Disconnect the degas hose retainer from the fan shroud.
30. Remove the fan shroud, the fan, and the fan clutch.
31. Remove the bolts and the radiator support brackets.
32. Remove the radiator from the vehicle.
33. Disconnect the A/C pressure cutoff switch electrical connector.

> ❊❊ **CAUTION**
>
> **Use a wrench on each side of the fitting to prevent damage to the A/C fitting.**

34. Disconnect the compressor suction tube.

> ❊❊ **CAUTION**
>
> **Use a wrench on each side of the fitting to prevent damage to the A/C fitting.**

35. Disconnect the compressor discharge tube.
36. Disconnect the condenser-to-evaporator tube.
37. Remove the A/C condenser core.
38. Set the hood latch aside.
39. Remove the bolts and set the power steering reservoir aside.
40. Remove the nuts and the battery feed cable at the power distribution box.
41. Set aside the battery feed wiring harness to the power distribution box. Disengage the routing clips.

42. Remove the eight bolts and the upper radiator support.
43. Remove the pin-type retainers and the right and left air deflectors.
44. Set aside the left side of the headlamp dash panel junction wiring harness.
45. Set aside the right side of the headlamp dash panel junction wiring harness.
46. Remove the 12 bolts and the lower radiator support.
47. Disconnect the lower radiator hose from the oil filter adapter water inlet and set aside.
48. Rotate the tensioner clockwise to release belt tension and remove the drive belt.
49. Disconnect the alternator electrical connections.
50. Remove the bolts and the alternator.
51. Disconnect the electrical connectors, remove the nut, and remove the ground strap and mounting bracket.
52. Remove the engine oil filler tube support strap bolt.
53. Remove the fluid level indicator and disconnect the attachments at the transmission fluid filler tube.
54. Disconnect the evaporative emission canister purge valve electrical connector.
55. Remove the nut and the transmission fluid filler tube, and allow the fluid to drain into a suitable container.
56. Release the wiring retainers from the heater outlet tube bracket.
57. Disconnect the hose from the heater outlet tube.
58. Remove the heater outlet tube studs.
59. Remove the heater outlet tube.
60. Release the transmission wiring harness connector retainer from the bracket.
61. Disconnect the transmission wiring harness and the left and right heated oxygen sensor (HO$_2$S) electrical connectors.
62. Remove the four upper transmission-to-engine bolts and the fuel line, and the left HO$_2$S brackets.
63. Install a lifting tool.
64. Support the transmission with a jack.
65. Remove the engine from the vehicle.

To install:

66. Position the engine in the vehicle.
67. Remove the floor crane and the jack supporting the transmission.
68. With the vehicle in **Neutral**, position it on a hoist.

➡**Align the engine-to-transmission dowels before installing the engine-to-transmission bolts.**

69. Position the shifter cable support bracket and install the two transmission-to-engine bolts. Torque to 44 ft. lbs. (60 Nm).

70. Install the right lower transmission-to-engine bolt. Torque to 44 ft. lbs. (60 Nm).

Vehicles equipped with 4R70E transmission

71. Install the mounting bracket and connect the shift cable. Torque to 18 ft. lbs. (25 Nm).

All engines

72. Install four new nuts to retain the torque converter to the flexplate. Rotate the crankshaft to access all of the torque converter nuts. Torque to 26 ft. lbs. (35 Nm).

73. Install the cylinder block opening cover.

74. Install the flexplate inspection cover. Torque to 26 ft. lbs. (35 Nm).

75. Install the four engine mount nuts. Torque to 66 ft. lbs. (90 Nm).

76. Install the starter motor.

77. Connect the starter motor electrical connections.

78. Install the starter motor solenoid terminal cover.

79. Mount the exhaust system to the left and right exhaust manifolds. Torque to 30 ft. lbs. (40 Nm).

➡**Make sure the tab on the oil filter adapter nests into the notch in the oil cooler.**

80. Position the oil cooler on the oil filter adapter and install the threaded insert.

81. Install a new oil filter.

82. Connect the oil cooler hoses.

Romeo engine (4.6L)

83. Position the transmission fluid cooler tube support bracket and install the nut.

Windsor engine (5.4L)

84. Position the fluid cooler tube support bracket and install the nut.

All engines

85. Using a suitable tool, install a new Teflon® seal on the power steering pressure tube.

86. Connect the power steering pressure tube and the power steering reservoir hose to the power steering pump.

87. Install and tighten the oil drain plug.

88. Position the fuel line and the left heated oxygen sensor (HO2S) brackets. Install the four upper transmission-to-engine bolts. Torque to 44 ft. lbs. (60 Nm).

89. Connect the transmission wiring harness and the left and right HO2S electrical connectors. Install the transmission wiring harness connector retainer in the bracket.

➡**Do not reuse the O-ring seals. Lubricate the new O-ring seals with clean engine coolant before installing the heater outlet tube.**

90. Insert the heater outlet tube over the new seals.

Romeo engines (4.6L)

91. Install the heater outlet tube studs. Torque to 18 ft. lbs. (25 Nm).

➡**Lubricate the O-ring seals with clean transmission fluid before installing the transmission fluid filler tube.**

92. Install the transmission fluid filler tube.

Windsor engine (5.4L)

93. Install the heater outlet tube studs.

➡**Lubricate the O-ring seals with clean transmission fluid before installing the transmission fluid filler tube.**

94. Install the transmission fluid filler tube.

All engines

95. Connect the hose to the heater outlet tube.

96. Install the wiring retainers in the heater outlet tube bracket.

97. Connect the evaporative emission canister purge valve electrical connector.

98. Connect the attachments to the transmission fluid filler tube and install the fluid level indicator.

99. Install the engine oil filler tube support strap bolt.

100. Position the mounting bracket, install the ground strap and nut, and connect the electrical connectors.

101. Position the alternator and install the bolts.

102. Connect the alternator electrical connections.

103. Rotate the tensioner clockwise and install the drive belt. Refer to the decal on the upper radiator air deflector for belt routing.

104. Connect the lower radiator hose to the oil filter adapter coolant inlet.

105. Position the lower radiator support and install the twelve bolts.

106. Install the right side of the headlamp dash panel junction wiring harness.

107. Install the left side of the headlamp dash panel junction wiring harness.

108. Position the right and left air deflectors and install the pin-type retainers.

109. Position the upper radiator support and install the eight bolts.

110. Route the battery feed wiring harness to the power distribution box and insert the routing clips.

111. Install the battery feed cable to the power distribution box.

112. Install the power steering reservoir.

113. Install the hood latch.

114. Install the A/C condenser core.

✳✳ CAUTION
Use a wrench on each side of the fitting to prevent damage to the A/C fitting.

115. Connect the condenser core refrigerant tubes. Torque the condenser-to-evaporator fitting to 13 ft. lbs. (18 Nm); the compressor discharge tube to 29 ft. lbs. (39 Nm).

✳✳ CAUTION
Use a wrench on each side of the fitting to prevent damage to the A/C fitting.

116. Connect the compressor suction tube. Torque to 35 ft. lbs. (47 Nm).

117. Connect the A/C pressure cutoff switch electrical connector.

118. Position the radiator in the vehicle.

119. Position the radiator support brackets and install the bolts.

120. Position the fan shroud and the fan and fan clutch in the vehicle, and install the bolts.

121. Insert the degas hose retainer in the fan shroud.

122. Install the fan blade assembly and fan clutch.

123. Connect the upper radiator hose and the degas hose to the radiator.

124. Install the valance panel.

125. Connect the transmission cooler tubes.

126. Position the splash shield and install the pushpin retainers.

127. Connect the lower radiator hose to the radiator.

128. Install the front bumper.

✳✳ CAUTION
The oil pump must be primed prior to starting the engine.

129. Fill the engine with clean engine oil.

130. Install the intake manifold.

131. Fill all fluids to the correct levels.

132. Start the engine and check for leaks. Stop the engine and recheck the fluid levels.

133. Evacuate and recharge the air conditioning system.

6.8L Engine

1. Before servicing the vehicle, refer to the Precautions Section.

2. Discharge and recover the air conditioning system.

3. Disconnect the 42-pin and the two 16-pin connectors and remove the nut and the harness mounting bracket.

4. Remove the intake manifold.

5. Remove the radiator right and left air deflector, the radiator grille support, the valance panel and the upper and lower radiator supports.

6. Remove the radiator, fan shroud and engine cooling fan.

7. Remove the headlamps and side marker lamps.

8. Remove the A/C condenser core.

9. Remove the drive belt.

10. Disconnect the power steering reservoir hose at the power steering pump and let drain into a drain pan.

11. Disconnect the power steering pressure hose.

12. At the oil cooler water inlet, disconnect and set aside the lower radiator hose.

13. Disconnect the suction hose at the accumulator.

14. Disconnect the transmission harness and the left and right heated exhaust gas oxygen sensor connectors.

15. Remove the upper transmission-to-engine bolts and the fuel tube bracket.

16. Raise and support the vehicle.

17. Remove the nuts.

18. Drain the engine oil and remove the oil filter.

19. Disconnect the oil cooler hoses and position aside.

20. Loosen the threaded shaft and remove the oil cooler from the oil filter adapter.

21. Remove the starter motor.

22. Remove the bolt from the A/C compressor manifold and position the manifold aside.

23. Remove the bolts and position the shift cable and bracket aside.

24. Remove and discard the six nuts retaining the torque converter to the flexplate.

25. Remove the engine support insulator nuts.

26. Remove the remaining transmission to engine bolts.

27. Lower the vehicle.

28. Install the Modular Engine Lift Bracket.

29. Support the transmission with a jack.

30. Remove the engine from the vehicle.

To install:

31. Position the engine in the vehicle and remove the Modular Engine Lift Bracket and the jack supporting the transmission.

32. Raise and support the vehicle.

33. Install and tighten the nuts.

34. Install the fuel tube line bracket and the remaining transmission to engine bolts.

35. Install and tighten the six new nuts retaining the torque converter.

36. Install the starter motor.

37. Position the A/C compressor manifold assembly and install the bolt.

38. Install and tighten the nuts.

39. Connect the power steering pressure hose.

40. Install the oil cooler to the oil filter adapter and install the oil filter.

41. Position the oil cooler hoses and install the hose clamps.

42. Connect the lower radiator hose.

43. Lower the vehicle.

44. Connect the transmission wiring harness and the left and right heated exhaust gas oxygen sensor connectors.

45. Install the intake manifold.

46. Install the suction line to the accumulator.

47. Install the power steering reservoir hose at the power steering pump.

48. Connect the 16 and 42-pin connectors.

49. Install the drive belt.

50. Install the upper and lower radiator supports, valance panel, radiator grille support and the radiator right and left air deflectors.

51. Install the A/C condenser core.

52. Install the radiator.

53. Install the side marker lamps and headlamps.

54. Install the engine air cleaner assembly and tubes.

55. Fill all fluids to the correct levels.

56. Connect the battery ground cable.

57. Start the engine and check for leaks. Stop the engine and recheck the fluid levels.

58. Evacuate and recharge the A/C system.

6.0L Diesel Engine

1. Before servicing the vehicle, refer to the Precautions Section.

2. With the vehicle in **Neutral**, position it on a hoist.

3. Disconnect the battery ground cable.

4. Remove the A/C condenser assembly.

5. Remove the front bumper.

6. Remove the radiator grille support.

7. Remove the bolts, disconnect and remove the air bag sensor. Position the headlamp wiring harness aside.

➡**Mark the latch before removal.**

8. Remove the bolts and hood latch.

9. Remove the bolts and the radiator core supports.

10. Remove the intake manifold.

11. Remove the right fan stator stand-off. Remove the bolt and position the cable aside.

12. Remove the bolt and disconnect the A/C manifold. Disconnect the A/C electrical connector.

13. Remove and discard the O-ring seals.

14. Cap or plug the A/C openings as needed.

15. Disconnect the A/C pressure switch and remove the A/C manifold from the tee block.

16. Remove and discard the O-ring seals.

17. Cap or plug the A/C openings as needed.

18. Remove the bolts and A/C compressor.

19. Disconnect the heater hose. Position the heater hose and tube aside.

20. Remove the bolt and idler pulley.

21. Disconnect the engine coolant fill hose from the retaining clip. Loosen the clamp and remove the engine coolant fill hose.

22. Disconnect the vacuum pump hose and remove the engine coolant fill hose clip.

➡**The bolt behind the pulley is accessed through the pulley with an extension and a short socket.**

23. Remove the bolts and the vacuum pump.

24. Remove the power steering upper mounting bolt.

25. Remove the left fan stator stand-off.

➡**The front bolt will remain in the power steering pump.**

26. Remove the bolts and position the power steering pump aside.

27. Remove the lower radiator hose.

28. Disconnect the fuel lines.

29. Disconnect the crankshaft position (CKP) sensor electrical connector and retaining clips.

30. Disconnect the injection control pressure (ICP) sensor electrical connector.

31. Disconnect the glow plug electrical connector and wire retainers.

32. Disconnect the camshaft position sensor electrical connector and retaining clips.

33. Disconnect the two electrical connectors and wire retainers at the transmission.

34. Disconnect the glow plug module electrical connectors.

✻✻ WARNING

Do not use power tools when removing the nut.

35. Position back the boot and disconnect the B+ wire.

36. Disconnect the exhaust back pressure sensor electrical connector and push-pin retainer.

37. Disconnect the left glow plug electrical connector.

38. Disconnect the two electrical connectors.

39. Disconnect the two powertrain control module (PCM) electrical connectors and position the engine wiring harness aside.

40. Remove the bolts and the oil filter assembly.

41. Remove the bolt at the transmission filter housing.

42. Remove the retaining nut and remove the transmission cooling tubes.

43. Remove the torque converter cover.

44. Remove and discard the torque converter nuts.

45. Disconnect the block heater electrical connector.

46. Remove the retaining nut and position the cable bracket aside.

47. Remove the starter solenoid protective cap.

48. Disconnect the starter motor electrical connections.

49. Remove the bolts and the starter motor.

50. Remove the cylinder block drain plugs and drain the coolant from the block.

➡**Apply clean engine oil to the O-ring seal prior to installing.**

51. Install the cylinder block drain plugs.

52. Remove the motor mount nuts.

53. Remove the lower engine-to-transmission bolts.

54. Remove the mounting bolts from the lifting bracket and remove the tubes.

55. Disconnect the glow plug wire retainer. Remove the retaining nut and the oil indicator and tube.

56. Remove and discard the O-ring seal.

57. Disconnect the exhaust back pressure tube at the exhaust manifold.

58. Remove the retaining nuts and glow plug module.

➡**Power stud removed for clarity.**

59. Remove the retaining nuts and the glow plug module mounting bracket.

➡**Mark the location of the studs prior to removal.**

60. Remove the bolts and the left valve cover.

61. Remove the valve cover gasket.

62. Cover the cylinder head after the valve cover is removed.

63. Remove the ICP sensor.

64. Plug or cap the opening as needed.

➡**Do not tighten the bolts at this time.**

65. Install the special tools.

66. Remove the turbocharger exhaust pipe.

67. Remove the factory installed engine lifting bracket.

68. Install the special tool.

69. Install the engine lifting attachment and lifting crane.

70. Remove the oil pan drain plug and drain the engine oil.

➡**It may be necessary to raise the engine for oil pan removal. Disconnect the linkage from the engine lifting attachment to raise the engine.**

71. Remove the bolts and position back the oil pan until the oil pick up tube bolts are accessible.

72. Remove the bolts and let the oil pick-up tube go into the oil pan. Remove the oil pan.

73. Remove the press-in-place gasket and discard.

74. Remove and discard the oil pick-up tube O-ring seal.

75. Position a suitable transmission jack under the transmission.

76. Remove the upper engine-to-transmission bolts.

77. Raise the engine. Remove the four bolts and left motor mount.

78. Remove the bolts and the right motor mount.

➡**The engine must be moved to the driver's side for removal.**

79. Remove the engine from the vehicle.

To install:

80. With the vehicle in **Neutral**, position it on a hoist.

➡**The engine will need to be to the left of the center line to install.**

81. Raise the engine high enough to clear the No.1 crossmember, and position the engine into the vehicle.

82. Position the motor mounts in the vehicle.

83. Align the torque converter studs with the holes in the flywheel and push the engine in. Install the top engine-to-transmission bolts. Torque to 35 ft. lbs. (47 Nm).

84. Lower the engine until it is just

above the motor mounts. Install the retaining bolts in the right motor mount. Torque to 59 ft. lbs. (80 Nm).

85. Install the four retaining bolts in the left motor mount. Torque to 59 ft. lbs. (80 Nm).

86. Remove the transmission jack.

87. Install a new O-ring seal on the oil pick-up tube and position the oil pick-up tube in the oil pan.

88. Install a new press-in-place gasket into the upper oil pan.

89. Position the oil pan in the vehicle.

90. Install the oil pick-up tube and bolts.

91. Position the oil pan and install the bolts.

92. Clean and inspect the oil pan drain plug and gasket. Install new, if necessary.

93. Install the oil pan drain plug.

94. Lower the engine. Remove the lifting crane and the engine lifting attachment.

95. Remove the special tool.

96. Install the factory engine lifting bracket.

97. Loosely install the turbocharger exhaust pipe.

98. Remove the special tools.

➡**Remove the plug or cap as needed.**

99. Install the injection control pressure (ICP) sensor.

➡**Remove the protective covering from the cylinder head.**

100. Install the left valve cover gasket, valve cover and bolts.

101. Install the glow plug module mounting bracket and retaining nuts.

102. Install the glow plug module and retaining nuts.

103. Connect the exhaust back pressure tube at the exhaust manifold.

➡**Install a new O-ring seal and coat with clean engine oil.**

104. Install the oil indicator and tube. Install the retaining nut. Connect the glow plug wire retainer.

105. Position the fuel tubes and install the mounting bolts for the fuel tube bracket.

106. Install the lower engine-to-transmission bolts. Torque to 35 ft. lbs. (47 Nm).

➡**The top retaining nut must be tightened first.**

107. Install the motor mount nuts. Torque to 66 ft. lbs. (90 Nm).

108. Install the starter motor and bolts.

109. Connect the starter motor electrical connections.

110. Install the starter motor solenoid protective cap.

111. Position the cable bracket and install the retaining nut.

112. Connect the block heater electrical connector.

113. Install the new torque converter nuts. Torque to 26 ft. lbs. (35 Nm).

114. Install the torque converter cover.

➡**Inspect the O-ring seals. Install new seals, if necessary.**

115. Position the transmission cooler tubes and install the retaining nut.

116. Position the tube lock and install the retaining bolt.

117. Install the oil filter assembly and bolts. Torque to 18 ft. lbs. (25 Nm).

118. Position the engine wiring harness and connect the powertrain control module (PCM) electrical connectors.

119. Connect the two electrical connectors.

120. Connect the left glow plug electrical connector.

121. Connect the push pin retainer and exhaust back pressure sensor electrical connector.

✳✳ WARNING

Do not use power tools when installing the nut. Use care not to overtighten the nut during installation.

122. Connect the B+ wire and reposition the boot.

123. Connect the two electrical connectors and wire retainers at the transmission.

124. Connect the glow plug module electrical connectors.

125. Connect the camshaft position sensor electrical connector and retaining clips.

126. Position the wiring and connect the glow plug electrical connector. Connect the ICP sensor electrical connector.

127. Connect the crankshaft position (CKP) sensor electrical connector and retaining clips.

128. Connect the fuel lines and install the retaining clips.

129. Install the lower radiator hose.

130. Position the power steering pump and install the bolts. Torque to 18 ft. lbs. (25 Nm).

131. Install the left fan stator stand-off.

132. Install the power steering upper mounting bolt. Torque to 18 ft. lbs. (25 Nm).

➡**The bolt behind the pulley is accessed through the pulley with an extension and a short socket.**

133. Install the vacuum pump and bolts. Torque to 35 ft. lbs. (47 Nm).

134. Connect the vacuum pump hose and install the engine coolant fill hose clip.

135. Install the engine coolant fill hose and tighten the clamp. Connect the engine fill hose into the retaining clip.

136. Install the idler pulley and bolt. Torque to 35 ft. lbs. (47 Nm).

137. Position the heater hose back and connect.

138. Install the A/C compressor and bolts. Torque to 18 ft. lbs. (25 Nm).

➡**Remove the caps or plugs as needed. Install new O-ring seals and lubricate with PAG oil.**

139. Install the A/C manifold at the tee block. Torque to 35 ft. lbs. (47 Nm).Connect the high pressure switch electrical connector.

➡**Remove the caps or plugs as needed. Install new O-ring seals and lubricate with PAG oil.**

140. Position the A/C manifold and install the bolt. Connect the A/C clutch electrical connector.

141. Position back the cable and install the bolt. Install the right fan stator stand-off.

142. Install the intake manifold.

143. Install the radiator core supports and bolts.

144. Position the hood latch and install the bolts.

145. Position the headlamp wiring harness and connect the air bag sensor. Install the bolts for the air bag sensor.

146. Install the valance panel, radiator grille support and grille opening panel reinforcement.

147. Install the front bumper.

148. Install the A/C condenser assembly.

149. Fill the engine with clean engine oil.

150. Connect the battery ground cable.

151. Check and top off the transmission fluid level.

EXHAUST MANIFOLD

REMOVAL & INSTALLATION

4.6L and 5.4L Engines

Left Side

See Figure 156.

1. Before servicing the vehicle, refer to the Precautions Section.

All engines

2. With the vehicle in **Neutral**, position it on a hoist.

3. Remove the engine cover.

Romeo engine (4.6L)

4. Disconnect the differential pressure feedback exhaust gas recirculation (EGR) sensor hoses from the EGR valve tube.

5. Remove the EGR valve tube.

Windsor engine (5.4L)

6. Disconnect the differential pressure feedback EGR sensor hoses from the EGR valve tube.

7. Disconnect the upper and lower fittings and remove the EGR valve tube.

8. Remove the front fender splash shield.

9. Remove the nuts.

10. Remove the nuts and the exhaust manifold.

11. Remove and discard the exhaust manifold gasket.

12. Clean and inspect the exhaust manifold.

To install:
All engines

13. Position the exhaust manifold gasket.

14. Position the exhaust manifold and loosely install the nuts.

15. Tighten the nuts in the sequence shown.

16. Install the three-way catalytic converter to exhaust manifold nuts.

Windsor engine (5.4L)

17. Install the EGR valve fittings in two steps.

   a. Step 1: Hand-tighten the fittings.

   b. Step 2: Tighten the lower fitting to 50 Nm (37 ft. lbs.).

18. Connect the differential pressure feedback EGR sensor hoses to the EGR valve tube.

Romeo engine (4.6L)

19. Install the EGR valve tube in two steps.

   a. Step 1: Connect the upper and lower fittings and hand-tighten.

   b. Step 2: Tighten the fittings to 40 Nm (30 ft. lbs.).

20. Install the differential feedback EGR sensor hoses to the EGR valve tube.

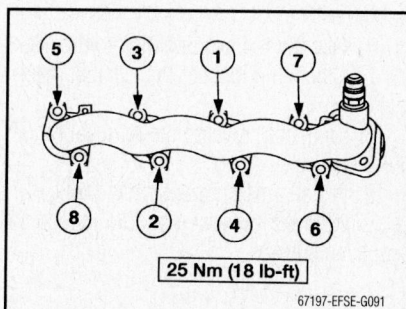

25 Nm (18 lb-ft)

67197-EFSE-G091

Fig. 156 Left exhaust manifold torque sequence—4.6L or 5.4L engine

All engines

21. Install the front fender splash shield.
22. Install the engine cover.

Right Side

See Figure 157.

1. Before servicing the vehicle, refer to the Precautions Section.
2. With the vehicle in **Neutral**, position it on a hoist.
3. Remove the front fender splash shield.
4. Remove the three-way catalytic converter to exhaust manifold nuts.
5. Remove the eight nuts and the exhaust manifold.
6. Remove and discard the exhaust manifold gasket.
7. Clean and inspect the exhaust manifold.
8. To install, reverse the removal procedure. Tighten the exhaust manifold nuts in the sequence shown.

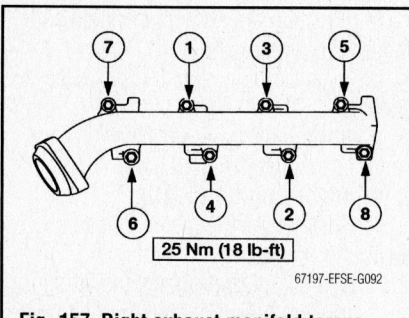

Fig. 157 Right exhaust manifold torque sequence—4.6L or 5.4L engine

6.8L Engine

Right Side

1. Before servicing the vehicle, refer to the Precautions Section.
2. With the vehicle in **Neutral**, position it on a hoist.
3. Remove the engine cover.
4. Remove the nuts.
5. Remove the 10 nuts, the exhaust manifold, and the exhaust manifold gasket.
6. Discard the exhaust manifold gasket.
7. Clean and inspect the exhaust manifold.
8. To install, reverse the removal procedure.
9. Install a new exhaust manifold gasket. Tighten the exhaust manifold nuts in the sequence shown.

Left Side

1. Before servicing the vehicle, refer to the Precautions Section.

2. With the vehicle in **Neutral**, position it on a hoist.
3. Remove the engine cover.
4. Remove the nuts.
5. Remove the exhaust manifold nuts and the exhaust manifold. Discard the exhaust manifold gaskets.
6. Clean and inspect the exhaust manifold.
7. To install, reverse the removal procedure. Tighten the exhaust manifold nuts in the sequence shown.

6.0L Diesel Engine

Left Side

See Figure 158.

1. Before servicing the vehicle, refer to the Precautions Section.
2. With the vehicle in **Neutral**, position it on a hoist.
3. Remove the engine cover.
4. Prior to removing the exhaust manifold, inspect the exhaust manifold for warpage with a feeler gauge between the manifold and the cylinder head. Record the measurement and compare with the specifications.
5. Remove the left bolts for the turbocharger adapter pipe.
6. Disconnect the exhaust back pressure tube.
7. Remove the bolts and the left exhaust manifold.

To install:

➡ **Start installing the bolts with the second bolt from the rear on the top. The hole diameter is smaller, therefore allowing alignment of the remaining bolts.**

➡ **Apply anti-seize lubricant to the bolt threads prior to installing the bolts.**

8. Install the left exhaust manifold and bolts. Tighten the bolts in the sequence shown.
9. Connect the exhaust back pressure tube at the exhaust manifold.

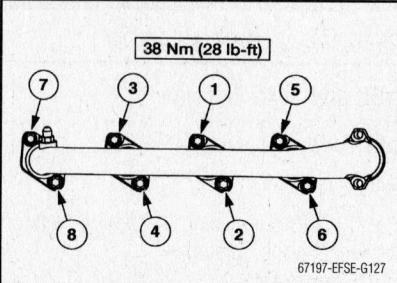

Fig. 158 Left exhaust manifold torque sequence—6.0L engine

10. Install the left bolts for the turbocharger adapter pipe.
11. Install the engine cover.

Right Side

See Figure 159.

1. Before servicing the vehicle, refer to the Precautions Section.
2. With the vehicle in **Neutral**, position it on a hoist.
3. Disconnect the battery ground cable.
4. Remove the engine cover.
5. Prior to removing the exhaust manifold, inspect the exhaust manifold for warpage with a feeler gauge between the manifold and the cylinder head. Record the measurement and compare with the specifications.
6. Remove the right bolts for the turbocharger adapter pipe.
7. Remove the bolts and the right exhaust manifold.

To install:

➡ **Start installing the bolts with the second bolt from the rear on the top. The hole diameter is smaller, therefore allowing alignment of the remaining bolts.**

➡ **Apply anti-seize lubricant to the bolt threads prior to installing the bolts.**

8. Install the right exhaust manifold and bolts. Tighten the bolts in the sequence shown.

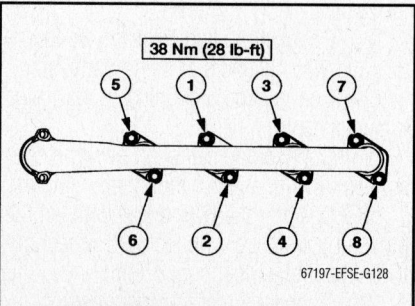

Fig. 159 Right exhaust manifold torque sequence—6.0L engine

9. Install the right bolts for the turbocharger adapter pipe.
10. Install the engine cover.
11. Connect the battery ground cable.

INTAKE MANIFOLD

REMOVAL & INSTALLATION

4.6L Engine

Removal

See Figure 160.

1. Before servicing the vehicle, refer to the Precautions Section.

2. Disconnect the battery ground cable.

3. Remove the air cleaner outlet pipe.

4. Drain the engine cooling system.

5. Compress and slide the hose clamp and disconnect the upper radiator hose.

6. Disconnect the accelerator cable.

7. Disconnect the speed control actuator cable.

8. Remove the accelerator return spring.

9. Remove the accelerator cable bracket bolts and position the bracket and cables aside.

10. Disconnect the main vacuum harness.

11. Remove the idle air control (IAC) fresh air hose.

12. Disconnect the exhaust gas recirculation (EGR) vacuum regulator solenoid connections.

13. Disconnect the IAC and throttle position (TP) sensor electrical connectors.

14. Disconnect the EGR valve vacuum hose and the evaporative emission canister purge valve hose and position them aside.

15. Disconnect the fuel pressure regulator vacuum hose.

16. Disconnect the differential pressure feedback EGR system electrical connector.

17. Disconnect the evaporative emission canister purge valve vacuum hose.

18. Remove the nut. Disconnect the brake booster vacuum tube and position the bracket and tube aside.

19. Position the crankcase ventilation hose aside.

20. Position the exhaust manifold to EGR valve tube aside.

21. Disconnect the fuel hose spring lock couplings.

22. Disconnect the heater hose and the heated throttle body inlet hose.

23. Disconnect the positive crankcase ventilation (PCV) hose.

24. Remove the four bolts and move the throttle body adapter forward slightly.

25. Disconnect the heated throttle body hose and remove the throttle body adapter.

26. Discard the throttle body adapter-to-intake manifold gasket. Inspect the throttle body and adapter for damage.

27. Remove the power steering reservoir upper mounting bracket.

28. Disconnect and remove the eight ignition coils.

29. Disconnect the eight fuel injectors.

30. Rotate the belt tensioner clockwise and detach the drive belt from the alternator pulley.

31. Remove the bolts and the generator upper mounting bracket.

32. Remove the generator lower mounting bolts and position the generator aside.

33. Remove the bolts, thermostat housing and thermostat. Discard the O-ring seal.

34. Remove the nine bolts.

35. Lift the intake manifold. Disconnect the intake manifold tuning valve electrical connector. Remove the intake manifold and discard the gaskets. Inspect the intake manifold assembly for damage.

Disassembly

See Figure 160.

1. Before servicing the vehicle, refer to the Precautions Section.

2. Remove the fuel infection supply manifold.

3. Remove the fuel injectors from the fuel injection supply manifold.

4. Inspect the two O-ring seals from each fuel injector. Install new O-ring seals as needed.

5. Remove the engine noise shield.

6. Remove the bolts.

7. Separate the upper and lower intake manifolds and discard the lower intake manifold gasket.

❋❋ **WARNING**

If the engine has been internally damaged and metal or other foreign material has entered the manifold, it is recommended the manifold be discarded.

➡**If there is no residual gasket material present, metal surface prep can be used to clean and prepare the sealing surfaces.**

8. Inspect all external and internal surfaces of the upper intake manifold. Inspect for cracks or other damage. Inspect for foreign material inside of the manifold. Clean the upper intake manifold sealing surfaces with silicone gasket remover and metal surface prep. Follow the directions on the packaging.

9. Allow the upper and lower intake manifolds to dry completely.

Assembly

See Figure 161.

1. Before servicing the vehicle, refer to the Precautions Section.

2. Position a new lower intake manifold gasket and the upper intake manifold on the lower intake manifold and loosely install the bolts.

3. Tighten the bolts in two stages using the sequence shown.
   - Stage 1: Tighten to 2 Nm (18 inch lbs.).
   - Stage 2: Tighten to 10 Nm (89 inch lbs.).
4. Install the engine noise shield.

➡**Lubricate the O-ring seals with clean engine oil, to aid installation.**

5. Install the fuel injectors into the fuel injection supply manifold.

6. Install the fuel injection supply manifold. Torque to 89 inch lbs. (10 Nm).

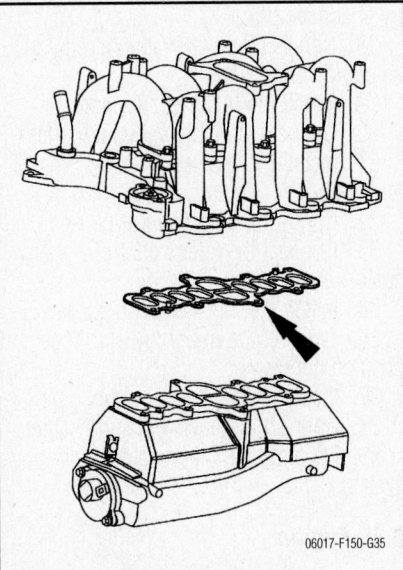

06017-F150-G35

Fig. 160 Upper and lower intake manifolds—4.6L Engine

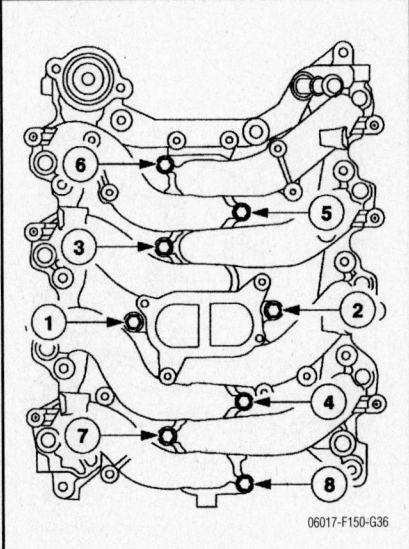

06017-F150-G36

Fig. 161 Upper-to-lower intake manifold torque sequence—4.6L Engine

Installation

See Figure 162.

> ※※ **WARNING**
>
> **Do not use metal scrapers, power abrasive discs or any abrasive means to clean the sealing surfaces, these tools cause scratches and gouges that make leak paths. Use a plastic scraper only.**

1. Before servicing the vehicle, refer to the Precautions Section.
2. Clean all the sealing surfaces.
3. Position new gaskets and install the intake manifold assembly. Loosely install the nine bolts.
4. Connect the intake manifold tuning valve electrical connector.
5. Install the thermostat.
6. Install the thermostat.
7. Install a new O-ring seal.

➡ **The thermostat housing bolts are tightened in sequence with the intake manifold bolts.**

8. Install the thermostat housing and loosely install the bolts.
9. Tighten the 11 bolts in two stages in the sequence shown.
   - Stage 1: Tighten to 2 Nm (18 inch lbs.).
   - Stage 2: Tighten to 25 Nm (18 ft. lbs.).
10. Position the generator and install the lower mounting bolts.
11. Install the generator upper mounting bracket. Torque to 89 inch lbs. (10 Nm).

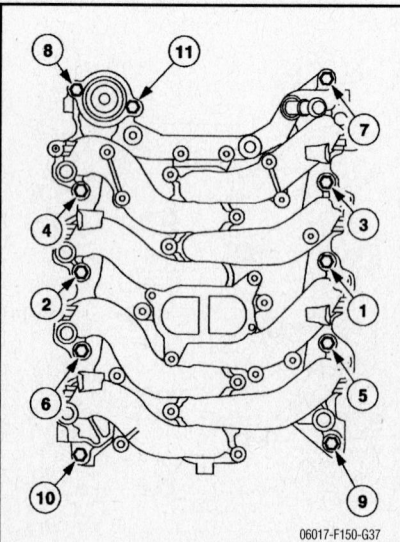

Fig. 162 Intake manifold assembly installation torque sequence—4.6L Engine

06017-F150-G37

12. Rotate the belt tensioner clockwise and install the drive belt. Refer to the decal on the radiator upper air deflector for belt routing.
13. Connect the eight fuel injector electrical connectors.
14. Install and connect eight ignition coils.
15. Install the power steering reservoir upper mounting bracket. Torque the 2 upper bolts to 13 ft. lbs. (17 Nm); the one lower bolt to 96 inch lbs. (11 Nm).
16. Roughly position the throttle body adapter in the vehicle and connect the heated throttle body hose.
17. Install a new gasket, the throttle body adapter and the bolts. Torque to 89 inch lbs. (10 Nm).
18. Connect the PCV hose.
19. Connect the heater hose and the heated throttle body inlet hose.
20. Install the exhaust manifold to EGR valve tube. Hand-tighten the fittings. Tighten the upper and lower fittings to 26–33 ft. lbs. (35–45 Nm).
21. Connect the fuel hose spring lock couplings.
22. Connect the brake booster vacuum tube and bracket and install the nut.
23. Roughly position the vacuum harness and connect the evaporative emission canister purge valve vacuum hose.
24. Connect the differential pressure feedback EGR system electrical connector.
25. Connect the fuel pressure regulator vacuum hose.
26. Connect the evaporative emission canister purge valve hose and the EGR valve vacuum hose.
27. Connect the TP sensor and IAC electrical connectors.
28. Connect the EGR vacuum regulator solenoid connections.
29. Install the IAC fresh air hose.
30. Connect the main vacuum harness.
31. Install the accelerator cable bracket and the bolts.
32. Connect the accelerator cable.
33. Connect the speed control actuator cable.
34. Install the throttle return spring.
35. Connect the upper radiator hose and position the clamp.
36. Install the air cleaner outlet pipe.
37. Connect the battery ground cable.
38. Fill and bleed the engine cooling system.

6.8L Engine

Removal

See Figure 163.

1. Before servicing the vehicle, refer to the Precautions Section.
2. Relieve the fuel system pressure.
3. Disconnect the battery ground cable.
4. Drain the coolant system.
5. Remove the air cleaner outlet tube.
6. Remove the generator.
7. Disconnect the fuel line spring lock couplings.
8. Compress and slide the hose clamp and disconnect the water outlet hose.
9. Remove the accelerator cable splash shield.
10. Disconnect the accelerator and speed control cables and remove the return spring.
11. Position the accelerator cable bracket aside.
12. Disconnect the positive crankcase ventilation (PCV) tube and the vacuum lines.
13. Disconnect the heated PCV coolant hose.
14. Disconnect the vacuum line.
15. Disconnect the five RH fuel injector electrical connectors and five ignition coil electrical connectors.
16. Disconnect the idle air control (IAC) motor electrical connector and the bypass hose.
17. Disconnect the heater hose.
18. If equipped, disconnect the exhaust gas recirculation (EGR) transducer and disconnect the throttle position (TP) sensor connectors.
19. If equipped, disconnect the EGR transducer vacuum lines.
20. If equipped, remove the EGR transducer bracket.
21. If equipped, position the EGR valve to exhaust manifold tube aside.
22. If equipped, disconnect the EGR valve vacuum line.
23. If equipped, disconnect the EGR vacuum regulator valve solenoid electrical and vacuum harness.
24. If equipped, remove the EGR vacuum regulator valve bracket.
25. Disconnect the five LH fuel injector and TP sensor electrical connectors and ignition coil connectors.
26. Remove the ignition coils.
27. Disconnect the vacuum connector from the fuel pressure regulator.
28. Remove the thermostat housing.
29. Remove the bolts, the upper intake manifold and the intake manifold gaskets.
30. Discard the intake manifold gaskets.

Do not use metal scrapers, wire brushes, power abrasive discs or other abrasive means to clean the aluminum retainer plate. These tools cause scratches and gouges, which make leak paths.

31. Clean all mating surfaces.

Disassembly

See Figure 163.

1. Before servicing the vehicle, refer to the Precautions Section.
2. Disconnect the heated positive crankcase valve (PCV) coolant hose.
3. Remove the coolant thermostat and the O-ring seal. Discard the O-ring seal.
4. Remove the throttle body (TB) adapter. Remove the TB adapter. Discard the TB adapter press-in-place gasket.
5. Remove the five bolts holding the fuel injection supply manifold assembly and the fuel injectors. Discard the fuel injector O-ring seals.
6. Separate the upper and lower intake manifolds. Remove the bolts. Discard the intake manifold gasket.
7. Using clean metal surface cleaner, clean and inspect the upper and lower manifold internal passages and mating surfaces.
8. Allow the upper and lower intake manifolds to dry completely.

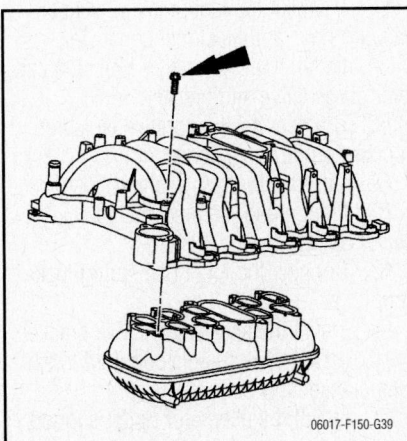

Fig. 163 Upper and lower intake manifolds—6.8L engine

Assembly

See Figure 164.

1. Before servicing the vehicle, refer to the Precautions Section.
2. Position a new lower intake manifold

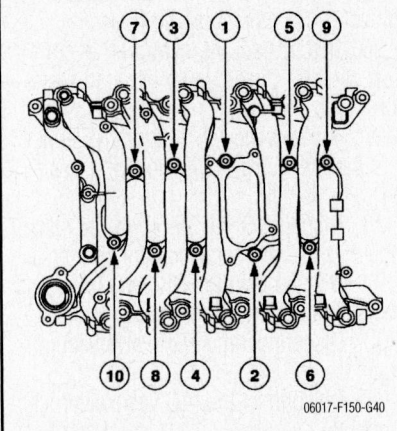

06017-F150-G40

Fig. 164 Upper-to-lower intake manifold bolt torque sequence—6.8L engine

gasket and the upper intake manifold on the lower intake manifold and loosely install the bolts.

3. Tighten the bolts in two stages using the sequence shown.
- Stage 1: Tighten to 2 Nm (18 inch lbs.).
- Stage 2: Tighten to 10 Nm (89 inch lbs.).

Check for leakage after installation is complete.

➡**Be sure fuel injectors and fuel rail are fully seated.**

4. Lubricate the new fuel injector O-ring seals with clean engine oil prior to installation.
5. Install the fuel rail.
6. Position a new TB adapter press-in-place gasket.
7. Position the TB adapter.
8. Install the four bolts in 2 stages:
- Stage 1: Tighten to 9 Nm (80 inch lbs.).
- Stage 2: Tighten an additional 90 degrees.

➡**Thermostat must be installed as illustrated.**

9. Use a new O-ring seal to position the coolant thermostat in the upper intake manifold.
10. Connect the heated PCV hose.

Installation

See Figure 165.

1. Before servicing the vehicle, refer to the Precautions Section.
2. Position the thermostat housing.
3. Position the upper intake manifold

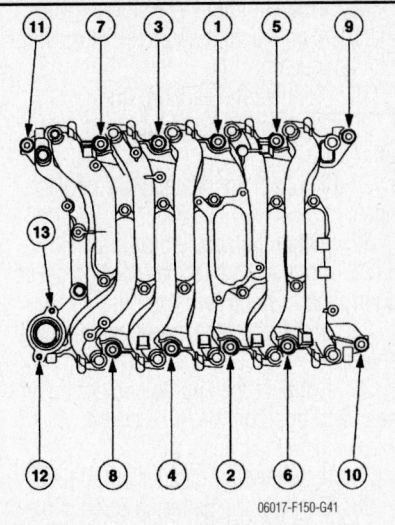

06017-F150-G41

Fig. 165 Intake manifold assembly installation tightening sequence—6.8L engine

gaskets and the intake manifold, and loosely install the bolts.

4. Tighten the bolts in two stages, in the sequence shown.
- Stage 1: Tighten to 2 Nm (18 inch lbs.).
- Stage 2: Tighten to 25 Nm (18 ft. lbs.).
5. Connect the fuel line spring lock coupling.
6. Connect the vacuum line to the fuel injection supply manifold.
7. Install the ignition coils. Torque to 53 inch lbs. (6 Nm).
8. Connect the five LH fuel injector electrical connectors and five LH ignition coil connectors.
9. If equipped, install the EGR vacuum regulator valve solenoid bracket.
10. If equipped, connect the EGR vacuum regulator valve solenoid vacuum and electrical connectors.
11. If equipped, connect the EGR valve vacuum line.
12. If equipped, install the EGR valve-to-exhaust manifold tube. Hand-tighten the fittings. Tighten the upper and lower fittings to 40–60 Nm (30–44 ft. lbs.).
13. If equipped, install the EGR transducer bracket. Torque to 106 inch lbs. (12 Nm).
14. If equipped, connect the vacuum lines.
15. If equipped, connect the EGR transducer and throttle position sensor electrical connectors.
16. Connect the heater hose.
17. Connect the idle air control (IAC) motor bypass hose and connector.

18. Connect the five RH fuel injector electrical connectors and five RH ignition coil connectors.

19. Connect the vacuum line.

20. Connect the PCV tube and the vacuum lines.

21. Connect the heated PCV coolant hose.

22. Install the accelerator bracket.

23. Connect the accelerator and speed control cables and return spring.

24. Install the accelerator cable splash shield.

25. Connect the engine coolant outlet hose and position the hose clamp.

26. Install the generator.

27. Install the air cleaner outlet tube.

28. Connect the battery ground cable.

29. Fill the cooling system.

5.4L Engine

1. Before servicing the vehicle, refer to the Precautions Section.

2. Disconnect the battery ground cable.

3. Remove the interior engine cover.

4. Disconnect the fuel hose spring lock couplings.

5. Drain the cooling system.

6. Position the engine air cleaner (ACL).

7. Disconnect the MAF sensor electrical connector and remove the ACL.

8. Disconnect the two hoses.

9. Loosen the clamp and remove the air cleaner outlet pipe.

10. Remove the accelerator cable snow shield.

11. Disconnect the accelerator cable.

12. Disconnect the speed control actuator cable.

13. Remove the throttle return spring.

14. Compress and slide the hose clamp and disconnect the upper radiator hose.

15. Disconnect the coolant hose.

16. Disconnect the coolant hose.

17. Disconnect the throttle position (TP) sensor.

18. Disconnect the differential pressure feedback exhaust gas recirculation (EGR) system.

19. Remove the differential pressure feedback EGR system bracket.

20. Remove the bolt and the bracket.

21. Remove the bolts and the alternator upper support bracket.

22. Remove the bolt retaining the transmission fluid filler tube support bracket.

23. Remove the bolts and position the accelerator cable bracket and cables aside.

24. If equipped, disconnect the auxiliary heater hoses and position aside.

25. Disconnect and remove the idle air control (IAC) valve fresh air hose.

26. Disconnect the evaporative emission canister purge valve hose and vacuum hose.

27. Remove the two evaporative emission canister purge valve nuts and position the valve aside.

28. Disconnect the fuel pressure sensor vacuum hose and the electrical connector.

29. Disconnect the EGR vacuum regulator solenoid connections.

30. Disconnect the EGR valve vacuum hose.

31. Disconnect the IAC valve electrical connector.

32. Disconnect the brake booster and main engine vacuum harness and position aside.

33. Disconnect the differential pressure feedback EGR sensor hoses from the EGR valve.

34. Remove the exhaust manifold-to-EGR valve tube.

35. Remove the four bolts, and the throttle body and adapter as an assembly. Discard the throttle body adapter gasket.

36. Disconnect and remove the positive crankcase ventilation hose.

37. Disconnect the eight ignition coil electrical connectors.

38. Disconnect the eight fuel injector electrical connectors.

39. Remove the eight bolts and the eight ignition coils.

40. Remove the bolts, the thermostat housing and the thermostat. Disconnect the O-ring seal.

41. Remove the nine bolts retaining the intake manifold.

42. Remove the intake manifold. Discard the intake manifold gaskets.

43. Inspect the throttle body, the intake manifold, and their sealing surfaces for damage.

To install:

➡Do not use metal scrapers, wire brushes, power abrasive discs or any other abrasive means to clean the sealing surfaces. These tools cause scratches and gouges which can cause leak paths. Use a plastic scraping tool to clean these surfaces.

44. Clean and inspect all sealing surfaces.

45. Position the intake manifold gaskets and the intake manifold.

46. Loosely install the nine bolts.

47. Install the thermostat.

48. Install a new O-ring seal.

➡The thermostat housing bolts are tightened in sequence with the intake manifold bolts.

49. Loosely install the thermostat housing and bolts.

50. Tighten the bolts in two steps, in the sequence shown.

   a. Step 1: Tighten to 2 Nm (18 inch lbs.).

   b. Step 2: Tighten to 25 Nm (18 ft. lbs.).

51. Install the eight ignition coils and bolts.

52. Connect the eight fuel injector electrical connectors.

53. Connect the eight ignition coil electrical connectors.

54. Install the PCV hose and valve.

55. Install the new throttle body adapter gasket.

56. Install the throttle body and adapter assembly.

57. Install the exhaust manifold-to-EGR valve tube and tighten the fitting in two steps.

   a. Hand-tighten the fittings.

   b. Tighten the fittings to 50 Nm (37 ft. lbs.).

58. Connect the differential pressure EGR sensor hoses to the EGR valve tube.

59. Connect the brake booster and the main engine vacuum harnesses.

60. Connect the IAC electrical connector.

61. Connect the EGR vacuum hose.

62. Connect the EGR vacuum regulator solenoid connections.

63. Connect the fuel pressure sensor vacuum hose and electrical connector.

64. Install the evaporative emission canister purge valve and bracket.

65. Connect the evaporative emission canister purge valve hoses.

66. Connect the IAC fresh air hose.

67. If equipped, connect the auxiliary heater hoses.

68. Connect the fuel hose spring lock couplings.

69. Install the accelerator cable bracket.

70. Install the transmission fluid filler tube bracket and bolt.

71. Install the alternator upper support bracket.

72. Install the accelerator cable routing bracket.

73. Install the differential pressure feedback EGR system bracket.

74. Connect the differential pressure feedback EGR sensor.

75. Connect the TP sensor.

76. Connect the coolant hose.

77. Connect the coolant hose.

78. Connect the upper radiator hose.
79. Connect the accelerator cable.
80. Connect the speed control actuator cable.
81. Install the throttle return spring.
82. Install the accelerator cable snow shield.
83. Install the air cleaner outlet pipe and tighten the clamp.
84. Connect the two hoses to the air cleaner outlet pipe.
85. Connect the MAF sensor and position the ACL.
86. Install the ACL.
87. Install the interior engine cover.
88. Connect the battery ground cable.
89. Fill and bleed the engine cooling system.

6.0L Diesel Engine

See Figures 166 and 167.

1. Before servicing the vehicle, refer to the Precautions Section.

All vehicles
2. Disconnect the battery ground cable.
3. Remove the cooling fan stator.
4. Remove the turbocharger pedestal.

Vehicles with dual alternator
5. Remove the accessory drive belt.
6. Remove the bolt and the accessory drive belt tensioner.
7. Remove the accessory drive belt.
8. Remove the bolts, bracket and accessory drive belt idler pulley.
9. Remove the bolts and the accessory drive belt tensioner.
10. Disconnect the alternator electrical connector and the B+ wire.
11. Remove the bolts and the alternator with mounting bracket.

Vehicles with single alternator
12. Remove the accessory drive belt.

All vehicles
13. Remove the bolt and position the ground wire aside. Disconnect the electrical connector push pin.
14. Remove the conduit and position the wiring aside.
15. Disconnect the locking tab.
16. Remove the bolts.
17. Disconnect the push pin and remove the wiring harness from the conduit.
18. Remove the bolts for the charge air cooler tube and oil fill tube.
19. Disconnect the oil fill tube at the valve cover.
20. Remove the retaining nuts, charge air cooler tube, oil fill tube and bracket.
21. Disconnect the alternator electrical connector and the B+ wire. Disconnect the wiring push pin.

22. Remove the retaining nut for the transmission fluid indicator and tube.
23. Disconnect the push pin retainer. Remove the retaining nut and position the transmission fluid indicator and tube aside.
24. Remove the three bolts, ground wire and the alternator.
25. Remove the bolts and position the heater hose tube aside.
26. Remove and discard the O-ring.

➡ **It will be necessary to position back or remove the heat insulating wrap.**

27. Remove the retaining nut and disconnect the wiring retainer and the injection pressure regulator valve electrical connector.
28. Disconnect the exhaust gas recirculation (EGR) valve electrical connector.
29. Disconnect the engine oil pressure (EOP) sensor electrical connector.
30. Disconnect the engine oil temperature (EOT) sensor electrical connector.
31. Disconnect the EGR throttle position control module electrical connector.
32. Disconnect the EGR throttle position sensor electrical connector.
33. Disconnect the pin-type retainer and engine coolant temperature (ECT) sensor.
34. Remove the ECT sensor.
35. Plug or cap the opening as needed.
36. Disconnect the intake air temperature (IAT2) sensor electrical connector.
37. Remove the IAT2 sensor.
38. Plug or cap the opening as needed.
39. Disconnect the eight fuel injector electrical connectors and wiring connectors.
40. Disconnect the harness retainers. Position the engine wiring harness as needed for intake manifold removal.
41. Disconnect the manifold absolute pressure (MAP) sensor hose.
42. Disconnect the engine coolant vent hose.
43. Remove the secondary fuel filter and remove all fuel from the filter housing.
44. Disconnect the fuel tube fittings at the secondary fuel filter.
45. Remove and discard the copper sealing washers.
46. Disconnect the fuel tube at the fuel filter housing. Remove the retaining nut.
47. Remove the banjo bolt and fuel tube.
48. Discard the copper sealing washers.
49. Remove the bolts and the secondary fuel filter assembly.
50. Remove the nuts and turbocharger heat shield.

➡ **Align the flat edge with the index feature located on the coolant supply port.**

51. Pull the EGR cooler clamp forward, twist and then slide the EGR cooler hose rearward to remove.
52. Remove the bolts and the intake manifold.
53. Remove the intake manifold gaskets.
54. Clean and inspect the gaskets. Install new gaskets if necessary.
55. Clean and inspect the sealing surfaces.
56. Remove and discard the front module O-ring seal.

To install:

➡ **The locating tabs on the gaskets must be positioned upward and toward the center of the engine, or a leak will occur.**

57. Install the intake manifold gaskets. Install a new front module O-ring seal.

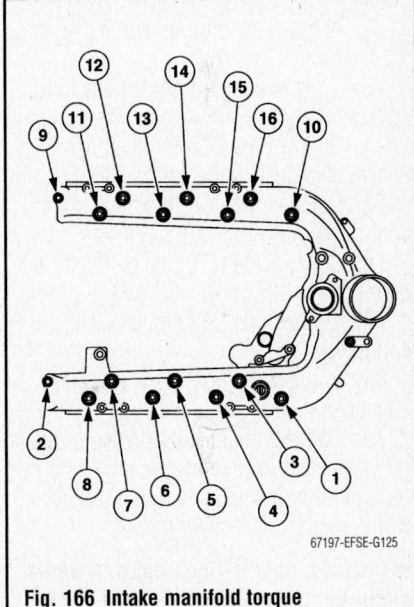

67197-EFSE-G125

Fig. 166 Intake manifold torque sequence—6.0L engine

58. Install the intake manifold and bolts and tighten in the following sequence.
   a. Loosely install bolts 1–8.
   b. Tighten bolts 9–16 to 11 Nm (8 ft. lbs.).
   c. Tighten all bolts to 11 Nm (8 ft. lbs.).
59. Slide the EGR cooler hose forward and rotate the flat to lock.
60. Install the turbocharger heat shield and nuts.
61. Install the secondary fuel filter assembly and bolts. Toque to 18 ft. lbs. (25 Nm).

➡ **Install new copper sealing washers.**

62. Install the fuel line and banjo bolt. Torque to 28 ft. lbs. (38 Nm).

63. Install the retaining nut and connect the fuel tube at the fuel filter assembly. Torque to 19 ft. lbs. (26 Nm).

➡**Install new copper sealing washers on the banjo fitting.**

64. Reposition and connect the fuel tubes at the fuel filter housing.

65. Install the secondary fuel filter and cover. Torque to 10 ft. lbs. (14 Nm).

66. Connect the engine coolant vent hose.

67. Connect the MAP sensor hose.

68. Position back the engine wiring harness as needed. Connect the harness retainers.

69. Connect the eight fuel injector electrical connectors.

70. Remove the plug or cap. Install the IAT2 sensor.

71. Connect the IAT2 sensor electrical connector.

72. Remove the plug or cap. Install the ECT sensor.

73. Connect the ECT sensor electrical connector and the pin-type retainer.

74. Connect the EGR throttle position sensor electrical connector.

75. Connect the EGR throttle position control module electrical connector.

76. Connect the EOT sensor electrical connector.

77. Connect the EOP sensor electrical connector.

78. Connect the EGR valve electrical connector.

79. Connect the injector pressure regulator valve electrical connector and position back the heat insulating wrap. Install the wiring retainer and retaining nut.

➡**Install a new O-ring seal and apply clean engine coolant**

80. Install the heater tube and bolts.

81. Install the alternator, ground wire and the three bolts.

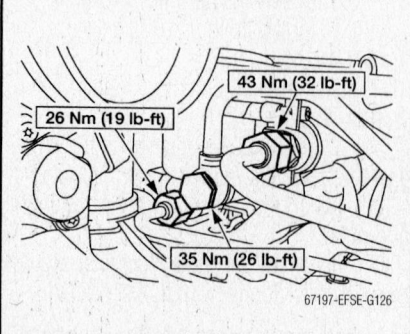

Fig. 167 Reposition and connect the fuel tubes at the fuel filter housing

82. Position back the transmission fluid indicator and tube and install the retaining nut.

83. Connect the push pin retainer.

84. Install the retaining nut for the transmission fluid indicator and tube.

85. Connect the alternator B+ wire and electrical connector. Position back the boot. Connect the wiring push pin.

86. Position the charge air cooler tube, oil fill tube and bracket. Install the retaining nuts.

87. Connect the oil fill tube at the valve cover.

88. Install the bolts for the charge air cooler tube and oil fill tube.

89. Install the conduit and bolts.

90. Install the wiring harness into the conduit and connect the push pin.

91. Install the bolts.

92. Connect the locking tab.

93. Connect the electrical connector push pin. Position back the ground wire and install the bolt.

Vehicles with single alternator

94. Install the accessory drive belt.

Vehicles with dual alternator

95. Install the alternator with mounting bracket and bolts.

96. Connect the alternator B+ wire and electrical connector. Position the boot.

97. Install the accessory drive belt tensioner and bolts.

98. Position the accessory drive belt idler pulley. Install the bracket and bolts.

99. Install the accessory drive belt.

100. Install the accessory drive belt tensioner and bolt.

101. Install the accessory drive belt.

All vehicles

102. Install the cooling fan stator.

103. Install the turbocharger pedestal and turbocharger.

104. Connect the battery ground cable.

OIL PAN

REMOVAL & INSTALLATION

4.6L and 5.4L Engines

See Figures 168 through 171.

1. Before servicing the vehicle, refer to the Precautions Section.

2. Remove the intake manifold.

3. Remove the fan shroud and the engine cooling fan.

4. Remove the retainers and the shield.

5. Remove the nut and position the transmission fluid filler tube aside.

6. Release the wiring retainers from the heater outlet tube bracket.

7. Release the knock sensor electrical connector retainer.

8. Release the engine harness routing clip retainer.

9. Disconnect the hose from the heater outlet tube.

10. Remove the heater outlet tube studs.

11. Remove the heater outlet tube.

12. Remove the two transmission-to-engine bolts.

13. Assemble the lifting tools, 303-F047 and 303-F694, or equivalent.

14. Install the lifting tools.

15. Install the special tool and support the engine.

16. Raise and support the vehicle.

17. Drain the engine oil, and remove the oil filter.

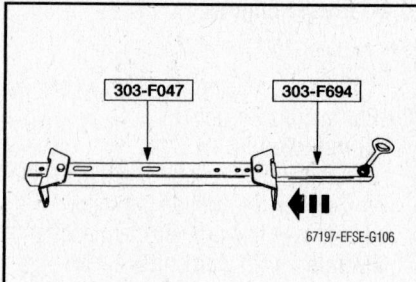

Fig. 168 Assemble the lifting tools, 303-F047 and 303-F694, or equivalent—4.6L and 5.4L Engines

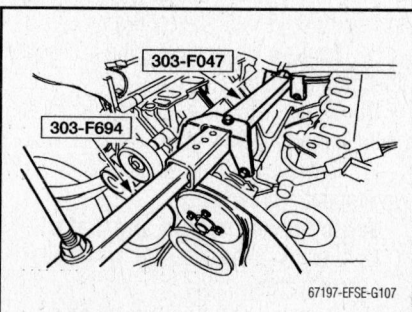

Fig. 169 Install the lifting tools—4.6L and 5.4L Engines

Fig. 170 Install the support tools—4.6L and 5.4L Engines

18. Remove the four engine mount nuts.

19. Remove the flexplate inspection plate.

20. Lower the vehicle.

21. Using the Heavy Duty Engine Support, raise the engine 10¼ inches from the crankshaft pulley to the lower edge of the No. 1 crossmember.

22. Raise the vehicle.

23. Remove the bolts and partially lower the oil pan.

24. Remove the bolts retaining the oil pump screen cover and pickup tube and let the bolts drop into the oil pan.

25. Remove the oil pan at the rear of the engine.

26. Clean the oil pan thoroughly and inspect the oil pan gasket.

27. Clean the mating surfaces for the oil pan with silicone gasket remover and metal surface prep. Follow the directions on the packaging.

To install:
All engines

❋❋ WARNING

Make sure the O-ring is in place and not damaged. A missing or damaged O-ring can cause foam in the lubrication system, low oil pressure and severe engine damage.

➡**Clean and inspect the mating surfaces and install a new O-ring. Lubricate the O-ring with clean engine oil.**

28. Install the oil pump screen and pickup tube. Torque the tube base bolts to 89 inch lbs. (10 Nm); the bracket bolt to 18 ft. lbs. (25 Nm).

➡**If not secured within four minutes, the sealant must be removed and the sealing area cleaned. To clean the sealing area, use silicone gasket remover and metal surface prep. Follow the directions on the packaging. Failure to follow this procedure can cause future oil leakage.**

29. Apply a bead of silicone gasket and sealant at the crankshaft rear seal retainer-to-cylinder block surface.

30. Apply a bead of silicone gasket and sealant at the engine front cover-to-cylinder block surface.

31. Position the pan. Tighten the bolts in three steps, in the sequence shown.

    d. Stage 1: Tighten to 2 Nm (18 inch lbs.).

    e. Stage 2: Tighten to 20 Nm (15 ft. lbs.).

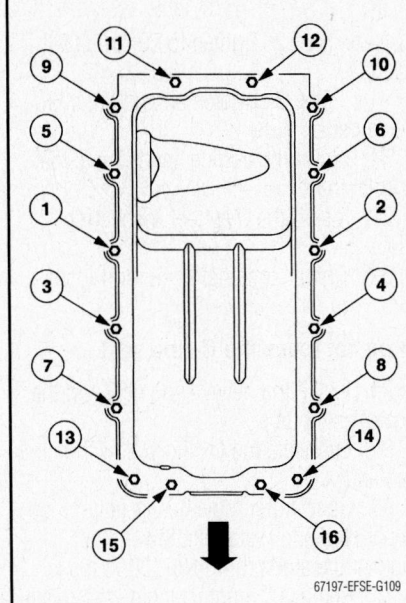

Fig. 171 Oil pan torque sequence—4.6L or 5.4L engine

    f. Stage 3: Tighten an additional 90 degrees.

32. Install a new oil filter.

33. Lower the vehicle.

34. Lower the engine and remove the special tools.

35. Raise the vehicle.

36. Install the four engine mount nuts. Torque to 66 ft. lbs. (90 Nm).

37. Install the flexplate inspection plate. Torque to 25 ft. lbs. (34 Nm).

38. Lower the vehicle.

39. Install the transmission-to-engine bolts. Torque to 44 ft. lbs. (60 Nm).

➡**Do not reuse the O-ring seals. Lubricate the new O-ring seals with clean engine coolant before installing the heater outlet tube.**

40. Insert the heater outlet tube over the new seals.
Romeo engines (4.6L)

41. Install the heater outlet tube studs.

42. Position the transmission fluid filler tube and install the nut.
Windsor engine (5.4L)

43. Install the heater outlet tube studs.

44. Position the transmission fluid filler tube and install the nut.
All engines

45. Connect the hose to the heater outlet tube.

46. Install the wiring retainers in the heater outlet tube bracket.

47. Install the knock sensor electrical connector retainer.

48. Install the engine harness routing clip retainer.

49. Install the retainers and the shield.

50. Install the fan shroud and the engine cooling fan.

51. Install the intake manifold.

❋❋ WARNING

The oil pump must be primed prior to starting the engine.

52. Fill the engine with clean engine oil.

53. Start the engine and check for leaks.

6.8L Engines

1. Before servicing the vehicle, refer to the Precautions Section.

2. With the vehicle in **Neutral**, position it on a hoist.

3. Remove the intake manifold.

4. Remove the engine cooling fan and fan shroud.

5. Remove the retainers and the shield.

6. Remove the nut attaching the transmission oil level tube.

7. Disconnect the wiring harness retainer.

8. Remove the stud bolts and position the heater outlet tube aside.

9. Remove the two transmission-to-engine bolts.

10. Disconnect the oil fill tube from the right valve cover.

11. Remove the bolt and the oil fill tube.

12. Assemble the special tools.

13. Install the special tools.

14. Install the special tool and support the engine.

15. Drain the engine oil and remove the oil filter.

16. Remove the right and left nuts retaining the front engine support insulators to the front engine support bracket.

17. Remove the flywheel inspection plate.

18. Using the special tool, raise the engine.

19. Remove the bolts and partially lower the oil pan.

20. Remove the bolts retaining the oil pump screen cover and pickup tube and allow it to drop into the oil pan. Also remove the tube and spacer and allow it to drop into the oil pan.

21. Remove the oil pan.

> ### ✳ WARNING
>
> **Do not use metal scrapers, wire brushes, power abrasive discs or other abrasive means to clean the sealing surfaces. These tools cause scratches and gouges, which make leak paths. Use a plastic scraping tool to remove all traces of sealant.**

22. Clean the mating surfaces for the oil pan and the engine with silicone gasket remover and metal surface prep. Follow the directions on the packaging.

To install:

➡**The oil pump screen and pickup tube must be in the oil pan when the oil pan is positioned in the vehicle.**

23. Position the oil pan gasket and the oil pan in the vehicle from the rear of the engine.

> ### ✳ WARNING
>
> **Make sure the O-ring is in place and not damaged. A missing or damaged O-ring can cause foam in the lubrication system, low oil pressure and severe engine damage.**

➡**Clean and inspect the mating surfaces and install a new O-ring. Lubricate the O-ring with clean engine oil.**

24. Position the oil pump screen cover and pickup tube.
25. Install and tighten the spacer. Torque to 18 ft. lbs. (25 Nm).
26. Insert the oil pump screen pickup tube into the oil pump and position the support bracket over the spacer.
27. Install and tighten the bolts. Torque the tube base bolts to 89 inch lbs. (10 Nm); the bracket bolt to 18 ft. lbs. (25 Nm).
28. Apply a bead of silicone gasket and sealant at the crankshaft rear seal retainer-to-cylinder block surface.

➡**If not secure within four minutes, the sealant must be removed and the sealing area cleaned. To clean the sealing area, follow the directions provided on the packaging of the silicone gasket remover and the metal surface prep. Failure to follow this procedure can cause future oil leakage.**

29. Apply a bead of silicone gasket and sealant at the engine front cover-to-cylinder block surface.

➡**Position the oil pan. Tighten the bolts in three steps.**

30. Tighten the bolts in the sequence shown.

a. Step 1: Tighten to 2 Nm (18 inch lbs.).
b. Step 2: Tighten to 20 Nm (15 ft. lbs.).
c. Step 3: Tighten an additional 90 degrees.
31. Lower the engine and remove the special tools.
32. Install the flywheel inspection plate.
33. Tighten the engine support insulators.

➡**Do not reuse the O-ring seal.**

34. Install the new O-ring seal and the heater outlet tube.
35. Lubricate the O-ring seal with engine coolant.
36. Hand-tighten the heater outlet tube upper stud and install the lower stud. Tighten the studs to 40 Nm (30 ft. lbs.).
37. Remove the nut attaching the transmission oil level tube.
38. Connect the wiring harness retainer.
39. Connect the oil fill tube to the right valve cover.
40. Install the oil fill tube support bracket bolt.
41. Install the transmission-to-engine bolts.
42. Install the shield and the retainers.
43. Install the intake manifold.
44. Fill the engine with clean engine oil.
45. Install the engine cooling fan and fan shroud.
46. Fill and bleed the engine cooling system.

6.0L Diesel Engine

Lower Pan

1. Before servicing the vehicle, refer to the Precautions Section.
2. With the vehicle in **Neutral**, position it on a hoist.
3. Disconnect the battery ground cable.
4. Remove the engine cover.
5. Remove the cooling fan stator.
6. Remove the A/C compressor.
7. Remove the power steering pump upper mounting bolt.
8. Remove the left fan stator stand-off.

➡**The front bolt will remain in the power steering pump.**

9. Remove the bolts and position the power steering pump aside.
10. Remove the oil pan drain plug.
11. Loosen the exhaust pipe retaining nuts.
12. Remove the motor mount retaining nuts.

13. Remove the right fan stator stand-off. Remove the bolt and position the cable aside.
14. Install the special tools.
15. Install the engine lifting attachment and floor crane.

> ### ✳✳ CAUTION
>
> **Use care when raising the engine to avoid engine or body damage**

16. Raise the engine.
17. Remove the bolts and position back the oil pan until the oil pick up tube bolts are accessible.
18. Remove the bolts and let the oil pick-up tube go into the oil pan. Remove the oil pan.
19. Remove and discard the oil pick-up tube O-ring seal.
20. Remove the press-in-place gasket and discard.
21. Clean and inspect the sealing surfaces.

To install:

22. Install a new press-in-place gasket into the upper oil pan.
23. Install a new O-ring seal on the oil pick-up tube and position the oil pick-up tube in the oil pan.
24. Position the oil pan in the vehicle.
25. Install the oil pan pick-up tube and bolts.
26. Install the oil pan and bolts.
27. Lower the engine.
28. Remove the floor crane and engine lifting attachment.
29. Remove the special tools.
30. Position back the cable and install the bolt. Install the right fan stator stand-off.

➡**Tighten the top retaining nut first.**

31. Install the motor mount retaining nuts.
32. Tighten the exhaust pipe retaining nuts.
33. Clean and inspect the oil pan drain plug and gasket. Install new, if necessary.
34. Install the oil drain plug.
35. Reposition the power steering pump and install the power steering pump bolts.
36. Install the left fan stator stand-off.
37. Install the upper power steering mounting bolt.
38. Fill the engine with clean engine oil.
39. Install the engine cover.
40. Connect the battery ground cable.
41. Install the A/C compressor.
42. Install the cooling fan stator.
43. Run the engine and check for leaks.

Upper Oil Pan

1. Before servicing the vehicle, refer to the Precautions Section.
2. Remove the oil pan.
3. Remove the bolts and the upper oil pan. Remove and discard the press-in-place gasket.
4. Clean and inspect the sealing surfaces.

To install:

➡Install a new press-in-place gasket.

5. Install the upper oil pan and bolts.
6. Install the lower oil pan.

OIL PUMP

REMOVAL & INSTALLATION

4.6L, 5.4L and 6.8L Engines

See Figures 172 and 173.

1. Before servicing the vehicle, refer to the Precautions Section.
2. Raise and safely support the vehicle.
3. Remove the timing drive components.
4. Remove the oil pan.
5. Remove the 3 bolts, the oil pump screen and pickup tube and the spacer.
6. Remove the 3 bolts and the oil pump.

To install:

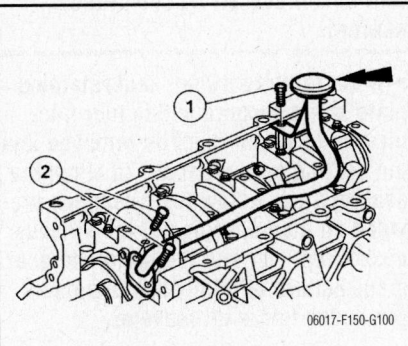

Fig. 172 Pickup tube and spacer—4.6L, 5.4L and 6.8L engines

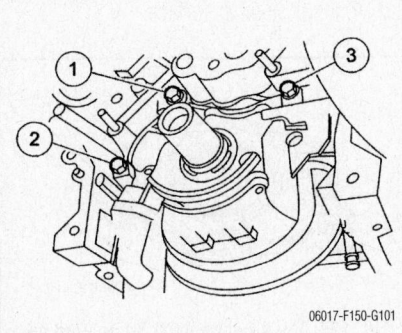

Fig. 173 Oil pump fasteners—4.6L, 5.4L and 6.8L engines

➡Lubricate the new O-ring seal with clean engine oil.

7. Clean and inspect the mating surfaces and install a new O-ring seal.

✳✳ WARNING

The oil pump must be primed prior to starting the engine.

8. Install the oil pump and loosely install the 3 bolts. Tighten the bolts in the sequence shown to 10 Nm (89 inch lbs.).

✳✳ WARNING

Make sure the O-ring is in place and not damaged. A missing or damaged O-ring can cause foam in the lubrication system, low oil pressure and severe engine damage.

➡Install a new O-ring and lubricate with clean engine oil.

9. Install the pickup tube spacer, oil pump screen and pickup tube and the 3 bolts. Tighten bolt 1 to 25 Nm (18 ft. lbs.). Tighten bolts 2 to 10 Nm (89 inch lbs.).
10. Install the oil pan.
11. Install the timing drive components.

6.0L Diesel Engine

See Figure 174.

1. Before servicing the vehicle, refer to the Precautions Section.
2. With the vehicle in **Neutral**, position it on a hoist.
3. Disconnect the battery ground cable(s).
4. Remove the cooling fan.
5. On vehicles with dual alternator, perform the following:
    a. Remove the dual alternator accessory drive belt.
    b. Remove the bolts and the dual alternator pulley.
6. Remove the accessory drive belt.
7. Check the crankshaft vibration damper runout.
8. Remove the paint from the face of the crankshaft vibration damper at four points 90 degrees apart.
9. Attach dial indicator 100-002 to the cylinder block. Position the tool on one of the unpainted surfaces.
10. Using a suitable tool, pry the crankshaft forward. Zero the dial indicator.

➡ Pry the crankshaft forward only to eliminate possible error caused by crankshaft end play.

11. Rotate the crankshaft 90 degrees. Pry

the crankshaft forward. Record the measurement. Repeat at each unpainted surface.
12. If the runout exceeds specification, install a new crankshaft vibration damper.

✳✳ CAUTION

To avoid personal injury, support the vibration damper during mounting bolt removal. The damper can slide off the nose of the crankshaft very easily.

13. Remove the bolts and the crankshaft vibration damper.
14. Discard the bolts.
15. Punch two holes in the seal.
16. Using the special tool 303-D060, remove the crankshaft seal.

➡Production engine will not have a wear sleeve.

17. If equipped, remove the crankshaft damper wear sleeve using tool 303-762.
18. Remove the bolts and the gerotor cover. Remove and discard the O-ring seal.

➡Mark the front of the inner and outer gerotor for correct reassembly.

19. Remove the inner and outer gerotors.
20. Inspect the oil pump components and replace as necessary.
21. Inspect the oil pump for excessive metal particles.
22. Inspect the oil pump for gouging, cracks or deep scratches.
23. Inspect the oil pump inner and outer gear rotors for damage or excessive wear.

To install:

➡Install the gears with marks pointing outward.

24. Lubricate the inner gear with lithium assembly grease and install onto the crankshaft. Lubricate the outer gear with lithium assembly grease and mesh with the inner gear rotor in the oil pump housing. Wipe off the excess assembly grease.
25. Install a new O-ring seal.
26. Install the gerotor cover and bolts. Tighten to 71 inch lbs. (8 Nm).
27. Thoroughly clean the crankshaft front seal mounting surface.
28. Apply Threadlock 262® to the outer circumference of the leading edge of the crankshaft.

➡ New seal and wear sleeve must not be separated.

29. Using the special tool 303-361, install the oil seal and wear sleeve assembly.

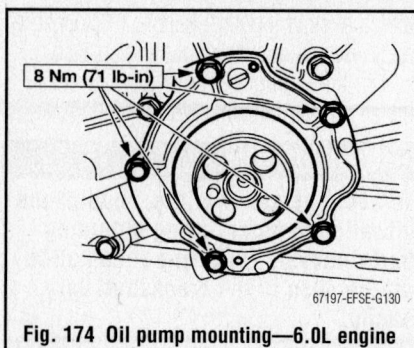

Fig. 174 Oil pump mounting—6.0L engine

※ CAUTION

To prevent engine damage, you must always install four new bolts when installing the vibration damper.

➡Do not use anti-seize compounds, grease or any lubricants. Lubricants have an adverse effect on the torque results.

30. Install the crankshaft vibration damper and bolts.
31. Tighten the bolts in a criss-cross sequence as follows:
   a. Tighten the bolts to 50 ft. lbs. (68 Nm).
   b. Tighten the bolts an additional 90 degrees.
32. Install the accessory drive belt.
33. On vehicles with dual alternator, perform the following:
   a. Install the dual alternator pulley and bolts. Tighten to 35 ft. lbs. (47 Nm).
   b. Install the dual alternator accessory drive belt.
34. Install the cooling fan stator
35. Connect the battery ground cables.

PISTON AND RING

POSITIONING
See Figures 175 through 178.

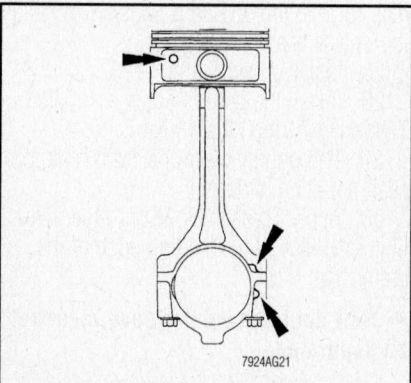

Fig. 175 4.6L engine—piston and connecting rod front mark locations

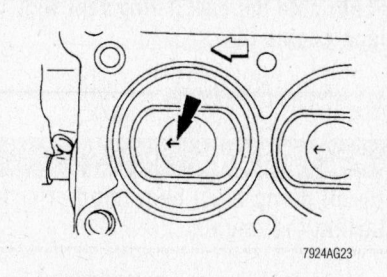

Fig. 176 4.6L engine—piston-to-engine orientation

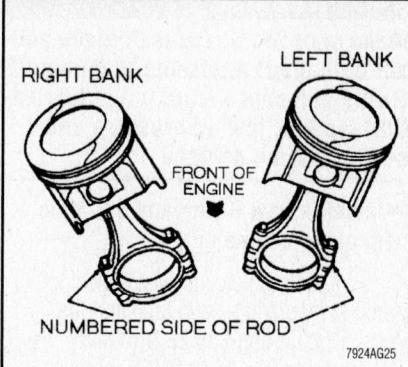

Fig. 177 5.4L and 6.8L engines—piston and connecting rod assembly positioning

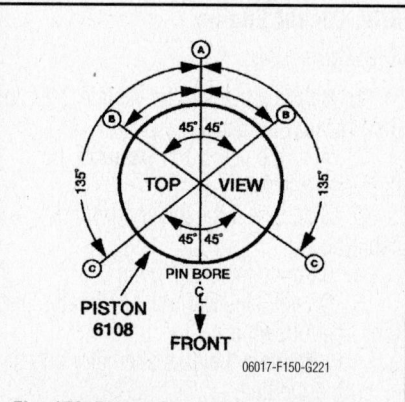

Fig. 178 Piston ring arrangement—all gasoline engines

REAR MAIN SEAL

REMOVAL & INSTALLATION

4.6L, 5.4L and 6.8L Engines
See Figures 179 through 182.

1. Before servicing the vehicle, refer to the Precautions Section.
2. Remove the oil pan.
3. Remove the flexplate.
4. Using a puller set, remove the crankshaft rear oil seal slinger.
5. Using a puller set, remove the crankshaft rear seal.

6. Remove the six bolts and the crankcase rear seal retainer.

To install:

※ CAUTION

Do not use metal scrapers, wire brushes, power abrasive discs or other abrasive means to clean the sealing surfaces. These tools cause scratches and gouges which make leak paths. Use a plastic scraping tool to remove all traces of old sealant.

➡Clean the sealing surfaces with silicone gasket remover and metal surface prep.

7. Follow the directions on the packaging. Failure to follow this procedure can cause future oil leakage.
8. Clean and inspect the mating surface.

※ CAUTION

Do not use metal scrapers, wire brushes, power abrasive discs or other abrasive means to clean the sealing surfaces. These tools cause scratches and gouges which make leak paths. Use a plastic scraping tool to remove all traces of old sealant.

➡If the rear crankshaft seal retaining plate is not secured within four minutes, the sealant must be removed and the sealing area cleaned. To clean the sealing area, follow the directions provided on the packaging of the silicone gasket remover and the metal surfacer prep. Failure to follow this procedure can cause future oil leakage.

➡The silicone must be applied on the groove along the retainer plate.

9. Apply a 4 mm (0.16 in.) bead of silicone gasket and sealant around the rear oil seal retainer sealing surface.

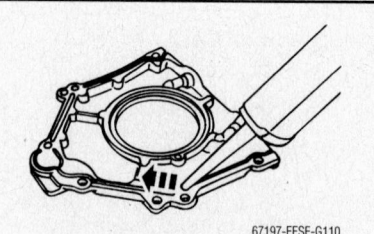

Fig. 179 The silicone must be applied on the groove along the retainer plate—4.6L, 5.4L and 6.8L Engines

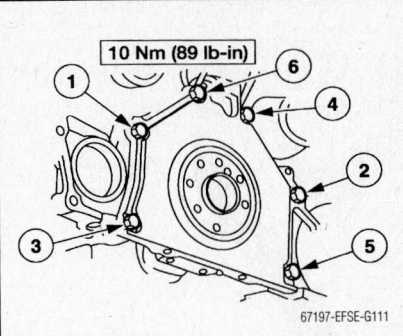

Fig. 180 Tighten the bolts in the sequence shown—4.6L, 5.4L and 6.8L Engines

10. Install the rear seal retainer and loosely install the six bolts. Tighten the bolts in the sequence shown.

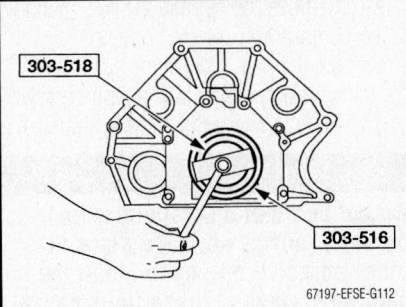

Fig. 181 Using the special tools, install the crankshaft rear seal—4.6L, 5.4L and 6.8L Engines

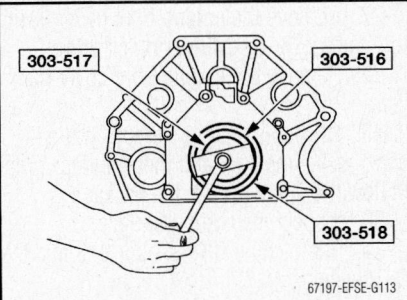

Fig. 182 Using the special tools, install the crankshaft rear oil slinger—4.6L, 5.4L and 6.8L Engines

➡**Lubricate the inner lip of the rear crankshaft seal with clean engine oil.**

11. Using the special tools, install the crankshaft rear seal.
12. Using the special tools, install the crankshaft rear oil slinger.
13. Install the oil pan.
14. Install the flexplate.

6.0L Diesel Engine

See Figures 183 through 185.

1. Before servicing the vehicle, refer to the Precautions Section.
2. Remove the transmission.
3. Remove the bolts.
4. Remove the flexplate or flywheel.

➡**Use extreme care when removing the flywheel front adapter to prevent damage to the alignment dowel pin.**

5. Remove the flywheel front adapter.

✳✳ CAUTION

To prevent engine damage, do not remove the rear primary crankshaft flange bolts under any circumstances. If the flange is removed and reinstalled, it will result in engine vibration and premature transmission component wear.

6. Punch two holes in the rear main seal, across from each other.
7. Using the puller tool 100-001, remove the rear main seal.

➡**Production engines will not have a wear sleeve.**

8. If equipped with a crankshaft wear sleeve, use the tool 303-771 to remove the crankshaft rear wear sleeve.1

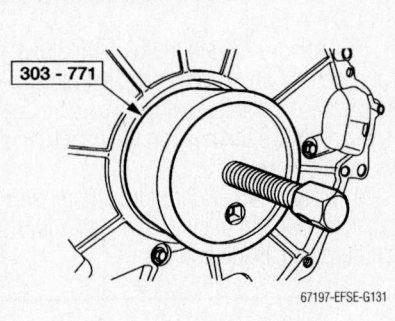

Fig. 183 Rear main seal wear sleeve removal—6.0L engine

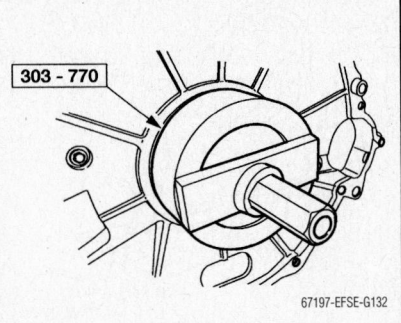

Fig. 184 Rear main seal installation—6.0L engine

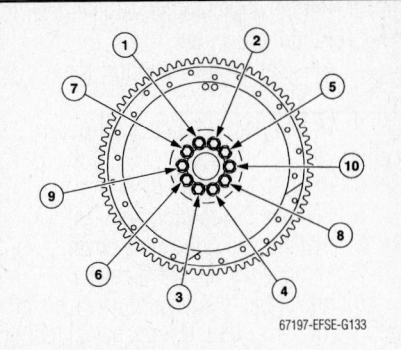

Fig. 185 Flywheel installation torque sequence—6.0L engine

9. Clean and inspect the crankshaft sealing surface.

To install:

➡**The crankshaft rear oil seal and wear sleeve are installed as an assembly.**

➡ **Lubricate the outer diameter of the rubber seal with a solution of dish soap and water (approximately 50/50 mix) prior to assembly. Do not use any other type of lubricant.**

10. Apply a bead of Threadlock 262® around the circumference of the outer rear edge of the secondary crankshaft flange.
11. Using tool 303-770, install the crankshaft rear oil seal.
12. Install the flywheel front adapter.
13. Install the flexplate or flywheel.
14. Install the bolts. Snug all bolts to 44 inch lbs. (5 Nm), then tighten all bolts to 69 ft. lbs. (94 Nm) in the sequence illustrated.
15. Install the transmission.

TIMING COVER, TIMING CHAIN, AND SPROCKETS

REMOVAL & INSTALLATION

4.6L and 5.4L Engines

See Figures 186 through 216.

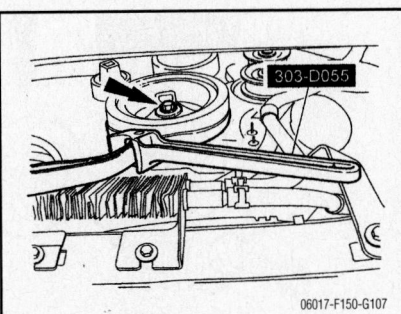

Fig. 186 Using special tool 303-D055, remove the bolt and washer—4.6L and 5.4L engines

1. Before servicing the vehicle, refer to the Precautions Section.
2. Raise and safely support the vehicle.
3. Disconnect the battery ground cable.
4. Drain the engine oil.
5. Remove the cooling fan.
6. Remove the right valve cover.
7. Remove the left valve cover.
8. Rotate the tensioner clockwise and remove the drive belt. Using special tool 303-D055, remove the bolt and washer and discard the bolt.

❊❊ WARNING

This bolt is torque-to-yield and cannot be reused.

9. Using special tool 303-099, remove the crankshaft pulley.
10. Using special tool 303-107, remove the crankshaft front seal.
11. Remove the 4 coolant pump pulley bolts and the coolant pump pulley.

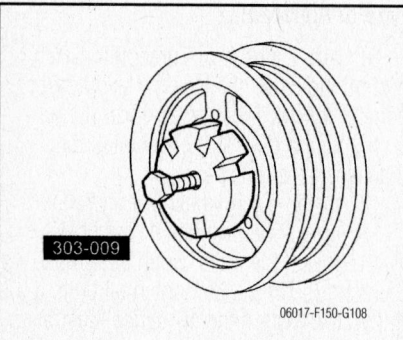

Fig. 187 Using special tool 303-099, remove the crankshaft pulley—4.6L and 5.4L engines

Fig. 189 Using special tool 211-016, remove the power steering pump pulley—4.6L and 5.4L engines

12. Remove the accessory drive belt idler pulley bolt and the accessory drive belt idler pulley.
13. Using special tool 211-016, remove the power steering pump pulley.
14. Disconnect the power steering pressure tube. Drain the power steering fluid into a suitable container.
15. Remove the nut and position aside the power steering pressure tube.
16. Remove the power steering pump bolts and position the power steering pump assembly aside.
17. Disconnect the camshaft position (CMP) sensor electrical connector.
18. Remove the CMP sensor bolt and the CMP sensor.
19. Remove the left radio interference capacitor nut and position the left radio interference capacitor aside.
20. Remove the nut and the upper radiator hose bracket.
21. Remove the right radio interference capacitor nut and position the right radio interference capacitor aside.

22. Disconnect the crankshaft position (CKP) sensor electrical connector.
23. Remove the 4 oil pan bolts.
24. Remove the nut and the A/C manifold and tube assembly support bracket.
25. If equipped, remove the nut and the transmission cooler tube support bracket.
26. Remove the bolts and the studs.

❊❊ WARNING

Do not use metal scrapers, wire brushes, power abrasive discs or other abrasive means to clean the sealing surfaces. These tools cause scratches and gouges which make leak paths. Use a plastic scraping tool to remove all traces of old sealant.

27. Remove the engine front cover from the front cover-to-cylinder block dowel.
28. Remove the engine front cover gaskets.
29. Clean the mating surfaces with silicone gasket remover and metal surface prep. Follow the directions on the packaging.
30. Inspect the mating surfaces.
31. Remove the CKP sensor bolt and the CKP sensor.

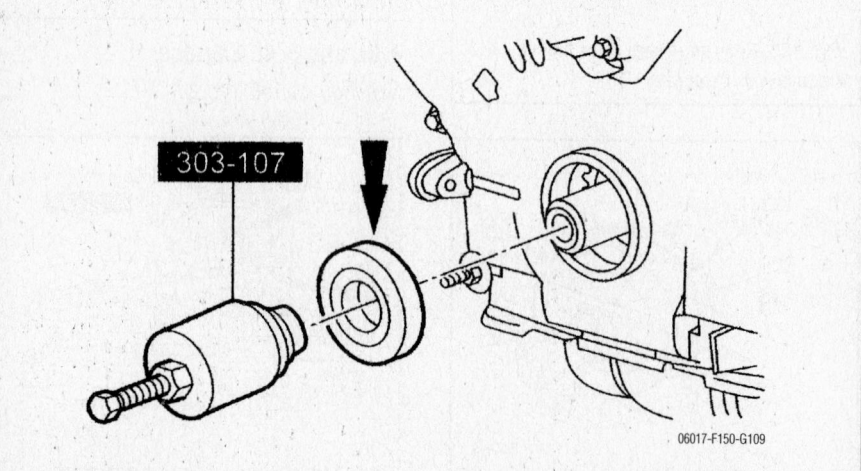

Fig. 188 Using special tool 303-107, remove the crankshaft front seal—4.6L and 5.4L engines

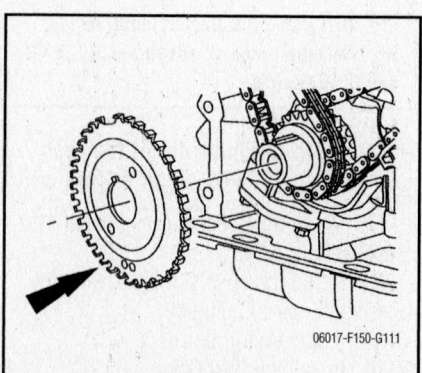

Fig. 190 Crankshaft sensor ring—4.6L and 5.4L engines

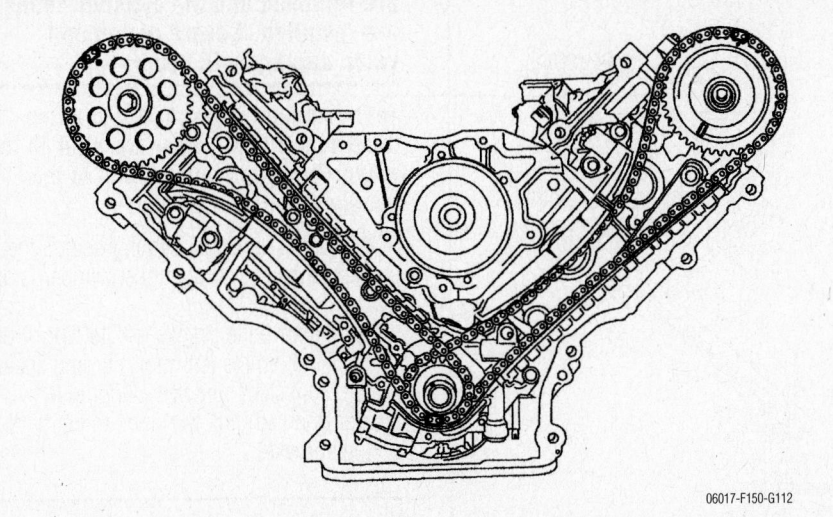

Fig. 191 Rotate the crankshaft until the timing mark on the right camshaft sprocket is approximately at the 11 o'clock position and the timing mark on the left camshaft sprocket is approximately at the 12 o'clock position—4.6L and 5.4L engines

32. Remove the crankshaft sensor ring from the crankshaft.

33. Rotate the crankshaft until the timing mark on the right camshaft sprocket is approximately at the 11 o'clock position and the timing mark on the left camshaft sprocket is approximately at the 12 o'clock position.

34. Install the special tools on the camshaft as shown.

> ※※ **WARNING**
>
> **If one or both of the tensioner mounting bolts are loosened or removed, the tensioner-sealing bead must be inspected for seat integrity. If cracks, tears or separation from the tensioner body or permanent compression of the seal bead is observed, install a new tensioner.**

35. Remove the bolts (1). Remove the timing chain tensioners (2). Remove the timing chain tensioner arms (3).

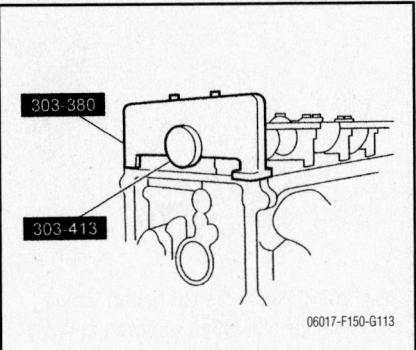

Fig. 192 Install the special tools on the camshaft—4.6L engine

36. Remove the timing chains and crankshaft sprocket.

37. Remove the bolts (1). Remove the left timing chain guide (2).

38. Remove the bolts (3). Remove the right timing chain guide (4).

To install:

> ※※ **WARNING**
>
> **Timing chain procedures must be followed exactly or damage to valves and pistons will result.**

> ※※ **WARNING**
>
> **Prior to installation, inspect the tensioner-sealing bead for seal integrity. If cracks, tears, separation from the tensioner body or permanent compression of the seal bead is observed, install a new tensioner.**

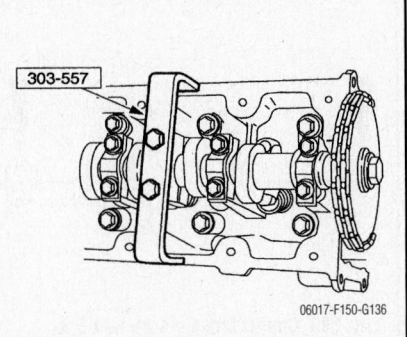

Fig. 193 Install the special tool on the camshaft—5.4L engine

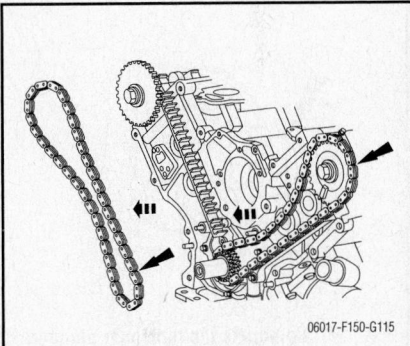

Fig. 195 Timing chain and sprocket removal—4.6L and 5.4L engines

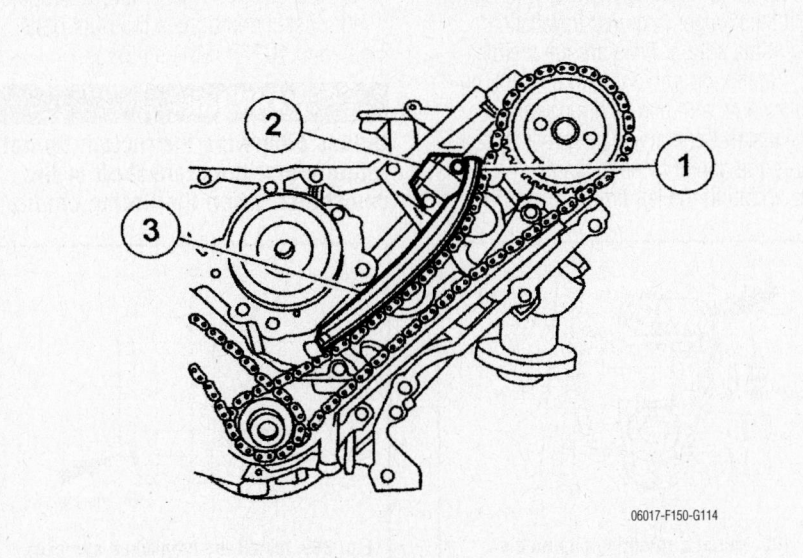

Fig. 194 Removing the tensioners and tensioner arms—4.6L and 5.4L engines

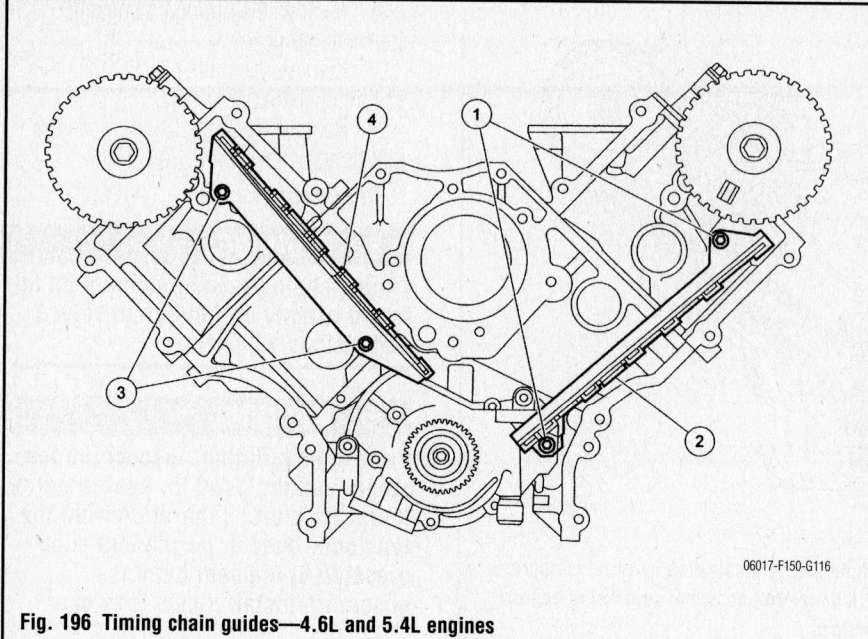

Fig. 196 Timing chain guides—4.6L and 5.4L engines

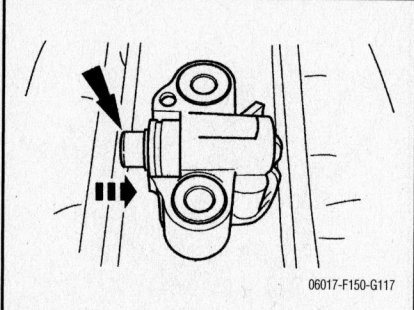

Fig. 197 Compress the tensioner plunger, using a vise—4.6L and 5.4L engines

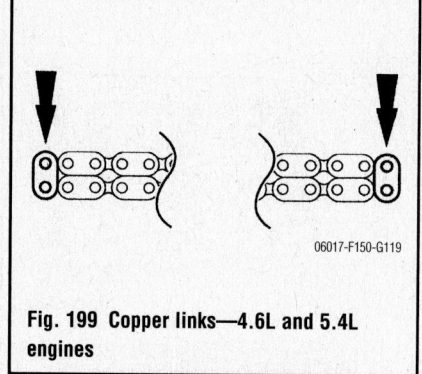

Fig. 199 Copper links—4.6L and 5.4L engines

39. Compress the tensioner plunger, using a vise.

40. Install a retaining clip on the tensioner to hold the plunger in during installation.

41. If the copper links are not visible, mark one link on one end and one link on the other end, and use as timing marks.

42. Install the crankshaft sprocket, making sure the flange faces forward.

43. Position the left timing chain guide.

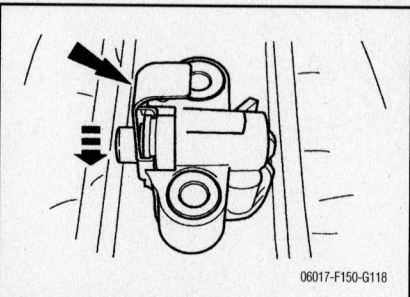

Fig. 198 Install a retaining clip on the tensioner to hold the plunger in during installation—4.6L and 5.4L engines

44. Install and tighten the left bolts. Tighten to 10 Nm (89 inch lbs.).

45. Position the right timing chain guide.

46. Install and tighten the right bolts. Tighten to 10 Nm (89 inch lbs.).

✻✻ WARNING

Unless otherwise instructed, do not rotate either the crankshaft or the camshafts, when the timing chains

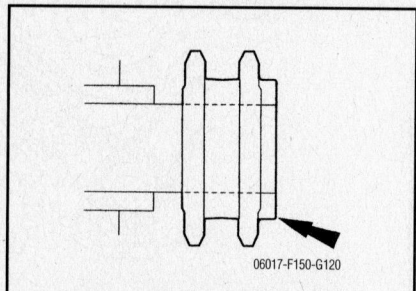

Fig. 200 Install the crankshaft sprocket, making sure the flange faces forward—4.6L and 5.4L engines

are removed and the cylinder heads are installed. Severe piston and valve damage will occur.

➡ The number one cylinder is at top dead center (TDC) when the stud on the engine block fits into the slot in the handle of the special tool.

47. Using the special tool, position the crankshaft so the number one cylinder is at TDC.

48. Remove the Crankshaft Holding Tool.

49. Position the left (inner) timing chain on the crankshaft sprocket, aligning the copper (marked) link with the timing mark on the sprocket.

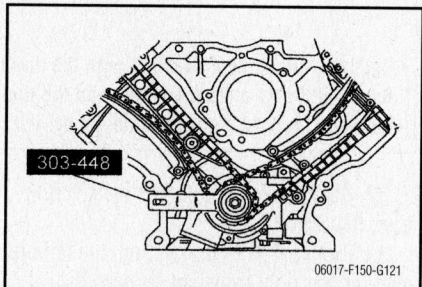

Fig. 201 Using the special tool, position the crankshaft so the number one cylinder is at TDC—4.6L and 5.4L engines

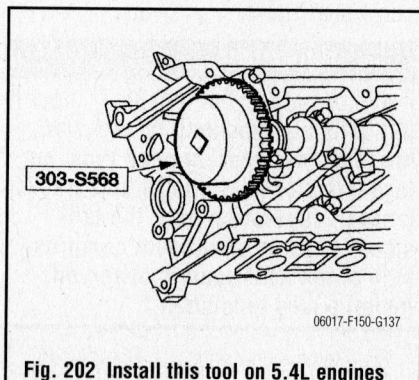

Fig. 202 Install this tool on 5.4L engines

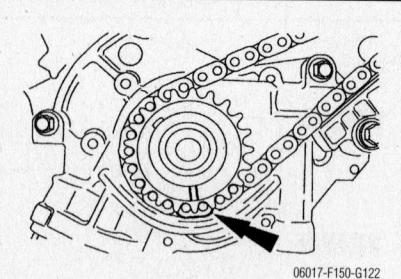

Fig. 203 Position the left (inner) timing chain on the crankshaft sprocket, aligning the copper (marked) link with the timing mark on the sprocket—4.6L and 5.4L engines

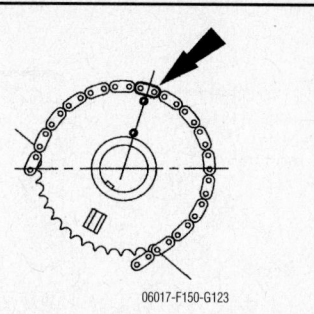

Fig. 204 Install the left timing chain on the camshaft sprocket, aligning the copper (marked) link with the timing marks on the sprocket—4.6L and 5.4L engines

50. Install the left timing chain on the camshaft sprocket, aligning the copper (marked) link with the timing marks on the sprocket.

➡**The left timing chain tensioner arm has a bump near the dowel hole for identification.**

51. Position the left timing chain tensioner arm on the dowel pin and install the left timing chain tensioner. Tighten to 25 Nm (18 ft. lbs.).

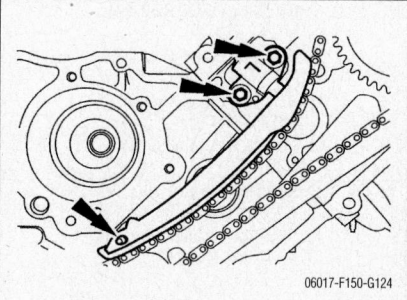

Fig. 205 Position the left timing chain tensioner arm on the dowel pin and install the left timing chain tensioner—4.6L and 5.4L engines

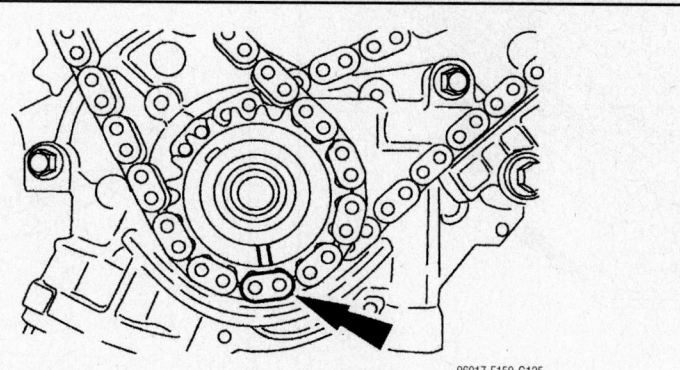

Fig. 206 Position the right (outer) timing chain on the crankshaft sprocket, aligning the copper (marked) link with the timing mark on the sprocket—4.6L and 5.4L engines

52. Remove the retaining clip from the left timing chain tensioner.

53. Position the right (outer) timing chain on the crankshaft sprocket, aligning the copper (marked) link with the timing mark on the sprocket.

55. Install the right timing chain on the camshaft sprocket, aligning the copper (marked) link with the timing marks on the sprocket.

56. Position the right timing chain tensioner arm on the dowel pin and install the right timing chain tensioner. Tighten to 25 Nm (18 ft. lbs.).

57. Remove the retaining clip from the right timing chain tensioner.

58. Make sure that the copper (marked) chain links are lined up with the dots on the crankshaft sprockets and the camshaft sprocket.

59. Remove the special tools from the camshaft.

60. Install the crankshaft sensor ring on the crankshaft.

61. Install the CKP sensor and the CKP sensor bolt. Tighten to 10 Nm (89 inch lbs.).

❋❋ WARNING

Do not use metal scrapers, wire brushes, power abrasive discs or other abrasive means to clean the sealing surfaces. These tools cause scratches and gouges which make leak paths. Use a plastic scraping tool to remove all traces of old sealant.

➡**If the engine front cover is not secured within 4 minutes, the sealant must be removed and the sealing area cleaned. To clean the sealing area, use silicone gasket remover and metal surface prep. Follow the directions on the packaging. Failure to follow this procedure can cause future oil leakage.**

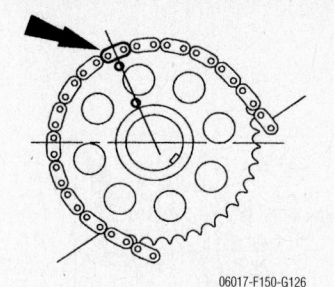

Fig. 207 Install the right timing chain on the camshaft sprocket, aligning the copper (marked) link with the timing marks on the sprocket—4.6L and 5.4L engines

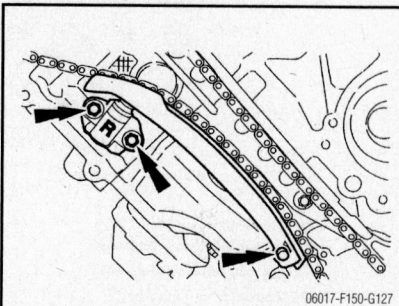

Fig. 208 Position the right timing chain tensioner arm on the dowel pin and install the right timing chain tensioner—4.6L and 5.4L engines

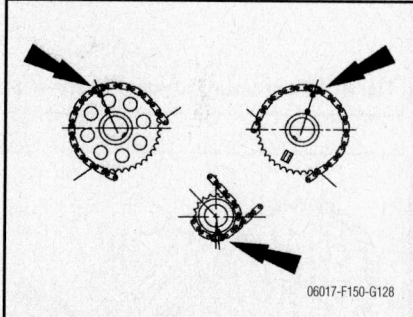

Fig. 209 Make sure that the copper (marked) chain links are lined up with the dots on the crankshaft sprockets and the camshaft sprocket—4.6L and 5.4L engines

➡**Make sure that the engine front cover gasket is in place on the engine front cover before installation.**

62. Apply a bead of silicone gasket and sealant along the cylinder head-to-cylinder block surface and the oil pan-to-cylinder block surface, at the locations shown.

63. Install the engine front cover with the engine front cover gasket on the front cover-to-cylinder block dowel and loosely install the bolts.

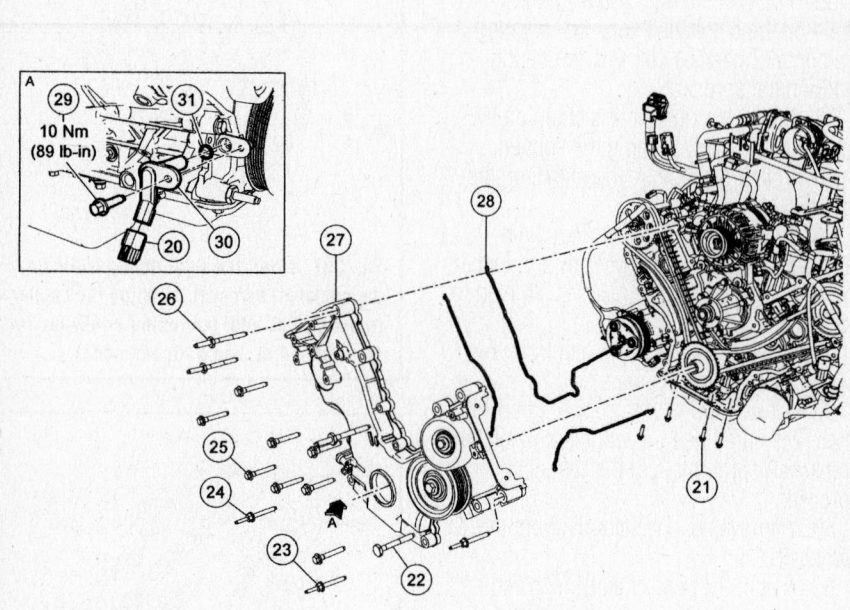

20 Crankshaft position (CKP) sensor electrical connector
21 Oil pan bolts (4 required)
22 Engine front cover bolt
23 Engine front cover lower stud bolt
24 Engine front cover lower stud bolt
25 Engine front cover bolts (8 required)
26 Engine front cover upper stud bolts (4 required)
27 Engine front cover
28 Engine front cover gaskets (3 required)
29 CKP sensor bolt
30 CKP sensor
31 CKP sensor O-ring seal

06017-F150-G129

Fig. 210 Front cover and related parts—4.6L and 5.4L engines

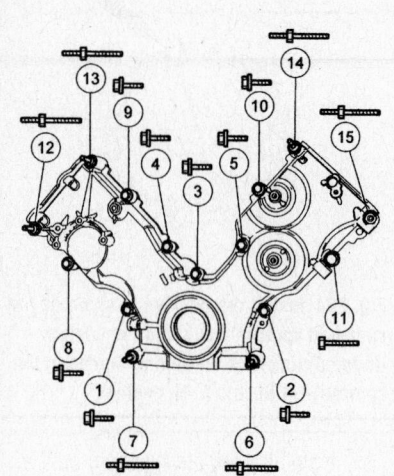

1 Bolt, Hex Flange Head Pilot, M8 x 1.25 x 53
2 Bolt, Hex Flange Head Pilot, M8 x 1.25 x 53
3 Bolt, Hex Flange Head Pilot, M8 x 1.25 x 53
4 Bolt, Hex Flange Head Pilot, M8 x 1.25 x 53
5 Bolts, Hex Flange Head Pilot, M8 x 1.25 x 53
6 Stud Hex Shoulder Pilot, M8 x 1.25 x 50— M6 x 1 x 10
7 Stud and Washer, Hex Head Pilot, M8 x 1.25 — M6 x 1 x 86.35
8 Bolt, Hex Flange Head Pilot, M8 x 1.25 x 53
9 Bolt, Hex Flange Head Pilot, M8 x 1.25 x 53
10 Bolt, Hex Flange Head Pilot, M8 x 1.25 x 53
11 Bolt, Hex Head Pilot, M8 x 1.25 x 53
12 Stud Hex Shoulder Pilot, M8 x 1.25 x 1.25 x 91.1
13 Stud Hex Shoulder Pilot, M8 x 1.25 x 1.25 x 91.1

06017-F150-G131

Fig. 212 Front cover fastener identification—4.6L and 5.4L engines

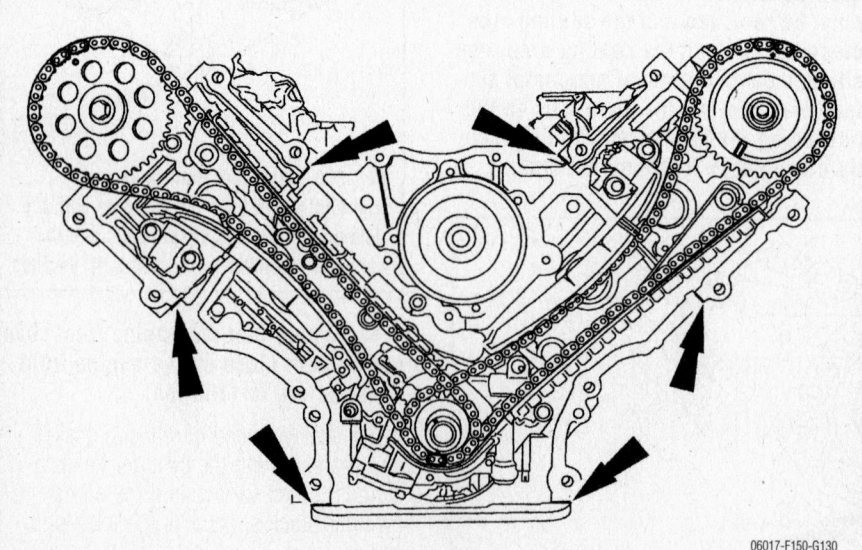

06017-F150-G130

Fig. 211 Apply a bead of silicone gasket and sealant along the cylinder head-to-cylinder block surface and the oil pan-to-cylinder block surface, at the locations indicated—4.6L and 5.4L engines

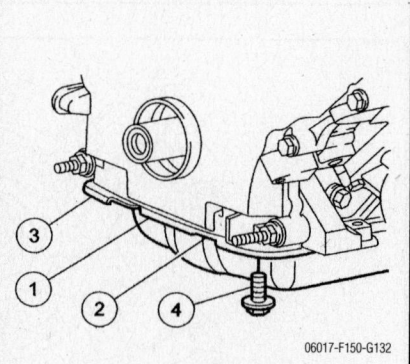

06017-F150-G132

Fig. 213 Oil pan-to-front cover bolt torque sequence—4.6L and 5.4L engines

64. Tighten the engine front cover fasteners in the sequence shown.

65. Loosely install the oil pan-to-front cover bolts, then tighten the bolts in 2 steps, in the sequence shown.
- Step 1: Tighten to 20 Nm (15 ft. lbs.).
- Step 2: Tighten an additional 60 degrees.

66. If equipped, install the transmission cooler tube support bracket and nut. Tighten to 10 Nm (89 inch lbs.).

67. Install the A/C manifold and tube assembly support bracket and nut. Tighten to 10 Nm (89 inch lbs.).

68. Connect the CKP sensor electrical connector.

69. Position the right radio interference capacitor and install the nut. Tighten to 10 Nm (89 inch lbs.).

70. Position the upper radiator hose bracket and install the nut. Tighten to 10 Nm (89 inch lbs.).

71. Install the left radio interference capacitor and install the left radio interference capacitor nut. Tighten to 10 Nm (89 inch lbs.).

72. Install the CMP sensor and the bolt. Tighten to 10 Nm (89 inch lbs.).

73. Connect the CMP sensor electrical connector.

74. Position the power steering pump and install the bolts. Tighten to 25 Nm (18 ft. lbs.).

75. Using special tool 211-D207, install a new O-ring seal on the pressure line fitting.

76. Connect the power steering pressure tube. Tighten to 65 Nm (48 ft. lbs.).

77. Position the power steering pressure tube support bracket and install the nut. Tighten to 10 Nm (89 inch lbs.).

✷✷ WARNING

If the pulley has been removed and installed twice, install a new power steering pump pulley.

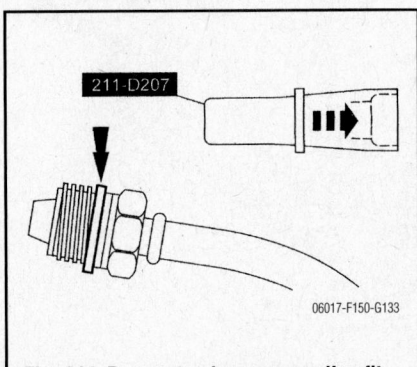

Fig. 214 Power steering pressure line fitting connection—4.6L and 5.4L engines

78. Using special tool 211-185, install the power steering pump pulley. Inspect the pulley for paint marks in the web area near the hub. If there are 2 paint marks, install a new pulley. If there is 1 paint mark or none at all, use a pencil to mark the web area of the pulley near the hub.

79. Install the accessory drive belt idler pulley and the 3 bolts. Tighten to 25 Nm (18 ft. lbs.).

80. Install the coolant pump pulley and the 4 bolts. Tighten to 25 Nm (18 ft. lbs.).

81. Lubricate the engine front cover and the crankshaft front seal inner lip with clean engine oil.

82. Using the special tools shown, install the crankshaft front seal.

➡**If not secured within 4 minutes, the sealant must be removed and the sealing area cleaned. To clean the sealing area, use silicone gasket remover and metal surface prep. Follow the directions on the packaging. Failure to follow this procedure can cause future oil leakage.**

83. Apply silicone gasket and sealant to the Woodruff key slot on the crankshaft pulley.

84. Using special tool 303-102, install the crankshaft pulley.

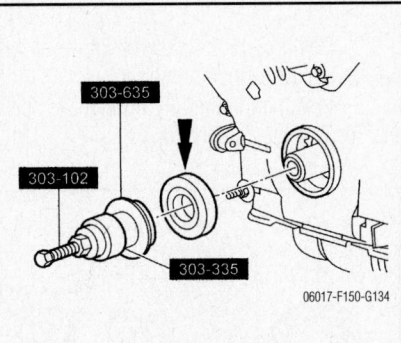

Fig. 215 Crankshaft front seal installation—4.6L and 5.4L engines

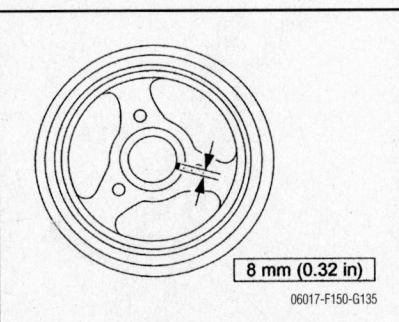

Fig. 216 Apply silicone gasket and sealant to the Woodruff key slot on the crankshaft pulley—4.6L and 5.4L engines

85. Using a new crankshaft pulley bolt, install the crankshaft pulley bolt and washer.

86. Using the special tool to hold the crankshaft pulley, tighten the bolt in 4 steps:
- Step 1: Tighten the bolt to 90 Nm (66 ft. lbs.).
- Step 2: Loosen the bolt one full turn.
- Step 3: Tighten the bolt to 50 Nm (37 ft. lbs.).
- Step 4: Tighten the bolt an additional 90 degrees without exceeding 200 Nm (148 ft. lbs.).

87. Rotate the tensioner clockwise and install the drive belt.

88. Install the left valve cover.

89. Install the right valve cover.

90. Install the cooling fan.

91. Connect the battery ground cable.

92. Fill the engine with clean engine oil.

6.8L Engine

See Figures 217 through 241.

1. Before servicing the vehicle, refer to the Precautions Section.

2. Disconnect the battery ground cable.

3. Remove both of the valve covers.

4. Remove the radiator.

5. Remove the water pump.

6. Raise and support the vehicle.

7. Remove the top bolts and the lower bolt and position the power steering pump aside.

8. Disconnect the crankshaft position (CKP) sensor electrical connector.

9. Remove the drain plug and drain the engine oil.

10. Remove the four front oil pan bolts.

11. Lower the vehicle.

12. Remove the crankshaft front seal.

13. Disconnect the camshaft position (CMP) sensor electrical connection.

14. Remove the bolt and the belt idler pulley.

15. Remove the bolts.

✷✷ WARNING

Do not use metal scrapers, wire brushes, power abrasive discs or other abrasive means to clean the sealing surfaces. These tools cause scratches and gouges which make leak paths. Use a plastic scraping tool to remove all traces of old sealant.

16. Remove the engine front cover from the front cover to cylinder block dowel.

17. Remove the engine front cover gasket and clean and inspect the mating surfaces.

❊❊ WARNING

Since the engine is not free-wheeling, if the crankshaft or the camshafts are moved in any manner during removal and installation the crankshaft and camshaft must be resynchronized.

18. Remove the engine front cover.
19. Remove the crankshaft sensor ring from the crankshaft.

❊❊ WARNING

The caps must be marked for installation in their original location or damage to the engine can occur.

20. Remove the six bolts and remove the balance shaft bearing caps.
21. Remove the balance shaft.

❊❊ WARNING

Unless otherwise instructed, at no time when the timing chain are removed and the cylinder heads are installed may the crankshaft or camshaft be rotated. Severe piston and valve damage will occur.

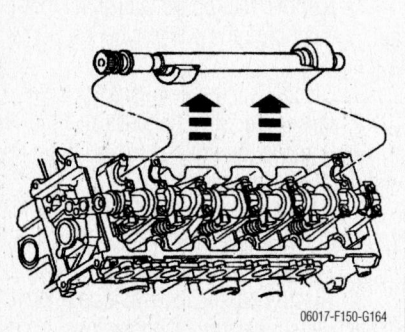

Fig. 217 Remove the balance shaft—6.8L Engine

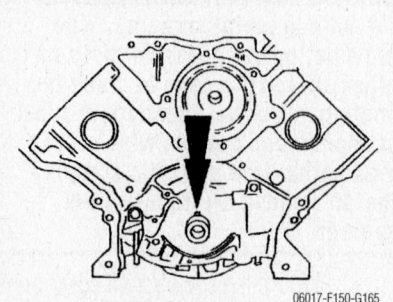

Fig. 218 Position the crankshaft with the keyway at the 12 o'clock position—6.8L Engine

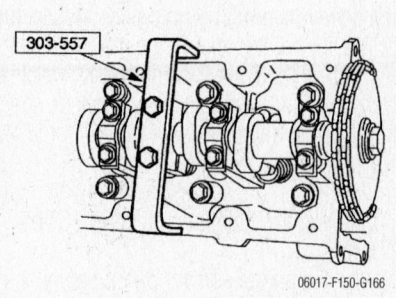

Fig. 219 Install and carefully tighten the special tool on the camshafts—6.8L Engine

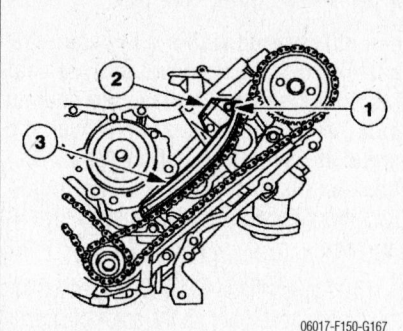

Fig. 220 Remove the timing chain tensioners and arms—6.8L Engine

22. Position the crankshaft with the keyway at the 12 o'clock position.
23. Install and carefully tighten the special tool on the camshafts.

24. Remove the bolts. Remove the timing chain tensioners.
25. Remove the timing chain tensioner arms.
26. Remove the right timing chain from the camshaft sprocket.
27. Remove the right timing chain from the crankshaft sprocket.
28. Remove the left timing chain from the camshaft sprocket.
29. Remove the left timing chain from the crankshaft sprocket.
30. Remove the bolts. Remove the timing chain guides.
31. On engine with bolt-on sprockets, remove the camshaft sprocket.
32. Remove the bolt.
33. Remove the camshaft sprocket.

To install:

❊❊ WARNING

Timing chain procedures must be followed exactly or damage to valves and pistons will result.

34. Compress the tensioner using a soft-jawed vice.
35. While holding the ratchet mechanism with a pick, push the ratchet arm back into the tensioner housing.
36. Install a paper clip on the tensioner to hold the plunger in during installation.

➡ **There are 61 links in each timing chain.**

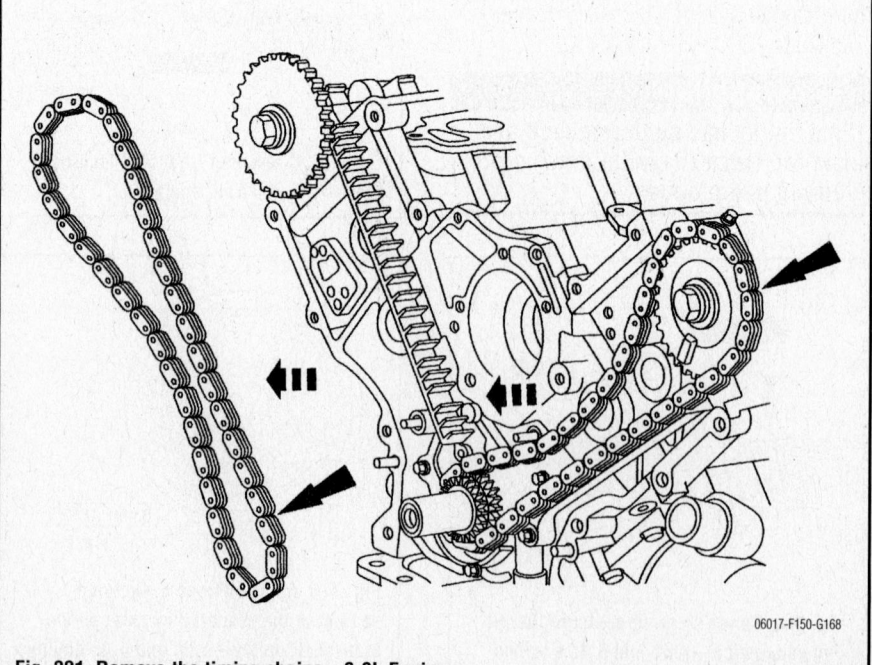

Fig. 221 Remove the timing chains—6.8L Engine

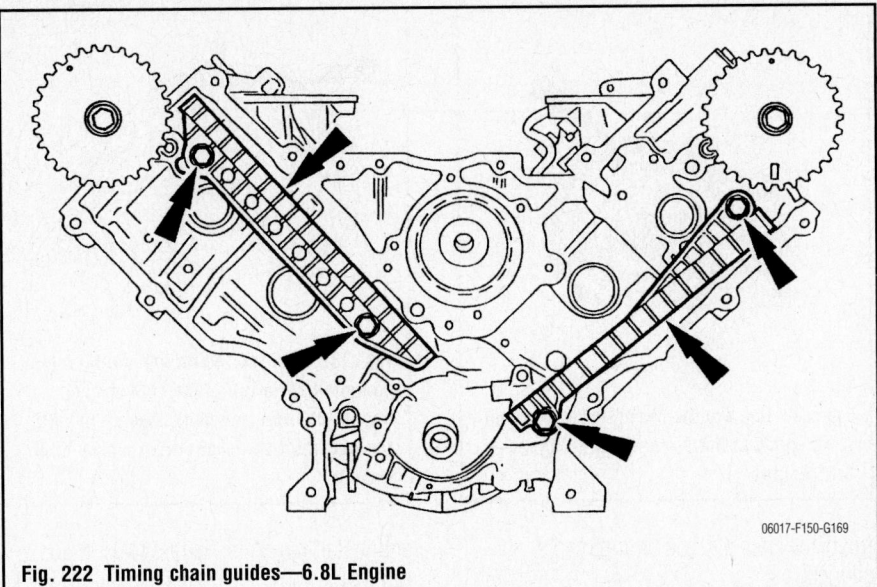

Fig. 222 Timing chain guides—6.8L Engine

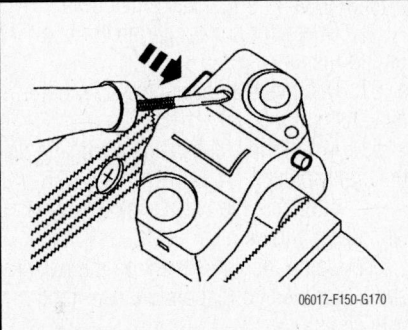

Fig. 223 While holding the ratchet mechanism with a pick, push the ratchet arm back into the tensioner housing—6.8L Engine

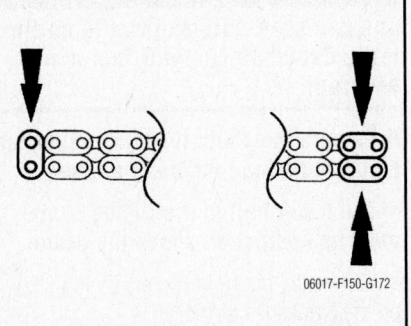

Fig. 225 If copper links are not visible, mark two links on one end and one link on the other end, and use as timing marks—6.8L Engine

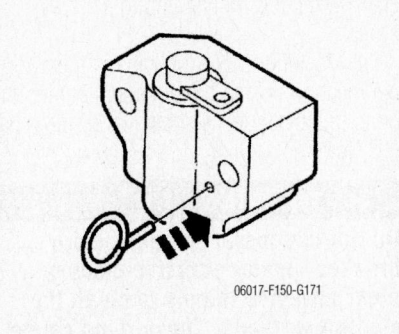

Fig. 224 Install a paper clip on the tensioner to hold the plunger in during installation—6.8L Engine

37. If copper links are not visible, mark two links on one end and one link on the other end, and use as timing marks.

38. On engines equipped with bolt-on sprockets, install the camshaft sprocket bolt. Tighten the bolt as follows:

a. M10 bolt: Tighten in two stages.
- Stage 1: Tighten to 40 Nm (30 ft. lbs.).
- Stage 2: Tighten an additional 90 degrees.

b. M12 bolt: Tighten to 120 Nm (90 ft. lbs.).

39. Install the timing chain guides. Torque to 89 inch lbs. (10 Nm).

➡ **Slightly loosen the Camshaft Holding Tool to allow slight camshaft movement.**

40. Rotate the left camshaft with the Camshaft Positioning Tool until the timing mark is approximately at 12 o'clock.

41. Rotate the right camshaft with the Camshaft Positioning Tool until the timing mark is approximately at 11 o'clock.

42. Tighten the Camshaft Holding Tool to maintain camshaft pre-positioning.

❊❊ WARNING

Rotate the crankshaft counterclockwise only. Do not rotate past the position shown or severe piston and/or valve damage can occur.

43. Position the crankshaft with the special tool, remove the tool.

44. Install the crankshaft sprocket, making sure the flange faces forward.

45. Install the lower end of the left (inner) timing chain, aligning the timing marks.

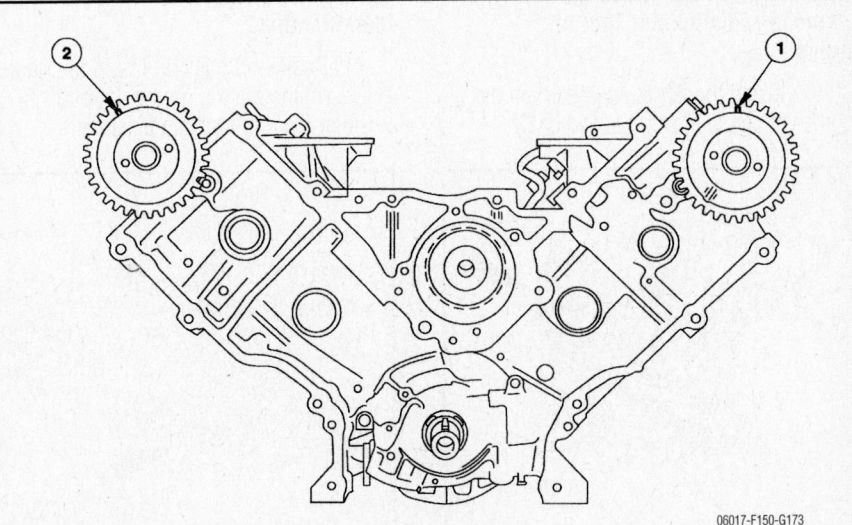

Fig. 226 Rotate the left camshaft with the Camshaft Positioning Tool until the timing mark is approximately at 12 o'clock. Rotate the right camshaft with the Camshaft Positioning Tool until the timing mark is approximately at 11 o'clock—6.8L Engine

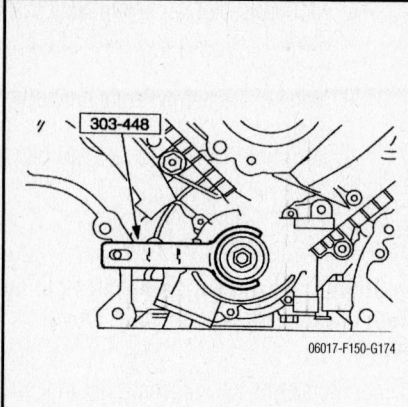

Fig. 227 Position the crankshaft with the special tool—6.8L Engine

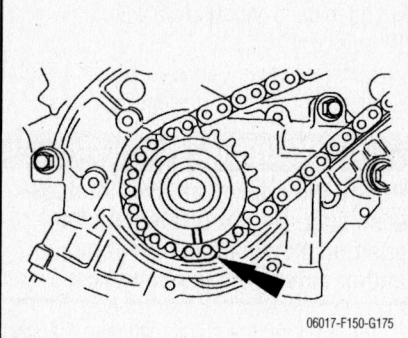

Fig. 228 Install the lower end of the left (inner) timing chain, aligning the timing marks—6.8L Engine

➡Be sure the upper half of the timing chain is below the tensioner guide dowel. If necessary, use the Camshaft Positioning Tool to adjust.

46. Install the left timing chain on the camshaft sprocket with the two chain

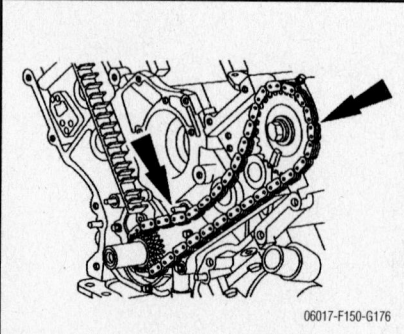

Fig. 229 Install the left timing chain on the camshaft sprocket with the two chain (marked) links and the timing marks aligned—6.8L Engine

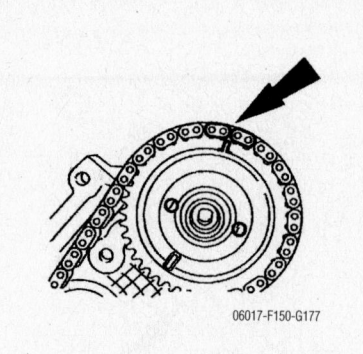

Fig. 230 Be sure the chain link and crankshaft sprocket timing marks are aligned—6.8L Engine

(marked) links and the timing marks aligned.

✳✳ WARNING

The camshaft sprocket can jump time if the Camshaft Holding Tool is not secured.

➡Be sure the chain link and crankshaft sprocket timing marks are aligned.

➡The lower half of the timing chain must be positioned above the dowel.

47. Install the right (outer) timing chain on the crankshaft sprocket.

48. Position the timing chain on the camshaft sprocket. Make sure the two copper-colored (marked) links align with the camshaft sprocket timing mark.

➡The left timing chain tensioner arm has a bump near the dowel hole, for identification.

49. Position the left and right timing chain tensioner arms on the dowel pins. Position the timing chain tensioners

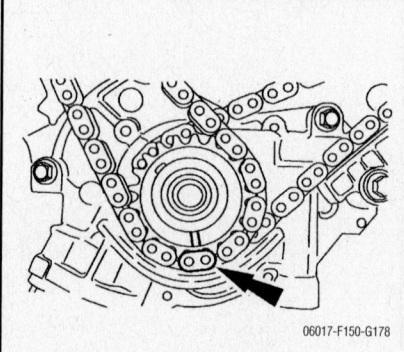

Fig. 231 Install the right (outer) timing chain on the crankshaft sprocket—8L Engine

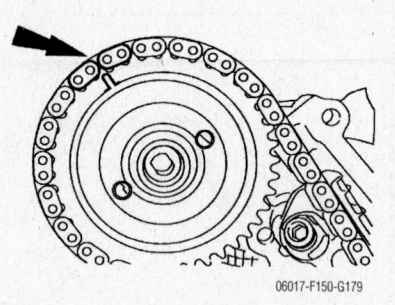

Fig. 232 Position the timing chain on the camshaft sprocket. Make sure the two copper-colored (marked) links align with the camshaft sprocket timing mark—6.8L Engine

and install the bolts. Torque to 18 ft. lbs. (25 Nm).

50. Remove the retaining clips from the right and left timing chain tensioners.

51. Check for correct alignment of all timing marks.

52. Remove the special tools from the camshafts.

53. Install the crankshaft sensor ring on the crankshaft.

54. Lubricate the balance shaft journals with clean engine oil.

55. Using the index mark on the balance shaft, mark the corresponding gear tooth with chalk.

56. Position the balance shaft on the journals.

➡It may be necessary to use an inspection mirror to see the marks.

57. Align the chalk mark on the balance shaft with the camshaft timing mark as shown.

58. Install the bearing caps in their original location. Install the bolts and tighten the bolts in the sequence shown to 89 inch lbs. (10 Nm).

✳✳ WARNING

Do not use metal scrapers, wire brushes, power abrasive discs or other abrasive means to clean the sealing surfaces. These tools cause scratches and gouges which make leak paths. Use a plastic scraping tool to remove all traces of old sealant.

➡If the engine front cover is not secured within four minutes, the sealant must be removed and the sealing area cleaned with metal surface cleaner. Allow to dry until there is no sign of wetness, or four minutes,

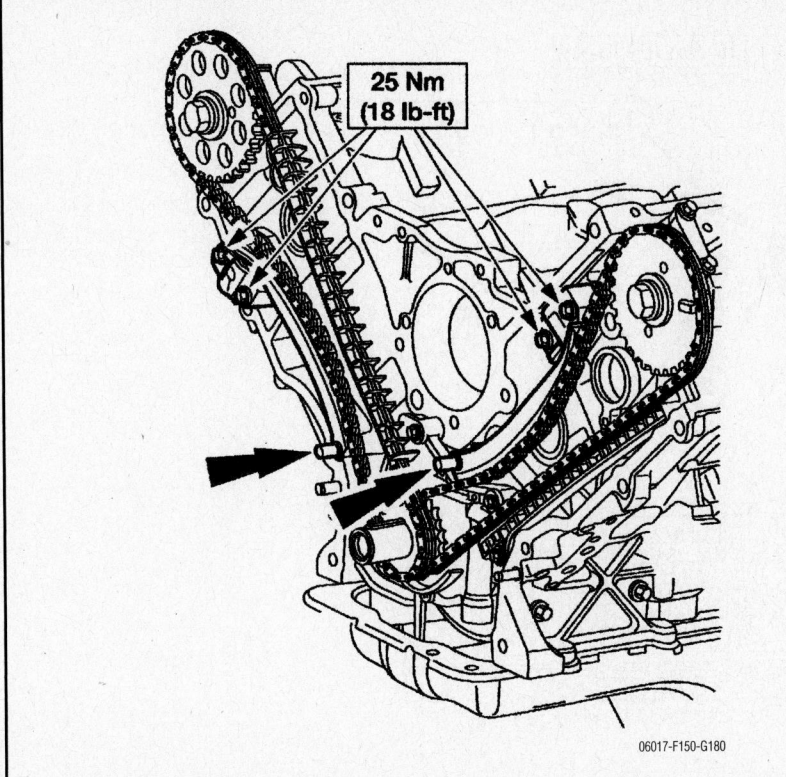

25 Nm (18 lb-ft)

06017-F150-G180

Fig. 233 Position the left and right timing chain tensioner arms on the dowel pins—6.8L Engine

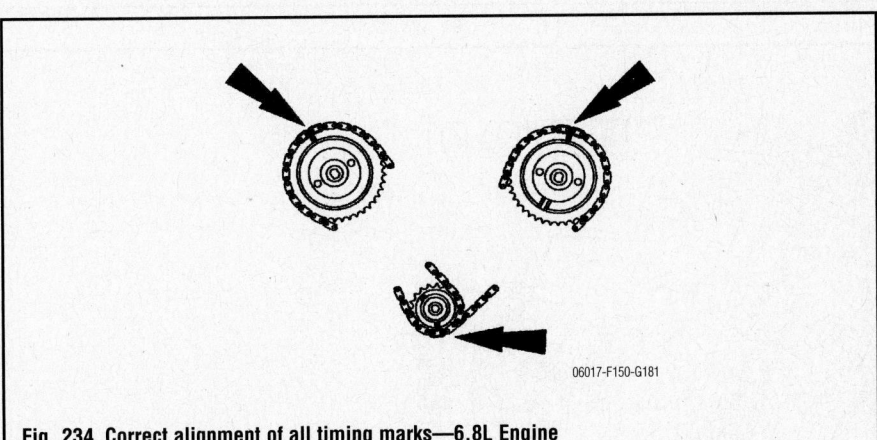

06017-F150-G181

Fig. 234 Correct alignment of all timing marks—6.8L Engine

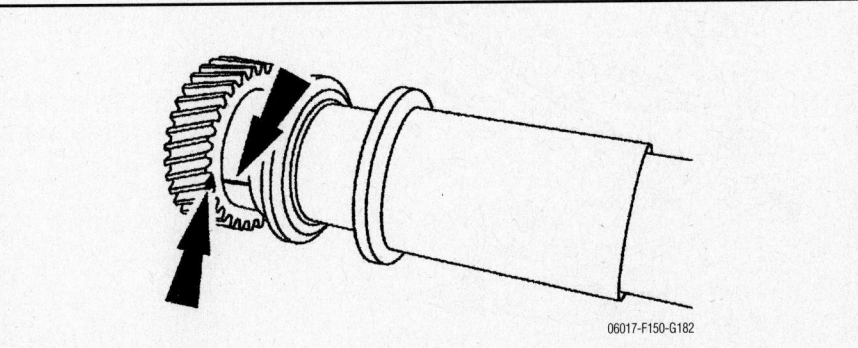

06017-F150-G182

Fig. 235 Using the index mark on the balance shaft, mark the corresponding gear tooth with chalk—6.8L Engine

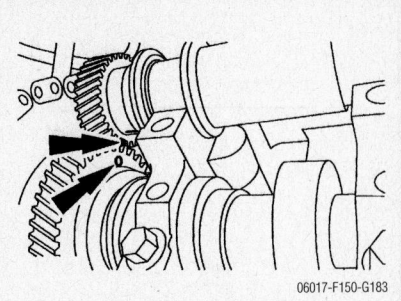

06017-F150-G183

Fig. 236 Align the chalk mark on the balance shaft with the camshaft timing—6.8L Engine

whichever is longer. Failure to follow this procedure can cause future oil leakage.

➡**Make sure that the engine front cover gasket is in place on the engine front cover before installation.**

59. Apply silicone gasket and sealant along the cylinder head to cylinder block surface and the oil pan to cylinder block surface.

60. Install the engine front cover with engine front cover gasket on the front cover to cylinder block dowel and loosely install the bolts.

61. Tighten the engine front cover fasteners in sequence in two stages.
- Stage 1: Tighten fasteners 1 through 7 to 20–30 Nm (15–22 ft. lbs.).
- Stage 2: Tighten fasteners 6 through 15 to 40–55 Nm (30–41 ft. lbs.).

62. Connect the CMP electrical connection.

63. Install a new crankshaft front seal.

64. Raise and support the vehicle.

65. Loosely install the oil pan-to-front cover bolts, then tighten the bolts in the two stages, in the sequence shown.
- Stage 1: Tighten to 20 Nm (15 ft. lbs.).
- Stage 2: Tighten an additional 60 degrees.

66. Connect the crankshaft position sensor electrical connector.

➡**The front lower hole in the power steering pump is not used.**

67. Position the power steering pump and install the bolts. Torque to 15–22 ft. lbs. (20–30 Nm).

68. Install the drain plug.

69. Lower the vehicle.

70. Install the valve covers.

71. Install the water pump.

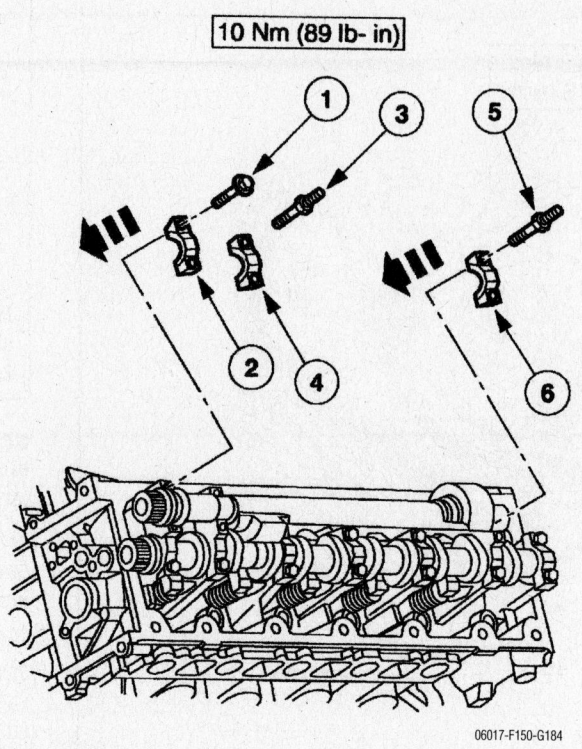

10 Nm (89 lb- in)

06017-F150-G184

Fig. 237 Bearing cap torque sequence—6.8L Engine

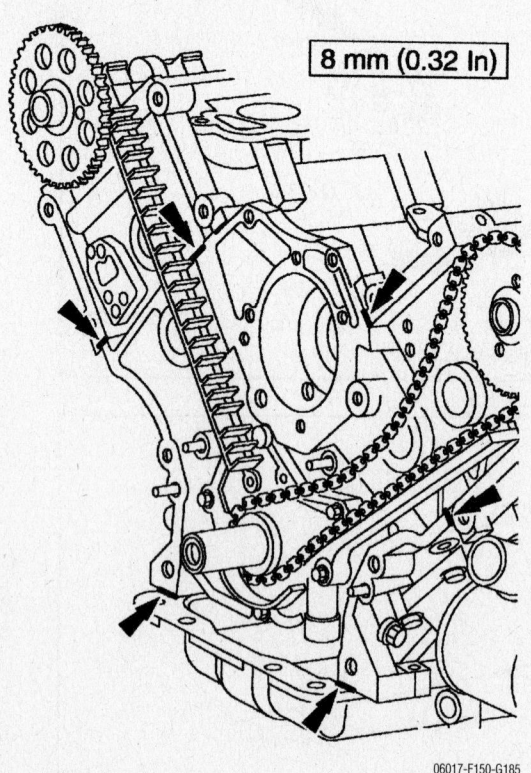

8 mm (0.32 In)

06017-F150-G185

Fig. 238 Apply silicone gasket and sealant along the cylinder head to cylinder block surface and the oil pan to cylinder block surface—6.88L Engine

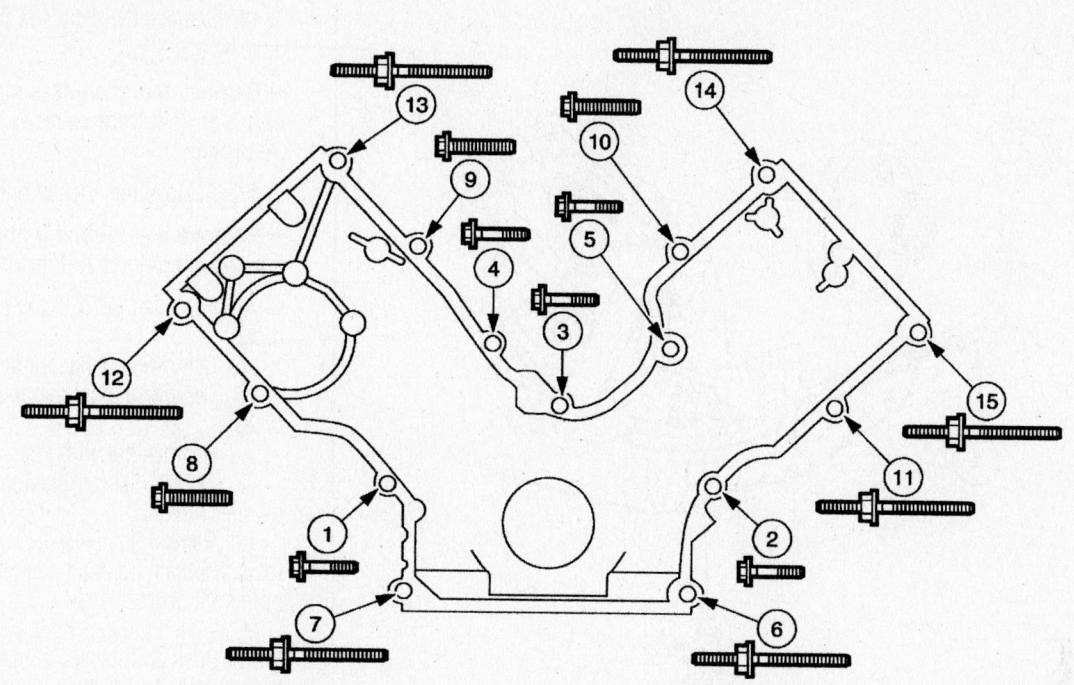

1	Bolt, Hex Flange Head Pilot, M8 x 1.25 x 53	10	Screw and Washer, Hex Pilot, M10 x 1.5 x 57.5
2	Bolt, Hex Flange Head Pilot, M8 x 1.25 x 53	11	Stud and Washer, Hex Head Pilot, M10 x 1.5 x M8 x 1.25 x 109.6
3	Bolt, Hex Flange Head Pilot, M8 x 1.25 x 53	12	Stud and Washer, Hex Head Pilot, M10 x 1.5 x M8 x 1.25 x 109.6
4	Bolt, Hex Flange Head Pilot, M8 x 1.25 x 53	13	Stud and Washer, Hex Head Pilot, M10 x 1.5 x M8 x 1.25 x 109.6
5	Bolts, Hex Flange Head Pilot, M8 x 1.25 x 53	14	Stud and Washer, Hex Head Pilot, M10 x 1.5 x M8 x 1.25 x 109.6
6	Stud, Hex-Head Pilot, M10 x 1.5 x 1.5 x 103.1	15	Stud and Washer, Hex Head Pilot, M10 x 1.5 x M8 x 1.25 x 109.6
7	Stud, Hex-Head Pilot, M10 x 1.5 x 1.5 x 103.1		
8	Screw and Washer, Hex Pilot, M10 x 1.5 x 57.5		
9	Screw and Washer, Hex Pilot, M10 x 1.5 x 57.5		

06017-F150-G186

Fig. 239 Front cover fastener identification—6.8L Engine

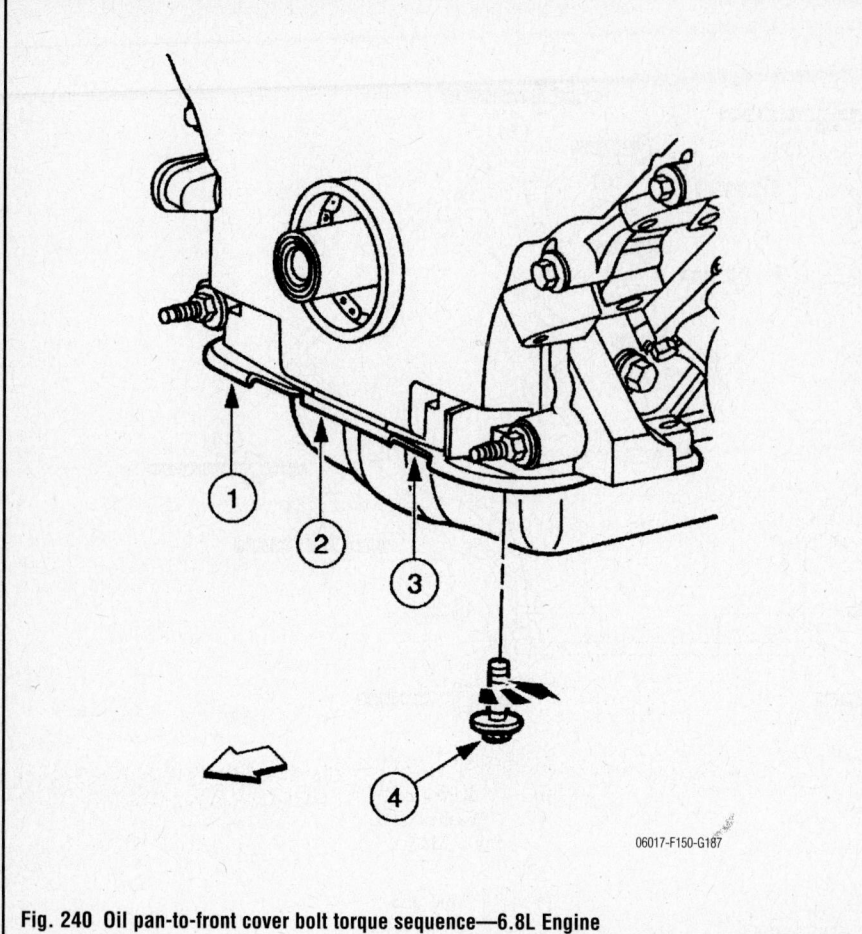

Fig. 240 Oil pan-to-front cover bolt torque sequence—6.8L Engine

06017-F150-G187

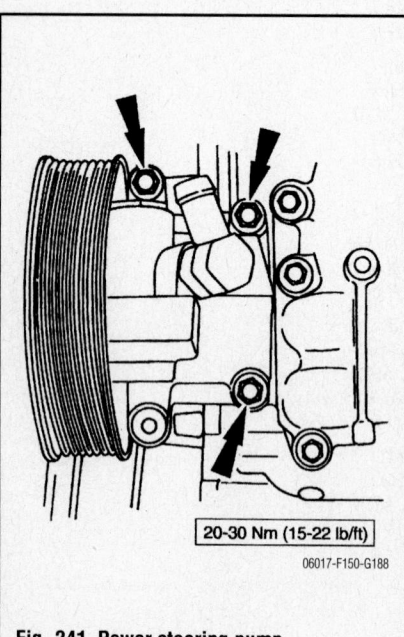

20-30 Nm (15-22 lb/ft)

06017-F150-G188

Fig. 241 Power steering pump installation—6.8L Engine

72. Install the radiator.
73. Fill the engine with clean engine oil.
74. Connect the battery ground cable.

TIMING FRONT COVER, SEAL AND TIMING GEARS

REMOVAL & INSTALLATION

6.0L Diesel Engine

1. Before servicing the vehicle, refer to the Precautions Section.
2. Remove the intake manifold.
3. Disconnect the exhaust pressure tube at the exhaust.
4. Remove the nuts and the exhaust pressure bracket assembly.

➡ Remove the thermostat housing only if a new front cover is being installed.

5. Remove the stud bolts and the thermostat housing.
6. Remove and discard the O-ring.
7. Disconnect the engine coolant fill hose.
8. Disconnect the lower radiator hose.
9. Remove the stator stand-off bolt.

➡ Upper bolts shown, lower bolts similar.

10. Remove the four bolts and position aside the power steering pump.

11. Remove the bolts and the accessory drive belt tensioner.
12. Remove the bolts and the accessory drive idler pulleys.

➡ Remove the coolant pump pulley only if a new front cover is being installed.

13. Remove the coolant pump pulley.

➡ Remove the coolant pump only if a new front cover is being installed.

14. Remove the bolts and the coolant pump.
15. Remove and discard the O-ring.
16. Remove the nut and the battery cable bracket.
17. Remove the oil pump.
18. Check the crankshaft vibration damper runout.
19. Remove the paint from the face of the crankshaft vibration damper at four points 90 degrees apart.
20. Attach the special tool to the cylinder block. Position the special tool on one of the unpainted surfaces.
21. Using a suitable tool, pry the crankshaft forward. Zero the dial indicator.

➡ Pry the crankshaft forward at the same point to eliminate possible error caused by crankshaft end play.

22. Rotate the crankshaft 90 degrees. Pry the crankshaft forward. Record the measurement. Repeat at each unpainted surface. If the runout exceeds specification, install a new crankshaft vibration damper.

✳✳ WARNING

To prevent engine damage, you must always install four new bolts when installing the vibration damper.

✳✳ WARNING

To avoid personal injury, support the vibration damper during mounting bolt removal. The damper can slide off the nose of the crankshaft very easily.

23. Remove the bolts and the crankcase vibration damper.
24. Discard the bolts.
25. Remove the bolts and the front cover.

✳✳ WARNING

Sealant is used where the crankcase and lower crankcase meet. Failure to cut the sealant could result in pulling the lower crankcase seal out while removing the front cover gasket.

26. Use a thin blade scraper to cut the sealant where the crankcase and the lower crankcase meet. Remove and discard the front cover gasket.

27. Clean and inspect the sealing surfaces.

28. Punch two holes in the seal.

29. Using the special tool, remove the crankshaft seal.

➡ **Production engine will not have a wear sleeve.**

30. If equipped, remove the crankshaft damper wear sleeve.

31. Remove the thrust plate mounting bolts and remove the camshaft and gear.

To install:

32. Install the camshaft and gear assembly. Using the special tool, align the camshaft timing mark as shown. Install the thrust plate mounting bolts.

33. Thoroughly clean the crankshaft front seal mounting surface.

34. Apply Threadlock 262® to the outer circumference of the leading edge of the crankshaft.

➡ **New seal and wear sleeve must not be separated.**

35. Using the special tool, install the oil seal and wear sleeve assembly.

36. If removed, install the front cover crankcase dowels into the cylinder block.

➡ **Use guide studs to aid in installation. Studs must be fabricated locally.**

37. Install the guide studs.

38. Apply a bead of sealant at the seam where the crankcase and the lower crankcase meet.

39. Install a new engine front cover gasket.

40. Install the engine front cover and bolts.

✳✳ WARNING

To prevent engine damage, you must always install four new bolts when installing the vibration damper.

➡ **Do not use anti-seize compounds, grease or any lubricants. Lubricants have an adverse effect on the torque results.**

41. Install the crankshaft vibration damper and bolts.

42. Tighten the bolts in the sequence shown.

   a. Tighten the bolts to 68 Nm (50 ft. lbs.).

   b. Tighten the bolts an additional 90 degrees.

43. Install the oil pump.

44. Install the battery cable bracket and nut.

➡ **Install a new O-ring on the coolant pump pulley.**

45. If removed, install the coolant pump and bolts.

46. If removed, install the coolant pump pulley and bolts.

47. Install the accessory drive idler pulleys and bolts.

48. Install the accessory drive belt tensioner and bolts.

49. Position back the power steering pump and install the bolts.

50. Install the stator stand-off bolt.

51. Connect the lower radiator coolant hose.

52. Connect the engine coolant hose.

➡ **Install a new O-ring.**

53. If removed, install the thermostat housing and stud bolts.

54. Install the exhaust pressure bracket assembly and retaining nuts.

55. Connect the exhaust pressure tube fitting at the exhaust manifold.

56. Install the intake manifold.

TURBOCHARGER

REMOVAL & INSTALLATION

6.0L Diesel Engines

1. Before servicing the vehicle, refer to the Precautions Section.

2. Remove the engine cover.

3. Remove the retainers and the air deflector.

4. Remove the power steering reservoir bracket retainers.

5. Remove the power steering fluid indicator and retainers. Remove the power steering mounting bracket. Install the power steering fluid indicator and position the power steering reservoir aside.

6. Disconnect the coolant hoses from the air cleaner outlet pipe.

7. Loosen the clamps and remove the air cleaner outlet pipe.

8. Disconnect the turbocharger intake tube breather hose.

9. Loosen the clamp at the turbocharger.

10. Remove the retaining nuts and position the heater hose bracket aside.

11. Remove the stud bolts and the turbocharger intake tube.

12. Loosen the turbocharger outlet clamp.

13. Remove the turbocharger outlet clamp.

14. Loosen the pipe at the exhaust clamp and position aside.

15. Remove the left bolts for the turbocharger adapter pipe.

16. Remove the right bolts for the turbocharger adapter pipe.

17. Remove the exhaust gas recirculation (EGR) cooler clamp.

18. Remove the turbocharger inlet clamp and turbocharger adapter pipe.

19. Disconnect the VGT actuator electrical connector and retaining clip.

20. Remove the bolts from the turbocharger oil feed tube.

21. Remove and discard the gasket.

22. Remove the bolt and turbocharger oil feed tube.

23. Remove and discard the O-ring seals.

24. Remove the right turbocharger mounting bolts.

25. Remove the left turbocharger mounting bolts.

✳✳ WARNING

Use care not to damage the turbocharger outlet hose when removing the turbocharger.

26. Position the turbocharger to remove the turbocharger drain tube. Remove the turbocharger from the vehicle.

27. Remove and discard the O-ring seals.

28. Remove the plug and drain the oil filter assembly and tubes.

29. Disconnect the wiring push-pin retainer.

30. Remove the bolt and retaining clamp at the oil filter adapter.

31. Remove the bolt and retaining clamp at the oil filter assembly.

➡ **Use care not to bend the tubes, when removing the oil filter tubes.**

32. Remove the bolt and retaining clamp. Remove the oil filter tubes.

33. Remove the bolts and turbocharger pedestal.

To install:

➡ **Install new drain tube O-ring seals and apply clean engine oil.**

➡ **Position the turbocharger outlet flange into the outlet hose as the turbocharger is positioned on the engine.**

34. Position the turbocharger in the vehicle. Install the turbocharger drain tube and turbocharger.

35. Install the left turbocharger mounting bolts. Torque to 28 ft. lbs. (38 Nm).

36. Install the right turbocharger mounting bolts. Torque to 28 ft. lbs. (38 Nm).

37. Prelubricate the oil inlet hole of the turbocharger assembly with clean engine oil and spin the compressor wheel several times to coat the bearings with oil.

➡ **Use a new gasket when installing the oil feed tube.**

38. Install the turbocharger oil feed tube, gasket and bolts. Torque to 18 ft. lbs. (25 Nm).

➡ **Install a new O-ring seal and apply clean engine oil.**

39. Install the turbocharger oil feed tube. Position the clamp and install the bolt.

40. Connect the VGT actuator electrical connector and retaining clip.

41. Position the turbocharger adapter pipe and install the turbocharger inlet clamp.

42. Install the EGR cooler clamp.

43. Install the right bolts for the turbocharger adapter pipe. Torque to 20 ft. lbs. (27 Nm).

44. Install the left bolts for the turbocharger adapter pipe.

45. Position back the turbocharger exhaust pipe. Install the turbocharger exhaust clamp.

46. Tighten the retaining nuts at the exhaust clamp.

47. Tighten the turbocharger outlet clamp.

48. Install the turbocharger intake tube.

49. Inspect the O-ring seals for the oil filter tube ends, replace as necessary.

50. Check and top off the engine oil after the engine is running.

VALVE LASH

ADJUSTMENT

The 4.6L, 5.4L and 6.8L engines utilize hydraulic lash adjusters, which automatically adjust the valve lash. No valve lash adjustment is necessary.

Valve lash on the diesel engine is not adjustable.

ENGINE PERFORMANCE & EMISSION CONTROL

COMPONENT LOCATIONS

See Figures 242 through 257.

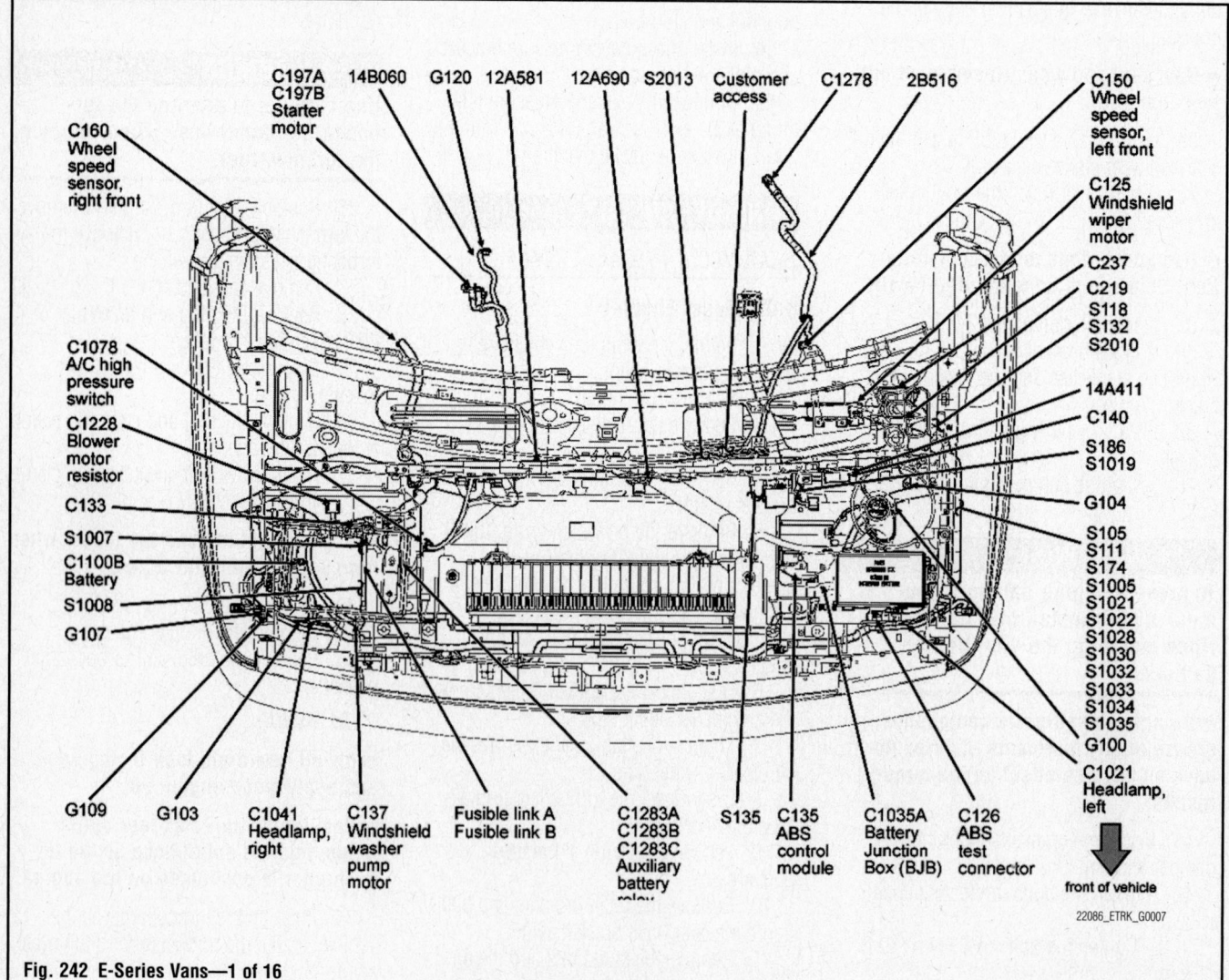

Fig. 242 E-Series Vans—1 of 16

22086_ETRK_G0007

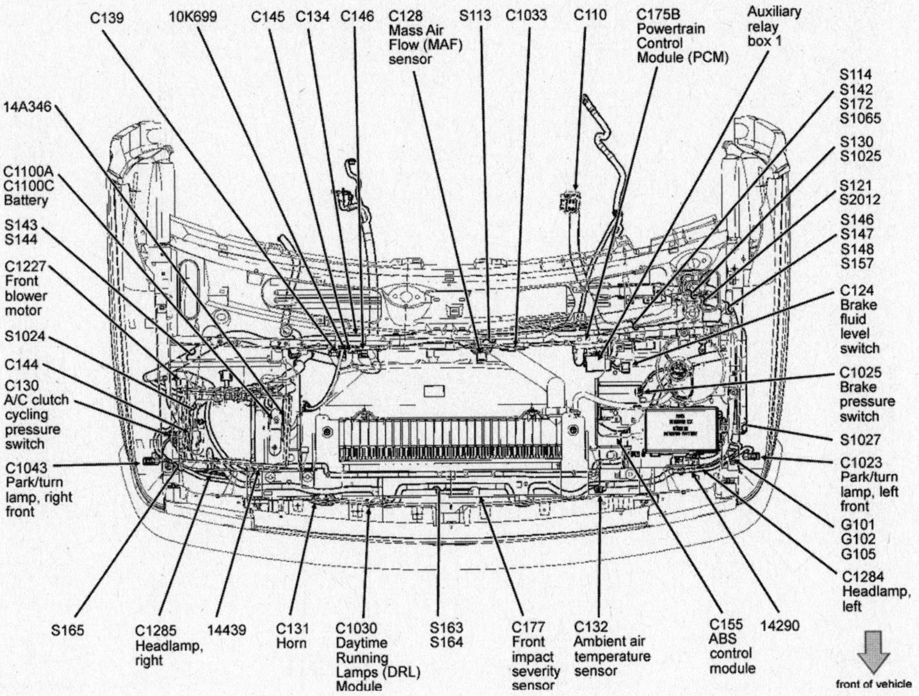

C139 10K699 C145 C134 C146 C128 Mass Air Flow (MAF) sensor S113 C1033 C110 C175B Powertrain Control Module (PCM) Auxiliary relay box 1

14A346

C1100A C1100C Battery

S143 S144

C1227 Front blower motor

S1024

C144

C130 A/C clutch cycling pressure switch

C1043 Park/turn lamp, right front

S114 S142 S172 S1065

S130 S1025

S121 S2012

S146 S147 S148 S157

C124 Brake fluid level switch

C1025 Brake pressure switch

S1027

C1023 Park/turn lamp, left front

G101 G102 G105

C1284 Headlamp, left

S165 C1285 Headlamp, right 14439 C131 Horn C1030 Daytime Running Lamps (DRL) Module S163 S164 C177 Front impact severity sensor C132 Ambient air temperature sensor C155 ABS control module 14290

front of vehicle

22086_ETRK_G0008

Fig. 243 E-Series Vans—2 of 16

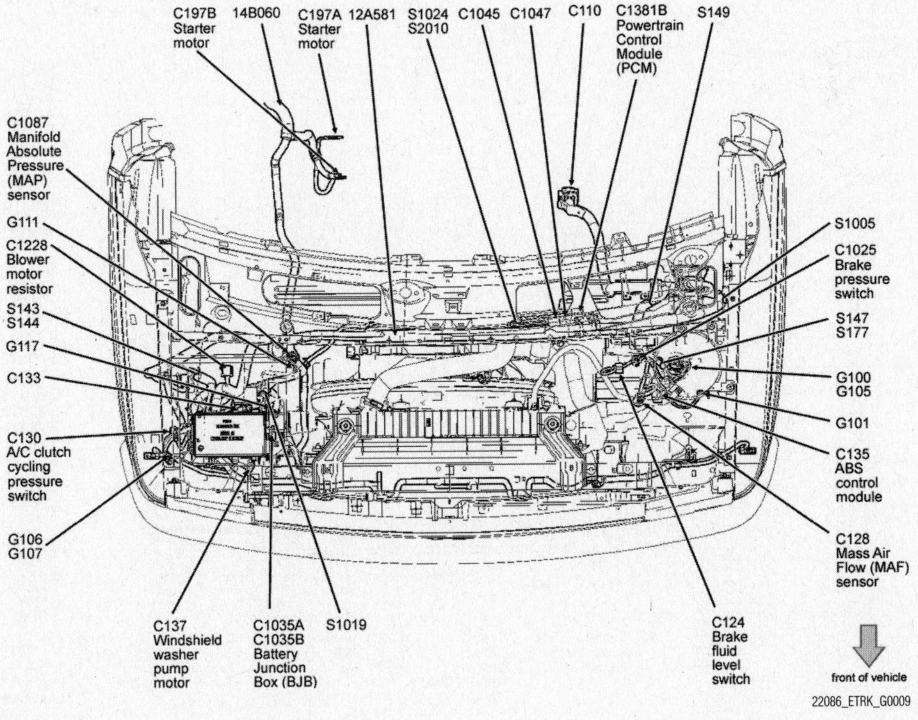

C197B Starter motor 14B060 C197A Starter motor 12A581 S1024 S2010 C1045 C1047 C110 C1381B Powertrain Control Module (PCM) S149

C1087 Manifold Absolute Pressure (MAP) sensor

G111

C1228 Blower motor resistor

S143 S144

G117

C133

C130 A/C clutch cycling pressure switch

G106 G107

S1005

C1025 Brake pressure switch

S147 S177

G100 G105

G101

C135 ABS control module

C128 Mass Air Flow (MAF) sensor

C124 Brake fluid level switch

C137 Windshield washer pump motor C1035A C1035B Battery Junction Box (BJB) S1019

front of vehicle

22086_ETRK_G0009

Fig. 244 E-Series Vans—3 of 16

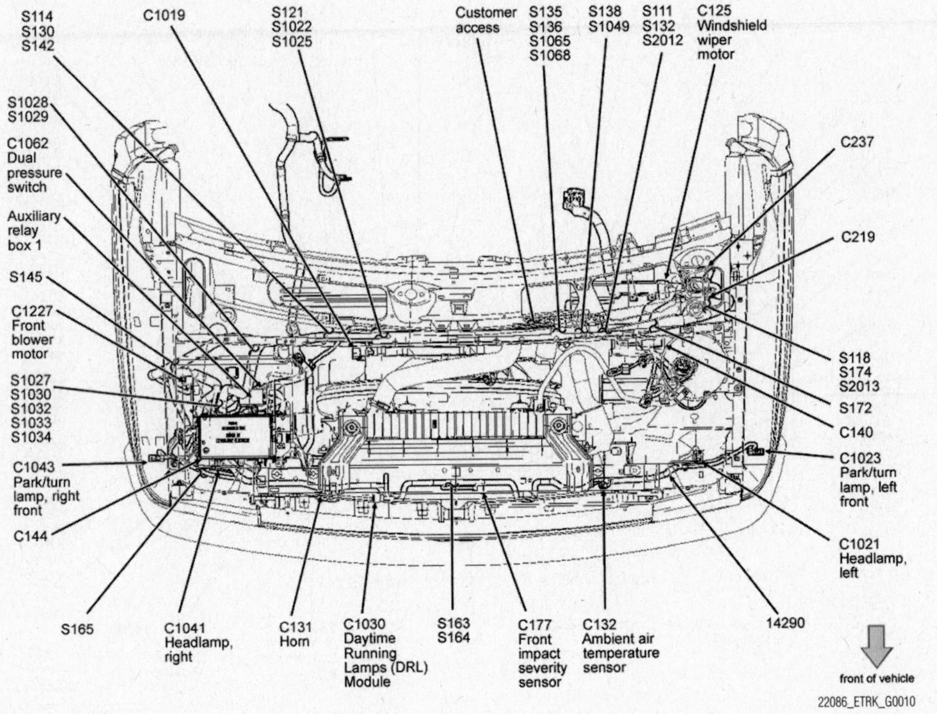

S114
S130
S142

C1019

S121
S1022
S1025

Customer access

S135
S136
S1065
S1068

S138
S1049

S111
S132
S2012

C125
Windshield wiper motor

C237

C219

S1028
S1029

C1062
Dual pressure switch

Auxiliary relay box 1

S145

C1227
Front blower motor

S118
S174
S2013

S172

C140

S1027
S1030
S1032
S1033
S1034

C1043
Park/turn lamp, right front

C144

C1023
Park/turn lamp, left front

C1021
Headlamp, left

S165

C1041
Headlamp, right

C131
Horn

C1030
Daytime Running Lamps (DRL) Module

S163
S164

C177
Front impact severity sensor

C132
Ambient air temperature sensor

14290

front of vehicle

22086_ETRK_G0010

Fig. 245 E-Series Vans—4 of 16

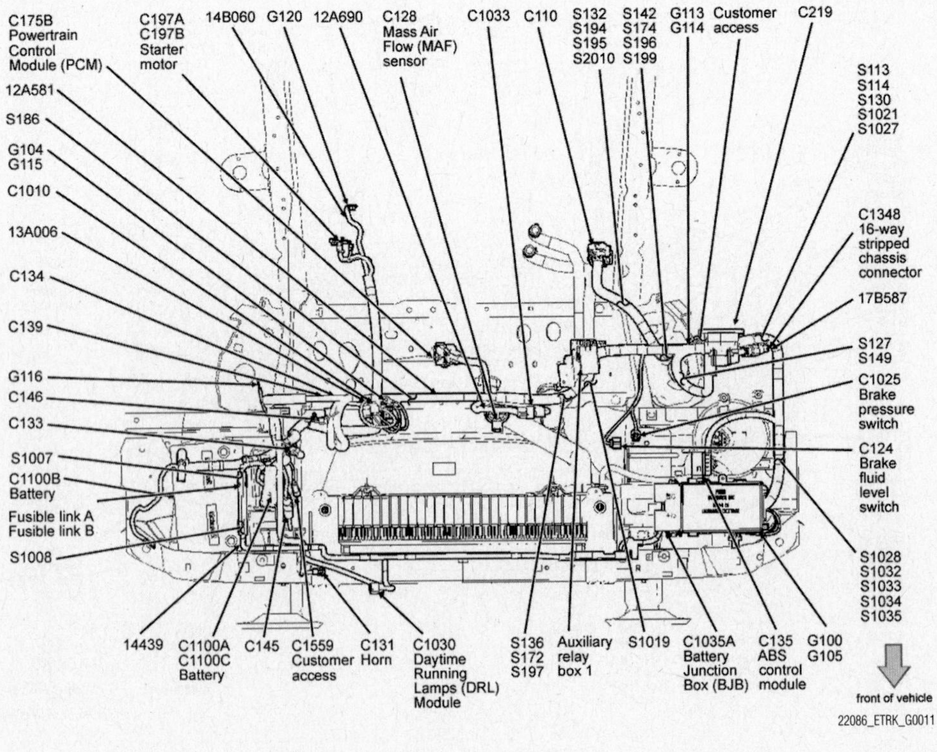

C175B
Powertrain Control Module (PCM)

C197A
C197B
Starter motor

14B060

G120

12A690

C128
Mass Air Flow (MAF) sensor

C1033

C110

S132
S194
S195
S2010

S142
S174
S196
S199

G113
G114

Customer access

C219

S113
S114
S130
S1021
S1027

12A581

S186

G104
G115

C1010

13A006

C134

C139

G116

C146

C133

S1007

C1100B
Battery

Fusible link A
Fusible link B

S1008

C1348
16-way stripped chassis connector

17B587

S127
S149

C1025
Brake pressure switch

C124
Brake fluid level switch

S1028
S1032
S1033
S1034
S1035

14439

C1100A
C1100C
Battery

C145

C1559
Customer access

C131
Horn

C1030
Daytime Running Lamps (DRL) Module

S136
S172
S197

S1019

Auxiliary relay box 1

C1035A
Battery Junction Box (BJB)

C135
ABS control module

G100
G105

front of vehicle

22086_ETRK_G0011

Fig. 246 E-Series Vans—5 of 16

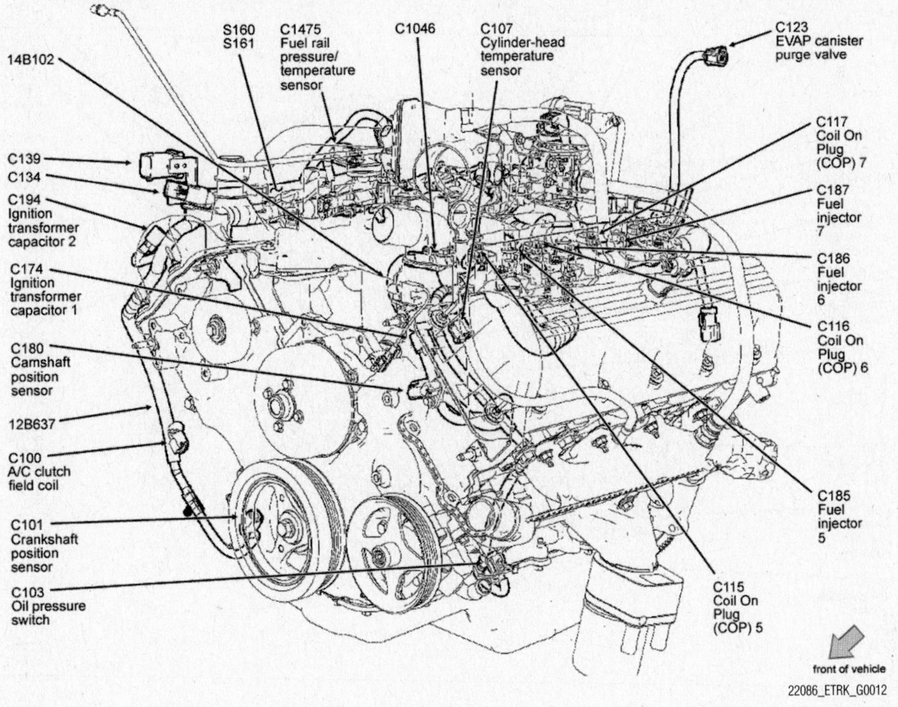

14B102

S160
S161

C1475
Fuel rail
pressure/
temperature
sensor

C1046

C107
Cylinder-head
temperature
sensor

C123
EVAP canister
purge valve

C139

C134

C194
Ignition
transformer
capacitor 2

C174
Ignition
transformer
capacitor 1

C180
Camshaft
position
sensor

12B637

C100
A/C clutch
field coil

C101
Crankshaft
position
sensor

C103
Oil pressure
switch

C117
Coil On
Plug
(COP) 7

C187
Fuel
injector
7

C186
Fuel
injector
6

C116
Coil On
Plug
(COP) 6

C185
Fuel
injector
5

C115
Coil On
Plug
(COP) 5

front of vehicle

22086_ETRK_G0012

Fig. 247 E-Series Vans—6 of 16

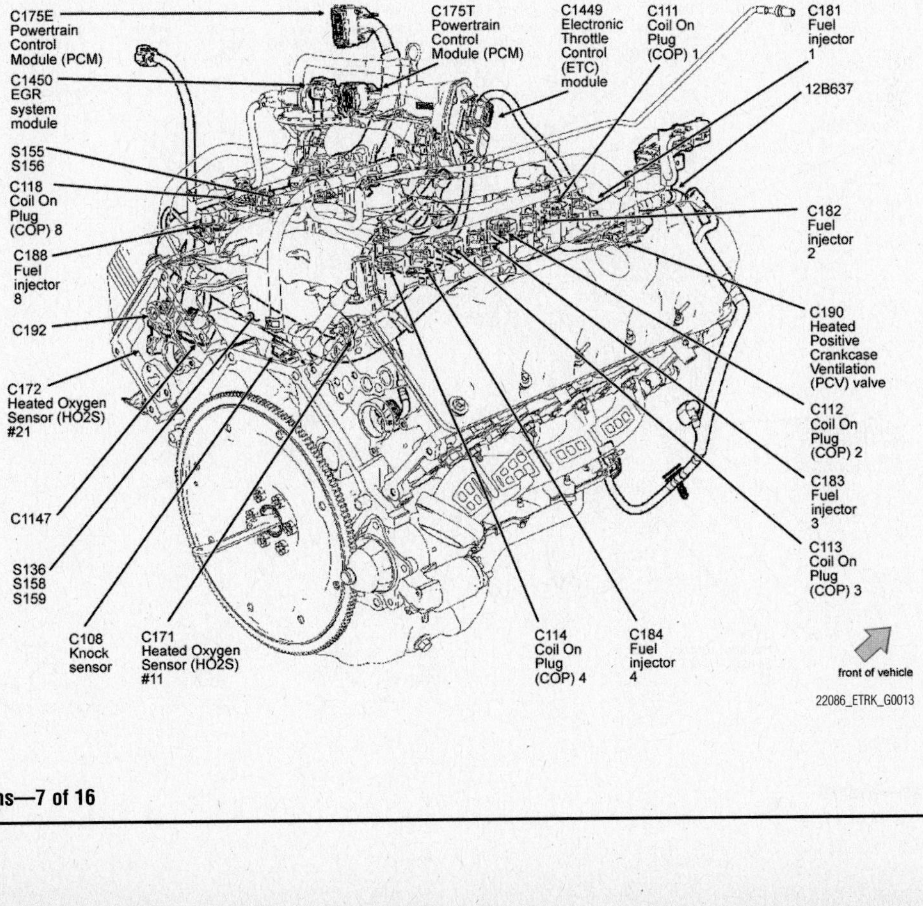

C175E
Powertrain
Control
Module (PCM)

C1450
EGR
system
module

S155
S156

C118
Coil On
Plug
(COP) 8

C188
Fuel
injector
8

C192

C172
Heated Oxygen
Sensor (HO2S)
#21

C1147

S136
S158
S159

C108
Knock
sensor

C171
Heated Oxygen
Sensor (HO2S)
#11

C175T
Powertrain
Control
Module (PCM)

C1449
Electronic
Throttle
Control
(ETC)
module

C111
Coil On
Plug
(COP) 1

C181
Fuel
injector
1

12B637

C182
Fuel
injector
2

C190
Heated
Positive
Crankcase
Ventilation
(PCV) valve

C112
Coil On
Plug
(COP) 2

C183
Fuel
injector
3

C113
Coil On
Plug
(COP) 3

C114
Coil On
Plug
(COP) 4

C184
Fuel
injector
4

front of vehicle

22086_ETRK_G0013

Fig. 248 E-Series Vans—7 of 16

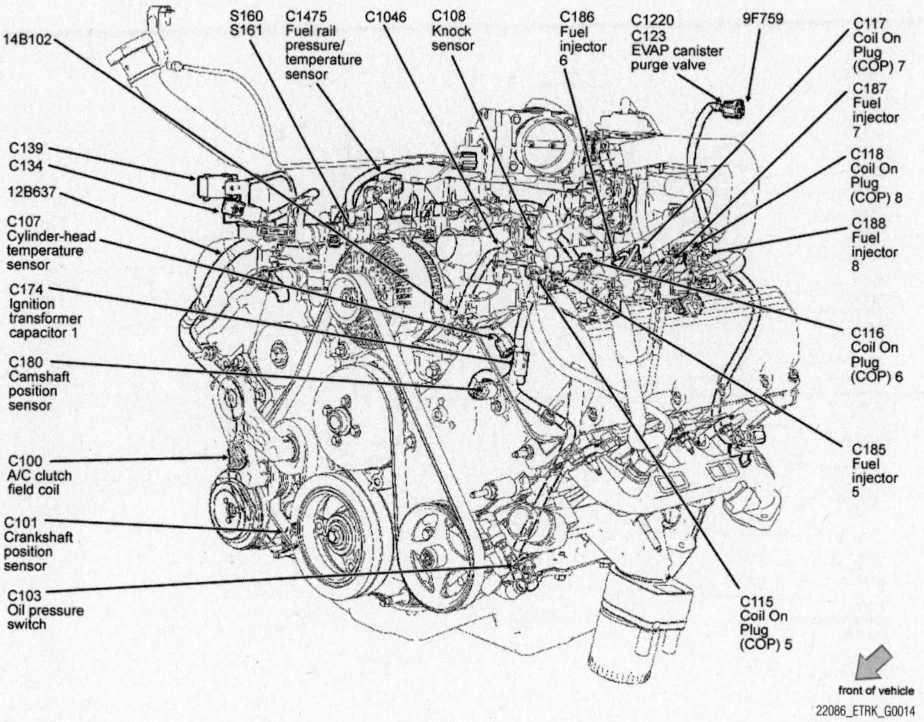

14B102

S160
S161

C1475
Fuel rail
pressure/
temperature
sensor

C1046

C108
Knock
sensor

C186
Fuel
injector
6

C1220
C123
EVAP canister
purge valve

9F759

C117
Coil On
Plug
(COP) 7

C187
Fuel
injector
7

C118
Coil On
Plug
(COP) 8

C188
Fuel
injector
8

C116
Coil On
Plug
(COP) 6

C185
Fuel
injector
5

C139
C134
12B637
C107
Cylinder-head
temperature
sensor

C174
Ignition
transformer
capacitor 1

C180
Camshaft
position
sensor

C100
A/C clutch
field coil

C101
Crankshaft
position
sensor

C103
Oil pressure
switch

C115
Coil On
Plug
(COP) 5

front of vehicle
22086_ETRK_G0014

Fig. 249 E-Series Vans—8 of 16

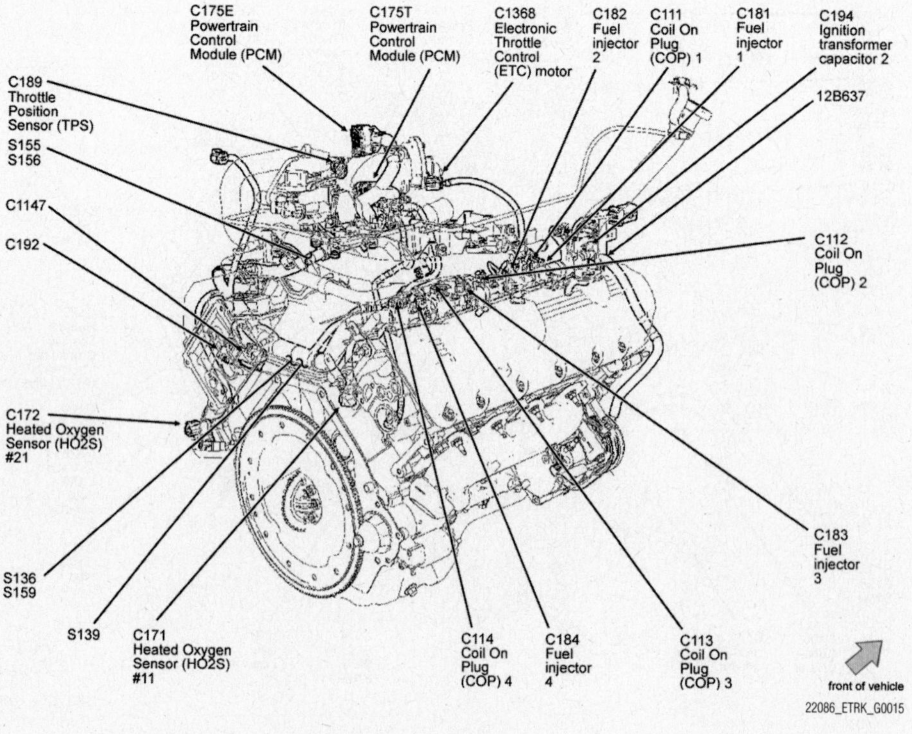

C175E
Powertrain
Control
Module (PCM)

C175T
Powertrain
Control
Module (PCM)

C1368
Electronic
Throttle
Control
(ETC) motor

C182
Fuel
injector
2

C111
Coil On
Plug
(COP) 1

C181
Fuel
injector
1

C194
Ignition
transformer
capacitor 2

12B637

C189
Throttle
Position
Sensor (TPS)

S155
S156

C1147

C192

C112
Coil On
Plug
(COP) 2

C172
Heated Oxygen
Sensor (HO2S)
#21

C183
Fuel
injector
3

S136
S159

S139

C171
Heated Oxygen
Sensor (HO2S)
#11

C114
Coil On
Plug
(COP) 4

C184
Fuel
injector
4

C113
Coil On
Plug
(COP) 3

front of vehicle
22086_ETRK_G0015

Fig. 250 E-Series Vans—9 of 16

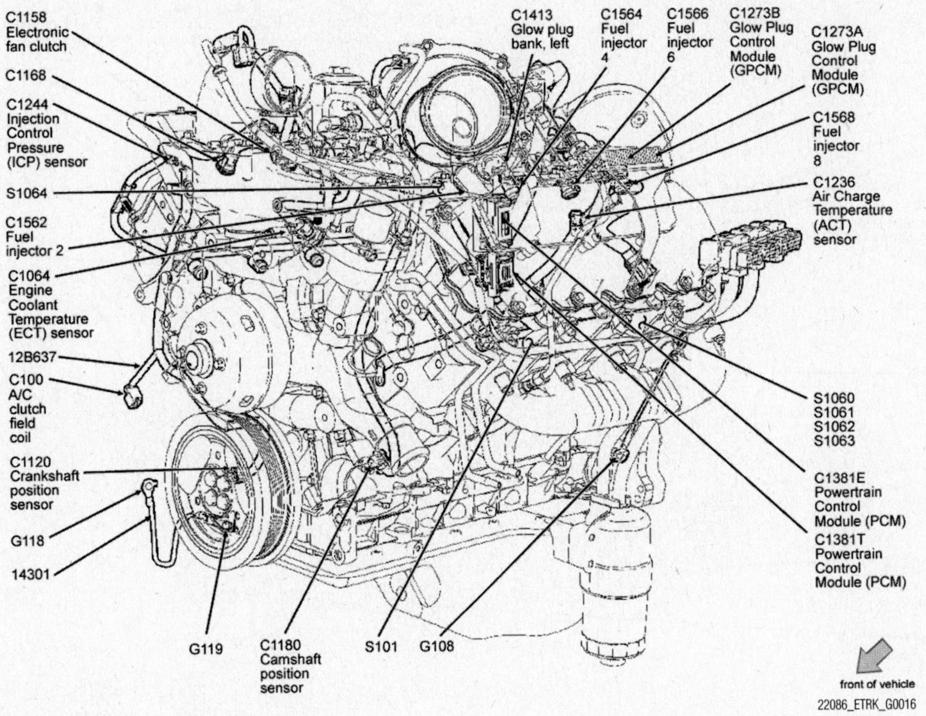

C1158
Electronic
fan clutch

C1168

C1244
Injection
Control
Pressure
(ICP) sensor

S1064

C1562
Fuel
injector 2

C1064
Engine
Coolant
Temperature
(ECT) sensor

12B637

C100
A/C
clutch
field
coil

C1120
Crankshaft
position
sensor

G118

14301

G119

C1180
Camshaft
position
sensor

S101

G108

C1413
Glow plug
bank, left

C1564
Fuel
injector
4

C1566
Fuel
injector
6

C1273B
Glow Plug
Control
Module
(GPCM)

C1273A
Glow Plug
Control
Module
(GPCM)

C1568
Fuel
injector
8

C1236
Air Charge
Temperature
(ACT)
sensor

S1060
S1061
S1062
S1063

C1381E
Powertrain
Control
Module
(PCM)

C1381T
Powertrain
Control
Module
(PCM)

front of vehicle
22086_ETRK_G0016

Fig. 251 E-Series Vans—10 of 16

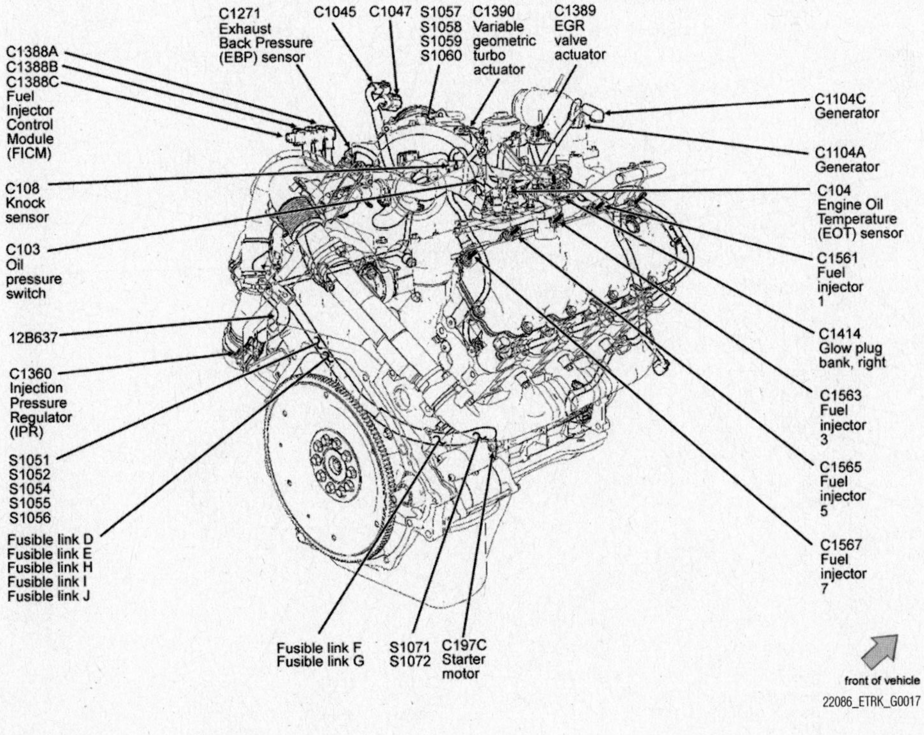

C1388A
C1388B
C1388C
Fuel
Injector
Control
Module
(FICM)

C108
Knock
sensor

C103
Oil
pressure
switch

12B637

C1360
Injection
Pressure
Regulator
(IPR)

S1051
S1052
S1054
S1055
S1056

Fusible link D
Fusible link E
Fusible link H
Fusible link I
Fusible link J

Fusible link F
Fusible link G

S1071
S1072

C197C
Starter
motor

C1271
Exhaust
Back Pressure
(EBP) sensor

C1045

C1047

S1057
S1058
S1059
S1060

C1390
Variable
geometric
turbo
actuator

C1389
EGR
valve
actuator

C1104C
Generator

C1104A
Generator

C104
Engine Oil
Temperature
(EOT) sensor

C1561
Fuel
injector
1

C1414
Glow plug
bank, right

C1563
Fuel
injector
3

C1565
Fuel
injector
5

C1567
Fuel
injector
7

front of vehicle
22086_ETRK_G0017

Fig. 252 E-Series Vans—11 of 16

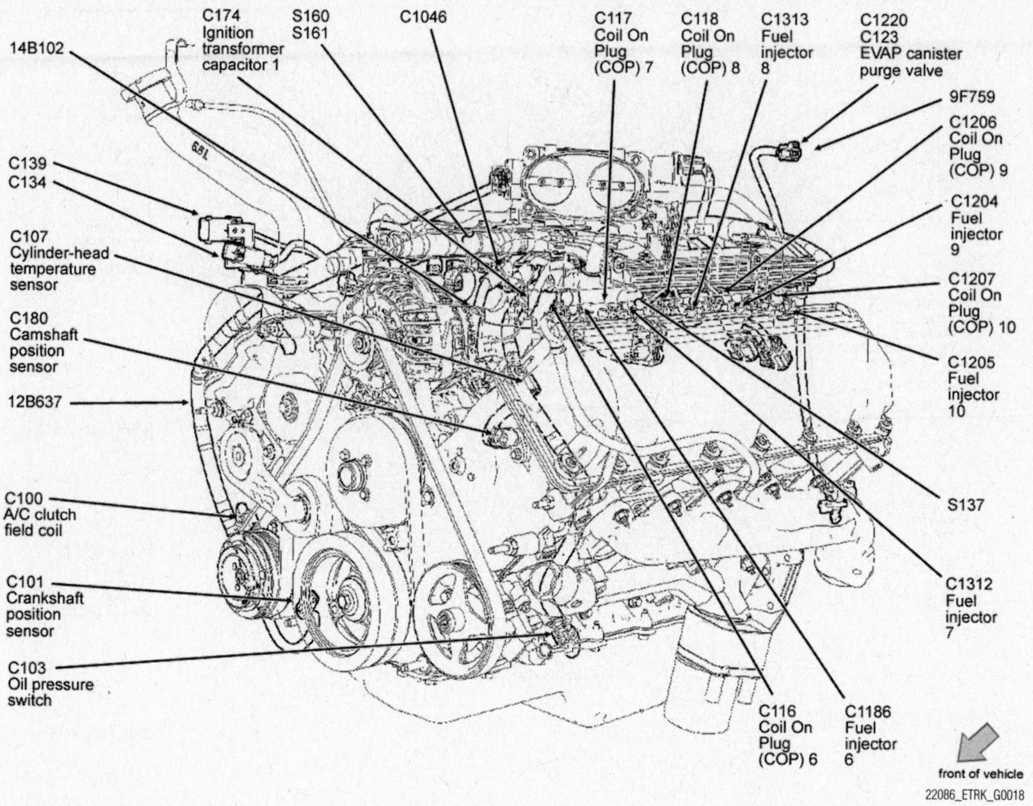

C174
Ignition
transformer
capacitor 1

S160
S161

C1046

C117
Coil On
Plug
(COP) 7

C118
Coil On
Plug
(COP) 8

C1313
Fuel
injector
8

C1220
C123
EVAP canister
purge valve

14B102

9F759

C1206
Coil On
Plug
(COP) 9

C139
C134

C107
Cylinder-head
temperature
sensor

C1204
Fuel
injector
9

C180
Camshaft
position
sensor

C1207
Coil On
Plug
(COP) 10

12B637

C1205
Fuel
injector
10

C100
A/C clutch
field coil

S137

C101
Crankshaft
position
sensor

C1312
Fuel
injector
7

C103
Oil pressure
switch

C116
Coil On
Plug
(COP) 6

C1186
Fuel
injector
6

front of vehicle
22086_ETRK_G0018

Fig. 253 E-Series Vans—12 of 16

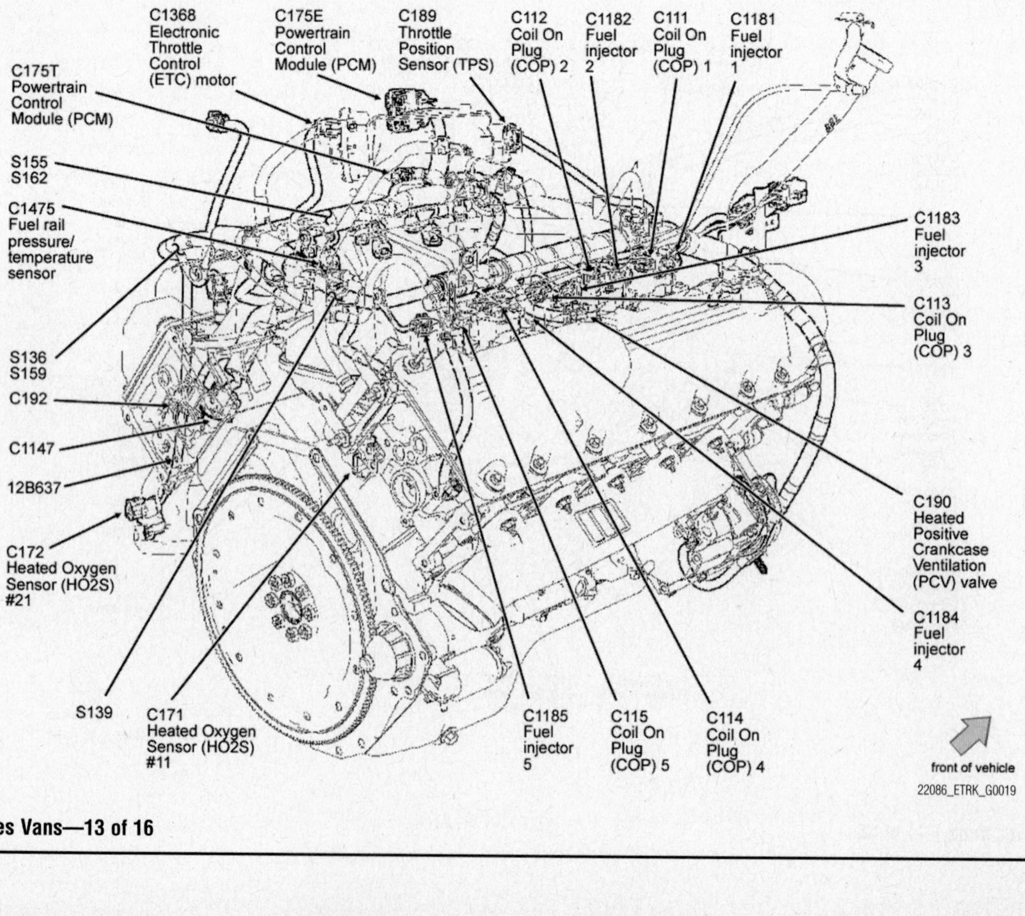

C1368
Electronic
Throttle
Control
(ETC) motor

C175E
Powertrain
Control
Module (PCM)

C189
Throttle
Position
Sensor (TPS)

C112
Coil On
Plug
(COP) 2

C1182
Fuel
injector
2

C111
Coil On
Plug
(COP) 1

C1181
Fuel
injector
1

C175T
Powertrain
Control
Module (PCM)

S155
S162

C1183
Fuel
injector
3

C1475
Fuel rail
pressure/
temperature
sensor

C113
Coil On
Plug
(COP) 3

S136
S159

C192

C1147

C190
Heated
Positive
Crankcase
Ventilation
(PCV) valve

12B637

C172
Heated Oxygen
Sensor (HO2S)
#21

C1184
Fuel
injector
4

S139

C171
Heated Oxygen
Sensor (HO2S)
#11

C1185
Fuel
injector
5

C115
Coil On
Plug
(COP) 5

C114
Coil On
Plug
(COP) 4

front of vehicle
22086_ETRK_G0019

Fig. 254 E-Series Vans—13 of 16

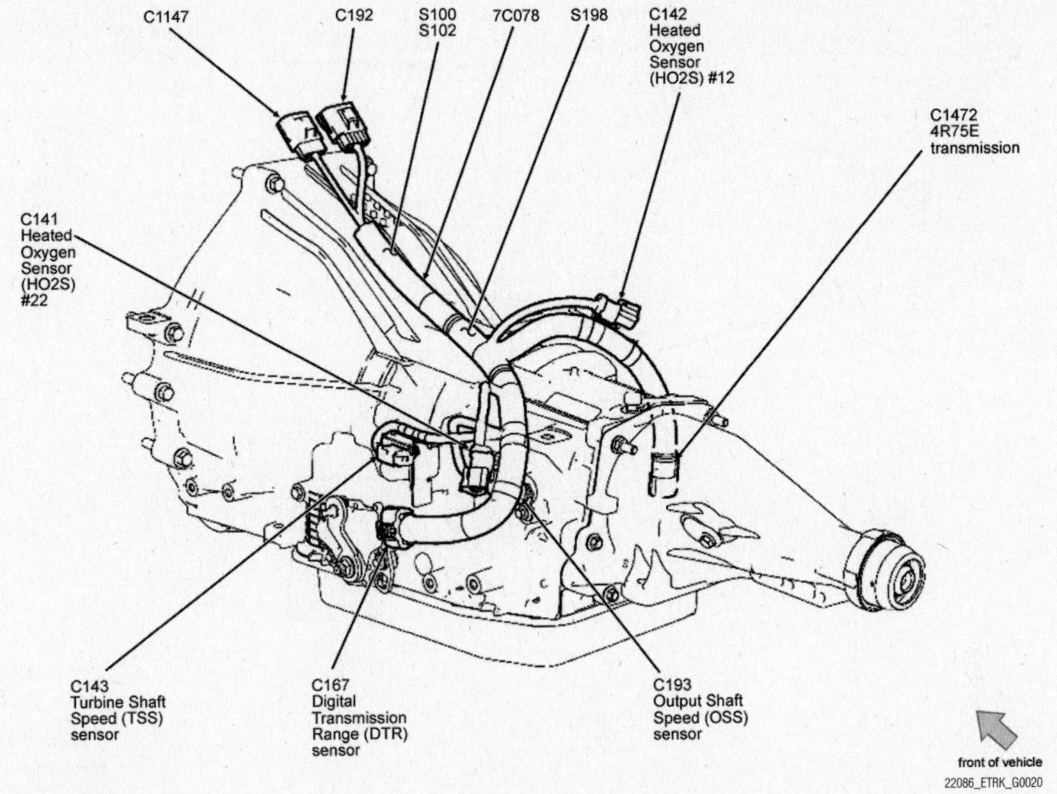

C1147   C192   S100   7C078   S198   C142
S102   Heated
                                 Oxygen
                                 Sensor
                                 (HO2S) #12

C1472
4R75E
transmission

C141
Heated
Oxygen
Sensor
(HO2S)
#22

C143   C167   C193
Turbine Shaft   Digital   Output Shaft
Speed (TSS)   Transmission   Speed (OSS)
sensor   Range (DTR)   sensor
                    sensor

front of vehicle
22086_ETRK_G0020

Fig. 255 E-Series Vans—14 of 16

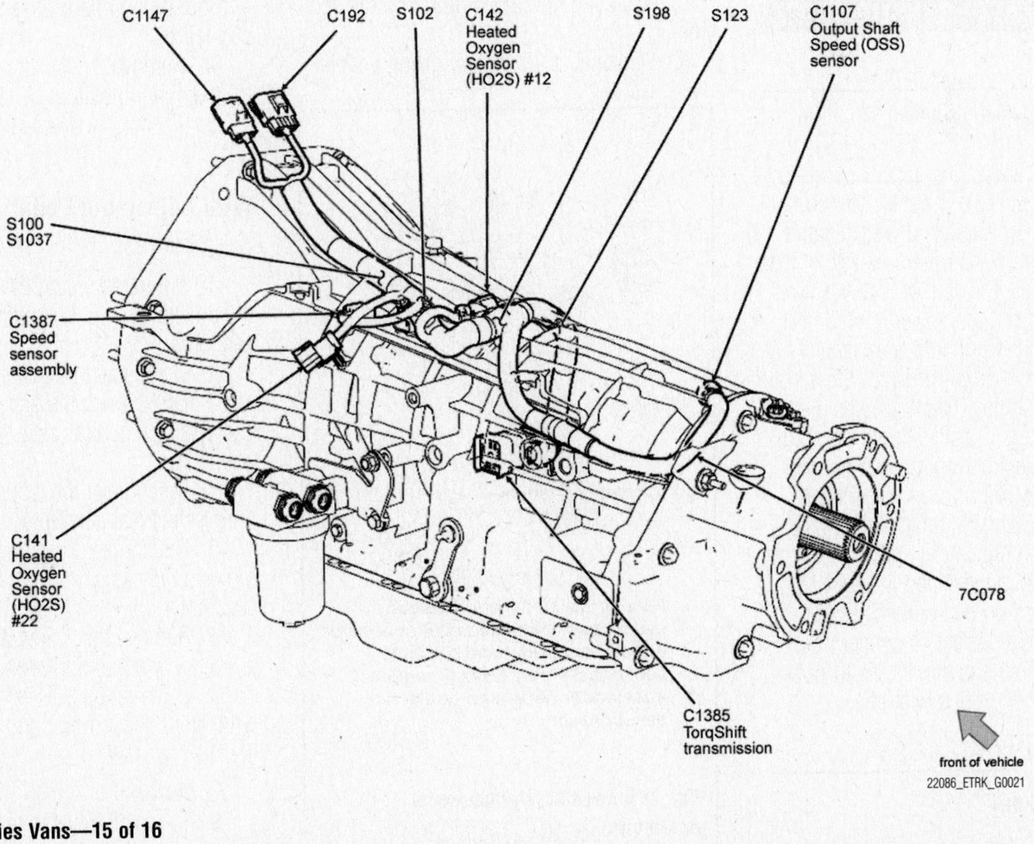

C1147   C192   S102   C142   S198   S123   C1107
                             Heated   Output Shaft
                             Oxygen   Speed (OSS)
                             Sensor   sensor
                             (HO2S) #12

S100
S1037

C1387
Speed
sensor
assembly

C141
Heated
Oxygen
Sensor
(HO2S)
#22

7C078

C1385
TorqShift
transmission

front of vehicle
22086_ETRK_G0021

Fig. 256 E-Series Vans—15 of 16

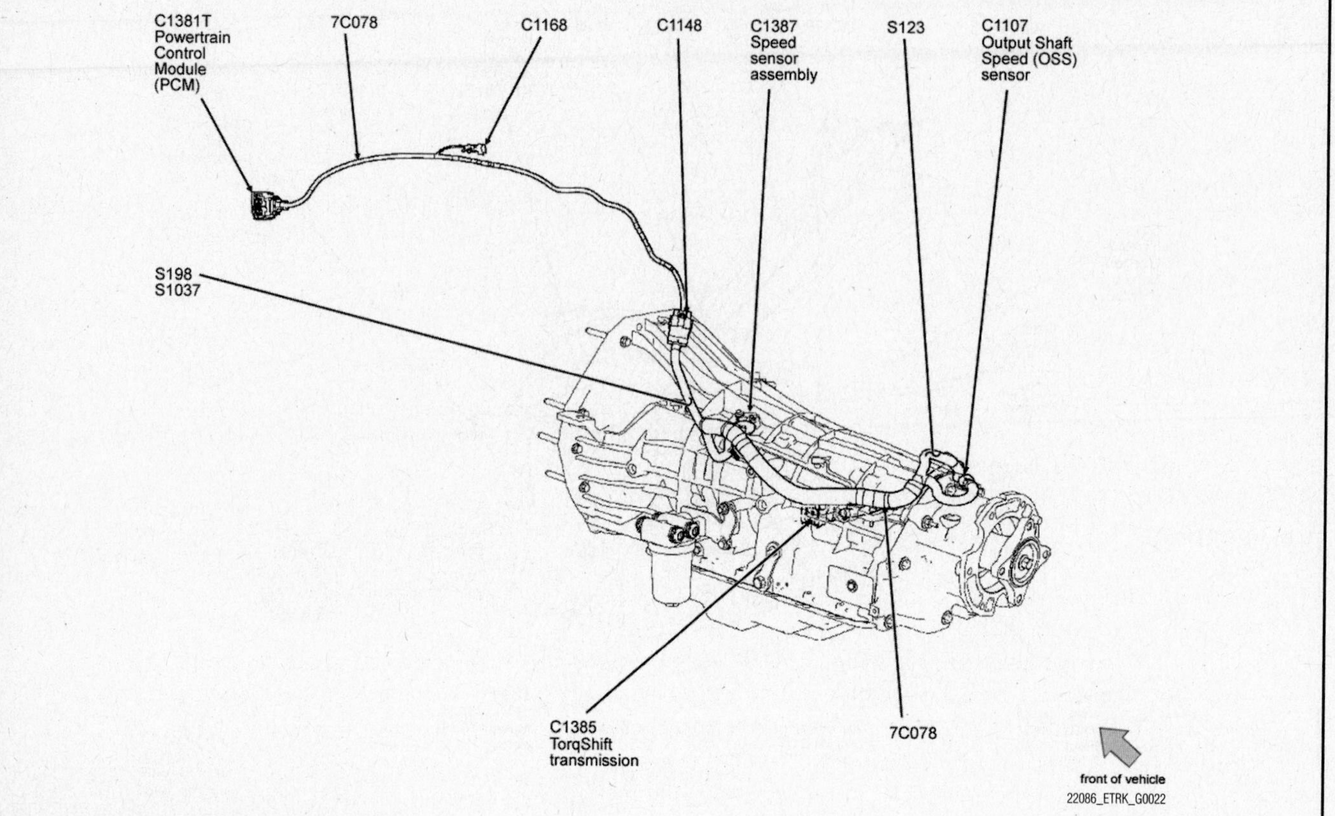

C1381T
Powertrain
Control
Module
(PCM)

7C078

C1168

C1148

C1387
Speed
sensor
assembly

S123

C1107
Output Shaft
Speed (OSS)
sensor

S198
S1037

C1385
TorqShift
transmission

7C078

front of vehicle
22086_ETRK_G0022

Fig. 257 E-Series Vans—16 of 16

ACCELERATOR PEDAL POSITION (APP) SENSOR

LOCATION

Part of the accelerator pedal assembly.

OPERATION

The APP sensor is a 3-track potentiometer that is used to calculate driver demand for power based on the rotation angle of the accelerator pedal. The sensor receives a reference voltage from the powertrain control module (PCM) and provides a variable voltage signal directly proportional to the accelerator pedal position. The PCM uses the 3 APP sensor inputs to calculate the desired fuel quantity, injection timing, and the correct injection control pressure. A concern with the APP sensor illuminates the powertrain malfunction indicator (wrench). Normal engine operation is permitted if the PCM detects a concern on one of the 3 sensor signals. If the PCM detects a concern on two of the 3 sensor signals, the PCM only allows the engine to operate at idle.

REMOVAL & INSTALLATION

With Fixed Pedal
See Figure 258.

1. Before servicing the vehicle, refer to the precautions in the beginning of this section.
2. Disconnect the battery ground cable.

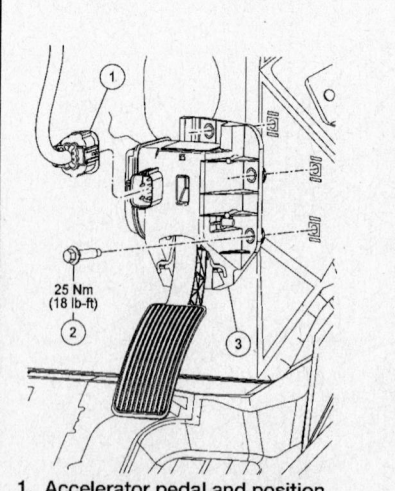

25 Nm
(18 lb-ft)

1. Accelerator pedal and position sensor assembly electrical connector
2. Accelerator pedal and position sensor assembly bolts (3 required)
3. Accelerator pedal and position sensor assembly

22086_ETRK_G0023

Fig. 258 Fixed Accelerator Pedal Assembly

3. Disconnect the accelerator pedal and position sensor assembly electrical connector.
4. Remove the 3 bolts and the accelerator pedal and position sensor assembly.
5. To install, reverse the removal procedure.

With Adjustable Pedal
See Figure 259.

1. Before servicing the vehicle, refer to the precautions in the beginning of this section.
2. Disconnect the battery ground cable.
3. Disconnect the accelerator pedal and position sensor assembly electrical connector.
4. Disconnect the adjustable pedal motor electrical connector.
5. Disconnect the adjustable pedal motor drive cable from the brake pedal assembly.
6. Remove the 3 nuts and the accelerator pedal and position sensor assembly.
7. Remove the 3 bolts and the adjustable pedal motor and bracket assembly.

To install:
8. To install, reverse the removal procedure.

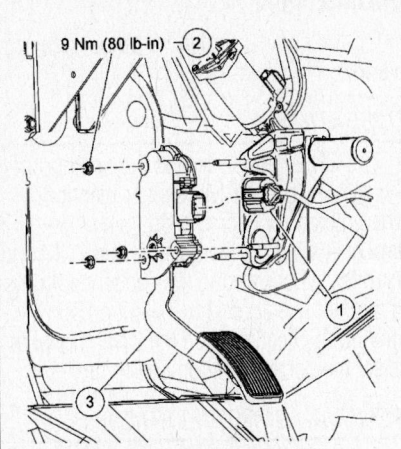

1. Accelerator pedal and position sensor assembly electrical connector
2. Accelerator pedal and position sensor assembly nuts (3 required)
3. Accelerator pedal and position sensor assembly

22086_ETRK_G0024

Fig. 259 Adjustable Accelerator Pedal Assembly

✳✳ CAUTION

The adjustable pedal system must be indexed whenever the brake pedal assembly or accelerator pedal assembly is installed.

➡ **Make sure the electrical connector is connected to the adjustable pedal motor.**

9. Disconnect the adjustable pedal motor drive cable from the brake pedal drive.
10. Operate the accelerator pedal to the full rearward position.
11. Connect the adjustable pedal motor drive cable to the adjustable brake pedal drive.
12. Operate the adjustable pedals to the full forward position.
13. Disconnect the adjustable pedal motor drive cable from the adjustable brake pedal assembly.
14. Operate the adjustable accelerator pedal to the full forward position.
15. Connect the adjustable pedal motor drive cable to the adjustable brake pedal drive.
16. Check that the brake and accelerator pedals can be fully adjusted forward and rearward.

TESTING

See Figures 260 and 261.

1. Before servicing the vehicle, refer to the precautions in the beginning of this section.

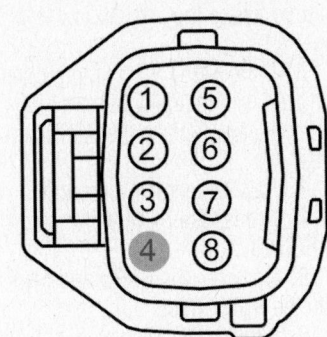

1. Accelerator pedal sensor 3 return
2. PCM accelerator pedal sensor
3. Accelerator pedal sensor 2 return
4. Not used
5. Accelerator pedal sensor 2 signal
6. Accelerator pedal sensor 3 signal
7. Accelerator pedal sensor 2 power
8. Accelerator pedal sensor 3 power

22086_ETRK_G0025

Fig. 260 Accelerator Pedal Position Sensor Connector—Gasoline Engines

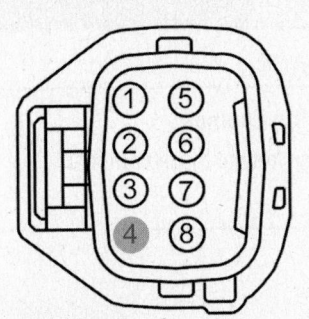

1. Signal return
2. PCM accelerator pedal sensor
3. Accelerator pedal sensor 2 return
4. Not used
5. Accelerator pedal sensor 2 signal
6. Accelerator pedal sensor 2 power
7. Reference voltage
8. Accelerator pedal sensor 3 power

22086_ETRK_G0026

Fig. 261 Accelerator Pedal Position Sensor Connector—Diesel Engine

✳✳ WARNING

Use only a high-impedance multimeter, otherwise damage to the PCM and/or sensors can result.

2. With the key **ON** and the engine **OFF**, check pins 6 and 7 for reference voltage (4.5–5.5 VDC).
3. Check pins 1 and 3 for ground.
4. Check the voltage at pins 2, 5, and 8 while moving the accelerator pedal. The voltage should rise and fall smoothly with pedal movement.
5. If any measurement falls outside the range given, replace the APP sensor.

BAROMETRIC PRESSURE (BARO) SENSOR

LOCATION

Under the instrument panel behind the lower steering column cover.

OPERATION

The BARO pressure sensor is a variable capacitor sensor that processes a signal indicating atmospheric pressure. This allows the PCM to compensate for altitude. The PCM uses this information to calculate injection timing and glow plug control. At higher altitudes, glow plug on time is increased to reduce start-up smoke. The BARO sensor is located behind the lower steering column opening finish panel.

REMOVAL & INSTALLATION

6.0L Diesel Engine

✳✳ CAUTION

Make sure the ignition switch is in the OFF position prior to working on the electronic engine controls.

1. Before servicing the vehicle, refer to the precautions in the beginning of this section.
2. Turn the ignition switch to the OFF position.

✳✳ CAUTION

Use care when removing the instrument panel steering column cover or damage to the cover locating tab can occur.

3. Remove the instrument panel steering column cover.
4. Unlock the retainers.
5. Remove the instrument panel steering column cover.
6. Disconnect the BARO sensor electrical connector.
7. Release the clip and remove the BARO sensor.
8. To install, reverse the removal procedure.

TESTING

6.0L Diesel Engine
See Figure 262.

➡ Most weather reports include a local barometric pressure that has been corrected to factor in sea level. However, the BARO PID reports the barometric pressure for the vehicle's actual altitude. Local weather conditions (high or low pressure) change the local barometric pressure by several inches of mercury.

1. Before servicing the vehicle, refer to the precautions in the beginning of this section.
2. Key ON, engine OFF.
3. Access the PCM and monitor the BARO and MAP PIDs.
4. Record the BARO and MAP values.
5. Verify that the BARO PID reading is approximately the same as the barometric pressure reading for the location, day, and altitude where the vehicle is being repaired.
6. If the BARO PID reading does not compare with the daily barometric report for the local area, replace the BARO sensor and retest.
7. Key ON, engine running.
8. Access the PCM and monitor the BARO PID.
9. Compare the BARO and MAP value with the KOEO value.
10. If the BARO PID value is not equal to the recorded value, replace the BARO sensor and retest.

CAMSHAFT POSITION (CMP) SENSOR

LOCATION

Gasoline Engines

At the front of the left cylinder head.

Diesel Engine

On the engine, under the power steering pump.

OPERATION

The CMP sensor detects the position of the camshaft. The CMP sensor identifies when piston number 1 is on its compression stroke. A signal is then sent to the PCM and used for synchronizing the sequential firing of the fuel injectors. Coil-on-plug (COP) ignition applications use the CMP signal to select the correct ignition coil to fire.

REMOVAL & INSTALLATION

4.6L Engine

See Figure 263.

1. Before servicing the vehicle, refer to the precautions in the beginning of this section.
2. Disconnect the battery ground cable.
3. Disconnect the camshaft position sensor (CMP) sensor electrical connector.

C2256 (BK)

Barometric
Absolute
Pressure
(BAP) switch

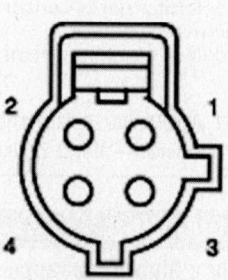

FEMALE

Pin	Circuit	Circuit function
1	3011 (BK/OG)	Signal return
2	3010 (TN)	Reference voltage
3	356 (DB/LG)	Sensor signal
4	–	not used

22086_ETRK_G0027

Fig. 262 BARO sensor connector—6.0L Diesel Engine

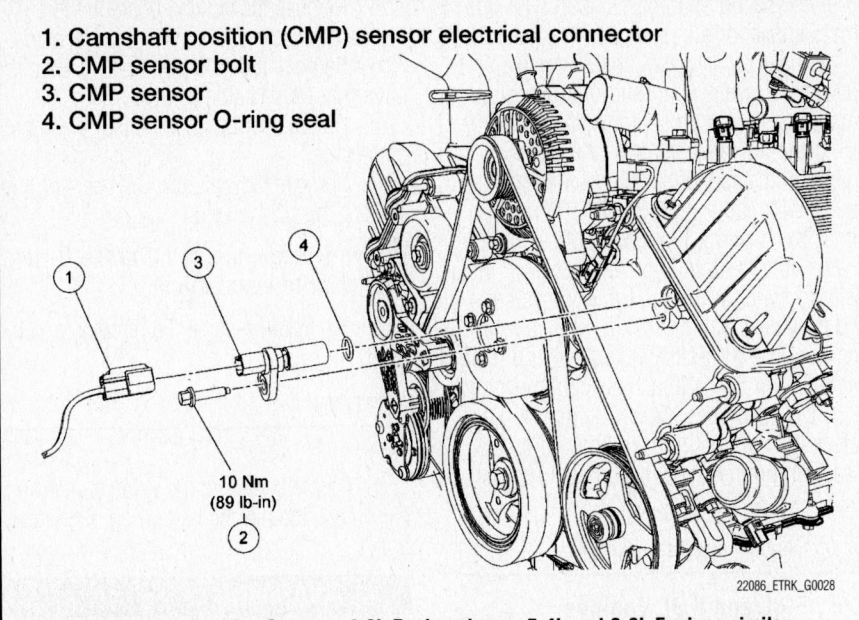

1. Camshaft position (CMP) sensor electrical connector
2. CMP sensor bolt
3. CMP sensor
4. CMP sensor O-ring seal

10 Nm
(89 lb-in)

22086_ETRK_G0028

Fig. 263 Camshaft Position Sensor—4.6L Engine shown, 5.4L and 6.8L Engines similar

4. Remove the bolt and the CMP sensor.
5. To install, reverse the removal procedure.

5.4L Engine

See Figure 263.

1. Before servicing the vehicle, refer to the precautions in the beginning of this section.
2. Disconnect the battery ground cable.
3. For the left camshaft position (CMP) sensor, remove the air cleaner inlet pipe and resonator.
4. Disconnect the CMP sensor electrical connector.
5. Remove the bolt and the CMP sensor.
6. To install, reverse the removal procedure.

6.8L Engine

See Figure 263.

1. Before servicing the vehicle, refer to the precautions in the beginning of this section.
2. Disconnect the battery ground cable.
3. Disconnect the camshaft position (CMP) sensor electrical connector.
4. Remove the bolt and the CMP sensor. Discard the O-ring seal.
5. Lubricate a new O-ring seal with clean engine oil prior to installation.
6. To install, reverse the removal procedure.

6.0L Diesel Engine

See Figure 264.

1. Before servicing the vehicle, refer to

the precautions in the beginning of this section.
2. With the vehicle in NEUTRAL, position it on a hoist.

❊❊ CAUTION

Make sure the ignition switch is in the OFF position prior to working on the electronic engine controls.

3. Turn the ignition switch to the OFF position.
4. Rotate the accessory drive belt tensioner clockwise and remove the accessory

drive belt from the power steering pump pulley.
5. Remove the 3 bolts and position the power steering pump aside.

➡**The camshaft position (CMP) sensor is located behind the power steering pump.**

6. Disconnect the CMP sensor electrical connector.
7. Remove the bolt, the CMP sensor and discard the O-ring seal.

➡ **Apply clean engine oil to the new O-ring seal prior to installation.**

8. To install, reverse the removal procedure.
9. Verify that the accessory drive belt is correctly seated on the pulleys.

TESTING

4.6L, 5.4L and 6.8L Engines

See Figure 265.

1. Before servicing the vehicle, refer to the precautions in the beginning of this section.

❊❊ WARNING

Use only a high-impedance multimeter, otherwise damage to the PCM and/or sensors can result.

2. With the key **OFF**, disconnect the CMP sensor harness connector.
3. Measure the resistance of the CMP sensor. Specification is 2 50–1000 ohms.

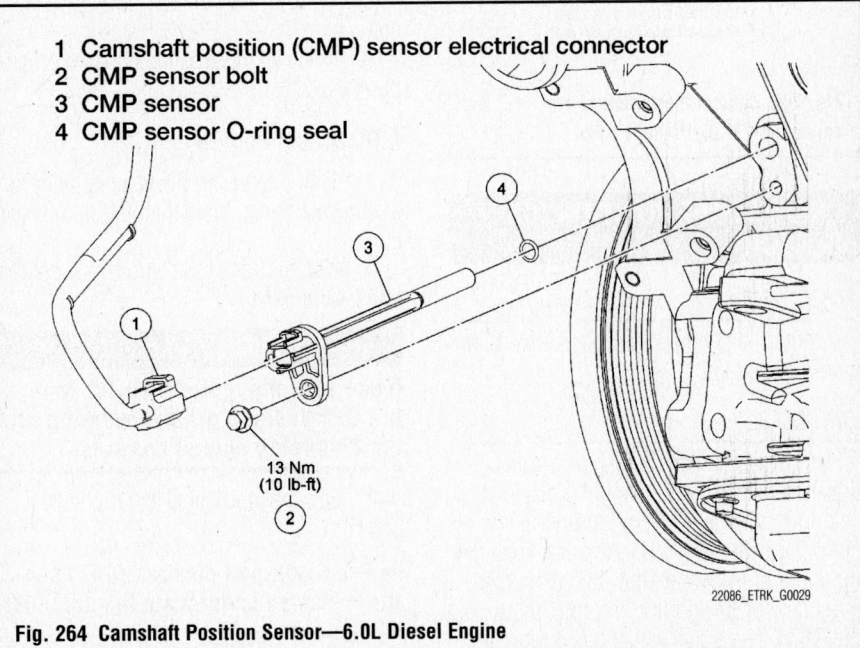

1 Camshaft position (CMP) sensor electrical connector
2 CMP sensor bolt
3 CMP sensor
4 CMP sensor O-ring seal

13 Nm
(10 lb-ft)

22086_ETRK_G0029

Fig. 264 Camshaft Position Sensor—6.0L Diesel Engine

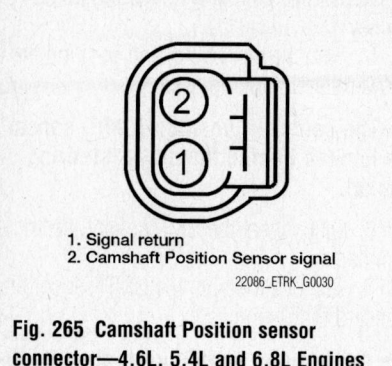

1. Signal return
2. Camshaft Position Sensor signal

22086_ETRK_G0030

Fig. 265 Camshaft Position sensor connector—4.6L, 5.4L and 6.8L Engines

6.0L Diesel Engine

See Figure 266.

1. Before servicing the vehicle, refer to the precautions in the beginning of this section.

❊❊ WARNING

Use only a high-impedance multimeter, otherwise damage to the PCM and/or sensors can result.

2. With the key **OFF**, disconnect the CMP sensor harness connector.
3. Measure the resistance of the CMP sensor. Specification is 800–1000 ohms.

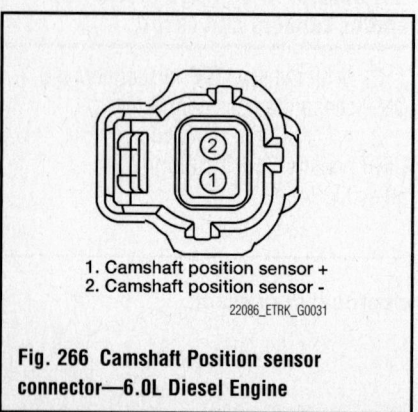

1. Camshaft position sensor +
2. Camshaft position sensor -

22086_ETRK_G0031

Fig. 266 Camshaft Position sensor connector—6.0L Diesel Engine

CRANKSHAFT POSITION (CKP) SENSOR

LOCATION

Front of the engine, passenger side of the crankshaft pulley.

OPERATION

The CKP sensor is a magnetic transducer mounted on the engine block adjacent to a pulse wheel located on the crankshaft. By monitoring the crankshaft mounted pulse wheel, the CKP is the primary sensor for ignition information to the PCM. The pulse wheel has a total of 35 teeth spaced 10 degrees apart with one empty space for a missing tooth. The 6.8L 10-cylinder pulse wheel has 39 teeth spaced 9 degrees apart and one 9 degree empty space for a missing tooth. By monitoring the pulse wheel, the CKP sensor signal indicates crankshaft position and speed information to the PCM. By monitoring the missing tooth, the CKP sensor is also able to identify piston travel in order to synchronize the ignition system and provide a way of tracking the angular position of the crankshaft relative to a fixed reference for the CKP sensor configuration. The PCM also uses the CKP signal to determine if a misfire has occurred by measuring rapid decelerations between teeth.

REMOVAL & INSTALLATION

4.6L, 5.4L and 6.8L Engines

1. Before servicing the vehicle, refer to the precautions in the beginning of this section.
2. With the vehicle in NEUTRAL, position it on a hoist.
3. Disconnect the battery ground cable.
4. Remove the accessory drive belt.
5. If equipped, remove the 2 bolts and position the power steering fluid cooler aside.
6. Loosen the A/C compressor bolts enough to slide the A/C compressor down 25 mm (1 in), to allow access to the crankshaft position (CKP) sensor.
7. Disconnect the CKP sensor electrical connector.
8. Remove the bolt and the CKP sensor.
9. To install, reverse the removal procedure.

6.0L Diesel Engine

1. Before servicing the vehicle, refer to the precautions in the beginning of this section.
2. With the vehicle in NEUTRAL, position it on a hoist.

❊❊ CAUTION

Make sure the ignition switch is in the OFF position prior to working on the electronic engine controls.

3. Turn the ignition switch to the OFF position.

➡ **The crankshaft position (CKP) sensor is located underneath the air conditioning compressor.**

4. Remove the nut and position the positive battery cable and support bracket aside.
5. Remove the stud bolt and position the battery negative cable aside.
6. Disconnect the CKP sensor electrical connector.
7. Remove the bolt, the CKP sensor and discard the O-ring seal.

➡ **Apply clean engine oil to the O-ring seal prior to installation.**

8. To install, reverse the removal procedure.

TESTING

See Figures 267 and 268.

1. Before servicing the vehicle, refer to the precautions in the beginning of this section.

❊❊ WARNING

Use only a high-impedance multimeter, otherwise damage to the PCM and/or sensors can result.

2. With the key **OFF**, disconnect the CKP sensor harness connector.
3. Measure the resistance of the CKP sensor. Specification is 300–400 ohms for the 6.0L diesel engine, and 250–1000 ohms for all gasoline engines.

1. Crankshaft position sensor -
2. Crankshaft position sensor +

22086_ETRK_G0033

Fig. 267 Crankshaft Position sensor connector—Gasoline Engines

1. Crankshaft position sensor +
2. Crankshaft position sensor -

22086_ETRK_G0032

Fig. 268 Crankshaft Position sensor connector—Diesel Engine

CYLINDER HEAD TEMPERATURE SENSOR (CHT)

LOCATION

Front of the left cylinder head.

OPERATION

The CHT sensor is a thermistor device in which resistance changes with the temperature. The electrical resistance of a thermistor decreases as temperature increases, and the resistance increases as the temperature decreases. The varying resistance affects the voltage drop across the sensor terminals and provides electrical signals to the PCM corresponding to temperature.

The CHT sensor is installed in the cylinder head and measures the metal temperature. The CHT sensor can provide complete engine temperature information and can be used to infer coolant temperature. If the CHT sensor conveys an overheating condition to the PCM, the PCM initiates a fail-safe cooling strategy based on information from the CHT sensor. A cooling system concern such as low coolant or coolant loss could cause an overheating condition. As a result, damage to major engine components could occur. Using both the CHT sensor and fail-safe cooling strategy, the PCM prevents damage by allowing air cooling of the engine and limp home capability.

REMOVAL & INSTALLATION

1. Before servicing the vehicle, refer to the precautions in the beginning of this section.
2. Remove the alternator.
3. Disconnect the cylinder head temperature (CHT) sensor electrical connector.
4. Remove the CHT sensor.
5. To install, reverse the removal procedure.
6. Coat the CHT sensor threads with high temperature nickel anti-seize lubricant prior to installation.

TESTING

See Figures 269 and 270.

→The CHT sensor is used to determine the engine coolant temperature. To cover the entire temperature range of both the CHT and ECT sensors, the PCM has a dual switching resistor circuit on the CHT input. A graph showing the temperature switching from the COLD END line to the HOT END line, with increasing temperature and back with decreasing temperature is included. Note the temperature to voltage overlap zone. Within this zone it is

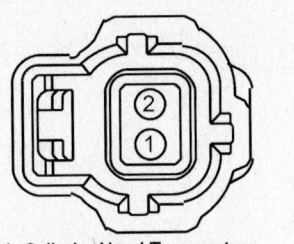

1. Cylinder Head Temperature sensor signal
2. Signal return

22086_ETRK_G0034

Fig. 269 Cylinder Head Temperature Sensor Connector

possible to have either a COLD END or HOT END voltage at the same temperature. For example, at 90°C (194°F) the voltage could read either 0.60 volt or 3.71 volts. Refer to the table for the temperature to voltage expected values.

1. Before servicing the vehicle, refer to the precautions in the beginning of this section.

✳✳ WARNING

Use only a high-impedance multimeter, otherwise damage to the PCM and/or sensors can result.

CYLINDER HEAD TEMPERATURE SENSOR EXPECTED VALUES

Temperature		CHT Sensor Values		
°C	°F	COLD END (volts)	HOT END (volts)	Resistance (K ohms)
-40	-40	4.89	-	965.808
-30	-22	4.81	-	513.019
-20	-4	4.67	-	283.664
-10	14	4.45	-	162.584
0	32	4.14	-	96.255
10	50	3.73	-	59.175
20	68	3.26	-	37.387
30	86	2.74	-	24.215
40	104	2.23	-	16.043
50	122	1.76	-	10.85
60	140	1.36	-	7.487
70	158	1.04	-	5.268
80	176	0.79	3.99	3.775
85	185	0.69	3.86	3.215
90	194	0.60	3.71	2.75
95	203	0.53	3.56	2.361
100	212	0.46	3.41	2.034
110	230	-	3.07	1.523
120	248	-	2.74	1.155
130	266	-	2.41	0.8866
140	284	-	2.10	0.6891
150	302	-	1.81	0.5417
160	320	-	1.55	0.4301
170	338	-	1.33	0.3449
180	356	-	1.13	0.2791
190	374	-	0.96	0.2278
200	392	-	0.82	0.1875
210	410	-	0.70	0.155
220	428	-	0.60	0.130
230	446	-	0.51	0.109
240	464	-	0.44	0.092
250	482	-	0.35	0.078
260	500	-	0.33	0.067

22086_ETRK_G0035

Fig. 270 CHT Temperature, Resistance and Voltage Table

2. With the key **OFF**, disconnect the CHT sensor harness connector and measure the resistance of the sensor. Compare the resistance and the temperature with the illustration.

3. Connect the CHT sensor harness and backprobe the connection.

4. With the key **ON**, compare the voltage measurement and the temperature with the illustration.

5. If the measurements are not as listed, replace the CHT sensor.

ENGINE COOLANT TEMPERATURE (ECT) SENSOR

LOCATION

Front and top of engine, near thermostat housing.

OPERATION

The ECT sensor is a thermistor device in which resistance changes with temperature. The electrical resistance of a thermistor decreases as the temperature increases, and resistance increases as the temperature decreases. The varying resistance affects the voltage drop across the sensor terminals and provides electrical signals to the PCM corresponding to temperature.

If the PCM receives a high engine temperature signal from the ECT, it adjusts fueling rates to protect the engine from damage due to overheating.

REMOVAL & INSTALLATION

6.0L Diesel Engine

See Figure 271.

�֎ CAUTION

Make sure the ignition switch is in the OFF position prior to working on the electronic engine controls.

1. Before servicing the vehicle, refer to the precautions in the beginning of this section.

2. Turn the ignition switch to the OFF position.

3. Drain the engine cooling system.

4. Disconnect the cooling fan electrical connector.

5. Disconnect the engine coolant temperature (ECT) electrical connector.

6. Remove the ECT sensor and discard the O-ring seal.

To install:

➡ **Apply clean engine oil to the new O-ring seal prior to installation.**

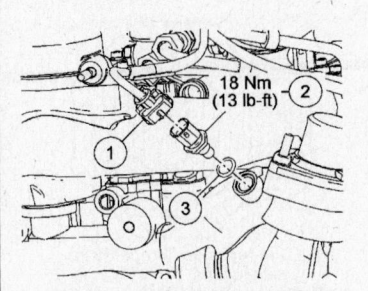

1. Engine coolant temperature (ECT) sensor electrical connector
2. ECT sensor
3. ECT sensor O-ring seal

22086_ETRK_G0036

Fig. 271 Engine Coolant Temperature sensor

7. Using a new O-ring seal, install the ECT sensor.

8. Tighten to 18 Nm (13 lb-ft).

9. Connect the ECT sensor electrical connector.

10. Connect the cooling fan electrical connector.

11. Fill and bleed the engine cooling system.

TESTING

See Figures 272 and 273.

1. Before servicing the vehicle, refer to the precautions in the beginning of this section.

�֎ WARNING

Use only a high-impedance multimeter, otherwise damage to the PCM and/or sensors can result.

2. With the key **OFF**, disconnect the ECT sensor harness connector and measure the

resistance of the sensor. Compare the resistance and the temperature with the illustration.

3. If the measurements are not as listed, replace the ECT sensor.

TEMPERATURE VS. RESISTANCE VALUES (APPROXIMATE)

Degrees C	Degrees F	Ohms
100	212	2,080
90	194	2,803
80	176	3,836
70	158	5,337
60	140	7,556
50	122	10,908
45	113	13,216
40	104	16,092
35	95	19,696
30	86	24,329
25	77	30,000
20	68	37,352
15	59	46,797
10	50	59,016
5	41	79,940
0	32	95,851
-5	23	124,485
-10	14	160,313
-15	5	209,816
-20	-4	276,959
-30	-22	496,051
-40	-40	925,021

22086_ETRK_G0038

Fig. 273 Engine Coolant Temperature Sensor resistance and temperature table— 6.0L Diesel Engine

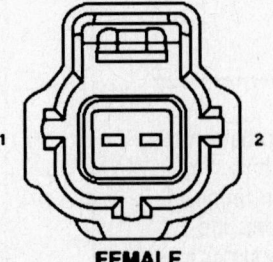

C1064 (GY)

Engine Coolant Temperature (ECT) sensor

1   2

FEMALE

Pin	Circuit	Circuit function
1	359 (GY/RD)	Signal return
2	3076 (YE/WH)	Reference voltage

22086_ETRK_G0037

Fig. 272 Engine Coolant Temperature sensor connector—6.0L Diesel Engine

ENGINE OIL TEMPERATURE (EOT) SENSOR

LOCATION

Right side of engine, near the starter.

OPERATION

The EOT sensor is a thermistor device in which resistance changes with temperature. The electrical resistance of a thermistor decreases as the temperature increases and the resistance increases as the temperature decreases. The varying resistance changes the voltage drop across the sensor terminals and provides electrical signals to the PCM corresponding to temperature.

Thermistor-type sensors are considered passive sensors. A passive sensor is connected to a voltage divider network so that varying the resistance of the passive sensor causes a variation in total current flow. Voltage that is dropped across a fixed resistor in a series with the sensor resistor determines the voltage signal at the PCM. This voltage signal is equal to the reference voltage minus the voltage drop across the fixed resistor.

REMOVAL & INSTALLATION

6.8L Engine

See Figure 274.

1. Before servicing the vehicle, refer to the precautions in the beginning of this section.

2. With the vehicle in NEUTRAL, position it on a hoist.

3. Disconnect the battery ground cable.

4. Drain the engine oil.

5. Disconnect the engine oil temperature (EOT) sensor electrical connector.

6. Remove the EOT sensor. Discard the O-ring seal.

7. Install a new O-ring seal. Lubricate the new O-ring seal with clean engine oil prior to installation.

8. To install, reverse the removal procedure.

6.0L Diesel Engine

See Figure 275.

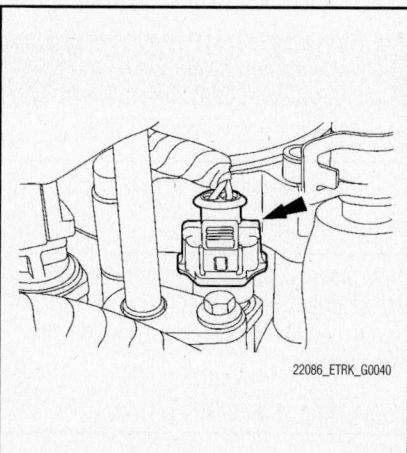

Fig. 275 Engine Oil Temperature sensor— 6.0L Diesel Engine

22086_ETRK_G0040

✳✳ CAUTION

Make sure the ignition switch is in the OFF position prior to working on the electronic engine controls.

1. Before servicing the vehicle, refer to the precautions in the beginning of this section.

2. Turn the ignition switch to the OFF position.

3. Disconnect the engine oil temperature (EOT) sensor.

4. Remove the EOT sensor.

5. To install, reverse the removal procedure. Tighten the EOT sensor to 18 Nm (13 lb-ft).

TESTING

See Figures 276 and 277.

1. Before servicing the vehicle, refer to the precautions in the beginning of this section.

✳✳ WARNING

Use only a high-impedance multimeter, otherwise damage to the PCM and/or sensors can result.

2. With the key **OFF**, disconnect the EOT sensor harness connector and measure the resistance of the sensor. Compare the resistance and the temperature with the illustration.

3. If the measurements are not as listed, replace the EOT sensor.

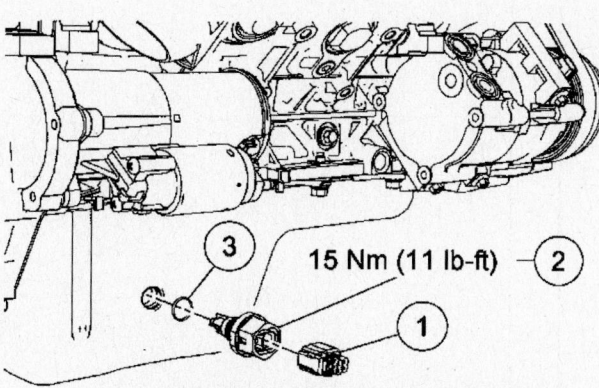

15 Nm (11 lb-ft)

1. **Engine oil temperature (EOT) sensor electrical connector**
2. **EOT sensor**
3. **EOT sensor O-ring seal**

22086_ETRK_G0039

Fig. 274 Engine Oil Temperature sensor—6.8L Engine

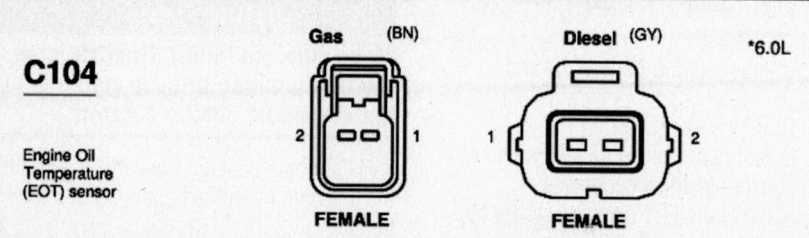

C104

Engine Oil Temperature (EOT) sensor

Gas (BN)   Diesel (GY)   *6.0L

FEMALE   FEMALE

Pin	Circuit	Circuit function
1	263 (YE/LB)	Engine Oil Temperature (EOT) sensor,signal
*1	359 (GY/RD)	Signal return
2	359 (GY/RD)	Signal return
*2	354 (LG/RD)	Engine Oil Temperature (EOT) sensor,signal

22086_ETRK_G0041

Fig. 276 Engine Oil Temperature sensor connector

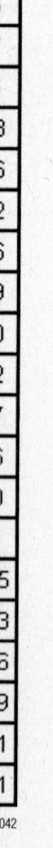

TEMPERATURE VS. RESISTANCE VALUES (APPROXIMATE)

°C	°F	Ohms
100	212	2,080
90	194	2,083
90	176	2,836
70	158	5,337
60	140	7,556
50	122	10,908
45	113	13,216
40	104	16,092
35	95	19,696
30	86	24,329
25	77	30,000
20	68	37,352
15	59	46,797
10	50	59,016
5	41	79,940
0	32	95,851
-5	23	124,485
-10	14	160,313
-15	5	209,816
-20	-4	276,959
-30	-22	496,051
-40	-40	925,021

22086_ETRK_G0042

Fig. 277 Engine Oil Temperature Sensor resistance and temperature table

EXHAUST BACKPRESSURE SENSOR

LOCATION

Front of the engine, left side.

OPERATION

Measures analog output indicating exhaust back pressure. PCM uses information to control back pressure under cold conditions.

REMOVAL & INSTALLATION

6.0L Diesel Engine

See Figure 278.

✳✳ CAUTION

Make sure the ignition switch is in the OFF position prior to working on the electronic engine controls.

1. Before servicing the vehicle, refer to the precautions in the beginning of this section.
2. Turn the ignition switch to the OFF position.
3. Disconnect the exhaust pressure (EP) sensor electrical connector.

➡ **Support the EP sensor tube flange nut when removing the EP sensor.**

4. Remove the EP sensor.
5. To install, reverse the removal procedure. Tighten to 20 Nm (15 lb-ft).

TESTING

See Figures 279 and 280.

1. Before servicing the vehicle, refer to the precautions in the beginning of this section.
2. With the key **OFF**, disconnect the EP sensor.
3. Install the ICP/EBC Adapter Cable D94T-50-A or equivalent between the EP sensor and the vehicle harness.
4. Start the engine and measure the voltage between the EP signal circuit and ground on the ICP/EBC Adapter Cable D94T-50-A.
5. Accelerate the engine to wide open throttle (WOT) several times. The voltage should be above 1.35 VDC during acceleration.

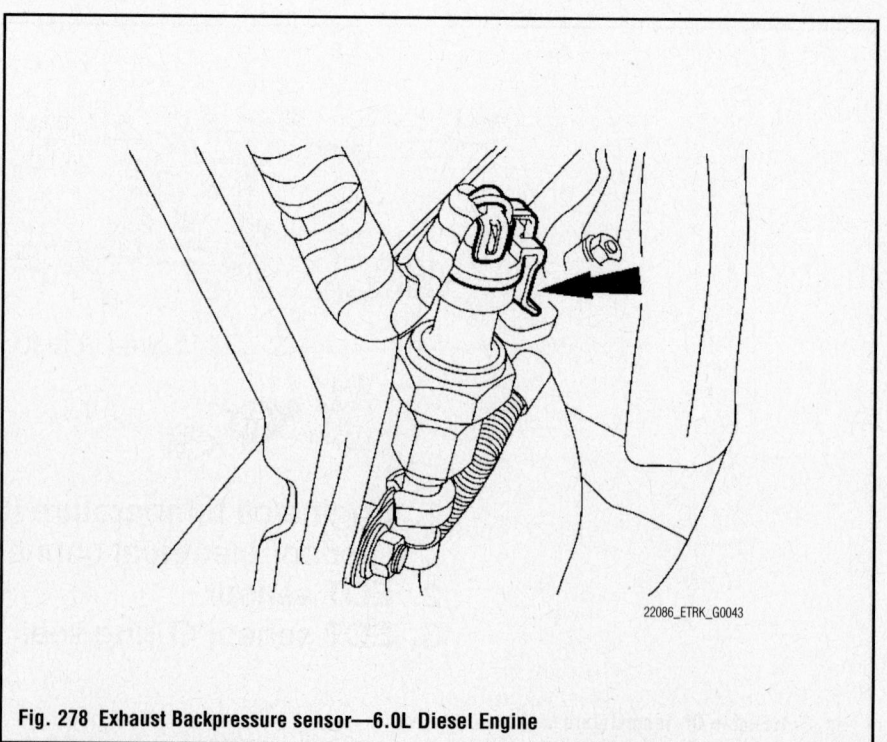

22086_ETRK_G0043

Fig. 278 Exhaust Backpressure sensor—6.0L Diesel Engine

C1271 (BK)

Exhaust Back
Pressure
(EBP) sensor

FEMALE

Pin	Circuit	Circuit function
1	359 (GY/RD)	Signal return
2	351 (BN/WH)	Reference voltage
3	553 (VT/LB)	Pressure sense

22086_ETRK_G0044

Fig. 279 Exhaust Backpressure sensor connector—6.0L Diesel Engine

kPa	psi	EP (volts)
43.8	6.4	0.05
70.5	10.2	0.45
101.5	14.7	0.90
325.5	47.2	4.14
365.4	53	4.75

22086_ETRK_G0045

Fig. 280 Exhaust Pressure Sensor pressure and voltage table

HEATED OXYGEN (HO2S) SENSOR

LOCATION

See Figure 281.

OPERATION

The HO2S detects the presence of oxygen in the exhaust and produces a variable voltage according to the amount of oxygen detected. A high concentration of oxygen (lean air/fuel ratio) in the exhaust produces a voltage signal less than 0.4 volt. A low concentration of oxygen (rich air/fuel ratio) produces a voltage signal greater than 0.6 volt. The HO2S provides feedback to the PCM indicating air/fuel ratio in order to achieve a near stoichiometric air/fuel ratio of 14.7:1 during closed loop engine operation. The HO2S generates a voltage between 0.0 and 1.1 volts.

Embedded with the sensing element is the HO2S heater. The heating element heats the sensor to a temperature of 800°C (1,472°F). At approximately 300°C (572°F) the engine can enter closed loop operation. The VPWR circuit supplies voltage to the heater. The PCM turns the heater on by providing the ground when the correct conditions occur. The heater allows the engine to enter closed loop operation sooner. The use of this heater requires the HO2S heater control to be duty cycled, to prevent damage to the heater.

REMOVAL & INSTALLATION

4.6L, 5.4L and 6.8L Engines

See Figure 282.

1. Before servicing the vehicle, refer to the precautions in the beginning of this section.
2. With the vehicle in NEUTRAL, position it on a hoist.
3. Disconnect the battery ground cable.

➡ **If necessary, lubricate the HO2S with penetrating and lock lubricant to assist in removal.**

4. Remove the HO2S.
5. To install, reverse the removal procedure.

➡**Apply anti-seize to the threads of the HO2S.**

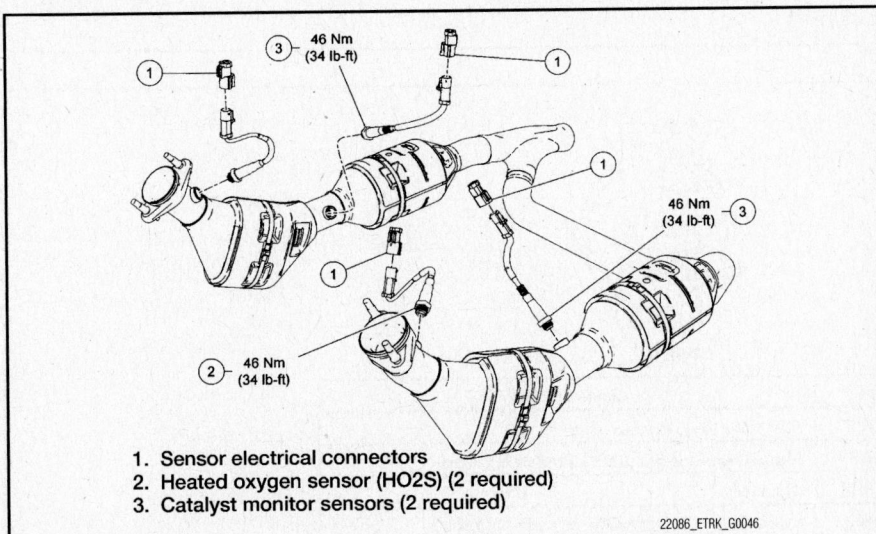

1. Sensor electrical connectors
2. Heated oxygen sensor (HO2S) (2 required)
3. Catalyst monitor sensors (2 required)

22086_ETRK_G0046

Fig. 281 Heated Oxygen Sensors—5.4L Engine shown, 4.6L and 6.8L Engines similar

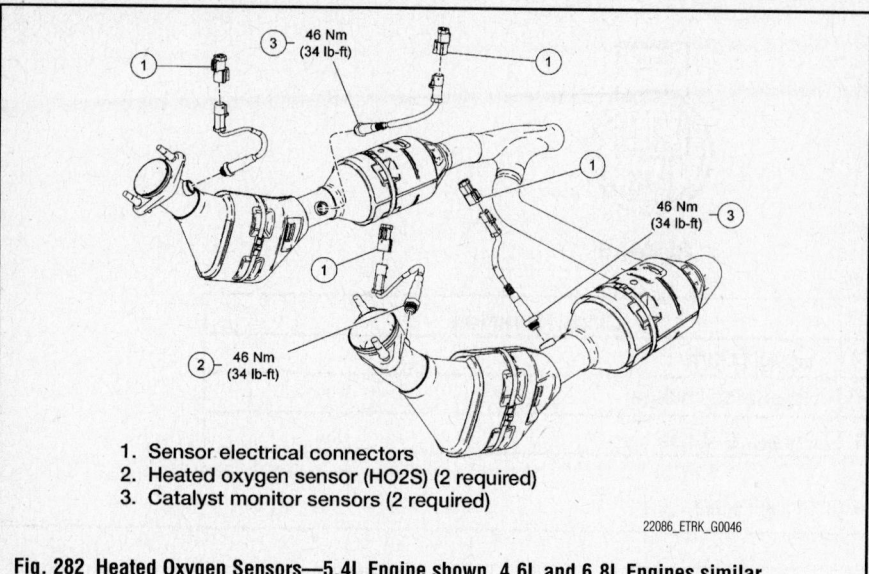

1. Sensor electrical connectors
2. Heated oxygen sensor (HO2S) (2 required)
3. Catalyst monitor sensors (2 required)

22086_ETRK_G0046

Fig. 282 Heated Oxygen Sensors—5.4L Engine shown, 4.6L and 6.8L Engines similar

⁕⁕ WARNING

Use only a high-impedance multimeter, otherwise damage to the PCM and/or sensors can result.

⁕⁕ WARNING

Do not measure resistance between pins 3 and 4. Damage to the HO2S will result.

2. With the key **OFF**, disconnect the HO2S harness connector.
3. Measure the HO2S sensor resistances as follows:
 - Pins 1 and 2: 3–30 ohms
 - Pins 1 and 4: Greater than 10M ohms
 - Pin 1 and battery negative: Greater than 10M ohms.
4. If any measurement is outside the range given, replace the HO2S.

TESTING

See Figures 283 through 286.

1. Before servicing the vehicle, refer to the precautions in the beginning of this section.

C171 (BK)

Heated Oxygen Sensor
(HO2S) #11

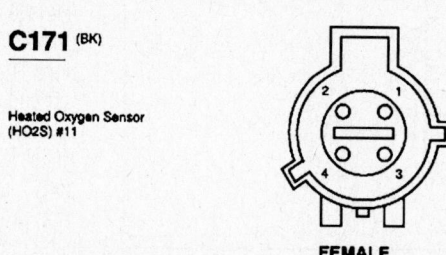

FEMALE

Pin	Circuit	Circuit function
1	391 (RD/YE)	PCM power relay, switched power
2	387 (RD/WH)	Heated Oxygen Sensor (HO2S) #11 (9F472), heater
3	359 (GY/RD)	Signal return
4	74 (GY/LB)	Heated Oxygen Sensor (HO2S) #11 (9F472), input

22086_ETRK_G0047

Fig. 283 Heated Oxygen Sensor Connector—Bank 1 Sensor 1

C172 (BK)

Heated Oxygen Sensor
(HO2S) #21

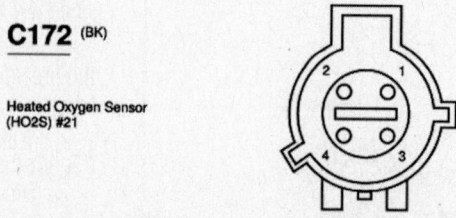

FEMALE

Pin	Circuit	Circuit function
1	391 (RD/YE)	PCM power relay, switched power
2	388 (YE/LB)	Heated Oxygen Sensor (HO2S) #21 (9F472), heater
3	359 (GY/RD)	Signal return
4	94 (RD/BK)	Heated Oxygen Sensor (HO2S) #21 (9F472), input

22086_ETRK_G0048

Fig. 284 Heated Oxygen Sensor Connector—Bank 2 Sensor 1

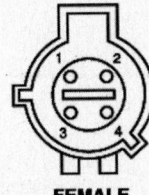

C142 (BU)

Heated Oxygen Sensor
(HO2S) #12

FEMALE

Pin	Circuit	Circuit function
1	389 (WH/BK)	Heated Oxygen Sensor (HO2S) #12 (9G444), heater
2	391 (RD/YE)	PCM power relay, switched power
3	392 (RD/LG)	Heated Oxygen Sensor (HO2S) #12 (9G444), input
4	1704 (VT/LG)	Signal return

22086_ETRK_G0049

Fig. 285 Heated Oxygen Sensor Connector—Bank 1 Sensor 2

C141 (BU)

Heated Oxygen
Sensor (HO2S)
#22

FEMALE

Pin	Circuit	Circuit function
1	390 (TN/YE)	Heated Oxygen Sensor (HO2S) #22 (9G444), heater
2	391 (RD/YE)	PCM power relay, switched power
3	393 (VT/LG)	Heated Oxygen Sensor (HO2S) #22 (9G444), input
4	1704 (VT/LG)	Signal return

22086_ETRK_G0050

Fig. 286 Heated Oxygen Sensor Connector—Bank 2 Sensor 2

INJECTOR DRIVER MODULE (IDM)

LOCATION

Left side of engine, above valve cover.

OPERATION

Also referred to as the Fuel Injector Control Module (FICM).

The FICM requires a 12-volt power source. The FICM receives power from the vehicle batteries through the FICM relay contacts each time the key is turned to the ON position. As the key is turned to the ON position, the FICM provides an internal ground to the coil side of the FICM relay. This closes the relay contacts and provides the FICM with the necessary power. The PCM communicates with the FICM using the CAN protocol. The CAN protocol is an international standards organization (ISO) standard for serial data communication. The CAN protocol standard includes a physical layer using differential transmission on a twisted pair of wires and a data link layer that defines different message types, arbitration rules for bus access, methods for concern detection and concern confinement. The FICM receives information from the PCM, including the volume of fuel desired, RPM, engine oil temperature, injection control pressure, and others. The FICM uses those signals to calculate fuel injection and duration. After calculating injector fuel delivery time, the FICM sends 48 volts at a 20-amp pulse to the correct injector so that the correct amount of fuel is delivered to the cylinder at the correct time.

REMOVAL & INSTALLATION

❋❋ CAUTION

Make sure the ignition switch is in the OFF position prior to working on the electronic engine controls.

1. Before servicing the vehicle, refer to the precautions in the beginning of this section.
2. Turn the ignition switch to the OFF position.

❋❋ WARNING

Never remove the pressure relief cap while the engine is operating or when the cooling system is hot. Failure to follow these instructions can result in damage to the cooling system or engine or result in personal injury. To avoid having scalding hot coolant or steam blow out of the degas bottle when removing the pressure relief cap, wait until the engine has cooled, then wrap a thick cloth around the pressure relief cap and turn it slowly. Step back while the pressure is released from the cooling system. When certain all the pressure has been released, (still with a cloth) turn and remove the pressure relief cap. Failure to follow these instructions can result in personal injury.

3. Relieve the cooling system pressure. Disconnect and plug or cap the engine vent hose and radiator vent hose.
4. Remove the 2 bolts and position the degas bottle aside.
5. Release the 2 exhaust pressure (EP) sensor harness pin-type retainers.
6. Disconnect the EP sensor electrical connector and position the harness aside.
7. Remove the fuel injector control module (FICM) nuts and bracket.
8. Remove the FICM bolts.

❋❋ CAUTION

Make sure both latches are released before removing the electrical connectors or connector damage can occur.

9. Position out the FICM and disconnect the electrical connectors. Remove the FICM.

❋❋ CAUTION

With the engine cold, fill vehicles with a yellow fill level decal to within the yellow cold fill range shown on the decal. If the decal is missing, fill the degas bottle only to the molded line. The correct fill level on these vehicles is between the molded line and 15 mm (0.59 inch) below the line. These fill levels will allow for coolant expansion. Overfilling the degas bottle may result in damage to the pressure cap, which can cause the engine to overheat.

10. To install, reverse the removal procedure.

TESTING

See Figure 287.

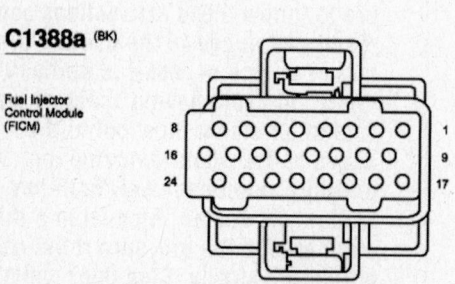

C1388a (BK)

Fuel Injector
Control Module
(FICM)

8 ... 1
16 ... 9
24 ... 17

FEMALE

Pin	Circuit	Circuit function
1	7 (LG/YE)	Fuel injector 4, open coil, Ground
2	3 (LG/WH)	Fuel injector 1, open coil, Ground
3	11 (TN/YE)	Fuel injector 7, open coil, Ground
4	15 (RD/YE)	Fuel injector 6, open coil, Ground
5	2 (WH/LB)	Fuel injector 1, close coil, Ground
6	6 (YE/LG)	Fuel injector 4, close coil, Ground
7	14 (BN)	Fuel injector 6, close coil, Ground
8	10 (LG/RD)	Fuel injector 7, close coil, Ground
9	–	not used
10	–	not used
11	–	not used
12	–	not used
13	–	not used
14	–	not used
15	–	not used
16	–	not used
17	12 (LG/BK)	Fuel injector 7, open coil, Power
18	9 (LG/OG)	Fuel injector 7, close coil, Power
19	4 (WH/BK)	Fuel injector 1, open coil, Power
20	1 (DB)	Fuel injector 1, close coil, Power
21	16 (RD/LG)	Fuel injector 6, open coil, Power
22	13 (RD/BK)	Fuel injector 6, close coil, Power
23	33 (WH/PK)	Fuel injector 4, open coil, Power
24	5 (OG/LB)	Fuel injector 4, close coil, Power

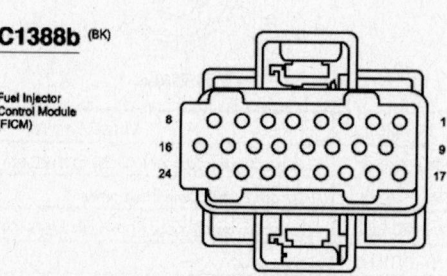

C1388b (BK)

Fuel Injector
Control Module
(FICM)

8 ... 1
16 ... 9
24 ... 17

FEMALE

Pin	Circuit	Circuit function
1	23 (TN/LG)	Fuel injector 5, open coil, Ground
2	19 (LB/RD)	Fuel injector 2, open coil, Ground
3	31 (WH/RD)	Fuel injector 8, open coil, Ground
4	27 (OG/LG)	Fuel injector 3, open coil, Ground
5	22 (LB/BK)	Fuel injector 5, close coil, Ground
6	18 (OG/YE)	Fuel injector 2, close coil, Ground
7	30 (BK/LG)	Fuel injector 8, close coil, Ground
8	26 (WH/VT)	Fuel injector 3, close coil, Ground
9	–	not used
10	–	not used
11	–	not used
12	–	not used
13	–	not used
14	–	not used
15	–	not used
16	–	not used
17	20 (WH/LB)	Fuel injector 2, open coil, Power
18	17 (WH)	Fuel injector 2, close coil, Power
19	28 (BK/PK)	Fuel injector 3, open coil, Power
20	25 (DG/VT)	Fuel injector 3, close coil, Power
21	24 (DB/OG)	Fuel injector 5, open coil, Power
22	21 (DG/LG)	Fuel injector 5, close coil, Power
23	32 (RD/LB)	Fuel injector 8, open coil, Power
24	29 (YE/WH)	Fuel injector 8, close coil, Power

22086_ETRK_G0051

Fig. 287 Injector Driver Module connectors—6.0L Diesel Engine

INJECTION CONTROL PRESSURE (ICP) SENSOR

LOCATION

5.4L Engines

Attached to the left fuel rail.

4.6L and 6.8L Engines

Attached to the right fuel rail.

OPERATION

The FRPT sensor measures the pressure and temperature of the fuel in the fuel rail and sends these signals to the PCM. The sensor uses the intake manifold vacuum as a reference to determine the pressure difference between the fuel rail and the intake manifold. The relationship between fuel pressure and fuel temperature is used to determine the possible presence of fuel vapor in the fuel rail.

The temperature sensing portion of the FRPT sensor is a thermistor device in which resistance changes with temperature. The electrical resistance of the thermistor decreases as the temperature increases, and the resistance increases as the temperature decreases. The varying resistance changes the voltage drop across the sensor terminals and provides electrical signals to the PCM corresponding to temperature.

Both the pressure and temperature signals are used to control the speed of the fuel pump. The speed of the fuel pump sustains fuel rail pressure which preserves fuel in its liquid state. The dynamic range of the fuel injectors increase because of the higher rail pressure, which allows the injector pulse width to decrease.

REMOVAL & INSTALLATION

4.6L Engine

See Figure 288.

✳✳ WARNING

Do not smoke or carry lighted tobacco or open flame of any type when working on or near any fuel-related components. Highly flammable mixtures are always present and can be ignited. Failure to follow these instructions may result in personal injury.

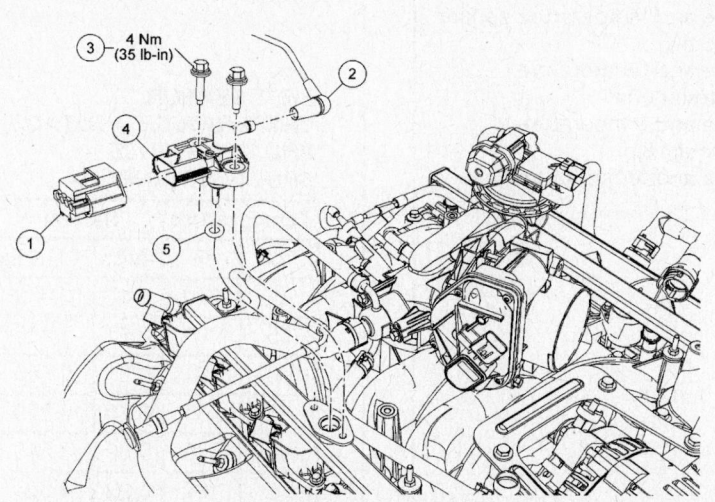

1. Fuel pressure and temperature sensor electrical connector
2. Fuel pressure and temperature sensor vacuum connector
3. Fuel pressure and temperature sensor bolt (2 required)
4. Fuel pressure and temperature sensor
5. Fuel pressure and temperature sensor O-ring seal

22086_ETRK_G0052

Fig. 288 Fuel Rail Pressure and Temperature Sensor—4.6L Engine

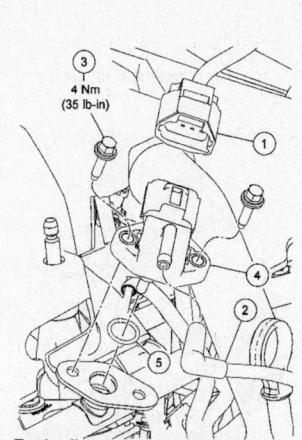

1. Fuel rail pressure and temperature sensor electrical connector
2. Fuel rail pressure and temperature sensor vacuum connector
3. Fuel rail pressure and temperature sensor bolts
4. Fuel rail pressure and temperature sensor

22086_ETRK_G0053

Fig. 289 Fuel Rail Pressure and Temperature Sensor—5.4L Engine

✳✳ WARNING

Fuel in the fuel system remains under high pressure even when the engine is not running. Before working on or disconnecting any of the fuel lines or fuel system components, the fuel system pressure must be relieved. Failure to follow these instructions may result in personal injury.

1. Before servicing the vehicle, refer to the precautions in the beginning of this section.
2. Release the fuel system pressure.
3. Disconnect the fuel pressure and temperature sensor electrical connector.
4. Disconnect the fuel pressure and temperature sensor vacuum connector.
5. Remove the bolts and the fuel pressure and temperature sensor.
6. Remove and discard the O-ring seal.
7. Install a new O-ring seal and lubricate with clean engine oil prior to installation.
8. To install, reverse the removal procedure.

5.4L Engine

See Figure 289.

✳✳ WARNING

Do not smoke or carry lighted tobacco or open flame of any type when working on or near any fuel-related components. Highly flammable mixtures are always present and can be ignited. Failure to follow these instructions may result in personal injury.

✳✳ WARNING

Fuel in the fuel system remains under high pressure even when the engine is not running. Before working on or disconnecting any of the fuel lines or fuel system components, the fuel system pressure must be relieved. Failure to follow these instructions may result in personal injury.

1. Before servicing the vehicle, refer to the precautions in the beginning of this section.
2. Release the fuel system pressure.
3. Disconnect the battery ground cable.
4. Disconnect the fuel rail pressure and temperature sensor electrical connector.
5. Disconnect the fuel rail pressure and temperature sensor vacuum connector.
6. Remove the bolts and the fuel rail pressure and temperature sensor.
7. Remove and discard the O-ring seal.
8. Install a new O-ring seal and lubricate it with clean engine oil.
9. To install, reverse the removal procedure.

6.8L Engine

See Figure 290.

✳✳ WARNING

Do not smoke or carry lighted tobacco or open flame of any type when working on or near any fuel-related components. Highly flammable mixtures are always present and can be ignited. Failure to follow these instructions may result in personal injury.

✳✳ WARNING

Fuel in the fuel system remains under high pressure even when the engine is not running. Before working on or disconnecting any of the fuel lines or fuel system components, the fuel system pressure must be relieved. Failure to follow these instructions may result in personal injury.

1. Before servicing the vehicle, refer to the precautions in the beginning of this section.
2. Release the fuel system pressure.
3. Disconnect the battery ground cable.
4. Disconnect the fuel rail pressure and temperature sensor electrical and vacuum connectors.

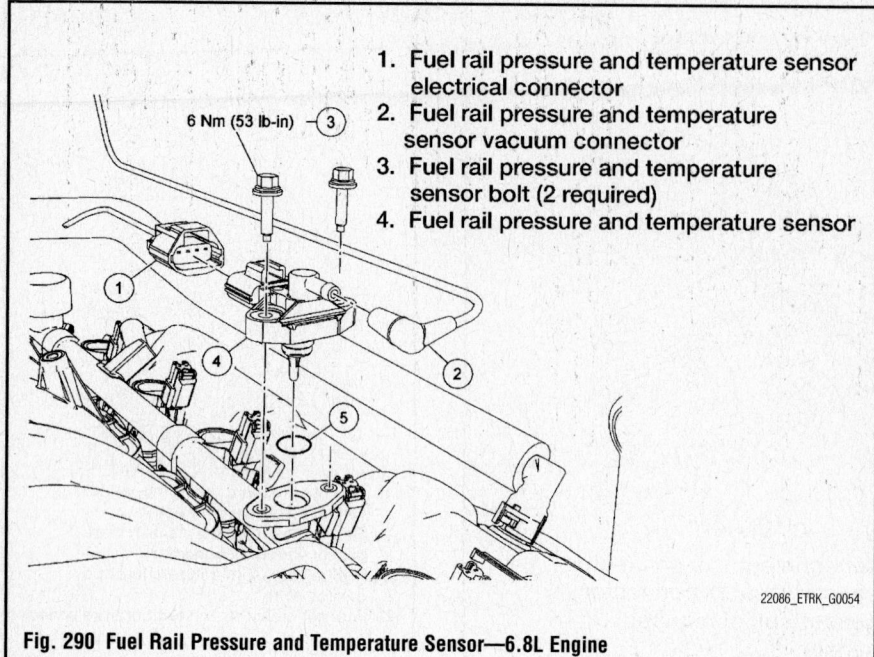

1. Fuel rail pressure and temperature sensor electrical connector
2. Fuel rail pressure and temperature sensor vacuum connector
3. Fuel rail pressure and temperature sensor bolt (2 required)
4. Fuel rail pressure and temperature sensor

6 Nm (53 lb-in) — 3

22086_ETRK_G0054

Fig. 290 Fuel Rail Pressure and Temperature Sensor—6.8L Engine

5. Remove the 2 bolts and the fuel rail pressure and temperature sensor and discard the O-ring seal.

6. Lubricate the new O-ring seal with clean engine oil prior to installation.

7. To install, reverse the removal procedure.

TESTING

See Figures 291 through 293.

1. Before servicing the vehicle, refer to the precautions in the beginning of this section.

2. Connect a mechanical fuel pressure gauge.

3. With the key **ON** and engine running, backprobe the FRPT sensor pins 1 and 4.

Voltage	Pressure (kPa)	Pressure (psi)
4.5	482	70
3.9	413	60
3.4	344	50
2.8	275	40
2.2	207	30
1.6	138	20
1.1	69	10
0.5	0	0

22086_ETRK_G0056

Fig. 292 FRPT sensor pressure specification table

FRPT SENSOR TEMPERATURE, VOLTAGE, AND RESISTANCE SPECIFICATIONS

Temperature		Sensor	
°C	°F	Volts	K Ohms
100	212	0.47	2.073
95	203	0.54	2.405
90	194	0.61	2.800
85	185	0.70	3.273
80	176	0.80	3.840
75	167	0.92	4.524
70	158	1.06	5.351
65	149	1.21	6.356
60	140	1.38	7.584
55	131	1.56	9.091
50	122	1.77	10.949
45	113	1.99	13.252
40	104	2.23	16.123
35	95	2.48	19.720
30	86	2.74	24.253
25	77	3.00	30.000
20	68	3.26	37.332
15	59	3.50	46.745
10	50	3.73	58.911
5	41	3.95	74.745
0	32	4.13	95.501

22086_ETRK_G0057

Fig. 293 FRPT sensor temperature specification table

4. Compare the voltage and pressure readings with the specifications table.

5. Backprobe FRPT sensor pins 3 and 4.

6. Compare the voltage and temperature with the specification table.

INJECTION PRESSURE REGULATOR (IPR)

LOCATION

Rear center of the engine.

OPERATION

Regulates high pressure oil used for controlling fuel injectors.

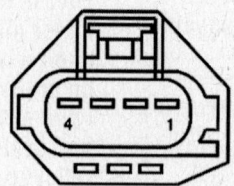

C1073 (BK)

Injector Pressure Sensor (IPS)

FEMALE

Pin	Circuit	Circuit function
1	1289 (OG/LG)	Fuel rail pressure sensor signal
2	3073 (RD/WH)	Fuel rail pressure sensor reference voltage
3	225 (BK/YE)	Fuel rail temperature sensor signal
4	359 (GY/RD)	Signal return

22086_ETRK_G0055

Fig. 291 Fuel Rail Pressure and Temperature sensor connector

TESTING

See Figure 294.

C1360 (BK)

Injection
Pressure
Regulator
(IPR)

FEMALE

Pin	Circuit	Circuit function
A	361 (RD)	PCM power relay, switched power
B	552 (YE/RD)	Switched ground

22086_ETRK_G0058

Fig. 294 Injection Pressure Regulator connector—6.0L Diesel Engine

INTAKE AIR TEMPERATURE (IAT) SENSOR

Part of the Mass Air Flow Sensor.

KNOCK SENSOR (KS)

LOCATION

Under the intake manifold.

OPERATION

The KS is a tuned accelerometer on the engine which converts engine vibration to an electrical signal. The PCM uses this signal to determine the presence of engine knock and to retard spark timing.

REMOVAL & INSTALLATION

See Figure 295.

1. Before servicing the vehicle, refer to the precautions in the beginning of this section.
2. Remove the intake manifold.
3. Disconnect the knock sensor (KS) electrical connector.

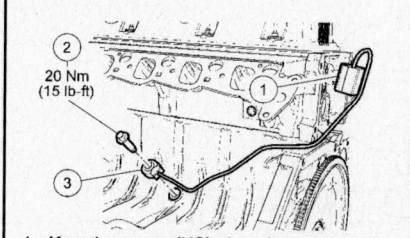

1. Knock sensor (KS) electrical connector
2. KS bolt
3. KS

22086_ETRK_G0060

Fig. 295 Knock Sensor—4.6L Engine shown, 5.4L and 6.8L similar

4. Remove the bolt and the KS.
5. To install, reverse the removal procedure.

TESTING

See Figure 296.

1. Before servicing the vehicle, refer to the precautions in the beginning of this section.

❄❄ WARNING

Use only a high-impedance multimeter, otherwise damage to the PCM and/or sensors can result.

2. With the key **ON** and the engine **OFF**, disconnect the knock sensor.
3. Measure resistance of the knock sensor. Standard value is 4.39M ohms—5.35M ohms. If not, replace the knock sensor.

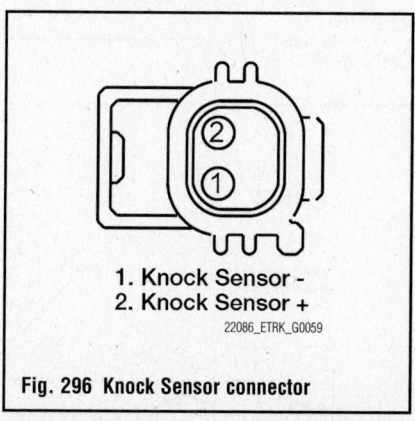

1. Knock Sensor -
2. Knock Sensor +

22086_ETRK_G0059

Fig. 296 Knock Sensor connector

MASS AIR FLOW (MAF) SENSOR

LOCATION

Attached to the air filter assembly.

OPERATION

The MAF sensor uses a hot wire sensing element to measure the amount of air entering the engine. Air passing over the hot wire causes it to cool. This hot wire is maintained at 200°C (392°F) above the ambient temperature as measured by a constant cold wire. The current required to maintain the temperature of the hot wire is proportional to the mass air flow. The MAF sensor then outputs an analog voltage signal to the PCM proportional to the intake air mass. The PCM calculates the required fuel injector pulse width in order to provide the desired air/fuel ratio. This input is also used in determining transmission electronic pressure control (EPC), shift and torque converter clutch scheduling.

The MAF sensor is located between the air cleaner and the throttle body or inside the air cleaner assembly. Most MAF sensors have integrated bypass technology with an integrated intake air temperature (IAT) sensor. The hot wire electronic sensing element must be replaced as an assembly. Replacing only the element may change the air flow calibration.

REMOVAL & INSTALLATION

See Figure 297.

1. Before servicing the vehicle, refer to the precautions in the beginning of this section.
2. Open the clamp on the air cleaner and separate the tray from the cover.
3. Disconnect the mass air flow (MAF) sensor electrical connector and detach the connector retainer.
4. Remove the grommet from the air cleaner cover and slide it down the electrical harness.

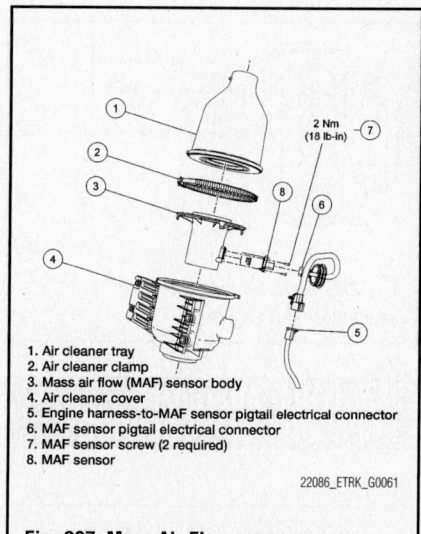

1. Air cleaner tray
2. Air cleaner clamp
3. Mass air flow (MAF) sensor body
4. Air cleaner cover
5. Engine harness-to-MAF sensor pigtail electrical connector
6. MAF sensor pigtail electrical connector
7. MAF sensor screw (2 required)
8. MAF sensor

22086_ETRK_G0061

Fig. 297 Mass Air Flow sensor

5. Pull the air cleaner inner cover and MAF sensor out of the air cleaner cover.

6. Disconnect the MAF sensor electrical connector and remove the inner cover and MAF sensor assembly.

7. Remove the bolts and the MAF sensor.

8. To install, reverse the removal procedure.

TESTING

See Figure 298.

1. Before servicing the vehicle, refer to the precautions in the beginning of this section.

✳✳ WARNING

Use only a high-impedance multimeter, otherwise damage to the PCM and/or sensors can result.

2. Check the air inlet system (air cleaner, housing, ductwork) for obstructions or blockage.

3. Check for broken/loose air outlet tube clamps (throttle body and air cleaner assembly ends), cracks/holes in the air outlet tube, and worn gaskets between the MAF sensor and the air cleaner assembly. Check throttle body bore for sludge. Verify the MAF sensor is connected. Repair as necessary.

4. Disconnect the MAF harness connector.

5. With the key **ON** and engine **OFF**, check the following connector pin values:
- Pins 2, 4, and 5 should be ground.
- Pin 6 should be B+ voltage.

6. Turn the key **OFF** and reconnect the MAF harness connector.

7. Start the engine and backprobe pin 1. This voltage should change with the intake air temperature.

8. Start the engine and backprobe pin 3. This voltage should rise with the engine rpm.

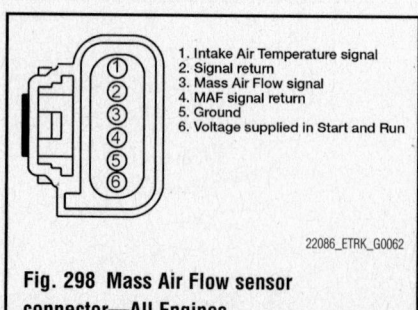

1. Intake Air Temperature signal
2. Signal return
3. Mass Air Flow signal
4. MAF signal return
5. Ground
6. Voltage supplied in Start and Run

22086_ETRK_G0062

Fig. 298 Mass Air Flow sensor connector—All Engines

MANIFOLD ABSOLUTE PRESSURE (MAP) SENSOR

LOCATION

Passenger side of the engine, near the cowl.

OPERATION

The MAP sensor is a variable capacitor sensor that is supplied a 5-volt reference signal by the PCM and returns a voltage signal to the PCM relative to the intake manifold pressure. The sensor voltage increases as the pressure increases. The MAP sensor allows the PCM to determine the engine boost to calculate fuel quantity. In addition, the MAP signal is used to control smoke by limiting fuel quantity during acceleration until a specified boost pressure is obtained, and is used by the PCM for EGR system calculations and control.

A MAP signal concern detected by the PCM causes the PCM to calculate an estimated manifold pressure based on known engine conditions.

REMOVAL & INSTALLATION

✳✳ CAUTION

Make sure the ignition switch is in the OFF position prior to working on the electronic engine controls.

1. Before servicing the vehicle, refer to the precautions in the beginning of this section.

2. Turn the ignition switch to the OFF position.

3. Disconnect the manifold absolute pressure (MAP) sensor.

4. Disconnect the pressure hose.

5. Disconnect the electrical connector.

6. Remove the mounting screws and the MAP sensor.

7. To install, reverse the removal procedure.

TESTING

See Figures 299 and 300.

MAP Sensor		
Volts	kPa	psi
0.02	20	2.9
0.5	50	7.25
0.92	76.6	11.1
3.8	255.9	37.1
4.49	299	43.4
5	300	43.5

22086_ETRK_G0064

Fig. 300 MAP sensor pressure/voltage table

1. Before servicing the vehicle, refer to the precautions in the beginning of this section.

✳✳ WARNING

Use only a high-impedance multimeter, otherwise damage to the PCM and/or sensors can result.

2. Disconnect the pressure hose from the MAP sensor.

3. With the key ON, engine OFF, connect the Pressure Adapter Kit 014-00761, or equivalent (gauge bar), and apply pressure to the MAP sensor.

4. Backprobe MAP sensor connector pin 2 and measure the voltage between pin 2 and ground.

5. Compare the values with the pressure/voltage table.

POWERTRAIN CONTROL MODULE (PCM)

LOCATION

Except 6.0L Diesel Engine

Mounted to the cowl, next to the brake booster.

C1087 (BK)

Manifold Absolute
Pressure (MAP)
sensor

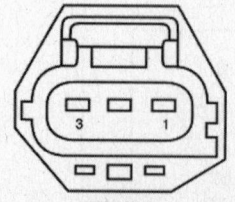

FEMALE

Pin	Circuit	Circuit function
1	351 (BN/WH)	Reference voltage
2	358 (LG/BK)	Manifold Absolute Pressure (MAP) sensor, to, Powertrain Control Module (PCM)
3	359 (GY/RD)	Signal return

22086_ETRK_G0063

Fig. 299 Manifold Absolute Pressure sensor connector—6.0L Diesel Engine

6.0L Diesel Engine

Under the air cleaner outlet pipe.

OPERATION

The center of the electronic engine control (EEC) system is a microprocessor called the PCM. The PCM receives input from sensors and other electronic components (switches, relays). Based on the information received and programmed into its memory, the PCM generates output signals to control various relays, solenoids and actuators.

REMOVAL & INSTALLATION

Gasoline Engines

1. Before servicing the vehicle, refer to the precautions in the beginning of this section.

2. Retrieve the module configuration. Carry out the module configuration retrieval steps of the Programmable Module Installation procedure.

3. Remove the air cleaner assembly and air cleaner outlet tube.

4. Disconnect the 3 powertrain control module (PCM) electrical connectors.

5. Remove the 2 retaining nuts and PCM.

6. To install, reverse the removal procedure.

Diesel Engine

✳✳ CAUTION

Make sure the ignition switch is in the OFF position prior to working on the electronic engine controls.

1. Before servicing the vehicle, refer to the precautions in the beginning of this section.

2. Turn the ignition switch to the OFF position.

3. Remove the retainers and the air deflector.

4. Remove the power steering reservoir bracket retainers.

5. Remove the power steering fluid indicator and retainers. Remove the power steering reservoir bracket.

6. Install the power steering indicator and position aside.

7. Disconnect the coolant hoses from the air cleaner outlet pipe.

8. Loosen the clamps and remove the air cleaner outlet pipe.

9. Unlatch and disconnect the powertrain control module (PCM) electrical connectors.

10. Remove the bolt and PCM.

11. To install, reverse the removal procedure.

PROGRAMMABLE MODULE INSTALLATION (PMI) USING THE INTEGRATED DIAGNOSTIC SYSTEM (IDS)

When The Original Module Is Available

➡**If PMI fails on the first attempt, exit the diagnostic tool PMI application and carry out the procedure again.**

1. Connect the IDS and ID the vehicle as normal.

2. From the Toolbox icon, select and highlight Module Programming and press the check mark.

3. Select and highlight Programmable Module Installation.

4. Follow the on-screen instructions, turn the ignition key to the OFF position, and press the check mark.

5. INSTALL the new module and press the check mark.

6. Turn the headlamp switch to the OFF position.

7. Turn the ignition key to the RUN position.

8. Open the driver's door.

9. Unlock the doors using the interior trim switch.

10. Follow the on-screen instructions, turn the ignition key to the ON position, and press the check mark.

11. The module configuration is complete.

12. Test the module for correct operation.

When The Original Module Is Not Available

➡**If PMI fails on the first attempt, exit the diagnostic tool PMI application and carry out the procedure again.**

1. Install the new module.

2. Connect the IDS and ID the vehicle as normal.

3. From the Toolbox icon, select and highlight Module Programming. Then highlight the module that was installed and press the check mark.

4. Select and highlight Programmable Module Installation. Then highlight the module that was installed and press the check mark.

5. Turn the headlamp switch to the OFF position.

6. Turn the ignition key to the RUN position.

7. Open the driver's door.

8. Unlock the doors using the interior trim switch.

9. Follow the on-screen instructions, turn the ignition key to the RUN position and press the check mark.

10. The IDS retrieves the module data, automatically downloads the data into the new module, and displays Module Configuration Complete.

11. If the data is not available in the module, the IDS displays a screen stating to contact the As-Built Data Center. Retrieve the data from WWW.FMCDEALER.COM at this time and press the check mark.

12. Enter the module data (the module address and line are displayed to the left of the 3 entry boxes) and press the check mark.

13. The IDS downloads the data into the new module and displays Operation Successful—Programming Complete.

14. Test the module for correct operation.

KEY PROGRAMMING USING TWO PROGRAMMED KEYS

➡ **This procedure works only if 2 or more programmed ignition keys are available.**

➡ **If the programming procedure is successful, the new key(s) will start the vehicle and the anti-theft indicator will prove-out for approximately 3 seconds. If the programming procedure is not successful and the new key(s) does not start the engine, leave the key in the ON position for at least 3 seconds, then turn the key off. Repeat the key programming procedure from Step 1.**

➡ **A minimum of 2 PATS keys must be programmed into the PCM before the vehicle will start.**

➡ **If the vehicle is in unlimited key mode, this spare key programming procedure still functions. Any 2 keys that can start the vehicle can be used to program an additional unlimited key.**

➡ **If additional keys are to be programmed, and the remaining keys are with the customer, or are not available, instruct the customer to refer to the Owner's Literature for instructions on programming the remaining keys.**

➡ **If the steps are not carried out as outlined, the programming procedure will end.**

➡ **Ignition keys must have a correct mechanical key cut for the vehicle and must be PATS encoded keys (contain a transponder).**

1. Insert the first programmed key into the ignition lock cylinder and turn the key from the OFF position to the ON position (maintain the key in the ON position for a minimum of 3 seconds and less than 10 seconds).

2. Turn the key to the OFF position and remove the first key from the ignition lock cylinder.

3. Within 5 seconds of turning the key to the OFF position, insert the second programmed key into the ignition lock cylinder and turn the key from the OFF position to the ON position (maintain the key in the ON position for a minimum of 3 seconds and less than 10 seconds).

4. Turn the key to the OFF position and remove the key from the ignition lock cylinder.

5. Within 10 seconds of turning the key to the OFF position, insert the unprogrammed key (the new key) into the ignition lock cylinder and turn the key from the OFF position to the ON position (maintain the key in the ON position for a minimum of 3 seconds and less than 10 seconds).

6. If it is desired to program additional key(s) (only up to 8 keys total can be programmed into the PCM), repeat Steps 1 - 5 for each additional key that needs to be programmed.

7. Start the vehicle with the new key(s).

THROTTLE POSITION SENSOR (TPS)

LOCATION

Mounted on the throttle body.

OPERATION

As resistance varies according to accelerator pedal angle, PCM applies voltage to sensor and measures voltage drop to calculate fuel delivery.

REMOVAL & INSTALLATION

5.4L Engine

See Figure 301.

1. Before servicing the vehicle, refer to the precautions in the beginning of this section.

2. Disconnect the throttle position (TP) sensor electrical connector.

> **※ CAUTION**
>
> **Failure to remove the TP sensor screws in the following manner will result in damage to the screws.**

3. First loosen the screws 1-2 full turns using a hand tool and then use a suitable high speed driver to complete the removal.

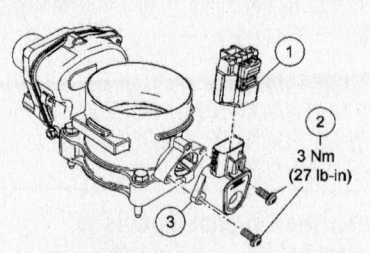

1. **Throttle position (TP) sensor electrical connector**
2. **TP sensor screws (2 required)**
3. **TP sensor**

22086_ETRK_G0066

Fig. 301 Throttle Position Sensor—5.4L Engine

4. Remove and discard the 2 screws and the TP sensor.

To install:

> **※ CAUTION**
>
> **Do not reuse the TP sensor and screws. A new TP sensor and screws must be installed.**

> **※ CAUTION**
>
> **Do not use a high speed driver to install the new screws or damage to the TP sensor can occur.**

➡ When installing the new TP sensor, make sure that the radial locator tab on the TP sensor is aligned with the radial locator hole on the throttle body (TB).

5. Position the new TP sensor and install the 2 new screws.

6. Tighten to 3 Nm (27 lb-in).

7. Connect the TP sensor electrical connector.

6.8L Engine

See Figure 302.

1. Before servicing the vehicle, refer to the precautions in the beginning of this section.

2. Disconnect the throttle position (TP) sensor electrical connector.

> **※ CAUTION**
>
> **Failure to remove the TP sensor screws in the following manner will result in damage to the screws.**

3. First loosen the screws 1-2 full turns using a hand tool and then use a suitable high speed driver to complete the removal.

4. Remove and discard the 2 screws and the TP sensor.

To install:

> **※ CAUTION**
>
> **Do not reuse the TP sensor and screws. A new TP sensor and screws must be installed.**

> **※ CAUTION**
>
> **Do not use a high speed driver to install the new screws or damage to the TP sensor can occur.**

➡ When installing the new TP sensor, make sure that the radial locator tab on the TP sensor is aligned with the radial locator hole on the throttle body (TB).

5. Position the new TP sensor and install the 2 new screws.

6. Tighten to 3 Nm (27 lb-in).

7. Connect the TP sensor electrical connector.

TESTING

See Figure 303.

1. Before servicing the vehicle, refer to the precautions in the beginning of this section.

> **※ WARNING**
>
> **Use only a high-impedance multimeter, otherwise damage to the PCM and/or sensors can result.**

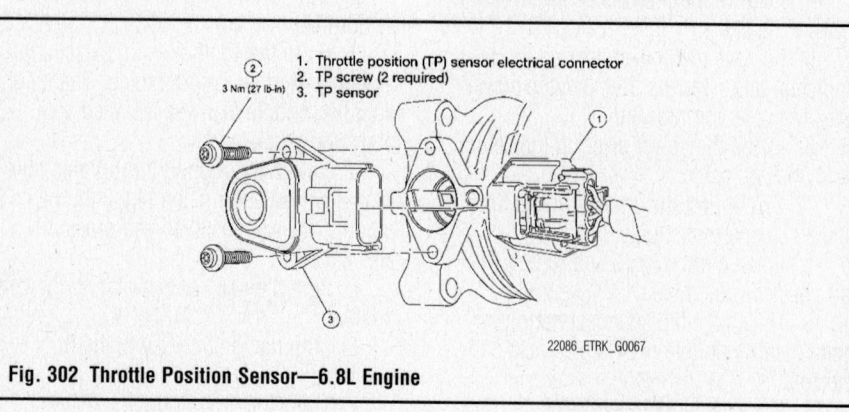

1. Throttle position (TP) sensor electrical connector
2. TP screw (2 required)
3. TP sensor

3 Nm (27 lb-in)

22086_ETRK_G0067

Fig. 302 Throttle Position Sensor—6.8L Engine

C1189 (BK)

**Throttle Position
Sensor (TPS)**

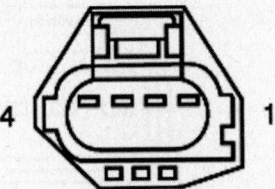

FEMALE

Pin	Circuit	Circuit function
1	357 (YE/WH)	Throttle Position Sensor (TPS) signal 2
2	1945 (VT/WH)	Throttle Position Sensor (TPS) Reference voltage
3	1946 (OG/LB)	Throttle Position Sensor (TPS) Signal return
4	355 (GY/WH)	Throttle Position Sensor (TPS) signal 1

22086_ETRK_G0068

Fig. 303 Throttle Position sensor connector—5.4L and 6.8L Engines

2. With the key **ON** and engine **OFF**, backprobe the TPS connector and check for the following values:
- Pin 2: 5 volt reference voltage
- Pins 1 and 4: Change with throttle position
- Pin 3: Signal return

VEHICLE SPEED SENSOR (VSS)

LOCATION

Rear of the transmission, near the output shaft.

OPERATION

Also called the Output Shaft Speed (OSS) Sensor.

The Output Shaft Speed (OSS) sensor is a Hall effect type sensor located on the extension housing. The OSS input to the PCM is used for shift scheduling, timing, and TCC operation. The OSS has bi-directional capability and has a digital output.

REMOVAL & INSTALLATION

See Figure 304.

1. Before servicing the vehicle, refer to the precautions in the beginning of this section.
2. With the vehicle in NEUTRAL, position it on a hoist.
3. Disconnect the output shaft speed (OSS) sensor electrical connector.

➡ **Prior to removing the speed sensor, make sure that the area around the sensor is free of foreign material to prevent contamination of the transmission.**

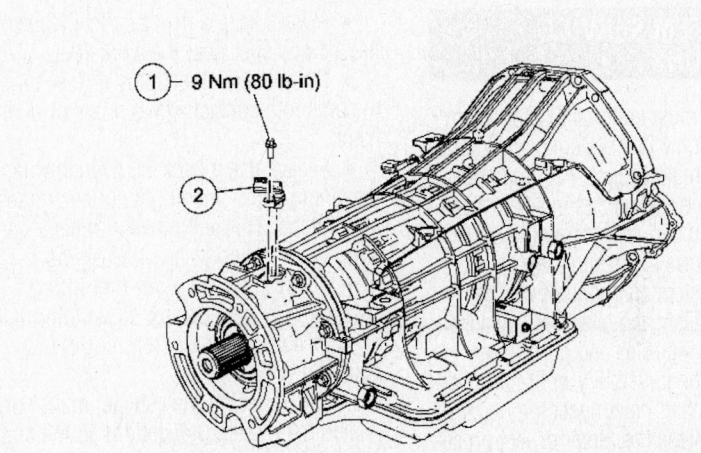

1. Output shaft speed (OSS) sensor retaining bolt
2. OSS sensor

22086_ETRK_G0069

Fig. 304 Output Shaft Speed sensor

4. Remove the OSS sensor.

To install:

5. Lubricate the O-ring with clean automatic transmission fluid and install the OSS sensor.
6. Install the bolt and tighten to 9 Nm (80 lb-in).
7. Connect the OSS sensor electrical connector.

TESTING

See Figure 305.

1. Before servicing the vehicle, refer to the precautions in the beginning of this section.
2. Disconnect the Output Shaft Speed (OSS) sensor harness connector.
3. Measure the resistance between sensor pins 2 and 1, 3 and ground. Specification is no continuity.
4. Measure the resistance between pins 2 and 3. Specification is 400–1250 ohms.
5. If any measurement is outside specifications, replace the OSS sensor.

C1107 (BK)

Output Shaft
Speed (OSS)
sensor

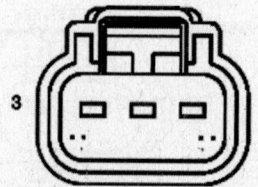

3   1

FEMALE

*Diesel

**Gas

Pin	Circuit	Circuit function
1	*371 (PK/WH)	Reference voltage
	**3087 (DG/VT)	Reference voltage
2	136 (DB/YE)	Output Shaft Speed (OSS) sensor (7H103), signal
3	*570 (BK/WH)	Signal return
	**1704 (VT/LG)	Signal return

22086_ETRK_G0070

Fig. 305 Output Shaft Speed sensor connector

FUEL

GASOLINE FUEL INJECTION SYSTEM

FUEL SYSTEM SERVICE PRECAUTIONS

Safety is the most important factor when performing not only fuel system maintenance but any type of maintenance. Failure to conduct maintenance and repairs in a safe manner may result in serious personal injury or death. Maintenance and testing of the vehicle's fuel system components can be accomplished safely and effectively by adhering to the following rules and guidelines.

• To avoid the possibility of fire and personal injury, always disconnect the negative battery cable unless the repair or test procedure requires that battery voltage be applied.

• Always relieve the fuel system pressure prior to disconnecting any fuel system component (injector, fuel rail, pressure regulator, etc.), fitting or fuel line connection. Exercise extreme caution whenever relieving fuel system pressure to avoid exposing skin, face and eyes to fuel spray. Please be advised that fuel under pressure may penetrate the skin or any part of the body that it contacts.

• Always place a shop towel or cloth around the fitting or connection prior to loosening to absorb any excess fuel due to spillage. Ensure that all fuel spillage (should it occur) is quickly removed from engine surfaces. Ensure that all fuel soaked cloths or towels are deposited into a suitable waste container.

• Always keep a dry chemical (Class B) fire extinguisher near the work area.

• Do not allow fuel spray or fuel vapors to come into contact with a spark or open flame.

• Always use a back-up wrench when loosening and tightening fuel line connection fittings. This will prevent unnecessary stress and torsion to fuel line piping.

• Always replace worn fuel fitting O-rings with new Do not substitute fuel hose or equivalent where fuel pipe is installed.

Before servicing the vehicle, make sure to also refer to the precautions in the beginning of this section as well.

RELIEVING FUEL SYSTEM PRESSURE

RELIEVING

1. Before servicing the vehicle, refer to the Precautions Section.
2. Remove the fuel pump fuse from the engine compartment fuse box.
3. Start the engine and allow it to idle until it stalls.
4. After the engine stalls, crank the engine for approximately 5 seconds to make sure the fuel injection supply manifold pressure has been relieved.
5. Turn the ignition switch to the OFF position.
6. When fuel system service is complete, install the fuel pump fuse.

➡It may take more than one key cycle to pressurize the fuel system. Cycle the ignition key and wait three seconds to pressurize the fuel system. Check for leaks before starting the engine.

7. Start the vehicle and check the fuel system for leaks.

FUEL FILTER

REMOVAL & INSTALLATION

1. Before servicing the vehicle, refer to the Precautions Section.
2. Relieve the fuel system pressure.
3. Disconnect the fuel lines from the fuel filter.
4. Remove the fuel filter.
5. Loosen the fuel filter clamp screw.

➡Make sure that an audible click is heard when installing the fuel lines. Pull back on the fuel lines to confirm engagement.

6. To install, reverse the removal procedure.

FUEL INJECTORS

REMOVAL & INSTALLATION

4.6L Engines
See Figure 306.

1. Before servicing the vehicle, refer to the Precautions Section.

2. Disconnect the battery ground cable.

3. Partially drain the engine cooling system.

4. Remove the air cleaner outlet pipe.

5. Disconnect the exhaust gas recirculation (EGR) valve vacuum hose and the evaporative emission canister purge valve hose and position them aside.

6. Disconnect the evaporative emission canister purge valve vacuum hose.

7. Disconnect the fuel pressure regulator valve vacuum hose.

8. Remove the crankcase ventilation tube.

9. Remove the power steering reservoir upper bracket.

✳✳ WARNING

After disconnecting, plug the fuel tubes to prevent leakage.

10. Disconnect the fuel hose spring lock couplings.

11. Disconnect the eight ignition coil electrical connectors.

12. Disconnect the eight fuel injector electrical connectors.

13. Disconnect the EGR vacuum regulator solenoid connections.

14. Disconnect the idle air control (IAC) valve and throttle position (TP) sensor electrical connectors.

15. Remove the nut and disconnect the brake booster vacuum tube and bracket.

16. Disconnect and remove the positive crankcase ventilation (PCV) hose.

➡**The throttle body adapter is shown slightly displaced for clarity.**

17. Disconnect the heated throttle body hose and position aside.

18. Disconnect the exhaust manifold to EGR valve tube upper fitting.

19. Disconnect the differential pressure feedback EGR system electrical connector.

20. Disconnect the exhaust manifold to EGR valve tube lower fitting.

21. Disconnect the heater hose and position aside.

22. Disconnect the climate control vacuum connector.

➡**Release any wiring harnesses or vacuum hoses which are attached to the fuel injection supply manifold, before removing the manifold.**

23. Remove the bolts and lift the fuel injection supply manifold and injectors upward, out of the intake manifold.

24. Remove the fuel injectors from the fuel injection supply manifold.

25. Inspect the two O-ring seals from

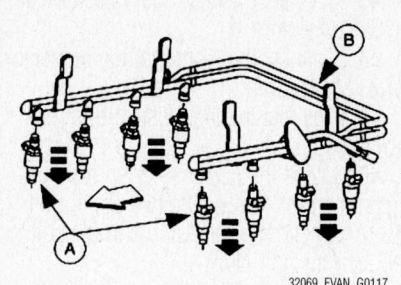

Fig. 306 Fuel rail and injectors—4.6L engine

32069_EVAN_G0117

each fuel injector. New O-ring seals will be installed as needed.

To install:

➡**Lubricate the new O-ring seals with clean engine oil to aid installation.**

26. Install new O-ring seals, as required.

27. Install the fuel injectors into the fuel injection supply manifold.

28. Position the fuel injection supply manifold and install the four bolts. Torque to 89 inch lbs. (10 Nm).

29. Connect the climate control vacuum connector.

30. Connect the heater hose.

31. Install the exhaust manifold to EGR valve tube. Torque the fittings to 26–33 ft. lbs. (35–45 Nm).

32. Connect the differential pressure feedback EGR system electrical connector.

➡**The throttle body adapter is shown slightly displaced for clarity.**

33. Connect the heated throttle body hose.

34. Install the PCV hose.

35. Connect the brake booster vacuum tube and bracket and install the nut. Torque to 89 inch lbs. (10 Nm).

36. Connect the TP sensor and IAC valve electrical connectors.

37. Connect the EGR vacuum regulator solenoid connections.

38. Connect the eight fuel injector electrical connectors.

39. Connect the eight ignition coil electrical connectors.

40. Connect the fuel hose spring lock couplings.

41. Install the power steering reservoir upper bracket. Torque the two upper bolts to 13 ft. lbs. (17 Nm); the single lower bolt to 96 inch lbs. (11 Nm).

42. Install the crankcase ventilation tube.

43. Connect the fuel pressure regulator valve vacuum hose.

44. Connect the evaporative emission canister purge valve vacuum hose.

45. Connect the evaporative emission canister purge valve hose and the EGR valve vacuum hose.

46. Install the air cleaner outlet pipe.

47. Connect the battery ground cable.

48. Fill and bleed the engine cooling system.

5.4L Engines

See Figure 307.

1. Before servicing the vehicle, refer to the Precautions Section.

2. Disconnect the battery ground cable.

3. Partially drain the engine cooling system.

4. Remove the air cleaner outlet pipe.

5. Disconnect the exhaust gas recirculation (EGR) valve vacuum hose and the evaporative emission canister purge valve hose and position them aside.

6. Disconnect the evaporative emission canister purge valve vacuum hose.

7. Disconnect the fuel pressure regulator valve vacuum hose.

8. Remove the crankcase ventilation tube.

9. Remove the power steering reservoir upper bracket.

✳✳ WARNING

After disconnecting, plug the fuel tubes to prevent leakage.

10. Disconnect the fuel hose spring lock couplings.

11. Disconnect the eight ignition coil electrical connectors.

12. Disconnect the eight fuel injector electrical connectors.

13. Remove the IAC valve fresh air tube.

14. Disconnect the IAC electrical connector.

15. Disconnect the differential pressure feedback EGR system electrical connector.

16. Remove the brake booster bracket and tube.

17. Disconnect the two differential pressure feedback EGR system hoses.

18. Disconnect the exhaust manifold to EGR valve tube upper fitting.

19. Disconnect the exhaust manifold to EGR valve tube lower fitting.

20. Disconnect the PCV hose from the throttle body adapter.

21. Disconnect the heated throttle body outlet hose from the throttle body adapter.

22. Disconnect the PCV hose from the intake manifold.

23. Remove the PCV valve and position the harness aside.

24. Disconnect the heater hose and position aside.

25. Disconnect the climate control vacuum connector.

➡ **Release any wiring harnesses or vacuum hoses which are attached to the fuel injection supply manifold, before removing the manifold.**

26. Remove the bolts and lift the fuel injection supply manifold and injectors upward, out of the intake manifold.

27. Remove the fuel injectors from the fuel injection supply manifold.

28. Inspect the two O-ring seals from each fuel injector. New O-ring seals will be installed as needed.

To install:

➡ **Lubricate the new O-ring seals with clean engine oil to aid installation.**

29. Install new O-ring seals, as required.

30. Install the fuel injectors into the fuel injection supply manifold.

31. Position the fuel injection supply manifold and install the four bolts. Torque to 89 inch lbs. (10 Nm).

32. Connect the climate control vacuum connector.

33. Connect the heater hose.

34. Install the PCV valve.

35. Connect the PCV hose to the intake manifold.

36. Connect the heated throttle body outlet hose.

37. Connect the PCV hose to the throttle body adapter.

38. Install the exhaust manifold to EGR valve tube and connect the differential pressure feedback EGR system hoses. Torque the fittings to 30–44 ft. lbs. (40–60 Nm).

39. Install the brake booster vacuum tube and bracket.

40. Connect the differential pressure feedback EGR system electrical connector.

41. Connect the IAC valve electrical connector.

42. Install the IAC valve fresh air tube.

43. Connect the eight fuel injector electrical connectors.

44. Connect the eight ignition coil electrical connectors.

45. Connect the fuel hose spring lock couplings.

46. Install the power steering reservoir upper bracket. Torque the two upper bolts to 13 ft. lbs. (17 Nm); the single lower bolt to 96 inch lbs. (11 Nm).

47. Install the crankcase ventilation tube.

48. Connect the fuel pressure regulator valve vacuum hose.

49. Connect the evaporative emission canister purge valve vacuum hose.

50. Connect the evaporative emission canister purge valve hose and the EGR valve vacuum hose.

51. Install the air cleaner outlet pipe.

52. Connect the battery ground cable.

53. Fill and bleed the engine cooling system.

6.8L Engine

See Figure 308.

1. Before servicing the vehicle, refer to the Precautions Section.

2. Release the fuel system pressure.

3. Disconnect the battery ground cable.

4. Remove the air cleaner outlet pipe.

5. Disconnect the fuel supply tube spring lock coupling.

6. Disconnect the 2 electrical connectors from the throttle body (TB).

7. Disconnect the positive crankcase ventilation (PCV) tube from the TB spacer.

8. Disconnect the 2 vacuum lines from the TB spacer.

9. Disconnect the fuel rail pressure and temperature sensor electrical and vacuum connectors.

10. Disconnect the 10 fuel injector electrical connectors.

11. Detach the main engine wiring harness retainer from the RH valve cover.

12. Detach the 2 main engine wiring harness retainers from the intake manifold and position the harness for access to remove the fuel rail.

➡ **When removing the fuel rail, leave the fuel injectors in the intake manifold. This will make removal of the fuel rail easier.**

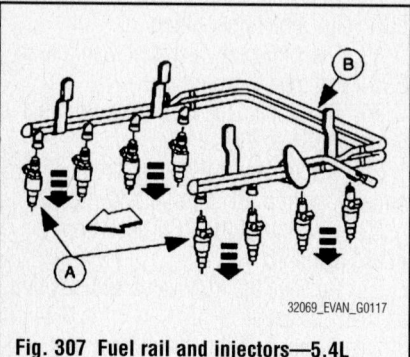

Fig. 307 Fuel rail and injectors—5.4L engine

32069_EVAN_G0117

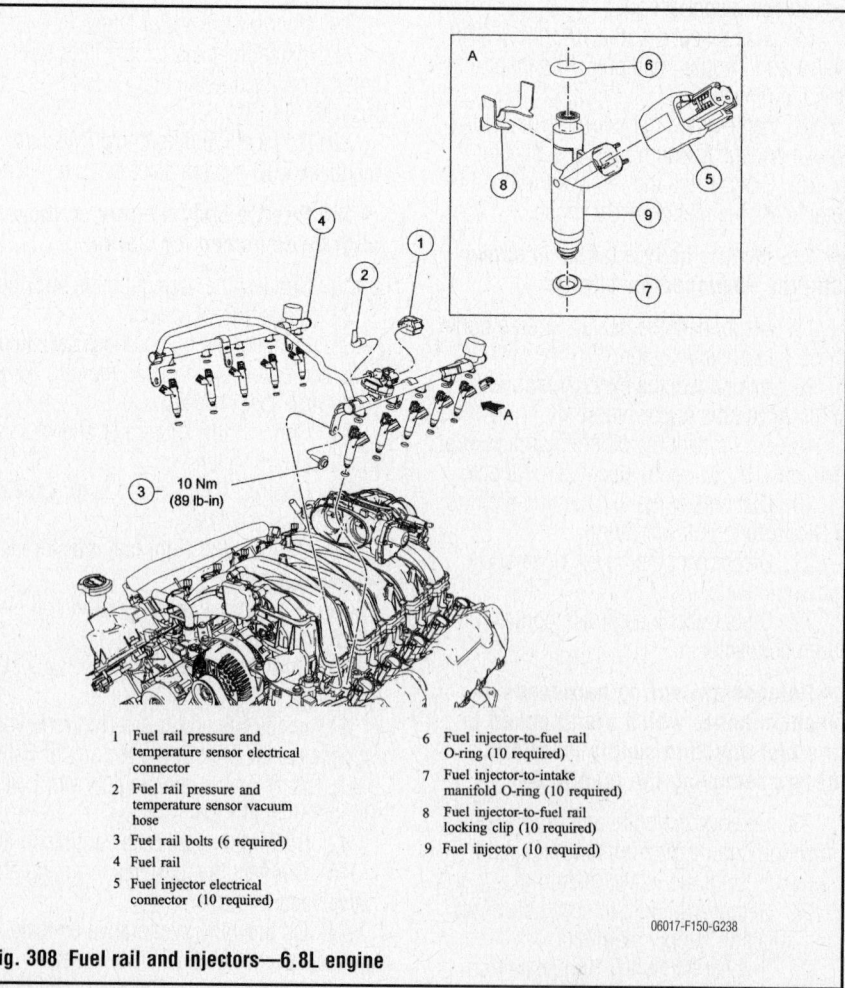

1 Fuel rail pressure and temperature sensor electrical connector
2 Fuel rail pressure and temperature sensor vacuum hose
3 Fuel rail bolts (6 required)
4 Fuel rail
5 Fuel injector electrical connector (10 required)
6 Fuel injector-to-fuel rail O-ring (10 required)
7 Fuel injector-to-intake manifold O-ring (10 required)
8 Fuel injector-to-fuel rail locking clip (10 required)
9 Fuel injector (10 required)

06017-F150-G238

Fig. 308 Fuel rail and injectors—6.8L engine

13. Remove the 6 fuel rail bolts and the fuel rail.

⁑ WARNING

Use O-ring seals that are made of special fuel-resistant material. Use of ordinary O-rings can cause the fuel system to leak. Do not reuse the O-ring seals. Lubricate the O-ring seals with clean engine oil prior to installation.

14. Remove the fuel injectors and the fuel injector O-ring seals. Discard the O-ring seals.

15. To install, reverse the removal procedure. Torque the 6 fuel rail bolts to 10 Nm (89 inch lbs.)

FUEL PUMP

REMOVAL & INSTALLATION

See Figure 309.

⁑ CAUTION

Fuel injection systems remain under pressure, even after the engine has been turned OFF. The fuel system pressure must be relieved before disconnecting any fuel lines. Failure to do so may result in fire and/or personal injury.

1. Before servicing the vehicle, refer to the Precautions Section.
2. Remove or disconnect the following:
   - Negative battery cable
   - Fuel system pressure
   - Fuel tank
   - Fuel tank filler pipe vent hose and fuel tank filler pipe from the tank
3. Support the fuel tank with a jack.
   - The 2 fuel tank support strap nuts
   - 2 fuel tank support straps
4. Lower the fuel tank to allow access to the electrical connections
   - Fuel tank connections
   - Fuel and electrical connections from the fuel pump
   - Fuel tank
   - Fuel tank screws/nuts, fuel pump and sender

To install:

5. Install or connect the following:
   - Fuel sender and fuel pump into the fuel tank. Tighten the screws/nuts to 89 inch lbs. (10 Nm).
6. Raise the fuel tank.
   - Fuel and electrical connections to the fuel pump
   - Fuel tank connections

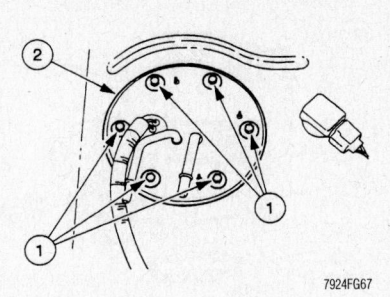

Fig. 309 Remove the mounting bolts (1), then lift the fuel pump assembly (2) out of the tank

- Fuel tank support straps and tighten the nuts to
- Mid-ships tank: 18 ft. lbs. (25 Nm)
- Aft-of-axle tank: bolts 76 ft. lbs. (103 Nm); nuts 66 ft. lbs. (90 Nm)
- Fuel tank filler pipe vent hose and the fuel tank filler pipe to the tank
- Negative battery cable

IDLE SPEED

ADJUSTMENT

Idle speed is maintained by the Powertrain Control Module (PCM). No adjustment is necessary or possible.

THROTTLE BODY

REMOVAL & INSTALLATION

4.6L Engine

See Figure 310.

1. Before servicing the vehicle, refer to the Precautions Section.

➡The throttle body bore and plate area have a special coating and cannot be cleaned.

2. Disconnect the battery ground.
3. Remove the air cleaner outlet pipe.
4. Disconnect the TP sensor electrical connector.
5. Disconnect the electronic throttle control electrical connector.
6. Remove the TB bolts and the TB and discard the gasket.
7. To install, reverse the removal procedure. Install a new TB gasket. To install, tighten t0 9 Nm (80 inch lbs.). Tighten an additional 90 degrees.

5.4L Engine

See Figure 311.

1. Before servicing the vehicle, refer to the Precautions Section.

➡The throttle body bore and plate area have a special coating and cannot be cleaned.

2. Disconnect the battery ground cable.
3. Remove the air cleaner and air cleaner intake pipe.
4. Disconnect the electronic throttle control electrical connector.
5. Disconnect the throttle position (TP) sensor electrical connector.
6. Remove the 4 throttle body (TB) bolts and the TB and discard the TB O-ring seal.
7. To install, reverse the removal procedure. Install a new TB gasket. To install,

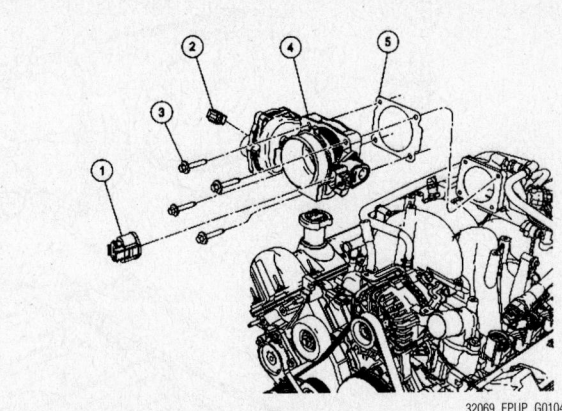

Fig. 310 1. Throttle position (TP) sensor electrical connector
2. Electronic throttle control electrical connector
3. Throttle body (TB) bolts
4. Throttle body
5. Throttle body gasket
Throttle body and related parts—4.6L engine

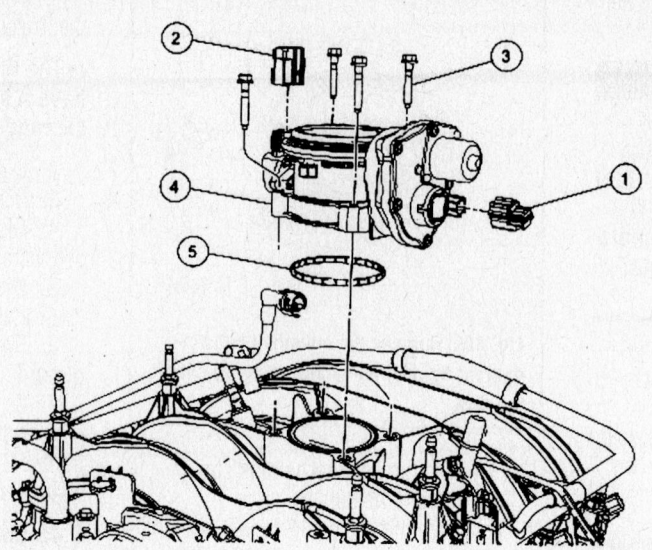

Fig. 311 1. Electronic throttle control electrical connector
2. Throttle position (TP) sensor electrical connector
3. Throttle body (TB) bolts
4. TB
5. TB O-ring seal
Throttle body and related parts—5.4L engine

tighten to 9 Nm (80 inch lbs.). Tighten an additional 90 degrees.

6.8L Engine

See Figure 312.

1. Before servicing the vehicle, refer to the Precautions Section.

2. Disconnect the battery ground cable.

3. Remove the air cleaner outlet tube.

4. Disconnect the electronic throttle control electrical connector.

5. Disconnect the TP sensor electrical connector.

6. Remove the 4 throttle body bolts and the throttle body and discard the throttle body gasket.

7. To install, reverse the removal procedure. To install, tighten to 9 Nm (80 inch lbs.). Tighten an additional 90 degrees.

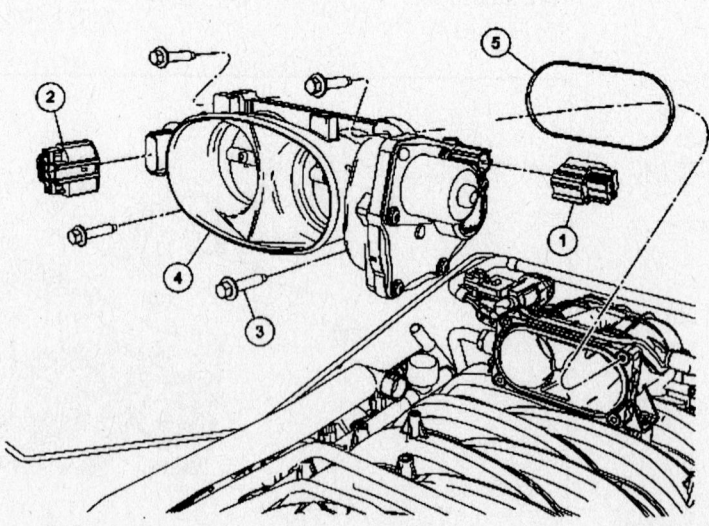

Fig. 312 1. Electronic throttle control electrical connector
2. Throttle position (TP) sensor electrical connector
3. Throttle body bolts
4. Throttle body
5. Throttle body gasket
Throttle body and related parts—6.8L engine

FUEL

FUEL SYSTEM SERVICE PRECAUTIONS

Safety is the most important factor when performing not only fuel system maintenance but any type of maintenance. Failure to conduct maintenance and repairs in a safe manner may result in serious personal injury or death. Maintenance and testing of the vehicle's fuel system components can be accomplished safely and effectively by adhering to the following rules and guidelines.

• To avoid the possibility of fire and personal injury, always disconnect the negative battery cable unless the repair or test procedure requires that battery voltage be applied.

• Always relieve the fuel system pressure prior to disconnecting any fuel system component (injector, fuel rail, pressure regulator, etc.), fitting or fuel line connection. Exercise extreme caution whenever relieving fuel system pressure to avoid exposing skin, face and eyes to fuel spray. Please be advised that fuel under pressure may penetrate the skin or any part of the body that it contacts.

• Always place a shop towel or cloth around the fitting or connection prior to loosening to absorb any excess fuel due to spillage. Ensure that all fuel spillage (should it occur) is quickly removed from engine surfaces. Ensure that all fuel soaked cloths or towels are deposited into a suitable waste container.

• Always keep a dry chemical (Class B) fire extinguisher near the work area.

• Do not allow fuel spray or fuel vapors to come into contact with a spark or open flame.

• Always use a back-up wrench when loosening and tightening fuel line connection fittings. This will prevent unnecessary stress and torsion to fuel line piping.

• Always replace worn fuel fitting O-rings with new. Do not substitute fuel hose or equivalent where fuel pipe is installed.

Before servicing the vehicle, make sure to also refer to the precautions in the beginning of this section as well.

RELIEVING FUEL SYSTEM PRESSURE

RELIEVING

6.0L Diesel Engine

1. Before servicing the vehicle, refer to the Precautions Section.

2. Raise and safely support the vehicle.
3. Disconnect both battery ground cables.
4. Open the fuel/water separator drain valve to release the fuel pressure.

ELECTRIC FUEL PUMP

REMOVAL & INSTALLATION

6.0L Diesel Engine

The fuel pump is located in the fuel conditioning module.

FUEL CONDITIONING MODULE

The Fuel Condition Module contains the fuel pump and water separator.

DRAINING

6.0L Diesel Engine
See Figure 313.

1. Before servicing the vehicle, refer to the Precautions Section.

✳✳ CAUTION

Smoking or open flame of any type must not be present when working near fuel or fuel vapor.

2. Disconnect both battery ground cables.
3. Raise and support the vehicle.
4. Open the fuel/water separator drain valve to release the fuel pressure.

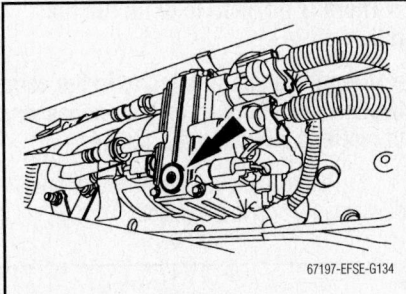

Fig. 313 Fuel/water separator drain valve—6.0L engine

67197-EFSE-G134

REMOVAL & INSTALLATION

6.0L Diesel Engine

1. Before servicing the vehicle, refer to the Precautions Section.

✳✳ CAUTION

Smoking or open flame of any type must not be present when working near fuel or fuel vapor.

2. Disconnect both battery ground cables.
3. Raise and support the vehicle.
4. Open the fuel/water separator drain valve to release the fuel pressure.
5. Disconnect the electrical connectors.
6. Disconnect the fuel pump electrical connector.
7. Disconnect the fuel warmer electrical connector.
8. Disconnect the water-in-fuel electrical connector.
9. Disconnect the fuel hoses.
10. Remove the fuel hose retaining clips and discard. Disconnect the fuel hoses from the fuel pump.
11. Press in the retaining clips and release the fuel hoses.
12. Remove the mounting nuts and the fuel conditioning module.
13. To install, reverse the removal procedure. Torque the nuts to 11 ft. lbs. (15 Nm).

FUEL FILTER

REMOVAL & INSTALLATION

6.0L Diesel Engine
See Figure 314.

1. Before servicing the vehicle, refer to the Precautions Section.

✳✳ CAUTION

Do not smoke or carry lighted tobacco or open flame of any type when working on or near any fuel related component. Highly flammable mixtures are always present and can be ignited, resulting in possible personal injury.

2. Relieve the fuel system pressure.
3. Disconnect the fuel lines from the fuel filter.
4. Remove the fuel filter.
5. Loosen the fuel filter clamp screw.

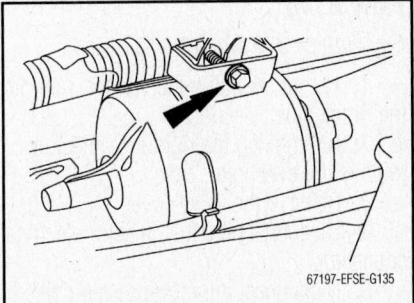

67197-EFSE-G135

Fig. 314 Fuel filter—6.0L engine

➡Make sure that an audible click is heard when installing the fuel lines. Pull back on the fuel lines to confirm engagement.

6. To install, reverse the removal procedure.

DRAINING WATER FROM THE SYSTEM

6.0L Diesel Engine

See Figure 315.

1. Before servicing the vehicle, refer to the Precautions Section.

❉❉ CAUTION

Smoking or open flame of any type must not be present when working near fuel or fuel vapor.

2. Disconnect both battery ground cables.
3. Raise and support the vehicle.
4. Open the fuel/water separator drain valve to release the fuel pressure.

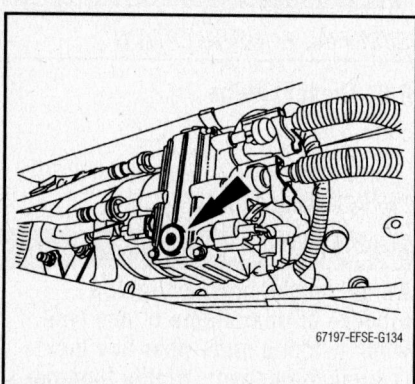

67197-EFSE-G134

Fig. 315 Fuel/water separator drain valve—6.0L engine

FUEL INJECTORS

REMOVAL & INSTALLATION

6.0L Diesel Engine

Early Build

See Figures 316 through 318.

1. Before servicing the vehicle, refer to the Precautions Section.
2. If removing the right fuel injectors, remove the evaporator case.
3. Remove the valve cover.
4. Disconnect the fuel injector electrical connector.
5. Disconnect the high-pressure oil rail supply line at the high-pressure oil rail.

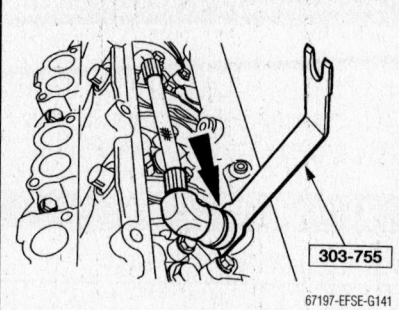

303-755

67197-EFSE-G141

Fig. 316 Disconnect the high-pressure oil rail supply line at the high-pressure oil rail—6.0L engine

6. Remove the bolts and the high-pressure oil rail.
7. Disconnect and remove the high-pressure oil supply line.

❉❉ WARNING

Do not attempt to apply battery voltage to the fuel injector or damage to the fuel injector will occur.

8. Using a 19 mm socket, push the fuel injector electrical connector out of the rocker arm carrier.

❉❉ WARNING

To prevent engine damage, do not use air tools to remove the fuel injectors. The clip that extracts the injector can dislodge and fall into the oil drain hole.

➡There is no need to drain the fuel rail.

➡If engine coolant is found in the combustion chambers, It may be necessary to install a new injector sleeve.

9. Remove the bolt, fuel injector hold-down clamp and fuel injector.

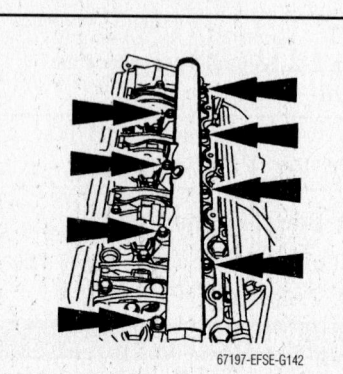

67197-EFSE-G142

Fig. 317 Remove the bolts and the high-pressure oil rail

To install:

❉❉ WARNING

If the fuel injector oil inlet D-shaped O-ring is damaged, a new fuel injector must be installed.

10. Install new O-ring seals and copper washer on the fuel injector. Lubricate the fuel injector and O-ring seals liberally with clean engine oil.

❉❉ WARNING

To prevent engine damage, do not use air tools to install the fuel injectors. The clip that extracts the injector can dislodge and fall into the oil drain hole.

11. Install the fuel injector, fuel injector hold-down clamp and bolt. Torque to 24 ft. lbs. (33 Nm).
12. Install the fuel injector electrical connector into the rocker carrier.
13. Apply engine oil to the top fuel injector O-ring seals.
14. Install the high-pressure oil rail and bolts.
15. Install the high-pressure oil rail.
16. Install the bolts finger tight.
17. Tighten the bolts in the sequence shown.
18. Install the high-pressure oil line.
19. Connect the fuel injector electrical connector.
20. Install the valve covers.
21. If removed, install the evaporator case.

Late Build

See Figures 319 through 321.

1. Before servicing the vehicle, refer to the Precautions Section.
2. Remove the valve cover.
3. Disconnect the fuel injector electrical connector.

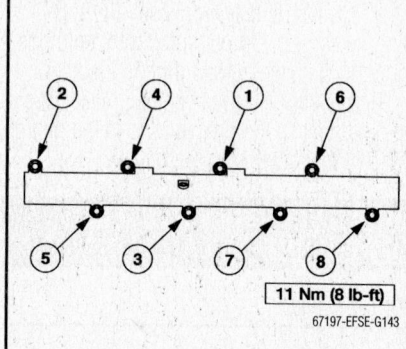

11 Nm (8 lb-ft)

67197-EFSE-G143

Fig. 318 High pressure oil rail torque sequence—early build 6.0L engine

⁂ **WARNING**

To prevent engine damage, it is recommended that a new crankcase-to-head tube to installed each time it is removed. The D-rings are not replaceable. If you reuse the crankcase-to-head tube, you assume the risk for leakage. You must inspect each D-ring carefully for evidence of cutting, abrasion or twisting and never reuse a tube exhibiting any of these conditions.

4. Remove the crankcase-to-head tube assembly.

➡Do not remove the oil rail end plugs or acoustic wave attenuator port fitting. Service parts are not available to support the components.

5. Remove the bolts and the high-pressure oil rail.

➡Use a shop towel and brake parts cleaner to remove the oil residue prior to removal.

6. If the crankcase-to-head tube separated, use the special tool to remove the lower crankcase-to-head tube.

⁂ **WARNING**

Do not attempt to apply battery voltage to the fuel injector or damage to the fuel injector will occur.

7. Using the special tool, push the fuel injector electrical connector out of the rocker arm carrier.

8. Prior to removing the injector assembly, insert clean shop towels in the oil drain holes adjacent to each glow plug.

⁂ **WARNING**

Failure to account for all snaprings or pieces prior to placing the vehicle back in service can cause engine damage. A missing snapring can be ingested into the lube oil system, causing severe engine damage.

⁂ **WARNING**

To prevent engine damage, do not use air tools to remove the fuel injectors. The snapring that extracts the injector can dislodge and fall into the oil drain hole.

➡There is no need to drain the fuel rail.

➡If engine coolant is found in the combustion chambers, it may be necessary to install a new injector sleeve.

➡Use a tool like Snap-On® SDMT440 Torx®to avoid damaging the fuel injector plastic and to avoid interference with the evaporator case.

9. Remove the bolt, fuel injector hold-down clamp and fuel injector.

➡If a snapring or piece of a snapring is missing from the injector hold-down assembly, it must be located prior to removing the shop towels.

10. Remove the shop towels.

To install:

⁂ **WARNING**

If the fuel injector oil inlet D-shaped O-ring is damaged, a new fuel injector must be installed.

11. Install new O-ring seals and copper washer on the fuel injector. Lubricate the fuel injector and O-ring seals liberally with clean engine oil.

⁂ **WARNING**

Failure to tighten the injector correctly can lead to engine failure.

⁂ **WARNING**

To prevent engine damage, do not use air tools to install the fuel injectors. The snapring that extracts the injector can dislodge and fall into the oil drain hole.

12. Install the fuel injector, fuel injector hold-down clamp and bolt. Torque to 24 ft. lbs. (33 Nm).

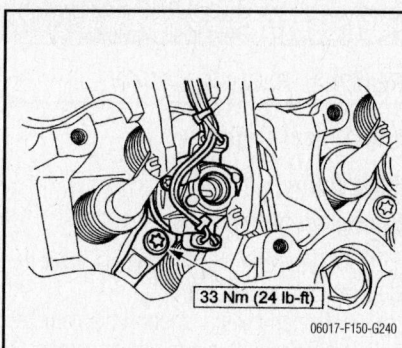

33 Nm (24 lb-ft)

06017-F150-G240

Fig. 319 Injector installation—6.0L engine

⁂ **WARNING**

Make sure the injector wiring is clear of all moving parts or engine damage can occur.

13. Install the fuel injector electrical connector into the rocker carrier.

14. Apply engine oil to the top fuel injector O-ring seals.

➡Apply clean engine oil on the tubes prior to installing the oil manifold.

15. Position the oil rail on the fuel injectors.

a. Place the oil rail on top of the carrier so that the four single ball tubes are engaging the injector lead angle.

b. Insert three bolts, two on the ends of the straight side of the oil rail and one in the middle of the wavy side of the rail. Install the guide studs six to seven turns.

c. Press the oil rail into the fuel injectors.

d. Make sure that the oil rail mounting feet are flat against the mounting surface.

e. Loosely install the six bolts.

16. Install the oil rail retaining bolts.

a. Remove the three guide bolts.

b. Loosely install three remaining bolts.

c. Tighten the nine bolts in the sequence shown to 10 ft. lbs. (13 Nm).

⁂ **WARNING**

To prevent engine damage, it is recommended that a new crankcase-to-head tube to installed each time it is removed. The D-rings are not replaceable. If you reuse the crankcase-to-head tube, you assume the risk for leakage. You must inspect each D-ring carefully for evidence of cutting, abrasion or twisting and never reuse a tube exhibiting any of these conditions.

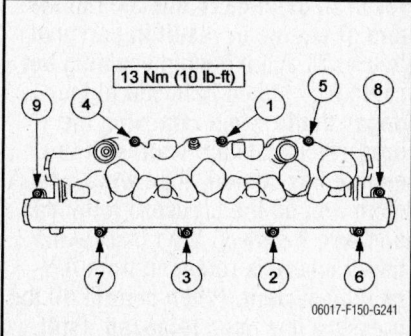

13 Nm (10 lb-ft)

06017-F150-G241

Fig. 320 Oil rail bolt torque sequence—late build 6.0L engine

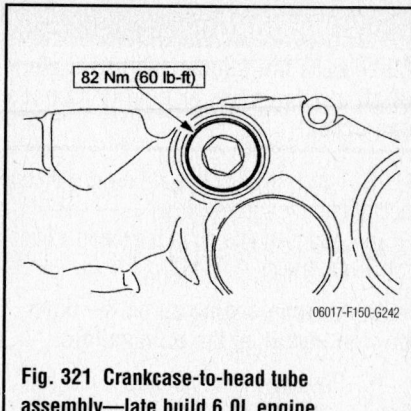

Fig. 321 Crankcase-to-head tube assembly—late build 6.0L engine

➡ **Apply clean engine oil to the crankcase-to-head tube prior to installation.**

17. Install the crankcase-to-head tube assembly. Torque to 60 ft. lbs. (82 Nm).

18. Connect the fuel injector electrical connector.

19. Install the valve covers.

FUEL INJECTOR CONTROL MODULE

REMOVAL & INSTALLATION

6.0L Diesel Engine

See Figure 322.

> ❄ **WARNING**
>
> **Make sure the ignition switch is in the OFF position prior to working on the electronic engine controls.**

1. Turn the ignition switch to the OFF position.

> ❄ **CAUTION**
>
> **Never remove the pressure relief cap while the engine is operating or when the cooling system is hot. Failure to follow these instructions can result in damage to the cooling system or engine or result in personal injury. To avoid having scalding hot coolant or steam blow out of the degas bottle when removing the pressure relief cap, wait until the engine has cooled, then wrap a thick cloth around the pressure relief cap and turn it slowly. Step back while the pressure is released from the cooling system. When certain all the pressure has been released, (still with a cloth) turn and remove the pressure relief cap. Failure to follow**

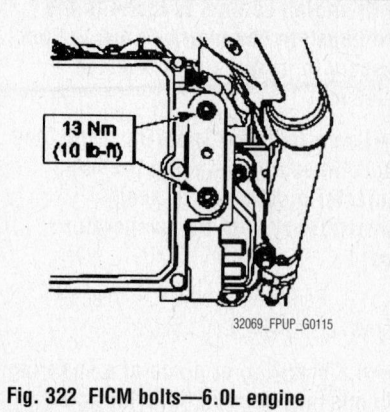

Fig. 322 FICM bolts—6.0L engine

these instructions can result in personal injury.

2. Before servicing the vehicle, refer to the Precautions Section.

3. Relieve the cooling system pressure. Disconnect and plug or cap the engine vent hose and radiator vent hose.

4. Remove the bolts and position the degas (coolant reservoir) bottle aside.

5. On late build vehicles: Disconnect the two exhaust pressure (EP) sensor harness pin-type retainers. Disconnect the EP sensor electrical connector and position the harness aside.

6. Remove the two bolts, two nuts and turbocharger intake tube bracket.

7. Remove the fuel injector control module (FICM) bolts.

> ❄ **WARNING**
>
> **Make sure both latches are released before removing the electrical connectors or connector damage can occur.**

8. Position out the FICM and disconnect the electrical connectors. Remove the FICM. To install, reverse the removal procedure.

FUEL INJECTION PRESSURE REGULATOR

REMOVAL & INSTALLATION

6.0L Diesel Engine

Early Build

See Figures 323 and 324.

1. Before servicing the vehicle, refer to the Precautions Section.

2. Raise and safely support the vehicle.

3. Vehicles with automatic transmission: Remove the fluid level indicator. Remove the transmission fluid fill tube nut.

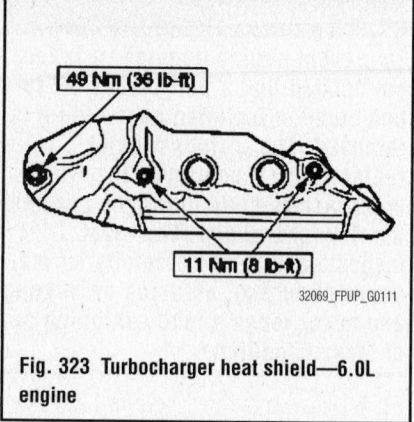

Fig. 323 Turbocharger heat shield—6.0L engine

Position aside the transmission fluid filler tube.

4. Remove the turbocharger heat shield.

➡ **It will be necessary to position aside or remove the heat insulating wrap.**

5. Disconnect the injector pressure regulator (IPR) valve electrical connector.

➡ **Use a 1⅜ inch 12-point deep flare nut crowfoot wrench to remove the valve.**

6. Remove the IPR valve.

7. To install, reverse the removal procedure. Apply clean engine oil to the IPR valve prior to installing it. Torque the IPR to 50 Nm (37 ft. lbs.).

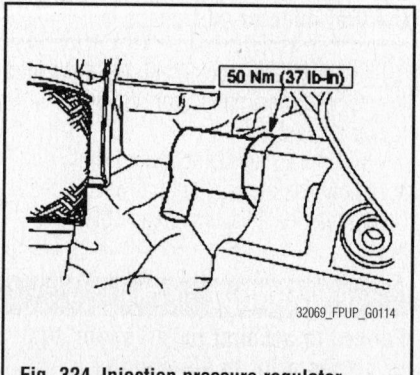

Fig. 324 Injection pressure regulator valve—early build 6.0L engines

Late Build

See Figures 325 and 326.

1. Before servicing the vehicle, refer to the Precautions Section.

2. Remove the turbocharger intake tube.

3. Remove the fuel injector control module (FICM). For additional information, refer to the procedure in this section.

4. Remove the retaining nuts and the rear FICM bracket.

5. Remove the retaining nuts from the heat shield bracket. Position the ground wire aside.

6. Disconnect the wiring retainer from the back of the heat shield bracket.

7. Remove the bolts and the heat shield bracket.

8. Remove the intake manifold stud.

9. Position back the injection pressure regulator (IPR) valve electrical connector heat insulating wrap.

10. Disconnect the IPR valve electrical connector.

11. Disconnect the snap and remove the heat insulating wrap.

12. Remove the IPR valve.

➡ **It is necessary to re-install the heat insulating wrap on the IPR valve.**

13. To install, reverse the removal procedure. Apply clean engine oil to the IPR valve prior to installing. Observe the following torques:

- IPR: 50 Nm (37 ft. lbs.)
- Intake manifold stud: 11 Nm (8 ft. lbs.)
- FICM bracket: 8 Nm (71 inch lbs.)

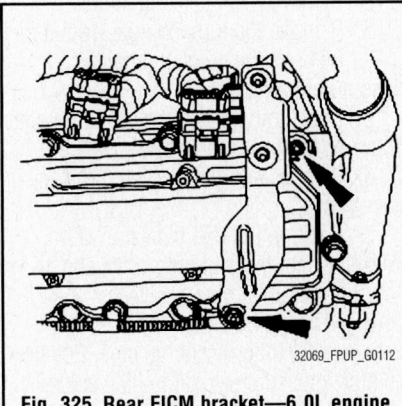

Fig. 325 Rear FICM bracket—6.0L engine

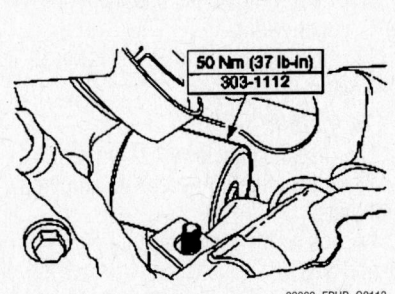

Fig. 326 Injection pressure regulator valve—late build 6.0L engines

FUEL PRESSURE REGULATOR

REMOVAL & INSTALLATION

6.0L Diesel Engine

See Figure 327.

1. Before servicing the vehicle, refer to the Precautions Section.

2. Remove the secondary fuel filter and remove all fuel from the fuel filter housing.

3. Disconnect the fuel return tube from the regulator cover.

> ※ **CAUTION**
>
> **Clean all fuel residue from the engine compartment. Failure to follow these instructions may result in personal injury.**

4. Remove the screws and the fuel pressure regulator cover.

5. Remove and discard the fuel pressure regulator cover O-ring seal.

6. Remove the restrictor, spring and poppet valve.

7. Clean the fuel pressure regulator bore in the fuel filter housing.

8. To install, reverse the removal procedure. Tighten the fuel line fitting to 43 Nm (32 ft. lbs.).

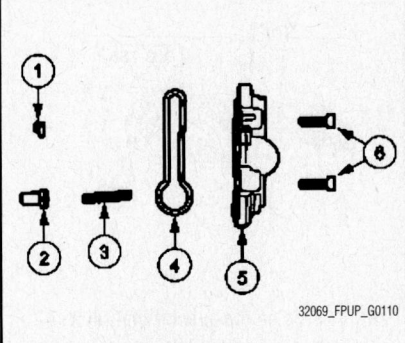

Fig. 327 1. Fixed orifice
2. Poppet valve and O-ring seal
3. Spring
4. O-ring seal
5. Cover
6. Screw, Torx®M5
Fuel pressure regulator—6.0L engine

GLOW PLUGS

REMOVAL & INSTALLATION

6.0L Diesel Engine

See Figure 328.

1. Before servicing the vehicle, refer to the Precautions Section.

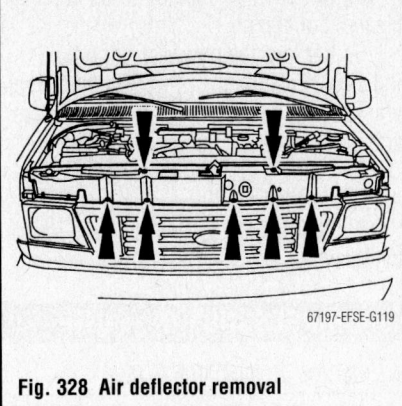

Fig. 328 Air deflector removal

Number 2 glow plug

2. Remove the retainers and the air deflector.

3. Remove the power steering reservoir bracket retainers.

4. Remove the power steering fluid indicator and retainers. Remove the power steering reservoir mounting bracket. Install the power steering fluid indicator and position the power steering reservoir aside.

5. Disconnect the coolant hoses from the air cleaner outlet pipe.

6. Loosen the clamps and remove the air cleaner outlet pipe.

Number 1, 3-8 glow plugs

7. Remove the engine cover.

All glow plugs

> ※ **WARNING**
>
> **Do not pull on the wiring to remove the glow plug connector or damage may occur.**

➡ **Only the number 2 glow plug is accessed from under the hood, all others are accessed from inside the cab.**

8. Remove the glow plug harness as needed.

➡ **If coolant residue is found on the glow plug, a new glow plug sleeve may have to be installed.**

9. Remove the glow plug.

To install:

All glow plugs

10. Install the glow plug.

11. Clean and inspect the O-ring seals and install new if necessary. Apply clean engine oil to the O-ring seals.

12. Install the glow plug harness.

Number 1, 3-8 glow plug

13. Install the engine cover.

Number 2 glow plug

14. Install the air cleaner outlet pipe and tighten the clamps.

15. Connect the coolant hoses to the air cleaner outlet pipe.

16. Remove the power steering fluid indicator. Position the power steering reservoir mounting bracket. Install the retainers and power steering fluid indicator.

17. Install the power steering reservoir bracket retainers.

18. Position the air deflector and install the retainers.

HIGH PRESSURE OIL PUMP

REMOVAL & INSTALLATION

6.0L Diesel Engine

Early Build

See Figures 329 through 333.

1. Before servicing the vehicle, refer to the Precautions Section.

2. Remove the intake manifold.

3. Remove the turbocharger heat shield.

4. Remove the bolts and the high-pressure oil pump cover. Use a thin gasket scraper to separate the cover from the crankcase.

5. Remove and discard the press-in-place gasket.

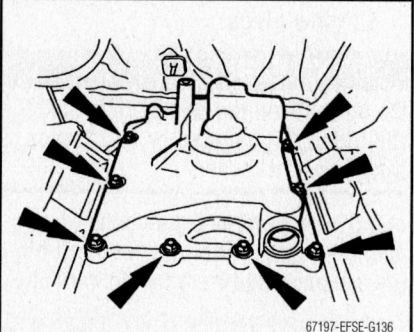

Fig. 329 Remove the high-pressure oil pump cover

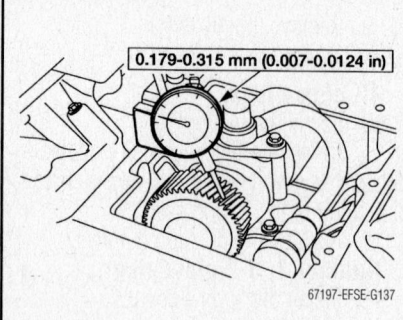

Fig. 330 Check the oil pump drive gear backlash

6. Position the dial indicator with bracketry onto the oil pump drive and check the oil pump drive gear backlash.

7. Remove the bolts from the high-pressure oil pump discharge pipe.

8. Using the special tool, disconnect and remove the high-pressure oil pump discharge pipe.

9. Remove and discard the D-shaped O-ring seal.

10. Remove and discard the high-pressure pump O-ring seal.

11. Remove the bolts and the high-pressure oil pump.

12. Remove and discard the lower O-ring seal.

To install:

13. Install a new lower O-ring seal.

14. Install the high-pressure oil pump and bolts. Torque to 18 ft. lbs. (24 Nm).

15. Install the high-pressure pump O-ring seal.

16. Install the oil pump discharge pipe.

17. Install the bolts for the oil discharge pipe.

18. Position the dial indicator with bracketry onto the oil pump drive and check the oil pump drive gear backlash.

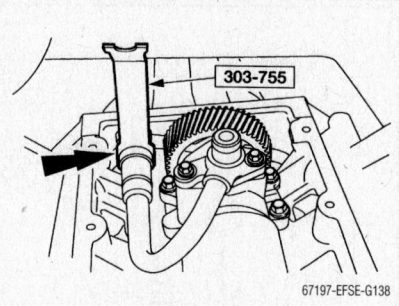

Fig. 331 Using the special tool, disconnect and remove the high-pressure oil pump discharge pipe

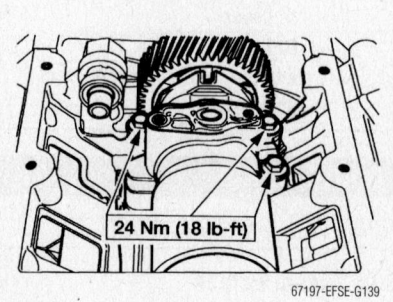

Fig. 332 Install the high pressure oil pump

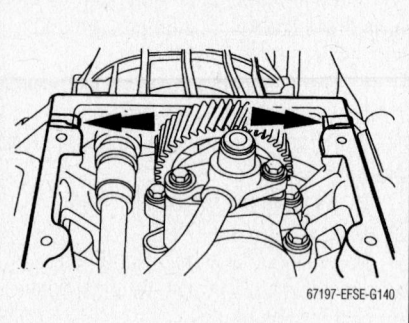

Fig. 333 Clean the cover mounting surface and apply sealer at the seams

19. Install a new D-ring seal on the high-pressure discharge pipe. Torque to 71 inch lbs. (8 Nm).

20. Install a new press-in-place gasket in the high-pressure pump cover.

21. Clean the cover mounting surface and apply sealer at the seams.

22. Install the high-pressure pump cover and bolts. Torque to 8 ft. lbs. (11 Nm).

23. Install the turbocharger heat shield.

24. Install the intake manifold.

Late Build

1. Before servicing the vehicle, refer to the Precautions Section.

2. Remove the intake manifold.

3. Remove the turbocharger heat shield.

4. Remove the bolts and the high-pressure oil pump cover.

5. Use a thin gasket scraper to separate the cover from the crankcase.

6. Remove and discard the press-in-place gasket.

7. Position the dial indicator with bracketry onto the oil pump drive and check the oil pump drive gear backlash.

8. Remove the bolts from the high-pressure oil pump discharge pipe. Position the high-pressure discharge pipe aside.

9. Remove and discard the high-pressure pump O-ring seal.

10. Remove the bolts and the high-pressure oil pump.

11. Remove and discard the lower O-ring seal.

To install:

12. Install a new lower O-ring seal.

13. Install the high-pressure oil pump and bolts.

14. Install the high-pressure pump O-ring seal.

15. Position back the high-pressure discharge tube and install the bolts.

16. Position the dial indicator with bracketry onto the oil pump drive and check the oil pump drive gear backlash.

17. Install a new D-ring seal on the high-pressure discharge pipe.

18. Install a new press-in-place gasket in the high-pressure pump cover. Clean the cover mounting surface and apply sealer at the seams.

19. Install the high-pressure pump cover and bolts.

20. Install the turbocharger heat shield.

21. Install the intake manifold.

IDLE SPEED

ADJUSTMENT

The fuel system is controlled by the PCM. No adjustments are necessary or possible.

INJECTION TIMING

ADJUSTMENT

The injection timing is controlled by the Powertrain Control Module (PCM). No adjustment is necessary or possible.

HEATING & AIR CONDITIONING SYSTEM

BLOWER MOTOR

REMOVAL & INSTALLATION

See Figure 334 and 335.

WARNING

To avoid accidental deployment and possible injury, the air bag system backup power supply must be depleted before repairing any climate control components. To deplete the backup power supply, disconnect the battery-to-starter cable and wait one minute.

1. Remove the battery.
2. Remove the battery tray.
3. If equipped with air conditioning, loosen and move the suction accumulator/drier to access the blower motor. It is not necessary to discharge the refrigerant system.
4. Disconnect the electrical hardshell connector.
5. Remove the blower motor housing tube.
6. Remove four screws.
7. Remove the retaining clip.
8. To ease removal, align the flat spot on the blower motor mounting plate with the accumulator.
9. Remove the blower motor.
10. Remove the retaining clip.
11. Remove the blower motor wheel.

To install:

12. Follow the disassembly procedure in reverse order.

➡When the battery has been disconnected and reconnected, some abnormal drive symptoms may occur while the powertrain control module relearns its adaptive strategy. The vehicle may need to be driven 16 km (10 miles) or more to relearn the strategy.

13. Follow the removal procedure in reverse order.

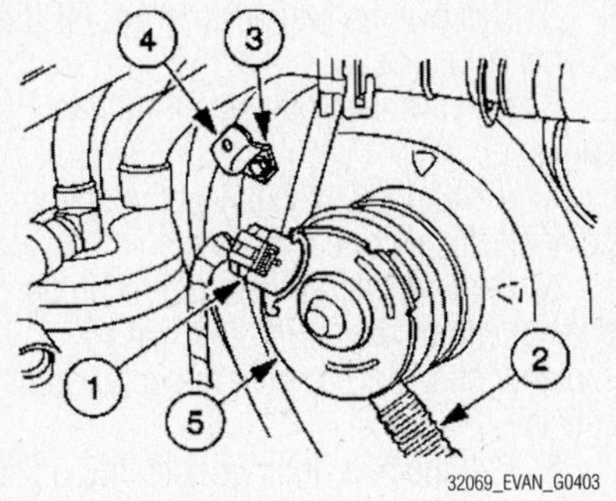
4
3
1
5
2
32069_EVAN_G0403

Fig. 334 Blower Motor

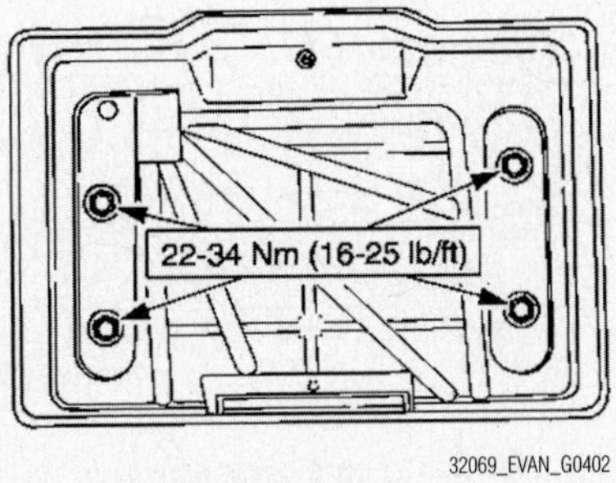
22-34 Nm (16-25 lb/ft)
32069_EVAN_G0402

Fig. 335 Battery tray fastener torque

HEATER CORE

REMOVAL & INSTALLATION

See Figure 336.

1. Before servicing the vehicle, refer to the Precautions Section.
2. Clamp off and disconnect the heater hoses at the heater core.
3. Remove the instrument panel finish panel.
4. Remove the bolts and the instrument panel reinforcement.
5. Remove the bolts and the instrument panel reinforcement bracket.
6. Remove the screws and position the wire harness aside.
7. Remove the screws and the heater core cover.

➡Use care not to spill the coolant remaining in the heater core during removal.

8. Remove the heater core.
9. To install, reverse the removal procedure. Clean and lubricate the coolant hoses with plain water only, if needed.
10. Fill the engine cooling system.

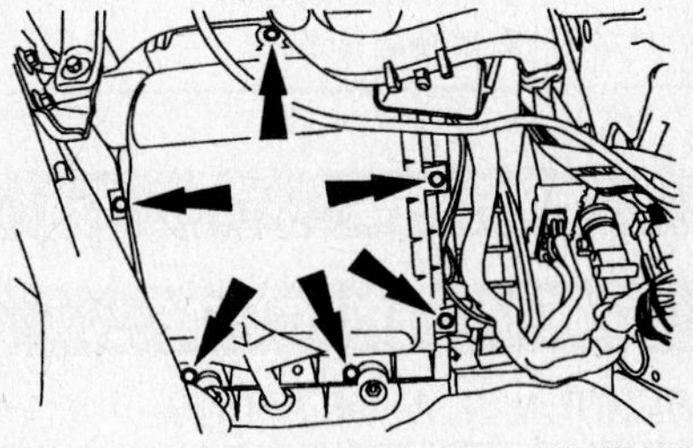
67197-EFSE-G031

Fig. 336 Heater core cover screw locations—E-Series primary system

AUXILIARY HEATING & AIR CONDITIONING SYSTEM

BLOWER MOTOR

REMOVAL & INSTALLATION

See Figure 337.

1. If equipped, remove the third, fourth, and fifth bench seats as necessary.
2. Remove the left center bolster trim panel.
3. Remove the quarter trim rear upper panel.
4. Remove the lower rear body side trim panel.
5. Disconnect the electrical connector.
6. Remove the blower motor housing tube.
7. Remove the screws.
8. Remove the blower motor.
9. Note the location of the blower motor wheel on the blower motor.
10. Remove the retaining clip.

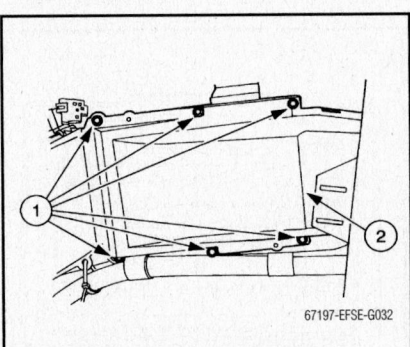

32069_EVAN_G0409

Fig. 337 1: Electrical Connector
2: Housing Tube
3: Mounting Screws
4: Blower Motor

11. Remove the blower motor wheel.
12. To install, reverse the removal procedure.

HEATER CORE

REMOVAL & INSTALLATION

See Figure 338.

1. Before servicing the vehicle, refer to the Precautions Section.
2. Remove the rear seats to access the quarter trim panels.
3. Remove the body side trim finish panel.
4. If equipped, disconnect the power-point electrical connector.
5. Remove the rear seat belt shoulder strap opening covers. Pry the seat belt shoulder strap covers from the upper trim panels.
6. Pull the rear door weatherstrip off at the rear door opening to access the trim panel pin-type retainers.

67197-EFSE-G032

Fig. 338 Heater core cover screw locations—E-Series auxiliary system

7. Remove the rear upper body side trim panel.
8. Remove the rear lower body side trim panel.
9. Remove the window latches, if so equipped.
10. Position the driver seat to the full forward position.
11. Remove the front seat belt guide cover.
12. Remove the nut and front safety belt guide.
13. Remove the front upper body side trim panel.
14. Remove the front lower body side trim panel.
15. To install, reverse the removal procedure.
    a. To install the front upper body side trim panel, start at the lower pillar, then work to the second lower pillar.
    b. To install the rear lower body side trim panel, start with the clip to the heater housing, then snap the trim panel into the panel clips.
    c. To install the rear upper body side trim panel, start with the rear lower portion of the panel at the pillar.
16. Remove the heater core cover.
17. Clamp off and disconnect the heater hoses.
18. Remove the heater core case seal.
19. Remove the heater core.
20. To install, reverse the removal procedure. Lubricate the coolant hoses with plain water, if needed.
21. Fill the engine cooling system.

STEERING

POWER STEERING GEAR

REMOVAL & INSTALLATION

1. Before servicing the vehicle, refer to the Precautions Section.

➡**New O-ring seals must be installed any time the lines are disconnected from the steering gear.**

2. Place the front wheels in the straight-ahead position and the ignition switch in the OFF position.

✳✳ WARNING

Do not allow the steering column shaft to rotate while the intermediate shaft is disconnected or damage to the clockspring can result. If there is evidence that the shaft has rotated, the clockspring must be removed and recentered.

3. Remove the bolt and detach the intermediate shaft from the gear.
4. Disconnect the lines. Discard the O-ring seals.
5. With vehicle in **Neutral**, place on a hoist.
6. Remove and discard the cotter pin and nut.
7. Using a puller, separate the drag link.
8. Remove the bolts and the steering gear.
9. Secure the steering gear in a vise and remove the nut and lockwasher.
10. Using the special tool, remove the steering gear sector shaft arm.
11. To install, reverse the removal procedure.
12. Note the following torques:
    - Pinch bolt: 18 ft. lbs. (25 Nm)
    - Steering gear mounting bolts: 60 ft. lbs. (81 Nm)
    - Power steering lines: 15 ft. lbs. (20 Nm)
    - Drag link-to-Pitman arm: 68 ft. lbs. (92 Nm)
    - Pitman arm-to-gear: 199 ft. lbs. (270 Nm)
13. Install a new high pressure hose

O-ring seal and a new return hose O-ring seal.

14. Fill and leak check the system.

POWER STEERING PUMP

REMOVAL & INSTALLATION

1. On 6.0L engines, remove the engine cooling fan.

2. On all models, rotate the tensioner clockwise and remove the belt from the power steering pump pulley.

3. With the vehicle in NEUTRAL, position it on a hoist.

4. If equipped, remove the deflector shield.

5. Using pulley remover tool, remove the pump pulley.

6. Disconnect the power steering reservoir pump hose and pressure line from the power steering pump.

7. Drain the power steering oil reservoir.

8. Remove the bolts and the pump.

9. To install, reverse the removal procedure.

10. Install a new power steering seal on the power steering pressure fitting by stretching the seal over the seal replacer until it is large enough to slip over the threads of the fitting.

11. Tighten the pump mounting bolts to 19 ft. lbs. (26 Nm).

BLEEDING

1. Remove the powertrain control module (PCM) relay to disable the vehicle.

2. Fill the power steering pump reservoir.

3. Crank the engine with the starter motor no more than 15 seconds and add fluid until the level remains constant.

➡ **Front wheels must be off the floor during lock-to-lock rotation of the steering wheel.**

4. Raise and support the vehicle

✳✳ CAUTION

Do not hold the steering wheel against the stops for an extended period of time. Damage to the pump can occur.

5. While cranking the engine, rotate the steering wheel from lock to lock.

6. Check the fluid level and add fluid if necessary.

7. Install the powertrain control module (PCM) relay.

8. Start the engine and allow it to run for several minutes.

9. Rotate the steering wheel from lock to lock.

10. Turn off the engine and check the fluid level. Add fluid if necessary.

11. Lower the vehicle.

AIR PURGING

1. Remove the power steering pump reservoir cap. Check the fluid.

2. Raise the front wheels off the floor.

3. Tightly insert the stopper of the vacuum pump into the reservoir.

4. Start the engine.

5. Install the vacuum pump, apply vacuum, and maintain the maximum vacuum of 68-85 kPa (20-25 in-Hg).

6. If equipped with Hydro-Boost®, apply the brake pedal twice.

✳✳ CAUTION

Do not hold the steering wheel against the stops for more than 3 to 5 seconds at a time. Damage to the power steering pump can occur.

7. Cycle the steering wheel fully from stop-to-stop 10 times.

8. Stop the engine.

9. Release the vacuum and remove the vacuum pump.

10. Fill the reservoir.

11. Start the engine.

12. Install the vacuum pump. Apply and maintain the maximum vacuum of 68-85 kPa (20-25 in-Hg).

13. Cycle the steering wheel fully from stop-to-stop 10 times.

14. Stop the engine, release the vacuum and remove the vacuum pump.

15. Fill the reservoir as needed and install the reservoir cap.

16. Visually inspect the power steering system for leaks.

17. Install the reservoir cap.

SUSPENSION

FRONT SUSPENSION

BALL JOINTS

REMOVAL & INSTALLATION

Upper And Lower

See Figure 339.

1. Before servicing the vehicle, refer to the Precautions Section.

2. Remove the brake disc.

3. Remove the wheel speed sensor.

4. Remove and discard the cotter pin and nut.

5. Using the special tool, disconnect the tie-rod end.

6. Remove and discard the cotter pin and the nut.

7. Remove the pinch bolt adjuster.

✳✳ WARNING

To prevent damage to the ball joint seal and the ball joint socket, do not use a pickle fork-type remover to loosen the ball joints.

8. Remove the front wheel spindle.
   a. Strike the lower end of the front axle to loosen the ball joint.
   b. Remove the front wheel spindle.

9. Position the front wheel spindle in a vise, and remove the snapring from the lower ball joint.

✳✳ WARNING

To avoid damage to the components, do not use heat to aid ball joint removal.

10. Using a U-Joint C-Clamp tool and suitable receiver cup, remove the lower ball joint from the front wheel spindle.

11. Using a U-Joint C-Clamp tool and suitable receiver cup, remove the upper ball joint.

To install:

✳✳ WARNING

To avoid damage to components, do not use heat to aid installation.

➡ **Clean the wheel knuckle ball joint bores.**

➡ **The lower ball joint must be installed first.**

12. Using a U-Joint C-Clamp tool with suitable receiver cups, install the lower ball joint.

13. Using a U-Joint C-Clamp tool with suitable receiver cups, install the upper ball joint.

14. Install the snapring in the groove at the bottom of the ball joint.

15. To install, reverse the removal procedure.

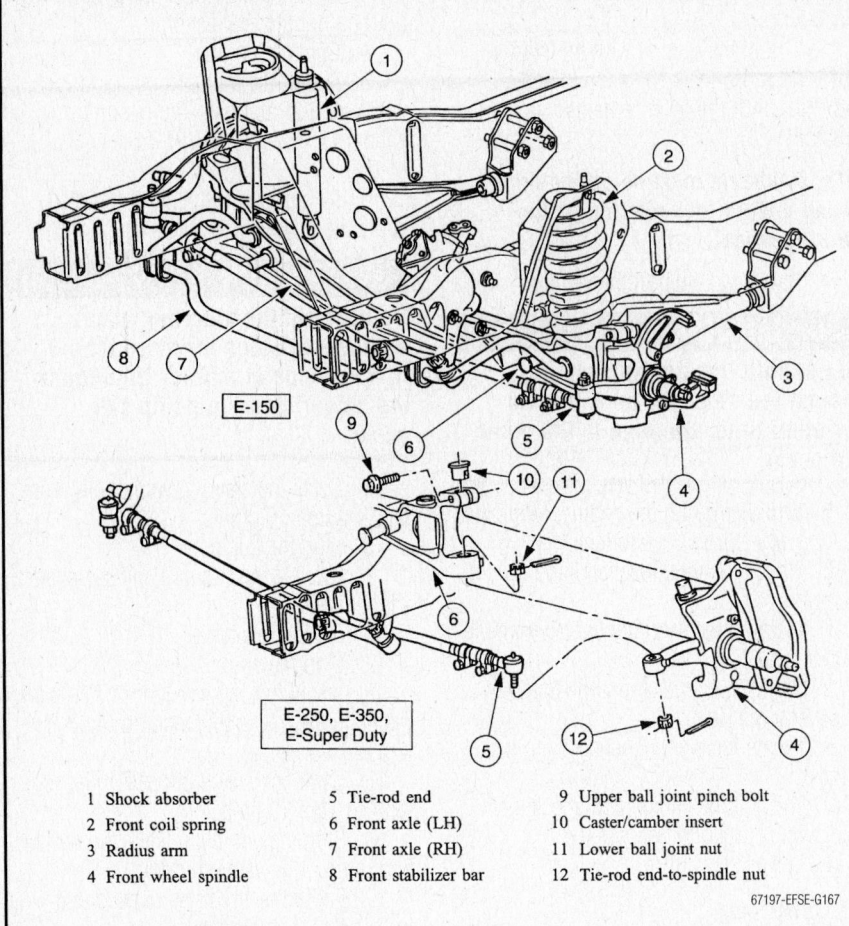

Fig. 339 Front suspension—E-Series

1	Shock absorber	5	Tie-rod end	9	Upper ball joint pinch bolt
2	Front coil spring	6	Front axle (LH)	10	Caster/camber insert
3	Radius arm	7	Front axle (RH)	11	Lower ball joint nut
4	Front wheel spindle	8	Front stabilizer bar	12	Tie-rod end-to-spindle nut

67197-EFSE-G167

16. Observe the following torques:
- Pinch bolt: 77 ft. lbs. (104 Nm)
- Lower ball stud nut: 130 ft. lbs. (176 Nm)
- Toe rod end nut: 66 ft. lbs. (90 Nm)

17. Check and, if necessary, align the front end.

COIL SPRING

REMOVAL & INSTALLATION

See Figure 339.

1. Before servicing the vehicle, refer to the Precautions Section.
2. Remove the stabilizer bar.

✱✱ WARNING

The axle must be supported throughout the procedure to prevent strain on the front brake hose.

3. Using a suitable jack, support the front axle.
4. Loosen the shock absorber upper nut. Loosen the nut to the top of the threads.

5. Remove the front spring upper retainer bolt and the upper spring retainer.

➡ **It may be necessary to loosen the radius arm-to-axle nut to remove the spring.**

6. Lower the jack supporting the front axle, then remove the front coil spring from the lower retainer. Using a suitable spray lubricant, spray the lower spring and spring retainer. Rotate the spring 180 degrees counterclockwise, tilt the spring outward and remove.

7. To install, reverse the removal procedure. Tighten the upper spring retainer to 22 ft. lbs. (30 Nm). Tighten the upper shock nut to 30 ft. lbs. (40 Nm).

RADIUS ARM

REMOVAL & INSTALLATION

See Figure 339.

1. Before servicing the vehicle, refer to the Precautions Section.
2. Remove the front coil spring.

3. Remove the radius arm-to-axle nut and bolt.
4. Remove the spring retainer and insulator.
5. Remove the radius arm.
   a. Remove the nut.
   b. Remove the washer and rear insulator.
   c. Pull the radius arm from the bracket, and remove the spacer, insulator and washer.

➡ **Inspect the bushings and install new as necessary.**

6. To install, reverse the removal procedure. Torque the pivot nut to 221 ft. lbs. (300 Nm); the bracket end nut to 98 ft. lbs. (133 Nm).

SHOCK ABSORBERS

REMOVAL & INSTALLATION

See Figure 339.

1. Before servicing the vehicle, refer to the Precautions Section.
2. Raise the vehicle and secure on support stands.
3. Remove the self-locking nut, steel washer, and rubber bushings at the upper end of the shock absorber.
4. Remove the bolt and nut at the lower end and remove the shock absorber.

To install:

5. When installing a new shock absorber, use new rubber bushings. Position the shock absorber on the mounting brackets with the stud end at the top. Install the upper bushing, steel washer and self-locking nut at the upper end, and the bolt and nut at the lower end.
6. Tighten the upper mounting studs to 30 ft. lbs. (41 Nm) and the lower mounting nuts to 59 ft. lbs. (80 Nm).

SPINDLE

REMOVAL & INSTALLATION

See Figure 340.

1. Before servicing the vehicle, refer to the Precautions Section.
2. Remove the brake disc.
3. Remove the wheel speed sensor.
4. Remove and discard the cotter pin and nut.
5. Disconnect the tie-rod end.
6. Remove and discard the cotter pin and the nut.
7. Remove the pinch bolt adjuster.

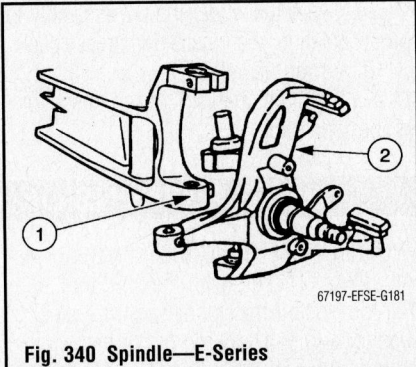

Fig. 340 Spindle—E-Series

❊ WARNING

To prevent damage to the ball joint seal and the ball joint socket, do not use a pickle fork-type remover to loosen the ball joints.

8. Strike the lower end of the front axle to loosen the ball joint.

9. Remove the front wheel spindle.

10. To install, reverse the removal procedure. Observe the following torques:

- Tie rod ball stud nut: 66 ft. lbs. (90 Nm)
- Lower ball joint nut: 130 ft. lbs. (176 Nm)
- Pinch bolt adjuster bolt: 77 ft. lbs. (104 Nm)

11. Check and, if necessary, align the front end.

STABILIZER BAR

REMOVAL & INSTALLATION

1. Before servicing the vehicle, refer to the Precautions Section.

2. Remove the wheel and tire assembly.

3. Remove the four bolts and the stabilizer bar.

4. To install, reverse the removal procedure. Torque the bolts to 18 ft. lbs. (25 Nm).

WHEEL BEARINGS

ADJUSTMENT

1. Before servicing the vehicle, refer to the Precautions Section.

2. Raise and safely support the vehicle.

3. Support the front end.

4. Remove the wheel cover, if equipped.

5. Remove the grease cap.

➡**Check the wheel bearings for sufficient grease.**

6. Remove the cotter pin and retaining washer. Back off the spindle nut. Discard the cotter pin.

7. Adjust the wheel bearings as follows:

a. Tighten the spindle nut to 30 ft. lbs. (40 Nm) while rotating the brake disc clockwise to seat the wheel bearings.

b. Back off the nut 2 full turns.

c. While rotating the disc counterclockwise, tighten the nut to 17–24 ft. lbs. (23–34 Nm).

d. Back off the spindle nut about ½ turn.

e. Tighten the spindle nut to 17 inch lbs. (2 Nm).

8. Install the retaining washer so the castellations are aligned with the cotter pin hole. Install a new cotter pin.

9. Check the wheel and tire assembly for proper rotation, then install the grease cap. If the wheel still does not rotate properly, inspect and clean or replace the wheel bearings and cups.

10. Install the wheel cover, if equipped.

11. Lower the vehicle.

12. Road test the vehicle and check for proper operation.

REMOVAL & INSTALLATION

See Figure 341.

The hub is part of the disc brake rotor and cannot be serviced separately. The inner and outer wheel bearing and races are serviced individually. Be sure to have a new hub grease seal when servicing the wheel bearings.

1. Before servicing the vehicle, refer to the Precautions Section.

2. Remove or disconnect the following:

- Wheels
- Caliper
- Brake pads and anti-rattle clips
- Hub grease cap, cotter pin, retainer washer and the spindle nut
- Wheel bearing retainer washer and the outer wheel bearing
- Brake hub and rotor assembly
- Grease seal
- Inner wheel bearing

3. Clean and inspect the wheel bearings and races for unusual wear or damage. Replace parts as necessary.

4. Inspect the hub and brake rotor assembly. If required, the hub and brake rotor assembly must be replaced as a unit.

To install:

5. If needed, pack the wheel bearing with a suitable high temperature wheel bearing grease before assembly.

6. Install or connect the following:

- Inner wheel bearing in the hub and brake rotor assembly
- New grease seal
- Hub and rotor assembly on the wheel spindle and install the outer wheel bearing.
- Retainer washer and the spindle nut

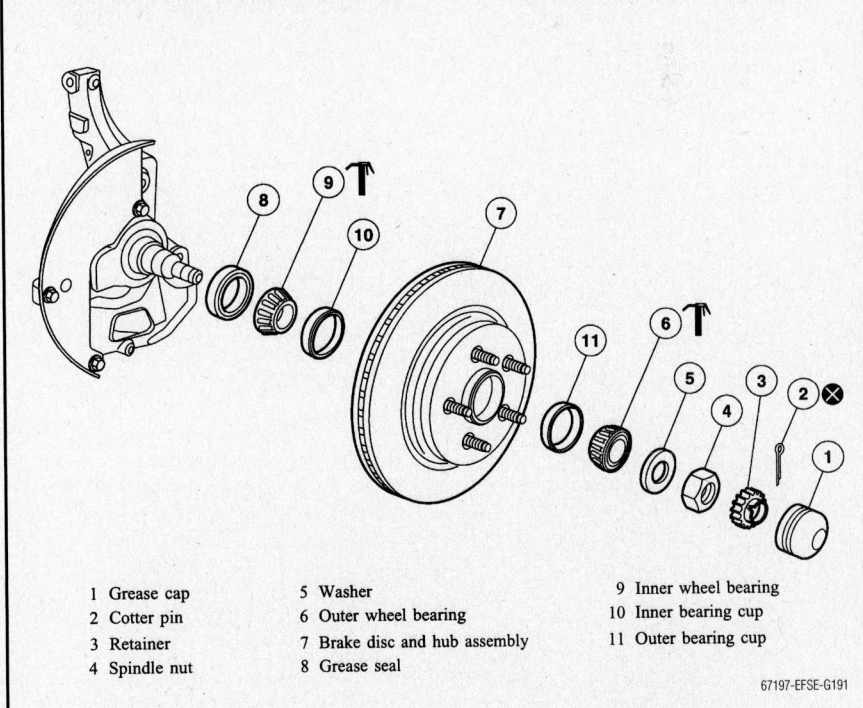

1 Grease cap	5 Washer	9 Inner wheel bearing
2 Cotter pin	6 Outer wheel bearing	10 Inner bearing cup
3 Retainer	7 Brake disc and hub assembly	11 Outer bearing cup
4 Spindle nut	8 Grease seal	

Fig. 341 Front hub and bearings

7. Adjust the wheel bearings.
8. Install or connect the following:
   - Retaining washer, so the castellations are aligned with the cotter pin hole. Install a new cotter pin.

- Anti-rattle clips
- Disc brake pads
- Caliper
- Wheels. Tighten the lug nuts to 83–112 ft. lbs. (113–153 Nm).

9. Check the wheel and tire assembly for proper rotation, then install the grease cap.
10. Lower the vehicle.
11. Road test the vehicle and check for proper operation.

SUSPENSION

LEAF SPRING

REMOVAL & INSTALLATION

1. Before servicing the vehicle, refer to the Precautions Section.
2. Remove the wheel and tire assembly.
3. Support the rear axle with a suitable jack.
4. Disconnect the lower end of the rear shock absorber.
5. Remove the nuts. Remove the U-bolts. Remove the rear spring plate.
6. Remove the front shackle bolt and nut.
7. Remove the rear shackle bolt and nut.
8. Remove the rear spring.
9. Installation is the reverse of removal. Observe the following torques:
   - E-150 U-bolt nuts: 85 ft. lbs. (115 Nm)
   - E-250/350 U-bolt nuts: 130 ft. lbs. (176 Nm)
   - E-150 spring-to-front shackle bolt/nut: 148 ft. lbs. (200 Nm)

- E-250/350 spring-to-front shackle bolt/nut: 295 ft. lbs. (400 Nm)
- Spring-to-rear shackle bolt/nut, all: 85 ft. lbs. (115 Nm)
- E-150 rear shackle-to-frame: 98 ft. lbs. (133 Nm)
- E-250/350 rear shackle-to-frame: 111 ft. lbs. (150 Nm)

SHOCK ABSORBER

REMOVAL & INSTALLATION

1. Before servicing the vehicle, refer to the Precautions Section.
2. Raise the vehicle and secure on support stands.
3. Remove the self-locking nut, steel washer, and rubber bushings at the upper end of the shock absorber.
4. Remove the bolt and nut at the lower end and remove the shock absorber. If needed, raise the rear axle assembly slightly with a jack.

To install:

5. When installing a new shock absorber, use new rubber bushings.

REAR SUSPENSION

Position the shock absorber on the mounting brackets with the stud end at the top. Install the upper bushing, steel washer and self-locking nut at the upper end, and the bolt and nut at the lower end.

6. Tighten the upper mounting studs to:
   - Upper end 30 ft. lbs. (40 Nm)
   - Lower end 52 ft. lbs. (70 Nm)

STABILIZER BAR

REMOVAL & INSTALLATION

1. Before servicing the vehicle, refer to the Precautions Section.
2. Remove the lower nut, washer and insulator.
3. Remove the upper bolt and washer.
4. Remove the rear stabilizer bar.
5. Remove the bolt and the stabilizer bar. Discard the bolts.
6. To install, reverse the removal procedure. Torque the bracket bolts to 30 ft. lbs. (40 Nm); the link-to-bar nuts to 21 ft. lbs. (28 Nm); the link-to-frame bolts to 60 ft. lbs. (81 Nm).

FORD AND MERCURY

Escape • Mariner

6

SPECIFICATIONS AND MAINTENANCE CHARTS

ENGINE AND VEHICLE IDENTIFICATION

			Engine						Model Year	
Code ①	Liters	Cu. In.	Cyl.	Fuel Sys.	Engine Type	Eng. Mfg.		Code ②		Year
Z	2.3	137	4	SFI	DOHC	Ford		5		2005
1	3.0	182	6	SFI	DOHC	Ford		6		2006
								7		2007
								8		2008

SFI: Multi-port Fuel Injection

DOHC: Double Overhead Camshafts

① 8th digit of VIN

② 10th digit of VIN

22086_ESCA_C0001

GENERAL ENGINE SPECIFICATIONS

Year	Model	Engine Displacement Liters	Engine VIN	Net Horsepower @ rpm	Net Torque @ rpm (ft. lbs.)	Bore x Stroke (in.)	Com- pression Ratio	Oil Pressure @ rpm
2005	Escape/Mariner	2.3	Z	153@5800	152@4250	3.44x3.70	9.7:1	29-39@2000
	Escape/Mariner	3.0	1	200@5500	200@4500	3.50x3.13	10.0:1	11@1500 ①
2006	Escape/Mariner	2.3	Z	153@5800	152@4250	3.44x3.70	9.7:1	29-39@2000
	Escape/Mariner	3.0	1	200@5500	200@4500	3.50x3.13	10.0:1	11@1500 ①
2007	Escape/Mariner	2.3	Z	153@5800	152@4250	3.44x3.70	9.7:1	29-39@2000
	Escape/Mariner	3.0	1	200@5500	200@4500	3.50x3.13	10.0:1	11@1500 ①
2008	Escape/Mariner	2.3	Z	153@5800	152@4250	3.44x3.70	9.7:1	29-39@2000
	Escape/Mariner	3.0	1	200@5500	200@4500	3.50x3.13	10.0:1	11@1500 ①

SFI: Multi-port Fuel Injection

① Minimum hot

22086_ESCA_C0002

ENGINE TUNE-UP SPECIFICATIONS

Year	Engine Displacement Liters	Engine VIN	Spark Plug Gap (in.)	Ignition Timing (deg.) MT	AT	Fuel Pump (psi) ①	Idle Speed (rpm) MT	AT	Valve Clearance Intake	Exhaust
2005	2.3	Z	0.049-0.053	10 BTDC	10 BTDC	39	②	②	HYD.	HYD.
	2.3	H	0.049-0.053	—	NA	39	②	②	HYD.	HYD.
	3.0	1	0.052-0.056	10 BTDC	10 BTDC	39	②	②	HYD.	HYD.
2006	2.3	Z	0.049-0.053	10 BTDC	10 BTDC	39	②	②	HYD.	HYD.
	2.3	H	0.049-0.053	—	NA	39	②	②	HYD.	HYD.
	3.0	1	0.052-0.056	10 BTDC	10 BTDC	39	②	②	HYD.	HYD.
2007	2.3	Z	0.049-0.053	10 BTDC	10 BTDC	39	②	②	HYD.	HYD.
	2.3	H	0.049-0.053	—	NA	39	②	②	HYD.	HYD.
	3.0	1	0.052-0.056	10 BTDC	10 BTDC	39	②	②	HYD.	HYD.
2008	2.3	Z	0.049-0.053	10 BTDC	10 BTDC	39	②	②	HYD.	HYD.
	2.3	H	0.049-0.053	—	NA	39	②	②	HYD.	HYD.
	3.0	1	0.052-0.056	10 BTDC	10 BTDC	39	②	②	HYD.	HYD.

BTDC: Before Top Dead Center

HYD: Hydraulic lash adjusters

NA: Information not available

① Key on; engine off

② Refer to Vehicle Emission Control Information Label

22086_ESCA_C0003

CAPACITIES

Year	Model	Engine Displacement Liters	Engine VIN	Engine Oil with Filter (qts.)	Transmission (pts.) Manual	Auto ①	Transfer Case (pts.)	Drive Axle Front (pts.)	Rear (pts.)	Fuel Tank (gal.)	Cooling System (qts.)
2005	Escape/Mariner	2.3	Z	4.5	5.0	—	—	—	3.0	16.5	①
	Escape/Mariner	3.0	1	6.0	5.0	20.4	0.75	2.95	3.0	16.5	10.5
2006	Escape/Mariner	2.3	Z	4.5	5.0	—	—	—	3.0	16.5	①
	Escape/Mariner	3.0	1	6.0	5.0	20.4	0.75	2.95	3.0	16.5	10.5
2007	Escape/Mariner	2.3	Z	4.5	5.0	—	—	—	3.0	16.5	①
	Escape/Mariner	3.0	1	6.0	5.0	20.4	0.75	2.95	3.0	16.5	10.5
2008	Escape/Mariner	2.3	Z	4.5	5.0	—	—	—	3.0	16.5	①
	Escape/Mariner	3.0	1	6.0	5.0	20.4	0.75	2.95	3.0	16.5	10.5

NOTE: All capacities are approximate. Add fluid gradually and check to be sure a proper fluid level is obtained.

① Dry fill

② With manual transaxle: 6.9 qts; with automatic transaxle: 8.0 qts.

22086_ESCA_C0004

FLUID SPECIFICATIONS

Year	Model	Engine Displacement Liters	Engine ID/VIN	Engine Oil	Auto. Trans. ①	Drive Axle	Power Steering Fluid	Brake Master Cylinder
2005	Escape/	2.3	Z	5W-20	Mercon®V	80W-90	Mercon®V	DOT 3
	Mariner	3.0	1	5W-20	Mercon®V	80W-90	Mercon®V	DOT 3
2006	Escape/	2.3	Z	5W-20	Mercon®V	80W-90	Mercon®V	DOT 3
	Mariner	3.0	1	5W-20	Mercon®V	80W-90	Mercon®V	DOT 3
2007	Escape/	2.3	Z	5W-20	Mercon®V	80W-90	Mercon®V	DOT 3
	Mariner	3.0	1	5W-20	Mercon®V	80W-90	Mercon®V	DOT 3
2008	Escape/	2.3	Z	5W-20	Mercon®V	80W-90	NA	DOT 3
	Mariner	3.0	1	5W-20	Mercon®V	80W-90	NA	DOT 3

NA - Not Available

DOT: Department Of Transpotation

®: Registerd Trademark

22086_ESCA_C0005

VALVE SPECIFICATIONS

Year	Engine Displacement Liters	Engine VIN	Seat Angle (deg.)	Face Angle (deg.)	Spring Test Pressure (lbs. @ in.)	Spring Installed Height (in.)	Stem-to-Guide Clearance (in.) Intake	Stem-to-Guide Clearance (in.) Exhaust	Stem Diameter (in.) Intake	Stem Diameter (in.) Exhaust
2005	2.3	Z	45	45	38.6@1.49	1.492	0.0010	0.0011	0.2153-0.2159	0.2151-0.2157
	3.0	1	44.75	45.5	153@ 1.18	1.57	0.0008-0.0027	0.0018-0.0037	0.2352-0.2360	0.2343-0.2350
2006	2.3	Z	45	45	38.6@1.49	1.492	0.0010	0.0011	0.2153-0.2159	0.2151-0.2157
	3.0	1	44.75	45.5	153@ 1.18	1.57	0.0008-0.0027	0.0018-0.0037	0.2352-0.2360	0.2343-0.2350
2007	2.3	Z	45	45	38.6@1.49	1.492	0.0010	0.0011	0.2153-0.2159	0.2151-0.2157
	3.0	1	44.75	45.5	153@ 1.18	1.57	0.0008-0.0027	0.0018-0.0037	0.2352-0.2360	0.2343-0.2350
2008	2.3	Z	45	45	38.6@1.49	1.492	0.0010	0.0011	0.2153-0.2159	0.2151-0.2157
	3.0	1	44.75	45.5	153@ 1.18	1.57	0.0008-0.0027	0.0018-0.0037	0.2352-0.2360	0.2343-0.2350

22086_ESCA_C0006

CAMSHAFT AND BEARING SPECIFICATIONS CHART

All measurements are given in inches.

Year	Engine Displ. Liters	Engine ID/VIN	Journal Dia.	Brg. Oil Clearance	Shaft End-play	Runout	Journal Bore	Lobe Height Intake	Lobe Height Exhaust
2005	2.3	Z	0.982-0.983	0.001-0.003	0.003-0.009	0.001	0.001-0.003	0.324	0.307
	3.0	1	1.061-1.060	0.001-0.00029	0.00748	—	1.063-1.062	0.189	0.189
2006	2.3	Z	0.982-0.983	0.001-0.003	0.003-0.009	0.001	0.001-0.003	0.324	0.307
	3.0	1	1.061-1.060	0.001-0.00029	0.00748	—	1.063-1.062	0.189	0.189
2007	2.3	Z	0.982-0.983	0.001-0.003	0.003-0.009	0.001	0.001-0.003	0.324	0.307
	3.0	1	1.061-1.060	0.001-0.00029	0.00748	—	1.063-1.062	0.189	0.189
2008	2.3	Z	0.982-0.983	0.001-0.003	0.003-0.009	0.001	0.001-0.003	0.324	0.307
	3.0	1	1.061-1.060	0.001-0.00029	0.00748	—	1.063-1.062	0.189	0.189

22086_HYBR_C0007

CRANKSHAFT AND CONNECTING ROD SPECIFICATIONS

All measurements are given in inches.

Year	Engine Displacement Liters	Engine VIN	Crankshaft Main Brg. Journal Dia.	Crankshaft Main Brg. Oil Clearance	Crankshaft Shaft End-play	Crankshaft Thrust on No.	Connecting Rod Journal Diameter	Connecting Rod Oil Clearance	Connecting Rod Side Clearance
2005	2.3	Z	2.0460-2.0470	0.0007-0.0013	0.0080-0.0160	NA	1.9673-1.9681	0.0011-0.0026	0.0760-0.1200
	3.0	1	2.4791-2.4800	0.0010-0.0018	0.0043-0.0091	3	1.9673-1.9681	0.0011-0.0026	0.0039-0.0118
2006	2.3	Z	2.0460-2.0470	0.0007-0.0013	0.0080-0.0160	NA	1.9673-1.9681	0.0011-0.0026	0.0760-0.1200
	3.0	1	2.4791-2.4800	0.0010-0.0018	0.0043-0.0091	3	1.9673-1.9681	0.0011-0.0026	0.0039-0.0118
2007	2.3	Z	2.0460-2.0470	0.0007-0.0013	0.0080-0.0160	NA	1.9673-1.9681	0.0011-0.0026	0.0760-0.1200
	3.0	1	2.4791-2.4800	0.0010-0.0018	0.0043-0.0091	3	1.9673-1.9681	0.0011-0.0026	0.0039-0.0118
2008	2.3	Z	2.0460-2.0470	0.0007-0.0013	0.0080-0.0160	NA	1.9673-1.9681	0.0011-0.0026	0.0760-0.1200
	3.0	1	2.4791-2.4800	0.0010-0.0018	0.0043-0.0091	3	1.9673-1.9681	0.0011-0.0026	0.0039-0.0118

NA: Not Available

22086_ESCA_C0008

PISTON AND RING SPECIFICATIONS
All measurements are given in inches.

Year	Engine Displacement Liters	Engine VIN	Piston Clearance	Ring Gap			Ring Side Clearance		
				Top Compression	Bottom Compression	Oil Control	Top Compression	Bottom Compression	Oil Control
2005	2.3	Z	0.0009-0.0017	0.0060-0.0120	0.0120-0.0180	0.0070-0.0270	NA	NA	NA
	3.0	1	0.0005-0.0009	0.0039-0.0098	0.0106-0.0165	0.0059-0.0256	0.0016-0.0030	0.0016-0.0033	snug
2006	2.3	Z	0.0009-0.0017	0.0060-0.0120	0.0120-0.0180	0.0070-0.0270	NA	NA	NA
	3.0	1	0.0005-0.0009	0.0039-0.0098	0.0106-0.0165	0.0059-0.0256	0.0016-0.0030	0.0016-0.0033	snug
2007	2.3	Z	0.0009-0.0017	0.0060-0.0120	0.0120-0.0180	0.0070-0.0270	NA	NA	NA
	3.0	1	0.0005-0.0009	0.0039-0.0098	0.0106-0.0165	0.0059-0.0256	0.0016-0.0030	0.0016-0.0033	snug
2008	2.3	Z	0.0009-0.0017	0.0060-0.0120	0.0120-0.0180	0.0070-0.0270	NA	NA	NA
	3.0	1	0.0005-0.0009	0.0039-0.0098	0.0106-0.0165	0.0059-0.0256	0.0016-0.0030	0.0016-0.0033	snug

NA: Not Available

22086_ESCA_C0009

TORQUE SPECIFICATIONS
All readings in ft. lbs.

Year	Engine Displacement Liters	Engine VIN	Cylinder Head Bolts	Main Bearing Bolts	Rod Bearing Bolts	Crankshaft Damper Bolts	Flywheel Bolts	Manifold		Spark Plugs	Oil Pan Drain Plug
								Intake	Exhaust		
2005	2.3	Z	①	NA	NA	②	③	13	35	11	21
	3.0	1	④	⑤	⑥	⑦	59	⑧	15	11	19
2006	2.3	Z	①	NA	NA	②	③	13	35	11	21
	3.0	1	④	⑤	⑥	⑦	59	⑧	15	11	19
2007	2.3	Z	①	NA	NA	②	③	13	35	11	21
	3.0	1	④	⑤	⑥	⑦	59	⑧	15	11	19
2008	2.3	Z	①	NA	NA	②	③	13	35	11	21
	3.0	1	④	⑤	⑥	⑦	59	⑧	15	11	19

NA: Information not available

① Step 1: 44 inch lbs.
  Step 2: 11 ft. lbs.
  Step 3: 33 ft. lbs.
  Step 4: +90 degrees
  Step 5: Plus 90 degrees

② Step2: 74 ft. lbs.
  Step 2: plus 90 degrees

③ Step 1: 37 ft. lbs.
  Step 2: 50 ft. lbs
  Step 3: 83 ft. lbs.

④ Step 1: 30 ft. lbs. (40 Nm).
  Step 2: Tighten the bolts 90 degrees.
  Step 3: Loosen the bolts one full turn.
  Step 4: 30 ft. lbs. (40 Nm).
  Step 5: Tighten the bolts 90 degrees.
  Step 6: Tighten the bolts 90 degrees.

⑤ Step 1: Fasteners 1-8: 18 ft. lbs.
  Step 2: Fasteners 9-19: 30 ft. lbs.
  Step 3: Fasteners 1-16: +90 degrees
  Step 4: fasteners 17-22: 18 ft. lbs.

⑥ Step 1: 17 ft. lbs.
  Step 2: 32 ft. lbs.

⑦ Step1: 86 ft. lbs
  Step 2: Loosen 1 full turn
  Step 3: 37 ft. lbs.
  Step 4: plus 90 degrees

⑧ 89 inch lbs.

22086_ESCA_C0010

WHEEL ALIGNMENT

Year	Model		Caster Range (+/-Deg.)	Caster Preferred Setting (Deg.)	Camber Range (+/-Deg.)	Camber Preferred Setting (Deg.)	Toe-in (in.)
2005	2.3L	F	1.00	+1.60	1.00	-1.00	0.23+/-0.32
		R	NA	NA	0.75	①	0.03+/-0.20
	3.0L	F	1.00	+1.60	1.00	-1.00	0.23+/-0.32
		R	NA	NA	0.75	①	0.03+/-0.20
2006	2.3L	F	1.00	+1.50 ②	1.00	-1.00	0.23+/-0.32
		R	NA	NA	0.75	0.00	-0.14+/-0.20
	3.0L	F	1.00	+1.50 ②	1.00	-1.00	0.23+/-0.32
		R	NA	NA	0.75	0.00	-0.14+/-0.20
2007	2.3L	F	1.00	+1.50 ②	1.00	-1.00	0.23+/-0.32
		R	NA	NA	0.75	0.00	-0.14+/-0.20
	3.0L	F	1.00	+1.50 ②	1.00	-1.00	0.23+/-0.32
		R	NA	NA	0.75	0.00	-0.14+/-0.20
2008	2.3L	F	1.00	+1.50 ②	1.00	-1.00	0.23+/-0.32
		R	NA	NA	0.75	0.00	-0.18+/-0.20 ③
	3.0L	F	1.00	+1.50 ②	1.00	-1.00	0.23+/-0.32
		R	NA	NA	0.75	0.00	-0.18+/-0.20 ③

Early build vehicles are those built before 8/02/04 at Kansas City, or, before 8/16/04 at Ohio.

NA: Information not available

① Early build: +20 degrees
  Late build: 0

② Left side 1.80 degrees

③ AWD -0.12 +/- 0.20

22086_ESCA_C0011

TIRE, WHEEL AND BALL JOINT SPECIFICATIONS

Year	Model	OEM Tires Standard	OEM Tires Optional	Tire Pressures (psi) Front	Tire Pressures (psi) Rear	Wheel Size	Ball Joint Inspection	Lug Nuts (ft. lbs.)
2005	Escape XLS Value	P225/70R15	none	①	①	6.5	0.008 in.	98
	Escape XLS	P235/70R16	none	①	①	7.5	0.008 in.	98
	Mariner	P235/70R16	none	①	①	7.5	0.008 in.	98
2006	Escape	P235/70R16	none	①	①	NA	0.008 in.	98
	Mariner	P235/70R16	none	①	①	NA	0.008 in.	98
2007	Escape	P235/70R16	none	①	①	NA	0.008 in.	98
	Mariner	P235/70R16	none	①	①	NA	0.008 in.	98
2008	Escape	P235/70R16	none	①	①	NA	0.008 in.	98
	Mariner	P235/70R16	none	①	①	NA	0.008 in.	98

OEM: Original Equipment Manufacturer

PSI: Pounds Per Square Inch

STD: Standard

OPT: Optional

① See safety certification on driver's door jam

22086_ESCA_C0012

BRAKE SPECIFICATIONS

All measurements in inches unless noted

Year	Model		Brake Disc Original Thickness	Brake Disc Minimum Thickness	Brake Disc Maximum Run-out	Brake Drum Original Inside Diameter	Brake Drum Maximum Machine Diameter	Minimum Lining Thickness	Brake Caliper Bracket Bolts (ft. lbs.)	Brake Caliper Mounting Bolts (ft. lbs.)
2005	Escape/Mariner	F	NA	①	0.004	—	—	0.118	111	②
		R	NA	0.430	0.004	NA	9.05	0.118	—	26
2006	Escape/Mariner	F	NA	①	0.004	—	—	0.118	111	②
		R	NA	0.430	0.004	NA	9.05	0.118	—	26
2007	Escape/Mariner	F	NA	①	0.004	—	—	0.118	111	②
		R	NA	0.430	0.004	NA	9.05	0.118	—	26
2008	Escape/Mariner	F	NA	0.950	0.004	—	—	0.118	111	②
		R	NA	0.430	0.004	NA	10.0.	0.118	—	26

NA: Not Available

① Base brakes: 0.86 in.

   With 4-wheel discs: 0.95 in.

② With disc/drum: 26 ft. lbs.

   With 4-wheel disc: 33 ft. lbs.

   Escape Hybrid: 33 ft. lbs.

22086_ESCA_C0013

SCHEDULED MAINTENANCE INTERVALS
2005-06 Ford Escape/Mercury Mariner

TO BE SERVICED	TYPE OF SERVICE	VEHICLE MILEAGE INTERVAL (x1000)												
		5	10	15	20	25	30	35	40	45	50	55	60	65
Air cleaner filter	R						✓						✓	
Accessory drive belt	I ⑤	Every 100,000 miles												
Auto. Trans. fluid level	I		✓				✓			✓			✓	
Auto. Trans. Fluid	③ ④						✓						✓	
Ball joints (2wd)	L			✓			✓			✓			✓	
Brake system ①	S/I			✓			✓			✓			✓	
Cabin air filter	R			✓			✓			✓			✓	
Cooling system hoses and clamps	S/I			✓			✓			✓			✓	
Driveshafts & halfshafts	S/I			✓			✓			✓			✓	
Engine coolant (Premium Gold)	R	Five years or 100,000 miles, then every 3 years or 50,000 miles												
Engine coolant (exc. Premium Gold)	R	Every 105,000 miles												
Engine oil & filter	R	✓	✓	✓	✓	✓	✓	✓	✓	✓	✓	✓	✓	✓
Front wheel bearings and seals (2wd)	R	Every 150,000 miles, if not previously done												
Fuel filter	R						✓						✓	
Man. Trans. Fluid	R	Every 120,000 miles												
PCV valve	S/I	Every 100,000 miles												
Exhaust system & heat shields	S/I						✓						✓	
Rear axle lubricant (4wd)	R	Every 150,000 miles												
Rotate tires	S/I	✓	✓	✓	✓	✓	✓	✓	✓	✓	✓	✓	✓	✓
Steering linkage	S/I			✓			✓			✓			✓	
Spark plugs	R	Change at 100,000 miles												
Suspension components	S/I			✓			✓			✓			✓	
Wheels ②	I			✓			✓			✓			✓	
Multi-Point inspection	⑥	✓	✓	✓	✓	✓	✓	✓	✓	✓	✓	✓	✓	✓

R: Replace   S/I: Inspect and service, if necessary   L: Lubricate   A: Adjust   C: Clean

① Inspect the reservoir fluid level, rotor and or drum, brake lines, hoses, calipers and or wheel cylinders

② Inspect for end play and noise

③ Change automatic transmission/transaxle fluid and filter on all vehicles equipped with 4F50N, 4R100 and 4F27E.

④ Change every 150,000 miles for all transaxles

⑤ Replace at 150,000 miles, if not previously done

22086_ESCA_C0014

SCHEDULED MAINTENANCE INTERVALS
2005-06 Ford Escape/Mercury Mariner

⑥ **Multi-Point inspection**

The following inspections are recommended at every service interval:

Check and top off brake, coolant, manual and automatic transmission fluid power steering and washer fluid

Inspect tires for wear and correct air pressure, including spare tire

Check exhaust system for leaks, damage, loose parts and foreighn material

Check battery performance

Check operation of horn, exterior lamps, turn signals and hazard warning lights

Check radiator, coolers, heater and airconditioning hoses

Inspect tires for wear and correct air pressure, including spare tire

Inspect windshield wiper spray and wiper operation

Check windshield for cracks, chips and pitting

Inspect for oil and fluid leaks

Inspect air filter

Inspect halfshaft dust boots

Check shocks struts and other suspension components for leaks and damage

Inspect steering linkage

Inspect accesory drive belts

Inspect clutck operation (if equipped)

When operating in dusty conditions such as unpaved or dusty roads:

Change engine oil and install a new oil filter every 4,800 km (3,000 miles) or 3 months.

Install a new fuel filter every 24,000 km (15,000 miles).

Change automatic transmission fluid every 48,000 km (30,000 miles).

Change transfer case fluid every 96,000 km (60,000 miles).

Install a new engine air filter as required.

Install a new cabin air filter as required.

When operating in off-road conditions:

Change automatic transmission fluid every 48,000 km (30,000 miles).

Change transfer case fluid every 96,000 km (60,000 miles).

Install a new cabin air filter as required.

Inspect and lubricate U-joints.

Inspect and lubricate steering linkage ball joints with zerk fittings.

Special Operating Condition Requirements

When towing a trailer or using a camper or car-top carrier:

Change engine oil and install a new oil filter every 4,800 km (3,000 miles) or 3 months.

Change transfer case fluid every 96,000 km (60,000 miles).

Change manual transmission fluid as required.

Inspect and lubricate U-joints as required.

During extensive idling and/or low speed driving for long distances, as in heavy commercial use such as delivery, taxi, patrol car or livery:

Change engine oil and install a new oil filter, lube front lower control arm and steering linkage ball joints with zerk fittings (if equipped) every 4,800 km (3,000 miles) or 3 months.

Inspect brake system and check battery electrolyte level (Patrol cars) every 8,000 km (5,000 miles).

Install a new fuel filter every 24,000 km (15,000 miles).

Change automatic transmission fluid, lubricate 4x2 wheel bearings,

Install new grease seals and adjust bearings every 48,000 km (30,000 miles).

Install new spark plugs and change transfer case fluid every 96,000 km (60,000 miles).

Install a new cabin air filter as required.

22086_ESCA_C0014A

SCHEDULED MAINTENANCE INTERVALS
2007 Ford Escape/Mercury Mariner

TO BE SERVICED	TYPE OF SERVICE	VEHICLE MILEAGE INTERVAL (x1000)												
		5	10	15	20	25	30	35	40	45	50	55	60	65
Air cleaner filter	R						✓						✓	
Accessory drive belt	I ⑤					Every 100,000 miles								
Auto. Trans. fluid level	I			✓			✓			✓			✓	
Auto. Trans. Fluid	③ ④						✓						✓	
Ball joints (2wd)	L			✓			✓			✓			✓	
Brake system ①	S/I			✓			✓			✓			✓	
Cabin air filter	R			✓			✓			✓			✓	
Cooling system hoses and clamps	S/I			✓			✓			✓			✓	
Driveshafts & halfshafts	S/I			✓			✓			✓			✓	
Engine coolant (Premium Gold)	R		5 years or 100,000 miles, then every 3 years or 50,000 miles											
Engine coolant (exc. Premium Gold)	R		Every 105,000 miles											
Engine oil & filter	R	✓	✓	✓	✓	✓	✓	✓	✓	✓	✓	✓	✓	✓
Front wheel bearings and seals (2wd)	R		Every 150,000 miles, if not previously done											
Fuel filter	R						✓						✓	
Man. Trans. Fluid	R		Every 120,000 miles											
PCV valve	S/I		Every 100,000 miles											
Exhaust system & heat shields	S/I						✓						✓	
Rear axle lubricant (4wd)	R		Every 150,000 miles											
Rotate tires	S/I	✓	✓	✓	✓	✓	✓	✓	✓	✓	✓	✓	✓	✓
Steering linkage	S/I			✓			✓			✓			✓	
Spark plugs	R		Change at 100,000 miles											
Suspension components	S/I			✓			✓			✓			✓	
Wheels ②	I			✓			✓			✓			✓	
Multi-Point inspection	⑥	✓	✓	✓	✓	✓	✓	✓	✓	✓	✓	✓	✓	✓

R: Replace   S/I: Inspect and service, if necessary   L: Lubricate   A: Adjust   C: Clean

① Inspect the reservoir fluid level, rotor and or drum, brake lines, hoses, calipers and or wheel cylinders

② Inspect for end play and noise

③ Change automatic transmission/transaxle fluid on TorqShift transmissions and externally mounted filter if equipped.

④ Change every 150,000 miles for all transaxles

⑤ Replace at 150,000 miles, if not previously done

22086_ESCA_C0015

SCHEDULED MAINTENANCE INTERVALS
2007 Ford Escape/Mercury Mariner

⑥ Multi-Point inspection

The following inspections are recommended at every service interval:

Check and top off brake, coolant, manual and automatic transmission fluid power steering and washer fluid

Inspect tires for wear and correct air pressure, including spare tire

Check exhaust system for leaks, damage, loose parts and foreighn material

Check battery performance

Check operation of horn, exterior lamps, turn signals and hazard warning lights

Check radiator, coolers, heater and airconditioning hoses

Inspect tires for wear and correct air pressure, including spare tire

Inspect windshield wiper spray and wiper operation

Check windshield for cracks, chips and pitting

Inspect for oil and fluid leaks

Inspect air filter

Inspect halfshaft dust boots

Check shocks struts and other suspension components for leaks and damage

Inspect steering linkage

Inspect accesory drive belts

Inspect clutck operation (if equipped)

When operating in dusty conditions such as unpaved or dusty roads:

Change engine oil and install a new oil filter every 4,800 km (3,000 miles) or 3 months.

Install a new fuel filter every 24,000 km (15,000 miles).

Change automatic transmission fluid every 48,000 km (30,000 miles).

Change transfer case fluid every 96,000 km (60,000 miles).

Install a new engine air filter as required.

Install a new cabin air filter as required.

When operating in off-road conditions:

Change automatic transmission fluid every 48,000 km (30,000 miles).

Change transfer case fluid every 96,000 km (60,000 miles).

Install a new cabin air filter as required.

Inspect and lubricate U-joints.

Inspect and lubricate steering linkage ball joints with zerk fittings.

Special Operating Condition Requirements

When towing a trailer or using a camper or car-top carrier:

Change engine oil and install a new oil filter every 8,000 km (5,000 miles) or 3 months.

Change automatic transmission fluid every 48,000 km (30,000 miles). (not required on 6R60/6R75 transmissions).

Inspect and rotate tires 8,000 km (5,000 miles)

Change transfer case fluid every 96,000 km (60,000 miles).

Change manual transmission fluid as required.

Inspect and lubricate U-joints and half shafts as required.

During extensive idling and/or low speed driving for long distances, as in heavy commercial use such as delivery, taxi, patrol car or livery:

Change engine oil and install a new oil filter, lube front lower control arm and steering linkage ball joints with

zerk fittings (if equipped) every 8,000 km (5,000 miles) or 3 months.

Inspect brake system and check battery electrolyte level (Patrol cars) every 8,000 km (5,000 miles).

Install a new fuel filter every 24,000 km (15,000 miles).

Change automatic transmission fluid, lubricate 4x2 wheel bearings,

Lubricate rear wheel drive (RWD) front wheel bearings, install new grease seals and adjust every 48,000 km (30,000 miles).

Install new spark plugs and change transfer case fluid every 96,000 km (60,000 miles).

Install a new cabin air filter as required.

SCHEDULED MAINTENANCE INTERVALS
2008 Ford Escape/Mercury Mariner

TO BE SERVICED	OF SERVIC	VEHICLE MILEAGE INTERVAL (x1000)												
		7.5	15	22.5	30	37.5	45	52.5	60	67.5	75	82.5	90	97.5
Air cleaner filter	R			✓			✓			✓			✓	
Auto. Trans. fluid level	I		✓		✓		✓		✓		✓		✓	
Auto. Trans. Fluid	R				✓				✓				✓	
Accessory drive belt	I ①	✓	✓	✓	✓	✓	✓	✓	✓	✓	✓	✓	✓	
Brake system ②	S/I		✓		✓		✓		✓		✓		✓	
Cabin air filter	R				✓				✓				✓	
Cooling system hoses and clamps	S/I		✓		✓		✓		✓		✓		✓	
Driveshafts & halfshafts	S/I		✓		✓		✓		✓		✓		✓	
Engine coolant	R	At 6 years or 100,000 miles; then every 3 years or 50,000 miles												
Engine oil & filter	R	✓	✓	✓	✓	✓	✓	✓	✓	✓	✓	✓	✓	✓
Exhaust system & heat shields	I		✓		✓		✓		✓		✓		✓	
Man. Trans. Fluid	R	Every 120,000 miles												
Fuel filter	R				✓				✓				✓	
PCV valve	S/I	Every 150,000 miles												
Rear axle lubricant (4wd)	R	Every 150,000 miles												
Rear (high voltage) battery A/C filter	I	✓	✓	✓	✓	✓	✓	✓	✓	✓	✓	✓	✓	
Rear (high voltage) battery A/C filter	R		✓		✓		✓		✓		✓		✓	
Tires	Rotate	Every 7,500 miles												
Steering linkage	S/I		✓		✓		✓		✓		✓		✓	
Spark plugs	R	Every 90,000 miles												
Suspension components and ball joints	S/I		✓		✓		✓		✓		✓		✓	
Multi-Point inspection	③	✓	✓	✓	✓	✓	✓	✓	✓	✓	✓	✓	✓	✓

R: Replace   S/I: Inspect and service, if necessary   L: Lubricate   A: Adjust   C: Clean

① Replace at 150,000 miles, if not previously done

② Inspect the reservoir fluid level, rotor and or drum, brake lines, hoses, calipers and or wheel cylinders

Monthly Checks
Check each of the following items every month:

All interior and exterior lights

Tires for wear and correct air pressure, including spare tire

Engine oil fluid level

Windshield washer solvent fluid level

Six Month Checks
Check each of the following items at least every 6 months:

Lap/shoulder belts and seat latches for wear and function

External mounted spare is stowed correctly (tight to body)

Parking brake for correct operation

Safety warning lamps (brake, ABS, air bag, safety belt) for correct operation

Clutch fluid level (if equipped)

Engine coolant system fluid level and correct strength

Power steering fluid

Battery 12-volt connections. Clean if necessary

Windshield washer spray, wiper operation, clean all wiper blades

Lubricate all hinges, latches and outside locks. Inspect for correct operation

Lubricate door rubber weatherstrips. Inspect for excessive wear

Clean body and door drain holes. Inspect for clogs and obstructions

SCHEDULED MAINTENANCE INTERVALS
2008 Ford Escape/Mercury Mariner
SCHEDULED MAINTENANCE INTERVALS
2008 Ford Escape/Mercury Mariner
(Footnotes continued)

③ **Multi-Point inspection**

The following inspections are recommended at every service interval:

Check and top off brake, coolant, manual and automatic transmission fluid power steering and washer fluid

Inspect tires for wear and correct air pressure, including spare tire

Check exhaust system for leaks, damage, loose parts and foreighn material

Check battery performance

Check operation of horn, exterior lamps, turn signals and hazard warning lights

Check radiator, coolers, heater and airconditioning hoses

Inspect tires for wear and correct air pressure, including spare tire

Inspect windshield wiper spray and wiper operation

Check windshield for cracks, chips and pitting

Inspect for oil and fluid leaks

Inspect air filter

Inspect halfshaft dust boots

Check shocks struts and other suspension components for leaks and damage

Inspect steering linkage

Inspect accesory drive belts

Inspect clutck operation (if equipped)

When operating in dusty conditions such as unpaved or dusty roads:

Change engine oil and install a new oil filter every 4,800 km (3,000 miles) or 3 months.

Install a new fuel filter every 24,000 km (15,000 miles).

Change automatic transmission fluid every 48,000 km (30,000 miles).

Change transfer case fluid every 96,000 km (60,000 miles).

Install a new engine air filter as required.

Install a new cabin air filter as required.

When operating in off-road conditions:

Change automatic transmission fluid every 48,000 km (30,000 miles).

Change transfer case fluid every 96,000 km (60,000 miles).

Install a new cabin air filter as required.

Inspect and lubricate U-joints.

Inspect and lubricate steering linkage ball joints with zerk fittings.

Special Operating Condition Requirements

When towing a trailer or using a camper or car-top carrier:

Change engine oil and install a new oil filter every 8,000 km (5,000 miles) or 3 months.

Change automatic transmission fluid every 48,000 km (30,000 miles). (not required on 6R60/6R75 transmissions).

Inspect and rotate tires 8,000 km (5,000 miles)

Change transfer case fluid every 96,000 km (60,000 miles).

Change manual transmission fluid as required.

Inspect and lubricate U-joints and half shafts as required.

During extensive idling and/or low speed driving for long distances, as in heavy commercial use such as delivery, taxi, patrol car or livery:

Change engine oil and install a new oil filter, lube front lower control arm and steering linkage ball joints with

zerk fittings (if equipped) every 8,000 km (5,000 miles) or 3 months.

Inspect brake system and check battery electrolyte level (Patrol cars) every 8,000 km (5,000 miles).

Install a new fuel filter every 24,000 km (15,000 miles).

Change automatic transmission fluid, lubricate 4x2 wheel bearings,

Lubricate rear wheel drive (RWD) front wheel bearings, install new grease seals and adjust every 48,000 km (30,000 miles).

Install new spark plugs and change transfer case fluid every 96,000 km (60,000 miles).

Install a new cabin air filter as required.

PRECAUTIONS

Before servicing any vehicle, please be sure to read all of the following precautions, which deal with personal safety, prevention of component damage, and important points to take into consideration when servicing a motor vehicle:

• Never open, service or drain the radiator or cooling system when the engine is hot; serious burns can occur from the steam and hot coolant.

• Observe all applicable safety precautions when working around fuel. Whenever servicing the fuel system, always work in a well-ventilated area. Do not allow fuel spray or vapors to come in contact with a spark, open flame, or excessive heat (a hot drop light, for example). Keep a dry chemical fire extinguisher near the work area. Always keep fuel in a container specifically designed for fuel storage; also, always properly seal fuel containers to avoid the possibility of fire or explosion. Refer to the additional fuel system precautions later in this section.

• Fuel injection systems often remain pressurized, even after the engine has been turned **OFF**. The fuel system pressure must be relieved before disconnecting any fuel lines. Failure to do so may result in fire and/or personal injury.

• Brake fluid often contains polyglycol ethers and polyglycols. Avoid contact with the eyes and wash your hands thoroughly after handling brake fluid. If you do get brake fluid in your eyes, flush your eyes with clean, running water for 15 minutes. If eye irritation persists, or if you have taken brake fluid internally, IMMEDIATELY seek medical assistance.

• The EPA warns that prolonged contact with used engine oil may cause a number of skin disorders, including cancer. You should make every effort to minimize your exposure to used engine oil. Protective gloves should be worn when changing oil. Wash your hands and any other exposed skin areas as soon as possible after exposure to used engine oil. Soap and water, or waterless hand cleaner should be used.

• All new vehicles are now equipped with an air bag system, often referred to as a Supplemental Restraint System (SRS) or Supplemental Inflatable Restraint (SIR) system. The system must be disabled before performing service on or around system components, steering column, instrument panel components, wiring and sensors. Failure to follow safety and disabling procedures could result in accidental air bag deployment, possible personal injury and unnecessary system repairs.

• Always wear safety goggles when working with, or around, the air bag system. When carrying a non-deployed air bag, be sure the bag and trim cover are pointed away from your body. When placing a non-deployed air bag on a work surface, always face the bag and trim cover upward, away from the surface. This will reduce the motion of the module if it is accidentally deployed. Refer to the additional air bag system precautions later in this section.

• Clean, high quality brake fluid from a sealed container is essential to the safe and proper operation of the brake system. You should always buy the correct type of brake fluid for your vehicle. If the brake fluid becomes contaminated, completely flush the system with new fluid. Never reuse any brake fluid. Any brake fluid that is removed from the system should be discarded. Also, do not allow any brake fluid to come in contact with a painted surface; it will damage the paint.

• Never operate the engine without the proper amount and type of engine oil; doing so WILL result in severe engine damage.

• Timing belt maintenance is extremely important. Many models utilize an interference-type, non-freewheeling engine. If the timing belt breaks, the valves in the cylinder head may strike the pistons, causing potentially serious (also time-consuming and expensive) engine damage. Refer to the maintenance interval charts for the recommended replacement interval for the timing belt, and to the timing belt section for belt replacement and inspection.

• Disconnecting the negative battery cable on some vehicles may interfere with the functions of the on-board computer system(s) and may require the computer to undergo a relearning process once the negative battery cable is reconnected.

• When servicing drum brakes, only disassemble and assemble one side at a time, leaving the remaining side intact for reference.

• Only an MVAC-trained, EPA-certified automotive technician should service the air conditioning system or its components.

BRAKES

GENERAL INFORMATION

The Anti-lock Brake System (ABS) module simultaneously manages the anti-lock braking, traction control and engine control systems to maintain vehicle control during deceleration and acceleration.

When the ignition switch is in the **RUN** position, the module carries out a preliminary electrical check and, at approximately 12 mph (20 km/h), the hydraulic pump motor is turned on for approximately one half-second. Any malfunction of the anti-lock brake system disables the traction control and stability assist (if equipped) and the anti-lock brake warning indicator illuminates. However, the power-assist braking system functions normally.

The Anti-lock Brake System (ABS) consists of the following components:
• Hydraulic Control Unit (HCU)
• ABS control module
• Rear anti-lock brake sensor
• Rear anti-lock brake sensor indicator
• Front anti-lock brake sensor
• Front anti-lock brake sensor indicator
• Yellow ABS warning indicator
• Red brake warning indicator

SPEED SENSORS

REMOVAL & INSTALLATION

Front

See Figure 1.

1. Raise and safely support the vehicle.

ANTI-LOCK BRAKE SYSTEM (ABS)

➡The harness connector is located in the engine compartment.

2. Disconnect the electrical connector.

❋❋ WARNING

Care must be taken during the removal of the plug to prevent damage. If the plug is damaged, a new sensor may need to be installed, even though the sensor is functional in all other aspects.

3. Remove the grommet from the body.

4. When removing the body plug, rotate the plug into a position which allows the use of a small screwdriver to release the tabs on the underside of the body plug. These 2 tabs are located at right angles to the sensor wire.

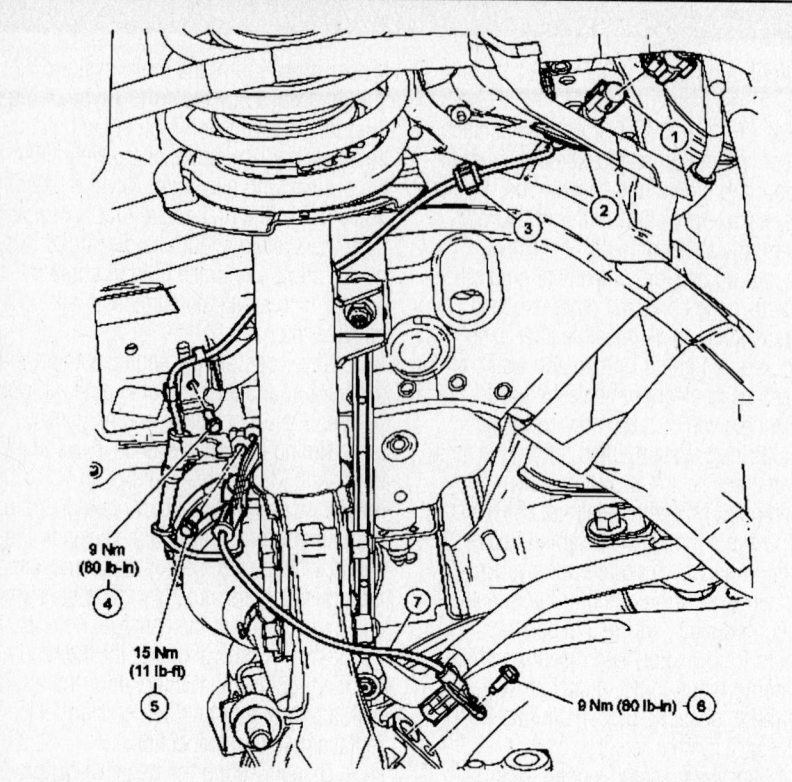

Fig. 1 View of the front wheel speed sensor wire connector (1), grommet (2), front wheel speed sensor wire retainer (3), front wheel speed sensor wire-to-body bolts (4), front wheel speed sensor bolts (5, 6) and front wheel speed sensor (7)

5. Remove the front wheel speed sensor wire from the retainer.

6. Remove the front wheel speed sensor wire-to-body bolt.

7. Remove the front wheel speed sensor wire bolt.

8. Remove the front wheel speed sensor bolt from the wheel knuckle.

➡Clean off any foreign material that may have collected around the sensor before removal.

9. Remove the front wheel speed sensor.

➡Thoroughly clean the mounting surface.

10. Installation is the reverse of the removal procedure, noting the following tightening specifications:

   a. Front wheel speed sensor-to-knuckle bolt: 80 inch lbs. (9 Nm)

   b. Front wheel speed sensor wire bolt: 11 ft. lbs. (15 Nm)

   c. Front wheel speed sensor wire-to-body bolt: 80 inch lbs. (9 Nm)

Rear

1. Remove the wheel and tire.

✳✳ WARNING

Care must be taken during the removal of the plug to prevent damage. If the plug is damaged, a new sensor may need to be installed even though the sensor is functional in all other aspects.

2. Remove the grommet from the body.

3. When removing the body plug, rotate the plug into a position which allows the use of a small screwdriver to release the tabs on the underside of the body plug. These 2 tabs are located at right angles to the sensor wire.

4. Disconnect the sensor wiring.

5. Detach the sensor wiring bolts.

➡Clean off any dirt that may have collected around the sensor before removal.

6. Remove the bolt and the sensor.

➡Thoroughly clean the mounting surface.

7. Installation is the reverse of the removal procedure. Tighten all retainers to 80 inch lbs. (9 Nm).

BRAKES

BLEEDING PROCEDURE

BLEEDING PROCEDURE

• Use of any other than the approved DOT 3 brake fluid will cause permanent damage to brake components and will render the brakes inoperative. Failure to follow these instructions may result in personal injury.

• Brake fluid contains polyglycol ethers and polyglycols. Avoid contact with eyes. Wash hands thoroughly after handling. If brake fluid contacts eyes, flush eyes with running water for 15 minutes. Get medical attention if irritation persists. If taken internally, drink water and induce vomiting. Get medical attention immediately. Failure to follow these instructions may result in personal injury.

• Do not allow the brake master cylinder reservoir to run dry during the bleeding operation. Keep the master cylinder reservoir filled with the specified brake fluid. Never reuse the brake fluid that has been drained from the hydraulic system.

• Brake fluid is harmful to painted and plastic surfaces. If brake fluid is spilled onto a painted or plastic surface, immediately wash it with water.

• When any part of the hydraulic system has been disconnected or a new component is installed, air may enter the system, causing spongy brake pedal action. This requires the bleeding of the hydraulic system after it has been correctly connected.

BLEEDING THE BRAKE SYSTEM

Manual Bleeding

1. Before servicing the vehicle, refer to the Precautions Section.

✳✳ WARNING

Be sure to check the brake fluid level in the brake master cylinder reservoir often. Do not let it run dry.

2. Fill the brake master cylinder reservoir with the specified brake fluid.

3. Begin bleeding the system, going in order from the right rear wheel, to the left rear wheel, to the right front wheel, and ending with the left front wheel.

4. Attach a rubber drain hose to the rear bleeder screw and submerge the free end in a container partially filled with clean brake fluid.

5. Have an assistant pump the brake pedal 10 times and then hold firm pressure on the brake pedal.

6. Loosen the bleeder screw until the fluid flow stops. Maintain pressure on the brake pedal and tighten the bleeder screw.

7. Repeat Steps 4 and 5 until clear, bubble-free brake fluid flows.

8. Tighten the bleeder screw to 12 ft. lbs. (16 Nm).

9. Refill the brake master cylinder reservoir as necessary.

10. Continue bleeding the brake hydraulic system at each wheel.

11. Fill the brake master cylinder reservoir with the specified brake fluid.

ABS BLEEDING

➡ Bleeding the Hydraulic Control Unit (HCU) is required only when removing or installing the HCU or master cylinder, or opening the lines to the HCU.

➡ Carrying out the System Bleed function drives trapped air from the HCU. Subsequent bleeding removes the air from the brake hydraulic system through the bleeder screws.

➡ Adequate voltage to the HCU module is required during the anti-lock control portion of the system bleed.

1. Connect a suitable scan/diagnostic tool.

2. Access the SYSTEM BLEED FUNCTION. Go to the Tool Tab-Chassis-Braking-ABS Service Bleed and follow the directions on the diagnostic tool.

3. Manually bleed the brake hydraulic system. For additional information, refer to Manual Bleed in this section.

4. Repeat the procedure carrying out a total of two diagnostic tool cycles and two manual bleed cycles.

BRAKES

FRONT DISC BRAKES

✳✳ CAUTION

Dust and dirt accumulating on brake parts during normal use may contain asbestos fibers from production or aftermarket brake linings. Breathing excessive concentrations of asbestos fibers can cause serious bodily harm. Exercise care when servicing brake parts. Do not sand or grind brake lining unless equipment used is designed to contain the dust residue. Do not clean brake parts with compressed air or by dry brushing. Cleaning should be done by dampening the brake components with a fine mist of water, then wiping the brake components clean with a dampened cloth. Dispose of cloth and all residue containing asbestos fibers in an impermeable container with the appropriate label. Follow practices prescribed by the Occupational Safety and Health Administration (OSHA) and the Environmental Protection Agency (EPA) for the handling, processing, and disposing of dust or debris that may contain asbestos fibers.

BRAKE CALIPER

REMOVAL & INSTALLATION
See Figure 2.

1. Before servicing the vehicle, refer to the Precautions Section.

2. Remove the wheel and tire assembly.

3. Remove the brake caliper clip.

4. Remove the brake caliper dust boot caps.

5. Remove the brake caliper guide bolts.

6. Remove the brake caliper.

✳✳ CAUTION

Do not allow the brake caliper to hang by the flexible brake hose.

7. Remove the disc brake pads.

8. Remove the brake caliper jounce hose. Loosen the jounce hose fitting prior to removing the brake caliper.

To install:

9. To install, reverse the removal procedure.

10. Torque the caliper pin bolts to 26 ft. lbs. (35 Nm) on disc/drum systems; 33 ft. lbs. (45 Nm) on 4-wheel disc systems.

11. If the hydraulic system was opened, bleed the brake system.

➡ Thread the brake caliper jounce hose onto the brake caliper before installing the brake caliper.

➡ Make sure that the brake caliper jounce hose is not twisted.

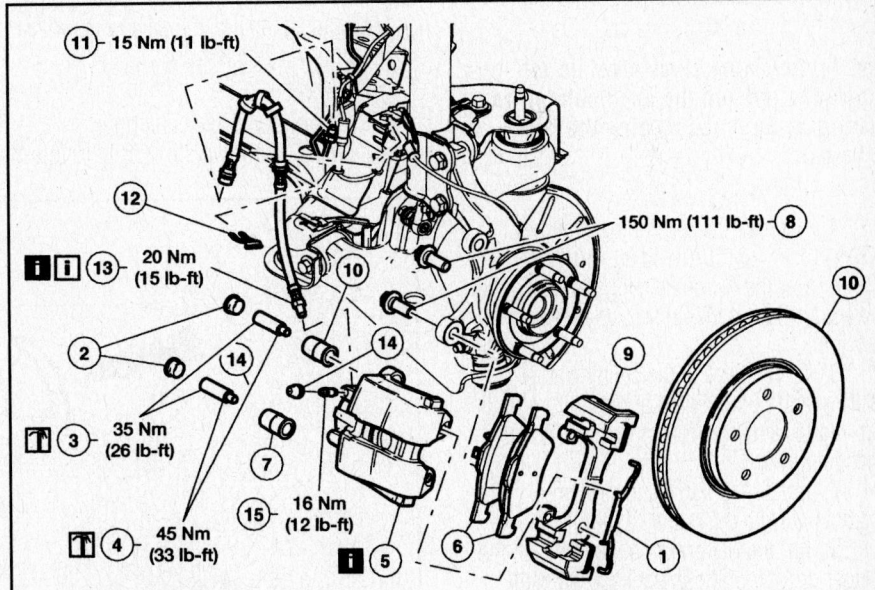

1 Brake caliper clip	9 Brake caliper anchor plate
2 Brake caliper dust boot caps	10 Brake disc
3 Brake caliper guide bolts (disc-drum system)	11 Brake line fitting nut
4 Brake caliper guide bolts (4-wheel disc brake system)	12 Brake caliper jounce hose retaining clip
5 Brake caliper (RH/LH)	13 Brake caliper jounce hose
6 Disc brake pads (kit)	14 Bleeder screw cap
7 Brake caliper dust boots	15 Bleeder screw
8 Brake caliper anchor plate bolts	

67197-ESCA-G49

Fig. 2 Front caliper installation—2005 model shown

12. Position the brake caliper to the anchor plate and tighten the brake caliper jounce hose.

DISC BRAKE PADS

REMOVAL AND INSTALLATION

2005–07 Models

1. Before servicing the vehicle, refer to the Precautions Section.
2. Remove the wheel and tire assembly.
3. Remove the brake caliper clip.
4. Position the caliper aside.
5. Remove brake caliper bolt caps and the bolts.
6. Position the caliper aside and support.
7. Remove the brake pads.
8. Remove the outer brake pad from the anchor.
9. Remove the inner brake pad from the caliper piston.
10. To install, reverse the removal procedure.

2008 Models

See Figures 3 and 4.

1. Before servicing the vehicle, refer to the Precautions Section.
2. With the vehicle in NEUTRAL, position it on a hoist.

➡**The following steps must be followed to prevent the accumulator from charging and pressurizing the brake system.**

3. Disconnect the battery.
4. Remove the battery junction box (BJB) fuses 24 (50A) and 31 (50A).
5. For the LH brake caliper, release the lower portion of the brake pad anti-rattle spring.
6. Apply force to the center of the spring and pull outward at the bottom of the spring to remove it from the lower brake caliper cavity.
7. Rotate the spring upward and remove it from the brake caliper.
8. For the RH brake caliper, release the upper portion of the brake pad anti-rattle spring.
9. Apply force to the center of the spring and pull outward at the top of the spring to remove it from the upper brake caliper cavity.
10. Rotate the spring downward and remove it from the brake caliper.
11. Remove the 2 guide pin bushing caps and the 2 brake caliper guide pin bolts, position the caliper aside.

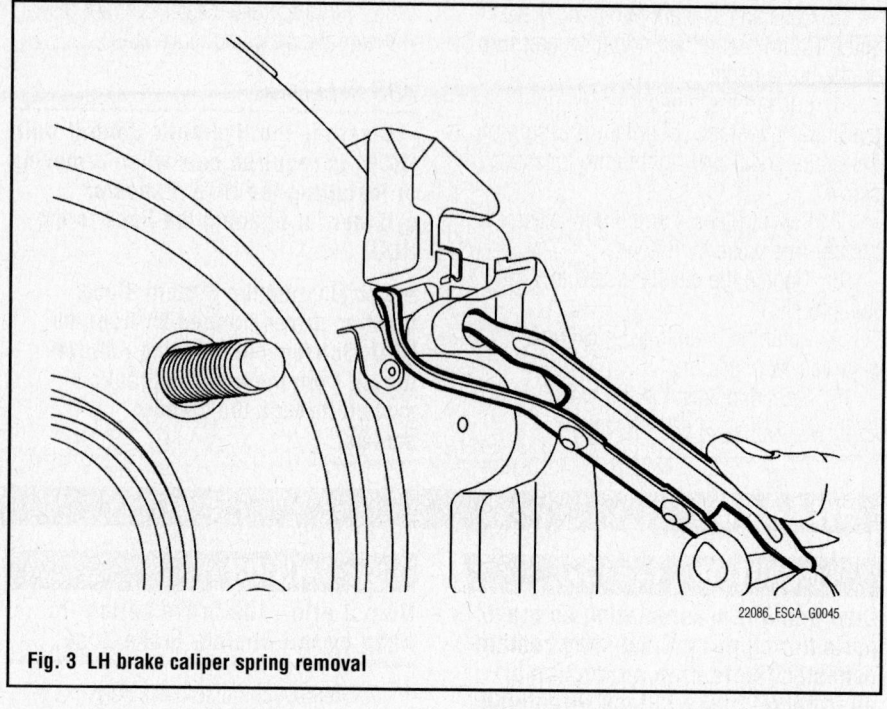

Fig. 3 LH brake caliper spring removal

22086_ESCA_G0045

12. Support the caliper using mechanic's wire.
13. Remove the 2 brake pads from the caliper.
14. Use a suitable tool to protect the brake caliper piston and compress the brake caliper piston into the brake caliper.
15. Inspect the brake disc and resurface or install new as necessary

To install:

16. Clean, dry and inspect the brake caliper anchor plate. Apply a light coat of specified lubricant to the 4 brake pad

➡**Make sure that the brake flexible hose is not twisted.**

17. Install the brake pads onto the caliper and position the brake caliper onto the anchor plate.
18. Install the 2 brake caliper guide pin bolts and tighten to 26 ft. lbs. (35 Nm) install the 2 bushing caps.

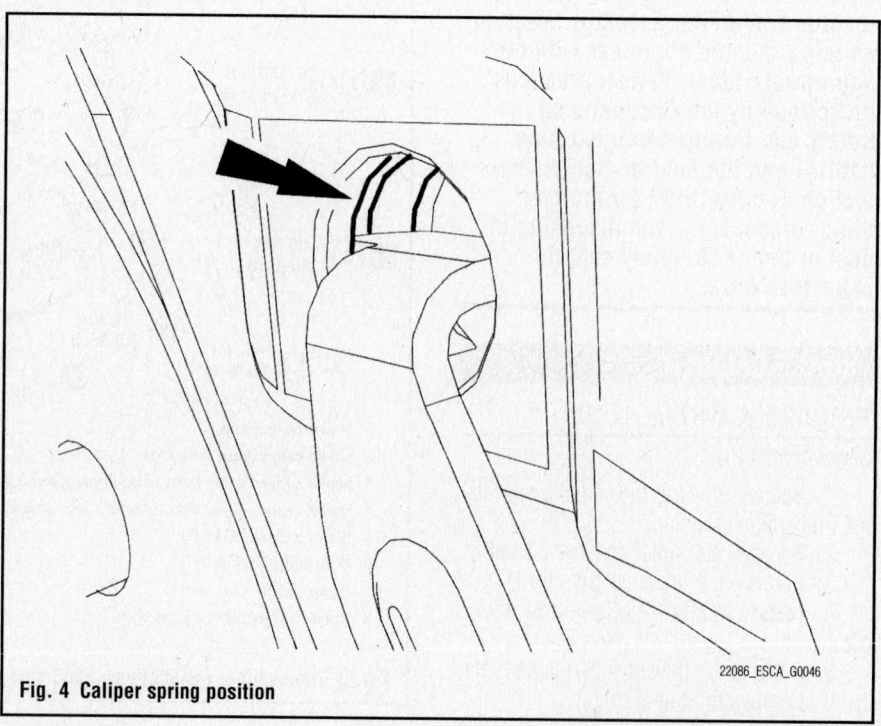

Fig. 4 Caliper spring position

22086_ESCA_G0046

➥ The 2-tabbed end of the brake pad anti-rattle spring must be installed first.

19. Install the brake pad anti-rattle spring using the following procedure:
- Insert the tab of the spring into the brake caliper cavity.
- Twist the tab into the cavity (LH side in the upper brake caliper cavity, RH side in the lower brake caliper cavity).
- Rotate the brake pad anti-rattle spring and position the upper portion onto the anchor plate.

- Position the lower portion of the brake pad anti-rattle spring onto the anchor plate.
- Push down and inward until the upper and lower ends of the brake pad anti-rattle spring are latched and seated in the brake caliper cavities.

✱✱ WARNING

The latch MUST be positioned as shown, or damage to component may occur.

➥ Verify that the brake pad anti-rattle spring is correctly latched by pulling on the spring.

20. Install the wheel and tire.
21. Install the battery junction box (BJB) fuses 24 (50A) and 31 (50A).
22. Connect the battery.
23. Fill the brake master cylinder reservoir with clean, specified brake fluid.
24. Test the brakes for normal operation.

BRAKES

REAR DISC BRAKES

✱✱ CAUTION

Dust and dirt accumulating on brake parts during normal use may contain asbestos fibers from production or aftermarket brake linings. Breathing excessive concentrations of asbestos fibers can cause serious bodily harm. Exercise care when servicing brake parts. Do not sand or grind brake lining unless equipment used is designed to contain the dust residue. Do not clean brake parts with compressed air or by dry brushing. Cleaning should be done by dampening the brake components with a fine mist of water, then wiping the brake components clean with a dampened cloth. Dispose of cloth and all residue containing asbestos fibers in an impermeable container with the appropriate label. Follow practices prescribed by the Occupational Safety and Health Administration (OSHA) and the Environmental Protection Agency (EPA) for the handling, processing, and disposing of dust or debris that may contain asbestos fibers.

BRAKE CALIPER

REMOVAL & INSTALLATION
See Figure 5.

1. Before servicing the vehicle, refer to the Precautions Section.
2. Remove the wheel and tire assembly.
3. Remove the brake caliper guide bolts.
4. Remove the caliper.

✱✱ CAUTION

Do not allow the brake caliper to hang by the flexible brake hose.

5. Remove the brake disc pads.
6. Remove the brake caliper hose flow bolt.
7. Remove and discard the copper washers.
8. To install, reverse the removal procedure. Use new copper washers. Torque the caliper pin bolts to 26 ft. lbs. (35 Nm); torque the flow bolt to 26 ft. lbs. (35 Nm).

9. If the hydraulic system was opened, bleed the brake system.

DISC BRAKE PADS

REMOVAL & INSTALLATION

1. Before servicing the vehicle, refer to the Precautions Section.

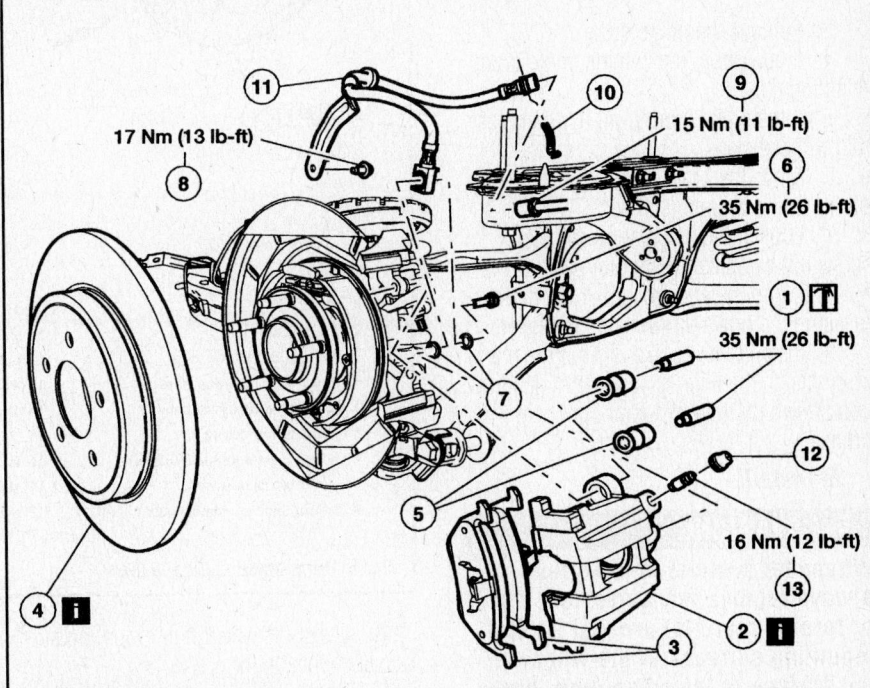

1 Brake caliper guide bolts	8 Brake caliper jounce hose bracket bolt
2 Caliper (RH/LH)	9 Brake line fitting nut
3 Brake disc pads	10 Brake caliper jounce hose retaining clip
4 Brake disc	11 Jounce hose (RH/LH)
5 Brake caliper guide bolt	12 Bleeder screw cap
6 Brake caliper hose flow bolt	13 Bleeder screw
7 Copper washers	

67197-ESCA-G50

Fig. 5 Rear caliper installation—2005 model shown

2. Remove the wheel and tire assembly.

3. Remove the brake caliper guide bolts.

4. Remove the caliper.

BRAKES

BRAKE DRUM

REMOVAL & INSTALLATION

See Figure 6.

1. Before servicing the vehicle, refer to the Precautions Section.

2. Remove the tire and wheel assembly.

✳✳ CAUTION

Use of a brake drum puller or a torch is not recommended. Brake drum distortion can result.

➡ If the brake drum is rusted to the axle shaft pilot diameter, tap the center of the brake drum between the wheel studs.

3. Remove the brake drum.

4. If equipped, remove the brake drum retaining clips.

5. If the brake drums will not come off, follow these steps.

6. Move the brake shoe adjusting lever off the brake adjuster screw.

7. Loosen the brake shoe adjuster screw nut by adjusting the nut upward.

8. Using the special tool, 134-R0191, measure the brake drum inside diameter.

9. Install a new brake drum if the maximum inside diameter exceeds the specification shown on the outside of the brake drum.

To install:

✳✳ WARNING

Whenever a wheel is installed, always remove any corrosion, dirt or foreign material present on the mounting surfaces of the wheel or the surface of the wheel hub, brake drum or brake disc that contacts the wheel. Installing wheels without correct metal-to-metal contact at the wheel mounting surfaces can cause the wheel nuts to loosen and the wheel to come off while the vehicle is in motion, causing loss of control. Failure to follow these instructions may result in personal injury.

✳✳ CAUTION

Do not allow the brake caliper to hang by the flexible brake hose.

5. Remove the brake disc pads.

6. To install, reverse the removal procedure.

7. If the hydraulic system was opened, bleed the brake system.

REAR DRUM BRAKES

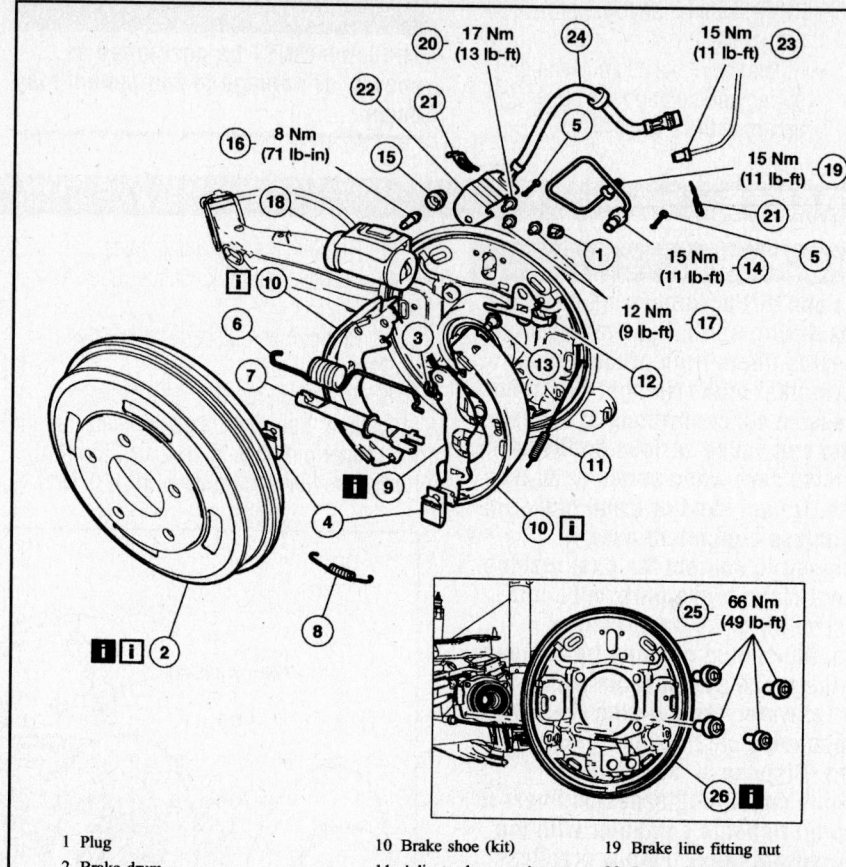

1 Plug	10 Brake shoe (kit)
2 Brake drum	11 Adjuster lever spring
3 Parking brake lever clip	12 Adjuster lever (LH/RH)
4 Brake shoe retaining clips	13 Pivot pin (part of 2200)
5 Brake shoe retaining pins	14 Brake line fitting nut
6 Upper return spring	15 Bleeder screw cap
7 Adjuster assembly (LH/RH)	16 Bleeder screw
8 Lower return spring	17 Wheel cylinder bolts
9 Parking brake actuator lever (LH/RH)	18 Wheel cylinder

19 Brake line fitting nut
20 Jounce hose bracket bolt
21 Jounce hose retaining clips
22 Jounce hose bracket
23 Brake line fitting nut
24 Jounce hose (LH/RH)
25 Backing plate bolts
26 Backing plate

67197-ESCA-G51

Fig. 6 Drum brake exploded view

10. Clean the wheel hub mounting surface and wheel pilot.

11. Install the tire and wheel assembly.

BRAKE SHOES

REMOVAL & INSTALLATION

1. Before servicing the vehicle, refer to the Precautions Section.

2. Remove the brake drum.

3. Use the Brake/Clutch/Service Vacuum to remove brake dust and dirt from the brake assemblies.

➡ If new rear brake shoes and linings are being installed, resurface the brake drums to remove glazing and to ensure an equal friction surface from side-to-side. Resurfacing will also correct out-of-round and bell conditions.

4. Using the special tool, measure the braking surface diameter. If the inside diameter measures more than the maximum specification shown on the outside of the brake drum, install a new brake drum.

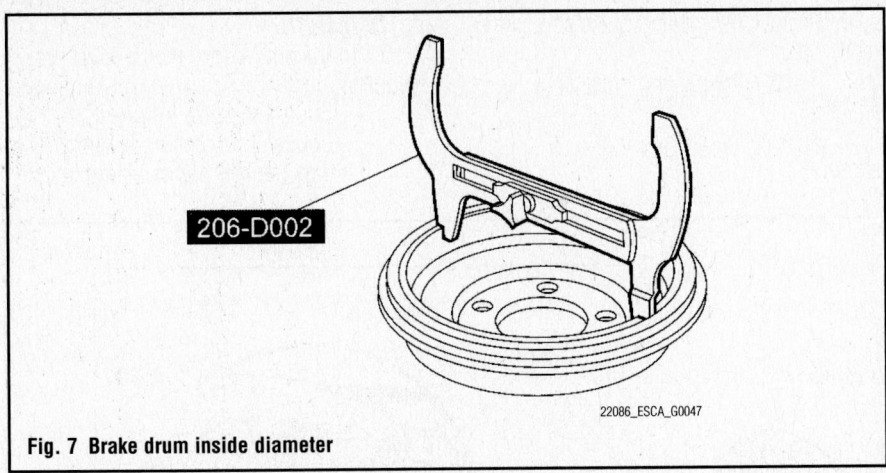

Fig. 7 Brake drum inside diameter

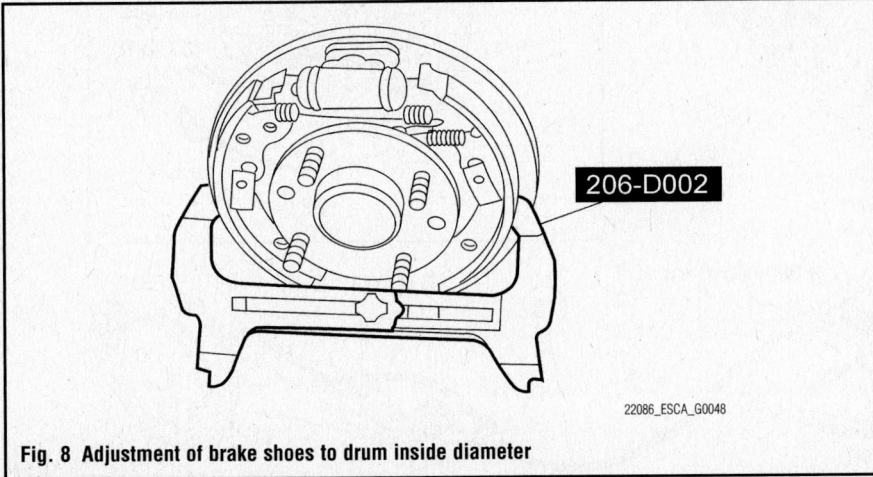

Fig. 8 Adjustment of brake shoes to drum inside diameter

5. Remove the parking brake cable from the parking brake cable lever.

6. Remove the hold-down clips and pins.

7. Remove the lower spring.

8. Remove the rear brake shoes.

9. Pull the bottom of the brake shoe forward.

10. Release the upper return spring.

11. Remove both brake shoes together.

12. Remove the self adjuster lever.

13. Remove the self adjuster and spring assembly.

14. Return the self adjuster to the fully seated position.

15. Remove the parking brake lever.

16. Remove the horseshoe clip.

17. Remove the parking brake lever.

18. Inspect the rear brake shoes for minimum thickness above the backing plate, and install new as necessary.

19. To install, reverse the removal procedure.

ADJUSTMENT

See Figures 7 and 8.

1. Remove the brake drum.

2. Using the special tool, 134-R0191, measure the brake drum inside diameter.

3. Position the special tool on the brake shoes and linings and adjust accordingly.

4. Install the brake drum

BRAKES

PARKING BRAKE CABLES

ADJUSTMENT

See Figure 9.

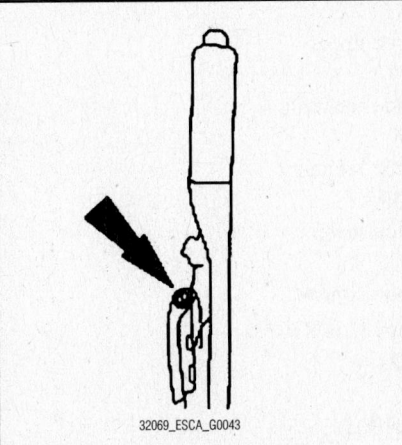

Fig. 9 Turn the parking brake control adjustment nut so that the parking brake control stroke is three to five notches when pulled

1. On vehicle with low series floor console:

   a. If equipped, remove the manual transmission shift knob by turning counterclockwise.

   b. Remove the floor console front finish panel.

   c. Apply the parking brake, then remove the floor console rear finish panel.

2. On vehicle with high series floor console:

   a. Apply the parking brake.

   b. Remove the floor console finish panel.

3. Remove the adjustment nut clip.

4. Turn the parking brake control adjustment nut so that the parking brake control stroke is three to five notches when pulled.

5. Confirm the parking brake is applied.

6. Install the adjustment nut clip.

7. On vehicles with high series floor console:

PARKING BRAKE

   a. Install the floor console rear finish panel.

8. On vehicles with low series floor console:

   a. Install the floor console rear finish panel.

   b. Install the floor console front finish panel. If equipped, install the manual transmission shifter knob by turning clockwise.

PARKING BRAKE SHOES

REMOVAL & INSTALLATION

With Rear Drum Brakes

The rear drum brake shoes serve as the parking brakes. Refer to the procedures under Rear Drum Brakes.

With Rear Disc Brakes

See Figure 10.

1. Before servicing the vehicle, refer to the Precautions Section.

2. Remove the rear brake disc.

3. Remove the parking brake shoe upper return spring.

4. Remove the 2 parking brake shoe retaining pins.

5. Remove the 2 parking brake shoe retaining springs.

6. Remove the parking brake shoe lower return spring.

7. Remove the parking brake shoe adjuster.

8. Remove the parking brake shoes.

To install:

9. To install, reverse the removal procedure.

• Using anti-seize lubricant, lubricate the parking brake shoe contact points before instal-

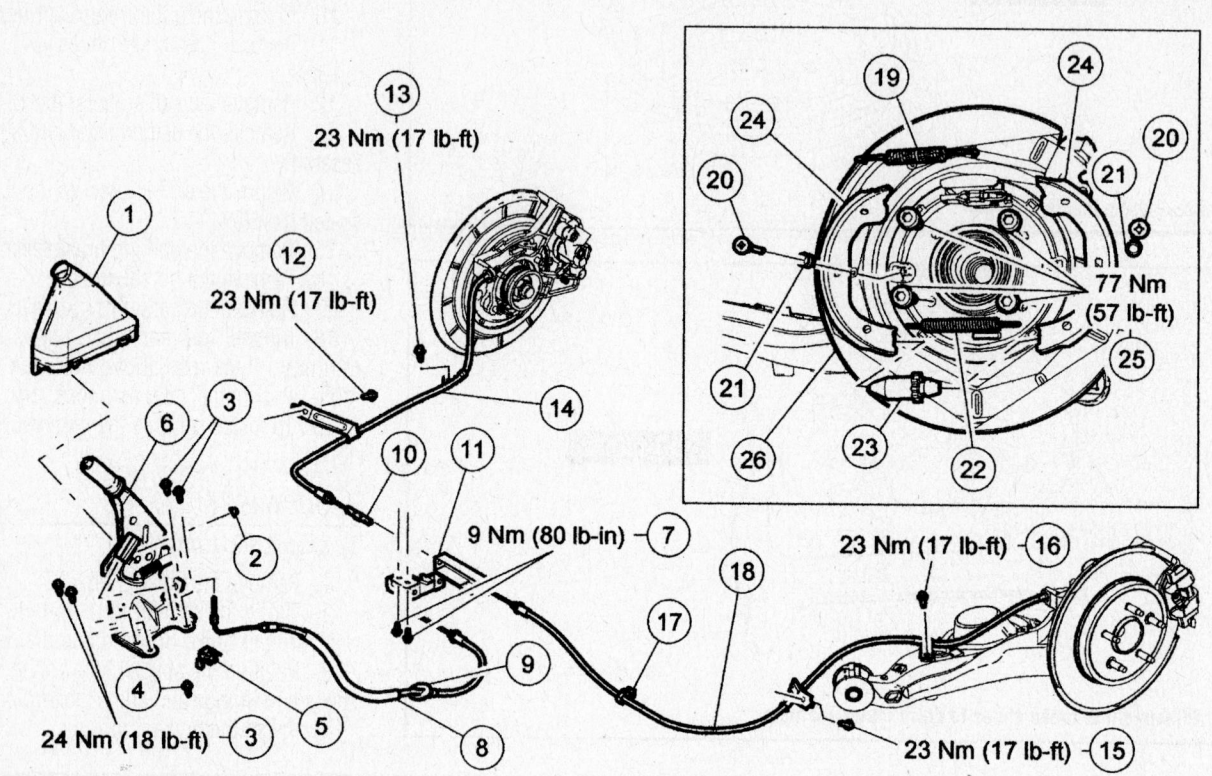

1 Parking brake control boot
2 Front cable adjuster nut
3 Parking brake control bolts (4 required)
4 Warning indicator switch screw
5 Warning indicator switch
6 Parking brake control
7 Parking brake equalizer bracket bolts (2 required)
8 Front parking brake cable
9 Grommet
10 Cable connector
11 Parking brake equalizer and bracket
12 Cable bracket-to-body bolt
13 Cable bracket-to-trailing arm bolt
14 Rear parking brake cable (RH)
15 Cable bracket-to-body bolt
16 Cable bracket-to-trailing arm bolt
17 Cable-to-fuel tank strap clip
18 Rear parking brake cable (LH)
19 Parking brake shoe upper return spring
20 Parking brake shoe retaining pins (2 required)
21 Parking brake shoe retaining springs (2 required)
22 Parking brake shoe lower return spring
23 Parking brake shoe adjuster
24 Parking brake shoe (LH/RH)
25 Support plate bolts (4 required)
26 Support plate (LH/RH)

06017-ESCA-G99

Fig. 10 Parking brake system—with rear disc brakes

lation of the rear parking brake shoes.
- Lubricate the adjust screw threads with anti-seize lubricant.
- Adjust the parking brake shoe and lining.
- Check the parking brake for normal operation.

ADJUSTMENT

See Figures 11 and 12.

1. Before servicing the vehicle, refer to the Precautions Section.
2. With the vehicle in NEUTRAL, position it on a hoist.

➡**Make sure the parking brake is fully released.**

3. Using the release handle, release the parking brake control.
4. Remove the rear brake disc.

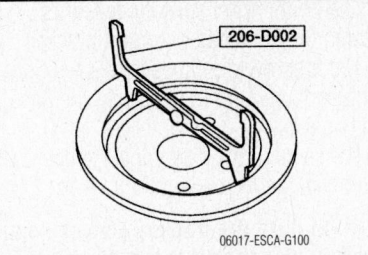

Fig. 11 Using the special tool, measure the inside diameter of the drum portion of the rear brake disc and set the locking screw

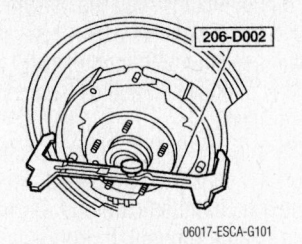

Fig. 12 Place the special tool over the widest diameter of the parking brake shoes

5. Using the special tool, measure the inside diameter of the drum portion of the rear brake disc and set the locking screw. Record the measurement.
6. Place the special tool over the widest diameter of the parking brake shoes.
7. Adjust the parking brake shoe clearance to 1.07 mm (0.04 in) less than the inside diameter of the drum portion of the rear brake disc. Rotate the parking brake shoe adjuster to achieve the correct parking brake shoe-to-brake disc clearance.
8. Install the rear brake disc.
9. Test the parking brake for normal operation.

CHASSIS ELECTRICAL   AIR BAG (SUPPLEMENTAL RESTRAINT SYSTEM)

GENERAL INFORMATION

✳✳ CAUTION

These vehicles are equipped with an air bag system. The system must be disarmed before performing service on, or around, system components, the steering column, instrument panel components, wiring and sensors. Failure to follow the safety precautions and the disarming procedure could result in accidental air bag deployment, possible injury and unnecessary system repairs.

SERVICE PRECAUTIONS

Disconnect and isolate the battery negative cable before beginning any airbag system component diagnosis, testing, removal, or installation procedures. Allow system capacitor to discharge for two minutes before beginning any component service. This will disable the airbag system. Failure to disable the airbag system may result in accidental airbag deployment, personal injury, or death.

Do not place an intact undeployed airbag face down on a solid surface. The airbag will propel into the air if accidentally deployed and may result in personal injury or death.

When carrying or handling an undeployed airbag, the trim side (face) of the airbag should be pointing towards the body to minimize possibility of injury if accidental deployment occurs. Failure to do this may result in personal injury or death.

Replace airbag system components with OEM replacement parts. Substitute parts may appear interchangeable, but internal differences may result in inferior occupant protection. Failure to do so may result in occupant personal injury or death.

Wear safety glasses, rubber gloves, and long sleeved clothing when cleaning powder residue from vehicle after an airbag deployment. Powder residue emitted from a deployed airbag can cause skin irritation. Flush affected area with cool water if irritation is experienced. If nasal or throat irritation is experienced, exit the vehicle for fresh air until the irritation ceases. If irritation continues, see a physician.

Do not use a replacement airbag that is not in the original packaging. This may result in improper deployment, personal injury, or death.

The factory installed fasteners, screws and bolts used to fasten airbag components have a special coating and are specifically designed for the airbag system. Do not use substitute fasteners. Use only original equipment fasteners listed in the parts catalog when fastener replacement is required.

During, and following, any child restraint anchor service, due to impact event or vehicle repair, carefully inspect all mounting hardware, tether straps, and anchors for proper installation, operation, or damage. If a child restraint anchor is found damaged in any way, the anchor must be replaced. Failure to do this may result in personal injury or death.

Deployed and non-deployed airbags may or may not have live pyrotechnic material within the airbag inflator.

Do not dispose of driver/passenger/curtain airbags or seat belt tensioners unless you are sure of complete deployment. Refer to the Hazardous Substance Control System for proper disposal.

Dispose of deployed airbags and tensioners consistent with state, provincial, local, and federal regulations.

After any airbag component testing or service, do not connect the battery negative cable. Personal injury or death may result if the system test is not performed first.

If the vehicle is equipped with the Occupant Classification System (OCS), do not connect the battery negative cable before performing the OCS Verification Test using the scan tool and the appropriate diagnostic information. Personal injury or death may result if the system test is not performed properly.

Never replace both the Occupant Restraint Controller (ORC) and the Occupant Classification Module (OCM) at the same time. If both require replacement, replace one, then perform the Airbag System test before replacing the other.

Both the ORC and the OCM store Occupant Classification System (OCS) calibration data, which they transfer to one another when one of them is replaced. If both are replaced at the same time, an irreversible fault will be set in both modules and the OCS may malfunction and cause personal injury or death.

If equipped with OCS, the Seat Weight Sensor is a sensitive, calibrated unit and must be handled carefully. Do not drop or handle roughly. If dropped or damaged, replace with another sensor. Failure to do so may result in occupant injury or death.

If equipped with OCS, the front passenger seat must be handled carefully as well. When removing the seat, be careful when setting on floor not to drop. If dropped, the sensor may be inoperative, could result in occupant injury, or possibly death.

If equipped with OCS, when the passenger front seat is on the floor, no one should sit in the front passenger seat. This uneven force may damage the sensing ability of the seat weight sensors. If sat on and damaged, the sensor may be inoperative, could result in occupant injury, or possibly death.

DISARMING THE SYSTEM

1. Before servicing the vehicle, refer to the Precautions Section.
2. Turn all vehicle accessories OFF.
3. Turn the ignition switch to OFF.
4. At the central junction box (CJB), located below the left side of the instrument panel, remove the cover and the restraints control module (RCM) fuse(s) from the CJB. See the Owner's Manual.
5. Turn the ignition ON and visually monitor the air bag indicator for at least 30 seconds. The air bag indicator will remain lit continuously (no flashing) if the correct RCM fuse has been removed. If the air bag indicator does not remain lit continuously, remove the correct RCM fuse before proceeding.
6. Turn the ignition OFF.

※※ CAUTION

To avoid accidental deployment and possible personal injury, the backup power supply must be depleted before repairing or replacing any front or side air bag Supplemental Restraint System (SRS) components and before servicing, replacing, adjusting or striking components near the front or side air bag sensors, such as doors, instrument panel, console, door latches, strikers, seats and hood latches.

The front impact severity sensor is located on the radiator support bracket.

The first row side impact sensors (if equipped) are located at or near the base of the B-pillars.

The second row side impact sensors (if equipped) are located on the C-pillar.

➡**To deplete the backup power supply energy, disconnect the battery ground cable and wait at least one minute. Be sure to disconnect auxiliary batteries and power supplies (if equipped).**

7. Disconnect the battery ground cable and wait at least one minute

ARMING THE SYSTEM

1. Before servicing the vehicle, refer to the Precautions Section.

※※ CAUTION

The restraint system diagnostic tool is for restraint system service only. Remove from vehicle prior to road use. Failure to remove could result in injury and possible violation of vehicle safety standards.

2. Make sure all restraint system diagnostic tool(s) that may have been installed during the repair have been removed from the vehicle and all SRS components are connected.
3. Turn the ignition switch from OFF to ON.
4. Install RCM fuse(s) to the CJB and close the cover.

※※ CAUTION

Be sure that nobody is in the vehicle and that there is nothing blocking or set in front of any air bag module when the battery ground cable is connected.

5. Connect the battery ground cable.
6. Prove out the Supplemental Restraint System (SRS) as follows:
   a. Turn the ignition key from ON to OFF. Wait 10 seconds, then turn the key back to ON and visually monitor the air bag indicator with the air bag modules installed. The air bag indicator will light continuously for approximately six seconds and then turn off. If an air bag Supplemental Restraint System (SRS) fault is present, the air bag indicator will either:
   • fail to light.
   • remain lit continuously.
   • flash.

   b. The flashing might not occur until approximately 30 seconds after the ignition switch has been turned from the OFF to the ON position. This is the time required for the restraints control module (RCM) to complete the testing of the SRS. If the air bag indicator is inoperative and a SRS fault exists, a chime will sound in a pattern of five sets of five beeps. If this occurs, the air bag indicator and any SRS fault discovered must be diagnosed and repaired.
7. Clear all continuous DTCs from the restraints control module using a scan tool.

CLOCKSPRING CENTERING

See Figure 13.

1. Before servicing the vehicle, refer to the Precautions Section.

※※ CAUTION

Incorrect centralization may result in premature component failure. If in doubt when centralizing the clockspring, repeat the centralizing procedure. Failure to follow this instruction may result in personal injury.

➡**Make sure the road wheels are in the straight-ahead position.**

2. If the vehicle's clockspring has rotated out of center, follow these steps to center the clockspring.
   c. Hold the clockspring outer housing stationary.

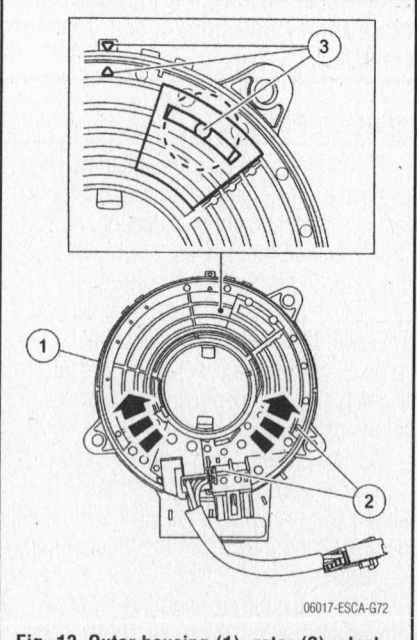

06017-ESCA-G72

Fig. 13 Outer housing (1), rotor (2), clockspring aligning

✳ WARNING

Overturning will destroy the clockspring. The internal ribbon wire acts as the stop and can be broken from its internal connection.

   d. While turning the rotor clockwise, carefully feel for the ribbon wire to run out of length and for a slight resistance. Stop turning at this point.

   e. Turn the clockspring counterclockwise until the yellow indicator shows anywhere in the window (window will be near the 1 o'clock position) and the arrow on the rotor lines up with the arrow on the top of the housing. The clockspring is now centered. Do not allow the rotor to turn from this position.

CLOCKSPRING REMOVAL & INSTALLATION

See Figures 14 through 17.

   1. Before servicing the vehicle, refer to the Precautions Section.

   2. Disarm the Supplemental Restraint System (SRS). Refer to the Chassis Electrical Section.

   3. Make sure the road wheels are in the straight-ahead position.

   4. Position the steering wheel in the straight-ahead position and remove the ignition key. Rotate the steering wheel until the steering column locks into position.

   5. Open the cover on the underside of the steering wheel.

   6. Remove the steering wheel pinion bolt.

   7. Remove the steering wheel. Position the steering wheel rearward. Disconnect the 2 electrical connectors.

   8. If equipped with tilt steering, position the steering column completely downward and lock in place.

   9. Push in where indicated, releasing the retaining tabs, and remove the upper steering column shroud.

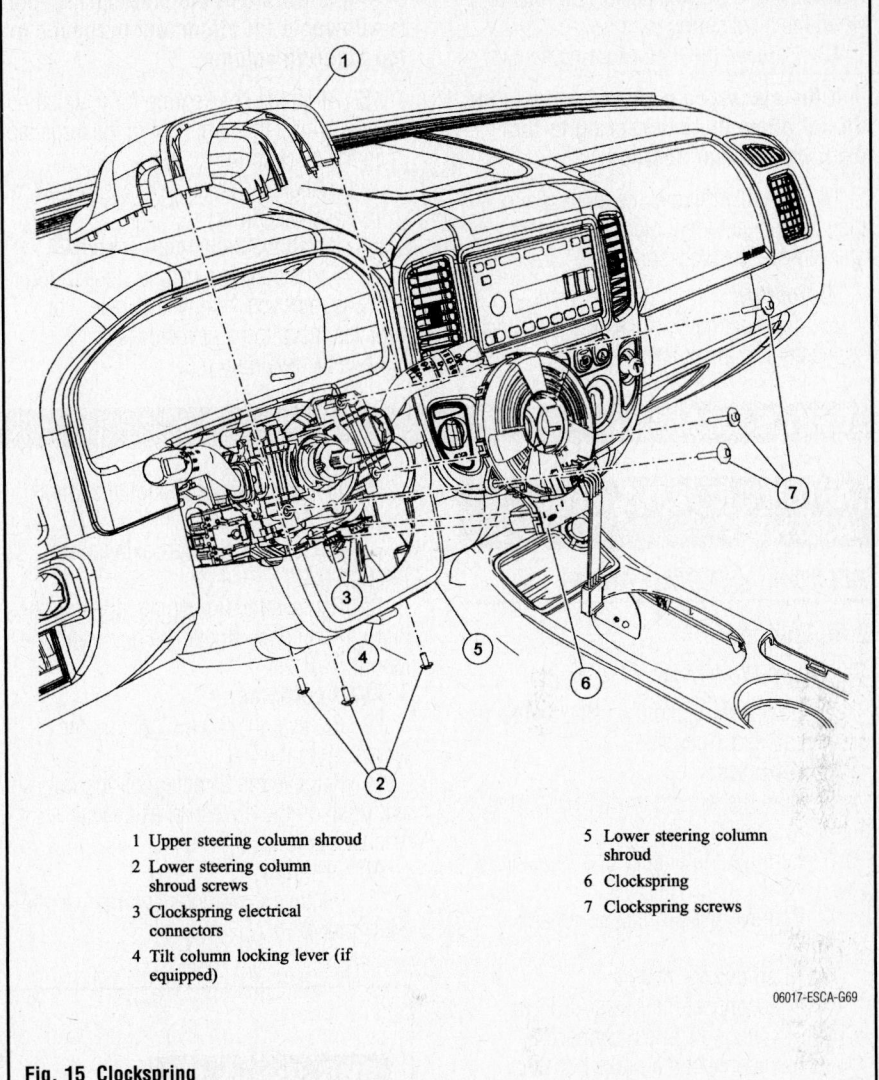

1 Upper steering column shroud
2 Lower steering column shroud screws
3 Clockspring electrical connectors
4 Tilt column locking lever (if equipped)
5 Lower steering column shroud
6 Clockspring
7 Clockspring screws

06017-ESCA-G69

Fig. 15 Clockspring

   10. Release the tilt column locking lever, allowing the steering column to move upward. Do not lock the tilt column locking lever back in place.

   11. Remove the 3 screws and position the lower steering column shroud aside.

   12. If installing the same clockspring, apply 2 strips of masking tape across the

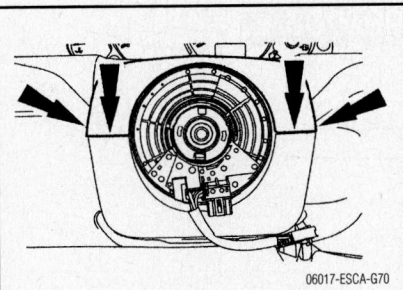

06017-ESCA-G70

Fig. 14 Push in where indicated, releasing the retaining tabs, and remove the upper steering column shroud

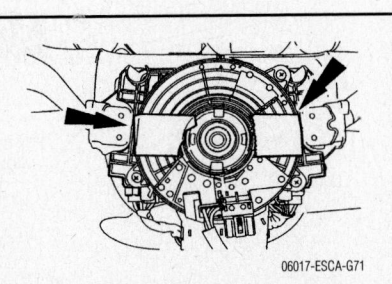

06017-ESCA-G71

Fig. 16 If installing the same clockspring, apply 2 strips of masking tape across the clockspring to prevent accidental rotation when the clockspring is removed

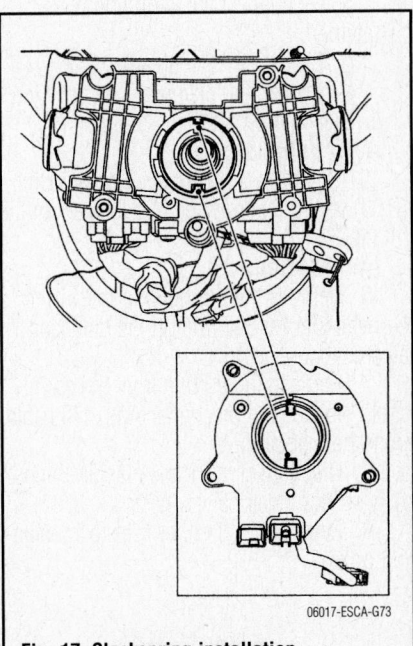

06017-ESCA-G73

Fig. 17 Clockspring installation

clockspring to prevent accidental rotation when the clockspring is removed.

13. Remove the 3 clockspring screws.

➡**If the clockspring is to be reinstalled, do not allow the clockspring to turn from its removal position.**

14. Partially remove the clockspring, then disconnect the 2 electrical connectors and remove the clockspring.

To install:

15. Connect the 2 clockspring electrical connectors to the clockspring.

➡**Slight turning of the clockspring rotor is allowable for alignment purposes to the steering column.**

16. Align the clockspring for installation.
  a. Align the large slot to the large tab in the clockspring.
  b. Align the small slot to the small tab in the clockspring.
17. Install the 3 clockspring screws.
18. For vehicles reusing a clockspring that was removed, remove the tape. For vehicles installing a new clockspring, remove the retaining pin.

19. Install the lower steering column shroud and the 3 screws.
20. Position the steering column completely downward and lock in place.
21. Install the upper steering column shroud and engage the retaining tabs.
22. Install the steering wheel. Torque the steering wheel pinion bolt to 9 ft. lbs. (12 Nm).
23. Rearm the Supplemental Restraint System (SRS).

DRIVE TRAIN

AUTOMATIC TRANSAXLE ASSEMBLY

REMOVAL & INSTALLATION

2.3L Engines

See Figures 18 through 21.

1. Before servicing the vehicle, refer to the Precautions Section.

All vehicles:

2. With the vehicle in NEUTRAL, position it on a hoist.
3. Remove the battery and the battery tray.
4. Remove the air cleaner as an assembly.
  a. Remove the bolt.
  b. Disconnect the Mass Air Flow (MAF) sensor electrical connector.
  c. Disconnect the brake booster vacuum hose.
  d. Disconnect the wiring harness retainer
  e. Disconnect the breather tube.
  f. Loosen the clamp and remove the air cleaner assembly.

AWD vehicles:

5. Disconnect the Power Transfer Unit (PTU) vent hose from the clip located on the fill tube

All vehicles:

6. Remove the nut holding the wiring harness bracket and unplug the bulkhead electrical connector.
7. Remove the 2 bolts from the shift cable bracket and disconnect the shift cable from the manual lever.
8. Disconnect the Transmission Range (TR) sensor electrical connector.
9. Remove the 3 upper transaxle retaining bolts.

10. Install the suitable engine support tools.
11. Remove the LH transaxle mount through bolt.
12. Remove the 2 nuts, the bolt and the through bolt and remove the rear transaxle mount.

AWD vehicles:

13. Remove the 6 bolts holding the driveshaft to the PTO.
14. Remove the 2 center bearing nuts and position the driveshaft aside with mechanic's wire

All vehicles:

15. Remove the 4 bolts and remove the cross brace.

16. Remove the 7 retainers and the LH splash shield.
17. Remove the 5 retainers and the RH splash shield.
18. Remove the bolt for the mount and the 2 bolts from the cross brace.
19. Remove and discard the nut and remove the cross brace.

➡**If transmission disassembly or installation of a new transmission is necessary, the transmission fluid will need to be drained.**

20. Remove the drain plug and drain the fluid.
21. Remove and discard the LH front axle wheel hub nut.

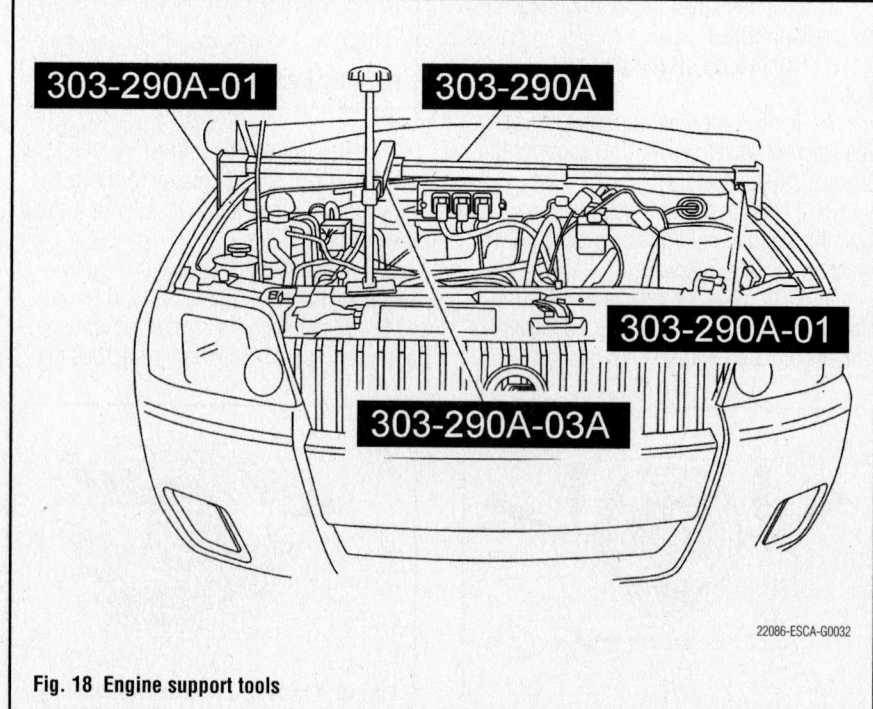

303-290A-01   303-290A

303-290A-01

303-290A-03A

22086-ESCA-G0032

Fig. 18 Engine support tools

22. Remove the frame bolt from the LH and RH control arms.

23. Using a suitable tool, separate the LH halfshaft from the front wheel knuckle.

24. Using a suitable tool, remove the LH halfshaft and disconnect the RH halfshaft from the intermediate shaft.

25. Remove the 2 intermediate shaft retaining nuts.

26. Remove the intermediate shaft.

27. Remove the 2 bolts which hold the exhaust bracket to the intermediate shaft bracket.

28. Remove the 2 nuts on the other end of the exhaust-to-intermediate shaft bracket and remove the bracket.

29. Remove the 3 nuts and separate the flexpipe from the exhaust manifold.

AWD vehicles:

30. Remove the 6 bolts holding the engine bracket to the PTU and remove the bracket.

31. Remove the 3 bolts and the PTU assembly.

Front wheel drive (FWD) vehicles:

32. Remove the 3 bolts and the dampener.

All vehicles:

33. Remove the 3 bolts holding the transaxle front mount plate.

34. Remove the fluid cooler line.

35. Remove the fluid cooler tube.

   a. Disconnect the Output Shaft Sensor (OSS) sensor electrical connector (black).

   b. Disconnect the Transmission Shaft Sensor (TSS) sensor electrical connector (white).

   c. Disconnect the wiring harness retainer from the transmission case and position the harness aside

   d. Remove the transmission fluid cooler line retaining bracket bolt.

   e. Remove the fluid cooler tube and position it aside.

36. Remove the OSS sensor.

37. Disconnect the starter terminals.

38. Remove the wire harness clip retainer and the ground wire from the starter bolts.

39. Remove the 3 bolts and remove the starter.

40. Remove the starter motor isolator.

41. Remove and discard the 4 torque converter nuts.

42. Using a suitable tool, lower the transmission.

43. Push the converter back from the flexplate. Use a suitable transmission jack to support the transaxle and remove the 3 rear bell housing bolts.

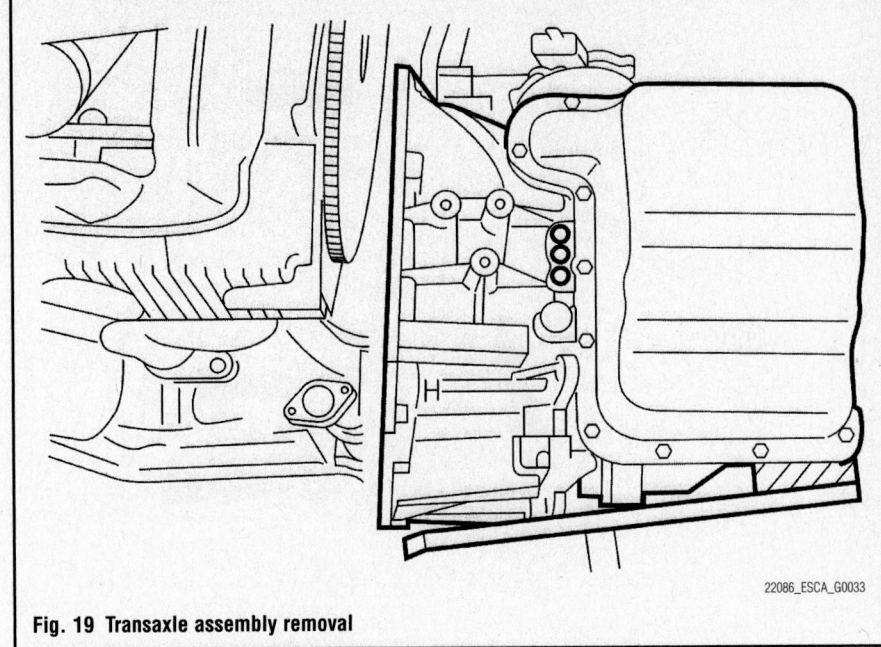

Fig. 19 Transaxle assembly removal

22086_ESCA_G0033

44. Remove the 4 remaining transaxle-to-engine bolts.

➡**The torque converter is heavy. Secure torque converter before lowering the transaxle.**

45. Lower the transaxle from the engine compartment.

To install:

❊❊ **WARNING**

Carry out the transmission fluid cooler back flushing and cleaning if the transaxle is being overhauled or installing a new or remanufactured transaxle. Carry out the transmission fluid cooler flow test if the transaxle is being overhauled or installing a new or remanufactured transaxle.

All vehicles:

46. Lubricate the torque converter pilot hub with grease.

47. Rotate the torque converter to place the paint dot in the 6 o'clock position.

48. Position the transaxle in place.

49. Move the transaxle assembly toward the engine assembly and install the 4 bolts.

50. Tighten the transaxle mounting bolts to 30 ft. lbs. (40 Nm).

51. Install the transaxle retaining bolts and tighten to 30 ft. lbs. (40 Nm).

52. Install 4 new torque converter nuts and tighten to 30 ft. lbs. (40 Nm).

53. Install the transmission fluid cooler tube and tighten to 17 ft. lbs. (23 Nm).

54. Install the OSS sensor and tighten to 9 ft. lbs. (12 Nm).

55. Install the fluid cooler tube.

   a. Connect the OSS sensor.

   b. Connect the TSS sensor (white connector).

   c. Connect the wiring harness retainer to the transmission case.

   d. Install the fluid cooler tube and tighten to 17 ft. lbs. (23 Nm).

   e. Install fluid cooler bolt and tighten to 10 ft. lbs. (13 Nm).

56. Install the starter motor isolator.

57. Install the starter motor and mounting bolts, tighten to 26 ft. lbs. (35 Nm).

58. Connect starter terminals and tighten nuts to 89 inch lbs. (10 Nm) for battery cable. And 62 inch lbs. (7 Nm). for solenoid wire nut.

59. Install the wire harness clip retainer and the ground wire to starter bolts.

60. Install the lower front mount bracket and tighten to 41 ft. lbs. (55 Nm).

61. Using a suitable tool, raise the transaxle.

62. Install the LH upper transaxle mount through bolt and tighten to 76 ft. lbs. (103 Nm).

63. Remove engine support tools.

64. Install the upper transaxle bolts and tighten to 30 ft. lbs. (40 Nm).

65. Connect the TR sensor electrical connector.

66. Connect the shift cable to the manual lever and install the 2 bolts then, tighten to 17 ft. lbs. (23 Nm).

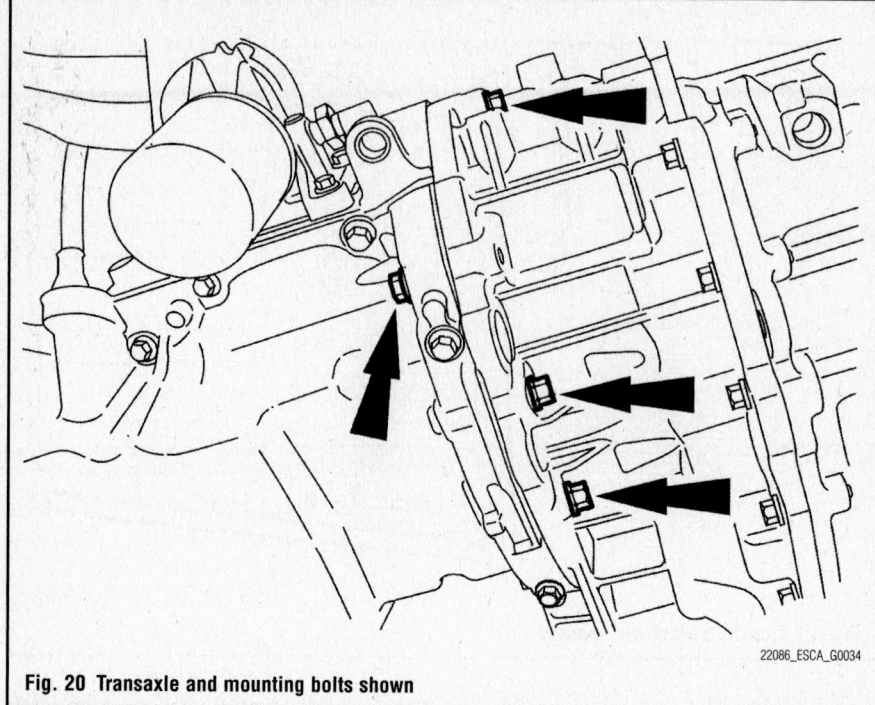

Fig. 20 Transaxle and mounting bolts shown

22086_ESCA_G0034

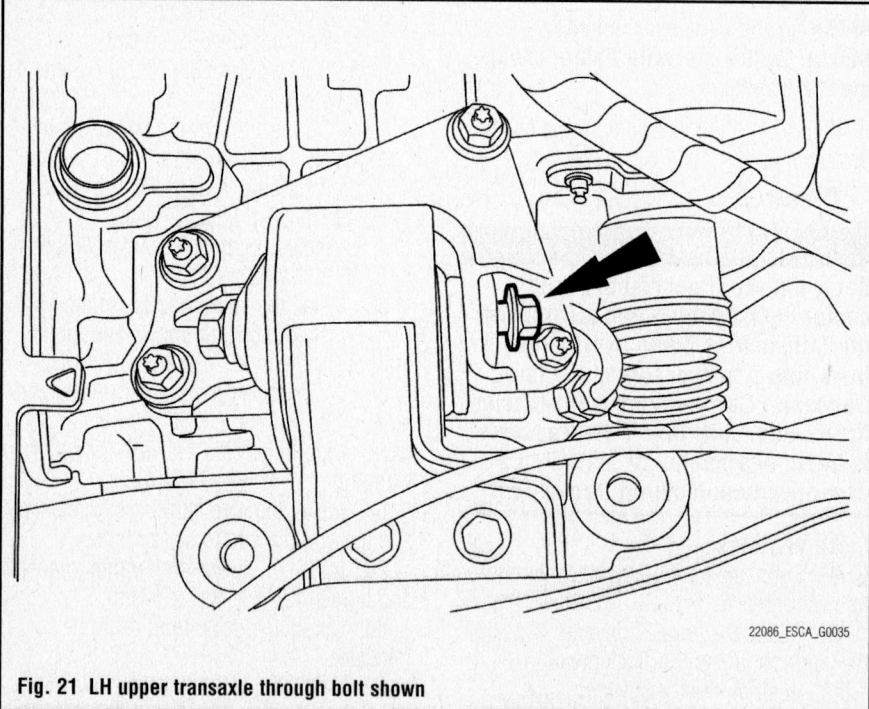

Fig. 21 LH upper transaxle through bolt shown

22086_ESCA_G0035

67. Install the wire harness bracket nut and tighten to 89 inch lbs. (10 Nm). Plug in the bulkhead electrical connector.

68. Install the rear transmission mount and tighten to 59 ft. lbs. (80 Nm).

69. Install the rear transaxle mount through bolt and tighten to 89 ft. lbs. (120 Nm).

FWD vehicles:

70. Install the dampener and tighten bolts to 30 ft. lbs. (40 Nm).

AWD vehicles:

71. Install the PTU assembly and tighten to 33 ft. lbs. (45 Nm).

72. Position the driveshaft in place and install the nuts. Tighten nuts to 35 ft. lbs. (48 Nm).

73. Install the driveshaft and tighten mounting bolts to 15 ft. lbs. (20 Nm).

All vehicles

74. Install the bracket and tighten to 41 ft. lbs. (55 Nm).

75. Install the front nuts on the exhaust-to-intermediate shaft bracket and tighten to 22 ft. lbs. (30 Nm).

76. Install the bolts on the rear of the exhaust-to-intermediate shaft bracket and tighten to 22 ft. lbs. (30 Nm).

77. Install the flexpipe on the exhaust manifold, and tighten the mounting nuts to 18 ft. (25 Nm).

78. Install the intermediate shaft.

79. Install the intermediate shaft retaining nuts and tighten to 20 ft. lbs. (27 Nm).

80. Install the LH and RH halfshafts and frame bolts and tighten to 85 ft. lbs. (115 Nm).

81. Install the LH halfshaft into the wheel knuckle.

82. Install the LH hub nut and tighten to 214 ft. lbs. (290 Nm).

83. Install the cross brace and tighten rear nut to 129 ft. lbs. (175 Nm).

84. Tighten front cross brace bolts to 66 ft. lbs. (90 Nm).

85. Install the bolt for the mount and tighten to 85 ft. lbs. (115 Nm).

86. Install the cross brace and the 4 bolts, tighten bolts to 85 ft. lbs. (115 Nm).

87. Install the LH splash shield and the 7 retainers.

88. Install the RH splash shield and the 5 retainers.

AWD vehicles:

89. Install the vent tube to the fluid level indicator.

All vehicles:

90. Install the air cleaner assembly.

  a. Install the bolt and tighten to 89 inch lbs. (10 Nm).

  b. Reconnect the MAF sensor electrical connector.

  c. Reconnect the brake booster vacuum hose.

  d. Reconnect the wiring harness retainer.

  e. Reconnect the breather tube.

  f. Tighten the clamp and install the air cleaner assembly.

91. Install the battery tray.

92. Fill the transaxle with clean automatic transmission fluid.

93. Check the fluid level and correct as necessary.

➡**Verify that the shift cable is correctly adjusted. The vehicle should start in PARK and REVERSE and the reverse lamps should illuminate in REVERSE.**

3.0L Engines

See Figures 22 through 26.

1. Before servicing the vehicle, refer to the Precautions Section.

All vehicles:

2. Remove the battery and the battery tray.

3. Remove the air cleaner as an assembly.

    a. Disconnect the breather tube.

    b. Disconnect the Mass Air Flow (MAF) sensor electrical connector and the wiring harness fastener.

    c. Remove the air intake tube.

    d. Remove the air cleaner assembly retaining bolt.

    e. Remove the air cleaner assembly

4. Disconnect the Transmission Range (TR) sensor.

5. Disconnect the transaxle harness connector, remove the wire harness bracket nut and position the harness bracket aside

6. Remove the main control cover vent tube.

AWD vehicles:

7. Disconnect the Power Transfer Unit (PTU) vent hose from the transmission fluid filler tube.

All vehicles:

8. Disconnect the Power Transfer Unit (PTU) vent hose from the transmission fluid filler tube.

All vehicles:

9. Disconnect the wire harness from the battery tray hold-down bracket.

10. Disconnect the shift cable from the manual lever

11. Disconnect the wire harness retainer from the shift cable bracket, remove the 2 retaining bolts, and position the cable and bracket aside.

12. Remove the selector lever cable retainer from the transmission fluid filler tube

13. Disconnect the starter motor harness connector.

14. Disconnect the ground wire

15. Remove the 2 starter bolts and remove the starter motor.

16. Remove and disconnect both electrical connectors from the upper intake to gain access to the engine for installing the lifting bracket

17. Install suitable engine support system and secure engine with proper adapters.

18. Remove the 4 upper transaxle retaining bolts

19. Loosen, but do not remove, the 4 retaining nuts holding the bracket to the transaxle case. Remove the LH upper transaxle mount bolt.

20. Remove the RH upper engine mount bolt.

21. Remove the front wheels and tires.

22. Remove the 7 retainers and the LH splash shield.

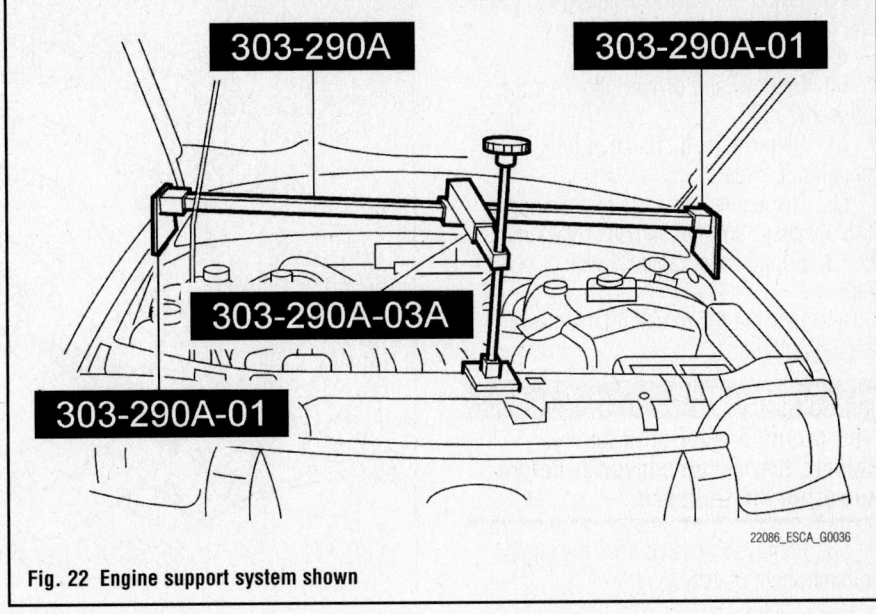

Fig. 22 Engine support system shown

22086_ESCA_G0036

23. Remove the 6 retainers and the RH splash shield.

24. If transaxle disassembly is necessary, remove the drain plug and drain the transmission fluid. After the fluid has drained, install the drain plug.

25. Disconnect the LH and RH suspension.

    a. Disconnect the sway bar link.

    b. Remove the tie-rod end retaining nut

    c. Remove the lower control arm knuckle bolt.

26. Using a suitable tool, disconnect the LH and RH tie-rod end from the steering knuckle.

27. Carefully pry down on the LH and RH lower control arms and disconnect the steering knuckle from the lower ball joint and position the steering knuckle aside.

28. Remove the brake hose retainer and the ABS sensor retaining bolt from the RH strut.

29. Using a suitable tool, remove the RH halfshaft from the intermediate shaft and secure the halfshaft aside.

30. Remove the brake hose retainer and the ABS sensor retaining bolt from the LH strut.

31. Using a pry bar between the transaxle case and the LH halfshaft, carefully disconnect the halfshaft from the transaxle case and secure the halfshaft aside.

32. Disconnect the heated oxygen sensor (HO2S) connector and remove the 2 clips from the oil pan bolt studs.

33. Remove the 2 intermediate shaft retaining nuts.

34. Remove the intermediate shaft.

35. Remove the cross brace.

36. Disconnect and remove the exhaust Y-pipe and hanger.

AWD vehicles:

37. Index the driveshaft to the yoke and remove the 6 bolts holding the driveshaft to the PTU

38. Remove the 2 center bearing nuts and position the driveshaft aside with mechanic's wire.

39. Remove the RH catalytic converter to gain access to the PTU bracket.

40. Remove the bolts and the PTU support bracket.

All vehicles:

41. Remove the bolt for the mount and the 2 bolts for the cross brace.

42. Remove and discard the nut and remove the cross brace.

43. Remove the electrical connectors and harness fastener from the lower mount bracket.

AWD vehicles:

44. Remove the bolts from the PTU and remove the PTU.

All vehicles:

45. Remove the through bolt from the rear transaxle mount.

46. Disconnect the electrical connector and remove the bolt and output shaft speed (OSS) sensor.

➡ **It is necessary to raise the engine a couple of inches in order to remove the transaxle.**

47. Using the engine support system, raise the front of the engine.

➡ **It is necessary to lower the transaxle in order to clear the subframe to remove the transaxle.**

48. Lower the transaxle enough to clear the frame.

49. Remove the access cover.

50. Remove and discard the 4 torque converter nuts.

51. Remove the fluid cooler tube and position it aside.

52. Disconnect the turbine shaft speed (TSS) sensor and the harness retainers.

53. Support the transaxle with a high-lift jack.

54. Remove the remaining transaxle mounting bolts.

> **⁜ WARNING**
>
> **The torque converter is heavy. Secure the torque converter before lowering the transaxle.**

55. Remove transaxle from the engine compartment of vehicle.

To install:

> **⁜ WARNING**
>
> **Carry out the transmission fluid cooler back flushing and cleaning if the transaxle is being overhauled or installing a new or remanufactured transaxle. Carry out the transmission fluid cooler flow test if the transaxle is being overhauled or installing a new or remanufactured transaxle.**

All vehicles:

56. Lubricate the torque converter pilot hub with grease.

57. Position the transaxle in place.

58. Move the transaxle assembly toward the engine assembly and install the bolt.

59. Install the 2 nuts and the stud tighten all the bolts to 35 ft. lbs. (48 Nm).

60. Install lower transaxle bolts and tighten to 35 ft. lbs. (48 Nm).

61. Install the mount bracket and tighten to 41 ft. lbs. (55 Nm).

62. Loosely install the rear transaxle mount bolt.

63. Install the LH transaxle mount through bolt

64. Tighten the rear transaxle mount bolt to 89 ft. lbs. (120 Nm).

65. Install the transmission fluid cooler tubes and tighten to 18 ft. lbs. (25 Nm).

66. Install the output shaft speed (OSS) sensor and tighten the bolt to 9 ft. lbs. (12 Nm).

67. Connect the OSS speed sensor and the turbine shaft speed (TSS) sensor electrical connectors and connect the wiring harness fasteners.

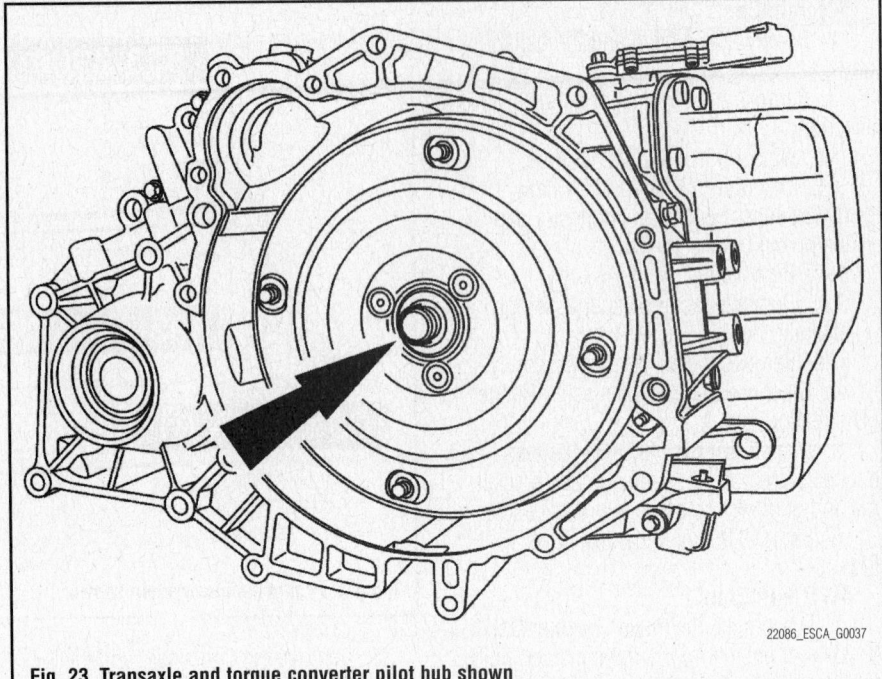

Fig. 23 Transaxle and torque converter pilot hub shown

22086_ESCA_G0037

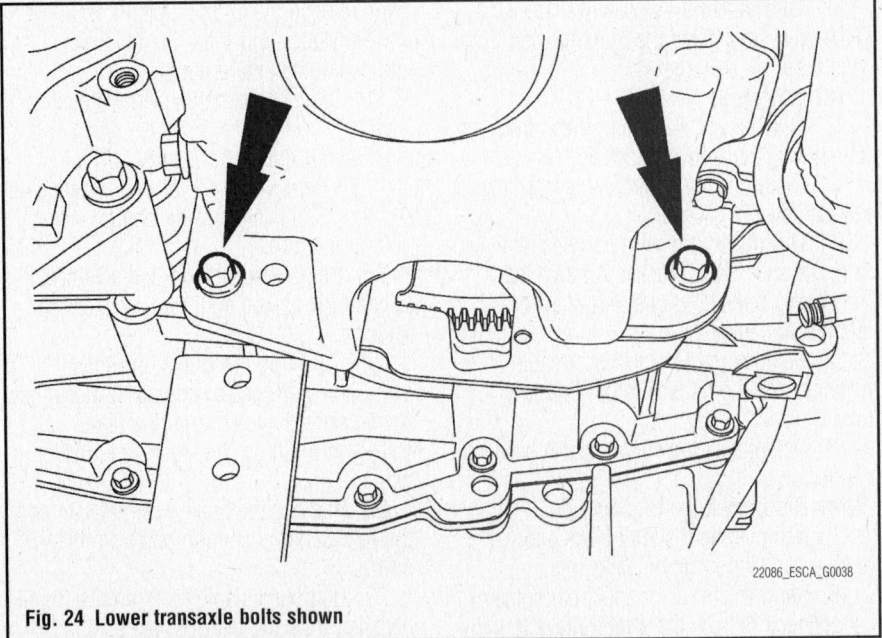

Fig. 24 Lower transaxle bolts shown

22086_ESCA_G0038

68. Install 4 new torque converter nuts and tighten to 30 ft. lbs. (40 Nm).

69. Install the access cover.

AWD vehicles:

70. Position the Power Transfer Unit (PTU) in place and install the bolt and tighten to 35 ft. lbs. (37 Nm).

71. Install the PTU-to-transaxle bolts and tighten to 52 ft. lbs. (70 Nm).

All vehicles:

72. Connect the electrical connector fasteners to the lower mount bracket.

73. Install the cross brace and the rear nut. Tighten the rear nut to 129 ft. lbs.

(175 Nm). and the front bolts to 66 ft. lbs. (90 Nm).

74. Install the bolt for the mount and tighten to 85 ft. lbs. (115 Nm).

AWD vehicles:

75. Install the PTU support bracket and tighten mounting bolts to 41 ft. lbs. (55 Nm).

76. Install the RH catalytic converter.

77. Position the driveshaft in place and install the nuts. Tighten to 35 ft. lbs. (48 Nm).

78. Connect the rear driveshaft to the PTU. Install the PTU bolts and tighten to 27 ft. lbs. (37 Nm).

All vehicles:

79. Install the exhaust Y-pipe with new gaskets and tighten mounting nuts to 21 ft. lbs. (29 Nm).

80. Install the exhaust rubber hanger.

81. Install the cross brace and tighten to 85 ft. lbs. (115 Nm).

82. Install the intermediate shaft and retaining nuts. Tighten nuts to 20ft. lbs. (27 Nm).

83. Connect the heated oxygen sensor (HO2S) wire to the oil pan bolt studs and connect the connector.

84. Install the LH halfshaft into the transaxle and the RH halfshafts in the intermediate shaft and install the ball joints in the knuckles

85. Install the LH and RH brake hose retainer and the ABS sensor bolt. Tighten bolt to 11 ft. lbs. (15 Nm).

86. Reconnect the LH and RH suspension.

　a. Reconnect the sway bar link and tighten nuts to 46 ft. lbs. (63 Nm).

　b. Install the tie-rod end retaining nut and tighten to 41 ft. lbs. (55 Nm).

　c. Install the lower control arm knuckle bolt and tighten to 46 ft. lbs. (63 Nm).

87. Install the LH splash shield, the retainer and the 5 bolts.

88. Install the RH splash shield, the retainer and the 5 bolts.

89. Install the front wheels and tires.

90. Using the engine support system, lower the engine onto the RH engine mount.

91. Install the bolt for the RH engine mount and tighten to 89 ft. lbs. (120 Nm).

92. Tighten the LH upper transaxle mount assembly.

　a. Tighten the 4 nuts for the bracket to 30 ft. lbs. (40 Nm).

　b. Tighten the through bolt to 76 ft. lbs. (104 Nm).

93. Install the upper transaxle retaining bolts and tighten to 35 ft. lbs. (48 Nm).

94. Remove the engine support system tool.

95. Connect the electrical connectors together and then connect them to the upper intake manifold.

96. Install the starter motor and bolts. Tighten the bolts to 18 ft. lbs. (25 Nm).

97. Install and tighten the ground cable to 20 ft. lbs. (27 Nm).

98. Reconnect the starter cables. Tighten battery cable to 20 ft. lbs. (27 Nm), and the solenoid nut to 44 inch lbs. (5 Nm).

99. Position the shift cable and bracket in place, install the bolts and install the wiring harness retainer. Tighten bolts to 17 ft. lbs. (23 Nm).

100. Connect the shift cable to the manual lever.

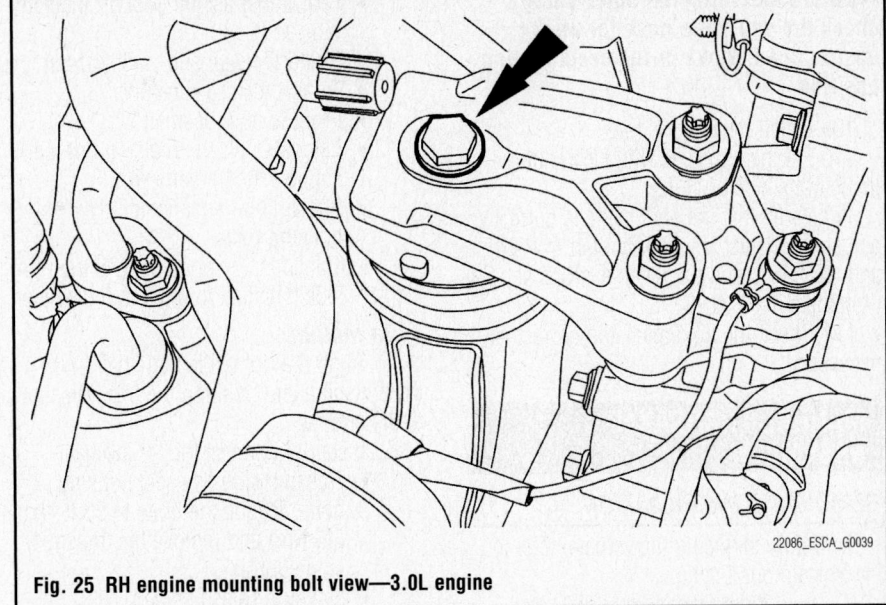

Fig. 25 RH engine mounting bolt view—3.0L engine

101. Install the selector lever cable retainer on the transmission fluid filler tube.

102. Connect the wire harness to the battery hold-down bracket.

AWD vehicles:

103. Connect the evaporative emissions (EVAP) and PTU vent hose to the transmission filler tube bracket.

All vehicles:

104. Install the main control cover vent tube.

105. Position the bracket in place and install and tighten the nut to 18 ft. lbs. (25 Nm). Connect the transaxle harness connector.

106. Connect the Transmission Range (TR) sensor.

➡ **If installing an exchange transaxle, the digital TR sensor must be aligned.**

107. Using the special tool, align the digital TR sensor.

108. Install the air cleaner as an assembly.

　a. Install the air cleaner assembly.

　b. Connect the air intake tube.

　c. Install the retaining bolt and tighten to 89 inch lbs. (10 Nm).

　d. Install the breather tube

　e. Connect the MAF sensor electrical connector.

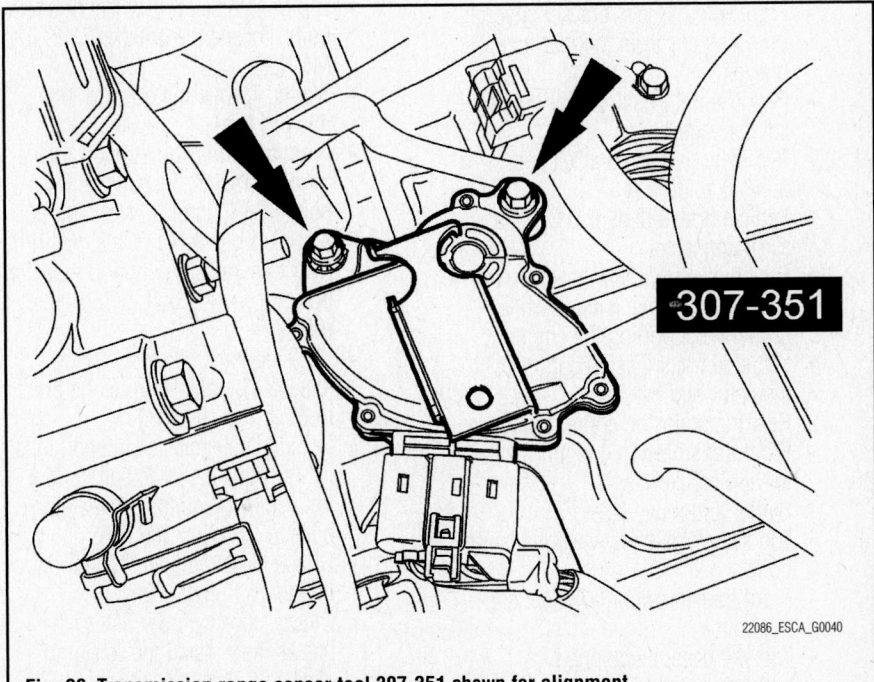

Fig. 26 Transmission range sensor tool 307-351 shown for alignment

➡**Before installing the battery tray, check the vent tube hose for any obstructions, kinks or incorrect routing position**

109. Install the battery tray.

110. Fill the transaxle with clean automatic transmission fluid.

111. Verify that the shift cable is correctly adjusted. The vehicle should start in PARK and NEUTRAL and the reverse lamps should illuminate in REVERSE.

112. Check the fluid level and correct as necessary.

MANUAL TRANSAXLE ASSEMBLY

REMOVAL & INSTALLATION

1. Before servicing the vehicle, refer to the Precautions Section.

2. Drain the transmission fluid.

3. Remove or disconnect the following:
- Battery cables
- Battery and tray
- Mass Air Flow (MAF) sensor electrical connector
- Accelerator cable from the air cleaner outlet tube
- Emission management tube and hose
- Crankcase ventilation hose
- Air cleaner outlet tube
- Air cleaner housing
- Back-up lamp switch electrical connector
- Front wire harness bracket and move it aside
- Front wire harness bracket spacer
- Wire harness from the rear harness bracket
- Park Neutral Position (PNP) electrical connector
- Rear wire harness bracket and move it aside
- Vehicle Speed Sensor (VSS) electrical connector
- Clutch slave cylinder line from the bracket and move it aside while properly supporting the engine
- Left side transmission support insulator and bracket
- Rear transmission support insulator
- Front transmission support insulator and bracket
- Starter and move it aside
- Top transmission flywheel housing bolts
- Front transmission flywheel housing bolts
- Transfer case, if equipped
- Left side halfshaft

- Rear transmission support insulator bracket
- Shifter linkage and stabilizer bar
- Transverse crossmember
- Front to aft crossmember
- Left side splash shield and properly support the transmission
- Remaining transmission flywheel housing bolts
- Transmission and separate the right side halfshaft from the transmission

To install:

4. Align the right side half shaft to the transmission and position the transmission to the engine.

5. Install or connect the following:
- Transmission flywheel housing bolts. Torque the bolts to 33 ft. lbs. (45 Nm) and remove the transmission support
- Left side splash shield
- Front-to-aft crossmember. Torque the bolts to 66 ft. lbs. (90 Nm).
- Transverse crossmember. Torque the bolts to 85 ft. lbs. (115 Nm).
- Shifter linkage. Torque the bolt to 15 ft. lbs. (20 Nm).
- Stabilizer bar. Torque the bolt to 30 ft. lbs. (40 Nm).
- Rear transmission support bracket. Torque the bolts to 66 ft. lbs. (90 Nm).
- Left side halfshaft
- Transfer case, if equipped
- Front transmission flywheel housing bolts. Torque the bolts to 33 ft. lbs. (45 Nm).
- Top transmission flywheel housing bolts. Torque the bolts to 33 ft. lbs. (45 Nm).
- Starter. Torque the bolts to 33 ft. lbs. (45 Nm).
- Front transmission support insulator and bracket. Torque the lower bolt to 66 ft. lbs. (90 Nm) and the 3 upper bolts to 41 ft. lbs. (55 Nm).
- Rear transmission support insulator bolt. Torque the bolt to 66 ft. lbs. (90 Nm).
- Left side transmission support insulator bracket. Torque the bolts to 66 ft. lbs. (90 Nm).
- Left side transmission support insulator. Torque the large bolt to 66 ft. lbs. (90 Nm) and the 3 remaining bolts to 41 ft. lbs. (55 Nm).
- Clutch slave cylinder. Torque the bolt to 15 ft. lbs. (20 Nm).
- Clutch slave cylinder line to the bracket and install the retaining clip

- VSS electrical connector
- Rear wire harness bracket. Torque the bolts to 80 inch lbs. (9 Nm).
- PNP switch electrical connector
- Wire harness to the rear bracket
- Front wire harness bracket spacer and bracket. Torque the bolt to 9 ft. lbs. (12 Nm).
- Back-up lamp switch electrical connector
- Air cleaner housing
- MAF sensor electrical connector
- Air cleaner outlet tube
- Crankcase ventilation hose
- Emission management tube and hose
- Accelerator cable to the air cleaner outlet tube
- Battery and tray
- Both battery cables

6. Fill the transmission to the proper level.

7. Start the vehicle and check for leaks, repair if necessary.

CLUTCH

REMOVAL & INSTALLATION

See Figures 27 and 28.

1. Before servicing the vehicle, refer to the Precautions Section.

2. Remove or disconnect the following:
- Negative battery cable
- Transmission and lock the flywheel to the engine with special tool 303-103
- Pressure plate bolts by loosening them evenly
- Clutch pressure plate and disc

3. Clean the pressure plate and inspect it for burn marks, scores, flatness or ridges, replace if damaged.

4. Inspect the pressure plate diaphragm finger for wear, replace if damaged.

5. Measure the depth of the rivet heads. Minimum depth is 0.012 inch (0.3mm).

6. Inspect the clutch disc for signs of wear and replace if needed.

7. Check the clutch disc runout. Replace the disc if not with specification: 0.027 inch (0.7mm).

To install:

8. Install or connect the following:
- Clutch disc to the flywheel
- Pressure plate to the flywheel. Torque the bolts in sequence to 21 ft. lbs. (29 Nm).
- Transmission
- Negative battery cable

9. Check the transmission fluid level and top off if necessary.

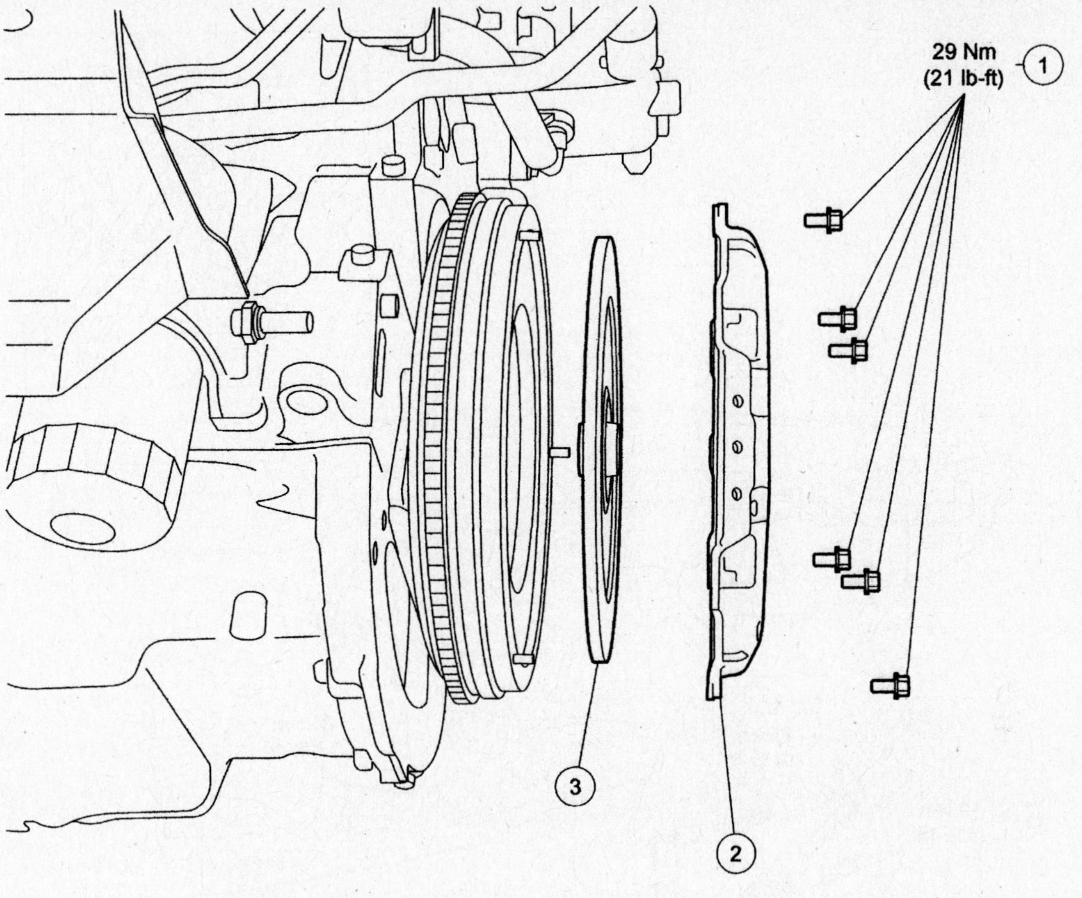

29 Nm
(21 lb-ft) ①

1 Clutch pressure plate bolts (6
required)
2 Clutch pressure plate
3 Clutch disc

06017-ESCA-G49

Fig. 27 Clutch components

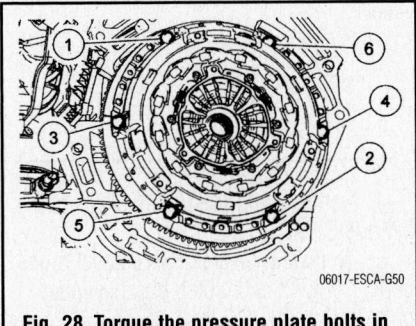

06017-ESCA-G50

**Fig. 28 Torque the pressure plate bolts in
the proper sequence**

HYDRAULIC CLUTCH SYSTEM

BLEEDING

The following procedure is recommended for bleeding the clutch hydraulic
system installed on the vehicle. It is recommended that the original clutch tube,
with quick-connect fitting be replaced
when servicing the hydraulic system,
because air can be trapped in the quick-
connect fitting and prevent complete
bleeding of the system.

1. Before servicing the vehicle, refer to
the Precautions Section.
2. Clean the dirt and grease from the
dust cap.
3. Remove the cap and diaphragm
and fill the reservoir 3/4 of the way with
approved brake fluid C6AZ-19542-AB
or DOT 3 equivalent fluid (ESA-M6C25-A).
4. Loosen the bleeder screw cover from
the slave cylinder and attach a hose to the
screw.
5. Place the hose in a container and
slowly pump the clutch pedal several
times.
6. With the clutch pedal depressed,
loosen the bleeder screw to release the fluid
and air.
7. Remove the hose and tighten the
bleeder screw.

8. Repeat this procedure until all the air
is removed from the hydraulic system

REMOVAL & INSTALLATION

Master Cylinder

See Figure 29.

1. Before servicing the vehicle, refer to
the Precautions Section.

※※ WARNING

**Brake fluid is harmful to painted and
plastic surfaces. If brake fluid is
spilled onto a painted or plastic
surface, wash it immediately with
water.**

➡**If removing the clutch line, remove
the engine air cleaner.**

➡**If removing the clutch slave cylinder
or the clutch slave cylinder-to-clutch
line adapter, remove the transaxle.**

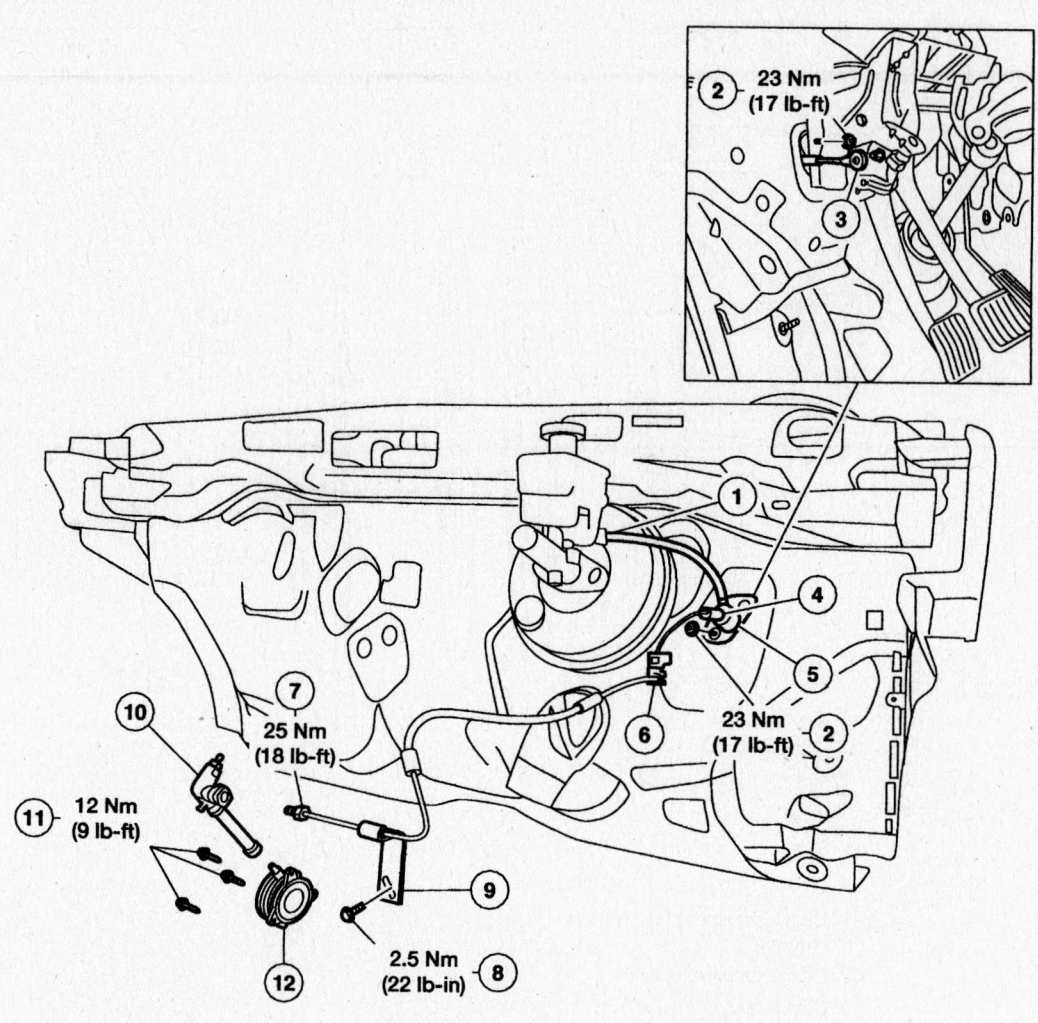

1 Clutch master cylinder hose   5 Clutch master cylinder   9 Clutch line bracket
2 Nut   6 Clutch line   10 Clutch slave cylinder to clutch line adapter
3 Clutch master cylinder push rod   7 Fitting   11 Bolt
4 Fitting   8 Bolt   12 Clutch slave cylinder

67197-ESCA-G60

Fig. 29 Hydraulic clutch components—2005 models shown, other years similar

2. Remove the clutch master cylinder hose

3. Remove the clutch master cylinder push rod

4. Remove the fitting at the master cylinder.

5. Remove the clutch master cylinder

✳✳ WARNING

Make sure the O-rings are properly positioned on the hydraulic line fittings or leaks may occur.

6. To install, reverse the removal procedure. Torque the mounting nuts to 17 ft. lbs. (23 Nm).

7. Fill and bleed the system.

Slave Cylinder

See Figure 29.

1. Before servicing the vehicle, refer to the Precautions Section.

✳✳ WARNING

Brake fluid is harmful to painted and plastic surfaces. If brake fluid is spilled onto a painted or plastic surface, wash it immediately with water.

2. Remove the transaxle.
3. Disconnect the clutch slave cylinder-to-clutch hydraulic fluid tube adapter.

4. Remove and the clutch slave cylinder.

5. To install, reverse the removal procedure. Tighten the 3 clutch slave cylinder bolts to 9 ft. lbs. (12 Nm)

6. Bleed the air from the system.

TRANSFER CASE ASSEMBLY

REMOVAL & INSTALLATION

With Manual Transaxle

See Figure 30.

1. Before servicing the vehicle, refer to the Precautions Section.
2. Remove the driveshaft.

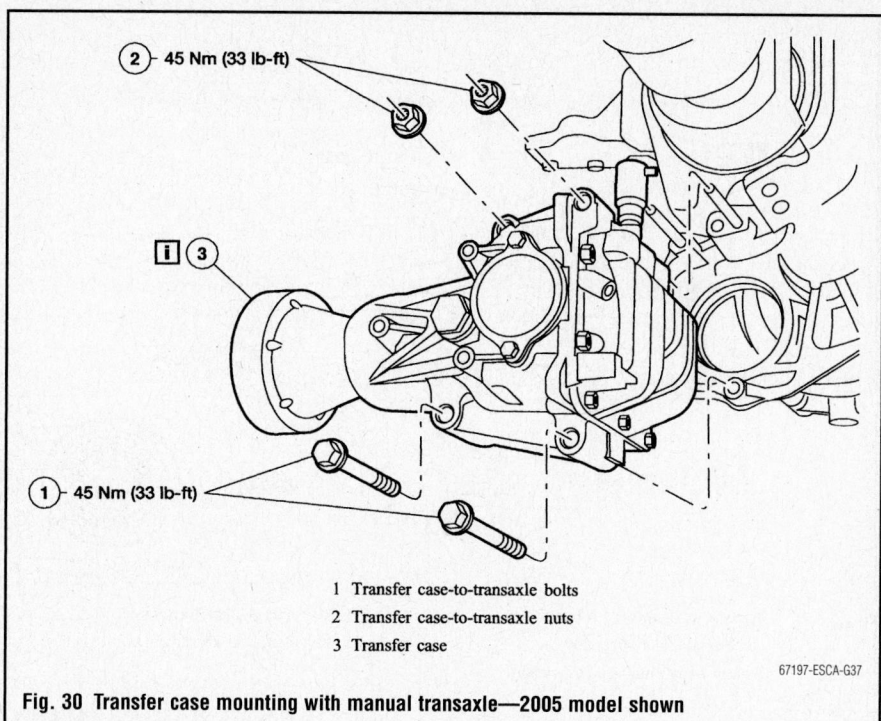

1 Transfer case-to-transaxle bolts
2 Transfer case-to-transaxle nuts
3 Transfer case

67197-ESCA-G37

Fig. 30 Transfer case mounting with manual transaxle—2005 model shown

3. Remove the 4 bolts and the cross-member brace.

4. Remove the transfer case-to-transaxle bolts.

5. Remove the transfer case-to-transaxle nut.

6. Remove the transfer case.

7. To install, reverse the removal procedure.

※ WARNING

The O-ring must be properly installed before mating the transfer case to the manual transaxle. Failure to properly install the O-ring may cause the O-ring to be damaged resulting in transaxle oil leak.

8. Install a new O-ring seal. Observe the following torques:
- Crossmember bolts: 30 ft. lbs. (40 Nm).
- Transfer case mounting nuts: 33 ft. lbs. (45 Nm).
- Transfer case mounting bolts: 33 ft. lbs. (45 Nm).

With Automatic Transaxle

See Figure 31.

1. Before servicing the vehicle, refer to the Precautions Section.

2. Disconnect the battery.

3. Drain the transfer case.

4. Remove the front right intermediate shaft.

5. Remove the driveshaft.

6. Remove the 4 bolts and the cross-member brace.

7. Remove the alternator.

8. Remove the exhaust as required.

9. Remove the heat shield.

10. Remove the transfer case-to-transaxle bolts.

11. Remove the transfer case.

※ WARNING

A new transfer case driven gear seal must be installed whenever the intermediate shaft or transfer case is removed from the vehicle.

➡**If necessary, replace the right differential fluid seal.**

12. To install, reverse the removal procedure. Observe the following torques:
- Crossmember bolts: 30 ft. lbs. (40 Nm).
- Transfer case-to-transaxle bolts: 33 ft. lbs. (45 Nm).

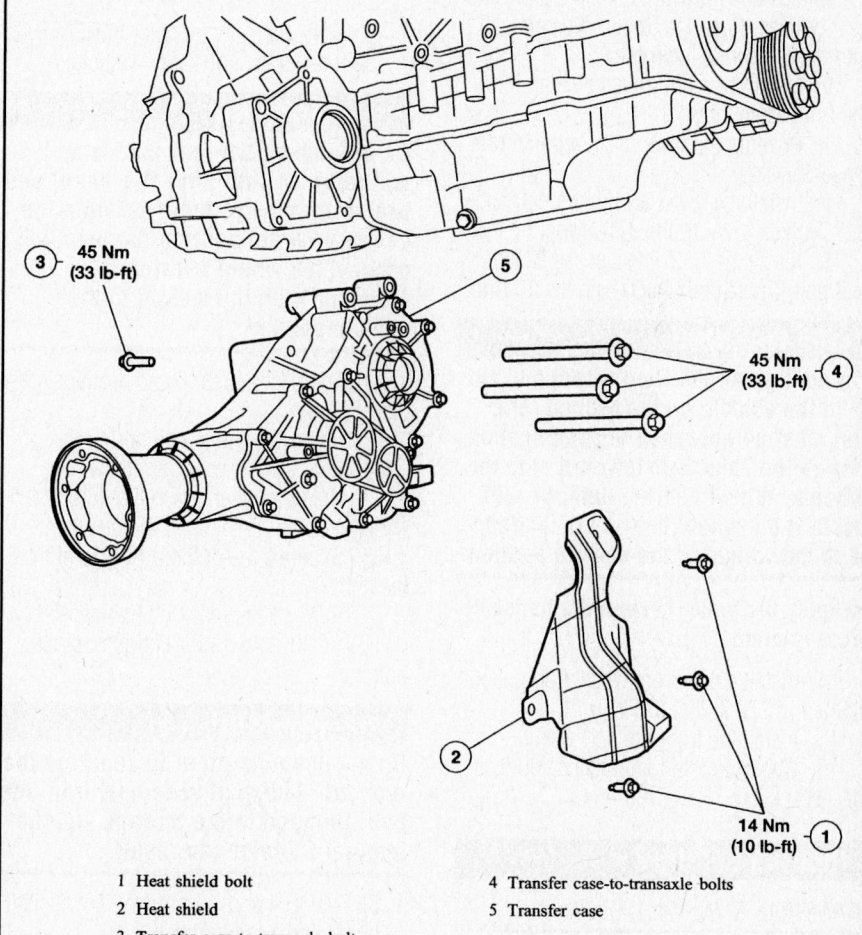

1 Heat shield bolt
2 Heat shield
3 Transfer case-to-transaxle bolts
4 Transfer case-to-transaxle bolts
5 Transfer case

67197-ESCA-G38

Fig. 31 Transfer case mounting with automatic transaxle—2005 model shown, other years similar

FRONT HALFSHAFT

REMOVAL & INSTALLATION

1. With the vehicle in NEUTRAL, position it on a hoist.
2. Remove the front tire and wheel.
3. Remove and discard the front wheel hub nut.
4. Remove the ABS wheel speed sensor bolt and position the sensor aside.
5. Remove the lower arm pinch bolt and nut from the lower arm.
6. Separate the lower arm from the front wheel knuckle.
7. Separate the front drive halfshaft from the front wheel hub using a suitable tool.
8. Remove the front drive halfshaft from the differential.

To install:

➡**When seated correctly, the front drive half shaft bearing retainer circlip can be felt as it snaps into the differential side gear groove.**

9. Position the front drive halfshaft so the splines line up with the differential side gear splines. Push the front drive halfshaft into the differential side gear.
10. Install the front drive halfshaft into the front wheel hub.
11. Position the lower arm into the front wheel knuckle.
12. Install the lower arm pinch bolt and nut. Tighten to 52 ft. lbs. (70 Nm).
13. Install the ABS wheel speed sensor and bolt. Tighten bolt to 80 inch lbs. (9 Nm).

✳ WARNING

Do not tighten the front wheel hub nut with the vehicle on the ground. The nut must be tightened to specification before the vehicle is lowered onto the wheels. Wheel bearing damage will occur if the wheel bearing is loaded with the weight of the vehicle applied.

➡**Apply the brake to keep the halfshaft from rotating.**

14. Install a new front wheel hub nut and tighten to 222 ft. lbs. (300 Nm).
15. Install the front tire and wheel.
16. Check and fill the transaxle fluid as necessary.

REAR HALFSHAFT

REMOVAL & INSTALLATION

See Figure 32.

1. Before servicing the vehicle, refer to the Precautions Section.

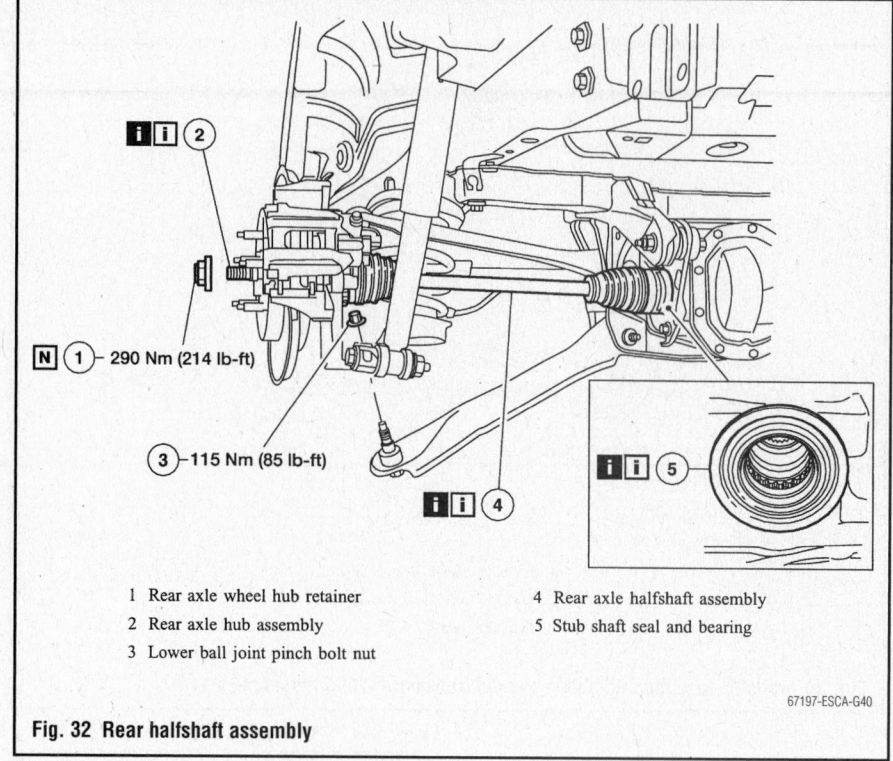

1 Rear axle wheel hub retainer
2 Rear axle hub assembly
3 Lower ball joint pinch bolt nut
4 Rear axle halfshaft assembly
5 Stub shaft seal and bearing

N **1** — 290 Nm (214 lb-ft)
3 — 115 Nm (85 lb-ft)

67197-ESCA-G40

Fig. 32 Rear halfshaft assembly

2. Place the selector lever in NEUTRAL.
3. Raise and support the vehicle.

✳✳ WARNING

Do not loosen the rear axle wheel hub retainer until after the wheel and tire assembly are removed from the vehicle. Wheel bearing damage will occur if the wheel bearing is unloaded with the weight of the vehicle applied.

4. Remove the rear brake drum or brake disc.
5. Remove the rear coil spring.
6. Rear axle wheel hub retainer.
7. Using a puller, press the outboard CV joint until it is loose in the hub.
8. Separate the outboard CV joint from the hub.
9. Remove the rear axle hub assembly.
10. Remove the lower ball joint pinch bolt nut.

✳✳ WARNING

Do not use a hammer to separate the rear axle halfshaft assembly from the hub. Damage to the threads and the internal CV joint can result.

11. Using a prybar, remove the halfshaft.
12. Using a puller, remove the stub and shaft seal.
13. Using a slidehammer and adapter, remove the stub shaft pilot bearing and seal.

14. To install, reverse the removal procedure.
15. Fill the axle with the specified quantity of the specified lubricant.

➡**Lubricate the new stub shaft pilot bearing with rear axle lubricant.**

16. Using suitable drivers, install the stub shaft pilot bearing.

➡**Lubricate the new stub shaft pilot bearing housing seal with grease.**

17. Using the special tools, install the stub shaft pilot bearing housing seal.
18. Install a new circlip on the inboard CV joint.
19. Install the halfshaft end into the hub assembly.
20. Observe the following torques:
   • Lower ball joint: 85 ft. lbs. (115 Nm).
   • Halfshaft nut: 221 ft. lbs. (300 Nm).

CV-JOINTS

OVERHAUL

See Figures 33 through 38.

1. Before servicing the vehicle, refer to the Precautions Section. Observe the following cautionary notes:
   • Never pick up or hold the halfshaft by only the inner or outboard CV joint.
   • Handle the halfshaft by only the interconnecting shaft to avoid pull-apart and potential damage to the CV joints.

- Do not over-angle the CV joints.
- Damage will occur to an assembled inner CV joint if it is over-plunged outward from the joint housing.
- Never use a hammer to remove or install the halfshafts.
- Never use the halfshaft assembly as a lever to position other components. Always support the free-ends of the half-shaft.
- Do not allow the boots to contact sharp edges or hot exhaust components.
- Do not drop assembled halfshafts. The impact may cut the boots from the inside without evidence of external damage.

2. Before servicing the vehicle, refer to the Precautions Section.

3. Remove or disconnect the following:
- Negative battery cable
- Halfshaft and secure it in a soft-jawed vise
- Inboard halfshaft boot clamp
- Boot from the inboard CV-joint housing
- Tripod joint from the CV-joint housing and matchmark the tripod joint to the halfshaft
- Snapring and boot from the half-shaft
- Outboard halfshaft boot clamps
- Outboard boot back to expose the CV-joint and matchmark the joint to the halfshaft
- Outboard CV-joint from the half-shaft

- Halfshaft retainer circlip and dis-card it
- Boot from the halfshaft

To install:
4. Lubricate the outer CV-joint with grease.

5. Install or connect the following:
- Outboard CV-joint and boot
- New halfshaft bearing circlip
- Inboard CV-joint to the halfshaft
- Outboard halfshaft boot forward on to the outboard CV-joint
- New outboard halfshaft boot clamps
- Inboard halfshaft boot
- Tripod joint on the halfshaft by aligning the matchmarks
- New snapring to the tripod joint and lubricate the needle bearings while filling the housing with CV-joint grease, E43Z–19590–A
- Inboard halfshaft boot with new clamps
- Halfshaft
- Negative battery cable

REAR DIFFERENTIAL MASS DAMPER

REMOVAL & INSTALLATION

See Figures 39 and 40.

1. Before servicing the vehicle, refer to the Precautions Section.

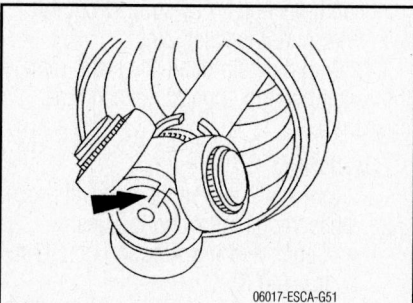

Fig. 33 Matchmark the tripod joint to the halfshaft—front shaft

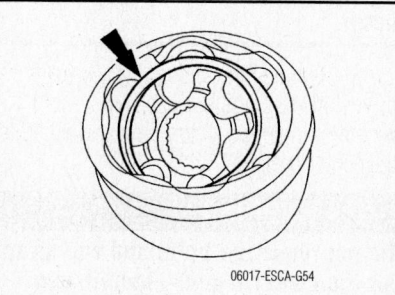

Fig. 36 Lubricate the outer CV-joint with grease—front shaft

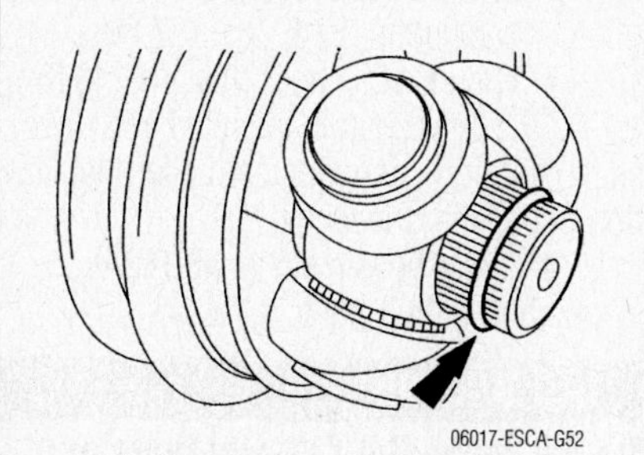

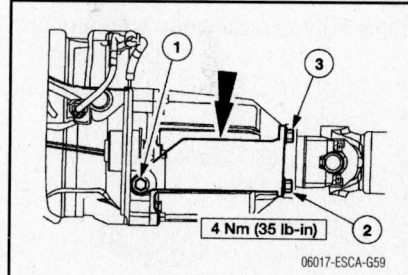

Fig. 39 Tighten the rear differential mass damper bolts to 35 inch lbs. in the sequence shown

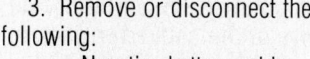

Fig. 34 Remove the snapring from the from the shaft end—front shaft

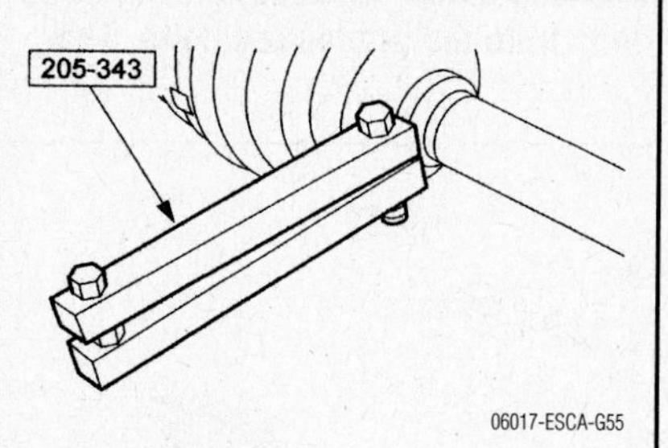

205-343

Fig. 37 Installing new outer CV-joint boot clamps—front shaft

Fig. 35 Halfshaft retainer circlip—front shaft

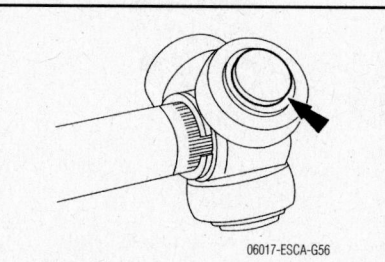

Fig. 38 Lubricate the needle bearings while filling the housing with CV-joint grease—front shaft

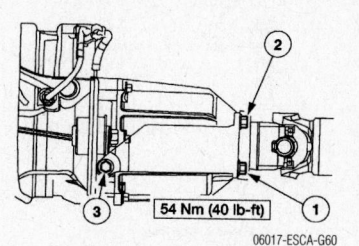

54 Nm (40 lb-ft)

Fig. 40 Tighten the rear differential mass damper bolts to 40 ft. lbs. in the sequence shown

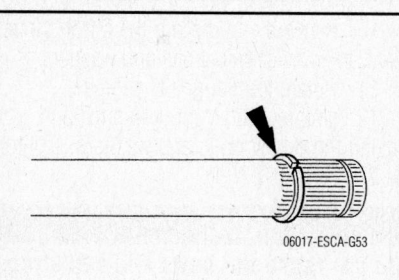

2. Remove the rear differential mass damper.

3. Remove the bolts.

4. Remove the rear differential mass damper.

✳ WARNING

The mass damper bolts must be installed in the sequence shown or damage to the vehicle may occur.

➡**Install the mass damper bolts by hand until finger tight.**

5. Install the rear differential mass damper.

6. Position the rear differential mass damper and install the bolts in the sequence shown to 35 inch lbs. (4 Nm).

7. Final torque the mass damper bolts in the sequence shown to 40 ft. lbs. (54 Nm).

REAR DRIVESHAFT

REMOVAL & INSTALLATION

See Figure 41.

1. Before servicing the vehicle, refer to the Precautions Section.

✳✳ CAUTION

The normal operating temperature of the exhaust system is very high. Never attempt to remove any part of the system until it has cooled. Be especially careful when working around the catalytic converters. The temperature of the converter rises to a high level after only a few minutes of engine operation. Failure to follow these instructions may result in personal injury.

➡**Do not swap driveshaft assembles from different vehicles. The Escape Hybrid drive shaft is longer than the driveshaft in the Escape/Mariner and is not interchangeable. With the vehicle in NEUTRAL, position it on a hoist.**

2. Remove the ground strap bolt.

✳✳ WARNING

Do not reuse the CV-joint bolts and washers. Install new bolts and washers or damage to the vehicle may occur.

3. Remove and discard the 6 front driveshaft-to-transfer case bolts and washers. Index-mark the front driveshaft to the center bearing.

✳✳ WARNING

Do not reuse the bolts and cap straps for the center U-joint. Install new bolts and cap straps or damage to the vehicle may occur.

➡**There is a difference in the length of the head of the replacement cap strap bolts from the production bolts. The** longer head pinion bolts can be used in either location.

4. Remove and discard the 4 universal joint cap strap bolts and 2 cap straps and remove the front driveshaft.

5. Index-mark the pinion and yoke to the driveshaft.

✳✳ WARNING

Do not reuse the bolts and cap straps for the rear U-joint. Install new bolts and cap straps.

➡**There is a difference in the length of the head of the replacement strap bolts from the production bolts. The longer head pinion bolts can be used in either location.**

6. Remove and discard the 4 universal joint cap bolts and 2 cap straps from the rear driveshaft universal joint.

7. With the help of an assistant, remove the center bearing support nuts and the driveshaft.

To install:

8. To install, reverse the removal procedure. Observe the following torques:

- Center bearing support nuts: 35 ft. lbs. (48 Nm)
- Rear universal joint cap bolts: 17 ft. lbs. (23 Nm)
- Front universal joint cap strap bolts: 17 ft. lbs. (23 Nm)
- The 6 front driveshaft-to-transfer case bolts: 27 ft. lbs. (37 Nm)
- Ground strap bolt: 30 ft. lbs. (40 Nm)

9. If a driveshaft is installed and driveshaft vibration is encountered after installation, index the driveshaft.

a. With the vehicle in NEUTRAL, position it on a hoist.

✳✳ WARNING

Do not reuse the CV-joint bolts and washers. Install new bolts and washers or damage to the vehicle may occur.

10. Remove and discard the 6 front driveshaft-to-transfer case bolts and washers.

11. Rotate the flange 60 degrees.

12. Connect the front driveshaft and install the 6 new bolts and washers. Tighten to 27 ft. lbs. (37 Nm).

✳✳ WARNING

Do not reuse the bolts and cap straps for the pinion yoke. Install new bolts and cap straps or damage to the vehicle may occur.

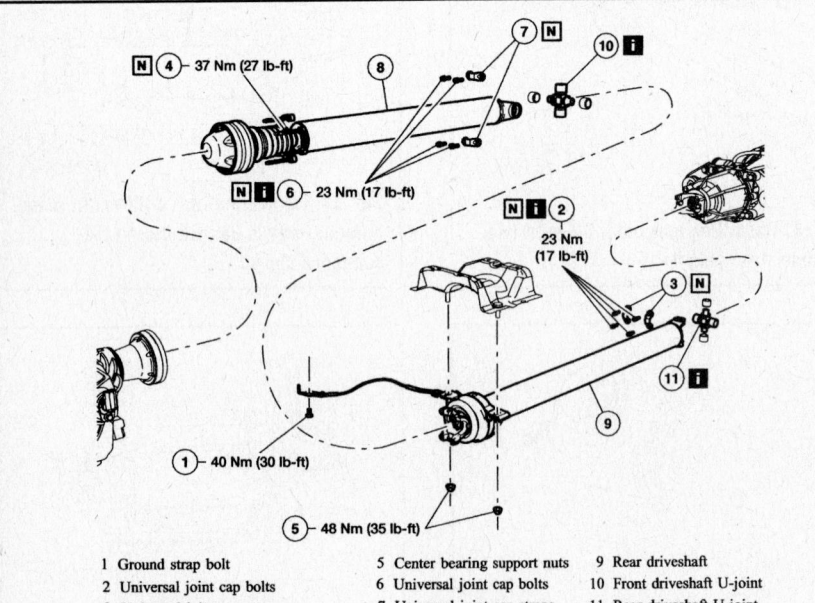

1 Ground strap bolt	5 Center bearing support nuts
2 Universal joint cap bolts	6 Universal joint cap bolts
3 Universal joint cap straps	7 Universal joint cap straps
4 Front driveshaft-to-transfer case bolts	8 Front driveshaft

9 Rear driveshaft
10 Front driveshaft U-joint
11 Rear driveshaft U-joint

67197-ESCA-G42

Fig. 41 Rear driveshaft assembly

13. Disconnect the rear driveshaft universal joint. Discard the 4 bolts and the 2 cap straps.

14. Rotate the rear pinion 180 degrees.

15. Connect the rear driveshaft and install 4 new bolts and 2 new cap straps. Tighten to 17 ft. lbs. (23 Nm).

16. Lower the vehicle and test drive.

17. Repeat the procedure if necessary.

REAR PINION SEAL

REMOVAL & INSTALLATION

See Figures 42 through 45.

1. Before servicing the vehicle, refer to the Precautions Section.

2. With the vehicle in NEUTRAL, position it on a hoist.

3. Index-mark the pinion and pinion flange to the rear of the driveshaft.

4. Remove the 4 bolts and the 2 cap straps. Disconnect and support the driveshaft.

➡**Discard the nut after removing it. Install a new nut during installation.**

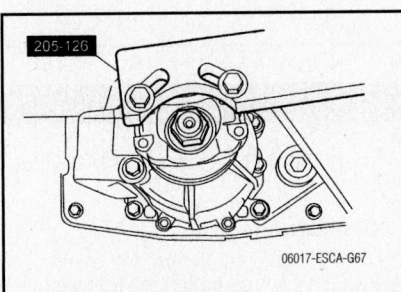

Fig. 42 Flange holding tool

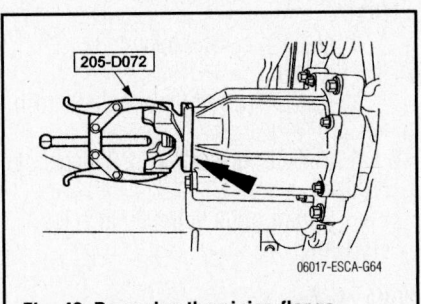

Fig. 43 Removing the pinion flange

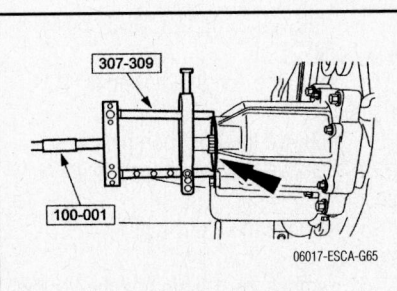

Fig. 44 Removing the pinion seal

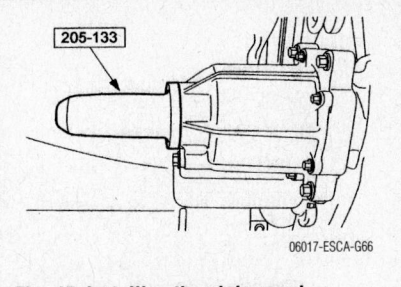

Fig. 45 Installing the pinion seal

5. Using the special tool, hold the pinion flange while removing the nut. Remove the nut.

6. Index-mark the location of the pinion to the yoke.

7. Using a puller, remove the pinion flange.

8. Using the special tool, remove the seal.

To install:

➡**Make sure that the mating surface is clean before installing the new seal.**

9. Using a seal driver, install the seal.

➡**Lubricate the pinion flange with premium long-life grease.**

10. Line up the index marks and position the pinion flange.

11. Using the special tool, install the pinion nut. Tighten to 180 ft. lbs. (244 Nm).

12. Line up the index marks and position the rear driveshaft.

13. Install the 2 cap straps and the 4 bolts. Tighten to 17 ft. lbs. (23 Nm).

REAR AXLE HOUSING

REMOVAL & INSTALLATION

See Figure 46.

1. Before servicing the vehicle, refer to the Precautions Section.

2. Remove the spare tire.

3. Remove the rear driveshaft assembly.

4. Remove the rear halfshafts.

5. Position a suitable transmission hydraulic jack to the axle housing. Securely strap the jack to the housing.

6. Remove the electrical connector at the axle.

7. Remove the rear axle differential housing-to-front insulator bracket bolts.

8. Remove the front insulator-to-bracket subframe bolts.

9. Remove the front insulator brackets.

10. Remove the side insulator bracket-to-subframe nut.

11. Remove the side insulator bracket-to-subframe bolt.

12. Remove the rear axle assembly.

13. Remove the side insulator bracket-to-rear axle differential bolts.

14. Remove the side insulator bracket.

To install:

15. To install, reverse the removal procedure. Observe the following torques:
- Axle housing-to-front insulator bracket: 59 ft. lbs. (80 Nm)

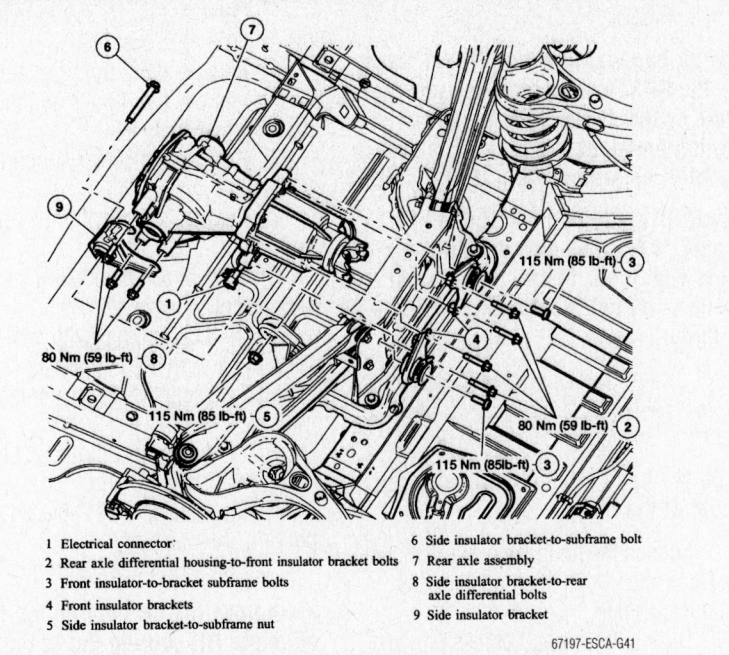

1 Electrical connector
2 Rear axle differential housing-to-front insulator bracket bolts
3 Front insulator-to-bracket subframe bolts
4 Front insulator brackets
5 Side insulator bracket-to-subframe nut
6 Side insulator bracket-to-subframe bolt
7 Rear axle assembly
8 Side insulator bracket-to-rear axle differential bolts
9 Side insulator bracket

Fig. 46 Rear drive axle removal—2005 models shown, other years similar

- Front insulator-to-bracket subframe bolts: 85 ft. lbs. (115 Nm)
- Side insulator bracket-to-subframe nut: 85 ft. lbs. (115 Nm)
- Side insulator bracket-to-differential bolts: 59 ft. lbs. (80 Nm)

INTERMEDIATE SHAFT

REMOVAL & INSTALLATION

See Figure 47.

1. Before servicing the vehicle, refer to the Precautions Section.

➡**If removing the intermediate shaft in order to repair a separate component, it should only be removed as an assembly with the right front halfshaft.**

2. Remove the right front halfshaft.
3. Remove the inner halfshaft bearing retainer nuts
4. Remove the intermediate shaft
5. To install, reverse the removal procedure. Apply a thin coat of grease to the splines of the intermediate shaft.
6. Verify the front axle lubricant level is to specifications.

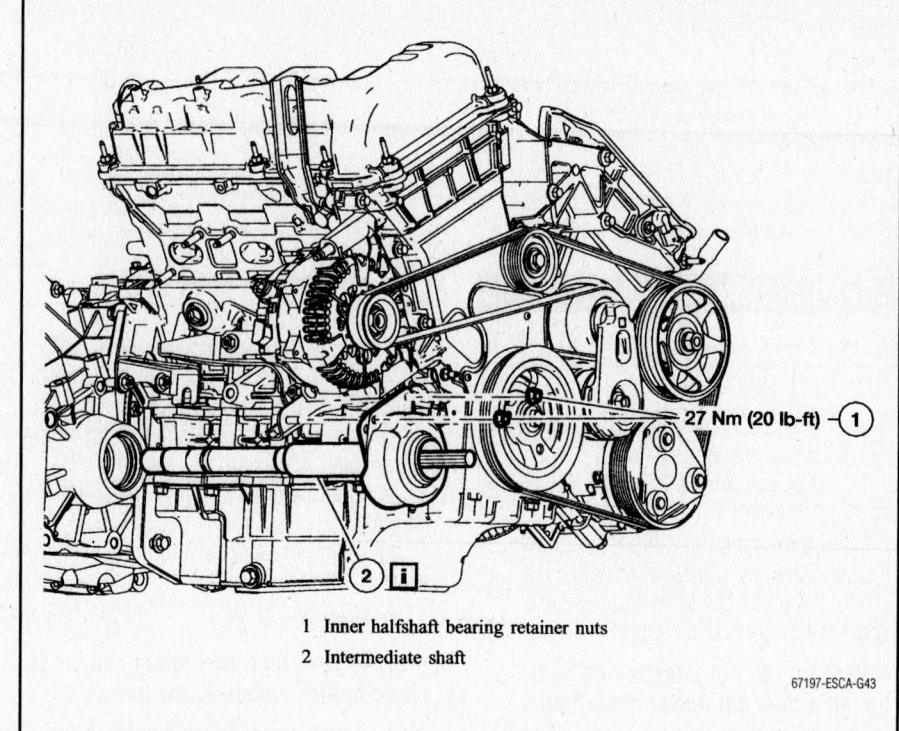

27 Nm (20 lb-ft) — ①

1 Inner halfshaft bearing retainer nuts
2 Intermediate shaft

67197-ESCA-G43

Fig. 47 Intermediate shaft

ENGINE COOLING

ENGINE FAN

REMOVAL & INSTALLATION

2005–07 Models

1. Raise and support the vehicle.
2. Remove the front impact severity sensor, as follows:

➡**The air bag warning lamp illuminates when the RCM fuse is removed and the ignition switch is ON. This is normal operation and does not indicate a supplemental restraint system (SRS) fault.**

➡**Repair is made by installing a new part only. If the new part does not correct the condition, install the original part and carry out the diagnostic procedure again.**

b. Disarm the Supplemental Restraint System (SRS), as outlined in the Chassis Electrical Section.

➡**Mark the hood latch position prior to removal of the bolts.**

c. Loosen the hood latch nut, remove the hood latch bolts, then position the hood latch aside.
d. Detach the wiring harness pin-type retainers.

e. Remove the radiator support bracket bolt.
f. Remove the front impact severity sensor bolt.
g. Disconnect the electrical connector and remove the front impact severity sensor.
3. Remove the 2 pushpin retainers from the front bumper bracket.
4. Remove the 2 front grille bolts.
5. Remove the 4 bolts and the 2 radiator brackets.
6. Remove the center support lower bolt.
7. Remove the nut and the center support.
8. Disconnect the cooling fan electrical connectors
9. On 3.0L engines with 1-piece fan shroud, perform the following:
   a. Disconnect the transmission cooler hose.
   b. Remove the 2 bolts and the cooling fan motor and shroud.
10. On vehicles with 2-piece fan shroud, perform the following:
   a. Remove the 6 cooling fan bolts.

➡**Remove the LH cooling fan first and slide the RH cooling fan to the left side to remove.**

11. Remove the LH and the RH cooling fans.

To install:

12. Installation is the reverse of the removal procedure, noting the following tightening specifications:
   a. Cooling fan bolts: 89 inch lbs. (10 Nm).
   b. Nut and center support: 89 inch lbs. (10 Nm).
   c. Center support lower bolt: 89 inch lbs. (10 Nm).
   d. Radiator bracket bolts: 89 inch lbs. (10 Nm).
   e. 2 front grille bolts: 89 inch lbs. (10 Nm).

2008 Models

See Figure 48.

1. With vehicle in NEUTRAL, position it on a hoist.
2. Drain the cooling system for 2.3L engines.
3. Remove the front bumper cover.
4. Remove the front impact severity sensor
5. Remove the 2 pin-type retainers.
6. Remove the 4 bolts and the 2 radiator brackets.

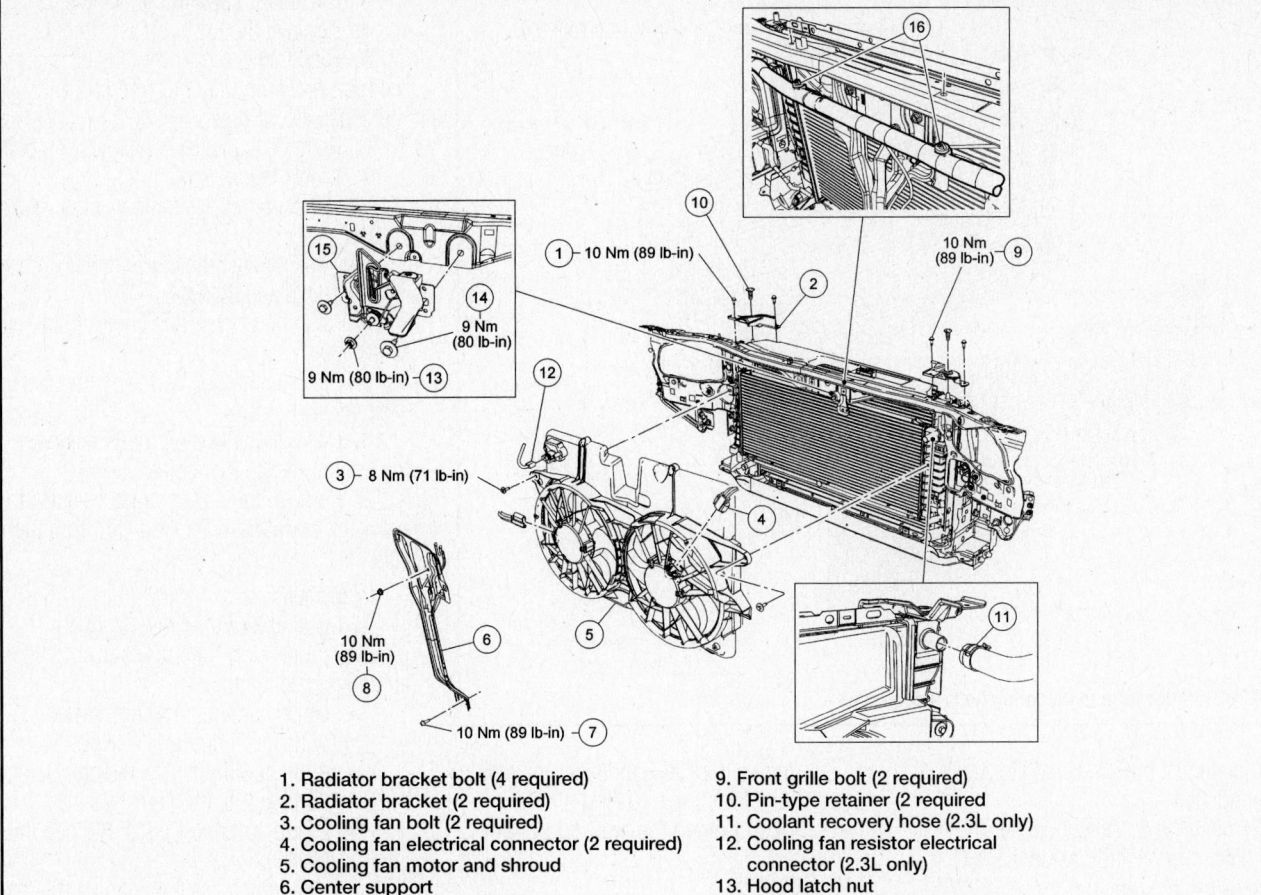

1. Radiator bracket bolt (4 required)
2. Radiator bracket (2 required)
3. Cooling fan bolt (2 required)
4. Cooling fan electrical connector (2 required)
5. Cooling fan motor and shroud
6. Center support
7. Center support lower bolt
8. Center support nut
9. Front grille bolt (2 required)
10. Pin-type retainer (2 required
11. Coolant recovery hose (2.3L only)
12. Cooling fan resistor electrical
    connector (2.3L only)
13. Hood latch nut
14. Hood latch bolt (2 required)
15. Hood latch
16. Wiring harness retainers (2 required)

22086_ESCA_G0021

Fig. 48 Cooling fan motor and shroud—2008 models

➡**Mark the hood latch position prior to removal of the bolts.**

7. Loosen the nut, remove the 2 bolts and position aside the hood latch.

8. Remove the 2 wiring harness retainers from the front bumper bracket

9. Remove the center support bolt.

10. For 2.3L engines, perform the following:

   a. Disconnect the cooling fan resistor electrical connector.

   b. Disconnect the coolant recovery hose from the radiator and position it aside.

11. For 3.0L engines, detach the lower degas bottle hose from the cooling fan motor and shroud.

12. Disconnect the cooling fan electrical connectors.

13. Remove the 2 cooling fan bolts and the cooling fan motor and shroud.

To install:

14. To install, reverse the removal procedure and note the following:

   a. Tighten the cooling fan bolts, the cooling fan motor and shroud bolts to 71 inch. lbs. (8 Nm).

   b. Tighten the center support bolt to 89 inch lbs. (10 Nm).

   c. Tighten the hood latch bolts to 80 inch lbs. (9 Nm).

   d. Tighten the radiator bracket bolts to 89 inch lbs. (10 Nm).

RADIATOR

REMOVAL & INSTALLATION

2.3L Engine
2005–07 Models

1. Raise and 7safely support the vehicle.

2. Drain the cooling system.

3. Remove the cooling fan motor and shroud.

4. Disconnect the upper radiator-to-degas bottle hose from the radiator.

5. Disconnect the upper radiator hose from the radiator.

6. Disconnect the lower degas bottle-to-radiator hose from the radiator.

7. Disconnect the lower radiator hose from the radiator.

8. Disconnect the 2 transaxle cooling hoses from the radiator.

9. Remove the radiator.

10. To install, reverse the removal procedure.

11. Fill and bleed the cooling system.

2008 Models

See Figures 49 and 50.

1. With vehicle in NEUTRAL, position it on a hoist.

2. Remove the cooling fan motor and shroud.

3. Disconnect the upper radiator hose from the radiator.

4. Disconnect the lower degas bottle-to-radiator hose from the radiator.

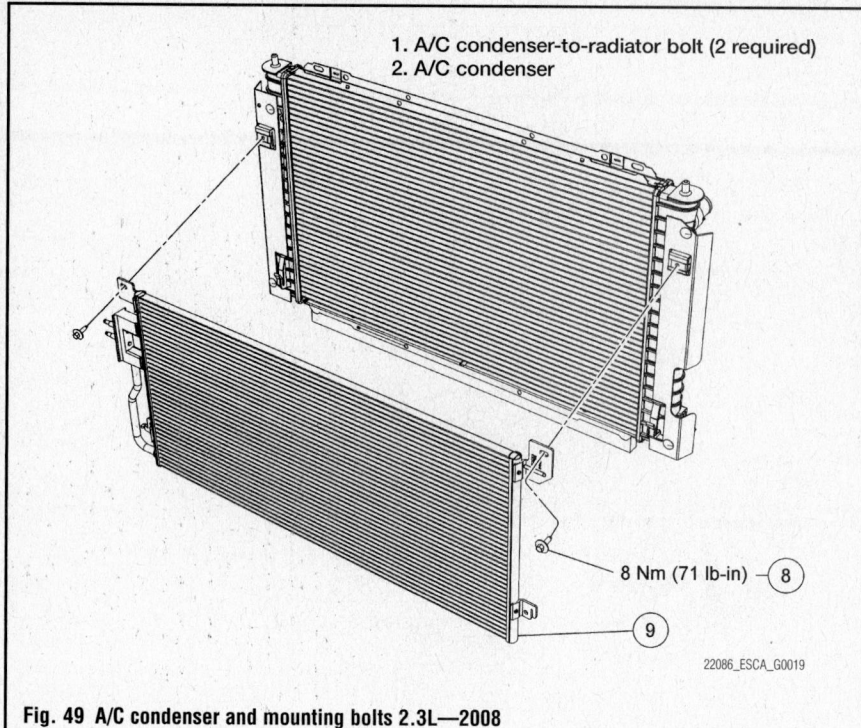

1. A/C condenser-to-radiator bolt (2 required)
2. A/C condenser

8 Nm (71 lb-in) — 8

9

22086_ESCA_G0019

Fig. 49 A/C condenser and mounting bolts 2.3L—2008

5. Disconnect the lower radiator hose from the radiator.

6. Remove the 2 A/C condenser-to-radiator bolts and position aside the A/C condenser from the radiator.

7. Remove the radiator.

To install:

8. To install, reverse the removal procedure.

9. Tighten the A/C condenser-to-radiator bolts to 71 inch lbs. (8 Nm).

10. Fill and bleed the cooling system.

3.0L Engines
2005–07 Models

1. Disconnect the negative battery cable.

2. Drain the engine cooling system.

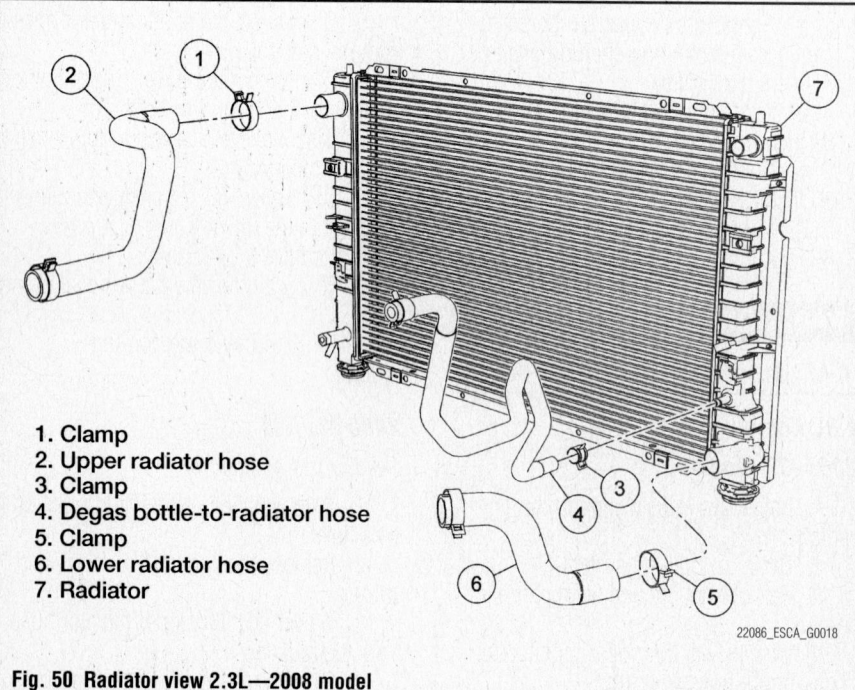

1. Clamp
2. Upper radiator hose
3. Clamp
4. Degas bottle-to-radiator hose
5. Clamp
6. Lower radiator hose
7. Radiator

22086_ESCA_G0018

Fig. 50 Radiator view 2.3L—2008 model

3. Raise and support the vehicle.

4. Remove the lower splash shields.

5. Disconnect the lower radiator hose, the high pressure transmission line and the degas return hose.

6. Remove the lower center support bolt.

7. Lower the vehicle.

   a. Disconnect the transmission return line.

   b. Disconnect the upper radiator hose and degas supply hose.

8. Position the hood latch assembly out of the way.

9. Remove the two bolts and the center support.

10. Remove the two top bolts retaining the cooling fan to the radiator.

11. Remove the upper radiator support brackets, and remove the radiator from the vehicle.

To install:

12. Installation is the reverse of the removal procedure. Note the following tightening specifications:

- Upper radiator support bracket bolts: 89 inch lbs. (10 Nm).
- 2 top cooling fan-to-radiator bolts: 89 inch lbs. (10 Nm).
- 2 center support bolts: 89 inch lbs. (10 Nm).
- Hood latch assembly bolts: 89 inch lbs. (10 Nm).
- Lower center support bolt: 89 inch lbs. (10 Nm).

13. Fill and bleed the cooling system.

2008 Models

See Figure 51.

1. With vehicle in NEUTRAL, position it on a hoist.

2. Drain the cooling system.

3. Remove the cooling fan motor and shroud.

4. Disconnect the radiator-to-degas bottle hose and upper radiator hose from the radiator.

5. Disconnect the lower degas bottle-to-radiator hose from the radiator.

6. Disconnect the lower radiator hose from the radiator.

7. Remove the 2 A/C condenser-to-radiator bolts and position aside the A/C condenser from the radiator.

8. Remove the radiator.

To install:

9. To install, reverse the removal procedure.

10. Tighten the A/C condenser-to-radiator bolts to 71 inch lbs. (8 Nm).

11. Fill and bleed the cooling system

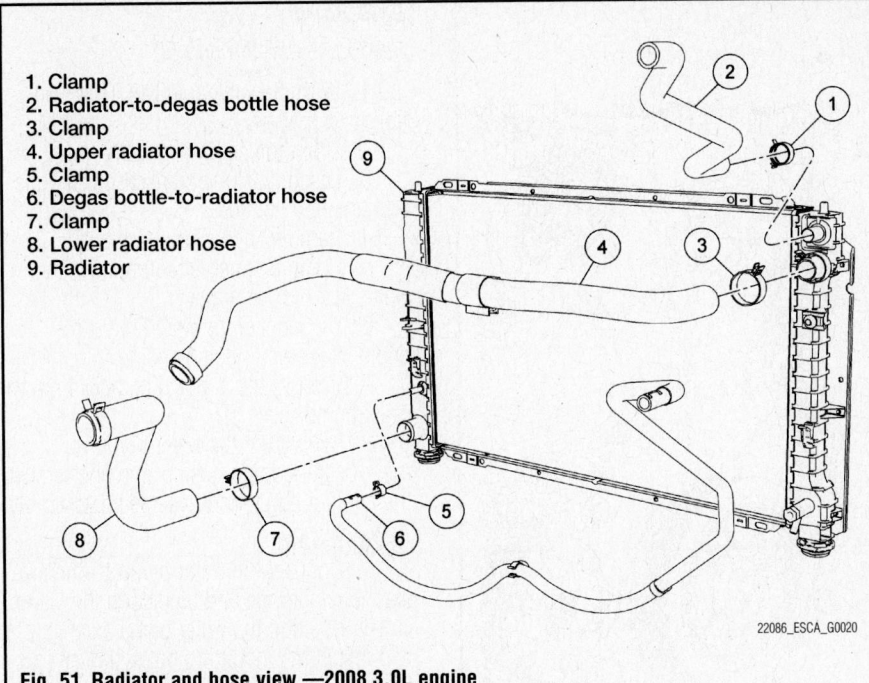

1. Clamp
2. Radiator-to-degas bottle hose
3. Clamp
4. Upper radiator hose
5. Clamp
6. Degas bottle-to-radiator hose
7. Clamp
8. Lower radiator hose
9. Radiator

22086_ESCA_G0020

Fig. 51 Radiator and hose view —2008 3.0L engine

THERMOSTAT

REMOVAL & INSTALLATION

2.3L Engine

➡**On the 2.3L engine, the thermostat and thermostat housing are serviced as an assembly.**

1. Raise and safely support the vehicle.
2. Drain the cooling system.
3. Remove the accessory drive belt tensioner.
4. Disconnect the heater hose at the thermostat housing.
5. Disconnect the lower radiator hose at the thermostat housing.
6. Remove the 3 bolts, thermostat housing and gasket.
7. Clean and inspect the gasket, replace if necessary.
8. To install, reverse the removal procedure. Tighten the thermostat housing bolts to 89 inch lbs. (10 Nm).

3.0L Engine

See Figure 52.

1. With the vehicle in NEUTRAL, position it on a hoist.
2. Drain the cooling system.
3. Remove the air cleaner outlet pipe.
4. Disconnect the lower radiator hose from the thermostat housing.
5. Remove the 3 bolts, thermostat housing cover, O-ring seal and thermostat.

To install:

6. Install thermostat a new O-ring seal.
7. Install thermostat housing and mounting bolts tighten to 89 inch lbs. (10 Nm).

➡**To install, lubricate the thermostat housing O-ring seal with clean engine coolant**

8. Reconnect lower radiator hose.
9. Install air cleaner outlet pipe.
10. Fill and bleed the cooling system.

WATER PUMP

REMOVAL & INSTALLATION

2.3L Engine

See Figure 53.

1. Before servicing the vehicle, refer to the Precautions Section.
2. With the vehicle in NEUTRAL, position it on a hoist.
3. Drain the cooling system.
4. Remove the accessory drive belt.
5. Remove the coolant pump pulley bolts.
6. Remove the coolant pump pulley.
7. Remove the coolant pump bolts.
8. Remove the coolant pump.
9. Remove the coolant pump O-ring seal.

To install:

10. To install, reverse the removal procedure. Torque the water pump bolts to 89 inch lbs. (10 Nm). Torque the pulley bolts to 15 ft. lbs. (20 Nm).
11. Fill and bleed the cooling system.

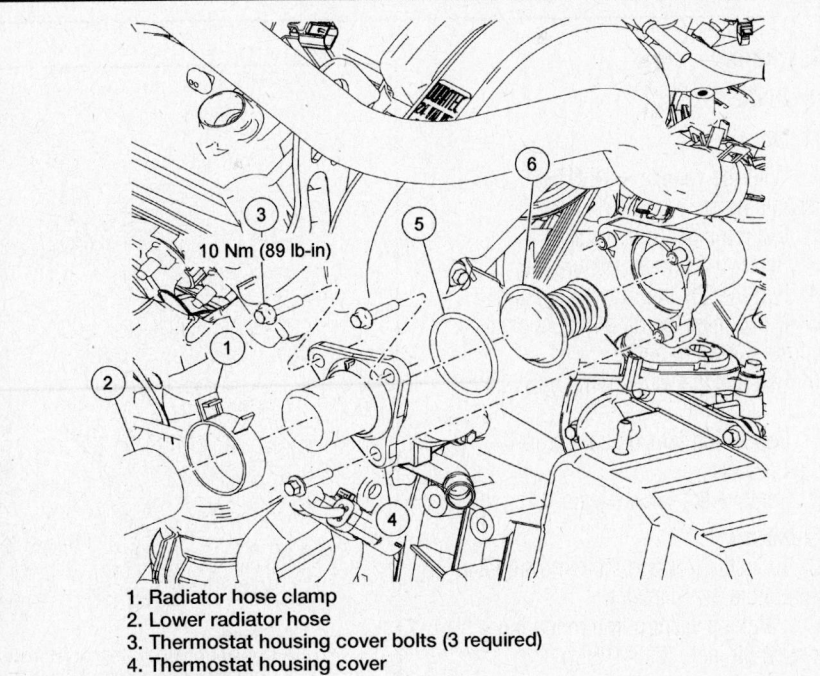

10 Nm (89 lb-in)

1. Radiator hose clamp
2. Lower radiator hose
3. Thermostat housing cover bolts (3 required)
4. Thermostat housing cover
5. O-ring seal
6. Thermostat

22086_ESCA_G0026

Fig. 52 Thermostat view and related parts—3.0L engine

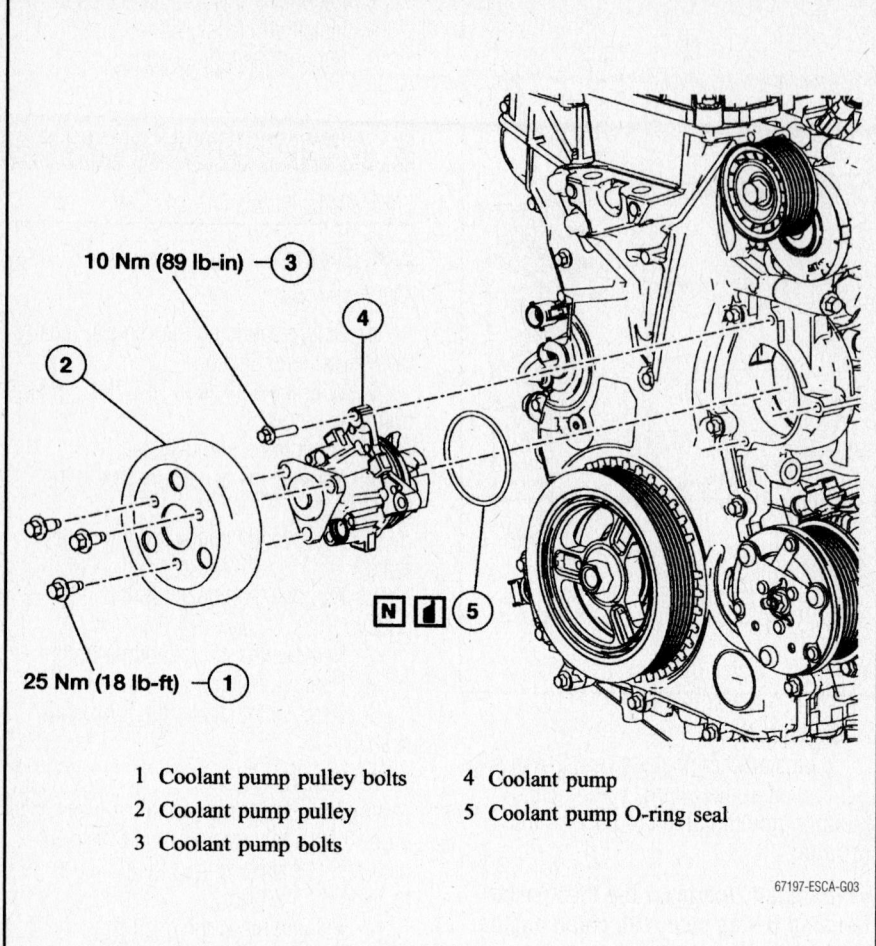

1 Coolant pump pulley bolts
2 Coolant pump pulley
3 Coolant pump bolts
4 Coolant pump
5 Coolant pump O-ring seal

67197-ESCA-G03

Fig. 53 Water pump mounting—2.3L engine

3.0L Engine

Early Build

See Figure 54.

1. With the vehicle in NEUTRAL, position it on a hoist.
2. Drain the cooling system
3. Remove the water pump belt.
4. Remove the thermostat housing.
5. Disconnect the oil cooler coolant hose from the water pump.
6. Remove the water pump mounting bolts.
7. Reposition the coolant pump-to-engine hose clamp.
8. Remove the water pump.

To install:

9. To install, reverse the removal procedure and note the following:
   a. Tighten water pump mounting bolts to 89 inch. lbs (10 Nm).
   b. Tighten the water pump mounting bolts an additional 90 degrees.
10. Fill and bleed the cooling system.

Late Build

See Figures 55 through 57.

1. With the vehicle in NEUTRAL, position it on a hoist.
2. Drain the cooling system.
3. Disconnect the crankcase vent tube and position it aside.
4. Remove the water pump belt.
5. Using a suitable tool, remove the water pump drive pulley.
6. Disconnect the water pump-to-engine hose and position aside.
7. Remove the 3 mounting bolts from the water pump assembly.
8. Reposition the water pump-to-thermostat housing hose clamp and remove the coolant pump and hose as an assembly.

To install:

9. Connect the water pump-to-thermostat housing hose and reposition the clamp.
10. Position the water pump assembly and install the mounting bolts, tighten to 89 inch lbs. (10 Nm).
11. Tighten the water pump mounting bolts an additional 90 degrees.
12. Connect the coolant pump-to-engine hose and the heater hose.

➡ **Install the water pump drive pulley flush with the end of the camshaft.**

13. Using a suitable tool, install the coolant pump drive pulley.
14. Install the coolant pump belt.
15. Connect the crankcase vent tube.
16. Fill and bleed the cooling system.

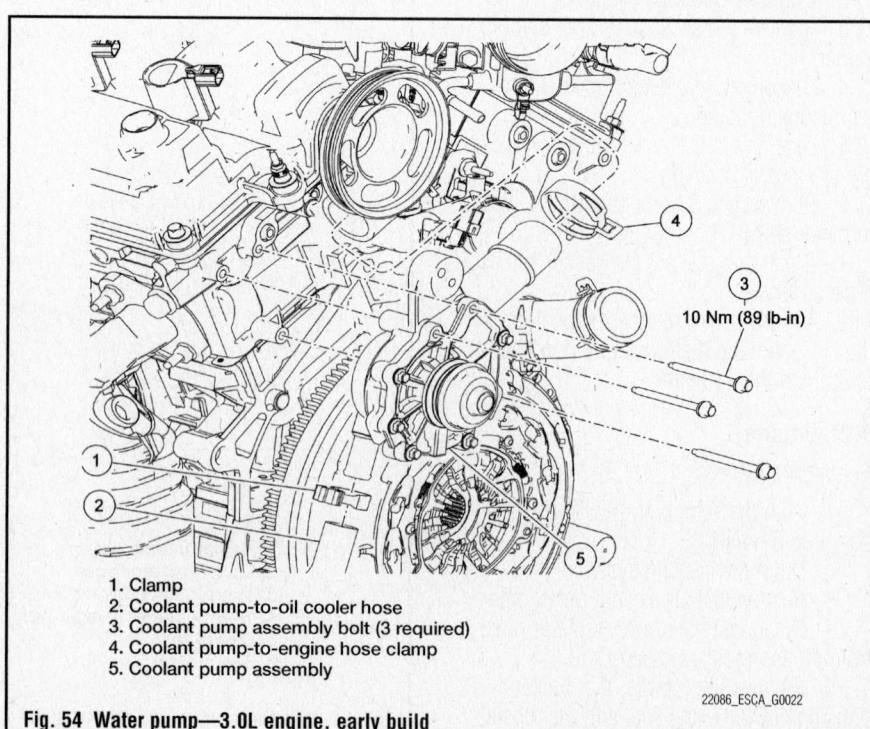

1. Clamp
2. Coolant pump-to-oil cooler hose
3. Coolant pump assembly bolt (3 required)
4. Coolant pump-to-engine hose clamp
5. Coolant pump assembly

22086_ESCA_G0022

Fig. 54 Water pump—3.0L engine, early build

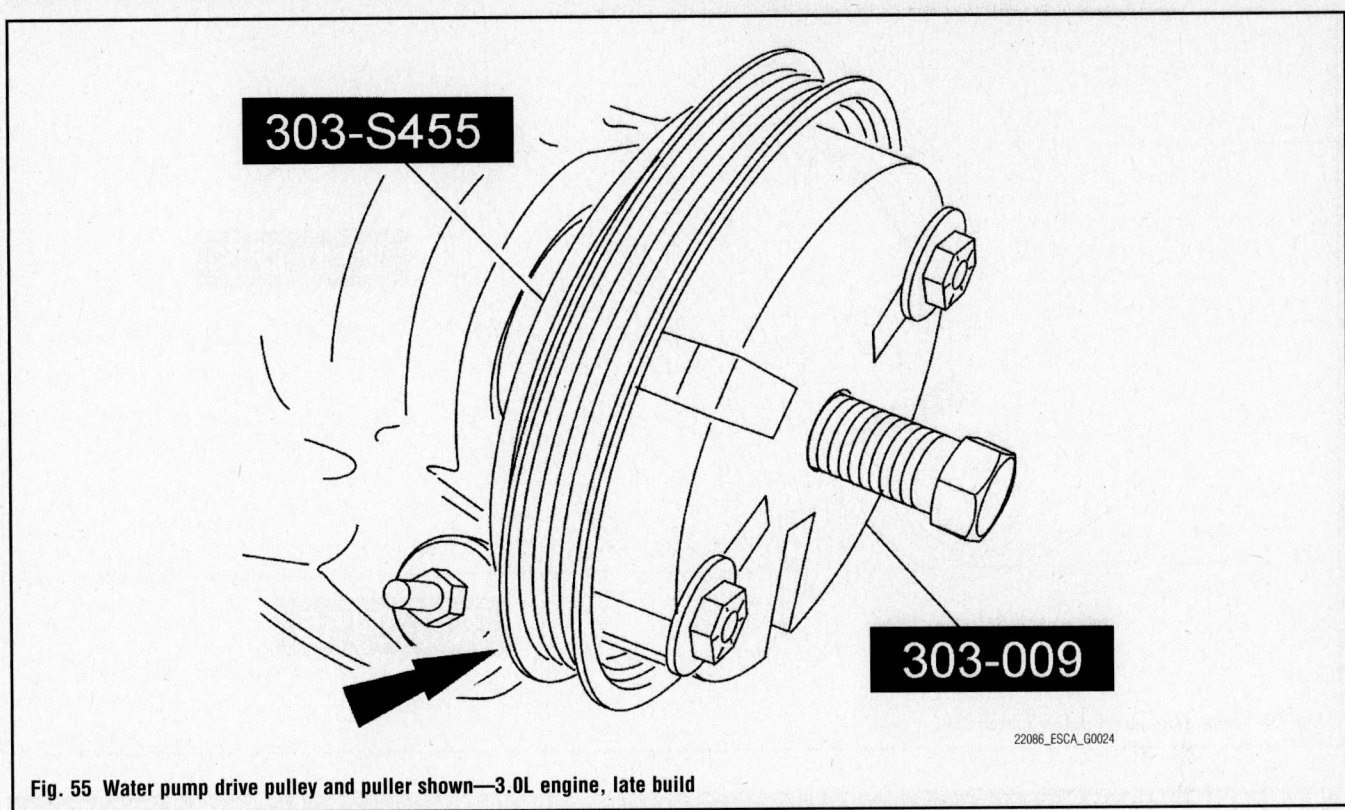

303-S455

303-009

22086_ESCA_G0024

Fig. 55 Water pump drive pulley and puller shown—3.0L engine, late build

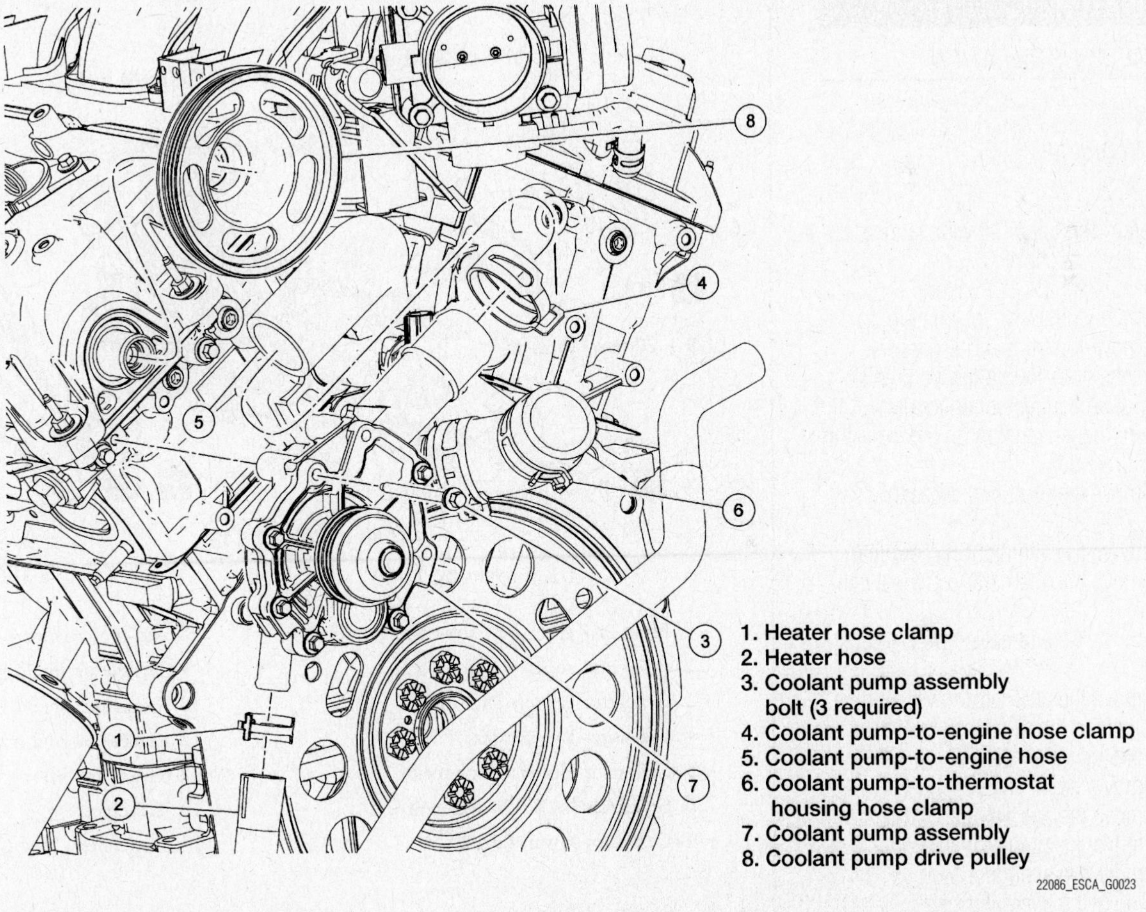

1. Heater hose clamp
2. Heater hose
3. Coolant pump assembly
   bolt (3 required)
4. Coolant pump-to-engine hose clamp
5. Coolant pump-to-engine hose
6. Coolant pump-to-thermostat
   housing hose clamp
7. Coolant pump assembly
8. Coolant pump drive pulley

22086_ESCA_G0023

Fig. 56 Water pump—3.0L engine, late build

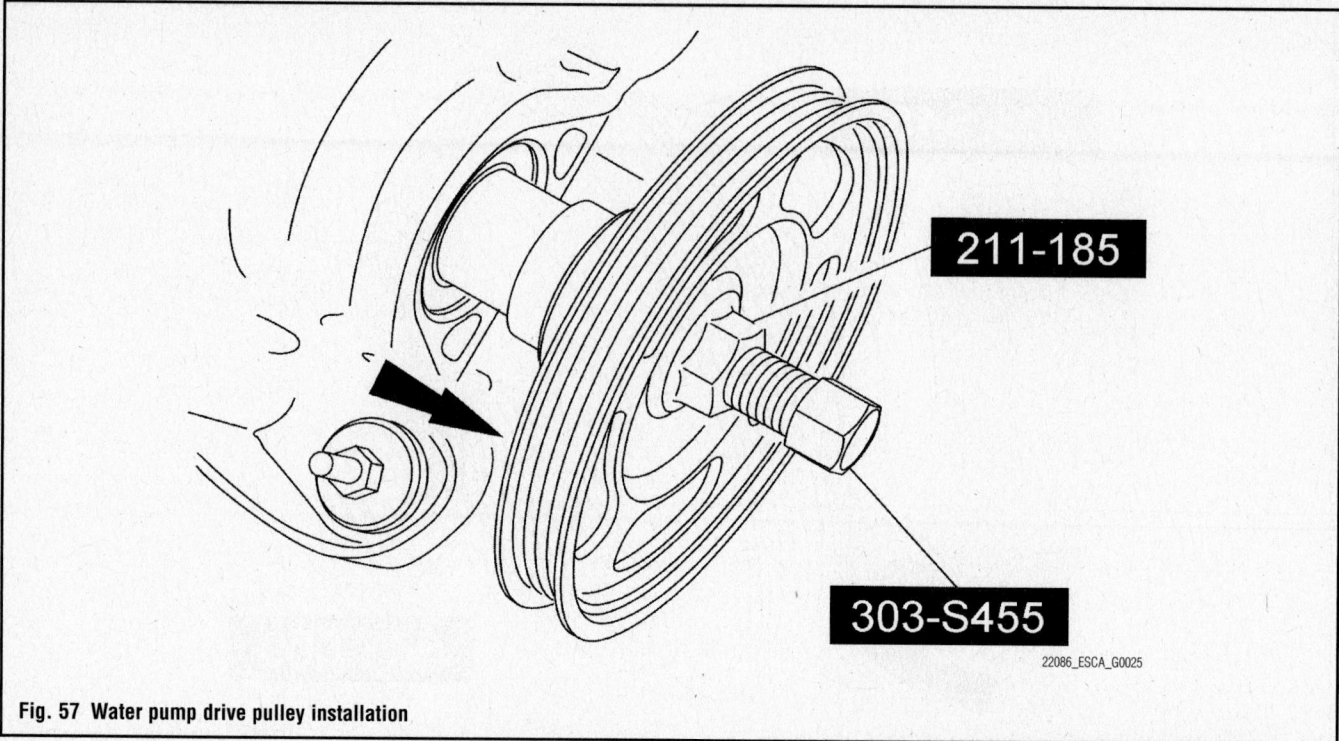

Fig. 57 Water pump drive pulley installation

22086_ESCA_G0025

ENGINE ELECTRICAL

CHARGING SYSTEM

ALTERNATOR

REMOVAL & INSTALLATION

2.3L Engine

2005–07 Models

See Figure 58.

1. Before servicing the vehicle, refer to the Precautions Section.
2. Disconnect the 12v battery.
3. Remove the lower splash shield.
4. Remove the front end accessory drive belt tensioner. Rotate the front end accessory drive belt tensioner counterclockwise to loosen tension on the front end accessory drive belt.
5. Remove the front end accessory drive belt.
6. Remove the alternator B+ terminal.
7. Remove the alternator electrical connector.
8. Remove the alternator lower air duct bolt.
9. Remove the alternator lower air duct. Press the locking tab to release the lower air duct from the upper air duct.
10. Remove the pin-type retainer.
11. Remove the alternator shield .
12. Remove the alternator stud nut.
13. Remove the alternator stud.
14. Remove the alternator bolts.
15. Remove the alternator.

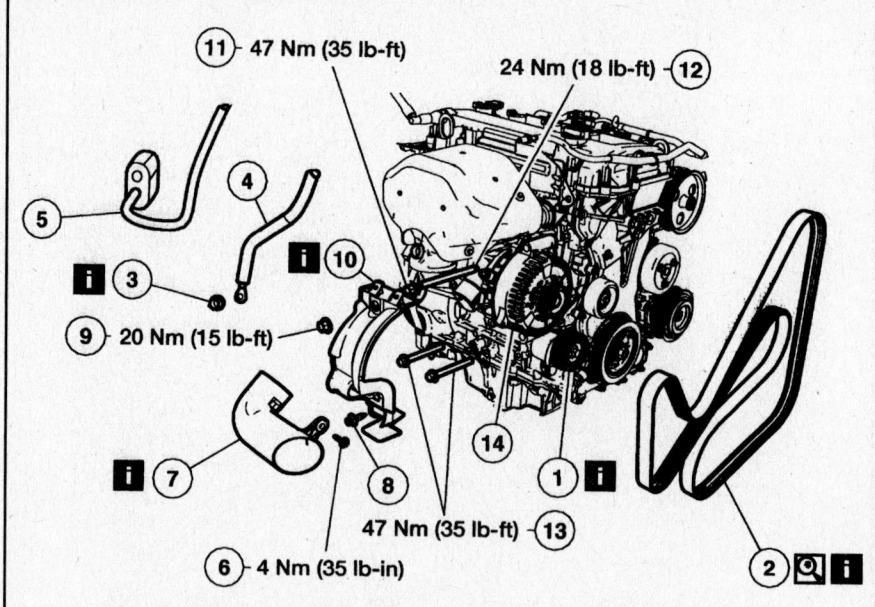

1	Front end accessory drive belt tensioner	8	Pin-type retainer
2	Front end accessory drive belt	9	Generator shield nut
3	Generator B+ terminal nut	10	Generator shield
4	Generator B+ terminal	11	Generator stud nut
5	Generator electrical connector	12	Generator stud
6	Generator lower air duct bolt	13	Generator bolts
7	Generator lower air duct	14	Generator

67197-ESCA-G01

Fig. 58 Alternator mounting—2005–07 2.3L Engine

To install:

16. To install, reverse the removal procedure. Observe the following torques:
- Alternator mounting bolts: 35 ft. lbs. (47 Nm)
- Alternator stud: 18 ft. lbs. (24 Nm)
- Stud nut: 35 ft. lbs. (47 Nm)
- Shield nut: 15 ft. lbs. (20 Nm)
- Lower air duct bolt: 35 inch lbs. (4 Nm)

2008 Models

See Figure 59.

1. Before servicing the vehicle, refer to the Precautions Section.

2. With the vehicle in NEUTRAL, position it on a hoist.

3. Disconnect the negative battery cable.

4. Remove the bolts and the RH lower splash shield.

5. Rotate the front end accessory drive belt tensioner clockwise and position the accessory drive belt aside.

6. Press the locking tab to release the alternator lower air duct from the alternator and remove the lower air duct.

7. Remove the battery harness locators from the alternator shield.

8. Remove the heated oxygen sensor (HO2S) harness locator from the lower part of the alternator. shield.

9. Position the alternator B+ protective cover aside and remove the alternator B+ terminal nut.

10. Position the alternator B+ cable aside

11. Disconnect the alternator electrical connector.

12. Remove the alternator shield nuts.

13. Remove the pin-type retainer from the bottom of the alternator and the alternator shield.

14. Remove the alternator bolt.

15. Remove the alternator stud nuts.

16. Remove the alternator studs.

17. Remove the screws and the alternator upper air duct.

➡ **Lower the vehicle on the hoist to remove the alternator.**

18. Remove the alternator..

To install:

19. Install alternator and upper air duct screws tighten screws to 35 inch. lbs (4 Nm).

20. Install and tighten alternator studs to 18 ft. lbs. (25 Nm).

21. Install alternator stud nuts and tighten to 35 ft. lbs. (47 Nm).

22. Install alternator bolt and tighten to 35 ft. lbs. (47 Nm).

23. Install pin-type retainers to bottom of alternator and shield.

24. Install alternator shield nuts and tighten to 15 ft. lbs. (20 Nm).

25. Reconnect the alternator electrical connector.

26. Reposition the alternator B+ protective cover and tighten the alternator B+ terminal nut to 9 ft. lbs. (12 Nm).

27. Install the heated oxygen sensor (HO2S) harness locator to the lower part of the alternator shield.

28. Install the battery harness locators to the alternator shield.

29. Install the lower air duct.

30. Install drive belt

31. Install bolts and the RH lower splash shield. Tighten bolts to 71 inch lbs. (8 Nm).

32. Connect the negative battery cable.

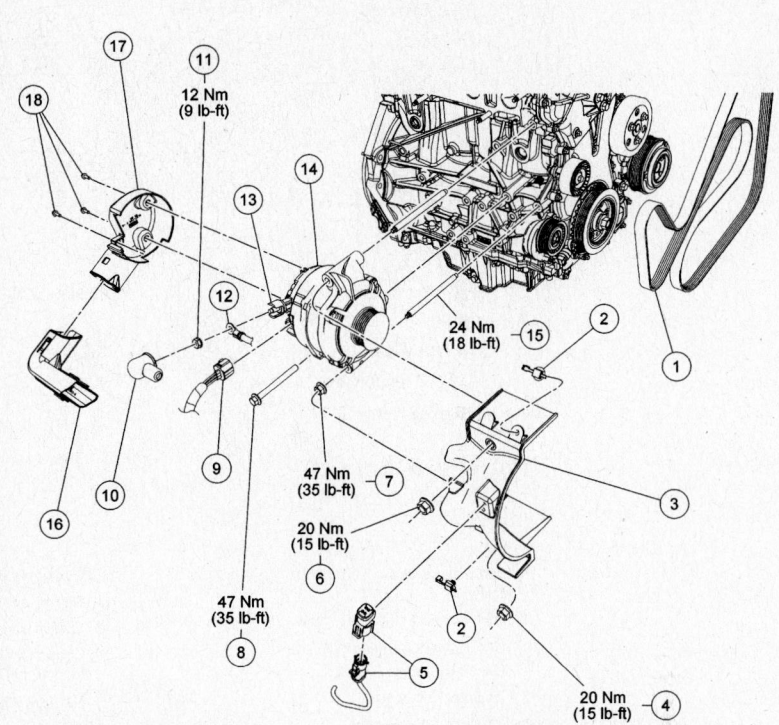

1. Front end accessory drive belt
2. Harness locators
3. Generator shield
4. Generator shield nut
5. Heated oxygen sensor (HO2S) harness connector/harness locator
6. Generator shield nut
7. Generator stud nut
8. Generator bolt
9. Generator electrical connector
10. B+ protective cover
11. Generator B+ terminal nut
12. Generator B+ cable
13. Generator B+ terminal
14. Generator
15. Generator stud (2 required-upper/lower)
16. Generator lower air duct
17. Generator upper air duct
18. Generator upper air duct screws (3 required)

22086_ESCA_G0002

Fig. 59 Alternator mounting—2008 2.3L Engine

3.0L Engine

2005–07 Models

See Figure 60.

1. Before servicing the vehicle, refer to the Precautions Section.

2. Remove or disconnect the following:
- Negative battery cable
- Right side intermediate axle shaft
- Right side splash shield and retainers
- Drive belt
- Alternator electrical connectors
- Alternator. Torque the mounting and adjusting bolts to 35 ft. lbs. (48Nm).

To install:

3. Install or connect the following:
- Alternator. Torque the bolts to 35 ft. lbs. (48 Nm).
- Alternator electrical connectors

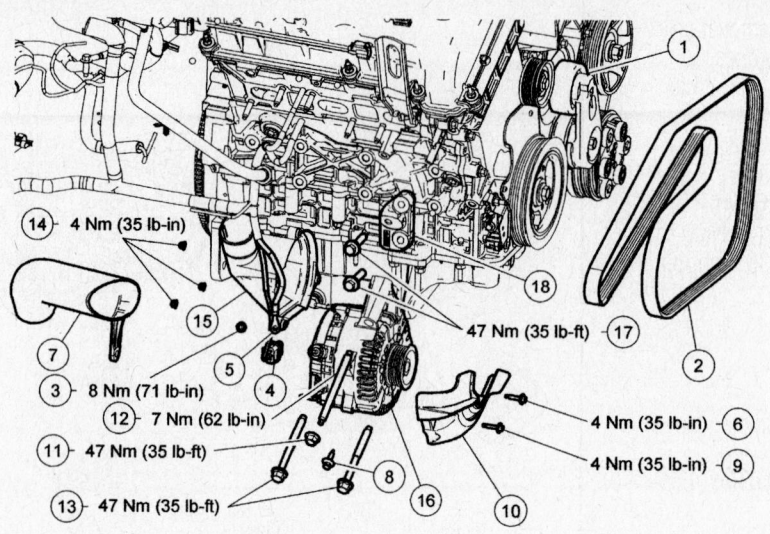

1 Front end accessory drive belt tensioner	11 Generator stud nut
2 Front end accessory drive belt	12 Generator stud
3 Generator B+ terminal nut	13 Generator bolts (2 required)
4 Generator electrical connector	14 Generator lower air duct nuts (3 required)
5 Generator B+ cable	15 Generator lower air duct
6 Generator upper air duct bolt	16 Generator
7 Generator upper air duct	17 Generator bracket bolts (2 required)
8 Pin-type retainer	18 Generator bracket
9 Generator shield bolt	
10 Generator shield	

06017-ESCA-G03

Fig. 60 Alternator mounting—2005–07 3.0L engine

- Drive belt
- Negative battery cable

2008 Models

See Figure 61.

⁂ WARNING

Do not allow any metal object to come in contact with the alternator housing and internal diode cooling fins. A short circuit may result and burn out the diodes. Failure to follow this instruction may result in component damage.

1. Disconnect the negative battery cable.

2. Remove the lower splash shield bolts and the pin-type retainers.

➥The LH lower splash shield must be removed before the RH lower splash shield.

3. Remove the lower splash shields.

4. Rotate the front end accessory drive tensioner counterclockwise and position the accessory drive belt aside

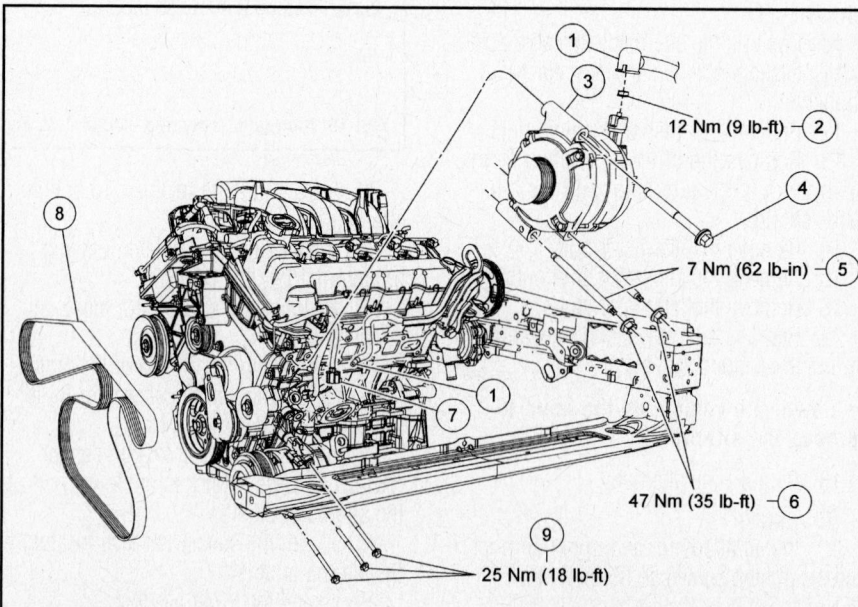

1. Generator B+ cable and B+ protective cover	6. Generator stud nuts (2 required)
2. Generator B+ terminal nut	7. Generator electrical connector
3. Generator	8. Front end accessory drive belt
4. Generator bolt	9. Air conditioning (A/C) compressor bolts (3 required)
5. Generator studs (2 required)	

22086_ESCA_G0003

Fig. 61 Alternator mounting—2008 3.0L engine

5. Disconnect the alternator electrical connector.

6. Position the alternator B+ protective cover aside and remove the alternator B+ terminal nut.

7. Remove the A/C compressor bolts. Use a tie-strap and position A/C compressor aside.

8. Loosen the alternator nuts.

9. Remove the lower alternator studs.

10. Remove the upper alternator bolt and the alternator.

To install:

11. Install alternator and upper bolt.

12. Tighten upper bolt to 35 ft. lbs. (47 Nm) with the vehicle on the ground.

13. Install the lower alternator studs and tighten to 62 inch lbs. (7 Nm).

14. Install and tighten the alternator nuts to 35 ft. lbs. (47 Nm).

15. Reposition and install A/C compressor bolts. Tighten to 18 ft. lbs. (25 Nm).

16. Reposition the alternator B+ protective cover and tighten terminal nut to 9 ft. lbs. (12 Nm).

17. Reconnect the alternator electrical connector.

18. Install accessory drive belt.

19. Install the splash shields and bolts and the 2 pin-type retainers.

20. Tighten the splash shield bolts to 71 inch lbs. (8 Nm).

21. Connect the negative battery cable.

ENGINE ELECTRICAL

FIRING ORDER

See Figures 62 and 63.

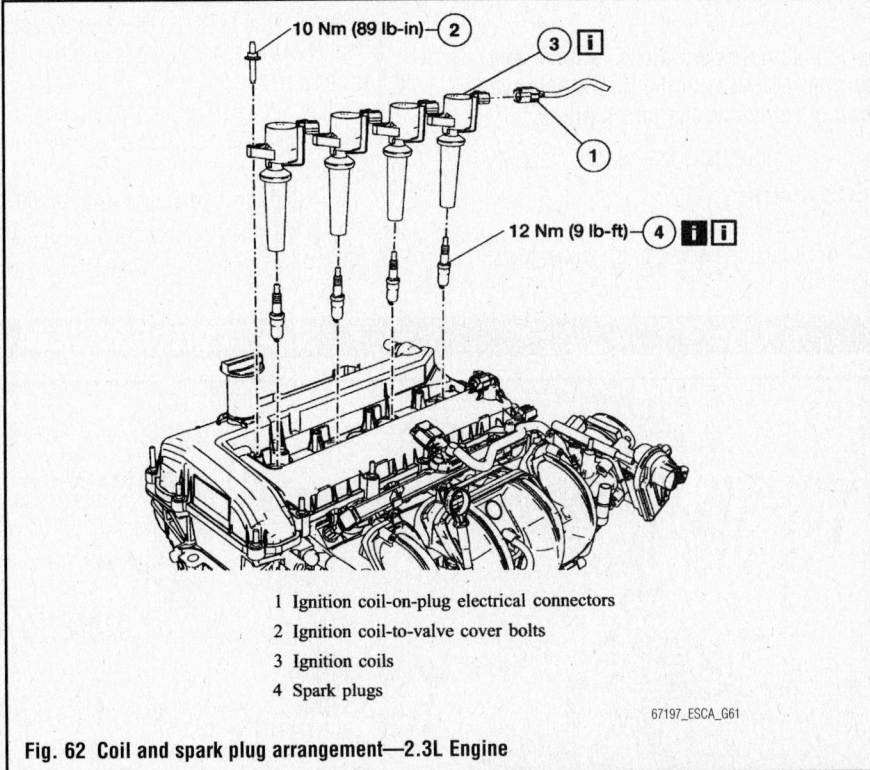

1 Ignition coil-on-plug electrical connectors
2 Ignition coil-to-valve cover bolts
3 Ignition coils
4 Spark plugs

67197_ESCA_G61

Fig. 62 Coil and spark plug arrangement—2.3L Engine

Fig. 63 3.0L engine
Firing order: 1-4-2-5-3-6
Distributorless ignition

79223G26

FRONT OF VEHICLE

IGNITION COIL

REMOVAL & INSTALLATION

2.3L Engine

The 2.3L engine uses an ignition coil-on-plug type of ignition coil.

1. Disconnect the negative battery cable.

2. Disconnect the ignition coil electrical connectors.

3. Remove the bolts and the ignition coils.

To install:

4. Install the ignition coils. Tighten the bolts to 71 inch lbs. (8 Nm).

IGNITION SYSTEM

5. Apply a small amount of dielectric grease to the inside of the ignition coil boots before attaching to the spark plugs.

3.0L Engine

Left Side

See Figure 64.

➡ **The 3.0L engine uses an ignition coil-on-plug type of ignition coil.**

1. Disconnect the negative battery cable.

2. Disconnect the ignition coil-on-plug electrical connector.

3. Remove the bolt, then remove the coil-on-plug.

To install:

4. Install the coil-on-plug. Tighten the coil-on-plug bolt to 11 ft. lbs. (15 Nm).

5. Attach the electrical connector.

➡ **Apply a light film of silicone brake caliper grease and dielectric compound to the interior of the spark plug boot prior to installation.**

6. Connect the negative battery cable.

Right Side

See Figure 65.

➡ **The 3.0L engine uses and ignition coil-on-plug type of ignition coil.**

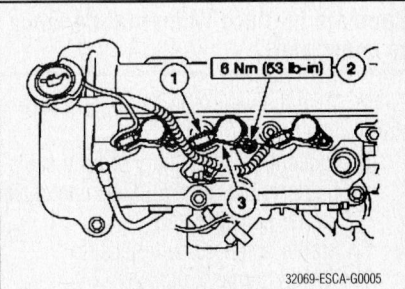

32069-ESCA-G0005

Fig. 64 Detach the electrical connector (1), remove the bolt (2) and the left side ignition coil-on-plug (3)—3.0L engine

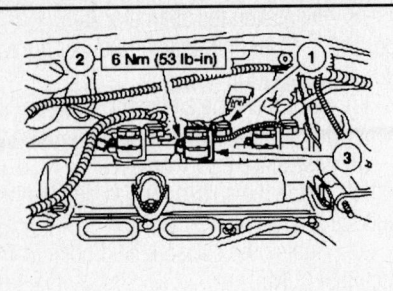

Fig. 65 View of the right side ignition coil-on-plug (3), electrical connector (1) and bolt (2)—3.0L engine

1. Remove the upper intake manifold. Refer to the Engine Mechanical Section.
2. Disconnect the electrical connector.
3. Remove the bolt, then remove the coil-on-plug.

To install:

4. Install the coil-on-plug. Tighten the coil-on-plug bolt to 11 ft. lbs. (15 Nm).
5. Attach the electrical connector.

➡**Apply a light film of silicone brake caliper grease and dielectric compound to the interior of the spark plug boot prior to installation.**

6. Install the upper intake manifold.
7. Connect the negative battery cable.

IGNITION TIMING

ADJUSTMENT

Ignition timing is controlled by the Powertrain Control Module (PCM). No adjustment is necessary or possible.

SPARK PLUGS

REMOVAL & INSTALLATION

2.3L Engine

1. Disconnect the negative battery cable.
2. Disconnect the ignition coil electrical connectors.
3. Remove the bolts and the ignition coils.

➡**Use compressed air to remove any foreign material in the spark plug well before removing the spark plugs.**

4. Remove the spark plugs.

To install:

5. Inspect the spark plugs.
6. Adjust the spark plug gap as neces-

sary. The proper gap is 0.049–0.053 in. (1.25–1.35mm).

7. Install the spark plugs and tighten to 9 ft. lbs. (12 Nm).
8. Apply a small amount of dielectric grease to the inside of the ignition coil boots before attaching to the spark plugs.
9. Install the ignition coils and bolts. Tighten to 89 inch lbs. (10 Nm).
10. Connect the ignition coil electrical connectors.
11. Connect the negative battery cable.

3.0L Engine

➡**The upper intake manifold must be removed to access the RH spark plugs only.**

1. Remove the ignition coil-on-plugs, as outlined in this section.
2. Remove the LH and RH spark plugs.
3. Inspect the spark plugs, as outlined in this section.
4. Adjust the spark plug gap as necessary. The proper gap is 0.052–0.056 in. (1.32–1.42mm).
5. To install, reverse the removal procedure. Tighten the spark plugs to 11 ft. lbs. (15 Nm).

ENGINE ELECTRICAL

STARTER

REMOVAL & INSTALLATION

2.3L Engine
2005–07 Models

See Figure 66.

1. Before servicing the vehicle, refer to the Precautions Section.

✳✳ WARNING

When performing maintenance on the starting system, be aware that heavy gauge leads are connected directly to the battery. Make sure protective caps are in place when maintenance is completed.

2. With the vehicle in NEUTRAL, position it on a hoist
3. Disconnect the battery ground cable.
4. Starter motor solenoid terminal cover
5. Starter solenoid wire
6. Starter solenoid battery cable
7. Wiring harness retainer
8. Ground strap
9. Starter motor stud bolts
10. Starter motor bracket bolt

STARTING SYSTEM

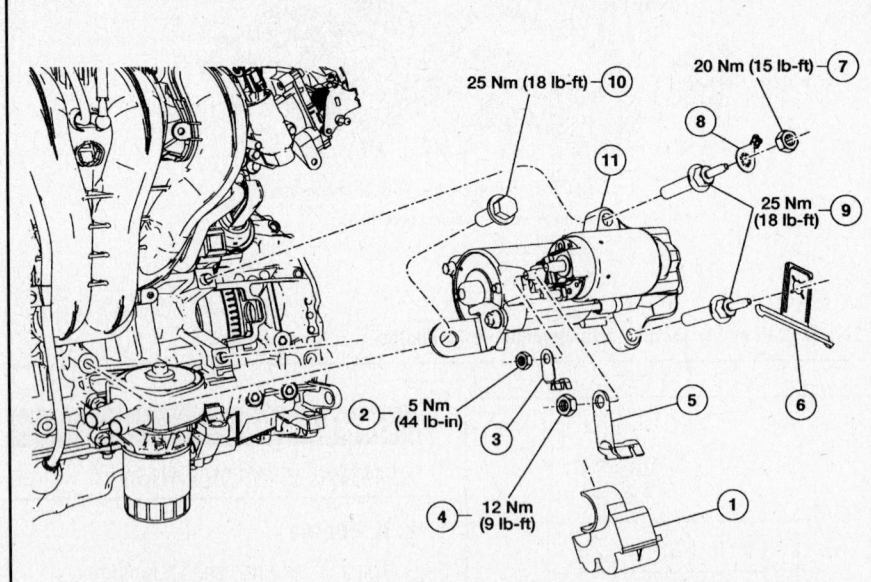

1 Starter motor solenoid terminal cover	5 Starter solenoid battery cable	9 Starter motor stud bolts
2 Starter solenoid wire nut	6 Wiring harness retainer	10 Starter motor bracket bolt
3 Starter solenoid wire	7 Ground strap nut	11 Starter motor
4 Starter solenoid battery cable nut	8 Ground strap	

Fig. 66 Starter mounting—2005–07 2.3L engine

11. Starter motor

12. To install, reverse the removal procedure. Torque the starter and bracket bolts to 18 ft. lbs. (25 Nm).

2008 Models

1. With the vehicle in NEUTRAL, position it on a hoist.

2. Disconnect the negative battery cable.

3. Remove the starter solenoid wire nut.

4. Remove the starter solenoid battery cable nut and disconnect the starter motor solenoid terminal cover and cables.

5. Disconnect the wiring harness retainer and position aside the wiring harness.

6. Remove the ground strap nut and position aside the strap.

7. Remove the stud bolts and the starter motor.

To install:

8. Install starter motor and mounting stud bolts, tighten bolts to 26 ft. lbs. (35 Nm).

9. Reposition ground strap and tighten ground strap nut to 18 ft. lbs. (25 Nm).

10. Install battery cable and tighten nut to 9 ft. lbs (12 Nm).

11. Install solenoid wire and tighten nut to 44 inch lbs. (5 Nm).

12. Secure all retainers, wires and cover.

13. Connect the negative battery cable.

3.0L Engine

2005–07 Models

1. Before servicing the vehicle, refer to the Precautions Section.

2. Drain the cooling system.

3. Remove or disconnect the following:
- Negative battery cable
- Air cleaner outlet tube
- Coolant hoses and move the thermostat aside
- Starter electrical connectors
- Starter

To install:

4. Install or connect the following:

- Starter. Torque bolts to 20 ft. lbs. (27 Nm).
- Starter electrical connectors and reposition the thermostat
- Connect the 4 coolant hoses
- Air cleaner outlet tube
- Negative battery cable

5. Fill the cooling system to the proper level.

6. Start the vehicle and check for leaks, repair if necessary.

2008 Models

See Figure 67.

1. Disconnect the negative battery cable.

2. Remove the air cleaner.

3. Disconnect the transmission shift cable-to-manual lever.

4. Remove the transmission cable bracket bolts and detach the wire harness retainer and position aside the transmission cable and bracket.

5. Remove the starter motor solenoid wire nut.

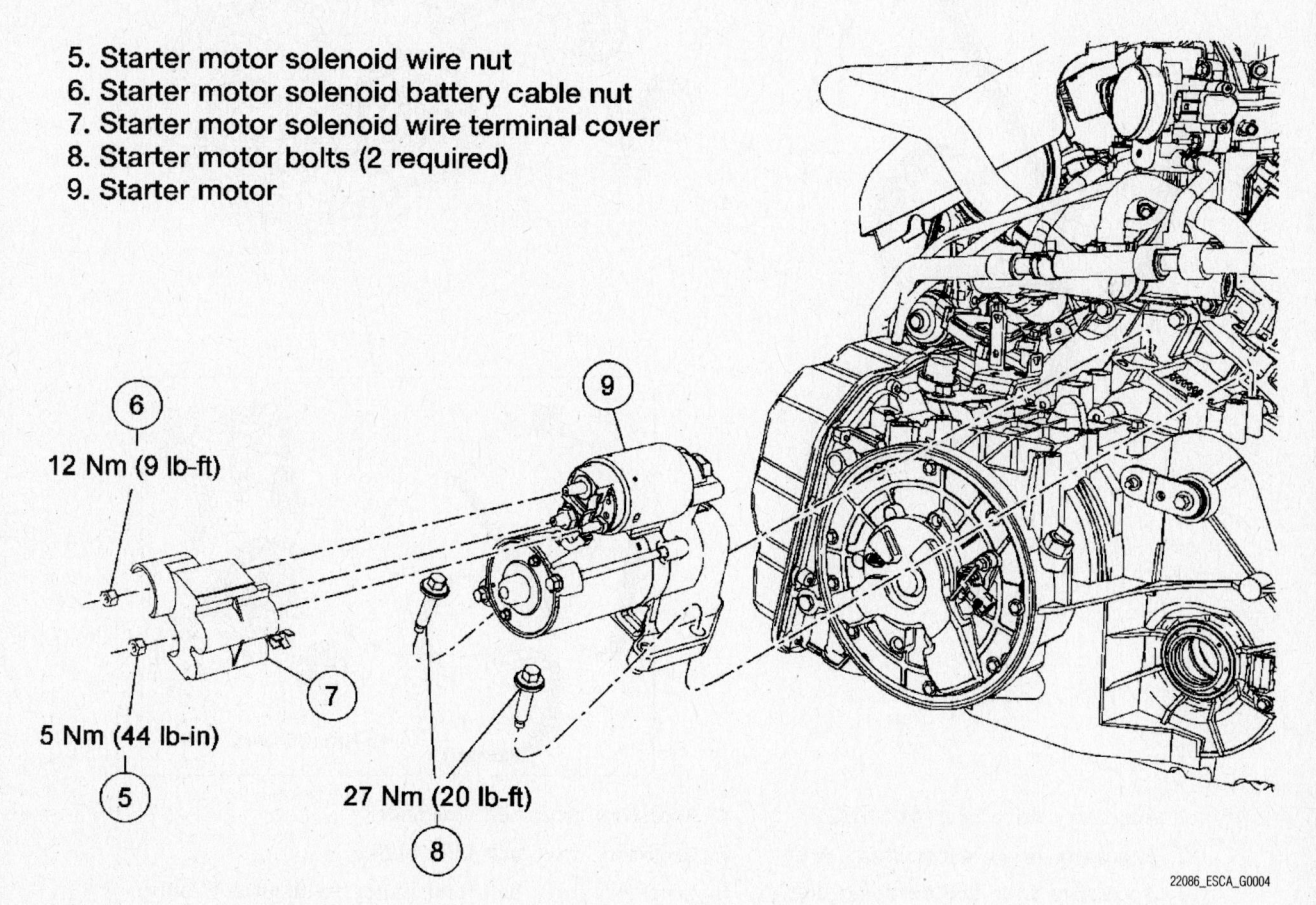

5. Starter motor solenoid wire nut
6. Starter motor solenoid battery cable nut
7. Starter motor solenoid wire terminal cover
8. Starter motor bolts (2 required)
9. Starter motor

12 Nm (9 lb-ft)

5 Nm (44 lb-in)

27 Nm (20 lb-ft)

Fig. 67 Starter mounting—2008 3.0L engine

22086_ESCA_G0004

6. Remove the starter motor solenoid battery cable nut and position aside the cables.

7. Remove the bolts and the starter motor.

To install:

8. Install starter motor and

mounting bolts, tighten bolts to 20 ft. lbs. (27 Nm).

9. Reposition battery cable and tighten cable nut to 9 ft. lbs. (12 Nm).

10. Install solenoid wire and tighten nut to 44 inch lbs. (5 Nm).

11. Install transmission shift cable

bracket, tighten mounting bolts to 17 ft. lbs. (23 Nm).

12. Reconnect the transmission shift cable-to-manual lever.

13. Install the air cleaner.

14. Connect the negative battery cable.

ENGINE MECHANICAL

➡Disconnecting the negative battery cable may interfere with the functions of the on board computer systems and may require the computer to

undergo a relearning process, once the negative battery cable is reconnected.

ACCESSORY DRIVE BELTS

ACCESSORY BELT ROUTING

See Figures 68 through 70.

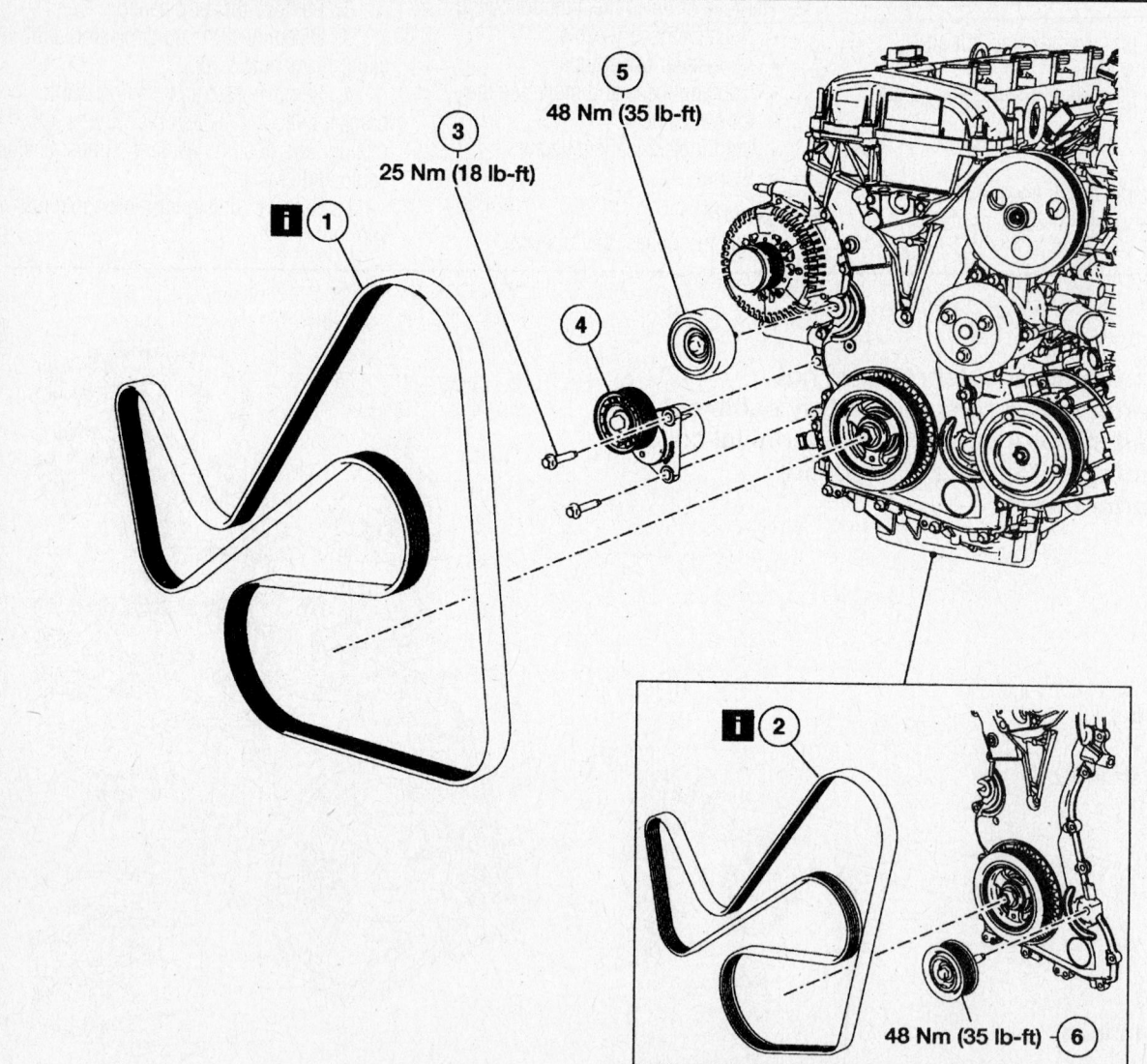

1 Accessory drive belt (with A/C)
2 Accessory drive belt (without A/C)
3 Accessory drive belt tensioner bolts
4 Accessory drive belt tensioner
5 Accessory drive belt idler pulley
6 Accessory drive belt idler pulley (without A/C only)

67197-ESCA-G62

Fig. 68 Accessory drive belt routings—2.3L engine

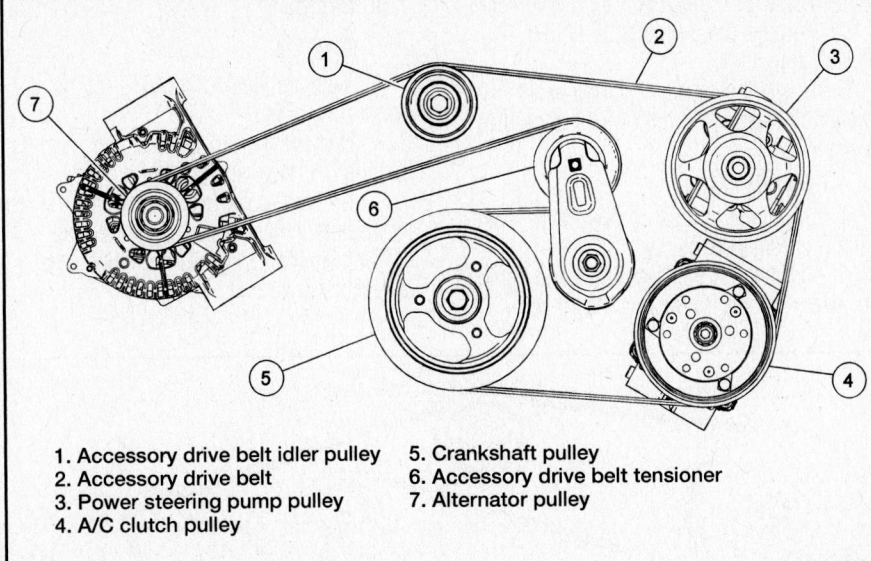

1. Accessory drive belt idler pulley
2. Accessory drive belt
3. Power steering pump pulley
4. A/C clutch pulley
5. Crankshaft pulley
6. Accessory drive belt tensioner
7. Alternator pulley

22086_ESCA_G0076

Fig. 69 Accessory drive belt routing—3.0L engine

1. Camshaft drive pulley
2. Water pump drive belt
3. Water pump pulley

22086_ESCA_G0077

Fig. 70 Water pump drive belt—3.0L engine

INSPECTION

❊❊ WARNING

Under no circumstances should the accessory drive belt, tensioner or pulleys be lubricated as potential damage to the belt material and tensioner damping mechanism will occur. Do not apply any fluids or belt dressing to the accessory drive belt or pulleys.

The water pump drive belt is on back of engine. It is driven off the rear cam pulley and doesn't have any adjustments.

Visual Inspection

Visually inspect the belt for obvious signs of mechanical damage:
- Drive belt cracking/chunking/wear
- Belt/pulley contamination
- Incorrectly routed belt

- Pulley misalignment or excessive pulley runout
- Loose or mislocated hardware
- Incorrectly routed power steering tubes (rubbing)

Eliminate all other non-belt related noises that could cause belt misdiagnosis, such as A/C compressor engagement chirp, power steering cavitations at low temperatures, variable camshaft timing (VCT) tick or alternator whine.

If a concern is found, correct the condition before proceeding to the next section.

V-Ribbed Serpentine Drive Belt With Cracks Across Ribs

See Figure 71.

➡**Up to 15 cracks in a rib over a distance of 4 inches (100mm) can be considered acceptable. If damage exceeds the acceptable limit or any chunks are**

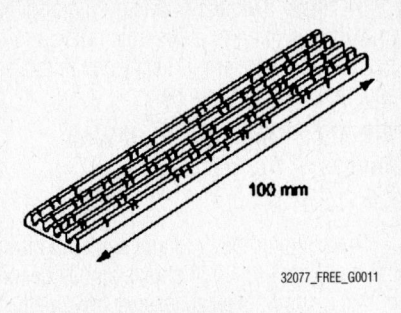

100 mm

32077_FREE_G0011

Fig. 71 Up to 15 cracks in a rib over a distance of 4 inches (100mm) can be considered acceptable. If cracks exceed this standard, install a new belt

found to be missing from the ribs, a new belt must be installed.

1. Check the belt for cracks. Up to 15 cracks in a rib over a distance of 4 inches (100mm) can be considered acceptable. If cracks exceed this standard, install a new belt.

V- Ribbed Serpentine Belt With Piling

See Figure 72.

➡**Piling is an excessive buildup in the V-grooves of the belt.**

The condition of the V-ribbed drive belt should be compared against the illustration and appropriate action taken.

1. Small scattered deposits of rubber material. This is not a concern, therefore, installation of a new belt is not required.

2. Longer deposit areas building up to 50 percent of the rib height. This is not considered a concern but it can result in excessive noise. If noise is apparent, install a new belt.

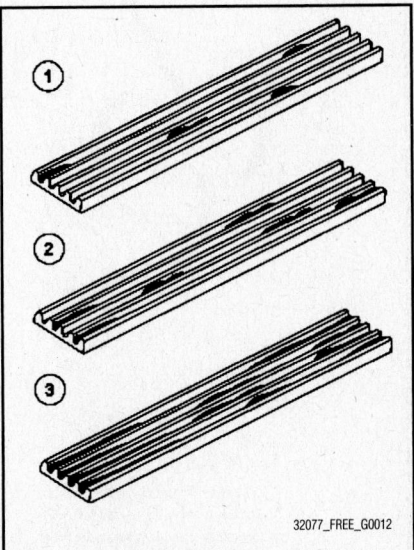

32077_FREE_G0012

Fig. 72 Compare the condition of the belt with the accompanying text

3. Heavy deposits building up along the grooves resulting in a possible noise and belt stability concern. If heavy deposits are apparent, install a new belt.

V-Ribbed Serpentine Belt With Chunks of Rib Missing

See Figure 73.

There should be no chunks missing from the belt ribs. If the belt shows any evidence of this, install a new accessory drive belt.

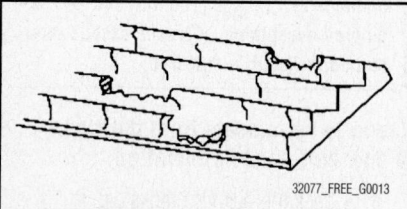

32077_FREE_G0013

Fig. 73 Replace the belt if missing chunks are found during inspection

ADJUSTMENT

The belts used on these vehicle are equipped with automatic (spring load) tensioners which maintain tension. No adjustment is necessary or possible.

REMOVAL & INSTALLATION

2.3L Engine

See Figure 74.

1. Raise and safely support the vehicle..
2. Remove the 5 bolts and the RH splash shield.
3. Rotate the accessory drive belt tensioner clockwise and remove the accessory drive belt.

To install:

4. Install the accessory drive belt. Make sure it is routed correctly.
5. Install the RH splash shield and tighten the retaining bolts to 80 inch lbs. (9 Nm).

3.0L Engine

See Figure 75.

1. With the vehicle in NEUTRAL, position it on a hoist.
2. Remove the pin-type retainer, 5 bolts and the RH lower splash shield.
3. Using a suitable belt tensioner release tool, rotate the accessory drive belt tensioner counterclockwise and remove the accessory drive belt.

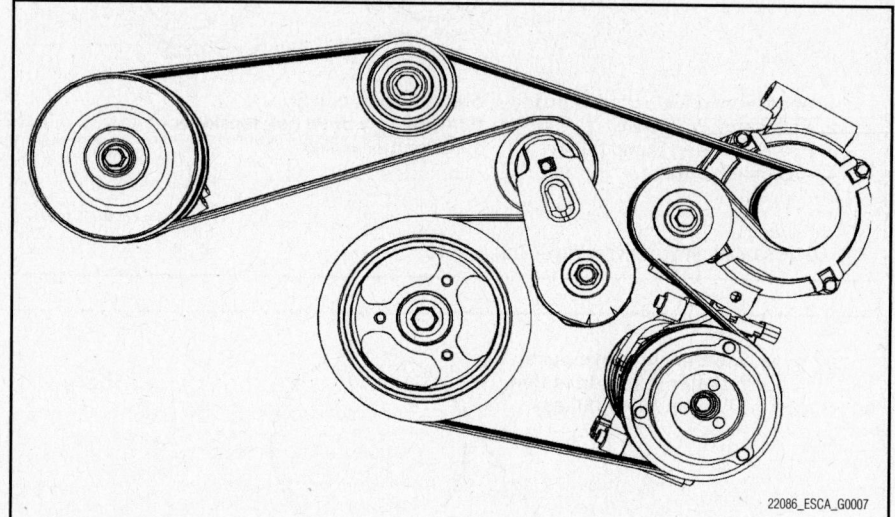

22086_ESCA_G0007

Fig. 75 Accessory drive belt routing—2008 3.0L engines with A/C and hydraulic power steering shown, other years similar

➡️Refer to the illustration for correct drive belt routing.

4. Installation is the reverse of the removal procedure. Make sure the belt is properly routed.

Water Pump Belt

See Figures 76 and 77.

1. With the vehicle in NEUTRAL, position it on a hoist.
2. Cut and remove the coolant pump belt.

To install:

3. Install the coolant pump belt on the coolant pump pulley and position it on the camshaft pulley.

➡️This belt does not have any adjustments.

❊❊ WARNING

Do not use any screwdrivers, pliers or other metal objects that could cause damage to the belt or camshaft pulley while installing the belt.

4. Remove the pin-type retainer, 5 bolts and the RH lower splash shield.

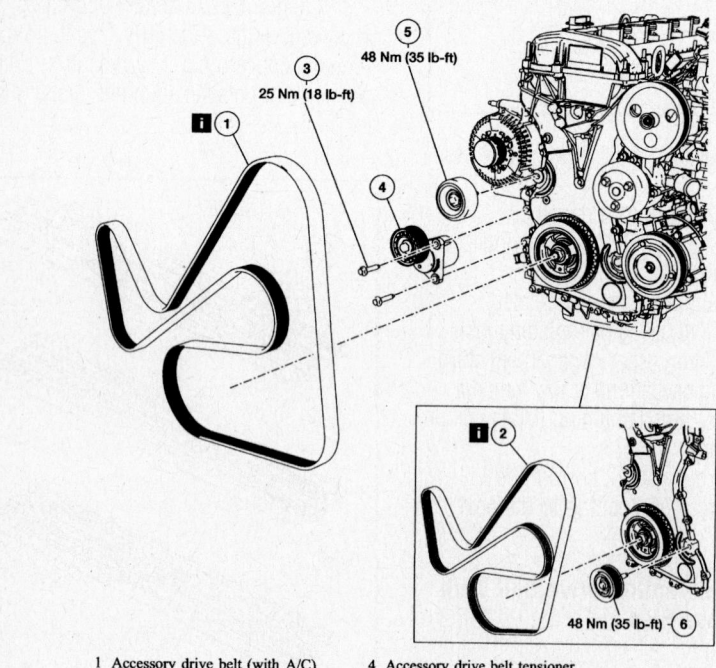

| ⑤ 48 Nm (35 lb-ft) |
| ③ 25 Nm (18 lb-ft) |
| ⓘ ① |
| ④ |
| ⓘ ② |
| 48 Nm (35 lb-ft) ⑥ |

1 Accessory drive belt (with A/C)
2 Accessory drive belt (without A/C)
3 Accessory drive belt tensioner bolts
4 Accessory drive belt tensioner
5 Accessory drive belt idler pulley
6 Accessory drive belt idler pulley (without A/C only)

67197-ESCA-G62

Fig. 74 Accessory drive belt routings—2.3L engine

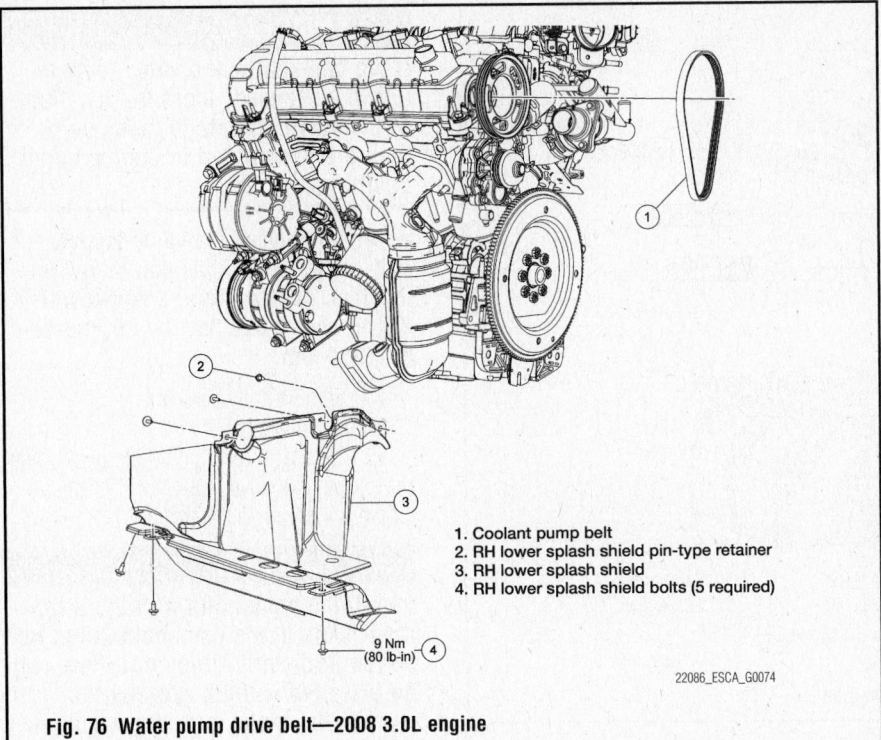

1. Coolant pump belt
2. RH lower splash shield pin-type retainer
3. RH lower splash shield
4. RH lower splash shield bolts (5 required)

9 Nm
(80 lb-in)

22086_ESCA_G0074

Fig. 76 Water pump drive belt—2008 3.0L engine

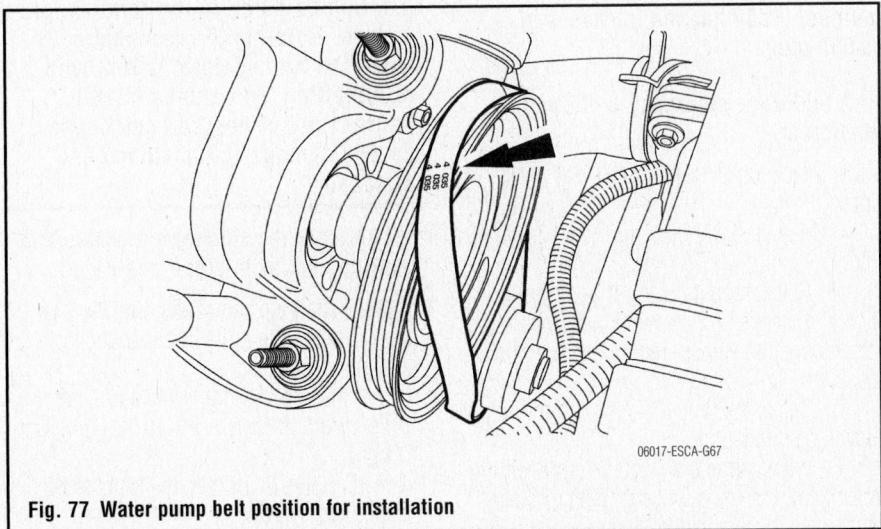

06017-ESCA-G67

Fig. 77 Water pump belt position for installation

5. Rotate the crankshaft clockwise to seat the coolant pump belt on the camshaft pulley.

CAMSHAFT AND VALVE LIFTERS

REMOVAL & INSTALLATION

2.3L Engine

See Figures 78 through 82.

1. Before servicing the vehicle, refer to the Precautions Section.

✳✳ WARNING

During engine repair procedures, cleanliness is extremely important.

Any foreign material, including any material created while cleaning gasket surfaces that enters the oil passages, coolant passages or the oil pan can cause engine failure.

✳✳ WARNING

The crankshaft, the crankshaft sprocket and the pulley are fitted together by friction, using diamond washers between the flange faces on each part. For that reason, the crankshaft sprocket is also unfastened if you loosen the pulley. Therefore, the engine must be retimed

each time the damper is removed. Otherwise severe engine damage can occur.

2. With the vehicle in NEUTRAL, position it on a hoist.

➡Valve tappets are select fit and the valve clearance must be checked before removing the tappets.

✳✳ WARNING

Turn the engine clockwise only, and only use the crankshaft bolt.

➡Before removing the camshafts, measure the clearance of each valve at base circle, with the lobe pointed away from the tappet. Failure to measure all clearances prior to removing the camshafts will necessitate repeated removal and installation and wasted labor time.

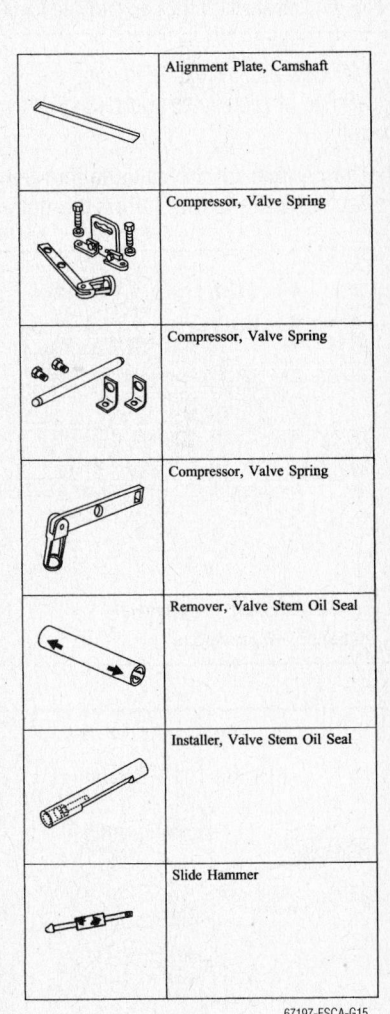

	Alignment Plate, Camshaft
	Compressor, Valve Spring
	Compressor, Valve Spring
	Compressor, Valve Spring
	Remover, Valve Stem Oil Seal
	Installer, Valve Stem Oil Seal
	Slide Hammer

67197-ESCA-G15

Fig. 78 Tools necessary for camshaft and lifter removal—2.3L engine

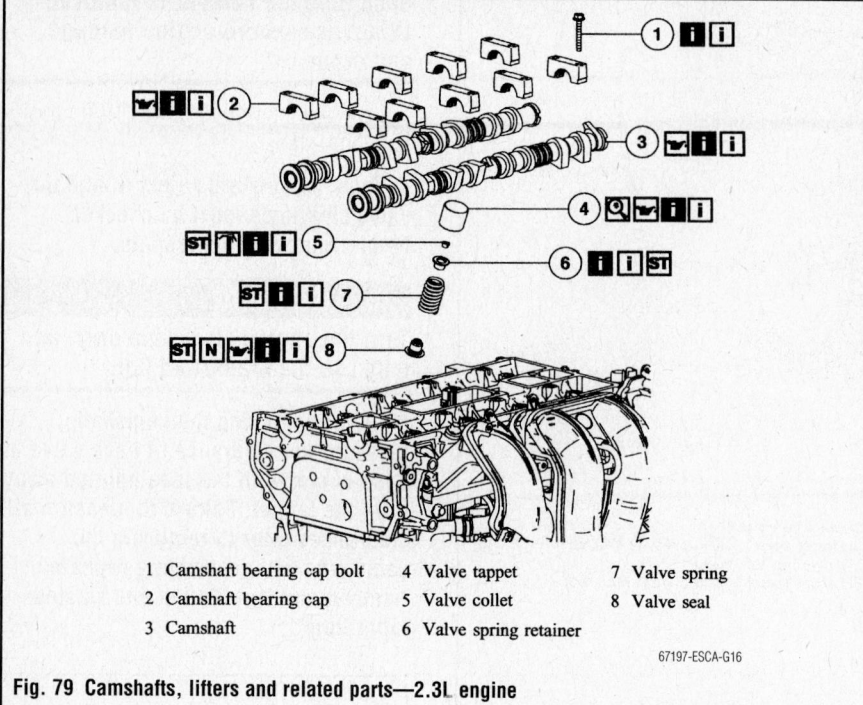

1 Camshaft bearing cap bolt   4 Valve tappet   7 Valve spring
2 Camshaft bearing cap   5 Valve collet   8 Valve seal
3 Camshaft   6 Valve spring retainer

67197-ESCA-G16

Fig. 79 Camshafts, lifters and related parts—2.3L engine

3. Use a feeler gauge to measure the clearance of each valve and record its location.

➡The number on the valve tappet only reflects the digits that follow the deci-

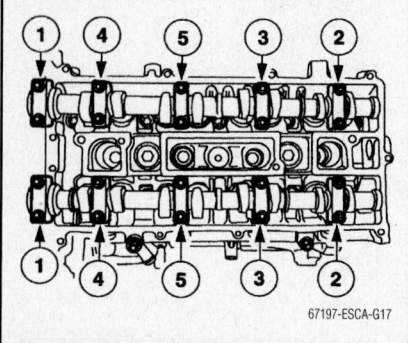

67197-ESCA-G17

Fig. 80 Camshaft cap removal sequence—2.3L engine

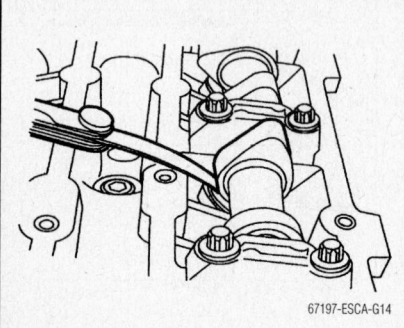

67197-ESCA-G14

Fig. 81 Valve clearance check—2.3L engine

mal. For example, a tappet with the number 0.650 has the thickness of 3.650 mm.

➡A midrange clearance is the most desirable:

- Intake: 0.22–0.28 mm (0.008–0.011 inch)
- Exhaust: 0.27–0.33 mm (0.010–0.013 inch)

4. Select tappets using this formula: tappet thickness = measured clearance + the base tappet thickness–most desirable thickness.

5. Select the tappets and mark the installation location.

6. If any tappets do not measure within specifications, install new tappets in these locations.

7. Remove the timing chain and sprockets.

8. Mark the position of the camshaft lobes on the No. 1 cylinder for assembly reference.

✳✳ WARNING

Failure to follow the camshaft loosening procedure can result in damage to the camshafts.

9. Loosen the camshaft bearing bolts in the sequence shown, one turn at a time. Repeat until all the tension is released.

10. Remove the camshaft bearing caps.

✳✳ WARNING

If the camshafts and valve tappets are to be reused, mark the location of the valve tappets to make sure they are assembled in their original positions.

➡The number on the valve tappets only reflects the digits that follow the decimal. For example, a tappet with the number 0.650 has the thickness of 3.650 mm.

11. Remove the camshafts.
12. Valve tappets.
13. To install, reverse the removal procedure. Coat the valve tappets with clean engine oil and insert them.

✳✳ WARNING

Install the camshafts with the alignment slots in the camshafts lined up so the Camshaft Alignment Plate can be installed without rotating the camshafts. Make sure the lobes on the No. 1 cylinder are in the same position as noted in the removal procedure. Rotating the camshafts when the timing chain is removed, or installing the camshafts 180 degrees out of position can cause severe damage to the valves and pistons.

➡Lubricate the camshaft journals and bearing caps with clean engine oil.

14. Install the camshafts and bearing caps. Tighten the bolts in the sequence shown in three stages.

  a. Stage 1: Tighten the camshaft bearing bolt caps one turn at a time until tight.

  b. Stage 2: Tighten the bolts to 62 inch lbs. (7 Nm).

  c. Stage 3: Tighten the bolts to 12 ft. lbs. (16 Nm).

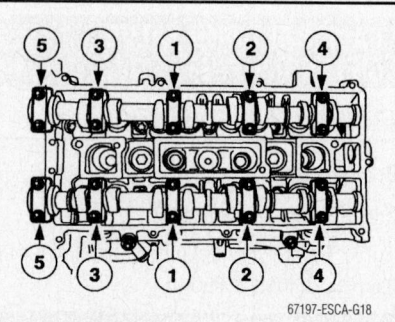

67197-ESCA-G18

Fig. 82 Camshaft cap torque sequence—2.3L engine

3.0L Engine

Left Side

See Figure 83.

1. Before servicing the vehicle, refer to the Precautions Section.
2. Remove or disconnect the following:
   - Negative battery cable
   - Water pump belt
   - Timing drive components
   - Camshaft oil seal
   - Camshaft oil seal retainer
   - Camshaft cap bolts by loosening them in sequence
   - Camshafts

To install:

3. Install or connect the following:
   - Camshaft bearing caps in their original position
   - Align the camshafts
   - Bearing thrust caps and hand tighten the bolts. When aligned properly, torque the bolts to 89 inch lbs. (10 Nm).
   - Timing drive components
   - Camshaft oil seal retainer
   - Crankshaft oil seal
   - Water pump drive pulley
   - Water pump belt
   - Negative battery cable

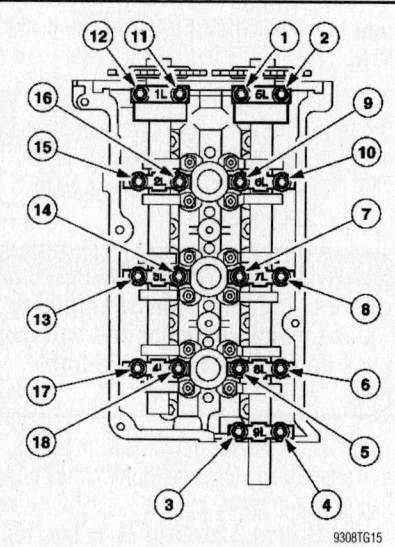

Fig. 83 Remove and install the left side camshaft bearing caps in sequence–3.0L engine

Right Side

See Figure 84.

1. Before servicing the vehicle, refer to the Precautions Section.
2. Remove or disconnect the following:
   - Negative battery cable

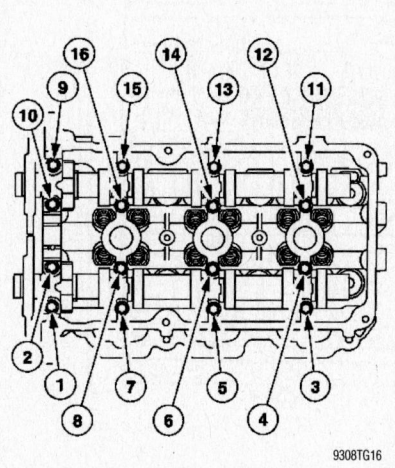

Fig. 84 Remove and install the right side camshaft bearing caps in sequence–3.0L engine

   - Timing drive components
   - Camshaft cap bolts by loosening them in sequence
   - Camshafts caps
   - Camshafts

To install:

3. Install or connect the following:
   - Camshaft bearing caps in their original position
   - Align the camshafts
   - Bearing caps and hand tighten the bolts
   - Bearing thrust caps and hand tighten the bolts. When aligned properly, torque the bolts to 89 inch lbs. (10 Nm).
   - Timing drive components
   - Negative battery cable

CRANKSHAFT DAMPER

REMOVAL & INSTALLATION

See Figures 85 through 88.

➡The following special tools, or their equivalents, are required for this procedure. Camshaft Alignment Plate 303-465 (T94P-6256-CH), Crankshaft Timing Peg 303-057, Drive Pinion Flange Holding Fixture 205-126 (T78P-4851-A), Adapter for 205-126 (205-072-02).

❊❊ WARNING

During engine repair procedures, cleanliness is extremely important. Any foreign material, including any material created while cleaning gas- ket surfaces, that enters the oil passages, coolant passages or the oil pan can cause engine failure.

❊❊ WARNING

The crankshaft, the crankshaft sprocket and the pulley are fitted together by friction, using diamond washers between the flange faces on each part. For that reason, the crankshaft sprocket is also unfastened if you loosen the pulley. Therefore, the engine must be retimed each time the damper is removed. Otherwise severe engine damage can occur.

1. Raise and safely support the vehicle.
2. Remove the accessory drive belt.
3. Remove the valve cover, as outlined in this section.

❊❊ WARNING

Failure to position the No. 1 piston at top dead center (TDC) can result in damage to the engine. Turn the engine in the normal direction of rotation only.

4. Using the crankshaft pulley bolt, turn the crankshaft clockwise to position the No. 1 piston at TDC. The hole in the crankshaft pulley should be in the 6 o'clock position.

❊❊ WARNING

The special tool 303-465 is for camshaft alignment only. Using this tool to prevent engine rotation can result in engine damage.

➡The camshaft timing slots are offset. If the special tool cannot be installed, rotate the crankshaft one complete

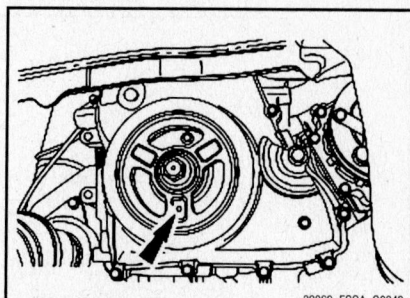

Fig. 85 Using the crankshaft pulley bolt, turn the crankshaft clockwise to position the No. 1 piston at TDC. The hole in the crankshaft pulley should be in the 6 o'clock position

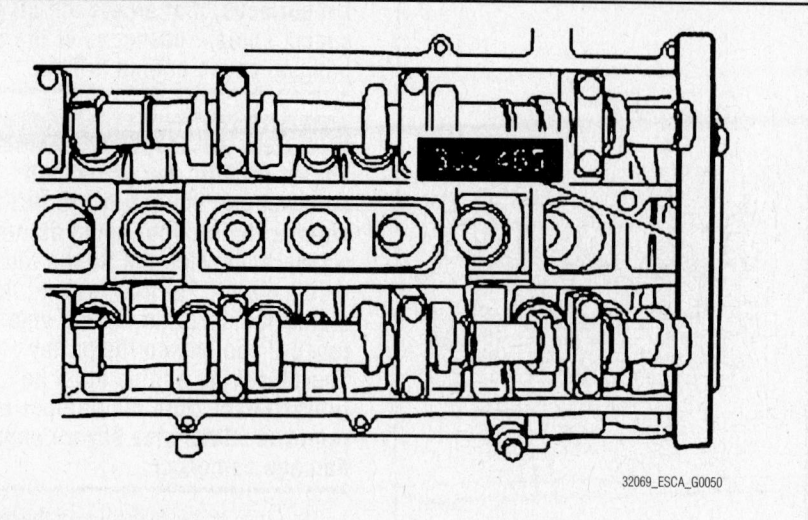

Fig. 86 Install the camshaft alignment plate special tool in the slots on the rear of both camshafts

revolution clockwise to correctly position the camshafts.

5. Install Camshaft Alignment Plate 303-465, or equivalent special tool in the slots on the rear of both camshafts.

6. Remove the engine plug bolt.

➡**The special tool will contact the crankshaft and prevent it from turning** past TDC. However, the crankshaft can still be rotated in the counterclockwise direction. The crankshaft must remain at the TDC position during the crankshaft pulley removal and installation.

7. Install Crankshaft Timing Peg 303-057 or equivalent special tool.

8. Install Drive Pinion Flange Holding Fixture 205-126 (T78P-4851-A)

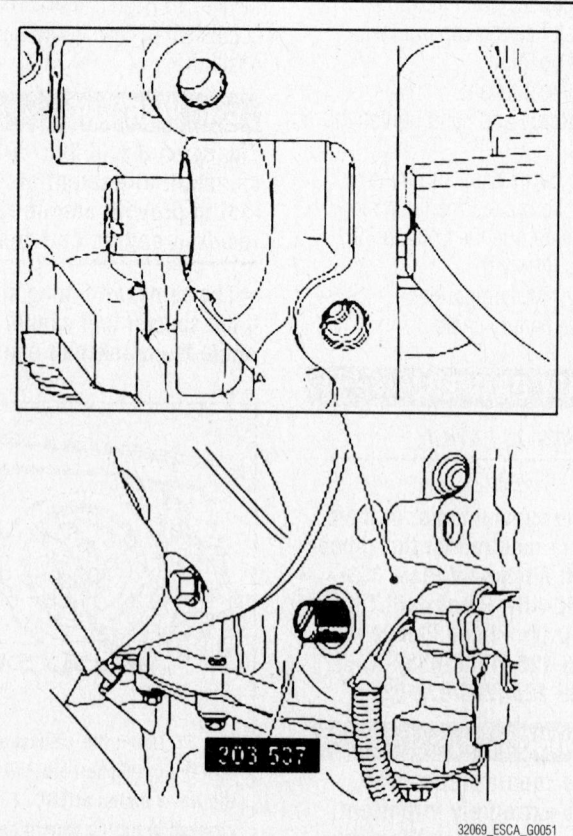

Fig. 87 Install Crankshaft Timing Peg 303-057 or equivalent special tool

and Adapter for 205-126 (205-072-02) or equivalent special tools.

✲✲ WARNING

Failure to hold the crankshaft pulley in place while loosening the bolt can result in damage to the engine.

✲✲ WARNING

If the crankshaft sprocket diamond washer comes off with the crankshaft pulley it must be installed back onto the crankshaft.

9. Remove the crankshaft pulley bolt and washer. Discard the bolt.

10. Remove the crankshaft pulley.

To install:

➡**Do not reuse the crankshaft pulley bolt.**

➡**Apply clean engine oil on the seal area before installing.**

11. Install the crankshaft pulley and hand-tighten the bolt.

✲✲ WARNING

Only hand-tighten the bolt or damage to the front cover can occur.

➡**The following 2 steps will correctly align the crankshaft pulley to the crankshaft.**

12. Install a standard 6-mm (0.23-in.) × 18-mm (0.7-in.) bolt through the crankshaft pulley and thread it into the front cover.

13. Rotate the pulley as necessary to align the bolt holes.

✲✲ WARNING

Failure to hold the crankshaft pulley in place while tightening the bolt can cause damage to the engine front cover.

14. Using the special tools to hold the crankshaft pulley in place, tighten the crankshaft pulley bolt in 2 stages:

   a. Stage 1: Tighten to 74 ft. lbs. (100 Nm).

   b. Stage 2: Tighten an additional 90 degrees (1/4 turn).

15. Remove the 6-mm (0.23-in.) × 18-mm (0.7-in.) bolt.

16. Remove the special tools.

➡**Only turn the engine in the normal direction of rotation.**

17. Turn the engine 2 complete revolutions.

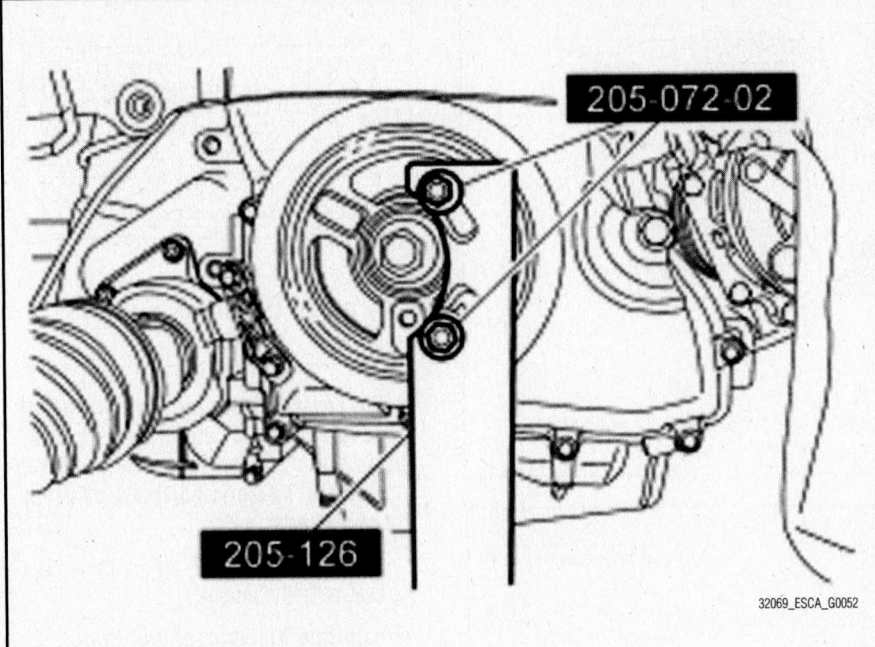

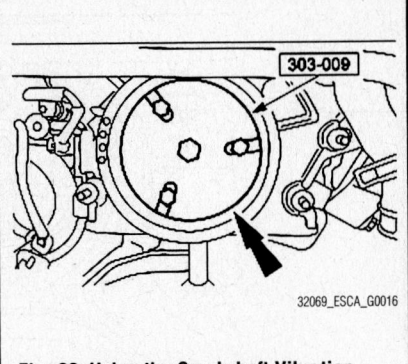

Fig. 90 Using the Crankshaft Vibration Damper Remover tool to remove the crankshaft pulley

Fig. 88 Install Drive Pinion Flange Holding Fixture and Adapter special tools

➡Only turn the engine in the normal direction of rotation.

18. Turn the crankshaft until the No. 1 piston is at TDC.

➡The following special tools, or their equivalents, are required for this procedure. Camshaft Alignment Plate 303-465 (T94P-6256-CH), Crankshaft Timing Peg 303-057, Drive Pinion Flange Holding Fixture 205-126 (T78P-4851-A), Adapter for 205-126 (205-072-02).

19. Install the special crankshaft timing peg tool.

✳✳ WARNING

Only hand-tighten the bolt or damage to the front cover can occur. Using the 6-mm (0.23-in.) x 18-mm (0.7-in.) bolt, check the position of the crankshaft pulley. If it is not possible to install the bolt, correct the engine timing.

20. Using the camshaft alignment plate special tool, check the position of the camshafts. If it is not possible to install the special tool, correct the engine timing.
21. Remove the 6-mm (0.23-in.) x 18-mm (0.7-in.) bolt.
22. Install the engine plug bolt and tighten to 15 ft. lbs. (20 Nm).
23. Install the accessory drive belt.
24. Install the valve cover.

3.0L Engine

See Figures 89 through 92.

1. Remove the accessory drive belt.
2. Remove the splash shield.
3. Install the Strap Wrench 303-D055 (D85L-6000-A), or equivalent special tool.
4. Remove the crankshaft pulley bolt and washer.
5. Using the Crankshaft Vibration Damper Remover 303-009 (T58P-6316-D) or equivalent special tool, remove the crankshaft pulley.

To install:

➡Clean the keyway and slot using metal surface cleaner before applying silicone gasket and sealer.

➡The crankshaft pulley must be installed and the bolt tightened within

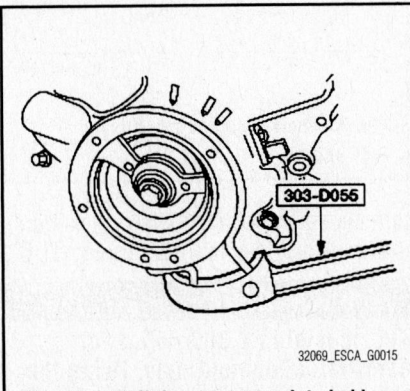

Fig. 89 Install the strap wrench to hold the crankshaft pulley stationary

four minutes of applying the silicone gasket and sealer.

6. Apply silicone gasket and sealant to the end of the keyway slot.

➡Lubricate the outside diameter sealing surface of the crankshaft pulley with clean engine oil.

7. Using Crankshaft Vibration Damper Installer 303-102 (T74P-6316-B) or equivalent special tool, install the crankshaft pulley.

➡Use an appropriate strap wrench to hold the crankshaft pulley.

8. Install the bolt and the washer and tighten in four stages.
   a. Stage 1: Tighten to 89 ft. lbs. (120 Nm).
   b. Stage 2: Loosen 360 degrees.
   c. Stage 3: Tighten to 37 ft. lbs. (50 Nm).
   d. Stage 4: Tighten an additional 90 degrees.
9. Install RH front inner splash shield. Tighten the retainers to 80 inch lbs. (9 Nm).
10. Install the accessory drive belt.

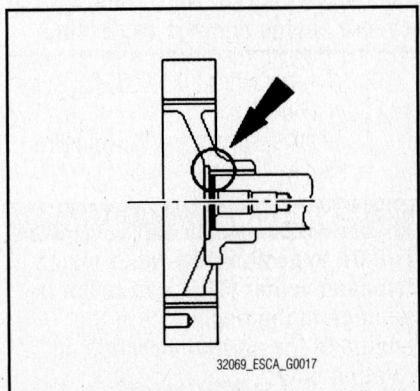

Fig. 91 Apply silicone gasket and sealant to the end of the keyway slot

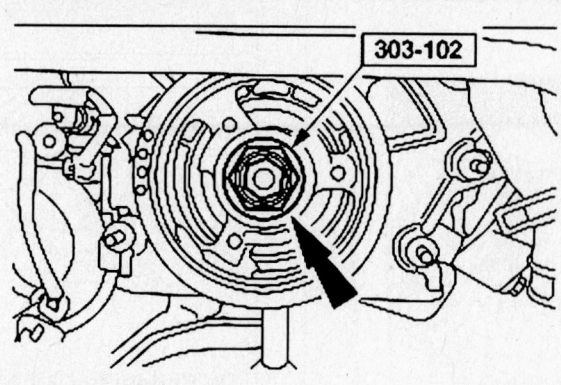

Fig. 92 Using Crankshaft Vibration Damper Installer 303-102 (T74P-6316-B) or equivalent special tool, install the crankshaft pulley

CRANKSHAFT FRONT SEAL

REMOVAL & INSTALLATION

2.3L Engine

See Figures 93 through 98.

1. Before servicing the vehicle, refer to the Precautions Section.

✳✳ WARNING

During engine repair procedures, cleanliness is extremely important. Any foreign material, including any material created while cleaning gasket surfaces that enters the oil passages, coolant passages or the oil pan can cause engine failure.

✳ WARNING

The crankshaft, the crankshaft sprocket and the pulley are fitted together by friction, using diamond washers between the flange faces on each part. For that reason, the crankshaft sprocket is also unfastened if you loosen the pulley. Therefore, the engine must be retimed each time the damper is removed. Otherwise severe engine damage can occur.

2. With the vehicle in NEUTRAL, position it on a hoist.
3. Remove the accessory drive belt.
4. Remove the valve cover.

✳ WARNING

Failure to position the No. 1 piston at top dead center (TDC) can result in damage to the engine. Turn the engine in the normal direction of rotation only.

5. Using the crankshaft pulley bolt,

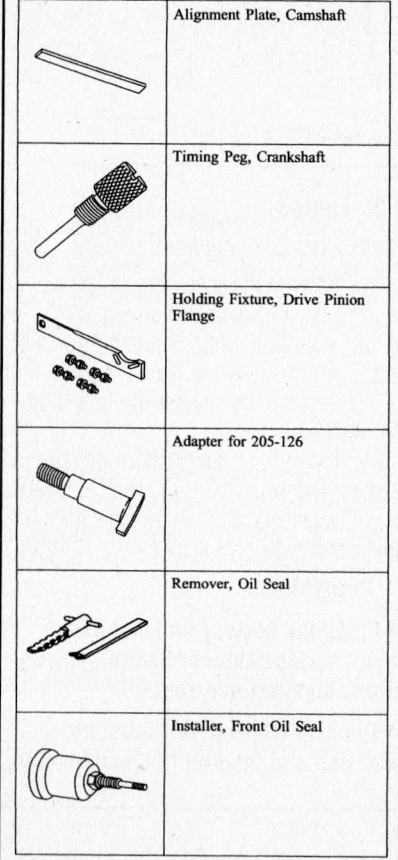

	Alignment Plate, Camshaft
	Timing Peg, Crankshaft
	Holding Fixture, Drive Pinion Flange
	Adapter for 205-126
	Remover, Oil Seal
	Installer, Front Oil Seal

Fig. 93 Tools necessary for this job— 2.3L engine

turn the crankshaft clockwise to position the No. 1 piston at top dead center (TDC).

✳✳ WARNING

The special tool 303-465 is for camshaft alignment only. Using this tool to prevent engine rotation can result in engine damage.

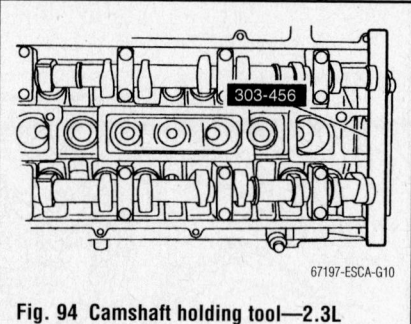

Fig. 94 Camshaft holding tool—2.3L engine

➡ The camshaft timing slots are offset. If the special tool cannot be installed, rotate the crankshaft one complete revolution clockwise to correctly position the camshafts.

6. Install the special tool in the slots on the rear of both camshafts.

➡ Installing the special tool in this step will prevent the engine from being rotated in the clockwise direction.

7. Install special tool 303-507.
8. Remove the crankshaft pulley bolt and washer.
9. Remove the engine plug bolt.
10. Install the crankshaft holding tools.

✳✳ WARNING

Failure to hold the crankshaft pulley in place while loosening the bolt can result in damage to the engine.

11. Remove the crankshaft pulley.

✳✳ WARNING

Use care not to damage the engine front cover or the crankshaft when removing the seal.

12. Using the special tool, remove the crankshaft front oil seal.

➡ Remove the through-bolt from the special tool.

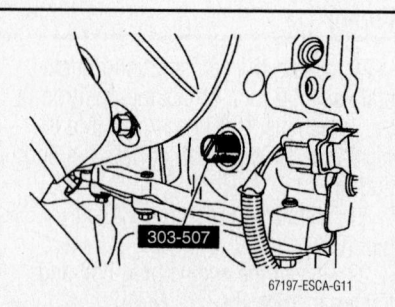

Fig. 95 Install special tool 303-507—2.3L engine

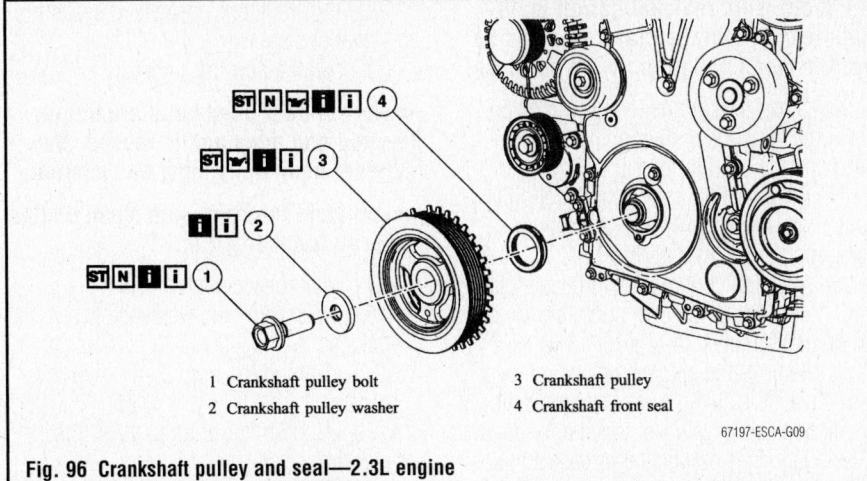

1 Crankshaft pulley bolt
2 Crankshaft pulley washer
3 Crankshaft pulley
4 Crankshaft front seal

67197-ESCA-G09

Fig. 96 Crankshaft pulley and seal—2.3L engine

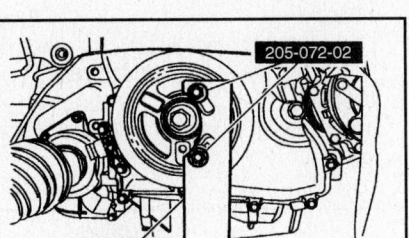

67197-ESCA-G12

Fig. 97 Install the crankshaft holding tools—2.3L engine

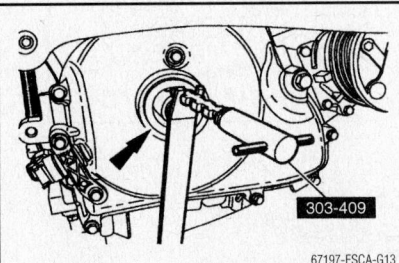

67197-ESCA-G13

Fig. 98 Using the special tool, remove the crankshaft front oil seal —2.3L engine

To install:

➡**Lubricate the oil seal with clean engine oil.**

13. Using the a seal driver, install the crankshaft front oil seal.

➡**Do not reuse the crankshaft damper bolt.**

➡**Apply clean engine oil on the seal area before installing.**

14. Install the crankshaft pulley and hand-tighten the bolt.

> ✳✳ **WARNING**
> **Only hand-tighten the bolt or damage to the front cover can occur.**

➡**This step will correctly align the crankshaft pulley to the crankshaft.**

15. Install a standard 6 mm × 18 mm bolt through the crankshaft pulley and thread it into the front cover. Rotate the pulley as necessary to align the bolt holes.

> ✳✳ **WARNING**
> **Failure to hold the crankshaft pulley in place while tightening the bolt can cause damage to the engine front cover.**

16. Using the special tools to hold the crankshaft pulley in place, tighten the crankshaft pulley bolt in two stages:
   a. Stage 1: Tighten to 74 ft. lbs. (100 Nm).
   b. Stage 2: Tighten an additional 90 degrees (1/4 turn).
17. Remove the 6 mm x 18 mm bolt.
18. Remove the special tools.

➡**Only turn the engine in the normal direction of rotation.**

19. Turn the engine two complete revolutions.
20. Turn the crankshaft until the No. 1 piston is at TDC.
21. Install special tool 303-507.

> ✳✳ **WARNING**
> **Only hand-tighten the bolt or damage to the front cover can occur.**

22. Using the 6 mm × 18 mm bolt, check the position of the crankshaft pulley. If it is not possible to install the bolt, correct the engine timing.
23. Using special tool 303-465, check the position of the camshafts. If it is not possible to install the special tool, correct the engine timing.

24. Remove the 6 mm × 18 mm bolt.
25. Install the engine plug bolt.

3.0L Engine

1. Before servicing the vehicle, refer to the Precautions Section.
  2. Remove or disconnect the following:
    • Negative battery cable
    • Crankshaft pulley
    • Front oil seal

To install:

3. Install or connect the following:
    • New front crankshaft oil seal
    • Crankshaft pulley. See the Torque Specifications Chart for the tightening torques.
    • Negative battery cable
  4. Start the vehicle and check for leaks, repair if necessary.

CYLINDER HEAD

REMOVAL & INSTALLATION

2.3L Engine

See Figures 99 through 101.

1. Before servicing the vehicle, refer to the Precautions Section.

> ✳✳ **WARNING**
> **During engine repair procedures, cleanliness is extremely important. Any foreign material, including any material created while cleaning gasket surfaces that enters the oil passages, coolant passages or the oil pan can cause engine failure.**

> ✳✳ **WARNING**
> **The crankshaft, the crankshaft sprocket and the pulley are fitted together by friction, using diamond washers between the flange faces on each part. For that reason, the crankshaft sprocket is also unfastened if you loosen the pulley. Therefore, the engine must be retimed each time the damper is removed. Otherwise severe engine damage can occur.**

> ✳✳ **WARNING**
> **Do not loosen or remove the crankshaft pulley bolt without first installing the special tools as instructed in the timing chain section. The crankshaft pulley and the crankshaft timing sprocket are not keyed to the crankshaft.**

2. With the vehicle in NEUTRAL, position it on a hoist.

3. Release the fuel system pressure.

4. Drain the engine cooling system.

5. Remove the timing drive components. For additional information, refer to Timing Drive Components in this section.

6. Mark the position of the camshaft lobes on the No. 1 cylinder for installation reference.

7. Loosen the camshaft bearing cap bolts, in sequence, one turn at a time until all tension is released from the camshaft bearing caps.

✳✳ WARNING

If the camshafts and valve tappets are to be reused, mark the location of the valve tappets to make sure they are assembled in their original positions.

8. Remove the camshafts.

9. Remove the intake manifold.

10. Remove the catalytic converter/manifold.

11. Disconnect the radio ignition interference capacitor electrical connector

12. Disconnect the exhaust gas recirculation (EGR) valve electrical connector

13. Remove the upper radiator hose.

14. Remove the EGR coolant tube clamp.

15. Remove the EGR coolant hose.

16. Remove the engine coolant vent hose.

17. Remove the heater hose.

18. Remove the bypass hose.

19. Remove and discard the cylinder head bolts.

20. Remove the cylinder head.

21. Remove the cylinder head gasket.

22. Inspect the cylinder head for distortion.

✳✳ WARNING

Do not use metal scrapers, wire brushes, power abrasive discs or other abrasive means to clean the sealing surfaces. These tools cause scratches and gouges that make leak paths. Use a plastic scraping tool to remove all traces of the head gasket.

✳✳ WARNING

Observe all warnings or cautions and follow all application directions contained on the packaging of the silicone gasket remover and the metal surface prep.

➡**If there is no residual gasket material present, metal surface prep can be used to clean and prepare the surfaces.**

23. Clean the cylinder head-to-cylinder block mating surface of both the cylinder head and the cylinder block.

24. Remove any large deposits of silicone or gasket material with a plastic scraper.

25. Apply silicone gasket remover, following package directions, and allow to set for several minutes.

26. Remove the silicone gasket remover with a plastic scraper. A second application of silicone gasket remover may be required if residual traces of silicone or gasket material remain.

27. Apply metal surface prep, following package directions, to remove any traces of oil or coolant, and to prepare the surfaces to bond with the new gasket. Do not attempt to make the metal shiny. Some staining of the metal surfaces is normal.

28. Apply silicone gasket and sealant to the locations shown.

29. Install a new head gasket.

➡**The cylinder head bolts are torque-to-yield and must not be reused. New cylinder head bolts must be installed.**

➡**Lubricate the bolts with clean engine oil prior to installation.**

30. Install new cylinder head bolts. Tighten the bolts in the sequence shown in five stages.

   a. Tighten the bolts to 44 inch lbs. (5 Nm).

   b. Tighten the bolts to 11 ft. lbs. (15 Nm).

   c. Tighten the bolts to 33 ft. lbs. (45 Nm).

   d. Turn the bolts 90 degrees.

   e. Turn the bolts an additional 90 degrees.

31. To install, reverse the removal procedure.

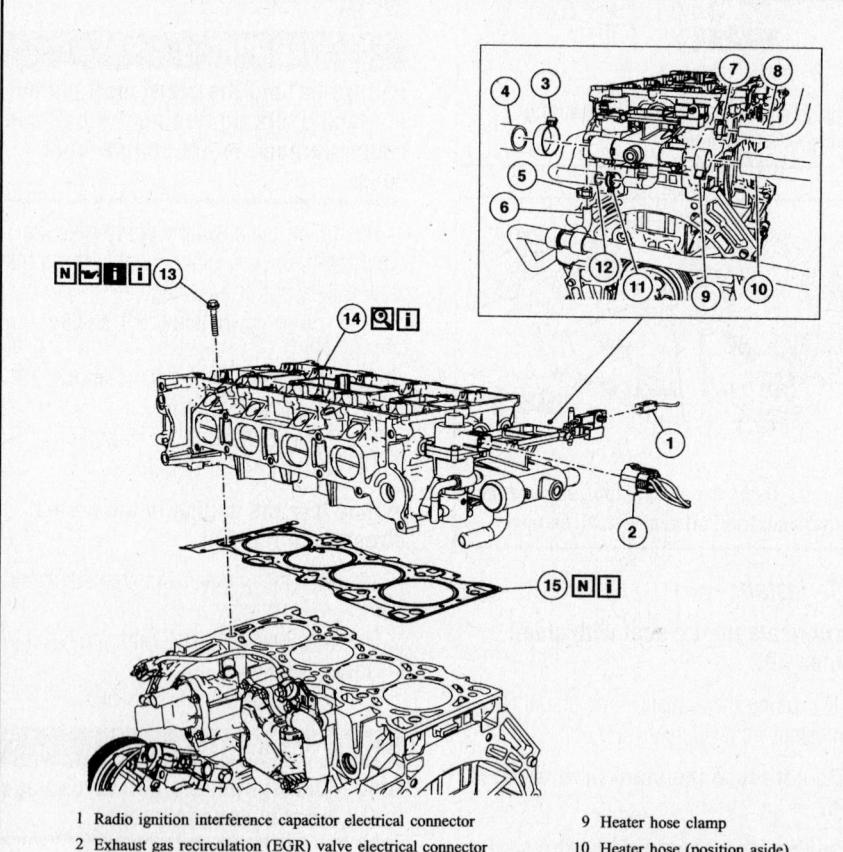

1 Radio ignition interference capacitor electrical connector
2 Exhaust gas recirculation (EGR) valve electrical connector
3 Upper radiator hose clamp
4 Upper radiator hose (position aside)
5 EGR coolant tube clamp
6 EGR coolant hose (part of heater hose) (position aside)
7 Engine coolant vent hose clamp
8 Engine coolant vent hose (position aside)
9 Heater hose clamp
10 Heater hose (position aside)
11 Bypass hose clamp
12 Bypass hose (position aside)
13 Cylinder head bolt
14 Cylinder head
15 Cylinder head gasket

67197-ESCA-G04

Fig. 99 Cylinder head removal—2.3L engine

Fig. 100 Apply silicone gasket and sealant to the locations shown—2.3L engine

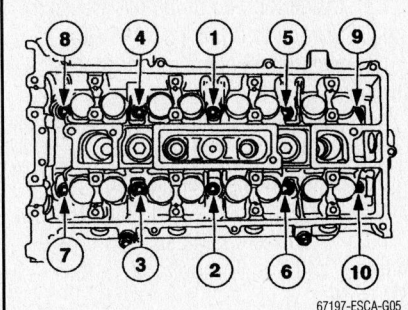

Fig. 101 Cylinder head bolt torque sequence—2.3L engine

3.0L Engine

See Figures 102 through 104.

The procedure for the left side cylinder head and right side are similar. Changes in the procedure will be noted for either side cylinder head.

1. Before servicing the vehicle, refer to the Precautions Section.
2. Properly relieve the fuel system pressure.
   • Drain the cooling system.
3. Remove or disconnect the following:
   • Negative battery cable
   • lower intake manifold
   • coolant bypass tube

✲✲ WARNING

The hydraulic lash adjusters must be installed in their original positions.

   • Camshaft
   • Exhaust Gas Recirculation (EGR) tube, right side only
   • Exhaust manifold
   • Camshaft followers
   • Hydraulic lash adjusters and matchmark them for proper installation
   • Cylinder head bolts in sequence and discard them
   • Cylinder head and discard the gasket

To install:

4. Install a new head gasket and the cylinder head.
5. Lubricate the cylinder head bolt threads.
6. Torque the cylinder head bolts in the proper sequence as follows:
   a. Step 1: 30 ft. lbs. (40 Nm).
   b. Step 2: Additional 90 degrees.
   c. Step 3: Loosen the bolts one full turn.
   d. Step 4: 30 ft. lbs. (40 Nm).
   e. Step 5: Plus an additional 90 degrees.
   f. Step 6: Plus an additional 90 degrees.

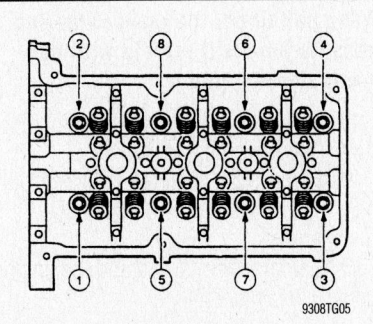

Fig. 102 Left side cylinder head bolt torque sequence 3.0L engine

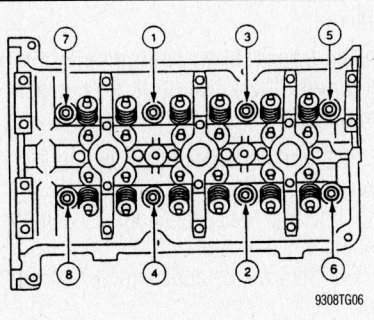

Fig. 103 Right side cylinder head bolt torque sequence 3.0L engine

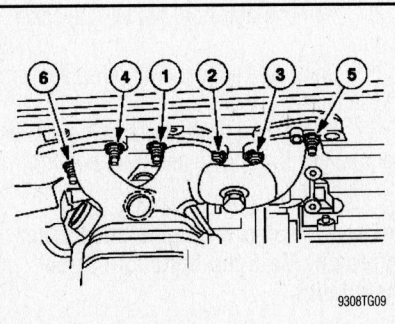

Fig. 104 Right side exhaust manifold bolt torque sequence—3.0L engine

7. Install or connect the following:
   • Hydraulic lash adjusters
   • Camshaft followers
   • Camshaft
   • Exhaust manifold. Torque the bolts in sequence to 15 ft. lbs. (20 Nm), right side only
   • EGR tube, right side only
   • Coolant bypass tube
   • Negative battery cable
8. Fill the coolant to the proper level.
9. Start the vehicle and check for leaks, repair if necessary.

ENGINE ASSEMBLY

REMOVAL & INSTALLATION

2.3L Engine—2005–07 models

Manual Transaxle

See Figure 105.

1. Before servicing the vehicle, refer to the Precautions Section.

All vehicles:
2. With the vehicle in NEUTRAL, position it on a hoist.
3. Release the fuel system pressure.
4. Remove the engine air cleaner and air cleaner outlet pipe.
5. Remove the battery tray.
6. Drain the engine oil.
7. Drain the cooling system.
8. Remove the starter.
9. Remove the catalytic converter.
10. Remove the accessory drive belt.
11. Remove the bolts and the lateral support crossmember.
12. Remove the left front drive halfshaft.
13. Remove the front drive intermediate halfshaft

4WD vehicles
14. Remove the six bolts holding the driveshaft to the transfer case.
15. Position the driveshaft aside.

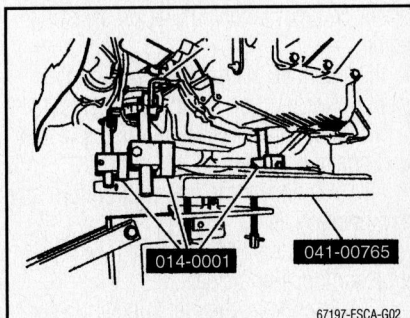

Fig. 105 Engine secured to lift table— 2.3L engine w/manual transaxle

All vehicles:

16. If equipped, remove the bolt and ground eyelet.

17. Remove the power distribution box cover.

18. Remove the nuts and disconnect the cables.

19. Disconnect the electrical connector from the power distribution box.

20. Remove the bolt and disconnect the ground strap. Loosen the bolt and disconnect the 42-pin electrical connector.

21. Detach the wiring harness retainers from the battery tray bracket and position the wiring harness out of the way.

22. Disconnect the clutch hydraulic tube fitting. Detach the tube from the spring clip and position aside.

23. Remove the retaining clips and disconnect the transaxle control cable.

24. Remove the retaining clips and disconnect the transaxle control cable.

25. Disconnect the vehicle speed sensor electrical connector and pin-type retainer.

26. Disconnect the reversing lamp indicator switch and detach the wiring harness retainers.

27. If equipped, disconnect the block heater electrical connector. Detach all the block heater wiring harness retainers and position the wiring harness aside.

28. Disconnect the upper radiator and coolant vent hoses.

29. Remove the nuts and the coolant vent hose brackets. Position the coolant vent hose aside.

30. Detach the heater hose support strap from the stud.

31. Disconnect the heater hoses from the heater core.

32. Remove the retainers and the accelerator cable snow shield.

33. Disconnect the accelerator cable and speed control cable (if equipped).

34. Remove the nut from the accelerator control cable bracket.

35. Remove the nut from the accelerator control cable bracket and position the accelerator control cable and bracket assembly aside.

36. Remove the nut and position the power steering tube and bracket aside.

37. Disconnect the vacuum supply tube and position aside.

38. Disconnect the fuel vapor return tube and position aside.

39. Disconnect the vacuum reservoir tube and position aside.

40. Disconnect the fuel supply tube and retainer and position aside.

41. Detach the electrical connector retainers.

42. Disconnect the Powertrain Control Module (PCM) electrical connectors. Remove the nut and position the harness aside.

43. Remove the bolt and detach the ground wire.

44. Remove the two power steering pump bolts.

45. Disconnect the lower radiator hose from the radiator.

46. Disconnect the A/C compressor electrical connector and remove the four bolts. Position the A/C compressor aside and support the compressor with a length of mechanics wire.

47. Disconnect the power steering pressure (PSP) sensor electrical connector.

➡ **The bolt under the power steering pressure tube will remain with the power steering pump.**

48. Remove the bolts and position the power steering pump aside.

49. Remove the front roll restrictor bolt and the two bolts for the engine support crossmember.

50. Remove the rear nut and the engine support crossmember.

➡ **The transaxle-to-engine bolts differ in length. Mark the bolts for correct installation.**

51. Remove the two transaxle-to-engine bolts.

➡ **The transaxle-to-engine bolts differ in length. Mark the bolts for correct installation.**

52. Remove the two transaxle-to-engine bolts.

53. Using the special tools, secure the engine to the lift table.

54. Remove the engine mount bracket bolt.

55. Remove the nuts and the engine mount bracket.

56. Remove the bolt from the transaxle rear mount.

57. Remove bolt from the left transaxle mount.

58. Lower the engine and transaxle from the vehicle.

59. Using the engine crane and spreader bar, remove the engine and transaxle from the lift table.

➡ **The transaxle-to-engine bolts differ in length. Mark the bolts for correct installation.**

60. Remove the remaining six engine-to-transaxle bolts and separate the engine and transaxle.

To install:
All vehicles

61. Using the engine crane and spreader bar, position the engine and transaxle together. Install the six upper transaxle-to-engine bolts. Torque to 35 ft. lbs. (48 Nm).

62. Using the engine crane and spreader bar, position the engine and transaxle onto the lift table.

63. Using the special tools, secure the engine to the lift table.

64. Raise the engine and transaxle into the vehicle.

65. Install the bolt in the left transaxle mount. Torque to 76 ft. lbs. (103 Nm).

66. Install the bolt in the rear transaxle mount. Torque to 85 ft. lbs. (115 Nm).

67. Install the engine mount bracket. Torque to 66 ft. lbs. (90 Nm).

68. Install the engine mount bracket bolt. Torque to 66 ft. lbs. (90 Nm).

69. Install the 4 lower transaxle-to-engine bolts. Torque to 35 ft. lbs. (48 Nm).

70. Install the engine support crossmember and nut. Torque to 66 ft. lbs. (90 Nm).

71. Install the two bolts for the engine support crossmember. Torque to 66 ft. lbs. (90 Nm).

72. Install the front roll restrictor bolt. Torque to 85 ft. lbs. (115 Nm).

➡ **The bolt under the power steering pressure tube will remain with the power steering pump.**

73. Position the power steering pump and install the bolts. Torque to 18 ft. lbs. (25 Nm).

74. Connect the power steering pressure (PSP) sensor electrical connector.

75. Install the A/C compressor and connect the A/C compressor electrical connector. Torque to 18 ft. lbs. (25 Nm).

76. Connect the lower radiator hose to the radiator.

77. Install the two lower power steering pump bolts. Torque to 18 ft. lbs. (25 Nm).

78. Install the ground wire and bolt.

79. Connect the Powertrain Control Module (PCM) electrical connectors. Position the harness and install the nut.

80. Attach the electrical connector retainers.

81. Connect the fuel supply tube.

82. Connect the vacuum reservoir tube.

83. Connect the fuel vapor return tube and retainer.

84. Connect the vacuum supply tube.

85. Install the power steering tube and bracket.

86. Position the accelerator control cable and bracket and install the nut.

87. Install the accelerator control cable and bracket and nut.

88. Install the accelerator cable and speed control cable (if equipped).

89. Install the accelerator cable snow shield and retainers.

90. Connect the heater hoses to the heater core.

91. Attach the heater hose support strap to the stud.

92. Position the coolant vent hose and install the coolant vent hose brackets and nuts.

93. Connect the upper radiator and coolant vent hoses.

94. If equipped, route the block heater wiring harness and attach all retainers. Connect the block heater electrical connector.

95. Connect the reversing lamp indicator switch and attach the wiring harness retainers.

96. Connect the vehicle speed sensor (VSS) electrical connector and pin-type retainer.

97. Connect the transaxle control cable and install the retaining clips.

98. Connect the transaxle control cable and install the retaining clips.

99. Connect the clutch hydraulic tube fitting. Attach the tube to the spring clip.

100. Attach the wiring harness retainers to the battery tray bracket.

101. Connect the 42-pin electrical connector and tighten the bolt. Install the ground strap and bolt.

102. Connect the electrical connector to the power distribution box.

103. Connect the cables and install the nuts.

104. Install the power distribution box cover.

105. If equipped, install the ground eyelet and bolt.

4WD vehicles

106. Install the driveshaft. Torque to 15 ft. lbs. (20 Nm).

All vehicles

107. Install the front drive intermediate halfshaft.

108. Install the left front drive halfshaft.

109. Install the lateral support crossmember. Torque to 85 ft. lbs. (115 Nm).

110. Install the accessory drive belt.

111. Install the catalytic converter.

112. Install the starter.

113. Install the battery tray and battery.

114. Install the engine air cleaner and air cleaner outlet pipe.

115. Fill the engine with clean engine oil.

116. Fill and bleed the cooling system.

117. Bleed the clutch system.

Automatic Transaxle

1. Before servicing the vehicle, refer to the Precautions Section.

All vehicles:

2. With the vehicle in NEUTRAL, position it on a hoist.

3. Release the fuel system pressure.

4. Remove the engine air cleaner and air cleaner outlet pipe.

5. Remove the battery tray.

6. Drain the engine oil.

7. Drain the cooling system.

8. Remove the starter.

9. Remove the catalytic converter.

10. Remove the accessory drive belt.

11. Remove the left front drive halfshafts.

4WD vehicles:

12. Remove the transfer case.

2WD vehicles:

13. Remove the bolts and the lateral support crossmember.

14. Remove the front drive intermediate halfshaft.

All vehicles:

15. If equipped, remove the bolt and ground eyelet.

16. Remove the power distribution box cover.

17. Remove the nuts and disconnect the cables.

18. Disconnect the electrical connector from the power distribution box.

19. Remove the bolt and disconnect the ground strap. Loosen the bolt and disconnect the 42-pin electrical connector.

20. Detach the wiring harness retainers from the battery tray bracket and position the wiring harness out of the way.

21. Disconnect the transaxle electrical connector.

22. Disconnect the shift cable from the transaxle manual lever.

23. Position the transaxle control cable and bracket aside.

24. Disconnect the transmission range (TR) sensor electrical connector.

25. Detach the transaxle control harness from the brackets.

26. Disconnect the fluid cooler tube.

27. Disconnect the output shaft speed (OSS) sensor electrical connector (black).

28. Disconnect the turbine shaft speed (TSS) sensor electrical connector (white connector).

29. Remove the transmission fluid cooler retaining bracket bolt.

30. Position the fluid cooler tube aside.

31. Remove the bolt and the OSS sensor.

32. Detach the transaxle control harness from the retaining clip.

33. If equipped, disconnect the block heater electrical connector. Detach all the block heater wiring harness retainers and position the wiring harness aside.

34. Disconnect the upper radiator and coolant vent hoses.

35. Remove the nuts and the coolant vent hose brackets. Position the coolant vent hose aside.

36. Detach the heater hose support strap from the stud.

37. Disconnect the heater hoses from the heater core.

38. Remove the retainers and the accelerator cable snow shield.

39. Disconnect the accelerator cable and speed control cable (if equipped).

40. Remove the nut from the accelerator control cable bracket.

41. Remove the nut from the accelerator control cable bracket and position the accelerator control cable and bracket assembly aside.

42. Remove the nut and position the power steering tube and bracket aside.

43. Disconnect the vacuum supply tube and position aside.

44. Disconnect the fuel vapor return tube and retainer and position aside.

45. Disconnect the vacuum reservoir tube and position aside.

46. Disconnect the fuel supply tube and position aside.

47. Detach the electrical connector retainers.

48. Disconnect the Powertrain Control Module (PCM) electrical connectors. Remove the nut and position the harness aside.

49. Remove the bolt and detach the ground wire.

50. Remove the two power steering pump bolts.

51. Disconnect the lower radiator hose from the radiator.

52. Disconnect the A/C compressor electrical connector and remove the four bolts. Position the A/C compressor aside and support the compressor with a length of mechanics wire.

53. Disconnect the power steering pressure (PSP) sensor electrical connector.

➡**The bolt under the power steering pressure tube will remain with the power steering pump.**

54. Remove the bolts and position the power steering pump aside.

55. Remove the front roll restrictor bolt and the two bolts for the engine support crossmember.

56. Remove the rear nut and the engine support crossmember.

➡ **The transaxle-to-engine bolts differ in length. Mark the bolts for correct installation.**

57. Remove the two transaxle-to-engine bolts.

➡ **The transaxle-to-engine bolts differ in length. Mark the bolts for correct installation.**

58. Remove the two transaxle-to-engine bolts.

59. Using the special tools, secure the engine to the lift table.

60. Remove the engine mount bracket bolt.

61. Remove the nuts and the engine mount bracket.

62. Remove the bolt from the transaxle rear mount.

63. Remove the bolt from the left transaxle mount.

64. Lower the engine and transaxle from the vehicle.

65. Using the engine crane and spreader bar remove the engine and transaxle from the lift table.

66. Remove the starter motor isolator.

67. Remove and discard the four torque converter nuts.

➡ **The transaxle-to-engine bolts differ in length. Mark the bolts for correct installation.**

68. Remove the remaining six engine-to-transaxle bolts and separate the engine and transaxle.

To install:
All vehicles:
69. Using the engine crane and spreader bar, position the engine and transaxle together. Install the six upper transaxle-to-engine bolts. Torque to 35 ft. lbs. (48 Nm).

70. Install new torque converter nuts. Torque to 26 ft. lbs. (35 Nm).

71. Install the starter motor isolator.

72. Using the engine crane and spreader bar, position the engine and transaxle onto the lift table.

73. Using the special tools, secure the engine to the lift table.

74. Raise the engine and transaxle into the vehicle.

75. Install the bolt in the left transaxle mount. Torque to 76 ft. lbs. (103 Nm).

76. Install the bolt in the rear transaxle mount. Torque to 85 ft. lbs. (115 Nm).

77. Install the engine mount bracket. Torque to 66 ft. lbs. (90 Nm).

78. Install the engine mount bracket bolt. Torque to 66 ft. lbs. (90 Nm).

79. Install the 4 transaxle-to-engine bolts. Torque to 35 ft. lbs. (48 Nm).

80. Install the engine support crossmember and nut. Torque to 66 ft. lbs. (90 Nm).

81. Install the two bolts for the engine support crossmember. Torque to 66 ft. lbs. (90 Nm).

82. Install the front roll restrictor bolt . Torque to 85 ft. lbs. (115 Nm).

83. Position the power steering pump and install the upper bolts. Torque to 18 ft. lbs. (25 Nm).

84. Connect the power steering pressure (PSP) sensor electrical connector.

85. Install the A/C compressor and connect the A/C compressor electrical connector. Torque to 18 ft. lbs. (25 Nm).

86. Connect the lower radiator hose to the radiator.

87. Install the two lower power steering pump bolts. Torque to 18 ft. lbs. (25 Nm).

88. Install the ground wire and bolt.

89. Connect the Powertrain Control Module (PCM) electrical connectors. Position the harness and install the nut.

90. Attach the electrical connector retainers.

91. Connect the fuel supply tube.

92. Connect the vacuum reservoir tube.

93. Connect the fuel vapor return tube and retainer.

94. Connect the vacuum supply tube.

95. Position the power steering tube and bracket and install the nut.

96. Position the accelerator control cable and bracket and install the nut.

97. Install the accelerator control cable and bracket and nut.

98. Install the accelerator cable and speed control cable (if equipped).

99. Install the accelerator cable snow shield and the retainers.

100. Connect the heater hoses to the heater core.

101. Attach the heater hose support strap to the stud.

102. Position the coolant vent hose and install the coolant vent hose brackets and nuts.

103. Connect the upper radiator and coolant vent hoses.

104. If equipped, route the block heater wiring harness and attach all retainers. Connect the block heater electrical connector.

105. Attach the transaxle control harness to the retaining clip.

106. Install the output shaft speed (OSS) sensor and bolt.

107. Install the fluid cooler tube.

108. Connect the transmission fluid cooler tube.

109. Attach the transaxle control harness to the brackets.

110. Connect the transmission range (TR) sensor electrical connector.

111. Install the transaxle control cable and bracket.

112. Connect the shift cable to the transaxle manual lever.

113. Connect the transaxle electrical connector.

114. Attach the wiring harness retainers to the battery tray bracket.

115. Connect the 42-pin electrical connector and tighten the bolt. Install the ground strap and bolt.

116. Connect the electrical connector to the power distribution box.

117. Connect the cables and install the nuts.

118. Install the power distribution box cover.

119. If equipped, install the ground eyelet and bolt.

2WD vehicles:
120. Install the front drive intermediate halfshaft.

121. Install the lateral support crossmember. Torque to 85 ft. lbs. (115 Nm).

4WD vehicles:
122. Install the transfer case.

All vehicles:
123. Install the left front drive halfshaft.

124. Install the accessory drive belt.

125. Install the catalytic converter.

126. Install the starter.

127. Install the battery tray and battery.

128. Install the engine air cleaner and air cleaner outlet pipe.

129. Fill the engine with clean engine oil.

130. Fill and bleed the cooling system.

2.3L Engine—2008 models

Manual Transaxle

See Figure 106.

1. With the vehicle in NEUTRAL, position it on a hoist.

2. Release the fuel system pressure.

3. Remove the engine air cleaner and air cleaner outlet pipe.

4. Remove the battery tray.

5. Drain the engine oil.

6. Remove the front wheels and tires.

7. Drain the cooling system.

8. Remove the exhaust flexible pipe.

9. Disconnect the heated oxygen sensor (HO2S) and the catalyst monitor sensor electrical connectors.

10. Remove the accessory drive belt and tensioner.

11. Press the 2 locking tabs (1 shown) to release the lower air duct from the upper air duct

12. Detach the wire retainers from the alternator shield and remove the nut and pin-type retainer, remove shield.

13. Remove the 4 bolts and the lateral support crossmember.

14. Remove the brake hose retainer and the ABS sensor retaining bolt from the LH strut.

15. Disconnect the LH stabilizer bar link.

16. Remove the LH tie rod end retaining nut.

17. Remove the LH lower control arm knuckle bolt.

18. Remove the brake hose retainer and the ABS sensor retaining bolt from the RH strut

19. Disconnect the RH stabilizer bar link.

20. Remove the RH tie rod end retaining nut.

21. Remove the RH lower control arm knuckle bolt.

22. Using Removal tool, disconnect the LH and RH tie rod end from the steering knuckle.

23. Separate the LH and RH lower control arms and disconnect the steering knuckle from the lower ball joint and position the steering knuckle aside.

24. Using a suitable tool, separate the LH halfshaft from the transaxle and secure the halfshaft aside.

25. Using the suitable tools, remove the RH halfshaft from the intermediate shaft and secure the halfshaft aside.

26. Remove the 2 intermediate shaft retaining nuts.

27. Remove the intermediate shaft

28. Remove the Power Distribution Box (PDB) cover.

29. Remove the nut and the cable from the PDB.

30. Disconnect the electrical connector from the PDB.

31. Remove the bolt and ground strap.

32. Disconnect the 34-pin electrical connector.

33. Detach the wiring harness retainers from the battery tray bracket and position the wiring harness aside

34. Position the clutch hydraulic line aside.

35. Remove the clutch hydraulic line bracket-to-transaxle bolt.

36. Disconnect the clutch hydraulic line from the clutch slave cylinder.

37. Plug the hydraulic line.

38. Position the clutch hydraulic line aside.

39. Remove the wiring harness bracket nut and position aside

40. Disconnect the vehicle speed sensor (VSS) electrical connector and pin-type retainers

41. Disconnect the reversing lamp indicator switch.

42. Disconnect the shift cables.

43. Remove the 3 shift cable bracket bolts.

44. Position the bracket aside.

45. If equipped, disconnect the block heater electrical connector.

46. Detach all the block heater wiring harness retainers and position the wiring harness aside.

47. Disconnect the upper radiator hose.

48. Detach the heater hose support strap from the stud.

49. Disconnect the heater hoses from the heater core.

50. Remove the retainers and the accelerator cable snow shield

51. Disconnect the accelerator cable and speed control cable (if equipped).

52. Disconnect the accelerator and speed control cable (if equipped) from the throttle body.

53. Remove the bolts from the accelerator cable bracket.

54. Remove the nut from the accelerator control cable bracket.

55. Position the accelerator control cable and bracket assembly aside.

56. Remove the nut from the accelerator control cable bracket.

57. Disconnect the vacuum supply tube and position aside.

58. Disconnect the fuel vapor return tube and position aside.

59. Disconnect the fuel supply tube.

60. Detach the electrical connector retainers.

61. Remove the bolt and detach the ground wire.

62. Disconnect the PCM electrical connectors.

63. Remove the wiring harness retainer nut.

64. Disconnect the lower radiator hose from the radiator.

65. Disconnect the A/C compressor electrical connector and remove the 3 bolts.

66. Position the A/C compressor aside and support the compressor with a length of mechanic's wire.

67. Remove the front roll restrictor bolt and the 2 bolts for the engine support crossmember.

68. Remove the rear nut and the engine support crossmember.

➡**The transaxle-to-engine bolts differ in length. Mark the bolts for correct installation.**

69. Remove the transaxle-to-engine bolts.

70. Remove the engine-to-transaxle bolts

71. Using the special tools, secure the engine to the lift table

72. Remove the engine mount bracket bolt.

73. Remove the nuts and the engine mount bracket.

74. Remove the bolt from the transaxle rear mount.

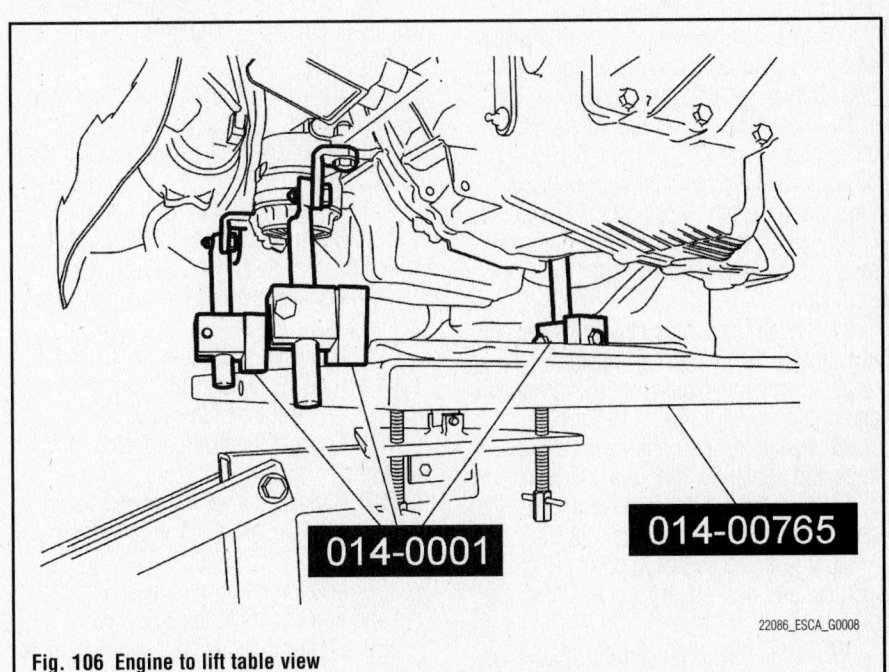

Fig. 106 Engine to lift table view

22086_ESCA_G0008

75. Remove bolt from the LH transaxle mount.

76. Lower the engine and transaxle from the vehicle.

77. Remove the battery cable nut.

78. Remove the starter solenoid terminal nut.

79. Remove the wire harness clip retainer and the ground wire from the starter bolts.

80. Remove the 2 stud bolts and remove the starter.

81. Using the engine crane and spreader bar, remove the engine and transaxle from the lift table.

➡ **The transaxle-to-engine bolts differ in length. Mark the bolts for correct installation.**

82. Remove the remaining 5 engine-to-transaxle bolts and separate the engine and transaxle.

To install:

83. Using the engine crane and spreader bar, position the engine and transaxle together. Install the 5 transaxle-to-engine bolts.

84. Using the engine crane and spreader bar, position the engine and transaxle onto the lift table.

85. Using the special tools, secure the engine to the lift table.

86. Install the starter motor and tighten bolts to 26 ft. lbs. (35 Nm).

87. Install the starter motor harness connector.

88. Install the starter motor solenoid battery nut and tighten to 9 ft. lbs. (12 Nm).

89. Install the starter motor solenoid nut and tighten to 44 inch. lbs (5 Nm).

90. Install the wire harness clip retainer and the ground wire and nut to the starter bolts tighten to 18 ft. lbs. (25 Nm).

91. Raise the engine and transaxle into the vehicle.

92. Install the bolt in the LH transaxle mount and tighten to 76 ft. lbs. (23 Nm).

93. Install the bolt in the rear transaxle mount and tighten to 85 ft. lbs. (115 Nm).

94. Install the engine mount bracket and nuts tighten to 85 ft. lbs. (115 Nm).

95. Install the engine mount bracket bolt and tighten to 85 ft. lbs. (115 Nm).

96. Install the 2 engine-to-transaxle bolts and tighten to 35 ft. lbs. (48 Nm).

97. Install the 2 transaxle-to-engine bolts and tighten to 35 ft. lbs. (48 Nm).

98. Install the engine support crossmember and new nut, tighten to 129 ft. lbs. (175 Nm).

99. Install the 2 bolts for the engine sup-

port crossmember and the front roll restrictor bolt.

100. Tighten the engine support crossmember bolts to 66 ft. lbs. (90 Nm).

101. Tighten the front roll restrictor bolt to 85 ft. lbs. (115 Nm).

102. Position the A/C compressor and install the bolts.

103. Tighten the bolts to 18 ft. lbs. (25 Nm).

104. Connect the A/C compressor electrical connector.

105. Connect the lower radiator hose to the radiator.

106. Connect the PCM electrical connectors.

107. Position the harness, install the nut and tighten to 53 inch. lbs (6 Nm).

108. Install the ground wire and bolt, tighten to 89 inch. lbs (10 Nm).

109. Attach the electrical connector retainers.

110. Connect the fuel supply tube quick connect coupling.

111. Connect the fuel vapor return tube and retainer.

112. Connect the vacuum supply tube.

113. Position the accelerator control cable and bracket and install the nut.

114. Tighten the bracket nut to 53 inch. lbs (6 Nm).

115. Install the accelerator cable and speed control cable (if equipped).

116. Connect the accelerator and speed control cable (if equipped) to the throttle body.

117. Install the accelerator cable bracket and bolts. Tighten to 89 inch. lbs (10 Nm).

118. Install the accelerator cable snow shield and retainers. Tighten to 35 inch. lbs (4 Nm).

119. Connect the heater hoses to the heater core.

120. Attach the heater hose support strap to the stud.

121. Connect the upper radiator hose.

122. If equipped, route the block heater wiring harness and attach all retainers.

123. Connect the block heater electrical connector.

124. Install the shift cable bracket and tighten mounting bolts to 16 ft. lbs. (22 Nm).

125. Connect the shift cables.

126. Connect the reversing lamp indicator switch.

127. Connect the vehicle speed sensor (VSS) electrical connector and pin-type retainer.

128. Install the wiring harness bracket nut and tighten to 9 ft. lbs. (12 Nm).

129. Connect the clutch hydraulic line to

the clutch slave cylinder and tighten to 18 ft. lbs. (25 Nm).

130. Install the clutch hydraulic line bracket-to-transaxle bolt and tighten to 27 inch lbs. (3 Nm).

131. Attach the wiring harness retainers to the battery tray bracket.

132. Connect the 34-pin electrical connector.

133. Install the ground strap and bolt. Tighten to 89 inch lbs. (10 Nm).

134. Connect the electrical connector to the power distribution box (PDB).

135. Connect the cable to the PDB and install and tighten the nut to 9 ft. lbs. (12 Nm).

136. Install the PDB cover.

137. Install the intermediate shaft.

138. Install the intermediate shaft retaining nuts and tighten to 20 ft. lbs. (27 Nm).

139. Install the LH half shaft in the transaxle and the RH half shaft to the intermediate shaft.

140. Install the ball joints in the knuckles.

141. Install the LH lower ball joint-to-knuckle bolt and tighten to 46 ft. lbs. (63 Nm).

142. Position the RH tie-rod end, install the retaining nut and tighten to 41 ft. lbs. (55 Nm).

143. Connect the stabilizer bar link and tighten to 46 ft. lbs. (63 Nm).

144. Install the RH brake hose retainer and the anti-lock brake system (ABS) sensor bolt. Tighten to 11 ft. lbs. (15 Nm).

145. Install the RH half shaft in the transaxle and the RH half shaft to the intermediate shaft.

146. Install the ball joints in the knuckles.

147. Install the RH lower ball joint-to-knuckle bolt and tighten to 46 ft. lbs. (63 Nm).

148. Position the RH tie-rod end, install the retaining nut and tighten to 41 ft. lbs. (55 Nm).

149. Connect the stabilizer bar link and tighten to 46 ft. lbs. (63 Nm).

150. Install the LH brake hose retainer and the ABS sensor bolt. Tighten to 11 ft. lbs. (15 Nm).

151. Install the lateral support crossmember and bolts. Tighten bolts to 85 ft. lbs. (115 Nm).

152. Install the alternator shield, the nut and the pin-type retainer.

153. Tighten to15 ft. lbs. (20 Nm).

154. Attach the wire retainers.

155. Install the lower air duct.

156. Install the accessory drive belt tensioner

157. Connect the heated oxygen sensor (HO2S) and the catalyst monitor sensor electrical connectors.

158. Install the exhaust flexible pipe.

159. Install the front wheels and tires.

160. Install the battery tray.

161. Install the engine air cleaner and air cleaner outlet pipe.

162. Fill the engine with clean engine oil.

163. Fill and bleed the cooling system.

164. Bleed the clutch system.

Automatic Transaxle

See Figure 107.

All vehicles:

1. Disconnect the negative battery cable.

2. With the vehicle in NEUTRAL, position it on a hoist.

3. Release the fuel system pressure.

4. Remove the engine air cleaner and air cleaner outlet pipe.

5. Remove the battery tray.

6. Drain the engine oil.

7. Remove the front wheels and tires.

8. Drain the cooling system.

9. Remove the exhaust flexible pipe.

10. Remove the accessory drive belt and tensioner.

11. Press the 2 locking tabs to release the lower air duct from the upper air duct.

12. Detach the wire retainers from the alternator shield and remove the nut and pin-type retainer.

13. Remove the alternator shield.

14. Remove the bolts and the lateral support crossmember.

15. Remove the brake hose retainer and the ABS sensor retaining bolt from the LH strut

16. Disconnect the LH stabilizer bar link.

17. Remove the LH tie rod end retaining nut.

18. Remove the LH lower control arm knuckle bolt.

19. Remove the brake hose retainer and the ABS sensor retaining bolt from the RH strut.

20. Disconnect the RH stabilizer bar link.

21. Remove the RH tie rod end retaining nut.

22. Remove the RH lower control arm knuckle bolt.

23. Using a suitable tool, disconnect the LH and RH tie rod end from the steering knuckle.

24. Separate the LH and RH lower control arms from the lower ball joints and position the steering knuckles aside.

25. Using a suitable tool, separate the LH halfshaft from the transaxle and secure the halfshaft aside.

26. Using the suitable tools, remove the RH halfshaft from the intermediate shaft and secure the halfshaft aside.

27. Remove the 2 intermediate shaft retaining nuts.

28. Remove the intermediate shaft.

AWD vehicles:

➡ **Index-mark the driveshaft to the yoke for installation.**

29. Remove the 6 bolts holding the driveshaft to the PTU and position aside with mechanic's wire.

All vehicles:

30. If equipped, remove the bolt and ground eyelet.

31. Remove the Power Distribution Box (PDB) cover.

32. Remove the nut and disconnect the cable from the PDB.

33. Disconnect the electrical connector from the PDB.

34. Remove the bolt and the ground strap.

35. Disconnect the 34-pin electrical connector.

36. Detach the wiring harness retainers from the battery tray bracket.

37. Detach the transaxle vent tube retaining clip from the engine wiring harness.

38. Remove the nut holding the wiring harness bracket and unplug the transaxle electrical connector.

39. Disconnect the shift cable from the transaxle manual lever.

40. Detach the wiring harness pin-type retainer and remove the 2 bolts.

41. Position the transaxle cable and bracket aside.

42. Disconnect the transaxle range sensor electrical connector.

43. Disconnect the front transaxle fluid cooler tube.

44. Disconnect the rear transaxle fluid cooler tube.

45. Disconnect the transaxle fluid cooler tube.

   a. Disconnect the Output Shaft Speed (OSS) sensor electrical connector (black).

   b. Disconnect the Turbine Shaft Speed (TSS) sensor electrical connector (white).

   c. Disconnect the wiring harness retainer from the transaxle case and position the harness aside.

   d. Remove the transaxle fluid cooler retaining bracket bolt.

   e. Position the fluid cooler tube aside.

46. Remove the bolt and the OSS sensor.

47. If equipped, disconnect the block heater electrical connector.

48. Detach all the block heater wiring harness retainers and position the wiring harness aside.

49. Disconnect the upper radiator hose.

50. Detach the heater hose support strap from the stud.

51. Disconnect the heater hoses from the heater core.

52. Remove the retainers and the accelerator cable snow shield.

53. Disconnect the accelerator and speed control cable (if equipped) from the throttle body.

54. Remove the bolts from the accelerator cable bracket.

55. Remove the nut from the accelerator control cable bracket.

56. Remove the nut from the accelerator control cable bracket.

57. Disconnect the vacuum supply tube and position aside.

58. Disconnect the fuel vapor return tube and retainer and position aside.

59. Disconnect the fuel supply tube quick connect coupling.

60. Detach the electrical connector retainers.

61. Remove the bolt and detach the ground wire.

62. Disconnect the Power Control Module (PCM) electrical connectors.

63. Remove the wiring harness retainer nut.

64. Disconnect the lower radiator hose from the radiator.

65. Disconnect the A/C compressor electrical connector and remove the 4 bolts.

66. Position the A/C compressor aside and support the compressor with a length of mechanic's wire.

67. Remove the front roll restrictor bolt and the 2 bolts for the engine support crossmember.

68. Remove the rear nut and the engine support crossmember.

Front wheel drive (FWD) vehicles:

69. Remove the 3 bolts and the damper.

All vehicles:

➡ **The transaxle-to-engine bolts differ in length. Mark the bolts for correct installation.**

70. Remove the 4 transaxle-to-engine bolts.

71. Using the suitable tools, secure the engine to the lift table.

72. Remove the engine mount bracket bolt.

73. Remove the nuts and the engine mount bracket

74. Remove the bolt from the transaxle rear mount.

75. Remove the bolt from the LH transaxle mount.

76. Lower the engine and transaxle from the vehicle.

77. Disconnect the starter battery cable, solenoid wire nuts and remove.

78. Remove the wire harness clip retainer and the ground wire from the starter bolts.

79. Remove the 2 stud bolts and remove the starter.

80. Remove the starter motor isolator.

AWD vehicles:

81. Remove the 2 lower catalytic converter bolts.

82. Remove the 6 bolts and the catalytic converter heat shield.

83. Remove and discard the 7 exhaust manifold nuts.

84. Remove the catalytic converter and discard the exhaust manifold gasket.

85. Remove and discard the 7 exhaust manifold studs.

86. Remove the 3 PTU bracket-to-engine bolts.

87. Remove the 2 PTU bracket-to-PTU bolts and remove the bracket.

88. Detach the PTU vent hose retainer.

89. Remove the transaxle-to-PTU bolt.

90. Remove the 3 PTU-to-transaxle bolts and the PTU.

All vehicles:

91. Remove and discard the 4 torque converter nuts.

92. Using the engine crane and spreader bar, remove the engine and transaxle from the lift table.

➡ **The transaxle-to-engine bolts differ in length. Mark the bolts for correct installation.**

93. Remove the remaining 6 engine-to-transaxle bolts and separate the engine and transaxle.

To install:
All vehicles:

94. Using the engine crane and spreader bar, position the engine and transaxle together. Install the 6 transaxle-to-engine bolts and tighten to 35 ft. lbs. (48 Nm).

95. Using the engine crane and spreader bar, position the engine and transaxle onto the lift table.

96. Using suitable tools, secure the engine to the lift table.

97. Install new torque converter nuts and tighten to 26 ft. lbs. (35 Nm).

AWD vehicles:

98. Install the Power Transfer Unit (PTU) and the 3 PTU-to-transaxle bolts. Tighten bolts to 52 ft. lbs. (70 Nm).

99. Install the 1 transaxle-to-PTU bolt and tighten to 35 ft. lbs. (48 Nm).

100. Attach the PTU vent hose.

101. Install the PTU bracket and the 2 bolts and tighten to 33 ft. lbs. (45 Nm).

102. Install the 3 PTU bracket-to-engine bolts and tighten to 30 ft. lbs. (40 Nm).

103. Install 7 new exhaust manifold studs in the cylinder head and tighten to 13 ft. lbs. (17 Nm).

104. Position the catalytic converter and tighten the 7 new exhaust manifold nuts in 2 stages:

    a. Snug all nuts down evenly.

    b. Tighten nuts to 35 ft. lbs. (47 Nm).

105. Install the heat shield and the 6 bolts and tighten to 89 inch lbs. (10 Nm).

106. Install the 2 lower catalytic converter bolts and tighten to 18 ft. lbs. (25 Nm).

All vehicles:

107. Install the starter motor isolator.

108. Install the starter motor tighten mounting bolts to 26 ft. lbs. (35 Nm).

109. Install starter cable harness tighten battery cable nut to 9 ft. lbs (12 Nm).

110. Tighten solenoid wire nut to 44 inch lbs. (5 Nm).

111. Install the wire harness clip retainer and the ground wire and nut to the starter bolts. Tighten nut to 18 ft. lbs. (25 Nm).

112. Raise the engine and transaxle into the vehicle.

113. Install the bolt in the LH transaxle mount and tighten to 76 ft. lbs. (103 Nm).

114. Install the bolt in the rear transaxle mount and tighten to 85 ft. lbs. (115 Nm).

115. Install the engine mount bracket and nuts. Tighten to 85 ft. lbs. (115 Nm).

116. Install the engine mount bracket bolt and tighten to 85 ft. lbs. (115 Nm).

117. Install the 4 transaxle-to-engine bolts and tighten to 35 ft. lbs. (38 Nm).

FWD vehicles:

118. Install the damper and the 3 bolts. Tighten to 30 ft. lbs. (40 Nm).

All vehicles:

119. Install the engine support cross-member and new nut. Tighten to 129 ft. lbs. (175 Nm).

120. Install the 2 bolts for the engine support crossmember and the front roll restrictor bolt.

    a. Tighten the engine support cross-member bolts to 66 ft. lbs. (90 Nm).

    b. Tighten the front roll restrictor bolt to 85 ft. lbs. (115 Nm).

121. Install the A/C compressor and connect the A/C compressor electrical connector.

122. Tighten A/C bolts to 18 ft. lbs. (25 Nm).

123. Connect the lower radiator hose to the radiator.

124. Connect the PCM electrical connectors.

125. Position the harness and install the nut. Tighten nut to 53 inch lbs. (6 Nm).

126. Install the ground wire and bolt. Tighten to 89 inch lbs. (10 Nm).

127. Attach the electrical connector retainers.

128. Connect the fuel supply tube quick connect coupling.

129. Connect the fuel vapor return tube and retainer.

130. Connect the vacuum supply tube.

131. Position the accelerator control

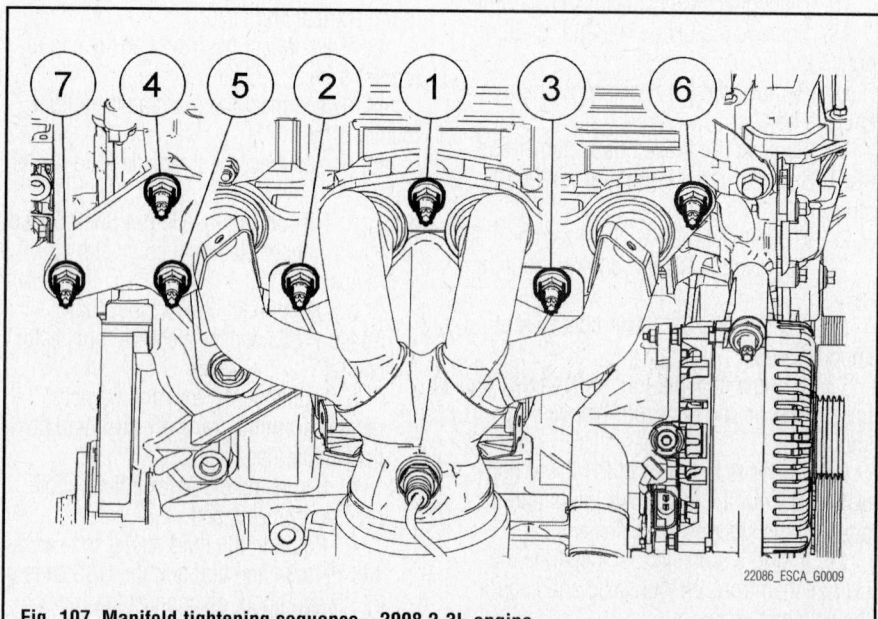

Fig. 107 Manifold tightening sequence—2008 2.3L engine

22086_ESCA_G0009

cable and bracket and install the nut. Tighten nut to 53 inch lbs. (6 Nm).

132. Install the accelerator cable and speed control cable (if equipped).

133. Connect the accelerator and speed control cable (if equipped) to the throttle body.

134. Install the accelerator cable bracket and bolts. Tighten to 89 inch lbs. (10 Nm).

135. Install the accelerator cable snow shield and retainers. Tighten to 35 inch lbs. (4 Nm).

136. Connect the heater hoses to the heater core.

137. Attach the heater hose support strap to the stud.

138. Connect the upper radiator hose.

139. If equipped, route the block heater wiring harness and attach all retainers.

140. Connect the block heater electrical connector.

141. Install the Output Shaft Speed (OSS) sensor tighten mounting bolt to 10 ft. lbs. (13 Nm).

142. Install the fluid cooler tube.

a.Connect the OSS sensor.

b.Connect the turbine shaft speed (TSS) sensor (white connector).

c.Connect the wiring harness retainer to the transaxle case.

d.Position the bracket and install the bolt. Tighten to 10 ft. lbs. (13 Nm).

e.Install the fluid cooler tube fitting and tighten to 17 ft. lbs. (23 Nm).

143. Connect the rear transaxle fluid cooler tube and tighten to 17 ft. lbs. (23 Nm).

144. Connect the front transaxle fluid cooler tube and tighten to 17 ft. lbs. (23 Nm).

145. Connect the transaxle range sensor electrical connector.

146. Install the transaxle control cable, bracket and tighten bolts to 14 ft. lbs. (19 Nm).

147. Attach the wiring harness pin-type retainers.

148. Connect the shift cable to the transaxle manual lever.

149. Install the transaxle wiring harness bracket and nut and connect the transaxle electrical connector. Tighten bracket nut to 89 inch lbs. (10 Nm).

150. Attach the transaxle vent tube retaining clip to the engine wiring harness.

151. Attach the wiring harness retainers to the battery tray bracket.

152. Connect the 34-pin electrical connector.

153. Install the ground strap and tighten bolt to 89 inch lbs. (10 Nm).

154. Connect the electrical connector to the Power Distribution Box (PDB).

155. Connect the cable to the PDB and

install and tighten the nut to 9 ft. lbs. (12 Nm).

156. Install the PDB cover.

157. If equipped, install the ground eyelet and bolt. Tighten to 89 inch lbs. (10 Nm).

AWD vehicles:

158. Align index mark and position the driveshaft to the PTU and install the 6 bolts.

159. Tighten driveshaft mounting bolts to 27 ft. lbs. (37 Nm).

All vehicles:

160. Install the intermediate shaft.

161. Install the intermediate shaft retaining nuts and tighten to 20 ft. lbs. (27 Nm).

162. Install the LH halfshaft in the transaxle and the RH halfshaft to the intermediate shaft.

163. Install the ball joints in the knuckles.

164. Install the RH lower ball joint-to-knuckle bolt and tighten to 46 ft. lbs. (63 Nm).

165. Position the RH tie-rod end and install the retaining nut. Tighten to 41 ft. lbs. (55 Nm).

166. Connect the RH stabilizer bar link and tighten to 46 ft. lbs. (63 Nm).

167. Install the RH brake hose retainer and the ABS sensor bolt. Tighten to 11 ft. lbs. (15 Nm).

168. Install the LH lower ball joint-to-knuckle bolt and tighten to 46 ft. lbs. (63 Nm).

169. Position the LH tie-rod end and install the retaining nut. Tighten to 41 ft. lbs. (55 Nm).

170. Connect the LH stabilizer bar link and tighten to 46 ft. lbs. (63 Nm).

171. Install the LH brake hose retainer and the ABS sensor bolt. Tighten to 11 ft. lbs. (15 Nm).

172. Install the lateral support crossmember and tighten bolts to 85 ft. lbs. (115 Nm).

173. Install the alternator shield and the pin-type retainer, tighten the nut to 15 ft. lbs. (20 Nm).

174. Install the lower air duct.

175. Install the accessory drive belt and tensioner.

176. Connect the heated oxygen sensor (HO2S) and the catalyst monitor sensor electrical connectors.

177. Install the exhaust flexible pipe.

178. Install the front wheels and tires.

179. Install the battery tray.

180. Install the engine air cleaner and air cleaner outlet pipe.

181. Fill the engine with clean engine oil.

182. Fill and bleed the cooling system.

3.0L Engine—2005–07 models

1. Before servicing the vehicle, refer to the Precautions Section.

2. Properly recover the air conditioning system refrigerant.

3. Properly relieve the fuel system pressure.

4. Drain the cooling system.

5. Drain the engine oil.

6. Remove or disconnect the following:
- Hood
- Battery and battery tray
- Air cleaner outlet tube and housing
- Lower radiator air deflectors
- Fuel lines
- Water pump drive belt
- Accelerator cable and speed control cable, if equipped
- Vapor Management Valve (VMV)
- Powertrain Control Module (PCM)
- PCM ground wire
- Thermostat housing and hose assembly and move them aside
- Power distribution box electrical connector
- Power distribution box cover
- Nuts and cables from inside the power distribution box
- Transmission linkage
- Brake booster vacuum hose
- Heater hoses
- Power steering return line
- Power Steering Pressure (PSP) switch electrical connector
- Power steering supply line
- Oil level indicator
- Catalytic converter
- A/C compressor
- Both front wheels
- Intermediate drive shaft, if equipped

7. Separate both side ball joints.

8. Separate both side tie rod ends from the steering knuckles.

9. Separate both sway bar links from the strut mounts.

10. Separate the struts from the steering knuckles.

11. Remove or disconnect the following:
- Both wheel speed sensors, if equipped
- Brake calipers from the steering knuckles and properly support the struts
- Steering shaft from the rack
- Transmission line bracket bolt
- Transmission cooler lines
- Torque converter inspection cover
- Torque converter nuts
- Block heater wiring, if equipped

12. Install a powertrain lifting devise and raise the vehicle.
- Engine support bracket
- Transmission support
- 2 rear subframe bolts
- 2 subframe side bolts

- Motor mount support bolts
- Engine and transmission as an assembly
- Heated Oxygen (HO2S) sensor
- Transmission Range (TR) sensor
- Transmission harness electronic control switch
- Transmission control harness from the bracket
- Starter and wire harness
- Knock Sensor (KS) electrical connector
- Output Shaft Speed (OSS) sensor electrical connector
- HO2S sensor and Exhaust Gas Recirculation (EGR) tube from the exhaust manifold
- Alternator and electrical connectors
- Right side exhaust manifold and gasket
- Halfshaft support bracket and move it aside

13. Separate the engine from the transmission assembly

To install:

14. Install or connect the following:
   - Powertrain assembly on the subframe
   - Transmission-to-engine bolts. Torque the bolts to 30 ft. lbs. (40 Nm).
   - Halfshaft bracket. Torque the bolts to 18 ft. lbs. (25 Nm).
   - Right side exhaust manifold and new gasket. Torque the bolts to 15 ft. lbs. (25 Nm).
   - Alternator. Torque the larger bolts to 18 ft. lbs. (25 Nm) and smaller bolt to 89 inch lbs. (10 Nm).
   - EGR tube and HO2S sensor electrical connectors
   - OSS sensor electrical connector
   - KS jumper electrical connector
   - Starter. Torque the bolts to 18 ft. lbs. (25 Nm).
   - Transmission control harness to the bracket. Torque the bolt to 18 ft. lbs. (25 Nm).
   - Transmission harness
   - Transmission range sensor
   - Powertrain assembly
   - Motor mount support. Torque the bolts to 66 ft. lbs. (90 Nm).
   - Subframe side nuts. Torque the nuts to 76 ft. lbs. (103 Nm). Raise the vehicle and support the powertrain assembly with a lifting device.
   - Transmission mount. Torque the bolts to side bolts to 66 ft. lbs. (90 Nm) and the other bolts to 76 ft. lbs. (103 Nm).

- Motor mount. Torque the bolts to side bolts to 66 ft. lbs. (90 Nm) and the other bolts to 76 ft. lbs. (103 Nm). Remove the powertrain lift.
- Block heater electrical connector, if equipped
- Torque converter. Torque the nuts to 27 ft. lbs. (37 Nm).
- Transmission cover plate and plug
- Transmission cooler lines
- Transmission cooler line bracket. Torque the bolt to 15 ft. lbs. (20 Nm).
- Steering shaft to the rack. Torque the bolt to 18 ft. lbs. (25 Nm).
- Struts to the steering knuckles. Torque the bolts to 75 ft. lbs. (102 Nm).
- Brake calipers to the steering knuckles
- Wheel speed sensors, if equipped. Torque the bolts to 89 inch lbs. (10 Nm).
- Sway bar links to the strut mount. Torque the bolts to 41 ft. lbs. (55 Nm).
- Tie rods to the steering knuckles. Torque the bolts to 41 ft. lbs. (55 Nm).
- Ball joints. Torque the bolts to 52 ft. lbs. (70 Nm).
- Intermediate drive shaft, if equipped
- Both front wheels
- A/C compressor
- Lower radiator air deflectors
- Catalytic converter
- Oil level indicator dipstick tube
- Power steering line and bracket. Torque the bolt to 13 ft. lbs. (17 Nm).
- PSP switch electrical connector
- Power steering return line
- Heater hoses
- Vacuum lines
- Transmission linkage
- Wire harness cables and nuts to the power distribution box. Torque the nuts to 89 inch lbs. (10 Nm).
- Power distribution box wire harness
- Thermostat housing and connect the hoses
- Ground wire. Torque the bolt to 89 inch lbs. (10 Nm).
- PCM electrical connector
- VMV electrical connector
- Accelerator cable and speed control cable, if equipped
- Air cleaner assembly
- Water pump drive belt
- Battery and tray

15. Fill and bleed the cooling system.
16. Fill the engine with clean oil.
17. Recharge the A/C system.
18. Inspect and top off the power steering fluid.
19. Start the vehicle, check for leaks and repair if necessary.

3.0L Engine—2008 models

See Figures 108 through 110.

1. Disconnect the negative battery cable.
2. With the vehicle in NEUTRAL, position it on a hoist.
3. Release the fuel system pressure.
4. Remove the battery tray.
5. Remove the air cleaner outlet pipe and air cleaner.
6. Remove the front wheels and tires.
7. Remove the lower splash shields.
8. Disconnect the catalyst monitor sensor electrical connector and the 2 wiring harness retainers.
9. Remove the 4 bolts and the lateral support crossmember.
10. Remove and discard the 6 exhaust Y-pipe-to-catalytic converter nuts.
11. Detach the exhaust hanger and remove the exhaust Y-pipe.
12. Remove the LH and RH brake hose retainers and ABS sensor wiring harness bolts.
13. Remove the LH and RH stabilizer link-to-strut nuts.
14. Remove the LH and RH tie-rod end nuts.
15. Using the suitable tool, separate the LH and RH tie-rod ends from the steering knuckles.
16. Remove the LH and RH lower ball joint pinch bolts and nuts.
17. Separate the steering knuckles from the lower ball joints.
18. Using a suitable tool, separate the LH halfshaft from the transaxle.
19. Support the halfshaft with a length of mechanic's wire.
20. Using the special tools, separate the RH halfshaft from the intermediate shaft.
21. Support the halfshaft with a length of mechanic's wire.
22. Remove the 2 intermediate shaft retaining nuts.
23. Remove the intermediate shaft.
All wheel drive (AWD) vehicles

✳✳ WARNING

Do not reuse the driveshaft flange bolts and washers. Install new bolts and washers or damage to the vehicle may occur.

→**Index-mark the drive shaft flange and Power Transfer Unit (PTU) flange for installation.**

24. Remove and discard the 6 front driveshaft-to-PTU bolts and washers.

25. Position the driveshaft aside and support with mechanic's wire.

26. Rotate the accessory drive belt tensioner counterclockwise and remove the accessory drive belt.

27. Drain the engine coolant.

28. Drain the engine oil and install the drain plug.

29. Disconnect the A/C clutch field coil electrical connector.

30. Remove the 3 bolts and position the A/C compressor aside.

31. Remove the 3 accessory drive belt idler pulley assembly bolts.

32. Detach the wiring harness retainer and remove the idler pulley assembly.

33. Remove the front roll restrictor bolt and the 2 bolts for the engine support cross brace.

34. Remove the rear nut and the engine support crossmember.

35. Disconnect the 2 transmission cooler tubes (1 shown).

36. Loosen the transaxle cooler tube fitting.

37. Remove the bracket bolt and the transaxle cooler tube.

38. Disconnect the EGR tube fitting from the converter.

39. Remove the 2 bolts and the accelerator cable snow shield.

40. Disconnect the accelerator cable and the speed control actuator cable.

41. Remove the 2 accelerator cable bracket bolts.

42. Remove the bolt and position the cables and brackets aside.

43. Disconnect the upper and lower radiator hoses.

44. Disconnect the heater hoses and the throttle body coolant hose.

45. Detach the transaxle vent tube retainer from the throttle body.

46. Disconnect the fuel supply tube quick connect coupling.

47. Disconnect the gearshift cable from the transaxle.

48. Disconnect the wire harness retainer from the shift cable bracket, remove the 2 remaining bolts, and position the cable and bracket aside.

49. Disconnect the differential pressure feedback EGR sensor electrical connector and detach the pin-type retainer.

50. Disconnect the EGR tube fitting and remove the EGR tube and the differential

pressure feedback EGR sensor as an assembly.

51. Disconnect the evaporative emissions (EVAP) canister purge valve tube from the intake manifold.

52. Disconnect the brake booster vacuum tube from the intake manifold.

53. Disconnect the manifold absolute pressure (MAP) sensor vacuum tube and electrical connector.

54. Disconnect the PCM electrical connectors and remove the nut.

55. Remove the bolt and detach the ground wire.

56. Remove the nut and disconnect the cable from the power distribution box.

57. Disconnect the electrical connector from the power distribution box.

58. Remove the bolt and disconnect the ground wire and the electrical connector.

59. Detach the wiring harness retainers from the battery tray bracket

60. Remove the nut and disconnect the wire from the battery cable.

61. Remove the nut and the ground wire from the engine mount stud.

62. If equipped, disconnect the engine block heater electrical connector.

63. Disconnect the output shaft speed (OSS) sensor electrical connector and remove the bolt and the OSS sensor.

64. Remove the torque converter inspection cover.

65. Remove the 4 torque converter nuts.

66. Remove the 2 oil pan-to-transaxle bolts.

67. Remove the 2 nuts and the transaxle-to-engine stud.

✳✳ WARNING

Do not allow the engine oil pan to rest on the power train lift. Doing so may cause damage to the oil pan.

68. Using the suitable tools, secure the engine and transaxle to the powertrain lift.

→**The next 5 steps must be carried out with the vehicle raised and the powertrain lift in position.**

69. Remove the RH transaxle support insulator bolt.

70. Remove the bolt, nuts and the RH transaxle support insulator.

71. Remove the rear transaxle support bolt.

72. Remove the 3 engine support bracket nuts and the bolt.

73. Remove the engine support bracket.

74. Lower the powertrain from the vehicle.

75. Disconnect the LH Heated Exhaust Gas Oxygen (HEGO) sensor and LH catalyst monitor sensor electrical connectors.

76. Detach the 3 pin-type retainers from the transaxle support bracket.

77. Disconnect the transmission range (TR) sensor electrical connector

78. Disconnect the transaxle electronic control switch electrical connector.

79. Detach the wiring harness from the bracket.

80. Disconnect the turbine speed sensor (TSS) electrical connector.

81. Detach the 2 wiring harness retainer.

AWD vehicles:

82. Disconnect the RH HO2S electrical connector

83. Remove the 6 RH exhaust manifold nuts and the manifold.

84. Discard the nuts and gasket.

85. Remove and discard the 6 RH exhaust manifold studs.

86. Remove the 6 bolts and the half-shaft support bracket.

87. Remove the bolt, detach the pin-type retainer and position the Power Transfer Unit (PTU) vent tube aside.

88. Remove the 3 PTU bolts.

89. Remove the bolt and the PTU.

All vehicles:

90. Remove the nut and detach wiring harness retainer.

91. Remove the 2 stud bolts and position the EGR regulator aside.

92. Install engine lifting brackets to engine.

93. Using the suitable tools and a suitable engine crane, remove the engine and transaxle from the lift table.

94. Remove the 5 remaining transaxle-to-engine bolts.

95. Using the suitable tools and a suitable engine crane, separate the engine and transaxle.

To install:
All vehicles:

96. Using the special tools, align the engine with the transaxle.

97. Install the 5 transaxle-to-engine bolts and tighten to 35 ft. lbs. (48 Nm).

98. Using the suitable tools, secure the engine and transaxle to the powertrain lift.

99. Install the EGR regulator and the 2 stud bolts. Tighten to 53 inch lbs. (6 Nm).

100. Attach the wiring harness retainer and install the nut. Tighten to 53 inch lbs. (6 Nm).

AWD vehicles:

101. Position the Power Transfer Unit (PTU) and install the bolt. Tighten to 33 ft. lbs. (45 Nm).

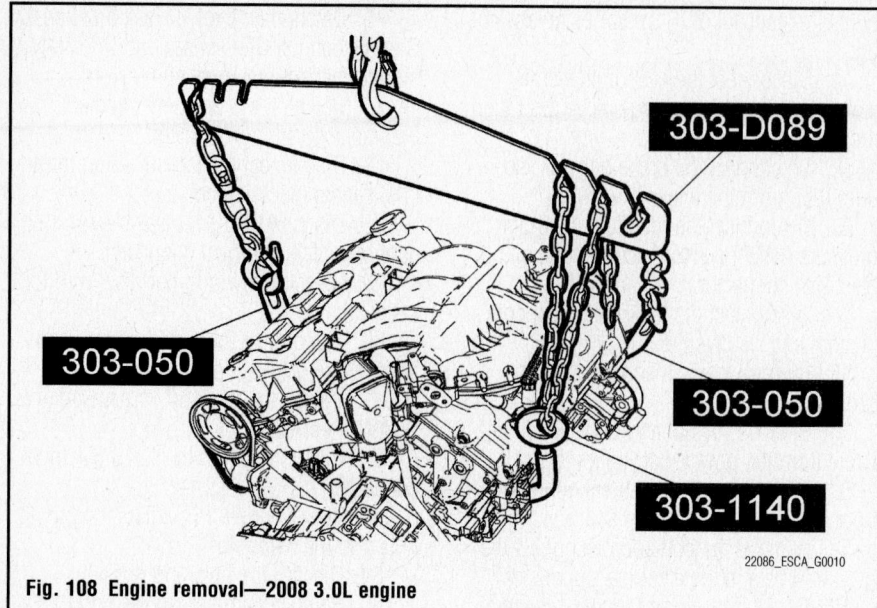

Fig. 108 Engine removal—2008 3.0L engine

102. Install the 3 PTU bolts and tighten to 33 ft. lbs. (45 Nm).

103. Install the PTU vent tube, the pin-type retainer and the bolt. Tighten to 20 ft. lbs. (14 Nm).

104. Install the halfshaft support bracket and the 6 bolts. Tighten bolts to 35 ft. lbs. (48 Nm).

105. Install 6 new RH exhaust manifold studs and tighten to 9 ft. lbs. (12 Nm).

106. Using a new gasket, install the RH exhaust manifold and 6 new nuts.

107. Tighten the manifold nuts to 15 ft. lbs. (20 Nm).

108. Connect the RH heated oxygen sensor (HO2S) electrical connector.

All vehicles:

109. Connect the turbine speed sensor (TSS) electrical connector.

110. Attach the wiring harness retainer.

111. Attach the transaxle control harness to the bracket.

112. Connect the transaxle wiring harness electronic control switch electrical connector.

113. Connect the transmission range (TR) sensor electrical connector

114. Attach the pin-type retainers to the transaxle support bracket and connect the HO2S and catalyst monitor sensor electrical connectors.

115. Position the powertrain into the vehicle

116. Install the engine support bracket, the bolt and the 3 nuts. Tighten the nuts to 56 ft. lbs. (41 Nm). And the bolts to 66 ft. lbs. (90 Nm).

117. Install the rear transaxle support through bolt and tighten to 76 ft. lbs. (103 Nm).

118. Position the RH transaxle support insulator and install the bolt and nuts. Tighten to 59 ft. lbs. (80 Nm).

119. Install the RH transaxle support insulator through bolt and tighten to 85 ft. lbs. (115 Nm).

120. Install the transaxle-to-engine stud and 2 nuts. Tighten to 35 ft. lbs. (48 Nm).

➡Clean and degrease all sealing surfaces with metal surface cleaner. The oil pan must be installed and the bolts tightened within 4 minutes of the sealant application.

121. Apply a 10 mm (0.39 in) dot of silicone gasket and sealant to the front cover-to-cylinder block sealing surface.

122. Install a new oil pan gasket.

123. Position the oil pan and gasket and loosely install the bolts and stud bolts.

124. Install the 2 oil pan-to-transaxle bolts. Tighten to 30 ft. lbs. (40 Nm).

125. Tighten the oil pan bolts in sequence to 18 ft. lbs. (25 Nm).

126. Install the 4 torque converter nuts and tighten to 30 ft. lbs. (40 Nm).

127. Install the torque converter inspection cover.

128. Install the output shaft speed (OSS) sensor and the bolt and connect the electrical connector. Tighten mounting bolt to 10 ft. lbs. (13 Nm).

129. If equipped, connect the engine block heater electrical connector.

130. Install the ground wire eyelet and nut to the engine mount stud. Tighten to 18 ft. lbs. (25 Nm).

131. Install the wire and nut to the battery cable. Tighten to 89 inch lbs. (10 Nm).

132. Attach the wiring harness retainers from the battery tray bracket.

133. Position the ground strap and the electrical connector and install the bolts. Tighten to 89 inch lbs. (10 Nm).

134. Connect the electrical connector to the power distribution box.

135. Install the cable and the nut. Tighten to 9 ft. lbs. (12 Nm).

136. Attach the ground wire and install the bolt. Tighten to 89 inch lbs. (10 Nm).

137. Position the wiring and install the nut. Tighten to 71 inch lbs. (8 Nm). Connect the PCM electrical connectors.

138. Connect the manifold absolute

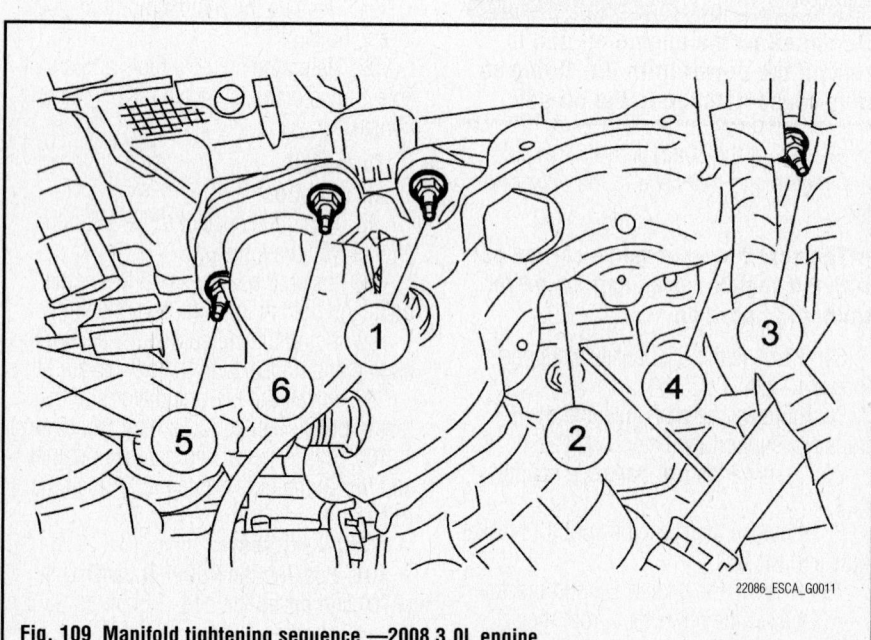

Fig. 109 Manifold tightening sequence —2008 3.0L engine

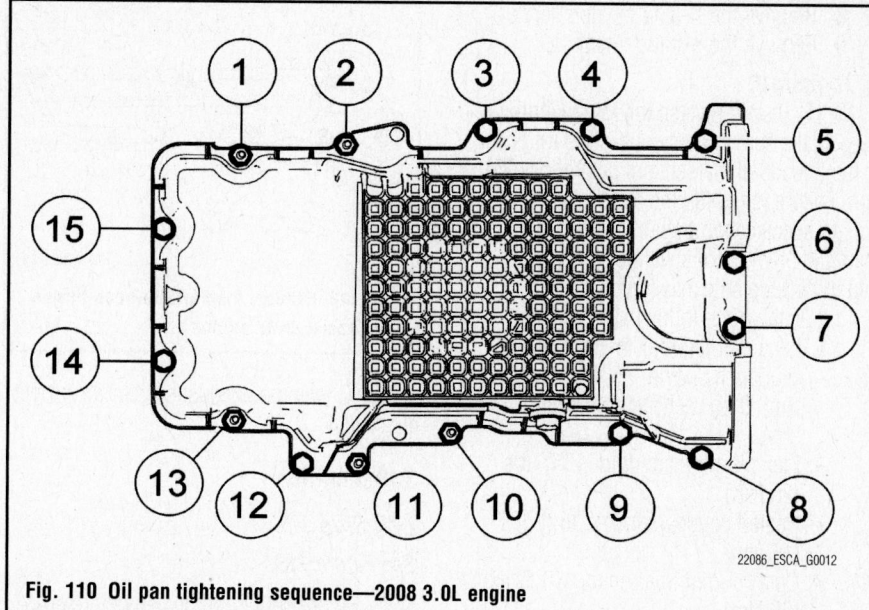

Fig. 110 Oil pan tightening sequence—2008 3.0L engine

22086_ESCA_G0012

pressure (MAP) sensor electrical connector and vacuum tube.

139. Connect the brake booster vacuum tube

140. Connect the evaporative emissions (EVAP) purge valve tube to the intake manifold.

141. Position the EGR tube and loosely install the fittings.

142. Tighten the EGR tube-to-EGR valve fitting to 30 ft. lbs. (40 Nm).

143. Connect the differential pressure feedback EGR sensor electrical connector and attach the pin-type retainer.

144. Position the shift cable and bracket in place, install the bolts and tighten to 17 ft. lbs. (23 Nm). Install the wiring harness retainer.

145. Connect the gearshift cable to the transaxle.

146. Attach the wiring harness pin-type retainer to the gearshift cable bracket.

147. Connect the fuel supply tube quick connect coupling at the fuel rail

148. Attach the transaxle vent tube retainer to the throttle body.

149. Connect the heater hoses and the throttle body coolant hose

150. Connect the upper and lower radiator hoses.

151. Position the accelerator and speed control cables and bracket. Install the nut and tighten to 89 inch lbs. (10 Nm).

152. Position the bracket and install and tighten the bolts to 89 inch lbs. (10 Nm).

153. Connect the accelerator cable and the speed control actuator cable

154. Position the accelerator cable snow shield, install and tighten the bolts to 89 inch lbs. (10 Nm).

155. Tighten the EGR tube-to-RH catalytic converter fitting to 30 ft. lbs. (40 Nm).

156. Install the transaxle cooler tube and the bracket bolt.

157. Tighten the bolt to 10 ft. lbs. (13 Nm), tighten the fitting to 17 ft. lbs. (23 Nm).

158. Connect the 2 transmission cooler tubes.

159. Install the cross brace and the new nut finger tight.

160. Install the 2 bolts for the cross brace and the bolt for the front roll restrictor.

  a. Tighten the 2 cross brace bolts to 66 ft. lbs. (90 Nm).

  b. Tighten the front roll restrictor bolt to 85 ft. lbs. (115 Nm).

161. Tighten the cross brace nut to 129 ft. lbs. (175 Nm).

162. Position the RH accessory drive belt idler pulley and bracket and attach the wiring harness retainer. Install the bolts and tighten to 18 ft. lbs. (25 Nm).

163. Install the A/C compressor and bolts, tighten to 18 ft. lbs. (25 Nm).

164. Connect the A/C clutch field coil electrical connector

165. Rotate the accessory drive belt tensioner counterclockwise and install the accessory drive belt.

AWD vehicles:

> ※※ **WARNING**
>
> **Do not reuse the driveshaft flange bolts and washers. Install new bolts and washers or damage to the vehicle may occur.**

166. Align the index-marks made during removal and install 6 new front

driveshaft-to-PTU bolts and washers. Tighten to 27 ft. lbs. (37 Nm).

All vehicles:

167. Install the intermediate shaft and the 2 nuts. Tighten to 20 ft. lbs. (27 Nm).

168. Install the RH halfshaft onto the intermediate shaft.

169. Install the LH halfshaft into the transaxle.

170. Attach the LH and RH lower ball joints to the steering knuckles and install the pinch bolts and nuts. Tighten to 46 ft. lbs (63 Nm).

171. Install the LH and RH tie-rod ends and nuts. Tighten to 41 ft. lbs. (55 Nm).

172. Install the LH and RH stabilizer link-to-strut nuts. Tighten to 46 ft. lbs (63 Nm).

173. Install the LH and RH brake hose retainers and ABS sensor wiring harness bolts. Tighten to 11 ft. lbs. (15 Nm).

174. Install the Y-pipe and the 2 exhaust flange-to-RH catalytic converter nuts. Tighten to 21 ft. lbs. (29 Nm).

175. Install the 2 exhaust flange-to-LH catalytic converter nuts. Tighten to 21 ft. lbs. (29 Nm).

176. Attach the Y-pipe to the rear catalytic converter.

177. Attach the exhaust hanger.

178. Install the 2 exhaust flange-to-rear catalytic converter nuts and tighten to 21 ft. lbs. (29 Nm).

179. Install the lateral support crossmember and the 4 bolts. Tighten to 85 ft. lbs. (115 Nm).

180. Connect the catalyst monitor sensor electrical connector and the 2 wiring harness retainers

181. Install the lower splash shields.

182. Install the front wheels and tires.

183. Install the air cleaner outlet pipe and air cleaner

184. Install the battery tray.

185. Fill the engine with clean engine oil.

186. Fill and bleed the cooling system.

187. Connect the negative battery cable.

EXHAUST MANIFOLD

REMOVAL & INSTALLATION

2.3L Engine

See Figures 111 and 112.

1. Before servicing the vehicle, refer to the Precautions Section.

> ※※ **WARNING**
>
> **Do not use oil or grease-based lubricants on the insulators. They may cause deterioration of the rubber.**

⚹⚹ **WARNING**

Oil or grease-based lubricants on the insulators may cause the exhaust hanger insulator to separate from the exhaust hanger bracket during vehicle operation.

➡**Exhaust fasteners are of a torque prevailing design. Use only new fasteners with the same part number as the original. Torque values must be used as specified during reassembly to make sure of correct retention of exhaust components.**

2. Remove the flex pipe nuts.
3. Remove the flex pipe gasket.
4. Remove the manifold bracket bolts.
5. Remove the heat shield.
6. Remove the exhaust manifold nuts.
7. Remove the catalyst monitor sensor.

8. Remove the heated oxygen sensor.
9. Remove the exhaust manifold.

To install:

10. To install, reverse the removal procedure. Make sure to apply anti-seize lubricant to the threads of the sensors before installation. Failure to tighten the exhaust manifold nuts to specification before installing the manifold bracket bolts will cause the manifold to develop an exhaust gas leak.
11. Observe the following torques:
- Exhaust manifold-to-head, in the sequence shown: 35 ft. lbs. (47 Nm), then recheck at 35 ft. lbs. (47 Nm)
- Flex pipe-to-manifold: 18 ft. lbs. (25 Nm)
- Heated oxygen sensor: 35 ft. lbs. (47 Nm)
- Catalyst monitor sensor: 30 ft. lbs. (40 Nm)

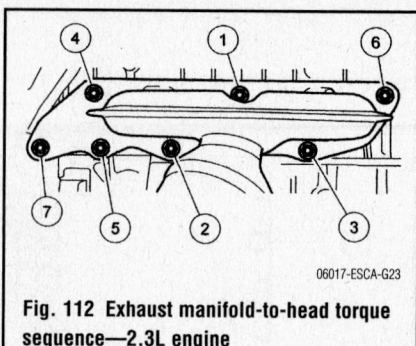

Fig. 112 Exhaust manifold-to-head torque sequence—2.3L engine

12. Check the exhaust system for proper alignment.

3.0L Engine

Left Side

See Figure 113.

1. Before servicing the vehicle, refer to the Precautions Section.
2. Remove or disconnect the following:
- Negative battery cable
- Heated Oxygen (HO2S) sensor and catalyst monitor
- Splash shield
- Exhaust crossover pipe
- Drive belt—2005–07 models
- A/C compressor and move it aside—2005–07 models
- Exhaust manifold and discard the gasket

To install:

3. Clean the sealing surfaces of any old gasket material.
4. Install or connect the following:
- Exhaust manifold and new gasket. Torque the bolts to 15 ft. lbs. (20 Nm).
- A/C compressor—2005–07 models. Torque the bolts to 18 ft. lbs. (20 Nm).
- Drive belt—2005–07 models
- Exhaust crossover pipe. Torque the bolts to 30 ft. lbs. (40 Nm).
- Splash shield. Torque the bolts to 80 inch lbs. (9 Nm).

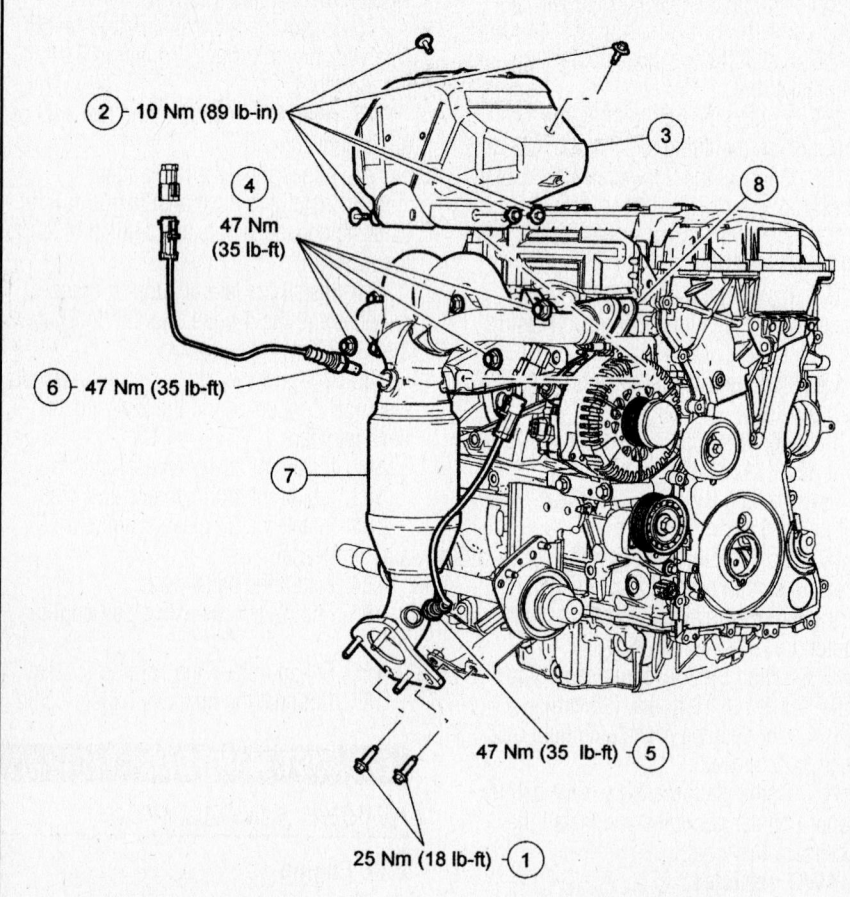

1 Catalytic converter bracket bolts (2 required)	5 Catalyst monitor sensor
2 Heat shield bolts (6 required)	6 Heated oxygen sensor (HO2S)
3 Heat shield	7 Catalytic converter
4 Exhaust manifold nuts (7 required)	8 Exhaust manifold gasket

Fig. 111 Catalytic converter/exhaust manifold—2.3L engine

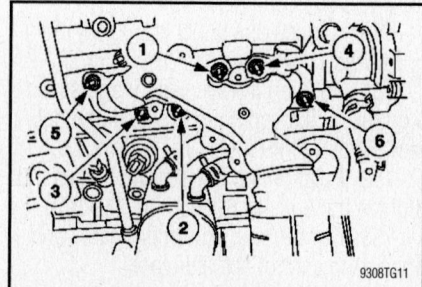

Fig. 113 Left side exhaust manifold bolt torque sequence—3.0L engine

- Left side HO₂S sensor and catalyst monitor
- Negative battery cable

5. Start the vehicle and check for leaks, repair if necessary.

Right Side

See Figure 114.

1. Before servicing the vehicle, refer to the Precautions Section.

2. Remove or disconnect the following:
- Negative battery cable
- Exhaust Gas Recirculation (EGR) tube
- Alternator
- Right side Heated Oxygen (HO₂S) sensor
- Right side exhaust manifold and discard the gasket

To install:

3. Clean the sealing surfaces of any old gasket material.

4. Install or connect the following:
- Exhaust manifold and new gasket. Torque the bolts to 15 ft. lbs. (20 Nm).
- Right side HO₂S sensor

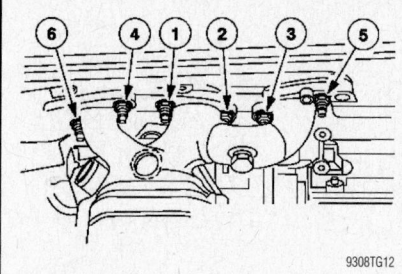

Fig. 114 Right side exhaust manifold bolt torque sequence—3.0L engine

- Alternator
- EGR tube
- Negative battery cable

5. Start the vehicle and check for leaks, repair if necessary.

INTAKE MANIFOLD

REMOVAL & INSTALLATION

2.3L Engine

See Figures 115 and 116.

1. Before servicing the vehicle, refer to the Precautions Section.

2. With the vehicle in NEUTRAL, position it on a hoist.
3. Remove the throttle body.
4. Remove the fuel rail.
5. Remove the oil level indicator tube.
6. Remove the vacuum tube.
7. Remove the vacuum supply hose.
8. Remove the fuel vapor return hose.
9. Remove the idle air control (IAC) motor electrical connector.
10. Remove the swirl control valve electrical connector.
11. Remove the knock sensor (KS) electrical connector.
12. Remove the temperature manifold absolute pressure (TMAP) sensor electrical connector.
13. Remove the oil pressure sender electrical connector.
14. Remove the engine control wiring harness.
15. Remove the intake manifold bolts.

➡**There are three different size bolts used. Mark the location of the bolts to make sure they are installed in the correct location.**

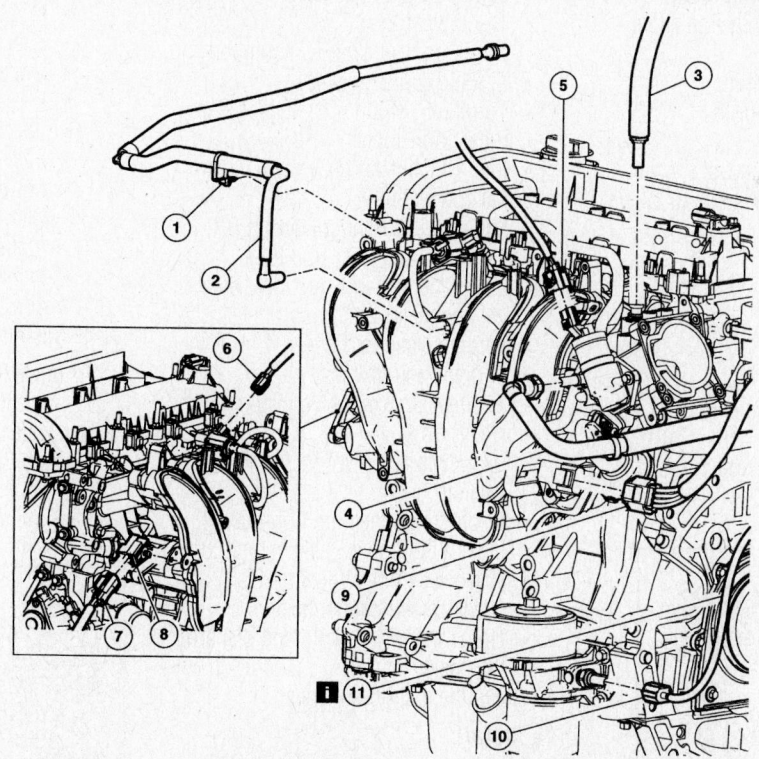

1 Vacuum tube retainer
2 Vacuum tube
3 Vacuum supply hose
4 Fuel vapor return hose
5 Idle air control (IAC) motor electrical connector
6 Swirl control valve electrical connector
7 Knock sensor (KS) electrical connector
8 Pin-type retainer
9 Temperature manifold absolute pressure (TMAP) sensor electrical connector
10 Oil pressure sender electrical connector
11 Engine control wiring harness

Fig. 115 Intake manifold and related parts—2.3L engine

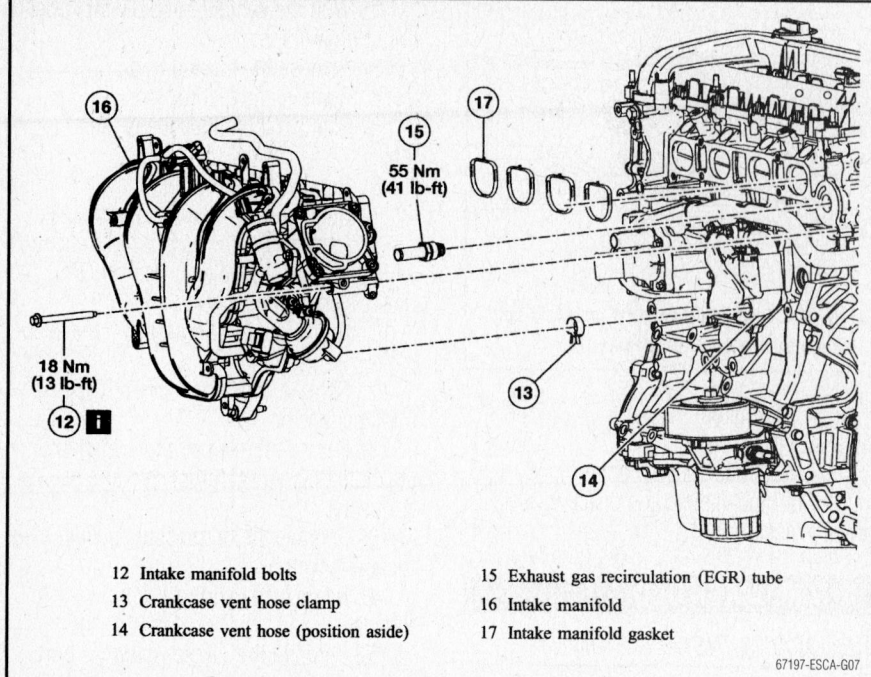

12 Intake manifold bolts
13 Crankcase vent hose clamp
14 Crankcase vent hose (position aside)
15 Exhaust gas recirculation (EGR) tube
16 Intake manifold
17 Intake manifold gasket

67197-ESCA-G07

Fig. 116 Intake manifold installation—2.3L engine

16. Remove the bolts and position the intake manifold aside to access the crankcase vent hose clamp and the EGR tube.

17. Remove the crankcase vent hose.

18. Remove the exhaust gas recirculation (EGR) tube.

19. Remove the intake manifold.

20. Remove the intake manifold gasket.

21. To install, reverse the removal procedure. Torque the intake manifold bolts to 13 ft. lbs. (18 Nm).

3.0L Engine

Upper

See Figure 117.

1. Before servicing the vehicle, refer to the Precautions Section.

2. Properly relieve the fuel system pressure. Drain the coolant system.

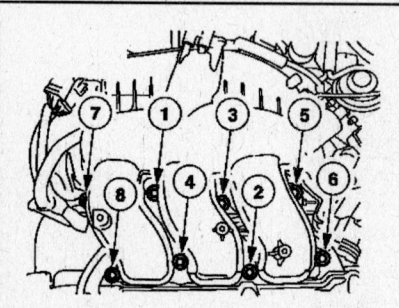

9308TG02

Fig. 117 Tighten the upper intake manifold bolts in the sequence shown—3.0L engine

3. Remove or disconnect the following:
- Negative battery cable
- Air cleaner outlet tube
- Engine appearance cover
- Throttle cable
- Speed control cable, if equipped
- Throttle cable bracket
- Throttle Position (TP) sensor electrical connector
- Idle Air Control (IAC) valve electrical connector
- Exhaust Gas Recirculation (EGR) valve vacuum hose and tube
- EGR vacuum regulator valve electrical connector and hose
- Chassis vacuum hose
- Engine vacuum hose
- Positive Crankcase Ventilation (PCV) hose
- Vapor Management Valve (VMV) vacuum hose
- Electrical connectors from the left side of the upper intake manifold
- Power Steering Pressure (PSP) sensor electrical connector
- Upper intake manifold and discard the gasket

4. Clean the mating surfaces.

To install:

5. Install or connect the following:
- New gasket
- Intake manifold. Torque the bolts, in sequence, to 89 inch lbs. (10 Nm).
- PSP electrical connector

- Electrical connectors on the left side of the upper intake manifold
- VMV vacuum hose
- Chassis, engine and PCV hoses
- EGR valve vacuum regulator
- EGR valve vacuum hose and tube. Torque the nut to 30 ft. lbs. (40 Nm).
- TP sensor electrical connector
- IAC valve electrical connector
- Throttle cable and speed control cable, if equipped. Torque the bracket bolts to 89 inch lbs. (10 Nm).
- Air cleaner outlet tube
- Engine appearance cover. Torque the bolts to 53 inch lbs. (6 Nm).
- Negative battery cable

6. Fill the coolant system to the proper level.

7. Start the vehicle and check for leaks, repair if necessary.

Lower

See Figure 118.

1. Before servicing the vehicle, refer to the Precautions Section.

2. Properly relieve the fuel system pressure.

3. Remove or disconnect the following:
- Negative battery cable
- Fuel line spring lock coupling
- Upper intake manifold
- Fuel rail
- Fuel injector electrical connectors
- Fuel pressure damper vacuum line
- Lower intake manifold
- Lower intake manifold from the fuel rail
- Fuel injectors from the manifold and discard the gasket

4. Clean the mating surfaces.

To install:

5. Inspect the fuel injector O-rings and replace if necessary.

6. Install or connect the following:
- Fuel injectors into the lower intake manifold

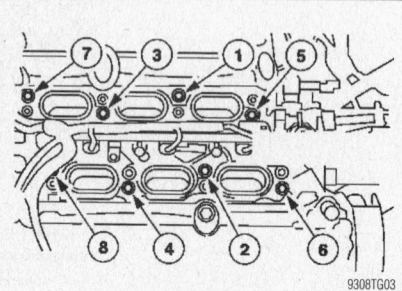

9308TG03

Fig. 118 Tighten the lower intake manifold bolts in the sequence shown—3.0L engine

- Fuel rail. Torque the bolts to 89 inch lbs. (10 Nm).
- New gasket
- Intake manifold. Torque the bolts, in sequence, to 89 inch lbs. (10 Nm).
- Fuel rail electrical connectors
- Fuel injector electrical connectors
- Fuel pressure damper vacuum line
- Upper intake manifold
- Fuel line spring lock coupling
- Negative battery cable

7. Start the vehicle and check for leaks, repair if necessary.

MAIN BEARING TORQUE SEQUENCE

See Figure 119.

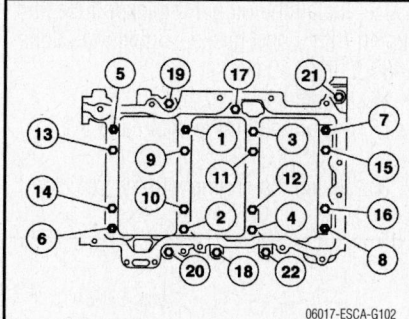

06017-ESCA-G102

Fig. 119 3.0L engine main bearing (bed plate) torque sequence

OIL PAN

REMOVAL & INSTALLATION

2.3L Engine

See Figures 120 and 121.

All vehicles:

1. With the vehicle in NEUTRAL, position it on a hoist.
2. Remove the air cleaner outlet pipe.

✳✳ WARNING

To prevent damage to the transmission, do not loosen the transmission-to-engine bolts more than 0.19 inch (5mm).

3. Loosen the 2 top bell housing-to-engine bolts 0.19 inch (5mm).

AWD vehicles:

4. Working from the top of the vehicle, loosen the 2 rear lower engine-to-bell housing bolts 0.19 inch (5mm).
5. Working from under the vehicle, loosen the 2 upper engine bracket-to-Power Transfer Unit (PTU) bolts 0.19 inch (5mm).

All vehicles:

6. Remove the 7 retainers and the LH splash shield.
7. Remove the oil level indicator and tube
8. Loosen the 2 front lower bell housing-to-engine bolts 0.19 inch (5mm).

FWD vehicles:

9. Loosen the 1 (manual transmission) and 2 (automatic transmission) rear lower engine-to-bell housing bolt 0.19 inch (5mm).

All vehicles:

10. Remove the 2 oil pan-to-bell housing bolts.
11. Remove the 2 bell housing-to-oil pan bolt.

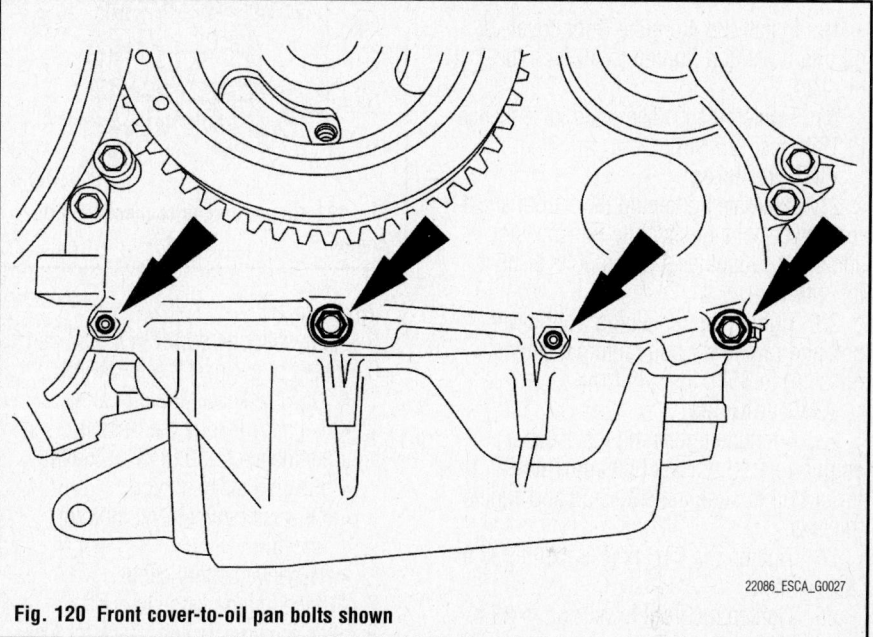

22086_ESCA_G0027

Fig. 120 Front cover-to-oil pan bolts shown

12. Slide the transmission rearward 5 mm (0.19 in).
13. Drain the engine oil.
14. Remove the 4 engine front cover-to-oil pan bolts.
15. Remove the 13 bolts and the oil pan.

To install:
All vehicles:

16. Clean and inspect all mating surfaces.

➡**If the oil pan is not secured within 10 minutes of sealant application, the sealant must be removed and the sealing area cleaned with metal surface cleaner. Allow to dry until there is no sign of wetness, or 10 minutes,**

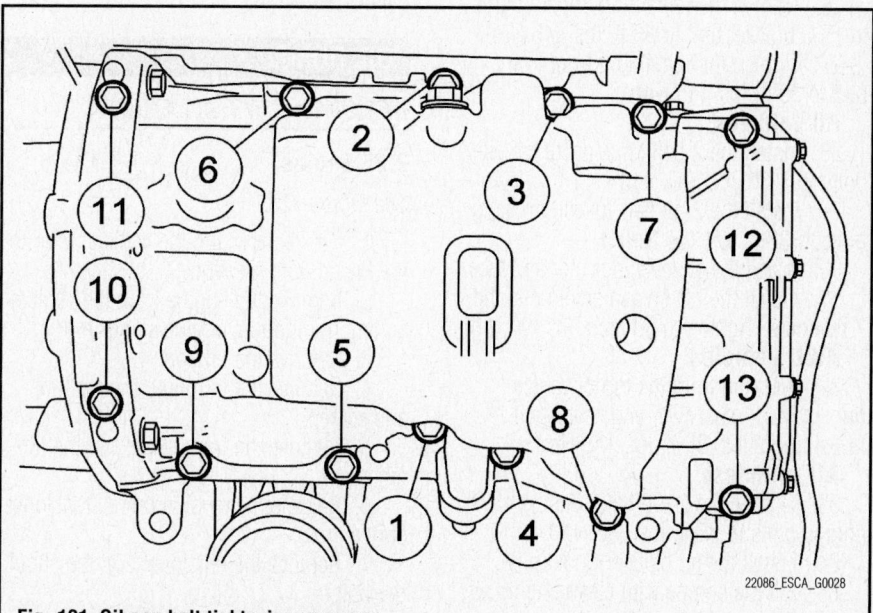

22086_ESCA_G0028

Fig. 121 Oil pan bolt tightening sequence

whichever is longer. Failure to follow this procedure can cause future oil leakage.

17. Apply a 0.09 inch. (2.5mm) bead of silicone gasket and sealant to the oil pan-to-engine block and to the oil pan-to-engine front cover mating surface.

18. Position the oil pan onto the engine and install the oil pan bolts finger-tight.

☀☀ WARNING

The engine front cover-to-oil pan bolts must be tightened first to align the front surface of the oil pan flush with the front surface of the engine block.

19. Install the 4 engine front cover-to-oil pan bolts and tighten to 89 inch lbs. (10 Nm).

20. Tighten the oil pan bolts in sequence to 18 ft. lbs. (25 Nm).

FWD vehicles:

21. Alternate tightening the 1 front and 1 rear lower bolts to slide the transmission and engine together. Tighten bolts to 35 ft. lbs. (48 Nm).

22. Tighten the remaining front lower bolt and rear lower bolt (automatic transmission) to 35 ft. lbs. (48 Nm).

AWD vehicles:

23. Alternate tightening the 1 upper engine-to-PTU bracket bolt and 1 front lower bolt to slide transmission and engine together.

24. Tighten the PTU bracket bolt to 33 ft. lbs. (45 Nm).

25. Tighten the front lower bolt to 33 ft. lbs. (45 Nm).

26. Tighten the remaining upper engine-to-PTU bracket bolt to 33 ft. lbs. (45 Nm).

27. Tighten the remaining front lower bolt to 33 ft. lbs. (45 Nm).

All vehicles:

28. Install the 2 bell housing-to-oil pan bolts to 33 ft. lbs. (45 Nm).

29. Install the 2 oil pan-to-bell housing bolts to 33 ft. lbs. (45 Nm).

30. Install the oil level indicator and tube.

31. Install the LH splash shield and the 7 retainers. Tighten to 80 inch. lbs (90 Nm).

AWD vehicles:

32. Working from the top of vehicle, tighten the 2 rear lower engine-to-bell housing bolts to 35 ft. lbs. (48 Nm).

All vehicles:

33. Tighten the 2 top bell housing-to-engine bolts to 35 ft. lbs. (48 Nm).

34. Install the air cleaner outlet pipe.

35. Fill the engine with clean engine oil.

36. Recheck for leaks.

3.0L Engine

See Figure 122.

1. Before servicing the vehicle, refer to the Precautions Section.

2. Drain the engine oil.

3. Remove or disconnect the following:
- Negative battery cable
- Flexible exhaust pipe
- Downstream catalyst monitor sensor
- Oil pan and gasket

4. Thoroughly clean the gasket mating surfaces.

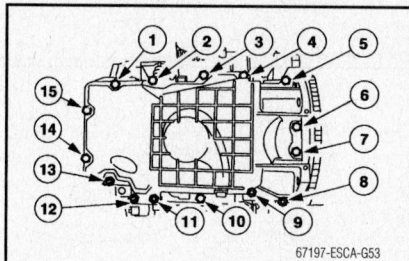

Fig. 122 Oil pan torque sequence—3.0L engine

To install:

5. Apply silicone sealer to the oil pan.

6. Install or connect the following:
- New gasket on the oil pan
- Oil pan. Torque the bolts in sequence to 19 ft. lbs. (26 Nm).
- Flexible exhaust pipe
- Downstream catalyst monitor sensor
- Negative battery cable

7. Fill the engine with clean oil.

8. Start the vehicle and check for leaks, repair if necessary.

OIL PUMP

REMOVAL & INSTALLATION

2.3L Engine

See Figure 123.

1. Before servicing the vehicle, refer to the Precautions Section.

2. Remove the engine from the vehicle and mount it on an engine stand.

3. Remove the oil pan.

4. Remove the oil pump pickup tube and screen.

5. Remove the front cover and the timing chain.

6. Release the tension on the tensioner spring.

7. Remove the tensioner and the shoulder bolt.

8. Remove the guide.

➡**The oil pump chain sprocket must be held in place.**

9. Remove the oil pump chain and sprockets.

10. Remove the oil pump assembly and gasket.

To install:

11. Install the oil pump with a new gasket. Tighten the bolts in sequence as follows:
   a. Step 1: 89 inch lbs. (10 Nm).
   b. Step 2: 17 ft. lbs. (23 Nm).

12. Install the pump chain and sprockets. Tighten the pump sprocket bolt to 18 ft. lbs. (25 Nm).

13. Install the chain guide, tensioner, and shoulder bolt. Tighten the bolts to 89 inch lbs. (10 Nm).

14. Hook the tensioner spring around the shoulder bolt.

15. Install the oil pump pickup tube and screen with a new gasket. Tighten the bolts to 89 ft. lbs. (10 Nm).

16. Install the oil pan.

17. Install the timing chain and front cover.

18. Install the engine into the vehicle.

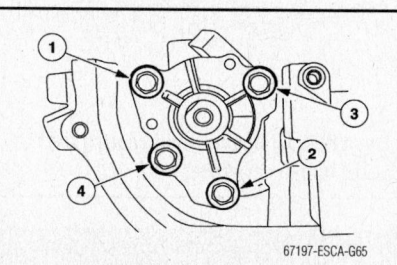

Fig. 123 Oil pump torque sequence—2.3L engine

3.0L Engine

See Figures 124 and 125.

1. Before servicing the vehicle, refer to the Precautions Section.

2. Drain the engine oil.

3. Remove or disconnect the following:
- Negative battery cable
- Timing drive components
- Oil pump screen cover and tube
- Damper bolt and crankshaft sprockets
- Oil pump bolts in the proper sequence

4. Thoroughly clean the gasket mating surfaces.

To install:

5. Install or connect the following:
- Oil pump and bolts in the proper sequence. Torque the bolts to 89 inch lbs. (10 Nm).

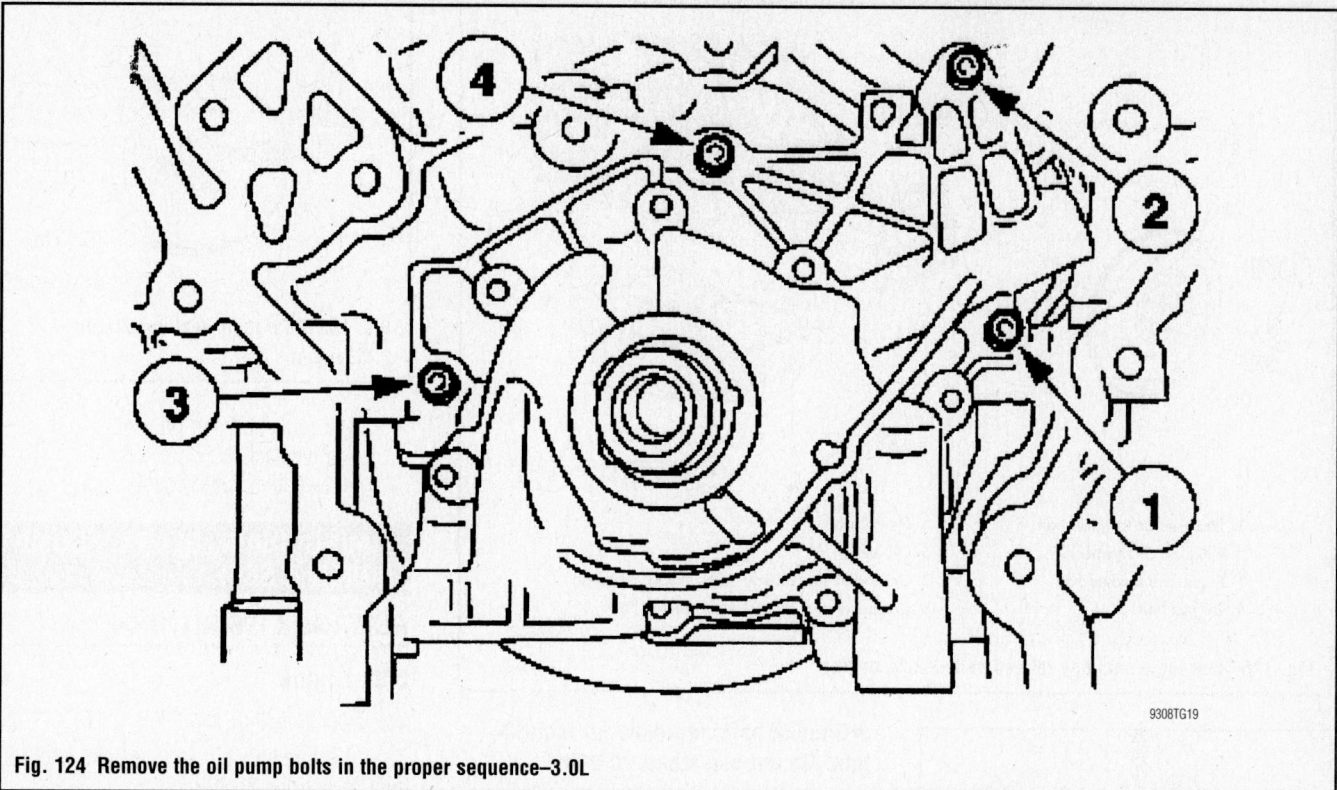

Fig. 124 Remove the oil pump bolts in the proper sequence–3.0L

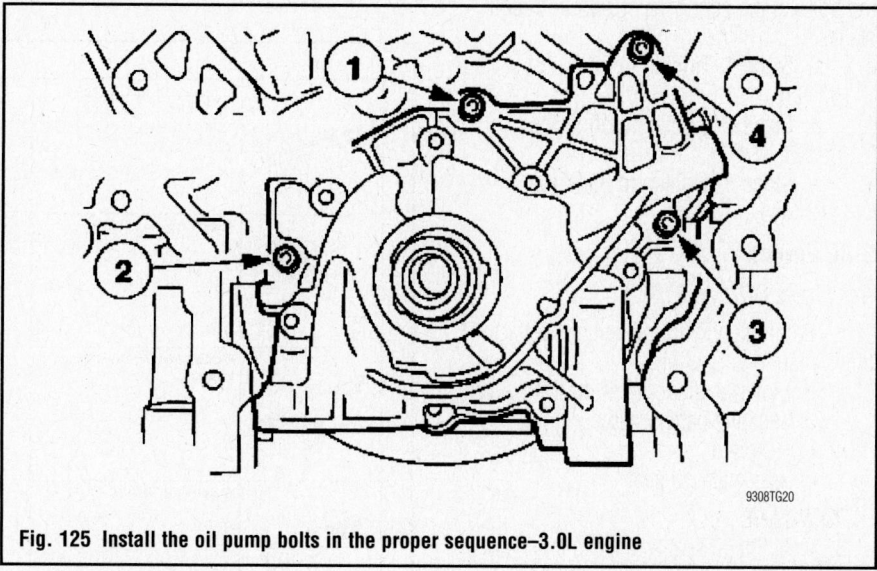

Fig. 125 Install the oil pump bolts in the proper sequence–3.0L engine

- Crankshaft sprockets
- Oil pump screen cover and tube
- Timing drive components
- Negative battery cable
6. Refill the engine with clean oil.
7. Start the engine and check for leaks; repair if necessary.

PISTON AND RING

POSITIONING

See Figures 126 and 127.

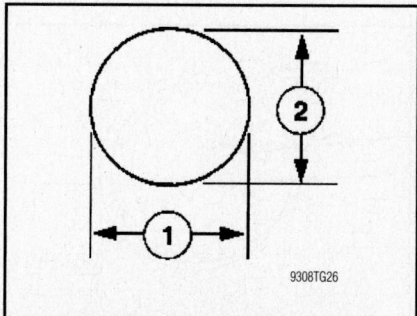

Fig. 126 2.3L engine —piston ring end-gap spacing

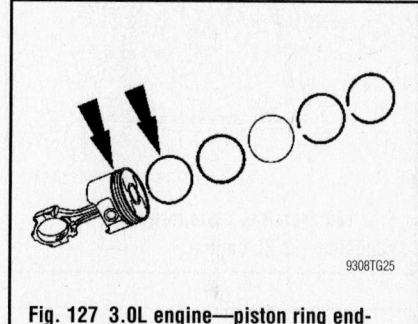

Fig. 127 3.0L engine—piston ring end-gap spacing

REAR MAIN SEAL

REMOVAL & INSTALLATION

2.3L Engine

See Figures 128 through 130.

1. Before servicing the vehicle, refer to the Precautions Section.
2. With the vehicle in NEUTRAL, position it on a hoist.
3. If equipped, remove the automatic transaxle.
4. If equipped, remove the manual transaxle and clutch.
5. Remove the flexplate or flywheel.
6. Remove the oil pan.
7. Remove the crankshaft rear oil seal with retainer plate

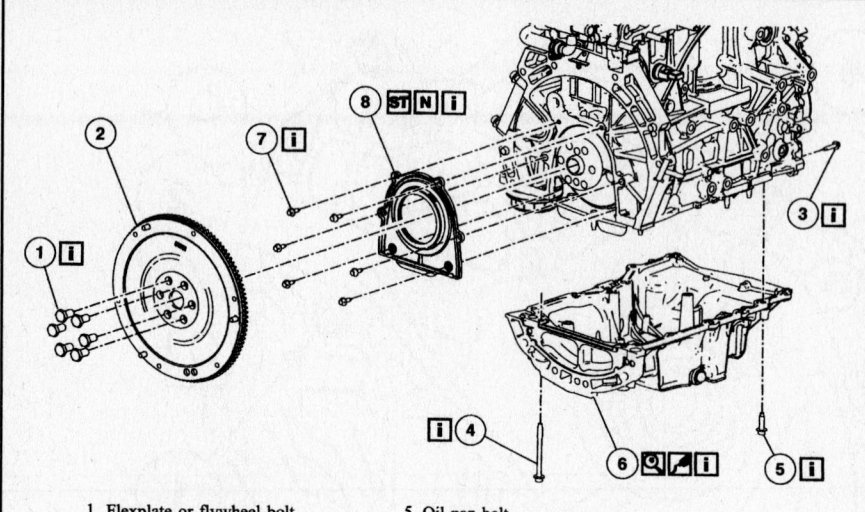

1 Flexplate or flywheel bolt
2 Flexplate or flywheel
3 Engine front cover bolt
4 Oil pan bolt

5 Oil pan bolt
6 Oil pan
7 Crankshaft rear oil seal with retainer plate bolt
8 Crankshaft rear oil seal with retainer plate

67197-ESCA-G22

Fig. 128 Rear main seal and related parts—2.3L engine

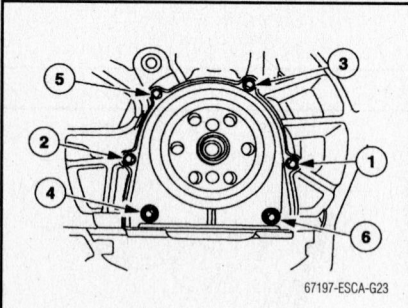

67197-ESCA-G23

Fig. 129 Retainer plate torque sequence—2.3L engine

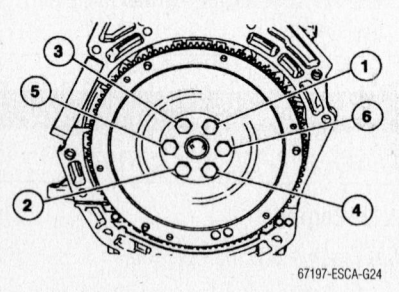

67197-ESCA-G24

Fig. 130 Flywheel torque sequence—2.3L engine

To install:

8. Using a seal installer, position the crankshaft rear oil seal with retainer plate onto the crankshaft.

9. Install the crankshaft rear oil seal with retainer plate. Tighten the bolts in the sequence shown to 89 inch lbs. (10 Nm).

10. Install the oil pan.

➡**Special bolts are used for installation. Do not use standard bolts.**

11. Install the flywheel/flexplate. Tighten the bolts in the sequence shown in three stages.

   a. Stage 1: Tighten to 37 ft. lbs. (50 Nm).
   b. Stage 2: Tighten to 50 ft. lbs. (80 Nm).
   c. Stage 3: Tighten to 83 ft. lbs. (112 Nm).

3.0L Engine

See Figures 131 and 132.

1. Before servicing the vehicle, refer to the Precautions Section.

2. Remove or disconnect the following:
- Negative battery cable
- Flexplate
- Rear main oil seal

To install:

3. Coat the oil seal with clean engine oil.
4. Install or connect the following:

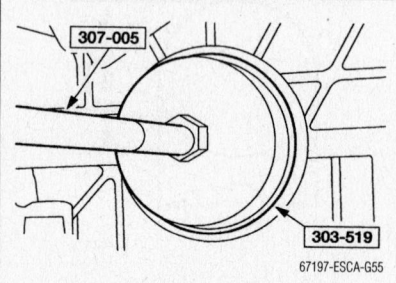

307-005

303-519

67197-ESCA-G55

Fig. 131 Rear main seal removal—3.0L engine

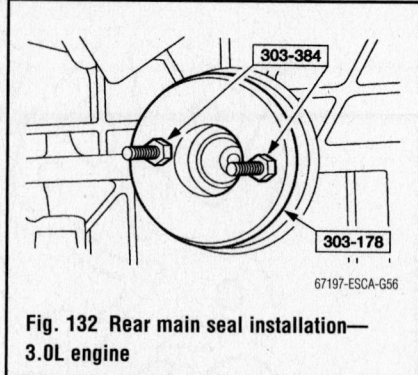

303-384

303-178

67197-ESCA-G56

Fig. 132 Rear main seal installation—3.0L engine

- Crankshaft rear oil seal
- Flywheel
- Negative battery cable

TIMING CHAIN, GEARS, FRONT COVER & SEAL

REMOVAL & INSTALLATION

2.3L Engine

See Figures 133 through 141.

1. Before servicing the vehicle, refer to the Precautions Section.

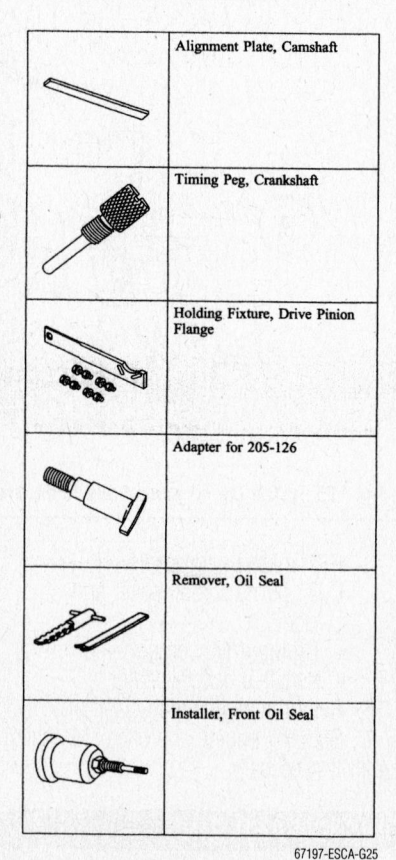

	Alignment Plate, Camshaft
	Timing Peg, Crankshaft
	Holding Fixture, Drive Pinion Flange
	Adapter for 205-126
	Remover, Oil Seal
	Installer, Front Oil Seal

67197-ESCA-G25

Fig. 133 Tools needed for timing chain and gears replacement—2.3L engine

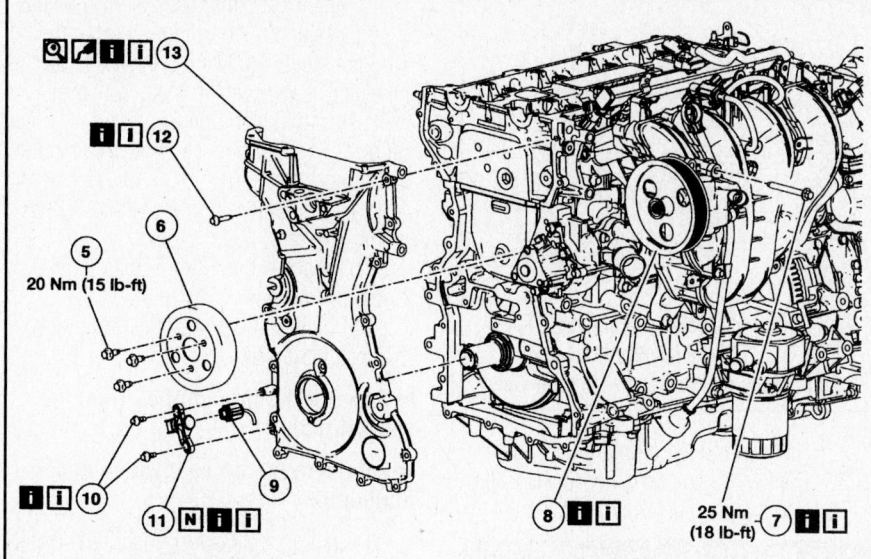

5 Coolant pump pulley bolt
6 Coolant pump pulley
7 Power steering pump bolt
8 Power steering pump (position aside)
9 Crankshaft position (CKP) sensor electrical connector

10 CKP sensor bolts
11 CKP sensor
12 Engine front cover bolt
13 Engine front cover

67197-ESCA-G26

Fig. 134 Front cover and related parts—2.3L engine

※※ **CAUTION**

During engine repair procedures, cleanliness is extremely important. Any foreign material, including any material created while cleaning gasket surfaces that enters the oil passages, coolant passages or the oil pan can cause engine failure.

※※ **CAUTION**

The crankshaft, the crankshaft sprocket and the pulley are fitted together by friction, using diamond washers between the flange faces on each part. For that reason, the crankshaft sprocket is also unfastened if you loosen the pulley. Therefore, the engine must be retimed each

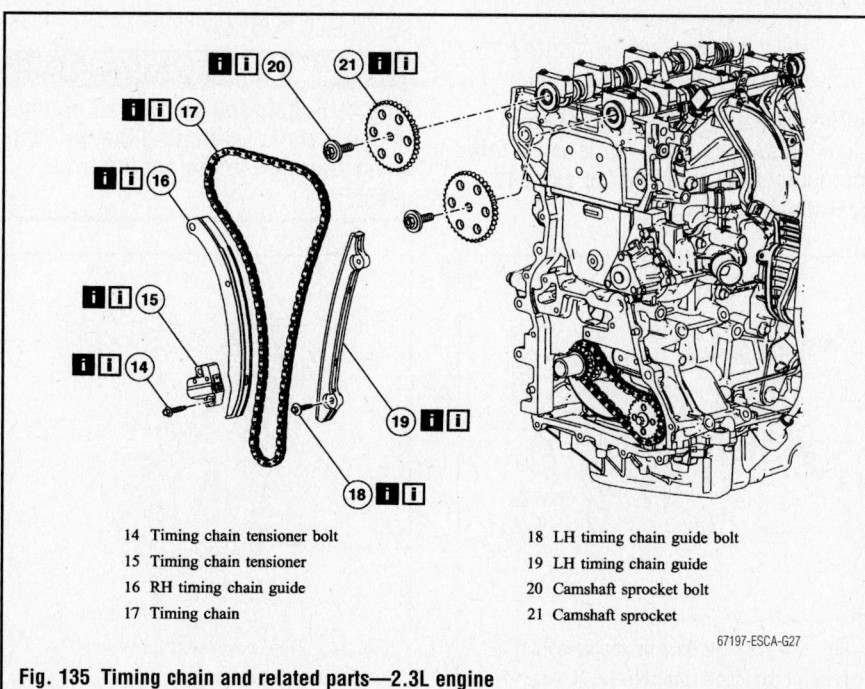

14 Timing chain tensioner bolt
15 Timing chain tensioner
16 RH timing chain guide
17 Timing chain

18 LH timing chain guide bolt
19 LH timing chain guide
20 Camshaft sprocket bolt
21 Camshaft sprocket

67197-ESCA-G27

Fig. 135 Timing chain and related parts—2.3L engine

time the damper is removed. Otherwise severe engine damage can occur.

2. With the vehicle in NEUTRAL, position it on a hoist.
3. Remove the accessory drive belt and idler pulleys.
4. Remove the engine mount.
5. Remove the valve cover.

※※ **CAUTION**

Failure to position the No. 1 piston at top dead center (TDC) can result in damage to the engine. Turn the engine in the normal direction of rotation only.

6. Using the crankshaft pulley bolt, turn the crankshaft clockwise to position the No. 1 piston at TDC.

※※ **CAUTION**

The special tool 303-465 is for camshaft alignment only. Using this tool to prevent engine rotation can result in engine damage.

➡The camshaft timing slots are offset. If the special tool cannot be installed, rotate the crankshaft one complete revolution clockwise to correctly position the camshafts.

7. Install special tool 303-465 in the slots on the rear of both camshafts.
8. Remove the engine plug bolt.

➡Only turn the engine in the normal direction of rotation.

➡Installing the special tool in this step will prevent the engine from being rotated in the clockwise direction.

9. Install special tool 303-507.
10. Install the special tools 205-126 and 205-072-02.

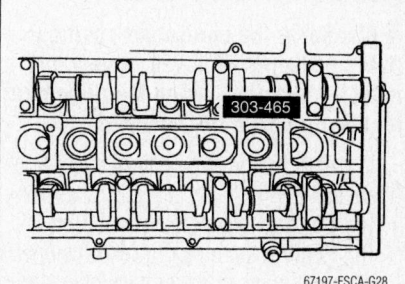

67197-ESCA-G28

Fig. 136 Install special tool 303-465 in the slots on the rear of both camshafts—2.3L engine

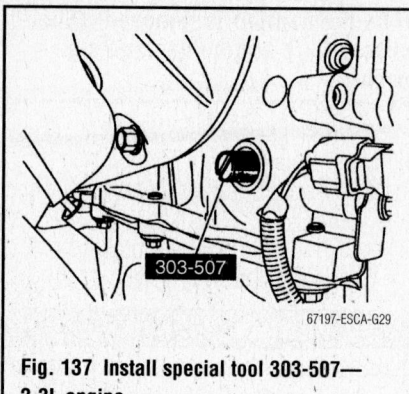

Fig. 137 Install special tool 303-507—2.3L engine

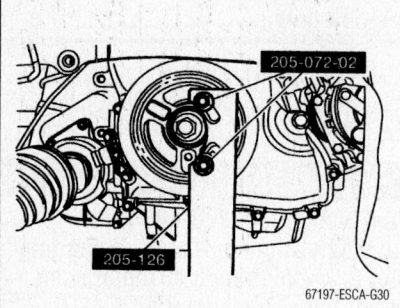

Fig. 138 Install the special tools 205-126 and 205-072-02—2.3L engine

※ CAUTION

Failure to hold the crankshaft pulley in place while loosening the bolt can result in damage to the engine.

11. Remove the crankshaft pulley bolt and washer.
12. Remove the crankshaft pulley.
13. Remove the crankshaft front seal.
14. Remove the coolant pump pulley.
15. Remove the power steering pump and position it aside.

➡ **The bolt under the power steering pressure tube will remain with the power steering pump.**

16. Remove the CKP sensor.

➡ **Whenever the crankshaft position (CKP) sensor is removed, a new one must be installed, using the alignment jig supplied with the new part.**

17. Remove the engine front cover bolts (there are 22).
18. Remove the engine front cover.
19. Remove the timing chain tensioner. Compress the timing chain tensioner, and insert a paper clip into the hole to retain the tensioner.
20. Remove the right timing chain guide.
21. Remove the timing chain.

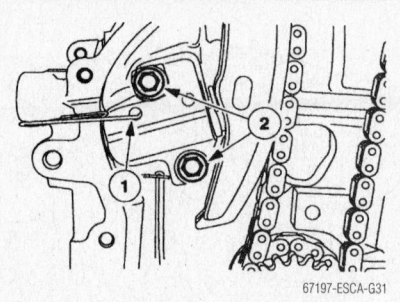

Fig. 139 Compress the timing chain tensioner, and insert a paper clip into the hole to retain the tensioner—2.3L engine

22. Remove the left timing chain guide.
23. Remove the camshaft sprocket bolts.
24. Remove the camshaft sprockets.

※ CAUTION

Do not rely on the Camshaft Alignment Plate to prevent camshaft rotation. Damage to the tool or the camshaft can occur. Use the flats on the camshaft to prevent camshaft rotation.

To install:
25. Installation is the reverse of removal. Note the following:

※ CAUTION

Do not use metal scrapers, wire brushes, power abrasive disks or other abrasive means to clean sealing surfaces. These tools cause scratches and gouges which make leak paths.

26. Clean and inspect the mounting surfaces of the engine and the front cover.

➡ **The engine front cover must be installed and the bolts tightened within four minutes of applying the silicone gasket and sealant.**

Fig. 140 Use the flats on the camshaft to prevent camshaft rotation—2.3L engine

27. Apply a 2.5 mm bead of silicone gasket and sealant to the cylinder head and oil pan joint areas. Apply a 2.5 mm bead of silicone gasket and sealant to the front cover.
28. Install the engine front cover. Tighten the bolts in the sequence shown, to the following specifications:
   a. Tighten the 8 mm bolts to 89 inch lbs. (10 Nm).
   b. Tighten the 13 mm bolts to 35 ft. lbs. (48 Nm).
29. Position the power steering pump and install the bolts.

➡ **Remove the through-bolt from the special tool.**

➡ **Lubricate the oil seal with clean engine oil.**

30. Using a seal driver, install the crankshaft front oil seal.

➡ **Do not reuse the crankshaft damper bolt.**

➡ **Apply clean engine oil on the seal area before installing.**

31. Install the crankshaft pulley and hand-tighten the bolt.

※ CAUTION

Only hand-tighten the bolt or damage to the front cover can occur.

➡ **This step will correctly align the crankshaft pulley to the crankshaft.**

32. Install a standard 6 mm × 18 mm bolt through the crankshaft pulley and thread it into the front cover. Rotate the pulley as necessary to align the bolt holes.

※ CAUTION

Failure to hold the crankshaft pulley in place while tightening the bolt can cause damage to the engine front cover.

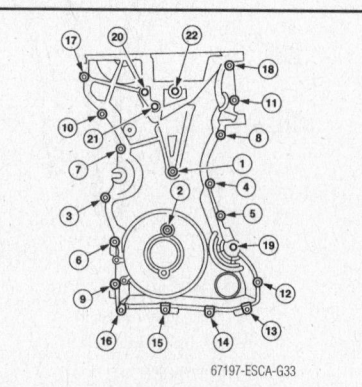

Fig. 141 Front cover bolt torque sequence—2.3L engine

33. Using the special tools to hold the crankshaft pulley in place, tighten the crankshaft pulley bolt in two stages:

    a. Stage 1: Tighten to 74 ft. lbs. (100 Nm).

    b. Stage 2: Tighten an additional 90 degrees (1/4 turn).

34. Remove the 6 mm × 18 mm bolt.

35. Remove special tool 303-507.

36. Remove special tool 303-465.

➡ **Only turn the engine in the normal direction of rotation.**

37. Turn the engine two complete revolutions.

➡ **Only turn the engine in the normal direction of rotation.**

38. Turn the crankshaft until the No. 1 piston is at TDC.

39. Install special tool 303-507.

✳✳ CAUTION

Only hand-tighten the bolt or damage to the front cover can occur.

40. Using the 6 mm × 18 mm bolt, check the position of the crankshaft pulley. If it is not possible to install the bolt, correct the engine timing.

41. Using special tool 303-465, check the position of the camshafts. If it is not possible to install the special tool, correct the engine timing.

42. Install the CKP sensor. Do not tighten the bolts at this time.

43. Adjust the CKP sensor alignment jig and tighten the bolts.

44. Remove the 6 mm × 18 mm bolt.

45. Install the engine plug bolt.

3.0L Engine

See Figures 142 through 153.

1. Before servicing the vehicle, refer to the Precautions Section.

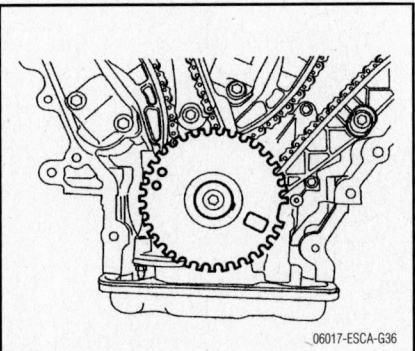

Fig. 142 Ignition pulse wheel—3.0L engine

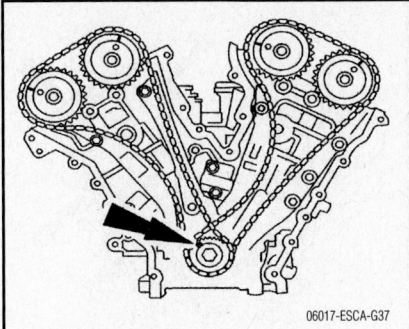

Fig. 143 Rotate the crankshaft clockwise to position the keyway at the 11 o'clock position—3.0L engine

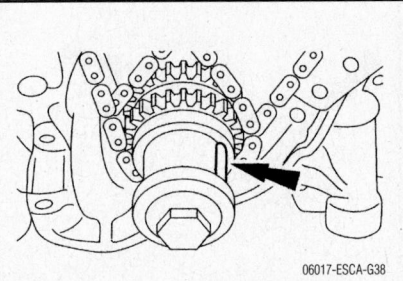

Fig. 144 Rotate the crankshaft clockwise 120 degrees to the 3 o'clock position to locate the right side camshafts in the neutral position—3.0L engine

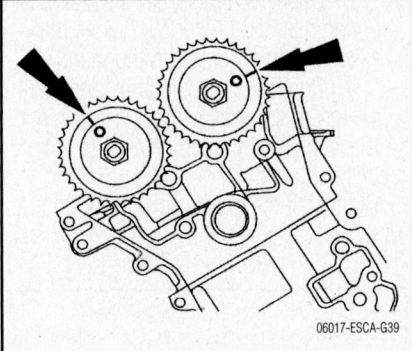

Fig. 145 Verify that the right camshafts are in the neutral position—3.0L engine

2. Remove or disconnect the following:
- Negative battery cable
- Engine front cover

➡ **This pulse wheel is used in several different engines. Install the pulse wheel with the keyway in the slot stamped "30" or "30RFF" (orange in color).**

- Ignition pulse wheel and install the damper bolt
- Spark plugs

3. Rotate the crankshaft clockwise to position the keyway at the 11 o'clock

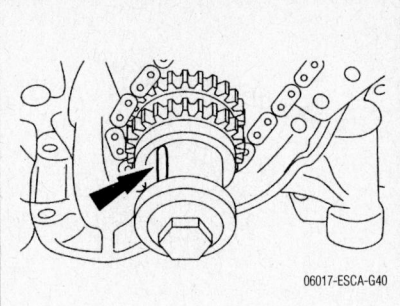

Fig. 146 Rotate the crankshaft clockwise 1 2/3 times to position the keyway at the 11 o'clock position—3.0L engine

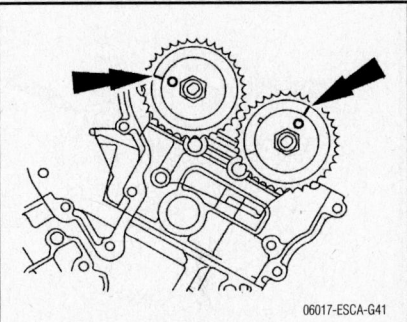

Fig. 147 Verify that the left side camshafts are in the neutral position—3.0L engine

position and the camshafts in the correct positions. The No. 1 cylinder will be at Top Dead Center (TDC).

4. Rotate the crankshaft clockwise 120 degrees to the 3 o'clock position to locate the right side camshafts in the neutral position. Verify that the right camshafts are in the neutral position.

5. Remove or disconnect the following:
- Right side timing chain and tensioner
- Tensioner arm and timing chain guide

6. Rotate the crankshaft clockwise 1 2/3 times to position the keyway at the 11 o'clock position. This will position the left side camshafts in the neutral position.

7. Verify that the left side camshafts are in the neutral position and mark the link position on the crankshaft sprocket.

8. Remove or disconnect the following:
- Left side timing chain and tensioner
- Tensioner arm and timing chain guide
- Damper bolt and crankshaft sprockets

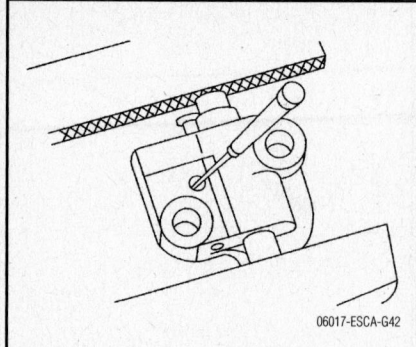

Fig. 148 Hold the ratchet lock mechanism away from the ratchet stem—3.0L engine

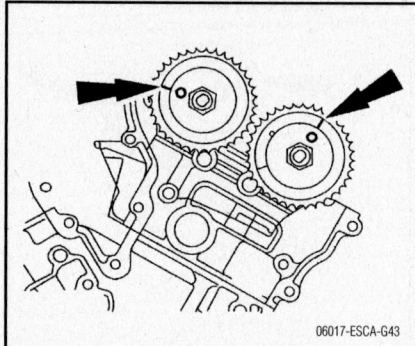

Fig. 149 Verify that the left camshafts are correctly positioned–3.0L engine

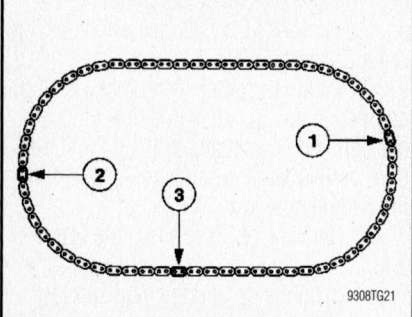

Fig. 150 Mark the timing chain in the proper sequence–3.0L engine

To install:

9. Install the crankshaft sprockets.

10. Position the timing chain tensioner in a soft jaw vise. Hold the ratchet lock mechanism away from the ratchet stem and slowly compress the timing chain tensioner. Retain the piston with a 1.5mm wire or paper clip.

11. If the timing marks on the chain are not visible, use a permanent marker to mark the left and right side timing chains. Mark the timing chains in the following sequence:

a. Mark any link to use as the crank-shaft timing mark.

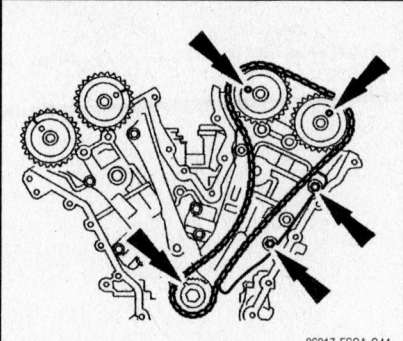

Fig. 151 Left side timing chain installed—3.0L engine

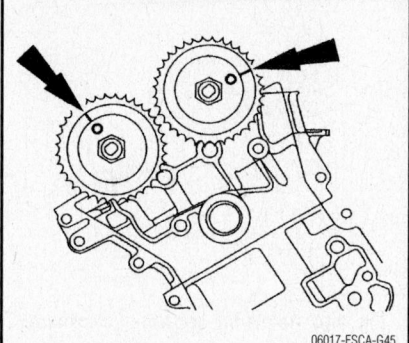

Fig. 152 Verify that the right camshafts are correctly positioned–3.0L engine

b. Count 29 links from the crankshaft timing mark and mark the link as the exhaust cam sprocket timing mark.

c. Continue counting to 42 and mark the link as the intake sprocket timing mark.

12. Verify that the left camshafts are correctly positioned.

13. Install the guide. Torque the bolts to 18 ft. lbs. (25 Nm).

14. Install the left side timing chain and align the chain in the following sequence:

a. Mark any link to use as the crank-shaft timing mark.

b. Count 29 links from the crank-shaft timing mark and mark the link as the exhaust cam sprocket timing mark.

c. Continue counting to 42 and mark the link as the intake sprocket timing mark

15. Install or connect the following:
- Left side timing chain and tensioner arm. Torque the bolts to 18 ft. lbs. (25 Nm).
- Crankshaft damper bolt and rotate the keyway to the 3 o'clock position.

16. Verify that the right side camshafts are properly positioned and install the right side timing chain and guide. Torque the bolts to 18 ft. lbs. (25 Nm).

17. Make certain that the timing chain aligns with the marks on the camshaft and crankshaft sprockets

✳✳ CAUTION

Install the pulse wheel with the keyway in the slot stamped 20–25–34Y–30M (Color Blur).

18. Install or connect the following:
- Right side timing chain tensioner and arm. Torque the bolts to 18 ft. lbs. (25 Nm) and remove the damper bolt
- Ignition pulse wheel
- Spark plugs
- Engine front cover
- Negative battery cable

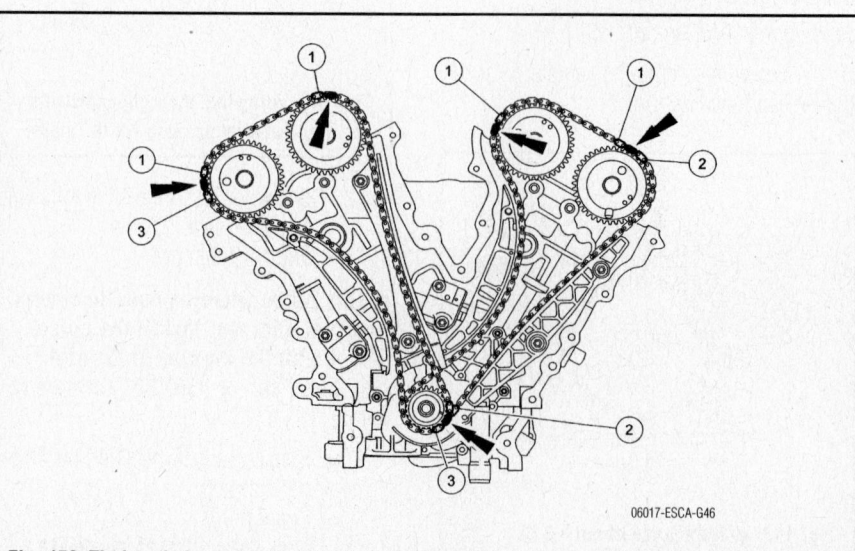

Fig. 153 Timing chains correctly installed—3.0L engine

ENGINE PERFORMANCE & EMISSION CONTROL

COMPONENT LOCATIONS

See Figures 154 through 157.

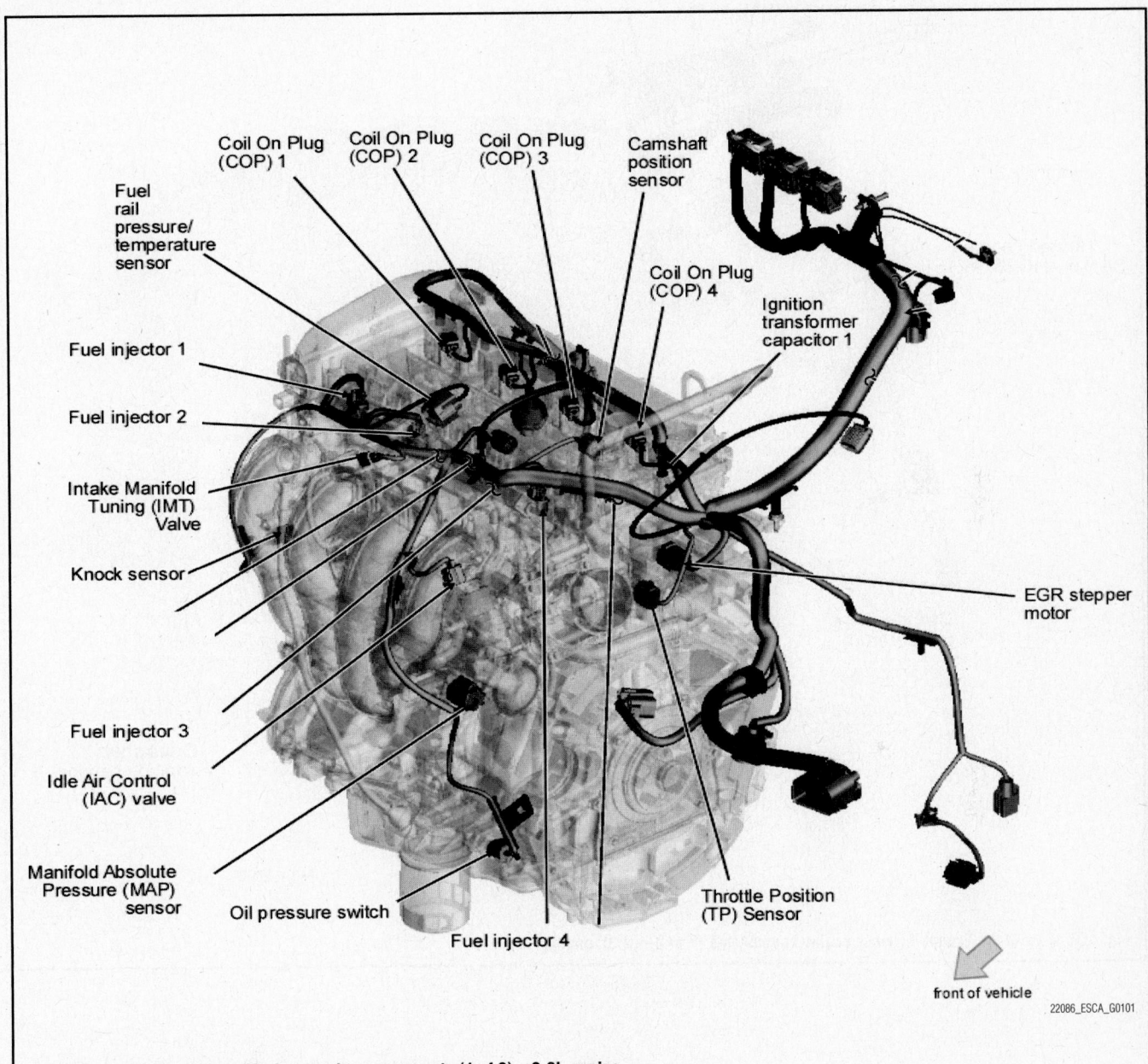

Fuel rail pressure/temperature sensor

Coil On Plug (COP) 1

Coil On Plug (COP) 2

Coil On Plug (COP) 3

Camshaft position sensor

Coil On Plug (COP) 4

Ignition transformer capacitor 1

Fuel injector 1

Fuel injector 2

Intake Manifold Tuning (IMT) Valve

Knock sensor

EGR stepper motor

Fuel injector 3

Idle Air Control (IAC) valve

Manifold Absolute Pressure (MAP) sensor

Oil pressure switch

Fuel injector 4

Throttle Position (TP) Sensor

front of vehicle

22086_ESCA_G0101

Fig. 154 View of the Escape/Mariner engine components (1 of 2)—2.3L engine

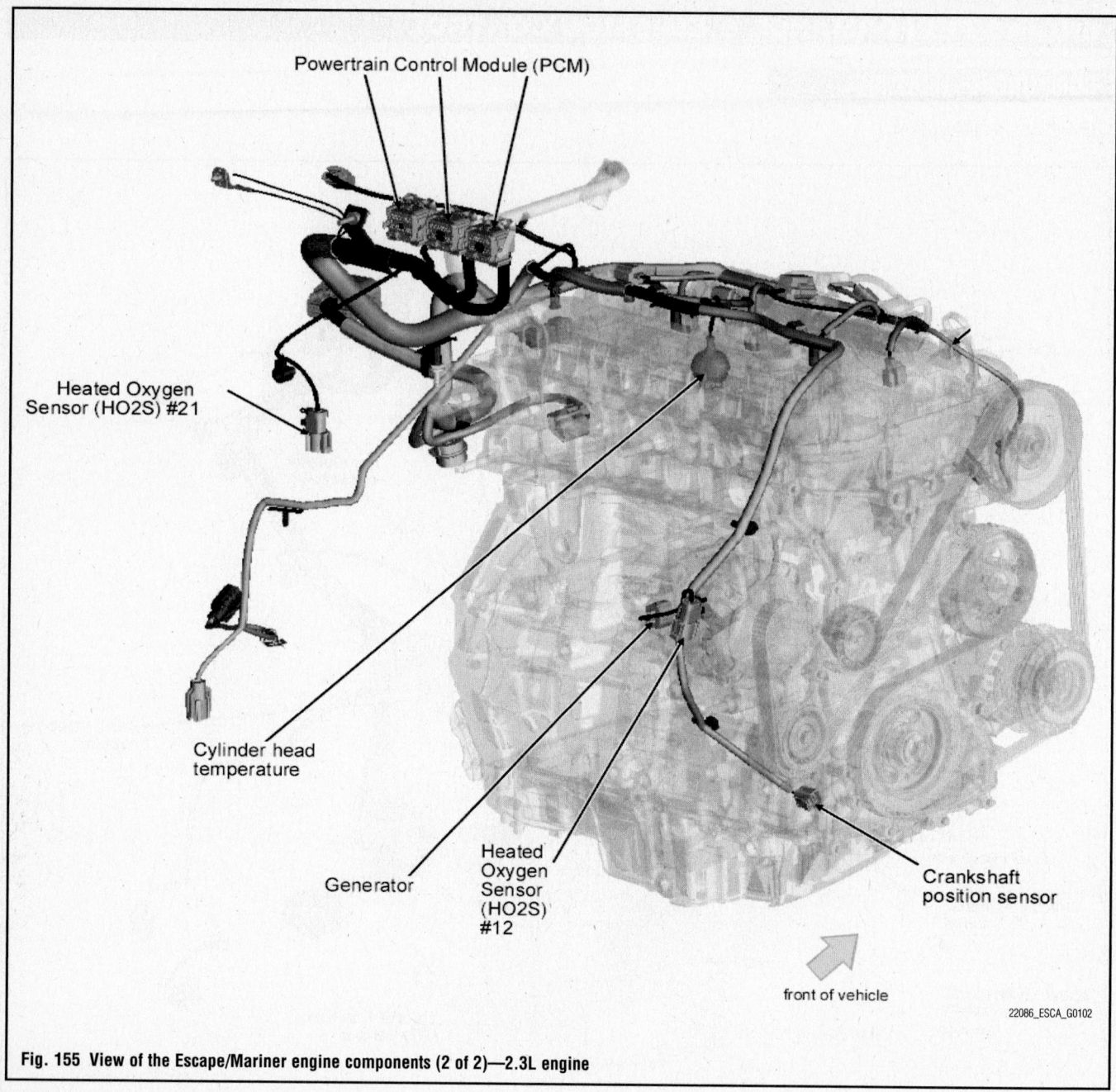

Fig. 155 View of the Escape/Mariner engine components (2 of 2)—2.3L engine

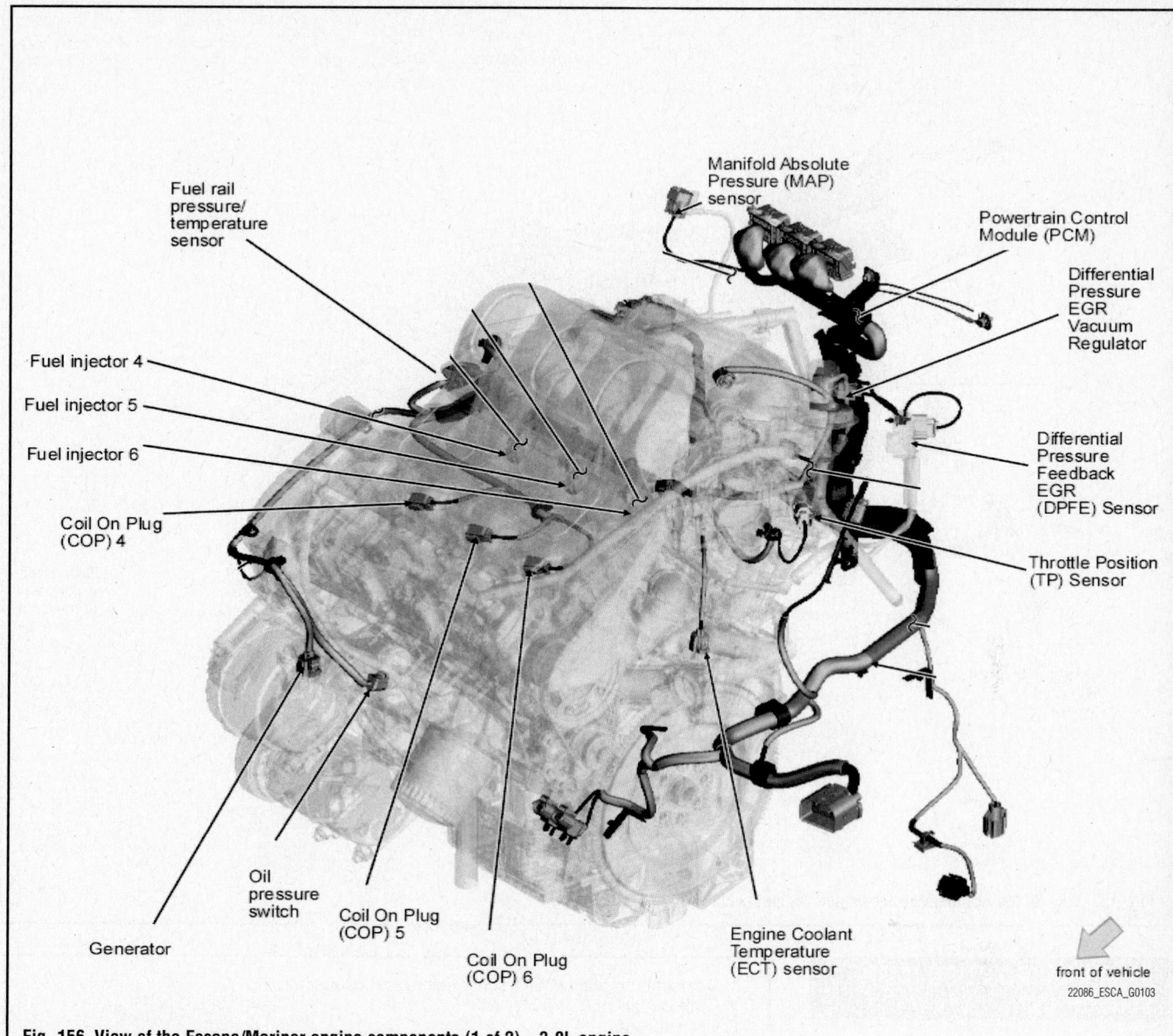

Fuel rail pressure/temperature sensor

Fuel injector 4

Fuel injector 5

Fuel injector 6

Coil On Plug (COP) 4

Oil pressure switch

Generator

Coil On Plug (COP) 5

Coil On Plug (COP) 6

Manifold Absolute Pressure (MAP) sensor

Powertrain Control Module (PCM)

Differential Pressure EGR Vacuum Regulator

Differential Pressure Feedback EGR (DPFE) Sensor

Throttle Position (TP) Sensor

Engine Coolant Temperature (ECT) sensor

front of vehicle

22086_ESCA_G0103

Fig. 156 View of the Escape/Mariner engine components (1 of 2)—3.0L engine

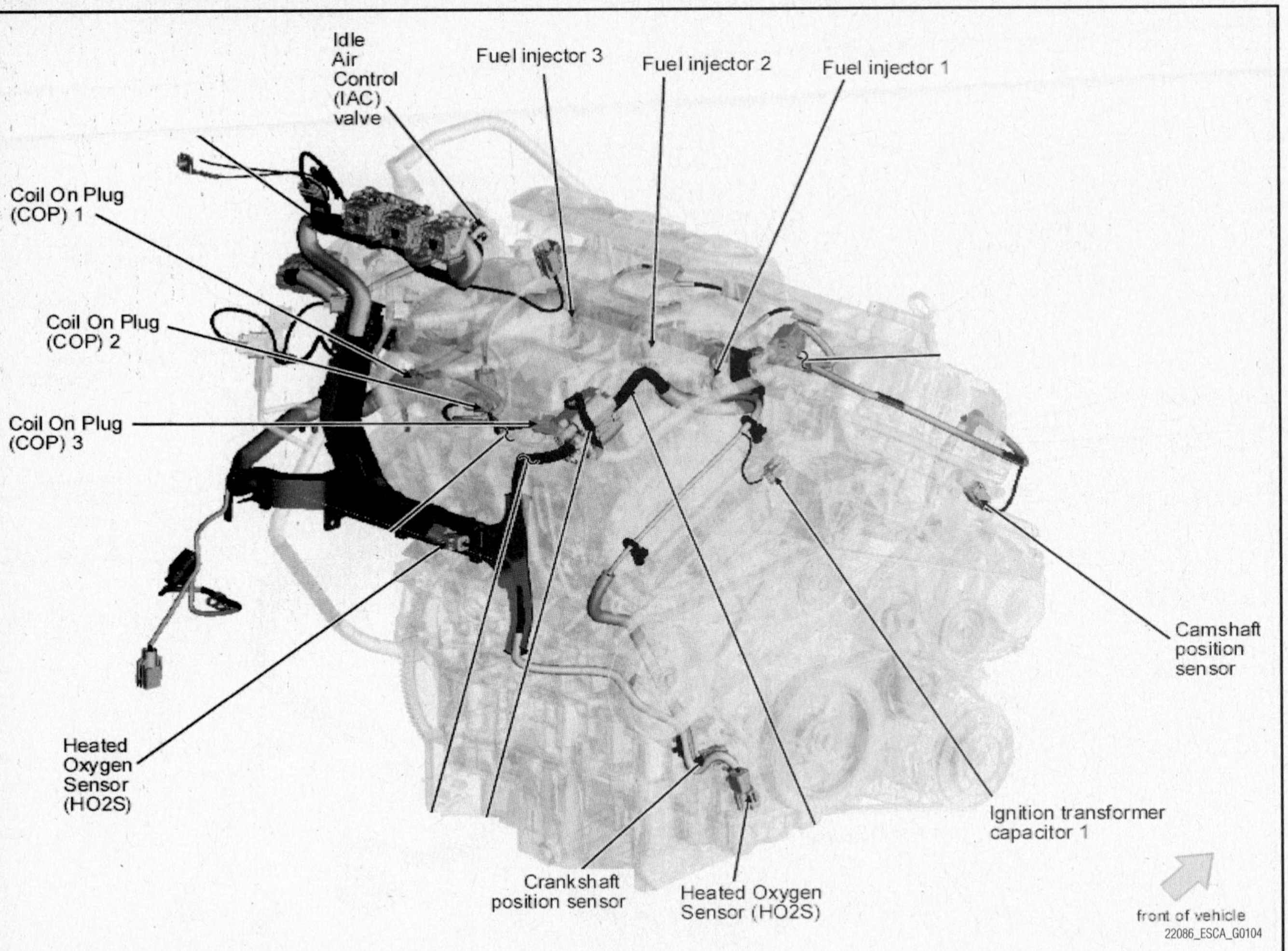

Idle Air Control (IAC) valve

Fuel injector 3

Fuel injector 2

Fuel injector 1

Coil On Plug (COP) 1

Coil On Plug (COP) 2

Coil On Plug (COP) 3

Heated Oxygen Sensor (HO2S)

Crankshaft position sensor

Heated Oxygen Sensor (HO2S)

Camshaft position sensor

Ignition transformer capacitor 1

front of vehicle
22086_ESCA_G0104

Fig. 157 View of the Escape/Mariner engine components (2 of 2)—3.0L engine

CAMSHAFT POSITION (CMP) SENSOR

LOCATION

2.3L Engine

See Figure 158.

The Camshaft Position (CMP) sensor is located on top the valve cover towards the front of the vehicle

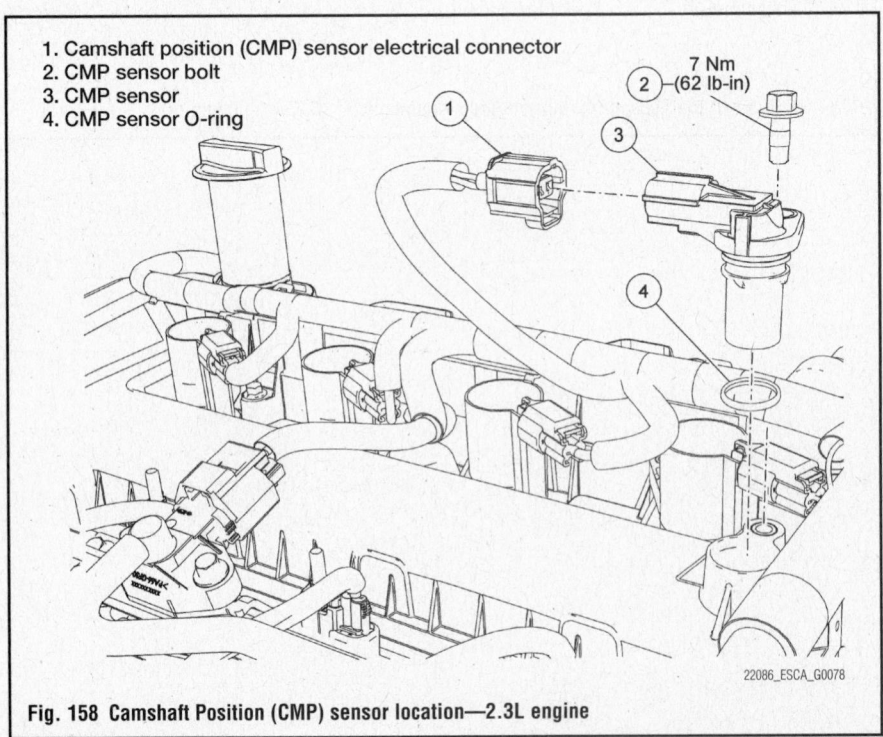

1. Camshaft position (CMP) sensor electrical connector
2. CMP sensor bolt
3. CMP sensor
4. CMP sensor O-ring

2. 7 Nm (62 lb-in)

22086_ESCA_G0078

Fig. 158 Camshaft Position (CMP) sensor location—2.3L engine

3.0L Engine

See Figure 159.

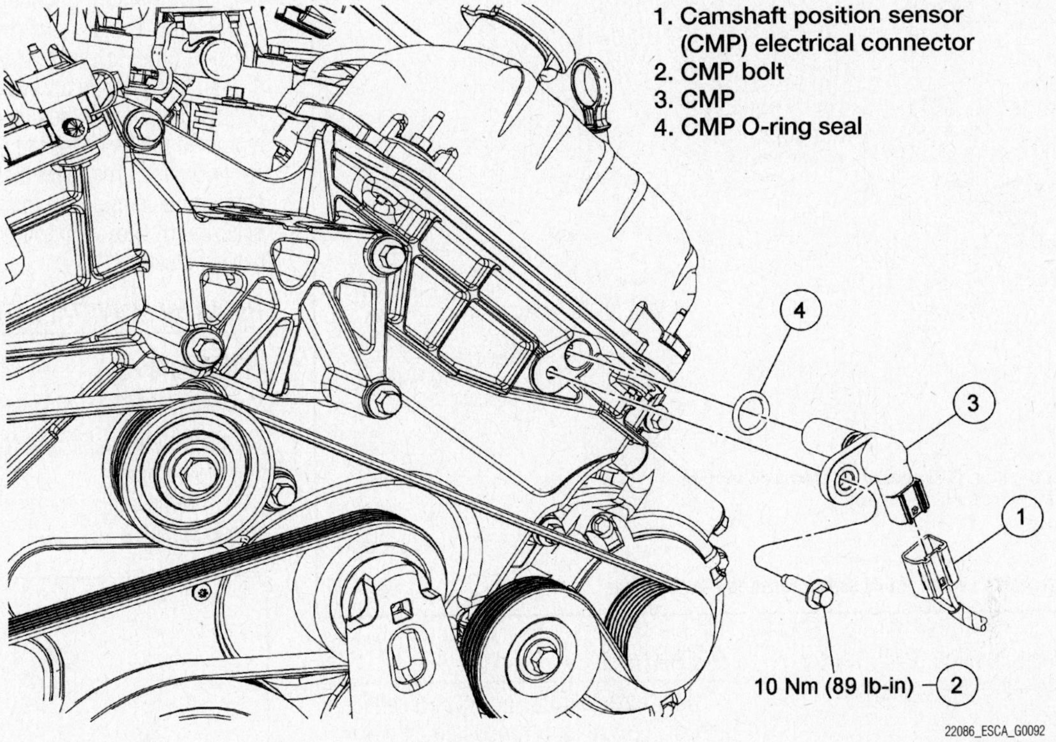

1. Camshaft position sensor (CMP) electrical connector
2. CMP bolt
3. CMP
4. CMP O-ring seal

10 Nm (89 lb-in)

22086_ESCA_G0092

Fig. 159 Camshaft Position (CMP) sensor location—3.0L engine

The Camshaft Position (CMP) sensor is located on left cylinder head just below the valve cover.

OPERATION

The Camshaft Position (CMP) sensor detects the position of the camshaft. The CMP sensor identifies when piston number 1 is on its compression stroke. A signal is then sent to the PCM and used for synchronizing the sequential firing of the fuel injectors. Coil-on-plug (COP) ignition applications use the CMP signal to select the correct ignition coil to fire. Vehicles with 2 CMP sensors are equipped with Variable Camshaft Timing (VCT). They use the second sensor to identify the position of the camshaft on bank 2 as an input to the PCM.

REMOVAL & INSTALLATION

2.3L Engine

1. Disconnect the Camshaft Position (CMP) sensor electrical connector.
2. Remove the bolt and the CMP sensor.

To install:

➡ Lubricate the CMP sensor O-ring seal with clean engine oil.

3. To install, reverse the removal procedure.
4. Tighten the mounting bolt to 62 inch lbs. (7 Nm)

3.0L Engine

1. Disconnect the Camshaft Position (CMP) sensor electrical connector.
2. Remove the bolt and the CMP sensor.

To install:

➡ Lubricate the CMP O-ring seal with clean engine oil.

3. To install, reverse the removal procedure and tighten the mounting bolt to 89 inch lbs. (10 Nm).

TESTING

See Figure 160.

1. Turn the ignition to the **OFF** position.
2. Disconnect the Camshaft Position Sensor (CMP) electrical connector.
3. Using a digital multimeter, measure the resistance between the CMP + and CMP- at component side of the connector.

4. The resistance should fall between 250—1,000 ohms.
5. If resistance is not within specification the CMP sensor may be faulty.

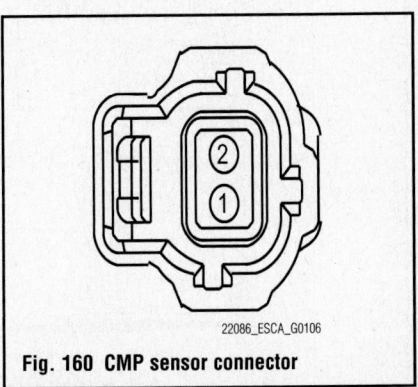

22086_ESCA_G0106

Fig. 160 CMP sensor connector

CRANKSHAFT POSITION (CKP) SENSOR

LOCATION

2.3L Engine

See Figure 161.

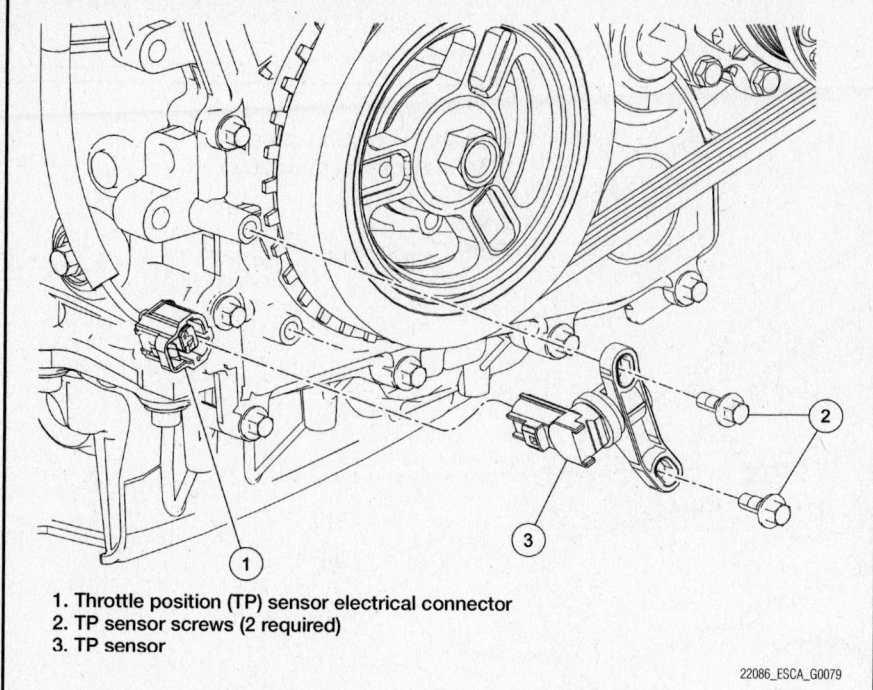

1. Throttle position (TP) sensor electrical connector
2. TP sensor screws (2 required)
3. TP sensor

22086_ESCA_G0079

Fig. 161 Crankshaft Position (CKP) sensor location—2.3L engine

The Crankshaft Position (CKP) sensor is located to the left of the crankshaft pulley.

3.0L Engine

See Figure 162.

The Crankshaft Position (CKP) sensor is located just behind the crankshaft pulley on engine block.

OPERATION

The Crankshaft Position (CKP) sensor is a magnetic transducer mounted on the engine block adjacent to a pulse wheel located on the crankshaft. By monitoring the crankshaft mounted pulse wheel, the CKP is the primary sensor for ignition information to the PCM. The pulse wheel has a total of 35 teeth spaced 10 degrees apart with one empty space for a missing tooth. By monitoring the pulse wheel, the CKP sensor signal indicates crankshaft position and speed information to the PCM. By monitoring the missing tooth, the CKP sensor is also able to identify piston travel in order to synchronize the ignition system and provide a way of tracking the angular position of the crankshaft relative to a fixed reference for the CKP sensor configuration. The PCM also uses the CKP signal to determine if a misfire has occurred by measuring rapid decelerations between teeth.

REMOVAL & INSTALLATION

2.3L Engine

See Figures 163 through 167.

1. With the vehicle in NEUTRAL, position it on a hoist.
2. Remove the 5 bolts and the RH splash shield.

22086_ESCA_G0081

Fig. 163 Engine plug bolt view—2.3L engine

3. Remove the engine plug bolt.
4. Turn the crankshaft pulley bolt to position the number one cylinder at Top Dead Center (TDC) and install the special tool.

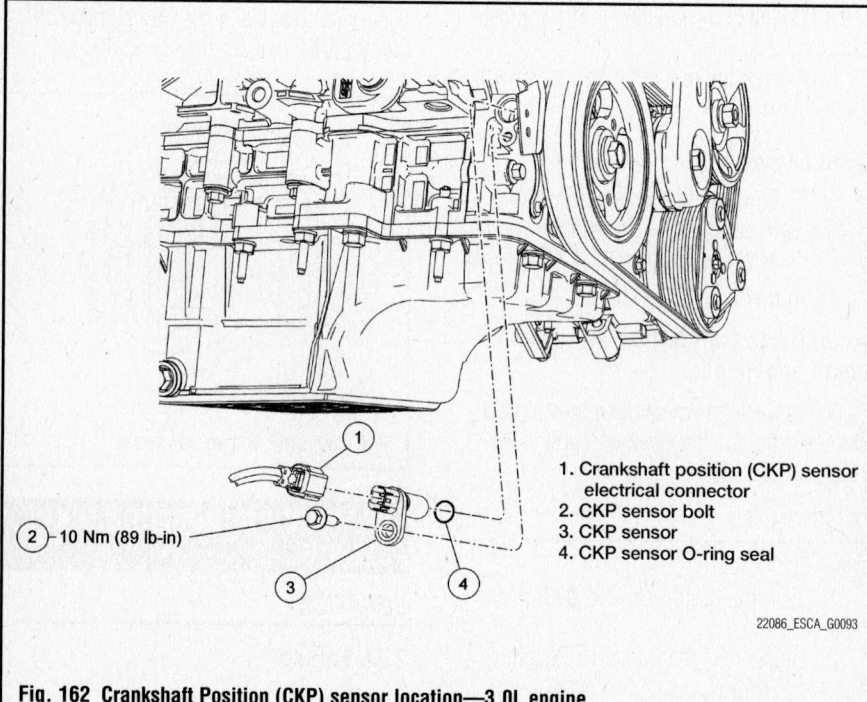

2 — 10 Nm (89 lb-in)

1. Crankshaft position (CKP) sensor electrical connector
2. CKP sensor bolt
3. CKP sensor
4. CKP sensor O-ring seal

22086_ESCA_G0093

Fig. 162 Crankshaft Position (CKP) sensor location—3.0L engine

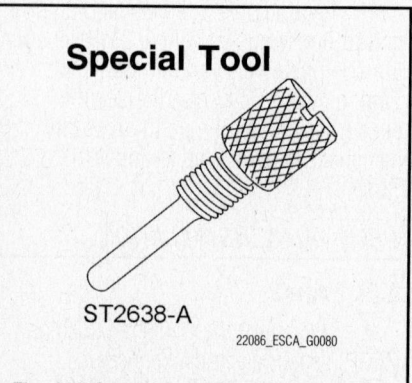

Special Tool

ST2638-A

22086_ESCA_G0080

Fig. 164 Special tool 303-507 timing peg, crankshaft

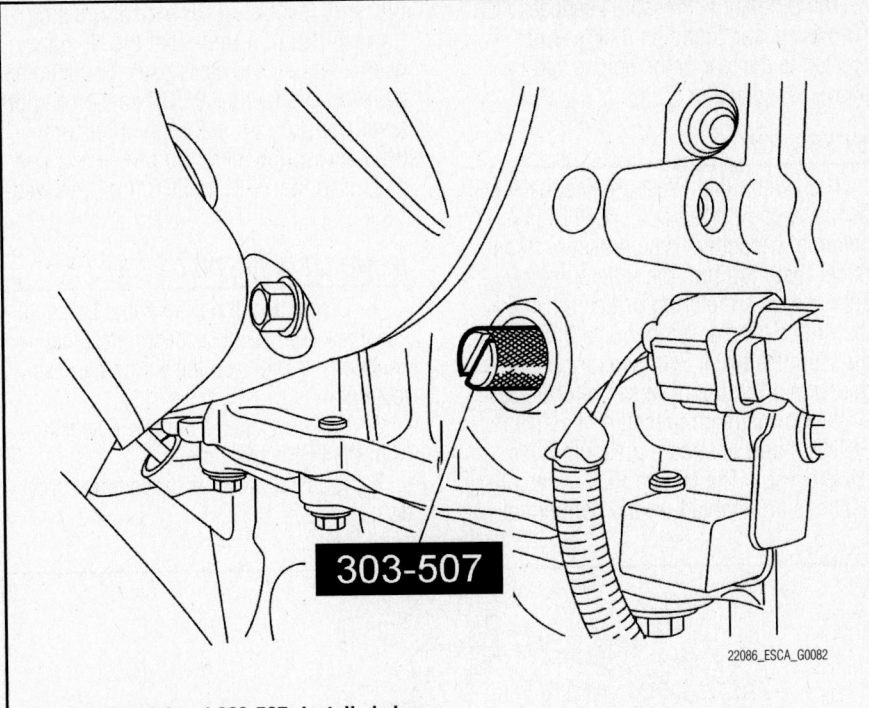

Fig. 165 Special tool 303-507, installed view

5. Disconnect the Crankshaft Position (CKP) sensor electrical connector.

6. Remove the bolts and the CKP sensor.

To install:

7. Install a (6mm) 0.23 inch. × (18mm) 0.7 inch standard bolt in the crankshaft pulley.

✳✳ WARNING

Only hand-tighten the bolt or damage to the front cover can occur.

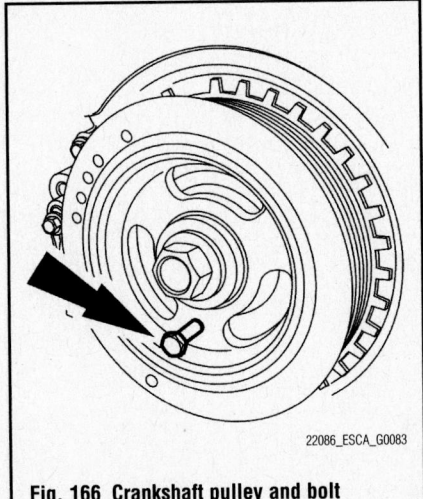

Fig. 166 Crankshaft pulley and bolt view—2.3L engine

➡**Whenever the CKP sensor is removed, a new one must be installed using the alignment tool supplied with the new part.**

8. Install a new CKP sensor and the bolts. Do not tighten the bolts at this time.

➡**The CKP sensor alignment tool is supplied with the new sensor and is not available separately.**

9. Adjust the CKP sensor with the alignment tool and tighten mounting bolts to 62 inch lbs. (7 Nm).

10. Connect the CKP sensor electrical connector.

11. Remove the (6mm) 0.23 inch bolt from the crankshaft pulley.

12. Install the engine plug bolt and tighten to 15 ft. lbs. (20 Nm).

13. Install the RH splash shield and tighten the bolts to 80 inch lbs. (9 Nm).

3.0L Engine

1. With the vehicle in NEUTRAL, position it on a hoist.

2. Remove the 5 bolts and the RH splash shield.

3. Disconnect the Crankshaft Position (CKP) sensor electrical connector.

➡**Lubricate the CKP O-ring seal with clean engine oil.**

4. Remove the bolt and the CKP sensor.

5. To install, reverse the removal procedure and tighten sensor mounting bolt to 89 inch lbs. (10 Nm).

TESTING

See Figure 168.

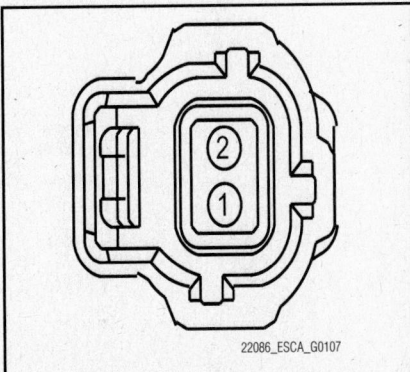

Fig. 168 Crankshaft position sensor connector

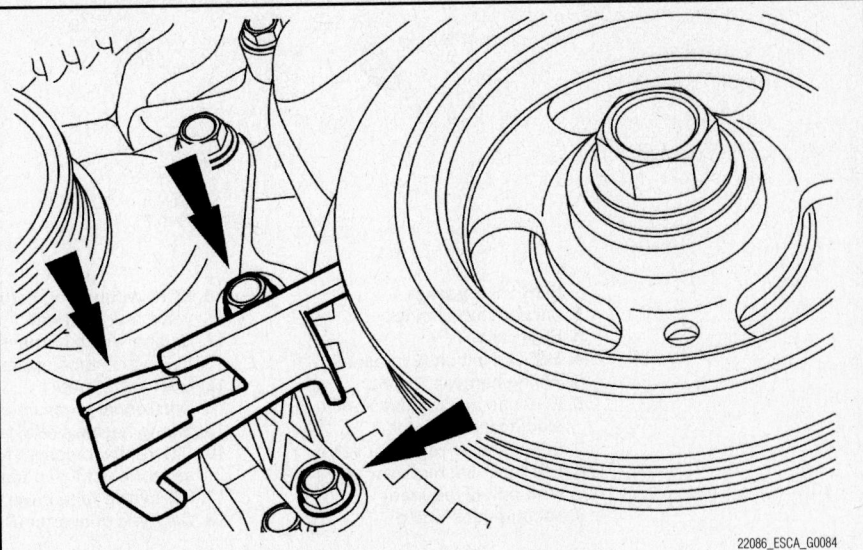

Fig. 167 Crankshaft sensor and alignment tool shown—2.3L engine

1. Turn the ignition to the **OFF** position.

2. Disconnect the Crankshaft Position Sensor (CKP) electrical connector.

3. Using a digital multimeter measure the resistance between the CKP + and CKP - at component side of the connector.

4. The resistance should fall between 250—1,000 ohms.

5. If resistance is not within specification the CKP sensor may be faulty.

DIFFERENTIAL PRESSURE FEEDBACK EGR (DPFE) SENSOR

LOCATION

See Figure 169.

The Differential Pressure Feedback EGR (DPFE) sensor, found on 3.0L engines, is located to the rear of the engine and is above RH converter.

OPERATION

The Differential Pressure Feedback EGR sensor also referred to as (DPFE) is a ceramic, capacitive-type pressure transducer that monitors the differential pressure across a metering orifice located in the orifice tube assembly. The differential pressure feedback EGR sensor receives this signal through 2 hoses referred to as the downstream pressure hose (REF SIGNAL) and upstream pressure hose (HI SIGNAL). The HI and REF hose connections are marked on the differential pressure feedback EGR sensor housing for identification (note that the HI signal uses a larger diameter hose). The differential pressure feedback EGR sensor outputs a voltage proportional to the pressure drop across the metering orifice and supplies it to the PCM as EGR flow rate feedback.

REMOVAL & INSTALLATION

1. Disconnect the Differential Pressure Feedback EGR (DPFE) sensor electrical connector and detach the wiring harness retainer.

2. Carefully detach the DPFE sensor from the EGR valve tube

3. To install, reverse the removal procedure.

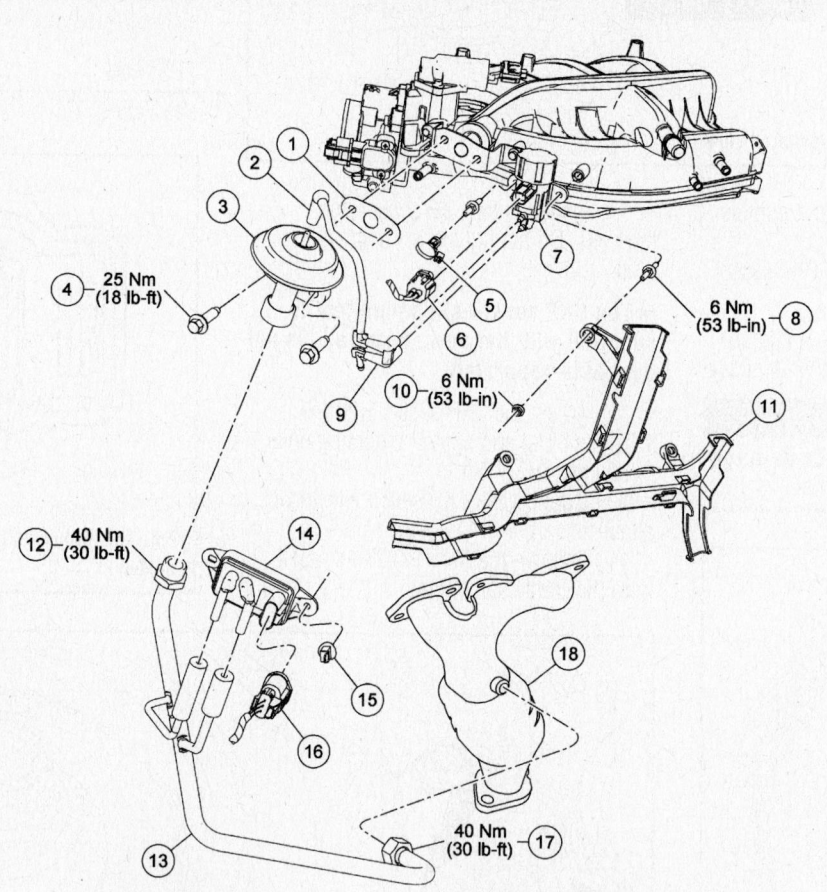

1. EGR valve gasket
2. Vacuum tube fitting
3. EGR valve
4. EGR valve bolt (2 required)
5. Wiring harness retainer
6. EGR vacuum regulator valve electrical connector
7. EGR vacuum regulator valve
8. EGR vacuum regulator valve stud bolt (2 required)
9. Vacuum tube fitting
10. EGR vacuum regulator valve stud bolt nut
11. Engine wiring harness bracket
12. EGR valve tube upper fitting
13. EGR valve tube
14. Differential pressure feedback EGR sensor
15. Wiring harness retainer
16. Differential pressure feedback EGR sensor electrical connector
17. EGR valve tube lower fitting
18. Catalytic converter (RH)

22086_ESCA_G0099

Fig. 169 Differential Pressure Feedback EGR (DPFE) sensor and EGR system view—3.0L engine

TESTING

See Figures 170 and 171.

1. Disconnect the DPFE sensor harness connector. With the ignition on and engine off, measure the voltage between VREF and SIGRTN terminals of the DPFE harness connector. If the voltage is 4—5.5V, the power circuits to the sensor are okay.

➤ Typical sensor voltage with no EGR flow is between 0.25 volt and 1.3 volts. A higher voltage at idle may be due to a non-seating or heavily carboned EGR valve pintle. DPFEGR PID voltage must increase as the valve opens and decrease as the valve closes. A slow return voltage is an indication of a binding or slow closing EGR valve.

ENGINE COOLANT TEMPERATURE (ECT) SENSOR

LOCATION

2.3L Engine

See Figure 172.

➤ On 2.3L engine, this sensor is referred to as the Cylinder Head Temperature (CHT) sensor.

The Cylinder Head Temperature (CHT) sensor is located between the two center ignition coils.

3.0L Engine

See Figure 173.

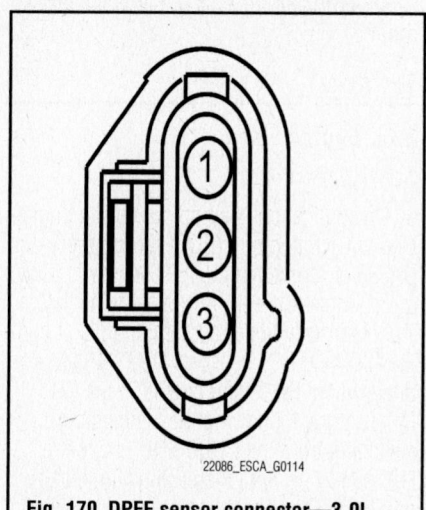

Fig. 170 DPFE sensor connector—3.0L engine

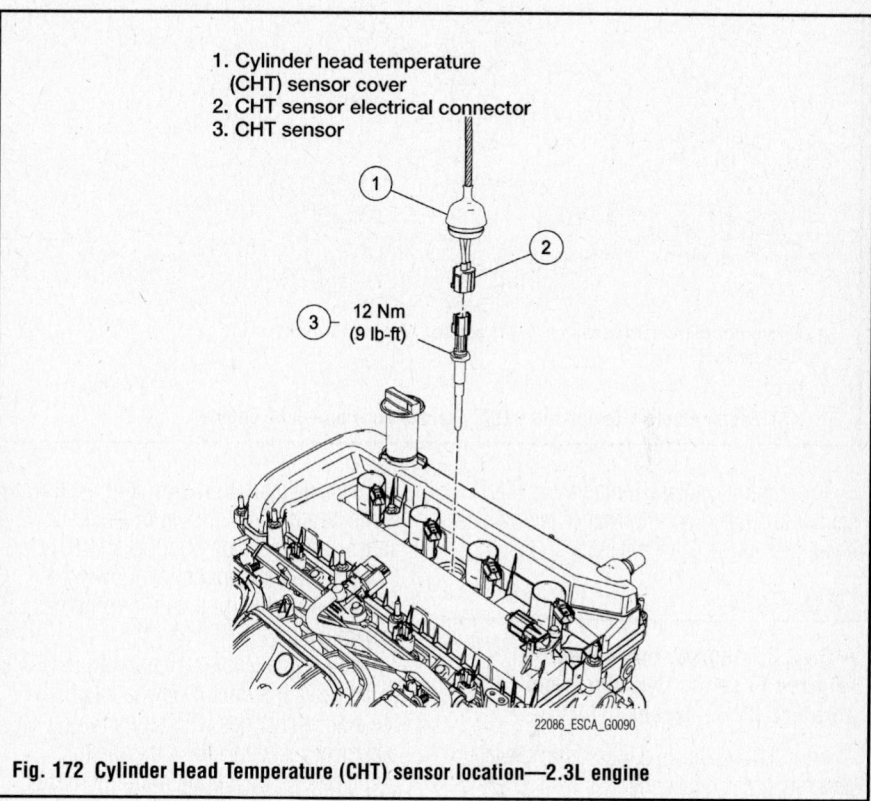

1. Cylinder head temperature (CHT) sensor cover
2. CHT sensor electrical connector
3. CHT sensor

12 Nm (9 lb-ft)

22086_ESCA_G0090

Fig. 172 Cylinder Head Temperature (CHT) sensor location—2.3L engine

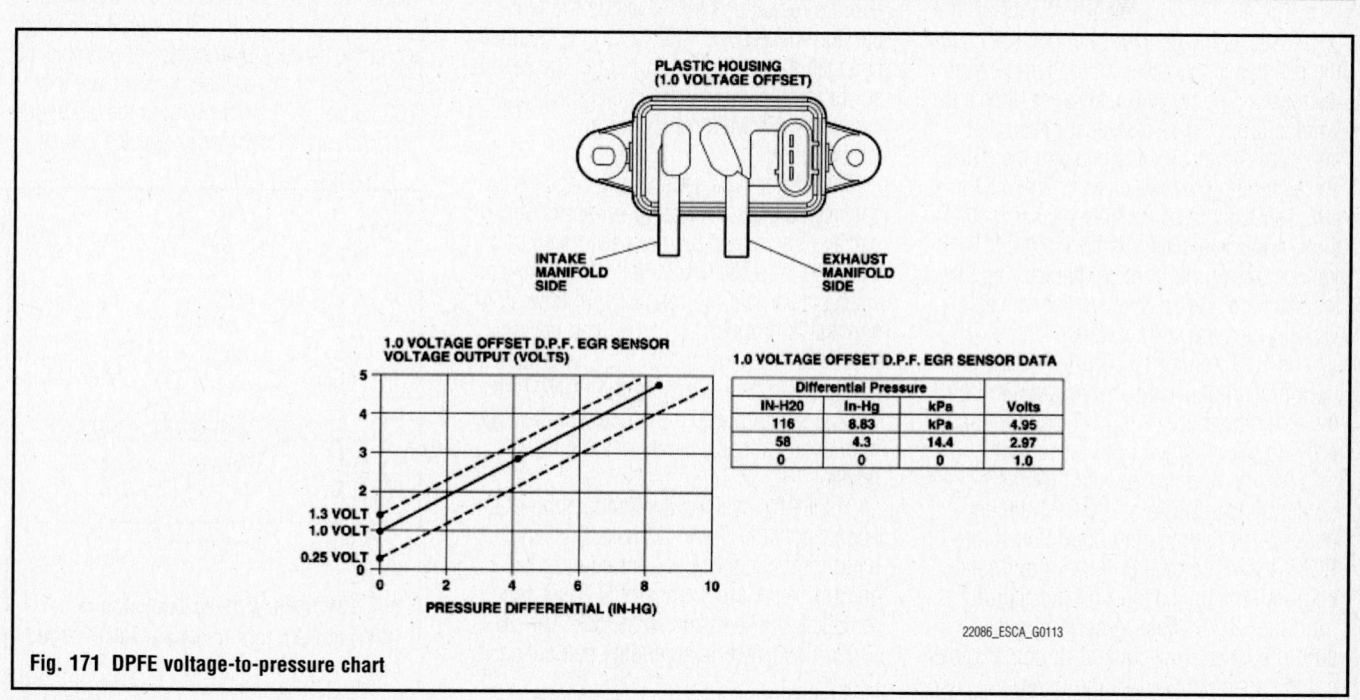

PLASTIC HOUSING (1.0 VOLTAGE OFFSET)

INTAKE MANIFOLD SIDE

EXHAUST MANIFOLD SIDE

1.0 VOLTAGE OFFSET D.P.F. EGR SENSOR VOLTAGE OUTPUT (VOLTS)

1.3 VOLT
1.0 VOLT
0.25 VOLT

PRESSURE DIFFERENTIAL (IN-HG)

1.0 VOLTAGE OFFSET D.P.F. EGR SENSOR DATA

Differential Pressure			
IN-H20	In-Hg	kPa	Volts
116	8.83	kPa	4.95
58	4.3	14.4	2.97
0	0	0	1.0

22086_ESCA_G0113

Fig. 171 DPFE voltage-to-pressure chart

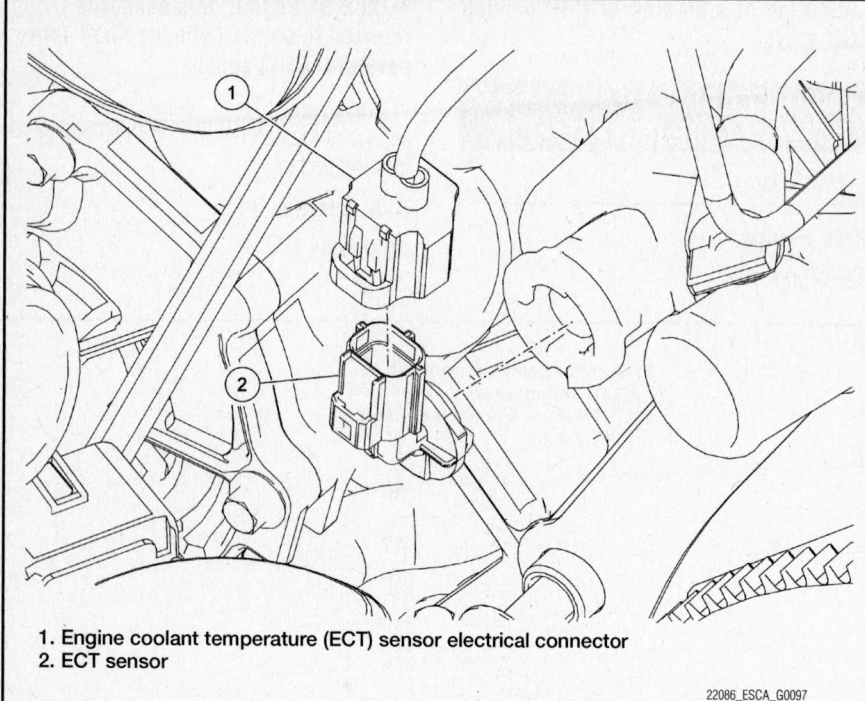

1. Engine coolant temperature (ECT) sensor electrical connector
2. ECT sensor

22086_ESCA_G0097

Fig. 173 Engine Coolant Temperature (ECT) sensor location—3.0L engine

The Engine Coolant Temperature (ECT) sensor is located on the front of left cylinder head, just under valve cover.

OPERATION

➡ **On 2.3L engine, this sensor is referred to as the Cylinder Head Temperature (CHT) sensor.**

The CHT sensor is a thermistor device in which the resistance changes with temperature. The electrical resistance of a thermistor decreases as the temperature increases, and the resistance increases as the temperature decreases. The varying resistance affects the voltage drop across the sensor terminals and provides electrical signals to the PCM corresponding to temperature. Thermistor type sensors are considered passive sensors. A passive sensor is connected to a voltage divider network so that varying the resistance of the passive sensor causes a variation in total current flow.

The CHT sensor is installed in the aluminum cylinder head and measures the metal temperature. The CHT sensor can provide complete engine temperature information and can be used to infer coolant temperature. If the CHT sensor conveys an overheating condition to the PCM, the PCM then initiates a fail-safe cooling strategy based on information from the CHT sensor. A cooling system failure such as low coolant or coolant loss could cause an overheating condition. As a result, damage to major engine components could occur. Using both the CHT sensor and fail-safe cooling strategy, the PCM prevents damage by allowing air cooling of the engine and limp home capability.

The Engine Coolant Temperature (ECT) sensor is a thermistor device in which resistance changes with temperature. The electrical resistance of a thermistor decreases as the temperature increases, and the resistance increases as the temperature decreases. The varying resistance changes the voltage drop across the sensor terminals and provides electrical signals to the PCM corresponding to temperature.

Thermistor-type sensors are considered passive sensors. A passive sensor is connected to a voltage divider network so that varying the resistance of the passive sensor causes a variation in total current flow. Voltage that is dropped across a fixed resistor in a series with the sensor resistor determines the voltage signal at the PCM. This voltage signal is equal the reference voltage minus the voltage drop across the fixed resistor.

The ECT measures the temperature of the engine coolant. The PCM uses the ECT input for fuel control and for cooling fan control. There are 3 types of ECT sensors, threaded, push-in, and twist-lock. The ECT sensor is located in an engine coolant passage.

REMOVAL & INSTALLATION

2.3L Engine

1. Detach the Cylinder Head Temperature (CHT) sensor cover and position aside.
2. Disconnect the CHT sensor electrical connector.
3. Remove and discard the CHT sensor.
4. To install, reverse the removal procedure and tighten the CHT sensor to 9 ft. lbs. (12 Nm).

3.0L Engine

1. Drain the cooling system.
2. Disconnect the Engine Coolant Temperature (ECT) sensor electrical connector.
3. To remove the ECT sensor, pull up on locking tab and rotate the sensor clockwise.
4. To install, reverse the removal procedure.

TESTING

2.3L Engine

See Figures 174 and 175.

On applications that do not use an Engine Coolant Temperature (ECT) sensor, the Cylinder Head Temperature (CHT) sensor is used to determine the engine coolant temperature. To cover the entire temperature range of both the CHT and ECT sensors, the PCM has a dual switching resistor circuit on the CHT input. A graph showing the temperature switching from the COLD END line to the HOT END line, with increasing temperature and back with decreasing temperature is included. Note the temperature to voltage overlap zone. Within this zone it is possible to have either a COLD END or HOT END voltage at the same temperature. For example, at 90°C (194°F) the voltage could read either 0.60 volt or 3.71 volts. Refer to the table for the temperature to voltage expected values.

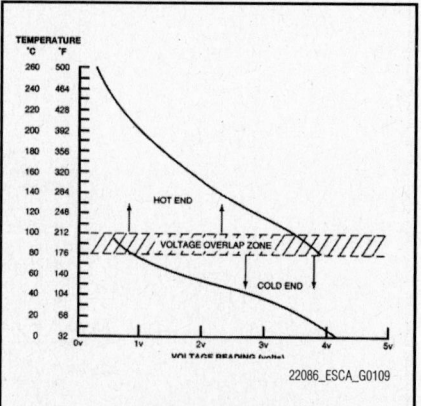

22086_ESCA_G0109

Fig. 174 Cylinder Head Temperature (CHT) temperature-to-voltage table—2.3L engine

1. Turn the ignition switch to the **OFF** position.

2. Disconnect the CHT sensor electrical connector.

3. Measure the resistance between CHT + pin 1 and CHT - pin 2 on sensor side of connector.

4. If resistance is not within specification replace sensor.

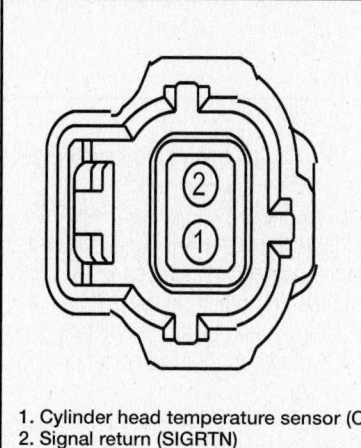

1. Cylinder head temperature sensor (CHT)
2. Signal return (SIGRTN)

22086_ESCA_G0108

Fig. 175 CHT sensor connector—2.3L engine

3.0L Engine

See Figures 176 through 178.

1. Turn the ignition switch to the **OFF** position.

2. Disconnect the Engine Coolant Temperature (ECT) sensor electrical connector.

3. Measure the resistance between ECT + pin 1 and ECT - pin 2 on sensor side of connector.

4. If resistance is not within specification replace sensor.

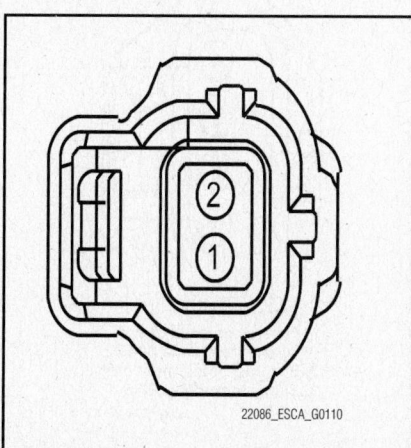

22086_ESCA_G0110

Fig. 176 ECT sensor connector—3.0L engine

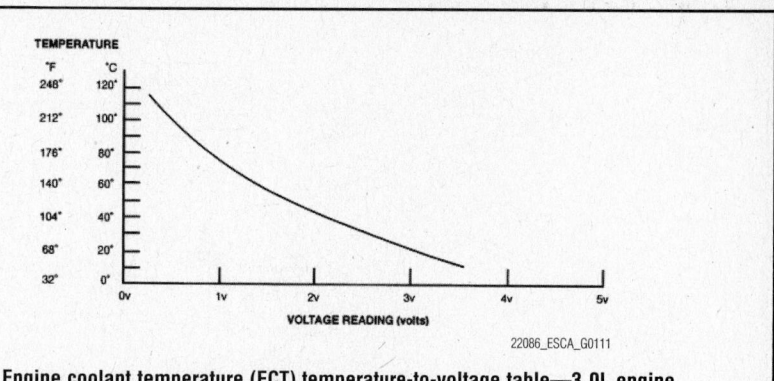

22086_ESCA_G0111

Fig. 177 Engine coolant temperature (ECT) temperature-to-voltage table—3.0L engine

TEMPERATURE SENSOR VOLTAGE AND RESISTANCE SPECIFICATIONS

Temperature		Temperature Sensor Values	
°C	°F	Voltage	Resistance (K ohms)
120	248	0.28	1.18
110	230	0.36	1.55
100	212	0.47	2.07
90	194	0.61	2.80
80	176	0.80	3.84
70	158	1.05	5.37
60	140	1.37	7.70
50	122	1.77	10.97
40	104	2.23	16.15
30	86	2.74	24.27
20	68	3.26	37.30
10	50	3.73	58.75
0	32	4.14	95.85
-10	14	4.45	160.31

22086_ESCA_G0112

Fig. 178 Temperature voltage and resistance specification chart—3.0L engine

FUEL RAIL TEMPERATURE PRESSURE (FRPT) SENSOR

LOCATION

See Figures 179 and 180.

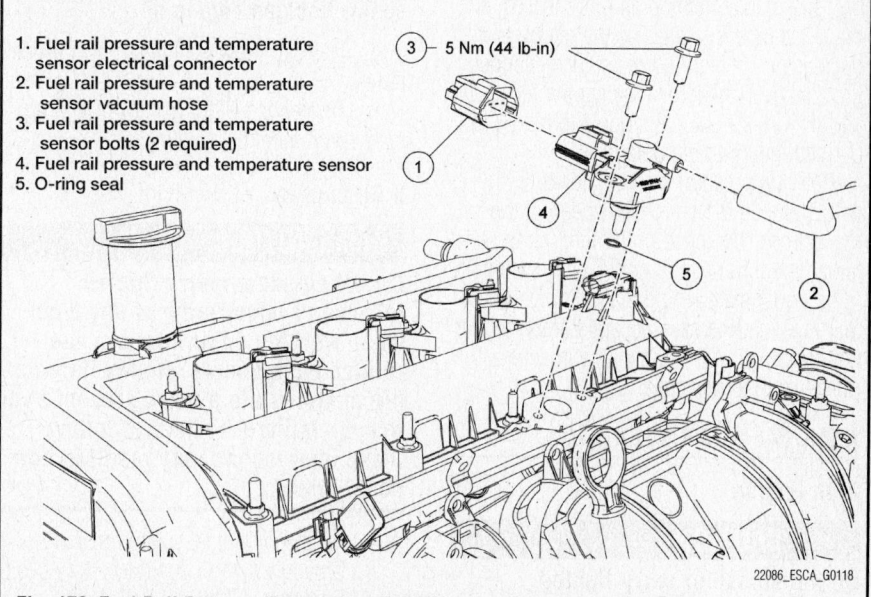

1. Fuel rail pressure and temperature sensor electrical connector
2. Fuel rail pressure and temperature sensor vacuum hose
3. Fuel rail pressure and temperature sensor bolts (2 required)
4. Fuel rail pressure and temperature sensor
5. O-ring seal

3 - 5 Nm (44 lb-in)

22086_ESCA_G0118

Fig. 179 Fuel Rail Pressure Temperature (FRPT) sensor location—2.3L engine

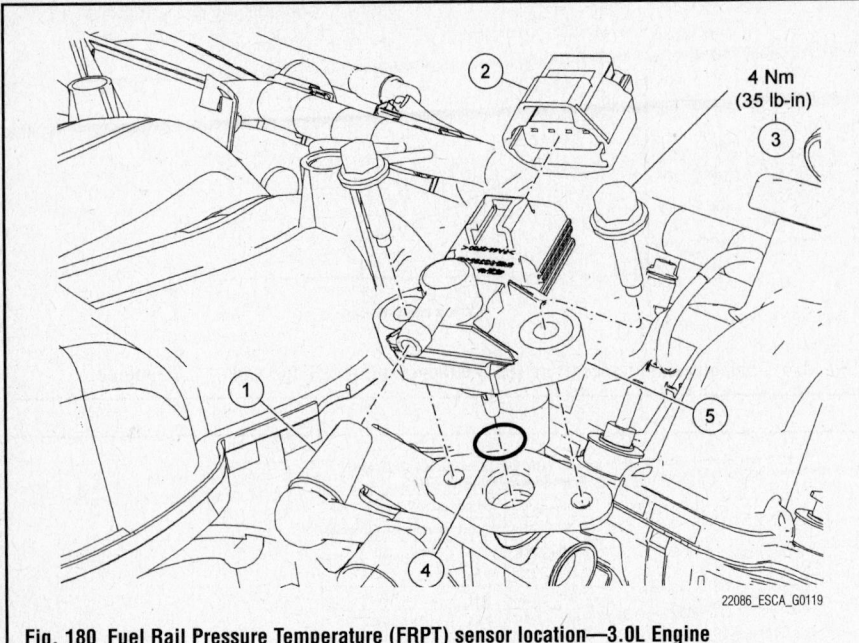

Fig. 180 Fuel Rail Pressure Temperature (FRPT) sensor location—3.0L Engine

OPERATION

The Fuel Rail Pressure Temperature (FRPT) sensor measures the pressure and temperature of the fuel in the fuel rail and sends these signals to the PCM. The sensor uses the intake manifold vacuum as a reference to determine the pressure difference between the fuel rail and the intake manifold. The relationship between fuel pressure and fuel temperature is used to determine the possible presence of fuel vapor in the fuel rail

The temperature sensing portion of the FRPT sensor is a thermistor device in which resistance changes with temperature. The electrical resistance of the thermistor decreases as the temperature increases, and the resistance increases as the temperature decreases. The varying resistance changes the voltage drop across the sensor terminals and provides electrical signals to the PCM corresponding to temperature.

Both the pressure and temperature signals are used to control the speed of the fuel pump. The speed of the fuel pump sustains fuel rail pressure which preserves fuel in its liquid state. The dynamic range of the fuel injectors increase because of the higher rail pressure, which allows the injector pulse width to decrease.

REMOVAL & INSTALLATION

2.3L Engine

✵✵ CAUTION

Do not smoke or carry lighted tobacco or open flame of any type

when working on or near any fuel-related components. Highly flammable mixtures are always present and may be ignited. Failure to follow these instructions may result in personal injury.

1. Release the fuel system pressure.
2. Disconnect the negative battery cable.
3. Disconnect the Fuel Rail Pressure Temperature (FRPT) sensor electrical connector and vacuum tube.
4. Remove the 2 bolts and the FRPT sensor.

To install:

➡Lubricate the FRPT sensor O-ring seal with clean engine oil.

5. To install, reverse the removal procedure.
6. Tighten the FRPT sensor mounting bolts to 44 inch lbs. (5 Nm).

3.0L Engine

✵✵ CAUTION

Do not smoke or carry lighted tobacco or open flame of any type when working on or near any fuel-related components. Highly flammable mixtures are always present and may be ignited. Failure to follow these instructions may result in personal injury.

1. Release the fuel system pressure.
2. Disconnect the negative battery cable.
3. Disconnect the Fuel Rail Pressure

Temperature (FRPT) sensor electrical connector and vacuum tube.
4. Remove the 2 bolts and the FRPT sensor.

To install:

➡Lubricate the FRPT sensor O-ring seal with clean engine oil.

5. To install, reverse the removal procedure.
6. Tighten the FRPT sensor mounting bolts to 35 inch lbs. (4 Nm).

TESTING

See Figure 181.

1. Turn the ignition key to the **OFF** position.
2. Disconnect the Fuel Rail Pressure Temperature sensor (FRPT) and measure the resistance between sensor connector component side FRT pin 3 and SIGRTN pin 4. The reading should be approximately 2K—96K ohms. If not, suspect a faulty FRPT sensor.
3. With the key on engine running, idle the engine for two minutes. Inspect the FRPT vacuum hose between the intake manifold and the FRPT sensor for air leaks and correct connection.

✵✵ CAUTION

Fuel in the fuel system remains under high pressure even when the engine is not running. Before working on or disconnecting any of the fuel tubes or fuel system components, the fuel system pressure must be relieved. Failure to follow these instructions may result in personal injury.

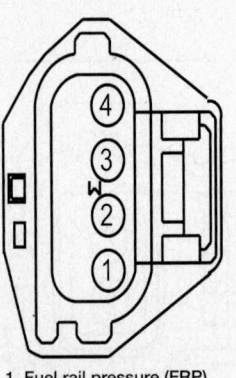

1. Fuel rail pressure (FRP)
2. Voltage reference (VREF)
3. Fuel rail temperature (FRT)
4. Signal return (SIGRTN)

22086_ESCA_G0117

Fig. 181 Fuel Rail Pressure Temperature (FRPT) sensor connector

HEATED OXYGEN SENSOR (HO2S)

LOCATION

2.3L Engine

See Figure 182.

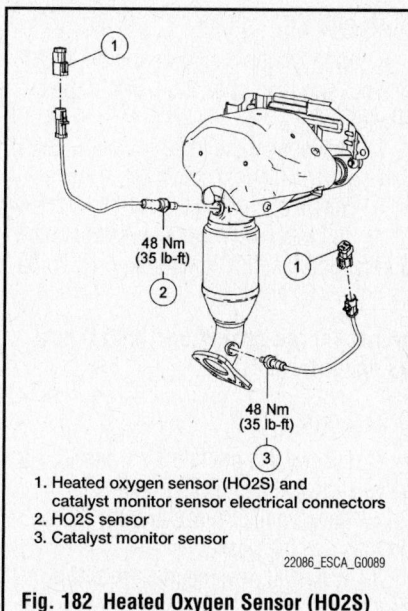

1. Heated oxygen sensor (HO2S) and catalyst monitor sensor electrical connectors
2. HO2S sensor
3. Catalyst monitor sensor

22086_ESCA_G0089

Fig. 182 Heated Oxygen Sensor (HO2S) location—2.3L engine

The Heated Oxygen Sensor (HO2S) is located just below exhaust manifold shield.

3.0L Engine

See Figure 183.

The Heated Oxygen Sensors (HO2S) are located at the top of the LH and RH converters.

OPERATION

The Heated Oxygen Sensor (HO2S) detects the presence of oxygen in the exhaust and produces a variable voltage according to the amount of oxygen detected. A high concentration of oxygen (lean air/fuel ratio) in the exhaust produces a voltage signal less than 0.4 volt. A low concentration of oxygen (rich air/fuel ratio) produces a voltage signal greater than 0.6 volt. The HO2S provides feedback to the PCM indicating air/fuel ratio in order to achieve a near stoichiometric air/fuel ratio of 14.7:1 during closed loop engine operation. The HO2S generates a voltage between 0.0 and 1.1 volts.

Embedded with the sensing element is the HO2S heater. The heating element heats the sensor to a temperature of 800°C (1,472°F). At approximately 300°C (572°F) the engine can enter closed loop operation. The VPWR circuit supplies voltage to the heater. The PCM turns the heater on by providing the ground when the correct conditions occur. The heater allows the engine to enter closed loop operation sooner. The use of this heater requires the HO2S heater control to be duty cycled, to prevent damage to the heater.

REMOVAL & INSTALLATION

2.3L Engine

1. With the vehicle in NEUTRAL, position it on a hoist.
2. Disconnect the Heated Oxygen Sensor (HO2S) electrical connector.
3. Using a suitable tool, remove the HO2S.

➡**Apply a light coat of anti-seize lubricant to the threads of the HO2S.**

4. To install, reverse the removal procedure and tighten HO2S to 35 ft. lbs. (48 Nm).

3.0L Engine

1. With the vehicle in NEUTRAL, position it on a hoist.
2. Remove the 7 bolts (5 shown) and the LH splash shield.
3. Disconnect the Heated Oxygen Sensor (HO2S) electrical connector.

➡**If necessary, lubricate the sensor threads with penetrating and lock lubricant to assist in removal.**

4. Using a suitable tool, remove the HO2S.

➡**Apply a light coat of anti-seize lubricant to the threads of the HO2S.**

5. To install, reverse the removal procedure and tighten HO2S to 35 ft. lbs. (38 Nm).

TESTING

See Figure 184.

1. Disconnect the Heated Oxygen Sensor (HO2S) connector. Measure the resistance between the HO2S heater and VPWR on sensor side of harness. The reading should be approximately 3—30 ohms. If resistance is not within specifications, the sensor may be faulty.
2. With the engine running and HO2S sensor in place measure the voltage with digital multimeter between terminals HO2S and SIGRTN at the sensor harness. The voltage should read approximately 0.01—1.0V. If the reading is off or the voltage fluctuation is very slow suspect faulty sensor.
3. Check for unmetered air leaks at intake manifold gasket leaks, hoses connecting to the mass air flow (MAF) sensor assembly, PCV system. Fuel calculations can be affected by unmetered air leaks.

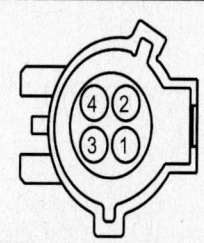

1. Fuse or circuit breaker
2. Heater oxygen sensor (HTR21)
3. Signal return (SIGRTN)
4. Heated oxygen pre-cat (HO2S21)

22086_ESCA_G0115

Fig. 184 Heated Oxygen Sensor (HO2S) connector

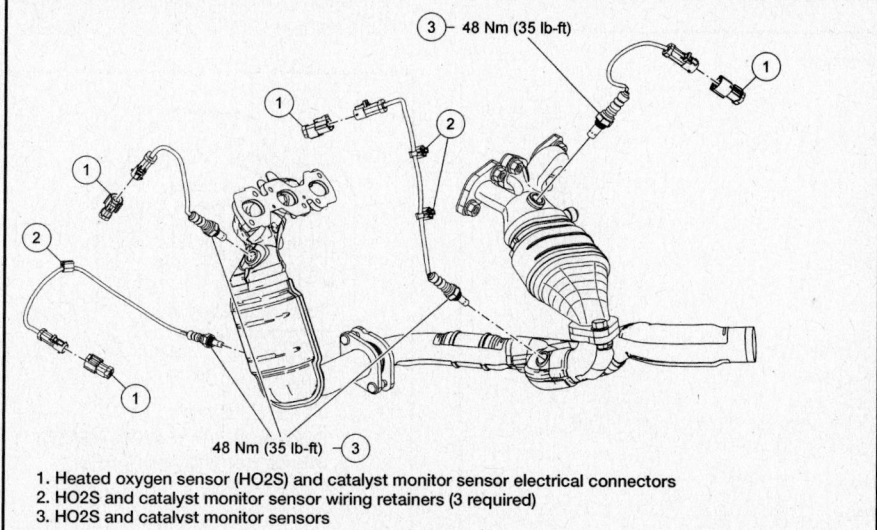

1. Heated oxygen sensor (HO2S) and catalyst monitor sensor electrical connectors
2. HO2S and catalyst monitor sensor wiring retainers (3 required)
3. HO2S and catalyst monitor sensors

22086_ESCA_G0098

Fig. 183 Heated Oxygen Sensor (HO2S) locations—3.0L engine

IDLE AIR CONTROL (IAC) VALVE

LOCATION

2.3L Engine

See Figure 185.

The Idle Air Control (IAC) valve is located just behind the throttle body on the intake manifold.

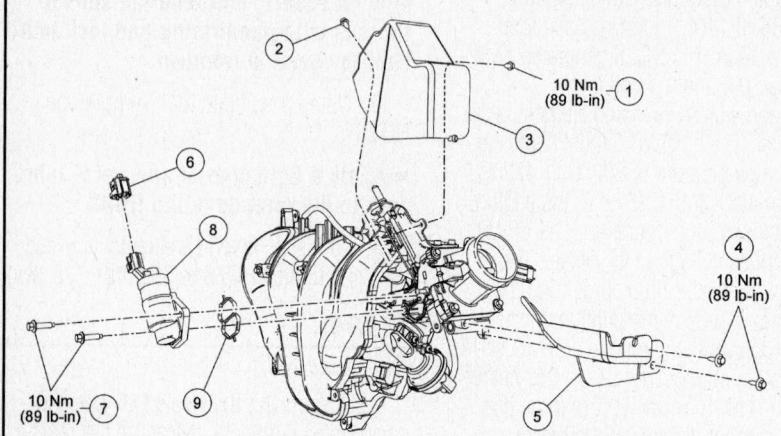

1. Upper snow shield-to-intake manifold screw
2. Upper snow shield-to-intake manifold pin-type retainer
3. Upper snow shield
4. Lower snow shield-to-intake manifold screws (2 required)
5. Lower snow shield
6. Idle air control (IAC) valve electrical connector
7. IAC valve bolts (2 required)
8. IAC valve
9. IAC valve gasket

22086_ESCA_G0087

Fig. 185 Idle Air Control (IAC) valve location—2.3L engine

3.0L Engine

See Figure 186.

The Idle Air Control (IAC) valve is located just behind the throttle body on the top of the intake manifold.

OPERATION

The Idle Air Control (IAC) valve assembly controls the engine idle speed and provides a dashpot function. The IAC valve assembly meters intake air around the throttle plate through a bypass within the IAC valve assembly and throttle body. The PCM determines the desired idle speed or bypass air and signals the IAC valve assembly through a specified duty cycle. The IAC valve responds by positioning the IAC valve to control the amount of bypassed air. The PCM monitors engine RPM and increases or decreases the IAC duty cycle in order to achieve the desired RPM.

➡The IAC valve assembly is not adjustable and cannot be cleaned, also some IAC valves are normally open and others are normally closed. Some IAC valves require engine vacuum to operate.

REMOVAL & INSTALLATION

2.3L Engine

1. Remove the 3 screws, the pin-type retainer and the upper and lower snow shield.
2. Disconnect the Idle Air Control (IAC) valve electrical connector.
3. Remove the 2 bolts and the IAC valve.
4. To install, reverse the removal procedure and tighten IAC mounting bolts to 89 inch lbs. (10 Nm).

➡**Inspect the gasket and install new as necessary.**

3.0L Engine

1. Disconnect the Idle Air Control (IAC) valve electrical connector.
2. Remove the 2 bolts and the IAC valve and discard the gasket.
3. To install, reverse the removal procedure.
4. Clean and inspect all sealing surfaces. Install new gasket.
5. Tighten IAC mounting bolts to 89 inch lbs. (10 Nm).

TESTING

See Figure 187.

1. To check for voltage to the Idle Air Control (IAC) valve, disconnect the IAC valve electrical connector. With the key **ON** and engine **OFF**, measure the voltage between IAC harness PWR and battery ground. The voltage reading should be greater than 10V.

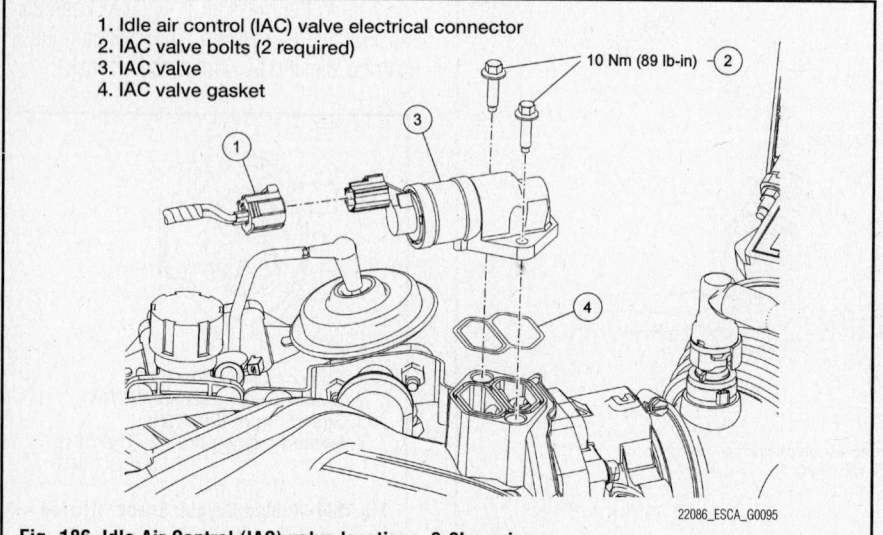

1. Idle air control (IAC) valve electrical connector
2. IAC valve bolts (2 required)
3. IAC valve
4. IAC valve gasket

22086_ESCA_G0095

Fig. 186 Idle Air Control (IAC) valve location—3.0L engine

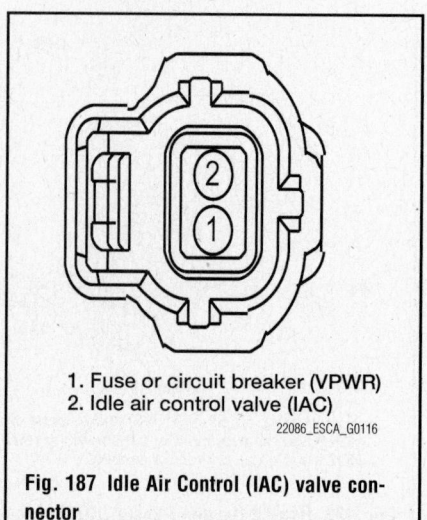

1. Fuse or circuit breaker (VPWR)
2. Idle air control valve (IAC)

22086_ESCA_G0116

Fig. 187 Idle Air Control (IAC) valve connector

2. Check the resistance of the IAC valve. With the key in the off position disconnect the IAC valve harness connector. Measure the resistance PWR and IAC (GRD) at the sensor. If the reading is not within specification 6—15 ohms suspect faulty IAC valve.

3. With the engine running at idle (if possible), listen for vacuum leaks. Inspect the entire intake air system from the Mass Air Flow (MAF) sensor to the intake manifold for leaks.

INTAKE AIR TEMPERATURE (IAT) SENSOR

LOCATION

The Intake Air Temperature (IAT) sensor is incorporated in the Mass Air Flow assembly. Refer to the Mass Air Flow (MAF) sensor.

KNOCK SENSOR (KS)

LOCATION

2.3L Engine

See Figure 188.

The Knock Sensor (KS) is located behind the intake manifold to the rear of engine block.

OPERATION

The Knock Sensor (KS) is a tuned accelerometer on the engine which converts engine vibration to an electrical signal. The PCM uses this signal to determine the presence of engine knock and to retard spark timing.

REMOVAL & INSTALLATION

1. With the vehicle in NEUTRAL, position it on a hoist.
2. Remove the intake manifold.
3. Remove the bolt and the Knock Sensor (KS).
4. To install, reverse the removal procedure and tighten the sensor mounting bolt to 15ft. lbs. (20 Nm).

TESTING

See Figure 189.

➡Appropriate repair methods and procedures are essential for the safe, reliable operation of all motor vehicles, as well as the personal safety of the individual doing the work. This procedure provides general directions for repairing vehicles with tested, effective techniques. Following them helps to establish reliability. There are numerous variations in procedures, techniques, tools, and parts for repairing vehicles, as well as in the skill of the individual doing the work. This manual cannot possibly anticipate all such variations and provide advice or cautions as to each. Accordingly, anyone who departs from the instructions provided in this procedure must first establish that they compromise neither their personal safety nor the vehicle integrity by their choice of methods, tools, or parts.

1. Disconnect the Knock Sensor (KS) harness connector and measure the resistance between KS + and KS - on the component side. The resistance should read between 4.39M—5.35M ohms. If resistance reading is not within specifications suspect a faulty KS.

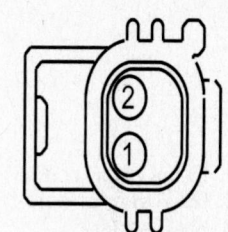

1. Knock sensor KS-1
2. Knock sensor KS+2

22086_ESCA_G0120

Fig. 189 Knock Sensor (KS) connector view—2.3L engine

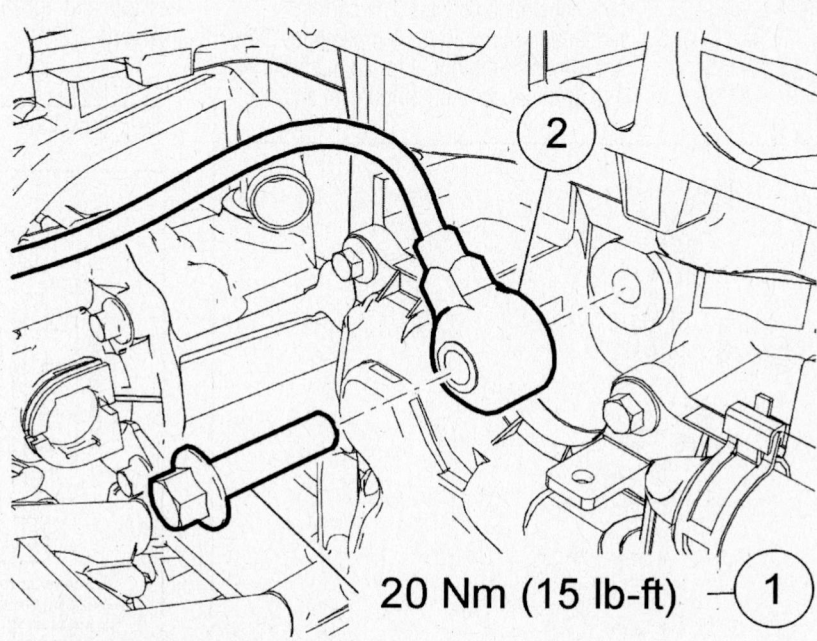

20 Nm (15 lb-ft)

1. Knock sensor bolt
2. Knock sensor

22086_ESCA_G0091

Fig. 188 Knock Sensor (KS) location—2.3L engine

MASS AIR FLOW (MAF) SENSOR

LOCATION

2.3L Engine

See Figure 190.

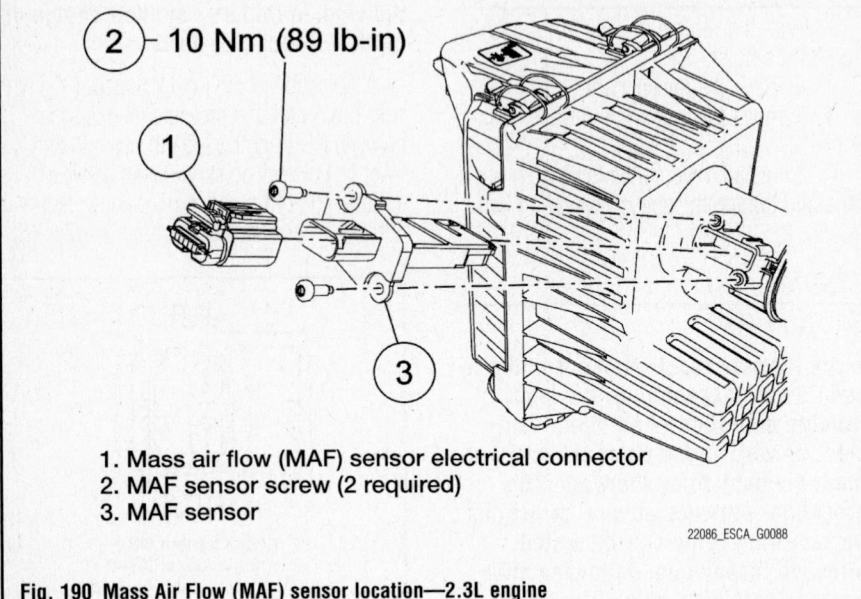

1. Mass air flow (MAF) sensor electrical connector
2. MAF sensor screw (2 required)
3. MAF sensor

22086_ESCA_G0088

Fig. 190 Mass Air Flow (MAF) sensor location—2.3L engine

The Mass Air Flow (MAF) sensor is located on air supply tube at air filter housing.

3.0L Engine

See Figure 191.

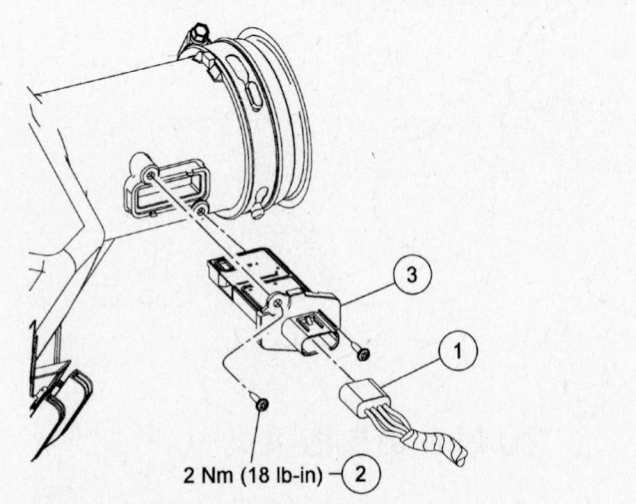

2 Nm (18 lb-in)

1. Mass air flow (MAF) sensor electrical connector
2. MAF sensor screw (2 required)
3. MAF sensor

22086_ESCA_G0096

Fig. 191 Mass Air Flow (MAF) sensor location—3.0L engine

The Mass Air Flow (MAF) sensor is located on air supply tube before throttle body.

OPERATION

The Mass Air Flow (MAF) sensor uses a hot wire sensing element to measure the amount of air entering the engine. Air passing over the hot wire causes it to cool. This hot wire is maintained at 200°C (392°F) above the ambient temperature as measured by a constant cold wire. The current required to maintain the temperature of the hot wire is proportional to the mass air flow. The MAF sensor then outputs an analog voltage signal to the PCM proportional to the intake air mass. The PCM calculates the required fuel injector pulse width in order to provide the desired air/fuel ratio. This input is also used in determining transmission electronic pressure control (EPC), shift and torque converter clutch scheduling.

The MAF sensor is located between the air cleaner and the throttle body or inside the air cleaner assembly. Most MAF sensors have integrated bypass technology with an integrated Intake Air Temperature (IAT) sensor. The hot wire electronic sensing element must be replaced as an assembly. Replacing only the element may change the air flow calibration.

REMOVAL & INSTALLATION

2.3L Engine

1. Disconnect the Mass Air Flow (MAF) sensor electrical connector.
2. Remove the 2 screws and the MAF sensor.
3. To install, reverse the removal procedure and tighten MAF sensor mounting screws to 89 inch lbs. (10 Nm).

3.0L Engine

1. Disconnect the Mass Air Flow (MAF) sensor electrical connector.
2. Remove the 2 screws and the MAF sensor.
3. To install, reverse the removal procedure and tighten screws to 18 inch lbs. (2 Nm).

TESTING

See Figure 192.

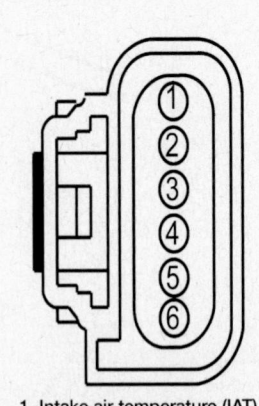

1. Intake air temperature (IAT)
2. Signal return (SIGRTN)
3. Mass air flow (MAF)
4. Power train mass air flow (MAFR TN)
5. Ground (GRND)
6. Fuse or circuit breaker

22086_ESCA_G0121

Fig. 192 Mass Air Flow (MAF) sensor connector

1. Using a multimeter, check for voltage by back probing the Mass Air Flow (MAF) sensor connector being careful not to cause connector damage. With the engine running verify that there is at least 10.5V between the VPWR and PWRGND terminals of the MAF sensor connector. If voltage is not within specifications check the power and ground circuits and repair as needed.

➡**A MAF sensor PID value of less than 0.6 volt may indicate an incorrectly installed air cleaner or a leak in the air inlet system.**

2. With the key on engine running allow engine to stabilize at correct operating temperature. Scan the MAF PID at idle in neutral and check that the reading is not greater than 1.3 volts. If so, suspect a faulty MAF sensor.

MANIFOLD ABSOLUTE PRESSURE (MAP) SENSOR

LOCATION
See Figure 193.

OPERATION

1. The Manifold Absolute Pressure (MAP) sensor measures intake manifold absolute pressure. The PCM uses information from the MAP sensor to measure how much exhaust gas is introduced into the intake manifold. The MAP sensor may also be referred to as TMAP sensor.

REMOVAL & INSTALLATION

1. Disconnect the electrical connector from the Manifold Absolute Pressure (MAP) sensor.
2. Remove the MAP sensor mounting screws.
3. To install, reverse the removal procedure

TESTING
See Figure 194.

1. Check the voltage supply to the Manifold Absolute Pressure (MAP) sensor by measuring the MAP sensor harness side VREF to SIGRTN The voltage reading should read 4.5—5.5 volts. If reading is not as

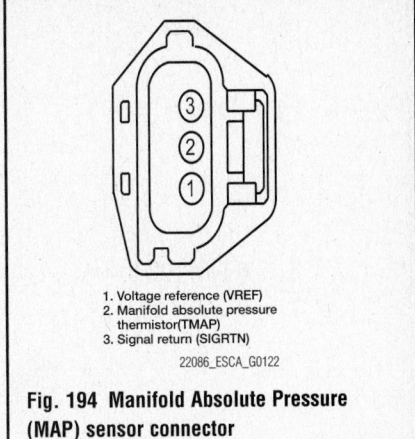

1. Voltage reference (VREF)
2. Manifold absolute pressure thermistor(TMAP)
3. Signal return (SIGRTN)

22086_ESCA_G0122

Fig. 194 Manifold Absolute Pressure (MAP) sensor connector

specified check the VREF to battery ground. If the voltage reading is present 4.5—5.5 volts. Check for open in SIGRTN circuit.

POWERTRAIN CONTROL MODULE (PCM)

LOCATION
See Figure 195.

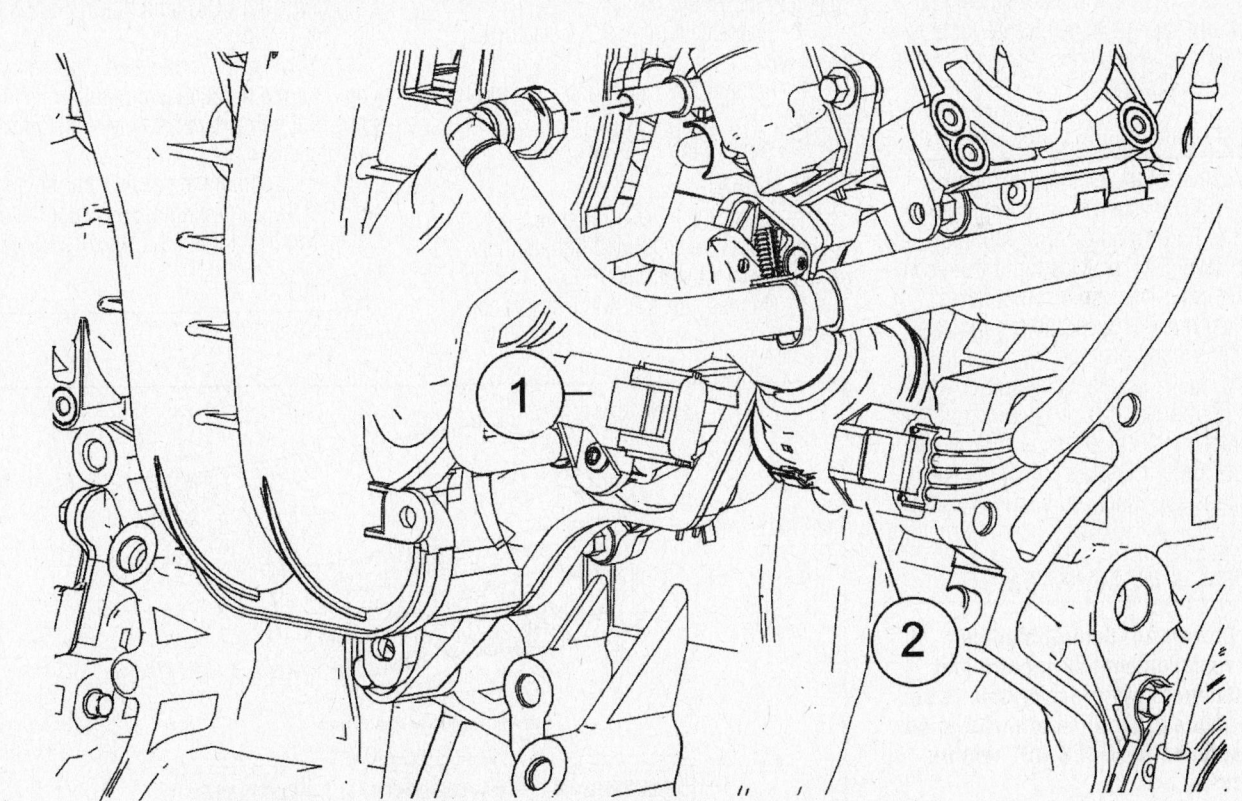

1. **Map sensor**
2. **Map sensor electrical connector**

22086_ESCA_G0105

Fig. 193 Manifold Absolute Pressure (MAP) sensor locations—2.3L engine

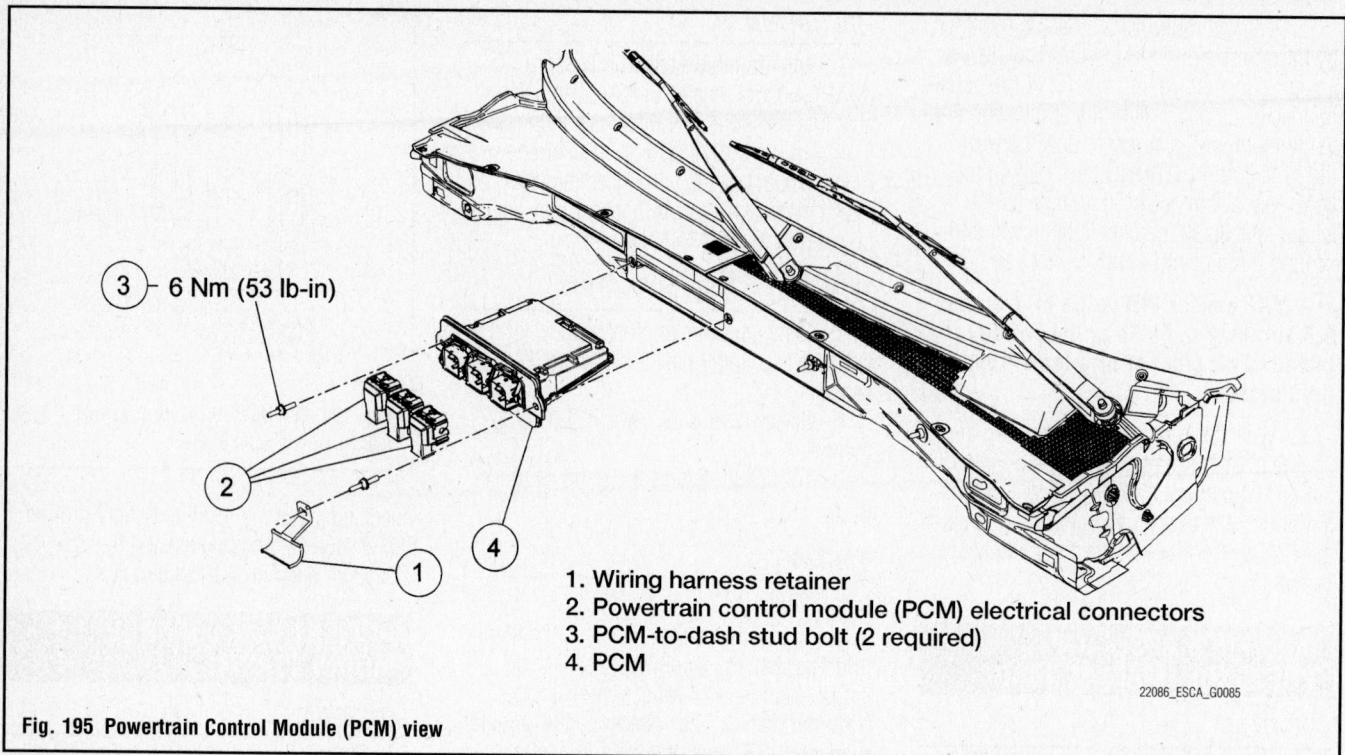

Fig. 195 Powertrain Control Module (PCM) view

3 — 6 Nm (53 lb-in)

1. Wiring harness retainer
2. Powertrain control module (PCM) electrical connectors
3. PCM-to-dash stud bolt (2 required)
4. PCM

22086_ESCA_G0085

For Escape and Mariner, the Powertrain Control Module (PCM) is located behind the instrument panel (cowl), center to both driver and passenger sides (access from the engine compartment).

OPERATION

The center of the Electronic Engine Control (EEC) system is a microprocessor called the Powertrain Control Module (PCM). The PCM receives input from sensors and other electronic components (switches, relays). Based on the information received and programmed into its memory, the PCM generates output signals to control various relays, solenoids and actuators. There are several different types of PCMs in use for this model year. The Escape and Mariner use the 150-pin PCM.

REMOVAL & INSTALLATION

➡**Any Powertrain Control Module (PCM) replacement will require that ALL customer keys are available to be programmed at the time of installation. PCM replacement DOES NOT require new keys.**

1. Retrieve the module configuration. Carry out the module configuration retrieval steps of the Programmable Module Installation procedure.
2. Disconnect the negative battery cable.

3. Remove the PCM stud bolt nut and position the wiring harness aside.
4. Disconnect the 3 PCM electrical connectors.
5. Remove the 2 stud bolts and the PCM
6. Remove the PCM cowl seal.

To install:
7. Install the PCM cowl seal.
8. Install the PCM and tighten the 2 stud bolts to 53 inch lbs. (6 Nm).
9. Connect the 3 PCM electrical connectors.

10. Position the wiring harness. Install and tighten the PCM stud bolt nut to 53 inch lbs. (6 Nm).
11. Restore the module configuration. Carry out the module configuration restore steps of the Programmable Module Installation procedure.
12. Reprogram the passive anti-theft system (PATS). Carry out the Key Programming Using Two Programmed Keys procedure.

TESTING

See Figures 196 and 197.

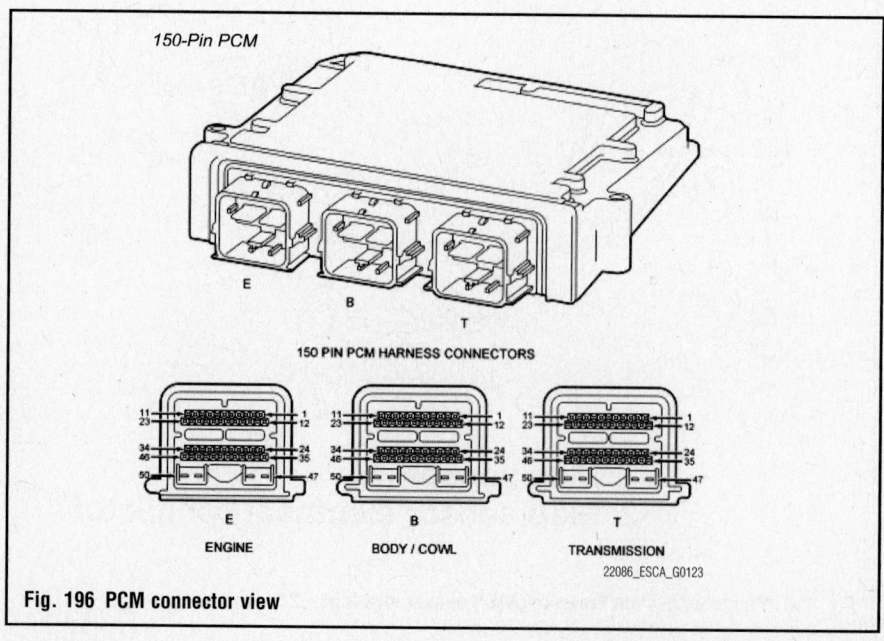

150-Pin PCM

150 PIN PCM HARNESS CONNECTORS

E ENGINE
B BODY / COWL
T TRANSMISSION

22086_ESCA_G0123

Fig. 196 PCM connector view

TABLE 1 — 150-PIN PCM POWER AND GROUNDS		
Function	Description	Connector/Pin
VPWR	Voltage input to module	B35
VPWR	Voltage input to module	B36
PWRGND	Power ground	B47
PWRGND	Power ground	B48
PWRGND	Power ground	B49
CSEGND	Case ground	B10
SIGRTN	Connector B signal return	B41
SIGRTN	Connector T signal return	T41
SIGRTN	Connector E signal return	E41
VREF	Connector buffered 5.0-volt reference	B40
VREF	Connector E buffered 5.0-volt reference	E40
KAPWR	Keep alive power	B45

22086_ESCA_G0124

Fig. 197 PCM voltage and power pin location chart

1. Check the power and grounds for the Powertrain Control Module (PCM). Check all the connector pins for corrosion or contact problems. Refer to PCM connectors, power and ground chart.

THROTTLE POSITION SENSOR (TPS)

LOCATION

2.3L Engine

See Figure 198.

The Throttle Position Sensor (TPS) is located to the right of throttle plate.

3.0L Engine

See Figure 199.

The Throttle Position Sensor (TPS) is located on the throttle body just behind the EGR valve tube.

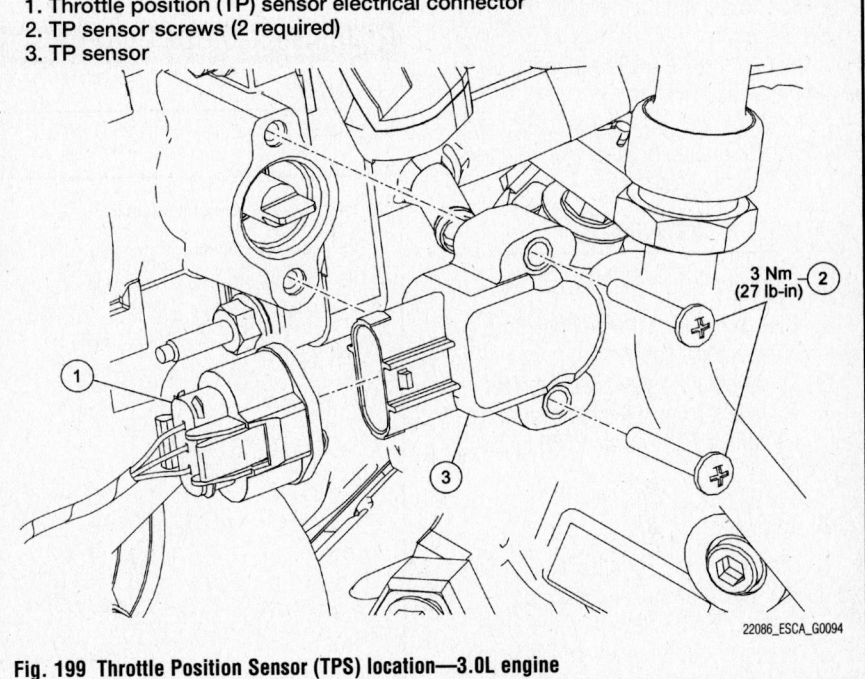

1. Throttle position (TP) sensor electrical connector
2. TP sensor screws (2 required)
3. TP sensor

3 Nm (27 lb-in)

22086_ESCA_G0094

Fig. 199 Throttle Position Sensor (TPS) location—3.0L engine

OPERATION

The Throttle Position Sensor (TPS) is a rotary potentiometer sensor that provides a signal to the PCM that is linearly proportional to the throttle plate/shaft position. The sensor housing has a 3-blade electrical

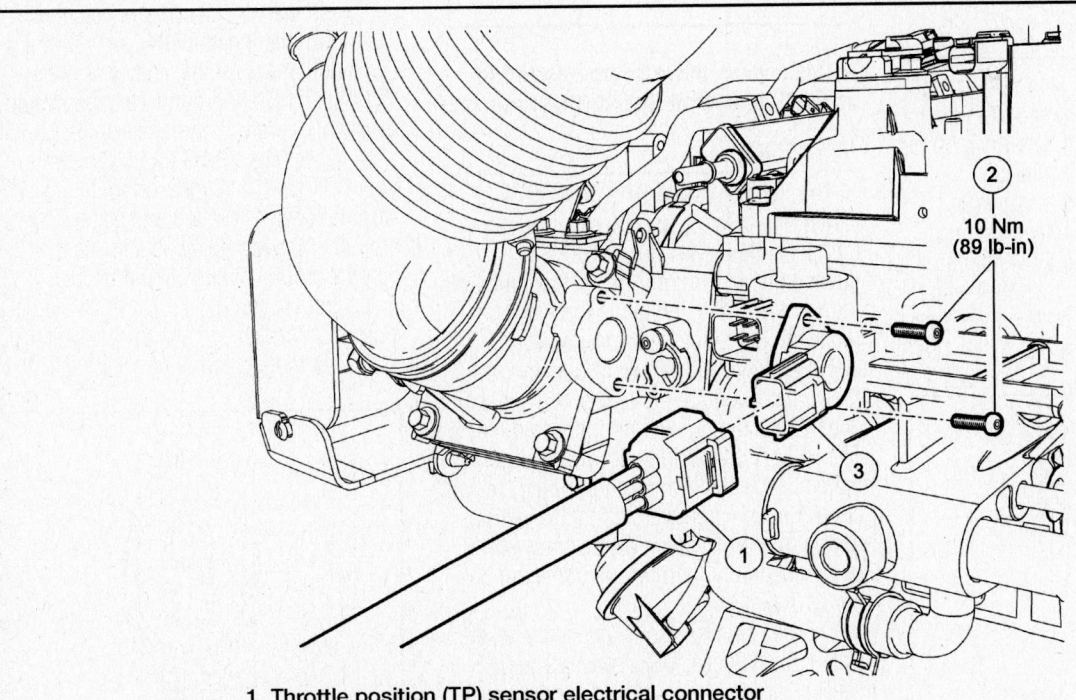

1. Throttle position (TP) sensor electrical connector
2. TP sensor screws (2 required)
3. TP sensor

10 Nm (89 lb-in)

22086_ESCA_G0086

Fig. 198 Throttle Position Sensor (TPS) location—2.3L engine

connector that may be gold plated. The gold plating increases the corrosion resistance on the terminals and increases the connector durability. The TPS is mounted on the throttle body. As the TPS is rotated by the throttle shaft, 4 operating conditions are determined by the PCM from the TPS.

1. The operating conditions are:
   a. Closed throttle (includes idle or deceleration)
   b. Part throttle (includes cruise or moderate acceleration)
   c. Wide open throttle (includes maximum acceleration or de-choke on crank)
   d. Throttle angle rate

REMOVAL & INSTALLATION

2.3L Engine

1. Disconnect the Throttle Position Sensor (TPS) electrical connector.
2. Remove the 2 screws and the TPS.
3. To install, reverse the removal procedure and tighten TPS screws to 89 inch lbs. (10 Nm).

3.0L Engine

1. Disconnect the Throttle Position Sensor (TPS) sensor electrical connector.
2. Remove the 2 screws and the TPS.
3. To install, reverse the removal procedure and tighten mounting screws to 27 inch lbs. (3 Nm).

TESTING

See Figure 200.

1. Check for voltage between VREF and SIGRTN at Throttle Position Sensor (TPS) harness. With the harness connector unplugged from sensor and the ignition switch on engine off. The voltage reading should be between 4.5v—5.5v. If not check circuits for power and or ground problems.
2. With the ignition on engine off, check the voltage at the SIGRTN circuit of the TPS

by carefully backprobing the connector using a multimeter. The voltage should be between 0.2 and 1.4 volts at idle. Slowly open the throttle plate and carefully watch the readings. The voltage should rise to approximately 4.8v at wide open throttle, and should not jump erratically but in a smooth motion.

VEHICLE SPEED SENSOR (VSS)

LOCATION

See Figure 201.

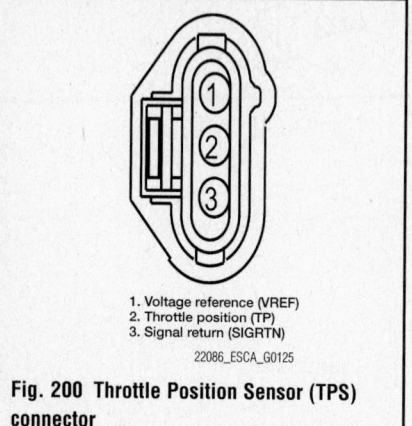

Fig. 201 Vehicle Speed Sensor (VSS) location

➡ This sensor may also be referred to as the Output Shaft Speed (OSS) sensor.

OPERATION

The Vehicle Speed Sensor (VSS) is a variable reluctance or hall-effect sensor that generates a waveform with a frequency that is proportional to the speed of the vehicle. If the vehicle is moving at a relatively low velocity, the sensor produces a signal with a low frequency. As the vehicle velocity increases, the sensor generates a signal with a higher frequency. The PCM uses the frequency signal generated by the VSS (and other inputs) to control such parameters as fuel injection, ignition control, transmission/transaxle shift scheduling, and torque converter clutch scheduling.

This sensor may also be referred to as the Output Shaft Speed (OSS) sensor. The OSS sensor provides the PCM with information about the rotational speed of an output shaft. The PCM uses the information to control and diagnose powertrain behavior. In some applications, the sensor is also used as the source of vehicle speed. The sensor may be physi-

cally located in different places on the vehicle, depending upon the specific application. The design of each speed sensor is unique and depends on which powertrain control feature uses the information that is generated.

REMOVAL & INSTALLATION

1. With the vehicle in NEUTRAL, position it on a hoist.
2. Remove the 7 retainers and the LH splash shield.
3. Disconnect the Vehicle Speed Sensor (VSS)/Output Shaft Speed (OSS) sensor electrical connector.
4. Remove the sensor bolt.
5. Remove the sensor.

To install:

➡ **When installing the sensor, lubricate the O-ring seal with clean transmission fluid.**

6. To install, reverse the removal procedure and note the following:
   a. Tighten the sensor mounting bolt to 9 ft. lbs. (12 Nm).

TESTING

See Figure 202.

1. Check the voltage to the Vehicle Speed Sensor (VSS)/Output Shaft Speed (OSS) sensor. Turn the ignition switch **OFF** and disconnect the sensor connector.
2. Turn the ignition **ON**, and with the engine off, measure the voltage between VPWR and battery ground. Voltage should read 10v or more if not repair power circuit.
3. Check the VPWR ground to the VSS/OSS sensor by measuring the resistance between PWRGND and battery ground. If the resistance is less than 5 ohms ground circuit should be okay.
4. Inspect the VSS/OSS vehicle harness connector for damage and proper seating.
5. If possible, carry out a wiggle test.

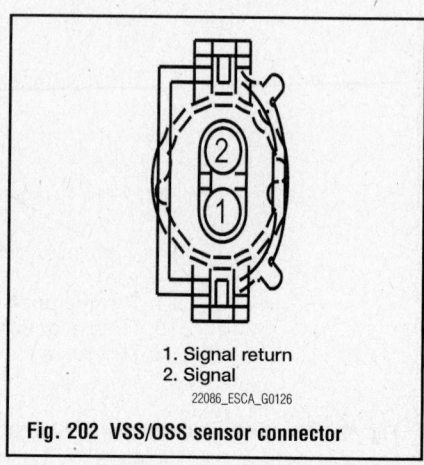

1. Signal return
2. Signal

22086_ESCA_G0126

Fig. 202 VSS/OSS sensor connector

1. Voltage reference (VREF)
2. Throttle position (TP)
3. Signal return (SIGRTN)

22086_ESCA_G0125

Fig. 200 Throttle Position Sensor (TPS) connector

FUEL SYSTEMS

GASOLINE FUEL INJECTION SYSTEM

FUEL SYSTEM SERVICE PRECAUTIONS

Safety is the most important factor when performing not only fuel system maintenance but any type of maintenance. Failure to conduct maintenance and repairs in a safe manner may result in serious personal injury or death. Maintenance and testing of the vehicle's fuel system components can be accomplished safely and effectively by adhering to the following rules and guidelines.

• To avoid the possibility of fire and personal injury, always disconnect the negative battery cable unless the repair or test procedure requires that battery voltage be applied.

• Always relieve the fuel system pressure prior to disconnecting any fuel system component (injector, fuel rail, pressure regulator, etc.), fitting or fuel line connection. Exercise extreme caution whenever relieving fuel system pressure to avoid exposing skin, face and eyes to fuel spray. Please be advised that fuel under pressure may penetrate the skin or any part of the body that it contacts.

• Always place a shop towel or cloth around the fitting or connection prior to loosening to absorb any excess fuel due to spillage. Ensure that all fuel spillage (should it occur) is quickly removed from engine surfaces. Ensure that all fuel soaked cloths or towels are deposited into a suitable waste container.

• Always keep a dry chemical (Class B) fire extinguisher near the work area.

• Do not allow fuel spray or fuel vapors to come into contact with a spark or open flame.

• Always use a back-up wrench when loosening and tightening fuel line connection fittings. This will prevent unnecessary stress and torsion to fuel line piping.

• Always replace worn fuel fitting O-rings with new Do not substitute fuel hose or equivalent where fuel pipe is installed.

Before servicing the vehicle, make sure to also refer to the precautions in the beginning of this section as well.

FUEL SYSTEM PRESSURE

RELIEVING

1. Before servicing the vehicle, refer to the Precautions Section.
2. Remove the fuel pump relay.

3. Start the engine and allow it to idle until it stalls.
4. After the engine stalls, crank the engine for approximately 5 seconds to make sure the fuel injection supply manifold pressure has been released.
5. Turn the ignition switch to the OFF position.
6. When fuel system service is complete, install the fuel pump relay.

➡ **It may take more than one key cycle to pressurize the fuel system.**

7. Cycle the ignition key and wait three seconds to pressurize the fuel system. Check for leaks before starting the engine.
8. Start the vehicle and check the fuel system for leaks.

FUEL FILTER

REMOVAL & INSTALLATION

1. Before servicing the vehicle, refer to the Precautions Section.

2. Properly relieve the fuel system pressure.
3. Remove or disconnect the following:
   • Negative battery cable
   • Fuel line to the fuel filter
4. Loosen the clamp and remove the filter

To install:

5. Install or connect the following:
   • New clips to the fuel lines
   • Fuel filter and tighten the clamp
   • Fuel lines to the fuel filter
   • Negative battery cable
6. Start the vehicle and check for leaks, repair if necessary.

FUEL INJECTORS

REMOVAL & INSTALLATION

2.3L Engine

See Figure 203.

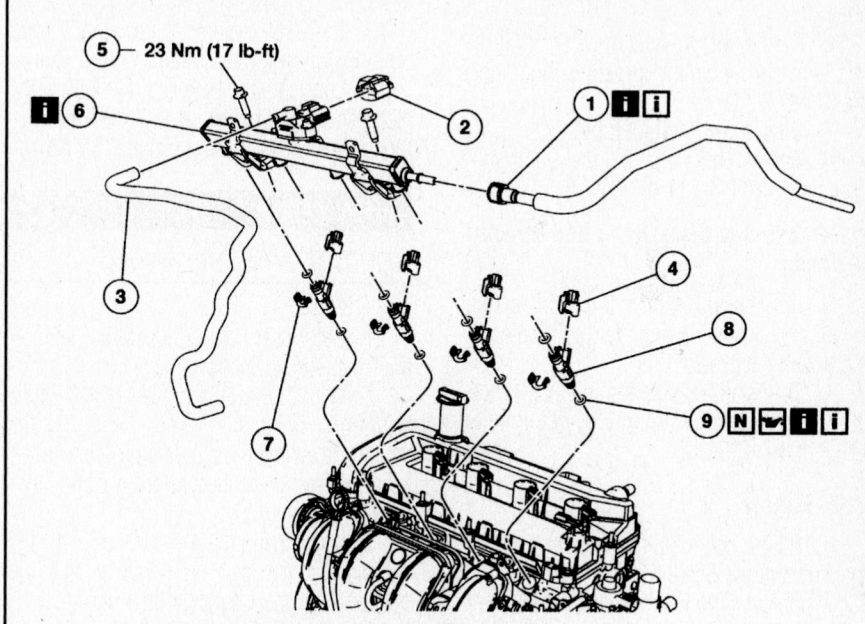

1 Fuel tube quick release coupling (position aside)
2 Fuel rail pressure and temperature sensor electrical connector
3 Fuel rail pressure and temperature sensor vacuum tube (position aside)
4 Fuel injector electrical connectors
5 Fuel rail bolts
6 Fuel rail
7 Fuel injector clips
8 Fuel injectors
9 Fuel injector O-ring seals

67197-ESCA-G35

Fig. 203 Fuel rail and injectors—2.3L engine

✳✳ WARNING

Do not smoke or carry lighted tobacco or open flame of any type when working on or near fuel-related components. Highly flammable vapors are always present and can ignite. Failure to follow these instructions can result in personal injury.

✳✳ WARNING

This procedure involves fuel handling. Be prepared for fuel spillage at all times and always observe fuel handling precautions. Failure to follow these instructions can result in personal injury.

1. Before servicing the vehicle, refer to the Precautions Section.
2. Disconnect the battery ground cable.
3. Release the fuel pressure.
4. Disconnect the fuel injector electrical connectors.
5. Disconnect the fuel pressure regulator electrical connector and the vacuum hose.
6. Disconnect the fuel injector harness retaining clips from the fuel injection supply manifold.
7. Disconnect the fuel tube.
8. Remove the bolts and the fuel injection supply manifold.

➡**Remove and discard the fuel injector O-rings.**

9. If necessary, remove the fuel injectors.
10. Install new O-rings and lubricate them with clean engine oil.
11. To install, reverse the removal procedure. Tighten the fuel supply manifold bolts to 18 ft. lbs. (25 Nm).

3.0L Engine

1. Before servicing the vehicle, refer to the Precautions Section.
2. Release the fuel system pressure
3. Disconnect the battery ground cable.
4. Remove the upper intake manifold.
5. Disconnect the fuel tube quick release coupling.
6. Disconnect the fuel rail pressure and temperature sensor vacuum tube
7. Disconnect the fuel rail pressure and temperature sensor electrical connector.
8. Disconnect the fuel injector electrical connectors.
9. Remove the fuel rail bolts.
10. Remove the fuel rail.

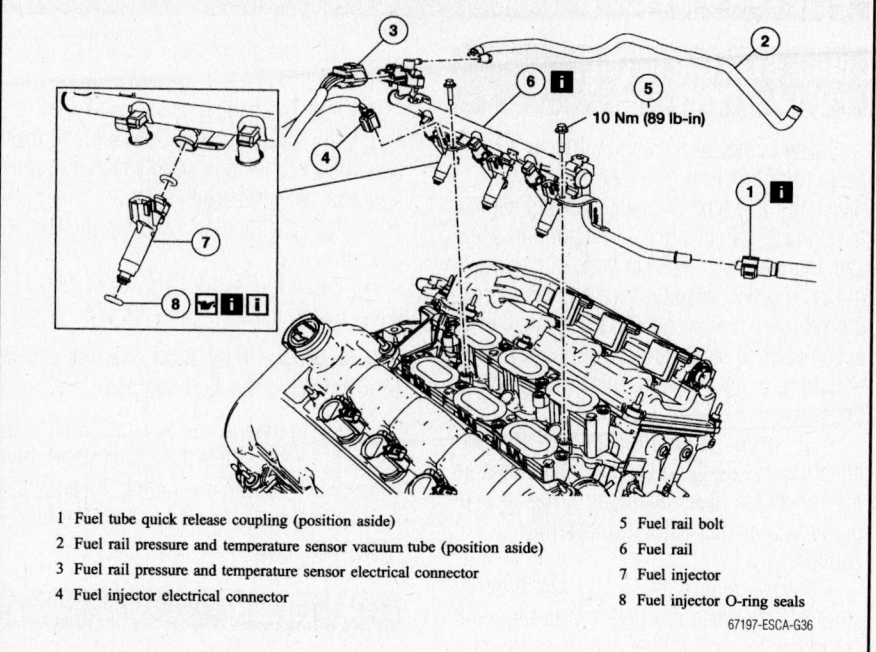

1   Fuel tube quick release coupling (position aside)
2   Fuel rail pressure and temperature sensor vacuum tube (position aside)
3   Fuel rail pressure and temperature sensor electrical connector
4   Fuel injector electrical connector
5   Fuel rail bolt
6   Fuel rail
7   Fuel injector
8   Fuel injector O-ring seals

67197-ESCA-G36

Fig. 204 Fuel rail and injectors—3.0L engine

11. Remove the fuel injector.
12. Remove the fuel injector O-ring seals.
13. To install, reverse the removal procedure. Install new fuel injector O-ring seals.
14. Lubricate the new O-ring seals with clean engine oil before installing. Torque the fuel rail bolts to 89 inch lbs. (10 Nm).

FUEL PUMP

REMOVAL & INSTALLATION

See Figure 205.

1. Before servicing the vehicle, refer to the Precautions Section.
2. With the vehicle in NEUTRAL, position it on a hoist.
3. Release the fuel system pressure.
4. Disconnect the battery ground cable.
5. If removing the fuel tank on a 4WD vehicle, it is necessary to lower the exhaust system from the catalytic converter back. Support the exhaust system with a suitable stand, release the three rear exhaust hangers and carefully lower the exhaust system to allow enough clearance to remove the fuel tank.
6. If removing the fuel tank on a four wheel drive vehicle, remove the rear driveshaft..
7. Lift the left rear seat cushion, position the carpet aside and remove the screws and the fuel pump module access cover.

8. Disconnect the fuel pump module electrical connector.
9. Fuel vapor control tube assembly valve electrical connector.
10. Using a suitable fuel pump lock ring remover, rotate the lock ring counterclockwise and remove.

✳✳ WARNING

The fuel pump module must be handled carefully to avoid damage to the float arm and filter.

✳✳ WARNING

Some fuel will remain in the fuel pump module after draining the fuel tank. Carefully drain the fuel pump module into a suitable container.

11. Prior to completely removing the fuel pump, position it aside and using the special tool and a suitable fuel recovery system, drain the fuel tank.
12. To release the bottom-mounted fuel pump module, reach into the fuel pump module opening and squeeze the retainer tabs on the pump module housing and pull upward.
13. Remove the fuel pump module O-ring seal.

To install:

14. Turn the ignition key to the ON position to pressurize the fuel system.
15. Visually inspect the fuel system for leaks.

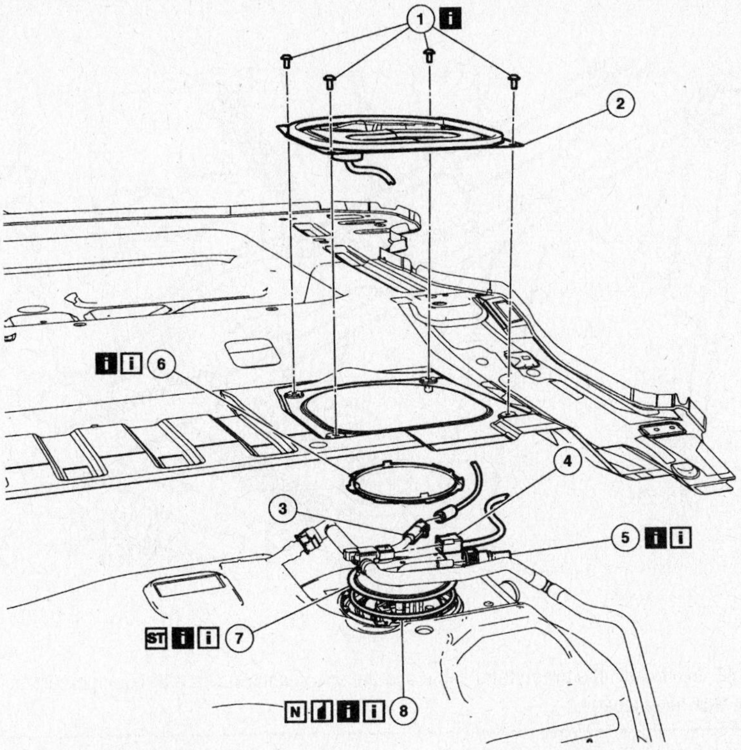

1 Fuel pump module access cover screws
2 Fuel pump module access cover
3 Fuel pump module electrical connector
4 Fuel vapor control tube assembly valve electrical connector
5 Fuel supply tube quick connect coupling
6 Fuel pump module lock ring
7 Fuel pump module
8 Fuel pump module O-ring seal

67197-ESCA-G34

Fig. 205 Access to fuel pump module—2005 model shown, other years similar

❋❋ WARNING

Make sure the fuel tube clicks into place when installing the tube. To make sure the tube is fully seated, pull on the tube.

➡**Apply clean engine oil to the end of the tube before inserting the tube into the connector.**

16. Install the fuel tube quick release coupling.

❋❋ WARNING

Inspect the surfaces of the fuel pump module flange and fuel tank O-ring contact surfaces. Do not polish or adjust the O-ring contact area of the fuel pump flange or fuel tank. Install a new fuel pump module or fuel tank if the O-ring contact area is bent, scratched or corroded.

❋❋ WARNING

Make sure to install a new fuel pump module O-ring and lock ring.

17. Lubricate and install a new fuel pump module O-ring seal upon installing the fuel pump module.

18. When installing the fuel pump module, make sure to align the locator tabs on the fuel tank mounting flange.

➡**Be sure the aligning tabs of the fuel pump module unit are positioned in the slot before tightening the lock ring.**

19. Holding the fuel pump module O-ring seal in place, rotate the lock ring clockwise until it stops against the retainer tabs.

➡**Make sure the collar on the fuel tube is inserted fully into the quick release coupling before the locking tab is locked.**

20. Connect the fuel supply quick connect coupling to the fuel supply manifold.

21. Press the fuel supply quick connect coupling locking tab into position.

22. Pull on the fitting to make sure it is fully engaged.

FUEL TANK

REMOVAL & INSTALLATION

1. Disconnect the negative battery cable.
2. With the vehicle in NEUTRAL, position it on a hoist.
3. Drain the fuel tank.

➡**All wheel drive (AWD) vehicles, remove the exhaust muffler and resonator and rear driveshaft.**

4. Release the clamp and remove the fuel tank filler pipe hose from the fuel tank.
5. Position a suitable lifting device under the fuel tank.
6. Detach the 2 retainer clips from the LH fuel tank strap.
7. Remove the 2 bolts and position the 2 fuel tank straps aside
8. Partially lower the fuel tank enough to disconnect the fuel vapor tube assembly-to-fuel tank quick connect coupling.
9. Remove the fuel tank.

To install:

10. Install fuel tank.
11. Connect fuel vapor tube assembly to fuel tank before completely raising fuel tank.
12. support fuel tank.
13. Reposition fuel tank straps and tighten bolts to 41 ft. lbs. (55 Nm).
14. Remove fuel tank support.
15. Install retainer clips to LH fuel strap.
16. Install fuel tank filler pipe and tighten hose clamp.
17. Connect the negative battery cable.
18. Install exhaust and rear drive shaft if they were removed for (AWD) models.
19. Lower vehicle and refill fuel tank
20. Connect the negative battery cable.

IDLE SPEED

ADJUSTMENT

Idle speed is maintained by the Powertrain Control Module (PCM). No adjustment is necessary or possible

THROTTLE BODY

REMOVAL & INSTALLATION

2.3L Engine

❋❋ WARNING

Throttle body bore and plate area have a special coating and cannot be cleaned, or possible damage to the throttle body can occur.

1. Disconnect the negative battery cable.

2. Remove the air cleaner outlet pipe.

3. Remove the upper snow shield screw and pin-type retainer.

4. Remove the upper snow shield.

5. Detach the accelerator and speed control cables from the throttle body.

6. Disconnect the throttle position sensor electrical connector.

7. Remove the 4 bolts and the throttle body.

8. Inspect the throttle body gasket and install new as necessary.

To install:

9. To install, reverse the removal procedure. Note the following tightening specifications:

    a. Throttle body bolts: 89 inch lbs. (10 Nm).

    b. Upper snow shield: 89 inch lbs. (10 Nm).

3.0L Engine

See Figures 206 and 207.

❋❋ CAUTION

Do not smoke or carry lighted tobacco or open flame of any type when working on or near any fuel-related components. Highly flammable mixtures are always present and may be ignited. Failure to follow these instructions may result in personal injury.

❋❋ WARNING

Throttle body bore and plate area have a special coating and should not be cleaned.

1. Remove the air cleaner outlet tube.

2. Disconnect the accelerator cable and the speed control cable (if equipped) from the throttle body lever.

3. Disconnect the Throttle Position (TP) sensor electrical connector.

4. Remove the bolt and position the transmission vent tube and bracket aside.

5. Disconnect and plug the 2 throttle body coolant hoses.

6. Remove the bolt, the stud bolt and the throttle body.

7. Discard the gasket.

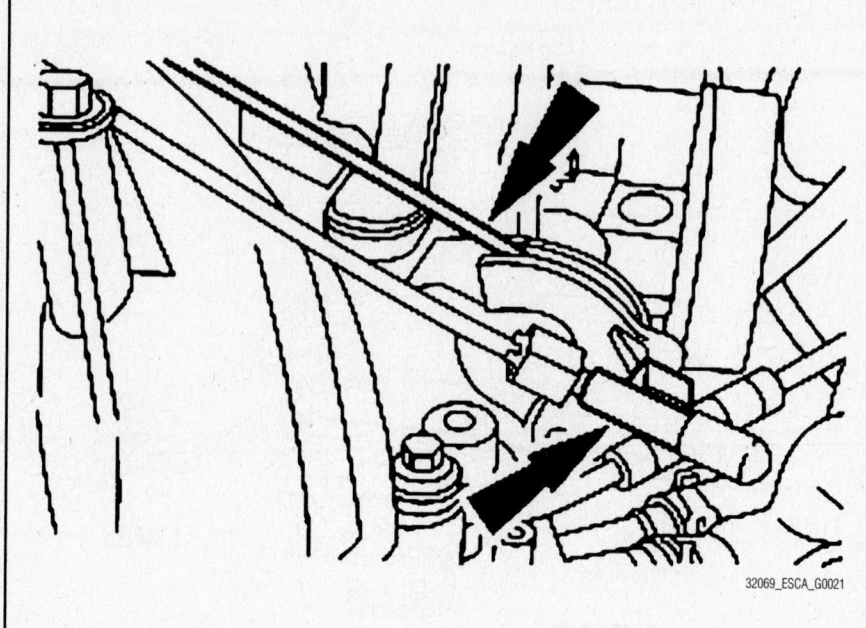

Fig. 206 Disconnect the accelerator cable and the speed control cable (if equipped) from the throttle body lever

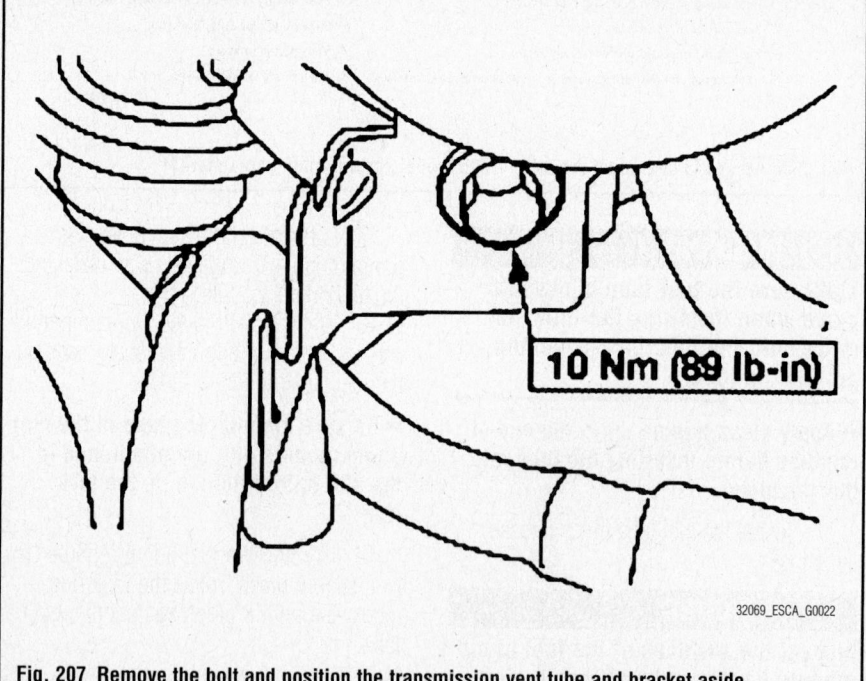

Fig. 207 Remove the bolt and position the transmission vent tube and bracket aside

To install:

8. Installation is the reverse of the removal procedure, noting the following:

  • Install a new gasket

  • Tighten the throttle body retainers to 89 inch lbs. (10 Nm).

  • Tighten the transmission vent tube and bracket bolt to 89 inch lbs. (10 Nm).

HEATING & AIR CONDITIONING SYSTEM

BLOWER MOTOR

REMOVAL & INSTALLATION

2005–07 Models

See Figure 208.

1. Remove the RH A-pillar lower trim.
2. Disconnect the blower motor electrical connector.
3. Remove the washer screws.
4. Remove the blower motor and cover, lower the assembly from the housing.
5. Installation is the reverse of the removal procedure.

2008 Models

1. Disconnect the blower motor electrical connector.
2. Release the 2 blower motor vent tube clips and pull the vent tube down until it is disengaged from the heater core and evaporator core housing.
3. The carpet below the blower motor must be slightly repositioned to remove the blower motor.
4. Rotate the blower motor counterclockwise to disengage it from the housing and remove the blower motor.
5. To install, reverse the removal procedure

HEATER CORE

REMOVAL & INSTALLATION

2005–07 Models

1. Before servicing the vehicle, refer to the Precautions Section.
2. Drain the engine coolant.
3. Release the 2 clamps and disconnect the 2 heater hoses from the heater core.
4. Disarm the Supplemental Restraint System (SRS), as outlined in the Chassis Electrical Section.
5. Position the seats forward and remove the 2 rear bolts.
6. Position the seats rearward and disconnect the battery.
7. Position the parking brake handle to the full-up position.
8. Remove the transmission selector lever bezel.
9. Release the parking brake handle boot from the floor console finish panel.
10. On the Mariner, remove the floor console top panel.

➥On Escape, if removing the floor console storage bin, squeeze the front and rear of the storage bin to release the retaining tabs from the floor console finish panel.

11. Remove the floor console finish panel. Disconnect the electrical connectors.
12. Remove the 6 bolts and remove the floor console.
13. Remove the 4 pin-type retainers and the 2 front door scuff plates.
14. Remove the 2 pin-type retainers and the 2 A-pillar lower trim panels.
15. Remove the instrument panel steering column opening cover.
16. Remove the left and right instrument panel end trim panels.
17. Lower the tilt steering column to the lowest position.
18. Remove the 2 screws and the instrument cluster finish panel.
19. Remove the 4 instrument cluster screws and the instrument cluster. Disconnect the electrical connector.
20. Disconnect the main electrical connector.

21. Remove the ground wire bolt and position the ground wire aside.
22. Remove the 2 bolts and position the hood release handle aside.
23. Remove the steering column coupler access cover.
24. Remove the steering column pinch bolt and disconnect the intermediate shaft.
25. Remove the cover panel pin-type retainer and the cover panel. Release the retaining clip from the instrument panel center brace.
26. Disconnect the climate control vacuum harness connector.
27. Disconnect the Restraint Control Module (RCM) electrical connector.
28. Disconnect the temperature control cable from the blend door shaft.
   a. Align the locator holes.
   b. Release the locking tab.
   c. Disconnect the temperature control cable.

➥Automatic transmission selector lever is shown; the manual transmission selector lever is similar.

1   Temperature blend door lever
2   Heater core cover screws (3 required)
3   Heater core cover
4   Heater core

06017-ESCA-G17

Fig. 208 Heater core

29. Remove the 4 transmission selector lever bolts and position the transmission selector lever aside. Disconnect the electrical connectors.

30. Remove the bolts and position the parking brake control aside Disconnect the electrical connectors.

31. Open the glove compartment. Press the release tabs inward while lowering the glove compartment.

32. Disconnect the blower motor electrical connectors.

33. Disconnect the antenna cable in-line connector.

34. Remove the cover and the instrument panel cowl top bolt.

35. Remove the 4 instrument panel center brace bolts.

36. Remove the instrument panel cluster opening nut through the instrument cluster opening.

37. Remove the 4 instrument panel cowl side bolts.

➡**This step requires an assistant.**

38. Remove the instrument panel.

39. Remove the screw and the temperature blend door lever.

40. Remove the 3 screws and the heater core cover.

41. Remove the heater core from the housing.

➡**Make sure the temperature blend door actuator and switch are in the correct position when installing the temperature blend door lever.**

➡**Lubricate the coolant hoses with plain water only if needed.**

To install:

42. To install, reverse the removal procedure. Observe the following torques:
- the 4 instrument panel cowl side bolts: 80 inch lbs. (9 Nm).
- the instrument panel cluster opening nut: 80 inch lbs. (9 Nm).
- The 4 instrument panel center brace bolts: 18 ft. lbs. (25 Nm).
- The instrument panel cowl top bolt: 53 inch lbs. (6 Nm).
- The parking brake control: 18 ft. lbs. (24 Nm).
- The 4 transmission selector lever bolts: 16 ft. lbs (22 Nm). for automatic transaxle; 15 ft. lbs. (20 Nm). for manual transaxle.
- The steering column pinch bolt: 17 ft. lbs. (23 Nm).
- The hood release handle: 53 inch lbs. (6 Nm).

43. Fill and bleed the engine cooling system.

44. If equipped with automatic transmission, adjust the linkage.

45. Rearm the supplemental restraint system.

46. Following installation of the new instrument cluster, download the module configuration information from the diagnostic tool into the new module as follows:

Using the Vehicle Communication Module (VCM) When the Original Body Chassis Electrical Module is Not Available

47. Install the new module.

48. Using the VCM and the latest version of the service function card, SELECT: Programmable Module Installation.

49. Select the module being installed.

50. Follow the on-screen instructions.

51. SELECT: Retrieve Module Configuration—Old ECU and press trigger.

52. Follow the on-screen instructions.

53. The VCM attempts to retrieve the module data from the Powertrain Control Module (PCM). If the module data is available, go to Step A. If the VCM displays: Call As-Built Data Center, go to Step B.

Step A

54. SELECT: Restore Configuration—New ECU. Press trigger.

55. The VCM completes loading the retrieved data and displays Module Download Successful.

56. Test the module for correct operation.

Step B

57. Press the trigger.

58. If the VCM asks for vehicle data, enter the vehicle data, then press store.

59. The VCM asks for module data line 1. Enter the data and press store.

60. The VCM then asks if there is an additional line of data available for that address. Select YES or NO depending on the information in the As Built Data Sheet.

61. Repeat Steps 3 and 4 until the answer is NO for Step 4.

62. The VCM should show a screen stating that the module data was stored. Press the trigger.

63. Follow the on-screen instructions.

64. SELECT: Restore Configuration—New ECU. Press the trigger.

65. The VCM completes loading the retrieved data and displays Module Download Successful.

66. Test the module for correct operation.

Using the Vehicle Communication Module (VCM) When the Original Body Chassis Electrical Module is Available

67. With the original module still installed, using the VCM and the latest version of the service function card, SELECT: Programmable Module Installation.

68. Select the module being installed and press the trigger.

69. Follow the on-screen instructions.

70. SELECT: Retrieve Module Configuration—Old ECU. Press the trigger.

71. Follow the on-screen instructions.

72. INSTALL new module, SELECT: Restore Configuration—New ECU. Press the trigger.

73. The VCM completes loading the retrieved data and displays Module Download Successful.

74. Test the module for correct operation.

Using the Worldwide Diagnostic System (WDS) When the Original Body Chassis Electrical Module is Not Available

75. Install the new module.

76. Connect the WDS and ID the vehicle as normal.

77. From the Toolbox icon, select and highlight Module Programming. Then highlight the module that was installed and press the check mark.

78. Select and highlight Programmable Module Installation. Then highlight the module that was installed and press the check mark.

79. Follow the on-screen instructions, turn the ignition key to the OFF position and press the check mark.

80. The WDS retrieves the module data from the PCM, automatically downloads the data into the new module, and displays Module Configuration Complete.

81. If the data is not available in the PCM, the WDS displays a screen stating to contact the As-Built Data Center. Retrieve the data from WWW.FMCDEALER.COM at this time and press the check mark.

82. Enter the module data (the module address and line are displayed to the left of the 3 entry boxes) and press the check mark.

83. The WDS downloads the data into the new module and displays Operation Successful—Programming Complete.

84. Test the module for correct operation.

Using the Worldwide Diagnostic System (WDS) When the Original Body Chassis Electrical Module is Available

85. Connect the WDS and ID the vehicle as normal.

86. From the Toolbox icon, select and highlight Module Programming and press the check mark.

87. Select and highlight Programmable Module Installation.

88. Follow the on-screen instructions, turn the ignition key to the OFF position, and press the check mark.

89. Install the new module and press the check mark.

90. Follow the on-screen instructions, turn the ignition key to the ON position, and press the check mark.

91. The module configuration is complete.

92. Test the module for correct operation.

2008 Models

See Figures 209 and 210.

1. Before servicing the vehicle, refer to the Precautions Section.

2. Drain the engine coolant.

3. Recover the refrigerant.

4. Position the seats forward and remove the 2 floor console rear bolts

5. Position the seats rearward.

6. Remove the transmission selector lever trim ring.

7. Remove the floor console storage bin.

8. Remove the floor console finish panel.

9. Remove the 8 floor console bolts and remove the floor console.

10. Disarm the supplemental restraint system (SRS).

11. Remove the RH and LH A-pillar trim panels.

12. Remove the 4 pin-type retainers and the RH and LH front door opening scuff plates.

13. Remove the RH and LH lower A-pillar trim panels.

14. Remove the steering column opening cover.

15. Remove the RH and LH instrument panel side finish panels.

16. Disconnect the 2 electrical connectors at the LH side of the instrument panel.

17. Disconnect the main steering module electrical connector.

18. Remove the bolts and position aside the hood release handle and parking brake release handle.

19. Remove and slide the steering column intermediate shaft access cover and weather shield up the steering column intermediate shaft.

✳✳ WARNING

Do not allow the steering column shaft to rotate while the lower shaft is disconnected or damage to the clockspring can result. If there is evidence that the shaft has rotated, the clockspring must be removed and re-centered.

20. Remove and discard the steering column intermediate shaft-to-coupling bolt and slide the steering column intermediate shaft up.

21. Remove scrivet and the Restraints Control Module (RCM) access cover.

22. Disconnect the LH RCM electrical connector.

23. For vehicles with automatic transmissions remove the selector lever cable from the selector lever assembly.

24. For vehicles with manual transmissions remove the shift cables from the shift lever assembly.

25. Disconnect the selector lever electrical connector and wiring harness pin-type retainers from the selector lever assembly.

26. If equipped, remove and position aside the Four Wheel Drive (4WD) control module and bracket from the selector lever assembly.

27. Remove the 4 selector lever assembly bolts and remove the selector lever assembly.

28. Disconnect the electrical connectors from the Smart Junction Box (SJB).

29. Disconnect the wiring harness pin-type retainers.

30. Remove the SJB lower bolts and the SJB.

31. Disconnect the 2 electrical connectors at the RH side of the instrument panel.

32. Disconnect the antenna cable in-line connector

33. Remove the LH and RH windshield wiper pivot arms.

34. Remove the cowl panel cover

35. Remove the 3 windshield wiper mounting arm and pivot shaft assembly bolts and position aside the windshield wiper mounting arm and pivot shaft assembly.

36. Remove the 3 instrument panel upper cowl bolts.

37. Remove the 4 instrument panel center brace bolts

38. Remove the 4 instrument panel side bolts.

➡**To avoid damage to the instrument panel, an assistant is required for this step.**

➡**Before removing the instrument panel, make sure that all electrical wiring is free and not hindered**

39. Remove the instrument panel.

40. Remove the Thermostatic Expansion Valve (TXV) fitting nut and disconnect the fitting.

41. Release the clamps and disconnect the heater inlet and outlet hoses from the heater core.

42. Remove the 6 heater core and evaporator core housing nuts.

43. Detach the heater core and evaporator core housing from the dash panel studs

44. Rotate the RH side of the heater core and evaporator core housing toward the rear of the vehicle while pulling the housing toward the RH door opening to detach it from the rear footwell duct.

45. Remove the heater core and evaporator core housing

46. Remove the dash panel seal.

47. Remove the heater core bracket screw and the heater core bracket

48. Remove the heater core.

To install:

49. Install heater core

50. Install heater core bracket screws and tighten to 27 inch lbs. (3 Nm).

51. Install the dash panel seal.

52. Install heater core and evaporator core housing.

53. Tighten core housing nuts to 80 inch lbs. (9 Nm).

54. Connect and tighten the heater inlet and outlet hoses to the heater core.

55. Install the thermostatic expansion valve (TXV) fitting nut and disconnect the fitting.

56. Install the instrument panel.

57. Install 2 instrument panel side bolts, one on each side, to hold the instrument panel in place.

58. Install the 3 instrument panel upper cowl bolts and tighten to 15 ft. lbs. (20 Nm).

59. Install the windshield wiper mounting arm and pivot shaft assembly and the 3 windshield wiper mounting arm and pivot shaft assembly bolts tighten to 9 ft. lbs. (12 Nm).

60. Install the cowl panel cover.

61. Install the LH and RH windshield wiper pivot arms.

62. Install the instrument panel side bolts and tighten to 8 ft. lbs. (11 Nm).

63. Install the instrument panel center brace bolts and tighten to 15 ft. lbs. (20 Nm).

64. Connect the antenna cable in-line connector.

65. Connect the electrical connectors at the RH side of the instrument panel

66. Install the SJB, bolts and connect the wiring harness pin-type retainers.

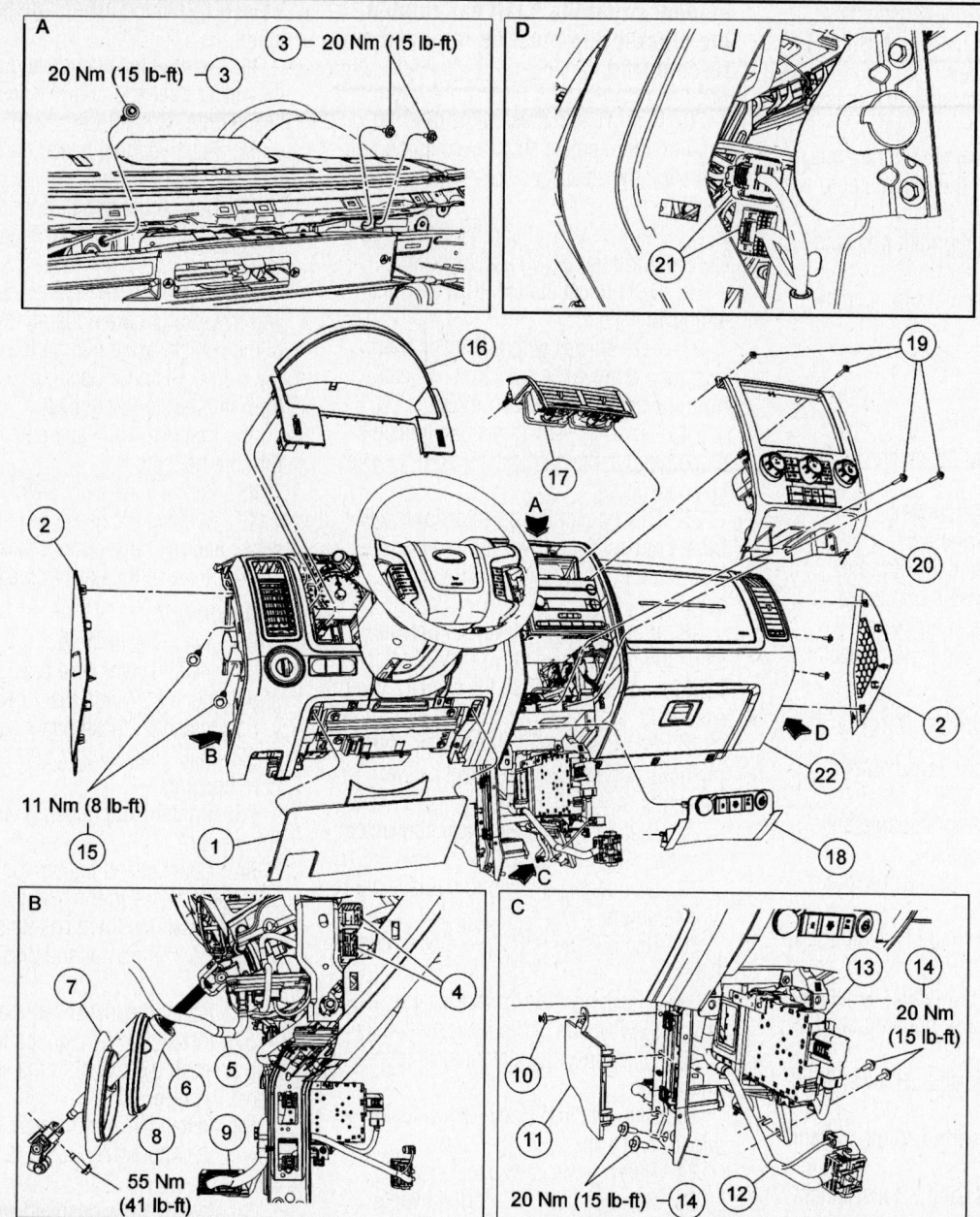

1. Steering column opening cover
2. Instrument panel side finish panel
3. Instrument panel upper cowl bolts (3 required)
4. LH side instrument panel electrical connectors
5. Steering module electrical connector
6. Steering column shaft access cover
7. Steering column shaft weather shield
8. Steering column intermediate shaft-to-coupling bolt
9. Restraints control module (RCM) electrical wiring harness
10. Scrivet
11. RCM access cover
12. Floor console electrical wiring harness
13. Smart junction box (SJB)
14. Instrument panel center brace bolts (4 required)
15. Instrument panel side bolts (4 required)
16. Instrument cluster finish panel
17. Upper instrument panel center finish panel
18. Lower instrument panel center finish panel
19. Middle instrument panel center finish panel screws (4 required)
20. Middle instrument panel center finish panel
21. RH side instrument panel electrical connectors
22. Instrument panel

22086_ESCA_G0049

Fig. 209 Instrument panel exploded view

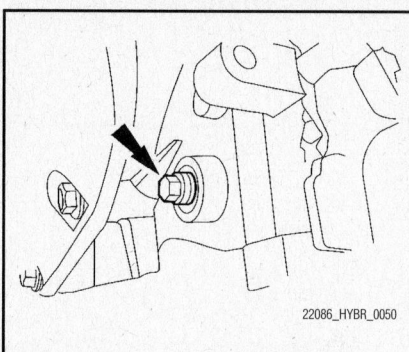

Fig. 210 Heater core and related parts

67. Connect the electrical connectors to the SJB.

68. Install the selector lever assembly and the 4 selector assembly bolts and tighten to 18 ft. lbs (25 Nm).

69. If equipped, install the 4WD control module and bracket onto the selector lever assembly.

70. Connect the selector lever electrical connector.

71. Install the wiring harness pin-type retainers to the selector lever assembly.

72. Vehicles with automatic transmissions, install the selector lever cable to the selector lever assembly.

73. Vehicles with manual transmissions, install the shift cables to the shift lever assembly.

74. Connect the LH RCM electrical connector

75. Install the RCM access cover and scrivet

76. Slide the steering column intermediate shaft down onto the coupling and install a new steering column intermediate shaft-to-coupling bolt, tighten to 42 ft. lbs. (55 Nm).

77. Install the steering column intermediate shaft access cover and weather shield.

78. Install the hood release and parking brake release handles and bolts.

79. Connect the main steering module electrical connector.

80. Connect the electrical connectors at the LH side of the instrument panel

81. Install the RH and LH instrument panel side finish panels

82. Install the steering column opening cover.

83. Install the RH and LH lower A-pillar trim panels.

84. Install the RH and LH A-pillar trim panels

85. Install the RH and LH front door opening scuff plates and the 4 pin-type retainers.

86. Rearm the SRS.

87. Install the 8 floor console bolts and the floor console.

88. Install the floor console finish panel.

89. Install the floor console storage bin.

90. Install the transmission selector lever trim ring.

91. Install and tighten the floor console rear bolts to 62 inch. lbs (7 Nm).

92. Evacuate, leak test and charge the refrigerant system.

93. Refill and bleed cooling system.

STEERING

POWER STEERING GEAR

REMOVAL & INSTALLATION

2005–07 Models

See Figure 211.

1. Before servicing the vehicle, refer to the Precautions Section.

2. With the vehicle in NEUTRAL, position it on a hoist.

3. Vehicles equipped with 3.0L engine, remove the EGR valve.

   a. Disconnect the exhaust manifold-to-exhaust gas recirculation (EGR) tube fitting from the EGR valve.

   b. Disconnect the vacuum tube fitting from the EGR valve.

➡**The EGR valve sealing surfaces are soft metals. Do not reuse the EGR valve gasket.**

   c. Remove the 2 bolts and the EGR valve. Remove and discard the EGR valve gasket.

4. Carefully clean the EGR valve sealing surfaces.

5. Remove the rear transaxle insulator bracket.

6. Remove the 3 bolts and the rear transaxle mounting plate.

➡**Do not loosen the tie-rod end nut to align the slot in the nut with the tie-rod end stud through-hole.**

7. Remove the 2 outer tie-rod end cotter pins and the 2 tie-rod end nuts.

8. Separate the tie-rod end from the knuckle.

✳✳ WARNING

Do not allow the steering wheel to rotate while the intermediate shaft is disconnected or damage to the clockspring can result. If there is evidence that the shaft has rotated, the clockspring must be removed and re-centered.

9. Hold the steering wheel in a straight-ahead position using a suitable tool.

10. Remove the nuts and the steering column boot.

11. Remove the steering column coupling-to-steering gear pinch bolt.

12. Remove the steering gear-to-fluid cooler return hose bracket-to-subframe bolt.

13. Remove the power steering pressure line bracket-to-steering gear bolt.

14. Remove the steering gear-to-fluid return hose bracket-to-steering gear stud.

15. Remove the power steering line clamp plate bolt.

➡**Install a new high pressure hose O-ring seal and a new return hose O-ring seal.**

16. Remove the power steering pressure and return lines.

17. Remove the 2 steering gear mounting bolts.

➡**Remove the steering gear from the right side of the vehicle.**

18. Remove the steering gear.

19. To install, reverse the removal procedure. Observe the following torques:

- Steering gear mounting bolts: 93 ft. lbs. (126 Nm)
- Power steering line clamp plate bolt: 18 ft. lbs. (25 Nm)
- Steering gear-to-fluid return hose bracket-to-steering gear stud: 89 inch lbs. (10 Nm)
- Power steering pressure line bracket-to-steering gear bolt: 89 inch lbs. (10 Nm)
- Steering gear-to-fluid cooler return hose bracket-to-subframe bolt: 89 inch lbs. (10 Nm)
- Steering column coupling-to-steering gear pinch bolt: 30 ft. lbs. (40 Nm)
- Outer tie-rod end cotter pins and the 2 tie-rod end nuts: 41 ft. lbs. (55 Nm). If necessary, continue to tighten the tie-rod end nut until the slot in the nut aligns with the tie-rod end stud through-hole.
- Rear transaxle mounting plate: 66 ft. lbs. (90 Nm)
- Rear transaxle insulator-to-bracket through-bolt: 66 ft. lbs. (90 Nm)

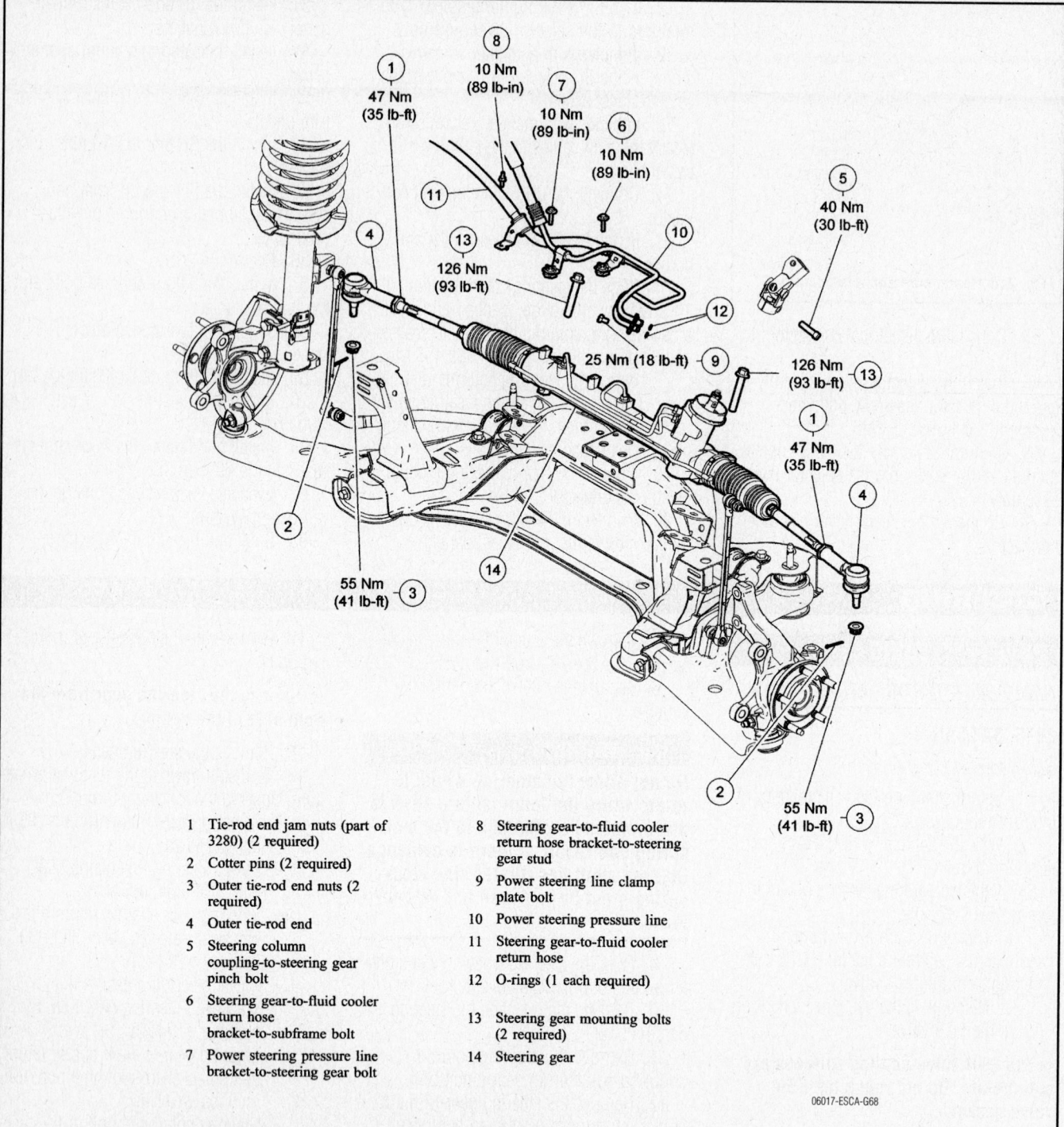

Fig. 211 Steering gear mounting—2005 models shown, other years similar

1. Tie-rod end jam nuts (part of 3280) (2 required)
2. Cotter pins (2 required)
3. Outer tie-rod end nuts (2 required)
4. Outer tie-rod end
5. Steering column coupling-to-steering gear pinch bolt
6. Steering gear-to-fluid cooler return hose bracket-to-subframe bolt
7. Power steering pressure line bracket-to-steering gear bolt
8. Steering gear-to-fluid cooler return hose bracket-to-steering gear stud
9. Power steering line clamp plate bolt
10. Power steering pressure line
11. Steering gear-to-fluid cooler return hose
12. O-rings (1 each required)
13. Steering gear mounting bolts (2 required)
14. Steering gear

06017-ESCA-G68

- Rear transaxle insulator bracket nuts: 66 ft. lbs. (90 Nm)
- Rear transaxle insulator bracket bolt: 66 ft. lbs. (90 Nm)
- EGR valve: 18 ft. lbs. (25 Nm)
- EGR tube fitting: 30 ft. lbs. (40 Nm)

20. Fill the power steering system.

21. Check and, if necessary, align the front end.

2008 Models

See Figures 212 and 213.

1. Remove the front wheels and tires.

2. Turn the ignition key to the OFF position. Remove the ignition key.

❊❊ WARNING

Do not allow the steering wheel to rotate while the intermediate shaft is disconnected or damage to the clock-spring can result. If there is evidence that the shaft has rotated, the clock-spring must be removed and re-centered

3. Remove and discard the steering column coupling-to-steering gear bolt and disconnect the coupling from the steering gear.

4. From the engine compartment, loosen the 2 steering gear bolts.

22086_ESCA_G0072

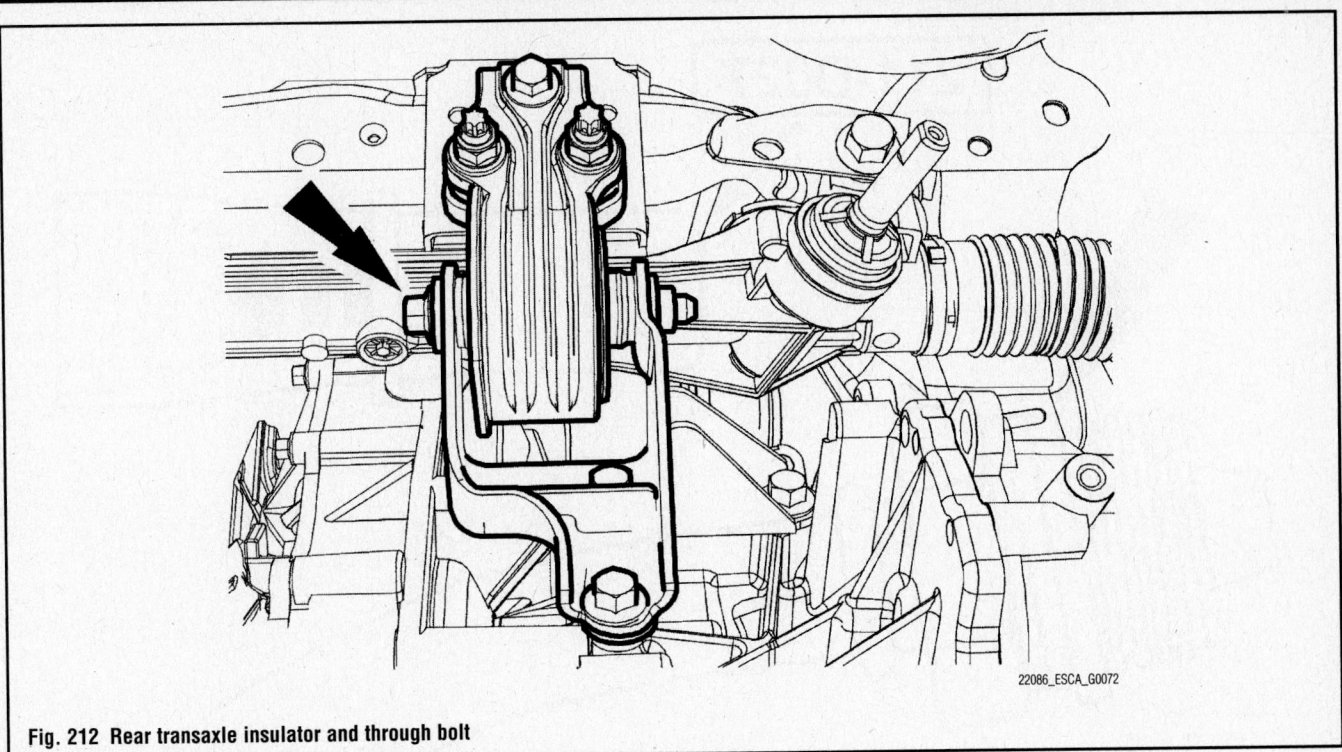

Fig. 212 Rear transaxle insulator and through bolt

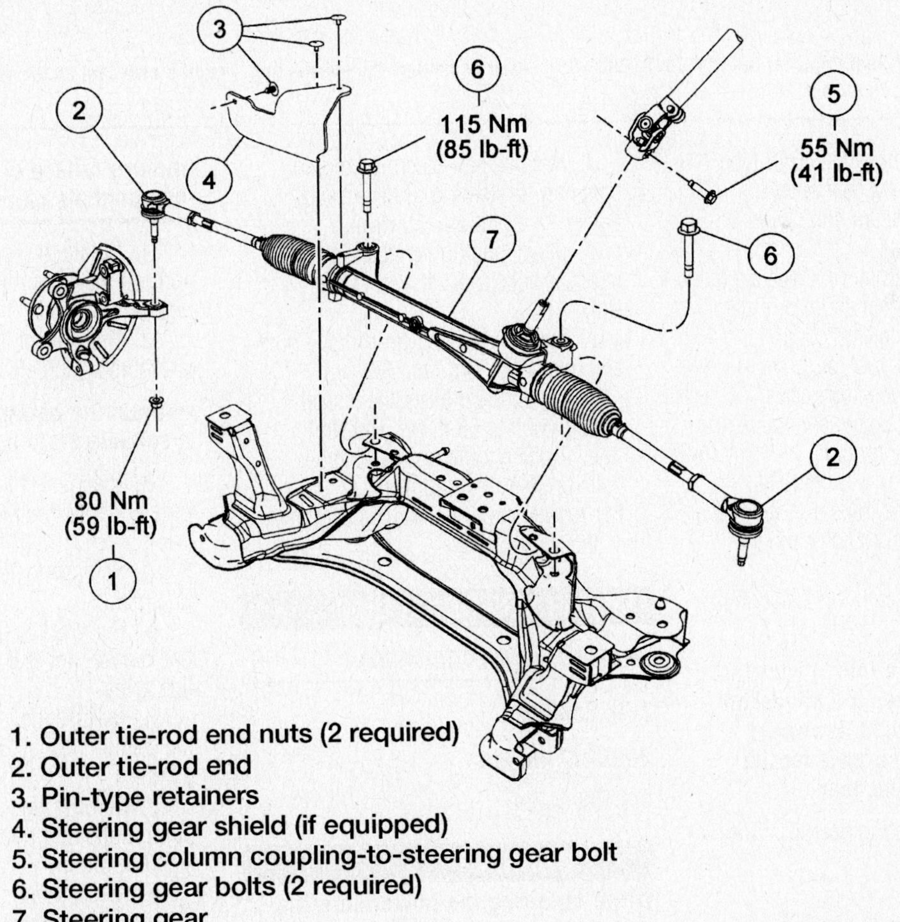

3
6
115 Nm
(85 lb-ft)
5
55 Nm
(41 lb-ft)
2
4
7
6
2
80 Nm
(59 lb-ft)
1
1. Outer tie-rod end nuts (2 required)
2. Outer tie-rod end
3. Pin-type retainers
4. Steering gear shield (if equipped)
5. Steering column coupling-to-steering gear bolt
6. Steering gear bolts (2 required)
7. Steering gear
22086_ESCA_G0073

Fig. 213 Steering gear exploded view—2008 model

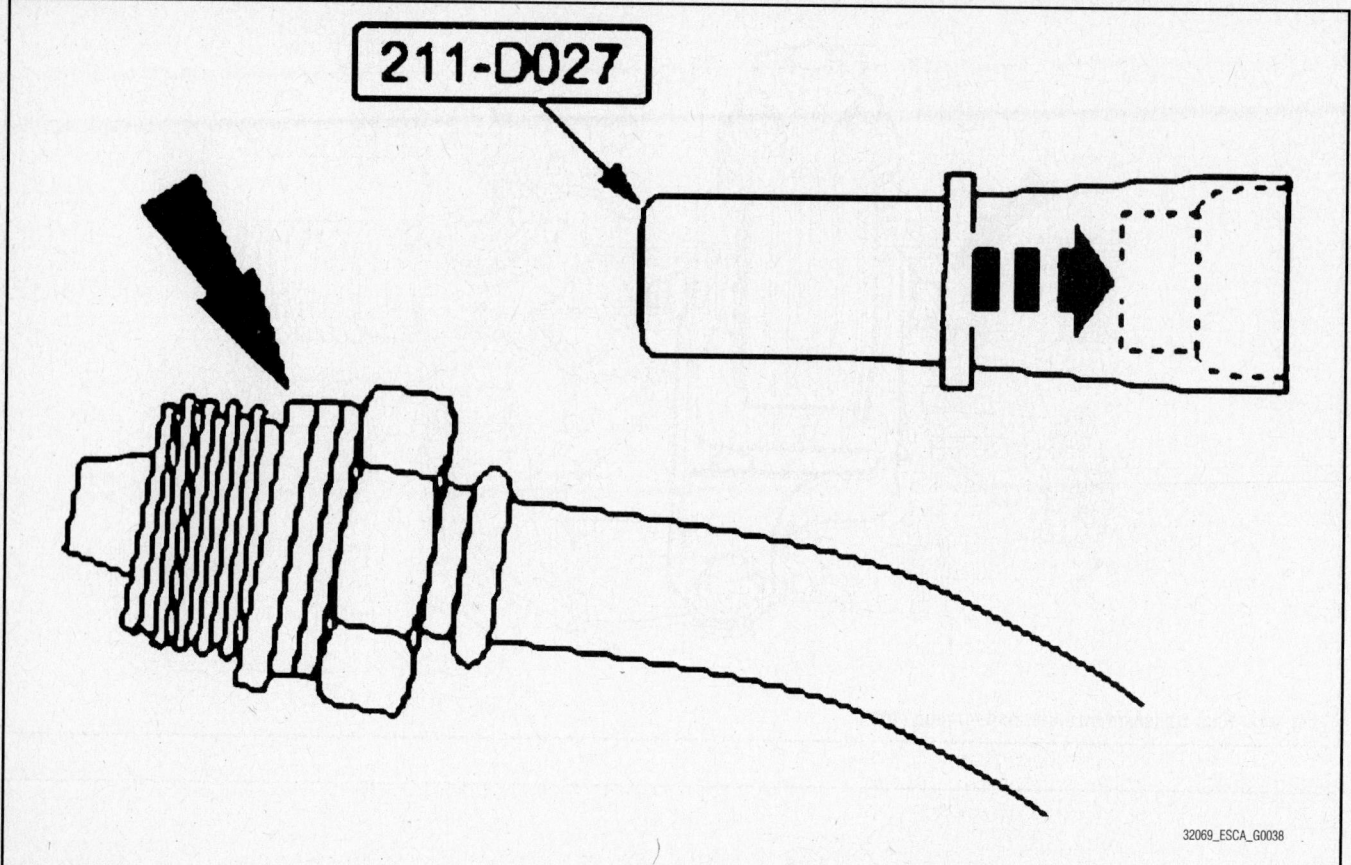

211-D027

Fig. 214 Using Teflon® Seal Replacer Set 211-D027 (D90P-3517-A) or equivalent the special tool, install a new seal on the power steering pressure hose fitting

5. If equipped, remove the 3 pin-type retainers and the steering gear shield.

6. Remove and discard the 2 outer tie-rod end nuts.

7. Do not use a hammer to separate the tie-rod end from the wheel knuckle or damage to the wheel knuckle can result.

8. Using a suitable tool, separate the tie-rod ends from the wheel knuckles.

9. For AWD vehicles, remove the rear transaxle insulator through bolt.

10. For FWD vehicles with the 2.3L engine and an automatic transaxle, remove the 3 transmission damper bolts and the transmission damper.

11. Remove and discard the 2 steering gear bolts.

➡For All Wheel Drive (AWD) vehicles, it is necessary to grasp the driveshaft by hand and apply slight downward pressure to obtain clearance for the removal of the steering gear.

12. Remove the steering gear from the LH side of the vehicle.

To install:

13. To install, reverse the removal procedure and note the following:

a. Install a new steering column coupling-to-steering gear bolt and tighten to 41 ft. lbs. (55 Nm).

b. Install and tighten the 2 steering gear bolts to 85 ft. lbs. (115 Nm).

c. Install new outer tie-rod end nuts and tighten to 59 ft. lbs. (80 Nm).

d. Tighten rear transaxle insulator through bolt to 66 ft. lbs. (90 Nm).

e. Tighten transmission damper bolts to 30 ft. lbs. (40 Nm).

14. Check and, if necessary, align the front end.

POWER STEERING PUMP

REMOVAL & INSTALLATION

2.3L Engine

2005–07 Models

See Figure 214.

❋❋ WARNING

While repairing the power steering system, care should be taken to prevent the entry of contaminants or pre-mature failure of the power steering components can result.

1. Rotate the tensioner clockwise and remove the belt from the power steering pump pulley.

2. Disconnect the power steering pressure switch electrical connector.

➡Drain the power steering fluid into a suitable drain pan.

3. Disconnect the power steering pressure line fitting nut from the power steering pump.

4. Remove the 2 lower power steering pump bolts.

5. Remove the power steering pressure line bracket nut and position the pressure line aside.

6. Release the clamp and disconnect the suction hose from the power steering pump.

7. Remove the 2 upper power steering pump bolts and remove the power steering pump.

8. If necessary, use Power Steering Pump Pulley Removal tool 211-016 (T69-10300B), or equivalent, to remove the steering pump pulley.

To install:

⁂ WARNING

Install a new power steering pump pulley after the second removal and installation. Inspect the pulley for paint marks in the web area near the hub. If there are no paint marks, or one paint mark, use a paint pencil to mark the web area of the pulley near the hub. Using Pump Pulley Replacer 211-185 (T91P-3A733-A), or equivalent special tool, install the power steering pump pulley.

9. Using Teflon® Seal Replacer Set 211-D027 (D90P-3517-A) or equivalent the special tool, install a new seal on the power steering pressure hose fitting:
   a. Remove and discard the original seal.
   b. Stretch the seal over the seal replacer and slide it onto the tube nut.
10. Position the power steering pump and install the upper bolts. Tighten to 18 ft. lbs. (25 Nm).
11. Connect the power steering suction hose and clamp.
12. Position the power steering pressure line bracket and install the nut. Tighten to 89 inch lbs. (10 Nm).
13. Raise the vehicle.
14. Install the lower power steering bolts. Tighten to 18 ft. lbs. (25 Nm).
15. Connect the power steering line fitting nut. Tighten to 48 ft. lbs. (65 Nm).
16. Connect the power steering pressure switch electrical connector.
17. Install the drive belt.
18. Fill and leak check the power steering system.

3.0L Engine

2005–07 Models

See Figure 215.

⁂ WARNING

While repairing the power steering system, care should be taken to prevent the entry of contaminants or premature failure of the power steering components can result.

1. Remove the power steering pump pulley.
2. Rotate the accessory drive belt tensioner counterclockwise and position the accessory drive belt aside.

➡Drain the power steering fluid into a suitable drain pan.

3. Release the clamp and remove the power steering fluid suction hose from the power steering pump.
4. Disconnect the power steering pressure line fitting nut from the power steering pump.
5. Remove the 3 power steering pump bolts.

⁂ WARNING

Do not let the flow control valve fall out of the power steering pump.

6. Remove the power steering pump.

➡A new power steering pump will be equipped with a power steering pressure line fitting (production purposes only) that must be removed and discarded to allow for connecting the existing fitting on the power steering pressure line.

To install:

7. To install, reverse the removal procedure and note the following:
   a. Tighten power steering pump pulley to 45 ft. lbs. (61 Nm).
   b. Tighten power steering pump mounting bolts 18 ft. lbs. (25 Nm).
   c. Tighten power steering pressure line fitting nut to 54 ft. lbs. (73 Nm).
8. Fill the power steering system and bleed out air.

BLEEDING

Power Steering System Filling

This procedure requires the use of the following special tools, or their equivalents:

- Vacuum Pump Kit 416-D002 (D95L-7559-A)
- Power Steering Evacuation Cap 211-265
- Power Steering Fill Adapter Manifold 211-327

⁂ WARNING

If the air is not purged from the power steering system correctly, premature power steering pump failure can result. The condition can occur on pre-delivery vehicles with evidence of aerated fluid or on vehicles that have had steering component repairs.

1. Remove the power steering pump reservoir cap.
2. Tightly install the evacuation cap to the power steering pump reservoir.
3. Install the hose from the fill adapter manifold tee to the evacuation cap on the power steering pump reservoir.
4. Install the vacuum pump to the fill adapter manifold control valve.
5. Install the hose to the opposite fill adapter manifold control valve and submerge the open end of the hose into a container of new power steering fluid.

➡The fill adapter manifold control valves are in the open position when the point of the handles face the center of the fill adapter manifold.

6. Close the fill adapter manifold control valve connected to the power steering fluid container.
7. Open the fill adapter manifold control valve connected to the vacuum pump.
8. Using the vacuum pump, apply 68-85 kPa (20-25 in-Hg) of vacuum to the power steering system.
9. Observe the vacuum gauge for 30 seconds.
10. If the vacuum gauge reading drops more than 3 kPa (0.88 in-Hg), correct any leaks in the power steering system or the filling tools before proceeding.

➡The vacuum pump gauge reading will drop slightly during this step. Slowly open the fill adapter manifold control valve connected to the power steering fluid container until power steering fluid completely fills the hose.

11. Close the fill adapter manifold control valve connected to the power steering fluid container.
12. Using the vacuum pump, apply 68-85 kPa (20-25 in-Hg) of vacuum to the power steering system.
13. Close the fill adapter manifold control valve connected to the vacuum pump.
14. Slowly open the fill adapter manifold control valve connected to the power steering fluid container.
15. When the power steering fluid has drained from the hose connected to the power steering fluid container, close the fill adapter manifold control valve connected to the power steering fluid container.
16. Remove the tools from the vehicle.
17. Install the power steering reservoir cap.

⁂ WARNING

Do not hold the steering wheel against the stops for more than 3 to 5 seconds at a time. Damage to the power steering pump can occur.

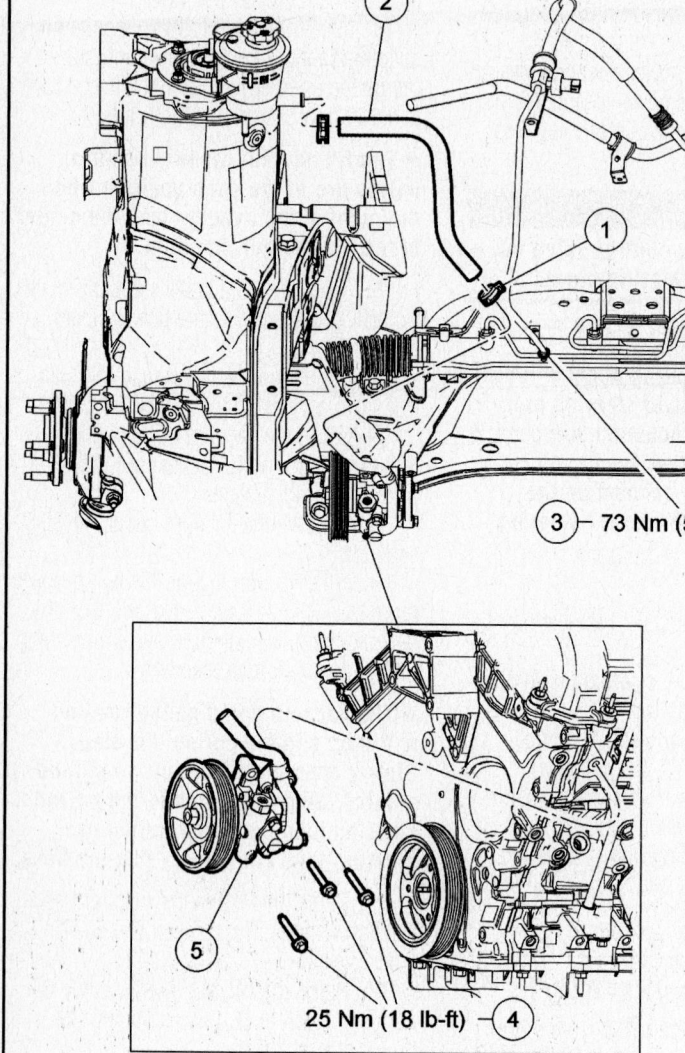

3 — 73 Nm (54 lb-ft)

5

25 Nm (18 lb-ft) — 4

1. Suction hose-to-power steering pump hose clamp
2. Suction hose
3. Power steering pressure line fitting nut
4. Power steering pump bolts (3 required)
5. Power steering pump

22086_ESCA_G0071

Fig. 215 Power steering view— 2005–07 models with 3.0L engine

➡There will be a slight drop in the power steering fluid level in the power steering fluid reservoir when the engine is started.

18. Start the engine and turn the steering wheel from stop-to-stop.

19. If equipped with Hydro-Boost®, apply the brake pedal twice.

20. Turn the ignition switch to the **OFF** position.

❊❊ **WARNING**

Do not overfill the reservoir.

21. Remove the power steering reservoir cap and fill the reservoir.

22. Install the power steering reservoir cap.

Power Steering System Purging

This procedure requires the use of the following special tools, or their equivalents:

• Vacuum Pump Kit 416-D002 (D95L-7559-A)

• Power Steering Evacuation Cap 211-265

❊❊ **WARNING**

If the air is not purged from the power steering system correctly, premature power steering pump failure

can result. The condition can occur on pre-delivery vehicles with evidence of aerated fluid or on vehicles that have had steering component repairs.

➡A whine heard from the power steering pump can be caused by air in the system. The power steering purge procedure must be carried out prior to any component repair for which power steering noise complaints are accompanied by evidence of aerated fluid.

1. Remove the power steering pump reservoir cap. Check the fluid.

2. Raise the front wheels off the floor.

3. Tightly insert the stopper of the vacuum pump into the reservoir.

4. Start the engine.

5. Install the vacuum pump, apply vacuum, and maintain the maximum vacuum of 68-85 kPa (20-25 in-Hg).

6. If equipped with Hydro-Boost®, apply the brake pedal twice.

✳ WARNING

Do not hold the steering wheel against the stops for more than 3 to 5 seconds at a time. Damage to the power steering pump can occur.

7. Cycle the steering wheel fully from stop-to-stop 10 times.

8. Stop the engine.

9. Release the vacuum and remove the vacuum pump.

✳✳ WARNING

Do not overfill the reservoir.

10. Fill the reservoir using the approved transmission fluid.

11. Start the engine.

12. Install the vacuum pump. Apply and maintain the maximum vacuum of 68-85 kPa (20-25 in-Hg).

✳✳ WARNING

Do not hold the steering wheel against the stops for more than 3 to 5 seconds at a time. Damage to the power steering pump can occur.

13. Cycle the steering wheel fully from stop-to-stop 10 times.

14. Stop the engine, release the vacuum and remove the vacuum pump.

✳✳ WARNING

Do not overfill the reservoir.

15. Fill the reservoir as needed and install the reservoir cap.

16. Visually inspect the power steering system for leaks.

✳✳ WARNING

Do not overfill the reservoir.

17. Fill the reservoir as needed and visually inspect the power steering system for leaks.

18. Install the reservoir cap.

SUSPENSION   FRONT SUSPENSION

COIL SPING

REMOVAL & INSTALLATION

See Figure 216.

1. Before servicing the vehicle, refer to the Precautions Section.

✳ CAUTION

Always wear safety goggles when using a spring compressor. Failure to follow these instructions may result in personal injury.

➡**Do not use an impact wrench on the nut.**

2. Mount the strut and spring assembly in a suitable spring compressor.

3. Compress the coil spring enough to relieve the tension on the strut assembly.

4. Remove the strut piston rod-to-bushing nut.

5. Remove the strut.

6. Remove the lower coil spring insulator.

7. Remove the coil spring.

8. Remove the upper coil spring insulator.

➡**During assembly, assemble the bearing plate to the strut so the arrow on the bearing plate points to the outboard side of the vehicle when the strut is installed.**

9. Remove the bearing plate.
10. Remove the bearing.
11. Remove the strut upper bushing.

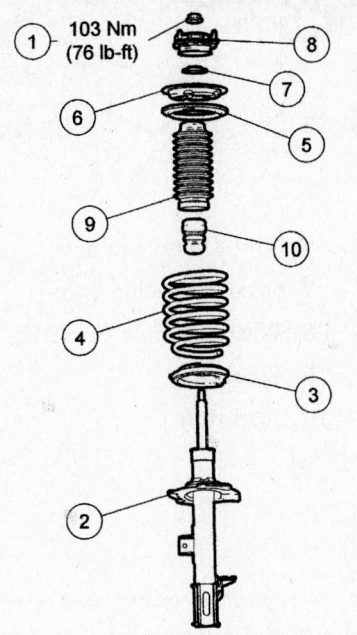

1   Strut piston rod-to-bushing nut
2   Strut (LH/RH)
3   Lower coil spring insulator
4   Coil spring
5   Upper coil spring insulator
6   Bearing plate
7   Bearing
8   Strut upper bushing
9   Dust boot
10 Bumper

06017-ESCA-G76

Fig. 216 Strut/spring disassembly— 2005 models shown, other years similar

12. Remove the dust boot and the bumper.

13. To assemble, reverse the disassembly procedure. Tighten the strut piston rod-to-bushing nut to 76 ft. lbs. (103 Nm).

LOWER BALL JOINT

REMOVAL & INSTALLATION

The lower ball joint is part of the lower control arm assembly.

LOWER CONTROL ARM

REMOVAL AND & INSTALLATION

See Figure 217.

1. Before servicing the vehicle, refer to the Precautions Section.

2. Remove the wheel.

3. Lift the lower arm with a floor jack until the vehicle starts to lift.

4. Record the ride height. It's measure from the center of the halfshaft to the fender lip.

5. Remove the floor jack.

6. Disconnect the ball joint from the knuckle.

7. Support the sub-frame and remove the lower arm.

To install:

8. Install the lower arm, with the bolts loose.

9. Connect the ball joint. Torque the bolt to 52 ft. lbs. (70 Nm).

10. Remove the support.

11. Position the jack under the ball joint

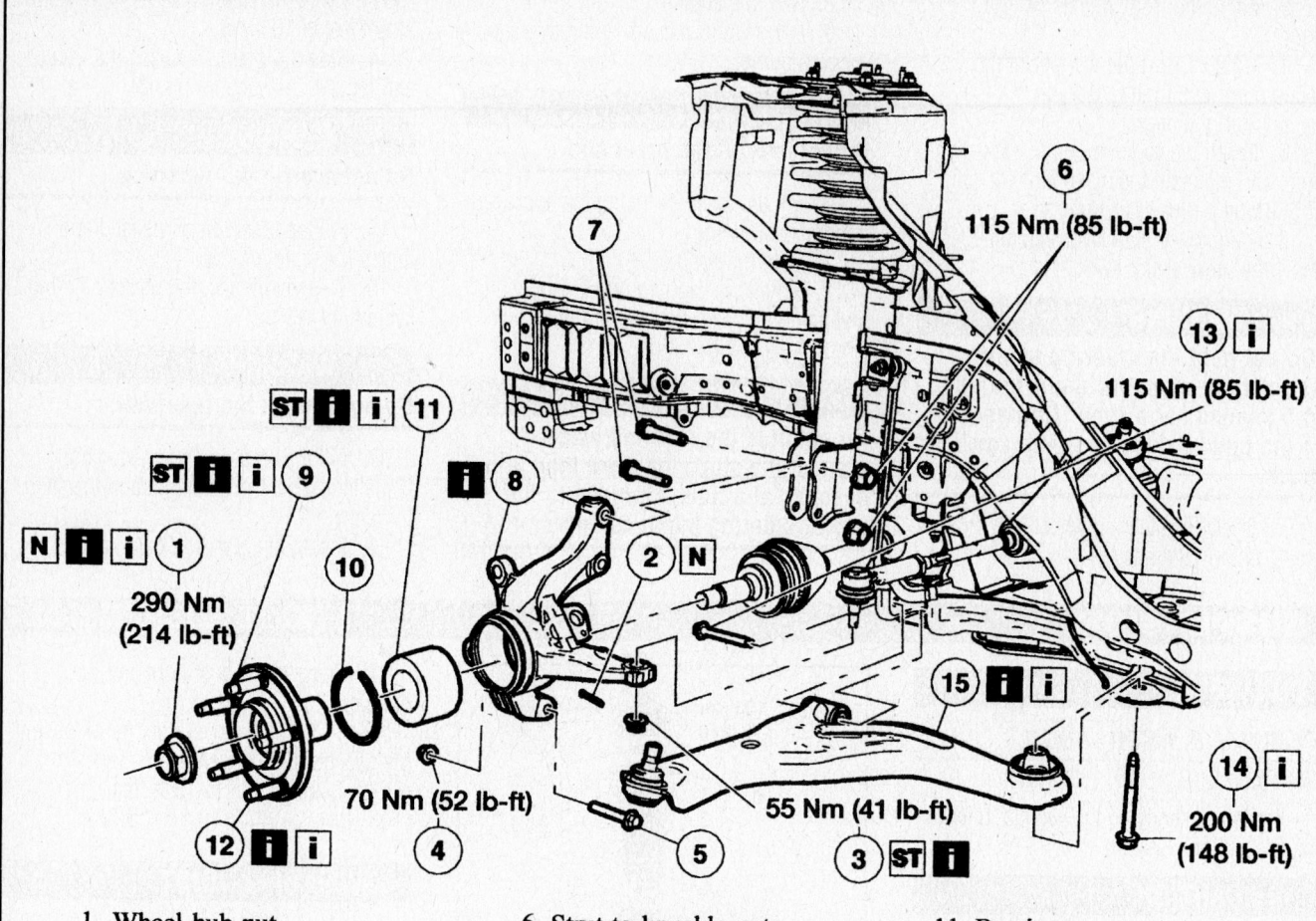

1 Wheel hub nut
2 Cotter pin
3 Tie rod end-to-knuckle nut
4 Lower ball joint pinch bolt
5 Lower ball joint pinch bolt

6 Strut-to-knuckle nuts
7 Strut-to-knuckle bolts
8 Wheel knuckle (LH/RH)
9 Wheel hub
10 Snap ring

11 Bearing
12 Wheel stud
13 Lower arm bolt (front)
14 Lower arm bolt (rear)
15 Lower arm

67197-ESCA-G48

Fig. 217 Front lower control arm assembly

and raise the arm to the previously recorded ride height.

12. Tighten the lower arm bolts. Horizontal 85 ft. lbs. (115 Nm); vertical 148 ft. lbs. (200 Nm).

MACPHERSON STRUT

REMOVAL & INSTALLATION

See Figure 218.

1. Before servicing the vehicle, refer to the Precautions Section.

➡**Make sure the steering wheel is in the unlocked position.**

➡**Use the hex holding feature to prevent the ball studs from turning while removing or installing the stabilizer bar link nuts.**

2. Raise and support the vehicle.
3. Remove the brake jounce hose clip.
4. Remove the brake jounce hose. Pull the brake jounce hose downward slightly to remove the hose from the bracket.
5. Remove the ABS sensor harness bolt.
6. Remove the stabilizer bar link nut.
7. Remove the strut-to-knuckle nuts.
8. Remove the strut-to-knuckle bolts.
9. Remove the strut upper bushing

nuts. Reference mark the strut mounting plate nuts.

10. Remove the strut and spring assembly.

✳ WARNING

Do not allow the axle shaft to move outboard. Over-extension of the tripod CV joint can result in separation of internal parts, causing failure of the axle shaft.

11. To install, reverse the removal procedure. See the illustration for the appropriate torque values.

12. Align the strut mounting plate nuts to the reference marks.

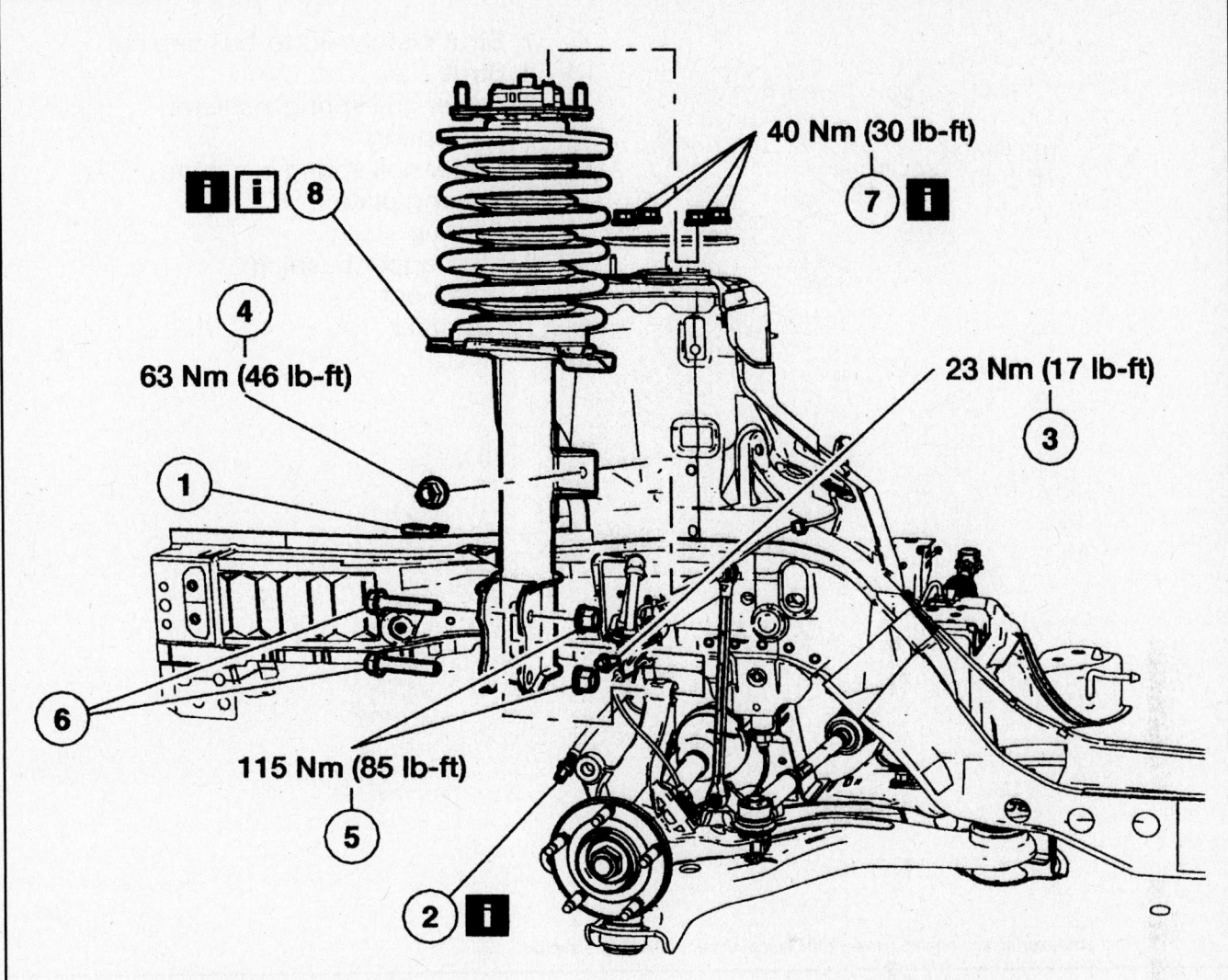

40 Nm (30 lb-ft)

63 Nm (46 lb-ft)

23 Nm (17 lb-ft)

115 Nm (85 lb-ft)

1 Brake jounce hose clip
2 Brake jounce hose (LH/RH)
3 ABS sensor harness bolt
4 Stabilizer bar link nut
5 Strut-to-knuckle nuts
6 Strut-to-knuckle bolts
7 Strut upper bushing nuts
8 Strut and spring assembly

67197-ESCA-G45

Fig. 218 Front strut installation—2005 model shown, other years similar

13. Check the front end alignment and adjust as necessary.

OVERHAUL

See Figure 219.

❊❊ CAUTION

Always wear safety goggles when using a spring compressor. Failure to follow these instructions may result in personal injury.

➡**Do not use an impact wrench on the nut. Mount the strut and spring assembly in a suitable spring compressor.**

1. Compress the coil spring enough to relieve the tension on the strut assembly.
2. Remove the strut piston rod-to-bushing nut.
3. Remove the strut.
4. Remove the lower coil spring insulator.
5. Remove the coil spring.

6. Remove the upper coil spring insulator.

➡**During assembly, assemble the bearing plate to the strut so the arrow on the bearing plate points to the outboard side of the vehicle when the strut is installed.**

7. Remove the bearing plate.
8. Remove the bearing.
9. Remove the strut upper bushing.
10. Remove the dust boot and the bumper.

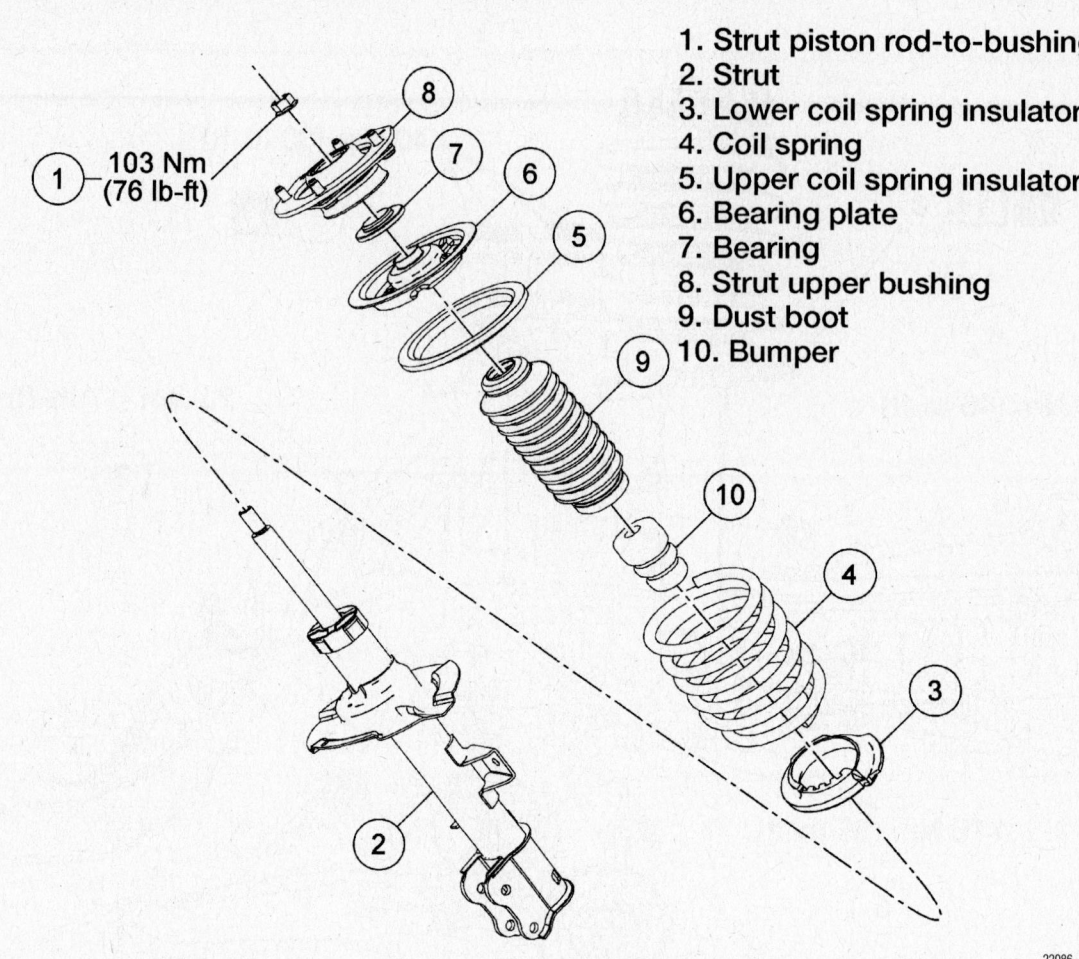

1. Strut piston rod-to-bushing nut
2. Strut
3. Lower coil spring insulator
4. Coil spring
5. Upper coil spring insulator
6. Bearing plate
7. Bearing
8. Strut upper bushing
9. Dust boot
10. Bumper

① 103 Nm (76 lb-ft)

22086_ESCA_G0041

Fig. 219 Front strut, spring and related parts—2008 model shown, other years similar

11. To assemble, reverse the disassembly procedure.

12. Replace any parts that show excessive wear or defects.

13. Tighten the strut piston rod-to-bushing nut to 76 ft. lbs. (103 Nm).

STABILIZER BAR

REMOVAL & INSTALLATION

1. Before servicing the vehicle, refer to the Precautions Section.

2. Remove the stabilizer bar bushing bracket bolts.

➡**Use the hex holding feature to prevent the ball stud from turning while removing or installing the stabilizer link nut.**

3. Remove the 2 lower stabilizer bar link nuts.

➡**Access the stabilizer bar through the left wheel opening.**

4. Remove the stabilizer bar.

5. To install, reverse the removal procedure. Observe the following torques:

- Link nuts: 41 ft. lbs. (55 Nm)
- Bushing bracket bolts: 52 ft. lbs. (70 Nm)

STABILIZER LINKS

REMOVAL & INSTALLATION

1. Before servicing the vehicle, refer to the Precautions Section.

2. Raise and support vehicle

3. Remove the wheel and tire.

➡**Use the hex holding feature to prevent the ball stud from turning while removing or installing the stabilizer bar link nut.**

4. Remove the upper stabilizer bar link nut.

5. Remove the lower stabilizer bar link nut.

6. Remove the stabilizer bar link.

7. Inspect the stabilizer bar link ball joints and boots for wear. If necessary, install new parts.

To install:

8. Install the stabilizer bar link.

9. Tighten the upper and lower stabilizer bar link nut to 41 ft. lbs. (55 Nm).

10. Install the wheel and tire.

11. Lower vehicle

STEERING KNUCKLE

REMOVAL & INSTALLATION

See Figures 220 and 221.

1. Before servicing the vehicle, refer to the Precautions Section.

2. Remove the brake disc.

3. Remove and discard the wheel hub nut.

4. Separate the outer CV-joint spindle from the wheel hub.

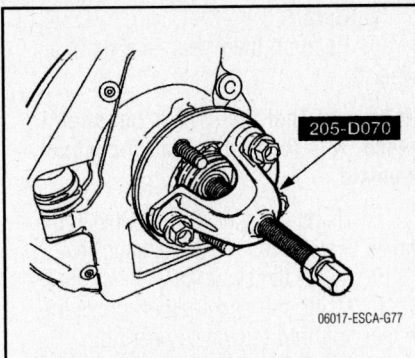

Fig. 220 Separate the outer CV-joint spindle from the wheel hub

5. Remove the cotter pin and the tie-rod end-to-knuckle nut.

✳✳ WARNING

Do not use a hammer to separate the tie-rod end from the wheel knuckle or damage to the wheel knuckle can result. Do not damage the tie-rod end boot while installing the special tool.

6. Separate the tie-rod from the wheel knuckle.

7. Remove the lower ball joint pinch bolt nut and the pinch bolt.

8. Remove the anti-lock brake system (ABS) wheel speed sensor bolt and position the sensor aside. Separate the lower ball joint from the wheel knuckle.

9. Remove the 2 strut-to-knuckle nuts, bolts and the wheel knuckle.

To install:

10. Position the wheel knuckle and install the 2 strut-to-knuckle bolts and nuts. Tighten to 85 ft. lbs. (115 Nm).

11. Position and align the ball joint stud into the wheel knuckle.

12. Install the lower ball joint pinch bolt and nut. Tighten to 52 ft. lbs. (70 Nm).

13. Install the ABS wheel speed sensor and the bolt. Tighten to 80 inch lbs.(9 Nm).

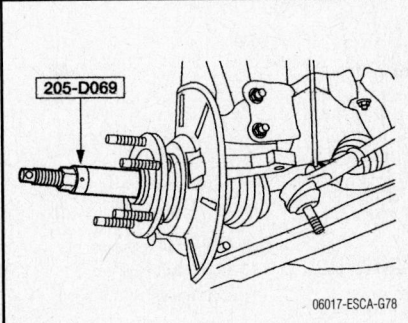

Fig. 221 Insert the halfshaft into the wheel hub

14. Position the tie rod-end into the wheel knuckle and install the tie-rod end-to-knuckle nut and a new cotter pin. Tighten to 41 ft. lbs. (55 Nm).

15. Insert the halfshaft into the wheel hub.

16. Install the wheel hub nut. Tighten to 221 ft. lbs. (300 Nm).

17. Install the brake disc.

18. Check and, if necessary, align the front end.

WHEEL BEARINGS

REMOVAL & INSTALLATION
See Figures 222 through 227.

1. Before servicing the vehicle, refer to the Precautions Section.

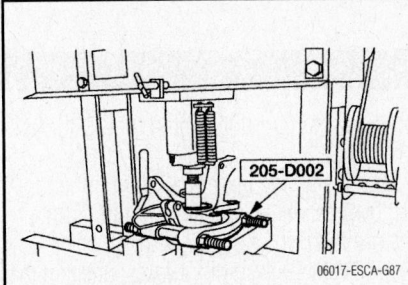

Fig. 222 Using the special tool, press the wheel hub from the wheel bearing—front hub/bearing

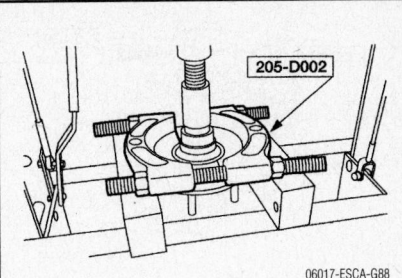

Fig. 223 Using the special tool, press the inner wheel bearing race from the wheel hub—front hub/bearing

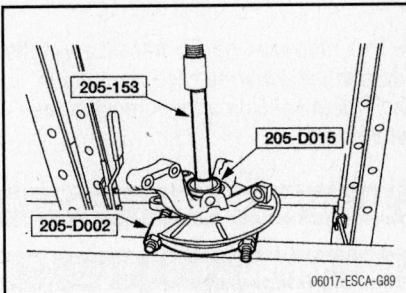

Fig. 224 Using the special tools, press the outer wheel bearing race from the wheel knuckle—front hub/bearing

➡ **If removing the wheel hub, the wheel bearing must be replaced.**

2. Remove the wheel knuckle.

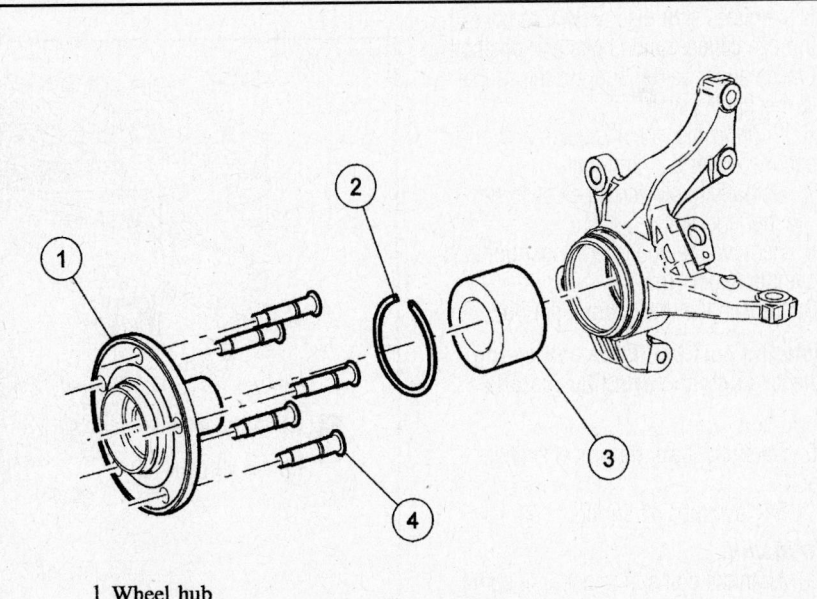

1 Wheel hub
2 Snap ring
3 Wheel bearing
4 Wheel studs (5 required)

Fig. 225 Front hub and bearing

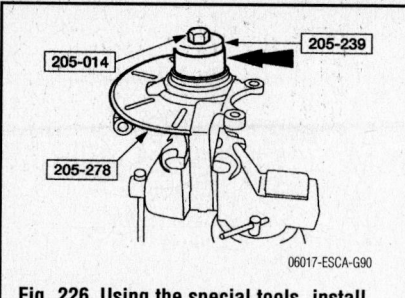

Fig. 226 Using the special tools, install the wheel bearing into the wheel knuckle—front hub/bearing

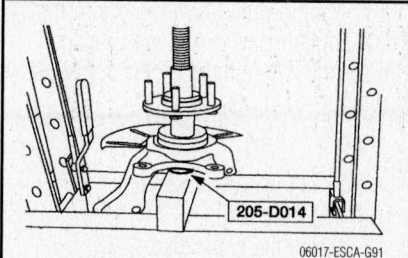

Fig. 227 Using the special tool, press the wheel hub into the wheel bearing—front hub/bearing

3. Using the special tool, press the wheel hub from the wheel bearing.

➡ **This step may not be necessary if the inner wheel bearing race remains in the wheel knuckle after removing the wheel hub.**

4. Using the special tool, press the inner wheel bearing race from the wheel hub.
5. Remove the snapring.
6. Using the special tools, press the outer wheel bearing race from the wheel knuckle.

To install:

7. Position the wheel knuckle in a vise.

➡ **Special Tool 205-278 is not seen in place. It is located behind the wheel knuckle.**

8. Using the special tools, install the wheel bearing into the wheel knuckle.
9. Install the snapring.
10. Using the special tool, press the wheel hub into the wheel bearing.
11. Install the wheel knuckle.

ADJUSTMENT

No adjustment is required or possible.
1. If the tire and wheel (hub) is loose on the spindle, does not rotate freely, or has a rough feeling when spun, install a new wheel bearing.

SUSPENSION

COIL SPRING

REMOVAL & INSTALLATION

1. Before servicing the vehicle, refer to the Precautions Section.
2. With the vehicle in NEUTRAL, position it on a hoist.
3. Remove the brake hose bracket-to-wheel knuckle bolt.
4. Vehicles with drum brakes, disconnect the brake line from the wheel cylinder.
5. Vehicles with disc brakes, remove the 2 brake caliper guide bolts and position the brake caliper aside. Support the caliper using mechanic's wire.
6. Support the wheel knuckle and remove the upper ball joint nut.
7. Remove the lower shock absorber nut, washer and bolt.
8. Remove the upper arm inner bolt and remove the upper arm.
9. Loosen the lower arm inner bolt.

➡ **Note the position of the coil spring insulator and coil spring for installation.**

10. Carefully lower the wheel knuckle support.
11. Remove the coil spring.

To install:

12. Align the coil spring and coil spring insulator to the previously noted position.
13. Carefully raise the wheel knuckle support.
14. Position the upper control arm and install the upper arm inner bolt tighten to 85 ft. lbs. (115 Nm).
15. Install the lower shock absorber

bolt, washer and nut tighten to 129 ft. lbs. (175 Nm).
16. Install the upper ball joint nut and remove the wheel knuckle support tighten the nut to 76 ft. lbs. (103 Nm).
17. Vehicles with disc brakes, position the brake caliper and install the 2 caliper guide bolts. Tighten bolts to 26 ft. lbs (35 Nm).
18. Vehicles with drum brakes, connect the brake line fitting to the wheel cylinder. Tighten the nut to 11 ft. lbs. (15 Nm).

19. Position the brake hose and install the brake hose bracket-to-wheel knuckle bolt. Tighten the nut to 13 ft. lbs (17 Nm).
20. Bleed the brake hydraulic system if line was removed.

REAR SUSPENSION

SHOCK ABSORBER

REMOVAL & INSTALLATION

See Figure 228.

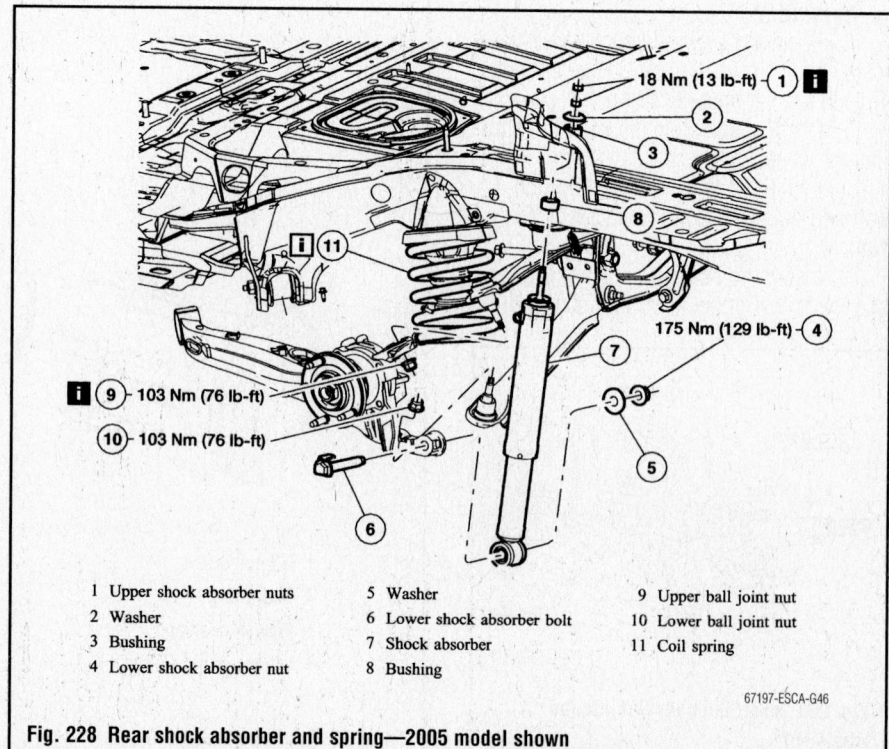

1 Upper shock absorber nuts	5 Washer	9 Upper ball joint nut
2 Washer	6 Lower shock absorber bolt	10 Lower ball joint nut
3 Bushing	7 Shock absorber	11 Coil spring
4 Lower shock absorber nut	8 Bushing	

Fig. 228 Rear shock absorber and spring—2005 model shown

1. Remove the wheel and tire assemblies.

2. Remove the rear quarter trim panel. Remove the upper shock absorber nut, bushing and washer.

3. Remove the lower shock absorber nut, bolt and washer.

4. Remove the shock absorber and bushing.

5. To install, reverse the removal procedure. Torque the upper nut to 13 ft. lbs.; the lower nut to 129 ft. lbs. (175 Nm).

TESTING

1. Road test the vehicle.

2. On a smooth road see if any vibrations are present.

3. Use your hands in order to lift up and push down each corner of the vehicle 3 times.

4. Remove your hands from the vehicle.

5. Replace any shock that exceeds more than two bounces.

6. Raise vehicle for inspection

7. Inspect each shock absorber for external fluid leakage.

8. Inspect for deformation or damage.

9. Inspect bushings for wear or damage.

10. Replace as necessary.

LOWER CONTROL ARM

REMOVAL & INSTALLATION

See Figure 229.

1. Before servicing the vehicle, refer to the Precautions Section.

2. Remove or disconnect the following:
  - Negative battery cable
  - Lower ball joint from the knuckle while holding the ball joint stud from moving
  - Lower ball joint nut
  - Lower control arm
  - Lower control arm inner bolt

To install:

3. Install or connect the following:
  - Lower control arm inner bolt
  - Lower control arm. Torque the bolts to 85 ft. lbs. (115 Nm).
  - Lower ball joint nut
  - Lower ball joint the knuckle. Torque the ball joint nut to 76 ft. lbs. (103 Nm).
  - Rear wheel

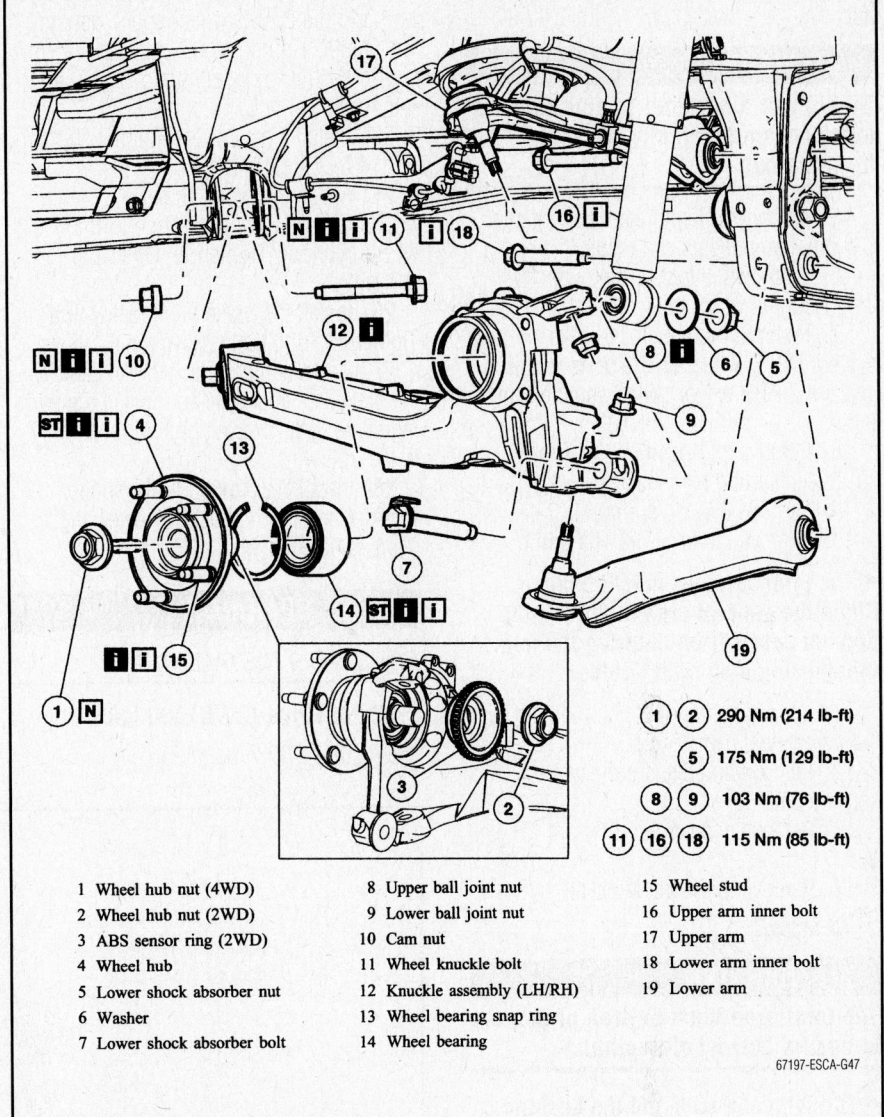

1 Wheel hub nut (4WD)
2 Wheel hub nut (2WD)
3 ABS sensor ring (2WD)
4 Wheel hub
5 Lower shock absorber nut
6 Washer
7 Lower shock absorber bolt
8 Upper ball joint nut
9 Lower ball joint nut
10 Cam nut
11 Wheel knuckle bolt
12 Knuckle assembly (LH/RH)
13 Wheel bearing snap ring
14 Wheel bearing
15 Wheel stud
16 Upper arm inner bolt
17 Upper arm
18 Lower arm inner bolt
19 Lower arm

① ②	290 Nm (214 lb-ft)
⑤	175 Nm (129 lb-ft)
⑧ ⑨	103 Nm (76 lb-ft)
⑪ ⑯ ⑱	115 Nm (85 lb-ft)

67197-ESCA-G47

Fig. 229 Rear lower control arm and related parts

UPPER CONTROL ARM

REMOVAL & INSTALLATION

1. Before servicing the vehicle, refer to the Precautions Section.

2. Remove the wheel and tire.

➡**It may be necessary to hold the ball joint stud to keep it from turning while removing the nut.**

3. Separate the upper arm from the wheel knuckle. Remove the upper ball joint nut.

4. Remove the upper arm inner bolt.

5. Remove the upper arm.

6. To install, reverse the removal procedure. Observe the following torques:
  - Ball joint nut: 76 ft. lbs. (103 Nm)

- Lower arm bolts: 85 ft. lbs. (115 Nm)

KNUCKLE

REMOVAL & INSTALLATION

1. Before servicing the vehicle, refer to the Precautions Section.

2. Drum brake vehicles:

  a. Remove the brake shoes.

  b. Disconnect the parking brake cable from the brake backing plate. Remove the parking brake cable from the brake backing plate.

  c. Disconnect the brake line from the wheel cylinder and remove the brake line bracket bolt.

3. Disc brake vehicles, remove the parking brake shoes.

4. Remove and discard the wheel hub nut.

> ### ✳✳ WARNING
> **Do not use a hammer to separate the outer constant velocity (CV) joint from the hub.**

5. Damage to the threads and internal CV joint components can result.

6. With 4wd, separate the outer CV-joint from the wheel hub.

7. Remove the anti-lock brake system (ABS) wheel speed sensor bolt and the 2 ABS wheel speed sensor wire bolts.

8. Remove and position the wheel speed sensor and harness aside.

9. Remove the coil spring.

10. Remove the lower ball joint nut.

➡ **The joint surfaces must be clean. Clean the general area of the joint to prevent debris from entering the joint. Clean using only mild liquids.**

11. Reference mark the notch on the cam nut adjustment cam.

12. Remove and discard the wheel knuckle bolt.

13. Remove and discard the cam nut.

14. Remove the wheel knuckle.

To install:

> ### ✳✳ WARNING
> **The joint area must be free of debris to ensure correct clamping.**

➡ **The joint surfaces and the bushing sleeve serrations must be clean before assembly.**

15. Clean the joint surfaces and the bushing sleeve serrations with a wire brush.

➡ **Align the notch on the cam nut with the reference marks.**

16. Position the wheel knuckle and install a new wheel knuckle bolt and cam nut.

17. Using a suitable tool, hold the cam nut stationary while tightening the wheel knuckle bolt. Tighten to 111 ft. lbs. (150 Nm).

18. Position the ABS wheel speed sensor harness and the sensor.

19. Position the lower ball joint into the wheel knuckle and install the lower ball joint nut. Tighten to 76 ft. lbs. (103 Nm).

20. Install the coil spring.

21. Install the ABS wheel speed sensor bolt and the 2 ABS wheel speed sensor wire bolts. Tighten to 80 inch lbs. (9 Nm).

22. With 4wd, install the outer CV joint into the wheel hub.

23. Install a new wheel hub nut. Tighten to 214 ft. lbs. (290 Nm).

24. Install the brake shoes.

25. Connect the brake line to the wheel cylinder. Tighten to 13 ft. lbs. (17 Nm).

26. Install the brake line bracket bolt. Tighten to 16 ft. lbs. (22 Nm).

27. Connect the parking brake cable to the brake backing plate and install the parking brake cable bracket bolt. Tighten to 17 ft. lbs. (23 Nm).

28. Install the parking brake shoes.

29. Check and adjust the wheel alignment as necessary.

WHEEL BEARINGS

REMOVAL & INSTALLATION

2-Wheel Drive (2WD) Vehicles

See Figures 230 through 236.

1. Before servicing the vehicle, refer to the Precautions Section.

2. Remove or disconnect the following:
   - Negative battery cable
   - Rear wheel
   - Rear brake drum
   - Wheel hub nut
   - Wheel hub
   - Inner wheel bearing race from the hub
   - Snapring
   - Wheel bearing outer race from the knuckle

To install:

3. Install or connect the following:
   - Wheel bearing in to the knuckle
   - Snapring
   - Wheel hub into the wheel bearing
   - Wheel hub nut. Torque the nut to 214 ft. lbs. (290 Nm).
   - Brake drum
   - Rear wheel
   - Negative battery cable

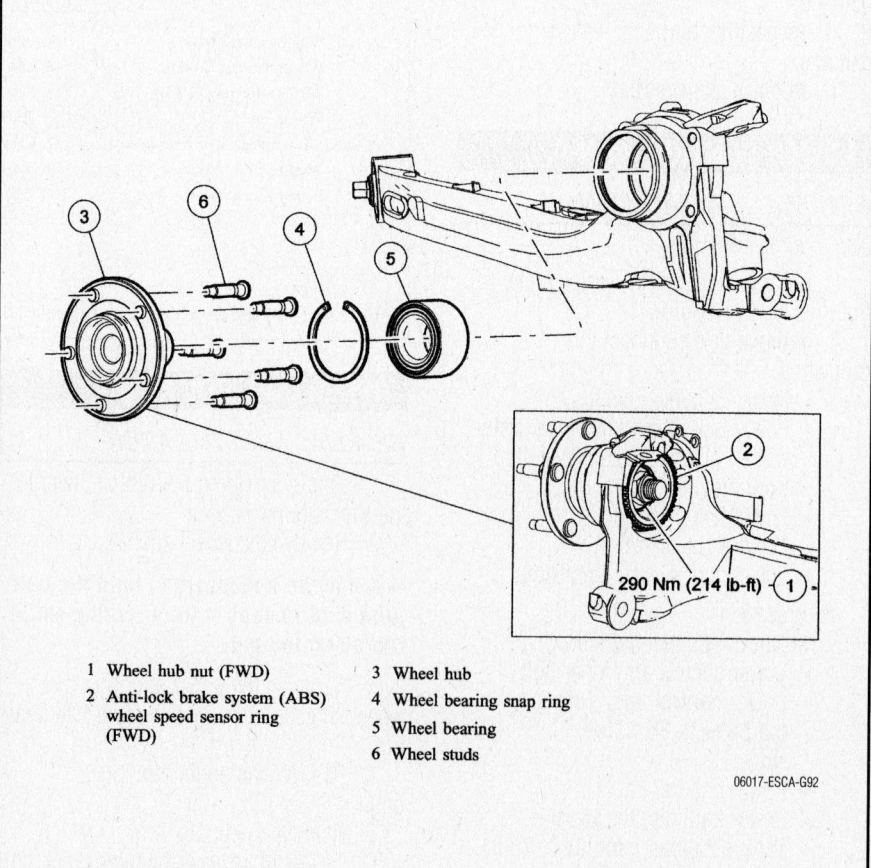

1 Wheel hub nut (FWD)	3 Wheel hub
2 Anti-lock brake system (ABS) wheel speed sensor ring (FWD)	4 Wheel bearing snap ring
	5 Wheel bearing
	6 Wheel studs

06017-ESCA-G92

Fig. 230 Rear hub and bearing

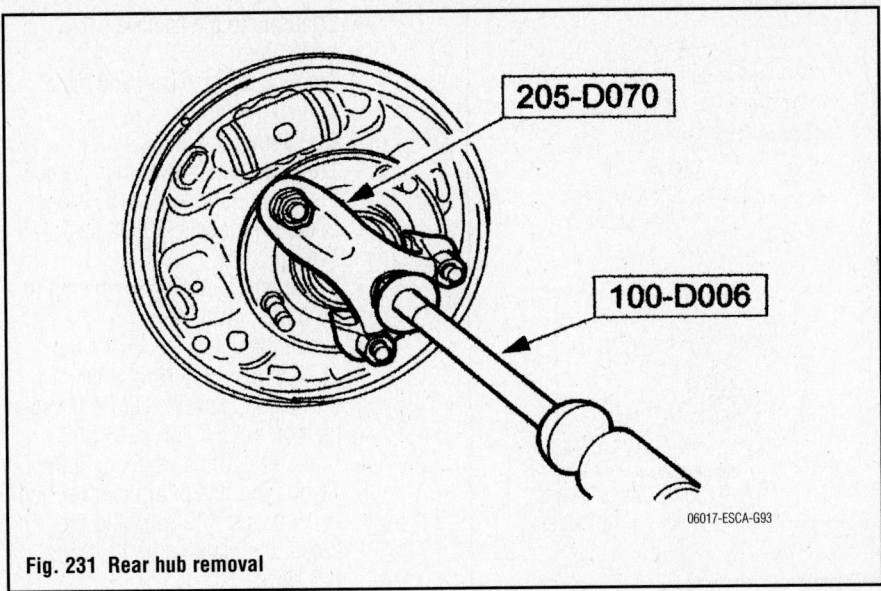

Fig. 231 Rear hub removal

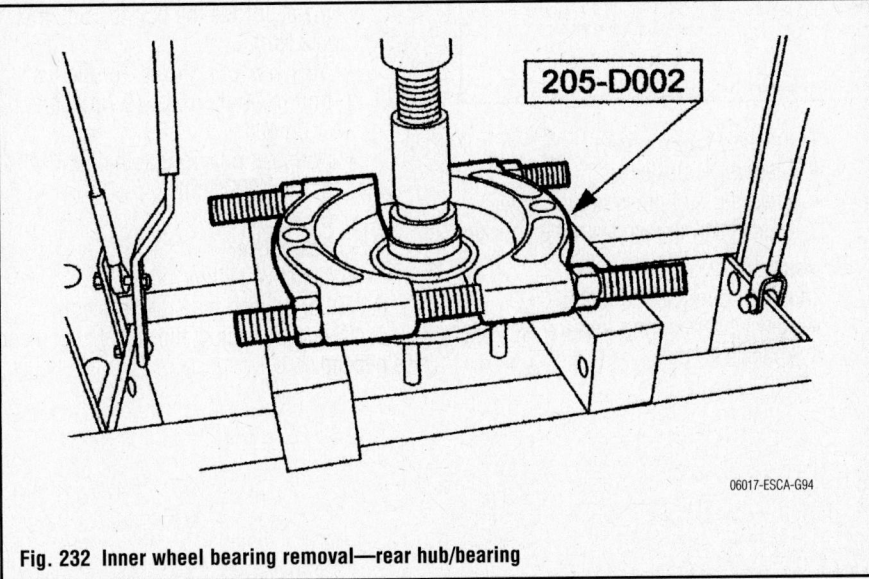

Fig. 232 Inner wheel bearing removal—rear hub/bearing

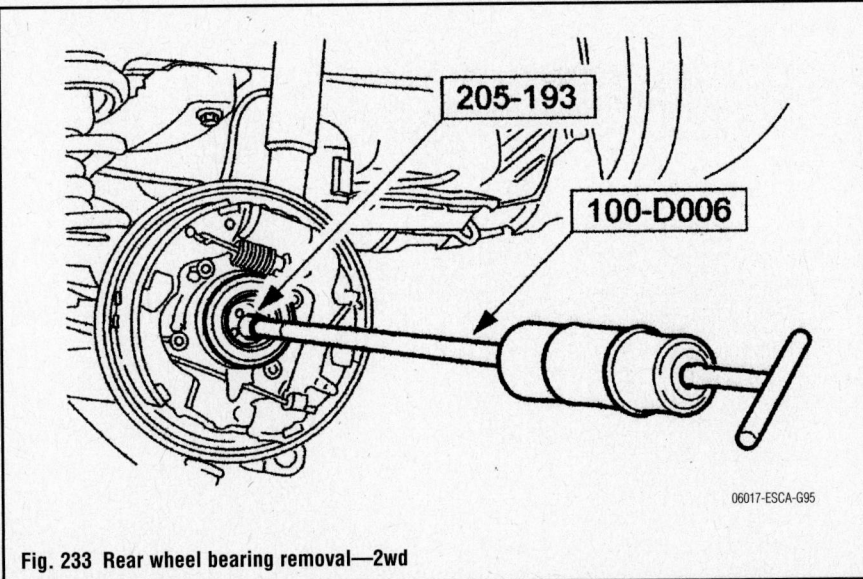

Fig. 233 Rear wheel bearing removal—2wd

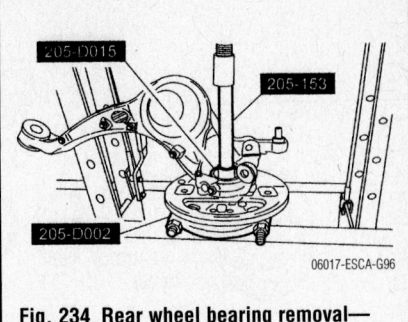

Fig. 234 Rear wheel bearing removal—4wd

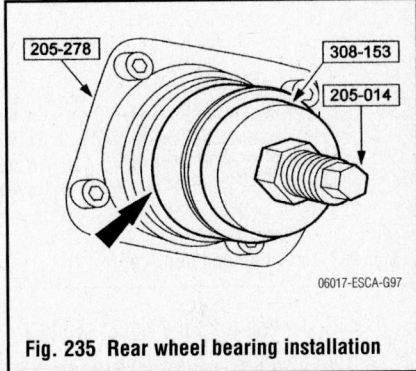

Fig. 235 Rear wheel bearing installation

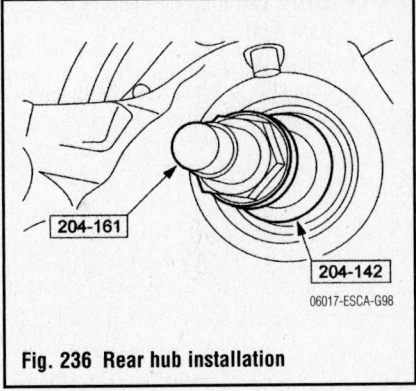

Fig. 236 Rear hub installation

4-Wheel Drive (4WD) Vehicles

See Figure 237.

1. Before servicing the vehicle, refer to the Precautions Section.
2. Remove or disconnect the following:

- Negative battery cable
- Rear wheel
- Rear brake shoes
- Rear halfshaft nut and loosen the halfshaft from the hub
- Wheel hub and place it in a vise
- Inner wheel bearing race from the hub
- Antilock Brake System (ABS) sensor bracket and move the sensor aside, if equipped
- Parking brake cable from the steering knuckle

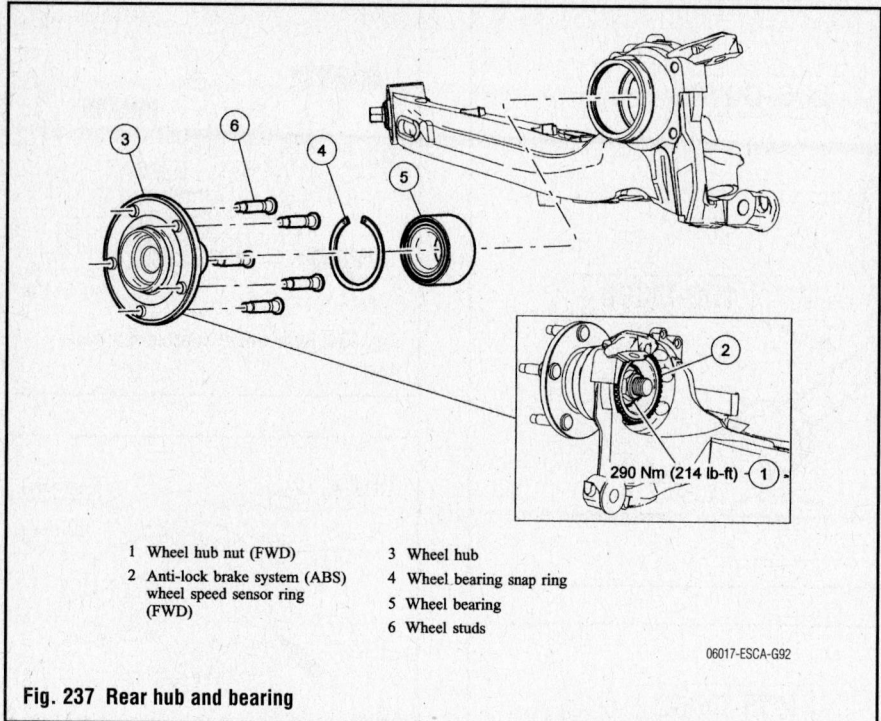

1 Wheel hub nut (FWD)
2 Anti-lock brake system (ABS) wheel speed sensor ring (FWD)
3 Wheel hub
4 Wheel bearing snap ring
5 Wheel bearing
6 Wheel studs

290 Nm (214 lb-ft)

06017-ESCA-G92

Fig. 237 Rear hub and bearing

- Brake line from the wheel cylinder and support the knuckle
- Lower shock absorber nut
- Lower ball joint by holding the ball joint stud
- Upper ball joint
- Coil spring while noting the location of the insulator

- Steering knuckle cam
- Steering knuckle
- Snapring and press out the outer wheel bearing race from the knuckle

To install:
3. Install or connect the following:
  - New wheel bearing into the steering knuckle

- Snapring to the knuckle
- Wheel hub
- Steering knuckle cam and hand tighten the bolt
- Coil spring
- Shock absorber lower nut. Torque the nut to 85 ft. lbs. (115 Nm) for 2002–04 models; 129 ft. lbs. (175 Nm).
- Upper ball joint. Torque the nut to 76 ft. lbs. (103 Nm).
- Lower ball joint. Torque the nut to 76 ft. lbs. (103 Nm). Align the steering knuckle cam and torque the bolt to 85 ft. lbs. (115 Nm).
- Brake line to the wheel cylinder. Torque the brake line bracket bolt to 15 ft. lbs. (20 Nm) and the brake line fastener to 11 ft. lbs. (15 Nm).
- Parking brake cable to the backing plate. Torque the bolt to 16 ft. lbs. (22 Nm).
- ABS sensor bracket. Torque the bolt to 80 inch lbs. (9 Nm), if equipped
- Halfshaft nut. Torque the nut to 214 ft. lbs. (290 Nm).
- Brake shoes
- Rear wheel
- Negative battery cable
4. Fill and bleed the brake system.
5. Check and adjust the wheel alignment as needed.

FORD AND MERCURY

Escape Hybrid • Mariner Hybrid

SPECIFICATIONS AND MAINTENANCE CHARTS

ENGINE AND VEHICLE IDENTIFICATION

Engine								Model Year	
Code ①	Liters	Cu. In.	Cyl.	Fuel Sys.	Engine Type	Eng. Mfg.		Code ②	Year
H	2.3	137	4	SFI/Hybrid	DOHC	Ford		5	2005
								6	2006
								7	2007
								8	2008

SFI: Multi-port Fuel Injection

DOHC: Double Overhead Camshafts

① 8th digit of VIN

② 10th digit of VIN

22086_HYBR_C0001

GENERAL ENGINE SPECIFICATIONS

Year	Model	Engine Displacement Liters	Engine VIN	Net Horsepower @ rpm	Net Torque @ rpm (ft. lbs.)	Bore x Stroke (in.)	Compression Ratio	Oil Pressure @ rpm
2005	Escape Hybrid	2.3	H	133@6000 ①	129@4500	3.44x3.70	12.3:1	29-39@2000
2006	Escape Hybrid	2.3	H	133@6000 ①	129@4500	3.44x3.70	12.3:1	29-39@2000
	Mariner Hybrid	2.3	H	133@6000 ①	129@4500	3.44x3.70	12.3:1	29-39@2000
2007	Escape Hybrid	2.3	H	133@6000 ①	129@4500	3.44x3.70	12.3:1	29-39@2000
	Mariner Hybrid	2.3	H	133@6000 ①	129@4500	3.44x3.70	12.3:1	29-39@2000
2008	Escape Hybrid	2.3	H	133@6000 ①	129@4500	3.44x3.70	12.3:1	29-39@2000
	Mariner Hybrid	2.3	H	133@6000 ①	129@4500	3.44x3.70	12.3:1	29-39@2000

① Combined horsepower of gasoline engine and electric motor: 155 hp

22086_HYBR_C0002

ENGINE TUNE-UP SPECIFICATIONS

Year	Engine Displacement Liters	Engine VIN	Spark Plug Gap (in.)	Ignition Timing (deg.) MT	AT	Fuel Pump (psi) ①	Idle Speed (rpm) MT	AT	Valve Clearance Intake	Exhaust
2005	2.3	H	0.049-0.053	—	NA	39	②	②	HYD	HYD
2006	2.3	H	0.049-0.053	—	NA	39	②	②	HYD	HYD
2007	2.3	H	0.049-0.053	—	NA	39	②	②	HYD	HYD
2008	2.3	H	0.049-0.053	—	NA	39	②	②	HYD	HYD

HYD: Hydraulic lash adjusters

① Key on; engine off

② Refer to Vehicle Emission Control Information Label

22086_HYBR_C0003

CAPACITIES

Year	Model	Engine Displacement Liters	Engine VIN	Engine Oil with Filter (qts.)	Transmission (pts.) Manual	Transmission (pts.) Auto ①	Transfer Case (pts.)	Drive Axle Front (pts.)	Drive Axle Rear (pts.)	Fuel Tank (gal.)	Cooling System (qts.)
2005	Escape Hybrid	2.3	H	4.5	—	10.6 ②	0.75	—	3.0	15.0	8.5
2006	Escape Hybrid	2.3	H	4.5	—	10.6 ②	0.75	—	3.0	15.0	8.5
	Mariner Hybrid	2.3	H	4.5	—	10.6 ②	0.75	—	3.0	15.0	8.5
2007	Escape Hybrid	2.3	H	4.5	—	10.6 ②	0.75	—	3.0	15.0	8.5
	Mariner Hybrid	2.3	H	4.5	—	10.6 ②	0.75	—	3.0	15.0	8.5
2008	Escape Hybrid	2.3	H	4.5	—	10.6 ②	0.75	—	3.0	15.0	8.5
	Escape Hybrid	2.3	H	4.5	—	10.6 ②	0.75	—	3.0	15.0	8.5

NOTE: All capacities are approximate. Add fluid gradually and check to be sure a proper fluid level is obtained.

① Dry fill

② Motor electronics cooling system dry fill: 7.4 pts.

22086_HYBR_C0004

FLUID SPECIFICATIONS

Year	Model	Engine Displacement Liters	Engine ID/VIN	Engine Oil	Auto. Trans.	Drive Axle	Power Steering Fluid	Brake Master Cylinder
2005	Escape Hybrid	2.3	H	5W-20	Mercon®V	80W-90	NA	DOT 3
2006	Escape Hybrid	2.3	H	5W-30	Mercon®V	80W-90	NA	DOT 3
	Mariner Hybrid	2.3	H	5W-30	Mercon®V	80W-90	NA	DOT 3
2007	Escape Hybrid	2.3	H	5W-30	Mercon®V	80W-90	NA	DOT 3
	Mariner Hybrid	2.3	H	5W-30	Mercon®V	80W-90	NA	DOT 3
2008	Escape Hybrid	2.3	H	5W-30	Mercon®V	80W-90	NA	DOT 3
	Mariner Hybrid	2.3	H	5W-30	Mercon®V	80W-90	NA	DOT 3

DOT: Department Of Transpotation

® Registerd Trademark

22086_HYBR_C0005

VALVE SPECIFICATIONS

Year	Engine Displacement Liters	Engine VIN	Seat Angle (deg.)	Face Angle (deg.)	Spring Test Pressure (lbs. @ in.)	Spring Installed Height (in.)	Stem-to-Guide Clearance (in.) Intake	Stem-to-Guide Clearance (in.) Exhaust	Stem Diameter (in.) Intake	Stem Diameter (in.) Exhaust
2005	2.3	H	45	45	38.6@1.49	1.492	0.0010	0.0011	0.2153-0.2159	0.2151-0.2157
2006	2.3	H	45	45	38.6@1.49	1.492	0.0010	0.0011	0.2153-0.2159	0.2151-0.2157
2007	2.3	H	45	45	38.6@1.49	1.492	0.0010	0.0011	0.2153-0.2159	0.2151-0.2157
2008	2.3	H	45	45	38.6@1.49	1.492	0.0010	0.0011	0.2153-0.2159	0.2151-0.2157

22086_HYBR_C0006

CAMSHAFT AND BEARING SPECIFICATIONS

All measurements are given in inches.

Year	Engine Displacement Liters	Engine ID/VIN	Journal Dia.	Brg. Oil Clearance	Shaft End-play	Runout	Journal Bore	Lobe Height Intake	Lobe Height Exhaust
2005	2.3	H	0.9820-0.9830	NA	0.0016-0.0035	0.001	0.001-0.0030	—	0.3070
2006	2.3	H	0.9820-0.9830	NA	0.0016-0.0035	0.001	0.001-0.0030	—	0.3070
2007	2.3	H	0.9820-0.9830	NA	0.0016-0.0035	0.001	0.001-0.0030	—	0.3070
2008	2.3	H	0.9820-0.9830	NA	0.0016-0.0035	0.001	0.001-0.0030	—	0.3070

NA: Not Available

22086_HYBR_C0007

CRANKSHAFT AND CONNECTING ROD SPECIFICATIONS

All measurements are given in inches.

Year	Engine Displacement Liters	Engine VIN	Crankshaft Main Brg. Journal Dia.	Crankshaft Main Brg. Oil Clearance	Crankshaft Shaft End-play	Thrust on No.	Connecting Rod Journal Diameter	Connecting Rod Oil Clearance	Connecting Rod Side Clearance
2005	2.3	H	2.0460-2.0470	0.0007-0.0013	0.0080-0.0160	NA	1.9673-1.9681	0.0011-0.0026	0.0760-0.1200
	2.3	H	2.0460-2.0470	0.0007-0.0013	0.0080-0.0160	NA	1.9673-1.9681	0.0011-0.0026	0.0760-0.1200
2006	2.3	H	2.0460-2.0470	0.0007-0.0013	0.0080-0.0160	NA	1.9673-1.9681	0.0011-0.0026	0.0760-0.1200
	2.3	H	2.0460-2.0470	0.0007-0.0013	0.0080-0.0160	NA	1.9673-1.9681	0.0011-0.0026	0.0760-0.1200
2007	2.3	H	2.0460-2.0470	0.0007-0.0013	0.0080-0.0160	NA	1.9673-1.9681	0.0011-0.0026	0.0760-0.1200
	2.3	H	2.0460-2.0470	0.0007-0.0013	0.0080-0.0160	NA	1.9673-1.9681	0.0011-0.0026	0.0760-0.1200
2008	2.3	H	2.0460-2.0470	0.0007-0.0013	0.0080-0.0160	NA	1.9673-1.9681	0.0011-0.0026	0.0760-0.1200
	2.3	H	2.0460-2.0470	0.0007-0.0013	0.0080-0.0160	NA	1.9673-1.9681	0.0011-0.0026	0.0760-0.1200

NA: Not Available

22086_HYBR_C0008

PISTON AND RING SPECIFICATIONS

All measurements are given in inches.

Year	Engine Displacement Liters	Engine VIN	Piston Clearance	Ring Gap			Ring Side Clearance		
				Top Compression	Bottom Compression	Oil Control	Top Compression	Bottom Compression	Oil Control
2005	2.3	H	0.0009-0.0017	0.0060-0.0120	0.0120-0.0180	0.0070-0.0270	NA	NA	NA
	2.3	H	0.0009-0.0017	0.0060-0.0120	0.0120-0.0180	0.0070-0.0270	NA	NA	NA
2006	2.3	H	0.0009-0.0017	0.0060-0.0120	0.0120-0.0180	0.0070-0.0270	NA	NA	NA
	2.3	H	0.0009-0.0017	0.0060-0.0120	0.0120-0.0180	0.0070-0.0270	NA	NA	NA
2007	2.3	H	0.0009-0.0017	0.0060-0.0120	0.0120-0.0180	0.0070-0.0270	NA	NA	NA
	2.3	H	0.0009-0.0017	0.0060-0.0120	0.0120-0.0180	0.0070-0.0270	NA	NA	NA
2008	2.3	H	0.0009-0.0017	0.0060-0.0120	0.0120-0.0180	0.0070-0.0270	NA	NA	NA
	2.3	H	0.0009-0.0017	0.0060-0.0120	0.0120-0.0180	0.0070-0.0270	NA	NA	NA

NA: Not Available

22086_HYBR_C0009

TORQUE SPECIFICATIONS

All readings in ft. lbs.

Year	Engine Displacement Liters	Engine VIN	Cylinder Head Bolts	Main Bearing Bolts	Rod Bearing Bolts	Crankshaft Damper Bolts	Flywheel Bolts	Manifold		Spark Plugs	Oil Pan Drain Plug
								Intake	Exhaust		
2005	2.3	H	①	NA	NA	②	③	13	35	11	21
	2.3	H	①	NA	NA	②	③	13	35	11	21
2006	2.3	H	①	NA	NA	②	③	13	35	11	21
	2.3	H	①	NA	NA	②	③	13	35	11	21
2007	2.3	H	①	NA	NA	②	③	13	35	11	21
	2.3	H	①	NA	NA	②	③	13	35	11	21
2008	2.3	H	①	NA	NA	②	③	13	35	11	21
	2.3	H	①	NA	NA	②	③	13	35	11	21

NA: Not Available

① Step 1: 44 inch lbs.
  Step 2: 11 ft. lbs.
  Step 3: 33 ft. lbs.
  Step 4: +90 degrees
  Step 5: Plus 90 degrees

② Step 1: 74 ft. lbs.
  Step 2: plus 90 degrees

③ Step 1: 37 ft. lbs.
  Step 2: 59 ft. lbs
  Step 3: 83 ft. lbs.

22086_HYBR_C0010

WHEEL ALIGNMENT

Year	Model		Caster Range (+/-Deg.)	Caster Preferred Setting (Deg.)	Camber Range (+/-Deg.)	Camber Preferred Setting (Deg.)	Toe-in (in.)
2005	Escape Hybrid	F	1.00	+1.60	0.75	-1.00	0.23+/-0.23
		R	NA	NA	0.75	①	-0.06+/-0.20
2006	Escape/Mariner	F	1.00	+1.50 ②	0.75	-1.00	0.23+/-0.23
	Hybrid	R	NA	NA	0.75	0.00	-0.14+/-0.20
2007	Escape/Mariner	F	1.00	+1.50 ②	0.75	-1.00	0.23+/-0.23
	Hybrid	R	NA	NA	0.75	0.00	-0.14+/-0.20
2008	Escape/Mariner	F	1.00	+1.50 ②	0.75	-1.00	0.23+/-0.23
	Hybrid	R	NA	NA	0.75	0.00	-0.18+/-0.20 ③

Early build vehicles are those built before 8/02/04 at Kansas City, or, before 8/16/04 at Ohio.

NA: Information not available

① Early build: 0.20 degrees +/- 0.75
   Late build: -0.00 degrees +/- 0.75

② Left side 1.80 degrees

③ AWD -0.12 +/- 0.20

22086_HYBR_C0011

TIRE, WHEEL AND BALL JOINT SPECIFICATIONS

Year	Model	OEM Tires Standard	OEM Tires Optional	Tire Pressures (psi) Front	Tire Pressures (psi) Rear	Wheel Size	Ball Joint Inspection	Lug Nuts (ft. lbs.)
2005	Escape Hybrid	P235/70R16	none	①	①	NA	0.008 in.	98
2006	Escape Hybrid	P235/70R16	none	①	①	NA	0.008 in.	98
	Mariner Hybrid	P235/70R16	none	①	①	NA	0.008 in.	98
2007	Escape Hybrid	P235/70R16	none	①	①	NA	0.008 in.	98
	Mariner Hybrid	P235/70R16	none	①	①	NA	0.008 in.	98
2008	Escape Hybrid	P235/70R16	none	①	①	NA	0.008 in.	98
	Mariner Hybrid	P235/70R16	none	①	①	NA	0.008 in.	98

NA: Not Available

PSI: Pounds Per Square Inch

① See safety cirtification on drivers door jam

22086_HYBR_C00012

BRAKE SPECIFICATIONS

All measurements in inches unless noted

Year	Model		Brake Disc			Brake Drum		Minimum Lining Thickness	Brake Caliper	
			Original Thickness	Minimum Thickness	Maximum Run-out	Original Inside Diameter	Maximum Machine Diameter		Bracket Bolts (ft. lbs.)	Mounting Bolts (ft. lbs.)
2005	Escape Hybrid	F	NA	①	0.004	—	—	0.118	111	②
		R	NA	0.430	0.004	NA	9.05	0.118	—	26
2006	Escape Hybrid/	F	NA	①	0.004	—	—	0.118	111	②
	Mariner Hybrid	R	NA	0.430	0.004	NA	9.05	0.118	—	26
2007	Escape Hybrid/	F	NA	①	0.004	—	—	0.118	111	②
	Mariner Hybrid	R	NA	0.430	0.004	NA	9.05	0.118	—	26
2008	Escape Hybrid/	F	NA	0.950	0.004	—	—	0.118	111	②
	Mariner Hybrid	R	NA	0.430	0.004	NA	10.0	0.118	—	26

NA: Not Available

① Base brakes: 0.86 in.

   With 4-wheel discs: 0.95 in.

② With disc/drum: 26 ft. lbs.

   With 4-wheel disc: 33 ft. lbs.

22086_HYBR_C0013

SCHEDULED MAINTENANCE INTERVALS
2005-06 Ford Escape Hybrid/Mercury Mariner Hybrid

TO BE SERVICED	TYPE OF SERVICE	Vehicle mileage intervals (x1000)											
		10	20	30	40	50	60	70	80	90	100	110	120
Air cleaner filter	R			✓			✓			✓			✓
Accessory drive belt	I ①										✓		
Brake system ②	S/I		✓		✓		✓		✓		✓		✓
Cooling system hoses and clamps	S/I		✓		✓		✓		✓		✓		✓
Driveshafts & halfshafts	S/I		✓		✓		✓		✓		✓		✓
Engine coolant	R	At 5 years or 100,000 miles; then every 3 years or 50,000 miles											
Engine oil & filter	R	✓	✓	✓	✓	✓	✓	✓	✓	✓	✓	✓	✓
Exhaust system & heat shields					✓				✓				✓
Fuel filter	R										✓		
PCV valve	S/I	Every 150,000 miles											
Rear axle lubricant (4wd)	R	Every 150,000 miles											
Rear (high voltage) battery A/C filter	I	✓	✓	✓	✓	✓	✓	✓	✓	✓	✓	✓	✓
Rear (high voltage) battery A/C filter	R		✓		✓		✓		✓		✓		✓
Tires	Rotate	Every 5,000 miles											
Steering linkage	S/I		✓		✓		✓		✓		✓		✓
Spark plugs	R										✓		
Suspension components and ball joints	S/I		✓		✓		✓		✓		✓		✓

R: Replace   S/I: Inspect and service, if necessary   L: Lubricate   A: Adjust   C: Clean

① Replace at 150,000 miles, if not previously done

② Inspect the reservoir fluid level, rotor and or drum, brake lines, hoses, calipers and or wheel cylinders

Monthly Checks

Check each of the following items every month:

    All interior and exterior lights

    Tires for wear and correct air pressure, including spare tire

    Engine oil fluid level

    Windshield washer solvent fluid level

Six Month Checks

Check each of the following items at least every 6 months:

    Lap/shoulder belts and seat latches for wear and function

    Parking brake for correct operation

    Safety warning lamps (brake, ABS, air bag, safety belt) for correct operation

    Engine coolant system fluid level and correct strength

    Motor/electrical cooling system fluid level and correct strength

    Battery 12-volt connections. Clean if necessary

    Windshield washer spray, wiper operation, clean all wiper blades

    Lubricate all hinges, latches and outside locks. Inspect for correct operation

    Lubricate door rubber weatherstrips. Inspect for excessive wear

    Clean body and door drain holes. Inspect for clogs and obstructions

22086_HYBR_C0014

SCHEDULED MAINTENANCE INTERVALS
2007-08 Ford Escape Hybrid/Mercury Mariner Hybrid

TO BE SERVICED	TYPE OF SERVICE	Vehicle mileage intervals (x1000)											
		10	20	30	40	50	60	70	80	90	100	110	120
Air cleaner filter	R			✓			✓			✓			✓
Accessory drive belt	I ①										✓		
Brake system ②	S/I		✓		✓		✓		✓		✓		✓
Cooling system hoses and clamps	S/I		✓		✓		✓		✓		✓		✓
Driveshafts & halfshafts	S/I		✓		✓		✓		✓		✓		✓
Engine coolant	R	At 5 years or 100,000 miles; then every 3 years or 50,000 miles											
Engine oil & filter	R	✓	✓	✓	✓	✓	✓	✓	✓	✓	✓	✓	✓
Exhaust system & heat shields				✓					✓				✓
Fuel filter	R										✓		
PCV valve	S/I	Every 150,000 miles											
Rear axle lubricant (4wd)	R	Every 150,000 miles											
Rear (high voltage) battery A/C filter	I	✓	✓	✓	✓	✓	✓	✓	✓	✓	✓	✓	✓
Rear (high voltage) battery A/C filter	R		✓		✓		✓		✓		✓		✓
Tires	Rotate	Every 5,000 miles											
Steering linkage	S/I		✓		✓		✓		✓		✓		✓
Spark plugs	R									✓			
Suspension components and ball joints	S/I		✓		✓		✓		✓		✓		✓
Multi-Point inspection	③	✓	✓	✓	✓	✓	✓	✓	✓	✓	✓	✓	✓

R: Replace   S/I: Inspect and service, if necessary   L: Lubricate   A: Adjust   C: Clean

① Replace at 150,000 miles, if not previously done

② Inspect the reservoir fluid level, rotor and or drum, brake lines, hoses, calipers and or wheel cylinders

Monthly Checks

Check each of the following items every month:

    All interior and exterior lights

    Tires for wear and correct air pressure, including spare tire

    Engine oil fluid level

    Windshield washer solvent fluid level

Six Month Checks

Check each of the following items at least every 6 months:

    Lap/shoulder belts and seat latches for wear and function

    Parking brake for correct operation

    Safety warning lamps (brake, ABS, air bag, safety belt) for correct operation

    Engine coolant system fluid level and correct strength

    Motor/electrical cooling system fluid level and correct strength

    Battery 12-volt connections. Clean if necessary

    Windshield washer spray, wiper operation, clean all wiper blades

    Lubricate all hinges, latches and outside locks. Inspect for correct operation

    Lubricate door rubber weatherstrips. Inspect for excessive wear

    Clean body and door drain holes. Inspect for clogs and obstructions

SCHEDULED MAINTENANCE INTERVALS
2007-08 Ford Escape Hybrid/Mercury Mariner Hybrid
(Footnotes continued)

③ **Multi-Point inspection**

The following inspections are recommended at every service interval:

Check and top off brake, coolant, manual and automatic transmission fluid power steering and washer fluid

Inspect tires for wear and correct air pressure, including spare tire

Check exhaust system for leaks, damage, loose parts and foreighn material

Check battery performance

Check operation of horn, exterior lamps, turn signals and hazard warning lights

Check radiator, coolers, heater and airconditioning hoses

Inspect tires for wear and correct air pressure, including spare tire

Inspect windshield wiper spray and wiper operation

Check windshield for cracks, chips and pitting

Inspect for oil and fluid leaks

Inspect air filter

Inspect halfshaft dust boots

Check shocks struts and other suspension components for leaks and damage

Inspect steering linkage

Inspect accesory drive belts

Inspect clutck operation (if equipped)

When operating in dusty conditions such as unpaved or dusty roads:

Change engine oil and install a new oil filter every 8,000 km (5,000 miles) or 3 months.

Install a new high voltage battery A/C filter as required

Inspect and rotate tires every 8,000 km (5,000 miles)

Install a new engine air filter as required.

Install a new cabin air filter as required.

When operating in off-road conditions:

Change engine oil and install a new oil filter every 8,000 km (5,000 miles) or 12 months or 200 hours of engine operation.

Inspect and rotate tires every 8,000 km (5,000miles).

Install a new cabin air filter as required.

Install a new high voltage battery A/C filter as required

Inspect and lubricate U-joints.

Inspect and lubricate steering linkage ball joints with zerk fittings.

Special Operating Condition Requirements

When towing a trailer or using a camper or car-top carrier:

Change engine oil and install a new oil filter every 8,000 km (5,000 miles) or 12months or 200 hours of engine operation.

Change automatic transmission fluid every 48,000 km (30,000 miles). (not required on 6R60/6R75 transmissions).

Inspect and rotate tires 8,000 km (5,000 miles)

Change manual transmission fluid as required.

Inspect and lubricate U-joints and half shafts as required.

During extensive idling and/or low speed driving for long distances, as in heavy commercial use such as delivery, taxi, patrol car or livery:

Change engine oil and install a new oil filter, lube front lower control arm and steering linkage ball joints with

zerk fittings (if equipped) every 8,000 km (5,000 miles) or 12 months or 200 hours of engine operation.

Inspect brake system and check battery electrolyte level (Patrol cars) every 8,000 km (5,000 miles).

Install a new fuel filter every 24,000 km (15,000 miles).

Change automatic transmission fluid, lubricate 4x2 wheel bearings,

Lubricate rear wheel drive (RWD) front wheel bearings, install new grease seals and adjust every 48,000 km (30,000 miles).

Install new spark plugs and change transfer case fluid every 96,000 km (60,000 miles).

Install a new cabin air filter as required.

PRECAUTIONS

Before servicing any vehicle, please be sure to read all of the following precautions, which deal with personal safety, prevention of component damage, and important points to take into consideration when servicing a motor vehicle:

• Never open, service or drain the radiator or cooling system when the engine is hot; serious burns can occur from the steam and hot coolant.

• Observe all applicable safety precautions when working around fuel. Whenever servicing the fuel system, always work in a well-ventilated area. Do not allow fuel spray or vapors to come in contact with a spark, open flame, or excessive heat (a hot drop light, for example). Keep a dry chemical fire extinguisher near the work area. Always keep fuel in a container specifically designed for fuel storage; also, always properly seal fuel containers to avoid the possibility of fire or explosion. Refer to the additional fuel system precautions later in this section.

• Fuel injection systems often remain pressurized, even after the engine has been turned **OFF**. The fuel system pressure must be relieved before disconnecting any fuel lines. Failure to do so may result in fire and/or personal injury.

• Brake fluid often contains polyglycol ethers and polyglycols. Avoid contact with the eyes and wash your hands thoroughly after handling brake fluid. If you do get brake fluid in your eyes, flush your eyes with clean, running water for 15 minutes. If eye irritation persists, or if you have taken brake fluid internally, IMMEDIATELY seek medical assistance.

• The EPA warns that prolonged contact with used engine oil may cause a number of skin disorders, including cancer. You should make every effort to minimize your exposure to used engine oil. Protective gloves should be worn when changing oil. Wash your hands and any other exposed skin areas as soon as possible after exposure to used engine oil. Soap and water, or waterless hand cleaner should be used.

• All new vehicles are now equipped with an air bag system, often referred to as a Supplemental Restraint System (SRS) or Supplemental Inflatable Restraint (SIR) system. The system must be disabled before performing service on or around system components, steering column, instrument panel components, wiring and sensors. Failure to follow safety and disabling procedures could result in accidental air bag deployment, possible personal injury and unnecessary system repairs.

• Always wear safety goggles when working with, or around, the air bag system. When carrying a non-deployed air bag, be sure the bag and trim cover are pointed away from your body. When placing a non-deployed air bag on a work surface, always face the bag and trim cover upward, away from the surface. This will reduce the motion of the module if it is accidentally deployed. Refer to the additional air bag system precautions later in this section.

• Clean, high quality brake fluid from a sealed container is essential to the safe and proper operation of the brake system. You should always buy the correct type of brake fluid for your vehicle. If the brake fluid becomes contaminated, completely flush the system with new fluid. Never reuse any brake fluid. Any brake fluid that is removed from the system should be discarded. Also, do not allow any brake fluid to come in contact with a painted surface; it will damage the paint.

• Never operate the engine without the proper amount and type of engine oil; doing so WILL result in severe engine damage.

• Timing belt maintenance is extremely important. Many models utilize an interference-type, non-freewheeling engine. If the timing belt breaks, the valves in the cylinder head may strike the pistons, causing potentially serious (also time-consuming and expensive) engine damage. Refer to the maintenance interval charts for the recommended replacement interval for the timing belt, and to the timing belt section for belt replacement and inspection.

• Disconnecting the negative battery cable on some vehicles may interfere with the functions of the on-board computer system(s) and may require the computer to undergo a relearning process once the negative battery cable is reconnected.

• When servicing drum brakes, only disassemble and assemble one side at a time, leaving the remaining side intact for reference.

• Only an MVAC-trained, EPA-certified automotive technician should service the air conditioning system or its components.

BRAKES

GENERAL INFORMATION

The Anti-lock Brake System (ABS) module simultaneously manages the anti-lock braking, traction control and engine control systems to maintain vehicle control during deceleration and acceleration.

When the ignition switch is in the **RUN** position, the module carries out a preliminary electrical check and, at approximately 12 mph (20 km/h), the hydraulic pump motor is turned on for approximately one half-second. Any malfunction of the anti-lock brake system disables the traction control and stability assist (if equipped) and the anti-lock brake warning indicator illuminates. However, the power-assist braking system functions normally.

The Anti-lock Brake System (ABS) consists of the following components:
• Hydraulic Control Unit (HCU)
• ABS control module
• Rear anti-lock brake sensor
• Rear anti-lock brake sensor indicator
• Front anti-lock brake sensor
• Front anti-lock brake sensor indicator
• Yellow ABS warning indicator
• Red brake warning indicator

SPEED SENSORS

REMOVAL & INSTALLATION

Front

See Figure 1.

1. Raise and safely support the vehicle.

ANTI-LOCK BRAKE SYSTEM (ABS)

➡ The harness connector is located in the engine compartment.

2. Disconnect the electrical connector.

✳✳ WARNING

Care must be taken during the removal of the plug to prevent damage. If the plug is damaged, a new sensor may need to be installed, even though the sensor is functional in all other aspects.

3. Remove the grommet from the body.
4. When removing the body plug, rotate the plug into a position which allows the use of a small screwdriver to release the tabs on the underside of the body plug. These 2 tabs are located at right angles to the sensor wire.

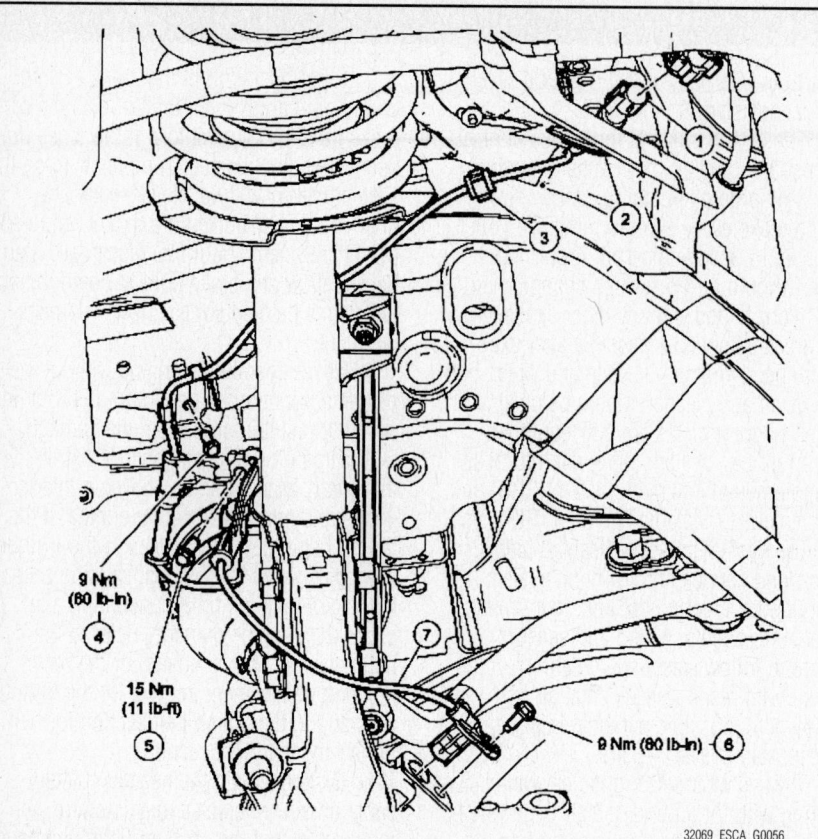

Fig. 1 View of the front wheel speed sensor wire connector (1), grommet (2), front wheel speed sensor wire retainer (3), front wheel speed sensor wire-to-body bolts (4), front wheel speed sensor bolts (5, 6) and front wheel speed sensor (7)

5. Remove the front wheel speed sensor wire from the retainer.

6. Remove the front wheel speed sensor wire-to-body bolt.

7. Remove the front wheel speed sensor wire bolt.

8. Remove the front wheel speed sensor bolt from the wheel knuckle.

➡ Clean off any foreign material that may have collected around the sensor before removal.

9. Remove the front wheel speed sensor.

➡ Thoroughly clean the mounting surface.

10. Installation is the reverse of the removal procedure, noting the following tightening specifications:

   a. Front wheel speed sensor-to-knuckle bolt: 80 inch lbs. (9 Nm)

   b. Front wheel speed sensor wire bolt: 11 ft. lbs. (15 Nm)

   c. Front wheel speed sensor wire-to-body bolt: 80 inch lbs. (9 Nm)

Rear

1. Remove the wheel and tire.

✳✳ WARNING

Care must be taken during the removal of the plug to prevent damage. If the plug is damaged, a new sensor may need to be installed even though the sensor is functional in all other aspects.

2. Remove the grommet from the body.

3. When removing the body plug, rotate the plug into a position which allows the use of a small screwdriver to release the tabs on the underside of the body plug. These 2 tabs are located at right angles to the sensor wire.

4. Disconnect the sensor wiring.

5. Detach the sensor wiring bolts.

➡ Clean off any dirt that may have collected around the sensor before removal.

6. Remove the bolt and the sensor.

➡ Thoroughly clean the mounting surface.

7. Installation is the reverse of the removal procedure. Tighten all retainers to 80 inch lbs. (9 Nm).

BRAKES

BLEEDING PROCEDURE

BLEEDING PROCEDURE

• Use of any other than the approved DOT 3 brake fluid will cause permanent damage to brake components and will render the brakes inoperative. Failure to follow these instructions may result in personal injury.

• Brake fluid contains polyglycol ethers and polyglycols. Avoid contact with eyes. Wash hands thoroughly after handling. If brake fluid contacts eyes, flush eyes with running water for 15 minutes. Get medical attention if irritation persists. If taken internally, drink water and induce vomiting. Get medical attention immediately. Failure to

follow these instructions may result in personal injury.

• Do not allow the brake master cylinder reservoir to run dry during the bleeding operation. Keep the master cylinder reservoir filled with the specified brake fluid. Never reuse the brake fluid that has been drained from the hydraulic system.

• Brake fluid is harmful to painted and plastic surfaces. If brake fluid is spilled onto a painted or plastic surface, immediately wash it with water.

• When any part of the hydraulic system has been disconnected or a new component is installed, air may enter the system, causing spongy brake pedal action.

BLEEDING THE BRAKE SYSTEM

This requires the bleeding of the hydraulic system after it has been correctly connected.

Manual Bleeding

1. Before servicing the vehicle, refer to the Precautions Section.

✳✳ WARNING

Be sure to check the brake fluid level in the brake master cylinder reservoir often. Do not let it run dry.

2. Fill the brake master cylinder reservoir with the specified brake fluid.

3. Begin bleeding the system, going in order from the right rear wheel, to the left

rear wheel, to the right front wheel, and ending with the left front wheel.

4. Attach a rubber drain hose to the rear bleeder screw and submerge the free end in a container partially filled with clean brake fluid.

5. Have an assistant pump the brake pedal 10 times and then hold firm pressure on the brake pedal.

6. Loosen the bleeder screw until the fluid flow stops. Maintain pressure on the brake pedal and tighten the bleeder screw.

7. Repeat Steps 4 and 5 until clear, bubble-free brake fluid flows.

8. Tighten the bleeder screw to 12 ft. lbs. (16 Nm).

9. Refill the brake master cylinder reservoir as necessary.

10. Continue bleeding the brake hydraulic system at each wheel.

11. Fill the brake master cylinder reservoir with the specified brake fluid.

ABS BLEEDING

➡ **Bleeding the Hydraulic Control Unit (HCU) is required only when removing or installing the HCU or master cylinder, or opening the lines to the HCU.**

➡ **Carrying out the System Bleed function drives trapped air from the HCU. Subsequent bleeding removes the air from the brake hydraulic system through the bleeder screws.**

➡ **Adequate voltage to the HCU module is required during the anti-lock control portion of the system bleed.**

1. Connect a suitable scan/diagnostic tool.

2. Access the SYSTEM BLEED FUNCTION. Go to the Tool Tab-Chassis-Braking-ABS Service Bleed and follow the directions on the diagnostic tool.

3. Manually bleed the brake hydraulic system. For additional information, refer to Manual Bleed in this section.

4. Repeat the procedure carrying out a total of two diagnostic tool cycles and two manual bleed cycles.

BRAKES

FRONT DISC BRAKES

❊❊ CAUTION

Dust and dirt accumulating on brake parts during normal use may contain asbestos fibers from production or aftermarket brake linings. Breathing excessive concentrations of asbestos fibers can cause serious bodily harm. Exercise care when servicing brake parts. Do not sand or grind brake lining unless equipment used is designed to contain the dust residue. Do not clean brake parts with compressed air or by dry brushing. Cleaning should be done by dampening the brake components with a fine mist of water, then wiping the brake components clean with a dampened cloth. Dispose of cloth and all residue containing asbestos fibers in an impermeable container with the appropriate label. Follow practices prescribed by the Occupational Safety and Health Administration (OSHA) and the Environmental Protection Agency (EPA) for the handling, processing, and disposing of dust or debris that may contain asbestos fibers.

BRAKE CALIPER

REMOVAL & INSTALLATION

1. Before servicing the vehicle, refer to the Precautions Section.

➡ **The rear brake pads will wear at approximately twice the rate of the front brake pads. With the vehicle in NEUTRAL, position it on a hoist.**

➡ **The following steps must be followed to prevent the accumulator from charging and pressurizing the brake system.**

2. Disconnect the battery.

3. Remove the battery junction box (BJB) fuses 24 (50A) and 31 (50A).

4. Remove the brake caliper clip.

5. Loosen the brake caliper jounce hose at the brake caliper.

6. Remove the 2 brake caliper dust boot caps.

7. Remove the 2 brake caliper guide bolts.

8. Unthread the brake caliper from the brake caliper jounce hose. Remove the brake caliper.

➡ **Make sure that the brake caliper jounce hose is not twisted.**

9. To install, reverse the removal procedure. Observe the following torques:
- Brake caliper guide bolts: 33 ft. lbs. (45 Nm)
- Brake hose at the brake caliper: 15 ft. lbs. (20 Nm)

10. Bleed the brake system.

DISC BRAKE PADS

REMOVAL & INSTALLATION

2005–07 Models

1. Before servicing the vehicle, refer to the Precautions Section.

2. With the vehicle in NEUTRAL, position it on a hoist.

➡ **The following steps must be followed to prevent the accumulator from charging and pressurizing the brake system.**

3. Disconnect the battery.

4. Remove the battery junction box (BJB) fuses 24 (50A) and 31 (50A).

5. Remove the brake caliper clip.

6. Remove the 2 brake caliper dust boot caps.

7. Remove the 2 brake caliper guide bolts.

❊❊ WARNING

Do not allow the brake caliper to hang by the brake caliper jounce hose.

8. Remove the brake caliper and support the brake caliper to the vehicle.

9. Remove the inboard brake pad from the brake caliper.

10. Remove the outboard brake pad from the brake caliper anchor plate.

11. To install, reverse the removal procedure. Torque the caliper pin bolts to 33 ft. lbs. (45 Nm).

2008 Models

See Figures 2 and 3.

1. Before servicing the vehicle, refer to the Precautions Section.

2. With the vehicle in NEUTRAL, position it on a hoist.

➡ **The following steps must be followed to prevent the accumulator from charging and pressurizing the brake system.**

3. Disconnect the battery.

4. Remove the battery junction box (BJB) fuses 24 (50A) and 31 (50A).

5. For the LH brake caliper, release the lower portion of the brake pad anti-rattle spring.

6. Apply force to the center of the spring and pull outward at the bottom of the spring to remove it from the lower brake caliper cavity.

7. Rotate the spring upward and remove it from the brake caliper.

8. For the RH brake caliper, release the upper portion of the brake pad anti-rattle spring.

9. Apply force to the center of the spring and pull outward at the top of the spring to remove it from the upper brake caliper cavity.

10. Rotate the spring downward and remove it from the brake caliper.

11. Remove the 2 guide pin bushing caps and the 2 brake caliper guide pin bolts, position the caliper aside.

12. Support the caliper using mechanic's wire.

13. Remove the 2 brake pads from the caliper.

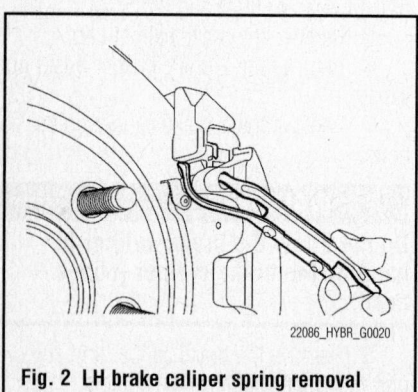

Fig. 2 LH brake caliper spring removal

14. Use a suitable tool to protect the brake caliper piston and compress the brake caliper piston into the brake caliper.

15. Inspect the brake disc and resurface or install new as necessary

To install:

16. Clean, dry and inspect the brake caliper anchor plate. Apply a light coat of specified lubricant to the 4 brake pad

➡**NOTE: Make sure that the brake flexible hose is not twisted.**

17. Install the brake pads onto the caliper and position the brake caliper onto the anchor plate.

18. Install the 2 brake caliper guide pin bolts and tighten to 26 ft. lbs. (35 Nm) install the 2 bushing caps.

➡**The 2-tabbed end of the brake pad anti-rattle spring must be installed first.**

19. Install the brake pad anti-rattle spring using the following procedure:

- Insert the tab of the spring into the brake caliper cavity.
- Twist the tab into the cavity (LH side in the upper brake caliper cavity, RH side in the lower brake caliper cavity).
- Rotate the brake pad anti-rattle spring and position the upper portion onto the anchor plate.
- Position the lower portion of the brake pad anti-rattle spring onto the anchor plate.

- Push down and inward until the upper and lower ends of the brake pad anti-rattle spring are latched and seated in the brake caliper cavities.

❋❋ WARNING

The latch MUST be positioned as shown, or damage to component may occur.

➡**Verify that the brake pad anti-rattle spring is correctly latched by pulling on the spring.**

20. Install the wheel and tire.

21. Install the battery junction box (BJB) fuses 24 (50A) and 31 (50A).

22. Connect the battery.

23. Fill the brake master cylinder reservoir with clean, specified brake fluid.

24. Test the brakes for normal operation.

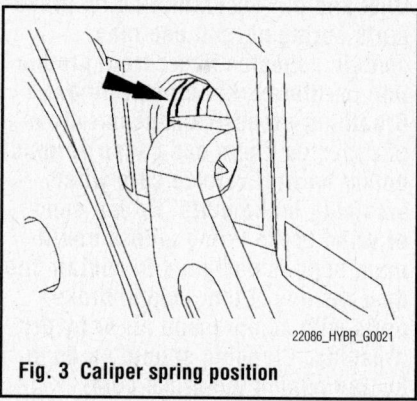

Fig. 3 Caliper spring position

BRAKES

❋❋ CAUTION

Dust and dirt accumulating on brake parts during normal use may contain asbestos fibers from production or aftermarket brake linings. Breathing excessive concentrations of asbestos fibers can cause serious bodily harm. Exercise care when servicing brake parts. Do not sand or grind brake lining unless equipment used is designed to contain the dust residue. Do not clean brake parts with compressed air or by dry brushing. Cleaning should be done by dampening the brake components with a fine mist of water, then wiping the brake components clean with a dampened cloth. Dispose of cloth and all residue containing asbestos fibers in an impermeable container with the appropriate label. Follow practices

prescribed by the Occupational Safety and Health Administration (OSHA) and the Environmental Protection Agency (EPA) for the handling, processing, and disposing of dust or debris that may contain asbestos fibers.

BRAKE CALIPER

REMOVAL & INSTALLATION

1. Before servicing the vehicle, refer to the Precautions Section.

➡**The rear brake pads will wear at approximately twice the rate of the front brake pads.**

2. With the vehicle in NEUTRAL, position it on a hoist.

➡**The following steps must be followed to prevent the accumulator**

REAR DISC BRAKES

from charging and pressurizing the brake system.

3. Disconnect the battery.

4. Remove the battery junction box (BJB) fuses 24 (50A) and 31 (50A).

➡**Install new copper washers.**

5. Remove the brake caliper jounce hose flow bolt and discard the 2 copper washers.

6. Remove the 2 brake caliper guide bolts.

7. Remove the brake caliper.

8. To install, reverse the removal procedure. Observe the following torques:

- Brake caliper guide bolts: 26 ft. lbs. (35 Nm)
- Brake caliper hose flow bolt: 26 ft. lbs. (35 Nm)

9. Bleed the brake system.

DISC BRAKE PADS

REMOVAL & INSTALLATION

1. Before servicing the vehicle, refer to the Precautions Section.

➡ **The rear brake pads will wear at approximately twice the rate of the front brake pads.**

2. With the vehicle in NEUTRAL, position it on a hoist.

➡ **The following steps must be followed to prevent the accumulator from charging and pressurizing the brake system.**

3. Disconnect the battery.

4. Remove the battery junction box (BJB) fuses 24 (50A) and 31 (50A).

5. Remove the 2 brake caliper guide bolts.

✳✳ WARNING

Do not allow the brake caliper to hang by the brake caliper jounce hose.

6. Remove the brake caliper and secure the brake caliper to the vehicle.

7. Remove the inboard and outboard brake pads from the brake caliper. Torque the 2 brake caliper guide bolts to 26 ft. lbs. (35 Nm).

BRAKES

✳✳ CAUTION

Dust and dirt accumulating on brake parts during normal use may contain asbestos fibers from production or aftermarket brake linings. Breathing excessive concentrations of asbestos fibers can cause serious bodily harm. Exercise care when servicing brake parts. Do not sand or grind brake lining unless equipment used is designed to contain the dust residue. Do not clean brake parts with compressed air or by dry brushing. Cleaning should be done by dampening the brake components with a fine mist of water, then wiping the brake components clean with a dampened cloth. Dispose of cloth and all residue containing asbestos fibers in an impermeable container with the appropriate label. Follow practices prescribed by the Occupational Safety and Health Administration (OSHA) and the Environmental Protection Agency (EPA) for the handling, processing, and disposing of dust or debris that may contain asbestos fibers.

BRAKE DRUM

REMOVAL & INSTALLATION

See Figure 4.

1. Before servicing the vehicle, refer to the Precautions Section.

2. Remove the tire and wheel assembly.

✳✳ CAUTION

Use of a brake drum puller or a torch is not recommended. Brake drum distortion can result.

➡ **If the brake drum is rusted to the axle shaft pilot diameter, tap the center** of the brake drum between the wheel studs.

3. Remove the brake drum.

4. If equipped, remove the brake drum retaining clips.

5. If the brake drums will not come off, follow these steps.

6. Move the brake shoe adjusting lever off the brake adjuster screw.

REAR DRUM BRAKES

7. Loosen the brake shoe adjuster screw nut by adjusting the nut upward.

8. Using the special tool, 134-R0191, measure the brake drum inside diameter.

9. Install a new brake drum if the maximum inside diameter exceeds the specification shown on the outside of the brake drum.

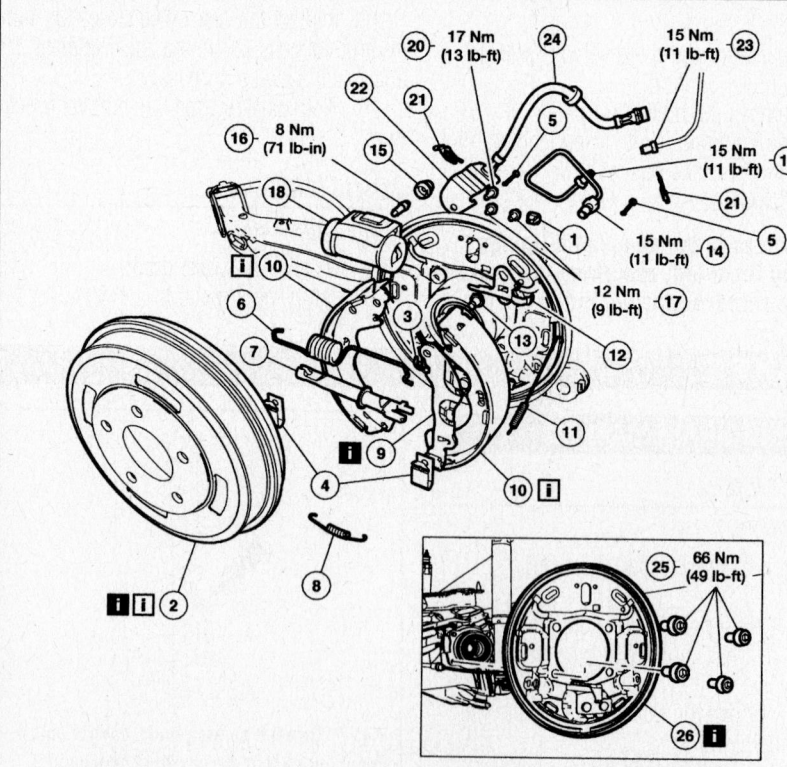

1 Plug	10 Brake shoe (kit)	19 Brake line fitting nut
2 Brake drum	11 Adjuster lever spring	20 Jounce hose bracket bolt
3 Parking brake lever clip	12 Adjuster lever (LH/RH)	21 Jounce hose retaining clips
4 Brake shoe retaining clips	13 Pivot pin (part of 2200)	22 Jounce hose bracket
5 Brake shoe retaining pins	14 Brake line fitting nut	23 Brake line fitting nut
6 Upper return spring	15 Bleeder screw cap	24 Jounce hose (LH/RH)
7 Adjuster assembly (LH/RH)	16 Bleeder screw	25 Backing plate bolts
8 Lower return spring	17 Wheel cylinder bolts	26 Backing plate
9 Parking brake actuator lever (LH/RH)	18 Wheel cylinder	

67197-ESCA-G51

Fig. 4 Drum brake exploded view

To install:

※※ WARNING

Whenever a wheel is installed, always remove any corrosion, dirt or foreign material present on the mounting surfaces of the wheel or the surface of the wheel hub, brake drum or brake disc that contacts the wheel. Installing wheels without correct metal-to-metal contact at the wheel mounting surfaces can cause the wheel nuts to loosen and the wheel to come off while the vehicle is in motion, causing loss of control. Failure to follow these instructions may result in personal injury.

10. Clean the wheel hub mounting surface and wheel pilot.
11. Install the tire and wheel assembly.

BRAKE SHOES

REMOVAL & INSTALLATION

See Figure 4.

1. Before servicing the vehicle, refer to the Precautions Section.
2. Remove the brake drum.
3. Use the Brake/Clutch/Service Vacuum to remove brake dust and dirt from the brake assemblies.

➡ If new rear brake shoes and linings are being installed, resurface the brake drums to remove glazing and to ensure an equal friction surface from side-to-side. Resurfacing will also correct out-of-round and bell conditions.

4. Using the special tool, measure the braking surface diameter. If the inside diameter measures more than the maximum specification shown on the outside of the brake drum, install a new brake drum.
5. Remove the parking brake cable from the parking brake cable lever.
6. Remove the hold-down clips and pins.
7. Remove the lower spring.
8. Remove the rear brake shoes.
9. Pull the bottom of the brake shoe forward.
10. Release the upper return spring.
11. Remove both brake shoes together.
12. Remove the self adjuster lever.
13. Remove the self adjuster and spring assembly.
14. Return the self adjuster to the fully seated position.
15. Remove the parking brake lever.
16. Remove the horseshoe clip.
17. Remove the parking brake lever.
18. Inspect the rear brake shoes for minimum thickness above the backing plate, and install new as necessary.
19. To install, reverse the removal procedure.

ADJUSTMENT

See Figures 5 and 6.

1. Remove the brake drum.
2. Using the special tool, 134-R0191, measure the brake drum inside diameter.
3. Position the special tool on the brake shoes and linings and adjust accordingly.
4. Install the brake drum

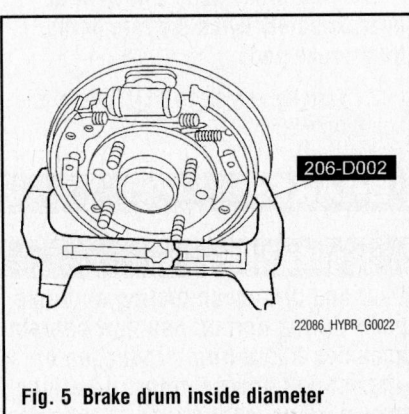

Fig. 5 Brake drum inside diameter

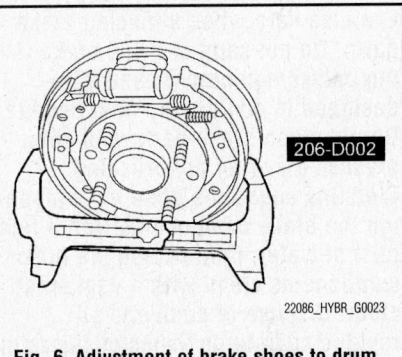

Fig. 6 Adjustment of brake shoes to drum inside diameter

BRAKES

PARKING BRAKE CABLES

ADJUSTMENT

See Figure 7:

1. On vehicle with low series floor console:
    a. If equipped, remove the manual transaxle shift knob by turning counterclockwise.
    b. Remove the floor console front finish panel.
    c. Apply the parking brake, then remove the floor console rear finish panel.
2. On vehicle with high series floor console:
    a. Apply the parking brake.
    b. Remove the floor console finish panel.
3. Remove the adjustment nut clip.
4. Turn the parking brake control adjustment nut so that the parking brake control stroke is three to five notches when pulled.

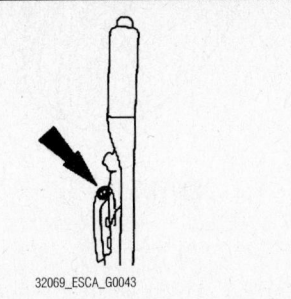

Fig. 7 Turn the parking brake control adjustment nut so that the parking brake control stroke is three to five notches when pulled

5. Confirm the parking brake is applied.
6. Install the adjustment nut clip.
7. On vehicles with high series floor console:
    a. Install the floor console rear finish panel.
8. On vehicles with low series floor console:

PARKING BRAKE

    a. Install the floor console rear finish panel.
    b. Install the floor console front finish panel. If equipped, install the manual transaxle shifter knob by turning clockwise.

PARKING BRAKE SHOES

REMOVAL & INSTALLATION

With Rear Drum Brakes

The rear drum brake shoes serve as the parking brakes. Refer to the procedures under Rear Drum Brakes.

With Rear Disc Brakes

See Figure 8.

1. Before servicing the vehicle, refer to the Precautions Section.
2. Remove the rear brake disc.
3. Remove the parking brake shoe upper return spring.

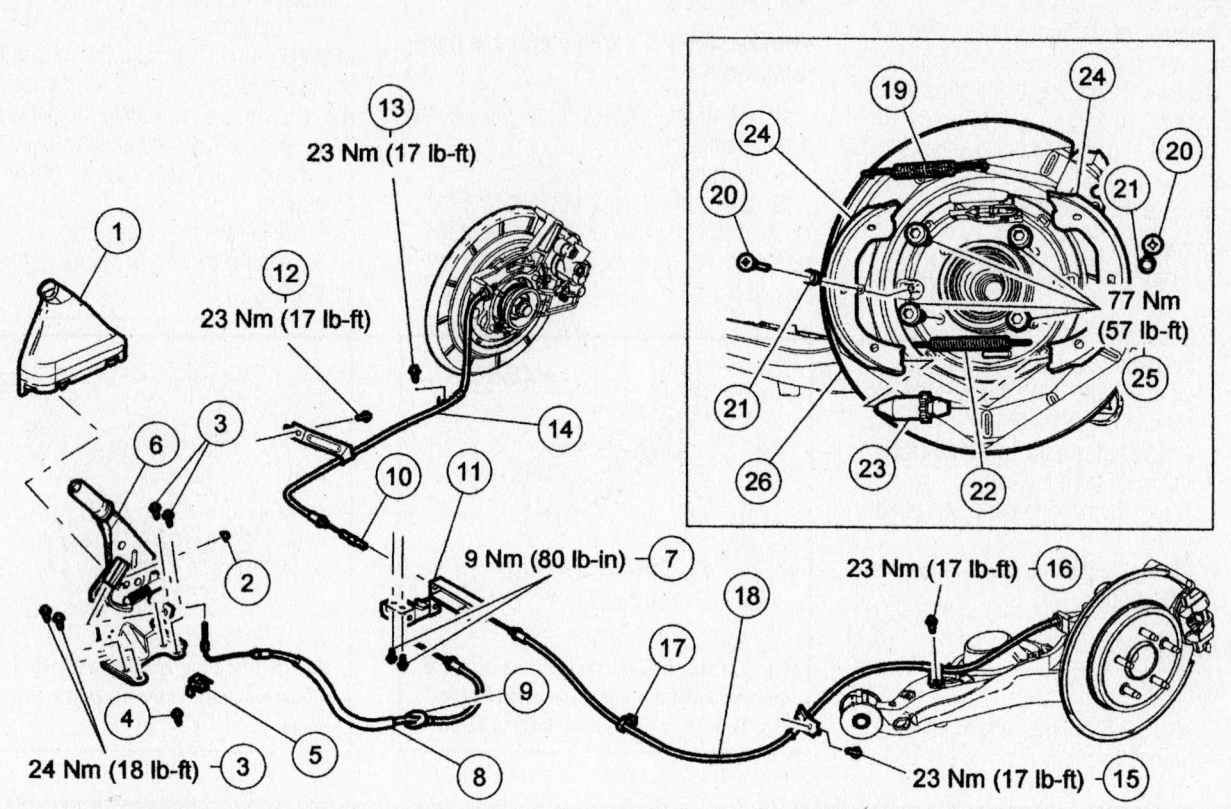

23 Nm (17 lb-ft)

23 Nm (17 lb-ft)

77 Nm (57 lb-ft)

9 Nm (80 lb-in)

23 Nm (17 lb-ft)

24 Nm (18 lb-ft)

23 Nm (17 lb-ft)

1 Parking brake control boot	15 Cable bracket-to-body bolt
2 Front cable adjuster nut	16 Cable bracket-to-trailing arm bolt
3 Parking brake control bolts (4 required)	17 Cable-to-fuel tank strap clip
4 Warning indicator switch screw	18 Rear parking brake cable (LH)
5 Warning indicator switch	19 Parking brake shoe upper return spring
6 Parking brake control	20 Parking brake shoe retaining pins (2 required)
7 Parking brake equalizer bracket bolts (2 required)	21 Parking brake shoe retaining springs (2 required)
8 Front parking brake cable	22 Parking brake shoe lower return spring
9 Grommet	23 Parking brake shoe adjuster
10 Cable connector	24 Parking brake shoe (LH/RH)
11 Parking brake equalizer and bracket	25 Support plate bolts (4 required)
12 Cable bracket-to-body bolt	26 Support plate (LH/RH)
13 Cable bracket-to-trailing arm bolt	
14 Rear parking brake cable (RH)	

06017-ESCA-G99

Fig. 8 Parking brake system—with rear disc brakes

4. Remove the 2 parking brake shoe retaining pins.

5. Remove the 2 parking brake shoe retaining springs.

6. Remove the parking brake shoe lower return spring.

7. Remove the parking brake shoe adjuster.

8. Remove the parking brake shoes.

To install:

9. To install, reverse the removal procedure.

- Using anti-seize lubricant, lubricate the parking brake shoe contact points before installation of the rear parking brake shoes.
- Lubricate the adjust screw threads with anti-seize lubricant.
- Adjust the parking brake shoe and lining.
- Check the parking brake for normal operation.

ADJUSTMENT

See Figures 9 and 10.

1. Before servicing the vehicle, refer to the Precautions Section.

2. With the vehicle in NEUTRAL, position it on a hoist.

➡**Make sure the parking brake is fully released.**

3. Using the release handle, release the parking brake control.

4. Remove the rear brake disc.

5. Using the special tool, measure the inside diameter of the drum portion of the rear brake disc and set the locking screw. Record the measurement.

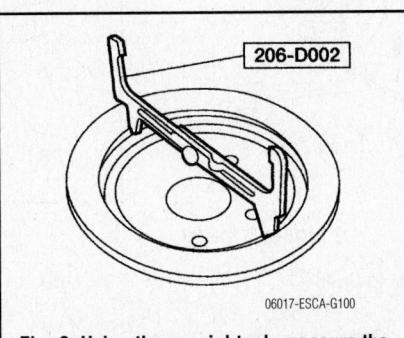

Fig. 9 Using the special tool, measure the inside diameter of the drum portion of the rear brake disc and set the locking screw

6. Place the special tool over the widest diameter of the parking brake shoes.

7. Adjust the parking brake shoe clearance to 1.07 mm (0.04 in) less than the inside diameter of the drum portion of the rear brake disc. Rotate the parking brake shoe adjuster to achieve the correct parking brake shoe-to-brake disc clearance.

8. Install the rear brake disc.

9. Test the parking brake for normal operation.

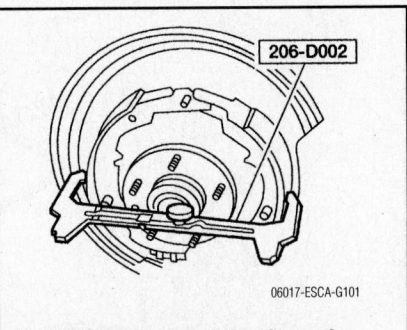

Fig. 10 Place the special tool over the widest diameter of the parking brake shoes

CHASSIS ELECTRICAL

AIR BAG (SUPPLEMENTAL RESTRAINT SYSTEM)

GENERAL INFORMATION

✳✳ CAUTION

These vehicles are equipped with an air bag system. The system must be disarmed before performing service on, or around, system components, the steering column, instrument panel components, wiring and sensors. Failure to follow the safety precautions and the disarming procedure could result in accidental air bag deployment, possible injury and unnecessary system repairs.

SERVICE PRECAUTIONS

Disconnect and isolate the battery negative cable before beginning any airbag system component diagnosis, testing, removal, or installation procedures. Allow system capacitor to discharge for two minutes before beginning any component service. This will disable the airbag system. Failure to disable the airbag system may result in accidental airbag deployment, personal injury, or death.

Do not place an intact undeployed airbag face down on a solid surface. The airbag will propel into the air if accidentally deployed and may result in personal injury or death.

When carrying or handling an undeployed airbag, the trim side (face) of the airbag should be pointing towards the body to minimize possibility of injury if accidental deployment occurs. Failure to do this may result in personal injury or death.

Replace airbag system components with OEM replacement parts. Substitute parts may appear interchangeable, but internal differences may result in inferior occupant protection. Failure to do so may result in occupant personal injury or death.

Wear safety glasses, rubber gloves, and long sleeved clothing when cleaning powder residue from vehicle after an airbag deployment. Powder residue emitted from a deployed airbag can cause skin irritation. Flush affected area with cool water if irritation is experienced. If nasal or throat irritation is experienced, exit the vehicle for fresh air until the irritation ceases. If irritation continues, see a physician.

Do not use a replacement airbag that is not in the original packaging. This may result in improper deployment, personal injury, or death.

The factory installed fasteners, screws and bolts used to fasten airbag components have a special coating and are specifically designed for the airbag system. Do not use substitute fasteners. Use only original equipment fasteners listed in the parts catalog when fastener replacement is required.

During, and following, any child restraint anchor service, due to impact event or vehicle repair, carefully inspect all mounting hardware, tether straps, and anchors for proper installation, operation, or damage. If a child restraint anchor is found damaged in any way, the anchor must be replaced. Failure to do this may result in personal injury or death.

Deployed and non-deployed airbags may or may not have live pyrotechnic material within the airbag inflator.

Do not dispose of driver/passenger/curtain airbags or seat belt tensioners unless you are sure of complete deployment. Refer to the Hazardous Substance Control System for proper disposal.

Dispose of deployed airbags and tensioners consistent with state, provincial, local, and federal regulations.

After any airbag component testing or service, do not connect the battery negative cable. Personal injury or death may result if the system test is not performed first.

If the vehicle is equipped with the Occupant Classification System (OCS), do not connect the battery negative cable before

performing the OCS Verification Test using the scan tool and the appropriate diagnostic information. Personal injury or death may result if the system test is not performed properly.

Never replace both the Occupant Restraint Controller (ORC) and the Occupant Classification Module (OCM) at the same time. If both require replacement, replace one, then perform the Airbag System test before replacing the other.

Both the ORC and the OCM store Occupant Classification System (OCS) calibration data, which they transfer to one another when one of them is replaced. If both are replaced at the same time, an irreversible fault will be set in both modules and the OCS may malfunction and cause personal injury or death.

If equipped with OCS, the Seat Weight Sensor is a sensitive, calibrated unit and must be handled carefully. Do not drop or handle roughly. If dropped or damaged, replace with another sensor. Failure to do so may result in occupant injury or death.

If equipped with OCS, the front passenger seat must be handled carefully as well. When removing the seat, be careful when setting on floor not to drop. If dropped, the sensor may be inoperative, could result in occupant injury, or possibly death.

If equipped with OCS, when the passenger front seat is on the floor, no one should sit in the front passenger seat. This uneven force may damage the sensing ability of the seat weight sensors. If sat on and damaged, the sensor may be inoperative, could result in occupant injury, or possibly death.

DISARMING THE SYSTEM

1. Before servicing the vehicle, refer to the Precautions Section.
2. Turn all vehicle accessories OFF.
3. Turn the ignition switch to OFF.
4. At the central junction box (CJB), located below the left side of the instrument panel, remove the cover and the restraints control module (RCM) fuse(s) from the CJB. See the Owner's Manual.
5. Turn the ignition ON and visually monitor the air bag indicator for at least 30 seconds. The air bag indicator will remain lit continuously (no flashing) if the correct RCM fuse has been removed. If the air bag indicator does not remain lit continuously, remove the correct RCM fuse before proceeding.
6. Turn the ignition OFF.

✳✳ CAUTION

To avoid accidental deployment and possible personal injury, the backup

power supply must be depleted before repairing or replacing any front or side air bag Supplemental Restraint System (SRS) components and before servicing, replacing, adjusting or striking components near the front or side air bag sensors, such as doors, instrument panel, console, door latches, strikers, seats and hood latches.

The front impact severity sensor is located on the radiator support bracket.

The first row side impact sensors (if equipped) are located at or near the base of the B-pillars.

The second row side impact sensors (if equipped) are located on the C-pillar.

➡**To deplete the backup power supply energy, disconnect the battery ground cable and wait at least one minute. Be sure to disconnect auxiliary batteries and power supplies (if equipped).**

7. Disconnect the battery ground cable and wait at least one minute

ARMING THE SYSTEM

1. Before servicing the vehicle, refer to the Precautions Section.

✳✳ CAUTION

The restraint system diagnostic tool is for restraint system service only. Remove from vehicle prior to road use. Failure to remove could result in injury and possible violation of vehicle safety standards.

2. Make sure all restraint system diagnostic tool(s) that may have been installed during the repair have been removed from the vehicle and all SRS components are connected.
3. Turn the ignition switch from OFF to ON.
4. Install RCM fuse(s) to the CJB and close the cover.

✳✳ CAUTION

Be sure that nobody is in the vehicle and that there is nothing blocking or set in front of any air bag module when the battery ground cable is connected.

5. Connect the battery ground cable.
6. Prove out the Supplemental Restraint System (SRS) as follows:
   a. Turn the ignition key from ON to OFF. Wait 10 seconds, then turn the key back to ON and visually monitor the air

bag indicator with the air bag modules installed. The air bag indicator will light continuously for approximately six seconds and then turn off. If an air bag Supplemental Restraint System (SRS) fault is present, the air bag indicator will either:
   • fail to light.
   • remain lit continuously.
   • flash.
   b. The flashing might not occur until approximately 30 seconds after the ignition switch has been turned from the OFF to the ON position. This is the time required for the restraints control module (RCM) to complete the testing of the SRS. If the air bag indicator is inoperative and a SRS fault exists, a chime will sound in a pattern of five sets of five beeps. If this occurs, the air bag indicator and any SRS fault discovered must be diagnosed and repaired.
7. Clear all continuous DTCs from the restraints control module using a scan tool.

CLOCKSPRING CENTERING

See Figure 11.

1. Before servicing the vehicle, refer to the Precautions Section.

✳✳ CAUTION

Incorrect centralization may result in premature component failure. If in doubt when centralizing the clockspring, repeat the centralizing procedure. Failure to follow this instruction may result in personal injury.

➡**Make sure the road wheels are in the straight-ahead position.**

2. If the vehicle's clockspring has rotated out of center, follow these steps to center the clockspring.
   c. Hold the clockspring outer housing stationary.

✳✳ WARNING

Overturning will destroy the clockspring. The internal ribbon wire acts as the stop and can be broken from its internal connection.

   d. While turning the rotor clockwise, carefully feel for the ribbon wire to run out of length and for a slight resistance. Stop turning at this point.
   e. Turn the clockspring counterclockwise until the yellow indicator shows anywhere in the window (window

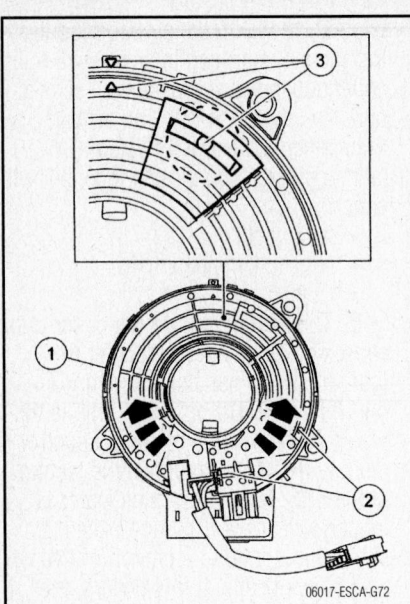

Fig. 11 Outer housing (1), rotor (2), clockspring aligning

will be near the 1 o'clock position) and the arrow on the rotor lines up with the arrow on the top of the housing. The clockspring is now centered. Do not allow the rotor to turn from this position.

CLOCKSPRING REMOVAL & INSTALLATION

See Figures 12 through 15.

1. Before servicing the vehicle, refer to the Precautions Section.
2. Disarm the Supplemental Restraint System (SRS). Refer to the Chassis Electrical Section.
3. Make sure the road wheels are in the straight-ahead position.
4. Position the steering wheel in the

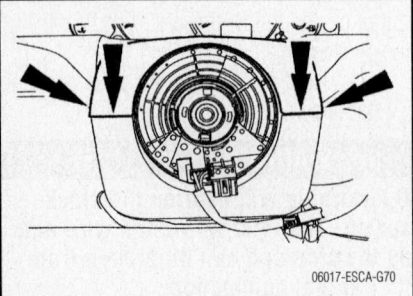

Fig. 12 Push in where indicated, releasing the retaining tabs, and remove the upper steering column shroud

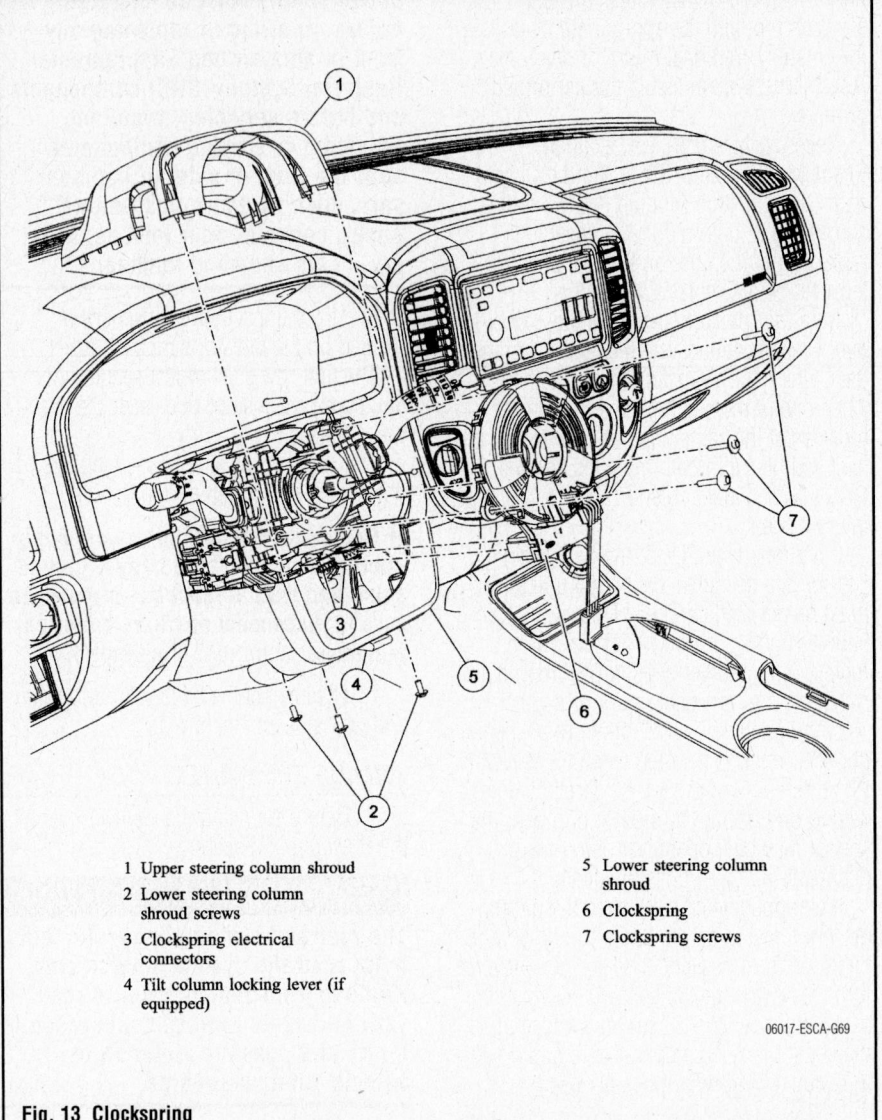

1 Upper steering column shroud	5 Lower steering column shroud
2 Lower steering column shroud screws	6 Clockspring
3 Clockspring electrical connectors	7 Clockspring screws
4 Tilt column locking lever (if equipped)	

Fig. 13 Clockspring

straight-ahead position and remove the ignition key. Rotate the steering wheel until the steering column locks into position.

5. Open the cover on the underside of the steering wheel.
6. Remove the steering wheel pinion bolt.
7. Remove the steering wheel. Position the steering wheel rearward. Disconnect the 2 electrical connectors.
8. If equipped with tilt steering, position the steering column completely downward and lock in place.
9. Push in where indicated, releasing the retaining tabs, and remove the upper steering column shroud.
10. Release the tilt column locking lever,

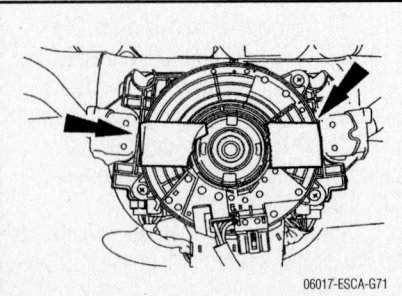

Fig. 14 If installing the same clockspring, apply 2 strips of masking tape across the clockspring to prevent accidental rotation when the clockspring is removed

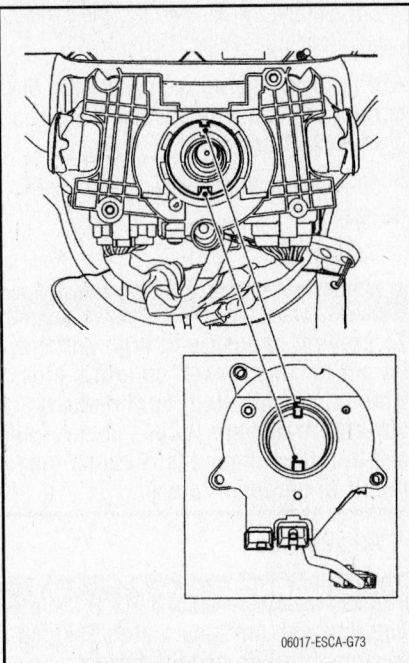

06017-ESCA-G73

Fig. 15 Clockspring installation

allowing the steering column to move upward. Do not lock the tilt column locking lever back in place.

11. Remove the 3 screws and position the lower steering column shroud aside.

12. If installing the same clockspring, apply 2 strips of masking tape across the clockspring to prevent accidental rotation when the clockspring is removed.

13. Remove the 3 clockspring screws.

➡**If the clockspring is to be reinstalled, do not allow the clockspring to turn from its removal position.**

14. Partially remove the clockspring, then disconnect the 2 electrical connectors and remove the clockspring.

To install:

15. Connect the 2 clockspring electrical connectors to the clockspring.

➡**Slight turning of the clockspring rotor is allowable for alignment purposes to the steering column.**

16. Align the clockspring for installation.
   a. Align the large slot to the large tab in the clockspring.
   b. Align the small slot to the small tab in the clockspring.

17. Install the 3 clockspring screws.

18. For vehicles reusing a clockspring that was removed, remove the tape. For vehicles installing a new clockspring, remove the retaining pin.

19. Install the lower steering column shroud and the 3 screws.

20. Position the steering column completely downward and lock in place.

21. Install the upper steering column shroud and engage the retaining tabs.

22. Install the steering wheel. Torque the steering wheel pinion bolt to 9 ft. lbs. (12 Nm).

23. Rearm the Supplemental Restraint System (SRS). Refer to the Chassis Electrical Section.

DRIVE TRAIN

AUTOMATIC TRANSAXLE ASSEMBLY

REMOVAL & INSTALLATION

eCVT Transaxle

1. Before servicing the vehicle, refer to the Precautions Section.

❊❊ **CAUTION**

Before proceeding, read and observe all of the High Voltage System Precautions.

❊❊ **CAUTION**

To prevent exposure to high voltage, do not for any reason open the electronically controlled, continuously variable transaxle (eCVT) cover. Failure to follow these instructions may result in personal injury.

All vehicles

2. With the vehicle in DRIVE, position it on a hoist.

3. Release the fuel system pressure.

4. Disconnect the battery ground cable.

❊❊ **WARNING**

Before removing the high voltage cables, the vehicle electrical system must be completely shut down for at least 10 minutes to allow for the high voltage capacitors to discharge.

5. Disarm the high voltage traction battery. Establish a buffer zone. See the procedure under Disarming the High Voltage Traction Battery.

6. Drain the engine cooling system.

❊❊ **WARNING**

The coolant must be recovered in a suitable, clean container for reuse. If the coolant is contaminated, it must be recycled or disposed of correctly.

❊❊ **WARNING**

Always refill the motor electronics cooling system (MECS) with the same type of coolant that was drained from the system. Do not mix coolant types.

7. Turn the ignition to the OFF position.

8. Remove the left splash shield.

9. Place a suitable container below the transaxle.

10. Loosen the hose clamps at the transaxle, then pull the hoses off to allow the coolant to drain.

11. Remove the upper and lower intake manifold.

12. Remove the engine air cleaner.

13. Remove the exhaust manifold/catalytic converter.

14. Disconnect the motor electronics coolant vent hose.

15. Disconnect the 2 engine coolant vent hoses.

16. Remove the degas bottle bolt and nut.

17. Lift the degas bottle up and disconnect the engine coolant and motor electronics coolant return hoses.

18. Remove the degas bottle.

19. Remove the accessory drive belt.

20. Remove the left front drive halfshaft.

4WD vehicles

21. Remove the transfer case.

2WD vehicles

22. Remove the front drive intermediate halfshaft.

23. Remove the bolts and the lateral support crossmember.

All vehicles

24. Drain the engine oil.

25. Disconnect the heater hoses from the heater core.

26. Detach the heater hose retaining clip from the transaxle mount stud.

27. Disconnect the upper radiator and coolant vent hoses.

28. Disconnect the following electrical connectors:
   • Secondary Air Injection (AIR) solenoid
   • Transaxle mount control solenoid
   • Purge valve

29. Disconnect the engine control harness.

30. Disconnect the 2 engine control harness electrical connectors and the 2 pin-type retainers.

31. Remove the bolt and disconnect the transaxle harness electrical connector.

32. Disconnect the DC-to-DC converter electrical connector and pin-type retainer.

33. Disconnect and remove the fuel supply tube and evaporative emissions (EVAP) tube.

34. If equipped, position the block heater wiring harness aside. Detach the 3 harness retainer clips. Route the harness through the radiator support into the engine compartment.

35. Remove the 2 bolts and disconnect the auxiliary coolant pump electrical connector.

36. Position the auxiliary coolant pump aside.

37. Remove the bolts and the transaxle control splash shield.

38. Disconnect the transaxle control cable.

39. Disconnect the pin-type retainer.

40. Disconnect the pin-type retainer and position the transaxle control cable aside.

41. Disconnect the motor electronics coolant temperature sensor electrical connector and pin-type retainer.

42. Disconnect the transaxle coolant hoses.

43. Remove the nut and the ground cable.

44. Remove the 2 bolts and position the motor electronics coolant pump aside.

45. Disconnect the lower radiator hose from the radiator.

46. Disconnect the A/C compressor electrical connector and remove the 3 bolts. Position the A/C compressor aside and support the compressor with a length of mechanic's wire.

47. Remove the front roll restrictor bolt.

48. Remove the rear roll restrictor bolt.

49. Remove the nut, bolts and the engine support crossmember.

➡ **The transaxle-to-engine bolts differ in length. Mark the bolts for correct installation.**

50. Remove the 2 transaxle-to-engine bolts.

➡ **The transaxle-to-engine bolts differ in length. Mark the bolts for correct installation.**

51. Remove the 2 transaxle-to-engine bolts.

➡ **Due to the weight of the transaxle, special care should be taken to mount the powertrain securely to the lift table.**

52. Using the special tools, secure the engine to the lift table.

53. Remove the engine mount bracket bolt.

54. Remove the nuts and the engine mount bracket.

55. Remove the right transaxle mount bracket nut.

56. Remove the bolts and the right transaxle mount bracket.

57. Remove the bolts and the rear transaxle mount brace.

58. Remove the nuts, bolt and rear transaxle mount.

59. Lower the engine and transaxle from the vehicle.

60. Using the engine crane and spreader bar, remove the engine and transaxle from the lift table.

61. Disconnect the high voltage wiring harness electrical connector.

62. Disconnect the 2 low voltage wiring harness electrical connectors and position the harness aside.

➡ **The transaxle-to-engine bolts differ in length. Mark the bolts for correct installation.**

63. Remove the remaining 6 engine-to-transaxle bolts and separate the engine and transaxle.

✳✳ WARNING

The damper contains a clutch which designed to slip briefly during vehicle operation. It is essential that no grease, oil or cleaning solvents be allowed to contaminate the slip clutch. Do not use grease on transaxle input shaft or input shaft splines.

64. Should the damper become contaminated it must be replaced.

➡ **Due to packaging requirements, the correct bolt must be used at the damper locations.**

65. Remove the bolts and the transaxle damper.

To install:

✳✳ CAUTION

To prevent exposure to high voltage, do not for any reason open the electronically controlled, continuously variable transaxle (eCVT) cover. Failure to follow these instructions may result in personal injury.

All vehicles

✳✳ WARNING

The damper contains a clutch which designed to slip briefly during vehicle operation. It is essential that no grease, oil or cleaning solvents be allowed to contaminate the slip clutch. Do not use grease on transaxle input shaft or input shaft splines.

66. Should the damper become contaminated it must be replaced.

➡ **Due to packaging requirements, the correct bolt must be used at the damper locations.**

67. Install the transaxle damper. Tighten to 21 ft. lbs. (29 Nm).

✳✳ WARNING

When positioning the engine to the transaxle, care must be taken to maintain alignment of the damper spline with the transaxle input shaft.

➡ **Transaxle removed from view for clarity.**

68. Using the engine crane and spreader bar, position the engine and transaxle together.

69. Install the 6 transaxle-to-engine bolts. Tighten to 35 ft. lbs. (47 Nm).

70. Position the low voltage wiring harness and connect the 2 transaxle electrical connectors.

71. Connect the high voltage wiring harness electrical connector.

72. Using the engine crane and spreader bar, position the engine and transaxle onto the lift table.

✳✳ WARNING

Due to the weight of the transaxle, special care should be taken to mount the powertrain securely to the lift table.

73. Using the special tools, secure the engine to the lift table.

74. Raise the engine and transaxle into the vehicle.

75. Install the rear transaxle mount. Tighten to 66 ft. lbs. (90 Nm).

76. Install the rear transaxle mount bracket. Tighten to 18 ft. lbs. (25 Nm).

77. Install the right transaxle mount bracket. Tighten to 66 ft. lbs. (90 Nm).

78. Install the right transaxle mount bracket nut. Tighten to 66 ft. lbs. (90 Nm).

79. Install the engine mount bracket. Tighten to 66 ft. lbs. (90 Nm).

80. Install the engine mount bracket bolt. Tighten to 66 ft. lbs. (90 Nm).

81. Install the 2 transaxle-to-engine bolts. Tighten to 35 ft. lbs. (47 Nm).

82. Install the 2 transaxle-to-engine bolts. Tighten to 35 ft. lbs. (47 Nm).

83. Install the engine support cross-member nut and bolts. Tighten to 129 ft. lbs. (175 Nm).

84. Install the rear roll restrictor bolt. Tighten to 66 ft. lbs. (90 Nm).

85. Install the front roll restrictor bolt. Tighten to 85 ft. lbs. (115 Nm).

86. Install the A/C compressor and connect the A/C compressor electrical connector. Tighten to 18 ft. lbs. (25 Nm).

87. Connect the lower radiator hose to the radiator.

88. Install the motor electronics coolant pump. Tighten to 18 ft. lbs. (25 Nm).

89. Install the ground cable and nut. Tighten to 15 ft. lbs. (20 Nm).

90. Connect the transaxle coolant hoses.

91. Connect the motor electronics coolant temperature sensor electrical connector and pin-type retainer.

92. Position the transaxle control cable and connect the pin-type retainer.

93. Connect the pin-type retainer.

94. Connect the transaxle control cable. Install the transaxle control cable bracket and the 2 nuts finger tight. Attach the transaxle control cable to the control lever. Tighten to 16 ft. lbs. (22 Nm).

95. Position the control lever between the 2 casting ribs on the transaxle case.

96. Place the selector lever in the D position.

97. Tighten the transaxle control cable bracket nuts to 16 ft. lbs. (22 Nm).

98. To verify the correct cable adjustment, observe the control lever on the transaxle while an assistant shifts the selector lever to each range position ending in the D position.

99. Install the transaxle control splash shield. Tighten to 11 ft. lbs. (15 Nm).

100. Install the motor auxiliary coolant pump and connect the electrical connector. Tighten to 89 inch lbs. (10 Nm).

➡ **Parts removed from view for clarity.**

101. If equipped, install the block heater wiring harness. Route the harness through the radiator support. Attach the 3 harness retainer clips.

102. Install the fuel supply tube and evaporative emissions (EVAP) tube.

103. Connect the DC-to-DC converter electrical connector and pin-type retainer.

104. Connect the transaxle harness electrical connector and install the bolt. Tighten to 18 ft. lbs. (25 Nm).

105. Connect the 2 engine control harness electrical connectors and the 2 pin-type retainers.

106. Connect the engine control harness. Engage the Powertrain Control Module (PCM) connector. Install the harness retaining nut. Tighten to 53 inch lbs. (6 Nm).

107. Connect the following electrical connectors:

- Secondary Air Injection (AIR) solenoid
- Transaxle mount control solenoid
- Purge valve

108. Connect the upper radiator and coolant vent hoses.

109. Attach the heater hose retaining clip to the transaxle mount stud.

110. Connect the heater hoses to the heater core.

2WD vehicles

111. Install the lateral support crossmember. Tighten to 85 ft. lbs. (115 Nm).

112. Install the front drive intermediate halfshaft.

4WD vehicles

113. Install the transfer case.

All vehicles

114. Install the left front drive halfshaft.

115. Install the accessory drive belt.

116. Install the engine coolant degas bottle.

117. Install the exhaust manifold/catalytic converter.

118. Install the engine air cleaner.

119. Install the intake manifold.

120. Enable the vehicle high voltage electrical system. See the procedure under High Voltage Traction Battery.

121. Connect the battery ground cable.

122. Fill the engine with clean engine oil.

123. Connect the hoses to the transaxle and install the hose clamps.

✳✳ WARNING

Adhesives, stop-leak pellets or small debris in the Motor electronics cooling system (MECS) can cause poor performance or temporary blockage of the motor electronics pump. Only use clean, approved coolant when filling the system.

124. Loosen the bleed screw and fill the degas bottle with coolant until it begins to flow out of the bleed hole. Then, close the bleed screw.

125. Turn the ignition to the ON position to actuate the motor electronics cooling pump and continue to fill the degas bottle to the correct level.

➡ **Most of the MECS air bleeding occurs as a normal process at the degas bottle through the vent tube; very little occurs at the bleed screw.**

126. To bleed air from the system, loosen the bleed screw and allow air to escape while the M/E coolant pump is operating. Fill and bleed the motor electronics cooling system.

127. Fill and bleed the engine cooling system.

Upper Transaxle Insulator and Retainer

1. Before servicing the vehicle, refer to the Precautions Section.

2. Remove the air cleaner assembly.

3. Support the transaxle with a suitable floor jack.

4. Remove the bolts and the bracket.

5. Remove the nuts, bolt and the insulator.

6. To install, reverse the removal procedure. Torque the insulator bracket bolts to 18 ft. lbs. (25 Nm); the insulator bolts/nuts to 66 ft. lbs. (90 Nm).

Lower Transaxle Insulator and Retainer

1. Before servicing the vehicle, refer to the Precautions Section.

2. With the vehicle in DRIVE, position it on a hoist.

3. Turn the ignition to the OFF position.

4. Remove the splash shield retainers and remove the left splash shield.

5. Remove the bolts and the lateral support crossmember.

6. Remove the front insulator bolt.

7. Remove the rear insulator bolt.

8. Remove the nut, bolts and the cross-member.

9. Remove the lower rear insulator bolt and remove it from the bracket.

10. To install, reverse the removal procedure. Observe the following torques:

- Lower rear insulator bolt: 66 ft. lbs. (90 Nm)
- Crossmember front bolts: 66 ft. lbs. (90 Nm)
- Crossmember rear nut: 111 ft. lbs. (150 Nm)
- Front and rear insulator bolts: 66 ft. lbs. (90 Nm)
- Lateral support crossmember bolts: 85 ft. lbs. (115 Nm)

Rear Transaxle Insulator and Retainer

1. Before servicing the vehicle, refer to the Precautions Section.

2. With the vehicle in DRIVE, position it on a hoist.

3. Turn the ignition to the OFF position.

4. Disconnect the heater hose retaining clip from the transaxle mount stud.

5. Remove insulator nut.

6. Remove the nuts and the bracket.

7. Remove the nuts, heat shield, and insulator.

8. To install, reverse the removal procedure. Tighten all fasteners to 66 ft. lbs. (90 Nm).

Motor Electronics Cooler

See Figures 16 and 17.

1. Before servicing the vehicle, refer to the Precautions Section.

➡**Always refill the motor electronics cooling system (MECS) with the same type of coolant that was drained from the system. Do not mix coolant types.**

2. With the vehicle in DRIVE, position it on a hoist.

3. Turn the ignition to the OFF position.

4. Remove the left splash shield.

5. Place a suitable container below the transaxle.

6. Loosen the hose clamps at the transaxle, then, pull the hoses off to allow the coolant to drain.

7. Remove the front bumper cover.

a. Remove the 6 pin-type retainers (3 each side).

b. Remove the 4 fender splash shield bolts (2 each side).

c. Remove the 4 air deflector bolts.

d. Remove the 2 center front bumper cover pin-type retainers.

e. Remove the 2 front bumper cover outer pin-type retainers (1 each side).

f. If equipped, disconnect the fog lamp electrical connectors.

g. Remove the 2 upper bolts and the front bumper cover.

8. Loosen the hose clamp and disconnect the inlet hose.

9. Loosen the hose clamp and disconnect the outlet hose.

10. Remove the motor electronics (M/E) cooler bolts.

11. To install, reverse the removal procedure. Observe the following torques:

- Motor electronics (M/E) cooler bolts: 53 inch lbs. (6 Nm)
- Front bumper cover bolts: 71 inch lbs. (8 Nm)
- Air deflector bolts: 71 inch lbs. (8 Nm)
- Fender splash shield bolts: 71 inch lbs. (8 Nm)

12. Connect the hoses to the transaxle and install the hose clamps.

❋❋ WARNING

Adhesives, stop-leak pellets or small debris in the Motor electronics cooling system (MECS) can cause poor performance or temporary blockage of the motor electronics pump. Only use clean, approved coolant when filling the system.

13. Loosen the bleed screw and fill the degas bottle with coolant until it begins to flow out of the bleed hole. Then, close the bleed screw.

14. Turn the ignition to the ON position to actuate the motor electronics cooling pump and continue to fill the degas bottle to the correct level.

➡**Most of the MECS air bleeding occurs as a normal process at the degas bottle through the vent tube; very little occurs at the bleed screw.**

15. To bleed air from the system, loosen the bleed screw and allow air to escape while the M/E coolant pump is operating.

Motor Electronics Pump

1. Before servicing the vehicle, refer to the Precautions Section.

➡**Always refill the motor electronics cooling system (MECS) with the same type of coolant that was drained from the system. Do not mix coolant types.**

2. With the vehicle in DRIVE, position it on a hoist.

3. Turn the ignition to the OFF position.

4. Remove the left splash shield.

5. Place a suitable container below the transaxle.

6. Disconnect the inlet and outlet hoses.

7. Remove the bolts.

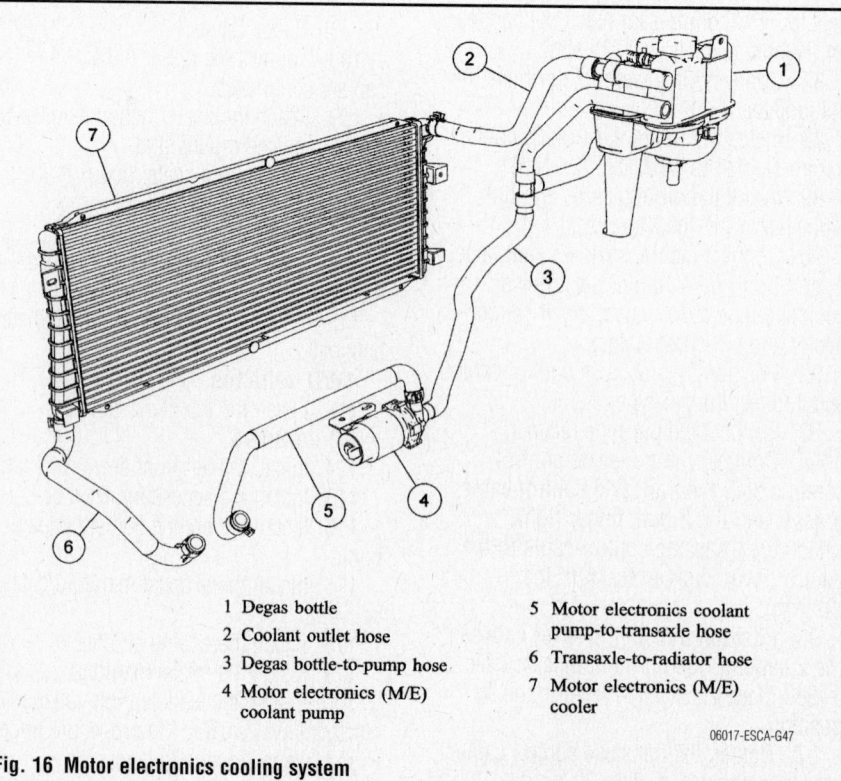

1 Degas bottle
2 Coolant outlet hose
3 Degas bottle-to-pump hose
4 Motor electronics (M/E) coolant pump
5 Motor electronics coolant pump-to-transaxle hose
6 Transaxle-to-radiator hose
7 Motor electronics (M/E) cooler

06017-ESCA-G47

Fig. 16 Motor electronics cooling system

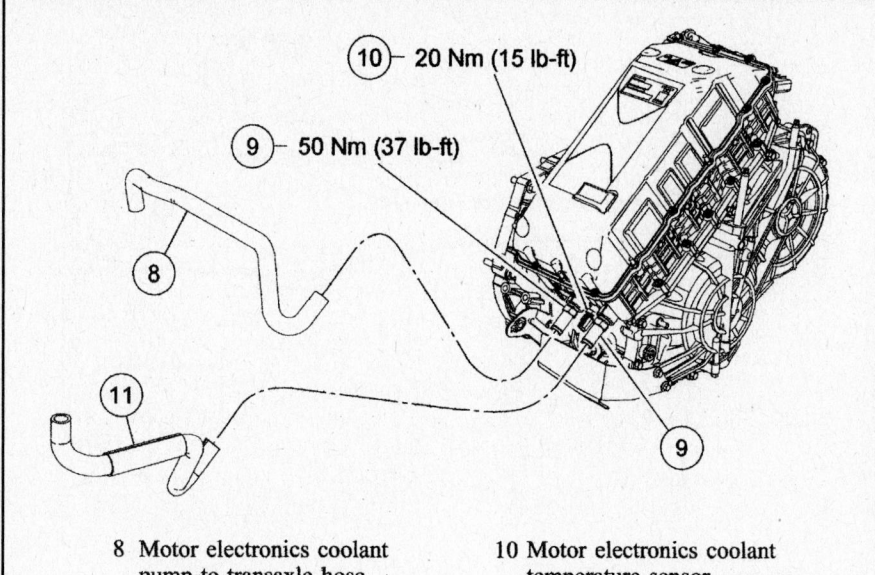

8 Motor electronics coolant
   pump-to-transaxle hose
9 Coolant tube (inlet/outlet)

10 Motor electronics coolant
    temperature sensor
11 Transaxle-to-radiator hose

06017-ESCA-G48

Fig. 17 Motor electronics cooler hose connections

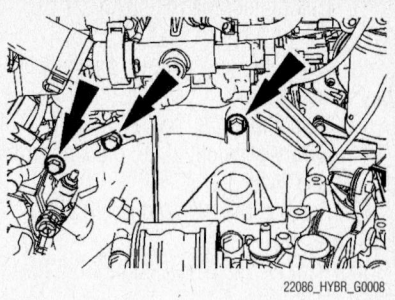

22086_HYBR_G0008

Fig. 19 Engine to transaxle mounting bolts

8. To install, reverse the removal procedure. Tighten to 15 ft. lbs. (20 Nm).

✳✳ WARNING

Adhesives, stop-leak pellets or small debris in the Motor electronics cooling system (MECS) can cause poor performance or temporary blockage of the motor electronics pump. Only use clean, approved coolant when filling the system.

9. Loosen the bleed screw and fill the degas bottle with coolant until it begins to flow out of the bleed hole. Then, close the bleed screw.

10. Turn the ignition to the ON position to actuate the motor electronics cooling pump and continue to fill the degas bottle to the correct level.

➡**Most of the MECS air bleeding occurs as a normal process at the degas bottle through the vent tube; very little occurs at the bleed screw.**

11. To bleed air from the system, loosen the bleed screw and allow air to escape while the M/E coolant pump is operating.

MANUAL TRANSAXLE ASSEMBLY

REMOVAL & INSTALLATION

See Figures 18 through 21.

1. Disconnect the negative battery cable.

2. With the vehicle in NEUTRAL, position it on a hoist

3. Remove the air cleaner assembly.

4. Remove the battery tray.

5. Remove the wiring harness bracket nut.

6. Disconnect the reverse switch and vehicle speed sensor (VSS) connectors.

7. Disconnect the shift cables.

8. Remove the 3 shift cable bracket bolts.

9. Position the clutch hydraulic tube aside.

10. Remove the clutch hydraulic tube bracket-to-transaxle bolt.

11. Disconnect the clutch hydraulic tube from the clutch slave cylinder.

12. Plug the hydraulic tube.

13. Position the clutch hydraulic tube aside.

14. Using the special tool, support the engine.

15. Remove the 3 LH transaxle support

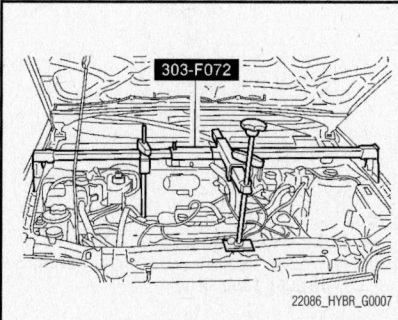

303-F072

22086_HYBR_G0007

Fig. 18 Engine and support tool shown

insulator bracket nuts. Loosen, but do not remove the through bolt.

16. Remove the transaxle rear support insulator bolt and the 2 nuts.

17. Using the 3-Bar Engine Support, raise the engine up 1.0 inch. 25.4 mm, lower the transaxle side downward.

18. Remove the RH engine mount bolt.

19. Remove the 3 upper transaxle-to-engine bolts.

20. With the weight of the vehicle on the wheels, loosen the wheel nuts.

21. With the vehicle in NEUTRAL, position it on a hoist.

22. Remove the wheel and tire assembly.

23. Remove the 6 LH splash shield screws.

24. Remove the 6 screws and a push-pin.

25. Remove the LH splash shield.

26. Drain the transaxle fluid.

27. Remove the crossmember bolts.

28. Remove the crossmember.

29. Remove the 3 front-to-aft crossmember bolts.

30. Remove the LH transaxle support insulator through bolt.

31. Remove the front-to-aft crossmember and the LH transaxle support insulator.

32. Working in the engine compartment, use the 3-Bar Engine Support to raise the engine up 1.0 inch. 25.4 mm, lowering the transaxle side downward.

33. Remove the transaxle right support insulator through bolt and the mount.

34. Remove the starter motor assembly.

35. Disconnect the LH stabilizer bar link.

36. Disconnect the LH tie rod-end.

37. Disconnect the ball joint.

38. Remove the clip, then disconnect the brake hose.

39. Remove the bolt and position the ABS wire aside.

40. Remove the LH halfshaft from the transaxle.

41. Disconnect the RH stabilizer bar link.

42. Using the special tool, disconnect the RH tie-rod end.

43. Disconnect the RH ball joint.

44. Remove the clip, then disconnect the brake hose.

45. Remove the bolt and position the ABS wire aside.

46. Remove the RH halfshaft from the transaxle.

47. Remove the intermediate shaft.

48. If equipped, remove the power transfer unit (PTU).

49. Remove 2 lower transaxle-to-engine bolts.

❊❊ CAUTION

Secure the assembly to the jack. Avoid any obstructions while lowering and raising the jack. Contact with obstructions may cause the assembly to fall off the jack, which may result in serious personal injury.

50. Position the transaxle jack under the transaxle.

51. Remove the remaining 4 transaxle-to-engine bolts.

52. Remove the transaxle.

To install:

53. Do not lubricate the splines on the input shaft.

54. Raise and position the transaxle to the engine.

55. Install the 2 short transaxle-to-engine bolts and tighten to 35 ft. lbs. (47Nm).

56. Install the LH transaxle support insulator bracket.

57. Raise the transaxle, aligning the bracket to the insulator. Install the 3 nuts and tighten to 30 ft. lbs. (40 Nm).

58. Install the rear transaxle support insulator. Install the nuts, the bolt and through bolt. Tighten the through bolt to 76 ft. lbs. (103 Nm). Do not tighten the nuts and bolt at this time.

59. After removing the transaxle jack, install 4 long transaxle-to-engine bolts and tighten to 35 ft. lbs. (47Nm).

60. If equipped, install the power transfer unit (PTU).

61. Install the intermediate shaft.

62. Install the RH halfshaft.

63. Connect the RH ball joint and tighten to 46 ft lbs. (63 Nm).

64. Connect the RH stabilizer bar link and tighten to 41 ft. lbs. (55 Nm).

65. Connect the RH tie-rod end and tighten to 41 ft. lbs. (55 Nm).

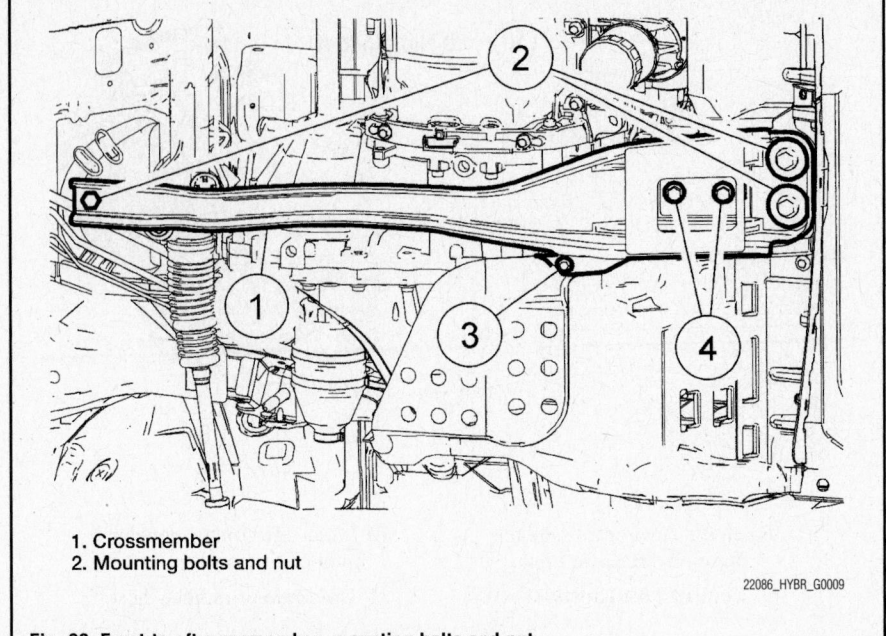

1. Crossmember
2. Mounting bolts and nut

22086_HYBR_G0009

Fig. 20 Front-to-aft crossmember, mounting bolts and nut

66. Install the brake hose and the clip.

67. Position the ABS wire then install the bolt.

68. Install the LH halfshaft.

69. Connect the LH ball joint and tighten to 46 ft lbs. (63 Nm).

70. Connect the LH stabilizer bar link and tighten to 41 ft. lbs. (55 Nm).

71. Connect the LH tie-rod end and tighten to 41 ft. lbs. (55 Nm).

72. Install the brake hose and the clip.

73. Position the ABS wire then install the bolt.

74. Install the starter motor assembly.

75. Install the front-to-aft crossmember.

76. Install the front-to-aft crossmember and install the 2 bolts and tighten to 66 ft. lbs. (90 Nm).

77. Tighten the nut to 129 ft. lbs. (175 Nm).

78. Position and install crossmember and bolts tighten bolts to 85 ft. lbs. (115 Nm).

79. Install the front transaxle mount through bolt.

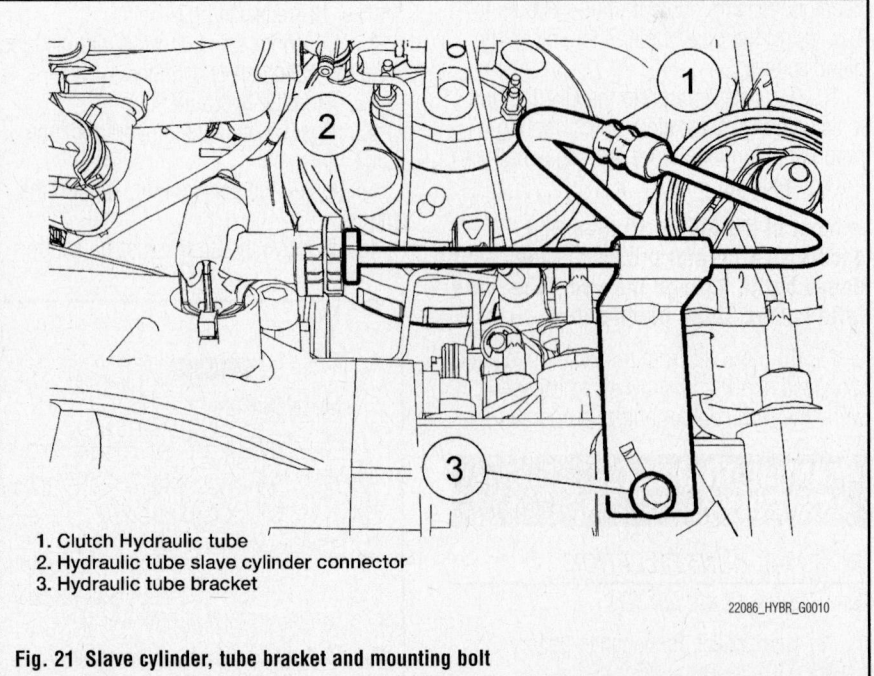

1. Clutch Hydraulic tube
2. Hydraulic tube slave cylinder connector
3. Hydraulic tube bracket

22086_HYBR_G0010

Fig. 21 Slave cylinder, tube bracket and mounting bolt

80. Tighten the LH transaxle mount fasteners to 30 ft. lbs. (40 Nm).

81. Tighten the transaxle rear support insulator fasteners to 59 ft. lbs. (80 Nm).

82. Remove the 3-Bar Engine Support.

83. Install the RH engine support bolt and tighten to 66 ft. lbs. (90 Nm).

84. Install the 3 upper transaxle-to-engine bolts. Tighten the bolts to 33 ft. lbs. (45 Nm).

85. Connect the clutch hydraulic tube.

86. Position the clutch hydraulic tube.

87. Connect the clutch hydraulic tube from the clutch slave cylinder.

88. Install the clutch hydraulic tube bracket-to-transaxle bolt and tighten to 22 inch lbs. (2.5 Nm).

89. Install shift cable bracket and tighten bolts to 16 ft. lbs. (22 Nm).

90. Connect the shift cables

91. Connect the reverse switch and vehicle speed sensor (VSS) connectors.

92. Install the wiring harness bracket nut and tighten to 9 ft. lbs (12 Nm).

93. Install the battery tray.

94. Install the air cleaner assembly.

95. Fill the transaxle fluid.

96. Fill and bleed the clutch.

97. Install the RH and LH side splash shields and screws.

98. Install the wheel and tire assembly.

99. Connect the negative battery cable.

CLUTCH

REMOVAL & INSTALLATION

See Figure 22.

1. Before servicing the vehicle, refer to the Precautions Section.

2. Remove or disconnect the following:
   - Negative battery cable
   - Transaxle and lock the flywheel to the engine with special tool 303–103
   - Pressure plate bolts by loosening them evenly
   - Clutch pressure plate and disc

3. Clean the pressure plate and inspect it for burn marks, scores, flatness or ridges, replace if damaged.

4. Inspect the pressure plate diaphragm finger for wear, replace if damaged.

5. Measure the depth of the rivet heads. Minimum depth is 0.012 inch (0.3mm).

6. Inspect the clutch disc for signs of wear and replace if needed.

7. Check the clutch disc runout. Replace the disc if not with specification: 0.027 inch (0.7mm).

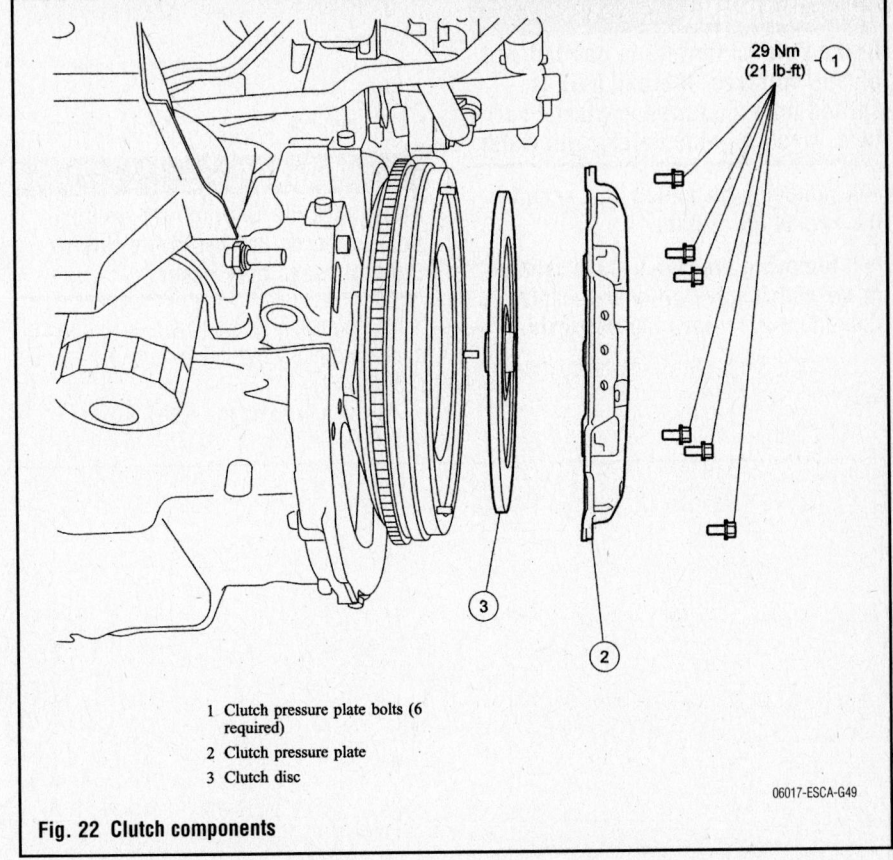

1 Clutch pressure plate bolts (6 required)
2 Clutch pressure plate
3 Clutch disc

06017-ESCA-G49

Fig. 22 Clutch components

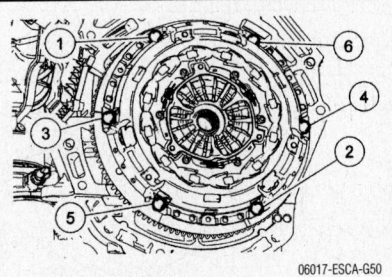

06017-ESCA-G50

Fig. 23 Torque the pressure plate bolts in the proper sequence

To install:

8. Install or connect the following:
   - Clutch disc to the flywheel
   - Pressure plate to the flywheel. Torque the bolts in sequence to 21 ft. lbs. (29 Nm).
   - Transaxle
   - Negative battery cable

9. Check the transaxle fluid level and top off if necessary.

CLUTCH HYDRAULIC SYSTEM

BLEEDING

The following procedure is recommended for bleeding the clutch hydraulic system installed on the vehicle. It is recommended that the original clutch tube, with quick-connect fitting be replaced when servicing the hydraulic system, because air can be trapped in the quick-connect fitting and prevent complete bleeding of the system.

1. Before servicing the vehicle, refer to the Precautions Section.

2. Clean the dirt and grease from the dust cap.

3. Remove the cap and diaphragm and fill the reservoir ¾ of the way with approved brake fluid C6AZ-19542-AB or DOT 3 equivalent fluid (ESA-M6C25-A).

4. Loosen the bleeder screw cover from the slave cylinder and attach a hose to the screw.

5. Place the hose in a container and slowly pump the clutch pedal several times.

6. With the clutch pedal depressed, loosen the bleeder screw to release the fluid and air.

7. Remove the hose and tighten the bleeder screw.

8. Repeat this procedure until all the air is removed from the hydraulic system

REMOVAL & INSTALLATION

Master Cylinder

See Figure 24.

1. Before servicing the vehicle, refer to the Precautions Section.

⁕⁕ WARNING

Brake fluid is harmful to painted and plastic surfaces. If brake fluid is spilled onto a painted or plastic surface, wash it immediately with water.

➡ If removing the clutch line, remove the engine air cleaner.

➡ If removing the clutch slave cylinder or the clutch slave cylinder-to-clutch line adapter, remove the transaxle.

2. Remove the clutch master cylinder hose

3. Remove the clutch master cylinder push rod
4. Remove the fitting at the master cylinder.
5. Remove the clutch master cylinder

⁕⁕ WARNING

Make sure the O-rings are properly positioned on the hydraulic line fittings or leaks may occur.

6. To install, reverse the removal procedure. Torque the mounting nuts to 17 ft. lbs. (23 Nm).
7. Fill and bleed the system.

Slave Cylinder

See Figure 24.

1. Before servicing the vehicle, refer to the Precautions Section.

⁕⁕ WARNING

Brake fluid is harmful to painted and plastic surfaces. If brake fluid is spilled onto a painted or plastic surface, wash it immediately with water.

2. Remove the transaxle.
3. Disconnect the clutch slave cylinder-to-clutch hydraulic fluid tube adapter.

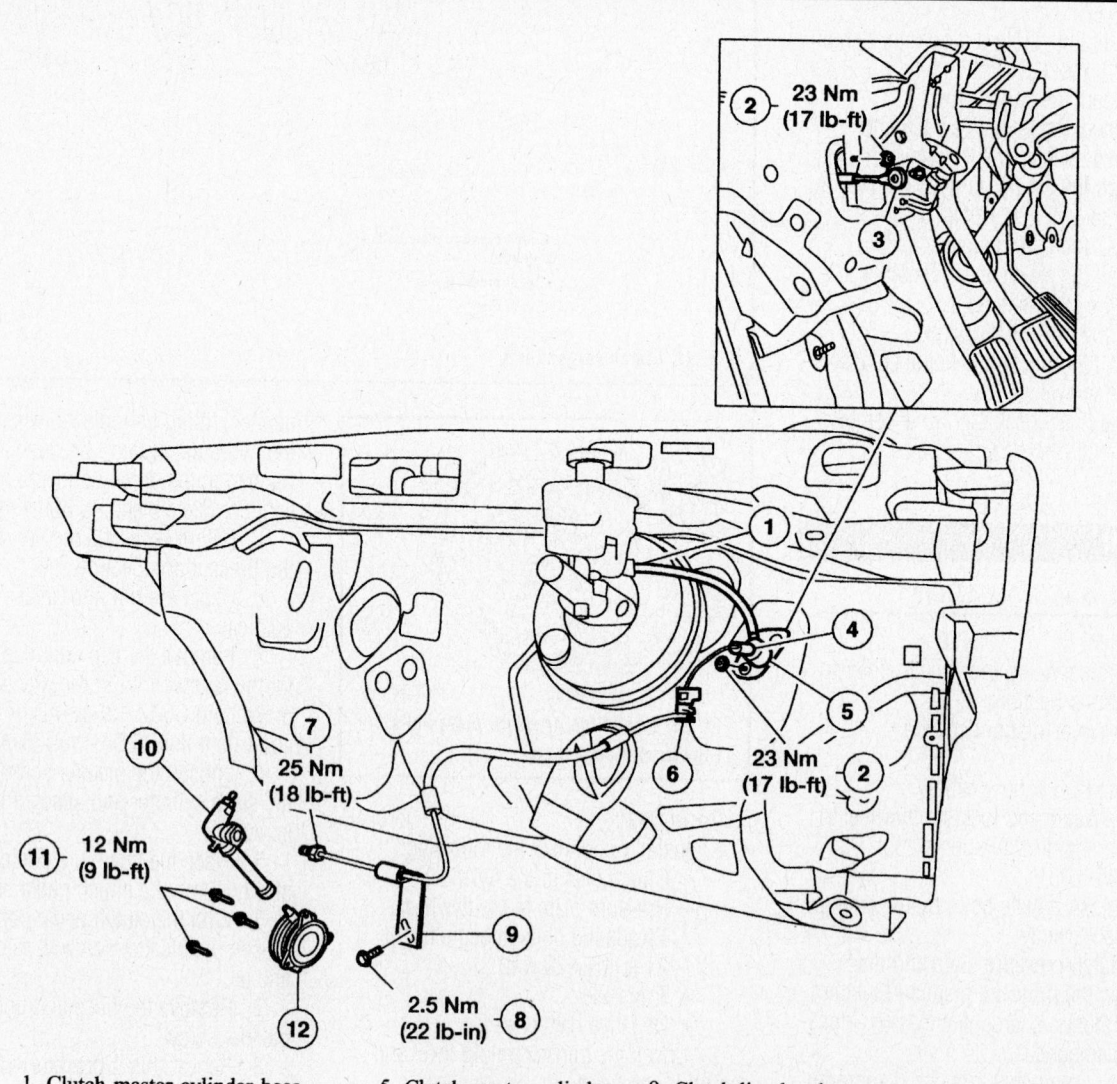

1	Clutch master cylinder hose	5	Clutch master cylinder	9	Clutch line bracket
2	Nut	6	Clutch line	10	Clutch slave cylinder to clutch line adapter
3	Clutch master cylinder push rod	7	Fitting	11	Bolt
4	Fitting	8	Bolt	12	Clutch slave cylinder

67197-ESCA-G60

Fig. 24 Hydraulic clutch components—2005 models shown, other years similar

4. Remove and the clutch slave cylinder.

5. To install, reverse the removal procedure. Tighten the 3 clutch slave cylinder bolts to 9 ft. lbs. (12 Nm)

6. Bleed the air from the system.

FRONT HALFSHAFT

REMOVAL & INSTALLATION

1. With the vehicle in NEUTRAL, position it on a hoist.

2. Remove the front tire and wheel.

3. Remove and discard the front wheel hub nut.

4. Remove the ABS wheel speed sensor bolt and position the sensor aside.

5. Remove the lower arm pinch bolt and nut from the lower arm.

6. Separate the lower arm from the front wheel knuckle.

7. Separate the front drive halfshaft from the front wheel hub using a suitable tool.

8. Remove the front drive halfshaft from the differential.

To install:

➡**When seated correctly, the front drive half shaft bearing retainer cir-clip can be felt as it snaps into the differential side gear groove.**

9. Position the front drive halfshaft so the splines line up with the differential side gear splines. Push the front drive halfshaft into the differential side gear.

10. Install the front drive halfshaft into the front wheel hub.

11. Position the lower arm into the front wheel knuckle.

12. Install the lower arm pinch bolt and nut. Tighten to 52 ft. lbs. (70 Nm).

13. Install the ABS wheel speed sensor and bolt. Tighten bolt to 80 inch lbs. (9 Nm).

✲✲ WARNING

Do not tighten the front wheel hub nut with the vehicle on the ground. The nut must be tightened to specification before the vehicle is lowered onto the wheels. Wheel bearing damage will occur if the wheel bearing is loaded with the weight of the vehicle applied.

➡**Apply the brake to keep the halfshaft from rotating.**

14. Install a new front wheel hub nut and tighten to 222 ft. lbs. (300 Nm).

15. Install the front tire and wheel.

16. Check and fill the transaxle fluid as necessary.

CV-JOINTS OVERHAUL

See Figures 25 through 30.

1. Before servicing the vehicle, refer to the Precautions Section.

Observe the following cautionary notes:

• Never pick up or hold the halfshaft by only the inner or outboard CV joint.

• Handle the halfshaft by only the interconnecting shaft to avoid pull-apart and potential damage to the CV joints.

• Do not over-angle the CV joints.

• Damage will occur to an assembled inner CV joint if it is over-plunged outward from the joint housing.

• Never use a hammer to remove or install the halfshafts.

• Never use the halfshaft assembly as a lever to position other components. Always support the free-ends of the halfshaft.

• Do not allow the boots to contact sharp edges or hot exhaust components.

• Do not drop assembled halfshafts. The impact may cut the boots from the inside without evidence of external damage.

2. Before servicing the vehicle, refer to the Precautions Section.

3. Remove or disconnect the following:

• Negative battery cable
• Halfshaft and secure it in a soft-jawed vise
• Inboard halfshaft boot clamp
• Boot from the inboard CV-joint housing
• Tripod joint from the CV-joint housing and matchmark the tripod joint to the halfshaft
• Snapring and boot from the halfshaft
• Outboard halfshaft boot clamps
• Outboard boot back to expose the CV-joint and matchmark the joint to the halfshaft
• Outboard CV-joint from the halfshaft

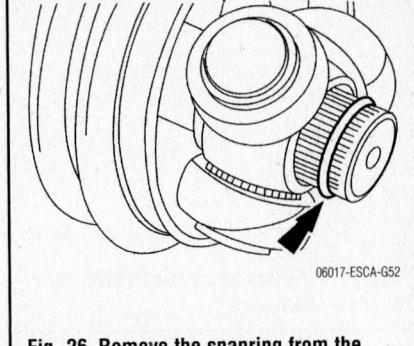

Fig. 26 Remove the snapring from the from the shaft end—front shaft

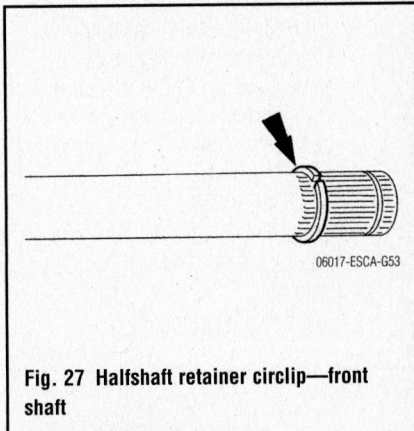

Fig. 27 Halfshaft retainer circlip—front shaft

• Halfshaft retainer circlip and discard it
• Boot from the halfshaft

To install:

4. Lubricate the outer CV-joint with grease.

5. Install or connect the following:

• Outboard CV-joint and boot
• New halfshaft bearing circlip
• Inboard CV-joint to the halfshaft
• Outboard halfshaft boot forward on to the outboard CV-joint

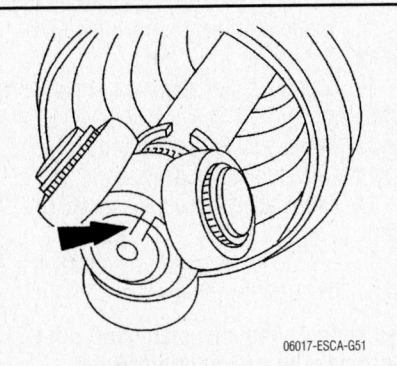

Fig. 25 Matchmark the tripod joint to the halfshaft—front shaft

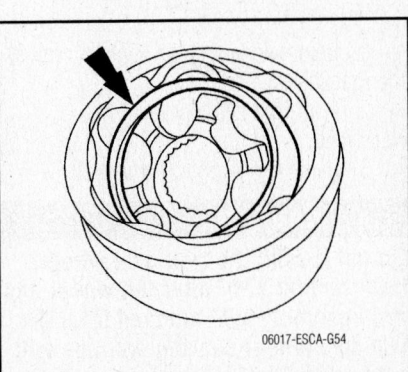

Fig. 28 Lubricate the outer CV-joint with grease—front shaft

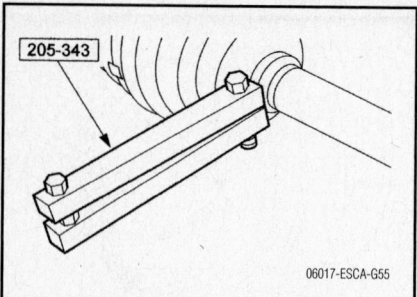

Fig. 29 Installing new outer CV-joint boot clamps—front shaft

- New outboard halfshaft boot clamps
- Inboard halfshaft boot
- Tripod joint on the halfshaft by aligning the matchmarks
- New snapring to the tripod joint and lubricate the needle bearings while filling the housing with CV-joint grease, E43Z–19590–A
- Inboard halfshaft boot with new clamps
- Halfshaft
- Negative battery cable

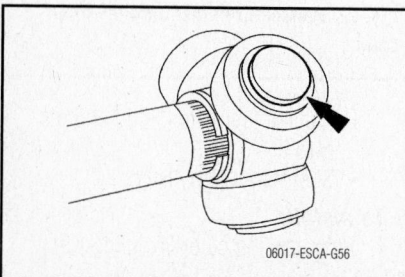

Fig. 30 Lubricate the needle bearings while filling the housing with CV-joint grease—front shaft

REAR HALFSHAFT

REMOVAL & INSTALLATION

See Figure 31.

1. Before servicing the vehicle, refer to the Precautions Section.
2. Place the selector lever in NEUTRAL.
3. Raise and support the vehicle.

※※ WARNING

Do not loosen the rear axle wheel hub retainer until after the wheel and tire assembly are removed from the vehicle. Wheel bearing damage will occur if the wheel bearing is unloaded with the weight of the vehicle applied.

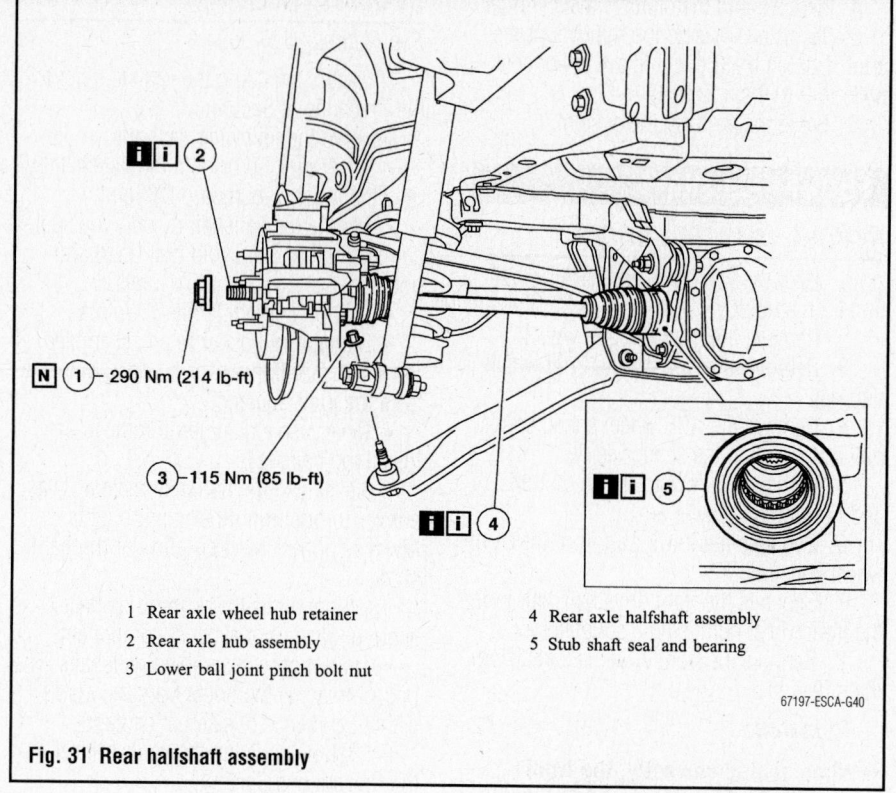

1 Rear axle wheel hub retainer
2 Rear axle hub assembly
3 Lower ball joint pinch bolt nut
4 Rear axle halfshaft assembly
5 Stub shaft seal and bearing

Fig. 31 Rear halfshaft assembly

4. Remove the rear brake drum or brake disc.
5. Remove the rear coil spring.
6. Rear axle wheel hub retainer.
7. Using a puller, press the outboard CV joint until it is loose in the hub.
8. Separate the outboard CV joint from the hub.
9. Remove the rear axle hub assembly.
10. Remove the lower ball joint pinch bolt nut.

※※ WARNING

Do not use a hammer to separate the rear axle halfshaft assembly from the hub. Damage to the threads and the internal CV joint can result.

11. Using a prybar, remove the halfshaft.
12. Using a puller, remove the stub and shaft seal.
13. Using a slidehammer and adapter, remove the stub shaft pilot bearing and seal.
14. To install, reverse the removal procedure.
15. Fill the axle with the specified quantity of the specified lubricant.

➡**Lubricate the new stub shaft pilot bearing with rear axle lubricant.**

16. Using suitable drivers, install the stub shaft pilot bearing.

➡**Lubricate the new stub shaft pilot bearing housing seal with grease.**

17. Using the special tools, install the stub shaft pilot bearing housing seal.
18. Install a new circlip on the inboard CV joint.
19. Install the halfshaft end into the hub assembly.
20. Observe the following torques:
- Lower ball joint: 85 ft. lbs. (115 Nm).
- Halfshaft nut: 221 ft. lbs. (300 Nm).

CV-JOINTS OVERHAUL

1. Before servicing the vehicle, refer to the Precautions Section.

Observe the following cautionary notes:

- Never pick up or hold the halfshaft by only the inner or outboard CV joint.
- Handle the halfshaft by only the interconnecting shaft to avoid pull-apart and potential damage to the CV joints.
- Do not over-angle the CV joints.
- Damage will occur to an assembled inner CV joint if it is over-plunged outward from the joint housing.
- Never use a hammer to remove or install the halfshafts.
- Never use the halfshaft assembly as a lever to position other components. Always support the free-ends of the halfshaft.

• Do not allow the boots to contact sharp edges or hot exhaust components.

• Do not drop assembled halfshafts. The impact may cut the boots from the inside without evidence of external damage.

2. Before servicing the vehicle, refer to the Precautions Section.

3. Remove the halfshaft.

4. Secure the halfshaft in a vise using protective jaw covers.

5. Remove the 2 inner halfshaft boot clamps.

6. Slide the inner halfshaft boot off the inner CV-joint housing.

7. If reinstalling the original inner joint, mark the inner CV-joint and the halfshaft to be sure of correct installation.

8. Using a soft face hammer, separate the halfshaft from the inner joint housing.

9. Remove and discard the bearing retainer circlip.

10. Remove and discard the snap ring.

11. Remove the inner halfshaft boot from the halfshaft.

12. Remove the 2 outer halfshaft boot clamps.

13. Slide the outer halfshaft joint boot back out of the way exposing the outer CV-joint.

14. If reinstalling the original inner CV-joint, mark the outer CV-joint and the halfshaft to be sure of correct installation.

15. Using a soft-face hammer, separate the outer CV-joint by gently tapping it off the halfshaft.

16. Remove and discard the bearing retainer circlip.

17. Remove the snap ring from the halfshaft.

18. Slide the outer halfshaft boot off the halfshaft.

To assemble:

19. Lubricate the inner and outer CV-joints with joint grease.

20. Install the outer halfshaft boot.

21. Install the snap ring on the halfshaft.

22. Install a new halfshaft bearing retainer circlip.

23. Using a soft-face hammer, install the inner CV-joint by gently tapping it onto the halfshaft.

24. Remove any excess grease on the mating surfaces and slide the outer halfshaft joint boot forward onto the outer CV-joint.

25. Remove any excess air trapped in the outer halfshaft boot using a cloth-covered screwdriver after adjusting the outer halfshaft boot spacing.

26. Using a crimping tool, install 2 new outer halfshaft boot clamps.

27. Position the inner halfshaft boot.

28. Install the snap ring.

29. Install the bearing retainer circlip.

30. Using a soft face hammer, install the halfshaft on the inner CV-joint.

31. Position the inner halfshaft boot.

32. Remove any excess air trapped in the inner halfshaft boot using a cloth-covered screwdriver after adjusting the inner halfshaft boot spacing.

33. Using a crimping tool, install 2 new inner CV-joint boot clamps.

34. Install the halfshaft.

REAR DIFFERENTIAL MASS DAMPER

REMOVAL & INSTALLATION

See Figures 32 and 33.

1. Before servicing the vehicle, refer to the Precautions Section.

2. Remove the rear differential mass damper.

3. Remove the bolts.

4. Remove the rear differential mass damper.

To install:

✱✱ WARNING

The mass damper bolts must be installed in the sequence shown or damage to the vehicle may occur.

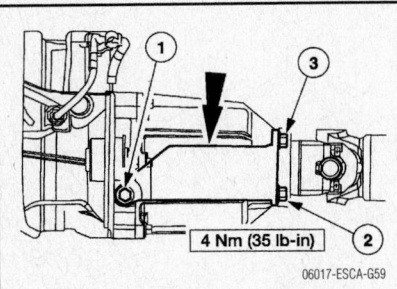

Fig. 32 Tighten the rear differential mass damper bolts to 35 inch lbs. in the sequence shown

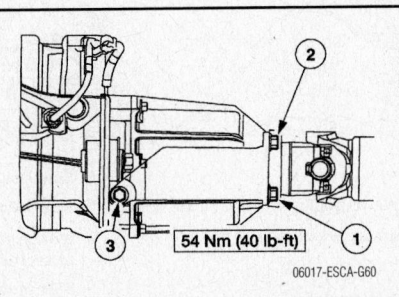

Fig. 33 Tighten the rear differential mass damper bolts to 40 ft. lbs. in the sequence shown

➡**Install the mass damper bolts by hand until finger tight.**

5. Install the rear differential mass damper.

6. Position the rear differential mass damper and install the bolts in the sequence shown to 35 inch lbs. (4 Nm).

7. Final torque the mass damper bolts in the sequence shown to 40 ft. lbs. (54 Nm).

REAR PINION SEAL

REMOVAL & INSTALLATION

See Figures 34 through 37.

1. Before servicing the vehicle, refer to the Precautions Section.

2. With the vehicle in NEUTRAL, position it on a hoist.

3. Index-mark the pinion and pinion flange to the rear of the driveshaft.

4. Remove the 4 bolts and the 2 cap straps. Disconnect and support the driveshaft.

➡**Discard the nut after removing it. Install a new nut during installation.**

5. Using the special tool, hold the pinion flange while removing the nut. Remove the nut.

6. Index-mark the location of the pinion to the yoke.

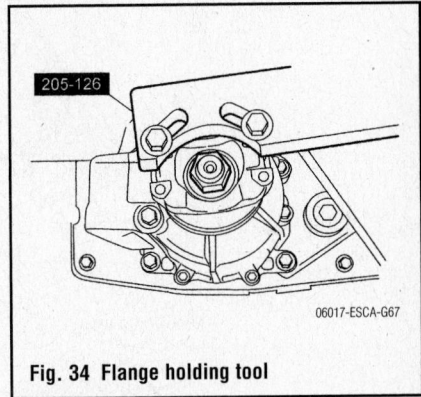

Fig. 34 Flange holding tool

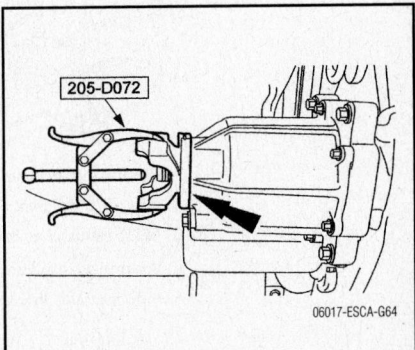

Fig. 35 Removing the pinion flange

7. Using a puller, remove the pinion flange.

8. Using the special tool, remove the seal.

To install:

➡**Make sure that the mating surface is clean before installing the new seal.**

9. Using a seal driver, install the seal.

➡**Lubricate the pinion flange with premium long-life grease.**

10. Line up the index marks and position the pinion flange.

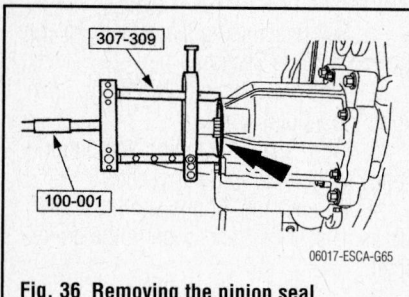

Fig. 36 Removing the pinion seal

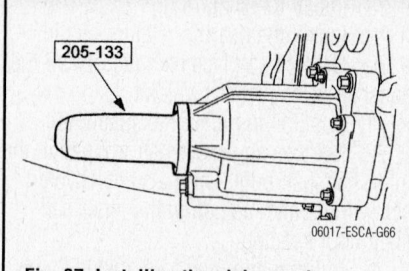

Fig. 37 Installing the pinion seal

11. Using the special tool, install the pinion nut. Tighten to 180 ft. lbs. (244 Nm).

12. Line up the index marks and position the rear driveshaft.

13. Install the 2 cap straps and the 4 bolts. Tighten to 17 ft. lbs. (23 Nm).

REAR AXLE HOUSING

REMOVAL & INSTALLATION

See Figure 38.

1. Before servicing the vehicle, refer to the Precautions Section.

2. Remove the spare tire.

3. Remove the rear driveshaft assembly.

4. Remove the rear halfshafts.

5. Position a suitable transaxle hydraulic jack to the axle housing. Securely strap the jack to the housing.

6. Remove the electrical connector at the axle.

7. Remove the rear axle differential housing-to-front insulator bracket bolts.

8. Remove the front insulator-to-bracket subframe bolts.

9. Remove the front insulator brackets.

10. Remove the side insulator bracket-to-subframe nut.

11. Remove the side insulator bracket-to-subframe bolt.

12. Remove the rear axle assembly.

13. Remove the side insulator bracket-to-rear axle differential bolts.

14. Remove the side insulator bracket.

To install:

15. To install, reverse the removal procedure. Observe the following torques:

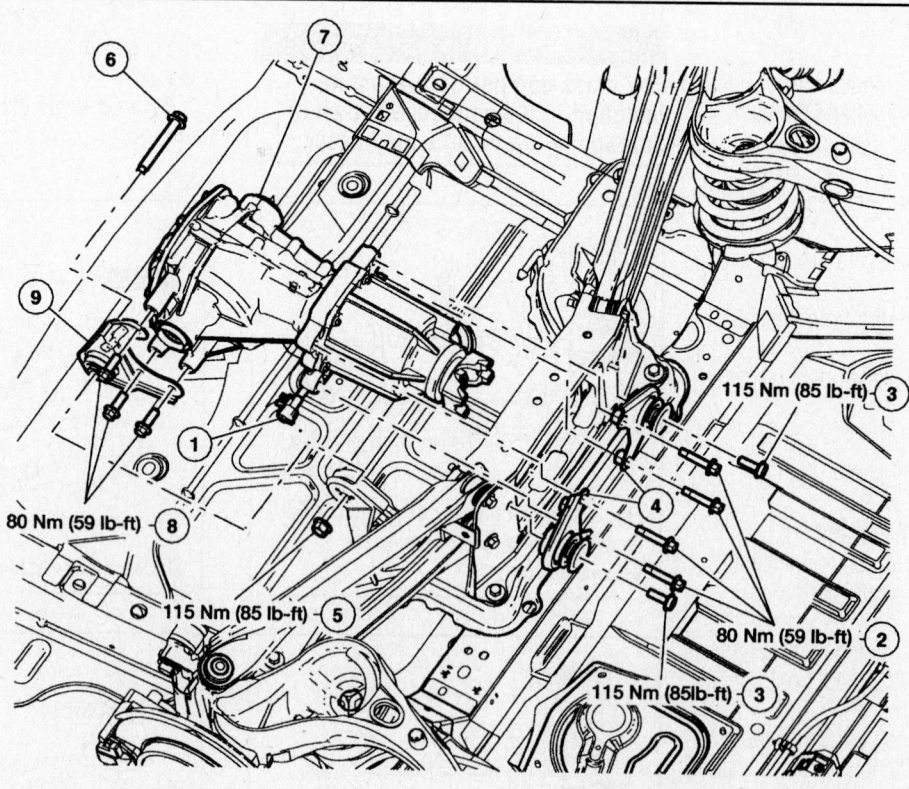

1 Electrical connector
2 Rear axle differential housing-to-front insulator bracket bolts
3 Front insulator-to-bracket subframe bolts
4 Front insulator brackets
5 Side insulator bracket-to-subframe nut
6 Side insulator bracket-to-subframe bolt
7 Rear axle assembly
8 Side insulator bracket-to-rear axle differential bolts
9 Side insulator bracket

Fig. 38 Rear drive axle removal—2005 models

- Axle housing-to-front insulator bracket: 59 ft. lbs. (80 Nm)
- Front insulator-to-bracket subframe bolts: 85 ft. lbs. (115 Nm)
- Side insulator bracket-to-subframe nut: 85 ft. lbs. (115 Nm)
- Side insulator bracket-to-differential bolts: 59 ft. lbs. (80 Nm)

REAR DRIVESHAFT

REMOVAL & INSTALLATION

See Figure 39.

1. Before servicing the vehicle, refer to the Precautions Section.

�֎ CAUTION

The normal operating temperature of the exhaust system is very high. Never attempt to remove any part of the system until it has cooled. Be especially careful when working around the catalytic converters. The temperature of the converter rises to a high level after only a few minutes of engine operation. Failure to follow these instructions may result in personal injury.

➡Do not swap driveshaft assembles from different vehicles. The Escape Hybrid drive shaft is longer than the driveshaft in the Escape/Mariner and is not interchangeable. With the vehicle in NEUTRAL, position it on a hoist.

2. Remove the ground strap bolt.

✖✖ WARNING

Do not reuse the CV-joint bolts and washers. Install new bolts and washers or damage to the vehicle may occur.

3. Remove and discard the 6 front driveshaft-to-transfer case bolts and washers. Index-mark the front driveshaft to the center bearing.

✖✖ WARNING

Do not reuse the bolts and cap straps for the center U-joint. Install new bolts and cap straps or damage to the vehicle may occur.

➡There is a difference in the length of the head of the replacement cap strap bolts from the production bolts. The

longer head pinion bolts can be used in either location.

4. Remove and discard the 4 universal joint cap strap bolts and 2 cap straps and remove the front driveshaft.

5. Index-mark the pinion and yoke to the driveshaft.

✖✖ WARNING

Do not reuse the bolts and cap straps for the rear U-joint. Install new bolts and cap straps.

➡There is a difference in the length of the head of the replacement strap bolts from the production bolts. The longer head pinion bolts can be used in either location.

6. Remove and discard the 4 universal joint cap bolts and 2 cap straps from the rear driveshaft universal joint.

7. With the help of an assistant, remove the center bearing support nuts and the driveshaft.

To install:

8. To install, reverse the removal procedure. Observe the following torques:

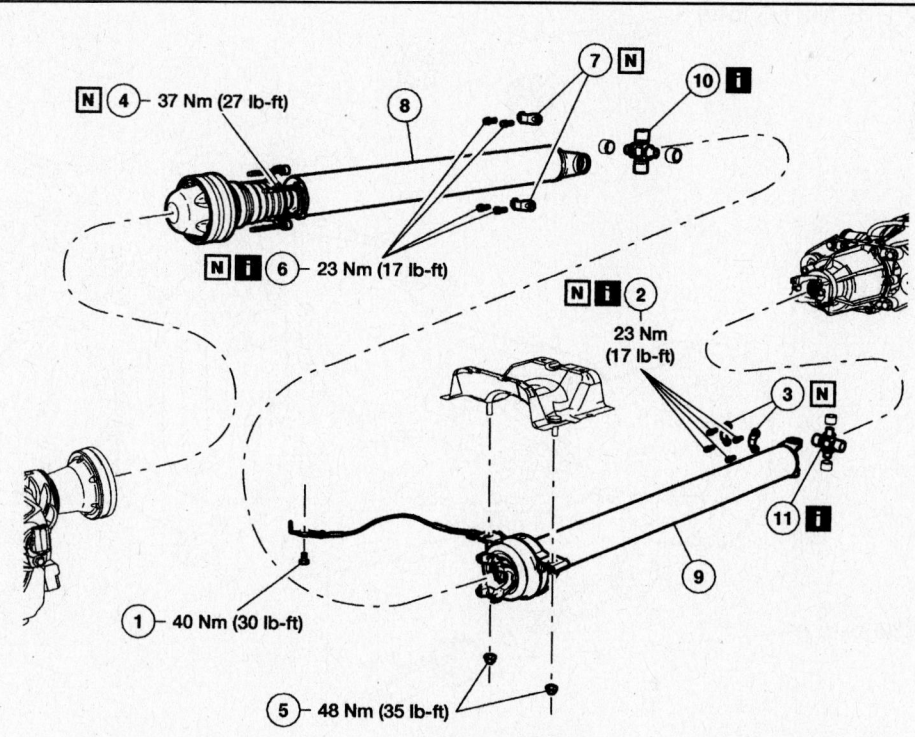

1 Ground strap bolt
2 Universal joint cap bolts
3 Universal joint cap straps
4 Front driveshaft-to-transfer case bolts
5 Center bearing support nuts
6 Universal joint cap bolts
7 Universal joint cap straps
8 Front driveshaft
9 Rear driveshaft
10 Front driveshaft U-joint
11 Rear driveshaft U-joint

67197-ESCA-G42

Fig. 39 Rear driveshaft assembly

- Center bearing support nuts: 35 ft. lbs. (48 Nm)
- Rear universal joint cap bolts: 17 ft. lbs. (23 Nm)
- Front universal joint cap strap bolts: 17 ft. lbs. (23 Nm)
- The 6 front driveshaft-to-transfer case bolts: 27 ft. lbs. (37 Nm)
- Ground strap bolt: 30 ft. lbs. (40 Nm)

9. If a driveshaft is installed and driveshaft vibration is encountered after installation, index the driveshaft.

a. With the vehicle in NEUTRAL, position it on a hoist.

✳✳ WARNING

Do not reuse the CV-joint bolts and washers. Install new bolts and washers or damage to the vehicle may occur.

10. Remove and discard the 6 front driveshaft-to-transfer case bolts and washers.

11. Rotate the flange 60 degrees.

12. Connect the front driveshaft and install the 6 new bolts and washers. Tighten to 27 ft. lbs. (37 Nm).

✳✳ WARNING

Do not reuse the bolts and cap straps for the pinion yoke. Install new bolts and cap straps or damage to the vehicle may occur.

13. Disconnect the rear driveshaft universal joint. Discard the 4 bolts and the 2 cap straps.

14. Rotate the rear pinion 180 degrees.

15. Connect the rear driveshaft and install 4 new bolts and 2 new cap straps. Tighten to 17 ft. lbs. (23 Nm).

16. Lower the vehicle and test drive.

17. Repeat the procedure if necessary.

TRANSFER CASE ASSEMBLY

REMOVAL & INSTALLATION

With Manual Transaxle

See Figure 40.

1. Before servicing the vehicle, refer to the Precautions Section.

2. Remove the driveshaft.

3. Remove the 4 bolts and the crossmember brace.

4. Remove the transfer case-to-transaxle bolts.

5. Remove the transfer case-to-transaxle nut.

6. Remove the transfer case.

7. To install, reverse the removal procedure.

✳✳ WARNING

The O-ring must be properly installed before mating the transfer case to the manual transaxle. Failure to properly install the O-ring may cause the O-ring to be damaged resulting in transaxle oil leak.

8. Install a new O-ring seal. Observe the following torques:

- Crossmember bolts: 30 ft. lbs. (40 Nm).
- Transfer case mounting nuts: 33 ft. lbs. (45 Nm).
- Transfer case mounting bolts: 33 ft. lbs. (45 Nm).

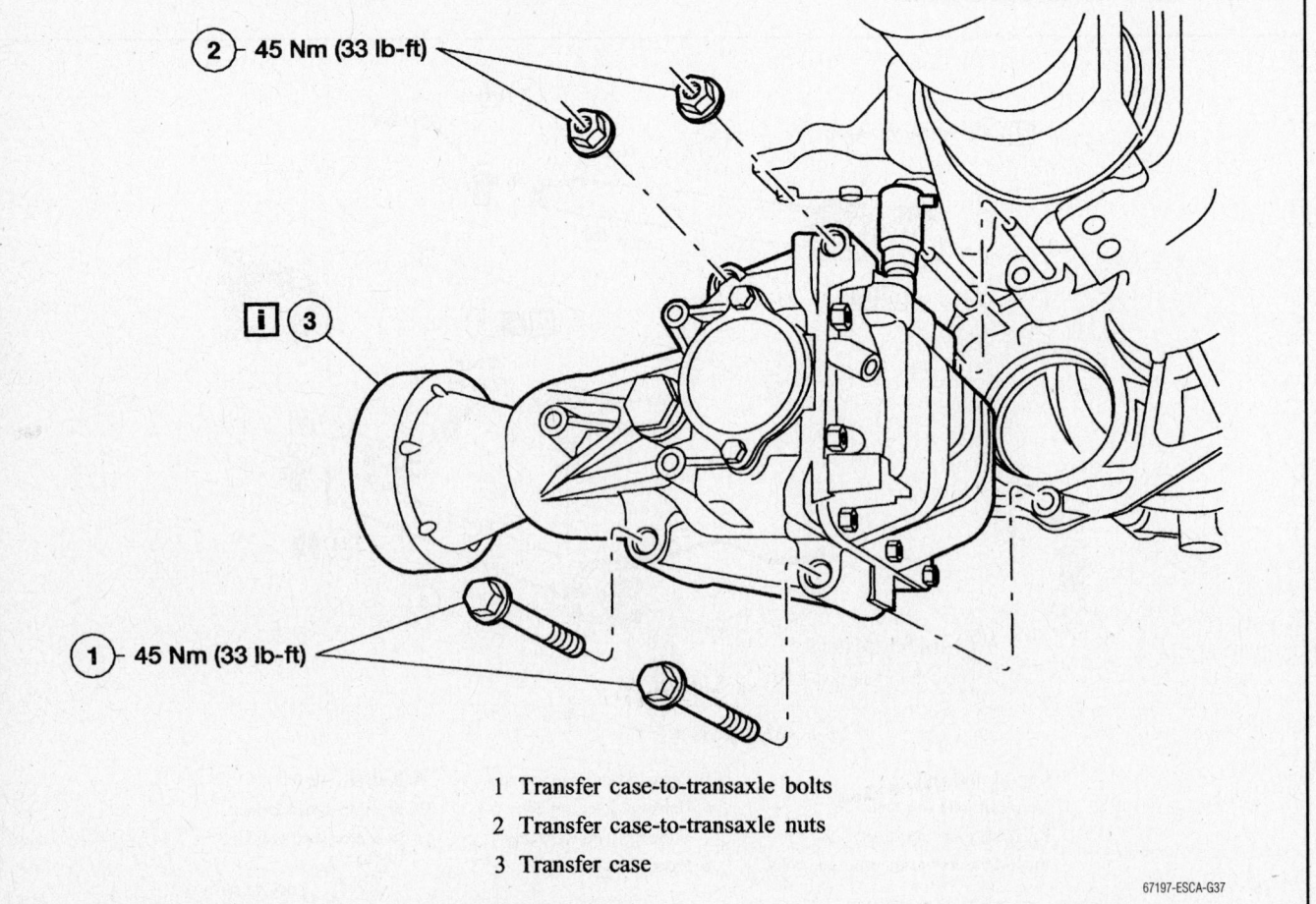

1 Transfer case-to-transaxle bolts

2 Transfer case-to-transaxle nuts

3 Transfer case

67197-ESCA-G37

Fig. 40 Transfer case mounting with manual transaxle—2005 model shown

With Automatic Transaxle

See Figure 41.

1. Before servicing the vehicle, refer to the Precautions Section.
2. Disconnect the battery.
3. Drain the transfer case.
4. Remove the front right intermediate shaft.
5. Remove the driveshaft.
6. Remove the 4 bolts and the crossmember brace.
7. Remove the generator.
8. Remove the exhaust as required.
9. Remove the heat shield.
10. Remove the transfer case-to-transaxle bolts.

11. Remove the transfer case.

✳✳ WARNING

A new transfer case driven gear seal must be installed whenever the intermediate shaft or transfer case is removed from the vehicle.

➡ **If necessary, replace the right differential fluid seal.**

12. To install, reverse the removal procedure. Observe the following torques:
   • Crossmember bolts: 30 ft. lbs. (40 Nm).
   • Transfer case-to-transaxle bolts: 33 ft. lbs. (45 Nm).

INTERMEDIATE SHAFT

REMOVAL & INSTALLATION

See Figure 42.

1. Before servicing the vehicle, refer to the Precautions Section.

➡ **If removing the intermediate shaft in order to repair a separate component, it should only be removed as an assembly with the right front halfshaft.**

2. Remove the right front halfshaft.
3. Remove the inner halfshaft bearing retainer nuts

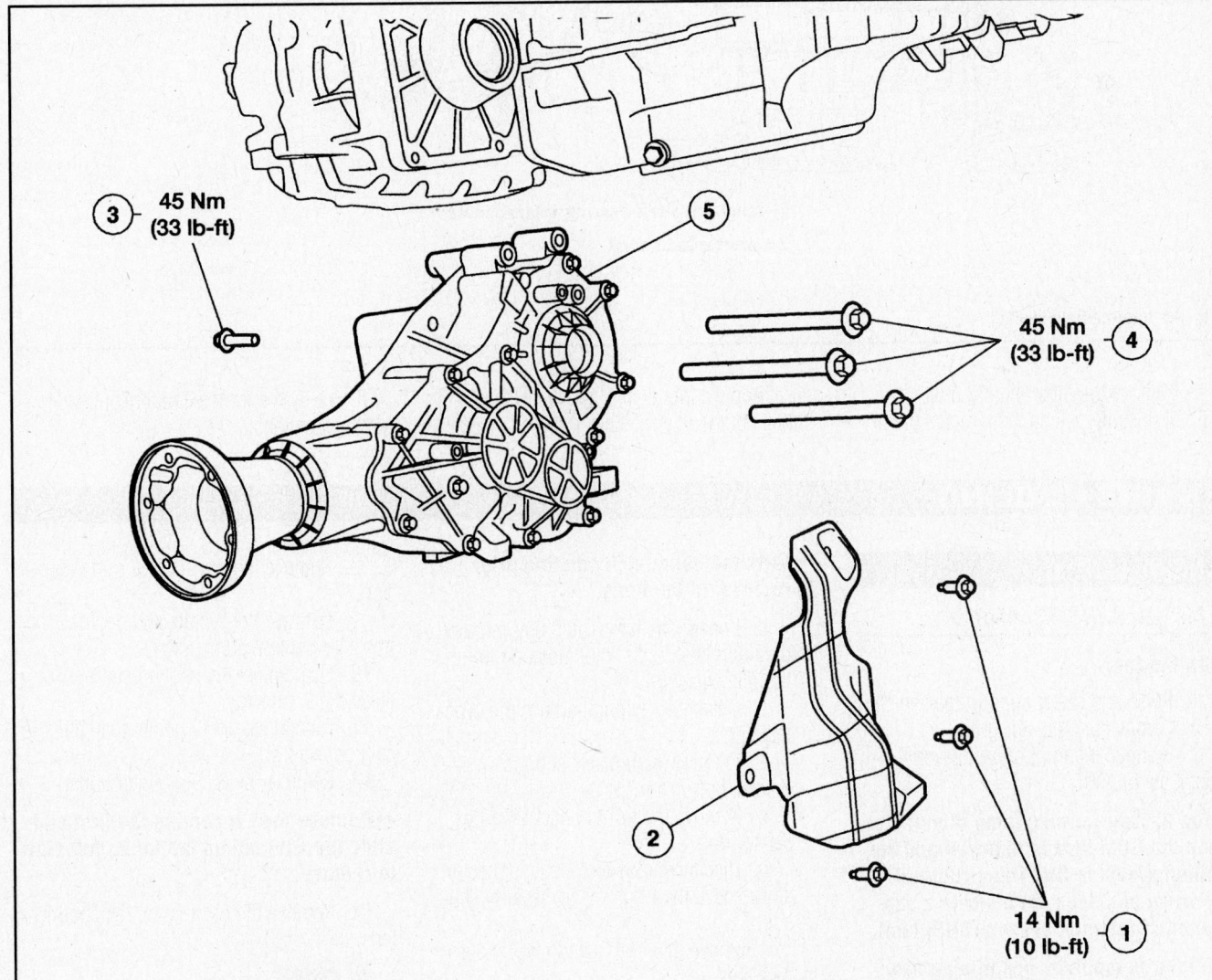

1 Heat shield bolt
2 Heat shield
3 Transfer case-to-transaxle bolts
4 Transfer case-to-transaxle bolts
5 Transfer case

67197-ESCA-G38

Fig. 41 Transfer case mounting with automatic transaxle—2005 model shown

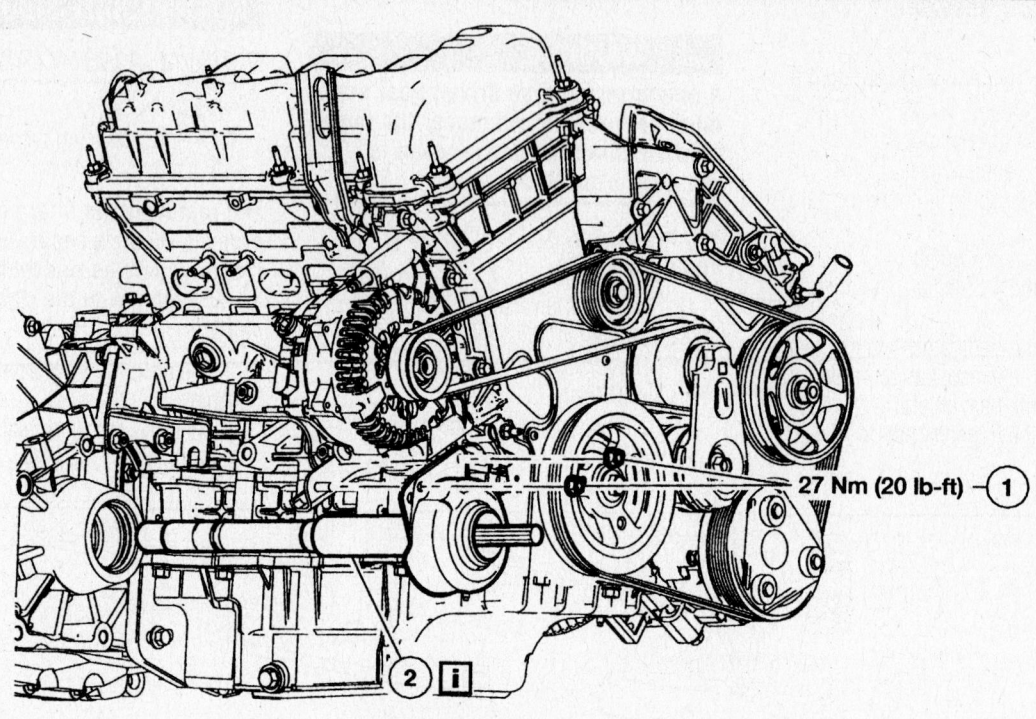

1 Inner halfshaft bearing retainer nuts
2 Intermediate shaft

67197-ESCA-G43

Fig. 42 Intermediate shaft

4. Remove the intermediate shaft
5. To install, reverse the removal procedure. Apply a thin coat of grease to the splines of the intermediate shaft.

6. Verify the front axle lubricant level is to specifications.

ENGINE COOLING

ENGINE FAN

REMOVAL & INSTALLATION

2005 Models

1. Raise and safely support the vehicle.
2. Remove the radiator grille.
3. Remove the front impact severity sensor, as follows:

➡The air bag warning lamp illuminates when the RCM fuse is removed and the ignition switch is ON. This is normal operation and does not indicate a supplemental restraint system (SRS) fault.

➡Repair is made by installing a new part only. If the new part does not correct the condition, install the original part and carry out the diagnostic procedure again.

   b. Disarm the Supplemental Restraint System (SRS), as outlined in the Chassis Electrical Section.

➡Mark the hood latch position prior to removal of the bolts.

   c. Loosen the hood latch nut, remove the hood latch bolts, then position the hood latch aside.
   d. Detach the wiring harness pin-type retainers.
   e. Remove the radiator support bracket bolt.
   f. Remove the front impact severity sensor bolt.
   g. Disconnect the electrical connector and remove the front impact severity sensor.
   4. Remove the 4 bolts and the 2 radiator brackets.
   5. Disconnect the hood switch electrical connector.
   6. Remove the 3 relay box bracket bolts and position the relay box and bracket aside.
   7. Remove the center support lower bolt.

   8. Remove the nut and the center support.
   9. Remove the 2 bolts and position the auxiliary coolant pump aside.
   10. Disconnect the cooling fan resistor electrical connector.
   11. Disconnect the 2 cooling fan electrical connectors
   12. Remove the 6 cooling fan bolts.

➡Remove the LH cooling fan first and slide the RH cooling fan to the left side to remove.

   13. Remove the LH and the RH cooling fans.

   To install:
   14. Installation is the reverse of the removal procedure, noting the following tightening specifications:
     a. Cooling fan bolts: 71 inch lbs. (8 Nm)
     b. Auxiliary coolant pump bolts: 62 inch lbs. (7 Nm).

c. Center support nut and lower bolt: 89 inch lbs. (10 Nm)

d. Relay box bracket bolts: 89 inch lbs. (10 Nm)

e. Radiator bracket bolts: 89 inch lbs. (10 Nm)

15. Install the front impact severity sensor, as follows:

a. Connect the electrical connector to the front impact severity sensor.

➡**Make sure the radiator support and front impact severity sensor mating surfaces are clean and free of foreign material.**

b. Align the locator tabs of the front impact severity sensor to the openings in the radiator support bracket.

⁂ CAUTION

The tightening torque of the air bag front impact severity sensor retaining bolt is critical for correct system operation.

c. Install the front impact severity sensor bolt. Tighten to 9 ft. lbs. (12 Nm).

d. Install the radiator support bracket bolt and tighten to 9 ft. lbs. (12 Nm)

e. Attach the wiring harness pin-type retainers.

➡**Align the hood latch position as previously marked during removal.**

f. Position the hood latch, install the hood latch bolts and nut and tighten to 80 inch lbs. (9 Nm).

⁂ WARNING

Make sure the hood latch is fully engaged.

g. Verify the hood latch striker is fully engaging the hood latch.

h. Rearm the SRS, as outlined in the Chassis Electrical Section.

2006–08 Models

See Figure 43.

1. With vehicle in neutral position it on a hoist.
2. Drain the cooling system.
3. Remove the front bumper cover.

4. Remove the front impact severity sensor.

5. Remove the 2 pin-type retainers.

6. Remove the 4 bolts and the 2 radiator brackets.

➡**Mark the hood latch position prior to removal of the bolts.**

7. Loosen the nut, remove the 2 bolts and position aside the hood latch.

8. Remove the center support bolt.

9. Disconnect the cooling fan resistor electrical connector.

10. Disconnect the coolant recovery bottle and set aside.

11. Disconnect the cooling fan electrical connectors.

12. Remove the cooling fan bolts and the cooling fan motor and shroud.

To install:

13. To Install reverse the removal procedure and not the following:

a. Tighten cooling fan bolts to 71 inch lbs. (8 Nm).

b. Tighten center support bolt to 89 inch lbs. (10 Nm).

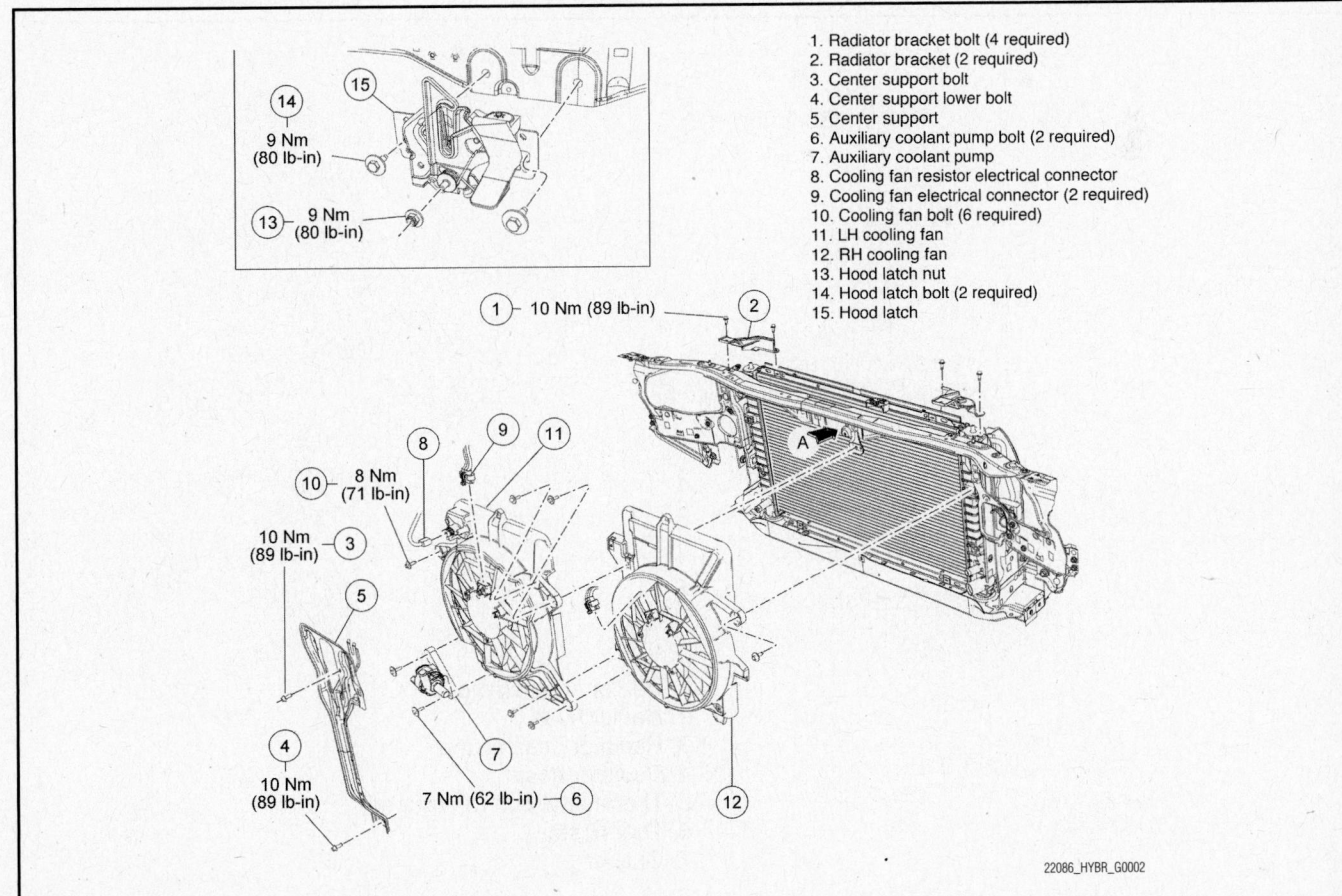

1. Radiator bracket bolt (4 required)
2. Radiator bracket (2 required)
3. Center support bolt
4. Center support lower bolt
5. Center support
6. Auxiliary coolant pump bolt (2 required)
7. Auxiliary coolant pump
8. Cooling fan resistor electrical connector
9. Cooling fan electrical connector (2 required)
10. Cooling fan bolt (6 required)
11. LH cooling fan
12. RH cooling fan
13. Hood latch nut
14. Hood latch bolt (2 required)
15. Hood latch

22086_HYBR_G0002

Fig. 43 Cooling fan motor, shroud and related parts

c. Tighten hood latch bolts to 80 inch lbs. (9 Nm).

d. Tighten 4 bolts to 2 radiator bracket to 89 inch lbs. (10 Nm).

e. Tighten impact severity sensor bolt. Tighten to 9 ft. lbs. (12 Nm).

14. Fill and bleed the cooling system.

15. Connect the negative battery cable.

RADIATOR

REMOVAL & INSTALLATION

1. Raise and safely support the vehicle.

2. Drain the cooling system.

3. Drain the motor electronics cooling system, as follows

a. With the vehicle in DRIVE, make sure the vehicle is raised and safely supported.

b. Turn the ignition to the OFF position.

c. Remove the LH splash shield.

d. Place a suitable container below the transaxle.

e. Loosen the hose clamps at the transaxle, then pull the hoses off to allow the coolant to drain.

4. Remove the cooling fan motor and shroud.

5. Disconnect the upper hose from the motor electronics radiator.

6. Remove the 2 motor electronics radiator-to-engine radiator bolts and position the motor electronics radiator aside.

7. Remove the 2 A/C condenser-to-radiator bolts and position the A/C condenser aside.

8. Disconnect the lower radiator hose from the radiator.

9. Disconnect the degas bottle return hose from the radiator.

10. Disconnect the engine coolant vent hose from the radiator.

11. Disconnect the upper radiator hose from the radiator.

12. Remove the radiator.

To install:

13. Installation is the reverse of the removal procedure, noting the following tightening specifications:

a. A/C condenser-to-radiator bolts: 71 inch lbs. (8 Nm)

b. Motor electronics radiator-to-engine radiator bolts: 53 inch lbs. (6 Nm).

14. Fill and bleed the cooling system.

15. Fill and bleed the motor electronics cooling system.

THERMOSTAT

REMOVAL & INSTALLATION

See Figure 44.

➡**The thermostat and thermostat housing are serviced as an assembly.**

1. Raise and safely support the vehicle.

2. Drain the cooling system.

3. Remove the accessory drive belt tensioner.

4. Disconnect the heater hose at the thermostat housing.

5. Disconnect the lower radiator hose at the thermostat housing.

6. Remove the 3 bolts, thermostat housing and gasket.

7. Clean and inspect the gasket, replace if necessary.

8. To install, reverse the removal procedure. Tighten the thermostat housing bolts to 89 inch lbs. (10 Nm).

9. Fill and bleed the cooling system.

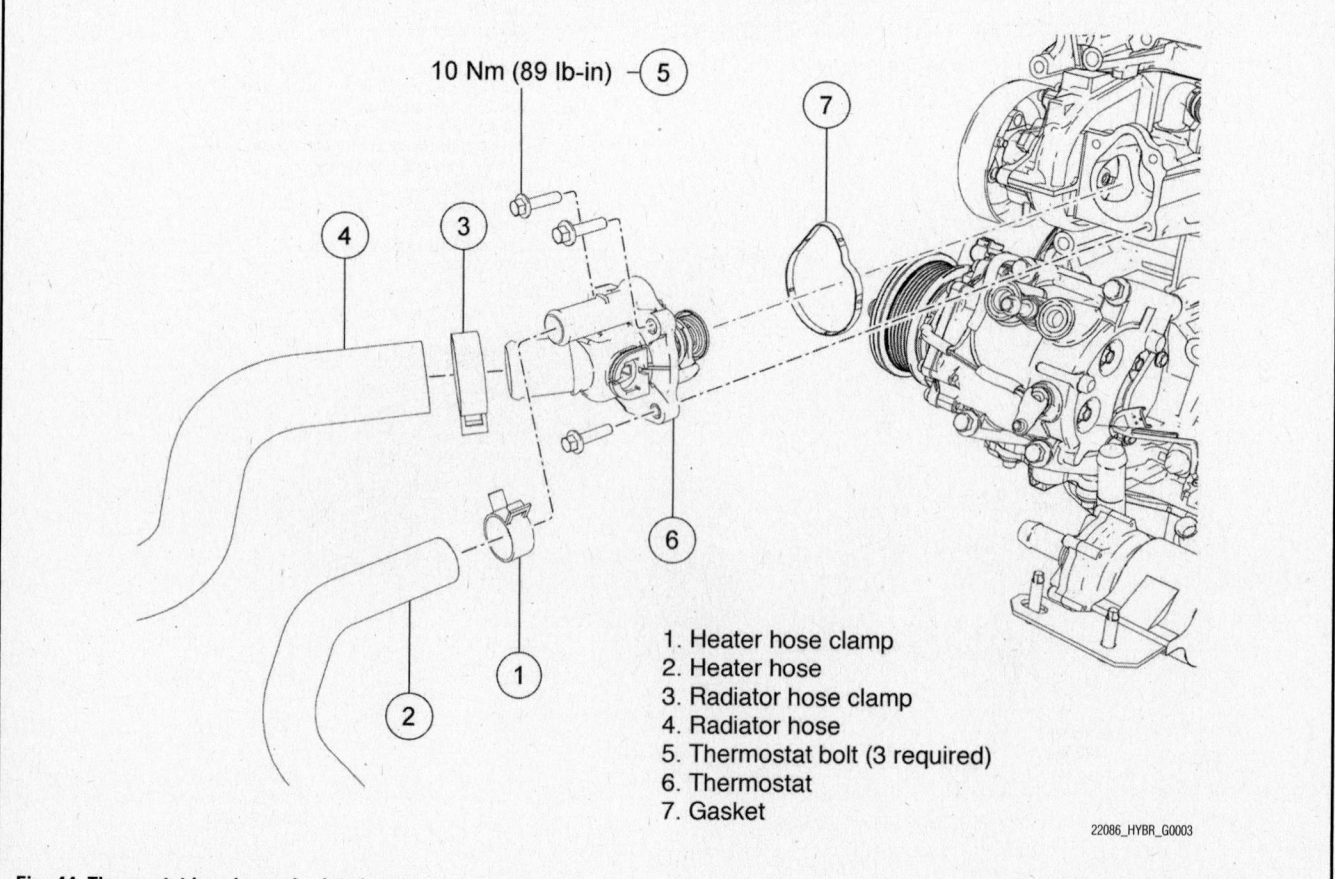

10 Nm (89 lb-in)

1. Heater hose clamp
2. Heater hose
3. Radiator hose clamp
4. Radiator hose
5. Thermostat bolt (3 required)
6. Thermostat
7. Gasket

22086_HYBR_G0003

Fig. 44 Thermostat housing and related parts

WATER PUMP

REMOVAL & INSTALLATION

See Figure 45.

1. Before servicing the vehicle, refer to the Precautions Section.
2. With the vehicle in NEUTRAL, position it on a hoist.
3. Drain the cooling system.
4. Remove the accessory drive belt.
5. Remove the coolant pump pulley bolts.
6. Remove the coolant pump pulley.
7. Remove the coolant pump bolts.
8. Remove the coolant pump.
9. Remove the coolant pump O-ring seal.
10. To install, reverse the removal procedure. Torque the water pump bolts to 89 inch lbs. (10 Nm). Torque the pulley bolts to 15 ft. lbs. (20 Nm).
11. Fill and bleed the cooling system.

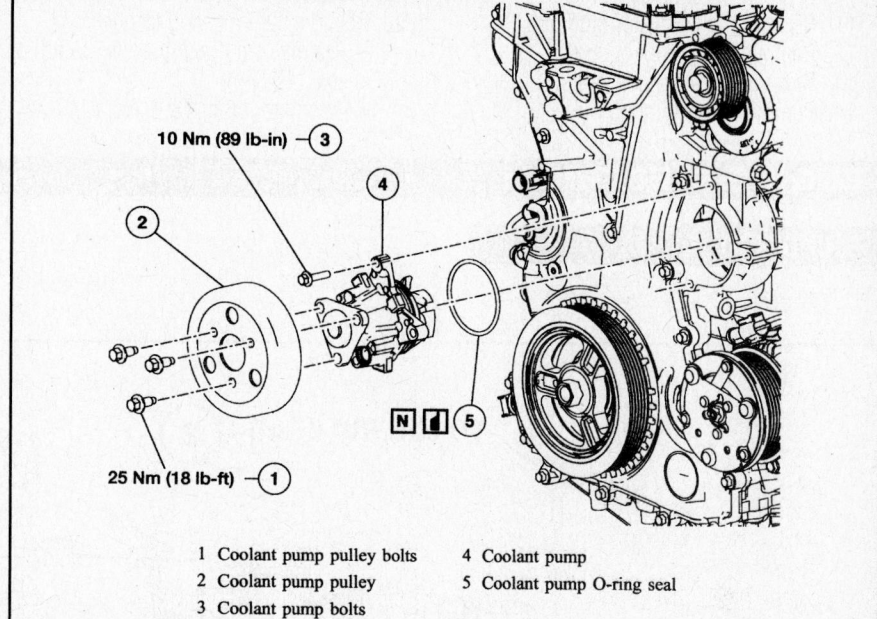

1	Coolant pump pulley bolts	4	Coolant pump
2	Coolant pump pulley	5	Coolant pump O-ring seal
3	Coolant pump bolts		

67197-ESCA-G03

Fig. 45 Water pump mounting—2.3L hybrid engine

ENGINE ELECTRICAL

CHARGING SYSTEM

ALTERNATOR

REMOVAL & INSTALLATION

See Figure 46.

1. Before servicing the vehicle, refer to the Precautions Section.
2. Disconnect the 12v battery.

➡**When the battery is disconnected and connected, the brake pedal needs to be calibrated. After the battery has been connected, with the vehicle in park, turn the key to the ON position. Press the brake pedal firmly, then fully release to calibrate the brake pedal.**

3. Remove the front end accessory drive belt tensioner. Rotate the front end accessory drive belt tensioner counterclockwise to loosen tension on the front end accessory drive belt.
4. Remove the front end accessory drive belt.
5. Remove the alternator B+ terminal.
6. Remove the alternator electrical connector.
7. Remove the alternator lower air duct bolt.
8. Remove the alternator lower air duct. Press the locking tab to release the lower air duct from the upper air duct.
9. Remove the pin-type retainer.

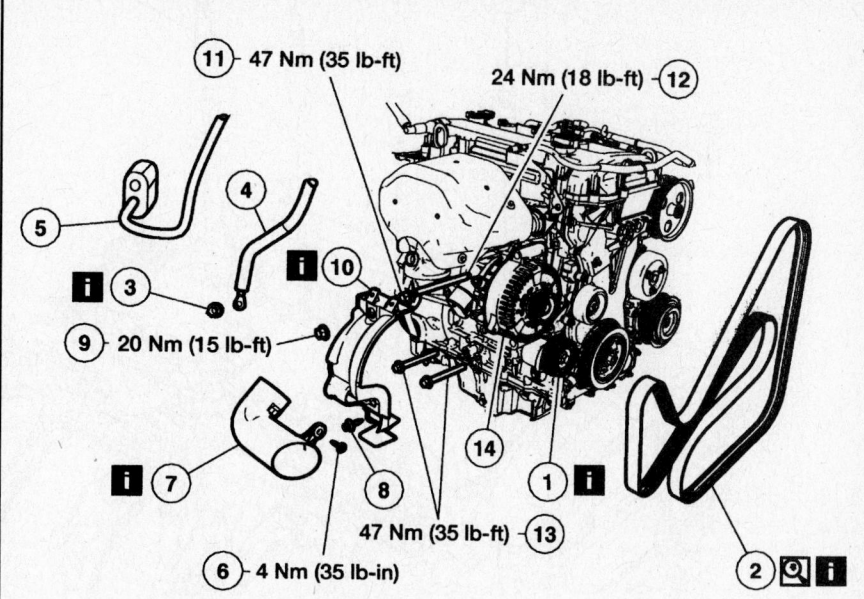

1	Front end accessory drive belt tensioner	8	Pin-type retainer
2	Front end accessory drive belt	9	Generator shield nut
3	Generator B+ terminal nut	10	Generator shield
4	Generator B+ terminal	11	Generator stud nut
5	Generator electrical connector	12	Generator stud
6	Generator lower air duct bolt	13	Generator bolts
7	Generator lower air duct	14	Generator

67197-ESCA-G01

Fig. 46 Alternator mounting—2.3L hybrid engine

10. Remove the alternator shield .
11. Remove the alternator stud nut.
12. Remove the alternator stud.
13. Remove the alternator bolts.
14. Remove the alternator.

15. To install, reverse the removal procedure. Observe the following torques:
- Alternator mounting bolts: 35 ft. lbs. (47 Nm)
- Alternator stud: 18 ft. lbs. (24 Nm)

- Stud nut: 35 ft. lbs. (47 Nm)
- Shield nut: 15 ft. lbs. (20 Nm)
- Lower air duct bolt: 35 inch lbs. (4 Nm)

ENGINE ELECTRICAL   IGNITION SYSTEM

FIRING ORDER

See Figure 47.

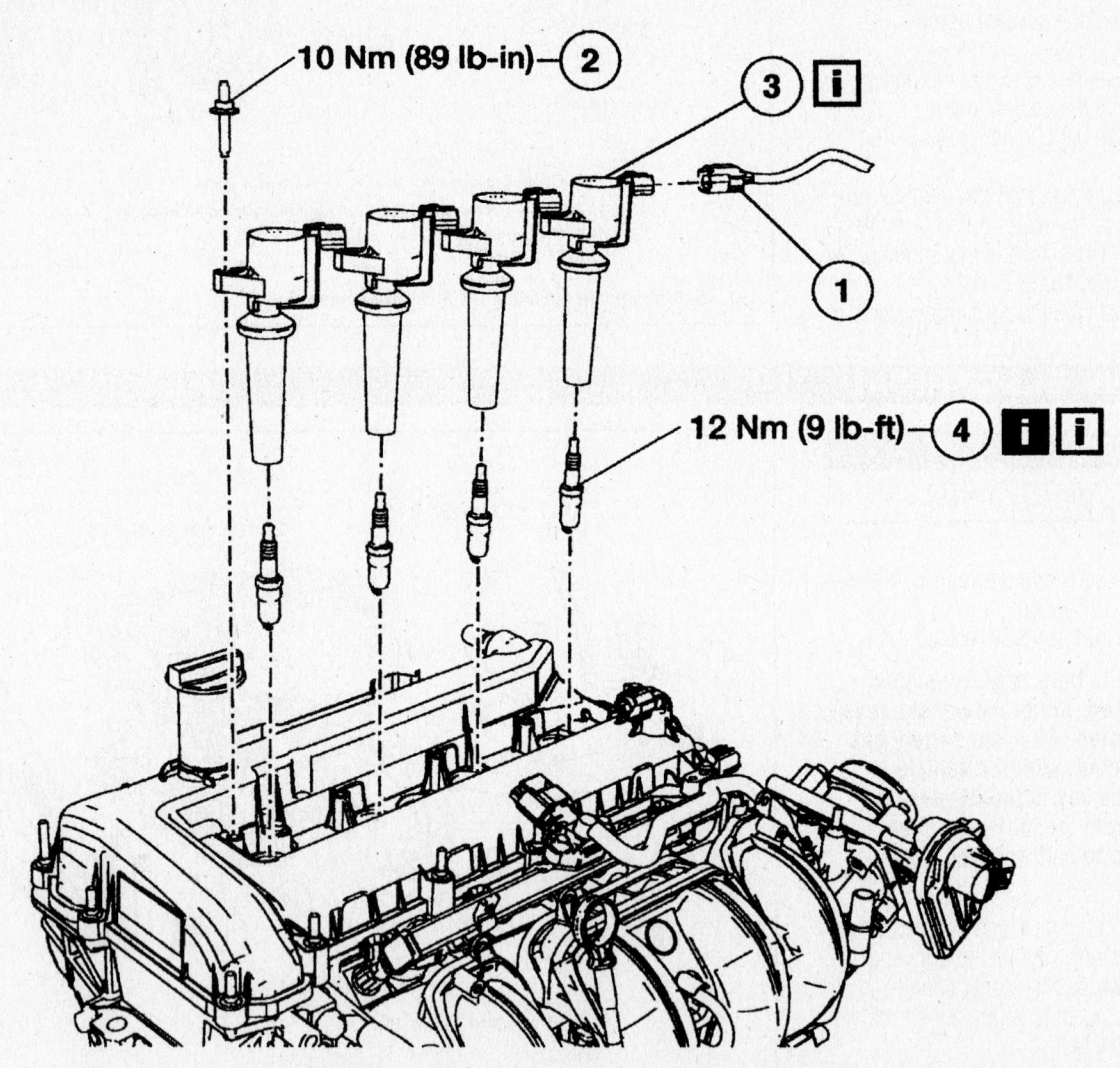

1 Ignition coil-on-plug electrical connectors

2 Ignition coil-to-valve cover bolts

3 Ignition coils

4 Spark plugs

67197-ESCA-G61

Fig. 47 Coil and spark plug arrangement—2.3L hybrid engine

GNITION COIL

REMOVAL & INSTALLATION

1. Disconnect the negative battery cable.
2. Disconnect the ignition coil electrical connectors.
3. Remove the bolts and the ignition coils.

To install:

4. Install the ignition coils. Tighten the bolts to 71 inch lbs. (8 Nm).
5. Apply a small amount of dielectric grease to the inside of the ignition coil boots before attaching to the spark plugs.

IGNITION TIMING

The ignition timing is controlled by the Powertrain Control Module (PCM). No adjustment is necessary or possible.

SPARK PLUGS

REMOVAL & INSTALLATION

1. Disconnect the negative battery cable.
2. Disconnect the ignition coil electrical connectors.
3. Remove the bolts and the ignition coils.

➡ **Use compressed air to remove any foreign material in the spark plug well before removing the spark plugs.**

4. Remove the spark plugs.

To install:

5. Inspect the spark plugs.
6. Adjust the spark plug gap as necessary. The proper gap is 0.049–0.053 in. (1.25–1.35mm).
7. Install the spark plugs and tighten to 9 ft. lbs. (12 Nm).
8. Apply a small amount of dielectric grease to the inside of the ignition coil boots before attaching to the spark plugs.
9. Install the ignition coils and bolts. Tighten to 71 inch lbs. (8 Nm).
10. Connect the ignition coil electrical connectors.
11. Connect the negative battery cable.

ENGINE ELECTRICAL   STARTING SYSTEM

STARTER

REMOVAL & INSTALLATION
See Figure 48.

1. Before servicing the vehicle, refer to the Precautions Section.

✳✳ WARNING

When performing maintenance on the starting system, be aware that heavy gauge leads are connected directly to the battery. Make sure protective caps are in place when maintenance is completed.

2. With the vehicle in NEUTRAL, position it on a hoist
3. Disconnect the battery ground cable.
4. Starter motor solenoid terminal cover

5. Starter solenoid wire
6. Starter solenoid battery cable
7. Wiring harness retainer
8. Ground strap
9. Starter motor stud bolts
10. Starter motor bracket bolt
11. Starter motor
12. To install, reverse the removal procedure. Torque the starter and bracket bolts to 26 ft. lbs. (35 Nm).

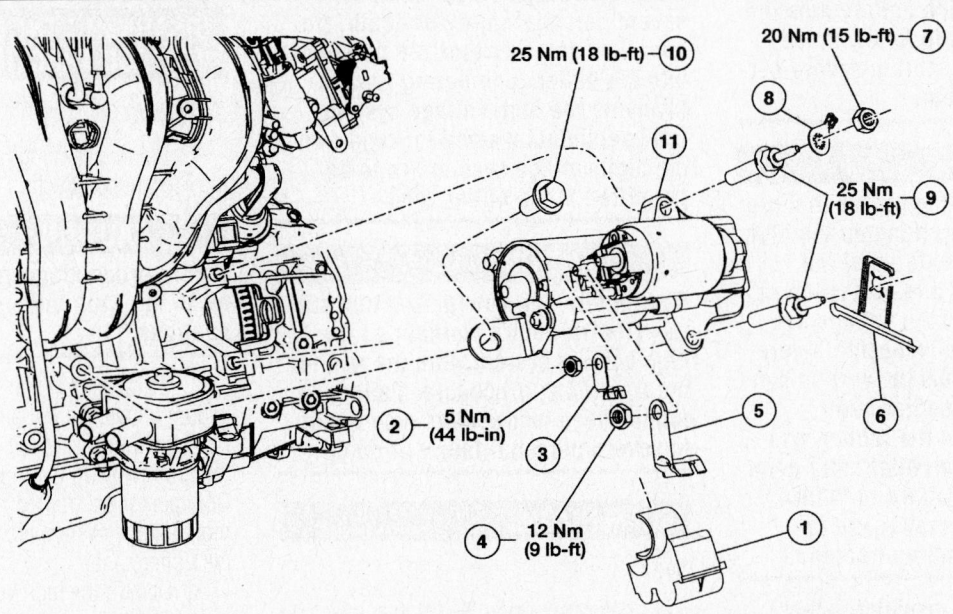

1 Starter motor solenoid terminal cover	5 Starter solenoid battery cable	9 Starter motor stud bolts
2 Starter solenoid wire nut	6 Wiring harness retainer	10 Starter motor bracket bolt
3 Starter solenoid wire	7 Ground strap nut	11 Starter motor
4 Starter solenoid battery cable nut	8 Ground strap	

67197-ESCA-G19

Fig. 48 Starter mounting—2.3L hybrid engine

HYBRID HIGH VOLTAGE ELECTRICAL SYSTEM

PRECAUTIONS

Before working on any part of the Escape Hybrid high voltage system, observe the following precautions:

✸ CAUTION

The nominal high voltage traction battery voltage is 330 volts DC. The buffer zone must be set up and insulated rubber gloves and a face shield must be worn. Failure to follow these instructions may result in severe injury or death.

✸ CAUTION

The high voltage traction battery and charging system contains high voltage components and wiring. High voltage insulated safety gloves and a face shield must be worn when carrying out any diagnostics on this vehicle. Failure to follow these instructions may result in severe personal injury or death.

✸ CAUTION

Before carrying out any removal and installation procedures of the high voltage traction battery system, the high voltage traction battery must be Disarmed. Failure to follow these instructions may result in severe personal injury or death.

✸✸ CAUTION

The rubber insulating gloves that are to be worn while working on the high voltage system should be of the appropriate safety and protection rating for use on the high voltage system. They must be inspected before use and must always be worn in conjunction with the leather outer gloves. Any hole in the rubber insulating glove is a potential entry point for high voltage. Failure to follow these instructions may result in severe personal injury or death.

➡ The high voltage insulated safety gloves must be re-certified every 6 months to remain within Occupational Safety and Health Administration (OSHA) guidelines:

• Roll the glove up from the open end until the lower portion of the glove begins to balloon from the resulting air pressure. If the glove leaks any air, it must not be used.

• The gloves should not be used if they exhibit any signs of wear and tear.

• The leather gloves must always be worn over the rubber insulating gloves in order to protect them.

• The rubber insulating gloves must be class "00" and meet all of the American Society for Testing and Materials (ASTM) standards

✸✸ CAUTION

High voltage insulated safety gloves and a face shield must be worn when working with high voltage cables. The ignition switch must be OFF for a minimum of 5 minutes before removing high voltage cables. Failure to follow these instructions may result in severe personal injury or death.

✸✸ CAUTION

Establish a buffer zone before servicing the high voltage system. The buffer zone is required only when working with the high voltage system. See the text for buffer zone establishment. Failure to follow these instructions may result in severe personal injury or death. Do not allow any unauthorized personnel into the buffer zone during repairs involving the high voltage system. Only personnel trained for repair on the high voltage system are to be permitted in the buffer zone.

✸✸ CAUTION

Disarm the high voltage traction battery (HVTB) before working on the high voltage system. See the text for the Disarming procedure. Failure to follow these instructions may result in severe personal injury or death.

BUFFER ZONE

See Figure 49.

1. Before servicing the vehicle, refer to the Precautions Section.

✸✸ CAUTION

Before proceeding, read and observe all of the High Voltage System Precautions.

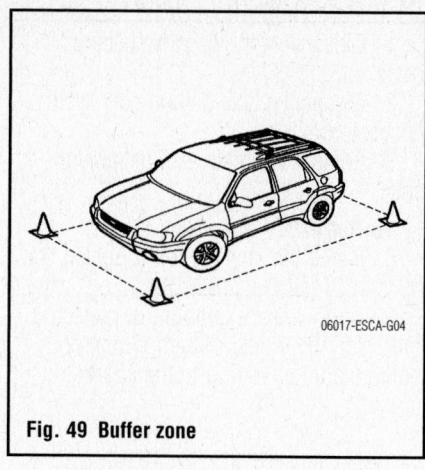

06017-ESCA-G04

Fig. 49 Buffer zone

2. Establish a buffer zone around the vehicle:

a. Position the vehicle in the repair bay.

b. Position 4 orange cones at the corners of the vehicle to mark off a 1 m (3 ft.) perimeter around the vehicle.

c. Do not allow any unauthorized personnel into the buffer zone during repairs involving the high voltage system. Only personnel trained for repair on the high voltage system are to be permitted in the buffer zone.

DISARMING THE HIGH VOLTAGE TRACTION BATTERY

See Figure 50.

1. Before servicing the vehicle, refer to the Precautions Section.

✸✸ CAUTION

Before proceeding, read and observe all of the High Voltage System Precautions.

2. Establish a buffer zone. See the procedure above. Do not allow any unauthorized personnel into the buffer zone during repairs involving the high voltage system. Only personnel trained for repair on the high voltage system are to be permitted in the buffer zone.

3. Disarm the high voltage traction battery (HVTB).

d. Rotate the service disconnect plug from the LOCK (1) position to the UNLOCK (2) position.

e. Remove the service disconnect plug and place in the SERVICING SHIPPING (3) position.

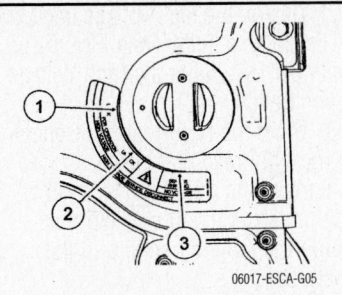

Fig. 50 Rotate the service disconnect plug from the LOCK (1) position to the UNLOCK (2) position

06017-ESCA-G05

❋❋ WARNING

Place the service disconnect plug into the SERVICING SHIPPING position while the high voltage traction battery (HVTB) is being removed and/or while the high voltage system is having repairs carried out. If the service disconnect plug is left out and placed on the bench or toolbox, dirt or other contaminants may enter the HVTB, which can cause damage.

4. Insert the service disconnect plug into the SERVICING SHIPPING position. This disconnects the HVTB.

5. To Rearm, reverse the Disarm procedure.

HIGH VOLTAGE TRACTION BATTERY

REMOVAL & INSTALLATION

See Figure 51.

1. Before servicing the vehicle, refer to the Precautions Section.

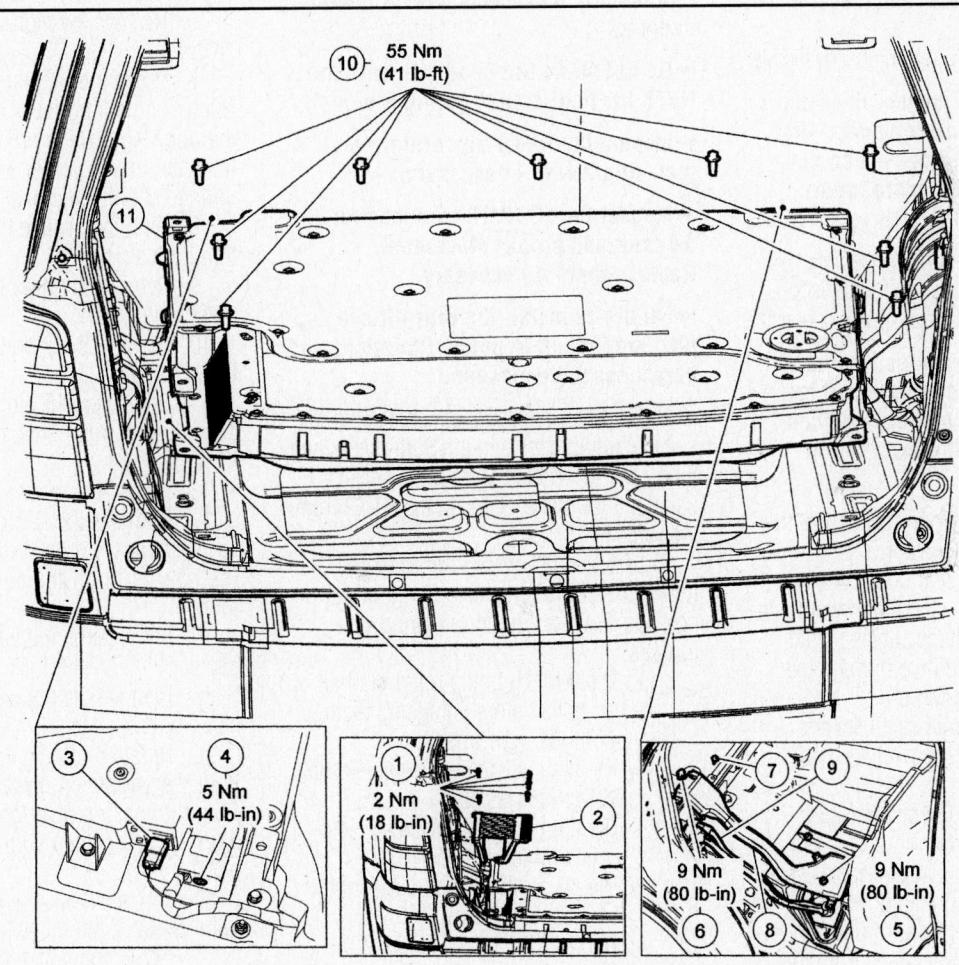

1 A/C return duct assembly screws (5 required)

2 A/C return duct assembly

3 6-pin low voltage electrical connector

4 40-pin low voltage electrical connector

5 High voltage cables shield nuts (2 required)

6 High voltage cables shield bolt

7 High voltage cables shield plastic rivet/screw

8 High voltage cables shield

9 High voltage cables electrical connector

10 High voltage traction battery bolts (9 required)

11 High voltage traction battery

06017-ESCA-G06

Fig. 51 High voltage traction battery

❄❄ CAUTION

Before proceeding, read and observe all of the High Voltage System Precautions.

2. Disarm the high voltage traction battery. Establish a buffer zone. See the procedure under Disarm the High Voltage Traction Battery.

3. Position the carpet aside.

➡**When installing, tighten the screws on the HVTB first or an air flow loss to the HVTB may occur.**

4. Remove the 5 A/C return duct assembly screws.

5. Remove the A/C return duct assembly.

➡**Due to clearance issues, the 6-pin connector must be disconnected first during the removal process and connected last during the installation process.**

6. From the left rear door opening, fold the left rear seat backrest down and disconnect the 6-pin low voltage electrical connector.

➡**Due to clearance issues, the 40-pin connector must be disconnected last during the removal process and connected first during the installation process.**

7. Loosen the bolt and disconnect the 40-pin low voltage connector.

8. From the right rear door opening, fold the right rear seat cushion forward and remove the 2 high voltage cables shield nuts (access the shield nuts through the slotted opening in the carpet).

9. Fold the right rear seat backrest down and remove the high voltage cables shield bolt.

10. Remove the high voltage cables shield plastic rivet/screw.

11. Remove the high voltage cables shield.

12. Press the locking tab down and rotate the locking lever upward until the aligning dowels are disengaged from the locking lever to remove the high voltage cables electrical connector.

➡**The attaching bolts have a conductive coating on them and are serrated under the head flange. These features ground the HVTB to the vehicle, which is required for electro-magnetic compatibility (EMC). The serration also helps the grounding effect. If a bolt(s) is lost or damaged, it must be replaced with the identical type of bolt.**

13. Remove the 9 HVTB bolts.

➡**The 2 front lift points are the eyelets on each front corner and the rear lift point is beneath the cap plug in the center rear of the HVTB.**

➡**Remove the cap plug to expose the center (rear) lifting attachment point.**

➡**Attach 3 M10×1.5×35 eyebolts to the 3 HVTB lift points. Obtain the eyebolts locally.**

➡**Make certain the HVTB does not mar or damage the interior panels during removal. There is only 6 mm (0.23 in) clearance on each side. Cover the battery mounting brackets with protective padding.**

➡**Do not strike the headliner with the HVTB (or floor crane) during removal.**

➡**Inspect the HVTB tray drain grommet. Replace it if necessary.**

➡**Inspect the 10 HVTB cushions for damage and proper placement. Replace them if necessary.**

➡**Failure to install the rear lift eye cap plug may result in noise, vibration, and harshness (NVH) issues.**

14. With an assistant, attach a chain or suitable lifting device to the 3 lift points and lift the HVTB off the 2 alignment dowels using a floor crane. Remove the HVTB from the vehicle.

15. To install, reverse the removal procedure. To Rearm, reverse the Disarm procedure. Observe the following torques:

- The 9 HVTB bolts. Hand-start all of the bolts before tightening them to: 41 ft. lbs. (55 Nm)
- The high voltage cables shield bolt: 80 inch lbs. (9 Nm).
- The 2 high voltage cables shield nuts: 80 inch lbs. (9 Nm)
- The 40-pin low voltage connector: 44 inch lbs. (5 Nm)
- The 5 A/C return duct assembly screws: 18 inch lbs. (2 Nm)

HIGH VOLTAGE CABLES

REMOVAL & INSTALLATION

See Figure 52.

1. Before servicing the vehicle, refer to the Precautions Section.

❄❄ CAUTION

Before proceeding, read and observe all of the High Voltage System Precautions.

2. Disarm the high voltage traction battery. Establish a buffer zone. See the procedure under Disarming the High Voltage Traction Battery.

3. From the right rear door opening, fold the right rear seat cushion forward and remove the 2 high voltage cables shield nuts (access the shield nuts through the slotted opening in the carpet).

4. Fold the right rear seat backrest down and remove the high voltage cables shield bolt.

5. Remove the high voltage cables shield plastic rivet/screw.

6. Remove the high voltage cables shield.

7. Press the locking tab down and rotate the locking lever upward until the aligning dowels are disengaged from the locking lever to remove the high voltage cables electrical connector.

8. With the vehicle in NEUTRAL, position it on a hoist.

9. Remove the high voltage cables floor pan grommet.

10. Remove the 2 bolts and the park brake cable bracket.

11. Remove the 5 high voltage cables conduit nuts (right side inner frame rail and floor pan).

12. Lower the vehicle.

13. Remove the 2 high voltage cables bracket nuts (bulkhead). (Access the nuts through the engine compartment.)

14. Remove the nut and the eCVT shift cable.

15. Remove the high voltage cables-to-eCVT bolt.

16. Rotate the locking lever rearward until the alignment dowels are disengaged from the locking lever and remove the high voltage cables connection to the eCVT.

17. To install, reverse the removal procedure. Observe the following torques:

- The high voltage cables-to-eCVT bolt: 9 Nm (80 lb-in)
- The eCVT shift cable: 8 Nm (71 lb-in)
- The 2 high voltage cables bracket nuts: 8 Nm (71 lb-in)
- The 5 high voltage cables conduit nuts: 8 Nm (71 lb-in)
- The park brake cable bracket: 8 Nm (71 lb-in).
- The high voltage cables shield bolt: 9 Nm (80 lb-in).
- The 2 high voltage cables shield nuts: 9 Nm (80 lb-in)

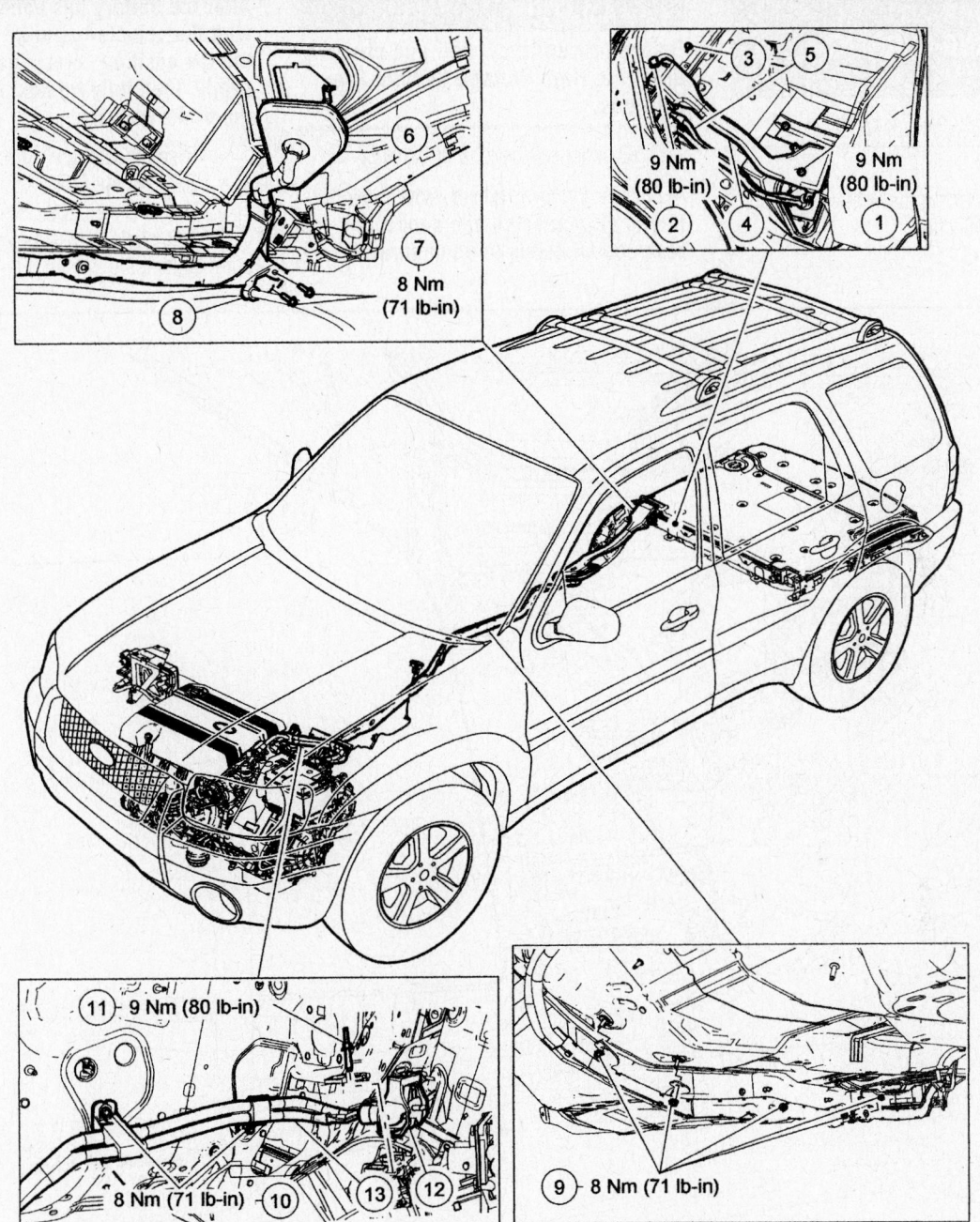

1 High voltage cables shield nuts (2 required)

2 High voltage cables shield bolt

3 High voltage cables shield plastic rivet/screw

4 High voltage cables shield

5 High voltage cables electrical connector

6 High voltage cables floorpan grommet

7 Park brake cable bracket bolts (2 required)

8 Park brake cable bracket

9 High voltage cables conduit nuts (right side inner frame rail and floorpan) (5 required)

10 High voltage cables bracket nuts (bulkhead) (2 required)

11 High voltage cables-to-electronically controlled continuously variable transmission (eCVT) bolt

12 High voltage cables connection to eCVT

13 High voltage cables

06017-ESCA-G07

Fig. 52 High Voltage Cables

DIRECT CURRENT/ ALTERNATING CURRENT INVERTER

REMOVAL & INSTALLATION

See Figure 53.

1. Before servicing the vehicle, refer to the Precautions Section.

⁑ CAUTION

Before proceeding, read and observe all of the High Voltage System Precautions.

2. Disconnect the 12 volt battery.

→**For the Escape Hybrid, when the battery is disconnected and connected, the brake pedal needs to be calibrated.**

After the battery has been connected, with the vehicle in park, turn the key to the ON position. Press the brake pedal firmly, then fully release to calibrate the brake pedal.

3. Disconnect the electrical connectors.
4. Remove the 2 DC/AC inverter nuts.
5. Remove the DC/AC inverter.
6. To install, reverse the removal procedure. Tighten the nuts to 80 inch lbs. (9 Nm).

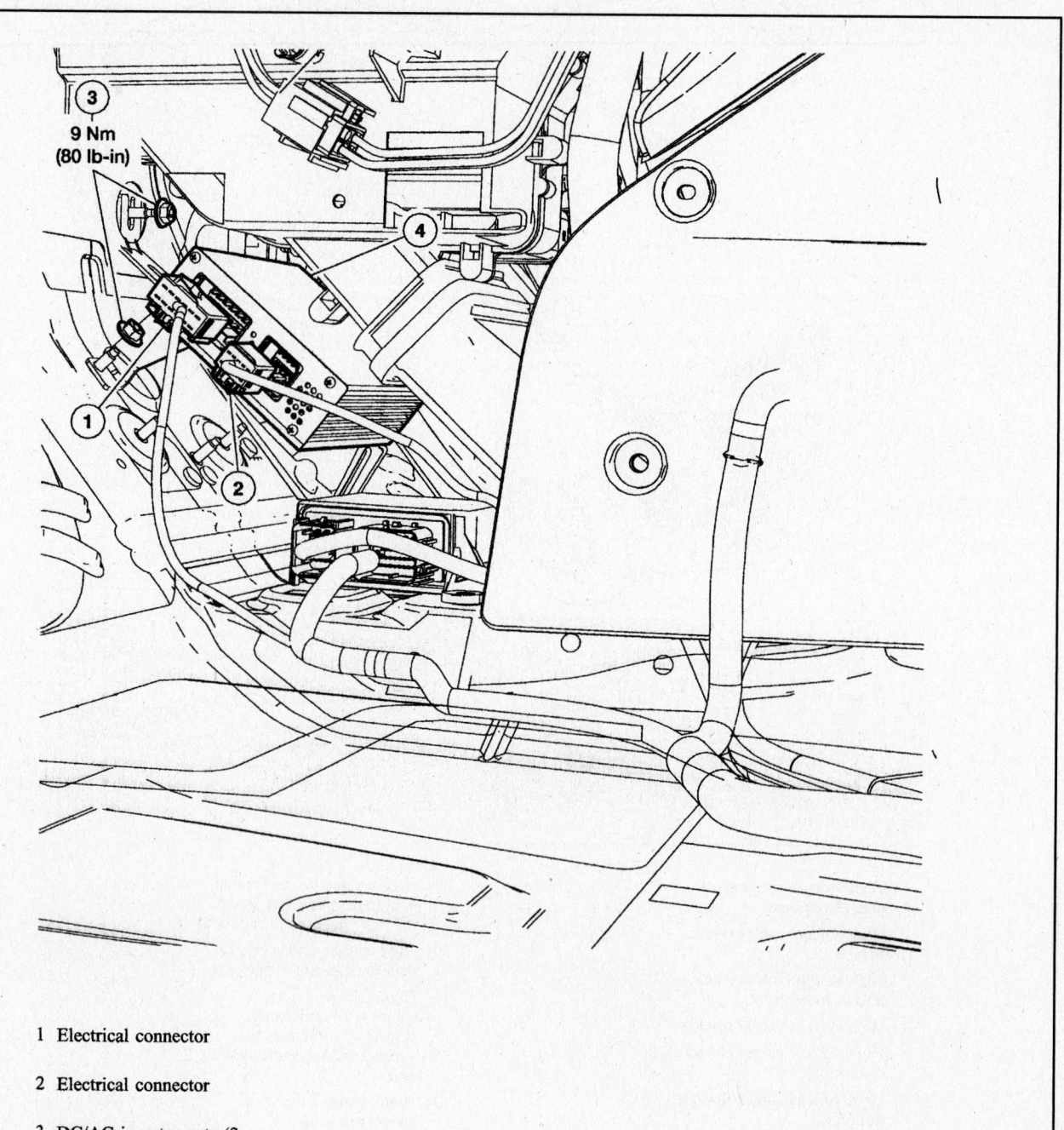

1 Electrical connector

2 Electrical connector

3 DC/AC inverter nuts (2 required)

4 DC/AC inverter

06017-ESCA-G08

Fig. 53 DC/AC Inverter

DIRECT CURRENT/DIRECT CURRENT CONVERTER

REMOVAL & INSTALLATION

See Figures 54 and 55.

1. Before servicing the vehicle, refer to the Precautions Section.

❈❈ CAUTION

Before proceeding, read and observe all of the High Voltage System Precautions.

2. Disarm the high voltage traction battery. Establish a buffer zone. See the procedure under Disarming the High Voltage Traction Battery.

3. Disconnect the 12 volt battery.

➡ **For the Escape Hybrid, when the battery is disconnected and connected, the brake pedal needs to be calibrated. After the battery has been connected, with the vehicle in park, turn the key to the ON position. Press the brake pedal firmly, then fully release to calibrate the brake pedal.**

4. With the vehicle in NEUTRAL, position it on a hoist.

5. Drain the cooling system.

❈❈ WARNING

Always refill the motor electronics cooling system (MECS) with the same type of coolant that was drained from the system. Do not mix coolant types.

6. Drain the motor electronics cooling system:

    a. With the vehicle in DRIVE, position it on a hoist.

    b. Turn the ignition to the OFF position.

    c. Remove the left splash shield.

    d. Place a suitable container below the transaxle.

    e. Loosen the hose clamps at the transaxle, then pull the hoses off to allow the coolant to drain.

7. Disconnect the motor electronics coolant vent hose.

8. Disconnect the 2 engine coolant vent hoses.

9. Remove the degas bottle bolt and nut.

10. Lift the degas bottle up and disconnect the engine coolant and motor electronics coolant return hoses.

11. Remove the degas bottle.

12. Disconnect the 2 female pin-type retainers.

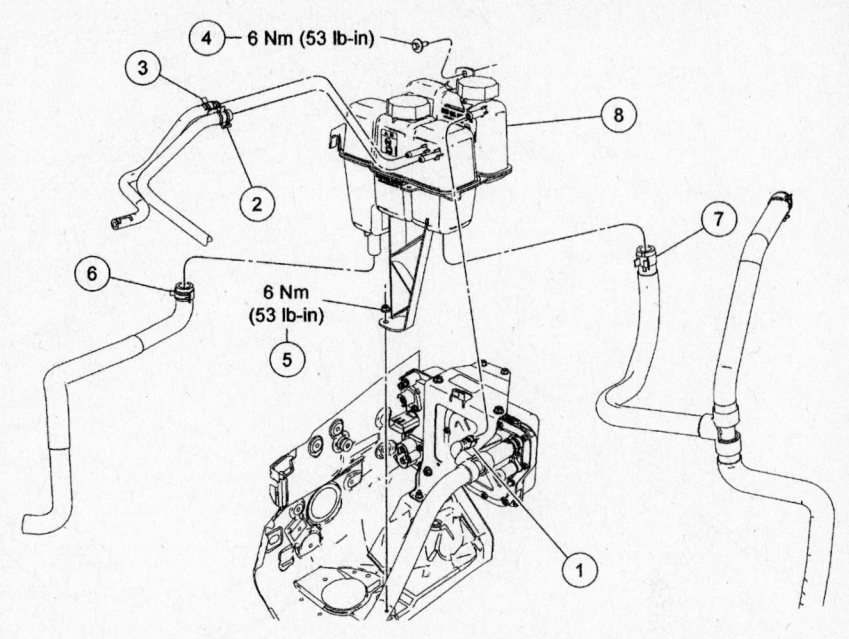

1 Motor electronics coolant vent hose and clamp	5 Degas bottle-to-fender nut
2 Engine coolant vent hose and clamp	6 Engine coolant return hose and clamp
3 Engine coolant vent hose and clamp	7 Motor electronics coolant return hose and clamp
4 Degas bottle-to-bracket bolt	8 Degas bottle

06017-ESCA-G10

Fig. 54 Degas bottle

➡ **Press the locking clip to release the connector.**

13. Disconnect the DC/DC converter high voltage connector.

14. Clamp the motor/electronics coolant (MECT) hoses to prevent coolant from leaking from the hoses during the repair.

15. Loosen the hose clamps and remove the MECT hoses from the DC/DC converter.

16. Remove the 2 DC/DC converter low voltage battery cable nuts and remove the low voltage battery cables.

17. Disconnect the DC/DC converter low voltage electrical connector.

18. Remove the 3 DC/DC converter nuts.

19. Remove the DC/DC converter assembly.

To install:

20. To install, reverse the removal procedure. Rearm the high voltage battery. Observe the following torques:

- The 3 DC/DC converter nuts: 9 ft. lbs. (12 Nm)
- The 2 DC/DC converter low voltage battery cable nuts: 9 ft. lbs. (12 Nm)

- The degas bottle bolt and nut: 53 inch lbs. (6 Nm)

21. Fill the Motor Electronics Cooling System as follows:

➡ **Vehicle cooling systems are filled with Motorcraft® Premium Gold Engine Coolant. Always fill the cooling system with the same coolant that is present in the system. Do not mix coolant types.**

    f. Connect the hoses to the transaxle and install the hose clamps.

❈❈ WARNING

Adhesives, stop-leak pellets or small debris in the Motor Electronics Cooling System (MECS) can cause poor performance or temporary blockage of the motor electronics pump. Only use clean, approved coolant when filling the system.

    g. Loosen the bleed screw and fill the degas bottle with coolant until it begins to flow out of the bleed hole. Then, close the bleed screw.

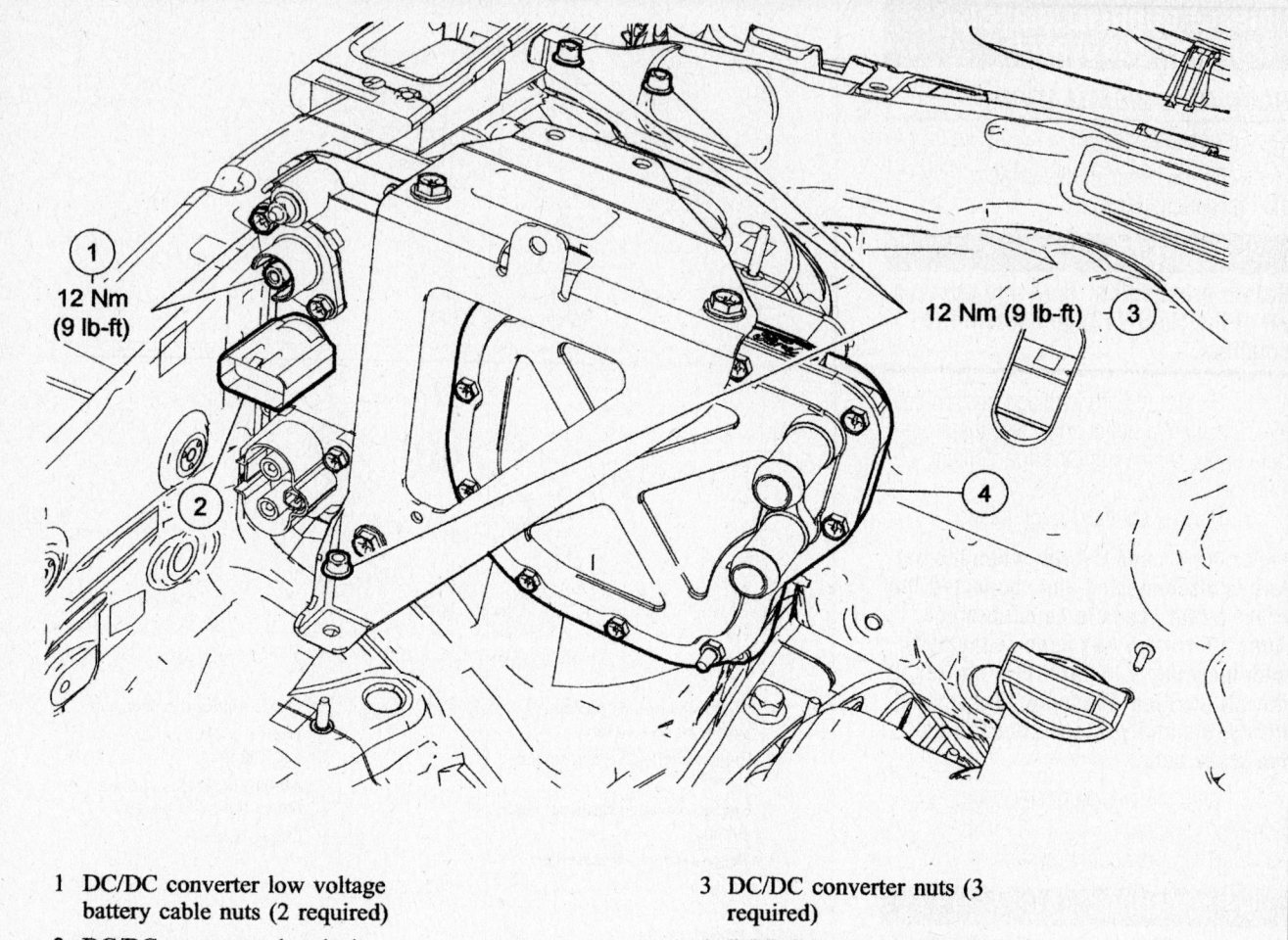

1 DC/DC converter low voltage
   battery cable nuts (2 required)
2 DC/DC converter electrical
   connector
3 DC/DC converter nuts (3
   required)
4 DC/DC converter assembly

06017-ESCA-G09

Fig. 55 DC/DC converter

h. Turn the ignition to the ON position to actuate the motor electronics cooling pump and continue to fill the degas bottle to the correct level.

➡**Most of the MECS air bleeding occurs as a normal process at the degas bottle through the vent tube; very little occurs at the bleed screw.**

i. To bleed air from the system, loosen the bleed screw and allow air to escape while the M/E coolant pump is operating.

DIRECT CURRENT/DIRECT CURRENT CONVERTER WIRING HARNESS

REMOVAL & INSTALLATION

See Figure 56.

1. Before servicing the vehicle, refer to the Precautions Section.

✳✳ CAUTION

Before proceeding, read and observe all of the High Voltage System Precautions.

2. Disarm the high voltage traction battery. Establish a buffer zone. See the procedure under Disarming the High Voltage Traction Battery.
3. Disconnect the 12 volt battery.

➡**For the Escape Hybrid, when the battery is disconnected and connected, the brake pedal needs to be calibrated. After the battery has been connected, with the vehicle in park, turn the key to the ON position. Press the brake pedal firmly, then fully release to calibrate the brake pedal.**

4. Remove the engine cover.
5. Disconnect the DC/DC converter harness connector from the electronically

controlled continuously variable transaxle (ECVT).

6. Drain the cooling system.

✳✳ WARNING

Always refill the motor electronics cooling system (MECS) with the same type of coolant that was drained from the system. Do not mix coolant types.

7. Drain the motor electronics cooling system:

a. With the vehicle in DRIVE, position it on a hoist.
b. Turn the ignition to the OFF position.
c. Remove the left splash shield.
d. Place a suitable container below the transaxle.
e. Loosen the hose clamps at the transaxle, then pull the hoses off to allow the coolant to drain.

8. Disconnect the motor electronics coolant vent hose.

9. Disconnect the 2 engine coolant vent hoses.

10. Remove the degas bottle bolt and nut.

11. Lift the degas bottle up and disconnect the engine coolant and motor electronics coolant return hoses.

12. Remove the degas bottle.

13. Disconnect the plastic loop.

14. Disconnect the 2 pin-type retainers.

15. Disconnect the 2 female pin-type retainers.

➡**Press the locking clip to release the connector.**

16. Disconnect the DC/DC converter high voltage electrical connector.

17. Remove the DC/DC converter wiring harness.

To install:

18. To install, reverse the removal procedure. Rearm the high voltage battery.

19. Fill the Motor Electronics Cooling System as follows:

➡**Vehicle cooling systems are filled with Motorcraft® Premium Gold Engine Coolant. Always fill the cooling**

system with the same coolant that is present in the system. Do not mix coolant types.

f. Connect the hoses to the transaxle and install the hose clamps.

❋❋ **WARNING**

Adhesives, stop-leak pellets or small debris in the Motor electronics cooling system (MECS) can cause poor performance or temporary blockage of the motor electronics pump. Only use clean, approved coolant when filling the system.

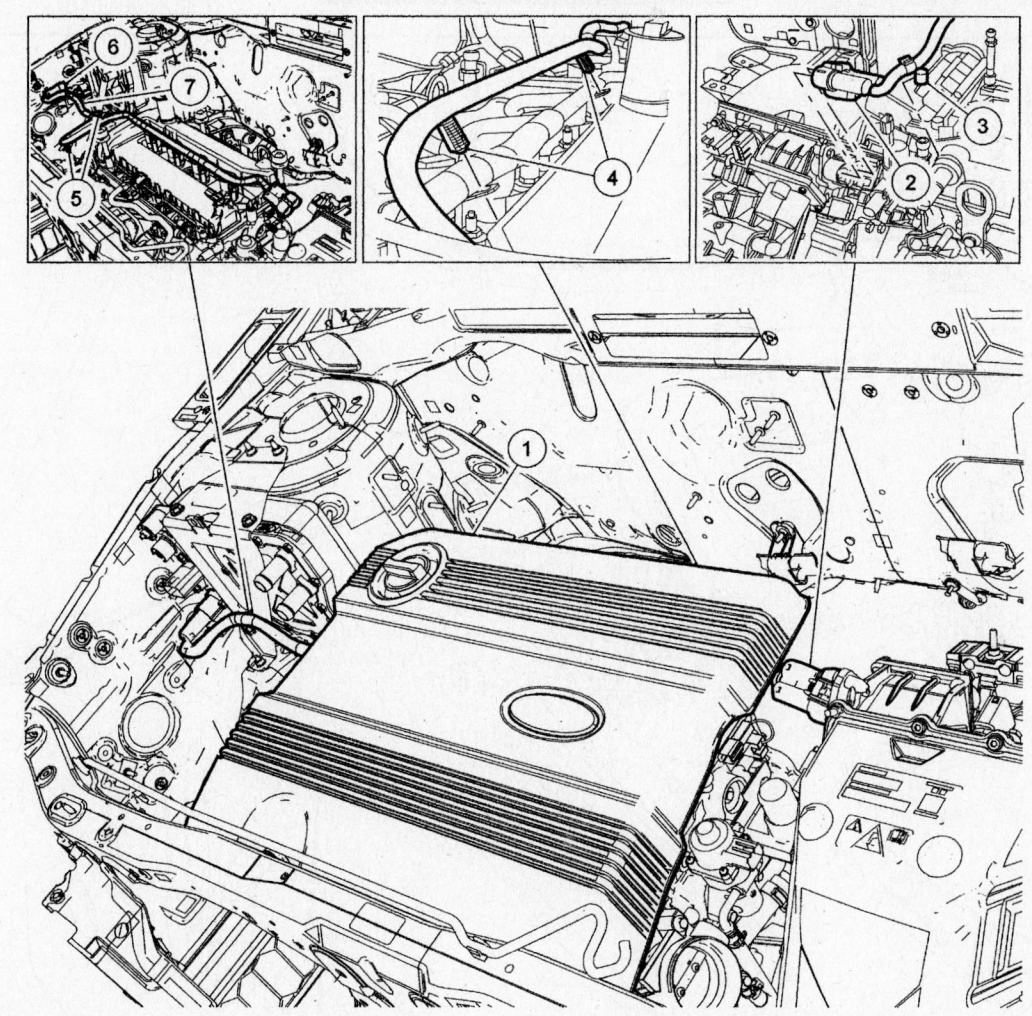

1 Engine cover
2 DC/DC converter high voltage electrical connector
3 Plastic loop
4 Pin-type retainers (part of 14B323) (2 required)
5 Pin-type retainers (female) (part of 14B323) (2 required)
6 DC/DC converter high voltage electrical connector (high voltage)
7 DC/DC converter wiring harness

06017-ESCA-G11

Fig. 56 DC/DC converter wiring harness

g. Loosen the bleed screw and fill the degas bottle with coolant until it begins to flow out of the bleed hole. Then, close the bleed screw.

h. Turn the ignition to the ON position to actuate the motor electronics cooling pump and continue to fill the degas bottle to the correct level.

➡ **Most of the MECS air bleeding occurs as a normal process at the degas bottle through the vent tube; very little occurs at the bleed screw.**

i. To bleed air from the system, loosen the bleed screw and allow air to escape while the M/E coolant pump is operating.

ALTERNATING CURRENT POWERPOINT

REMOVAL & INSTALLATION
See Figure 57.

1. Before servicing the vehicle, refer to the Precautions Section.

❊❊ CAUTION

Before proceeding, read and observe all of the High Voltage System Precautions.

2. Disconnect the 12 volt battery.

➡ **For the Escape Hybrid, when the battery is disconnected and connected, the brake pedal needs to be calibrated. After the battery has been connected, with the vehicle in park, turn the key to the ON position. Press the brake pedal firmly, then fully release to calibrate the brake pedal.**

3. Remove the console trim insert.

4. Disconnect the electrical connector and remove the AC powerpoint.

5. To install, reverse the removal procedure.

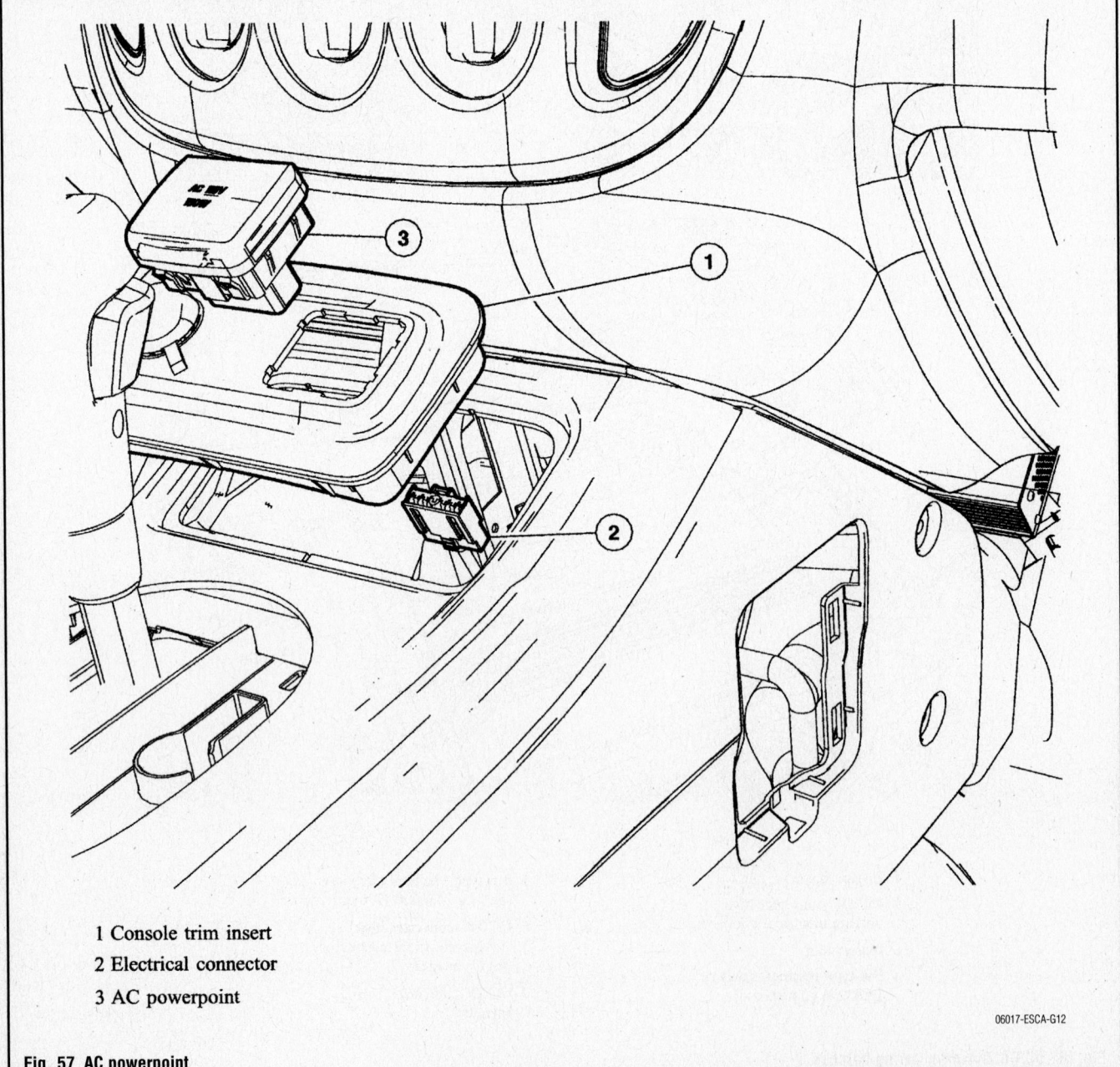

1 Console trim insert
2 Electrical connector
3 AC powerpoint

06017-ESCA-G12

Fig. 57 AC powerpoint

ENGINE MECHANICAL

➡Disconnecting the negative battery cable may interfere with the functions of the on board computer systems and may require the computer to undergo a relearning process, once the negative battery cable is reconnected.

ACCESSORY DRIVE BELTS

ACCESSORY BELT ROUTING

See Figure 58.

INSPECTION

✷✷ WARNING

Under no circumstances should the accessory drive belt, tensioner or pulleys be lubricated, as potential damage to the belt material and tensioner damping mechanism will occur. Do not apply any fluids or belt dressing to the accessory drive belt or pulleys.

Visual Inspection

Visually inspect the belt for obvious signs of mechanical damage:

- Drive belt cracking/chunking/wear
- Belt/pulley contamination
- Incorrectly routed belt
- Pulley misalignment or excessive pulley runout
- Loose or mislocated hardware
- Incorrectly routed power steering tubes (rubbing)

Eliminate all other non-belt related noises that could cause belt misdiagnosis, such as A/C compressor engagement chirp, power steering cavitations at low temperatures, variable camshaft timing (VCT) tick or generator whine.

If a concern is found, correct the condition before proceeding to the next section.

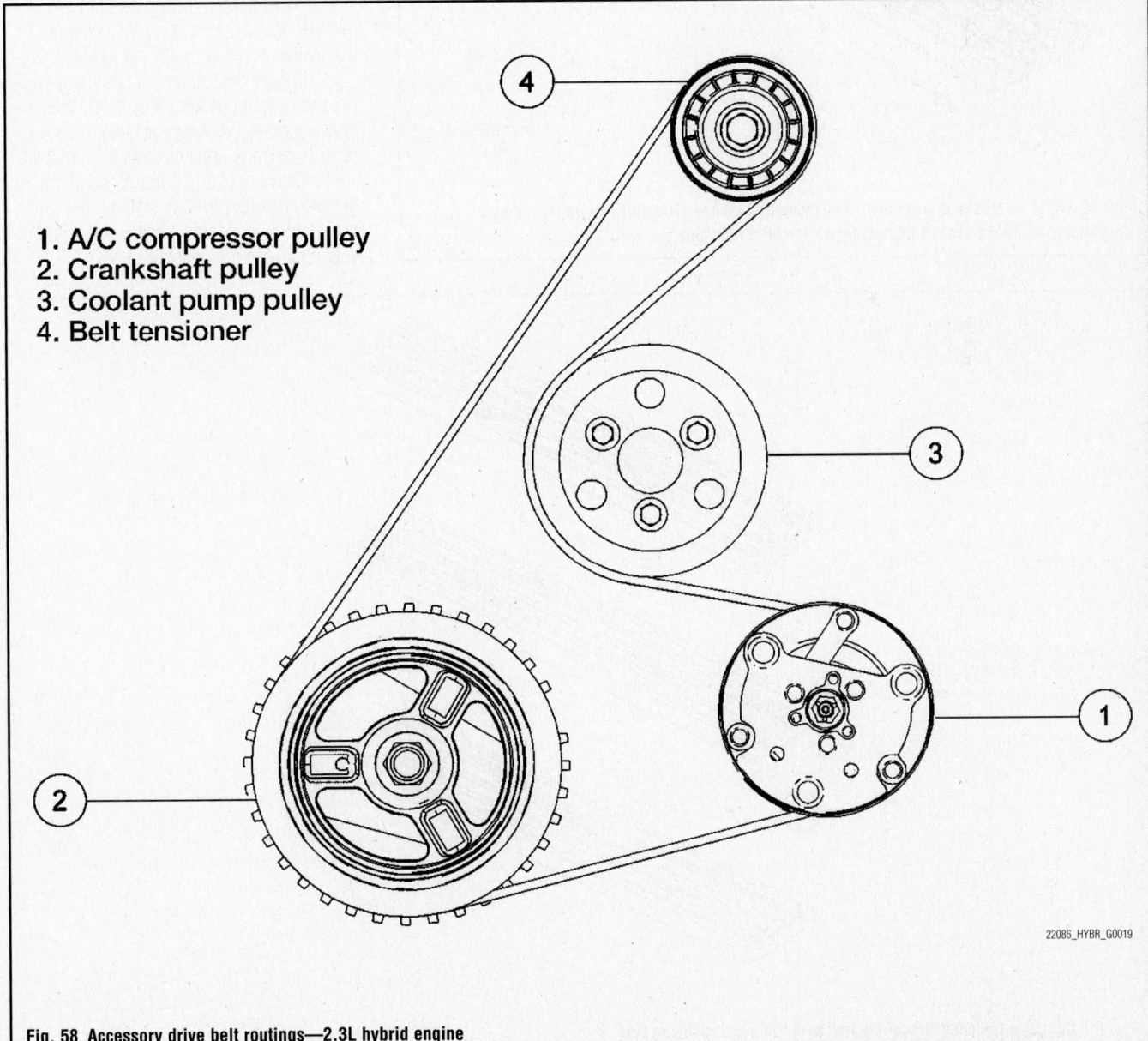

1. A/C compressor pulley
2. Crankshaft pulley
3. Coolant pump pulley
4. Belt tensioner

22086_HYBR_G0019

Fig. 58 Accessory drive belt routings—2.3L hybrid engine

V-Ribbed Serpentine Drive Belt With Cracks Across Ribs

See Figure 59.

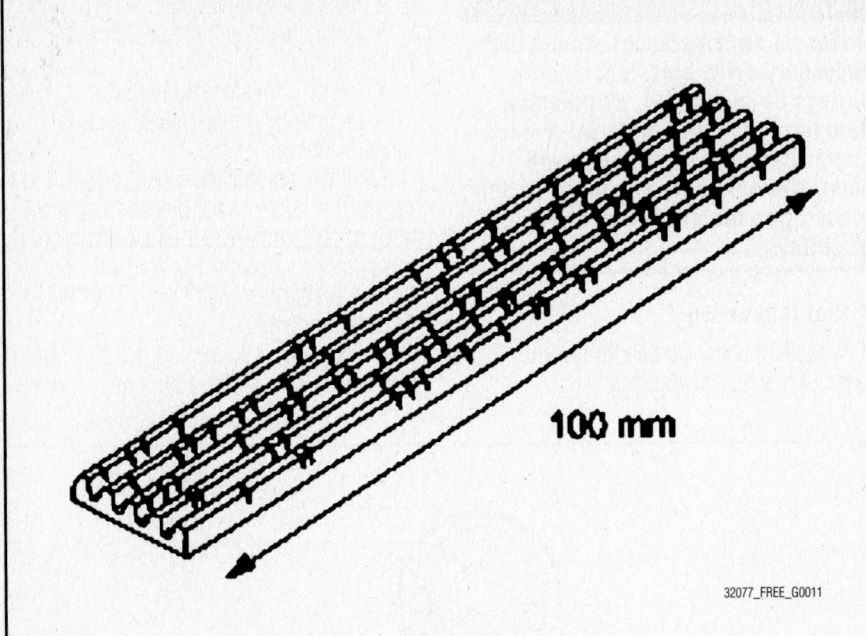

100 mm

32077_FREE_G0011

Fig. 59 Up to 15 cracks in a rib over a distance of 4 inches (100mm) can be considered acceptable. If cracks exceed this standard, install a new belt

➡Up to 15 cracks in a rib over a distance of 4 inches (100mm) can be considered acceptable. If damage exceeds the acceptable limit or any chunks are found to be missing from the ribs, a new belt must be installed.

1. Check the belt for cracks. Up to 15 cracks in a rib over a distance of 4 inches (100mm) can be considered acceptable. If cracks exceed this standard, install a new belt.

V- Ribbed Serpentine Belt With Piling

See Figure 60.

➡Piling is an excessive buildup in the V-grooves of the belt.

The condition of the V-ribbed drive belt should be compared against the illustration and appropriate action taken.

1. Small scattered deposits of rubber material. This is not a concern, therefore, installation of a new belt is not required.

2. Longer deposit areas building up to 50 percent of the rib height. This is not considered a concern but it can result in excessive noise. If noise is apparent, install a new belt.

3. Heavy deposits building up along the grooves resulting in a possible noise and belt stability concern. If heavy deposits are apparent, install a new belt.

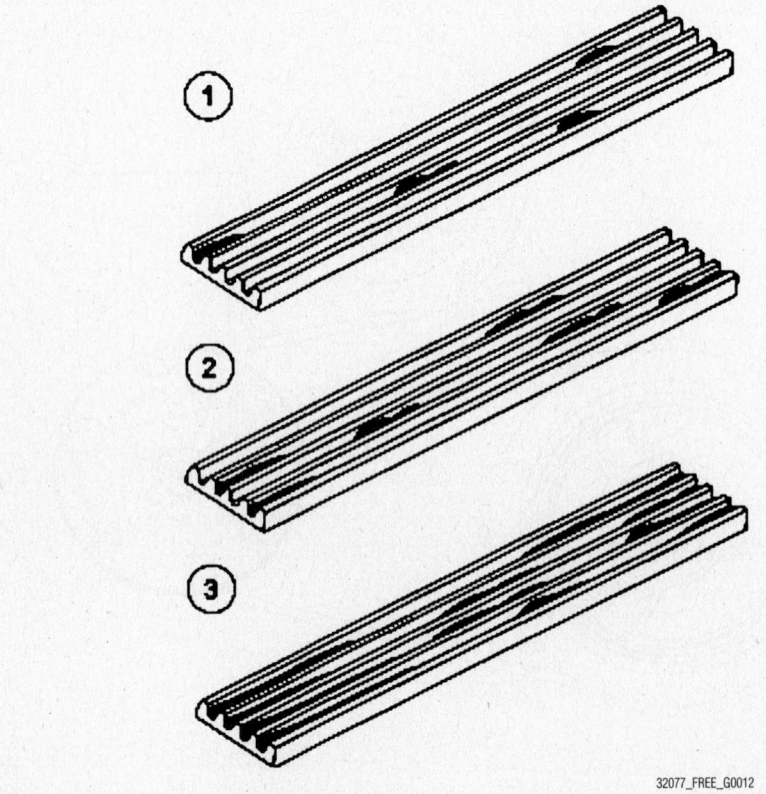

32077_FREE_G0012

Fig. 60 Compare the condition of the belt with the accompanying text

V-Ribbed Serpentine Belt With Chunks of Rib Missing

See Figure 61.

There should be no chunks missing from the belt ribs. If the belt shows any evidence of this, install a new accessory drive belt.

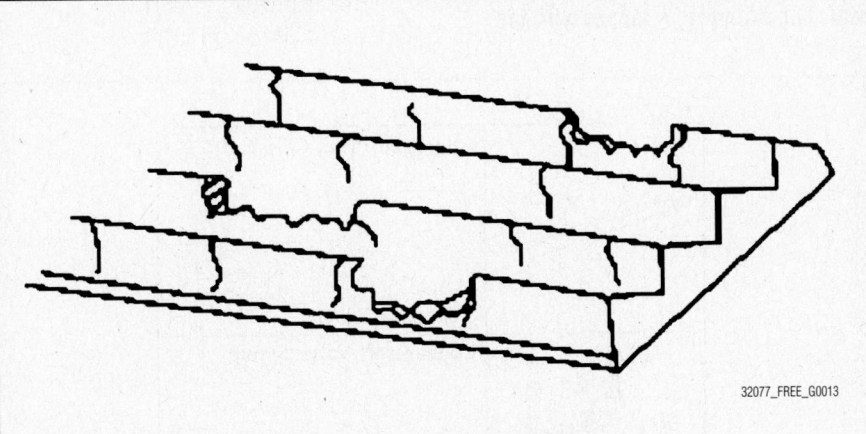

32077_FREE_G0013

Fig. 61 Replace the belt if missing chunks are found during inspection

ADJUSTMENT

The belts used on these vehicle are equipped with automatic (spring load) tensioners which maintain tension. No adjustment is necessary or possible.

REMOVAL & INSTALLATION

See Figure 62.

1. Raise and safely support the vehicle.
2. Remove the 5 bolts and the RH splash shield.
3. Rotate the accessory drive belt tensioner clockwise and remove the accessory drive belt.

To install:

4. Install the accessory drive belt. Make sure it is routed correctly.
5. Install the RH splash shield and tighten the retaining bolts to 80 inch lbs. (9 Nm).

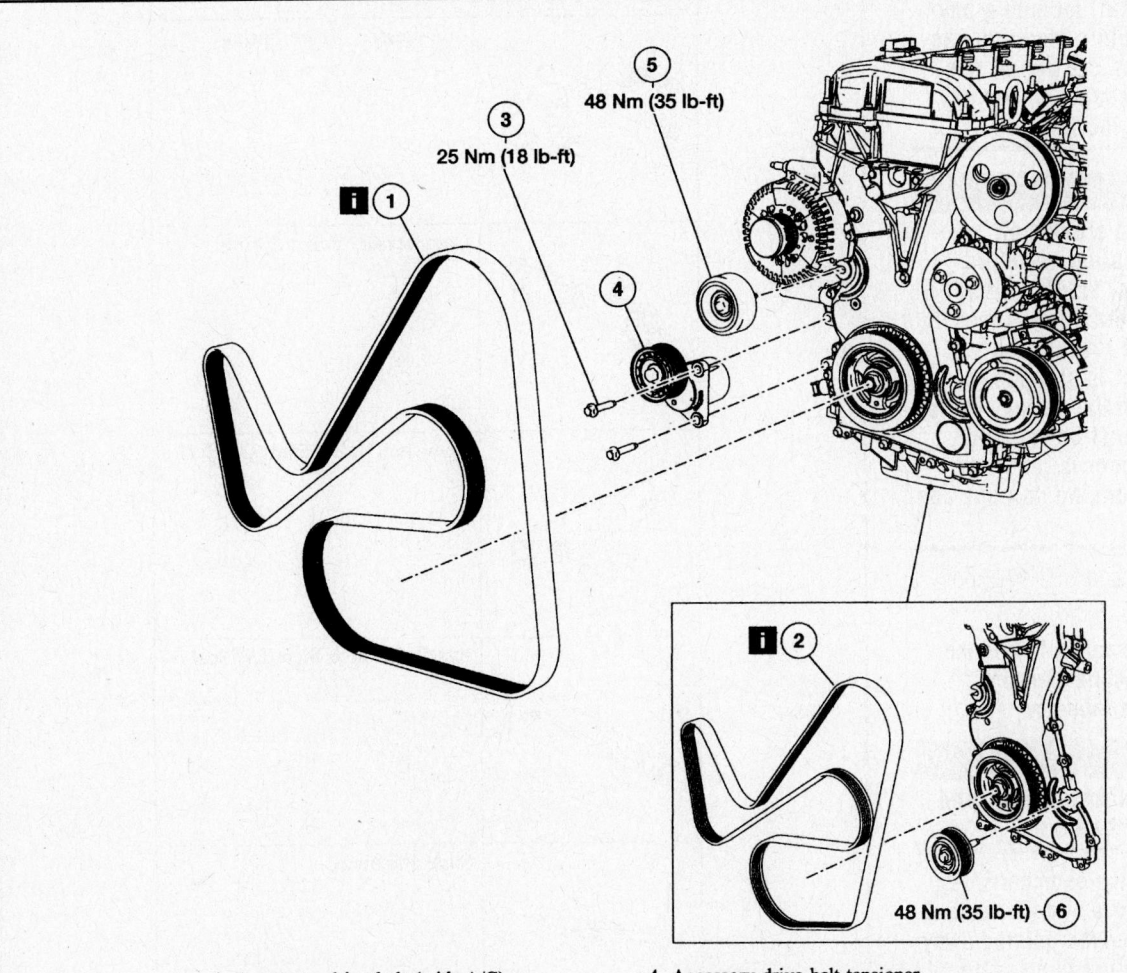

1 Accessory drive belt (with A/C)
2 Accessory drive belt (without A/C)
3 Accessory drive belt tensioner bolts
4 Accessory drive belt tensioner
5 Accessory drive belt idler pulley
6 Accessory drive belt idler pulley (without A/C only)

67197-ESCA-G62

Fig. 62 Accessory drive belt routings—2.3L hybrid engine

CAMSHAFT AND VALVE LIFTERS

INSPECTION

1. Inspect camshaft lobes for pitting or damage in the contact area. Minor pitting is acceptable outside the contact area. If excessive pitting or damage is present replace components as necessary.

2. Check for valve tappet face wear.

3. Check for excessive valve tappet clearance.

REMOVAL & INSTALLATION

See Figures 63 through 67.

1. Before servicing the vehicle, refer to the Precautions Section.

> **❊❊ WARNING**
>
> **During engine repair procedures, cleanliness is extremely important. Any foreign material, including any material created while cleaning gasket surfaces that enters the oil passages, coolant passages or the oil pan can cause engine failure.**

> **✪ WARNING**
>
> **The crankshaft, the crankshaft sprocket and the pulley are fitted together by friction, using diamond washers between the flange faces on each part. For that reason, the crankshaft sprocket is also unfastened if you loosen the pulley. Therefore, the engine must be retimed each time the damper is removed. Otherwise severe engine damage can occur.**

2. With the vehicle in NEUTRAL, position it on a hoist.

➥Valve tappets are select fit and the valve clearance must be checked before removing the tappets.

> **✪ WARNING**
>
> **Turn the engine clockwise only, and only use the crankshaft bolt.**

➥Before removing the camshafts, measure the clearance of each valve at base circle, with the lobe pointed away from the tappet. Failure to measure all clearances prior to removing the camshafts will necessitate repeated removal and installation and wasted labor time.

3. Use a feeler gauge to measure the clearance of each valve and record its location.

➥The number on the valve tappet only reflects the digits that follow the decimal. For example, a tappet with the number 0.650 has the thickness of 3.650 mm.

➥A midrange clearance is the most desirable:

- Intake: 0.22–0.28 mm (0.008–0.011 inch)

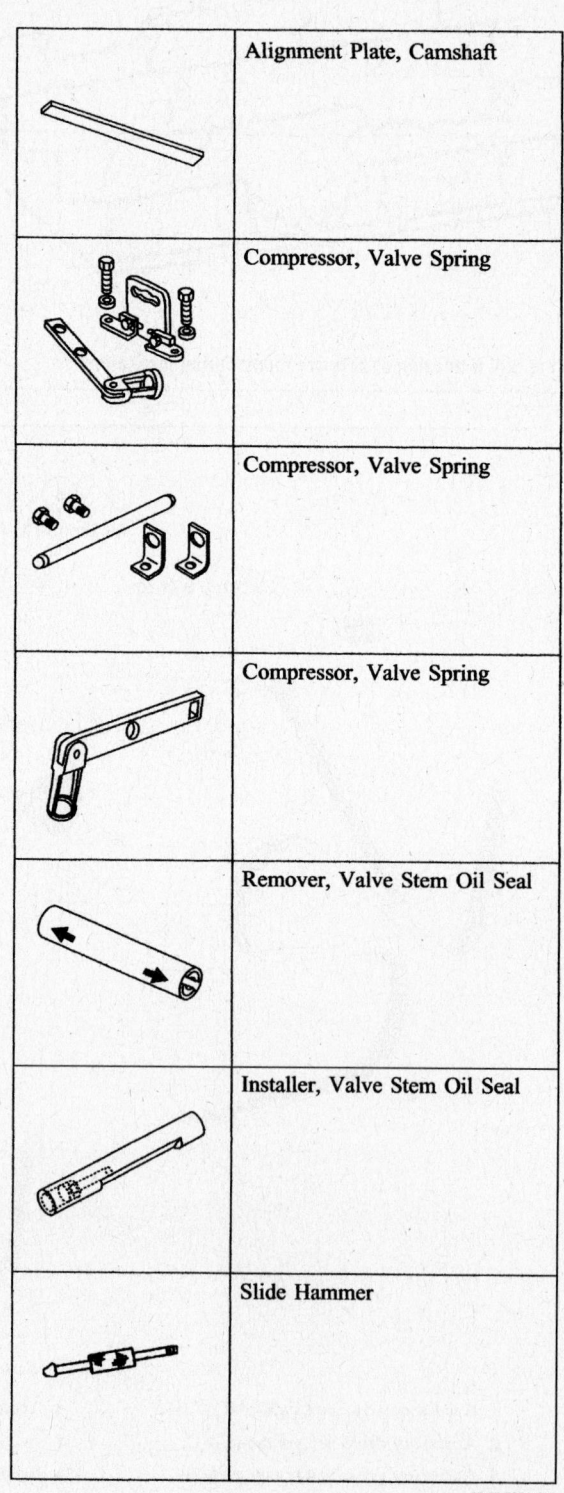

	Alignment Plate, Camshaft
	Compressor, Valve Spring
	Compressor, Valve Spring
	Compressor, Valve Spring
	Remover, Valve Stem Oil Seal
	Installer, Valve Stem Oil Seal
	Slide Hammer

67197-ESCA-G15

Fig. 63 Tools necessary for camshaft and lifter removal—2.3L hybrid engine

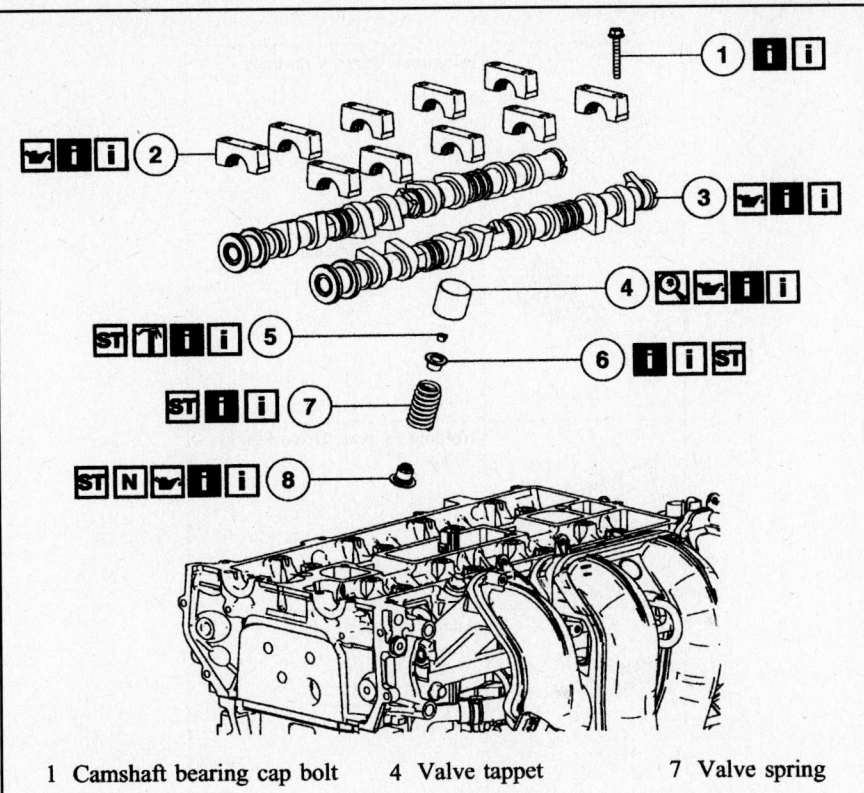

1 Camshaft bearing cap bolt
2 Camshaft bearing cap
3 Camshaft
4 Valve tappet
5 Valve collet
6 Valve spring retainer
7 Valve spring
8 Valve seal

67197-ESCA-G16

Fig. 64 Camshafts, lifters and related parts—2.3L hybrid engine

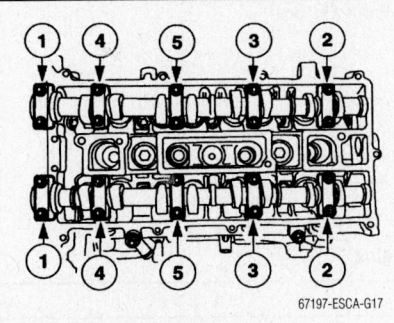

67197-ESCA-G17

Fig. 65 Camshaft cap removal sequence—2.3L hybrid engine

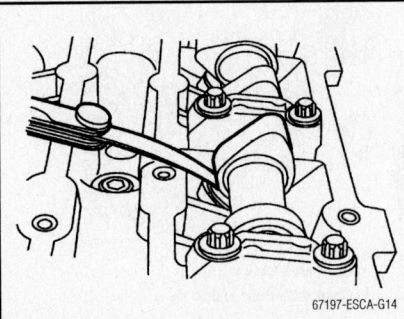

67197-ESCA-G14

Fig. 66 Valve clearance check—2.3L hybrid engine

• Exhaust: 0.27–0.33 mm (0.010–0.013 inch)

4. Select tappets using this formula: tappet thickness = measured clearance + the base tappet thickness—most desirable thickness.

5. Select the tappets and mark the installation location.

6. If any tappets do not measure within specifications, install new tappets in these locations.

7. Remove the timing chain and sprockets.

8. Mark the position of the camshaft lobes on the No. 1 cylinder for assembly reference.

✳✳ WARNING

Failure to follow the camshaft loosening procedure can result in damage to the camshafts.

9. Loosen the camshaft bearing bolts in the sequence shown, one turn at a time Repeat until all the tension is released.

10. Remove the camshaft bearing caps.

✳✳ WARNING

If the camshafts and valve tappets are to be reused, mark the location of the valve tappets to make sure they are assembled in their original positions.

➡The number on the valve tappets only reflects the digits that follow the decimal. For example, a tappet with the number 0.650 has the thickness of 3.650 mm.

11. Remove the camshafts.
12. Valve tappets.
13. To install, reverse the removal procedure. Coat the valve tappets with clean engine oil and insert them.

✳✳ WARNING

Install the camshafts with the alignment slots in the camshafts lined up so the Camshaft Alignment Plate can be installed without rotating the camshafts. Make sure the lobes on the No. 1 cylinder are in the same position as noted in the removal procedure. Rotating the camshafts when the timing chain is removed, or installing the camshafts 180 degrees out of position can cause severe damage to the valves and pistons.

➡Lubricate the camshaft journals and bearing caps with clean engine oil.

14. Install the camshafts and bearing caps. Tighten the bolts in the sequence shown in three stages.

   a. Stage 1: Tighten the camshaft bearing bolt caps one turn at a time until tight.

   b. Stage 2: Tighten the bolts to 62 inch lbs. (7 Nm).

   c. Stage 3: Tighten the bolts to 12 ft. lbs. (16 Nm).

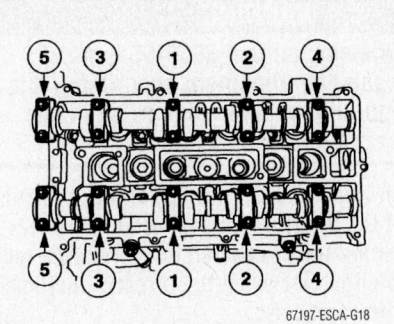

67197-ESCA-G18

Fig. 67 Camshaft cap torque sequence—2.3L hybrid engine

CRANKSHAFT FRONT SEAL

REMOVAL & INSTALLATION

See Figures 68 through 73.

1. Before servicing the vehicle, refer to the Precautions Section.

✳✳ WARNING

During engine repair procedures, cleanliness is extremely important. Any foreign material, including any material created while cleaning gasket surfaces that enters the oil passages, coolant passages or the oil pan can cause engine failure.

✳✳ WARNING

The crankshaft, the crankshaft sprocket and the pulley are fitted together by friction, using diamond washers between the flange faces on each part. For that reason, the crankshaft sprocket is also unfastened if you loosen the pulley. Therefore, the engine must be retimed each time the damper is removed. Otherwise severe engine damage can occur.

2. With the vehicle in NEUTRAL, position it on a hoist.
3. Remove the accessory drive belt.
4. Remove the valve cover.

✳✳ WARNING

Failure to position the No. 1 piston at top dead center (TDC) can result in damage to the engine. Turn the engine in the normal direction of rotation only.

5. Using the crankshaft pulley bolt, turn the crankshaft clockwise to position the No. 1 piston at top dead center (TDC).

✳✳ WARNING

The special tool 303-465 is for camshaft alignment only. Using this tool to prevent engine rotation can result in engine damage.

➡ The camshaft timing slots are offset. If the special tool cannot be installed, rotate the crankshaft one complete revolution clockwise to correctly position the camshafts.

6. Install the special tool in the slots on the rear of both camshafts.

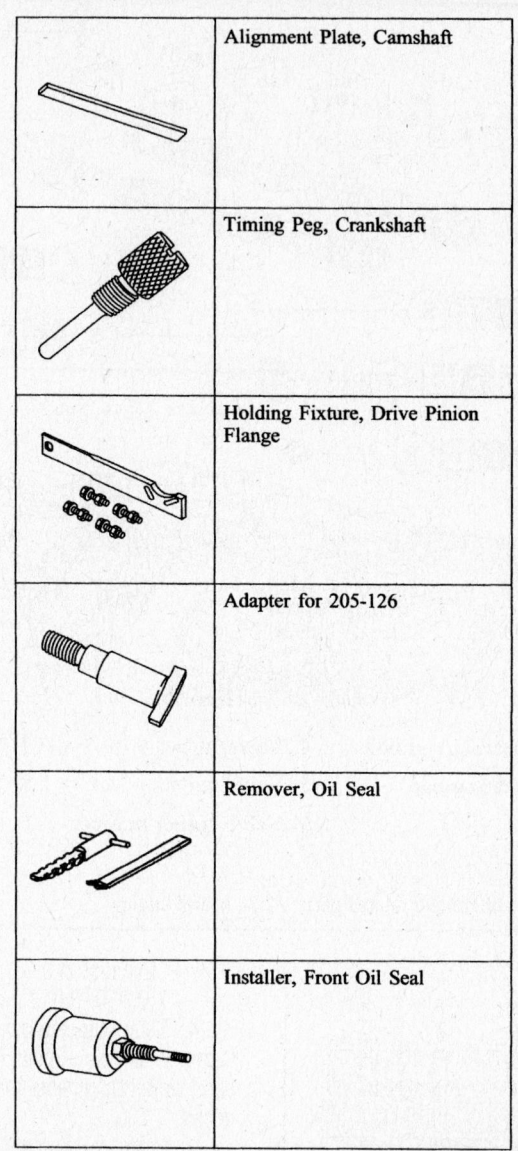

	Alignment Plate, Camshaft
	Timing Peg, Crankshaft
	Holding Fixture, Drive Pinion Flange
	Adapter for 205-126
	Remover, Oil Seal
	Installer, Front Oil Seal

67197-ESCA-G08

Fig. 68 Tools necessary for this job—2.3L hybrid engine

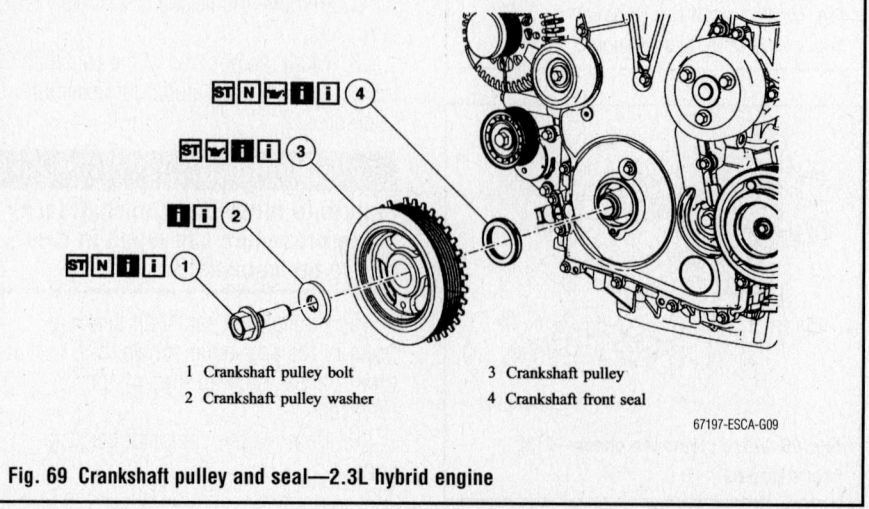

1 Crankshaft pulley bolt　　3 Crankshaft pulley
2 Crankshaft pulley washer　　4 Crankshaft front seal

67197-ESCA-G09

Fig. 69 Crankshaft pulley and seal—2.3L hybrid engine

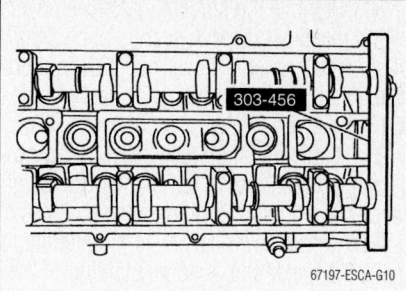

Fig. 70 Camshaft holding tool—2.3L hybrid engine

➡**Installing the special tool in this step will prevent the engine from being rotated in the clockwise direction.**

7. Install special tool 303-507.
8. Remove the crankshaft pulley bolt and washer.
9. Remove the engine plug bolt.
10. Install the crankshaft holding tools.

✳✳ WARNING

Failure to hold the crankshaft pulley in place while loosening the bolt can result in damage to the engine.

11. Remove the crankshaft pulley.

✳✳ WARNING

Use care not to damage the engine front cover or the crankshaft when removing the seal.

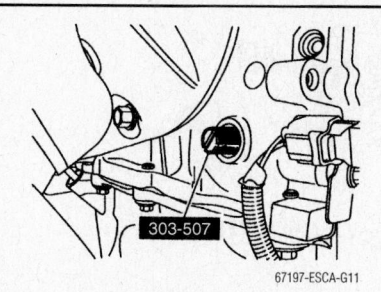

Fig. 71 Install special tool 303-507—2.3L hybrid engine

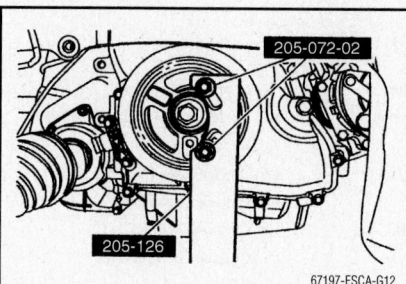

Fig. 72 Install the crankshaft holding tools—2.3L hybrid engine

12. Using the special tool, remove the crankshaft front oil seal.

➡**Remove the through-bolt from the special tool.**

To install:

➡**Lubricate the oil seal with clean engine oil.**

13. Using the a seal driver, install the crankshaft front oil seal.

➡**Do not reuse the crankshaft damper bolt.**

➡**Apply clean engine oil on the seal area before installing.**

14. Install the crankshaft pulley and hand-tighten the bolt.

✳✳ WARNING

Only hand-tighten the bolt or damage to the front cover can occur.

➡**This step will correctly align the crankshaft pulley to the crankshaft.**

15. Install a standard 6 mm × 18 mm bolt through the crankshaft pulley and thread it into the front cover. Rotate the pulley as necessary to align the bolt holes.

✳✳ WARNING

Failure to hold the crankshaft pulley in place while tightening the bolt can cause damage to the engine front cover.

16. Using the special tools to hold the crankshaft pulley in place, tighten the crankshaft pulley bolt in two stages:
   a. Stage 1: Tighten to 74 ft. lbs. (100 Nm).
   b. Stage 2: Tighten an additional 90 degrees (¼ turn).
17. Remove the 6 mm x 18 mm bolt.
18. Remove the special tools.

➡**Only turn the engine in the normal direction of rotation.**

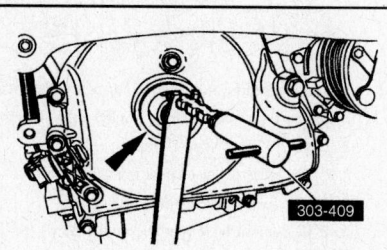

Fig. 73 Using the special tool, remove the crankshaft front oil seal—2.3L hybrid engine

19. Turn the engine two complete revolutions.
20. Turn the crankshaft until the No. 1 piston is at TDC.
21. Install special tool 303-507.

✳✳ WARNING

Only hand-tighten the bolt or damage to the front cover can occur.

22. Using the 6 mm x 18 mm bolt, check the position of the crankshaft pulley. If it is not possible to install the bolt, correct the engine timing.
23. Using special tool 303-465, check the position of the camshafts. If it is not possible to install the special tool, correct the engine timing.
24. Remove the 6 mm x 18 mm bolt.
25. Install the engine plug bolt.

CYLINDER HEAD

REMOVAL & INSTALLATION

See Figures 74 through 76.

✳✳ WARNING

Do not loosen or remove the crankshaft pulley bolt without first installing the special tools as instructed in this procedure. The crankshaft pulley and the crankshaft timing sprocket are not keyed to the crankshaft. The crankshaft, the crankshaft sprocket and the pulley are fitted together by friction, using diamond washers between the flange faces on each part. For that reason, the crankshaft sprocket is also unfastened if you loosen the pulley bolt. Before any repair requiring loosening or removal of the crankshaft pulley bolt, the crankshaft and camshafts must be locked in place by the special service tools, otherwise severe engine damage can occur.

1. Before servicing the vehicle, refer to the Precautions Section.

✳✳ WARNING

During engine repair procedures, cleanliness is extremely important. Any foreign material, including any material created while cleaning gasket surfaces that enters the oil passages, coolant passages or the oil pan can cause engine failure.

2. With the vehicle in NEUTRAL, position it on a hoist.

3. Release the fuel system pressure.

4. Drain the engine cooling system.

5. Remove the timing drive components. For additional information, refer to timing chain and components .

6. Remove the special tool.

7. Mark the position of the camshaft lobes on the No. 1 cylinder for installation reference.

❊❊ WARNING

Failure to follow the camshaft loosening procedure can result in damage to the camshafts.

8. Remove the camshafts from engine.

9. Loosen the camshaft bearing cap bolts, in sequence, one turn at a time until all tension is released from the camshaft bearing caps.

10. Remove the bolts and the camshaft bearing caps.

11. Remove the camshafts.

❊❊ WARNING

If the camshafts and valve tappets are to be reused, mark the location of the valve tappets to make sure they are assembled in their original positions.

12. Remove the valve tappets.

13. Remove the intake manifold.

14. Remove the catalytic converter.

15. Disconnect the radio ignition interference capacitor electrical connector

16. Disconnect the exhaust gas recirculation (EGR) valve electrical connector

17. Remove the upper radiator hose.

18. Remove the EGR coolant tube clamp.

19. Remove the EGR coolant hose.

20. Remove the engine coolant vent hose.

21. Remove the heater hose.

22. Remove the bypass hose.

23. Remove and discard the cylinder head bolts.

24. Remove the cylinder head.

25. Remove the cylinder head gasket.

26. Inspect the cylinder head for distortion.

❊❊ WARNING

Do not use metal scrapers, wire brushes, power abrasive discs or other abrasive means to clean the sealing surfaces. These tools cause scratches and gouges that make leak paths. Use a plastic scraping tool to remove all traces of the head gasket.

❊❊ WARNING

Observe all warnings or cautions and follow all application directions contained on the packaging of the silicone gasket remover and the metal surface prep.

➡**If there is no residual gasket material present, metal surface prep can be used to clean and prepare the surfaces.**

27. Clean the cylinder head-to-cylinder block mating surface of both the cylinder head and the cylinder block.

28. Remove any large deposits of silicone or gasket material with a plastic scraper.

29. Apply silicone gasket remover, following package directions, and allow to set for several minutes.

30. Remove the silicone gasket remover with a plastic scraper. A second application of silicone gasket remover may be required if residual traces of silicone or gasket material remain.

31. Apply metal surface prep, following package directions, to remove any traces of oil or coolant, and to prepare the surfaces to bond with the new gasket. Do not attempt to make the metal shiny. Some staining of the metal surfaces is normal.

32. Apply silicone gasket and sealant to the locations shown.

33. Install a new head gasket.

➡**The cylinder head bolts are torque-to-yield and must not be reused. New cylinder head bolts must be installed.**

➡**Lubricate the bolts with clean engine oil prior to installation.**

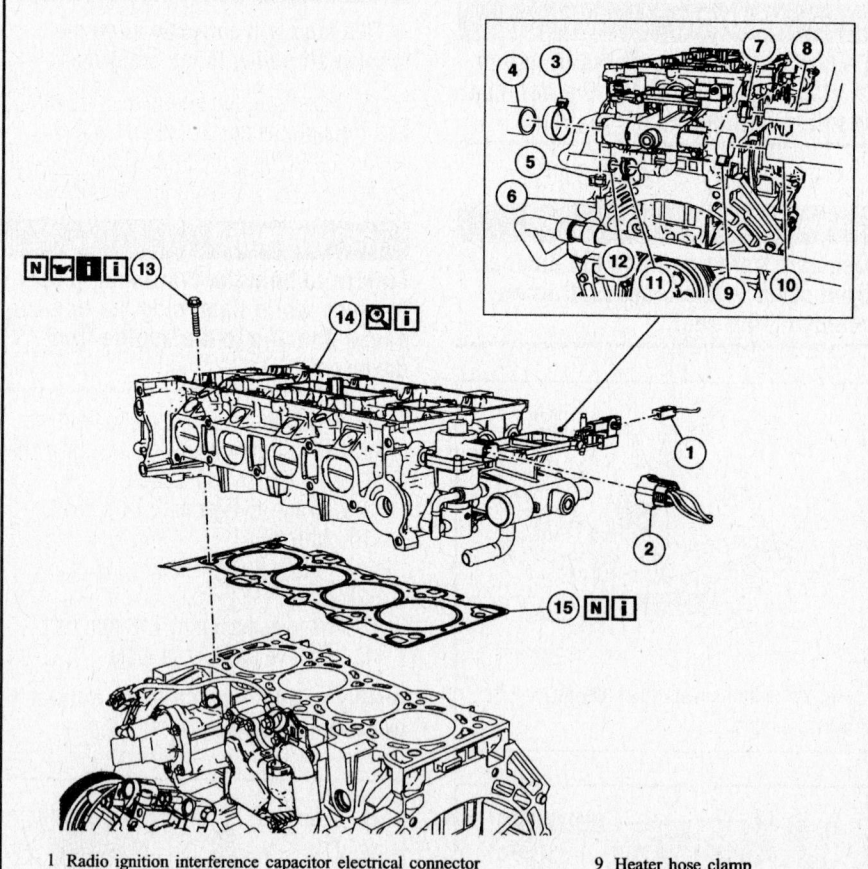

1 Radio ignition interference capacitor electrical connector
2 Exhaust gas recirculation (EGR) valve electrical connector
3 Upper radiator hose clamp
4 Upper radiator hose (position aside)
5 EGR coolant tube clamp
6 EGR coolant hose (part of heater hose) (position aside)
7 Engine coolant vent hose clamp
8 Engine coolant vent hose (position aside)
9 Heater hose clamp
10 Heater hose (position aside)
11 Bypass hose clamp
12 Bypass hose (position aside)
13 Cylinder head bolt
14 Cylinder head
15 Cylinder head gasket

67197-ESCA-G04

Fig. 74 Cylinder head removal—2.3L hybrid engine

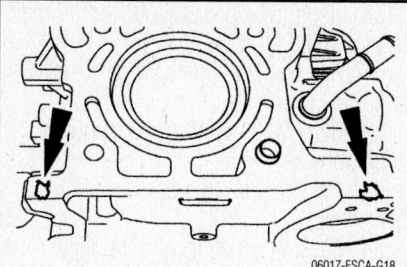

Fig. 75 Apply silicone gasket and sealant to the locations shown—2.3L hybrid engine

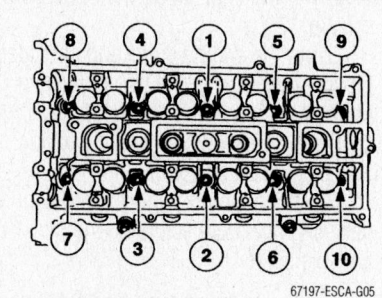

Fig. 76 Cylinder head bolt torque sequence—2.3L hybrid engine

34. Install new cylinder head bolts. Tighten the bolts in the sequence shown in five stages.

    a. Tighten the bolts to 44 inch lbs. (5 Nm).

    b. Tighten the bolts to 11 ft. lbs. (15 Nm).

    c. Tighten the bolts to 33 ft. lbs. (45 Nm).

    d. Turn the bolts 90 degrees.

    e. Turn the bolts an additional 90 degrees.

35. To install, reverse the removal procedure.

ENGINE ASSEMBLY

REMOVAL & INSTALLATION

See Figures 77 through 80.

1. Before servicing the vehicle, refer to the Precautions Section.

❊❊ CAUTION

Before proceeding, read and observe all of the High Voltage System Precautions.

All Vehicles

2. With the vehicle in NEUTRAL, position it on a hoist.

3. Release the fuel system pressure.

4. Disconnect the battery ground cable.

➥When the battery is disconnected and connected, the brake pedal needs to be calibrated. After the battery has been connected, with the vehicle in park, turn the key to the ON position. Press the brake pedal firmly, then fully release to calibrate the brake pedal.

5. Disarm the high voltage traction battery. Establish a buffer zone. See the procedure under Disarming the High Voltage Traction Battery.

6. Drain the cooling system.

❊❊ WARNING

Always refill the motor electronics cooling system (MECS) with the same type of coolant that was drained from the system. Do not mix coolant types.

7. Drain the motor electronics cooling system:

    a. With the vehicle in DRIVE, position it on a hoist.

    b. Turn the ignition to the OFF position.

    c. Remove the left splash shield.

    d. Place a suitable container below the transaxle.

    e. Loosen the hose clamps at the transaxle, then pull the hoses off to allow the coolant to drain.

8. Disconnect the motor electronics coolant vent hose.

9. Disconnect the 2 engine coolant vent hoses.

10. Remove the degas bottle bolt and nut.

11. Lift the degas bottle up and disconnect the engine coolant and motor electronics coolant return hoses.

12. Remove the degas bottle.

13. Remove the intake manifold.

14. Remove the engine air cleaner.

15. Remove the exhaust manifold/catalytic converter.

16. Remove the accessory drive belt.

17. Remove the left front drive halfshaft.

4WD vehicles

18. Remove the transfer case.

2WD vehicles

19. Remove the front drive intermediate halfshaft.

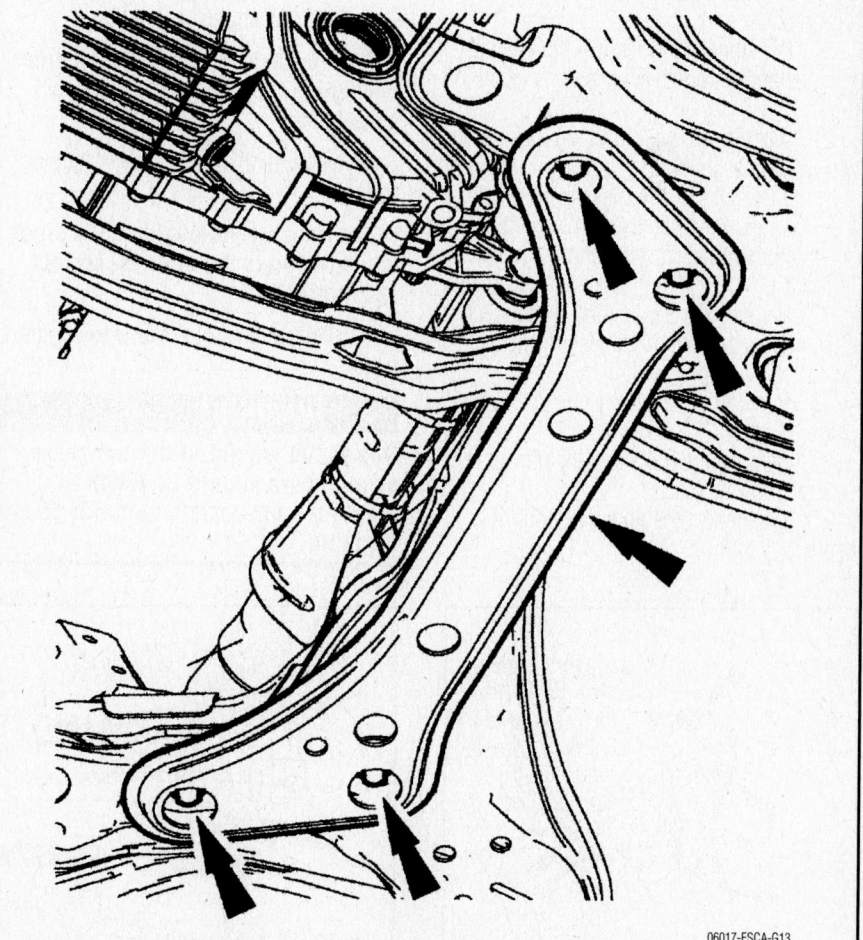

Fig. 77 Remove the bolts and the lateral support crossmember

20. Remove the bolts and the lateral support crossmember.

All vehicles

21. Drain the engine oil.

22. Disconnect the heater hoses from the heater core.

23. Detach the heater hose retaining clip from the transaxle mount stud.

24. Disconnect the upper radiator and coolant vent hoses.

25. Disconnect the following electrical connectors:
- Secondary Air Injection (AIR) solenoid
- Transaxle mount control solenoid
- Purge valve

26. Disconnect the engine control harness:

a. Release the Powertrain Control Module (PCM) connector.

b. Remove the harness retaining nut.

27. Disconnect the 2 engine control harness electrical connectors and the 2 pin-type retainers.

28. Remove the bolt and disconnect the transaxle harness electrical connector.

29. Disconnect the DC-to-DC converter electrical connector and pin-type retainer.

30. Disconnect and remove the fuel supply tube and evaporative emissions (EVAP) tube.

31. If equipped, position the block heater wiring harness aside.

a. Detach the 3 harness retainer clips.

b. Route the harness through the radiator support into the engine compartment.

32. Remove the 2 bolts and disconnect the auxiliary coolant pump electrical connector.

33. Position the auxiliary coolant pump aside.

34. Remove the bolts and the transaxle control snow shield.

35. Disconnect the transaxle control cable.

a. Release the transaxle control cable from the control lever.

b. Remove the nuts from the transaxle control cable bracket.

36. Disconnect the pin-type retainer.

37. Disconnect the pin-type retainer and position the transaxle control cable aside.

38. Disconnect the transaxle coolant temperature sensor electrical connector and pin-type retainer.

39. Disconnect the transaxle coolant hoses.

40. Remove the nut and the ground cable.

41. Remove the 2 bolts and position the motor electronics coolant pump aside.

42. Disconnect the lower radiator hose from the radiator.

43. Disconnect the A/C compressor electrical connector and remove the 3 bolts.

44. Position the A/C compressor aside and support the compressor with a length of mechanic's wire.

45. Remove the front roll restrictor bolt.

46. Remove the rear roll restrictor bolt.

47. Remove the nut, bolts and the engine support crossmember.

➡ **The transaxle-to-engine bolts differ in length. Mark the bolts for correct installation.**

48. Remove the 2 transaxle-to-engine bolts.

➡ **The transaxle-to-engine bolts differ in length, mark the bolts for correct installation.**

49. Remove the 2 transaxle-to-engine bolts.

⁂ **WARNING**

Due to the weight of the transaxle, special care should be taken to mount the powertrain securely to the lift table.

50. Using the special tools, secure the engine to the lift table.

51. Remove the engine mount bracket bolt.

52. Remove the nuts and the engine mount bracket.

53. Remove the right transaxle mount bracket nut.

54. Remove the bolts and the right transaxle mount bracket.

55. Remove the bolt, nut and the rear transaxle mount brace.

56. Remove the nuts, bolt and rear transaxle mount.

57. Lower the engine and transaxle from the vehicle.

58. Using the engine crane and spreader bar, remove the engine and transaxle from the lift table.

59. Disconnect the high voltage wiring harness electrical connector.

60. Disconnect the 2 high voltage wiring harness electrical connectors and position the harness aside.

➡ **The transaxle-to-engine bolts differ in length, mark the bolts for correct installation.**

61. Remove the remaining 6 engine-to-transaxle bolts and separate the engine and transaxle.

➡ **Due to packaging requirements the correct bolt must be used at the damper locations.**

➡ **The damper contains a clutch which is designed to slip briefly during vehicle operation. It is essential that no grease, oil or cleaning solvents be allowed to contaminate the slip clutch. Do not use grease on transaxle input shaft. Should the damper become contaminated, it must be replaced.**

62. Remove the bolts and the transaxle damper.

06017-ESCA-G14

Fig. 78 Motor electronics coolant pump

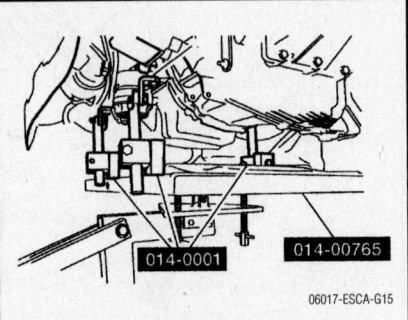

014-0001   014-00765

06017-ESCA-G15

Fig. 79 Using the special tools, secure the engine to the lift table

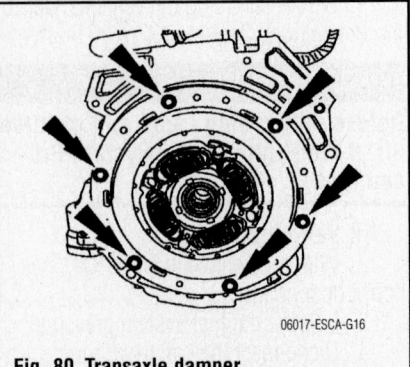

06017-ESCA-G16

Fig. 80 Transaxle damper

To install:
All vehicles

➡Due to packaging requirements the correct bolt must be used at the damper locations.

➡The damper contains a clutch which is designed to slip briefly during vehicle operation. It is essential that no grease, oil or cleaning solvents be allowed to contaminate the slip clutch. Do not use grease on transaxle input shaft. Should the damper become contaminated, it must be replaced.

63. Install the transaxle damper. Tighten to 21 ft. lbs. (29 Nm).

❋❋ WARNING

When positioning the engine to the transaxle, care must be taken to maintain alignment of the damper spline with the transaxle input shaft.

64. Using the engine crane and spreader bar, position the engine and transaxle together.
65. Install the 6 transaxle-to-engine bolts. Tighten to 35 ft. lbs. (48 Nm).
66. Position the high voltage wiring harness and connect the 2 transaxle electrical connectors.
67. Connect the high voltage wiring harness electrical connector.
68. Using the engine crane and spreader bar, position the engine and transaxle onto the lift table.

❋❋ WARNING

Due to the weight of the transaxle, special care should be taken to mount the powertrain securely to the lift table.

69. Using the special tools, secure the engine to the lift table.
70. Raise the engine and transaxle into the vehicle.
71. Install the rear transaxle mount. Tighten the nuts to 85 ft. lbs. (115 Nm). Tighten the bolt to 66 ft. lbs. (90 Nm).
72. Install the rear transaxle mount brace. Tighten to 18 ft. lbs. (25 Nm).
73. Install the right transaxle mount bracket. Tighten to 66 ft. lbs. (90 Nm).
74. Install the right transaxle mount bracket nut. Tighten to 66 ft. lbs. (90 Nm).
75. Install the engine mount bracket. Tighten to 66 ft. lbs. (90 Nm).
76. Install the engine mount bracket bolt. Tighten to 66 ft. lbs. (90 Nm).
77. Install the 2 transaxle-to-engine bolts. Tighten to 35 ft. lbs. (48 Nm).

78. Install the 2 transaxle-to-engine bolts. Tighten to 35 ft. lbs. (48 Nm).
79. Install the engine support crossmember. Tighten to the bolts to 66 ft. lbs. (90 Nm). Tighten to the nut to 129 ft. lbs. (175 Nm).
80. Install the rear roll restrictor bolt. Tighten to 66 ft. lbs. (90 Nm).
81. Install the front roll restrictor bolt. Tighten to 85 ft. lbs. (115 Nm).
82. Install the A/C compressor and connect the A/C compressor electrical connector. Tighten to 18 ft. lbs. (25 Nm).
83. Connect the lower radiator hose to the radiator.
84. Install the motor electronics coolant pump. Tighten to 62 inch lbs. (7 Nm).
85. Install the ground cable and nut. Tighten to 15 ft. lbs. (20 Nm).
86. Connect the transaxle coolant hoses.
87. Connect the transaxle coolant temperature sensor electrical connector and pin-type retainer.
88. Position the transaxle control cable and connect the pin-type retainer.
89. Connect the pin-type retainer.
90. Connect the transaxle control cable:
   a. Install the transaxle control cable bracket and the 2 nuts finger tight.
   b. Attach the transaxle control cable to the control lever.
91. Position the control lever between the 2 casting ribs on the transaxle case.
92. Place the gear selector lever in the **D** position.
93. Tighten the transaxle control cable bracket nuts to 16 ft. lbs. (22 Nm).
94. To verify the correct cable adjustment, observe the control lever on the transaxle while an assistant shifts the gear selector lever to each range position ending in the D position.
95. Install the transaxle control snow shield. Tighten to 16 ft. lbs. (22 Nm).
96. Install the auxiliary coolant pump and connect the electrical connector. Tighten to 89 inch lbs. (10 Nm).

➡**Parts removed from view for clarity.**

97. If equipped, install the block heater wiring harness.
   a. Route the harness through the radiator support.
   b. Attach the 3 harness retainer clips.
98. Install the fuel supply tube and evaporative emissions (EVAP) tube.
99. Connect the DC-to-DC converter electrical connector and pin-type retainer.
100. Connect the transaxle harness electrical connector and install the bolt. Tighten to 89 inch lbs. (10 Nm).

101. Connect the 2 engine control harness electrical connectors and the 2 pin-type retainers.
102. Connect the engine control harness.
   a. Engage the Powertrain Control Module (PCM) connector.
   b. Install the harness retaining nut.
   c. Tighten to 53 inch lbs. (6 Nm).
103. Connect the following electrical connectors:
   • Secondary Air Injection (AIR) solenoid
   • Transaxle mount control solenoid
   • Purge valve
104. Connect the upper radiator and coolant vent hoses.
105. Attach the heater hose retaining clip to the transaxle mount stud.
106. Connect the heater hoses to the heater core.

2WD vehicles
107. Install the lateral support crossmember. Tighten to 85 ft. lbs. (115 Nm).
108. Install the front drive intermediate halfshaft.

4WD vehicles
109. Install the transfer case.

All vehicles
110. Install the left front drive halfshaft.
111. Install the accessory drive belt.
112. Install the engine coolant degas bottle.
113. Install the catalytic converter.
114. Install the engine air cleaner.
115. Install the intake manifold.
116. Rearm the vehicle high voltage electrical system. For additional information, refer to the High Voltage Traction Battery procedure.
117. Connect the 12v battery ground cable.
118. Fill the engine with clean engine oil.
119. Fill the Motor Electronics Cooling System as follows:

➡**Vehicle cooling systems are filled with Motorcraft® Premium Gold Engine Coolant. Always fill the cooling system with the same coolant that is present in the system. Do not mix coolant types.**

   d. Connect the hoses to the transaxle and install the hose clamps.

❋❋ WARNING

Adhesives, stop-leak pellets or small debris in the Motor electronics cooling system (MECS) can cause poor performance or temporary blockage of the motor electronics pump. Only use clean, approved coolant when filling the system.

e. Loosen the bleed screw and fill the degas bottle with coolant until it begins to flow out of the bleed hole. Then, close the bleed screw.

f. Turn the ignition to the ON position to actuate the motor electronics cooling pump and continue to fill the degas bottle to the correct level.

➡**Most of the MECS air bleeding occurs as a normal process at the degas bottle through the vent tube; very little occurs at the bleed screw.**

g. To bleed air from the system, loosen the bleed screw and allow air to escape while the M/E coolant pump is operating.

120. Fill and bleed the cooling system.

EXHAUST MANIFOLD

REMOVAL & INSTALLATION

See Figure 81.

1. Before servicing the vehicle, refer to the Precautions Section.
2. Remove the exhaust flexible pipe.
3. Remove the 2 catalytic converter bracket bolts.

➡**If installing a new converter, remove the heated oxygen sensor (HO2S) and the catalyst monitoring sensor (CMS) for installation in the new converter.**

4. Disconnect the HO2S and the CMS electrical connectors.
5. Remove and discard the 7 exhaust manifold nuts.
6. Remove the catalytic converter from the vehicle. Discard the exhaust manifold gasket.

To install:

❈ WARNING

If the warpage is greater than 0.76 mm (0.03 inch) replace the catalytic converter.

7. Inspect the catalytic converter for warpage across the manifold flange area.
8. Position a new exhaust manifold gasket on the engine.

❈ WARNING

Failure to tighten the catalytic converter nuts to specification before installing the converter bracket bolts will cause the converter to develop an exhaust leak.

❈ WARNING

Failure to tighten the catalytic converter nuts to specification a second time will cause the converter to develop an exhaust leak.

9. Position the catalytic converter and tighten the 7 exhaust manifold nuts in the sequence shown.
- Step 1: Tighten to 35 ft. lbs. (47 Nm).
- Step 2: Retighten to 35 ft. lbs. (47 Nm).

➡**Apply anti-seize lubricant to the threads of the sensors before installation.**

10. If installing a new converter, install the HO2S and the CMS. Tighten to 35 ft. lbs. (47 Nm).
11. Connect the HO2S and the CMS electrical connectors.
12. Install the 2 catalytic converter bracket bolts. Tighten to 18 ft. lbs. (25 Nm).
13. Install the exhaust flexible pipe. Tighten to 18 ft. lbs. (25 Nm).

INTAKE MANIFOLD

REMOVAL & INSTALLATION

See Figures 82 through 84.

1. Before servicing the vehicle, refer to the Precautions Section.

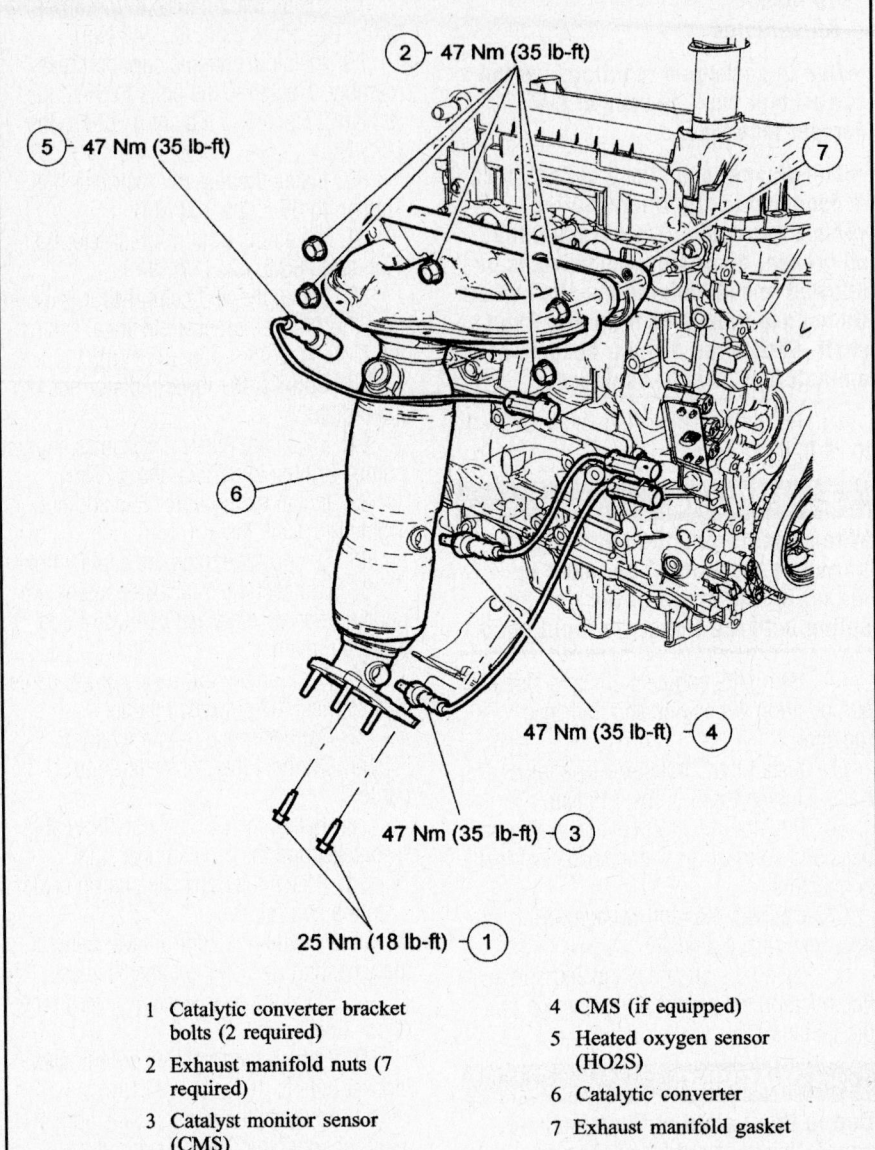

1 Catalytic converter bracket bolts (2 required)
2 Exhaust manifold nuts (7 required)
3 Catalyst monitor sensor (CMS)
4 CMS (if equipped)
5 Heated oxygen sensor (HO2S)
6 Catalytic converter
7 Exhaust manifold gasket

Fig. 81 Exhaust manifold/catalytic converter—2.3L hybrid engine

2. With vehicle in NEUTRAL, position it on a hoist.

3. Remove the throttle body.

4. Remove the fuel rail.

5. Loosen the clamp and disconnect the secondary air injection (AIR) tube from the AIR pump hose.

6. Remove the right and left splash shields.

7. Remove the 2 bolts and position the motor electronics coolant pump aside.

8. Disconnect the AIR pump electrical connector.

9. Remove the 2 bolts and the AIR pump.

10. Remove the 5 bolts and the right splash shield.

11. Remove the lower oil level indicator tube bolt.

12. Remove the oil level indictor.

13. Remove the upper bolt and the oil level indicator tube.

14. Remove and discard the oil level indicator tube O-ring seal.

15. Disconnect the oil pressure sender electrical connector.

16. Disconnect the TMAP sensor electrical connector.

17. Disconnect the swirl control valve electrical connector.

18. Disconnect the IMRC actuator electrical connector.

19. If equipped, disconnect the block heater electrical harness connector.

20. Disconnect the KS electrical connector and detach the pin-type retainer.

21. Disconnect the fuel vapor return hose from the intake manifold.

22. Disconnect the power brake booster vacuum tube. Depress the quick release

locking ring. Pull the vacuum tube out of the quick release fitting.

➡**There are 3 different size bolts used. Mark the location of the bolts to make sure they are installed in the correct location.**

23. Remove the 8 bolts and position the intake manifold aside to access the crankcase vent hose clamp and the EGR tube.

24. Release the clamp and disconnect the crankcase vent hose.

25. Remove the EGR tube.

26. Remove the intake manifold and gaskets.

To install:

27. To install, reverse the removal procedure. Inspect and install new intake manifold gaskets if necessary. Observe the following torques:

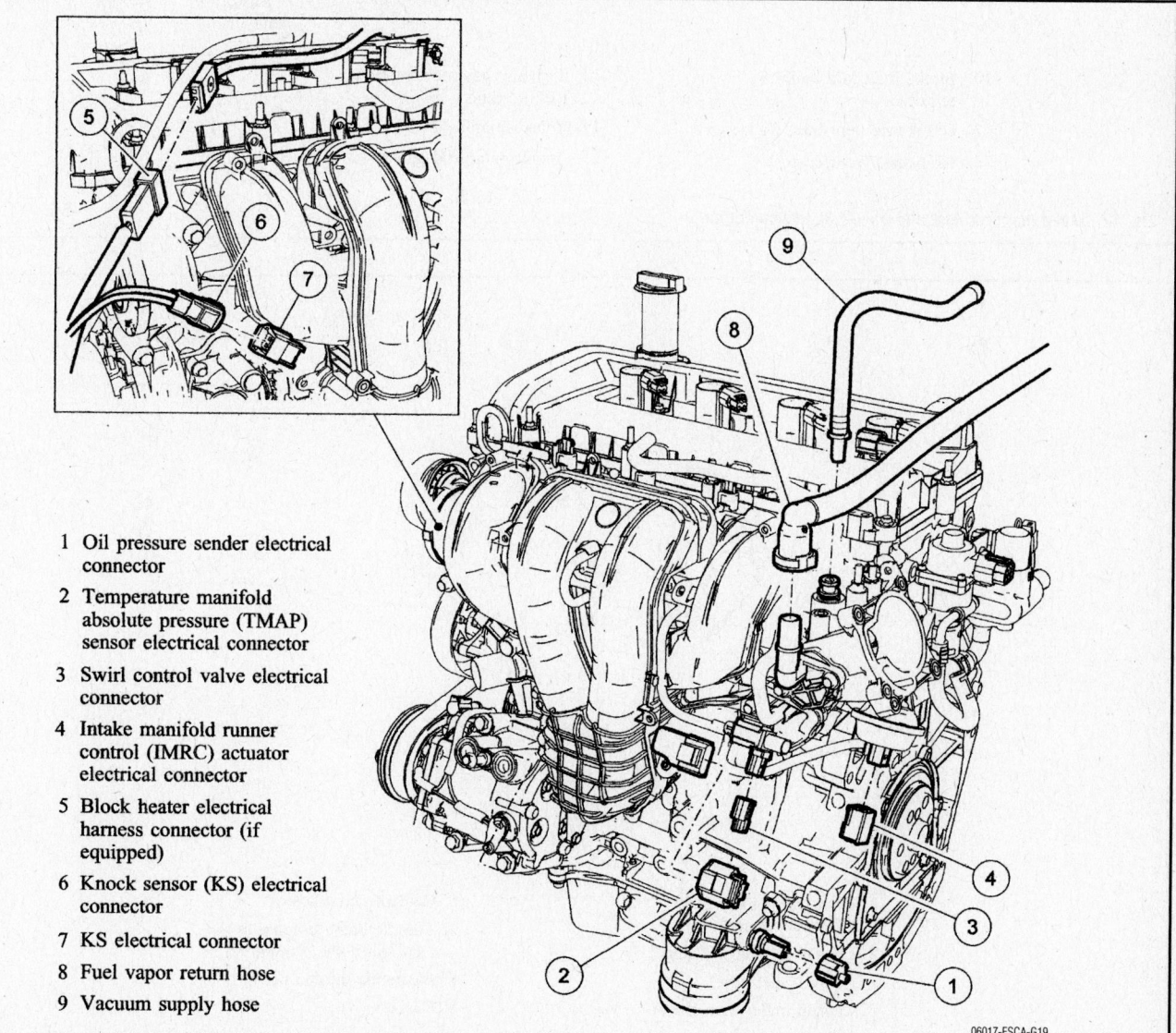

1 Oil pressure sender electrical connector

2 Temperature manifold absolute pressure (TMAP) sensor electrical connector

3 Swirl control valve electrical connector

4 Intake manifold runner control (IMRC) actuator electrical connector

5 Block heater electrical harness connector (if equipped)

6 Knock sensor (KS) electrical connector

7 KS electrical connector

8 Fuel vapor return hose

9 Vacuum supply hose

06017-ESCA-G19

Fig. 82 Intake manifold and related parts—2.3L hybrid engine

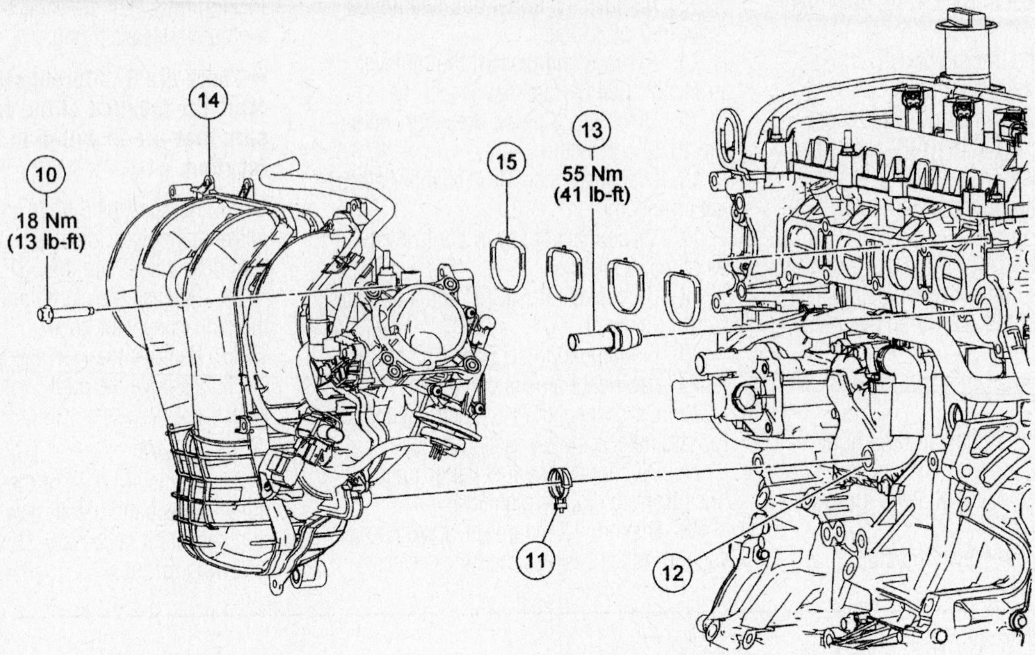

10 Intake manifold bolts (8 required)

11 Crankcase vent hose clamp

12 Crankcase vent hose

13 Exhaust gas recirculation (EGR) tube

14 Intake manifold

15 Intake manifold gasket

06017-ESCA-G20

Fig. 83 Intake manifold installation—2.3L hybrid engine

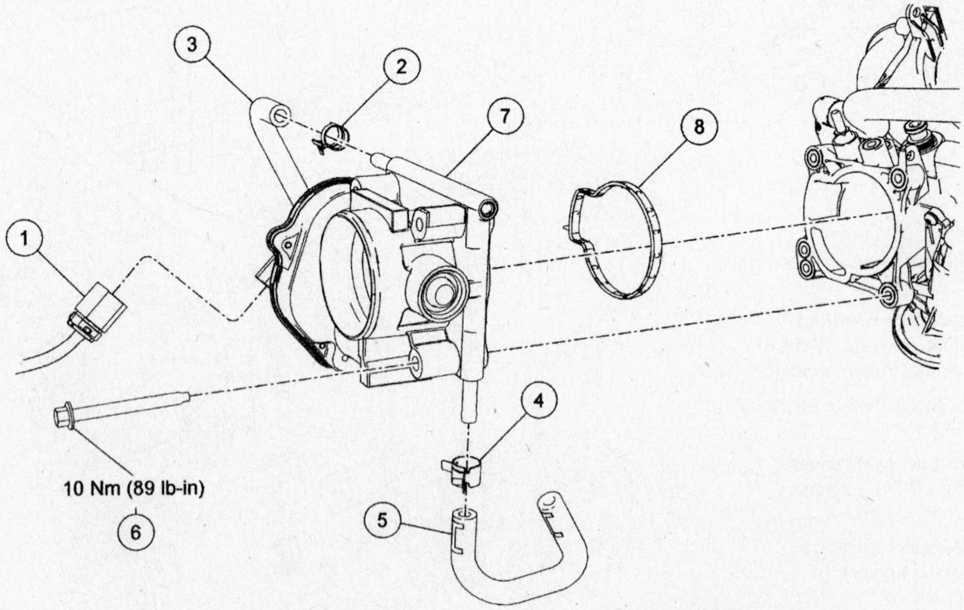

1 Electronic throttle body electrical connector

2 Coolant inlet hose clamp

3 Coolant inlet hose

4 Coolant outlet hose clamp

5 Coolant outlet hose

6 Throttle body-to-upper intake manifold bolts (4 required)

7 Electronic throttle body

8 Gasket

06017-ESCA-G21

Fig. 84 Throttle body—2.3L hybrid engine

- EGR tube: 41 ft. lbs. (55 Nm)
- Intake manifold: 13 ft. lbs. (18 Nm)
- Upper oil level indicator tube bolt: 89 inch lbs. (10 Nm)
- Lower oil level indicator tube bolt: 35 ft. lbs. (47 Nm)
- AIR pump: 22 ft. lbs. (30 Nm)
- Motor electronics coolant pump: 62 inch lbs. (7 Nm)

OIL PAN

REMOVAL & INSTALLATION

See Figures 85 and 86.

1. Before servicing the vehicle, refer to the Precautions Section.
2. With the vehicle in NEUTRAL, position it on a hoist.
3. Remove the oil level indicator and tube.
4. Drain the oil.
5. Remove the 4 front cover-to-oil pan bolts.
6. Remove the 4 oil pan-to-bell housing bolts.
7. Remove the 13 oil pan-to-block bolts.

To install:

✳✳ WARNING

Do not use metal scrapers, wire brushes, power abrasive discs or other abrasive means to clean the sealing surfaces. These tools cause scratches and gouges, which make leak paths. Use a plastic scraping tool to remove traces of sealant.

8. Clean and inspect all mating surfaces.

➡ If the oil pan is not secured within four minutes of sealant application the sealant must be removed and the sealing area cleaned with metal surface cleaner. Allow to dry until there is no sign of wetness, or four minutes, whichever is longer. Failure to follow this procedure can cause future oil leakage.

➡ The oil pan must be installed and the bolts tightened within four minutes of applying the silicone gasket and sealant.

9. Apply a 2.5 mm bead of silicone gasket and sealant to the oil pan. Install the

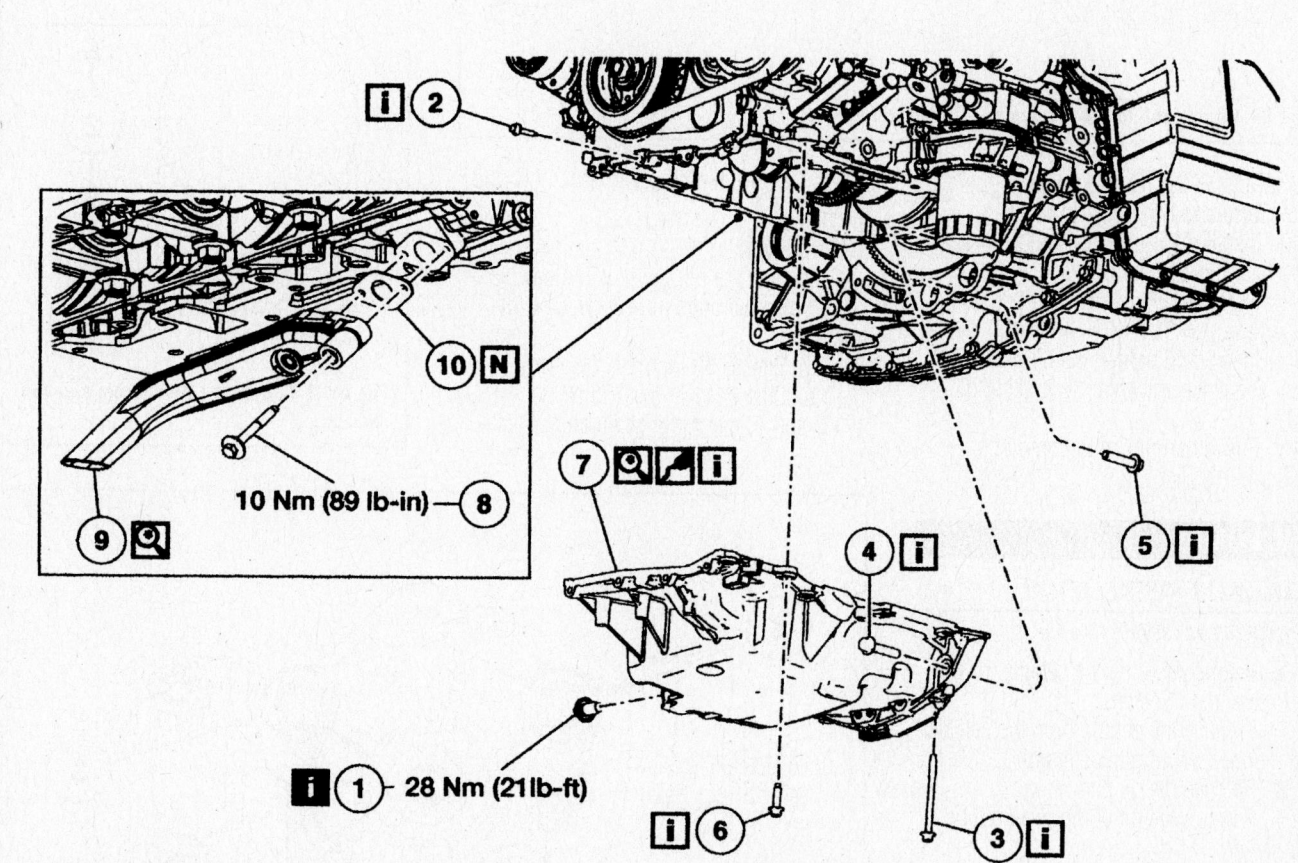

1 Drain plug
2 Engine front cover bolt
3 Oil pan bolt
4 Oil pan-to-bell housing bolt
5 Oil pan-to-bell housing bolt
6 Oil pan bolt
7 Oil pan
8 Oil pump screen and pickup tube bolt
9 Oil pump screen and pickup tube
10 Oil pump screen and pickup tube gasket

67197-ESCA-G20

Fig. 85 Oil pan, pump and related parts—2.3L hybrid engine

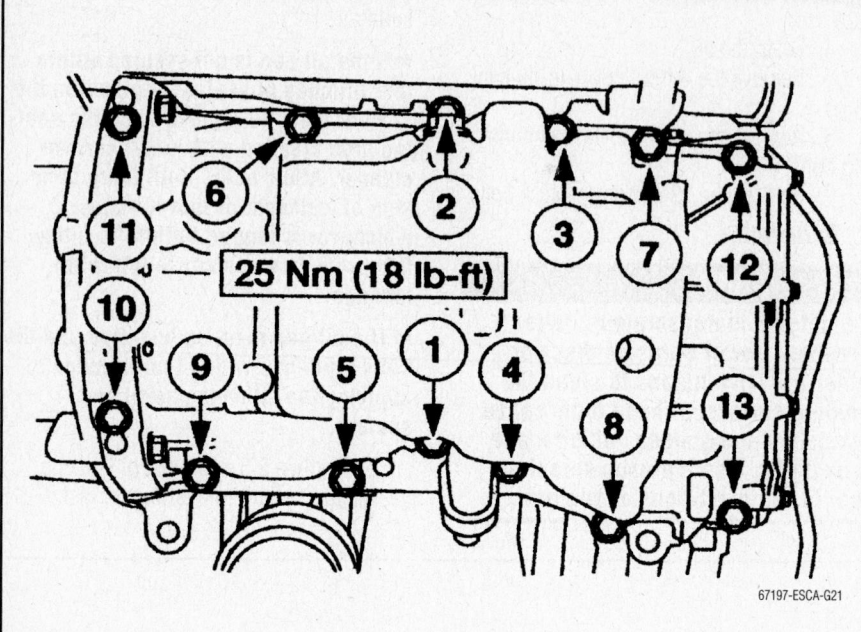

Fig. 86 Oil pan bolt torque sequence—2.3L hybrid engine

25 Nm (18 lb-ft)

67197-ESCA-G21

oil pan. Install the oil pan-to-bell housing bolts. Torque to 35 ft. lbs. (48 Nm).

10. Install the front cover bolts. Torque to 89 inch lbs. (10 Nm).

11. Install the oil pan-to-bell housing bolts. Torque to 35 ft. lbs. (48 Nm).

12. Install and tighten the oil pan bolts in the sequence shown to 18 ft. lbs. (25 Nm).

13. Fill the engine with clean engine oil.

OIL PUMP

REMOVAL & INSTALLATION

See Figures 85 and 87.

1. Before servicing the vehicle, refer to the Precautions Section.

2. Remove the engine from the vehicle and mount it on an engine stand.

3. Remove the oil pan.

4. Remove the oil pump pickup tube and screen.

5. Remove the front cover and the timing chain.

6. Release the tension on the tensioner spring.

7. Remove the tensioner and the shoulder bolt.

8. Remove the guide.

➡**The oil pump chain sprocket must be held in place.**

9. Remove the oil pump chain and sprockets.

10. Remove the oil pump assembly and gasket.

To install:

11. Install the oil pump with a new gasket. Tighten the bolts in sequence as follows:

  a. Step 1: 89 inch lbs. (10 Nm).
  b. Step 2: 17 ft. lbs. (23 Nm).

12. Install the pump chain and sprock-ets. Tighten the pump sprocket bolt to 18 ft. lbs. (25 Nm).

13. Install the chain guide, tensioner, and shoulder bolt. Tighten the bolts to 89 inch lbs. (10 Nm).

14. Hook the tensioner spring around the shoulder bolt.

15. Install the oil pump pickup tube and screen with a new gasket. Tighten the bolts to 89 ft. lbs. (10 Nm).

16. Install the oil pan.

17. Install the timing chain and front cover.

18. Install the engine into the vehicle.

PISTON AND RING

POSITIONING

See Figure 88.

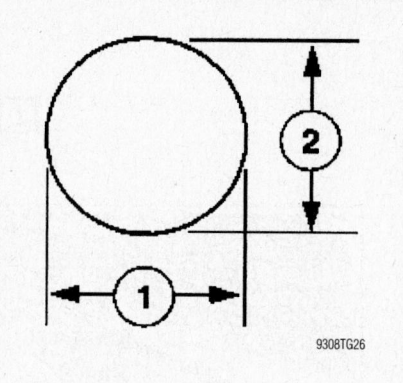

9308TG26

Fig. 88 2.3L engine—piston ring end-gap spacing

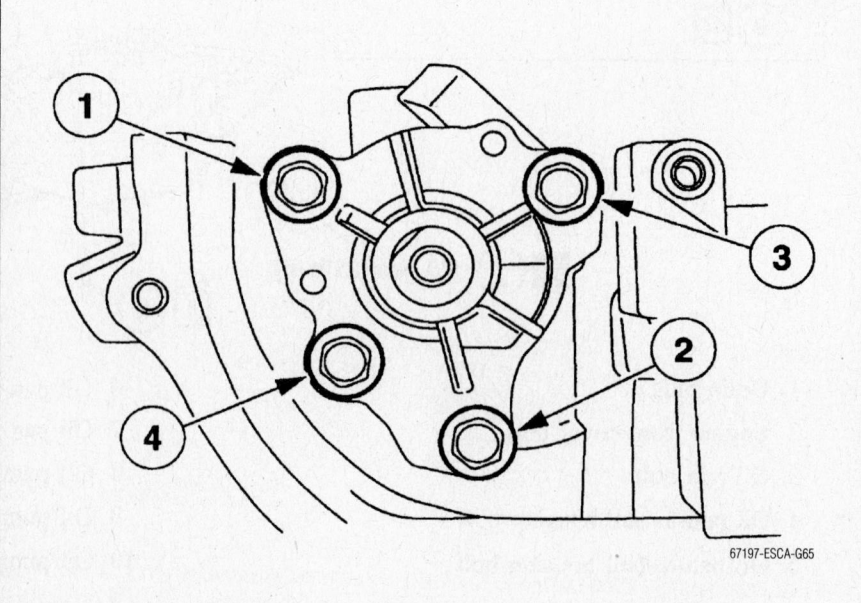

67197-ESCA-G65

Fig. 87 Oil pump torque sequence—2.3L hybrid engine

REAR MAIN SEAL

REMOVAL & INSTALLATION

See Figures 89 through 91.

1. Before servicing the vehicle, refer to the Precautions Section.

2. With the vehicle in NEUTRAL, position it on a hoist.

3. If equipped, remove the automatic transaxle.

4. If equipped, remove the manual transaxle and clutch.

5. Remove the flexplate or flywheel.

6. Remove the oil pan.

7. Remove the crankshaft rear oil seal with retainer plate

To install:

8. Using a seal installer, position the crankshaft rear oil seal with retainer plate onto the crankshaft.

9. Install the crankshaft rear oil seal with retainer plate. Tighten the bolts in the sequence shown to 89 inch lbs. (10 Nm).

10. Install the oil pan.

➡**Special bolts are used for installation. Do not use standard bolts.**

11. Install the flywheel/flexplate. Tighten

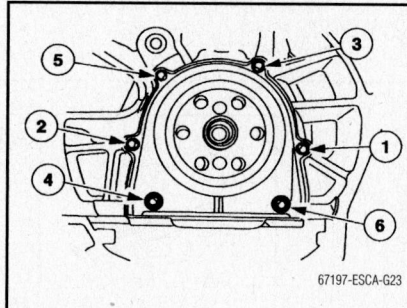

Fig. 90 Retainer plate torque sequence—2.3L hybrid engine

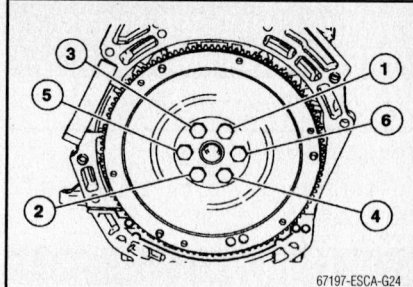

Fig. 91 Flywheel torque sequence—2.3L hybrid engine

the bolts in the sequence shown in three stages.

   a. Stage 1: Tighten to 37 ft. lbs. (50 Nm).

   b. Stage 2: Tighten to 50 ft. lbs. (80 Nm).

   c. Stage 3: Tighten to 83 ft. lbs. (112 Nm).

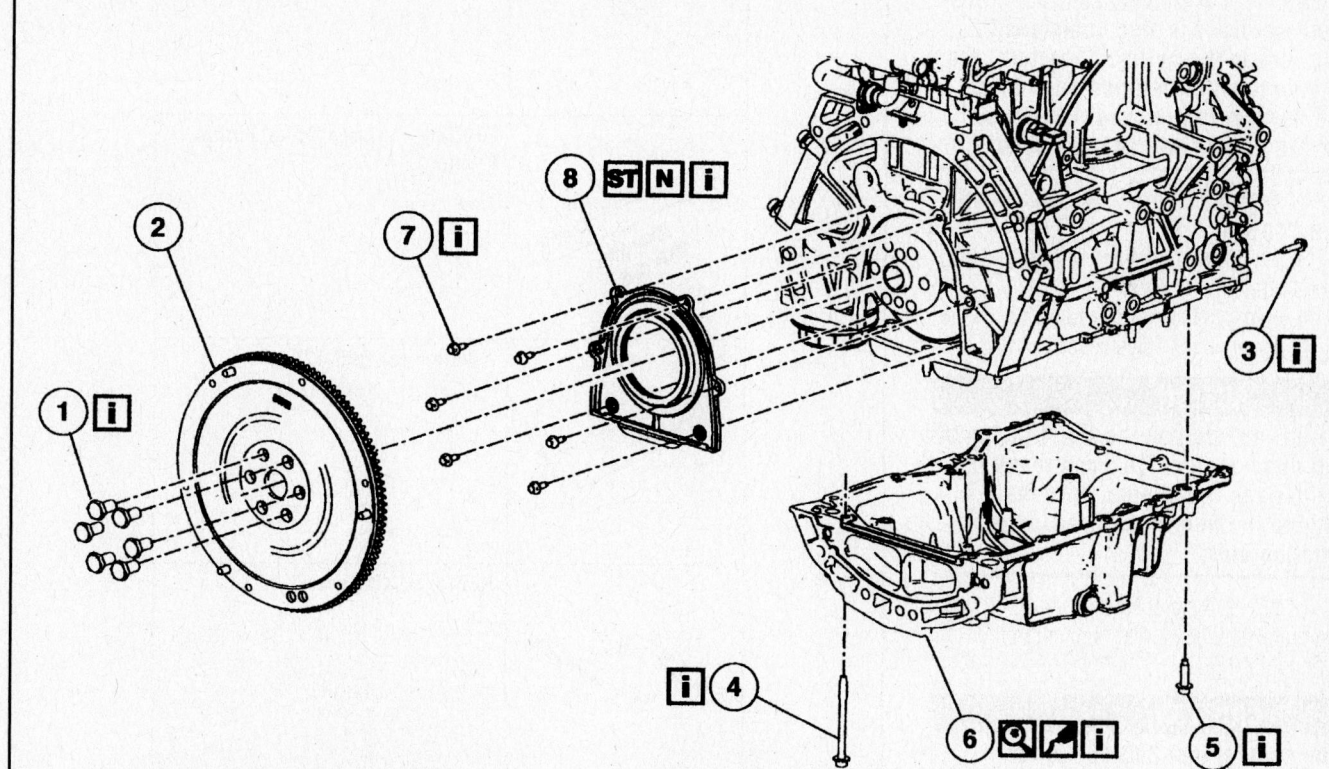

1	Flexplate or flywheel bolt	5	Oil pan bolt
2	Flexplate or flywheel	6	Oil pan
3	Engine front cover bolt	7	Crankshaft rear oil seal with retainer plate bolt
4	Oil pan bolt	8	Crankshaft rear oil seal with retainer plate

Fig. 89 Rear main seal and related parts—2.3L hybrid engine

TIMING CHAIN, SPROCKETS, FRONT COVER AND SEAL

REMOVAL & INSTALLATION

See Figures 92 through 100.

1. Before servicing the vehicle, refer to the Precautions Section.

✳✳ CAUTION

During engine repair procedures, cleanliness is extremely important. Any foreign material, including any material created while cleaning gasket surfaces that enters the oil passages, coolant passages or the oil pan can cause engine failure.

✸ CAUTION

The crankshaft, the crankshaft sprocket and the pulley are fitted together by friction, using diamond washers between the flange faces on each part. For that reason, the crankshaft sprocket is also unfastened if you loosen the pulley. Therefore, the engine must be retimed each time the damper is removed. Otherwise severe engine damage can occur.

2. With the vehicle in NEUTRAL, position it on a hoist.
3. Remove the accessory drive belt and idler pulleys.
4. Remove the engine mount.
5. Remove the valve cover.

✸ CAUTION

Failure to position the No. 1 piston at top dead center (TDC) can result in damage to the engine. Turn the engine in the normal direction of rotation only.

6. Using the crankshaft pulley bolt, turn the crankshaft clockwise to position the No. 1 piston at TDC.

✳✳ CAUTION

The special tool 303-465 is for camshaft alignment only. Using this tool to prevent engine rotation can result in engine damage.

➡ The camshaft timing slots are offset. If the special tool cannot be installed, rotate the crankshaft one complete revolution clockwise to correctly position the camshafts.

7. Install special tool 303-465 in the slots on the rear of both camshafts.

8. Remove the engine plug bolt.

➡ Only turn the engine in the normal direction of rotation.

➡ Installing the special tool in this step will prevent the engine from being rotated in the clockwise direction.

9. Install special tool 303-507.
10. Install the special tools 205-126 and 205-072-02.

✳✳ CAUTION

Failure to hold the crankshaft pulley in place while loosening the bolt can result in damage to the engine.

11. Remove the crankshaft pulley bolt and washer.
12. Remove the crankshaft pulley.
13. Remove the crankshaft front seal.

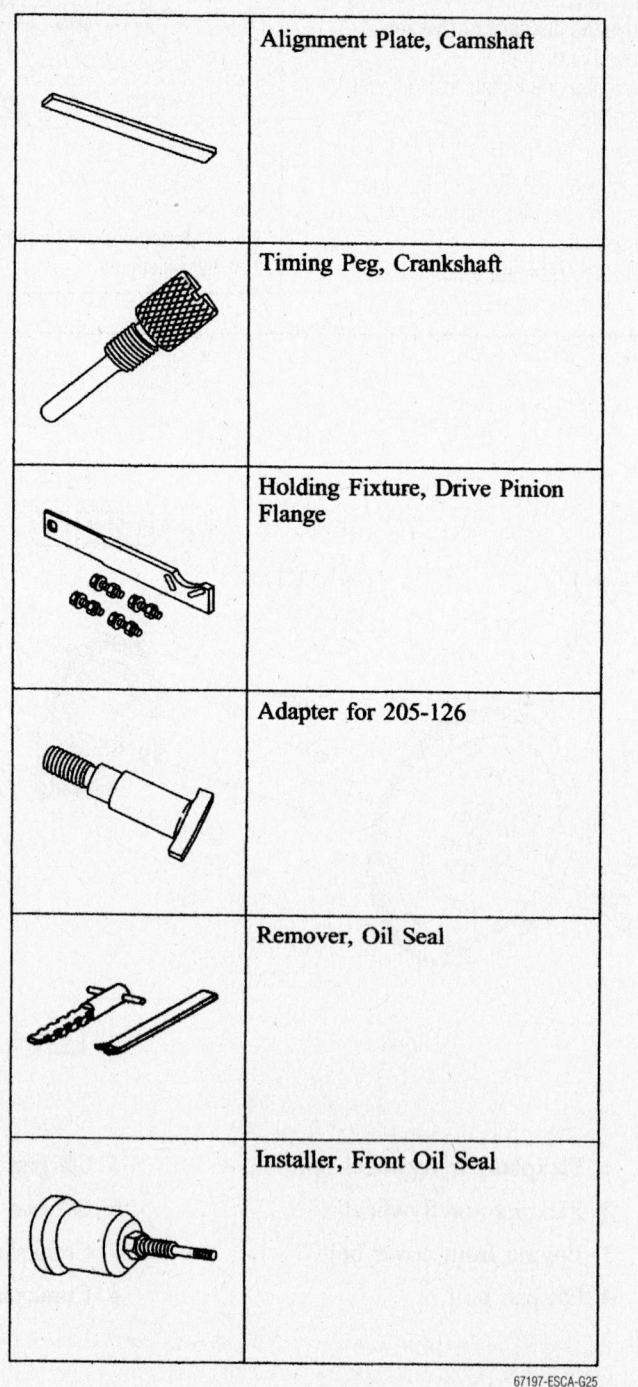

	Alignment Plate, Camshaft
	Timing Peg, Crankshaft
	Holding Fixture, Drive Pinion Flange
	Adapter for 205-126
	Remover, Oil Seal
	Installer, Front Oil Seal

67197-ESCA-G25

Fig. 92 Tools needed for timing chain and gears replacement—2.3L hybrid engine

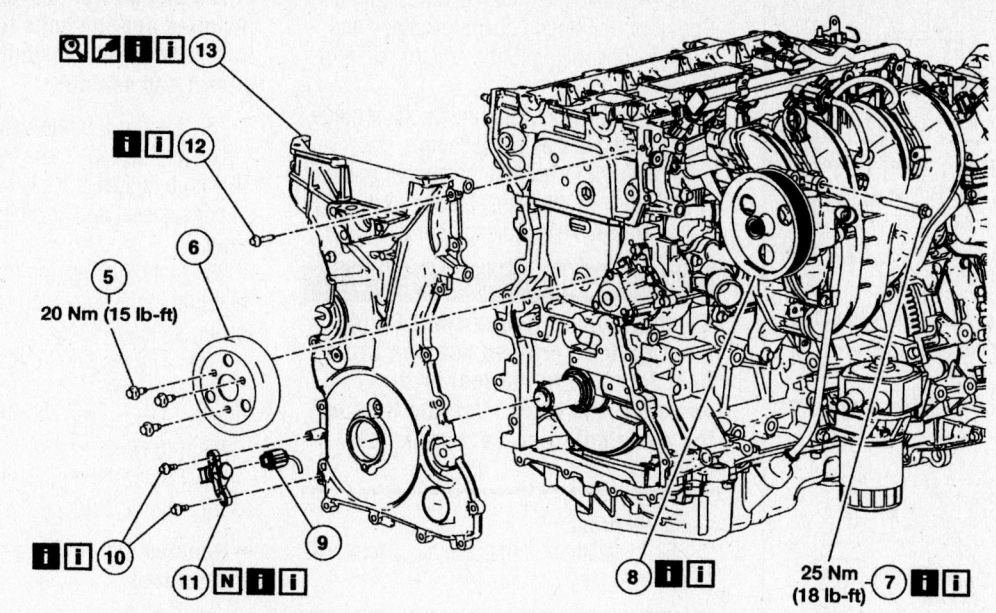

20 Nm (15 lb-ft)

25 Nm
(18 lb-ft)

5   Coolant pump pulley bolt
6   Coolant pump pulley
7   Power steering pump bolt
8   Power steering pump (position aside)
9   Crankshaft position (CKP) sensor electrical connector

10   CKP sensor bolts
11   CKP sensor
12   Engine front cover bolt
13   Engine front cover

67197-ESCA-G26

Fig. 93 Front cover and related parts—2.3L hybrid engine

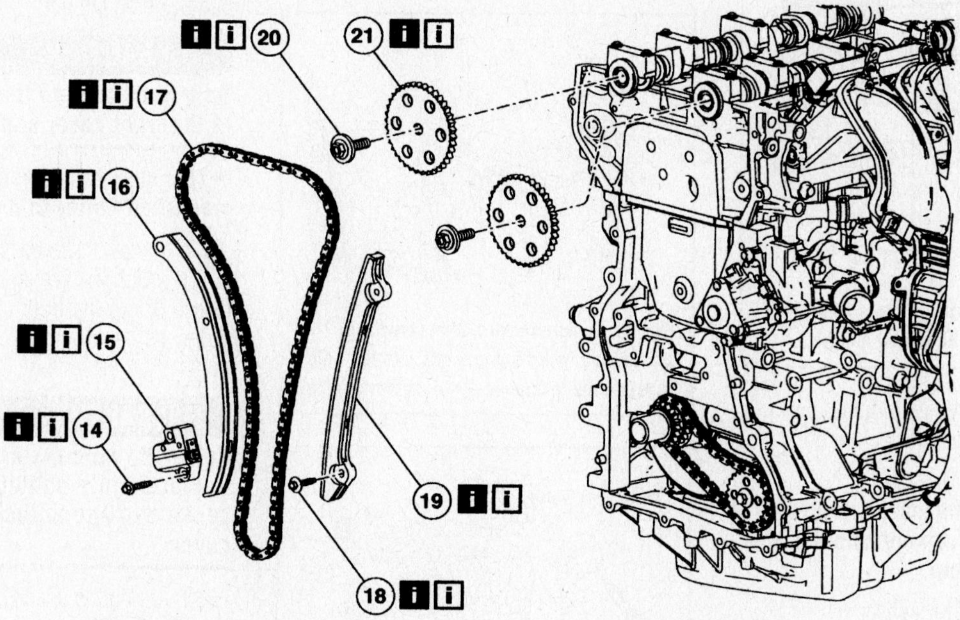

14   Timing chain tensioner bolt
15   Timing chain tensioner
16   RH timing chain guide
17   Timing chain

18   LH timing chain guide bolt
19   LH timing chain guide
20   Camshaft sprocket bolt
21   Camshaft sprocket

67197-ESCA-G27

Fig. 94 Timing chain and related parts—2.3L hybrid engine

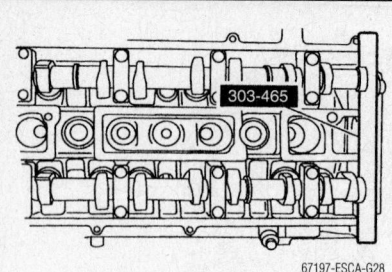

Fig. 95 Install special tool 303-465 in the slots on the rear of both camshafts—2.3L hybrid engine

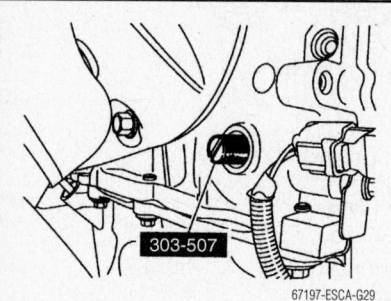

Fig. 96 Install special tool 303-507—2.3L hybrid engine

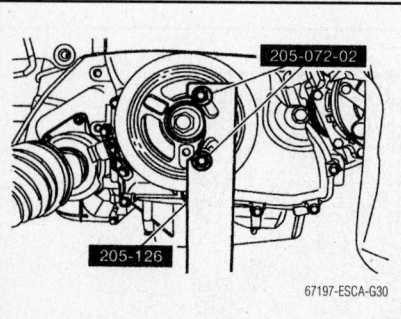

Fig. 97 Install the special tools 205-126 and 205-072-02—2.3L hybrid engine

14. Remove the coolant pump pulley.

15. Remove the power steering pump and position it aside.

➡**The bolt under the power steering pressure tube will remain with the power steering pump.**

16. Remove the CKP sensor.

➡**Whenever the crankshaft position (CKP) sensor is removed, a new one must be installed, using the alignment jig supplied with the new part.**

17. Remove the engine front cover bolts (there are 22).

18. Remove the engine front cover.

19. Remove the timing chain tensioner. Compress the timing chain tensioner, and insert a paper clip into the hole to retain the tensioner.

20. Remove the right timing chain guide.

21. Remove the timing chain.

22. Remove the left timing chain guide.

23. Remove the camshaft sprocket bolts.

24. Remove the camshaft sprockets.

✳✳ CAUTION

Do not rely on the Camshaft Alignment Plate to prevent camshaft rotation. Damage to the tool or the camshaft can occur. Use the flats on the camshaft to prevent camshaft rotation.

To install:

25. Installation is the reverse of removal. Note the following:

✳✳ CAUTION

Do not use metal scrapers, wire brushes, power abrasive disks or other abrasive means to clean sealing surfaces. These tools cause scratches and gouges which make leak paths.

26. Clean and inspect the mounting surfaces of the engine and the front cover.

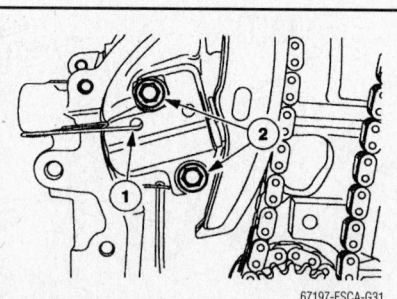

Fig. 98 Compress the timing chain tensioner, and insert a paper clip into the hole to retain the tensioner—2.3L hybrid engine

Fig. 99 Use the flats on the camshaft to prevent camshaft rotation—2.3L hybrid engine

➡**The engine front cover must be installed and the bolts tightened within four minutes of applying the silicone gasket and sealant.**

27. Apply a 2.5 mm bead of silicone gasket and sealant to the cylinder head and oil pan joint areas. Apply a 2.5 mm bead of silicone gasket and sealant to the front cover.

28. Install the engine front cover. Tighten the bolts in the sequence shown, to the following specifications:

   a. Tighten the 8 mm bolts to 89 inch lbs. (10 Nm).

   b. Tighten the 13 mm bolts to 35 ft. lbs. (48 Nm).

29. Position the power steering pump and install the bolts.

➡**Remove the through-bolt from the special tool.**

➡**Lubricate the oil seal with clean engine oil.**

30. Using a seal driver, install the crankshaft front oil seal.

➡**Do not reuse the crankshaft damper bolt.**

➡**Apply clean engine oil on the seal area before installing.**

31. Install the crankshaft pulley and hand-tighten the bolt.

✳✳ CAUTION

Only hand-tighten the bolt or damage to the front cover can occur.

➡**This step will correctly align the crankshaft pulley to the crankshaft.**

32. Install a standard 6 mm × 18 mm bolt through the crankshaft pulley and thread it into the front cover. Rotate the pulley as necessary to align the bolt holes.

✳✳ CAUTION

Failure to hold the crankshaft pulley in place while tightening the bolt can cause damage to the engine front cover.

33. Using the special tools to hold the crankshaft pulley in place, tighten the crankshaft pulley bolt in two stages:

   a. Stage 1: Tighten to 74 ft. lbs. (100 Nm).

   b. Stage 2: Tighten an additional 90 degrees (¼ turn).

34. Remove the 6 mm × 18 mm bolt.

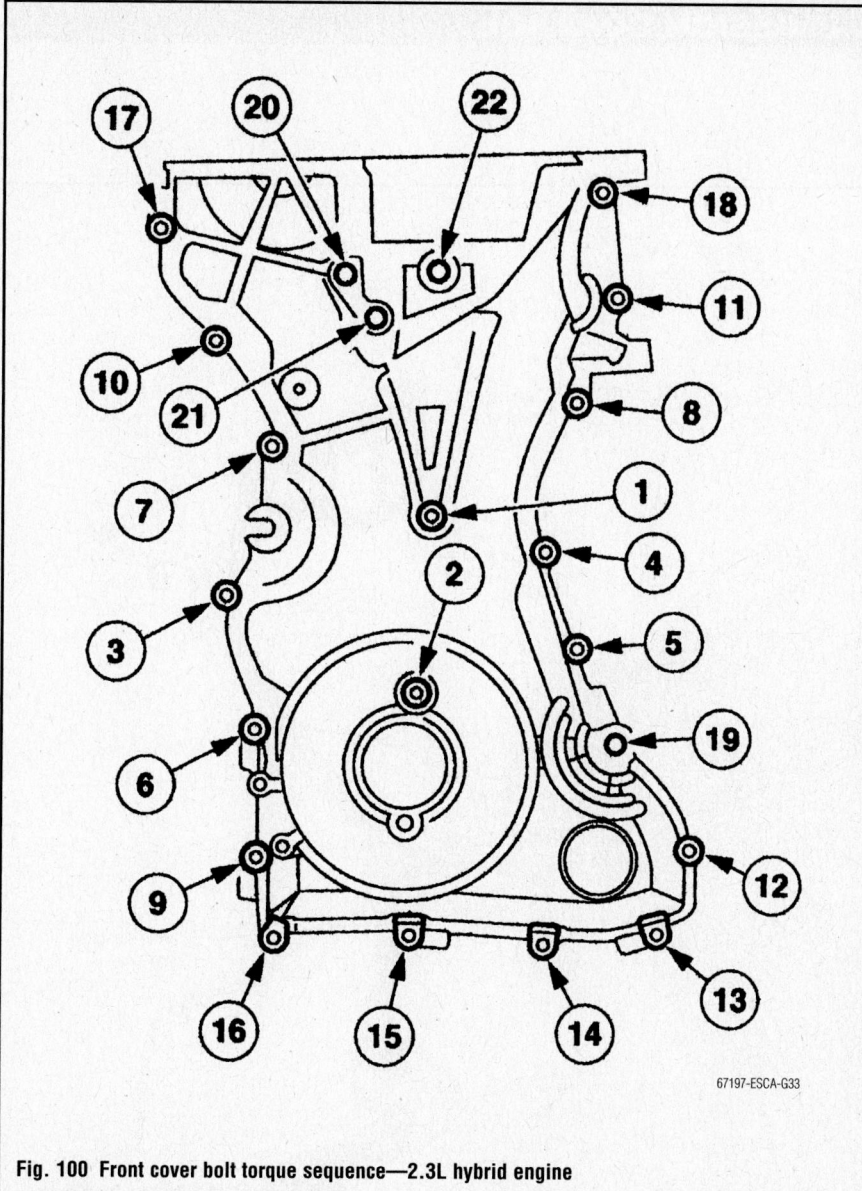

Fig. 100 Front cover bolt torque sequence—2.3L hybrid engine

35. Remove special tool 303-507.
36. Remove special tool 303-465.

➡**Only turn the engine in the normal direction of rotation.**

37. Turn the engine two complete revolutions.

➡**Only turn the engine in the normal direction of rotation.**

38. Turn the crankshaft until the No. 1 piston is at TDC.
39. Install special tool 303-507.

✳✳ CAUTION

Only hand-tighten the bolt or damage to the front cover can occur.

40. Using the 6 mm x 18 mm bolt, check the position of the crankshaft pulley. If it is not possible to install the bolt, correct the engine timing.

41. Using special tool 303-465, check the position of the camshafts. If it is not possible to install the special tool, correct the engine timing.

42. Install the CKP sensor. Do not tighten the bolts at this time.

43. Adjust the CKP sensor alignment jig and tighten the bolts.

44. Remove the 6 mm x 18 mm bolt.

45. Install the engine plug bolt.

VALVE LASH

ADJUSTMENT

1. Before servicing the vehicle, refer to the Precautions Section.

➡**Before removing the camshafts, measure the clearance of each valve at base circle, with the lobe pointed away from the tappet. Failure to measure all clearances prior to removing the camshafts will necessitate repeated removal and installation and wasted labor time.**

2. Use a feeler gauge to measure the clearance of each valve and record its location.

➡**The number on the valve tappet only reflects the digits that follow the decimal. For example, a tappet with the number 0.650 has the thickness of 3.650 mm.**

➡**A midrange clearance is the most desirable:**

- Intake: 0.22–0.28 mm (0.008–0.011 inch)
- Exhaust: 0.27–0.33 mm (0.010–0.013 inch)

3. Select tappets using this formula: tappet thickness = measured clearance + the base tappet thickness – most desirable thickness.

4. Select the tappets and mark the installation location.

5. If any tappets do not measure within specifications, install new tappets in these locations.

ENGINE PERFORMANCE & EMISSION CONTROL

COMPONENT LOCATIONS

See Figures 101 and 102.

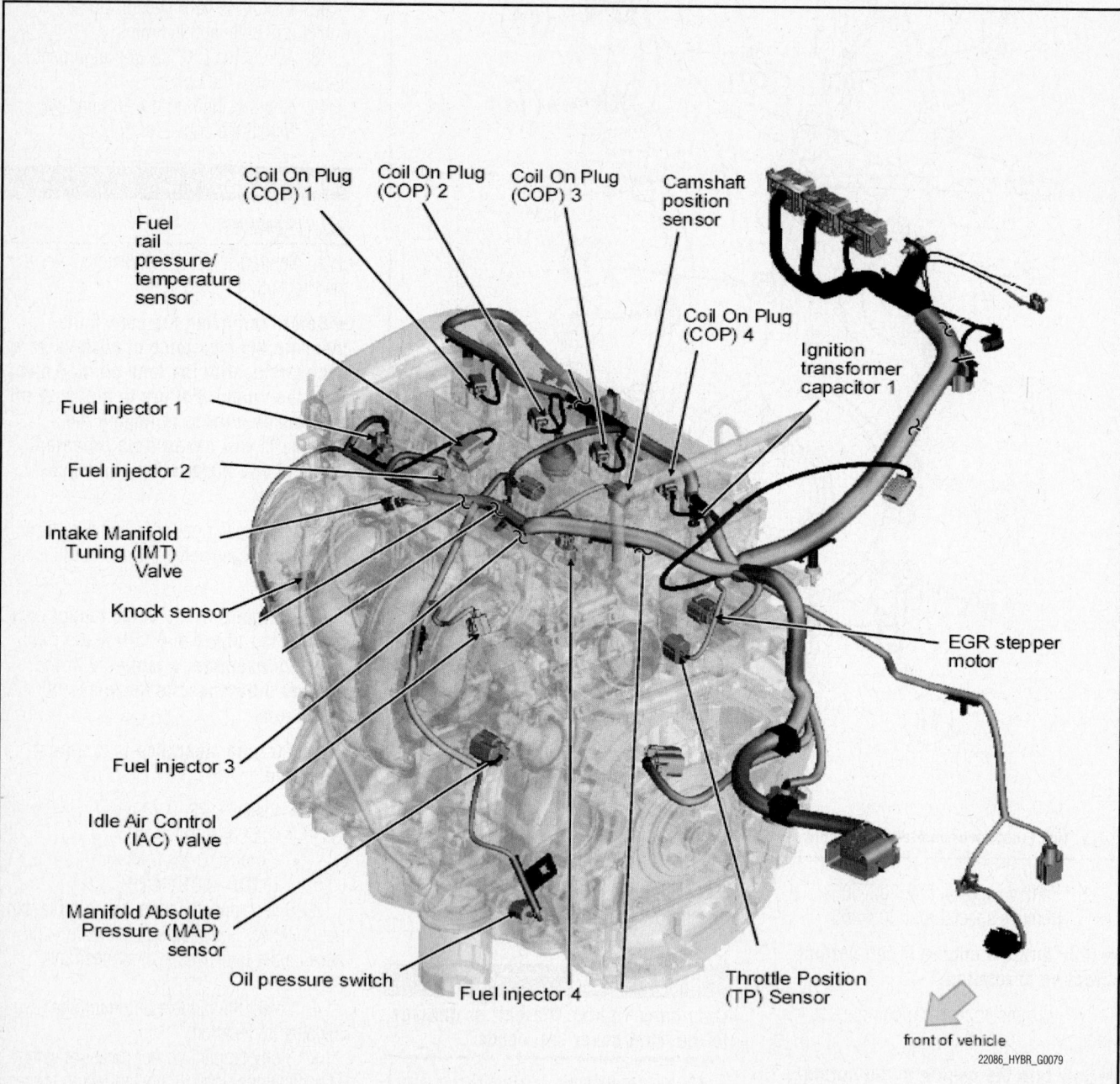

Fuel rail pressure/temperature sensor

Coil On Plug (COP) 1

Coil On Plug (COP) 2

Coil On Plug (COP) 3

Camshaft position sensor

Coil On Plug (COP) 4

Ignition transformer capacitor 1

Fuel injector 1

Fuel injector 2

Intake Manifold Tuning (IMT) Valve

Knock sensor

EGR stepper motor

Fuel injector 3

Idle Air Control (IAC) valve

Manifold Absolute Pressure (MAP) sensor

Oil pressure switch

Fuel injector 4

Throttle Position (TP) Sensor

front of vehicle

22086_HYBR_G0079

Fig. 101 Escape/Mariner Hybrid engine component (view 1)—2.3L hybrid engine

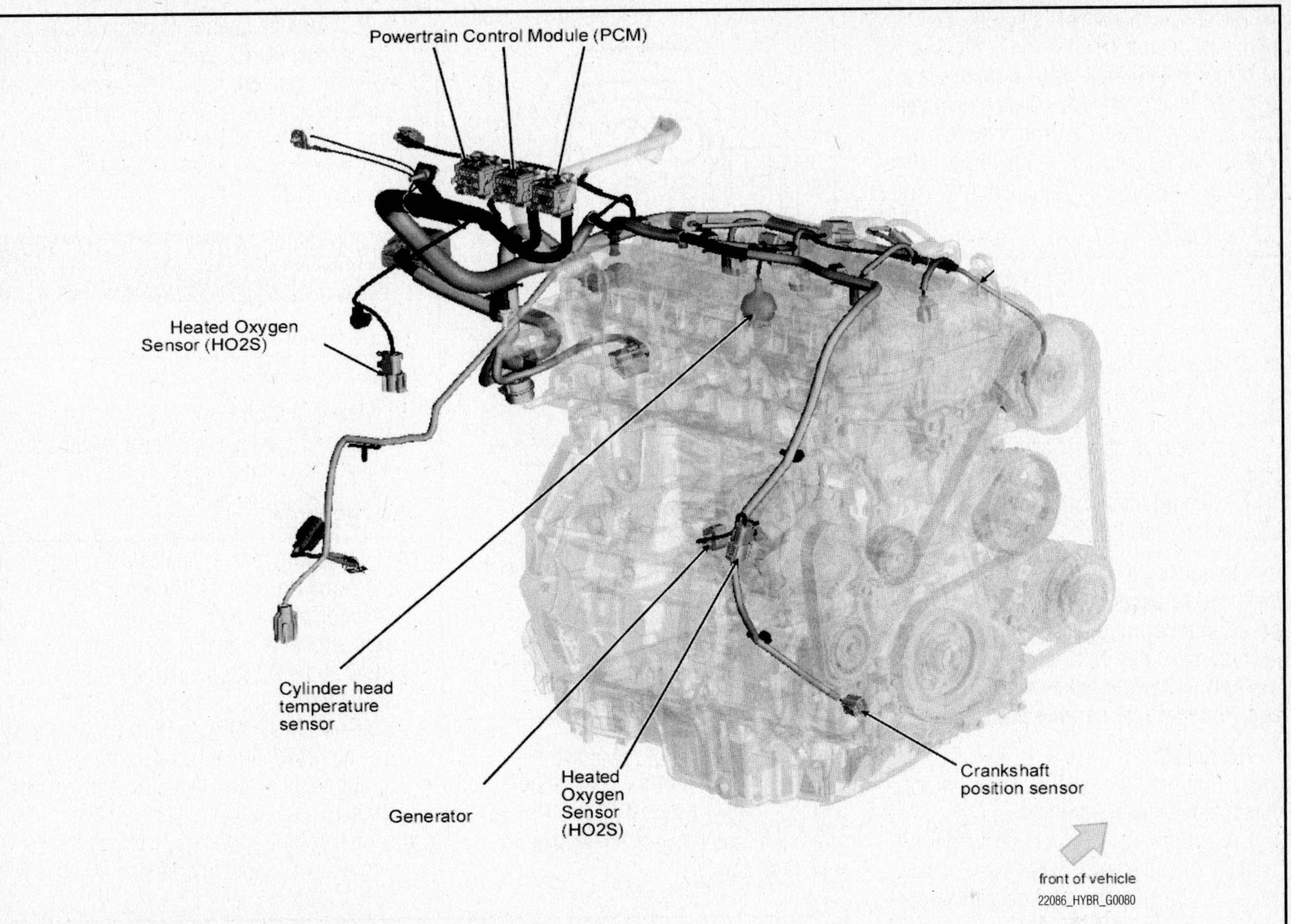

Powertrain Control Module (PCM)
Heated Oxygen Sensor (HO2S)
Cylinder head temperature sensor
Generator
Heated Oxygen Sensor (HO2S)
Crankshaft position sensor
front of vehicle
22086_HYBR_G0080

Fig. 102 Escape/Mariner Hybrid engine component (view 2)—2.3L hybrid engine

ACCELERATOR PEDAL POSITION (APP) SENSOR

LOCATION

See Figure 103.

The Accelerator Pedal Position (APP) sensor is inside of the vehicle and is part of the pedal assembly.

OPERATION

The Accelerator Pedal Position (APP) sensor is an input to the Powertrain Control Module (PCM) and is used to determine the torque demand. There are 3 pedal position signals in the sensor. Signal 1, APPS1, has a negative slope (increasing angle, decreasing voltage). Signals 2 and 3, APPS2 and APPS3, both have a positive slope (increasing angle, increasing voltage). During normal operation APPS1 is used as the indication of pedal position by the strategy. The 3 pedal position signals make sure the PCM receives a correct input even if a signal has a concern. There are 2 reference voltage circuits and 2 signal return circuits for the sensor.

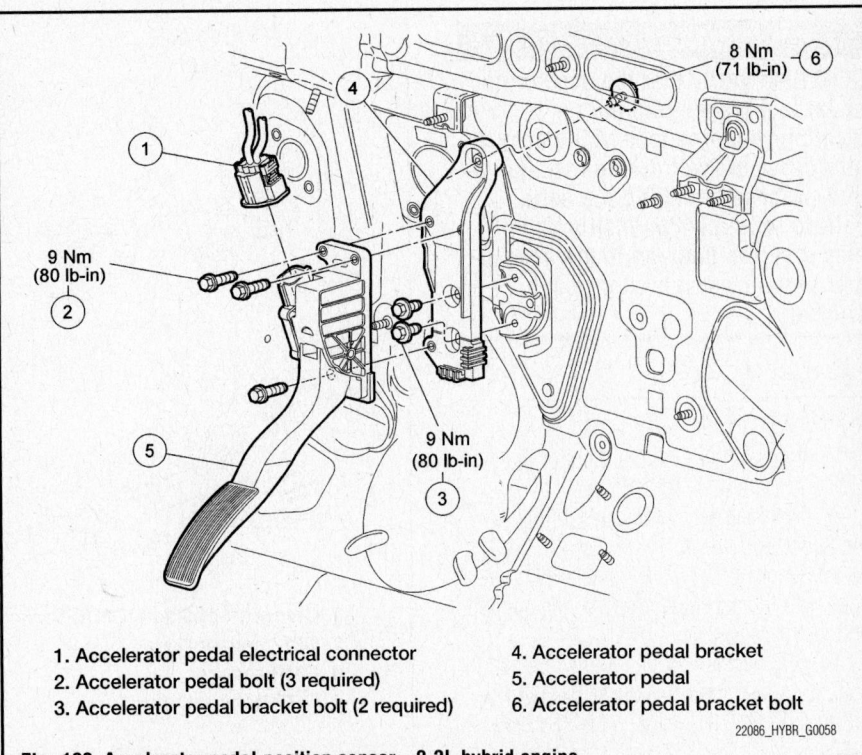

8 Nm (71 lb-in) 6
4
1
9 Nm (80 lb-in) 2
5
9 Nm (80 lb-in) 3
1. Accelerator pedal electrical connector
2. Accelerator pedal bolt (3 required)
3. Accelerator pedal bracket bolt (2 required)
4. Accelerator pedal bracket
5. Accelerator pedal
6. Accelerator pedal bracket bolt
22086_HYBR_G0058

Fig. 103 Accelerator pedal position sensor—2.3L hybrid engine

The engine management system electronically operates the throttle of the engine in response to throttle pedal movements initiated by the driver. In the event of a system failure, the engine management system provides a "limp home" mode which allows the car to be driven with limited performance.

REMOVAL & INSTALLATION

1. Disconnect the accelerator pedal electrical connector.

2. Remove the 3 bolts and release the accelerator pedal from the locating/retaining tabs on the lower RH corner of the accelerator pedal mounting bracket.

3. Remove the accelerator pedal bracket bolt.

4. Remove the 2 bolts and remove the accelerator pedal bracket.

➠If installing a new accelerator pedal and sensor assembly, the accelerator pedal bracket may also require replacement due to a different mounting bolt pattern between the original and replacement service parts.

To install:

5. To install, reverse the removal procedure and note the following:

   a. Tighten accelerator pedal bracket bolts to 80 inch lbs. (9 Nm).

   b. Tighten accelerator pedal bracket bolt to 71 inch lbs. (8 Nm).

   c. Tighten accelerator pedal mounting bracket to 80 inch lbs. (9 Nm).

✳✳ WARNING

CAUTION: Verify that the accelerator pedal is engaged into the locating/retaining tabs of the accelerator pedal bracket during installation, prior to installing the bolts. Failure to follow this instruction may result in damage to the accelerator pedal or accelerator pedal bracket.

TESTING

See Figure 104.

1. Access the PCM and monitor the APP1, APP2 and APP3 PIDs.

2. Press the accelerator pedal fully to the floor and release.

3. Record APP1, APP2 and APP3 voltages with the accelerator pedal fully applied and fully released.

4. With accelerator pedal fully applied voltage values should read (APP1) 0.48—1.76v, (APP2) 2.95—4.62v, (APP3) 2.43—4.02v.

5. With accelerator pedal released

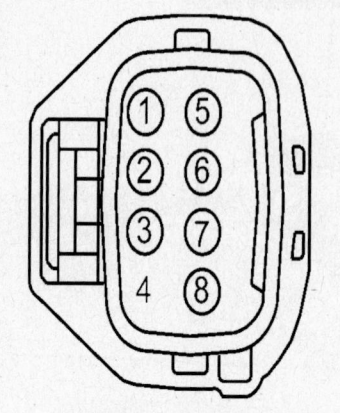

1. Accelerator Pedal Position 2 (APP2RTN)
2. Accelerator Pedal Position 1 (APP1)
3. Accelerator Pedal Position 1 (APP1 RTN)
4. Not used
5. Accelerator Pedal Position 2 (APP2)
6. Accelerator Pedal Position 2 (APP2VREF)
7. Accelerator Pedal Position 1 (APP1VREF)
8. Accelerator Pedal Position 3 (APP3)

22086_HYBR_G0082

Fig. 104 APP sensor—Escape/Mariner hybrid

Voltage values should read (APP1) 3.43—4.69v, (APP2), 1.13—1.18v, (APP3) 0.64—1.28v. If all 3 (APP) signals are out of range check the voltage to (APP) sensor.

6. Turn the ignition to off position and disconnect (APP) sensor harness connector. With the ignition on and the engine off measure the voltage between ETCREF1 Pin-7 and ETCRTN Pin-3 on the harness side. If measurement reads 4.5—5.5v The circuit is good.

CAMSHAFT POSITION (CMP) SENSOR

LOCATION

See Figure 105.

The Camshaft Position (CMP) sensor is located on top the valve cover towards the front.

OPERATION

The CMP sensor detects the position of the camshaft. The CMP sensor identifies when piston number 1 is on its compression stroke. A signal is then sent to the PCM and used for synchronizing the sequential firing of the fuel injectors. Coil-on-plug (COP) ignition applications use the CMP signal to select the correct ignition coil to fire. Vehicles with 2 CMP sensors are equipped with variable camshaft timing (VCT). They use the second sensor to identify the position of the

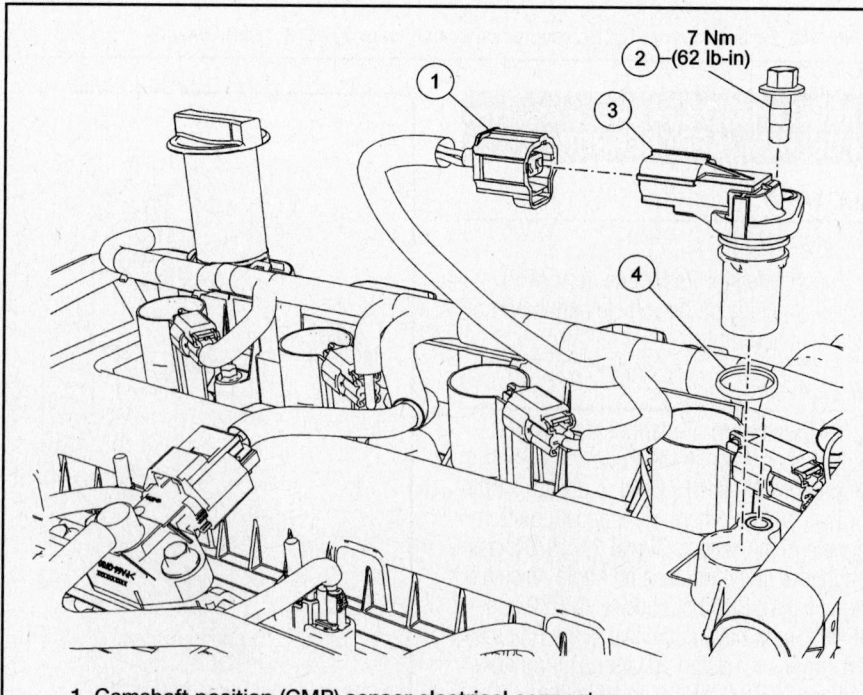

1. Camshaft position (CMP) sensor electrical connector
2. CMP sensor bolt
3. CMP sensor
4. CMP sensor O-ring

22086_HYBR_G0059

Fig. 105 Camshaft position sensor location—2.3L hybrid engine

camshaft on bank 2 as an input to the PCM.

REMOVAL & INSTALLATION

1. Disconnect the Camshaft Position (CMP) sensor electrical connector.
2. Remove the bolt and the CMP sensor.

➡**Lubricate the camshaft position (CMP) sensor O-ring seal with clean engine oil.**

3. To install, reverse the removal procedure.
4. Tighten the mounting bolt to 62 inch lbs. (7 Nm)

TESTING

See Figure 106.

1. Turn the ignition to the **OFF** position.
2. Disconnect the Camshaft Position Sensor (CMP) electrical connector.
3. Using a digital multimeter measure the resistance between the CMP + and CMP − at component side of the connector.
4. The resistance should fall between 250—1000 ohms.
5. If resistance is not within specification the CMP sensor may be faulty.

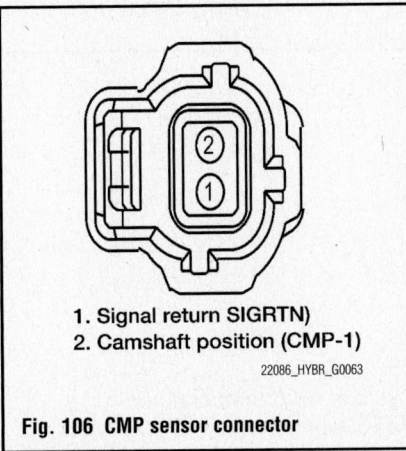

1. Signal return SIGRTN)
2. Camshaft position (CMP-1)

22086_HYBR_G0063

Fig. 106 CMP sensor connector

CRANKSHAFT POSITION (CKP) SENSOR

LOCATION

See Figure 107.

The Crankshaft Position (CKP) sensor is located to the left of the crankshaft pulley.

OPERATION

The CKP sensor is a magnetic transducer mounted on the engine block adjacent to a pulse wheel located on the crankshaft. By monitoring the crankshaft mounted pulse wheel, the CKP is the primary sensor for

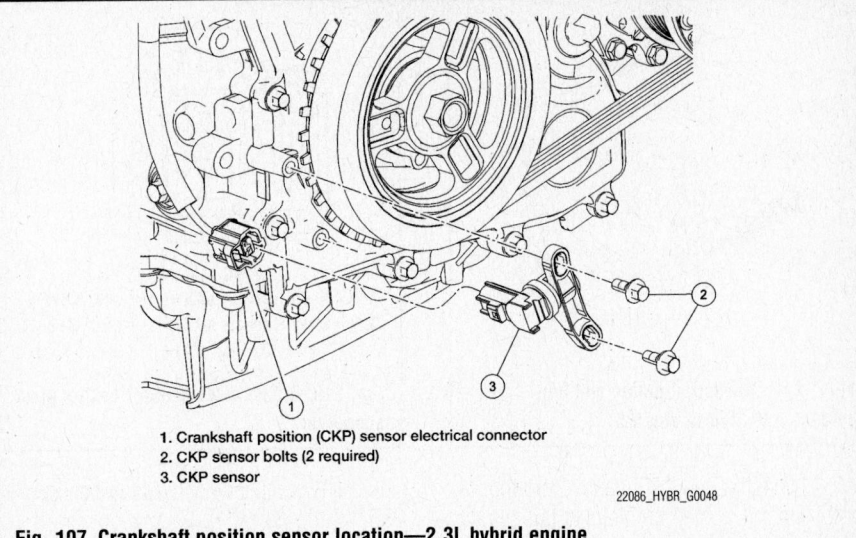

1. Crankshaft position (CKP) sensor electrical connector
2. CKP sensor bolts (2 required)
3. CKP sensor

22086_HYBR_G0048

Fig. 107 Crankshaft position sensor location—2.3L hybrid engine

ignition information to the PCM. The pulse wheel has a total of 35 teeth spaced 10 degrees apart with one empty space for a missing tooth. By monitoring the pulse wheel, the CKP sensor signal indicates crankshaft position and speed information to the PCM. By monitoring the missing tooth, the CKP sensor is also able to identify piston travel in order to synchronize the ignition system and provide a way of tracking the angular position of the crankshaft relative to a fixed reference for the CKP sensor configuration. The PCM also uses the CKP signal to determine if a misfire has occurred by measuring rapid decelerations between teeth.

REMOVAL & INSTALLATION

See Figures 108 through 112.

1. Raise and safely support the vehicle.
2. Remove the 5 bolts and the RH splash shield.
3. Remove the engine plug bolt.
4. Turn the crankshaft pulley bolt to position the number one cylinder at top dead center and install the special tool.
5. Disconnect the Crankshaft Position (CKP) sensor electrical connector.
6. Remove the bolts and the CKP sensor.

To install:

7. Install a 0.23 × 0.7 inch (6mm × 18mm) standard bolt in the crankshaft pulley.

❊❊ WARNING

Only hand-tighten the bolt or damage to the front cover can occur.

➡**Whenever the CKP sensor is removed, a new one must be installed using the alignment tool supplied with the new part.**

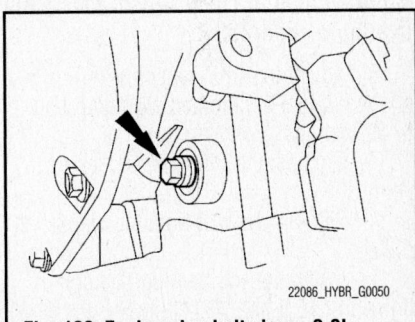

22086_HYBR_G0050

Fig. 108 Engine plug bolt view—2.3L hybrid engine

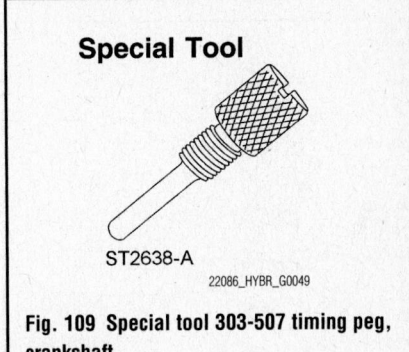

Special Tool

ST2638-A

22086_HYBR_G0049

Fig. 109 Special tool 303-507 timing peg, crankshaft

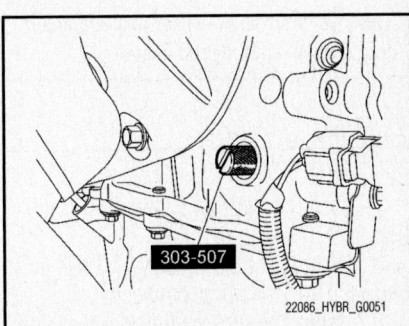

303-507

22086_HYBR_G0051

Fig. 110 Special tool 303-507 installation view

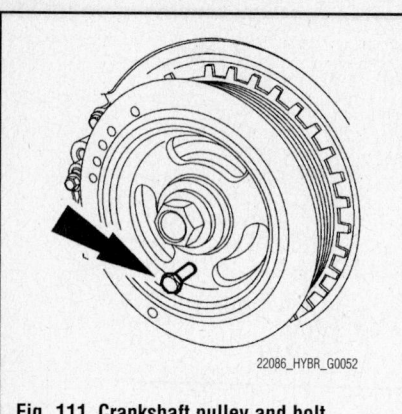

Fig. 111 Crankshaft pulley and bolt view—2.3L hybrid engine

8. Install a new CKP sensor and the bolts. Do not tighten the bolts at this time.

➡**The CKP sensor alignment tool is supplied with the new sensor and is not available separately.**

9. Adjust the CKP sensor with the alignment tool and tighten mounting bolts to 62 inch lbs. (7 Nm).

10. Connect the CKP sensor electrical connector.

11. Remove the bolt from the crankshaft pulley.

12. Install the engine plug bolt and tighten to 15 ft. lbs. (20 Nm).

13. Install the RH splash shield and tighten the bolts to 80 inch lbs. (9 Nm).

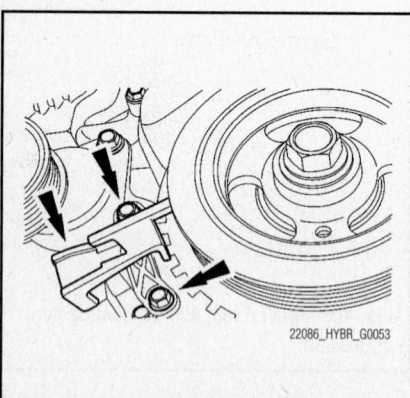

Fig. 112 Crankshaft sensor and alignment tool shown—2.3L hybrid engine

TESTING

See Figure 113.

1. Turn the ignition to the **OFF** position.

2. Disconnect the Crankshaft Position Sensor (CKP) electrical connector.

3. Using a digital multimeter measure the resistance between the CKP + and CKP − at component side of the connector.

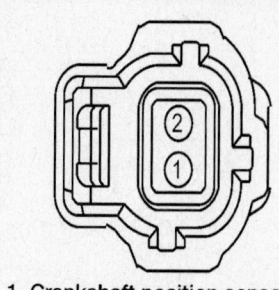

1. Crankshaft position sensor (CKP)
2. Crankshaft position sensor (CKPN)

Fig. 113 Crankshaft Position (CKP) sensor connector

4. The resistance should fall between 250—1000 ohms.

5. If resistance is not within specification the CKP sensor may be faulty.

CYLINDER HEAD TEMPERATURE (CHT) SENSOR

LOCATION

See Figure 114.

The Cylinder Head Temperature (CHT) sensor is located between the two center ignition coils.

OPERATION

The Cylinder Head Temperature (CHT) sensor is a thermistor device in which the resistance changes with temperature. The electrical resistance of a thermistor decreases as the temperature increases, and the resistance increases as the temperature decreases. The varying resistance affects the voltage drop across the sensor terminals and provides electrical signals to the PCM corresponding to temperature. Thermistor type sensors are considered passive sensors. A passive sensor is connected to a voltage divider network so that varying the resistance of the passive sensor causes a variation in total current flow.

The CHT sensor is installed in the aluminum cylinder head and measures the metal temperature. The CHT sensor can provide complete engine temperature information and can be used to infer coolant temperature. If the CHT sensor conveys an overheating condition to the PCM, the PCM then initiates a fail-safe cooling strategy based on information from the CHT sensor. A cooling system failure such as low coolant or coolant loss could cause an overheating condition. As a result, damage to major engine components could occur. Using both the CHT sensor and fail-safe cooling strategy, the PCM prevents

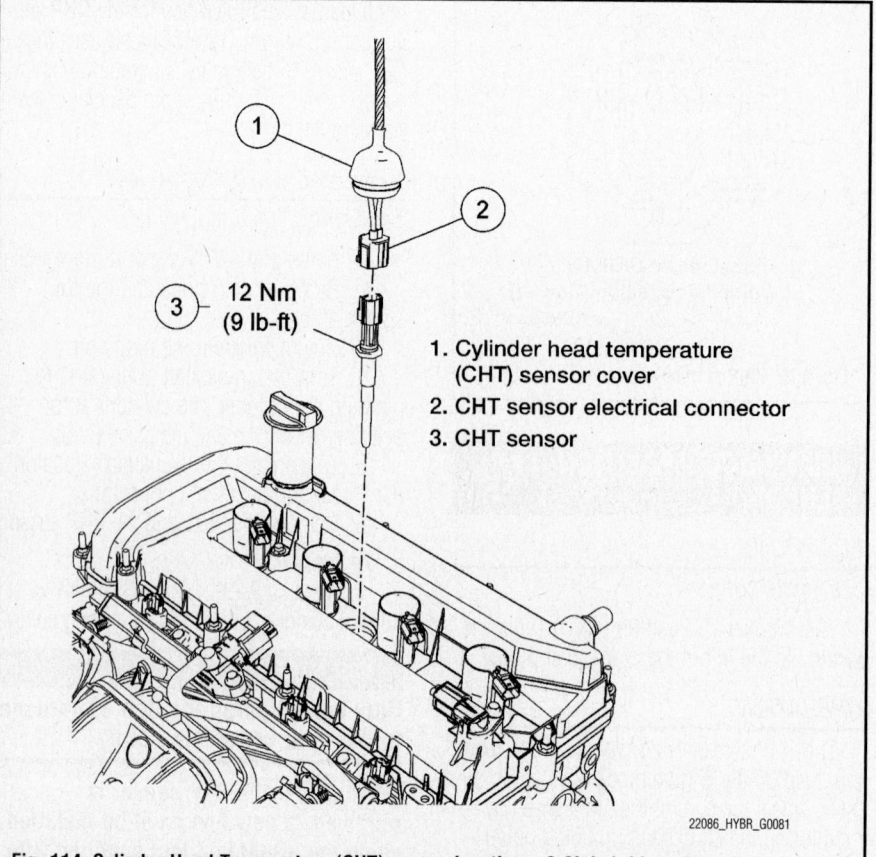

1. Cylinder head temperature (CHT) sensor cover
2. CHT sensor electrical connector
3. CHT sensor

Fig. 114 Cylinder Head Temperature (CHT) sensor location—2.3L hybrid engine

damage by allowing air cooling of the engine and limp home capability.

The MECT sensor is a thermistor device in which resistance changes with temperature. The electrical resistance of a thermistor decreases as the temperature increases, and the resistance increases as the temperature decreases. The varying resistance affects the voltage drop across the sensor terminals and provides electrical signals to the PCM corresponding to temperature. A thermistor type sensor is considered a passive sensor. A passive sensor is connected to a voltage divider network so that varying the resistance of the passive sensor causes a variation in total current flow. Voltage that is dropped across a fixed resistor in a series with the sensor resistor determines the voltage signal at the PCM. This voltage signal is equal to the reference voltage minus the voltage drop across the fixed resistor. The MECT provides motor electronics coolant system temperature information to the PCM. The PCM uses this information for determining when to activate the cooling system fans and indicate over-temperature.

REMOVAL & INSTALLATION

1. Detach the Cylinder Head Temperature (CHT) sensor cover and position aside.
2. Disconnect the CHT sensor electrical connector.
3. Remove and discard the CHT sensor.
4. To install, reverse the removal procedure and tighten the CHT sensor to 9 ft. lbs. (12 Nm).

TESTING

See Figures 115 and 116.

On applications that do not use an Engine Coolant Temperature (ECT) sensor, the Cylinder Head Temperature (CHT) sensor is used to determine the engine coolant temperature. To cover the entire temperature range of both the CHT and ECT sensors, the PCM has a dual switching resistor circuit on the CHT input. A graph showing the temperature switching from the COLD END line to the HOT END line, with increasing temperature and back with decreasing temperature is included. Note the temperature to voltage overlap zone. Within this zone it is possible to have either a COLD END or HOT END voltage at the same temperature. For example, at 90°C (194°F) the voltage could read either 0.60 volt or 3.71 volts. Refer to the table for the temperature to voltage expected values.

1. Turn the ignition switch to the **OFF** position.
2. Disconnect the CHT sensor electrical connector.

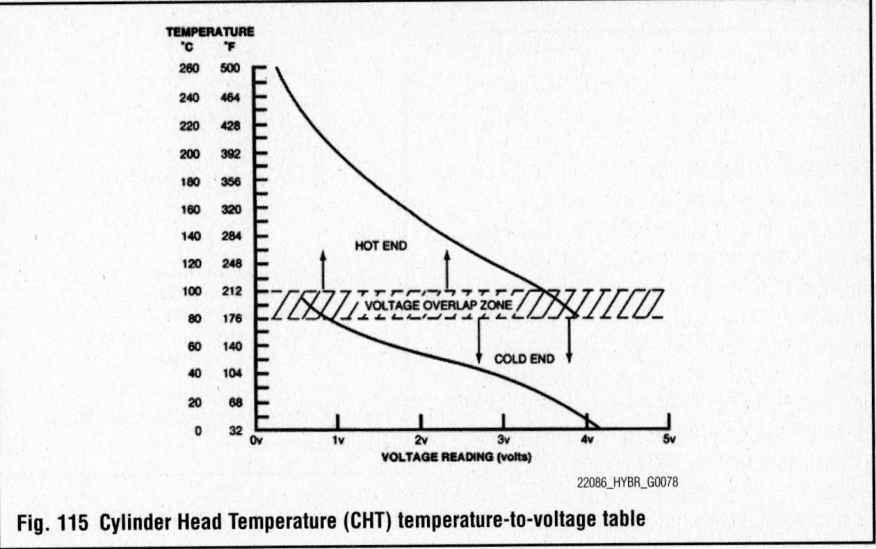

Fig. 115 Cylinder Head Temperature (CHT) temperature-to-voltage table

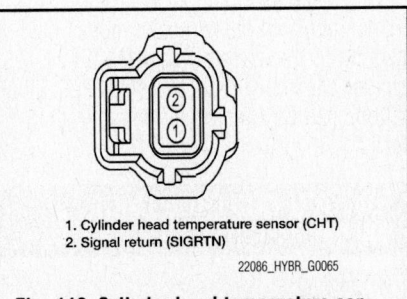

1. Cylinder head temperature sensor (CHT)
2. Signal return (SIGRTN)

22086_HYBR_G0065

Fig. 116 Cylinder head temperature sensor connector—2.3L hybrid engine

3. Measure the resistance between CHT + pin 1 and CHT − pin 2 on sensor side of connector.
4. If resistance is not within specification replace sensor.

HEATED OXYGEN (HO2S) SENSOR

LOCATION

See Figure 117.

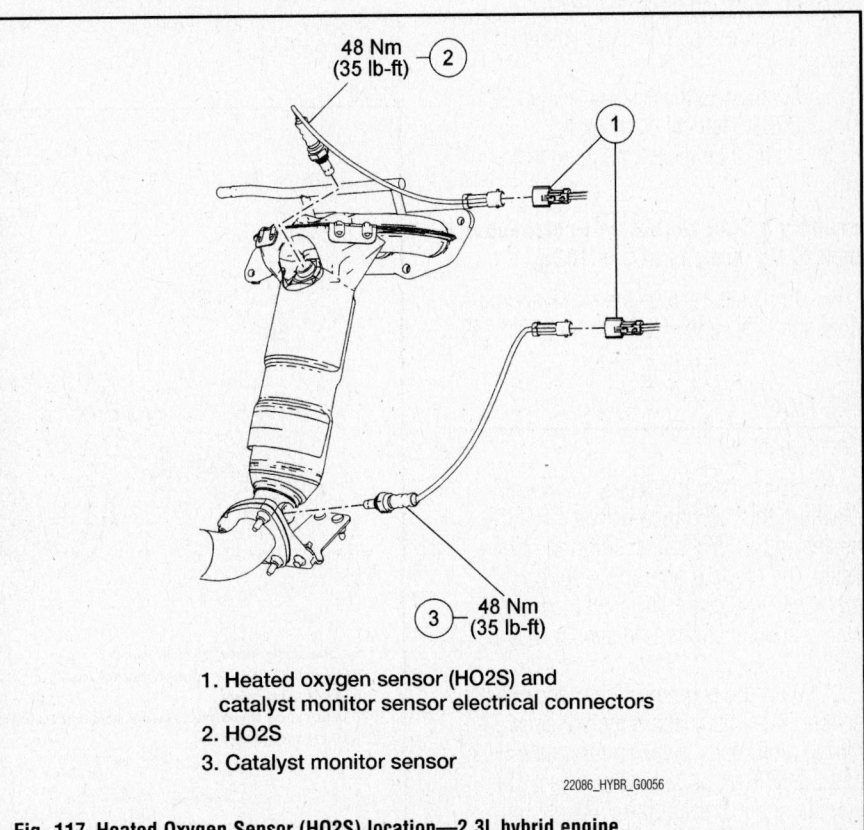

1. Heated oxygen sensor (HO2S) and catalyst monitor sensor electrical connectors
2. HO2S
3. Catalyst monitor sensor

22086_HYBR_G0056

Fig. 117 Heated Oxygen Sensor (HO2S) location—2.3L hybrid engine

OPERATION

The Heated Oxygen Sensor (HO2S) detects the presence of oxygen in the exhaust and produces a variable voltage according to the amount of oxygen detected. A high concentration of oxygen (lean air/fuel ratio) in the exhaust produces a voltage signal less than 0.4 volt. A low concentration of oxygen (rich air/fuel ratio) produces a voltage signal greater than 0.6 volt. The HO2S provides feedback to the PCM indicating air/fuel ratio in order to achieve a near stoichiometric air/fuel ratio of 14.7:1 during closed loop engine operation. The HO2S generates a voltage between 0.0 and 1.1 volts.

Embedded with the sensing element is the HO2S heater. The heating element heats the sensor to a temperature of 800°C (1,472°F). At approximately 300°C (572°F) the engine can enter closed loop operation. The VPWR circuit supplies voltage to the heater. The PCM turns the heater on by providing the ground when the correct conditions occur. The heater allows the engine to enter closed loop operation sooner. The use of this heater requires the HO2S heater control to be duty cycled, to prevent damage to the heater.

REMOVAL & INSTALLATION

1. Raise and safely support the vehicle.
2. Disconnect the Heated Oxygen Sensor (HO2S) electrical connector.
3. Using a suitable tool, remove the HO2S.

➡ **Apply a light coat of anti-seize lubricant to the threads of the HO2S.**

4. To install, reverse the removal procedure and tighten the HO2S to 35 ft. lbs. (48 Nm).

TESTING

See Figure 118.

1. Disconnect the HO2S connector. Measure the resistance between HO2S heater and VPWR on sensor side of harness. The reading should be approximately 3—30 ohms. If resistance is not within specifications, the sensor may be faulty.
2. With the engine running and HO2S sensor in place measure the voltage with digital multimeter between terminals HO2S and SIGRTN at the sensor harness. The voltage should read approximately 0.01—1.0V. If the reading is off or the voltage

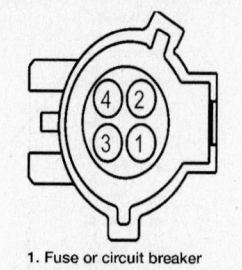

1. Fuse or circuit breaker
2. Heater oxygen sensor (HTR21)
3. Signal return (SIGRTN)
4. Heated oxygen pre-cat (HO2S21)

22086_HYBR_G0077

Fig. 118 Heated Oxygen Sensor (HO2S) connector

fluctuation is very slow suspect a faulty sensor.

3. Check for unmetered air leaks at intake manifold gasket leaks, hoses connecting to the mass air flow (MAF) sensor assembly, PCV system. Fuel calculations can be affected by unmetered air leaks.

IDLE AIR CONTROL (IAC) VALVE

LOCATION

See Figure 119.

The Idle Air Control (IAC) valve is located just behind the throttle body on the intake manifold.

OPERATION

The Idle Air Control (IAC) valve assembly controls the engine idle speed and provides a dashpot function. The IAC valve assembly meters intake air around the throttle plate through a bypass within the IAC valve assembly and throttle body. The PCM determines the desired idle speed or bypass air and signals the IAC valve assembly through a specified duty cycle. The IAC valve responds by positioning the IAC valve to control the amount of bypassed air. The PCM monitors engine RPM and increases or decreases the IAC duty cycle in order to achieve the desired RPM.

➡ **The IAC valve assembly is not adjustable and cannot be cleaned, also some IAC valves are normally open and others are normally closed. Some IAC valves require engine vacuum to operate.**

REMOVAL & INSTALLATION

1. Remove the 3 screws, the pin-type retainer and the upper and lower snow shield.
2. Disconnect the Idle Air Control (IAC) valve electrical connector.
3. Remove the 2 bolts and the IAC valve.

To install:

➡ **Inspect the gasket and install a new gasket as necessary.**

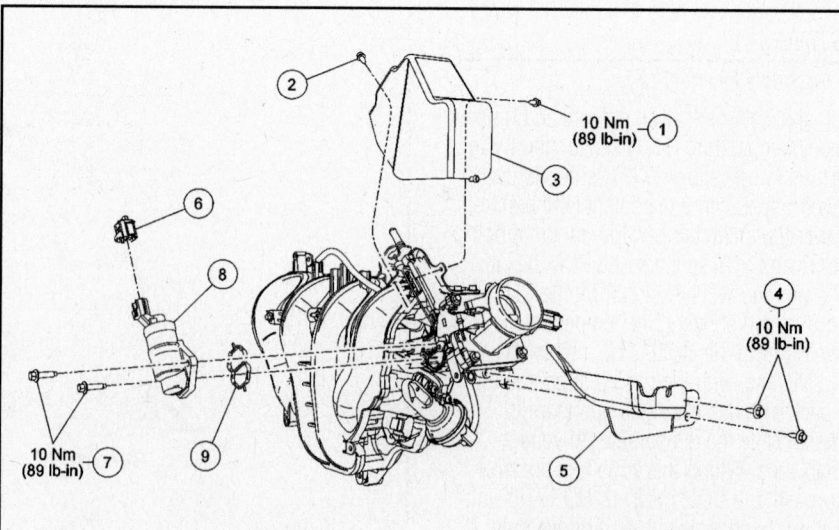

1. Upper snow shield-to-intake manifold screw
2. Upper snow shield-to-intake manifold pin-type retainer
3. Upper snow shield
4. Lower snow shield-to-intake manifold screws (2 required)
5. Lower snow shield
6. Idle air control (IAC) valve electrical connector
7. IAC valve bolts (2 required)
8. IAC valve
9. IAC valve gasket

22086_HYBR_G0076

Fig. 119 Idle Air Control (IAC) valve location—2.3L hybrid engine

4. To install, reverse the removal procedure and tighten the IAC valve mounting bolts to 89 inch lbs. (10 Nm).

TESTING

See Figure 120.

1. To check for voltage to the Idle Air Control (IAC) valve. Disconnect the IAC valve electrical connector. With the key on and engine off measure the voltage between the IAC harness PWR and battery ground. The voltage reading should be greater than 10V.

2. Check the resistance of the IAC valve. With the key in the off position disconnect the IAC valve harness connector. Measure the resistance PWR and IAC (GRD) at the sensor. If the reading is not within specification 6—15 ohms suspect a faulty IAC valve.

3. With the engine running at idle (if possible), listen for vacuum leaks. Inspect the entire intake air system from the Mass Air Flow (MAF) sensor to the intake manifold for leaks.

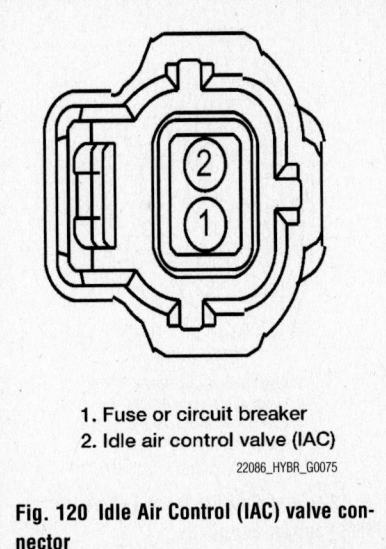

1. Fuse or circuit breaker
2. Idle air control valve (IAC)

22086_HYBR_G0075

Fig. 120 Idle Air Control (IAC) valve connector

FUEL RAIL PRESSURE TEMPERATURE (FRPT) SENSOR

LOCATION

See Figure 121.

OPERATION

The Fuel Rail Pressure Temperature (FRPT) sensor measures the pressure and temperature of the fuel in the fuel rail and sends these signals to the PCM. The sensor uses the intake manifold vacuum as a reference to determine the pressure difference between the fuel rail and the intake manifold. The relationship between fuel pressure and fuel temperature is used to determine the possible presence of fuel vapor in the fuel rail

The temperature sensing portion of the FRPT sensor is a thermistor device in which resistance changes with temperature. The electrical resistance of the thermistor decreases as the temperature increases, and the resistance increases as the temperature decreases. The varying resistance changes the voltage drop across the sensor terminals and provides electrical signals to the PCM corresponding to temperature.

Both the pressure and temperature signals are used to control the speed of the fuel pump. The speed of the fuel pump sustains fuel rail pressure which preserves fuel in its

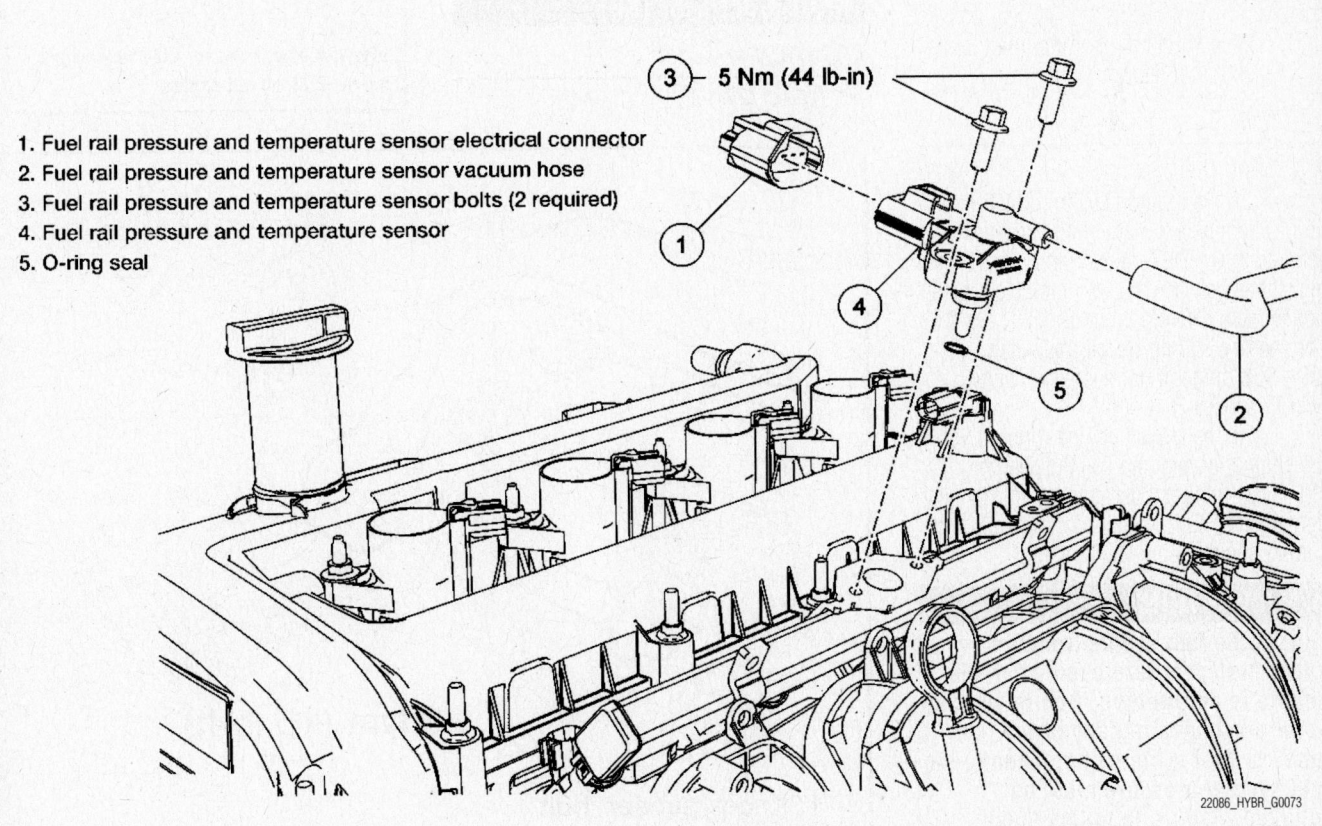

1. Fuel rail pressure and temperature sensor electrical connector
2. Fuel rail pressure and temperature sensor vacuum hose
3. Fuel rail pressure and temperature sensor bolts (2 required)
4. Fuel rail pressure and temperature sensor
5. O-ring seal

3 — 5 Nm (44 lb-in)

22086_HYBR_G0073

Fig. 121 Fuel Rail Pressure Temperature (FRPT) sensor location—2.3L hybrid engine

liquid state. The dynamic range of the fuel injectors increase because of the higher rail pressure, which allows the injector pulse width to decrease.

REMOVAL & INSTALLATION

※※ CAUTION

Do not smoke or carry lighted tobacco or open flame of any type when working on or near any fuel-related components. Highly flammable mixtures are always present and may be ignited. Failure to follow these instructions may result in personal injury.

1. Release the fuel system pressure.
2. Disconnect the battery ground cable.
3. Disconnect the Fuel Rail Pressure Temperature (FRPT) sensor electrical connector and vacuum tube.
4. Remove the 2 bolts and the fuel rail pressure and temperature sensor.

➡**Lubricate the FRPT sensor O-ring seal with clean engine oil.**

5. To install, reverse the removal procedure.
6. Tighten FRPT sensor mounting bolts to 44 inch lbs. (5 Nm).

TESTING

See Figure 122.

1. Turn the ignition key to the **OFF** position. Disconnect the Fuel Rail Pressure Temperature (FRPT) sensor and measure the resistance between sensor connector component side FRT pin 3 and SIGRTN pin 4. The reading should be approximately 2K—96K ohms. If not suspect a faulty (FRPT) sensor.
2. With the key on engine running, idle the engine for two minutes. Inspect the FRPT vacuum hose between the intake manifold and the FRPT sensor for air leaks and correct connection.

※※ CAUTION

Fuel in the fuel system remains under high pressure even when the engine is not running. Before working on or disconnecting any of the fuel tubes or fuel system components, the fuel system pressure must be relieved. Failure to follow these instructions may result in personal injury.

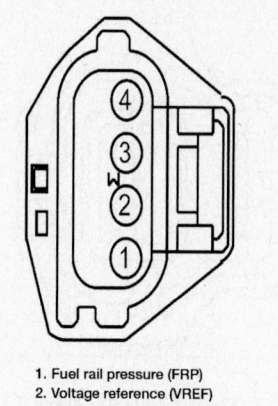

1. Fuel rail pressure (FRP)
2. Voltage reference (VREF)
3. Fuel rail temperature (FRT)
4. Signal return (SIGRTN)

22086_HYBR_G0074

Fig. 122 Fuel Rail Pressure Temperature (FRPT) sensor connector

INTAKE AIR TEMPERATURE (IAT) SENSOR

OPERATION

The Intake Air Temperature (IAT) sensor is part of the Mass Air Flow (MAF) sensor.

KNOCK SENSOR (KS)

LOCATION

See Figure 123.

The Knock Sensor (KS) is located behind the intake manifold to the rear of engine block.

OPERATION

The Knock Sensor (KS) is a tuned accelerometer on the engine which converts engine vibration to an electrical signal. The PCM uses this signal to determine the presence of engine knock and to retard spark timing.

REMOVAL & INSTALLATION

See Figure 124.

1. Raise and safely support the vehicle.
2. Remove the intake manifold.
3. Remove the bolt and the Knock Sensor (KS).

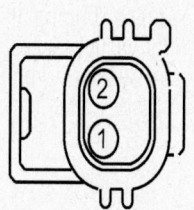

1. Knock sensor KS-1
2. Knock sensor KS+2

22086_HYBR_G0072

Fig. 124 Knock Sensor (KS) connector view—2.3L hybrid engine

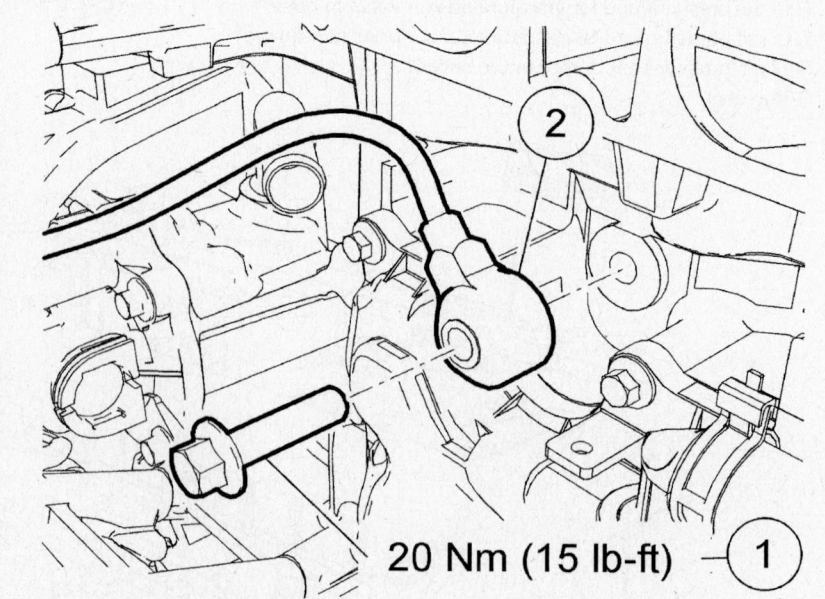

20 Nm (15 lb-ft)

1. **Knock sensor bolt**
2. **Knock sensor**

22086_HYBR_G0057

Fig. 123 Knock Sensor (KS) location—2.3L hybrid engine

4. To install, reverse the removal procedure and tighten mounting bolt to 15ft. lbs. (20 Nm).

TESTING

→**Appropriate repair methods and procedures are essential for the safe, reliable operation of all motor vehicles, as well as the personal safety of the individual doing the work. This manual provides general directions for repairing vehicles with tested, effective techniques. Following them helps to establish reliability. There are numerous variations in procedures, techniques, tools, and parts for repairing vehicles, as well as in the skill of the individual doing the work. This manual cannot possibly anticipate all such variations and provide advice or cautions as to each. Accordingly, anyone who departs from the instructions provided in this manual must first establish that they compromise neither their personal safety nor the vehicle integrity by their choice of methods, tools, or parts.**

1. Disconnect the Knock Sensor (KS) harness connector and measure the resistance between KS + and KS − on the component side. The resistance should read between 4.39M—5.35M ohms. If resistance reading is not within specifications suspect a faulty knock sensor.

MASS AIR FLOW (MAF) SENSOR

LOCATION

See Figure 125.

The Mass Air Flow (MAF) sensor is located in air filter housing lid.

OPERATION

The Mass Air Flow (MAF) sensor uses a hot wire sensing element to measure the amount of air entering the engine. Air passing over the hot wire causes it to cool. This hot wire is maintained at 200°C (392°F) above the ambient temperature as measured by a constant cold wire. The current required to maintain the temperature of the hot wire is proportional to the mass air flow. The MAF sensor then outputs an analog voltage signal to the PCM proportional to the intake air mass. The PCM calculates the required fuel injector pulse width in order to provide the desired air/fuel ratio. This input is also used in determining transmission Electronic Pressure Control (EPC), shift and torque converter clutch scheduling.

The MAF sensor is located between the air cleaner and the throttle body or inside the air cleaner assembly. Most MAF sensors have integrated bypass technology with an integrated Intake Air Temperature (IAT) sensor. The hot wire electronic sensing element must be replaced as an assembly. Replacing only the element may change the air flow calibration.

REMOVAL & INSTALLATION

1. Disconnect the Mass Air Flow (MAF) sensor electrical connector.
2. Remove the 2 screws and the MAF sensor.

3. To install, reverse the removal procedure and tighten mounting screws to 89 inch lbs. (10 Nm).

TESTING

See Figure 126.

1. Using a multimeter, check for voltage by back probing the Mass Air Flow (MAF) sensor connector being careful not to cause connector damage. With the engine running verify that there is at least 10.5V between the VPWR and PWRGND terminals of the MAF sensor connector. If voltage is not within specifications check the power and ground circuits and repair as needed.

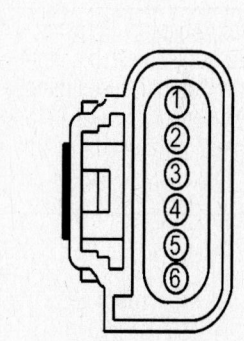

1. Intake air temperature (IAT)
2. Signal return (SIGRTN)
3. Mass air flow (MAF)
4. Power train mass air flow (MAFR TN)
5. Ground (GRND)
6. Fuse or circuit breaker

22086_HYBR_G0071

Fig. 126 MAF sensor connector

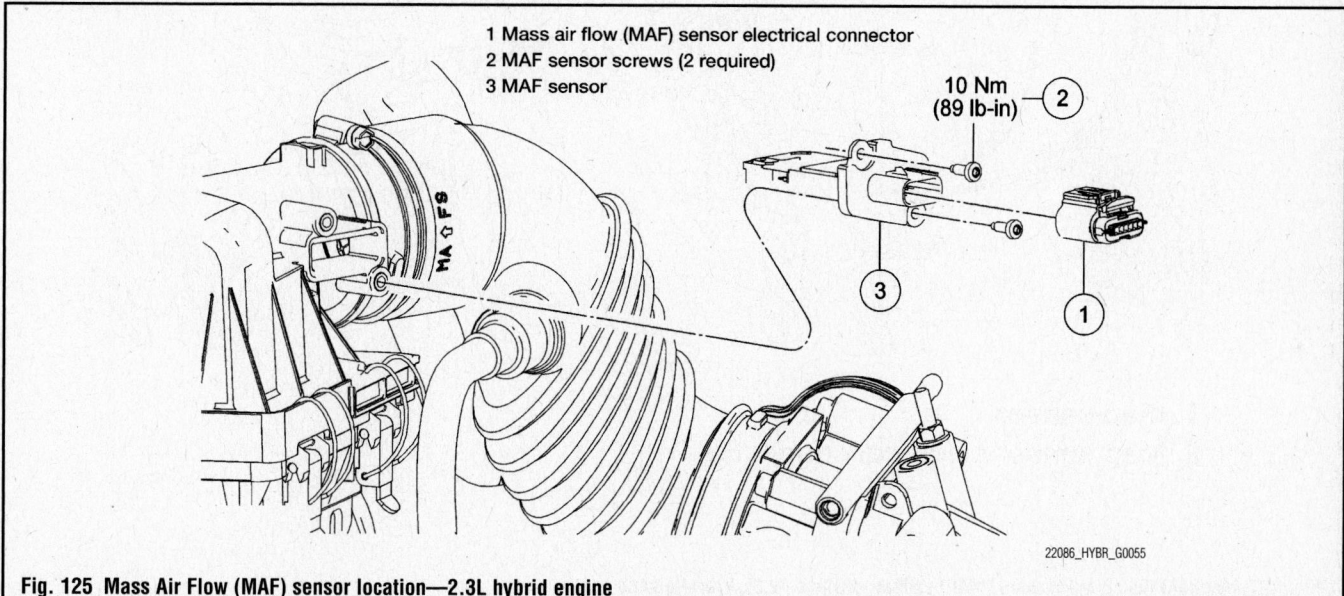

1 Mass air flow (MAF) sensor electrical connector
2 MAF sensor screws (2 required)
3 MAF sensor

10 Nm (89 lb-in)

22086_HYBR_G0055

Fig. 125 Mass Air Flow (MAF) sensor location—2.3L hybrid engine

➡A MAF PID value of less than 0.6 volt may indicate an incorrectly installed air cleaner or a leak in the air inlet system.

2. With the key **ON** and engine running, allow the engine to stabilize at correct operating temperature. Scan the MAF PID at idle in neutral and check that the reading is not greater than 1.3 volts. If so suspect a faulty MAF sensor.

MANIFOLD ABSOLUTE PRESSURE (MAP) SENSOR

LOCATION

See Figure 127.

OPERATION

1. The Manifold Absolute Pressure (MAP) sensor measures intake manifold absolute pressure. The PCM uses information from the MAP sensor to measure how much exhaust gas is introduced into the intake manifold. The MAP sensor may also be referred to as TMAP sensor.

REMOVAL & INSTALLATION

1. Disconnect the electrical connector from the Manifold Absolute Pressure (MAP) sensor.

2. Remove the mounting screws, then remove the MAP sensor.

3. To install, reverse the removal procedure.

TESTING

See Figure 128.

1. Check the voltage supply to the Manifold Absolute Pressure (MAP) sensor by measuring MAP sensor harness side VREF to SIGRTN The voltage reading should read 4.5—5.5 volts. If reading is not as specified check the VREF to battery ground. If the voltage reading is present 4.5—5.5 volts. Check for open in SIGRTN circuit.

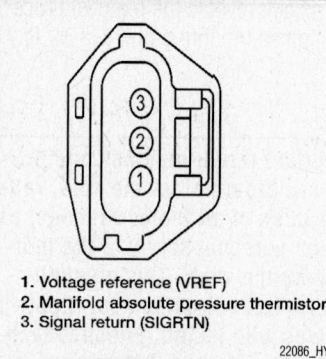

1. Voltage reference (VREF)
2. Manifold absolute pressure thermistor(TMAP)
3. Signal return (SIGRTN)

22086_HYBR_G0070

Fig. 128 MAP sensor connector

POWERTRAIN CONTROL MODULE (PCM)

LOCATION

See Figure 129.

For the Escape and Mariner hybrids, the Powertrain Control Module (PCM) is located behind the instrument panel (cowl),

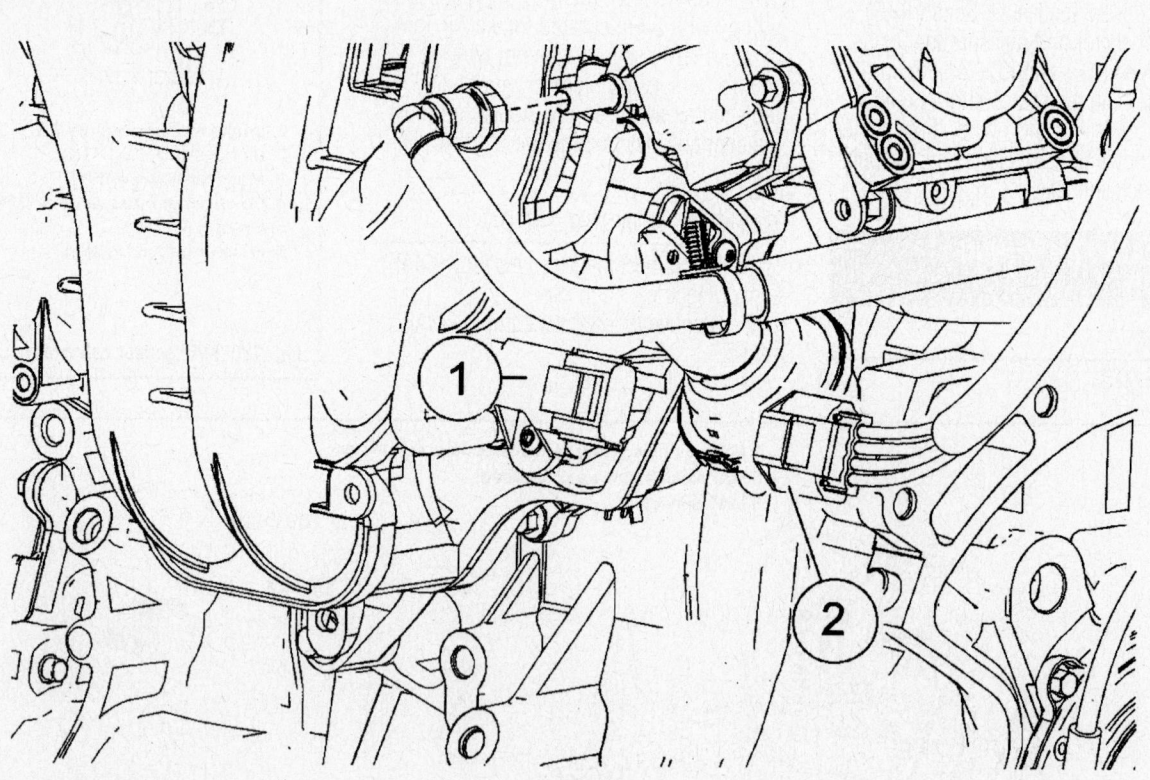

1. Map sensor
2. Map sensor electrical connector

22086_HYBR_G0061

Fig. 127 Manifold Absolute Pressure (MAP) sensor location—2.3L hybrid engine

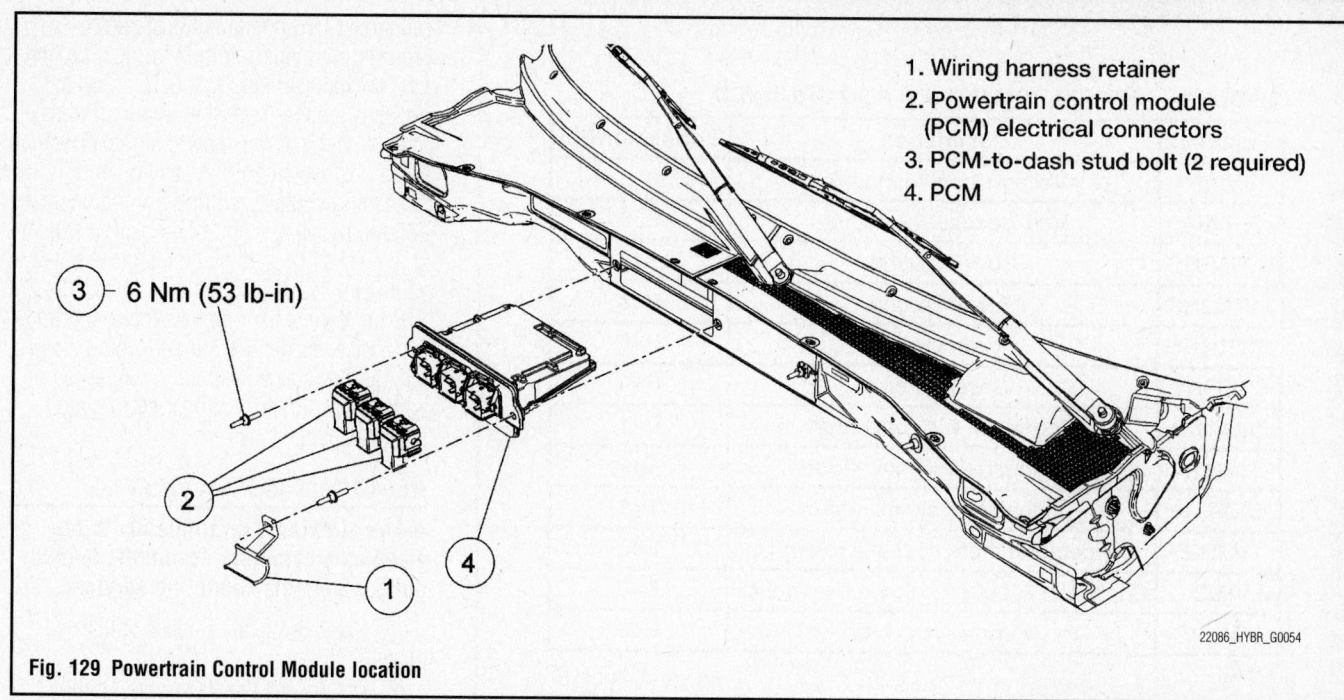

1. Wiring harness retainer
2. Powertrain control module (PCM) electrical connectors
3. PCM-to-dash stud bolt (2 required)
4. PCM

Fig. 129 Powertrain Control Module location

22086_HYBR_G0054

center to both driver and passenger sides (access from the engine compartment).

OPERATION

The center of the Electronic Engine Control (EEC) system is a microprocessor called the Powertrain Control Module (PCM). The PCM receives input from sensors and other electronic components (switches, relays). Based on the information received and programmed into its memory, the PCM generates output signals to control various relays, solenoids and actuators. There are several different types of PCMs in use for this model year. The Escape and Mariner use the 150-pin PCM.

REMOVAL & INSTALLATION

➡ **Any Powertrain Control Module (PCM) replacement will require that ALL customer keys are available to be programmed at the time of installation. PCM replacement DOES NOT require new keys.**

1. Retrieve the module configuration. Carry out the module configuration retrieval steps of the Programmable Module Installation procedure.
2. Disconnect the negative battery cable.
3. Remove the PCM stud bolt nut and position the wiring harness aside.
4. Disconnect the 3 PCM electrical connectors.
5. Remove the 2 stud bolts and the PCM
6. Remove the PCM cowl seal.

To install:
7. Install the PCM cowl seal.
8. Install the PCM and tighten the 2 stud bolts to 53 inch lbs. (6 Nm).
9. Connect the 3 PCM electrical connectors.
10. Position the wiring harness. Install and tighten the PCM stud bolt nut to 53 inch lbs. (6 Nm).
11. Restore the module configuration. Carry out the module configuration restore steps of the Programmable Module Installation procedure.

12. Reprogram the Passive Anti-Theft System (PATS). Carry out the Key Programming Using Two Programmed Keys procedure.

TESTING

See Figures 130 and 131.

1. Check the Power and grounds for the PCM. Check all the connector pins for corrosion or contact problems. Refer to PCM connectors, power and ground chart.

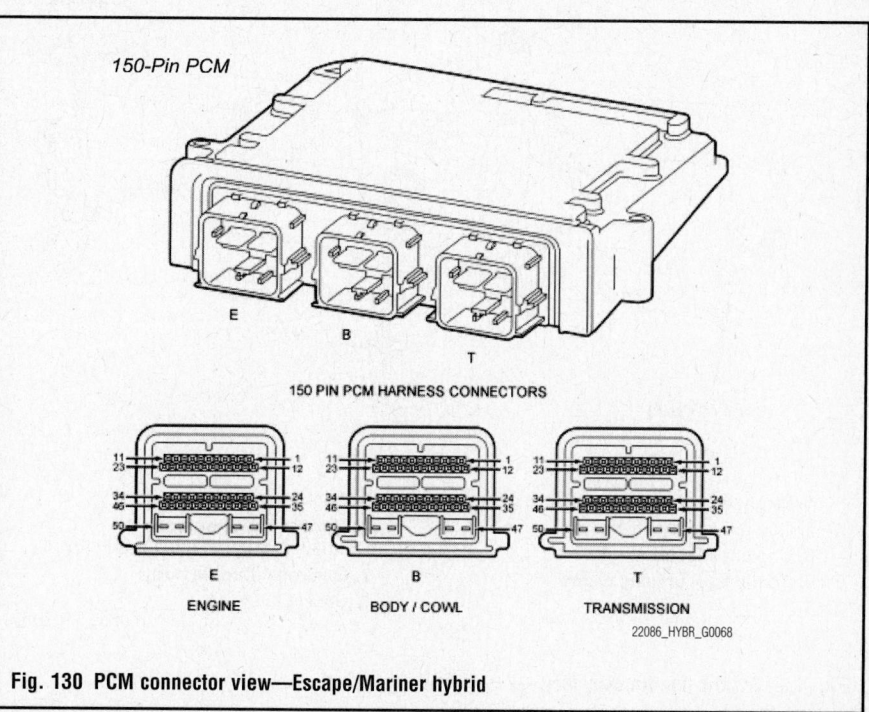

150-Pin PCM

150 PIN PCM HARNESS CONNECTORS

E — ENGINE
B — BODY / COWL
T — TRANSMISSION

22086_HYBR_G0068

Fig. 130 PCM connector view—Escape/Mariner hybrid

TABLE 1 — 150-PIN PCM POWER AND GROUNDS

Function	Description	Connector/Pin
VPWR	Voltage input to module	B35
VPWR	Voltage input to module	B36
PWRGND	Power ground	B47
PWRGND	Power ground	B48
PWRGND	Power ground	B49
CSEGND	Case ground	B10
SIGRTN	Connector B signal return	B41
SIGRTN	Connector T signal return	T41
SIGRTN	Connector E signal return	E41
VREF	Connector buffered 5.0-volt reference	B40
VREF	Connector E buffered 5.0-volt reference	E40
KAPWR	Keep alive power	B45

22086_HYBR_G0069

Fig. 131 PCM voltage and power pin location chart—Escape/Mariner hybrid

THROTTLE POSITION SENSOR (TPS)

LOCATION

See Figure 132.

The Throttle Position Sensor (TPS) is part of the Electric Throttle Body (ETB).

OPERATION

The ETB position sensor has 2 signal circuits in the sensor for redundancy. The redundant ETB position signals are required for increased monitoring. The first ETB position sensor signal (TP1) has a negative slope (increasing angle, decreasing voltage) and the second signal (TP2) has a positive slope (increasing angle, increasing voltage). During normal operation the negative slope ETB position sensor signal (TP1) is used by the control strategy as the indication of throttle position. The 2 ETB position sensor signals make sure the PCM receives a correct input even if a signal has a concern. There is 1 reference voltage circuit and 1 signal return circuit for the sensor.

REMOVAL & INSTALLATION

➡The electronic throttle body is serviced as a complete assembly. Individual components cannot be serviced.

1. Remove the air cleaner outlet pipe.
2. Disconnect the electronic throttle body coolant hoses.
3. Disconnect the electronic throttle body electrical connector.
4. Remove the 4 bolts and the electronic throttle body.
5. To install, reverse the removal procedure and note the following:
   a. Tighten the electronic throttle body bolts to 89 inch lbs. (10 Nm).
   b. Clean and inspect the electronic throttle body gasket and install new if necessary.

TESTING

See Figure 133.

The Throttle Position Sensor (TPS) is part of the Electric Throttle Body (ETB).

1. Check voltage reading at the TP sensor. Disconnect the Electronic Throttle Body

10 Nm (89 lb-in)

1. Electronic throttle body electrical connector
2. Coolant inlet hose clamp
3. Coolant inlet hose
4. Coolant outlet hose clamp
5. Coolant outlet hose
6. Throttle body-to-upper intake manifold bolt (4 required)
7. Electronic throttle body
8. Gasket

22086_HYBR_G0060

Fig. 132 Electric throttle body view—2.3L hybrid engine

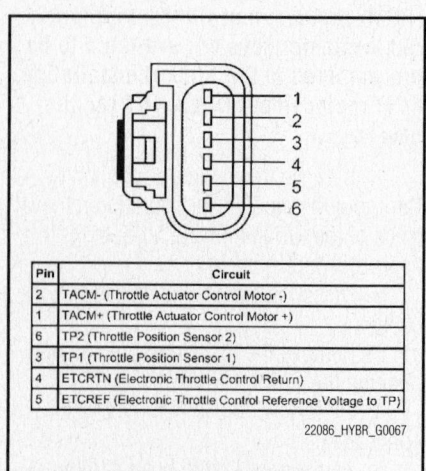

Pin	Circuit
2	TACM- (Throttle Actuator Control Motor -)
1	TACM+ (Throttle Actuator Control Motor +)
6	TP2 (Throttle Position Sensor 2)
3	TP1 (Throttle Position Sensor 1)
4	ETCRTN (Electronic Throttle Control Return)
5	ETCREF (Electronic Throttle Control Reference Voltage to TP)

22086_HYBR_G0067

Fig. 133 Electronic throttle body connector—Escape/Mariner hybrid

(ETB) connector. Measure the voltage between ETCREF pin 5 and ETCRTN pin 4 voltage should read between 4.5—5.5v. If so the circuit is okay.

2. With the key on and engine off access the PCM and monitor the TP1 and TP2 PIDs. Activate the engine cranking diagnostic mode, do not crank the engine. Apply the brake pedal and press the accelerator pedal to the floor and release. Check that the TP-1 voltage when pedal is fully applied should read between 0.7—2.9v and when released 3.7—4.7v. Check the TP-2 voltage when pedal is fully applied should read between 4.1—4.7v and when released 0.3—1.9v.

VEHICLE SPEED SENSOR (VSS)

LOCATION

See Figure 134.

➡ **This sensor may also be referred to as the Output Shaft Speed (OSS) sensor.**

OPERATION

The Vehicle Speed Sensor (VSS) is a variable reluctance or hall-effect sensor that generates a waveform with a frequency that is proportional to the speed of the vehicle. If the vehicle is moving at a relatively low velocity, the sensor produces a signal with a low frequency. As the vehicle velocity increases, the sensor generates a signal with a higher frequency. The PCM uses the frequency signal generated by the VSS (and other inputs) to control such parameters as fuel injection, ignition control, transmission/transaxle shift scheduling, and torque converter clutch scheduling.

This sensor may also be referred to as the Output Shaft Speed (OSS) sensor. The OSS sensor provides the PCM with information about the rotational speed of an output shaft. The PCM uses the information to control and diagnose powertrain behavior. In some applications, the sensor is also used as the source of vehicle speed. The sensor may be physically located in different places on the vehicle, depending upon the specific application. The design of each speed sensor is unique and depends on which powertrain control feature uses the information that is generated.

REMOVAL & INSTALLATION

1. Raise and safely support the vehicle.
2. Remove the 7 retainers and the LH splash shield.
3. Disconnect the Vehicle Speed Sensor (VSS)/Output Shaft Speed (OSS) electrical connector.

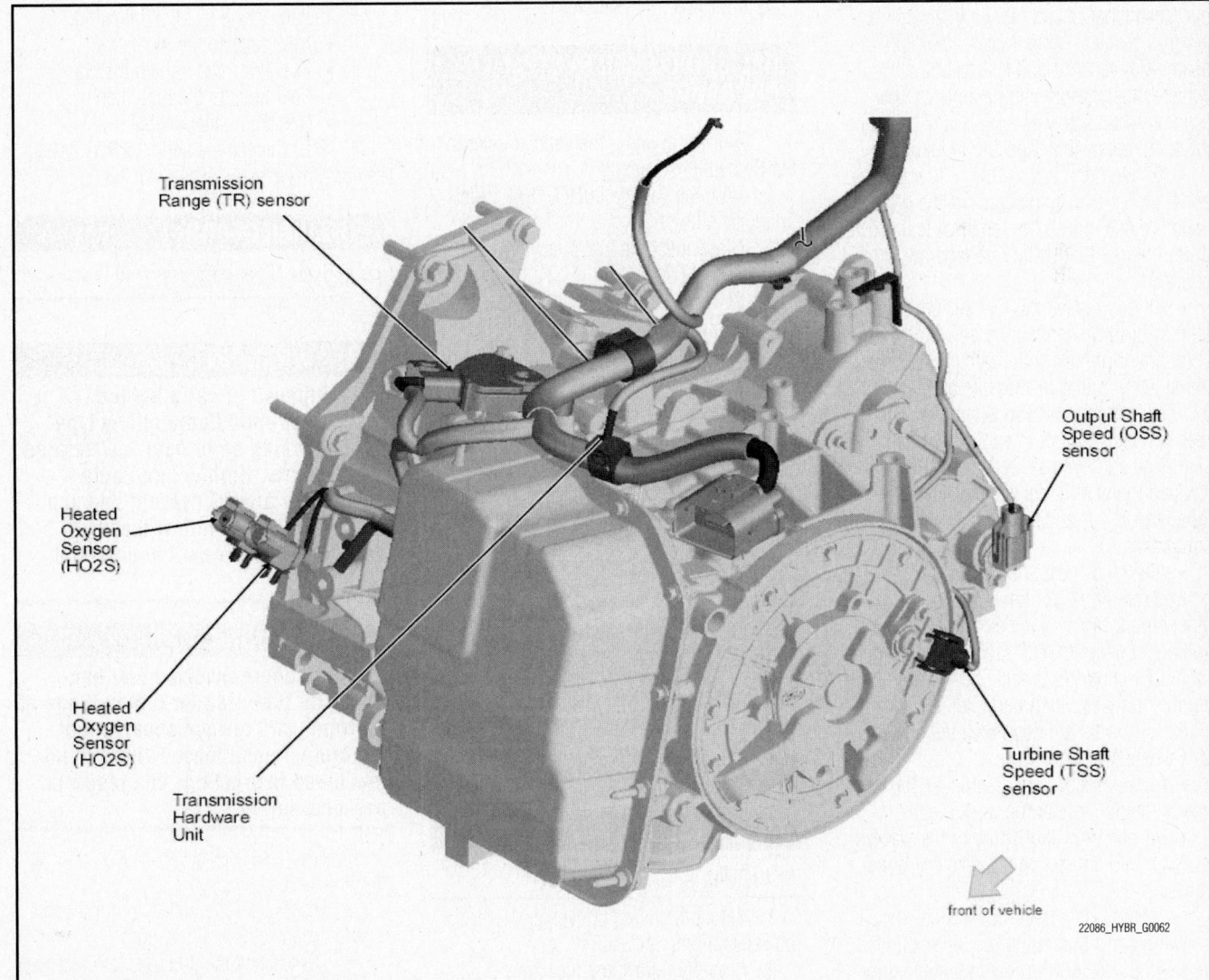

Fig. 134 VSS/OSS sensor and transaxle view

4. Remove the sensor bolt, then remove the sensor.

➡**When installing the sensor, lubricate the O-ring seal with clean transmission fluid.**

5. To install, reverse the removal procedure and note the following:

6. Tighten the sensor mounting bolt to 9 ft. lbs. (12 Nm).

TESTING

See Figure 135.

1. Check the voltage to the OSS/VSS sensor. Turn the ignition switch off disconnect the sensor connector. Turn the ignition on, with engine off measure the voltage between VPWR and battery ground. Voltage should read 10v or more if not repair power circuit.

2. Check the VPWR ground to the OSS/VSS sensor by measuring the resistance between PWRGND and battery ground. If the resistance is less than 5 ohms ground circuit should be okay.

3. Inspect the OSS/VSS vehicle harness connector for damage and proper seating.

4. If possible, carry out a wiggle test.

1. Signal return
2. Signal

22086_HYBR_G0066

Fig. 135 OSS/VSS sensor connector—Escape/Mariner hybrid

FUEL SYSTEMS

GASOLINE FUEL INJECTION SYSTEM

FUEL SYSTEM SERVICE PRECAUTIONS

Safety is the most important factor when performing not only fuel system maintenance but any type of maintenance. Failure to conduct maintenance and repairs in a safe manner may result in serious personal injury or death. Maintenance and testing of the vehicle's fuel system components can be accomplished safely and effectively by adhering to the following rules and guidelines.

• To avoid the possibility of fire and personal injury, always disconnect the negative battery cable unless the repair or test procedure requires that battery voltage be applied.

• Always relieve the fuel system pressure prior to disconnecting any fuel system component (injector, fuel rail, pressure regulator, etc.), fitting or fuel line connection. Exercise extreme caution whenever relieving fuel system pressure to avoid exposing skin, face and eyes to fuel spray. Please be advised that fuel under pressure may penetrate the skin or any part of the body that it contacts.

• Always place a shop towel or cloth around the fitting or connection prior to loosening to absorb any excess fuel due to spillage. Ensure that all fuel spillage (should it occur) is quickly removed from engine surfaces. Ensure that all fuel soaked cloths or towels are deposited into a suitable waste container.

• Always keep a dry chemical (Class B) fire extinguisher near the work area.

• Do not allow fuel spray or fuel vapors to come into contact with a spark or open flame.

• Always use a back-up wrench when loosening and tightening fuel line connection fittings. This will prevent unnecessary stress and torsion to fuel line piping.

• Always replace worn fuel fitting O-rings with new Do not substitute fuel hose or equivalent where fuel pipe is installed.

Before servicing the vehicle, make sure to also refer to the precautions in the beginning of this section as well.

RELIEVING FUEL SYSTEM PRESSURE

1. Before servicing the vehicle, refer to the Precautions Section.

2. With the vehicle in NEUTRAL, position it on a hoist.

3. Disconnect the fuel pump driver module electrical connector.

4. Start the engine and allow it to idle until it stalls.

5. After the engine stalls, crank the engine for approximately 5 seconds to make sure the fuel injection supply manifold pressure has been released.

6. Turn the ignition switch to the OFF position.

7. When fuel system service is complete, connect the fuel pump driver module electrical connector.

➡**It may take more than 1 key cycle to pressurize the fuel system.**

8. Cycle the ignition key and wait 3 seconds to pressurize the fuel system. Check for leaks before starting the engine.

9. Start the vehicle and check the fuel system for leaks.

FUEL FILTER

REMOVAL & INSTALLATION

1. Before servicing the vehicle, refer to the Precautions Section.

2. Properly relieve the fuel system pressure.

3. Remove or disconnect the following:
   • Negative battery cable
   • Fuel line to the fuel filter

4. Loosen the clamp and remove the filter

To install:

5. Install or connect the following:
   • New clips to the fuel lines
   • Fuel filter and tighten the clamp
   • Fuel lines to the fuel filter
   • Negative battery cable

6. Start the vehicle and check for leaks, repair if necessary.

FUEL INJECTORS

REMOVAL & INSTALLATION

See Figure 136.

✴✴ WARNING

Do not smoke or carry lighted tobacco or open flame of any type when working on or near fuel-related components. Highly flammable vapors are always present and can ignite. Failure to follow these instructions can result in personal injury.

✴✴ WARNING

This procedure involves fuel handling. Be prepared for fuel spillage at all times and always observe fuel handling precautions. Failure to follow these instructions can result in personal injury.

1. Before servicing the vehicle, refer to the Precautions Section.

2. Disconnect the battery ground cable.

3. Release the fuel pressure.

4. Disconnect the fuel injector electrical connectors.

5. Disconnect the fuel pressure regula-

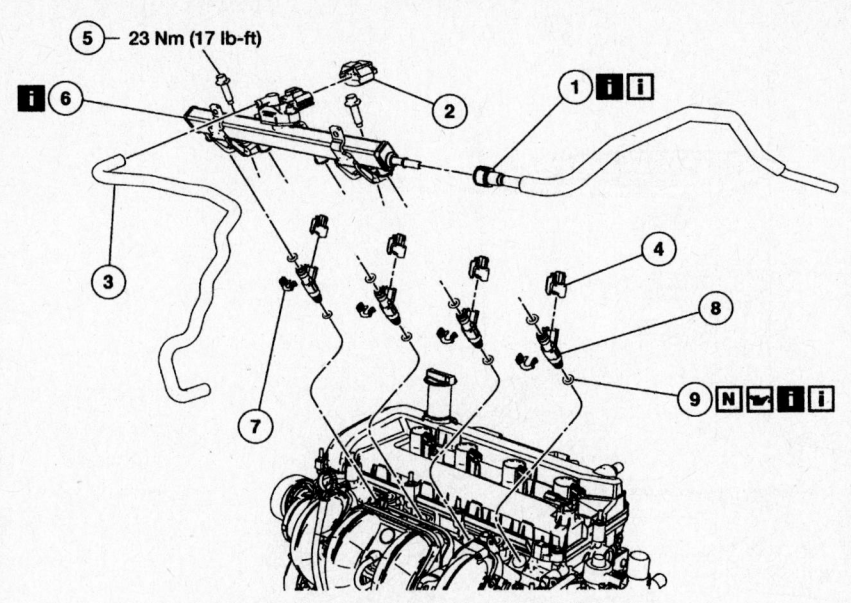

5 — 23 Nm (17 lb-ft)

1 Fuel tube quick release coupling (position aside)

2 Fuel rail pressure and temperature sensor electrical connector

3 Fuel rail pressure and temperature sensor vacuum tube (position aside)

4 Fuel injector electrical connectors

5 Fuel rail bolts

6 Fuel rail

7 Fuel injector clips

8 Fuel injectors

9 Fuel injector O-ring seals

67197-ESCA-G35

Fig. 136 Fuel rail and injectors—2.3L hybrid engine

tor electrical connector and the vacuum hose.

6. Disconnect the fuel injector harness retaining clips from the fuel injection supply manifold.

7. Disconnect the fuel tube.

8. Remove the bolts and the fuel injection supply manifold.

➡**Remove and discard the fuel injector O-rings.**

9. If necessary, remove the fuel injectors.

10. Install new O-rings and lubricate them with clean engine oil.

11. To install, reverse the removal procedure. Tighten the fuel supply manifold bolts to 18 ft. lbs. (25 Nm).

FUEL PUMP

REMOVAL & INSTALLATION

See Figure 137.

1. Before servicing the vehicle, refer to the Precautions Section.

2. With the vehicle in NEUTRAL, position it on a hoist.

3. Release the fuel system pressure.

4. Disconnect the battery ground cable.

5. If removing the fuel tank on a four wheel drive vehicle, it is necessary to lower the exhaust system from the catalytic converter back. Support the exhaust system with a suitable stand, release the three rear exhaust hangers and carefully lower the exhaust system to allow enough clearance to remove the fuel tank.

6. If removing the fuel tank on a four wheel drive vehicle, remove the rear driveshaft..

7. Lift the left rear seat cushion, position the carpet aside and remove the screws and the fuel pump module access cover.

8. Disconnect the fuel pump module electrical connector

9. Fuel vapor control tube assembly valve electrical connector

10. Using a suitable fuel pump lock ring remover, rotate the lock ring counterclockwise and remove.

> ✳✳ **WARNING**
>
> **The fuel pump module must be handled carefully to avoid damage to the float arm and filter.**

> ✳✳ **WARNING**
>
> **Some fuel will remain in the fuel pump module after draining the fuel tank. Carefully drain the fuel pump module into a suitable container.**

11. Prior to completely removing the fuel pump, position it aside and using the special tool and a suitable fuel recovery system, drain the fuel tank.

12. To release the bottom-mounted fuel pump module, reach into the fuel pump module opening and squeeze the retainer tabs on the pump module housing and pull upward.

13. Remove the fuel pump module O-ring seal

To install:

14. Turn the ignition key to the ON position to pressurize the fuel system.

15. Visually inspect the fuel system for leaks.

> ✳✳ **WARNING**
>
> **Make sure the fuel tube clicks into place when installing the tube. To make sure the tube is fully seated, pull on the tube.**

➡**Apply clean engine oil to the end of the tube before inserting the tube into the connector.**

16. Install the fuel tube quick release coupling.

> ✳✳ **WARNING**
>
> **Inspect the surfaces of the fuel pump module flange and fuel tank O-ring contact surfaces. Do not polish or adjust the O-ring contact area of the fuel pump flange or fuel tank. Install a new fuel pump module or fuel tank if the O-ring contact area is bent, scratched or corroded.**

> ✳✳ **WARNING**
>
> **Make sure to install a new fuel pump module O-ring and lock ring.**

17. Lubricate and install a new fuel pump module O-ring seal upon installing the fuel pump module.

18. When installing the fuel pump module, make sure to align the locator tabs on the fuel tank mounting flange.

➡**Be sure the aligning tabs of the fuel pump module unit are positioned in the slot before tightening the lock ring.**

19. Holding the fuel pump module O-ring seal in place, rotate the lock ring

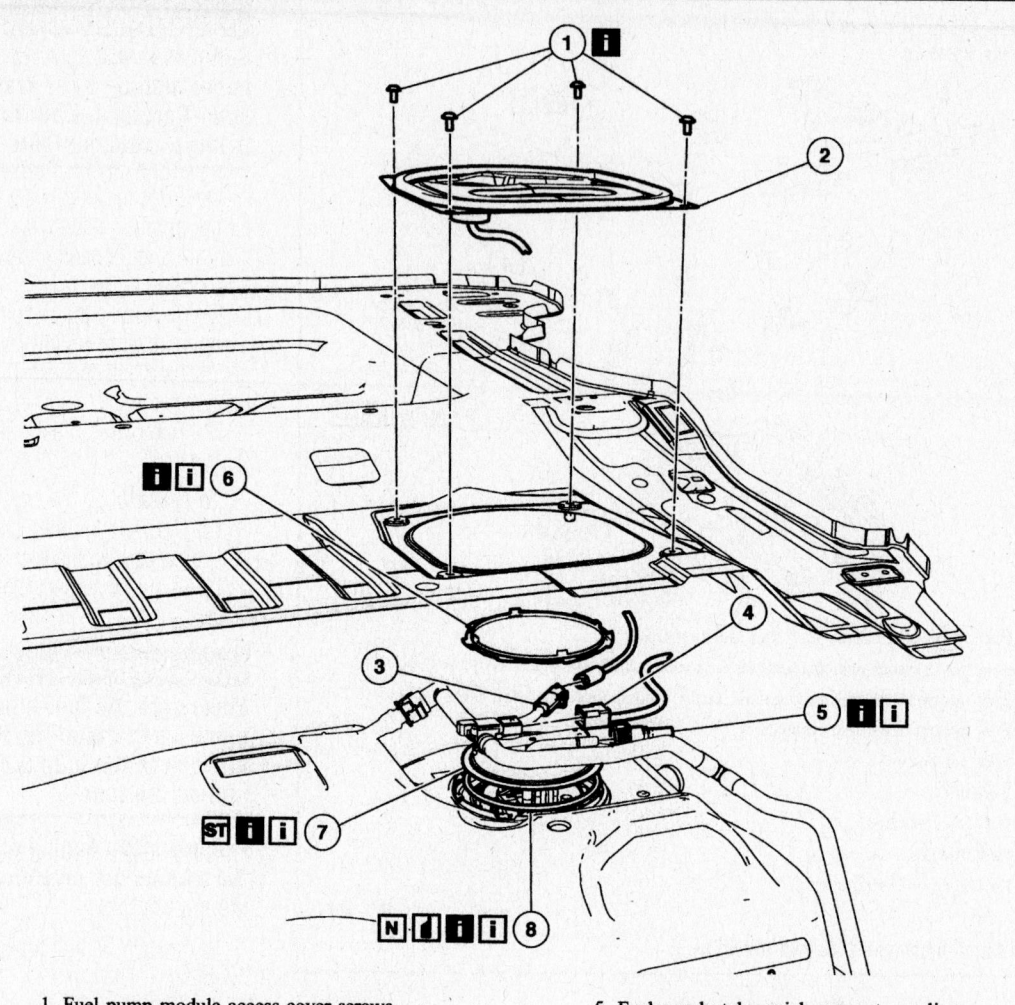

1 Fuel pump module access cover screws
2 Fuel pump module access cover
3 Fuel pump module electrical connector
4 Fuel vapor control tube assembly valve electrical connector
5 Fuel supply tube quick connect coupling
6 Fuel pump module lock ring
7 Fuel pump module
8 Fuel pump module O-ring seal

67197-ESCA-G34

Fig. 137 Access to fuel pump module—2005 models shown, others similar

clockwise until it stops against the retainer tabs.

➡**Make sure the collar on the fuel tube is inserted fully into the quick release coupling before the locking tab is locked.**

20. Connect the fuel supply quick connect coupling to the fuel supply manifold.

21. Press the fuel supply quick connect coupling locking tab into position.

22. Pull on the fitting to make sure it is fully engaged.

FUEL TANK

REMOVAL & INSTALLATION

1. Disconnect the negative battery cable.

2. With the vehicle in NEUTRAL, position it on a hoist.

3. Drain the fuel tank.

➡**For All Wheel Drive (AWD) vehicles, remove the exhaust muffler and resonator and rear driveshaft.**

4. Release the clamp and remove the fuel tank filler pipe hose from the fuel tank.

5. Position a suitable lifting device under the fuel tank.

6. Detach the 2 retainer clips from the LH fuel tank strap.

7. Remove the 2 bolts and position the 2 fuel tank straps aside

8. Partially lower the fuel tank enough to disconnect the fuel vapor tube assembly-to-fuel tank quick connect coupling.

9. Remove the fuel tank.

To install:

10. Install the fuel tank.

11. Connect the fuel vapor tube assembly to fuel tank before completely raising fuel tank.

12. Support fuel tank.

13. Reposition fuel tank straps and tighten bolts to 41 ft. lbs. (55 Nm).

14. Remove fuel tank support.

15. Install retainer clips to LH fuel strap.

16. Install fuel tank filler pipe and tighten hose clamp.

17. Connect the negative battery cable.

18. Install exhaust and rear drive shaft if they were removed for AWD models.

19. Lower vehicle and refill fuel tank

20. Connect the negative battery cable.

IDLE SPEED

ADJUSTMENT

Idle speed is maintained by the Powertrain Control Module (PCM). No adjustment is necessary or possible.

THROTTLE BODY

REMOVAL & INSTALLATION

See Figure 138.

✳ WARNING

Throttle body bore and plate area have a special coating and cannot be cleaned, or possible damage to the throttle body can occur.

➡**The electronic throttle body is serviced as a complete assembly. Individual components cannot be serviced.**

1. Remove the air cleaner outlet pipe.
2. Disconnect the electronic throttle body coolant hoses.

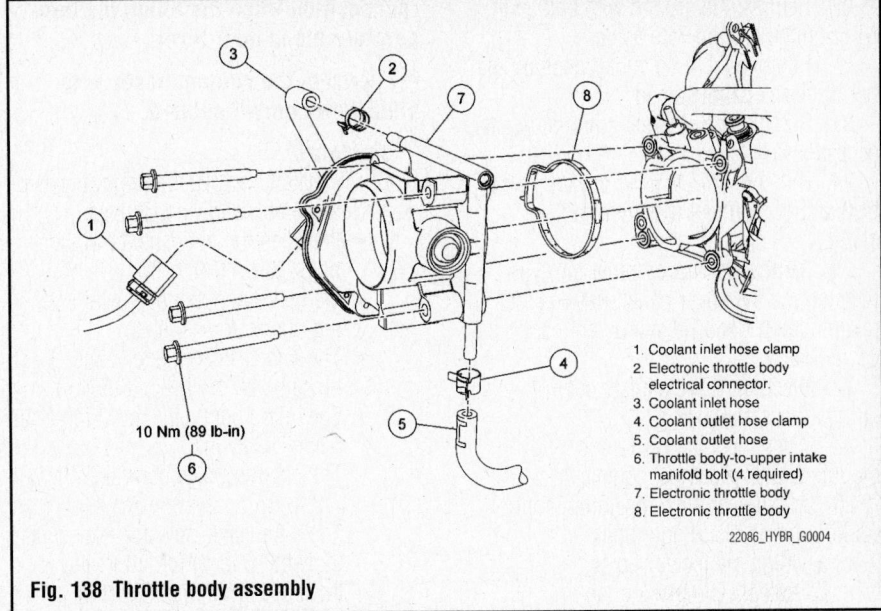

1. Coolant inlet hose clamp
2. Electronic throttle body electrical connector
3. Coolant inlet hose
4. Coolant outlet hose clamp
5. Coolant outlet hose
6. Throttle body-to-upper intake manifold bolt (4 required)
7. Electronic throttle body
8. Electronic throttle body

10 Nm (89 lb-in)

22086_HYBR_G0004

Fig. 138 Throttle body assembly

3. Disconnect and plug the coolant hoses.
4. Disconnect the electronic throttle body electrical connector.
5. Remove the 4 bolts and the electronic throttle body.

6. Clean and inspect the electronic throttle body gasket, replace if necessary.
7. Installation is the reverse of the removal procedure. Tighten the throttle body bolts to 89 inch lbs. (10 Nm).

HEATING & AIR CONDITIONING SYSTEM

BLOWER MOTOR

REMOVAL & INSTALLATION

2005–07 Models

1. Remove the RH A-pillar lower trim.
2. Disconnect the blower motor electrical connector.
3. Remove the washer screws.
4. Remove the blower motor and cover, lower the assembly from the housing.
5. Installation is the reverse of the removal procedure.

2008 Models

1. Disconnect the blower motor electrical connector.
2. Release the 2 blower motor vent tube clips and pull the vent tube down until it is disengaged from the heater core and evaporator core housing.
3. The carpet below the blower motor must be slightly repositioned to remove the blower motor.
4. Rotate the blower motor counterclockwise to disengage it from the housing and remove the blower motor.
5. To install, reverse the removal procedure

HEATER CORE

REMOVAL & INSTALLATION

2005–07 Models

See Figure 139.

1. Before servicing the vehicle, refer to the Precautions Section.
2. Drain the engine coolant.
3. Release the 2 clamps and disconnect the 2 heater hoses from the heater core.
4. Disarm the Supplemental Restraint System (SRS).
5. Position the seats forward and remove the 2 rear bolts.
6. Position the seats rearward and disconnect the battery.

➡**For the Escape Hybrid, when the battery is disconnected and connected, the brake pedal needs to be calibrated. After the battery has been connected, with the vehicle in park, turn the key to the ON position. Press the brake pedal firmly, then fully release to calibrate the brake pedal.**

7. Position the parking brake handle to the full-up position.
8. Remove the transaxle selector lever bezel.

9. Release the parking brake handle boot from the floor console finish panel.
10. On the Mariner, remove the floor console top panel.

➡**On Escape, if removing the floor console storage bin, squeeze the front and rear of the storage bin to release the retaining tabs from the floor console finish panel.**

11. Remove the floor console finish panel. Disconnect the electrical connectors.
12. Remove the 6 bolts and remove the floor console.
13. Remove the 4 pin-type retainers and the 2 front door scuff plates.
14. Remove the 2 pin-type retainers and the 2 A-pillar lower trim panels.
15. Remove the instrument panel steering column opening cover.
16. Remove the left and right instrument panel end trim panels.
17. Lower the tilt steering column to the lowest position.
18. Remove the 2 screws and the instrument cluster finish panel.
19. Remove the 4 instrument cluster screws and the instrument cluster. Disconnect the electrical connector.
20. Disconnect the main electrical connector.

21. Remove the ground wire bolt and position the ground wire aside.

22. Remove the 2 bolts and position the hood release handle aside.

23. Remove the steering column coupler access cover.

24. Remove the steering column pinch bolt and disconnect the intermediate shaft.

25. Remove the cover panel pin-type retainer and the cover panel. Release the retaining clip from the instrument panel center brace.

26. Disconnect the climate control vacuum harness connector.

27. Disconnect the restraint control module (RCM) electrical connector.

28. Disconnect the temperature control cable from the blend door shaft.

  a. Align the locator holes.
  b. Release the locking tab.
  c. Disconnect the temperature control cable.

→**Automatic transaxle selector lever is shown; the manual transaxle selector lever is similar.**

29. Remove the 4 transaxle selector lever bolts and position the transaxle selector lever aside. Disconnect the electrical connectors.

30. Remove the bolts and position the parking brake control aside Disconnect the electrical connectors.

31. Open the glove compartment. Press the release tabs inward while lowering the glove compartment.

32. Disconnect the blower motor electrical connectors.

33. Disconnect the antenna cable in-line connector.

34. Remove the cover and the instrument panel cowl top bolt.

35. Remove the 4 instrument panel center brace bolts.

36. Remove the instrument panel cluster opening nut through the instrument cluster opening.

37. Remove the 4 instrument panel cowl side bolts.

→**This step requires an assistant.**

38. Remove the instrument panel.

39. Remove the screw and the temperature blend door lever.

40. Remove the 3 screws and the heater core cover.

41. Remove the heater core from the housing.

→**Make sure the temperature blend door actuator and switch are in the cor-**

rect position when installing the temperature blend door lever.

→**Lubricate the coolant hoses with plain water only if needed.**

To install:

42. To install, reverse the removal procedure. Observe the following torques:

  • the 4 instrument panel cowl side bolts: 9 Nm (80 lb-in)
  • the instrument panel cluster opening nut: 9 Nm (80 lb-in)
  • The 4 instrument panel center brace bolts: 18 ft. lbs. (25 Nm)
  • The instrument panel cowl top bolt: 6 Nm (53 lb-in)
  • The parking brake control: 24 Nm (18 lb-ft)
  • The 4 transaxle selector lever bolts: 22 Nm (16 lb-ft) for automatic transaxle; 15 ft. lbs. (20 Nm) for manual transaxle
  • The steering column pinch bolt: 23 Nm (17 lb-ft)
  • The hood release handle: 6 Nm (53 lb-in)

43. Fill and bleed the engine cooling system.

44. If equipped with automatic transaxle, adjust the linkage.

45. Rearm the Supplemental Restraint System (SRS).

46. Following installation of the new instrument cluster, download the module configuration information from the diagnostic tool into the new module as follows:

Using the Vehicle Communication Module (VCM) When the Original Body Chassis Electrical Module is Not Available

47. Install the new module.

48. Using the VCM and the latest version of the service function card, SELECT: Programmable Module Installation.

49. Select the module being installed.

50. Follow the on-screen instructions.

51. SELECT: Retrieve Module Configuration—Old ECU and press trigger.

52. Follow the on-screen instructions.

53. The VCM attempts to retrieve the module data from the Powertrain Control Module (PCM). If the module data is available, go to Step A. If the VCM displays: Call As-Built Data Center, go to Step B.

Step A

54. SELECT: Restore Configuration—New ECU. Press trigger.

55. The VCM completes loading the retrieved data and displays Module Download Successful.

56. Test the module for correct operation.

Step B

57. Press the trigger.

58. If the VCM asks for vehicle data, enter the vehicle data, then press store.

59. The VCM asks for module data line 1. Enter the data and press store.

60. The VCM then asks if there is an additional line of data available for that address. Select YES or NO depending on the information in the As Built Data Sheet.

61. Repeat Steps 3 and 4 until the answer is NO for Step 4.

62. The VCM should show a screen stating that the module data was stored. Press the trigger.

63. Follow the on-screen instructions.

64. SELECT: Restore Configuration—New ECU. Press the trigger.

65. The VCM completes loading the retrieved data and displays Module Download Successful.

66. Test the module for correct operation.

Using the Vehicle Communication Module (VCM) When the Original Body Chassis Electrical Module is Available

67. With the original module still installed, using the VCM and the latest version of the service function card, SELECT: Programmable Module Installation.

68. Select the module being installed and press the trigger.

69. Follow the on-screen instructions.

70. SELECT: Retrieve Module Configuration—Old ECU. Press the trigger.

71. Follow the on-screen instructions.

72. INSTALL new module, SELECT: Restore Configuration—New ECU. Press the trigger.

73. The VCM completes loading the retrieved data and displays Module Download Successful.

74. Test the module for correct operation.

Using the Worldwide Diagnostic System (WDS) When the Original Body Chassis Electrical Module is Not Available

75. Install the new module.

76. Connect the WDS and ID the vehicle as normal.

77. From the Toolbox icon, select and highlight Module Programming. Then highlight the module that was installed and press the check mark.

78. Select and highlight Programmable Module Installation. Then highlight the module that was installed and press the check mark.

79. Follow the on-screen instructions, turn the ignition key to the OFF position and press the check mark.

1 Temperature blend door lever
2 Heater core cover screws (3 required)
3 Heater core cover
4 Heater core

06017-ESCA-G17

Fig. 139 Heater core—2005–07 models

80. The WDS retrieves the module data from the PCM, automatically downloads the data into the new module, and displays Module Configuration Complete.

81. If the data is not available in the PCM, the WDS displays a screen stating to contact the As-Built Data Center. Retrieve the data from WWW.FMCDEALER.COM at this time and press the check mark.

82. Enter the module data (the module address and line are displayed to the left of the 3 entry boxes) and press the check mark.

83. The WDS downloads the data into the new module and displays Operation Successful—Programming Complete.

84. Test the module for correct operation.

Using the Worldwide Diagnostic System (WDS) When the Original

Body Chassis Electrical Module is Available

85. Connect the WDS and ID the vehicle as normal.

86. From the Toolbox icon, select and highlight Module Programming and press the check mark.

87. Select and highlight Programmable Module Installation.

88. Follow the on-screen instructions, turn the ignition key to the OFF position, and press the check mark.

89. Install the new module and press the check mark.

90. Follow the on-screen instructions, turn the ignition key to the ON position, and press the check mark.

91. The module configuration is complete.

92. Test the module for correct operation.

2008 Models

See Figures 140 and 141.

1. Before servicing the vehicle, refer to the Precautions Section.

2. Drain the engine coolant.

3. Recover the refrigerant.

4. Position the seats forward and remove the 2 floor console rear bolts

5. Position the seats rearward

6. Remove the transaxle selector lever trim ring.

7. Remove the floor console storage bin.

8. Remove the floor console finish panel.

9. Remove the 8 floor console bolts and remove the floor console

10. Disarm the Supplemental Restraint System (SRS).

11. Remove the RH and LH A-pillar trim panels.

12. Remove the 4 pin-type retainers and the RH and LH front door opening scuff plates

13. Remove the RH and LH lower A-pillar trim panels

14. Remove the steering column opening cover.

15. Remove the RH and LH instrument panel side finish panels.

16. Disconnect the 2 electrical connectors at the LH side of the instrument panel.

17. Disconnect the main steering module electrical connector.

18. Remove the bolts and position aside the hood release handle and parking brake release handle.

19. Remove and slide the steering column intermediate shaft access cover and weather shield up the steering column intermediate shaft.

※※ WARNING

Do not allow the steering column shaft to rotate while the lower shaft is disconnected or damage to the clockspring can result. If there is evidence that the shaft has rotated, the clockspring must be removed and recentered.

20. Remove and discard the steering column intermediate shaft-to-coupling bolt and slide the steering column intermediate shaft up.

21. Remove scrivet and the Restraints Control Module (RCM) access cover.

22. Disconnect the LH RCM electrical connector.

23. For vehicles with automatic transaxles remove the selector lever cable from the selector lever assembly.

24. For vehicles with manual transaxles remove the shift cables from the shift lever assembly.

25. Disconnect the selector lever electrical connector and wiring harness pin-type retainers from the selector lever assembly.

26. equipped, remove and position aside the Four Wheel Drive (4WD) control module and bracket from the selector lever assembly.

27. Remove the 4 selector lever assembly bolts and remove the selector lever assembly.

28. Disconnect the electrical connectors from the Smart Junction Box (SJB).

29. Disconnect the wiring harness pin-type retainers.

30. Remove the SJB lower bolts and the SJB.

31. Disconnect the 2 electrical connectors at the RH side of the instrument panel.

32. Disconnect the antenna cable in-line connector

33. Remove the LH and RH windshield wiper pivot arms.

34. Remove the cowl panel cover

35. Remove the 3 windshield wiper mounting arm and pivot shaft assembly bolts and position aside the windshield wiper mounting arm and pivot shaft assembly.

36. Remove the 3 instrument panel upper cowl bolts.

37. Remove the 4 instrument panel center brace bolts

38. Remove the 4 instrument panel side bolts.

➡**To avoid damage to the instrument panel, an assistant is required for this step.**

➡**Before removing the instrument panel, make sure that all electrical wiring is free and not hindered**

39. Remove the instrument panel.

40. Remove the Thermostatic Expansion Valve (TXV) fitting nut and disconnect the fitting.

41. Release the clamps and disconnect the heater inlet and outlet hoses from the heater core.

42. Remove the 6 heater core and evaporator core housing nuts.

43. Detach the heater core and evaporator core housing from the dash panel studs

44. Rotate the RH side of the heater core and evaporator core housing toward the rear of the vehicle while pulling the housing toward the RH door opening to detach it from the rear footwell duct.

45. Remove the heater core and evaporator core housing

46. Remove the dash panel seal.

47. Remove the heater core bracket screw and the heater core bracket

48. Remove the heater core.

To install:

49. Install heater core

50. Install heater core bracket screws and tighten to 27 inch lbs. (3 Nm).

51. Install the dash panel seal.

52. Install heater core and evaporator core housing.

53. Tighten core housing nuts to 80 inch lbs. (9 Nm).

54. Connect and tighten the heater inlet and outlet hoses to the heater core.

55. Install the thermostatic expansion valve (TXV) fitting nut and disconnect the fitting.

56. Install the instrument panel.

57. Install 2 instrument panel side bolts, one on each side, to hold the instrument panel in place.

58. Install the 3 instrument panel upper cowl bolts and tighten to 15 ft. lbs. (20 Nm).

59. Install the windshield wiper mounting arm and pivot shaft assembly and the 3 windshield wiper mounting arm and pivot shaft assembly bolts tighten to 9 ft. lbs. (12 Nm).

60. Install the cowl panel cover.

61. Install the LH and RH windshield wiper pivot arms.

62. Install the instrument panel side bolts and tighten to 8 ft. lbs. (11 Nm).

63. Install the instrument panel center brace bolts and tighten to 15 ft. lbs. (20 Nm).

64. Connect the antenna cable in-line connector.

65. Connect the electrical connectors at the RH side of the instrument panel

66. Install the SJB, bolts and connect the wiring harness pin-type retainers.

67. Connect the electrical connectors to the SJB.

68. Install the selector lever assembly and the 4 selector assembly bolts and tighten to 18 ft. lbs (25 Nm).

69. If equipped, install the 4WD control module and bracket onto the selector lever assembly.

70. Connect the selector lever electrical connector.

71. Install the wiring harness pin-type retainers to the selector lever assembly.

72. Vehicles with automatic transaxles, install the selector lever cable to the selector lever assembly.

73. Vehicles with manual transaxles, install the shift cables to the shift lever assembly.

74. Connect the LH RCM electrical connector

75. Install the RCM access cover and scrivet

76. Slide the steering column intermediate shaft down onto the coupling and install a new steering column intermediate shaft-to-coupling bolt, tighten to 42 ft. lbs. (55 Nm).

77. Install the steering column intermediate shaft access cover and weather shield.

78. Install the hood release and parking brake release handles and bolts.

79. Connect the main steering module electrical connector.

80. Connect the electrical connectors at the LH side of the instrument panel

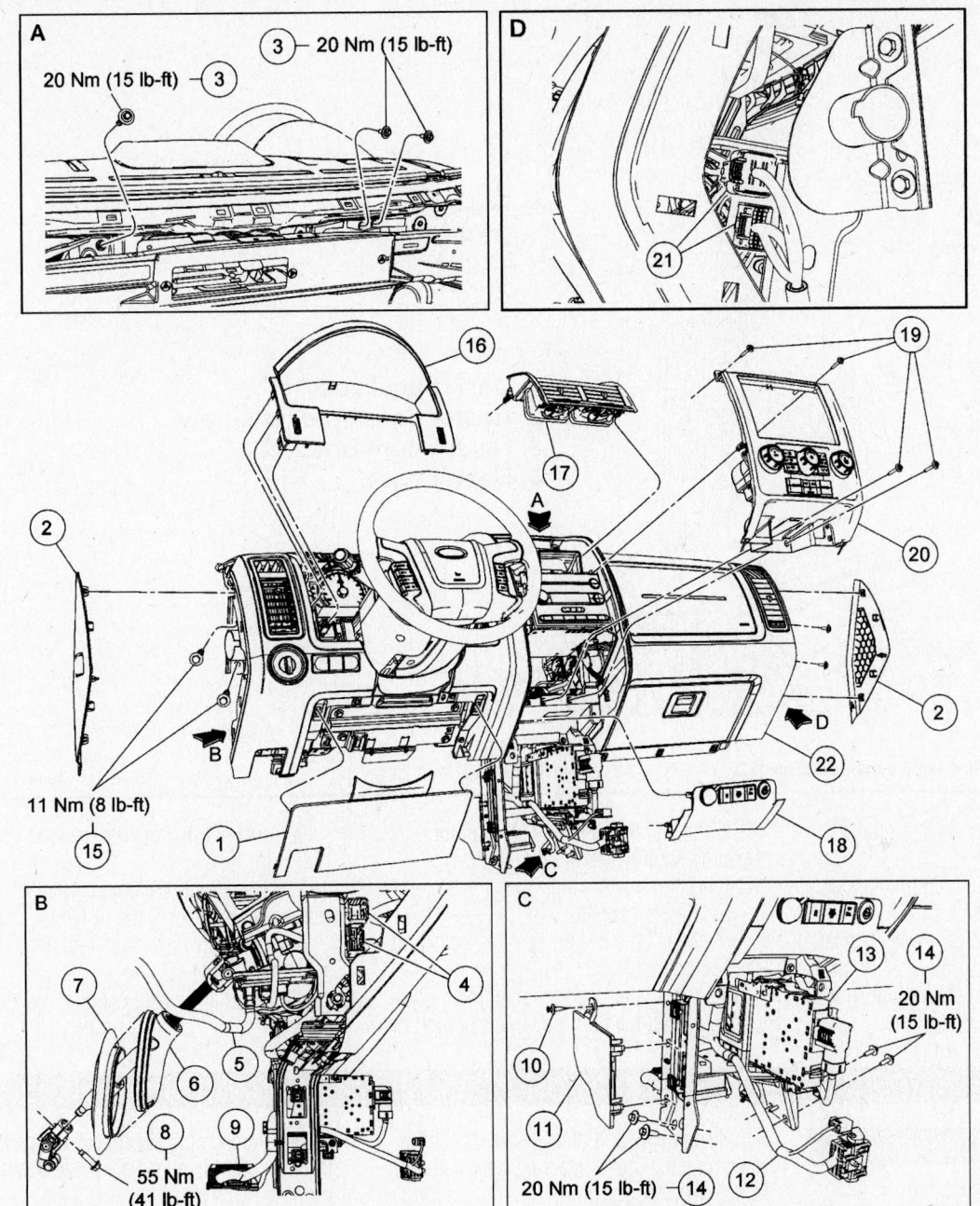

1. Steering column opening cover
2. Instrument panel side finish panel
3. Instrument panel upper cowl bolts (3 required)
4. LH side instrument panel electrical connectors
5. Steering module electrical connector
6. Steering column shaft access cover
7. Steering column shaft weather shield
8. Steering column intermediate
   shaft-to-coupling bolt
9. Restraints control module
   (RCM) electrical wiring harness
10. Scrivet
11. RCM access cover
12. Floor console electrical wiring harness
13. Smart junction box (SJB)
14. Instrument panel center brace bolts (4 required)
15. Instrument panel side bolts (4 required)
16. Instrument cluster finish panel
17. Upper instrument panel center finish panel
18. Lower instrument panel center finish panel
19. Middle instrument panel center
    finish panel screws (4 required)
20. Middle instrument panel center finish panel
21. RH side instrument panel electrical connectors
22. Instrument panel

22086_HYBR_G0025

Fig. 140 Instrument panel exploded view—2008 models

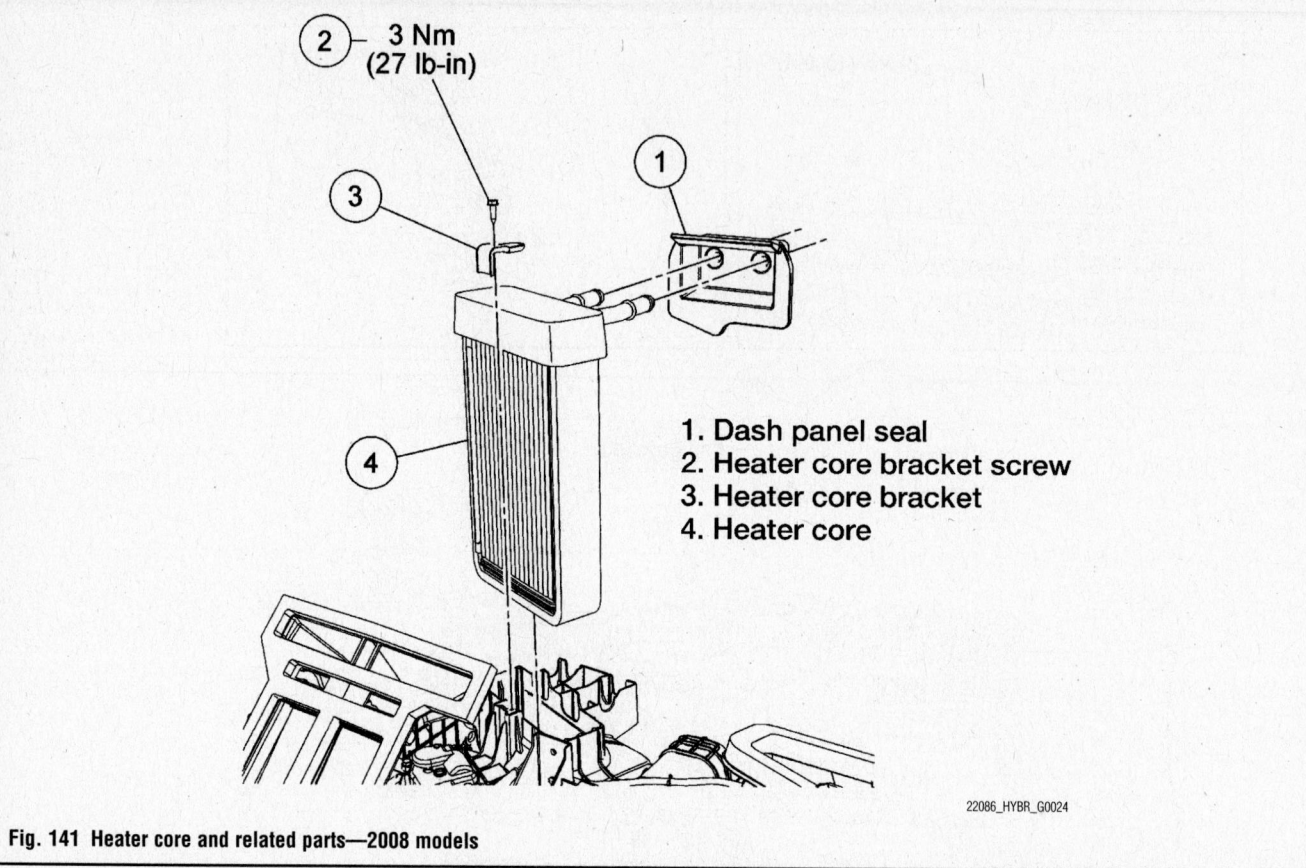

2 — 3 Nm
(27 lb-in)

1. Dash panel seal
2. Heater core bracket screw
3. Heater core bracket
4. Heater core

22086_HYBR_G0024

Fig. 141 Heater core and related parts—2008 models

81. Install the RH and LH instrument panel side finish panels

82. Install the steering column opening cover.

83. Install the RH and LH lower A-pillar trim panels.

84. Install the RH and LH A-pillar trim panels

85. Install the RH and LH front door opening scuff plates and the 4 pin-type retainers.

86. Rearm the SRS.

87. Install the 8 floor console bolts and the floor console.

88. Install the floor console finish panel.

89. Install the floor console storage bin.

90. Install the transaxle selector lever trim ring.

91. Install and tighten the floor console rear bolts to 62 inch. lbs (7 Nm).

92. Evacuate, leak test and charge the refrigerant system.

93. Refill and bleed cooling system.

STEERING

POWER STEERING GEAR

REMOVAL & INSTALLATION

See Figures 142 through 144.

1. Before servicing the vehicle, refer to the Precautions Section.

2. Remove the front wheels and tires.

3. Turn the ignition key to the OFF position and remove the ignition key.

✵✵ WARNING

Do not allow the steering wheel to rotate while the intermediate shaft is disconnected or damage to the clockspring can result. If there is evidence that the shaft has rotated, the clockspring must be removed and recentered

4. Remove and discard the steering column coupling-to-steering gear bolt and disconnect the coupling from the steering gear.

5. From the engine compartment, loosen the 2 steering gear bolts.

6. If equipped, remove the 3 pin-type retainers and the steering gear shield.

7. Remove and discard the 2 outer tie-rod end nuts.

8. Using the special tool, separate the tie-rod ends from the wheel knuckles.

✵✵ WARNING

Do not use a hammer to separate the tie-rod end from the wheel knuckle or damage to the wheel knuckle can result.

9. Remove the rear transaxle insulator through bolt for All Wheel Drive (AWD) vehicles.

10. Remove the 3 transaxle damper bolts and the transaxle damper for Front Wheel Drive (FWD) 2.3L models.

11. Remove and discard the 2 steering gear bolts.

➡**For All Wheel Drive (AWD) vehicles, it is necessary to grasp the driveshaft by hand and apply slight downward pressure to obtain clearance for the removal of the steering gear.**

12. Remove the steering gear from the LH side of the vehicle.

13. To install, reverse the removal procedure and note the following:

   a. Tighten the outer tie-rod end nuts to 59 ft. lbs. (80 Nm).

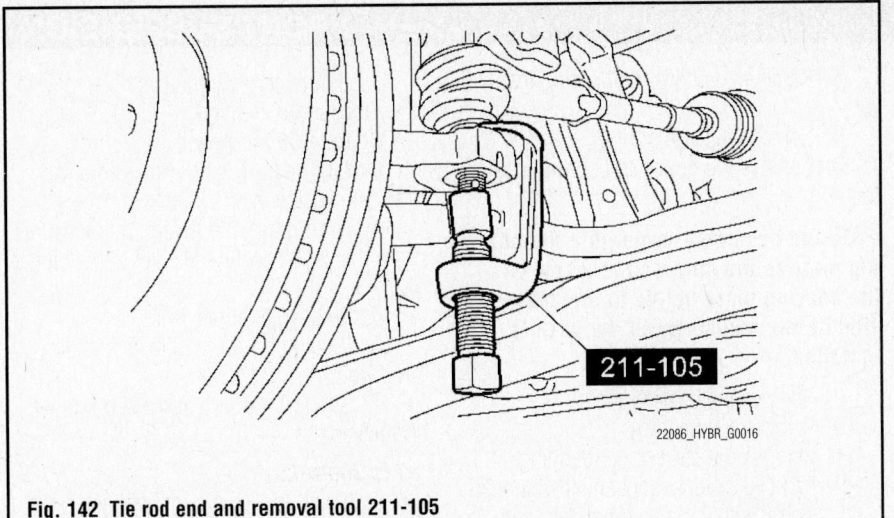

Fig. 142 Tie rod end and removal tool 211-105

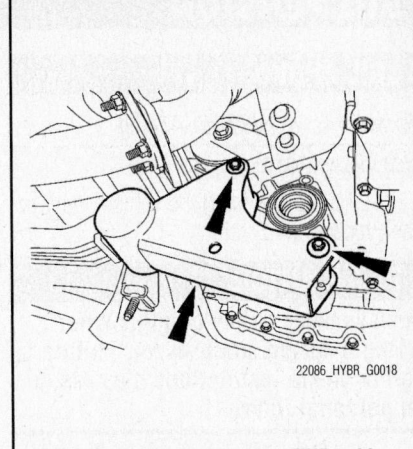

Fig. 144 Transaxle damper—FWD vehicles

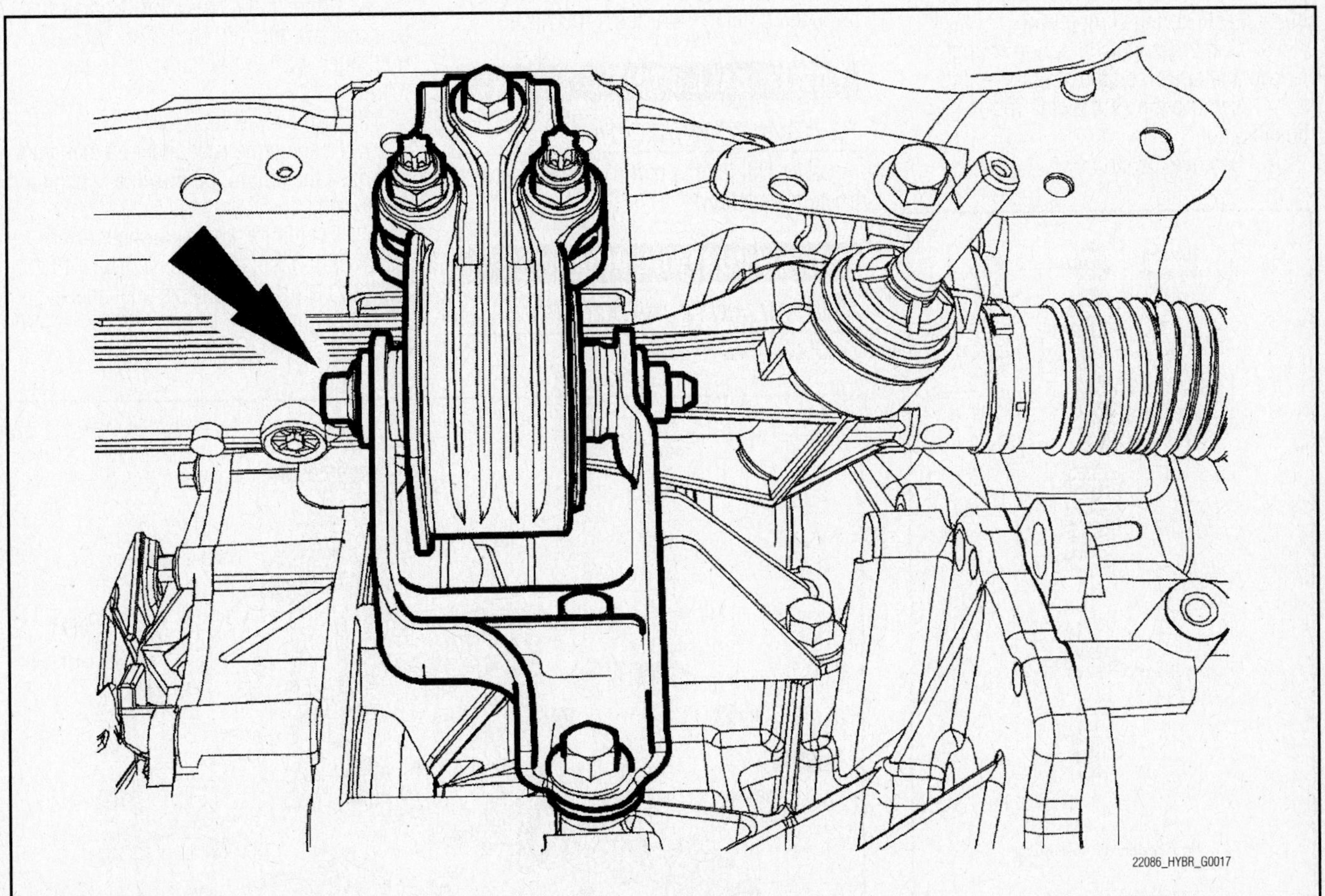

Fig. 143 Rear transaxle insulator—AWD vehicles

b. Tighten steering gear bolts to 85 ft. lbs. (115 Nm).

c. Tighten steering column coupling-to-steering gear bolt to 41 ft. lbs. (55 Nm).

d. Tighten rear transaxle insulator through bolt to 66 ft. lbs (90 Nm).

e. Tight transaxle damper bolts to 30 ft. lbs. (40 Nm).

POWER STEERING PUMP

REMOVAL & INSTALLATION

Instead of a conventional power steering pump, these vehicles have an electric power steering system, which provides power steering assist to the driver by replacing the conventional hydraulic valve system with an electric motor coupled to the steering gear. The motor is controlled by an electronic control unit that senses the steering effort through the use of a torque sensor mounted between the steering column shaft and the steering gear. Steering assist is provided in proportion to the steering input effort and vehicle speed.

SUSPENSION

FRONT SUSPENSION

COIL SPRING

REMOVAL & INSTALLATION

See Figure 145.

1. Before servicing the vehicle, refer to the Precautions Section.

❊❊ CAUTION

Always wear safety goggles when using a spring compressor. Failure to follow these instructions may result in personal injury.

➡**Do not use an impact wrench on the nut.**

2. Mount the strut and spring assembly in a suitable spring compressor.
3. Compress the coil spring enough to relieve the tension on the strut assembly.
4. Remove the strut piston rod-to-bushing nut.
5. Remove the strut.

6. Remove the lower coil spring insulator.
7. Remove the coil spring.
8. Remove the upper coil spring insulator.

➡**During assembly, assemble the bearing plate to the strut so the arrow on the bearing plate points to the outboard side of the vehicle when the strut is installed.**

9. Remove the bearing plate.
10. Remove the bearing.
11. Remove the strut upper bushing.
12. Remove the dust boot and the bumper.
13. To assemble, reverse the disassembly procedure. Tighten the strut piston rod-to-bushing nut to 76 ft. lbs. (103 Nm).

LOWER BALL JOINT

REMOVAL & INSTALLATION

Lower ball joint is part of the lower control arm assembly.

LOWER CONTROL ARM

REMOVAL AND & INSTALLATION

See Figure 146.

1. Before servicing the vehicle, refer to the Precautions Section.
2. Remove the wheel.
3. Lift the lower arm with a floor jack until the vehicle starts to lift.
4. Record the ride height. It's measure from the center of the halfshaft to the fender lip.
5. Remove the floor jack.
6. Disconnect the ball joint from the knuckle.
7. Support the sub-frame and remove the lower arm.

To install:

8. Install the lower arm, with the bolts loose.
9. Connect the ball joint. Tighten the bolt to 52 ft. lbs. (70 Nm). For vehicles built after 9/2005 tighten to 46 ft. lbs. (63 Nm).
10. Remove the support.
11. Position the jack under the ball joint and raise the arm to the previously recorded ride height.
12. Tighten the lower arm bolts. Horizontal 85 ft. lbs. (115 Nm); vertical 148 ft. lbs. (200 Nm). For vehicles built after 9/2005) tighten vertical to129 ft. lbs. (175 Nm).

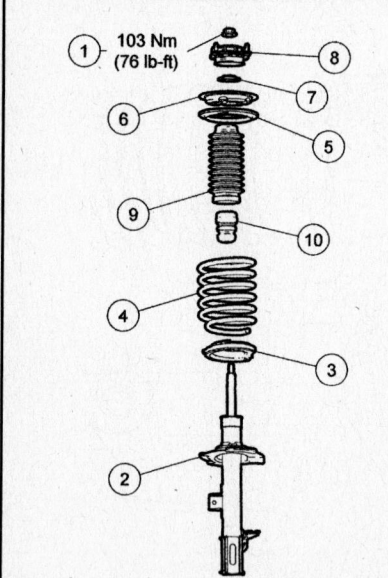

1	Strut piston rod-to-bushing nut
2	Strut (LH/RH)
3	Lower coil spring insulator
4	Coil spring
5	Upper coil spring insulator
6	Bearing plate
7	Bearing
8	Strut upper bushing
9	Dust boot
10	Bumper

06017-ESCA-G76

Fig. 145 Strut/spring disassembly—2005 models shown, others similar

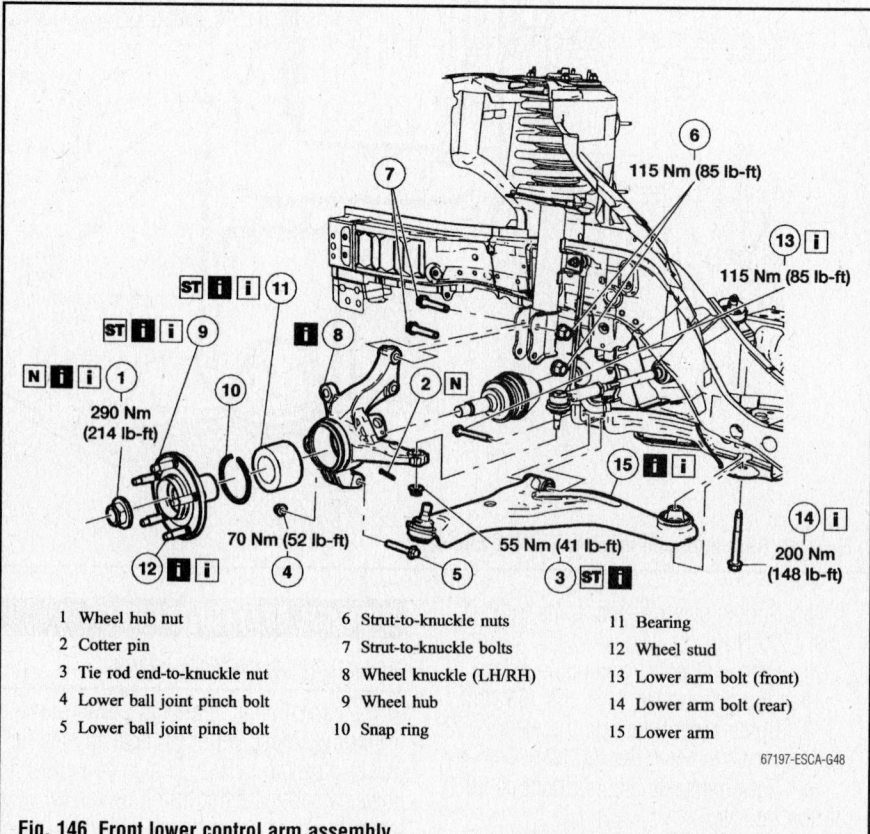

1	Wheel hub nut	6	Strut-to-knuckle nuts	11	Bearing
2	Cotter pin	7	Strut-to-knuckle bolts	12	Wheel stud
3	Tie rod end-to-knuckle nut	8	Wheel knuckle (LH/RH)	13	Lower arm bolt (front)
4	Lower ball joint pinch bolt	9	Wheel hub	14	Lower arm bolt (rear)
5	Lower ball joint pinch bolt	10	Snap ring	15	Lower arm

67197-ESCA-G48

Fig. 146 Front lower control arm assembly

MACPHERSON STRUT

REMOVAL & INSTALLATION

See Figure 147.

1. Before servicing the vehicle, refer to the Precautions Section.

➡ **Make sure the steering wheel is in the unlocked position.**

➡ **Use the hex holding feature to prevent the ball studs from turning while removing or installing the stabilizer bar link nuts.**

2. Raise and support the vehicle.
3. Remove the brake jounce hose clip.
4. Remove the brake jounce hose. Pull the brake jounce hose downward slightly to remove the hose from the bracket.
5. Remove the ABS sensor harness bolt.
6. Remove the stabilizer bar link nut.
7. Remove the strut-to-knuckle nuts.
8. Remove the strut-to-knuckle bolts.
9. Remove the strut upper bushing nuts. Reference mark the strut mounting plate nuts.
10. Remove the strut and spring assembly.

✻✻ WARNING

Do not allow the axle shaft to move outboard. Over-extension of the tripod CV joint can result in separation of internal parts, causing failure of the axle shaft.

11. To install, reverse the removal procedure. See the illustration for the appropriate torque values.

12. Align the strut mounting plate nuts to the reference marks.
13. Check the front end alignment and adjust as necessary.

OVERHAUL

See Figure 148.

✻✻ CAUTION

Always wear safety goggles when using a spring compressor. Failure to follow these instructions may result in personal injury.

➡ **Do not use an impact wrench on the nut. Mount the strut and spring assembly in a suitable spring compressor.**

1. Compress the coil spring enough to relieve the tension on the strut assembly.

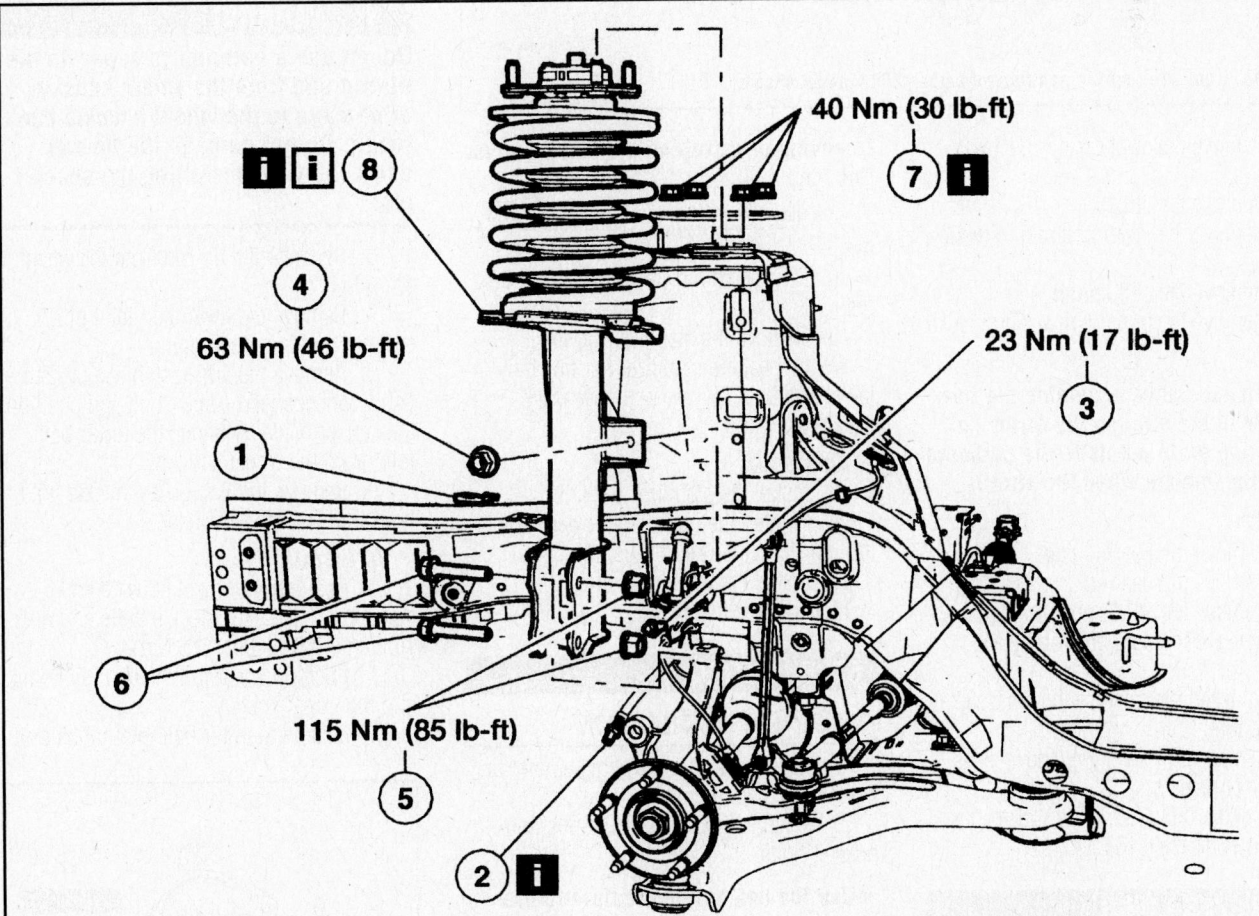

40 Nm (30 lb-ft)
63 Nm (46 lb-ft)
23 Nm (17 lb-ft)
115 Nm (85 lb-ft)

1 Brake jounce hose clip	5 Strut-to-knuckle nuts
2 Brake jounce hose (LH/RH)	6 Strut-to-knuckle bolts
3 ABS sensor harness bolt	7 Strut upper bushing nuts
4 Stabilizer bar link nut	8 Strut and spring assembly

67197-ESCA-G45

Fig. 147 Front strut installation—2005 model shown, others similar

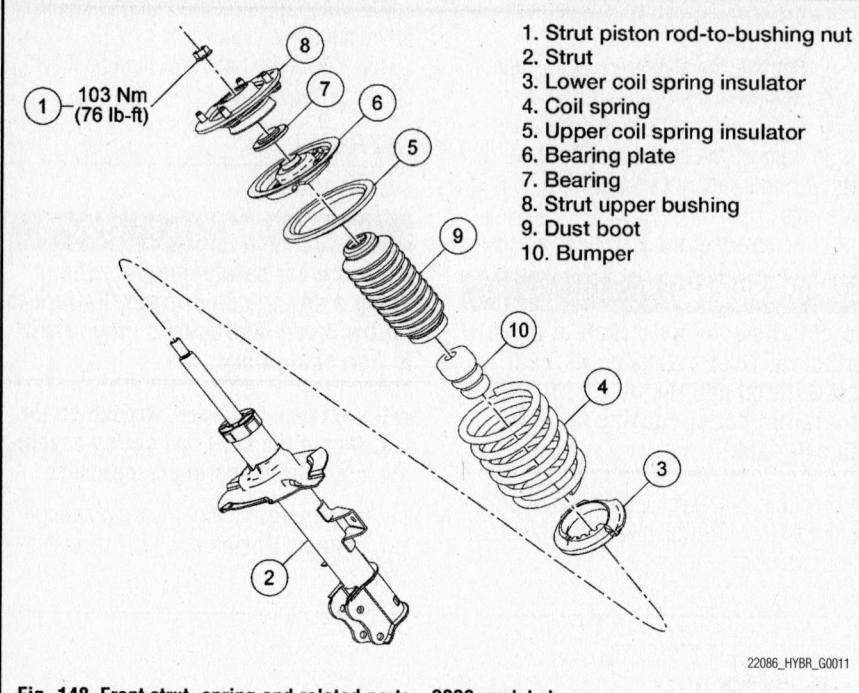

1. Strut piston rod-to-bushing nut
2. Strut
3. Lower coil spring insulator
4. Coil spring
5. Upper coil spring insulator
6. Bearing plate
7. Bearing
8. Strut upper bushing
9. Dust boot
10. Bumper

22086_HYBR_G0011

Fig. 148 Front strut, spring and related parts—2008 model shown

2. Remove the strut piston rod-to-bushing nut.
3. Remove the strut.
4. Remove the lower coil spring insulator.
5. Remove the coil spring.
6. Remove the upper coil spring insulator.

➡ **During assembly, assemble the bearing plate to the strut so the arrow on the bearing plate points to the outboard side of the vehicle when the strut is installed.**

7. Remove the bearing plate.
8. Remove the bearing.
9. Remove the strut upper bushing.
10. Remove the dust boot and the bumper.
11. To assemble, reverse the disassembly procedure.
12. Replace any parts that show excessive wear or defects.
13. Tighten the strut piston rod-to-bushing nut to 76 ft. lbs. (103 Nm).

STABILIZER LINKS

REMOVAL & INSTALLATION

1. Before servicing the vehicle, refer to the Precautions Section.
2. Raise and support vehicle.
3. Remove the wheel and tire.

➡ **Use the hex holding feature to prevent the ball stud from turning while**

removing or installing the stabilizer bar link nut.

4. Remove the upper stabilizer bar link nut.
5. Remove the lower stabilizer bar link nut.
6. Remove the stabilizer bar link.
7. Inspect the stabilizer bar link ball joints and boots for wear. If necessary, install new parts.

To install:
8. Install the stabilizer bar link.
9. Tighten the upper and lower stabilizer bar link nut to 41 ft. lbs. (55 Nm).
10. Install the wheel and tire.
11. Lower vehicle.

STABILIZER BAR

REMOVAL & INSTALLATION

1. Before servicing the vehicle, refer to the Precautions Section.
2. Remove the stabilizer bar bushing bracket bolts.

➡ **Use the hex holding feature to prevent the ball stud from turning while removing or installing the stabilizer link nut.**

3. Remove the 2 lower stabilizer bar link nuts.

➡ **Access the stabilizer bar through the left wheel opening.**

4. Remove the stabilizer bar.

5. To install, reverse the removal procedure. Observe the following torques:
   • 2005–08 link nuts: 41 ft. lbs. (55 Nm)
   • Bushing bracket bolts: 52 ft. lbs. (70 Nm)

STEERING KNUCKLE

REMOVAL & INSTALLATION

See Figure 149.

1. Before servicing the vehicle, refer to the Precautions Section.
2. Remove the brake disc.
3. Remove and discard the wheel hub nut.
4. Separate the outer CV-joint spindle from the wheel hub.
5. Remove the cotter pin and the tie-rod end-to-knuckle nut.

✳✳ WARNING

Do not use a hammer to separate the tie-rod end from the wheel knuckle or damage to the wheel knuckle can result. Do not damage the tie-rod end boot while installing the special tool.

6. Separate the tie-rod from the wheel knuckle.
7. Remove the lower ball joint pinch bolt nut and the pinch bolt.
8. Remove the anti-lock brake system (ABS) wheel speed sensor bolt and position the sensor aside. Separate the lower ball joint from the wheel knuckle.
9. Remove the 2 strut-to-knuckle nuts, bolts and the wheel knuckle.

To install:
10. Position the wheel knuckle and install the 2 strut-to-knuckle bolts and nuts. Tighten to 85 ft. lbs. (115 Nm).
11. Position and align the ball joint stud into the wheel knuckle.
12. Install the lower ball joint pinch bolt

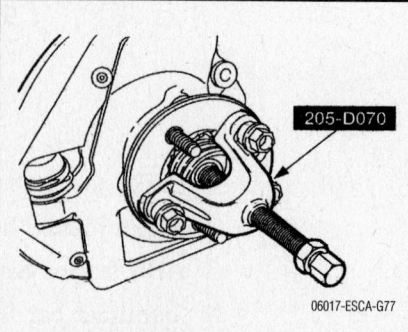

205-D070

06017-ESCA-G77

Fig. 149 Separate the outer CV-joint spindle from the wheel hub

and nut. Tighten to 52 ft. lbs. (70 Nm). For vehicles built after 9/2005 tighten to 46 ft. lbs. (63 Nm).

13. Install the ABS wheel speed sensor and the bolt. Tighten to 80 inch lbs. (9 Nm).

14. Position the tie rod-end into the wheel knuckle and install the tie-rod end-to-knuckle nut and a new cotter pin. Tighten to 41 ft. lbs. (55 Nm).

15. Insert the halfshaft into the wheel hub.

16. Install the wheel hub nut. Tighten to 221 ft. lbs. (300 Nm).

17. Install the brake disc.

18. Check and, if necessary, align the front end.

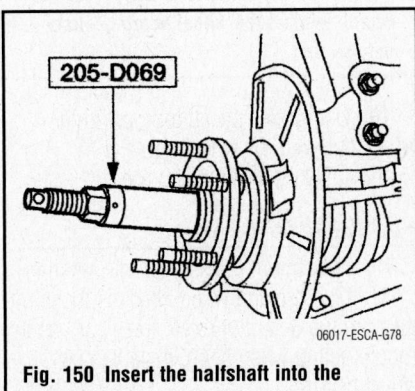

Fig. 150 Insert the halfshaft into the wheel hub

WHEEL BEARINGS

REMOVAL & INSTALLATION

See Figures 151 through 156.

1. Before servicing the vehicle, refer to the Precautions Section.

➡**If removing the wheel hub, the wheel bearing must be replaced.**

2. Remove the wheel knuckle.
3. Using the special tool, press the wheel hub from the wheel bearing.

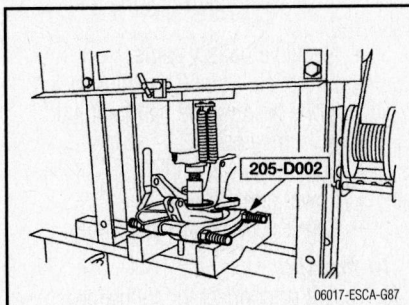

Fig. 151 Using the special tool, press the wheel hub from the wheel bearing—front hub/bearing

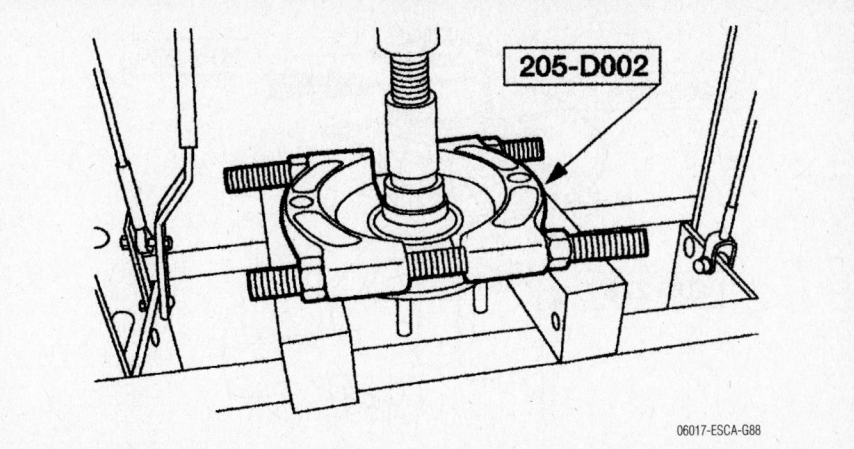

Fig. 152 Using the special tool, press the inner wheel bearing race from the wheel hub—front hub/bearing

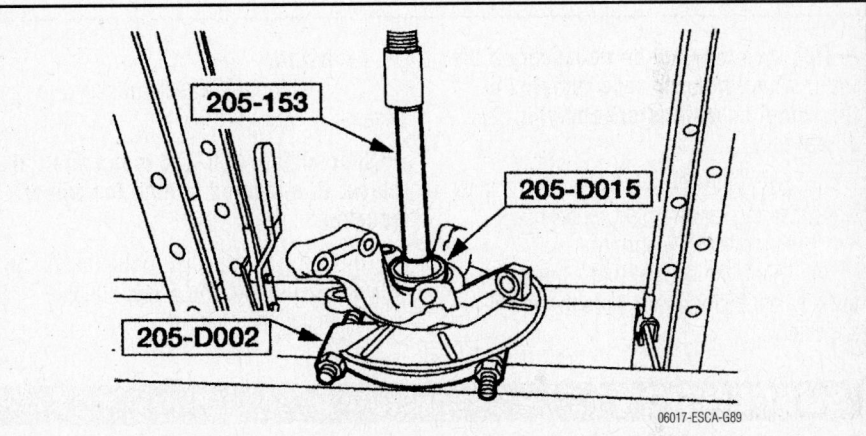

Fig. 153 Using the special tools, press the outer wheel bearing race from the wheel knuckle—front hub/bearing

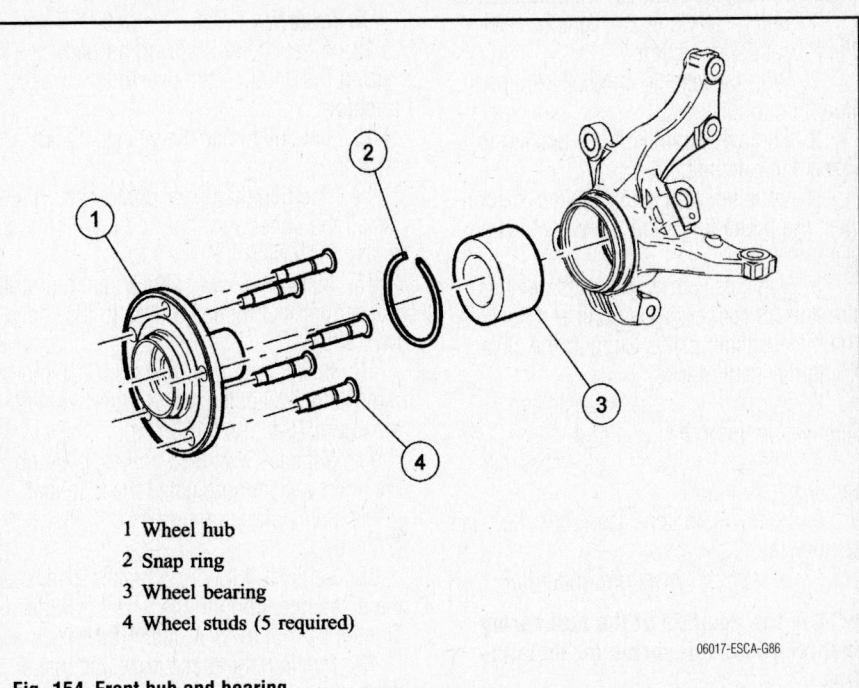

1 Wheel hub
2 Snap ring
3 Wheel bearing
4 Wheel studs (5 required)

Fig. 154 Front hub and bearing

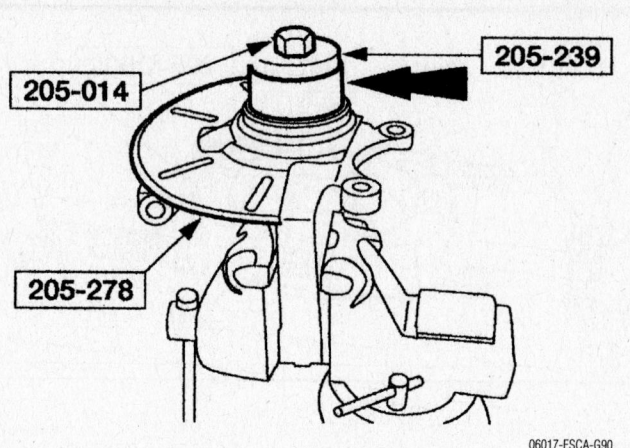

Fig. 155 Using the special tools, install the wheel bearing into the wheel knuckle—front hub/bearing

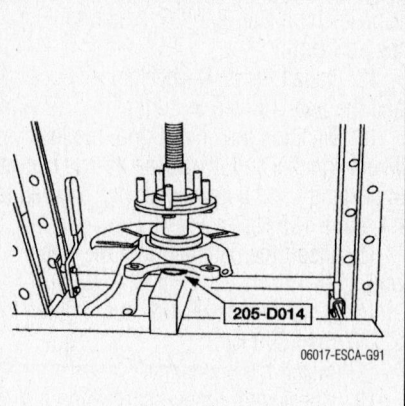

Fig. 156 Using the special tool, press the wheel hub into the wheel bearing—front hub/bearing

➡**This step may not be necessary if the inner wheel bearing race remains in the wheel knuckle after removing the wheel hub.**

4. Using the special tool, press the inner wheel bearing race from the wheel hub.

5. Remove the snapring.

6. Using the special tools, press the outer wheel bearing race from the wheel knuckle.

To install:

7. Position the wheel knuckle in a vise.

➡**Special Tool 205-278 is not seen in place. It is located behind the wheel knuckle.**

8. Using the special tools, install the wheel bearing into the wheel knuckle.

9. Install the snapring.

10. Using the special tool, press the wheel hub into the wheel bearing.

11. Install the wheel knuckle.

ADJUSTMENT

No adjustment is required or possible.

1. If the tire and wheel (hub) is loose on the spindle, does not rotate freely, or has a rough feeling when spun, install a new wheel bearing.

SUSPENSION

COIL SPRING

REMOVAL & INSTALLATION

1. Before servicing the vehicle, refer to the Precautions Section.

2. With the vehicle in NEUTRAL, position it on a hoist.

3. Remove the brake hose bracket-to-wheel knuckle bolt.

4. Vehicles with drum brakes, disconnect the brake line from the wheel cylinder.

5. Vehicles with disc brakes, remove the 2 brake caliper guide bolts and position the brake caliper aside. Support the caliper using mechanic's wire.

6. Support the wheel knuckle and remove the upper ball joint nut.

7. Remove the lower shock absorber nut, washer and bolt.

8. Remove the upper arm inner bolt and remove the upper arm.

9. Loosen the lower arm inner bolt.

➡**Note the position of the coil spring insulator and coil spring for installation.**

10. Carefully lower the wheel knuckle support.

11. Remove the coil spring.

To install:

12. Align the coil spring and coil spring insulator to the previously noted position.

13. Carefully raise the wheel knuckle support.

14. Position the upper control arm and install the upper arm inner bolt tighten to 85 ft. lbs. (115 Nm).

15. Install the lower shock absorber bolt, washer and nut tighten to 129 ft. lbs. (175 Nm).

16. Install the upper ball joint nut and remove the wheel knuckle support tighten the nut to 76 ft. lbs. (103 Nm).

17. Vehicles with disc brakes, position the brake caliper and install the 2 caliper guide bolts. Tighten bolts to 26 ft. lbs (35 Nm).

18. Vehicles with drum brakes, connect the brake line fitting to the wheel cylinder. Tighten the nut to 11 ft. lbs. (15 Nm).

19. Position the brake hose and install the brake hose bracket-to-wheel knuckle

REAR SUSPENSION

bolt. Tighten the nut to 13 ft. lbs (17 Nm).

20. Bleed the brake hydraulic system if line was removed.

LOWER CONTROL ARM

REMOVAL & INSTALLATION

See Figure 157.

1. Before servicing the vehicle, refer to the Precautions Section.

2. Remove or disconnect the following:
   - Negative battery cable
   - Lower ball joint from the knuckle while holding the ball joint stud from moving
   - Lower ball joint nut
   - Lower control arm
   - Lower control arm inner bolt

To install:

3. Install or connect the following:
   - Lower control arm inner bolt
   - Lower control arm. Torque the bolts to 85 ft. lbs. (115 Nm).
   - Lower ball joint nut

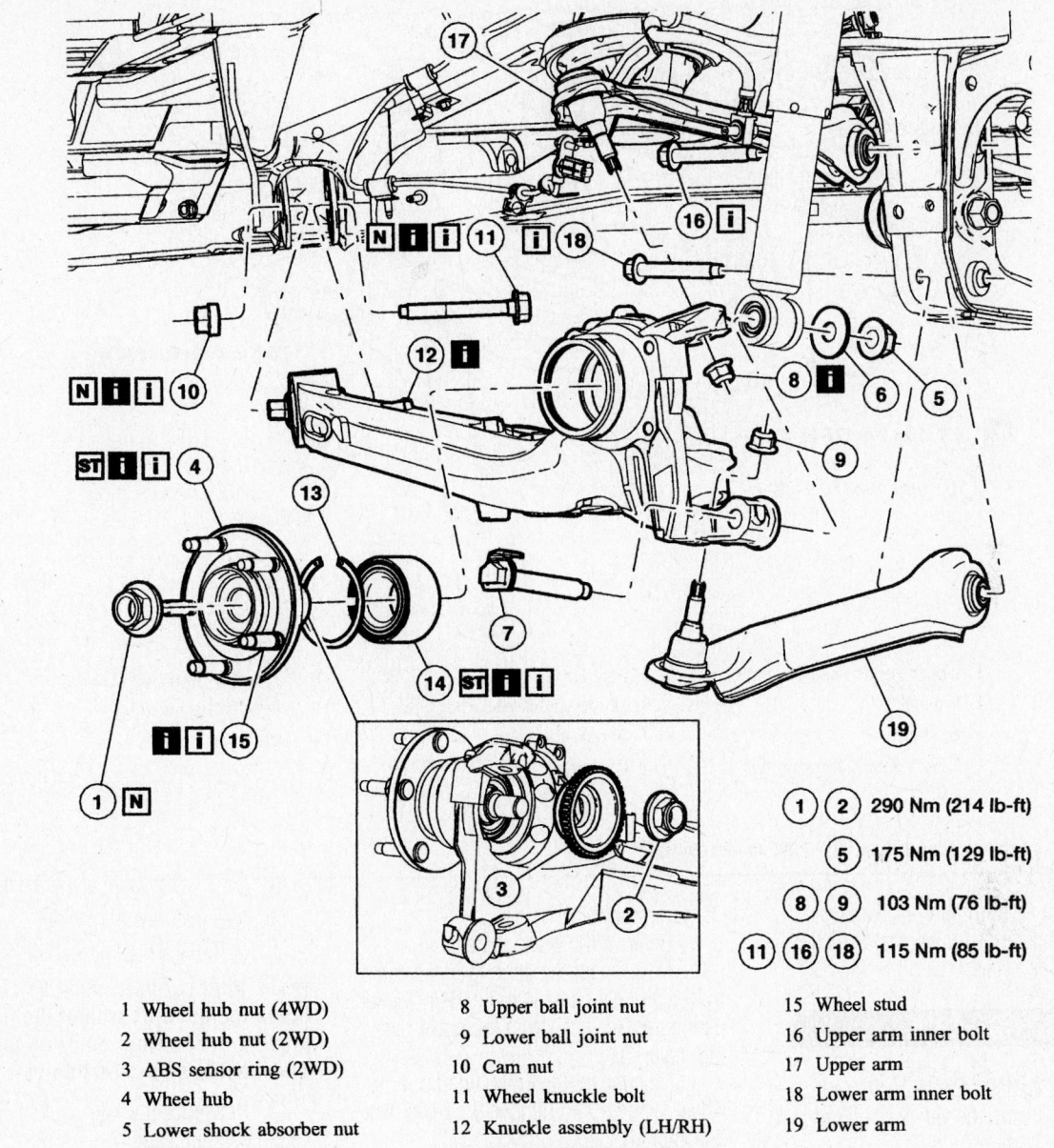

1 Wheel hub nut (4WD)
2 Wheel hub nut (2WD)
3 ABS sensor ring (2WD)
4 Wheel hub
5 Lower shock absorber nut
6 Washer
7 Lower shock absorber bolt
8 Upper ball joint nut
9 Lower ball joint nut
10 Cam nut
11 Wheel knuckle bolt
12 Knuckle assembly (LH/RH)
13 Wheel bearing snap ring
14 Wheel bearing
15 Wheel stud
16 Upper arm inner bolt
17 Upper arm
18 Lower arm inner bolt
19 Lower arm

(1) (2) 290 Nm (214 lb-ft)
(5) 175 Nm (129 lb-ft)
(8) (9) 103 Nm (76 lb-ft)
(11) (16) (18) 115 Nm (85 lb-ft)

67197-ESCA-G47

Fig. 157 Rear lower control arm and related parts

- Lower ball joint the knuckle. Torque the ball joint nut to 76 ft. lbs. (103 Nm).
- Rear wheel

SHOCK ABSORBER

REMOVAL & INSTALLATION

See Figure 158.

1. Before servicing the vehicle, refer to the Precautions Section.

2. Remove the wheel and tire assemblies.

3. Remove the rear quarter trim panel. Remove the upper shock absorber nut, bushing and washer.

4. Remove the lower shock absorber nut, bolt and washer.

5. Remove the shock absorber and bushing.

6. To install, reverse the removal procedure. Torque the upper nut to 13 ft. lbs.; the lower nut to 129 ft. lbs. (175 Nm).

TESTING

1. Road test the vehicle.

2. On a smooth road see if any vibrations are present.

3. Use your hands in order to lift up and push down each corner of the vehicle 3 times.

4. Remove your hands from the vehicle.

5. Replace any shock that exceeds more than two bounces.

6. Raise vehicle for inspection

7. Inspect each shock absorber for external fluid leakage.

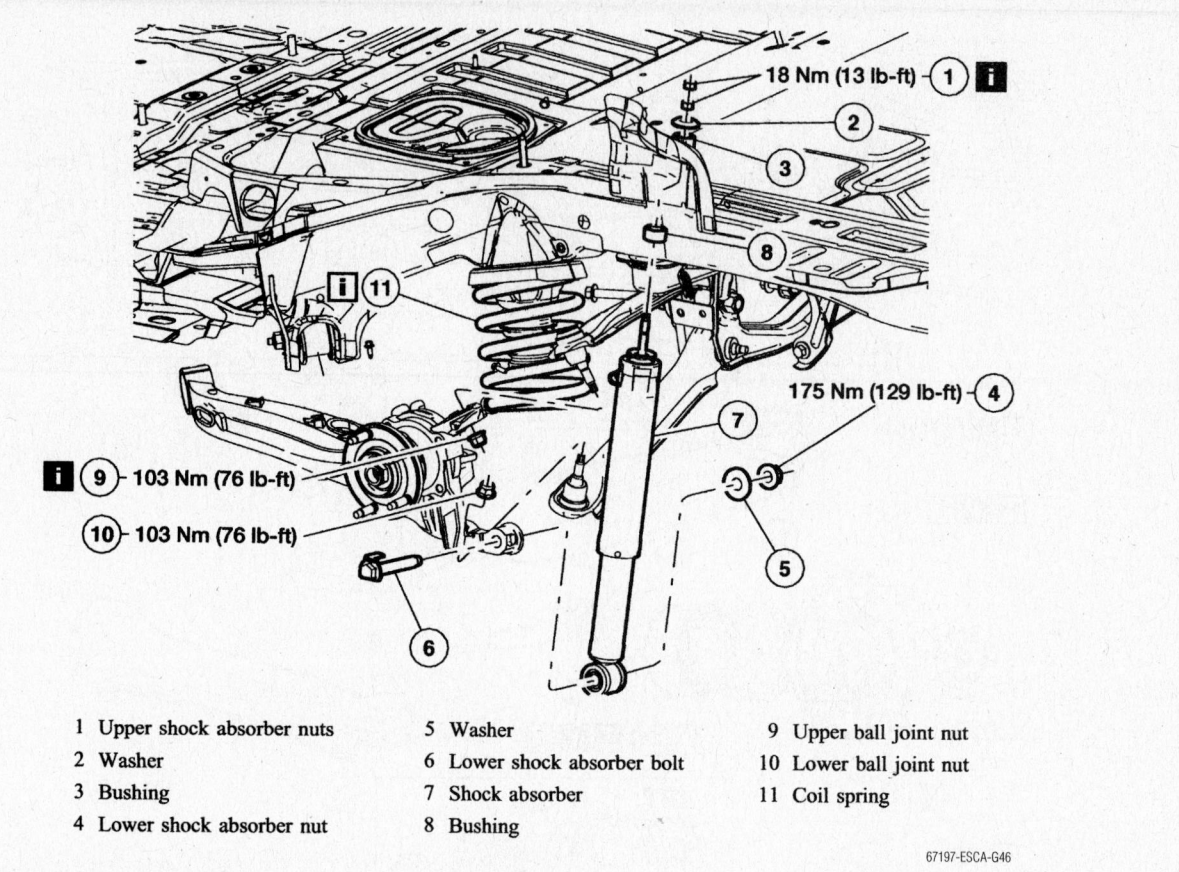

1 Upper shock absorber nuts
2 Washer
3 Bushing
4 Lower shock absorber nut

5 Washer
6 Lower shock absorber bolt
7 Shock absorber
8 Bushing

9 Upper ball joint nut
10 Lower ball joint nut
11 Coil spring

67197-ESCA-G46

Fig. 158 Rear shock absorber and spring—2005 model shown

8. Inspect for deformation or damage.
9. Inspect bushings for wear or damage.
10. Replace as necessary.

UPPER CONTROL ARM

REMOVAL & INSTALLATION

1. Before servicing the vehicle, refer to the Precautions Section.
2. Remove the wheel and tire.

➥It may be necessary to hold the ball joint stud to keep it from turning while removing the nut.

3. Separate the upper arm from the wheel knuckle. Remove the upper ball joint nut.
4. Remove the upper arm inner bolt.
5. Remove the upper arm.
6. To install, reverse the removal procedure. Observe the following torques:
   • Ball joint nut: 76 ft. lbs. (103 Nm)
   • Lower arm bolts: 85 ft. lbs. (115 Nm)

KNUCKLE

REMOVAL & INSTALLATION

1. Before servicing the vehicle, refer to the Precautions Section.

2. Drum brake vehicles:
   a. Remove the brake shoes.
   b. Disconnect the parking brake cable from the brake backing plate. Remove the parking brake cable from the brake backing plate.
   c. Disconnect the brake line from the wheel cylinder and remove the brake line bracket bolt.
3. Disc brake vehicles, remove the parking brake shoes.
4. Remove and discard the wheel hub nut.

✳✳ WARNING

Do not use a hammer to separate the outer constant velocity (CV) joint from the hub.

5. Damage to the threads and internal CV joint components can result.
6. With 4wd, separate the outer CV-joint from the wheel hub.
7. Remove the anti-lock brake system (ABS) wheel speed sensor bolt and the 2 ABS wheel speed sensor wire bolts.
8. Remove and position the wheel speed sensor and harness aside.

9. Remove the coil spring.
10. Remove the lower ball joint nut.

➥The joint surfaces must be clean. Clean the general area of the joint to prevent debris from entering the joint. Clean using only mild liquids.

11. Reference mark the notch on the cam nut adjustment cam.
12. Remove and discard the wheel knuckle bolt.
13. Remove and discard the cam nut.
14. Remove the wheel knuckle.

To install:

✳✳ WARNING

The joint area must be free of debris to ensure correct clamping.

➥The joint surfaces and the bushing sleeve serrations must be clean before assembly.

15. Clean the joint surfaces and the bushing sleeve serrations with a wire brush.

➥Align the notch on the cam nut with the reference marks.

16. Position the wheel knuckle and install a new wheel knuckle bolt and cam nut.

17. Using a suitable tool, hold the cam nut stationary while tightening the wheel knuckle bolt. Tighten to 111 ft. lbs. (150 Nm).

18. Position the ABS wheel speed sensor harness and the sensor.

19. Position the lower ball joint into the wheel knuckle and install the lower ball joint nut. Tighten to 76 ft. lbs. (103 Nm).

20. Install the coil spring.

21. Install the ABS wheel speed sensor bolt and the 2 ABS wheel speed sensor wire bolts. Tighten to 80 inch lbs. (9 Nm).

22. With 4wd, install the outer CV joint into the wheel hub.

23. Install a new wheel hub nut. Tighten to 214 ft. lbs. (290 Nm).

24. Install the brake shoes.

25. Connect the brake line to the wheel cylinder. Tighten to 13 ft. lbs. (17 Nm).

26. Install the brake line bracket bolt. Tighten to 16 ft. lbs. (22 Nm).

27. Connect the parking brake cable to the brake backing plate and install the parking brake cable bracket bolt. Tighten to 17 ft. lbs. (23 Nm).

28. Install the parking brake shoes.

29. Check and adjust the wheel alignment as necessary.

WHEEL BEARINGS

REMOVAL & INSTALLATION

2-Wheel Drive Vehicles

See Figures 159 through 165.

1. Before servicing the vehicle, refer to the Precautions Section.

2. Remove or disconnect the following:
   • Negative battery cable
   • Rear wheel
   • Rear brake drum
   • Wheel hub nut
   • Wheel hub
   • Inner wheel bearing race from the hub
   • Snapring
   • Wheel bearing outer race from the knuckle

To install:

3. Install or connect the following:
   • Wheel bearing in to the knuckle
   • Snapring
   • Wheel hub into the wheel bearing
   • Wheel hub nut. Torque the nut to 214 ft. lbs. (290 Nm).
   • Brake drum
   • Rear wheel
   • Negative battery cable

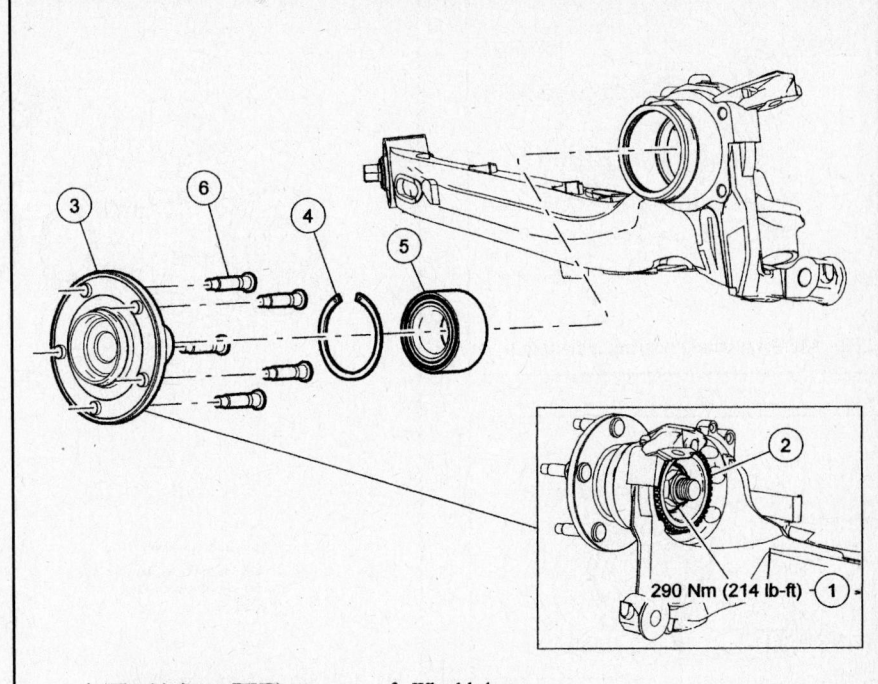

1 Wheel hub nut (FWD)
2 Anti-lock brake system (ABS) wheel speed sensor ring (FWD)
3 Wheel hub
4 Wheel bearing snap ring
5 Wheel bearing
6 Wheel studs

06017-ESCA-G92

Fig. 159 Rear hub and bearing

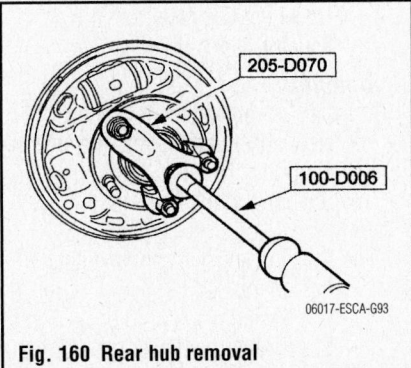

06017-ESCA-G93

Fig. 160 Rear hub removal

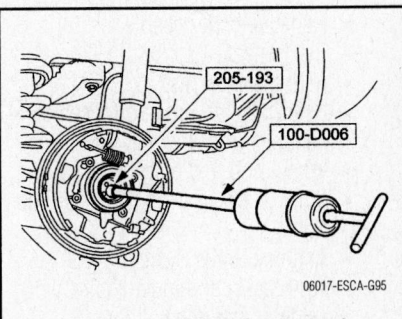

06017-ESCA-G95

Fig. 162 Rear wheel bearing removal— 2wd

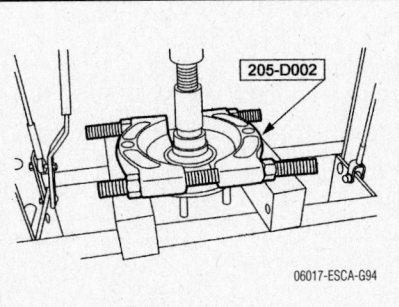

06017-ESCA-G94

Fig. 161 Inner wheel bearing removal— rear hub/bearing

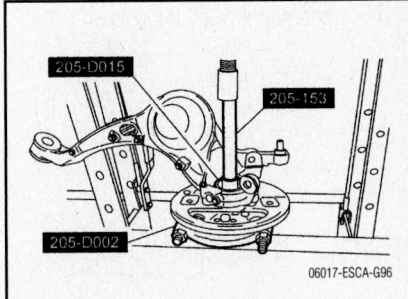

06017-ESCA-G96

Fig. 163 Rear wheel bearing removal—4wd

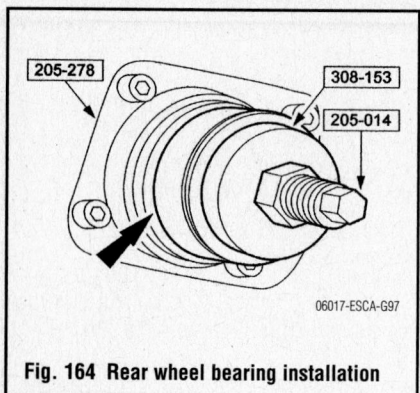

Fig. 164 Rear wheel bearing installation

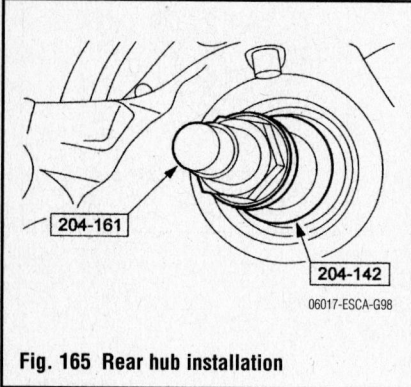

Fig. 165 Rear hub installation

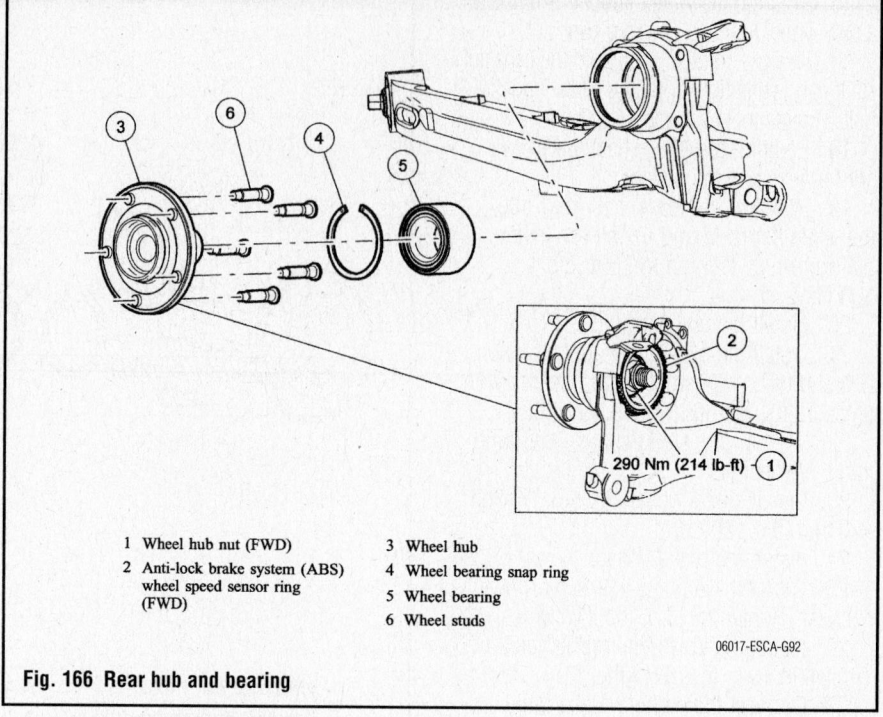

1 Wheel hub nut (FWD)
2 Anti-lock brake system (ABS) wheel speed sensor ring (FWD)
3 Wheel hub
4 Wheel bearing snap ring
5 Wheel bearing
6 Wheel studs

Fig. 166 Rear hub and bearing

4-Wheel Drive Vehicles

See Figure 166.

1. Before servicing the vehicle, refer to the Precautions Section.

2. Remove or disconnect the following:
   - Negative battery cable
   - Rear wheel
   - Rear brake shoes
   - Rear halfshaft nut and loosen the halfshaft from the hub
   - Wheel hub and place it in a vise
   - Inner wheel bearing race from the hub
   - Antilock Brake System (ABS) sensor bracket and move the sensor aside, if equipped
   - Parking brake cable from the steering knuckle
   - Brake line from the wheel cylinder and support the knuckle
   - Lower shock absorber nut
   - Lower ball joint by holding the ball joint stud
   - Upper ball joint
   - Coil spring while noting the location of the insulator
   - Steering knuckle cam
   - Steering knuckle
   - Snapring and press out the outer wheel bearing race from the knuckle

To install:

3. Install or connect the following:
   - New wheel bearing into the steering knuckle
   - Snapring to the knuckle
   - Wheel hub
   - Steering knuckle cam and hand tighten the bolt
   - Coil spring
   - Shock absorber lower nut. Torque the nut to 85 ft. lbs. (115 Nm) for 2002–04 models; 129 ft. lbs. (175 Nm).
   - Upper ball joint. Torque the nut to 76 ft. lbs. (103 Nm).
   - Lower ball joint. Torque the nut to 76 ft. lbs. (103 Nm). Align the steering knuckle cam and torque the bolt to 85 ft. lbs. (115 Nm).
   - Brake line to the wheel cylinder. Torque the brake line bracket bolt to 15 ft. lbs. (20 Nm) and the brake line fastener to 11 ft. lbs. (15 Nm).
   - Parking brake cable to the backing plate. Torque the bolt to 16 ft. lbs. (22 Nm).
   - ABS sensor bracket. Torque the bolt to 80 inch lbs. (9 Nm), if equipped
   - Halfshaft nut. Torque the nut to 214 ft. lbs. (290 Nm).
   - Brake shoes
   - Rear wheel
   - Negative battery cable

4. Fill and bleed the brake system.

5. Check and adjust the wheel alignment as needed.

FORD, LINCOLN AND MERCURY

Diagnostic Trouble Codes

DIAGNOSTIC TROUBLE CODES

OBD II VEHICLE APPLICATIONS

FORD

Crown Victoria
2005–2007
- 4.6L . . . . .VIN V, W

Edge
2006–2007
- 3.5L . . . . .VIN C

Explorer & Explorer Sport-Trac
2005–2007
- 4.0L . . . . .VIN E
- 4.0L . . . . .VIN K
- 4.6L . . . . .VIN W
- 4.6L . . . . .VIN 8

F-150, F-250, F-350
2005–2007
- 4.2L . . . . .VIN 2
- 4.6L . . . . .VIN W
- 5.4L . . . . .VIN 5
- 5.4L . . . . .VIN L
- 5.4L . . . . .VIN V
- 6.8L . . . . .VIN S
- 6.8L . . . . .VIN V
- 6.8L . . . . .VIN W

E-150, E-250, E-350
2005–2007
- 4.6L . . . . .VIN W
- 5.4L . . . . .VIN L
- 6.8 L . . . . .VIN S

Escape
2005–2007
- 2.3L . . . . .VIN Z
- 3.0L . . . . .VIN 1

Escape Hybrid
2005–2007
- 2.3L . . . . .VIN H

LINCOLN

Aviator
2005
- 4.6L . . . . .VIN H

Mark LT
2006–2007
- 5.4L . . . . .VIN 5

MKX
2006–2007
- 3.5L . . . . .VIN C

Town car
2005–2007
- 4.6L . . . . .VIN V, W

MERCURY

Grand Marquis
2005–2007
- 4.6L . . . . .VIN V, W

Mariner
2005–2007
- 2.3L . . . . .VIN ZH
- 3.0L . . . . .VIN 1

Mariner Hybrid
2005–2007
- 2.3L . . . . .VIN H

Mountaineer
2005–2007
- 4.0L . . . . .VIN E
- 4.0L . . . . .VIN K
- 4.6L . . . . .VIN W
- 4.6L . . . . .VIN 8

INTRODUCTION

To use this information, first read and record all codes in memory along with any Freeze Frame data. *If the PCM reset function is done prior to recording any data, all codes and freeze frame data will be lost!* Look up the desired code by DTC number, Code Title and Conditions (enable criteria) that indicate why a code set, and how to drive the vehicle. **1T and 2T** indicate a 1-trip or 2-trip fault and the Monitor type.

Gas Engine OBD II Trouble Code List (P0xxx Codes)

DTC	Trouble Code Title, Conditions & Possible Causes
DTC: P0010 **2T CCM, MIL: Yes** **Years:** 2005, 2006, 2007 **Models:** All Models **Engines:** All **Transmissions:** All	**Variable Cam Timing Solenoid 'A' Circuit Malfunction** Key on or engine running; and the PCM detected an unexpected high voltage or low voltage condition on the Variable Cam Timing (VCT) Solenoid 'A' control circuit during testing. **Possible Causes:** • VCT 'A' solenoid connector is damaged, loose or shorted • VCT 'A' solenoid control circuit is open, shorted to ground or shorted to power • VCT 'A' solenoid is damaged or the PCM has failed
DTC: P0011 **2T CCM, MIL: Yes** **Years:** 2005, 2006, 2007 **Models:** All Models **Engines:** All **Transmissions:** All	**Variable Cam Timing Over Advanced (Bank 1)** Engine started; and the PCM detected the camshaft timing exceeded the maximum calibrated advance value, or the camshaft remained in an advanced position during the CCM test. **Possible Causes:** • Camshaft timing improperly set, or continuous oil flow to the VCT piston chamber • Camshaft advance mechanism (the VCT unit) is sticking or binding mechanically • VCT solenoid valve is stuck in open position
DTC: P0012 **2T CCM, MIL: Yes** **Years:** 2005, 2006, 2007 **Models:** All Models **Engines:** All **Transmissions:** All	**Variable Cam Timing Over Retarded (Bank 1)** Engine started; and the PCM detected the camshaft timing exceeded the maximum calibrated retard value, or the camshaft remained in a retarded position during the CCM test. **Possible Causes:** • Camshaft timing improperly set, or continuous oil flow to the VCT piston chamber • Camshaft advance mechanism (the VCT unit) is sticking or binding mechanically • VCT solenoid valve is stuck in open position
DTC: P0020 **2T CCM, MIL: Yes** **Years:** 2005, 2006, 2007 **Models:** All Models **Engines:** All **Transmissions:** All	**Variable Cam Timing Solenoid 'B' Circuit Malfunction** Key on or engine running; and the PCM detected an unexpected high or low voltage condition on the Variable Cam Timing (VCT) Solenoid 'B' control circuit during testing. **Possible Causes:** • VCT 'B' solenoid connector is damaged, loose or shorted • VCT 'B' solenoid control circuit is open, shorted to ground or shorted to power • VCT 'B' solenoid is damaged or the PCM has failed
DTC: P0020 **2T CCM, MIL: Yes** **Years:** 2005, 2006, 2007 **Models:** All Models **Engines:** All **Transmissions:** All	**Variable Cam Timing Over Advanced (Bank 2)** Engine started; and the PCM detected the camshaft timing exceeded the maximum calibrated advance value, or the camshaft remained in an advanced position during the CCM test. **Possible Causes:** • Camshaft timing improperly set, or continuous oil flow to the VCT piston chamber • Camshaft advance mechanism (the VCT unit) is sticking or binding mechanically • VCT solenoid valve is stuck in open position
DTC: P0022 **2T CCM, MIL: Yes** **Years:** 2005, 2006, 2007 **Models:** All Models **Engines:** All **Transmissions:** All	**Variable Cam Timing Over Retarded (Bank 2)** Engine started; and the PCM detected the camshaft timing exceeded the maximum calibrated retard value, or the camshaft remained in a retarded position during the CCM test. **Possible Causes:** • Camshaft timing improperly set, or continuous oil flow to the VCT piston chamber • Camshaft advance mechanism (the VCT unit) is sticking or binding mechanically • VCT solenoid valve is stuck in open position
DTC: P0040 **2T CCM, MIL: Yes** **Years:** 2005, 2006, 2007 **Models:** Crown Victoria, Grand Marquis, Town Car **Engines:** 4.6L VIN V, W **Transmissions:** All	**Upstream Oxygen Sensors Swapped From Bank To Bank** Engine started; and after the PCM performed a brief fuel shift in engine Bank 1, it did not detect the correct response in the HO2S-11 and/or HO2S-21 (sensors) during testing. **Possible Causes:** • HO2S-11 and HO2S-21 harness connectors are swapped • HO2S-11 and HO2S-21 wiring is crossed inside the harness • HO2S-11 and HO2S-21 wires are crossed at 104-pin connector
DTC: P0041 **2T CCM, MIL: Yes** **Years:** 2005, 2006, 2007 **Models:** Crown Victoria, Grand Marquis, Town Car **Engines:** 4.6L VIN V, W **Transmissions:** All	**Downstream Oxygen Sensors Swapped Bank To Bank** Engine started; and after the PCM performed a brief fuel shift in engine Bank 1, it did not detect the correct response in the HO2S-12 and/or HO2S-22 (sensors) during testing. **Possible Causes:** • HO2S-12 and HO2S-22 harness connectors are swapped • HO2S-12 and HO2S-22 wiring is crossed inside the harness • HO2S-12 and HO2S-22 wires are crossed at 104-pin connector

DTC	Trouble Code Title, Conditions & Possible Causes
DTC: P0041 **2T CCM, MIL: Yes** **Years:** 2005, 2006, 2007 **Models:** Crown Victoria, Grand Marquis, Town Car **Engines:** 4.6L VIN V, W **Transmissions:** All	**TP Sensor, ETC TP Sensor Inconsistent With MAF Sensor** Engine started, KOER Self Test enabled, and the PCM detected the MAF and ETC TP sensor signals were not consistent with the calibrated values expected for these sensors in the test. TP Sensor: Drive the vehicle and then monitor the TPNS PID in all gears. A TP PID under 0.24v (4.82%) with a LOAD PID over 55%, or a TP V PID over 2.44v (49.05%) with a LOAD PID under 30% will set this code. ETC TP: Drive the vehicle and then monitor the TPNS PID in all gears. A TPNS PID under 0.24v (4.82%) with a LOAD PID over 55% or TPNS PID over 2.44v (49.05%) with LOAD PID under 30% will set a code. **Possible Causes:** • Air leak exists between MAF sensor and the throttle body • MAF sensor is out-of-calibration or it has failed • TP sensor is not seated properly or the TP sensor is damaged
DTC: P0102 **2T CCM, MIL: Yes** **Years:** 2005, 2006, 2007 **Models:** All Models **Engines:** All **Transmissions:** All	**MAF Sensor Circuit Low Input** DTC P0505 not set, engine started, and the PCM detected the MAF sensor signal was less than 0.23v during the CCM test period. **Possible Causes:** • Check for leaks at air outlet tube • Sensor power circuit open, sensor ground circuit open • Sensor signal circuit open (may be disconnected) • Check for loose tube clamps near the MAF sensor
DTC: P0103 **2T CCM, MIL: Yes** **Years:** 2005, 2006, 2007 **Models:** All Models **Engines:** All **Transmissions:** All	**MAF Sensor Circuit High Input** DTC P0505 not set, engine started, and the PCM detected the MAF sensor signal was more than 4.60v during the CCM test period. **Possible Causes:** • Check for a restricted inlet screen on the MAF sensor. • MAF sensor signal circuit is shorted to system power (B+) • MAF sensor is damaged or the PCM has failed
DTC: P0106 **2T CCM, MIL: Yes** **Years:** 2005, 2006, 2007 **Models:** All Models **Engines:** All **Transmissions:** All	**Barometric Pressure Sensor Circuit Performance** Engine started, and the PCM detected the BARO sensor was out of range during the CCM test. The BARO sensor signal should be in a range of 4.0-6.0v. The Scan Tool displays the sensor reading as a frequency. **Note: The sensor VREF should be less than 6.0v at all times.** **Possible Causes:** • Sensor has deteriorated (response time too slow) or has failed • PCM has failed
DTC: P0107 **2T CCM, MIL: Yes** **Years:** 2005, 2006, 2007 **Models:** All Models **Engines:** All **Transmissions:** All	**Barometric Pressure Sensor Circuit Low Input** Engine started, and the PCM detected the BARO sensor indicated less than the minimum calibrated parameter. The BARO sensor is a variable capacitance unit used to detect altitude. **Possible Causes:** • BARO sensor signal circuit is shorted to ground • BARO sensor VREF circuit (5v) is open • BARO sensor is damaged or it has failed • PCM has failed
DTC: P0108 **2T CCM, MIL: Yes** **Years:** 2005, 2006, 2007 **Models:** All Models **Engines:** All **Transmissions:** All	**Barometric Sensor Circuit High Input** Engine started, and the PCM detected the BARO sensor signal was more than the maximum calibrated parameter of 5.0v. **Note: The sensor VREF should be 4.0v to 6.0v at all times.** **Possible Causes:** • BARO sensor connector is damaged, open or shorted • BARO sensor signal circuit is open or shorted to VREF (5v) • BARO sensor is damaged or it has failed • PCM has failed
DTC: P0109 **2T CCM, MIL: Yes** **Years:** 2005, 2006, 2007 **Models:** All Models **Engines:** All **Transmissions:** All	**Barometric Sensor Circuit Intermittent Input** Engine started, and the PCM detected the BARO sensor signal had an intermittent failure during normal engine operation. **Possible Causes:** • BARO sensor signal circuit is open or shorted to ground (intermittent) • BARO sensor VREF circuit (5v) is open • BARO sensor signal circuit is shorted to ground (Intermittent) • BARO sensor is damaged or it has failed

DTC	Trouble Code Title, Conditions & Possible Causes
DTC: P0112 **2T CCM, MIL: Yes** **Years:** 2005, 2006, 2007 **Models:** All Models **Engines:** All **Transmissions:** All	**Intake Air Temperature Sensor Circuit Low Input** Key on or engine running; and the PCM detected the IAT sensor signal was less than the self-test minimum of 0.20v (Scan Tool reads over 250°F). This is a thermistor-type sensor with a variable resistance that changes when exposed to different temperatures. **Possible Causes:** • IAT sensor signal circuit is grounded (check wiring & connector) • IAT sensor is damaged or it has failed • PCM has failed
DTC: P0113 **2T CCM, MIL: Yes** **Years:** 2005, 2006, 2007 **Models:** All Models **Engines:** All **Transmissions:** All	**Intake Air Temperature Sensor Circuit High Input** Key on or engine running; and the PCM detected the IAT sensor signal was more than the self-test maximum 4.60v (Scan Tool reads under −46°F). This is a thermistor-type sensor with a variable resistance that changes when exposed to different temperatures. **Possible Causes:** • IAT sensor signal circuit is open (inspect wiring & connector) • IAT sensor signal circuit is shorted to VREF (5v) • IAT sensor is damaged or it has failed • PCM has failed
DTC: P0116 **2T ECT, MIL: Yes** **Years:** 2005, 2006, 2007 **Models:** All Models **Engines:** All **Transmissions:** All	**ECT Sensor / CHT Sensor Signal Range/Performance** Engine off for a calibrated period of time after an engine cold soak period over 6 hours, engine started, and the PCM detected the ECT sensor exceeded the IAT sensor by more than a calibrated value (e.g., 30°F), or the ECT sensor was more than a calibrated value of 225°F; the Catalyst, Fuel System, HO2S and Misfire Monitor did not complete, or the timer expired. **Possible Causes:** • Check for low coolant level or incorrect coolant mixture • CHT sensor is out-of-calibration or it has failed • ECT sensor is out-of-calibration or it has failed
DTC: P0117 **2T CCM, MIL: Yes** **Years:** 2005, 2006, 2007 **Models:** All Models **Engines:** All **Transmissions:** All	**ECT Sensor Circuit Low Input** Key on or engine running; and the PCM detected the ECT sensor signal was less than the self-test minimum of 0.20v (Scan Tool reads over 250°F). This is a thermistor-type sensor with a variable resistance that changes when exposed to different temperatures **Possible Causes:** • ECT sensor signal circuit is grounded in the wiring harness • ECT sensor is damaged or the PCM has failed
DTC: P0118 **2T CCM, MIL: Yes** **Years:** 2005, 2006, 2007 **Models:** All Models **Engines:** All **Transmissions:** All	**ECT Sensor Circuit High Input** Key on or engine running; and the PCM detected the ECT sensor signal was more than the self-test maximum of 4.60v (Scan Tool reads under −46°F). This is a thermistor-type sensor with a variable resistance that changes when exposed to different temperatures **Possible Causes:** • ECT sensor signal circuit is open (inspect wiring & connector) • ECT sensor signal circuit is shorted to VREF (5v) • ECT sensor is damaged or it has failed • PCM has failed
DTC: P0121 **2T CCM, MIL: Yes** **Years:** 2005, 2006, 2007 **Models:** All Models Except Crown Victoria, Grand Marquis & Town Car **Engines:** All **Transmissions:** All	**TP Sensor Signal Range/Performance** Engine started; then immediately following a condition where the engine was running under at off-idle, the PCM detected the TP sensor signal indicated the throttle did not return to its previous closed position during the CCM Rationality test. **Possible Causes:** • Throttle plate is binding, dirty or sticking • TP sensor signal circuit open (inspect wiring & connector) • TP sensor ground circuit open (inspect wiring & connector) • TP Sensor is damaged or has failed
DTC: P0121 **2T CCM, MIL: Yes** **Years:** 2005, 2006, 2007 **Models:** Crown Victoria, Grand Marquis, Town Car **Engines:** 4.6L VIN V, W **Transmissions:** All	**ETC Throttle Position Sensor Signal Range/Performance** Key on or engine running; then immediately after the throttle is open or following a closed throttle (deceleration) event, the PCM detected the TP2 PID (TP Sensor 2) signal indicated more than 93% (4.65v) from its previous closed position during the CCM Rationality test. **Possible Causes:** • ECT TP sensor connector is damaged, loose or shorted • ETC TP sensor signal circuit is open • ETC TP sensor ground circuit is open • ETC TP sensor circuit VREF (5v) is open • ECT TP sensor is not seated properly, or it is sticking • ETC TP Sensor is damaged or it has failed

DTC	Trouble Code Title, Conditions & Possible Causes
DTC: P0122 **2T CCM, MIL: Yes** **Years:** 2005, 2006, 2007 **Models:** All Models Except Crown Victoria, Grand Marquis & Town Car **Engines:** All **Transmissions:** All	**TP Sensor Circuit Low Input** Key on or engine running; and the PCM detected the TP sensor was less than 0.17v (Scan Tool TP PID reads under 3.42%) in the test. **Possible Causes:** • TP sensor signal circuit open (inspect wiring & connector) • TP sensor signal shorted to ground (inspect wiring & connector) • TP sensor VREF circuit is open (between the sensor and PCM) • TP sensor is damaged or has failed • PCM has failed
DTC: P0122 **2T CCM, MIL: Yes** **Years:** 2005, 2006, 2007 **Models:** Crown Victoria, Grand Marquis, Town Car **Engines:** 4.6L VIN V, W **Transmissions:** All	**ETC Throttle Position Sensor Circuit Low Input** Key on or engine running; and the PCM detected the ETC TP sensor was below the self-test minimum of 0.17v (Scan Tool below 3.42%). **Possible Causes:** • TP sensor signal circuit open (inspect wiring & connector) • TP sensor signal shorted to ground (inspect wiring & connector) • TP sensor VREF circuit is open (between the sensor and PCM) • TP sensor is damaged or has failed • PCM has failed
DTC: P0122 **2T CCM, MIL: Yes** **Years:** 2005, 2006, 2007 **Models:** Crown Victoria, Grand Marquis, Town Car **Engines:** 4.6L VIN V, W **Transmissions:** All	**ETC Throttle Position Sensor Circuit High Input** Key on or engine running; and the PCM detected the ETC TP sensor was less than the self-test maximum of 4.65v (Scan Tool TP PID reads more than 93%) during the CCM test. **Possible Causes:** • TP sensor connector is damaged, loose or shorted • TP sensor signal circuit is open or shorted to ground • TP sensor VREF circuit is open (between the sensor and PCM) • TP sensor is damaged or has failed • PCM has failed
DTC: P0123 **2T CCM, MIL: Yes** **Years:** 2005, 2006, 2007 **Models:** All Models **Engines:** All **Transmissions:** All	**TP Sensor Circuit High Input** Engine started, and the PCM detected the TP sensor signal was more than the self-test maximum of 4.65v (equivalent to a Scan Tool TP PID of more than 93%) during testing. **Possible Causes:** • TP sensor not seated correctly in housing (may be damaged) • TP sensor signal is circuit shorted to VREF or system voltage • TP sensor ground circuit is open (check the wiring harness) • Perform a "sensor sweep test" and monitor for any glitches • PCM has failed
DTC: P0125 **2T ECT, MIL: Yes** **Years:** 2005, 2006, 2007 **Models:** All Models **Engines:** All **Transmissions:** All	**Insufficient Coolant Temperature For Closed Loop** Engine runtime at road load more than 6 minutes, and the PCM detected that the ECT sensor (or CHT sensor) signal did not indicate the required engine temperature value to enter closed loop within a specified amount of time. The amount of time is calculated from the point at which the engine is started, and depends upon the ECT or CHT sensor signal value at startup. **Possible Causes:** • Check the coolant mixture for an incorrect mixture • Check the operation of the thermostat (it may be stuck open) • ECT sensor (or the CHT sensor) has failed • Inspect for low coolant level
DTC: P0127 **2T CCM, MIL: Yes** **Years:** 2005, 2006, 2007 **Models:** All Models **Engines:** All **Transmissions:** All	**IAT Sensor 2 Circuit High Input** Engine started, engine running for a calibrated period of time, and the PCM detected the IAT Sensor 2 (PID IAT2) signal was too high. This code indicates a potential fault present in the Intercooler system (the Supercharger Boost is bypassed when this code is set). **Possible Causes:** • Blockage present in the Heat Exchangers • Low fluid level, or a fluid leak is present • Intercooler pump or relay has failed • Intercooler coolant lines may be crossed

DTC	Trouble Code Title, Conditions & Possible Causes
DTC: P0128 **2T CCM, MIL: Yes** **Years:** 2005, 2006, 2007 **Models:** All Models **Engines:** All **Transmissions:** All	**Intake Air Temperature Sensor 2 Circuit High Input** Engine started, vehicle driven for over 10 minutes, and the PCM detected the engine did not reach an engine operating temperature of 160°F after an additional runtime of 2 minutes. **Possible Causes:** • Check the operation of the thermostat (it may be stuck open) • ECT sensor or CHT sensor is out-of-calibration, or has failed • Inspect for low coolant level or an incorrect coolant mixture
DTC: P0131 **2T CCM, MIL: Yes** **Years:** 2005, 2006, 2007 **Models:** All Models **Engines:** All **Transmissions:** All	**HO2S-11 (Bank 1 Sensor 1) Circuit Low Input** Engine running for more than 5 minutes, and the PCM detected the HO2S signal was in a negative voltage range referred to as "character shift downward". This code sets when the HO2S signal remains in a low state (usually less than 156 mv). In effect, it does not switch properly between 0.1v and 1.1v in closed loop operation. **Possible Causes:** • HO2S is contaminated (due to presence of silicone in fuel) • HO2S signal and ground circuit wires crossed in wiring harness • HO2S signal circuit is shorted to sensor or chassis ground • HO2S element has failed (internal short condition) • PCM has failed
DTC: P0132 **2T CCM, MIL: Yes** **Years:** 2005, 2006, 2007 **Models:** All Models **Engines:** All **Transmissions:** All	**HO2S-11 (Bank 1 Sensor 1) Circuit High Input** Engine running for more than 5 minutes, and the PCM detected the HO2S signal remained in a high state (i.e., more than 1.5v). **Note: The HO2S signal circuit may be shorted to the heater power circuit due to tracking inside of the HO2S connector. Remove the connector and visually inspect the connector for signs of oil or water.** **Possible Causes:** • HO2S signal shorted to heater power circuit inside connector • HO2S signal circuit shorted to VREF or to system voltage • PCM has failed
DTC: P0133 **2T O2S, MIL: Yes** **Years:** 2005, 2006, 2007 **Models:** All Models **Engines:** All **Transmissions:** All	**HO2S-11 (Bank 1 Sensor 1) Circuit Slow Response** Engine started, engine running in closed loop for over 5 minutes, and the PCM detected the HO2S amplitude and frequency were out of the normal range (e.g., the HO2S rich to lean switch time was more than 100 ms) during the HO2S Monitor test. **Possible Causes:** • HO2S is contaminated (due to presence of silicone in fuel) • HO2S signal circuit open • Leaks present in the exhaust manifold or exhaust pipes • HO2S is damaged or has failed • PCM has failed
DTC: P0135 **2T O2HTR, MIL: Yes** **Years:** 2005, 2006, 2007 **Models:** All Models **Engines:** All **Transmissions:** All	**HO2S-11 (Bank 1 Sensor 1) Heater Circuit Malfunction** Engine started, engine running for 5 minutes, and the PCM detected an unexpected voltage condition, or it detected excessive current draw in the heater circuit during the CCM test. **Possible Causes:** • HO2S heater power circuit is open or heater ground circuit open • HO2S signal tracking (due to oil or moisture in the connector) • HO2S is damaged or has failed • PCM has failed
DTC: P0136 **2T O2S, MIL: Yes** **Years:** 2005, 2006, 2007 **Models:** All Models **Engines:** All **Transmissions:** All	**HO2S-12 (Bank 1 Sensor 1) Circuit No Activity** Engine started, engine running in closed loop for over 5 minutes, and the PCM detected the HO2S signal failed to meet the maximum or minimum voltage levels (i.e., it failed the voltage range check). **Possible Causes:** • Leaks present in the exhaust manifold or exhaust pipes • HO2S signal wire and ground wire crossed in connector • HO2S element is fuel contaminated or has failed • PCM has failed
DTC: P0138 **2T CCM, MIL: Yes** **Years:** 2005, 2006, 2007 **Models:** All Models **Engines:** All **Transmissions:** All	**HO2S-12 (Bank 1 Sensor 2) Circuit High Input** Engine running for more than 5 minutes, and the PCM detected the HO2S signal remained in a high state (i.e., more than 1.5v). **Note: The HO2S signal circuit may be shorted to the heater power circuit due to tracking inside of the HO2S connector. Remove the connector and visually inspect the connector for signs of oil or water.** **Possible Causes:** • HO2S signal shorted to heater power circuit in the connector • HO2S signal circuit shorted to VREF or to system voltage • PCM has failed

DTC	Trouble Code Title, Conditions & Possible Causes

DTC: P0141
2T O2HTR, MIL: Yes
Years: 2005, 2006, 2007
Models: All Models
Engines: All
Transmissions: All
	HO2S-12 (Bank 1 Sensor 2) Heater Circuit Malfunction
	Engine running for 5 minutes, and the PCM detected an open or shorted condition, or excessive current draw in the heater circuit.
	Possible Causes:
	  • HO2S heater power circuit is open or heater ground circuit open
	  • HO2S signal tracking (due to oil or moisture in the connector)
	  • HO2S is damaged or has failed
	  • PCM has failed

DTC: P0148
2T CCM, MIL: Yes
Years: 2005, 2006, 2007
Models: All Models
Engines: All
Transmissions: All
	Fuel Delivery Error
	Engine started, engine running for a specified period of time in closed loop, then after at least one WOT event was recorded, the PCM detected a lean air/fuel condition in at least one engine bank during the wide-open throttle event.
	Possible Causes:
	  • Severely restricted fuel filter
	  • Severely pinched or restricted fuel delivery line

DTC: P0151
2T CCM, MIL: Yes
Years: 2005, 2006, 2007
Models: All Models with a 4-Cyl, V6 or V8 engine
Engines: All Except V10
Transmissions: All
	HO2S-21 (Bank 2 Sensor 1) Circuit Low Input
	Engine started, engine running for over 5 minutes, and the PCM detected the HO2S signal was in a negative voltage range referred to as "character shift downward". This code sets when the HO2S signal remains in a low state (less than 156 mv). In effect, the sensor did not switch properly between 0.1v and 1.1v in closed loop.
	Possible Causes:
	  • HO2S connector is damaged or shorted
	  • HO2S signal and ground circuit wires crossed in wiring harness
	  • HO2S signal circuit is shorted to sensor or chassis ground
	  • HO2S element has failed (internal short condition)
	  • PCM has failed

DTC: P0152
2T CCM, MIL: Yes
Years: 2005, 2006, 2007
Models: All Models with a 4-Cyl, V6 or V8 engine
Engines: All Except V10
Transmissions: All
	HO2S-21 (Bank 2 Sensor 1) Circuit High Input
	Engine started, engine runtime over 5 minutes, and the PCM detected the HO2S signal remained in a high state (more than 1.5v).
	Note: The HO2S signal circuit may be shorted to the heater power circuit due to tracking inside of the HO2S connector. Remove the connector and visually inspect the connector for signs of oil or water.
	Possible Causes:
	  • HO2S is contaminated (due to presence of silicone in fuel)
	  • HO2S signal tracking (due to oil or moisture in the connector)
	  • HO2S signal circuit is open or shorted to VREF
	  • PCM has failed

DTC: P0153
2T O2S, MIL: Yes
Years: 2005, 2006, 2007
Models: All Models with a 4-Cyl, V6 or V8 engine
Engines: All Except V10
Transmissions: All
	HO2S-21 (Bank 2 Sensor 1) Circuit Slow Response
	Engine started, engine running in closed loop for over 5 minutes, and the PCM detected the HO2S amplitude and frequency were out of the normal range (e.g., the HO2S rich to lean switch time was more than 100 ms) during the HO2S Monitor test.
	Possible Causes:
	  • HO2S is contaminated (due to presence of silicone in fuel)
	  • Leaks present in the exhaust manifold or exhaust pipes
	  • HO2S is damaged or has failed
	  • PCM has failed

DTC: P0155
2T O2HTR, MIL: Yes
Years: 2005, 2006, 2007
Models: All Models with a 4-Cyl, V6 or V8 engine
Engines: All Except V10
Transmissions: All
	HO2S-21 (Bank 2 Sensor 1) Heater Circuit Malfunction
	Engine running for 5 minutes, and the PCM detected an open or shorted condition, or excessive current draw in the heater circuit.
	Possible Causes:
	  • HO2S heater power circuit is open
	  • HO2S heater ground circuit is open
	  • HO2S signal tracking (due to oil or moisture in the connector)
	  • HO2S is damaged or has failed
	  • PCM has failed

DTC: P0156
2T O2S, MIL: Yes
Years: 2005, 2006, 2007
Models: All Models with a 4-Cyl, V6 or V8 engine
Engines: All Except V10
Transmissions: All
	HO2S-22 (Bank 2 Sensor 2) Circuit No Activity
	Engine running in closed loop for more than 5 minutes, and the PCM detected the HO2S signal failed to meet the maximum or minimum voltage (i.e., it failed the voltage check).
	Possible Causes:
	  • Leaks present in the exhaust manifold or exhaust pipes
	  • HO2S signal wire and ground wire crossed in connector
	  • HO2S element is fuel contaminated or has failed
	  • PCM has failed

DTC	Trouble Code Title, Conditions & Possible Causes
DTC: P0158 **2T CCM, MIL: Yes** **Years:** 2005, 2006, 2007 **Models:** All Models with a 4-Cyl, V6 or V8 engine **Engines:** All Except V10 **Transmissions:** All	**HO2S-22 (Bank 2 Sensor 2) Circuit High Input** Engine running for more than 5 minutes, and the PCM detected the HO2S signal remained in a high state (i.e., more than 1.5v). **Note: The HO2S signal circuit may be shorted to the heater power circuit due to tracking inside of the HO2S connector. Remove the connector and visually inspect the connector for signs of oil or water.** **Possible Causes:** • HO2S signal shorted to the heater power circuit (due to oil or moisture in the connector) • HO2S signal circuit shorted to VREF or to system voltage • PCM has failed
DTC: P0161 **2T O2HTR, MIL: Yes** **Years:** 2005, 2006, 2007 **Models:** All Models with a 4-Cyl, V6 or V8 engine **Engines:** All Except V10 **Transmissions:** All	**HO2S-22 (Bank 2 Sensor 2) Heater Circuit Malfunction** Engine running for 5 minutes, and the PCM detected an open or shorted condition, or excessive current draw in the heater circuit. **Possible Causes:** • HO2S heater power circuit or the heater ground circuit is open • HO2S signal tracking (due to oil or moisture in the connector) • HO2S has failed, or the PCM has failed
DTC: P0171 **2T FUEL, MIL: Yes** **Years:** 2005, 2006, 2007 **Models:** All Models **Engines:** All **Transmissions:** All	**Fuel System Too Lean (Cylinder Bank 1)** Engine started, engine running at cruise speed for 3 to 4 minutes, and the PCM detected the Bank 1 Adaptive Fuel Control System reached its rich correction limit (a lean A/F condition). **Possible Causes:** • Air leaks after the MAF sensor, or leaks in the PCV system • Exhaust leaks before or near where the HO2S is mounted • Fuel injector(s) restricted or not supplying enough fuel • Fuel pump not supplying enough fuel during high fuel demand conditions • Leaking EGR gasket, or leaking EGR valve diaphragm • MAF sensor dirty (causes PCM to underestimate airflow) • Vehicle running out of fuel or engine oil dip stick not seated • TSB 01-20-5 contains a repair procedure for this trouble code
DTC: P0172 **2T FUEL, MIL: Yes** **Years:** 2005, 2006, 2007 **Models:** All Models **Engines:** All **Transmissions:** All	**Fuel System Too Rich (Cylinder Bank 1)** Engine started, engine running at cruise speed for 3 to 4 minutes, and the PCM detected the Bank 1 Adaptive Fuel Control System reached its rich correction limit (a rich A/F condition). **Possible Causes:** • Camshaft timing is incorrect, or the engine has an oil overfill condition • EVAP vapor recovery system failure (may be pulling vacuum) • Fuel pressure regulator is damaged or leaking • HO2S element is contaminated with alcohol or water • MAF or MAP sensor values are incorrect or out-of-range • One of more fuel injectors is leaking
DTC: P0174 **2T FUEL, MIL: Yes** **Years:** 2005, 2006, 2007 **Models:** All Models With V6 Or V8 engine **Engines:** All V6, V8 **Transmissions:** All	**Fuel System Too Lean (Cylinder Bank 2)** Engine started, engine running at cruise speed for 3 to 4 minutes, and the PCM detected the Bank 2 Adaptive Fuel Control System reached its rich correction limit (a lean A/F condition). **Possible Causes:** • Air leaks after the MAF sensor, or leaks in the PCV system • Exhaust leaks before or near where the HO2S is mounted • Fuel injector(s) restricted or not supplying enough fuel • Fuel system not supplying enough fuel during high fuel demand conditions (e.g., the fuel pump may not supply enough fuel) • Leaking EGR gasket, or leaking EGR valve diaphragm • MAF sensor dirty (causes PCM to underestimate airflow) • Vehicle running out of fuel or engine oil dip stick not seated • TSB 1-20-5 contains a repair procedure for this trouble code
DTC: P0175 **2T FUEL, MIL: Yes** **Years:** 2005, 2006, 2007 **Models:** All Models With V6 Or V8 engine **Engines:** All V6, V8 **Transmissions:** All	**Fuel System Too Rich (Cylinder Bank 2)** Engine started, engine running at cruise speed for 3 to 4 minutes, and the PCM detected the Bank 2 Adaptive Fuel Control System reached its rich correction limit (a rich A/F condition). **Possible Causes:** • Camshaft timing is incorrect • Engine oil overfill condition • EVAP vapor recovery system failure (may be pulling vacuum) • Fuel pressure regulator is damaged or leaking • HO2S element is contaminated with alcohol or water • MAF or MAP sensor values are incorrect or out-of-range • One of more fuel injectors is leaking

DTC	Trouble Code Title, Conditions & Possible Causes
DTC: P0180 **2T CCM, MIL: Yes** **Years:** 2005, 2006, 2007 **Models:** All Models **Engines:** All **Transmissions:** All	**Engine Fuel Temperature Sensor 'A' Circuit Malfunction** Engine runtime over 2 minutes, and the PCM detected the Engine Fuel Temperature (EFT) sensor 'A' signal was out-of-range (i.e., it was more than 4.54v [−46°F] or less than 0.21v [275°F]. **Note: Monitor the EFT PID value to identify an open or short circuit.** **Possible Causes:** • Engine operating under "low" ambient temperature conditions • EFT sensor signal circuit open or shorted in the wiring harness • EFT sensor is damaged or it has failed • PCM has failed
DTC: P0181 **2T CCM, MIL: Yes** **Years:** 2005, 2006, 2007 **Models:** Crown Victoria, F-Series, E-Series, Grand Marquis, Mark LT, Town Car **Engines:** All **Transmissions:** All	**Fuel Temperature Sensor 'A' Signal Performance** Engine runtime over 2 minutes, and the PCM detected the Engine Fuel Temperature (EFT) sensor 'A' signal was more than 4.50v [−46°F] or less than 0.21v [275°F] the calibrated limit in the self-test. **Possible Causes:** • Engine operating under "low" ambient temperature conditions • EFT sensor signal circuit open or shorted in the wiring harness • EFT sensor is damaged or it has failed • PCM has failed
DTC: P0182 **2T CCM, MIL: Yes** **Years:** 2005, 2006, 2007 **Models:** Crown Victoria, F-Series, E-Series, Grand Marquis, Mark LT, Town Car **Engines:** All **Transmissions:** All	**Engine Fuel Temperature Sensor 'A' Circuit Low Input** Key on or engine running; and the PCM detected the Engine Fuel Temperature (EFT) Sensor 'A' signal was over 260°F in the self-test. **Possible Causes:** • EFT sensor connector is damaged or shorted • EFT sensor VREF circuit is open or shorted to ground • EFT sensor circuit is shorted to chassis or to sensor ground • EFT sensor is damaged or it has failed • PCM has failed
DTC: P0183 **2T CCM, MIL: Yes** **Years:** 2005, 2006, 2007 **Models:** Crown Victoria, F-Series, E-Series, Grand Marquis, Mark LT, Town Car **Engines:** All **Transmissions:** All	**Engine Fuel Temperature Sensor 'A' Circuit High Input** Key on or engine running; and the PCM detected the EFT sensor 'A' signal was more than the limit of 4.50v [−46°F] during the self-test. **Possible Causes:** • EFT sensor connector is damaged, loose or open • EFT sensor signal circuit is shorted to VREF (5v) • EFT sensor signal circuit is open • EFT sensor is damaged or it has failed • PCM has failed
DTC: P0186 **2T CCM, MIL: Yes** **Years:** 2005, 2006, 2007 **Models:** Crown Victoria, F-Series, E-Series, Grand Marquis, Mark LT, Town Car **Engines:** All **Transmissions:** All	**Engine Fuel Temperature Sensor 'B' Signal Performance** Engine started, engine runtime over 2 minutes, and the PCM detected the EFT sensor 'B' signal was more than 4.50v (Scan Tool reads less than −46°F) or less than 0.21v (Scan Tool reads more than 275°F) the calibrated limit during the self-test. **Possible Causes:** • Engine operating under "low" ambient temperature conditions • EFT sensor signal circuit open or shorted in the wiring harness • EFT sensor is damaged or it has failed • PCM has failed
DTC: P0187 **2T CCM, MIL: Yes** **Years:** 2005, 2006, 2007 **Models:** Crown Victoria, F-Series, E-Series, Grand Marquis, Mark LT, Town Car **Engines:** All **Transmissions:** All	**Engine Fuel Temperature Sensor 'B' Circuit Low Input** Engine started, engine runtime over 2 minutes, and the PCM detected the EFT Sensor 'B' signal was less than the calibrated limit of 0.21v (Scan Tool reads less than 275°F) during the self-test. **Possible Causes:** • Engine operating under "low" ambient temperature conditions • EFT sensor signal circuit shorted to ground in the harness • EFT sensor is damaged or it has failed • PCM has failed
DTC: P0188 **2T CCM, MIL: Yes** **Years:** 2005, 2006, 2007 **Models:** Crown Victoria, F-Series, E-Series, Grand Marquis, Mark LT, Town Car **Engines:** All **Transmissions:** All	**Engine Fuel Temperature Sensor 'B' Circuit High** Engine running for more than 2 minutes, and the PCM detected the EFT sensor 'A' signal was more than the calibrated limit of 4.50v [−46°F] during the self-test. **Possible Causes:** • EFT sensor signal circuit open in the wiring harness • EFT sensor signal circuit shorted to VREF in the wiring harness • EFT sensor is damaged or it has failed • PCM has failed

DTC	Trouble Code Title, Conditions & Possible Causes
DTC: P0190 **2T CCM, MIL: Yes** **Years:** 2005, 2006, 2007 **Models:** Crown Victoria, F-Series, E-Series, Grand Marquis, Mark LT, Town Car **Engines:** All **Transmissions:** All	**Fuel Rail Pressure Sensor Circuit Malfunction** Key on, and the PCM detected that the FRP sensor VREF was less than its acceptable range (minimum value of 4.0v) during the CCM test). The FRP sensor signal should be in a range of 4.0-6.0v during testing. **Note: The sensor VREF should be between 4.0 to 6.0v at all times.** **Possible Causes:** • Sensor VREF circuit open in the wiring harness • Sensor VREF circuit open at the sensor • Sensor VREF circuit open between the sensor and the PCM • PCM has failed
DTC: P0191 **2T CCM, MIL: Yes** **Years:** 2005, 2006, 2007 **Models:** Crown Victoria, F-Series, E-Series, Grand Marquis, Mark LT, Town Car **Engines:** All **Transmissions:** All	**Fuel Rail Pressure Sensor Range/Performance** Engine started, and the PCM detected the FRP sensor signal was less than the minimum acceptable range or was more than the maximum acceptable range. With the engine running, the FRP PID should read between 20 psi [138 kPa] and 60 psi [413 kPa] for gasoline powered vehicles, or between 85 psi [586 kPa] and 105 psi [725 kPa] for natural gas (NG) powered vehicles. **Possible Causes:** • Fuel pressure too high or too low during engine operation • FRP sensor signal circuit has high resistance • FRP sensor is damaged or has failed
DTC: P0192 **2T CCM, MIL: Yes** **Years:** 2005, 2006, 2007 **Models:** Crown Victoria, F-Series, E-Series, Grand Marquis, Mark LT, Town Car **Engines:** All **Transmissions:** All	**Fuel Rail Pressure Sensor Circuit Low** Engine started, and the PCM detected the FRP sensor signal was less than 0.3v for gasoline vehicles or less than 0.5v for NG vehicles during the self-test. **Possible Causes:** • FRP sensor signal shorted to chassis ground or sensor ground • FRP sensor signal circuit open (NG usage only) • FRP sensor is damaged or has failed • PCM has failed
DTC: P0193 **2T CCM, MIL: Yes** **Years:** 2005, 2006, 2007 **Models:** Crown Victoria, F-Series, E-Series, Grand Marquis, Mark LT, Town Car **Engines:** All **Transmissions:** All	**Fuel Absolute Pressure Sensor Circuit High Input** Engine started, and the PCM detected the FRP sensor was more than 4.5v for gasoline vehicles or more than 4.8v for NG vehicles. **Possible Causes:** • FRP sensor signal shorted to VREF or system voltage • FRP sensor signal circuit open (gasoline usage only) • Low fuel pressure (NG vehicle only) • FRP sensor is damaged or has failed • PCM has failed
DTC: P0196 **2T CCM, MIL: Yes** **Years:** 2005, 2006, 2007 **Models:** Crown Victoria, Grand Marquis, Town Car **Engines:** 4.6L VIN V, W **Transmissions:** All	**Engine Oil Temperature Sensor Signal Performance** Engine started, KOER Self Test enabled, and the PCM detected the Engine Oil Temperature (EOT) sensor signal was not within a calibrated amount of the ECT sensor signal during the test. The EOT sensor value should be close to the engine oil temperature. **Possible Causes:** • Cooling system malfunction, or the thermostat is stuck • Engine not operating at normal operating temperature • EOT sensor is damaged or it has failed • PCM has failed
DTC: P0197 **2T CCM, MIL: Yes** **Years:** 2005, 2006, 2007 **Models:** Crown Victoria, Grand Marquis, Town Car **Engines:** 4.6L VIN V, W **Transmissions:** All	**Engine Oil Temperature Sensor Circuit Low Input** Key on or engine running; and the PCM detected that the Engine Oil Temperature (EOT) sensor was less than 0.20v during the test. The EOT sensor value should be close to the engine oil temperature. **Possible Causes:** • EOT sensor connector is damaged or shorted • EOT sensor signal circuit shorted to chassis or sensor ground • EOT sensor is damaged or it has failed • PCM has failed
DTC: P0198 **2T CCM, MIL: Yes** **Years:** 2005, 2006, 2007 **Models:** Crown Victoria, Grand Marquis, Town Car **Engines:** 4.6L VIN V, W **Transmissions:** All	**Engine Oil Temperature Sensor Circuit High Input** Key on or engine running; and the PCM detected that the Engine Oil Temperature (EOT) sensor was less than 4.50v during the test. The EOT sensor value should be close to the engine oil temperature. **Possible Causes:** • EOT sensor connector is damaged or open • EOT sensor signal circuit is shorted to VREF (5v) • EOT sensor is damaged or it has failed • PCM has failed

DTC	Trouble Code Title, Conditions & Possible Causes

DTC: P0201
2T CCM, MIL: Yes
Years: 2005, 2006, 2007
Models: All Models
Engines: All
Transmissions: All
	Cylinder 1 Injector Circuit Malfunction
	Engine started, and the PCM detected the fuel injector "1" control circuit was in a high state when it should have been low, or in a low state when it should have been high (wiring harness & injector okay).
	Note: Monitor the INJIF PID Fault "flags" with the Scan Tool. The appropriate INJF PID "flag" will read Yes when this code is set.
	Possible Causes:
	   • Injector 1 connector is damaged, open or shorted
	   • Injector 1 control circuit is open, shorted to ground or to power
	   • PCM has failed (the injector driver circuit may be damaged)

DTC: P0202
2T CCM, MIL: Yes
Years: 2005, 2006, 2007
Models: All Models
Engines: All
Transmissions: All
	Cylinder 2 Injector Circuit Malfunction
	Engine started, and the PCM detected the fuel injector "2" control circuit was in a high state when it should have been low, or in a low state when it should have been high (wiring harness & injector okay).
	Note: Monitor the INJIF PID Fault "flags" with the Scan Tool. The appropriate INJF PID "flag" will read Yes when this code is set.
	Possible Causes:
	   • Injector 2 connector is damaged, open or shorted
	   • Injector 2 control circuit is open, shorted to ground or to power
	   • PCM has failed (the injector driver circuit may be damaged)

DTC: P0203
2T CCM, MIL: Yes
Years: 2005, 2006, 2007
Models: All Models
Engines: All
Transmissions: All
	Cylinder 3 Injector Circuit Malfunction
	Engine started, and the PCM detected the fuel injector "3" control circuit was in a high state when it should have been low, or in a low state when it should have been high (wiring harness & injector okay).
	Note: Monitor the INJIF PID Fault "flags" with the Scan Tool. The appropriate INJF PID "flag" will read Yes when this code is set.
	Possible Causes:
	   • Injector 3 connector is damaged, open or shorted
	   • Injector 3 control circuit is open, shorted to ground or to power
	   • PCM has failed (the injector driver circuit may be damaged)

DTC: P0204
2T CCM, MIL: Yes
Years: 2005, 2006, 2007
Models: All Models
Engines: All
Transmissions: All
	Cylinder 4 Injector Circuit Malfunction
	Engine started, and the PCM detected the fuel injector "4" control circuit was in a high state when it should have been low, or in a low state when it should have been high (wiring harness & injector okay).
	Note: Monitor the INJIF PID Fault "flags" with the Scan Tool. The appropriate INJF PID "flag" will read Yes when this code is set.
	Possible Causes:
	   • Injector 4 connector is damaged, open or shorted
	   • Injector 4 control circuit is open, shorted to ground or to power
	   • PCM has failed (the injector driver circuit may be damaged)

DTC: P0205
2T CCM, MIL: Yes
Years: 2005, 2006, 2007
Models: All Models With V6, V8 or V10 Engine
Engines: All V6, V8, V10
Transmissions: All
	Cylinder 5 Injector Circuit Malfunction
	Engine started, and the PCM detected the fuel injector "5" control circuit was in a high state when it should have been low, or in a low state when it should have been high (wiring harness & injector okay).
	Note: Monitor the INJIF PID Fault "flags" with the Scan Tool. The appropriate INJF PID "flag" will read Yes when this code is set.
	Possible Causes:
	   • Injector 5 connector is damaged, open or shorted
	   • Injector 5 control circuit is open, shorted to ground or to power
	   • PCM has failed (the injector driver circuit may be damaged)

DTC: P0206
2T CCM, MIL: Yes
Years: 2005, 2006, 2007
Models: All Models With V6, V8 or V10 Engine
Engines: All V6, V8, V10
Transmissions: All
	Cylinder 6 Injector Circuit Malfunction
	Engine started, and the PCM detected the fuel injector control circuit was in a high state when it should have been low, or in a low state when it should have been high (wiring harness & injector okay).
	Note: Monitor the INJIF PID Fault "flags" with the Scan Tool. The appropriate INJF PID "flag" will read Yes when this code is set.
	Possible Causes:
	   • Injector 6 connector is damaged, open or shorted
	   • Injector 6 control circuit is open, shorted to ground or to power
	   • PCM has failed (the injector driver circuit may be damaged)

DTC	Trouble Code Title, Conditions & Possible Causes

DTC: P0207
2T CCM, MIL: Yes
Years: 2005, 2006, 2007
Models: All Models With V8 or V10 Engine
Engines: All V8, V10
Transmissions: All
	Cylinder 7 Injector Circuit Malfunction
	Engine started, and the PCM detected the fuel injector "7" control circuit was in a high state when it should have been low, or in a low state when it should have been high (wiring harness & injector okay).
	Note: Monitor the INJIF PID Fault "flags" with the Scan Tool. The appropriate INJF PID "flag" will read Yes when this code is set.
	Possible Causes:
	   • Injector 7 connector is damaged, open or shorted
	   • Injector 7 control circuit is open, shorted to ground or to power
	   • PCM has failed (the injector driver circuit may be damaged)

DTC: P0208
2T CCM, MIL: Yes
Years: 2005, 2006, 2007
Models: All Models With V8 or V10 Engine
Engines: All V8, V10
Transmissions: All
	Cylinder 8 Injector Circuit Malfunction
	Engine started, and the PCM detected the fuel injector "8" control circuit was in a high state when it should have been low, or in a low state when it should have been high (wiring harness & injector okay).
	Note: Monitor the INJIF PID Fault "flags" with the Scan Tool. The appropriate INJF PID "flag" will read Yes when this code is set.
	Possible Causes:
	   • Injector 8 connector is damaged, open or shorted
	   • Injector 8 control circuit is open, shorted to ground or to power
	   • PCM has failed (the injector driver circuit may be damaged)

DTC: P0209
2T CCM, MIL: Yes
Years: 2005, 2006, 2007
Models: All Models With V10 Engine
Engines: All V10
Transmissions: All
	Cylinder 9 Injector Circuit Malfunction
	Engine started, and the PCM detected the fuel injector "9" control circuit was in a high state when it should have been low, or in a low state when it should have been high (wiring harness & injector okay).
	Note: Monitor the INJIF PID Fault "flags" with the Scan Tool. The appropriate INJF PID "flag" will read Yes when this code is set.
	Possible Causes:
	   • Injector 9 connector is damaged, open or shorted
	   • Injector 9 control circuit is open, shorted to ground or to power
	   • PCM has failed (the injector driver circuit may be damaged)

DTC: P0210
2T CCM, MIL: Yes
Years: 2005, 2006, 2007
Models: All Models With V10 Engine
Engines: All V10
Transmissions: All
	Cylinder 10 Injector Circuit Malfunction
	Engine started, and the PCM detected the fuel injector "10" control circuit was in a high state when it should have been low, or in a low state when it should have been high (wiring harness & injector okay).
	Note: Monitor the INJIF PID Fault "flags" with the Scan Tool. The appropriate INJF PID "flag" will read Yes when this code is set.
	Possible Causes:
	   • Injector 10 connector is damaged, open or shorted
	   • Injector 10 control circuit is open, shorted to ground or to power
	   • PCM has failed (the injector driver circuit may be damaged)

DTC: P0219
2T CCM, MIL: Yes
Years: 2005, 2006, 2007
Models: All Models
Engines: All
Transmissions: All
	Engine Over-Speed Condition
	Engine started, and the PCM determined the vehicle had been driven in a manner that caused the engine to over-speed, and to exceed the engine speed calibration limit stored in memory.
	Possible Causes:
	   • Engine operated in the wrong transmission gear position
	   • Excessive engine speed with gear selector in Neutral position
	   • Wheel slippage due to wet, muddy or snowing conditions

DTC: P0221
2T CCM, MIL: Yes
Years: 2005, 2006, 2007
Models: Crown, Victoria, Grand Marquis, Town Car
Engines: 4.6L VIN V, W
Transmissions: All
	Throttle Position Sensor 'B' Signal Performance
	Engine started; and the PCM detected the TP Sensor 'B' circuit was out of its normal operating range during a condition with the throttle wide open, or with it completely closed.
	Possible Causes:
	   • Throttle body is damaged
	   • Throttle linkage is binding or sticking
	   • ETC TP Sensor 'B' signal circuit to the PCM is open
	   • ETC TP Sensor 'B' ground circuit is open
	   • ETC TP Sensor 'B' is damaged or it has failed

DTC: P0222
2T CCM, MIL: Yes
Years: 2005, 2006, 2007
Models: Crown, Victoria, Grand Marquis, Town Car
Engines: 4.6L VIN V, W
Transmissions: All
	Throttle Position Sensor 'B' Circuit Low Input
	Key on or engine running; and the PCM detected the TP Sensor 'B' indicated less than 0.17v (Scan Tool reads less than 3.42%).
	Possible Causes:
	   • ETC TP Sensor 'B' connector is damaged or shorted
	   • ETC TP Sensor 'B' signal circuit is shorted to ground
	   • ETC TP Sensor 'B' is damaged or it has failed
	   • PCM has failed

DTC	Trouble Code Title, Conditions & Possible Causes
DTC: P0223 **2T CCM, MIL: Yes** **Years:** 2005, 2006, 2007 **Models:** Crown, Victoria, Grand Marquis, Town Car **Engines:** 4.6L VIN V, W **Transmissions:** All	**Throttle Position Sensor 'B' Circuit High Input** Key on or engine running; and the PCM detected the TP Sensor 'B' indicated more than 4.65v (Scan Tool reads more than 93%) during the CCM test period. **Possible Causes:** • ETC TP Sensor 'B' connector is damaged or open • ETC TP Sensor 'B' signal circuit is open • ETC TP Sensor 'B' signal circuit is shorted to VREF (5v) • ETC TP Sensor 'B' is damaged or it has failed
DTC: P0230 **2T CCM, MIL: Yes** **Years:** 2005, 2006, 2007 **Models:** All Models **Engines:** All **Transmissions:** All	**Fuel Pump Primary Circuit Malfunction** Key on, and the PCM detected high current in fuel pump or fuel shutoff valve (FSV) circuit (NG only), or it detected voltage with the valve off, or it did not detect voltage on the circuit. The circuit is used to energize the fuel pump relay for 20 seconds at key on or while running. **Possible Causes:** • FP or FSV circuit is open or shorted • Fuel pump relay VPWR circuit open • Fuel pump relay is damaged or has failed • PCM has failed
DTC: P0231 **2T CCM, MIL: Yes** **Years:** 2005, 2006, 2007 **Models:** All Models **Engines:** All **Transmissions:** All	**Fuel Pump Primary Circuit Low Input** Key on, and the PCM detected a lack of voltage on the FP Monitor circuit with the fuel pump commanded on. The fuel pump control circuit is used by the PCM to energize the fuel pump relay. At key on, the relay is energized for 20 seconds, and all the time the engine is running. **Possible Causes:** • FP or FSV circuit is open or shorted to ground • Fuel pump relay VPWR circuit open or fuel pump relay failed • PCM has failed
DTC: P0232 **2T CCM, MIL: Yes** **Years:** 2005, 2006, 2007 **Models:** All Models **Engines:** All **Transmissions:** All	**Fuel Pump Secondary Circuit High Input** Key on, and the PCM detected voltage on the FP Monitor circuit with fuel pump "off". The PCM uses the fuel pump control circuit to energize the fuel pump relay. At key on, the relay is "on" for 20 seconds or while running. This circuit is used to check voltage to the pump. **Possible Causes:** • Fuel pump relay contacts always closed • Fuel pump ground circuit has high resistance • Fuel pump secondary circuit is shorted to power • Low speed fuel pump relay damaged or related circuit problem
DTC: P0297 **2T CCM, MIL: Yes** **Years:** 2005, 2006, 2007 **Models:** All Models **Engines:** All **Transmissions:** All	**Vehicle Over-Speed Condition** Engine started, vehicle driven at a very high engine speed, and the PCM detected the vehicle speed exceeded the calibration limit, and then enabled the High Vehicle Speed Strategy to control the speed. **Possible Causes:** • The code indicates the vehicle was driven at very high engine speed (rpm) for too long. The PCM temporarily prohibits high engine speed by disabling the fuel injectors with this code set.
DTC: P0300 2T MISFIRE **MIL: Yes** **Years:** 2005, 2006, 2007 **Models:** All Models **Engines:** All **Transmissions:** All	**Random Misfire Detected** DTC P0136, P0156, P0171, P0172, P0175, P1130 and P1150 not set, engine running under positive torque conditions, and the PCM detected a misfire in 1000 revolution (High Emissions) or the 200 revolution (Catalyst Damaging 1T) range in two or more cylinders. **Note: If the misfire is severe, the MIL will flash on/off on the 1st trip!** **Possible Causes:** • Base engine mechanical fault that affects two or more cylinders • Fuel metering fault that affects two or more cylinders • Fuel pressure too low or too high, fuel supply contaminated • EVAP system problem or the EVAP canister is fuel saturated • EGR valve is stuck open or the PCV system has a vacuum leak • Ignition system fault (coil, plug) affecting two or more cylinders • MAF sensor contamination (it can cause a very lean condition) • Vehicle driven while very low on fuel (less than 1/8 of a tank) • TSB 03-14-4 contains repair help for this code for COP ignition

DTC	Trouble Code Title, Conditions & Possible Causes
DTC: P0301 2T MISFIRE **MIL: Yes** **Years:** 2005, 2006, 2007 **Models:** All Models **Engines:** All **Transmissions:** All	**Cylinder Number 1 Misfire Detected** DTC P0136, P0156, P0171, P0172, P0175, P1130 and P1150 not set, engine started, engine running under positive torque conditions, and the PCM detected a misfire a misfire in Cylinder 1 during the 200 revolution (Catalyst) or 1000 revolution (High Emissions) period. **Note: If the misfire is severe, the MIL will flash on/off on the 1st trip!** **Possible Causes:** • Air leak in the intake manifold, or in the EGR or PCM system • Base engine mechanical problem that affects only Cylinder 1 • Fuel delivery component problem that affects only Cylinder 1 (i.e., a contaminated, dirty or sticking fuel injector) • Ignition system problem (coil, plug) that affects only Cylinder 1 • TSB 02-16-2 contains repair help for this code (LS & T-Bird) • TSB 03-14-4 contains repair help for this code for COP ignition
DTC: P0302 2T MISFIRE **MIL: Yes** **Years:** 2005, 2006, 2007 **Models:** All Models **Engines:** All **Transmissions:** All	**Cylinder Number 2 Misfire Detected** DTC P0136, P0156, P0171, P0172, P0175, P1130 and P1150 not set, engine started, engine running under positive torque conditions, and the PCM detected a misfire a misfire in Cylinder 2 during the 200 revolution (Catalyst) or 1000 revolution (High Emissions) period. **Note: If the misfire is severe, the MIL will flash on/off on the 1st trip!** **Possible Causes:** • Air leak in the intake manifold, or in the EGR or PCM system • Base engine mechanical problem that affects only Cylinder 2 • Fuel delivery component problem that affects only Cylinder 2 (i.e., a contaminated, dirty or sticking fuel injector) • Ignition system problem (coil, plug) that affects only Cylinder 2 • TSB 02-16-2 contains repair help for this code (LS & T-Bird) • TSB 03-14-4 contains repair help for this code for COP ignition
DTC: P0303 2T MISFIRE **MIL: Yes** **Years:** 2005, 2006, 2007 **Models:** All Models **Engines:** All **Transmissions:** All	**Cylinder Number 3 Misfire Detected** DTC P0136, P0156, P0171, P0172, P0175, P1130 and P1150 not set, engine started, engine running under positive torque conditions, and the PCM detected a misfire a misfire in Cylinder 3 during the 200 revolution (Catalyst) or 1000 revolution (High Emissions) period. **Note: If the misfire is severe, the MIL will flash on/off on the 1st trip!** **Possible Causes:** • Air leak in the intake manifold, or in the EGR or PCM system • Base engine mechanical problem that affects only Cylinder 3 • Fuel delivery component problem that affects only Cylinder 3 (i.e., a contaminated, dirty or sticking fuel injector) • Ignition system problem (coil, plug) that affects only Cylinder 3 • TSB 02-16-2 contains repair help for this code (LS & T-Bird) • TSB 03-14-4 contains repair help for this code for COP ignition
DTC: P0304 2T MISFIRE **MIL: Yes** **Years:** 2005, 2006, 2007 **Models:** All Models **Engines:** All **Transmissions:** All	**Cylinder Number 4 Misfire Detected** DTC P0136, P0156, P0171, P0172, P0175, P1130 and P1150 not set, engine started, engine running under positive torque conditions, and the PCM detected a misfire a misfire in Cylinder 4 during the 200 revolution (Catalyst) or 1000 revolution (High Emissions) period. **Note: If the misfire is severe, the MIL will flash on/off on the 1st trip!** **Possible Causes:** • Air leak in the intake manifold, or in the EGR or PCM system • Base engine mechanical problem that affects only Cylinder 4 • Fuel delivery component problem that affects only Cylinder 4 (i.e., a contaminated, dirty or sticking fuel injector) • Ignition system problem (coil, plug) that affects only Cylinder 4 • TSB 02-16-2 contains repair help for this code (LS & T-Bird) • TSB 03-14-4 contains repair help for this code for COP ignition
DTC: P0305 2T MISFIRE **MIL: Yes** **Years:** 2005, 2006, 2007 **Models:** All Models With V6, V8 or V10 Engine **Engines:** All V6, V8, V10 **Transmissions:** All	**Cylinder Number 5 Misfire Detected** DTC P0136, P0156, P0171, P0172, P0175, P1130 and P1150 not set, engine started, engine running under positive torque conditions, and the PCM detected a misfire a misfire in Cylinder 5 during the 200 revolution (Catalyst) or 1000 revolution (High Emissions) period. **Note: If the misfire is severe, the MIL will flash on/off on the 1st trip!** **Possible Causes:** • Air leak in the intake manifold, or in the EGR or PCM system • Base engine mechanical problem that affects only Cylinder 5 • Fuel delivery component problem that affects only Cylinder 5 (i.e., a contaminated, dirty or sticking fuel injector) • Ignition system problem (coil, plug) that affects only Cylinder 5 • TSB 02-16-2 contains repair help for this code (LS & T-Bird) • TSB 03-14-4 contains repair help for this code for COP ignition

DTC	Trouble Code Title, Conditions & Possible Causes
DTC: P0306 2T MISFIRE **MIL: Yes** **Years:** 2005, 2006, 2007 **Models:** All Models With V6, V8 or V10 Engine **Engines:** All V6, V8, V10 **Transmissions:** All	**Cylinder Number 6 Misfire Detected** DTC P0136, P0156, P0171, P0172, P0175, P1130 and P1150 not set, engine started, engine running under positive torque conditions, and the PCM detected a misfire a misfire in Cylinder 6 during the 200 revolution (Catalyst) or 1000 revolution (High Emissions) period. **Note: If the misfire is severe, the MIL will flash on/off on the 1st trip!** **Possible Causes:** • Air leak in the intake manifold, or in the EGR or PCM system • Base engine mechanical problem that affects only Cylinder 6 • Fuel delivery component problem that affects only Cylinder 6 (i.e., a contaminated, dirty or sticking fuel injector) • Ignition system problem (coil, plug) that affects only Cylinder 6 • TSB 02-16-2 contains repair help for this code (LS & T-Bird) • TSB 03-14-4 contains repair help for this code for COP ignition
DTC: P0307 2T MISFIRE **MIL: Yes** **Years:** 2005, 2006, 2007 **Models:** Models equipped with V8 or V10 engine **Engines:** All V8, V10 **Transmissions:** All	**Cylinder Number 7 Misfire Detected** DTC P0136, P0156, P0171, P0172, P0175, P1130 and P1150 not set, engine started, engine running under positive torque conditions, and the PCM detected a misfire a misfire in Cylinder 7 during the 200 revolution (Catalyst) or 1000 revolution (High Emissions) period. **Note: If the misfire is severe, the MIL will flash on/off on the 1st trip!** **Possible Causes:** • Air leak in the intake manifold, or in the EGR or PCM system • Base engine mechanical problem that affects only Cylinder 7 • Fuel delivery component problem that affects only Cylinder 7 (i.e., a contaminated, dirty or sticking fuel injector) • Ignition system problem (coil, plug) that affects only Cylinder 7 • TSB 02-16-2 contains repair help for this code (LS & T-Bird) • TSB 03-14-4 contains repair help for this code for COP ignition
DTC: P0308 2T MISFIRE **MIL: Yes** **Years:** 2005, 2006, 2007 **Models:** Models equipped with V8 or V10 engine **Engines:** All V8, V10 **Transmissions:** All	**Cylinder Number 8 Misfire Detected** DTC P0136, P0156, P0171, P0172, P0175, P1130 and P1150 not set, engine started, engine running under positive torque conditions, and the PCM detected a misfire a misfire in Cylinder 8 during the 200 revolution (Catalyst) or 1000 revolution (High Emissions) period. **Note: If the misfire is severe, the MIL will flash on/off on the 1st trip!** **Possible Causes:** • Air leak in the intake manifold, or in the EGR or PCM system • Base engine mechanical problem that affects only Cylinder 8 • Fuel delivery component problem that affects only Cylinder 8 (i.e., a contaminated, dirty or sticking fuel injector) • Ignition system problem (coil, plug) that affects only Cylinder 8 • TSB 02-16-2 contains repair help for this code (LS & T-Bird) • TSB 03-14-4 contains repair help for this code for COP ignition
DTC: P0309 2T MISFIRE **MIL: Yes** **Years:** 2005, 2006, 2007 **Models:** Models equipped with a V10 engine **Engines:** All V10 **Transmissions:** All	**Cylinder Number 9 Misfire Detected** DTC P0136, P0156, P0171, P0172, P0175, P1130 and P1150 not set, engine started, engine running under positive torque conditions, and the PCM detected a misfire a misfire in Cylinder 9 during the 200 revolution (Catalyst) or 1000 revolution (High Emissions) period. **Note: If the misfire is severe, the MIL will flash on/off on the 1st trip!** **Possible Causes:** • Air leak in the intake manifold, or in the EGR or PCM system • Base engine mechanical problem that affects only Cylinder 9 • Fuel delivery component problem that affects only Cylinder 9 (i.e., a contaminated, dirty or sticking fuel injector) • Ignition system problem (coil, plug) that affects only Cylinder 9 • TSB 03-14-4 contains repair help for this code for COP ignition
DTC: P0310 2T MISFIRE **MIL: Yes** **Years:** 2005, 2006, 2007 **Models:** Models equipped with a V10 engine **Engines:** All V10 **Transmissions:** All	**Cylinder Number 10 Misfire Detected** DTC P0136, P0156, P0171, P0172, P0175, P1130 and P1150 not set, engine started, engine running under positive torque conditions, and the PCM detected a misfire a misfire in Cylinder 10 during the 200 revolution (Catalyst) or 1000 revolution (High Emissions) period. **Note: If the misfire is severe, the MIL will flash on/off on the 1st trip!** **Possible Causes:** • Air leak in the intake manifold, or in the EGR or PCM system • Base engine mechanical problem that affects only Cylinder 10 • Fuel delivery component problem that affects only Cylinder 10 i.e., a contaminated, dirty or sticking fuel injector) • Ignition system problem (coil, plug) that affects only Cylinder 10 • TSB 03-14-4 contains repair help for this code for COP ignition

DTC	Trouble Code Title, Conditions & Possible Causes
DTC: P0315 **2T CCM, MIL: Yes** **Years:** 2005, 2006, 2007 **Models:** All Models **Engines:** All **Transmissions:** All	**Unable to Learn Crankshaft Variation** Engine started, and the PCM determined that it was unable to correct for mechanical inaccuracies in the CKP wheel tooth spacing. **Note: The Misfire Monitor will be disabled.** **Possible Causes:** • Inspect the CKP sensor for damage • Inspect the CKP sensor for debris on the rotor • Inspect the crankshaft pulse wheel for damaged teeth • Inspect the crankshaft pulse wheel for wobble (loose condition)
DTC: P0316 2T MISFIRE **MIL: Yes** **Years:** 2005, 2006, 2007 **Models:** All Models **Engines:** All **Transmissions:** All	**Misfire in the First 1000 Revolutions** Engine started, and the PCM detected a severe misfire within the first 1000 engine revolutions. **Possible Causes:** • Check for CMC DTC P0136, P0156, P0171, P0172, P0175, P1130 and P1150. Repair these adaptive fuel and HO2S codes • Check for any other CMC in memory. Repair these codes first! • Ignore P1000 codes that set during KOEO and KOER Self-Test
DTC: P0320 **2T CCM, MIL: Yes** **Years:** 2005, 2006, 2007 **Models:** E-Series, F-Series, Mark LT **Engines:** All **Transmissions:** All	**Ignition Engine Speed Input Circuit Malfunction** Engine started, and the PCM detected two or more successive erratic PIP signals during the self-test. **Possible Causes:** • Verify that the vehicle Antitheft system is operational • Inspect for any Aftermarket 2-way radio problems • Inspect for signs of "arcing" at one or more of the ignition coils • Verify that the Inertia Fuel Switch (IFS) is set properly (reset)
DTC: P0320 **2T CCM, MIL: Yes** **Years:** 2005, 2006, 2007 **Models:** All Models **Engines:** All **Transmissions:** All	**Ignition Engine Speed Input Circuit Malfunction** Engine started, and the PCM detected 2 or more successive erratic PIP signals during testing. **Possible Causes:** • Inspect for problems with an Aftermarket 2-way radio • Inspect for signs of "arcing" at one or more of the ignition coils • Inspect the Profile Ignition Pickup (PIP) unit inside distributor (check for damage or corrosion at the PIP sensor connector) • PIP sensor is damaged or it has failed (distributor models) • Ignition control module (ICM) has failed (Distributorless models)
DTC: P0325 **2T CCM, MIL: Yes** **Years:** 2005, 2006, 2007 **Models:** All Models **Engines:** All **Transmissions:** All	**Knock Sensor 1 Circuit Malfunction** Key on or engine running; and the PCM detected the knock Sensor 1 (KS1) signal was more than 0.5v at key on, engine off, or the KS1 signal was out of normal range (engine running). **Possible Causes:** • Knock sensor circuit is open • Knock sensor circuit is shorted to ground, or shorted to power • Knock sensor is damaged or it has failed • PCM has failed
DTC: P0326 **2T CCM, MIL: Yes** **Years:** 2005, 2006, 2007 **Models:** All Models **Engines:** All **Transmissions:** All	**Knock Sensor 1 Signal Range/Performance** Engine started, vehicle driven, and the PCM detected the Knock Sensor 1 (KS1) signal was more than the calibrated value. This code can set at key on, engine off, if the KS 1 signal is more than 0.5v. **Possible Causes:** • Knock sensor circuit is open • Knock sensor circuit is shorted to ground, or shorted to power • Knock sensor is damaged or it has failed • PCM has failed
DTC: P0330 **2T CCM, MIL: Yes** **Years:** 2005, 2006, 2007 **Models:** All Models **Engines:** All **Transmissions:** All	**Knock Sensor 2 Circuit Malfunction** Key on or engine running; and the PCM detected the knock Sensor 2 (KS2) signal was more than 0.5v at key on, engine off, or that the KS2 signal was out of the normal range with the engine running. **Possible Causes:** • Knock sensor circuit is open • Knock sensor circuit is shorted to ground, or shorted to power • Knock sensor is damaged or it has failed • PCM has failed

DTC	Trouble Code Title, Conditions & Possible Causes

DTC: P0331
2T CCM, MIL: Yes
Years: 2005, 2006, 2007
Models: All Models
Engines: All
Transmissions: All
	Knock Sensor 2 Signal Range/Performance
	Engine started, vehicle driven, and the PCM detected that the Knock Sensor 2 (KS2) signal was more than the calibrated value. This code can set at key on, engine off, if the KS2 signal is more than 0.5v.
	Possible Causes:
	    • Knock sensor circuit is open
	    • Knock sensor circuit is shorted to ground, or shorted to power
	    • Knock sensor is damaged or it has failed
	    • PCM has failed

DTC: P0340
2T CCM, MIL: Yes
Years: 2005, 2006, 2007
Models: All Models
Engines: All
Transmissions: All
	Camshaft Position Sensor Circuit Malfunction
	Engine started, and the PCM detected the CMP sensor signal was missing or it was erratic.
	Possible Causes:
	    • CMP sensor circuit is open or shorted to ground
	    • CMP sensor circuit is shorted to power
	    • CMP sensor ground (return) circuit is open
	    • CMP sensor installation incorrect (Hall-effect type)
	    • CMP sensor is damaged or CMP sensor shielding damaged
	    • PCM has failed
	    • TSB 02-22-1 contains repair information for this trouble code

DTC: P0350
2T CCM, MIL: Yes
Years: 2005, 2006, 2007
Models: All Models
Engines: All
Transmissions: All
	Ignition Coil (Undetermined) Primary/Secondary Circuit Malfunction
	Engine started, and the PCM did not receive valid IDM pulses from the ignition module. The PCM did not identify the coil with a problem.
	Possible Causes:
	    • Ignition START/RUN circuit is open or shorted to ground
	    • Ignition coil driver circuit is open or shorted to ground
	    • Ignition coil circuit is shorted to power
	    • Ignition coil damaged or it has failed
	    • PCM has failed

DTC: P0350
2T CCM, MIL: Yes
Years: 2005, 2006, 2007
Models: Crown Victoria, F-Series, E-Series, Grand Marquis, Mark LT, Town Car
Engines: All
Transmissions: All
	Ignition Coil Primary/Secondary Circuit Malfunction
	Engine started, and the PCM did not receive valid IDM pulses from the ignition module. The PCM did not identify the coil with a problem.
	Possible Causes:
	    • Ignition START/RUN circuit is open or shorted to ground
	    • Ignition coil driver circuit is open
	    • Ignition coil driver circuit is shorted to ground
	    • Ignition coil driver circuit is shorted to system power (B+)
	    • Ignition coil damaged or it has failed
	    • PCM has failed
	    • TSB 01-1-6 contains a repair procedure for this trouble code

DTC: P0351-P0310
2T CCM, MIL: Yes
Years: 2005, 2006, 2007
Models: Aviator, Crown Victoria, E-Series, Explorer, Explorer Sport-Trac, Explorer Sport-Trac, F-Series, Grand Marquis, Town Car With Coil On Plug (COP)
Engines: All
Transmissions: All
	Ignition Coil 1-10 Primary/Secondary Circuit Malfunction
	Engine started, and the PCM did not receive any valid IDM pulses from the ignition module for the Ignition Coil 1-10 primary circuit.
	Possible Causes:
	    • Ignition START/RUN circuit is open or shorted to ground
	    • Ignition coil driver 1-10 circuit is open or shorted to ground
	    • Ignition coil 1-10 circuit is shorted to power
	    • Ignition coil -101 damaged or it has failed
	    • PCM has failed

DTC: P0351-P0358
2T CCM, MIL: Yes
Years: 2005, 2006, 2007
Models: Escape, Mariner With Coil On Plug (COP)
Engines: All
Transmissions: All
	Ignition Coil 1-8 Primary/Secondary Circuit Malfunction
	Engine started, and the PCM did not receive any valid IDM pulses from the ignition module for the Ignition Coil 1-8 primary circuit.
	Possible Causes:
	    • Ignition START/RUN circuit is open or shorted to ground
	    • Ignition coil driver 1-8 circuit is open or shorted to ground
	    • Ignition coil 1-8 circuit is shorted to power
	    • Ignition coil 1-8 damaged or it has failed
	    • PCM has failed

DTC	Trouble Code Title, Conditions & Possible Causes
DTC: P0351-P0310 **2T CCM, MIL: Yes** **Years:** 2005, 2006, 2007 **Models:** Aviator, E-Series, Explorer, Explorer Sport-Trac, Explorer Sport-Trac, F-Series, Mountaineer **Engines:** All **Transmissions:** All	**Ignition Coil 1-10 Primary/Secondary Circuit Malfunction** Engine started, and the PCM did not receive any valid IDM pulses from the ignition module for the Ignition Coil 1-10 primary circuit. **Possible Causes:** • Ignition START/RUN circuit is open or shorted to ground • Ignition coilpack or COP 1-10 circuit is open or shorted to ground • Ignition coilpack or COP 1-10 circuit is shorted to power • Ignition coilpack or COP 1-10 damaged or it has failed • PCM has failed
DTC: P0351-P0358 **2T CCM, MIL: Yes** **Years:** 2005, 2006, 2007 **Models:** Crown Victoria, Grand Marquis, Town Car With Coilpack **Engines:** 4.6L VIN V, W **Transmissions:** All	**Ignition Coil 1-8 Primary/Secondary Circuit Malfunction** Engine started, and the PCM did not receive any valid IDM pulses from the ignition module for the Ignition Coil 1-8 primary circuit. **Possible Causes:** • Ignition START/RUN circuit is open or shorted to ground • Ignition coil driver 1-8 circuit open, shorted to ground or to power • Ignition coil 1-8 is damaged or it has failed • PCM has failed • TSB 01-1-6 contains a repair procedure for this trouble code
DTC: P0400 **2T EGR, MIL: Yes** **Years:** 2005, 2006, 2007 **Models:** Aviator, E-Series, Escape, Explorer, Explorer Sport-Trac, Explorer Sport-Trac, F-Series, Mountaineer **Engines:** All **Transmissions:** All	**Exhaust EGR System Malfunction** DTC P0102, P0103, P0107, P0108, P1100 and P1101 not set, vehicle driven at over 48 mph at a steady speed in closed loop for 1 minute, and the PCM detected the EGR flow rate was less than or more than the calibrated flow rate limits during the EGR test period. **Possible Causes:** • DPFE EGR sensor connector is damaged, loose or shorted • EGR valve is sticking, damaged or it has failed • MAP sensor is damaged or out of calibration • PCM has failed • TSB 03-31-3 contains repair information for this trouble code
DTC: P0400 **2T EGR, MIL: Yes** **Years:** 2005, 2006, 2007 **Models:** Aviator, Crown Victoria, Grand Marquis, Town Car **Engines:** 4.6L VIN H, V, W **Transmissions:** All	**Exhaust EGR System Malfunction (ESM System)** DTC P0102, P0103, P0107, P0108, P1100 and P1101 not set, vehicle driven at over 48 mph at a steady speed in closed loop for 1 minute, and the PCM detected the EGR flow rate was less than or more than the calibrated flow rate limits during the EGR test period. **Possible Causes:** • DPFE EGR sensor connector is damaged, loose or shorted • EGR valve is sticking, damaged or it has failed • MAP sensor is damaged or out of calibration • PCM has failed
DTC: P0401 **2T EGR, MIL: Yes** **Years:** 2005, 2006, 2007 **Models:** All Models **Engines:** All **Transmissions:** All	**Insufficient EGR Flow Detected** Engine started, engine running in closed loop under steady cruise conditions, and the PCM detected the DPFE sensor input indicated insufficient EGR gas flow. Run the KOER Self-Test, and if DTC P1408 is present, the fault is currently present. **Possible Causes:** • DPFE sensor signal circuit is shorted to ground • DPFE sensor VREF circuit is open between sensor and PCM • DPFE sensor downstream hose off or plugged • DPFE sensor hoses both off, loose or damaged • DPFE sensor hoses connected wrong (reversed) • EGR orifice tube is damaged or restricted • TSB 03-31-3 contains repair information for this trouble code
DTC: P0401 **2T EGR, MIL: Yes** **Years:** 2005, 2006, 2007 **Models:** E-Series, Escape, Explorer, Explorer Sport-Trac, F-Series, Mountaineer **Engines:** All **Transmissions:** All	**Exhaust Gas Recirculation Malfunction** Engine started, engine running under at cruise speed in closed loop, and the PCM detected a problem in the EGR system. Run the KOER self-test. If DTC P1406 is set, test the EGR valve operation. **Possible Causes:** • DPFE EGR valve hoses are damaged, leaking or restricted • DPFE EGR valve hoses may be reversed at the sensor • EGR valve connector is damaged, loose or shorted • EGR valve is damaged or it has failed • PCM has failed • TSB 4-3-1 contains repair information for this trouble code

DTC	Trouble Code Title, Conditions & Possible Causes
DTC: P0401 **2T EGR, MIL: Yes** **Years:** 2005, 2006, 2007 **Models:** Aviator, Crown Victoria, Grand Marquis, Town Car **Engines:** 4.6L VIN H, V, W **Transmissions:** All	**Exhaust Gas Recirculation Malfunction (ESM System)** Engine running under at cruise speed in closed loop, and the PCM detected a problem in the EGR ESM system. Run the KOER self-test. If DTC P1408 is present, inspect the EGR valve. **Possible Causes:** • DPFE EGR valve hoses are damaged, leaking or restricted • EGR valve connector is damaged, loose or shorted • EGR valve is damaged or it has failed • PCM has failed
DTC: P0402 **2T EGR, MIL: Yes** **Years:** 2005, 2006, 2007 **Models:** All Models **Engines:** All **Transmissions:** All	**Excessive EGR Flow Detected** Engine started, engine running in hot idle speed, and the PCM detected the Actual DPFE sensor value indicated more than the KOEO DPFE sensor value stored in the PCM memory. **Possible Causes:** • DPFE EGR valve source hoses loose or connected wrong • DPFE sensor slow to respond or sluggish (it may have failed) • DPFE sensor signal circuit is open or shorted to ground • DPFE EGR sensor is damaged or the PCM has failed
DTC: P0402 **2T EGR, MIL: Yes** **Years:** 2005, 2006, 2007 **Models:** Aviator, Crown Victoria, Grand Marquis, Town Car **Engines:** 4.6L VIN H, V, W **Transmissions:** All	**EGR Flow At Idle Speed Detected (ESM System)** Engine started, engine running in hot idle speed, and the PCM detected the Actual DPFE sensor value indicated more than the KOEO DPFE sensor value stored in the memory. If DTC P1405 is set, repair the cause of that trouble code prior to repairing P0402. **Possible Causes:** • DPFE EGR sensor is damaged • DPFE EGR valve source hoses loose or connected wrong • DPFE sensor slow to respond or sluggish (it may have failed) • DPFE sensor signal circuit is open or shorted to ground • PCM has failed • TSB 03-31-3 contains repair information for this trouble code
DTC: P0402 **2T EGR, MIL: Yes** **Years:** 2005, 2006, 2007 **Models:** E-Series, Escape, Explorer, Explorer Sport-Trac, F-Series **Engines:** All **Transmissions:** All	**EGR Flow At Idle Speed Detected (ESM System)** Engine started, engine running in hot idle speed, and the PCM detected the Actual DPFE sensor value indicated more than the KOEO DPFE sensor value stored in the memory. If DTC P1405 is set, repair the cause of that trouble code prior to repairing P0402. **Possible Causes:** • DPFE EGR sensor is damaged • DPFE EGR valve source hoses loose or connected wrong • DPFE sensor slow to respond or sluggish (it may have failed) • DPFE sensor signal circuit is open or shorted to ground • PCM has failed • TSB 03-31-3 contains repair information for this trouble code
DTC: P0403 **2T CCM, MIL: Yes** **Years:** 2005, 2006, 2007 **Models:** Aviator, Crown Victoria, Grand Marquis, Town Car **Engines:** 4.6L VIN H, V, W **Transmissions:** All	**EGR Solenoid Circuit Malfunction (ESM System)** Engine started, and the PCM detected an unexpected high or low voltage condition on the ESM EGR solenoid control circuit at idle. **Possible Causes:** • EGR solenoid connector is damaged, loose or shorted • EGR solenoid control circuit is open, or shorted to ground • EGR solenoid power circuit is open (check power to relay) • EGR solenoid is damaged or the PCM has failed
DTC: P0403 **2T CCM, MIL: Yes** **Years:** 2005, 2006, 2007 **Models:** Aviator, E-Series, Escape, Explorer, Explorer Sport-Trac, F-Series, Mountaineer **Engines:** All **Transmissions:** All	**EGR Solenoid Circuit Malfunction** Engine started, and the PCM detected an unexpected high or low voltage condition on the EGR solenoid control circuit at idle speed. **Possible Causes:** • EGR solenoid connector is damaged, loose or shorted • EGR solenoid control circuit is open, or shorted to ground • EGR solenoid power circuit is open (check power to relay) • EGR motor winding is open or shorted to power • EGR solenoid is damaged or has failed • PCM has failed
DTC: P0405 **2T CCM, MIL: Yes** **Years:** 2005, 2006, 2007 **Models:** Aviator, Crown Victoria, Grand Marquis, Town Car **Engines:** 4.6L VIN H, V, W **Transmissions:** All	**DPFE Sensor Circuit Low Input (ESM System)** Engine started, and the PCM detected an unexpected low voltage condition (less than 0.20v) on the ESM DPFE sensor circuit. **Possible Causes:** • DPFE sensor connector is damaged or shorted • DPFE sensor power supply circuit is open or shorted to ground • DPFE sensor signal circuit is shorted to ground • DPFE sensor is damaged or the PCM has failed

DTC	Trouble Code Title, Conditions & Possible Causes
DTC: P0405 **2T CCM, MIL: Yes** **Years:** 2005, 2006, 2007 **Models:** Aviator, E-Series, Escape, Explorer, Explorer Sport-Trac, F-Series, Mountaineer **Engines:** All **Transmissions:** All	**DPFE Sensor Circuit Low Input** Engine started, and the PCM detected an unexpected low voltage condition (less than 0.20v) on the ESM DPFE sensor circuit. **Possible Causes:** • DPFE sensor connector is damaged or shorted • DPFE sensor power supply circuit is open or shorted to ground • DPFE sensor signal circuit is shorted to ground • DPFE sensor is damaged or has failed • PCM has failed
DTC: P0406 **2T CCM, MIL: Yes** **Years:** 2005, 2006, 2007 **Models:** Aviator, Crown Victoria, Grand Marquis, Town Car **Engines:** 4.6L VIN H, V, W **Transmissions:** All	**DPFE Sensor Circuit High Input (ESM System)** Key on or engine running at idle speed, and the PCM detected an unexpected high voltage condition (more than 4.00v) on the ESM DPFE sensor circuit during the CCM test period. **Possible Causes:** • DPFE sensor connector is damaged or open • DPFE sensor signal circuit is open or it is shorted to VREF (5v) • DPFE sensor is damaged or has failed • PCM has failed
DTC: P0406 **2T CCM, MIL: Yes** **Years:** 2005, 2006, 2007 **Models:** Aviator, E-Series, Escape, Explorer, Explorer Sport-Trac, F-Series, Mountaineer **Engines:** All **Transmissions:** All	**DPFE Sensor Circuit High Input** Key on or engine running at idle speed, and the PCM detected an unexpected high voltage condition (more than 4.00v) on the ESM DPFE sensor circuit during the CCM test period. **Possible Causes:** • DPFE sensor connector is damaged or open • DPFE sensor signal circuit is shorted to VREF (5v) • DPFE sensor signal circuit is open • DPFE sensor is damaged or has failed • PCM has failed
DTC: P0411 **2T AIR, MIL: Yes** **Years:** 2005, 2006, 2007 **Models:** All Models **Engines:** All **Transmissions:** All	**Secondary AIR System Incorrect Upstream Flow Detected** Engine started, engine running at idle speed in closed loop, and the PCM detected the secondary AIR pump airflow was not diverted correctly when requested during the self-test. **Possible Causes:** • Air pump output is blocked • AIR bypass solenoid leaking or blocked • AIR bypass solenoid is stuck open or stuck closed • Air injection pump hose(s) leaking • PCM has failed
DTC: P0412 **2T CCM, MIL: Yes** **Years:** 2005, 2006, 2007 **Models:** All Models **Engines:** All **Transmissions:** All	**Secondary Air Injection Solenoid Circuit Malfunction** Engine started, and the PCM detected an unexpected low or high voltage condition on the AIR solenoid control circuit during testing. **Possible Causes:** • AIR solenoid power circuit (B+) is open (check dedicated fuse) • AIR bypass solenoid control circuit is open or shorted to ground • AIR diverter solenoid control circuit open or shorted to ground • AIR pump control circuit is open or shorted to ground • Check valve (one or more) is damaged or leaking • Solid State relay is damaged or it has failed • PCM has failed
DTC: P0413 **2T CCM, MIL: Yes** **Years:** 2005, 2006, 2007 **Models:** All Models **Engines:** All **Transmissions:** All	**Secondary AIR System Switching Valve 'A' Circuit Malfunction** Engine started; Air Injection solenoid commanded "on", and the PCM detected an unexpected "high" voltage condition on the Secondary AIR control circuit during the CCM test. **Possible Causes:** • AIR solenoid control circuit is shorted to system power • AIR pump solenoid is damaged or has failed • PCM has failed
DTC: P0414 **2T CCM, MIL: Yes** **Years:** 2005, 2006, 2007 **Models:** All Models **Engines:** All **Transmissions:** All	**Secondary AIR System Switching Valve 'A' Circuit Malfunction** Engine started; AIR solenoid disabled, and the PCM detected an unexpected low voltage condition on the AIR Solenoid control circuit **Possible Causes:** • AIR solenoid control circuit is shorted to ground • AIR solenoid power circuit is open (no power to the solenoid) • AIR pump solenoid is damaged or has failed • Solid State relay is damaged or the PCM has failed

DTC	Trouble Code Title, Conditions & Possible Causes
DTC: P0416 **2T CCM, MIL: Yes** **Years:** 2005, 2006, 2007 **Models:** All Models **Engines:** All **Transmissions:** All	**Secondary AIR System Switching Valve 'B' Circuit Fault** Engine started, AIR solenoid enabled, and the PCM detected an unexpected high voltage condition on AIR solenoid control circuit. **Possible Causes:** • AIR solenoid control circuit is open or it is shorted to system power • AIR pump is damaged or the Solid State relay is damaged or has failed • PCM has failed
DTC: P0417 **2T CCM, MIL: Yes** **Years:** 2005, 2006, 2007 **Models:** All Models **Engines:** All **Transmissions:** All	**Secondary AIR System Switching Valve 'B' Circuit Fault** Engine started; Air Injection solenoid commanded "on", and the PCM detected an unexpected "low" voltage condition on the AIR Solenoid control circuit during the CCM test. **Possible Causes:** • AIR solenoid control circuit is shorted to ground or there is no power to the circuit • AIR pump is damaged or the Solid State relay is damaged or has failed • PCM has failed
DTC: P0420 **2T CAT, MIL: Yes** **Years:** 2005, 2006, 2007 **Models:** All Models **Engines:** All **Transmissions:** All	**Catalyst System Efficiency Bank 1 Below Threshold** Vehicle driven at steady cruise speed for 5 minutes, and the PCM detected the switch rate of the rear HO2S-12 was close to the switch rate of front HO2S (it should be much slower). **Possible Causes:** • Air leaks at the exhaust manifold or in the exhaust pipes • Catalytic converter is damaged, contaminated or it has failed • ECT/CHT sensor has lost its calibration (the signal is incorrect) • Engine cylinders misfiring, or the ignition timing is over retarded • Engine oil is contaminated • Front HO2S or rear HO2S is contaminated with fuel or moisture • Front HO2S and/or the rear HO2S is loose in the mounting hole • Front HO2S much older than the rear HO2S (HO2S-11 is lazy) • Fuel system pressure is too high (check the pressure regulator) • Rear HO2S wires improperly connected or the HO2S has failed
DTC: P0430 **2T CAT, MIL: Yes** **Years:** 2005, 2006, 2007 **Models:** All Models **Engines:** All **Transmissions:** All	**Catalyst System Efficiency Bank 2 Below Threshold** Vehicle driven at steady cruise speed for 5 minutes, and the PCM detected the switch rate of the rear HO2S-12 was close to the switch rate of front HO2S (it should be much slower). **Possible Causes:** • Air leaks at the exhaust manifold or in the exhaust pipes • Catalytic converter is damaged, contaminated or it has failed • ECT/CHT sensor has lost its calibration (the signal is incorrect) • Engine cylinders misfiring, or the ignition timing is over retarded • Engine oil is contaminated • Front HO2S or rear HO2S is contaminated with fuel or moisture • Front HO2S and/or the rear HO2S is loose in the mounting hole • Front HO2S much older than the rear HO2S (HO2S-11 is lazy) • Fuel system pressure is too high (check the pressure regulator) • Rear HO2S wires improperly connected or the HO2S has failed
DTC: P0442 **2T EVAP, MIL: Yes** **Years:** 2005, 2006, 2007 **Models:** All Models **Engines:** All **Transmissions:** All	**EVAP Control System Small Leak Detected** ECT sensor less than 90°F at startup (cold engine), engine running in closed loop at a steady cruise speed, and the PCM detected a leak in the EVAP system as small as 0.040" in the test. **Possible Causes:** • Aftermarket EVAP parts that do not conform to specifications • CV solenoid stays partially open when commanded to close • EVAP component seals leaking (i.e., leaks in the Purge valve, fuel vapor control valve tube assembly or fuel vapor vent valve) • Fuel filler cap damaged, cross-threaded or loosely installed • Loose fuel vapor hose/tube connections to EVAP components • Small holes or cuts in fuel vapor hoses or EVAP canister tubes

DTC	Trouble Code Title, Conditions & Possible Causes
DTC: P0442 **2T EVAP, MIL: Yes** **Years:** 2005, 2006, 2007 **Models:** All Models **Engines:** All **Transmissions:** All	**EVAP Control System Small Leak (0.040") Detected** ECT sensor less than 90°F and within 10°F of the IAT sensor at startup (cold engine), engine started, the with the engine running in closed loop at a steady cruise speed, the PCM detected a leak in the EVAP system as small as 0.040" during the EVAP Monitor Test. **Possible Causes:** • Aftermarket EVAP parts that do not conform to specifications • CV solenoid remains partially open when commanded to close • EVAP component seals leaking (i.e., leaks in the Purge valve, fuel tank pressure sensor, canister vent solenoid, fuel vapor control valve tube assembly or fuel vapor vent valve). • Fuel filler cap damaged, cross-threaded or loosely installed • Loose fuel vapor hose/tube connections to EVAP components • Small holes or cuts in fuel vapor hoses or EVAP canister tubes • TSB 99-23-4, TSB 3-9-8 & TSB 3-20-3 contain a repair procedure for this trouble code
DTC: P0443 **2T CCM, MIL: Yes** **Years:** 2005, 2006, 2007 **Models:** All Models **Engines:** All **Transmissions:** All	**EVAP Canister Purge Solenoid Circuit Malfunction** Engine started, and the PCM detected an unexpected high or low voltage condition on the Purge solenoid control circuit when the device was cycled "on" and "off" during testing. **Possible Causes:** • EVAP purge solenoid supply circuit is open • EVAP purge solenoid control circuit open, shorted to ground • EVAP purge solenoid control circuit is shorted to power (B+) • EVAP canister purge solenoid valve is damaged or the PCM has failed
DTC: P0443 **2T CCM, MIL: Yes** **Years:** 2005, 2006, 2007 **Models:** All Models **Engines:** All **Transmissions:** All	**EVAP Canister Purge Solenoid Circuit Malfunction** Engine started, and the PCM detected an unexpected high or low voltage condition on the EVAP Purge solenoid control circuit when the device was cycled On/Off during testing. **Possible Causes:** • EVAP purge solenoid supply circuit is open • EVAP purge solenoid control circuit open, shorted to ground • EVAP purge solenoid control circuit is shorted to power (B+) • EVAP canister purge solenoid valve is damaged or it has failed • PCM has failed
DTC: P0446 **2T EVAP, MIL: Yes** **Years:** 2005, 2006, 2007 **Models:** All Models **Engines:** All **Transmissions:** All	**EVAP Canister Vent System Performance** ECT sensor less than 90°F, engine started, engine running at a steady cruise speed, and the PCM detected excessive vacuum was present in the EVAP system during the test period. **Possible Causes:** • Canister vent (CV) solenoid is stuck closed (partially or fully) • EVAP canister purge outlet tube blocked or kinked between the canister purge valve and the EVAP canister, or EVAP canister tube blocked between the fuel tank and canister • EVAP canister restricted, or plugged CV solenoid filter unit • Plugged or contaminated CV solenoid filter • EVAP canister purge valve stuck open • Fuel filler cap stuck closed (no vacuum relief) • FTP sensor VREF circuit open, or FTP sensor is damaged • Fuel vapor elbow at the EVAP canister contaminated
DTC: P0446 **2T EVAP, MIL: Yes** **Years:** 2005, 2006, 2007 **Models:** All Models **Engines:** All **Transmissions:** All	**EVAP Canister Vent Solenoid Circuit Malfunction** Engine started, and the PCM detected an unexpected high or low voltage condition on the EVAP Canister Vent solenoid control circuit after the device was cycled On/Off in the test. **Possible Causes:** • Canister vent solenoid supply circuit is open • Canister vent solenoid control circuit open, shorted to ground • Canister vent solenoid control circuit is shorted to power (B+) • Canister vent solenoid valve is damaged or the PCM has failed
DTC: P0451 **2T CCM, MIL: Yes** **Years:** 2005, 2006, 2007 **Models:** All Models **Engines:** All **Transmissions:** All	**Fuel Tank Pressure Sensor Intermittent Signal** Engine started, and the PCM detected the FTP sensor signal changed from over +15" H2O to under −15" H2O within 100 ms. **Possible Causes:** • FTP sensor signal circuit has an intermittent open condition • FTP sensor signal circuit has an intermittent shorted condition • FTP sensor is damaged or it has failed

DTC	Trouble Code Title, Conditions & Possible Causes
DTC: P0452 **2T CCM, MIL: Yes** **Years:** 2005, 2006, 2007 **Models:** All Models **Engines:** All **Transmissions:** All	**FTP Sensor Circuit Low Input** Key on or engine running; and the PCM detected the FTP sensor indicated less than the minimum calibrated limit of 0.22v in the test. **Possible Causes:** • FTP sensor connector has internal damage or contamination • FTP sensor signal circuit is shorted to chassis or signal ground • FTP sensor is damaged • PCM has failed
DTC: P0453 **2T CCM, MIL: Yes** **Years:** 2005, 2006, 2007 **Models:** All Models **Engines:** All **Transmissions:** All	**FTP Sensor Circuit High Input** Key on or engine running; and the PCM detected the FTP sensor indicated more than the maximum calibrated limit (4.50v) in the test. **Possible Causes:** • FTP sensor signal circuit is open or the ground circuit is open • FTP sensor signal circuit is shorted to VREF (5v) • FTP sensor is damaged or the PCM has failed
DTC: P0455 **2T EVAP, MIL: Yes** **Years:** 2005, 2006, 2007 **Models:** All Models **Engines:** All **Transmissions:** All	**EVAP Control System Large Leak Detected** ECT sensor less than 90°F at startup, engine running, and the PCM detected several small fuel vapor leaks or a large leak in the system. **Possible Causes:** • Aftermarket EVAP hardware non-conforming to specifications • Canister vent (CV) solenoid stuck open • EVAP canister purge valve stuck closed, or canister damaged • EVAP canister tube, EVAP canister purge outlet tube or EVAP return tube disconnected or cracked, or canister is damaged • Fuel filler cap missing, loose (not tightened) or the wrong part • Loose fuel vapor hose/tube connections to EVAP components • Purge sensor or FTP sensor is out of calibration or has failed
DTC: P0455 **2T EVAP, MIL: Yes** **Years:** 2005, 2006, 2007 **Models:** All Models **Engines:** All **Transmissions:** All	**EVAP Control System Large Leak (0.080") Detected** ECT sensor less than 90°F, engine running at a steady cruise speed, and the PCM detected multiple small fuel vapor leaks; or it detected a large leak in the system during the leak test. **Possible Causes:** • Aftermarket EVAP hardware non-conforming to specifications • EVAP canister tube, EVAP canister purge outlet tube or EVAP return tube disconnected or cracked, or canister is damaged • EVAP canister purge valve stuck closed, or canister damaged • Fuel filler cap missing, loose (not tightened) or the wrong part • Loose fuel vapor hose/tube connections to EVAP components • Canister vent (CV) solenoid stuck open • Fuel tank pressure (FTP) sensor has failed mechanically • TSB 99-23-4 contains a repair procedure for this trouble code • TSB 03-9-8 contains a repair procedure for this trouble code • TSB 3-20-3 contains a repair procedure for this trouble code
DTC: P0456 **2T EVAP, MIL: Yes** **Years:** 2005, 2006, 2007 **Models:** All Models **Engines:** All **Transmissions:** All	**EVAP Control System Very Small Leak (0.020") Detected** ECT sensor less than 90°F (cold engine), engine started, engine running at a steady cruise speed, and the PCM detected a very small fuel vapor leak (0.020") during the leak test. **Possible Causes:** • Canister tube, EVAP canister purge outlet tube or return tube disconnected or cracked • EVAP canister purge valve stuck closed, or canister damaged • Fuel vapor hoses/tubes that have very small holes and/or cuts • Fuel vapor hose/tube connections are loose or damaged • EVAP component seals are leaking (i.e., Purge valve, fuel tank pressure sensor, canister vent solenoid, fuel vapor control valve tube assembly or fuel vapor vent valve assembly) • TSB 03-9-8 contains a repair procedure for this trouble code • TSB 3-20-3 contains a repair procedure for this trouble code

DTC	Trouble Code Title, Conditions & Possible Causes
DTC: P0457 **2T EVAP, MIL: Yes** **Years:** 2005, 2006, 2007 **Models:** All Models **Engines:** All **Transmissions:** All	**EVAP Control System Leak Detected (Fuel Cap Missing)** ECT sensor less than 90°F at startup, engine running at a steady state cruise speed, and the PCM detected the fuel tank pressure changed more than minus (-) 7" H2O in 30 seconds, or excessive purge flow (over 0.06 pounds per minute) occurred in the EVAP Running Loss Monitor Test ("Check Fuel Cap" Lamp may be "on"). **Possible Causes:** • Fuel filler cap not installed after refueling (CMC P0457 is set) • Fuel filler cap missing, loose or cross-threaded • TSB 03-9-8 contains a repair procedure for this trouble code • TSB 3-20-3 contains a repair procedure for this trouble code
DTC: P0460 **2T CCM, MIL: Yes** **Years:** 2005, 2006, 2007 **Models:** All Models **Engines:** All **Transmissions:** All	**Fuel Level Sensor Signal Range/Performance** Engine started, and the PCM detected the FLI sensor did not match the fuel level (e.g., FLI V PID below 0.90v with FLI PID at 25%, or FLIV PID more than 2.45v with FLI PID at 75%). **Possible Causes:** • Fuel tank is empty • FP module is stuck open • Fuel gauge is incorrectly installed • Instrument cluster damaged • PCM Case ground circuit open • Fuel level indicator (FLI) circuit is shorted to power, or is open • Fuel tank has been overfilled, or fuel gauge is damaged • Fuel pump (FP) module is stuck closed, or is stuck open • Fuel level indicator circuit shorted to Case or to power ground • PCM Case ground shorted to VPWR (shorted to system power) • TSB 03-1-7 contains repair help for this code (LS & T-Bird)
DTC: P0462 **2T CCM, MIL: Yes** **Years:** 2005, 2006, 2007 **Models:** All Models **Engines:** All **Transmissions:** All	**Fuel Level Sensor Circuit Low Input** Key on or engine running; and the PCM detected the FLI sensor indicated less than 0.20v at any time during the CCM test period. **Possible Causes:** • Fuel tank is empty • FLI signal circuit is open • FLI signal circuit is shorted to case or chassis ground • PCM has failed
DTC: P0463 **2T CCM, MIL: Yes** **Years:** 2005, 2006, 2007 **Models:** All Models **Engines:** All **Transmissions:** All	**Fuel Level Sensor Circuit High Input** Key on or engine running; and the PCM detected that the FLI sensor indicated more than 4.50v at any time during the CCM test period. **Possible Causes:** • Fuel level sensor connector is damaged or shorted • Fuel tank has been over-filled • FLI signal circuit is shorted to VREF (5v or 12v) • PCM has failed
DTC: P0480 **2T CCM, MIL: Yes** **Years:** 2005, 2006, 2007 **Models:** Crown Victoria, Grand Marquis, Town Car **Engines:** 4.6L VIN V, W **Transmissions:** All	**Visctronic Drive Fan Primary Circuit Malfunction** Key on or engine running; and the PCM detected an unexpected high or low voltage condition on the Visctronic Drive Fan (VDF) primary circuit during the CCM test period. **Possible Causes:** • VDF variable control circuit is open • VDF variable control circuit is shorted to chassis ground • VDF variable control circuit shorted to Fan Speed Sensor circuit • VDF clutch power supply (VPWR) circuit is open • VDF clutch is damaged or it has failed • PCM has failed
DTC: P0480 **2T CCM, MIL: Yes** **Years:** 2005, 2006, 2007 **Models:** E-Series, Escape, Mountaineer **Engines:** All **Transmissions:** All	**Fan Control Relay Circuit Malfunction** Key on or engine running; and the PCM detected an unexpected high or low voltage condition on the Fan Control relay control circuit. **Possible Causes:** • High/Low/Medium FC relay control circuit is open • High/Low/Medium FC relay control circuit is shorted to ground • High/Low/Medium FC relay VPWR circuit is open • High/Low/Medium FC relay direct battery (B+) circuit is open • High/Low/Medium FC relay is damaged or it has failed • PCM has failed

DTC	Trouble Code Title, Conditions & Possible Causes

DTC: P0482
2T CCM, MIL: Yes
Years: 2005, 2006, 2007
Models: Aviator, Escape, Explorer, Explorer Sport-Trac, Mountaineer
Engines: All
Transmissions: All
	Constant Control Relay Module Circuit Malfunction
	Key on or engine running; and the PCM detected an unexpected high or low voltage condition on the High Fan Control (HFC) relay control circuit (located inside the CCRM) during the CCM test period.
	Possible Causes:
	  • FC relay control circuit is open
	  • FC relay control circuit is shorted to chassis ground
	  • FC relay power supply (VPWR) circuit is open
	  • FC relay direct battery (B+) circuit is open
	  • PCM has failed

DTC: P0500
2T CCM, MIL: Yes
Years: 2005, 2006, 2007
Models: All Models
Engines: All
Transmissions: All
	Vehicle Speed Sensor Malfunction
	Engine running, then with the engine speed more than the TCC stall speed, the PCM detected a lack of vehicle speed data occurred.
	Note: The PCM receives vehicle speed data from the VSS, TCSS, ABS module, CTM or GEM controller, depending up the application.
	Possible Causes:
	  • Modules connected to VSC/VSS harness circuits are damaged
	  • Mechanical drive mechanism for the VSS or TCSS is damaged
	  • VSS+ or VSS− harness circuit is open
	  • TCSS signal or TCSS signal return harness circuit is open
	  • VSS harness circuit, TCSS harness circuit is shorted to ground
	  • VSS harness circuit, CSS harness circuit is shorted to power
	  • VSS circuit open between the PCM and related control module
	  • VSS or TCSS, or wheel speed sensors circuits are damaged
	  • TSB 01-21-13 contains a repair procedure for this trouble code

DTC: P0500
2T CCM, MIL: Yes
Years: 2005, 2006, 2007
Models: All Models
Engines: All
Transmissions: All
	Vehicle Speed Sensor Circuit Malfunction
	Engine running, then with the engine speed more than the TCC stall speed, the PCM detected a lack of vehicle speed data occurred.
	Note: The PCM receives vehicle speed data from the Vehicle Speed Sensor on these vehicle applications.
	Possible Causes:
	  • VSS signal circuit is open or shorted to ground
	  • VSS ground circuit is open or VSS power circuit is open
	  • VSS is damaged or it has failed
	  • PSOM is damaged or it has failed (All Models)
	  • PCM has failed

DTC: P0500
2T CCM, MIL: Yes
Years: 2005, 2006, 2007
Models: Crown Victoria, Grand Marquis, Town Car
Engines: 4.6L VIN V, W
Transmissions: All
	Vehicle Speed Sensor Circuit Malfunction
	Engine running, then with the engine speed more than the TCC stall speed, the PCM detected a lack of vehicle speed data occurred.
	Note: The PCM receives vehicle speed data from the ABS module.
	Possible Causes:
	  • The vehicle speed information on this vehicle application is provided to the PCM by the Antilock Brake System module.
	  • Refer to the ABS diagnostics and trouble codes to diagnose this particular trouble code.

DTC: P0500
2T CCM, MIL: Yes
Years: 2005, 2006, 2007
Models: F-Series With 4WD
Engines: All
Transmissions: All
	Vehicle Speed Sensor Circuit Malfunction
	Engine running, then with the engine speed more than the TCC stall speed, the PCM detected a lack of vehicle speed data for a period of time.
	Note: The PCM receives vehicle speed data from the Transfer Case Speed Sensor on these vehicle applications.
	Possible Causes:
	  • TCSS signal circuit is open or shorted to ground
	  • TCSS ground circuit is open
	  • TCSS is damaged or it has failed
	  • PCM has failed

DTC: P0500
2T CCM, MIL: Yes
Years: 2005, 2006, 2007
Models: Aviator, Explorer, Explorer Sport-Trac, F-Series, Mountaineer
Engines: All
Transmissions: All
	Vehicle Speed Sensor Circuit Malfunction
	Engine started; then with the engine speed more than the TCC stall speed, the PCM detected a lack of vehicle speed data occurred.
	Note: The PCM receives vehicle speed data from the Rear Wheel ABS (RABS) or 4-Wheel ABS (4WABS) on these applications.
	Possible Causes:
	  • VSC positive signal circuit is open or shorted to ground
	  • VSC negative signal circuit is open
	  • RABS or 4WABS control unit is damaged or has failed
	  • One of the other modules (CTM or GEM) may be the cause of this trouble code. Diagnose other codes from these modules.

DTC	Trouble Code Title, Conditions & Possible Causes
DTC: P0501 **1T CCM, MIL: Yes** **Years:** 2005, 2006, 2007 **Models:** All Models **Engines:** All **Transmissions:** All	**Vehicle Speed Sensor or PSOM Range/Performance** Engine started; engine speed above the TCC stall speed, and the PCM detected a loss of the VSS signal over a period of time. **Note: The PCM receives vehicle speed data from the VSS, TCSS, ABS module, CTM or GEM controller, depending up the application.** **Possible Causes:** • VSS+ or VSS− signal circuit is open or shorted to ground • TCSS signal or TCSS signal return harness circuit is open • VSS harness circuit, TCSS harness circuit is shorted to ground • VSS harness circuit, CSS harness circuit is shorted to power • VSS circuit open between the PCM and related control module • VSS or TCSS, or wheel speed sensors circuits are damaged • Modules connected to VSC/VSS harness circuits are damaged • Mechanical drive mechanism for the VSS or TCSS is damaged
DTC: P0501 **1T CCM, MIL: Yes** **Years:** 2005, 2006, 2007 **Models:** All Models **Engines:** All **Transmissions:** All	**Vehicle Speed Sensor Range/Performance** Engine started; then with the engine speed more than the TCC stall speed, the PCM detected a problem with the vehicle speed data. **Note: The PCM receives vehicle speed data from the Vehicle Speed Sensor on these vehicle applications.** **Possible Causes:** • VSS signal circuit is open or shorted to ground • VSS ground circuit is open • VSS power circuit (VPWR) is open • VSS is damaged or it has failed • PCM has failed
DTC: P0500 **2T CCM, MIL: Yes** **Years:** 2005, 2006, 2007 **Models:** Crown Victoria, Grand Marquis, Town Car **Engines:** 4.6L VIN V, W **Transmissions:** All	**Vehicle Speed Sensor Signal Range/Performance** Engine started; then with the engine speed more than the TCC stall speed, the PCM detected a problem with the vehicle speed data. **Note: The PCM receives vehicle speed data from the ABS module.** **Possible Causes:** • The vehicle speed information on this vehicle application is provided to the PCM by the Antilock Brake System module. • Refer to the ABS diagnostics and trouble codes to diagnose this particular trouble code.
DTC: P0501 **2T CCM, MIL: Yes** **Years:** 2005, 2006, 2007 **Models:** F-Series Trucks With 4WD **Engines:** All **Transmissions:** All	**Vehicle Speed Sensor Signal Range/Performance** Engine running, then with the engine speed more than the TCC stall speed, the PCM detected a problem with the vehicle speed data. **Note: The PCM receives vehicle speed data from the Transfer Case Speed Sensor on these vehicle applications.** **Possible Causes:** • TCSS signal circuit is open or shorted to ground • TCSS ground circuit is open • TCSS is damaged or it has failed • PCM has failed
DTC: P0501 **2T CCM, MIL: Yes** **Years:** 2005, 2006, 2007 **Models:** Aviator, Explorer, Explorer Sport-Trac, F-Series, Mountaineer **Engines:** All **Transmissions:** All	**Vehicle Speed Sensor Signal Range/Performance** Engine running, then with the engine speed more than the TCC stall speed, the PCM detected a problem with the vehicle speed data. **Note: The PCM receives vehicle speed data from the Rear Wheel ABS (RABS) or 4-Wheel ABS (4WABS) on these applications.** **Possible Causes:** • VSC positive signal circuit is open or shorted to ground • VSC negative signal circuit is open • RABS or 4WABS control unit is damaged or has failed • One of the other modules (CTM or GEM) may be the cause of this trouble code. Diagnose other codes from these modules.
DTC: P0503 **2T CCM, MIL: Yes** **Years:** 2005, 2006, 2007 **Models:** All Models **Engines:** All **Transmissions:** A/T	**Vehicle Speed Sensor Signal Intermittent** Engine started, engine speed above the TCC stall speed, and the PCM detected the vehicle speed data was "noisy" or intermittent. **Note: The PCM receives vehicle speed data from the VSS, TCSS, ABS module, CTM or GEM controller, depending up the application.** **Possible Causes:** • Module or circuits connected to VSS/TCSS circuit are damaged • VSS/TCSS wiring harness or connector is damaged or loose • VSS/TCSS signal is "noisy" due to RFI or EMI interference from sources such as ignition components or charging system • VSS/TCSS gears are damaged or there is debris on the sensor

DTC	Trouble Code Title, Conditions & Possible Causes
DTC: P0503 **2T CCM, MIL: Yes** **Years:** 2005, 2006, 2007 **Models:** Aviator, Explorer, Explorer Sport-Trac, F-Series, Mountaineer **Engines:** All **Transmissions:** M/T	**Vehicle Speed Sensor Signal Intermittent** Engine started, engine speed above the TCC stall speed, and the PCM detected the vehicle speed data was "noisy" or intermittent. **Note: The PCM receives vehicle speed data from the VSS or TCSS.** **Possible Causes:** • TCSS or VSS signal circuit is open or shorted to ground • TCSS or VSS ground circuit is open (an intermittent problem) • TCSS or VSS power supply (VREF) circuit is open (intermittent) • TCSS or VSS is damaged or it has failed (intermittent problem) • PCM has failed
DTC: P0505 **2T CCM, MIL: Yes** **Years:** 2005, 2006, 2007 **Models:** All Models **Engines:** All **Transmissions:** All	**Idle Air Control System Malfunction** Engine started, engine running at hot idle speed, and the PCM detected the Actual Idle Speed was too low or too high when compared to the Target Idle Speed during the KOER self-test. Specification: The IAC valve resistance is 6-13 ohms at 68°F. **Possible Causes:** • Air inlet dirty, restricted or the air cleaner is severely restricted • IAC solenoid control circuit is open, shorted to ground or to B+ • IAC solenoid power circuit (VPWR) is open from the relay • IAC valve is damaged or has failed • PCM has failed • TSB 03-3-5 contains repair information for this trouble code
DTC: P0506 **2T CCM, MIL: Yes** **Years:** 2005, 2006, 2007 **Models:** All Models **Engines:** All **Transmissions:** All	**Idle Air Control System RPM Lower Than Expected** DTC P0402 not set, engine started, engine running in closed loop, and the PCM detected it could not control the idle speed correctly. **Possible Causes:** • Air inlet is plugged or the air filter element is severely clogged • IAC circuit is open or shorted to the VPWR circuit • IAC circuit VPWR circuit is open • IAC solenoid is damaged or has failed • PCM has failed • TSB 03-3-5 contains repair information for this trouble code
DTC: P0507 **2T CCM, MIL: Yes** **Years:** 2005, 2006, 2007 **Models:** All Models **Engines:** All **Transmissions:** All	**Idle Air Control System RPM Higher Than Expected** DTC P0402 not set, engine started, engine running in closed loop, and the PCM detected it could not control the idle speed correctly. **Possible Causes:** • Air intake leak located somewhere after the throttle body • IAC control circuit is shorted to chassis ground • IAC solenoid is damaged or has failed • PCM has failed • TSB 03-3-5 contains repair information for this trouble code
DTC: P0511 **2T CCM, MIL: Yes** **Years:** 2005, 2006, 2007 **Models:** All Models **Engines:** All **Transmissions:** All	**Idle Air Control Valve Circuit Malfunction** DTC P0402 not set, engine started, engine running in closed loop, and the PCM detected it could not control the idle speed correctly. **Possible Causes:** • IAC control circuit is open • IAC control circuit is shorted to power (B+) • IAC power supply circuit (VPWR) is open • IAC solenoid is damaged or the PCM has failed
DTC: P0528 **2T CCM, MIL: Yes** **Years:** 2005, 2006, 2007 **Models:** Crown Victoria, Grand Marquis, Town Car **Engines:** 4.6L VIN V, W **Transmissions:** All	**Visctronic Drive Fan Speed Sensor Circuit Malfunction** Engine started, Visctronic Drive Fan (VDF) commanded to a 100% duty cycle position, and the PCM detected the VDF Speed Sensor signal was less than a calibrated value in the test. **Possible Causes:** • VDF fan motor has a mechanical interference fault or is binding • VDF speed sensor circuit is open or shorted to ground • Vehicle Buffered Power (VBPWR) circuit is open or shorted • VDF speed sensor power ground circuit is open • VDF speed sensor is damaged or the PCM has failed

DTC	Trouble Code Title, Conditions & Possible Causes
DTC: P0534 **2T CCM, MIL: Yes** **Years:** 2005, 2006, 2007 **Models:** All Models **Engines:** All **Transmissions:** All	**Low Air Conditioning Cycle Period** Engine started; A/C enabled, and the PCM detected frequent A/C compressor clutch cycling during the CCM test period. Note that this trouble code and test was designed to protect the transmission. In some cases, the PCM will unlock TCC operation. **Possible Causes:** • A/C cycling pressure switch signal to PCM open (intermittent) • A/C cycling pressure switch IGN (B+) circuit open (intermittent) • A/C mechanical problem (low A/C refrigerant charge or a damaged A/C cycling switch)
DTC: P0537 **2T CCM, MIL: Yes** **Years:** 2005, 2006, 2007 **Models:** All Models **Engines:** All **Transmissions:** All	**A/C Evaporator Temperature Circuit Sensor Low Input** Engine started; A/C enabled, and the PCM detected an unexpected low voltage condition on the A/C Evaporator Temperature (ACET) sensor circuit during the CCM test period. **Possible Causes:** • ACET sensor signal circuit shorted to sensor or chassis ground • ACET sensor is damaged or it has failed • PCM has failed
DTC: P0538 **2T CCM, MIL: Yes** **Years:** 2005, 2006, 2007 **Models:** All Models **Engines:** All **Transmissions:** All	**A/C Evaporator Temperature Sensor Circuit High Input** Engine started; A/C enabled, and the PCM detected an unexpected high voltage condition on the A/C Evaporator Temperature (ACET) sensor circuit during the CCM test period. **Possible Causes:** • ACET sensor signal circuit is open • ACET sensor signal circuit is shorted to VREF (5v) • ACET sensor ground circuit is open • ACET sensor is damaged or it has failed • PCM has failed
DTC: P0552 **2T CCM, MIL: Yes** **Years:** 2005, 2006, 2007 **Models:** All Models **Engines:** All **Transmissions:** All	**Power Steering Pressure Sensor Circuit Low Input** Engine started, and the PCM detected an unexpected low voltage condition on the Power Steering Pressure (PSP) sensor circuit. **Possible Causes:** • PSP sensor signal circuit is shorted to sensor ground • PSP sensor signal circuit is shorted to chassis ground • PSP sensor VREF (5v) circuit is open • PSP sensor is damaged or it has failed • PCM has failed
DTC: P0553 **2T CCM, MIL: Yes** **Years:** 2005, 2006, 2007 **Models:** All Models **Engines:** All **Transmissions:** All	**Power Steering Pressure Sensor Circuit High Input** Engine started, and the PCM detected an unexpected high voltage condition on the Power Steering Pressure (PSP) sensor circuit. **Possible Causes:** • PSP sensor ground circuit is open • PSP sensor ground circuit is shorted to VREF (5v) • PSP sensor signal circuit is shorted to VREF (5v) • PSP sensor is damaged or the PCM has failed
DTC: P0602 **1T PCM, MIL: Yes** **Years:** 2005, 2006, 2007 **Models:** All Models **Engines:** All **Transmissions:** All	**Control Module Programming Error** Key on, and the PCM detected a programming error in the VID block. This fault requires that the VID Block be reprogrammed, or that the EEPROM be re-flashed. **Possible Causes:** • During the VID reprogramming function, the Vehicle ID (VID) data block failed during reprogramming wit the Scan Tool.
DTC: P0603 **1T PCM, MIL: Yes** **Years:** 2005, 2006, 2007 **Models:** All Models **Engines:** All **Transmissions:** All	**PCM Keep Alive Memory Test Error** Key on, and the PCM detected an internal memory fault. This code will set if KAPWR to the PCM is interrupted (at the initial key on). **Possible Causes:** • Battery terminal corrosion, or loose battery connection • KAPWR to PCM interrupted, or the circuit has been opened • Reprogramming error has occurred • PCM has failed and needs replacement. Remember to check for Aftermarket Performance Products before replacing a PCM.
DTC: P0605 **1T PCM, MIL: Yes** **Years:** 2005, 2006, 2007 **Models:** All Models **Engines:** All **Transmissions:** All	**PCM Read Only Memory Test Error** Key on, and the PCM detected a ROM test error (ROM inside PCM is corrupted). The PCM is normally replaced if this code has set. **Possible Causes:** • An attempt was made to change the module calibration, or a Module programming error may have occurred • Clear the trouble codes and then check for this trouble code. If it resets, the PCM has failed and needs replacement. • Remember to check for signs of Aftermarket Performance Products installation before replacing the PCM.

DTC	Trouble Code Title, Conditions & Possible Causes
DTC: P0606 **1T PCM, MIL: Yes** **Years:** 2005, 2006, 2007 **Models:** All Models **Engines:** All **Transmissions:** All	**PCM Internal Communication Error** Key on, and the PCM detected an internal communications register read back error during the initial key on check period. **Possible Causes:** • Clear the trouble codes and then check for this trouble code. If it resets, the PCM has failed and needs replacement. • Remember to check for signs of Aftermarket Performance Products installation before replacing the PCM.
DTC: P0622 **1T CCM, MIL: Yes** **Years:** 2005, 2006, 2007 **Models:** All Models **Engines:** All **Transmissions:** All	**Generator Regulator System Malfunction** Engine started; and the PCM detected an unexpected voltage condition on the Generator control circuit. **Possible Causes:** • Generator belt is loose or worn out • Generator or regulator is damaged or has failed • PCM has failed
DTC: P0645 **1T CCM, MIL: Yes** **Years:** 2005, 2006, 2007 **Models:** All Models **Engines:** All **Transmissions:** All	**Wide Open Throttle A/C Output Primary Circuit Malfunction** Key on or engine running; and the PCM detected an unexpected low or high voltage condition WAC output primary circuit during the test. **Possible Causes:** • WAC relay control circuit is open or shorted to ground • WAC relay power circuit (VPWR) is open • WAC relay is damaged or it has failed • PCM has failed
DTC: P0660 **1T CCM, MIL: Yes** **Years:** 2005, 2006, 2007 **Models:** E-Series, F-Series, Mark LT **Engines:** All **Transmissions:** All	**Intake Manifold Runner Control Valve Circuit Malfunction** Key on or engine running; and the PCM detected an unexpected low or high voltage condition on the Intake Manifold Runner Control (IMRC) signal circuit during the CCM test. **Possible Causes:** • IMRC signal circuit is open • IMRC signal circuit is shorted to chassis ground • IMRC actuator assembly is damaged or failed • PCM has failed
DTC: P0660 **1T CCM, MIL: Yes** **Years:** 2005, 2006, 2007 **Models:** Aviator **Engines:** 4.6L VIN H engine **Transmissions:** All	**Intake Manifold Communication Control Circuit Malfunction** Key on or engine running; and the PCM detected an unexpected low or high voltage condition on the Intake Manifold Communication Control (IMCC) signal circuit in the test. **Possible Causes:** • IMCC signal circuit is open • IMCC signal circuit is shorted to chassis ground • Long / Short actuator assembly is damaged or failed • PCM has failed
DTC: P0703 **2T CCM, MIL: Yes** **Years:** 2005, 2006, 2007 **Models:** All Models **Engines:** All **Transmissions:** A/T	**Brake Switch Circuit Malfunction** Engine started, and the PCM did not detect any change in the Brake Pedal Position (BPP) switch status, or with the vehicle at Cruise speed, followed by one or more short deceleration periods, the PCM did not detect any change in the Brake Pedal Position switch status. **Possible Causes:** • BPP switch circuit is open • BPP switch is damaged or it is out of adjustment • BPP switch power circuit is open (check the switch inline fuse)
DTC: P0704 **1T CCM, MIL: No** **Years:** 2005, 2006, 2007 **Models:** E-Series, F-Series, Mark LT **Engines:** All **Transmissions:** M/T	**Clutch Pedal Position Switch Circuit Malfunction** Engine running in gear, followed by several gearshift changes, and the PCM did not detect any change in the clutch switch status. **Note: The CCP PID should change (5v to 0v) with clutch depressed.** **Possible Causes:** • CPP switch signal circuit shorted to power • CPP switch ground (return) circuit is open • CPP switch is damaged or out of adjustment • PCM has failed

DTC	Trouble Code Title, Conditions & Possible Causes
DTC: P0705 **2T CCM, MIL: Yes** **Years:** 2005, 2006, 2007 **Models:** All Models **Engines:** All **Transmissions:** A/T	**DTR Sensor / TR Sensor Circuit Malfunction** Key on or engine running; and the PCM detected that one or more of the Digital Transmission Range (DTR) or Transmission Range sensor (TR) signals (TR4, TR3, TR2 and TR1) were invalid (e.g., two TR or DR sensor signals received at the same time). **Possible Causes:** • DTR or TR sensor connector is damaged or shorted • DTR or TR sensor signal circuit is open or shorted to ground • DTR or TR sensor signal circuit is shorted to VREF (5v) • DTR or TR sensor damaged • PCM has failed
DTC: P0707 **2T CCM, MIL: Yes** **Years:** 2005, 2006, 2007 **Models:** All Models **Engines:** All **Transmissions:** A/T	**DTR Sensor / TR Sensor Circuit Low Input** Key on or engine running; and the PCM detected the Digital Transmission Range (DTR) or Transmission Range sensor (TR) signal was less than the self-test minimum value in the test. **Possible Causes:** • DTR or TR sensor connector is damaged or it is shorted • DTR or TR sensor signal circuit is shorted to sensor ground • DTR or TR sensor damaged • PCM has failed
DTC: P0708 **2T CCM, MIL: Yes** **Years:** 2005, 2006, 2007 **Models:** All Models **Engines:** All **Transmissions:** A/T	**DTR Sensor or TR Sensor Circuit High Input** Key on or engine running; and the PCM detected the Digital Transmission Range (DTR) or Transmission Range sensor (TR) input was more than the self-test maximum range in the test. **Possible Causes:** • DTR or TR sensor connector is damaged or open • DTR or TR sensor signal circuit is open • DTR or TR sensor is shorted to VREF (5v) • DTR or TR sensor is damaged or the PCM has failed
DTC: P0711 **2T CCM, MIL: No** **Years:** 2005, 2006, 2007 **Models:** All Models **Engines:** All **Transmissions:** A/T	**TFT Sensor Signal Range/Performance** Engine started, KOER Self-Test enabled, engine running for over 10 minutes, and the PCM detected the Transmission Fluid Temperature (TFT) sensor value was not close its normal operating temperature. **Possible Causes:** • ATF is low, contaminated, dirty or burnt • TFT sensor signal circuit has a high resistance condition • TFT sensor is out-of-calibration ("skewed") or it has failed • PCM has failed
DTC: P0712 **2T CCM, MIL: No** **Years:** 2005, 2006, 2007 **Models:** All Models **Engines:** All **Transmissions:** A/T	**TFT Sensor Circuit Low Input** Key on or engine running; and the PCM detected the Transmission Fluid Temperature (TFT) sensor was less than its minimum self-test range (Scan Tool reads below −40°F) in the test. **Possible Causes:** • TFT sensor signal circuit is shorted to chassis ground • TFT sensor signal circuit is shorted to sensor ground • TFT sensor is damaged, or out-of-calibration, or has failed • PCM has failed
DTC: P0713 **2T CCM, MIL: No** **Years:** 2005, 2006, 2007 **Models:** All Models **Engines:** All **Transmissions:** A/T	**TFT Sensor Circuit High Input** Key on or engine running; and the PCM detected the Transmission Fluid Temperature (TFT) sensor was more than its maximum self-test range (Scan Tool reads over 315°F) in the test. **Possible Causes:** • TFT sensor signal circuit is open between the sensor and PCM • TFT sensor ground circuit is open between sensor and PCM • TFT sensor is damaged or has failed • PCM has failed
DTC: P0715 **2T CCM, MIL: No** **Years:** 2005, 2006, 2007 **Models:** All Models **Engines:** All **Transmissions:** A/T	**Transmission Speed Shaft Sensor Circuit Malfunction** Engine started, vehicle driven with the vehicle speed sensor indicating more than 1 mph, and the PCM detected the TSS signals were erratic, or that they were missing for a period of time. **Possible Causes:** • TSS signal circuit is open • TSS signal is shorted to chassis ground • TSS signal is shorted to sensor ground • TSS assembly is damaged or it has failed • PCM has failed

DTC	Trouble Code Title, Conditions & Possible Causes
DTC: P0717 **2T CCM, MIL: No** **Years:** 2005, 2006, 2007 **Models:** All Models **Engines:** All **Transmissions:** A/T	**Transmission Speed Shaft Sensor Signal Intermittent** Engine started, vehicle speed sensor indicating over 1 mph, and the PCM detected an intermittent loss of TSS signals (i.e., the TSS signals were erratic, irregular or missing). **Possible Causes:** • TSS connector is damaged, loose or shorted • TSS signal circuit has an intermittent open condition • TSS signal circuit has an intermittent short to ground condition • TSS assembly is damaged or is has failed • PCM has failed
DTC: P0718 **2T CCM, MIL: No** **Years:** 2005, 2006, 2007 **Models:** All Models **Engines:** All **Transmissions:** A/T	**Transmission Speed Shaft Sensor Signal Noisy** Engine started, vehicle speed sensor signal over 1 mph, and the PCM detected the "noise" interference on the TSS signal circuit. **Possible Causes:** • TSS signal is "noisy" due to RFI or EMI interference from sources such as ignition components or charging system • TSS signal wiring is damaged or contacting other signal wiring • PCM has failed
DTC: P0718 **2T CCM, MIL: Yes** **Years:** 2005, 2006, 2007 **Models:** All Models **Engines:** All **Transmissions:** A/T	**A/T Output Shaft Speed Sensor Insufficient Input** Engine started, VSS signal more than 1 mph, and the PCM detected the Output Shaft Speed signal did not correlate to the incoming signals received from the VSS or TCSS devices or related modules. **Possible Causes:** • OSS sensor signal circuit is shorted to ground or • OSS sensor signal circuit is open • OSS sensor circuit is shorted to power • OSS sensor is damaged or it has failed • PCM has failed
DTC: P0721 **2T CCM, MIL: No** **Years:** 2005, 2006, 2007 **Models:** All Models **Engines:** All **Transmissions:** A/T	**A/T Output Shaft Speed Sensor Noise Interference** Engine started, VSS signal more than 1 mph, and the PCM detected "noise" interference on the Output Shaft Speed (OSS) sensor circuit. **Possible Causes:** • After market add-on devices interfering with the OSS signal • OSS connector is damaged, loose or shorted, or the wiring is misrouted or it is damaged • OSS assembly is damaged or it has failed • PCM has failed
DTC: P0722 **2T CCM, MIL: No** **Years:** 2005, 2006, 2007 **Models:** All Models **Engines:** All **Transmissions:** A/T	**A/T Output Speed Sensor No Signal** Engine started, and the PCM did not detect any Output Shaft Speed (OSS) sensor signals upon initial vehicle movement. **Possible Causes:** • After market add-on devices interfering with the OSS signal • OSS sensor wiring is misrouted or damaged, or the OSS sensor is damaged • PCM has failed
DTC: P0723 **2T CCM, MIL: No** **Years:** 2005, 2006, 2007 **Models:** All Models **Engines:** All **Transmissions:** A/T	**A/T Output Speed Sensor Signal Intermittent** Engine started, and the PCM detected the Output Shaft Speed (OSS) sensor signal was interrupted or irregular during testing. **Possible Causes:** • OSS harness connector is damaged, loose or shorted, or the connector is not seated • OSS signal is open or it is shorted to ground (intermittent fault) • OSS assembly is damaged or it has failed
DTC: P0731 **2T CCM, MIL: No** **Years:** 2005, 2006, 2007 **Models:** All Models **Engines:** All **Transmissions:** A/T	**Incorrect First Gear Ratio** Engine started, vehicle operating with 1st Gear commanded "on", and the PCM detected an incorrect 1st gear ratio during the test. **Possible Causes:** • 1st Gear solenoid harness connector not properly seated • 1st Gear solenoid signal shorted to ground, or open • 1st Gear solenoid wiring harness connector is damaged • 1st Gear solenoid is damaged or not properly installed
DTC: P0731 **2T CCM, MIL: No** **Years:** 2005, 2006, 2007 **Models:** Escape, Mountaineer **Engines:** All **Transmissions:** A/T	**Incorrect First Gear Ratio** Engine started, vehicle operating with 1st Gear commanded "on", and the PCM detected an incorrect 1st gear ratio during the test. **Possible Causes:** • 1st Gear solenoid harness connector not properly seated • 1st Gear solenoid signal shorted to ground, or open • 1st Gear solenoid wiring harness connector is damaged • 1st Gear solenoid is damaged or not properly installed • TSB 02-2-4 contains a repair procedure for this trouble code

DTC	Trouble Code Title, Conditions & Possible Causes
DTC: P0732 **2T CCM, MIL: No** **Years:** 2005, 2006, 2007 **Models:** All Models **Engines:** All **Transmissions:** A/T	**Incorrect Second Gear Ratio** Engine started, vehicle operating with 2nd Gear commanded "on", and the PCM detected an incorrect 2nd gear ratio during the test. **Possible Causes:** • 2nd Gear solenoid harness connector not properly seated • 2nd Gear solenoid signal shorted to ground, or open • 2nd Gear solenoid wring harness connector is damaged • 2nd Gear solenoid is damaged or not properly installed
DTC: P0732 **2T CCM, MIL: No** **Years:** 2005, 2006, 2007 **Models:** Escape, Mountaineer **Engines:** All **Transmissions:** A/T	**Incorrect Second Gear Ratio** Engine started, vehicle operating with 2nd Gear commanded "on", and the PCM detected an incorrect 2nd gear ratio during the test. **Possible Causes:** • 2nd Gear solenoid harness connector not properly seated • 2nd Gear solenoid signal shorted to ground, or open • 2nd Gear solenoid wring harness connector is damaged • 2nd Gear solenoid is damaged or not properly installed • TSB 02-2-4 contains a repair procedure for this trouble code
DTC: P0733 **2T CCM, MIL: No** **Years:** 2005, 2006, 2007 **Models:** All Models **Engines:** All **Transmissions:** A/T	**Incorrect Third Gear Ratio** Engine started, vehicle operating with 3rd Gear commanded "on", and the PCM detected an incorrect 3rd gear ratio during the test. **Possible Causes:** • 3rd Gear solenoid harness connector not properly seated • 3rd Gear solenoid signal shorted to ground, or open • 3rd Gear solenoid wiring harness connector is damaged • 3rd Gear solenoid is damaged or not properly installed
DTC: P0734 **2T CCM, MIL: No** **Years:** 2005, 2006, 2007 **Models:** All Models **Engines:** All **Transmissions:** A/T	**Incorrect Fourth Gear Ratio** Engine started, vehicle operating with 4th Gear commanded "on", and the PCM detected an incorrect 4th gear ratio during the test. **Possible Causes:** • 4th Gear solenoid harness connector not properly seated • 4th Gear solenoid signal shorted to ground, or open • 4th Gear solenoid wiring harness connector is damaged • 4th Gear solenoid is damaged or not properly installed
DTC: P0734 **2T CCM, MIL: No** **Years:** 2005, 2006, 2007 **Models:** Escape, Mountaineer **Engines:** All **Transmissions:** A/T	**Incorrect Fourth Gear Ratio** Engine started, vehicle operating with 4th Gear commanded "on", and the PCM detected an incorrect 4th gear ratio during the test. **Possible Causes:** • 4th Gear solenoid harness connector not properly seated • 4th Gear solenoid signal shorted to ground, or open • 4th Gear solenoid wiring harness connector is damaged • 4th Gear solenoid is damaged or not properly installed • TSB 02-2-4 contains a repair procedure for this trouble code
DTC: P0735 **2T CCM, MIL: No** **Years:** 2005, 2006, 2007 **Models:** All Models **Engines:** All **Transmissions:** A/T	**Incorrect Fifth Gear Ratio** Engine started, vehicle operating with 5th Gear commanded "on", and the PCM detected an incorrect 5th gear ratio during the test. **Possible Causes:** • 5th Gear solenoid harness connector not properly seated • 5th Gear solenoid signal shorted to ground, or open • 5th Gear solenoid wiring harness connector is damaged • 5th Gear solenoid is damaged or not properly installed
DTC: P0736 **2T CCM, MIL: No** **Years:** 2005, 2006, 2007 **Models:** All Models **Engines:** All **Transmissions:** A/T	**Incorrect Reverse Gear Ratio** Engine started, vehicle operating with Reverse Gear commanded "on", and the PCM detected an incorrect reverse gear ratio occurred. **Possible Causes:** • Reverse Gear solenoid harness connector not properly seated • Reverse Gear solenoid signal shorted to ground, or open • Reverse Gear solenoid wiring harness connector is damaged • Reverse Gear solenoid is damaged or not properly installed
DTC: P0740 **2T CCM, MIL: No** **Years:** 2005, 2006, 2007 **Models:** All Models **Engines:** All **Transmissions:** A/T	**TCC Solenoid Circuit Malfunction** Engine started, KOER Self-Test enabled, vehicle driven at cruise speed, and the PCM did not detect any voltage drop across the TCC solenoid circuit during the test period. **Possible Causes:** • TCC solenoid control circuit is open or shorted to ground • TCC solenoid wiring harness connector is damaged • TCC solenoid is damaged or has failed • PCM has failed

DTC	Trouble Code Title, Conditions & Possible Causes
DTC: P0741 **2T CCM, MIL: No** **Years:** 2005, 2006, 2007 **Models:** All Models **Engines:** All **Transmissions:** A/T	**TCC Mechanical System Range/Performance** Engine started, vehicle driven in gear with VSS signals received, and the PCM detected excessive slippage while in normal operation. **Possible Causes:** • TCC solenoid has a mechanical failure • TCC solenoid has a hydraulic failure • PCM has failed
DTC: P0741 **2T CCM, MIL: No** **Years:** 2005, 2006, 2007 **Models:** Escape, Mountaineer **Engines:** All **Transmissions:** A/T	**TCC Mechanical System Range/Performance** Engine started, vehicle driven in gear with VSS signals received, and the PCM detected excessive slippage while in normal operation. **Possible Causes:** • TCC solenoid has a mechanical failure • TCC solenoid has a hydraulic failure • PCM has failed • TSB 02-2-4 contains a repair procedure for this trouble code
DTC: P0743 **2T CCM, MIL: Yes** **Years:** 2005, 2006, 2007 **Models:** All Models **Engines:** All **Transmissions:** A/T	**TCC Solenoid Circuit Malfunction** Key on, KOEO Self-Test enabled and the PCM did not detect any voltage drop across the TCC solenoid circuit during the test period. **Possible Causes:** • TCC solenoid control circuit is open • TCC solenoid control circuit is shorted to ground • TCC solenoid wiring harness connector is damaged • TCC solenoid is damaged or it has failed • PCM has failed
DTC: P0746 **2T CCM, MIL: No** **Years:** 2005, 2006, 2007 **Models:** All Models **Engines:** All **Transmissions:** A/T	**A/T EPC Solenoid Circuit Malfunction** Key on, KOEO Self-Test enabled and the PCM did not detect any voltage drop across the EPC solenoid circuit during the test period. **Possible Causes:** • EPC solenoid control circuit is open • EPC solenoid control circuit is shorted to ground • EPC solenoid wiring harness connector is damaged • EPC solenoid is damaged or it has failed • PCM has failed
DTC: P0750 **2T CCM, MIL: Yes** **Years:** 2005, 2006, 2007 **Models:** All Models **Engines:** All **Transmissions:** A/T	**A/T Shift Solenoid 1/A Circuit Malfunction** Engine started, vehicle driven with the solenoid applied, and the PCM detected an unexpected voltage condition on the SS1/A solenoid circuit was incorrect during the test. **Possible Causes:** • SS1/A solenoid control circuit is open • SS1/A solenoid control circuit is shorted to ground • SS1/A solenoid wiring harness connector is damaged • SS1/A solenoid is damaged or has failed • PCM has failed
DTC: P0751 **2T CCM, MIL: No** **Years:** 2005, 2006, 2007 **Models:** All Models **Engines:** All **Transmissions:** A/T	**A/T Shift Solenoid 1/A Function Range/Performance** Engine started, vehicle driven with the solenoid applied, and the PCM detected a mechanical failure while operating the Shift Solenoid 1/A during the CCM test period. **Possible Causes:** • SS1/A solenoid is stuck in the "off" position • SS1/A solenoid has a mechanical failure • SS1/A solenoid has a hydraulic failure • PCM has failed
DTC: P0752 **1T CCM, MIL: No** **Years:** 2005, 2006, 2007 **Models:** All Models **Engines:** All **Transmissions:** A/T	**A/T Shift Solenoid 1/A Function Range/Performance** Engine started, vehicle driven with the solenoid applied, and the PCM detected a mechanical failure while operating the Shift Solenoid 1/A during the CCM test period. **Possible Causes:** • SS1/A solenoid is stuck in the "on" position • SS1/A solenoid has a mechanical failure • SS1/A solenoid has a hydraulic failure • PCM has failed

DTC	Trouble Code Title, Conditions & Possible Causes
DTC: P0753 **1T CCM, MIL: Yes** **Years:** 2005, 2006, 2007 **Models:** All Models **Engines:** All **Transmissions:** A/T	**A/T Shift Solenoid 1/A Circuit Malfunction** Engine started, vehicle driven with the solenoid applied, and the PCM detected an unexpected voltage condition on the SS1/A solenoid circuit was incorrect during the test. **Possible Causes:** • SS1/A solenoid control circuit is open • SS1/A solenoid control circuit is shorted to ground • SS1/A solenoid wiring harness connector is damaged • SS1/A solenoid is damaged or has failed • PCM has failed
DTC: P0755 **1T CCM, MIL: Yes** **Years:** 2005, 2006, 2007 **Models:** All Models **Engines:** All **Transmissions:** A/T	**A/T Shift Solenoid 2/B Circuit Malfunction** Engine started, vehicle driven with the solenoid applied, and the PCM detected an unexpected voltage condition on the SS2/B solenoid circuit was incorrect during the test. **Possible Causes:** • SS2/B solenoid control circuit is open • SS2/B solenoid control circuit is shorted to ground • SS2/B solenoid wiring harness connector is damaged • SS2/B solenoid is damaged or has failed • PCM has failed
DTC: P0756 **1T CCM, MIL: Yes** **Years:** 2005, 2006, 2007 **Models:** All Models **Engines:** All **Transmissions:** A/T	**A/T Shift Solenoid 2/B Function Range/Performance** Engine started, vehicle driven with the solenoid applied, and the PCM detected a mechanical failure while operating the Shift Solenoid 2/B during the CCM test period. **Possible Causes:** • SS2/B solenoid is stuck in the "on" position • SS2/B solenoid has a mechanical failure • SS2/B solenoid has a hydraulic failure • PCM has failed
DTC: P0757 **1T CCM, MIL: Yes** **Years:** 2005, 2006, 2007 **Models:** All Models **Engines:** All **Transmissions:** A/T	**A/T Shift Solenoid 2/B Function Range/Performance** Engine started, vehicle driven with the solenoid applied, and the PCM detected a mechanical failure while operating the Shift Solenoid 2/B during the CCM test period. **Possible Causes:** • SS2/B solenoid is stuck in the "on" position • SS2/B solenoid has a mechanical failure • SS2/B solenoid has a hydraulic failure • PCM has failed
DTC: P0758 **1T CCM, MIL: Yes** **Years:** 2005, 2006, 2007 **Models:** All Models **Engines:** All **Transmissions:** A/T	**A/T Shift Solenoid 2/B Circuit Malfunction** Key on, KOEO Self-Test enabled, Shift Solenoid 2/B applied, and the PCM detected an unexpected voltage condition on the Shift Solenoid 2/B circuit during the CCM test period. **Possible Causes:** • Shift Solenoid 2/B connector is damaged, open or shorted • Shift Solenoid 2/B control circuit is open • Shift Solenoid 2/B control circuit is shorted to ground • Shift Solenoid 2/B is damaged or it has failed • PCM has failed
DTC: P0760 **1T CCM, MIL: Yes** **Years:** 2005, 2006, 2007 **Models:** All Models **Engines:** All **Transmissions:** A/T	**A/T Shift Solenoid 3/C Circuit Malfunction** Engine started, vehicle driven with Shift Solenoid 3/C applied, and the PCM detected an unexpected voltage condition on the Shift Solenoid 3/C circuit during the CCM test period. **Possible Causes:** • Shift Solenoid 3/C connector is damaged, open or shorted • Shift Solenoid 3/C control circuit is open • Shift Solenoid 3/C control circuit is shorted to ground • Shift Solenoid 3/C is damaged or it has failed • PCM has failed
DTC: P0761 **1T CCM, MIL: No** **Years:** 2005, 2006, 2007 **Models:** All Models **Engines:** All **Transmissions:** A/T	**A/T Shift Solenoid 3/C Function Range/Performance** Engine started, vehicle driven with Shift Solenoid 3/C applied, and the PCM detected a mechanical failure occurred (stuck "off") while operating Shift Solenoid 3/C during the test. **Possible Causes:** • SS3/C solenoid may be stuck "off" • SS3/C solenoid has a mechanical failure • SS3/C solenoid has a hydraulic failure • PCM has failed

DTC	Trouble Code Title, Conditions & Possible Causes
DTC: P0762 **1T CCM, MIL: No** **Years:** 2005, 2006, 2007 **Models:** All Models **Engines:** All **Transmissions:** A/T	**A/T Shift Solenoid 3/C Function Range/Performance** Engine started, vehicle driven with Shift Solenoid 3/C applied, and the PCM detected a mechanical failure occurred (stuck "on") while operating Shift Solenoid 3/C during the test. **Possible Causes:** • SS3/C solenoid may be stuck "on" • SS3/C solenoid has a mechanical failure • SS3/C solenoid has a hydraulic failure • PCM has failed
DTC: P0765 **1T CCM, MIL: Yes** **Years:** 2005, 2006, 2007 **Models:** All Models **Engines:** All **Transmissions:** A/T	**A/T Shift Solenoid 4/D Circuit Malfunction** Engine started, vehicle driven with Shift Solenoid 4/D applied, and the PCM detected an unexpected voltage condition on Shift Solenoid 4/D circuit during the CCM continuous test. **Possible Causes:** • Shift Solenoid 4/D wiring harness or connector is damaged • Shift Solenoid 4/D control circuit is open or shorted to ground • Shift Solenoid 4/D is damaged or it has failed • PCM has failed
DTC: P0781 **1T CCM, MIL: No** **Years:** 2005, 2006, 2007 **Models:** All Models **Engines:** All **Transmissions:** A/T	**A/T 1 to 2 Shift Error** Engine started, vehicle driven in gear with VSS signals received, and the PCM detected the engine speed (rpm) did not decrease properly (i.e., an incorrect 1-2 gear ratio was detected during a shift event). **Possible Causes:** • SS1/A solenoid may be stuck • SS1/A solenoid has a hydraulic problem • SS2/B solenoid may be stuck • SS2/B has a hydraulic problem • Transmission may have damaged friction material • Transmission has internal damage and needs replacement
DTC: P0782 **1T CCM, MIL: No** **Years:** 2005, 2006, 2007 **Models:** All Models **Engines:** All **Transmissions:** A/T	**A/T 2 to 3 Shift Error** Engine started, vehicle driven in gear with VSS signals received, and the PCM detected the engine speed (rpm) did not decrease properly (i.e., an incorrect 2-3 gear ratio was detected during a shift event). **Possible Causes:** • SS1/A solenoid may be stuck • SS1/A solenoid has a hydraulic problem • SS2/B solenoid may be stuck • SS2/B has a hydraulic problem • Transmission may have damaged friction material • Transmission has internal damage and needs replacement
DTC: P0783 **1T CCM, MIL: No** **Years:** 2005, 2006, 2007 **Models:** All Models **Engines:** All **Transmissions:** A/T	**A/T 3 to 4 Shift Error** Engine started, vehicle driven in gear with VSS signals received, and the PCM detected the engine speed (rpm) did not change properly (i.e., an incorrect 3-4 gear ratio was detected during the shift event). **Possible Causes:** • SS1/A solenoid may be stuck, or a hydraulic failure exists • SS2/B solenoid may be stuck, or a hydraulic failure exists • Transmission may have damaged friction material
DTC: P0784 **1T CCM, MIL: No** **Years:** 2005, 2006, 2007 **Models:** All Models **Engines:** All **Transmissions:** A/T	**A/T 4 to 5 Shift Error** Engine started, vehicle driven in gear with VSS signals received, and the PCM detected the engine speed (rpm) did not change properly (i.e., an incorrect 4-5 gear ratio was detected during a shift event). **Possible Causes:** • SS2/B solenoid may be stuck, or a hydraulic failure exists • SS3/C solenoid may be stuck, or a hydraulic failure exists • Transmission may have damaged friction material
DTC: P0812 **1T CCM, MIL: No** **Years:** 2005, 2006, 2007 **Models:** All Models **Engines:** All **Transmissions:** A/T	**A/T Reverse Switch Circuit Malfunction** Key on, engine off, KOEO Self Test enabled, and the PCM detected the reverse switch signal did not change as the selector was shifted in or out of reverse gear. **Note: The RS PID should change from ON to OFF while shifting.** **Possible Causes:** • Transmission shift not indicating neutral during the self-test • RS switch circuit shorted to VREF or VPWR • RS switch circuit is open or shorted to ground (signal return) • Reverse switch is damaged • PCM has failed

DTC	Trouble Code Title, Conditions & Possible Causes
DTC: P0813 **1T CCM, MIL: Yes** **Years:** 2005, 2006, 2007 **Models:** All Models **Engines:** All **Transmissions:** A/T	**Transmission Control System Malfunction** Engine started, vehicle speed more than 1 in gear, and the PCM detected a problem in the Transmission Control System operation. **Possible Causes:** • Refer to the information in the Transmission Section of the appropriate Workshop Repair manual (i.e., the information for the particular vehicle that set this trouble code).
DTC: P0815 **1T CCM, MIL: Yes** **Years:** 2005, 2006, 2007 **Models:** All Models **Engines:** All **Transmissions:** A/T	**Transmission Control System Malfunction** Key on, engine off, KOEO Self Test enabled, and the PCM detected the reverse switch input did not change as the selector was shifted in or out of reverse (i.e., it was high when it should have been low). **Note: The RS PID should change from ON to OFF while shifting.** **Possible Causes:** • Refer to the information in the Transmission Section of the appropriate Workshop Repair manual (i.e., the information for the particular vehicle that set this trouble code).

Gas Engine OBD II Trouble Code List (P1xxx Codes)

DTC	Trouble Code Title, Conditions & Possible Causes
DTC: P1000 **1T PCM, MIL: No** **Years:** 2005, 2006, 2007 **Models:** All Models **Engines:** All **Transmissions:** All	**OBD II Monitor Testing Not Complete** Key on or engine running; and the PCM detected one the conditions shown under Possible Causes (i.e., this code cannot be cleared manually - it must clear itself after all of the OBD II Monitors complete). **Note: This code must be cleared to pass an Inspection/Maintenance Test required to register a vehicle in certain states.** **Possible Causes:** • Battery keep alive power (KAPWR) was removed to the PCM • One or more OBD II Monitors did not complete during an official OBD II Drive Cycle • PCM Reset step was performed with an OBD II Scan Tool
DTC: P1001 **1T CCM, MIL: No** **Years:** 2005, 2006, 2007 **Models:** All Models **Engines:** All **Transmissions:** All	**KOER Self-Test Not Completed, KOER Test Aborted** Key on, engine running self-test not completed during the normal allowable time period. **Possible Causes:** • Engine speed (rpm) out of specification during the KOER test • Incorrect Self-Test Procedure • Scan Tool has a communication problem • Unexpected response from Self-Test monitors
DTC: P1100 **2T CCM, MIL: Yes** **Years:** 2005, 2006, 2007 **Models:** All Models **Engines:** All **Transmissions:** All	**MAF Sensor Signal Intermittent** Engine started, engine running at idle or cruise speed, and the PCM detected the MAF sensor signal above or below the calibrated limit. **Possible Causes:** • MAF sensor continuity problems at the connector • MAF sensor continuity through the wiring harness • MAF sensor circuit intermittent open inside the sensor • PCM has failed
DTC: P1101 **2T CCM, MIL: Yes** **Years:** 2005, 2006, 2007 **Models:** All Models **Engines:** All **Transmissions:** All	**MAF Sensor Out Of Self-Test Range** Key on and engine off, and the PCM detected the MAF sensor was more than 0.27v, or with the engine running, the MAF sensor voltage was not within a normal range of 0.46v to 2.44v. **Possible Causes:** • Low battery charge • MAF sensor partially connected, or the sensor is contaminated • MAF sensor power ground circuit or sensor signal (return) open • MAF sensor is damaged or it has failed • PCM has failed
DTC: P1112 **2T CCM, MIL: Yes** **Years:** 2005, 2006, 2007 **Models:** All Models **Engines:** All **Transmissions:** All	**IAT Sensor Circuit Intermittent** Engine started, and the PCM detected an intermittent condition in the IAT sensor signal during the self-test. **Note: Select the IAT PID and monitor the signal for sudden changes.** **Possible Causes:** • IAT sensor wiring harness is damaged (wire may be open) • IAT sensor harness connector is damaged • IAT sensor is damaged or the PCM has failed

DTC	Trouble Code Title, Conditions & Possible Causes
DTC: P1114 **2T CCM, MIL: Yes** **Years:** 2005, 2006, 2007 **Models:** All Models **Engines:** All **Transmissions:** All	**IAT Sensor Circuit Low Input** Engine started, and the PCM detected the IAT sensor signal was less than the self-test minimum of 0.20v (equivalent to 250°F). Monitor the IAT PID for very low signal. **Possible Causes:** • IAT sensor wiring harness is damaged (wire may be grounded) • IAT sensor harness connector is damaged (may be grounded) • IAT sensor is damaged or the PCM has failed
DTC: P1115 **2T CCM, MIL: Yes** **Years:** 2005, 2006, 2007 **Models:** All Models **Engines:** All **Transmissions:** All	**IAT Sensor 2 Circuit High Input** Engine started, and the PCM detected the IAT Sensor 2 signal was more than the self-test maximum of 4.60v (equivalent to 250°F). Monitor the IAT PID for very high signal. **Possible Causes:** • IAT sensor wiring harness or harness connector is damaged (wire may be open) • IAT sensor signal circuit is open, or the ground circuit is open • IAT sensor is damaged or has failed • PCM has failed
DTC: P1116 **1T CCM, MIL: Yes** **Years:** 2005, 2006, 2007 **Models:** All Models **Engines:** All **Transmissions:** All	**CHT or ECT Sensor Out Of Self-Test Range** Key on, KOEO Self-Test enabled, and the PCM detected the ECT sensor was more than the expected range (50°F), or engine running, KOER Self-Test enabled, and the PCM detected the ECT senor signal was less than 180°F during the self test period. The ECT PID must be above 50°F in the KOEO test or above 180°F in the KOER self-test to pass these parameters. **Possible Causes:** • ECT sensor harness connector is damaged, loose or shorted • ECT sensor is damaged • KOER or KOER Self-Test performed with the engine "too cold"
DTC: P1117 **2T CCM, MIL: Yes** **Years:** 2005, 2006, 2007 **Models:** All Models **Engines:** All **Transmissions:** All	**CHT or ECT Sensor Signal Intermittent** Engine started, and the PCM detected an intermittent loss of the CHT or ECT sensor signal (it may have an open circuit condition). **Note: Select the CHT or IAT PID and monitor the signal for sudden changes while wiggling the CHT or IAT sensor connector. On the 5.4L V8, if the temperature exceeds 258°F, the PCM disables four fuel injectors at a time. It alternates which four fuel injectors are disabled every 32-engine cycles. The cylinders that are disabled do not inject fuel, so they act as air pumps to aid in cooling the engine. If the temperature exceeds 310°F, the PCM disables all of the fuel injectors until the engine temperature drops below 310°F.** **Possible Causes:** • ECT sensor harness connector is damaged, loose or shorted • ECT sensor is damaged or it has failed • Engine overheating condition present • Thermostat is faulty, or engine coolant level is low
DTC: P1120 **2T CCM, MIL: Yes** **Years:** 2005, 2006, 2007 **Models:** All Models **Engines:** All **Transmissions:** All	**TP Sensor Signal Out-of-Range Low** Key on or engine running; and the PCM detected the TP sensor signal was between 0.17-0.49v (3.42-9.85%) with the signal within the calibrated self-test range. **Possible Causes:** • ECT sensor harness connector is damaged • ECT sensor is damaged • Engine coolant level is low • PCM has failed
DTC: P1121 **2T CCM, MIL: Yes** **Years:** 2005, 2006, 2007 **Models:** All Models **Engines:** All **Transmissions:** All	**TP Sensor Inconsistent With MAF Sensor** Engine started; and the PCM detected the MAF and TP sensor signals were not consistent the calibrated values expected for these two sensors during the self-test. **Note: Drive the vehicle and monitor the TP PID in all gears. A TP PID of less than 0.24v (4.82%) with a LOAD PID over 55%, or a TP PID over 2.44v (49.05%) with a LOAD PID under 30% will set this code.** **Possible Causes:** • Air leak exists between MAF sensor and the throttle body • MAF sensor is damaged or it has failed • TP sensor is not seated properly • TP sensor is damaged

DTC	Trouble Code Title, Conditions & Possible Causes
DTC: P1124 **1T CCM, MIL: Yes** **Years:** 2005, 2006, 2007 **Models:** All Models **Engines:** All **Transmissions:** All	**TP Sensor Out of Self-Test Range** Key on, KOEO Self-Test enabled, and the PCM detected the TP sensor signal was less than 0.66v (13.27%), or with the engine running, KOER Self-Test enabled, the PCM detected the TP sensor signal was approximately 1.17v (23.52%). **Note: A TP V PID less than 4.82 % (0.24 volt) with a LOAD PID more than 55%; or the TP V PID more than 49.05% (2.44 volts) with a LOAD PID less than 30% indicates a hard fault is present.** **Possible Causes:** • Throttle linkage is binding, or TP sensor is not seated properly • Throttle plate below closed throttle position • Throttle plate screw is misadjusted • TP sensor is damaged or it has failed • PCM has failed
DTC: P1125 **2T CCM, MIL: Yes** **Years:** 2005, 2006, 2007 **Models:** All Models **Engines:** All **Transmissions:** All	**TP Sensor Circuit Malfunction (Intermittent)** Engine started, and the PCM detected the TP sensor rotational angle changed beyond the minimum or maximum calibrated limit. **Note: Monitor the TP V PID, and tap lightly on the TP sensor housing and wiggle the wiring harness. Watch for the value to suddenly go below 0.49v or over 4.65v.** **Possible Causes:** • TP sensor wiring harness or connector has an intermittent open • TP sensor has an intermittent open or shorted condition
DTC: P1127 **2T CCM, MIL: Yes** **Years:** 2005, 2006, 2007 **Models:** All Models **Engines:** All **Transmissions:** All	**Exhaust Not Warm, Downstream Sensor Not Tested** Engine started, KOER Self-Test enabled, and the PCM detected the inferred exhaust temperature was less than a minimum value. **Note: Monitor the HO2S Heater PID to determine their ON/OFF status (the heaters must work properly in order to pass this test).** **Possible Causes:** • Engine not operating long enough prior to the KOER Self-Test • Exhaust system temperature too cold to run the self-test
DTC: P1128 **2T CCM, MIL: Yes** **Years:** 2005, 2006, 2007 **Models:** All Models **Engines:** All **Transmissions:** All	**Upstream Oxygen Sensors Swapped From Bank-to-Bank** Engine started, KOER Self-Test enabled, and the PCM detected the HO2S signal response to a related fuel shift did not correspond to the correct engine cylinder bank (e.g., the HO2S-11 and the HO2S-21 wires were crossed) during the test period. **Possible Causes:** • Upstream HO2S-11, HO2S-21 wiring crossed at the connector • Upstream HO2S-11, HO2S-21 crossed in the wiring harness • Upstream HO2S-11, HO2S-21 crossed at PCM pin connector
DTC: P1129 **2T CCM, MIL: Yes** **Years:** 2005, 2006, 2007 **Models:** All Models **Engines:** All **Transmissions:** All	**Downstream Oxygen Sensors Swapped From Bank-to-Bank** Engine started, KOER Self-Test enabled, and the PCM detected the HO2S signal response to a related fuel shift did not correspond to the correct engine cylinder bank (e.g., the HO2S-12 and HO2S-22 wires were crossed) during the test period. **Possible Causes:** • Upstream HO2S-12, HO2S-21 wiring crossed at the connector • Upstream HO2S-12, HO2S-21 crossed in the wiring harness • Upstream HO2S-12, HO2S-21 crossed at PCM pin connector
DTC: P1130 **2T O2S, MIL: Yes** **Years:** 2005, 2006, 2007 **Models:** All Models **Engines:** All **Transmissions:** All	**Lack of HO2S-11 Switching, Fuel Trim at Rich/Lean Limit** DTC P0300-P0310 not set, engine running in closed loop, and the PCM detected the HO2S circuit was too lean or too rich, or that it could no longer change Fuel Trim because it was at its rich limit or its lean limit. **Possible Causes:** • Air intake system leaking, vacuum hoses leaking or damaged • Air leaks located after the MAF sensor mounting location • EGR valve sticking, EGR diaphragm leaking, or gasket leaking • EVAP vapor recovery system has failed • Excessive fuel pressure, leaking or contaminated fuel injectors • Exhaust leaks before or near the HO2S(s) mounting location • Fuel pressure regulator is leaking or damaged • HO2S circuits wet or oily, corroded, or poor terminal contact • HO2S is damaged or it has failed • HO2S signal circuit open, shorted to ground, shorted to power • Low fuel pressure or vehicle driven until it was out of fuel • Oil dipstick not seated or engine oil level too high (overfilled)

DTC	Trouble Code Title, Conditions & Possible Causes
DTC: P1131 **2T O2S, MIL: Yes** **Years:** 2005, 2006, 2007 **Models:** All Models **Engines:** All **Transmissions:** All	**Lack of HO2S-11 Switching, HO2S Signal Low Input** DTC P0300-P0310 not set, engine started, engine running in closed loop, and the PCM detected the HO2S-11 was not switching (i.e., the HO2S-11 indicated a lean A/F mixture). **Possible Causes:** • Air intake system leaking, vacuum hoses leaking or damaged • Air leaks located after the MAF sensor mounting location • Base engine mechanical fault (i.e., compression, valve timing) • HO2S circuits wet or oily, corroded, or poor terminal contact • HO2S signal circuit open, shorted to ground, shorted to power, or the sensor has failed • Low fuel pressure or vehicle driven until it was out of fuel • Possible air leaks at the PCV valve or at the related hoses
DTC: P1132 **2T O2S, MIL: Yes** **Years:** 2005, 2006, 2007 **Models:** All Models **Engines:** All **Transmissions:** All	**Lack of HO2S-11 Switching, HO2S Signal High Input** DTC P0300-P0310 not set, engine started, engine running in closed loop, and the PCM detected the HO2S-11 was not switching (i.e., the HO2S-11 indicated a rich A/F mixture). **Possible Causes:** • Check air cleaner element and air cleaner housing for blockage • EVAP vapor recovery system has failed (canister full of fuel) • Fuel pressure too high, contaminated or leaking fuel injectors • HO2S is fuel contaminated, or coated with silicone or moisture
DTC: P1137 **2T O2S, MIL: Yes** **Years:** 2005, 2006, 2007 **Models:** All Models **Engines:** All **Transmissions:** All	**Lack of HO2S-12 Switching, HO2S Signal Low Input** DTC P0300-P0310 not set, engine started, engine running in closed loop, and the PCM detected the HO2S-12 was not switching (i.e., the HO2S-12 indicated a lean A/F mixture). **Possible Causes:** • Air intake system leaking, vacuum hoses leaking or damaged • Air leaks located after the MAF sensor mounting location • Base engine mechanical fault (i.e., compression, valve timing) • HO2S circuits wet or oily, corroded, or poor terminal contact • HO2S is damaged or it has failed • HO2S signal circuit open, shorted to ground, shorted to power • Low fuel pressure or vehicle driven until it was out of fuel • Possible air leaks at the PCV valve or at the related hoses
DTC: P1138 **2T O2S, MIL: Yes** **Years:** 2005, 2006, 2007 **Models:** All Models **Engines:** All **Transmissions:** All	**Lack of HO2S-12 Switching, HO2S Signal High Input** DTC P0300-P0310 not set, engine started, engine running in closed loop, and the PCM detected the HO2S-12 was not switching (i.e., the HO2S-12 indicated a rich A/F mixture). **Possible Causes:** • Check air cleaner element and air cleaner housing for blockage • EVAP vapor recovery system has failed (canister full of fuel) • Fuel pressure too high, contaminated or leaking fuel injectors • HO2S is fuel contaminated, or coated with silicone or moisture
DTC: P1150 **2T O2S, MIL: Yes** **Years:** 2005, 2006, 2007 **Models:** All Models **Engines:** All **Transmissions:** All	**Lack of HO2S-21 Switching, Fuel Trim At Rich/Lean Limit** DTC P0300-P0310 not set, engine running in closed loop, and the PCM detected the HO2S circuit was too lean or too rich, or that it could no longer correct Fuel Trim (i.e., the Fuel Trim was at its calibrated rich limit or its calibrated lean limit). **Possible Causes:** • Air intake system leaking, vacuum hoses leaking or damaged • Air leaks located after the MAF sensor mounting location • EGR valve sticking, EGR diaphragm leaking, or gasket leaking • EVAP vapor recovery system has failed • Excessive fuel pressure, leaking or contaminated fuel injectors • Exhaust leaks before or near the HO2S(s) mounting location • Fuel pressure regulator is leaking or damaged • HO2S circuits wet or oily, corroded, or poor terminal contact • HO2S signal circuit open, shorted to ground, shorted to power, or the sensor has failed • Low fuel pressure or vehicle driven until it was out of fuel • Oil dipstick not seated or engine oil level too high (overfilled)

DTC	Trouble Code Title, Conditions & Possible Causes
DTC: P1151 **2T O2S, MIL: Yes** **Years:** 2005, 2006, 2007 **Models:** All Models **Engines:** All **Transmissions:** All	**Lack of HO2S-21 Switching, HO2S Signal Low Input** DTC P0300-P0310 not set, engine started, engine running in closed loop, and the PCM detected the HO2S-21 was not switching (i.e., the HO2S-21 indicated a lean A/F mixture). **Possible Causes:** • Air intake system leaking, vacuum hoses leaking or damaged • Air leaks located after the MAF sensor mounting location or in the PCV system • Base engine mechanical fault (i.e., compression, valve timing) • HO2S circuits wet or oily, corroded, or poor terminal contact • HO2S signal circuit open, shorted to ground, shorted to power, or the sensor has failed • Low fuel pressure or vehicle driven until it was out of fuel
DTC: P1152 **2T O2S, MIL: Yes** **Years:** 2005, 2006, 2007 **Models:** All Models **Engines:** All **Transmissions:** All	**Lack of HO2S-21 Switching, HO2S Signal High Input** DTC P0300-P0310 not set, engine started, engine running in closed loop, and the PCM detected the HO2S-21 was not switching (i.e., the HO2S-21 indicated a rich A/F mixture). **Possible Causes:** • Check air cleaner element and air cleaner housing for blockage • EVAP vapor recovery system has failed (canister full of fuel) • Fuel pressure too high, contaminated or leaking fuel injectors • HO2S is fuel contaminated, or coated with silicone or moisture
DTC: P1157 **2T O2S, MIL: Yes** **Years:** 2005, 2006, 2007 **Models:** All Models **Engines:** All **Transmissions:** All	**Lack of HO2S-22 Switching, HO2S Signal Low Input** DTC P0300-P0310 not set, engine started, engine running in closed loop, and the PCM detected the HO2S-22 was not switching (i.e., the HO2S-22 indicated a lean A/F mixture). **Possible Causes:** • Air intake system leaking, vacuum hoses leaking or damaged • Air leaks located after the MAF sensor mounting location • Base engine mechanical fault (i.e., compression, valve timing) • HO2S circuits wet or oily, corroded, or poor terminal contact • HO2S is damaged or it has failed • HO2S signal circuit open, shorted to ground, shorted to power • Low fuel pressure or vehicle driven until it was out of fuel • Possible air leaks at the PCV valve or at the related hoses
DTC: P1158 **2T O2S, MIL: Yes** **Years:** 2005, 2006, 2007 **Models:** All Models **Engines:** All **Transmissions:** All	**Lack of HO2S-22 Switching, HO2S Signal High Input** DTC P0300-P0310 not set, engine started, engine running in closed loop, and the PCM detected the HO2S-22 was not switching (i.e., the HO2S-22 indicated a rich A/F mixture). **Possible Causes:** • Check air cleaner element and air cleaner housing for blockage • EVAP vapor recovery system has failed (canister full of fuel) • Fuel pressure too high, contaminated or leaking fuel injectors • HO2S is fuel contaminated, or coated with silicone or moisture
DTC: P1183 **2T CCM, MIL: Yes** **Years:** 2005, 2006, 2007 **Models:** All Models **Engines:** All **Transmissions:** All	**Engine Oil Temperature Sensor Circuit Malfunction** Engine started, and the PCM detected the engine oil temperature (EOT) sensor circuit was open or shorted to ground (i.e., this fault is usually caused by an interruption of the signal - intermittent fault). **Possible Causes:** • EOT sensor circuit is open or shorted to ground • EOT sensor has failed • PCM has failed
DTC: P1184 **2T CCM, MIL: Yes** **Years:** 2005, 2006, 2007 **Models:** All Models **Engines:** All **Transmissions:** All	**Engine Oil Temperature Sensor Out Of Self-Test Range** Engine started, and the PCM detected the engine oil temperature (EOT) sensor circuit was open or shorted to ground (i.e., this fault can be caused by an intermittent loss of this signal). **Possible Causes:** • EOT sensor circuit is open or shorted to ground (intermittent) • EOT sensor is corroded, damaged or it has failed • PCM has failed
DTC: P1231 **1T CCM, MIL: No** **Years:** 2005, 2006, 2007 **Models:** All Models **Engines:** All **Transmissions:** All	**Fuel Pump Secondary Low, High Speed Pump On** Key on, KOEO Self-Test enabled; High Speed Fuel Pump (HFP) relay energized, fuel pump driver in VLCM off (to VLCM Pin 7) off, the PCM detected voltage on the FPM circuit. **Possible Causes:** • HFP relay circuit to battery power (B+) is open • HFP relay is damaged or it has failed • Power-To-Pump circuit between HFP relay and splice is open

DTC	Trouble Code Title, Conditions & Possible Causes
DTC: P1232 **2T CCM, MIL: Yes** **Years:** 2005, 2006, 2007 **Models:** All Models **Engines:** All **Transmissions:** All	**Low Speed Fuel Pump Primary Circuit Malfunction** Engine started, Low Speed Fuel Pump (LFP) relay energized, the PCM detected excessive current on the LFP circuit; or with LFP commanded off it detected power on the LFP circuit. **Possible Causes:** • Low fuel pump (LFP) circuit open or shorted • Low speed fuel pump relay VPWR circuit open • Low speed fuel pump relay is damaged • PCM has failed
DTC: P1233 **2T CCM, MIL: Yes** **Years:** 2005, 2006, 2007 **Models:** All Models **Engines:** All **Transmissions:** All	**Fuel System Disabled Or Offline** Key on or engine running; and the PCM did not receive any diagnostic information (via duty cycle signals) from the FPDM. **Possible Causes:** • Inertia fuel shutoff (IFS) switch needs to be reset • FPDM ground circuit is open, or FPM circuit is open or shorted • Mark VIII: FPDM PWR circuit is open, the FPDM power supply relay VPWR circuit is opened or grounded, or power relay failed • Escort/Tracer: FPDM PWR circuit is open, or the CCRM pin 11 is open to power (B+), or the CCRM (relay) is damaged • Continental: FPDM circuit to VPWR is open, or the FPDM or the IFS is damaged • Refer to the GEM or REM controllers for related trouble codes
DTC: P1234 **1T CCM, MIL: Yes** **Years:** 2005, 2006, 2007 **Models:** All Models **Engines:** All **Transmissions:** All	**Fuel System Disabled Or Offline** Key on, and the PCM did not receive any diagnostic information from the FPDM. **Possible Causes:** • Inertia fuel shutoff (IFS) switch needs to be reset or has failed • FPDM ground circuit is open, or FPM circuit is open or shorted • Mark VIII: FPDM PWR circuit is open, the FPDM power supply relay VPWR circuit is opened or grounded, or power relay failed • Escort/Tracer: FPDM PWR circuit is open, or the CCRM pin 11 is open to power (B+), or the CCRM (relay) is damaged • Continental: FPDM circuit to VPWR is open, or the FPDM or the IFS is damaged • LS6, LS8 **Models** This code indicates the PCM is not receiving data about the fuel level on the SCP data line from the Rear Electronics Module (REM). Test the REM first! • PCM has failed
DTC: P1235 **2T CCM, MIL: Yes** **Years:** 2005, 2006, 2007 **Models:** All Models **Engines:** All **Transmissions:** All	**Fuel Pump Control Out Of Range** Key on or engine running; and the PCM received a signal from the FPM over the SCP bus that the FPDM had received an invalid or missing fuel pump command from the PCM. **Possible Causes:** • FP circuit is open or shorted • FPDM is damaged • PCM has failed
DTC: P1236 **2T CCM, MIL: No** **Years:** 2005, 2006, 2007 **Models:** All Models **Engines:** All **Transmissions:** All	**Fuel Pump Control Out Of Range** Key on or engine running; and the PCM received a signal (from the FPM over the SCP bus) that the FPDM had received an invalid or missing fuel pump command from the PCM. **Possible Causes:** • FP circuit is open or it is shorted • FPDM is damaged or the PCM has failed
DTC: P1237 **2T CCM, MIL: Yes** **Years:** 2005, 2006, 2007 **Models:** All Models **Engines:** All **Transmissions:** All	**Fuel Pump Secondary Circuit Malfunction** Key on or engine running; and the PCM received a signal from the FPDM that it had detected a fault in the fuel pump secondary circuit. **Possible Causes:** • FP PWR circuit is open or shorted • FPDM fuel pump return circuit is open • Fuel pump windings are open or shorted, or the rotor is locked • FPDM is damaged
DTC: P1238 **2T CCM, MIL: Yes** **Years:** 2005, 2006, 2007 **Models:** All Models **Engines:** All **Transmissions:** All	**Fuel Pump Secondary Circuit Malfunction** Key on or engine running; and the PCM received a signal from the FPDM that it had detected a fault in the fuel pump secondary circuit. **Possible Causes:** • FP PWR circuit is open or shorted • FPDM fuel pump return circuit is open • Fuel pump windings are open or shorted • Fuel pump rotor is locked • FPDM is damaged

DTC	Trouble Code Title, Conditions & Possible Causes
DTC: P1244 **2T CCM, MIL: Yes** **Years:** 2005, 2006, 2007 **Models:** All Models **Engines:** All **Transmissions:** All	**Generator Load Circuit Low Input** Engine started, and the PCM detected the GLI signal was less than the calibrated limit for a calibrated amount of time. **Possible Causes:** • GLI circuit is open or shorted • Voltage regulator/generator is damaged • PCM has failed
DTC: P1245 **2T CCM, MIL: Yes** **Years:** 2005, 2006, 2007 **Models:** All Models **Engines:** All **Transmissions:** All	**Generator Load circuit High Input** Engine started, and the PCM detected the GLI signal was more than the calibrated limit for a calibrated amount of time. **Possible Causes:** • GLI circuit is open or shorted • Voltage regulator/generator is damaged • PCM has failed
DTC: P1246 **2T CCM, MIL: Yes** **Years:** 2005, 2006, 2007 **Models:** All Models Except Crown Victoria, Grand Marquis & Town Car **Engines:** All **Transmissions:** All	**Generator Load Circuit Malfunction** Engine started, and the PCM detected the GLI was more than or less than a calibrated amount for too long a period of time. **Possible Causes:** • Generator circuit is open, shorted to ground or shorted to power • Generator drive mechanism has failed • Generator/regulator assembly is damaged or the PCM has failed
DTC: P1246 **2T CCM, MIL: Yes** **Years:** 2005, 2006, 2007 **Models:** Crown Victoria, Grand Marquis & Town Car **Engines:** 4.6L VIN V, W **Transmissions:** All	**Generator Load Circuit Malfunction** Engine started, and the PCM detected the GLI was more than or less than a calibrated amount for too long a period of time. **Possible Causes:** • Generator circuit is open, shorted to ground or shorted to power • Generator drive mechanism has failed • Generator/regulator assembly is damaged or the PCM has failed • TSB 03-14-2 contains repair information for this trouble code
DTC: P1260 **2T PCM, MIL: Yes** **Years:** 2005, 2006, 2007 **Models:** All Models **Engines:** All **Transmissions:** All	**Theft Detected, Vehicle Immobilized** Key on, and the PCM received a signal from the Anti-Theft System that a theft condition had occurred. The theft indicator on the dash will flash rapidly or remain on "solid" with the ignition switch in the "on" position. The engine may "start and stall", or may not crank if the vehicle is equipped with the PATS starter disable feature. **Possible Causes:** • A Previous theft condition has occurred • Anti-Theft System is damaged or has failed • TSB 01-6-2 (superseded from 76-65-4) contains an updated repair procedure
DTC: P1270 **1T CCM, MIL: Yes** **Years:** 2005, 2006, 2007 **Models:** All Models **Engines:** All **Transmissions:** All	**Engine Speed/Vehicle Speed Limiter Fault** Engine started, and after the PCM monitored the engine speed and VSS signals), it detected the vehicle was operated in a manner where the engine or vehicle speed to exceeded its limit. **Possible Causes:** • Excessive wheel slippage due to water, ice, mud and snow • Excessive engine speed (rpm) with the gearshift in Neutral • Vehicle driven at a high rate of speed
DTC: P1285 **2T CCM, MIL: Yes** **Years:** 2005, 2006, 2007 **Models:** All Models with CHT **Engines:** All With CHT **Transmissions:** All	**Cylinder Head Over-Temperature Sensed** Key on or engine running; and the PCM detected an engine overheat condition through inputs from the cylinder head temperature sensor. Engine started, and the PCM detected the CHT or ECT sensor signal was intermittent (it may have an intermittent open condition). **Note: Select the CHT or IAT PID and monitor the signal for sudden changes while wiggling the CHT or IAT sensor connector.** On the 5.4L V8, if the temperature exceeds 258°F, the PCM disables four fuel injectors at a time. It alternates which four fuel injectors are disabled every 32-engine cycles. The cylinders that are disabled do not inject fuel, so they act as air pumps to aid in cooling the engine. If the temperature exceeds 310°F, the PCM disables all of the fuel injectors until the engine temperature drops below 310°F. **Possible Causes:** • Base engine problems or related concerns • CHT sensor has deteriorated or it has failed • Engine coolant level is too low • Engine cooling system has a problem • TSB 10-29-1 contains repair help for this code (LS & T-Bird)

DTC	Trouble Code Title, Conditions & Possible Causes
DTC: P1288 **2T CCM, MIL: Yes** **Years:** 2005, 2006, 2007 **Models:** All Models with CHT **Engines:** All With CHT **Transmissions:** All	**Cylinder Head Temperature Sensor Out of Self-Test Range** Key on and KOEO Self-Test enabled, or engine running with the KOER Self-Test enabled, and the PCM detected the CHT sensor was out of its self-test range (i.e., the engine was too hot or it did not warm to its normal operating temperature) during the test period. **Possible Causes:** • CHT sensor harness connector is damaged • CHT sensor is damaged • Engine coolant level is too low • Engine is cold, or the engine is overheated
DTC: P1289 **2T CCM, MIL: Yes** **Years:** 2005, 2006, 2007 **Models:** All Models with CHT **Engines:** All With CHT **Transmissions:** All	**Cylinder Head Temperature Sensor Circuit High Input** Key on or engine running; and the PCM detected a Cylinder Head Temperature (CHT) sensor signal that was more than 4.60v. This code may be due to an intermittent fault. Wiggle the CHT sensor wiring and connector while monitoring the CHT PID for a sudden change in voltage. DTC P0118 may also be reported when this code is set, and either code will cause the PCM to activate the MIL. **Possible Causes:** • CHT sensor circuit is open in the wiring harness, or an open circuit exists in the CHT sensor circuit at the harness connector • CHT sensor is damaged or has failed • Engine coolant level is too low or the thermostat has failed • PCM has failed
DTC: P1290 **2T CCM, MIL: Yes** **Years:** 2005, 2006, 2007 **Models:** All Models with CHT **Engines:** All With CHT **Transmissions:** All	**Cylinder Head Temperature Sensor Circuit Low Input** Key on or engine running; and the PCM detected a Cylinder Head Temperature (CHT) sensor signal that was less than 0.2v. Note that this trouble code may be due to an intermittent type of fault. Wiggle the CHT sensor wiring and connector while monitoring the CHT V PID for signs of a sudden change in the voltage. DTC P0118 may also set along with this code (both codes will cause a MIL to be on). **Possible Causes:** • CHT sensor connector is damaged or a short circuit exists • CHT sensor signal circuit is shorted to sensor ground • CHT sensor is damaged or the PCM has failed
DTC: P1299 **2T CCM, MIL: Yes** **Years:** 2005, 2006, 2007 **Models:** All Models **Engines:** All **Transmissions:** All	**Cylinder Head Over-Temperature Protection Active** Engine started, and after a period of time with the engine running, the PCM detected the engine was in an overheated condition. **Note: The PCM enables the Fail-Safe Cooling whenever this code is set to cool the engine (a Failure Mode Effects Strategy or FMEM).** **Possible Causes:** • Cooling system has a problem • Engine coolant level is too low • A Base Engine problem may be present • TSB 10-29-1 contains repair help for this code (LS & T-Bird)
DTC: P1309 **1T MISFIRE** **MIL: Yes** **Years:** 2005, 2006, 2007 **Models:** All Models **Engines:** All **Transmissions:** All	**Misfire Monitor Disabled** DTC P0136, P0156, P0171, P0172, P0174, P0175, P1130 and P1150 not set, engine started, and the PCM disabled the Misfire Monitor in order to verify that the CMP sensor is synchronized. Note that this code can be caused by an incorrect input from the CMP sensor (i.e., it senses the passage of teeth from the CMP wheel). **Possible Causes:** • Camshaft position sensor is damaged or it has failed • CKP, ECT or MAF sensors may be out-of-calibration or failed • PCM has failed • TSB 02-22-1 contains repair information for this trouble code
DTC: P1336 **2T CCM, MIL: Yes** **Years:** 2005, 2006, 2007 **Models:** All Models **Engines:** All **Transmissions:** All	**CKP or CMP Signal Malfunction** Engine started, and the PCM detected an erratic signal from CKP sensor or the CMP sensor. It is possible for EMI/RFI interference to cause this code when they occur on these circuits. **Possible Causes:** • Base Engine problem or concern exists • CKP sensor or CMP signal circuit is open or shorted to ground • CKP sensor or CMP sensor is damaged or failed (check for EMI/RFI on this circuit). • PCM has failed • TSB 02-22-1 contains repair information for this trouble code

DTC	Trouble Code Title, Conditions & Possible Causes
DTC: P1351 **2T CCM, MIL: Yes** **Years:** 2005, 2006, 2007 **Models:** All Models **Engines:** All **Transmissions:** All	**Ignition Diagnostic Monitor Circuit Malfunction** Engine started, and the PCM detected a loss of the IDM circuit from the ignition module in the distributor (the fault may be intermittent). **Note: If DTC P0350, P0351, P0352, P0353 or P0354 is set, repair these trouble codes and then recheck to see if DTC P1351 resets.** **Possible Causes:** • Camshaft position sensor may have failed • IDM signal circuit may be open or grounded • CKP, ECT or MAF sensors may be damaged or have failed • PCM has failed
DTC: P1356 **1T CCM, MIL: No** **Years:** 2005, 2006, 2007 **Models:** All Models **Engines:** All **Transmissions:** All	**PIP Signals Present With Engine Off** Key on, and the PCM detected the presence of PIP signals, yet the Ignition Diagnostic Monitor (IDM) signals indicated the engine was not turning. **Possible Causes:** • Ignition Module has failed • PCM has failed
DTC: P1358 **2T CCM, MIL: Yes** **Years:** 2005, 2006, 2007 **Models:** All Models **Engines:** All **Transmissions:** All	**IDM Signals Out Of Self-Test Range** Engine started; and the PCM detected PIP signals that indicated that the Ignition Diagnostic Monitor signals were out of the self-test range under these operating conditions. **Possible Causes:** • Ignition Module has failed • PCM has failed
DTC: P1359 **2T CCM, MIL: Yes** **Years:** 2005, 2006, 2007 **Models:** All Models **Engines:** All **Transmissions:** All	**Spark Output Circuit Malfunction** Engine started, and the PCM did not detect any change in the Spark Output (SPOUT) signals during the test period. **Possible Causes:** • SPOUT signal circuit may be open (check the connector) • SPOUT signal circuit may be grounded • Ignition Module is damaged or has failed
DTC: P1390 **1T CCM, MIL: No** **Years:** 2005, 2006, 2007 **Models:** All Models **Engines:** All **Transmissions:** All	**Octane Adjust Circuit Malfunction** Key on, KOEO Self-Test enabled, and with the octane adjust software activated, the PCM detected a malfunction in the OCT circuit. **Possible Causes:** • OCT shorting bar removed • OCT circuit open • PCM has failed
DTC: P1400 **2T CCM, MIL: Yes** **Years:** 2005, 2006, 2007 **Models:** All Models Except Aviator, Crown Victoria, Grand Marquis & Town Car **Engines:** 4.6L VIN H, V, W **Transmissions:** All	**DPFE Sensor Circuit Low Input** Key on, and the PCM detected the DPF EGR sensor signal was less than the minimum calibrated value of 0.2v. **Note: The DPF EGR PID will read less than 0.2v with this code set.** **Possible Causes:** • DPF EGR signal circuit shorted to ground • DPF EGR signal VREF circuit open • DPF EGR sensor is damaged or has failed • PCM has failed • TSB 4-3-1 contains repair information for this trouble code
DTC: P1400 **2T CCM, MIL: Yes** **Years:** 2005, 2006, 2007 **Models:** Aviator, Crown Victoria, Grand Marquis, Town Car **Engines:** 4.6L VIN H, V, W **Transmissions:** All	**DPFE Sensor Circuit Low Input** Engine started, and the PCM detected the DPF EGR sensor signal was less than the minimum calibrated value of 0.2v. The DPFE, EGR valve and EVR solenoid are integrated into the ESM assembly. **Possible Causes:** • DPFE sensor signal circuit is shorted to ground • DPFE sensor VREF circuit (5v) is open • DPFE sensor is damaged or it has failed • PCM has failed

DTC	Trouble Code Title, Conditions & Possible Causes
DTC: P1401 **2T CCM, MIL: Yes** **Years:** 2005, 2006, 2007 **Models:** All Models Except Aviator, Crown Victoria, Grand Marquis & Town Car **Engines:** All **Transmissions:** All	**DPFE Sensor Circuit High Input** Key on; and the PCM detected the DPF EGR sensor signal was more than the maximum calibrated value of 4.5v. The DPF EGR PID will read more than 4.5v with this code set. **Possible Causes:** • DPF EGR signal circuit open, or sensor ground circuit open • DPF EGR signal shorted to VREF or to power • DPF EGR sensor is damaged or has failed • PCM has failed • TSB 4-3-1 contains repair information for this trouble code
DTC: P1401 **2T CCM, MIL: Yes** **Years:** 2005, 2006, 2007 **Models:** Aviator, Crown Victoria, Grand Marquis, Town Car **Engines:** 4.6L VIN H, V, W **Transmissions:** All	**DPFE Sensor Circuit High Input** Key on or engine running; and the PCM detected the DPF EGR sensor signal was more than the maximum calibrated value of 4.5v. On this vehicle application, the DPFE, EGR valve and EVR solenoid are integrated into the ESM assembly. **Possible Causes:** • DPFE sensor signal circuit is open • DPFE sensor ground circuit is open • DPFE sensor signal is shorted to VREF (5v) • DPFE sensor is damaged or it has failed • PCM has failed
DTC: P1405 **2T CCM, MIL: Yes** **Years:** 2005, 2006, 2007 **Models:** All Models **Engines:** All **Transmissions:** All	**DPFE Sensor Upstream Hose Off Or Plugged** Engine started; and the PCM detected the DPF EGR sensor indicated EGR flow in a negative direction (a closed EGR valve). Check for signs of icing in the hose, or wrong hose routing. **Possible Causes:** • DPF EGR sensor upstream hose is disconnected • DPF EGR sensor upstream hose is plugged (ice) • EGR tube is plugged or damaged
DTC: P1406 **2T CCM, MIL: Yes** **Years:** 2005, 2006, 2007 **Models:** All Models Except Aviator, Crown Victoria, Grand Marquis & Town Car **Engines:** All **Transmissions:** All	**DPFE Sensor Downstream Hose Off Or Plugged** Engine started; and the PCM detected the DPF EGR sensor signal indicated EGR flow existed with the EGR valve commanded closed. **Possible Causes:** • Check for signs of icing in the hose, or for a restricted tube • DPF EGR sensor downstream hose is disconnected • DPF EGR sensor downstream hose is plugged (ice) • EGR tube is plugged or damaged
DTC: P1406 **2T CCM, MIL: Yes** **Years:** 2005, 2006, 2007 **Models:** Aviator, Crown Victoria, Grand Marquis, Town Car **Engines:** 4.6L VIN H, V, W **Transmissions:** All	**DPFE Sensor Downstream Hose Off Or Plugged** Engine started, and the PCM detected the DPFE sensor indicated that EGR flow was present with the EGR valve commanded closed. On this vehicle application, the DPFE, EGR valve and EVR solenoid are integrated into the ESM assembly. **Possible Causes:** • Check for signs of icing in the hose, or for a restricted tube • DPF EGR sensor downstream hose is disconnected • DPF EGR sensor downstream hose is plugged (ice) • EGR tube is plugged or damaged
DTC: P1408 **1T EGR, MIL: Yes** **Years:** 2005, 2006, 2007 **Models:** All Models Except Aviator, Crown Victoria, Grand Marquis & Town Car **Engines:** All **Transmissions:** All	**EGR Flow Out Of Self-Test Range** KOER Self-Test enabled, and the PCM detected the EGR flow was out of the self-test range during the self-test with the engine running. **Possible Causes:** • EGR vacuum regulator solenoid vacuum supply problem • EVR valve stuck closed or iced up, or the flow path is restricted • EGR valve diaphragm leaking, hose is off, plugged or leaking • EGR VR solenoid open or the VPWR circuit is open • DPF EGR sensor pressure hoses connected wrong (reversed) • DPF EGR downstream hose connection leaking or plugged • EGR Orifice tube assembly is damaged • DPF EGR sensor or the EGR VR solenoid is damaged, or the PCM has failed

DTC	Trouble Code Title, Conditions & Possible Causes
DTC: P1408 **1T EGR, MIL: No** **Years:** 2005, 2006, 2007 **Models:** Aviator, Crown Victoria, Grand Marquis, Town Car **Engines:** 4.6L VIN H, V, W **Transmissions:** All	**EGR Flow Out Of Self-Test Range** Engine started, KOER Self-Test enabled, and the PCM detected the EGR flow was out of the self-test range during the self-test. On this vehicle application, the DPFE, EGR valve and EVR solenoid are integrated into the ESM assembly **Possible Causes:** • EGR vacuum regulator solenoid vacuum supply problem • EVR valve stuck closed or iced up, or the flow path is restricted • EGR valve diaphragm leaking, hose is off, plugged or leaking • EGR VR solenoid open or the VPWR circuit is open • DPF EGR sensor pressure hoses connected wrong (reversed) • DPF EGR sensor VREF circuit is open • DPF EGR downstream hose connection leaking or plugged • EGR Orifice tube assembly is damaged • DPF EGR sensor or the EGR VR solenoid is damaged • PCM has failed
DTC: P1409 **2T CCM, MIL: Yes** **Years:** 2005, 2006, 2007 **Models:** All Models Except Aviator, Crown Victoria, Grand Marquis & Town Car **Engines:** All **Transmissions:** All	**EGR Vacuum Regulator Solenoid Circuit Malfunction** Engine started, and the PCM detected a fault in the EGR VR solenoid circuit (i.e., the VR circuit was too high or low when compared to the expected range with the solenoid enabled). **Possible Causes:** • EGR VR solenoid circuit is open, or shorted to ground • EGR VR circuit is shorted to power or the VPWR circuit is open • EGR vacuum regulator solenoid is damaged or the PCM has failed
DTC: P1409 **1T CCM, MIL: Yes** **Years:** 2005, 2006, 2007 **Models:** Aviator, Crown Victoria, Grand Marquis, Town Car **Engines:** 4.6L VIN H, V, W **Transmissions:** All	**EGR Vacuum Regulator Solenoid Circuit Malfunction** Engine started, and the PCM detected a fault in the EGR VR solenoid circuit (i.e., the VR circuit was too high or low when compared to its expected range with the solenoid enabled). **Possible Causes:** • EGR VR solenoid circuit is open, or shorted to ground • EGR VR circuit is shorted to power or the VPWR circuit is open • EGR vacuum regulator solenoid is damaged or the PCM has failed
DTC: P1411 **2T AIR, MIL: Yes** **Years:** 2005, 2006, 2007 **Models:** All Models **Engines:** All **Transmissions:** All	**Secondary Air Injection System Downstream Flow** Engine started, engine running with AIR system "on", and the PCM detected the HO2S signal did not go lean with the AIR system "on". **Possible Causes:** • Secondary AIR System Electric Pump is damaged • Secondary AIR System Mechanical Pump is damaged • Secondary AIR pump hose is leaking • Secondary AIR pump hose is blocked • Secondary AIR Bypass solenoid passage leaking or blocked • Secondary AIR Bypass solenoid stuck open or stuck closed
DTC: P1413 **2T CCM, MIL: Yes** **Years:** 2005, 2006, 2007 **Models:** All Models **Engines:** All **Transmissions:** All	**Secondary AIR System Monitor Circuit Low Input** Engine started, engine running with AIR system "off", and the PCM detected an unexpected "low" voltage condition on the Secondary AIR monitor during the CCM test. **Possible Causes:** • AIR solenoid control circuit is open or it is shorted to ground • AIR pump is damaged or it has failed • Solid State relay is damaged or it has failed • Solid State relay battery power circuit (B+) is open • PCM has failed
DTC: P1414 **2T CCM, MIL: Yes** **Years:** 2005, 2006, 2007 **Models:** All Models **Engines:** All **Transmissions:** All	**Secondary AIR System Monitor Circuit High Input** Engine started, AIR system not active, and the PCM detected a high voltage signal present on the Secondary AIR monitor signal circuit. **Possible Causes:** • AIR Monitor circuit from the pump to the PCM is open • AIR solenoid control circuit is shorted to power • Solid State relay is damaged or has failed • AIR pump ground circuit is open • AIR pump is damaged or has failed • PCM has failed

DTC	Trouble Code Title, Conditions & Possible Causes
DTC: P1432 **1T CCM, MIL: Yes** **Years:** 2005, 2006, 2007 **Models:** All Models **Engines:** All **Transmissions:** All	**Thermostat Heater Control Circuit Malfunction** Engine started; and the PCM detected the Thermostat Heater Control circuit was less than or more than a calibrated limit for too long a period of time during the CCM self-test. **Possible Causes:** • Thermostat Heater Control (THTRC) circuit open or shorted • Thermostat Heater Control (THTRC) VPWR circuit open • Thermostat Heater assembly is damaged or has failed • PCM has failed
DTC: P1436 **2T CCM, MIL: Yes** **Years:** 2005, 2006, 2007 **Models:** All Models **Engines:** All **Transmissions:** All	**A/C Evaporator Temperature (ACET) Circuit Low Input** Key on or engine running; and the PCM detected the ACET signal was less than the self-test minimum amount of 0.13v in the self-test. **Possible Causes:** • ACET signal circuit shorted to sensor ground (return) • ACET signal circuit shorted to chassis ground • ACET sensor is damaged or has failed • PCM has failed
DTC: P1437 **2T CCM, MIL: Yes** **Years:** 2005, 2006, 2007 **Models:** All Models **Engines:** All **Transmissions:** All	**A/C Evaporator Temperature (ACET) Circuit High Input** Key on or engine running; and the PCM detected the ACET signal was more than the self-test maximum amount of 4.5v in the self-test. **Possible Causes:** • ACET signal circuit is open, or the ground circuit is open • ACET signal is shorted to VREF • ACET sensor is damaged or has failed • PCM has failed
DTC: P1442 **2T EVAP, MIL: Yes** **Years:** 2005, 2006, 2007 **Models:** All Models **Engines:** All **Transmissions:** All	**EVAP System Small Leak (0.040") Detected** Cold startup requirement met, engine running at Cruise speed in closed loop for 2-3 minutes, and the PCM detected a leak (as small as 0.040") in the EVAP system. **Note: Inspect the CV solenoid for contamination (as contamination can hold the CV open set DTC P0442 and also plugs the port to atmosphere enough to keep system from being vented quickly).** **Possible Causes:** • Fuel filler cap damaged, cross-threaded or loosely installed • Aftermarket EVAP parts that do not conform to specifications • Small holes or cuts in fuel vapor hoses or EVAP canister tubes • CV solenoid stays partially open when commanded closed • Loose fuel vapor hose/tube connections to EVAP components • EVAP component seals leaking (i.e., leaks in the Purge valve, fuel tank pressure sensor, canister vent solenoid, fuel vapor control valve tube assembly or fuel vapor vent valve) • TSB 03-9-8 contains a repair procedure for this trouble code • TSB 3-20-3 contains a repair procedure for this trouble code
DTC: P1443 **2T EVAP, MIL: Yes** **Years:** 2005, 2006, 2007 **Models:** All Models **Engines:** All **Transmissions:** All	**EVAP Canister Purge System Malfunction** Engine started, engine warmup completed engine running at a steady cruise speed, and the PCM detected a leak or blockage was present somewhere in the vapor line between the intake manifold, EVAP purge valve and the charcoal canister during the Continuous self test. **Possible Causes:** • EVAP canister purge valve is damaged or has failed • PF sensor is out-of-calibration or it is "skewed" • PCM has failed
DTC: P1443 **2T EVAP, MIL: Yes** **Years:** 2005, 2006, 2007 **Models:** All Models **Engines:** All **Transmissions:** All	**Low Purge Flow Or No Purge Flow Condition Detected** ECT sensor less than 90°F at startup (cold engine), engine running at a steady cruise speed, and the PCM detected a fuel tank pressure change occurred of more than −7" H2O within 30 seconds with the purge flow less than 0.02 pounds per minute during testing. **Possible Causes:** • EVAP canister purge valve stuck closed (mechanically) • Fuel vapor hose blocked between EVAP purge valve and FTP sensor, or blocked between purge valve and intake manifold, or vacuum hose blocked between purge valve and intake manifold

DTC	Trouble Code Title, Conditions & Possible Causes
DTC: P1444 **2T CCM, MIL: Yes** **Years:** 2005, 2006, 2007 **Models:** All Models **Engines:** All **Transmissions:** All	**Purge Flow Sensor Circuit Low Input** Key on or engine running; and the PCM detected the Purge Flow (PF) sensor signal was less than the minimum calibrated limit of 0.40v during the Continuous self test. **Possible Causes:** • PF sensor signal circuit is shorted to sensor or chassis ground • PF sensor is damaged or has failed • PCM has failed
DTC: P1445 **2T CCM, MIL: Yes** **Years:** 2005, 2006, 2007 **Models:** All Models **Engines:** All **Transmissions:** All	**Purge Flow Sensor Circuit High Input** Key on or engine running; and the PCM detected the Purge Flow (PF) sensor was more than the maximum calibrated limit of 4.80v. **Possible Causes:** • PF sensor signal circuit shorted to VREF or power (VPWR) • PF sensor signal circuit open or sensor ground circuit open • PF sensor is damaged or has failed • PCM has failed
DTC: P1450 **2T EVAP, MIL: Yes** **Years:** 2005, 2006, 2007 **Models:** All Models **Engines:** All **Transmissions:** All	**Unable to Bleed Up Fuel Tank Vacuum** ECT sensor less than 90°F at startup (cold engine), engine running at a steady cruise speed, and the PCM detected a high fuel tank vacuum condition was present during the EVAP test. **Possible Causes:** • CV solenoid is stuck partially or fully open or filter is plugged • EVAP canister tube or EVAP canister purge outlet tube blocked or kinked between fuel tank, purge valve and EVAP canister • Fuel filler cap stuck closed (vacuum relief cannot occur) • Contaminated fuel vapor elbow at the EVAP canister, or the EVAP canister is restricted or canister purge valve stuck open
DTC: P1450 **2T EVAP, MIL: Yes** **Years:** 2005, 2006, 2007 **Models:** All Models **Engines:** All **Transmissions:** All	**Unable to Bleed Up Fuel Tank Vacuum** ECT sensor less than 90°F at startup (cold engine), engine running at a steady cruise speed, and the PCM detected a high fuel tank vacuum condition was present during the EVAP test. **Possible Causes:** • CV solenoid is stuck partially or fully open or filter is plugged • EVAP canister tube or EVAP canister purge outlet tube blocked or kinked between fuel tank, purge valve and EVAP canister • Fuel filler cap stuck closed (vacuum relief cannot occur) • Contaminated fuel vapor elbow at the EVAP canister, or the EVAP canister is restricted or canister purge valve stuck open • FTP sensor is damaged
DTC: P1451 **2T CCM, MIL: Yes** **Years:** 2005, 2006, 2007 **Models:** All Models **Engines:** All **Transmissions:** All	**EVAP System Canister Vent Solenoid Circuit Malfunction** Engine started, engine running at a steady cruise speed, canister vent solenoid enabled, and the PCM detected an unexpected voltage condition on the Canister Vent solenoid circuit. **Possible Causes:** • CV solenoid circuit is open, shorted to ground or system power • CV solenoid is damaged or has failed • PCM has failed
DTC: P1452 **2T CCM, MIL: Yes** **Years:** 2005, 2006, 2007 **Models:** All Models **Engines:** All **Transmissions:** All	**Fuel Tank Pressure Sensor Circuit Malfunction** Key on or engine running; and the PCM detected that the Fuel Tank Pressure (FTP) sensor signal was less than or more than the calibrated amount during the self-test. Note that the FTP V PID should read from 2.40-2.80 with the cap off. **Possible Causes:** • FTP sensor signal circuit is open or shorted to ground • FTP sensor ground return circuit is open • FTP sensor is damaged or has failed • PCM has failed
DTC: P1455 **2T EVAP, MIL: Yes** **Years:** 2005, 2006, 2007 **Models:** All Models **Engines:** All **Transmissions:** All	**EVAP System Gross Leak Detected** ECT sensor less than 90°F at startup (cold engine), engine running at a steady cruise speed for 2-3 minutes, and the PCM detected a gross leak in the EVAP system during the test. **Possible Causes:** • Fuel filler cap missing, loose (not tightened) or the wrong part • FTP sensor signal circuit open or sensor ground circuit open • FTP sensor ground circuit open • FTP sensor is damaged or has failed • PCM has failed

DTC	Trouble Code Title, Conditions & Possible Causes
DTC: P1460 **1T CCM, MIL: Yes** **Years:** 2005, 2006, 2007 **Models:** All Models **Engines:** All **Transmissions:** All	**Wide Open Throttle A/C Cutout Relay Circuit Malfunction** Key on, and the PCM detected a malfunction in the A/C wide-open throttle (WOT) circuit during the test. **Note: If this code sets on vehicles without an A/C system, ignore this code.** **Possible Causes:** • WOT A/C Relay control circuit is open or shorted to ground • WOT A/C Relay VREF circuit is open • WOT A/C Relay is damaged or has failed • PCM has failed
DTC: P1461 **2T CCM, MIL: Yes** **Years:** 2005, 2006, 2007 **Models:** All Models **Engines:** All **Transmissions:** All	**A/C Pressure Sensor Circuit High Input** Engine started, and the PCM detected the A/C Pressure sensor signal was over the test limit. **Possible Causes:** • ACP sensor circuit shorted to VREF or to power (VPWR) • ACP sensor circuit is open, or the ground circuit is open • ACP sensor is damaged or has failed • PCM has failed
DTC: P1462 **2T CCM, MIL: Yes** **Years:** 2005, 2006, 2007 **Models:** All Models **Engines:** All **Transmissions:** All	**A/C Pressure Sensor Circuit Low Input** Engine started, and the PCM detected the A/C Pressure sensor signal was under the test limit. **Possible Causes:** • ACP sensor circuit shorted to VREF or to power (VPWR) • ACP sensor circuit is open, or the ground circuit is open • ACP sensor is damaged or has failed • PCM has failed
DTC: P1463 **2T CCM, MIL: Yes** **Years:** 2005, 2006, 2007 **Models:** All Models **Engines:** All **Transmissions:** All	**A/C Pressure Sensor Insufficient Pressure Change** Engine started, and with the A/C compressor operating, the PCM detected the A/C refrigerant pressure did not change as the compressor cycled during the self-test period. **Possible Causes:** • A/C system mechanical failure, or A/C clutch always engaged • ACP sensor signal open, or sensor ground circuit open • A/C sensor is damaged or the PCM has failed
DTC: P1464 **1T CCM, MIL: No** **Years:** 2005, 2006, 2007 **Models:** All Models **Engines:** All **Transmissions:** All	**A/C Demand Out of Self-Test Range** Key on, KOEO Self-Test enabled, or with the engine running, KOER Self-Test enabled, and the PCM detected the A/C demand switch signal was high during the self-test period. **Possible Causes:** • A/C switch was left "on" during the KOER self-test • A/C PWR circuit is shorted to power (N/C WAC relay contacts) • ACCS circuit is shorted to power • A/C Demand Switch, WAC relay or CCRM is damaged
DTC: P1469 **2T CCM, MIL: Yes** **Years:** 2005, 2006, 2007 **Models:** All Models **Engines:** All **Transmissions:** All	**Low A/C Cycling Period** Engine started, and with the A/C selected, PCM detected frequent cycling of the A/C compressor clutch. This test was designed to protect the transmission. In some strategies, the PCM will unlock the torque converter during A/C clutch engagement. If a concern is present that results in frequent A/C clutch cycling, damage could occur if the torque converter was cycled at these intervals. This test will detect this condition, set the code and prevent the torque converter from excessive cycling. **Possible Causes:** • Cycling pressure switch circuit open between pin 41 (ACCS) and the PCM, or the IGN RUN circuit is open to the cycling pressure switch circuit (if applicable) • Mechanical A/C system concern (i.e., low refrigerant charge, damaged A/C switch)
DTC: P1473 **2T CCM, MIL: Yes** **Years:** 2005, 2006, 2007 **Models:** All Models **Engines:** All **Transmissions:** All	**Fan Secondary High with Fan(s) Off** Key on, KOEO Self-Test enabled, and the PCM detected an unexpected voltage condition on the Power-To-Cooling fan circuit **Possible Causes:** • Power-to-Cooling fan circuit open in the wiring harness • Power-to-Cooling fan circuit shorted to power in wiring harness • Cooling fan motor windings open, or fan ground circuit is open • VLCM is damaged or has failed

DTC	Trouble Code Title, Conditions & Possible Causes

DTC: P1474
2T CCM, MIL: Yes
Years: 2005, 2006, 2007
Models: All Models
Engines: All
Transmissions: All
	Hydraulic Cooling Fan Primary Circuit Malfunction
	Key on or engine running; low cooling fan enabled, and the PCM detected the voltage to the Hydraulic Cooling Fan (HFC) motor was higher or lower than the expected range for the fan primary circuit.
	Possible Causes:
	  • FC circuit is open or shorted to power
	  • LFC circuit is open or shorted to power (CCRM models)
	  • FC or LFC relay VPWR circuit is open (Start/Run on Probe)

DTC: P1477
2T CCM, MIL: Yes
Years: 2005, 2006, 2007
Models: All Models
Engines: All
Transmissions: All
	Medium Fan Control Primary Circuit Malfunction
	Key on, medium cooling fan (MFC) enabled; and the PCM detected excessive current draw in the circuit; or with the MFC disabled (off), it detected voltage present on the MFC circuit.
	Possible Causes:
	  • MFC circuit is open
	  • MFC relay circuit to IGN START/RUN is open
	  • MFC relay is damaged or has failed
	  • PCM has failed

DTC: P1479
2T CCM, MIL: Yes
Years: 2005, 2006, 2007
Models: All Models
Engines: All
Transmissions: All
	High Fan Control Primary Circuit Malfunction
	Key on, high cooling fan (HFC) enabled, and the PCM detected excessive current draw in the circuit; or with the HFC commanded off, it detected voltage present on the HFC circuit.
	Possible Causes:
	  • HFC circuit is open
	  • HFC circuit is shorted to ground
	  • HFC relay power circuit (VPWR) is open
	  • High speed FC relay is damaged or it has failed
	  • PCM has failed

DTC: P1481
2T CCM, MIL: Yes
Years: 2005, 2006, 2007
Models: All Models
Engines: All
Transmissions: All
	Fan Secondary Low With High Fan On
	Key on or engine running; high speed cooling fan enabled, and the PCM detected the fan secondary circuit was low with the High Speed cooling fan commanded "on" during testing.
	Possible Causes:
	  • High speed cooling fan circuit is open
	  • High speed cooling fan circuit is shorted to ground
	  • High speed cooling fan relay power circuit (VPWR) is open
	  • High speed FC relay is damaged or has failed
	  • PCM has failed

DTC: P1483
2T CCM, MIL: Yes
Years: 2005, 2006, 2007
Models: All Models
Engines: All
Transmissions: All
	Power To Fan Circuit Over-Current Detected
	Key on or engine running; cooling fan enabled, and the PCM detected the current in the Fan PWR circuit exceeded the limit.
	Possible Causes:
	  • Power-to-Cooling Fan circuit shorted to ground
	  • Cooling fan motor is damaged or has failed
	  • VLCM is damaged or has failed
	  • PCM has failed

DTC: P1500
2T CCM, MIL: Yes
Years: 2005, 2006, 2007
Models: All Models
Engines: All
Transmissions: All
	VSS Signal Or POSM Signal Intermittent
	Engine running in gear with a VSS signal present, and the PCM detected that the VSS signal was intermittent
	Note: The VSS signal is received from the VSS, transfer case speed sensor, ABS Control module, the GEM or the Central Timer module (CTM), depending upon the vehicle application.
	Possible Causes:
	  • VSS pins damaged, loose or pushed in at the connector
	  • VSS circuit open or shorted in the wiring harness (insulation)
	  • VSS wiring harness routing incorrect or VSS mounting incorrect
	  • TSB 01-21-13 contains a repair procedure for this trouble code

DTC: P1501 **1T CCM, MIL: No** **Years:** 2005, 2006, 2007 **Models:** All Models **Engines:** All **Transmissions:** All	**VSS Signal Out Of Self-Test Range** Engine started, KOER Self-Test enabled, and the PCM detected a VSS signal during the self-test (i.e., with the vehicle not moving). **Possible Causes:** • VSS signal is noisy due to Radio Frequency Interference/ Electro-Magnetic Interference (RFI/EMI) from outside devices (ignition wires, charging circuit or aftermarket devices)

DTC	Trouble Code Title, Conditions & Possible Causes
DTC: P1501 **1T CCM, MIL: Yes** **Years:** 2005, 2006, 2007 **Models:** All Models **Engines:** All **Transmissions:** All	**VSS Signal Intermittent** Engine started, and the PCM detected the VSS signal dropped out. The TCIL will flash on the first trip this code sets. The speed signal is received from the VSS, transfer case speed sensor, ABS Control module, GEM or the Central Timer module (depends upon the vehicle). **Possible Causes:** • VSS signal is noisy due to Radio Frequency Interference/ Electro-Magnetic Interference (RFI/EMI) from outside devices (ignition wires, charging circuit or aftermarket devices)
DTC: P1502 **1T CCM, MIL: Yes** **Years:** 2005, 2006, 2007 **Models:** All Models **Engines:** All **Transmissions:** All	**VSS Signal Intermittent** Engine started, and the PCM detected an intermittent VSS signal. The TCIL will flash on the first trip that this code is set. The VSS signal is received from the VSS, transfer case speed sensor, ABS Control module, GEM or the Central Timer module (depends upon the vehicle). **Possible Causes:** • VSS+ or VSS− harness circuit is open • TCSS signal or TCSS signal return harness circuit is open • VSS harness circuit, TCSS harness circuit is shorted to ground • VSS harness circuit, CSS harness circuit is shorted to power • VSS circuit open between the PCM and related control module • VSS or TCSS, or wheel speed sensors circuits are damaged • Modules connected to VSC/VSS harness circuits are damaged • Mechanical drive mechanism for the VSS or TCSS is damaged
DTC: P1504 **2T CCM, MIL: Yes** **Years:** 2005, 2006, 2007 **Models:** All Models **Engines:** All **Transmissions:** All	**Idle Air Control Circuit Malfunction** Engine started, engine running for 1 minute, and the PCM detected an electrical load failure on the IAC motor circuit during the self-test. **Possible Causes:** • IAC circuit is open, shorted to ground or to the VPWR circuit • IAC solenoid VPWR circuit is open • IAC valve is damaged or has failed • PCM has failed
DTC: P1505 **2T CCM, MIL: Yes** **Years:** 2005, 2006, 2007 **Models:** All Models **Engines:** All **Transmissions:** All	**Idle Air Control System At Adaptive Clip** Engine running for over one minute, and the PCM detected the idle speed control had reached its "idle air trim limit" during the Continuous self test. **Possible Causes:** • Base engine air leaks are present • Air cleaner element is dirty, plugged or restricted • Throttle body/linkage is binding • IAC valve body is damaged or contaminated • Throttle body is damaged
DTC: P1506 **2T CCM, MIL: Yes** **Years:** 2005, 2006, 2007 **Models:** Crown Victoria, Grand Marquis Models **Engines:** 4.6L VIN V, W **Transmissions:** All	**Idle Air Control Overspeed Error** Engine started, engine running for 1 minute, and the PCM detected the idle speed was more than the desired engine Target Idle Speed. **Possible Causes:** • Base engine vacuum leaks present • EVAP system has a problem • IAC circuit shorted to ground • IAC valve is stuck open, or it is damaged • Throttle body or throttle plate is contaminated or very dirty • TSB 98-25-19 contains a repair procedure for this trouble code
DTC: P1506 **2T CCM, MIL: Yes** **Years:** 2005, 2006, 2007 **Models:** All Models Except Crown Victoria, Grand Marquis & Town Car **Engines:** All **Transmissions:** All	**Idle Air Control Overspeed Error** Engine started, engine running for 1 minute, and the PCM detected the idle speed was more than the desired engine Target Idle Speed. **Possible Causes:** • Base engine vacuum leaks present • EVAP system has a problem • IAC circuit shorted to ground • IAC valve is stuck open, or it is damaged • Throttle body or throttle plate is contaminated or very dirty

DTC	Trouble Code Title, Conditions & Possible Causes
DTC: P1507 **2T CCM, MIL: Yes** **Years:** 2005, 2006, 2007 **Models:** All Models **Engines:** All **Transmissions:** All	**Idle Air Control Underspeed Error** Engine started, engine running for 1 minute, and the PCM detected the idle speed was less than the desired engine Target Idle Speed. **Possible Causes:** • Air inlet is plugged or the air filter element is severely clogged • IAC circuit is open, or shorted to the VPWR circuit • IAC circuit VPWR circuit is open • IAC solenoid is damaged or has failed • Throttle body or throttle plate is contaminated or very dirty
DTC: P1512 **2T CCM, MIL: Yes** **Years:** 2005, 2006, 2007 **Models:** All Models **Engines:** All **Transmissions:** All	**Intake Manifold Runner Control System Malfunction** Engine started, and the PCM detected the IMRC Monitor indicated that the IMRC was stuck closed during the Continuous self test. **Possible Causes:** • Leaky vacuum reservoir, vacuum lines loose or damaged • Vacuum solenoid or vacuum actuator is damaged • IMRC actuator cable/gears are seized, or the cables are improperly routed or seized • IMRC housing return springs are damaged or disconnected • Lever/shaft return stop may be obstructed or bent, or the lever/shaft wide open stop may be obstructed or bent, or the IMRC lever/shaft may be sticking, binding or disconnected • IMRC control circuit open, shorted or the VPWR circuit is open • PCM has failed
DTC: P1513 **2T CCM, MIL: Yes** **Years:** 2005, 2006, 2007 **Models:** All Models **Engines:** All **Transmissions:** All	**Intake Manifold Runner Control Malfunction (Bank 1)** Engine started, and the PCM detected the IMRC Monitor indicated the IMRC was not functioning correctly during the self-test period. **Possible Causes:** • IMRC actuator cable/gears are seized, or the cables are improperly routed or seized • IMRC control circuit open, shorted or the VPWR circuit is open • IMRC housing return springs are damaged or disconnected • Leaky vacuum reservoir, vacuum lines loose or damaged • Lever/shaft return stop may be obstructed or bent, or the lever/shaft wide open stop may be obstructed or bent, or the IMRC lever/shaft may be sticking, binding or disconnected • Vacuum solenoid or vacuum actuator is damaged • PCM has failed
DTC: P1516 **2T CCM, MIL: Yes** **Years:** 2005, 2006, 2007 **Models:** All Models **Engines:** All **Transmissions:** All	**Intake Manifold Runner Control Input Error (Bank 1)** Key on or engine running; and the PCM detected the IMRC Monitor signal for Bank 1 was outside of its expected calibrated range during the Continuous self test. **Possible Causes:** • IMRC mechanical fault - the linkage may be bound or seized • Inspect for binding or improper routing. The cable core wire at the IMRC/IMSC housing attachment must have slack and lever must contact close plate stop screw
DTC: P1517 **2T CCM, MIL: Yes** **Years:** 2005, 2006, 2007 **Models:** All Models **Engines:** All **Transmissions:** All	**Intake Manifold Runner Control Input Error (Bank 2)** Key on or engine running; and the PCM detected the IMRC Monitor signal for Bank 2 was outside of its expected calibrated range during the Continuous self test. **Possible Causes:** • IMRC mechanical fault - the linkage may be bound or seized • Visually inspect for binding or improper routing. The cable core wire at the IMRC or IMSC housing attachment must have slack and lever must contact close plate stop screw
DTC: P1518 **2T CCM, MIL: Yes** **Years:** 2005, 2006, 2007 **Models:** All Models **Engines:** All **Transmissions:** All	**Intake Manifold Runner Control Malfunction (Stuck Open)** Engine started, and the PCM detected the IMRC Monitor signal was less than its expected calibrated range at closed throttle. An IMRCM PID of 1v at closed throttle indicates a fault. **Possible Causes:** • IMRC monitor signal circuit shorted to power ground • IMRC Monitor signal circuit shorted to signal ground (return) • IMRC actuator is damaged or has failed • PCM has failed

DTC	Trouble Code Title, Conditions & Possible Causes
DTC: P1519 **2T CCM, MIL: Yes** **Years:** 2005, 2006, 2007 **Models:** All Models **Engines:** All **Transmissions:** All	**Intake Manifold Runner Control Stuck Closed** Key on, and the PCM detected the IMRC Monitor was more than the expected calibrated range at closed throttle. **Note: An IMRCM PID of VREF at 3000 rpm may indicate a fault.** **Possible Causes:** • IMRC monitor signal circuit shorted to power ground • IMRC Monitor signal circuit shorted to signal ground (return) • IMRC actuator is damaged or has failed (e.g., there may be a small leak in the vacuum diaphragm of the actuator) • PCM has failed
DTC: P1520 **2T CCM, MIL: Yes** **Years:** 2005, 2006, 2007 **Models:** All Models **Engines:** All **Transmissions:** All	**Intake Manifold Runner Control Input Error** Key on or engine running; and the PCM detected the IMRC Monitor signal for was outside of its expected calibrated range. Use the Active Command or Output State Control on a Generic Scan Tool to help determine if an electrical fault is present. **Possible Causes:** • IMRC control circuit is open or shorted to ground • IMRC Monitor VREF circuit is open • IMRC is damaged or the PCM has failed
DTC: P1530 **2T CCM, MIL: Yes** **Years:** 2005, 2006, 2007 **Models:** All Models **Engines:** All **Transmissions:** All	**Air Conditioning Clutch Circuit Malfunction** Key on or engine running; and the PCM detected a circuit fault in the A/C Clutch power (Power To Clutch) circuit. **Possible Causes:** • A/C Clutch power circuit open or shorted to VPWR in harness • A/C clutch ground circuit is open • A/C clutch is open • VLCM is damaged or has failed
DTC: P1537 **2T CCM, MIL: Yes** **Years:** 2005, 2006, 2007 **Models:** All Models **Engines:** All **Transmissions:** All	**Intake Manifold Runner Control Malfunction (Bank 1 Stuck Open)** Key on or engine running; and the PCM detected the Bank 1 IMRC Monitor signal was less than its expected calibrated range at closed throttle (it may be stuck in open position). An IMRCM PID of 1v at closed throttle may indicate a fault is present. **Possible Causes:** • IMRC monitor signal circuit shorted to power ground • IMRC Monitor signal circuit shorted to signal ground (return) • IMRC actuator is damaged or the PCM has failed
DTC: P1538 **2T CCM, MIL: Yes** **Years:** 2005, 2006, 2007 **Models:** All Models **Engines:** All **Transmissions:** All	**Intake Manifold Runner Control Stuck Open (Bank 2)** Key on or engine running; and the PCM detected the Bank 2 IMRC Monitor signal was more than its expected calibrated range at closed throttle (it may be stuck in open position). An IMRCM PID of VREF at 3000 rpm may indicate a fault is present. **Possible Causes:** • IMRC monitor signal circuit shorted to power ground • IMRC Monitor signal circuit shorted to signal ground (return) • IMRC actuator is damaged or has failed • PCM has failed
DTC: P1539 **2T CCM, MIL: No** **Years:** 2005, 2006, 2007 **Models:** All Models **Engines:** All **Transmissions:** All	**Power To A/C Clutch Circuit Over-Current** Key on or engine running; and with the A/C switch "on", the PCM detected the current in the A/C Clutch power (PWR) circuit exceeded the normal current level during the self-test. **Possible Causes:** • A/C Clutch power circuit open or shorted to VPWR in harness • A/C clutch ground circuit is open • A/C clutch is open • VLCM is damaged or has failed
DTC: P1549 **1T CCM, MIL: No** **Years:** 2005, 2006, 2007 **Models:** Aviator **Engines:** 4.6L VIN H **Transmissions:** All	**Long / Short Runner Control Circuit Malfunction** Key on or engine running and the PCM detected an unexpected voltage on the Long / Short Runner Control (LSRC) circuit. An LSRC valve PID of YES status indicates a fault exists. **Possible Causes:** • LSRC circuit is open or shorted to ground • LSRC power circuit (VPWR) is open • LSRC assembly is damaged or it has failed • PCM has failed

DTC	Trouble Code Title, Conditions & Possible Causes
DTC: P1550 **1T CCM, MIL: No** **Years:** 2005, 2006, 2007 **Models:** All Models **Engines:** All **Transmissions:** All	**Power Steering Pressure Switch Circuit Malfunction** KOER Self-Test enabled, and the PCM detected the PSP switch signal did not change during the self-test. This code indicates the PSP input is out of its self-test range. **Possible Causes:** • PSP switch circuit open or shorted, or the ground circuit open • Steering wheel was not rotated during the KOER Self-Test • PCM has failed
DTC: P1572 **2T CCM, MIL: Yes** **Years:** 2005, 2006, 2007 **Models:** All Models **Engines:** All **Transmissions:** All	**Brake Pedal Switch Circuit Malfunction** Engine started, and the PCM detected the Brake Pedal switch and Brake Pressure switch inputs failed the Rationality test (i.e., one or both of these inputs did not change as expected). DTC P1572 is set when the PCM does not see the proper sequence of the brake pedal input signal from both the BPP and BPA when the brake pedal is pressed and released. **Possible Causes:** • BPP or BPA switches are out of adjustment (one or both) • Blown fuse to switch power circuit • BPP switch or BPA switch is damaged (one or both) • BPP or BPA switch circuit is open or shorted • PCM has failed
DTC: P1605 **1T PCM, MIL: Yes** **Years:** 2005, 2006, 2007 **Models:** All Models **Engines:** All **Transmissions:** All	**PCM Keep Alive Memory Test Error** Key on, and the PCM detected an internal memory fault. This code can be set if KAPWR to the PCM is interrupted. This trouble code will set at first key on if a battery circuit is opened. **Possible Causes:** • Battery terminals loose or corroded (high resistance in circuit) • Keep Alive Memory circuit to PCM interrupted or open • Reprogramming function not performed • PCM has failed
DTC: P1633 **1T PCM, MIL: Yes** **Years:** 2005, 2006, 2007 **Models:** All Models **Engines:** All **Transmissions:** All	**PCM Keep Alive Memory Voltage Too Low** Key on, and the PCM detected that the KAM power circuit to the battery was interrupted. **Possible Causes:** • KAPWR circuit has been interrupted (this problem may be an intermittent condition) • PCM has failed
DTC: P1635 **1T PCM, MIL: Yes** **Years:** 2005, 2006, 2007 **Models:** All Models **Engines:** All **Transmissions:** All	**Tire Axle/Ratio Out Of Acceptable Range** Key on, and the PCM detected the tire and axle information in the VID Block does not match the vehicle hardware. **Note: This code indicates that the PCM needs to be reprogrammed.** **Possible Causes:** • Incorrect tire size or Incorrect axle ratio • Incorrect VID configuration parameters • PCM need to be reprogrammed • TSB 02-23-4 contains repair information for this trouble code
DTC: P1636 **1T PCM, MIL: Yes** **Years:** 2005, 2006, 2007 **Models:** All Models **Engines:** All **Transmissions:** All	**Inductive Signature Chip Communication Error** Key on, and the PCM determined it had lost communication with the Inductive Signature Chip. The PCM has internal damage when this trouble code is present. **Possible Causes:** • PCM has failed and needs to be replaced
DTC: P1639 **1T PCM, MIL: Yes** **Years:** 2005, 2006, 2007 **Models:** All Models **Engines:** All **Transmissions:** All	**Vehicle ID Block Not Programmed Or Is Corrupt** Key on, and the PCM determined the Vehicle ID Block information was incorrect. **Possible Causes:** • PCM may not be the correct application • PCM may need to be reprogrammed • VID configuration may not be correct • TSB 02-23-4 contains repair information for this trouble code

DTC	Trouble Code Title, Conditions & Possible Causes
DTC: P1640 **1T PCM, MIL: Yes** **Years:** 2005, 2006, 2007 **Models:** All Models **Engines:** All **Transmissions:** All	**PCM Trouble Codes Available In Another Module** Engine started, and the PCM received a request from another module to turn on the MIL due to a fault that could affect emissions. **Note: Vehicles using a secondary Engine Control Module can request that the PCM turn on the Check Engine Light when a failure occurs that could affect emissions. Request PID 0946 to determine which module made the request. Then select that module to read the related trouble code(s).** **Possible Causes:** • Trouble codes are stored in a secondary module, which in turn, requested that the PCM turn on the MIL when this code is set.
DTC: P1650 **2T CCM, MIL: Yes** **Years:** 2005, 2006, 2007 **Models:** All Models **Engines:** All **Transmissions:** All	**Power Steering Pressure Switch Circuit Malfunction** Engine started, and the PCM detected the PSP switch signal did not change after a certain number of vehicle speed transitions. The PCM counts the number of times that the vehicle speed transitions from 0 mph to a calibrated speed. The PCM expects the PSP switch input to change after a certain number of transitions. **Possible Causes:** • Steering wheel must be turned during the KOER Self-Test • PSP switch/shorting bar is damaged • PSP signal circuit is open or shorted to ground • PSP switch ground (return) circuit is open • PCM has failed
DTC: P1651 **2T CCM, MIL: Yes** **Years:** 2005, 2006, 2007 **Models:** All Models **Engines:** All **Transmissions:** All	**Power Steering Pressure Switch Circuit Malfunction** Engine started, and the PCM detected the PSP switch signal did not change after a certain number of vehicle speed transitions. **Note: The PCM counts the number of times that the vehicle speed transitions from 0 mph to a calibrated speed. The PCM expects the PSP switch input to change after a certain number of transitions.** **Possible Causes:** • Steering wheel must be turned during the KOER Self-Test • PSP switch/shorting bar is damaged • PSP signal circuit is open or shorted to ground • PSP switch ground (return) circuit is open • PCM has failed
DTC: P1700 **1T CCM, MIL: No** **Years:** 2005, 2006, 2007 **Models:** All Models **Engines:** All **Transmissions:** A/T	**Transaxle Mechanical Malfunction** Engine started, vehicle driven in gear, and the PCM detected a transmission mechanical fault. **Possible Causes:** • This code can set due to low transmission fluid level • Refer to the appropriate Transmission Repair Manual or information in electronic media to perform a complete diagnosis of the automatic transmission when this code is set
DTC: P1701 **1T CCM, MIL: No** **Years:** 2005, 2006, 2007 **Models:** All Models **Engines:** All **Transmissions:** A/T	**Reverse Engagement Error** Engine started, and the PCM detected a Transmission Range (TR) sensor signal that indicated a reverse engagement error. **Possible Causes:** • Refer to the appropriate Transmission Repair Manual or information in electronic media to perform a complete diagnosis of the automatic transmission when this code is set
DTC: P1702 **1T CCM, MIL: No** **Years:** 2005, 2006, 2007 **Models:** All Models **Engines:** All **Transmissions:** A/T	**TR Sensor Signal Intermittent** Key on or engine running; and the PCM detected the failure Trouble Code Conditions for DTC P0705 or P0708 were met intermittently. **Possible Causes:** • Refer to the appropriate Transmission Repair Manual or information in electronic media to perform a complete diagnosis of the automatic transmission when this code is set
DTC: P1703 **1T CCM, MIL: No** **Years:** 2005, 2006, 2007 **Models:** All Models **Engines:** All **Transmissions:** A/T	**Brake Switch Circuit Out of Self-Test Range** Key on, KOEO Self-Test enabled; and the PCM detected the brake switch signal was high, or with the KOER Self-Test enabled, the PCM detected the switch signal did not cycle On / Off. **Possible Causes:** • BPP switch circuit open or shorted • Brake Switch is misadjusted, damaged or has failed • Stop lamp circuits open or shorted • Malfunction in the module(s) connected to BPP circuit (i.e., the Rear Electronic Module on Windstar and LS, or the Lighting Control Module on the Continental and Town Car) • PCM has failed

DTC	Trouble Code Title, Conditions & Possible Causes
DTC: P1704 **1T CCM, MIL: No** **Years:** 2005, 2006, 2007 **Models:** All Models **Engines:** All **Transmissions:** A/T	**Transmission Range Sensor Circuit Out Of Self-Test Range** Key on, KOEO Self Test enabled, and the PCM detected a Transmission Range (TR) sensor signal occurred in between gear positions. **Possible Causes:** • Digital TR sensor or shift cable misadjusted • Digital TR sensor circuit is open or shorted to ground • Digital TR sensor has failed
DTC: P1705 **1T CCM, MIL: No** **Years:** 2005, 2006, 2007 **Models:** All Models **Engines:** All **Transmissions:** A/T	**Transmission Range Sensor Out of Self-Test Range** Key on, KOEO Self Test enabled, and the PCM detected it did not receive a Transmission Range (TR) sensor signal in Park or Neutral position. **Possible Causes:** • Gear selector not in Park or Neutral during the self-test • Digital TR sensor circuit is open or shorted to ground • Digital TR sensor has failed • PCM has failed
DTC: P1708 **1T CCM, MIL: Yes** **Years:** 2005, 2006, 2007 **Models:** All Models **Engines:** All **Transmissions:** A/T	**Digital Transmission Range Sensor Circuit Malfunction** Engine started, and the PCM detected it did not receive a change in the Digital Transmission Range (TR) sensor signal after the vehicle was driven in gear. **Possible Causes:** • Digital TR sensor circuit open • Digital TR sensor ground circuit open • Digital TR sensor is damaged or has failed • PCM has failed
DTC: P1709 **1T CCM, MIL: No** **Years:** 2005, 2006, 2007 **Models:** All Models **Engines:** All **Transmissions:** A/T	**PNP Switch Out Of Self-Test Range** Key on, KOEO Self-Test enabled, and the PCM detected the PNP switch was high when is should have been low (wrong gearshift position). **Possible Causes:** • PNP switch ground circuit is open • PNP switch circuit short to power (VPWR) • PNP switch is damaged or has failed • PCM has failed
DTC: P1710 **2T CCM, MIL: Yes** **Years:** 2005, 2006, 2007 **Models:** All Models **Engines:** All **Transmissions:** A/T	**TFT Sensor In-Range Circuit Malfunction** Engine started, vehicle driven to a speed over 1 mph, TFT sensor signal in-range, and the PCM did not detect any change in the TFT signal in the self-test. **Possible Causes:** • Refer to the appropriate Transmission Repair Manual or information in electronic media to perform a complete diagnosis of the automatic transmission when this code is set
DTC: P1711 **1T CCM, MIL: No** **Years:** 2005, 2006, 2007 **Models:** All Models **Engines:** All **Transmissions:** A/T	**TFT Sensor Out of Self-Test Range** Key on, KOER Self Test enabled; or engine running with the KOER Self Test enabled, and the PCM detected the Transmission Fluid Temperature (TFT) sensor was more than or less than the calibrated range (25°F to 240°F) during the self-test. **Possible Causes:** • Refer to the appropriate Transmission Repair Manual or information in electronic media to perform a complete diagnosis of the automatic transmission when this code is set
DTC: P1712 **1T CCM, MIL: No** **Years:** 2005, 2006, 2007 **Models:** All Models **Engines:** All **Transmissions:** A/T	**TFT Sensor Circuit Low Input** Engine started, and the PCM detected the TFT sensor signal was less than 0.2v (equivalent to a temperature of more than 357°F). **Possible Causes:** • Refer to the appropriate Transmission Repair Manual or information in electronic media to perform a complete diagnosis of the automatic transmission when this code is set
DTC: P1713 **1T CCM, MIL: No** **Years:** 2005, 2006, 2007 **Models:** All Models **Engines:** All **Transmissions:** A/T	**TFT Sensor No Activity or TFT Sensor Circuit Low Input** Engine started, VSS over 1 mph, and the PCM did not detect any change in the TFT low range circuit during the self-test. **Possible Causes:** • Refer to the appropriate Transmission Repair Manual or information in electronic media to perform a complete diagnosis of the automatic transmission when this code is set

DTC	Trouble Code Title, Conditions & Possible Causes
DTC: P1714 **1T CCM, MIL: Yes** **Years:** 2005, 2006, 2007 **Models:** All Models **Engines:** All **Transmissions:** A/T	**Transmission Control System Malfunction** Engine started, VSS over 1 mph, and the PCM did not detect any change in the TFT low range circuit during the self-test. **Possible Causes:** • Refer to the appropriate Transmission Repair Manual or information in electronic media to perform a complete diagnosis of the automatic transmission when this code is set
DTC: P1715 **1T CCM, MIL: Yes** **Years:** 2005, 2006, 2007 **Models:** All Models **Engines:** All **Transmissions:** A/T	**Transmission Control System Malfunction** Engine started, VSS over 1 mph, and the PCM detected a mechanical problem in the Shift Solenoid 'B' (SSB) during the test. **Possible Causes:** • Refer to the appropriate Transmission Repair Manual or information in electronic media to perform a complete diagnosis of the automatic transmission when this code is set
DTC: P1716 **2T CCM, MIL: No** **Years:** 2005, 2006, 2007 **Models:** All Models **Engines:** All **Transmissions:** A/T	**Transmission Control System Malfunction** Engine started, VSS over 1 mph, and the PCM detected a problem in the Transmission Control system during the self-test. **Possible Causes:** • Refer to the appropriate Transmission Repair Manual or information in electronic media to perform a complete diagnosis of the automatic transmission when this code is set
DTC: P1717 **1T CCM, MIL: No** **Years:** 2005, 2006, 2007 **Models:** All Models **Engines:** All **Transmissions:** A/T	**Transmission Control System Malfunction** Engine started, VSS over 1 mph, and the PCM detected a problem in the Transmission Control system during the self-test. **Possible Causes:** • Refer to the appropriate Transmission Repair Manual or information in electronic media to perform a complete diagnosis of the automatic transmission when this code is set
DTC: P1718 **1T CCM, MIL: No** **Years:** 2005, 2006, 2007 **Models:** All Models **Engines:** All **Transmissions:** A/T	**TFT Sensor No Activity Or TFT Sensor Circuit High Input** Engine started, VSS over 1 mph, and the PCM did not detect any change in the TFT high range circuit during the self-test. **Possible Causes:** • Refer to the appropriate Transmission Repair Manual or information in electronic media to perform a complete diagnosis of the automatic transmission when this code is set
DTC: P1719 **1T CCM, MIL: No** **Years:** 2005, 2006, 2007 **Models:** All Models **Engines:** All **Transmissions:** A/T	**Transmission Control System Malfunction** Engine started, VSS over 1 mph, and the PCM detected a problem in the Transmission Control system during the self-test. **Possible Causes:** • Refer to the appropriate Transmission Repair Manual or information in electronic media to perform a complete diagnosis of the automatic transmission when this code is set
DTC: P1727 **1T CCM, MIL: No** **Years:** 2005, 2006, 2007 **Models:** All Models **Engines:** All **Transmissions:** A/T	**Transmission Coast Clutch Solenoid Slip Malfunction** Engine started, VSS over 1 mph in gear, and the PCM detected a signal that indicated the coast clutch solenoid had a slippage fault. **Possible Causes:** • Refer to the appropriate Transmission Repair Manual or information in electronic media to perform a complete diagnosis of the automatic transmission when this code is set
DTC: P1728 **1T CCM, MIL: No** **Years:** 2005, 2006, 2007 **Models:** All Models **Engines:** All **Transmissions:** A/T	**Transmission Slip Malfunction** Engine started, VSS over 1 mph in gear, and the PCM detected a signal that indicated the transmission was slipping while in gear. **Possible Causes:** • Refer to the appropriate Transmission Repair Manual or information in electronic media to perform a complete diagnosis of the automatic transmission when this code is set
DTC: P1729 **1T CCM, MIL: No** **Years:** 2005, 2006, 2007 **Models:** All Models **Engines:** All **Transmissions:** A/T	**4 x 4 Low Switch Circuit Malfunction** Engine started and the PCM detected the 4x4 switch did not go low after the switch was on. **Possible Causes:** • Speedometer out of calibration • 4x4L wiring harness is open or shorted, 4x4L switch is damaged or has failed • Electronic Shift Control Module is damaged or has failed, or the PCM has failed

DTC	Trouble Code Title, Conditions & Possible Causes
DTC: P1740 **1T CCM, MIL: Yes** **Years:** 2005, 2006, 2007 **Models:** All Models **Engines:** All **Transmissions:** A/T	**TCC Solenoid Mechanical Malfunction** Engine started, vehicle speed more than 20 mph, and the PCM detected that TCC lockup did not occur (the lockup event is inferred from other inputs). **Possible Causes:** • Refer to the appropriate Transmission Repair Manual or information in electronic media to perform a complete diagnosis of the automatic transmission when this code is set
DTC: P1741 **1T CCM, MIL: No** **Years:** 2005, 2006, 2007 **Models:** All Models **Engines:** All **Transmissions:** A/T	**TCC Engagement Error** Engine started, vehicle in gear at Cruise speed, and the PCM detected an error due to excessive TCC engagement. **Note: This problem can cause speed changes or vehicle surges.** **Possible Causes:** • Refer to the appropriate Transmission Repair Manual or information in electronic media to perform a complete diagnosis of the automatic transmission when this code is set
DTC: P1742 **1T CCM, MIL: Yes** **Years:** 2005, 2006, 2007 **Models:** All Models **Engines:** All **Transmissions:** A/T	**TCC Solenoid Failed On (Electrical Or Mechanical Fault)** Engine started, vehicle in gear at Cruise speed, and the PCM detected that the Torque Converter Clutch system had failed "on". **Possible Causes:** • Refer to the appropriate Transmission Repair Manual or information in electronic media to perform a complete diagnosis of the automatic transmission when this code is set.
DTC: P1744 **1T CCM, MIL: Yes** **Years:** 2005, 2006, 2007 **Models:** All Models **Engines:** All **Transmissions:** A/T	**TCC System Mechanically Stuck In Off Position** Engine started, vehicle in gear at Cruise speed, and the PCM detected the Torque Converter Clutch system had failed with the TCC in the mechanically "off" position. **Possible Causes:** • Refer to the appropriate Transmission Repair Manual or information in electronic media to perform a complete diagnosis of the automatic transmission when this code is set.
DTC: P1746 **1T CCM, MIL: No** **Years:** 2005, 2006, 2007 **Models:** All Models **Engines:** All **Transmissions:** A/T	**EPC Solenoid Circuit Malfunction** Engine started, vehicle in gear, and the PCM detected the Electronic Pressure Control (EPC) solenoid circuit indicated "open". This fault can cause harsh engagements and shifts. **Possible Causes:** • Refer to the appropriate Transmission Repair Manual or information in electronic media to perform a complete diagnosis of the automatic transmission when this code is set
DTC: P1747 **1T CCM, MIL: No** **Years:** 2005, 2006, 2007 **Models:** All Models **Engines:** All **Transmissions:** A/T	**A/T EPC Solenoid Circuit Malfunction** Engine started, vehicle in gear at Cruise speed, and the PCM detected a shorted output driver or the TCC solenoid was shorted. **Possible Causes:** • Refer to the appropriate Transmission Repair Manual or information in electronic media to perform a complete diagnosis of the automatic transmission when this code is set.
DTC: P1749 **1T CCM, MIL: No** **Years:** 2005, 2006, 2007 **Models:** All Models **Engines:** All **Transmissions:** A/T	**A/T EPC Solenoid Failed Low** Engine started, vehicle in gear at Cruise speed, and the PCM detected the Torque Converter Clutch solenoid had failed "low". **Possible Causes:** • Refer to the appropriate Transmission Repair Manual or information in electronic media to perform a complete diagnosis of the automatic transmission when this code is set.
DTC: P1751 **1T CCM, MIL: No** **Years:** 2005, 2006, 2007 **Models:** All Models **Engines:** All **Transmissions:** A/T	**A/T Shift Solenoid 1 Performance** Engine started, vehicle in gear at Cruise speed, and the PCM detected a mechanical fault in the Shift Solenoid 1 (SS1) operation. **Possible Causes:** • Refer to the appropriate Transmission Repair Manual or information in electronic media to perform a complete diagnosis of the automatic transmission when this code is set.
DTC: P1754 **1T CCM, MIL: No** **Years:** 2005, 2006, 2007 **Models:** All Models **Engines:** All **Transmissions:** A/T	**A/T Coast Clutch Solenoid Circuit Malfunction** Engine started, vehicle in gear at Cruise speed, and the PCM detected an unexpected voltage condition on the Coast Clutch Solenoid (CCS) circuit during the CCM test period. **Possible Causes:** • Refer to the appropriate Transmission Repair Manual or information in electronic media to perform a complete diagnosis of the automatic transmission when this code is set.

DTC	Trouble Code Title, Conditions & Possible Causes
DTC: P1756 **1T CCM, MIL: No** **Years:** 2005, 2006, 2007 **Models:** All Models **Engines:** All **Transmissions:** A/T	**A/T Shift Solenoid 2 Performance** Engine started, vehicle in gear at Cruise speed, and the PCM detected a mechanical fault in the Shift Solenoid 2 (SS2) operation. **Possible Causes:** • Refer to the appropriate Transmission Repair Manual or information in electronic media to perform a complete diagnosis of the automatic transmission when this code is set
DTC: P1760 **1T CCM, MIL: No** **Years:** 2005, 2006, 2007 **Models:** All Models **Engines:** All **Transmissions:** A/T	**A/T EPC Solenoid Circuit Malfunction** Engine started, vehicle in gear at Cruise speed, and the PCM detected a shorted output driver or the TCC solenoid was shorted. **Possible Causes:** • Refer to the appropriate Transmission Repair Manual or information in electronic media to perform a complete diagnosis of the automatic transmission when this code is set.
DTC: P1761 **1T CCM, MIL: No** **Years:** 2005, 2006, 2007 **Models:** All Models **Engines:** All **Transmissions:** A/T	**A/T Shift Solenoid 3 Performance** Engine started, vehicle in gear at Cruise speed, and the PCM detected a malfunction in the Shift Solenoid 3 (SS3) operation. **Possible Causes:** • Refer to the appropriate Transmission Repair Manual or information in electronic media to perform a complete diagnosis of the automatic transmission when this code is set.
DTC: P1762 **1T CCM, MIL: No** **Years:** 2005, 2006, 2007 **Models:** All Models **Engines:** All **Transmissions:** A/T	**Transmission System Malfunction** Engine started, vehicle in gear at Cruise speed, and the PCM detected a malfunction in the Transmission System operation. **Possible Causes:** • Refer to the appropriate Transmission Repair Manual or information in electronic media to perform a complete diagnosis of the automatic transmission when this code is set.
DTC: P1767 **1T CCM, MIL: No** **Years:** 2005, 2006, 2007 **Models:** All Models **Engines:** All **Transmissions:** A/T	**A/T Shift Solenoid Performance** Engine started, vehicle in gear at Cruise speed, and the PCM detected a malfunction in the Shift Solenoid operation. **Possible Causes:** • Refer to the appropriate Transmission Repair Manual or information in electronic media to perform a complete diagnosis of the automatic transmission when this code is set.
DTC: P1780 **1T CCM, MIL: No** **Years:** 2005, 2006, 2007 **Models:** All Models **Engines:** All **Transmissions:** A/T	**Transmission Control Switch Out of Self-Test Range** Engine started, KOER Self-Test enabled, and the PCM detected the Transmission Control Switch (TCS) was out of range during the test. **Possible Causes:** • TCS circuit open or shorted in the wiring harness • TCS not cycled during the self-test • TCS is damaged, or the PCM has failed
DTC: P1781 **1T CCM, MIL: No** **Years:** 2005, 2006, 2007 **Models:** All Models with 4WD **Engines:** All **Transmissions:** All	**4×4 Low Switch Out Of Self-Test Range** Key on, KOEO Self-Test enabled, and the PCM detected the 4x4 switch input was not low with the switch engaged or "on". **Possible Causes:** • 4x4L switch circuit is open or shorted in the wiring harness • Electronic Shift Module is damaged or has failed • PCM has failed
DTC: P1783 **1T CCM, MIL: No** **Years:** 2005, 2006, 2007 **Models:** All Models **Engines:** All **Transmissions:** A/T	**Transmission Over-Temperature Malfunction** Engine started, engine runtime more than 5 minutes, vehicle in gear at Cruise speed, and the PCM detected the TFT sensor signal was more than 300°F during the CCM test period. **Possible Causes:** • Refer to the appropriate Transmission Repair Manual or information in electronic media to perform a complete diagnosis of the automatic transmission when this code is set.
DTC: P1784 **1T CCM, MIL: No** **Years:** 2005, 2006, 2007 **Models:** All Models **Engines:** All **Transmissions:** A/T	**Transmission System First Or Reverse Gear Malfunction** Engine started, vehicle speed over 1 mph in gear, shift command received for First or Reverse gear, and the PCM detected a problem in the Transmission Control system. **Possible Causes:** • Refer to the appropriate Transmission Repair Manual or information in electronic media to perform a complete diagnosis of the automatic transmission when this code is set.

DTC	Trouble Code Title, Conditions & Possible Causes
DTC: P1785 **1T CCM, MIL: No** **Years:** 2005, 2006, 2007 **Models:** All Models **Engines:** All **Transmissions:** A/T	**Transmission System First Or Second Gear Malfunction** Engine started, vehicle speed over 1 mph in gear, shift command received for First or Second gear, and the PCM detected a problem in the Transmission Control system during the test. **Possible Causes:** • Refer to the appropriate Transmission Repair Manual or information in electronic media to perform a complete diagnosis of the automatic transmission when this code is set
DTC: P1786 **1T CCM, MIL: No** **Years:** 2005, 2006, 2007 **Models:** All Models **Engines:** All **Transmissions:** A/T	**Transmission System Second Or Third Gear Malfunction** Engine started, vehicle speed over 1 mph in gear, shift command received for Second or Third gear, and the PCM detected a problem in the Transmission Control system. **Possible Causes:** • Refer to the appropriate Transmission Repair Manual or information in electronic media to perform a complete diagnosis of the automatic transmission when this code is set.
DTC: P1787 **1T CCM, MIL: No** **Years:** 2005, 2006, 2007 **Models:** All Models **Engines:** All **Transmissions:** A/T	**Transmission System Third Or Fourth Gear Malfunction** Engine started, vehicle speed over 1 mph in gear, shift command received for Third or Fourth gear, and the PCM detected a problem in the Transmission Control system during the test. **Possible Causes:** • Refer to the appropriate Transmission Repair Manual or information in electronic media to perform a complete diagnosis of the automatic transmission when this code is set.
DTC: P1788 **1T CCM, MIL: No** **Years:** 2005, 2006, 2007 **Models:** All Models **Engines:** All **Transmissions:** A/T	**3-2 Timing/Coast Clutch Solenoid Signal High Input** Engine started, vehicle in gear at Cruise speed, and the PCM detected the malfunction 3-2 Timing or Coast Clutch solenoid circuit. **Possible Causes:** • 3-2 Timing or Coast Clutch solenoid circuit open or grounded, or the solenoid has failed • Coast Clutch solenoid is damaged or has failed
DTC: P1789 **1T CCM, MIL: No** **Years:** 2005, 2006, 2007 **Models:** All Models **Engines:** All **Transmissions:** A/T	**3-2 Timing/Coast Clutch Solenoid Signal Low Input** Engine started, vehicle in gear at Cruise speed, and the PCM detected the malfunction 3-2 Timing or Coast Clutch solenoid circuit. **Possible Causes:** • 3-2 Timing or Coast Clutch solenoid circuit is shorted • 3-2 Timing solenoid is damaged or has failed • Coast Clutch solenoid is damaged or has failed
DTC: P1900 **1T CCM, MIL: No** **Years:** 2005, 2006, 2007 **Models:** All Models **Engines:** All **Transmissions:** A/T	**Transmission System Malfunction** Engine started, vehicle in gear at Cruise speed, and the PCM detected a malfunction in the Transmission System operation. **Possible Causes:** • Refer to the appropriate Transmission Repair Manual or information in electronic media to perform a complete diagnosis of the automatic transmission when this code is set
DTC: P1901 **1T CCM, MIL: No** **Years:** 2005, 2006, 2007 **Models:** All Models **Engines:** All **Transmissions:** A/T	**Transmission System Malfunction** Engine started, vehicle in gear at Cruise speed, and the PCM detected a malfunction in the Transmission System operation. **Possible Causes:** • Refer to the appropriate Transmission Repair Manual or information in electronic media to perform a complete diagnosis of the automatic transmission when this code is set.

Gas Engine OBD II Trouble Code List (P2xxx Codes)

DTC	Trouble Code Title, Conditions & Possible Causes
DTC: P2004 **1T CCM, MIL: No** **Years:** 2005, 2006, 2007 **Models:** Aviator, E-Series, F-Series, Explorer, Explorer Sport-Trac, Mark LT, Mountaineer **Engines:** All **Transmissions:** All	**Intake Air System Malfunction** Engine started, engine running at hot idle speed for one minute, and the PCM detected a problem in the Intake Air System operation. It should be noted that the throttle bore cannot be cleaned as any attempt to clean it will damage the throttle bore and plate. **Possible Causes:** • Test for a sticking Accelerator or speed control cable condition: Turn the key off and disconnect accelerator and speed control cable from the throttle body. Rotate the throttle body linkage to determine if it rotates freely (the throttle body may have failed). • Check the air cleaner and air inlet assembly for restrictions • Check the IAC motor response (it may be damaged or sticking) • Check the PCV system (valve and hoses) for leaks or plugging • Check for signs of vacuum leaks in the engine or components • Test TP sensor signal (due a sweep test at key on, engine off)

DTC	Trouble Code Title, Conditions & Possible Causes
DTC: P2005 **1T CCM, MIL: No** **Years:** 2005, 2006, 2007 **Models:** Aviator, E-Series, F-Series, Explorer, Explorer Sport-Trac, Mark LT, Mountaineer **Engines:** All **Transmissions:** All	**Intake Air System Malfunction** Engine started, engine running at hot idle speed for one minute, and the PCM detected a problem in the Intake Air System operation. It should be noted that the throttle bore cannot be cleaned as any attempt to clean it will damage the throttle bore and plate. **Possible Causes:** • Test for a sticking Accelerator or speed control cable condition: Turn the key off and disconnect accelerator and speed control cable from the throttle body. Rotate the throttle body linkage to determine if it rotates freely (the throttle body may have failed). • Check the air cleaner and air inlet assembly for restrictions • Check the IAC motor response (it may be damaged or sticking) • Check the PCV system (valve and hoses) for leaks or plugging • Check for signs of vacuum leaks in the engine or components • Test TP sensor signal (due a sweep test at key on, engine off)
DTC: P2006 **1T CCM, MIL: No** **Years:** 2005, 2006, 2007 **Models:** Aviator, E-Series, F-Series, Explorer, Explorer Sport-Trac, Mark LT, Mountaineer **Engines:** All **Transmissions:** All	**Intake Air System Malfunction** Engine started, engine running at hot idle speed for one minute, and the PCM detected a problem in the Intake Air System operation. It should be noted that the throttle bore cannot be cleaned as any attempt to clean it will damage the throttle bore and plate. **Possible Causes:** • Test for a sticking Accelerator or speed control cable condition: Turn the key off and disconnect accelerator and speed control cable from the throttle body. Rotate the throttle body linkage to determine if it rotates freely (the throttle body may have failed). • Check the air cleaner and air inlet assembly for restrictions • Check the IAC motor response (it may be damaged or sticking) • Check the PCV system (valve and hoses) for leaks or plugging • Check for signs of vacuum leaks in the engine or components • Test TP sensor signal (due a sweep test at key on, engine off)
DTC: P2008 **1T CCM, MIL: No** **Years:** 2005, 2006, 2007 **Models:** Aviator, E-Series, F-Series, Explorer, Explorer Sport-Trac, Mark LT, Mountaineer **Engines:** All **Transmissions:** All	**Intake Air System Malfunction** Engine started, engine running at hot idle speed for one minute, and the PCM detected a problem in the Intake Air System operation. It should be noted that the throttle bore cannot be cleaned as any attempt to clean it will damage the throttle bore and plate. **Possible Causes:** • Accelerator or speed control cable sticking or binding. To test for this condition, turn the key off. Then disconnect the accelerator and speed control cable from the throttle body. Then rotate the throttle body linkage to determine if it rotates freely. If it is sticking, the throttle body may need replacement. • Check the air cleaner and air inlet assembly for restrictions • Check the IAC motor response (it may be damaged or sticking) • Check the PCV system (valve and hoses) for leaks or plugging • Check for signs of vacuum leaks in the engine or components • Test TP sensor signal (due a sweep test at key on, engine off)
DTC: P2014 **1T CCM, MIL: No** **Years:** 2005, 2006, 2007 **Models:** Aviator, E-Series, F-Series, Explorer, Explorer Sport-Trac, Mark LT, Mountaineer **Engines:** All **Transmissions:** All	**Intake Air System Malfunction** Engine started, engine running at hot idle speed for one minute, and the PCM detected a problem in the Intake Air System operation. It should be noted that the throttle bore cannot be cleaned as any attempt to clean it will damage the throttle bore and plate. **Possible Causes:** • Accelerator or speed control cable sticking or binding. To test for this condition, turn the key off. Then disconnect the accelerator and speed control cable from the throttle body. Then rotate the throttle body linkage to determine if it rotates freely. If it is sticking, the throttle body may need replacement. • Check the air cleaner and air inlet assembly for restrictions • Check the IAC motor response (it may be damaged or sticking) • Check the PCV system (valve and hoses) for leaks or plugging • Check for signs of vacuum leaks in the engine or components • Test TP sensor signal (due a sweep test at key on, engine off)

DTC	Trouble Code Title, Conditions & Possible Causes
DTC: P2019 **1T CCM, MIL: No** **Years:** 2005, 2006, 2007 **Models:** Aviator, E-Series, F-Series, Explorer, Explorer Sport-Trac, Mark LT, Mountaineer **Engines:** All **Transmissions:** All	**Intake Air System Malfunction** Engine started, engine running at hot idle speed for one minute, and the PCM detected a problem in the Intake Air System operation. It should be noted that the throttle bore cannot be cleaned as any attempt to clean it will damage the throttle bore and plate. **Possible Causes:** • Accelerator or speed control cable sticking or binding. To test these devices, turn the key off and disconnect the accelerator and speed control cable from the throttle body. Then rotate the throttle body linkage to determine if it rotates freely. • Check the air cleaner and air inlet assembly for restrictions • Check the IAC motor response (it may be damaged or sticking) • Check the PCV system (valve and hoses) for leaks or plugging • Check for signs of vacuum leaks in the engine or components • Test TP sensor signal (due a sweep test at key on, engine off)
DTC: P2070 **2T CCM, MIL: No** **Years:** 2005, 2006, 2007 **Models:** E-Series, F-Series **Engines:** 4.6L VIN W, 5.4L VIN L **Transmissions:** All	**Intake Manifold Runner Control Malfunction (Stuck Open)** Key on or engine running; and the PCM detected an unexpected low voltage condition on the Intake Manifold Runner Control circuit during the CCM test period (i.e., the valve may be stuck open). **Possible Causes:** • IMRC signal circuit shorted to chassis ground • IMRC signal circuit shorted to sensor ground • IMRC actuator is damaged or has failed • PCM has failed
DTC: P2070 **2T CCM, MIL: No** **Years:** 2005, 2006, 2007 **Models:** Aviator **Engines:** 4.6L VIN H **Transmissions:** All	**Long / Short Runner Control Circuit Malfunction (Open)** Key on or engine running; and the PCM detected an unexpected low voltage condition on the Long / Short Runner Control (LSRC) signal circuit during the test (i.e., the valve may be stuck open). The PCM uses the Intake Manifold Communication Control (IMCC) signal to monitor the status of the Long / Short Runner Control position. **Possible Causes:** • LSRC signal circuit is shorted to chassis ground • LSRC signal circuit is shorted to sensor ground • LSRC actuator assembly is damaged or failed • PCM has failed
DTC: P2071 **2T CCM, MIL: No** **Years:** 2005, 2006, 2007 **Models:** E-Series, F-Series **Engines:** 4.6L VIN W, 5.4L VIN L **Transmissions:** All	**Intake Manifold Runner Control Circuit Malfunction (Stuck Closed)** Key on or engine running; and the PCM detected an unexpected high voltage condition on the Intake Manifold Runner Control (IMRC) circuit during the CCM test (i.e., the valve may be stuck closed). **Possible Causes:** • IMRC monitor signal circuit is open • IMRC power circuit (VPWR) is open • IMRC actuator is damaged or has failed • PCM has failed
DTC: P2071 **2T CCM, MIL: No** **Years:** 2005, 2006, 2007 **Models:** Aviator **Engines:** 4.6L VIN H **Transmissions:** All	**Long / Short Runner Control Circuit Malfunction (Stuck Closed)** Key on or engine running; and the PCM detected an unexpected high voltage condition on the Long / Short Runner Control (LSRC) circuit (i.e., the valve may be stuck closed). The PCM uses the IMCC signal to monitor the status of the Long / Short Runner Control valve. **Possible Causes:** • LSRC control (signal) circuit is open • LSRC power circuit (VPWR) is open • LSRC actuator assembly is damaged or failed • PCM has failed
DTC: P2075 **12T CCM, MIL: No** **Years:** 2005, 2006, 2007 **Models:** F-Series **Engines:** 4.2L VIN 2 **Transmissions:** All	**Intake Manifold Tuning Valve Monitor Circuit Malfunction** Key on or engine running; and the PCM detected an unexpected low or high voltage condition on the Intake Manifold Tuning Valve Monitor circuit during the CCM test period. **Possible Causes:** • IMTV monitor signal circuit is open • IMTV monitor signal circuit shorted to chassis ground • IMTV actuator is damaged or has failed • PCM has failed

DTC	Trouble Code Title, Conditions & Possible Causes
DTC: P2075 **2T CCM, MIL: No** **Years:** 2005, 2006, 2007 **Models:** E-Series, F-Series **Engines:** 4.6L VIN W, 5.4L VIN L **Transmissions:** All	**Intake Manifold Runner Control Monitor Circuit Malfunction** Key on or engine running; and the PCM detected an unexpected high voltage condition on the Intake Manifold Runner Control (IMRC) Monitor circuit during the CCM test period. **Possible Causes:** • IMRC monitor signal circuit is open • IMRC monitor signal circuit shorted to chassis ground • IMRC actuator is damaged or has failed • PCM has failed
DTC: P2075 **2T CCM, MIL: No** **Years:** 2005, 2006, 2007 **Models:** Aviator **Engines:** 4.6L VIN H **Transmissions:** All	**Long / Short Runner Control Monitor Circuit Malfunction** Key on or engine running; and the PCM detected an unexpected low or high voltage condition on the Intake Manifold Communication Control (IMCC) Monitor circuit during the CCM test period. **Possible Causes:** • LSRC control (signal) circuit is open • LSRC control (signal) circuit is shorted to chassis ground • LSRC actuator assembly is damaged or failed • PCM has failed
DTC: P2195 **2T CCM, MIL: No** **Years:** 2005, 2006, 2007 **Models:** All Models **Engines:** All **Transmissions:** All	**Lack of HO2S-11 Switching, Sensor Indicates Lean** DTC P0300-P0310 not set, engine running in closed loop, and the PCM detected the HO2S indicated a lean signal, or it could no longer control Fuel Trim because it was at lean limit. **Possible Causes:** • Base engine problems: engine oil level high, camshaft timing error, cylinder compression low, exhaust leaks in front of HO2S • EGR System problem: EGR valve is stuck open, the gasket is leaking, or the EVR diaphragm is leaking • Fuel System problem: damaged fuel pressure regulator or extremely low fuel pressure • HO2S problems: HO2S circuit is open or shorted in the wiring harness or the HO2S is damaged or it has failed • Induction System problems: air leaks after the MAF sensor, PCV system leaks, engine vacuum leaks or dip stick not seated
DTC: P2196 **2T CCM, MIL: No** **Years:** 2005, 2006, 2007 **Models:** All Models **Engines:** All **Transmissions:** All	**Lack of HO2S-21 Switching, Sensor Indicates Rich** DTC P0300-P0310 not set, engine running in closed loop, and the PCM detected the HO2S indicated a rich signal, or it could no longer control Fuel Trim because it was at its rich limit. **Possible Causes:** • Base engine problems: engine oil level high, camshaft timing error, cylinder compression low, exhaust leaks in front of HO2S • Fuel System problem: excessive fuel pressure, leaking fuel injectors, fuel pressure regulator leaking • HO2S problems: HO2S circuit is open or shorted in the wiring harness, the HO2S signal circuit is contacting moisture in harness connector, or the HO2S is damaged or it has failed
DTC: P2197 **2T CCM, MIL: No** **Years:** 2005, 2006, 2007 **Models:** All Models **Engines:** All **Transmissions:** All	**Lack of HO2S-21 Switching, Sensor Indicates Lean** DTC P0300-P0310 not set, engine running in closed loop, and the PCM detected the HO2S indicated a lean signal, or it could no longer control Fuel Trim because it was at lean limit. **Possible Causes:** • Base engine problems: engine oil level high, camshaft timing error, cylinder compression low, exhaust leaks in front of HO2S • EGR System problem: EGR valve is stuck open, the gasket is leaking, or the EVR diaphragm is leaking • Fuel System problem: damaged fuel pressure regulator or extremely low fuel pressure • HO2S problems: HO2S circuit is open or shorted in the wiring harness or the HO2S is damaged or it has failed • Induction System problems: air leaks after the MAF sensor, PCV system leaks, engine vacuum leaks or dip stick not seated

DTC	Trouble Code Title, Conditions & Possible Causes
DTC: P2198 **2T CCM, MIL: No** **Years:** 2005, 2006, 2007 **Models:** All Models **Engines:** All **Transmissions:** All	**Lack of HO2S-21 Switching, Sensor Indicates Rich** DTC P0300-P0310 not set, engine running in closed loop, and the PCM detected the HO2S indicated a rich signal, or it could no longer control Fuel Trim because it was at its rich limit. **Possible Causes:** • Base engine problems: engine oil level high, camshaft timing error, cylinder compression low, exhaust leaks in front of HO2S • Fuel System problem: excessive fuel pressure, leaking fuel injectors, fuel pressure regulator leaking • HO2S problems: HO2S circuit is open or shorted in the wiring harness, the HO2S signal circuit is contacting moisture in harness connector, or the HO2S is damaged or it failed
DTC: P2270 **2T CCM, MIL: No** **Years:** 2005, 2006, 2007 **Models:** All Models **Engines:** All **Transmissions:** All	**Lack of HO2S-12 Switching, Sensor Indicates Lean** DTC P0300-P0310 not set, engine running in closed loop, and the PCM detected the HO2S indicated a lean signal, or it could no longer control Fuel Trim because it was at lean limit. **Possible Causes:** • Base engine problems: engine oil level high, camshaft timing error, cylinder compression low, exhaust leaks in front of HO2S • EGR System problem: EGR valve is stuck open, the gasket is leaking, or the EVR diaphragm is leaking • Fuel System problem: damaged fuel pressure regulator or extremely low fuel pressure • HO2S problems: HO2S circuit is open or shorted in the wiring harness or the HO2S is damaged or it has failed • Induction System problems: air leaks after the MAF sensor, PCV system leaks, engine vacuum leaks or dip stick not seated
DTC: P2271 **2T CCM, MIL: No** **Years:** 2005, 2006, 2007 **Models:** All Models **Engines:** All **Transmissions:** All	**Lack of HO2S-12 Switching, Sensor Indicates Rich** DTC P0300-P0310 not set, engine running in closed loop, and the PCM detected the HO2S indicated a rich signal, or it could no longer control Fuel Trim because it was at its rich limit. **Possible Causes:** • Base engine problems: engine oil level high, camshaft timing error, cylinder compression low, exhaust leaks in front of HO2S • Fuel System problem: excessive fuel pressure, leaking fuel injectors, fuel pressure regulator leaking • HO2S problems: HO2S circuit is open or shorted in the wiring harness, the HO2S signal circuit is contacting moisture in harness connector, or the HO2S is damaged or it failed
DTC: P2272 **2T CCM, MIL: No** **Years:** 2005, 2006, 2007 **Models:** All Models **Engines:** All **Transmissions:** All	**Lack of HO2S-22 Switching, Sensor Indicates Lean** DTC P0300-P0310 not set, engine running in closed loop, and the PCM detected the HO2S indicated a lean signal, or it could no longer control Fuel Trim because it was at lean limit. **Possible Causes:** • Base engine problems: engine oil level high, camshaft timing error, cylinder compression low, exhaust leaks in front of HO2S • EGR System problem: EGR valve is stuck open, the gasket is leaking, or the EVR diaphragm is leaking • Fuel System problem: damaged fuel pressure regulator or extremely low fuel pressure • HO2S problems: HO2S circuit is open or shorted in the wiring harness or the HO2S is damaged or it has failed • Induction System problems: air leaks after the MAF sensor, PCV system leaks, engine vacuum leaks or dip stick not seated
DTC: P2273 **2T CCM, MIL: No** **Years:** 2005, 2006, 2007 **Models:** All Models **Engines:** All **Transmissions:** All	**Lack of HO2S-22 Switching, Sensor Indicates Rich** DTC P0300-P0310 not set, engine running in closed loop, and the PCM detected the HO2S indicated a rich signal, or it could no longer control Fuel Trim because it was at its rich limit. **Possible Causes:** • Base engine problems: engine oil level high, camshaft timing error, cylinder compression low, exhaust leaks in front of HO2S • Fuel System problem: excessive fuel pressure, leaking fuel injectors, fuel pressure regulator leaking • HO2S problems: HO2S circuit is open or shorted in the wiring harness, the HO2S signal circuit is contacting moisture in harness connector, or the HO2S is damaged or it failed

Gas Engine OBD II Trouble Code List (Uxxxx Codes)

DTC	Trouble Code Title, Conditions & Possible Causes
DTC: U1011 **1T PCM, MIL: No** **Years:** 2005, 2006, 2007 **Models:** All Models **Engines:** All **Transmissions:** All	**Data Circuit Message** Key on, and the PCM detected that invalid or Missing Data from the Engine Air Intake system was received on the SCP data bus. **Note: Network codes occur during module-to-module communication failures. Invalid and Missing data network faults are outlined below.** **Possible Causes:** • Invalid Data: Data transferred in normal inter-module messages with known invalid data. Transmitting module will set the code. • Missing Network Data: Missing message fault logged by a module upon failure to receive a message from another module within a defined retry period.
DTC: U1020 **1T PCM, MIL: No** **Years:** 2005, 2006, 2007 **Models:** All Models **Engines:** All **Transmissions:** All	**Data Circuit Message** Key on, and the PCM detected that invalid or Missing Data from the Air Conditioning system was received on the SCP data bus. **Note: Network codes occur during module-to-module communication failures. Invalid and Missing data network faults are outlined below.** **Possible Causes:** • Invalid Data: Data transferred in normal inter-module messages with known invalid data. Transmitting module will set the code. • Missing Network Data: Missing message fault logged by a module upon failure to receive a message from another module within a defined retry period.
DTC: U1021 **1T PCM, MIL: No** **Years:** 2005, 2006, 2007 **Models:** All Models **Engines:** All **Transmissions:** All	**Data Circuit Message** Key on, and the PCM detected that invalid or Missing Data from the Air Conditioning Clutch status was received on the SCP data bus. **Note: Network codes occur during module-to-module communication failures. Invalid and Missing data network faults are outlined below.** **Possible Causes:** • Invalid Data: Data transferred in normal inter-module messages with known invalid data. Transmitting module will set the code. • Missing Network Data: Missing message fault logged by a module upon failure to receive a message from another module within a defined retry period.
DTC: U1037 **1T PCM, MIL: No** **Years:** 2005, 2006, 2007 **Models:** All Models **Engines:** All **Transmissions:** All	**Data Circuit Message** Key on, and the PCM detected that invalid or Missing Data from the Telltale Lamp Module was received on the SCP data bus. **Note: Network codes occur during module-to-module communication failures. Invalid and Missing data network faults are outlined below.** **Possible Causes:** • Invalid Data: Data transferred in normal inter-module messages with known invalid data. Transmitting module will set the code. • Missing Network Data: Missing message fault logged by a module upon failure to receive a message from another module within a defined retry period.
DTC: U1039 **1T PCM, MIL: No** **Years:** 2005, 2006, 2007 **Models:** All Models **Engines:** All **Transmissions:** All	**Data Circuit Message** Key on, and the PCM detected that invalid or Missing Data from the Vehicle Speed Sensor was received on the SCP data bus. **Note: Network codes occur during module-to-module communication failures. Invalid and Missing data network faults are outlined below.** **Possible Causes:** • Invalid Data: Data transferred in normal inter-module messages with known invalid data. Transmitting module will set the code. • Missing Network Data: Missing message fault logged by a module upon failure to receive a message from another module within a defined retry period. • TSB 01-21-13 contains a repair procedure for this trouble code
DTC: U1041 **1T PCM, MIL: No** **Years:** 2005, 2006, 2007 **Models:** All Models **Engines:** All **Transmissions:** All	**Data Circuit Message** Key on, and the PCM detected that invalid or Missing Data from the Vehicle Speed Sensor was received on the SCP data bus. **Note: Network codes occur during module-to-module communication failures. Invalid and Missing data network faults are outlined below.** **Possible Causes:** • Invalid Data: Data transferred in normal inter-module messages with known invalid data. Transmitting module will set the code. • Missing Network Data: Missing message fault logged by a module upon failure to receive a message from another module within a defined retry period.

DTC	Trouble Code Title, Conditions & Possible Causes
DTC: U1051 **1T PCM, MIL: No** **Years:** 2005, 2006, 2007 **Models:** All Models **Engines:** All **Transmissions:** All	**Data Circuit Message** Key on, and the PCM detected that invalid or Missing Data from the Antilock Brake System was received on the SCP data bus. **Note: Network codes occur during module-to-module communication failures. Invalid and Missing data network faults are outlined below.** **Possible Causes:** • Invalid Data: Data transferred in normal inter-module messages with known invalid data. Transmitting module will set the code. • Missing Network Data: Missing message fault logged by a module upon failure to receive a message from another module within a defined retry period.
DTC: U1071 **1T PCM, MIL: No** **Years:** 2005, 2006, 2007 **Models:** All Models **Engines:** All **Transmissions:** All	**Data Circuit Message** Key on, and the PCM detected that invalid or Missing Data from the Engine Sensor was received on the SCP data bus. **Note: Network codes occur during module-to-module communication failures. Invalid and Missing data network faults are outlined below.** **Possible Causes:** • Invalid Data: Data transferred in normal inter-module messages with known invalid data. Transmitting module will set the code. • Missing Network Data: Missing message fault logged by a module upon failure to receive a message from another module within a defined retry period.
DTC: U1073 **1T PCM, MIL: No** **Years:** 2005, 2006, 2007 **Models:** All Models **Engines:** All **Transmissions:** All	**Data Circuit Message** Key on, and the PCM detected that invalid or Missing Data from the Engine Coolant Fan Status was received on the SCP data bus. **Note: Network codes occur during module-to-module communication failures. Invalid and Missing data network faults are outlined below.** **Possible Causes:** • Invalid Data: Data transferred in normal inter-module messages with known invalid data. Transmitting module will set the code. • Missing Network Data: Missing message fault logged by a module upon failure to receive a message from another module within a defined retry period.
DTC: U1089 **1T PCM, MIL: No** **Years:** 2005, 2006, 2007 **Models:** All Models **Engines:** All **Transmissions:** All	**Data Circuit Message** Key on, and the PCM detected that invalid or Missing Data from the Suspension System Module was received on the SCP data bus. **Note: Network codes occur during module-to-module communication failures. Invalid and Missing data network faults are outlined below.** **Possible Causes:** • Invalid Data: Data transferred in normal inter-module messages with known invalid data. Transmitting module will set the code. • Missing Network Data: Missing message fault logged by a module upon failure to receive a message from another module within a defined retry period.
DTC: U1098 **1T PCM, MIL: No** **Years:** 2005, 2006, 2007 **Models:** All Models **Engines:** All **Transmissions:** All	**Data Circuit Message** Key on, and the PCM detected that invalid or Missing Data from the Vehicle Speed Control Module was received on the SCP data bus. **Note: Network codes occur during module-to-module communication failures. Invalid and Missing data network faults are outlined below.** **Possible Causes:** • Invalid Data: Data transferred in normal inter-module messages with known invalid data. Transmitting module will set the code. • Missing Network Data: Missing message fault logged by a module upon failure to receive a message from another module within a defined retry period.
DTC: U1130 **1T PCM, MIL: No** **Years:** 2005, 2006, 2007 **Models:** All Models **Engines:** All **Transmissions:** All	**Data Circuit Message** Key on, and the PCM detected that invalid or Missing Data from the Fuel System was received on the SCP data bus. **Note: Network codes occur during module-to-module communication failures. Invalid and Missing data network faults are outlined below.** **Possible Causes:** • Invalid Data: Data transferred in normal inter-module messages with known invalid data. Transmitting module will set the code. • Missing Network Data: Missing message fault logged by a module upon failure to receive a message from another module within a defined retry period.

DTC	Trouble Code Title, Conditions & Possible Causes
DTC: U1131 **1T PCM, MIL: No** **Years:** 2005, 2006, 2007 **Models:** All Models **Engines:** All **Transmissions:** All	**Data Circuit Message** Key on, and the PCM detected that invalid or Missing Data from the Fuel System was received on the SCP data bus. **Note: Network codes occur during module-to-module communication failures. Invalid and Missing data network faults are outlined below.** **Possible Causes:** • Invalid Data: Data transferred in normal inter-module messages with known invalid data. Transmitting module will set the code. • Missing Network Data: Missing message fault logged by a module upon failure to receive a message from another module within a defined retry period.
DTC: U1135 **1T PCM, MIL: No** **Years:** 2005, 2006, 2007 **Models:** All Models **Engines:** All **Transmissions:** All	**Data Circuit Message** Key on, and the PCM detected that invalid or Missing Data from the Ignition Switch Signal was received on the SCP data bus. **Note: Network codes occur during module-to-module communication failures. Invalid and Missing data network faults are outlined below.** **Possible Causes:** • Invalid Data: Data transferred in normal inter-module messages with known invalid data. Transmitting module will set the code. • Missing Network Data: Missing message fault logged by a module upon failure to receive a message from another module within a defined retry period.
DTC: U1147 **1T PCM, MIL: No** **Years:** 2005, 2006, 2007 **Models:** All Models **Engines:** All **Transmissions:** All	**Data Circuit Message** Key on, and the PCM detected that invalid or Missing Data from the Vehicle Security System was received on the SCP data bus. **Note: Network codes occur during module-to-module communication failures. Invalid and Missing data network faults are outlined below.** **Possible Causes:** • Invalid Data: Data transferred in normal inter-module messages with known invalid data. Transmitting module will set the code. • Missing Network Data: Missing message fault logged by a module upon failure to receive a message from another module within a defined retry period.
DTC: U1243 **1T PCM, MIL: No** **Years:** 2005, 2006, 2007 **Models:** All Models **Engines:** All **Transmissions:** All	**Data Circuit Message** Key on, and the PCM detected that invalid or Missing Data from the Exterior Environment System was received on the SCP data bus. **Note: Network codes occur during module-to-module communication failures. Invalid and Missing data network faults are outlined below.** **Possible Causes:** • Invalid Data: Data transferred in normal inter-module messages with known invalid data. Transmitting module will set the code. • Missing Network Data: Missing message fault logged by a module upon failure to receive a message from another module within a defined retry period.
DTC: U1256 **1T PCM, MIL: No** **Years:** 2005, 2006, 2007 **Models:** All Models **Engines:** All **Transmissions:** All	**Data Circuit Message** Key on, and the PCM detected a signal indicating a communication error had occurred with another module over the SCP data bus. **Note: Network codes occur during module-to-module communication failures. Invalid and Missing data network faults are outlined below.** **Possible Causes:** • Invalid Data: Data transferred in normal inter-module messages with known invalid data. Transmitting module will set the code. • Missing Network Data: Missing message fault logged by a module upon failure to receive a message from another module within a defined retry period.
DTC: U1260 **1T PCM, MIL: No** **Years:** 2005, 2006, 2007 **Models:** All Models **Engines:** All **Transmissions:** All	**Data Circuit Message** Key on, and the PCM detected a signal that indicated an open or shorted condition was present in the SCP (+) bus circuit. **Note: Network codes occur during module-to-module communication failures. Invalid and Missing data network faults are outlined below.** **Possible Causes:** • Invalid Data: Data transferred in normal inter-module messages with known invalid data. Transmitting module will set the code. • Missing Network Data: Missing message fault logged by a module upon failure to receive a message from another module within a defined retry period.

DTC	Trouble Code Title, Conditions & Possible Causes
DTC: U1261 **1T PCM, MIL: No** **Years:** 2005, 2006, 2007 **Models:** All Models **Engines:** All **Transmissions:** All	**Data Circuit Message** Key on, and the PCM detected a signal that indicated an open or shorted condition was present in the SCP (-) bus circuit. **Note: Network codes occur during module-to-module communication failures. Invalid and Missing data network faults are outlined below.** **Possible Causes:** • Invalid Data: Data transferred in normal inter-module messages with known invalid data. Transmitting module will set the code. • Missing Network Data: Missing message fault logged by a module upon failure to receive a message from another module within a defined retry period.
DTC: U1262 **1T PCM, MIL: No** **Years:** 2005, 2006, 2007 **Models:** All Models **Engines:** All **Transmissions:** All	**Data Circuit Message** Key on, and the PCM detected a signal that indicated a fault was present in the SCP bus (perform the network communication tests). **Note: Network codes occur during module-to-module communication failures. Invalid and Missing data network faults are outlined below.** **Possible Causes:** • Invalid Data: Data transferred in normal inter-module messages with known invalid data. Transmitting module will set the code. • Missing Network Data: Missing message fault logged by a module upon failure to receive a message from another module within a defined retry period.
DTC: U1341 **1T PCM, MIL: No** **Years:** 2005, 2006, 2007 **Models:** All Models **Engines:** All **Transmissions:** All	**Data Circuit Message** Key on, and the PCM detected that invalid or Missing Data from the Function Read Vehicle Speed was received on the SCP data bus. **Note: Network codes occur during module-to-module communication failures. Invalid and Missing data network faults are outlined below.** **Possible Causes:** • Invalid Data: Data transferred in normal inter-module messages with known invalid data. Transmitting module will set the code. • Missing Network Data: Missing message fault logged by a module upon failure to receive a message from another module within a defined retry period.
DTC: U1451 **1T PCM, MIL: No** **Years:** 2005, 2006, 2007 **Models:** All Models **Engines:** All **Transmissions:** All	**Data Circuit Message** Key on, and the PCM detected that invalid or Missing Data from the Vehicle Antitheft Module was received on the SCP data bus. **Note: Network codes occur during module-to-module communication failures. Invalid and Missing data network faults are outlined below.** **Possible Causes:** • Invalid Data: Data transferred in normal inter-module messages with known invalid data. Transmitting module will set the code. • Missing Network Data: Missing message fault logged by a module upon failure to receive a message from another module within a defined retry period.
DTC: U2015 **1T PCM, MIL: No** **Years:** 2005, 2006, 2007 **Models:** All Models **Engines:** All **Transmissions:** All	**Data Circuit Message** Key on, and the PCM detected that invalid or Missing Data from the Function Read Vehicle Speed was received on the SCP data bus. **Note: Network codes occur during module-to-module communication failures. Invalid and Missing data network faults are outlined below.** **Possible Causes:** • Invalid Data: Data transferred in normal inter-module messages with known invalid data. Transmitting module will set the code. • Missing Network Data: Missing message fault logged by a module upon failure to receive a message from another module within a defined retry period.
DTC: U2195 **1T PCM, MIL: No** **Years:** 2005, 2006, 2007 **Models:** All Models **Engines:** All **Transmissions:** All	**Data Circuit Message** Key on, and the PCM detected an open or shorted condition in the Signal Link circuit (not on the SCP data bus circuits). **Note: Network codes occur during module-to-module communication failures. Invalid and Missing data network faults are outlined below.** **Possible Causes:** • Invalid Data: Data transferred in normal inter-module messages with known invalid data. Transmitting module will set the code. • Missing Network Data: Missing message fault logged by a module upon failure to receive a message from another module within a defined retry period.

DTC	Trouble Code Title, Conditions & Possible Causes
DTC: U2243 **1T PCM, MIL: No** **Years:** 2005, 2006, 2007 **Models:** All Models **Engines:** All **Transmissions:** All	**Data Circuit Message** Key on, and the PCM detected that invalid or Missing Data from the SCLM Status was received on the SCP data bus. **Note: Network codes occur during module-to-module communication failures. Invalid and Missing data network faults are outlined below.** **Possible Causes:** • Invalid Data: Data transferred in normal inter-module messages with known invalid data. Transmitting module will set the code. • Missing Network Data: Missing message fault logged by a module upon failure to receive a message from another module within a defined retry period.

GLOSSARY

ABS: Anti-lock braking system. An electro-mechanical braking system which is designed to minimize or prevent wheel lock-up during braking.

ABSOLUTE PRESSURE: Atmospheric (barometric) pressure plus the pressure gauge reading.

ACCELERATOR PUMP: A small pump located in the carburetor that feeds fuel into the air/fuel mixture during acceleration.

ACCUMULATOR: A device that controls shift quality by cushioning the shock of hydraulic oil pressure being applied to a clutch or band.

ACTUATING MECHANISM: The mechanical output devices of a hydraulic system, for example, clutch pistons and band servos.

ACTUATOR: The output component of a hydraulic or electronic system.

ADVANCE: Setting the ignition timing so that spark occurs earlier before the piston reaches top dead center (TDC).

ADAPTIVE MEMORY (ADAPTIVE STRATEGY): The learning ability of the TCM or PCM to redefine its decision-making process to provide optimum shift quality.

AFTER TOP DEAD CENTER (ATDC): The point after the piston reaches the top of its travel on the compression stroke.

AIR BAG: Device on the inside of the car designed to inflate on impact of crash, protecting the occupants of the car.

AIR CHARGE TEMPERATURE (ACT) SENSOR: The temperature of the airflow into the engine is measured by an ACT sensor, usually located in the lower intake manifold or air cleaner.

AIR CLEANER: An assembly consisting of a housing, filter and any connecting ductwork. The filter element is made up of a porous paper, sometimes with a wire mesh screening, and is designed to prevent airborne particles from entering the engine through the carburetor or throttle body.

AIR INJECTION: One method of reducing harmful exhaust emissions by injecting air into each of the exhaust ports of an engine. The fresh air entering the hot exhaust manifold causes any remaining fuel to be burned before it can exit the tailpipe.

AIR PUMP: An emission control device that supplies fresh air to the exhaust manifold to aid in more completely burning exhaust gases.

AIR/FUEL RATIO: The ratio of air-to-gasoline by weight in the fuel mixture drawn into the engine.

ALDL (assembly line diagnostic link): Electrical connector for scanning ECM/PCM/TCM input and output devices.

ALIGNMENT RACK: A special drive-on vehicle lift apparatus/measuring device used to adjust a vehicle's toe, caster and camber angles.

ALL WHEEL DRIVE: Term used to describe a full time four wheel drive system or any other vehicle drive system that continuously delivers power to all four wheels. This system is found primarily on station wagon vehicles and SUVs not utilized for significant off road use.

ALTERNATING CURRENT (AC): Electric current that flows first in one direction, then in the opposite direction, continually reversing flow.

ALTERNATOR: A device which produces AC (alternating current) which is converted to DC (direct current) to charge the car battery.

AMMETER: An instrument, calibrated in amperes, used to measure the flow of an electrical current in a circuit. Ammeters are always connected in series with the circuit being tested.

AMPERAGE: The total amount of current (amperes) flowing in a circuit.

AMPLIFIER: A device used in an electrical circuit to increase the voltage of an output signal.

AMP/HR. RATING (BATTERY): Measurement of the ability of a battery to deliver a stated amount of current for a stated period of time. The higher the amp/hr. rating, the better the battery.

AMPERE: The rate of flow of electrical current present when one volt of electrical pressure is applied against one ohm of electrical resistance.

ANALOG COMPUTER: Any microprocessor that uses similar (analogous) electrical signals to make its calculations.

ANODIZED: A special coating applied to the surface of aluminum valves for extended service life.

ANTIFREEZE: A substance (ethylene or propylene glycol) added to the coolant to prevent freezing in cold weather.

ANTI-FOAM AGENTS: Minimize fluid foaming from the whipping action encountered in the converter and planetary action.

ANTI-WEAR AGENTS: Zinc agents that control wear on the gears, bushings, and thrust washers.

ANTI-LOCK BRAKING SYSTEM: A supplementary system to the base hydraulic system that prevents sustained lock-up of the wheels during braking as well as automatically controlling wheel slip.

ANTI-ROLL BAR: See stabilizer bar.

ARC: A flow of electricity through the air between two electrodes or contact points that produces a spark.

ARMATURE: A laminated, soft iron core wrapped by a wire that converts electrical energy to mechanical energy as in a motor or relay. When rotated in a magnetic field, it changes mechanical energy into electrical energy as in a generator.

ATDC: After Top Dead Center.

ATF: Automatic transmission fluid.

ATMOSPHERIC PRESSURE: The pressure on the Earth's surface caused by the weight of the air in the atmosphere. At sea level, this pressure is 14.7 psi at 32°F (101 kPa at 0°C).

ATOMIZATION: The breaking down of a liquid into a fine mist that can be suspended in air.

AUXILIARY ADD-ON COOLER: A supplemental transmission fluid cooling device that is installed in series with the heat exchanger (cooler), located inside the radiator, to provide additional support to cool the hot fluid leaving the torque converter.

AUXILIARY PRESSURE: An added fluid pressure that is introduced into a regulator or balanced valve system to control valve movement. The auxiliary pressure itself can be either a fixed or a variable value. (See balanced valve; regulator valve.)

AWD: All wheel drive.

AXIAL FORCE: A side or end thrust force acting in or along the same plane as the power flow.

AXIAL PLAY: Movement parallel to a shaft or bearing bore.

AXLE CAPACITY: The maximum load-carrying capacity of the axle itself, as specified by the manufacturer. This is usually a higher number than the GAWR.

AXLE RATIO: This is a number (3.07:1, 4.56:1, for example) expressing the ratio between driveshaft revolutions and wheel revolutions. A low numerical ratio allows the engine to work easier because it doesn't have to turn as fast. A high numerical ratio means that the engine has to turn more rpm's to move the wheels through the same number of turns.

BACKFIRE: The sudden combustion of gases in the intake or exhaust system that results in a loud explosion.

BACKLASH: The clearance or play between two parts, such as meshed gears.

BACKPRESSURE: Restrictions in the exhaust system that slow the exit of exhaust gases from the combustion chamber.

BAKELITE®: A heat resistant, plastic insulator material commonly used in printed circuit boards and transistorized components.

BALANCED VALVE: A valve that is positioned by opposing auxiliary hydraulic pressures and/or spring force. Examples include mainline regulator, throttle, and governor valves. (See regulator valve.)

BAND: A flexible ring of steel with an inner lining of friction material. When tightened around the outside of a drum, a planetary member is held stationary to the transmission/transaxle case.

BALL BEARING: A bearing made up of hardened inner and outer races between which hardened steel balls roll.

BALL JOINT: A ball and matching socket connecting suspension components (steering knuckle to lower control arms). It permits rotating movement in any direction between the components that are joined.

BARO (BAROMETRIC PRESSURE SENSOR): Measures the change in the intake manifold pressure caused by changes in altitude.

BAROMETRIC MANIFOLD ABSOLUTE PRESSURE (BMAP) SENSOR: Operates similarly to a conventional MAP sensor; reads intake manifold pressure and is also responsible for determining altitude and barometric pressure prior to engine operation.

BAROMETRIC PRESSURE: (See atmospheric pressure.)

BALLAST RESISTOR: A resistor in the primary ignition circuit that lowers voltage after the engine is started to reduce wear on ignition components.

BATTERY: A direct current electrical storage unit, consisting of the basic active materials of lead and sulfuric acid, which converts chemical energy into electrical energy. Used to provide current for the operation of the starter as well as other equipment, such as the radio, lighting, etc.

BEAD: The portion of a tire that holds it on the rim.

BEARING: A friction reducing, supportive device usually located between a stationary part and a moving part.

BEFORE TOP DEAD CENTER (BTDC): The point just before the piston reaches the top of its travel on the compression stroke.

BELTED TIRE: Tire construction similar to bias-ply tires, but using two or more layers of reinforced belts between body plies and the tread.

BEZEL: Piece of metal surrounding radio, headlights, gauges or similar components; sometimes used to hold the glass face of a gauge in the dash.

BIAS-PLY TIRE: Tire construction, using body ply reinforcing cords which run at alternating angles to the center line of the tread.

BI-METAL TEMPERATURE SENSOR: Any sensor or switch made of two dissimilar types of metal that bend when heated or cooled due to the different expansion rates of the alloys. These types of sensors usually function as an on/off switch.

BLOCK: See Engine Block.

BLOW-BY: Combustion gases, composed of water vapor and unburned fuel, that leak past the piston rings into the crankcase during normal engine operation. These gases are removed by the PCV system to prevent the buildup of harmful acids in the crankcase.

BOOK TIME: See Labor Time.

BOOK VALUE: The average value of a car, widely used to determine trade-in and resale value.

BOOST VALVE: Used at the base of the regulator valve to increase mainline pressure.

BORE: Diameter of a cylinder.

BRAKE CALIPER: The housing that fits over the brake disc. The caliper holds the brake pads, which are pressed against the discs by the caliper pistons when the brake pedal is depressed.

BRAKE HORSEPOWER (BHP): The actual horsepower available at the engine flywheel as measured by a dynamometer.

BRAKE FADE: Loss of braking power, usually caused by excessive heat after repeated brake applications.

BRAKE HORSEPOWER: Usable horsepower of an engine measured at the crankshaft.

BRAKE PAD: A brake shoe and lining assembly used with disc brakes.

BRAKE PROPORTIONING VALVE: A valve on the master cylinder which restricts hydraulic brake pressure to the wheels to a specified amount, preventing wheel lock-up.

BREAKAWAY: Often used by Chrysler to identify first-gear operation in D and 2 ranges. In these ranges, first-gear operation depends on a one-way roller clutch that holds on acceleration and releases (breaks away) on deceleration, resulting in a freewheeling coast-down condition.

BRAKE SHOE: The backing for the brake lining. The term is, however, usually applied to the assembly of the brake backing and lining.

BREAKER POINTS: A set of points inside the distributor, operated by a cam, which make and break the ignition circuit.

BRINNELLING: A wear pattern identified by a series of indentations at regular intervals. This condition is caused by a lack of lube, overload situations, and/or vibrations.

BTDC: Before Top Dead Center.

BUMP: Sudden and forceful apply of a clutch or band.

BUSHING: A liner, usually removable, for a bearing; an anti-friction liner used in place of a bearing.

CALIFORNIA ENGINE: An engine certified by the EPA for use in California only; conforms to more stringent emission regulations than Federal engine.

CALIPER: A hydraulically activated device in a disc brake system,

which is mounted straddling the brake rotor (disc). The caliper contains at least one piston and two brake pads. Hydraulic pressure on the piston(s) forces the pads against the rotor.

CAPACITY: The quantity of electricity that can be delivered from a unit, as from a battery in ampere-hours, or output, as from a generator.

CAMBER: One of the factors of wheel alignment. Viewed from the front of the car, it is the inward or outward tilt of the wheel. The top of the tire will lean outward (positive camber) or inward (negative camber).

CAMSHAFT: A shaft in the engine on which are the lobes (cams) which operate the valves. The camshaft is driven by the crankshaft, via a belt, chain or gears, at one half the crankshaft speed.

CAPACITOR: A device which stores an electrical charge.

CARBON MONOXIDE (CO): A colorless, odorless gas given off as a normal byproduct of combustion. It is poisonous and extremely dangerous in confined areas, building up slowly to toxic levels without warning if adequate ventilation is not available.

CARBURETOR: A device, usually mounted on the intake manifold of an engine, which mixes the air and fuel in the proper proportion to allow even combustion.

CASTER: The forward or rearward tilt of an imaginary line drawn through the upper ball joint and the center of the wheel. Viewed from the sides, positive caster (forward tilt) lends directional stability, while negative caster (rearward tilt) produces instability.

CATALYTIC CONVERTER: A device installed in the exhaust system, like a muffler, that converts harmful byproducts of combustion into carbon dioxide and water vapor by means of a heat-producing chemical reaction.

CENTRIFUGAL ADVANCE: A mechanical method of advancing the spark timing by using flyweights in the distributor that react to centrifugal force generated by the distributor shaft rotation.

CENTRIFUGAL FORCE: The outward pull of a revolving object, away from the center of revolution. Centrifugal force increases with the speed of rotation.

CETANE RATING: A measure of the ignition value of diesel fuel. The higher the cetane rating, the better the fuel. Diesel fuel cetane rating is roughly comparable to gasoline octane rating.

CHECK VALVE: Any one-way valve installed to permit the flow of air, fuel or vacuum in one direction only.

CHOKE: The valve/plate that restricts the amount of air entering an engine on the induction stroke, thereby enriching the air/fuel ratio.

CHUGGLE: Bucking or jerking condition that may be engine related and may be most noticeable when converter clutch is engaged; similar to the feel of towing a trailer.

CIRCLIP: A split steel snapring that fits into a groove to hold various parts in place.

CIRCUIT BREAKER: A switch which protects an electrical circuit from overload by opening the circuit when the current flow exceeds a pre-determined level. Some circuit breakers must be reset manually, while most reset automatically.

CIRCUIT: Any unbroken path through which an electrical current can flow. Also used to describe fuel flow in some instances.

CIRCUIT, BYPASS: Another circuit in parallel with the major circuit through which power is diverted.

CIRCUIT, CLOSED: An electrical circuit in which there is no interruption of current flow.

CIRCUIT, GROUND: The non-insulated portion of a complete circuit used as a common potential point. In automotive circuits, the ground is composed of metal parts, such as the engine, body sheet metal, and frame and is usually a negative potential.

CIRCUIT, HOT: That portion of a circuit not at ground potential. The hot circuit is usually insulated and is connected to the positive side of the battery.

CIRCUIT, OPEN: A break or lack of contact in an electrical circuit, either intentional (switch) or unintentional (bad connection or broken wire).

CIRCUIT, PARALLEL: A circuit having two or more paths for current flow with common positive and negative tie points. The same voltage is applied to each load device or parallel branch.

CIRCUIT, SERIES: An electrical system in which separate parts are connected end to end, using one wire, to form a single path for current to flow.

CIRCUIT, SHORT: A circuit that is accidentally completed in an electrical path for which it was not intended.

CLAMPING (ISOLATION) DIODES: Diodes positioned in a circuit to prevent self-induction from damaging electronic components.

CLEARCOAT: A transparent layer which, when sprayed over a vehicle's paint job, adds gloss and depth as well as an additional protective coating to the finish.

CLUTCH: Part of the power train used to connect/disconnect power to the rear wheels.

CLUTCH, FLUID: The same as a fluid coupling. A fluid clutch or coupling performs the same function as a friction clutch by utilizing fluid friction and inertia as opposed to solid friction used by a friction clutch. (See fluid coupling.)

CLUTCH, FRICTION: A coupling device that provides a means of smooth and positive engagement and disengagement of engine torque to the vehicle powertrain. Transmission of power through the clutch is accomplished by bringing one or more rotating drive members into contact with complementing driven members.

COAST: Vehicle deceleration caused by engine braking conditions.

COEFFICIENT OF FRICTION: The amount of surface tension between two contacting surfaces; identified by a scientifically calculated number.

COIL: Part of the ignition system that boosts the relatively low voltage supplied by the car's electrical system to the high voltage required to fire the spark plugs.

COMBINATION MANIFOLD: An assembly which includes both the intake and exhaust manifolds in one casting.

COMBINATION VALVE: A device used in some fuel systems that routes fuel vapors to a charcoal storage canister instead of venting them into the atmosphere. The valve relieves fuel tank pressure and allows fresh air into the tank as the fuel level drops to prevent a vapor lock situation.

COMBUSTION CHAMBER: The part of the engine in the cylinder head where combustion takes place.

COMPOUND GEAR: A gear consisting of two or more simple gears with a common shaft.

COMPOUND PLANETARY: A gearset that has more than the three elements found in a simple gearset and is constructed by combining members of two planetary gearsets to create additional gear ratio possibilities.

COMPRESSION CHECK: A test involving removing each spark plug and inserting a gauge. When the engine is cranked, the gauge will record a pressure reading in the individual cylinder. General operating condition can be determined from a compression check.

COMPRESSION RATIO: The ratio of the volume between the piston and cylinder head when the piston is at the bottom of its stroke (bottom dead center) and when the piston is at the top of its stroke (top dead center).

COMPUTER: An electronic control module that correlates input data according to prearranged engineered instructions; used for the management of an actuator system or systems.

CONDENSER: An electrical device which acts to store an electrical charge, preventing voltage surges.

2. A radiator-like device in the air conditioning system in which refrigerant gas condenses into a liquid, giving off heat.

CONDUCTOR: Any material through which an electrical current can be transmitted easily.

CONNECTING ROD: The connecting link between the crankshaft and piston.

CONSTANT VELOCITY JOINT: Type of universal joint in a halfshaft assembly in which the output shaft turns at a constant angular velocity without variation, provided that the speed of the input shaft is constant.

CONTINUITY: Continuous or complete circuit. Can be checked with an ohmmeter.

CONTROL ARM: The upper or lower suspension components which are mounted on the frame and support the ball joints and steering knuckles.

CONVENTIONAL IGNITION: Ignition system which uses breaker points.

CONVERTER: (See torque converter.)

CONVERTER LOCKUP: The switching from hydrodynamic to direct mechanical drive, usually through the application of a friction element called the converter clutch.

COOLANT: Mixture of water and anti-freeze circulated through the engine to carry off heat produced by the engine.

CORROSION INHIBITOR: An inhibitor in ATF that prevents corrosion of bushings, thrust washers, and oil cooler brazed joints.

COUNTERSHAFT: An intermediate shaft which is rotated by a mainshaft and transmits, in turn, that rotation to a working part.

COUPLING PHASE: Occurs when the torque converter is operating at its greatest hydraulic efficiency. The speed differential between the impeller and the turbine is at its minimum. At this point, the stator freewheels, and there is no torque multiplication.

CRANKCASE: The lower part of an engine in which the crankshaft and related parts operate.

CRANKSHAFT: Engine component (connected to pistons by connecting rods) which converts the reciprocating (up and down) motion of pistons to rotary motion used to turn the driveshaft.

CURB WEIGHT: The weight of a vehicle without passengers or payload, but including all fluids (oil, gas, coolant, etc.) and other equipment specified as standard.

CURRENT: The flow (or rate) of electrons moving through a circuit. Current is measured in amperes (amp).

CURRENT FLOW CONVENTIONAL: Current flows through a circuit from the positive terminal of the source to the negative terminal (plus to minus).

CURRENT FLOW, ELECTRON: Current or electrons flow from the negative terminal of the source, through the circuit, to the positive terminal (minus to plus).

CV-JOINT: Constant velocity joint.

CYCLIC VIBRATIONS: The off-center movement of a rotating object that is affected by its initial balance, speed of rotation, and working angles.

CYLINDER BLOCK: See engine block.

CYLINDER HEAD: The detachable portion of the engine, usually fastened to the top of the cylinder block and containing all or most of the combustion chambers. On overhead valve engines, it contains the valves and their operating parts. On overhead cam engines, it contains the camshaft as well.

CYLINDER: In an engine, the round hole in the engine block in which the piston(s) ride.

DATA LINK CONNECTOR (DLC): Current acronym/term applied to the federally mandated, diagnostic junction connector that is used to monitor ECM/PC/TCM inputs, processing strategies, and outputs including diagnostic trouble codes (DTCs).

DEAD CENTER: The extreme top or bottom of the piston stroke.

DECELERATION BUMP: When referring to a torque converter clutch in the applied position, a sudden release of the accelerator pedal causes a forceful reversal of power through the drivetrain (engine braking), just prior to the apply plate actually being released.

DELAYED (LATE OR EXTENDED): Condition where shift is expected but does not occur for a period of time, for example, where clutch or band engagement does not occur as quickly as expected during part throttle or wide open throttle apply of accelerator or when manually downshifting to a lower range.

DETENT: A spring-loaded plunger, pin, ball, or pawl used as a holding device on a ratchet wheel or shaft. In automatic transmissions, a detent mechanism is used for locking the manual valve in place.

DETENT DOWNSHIFT: (See kickdown.)

DETERGENT: An additive in engine oil to improve its operating characteristics.

DETONATION: An unwanted explosion of the air/fuel mixture in the combustion chamber caused by excess heat and compression, advanced timing, or an overly lean mixture. Also referred to as "ping".

DEXRON®: A brand of automatic transmission fluid.

DIAGNOSTIC TROUBLE CODES (DTCs): A digital display from the control module memory that identifies the input, processor, or output device circuit that is related to the powertrain emission/driveability malfunction detected. Diagnostic trouble codes can be read by the MIL to flash any codes or by using a handheld scanner.

DIAPHRAGM: A thin, flexible wall separating two cavities, such as in a vacuum advance unit.

DIESELING: The engine continues to run after the car is shut off; caused by fuel continuing to be burned in the combustion chamber.

DIFFERENTIAL: A geared assembly which allows the transmission of motion between drive axles, giving one axle the ability to rotate faster than the other, as in cornering.

DIFFERENTIAL AREAS: When opposing faces of a spool valve are acted upon by the same pressure but their areas differ in size, the face with the larger area produces the differential force and valve movement. (See spool valve.)

DIFFERENTIAL FORCE: (See differential areas)

DIGITAL READOUT: A display of numbers or a combination of numbers and letters.

DIGITAL VOLT OHMMETER: An electronic diagnostic tool used to measure voltage, ohms and amps as well as several other functions, with the readings displayed on a digital screen in tenths, hundredths and thousandths.

DIODE: An electrical device that will allow current to flow in one direction only.

DIRECT CURRENT (DC): Electrical current that flows in one direction only.

DIRECT DRIVE: The gear ratio is 1:1, with no change occurring in the torque and speed input/output relationship.

DISC BRAKE: A hydraulic braking assembly consisting of a brake disc, or rotor, mounted on an axle shaft, and a caliper assembly containing, usually two brake pads which are activated by hydraulic pressure. The pads are forced against the sides of the disc, creating friction which slows the vehicle.

DISPERSANTS: Suspend dirt and prevent sludge buildup in a liquid, such as engine oil.

DOUBLE BUMP (DOUBLE FEEL): Two sudden and forceful applies of a clutch or band.

DISPLACEMENT: The total volume of air that is displaced by all pistons as the engine turns through one complete revolution.

DISTRIBUTOR: A mechanically driven device on an engine which is responsible for electrically firing the spark plug at a pre-determined point of the piston stroke.

DOHC: Double overhead camshaft.

DOUBLE OVERHEAD CAMSHAFT: The engine utilizes two camshafts mounted in one cylinder head. One camshaft operates the exhaust valves, while the other operates the intake valves.

DOWEL PIN: A pin, inserted in mating holes in two different parts allowing those parts to maintain a fixed relationship.

DRIVELINE: The drive connection between the transmission and the drive wheels.

DRIVE TRAIN: The components that transmit the flow of power from the engine to the wheels. The components include the clutch, transmission, driveshafts (or axle shafts in front wheel drive), U-joints and differential.

DRUM BRAKE: A braking system which consists of two brake shoes and one or two wheel cylinders, mounted on a fixed backing plate, and a brake drum, mounted on an axle, which revolves around the assembly.

DRY CHARGED BATTERY: Battery to which electrolyte is added when the battery is placed in service.

DVOM: Digital volt ohmmeter

DWELL: The rate, measured in degrees of shaft rotation, at which an electrical circuit cycles on and off.

DYNAMIC: An application in which there is rotating or reciprocating motion between the parts.

EARLY: Condition where shift occurs before vehicle has reached proper speed, which tends to labor engine after upshift.

EBCM: See Electronic Control Unit (ECU).

ECM: See Electronic Control Unit (ECU).

ECU: Electronic control unit.

ELECTRODE: Conductor (positive or negative) of electric current.

ELECTROLYSIS: A surface etching or bonding of current conducting transmission/transaxle components that may occur when grounding straps are missing or in poor condition.

ELECTROLYTE: A solution of water and sulfuric acid used to activate the battery. Electrolyte is extremely corrosive.

ELECTROMAGNET: A coil that produces a magnetic field when current flows through its windings.

ELECTROMAGNETIC INDUCTION: A method to create (generate) current flow through the use of magnetism.

ELECTROMAGNETISM: The effects surrounding the relationship between electricity and magnetism.

ELECTROMOTIVE FORCE (EMF): The force or pressure (voltage) that causes current movement in an electrical circuit.

ELECTRONIC CONTROL UNIT: A digital computer that controls engine (and sometimes transmission, brake or other vehicle system) functions based on data received from various sensors. Examples used by some manufacturers include Electronic Brake Control Module (EBCM), Engine Control Module (ECM), Powertrain Control Module (PCM) or Vehicle Control Module (VCM).

ELECTRONIC IGNITION: A system in which the timing and firing of the spark plugs is controlled by an electronic control unit, usually called a module. These systems have no points or condenser.

ELECTRONIC PRESSURE CONTROL (EPC) SOLENOID: A specially designed solenoid containing a spool valve and spring assembly to control fluid mainline pressure. A variable current flow, controlled by the ECM/PCM, varies the internal force of the solenoid on the spool valve and resulting mainline pressure. (See variable force solenoid.)

ELECTRONICS: Miniaturized electrical circuits utilizing semiconductors, solid-state devices, and printed circuits. Electronic circuits utilize small amounts of power.

ELECTRONIFICATION: The application of electronic circuitry to a mechanical device. Regarding automatic transmissions, electrification is incorporated into converter clutch lockup, shift scheduling, and line pressure control systems.

ELECTROSTATIC DISCHARGE (ESD): An unwanted, high-voltage electrical current released by an individual who has taken on a static charge of electricity. Electronic components can be easily damaged by ESD.

ELEMENT: A device within a hydrodynamic drive unit designed with a set of blades to direct fluid flow.

ENAMEL: Type of paint that dries to a smooth, glossy finish.

END BUMP (END FEEL OR SLIP BUMP): Firmer feel at end of shift when compared with feel at start of shift.

END-PLAY: The clearance/gap between two components that allows for expansion of the parts as they warm up, to prevent binding and to allow space for lubrication.

ENERGY: The ability or capacity to do work.

ENGINE: The primary motor or power apparatus of a vehicle, which converts liquid or gas fuel into mechanical energy.

ENGINE BLOCK: The basic engine casting containing the cylinders, the crankshaft main bearings, as well as machined surfaces for the mounting of other components such as the cylinder head, oil pan, transmission, etc.

ENGINE BRAKING: Use of engine to slow vehicle by manually downshifting during zero-throttle coast down.

ENGINE CONTROL MODULE (ECM): Manages the engine and incorporates output control over the torque converter clutch solenoid. (Note: Current designation for the ECM in late model vehicles is PCM.)

ENGINE COOLANT TEMPERATURE (ECT) SENSOR: Prevents converter clutch engagement with a cold engine; also used for shift timing and shift quality.

EP LUBRICANT: EP (extreme pressure) lubricants are specially formulated for use with gears involving heavy loads (transmissions, differentials, etc.).

ETHYL: A substance added to gasoline to improve its resistance to knock, by slowing down the rate of combustion.

ETHYLENE GLYCOL: The base substance of antifreeze.

EXHAUST MANIFOLD: A set of cast passages or pipes which conduct exhaust gases from the engine.

FAIL-SAFE (BACKUP) CONTROL: A substitute value used by the PCM/TCM to replace a faulty signal from an input sensor. The temporary value allows the vehicle to continue to be operated.

FAST IDLE: The speed of the engine when the choke is on. Fast idle speeds engine warm-up.

FEDERAL ENGINE: An engine certified by the EPA for use in any of the 49 states (except California).

FEEDBACK: A circuit malfunction whereby current can find another path to feed load devices.

FEELER GAUGE: A blade, usually metal, of precisely predetermined thickness, used to measure the clearance between two parts.

FILAMENT: The part of a bulb that glows; the filament creates high resistance to current flow and actually glows from the resulting heat.

FINAL DRIVE: An essential part of the axle drive assembly where final gear reduction takes place in the powertrain. In RWD applications and north-south FWD applications, it must also change the power flow direction to the axle shaft by ninety degrees. (Also see axle ratio).

FIRING ORDER: The order in which combustion occurs in the cylinders of an engine. Also the order in which spark is distributed to the plugs by the distributor.

FIRM: A noticeable quick apply of a clutch or band that is considered normal with medium to heavy throttle shift; should not be confused with harsh or rough.

FLAME FRONT: The term used to describe certain aspects of the fuel explosion in the cylinders. The flame front should move in a controlled pattern across the cylinder, rather than simply exploding immediately.

FLARE (SLIPPING): A quick increase in engine rpm accompanied by momentary loss of torque; generally occurs during shift.

FLAT ENGINE: Engine design in which the pistons are horizontally opposed. Porsche, Subaru and some old VW are common examples of flat engines.

FLAT RATE: A dealership term referring to the amount of money paid to a technician for a repair or diagnostic service based on that particular service versus dealership's labor time (NOT based on the actual time the technician spent on the job).

FLAT SPOT: A point during acceleration when the engine seems to lose power for an instant.

FLOODING: The presence of too much fuel in the intake manifold and combustion chamber which prevents the air/fuel mixture from firing, thereby causing a no-start situation.

FLUID: A fluid can be either liquid or gas. In hydraulics, a liquid is used for transmitting force or motion.

FLUID COUPLING: The simplest form of hydrodynamic drive, the fluid coupling consists of two look-alike members with straight radial varies referred to as the impeller (pump) and the turbine. Input torque is always equal to the output torque.

FLUID DRIVE: Either a fluid coupling or a fluid torque converter. (See hydrodynamic drive units.)

FLUID TORQUE CONVERTER: A hydrodynamic drive that has the ability to act both as a torque multiplier and fluid coupling. (See hydrodynamic drive units; torque converter.)

FLUID VISCOSITY: The resistance of a liquid to flow. A cold fluid (oil) has greater viscosity and flows more slowly than a hot fluid (oil).

FLYWHEEL: A heavy disc of metal attached to the rear of the crankshaft. It smoothes the firing impulses of the engine and keeps the crankshaft turning during periods when no firing takes place. The starter also engages the flywheel to start the engine.

FOOT POUND (ft. lbs., lbs. ft. or sometimes, ft. lb.): The amount of energy or work needed to raise an item weighing one pound, a distance of one foot.

FREEZE PLUG: A plug in the engine block which will be pushed out if the coolant freezes. Sometimes called expansion plugs, they protect the block from cracking should the coolant freeze.

FRICTION: The resistance that occurs between contacting surfaces. This relationship is expressed by a ratio called the coefficient of friction (CL).

FRICTION, COEFFICIENT OF: The amount of surface tension between two contacting surfaces; expressed by a scientifically calculated number.

FRONT END ALIGNMENT: A service to set caster, camber and toe-in to the correct specifications. This will ensure that the car steers and handles properly and that the tires wear properly.

FRICTION MODIFIER: Changes the coefficient of friction of the fluid between the mating steel and composition clutch/band surfaces during the engagement process and allows for a certain amount of intentional slipping for a good "shift-feel".

FRONTAL AREA: The total frontal area of a vehicle exposed to air flow.

FUEL FILTER: A component of the fuel system containing a porous paper element used to prevent any impurities from entering the engine through the fuel system. It usually takes the form of a canister-like housing, mounted in-line with the fuel hose, located anywhere on a vehicle between the fuel tank and engine.

FUEL INJECTION: A system replacing the carburetor that sprays fuel into the cylinder through nozzles. The amount of fuel can be more precisely controlled with fuel injection.

FULL FLOATING AXLE: An axle in which the axle housing extends through the wheel giving bearing support on the outside of the housing. The front axle of a four-wheel drive vehicle is usually a full floating axle, as are the rear axles of many larger (1 ton and over) pick-ups and vans.

FULL-TIME FOUR-WHEEL DRIVE: A four-wheel drive system that continuously delivers power to all four wheels. A differential between the front and rear driveshafts permits variations in axle speeds to control gear wind-up without damage.

FULL THROTTLE DETENT DOWNSHIFT: A quick apply of accelerator pedal to its full travel, forcing a downshift.

FUSE: A protective device in a circuit which prevents circuit overload by breaking the circuit when a specific amperage is present. The device is constructed around a strip or wire of a lower amperage rating than the circuit it is designed to protect. When an amperage higher than that stamped on the fuse is present in the circuit, the strip or wire melts, opening the circuit.

FUSIBLE LINK: A piece of wire in a wiring harness that performs the same job as a fuse. If overloaded, the fusible link will melt and interrupt the circuit.

FWD: Front wheel drive.

GAWR: (Gross axle weight rating) the total maximum weight an axle is designed to carry.

GCW: (Gross combined weight) total combined weight of a tow vehicle and trailer.

GARAGE SHIFT: initial engagement feel of transmission, neutral to reverse or neutral to a forward drive.

GARAGE SHIFT FEEL: A quick check of the engagement quality and responsiveness of reverse and forward gears. This test is done with the vehicle stationary.

GEAR: A toothed mechanical device that acts as a rotating lever to transmit power or turning effort from one shaft to another. (See gear ratio.)

GEAR RATIO: A ratio expressing the number of turns a smaller gear will make to turn a larger gear through one revolution. The ratio is found by dividing the number of teeth on the smaller gear into the number of teeth on the larger gear.

GEARBOX: Transmission

GEAR REDUCTION: Torque is multiplied and speed decreased by the factor of the gear ratio. For example, a 3:1 gear ratio changes an input torque of 180 ft. lbs. and an input speed of 2700 rpm to 540 Ft. lbs. and 900 rpm, respectively. (No account is taken of frictional losses, which are always present.)

GEARTRAIN: A succession of intermeshing gears that form an assembly and provide for one or more torque changes as the power input is transmitted to the power output.

GEL COAT: A thin coat of plastic resin covering fiberglass body panels.

GENERATOR: A device which produces direct current (DC) necessary to charge the battery.

GOVERNOR: A device that senses vehicle speed and generates a hydraulic oil pressure. As vehicle speed increases, governor oil pressure rises.

GROUND CIRCUIT: (See circuit, ground.)

GROUND SIDE SWITCHING: The electrical/electronic circuit control switch is located after the circuit load.

GVWR: (Gross vehicle weight rating) total maximum weight a vehicle is designed to carry including the weight of the vehicle, passengers, equipment, gas, oil, etc.

HALOGEN: A special type of lamp known for its quality of brilliant white light. Originally used for fog lights and driving lights.

HARD CODES: DTCs that are present at the time of testing; also called continuous or current codes.

HARSH(ROUGH): An apply of a clutch or band that is more noticeable than a firm one; considered undesirable at any throttle position.

HEADER TANK: An expansion tank for the radiator coolant. It can be located remotely or built into the radiator.

HEAT RANGE: A term used to describe the ability of a spark plug to carry away heat. Plugs with longer nosed insulators take longer to carry heat off effectively.

HEAT RISER: A flapper in the exhaust manifold that is closed when the engine is cold, causing hot exhaust gases to heat the intake manifold providing better cold engine operation. A thermostatic spring opens the flapper when the engine warms up.

HEAVY THROTTLE: Approximately three-fourths of accelerator pedal travel.

HEMI: A name given an engine using hemispherical combustion chambers.

HERTZ (HZ): The international unit of frequency equal to one cycle per second (10,000 Hertz equals 10,000 cycles per second).

HIGH-IMPEDANCE DVOM (DIGITAL VOLT-OHMMETER): This styled device provides a built-in resistance value and is capable of limiting circuit current flow to safe milliamp levels.

HIGH RESISTANCE: Often refers to a circuit where there is an excessive amount of opposition to normal current flow.

HORSEPOWER: A measurement of the amount of work; one horsepower is the amount of work necessary to lift 33,000 lbs. one foot in one minute. Brake horsepower (bhp) is the horsepower delivered by an engine on a dynamometer. Net horsepower is the power remaining (measured at the flywheel of the engine) that can be used to turn the wheels after power is consumed through friction and running the engine accessories (water pump, alternator, air pump, fan etc.)

HOT CIRCUIT: (See circuit, hot; hot lead.)

HOT LEAD: A wire or conductor in the power side of the circuit. (See circuit, hot.)

HOT SIDE SWITCHING: The electrical/electronic circuit control switch is located before the circuit load.

HUB: The center part of a wheel or gear.

HUNTING (BUSYNESS): Repeating quick series of up-shifts and downshifts that causes noticeable change in engine rpm, for example, as in a 4-3-4 shift pattern.

HYDRAULICS: The use of liquid under pressure to transfer force of motion.

HYDROCARBON (HC): Any chemical compound made up of hydrogen and carbon. A major pollutant formed by the engine as a by-product of combustion.

HYDRODYNAMIC DRIVE UNITS: Devices that transmit power solely by the action of a kinetic fluid flow in a closed recirculating path. An impeller energizes the fluid and discharges the high-speed jet stream into the turbine for power output.

HYDROMETER: An instrument used to measure the specific gravity of a solution.

HYDROPLANING: A phenomenon of driving when water builds up under the tire tread, causing it to lose contact with the road. Slowing down will usually restore normal tire contact with the road.

HYPOID GEARSET: The drive pinion gear may be placed below or above the centerline of the driven gear; often used as a final drive gearset.

IDLE MIXTURE: The mixture of air and fuel (usually about 14:1) being fed to the cylinders. The idle mixture screw(s) are sometimes adjusted as part of a tune-up.

IDLER ARM: Component of the steering linkage which is a geometric duplicate of the steering gear arm. It supports the right side of the center steering link.

IMPELLER: Often called a pump, the impeller is the power input (drive) member of a hydrodynamic drive. As part of the torque converter cover, it acts as a centrifugal pump and puts the fluid in motion.

INCH POUND (inch lbs.; sometimes in. lb. or in. lbs.): One twelfth of a foot pound.

INDUCTANCE: The force that produces voltage when a conductor is passed through a magnetic field.

INDUCTION: A means of transferring electrical energy in the form of a magnetic field. Principle used in the ignition coil to increase voltage.

INITIAL FEEL: A distinct firmer feel at start of shift when compared with feel at finish of shift.

INJECTOR: A device which receives metered fuel under relatively low pressure and is activated to inject the fuel into the engine under relatively high pressure at a predetermined time.

INPUT: In an automatic transmission, the source of power from the engine is absorbed by the torque converter, which provides the power input into the transmission. The turbine drives the input(turbine)shaft.

INPUT SHAFT: The shaft to which torque is applied, usually carrying the driving gear or gears.

INTAKE MANIFOLD: A casting of passages or pipes used to conduct air or a fuel/air mixture to the cylinders.

INTERNAL GEAR: The ring-like outer gear of a planetary gearset with the gear teeth cut on the inside of the ring to provide a mesh with the planet pinions.

ISOLATION (CLAMPING) DIODES: Diodes positioned in a circuit to prevent self-induction from damaging electronic components.

IX ROTARY GEAR PUMP: Contains two rotating members, one shaped with internal gear teeth and the other with external gear teeth. As the gears separate, the fluid fills the gaps between gear teeth, is pulled across a crescent-shaped divider, and then is forced to flow through the outlet as the gears mesh.

IX ROTARY LOBE PUMP: Sometimes referred to as a gerotor type pump. Two rotating members, one shaped with internal lobes and the other with external lobes, separate and then mesh to cause fluid to flow.

JOURNAL: The bearing surface within which a shaft operates.

JUMPER CABLES: Two heavy duty wires with large alligator clips used to provide power from a charged battery to a discharged battery mounted in a vehicle.

JUMPSTART: Utilizing the sufficiently charged battery of one vehicle to start the engine of another vehicle with a discharged battery by the use of jumper cables.

KEY: A small block usually fitted in a notch between a shaft and a hub to prevent slippage of the two parts.

KICKDOWN: Detent downshift system; either linkage, cable, or electrically controlled.

KILO: A prefix used in the metric system to indicate one thousand.

KNOCK: Noise which results from the spontaneous ignition of a portion of the air-fuel mixture in the engine cylinder caused by overly advanced ignition timing or use of incorrectly low octane fuel for that engine.

KNOCK SENSOR: An input device that responds to spark knock, caused by over advanced ignition timing.

LABOR TIME: A specific amount of time required to perform a certain repair or diagnostic service as defined by a vehicle or after-market manufacturer.

LACQUER: A quick-drying automotive paint.

LATE: Shift that occurs when engine is at higher than normal rpm for given amount of throttle.

LIGHT-EMITTING DIODE (LED): A semiconductor diode that emits light as electrical current flows through it; used in some electronic display devices to emit a red or other color light.

LIGHT THROTTLE: Approximately one-fourth of accelerator pedal travel.

LIMITED SLIP: A type of differential which transfers driving force to the wheel with the best traction.

LIMP-IN MODE: Electrical shutdown of the transmission/ transaxle output solenoids, allowing only forward and reverse gears that are hydraulically energized by the manual valve. This permits the vehicle to be driven to a service facility for repair.

LIP SEAL: Molded synthetic rubber seal designed with an outer sealing edge (lip) that points into the fluid containing area to be sealed. This type of seal is used where rotational and axial forces are present.

LITHIUM-BASE GREASE: Chassis and wheel bearing grease using lithium as a base. Not compatible with sodium-base grease.

LOAD DEVICE: A circuit's resistance that converts the electrical energy into light, sound, heat, or mechanical movement.

LOAD RANGE: Indicates the number of plies at which a tire is rated. Load range B equals four-ply rating; C equals six-ply rating; and, D equals an eight-ply rating.

LOAD TORQUE: The amount of output torque needed from the transmission/transaxle to overcome the vehicle load.

LOCKING HUBS: Accessories used on part-time four-wheel drive systems that allow the front wheels to be disengaged from the drive train when four-wheel drive is not being used. When four-wheel drive is desired, the hubs are engaged, locking the wheels to the drive train.

LOCKUP CONVERTER: A torque converter that operates hydraulically and mechanically. When an internal apply plate (lockup plate) clamps to the torque converter cover, hydraulic slippage is eliminated.

LOCK RING: See Circlip or Snapring

MAGNET: Any body with the property of attracting iron or steel.

MAGNETIC FIELD: The area surrounding the poles of a magnet that is affected by its attraction or repulsion forces.

MAIN LINE PRESSURE: Often called control pressure or line pressure, it refers to the pressure of the oil leaving the pump and is controlled by the pressure regulator valve.

MALFUNCTION INDICATOR LAMP (MIL): Previously known as a check engine light, the dash-mounted MIL illuminates and signals the driver that an emission or driveability problem with the powertrain has been detected by the ECM/PCM. When this occurs, at least one diagnostic trouble code (DTC) has been stored into the control module memory.

MANIFOLD ABSOLUTE PRESSURE (MAP) SENSOR: Reads the amount of air pressure (vacuum) in the engine's intake manifold system; its signal is used to analyze engine load conditions.

MANIFOLD VACUUM: Low pressure in an engine intake manifold formed just below the throttle plates. Manifold vacuum is highest at idle and drops under acceleration.

MANIFOLD: A casting of passages or set of pipes which connect the cylinders to an inlet or outlet source.

MANUAL LEVER POSITION SWITCH (MLPS): A mechanical switching unit that is typically mounted externally to the transmission/transaxle to inform the PCM/ECM which gear range the driver has selected.

MANUAL VALVE: Located inside the transmission/transaxle, it is directly connected to the driver's shift lever. The position of the manual valve determines which hydraulic circuits will be charged with oil pressure and the operating mode of the transmission.

MANUAL VALVE LEVER POSITION SENSOR (MVLPS): The input from this device tells the TCM what gear range was selected.

MASS AIR FLOW (MAF) SENSOR: Measures the airflow into the engine.

MASTER CYLINDER: The primary fluid pressurizing device in a hydraulic system. In automotive use, it is found in brake and hydraulic clutch systems and is pedal activated, either directly or, in a power brake system, through the power booster.

MacPherson STRUT: A suspension component combining a shock absorber and spring in one unit.

MEDIUM THROTTLE: Approximately one-half of accelerator pedal travel.

MEGA: A metric prefix indicating one million.

MEMBER: An independent component of a hydrodynamic unit such as an impeller, a stator, or a turbine. It may have one or more elements.

MERCON: A fluid developed by Ford Motor Company in 1988. It contains a friction modifier and closely resembles operating characteristics of Dexron.

METAL SEALING RINGS: Made from cast iron or aluminum, their primary application is with dynamic components involving pressure sealing circuits of rotating members. These rings are designed with either butt or hook lock end joints.

METER (ANALOG): A linear-style meter representing data as lengths; a needle-style instrument interfacing with logical numerical increments. This style of electrical meter uses relatively low impedance internal resistance and cannot be used for testing electronic circuitry.

METER (DIGITAL): Uses numbers as a direct readout to show values. Most meters of this style use high impedance internal resistance and must be used for testing low current electronic circuitry.

MICRO: A metric prefix indicating one-millionth (0.000001).

MILLI: A metric prefix indicating one-thousandth (0.001).

MINIMUM THROTTLE: The least amount of throttle opening required for upshift; normally close to zero throttle.

MISFIRE: Condition occurring when the fuel mixture in a cylinder fails to ignite, causing the engine to run roughly.

MODULE: Electronic control unit, amplifier or igniter of solid state or integrated design which controls the current flow in the ignition primary circuit based on input from the pick-up coil. When the module opens the primary circuit, high secondary voltage is induced in the coil.

MODULATED: In an electronic-hydraulic converter clutch system (or shift valve system), the term modulated refers to the pulsing of a solenoid, at a variable rate. This action controls the buildup of oil pressure in the hydraulic circuit to allow a controlled amount of clutch slippage.

MODULATED CONVERTER CLUTCH CONTROL (MCCC): A pulse width duty cycle valve that controls the converter lockup apply pressure and maximizes smoother transitions between lock and unlock conditions.

MODULATOR PRESSURE (THROTTLE PRESSURE): A hydraulic signal oil pressure relating to the amount of engine load, based on either the amount of throttle plate opening or engine vacuum.

MODULATOR VALVE: A regulator valve that is controlled by engine vacuum, providing a hydraulic pressure that varies in relation to engine torque. The hydraulic torque signal functions to delay the shift pattern and provide a line pressure boost. (See throttle valve.)

MOTOR: An electromagnetic device used to convert electrical energy into mechanical energy.

MULTIPLE-DISC CLUTCH: A grouping of steel and friction lined plates that, when compressed together by hydraulic pressure acting upon a piston, lock or unlock a planetary member.

MULTI-WEIGHT: Type of oil that provides adequate lubrication at both high and low temperatures.

needed to move one amp through a resistance of one ohm.

MUSHY: Same as soft; slow and drawn out clutch apply with very little shift feel.

MUTUAL INDUCTION: The generation of current from one wire circuit to another by movement of the magnetic field surrounding a current-carrying circuit as its ampere flow increases or decreases.

NEEDLE BEARING: A bearing which consists of a number (usually a large number) of long, thin rollers.

NITROGEN OXIDE (NOx): One of the three basic pollutants found in the exhaust emission of an internal combustion engine. The amount of NOx usually varies in an inverse proportion to the amount of HC and CO.

NONPOSITIVE SEALING: A sealing method that allows some minor leakage, which normally assists in lubrication.

O2 SENSOR: Located in the engine's exhaust system, it is an input device to the ECM/PCM for managing the fuel delivery and ignition system. A scanner can be used to observe the fluctuating voltage readings produced by an O2 sensor as the oxygen content of the exhaust is analyzed.

O-RING SEAL: Molded synthetic rubber seal designed with a circular cross-section. This type of seal is used primarily in static applications.

OBD II (ON-BOARD DIAGNOSTICS, SECOND GENERATION): Refers to the federal law mandating tighter control of 1996 and newer vehicle emissions, active monitoring of related devices, and standardization of terminology, data link connectors, and other technician concerns.

OCTANE RATING: A number, indicating the quality of gasoline based on its ability to resist knock. The higher the number, the better the quality. Higher compression engines require higher octane gas.

OEM: Original Equipment Manufactured. OEM equipment is that furnished standard by the manufacturer.

OFFSET: The distance between the vertical center of the wheel and the mounting surface at the lugs. Offset is positive if the center is outside the lug circle; negative offset puts the center line inside the lug circle.

OHM'S LAW: A law of electricity that states the relationship between voltage, current, and resistance. Volts = amperes x ohms

OHM: The unit used to measure the resistance of conductor-to-electrical flow. One ohm is the amount of resistance that limits current flow to one ampere in a circuit with one volt of pressure.

OHMMETER: An instrument used for measuring the resistance, in ohms, in an electrical circuit.

ONE-WAY CLUTCH: A mechanical clutch of roller or sprag design that resists torque or transmits power in one direction only. It is used to either hold or drive a planetary member.

ONE-WAY ROLLER CLUTCH: A mechanical device that transmits or holds torque in one direction only.

OPEN CIRCUIT: A break or lack of contact in an electrical circuit, either intentional (switch) or unintentional (bad connection or broken wire).

ORIFICE: Located in hydraulic oil circuits, it acts as a restriction. It slows down fluid flow to either create back pressure or delay pressure buildup downstream.

OSCILLOSCOPE: A piece of test equipment that shows electric impulses as a pattern on a screen. Engine performance can be analyzed by interpreting these patterns.

OUTPUT SHAFT: The shaft which transmits torque from a device, such as a transmission.

OUTPUT SPEED SENSOR (OSS): Identifies transmission/transaxle output shaft speed for shift timing and may be used to calculate TCC slip; often functions as the VSS (vehicle speed sensor).

OVERDRIVE: (1.) A device attached to or incorporated in a transmission/transaxle that allows the engine to turn less than one full revolution for every complete revolution of the wheels. The net effect is to reduce engine rpm, thereby using less fuel. A typical overdrive gear ratio would be .87:1, instead of the normal 1:1 in high gear. (2.) A gear assembly which produces more shaft revolutions than that transmitted to it.

OVERDRIVE PLANETARY GEARSET: A single planetary gearset designed to provide a direct drive and overdrive ratio. When coupled to a three-speed transmission/transaxle configuration, a four-speed/overdrive unit is present.

OVERHEAD CAMSHAFT (OHC): An engine configuration in which the camshaft is mounted on top of the cylinder head and operates the valve either directly or by means of rocker arms.

OVERHEAD VALVE (OHV): An engine configuration in which all of the valves are located in the cylinder head and the camshaft is located in the cylinder block. The camshaft operates the valves via lifters and pushrods.

OVERRUNCLUTCH: Another name for a one-way mechanical clutch. Applies to both roller and sprag designs.

OVERSTEER: The tendency of some vehicles, when steering into a turn, to over-respond or steer more than required, which could result in excessive slip of the rear wheels. Opposite of under-steer.

OXIDATION STABILIZERS: Absorb and dissipate heat. Automatic transmission fluid has high resistance to varnish and sludge buildup that occurs from excessive heat that is generated primarily in the torque converter. Local temperatures as high as 6000F (3150C) can occur at the clutch plates during engagement, and this heat must be absorbed and dissipated. If the fluid cannot withstand the heat, it burns or oxidizes, resulting in an almost immediate destruction of friction materials, clogged filter screen and hydraulic passages, and sticky valves.

OXIDES OF NITROGEN: See nitrogen oxide (NOx).

OXYGEN SENSOR: Used with a feedback system to sense the presence of oxygen in the exhaust gas and signal the computer which can use the voltage signal to determine engine operating efficiency and adjust the air/fuel ratio.

PARALLEL CIRCUIT: (See circuit, parallel.)

PARTS WASHER: A basin or tub, usually with a built-in pump mechanism and hose used for circulating chemical solvent for the purpose of cleaning greasy, oily and dirty components.

PART-TIME FOUR WHEEL DRIVE: A system that is normally in the two wheel drive mode and only runs in four-wheel drive when the system is manually engaged because more traction is desired. Two or four wheel drive is normally selected by a lever to engage the front axle, but if locking hubs are used, these must also be manually engaged in the Lock position. Otherwise, the front axle will not drive the front wheels.

PASSIVE RESTRAINT: Safety systems such as air bags or automatic seat belts which operate with no action required on the part of the driver or passenger. Mandated by Federal regulations on all vehicles sold in the U.S. after 1990.

PAYLOAD: The weight the vehicle is capable of carrying in addition to its own weight. Payload includes weight of the driver, passengers and cargo, but not coolant, fuel, lubricant, spare tire, etc.

PCM: Powertrain control module.

PCV VALVE: A valve usually located in the rocker cover that vents crankcase vapors back into the engine to be reburned.

PERCOLATION: A condition in which the fuel actually "boils," due to excessive heat. Percolation prevents proper atomization of the fuel causing rough running.

PICK-UP COIL: The coil in which voltage is induced in an electronic ignition.

PING: A metallic rattling sound produced by the engine during acceleration. It is usually due to incorrect ignition timing or a poor grade of gasoline.

PINION: The smaller of two gears. The rear axle pinion drives the ring gear which transmits motion to the axle shafts.

PINION GEAR: The smallest gear in a drive gear assembly.

PISTON: A disc or cup that fits in a cylinder bore and is free to move. In hydraulics, it provides the means of converting hydraulic pressure into a usable force. Examples of piston applications are found in servo, clutch, and accumulator units.

PISTON RING: An open-ended ring which fits into a groove on the outer diameter of the piston. Its chief function is to form a seal between the piston and cylinder wall. Most automotive pistons have three rings: two for compression sealing; one for oil sealing.

PITMAN ARM: A lever which transmits steering force from the steering gear to the steering linkage.

PLANET CARRIER: A basic member of a planetary gear assembly that carries the pinion gears.

PLANET PINIONS: Gears housed in a planet carrier that are in constant mesh with the sun gear and internal gear. Because they have their own independent rotating centers, the pinions are capable of rotating around the sun gear or the inside of the internal gear.

PLANETARY GEAR RATIO: The reduction or overdrive ratio developed by a planetary gearset.

PLANETARY GEARSET: In its simplest form, it is made up of a basic assembly group containing a sun gear, internal gear, and planet carrier. The gears are always in constant mesh and offer a wide range of gear ratio possibilities.

PLANETARY GEARSET (COMPOUND): Two planetary gearsets combined together.

PLANETARY GEARSET (SIMPLE): An assembly of gears in constant mesh consisting of a sun gear, several pinion gears mounted in a carrier, and a ring gear. It provides gear ratio and direction changes, in addition to a direct drive and a neutral.

PLY RATING: A. rating given a tire which indicates strength (but not necessarily actual plies). A two-ply/four-ply rating has only two plies, but the strength of a four-ply tire.

POLARITY: Indication (positive or negative) of the two poles of a battery.

PORT: An opening for fluid intake or exhaust.

POSITIVE SEALING: A sealing method that completely prevents leakage.

POTENTIAL: Electrical force measured in volts; sometimes used interchangeably with voltage.

POWER: The ability to do work per unit of time, as expressed in horsepower; one horsepower equals 33,000 ft. lbs. of work per minute, or 550 ft. lbs. of work per second.

POWER FLOW: The systematic flow or transmission of power through the gears, from the input shaft to the output shaft.

POWER-TO-WEIGHT RATIO: Ratio of horsepower to weight of car.

POWERTRAIN: See Drivetrain.

POWERTRAIN CONTROL MODULE (PCM): Current designation for the engine control module (ECM). In many cases, late model vehicle control units manage the engine as well as the transmission. In other settings, the PCM controls the engine and is interfaced with a TCM to control transmission functions.

Ppm: Parts per million; unit used to measure exhaust emissions.

PREIGNITION: Early ignition of fuel in the cylinder, sometimes due to glowing carbon deposits in the combustion chamber. Preignition can be damaging since combustion takes place prematurely.

PRELOAD: A predetermined load placed on a bearing during assembly or by adjustment.

PRESS FIT: The mating of two parts under pressure, due to the inner diameter of one being smaller than the outer diameter of the other, or vice versa; an interference fit.

PRESSURE: The amount of force exerted upon a surface area.

PRESSURE CONTROL SOLENOID (PCS): An output device that provides a boost oil pressure to the mainline regulator valve to control line pressure. Its operation is determined by the amount of current sent from the PCM.

PRESSURE GAUGE: An instrument used for measuring the fluid pressure in a hydraulic circuit.

PRESSURE REGULATOR VALVE: In automatic transmissions, its purpose is to regulate the pressure of the pump output and supply the basic fluid pressure necessary to operate the transmission. The regulated fluid pressure may be referred to as mainline pressure, line pressure, or control pressure.

PRESSURE SWITCH ASSEMBLY (PSA): Mounted inside the transmission, it is a grouping of oil pressure switches that inputs to the PCM when certain hydraulic passages are charged with oil pressure.

PRESSURE PLATE: A spring-loaded plate (part of the clutch) that transmits power to the driven (friction) plate when the clutch is engaged.

PRIMARY CIRCUIT: The low voltage side of the ignition system which consists of the ignition switch, ballast resistor or resistance wire, bypass, coil, electronic control unit and pick-up coil as well as the connecting wires and harnesses.

PROFILE: Term used for tire measurement (tire series), which is the ratio of tire height to tread width.

PROM (PROGRAMMABLE READ-ONLY MEMORY): The heart of the computer that compares input data and makes the engineered program or strategy decisions about when to trigger the appropriate output based on stored computer instructions.

PULSE GENERATOR: A two-wire pickup sensor used to produce a fluctuating electrical signal. This changing signal is read by the controller to determine the speed of the object and can be used to measure transmission/transaxle input speed, output speed, and vehicle speed.

PSI: Pounds per square inch; a measurement of pressure.

PULSE WIDTH DUTY CYCLE SOLENOID (PULSE WIDTH MODULATED SOLENOID): A computer-controlled solenoid that turns on and off at a variable rate producing a modulated oil pressure; often referred to as a pulse width modulated (PWM) solenoid. Employed in many electronic automatic transmissions and transaxles, these solenoids are used to manage shift control and converter clutch hydraulic circuits.

PUSHROD: A steel rod between the hydraulic valve lifter and the valve rocker arm in overhead valve (OHV) engines.

PUMP: A mechanical device designed to create fluid flow and pressure buildup in a hydraulic system.

QUARTER PANEL: General term used to refer to a rear fender. Quarter panel is the area from the rear door opening to the tail light area and from rear wheel well to the base of the trunk and roof-line.

RACE: The surface on the inner or outer ring of a bearing on which the balls, needles or rollers move.

RACK AND PINION: A type of automotive steering system using a pinion gear attached to the end of the steering shaft. The pinion meshes with a long rack attached to the steering linkage.

RADIAL TIRE: Tire design which uses body cords running at right angles to the center line of the tire. Two or more belts are used to give tread strength. Radials can be identified by their characteristic sidewall bulge.

RADIATOR: Part of the cooling system for a water-cooled engine, mounted in the front of the vehicle and connected to the engine with rubber hoses. Through the radiator, excess combustion heat is dissipated into the atmosphere through forced convection using a water and glycol based mixture that circulates through, and cools, the engine.

RANGE REFERENCE AND CLUTCH/BAND APPLY CHART: A guide that shows the application of clutches and bands for each gear, within the selector range positions. These charts are extremely useful for understanding how the unit operates and for diagnosing malfunctions.

RAVIGNEAUX GEARSET: A compound planetary gearset that features matched dual planetary pinions (sets of two) mounted in a single planet carrier. Two sun gears and one ring mesh with the carrier pinions.

REACTION MEMBER: The stationary planetary member, in a planetary gearset, that is grounded to the transmission/transaxle case through the use of friction and wedging devices known as bands, disc clutches, and one-way clutches.

REACTION PRESSURE: The fluid pressure that moves a spool valve against an opposing force or forces; the area on which the opposing force acts. The opposing force can be a spring or a combination of spring force and auxiliary hydraulic force.

REACTOR, TORQUE CONVERTER: The reaction member of a fluid torque converter, more commonly called a stator. (See stator.)

REAR MAIN OIL SEAL: A synthetic or rope-type seal that prevents oil from leaking out of the engine past the rear main crankshaft bearing.

RECIRCULATING BALL: Type of steering system in which recirculating steel balls occupy the area between the nut and worm wheel, causing a reduction in friction.

RECTIFIER: A device (used primarily in alternators) that permits electrical current to flow in one direction only.

REDUCTION: (See gear reduction.)

REGULATOR VALVE: A valve that changes the pressure of the oil in a hydraulic circuit as the oil passes through the valve by bleeding off (or exhausting) some of the volume of oil supplied to the valve.

REFRIGERANT 12 (R-12) or 134 (R-134): The generic name of the refrigerant used in automotive air conditioning systems.

REGULATOR: A device which maintains the amperage and/or voltage levels of a circuit at predetermined values.

RELAY: A switch which automatically opens and/or closes a circuit.

RELAY VALVE: A valve that directs flow and pressure. Relay valves simply connect or disconnect interrelated passages without restricting the fluid flow or changing the pressure.

RELIEF VALVE: A spring-loaded, pressure-operated valve that limits oil pressure buildup in a hydraulic circuit to a predetermined maximum value.

RELUCTOR: A wheel that rotates inside the distributor and triggers the release of voltage in an electronic ignition.

RESERVOIR: The storage area for fluid in a hydraulic system; often called a sump.

RESIN: A liquid plastic used in body work.

RESIDUAL MAGNETISM: The magnetic strength stored in a material after a magnetizing field has been removed.

RESISTANCE: The opposition to the flow of current through a circuit or electrical device, and is measured in ohms. Resistance is equal to the voltage divided by the amperage.

RESISTOR SPARK PLUG: A spark plug using a resistor to shorten the spark duration. This suppresses radio interference and lengthens plug life.

RESISTOR: A device, usually made of wire, which offers a preset amount of resistance in an electrical circuit.

RESULTANT FORCE: The single effective directional thrust of the fluid force on the turbine produced by the vortex and rotary forces acting in different planes.

RETARD: Set the ignition timing so that spark occurs later (fewer degrees before TDC).

RHEOSTAT: A device for regulating a current by means of a variable resistance.

RING GEAR: The name given to a ring-shaped gear attached to a differential case, or affixed to a flywheel or as part of a planetary gear set.

ROADLOAD: grade.

ROCKER ARM: A lever which rotates around a shaft pushing down (opening) the valve with an end when the other end is pushed up by the pushrod. Spring pressure will later close the valve.

ROCKER PANEL: The body panel below the doors between the wheel opening.

ROLLER BEARING: A bearing made up of hardened inner and outer races between which hardened steel rollers move.

ROLLER CLUTCH: A type of one-way clutch design using rollers and springs mounted within an inner and outer cam race assembly.

ROTARY FLOW: The path of the fluid trapped between the blades of the members as they revolve with the rotation of the torque converter cover (rotational inertia).

ROTOR: (1.) The disc-shaped part of a disc brake assembly, upon which the brake pads bear; also called, brake disc. (2.) The device mounted atop the distributor shaft, which passes current to the distributor cap tower contacts.

ROTARY ENGINE: See Wankel engine.

RPM: Revolutions per minute (usually indicates engine speed).

RTV: A gasket making compound that cures as it is exposed to the atmosphere. It is used between surfaces that are not perfectly machined to one another, leaving a slight gap that the RTV fills and in which it hardens. The letters RTV represent room temperature vulcanizing.

RUN-ON: Condition when the engine continues to run, even when the key is turned off. See dieseling.

SEALED BEAM: A automotive headlight. The lens, reflector and filament from a single unit.

SEATBELT INTERLOCK: A system whereby the car cannot be started unless the seatbelt is buckled.

SECONDARY CIRCUIT: The high voltage side of the ignition system, usually above 20,000 volts. The secondary includes the ignition coil, coil wire, distributor cap and rotor, spark plug wires and spark plugs.

SELF-INDUCTION: The generation of voltage in a current-carrying wire by changing the amount of current flowing within that wire.

SEMI-CONDUCTOR: A material (silicon or germanium) that is neither a good conductor nor an insulator; used in diodes and transistors.

SEMI-FLOATING AXLE: In this design, a wheel is attached to the axle shaft, which takes both drive and cornering loads. Almost all solid axle passenger cars and light trucks use this design.

SENDING UNIT: A mechanical, electrical, hydraulic or electromagnetic device which transmits information to a gauge.

SENSOR: Any device designed to measure engine operating conditions or ambient pressures and temperatures. Usually electronic in nature and designed to send a voltage signal to an on-board computer, some sensors may operate as a simple on/off switch or they may provide a variable voltage signal (like a potentiometer) as conditions or measured parameters change.

SERIES CIRCUIT: (See circuit, series.)

SERPENTINE BELT: An accessory drive belt, with small multiple v-ribs, routed around most or all of the engine-powered accessories such as the alternator and power steering pump. Usually both the front and the back side of the belt comes into contact with various pulleys.

SERVO: In an automatic transmission, it is a piston in a cylinder assembly that converts hydraulic pressure into mechanical force and movement; used for the application of the bands and clutches.

SHIFT BUSYNESS: When referring to a torque converter clutch, it is the frequent apply and release of the clutch plate due to uncommon driving conditions.

SHIFT VALVE: Classified as a relay valve, it triggers the automatic shift in response to a governor and a throttle signal by directing fluid to the appropriate band and clutch apply combination to cause the shift to occur.

SHIM: Spacers of precise, predetermined thickness used between parts to establish a proper working relationship.

SHIMMY: Vibration (sometimes violent) in the front end caused by misaligned front end, out of balance tires or worn suspension components.

SHORT CIRCUIT: An electrical malfunction where current takes the path of least resistance to ground (usually through damaged insulation). Current flow is excessive from low resistance resulting in a blown fuse.

SHUDDER: Repeated jerking or stick-slip sensation, similar to chuggle but more severe and rapid in nature, that may be most noticeable during certain ranges of vehicle speed; also used to define condition after converter clutch engagement.

SIMPSON GEARSET: A compound planetary gear train that integrates two simple planetary gearsets referred to as the front planetary and the rear planetary.

SINGLE OVERHEAD CAMSHAFT: See overhead camshaft.

SKIDPLATE: A metal plate attached to the underside of the body to protect the fuel tank, transfer case or other vulnerable parts from damage.

SLAVE CYLINDER: In automotive use, a device in the hydraulic clutch system which is activated by hydraulic force, disengaging the clutch.

SLIPPING: Noticeable increase in engine rpm without vehicle speed increase; usually occurs during or after initial clutch or band engagement.

SLUDGE: Thick, black deposits in engine formed from dirt, oil, water, etc. It is usually formed in engines when oil changes are neglected.

SNAP RING: A circular retaining clip used inside or outside a shaft or part to secure a shaft, such as a floating wrist pin.

SOFT: Slow, almost unnoticeable clutch apply with very little shift feel.

SOFTCODES: DTCs that have been set into the PCM memory but are not present at the time of testing; often referred to as history or intermittent codes.

SOHC: Single overhead camshaft.

SOLENOID: An electrically operated, magnetic switching device.

SPALLING: A wear pattern identified by metal chips flaking off the hardened surface. This condition is caused by foreign particles, overloading situations, and/or normal wear.

SPARK PLUG: A device screwed into the combustion chamber of a spark ignition engine. The basic construction is a conductive core inside of a ceramic insulator, mounted in an outer conductive base. An electrical charge from the spark plug wire travels along the conductive core and jumps a preset air gap to a grounding point or points at the end of the conductive base. The resultant spark ignites the fuel/air mixture in the combustion chamber.

SPECIFIC GRAVITY (BATTERY): The relative weight of liquid (battery electrolyte) as compared to the weight of an equal volume of water.

SPLINES: Ridges machined or cast onto the outer diameter of a shaft or inner diameter of a bore to enable parts to mate without rotation.

SPLIT TORQUE DRIVE: In a torque converter, it refers to parallel paths of torque transmission, one of which is mechanical and the other hydraulic.

SPONGY PEDAL: A soft or spongy feeling when the brake pedal is depressed. It is usually due to air in the brake lines.

SPOOLVALVE: A precision-machined, cylindrically shaped valve made up of lands and grooves. Depending on its position in the valve bore, various interconnecting hydraulic circuit passages are either opened or closed.

SPRAG CLUTCH: A type of one-way clutch design using cams or contoured-shaped sprags between inner and outer races. (See one-way clutch.)

SPRUNG WEIGHT: The weight of a car supported by the springs.

SQUARE-CUT SEAL: Molded synthetic rubber seal designed with a square- or rectangular-shaped cross-section. This type of seal is used for both dynamic and static applications.

SRS: Supplemental restraint system

STABILIZER (SWAY) BAR: A bar linking both sides of the suspension. It resists sway on turns by taking some of added load from one wheel and putting it on the other.

STAGE: The number of turbine sets separated by a stator. A turbine set may be made up of one or more turbine members. A three-element converter is classified as a single stage.

STALL: In fluid drive transmission/transaxle applications, stall refers to engine rpm with the transmission/transaxle engaged and the vehicle stationary; throttle valve can be in any position between closed and wide open.

STALL SPEED: In fluid drive transmission/transaxle applications, stall speed refers to the maximum engine rpm with the transmission/transaxle engaged and vehicle stationary, when the throttle valve is wide open. (See stall; stall test.)

STALL TEST: A procedure recommended by many manufacturers to help determine the integrity of an engine, the torque converter stator, and certain clutch and band combinations. With the shift lever in each of the forward and reverse positions and with the brakes firmly applied, the accelerator pedal is momentarily pressed to the wide open throttle (WOT) position. The engine rpm reading at full throttle can provide clues for diagnosing the condition of the items listed above.

STALL TORQUE: The maximum design or engineered torque ratio of a fluid torque converter, produced under stall speed conditions. (See stall speed.)

STARTER: A high-torque electric motor used for the purpose of starting the engine, typically through a high ratio geared drive connected to the flywheel ring gear.

STATIC: A sealing application in which the parts being sealed do not move in relation to each other.

STATOR (REACTOR): The reaction member of a fluid torque converter that changes the direction of the fluid as it leaves the turbine to enter the impeller vanes. During the torque multiplication phase, this action assists the impeller's rotary force and results in an increase in torque.

STEERING GEOMETRY: Combination of various angles of suspension components (caster, camber, toe-in); roughly equivalent to front end alignment.

STRAIGHT WEIGHT: Term designating motor oil as suitable for use within a narrow range of temperatures. Outside the narrow temperature range its flow characteristics will not adequately lubricate.

STROKE: The distance the piston travels from bottom dead center to top dead center.

SUBSTITUTION: Replacing one part suspected of a defect with a like part of known quality.

SUMP: The storage vessel or reservoir that provides a ready source of fluid to the pump. In an automatic transmission, the sump is the oil pan. All fluid eventually returns to the sump for recycling into the hydraulic system.

SUN GEAR: In a planetary gearset, it is the center gear that meshes with a cluster of planet pinions.

SUPERCHARGER: An air pump driven mechanically by the engine through belts, chains, shafts or gears from the crankshaft. Two general types of supercharger are the positive displacement and centrifugal type, which pump air in direct relationship to the speed of the engine.

SUPPLEMENTAL RESTRAINT SYSTEM: See air bag.

SURGE: Repeating engine-related feeling of acceleration and deceleration that is less intense than chuggle.

SWITCH: A device used to open, close, or redirect the current in an electrical circuit.

SYNCHROMESH: A manual transmission/transaxle that is equipped with devices (synchronizers) that match the gear speeds so that the transmission/transaxle can be downshifted without clashing gears.

SYNTHETIC OIL: Non-petroleum based oil.

TACHOMETER: A device used to measure the rotary speed of an engine, shaft, gear, etc., usually in rotations per minute.

TDC: Top dead center. The exact top of the piston's stroke.

TEFLON SEALING RINGS: Teflon is a soft, durable, plastic-like material that is resistant to heat and provides excellent sealing. These rings are designed with either scarf-cut joints or as one-piece rings. Teflon sealing rings have replaced many metal ring applications.

TERMINAL: A device attached to the end of a wire or cable to make an electrical connection.

TEST LIGHT, CIRCUIT-POWERED: Uses available circuit voltage to test circuit continuity.

TEST LIGHT, SELF-POWERED: Uses its own battery source to test circuit continuity.

THERMISTOR: A special resistor used to measure fluid temperature; it decreases its resistance with increases in temperature.

THERMOSTAT: A valve, located in the cooling system of an engine, which is closed when cold and opens gradually in response to engine heating, controlling the temperature of the coolant and rate of coolant flow.

THERMOSTATIC ELEMENT: A heat-sensitive, spring-type device that controls a drain port from the upper sump area to the lower sump. When the transaxle fluid reaches operating temperature, the port is closed and the upper sump fills, thus reducing the fluid level in the lower sump.

THROTTLE POSITION (TP) SENSOR: Reads the degree of throttle opening; its signal is used to analyze engine load conditions. The ECM/PCM decides to apply the TCC, or to disengage it for coast or load conditions that need a converter torque boost.

THROTTLE PRESSURE/MODULATOR PRESSURE: A hydraulic signal oil pressure relating to the amount of engine load, based on either the amount of throttle plate opening or engine vacuum.

THROTTLE VALVE: A regulating or balanced valve that is controlled mechanically by throttle linkage or engine vacuum. It sends a hydraulic signal to the shift valve body to control shift timing and shift quality. (See balanced valve; modulator valve.)

THROW-OUT BEARING: As the clutch pedal is depressed, the throwout bearing moves against the spring fingers of the pressure plate, forcing the pressure plate to disengage from the driven disc.

TIE ROD: A rod connecting the steering arms. Tie rods have threaded ends that are used to adjust toe-in.

TIE-UP: Condition where two opposing clutches are attempting to apply at same time, causing engine to labor with noticeable loss of engine rpm.

TIMING BELT: A square-toothed, reinforced rubber belt that is driven by the crankshaft and operates the camshaft.

TIMING CHAIN: A roller chain that is driven by the crankshaft and operates the camshaft.

TIRE ROTATION: Moving the tires from one position to another to make the tires wear evenly.

TOE-IN (OUT): A term comparing the extreme front and rear of the front tires. Closer together at the front is toe-in; farther apart at the front is toe-out.

TOP DEAD CENTER (TDC): The point at which the piston reaches the top of its travel on the compression stroke.

TORQUE: Measurement of turning or twisting force, expressed as foot-pounds or inch-pounds.

TORQUE CONVERTER: A turbine used to transmit power from a driving member to a driven member via hydraulic action, providing changes in drive ratio and torque. In automotive use, it links the driveplate at the rear of the engine to the automatic transmission.

TORQUE CONVERTER CLUTCH: The apply plate (lockup plate) assembly used for mechanical power flow through the converter.

TORQUE PHASE: Sometimes referred to as slip phase or stall phase, torque multiplication occurs when the turbine is turning at a slower speed than the impeller, and the stator is reactionary (stationary). This sequence generates a boost in output torque.

TORQUE RATING (STALL TORQUE): The maximum torque multiplication that occurs during stall conditions, with the engine at wide open throttle (WOT) and zero turbine speed.

TORQUE RATIO: An expression of the gear ratio factor on torque effect. A 3:1 gear ratio or 3:1 torque ratio increases the torque input by the ratio factor of 3. Input torque (100 ft. lbs.) x 3 = output torque (300 ft. lbs.)

TRACTION: The amount of usable tractive effort before the drive wheels slip on the road contact surface.

TORSION BAR SUSPENSION: Long rods of spring steel which take the place of springs. One end of the bar is anchored and the other arm (attached to the suspension) is free to twist. The bars' resistance to twisting causes springing action.

TRACK: Distance between the centers of the tires where they contact the ground.

TRACTION CONTROL: A control system that prevents the spinning of a vehicle's drive wheels when excess power is applied.

TRACTIVE EFFORT: The amount of force available to the drive wheels, to move the vehicle.

TRANSAXLE: A single housing containing the transmission and differential. Transaxles are usually found on front engine/front wheel drive or rear engine/rear wheel drive cars.

TRANSDUCER: A device that changes energy from one form to another. For example, a transducer in a microphone changes sound energy to electrical energy. In automotive air-conditioning controls used in automatic temperature systems, a transducer changes an electrical signal to a vacuum signal, which operates mechanical doors.

TRANSMISSION: A powertrain component designed to modify torque and speed developed by the engine; also provides direct drive, reverse, and neutral.

TRANSMISSION CONTROL MODULE (TCM): Manages transmission functions. These vary according to the manufacturer's product design but may include converter clutch operation, electronic shift scheduling, and mainline pressure.

TRANSMISSION FLUID TEMPERATURE (TFT) SENSOR: Originally called a transmission oil temperature (TOT) sensor, this input device to the ECM/PCM senses the fluid temperature and provides a resistance value. It operates on the thermistor principle.

TRANSMISSION INPUT SPEED (TIS) SENSOR: Measures turbine shaft (input shaft) rpm's and compares to engine rpm's to determine torque converter slip. When compared to the transmission output speed sensor or VSS, gear ratio and clutch engagement timing can be determined.

TRANSMISSION OIL TEMPERATURE (TOT) SENSOR: (See transmission fluid temperature (TFT) sensor.)

TRANSMISSION RANGE SELECTOR (TRS) SWITCH: Tells the module which gear shift position the driver has chosen.

TRANSFER CASE: A gearbox driven from the transmission that delivers power to both front and rear driveshafts in a four-wheel drive system. Transfer cases usually have a high and low range set of gears, used depending on how much pulling power is needed.

TRANSISTOR: A semi-conductor component which can be actuated by a small voltage to perform an electrical switching function.

TREAD WEAR INDICATOR: Bars molded into the tire at right angles to the tread that appear as horizontal bars when 1/16 in. of tread remains.

TREAD WEAR PATTERN: The pattern of wear on tires which can be "read" to diagnose problems in the front suspension.

TUNE-UP: A regular maintenance function, usually associated with the replacement and adjustment of parts and components in the electrical and fuel systems of a vehicle for the purpose of attaining optimum performance.

TURBINE: The output (driven) member of a fluid coupling or fluid torque converter. It is splined to the input (turbine) shaft of the transmission.

TURBOCHARGER: An exhaust driven pump which compresses intake air and forces it into the combustion chambers at higher than atmospheric pressures. The increased air pressure allows more fuel to be burned and results in increased horsepower being produced.

TURBULENCE: The interference of molecules of a fluid (or vapor) with each other in a fluid flow.

TYPE F: Transmission fluid developed and used by Ford Motor Company up to 1982. This fluid type provides a high coefficient of friction.

TYPE 7176: The preferred choice of transmission fluid for Chrysler automatic transmissions and transaxles. Developed in 1986, it closely resembles Dexron and Mercon. Type 7176 is the recommended service fill fluid for all Chrysler products utilizing a lockup torque converter dating back to 1978.

U-JOINT (UNIVERSAL JOINT): A flexible coupling in the drive train that allows the driveshafts or axle shafts to operate at different angles and still transmit rotary power.

UNDERSTEER: The tendency of a car to continue straight ahead while negotiating a turn.

UNIT BODY: Design in which the car body acts as the frame.

UNLEADED FUEL: Fuel which contains no lead (a common gasoline additive). The presence of lead in fuel will destroy the functioning elements of a catalytic converter, making it useless.

UNSPRUNG WEIGHT: The weight of car components not supported by the springs (wheels, tires, brakes, rear axle, control arms, etc.).

UPSHIFT: A shift that results in a decrease in torque ratio and an increase in speed.

VACUUM: A negative pressure; any pressure less than atmospheric pressure.

VACUUM ADVANCE: A device which advances the ignition timing in response to increased engine vacuum.

VACUUM GAUGE: An instrument used for measuring the existing vacuum in a vacuum circuit or chamber. The unit of measure is inches (of mercury in a barometer).

VACUUM MODULATOR: Generates a hydraulic oil pressure in response to the amount of engine vacuum.

VALVES: Devices that can open or close fluid passages in a hydraulic system and are used for directing fluid flow and controlling pressure.

VALVE BODY ASSEMBLY: The main hydraulic control assembly of the transmission/transaxle that contains numerous valves, check balls, and other components to control the distribution of pressurized oil throughout the transmission.

VALVE CLEARANCE: The measured gap between the end of the valve stem and the rocker arm, cam lobe or follower that activates the valve.

VALVE GUIDES: The guide through which the stem of the valve passes.

The guide is designed to keep the valve in proper alignment.

VALVE LASH (clearance): The operating clearance in the valve train.

VALVE TRAIN: The system that operates intake and exhaust valves, consisting of camshaft, valves and springs, lifters, pushrods and rocker arms.

VAPOR LOCK: Boiling of the fuel in the fuel lines due to excess heat. This will interfere with the flow of fuel in the lines and can completely stop the flow. Vapor lock normally only occurs in hot weather.

VARIABLE DISPLACEMENT (VARIABLE CAPACITY) VANE PUMP: Slipper-type vanes, mounted in a revolving rotor and contained within the bore of a movable slide, capture and then force fluid to flow. Movement of the slide to various positions changes the size of the vane chambers and the amount of fluid flow. **Note:** GM refers to this pump design as variable displacement, and Ford terms it variable capacity.

VARIABLE FORCE SOLENOID (VFS): Commonly referred to as the electronic pressure control (EPC) solenoid, it replaces the cable/linkage style of TV system control and is integrated with a spool valve and spring assembly to control pressure. A variable computer-controlled current flow varies the internal force of the solenoid on the spool valve and resulting control pressure.

VARIABLE ORIFICE THERMAL VALVE: Temperature-sensitive hydraulic oil control device that adjusts the size of a circuit path opening. By altering the size of the opening, the oil flow rate is adapted for cold to hot oil viscosity changes.

VARNISH: Term applied to the residue formed when gasoline gets old and stale.

VCM: See Electronic Control Unit (ECU).

VEHICLE SPEED SENSOR (VSS): Provides an electrical signal to the computer module, measuring vehicle speed, and affects the torque converter clutch engagement and release.

VESPEL SEALING RINGS: Hard plastic material that produces excellent sealing in dynamic settings. These rings are found in late versions of the 4T60 and in all 4T60-E and 4T80-E transaxles.

VISCOSITY: The ability of a fluid to flow. The lower the viscosity rating, the easier the fluid will flow. 10 weight motor oil will flow much easier than 40 weight motor oil.

VISCOSITY INDEX IMPROVERS: Keeps the viscosity nearly constant with changes in temperature. This is especially important at low temperatures, when the oil needs to be thin to aid in shifting and for cold-weather starting. Yet it must not be so thin that at high temperatures it will cause excessive hydraulic leakage so that pumps are unable to maintain the proper pressures.

VISCOUS CLUTCH: A specially designed torque converter clutch apply plate that, through the use of a silicon fluid, clamps smoothly and absorbs torsional vibrations.

VOLT: Unit used to measure the force or pressure of electricity. It is defined as the pressure needed to move one amp through the resistance of one ohm.

VOLTAGE: The electrical pressure that causes current to flow. Voltage is measured in volts (V).

VOLTAGE, APPLIED: The actual voltage read at a given point in a circuit. It equals the available voltage of the power supply minus the losses in the circuit up to that point.

VOLTAGE DROP: The voltage lost or used in a circuit by normal loads such as a motor or lamp or by abnormal loads such as a poor (high-resistance) lead or terminal connection.

VOLTAGE REGULATOR: A device that controls the current output of the alternator or generator.

VOLTMETER: An instrument used for measuring electrical force in units called volts. Voltmeters are always connected parallel with the circuit being tested.

VORTEX FLOW: The crosswise or circulatory flow of oil between the blades of the members caused by the centrifugal pumping action of the impeller.

WANKEL ENGINE: An engine which uses no pistons. In place of pistons, triangular-shaped rotors revolve in specially shaped housings.

WATER PUMP: A belt driven component of the cooling system that mounts on the engine, circulating the coolant under pressure.

WATT: The unit for measuring electrical power. One watt is the product of one ampere and one volt (watts equals amps times volts). Wattage is the horsepower of electricity (746 watts equal one horsepower).

WHEEL ALIGNMENT: Inclusive term to describe the front end geometry (caster, camber, toe-in/out).

WHEEL CYLINDER: Found in the automotive drum brake assembly, it is a device, actuated by hydraulic pressure, which, through internal pistons, pushes the brake shoes outward against the drums.

WHEEL WEIGHT: Small weights attached to the wheel to balance the wheel and tire assembly. Out-of-balance tires quickly wear out and also give erratic handling when installed on the front.

WHEELBASE: Distance between the center of front wheels and the center of rear wheels.

WIDE OPEN THROTTLE (WOT): Full travel of accelerator pedal.

WORK: The force exerted to move a mass or object. Work involves motion; if a force is exerted and no motion takes place, no work is done. Work per unit of time is called power. Work = force x distance = ft. lbs. 33,000 ft. lbs. in one minute = 1 horsepower

ZERO-THROTTLE COAST DOWN: A full release of accelerator pedal while vehicle is in motion and in drive range.

Commonly Used Abbreviations

2

2WD	Two Wheel Drive

4

4WD	Four Wheel Drive

A

A/C	Air Conditioning
ABDC	After Bottom Dead Center
ABS	Anti-lock Brakes
AC	Alternating Current
ACL	Air cleaner
ACT	Air Charge Temperature
AIR	Secondary Air Injection
ALCL	Assembly Line Communications Link
ALDL	Assembly Line Diagnostic Link
AT	Automatic Transaxle/Transmission
ATDC	After Top Dead Center
ATF	Automatic Transmission Fluid
ATS	Air Temperature Sensor
AWD	All Wheel Drive

B

BAP	Barometric Absolute Pressure
BARO	Barometric Pressure
BBDC	Before Bottom Dead Center
BCM	Body Control Module
BDC	Bottom Dead Center
BPT	Backpressure Transducer
BTDC	Before Top Dead Center
BVSV	Bimetallic Vacuum Switching Valve

C

CAC	Charge Air Cooler
CARB	California Air Resources Board
CAT	Catalytic Converter
CCC	Computer Command Control
CCCC	Computer Controlled Catalytic Converter
CCCI	Computer Controlled Coil Ignition
CCD	Computer Controlled Dwell
CDI	Capacitor Discharge Ignition
CEC	Computerized Engine Control
CFI	Continuous Fuel Injection
CIS	Continuous Injection System
CIS-E	Continuous Injection System - Electronic
CKP	Crankshaft Position
CL	Closed Loop
CMP	Camshaft Position
CPP	Clutch Pedal Position
CTOX	Continuous Trap Oxidizer System
CTP	Closed Throttle Position
CVC	Constant Vacuum Control
CYL	Cylinder

D

DBC	Dual Bed Catalyst
DC	Direct Current
DFI	Direct Fuel Injection
DIS	Distributorless Ignition System
DLC	Data Link Connector
DMM	Digital Multimeter
DOHC	Double Overhead Camshaft
DRB	Diagnostic Readout Box
DTC	Diagnostic Trouble Code
DTM	Diagnostic Test Mode
DVOM	Digital Volt/Ohmmeter

E

EBCM	Electronic Brake Control Module
ECM	Engine Control Module
ECT	Engine Coolant Temperature
ECU	Engine Control Unit or Electronic Control Unit
EDIS	Electronic Distributorless Ignition System
EEC	Electronic Engine Control
EEPROM	Electrically Erasable Programmable Read Only Memory
EFE	Early Fuel Evaporation
EGR	Exhaust Gas Recirculation
EGRT	Exhaust Gas Recirculation Temperature
EGRVC	EGR Valve Control
EPROM	Erasable Programmable Read Only Memory
EVAP	Evaporative Emissions
EVP	EGR Valve Position

F

FBC	Feedback Carburetor
FEEPROM	Flash Electrically Erasable Programmable Read Only Memory
FF	Flexible Fuel
FI	Fuel Injection
FT	Fuel Trim
FWD	Front Wheel Drive

G

GND	Ground

H

HAC	High Altitude Compensation
HEGO	Heated Exhaust Gas Oxygen sensor
HEI	High Energy Ignition
HO2 Sensor	Heated Oxygen Sensor

I

IAC	Idle Air Control
IAT	Intake Air Temperature
ICM	Ignition Control Module
IFI	Indirect Fuel Injection
IFS	Inertia Fuel Shutoff
ISC	Idle Speed Control
IVSV	Idle Vacuum Switching Valve

Commonly Used Abbreviations

K

KOEO	Key On, Engine Off
KOER	Key ON, Engine Running
KS	Knock Sensor

M

MAF	Mass Air Flow
MAP	Manifold Absolute Pressure
MAT	Manifold Air Temperature
MC	Mixture Control
MDP	Manifold Differential Pressure
MFI	Multiport Fuel Injection
MIL	Malfunction Indicator Lamp or Maintenance
MST	Manifold Surface Temperature
MVZ	Manifold Vacuum Zone

N

| NVRAM | Nonvolatile Random Access Memory |

O

O2 Sensor	Oxygen Sensor
OBD	On-Board Diagnostic
OC	Oxidation Catalyst
OHC	Overhead Camshaft
OL	Open Loop

P

P/S	Power Steering
PAIR	Pulsed Secondary Air Injection
PCM	Powertrain Control Module
PCS	Purge Control Solenoid
PCV	Positive Crankcase Ventilation
PIP	Profile Ignition Pick-up
PNP	Park/Neutral Position
PROM	Programmable Read Only Memory
PSP	Power Steering Pressure
PTO	Power Take-Off
PTOX	Periodic Trap Oxidizer System

R

RABS	Rear Anti-lock Brake System
RAM	Random Access Memory
ROM	Read Only Memory
RPM	Revolutions Per Minute
RWAL	Rear Wheel Anti-lock Brakes
RWD	Rear Wheel Drive

S

SBC	Single Bed Converter
SBEC	Single Board Engine Controller
SC	Supercharger
SCB	Supercharger Bypass
SFI	Sequential Multiport Fuel Injection
SIR	Supplemental Inflatible Restraint
SOHC	Single Overhead Camshaft
SPL	Smoke Puff Limiter
SPOUT	Spark Output
SRI	Service Reminder Indicator
SRS	Supplemental Restraint System
SRT	System Readiness Test
SSI	Solid State Ignition
ST	Scan Tool
STO	Self-Test Output

T

TAC	Thermostatic Air Clearner
TBI	Throttle Body Fuel Injection
TC	Turbocharger
TCC	Torque Converter Clutch
TCM	Transmission Control Module
TDC	Top Dead Center
TFI	Thick Film Ignition
TP	Throttle Position
TR Sensor	Transaxle/Transmission Range Sensor
TVV	Thermal Vacuum Valve
TWC	Three-way Catalytic Converter

V

VAF	Volume Air Flow, or Vane Air Flow
VAPS	Variable Assist Power Steering
VRV	Vacuum Regulator Valve
VSS	Vehicle Speed Sensor
VSV	Vacuum Switching Valve

W

| WOT | Wide Open Throttle |
| WU-TWC | Warm Up Three-way Catalytic Converter |

ENGLISH TO METRIC CONVERSION: TORQUE

To convert foot-pounds (ft. lbs.) to Newton-meters (Nm), multiply the number of ft. lbs. by 1.36
To convert Newton-meters (Nm) to foot-pounds (ft. lbs.), multiply the number of Nm by 0.7376

ft. lbs.	Nm	ft. lbs.	Nm	ft. lbs.	Nm	ft. lbs.	Nm
0.1	0.1	34	46.2	76	103.4	118	160.5
0.2	0.3	35	47.6	77	104.7	119	161.8
0.3	0.4	36	49.0	78	106.1	120	163.2
0.4	0.5	37	50.3	79	107.4	121	164.6
0.5	0.7	38	51.7	80	108.8	122	165.9
0.6	0.8	39	53.0	81	110.2	123	167.3
0.7	1.0	40	54.4	82	111.5	124	168.6
0.8	1.1	41	55.8	83	112.9	125	170.0
0.9	1.2	42	57.1	84	114.2	126	171.4
1	1.4	43	58.5	85	115.6	127	172.7
2	2.7	44	59.8	86	117.0	128	174.1
3	4.1	45	61.2	87	118.3	129	175.4
4	5.4	46	62.6	88	119.7	130	176.8
5	6.8	47	63.9	89	121.0	131	178.2
6	8.2	48	65.3	90	122.4	132	179.5
7	9.5	49	66.6	91	123.8	133	180.9
8	10.9	50	68.0	92	125.1	134	182.2
9	12.2	51	69.4	93	126.5	135	183.6
10	13.6	52	70.7	94	127.8	136	185.0
11	15.0	53	72.1	95	129.2	137	186.3
12	16.3	54	73.4	96	130.6	138	187.7
13	17.7	55	74.8	97	131.9	139	189.0
14	19.0	56	76.2	98	133.3	140	190.4
15	20.4	57	77.5	99	134.6	141	191.8
16	21.8	58	78.9	100	136.0	142	193.1
17	23.1	59	80.2	101	137.4	143	194.5
18	24.5	60	81.6	102	138.7	144	195.8
19	25.8	61	83.0	103	140.1	145	197.2
20	27.2	62	84.3	104	141.4	146	198.6
21	28.6	63	85.7	105	142.8	147	199.9
22	29.9	64	87.0	106	144.2	148	201.3
23	31.3	65	88.4	107	145.5	149	202.6
24	32.6	66	89.8	108	146.9	150	204.0
25	34.0	67	91.1	109	148.2	151	205.4
26	35.4	68	92.5	110	149.6	152	206.7
27	36.7	69	93.8	111	151.0	153	208.1
28	38.1	70	95.2	112	152.3	154	209.4
29	39.4	71	96.6	113	153.7	155	210.8
30	40.8	72	97.9	114	155.0	156	212.2
31	42.2	73	99.3	115	156.4	157	213.5
32	43.5	74	100.6	116	157.8	158	214.9
33	44.9	75	102.0	117	159.1	159	216.2

METRIC TO ENGLISH CONVERSION: TORQUE

To convert foot-pounds (ft. lbs.) to Newton-meters (Nm), multiply the number of ft. lbs. by 1.36
To convert Newton-meters (Nm) to foot-pounds (ft. lbs.), multiply the number of Nm by 0.7376

Nm	ft. lbs.	Nm	ft. lbs.	Nm	ft. lbs.	Nm	ft. lbs.	Nm	ft. lbs.
0.1	0.1	34	25.0	76	55.9	118	86.8	160	117.6
0.2	0.1	35	25.7	77	56.6	119	87.5	161	118.4
0.3	0.2	36	26.5	78	57.4	120	88.2	162	119.1
0.4	0.3	37	27.2	79	58.1	121	89.0	163	119.9
0.5	0.4	38	27.9	80	58.8	122	89.7	164	120.6
0.6	0.4	39	28.7	81	59.6	123	90.4	165	121.3
0.7	0.5	40	29.4	82	60.3	124	91.2	166	122.1
0.8	0.6	41	30.1	83	61.0	125	91.9	167	122.8
0.9	0.7	42	30.9	84	61.8	126	92.6	168	123.5
1	0.7	43	31.6	85	62.5	127	93.4	169	124.3
2	1.5	44	32.4	86	63.2	128	94.1	170	125.0
3	2.2	45	33.1	87	64.0	129	94.9	171	125.7
4	2.9	46	33.8	88	64.7	130	95.6	172	126.5
5	3.7	47	34.6	89	65.4	131	96.3	173	127.2
6	4.4	48	35.3	90	66.2	132	97.1	174	127.9
7	5.1	49	36.0	91	66.9	133	97.8	175	128.7
8	5.9	50	36.8	92	67.6	134	98.5	176	129.4
9	6.6	51	37.5	93	68.4	135	99.3	177	130.1
10	7.4	52	38.2	94	69.1	136	100.0	178	130.9
11	8.1	53	39.0	95	69.9	137	100.7	179	131.6
12	8.8	54	39.7	96	70.6	138	101.5	180	132.4
13	9.6	55	40.4	97	71.3	139	102.2	181	133.1
14	10.3	56	41.2	98	72.1	140	102.9	182	133.8
15	11.0	57	41.9	99	72.8	141	103.7	183	134.6
16	11.8	58	42.6	100	73.5	142	104.4	184	135.3
17	12.5	59	43.4	101	74.3	143	105.1	185	136.0
18	13.2	60	44.1	102	75.0	144	105.9	186	136.8
19	14.0	61	44.9	103	75.7	145	106.6	187	137.5
20	14.7	62	45.6	104	76.5	146	107.4	188	138.2
21	15.4	63	46.3	105	77.2	147	108.1	189	139.0
22	16.2	64	47.1	106	77.9	148	108.8	190	139.7
23	16.9	65	47.8	107	78.7	149	109.6	191	140.4
24	17.6	66	48.5	108	79.4	150	110.3	192	141.2
25	18.4	67	49.3	109	80.1	151	111.0	193	141.9
26	19.1	68	50.0	110	80.9	152	111.8	194	142.6
27	19.9	69	50.7	111	81.6	153	112.5	195	143.4
28	20.6	70	51.5	112	82.4	154	113.2	196	144.1
29	21.3	71	52.2	113	83.1	155	114.0	197	144.9
30	22.1	72	52.9	114	83.8	156	114.7	198	145.6
31	22.8	73	53.7	115	84.6	157	115.4	199	146.3
32	23.5	74	54.4	116	85.3	158	116.2	200	147.1
33	24.3	75	55.1	117	86.0	159	116.9	201	147.8

ENGLISH/METRIC CONVERSION: TEMPERATURE

To convert Fahrenheit (F°) to Celsius (C°), take F° temperature and subtract 32, multiply the result by 5 and divide the result by 9

To convert Celsius (C°) to Fahrenheit (F°), take C° temperature and multiply it by 9, divide the result by 5 and add 32

F°	C°	F°	C°	C°	F°	C°	F°
-40	-40.0	150	65.6	-38	-36.4	46	114.8
-35	-37.2	155	68.3	-36	-32.8	48	118.4
-30	-34.4	160	71.1	-34	-29.2	50	122
-25	-31.7	165	73.9	-32	-25.6	52	125.6
-20	-28.9	170	76.7	-30	-22	54	129.2
-15	-26.1	175	79.4	-28	-18.4	56	132.8
-10	-23.3	180	82.2	-26	-14.8	58	136.4
-5	-20.6	185	85.0	-24	-11.2	60	140
0	-17.8	190	87.8	-22	-7.6	62	143.6
1	-17.2	195	90.6	-20	-4	64	147.2
2	-16.7	200	93.3	-18	-0.4	66	150.8
3	-16.1	205	96.1	-16	3.2	68	154.4
4	-15.6	210	98.9	-14	6.8	70	158
5	-15.0	212	100.0	-12	10.4	72	161.6
10	-12.2	215	101.7	-10	14	74	165.2
15	-9.4	220	104.4	-8	17.6	76	168.8
20	-6.7	225	107.2	-6	21.2	78	172.4
25	-3.9	230	110.0	-4	24.8	80	176
30	-1.1	235	112.8	-2	28.4	82	179.6
35	1.7	240	115.6	0	32	84	183.2
40	4.4	245	118.3	2	35.6	86	186.8
45	7.2	250	121.1	4	39.2	88	190.4
50	10.0	255	123.9	6	42.8	90	194
55	12.8	260	126.7	8	46.4	92	197.6
60	15.6	265	129.4	10	50	94	201.2
65	18.3	270	132.2	12	53.6	96	204.8
70	21.1	275	135.0	14	57.2	98	208.4
75	23.9	280	137.8	16	60.8	100	212
80	26.7	285	140.6	18	64.4	102	215.6
85	29.4	290	143.3	20	68	104	219.2
90	32.2	295	146.1	22	71.6	106	222.8
95	35.0	300	148.9	24	75.2	108	226.4
100	37.8	305	151.7	26	78.8	110	230
105	40.6	310	154.4	28	82.4	112	233.6
110	43.3	315	157.2	30	86	114	237.2
115	46.1	320	160.0	32	89.6	116	240.8
120	48.9	325	162.8	34	93.2	118	244.4
125	51.7	330	165.6	36	96.8	120	248
130	54.4	335	168.3	38	100.4	122	251.6
135	57.2	340	171.1	40	104	124	255.2
140	60.0	345	173.9	42	107.6	126	258.8
145	62.8	350	176.7	44	111.2	128	262.4

LENGTH CONVERSION

To convert inches (in.) to millimeters (mm), multiply the number of inches by 25.4

To convert millimeters (mm) to inches (in.), multiply the number of millimeters by 0.04

Inches	Millimeters	Inches	Millimeters	Inches	Millimeters	Inches	Millimeters
0.0001	0.00254	0.005	0.1270	0.09	2.286	4	101.6
0.0002	0.00508	0.006	0.1524	0.1	2.54	5	127.0
0.0003	0.00762	0.007	0.1778	0.2	5.08	6	152.4
0.0004	0.01016	0.008	0.2032	0.3	7.62	7	177.8
0.0005	0.01270	0.009	0.2286	0.4	10.16	8	203.2
0.0006	0.01524	0.01	0.254	0.5	12.70	9	228.6
0.0007	0.01778	0.02	0.508	0.6	15.24	10	254.0
0.0008	0.02032	0.03	0.762	0.7	17.78	11	279.4
0.0009	0.02286	0.04	1.016	0.8	20.32	12	304.8
0.001	0.0254	0.05	1.270	0.9	22.86	13	330.2
0.002	0.0508	0.06	1.524	1	25.4	14	355.6
0.003	0.0762	0.07	1.778	2	50.8	15	381.0
0.004	0.1016	0.08	2.032	3	76.2	16	406.4

ENGLISH/METRIC CONVERSION: LENGTH

To convert inches (in.) to millimeters (mm), multiply the number of inches by 25.4

To convert millimeters (mm) to inches (in.), multiply the number of millimeters by 0.04

Inches		Millimeters	Inches		Millimeters	Inches		Millimeters
Fraction	Decimal	Decimal	Fraction	Decimal	Decimal	Fraction	Decimal	Decimal
1/64	0.016	0.397	11/32	0.344	8.731	11/16	0.688	17.463
1/32	0.031	0.794	23/64	0.359	9.128	45/64	0.703	17.859
3/64	0.047	1.191	3/8	0.375	9.525	23/32	0.719	18.256
1/16	0.063	1.588	25/64	0.391	9.922	47/64	0.734	18.653
5/64	0.078	1.984	13/32	0.406	10.319	3/4	0.750	19.050
3/32	0.094	2.381	27/64	0.422	10.716	49/64	0.766	19.447
7/64	0.109	2.778	7/16	0.438	11.113	25/32	0.781	19.844
1/8	0.125	3.175	29/64	0.453	11.509	51/64	0.797	20.241
9/64	0.141	3.572	15/32	0.469	11.906	13/16	0.813	20.638
5/32	0.156	3.969	31/64	0.484	12.303	53/64	0.828	21.034
11/64	0.172	4.366	1/2	0.500	12.700	27/32	0.844	21.431
3/16	0.188	4.763	33/64	0.516	13.097	55/64	0.859	21.828
13/64	0.203	5.159	17/32	0.531	13.494	7/8	0.875	22.225
7/32	0.219	5.556	35/64	0.547	13.891	57/64	0.891	22.622
15/64	0.234	5.953	9/16	0.563	14.288	29/32	0.906	23.019
1/4	0.250	6.350	37/64	0.578	14.684	59/64	0.922	23.416
17/64	0.266	6.747	19/32	0.594	15.081	15/16	0.938	23.813
9/32	0.281	7.144	39/64	0.609	15.478	61/64	0.953	24.209
19/64	0.297	7.541	5/8	0.625	15.875	31/32	0.969	24.606
5/16	0.313	7.938	41/64	0.641	16.272	63/64	0.984	25.003
21/64	0.328	8.334	21/32	0.656	16.669	1/1	1.000	25.400
			43/64	0.672	17.066			

Manual Set ISBN 1-4180-6174-3/Part No. 136174

Benefits of Chilton Labor Data:

- hundreds of new labor operations, including maintenance services and electronic system diagnosis
- estimate with confidence using trusted Chilton labor times for 1981 through current domestic and imported vehicles that consider the real world environment in which technicians work
- reference any of three labor times: standard, severe, and warranty
- accepted by most insurance and extended warranty companies
- makes and models conform to current Automotive Aftermarket Industry Association (AAIA) Standard
- eliminate confusion by using standardized terms across different OEMs

Labor Guide Manual Benefits:

- save your wrists for wrenching and enjoy our perfectly sized, easy-to-handle manuals one for domestic vehicles, the other for imported vehicles
- find labor times faster with:
  - tabs that display contents by manufacturer and model
  - two indexes–labor operations and systems–in each model group
  - manufacturers arranged alphabetically, and page numbering that includes manufacturer code so you know where you are in the book

Hardcover Manuals are 8 1/2" x 11", ©2007

Labor Guide CD-ROM Benefits:

- save time with automatically calculated labor charges, taxes, and parts as total job estimates
- increase shop legitimacy with printable professional estimates for your customers and worksheets for your technicians
- keep track of customers, prior estimates, and your own parts or package jobs with less paperwork

CD ISBN 1-4180-6171-9/Part No. 136171
©2007

Previous Year Editions:

Chilton 2006 Labor Guide Manual, ISBN 1-4180-1688-8/Part No. 131688
Chilton 2006 Labor Guide CD-ROM, ISBN 1-4180-0605-X/Part No. 130605

Chilton 2008® Service Manuals include 12 manuals covering DaimlerChrysler, Ford, General Motors, Asian, and European vehicles. Users will be expertly provided with the most currently available information to assist in daily activities. These new, reliable, and comprehensive manuals provide essential information, allowing users to accurately and efficiently diagnose and repair. Step-by-step procedures and helpful illustrations provide easy references for jobs. These new service manuals cover 2006 and 2007 models, plus any available 2008 models.

Service Manual Benefits:

- twelve-volume manual set, organized by vehicle manufacturer, provides more than 2000 pages of expertly written content
- access new year, make, and model information without repeating previous edition's content
- comprehensive, technically detailed content—including exploded view illustrations, diagnostics and specification charts— arranged alphabetically by model group for quick, easy access

2008 Editions

Chilton 2008 DaimlerChrysler Service Manuals (2 volume set)—ISBN 1-4283-2204-3/Part No. 142204
Chilton 2008 Ford Service Manuals (2 volume set)—ISBN 1-4283-2208-6/Part No. 142208
Chilton 2008 General Motors Service Manuals (2 volume set)—ISBN 1-4283-2211-6/Part No. 142211
Chilton 2008 Asian Service Manuals (5 volume set)—ISBN 1-4283-2214-0/Part No. 142214
Chilton 2008 European Service Manual—ISBN 1-4283-2220-5/Part No. 142220

Domestic manuals available December 2007
Import manuals December 2008
Manuals are 8 1/2" x 11", ©2007

2006 Editions

Chilton 2006 DaimlerChrysler Mechanical Service Manual—ISBN 1-4180-0600-9/Part No. 130600
Chilton 2006 Ford Mechanical Service Manual—ISBN 1-4180-0601-7/Part No. 130601
Chilton 2006 General Motors Mechanical Service Manual—ISBN 1-4180-0602-5/Part No. 130602
Chilton 2006 Asian Mechanical Service Manual—Volume I—ISBN 1-4180-0947-4/Part No. 130947
Chilton 2006 Asian Mechanical Service Manual—Volume II—ISBN 1-4180-0948-2/Part No. 130948
Chilton 2006 Asian Mechanical Service Manual—Volume III—ISBN 1-4180-0949-0/Part No. 130949
Chilton 2006 Asian Mechanical Service Manual—3 Volume Set—ISBN 1-4180-0603-3/Part No. 130603
Chilton 2006 European Mechanical Service Manual—ISBN 1-4180-0604-1/Part No. 130604

Manuals are 8 1/2" x 11", ©2006

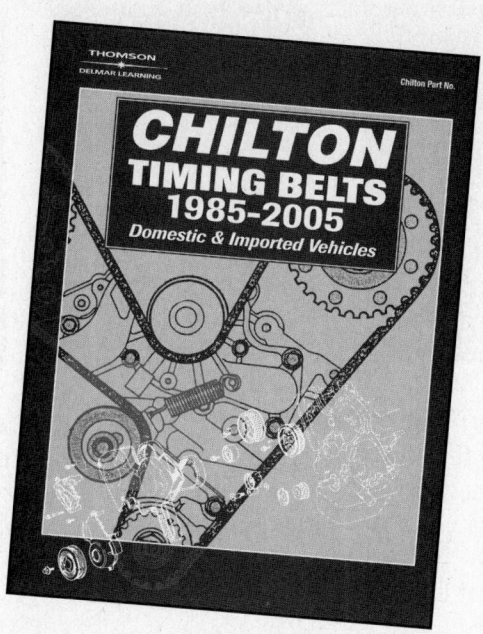

Chilton Timing Belts, 1985-2005

Chilton
ISBN 1-4018-9880-7/Part No. 129880

Timing belt procedures can represent increased profits for automotive repair shops and service stations, and this manual contains all the information automotive technicians need to properly service timing belts on domestic and imported cars, vans, and light trucks through 2005 models. Clear, straightforward procedures, illustrations, and specifications help to communicate 20 years of vehicle applications for fast, accurate inspection, replacement, and tensioning of timing belts. Readers will learn step-by-step how to perform key procedures both quickly and safely, while learning the correct labor time to charge for the service. OEM-recommended replacement intervals for proper maintenance of customer's vehicles are also featured.

Benefits
- detailed illustrations clearly demonstrate important concepts, such as how to correctly align camshaft and crankshaft timing marks, and how to simplify serpentine belt installation
- readers are made aware of potential hazards and time-wasting practices that can impede safe and profitable service procedures
- special tools are identified so that completing the service is as easy and quick as possible

544 pp, 8 1/2" x 11", softcover, ©2006

The *Chilton® Perennial Editions* contain repair and maintenance information for popular mechanical systems that may not be available elsewhere. They offer a wide range of repair information on cars, trucks, vans, and SUVs dating back to the early 1960s, and as current as 2002. Information for 1993 and later model years includes scheduled maintenance interval charts.

Benefits:

- covers the most common vehicle models found in the repair aftermarket today
- gain quick understanding of systems using exploded-view illustrations, diagrams, and charts
- simplify tough jobs with easy-to-follow removal and installation instructions for heater core and other components
- obtain complete coverage of repair procedures from drive train to chassis and associated components

Auto Repair Manual, 1998-2002, 1,426 pages
ISBN 0-8019-9362-8/Part No. 9362
Auto Repair Manual, 1993-1997, 2,064 pages
ISBN 0-8019-7919-6/Part No. 7919
Auto Repair Manual, 1988-1992, 1,284 pages
ISBN 0-8019-7906-4/Part No. 7906
Auto Repair Manual, 1980-1987, 1,344 pages
ISBN 0-8019-7670-7/Part No. 7670

Import Car Repair Manual, 1998-2002, 1,792 pps
ISBN 0-8019-9363-6/Part No. 9363
Import Car Repair Manual, 1993-1997, 2,080 pps
ISBN 0-8019-7920-X/Part No. 7920
Import Car Repair Manual, 1988-1992, 1,632 pages
ISBN 0-8019-7907-2/Part No. 7907
Import Car Repair Manual, 1980-1987, 1,488 pages
ISBN 0-8019-7672-3/Part No. 7672

Truck & Van Repair Manual, 1998-2002, 1,408 pages
ISBN 0-8019-9364-4/Part No. 9364
Truck & Van Repair Manual, 1993-1997, 2,096 pages
ISBN 0-8019-7921-8/Part No. 7921
Truck & Van Repair Manual, 1991-1995, 1,664 pages
ISBN 0-8019-7911-0/Part No. 7911
Truck & Van Repair Manual, 1986-1990, 1,536 pages
ISBN 0-8019-7902-1/Part No. 7902
Truck & Van Repair Manual, 1979-1986, 1,440 pages
ISBN 0-8019-7655-3/Part No. 7655

SUV Repair Manual, 1998-2002, 1,292 pages
ISBN 0-8019-9365-2/Part No. 9365

Hardcover manuals are 8 1/2" x 11".

Chilton Collector's Editions—*Reference Manuals for Vintage Vehicles*
Auto Repair Manual, 1964-1971, ISBN 0-8019-5974-8/Part No. 5974,
Truck & Van Repair Manual, 1961-1971, ISBN 0-8019-6198-X/Part No. 6198
Truck & Van Repair Manual, 1971-1978, ISBN 0-8019-7012-1/Part No. 7012

ASE Test Preparation Series, 4E
(A1-A8, L1, P2, X1, & C1)
ISBN 1-4180-3954-3
Part No. 133954

Each title in this popular series features the most up-to-date ASE task list available, along with practice test questions like those typically seen on an ASE certification exam to help users feel more comfortable and prepared to pass the actual test.

KEY FEATURES

- all ASE task lists are fully up-to-date, and completely current test preparation questions reflect the most recent ASE task changes for the broadest knowledge possible
- readers are given scores of opportunities to check their understanding of critical concepts through sample problems, refresher materials, and competency-specific test questions
- overviews of each task make an easy reference point for help in answering difficult ASE questions

Softcover manuals are 8½" x 11", SC, 1-Color, ©2006

(A1) Engine Repair, 4E
ISBN 1-4180-3878-4
Part No. 133878
The A1 manual covers the following topics: General Engine Diagnosis, Cylinder Head and Valve Train Diagnosis and Repair, Engine Block Diagnosis and Repair, Lubrication and Cooling Systems Diagnosis and Repair, Fuel, Electrical, Ignition and Exhaust Systems Inspection and Service.

(A2) Transmissions and Transaxles, 4E
ISBN 1-4180-3879-2
Part No. 133879
The A2 manual covers the following topics: General Transmission/ Transaxle Diagnosis (Mechanical/ Hydraulic Systems and Electronic Systems), Transmission/Transaxle Maintenance and Adjustment, In-Vehicle Transmission/ Transaxle Repair, Off-Vehicle Transmission/ Transaxle Repair.

(A3) Manual Drive Train and Axles, 4E
ISBN 1-4180-3880-6
Part No. 133880
The A3 manual covers the following topics: Clutch Diagnosis and Repair, Transmission Diagnosis and Repair, Transaxle Diagnosis and Repair, Drive Shaft/Half Shaft and Universal Joint/ Constant Velocity (CV) Joint Diagnosis and Repair (Front and Rear Wheel Drive), Rear Axle Diagnosis and Repair, Four Wheel Drive/All Wheel Drive Component Diagnosis and Repair.

(A4) Suspension and Steering, 4E
ISBN 1-4180-3881-4
Part No. 133881
The A4 manual covers the following topics: Steering Systems Diagnosis and Repair (Steering Columns and Manual Steering Gears, Power Assisted Steering Units, Steering Linkage), Suspension Systems Diagnosis and Repair (Front Suspensions, Rear Suspensions, Miscellaneous Services), Wheel Alignment Diagnosis, Adjustment and Repair, and Wheel and Tire Diagnosis and Repair.

(A5) Brakes, 4E
ISBN 1-4180-3882-2
Part No. 133882
The A5 manual covers the following topics: Hydraulic System Diagnosis and Repair, Drum Brake Diagnosis and Repair, Disc Brake Diagnosis and Repair, Power Assist Units Diagnosis and Repair, Miscellaneous Systems Diagnosis and Repair, Electronic Brake Control Systems, Antilock Brake Systems (ABS) Diagnosis and Repair.

(A6) Electrical-Electronic Systems, 4E
ISBN 1-4180-3883-0
Part No. 133883
The A6 manual covers the following topics: General Electrical/Electronic Systems Diagnosis, Battery Diagnosis and Service, Starting Systems Diagnosis and Repair, Charging Systems Diagnosis and Repair, Lighting Systems Diagnosis and Repair, Gauges, Warning Devices and Driver Information Systems Diagnosis and Repair, Horn and Wiper/ Washer Diagnosis and Repair, Accessories Diagnosis and Repair.

(A7) Heating and Air Conditioning, 4E
ISBN 1-4180-3884-9
Part No. 133884
The A7 manual covers the following topics: A/C System Service Diagnosis and Repair, Refrigeration System Component Diagnosis and Repair, Heating and Engine Cooling Systems Diagnosis and Repair, Operating Systems and Related Controls Diagnosis and Repair, Refrigerant Recovery, Recycling, Handling and Retrofit.

(A8) Engine Performance, 4E
ISBN 1-4180-3885-7
Part No. 133885
The A8 manual covers the following topics: General Engine Diagnosis, Ignition System Diagnosis and Repair, Fuel, Air Induction, and Exhaust Systems Diagnosis and Repair, Emissions Control Systems Diagnosis and Repair (Including OBDII), Computerized Engine controls Diagnosis and Repair (Including OBDII), Engine Electrical Systems diagnosis and Repair.

(L1) Advanced Engine Performance, 4E
ISBN 1-4180-3888-1
Part No. 133888
The L1 manual covers the following topics: General Powertrain Diagnosis, Computerized Powertrain Controls Diagnosis (Including OBDII), Ignition System Diagnosis, Fuel Systems and Air Induction Systems Diagnosis, Emission Control Systems Diagnosis, I/M Failure Diagnosis.

(X1) Exhaust Systems 4E
ISBN 1-4180-3886-5
Part No. 133886
The X1 manual covers the following topics: Exhaust Systems Inspection and Repair, Emissions Systems Diagnosis, Exhaust System Fabrication, Exhaust System Installation, Exhaust System Repair Regulations.

(P2) Automobile Parts Specialist, 4E
ISBN 1-4180-3887-3
Part No. 133887
The P2 manual covers the following topics: General Operations, Customer Relations and Sales Skills, Vehicle Systems Knowledge, Vehicle Identification, Cataloging Skills, Inventory Management, Merchandising.

(C1) Service Consultant, 4E
ISBN 1-4180-3889-X
Part No. 133889
The C1 manual covers the following topics: Communications, Product Knowledge, Sales Skills and Shop Operations.

Softcover Manuals are 8½" x 11", 1-Color, ©2006

ASE Test Preparation Series Español
(Complete Set Examenes A1-A8, L1, P2, X1)
ISBN 1-4018-1530-8
Part No. 21530

SPANISH AUTOMOTIVE SERIES
(A1) Reparación de Motores, 2a Edición
Part No. 21014
(10-Digit ISBN 1-4018-1014-4)
(A2) Transmission Automática/Eje de Transmission Automática, 2a Edición
Part No. 21015
(10-Digit ISBN 1-4018-1015-2)
(A3) Tren de y Mando Ejes Manuales, 2a Edición
Part No. 21016
(10-Digit ISBN 1-4018-1016-0)
(A4) Suspensión y Dirección, 2a Edición
Part No. 21017
(10-Digit ISBN 1-4018-1017-9)
(A5) Frenos, 2a Edición
Part No. 21018
(10-Digit ISBN 1-4018-1018-7)
(A6) Sistemas Eléctricos/ Electrónicos, 2a Edición
Part No. 21019
(10-Digit ISBN 1-4018-1019-5)
(A7) Calefacción y Aire Acondicionado, 2a Edición
Part No. 21020
(10-Digit ISBN 1-4018-1020-9)
(A8) Funcionamiento de Motores, 2a Edición
Part No. 21021
(10-Digit ISBN 1-4018-1021-7)
(L1)Especialista en el Funciommiato Avansado de Motores, 2a Edición
Part No. 21022
(10-Digit ISBN 1-4018-1022-5)
(P2) Especialista en Partes de Automovil, 2a Edición
Part No. 21023
(10-Digit ISBN 1-4018-1023-3)
(X1) Sistemas de Escape, 2a Edición
Part No. 21024
(10-Digit ISBN 1-4018-1024-1)

The ASE "Passing Lane" Package

(Complete Set A1-A8, L1, P2)
ISBN 0-7668-4338-6

The most comprehensive test preparation for Automotive Tests A1-A8, L1, and P2. Combining the most thorough ASE Test Preparation books with the latest in ASE videos, this package provides a comprehensive program of self-study for the automotive ASE Tests.

EACH BOOK IN THE SERIES FEATURES:
- test-taking strategies
- tasks lists and overview
- sample test questions
- ASE-style exams
- explanations to the answers
- glossary of terms

EACH VIDEO IN THE SERIES FEATURES:
- easy to follow videos emphasizing safety throughout
- major task areas and topics for each of the ASE exams
- Activity Sheets to help comprehend and retain information

(A1) Automotive Engine Repair Book/Video
ISBN 0-7668-4181-2
(A2) Automotive Transmissions and Transaxles Book/Video
ISBN 0-7668-4182-0
(A3) Automotive Manual Drive Trains and Axles Book/Video
ISBN 0-7668-4183-9
(A4) Automotive Suspension and Steering Book/Video
ISBN 0-7668-4184-7
(A5) Automotive Brakes Book/Video
ISBN 0-7668-4185-5
(A6) Automotive Electrical-Electronics Systems Book/Video
ISBN 0-7668-4186-3
(A7) Automotive Heating and Air Conditioning Book/Video
ISBN 0-7668-4187-1
(A8) Automotive Engine Performance Book/Video
ISBN 0-7668-4188-X
(L1) Automotive Advanced Engine Performance Book/Video
ISBN 0-7668-4189-8
(P2) Automobile Parts Specialist Book/Video
ISBN 0-7668-4190-1

ASE Test Preparation Series for Engine Machinist

(Complete Set M1-M3)
ISBN 0-7668-6283-6
Part No. 16283

These books are intended for automotive technicians who are preparing to take one or more of the Engine Machinist ASE examinations (for either gas or diesel engines). Each manual combines refresher materials with an abundance of sample test questions, as well as a wealth of information regarding test-taking strategies and the types of questions found in an ASE exam. In addition to the questions, thorough explanations are provided as to why each answer is correct or incorrect.

KEY FEATURES
- the History section explains why the exams are important to the industry
- test-taking strategies help prepare technicians for the environment they will encounter during the actual exam
- task lists and overviews help technicians focus their attention
- glossary of terms allows technicians to use the manual as a reference tool after they have passed the exam

(M1) Cylinder Head Specialist
ISBN 0-7668-6280-1
Part No. 16280

(M2) Cylinder Block Specialist
ISBN 0-7668-6281-X
Part No. 16281

(M3) Assembly Specialist
ISBN 0-7668-6282-8
Part No. 16282

Softcover manuals are 8½" x 11", 1-Color, ©2002

Automotive Technician Certification (ATC) Challenge CD-ROM Series

These exciting interactive CD-ROMs have been designed to prepare students and technicians for successful completion of the Collision or Automotive ASE task areas. This multimedia software assesses strengths and weaknesses by identifying topics needing further study while allowing users to review ASE task areas at their own pace. Not only are the *ATC Challenge 3.0* and *ATC Challenge for Collision Repair* the ultimate in test preparation, but they are also excellent learning tools!

KEY FEATURES
- explanation and hints for each answer aid in reader comprehension, critical thinking, and retention
- rationale for every answer, whether right or wrong
- "Notes" allow users to comment on any topic for future reference
- clear, detailed reports allow users to identify topics needing further review
- true ASE style questions
- LAN compatible

ATC Challenge 3.0 CD-ROM
ISBN 0-7668-2982-0
Part No. 12982
Covers tests A1 through A8, L1, P2, and X1. While all of the tests have been updated to the latest ASE task lists, particular attention has been paid to the L1 test and content on composite vehicles and related questions.
CD-ROM, ©2001

ATC Challenge for P2 CD-ROM
ISBN 0-7668-1827-6
CD-ROM, ©2000

ATC Challenge CD-ROM for Collision Repair
ISBN 0-7668-1511-0
Covers tests B2-B6.

Technician Test Preparation— Automotive Bilingual Series

Now both English and Spanish speaking technicians seeking ASE certification can access online test preparation material with ease! The *TTP-Automotive Bilingual* series for automotive training and certification provides up-to-date technology and content for tests A1-A8, L1, P2, X1, and C1. An easy-to-use format combined with helpful remediation addresses the unique needs of technicians by clearly demonstrating text-based theory for enhanced learning and retention. Not only is *TTP-Automotive Bilingual* the ultimate in test preparation, but it is also an excellent learning tool!

Technician Test Preparation Benefits:

- maps to the latest ASE task lists familiarize users with the actual work they should be able to do as technicians when taking the ASE tests
- well-illustrated remediation offered via digitized video clips, animations, and high impact graphics further explains key concepts for a more effective learning process
- practice questions provide helpful hints, insight into right and wrong answers, and links to further study specific task areas
- detailed reports provide accurate test results and instant feedback for selected test types so that users can pinpoint the task areas needing improvement
- switch between Spanish and English versions at the click of a button

Call Your Delmar Cengage Learning Sales Rep for Part Numbers & Pricing

Visit **www.TechnicianTestPrep.com** to see the latest modules and a free demo!

Automotive Technician Certification Test Preparation Manual, 3E
Don Knowles

ISBN 1-4180-4926-3
Part No. 134926

Filled with updated task list theory, practice tests, and abundant, demonstrative graphics, this revised edition provides all the latest information required to sufficiently prepare technicians to pass each of the A1-A8, and L1 ASE certification exams. Each chapter begins with a pretest that indicates the depth of preparation required to become familiar with the information in the chapter, followed by a description of each ASE task and the must-have information related to the task. ASE-type questions at the end of each chapter appear in the same format as on actual ASE tests to further prepare users to pass each exam.

KEY FEATURES

- current information provides practice questions which match the latest ASE task list
- answers to pretest questions and helpful analysis at the end of each chapter provide learners with faster access to accurate information
- supportive "Hints" throughout each chapter help users work through the process of determining the correct answers to the questions

CONTENTS

Engine Repair. Automatic Transmission/Transaxle. Manual Drive Train and Axles. Suspension and Steering. Brakes. Electrical/Electronic Systems. Heating, Ventilation, and Air Conditioning Systems. Engine Performance. Advanced Engine Performance.

656 pp, 8½" x 11", SC, 1-Color, ©2007

NATEF Standards Job Sheets
ISBN 0-7668-6375-1
(Complete Set: A1-A8)

Each of our eight *NATEF (National Automotive Technicians Education Foundation) Standards Job Sheets* workbooks has been thoughtfully designed to assist users in gaining valuable job preparedness skills and mastering specific technical competencies required for success as a professional automotive technician. The entire series is based on current NATEF standards.

Central to each manual are well-designed and easy-to-read job sheets, each of which contains specific, performance-based objectives, lists of required tools and materials, safety precautions, plus step-by-step procedures to lead users to completion of shop activities.

Key Features

- easy to use in any automotive education or training program in which NATEF coverage is desired
- completed Job Sheets may be kept as records, providing tangible evidence that instructors are addressing all NATEF tasks while paving the way for program certification

JOB SHEETS AVAILABLE FOR:
(A1) Automotive Engine Repair, 0-7668-6367-0
(A2) Automatic Transmissions and Transaxles, 0-7668-6368-9
(A3) Manual Drive Trains and Axles, 0-7668-6369-7
(A4) Automotive Suspension and Steering, 0-7668-6370-0
(A5) Automotive Brakes, 0-7668-6371-9
(A6) Automotive Electrical and Electronic Systems, 0-7668-6372-7
(A7) Automotive Heating and Air Conditioning, 0-7668-6373-5
(A8) Automotive Engine Performance, 0-7668-6374-3

All share the following information:
8½" x 11", softcover, ©2002

This pioneering eight-book series offers automotive service shop owners and those wanting to be shop owners the necessary business and customer service skills to run a successful automotive service facility.

The series covers three main topical areas: personnel management, business management, and sales and marketing. Each book provides a framework to help technicians make consistent, high-quality, and productive service a part of every day shop operations. According to the author, "Great performance coupled with increased customer loyalty, trust, and operational excellence will almost always result in increased profits."

Automotive Service Management Series Benefits:

- real-world approach reflects author's experience as a fourth generation technician, a repair & service company owner, and an automotive industry trainer
- all-inclusive coverage spans from designing an automotive repair facility floor plan through financial management techniques, customer/staff relations, and more
- length of each book makes it easy to incorporate this series into workshops, seminars, and training/education courses
- information is available "as is" or for customization

Total Customer Relationship Management
ISBN 1-4018-2657-1/Part No. 22657
From Intent to Implementation
ISBN 1-4018-2658-X/Part No. 22658
Operational Excellence
ISBN 1-4018-2659-8/Part No. 22659
Building a Team
ISBN 1-4018-2660-1/Part No. 22660
The High Performance Shop
ISBN 1-4018-2661-X/Part No. 22661
Safety Communications
ISBN 1-4018-2662-8/Part No. 22662
Managing Dollars with Sense
ISBN 1-4018-2663-6/Part No. 22663
Operations Management
ISBN 1-4018-2665-2/Part No. 22665
Entire Set of 8 Books
ISBN 1-4018-2499-4/Part No. 2499

Softcover manuals are 8 1/2" x 11", ©2003

ABOUT THE AUTHOR

Mitch Schneider is a fourth generation mechanic/technician and is a frequent speaker at major conventions and meetings of automotive industry trade organizations. Schneider is also an award-winning journalist and is a regular contributor and senior contributing editor for *Motor Age* magazine. He provides commentary on the evolving relationship between service dealers, jobbers, warehouse directors and manufacturers.

Schneider has also appeared on the TNN cable show "Truckin' USA" where he hosted the "Tech Tips" segment. In addition to operating the award-winning Schneider's Automotive for 22 years in Simi Valley, CA, he is also the president and founder of Schneider's Future-Tech, a service company specializing in conducting management seminars for automotive service dealers, jobbers, warehouse distribution companies, and manufacturers.

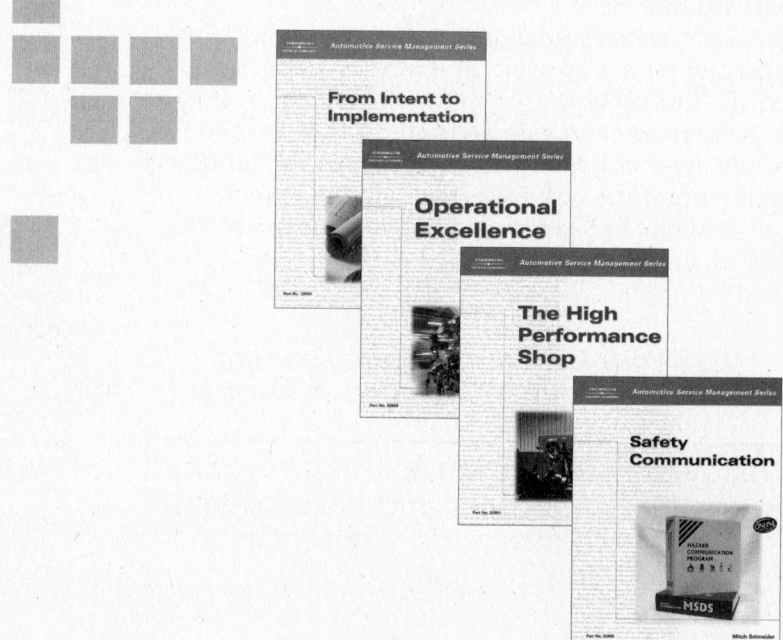

Introduction to OBDII
Roy Cox

ISBN 1-4180-1220-3/Part No. 131220

Here's an easy-to-understand, logical guide to the diagnosis and repair of today's complex and sophisticated automotive control systems! *Introduction to On-Board Diagnostics (OBD II)* readers will learn the fundamentals of how to perform diagnostic procedures, and be provided with valuable reference material for diagnosing and troubleshooting components and circuits. This book provides a simple, logical approach to explain the operation of the OBD II process and will teach the reader how to quickly spot problems and identify components that are not functioning correctly. In addition, the interrelationships between the fuel delivery, emission control, ignition, and accessory systems are clearly addressed and explained. This truly unique introduction to OBDII systems, and the troubleshooting of components and circuits, features an accompanying interactive diagnostic CD-ROM that leads readers through realistic trouble-code scenarios to reinforce its diagnostic and repair.

Benefits
- "quick hit" troubleshooting tricks teach readers how to diagnose problems when there is no stored OBDII trouble code, as well as how to handle situations where the trouble code is actually set by a basic mechanical problem rather than a failure of the indicated component
- information is useful for those who wish to expand their capabilities from more basic, mechanical repairs to complex electronics and drivability diagnosis and repair
- a substantial portion of the content focuses on logical troubleshooting that can be done without expensive, complicated test equipment and special tools
- also useful as a preparation manual for the ASE Certification exams

CONTENTS
Chapter 1- Introduction, Chapter 2- Evolution of OBD, Chapter 3- OBDII Terminology, Chapter 4- System Operating Protocols, Chapter 5- System Monitors, Chapter 6- Drive Cycles, Chapter 7- Diagnostic Trouble Codes (DTC's), Chapter 8- Diagnostic Routines

256 pp, 8 1/2" x 11", softcover, ©2006

SUPPLEMENTS
Diagnostic Tool CD-ROM 1-4180-1221-1/Part No. 131221
Instructor's Guide 1-4180-1222-X

TAKE YOUR TECHNICIAN TRAINING TO THE NEXT LEVEL

Comprehensive Skill Assessment Tool (CSAT) — Automotive

The online Comprehensive Skill Assessment Tool for Automotive helps instructors and trainers implement the necessary training programs for individual areas needing improvement over various key automotive topics. Within each key topic, strategic learning areas are measured to account for knowledge of theory, hands-on application, and diagnostics. Pre- and post-assessment phases assist with the identification of areas needing improvement. The combined phases of education and training, and post-assessment allow instructors to track skill level growth and target specific areas needing development and more teaching.

Benefits
- a low-cost solution benefiting trainers and students
- individual users can take tests online to identify areas of strength and areas needing improvement
- account set-up that enables instructors to assess and track the results of individual users

Call Your Delmar Cengage Learning Sales Rep for Part Numbers & Pricing

Visit **www.skillanalysis.com** to see the latest modules and a free demo!

CHILTON®PRO

ChiltonPRO is the new alternative for technicians who want a cost-effective electronic automotive repair system. It combines Chilton's famous automotive repair information into one solution covering more than 20 years of domestic and imported vehicles. The information is delivered online or on DVD-ROMs–your choice–updated regularly throughout the year.

Online Monthly Payment
Part No. 133002
13-Digit ISBN: 978-14180-3002-5
(10-Digit ISBN: 1-4180-3002-3)

DVD Monthly Payment
Part No. 133003
13-Digit ISBN: 978-1-4180-3003-2
(10-Digit ISBN: 1-4180-3003-1)

Online Annual Payment
Part No. 132876
13-Digit ISBN: 978-14180-2877-0
(10-Digit ISBN: 1-4180-2876-2)

DVD Annual Payment
Part No. 132877
13-Digit ISBN: 978-1-4180-2877-0
(10-Digit ISBN: 1-4180-2877-0)

Contact your sales representative for a free demo or visit www.chiltonpro.com

BENEFITS

- create better estimates using labor times developed with real-world factors
- save money by accurately identifying and solving engine performance problems
- save time with expert guidance through OBDII diagnostics
- increase efficiency by understanding system operation through detailed explanations and theory
- increase profits using Technical Service Bulletins to ensure that work is not going unperformed
- execute effective repairs by viewing cutaway diagrams and actual photos
- make better use of your time with information that can be found quicker using AAIA standards for year, make, and model
- increase confidence levels by always being able to print what you need
- eliminate guesswork with quick reference to critical specifications in helpful tables
- spend less on repair information

Automatically uploaded into online version or new DVD-ROM sets sent to customers. Initial content as follows:

- OEM recommended maintenance schedules, 1990–current
- trusted Chilton labor times, 1981–current
- step-by-step mechanical procedures, 1961–current
- diagnostics designed by instructors, 1990–current (Imported models through 2003)
- OEM Technical Service Bulletins, 1986–current

System Requirements:
Web browser

- Internet Explorer 5.0 or above (recommended)
- Firefox 1.5 or above
- High-speed internet connection
- Adobe Acrobat Reader 5.0 or above

DVD-ROMs:
The DVD versions of ChiltonPRO requires:

- Processor: Pentium II or equivalent
- Operating systems: Windows 2000, or Windows XP
- Memory: 128 RAM minimum
- Disk Space: 700 MB
- DVD-ROM drive
- Internet connection required for web authorization (product authorization also available via telephone)